LEXICON UNIVERSAL ENCYCLOPEDIA

Lexicon Publications, Inc.
New York, N.Y.

PHOENICIAN	**T** ETRUSCAN
EARLY HEBREW	**T** EARLY LATIN
EARLY ARAMAIC	**T** CLASSICAL LATIN
EARLY GREEK	**T** RUSSIAN-CYRILLIC
CLASSICAL GREEK	**T** GERMAN-GOTHIC

MODERN LATIN

T

T/t is the 20th letter of the English alphabet. Both the letter and its position in the alphabet were derived from the Latin, which derived it from the Greek by way of the Etruscan. The Greeks, who call the letter *tau,* took the name, form, and position of the letter from a Semitic writing system, in which the name of the sign was *taw;* it was the last letter of their alphabet. The sound of *T/t* is usually classified as a voiceless dental stop. In modern English speech it is the voiceless counterpart of *d* and is made not with the tongue against the upper front teeth but with the tongue against the ridge behind the teeth as in *top* or *post. T/t* also represents other sounds, such as *ch* in *nature* and *sh* in *partial* or *nation;* in some words, such as *listen,* it is silent. When *t* is followed by *h* in the same syllable, the combination is either voiceless or voiced; in a few words, such as *Thomas* or *Thames,* it is pronounced as simple *t,* and the *h* does not alter the pronunciation.

I. J. GELB AND R. M. WHITING

T Tauri stars [taw'-ree]

T Tauri stars are a class of VARIABLE STARS associated with nebulosity, having no regular period, and exhibiting spectra with emission lines. First recognized (1937) by the American astronomer Alfred H. Joy, they are thought to be stars that have recently formed and have not yet finished contracting onto the MAIN SEQUENCE. They seem to have a higher absolute brightness than main sequence stars of the same surface temperature. T Tauri stars are often found in groups, called T-associations.

R. H. GARSTANG

Bibliography: Hoffmeister, Cuno, et al., *Variable Stars* (1985).

t-test

The *t*-test is one of several statistical procedures used to test a NULL HYPOTHESIS. The *t*-test tests a hypothesis concerning the mean of a NORMAL DISTRIBUTION. If the null hypothesis states that the mean has the value *m,* and *n* observations are available that have sample mean *x* and sample STANDARD DEVIATION *s,* the *t*-test rejects the hypothesis when the *t*-statistic $\sqrt{n}(\bar{x} - m)/s$ is sufficiently far from 0. Because many populations have (at least approximately) a normal distribution, the *t*-test is one of the most common statistical procedures. Other *t*-tests are used to compare two means and in linear regression analysis. These use different statistics but have the same *t*-distribution.

DAVID S. MOORE

Bibliography: Weimer, Richard, *Introduction to Probability and Statistics* (1987).

Ta-lien (Dalian) [dah-lee-en]

Ta-lien, formerly known as Dairen (1983 est. pop., 1,270,000), is a component of the municipality of LÜ-TA, which encompasses Ta-lien and Lü-shun. Ta-lien occupies the eastern portion of the Liaotung Peninsula's tip at the entrance to the Po Hai (or Gulf of Chihli). The city serves as an entry port for Manchuria and is connected to the interior by rail. Ships, cement, steel, transportation equipment, and cotton textiles are produced. Soybean processing and petroleum refining are also important. New port facilities were completed in 1976.

The history of known settlement in Ta-lien dates from the 2d-century BC occupation by the Han dynasty. Subsequently, the area was occupied by the T'ang dynasty (7th century), Ming dynasty (15th century), and the Manchu dynasty (1633–1911). Russia occupied the city in 1897, renaming it Dalny, but Japan was awarded the area after the Russian defeat in the Russo-Japanese War (1904–05). After World War II, Ta-lien was returned to China. In 1984 it was among the coastal cities opened to foreign investment.

Taafe, Eduard, Graf von [tah'-fe]

During the reign of Austrian Emperor FRANCIS JOSEPH, the longest term as premier was served by Eduard, Graf von Taafe, b. Feb. 24, 1833, d. Nov. 29, 1895. Taking office in 1868, Taafe advocated political concessions to the Czechs similar to those accorded Poles and Hungarians within the Austro-Hungarian empire. This position lost him the support of the German majority of his government and led him to resign early in 1870. Taafe again became premier in 1879, and long held the support of the Catholic church and of Poles and Czechs in the Reichsrat. Later, however, his programs fell short of the demands of the nationalistic Czechs, and he was forced to resign in 1893.

K. M. SMOGORZEWSKI

Bibliography: Jenks, William A., *Austria under the Iron Ring* (1965).

Tabari, al- [tah-bah'-ree, ahl]

The Muslim scholar Abu Jafar Muhammad ibn Jarir al-Tabari, c.839–923, wrote a massive compendium, known as the *Tafsir,* of commentary on the Koran; his *Tarikh al-Rusul wa al-Mulak* (History of Prophets and Kings; portions of which have been translated into English) is the first history of the world in Arabic. Because they are an amalgam of the findings of earlier scholars, many of whose works are lost, al-Tabari's writings constitute a valuable record of Arabic literature.

Bibliography: Rosenthal, Franz, *A History of Muslim Historiography,* 2d ed. (1968).

Tabasco

Tabasco, a state in southeastern Mexico on the Bay of Campeche, has an area of 24,661 km² (9,522 mi²) and a population of 1,208,000 (1984 est.). The capital is VILLAHERMOSA. The low, flat territory is covered by swamps, lagoons, and rain forests and is crossed by numerous rivers. Predominantly agricultural, Tabasco is known for its tropical produce, which includes cacao, sugarcane, bananas, pineapple, vanilla, and chicle. Since the 1960s, petroleum extraction has become important. Explored by Juan de Grijalva in 1518, Tabasco was conquered by Francisco de Montejo in 1530. It became a state of independent Mexico in 1824.

LEON YACHER

Tabb, John B.

An American poet, Father John Banister Tabb, b. Richmond, Va., Mar. 22, 1845, d. Nov. 19, 1909, is remembered for the religious poems he wrote after his conversion to Roman Catholicism. In several volumes—*Poems* (1894), *Lyrics* (1897), and *The Rosary in Rhyme* (1904)—he displays a wit resembling that of the metaphysical poets.   JAMES HART

tabernacle

According to certain passages in the biblical Book of Exodus (chaps. 25–31, 35–40), the tabernacle was a portable sanctuary constructed by Moses where the Israelites worshiped during their wilderness wanderings. The most important part of the rectangular, hide-covered structure was the Holy of Holies, which held the sacred ARK OF THE COVENANT. Another passage in Exodus (33:7-10) describes it simply as a "tent of meeting" set up outside the camp as a place for consulting with Yahweh. Modern scholars attribute the first, more elaborate description to later priestly scribes (P) and view it as a postexilic attempt to project features of the later Temple and the ascending authority of Aaronic priests into Israel's early history. The priestly tradition may, however, preserve accurate elements from early cultic practice, which is presumed to be reflected in the second passage (attributed to the preexilic source E).   NORMAN K. GOTTWALD

Tabernacles, Feast of

The Feast of Tabernacles (or Booths), Sukkoth in Hebrew, is one of the three joyous pilgrim festivals of Judaism prescribed in Scripture. It marks the end of the harvest season—specifically, the vintage and fruit harvest in the Holy Land—and is celebrated for 8 or 9 days in late September or early October, Tishri 15–22 or 23 in the Jewish calendar. Its characteristic feature is the erection of a booth (sukkah) covered with greens and decorated with products of the harvest, the top of which is thatched lightly enough so that the sky is visible. (The Bible interprets the booth as a memorial to the shelters in which the Israelites camped during their wanderings in the desert.) Another characteristic observance is the use of four plants—citron, palm, myrtle, and willow—as a festal bouquet. They are carried in procession around the synagogue and are waved during the singing of psalms.

BERNARD J. BAMBERGER

Bibliography: Schauss, Hayyim, *The Jewish Festivals: From their Beginnings to Our Own Day,* rev. ed. (1969), and *Jewish Festivals: History and Observance* (1973).

tablature

Tablature is a system of notation using letters, numbers, or other signs with the purpose of showing the player of a musical instrument which string to stop, which hole to cover, or which key to depress. It is opposed to the staff system of notation, which has an alignment of notes showing duration and pitch. Various kinds of tablatures have been in use since the 14th century, when they were sometimes employed for keyboard music. In later periods, keyboard tablatures were common in most European countries, although different systems were in use simultaneously: the Germans favored letter-notation and the Spanish and Italian composers preferred figures.

Tablatures were indispensable for lute, vihuela, and guitar music. A six-line staff depicted the six courses or strings, finger positions being shown by letters or numbers. Some systems, especially German lute-tablature, were complex and cumbersome, but they served their purpose well. Tablatures also existed for other plucked instruments as well as the violin, lyra-viol, and certain wind instruments.   DENIS STEVENS

Bibliography: Apel, Willi, *The Notation of Polyphonic Music, 900-1600,* 2d ed. (1949).

Table Mountain

Table Mountain, 1,082 m (3,549 ft) high, lies south of Cape Town, South Africa. It is frequently shrouded by a cloud, "the Tablecloth," which is responsible for the heavy rainfall and luxuriant tropical growth on its flat summit. Antonio da Saldanha, who named it, was the first European to reach (1503) its summit.

table tennis

A table-tennis player (right) crouches in anticipation as his partner returns a shot during a doubles match. Coordination between partners is extremely important in doubles competition because the ball is returned alternately by each partner until a point is decided.

Table tennis, also known as Ping Pong, is a recreational and competitive game for singles or doubles competition. The object of the game is to hit a small ball over a net stretched across a table so that it hits the opposite side of the table. Points are scored when one player fails to return the ball over the net so that it bounces on the opponent's side. The ball is put into play with a serve, and each player has five consecutive turns serving.

A table-tennis table is 9 ft (2.7 m) long and 5 ft (1.5 m) wide, and 2.5 ft (76 cm) above the ground. The net is 6 in. (15.2 cm) high and stretches 6 ft (1.8 m) across the table so that it overlaps the edges 6 in. on each side. The table-tennis paddle may be any size, shape, or weight; the only restriction is on the thickness of the rubber-and-sponge striking surface. This may be no more than 2 mm (0.08 in) thick. Occasionally paddles are given a striking surface of pimpled rubber or sandpaper. The table-tennis ball has a diameter of 1.5 in. (3.8 cm) and should weigh 37–39 gr (2.4–2.5 g). The ball is made of celluloid (or a plastic material with similar characteristics) and has a white matte surface.

A game is to 21 points; if the score reaches a 20-point tie, then the first player to achieve a 2-point lead wins. In local competitions, a set is the best of three games; in international competitions, it is the best of five games.

Although it is a comparatively modern game, table tennis is

Table-tennis players use paddles to hit a small ball across a table divided by a fine mesh net. Analogous to that of a tennis court, the net extends beyond the side boundaries of the playing surface so that participants return wide-angle shots over the net.

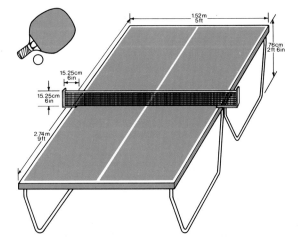

of obscure origin. The sound the ball makes in play led Parker Brothers to patent the name Ping Pong. The game enjoyed surges of popularity before and after World War I; the first world championships were held in London in 1926.

Bibliography: Barnes, Chester, *Table Tennis* (1977); Carr, Jack, *Advanced Table Tennis* (1979); Philip, David, and Cohen, Joel, *Table Tennis* (1975).

tabloids

Registered in 1884 as a trademark name for compressed drugs, the word *tabloid* began to be used in 1901 to identify a special type of newspaper. The tabloid was about 11 × 15 in. (28 × 63 cm) in page size (approximately half that of the standard newspaper), used a large number of pictures, presented brief news items in a sprightly style, ran features and some fiction, and blatantly appealed to the human interest in crime, sex, and disaster. Individually, each of these characteristics had been present much earlier. The *New York Evening Post* began in 1801 with a five-column, reduced-size format. The *New York Sun*, founded in 1833, combined a one-cent cost and criminal court coverage to attract mass circulation. The *Police Gazette*, particularly after it was taken over by Richard Fox in 1876, relied on illustrations and feature material. The *New York Daily Graphic* (1873–89), in fact, combined all these characteristics in a single publication, but came into existence before the term *tabloid* became current.

Credit for establishing the genre is usually given to Alfred Harmsworth (later Lord NORTHCLIFFE). In 1903 he founded the *London Daily Mirror*, which by 1914 had reached a circulation of 1 million and inspired several British imitators. In the United States the most successful and oldest surviving tabloid is the NEW YORK DAILY NEWS, started by Joseph Patterson in 1919. Its dramatic pictures and small size made it particularly popular among subway riders and helped boost its circulation to a 1947 peak of 2.4 million daily and 4.5 million on Sundays.

Some New York imitators of the *Daily News*, especially the *Evening Graphic* (1924–32) and the *Daily Mirror* (1924–63), placed such stress on the unusual and shocking that *tabloid* was often a synonym for *sensational;* however, most of the dailies using the compact format today differ from larger papers only in page size. Thus *tabloid* now refers more to format than to content; the format is used not only by dailies but also by many high school and college publications, religious and ethnic papers, and such specialized weeklies as *Variety* and the *Chronicle of Higher Education.*   WARREN G. BOVÉE

Bibliography: Bessie, Simon, *Jazz Journalism* (1938); Emery, Edwin, *The Press and America,* 3d ed. (1972).

taboo

Taboo is a powerful restriction or prohibition that regulates contacts between specific categories of individuals and things in particular circumstances. Taboos are backed by social sanctions or penalties. Some supernatural force is always invoked as authority for the sanction. Taboos reflect a society's understanding of its own order and that of the universe. They caution against contacts that might violate approved social behavior. There exists a nearly universal taboo against INCEST, and taboos concerning foods that are not to be eaten are common in all parts of the world. Other frequent subjects of taboo are menstrual blood and the dead.

The term *taboo* originated in POLYNESIA, where *tapu* (taboo) played a prominent part in the regulation of society. Among the New Zealand MAORI, taboos ranged from those intimately associated with spirit beings, such as the taboo concerning certain lizards believed to embody evil spirits, through those connected with the sanctity of chiefs, down to taboos placed on land or other possessions to ensure their treatment as the property of a particular individual or group.   CHRISTIAN CLERK

Bibliography: Browne, Ray B., *Forbidden Fruits* (1984); Douglas, Mary, *Purity and Danger* (1970); Frazer, J. G., *Taboo and the Powers of the Souls,* 3d ed. (1955); Freud, Sigmund, *Totem and Taboo,* trans. by Abraham A. Brill (1918; repr. 1960); Steiner, Franz, *Taboo* (1956; repr. 1967); Webster, Hutton, *Taboo: A Sociological Study* (1942; repr. 1973).

Tabor, Horace W. [tay'-bur]

Horace Warner Tabor, b. Holland, Vt., Nov. 26, 1830, d. Apr. 10, 1899, was a U.S. mining developer who made a fortune eventually worth $9 million from Colorado's Matchless Mine and other mining enterprises. Tabor first worked as a stonecutter and a farmer in Vermont. He joined (1859) the Pikes Peak gold rush, and opened a store in a Colorado mining area. There he grubstaked prospectors and became wealthy in 1878, when two men he had staked found a silver lode. He entered politics, becoming lieutenant governor of Colorado (1879–83). Tabor lost his fortune during the panic of 1893, and he became (1898) a postmaster in Denver. His widow, Elizabeth McCourt Tabor, known as Baby Doe, continued to live alone in a shack near the Matchless Mine, where she was found (1935) frozen to death. She is the subject of Douglas Moore's opera *The Ballad of Baby Doe* (1956).

Bibliography: Gandy, Lewis C., *The Tabors: A Footnote of Western History* (1934); Karsner, David, *Silver Dollar: The Story of the Tabors* (1932); Smith, Duane A., *Horace Tabor: His Life and Legend* (1973).

Tabor, Mount

Mount Tabor (Hebrew: Har Tavor) rises 588 m (1,929 ft) above the Plain of Esdraelon, 8 km (5 mi) east of Nazareth, in northern Israel. The stratified limestone mountain has been a landmark since ancient times. First referred to in the 13th century BC in Egyptian documents, it was frequently mentioned in the Old Testament. Christian tradition places the Transfiguration of Jesus there. A Franciscan church and a Greek Orthodox monastery are located on the slopes, which are popular with hikers.

Tabriz [tah-breez']

Tabriz, the capital of the province of East Azerbaijan, Iran, lies in the extreme northwest of the country, about 130 km (80 mi) south of the Soviet border. The population—852,296 (1982 est.)—is mostly Azerbaijani, although there is a Kurdish minority. Located at an altitude of about 1,370 m (4,490 ft) in an earthquake region, the city is said to have derived its name from the nearby hot springs. Famous for its carpets, Tabriz manufactures textiles, leather goods, soaps, paints, and dried fruits and nuts. A railroad connecting Tehran with the USSR passes through the city, which is also a highway junction. Landmarks include the 15th-century Blue Mosque and the citadel or Ark (actually the 14th-century mosque of Ali Shah). The University of Azarabadegan, founded in 1949, is located there.

Geology and geography have made Tabriz a victim of earthquakes (in 791, 858, 1041, 1721, and 1780) and of repeated conquests. Dating back to about the 3d century AD, the city was the capital of the Mongol khans in the 13th and early 14th centuries. In 1382, Tabriz was taken by Timur, the Turkic conqueror. Long disputed between the Ottoman and Persian empires, it became part of Persia in 1618, although the Turks occupied the city from 1721 to 1730, and the Russians from 1827 to 1828 and then from 1945 to 1946.   ARTHUR CAMPBELL TURNER

tacamahac [tak'-uh-muh-hak']

Native to the northernmost United States and Canada, tacamahac, *Populus balsamifera,* is a tall tree in the willow family, Salicaceae. The common name refers to the fragrant sticky resin exuded from its buds, similar to a substance from India used for incense and ointments. The wood is odorless, soft, light colored, and straight grained, making it indistinguishable from that of the other poplars. Tacamahac is used commercially for excelsior, plywood crates, and hidden parts of furniture.   JANE PHILPOTT

Tacca, Pietro [tahk'-kah]

The Mannerist sculptor Pietro Tacca, b. Sept. 6, 1577, d. Oct. 26, 1640, was the pupil of Giovanni da Bologna, whom he replaced in 1609 as sculptor to the Medici. His main works are the four bronze slaves at the foot of Bandini's statue of Ferdinand I de Medici at Livorno (1615–24); the grotesque fountain in the Piazza dell'Annunziata, Florence (1615–24); and the statues of Cosimo II and Ferdinand I de Medici (1627–34) for the Princes Chapel, Church of San Lorenzo, Florence. His style was conservative, but noteworthy for its virtuosity of execution, elegance, and ornamental complexity.

ROSA MARIA LETTS

Bibliography: Pope-Hennessy, John, *Italian High Renaissance and Baroque Sculpture* (1970); Wittkower, Rudolf, *Art and Architecture in Italy: 1600–1750,* rev. ed. (1973).

Taché, Sir Étienne Paschal   [tah-shay']

Sir Étienne Paschal Taché, b. Saint-Thomas, Lower Canada (now Montmagny, Quebec), Sept. 5, 1795, d. July 30, 1865, was a Canadian political leader. A War of 1812 veteran, he was a country doctor before being elected (1841) to the United Canada legislature. Appointed commissioner of public works in 1848, Taché was a member of the legislative council from then until 1864. He was copremier of Canada with Allan N. MacNab (1856) and John A. MacDonald (1856–57). In 1864, Taché, again copremier of a coalition government with Macdonald, presided over the Quebec Conference, which paved the way for confederation.

tachism: see ABSTRACT EXPRESSIONISM.

tachometer   [tak-ahm'-uh-tur]

A tachometer is an instrument that displays the speed of an engine (the angular rate at which the crankshaft is turning) in revolutions per minute (rpm), allowing the driver of an automobile to select the appropriate gear for a desired combination of road speed and engine speed. A tachometer dial's upper limit—called the redline—indicates the maximum speed at which the engine should be run. A tachometer is also useful in tuning an engine, because many engine parameters vary with varying rpm and should be set at a particular engine speed. Early tachometers were mechanically driven; modern ones are electric, obtaining their input from the vehicle's ignition system or an electronic sensor adjacent to the crankshaft.

DENNIS SIMANAITIS

See also: AUTOMOTIVE INSTRUMENTATION.

tachyon   [tak'-ee-ahn]

Named for a Greek word meaning "swift," a tachyon is a hypothetical particle, proposed independently by Gerald Feinberg and by George Sudarshan and coworkers, capable only of faster-than-light speeds. The tachyon theory is consistent with Einstein's theory of relativity. If tachyons exist, they would spontaneously emit light by a process similar to CHERENKOV RADIATION, even in a vacuum. Attempts to detect tachyons, by searching for suitable Cherenkov radiation and analyzing elementary-particle reactions that could give rise to tachyons, have yielded no evidence of them, and at present their existence is doubtful.

Bibliography: Feinberg, Gerald, "Particles that Go Faster than Light," *Scientific American,* February 1970.

Tacitus, Cornelius   [tas'-i-tuhs]

Cornelius Tacitus, AD c.56–c.115, a Roman senator and one of the greatest Roman historians, lived through the tyrannical rule of Domitian and the golden age of Trajan. He was praetor (88), consul (97), and governor of the province of Asia (c.112). His short monographs *Germany* (98) and *Dialogue on Orators* (between c.98 and 102) and the eulogy *Life of Agricola* (98) are important sources for knowledge about ancient Germany, Roman oratory, and Roman Britain. His two major works, the *Annals* and the *Histories,* cover the period from the death of Augustus (AD 14) to the death of Domitian (96). Today about one-third of the *Annals* is missing; the surviving four and one-half books of the *Histories* go only to the beginning (69–70) of Vespasian's reign and deal with the civil war after the death of Nero. In his succinct and pointed style, Tac-

itus contrasts the often imaginary liberty of the Roman republic and the tyranny of such emperors as Tiberius and Nero.

J. LINDERSKI

Bibliography: Chilver, G. E., *A Historical Commentary on Tacitus' Histories,* 4 vols. (1979–85); Dorey, T. A., ed., *Tacitus* (1969); Syme, Ronald, *Tacitus,* 2 vols. (1958; repr. 1980).

Tack, Augustus Vincent

Augustus Vincent Tack, b. Pittsburgh, Pa., Nov. 9, 1870, d. July 22, 1949, was an American painter of portraits, landscapes, and religious subjects. The figures in his freely interpreted religious scenes often have a wavering, flamelike character, as in the murals completed in 1928 for the governor's suite at the state capitol in Lincoln, Nebr.

ABRAHAM DAVIDSON

Tacna-Arica Dispute   [tahk'-nuh uh-ree'-kuh]

The Tacna-Arica Dispute was a long-standing quarrel between Peru and Chile over the ownership of two border provinces, Tacna and Arica. After Chile defeated Bolivia and Peru in the War of the Pacific (see PACIFIC, WAR OF THE), it controlled the southernmost portion of Peruvian territory. After the Treaty of Ancon, ratified in 1883, Peru and Chile agreed that a plebiscite would be held in Tacna and Arica after 10 years of Chilean occupation. The plebiscite never took place, however, because the two countries could not agree on terms. The resulting tension led to broken diplomatic relations in 1910. Finally, in 1928, Peru and Chile agreed to let U.S. secretary of state Frank Kellogg suggest an alternative to the plebiscite. The terms of the resulting agreement, signed June 3, 1929, assigned Tacna to Peru and Arica to Chile. In addition, Chile paid Peru an indemnity of $6 million and agreed to let Peru use Arica's port and transport facilities.

Bibliography: Dennis, William J., *Tacna and Arica: An Account of the Chile-Peru Boundary Dispute and of the Arbitrations by the United States* (1931; repr. 1967); Wilson, J. F., *The United States, Chile, and Peru in the Tacna and Arica Plebiscite* (1979).

Tacoma   [tuh-koh'-muh]

Tacoma is a city in west central Washington on Puget Sound where the Puyallup River enters Commencement Bay. The seat of Pierce County and the state's third largest city, Tacoma has a population of 158,501 (1980), with 485,643 persons in the metropolitan area. It is also a major seaport, with a fine natural harbor; a railroad terminus; and a major center for lumbering, forest products, and shipbuilding. Tacoma is linked to the Olympic Peninsula by the Tacoma Narrows Bridge (1950), one of the longest suspension bridges in the United States.

Although the site of Tacoma was settled in 1852, it was not until 1868 that Gen. Morton Matthew McCarver developed the settlement as Commencement City. It was later named Tacoma (Indian for "Mount Rainier"). Rapid growth followed the arrival of the Northern Pacific Railway in 1887.

tactics, military: see STRATEGY AND TACTICS, MILITARY.

Tadmor: see PALMYRA.

Tadzhik

The Tadzhik (Tajik), a people probably descended from the ancient Persians, are the oldest ethnic element in Central Asia, tracing their origins to 3000 BC. Speakers of Iranian variants of Indo-European languages, they were conquered by Arabs in the 7th century, Mongols in the 13th century, and Russians in the 19th century. In the 1980s they numbered 7,400,000, of whom 4,100,000 were in Afghanistan, 3,000,000 in the Tadzhik Soviet Socialist Republic, and 20,000 in Chinese Sinkiang (Xinjiang), working on family or collective farms. In physical type, the Tadzhik of Afghanistan are Mediterranean Caucasoid, but those of Soviet Central Asia and China appear more Mongoloid. Resulting genetic admixtures have yielded red or blond hair, blue or mixed eye colors, high cheekbones, and inner-eyelid skin folds.

Mountain farmers and herders, the Tadzhik are noted for their irrigated terraces, gristmills, and unirrigated grainfields. Bread, fish, fowl, nuts, fruits, rice, and dairy products are eaten. Tadzhik reputedly bake bread from almost anything, including peas and mulberries. In religion they are mostly Sunnite Muslim, but Shiite Muslim Tadzhik live in the Wakhan Corridor of Afghanistan. Although village of residence, lineage, and authority rest in the male line, women also play an important role. Few decisions are made without female advice, and veiling of women is uncommon. Also, it is rare for men to have multiple wives.   VICTOR L. MOTE

Bibliography: Dupree, Louis, *Afghanistan* (1973); Nove, Alec, and Newth, J. A., *The Soviet Middle East* (1967); Weekes, R. V., *Muslim Peoples: A World Ethnographic Survey* (1978); Wixman, Ronald, *The Peoples of the USSR* (1984).

Tadzhik Soviet Socialist Republic   [tuh-jik']

The Tadzhik Soviet Socialist Republic is one of the 15 constituent republics of the USSR. It is situated in Central Asia adjacent to Afghanistan and China. Tadzhikistan covers an area of 143,095 km^2 (55,251 mi^2) and has a population of 4,366,000 (1984 est.). The republic's capital is DUSHANBE.

Tadzhikistan is mountainous and encompasses the PAMIRS—the highest mountains in the USSR, including COMMUNISM PEAK. The climate varies with elevation from cold highlands to hot desert in the piedmont plains, where the population is concentrated.

The Tadzhik, who account for 56% of the population, are an Iranian-language group of Muslim religion, akin to the neighboring Afghans and to the Persians. They are traditionally cotton farmers, and 75% of the Tadzhik live in rural areas. Russians constitute 12% of the population and live almost entirely in cities. The second most populous city is Leninabad (1984 est. pop., 147,000). Other major cities are Kulyab and Kurgan-Tyube.

The Tadzhik republic is one of the USSR's uranium producers, with mines at Taboshar and processing at Chkalovsk near Leninabad. Cheap electric power generated by the Nurek hydroelectric station on the Vakhsh River supports an aluminum industry at Tursunzade (formerly Regar) and a chemical industry, producing chlorine and alkalis, at Yavan. The republic is also a major cotton-growing area, producing 10% of the nation's crop.

The region that is now Tadzhikistan belonged to the emir of Bukhara before passing to Russian control in the 1880s. After the assumption of power by the Soviets, it was constituted as an autonomous republic in 1924 and was raised to union republic status in 1929. Tadzhikistan encompasses a subsidiary ethnic area, the Gorno-Badakhshan Autonomous Oblast, with an area of about 63,700 km^2 (24,600 mi^2) and a population of 140,000 (1983 est.) mainly composed of Tadzhik mountain tribes.   THEODORE SHABAD

Taegu   [te'-goo]

Taegu (1983 est. pop., 1,958,800), the third largest city of South Korea, lies about 250 km (155 mi) southeast of Seoul. One of the country's main market cities and historically the economic and cultural center of southeastern Korea, Taegu manufactures textiles and metal products. Kyungpook National University (1946) and Yeungnam University (1967) are located there. During the Yi dynasty (1392–1910) Taegu was an administrative city, and in 1895 it became the provincial capital.

Taejon   [ty-juhn']

Taejon, a city in South Korea, lies about 140 km (90 mi) southwest of Seoul. The population is 800,000 (1983 est.). A rail junction since the early 20th century, the city is a rice-milling center and produces textiles, chemicals, and machinery. It served as the nation's temporary capital during the Korean War.

taffeta

Taffeta is a smooth and usually lustrous fabric made of silk or synthetic fibers. The fabric usually has ribs, made by using heavier or bulkier yarns for the filling, or weft. It was once impregnated with metallic salts to give it a characteristic stiffness. The term *taffeta*, from the Persian *taftah* meaning "to shine" or "to twist," originally described a silk fabric that was used as a luxurious cloth for women's wear. Moiré is taffeta with a watermarked finish.   ISABEL B. WINGATE

Taft, Lorado

Lorado Taft, b. Elmwood, Ill., Apr. 29, 1860, d. Oct. 30, 1931, was an American sculptor and writer who, after studying in Paris, established a studio in Chicago (1886) and also began lecturing and writing to defend sculpture against modernism. Yet he simplified nature to stress formal masses in the gigantic *Columbus* flanked by kneeling figures for his neo-Renaissance fountain (1912) in front of the railroad station in Washington, D.C. An enveloping robe curtailing literal details monumentalizes his enormous cast concrete *Time* (1922) on the fountain in Chicago's Washington Park. Taft's *History of American Sculpture* (1903) was the first to bring factual information and penetrating insights to the subject.   JOAN C. SIEGFRIED

Bibliography: Taft, Ada, *Lorado Taft: Sculptor and Citizen* (1946).

Taft, Robert A.

Sen. Robert A. Taft was known as "Mr. Republican" for his advocacy of conservative policies, including the Taft-Hartley Labor Relations Act (1947). His isolationist stance on foreign affairs contributed to his defeats in seeking the party nomination for president in 1940, 1948, and 1952.

Robert Alphonso Taft, b. Cincinnati, Ohio, Sept. 8, 1889, d. July 31, 1953, a son of President William Howard Taft, was a leader of the conservative Midwestern wing of the Republican party. After World War I, during which he had worked on European relief programs, he practiced law in Cincinnati and moved into Republican politics. He served in the Ohio house of representatives (1921–26), acting as speaker in 1926, and was a member of the state senate (1931–32). A vehement critic of Franklin Delano Roosevelt and New Deal welfare legislation, Taft won election to the U.S. Senate in 1938. Reelected in 1944 and 1950, he became known as "Mr. Republican."

An isolationist, Taft argued against most forms of U.S. diplomatic involvement outside the Western Hemisphere. He was a leading opponent of U.S. intervention in World War II before Pearl Harbor was attacked. During the postwar years he favored the containment of Soviet expansionism but opposed most of Harry S. Truman's cold-war measures as too costly and dangerous. Taft supported limited federal programs for health insurance, housing assistance, and aid to education and was cosponsor of the Taft-Hartley Act (1947; see LABOR-MANAGEMENT RELATIONS ACT), which placed some restrictions on labor unions. A candidate for the Republican presidential nomination in 1940, 1948, and 1952, he lost each time to a representative of northeastern, moderate, internationalist Republicans. He wrote *A Foreign Policy for Americans* (1951).

ALONZO L. HAMBY

Bibliography: Kirk, Russell, and McClellan, James, *The Political Principles of Robert A. Taft* (1967); Patterson, James T., *Mr. Republican: A Biography of Robert A. Taft* (1972); White, W. S., *The Taft Story* (1954).

Taft, William Howard

William Howard Taft was the 27th president (1909–13) of the United States and the nation's 10th chief justice (1921–30). His presidency was marked by controversy and turmoil amid a growing national reform movement, one that made him a bitter opponent of his old friend Theodore Roosevelt.

Early Life and Career. Taft was born in Cincinnati, Ohio, on Sept. 15, 1857. His family traced its origins to 17th-century Massachusetts. He was educated at Yale University, where he graduated (1878) second in his class, and at the Cincinnati Law School. In 1886 he married Helen W. Herron, a woman from Cincinnati who influenced his career considerably.

After practicing law and dabbling in Republican politics in Cincinnati, Taft was appointed (1887) to the Ohio Superior Court and won a 5-year term the next year. President Benjamin Harrison named him solicitor general in 1890. From 1892 to 1900 he served as a federal circuit judge of the newly created Sixth Circuit Court.

In 1900, Taft agreed—at the behest of President William McKinley—to head a commission to end U.S. military rule in the Philippines, which had been ceded to the United States after the Spanish-American War. In this capacity, and as civil governor (1901–04) of the islands, he headed an efficient and humane administration. He subordinated military to civil command, instituted land reform, sponsored a road-construction program, and, in general, prepared the Filipinos for self-government.

Taft's work in the Philippines resulted in his elevation (1904) to secretary of war in President Theodore Roosevelt's cabinet. The two became fast friends and confidants; by 1906, Roosevelt had chosen Taft as his successor. Reluctant at first, Taft yielded to pressure from his family and plunged headlong into the race. With Roosevelt's backing Taft won the Republican presidential nomination in 1908 and went on to defeat Democrat William Jennings Bryan in the fall election.

Presidency. Taft had been chosen by Roosevelt essentially to carry on Roosevelt's progressive policies. In a certain sense he did: he instituted and completed more antitrust cases than his "trust-busting" predecessor; he supported the proposed income-tax amendment to the U.S. Constitution; he helped enact a system of postal savings and a measure, the Mann-Elkins Bill, to regulate the railroads more effectively; and he backed several social reforms, including an employer's liability law for work done on government jobs and a mandatory 8-hour day in federal employment. The Taft administration was better known, however, for its troubles and failures—owing, in part, to Taft's limitations as a political leader and to the burgeoning progressive movement that threatened to fracture the Republican party. As the rift widened between the Eastern conservatives and the Midwestern progressives (sometimes called insurgents), Taft proved unable to mediate differences and find compromise solutions. Conservative by nature he drifted ever closer to the old guard.

Taft's troubles began with tariff reform, which he had promised in 1908. He called Congress into special session in 1909 and urged a reduction in duties. In the ensuing Senate battle, the House's moderate Payne Bill was altered so as to increase rates on manufactured goods, thus favoring the industrial Northeast and angering Midwestern progressives. Taft's clumsy intervention helped to reduce tariff levels once again, but hardly to the satisfaction of the progressives. Taft signed into law the Payne-Aldrich Tariff, still deemed a protectionist measure, acclaiming it a "really good bill."

Taft clashed with the progressives on other matters. He gave them the impression that he would support their rebellion against Speaker of the House Joseph Gurney CANNON but then abandoned them. He and the insurgents started out in

WILLIAM HOWARD TAFT
27th President of the United States (1909–13)

Born: Sept. 15, 1857, Cincinnati, Ohio
Education: Yale College (graduated 1878); Cincinnati Law School (LLB 1880)
Profession: Lawyer, Public Official
Religious Affiliation: Unitarian
Marriage: June 19, 1886, to Helen Herron (1861–1943)
Children: Robert Alphonso Taft (1889–1953); Helen Herron Taft (1891–   ); Charles Phelps Taft (1897–   )
Political Affiliation: Republican
Writings: *The Anti-Trust and the Supreme Court* (1914); *The United States and Peace* (1914); *Our Chief Magistrate and His Powers* (1916)
Died: Mar. 8, 1930, Washington, D.C.
Buried: Arlington National Cemetery, Arlington, Va.

Vice-President and Cabinet Members
Vice-President: James S. Sherman (1909–12)
Secretary of State: Philander C. Knox
Secretary of the Treasury: Franklin MacVeagh
Secretary of War: Jacob M. Dickinson (1909–11); Henry L. Stimson (1911–13)
Attorney General: George W. Wickersham
Postmaster General: Frank H. Hitchcock
Secretary of the Navy: George von L. Meyer
Secretary of the Interior: Richard A. Ballinger (1909–11); Walter Lowrie Fisher (1911–13)
Secretary of Agriculture: James Wilson
Secretary of Commerce and Labor: Charles Nagel

basic agreement on railroad legislation but wound up differing on details. Most important, they came to loggerheads on conservation policy. Chief Forester Gifford PINCHOT, a conservationist in the Roosevelt camp, accused Secretary of the Interior Richard A. BALLINGER of having turned over rich coal deposits in Alaska to a syndicate. A congressional investigation followed; Ballinger was exonerated, and Taft fired Pinchot.

Taft's battles with the progressives gradually drew Roosevelt into open opposition to the administration. In early 1912, Roosevelt, who had become more radical, decided to challenge Taft for the Republican presidential nomination. Although Roosevelt won most of the ensuing state primaries, Taft controlled the party machinery and defeated his former friend in the Chicago national convention. Roosevelt's creation of the PROGRESSIVE PARTY (or Bull Moose party) divided the Republican vote and resulted in the election of Democrat Woodrow Wilson. Taft finished a poor third.

Later Life. After his stormy presidency Taft settled into a professorship at the Yale Law School and served as cochairman of the National War Labor Board during World War I. In 1921, President Warren Harding appointed him chief justice of the United States. Although he was an able administrator of the Supreme Court, Taft never became a judicial giant. His essential conservatism was reflected in several of his opinions, although it was balanced by his more liberal postures on cases dealing with the minimum wage and interstate commerce. Serious illness forced him to leave the bench in early 1930; he died Mar. 8, 1930.   ROBERT F. WESSER

Bibliography: Anderson, Donald F., *William Howard Taft: A Conservative's Conception of the Presidency* (1973); Anderson, Judith I., *William Howard Taft: An Intimate History* (1981); Coletta, Paolo E., *Presidency of William Howard Taft* (1973); Mason, A. T., *William Howard Taft: Chief Justice* (1965; repr. 1983); Pringle, Henry F., *The Life and Times of William Howard Taft*, 2 vols. (1939).

Taft-Hartley Act: see LABOR-MANAGEMENT RELATIONS ACT.

Tagalog language: see MALAYO-POLYNESIAN LANGUAGES.

Taganrog   [tuh-guhn-rawk']

The city of Taganrog is located in Rostov oblast in the Russian republic of the USSR. The city has a population of 289,000 (1985 est.). Taganrog lies on the north shore of the Sea of Azov. Founded by Peter I in 1698 as a naval base, Taganrog developed under the tsars as a grain-shipping port and, after the 1890s, as a manufacturing center. During the Soviet period, Taganrog has been overshadowed by nearby Rostov-on-Don. The playwright Anton Chekhov was born in Taganrog.
                                        THEODORE SHABAD

Taglioni   (family)   [tah-lee-oh'-nee]

The Taglionis were a family of notable dancers and choreographers who flourished in the 19th century. A native of Italy, **Filippo Taglioni**, b. Nov. 5, 1777, d. Feb. 11, 1871, performed and staged ballets in many of the dance capitals of the Continent, Scandinavia, and Russia. He was a key figure in shaping the style of 19th-century romantic ballet, in which a light, ethereal quality in the technique and an atmosphere of spirituality is contrasted with earthier or exotic folk material, epitomized in his *La Sylphide* (1832). The airiness and delicacy of the technique and the chaste mood of the style he formed were in part created in conjunction with the virtues (and faults) of his daughter, **Marie Taglioni**, b. Apr. 23, 1804, d. Apr. 22, 1884, who became the most renowned ballerina of the romantic period, rivaled only by Fanny ELSSLER. He turned her frail body, with its disproportionately long limbs, and her lack of overt sensual appeal into a personal idiom and created ballets to enhance it. The title role of *La Sylphide* became Marie Taglioni's signature. The image it created of an idealized, unearthly being persists in ballet even today. Taglioni was a potent legend in her own time, feted in international dance capitals in the 1830s and '40s. In the late 1850s she emerged from retirement to teach at the Paris Opéra.

Paul Taglioni, b. Jan. 12, 1808, d. Jan. 6, 1888, the son of Filippo and brother of Marie Taglioni, was in his time a well-known dancer and choreographer, working primarily in London and Berlin. His daughter **Marie Paul Taglioni**, b. Oct. 27, 1833, d. Aug. 27, 1891, often confused with her more cele-

Marie Taglioni and her brother, Paul, danced together frequently in La Sylphide, *created for Marie by her father, Filippo Taglioni, in 1832.* La Sylphide, *the epitome of the romantic ballet, made her one of the great ballerinas of all time; it is still in the repertoires of major ballet companies.*

brated aunt, performed throughout Europe and was prima ballerina (1848–65) of the Berlin State Opera.

Salvatore Taglioni, 1790–1868, the brother of Filippo Taglioni, was for half a century principal dancer and ballet master at Naples, where he founded a school and staged more than 200 ballets, including his own version of *La Sylphide*. His daughter, **Louise Taglioni**, 1823–93, performed (1848–57) as a principal dancer at the Paris Opéra and appeared in the United States in 1855.   TOBI TOBIAS

Bibliography: Guest, Ivor, *The Romantic Ballet in England* (1954) and *The Romantic Ballet in Paris* (1966); Migel, Parmenia, *The Ballerinas, from the Court of Louis XIV to Pavlova* (1972).

Tagore, Sir Rabindranath   [tuh-gohr', ruh-bin'-druh-naht]

Sir Rabindranath Tagore, a major Indian poet and playwright, was awarded the Nobel Prize for literature in 1913 for his poetic work Gitanjali *(Song Offerings, 1910). Tagor wrote novels, stories, and songs as well as poems and plays dealing with philosophical and political subjects. His efforts to combine Eastern and Western traditions brought him international acclaim.*

The Indian poet and author Rabindranath Tagore, b. Calcutta, May 7, 1861, d. Aug. 7, 1941, won the Nobel Prize for literature in 1913 for his most famous collection, *Song Offerings* (1910; Eng. trans., 1912). A prolific writer (3,000 poems, 2,000 songs, 8 novels, 40 volumes of essays and short stories, 50 plays), he drew inspiration both from his native Bengal and from English literary tradition. His major theme was humanity's search for God and truth.

From 1878 to 1880 he studied law in England, and in 1890, having returned to India, took charge of his father's estates, where he saw firsthand the suffering and backwardness of India's rural poor and grew to love the serenity of the Indian countryside. Devoting himself to the agricultural development of the land and the health and education of the people, he founded, in 1901, Santiniketan ("Abode of Peace"), which became an international university with a wide-ranging curriculum. He was knighted in 1915, an honor he renounced 4 years later as a protest against British actions in the Punjab.

In 1890, Tagore published a volume of poetry, *Mānaśi* (The Mind's Embodiment), which foreshadowed the lyricism, eloquence, and grandeur of *Song Offerings* and *A Flight of Swans* (1914; Eng. trans., 1955). His profound symbolism, abetted by the free-flowing nature of his verse, create a universe of haunting beauty that expresses God's infinite love and humanity's deep compassion for all things beautiful.

Tagore's novels, particularly *Gora* (1910; Eng. trans., 1924), and short stories have strong underlying philosophical themes. The plays—notably *Sacrifice* (1890; Eng. trans., 1917), *The King of the Dark Chamber* (1910; Eng. trans., 1914), *Chitra* (1892; Eng. trans., 1913), and *Post Office* (1912; Eng. trans., 1914)—although allegorical in form and political in content, remain rich in characterization, sentiment, and spectacle. Tagore was also an accomplished composer, musician, and singer, as well as a painter and an actor. Later in life he wrote a number of experimental dance dramas, the best of which, *Shyama* (1939), deals with social and religious issues.

GAUTAM DASGUPTA

Bibliography: Hay, Stephen N., *Asian Ideas of East and West: Tagore and His Critics in Japan, China, and India* (1970); Lago, Mary M., *Rabindranath Tagore* (1976); Thompson, Edward J., *Rabindranath Tagore: Life and Work* (1974).

Tagus River [tay'-guhs]

The Tagus River, 1,000 km (625 mi) in length and with a drainage basin of 86,600 km² (33,400 mi²), is the longest river in the Iberian Peninsula. Rising at an elevation of 1,600 m (5,250 ft) in the Sierra de Albarracín about 130 km (80 mi) east of Madrid, the Tagus flows southwest past Toledo through mountainous Spanish terrain, forms the boundary between Spain and Portugal for about 50 km (30 mi), then enters Portugal, flowing west to Abrantes and finally southwest past Santarém to its estuary, Lisbon Bay, which in turn is linked to the Atlantic Ocean by a 13–km (8–mi) channel. In the vicinity of Santarém, annual spring floods deposit a fertile silt. The river's 59 tributaries include the Jamara, Tajuña, Alberche, Alagón, Tiétar, Guadiela, and Zêzere. Both the Tagus and its tributaries provide hydroelectric power and water for irrigation. Although navigable by small vessels from Lisbon to Abrantes, the Tagus does not allow commercial navigation beyond Santarém.

Taha Husayn [tah'-hah hoo-syn']

A dominant personality in politics, education, and literature in modern Egypt, Taha Husayn, b. Nov. 14, 1889, d. Oct. 28, 1973, was, though blind from youth, a distinguished writer and scholar. Because of his outspoken views on social and cultural matters, his career was rarely free of controversy. A prolific writer, he is best known for his autobiography and literary criticism, although he wrote a number of novels.

R. C. OSTLE

Bibliography: Cachia, P. J., *Taha Husayn* (1956).

Tahiti

Tahiti, the largest and most important of the Windward group of the SOCIETY ISLANDS, lies in the central South Pacific about 5,600 km (3,500 mi) east of Australia. With its capital at PAPEETE, and having an area of 1,041 km² (402 mi²) and a population of 107,000 (1983 est.), the island constitutes part of the overseas territory of FRENCH POLYNESIA. Two volcanic cones, Orohena (2,237 m/7,339 ft) and Roniu (1,332 m/4,369 ft), connected by the Isthmus of Taravao, give Tahiti a rugged landscape dissected by short, swift streams. Average annual rainfall varies from 1,750 mm (70 in) to more than 2,500 mm (100 in), but mean temperatures of 24° to 29° C (75° to 84° F) attract thousands of tourists every year. The island's exports include coconuts, sugarcane, vanilla, and coffee.

The first European to discover (1767) Tahiti, English navigator Samuel Wallis, was followed by James Cook (1769, 1773, 1777) and William Bligh (1786), commander of HMS *Bounty*. English missionaries began to convert the indigenous POLYNE-

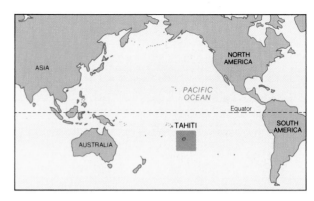

SIANS to Protestantism in 1797, but Louis Antoine de Bougainville had claimed the island for France in 1768, and during the early 19th century French missionaries won most inhabitants over to Catholicism. France established a protectorate in 1843 and annexed Tahiti in 1880. Paul Gauguin painted Tahitian landscapes, and Robert Louis Stevenson wrote about the island.

GARY A. KLEE

Bibliography: Putigny, Bob, *Tahiti and Its Islands*, 2d ed. (1976).

Tahltan bear dog

The Tahltan bear dog was developed by the Tahltan Indians of southwestern Canada. Its origins are unknown, but this little beagle-sized dog, now almost extinct, was used by the Tahltans in the hunting of grizzly bear, lynx, and other large or fierce game. When hunting, the dogs were carried in sacks until the game was sighted; then they were released, usually in pairs, to harass, distract, and hold the game until the hunters could approach close enough to make the kill. The Tahltan bear dog, as recognized by the Canadian Kennel Club, ranges from 30 to 40 cm (12 to 16 in) high at the shoulders and may be between 7 and 10 kg (16 to 22 lb) in weight. It has a moderately wide head, a pointed muzzle, and large, erect, batlike ears. Its tail is unique: it is between 13 and 20 cm (5 to 8 in) long, may be carried erect, or nearly so, and is equally thick from its base to its characteristically bushy tip. The Tahltan bear dog's double coat is dense and coarse and is usually black or blue gray, at least on the head, with varying amounts of white.

EDWIN E. ROSENBLUM

Tahoe, Lake [tah'-hoh]

Lake Tahoe, located on the border of California and Nevada at the eastern edge of the SIERRA NEVADA range, was named for the Washo Indian word meaning "lake." A freshwater body in a deep faulted trough, Lake Tahoe has an area of about 500 km² (195 mi²). Although its surface is 1,900 m (6,200 ft) above sea level, the lake's great depth of 500 m (1,600 ft) prevents it from freezing. Temperatures average about 21° C (70° F) in July and −4° C (24° F) in January. More than 30 mountain streams feed Lake Tahoe. The Truckee River drains the lake to the northwest into Pyramid Lake in Nevada and irrigates land around Carson City. Noted for the clarity of its waters and the beauty of its location, Lake Tahoe has become the focus of a popular year-round resort. The tourist towns of Chambers Lodge and Tahoe City are located on the lake's western shores.

Lake Tahoe was discovered in 1844 by the U.S. soldier-explorer John C. Frémont while he was conducting a government surveying assignment. Tahoe National Forest, near the lake, was the site of the 1960 Winter Olympic Games.

tahr [tawr]

A goatlike mammal in the genus *Hemitragus*, family Bovidae, the tahr is found in mountain forests of India, Nepal, and Oman. Standing about 1 m (40 in) at the shoulder, tahrs are about 1 m long, weigh up to 100 kg (220 lb), and typically have short, flattened horns that curve backwards. The brown-

The Himalayan tahr, H. jemlahicus, is native to mountainous areas in southern Asia from Kashmir to Sikkim. Related to the goat and the sheep, it often lives in groups of 30 to 40 animals.

ish hair is often shaggy, and the male Himalayan tahr, *H. jemlahicus,* bears a capelike mane hanging to the knees. Herds roam in search of any plant matter.   EVERETT SENTMAN

t'ai chi chuan: see MARTIAL ARTS.

Tai Chin   (Dai Jin)   [dy jin]

Tai Chin, 1388–1462, was a Chinese painter who founded the Che school of ink painting, which he established (after 1425) in his native Chekiang province. In works such as the *Fisherman's Scroll* (Freer Gallery, Washington, D.C.), he preserved faithfully the Ma-Hsia mode of landscape painting. Tai was often condemned by his rivals for his alleged professionalism, and his artistic achievements were belittled by Wu school painters.   LOUISA SHEN TING

Bibliography: Cahill, James, *Parting at the Shore: Chinese Painting of the Early and Middle Ming Dynasty, 1368–1580* (1978); Sirén, Osvald, *Chinese Painting: Leading Masters and Principles,* vol. 4 (1958).

T'ai-yüan   (Taiyuan)   [ty-yoo-ahn]

T'ai-yüan, the capital of Shansi (Shanxi) Province in northern China, has a population of 1,320,000 (1983 est.). Located on the Fen River, a tributary of the Hwang Ho (Huanghe), T'ai-yüan is surrounded by a rich coal- and iron-mining area. It is a great industrial city with a variety of heavy industries. Several institutions of higher learning are located there. The center of the ancient state of Chao (Zhao), T'ai-yüan was conquered by the Ch'in (Jin) in the 3d century BC. It was ruled by the warlord Yen Hsi-shan (Yan Xishan) from 1912 until the Communist takeover in 1948.

Taiga   [ty'-guh]

Ikeno Taiga, 1723–76, was a prolific painter of the Nanga school, a Japanese style derived from the Chinese school of landscape art. Taiga transformed techniques learned from Chinese painting manuals into animated, decorative landscapes notable for their wit and conceptual daring. Early in his career he did finger painting, a Chinese technique he learned from Yanagisawa Kien, a Nanga pioneer. He was also a skilled calligrapher.   BARBARA BRENNAN FORD

Bibliography: Yonezawa, Yoshio, and Yoshizawa, Chu, *Japanese Painting in the Literati Style,* trans. by B. I. Monroe (1974).

taiga climate

The taiga climate is a cold forest climate of subarctic latitudes in the Northern Hemisphere. Also known as the subarctic or boreal forest climate, it extends in a broad zone from western Alaska across Canada to Newfoundland in North America, and from northern Norway to the Kamchatka Peninsula in Eurasia. The forests typically consist of hardy trees such as spruce, pine, larch, birch, and aspen.

The influences of high latitude and continental air masses dominate the taiga climate for most of the year, producing large annual ranges of temperature and meager precipitation. Average July temperatures reach 10° C (50° F) in contrast to January averages as low as −40° C (−40° F) at some interior locations. Extreme minimums of −68° C (−90° F) at Verkhoyansk in eastern Siberia and −63° C (−81° F) at Snag in the Yukon Territory have been recorded. The subsoil remains frozen over large areas well into the summer season despite the high sun angle and long days.

Annual precipitation amounts vary from more than 1,000 mm (40 in) on the west coast of Norway, where the maximum falls in winter, to less than 200 mm (8 in) in northwestern Canada and eastern Siberia, which have summer maximums. A large proportion of winter precipitation falls as snow.
    HOWARD J. CRITCHFIELD

Bibliography: Trewartha, G., *An Introduction to Climate,* 5th ed. (1980).

tailorbird

The several species of tailorbirds comprise one or two genera in the Old World warbler subfamily, Sylviinae, family Muscicapidae. Found in southeast Asia and the Philippines, they are so named because they use their sharp, slender bills to pierce holes in the edges of large green leaves and to draw plant fibers through the holes, thus "sewing" a cone-shaped container to serve as a nest. They are usually from 10 to 15 cm (4 to 6 in) long and have olive green backs, reddish crowns, and grayish breasts. Tailorbirds feed on insects.

Taine, Hippolyte Adolphe   [ten]

The French historian and literary critic Hippolyte Adolphe Taine, b. Apr. 21, 1828, d. Mar. 5, 1893, was identified with POSITIVISM, an all-embracing philosophy that sought to apply the scientific method to such speculative fields as literary criticism, history, and religion. Taine first devoted himself to literature, writing several perceptive studies—of Jean de La Fontaine's fables, Livy, and a number of French philosophers. His mature work first appeared in 1863–64 in his four-volume *History of English Literature* (Eng. trans., 1871). Its introduction briefly sets forth Taine's philosophy and explains his method, which is primarily historical.

The defeat of France in the Franco-Prussian War (1870–71) challenged Taine's historical talents and forced him to reexamine the history of his country. His controversial analysis, which traced France's weakness to the divisive effects of the French Revolution, was published in six volumes as *The Origins of Contemporary France* (1876–93; Eng. trans., 1876–94). In 1878, Taine's stature as a writer and historian was recognized by his being elected to the Académie Française.
    JOEL COLTON

Bibliography: Gooch, G. P., *History and Historians in the Nineteenth Century,* 2d ed. (1952); Kahn, S. J., *Science and Aesthetic Judgment: A Study in Taine's Critical Method* (1953); Weinstein, Leo, *Hippolyte Taine* (1972).

Taipei   (Taibei)   [ty-pay']

Taipei is the capital, largest city, and educational, commercial, and industrial center of Taiwan. The city is situated on the east bank of the Tanshui River in northern Taiwan. Surrounded by mountains, it is located 24 km (15 mi) from the coast. The city of Chilung, a part of Taipei's metropolitan area, is Taipei's port. The metropolitan area covers 275 km² (105 mi²) and has a population of 5,050,000 (1981 est.). The city proper has a population of 2,483,900 (1985 est.). Taipei lies in the subtropical climate region. The annual average temperature is 19° C (67° F), and monthly averages vary between 28° C (83° F) in July and 14° C (58° F) in January. The annual average rainfall amounts to 2,108 mm (83 in), with most occurring during the summer months.

In the early 1980s two-fifths of the population were mainland-born Chinese who had migrated to Taiwan after the Communist takeover of China in 1949. Significant Buddhist, Taoist, and Christian communities exist. Major manufacturing industries include textiles and clothing, machinery, ships, transportation equipment, and handicraft items. The National Taiwan University (1928) is located there. The National Palace Museum houses an important collection of Chinese art.

The city, founded in the early 18th century, soon began to gain prominence as a market town. By the 19th century it had become an important center for overseas trade, and in 1891 it was officially designated the capital of Taiwan. Under Japanese control from 1895 to 1945, Taipei was renamed Taihoku. The city suffered heavy Allied bombing during World War II. It became the capital of the Republic of China in 1949, and in 1967 gained provincial status.   RICHARD ULACK

Taiping Rebellion   [ty-ping']

The Taiping Rebellion (1850–64), a radical Chinese revolution, cost about 20 million lives and permanently weakened the CH'ING (Qing; Manchu) dynasty. Its leader, Hung Hsiuch'üan (Hong Xiuchuan), who had come under Christian influence, experienced religious visions and vowed to overthrow the Ch'ing. After sweeping through southeastern China the rebels, ultimately one million strong, took Nanking (Nanjing) in 1853 and made it the capital of their Taiping (Great Peace) kingdom. This kingdom, although founded upon ideals of radical reform (puritanical moral precepts, primitive communism through equal distribution of land, full equality for women, and economic modernization), was weakened by leadership rivalries. Regional armies led by TSENG KUO-FAN (Zeng Guofan) and LI HUNG-CHANG (Li Hongzhang) and a Western-trained force led by Charles George GORDON gradually overcame the rebels, and Nanking fell in 1864.

Bibliography: Clarke, P., and Gregory, J. S., eds., *Western Reports on the Taiping* (1982); Michael, Franz, and Chang, Chung-li, *The Taiping Rebellion*, 3 vols. (1966–71); Teng, Ssu-yu, *New Light on the History of the Taiping Rebellion* (1950; repr. 1966).

Taïrov, Aleksandr Yakovlevich   [tah-ee'-ruhf]

The Russian producer and director Aleksandr Yakovlevich Taïrov, b. June 24 (N.S.), 1885, d. Sept. 25, 1950, founded the avant-garde Kamerny Theater in Moscow in 1914. He was, with Vsevolod Meyerhold and Eugene Vakhtangov, one of the great directors in the postrevolutionary Soviet theater. Opposing both naturalism and theatricalism in *Notes of a Director* (1921; Eng. trans., 1969), Taïrov proclaimed the theater to be its own art form.   MARJORIE L. HOOVER

Taiwan   [ty-wahn']

Taiwan, formerly also known as Formosa, is the main island of the Republic of China (Nationalist China). Located 185 km (115 mi) off the southeast coast of mainland China, it was a colony of Japan after 1895 and returned to Chinese sovereignty in 1945. In 1949 it became the last refuge for the government of the Republic of China under CHIANG KAI-SHEK and the KUOMINTANG (Nationalist party) when Communists took over mainland China and proclaimed the People's Republic of China. Both Nationalist and Communist China claim that Taiwan is a province of China and seek its reunification, on different terms, with the mainland. As presently constituted, the Republic of China includes the island of Taiwan, 15 nearby islands that are part of the Taiwan group, 64 small islands in the Pescadores (Penghu Islands), and the strategically important islands of QUEMOY and Ma-tsu near the mainland coast. Taiwan was modernized during the period of Japanese control and since 1949 has developed one of the world's fastest-growing industrial and export-oriented economies.

LAND AND RESOURCES
The island of Taiwan is about one-third the size of Ohio and has a north-south extent of about 400 km (245 mi) and an east-west extent of 145 km (90 mi). Two-thirds of the land is mountainous, and only one-third is lowland suitable for agricultural and industrial uses. The mountains rise abruptly along the east coast, reaching elevations of more than 3,050 m (10,000 ft) at more than 60 peaks. Hsin-kao, the highest peak on Taiwan, rises to 3,997 m (13,113 ft).

The climate is of the subtropical monsoon type and marked by seasonal wind changes. In winter, cold, dry winds, moist-

REPUBLIC OF CHINA (TAIWAN)

LAND. Area: 36,002 km² (13,900 mi²). Capital and largest city: Taipei (1986 est. pop., 2,507,620).
PEOPLE. Population (1988 est.): 19,800,000; density: 550 persons per km² (1,424 per mi²). Distribution (1988 est.): 67% urban, 33% rural. Annual growth (1979–86): 1.2%. Official language: Mandarin Chinese. Major religions: Taoism, Buddhism, Christianity.
EDUCATION AND HEALTH. Literacy (1985): 95% of adult population. Universities (1986): 16. Hospital beds (1987): 82,353. Physicians (1987): 17,641. Life expectancy (1985): women—75.8; men—70.8. Infant mortality (1987): 8.9 per 1,000 live births.
ECONOMY. GNP (1986): $73.25 billion; $3,468 per capita. Labor distribution (1987): commerce and services—35%; manufacturing—34%; agriculture and fishing—17%; construction—7%. Foreign trade (1987 est.): imports—$33.19 billion; exports—$52.04 billion; principal trade partners—United States, Japan, Hong Kong, West Germany, Canada. Currency: 1 new Taiwan dollar = 100 cents.
GOVERNMENT. Type: republic. Legislature: National Assembly. Political subdivisions: 16 counties, 2 special municipalities, 5 municipalities.
COMMUNICATIONS. Railroads (1986): 4,800 km (2,983 mi) total. Roads (1985): 19,676 km (12,226 mi) total. Major ports: 5. Major airfields: 2.

ened somewhat as they cross the East China Sea, blow out from Siberia toward Taiwan. In summer, hot, moist winds reach the island from the south and bring heavy rain. Rainfall is abundant and averages 2,590 mm (102 in) annually. Temperatures average 15° C (59° F) in winter (December to March) and 30° C (86° F) in summer (June to September). Typhoons occur at least once a year.

The natural resources of the island are limited. Approximately 70% of the land is unsuitable for farming, and the 25% used for agriculture is concentrated on the alluvial western plains and terraced hillsides. Forests cover about 55% of Taiwan but are mostly inaccessible for commercial development. Numerous rivers are harnessed for hydroelectric power, but such power resources are unable to meet the nation's fast-growing power needs. Principal minerals include small deposits of coal, petroleum, and natural gas; salt produced from seawater; and gold, copper, sulfur, marble, and limestone.

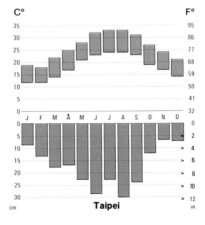

Bars indicate monthly ranges of temperatures (red) and precipitation (blue) in Taipei, the capital of Taiwan. The Pacific island has a subtropical humid climate.

PEOPLE

About 84% of the population are native Taiwanese, descended from Chinese immigrants in the 18th and 19th centuries; they continue to speak the dialect of their ancestors from Fukien (Fujian) province. The second largest group are the "mainlanders" and their descendants (about 14%) who arrived on Taiwan in 1949 and have strongly promoted Mandarin as Taiwan's official language. Non-Chinese aborigines constitute a small minority (about 2%); they are descended from a people of Indonesian origin who lived on the islands prior to Chinese immigration and were subsequently pushed inland to the mountains by the new arrivals. The aborigines speak some 13 different languages that are thought to be related to Malayo-Polynesian languages. Most Chinese follow the traditional religious beliefs and practices of Buddhism and Taoism and accept Confucianism as an ethical code. Animism is common among the aborigines, and Christianity is an important minority religion.

Taiwan's population has grown rapidly since 1956, but the proportion of adults and the elderly to the total population is increasing due to declining birth and death rates. Most people are concentrated in the western plains, where densities exceeding 1,040 per km² (2,700 per mi²) are common. TAIPEI and KAOHSIUNG are the principal cities.

Literacy is high, and 10 years of basic education are free and compulsory for all children six years of age and older. About 60% continue their education in secondary and vocational schools, and higher education is encouraged. National Taiwan (in Taipei) and National Taiwan Normal (in Taipei) rank among the leading universities. As diet and health care have improved during the last 30 years, the younger generation has grown significantly taller and heavier than their parents.

Taiwan considers itself the guardian of classical CHINESE ART AND ARCHITECTURE, CHINESE LITERATURE, and CHINESE MUSIC. The National Palace Museum outside Taipei reflects this conservative government policy and displays bronzes, paintings, and other treasures of China's artistic heritage. The traditional arts of Chinese opera, YÜAN DRAMA, and calligraphy are encouraged. Newspapers and radio and television are widely used to promote an appreciation of the Chinese classics.

ECONOMIC ACTIVITY

Agriculturally self-sufficient under the Chinese after the 17th century, Taiwan was developed (1895–1945) by the Japanese first as a rice-exporting colony and later as a supplier of sugarcane, bananas, pineapples, tea, and raw materials for Japan. Industrialization began after 1949, and by the early 1980s, Taiwan was a modern, industrial trading nation.

Most industries are labor intensive and benefit from Taiwan's literate and technically competent labor force. The major products are textiles, clothing, electronics, footwear, toys, ships, and such traditional handicrafts as ceramics, silks, and bamboo and paper items. In 1986, Taiwan produced 59 billion kW h of electricity. Domestic hydroelectric power resources are inadequate, and increasing amounts of electricity are generated from imported petroleum and nuclear power plants.

Rice is the principal crop, and increases in yield have kept pace with population growth so that Taiwan is self-sufficient with regard to rice. Widespread use of irrigation and chemical fertilizers, introduced (1895–1945) by the Japanese, land reforms under the Nationalists, and use of the new strains of "miracle rice" have contributed to this increase in rice output. The principal livestock are water buffalo, used as work animals, and pigs, chickens, and ducks, raised as much for their manure as for meat. Fishing is well developed on the west coast.

Most railroads and highways run north-south through the populous western lowlands, and communications are limited in an east-west direction. Chi-lung (Keelong), at the northern tip of the island, and Kaohsiung, on the southwest coast, are the leading seaports. The principal airport is near Taipei. Taiwan's foreign trade increased more than tenfold between 1964 and 1974 and continued to expand rapidly thereafter. The balance of trade is favorable, and additional revenues are derived from Chinese-owned shipping, remittances from overseas Chinese, and the tourist industry. The leading exports are electronics equipment, clothing, plastics, textiles, television and radio receivers, plywood, calculators, and toys. The major imports are crude petroleum, electronic components, foodstuffs, machinery, and iron and steel. In the 1980s, Taiwan faced increasing pressure to reduce its trade surplus with the United States, its chief trading partner.

GOVERNMENT

The Republic of China in Taiwan continues to be governed according to the constitution adopted on the Chinese mainland in 1946. The president and head of government is LEE TENG-HUI, who succeeded to the post following the death of president CHIANG CHING-KUO in 1988. Below the president, governmental authority rests with five yüans (councils)—the executive, legislative, judicial, examination, and control yüans. The legislative and control yüans are in theory elected, but members elected on the mainland hold power indefinitely, and only seats created since 1972 are filled through elections. Political power rests mainly with the "mainlanders" and members of the Kuomintang (Nationalist party). In 1988 the Kuomintang approved a plan calling for the gradual retirement of legislators elected on the mainland beginning in 1989. At the local level, Taiwan is also governed as a province of China and divided into 16 *hsien* (counties), 5 *shih* (municipalities), and two special municipalities (Taipei and Kaohsiung). The provincial governor and the mayor of Taipei are appointed by the central government; the provincial assembly is elected.

HISTORY

Taiwan first became known to the West in the 16th century by its Portuguese name, *Formosa*, "beautiful." In the 17th century, Spaniards and Dutch briefly controlled parts of the island until the Dutch were driven out in 1661 by the pirate Koxinga, who made Taiwan a refuge after 1644 for supporters of China's deposed Ming dynasty. In 1683, Taiwan surrendered to

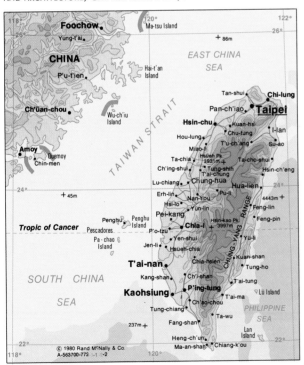

TAIWAN

	Meters	Feet
	4000	13124
—— Railroad	2000	6562
+ Spot Elevation	1000	3281
	500	1640
Scale 1:5,400,000	200	656
	0	0

Meters	Feet
0	0
200	656
Below 2000	Below 6562

0 25 50 75 100 125 km
0 25 50 75 mi

© 1980 Rand McNally & Co.
A-563700-772 -1 -2

the Ch'ing (Manchu) dynasty and became part of China's Fukien province. In 1895, Taiwan was ceded to Japan at the end of the first Sino-Japanese War and was developed as a Japanese colony. Reverting to Chinese sovereignty in 1945, it became a refuge for the Republic of China's ousted Nationalist government in 1949 following the Communist takeover of the Chinese mainland.

From their base on Taiwan, the Nationalists under Chiang Kai-shek continued to claim legal sovereignty over all China and seek "recovery of the mainland," a policy more popular with the "mainlander" minority than with the Taiwanese. The United States supported Taiwan's claims and in 1954 signed a mutual security pact for the defense of Taiwan and the Pescadores. Chiang Kai-shek died in 1975. He was succeeded as president by his vice-president Yen Chia-kan, but real power and leadership of the Kuomintang passed to Chiang's eldest son, Chiang Ching-kuo. In 1971, Taiwan lost its seat in the United Nations to the People's Republic of China. It lost additional international support in 1978 because of the unilateral termination of the United States–Taiwan security pact, although the United States and Taiwan continued to maintain unofficial ties. Domestically, Taiwan's economic success contributed to mounting demands for political liberalization. The desire for change was reflected in the Dec. 6, 1986, legislative elections, in which a technically illegal opposition party, the Democratic Progressive party, captured nearly 25% of the vote. Chiang Ching-kuo, who had been elected president in 1978 and reelected in 1984, launched a policy of gradual democratic reform. Martial law, in effect since 1949, was formally lifted on July 14, 1987. The role of the military was reduced, although many restrictions on political activity remained in effect under a new national security law. A ban on travel to the Chinese mainland was also eased in 1987.

Lee Teng-hui, who succeeded Chiang Ching-kuo as president and later as head of the Kuomintang, was Taiwan's first native-born president. He moved to increase the political voice of native-born Taiwanese.   JOHN E. MACDONALD

Bibliography: Ahern, E. M., and Gates, H., eds., *The Anthropology of Taiwanese Society* (1981); Barclay, G. W., *Colonial Development and Population in Taiwan* (1954; repr. 1971); Chiu, H., *China and the Taiwan Issue* (1979); Gold, T. B., *State and Society in the Taiwan Miracle* (1986); Harrell, S., *Plowshare Village* (1982); Ho, S. P., *Economic Development of Taiwan, 1860–1970* (1978); Hsiung, J., ed., *Contemporary Republic of China* (1981); Koenig, L. W., et al., *Congress, the Presidency, and the Taiwan Relations Act* (1980); Kuo, S. W. Y.,*The Taiwan Economy in Transition* (1983); Lau, L. J., *Models of Development* (1986); Li, V. C., ed., *The Future of Taiwan* (1980); Mendel, D. H., *The Politics of Formosan Nationalism* (1970); Pasternak, B., *Kinship and Community in Two Chinese Villages* (1972); Rabushka, A., *The New China* (1987).

Taj Mahal   [tahzh muh-hahl']

The Taj Mahal, located on the Jumna River in the city of Agra, India, is a monumental Islamic edifice built by Shah Jahan, Mogul emperor of India (r. 1628–58). Designed as an extraordinary representation of the throne of God in paradise, the structure also served as a mausoleum for the emperor's beloved consort Arjunand Banu Begum, who was also known by the title Taj Mahal ("crown of the palace"). It is widely acknowledged to be the greatest masterpiece of Indian Mogul architecture and one of the world's most beautiful buildings.

Work on the Taj Mahal was begun shortly after Arjunand's death (1631) and was completed in 1648. The mausoleum itself, which rises about 33 m (108 ft) from a platform of roughly 50 m² (165 ft²), is a domed building laid out in perfect symmetry along four axes. The composition and proportions of the mausoleum, as well as its use of such elements as a double dome, a high portal, and corner domes, represent the culmination of a tradition of secular mausoleums that had originated centuries earlier in Iran and Central Asia and was developed further in Mogul India by the emperor Humayun (r. 1530–56). The unique qualities of the Taj Mahal lie in the magnificent contrast between the white marble facade of the mausoleum and the red sandstone of the surrounding buildings, in the ethereal harmony of its parts, and in the rationally

(Above) *Rice is cultivated in alluvial lowlands near Taiwan's central mountain range. With rice paddies covering approximately half of the island's total arable land, the crop is Taiwan's principal agricultural product. Rice is grown chiefly for domestic consumption.*

(Right) *Balloons are released in Presidential Square during Nation Day festivities in Taipei. Nation Day, also called Double Tenth Day because it is observed on each October 10, celebrates the revolution of 1911, which established the Chinese republic.*

The Taj Mahal in India is one of the finest examples of Indo-Islamic architecture. The architectural symmetry of the white marble mausoleum is accentuated by its reflection in the pool before it.

thought-out proportions between its fulls and voids. The interior of the mausoleum is illuminated through carved-marble screens set near the tops of the walls.   OLEG GRABAR

Tajik: see TADZHIK.

Takeshita Noboru   [tah-keh-shee-tah]

Takeshita Noboru, b. Feb. 26, 1924, became head of Japan's ruling Liberal Democratic party in October 1987 and succeeded NAKASONE YASUHIRO as prime minister of Japan in November. First elected to parliament in 1958, Takeshita held cabinet posts under prime ministers SATO EISAKU, TANAKA KAKUEI, and Nakasone and served as party general secretary before becoming Nakasone's hand-chosen successor. As prime minister, he increased Japan's role on the world political and diplomatic stage.

Takla Makan Desert   [tah'-klah mah-kahn']

The Takla Makan (Takli Makan) is a mostly uninhabited desert in Sinkiang province, northwestern China, bordered on the north, south, and west by the Tien Shan, Kunlun, and Pamir ranges. It covers an area of about 323,740 km² (125,000 mi²). The desert is crossed by the TARIM RIVER, which disappears in the LOP NOR region to the east. The surface consists of shifting sand dunes with some exposed sandstone and clay. The Takla Makan is Asia's driest desert. Temperatures range from 38° C (100° F) in summer to −9° C (15° F) in winter. The sparse vegetation consists of tamarisk and grass. Indigenous animals include gazelles, wild boars, wolves, and foxes.

Talbot, William Henry Fox   [tal'-buht]

The English archaeologist, linguist, photochemist, and mathematician William Henry Fox Talbot, b. Feb. 11, 1800, d. Sept. 17, 1877, is best known for inventing the negative-positive process of PHOTOGRAPHY. His process, variously called photogenic drawing, CALOTYPE, and Talbotype, produced a negative, on paper, from which any number of paper positives could be made. This advantage over the daguerreotype, a unique picture on metal, was not immediately recognized, but it provided the basis of modern photography.

Talbot first fixed (1835) the camera image on paper made sensitive to light with silver halides. When L. J. M. Daguerre's process was announced (1839) in France, Talbot reported his work to the Royal Society in London. By 1841 he had perfected his process. Talbot also produced *The Pencil of Nature* (1844–46; facsimile repr. 1969), the first book illustrated with original photographs, at his own printing establishment.

Bibliography: Arnold, A. J. P., *Talbot: Pioneer of Photography and Man of Science* (1977); Buckland, Gail, *Fox Talbot and the Invention of Photography* (1979); Hannavy, J., *Fox Talbot* (1984).

talc

Talc [Mg₃ Si₄ O₁₀ (OH)₂] is a common, extremely soft, basic magnesium SILICATE MINERAL; compact aggregates are known as soapstone (steatite). Talc occurs as translucent, foliated or granular masses that vary in color from pale to dark green, with one perfect cleavage. Hardness is 1 (talc is a standard of hardness), streak is white, luster is pearly, and specific gravity is 2.7 to 2.8. Talc crystallizes in the monoclinic system. A low-grade metamorphic mineral, it forms when water and silica or carbon dioxide are added to extensively altered olivine- or pyroxene-rich igneous rocks and when water and silica are added to altered carbonate rocks. Talc is also found in crystalline schists. In most instances, talc is found associated with carbonate minerals, particularly dolomite.

Talc has been used since ancient times for carved and engraved ornaments and utensils. Modern industrial applications include use as chemical-resistant and moderate-heat-resistant fixtures, in lubricants, in roofing materials, in ceramics, and as toilet powders, insecticide carriers, and paint and paper fillers.

Talc is a very soft, translucent, white to green basic magnesium silicate with a characteristic soapy feel. It is usually found in foliated or compact fine-grained masses. Talc's most familiar use is in talcum powder, but one of its most important applications is in the production of glazed wall tiles, porcelain, and other ceramics. It is also used in insecticides, paints, paper, soaps, and rubber.

Tale of Genji, The

The most famous of all Japanese novels, *The Tale of Genji* was written early in the 11th century by a lady of the court, MURASAKI SHIKIBU, for the amusement of the emperor and his courtiers. Genji, the central character, is the indulged younger son of an ancient emperor, and his adventures, particularly the great loves of his life, are recounted in a style remarkable for its mixture of Japanese romanticism and worldly candor. The most notable female character is the beautiful child Murasaki, who is loved by Genji with all the tremulous yearning of a wooer and adopted by him for her protection. Genji's absence from the last ten chapters suggests that the novel was never finished. *The Tale of Genji* is valued not only for its picture of court life in Kyoto but for its depth of characterization and stylistic beauty. Lady Murasaki portrays the fogs, the clouds, the flowers, the meditating woman, the mountain, and the monk with all the simplicity and poignancy of traditional Japanese painting. The novel was first translated (1925–33) into English by Arthur Waley.   JANE COLVILLE BETTS

Bibliography: Morris, Ivan, *The World of the Shining Prince* (1964); Murase Miyeko, *Iconography of the Tale of the Genji* (1982); Seidensticker, E. G., *Genji Days* (1978).

Tale of a Tub, A

Jonathan SWIFT's *A Tale of a Tub*, written in 1697 but unpublished until 1704, was his first prose satire. The title refers to the nautical practice of throwing a tub into the water to distract a whale from attacking the ship. The whale is an allusion to Hobbes's *Leviathan* (1651)—a work of materialistic philosophy—and the ship to religion and government. Swift uses this vehicle to attack English religious and social excesses. The work's challenge for readers resides in its puns, learned wit, topicality, and chaotic form, itself a parody of the hack writing and PAMPHLET controversies of Swift's time.

Bibliography: Clark, John R., *Form and Frenzy in Swift's "Tale of a Tub"* (1970); Smith, Frederick N., *Language and Reality in Swift's "A Tale of the Tub"* (1979).

Tale of Two Cities, A

Charles DICKENS's historical novel of London and Paris before and during the French Revolution, *A Tale of Two Cities* (1859) describes social and psychological crises more accurately than historical events. Dickens's vision of the Terror encompasses aristocratic exploitation and neglect of the poor, public bloodshed, and private vengeance. Sydney Carton, a worthless, pleasure-loving English barrister, redeems himself by a heroic gesture of self-sacrifice—he allows himself to be executed in place of a French aristocrat, Charles Darnay.

Taliesin West   [tal-ee-es'-in]

Taliesin West, a complex of buildings, terraces, and pools near Phoenix, Ariz., evolved as the western home, workshop, and school of the architect Frank Lloyd WRIGHT. He first came to this area in 1927 and built a temporary camp. He so enjoyed the climate, however, that, beginning in 1937, he erected a permanent winter home for his Taliesin Fellowship at nearby Scottsdale, calling it Taliesin West (to distinguish it from Taliesin East at Spring Green, Wis.). It eventually consisted of a series of structures roofed in wood and canvas set upon massive sloping walls of desert boulders placed in forms filled with concrete.   ANN VAN ZANTEN

Talking Heads

The Talking Heads—whose albums include *Talking Heads:77* (1977), *Speaking in Tongues* (1983), and *Naked* (1988)—is an avant-garde U.S. rock band that fuses a distinctive musical style with band leader David Byrne's quirky, often enigmatic lyrics. Byrne and core band members Jerry Harrison, Tina Weymouth, and Chris Franz have expanded rock's range by drawing on polyrhythmic African melodies.

Byrne, b. Dumbarton, Scotland, May 14, 1942, has also directed films (*True Stories*—1986), designed album covers, and composed musical scores (for Twyla THARP's *The Catherine Wheel*, 1982, and Robert WILSON's CIVIL warS, 1986). Byrne earned an Academy Award for his contributions to the score of Bernardo Bertolucci's film *The Last Emperor* (1987).

Talladega College   [tal-uh-dee'-guh]

Established in 1867 by the American Missionary Association as a college for blacks, Talladega College (enrollment: 576; library: 86,000 volumes) is a coeducational liberal arts school in Talladega, Ala., affiliated with the United Church of Christ.

Tallahassee   [tal-uh-has'-ee]

Tallahassee, capital of Florida and seat of Leon County, is located in northern Florida, about 40 km (25 mi) from the Gulf of Mexico. The population is 81,548 (1980), and most workers are employed by the state and local governments. Tallahassee is the commercial service center of northern Florida's cattle raising, lumbering, and cotton and commercial truck-farming region. The state capitol building, begun in 1826, has undergone several renovations, the most recent in the mid-1970s. The city is the seat of Florida Agricultural and Mechanical University and Florida State University.

Hernando de Soto found an Indian village on the site in 1539, and the site was later a Spanish settlement. In 1824 it was selected as the state capital. During the Civil War, Tallahassee was the only Confederate state capital east of the Mississippi River to avoid capture.   TRUMAN A. HARTSHORN

Tallchief, Maria

Maria Tallchief, b. Fairfax, Okla., Jan. 24, 1925, was the star ballerina during the early years (1947–1965) of New York City Ballet and its forerunner, Ballet Society, and created many important parts in the works of George Balanchine, to whom she was married from 1946 to 1952. Trained by Bronislava Nijinska and at Balanchine's School of American Ballet, Tallchief was a brilliant technician. Her stage personality was mysterious and remote, yet she excelled in a wide variety of parts, from the cooly classical, in *Allegro Brillante,* to the romantic, in *Serenade,* and the exotic, in *Firebird* and as the Siren in *Prodigal Son.* From 1942 to 1947 she was a soloist with Ballet Russe de Monte Carlo, where she created important parts in Balanchine's *Danses Concertantes* and *Night Shadow.* From 1960 to 1962 she also appeared with American Ballet Theatre and various other companies. She now heads the Chicago City Ballet, which separated from the city's Lyric Opera company in 1980. She is the sister of the ballerina Marjorie Tallchief.   DALE HARRIS

Bibliography: Maynard, Olga, *Bird of Fire: The Story of Maria Tallchief* (1961); Tracy, R., and DeLano, S., *Balanchine's Ballerinas* (1983).

Talleyrand-Périgord, Charles Maurice de   [tahl-ay-rahn'-pay-ree-gohr']

Charles Maurice de Talleyrand-Périgord was a leading statesman under five different regimes in France. His capacity for political survival was matched by his political skill. At the Congress of Vienna (1814–15) he succeeded in playing Britain and Austria against Prussia and Russia to gain a moderate peace settlement and recognition of France as a great power.

Charles Maurice de Talleyrand-Périgord, b. Feb. 2, 1754, d. May 17, 1838, a French bishop, political leader, and diplomat, served in the top levels of most of the regimes that governed France between 1789 and 1848. He was the son of an old noble family. A physical disability precluded an army career, and he entered the church. Helped by the powerful archbishop of Reims, his uncle, he rose quickly to lucrative posts and in 1788 was named bishop of Autun. He sat in the First Estate of the States-General in 1789 and retained his seat when the States-General became the National Assembly. In October 1789 he proposed that the state take over the vast properties of the church; when this had been accomplished and the church reorganized as a virtual department of government, Talleyrand and one other bishop, in defiance of papal orders, consecrated the first new bishops of the constitutional church, thereby preserving the apostolic succession.

Talleyrand soon left the clergy and obtained diplomatic appointments abroad, which enabled him to escape the Terror. In 1797 he became minister of foreign affairs under the Directory. He resigned in 1799 and helped prepare the coup d'état that ended the Directory and made Napoléon Bonaparte (later Emperor NAPOLEON I) first consul. He was rewarded with the portfolio of foreign affairs. The emperor valued his services and rewarded him handsomely with property and titles, and Talleyrand used his office to increase his large personal fortune. After 1805, however, his views increasingly diverged from those of Napoleon, whose ambitions he regarded as dangerously excessive. Talleyrand resigned in 1807 and began intriguing with the emperor's foreign enemies.

In 1814, Talleyrand played the leading role in bringing the Bourbon LOUIS XVIII to the French throne. Again his reward was the ministry of foreign affairs. In that position he represented France at the Congress of Vienna (see VIENNA, CONGRESS OF) and, by taking advantage of rifts among the victors, won for France a role in the settlement and a fairly lenient peace. He resigned in 1815 and retired for 14 years.

A close advisor of LOUIS PHILIPPE, duc d'Orléans, Talleyrand helped persuade the duke to accept the crown in 1830. Louis Philippe appointed him ambassador to London to win British recognition of the new Orléanist regime. He succeeded not only in that but also in negotiating a Franco-British settlement of the Belgian independence problem, which for a time threatened to precipitate war between France and the conservative continental powers. Talleyrand retired from the London post in 1834, having served two Bourbon monarchies, the republic, the empire, and the July monarchy with cynical impartiality and effectiveness. His memoirs have been published in English translation (5 vols., 1891–92).   DAVID H. PINKNEY

Bibliography: Brinton, Crane, *The Lives of Talleyrand* (1963); Cooper, Duff, *Talleyrand* (1932; repr. 1986); Orieux, Jean, *Talleyrand: The Art of Survival* (1974).

Tallinn   [tal'-uhn]

Tallinn is the capital of the Estonian Soviet Socialist Republic of the USSR. The population is 464,000 (1985 est.). Tallinn's location on Tallinn Bay, an inlet of the Gulf of Finland, led to its prominence as a seaport and a manufacturing center specializing in the production of electric motors, cables, and other electrical goods. Fishing and fish processing are economically important.

The city, medieval in appearance and distinguished by Gothic architecture, consists of the hilltop fortress of Toompea, dating from the 13th–14th centuries; a lower town dating from the 14th–16th centuries; and more modern districts. The city's name, which means "Danish castle" in Estonian, refers to its settlement by Danes in 1219. The city was a major trade center of the Hanseatic League during the 13th and 14th centuries. It was annexed by Russia in the early 18th century and was then known as Revel. Modern industrial growth began during the late 19th century.   THEODORE SHABAD

Tallis, Thomas   [tal'-is]

Thomas Tallis, b. *c.*1505, d. Nov. 23, 1585, was an English organist and composer whose career spanned the reigns of four monarchs and a long period of religious change. He was organist of Dover Priory in 1532 but moved to London (Saint Mary-at-Hill) and then to Waltham Abbey, where the excellent choir and acoustics probably inspired him to compose his early Latin motets—*Ave Dei Patris, Gaude gloriosa,* and *Salve intemerata*—in the expansive and melismatic style then in favor. On the dissolution of the abbey, Tallis went to Canterbury for 2 years as a lay clerk at the cathedral but soon took up an appointment at the Chapel Royal, where he remained until his death. It was there that he met, taught, and befriended William BYRD, whose elegy "Ye sacred Muses" laments the death of his old and revered master. Tallis was indeed a master, not of one but of many styles, including the rich texture in the vein of Robert Fayrfax, the newer post-Reformation counterpoint exemplified in the motets and hymns in the *Cantiones sacrae* published jointly with Byrd in 1575, and the simpler, more homophonic style of the anthems written for the publications of John Day and Archbishop Parker. As an unrivaled example of a contrapuntal tour de force, Tallis's motet *Spem in alium* (for eight choirs of five voices) stands alone; it may have been written for some great ceremonial event at which the assembly of 40 highly trained voices would not be unusual. Many of his Latin motets were adapted

to English words, sometimes more than once; *Absterge Domine,* for instance, was sung to the tune of "Discomfit them" or "Wipe away my sins." As a virtuoso organist and virginalist, Tallis left a small but remarkable collection of antiphons and hymn verses that also included two massive settings of the offertory *Felix namque.*   DENIS STEVENS

Bibliography: Doe, Paul, *Thomas Tallis,* 2d ed. (1976).

tallow tree   [tal'-oh]

Tallow trees are three unrelated species of trees whose fruits or seeds yield an oily or fatty substance that suggests tallow, or animal fat, and that has been used in the making of candles and soap; the trees are also used for lumber. The Chinese tallow tree, *Sapium sebiferum,* of the spurge family, Euphorbiaceae, grows to 12 m (40 ft) high. The fruits of the Sierra Leone butter, or tallow, tree, *Pentadesma butyracea,* of the garcinia family, Guttiferae, yield an edible oil also used in making margarine. The African tallow tree, *Detarium senegalense,* of the pea family, Leguminosae, may exceed 30 m (100 ft) in height. The term *tallow wood,* which refers to trees and lumber having an oily or greasy quality, is most commonly used for the Australian eucalyptus tree, *Eucalyptus microcorys,* of the myrtle family, Myrtaceae.

Talma, François Joseph   [tahl-mah']

One of the greatest French actors, François Joseph Talma, b. Jan. 16, 1763, d. Oct. 19, 1826, was the shaping force of modern French theatrical technique. The first French actor to replace contemporary dress with period costuming, Talma substituted naturalness for exaggerated declamation in the speaking of theatrical verse. He made his debut (1787) in a Voltaire play and became famous in tragedies by Racine, Corneille, and Shakespeare.

Bibliography: Collins, Herbert F., *Talma, a Biography of an Actor* (1964).

Talmadge   (family)

The Talmadge family has been prominent in Georgia politics in the 20th century. **Eugene Talmadge**, b. Forsyth, Ga., Sept. 23, 1884, d. Dec. 21, 1946, served (1933–37, 1941–43) as Georgia's Democratic governor. A lawyer and farmer, he was Georgia's commissioner of agriculture (1927–33). As governor he advocated fiscally and racially conservative agrarian policies and opposed the New Deal. He died after winning (1946) the gubernatorial election for the fourth time. His son **Herman Talmadge**, b. McRae, Ga., Aug. 9, 1913, also served (1948–55) as governor of Georgia until he was elected (1956) Democratic U.S. senator from Georgia. He was reelected in 1962, 1968, and 1974. In 1979, Talmadge was officially denounced by the U.S. Senate for "reprehensible" official financial conduct. He lost his bid for reelection in 1980.

Bibliography: Anderson, William, *The Wild Man from Sugar Creek: The Political Career of Eugene Talmadge* (1975); Douth, George, *Leaders in Profile: The United States Senate* (1975).

Talmud   [tal'-mud]

The Talmud (Hebrew for "teaching" or "study"), a vast compendium of Jewish law and lore, is a unique literary document—a sequel to the Hebrew Bible—and the basis of Jewish religious life. It consists of the MISHNAH and lengthy, rambling commentary called Gemara (Aramaic for "learning" or "tradition"). There are two Gemaras—the Palestinian Gemara, a product of the 3d and 4th centuries AD, and the Babylonian Gemara, completed about 499, with some later additions. Hence, there are two Talmuds: the Talmud Yerushalmi and the Talmud Babli. The latter, the Babylonian Talmud, remains for traditional Jews the final authority on the law. The Mishnah is predominantly in Hebrew, the Gemaras largely in Aramaic. In addition to exhaustive and subtle discussions of civil, criminal, domestic, and ritual law, the Talmuds contain materials called haggadah ("narration")—statements on faith and morals, explanations of Bible verses, parables, and historical and legendary narratives.

Despite difficulties of language and content, the Talmud was for centuries the principal subject of Jewish study. It was provided with innumerable commentaries and annotations, the most important of which was by the 11th-century scholar RASHI. It was also the object of violent attacks by persons who had no knowledge of its contents, from medieval fanatics—24 cartloads of Talmud manuscripts were burned in Paris in 1242—to Nazi propagandists in the 1930s. Modern scholars have come increasingly to recognize its importance as a cultural monument. New Testament scholars in particular have used material from the Talmud and the related literature of MIDRASH for an understanding of Christian origins.

BERNARD J. BAMBERGER

Bibliography: Epstein, Isidore, ed., *The Babylonian Talmud,* 18 vols. (1961); Feinsilver, Alexander, ed., *The Talmud Today* (1980); Mielziner, Moses, *Introduction to the Talmud,* 4th ed. (1969); Strack, Hermann L., *Introduction to the Talmud and Midrash* (1969); Unterman, Isaac, *The Talmud: An Analytical Guide* (1985).

Talon, Jean [tah-lohn']

Jean Talon, b. c.1625, d. Nov. 24, 1694, was the first intendant (1665–68, 1670–72) of New France in Canada. As the effective ruler there, reporting directly to the French king, Talon promoted agricultural and commercial development, exploration of the interior, and immigration; under his administration the population almost doubled. After his final return to France, he became secretary to the king's privy chamber.

talus [tay'-lus]

Talus, or scree, is an accumulation of loose rock debris that slopes away from the foot of a cliff or steep slope. This landform is typical in high mountains and arctic regions where FROST ACTION dislodges rock material from fractured or jointed cliff faces. The spacing of these joints determines the particle size of the eroded material, which in turn establishes the slope angle of the deposit (angle of repose), ranging from 25° to 35°. Talus forms a cone where deposition is selectively concentrated in one area (narrow ravines), aprons where deposition is uniform, and undulating aprons (laterally connected cones) where the cliff face is notched.

Bibliography: Strahler, Arthur N. and Alan H., *Environmental Geoscience* (1973).

tamarack [tam'-uh-rak]

Tamarack is a common name of the conifer *Larix laricina,* of the pine family, Pinaceae. Other common names are American or black larch and hackmatack. Unlike most conifers, this tree has deciduous leaves, 2 to 3 cm (0.8 to 1.2 in) long. Tamarack grows to 15 to 18 m (50 to 60 ft) tall and to 45 to 50 cm (18 to 20 in) in diameter and bears small, upright cones. The tree is native to the cooler parts of North America and favors moist to boggy soils. The wood makes a strong and durable lumber.

The tamarack, L. laricina, *unlike most conifers, sheds its leaves, although not all at once. This tree grows in northern regions of North America.*

tamarin [tam'-uh-rin]

A tamarin is a small, diurnal, monkeylike marmoset found from Panama through South America. The approximately 20 species of true tamarins (genus *Saguinus*) and the 3 species of golden lion marmosets (*Leontideus*) differ from other marmosets in having the lower canine teeth longer than the incisors. Tamarins are from 15 to 35 cm (6 to 14 in) long and have a tail as long as or longer than the body. Whitish crests, moustaches, or other markings often contrast with the generally darkish coat.

EVERETT SENTMAN

tamarind [tam'-uh-rind]

The fruit-bearing tamarind is a tropical, old-world evergreen tree, *Tamarindus indica.* Believed to be native to eastern tropical Africa, it was later spread to India. During the Middle Ages, Arab traders introduced it to Europe. Its name is a contraction of the arabic *Tamr hindi,* which means "date of India." In India the tree is used for timber; its leaves furnish a yellow or red dye; and its fruit pulp is an ingredient in chutneys and is used as a mild laxative. Tamarind-flavored beverages are popular in Italy and Latin America. Most commercial exports of tamarind products come from the West Indies and Indonesia. In the United States, the tree is grown in Florida. The tamarind tree grows to a height of 24 m (80 ft) and has a trunk diameter of 1.8 to 2.4 m (6 to 8 ft). The pod that develops from the red to purplish, yellow-striped flowers is 80 to 200 mm (3 to 8 in) long. Within the pod is a brown, juicy, acid pulp and 1 to 12 seeds. The pulp is reputed to have more sugar and fruit acid per volume than any other fruit; it was once used by sailors to prevent scurvy.

tamarisk [tam'-uh-risk]

Tamarisk, or salt cedar, refers to 54 species of evergreen shrubs or small trees of the genus *Tamarix* of the family Tamaricaceae. Although they are native to Europe, Africa, and Asia, a few species have become naturalized to North America. They have small, scalelike leaves; long clusters of small white, pink, or rose flowers are borne on the ends of the branches or trunks, giving the trees an attractive feathery appearance. Tamarisks are useful ornamentals and windbreaks in desert and coastal regions because they can withstand drought and saline conditions. *T. ramosissima* and *T. chinensis* both grow in the arid southwest United States, where the latter often becomes an aggressive weed.

NATALIE UHL

Tamaulipas [tah-mow-lee'-pahs]

Tamaulipas is a mountainous state in northeastern Mexico, with an area of 79,598 km² (30,733 mi²) and a population of 2,148,000 (1984 est.). The most important resource is petroleum, discovered in the early 1900s, and the main agricultural crops are cotton, cereals, sugarcane, tobacco, and coffee. CIUDAD VICTORIA is the capital, and TAMPICO is the major port. Once inhabited by Tamaulipan Indians, the area was conquered by the Spanish early in the 16th century but was not colonized until 1747. In 1846 it was occupied by U.S. forces during the Mexican War.

LEON YACHER

Tamayo, Rufino [tah-mah'-yoh, roo-fee'-noh]

Rufino Tamayo, b. Oaxaca, Mexico, Aug. 26, 1899, is one of Mexico's leading painters and muralists. After studying (1917–21) at the Academy of San Carlos in Mexico City, he served as the head of ethnographic drawing at his native country's National Museum of Anthropology while pursuing his own art. He first rose to prominence in modernist art circles after moving (1936) to New York, and his European reputation was established during a 10-year (1954–64) sojourn in Paris. Unlike Diego RIVERA and David SIQUEIROS, he largely ignored social-purpose art in favor of exploring the aesthetic possibilities that he combined with elements taken from Mexico's folk heritage in paintings such as *Women of Tehuantepec* (1939; Albright-Knox Art Gallery, Buffalo).

In later years elements of abstract expressionism appeared

in Tamayo's works. His colors grew more intense, and the surfaces of his paintings became more richly textured. In 1964 he returned to Mexico. CARTER RATCLIFF

Bibliography: Genauer, E., *Rufino Tamayo* (1974); Lassaigne, J., *Rufino Tamayo* (1982); Reed, A. M., *The Mexican Muralists* (1960).

tambourine

A small, shallow drum with a single head, the tambourine has metallic ''jingles'' fitted into its rim. The instrument is played by shaking, striking it with the hand or a stick, or vibrating its head with a moistened thumb. The tambourine is of ancient origin and almost universal distribution. It is used to provide a Spanish or gypsy flavor in concert music or opera. It is also used by some rock music groups. ELWYN A. WIENANDT

Tamburlaine the Great   [tam'-bur-layn]

A two-part play by Christopher MARLOWE, *Tamburlaine the Great* (written c.1590) chronicles the rise and fall of an ambitious, monomaniacal conqueror, the historical Timur (or Tamerlane). From a lowly shepherd thief in Part 1, Tamburlaine rises to the apex of power, slashing his way through an increasingly bloody series of victories until he has achieved the conquest of Egypt and has married the Soldan's daughter Zenocrate. Part 2 dramatizes the death of Zenocrate and then of Tamburlaine. By employing his unique blank verse for Tamburlaine's high-flown bragging, Marlowe concentrates his play on the central figure, a technique that is a distinctive mark of his dramaturgy. W. L. GODSHALK

Bibliography: Battenhouse, Roy W., *Marlowe's ''Tamburlaine''* (1941); Fieler, Frank B., *Tamburlaine, Part I and Its Audience* (1962); Howe, James, *Marlowe, Tamburlaine, and Magic* (1976).

Tamerlane: see TIMUR.

Tamil   [tam'-ul]

The Tamil are an ethnic population of southern India, speaking a DRAVIDIAN LANGUAGE. They are concentrated in the southern Indian state of Tamil Nadu, where they number more than 32 million, and in northern Sri Lanka, where they number nearly 3 million (1984 est.). Large emigrant communities also live in southern Sri Lanka, Malaysia, Africa, Mauritius, and the West Indies. Like other Indian peoples, the Tamil are divided into CASTES. Caste is said to be more strictly observed in Tamil Nadu than in other parts of India.

In general, the Tamil trace descent through the male line and favor the marriage of close kin. Although today they are involved in numerous occupations—emigrant Tamil in particular being involved in estate work—the traditional mainstay of their economy is irrigated rice cultivation. The Tamil are particularly proud of their literary and architectural heritage. During the medieval period, Tamil literature was at its height, and some of the most famous Hindu temples in India are in Tamil Nadu. Tamil culture came under Western influence during the late 19th century; in Sri Lanka the minority Tamils dominated the civil service and various professions in the British colonial era. Tamil culture has experienced a resurgence in recent times in both India and Sri Lanka. The Tamils of Sri Lanka feel they have been systematically discriminated against by the Sinhalese majority since independence. In the 1980s a terrorist campaign by militant Sri Lankan Tamil separatists there led to outbreaks of communal violence.
HILLARY STANDING AND R. L. STIRRAT

Bibliography: Irschick, E. F., *Politics and Social Conflict in South India* (1969); Nagayam, X. T., *Tamil Culture and Civilization* (1971); Ponnambalam, S., *Sri Lanka: National Conflict and the Tamil Liberation Struggle* (1983); Ramchandran, K. S., *Archaeology of South India* (1980).

Tamil Nadu   [tam'-ul nah'-doo]

Tamil Nadu (formerly Madras) is a state in southeast India located on the Coromandel coast of the Bay of Bengal. It covers an area of 130,000 km² (50,000 mi²) and has a population of 48,408,077 (1981). Tamil Nadu is bounded by the Indian

Ocean on the east and south. The states of Kerala, Karnataka, and Andhra Pradesh surround Tamil Nadu on the west, northwest, and north, respectively. The capital is MADRAS. The eastern part of the state is a low-lying plain, and the northern and western regions are hilly. The important rivers are the Cauvery, Palar, Ponnaiyar, Tambraparni, and Vaigai. Three-fourths of the population, which is predominantly Tamil, engage in agriculture, growing rice, millet, peanuts, sugarcane, and cotton. Tamil Nadu's textile industry is important; cotton, including the distinctive dyed cloth called MADRAS, and silk fabrics are made. Food processing and the production of cars and motorcycles are also vital to the economy.

The seat of the Chola empire from AD 850, Tamil Nadu was part of the Hindu kingdom of VIJAYANAGAR (1336–1565). From 1639, when the British opened a trading post there, until 1947, when India gained independence, the area was almost continually under British control. The modern state was formed in 1956, and the name was changed from Madras in 1969.

Taming of the Shrew, The

William SHAKESPEARE's energetic, farcical comedy *The Taming of the Shrew* is an exuberant exploration of the male fantasy, common in folklore, of taming a headstrong, stubborn, and high-spirited woman so that she will make a docile wife. Petruchio and Kate contend with each other with tremendous vitality, and Petruchio seems to enjoy great success in his program of reeducation. In modern interpretations, however, Kate's submissiveness is made to seem ironic; she has finally discovered the secret of how women can dominate their men. The taming action actually constitutes a play-within-the-play performed for the benefit of Christopher Sly, a drunken tinker.
MAURICE CHARNEY

Tamiris, Helen

Helen Tamiris (Becker), b. New York City, Apr. 24, 1905, d. Aug. 4, 1966, was a dancer, choreographer, and teacher. Trained in ballet, she performed with the Metropolitan Opera Ballet Company and appeared in the *Music Box Revue* (1924). Turning her interest to the then-burgeoning field of modern dance choreography, she presented her first concert in 1927 and appeared annually in recitals with her own group from 1930 on. From 1930 to 1945 she maintained her School of American Dance. Her concert dance works, such as *Walt Whitman Suite* (1934) and *How Long Brethren?* (1937), were uncomplicated dances, attuned to American social currents and to her gifts as a performer, especially her forthright vitality. During the 1940s and '50s, Tamiris devoted herself to choreography for Broadway musicals. TOBI TOBIAS

Bibliography: Schlundt, C. L., *Tamiris: A Chronicle of Her Dance Career 1927–1955* (1973).

Tamm, Igor Yevgenievich   [tahm]

The Russian theoretical physicist Igor Yevgenievich Tamm, b. July 8, 1895, d. Apr. 12, 1971, was an outstanding scientist who shared (1958) the Nobel Prize for physics with P. A. Cherenkov and I. M. Frank for the theory explaining the nature of radiation of the electron. This in turn permitted an understanding of the CHERENKOV RADIATION effect earlier observed by Cherenkov. Tamm also investigated the photoelectric theory of metals, and electric discharges in plasmas.

Tammany Hall   [tam'-uh-nee]

A Democratic party organization in New York City, Tammany Hall frequently dominated city and even state politics in 19th- and 20th-century New York. Founded in 1789, the Society of St. Tammany or Columbian Order, named after a legendary Delaware chief, was an antiaristocratic fraternal order. Increasingly a partisan club from the 1790s onward, Tammany supported Thomas Jefferson's Democratic-Republican party in the early 1800s. With the establishment of universal white manhood suffrage in the 1820s and increased Irish immigration after 1830, Tammany's strength grew. It won support by helping immigrants find jobs and become citizens and by assisting the poor.

The Tammany tiger, symbol of New York's Democratic-party machine, mauls its defenseless victim, the Republic, in this 1871 Harper's Weekly *cartoon by Thomas Nast. Tammany's William M. "Boss" Tweed is depicted as a Roman emperor presiding over these "games."*

By mid-century, Tammany often controlled city and county politics in New York, organizing voters and electing its candidates with such efficiency that its methods were called machine politics. From the 1860s, Tammany was led by powerful political bosses—William M. TWEED in the 1860s and early 1870s, "Honest" John Kelly in the 1880s, Richard CROKER in the 1890s, and Charles ("Silent Charlie") Murphy in the early 1900s. Machine politics was frequently associated with corruption, and Tweed in particular became notorious for looting the city treasury. Murphy, on the other hand, sought respectability by endorsing working-class reform legislation and sponsoring outstanding young politicians, notably Robert F. WAGNER, Sr., and Alfred E. SMITH.

In the 1930s, Tammany was weakened by the election of antimachine candidate Fiorello LA GUARDIA as mayor and by the New Deal social-welfare programs that reduced the dependence of the poor on Tammany's services. Revived in the 1950s under Carmine G. De Sapio, the Tammany organization subsequently disappeared.   GERALD W. MCFARLAND

Bibliography: Connable, Alfred, and Silberfarb, Edward, *Tigers of Tammany* (1967); Mushkat, Jerome, *Tammany: The Evolution of a Political Machine, 1789–1865* (1971); Myers, Gustavus, *The History of Tammany Hall*, 2d rev. ed. (1917; repr. 1973); Werner, Morris R., *Tammany Hall* (1932; repr. 1968).

See also: BOSS, POLITICAL.

Tampa   [tam'-puh]

Tampa is a city in west central Florida, located on a peninsula across Tampa Bay from Saint Petersburg. The seat of Hillsbor-

ough County, Tampa has a population of 271,523 (1980), and the 3-county metropolitan area, 1,559,492. Tampa is Florida's leading industrial city, where plastics, food products, and cigars—made in the Latin quarter of Ybor City—are produced. Tampa is also a wholesale and retail distribution hub and service center. The city has an excellent harbor from which locally mined phosphates are exported. Tampa is the home of Busch Gardens theme park. Although Pánfilo de Narváez first saw Tampa Bay in 1528, the hostility of the local Indians was so intense that no permanent settlement was established until 1823, 4 years after the Florida territory became a U.S. possession. Growth was slow until a rail link joined the city with Jacksonville to the northeast in 1884, and Tampa became a popular tourist center.   TRUMAN A. HARTSHORN

Tampere   [tahm'-pair-ay]

Tampere, a city in Finland, lies in the southwestern part of the country, about 160 km (100 mi) northwest of Helsinki. It has a population of 168,150 (1984 est.). A major manufacturing hub and the textile center of Finland, Tampere also produces metals, heavy machinery, pulp, and paper. Noted for its lakes, gardens, and modern architecture, the city has educational institutions, museums, and a planetarium. Tampere was founded in 1779, and industrial growth began in 1821 when the Russian tsar Alexander I allowed tax-free imports.

Tampico   [tahm-pee'-koh]

The Mexican port of Tampico lies 10 km (6 mi) from the coast of the Gulf of Mexico in the southernmost part of Tamaulipas state. The population is 267,957 (1980). The center of a rich petroleum-producing area, both offshore and on land, Tampico has petroleum refineries and storage tanks, machine repair shops, shipyards, clothing factories, and canneries. Exports include petroleum, minerals, cotton, and sugar. It is also a popular resort, with tourist facilities centered on Playa Miramar. The swamps and lagoons around the city are good wildfowl-hunting and fishing areas. Tampico is connected by railroad and highway to the rest of Mexico.

Settled in 1823 on the site of a former Aztec village, Tampico became important after the discovery of petroleum there in 1911.

Tana, Lake   [tah'-nah]

Lake Tana, Ethiopia's largest lake, covers about 3,630 km^2 (1,400 mi^2) in the northwestern part of the country at an elevation of 1,850 m (6,000 ft). Fed by the Upper Nile and about 60 other streams, the lake is the source of the Blue Nile.
PETER SCHWAB

tanager   [tan'-uh-jur]

The western tanager, P. ludoviciana (left), feeds in the treetops of coniferous forests in western North America. Both the male (foreground) and the female are recognized by their distinctive wing bars. The scarlet tanager, P. olivacea (right), is commonly found in oak and pine forests in the east. The male (foreground) in breeding plumage is the only North American bird with a red body and black wings and tail.

Tanager is the common name for a subfamily, Thraupinae, family Emberizidae, of more than 220 species of typically brightly colored arboreal birds of the New World. Most species are tropical and subtropical, with only four species that winter in Central and South America venturing north of Mexico as summer visitors. Tanagers range in size from about 7.5 to 30 cm (3 to 12 in) long and usually have conical bills, short necks, rounded wings, and short-to-medium tails; some species are crested. Most feed on insects and fruit, with some species destroying insects harmful to trees and other plants. Some tanagers nest in trees and others in shrubs or ground crevices. During the breeding season, the male scarlet tanager, *Piranga olivacea*, found in the eastern United States and southern Canada, is strikingly beautiful, with a crimson red body and jet-black wings. The male summer tanager, *P. rubra*, of the southern United States, is all red.

WILLIAM F. SANFORD

Tanaka Giichi   [tah'-nah-kah gee-ee'-chee]

The Japanese general and statesman Tanaka Giichi, b. 1863, d. Sept. 28, 1929, was known as a mastermind of Japanese expansionism. Tanaka fought in the Russo-Japanese War (1904–05). Later, as minister of war (1918–21, 1923–24), he promoted both the Siberian expedition against Russia's Bolshevik regime and an aggressive China policy. He became head of the Seiyukai party in 1925. Prime minister from 1927 to 1929, he was forced to resign because of his inability to control army extremists.

Tanaka Kakuei   [tah-nah'-kah kah-koo'-ay]

Tanaka Kakuei, b. May 4, 1918, was prime minister of Japan from 1972 to 1974, when scandal forced his resignation. In 1983, following a 6-year trial, Tanaka was convicted of accepting bribes from the Lockheed Corporation while premier. Twice secretary general of the Liberal Democratic party (1965–66, 1968–71), Tanaka remains head of the party's largest faction and one of the most powerful politicians in Japan.

Tananarive: see ANTANANARIVO.

tanbark oak

Tanbark oak is the common name for *Lithocarpus densiflorus* of the beech family, Fagaceae, native to the coastal region of California and Oregon. Not a true oak but a related tree, it has leathery, evergreen leaves and a thick red bark rich in tannin; the hard wood is used for fuel and lumber.

Taney, Roger B.   [taw'-nee]

Roger Brooke Taney, b. Calvert County, Md., Mar. 17, 1777, d. Oct. 12, 1864, was the fifth chief justice of the U.S. Supreme Court, succeeding (1836) John Marshall. Reversing the trend that Marshall began of creating strong federal controls in government, Taney urged greater local controls. After graduating (1795) from Dickinson College and serving (1799–1800) as a Federalist in the Maryland House of Delegates, Taney practiced law in Frederick, Md. Later he served (1817–21) in the state senate, became a supporter of Andrew Jackson, and in 1827 was appointed attorney general of Maryland.

In 1831, President Jackson made Taney U.S. attorney general and sought his help in opposing the BANK OF THE UNITED STATES. Though he failed to gain in 1833 the Senate's approval as secretary of the Treasury and again in 1835 as an associate justice of the Supreme Court, Taney was confirmed a year later as chief justice because of changes in the Senate membership. In his most famous decision—DRED SCOTT V. SANDFORD (1857)—he ruled against congressional attempts to bar slavery from the territories and held that slaves or their free descendants were not citizens. In another controversial ruling (*Ex parte Merryman*, 1861) Taney declared President Lincoln's wartime suspension of habeas corpus unconstitutional.

Bibliography: Lewis, Walker, *Without Fear or Favor: A Biography of Chief Justice Roger Brooke Taney* (1965); Newmyer, R. Kent, *The Supreme Court under Marshall and Taney* (1969); Smith, Charles W., *Roger B. Taney: Jacksonian Jurist* (1936; repr. 1973).

Taneyev, Sergei Ivanovich   [tuhn-yay'-yuhf]

Sergei Ivanovich Taneyev, b. Nov. 25 (N.S.), 1856, d. June 19 (N.S.), 1915, was a distinguished Russian composer, pianist, and theorist. He entered the Moscow Conservatory of music at the age of 10 as a piano student and soon began studying composition with Tchaikovsky, whose close friend he became. Taneyev was the first pianist to receive the Conservatory's gold medal upon his graduation in 1875; in 1878 he succeeded Tchaikovsky as teacher of composition, later serving (1885–89) as director. Among his students were Aleksandr Scriabin, Sergei Rachmaninoff, and Nikolai Medtner. His polished compositions are perhaps lacking in warmth; they include symphonies, chamber music, and piano and choral works. He also wrote the influential textbook *Convertible Counterpoint in the Strict Style* (1909; Eng. trans. 1962).

MILOŠ VELIMIROVIĆ

Bibliography: Kocabelnikova, L. Z., *S. I. Taneyev at the Moscow Conservatory* (1974); Yakovlev, V., *S. I. Taneyev: His Musical Life* (1927).

T'ang   (Tang)   (dynasty)   [tahng]

This polychrome ink drawing, depicting a Chinese aristocrat and his attendant, dates from the early T'ang dynasty. The cultural vitality of the period was expressed in both the informal ''calligraphic'' style shown here and the developing court style of landscape painting.

One of the most glorious periods in the history of China was that of the T'ang dynasty (618–906), at whose zenith the Chinese empire was the largest, wealthiest, and most populous on earth. **Li Yüan**, the first T'ang emperor, came to power in 618 and abdicated in 626 in favor of his ambitious son, who reigned (627–49) as **T'ai-tsung**. This period marked the first great blossoming of the T'ang era, as Chinese suzerainty was extended west into Afghanistan and Turkistan as well as south to Tibet. T'ai-tsung's successor, **Kao-tsung** (r. 649–83), brought Korea and Japan into tributary relationship to China. Further consolidation was carried out by the Empress **Wu** (r. 690–705), one of China's few female sovereigns.

A massive bureaucracy was recruited by a perfected and increasingly used examination system. The T'ang government and the T'ang code of laws, based on Confucian thought, became models for neighboring states. Towns grew with the expansion of trade. Foreigners were welcome; they introduced new ideas and technology as well as new religions, such as Zoroastrianism and Nestorian Christianity.

In this tolerant atmosphere the arts flourished, culminating in the second blossoming of the T'ang dynasty during the reign (712–56) of the emperor **T'ang Hsüan-tsung**. The painter WU TAO-TZU and China's two famous poets, LI PO and TU FU, were active at this time. A little later, PO CHÜ-I began writing poetry in a near vernacular style, and the art of short-story writing was soon thriving. The advent of popular culture was foreshadowed by the printing of a Buddhist sutra (a collection of precepts) in 868 from wood blocks.

Under T'ang Hsüan-tsung, military commanders began to acquire independent authority and a decline of the central administration began. By the 9th century, T'ang power was spent, and the dynasty ended in a welter of rebellions and civil strife.

Bibliography: Bingham, W., *The Founding of the T'ang Dynasty* (1941; repr. 1970); Scott, Hugh D., *The Golden Age of Chinese Art* (1966; repr. 1981); Weschler, H. J., *Offerings of Jade and Silk* (1985); Wright, A. F., ed., *Perspectives on the T'ang*, rev. ed. (1981).

T'ang Hsüan-tsung   (Tang Xuanzong)   [tahng shwahn-tsung]

T'ang Hsüan-tsung, also known as Ming Huang (Enlightened or Lustrous Emperor), 685–762, 6th emperor (r. 712–56) of the T'ang dynasty, brought T'ang power and culture to their highest point. Successor to his father, Jui Tsung (r. 684–90, 710–12), he strengthened the central administration and fought successfully against the Turks and Tibetans. Under him China was open to foreign trade and ideas, and the arts flourished. In the latter years of T'ang Hsüan-tsung's rule, however, military commanders began to acquire independent political strength. One of them, An Lu-shan, feared a loss of influence when Yang Kuei-fei, the emperor's concubine, became a power at the imperial court. In 755 he began a revolt that forced T'ang Hsüan-tsung to abdicate in favor of Su Tsung (r. 756–62).

Bibliography: Pulleyblank, E. G., *The Background of the Rebellion of An Lu-shan* (1955); Reischauer, E. O., *Ennin's Travels in T'ang China* (1955).

Tanganyika: see TANZANIA.

Tanganyika, Lake   [tang-guh-nee'-kuh]

Lake Tanganyika, located in east central Africa in the Great Rift Valley, is the second largest lake in Africa and the second deepest lake in the world. About 680 km (420 mi) long and as much as 70 km (45 mi) wide, the body of water covers 32,900 km² (12,700 mi²). Depths reach 1,436 m (4,710 ft). An important waterway crossed by steamers, Lake Tanganyika is bounded by Tanzania in the east, Zaire in the west, Burundi in the northeast, and Zambia in the south. Its main port is BUJUMBURA, Burundi. The lake contains many fish and animal species; its shores support rice plantations.

The first Europeans to reach Lake Tanganyika were John Hanning Speke and Richard Burton in 1858. In 1871 the lake was explored by David Livingstone.   G. N. UZOIGWE

Tange, Kenzo   [tahng'-ee, kayn'-zoh]

The Japanese architect Kenzo Tange, b. Imabari, Shikoku, Japan, Sept. 4, 1913, has designed structures throughout Japan and in many other countries of the world. For his earliest design concepts he turned to the European influence of Le Corbusier. This influence is best seen in such examples as the facade of the Imabari Municipal Office Building (1957–58), which reflects aspects of the great French architect's work at Chandigarh, India. Other elements of Tange's work are more traditionally Japanese. The Kagawa Prefectural Offices at Takamatsu (1955–58) employs interlocking concrete beams arranged much like the lumber planks in Japanese temple shrines. A similar concern for the expressive use of structure may be seen in the Olympic Sports Stadia in Tokyo (1961–64), where cable roofs are suspended from concrete masts. After 1960, Tange's interests turned to urban planning. His concept for housing to be built over the Bay of Tokyo (1960) proposed temple-shaped clusters of apartments connected by vertebrae containing transportation links. The tendency to use repetitive units for evocative effect may be found in other projects, such as the Shizuoka Convention Hall (1955–57) or the Press Center in Kofu (1964–67). In 1987 he became the ninth recipient of the Pritzker Architecture Prize.   LEON SATKOWSKI

Bibliography: Boyd, Robin, *Kenzo Tange* (1962) and *New Directions in Japanese Architecture* (1969); Kulterman, Udo, and Tange, Kenzo, *Kenzo Tange* (1970).

tangent

In any right-angled triangle, the tangent of the acute angle θ is a ratio: the length of the side opposite θ divided by the length of the adjacent side. The tangent of θ is usually abbreviated as tan θ. *Tangent* is also often used as an adjective meaning "to touch." A tangent line is a line that touches a curve at a single point. A tangent plane is a plane that touches a surface at a single point. Tangent circles are those which have a common point; they touch each other at this point and only at this point. In Cartesian coordinates, tan θ is the ratio of the y-coordinate divided by the x-coordinate of point P (x, y) on the circumference of a unit circle, where the radius makes an angle θ with the positive x-axis. In this case, tan θ is a circular function that repeats every 180°.

tangerine

The tangerine, C. reticulata, is produced from a small, thorny tree that bears simple leaves and orangelike blossoms.

The tangerine, or mandarin, *Citrus reticulata* of the citrus family, is an orangelike fruit that, with its hybrids, ranks after the orange in worldwide economic importance among CITRUS FRUITS. Native to China, one variety, Dancy, was introduced to Europe via the Moroccan seaport of Tangier and was originally called the Tangiers orange. The names *tangerine* and *mandarin* are now used interchangeably, although the varieties produced in the United States and in southern Africa—called tangerines or mandarins—tend to have a deeper orange skin and pulp than those grown in other areas.

Most tangerine trees and their flowers and fruits resemble those of the orange, although tangerines are generally smaller. Tangerine peel adheres loosely to the flesh, and the segments are easy to separate. Although juice content and composition are similar, many tangerine varieties have a more deeply colored rind and flesh color than the orange.

About a third of the world production of tangerines is grown in Japan, which exports a variety called the Satsuma mandarin. Spain, Italy, the United States, and Brazil are also major producers. Most of the U.S. crop is grown in Florida.

Of the many tangerine hybrids, the most widely produced are the tangelos, hybrids of tangerines and grapefruits, and hybrids with the sweet orange, which include the tangor, king orange, and temple orange.   WALTER REUTHER

Bibliography: Hume, H. Harold, *Citrus Fruits*, rev. ed. (1957).

Tangier

Tangier is a seaport city on the northern coast of Morocco at the western end of the Strait of Gibraltar (see GIBRALTAR,

The city of Tangier, on the northern coast of Morocco, is situated on a bay of the Strait of Gibraltar and has been active as an international port for centuries. In 1923 it was recognized as an international neutral zone, and it was governed by representatives of various countries until its incorporation (1956) into Morocco.

STRAIT OF) about 30 km (18 mi) south of Spain. With a population of 312,227 (1982), it is the oldest continuously occupied city in Morocco and the principal port for passenger service. Tourism is the main industry. Roads and railroads connect Tangier with other tourist centers, including Casablanca, Fez, Meknès, and Rabat. Construction, textile industries and fishing supplement the economy. The old section of Tangier, surrounded by 15th-century fortifications, includes the former royal palace, the Grand Socco or main market area, and the 17th-century Great Mosque.

Settled as early as the 15th century BC by the Phoenicians, the city was occupied by the Carthaginians and, from 82 BC, by the Romans, who called it Tingis. Captured by the Arabs AD c.705, the city was ruled by Islamic dynasties until 1471, when the Portuguese seized control. After a brief period of English rule (1662–84), the city was restored to Morocco. Tangier acquired its international character in the 18th century when foreign ambassadors to the Moroccan court were housed there. Because of the strategic location at the entrance to the Mediterranean, the city and the surrounding area were given international status in 1923 and were governed by an international commission until 1956.

Tanglewood Festival: see BERKSHIRE MUSIC FESTIVAL.

tango

A dance that evolved in Buenos Aires at the end of the 19th century, the tango is probably derived from the *milonga,* a lively, suggestive Argentinian dance, and the *habanera* of Cuba and the West Indies. By the 1920s it had become a popular ballroom dance in Europe and the United States, and had been transformed into a flowing, elegant series of steps accompanied by somewhat melancholy music with a characteristic tango beat.

Tanguy, Yves   [tahn-gee', eev]

Yves Tanguy, b. Paris, Jan. 5, 1900, d. Jan. 15, 1955, a self-taught painter, became a leading figure in the French surrealist movement of the 1920s (see SURREALISM, art). Moved by the works of Giorgio de Chirico and stimulated by his friendship with the surrealist writer Jacques Prévert, he took up painting in 1923, joining André Breton's newly formed surrealist group in 1925. He then began to develop his peculiar vision of airless landscapes, such as *Indefinite Divisibility* (1942; Albright-Knox Art Gallery, Buffalo, N.Y.), in which strange, biomorphic objects hover in a strong, cold light. This dreamlike subject matter inspired most of his later work. Tanguy moved to the United States in 1939 and married the American surrealist painter Kay Sage in 1940.   IRMA B. JAFFE

Bibliography: Breton, André, *Surrealism and Painting,* trans. by Simon Watson Taylor (1972); Soby, James T., *Yves Tanguy* (1955; repr. 1972).

Tani Buncho: see BUNCHO.

Tanis   [tay'-nis]

Tanis, a city of ancient Egypt on the Nile's eastern delta, situated at present-day San al-Hajar al-Qibliyah, was a major seaport and the capital of Egypt under the kings of the 21st dynasty; since it stood near the border with Asia, it was also significant militarily. Under other dynasties it was the capital of a province. The city remained important until the flooding of Lake Tanis (now Lake Manzala) led to its gradual abandonment during the 4th century AD. In 1866 the German Egyptologist Karl Lepsius discovered at Tanis an inscription known as the Decree of Canopus. Like the ROSETTA STONE, it was written in hieroglyphics as well as two other scripts, including Greek. Temples and statuary as well as a necropolis were also found.
                                                              ROBIN BUSS

Tanizaki Junichiro   [tah-nee'-zah-kee jun-ee'-chee-roh]

The Japanese novelist Tanizaki Junichiro, b. July 24, 1886, d. July 30, 1965, was a versatile writer who employed a wealth of narrative techniques. His novels brilliantly probe the psychology of dependence and domination between the sexes and celebrate the eternal, ever-elusive image of feminine perfection and the complementary figure of the adolescent male. In such novels as *Some Prefer Nettles* (1929; Eng. trans., 1965) and *The Diary of a Mad Old Man* (1962; Eng. trans., 1965) Tanizaki draws exquisite portraits of traditional Japanese culture and conveys an infectious zest for life.
                                                        EDWARD B. FOWLER

Bibliography: Keene, Donald, *Modern Japanese Literature* (1956).

tank, military: see ARMORED VEHICLE.

tanker

A tanker is a ship designed to carry large volumes of oil or other liquid cargo. Basically, a tanker is a hollow shell in which one or more enormous oil tanks have been installed, each running the length of the ship. Overall, the tanker sector includes the largest vessels afloat and forms more than half the world's mercantile fleet capacity.

The four basic types of tanker are oil tankers, chemical carriers, liquefied-gas carriers, and OBO (ore/bulk/oil) tankers. The first oil tanker was built in 1886 in Germany and had a capacity of 300 deadweight tons (1 dwt = 2,240 lb). During the 1920s, cargo capacity increased to 12,000 dwt, and by 1939 it had increased to 16,000 dwt. World War II caused a massive increase in demand for petroleum. Five hundred tankers of the T-2 class, of 16,000-dwt capacity, were built by the United States. In 1947 oil tankers of 27,000 dwt emerged, and by 1970

The S.S. Manhattan, *an ice-breaking tanker, became the first merchant ship successfully to navigate (1969) the Northwest Passage, demonstrating the route's feasibility for transporting petroleum. The huge tankers built to convey petroleum are the largest ships afloat.*

the average tanker capacity worldwide had risen to 47,000 dwt. By the 1970s a few new vessels could hold more than 300,000 dwt. Most tankers are owned by oil companies, and transport petroleum and fuel from oil fields and refineries to distribution centers along a worldwide tanker network. The oil crisis of the 1970s created the need for larger tankers, and the largest today—the ultra large crude carriers (ULCC)—have capacities up to 500,000 dwt. Oil tankers have caused serious pollution problems, some because of accidents at sea (see OIL SPILLS), many because of the tanker's habitual method of cleaning their tanks—by flushing residual oil directly into the ocean.

The chemical-carrier division carries various types of chemicals for international distribution. The average chemical tanker capacity exceeds 20,000 dwt. The OBO tanker is a multipurpose bulk carrier designed for shipment of oil, bulk grain, fertilizers, or ores. The OBO tanker was introduced during the 1960s, and its average cargo capacity exceeds 200,000 dwt.

The volume of natural gas can be reduced from 17.56 m^3 (620 ft^3) to 0.028 m^3 (1 ft^3) when the gas is liquefied, so liquefaction is an economical state for transport and storage of the gas, which is composed mostly of methane. To liquefy, the gas is passed through refrigeration units, reaching a temperature of $-161°$ C ($-258°$ F). Tanker transport of liquefied natural gas (LNG) requires special, high-pressure tanks of stainless steel, aluminum, and nickel to hold the liquid at $-161°$ C; steel tanks cannot be used for LNG transport or storage, because the steel becomes brittle at low temperatures.

The Intergovernmental Maritime Consultative Organization (IMCO) studies some of the problems of tanker construction and operations. Areas being researched include control of sea pollution, development of adequate fire-fighting equipment, navigation safety, and special shipping lanes for tankers.

Since the early 1980s, as oil sales have slowed, many oil tankers have been retired. LNG and chemical-carrier tanker fleets, on the other hand, continue to expand as the demand for the products they carry grows.   ALAN E. BRANCH

Bibliography: McGuire, G., and White, B., *Liquefied Gas Handling Principles on Ships and in Terminals* (1986); Marks, Alex, *Elements of Oil Tanker Transportation* (1982); Mostert, N., *Supership* (1974); Ratcliffe, K. M., *Liquid Gold Ships: A History of the Tanker 1859–1984* (1985); Rutherford, D., *Tanker Cargo Handling* (1980); Sullivan, G., *Supertanker* (1978).

Tannenberg, Battles of   [tahn'-en-bairk]

Two famous battles were fought in the vicinity of Tannenberg (now Stębark, Poland; formerly in East Prussia) near the Baltic coast. The first, on July 15, 1410, sometimes called the Battle of Grünwald, was a Polish–Lithuanian victory over the TEUTONIC KNIGHTS. The clash halted the Knights' advance eastward along the Baltic and helped spur their decline.

The second battle, in late August 1914, was a German victory early in World War I over Russian armies that had invaded East Prussia. German commander Paul von HINDENBURG and Erich LUDENDORFF, his chief of staff, directed movements that encircled Gen. A. V. Samsonov's Second Russian Army. After the Germans took about 90,000 prisoners, Samsonov killed himself, and his remaining men were forced to retreat.
ROBIN BUSS

Tanner, Henry

The Banjo Lesson (c.1893), by the American artist Henry Tanner, is typical of the sensitive, naturalistic genre scenes for which he is best known. They were painted under the influence of his teacher and good friend Thomas Eakins. (Hampton Institute, Hampton, Va.)

A black American painter of genre and religious subjects, Henry Ossawa Tanner, b. Pittsburgh, Pa., June 21, 1859, d. May 26, 1937, spent most of his life in Europe. Having studied under Thomas Eakins at the Pennsylvania Academy of Fine Arts, Tanner emigrated to Paris in 1891, partly to escape racial prejudice. Among his most moving genre pieces is *The Banjo Lesson* (c.1893; Hampton Institute, Hampton, Va.), showing an old black man teaching a boy to play. Tanner made two trips to Palestine to research his scenes from the Old and New Testaments. These, sometimes set at night or in murky interiors, are dramatic and deeply felt.   ABRAHAM A. DAVIDSON

Bibliography: Mathews, Marcia M., *Henry Ossawa Tanner, American Artist* (1969).

Tannhäuser   [tahn'-hoy-zur]

Tannhäuser was a 13th-century German lyric poet and minnesinger (see MINSTRELS, MINNESINGERS, AND TROUBADOURS) whose adventures became legendary and inspired many ballads and other poems. His extant lyrics suggest that he had been in the service of many noble patrons and that he probably participated in one of the Crusades. In legend he is associated with the Venusberg story in which, after tearing himself away from a life of pleasure, he makes a pilgrimage to Rome for the pope's absolution for his sins. He is told that his sins will not be forgiven until his staff sprouts leaves. The best-known representation of the legend is the opera *Tannhäuser* (1845), by Richard Wagner.

Tanning, Dorothea

The surrealist painter Dorothea Tanning, b. Galesburg, Ill., 1910, was influenced by Max ERNST, whom she married in 1946. They lived first in Arizona and then in Touraine, France. Tanning's symbolism, based on her childhood with her two sisters, involves little girls: in *Eine Kleine Nachtmusik* (1946; Ronald Penrose Collection, London), they watch a giant sunflower creeping toward them in a corridor; in *Palaestra* (1947; William N. Copley Collection, New York City), they form a human pyramid up to the ceiling. In Tanning's works of the 1960s the clarity of forms and objects is sacrificed: nude figures, seemingly involved in orgies, are glimpsed through mists.   ABRAHAM A. DAVIDSON

tanning: see LEATHER AND HIDES.

Tannu Tuva: see TUVA.

tansy [tan'-zee]

The common tansy, or golden buttons, T. vulgare, *is an aromatic, perennial herb that flowers through most of the summer and into the early fall. Although its stem, leaves, flowers, and seeds contain tanacetin, a poisonous oil, the dried leaves have been used as a medicine and as a flavoring in cooking.*

Tansy is the common name for about 50 species of annual or perennial herbs of the genus *Tanacetum,* family Compositae. Common tansy, *T. vulgare,* has a pungent odor and aromatic juice, which is used as a flavoring but can be toxic in high doses. The dried leaves once were used for medicinal purposes.

tantalum [tan'-tuh-luhm]

Tantalum is a chemical element, a member of the third transition series of metals. Its symbol is Ta, its atomic number 73, and its atomic weight 180.9479. First discovered in 1802 by Gustav Ekeberg, it was confused with niobium until Heinrich Rose showed (1844) that niobic and tantalic acids were different.

Tantalum occurs mainly in the mineral columbite-tantalite. The pure metal is gray, heavy, and hard, is malleable and ductile, and can readily be drawn into fine wires. Tantalum is extremely resistant to chemical attack. Its high melting point (2,996° C) is exceeded only by that of tungsten and of rhenium. Most tantalum is used to make electrolytic capacitors and vacuum furnace parts, and it also replaces platinum in chemical, surgical, and dental apparatuses and instruments.   J. ALISTAIR KERR

Tantalus [tan'-tuh-luhs]

In Greek mythology, Tantalus was a son of Zeus and father of PELOPS and Niobe. He was admitted to the company of the gods and permitted to become immortal by eating their food. Depending on the story, Tantalus either stole ambrosia and nectar from the gods' table and fed the sacred food to mortals, or divulged divine secrets, or served his murdered son, Pelops, to the gods to test their omniscience. As punishment, he was condemned to stand eternally in water that receded when he tried to drink and to see beautiful boughs of fruit that bent just beyond his reach when he tried to eat. A great stone, hanging over his head, continuously threatened him. The word *tantalize* is derived from his name.

Tantra [tuhn'-truh]

An 18th-century Tibetan bronze portrays Yamataka, a fierce aspect of the bodhisattva Manjusri, vanquishing a demon and embracing his consort in the Tantric posture known as yab-yum. Tibetan Buddhism, also called Lamaism, is derived from the Indian Mahayana Buddhism and Bon, the traditional Tibetan religion. Tantric rituals and iconography are integral to Tibetan Buddhism. (Private collection.)

The term *Tantra* refers to a pan-Indian religious movement (also called Tantrism) that arose in about the 6th century AD within both BUDDHISM and HINDUISM and to the texts (either Buddhist or Hindu) setting forth its practices and beliefs. The main emphasis of Tantrism is on the development of the devotee's dormant psychophysical powers by means of special meditations and ritual techniques. These are essentially esoteric and must be passed on personally from master to initiate. Stressing the coordination of body, speech, and mind, they include the use of symbolic gestures (mudras); the uttering of potent formulas (MANTRAS); the entering (through meditation) of sacred diagrams (MANDALAS) and yantras; the meditator's creative visualization of and identification with specific divine forms; and the physical, iconographic, or mental use of sexual forces and symbols. Because of the last of these emphases, Tantra has sometimes been considered a degenerate form of religion rather than as the final outgrowth of trends whose roots reach deep into YOGA and Indian cosmology. Although the particulars of practice vary between the Buddhist and Hindu Tantras and within each of these traditions from one text or lineage to another, they all stress the realization, within the body, of the union of polar opposites, whether these be conceived of as devotee and goddess, the masculine principle (SHIVA) and the feminine (SHAKTI), reason and compassion, or samsara and nirvana. Tantrism is traditionally practiced in Tibet, Nepal, Bhutan, and other countries where TIBETAN BUDDHISM is followed, as well as in India.

JOSEPH M. KITAGAWA AND JOHN S. STRONG

Bibliography: Bharati, Agehananda, *The Tantric Tradition* (1965); Chattopadhyaya, Sudhakar, *Reflections on the Tantras* (1978); Wayman, Alex, *Yoga of the Guhyasamájatantra* (1977).

Tanyu [tahn'-yoo]

The Japanese painter Kano Tanyu, 1602–74, headed the main branch of the Kano school of official painters during the Tokugawa shogunate in Edo (modern Tokyo). His family's monopoly on official patronage was assured by his successful completion of the redecoration of Nijo Castle, undertaken by Tokugawa Iemitsu in preparation for the emperor's visit in 1626. Surviving portions of that project show the grandiose style of the day, which degenerated under Tanyu's descendants into academic formalism.   BARBARA BRENNAN FORD

Bibliography: Akiyama, Terukazu, *Japanese Painting* (1977).

Tanzania [tan-zuh-nee'-uh]

The United Republic of Tanzania is located in East Africa. Formed by a merger of the independent states of Tanganyika and the island of ZANZIBAR in April 1964, it is bordered by Mozambique and Malawi to the south; Zambia, Zaire, Burundi, and Rwanda to the west; Uganda and Kenya to the north; and the Indian Ocean to the east. Originally colonized by the Germans, the mainland of Tanganyika became a British colony after World War I, achieved independence in 1961, and came to be considered the model of African socialism.

LAND AND RESOURCES

Most of mainland Tanzania occupies a gently undulating plateau that averages above 1,050 m (3,500 ft) in elevation. The narrow coastal plain, with an average width of only about 30 km (20 mi), is backed by the edge of the plateau. A number of

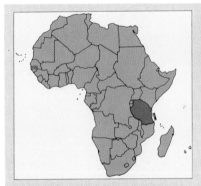

UNITED REPUBLIC OF TANZANIA

    LAND. Area: 945,087 km² (364,900 mi²). Capital and largest city: Dar es Salaam (1982 est. pop., 900,000).
    PEOPLE. Population (1987 est.): 23,500,000; density (1987 est.): 24.9 persons per km² (64.4 per mi²). Distribution (1986 est.): 18% urban, 82% rural. Annual growth (1987 est.): 3.5%. Official language: Swahili. Major religions: traditional religions, Islam, Roman Catholicism, Protestantism.
    EDUCATION AND HEALTH. Literacy (1983): 85% of adult population. Universities (1987): 1. Hospital beds (1984): 22,800. Physicians (1984): 1,065. Life expectancy (1984): women—53.0; men—50.0. Infant mortality (1986 est.): 111 per 1,000 live births.
    ECONOMY. GNP (1985): $5.84 billion; $270 per capita. Labor distribution (1983): agriculture—90%; industry, commerce, other—10%. Foreign trade (1984): imports—$831 million; exports—$396 million; principal trade partners—West Germany, United Kingdom, Japan. Currency: 1 Tanzania shilling = 100 cents.
    GOVERNMENT. Type: one-party state. Legislature: National Assembly. Political subdivisions: 25 regions.
    COMMUNICATIONS. Railroads (1986): 4,460 km (2,771 mi) total. Roads (1984 est.): 82,000 km (50,952 mi) total. Major ports: 3. Major airfields: 3.

small mountain ranges and isolated volcanoes cap the plateau. Mount KILIMANJARO, the highest peak in Africa, rises to 5,895 m (19,340 ft) along the Kenyan border. Lake Victoria (see VICTORIA, LAKE), the second largest lake in the world, is located in the northwest. Lake TANGANYIKA, the second deepest lake in the world, occupies the bottom of the East African Rift Valley (see EAST AFRICAN RIFT SYSTEM) along the western border. Lake NYASA (or Lake Malawi), also part of the rift system, is in the south.

Zanzibar, separated from the mainland by a 35-km-wide (22-mi) channel, has an area of 1,658 km² (640 mi²). PEMBA, another island, is located 48 km (30 mi) northwest of Zanzibar and covers 984 km² (380 mi²).

The best soils for agriculture are those of volcanic origin in the highlands and alluvial soils in river valleys. Most of the plateau surface is covered by deeply weathered red soils of moderate quality.

Because of Tanzania's tropical location temperature is largely a function of elevation. Greater rainfall (more than 1,420 mm/56 in) occurs in mountainous areas, whereas the central part of the country receives less than 610 mm (24 in). Average annual temperatures vary from 20° C (68° F) in the highlands to 32° C (90° F) on the coast.

Tanzanian rivers flow into four major drainage basins: the Indian Ocean, Lake Victoria, the Congo River, and an interior drainage basin. The Rufiji River, draining into the Indian Ocean, is the principal stream. Forests are found only in the uplands, although woodlands composed of shorter trees and a less-closed canopy cover most of the country. As rainfall diminishes, grasslands become dominant. Animals range from antelope to zebra, from dik-dik to elephant. Mineral deposits are widely scattered, but none are of major economic significance. Most important are the diamonds from Shinyanga. Arable land covers 60% of the country.

PEOPLE

Africans constitute about 99% of the population and are divided among approximately 120 different ethnic groups. Most of these groups are small; 97 of them account for only one-third of the total population. The largest ethnic group, the SUKUMA, constitute only 12.4% of the total. The country's people speak languages belonging to four distinct groups or families: the BANTU, accounting for about 95% of the total; Southern Cushitic; Nilotic; and Khoisan. Swahili, a trade language with elements of Arabic and Bantu languages, is the official language (see AFRICAN LANGUAGES). Although their numbers are declining, 30% of the inhabitants profess traditional religious beliefs. About 40% of the inhabitants are Christians; the remainder are Muslims.

Tanzania is a predominantly rural country. The capital and largest city is DAR ES SALAAM. Dodoma, a new capital city being built in central Tanzania and scheduled for completion in 1990, has a population of 100,000 (1984 est.).

The country is justly proud of its achievements in education and health care. The literacy rate, only 15% at independence, is now the highest in Africa, and education is free and compulsory for all children between the ages of 7 and 14. The University of Dar es Salaam was founded in 1961.

Contemporary art in Tanzania is exemplified by the abstract Makonde wood carvings, the Zaramo carvings of people and animals, and the famous wooden chests of Zanzibar. A resurgence of prose and poetry written in Swahili has taken place in recent years. Music, performed on drums and plucked instruments, is used primarily to accompany traditional dancing. (See AFRICAN ART; AFRICAN LITERATURE; AFRICAN MUSIC.)

ECONOMIC ACTIVITY

Tanzania's mineral and agricultural resources can be described as moderate at best. The agricultural sector provides more than 80% of all export earnings, although only 15% of the land is cultivated. Coffee, tea, cotton, sisal, pyrethrum, tobacco, and cashew nuts are the chief commercial crops; cloves provide about 45% of Zanzibar's export income. Cassava and corn are the primary subsistence crops. Manufacturing is overwhelmingly for domestic consumption and consists primarily of processing agricultural products. Some diamonds, gold, phosphates, tin, coal, and iron ore are mined.

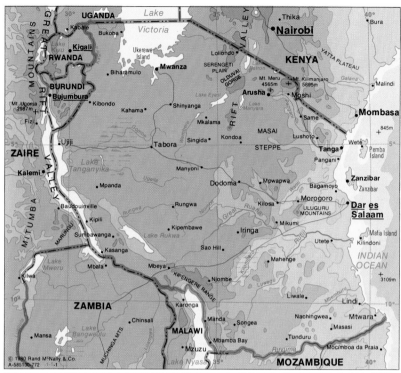

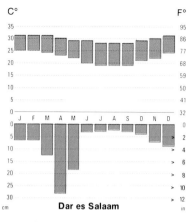

Bars indicate monthly ranges of temperatures (red) and precipitation (blue) of Dar es Salaam, the capital of Tanzania. Located on the Indian Ocean, Dar es Salaam has a tropical wet-dry climate.

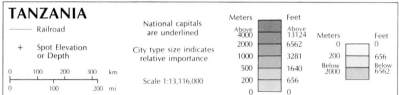

TANZANIA

— Railroad

+ Spot Elevation or Depth

National capitals are underlined

City type size indicates relative importance

Scale 1:13,116,000

Meters	Feet
Above 4000	Above 13124
2000	6562
1000	3281
500	1640
200	656
0	0

Meters	Feet
0	0
200	656
Below 2000	Below 6562

0 100 200 300 km
0   100   200 mi

© 1980 Rand McNally & Co.
A-585100-772

Large-scale socialization of the Tanzanian economy began with the Arusha Declaration in 1967. The keystone of this declaration was *ujamaa* (familyhood)—rural self-reliance and development based on collective activity. Banks, major industries, and trade were nationalized, and millions of peasants were resettled into agricultural cooperative villages. The economy grew steadily until 1977. From 1978 to 1984, however, per capita income declined 30%. The decline was due to a combination of factors, including rapid population growth, the breakup of the East African Community (1977), prolonged drought (1981–84), a growing trade deficit, inefficiency and corruption in state-run corporations, and the costs of Tanzania's 1979 invasion of Uganda. In the 1980s the government began to modify its strict socialist economic policies, providing a greater role for private enterprise and incentives to increase agricultural production. Attempts are also being made

Dar es Salaam, Tanzania's capital, largest city, and principal port on the Indian Ocean, was founded in 1862 by the sultan of Zanzibar. The city's initial growth dates from the colonial era, when Dar es Salaam prospered as the capital of German East Africa.

A herd of elephants forages for food along the grasslands, or savannas, of northeastern Tanzania near the Kenyan border. In the background lies Kilimanjaro, the tallest mountain of Africa. This snow-capped extinct volcano rises to a height of 5,895 m (19,340 ft).

to develop tourism, discouraged after independence, as a source of much-needed foreign exchange. The country is heavily dependent on foreign aid.

GOVERNMENT

According to the constitution of 1977, executive power of the united republic is vested in the president, who is advised by a cabinet and a vice-president; if the president is from Tanganyika, the vice-president must be from Zanzibar, and vice versa. The national assembly is composed of 165 members, 106 of whom are popularly elected. The sole legal political party is the Revolutionary party of Tanzania. Since 1965, Zanzibar has had control over internal affairs, with its own executive and legislature. Each of the 24 regions is headed by a commissioner appointed by the president.

HISTORY

By the Late Stone Age, people lived (c.500 BC) at various places along the Tanzanian coast. Accounts of the coastal area in the 1st century AD describe a number of settlements where commerce took place. For the next millennium Arab traders plied the coast, trading with Zanzibar and settlements on the Tanzanian mainland.

The principal settlement of Tanzania occurred by migrating waves of Bantu peoples. Probably originating about 2,000 years ago in eastern Nigeria, the proto-Bantu seem to have moved along the Congo River system into the southern portion of present-day Zaire. By the 10th century the areas around Lake Victoria and Lake Tanganyika had been settled. Bantu peoples continued to spread east and south in the 12th to the 15th centuries.

In 1498, Vasco da GAMA became the first European to visit the coast of Tanzania, and the Portuguese conducted trade along the coast until 1698 when they were expelled by Arabs from Oman. European missionaries and explorers such as David LIVINGSTONE entered the area in the 1850s. The Anglo-German Agreements (1886, 1900) divided spheres of influence along the present Kenya-Tanzania border, giving Germany control of the southern portion (today's Tanzania).

GERMAN EAST AFRICA was administered by the German East Africa Company. In 1891 the German government assumed control and the region became a protectorate. Opposition to foreign rule mounted, and the quasi-religious Maji Maji rebellion lasted from 1905 to 1907. In 1920, as a result of the German defeat in World War I, the British took over German East Africa. In 1954, Julius NYERERE was one of the founders of the Tanganyika African National Union (TANU), which led the nationalist movement. The well-organized movement won independence for Tanganyika in 1961, and Nyerere became head of state. Zanzibar, which gained independence in 1963, joined Tanganyika in 1964; in 1965 the nation was renamed Tanzania.

Nyerere, who became one of Africa's most respected leaders, unified the country and expanded education and health care. He supported black liberation movements in Mozambique, Rhodesia (now Zimbabwe), and South Africa and sent troops to Uganda in 1979 to help depose dictator Idi AMIN

DADA. The last Tanzanian forces withdrew from Uganda in 1981. Ideological differences led to the closing of the border between Tanzania and Kenya from 1977 to 1983. In 1984, mounting secessionist sentiments on Zanzibar forced the resignation of Zanzibar president Aboud Jumbe. His replacement, Ali Hassan Mwinyi, succeeded Nyerere when he retired as president of Tanzania in 1985. Nyerere retained his powerful position as party chairman and was reelected to another 5-year term as party leader in 1987.   RONALD D. GARST

Bibliography: Barkan, J. D., and Okumu, J. J., eds., *Politics and Public Policy in Kenya and Tanzania*, rev. ed. (1984); Bennett, N. R., *A History of the Arab State of Zanzibar* (1978); Bolton, D., *Nationalization: A Road to Socialism?* (1985); Clark, W. E., *Socialist Development and Public Investment in Tanzania, 1964–73* (1978); Coulson, A., *Tanzania: A Political Economy* (1982); Kahama, C. G., et al., *The Challenge for Tanzania's Economy* (1986); Resnick, I., *The Long Transition* (1982); Yeager, R., *Tanzania* (1982).

T'ao Ch'ien: see T'AO YÜAN-MING.

Tao-chi: see SHIH-T'AO.

Tao Te Ching   (Daode Jing)   [dow duh jing]

A philosophical classic by LAO-TZU, the *Tao Te Ching* is the single most important text of Chinese TAOISM. According to tradition, the sage composed its approximately 5,000 words in the 6th century BC at the request of a gatekeeper who wanted a record of his teachings. The book is now considered to date from the 4th century BC. Laced with richly poetic imagery, it counsels balance, restraint, simplicity, and the avoidance of activity and desire as the means of achieving harmony with the natural currents of the Tao, or universal way. In ancient China Lao-tzu's thoughts rivaled those of Confucius in popularity; hundreds of commentaries and translations exist.

Bibliography: Lao-tzu, *Tao Te Ching*, trans. by R. Wilhelm (1985); Sims, Bennett B., *Lao-tzu and the "Te Ching"* (1971).

T'ao Yüan-ming   (Tao Yuanming)   [tow yoo-ahn-ming]

The greatest of Chinese nature poets, T'ao Yüan-ming (courtesy name of T'ao Ch'ien), b. AD 365, d. 427, served as a magistrate in P'eng-tse, but after a tenure of only 83 days he resigned and returned to his farm to lead a life of freedom and frugality. T'ao Yüan-ming's poetical insight is rooted in the Taoist concept of oneness with nature. His poetry, which is marked by simplicity of diction and spontaneity of feeling, exercised an immense influence on later nature poets. He was also a skillful prose writer: *The Biography of Master Five Willows* is a charming self-portrait, and *The Peach-blossom Fountain* describes a utopian world according to the Taoist ideal.   ANGELA JUNG PALANDRI

Bibliography: Hightower, J. R., *The Poetry of T'ao Ch'ien* (1970).

Taoism   [dow'-izm]

The term *Taoism* refers to a movement that developed alongside CONFUCIANISM into both a philosophy and a religion, becoming one of the major belief systems in traditional China. The TAO TE CHING, sometimes called the *Lao-tzu* after its legendary author, and the *Chuang-tzu* stand as the core texts of Taoism.

Taoist Philosophy. The Taoist movement began during the Eastern Chou dynasty (c.770–256 BC) when religious hermits challenged Confucius's socially responsible *tao* (prescriptive doctrine, or way). Early Taoist iconoclasts advocated asceticism, hedonism, and egoism as the way. Mature Taoist theory, however, began with the slogan "abandon knowledge, discard self," as advocated by Shen Tao (c.4th century BC). He argued that there is only one actual *tao* and that to follow several prescriptive ways is a distraction from this natural, inevitable course of action.

The philosophy of the LAO-TZU (c.4th century BC) developed Shen Tao's slogan into a psycholinguistic theory in which doctrines were said to create "contrived" action *(wei)* by shaping desires *(yü)*. The process of learning the names *(ming)* used in the doctrines trained individuals to make distinctions between, for example, good and bad, beautiful and ugly, high and low, and "exists" *(yu)* and "exists-not" *(wu),* and thereby shaped desires. To abandon prescriptive knowledge, then, was to abandon names, distinctions, and socially induced tastes or desires. Thus spontaneous behavior, or non-contrived action *(wu-wei),* resulted.

Shen Tao's original prescription to give up all prescription and Lao-tzu's primitivism (his seeming advocacy of giving up name-motivated, conventionally conditioned action) are both virtually incoherent. To follow such advice is to ignore it. The analytic school, which advocated names in China, made this succinct criticism of early Taoism: to say "all language is perverse" is perverse. In other words, if what is said is acceptable then it is perverse.

CHUANG-TZU (*c.*399–*c.*295 BC), intimately familiar with the analytic arguments, constructed a more coherent version of Taoist theory. Rather than treating all language as perverse, he allowed that all language use was equally natural—all the disputing theorists were equally "pipes of heaven." Because all language expresses a contextual standpoint, or perspective, from which terms such as *this* or *that* (which have no fixed relation to the world) are used, any attempt to judge or rank perspectives itself must be from some perspective. Thus,

Taoists offer incense and food to their deified ancestors. True Taoist philosophy does not countenance ancestor worship, but the practice has been incorporated into religious rituals from Chinese folk tradition.

all ways of dividing the world into "things" remain equal. None has privileged status. None is uniquely the doctrine of heaven and nature.

It is not necessary, however, to give up language or to stop following doctrines. Humans naturally advocate and follow doctrines just as fledgling birds naturally tweet and twitter. Chuang-tzu advocted openness to all perspectives, suggesting myriad ways to evaluate one's way through life. Flute playing, butchering, and the analysis of names are among the traditional examples given for training responses. Taoist mastery can be achieved through any skill and can be characterized by the mystical sense of having transcended deliberate skill through guidance of the *tao.* Undiscovered ways may teach techniques of unimaginable power. Although Chuang-tzu argued against the preference for life over death, Taoist religion came to strive for a way, among the infinite number of undiscovered ways, that led to long life.

Taoist Religion. Religious Taoism was associated with legalism and the cult of the YELLOW EMPEROR, and it became popular after the suppression and decline of classical thought during the 3d century BC. Taoist experimenters in breathing practices and ALCHEMY caught the fancy of superstitious monarchs seeking immortality. These rulers promoted the compilation of such books as the *Lieh Tzu* (comp. during Han dynasty, 202 BC–AD 220) and the *Huai Nan Tzu* (*c.*100 BC), which cited fragments of the classical Taoist texts in support of every known occult practice.

Taoist sects based on the supposed *tao* of any one of thousands of local folk deities or archaic culture heroes (including Lao-tzu and the Yellow Emperor) spread throughout China. Experimentation continued in meditation, sexual practices, hygiene (internal alchemy), and travel in search of the secrets of long life. Still tinged with classical anarchist impulses, major sects—such as the Celestial Masters movement, headed by CHANG TAO-LING (*c.*2d century AD), and the Yellow Turban movement—often battled the imperial government.

Taoist religion provided a foothold for the introduction of Buddhism and influenced the form of its elaboration in China. Taoists developed a collection of over 1,400 scriptures known as *Tao-tsang.* Religious Taoism and Buddhism have blended in the minds of most ordinary Chinese believers, found now principally in Hong Kong and Taiwan.   CHAD HANSEN

Bibliography: Feng Gia-Ku, and English, Jane, *Lao Tzu: The Tao Te Ching* (1979); Graham, A. C., *Chuang Tzu: The Inner Chapters* (1981); Kaltenmark, Max, *Lao Tzu and Taoism,* trans. by R. Greaves (1969); Smullyan, Raymond M., *The Tao Is Silent* (1977); Welsh, Holmes, *Taoism: The Parting of the Way* (1957).

Taormina   [tah-ohr-mee'-nah]

Taormina is a town with a population of 10,085 (1981) on the east coast of Sicily, about 50 km (30 mi) south of Messina. On a hill overlooking the Ionian Sea and within view of Mount ETNA, Taormina is a popular winter resort. Landmarks include a Greek theater, Roman ruins, and the 14th-century Palazzo Corvaia. Founded in the 4th century BC by Dionysius the Elder of Syracuse, Taormina came under the Romans in 210 BC. It was seized by Arabs in the 10th century and fell to the Normans in 1079.   DANIEL R. LESNICK

Taos   [tows]

Taos (1980 pop., 3,369), officially known as Don Fernando de Taos, is a town in north central New Mexico. Located at an altitude of about 2,135 m (7,000 ft), 90 km (55 mi) north of Santa Fe, it is the seat of Taos County. The ancient Pueblo Indian village of San Geronimo de Taos lies north of the town, and the Spanish farming center, Ranchos de Taos, lies to the south. Founded about 1615, Taos is one of the oldest white settlements in the United States. It became an important trade center on the Santa Fe Trail in the 19th century. Since the early 1900s the town has been a noted artists' colony.

tap dancing

Except for the Indians' ritual dances, the first indigenous American art dance is tap dancing, whose roots lie in spirited Irish and English jigs and clog dances and in the rhythmic African improvisations that immigrants and free blacks combined spontaneously during the 1840s. Characterized by rapidly tapping toes and heels, usually in shoes fitted with metal tips, tap dancing evolved through both black and white minstrel shows, revues, vaudeville, musical comedy, and film, accumulating sophisticated new sounds for the feet, such as brushes, slides, hops, rolls, and complex new accents for the upper body as it went along. In 1900 the Floradora Sextet performed the first synchronized tap routine. The 50 girls of the first ZIEGFELD FOLLIES (1907) constituted the first tapping chorus line.   BARBARA NEWMAN

Bibliography: Ames, J., and Siegelman, J., *The Book of Tap* (1977).

tapaculo   [tap-uh-koo'-loh]

Tapaculos are a small-to-medium-sized, dull-colored, poor-flying ground birds found from Central America through

South America, mainly in forested regions. The more than 25 species make up the family Rhinocryptidae. Tapaculos have short, rounded wings, stout legs, and a distinctive flap of skin covering the nostrils. Their common name, of Spanish derivation, refers to their "immodest" habit of cocking the tail high over the back. They forage for seeds and insects.

JOSEPH R. JEHL

tape recording

Tape recording is the recording and the replaying of sound or video on magnetic tape. Magnetic recording requires both a recording medium, a thin, flexible substance capable of carrying magnetic signals equivalent to the aural or video signals being recorded; and a device for recording and playback (see SOUND RECORDING AND REPRODUCTION).

Although the idea of magnetic recording had been suggested by several inventors in the late 19th century, the first operating equipment was built by the Danish engineer Valdemar POULSEN, who patented his machine in 1898. Poulsen used steel wires or thin steel ribbon for the recording medium, and his invention met with some commercial success before World War I. Germany patented a new kind of tape, a strip of paper coated with iron particles, in 1928; and in 1935, BASF, a branch of the German chemical company I. G. Farben, produced a particle-coated plastic tape, which was recorded by and played on the Magnetophon, a machine developed by AEG Telefunken. The rest of the world was barely aware of these developments; during World War II, however, listeners to German radio were at a loss to explain how Hitler could be heard speaking in Bremen at 11AM and at 11:15 in Munich, hundreds of kilometers to the south. At war's end the Magnetophon became the model for new improvements outside Germany.

PRINCIPLES

In most of its forms the magnetic tape recorder employs the same basic principles. Aural or visual information is converted into an electrical signal, then mixed with a steady tone at a frequency higher than is required by the information itself. This tone, or AC bias, reduces distortion levels and allows for the recording of high-fidelity sound.

The combined signal is fed into the coil of a recording head, producing a fluctuating magnetic field that magnetizes the pigment (the iron oxide or other magnetic particles) on the tape as the tape moves past the head. During playback the tape is passed over the playback head, and the tape's magnetic field induces a current in the head's coil. This current is then amplified and converted into the final output—a replication of the original information.

Tape Speed and Composition. In general, the higher the tape's transport speed, the higher the frequencies that can be recorded on it; also, the wider the individual recording tracks on the tape, the lower the noise level in the final output. A major variable in both respects, however, is the pigment used in the tape. In the 1950s, with the tapes then in use, minimum standards for quality home-music reproduction dictated a transport speed of 7½ inches per second (ips; 19 cm/sec) and two tracks (one monaural track in each direction of tape travel) on ¼-in tape. Today's cassettes, which at their best offer comparable fidelity, run at only 1⅞ ips (4.75 cm/sec) and contain four tracks (a stereo pair in each direction) on a tape barely ⅛ in (3.81 mm) wide. Credit for maintaining good sound quality despite cutting back on tape width and speed can be ascribed to improved tape formulation, as in chromium-dioxide and metal-particle tapes, and also to improvements in head design and electronics. Some newer cassette machines offer automatic tape reversal and high-speed tape-to-tape dubbing.

Noise-Reduction Systems. The most obvious drawback to the use of tape as a recording medium is "tape hiss"—an audible sound composed of high frequencies picked up at random in the recording process. Several systems have been developed to suppress tape hiss (as well as the hiss that is often the background to FM signals, which are also accompanied by random, high-frequency noise). The systems operate in essentially the same manner: before they are recorded, audio signals are passed through an encoder that compresses one or more frequency bands. During playback, a decoder expands the signals. This compression-expansion process, for all practical purposes, eliminates tape and FM hiss.

The Dolby system, the original noise-reduction process, is used today in two versions for consumer equipment: Dolby B compresses the upper treble range, suppressing noise by about 10 decibels (dBs). Dolby C adds the mid-range bands, reducing noise by some 20 dBs. A second popular system, DBX, affects all frequency bands simultaneously.

TYPES OF RECORDERS

Originally, the standard tape format was the open-spool, or reel-to-reel, recorder, still used by professionals. Reel-to-reel tapes, however, have become increasingly elaborate. They may be as wide as 2 in (5.08 cm). The single track of the earlier monaural models has been replaced by 16, 24, or even more tracks, all of which can be recorded simultaneously.

The Introduction of Cassette Recorders. The compact cassette recorder, or tape deck, first introduced by Philips of the Netherlands in the early 1960s as a dictation machine, is now not only stereophonic but, within its rather stringent limitations of size, contains the technology for reproducing amaz-

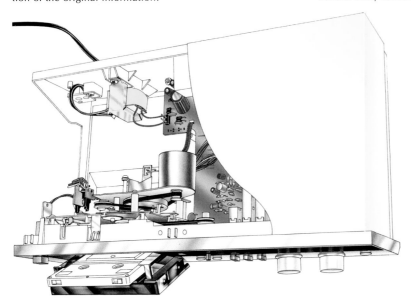

On the front end of a cassette tape recorder, or tape deck, settings provide for tape bias change and noise reduction. Sound level is controlled by knobs and can be read off a display. The tape transport system is controlled by gears and a motor inside the deck, and by knobs on the front end (hidden here by the open cassette carrier) that specify record, playback, and so forth. Recording and playback are achieved as the tape moves over a record/playback head. A counter tracks elapsed time or the amount of tape used.

ingly fine sound. Most recorders have switches to accommodate different tape formulations; noise-reduction switches; and dials to indicate frequency levels during recording and playback. Tape cassettes offer 30, 45, or 60 minutes of recording on each tape side.

Digital Systems. Digital tape systems use magnetic pulses representing a binary encoding of signals—that is, after recording, all the magnetized particles on the tape will point in one of two directions. Analog systems, on the other hand, represent a sound according to the percentage of particles pointing in one or the other direction. Although analog systems are highly successful, they reproduce any noise or distortion that happens to occur in the recorded signal. Digital signals eliminate almost all noise and distortion. Digital audio tape (DAT) recorders, a Japanese introduction, may well replace analog recorders, when enough digitally recorded tapes are available, and when the legal problems of tape and compact-disc copying are solved.

Videotape Recorders. Videotape recorders, or videocassette recorders (VCRs), use a fixed recording head to record sound. The picture—which requires much higher recorded frequencies and therefore much higher head-to-tape speeds—is recorded by heads that are rotated in the direction opposite to and on a bias with that of the tape motion. This "helical scan" uses more available tape space, allowing for the storage of larger amounts of information (see VIDEO RECORDING).

ROBERT LONG

Bibliography: Camras, M., ed., *Magnetic Tape Recording* (1985); Degen, Clara, *Understanding and Using Video* (1985); Hoagland, A. A., *Digital Magnetic Recording* (1963; repr. 1983); Jorgensen, F., *The Complete Handbook of Magnetic Recording*, 3d ed. (1986); Robinson, J. F., *Using Videotape* (1981); White, R. M., ed., *Introduction to Magnetic Recording* (1985).

tapestry

The term *tapestry* refers to hand-woven, figured fabrics—usually of silk or wool—used for wall hangings and furniture upholstery. A tapestry is composed of a foundation weave, the warp, across which are passed the different colored threads of the weft, which forms a decorative pattern. The warp is covered completely by the weft threads, which are taken across the width of the warp first in one direction and then in the other within the boundaries of the different zones of color (see LOOM; WEAVING).

TECHNIQUE

The colors and shapes of the pattern are indicated in a plan, or preliminary design, of the tapestry called the cartoon (see CARTOON, art). Tapestries are woven on either high-warp or low-warp looms. The high-warp loom is vertical, with the warp threads stretched vertically between two rollers. The warp threads, usually linen, wool, or cotton, are separated by a rounded rod into two sets, back and front, of odd and even threads. All the even-numbered threads are placed in front of the separating rod and remain free, and the odd-numbered threads remain at the back, each encircled by a short loop, or heddle. By pulling on the heddles, which are attached to bars, with the left hand, the weaver brings the back threads through to the front; at the same time, the right hand threads the weft in between the two series of warp threads with a shuttle. The weft thread is passed first over the back set of warp threads (half weft) and then in the other direction over the front set, making a complete weft. On a low-warp loom the warp threads are stretched horizontally between the two rollers. The threads, again divided into an odd and even series, are now all equipped with heddles, which are arranged underneath the warp threads and controlled by treadles. By pressing down with the foot alternately on the treadles, the weaver can lower first one and then the other series of warp threads, allowing more rapid progress than high-warp weaving in which the weaver works with the hands alone.

HISTORY

Both systems were known and used in the earliest tapestries: a painting (c.3000 BC) found in the necropolis of Beni Hasan in Egypt shows a high-warp loom; the finest and most interesting of ancient tapestries were also produced by this method in

Egypt by the Copts beginning in the 3d century AD. Excavations and research by archaeologists and historians have proved that the process of tapestry weaving was also known and practiced by the Hebrews, Greeks, Romans, Chinese, and Incas, among other ancient peoples.

Tapestries were not produced in Europe until about the 11th century. Thought to be the oldest surviving Western tapestry, the Cloth of Saint Gereon (originally in the Church of Saint Gereon in Cologne, Germany) is divided in fragments among the Kunstgewerbemuseum in Berlin, the Musée Historique des Tissus in Lyon, France, the Victoria and Albert Museum in London, and the Germanisches Museum in Nuremberg, Germany. Generally assumed to have been woven in Cologne in the early 11th century, it bears ornaments similar to those in illuminated manuscripts of the period. Germany, especially the region of Saxony, was a center for tapestries woven during the Romanesque period; examples are preserved in Halberstadt Cathedral.

By the 12th and 13th centuries, high- and low-warp weaving was practiced in France and Belgium, with centers of production established during the Gothic period in Paris and Ar-

(Above) *Symbolic floral and mythological motifs decorate the tapestries of the Copts, the native Christian people of Egypt, whose art flourished from the 3d to the 12th century. (Musée Historique des Tissus, Lyon.)*

(Left) *"The Great Whore that sitteth upon the waters," a figure from the Book of Revelation, is depicted in this detail from the Apocalypse of Angers. Commissioned by the duke of Anjou, it was woven in wool in 15 colors. (Musée des Tapisseries, Angers.)*

(Below) *A late-15th-century tapestry from Basel, Switzerland, portrays King Arthur and the emperor Charlemagne against a milles-fleurs ("thousand flowers") background. Unlike sophisticated Flemish and French tapestries, those of Basel have a simple figural style. (Historiches Museum, Basel.)*

"The Sense of Taste" (above) *is one of six celebrated tapestries from* The Lady and the Unicorn, *a set woven in the Loire Valley during the late 15th century. The symbolic figures are posed against a crimson background of* milles-fleurs *design. (Musée de Cluny, Paris.)*

ras in France and Tournai and Brussels in Belgium. The Parisian tapestry industry reached its height during the 14th century due to the royal patronage of Charles V of France and his brothers—Louis d'Anjou; Jean, Duc de Berry; and Philip the Bold, Duke of Burgundy. For Louis d'Anjou, the Parisian merchant and master weaver Nicolas Bataille supplied (1377–80) the seven immense *Apocalypse* tapestries (Musée des Tapisseries, Angers, France), the largest tapestry series

ever woven, from cartoons by Hennequin de Bruges inspired by illuminated manuscripts of the Book of Revelation. The Burgundian dukes—Philip the Bold and his descendants John the Fearless, Philip the Good, and Charles the Bold—to whom the province of Artois and its capital of Arras belonged, assured the commercial future of Arras during the 14th and 15th centuries by ordering their richest tapestries from workshops there. The only surviving documented work of the ear-

(Left) *A scene from the tapestry series* The Life of Louis XIV *shows the French king visiting the Gobelins tapestry works in Paris, where the work was woven from a design by Charles Le Brun. The king is accompanied by his minister Colbert, who established the factory. (Mobilier National, Paris.)*

lier period of Arras is the *Saint Piat and Saint Eleuthère* series presented to the Cathedral of Tournai in 1402. By the mid-15th century, Tournai had begun to replace Arras as a center of Burgundian patronage: from Pasquier Grenier, one of Tournai's master weavers, Philip the Good purchased (1459) a series of tapestries representing the *Story of Alexander the Great* (Galleria Doria Pamphili, Rome).

During the 16th and early 17th centuries, Brussels became the capital of European tapestry production with large factories established by Pieter van Aelst and Pieter Pannemaker. Among the Flemish weavers' great and noble clients were the Austrian Habsburgs, Sigismund II of Poland, and Pope Leo X, for whom van Aelst wove the *Acts of the Apostles* (1515–19; Victoria and Albert Museum), after cartoons by Raphael for the Sistine Chapel. With this series he introduced the Italian Renaissance style and the practice of copying paintings to European tapestry design.

Widely admired, Flemish weavers established workshops throughout Europe during the 16th and 17th centuries. At Ferrara, Italy, Jan and Nicolaus Carcher served Ercole II d'Este; Jan Rost, Nicolaus Carcher, and Jan van der Straet (Stradanus) supervised the tapestry workshop in Florence of Cosimo I de'Medici. The first series woven on the Florentine looms was the *History of Joseph* (1547–50; Palazzo Vecchio, Florence), designed by the Mannerist painter Angelo Bronzino. In the late 16th century Josse Jean Lanckeert and Frans Spierincx moved to Delft, the Netherlands, from Antwerp, Belgium; at about the same time Flemish weavers established workshops in Germany—at Stuttgart (Jakob de Carmes), Frankenthal (Pierre de Waeyere and Everard Van Orley), and Munich (Jan van der Biest). In 1620 a royal tapestry factory was established at Mortlake, England, with Josse Ampe of Bruges, Belgium, in charge of chiefly Flemish workers and weavers.

These provincial manufacturing centers did not (and could not) compete with the French royal factories founded by Louis XIV at GOBELINS (1662), Beauvais (1664), and AUBUSSON (1665). These factories dominated European production for nearly two centuries with tapestry series designed by France's greatest painters, including Charles Le Brun, Jean Baptiste Oudry, and François Boucher; the last two worked both for Gobelins and Beauvais. Among the series Oudry designed for Beauvais were *The New Indian Hunts* (1727), *Country Pleasures* (1730), and *Fine Verdures* (1736); for the same factory Boucher designed *Village Festivals* (1736), *The Story of Psyche*

A detail from the tapestry set Song of the World *(1957–64), by Jean Lurçat, shows a cosmos of animal and vegetable life surrounded by a ring of fire. (Musée des Tapisseries, Angers.)*

(1741), and *Loves of the Gods* (1749). During the 19th century, when tapestries were in less demand for wall hangings, Beauvais specialized in furniture covers, as Aubusson had since the 18th century (such as the covers with Oudry's scenes from the *Fables of La Fontaine*). When Beauvais was amalgamated with Gobelins in 1940, Aubusson became the major center for tapestry design and production in the 20th century—thanks to Jean Lurçat, who settled there for the purpose of creating a new tapestry industry at the request of the French Ministry of National Education in 1939. In 1945, Lurçat, with the artists Marc Saint-Saens and Jean Picart Le Doux, founded the Association of Tapestry Cartoon-Painters, which pioneered the revival of tapestry as modern architectural decoration, according to the principle that tapestries should be original works of art (not copies after paintings), intended for walls and designed for specific architectural spaces.

Reviewed by KATHRYN B. HIESINGER

Bibliography: Ackerman, Phyllis, *Tapestry, The Mirror of Civilization* (1933; repr. 1970); Bennett, Anna, *Five Centuries of Tapestry* (1976); Franses, Jack, *Tapestries and Their Mythology* (1973); Florisoone, Michel, et al., *The Book of Tapestry: History and Technique* (1978); Jobe, Joseph, ed., *The Art of Tapestry* (1965); Thomson, W. G., *A History of Tapestry* (1930); Weigert, R. A., *French Tapestry* (1963).

tapeworm

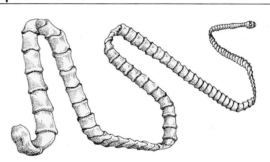

An adult pork tapeworm, T. solium, *lives in the intestines of humans, folding itself in accordion style to fit its long body into small spaces. A pork tapeworm, which grows up to 10 m (33 ft) long, can live in the small intestine, which is 6 m (20 ft) long. Humans get tapeworms by eating poorly cooked pork that is infested with tapeworm eggs.*

A tapeworm is a ribbonlike colony of parasitic flatworms, of the class Cestoda, that infest humans and other vertebrate animals. Species that most commonly infest humans are: the beef tapeworm, *Taenia saginata*, found worldwide; the pork tapeworm, *T. solium*, found mostly in Central and South America, Africa, and Asia; and the fish tapeworm, *Dibothriocephalus latus*, of parts of Europe, Africa, and the Americas.

A tapeworm consists of a head (scolex) that is equipped with hooks or suckers used to attach the parasite to the host's intestinal lining. The "body" is composed of segments known as proglottids, which are separate, sexually functional individuals that can synchronize their muscular activity to keep the colony mobile. The colony is looped back and forth so that the intestine remains unblocked; a 9-m (30-ft) tapeworm can inhabit a 3-m (10-ft) intestine.

Younger proglottids have testes; as they get older, the testes shrivel up and are replaced by ovaries and a uterus. Proglottids having male sex organs release sperm that travel to the older proglottids and fertilize the eggs. Proglottids that contain developing embryos break away and are excreted with feces. Larvae develop and, if the waste matter is eaten by an animal, become dormant and encysted in the animal's muscle tissue. Humans eating poorly cooked animal meat can then ingest the encysted larvae. Adult tapeworm infestations can be eliminated with chemotherapy. Humans, however, can also serve as intermediary hosts, the larvae forming cysts up to 25 cm (10 in) in diameter in the brain, lungs, liver, or other organs. Such infections can only be treated surgically, if at all.

LORUS J. AND MARGERY MILNE

Bibliography: Olsen, O. Wilford, *Animal Parasites*, 3d ed. (1974); Smyth, J. D., *The Physiology of Cestodes* (1969); Wardle, R. A., and McLeod, James A., *Zoology of Tapeworms* (1952; repr. 1968).

Tápies, Antonio   [tahp'-yes]

A leading abstract painter of postwar Spain, Tápies, b. Antonio Tápies Puig, Dec. 13, 1923, first exhibited his paintings in 1948. His early works, from 1949 and the early 1950s, show the influence of the surrealists, particularly Joan Miró. His later works focus on his materials; such paintings as *Swirling Sand* (1955; collection of Anthony Denney, London) and *Two Blankets Filled with Straw* (1968; Galerie Maeght, Paris) are mixed-media works combining such raw materials as sand, straw, and cloth with paint. Tápies had his first retrospective exhibition in the United States in 1953.   VALENTIN TATRANSKY

Bibliography: Linhartova, V., *Antonio Tápies*, trans. by A. Engel (1972).

tapioca: see MANIOC.

tapir   [tay'-pur]

An infant Malayan tapir, T. indicus, *has a patterned coat of spots and stripes that will fade by the time the animal is 1 year old.*

The tapir looks like a pig but is related to the rhinoceros and the horse. Four species make up the genus *Tapirus*, family Tapiridae. Tapirs are 1.8 to 2.4 m (6 to 8 ft) long, stand about 1 m (40 in) at the shoulder, and may weigh more than 270 kg (600 lb). The tapering and sloping face ends in a small, movable trunk. The eyes are small and the ears rounded and erect. The back is rounded, the legs short, and the tail stumpy. Each forefoot has four toes and each hind foot three. The Brazilian tapir, *T. terrestris*, ranges from Colombia and Venezuela to Brazil; Baird's tapir, *T. bairdi*, from southern Mexico to Ecuador; and the wooly Andean, or mountain, tapir, *T. roulini*, from Venezuela to Peru. These three species are reddish brown to black above, lighter below. The Asiatic, or Malayan, tapir, *T. indicus*, black on the front half and legs and white on the back and sides, is found in Thailand, Burma, Vietnam, Malaya, and Sumatra. Tapirs move quickly in open or jungle habitat and live from sea level to almost 4,575 m (15,000 ft). Also good swimmers, they feed on almost any plant and also raid farm crops. The female produces one young after a 400-day gestation period.   EVERETT SENTMAN

Tappan brothers   [tap'-uhn]

The Tappan brothers were U.S. businessmen and abolitionists. **Arthur Tappan**, b. Northampton, Mass., May 22, 1786, d. July 23, 1865, opened (1826) a silk-jobbing firm in New York City, which became successful because of its cash-and-carry and low-markup policies. In 1827 he began publishing the *N.Y. Journal of Commerce*, which carried both religious and business news. Six years later he cofounded the American Anti-Slavery Society. He also provided funds to help found Oberlin College.

   Lewis Tappan, b. Northampton, Mass., May 23, 1788, d. June 21, 1873, founded (1841) the first U.S. commercial credit rating agency (the Mercantile Agency), which became Dun and Bradstreet. He started his business career in Boston but soon joined his brother's silk firm in New York City. He also

helped to found (1833) the American Anti-Slavery Society but left it 7 years later, in protest against William Lloyd Garrison's radicalism, to form an abolitionist society of his own. Tappan also published *National Era*, a journal devoted to the cause of freeing the slaves.

Bibliography: Tappan, Lewis, *The Life of Arthur Tappan* (1870; repr. 1970); Winter, Rebecca J., *The Night Cometh: Two Wealthy Evangelicals Face the Nation* (1977); Wyatt-Brown, Bertram, *Lewis Tappan and the Evangelical War against Slavery* (1968).

taproot

A taproot is a root structure of higher PLANTS, used for anchorage, food storage, water and mineral absorption, and gaseous exchange with the surrounding soils. Developed as the primary or first root, it rapidly grows from the seed and enlarges considerably to remain the dominant feature of the root system. A taproot may be slender or thick, fleshy or woody; it often contains many comparatively small or fibrous root offshoots. Taproot systems exist in such dicotyledons as dandelions and carrots and in such gymnosperms as pines.

tar, pitch, and asphalt

Tar, pitch, and asphalt are viscous, sticky, dark brown or black substances that are composed primarily of carbon and hydrogen. Tar is produced as a by-product of the carbonization of coal and of such other organic substances as wood or peat. Pitch is produced from distilling coal tar, wood tar, or petroleum. Asphalt occurs naturally in large deposits, can be extracted from asphalt rock, and is also produced from petroleum. At room temperature, tar and asphalt vary from a solid to semisolid state, whereas pitch is a fluid or semifluid.

   Tar and pitch were once of great economic importance in naval stores because they are not soluble in water and were therefore used to caulk wooden ships. The manufacture of tar and pitch from pinewood was one of the earliest major export industries of the American colonies.

   Today tar, pitch, and asphalt are used for roofing, making road surfaces, lubricating, waterproofing, insulating, binding, making plastics, and preserving wood, among many other commercial uses.

tar sands

Tar, oil, or bituminous sands are loose or partly lithified freshwater or delta sands containing oil that is too viscous to be processed by conventional means. The most important deposits are found in Canada, Madagascar, the USSR, the United States, and Venezuela; the largest are in the northern part of the province of Alberta, Canada. The Alberta Oil Sands include the Athabasca deposit—the world's largest oil field—where commercial sand mining has been undertaken in the oil sands of the McMurray formation. Attempts have also been made to recover crude oil economically from tar sands of the Orinoco Petroleum Belt in Venezuela. Open-pit mining with hot-recovery, upgrading, and deep-oil extraction techniques has been used in Canada and Venezuela.

   Tar sands in the United States are found mainly in Utah, California, and Texas. The Utah tar sands are low in sulfur and are found mostly in the Uinta Basin of northeastern Utah, within 600 m (2,000 ft) of the surface. Although the U.S. deposits are much smaller than those found in Canada and Venezuela, their proximity to the land surface may soon allow oil to be extracted from them economically as oil prices rise.

Bibliography: Hills, L. V., ed., *Oil Sands: Fuel of the Future* (1974).

Tara   [tar'-uh]

The hill of Tara, traditionally considered to have been the seat of the high kings of ancient Ireland, is located 32 km (20 mi) northwest of Dublin. Documentary sources, notably the *Dindseanches* (*c.*1000), catalogue the individual sites on the hill together with their legendary associations. Among the surviving earthworks on the site, the so-called Banqueting Hall is most reminiscent of other elongated cult-enclosures built by Celtic peoples. The Rath of the Synods, where Saint Patrick reputedly held assembly, has yielded burials and evidence of occupation in the early centuries of the Christian era. The Rath of the Kings, which like other Irish royal sites is enclosed by an external bank with an internal ditch, itself encloses the Mound of the Hostages, shown by excavation to cover a Neolithic passage-grave, and the conjoined earthworks known as the House of Cormac and the House of the Kings. The site apparently was abandoned during the 6th century.   D. W. HARDING

tarantella   [tar-uhn-tel'-uh]

The tarantella is a rollicking Italian folk dance in 6/8 time in which a couple or several women teasingly pursue and court one another, twirling and capering with increasing speed to the music of a mandolin, guitar, castanets, or tambourine. Some authorities attribute its name to Taranto, the town of its supposed origin. Others refer to the dancing mania called Tarantism, allegedly caused by the bite of the venomous tarantula, which swept Italy in the 15th to 17th centuries. Because the frenzied tarantella was thought to cure the delirium tremens or melancholia that the bitten victims suffered, the dance's name may be derived from the spider's. The tarantella has often been used in ballet.

BARBARA NEWMAN

Taranto   [tah'-rahn-toh]

Taranto (ancient Tarentum), a port city in the Apulia region of southern Italy, is situated 430 km (270 mi) southeast of Rome on the Gulf of Taranto. With a population of 243,120 (1983 est.), the city has a naval base as well as shipbuilding, fishing, food-canning, and steel-manufacturing industries. Its historic monuments include the Romanesque Cathedral of Saint Cataldo (11th century) and a Byzantine castle rebuilt by the Aragonese (1480).

Taranto was founded by Greeks (8th century BC) and taken by the Romans (272 BC), Ostrogoths (AD 494), Byzantines (540), Lombards (675), Arabs (856), and Normans (1063). It was part of the Kingdom of Naples and then the Kingdom of the Two Sicilies before joining a newly united Italy in 1860. An important base for the Italian navy, Taranto was bombed by the British in 1940 and captured by the Allies in 1943.

DANIEL R. LESNICK

tarantula   [tuh-ran'-chuh-luh]

Aphonopelma chalcodes is a member of the genus of tarantulas of North America. This spider's bite is painful but not dangerous to humans, and some tarantulas can be trained as pets. The tarantula is able to live for long periods without food and water.

A tarantula is a hairy, long-legged, long-lived SPIDER found mostly in warm regions. Also sometimes known as bird spiders or monkey spiders, true tarantulas make up the family Theraphosidae; related forms, including funnel-web spiders and TRAP DOOR SPIDERS, are also sometimes grouped as tarantulas. Many species are about 2.5 to 7.5 cm (1 to 3 in) long, with a 13-cm (5-in) legspan, but some South American species are larger. Tarantulas inject a paralyzing venom into prey with their large fangs. They rarely bite humans, however, and although the bite is painful the venom is usually not seriously harmful to humans.

Bibliography: Lund, Dale, *All about Tarantulas* (1977); Perrero, Laurie and Louis, *Tarantulas: In Nature and as Pets* (1979).

Tarascan   [tuh-rahs'-kuhn]

The Tarascan Indians, who speak a language remotely connected to Macro-Mixtecan, live near Lake Patzcuaro in Michoacán, Mexico. In pre-Spanish times they numbered at least 200,000 and had their own empire. The Tarascan maintained a neutral position between the Spaniards and the AZTEC, by whom they had never been conquered. They were missionized by Vasco de Quiroga, Bishop of Michoacán (1537–65), whose ideas were influenced by Sir Thomas More's UTOPIA.

Contemporary Tarascan are field farmers who grow maize, beans, and squash, in addition to crops introduced by the Spaniards such as wheat, barley, oats, and fruits. They build their houses of wood, stone, and adobe and live in villages laid out in streets around a central plaza. The primary economic unit is the elementary family household, but large numbers of kinfolk are linked together by a ritual kin network of *compadrazgo* and *mayordomía*. Despite an outstanding pre-Christian feature, the *yácata*, a quasi-pyramidal temple, Tarascans have retained very few pre-Christian beliefs. Even ideas about witchcraft are European. As with many Mexican Indians, their Catholicism is rooted in a 16th-century folk ideology. Today they number about 60,000 (1980 est.).

LOUIS C. FARON

Bibliography: Beals, Ralph H., *Cherán, a Sierra Tarascan Village* (1946); Boyd, Maurice, *Tarascan Myths and Legends* (1969); Van Zantwijk, R. A. M., *Servants of the Saints* (1967).

Tarawa   [tuh-rah'-wuh]

Tarawa, a coral atoll in the west central Pacific, about 3,700 km (2,300 mi) northeast of Australia, is the capital of Kiribati. Covering approximately 23 km² (9 mi²), Tarawa has a population of 20,050 (1983 est.). The atoll is a commercial and educational center, with ports on several of its component islets. Mother-of-pearl and copra are exported. One of the fiercest battles in the Pacific theater of World War II was fought there in 1943.

Tarbell, Ida M.   [tahr'-bel]

A Pennsylvania journalist, editor, and biographer, Ida Minerva Tarbell, b. Erie County, Pa., Nov. 5, 1857, d. Jan. 6, 1944, became famous as a MUCKRAKER through her well-documented articles on political and corporate corruption in *McClure's Magazine* and *American Magazine*. Her two-volume *History of the Standard Oil Company* (1904) led to federal action against the giant corporation. She also wrote a biography (1900) of Abraham Lincoln and an autobiography, *All in a Day's Work* (1939).

Bibliography: Brady, Kathleen, *Ida Tarbell: Portrait of a Muckraker* (1984); Tomkins, Mary E., *Ida M. Tarbell* (1974).

Tardenoisian: see MESOLITHIC PERIOD.

Tardieu, Jean   [tahr-dee-u']

The experimental French poet, playwright, and radio producer Jean Tardieu, b. Nov. 1, 1903, has been associated with the THEATER OF THE ABSURD since the late 1940s. He explored the limits of theatrical possibility in sketches and one-act plays that were later collected in *Théâtre de Chambre* (Bedroom Theater, 1955) and *Poèmes à jouer* (Poems to Be Played, 1960). In verse—*Accents* (1939) and *Jours pétrifiés* (Petrified Days, 1948)—Tardieu also experimented with nontraditional forms, and in 1972 he received the Académie Française's poetry prize.

Bibliography: Tardieu, Jean, *The Underground Lovers and Experimental Plays*, trans. by U. C. Duckworth (1968).

tardigrade: see WATER BEAR.

tariff

A tariff is a tax levied on goods imported from abroad. A *specific* tariff is levied on each unit of an imported good. An *ad valorem* tariff is levied as a percentage of the value or wholesale price of the good.

Reasons for Tariffs. Historically, tariffs have been used as sources of government revenue in many countries. In the 19th century they were the principal source of revenue for the U.S. government. In recent decades the governments of industrially advanced countries have relied primarily on the income tax and other kinds of taxation for their revenue, although tariffs are still used for this purpose in many less-developed countries.

Tariffs are also used to protect domestic industries from lower-priced foreign competition. Many countries have low tariffs or none at all on imported raw materials, but place higher tariffs on more processed materials; this device is designed to protect established manufacturing industries without raising the price of raw materials used in production.

Tariffs are imposed for a variety of other reasons. Labor unions often favor tariffs because of the low-wage competition from abroad. A government may use tariffs in an effort to increase the country's gain from INTERNATIONAL TRADE, by keeping import prices lower than export prices. A tariff may be used to protect a particular industry or geographical area that is suffering unusual hardship; or it may be invoked for purposes of national defense, to make a country less dependent on foreign supplies of certain goods. Finally, there is the "infant industry" argument for tariffs: that new industries need protection from foreign competition until they are able to establish themselves.

Arguments against Tariffs. Arguments against tariffs have been enunciated since mercantilist times (see MERCANTILISM) and were stressed by classical economists, such as Adam Smith, who favored FREE TRADE. Each of the arguments for using tariffs has a counterargument. A tariff may enable workers to obtain higher wages by protecting them from foreign competition, but it will require consumers to pay higher prices for imports. It may also be costly if it serves to protect uneconomic, inefficient industries. If a country tries to use tariffs to give it a more favorable balance of trade than it would otherwise have, it runs the risk of retaliation from other countries, as happened in the 1930s when countries put up tariff barriers against each other. (The Reciprocal Trade Agreements Act of 1934 was enacted in the United States to attempt to reduce these barriers.) Such tariff warfare reduces the volume of international trade, to everyone's disadvantage. When workers in a particular geographic area or industry need assistance because they are unable to move to jobs elsewhere, it is less expensive to subsidize them directly than to protect their existing jobs with a tariff. If a government wishes to promote self-sufficiency for purposes of national defense, a tariff may be much less effective than other alternatives such as stockpiling critical raw materials or subsidizing their production directly. The same holds true for the case of an infant industry; it would be more efficient to subsidize the industry directly than to protect it by a tariff that imposes higher prices on consumers.

Other Ways of Limiting Imports. Tariffs are not the only way of controlling trade. A commonly used device is the import QUOTA, which specifies the maximum amount and sometimes the maximum value of a commodity that can be imported in a given period. The effects of a quota are different from those of a tariff; although the government receives the revenue from a tariff, in the case of a quota the increase in the selling price resulting from the limitation of supply is appropriated by the domestic importer or the foreign supplier, or is shared between them.

Another kind of nontariff measure, used increasingly by the United States, is the voluntary export restraint—the so-called orderly marketing agreement. This is an arrangement under which the foreign exporting country agrees to limit its exports of certain products for a specific period.

Attempts to Reduce Trade Barriers. After World War II the major trading countries established (1947) the GENERAL AGREEMENT ON TARIFFS AND TRADE (GATT) to oversee and limit the use of tariffs and other measures of trade control. This organization has served as a focal point for reducing tariffs and other trade barriers. In the course of a series of negotiations the member countries have agreed to liberalize their trade barriers in a manner that roughly balances the effects on their imports and exports. The Kennedy Round of tariff negotiations, completed in 1967 and implemented over the ensuing five years, resulted in substantial tariff reductions. This was followed by the Tokyo Round, a set of negotiations to reduce tariff and nontariff barriers to trade that was completed in 1979.

Along with the tariff reductions negotiated under GATT, several other, more limited initiatives have been undertaken to reduce trade barriers. These include the establishment of the EUROPEAN ECONOMIC COMMUNITY (1958), the EUROPEAN FREE TRADE ASSOCIATION (1959), the Canadian–U.S. Automotive Agreement (1965), and the extension by several industrialized countries, in the late 1960s and early 1970s, of a system of preferential tariffs designed to encourage imports from less-developed countries.

The Trade Reform Act of 1974, passed by the U.S. Congress, gave the president increased bargaining power on tariff and nontariff trade barrier negotiations. In addition, other provisions allowed for aid to U.S. workers and industries hurt by imports, permitted the extension of MOST-FAVORED-NATION STATUS to the USSR, and barred tariff preferences for members of the Organization of Petroleum Exporting Countries (OPEC).

In the United States, the U.S. International Trade Commission (established 1916) acts as an independent fact-finding and advisory agency for Congress and the president on tariff and trade affairs.   ROBERT M. STERN

Bibliography: Baldwin, R. E., *Non-Tariff Distortions of International Trade* (1970); Bergsten, C. Fred, ed., *Toward a New World Trade Policy* (1975); Bhagwati, Jagdish, *Trade, Tariffs, and Growth* (1969); Ellsworth, Paul T., and Leith, J. Clark, *The International Economy*, 5th ed. (1975); Johnson, Harry G., *Aspects of the Theory of Tariffs* (1971) and, as ed., *The New Mercantilism* (1975); Kostecki, M. M., *East-West Trade and the GATT System* (1979); Rom, Michael, *The Role of Tariff Quotas in Commercial Policy* (1978); U.S. Commission on International Trade and Investment Policy, *United States International Economic Policy in an Interdependent World* (1971).

See also: BALANCE OF PAYMENTS; CUSTOMS UNION; PROTECTIONISM.

tariff acts

In U.S. history, from 1789 to the early 20th century tariffs were the single most important source of federal government revenue and were increasingly used—at ever-higher rates—to protect domestic industry. Subsequently, as internal taxation was increased and mutual tariff reductions were negotiated with other countries to promote international trade, tariffs accounted for a declining share of the national government's revenue.

Because Britain's colonial trade policies had aroused American distrust of centralized tariff-levying authority, the Articles of Confederation vested only the individual states with the power to impose duties. Interstate trade warfare resulted. Furthermore, the central government lacked a vital source of revenue. Therefore delegates to the Constitutional Convention of 1787 produced a document—the U.S. Constitution—that returned authority to regulate commerce to the federal government while prohibiting export duties.

Tariffs were the national government's principal source of revenue until the income tax amendment (the 16th Amendment to the Constitution) was passed in 1913. But sectional and economic differences made them a source of contention from the outset. Northern manufacturers wanted protection for infant industries, but the agrarian South, dependent on cheap manufactures, favored tariffs for revenue only. A compromise was achieved by the first tariff law, passed in 1789. Ad valorem duties, based on assessed value of a commodity, ranged from 5 to 15 percent, the highest rates applying to luxury items and such manufactured goods as cordage, nails, iron, and glass.

New industries built up during the War of 1812 received protection in the increased rates of the 1816 tariff law. Southern leaders protested the even higher schedules of the "Tariff of Abominations" (1828), and South Carolina invoked John CALHOUN's doctrine of NULLIFICATION against the 1832 tariff. Henry CLAY's Compromise Tariff of 1833 set the pace for moderate duties until southern secession.

With the South's absence from Congress during the Civil War and the weakening of the Democratic party (historically favoring a low-tariff policy), the newly formed Republican party granted protection to northern manufacturers. The Morrill Tariff of 1861 and revisions (in 1862, 1864, 1867, and 1869) raised average rates on dutiable goods to 47 percent. In the late 19th century business interests were exerting increasing influence on government, and they secured record duties in the McKinley Tariff (1890) and Dingley Tariff (1897). In the Populist and Progressive eras farmers and small-business proprietors protested that protection was a major cause of monopoly formation. Woodrow Wilson campaigned against the special privileges of the so-called trust in 1912, then secured downward revision in the Underwood Act of 1913.

A desire for economic self-sufficiency among Europe's powers led to a worldwide high-tariff system after World War I. American farmers, faced by international competition, joined businesses in backing the restoration of a protective system with the high duties of the Fordney–McCumber Act (1922) and the Smoot–Hawley Act (1930). Intensified international trade warfare spurred even higher tariffs during the Great Depression of the 1930s. New Deal tariff policies were contradictory. President Franklin D. Roosevelt's recovery program required higher domestic prices, leading to protectionist measures to assist the process of reflation to 1929 price levels. Proponents of expanded foreign trade, however, secured passage of the Reciprocal Trade Agreements Act of 1934, which authorized the president to negotiate with foreign nations for mutual tariff reductions. This reciprocal trade measure promised a historic reversal in U.S. tariff policy.

The change came after World War II, with the emergence of the United States as the world's leading economic power, anxious for worldwide trade expansion. At Geneva in 1947, 23 governments, led by the United States, concluded the GENERAL AGREEMENT ON TARIFFS AND TRADE (GATT), resulting in a lowering of U.S. duties from an average of 54 percent in 1933 to 12 percent by 1963.

Faced by a recession and trade decline, President John F. Kennedy secured the Trade Expansion Act (TEA) of 1962. Congress reaffirmed a policy initiated in 1934 giving the president authority to negotiate downward revision in tariffs by as much as 50 percent in exchange for similar concessions. Under the Kennedy Round (1964–67), sixth in a series of trade conferences sponsored by GATT, duties were reduced by an average of about 35 percent on more than 5,000 items. The TEA allowed federal assistance to businesses, workers, and communities affected by tariff reductions.

Under the Carter and Reagan administrations, steps were again taken to protect U.S. industries from foreign competition, but the tendency was to use quotas and import-limitation agreements rather than tariffs.   ELLIOT A. ROSEN

Bibliography: Goss, John D., *History of Tariff Administration in the United States from Colonial Times to the McKinley Administrative Bill*, 2d ed. (1897; repr. 1968); Kenkel, Joseph, *Progressives and Protection: The Search for a Tariff Policy, 1866–1936* (1982); Kindleberger, Charles P., *Foreign Trade and the National Economy* (1962); Pincus, J. J., *Pressure Groups and Politics in Antebellum Tariffs* (1977); Rossides, Eugene T., *U.S. Customs, Tariffs, and Trade* (1977); Taussig, Frank W., *The Tariff History of the United States*, 8th ed. (1931); Thompson, R. W., *The History of Protective Tariff Laws* (1974).

Tariff Commission, U.S.: see INTERNATIONAL TRADE COMMISSION, U.S.

Tarim River [dah-reem']

The Tarim River rises as the Yarkand in the Karakoram Range on the Kashmir border and flows through the TAKLA MAKAN DESERT in the Sinkiang province of western China. It has a total length of about 2,028 km (1,260 mi). Fed by tributaries from the Tien Shan and the Kunlun mountains, the river often changes its course, flowing through lakes and swamps of the LOP NOR area, where nuclear testing is conducted. Waters from the Tarim irrigate nearby oases.

Tarkenton, Fran [tahr'-ken-tuhn]

Francis Asbury Tarkenton, b. Richmond, Va., Feb. 3, 1940, was an American football quarterback who holds virtually all of the career passing records in the National Football League (NFL). After a college career at the University of Georgia, Tarkenton was drafted (1961) by the Minnesota Vikings, and in his first appearance as quarterback he threw for four touchdowns and ran for a fifth. In 1967 he was traded to the New York Giants and played there for 5 years without distinction. Tarkenton was traded back to the Vikings, and between 1972 and 1977 he led them to five consecutive division titles and three Super Bowls. A highly mobile quarterback who "scrambled" out of the reach of pass rushers, Tarkenton gained more yards on the ground than any quarterback in NFL history. During his 17-year career Tarkenton completed 3,686 out of 6,467 attempted passes, gained 47,003 yd, and passed for 342 touchdowns, all NFL records. He retired in 1977 and became a sports commentator.

Bibliography: Sullivan, George, *Gamemakers: Pro Football's Great Quarterbacks* (1971); Yates, Brock, and Tarkenton, Fran, *Broken Patterns: The Education of a Quarterback* (1971).

Tarkington, Booth [tahr'-king-tuhn]

Newton Booth Tarkington, b. Indianapolis, Ind., July 29, 1869, d. May 19, 1946, was a prolific American novelist and playwright. He is well known for *Penrod* (1914) and *Seventeen* (1916), sentimental novels dealing with the throes of adolescence. His interest in American society, expressed in a short-lived career in Indiana politics, broadened into *The Magnificent Ambersons* (1918; film, 1942) and *Alice Adams* (1921; film, 1935), both Pulitzer Prize-winning novels. He also wrote plays, notably *The Man from Home* (1907), and the semiautobiographical *The World Does Move* (1928).   F. M. PAULSEN

Bibliography: Fennimore, Keith J., *Booth Tarkington* (1974); Woodress, James, *Booth Tarkington, Gentleman from Indiana* (1954).

Tarlton, Richard [tahrl'-tuhn]

An Elizabethan actor and clown, Richard "Dick" Tarlton, d. 1588, a member of the Queen's Men from 1583, was famous for his impromptu doggerel verse and may have been the model for the jester Yorick in Shakespeare's *Hamlet*. Anecdotes attributed to him may be found in *Tarlton's Jests* (c.1592–1611).

taro [tahr'-oh]

Taro, *Colocasia esculenta*, is a perennial tropical plant of the ARUM family, Araceae. Its large, starchy, tuberous roots are a staple food in Polynesia and East Asia. Roots from the wetland taro are heated to destroy their bitter taste, then ground and fermented into an edible paste called poi, an important food on many Polynesian islands. The upland (dry) taro, or dasheen, produces corms that are eaten like potatoes in Japan, China, and the West Indies. The dasheen is sometimes

Taro, C. esculenta, a tropical perennial herb, bears large, arrowhead-shaped leaves. It is cultivated in Asia and the Pacific Islands for its starchy, tuberous root (left), which is a staple food in many cultures.

grown as an ornamental houseplant called "elephant's ear" because of its large, heart-shaped leaves. FRANCES GIES

tarot [tar'-oh]

The oldest playing cards still in common use—both for CARD GAMES and as the basis of a branch of the fortune-telling art—the tarot was brought from the East to Italy in the 14th century by gypsies or returning Crusaders. The origin of the cards is obscure, and theories that the tarot is based on the Hebrew alphabet or on Egyptian or Hindu mythology have not been conclusively proved.

The tarot deck consists of 78 cards, which are divided into two distinct groups. The Minor, or Lesser, Arcana, the precursor of the modern deck, is made up of 56 cards divided into four suits. The wands suit corresponds with the modern suit clubs; cups with hearts; swords with spades; and pentacles with diamonds. Each suit has 14 cards, with numbered cards from ace to ten and four unnumbered face cards: king, queen, knight, and knave. (The four knave cards have been eliminated in the modern deck.)

The Major, or Greater, Arcana consists of 22 cards, each bearing a title and a picture. The symbolism of the Major Arcana has fascinated writers and psychologists, who assume that such pictures as the Hanged Man, the Wheel of Fortune, Judgment, and the Moon are medieval allegorical representations of virtues and vices, and life- and death-dealing forces. Twenty-one of the cards are numbered. The 22d card, the Fool, numbered 0, is analogous to the modern joker.

In fortune-telling, either the full pack or the Major Arcana alone is used. The relationship of one card to another, as laid out in a number of different configurations, is as important as the significance of each individual card. The Italian card game *tarrocchi* is still played in southern and central Europe.

A tarot reader is shown with a seven-card spread, one of the methods used in reading the tarot for divination. Each card of the Minor Arcana has a specific interpretation within the generic meaning of its suit, and the meanings of the cards of both the Minor and the Major Arcana may alter if the card is in a reversed position. In addition, the interpretation of each card is positively or negatively influenced by the cards surrounding it.

tarpan [tahr'-pan]

The tarpan, an extinct wild horse once native to Europe and parts of Asia, was probably domesticated as well as eaten by early humans. It is considered either an early ancestor of the modern horse, Equus caballus, *or a subspecies of the Asiatic wild horse,* E. przewalskii.

The tarpan is a wild horse that became extinct in Europe during the early 20th century. Also sometimes known as the European wild horse, the tarpan was short and had a long head, a thick neck, an upright mane, and a gray to brown coat with a dark back stripe. Once roaming by the thousands over Europe and parts of Asia, tarpans are believed to have been important sources of food for prehistoric humans. Horses much like the tarpan have been bred in Munich through selective breeding of horses with tarpan ancestry. EVERETT SENTMAN

Tarpeia [tahr-pee'-yuh]

In Roman legend, Tarpeia, the daughter of a commander in charge of ancient Rome, offered to open the citadel to the Sabines, who were attacking Rome, in exchange for their golden bracelets. Upon entering they crushed her with their shields. The Tarpeian rock at Rome, down which criminals were hurled to their death, took its name from her.

tarpon [tahr'-pahn]

The tarpon, *Megalops atlantica,* is the famous "silver king" of big-game anglers, noted for its spectacular leaps when hooked. It is found from Brazil to North Carolina and sometimes as far north as Cape Cod and off the Atlantic coast of Africa. A primitive bony fish, the tarpon can breathe with a gas bladder as well as with gills. It reaches more than 2.4 m (8 ft) and 135 kg (300 lb) and has a long, forked tail and a dorsal fin with an enlarged last ray; its color is blue on the back and silvery on the sides and belly. The larvae are transparent and ribbonlike. C. P. IDYLL

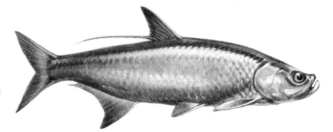

The tarpon, M. atlantica, is abundant near the Florida and Carolina coasts and ranges from Cape Cod to Brazil.

Tarquinia [tahr-kwin'-ee-uh]

According to Greek and Roman tradition, Tarquinia (Roman: Tarquinii)—in central Italy about 96 km (60 mi) north of Rome—was the foremost among ETRUSCAN cities in both wealth and age. Archaeological evidence has since shown that the city was already important in VILLANOVAN times (8th century BC), although it was later (c.600 BC) surpassed by its neighbors Caere and Vulci. A 6th- to 3d-century-BC Greek sanctuary unearthed (1969) at Tarquinia's port of Gravisca points to the city's close contact with Greece.

The town of Tarquinia was first uncovered in 1934–38, when its fortifications and a large 3d-century-BC temple were excavated. The terra-cotta sculpture of winged horses that was found adorning the temple is classed among the finest works of its time. Tarquinia is most famous for the paintings in the chamber tombs of its necropolis, which exemplify the evolution of the Etruscan style from the 6th century BC onward. Several examples of the archaic period (6th century BC) illustrate banquets, dances, athletic contests, and games featured at aristocratic funerals, thus providing insights into Etruscan daily life.   LARISSA BONFANTE

Bibliography: Banti, Luisa, *The Etruscan Cities and their Culture* (1974); Hencken, Hugh, *Tarquinia, Villanovans, and Early Etruscans* (1968).

Tarquinius Priscus, Etruscan King of Rome
[tahr-kwin'-ee-uhs pris'-kuhs]

Lucius Tarquinius Priscus, d. 578 BC, was an Etruscan who ruled (616–578 BC) Rome, according to Roman tradition, as its fifth king, following Ancus Marius (r. c.641–616 BC). Priscus is credited with subduing the Sabines and the Latins; draining the marshes; building the Circus Maximus, the Forum, and the Capitoline temple; and infusing Roman institutions with elements of Etruscan culture. Supposedly assassinated at the behest of Ancus's sons, he was succeeded by Servius Tullius (r. 578–534 BC).

Tarquinius Superbus, Etruscan King of Rome
[soo-pur'-buhs]

Lucius Tarquinius Superbus (Tarquin the Proud), the last of Rome's seven kings, ruled, according to tradition, from 534 to 510 BC. The son of Tarquinius Priscus, he supposedly murdered his father-in-law, Servius Tullius (r. 578–534), to succeed to the throne. According to tradition, he was expelled by a Senate-led revolt provoked by his son's rape of LUCRETIA. The Romans then established the republic. Superbus vainly sought to reinstate himself, aided by LARS PORSENA.

tarragon

Tarragon, A. dracunculus, a perennial herb, is an important seasoning in French cuisine and an ingredient of fines herbes (a finely chopped herb mixture). Its subtle flavor is used in egg dishes, butter, vinegar, soups, and a variety of other foods.

Tarragon is a perennial herb, *Artemisia dracunculus,* that is prized for its fragrant leaves, particularly in France. Native to the southwestern Asia region, the plant is now cultivated in sunny and dry locations throughout the temperate zones. It reaches a height of 90 cm (3 ft) and has many stems. The leaves are 25–100 mm (1–4 in) in length. It is usually propagated by stem cuttings or root divisions. Fresh leaves are used to flavor vinegar; dried leaves are used in pickles, prepared mustard, sauces, salads, and poultry, egg, and tomato dishes.
                    ARTHUR O. TUCKER

Tarragona [tah-rah-goh'-nah]

Tarragona, a port city in Catalonia, northeastern Spain, lies on the Mediterranean coast, about 80 km (50 mi) southwest of Barcelona. The population is 138,705 (1982 est.). Tarragona's industries process foods and tobacco; wine and olives are exported. Ruins of a Roman amphitheater, aqueduct, and forum as well as a Gothic cathedral (12th–13th century) are major landmarks. Captured by the Romans in 218 BC, the city was ruled by the Moors from AD 714 to 1120.

tarsier [tahr'-see-ur]

The tree-dwelling Philippine tarsier, T. syrichta, is a primitive relative of true monkeys. Its large eyes are adapted for seeing at night.

The tarsier is an arboreal, mainly nocturnal, rat-sized primate of the genus *Tarsius* found on southeastern Asian islands. It has a rounded head that can be turned almost in a circle, large ears, large staring eyes, and a pug nose. The small, gray brown body has long hind legs and a long, usually naked tail. Elongated digits tipped with rounded pads for gripping help the animal in its agile acrobatics. It preys on insects and other small animals.   EVERETT SENTMAN

Tarski, Alfred [tahr'-skee]

The Polish-American mathematician and logician Alfred Tarski, b. Jan. 14, 1902, d. Oct. 26, 1983, made important contributions in many areas of mathematics, including metamathematics (a branch of mathematical logic), set theory, measure theory, model theory, and general algebra. Formal scientific languages can be subjected to more thorough study by the semantic method that he developed. He wrote more than ten books in different areas of mathematics, and his teaching influenced many young mathematicians.

Tarski taught at the University of Warsaw and at Harvard University. He became (1942) a member of the faculty of the University of California at Berkeley and was emeritus professor there when he died.

Tarsus [tahr'-suhs]

Tarsus is an ancient port city on the Tarsus (Cydnus) River in southern Turkey, about 400 km (250 mi) southeast of Ankara. The population is 121,074 (1980). Located about 16 km (10 mi) inland, it serves fishing and coastal trading vessels at the east end of the Mediterranean. Tarsus is an agricultural and cotton-milling center in the heart of the fertile Cilician plain. A Roman temple and archaeological sites attract tourists. The prosperous city of Tarsus became capital of the Roman province of CILICIA in 67 BC. Mark Antony and Cleopatra first met

(41 BC) in Tarsus, and the Apostle Paul was born there. Located between the Mediterranean and the Cilician Gates—the major pass through the Taurus Mountains—it had strategic importance. Tarsus was controlled at various times by Assyrians, Persians, Greeks, Romans, Byzantines, Arabs, and Crusaders but finally fell to the Ottoman Turks in 1515.

Tartaglia, Niccolò   [tahr-tahl'-yah]

The Italian mathematician, Niccolò Tartaglia, b. c.1500, d. Dec. 13, 1557, developed a solution for cubic equations and first applied mathematics to gunnery. After solving cubic equations in 1535, independently of an earlier unpublished solution by Ferro in the early 16th century, he did not publish his solution but did confide it to Gerolamo CARDANO on the condition that it not be published. Cardano nonetheless published it in his *Ars Magna* (The Great Art, 1545), provoking a heated debate among Tartaglia, Cardano, and a student of his, Lodovico FERRARI. Tartaglia also wrote a popular arithmetic text, was the first Italian translator and publisher (1543) of EUCLID's *Elements*, and published Latin editions of ARCHIMEDES. His contributions to ballistics, published in his *Nova Scientia* (The New Science, 1537), include new methods and instruments, including the first firing tables.   STEVEN LUBAR

Bibliography: Sarton, George, *Six Wings: Men of Science in the Renaissance* (1957).

tartan

This print from a 19th-century book of tartans shows a plaid associated with the Buchanan clan. Many clan tartans date from the late 18th century, when a revival of the tartan for military dress prompted widespread interest in the distinctive patterns.

The Murray tartan is depicted in this 19th-century illustration. In addition to bold dress tartans, plaids in subdued hues, known as hunting tartans, often became associated with particular clans.

A tartan is a plaid pattern, now primarily associated with Scotland, that has come to be regarded as a heraldic device or badge that designates major Scottish CLANS, families, and districts. Such patterns, however, have existed for centuries in countries as disparate as Italy and Japan. The design, or sett, of a Scottish tartan consists of colored bands or lines of specific width and sequence crossing at right angles against a solid ground and usually woven into woolen cloth or wool and silk. Although the tartan may be made in any size, the proportions of the stripes must remain constant. Colors may vary from light to dark within a sett. Traditionally, extra lines have sometimes been added to indicate rank. The early setts were recorded by marking the number and color of each thread on a pattern stick in order to reproduce the design.

Tartans were originally worn by Scottish Highlanders as a single, large, rectangular cloth folded lengthwise and belted at the waist. The bottom portion fell in loose pleats, sometimes sewn; the upper and longer section was worn draped about the shoulders and pinned. During inclement weather it served as a protective cloak. When its wearer slept outdoors, it functioned as a blanket. The smaller kilt (knee-length pleated skirt) and plaid (rectangular length of tartan cloth placed over the left shoulder), now separate, were apparently derived from this costume sometime during the early 17th century.

The use of checkered garments is ancient. The Irish, Britons, Caledonians, and Celts wore them, and, formerly, they were appropriate for both male and female attire. In Scottish literature the earliest references to tartans date from the 13th century. At first tartans represented districts in Scotland. Later they became the badge of the chief clans or families of an area. A few patterns specify vocations, and different designs are sometimes worn for different occasions such as hunting or formal events. After the Jacobite Rebellion of 1745, Highland dress and the tartan were proscribed until 1782. Some old setts were lost in the intervening period, but many new ones were invented when military tartans for the Scottish regiments were subsequently approved by the government. Much of the present interest in tartan dress may be attributed to this official usage as well as to the pride inspired by the honors won by Highland regiments.

The tracing of specific tartans is difficult because references in the past have been meager, inconsistent, or both. More recently, portraits of chieftains, their pipers, and other household officers have been important sources for determining the history and genealogical relationships of clans and tartans. These portraits have proved more reliable than the tartan

Scottish tartans without clan associations include the Caledonia plaid (left) and the Jacobite plaid, worn by supporters of the Stuart cause (right). Like all authentic tartans, these are woven with identical patterns, or setts, for the warp and the weft.

books that began to appear in the 19th century. Another source, although limited, is the Public Register of All Arms and Bearings in Scotland. Today tartans are authorized and registered at Lyon Court in consultation with the Standing Council of Scottish Chiefs. As a result commercial manufacture of tartans has become relatively standardized. In the mid-1960s the Scottish Tartan Centre was founded at Stirling for tartan research. In the United States the word *tartan* refers to any cloth with a tartan design.

Bibliography: Grimble, Ian, *Scottish Clans and Tartans* (1982); Sutton, A., and Carr, R., *Tartans: Their Art and History* (1984).

Tartars: see TATAR.

Tartarus [tahr'-tuh-ruhs]

In Greek mythology, Tartarus was variously the lowest region of the underworld or synonymous with the underworld (HADES), where Uranus banished his rebellious sons, the Cyclopes, and according to Homer, Zeus later confined the defeated Titans. According to one creation myth, based on Hesiod, Tartarus was born of the union of air and mother earth; the giants, of the union of Tartarus and earth. A grove of black poplars along the ocean stream marks the entrance to Tartarus, which is bounded on the west by the Styx River.

Tartini, Giuseppe [tahr-tee'-nee]

Giuseppe Tartini, b. Apr. 8, 1692, d. Feb. 26, 1770, was an Italian violinist, composer, theorist, and founder (1728) of a school of violin playing in Padua that was famous throughout Europe. He studied at Padua and elsewhere, held various posts as violinist, and was conductor (1723–25) of Count Kinsky's orchestra in Prague. He improved the violin bow and wrote important treatises on playing the instrument and acoustics. His music for the violin in such works as the "Devil's Trill" sonata represents a significant advance in technique. His approximately 300 compositions include more than 100 concertos, numerous solo and trio sonatas, and some church music.   FARLEY K. HUTCHINS

Bibliography: Chapin, Victor, *The Violin and Its Masters* (1969).

Tartu [tahr'-too]

Tartu is the second largest city of the Estonian republic of the USSR. The population is 111,000 (1985 est.). In addition to its Estonian name of Tartu, the city was formerly known as Yur'yev (its historical Russian name) and Dorpat (its German name). Tartu is situated on the banks of the Emajogi River, midway between Estonia's largest lake, Võrtsjärv, and Lake Peipus. It is a manufacturing center, linked by railroad with Tallinn, and it produces tools, instruments, and farm machinery.

Its development as a major educational and cultural center has been associated mainly with the founding of the world-famous Tartu University (1802). Tartu also has a botanical garden, dating from the same period, and an agricultural academy. First mentioned in the 11th century, Tartu has the ruins of an ancient cathedral dating from the 13th century.
                                                   THEODORE SHABAD

Tartuffe [tahr-tuef']

One of MOLIÈRE's most biting comedies, *Tartuffe* (1669) in its original versions aroused vigorous opposition by its audacious portrayal of a religious imposter. An attack on hypocrisy, the play also satirizes the credulity and stubbornness of a society taken in by appearances. As in his other plays, Molière uses *Tartuffe* to plead for moderation and common sense. Although the play is a masterpiece of tightly knit classical drama, with all the main themes of the play introduced in act 1, the entrance of Tartuffe himself is suspensefully delayed until the third act, thus creating one of the great moments of French theater. *Tartuffe* shows Molière at the peak of his career, both in comic genius and poetic ability.   JOSEPH A. REITER

tarweed

Tarweed is the common name for about 18 species of herbs that compose the genus *Madia* of the sunflower family, Compositae. Native to western North America and Chile, these generally heavy-scented plants produce sticky, glandular hairs, linear to oblong leaves, and flower heads that close at midday in most species. The common tarweed, *M. elegans*, grows up to about 120 cm (4 ft), with conspicuous yellow ray flowers containing a brown red spot at the base.

Tarxien [tahx'-ee-uhn]

Tarxien, the largest of the approximately 30 identified prehistoric temples of Malta, is located just outside the capital city, Valetta. In its present form, which dates from c.1500 BC, Tarxien covers about 5,434 m² (6,500 yd²) and comprises three separate temples built atop the ruins of an earlier temple. Each component temple consists of two or three parallel, paved courtyards with semicircular ends. These courtyards, separated by enormous stone doorways, lead to a small inner shrine. Each temple is enclosed in a D-shaped wall of huge dressed-limestone blocks that is fronted by an elaborate masonry forecourt of concave shape. In the largest temple the distance from forecourt to shrine is 24.4 m (80 ft). Many of the stones are decorated with low-relief carvings that usually feature patterns of spirals but occasionally depict sacrificial animals. Cult figurines found at Tarxien suggest that the temple complex was dedicated to the worship of a mother goddess.
                                                   R. J. C. ATKINSON

Bibliography: Evans, J. D., *Malta* (1959); Trump, D. H., *Malta: An Archaeological Guide* (1972).

Tarzan of the Apes

A fictional hero created by Edgar Rice BURROUGHS in the 1912 novel *Tarzan of the Apes,* Tarzan has been the main character of 23 other novels Burroughs wrote periodically through 1944. Adopted and raised to adulthood in Africa by a tribe of great apes, Tarzan later discovers that he is a British lord and thereafter divides his life between London and Africa, where he is "the Lord of the Jungle." The hero of about three dozen movies, a radio series, a comic strip, and several television series, Tarzan is perhaps the most popular fictional character in the 20th-century United States.   JACK NACHBAR

Bibliography: Essoe, Gabe, *Tarzan of the Movies: A Pictorial History of More than Fifty Years of Edgar Rice Burroughs' Legendary Hero* (1973); Holtsmark, Erling B., *Tarzan and Tradition: Classical Myth in Popular Literature* (1981).

Tasaday [tahs-ah'-dy]

The Tasaday, a people of southern Mindanao in the Philippines, speak a distinct Filipino language affiliated with the Malayo-Polynesian (Austronesian) linguistic family. When contacted (1971) by government officials who reached their isolated rain forest by helicopter, the group consisted of about 25 men, women, and children living in three limestone caves. They appeared to have no knowledge of agriculture, weaving, or pottery. Their scant clothing was devised from leaves, and their tools were made of stone and bamboo. They collected wild yams, ferns, fruits, and the pith of the palm; trapped pigs, monkeys, and deer; and caught tadpoles, fish, and crabs by hand. Strict monogamy was practiced, with genealogical descent traced through both parents, and the spirits of the dead were believed to live in the tops of giant trees. In 1972 the Tasaday region was made a national preserve to protect the group's environment.

Subsequent dramatic changes in the group's way of life have led to charges that the Tasaday are a hoax perpetrated by government officials. Scientists who reinvestigated stated that the changes in what was thought to be a Stone Age culture could have resulted from the group's contacts with the outside world since 1971.   DONN V. HART

Bibliography: Nance, John, *The Gentle Tasaday* (1975).

Taschereau, Sir Henri   [tah-shuh-roh']

The Canadian jurist Sir Henri Elzéar Taschereau, b. Sainte
Marie de la Beauce, Oct. 7, 1836, d. Apr. 14, 1911, became
(1871) a judge of the Quebec Superior Court, a justice of Canada's Supreme Court (1878), and served (1902–06) as chief
justice of the Supreme Court.

Tashkent   [tash-kent']

Tashkent is the capital of the Uzbek Soviet Socialist Republic
of the USSR and the administrative center of Tashkent oblast.
The population is 1,986,000 (1984). Tashkent is the largest city
of Soviet Central Asia and is an important manufacturing and
transport center. It is situated in the foothills of the TIEN SHAN
system in an oasis irrigated by the Chirchik River.

The city's industries account for about a third of all the industrial output of the Uzbek republic. The city's leading manufacturing plants produce cotton harvesters and other agricultural equipment, excavators, compressors, hoisting machinery, ball bearings, light bulbs, and electric cables. Tashkent
also has Central Asia's largest cotton-textile mill, based on the
cotton-fiber production of the hinterland. Electricity for the
city's industries is provided by a chain of small hydroelectric
stations along the Chirchik River and by a gas-fired local power station. A subway was inaugurated in 1977.

A major cultural and educational center, Tashkent has a
university (1920), a conservatory, and specialized engineering
schools. An opera and ballet theater and both Uzbek and Russian drama theaters are based in Tashkent. The city's six museums include one on the history of Uzbekistan and an Uzbek
arts museum.

In existence since the 2d century BC, Tashkent became a
Muslim city in the 8th century AD, and was an important commercial center during the Middle Ages. Annexed by Russia in
1865, it now consists of an old Asian section, with winding
narrow streets, and a modern city, dating from the 19th century. Rail connections with Russia were completed in 1898, and
industrial development followed. The city's growth was
spurred in World War II, when many industries were evacuated there from the European part of the USSR. A devastating
earthquake in 1966 was followed by large-scale reconstruction.   THEODORE SHABAD

Tasman, Abel Janszoon   [taz'-muhn]

Abel Janszoon Tasman, c.1603–c.1659, a Dutch East India
Company navigator, was the first European to discover Tasmania, New Zealand, Tonga, and the Fiji Islands. In 1633 he
began a series of trading visits to the East Indies and later to
Japan. On his most famous mission (1642–43)—to the southern Pacific—he made his major discoveries, including Van
Diemen's Land (now Tasmania). He also sailed around the
continent called the Great South Land (later Australia), establishing that it was not connected to the polar continent. In
1644, having been sent out again to clarify Australia's relationship to Tasmania and New Guinea, Tasman found a passage
into the Pacific north of Australia's Gulf of Carpentaria. After
missions to Siam (1647) and against the Spaniards (1648), he
retired from the sea.   E. J. TAPP

Bibliography: Sharp, A., *Voyages of Abel Janszoon Tasman* (1968).

Tasman Sea

The Tasman Sea is a 2,250-km-wide (1,400-mi) arm of the Pacific bordered by Australia to the west, New Zealand to the
east, the Coral Sea to the north, and the Southern Ocean to
the south. Noted for strong winds and storms, it has a maximum depth of 5,200 m (17,000 ft). The sea, named for Abel
Janszoon Tasman, was explored by James Cook during the
1770s.

Tasmania   [taz-may'-nee-uh]

Tasmania, Australia's island state lying approximately 240 km
(150 mi) south of Victoria in the South Pacific Ocean, covers
68,329 km² (26,383 mi²) and has a population of 437,300 (1984
est.). Slightly smaller than the state of Maine, it accounts for

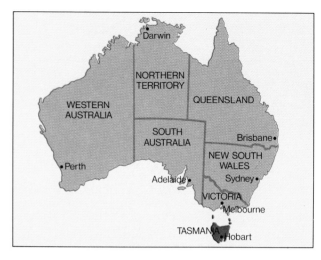

less than 1% of Australia's area. The capital is HOBART, located on the southeast coast. Mountainous, with peaks in the
west exceeding 1,500 m (5,000 ft), Tasmania is an extension of
the continent's Eastern Highlands. Annual rainfall ranges from
2,388 mm (94 in) in the west to less than 559 mm (22 in) elsewhere. January temperatures are about 16° C (60° F), and July
temperatures average about 7° C (45° F). Lakes are abundant,
especially in the wetter western areas. Natural vegetation is
dense forest, often composed of eucalyptus.

In contrast to other Australian states where a majority of the
people live in the capital, only a third of Tasmania's citizens
reside in Hobart. Launceston (1981 pop., 64,555), closer to the
mainland, is the second largest city. A fourth of the population is rural. Tasmania's English-speaking populace, overwhelmingly of British ancestry, has grown at a slower rate
during the 20th century than that of other states, and Tasmania has received few of Australia's recent immigrants.

The island has abundant hydroelectric power, and this
cheap energy source has attracted some major industries.
Lead, zinc, copper, and tin are mined. Industries manufacture
paper products, textiles, and candy. Mixed farming is found
throughout the island; wool, lamb, dairy products, potatoes,
berries, and apples are leading commodities.

Known as Van Diemen's Land until 1856, the island was renamed for Abel Janszoon Tasman, the Dutch navigator who
discovered it in 1642. Permanent European settlement consisting of both free persons and convicts dates from 1803 at Ris-
don. Initially part of New South Wales, the island became a
separate colony in 1825 and a state in 1901.

CALVIN WILVERT

Bibliography: Robson, Lloyd L., *A History of Tasmania*, vol. 1 (1983);
Roth, H. Ling, *The Aborigines of Tasmania*, 2d ed. (1968); Solomon,
Robert J., *Tasmania* (1972); West, John, *The History of Tasmania*, ed.
by A. G. L. Shaw (1971).

Tasmanian devil

The Tasmanian devil is a carnivorous marsupial, *Sarcophilus
harrisi* of the family Dasyuridae, now found only in Tasmania
but once widely distributed throughout Australia. The squat,
low-slung body with its squarish head may grow to 80 cm
(31.5 in) long and the tail to about 30 cm (12 in) long. Males
may weigh 9 kg (20 lb) or more. The coarse, brown black
coat has white patches on the face, sides, and chest. The jaws
and teeth are massive bone crushers. Tasmanian devils feed at
night on small animals and carrion. Up to four young are carried in the pouch for about 3½ months.   EVERETT SENTMAN

Tasmanian languages: see OCEANIC LANGUAGES.

Tasmanian wolf

The Tasmanian wolf, or thylacine, a carnivorous marsupial,
Thylacinus cynocephalus, was once common in Tasmania

The Tasmanian devil, S. harrisi, gained an undeserved reputation for bad temper from its early observers.

The Tasmanian wolf, or thylacine, T. cynocephalus, has a doglike head except for the wide gape of the jaws.

and Australia but was killed in large numbers because of its occasional attacks on sheep. The last known thylacine died in a zoo in 1936, but reports of sightings still occur. The animal is about 1 m (40 in) long, plus a thick-based tail of about 63 cm (25 in). Its tawny coat is marked with up to 19 dark bands on the back, giving it the alternative name of Tasmanian tiger. Few reliable observations of its behavior in the wild exist, but its prey is known to include small mammals and birds.

EVERETT SENTMAN

Tass News Agency: see PRESS AGENCIES AND SYNDICATES.

Tassili n'Ajjer [tah-see-lee' nahd-jair']

Tassili n'Ajjer, a plateau in the Saharan area of southern Algeria, is the site of a large group of prehistoric rock paintings, many of which were discovered (1956–57) by the French archaeologist Henri Lhote. The paintings found in Tassili n'Ajjer's rock shelters and caves date from the 4th–3d millennia BC, a time when hunter-gatherers and pastoralists flourished in a Sahara that enjoyed a much higher level of rainfall. Depicted in these works are the wild Saharan fauna and herds of domestic cattle and sheep in a wide variety of styles that range from naturalistic to abstract. The inhabitants of the cave used a distinctive type of pottery known as Dotted Wavy Line, as well as ground and polished stone axes and adzes. They cultivated some cereal crops but relied for much of their diet on hunting, gathering, and fishing in shallow lakes. The Tassili art is important for the light it throws on prehistoric migrations and economic practices in the Sahara before it dried up completely.

BRIAN FAGAN

Bibliography: Clark, J. Desmond, *The Prehistory of Africa* (1970; repr. 1984); Lajoux, J. D., and Elgar, Frank, *The Rock Paintings of Tassili* and *The Art of Tassili,* trans. by G. D. Liversage (1963); Lhote, Henri, *The Search for the Tassili Frescoes* (1959).

Tasso, Torquato [tahs'-soh, tohr-kwah'-toh]

The greatest poet of the Italian High Renaissance, Torquato Tasso, b. Sorrento, Mar. 11, 1544, d. Apr. 25, 1595, is known above all for his epic masterpiece, *Gerusalemme liberata* (1581; trans. as *Jerusalem Delivered,* 1594, 1600), and for the influence he exerted on English literature. The publication of a romantic narrative poem, *Rinaldo* (1562), when he was only 18 years old, gave early evidence of Tasso's genius.

In 1565 he entered the service of Cardinal Luigi d'Este, transferring in 1572 to the brilliant court of Duke Alfonso II d'Este in Ferrara; under their patronage he produced important *Discourses* on the art of poetry (1567; published 1587) and the charming pastoral drama (see PASTORAL LITERATURE) *Aminta* (performed 1573; published 1580; Eng. trans., 1591), the most influential Renaissance example of its genre.

Tasso's troubles began in 1575, after he had finished his greatest poem, *Gerusalemme liberata*; as the result of criticism voiced by friends, the first signs of a destructive perse-

cution mania became evident. Tasso submitted the work twice to the Inquisition; despite the fact that it was found without fault the poet remained unsatisfied—and the poem unpublished. His delusions worsened, and in 1577 he threw a knife at a servant he believed was spying. Put under surveillance, he fled only to return to Ferrara in 1579, when his violent railing at the duke led to his imprisonment in a hospital for nearly 7 years. Tasso nevertheless went on writing throughout this tortured period. When finally freed in 1586, he continued his restless peregrinations throughout Italy. Under the patronage of Pope Clement VIII during his final years, he died exhausted in Rome while preparations were in progress to crown him poet laureate.

A first ''authorized'' edition of *Gerusalemme liberata* appeared in 1581; although a heavily revised, much inhibited version bearing the title *Gerusalemme conquistata* (Jerusalem Conquered) was published by the poet in 1593, it is on the first that his high reputation in Italian letters is based. In this epic of the recapture of the Holy City from the Saracens during the First Crusade, Tasso attempted to fuse the epic form of Vergil with chivalric content and Christian morality; it is the beauty of the lyrical passages and the vitality of the characterization that give the work its enduring value.

Tasso is also admired for his love poetry in the Petrarchan tradition (*Rime,* 1591, 1593); for his *Dialoghi* (1585–89; trans. by Thomas Kyd as *The House-holder's Philosophy,* 1588) on philosophical, moral, literary, and aesthetic subjects; and for about 1,700 letters (*Lettere,* written 1579–86, published 1852–55).

OSCAR BÜDEL

Bibliography: Boulting, William, *Tasso and His Times* (1907; repr. 1968); Brand, Charles Peter, *Torquato Tasso: A Study of the Poet and of His Contribution to English Literature* (1965).

taste: see SENSES AND SENSATION; TONGUE.

taste buds: see TONGUE.

TAT: see PROJECTIVE TESTS.

Tatar [tah'-tur]

The Tatar, sometimes corrupted to *Tartar,* are descended from Caucasoid Volga Bulgars, but they became mingled with MONGOLS during the 13th century. They speak Kipchak Turkic, a URAL-ALTAIC LANGUAGE, and in physical type vary from blond, blue-eyed Finnic admixtures to people obviously Mongoloid. Ordinarily they have beardless, oval faces. In the early 1980s more than 6 million Tatar lived in the USSR; the remaining hundred thousand or so lived in China, the Balkans, and Anatolia. About half of the Tatar people are Hanafi-Sunni Muslims (see SUNNITES). Social structure remains based on the father's family, but such Muslim traditions as BRIDE-PRICE and marriage to multiple wives are virtually nonexistent; the DOWRY custom and year-long wedding rituals are disappearing. Most Tatar now live in cities, and urban Tatar often intermarry with Russians and Volga Finns.

Arriving from the southern steppes during the 7th century, Volga Bulgars mixed with local Finns, producing the Tatar people. During the 13th century hordes of Mongols suddenly appeared under the leadership of GENGHIS KHAN, terrifying and laying waste the civilized world. After the Mongol conquest of their land, the Tatar gradually assimilated with their conquerors, and the combined population kept the name *Tatar*, or *Tartar* (from a Greek word signifying hell and here used to describe the Mongol ruthlessness).

Bibliography: Katz, Zev, et al., *Handbook of Major Soviet Nationalities* (1975); Parker, E., *A Thousand Years of the Tartars*, 2d ed. (1924; repr. 1969); Poppe, N., *Tatar Manual* (1968); Symmons-Symonolewicz, K., ed., *The Non-Slavic Peoples of the Soviet Union* (1972).

Tate, Allen   [tayt]

An American poet and critic, John Orley Allen Tate, b. Winchester, Ky., Nov. 19, 1899, d. Feb. 9, 1979, was a founding member of the "Fugitives," a group of Vanderbilt University students and teachers who believed in the traditional values of the agrarian South. Tate's familiarity with Latin literature is suggested by his complex, ironic poems, many of which are collected in *Poems* (1960) and *The Swimmers and Other Selected Poems* (1970). He won the Bollingen Prize in poetry in 1956. His 1938 essay "Tension in Poetry" became an important statement of the principles of the NEW CRITICISM. *On the Limits of Poetry* (1948) and *Essays of Four Decades* (1969) are also notable among his critical works. His novel *The Fathers* (1938) elegizes the spiritual side of the antebellum South.

Bibliography: Allums, J. L., ed., *Allen Tate and the Poetic Way* (1984); Dupree, R. S., *Allen Tate and the Augustinian Imagination* (1983); Tate, Allen, *Memoirs and Opinions, 1926–1974* (1975).

Tate Gallery, The

The Tate Gallery in London, originally known as the National Gallery of British Art, was opened in July 1897 in a building designed (1894) by Sidney J. R. Smith and donated to the British government by Henry Tate, who also donated about 65 paintings and 3 sculptures to found the museum's collection. Originally conceived as a showplace for contemporary British art, the Tate gradually evolved into a more broadly based museum containing British paintings of all periods, the national collection of modern British and foreign sculpture, and the national collection of modern foreign paintings.

The holdings of the Tate cover the works of the British school of art from its beginnings in 16th-century works such as George Gower's portrait *Sir Thomas Kytson* (1573) through its 20th-century manifestations in the works of Ben Nicholson, Francis Bacon, and others. Strongly represented are such seminal British artists as William Hogarth, Sir Joshua Reynolds, William Blake, and John Constable. An added building (1987) designed by James STIRLING houses works by J. M. W. Turner.

The Hugh Lane bequest of French 19th-century paintings began (1915) the museum's National Gallery of Modern Foreign Art, which now includes a significant body of impressionist and postimpressionist works. The collection of modern sculpture, which originated in the acquisition of a group of bronzes by Auguste Rodin, has expanded to cover most of the principal modern sculptors.   MAGDALENA DABROWSKI

Bibliography: Chamot, Mary, et al., *Tate Gallery Catalogues: The Modern British Paintings, Drawings and Sculpture*, 2 vols. (1964); Compton, Michael, *Looking at Pictures in the Tate Gallery* (1985).

Tati, Jacques   [tah-tee']

The French film director Jacques Tati, b. Oct. 9, 1908, d. Nov. 5, 1982, began his career as a mime and established himself as an actor, writer, and director with *Jour de fête* (1947). Subsequently, he created the brilliant comic figure of Mr. Hulot, who appeared in *Mr. Hulot's Holiday* (1953), *Mon Oncle* (1958), and *Traffic* (1971). Hulot also appears as a background figure in Tati's masterpiece, *Playtime* (1967), a gently humorous study of contemporary civilization.   ROY ARMES

Bibliography: Cauliez, Armand J., *Jacques Tati* (1962); Gilliatt, Penelope, *Jacques Tati* (1976).

Tatian   [tay'-shuhn]

A Syrian writer of the 2d century AD, Tatian attended Saint Justin Martyr's school of philosophy in Rome and, after a long spiritual quest, was converted to Christianity. His *Diatessaron*, a synthesis of the four Gospels, and *Oratio ad Graecos* (Address to the Greeks), a reasoned defense of Christianity, were his most important works. He subsequently abandoned Christianity and founded the Encratites, a gnostic sect.

Tatlin, Vladimir Yevgrafovich   [taht-leen']

The Russian painter and sculptor Vladimir Yevgrafovich Tatlin, b. Dec. 28 (N.S.), 1885, d. May 31, 1953, was the founder of CONSTRUCTIVISM, which grew out of his interest in exploring the sculptural possibilities of various "modern" materials—such as glass, concrete, wire, and sheet metal—through abstract reliefs and constructions. In 1913, Tatlin, who had been conventionally trained at the Moscow School of Painting, Sculpture, and Architecture, visited Pablo Picasso in Paris. This encounter revolutionized his outlook and prompted him to launch his artistic experiments. In 1919 he began plans for a concert-lecture-exhibit hall to be called *Monument to the Third International* (never carried beyond a scale model). A union of architecture, sculpture, light, painting, and motion, it would have consisted of two cylinders and a glass pyramid rotating at different speeds and encircled by a spiral tower 400 m (1,312 ft) high. Abstract art was discredited by the Soviet government in 1920; Tatlin moved to Leningrad in 1921, where he taught the study of materials at the Research Institute for Artistic Culture.   BARBARA CAVALIERE

Bibliography: Gray, Camilla, *The Great Experiment: Russian Art, 1863–1922* (1962); Nakov, A. B., *Tatlin's Dream: Russian Suprematist and Constructivist Art, 1910–1923* (1973).

Tatti, Jacopo: see SANSOVINO, JACOPO.

tattoo: see BODY MARKING.

Tatum, Art   [tay'-tuhm]

The jazz pianist Arthur Tatum, b. Toledo, Ohio, Oct. 13, 1910, d. Nov. 4, 1956, was one of the first great virtuosos of the JAZZ keyboard and exerted a strong influence from the 1930s until his death. Tatum recorded and performed extensively both as a soloist and with his jazz trio. Although others before him, notably Fats Waller and Earl Hines, had done much to move jazz piano away from the old-time ragtime and stride styles, Tatum completed the process with his silky touch, fleetness, and harmonic imagination.   DONALD IVEY

Tatum, Edward L.

Edward Lawrie Tatum, b. Boulder, Colo., Dec. 14, 1909, d. Nov. 7, 1975, an American geneticist and biochemist, shared part of the 1958 Nobel Prize for physiology or medicine with Joshua LEDERBERG and George W. BEADLE for fundamental work in molecular genetics. Tatum, with Beadle, proved that genes regulate biochemical processes; with Lederberg, he demonstrated the existence of genetic recombination in bacteria and, as such, a form of sexual reproduction. He also helped elucidate genetic determination of inherited characteristics and the role of cytoplasmic inheritance.

Bibliography: Moore, Ruth, *The Coil of Life: The Story of the Great Discoveries in the Life Sciences* (1961).

Taube, Henry

American chemist Henry Taube, b. Neudorf, Saskatchewan, Nov. 30, 1915, was awarded the 1983 Nobel Prize for chemistry for his research on electron-transfer mechanisms in inorganic reactions. This work was central to the establishment of modern inorganic chemistry on a firm theoretical basis of kinetic and thermodynamic principles. Taube's studies of metal complexes are also important for understanding the catalytic functions of enzymes in biochemistry. Taube obtained his doctorate from the University of California in 1940, became a U.S. citizen two years later, and has served on the staff of Stanford University since 1961.

Tauler, Johannes   [tow'-lur]

A German Dominican preacher and mystic, Johannes Tauler, b. *c.*1300, d. June 16, 1361, was one of the greatest medieval preachers. His style was simple and direct, and the spiritual and intellectual content of his sermons, which called for detachment and abandonment to the Holy Spirit, met the needs of his listeners, often Dominican nuns. Like many Dominicans, Tauler was deeply influenced by the thought of Thomas Aquinas. In the 1320s, however, Tauler and his fellow Dominican Heinrich Suso came under the influence of Meister Eckhart. Commonly known as the Rhineland mystics, these three were the inspiration for the Friends of God and other late-medieval mystical movements.

Bibliography: Clark, James M., *Great German Mystics: Eckhart, Tauler, and Suso* (1949; repr. 1970); Tauler, Johannes, *History and Life of the Reverend Doctor John Tauler*, trans. by Susannah Winkworth (1962).

Taung skull   [towng]

The first fossil of the early humanlike genus AUSTRALOPITHECUS was identified (1924) by the South African anatomist Raymond DART from among fossil-filled rocks collected in a limestone quarry at Taung, in the Cape Province of South Africa. The quarry had already yielded the skull of a baboon encased in hardened sand and lime. Dart uncovered the skull and jaw of an infant primate that seemed to be anatomically more advanced than an ape. After careful study, Dart announced the discovery of *Australopithecus africanus*, a humanlike ape with small canine teeth, which the anatomist believed to be an ancestor of modern humans. Most scientists disagreed with Dart, until later discoveries of *Australopithecus* in the Transvaal and South Africa yielded sufficient specimens to confirm that *Australopithecus*, dating from between 5.5 and 1.5 million years ago, was indeed close to the main ancestry of humankind.

BRIAN FAGAN

Bibliography: Clark, J. Desmond, *The Prehistory of Africa* (1970).

Taurus   [taw'-ruhs]

Taurus, the Bull, is a zodiacal constellation that appears northwest of Orion high above the southern horizon on January evenings in mid-northern latitudes. One of the oldest of the star groups mentioned in ancient records, it marked the position of the Sun on the first day of spring more than 4,000 years ago. Taurus contains the orange-hued star Aldebaran, the 13th brightest star in the sky and 45 times larger than the Sun. The two most famous star clusters—the HYADES and the Pleiades (see PLEIADES, astronomy)—are located in Taurus. Along with numerous double stars, it also includes the CRAB NEBULA (M1), one of the strongest radio sources in the heavens.

ARTHUR F. CACELLA

Bibliography: Hogg, Helen S., *The Stars Belong to Everyone* (1976).

Taurus Mountains

The Taurus Mountains stretch for about 485 km (300 mi) along the southern rim of Turkey's Anatolian Plateau, parallel to the Mediterranean Sea, from Egridir Lake in the west to the Seyhan River in the east. Demirkazik (3,910 m/12,829 ft), in the easternmost part, is the highest peak in the main range. The rugged limestone terrain makes it difficult to exploit the mineral resources. The thinly populated region is crossed by the Cilician Gates and by four smaller passes used since ancient times.

Taverner, John   [tav'-ur-nur]

John Taverner, b. *c.*1495, d. Oct. 25, 1545, was an English composer of church music. His early musical upbringing was

at the collegiate church, Tattershall, in Lincolnshire. The bishop of Lincoln recommended Taverner as a singer and choirmaster to Cardinal Wolsey, whose splendid establishment Cardinal College (now Christ Church, Oxford) opened in 1526, the year in which the post was accepted. Taverner stayed for only three and a half years, returning to his native Boston, Lincolnshire, where he appears to have lived a less active musical life. His masses and motets span the earlier polyphonic style current in Henry VIII's reign, and the more modern quasi-homophonic vein of the reformers, with whom he was evidently in sympathy.   DENIS STEVENS

Bibliography: Josephson, David S., *John Taverner* (1979).

Tavernier, Jean Baptiste   [tah-vairn-ee-ay']

Jean Baptiste Tavernier, baron d'Aubonnes, 1605–89, was a French traveler and a trader in gems and other valuable items. Between 1630 and 1670, Tavernier made six voyages that took him to Turkey, Persia, central Asia, and the East Indies. He wrote *Six Voyages en Turquie, en Perse et aux Indes* (1676–77; trans. as *Travels in India*, 2 vols., 2d ed., 1925), providing Europeans with much new information on Asia.

Tawaraya Sotatsu: see SOTATSU.

Tawfiq Pasha   [tow-feek' pah-shah']

Muhammad Tawfiq Pasha, b. Apr. 30, 1852, d. Jan. 7, 1892, was Egypt's khedive (viceroy) from 1879 to 1892, during the establishment of Britain's protectorate over Egypt. He succeeded his father, Khedive ISMAIL PASHA, after the latter's deposition by his nominal Ottoman overlord at the urging of European financiers. Tawfiq, who had little political support, was a passive figurehead whose main ambition was to retain his throne. He was dominated successively by European financial advisors, by the ultranationalist minister of war Arabi Pasha (following an army rebellion led by Arabi), and finally by Lord CROMER's British occupation regime, established after the British invasion of 1882. Tawfiq was succeeded by Khedive Abbas Hilmi II (r. 1892–1914).   ROBERT G. LANDEN

Bibliography: al-Sayyid-Marsot, Afaf Lutfi, *Egypt and Cromer: A Study in Anglo-Egyptian Relations* (1968).

Tawney, Richard Henry   [taw'-nee]

The British economic historian Richard Henry Tawney, b. Nov. 30, 1880, d. Jan. 16, 1962, pioneered new theories on modern capitalism, contributing to the concept of the PROTESTANT ETHIC. Among his influential works were *The Agrarian Problem in the Sixteenth Century* (1912), *Religion and the Rise of Capitalism* (1926), and *Equality* (1931; 4th rev. ed., 1952). A socialist, Tawney pressed for such reforms as a minimum-wage law and increased educational opportunities.

Tax Court, U.S.

The United States Tax Court is a court of the federal government that hears cases brought by taxpayers who challenge decisions of the Internal Revenue Service (IRS) dealing with overpayment or underpayment of taxes. In many instances the decisions of the U.S. Tax Court can be appealed to the U.S. Court of Appeals and ultimately to the Supreme Court. When taxpayers exercise an option to agree to the use of simplified court procedures in disputes involving $5,000 or less, however, the cases tried under these procedures cannot be appealed to a higher court. The U.S. Tax Court also decides disputes over the rights of taxpayers to see documents and other materials that are related to their cases and that are contained in IRS files.

The court is composed of 19 judges appointed for life and 13 special trial judges who are appointed by the chief judge and serve at the pleasure of the court. It is augmented by retired judges when the case load is heavy. The court's offices are in Washington, D.C., but it holds trial sessions throughout the United States.

Bibliography: Huffman, William F., et al., *U.S. Tax Court Practice and Procedure Guide*, new ed. (1975).

taxation

Taxation is the imposition of a mandatory levy on the citizens of a country by their government. In almost all countries tax revenue is the major source of financing for public services.

History. Despite the adage that nothing is certain in the world but death and taxes, taxation has not always been the chief source of revenue for governments. The Athenians, for example, had use of the revenues from publicly owned mines and tribute from conquered countries. In the feudal hierarchy of the Middle Ages, funds flowed upward in the form of rent fees and fees paid in lieu of military services. Revenue from government-controlled resources also provides an alternative or supplement to taxation in some modern societies. Revenue from sales of petroleum and other natural resources provide notable examples in nations where such resources are publicly rather than privately owned.

During the Middle Ages, kings derived most of their income from their feudal holdings and generally needed to levy taxes only to pay for their expensive wars. Because ordinarily such taxes could be collected only with the consent and aid of nobles and other large landholders, monarchs found it necessary to call these landholders into session to approve such taxation. These sessions of landholders evolved into parliaments and other legislative bodies. Thus the need of the monarchy for tax revenues can be said to have been one of the causes of the rise of parliamentary government. In fact, many of the constitutional changes that have taken place in the modern world have resulted from the struggle between monarch and legislature over the collection of taxes. In Great Britain, the Glorious Revolution of 1688 established Parliament's authority over taxation.

''No taxation without representation'' was one of the rallying calls of the colonists in the American Revolution. After the United States achieved independence, the Articles of Confederation provided the framework for governing the new nation. A major weakness of the central government under the Articles was its inability to levy taxes. The U.S. Constitution, which replaced the Articles, gave the federal government power to levy TARIFFS (an exclusive right) and excises, but it required that direct taxes be apportioned among the states according to population. In 1913 ratification of the 16TH AMENDMENT to the Constitution made possible the adoption of the federal INCOME TAX, which is the mainstay of the modern federal revenue system. In 1985, $396 billion in federal personal and corporate income taxes accounted for 54 percent of the total federal revenue of $734 billion.

In the United States, state and local units of government also use the income tax but rely on other tax sources to a greater extent than the federal government. The PROPERTY TAX has traditionally been the backbone of the local revenue system. In addition, most states and many local units of government impose sales taxes. Taxes on tobacco, alcohol, gasoline, and amusement are levied by nearly all states. Most also impose INHERITANCE TAXES.

Classifying Taxes. Ultimately, taxes are the price paid for publicly provided services. In a democracy, a majority of citizens (or their representatives) vote to impose taxes on themselves in order to finance publicly services on which they place value but which they believe cannot be adequately provided by market processes.

Taxes, which drain money from the public sector, must ultimately be paid by a reduction in private consumption or investment expenditures. Determining which individuals or households actually reduce their private consumption or wealth as a consequence of a tax is not always straightforward. The economic units that are nominally assigned legal tax liability are often able to shift the actual burden of the tax onto other sources. Some taxes are not shifted at all; others may be only partially shifted.

Whether or not a tax is shifted provides one basis for classifying taxes. A tax is said to be direct if the economic unit that is legally assigned tax liability bears the full burden of the tax. The personal income tax, for example, is generally regarded by economists as a direct tax. An indirect tax is one that is shifted either wholly or in part. Any tax legally imposed on a commodity (see SALES TAX; VALUE-ADDED TAX) must be an indirect tax because ultimately only individuals can bear the burden of taxes. An indirect tax is said to be shifted forward if consumers of the taxed object bear the tax burden in the form of a higher price for the good. Backward shifting occurs when suppliers of productive resources to a taxed industry earn lower incomes as a result of the tax.

In addition to the direct-indirect classification, taxes are also classified as being either proportional, progressive, or regressive. This classification depends on the relationship between the size of the tax base (the value, income, or wealth being taxed) and the average tax rate applied to that base. If the average tax rate remains constant when the tax base varies in size, the tax is a proportional one. If the rate increases as the base increases, the tax is progressive. A regressive tax is characterized by the tax base and average tax rate varying in opposite directions. A slightly different definition of progressive, proportional, or regressive taxation is useful for analyzing indirect taxes. Under this definition, the tax burden is traced to the actual bearer and then related to income or wealth. A tax is progressive in this case if the tax burden expressed as a percentage of the income of the taxpaying unit rises with income. It is proportional if the tax burden is a constant proportion of income, and the tax is regressive if income received and the percentage of income paid in taxes vary in opposite directions.

Excess Burden. The direct burden of a tax borne by the individual taxpayer is the transfer of purchasing power from the individual to the public sector. If, in addition, the tax distorts taxpayers' choices in ways that prevent them from attaining maximum satisfaction with their remaining income, the tax is said to have generated an excess burden. The personal income tax can provide an example of this problem. Suppose an individual is earning an hourly wage of $5 and, given that wage, chooses to work 50 hours per week. In his or her opinion the $5 received for the 50th hour of work exactly compensates for the hour of leisure activity foregone in order to earn it. The additional $5 that could be earned by working a 51st hour is not enough in his or her view to compensate for that additional hour of leisure activity foregone. Now, suppose that an income tax of 10 percent is imposed. For each hour the individual works, the government collects $0.50 in tax revenue. At the lower net hourly wage of $4.50, the individual may choose to reduce his or her work effort to 42 hours per week. That individual's gross earnings are now $210, out of which $21.00 in tax revenue is collected.

To see how an excess burden may have been generated by the income tax, consider the following alternative way of collecting the same amount of tax revenue from the individual. Suppose that the taxing scheme simply assessed a fixed tax liability or lump-sum tax (also called a capitation, or head, tax) of $21.00 on the individual regardless of how large or how small his or her money income was. Now he or she might well choose to work more than 42 hours per week in this taxing scheme because the net monetary reward for the 43d and each successive hour of leisure foregone is now $5 rather than the $4.50 obtained under the income tax. Given the fixed tax liability of $21.00, the individual now possibly might choose to work the same 50 hours per week as he or she was working prior to imposition of any tax. Tax revenue and, implicitly, publicly provided services remain the same under both the income tax and the lump-sum tax, but with the latter tax, the individual is able to make a better allocation of time between work and leisure. The choice to work the extra 8 hours per week under the fixed tax indicates that he or she prefers 50 hours of work per week with a net income of $229 to 42 hours of work and a weekly income of $210. The inability to achieve this preferred position with an income tax is an indication of the excess burden of that tax.

Good and Bad Taxes. What constitutes a good tax? This issue has always stirred lively debate among tax scholars, legislators, and concerned taxpayers. Efficiency is one criterion against which a tax might be evaluated. The best tax by this standard is the one that generates the least excess burden.

Most experts would be unwilling to accept efficiency as the sole indicator of a good tax, however, because the most efficient tax is the lump-sum tax discussed above. Despite the desirable properties of this tax from the standpoint of efficiency, most people would undoubtedly disapprove of the inequity of a tax that imposed indentical tax burdens on the richest and poorest members of society. The best tax systems seek a balance between the often conflicting objectives of efficiency and equity.

The principle of horizontal equity is widely accepted as a desirable feature of a tax. Stated simply, this principle requires that equals be treated equally. Because the tax base determines circumstances under which individuals will be treated as equals for tax purposes, the horizontal equity norm is of primary relevance as a guide to defining the tax base. Generally, some measure of economic capacity or well-being has been sought as the relevant index of equality for tax purposes. The choice of the best measure, however, is subject to controversy. For example, a portion of the modern debate between proponents of income and consumption taxation, respectively, centers on whether a consumption tax can perform at least as well if not better from a horizontal equity perspective than the more traditional income tax.

A corollary to the principle that equals be treated equally is the principle of vertical equity, which suggests that unequals be treated unequally. According to this principle, individuals should be taxed in accordance with their ability to pay. Unfortunately, although the ability-to-pay principle generally requires that taxpayers with greater economic capacity pay a greater share of total tax burden, it is a subjective standard and does not provide clear guidelines with respect to the precise allocation of tax shares. A proportional, a progressive, or even, within limits, a regressive income tax, for example, can collect more in total tax revenue from the rich person than from the poor person.

One interpretation of the ability-to-pay principle, the concept of minimum aggregate sacrifice, seeks to allocate a given total tax burden among taxpayers in such a way as to minimize the total loss of welfare summed over all individuals. Based on the assumption that a $1 reduction in purchasing power entails a smaller loss of welfare to an individual the greater that individual's total income, minimum aggregate sacrifice requires extreme progression in the tax system in the form of a leveling off of after-tax incomes. Many scholars are uncomfortable with the concept of minimum aggregate sacrifice because they question the validity of comparing the welfare burden of taxes across individuals.

An alternative justification for progressive taxation is a desire to use the tax system to reduce inequality in the distribution of income. The extent to which the tax system can and should be used in this way is an important issue in tax policy. There are two types of progressive taxes. A degressive tax exempts some initial amount of the base from taxation and subjects all of the base in excess of this amount to a single flat rate. A graduated-rate progressive tax, on the other hand, subjects increments in the base to successively higher marginal rates—the marginal tax rate being the increment in tax liability divided by the increment in tax base. With respect to a personal tax such as the income tax, the minimal amount of progressivity embodied in the degressive tax is relatively uncontroversial. The initial exemption protects the poorest members of the society from tax burden. However, the issue of whether and to what degree a tax system ought to move beyond this minimal progressivity is a subject of ongoing debate. Is a graduated income tax appropriate, and, if so, how steeply should marginal rates rise? Graduated rate progressivity in the income tax concentrates a greater share of tax burden on upper-income groups than does the degressive tax. Even if this is viewed as a desirable distributional objective, steeply graduated rates can be discouraging to productive effort. The objective of achieving greater equality in the distribution of income can be achieved only if a price is paid in the form of lower total income for the society.

The ability-to-pay principle deals only with the allocation of a predetermined aggregate tax burden and thus fails to link the tax and expenditure sides of the public budget. An alternative tax principle that remedies this problem is the benefit principle of taxation. Under the benefit principle, an individual's tax burden is based on the benefits that he or she receives from public services. The benefit principle is, in most instances, difficult to follow with great precision because of difficulties with actually measuring individual benefits from public services and because the people who most need services are often those least able to pay. In some cases, however, the general guidelines of the benefit principle appear to underlie particular taxes, as, for example, an excise tax on gasoline, the proceeds of which are used to finance highway building and repair.

In addition to generating revenue to finance public services, taxation can be employed to serve other objectives, among the most important of which are income redistribution, economic stabilization, and the regulation of consumption of certain commodities or services. Altering the distribution of income in society is a function that many governments perform. Although it is not the only means of performing this function, taxation is the most explicit, with the revenue collected by taxing one group in society transferred directly to another group. The size of the government deficit—the difference between expenditures and tax revenue—is an important policy variable for purposes of economic stabilization (see FISCAL POLICY). Adjustments in tax rates are an important means of manipulating the deficit. Finally, excise taxes are often imposed on goods and services with the objective of reducing consumption by raising the price of taxed commodities. Tobacco and liquor are two commodities often subject to this sumptuary taxation.

MARILYN FLOWERS

Bibliography: Blum, Walter J., and Kalven, Harry, *The Uneasy Case for Progressive Taxation* (1953; repr. 1963); Break, George F., and Wallin, Bruce, *Taxation: Myths and Realities* (1978); Browning, Edgar K. and Jacquelene M., *Public Finance and the Price System*, 2d ed. (1983); Buchanan, James M., and Flowers, Marilyn R., *The Public Finances*, 5th ed. (1980); Coffield, James, *Popular History of Taxation* (1970); Groves, Harold M., *Tax Philosophers: Two Hundred Years of Thought in Great Britain and United States*, ed. by Donald J. Curran (1974); Rosen, Harvey S., *Public Finance* (1985).

See also: ECONOMY, NATIONAL; EXCESS PROFITS TAX; INCOME, NATIONAL; SINGLE TAX.

taxicab

The taxicab is a semiprivate means of transportation in which an automobile and its driver are available to the public for relatively short-term hire. The name is a condensation of taximeter cab, a type of horse-drawn vehicle that appeared in Europe in the late 19th century. It had a special meter device to indicate distance traveled and, hence the tax, or fare, due. Motorized cabs were first put into service in Paris. Early cabs were often specially designed and built for public hire, and London cabs are still built under regulations, determining their dimensions and operating performance. Most U.S. cabs are slightly modified conventional sedans.

GEORGE M. SMERK

Bibliography: Farris, Martin T., and Harding, Forrest E., *Passenger Transportation* (1976).

taxidermy

Taxidermy is the art of preparing, preserving, and mounting the skin, hair, feathers, or scales of animals in a lifelike position for study or display. The word *taxidermy* is derived from the Greek *taxis*, "to arrange," and *derma*, "skin." Taxidermy is used to mount hunting and fishing trophies, and many natural history museums have taxidermists on their staffs to prepare animal specimens for display.

Early cultures practiced a form of taxidermy in the preparing of skins and other parts of animals for clothing, ornamentation, or ritualistic accoutrements. Writings and existing specimens show that taxidermy, as it is known today, was practiced at least as early as the 16th century. The methods in current use, however, began in the late 19th century.

Techniques vary with the kind of animal, but in all cases the skin is removed, cleaned, chemically treated with a preservative, and placed on a prepared model made of a stable, strong material that will withstand insects and changes in humidity and temperature. The model is sculptured to reproduce the exact size and shape of the specimen and can be made from a material such as balsa wood, laminated paper, wire mesh with papier-mâché, foam plastic, or fiberglass. Treated fish skin is mounted over a mold made from the fish before it was skinned. Fish, reptile, and amphibian skins tend to lose color and must be painted after mounting.

Taxidermy is an exact, highly specialized art. Taxidermists must have a knowledge of anatomy, natural history, drawing, sculpture, mechanics, dyeing, and leather tanning.

DAVID SCHWENDEMAN

Bibliography: Grantz, Gerald J., *Home Book of Taxidermy and Tanning* (1970); Harrison, James M., *Bird Taxidermy* (1977); McFall, Waddy F., *Taxidermy Step by Step* (1975); Moyer, John W., *Practical Taxidermy* (1979); Tinsley, Russell, *Taxidermy Guide* (1977).

Taxila [tak'-sil-uh]

Taxila, or Takshasila, situated 32 km (20 mi) from Rawalpindi, Pakistan, is the archaeological site of three ancient cities that for centuries dominated the western Punjab. The remains of these separate ruined cities of the ancient province of GANDHARA are spread over an area of 64 km² (25 mi²). The oldest urban settlement, occupied from at least the 6th century BC to 185 BC, is represented by the remains in the Bhir Mound. Northeast of this, on the far side of the Tamranala River, are the remains of Sirkap, which may have been built by Bactrian Greeks and was occupied successively by Shakas (Scythians), Parthians, and Kushans. The last-named group sacked the city in AD 64, took possession of it, and from there launched their successful invasions of northwest India. The third city, Sirsukh, located about 1.6 km (1 mi) northeast of Sirkap, was a Kushan city built by Kanishka (fl. AD 120) with fortifications that differ markedly from those of Sirkap. Sirsukh flourished as a center of Kushan civilization until its destruction by the White Huns (Hephthalites) early in the 6th century. The construction of Sirsukh prompted the building in its suburbs of major shrines, the most significant of which are the great Dharmarajika stupa and the fire temple at Jandial. Also surviving from this period are the impressive remains of the monasteries at Mohra Moradu, Jaulian, Kalawan, Giri, and Bhamala. Excavations at the Taxila site were begun (1863) by Sir Alexander Cunningham and completed by Sir John Marshall.

DIRAN KAVORK DOHANIAN

Bibliography: Marshall, John Hubert, *A Guide to Taxila*, 3d ed. (1936) and *Taxila: An Illustrated Account of Archaeological Excavations* (1951).

taxis [tak'-sis]

Taxis, in biology, is the movement of an organism, such as a protozoan, in response to an orienting influence. Phototaxis is the response to light, geotaxis to gravity, thigmotaxis to contact, and chemotaxis to chemical substances. If the organism orients toward the stimuli, its response is called positive; if away, negative. Taxes may be governed by comparisons of the influence registered at separate sense organs or by a sense organ that registers changes of stimulation along a path of motion.

JULIAN LEWIS

Bibliography: Carlila, M. S., ed., *Primitive Sensory and Communication Systems* (1975).

taxonomy: see CLASSIFICATION, BIOLOGICAL.

Tay, River [tay]

The River Tay in Scotland, 188 km (117 mi) long, rises in the Grampian Mountains in two headstreams, the Lochay and Dochart, which join at Loch Tay. The river, Scotland's longest, then flows past Perth and Dundee to the 40-km-long (25-mi) Firth (estuary) of Tay on the North Sea. The firth is crossed by railway (1888) and road (1966) bridges; the original railway bridge collapsed during a storm in 1879, killing 90 people.

Tay-Sachs disease [tay-saks]

Tay-Sachs disease is a rare GENETIC DISEASE in which the lack of an enzyme (hexosaminidase A) involved in the metabolism of brain lipids causes a fatty substance called ganglioside to accumulate in nerve cells of the brain. The disease develops during infancy, primarily in babies of Jewish descent, and leads to blindness, dementia, convulsions, extensive paralysis, and death, usually in 2 to 4 years. The Tay-Sachs gene, which is carried by 4 percent of American Jews of European extraction, must be present in both parents for the child to develop the disease. A medical procedure called AMNIOCENTESIS allows detection of the disease before birth.

PETER L. PETRAKIS

Bibliography: Volk, Bruno W., ed., *Tay-Sachs' Disease* (1964).

Taylor, Bayard

A popular American poet and author of travel books during the Gilded Age, Bayard Taylor, b. Kennett Square, Pa., Jan. 11, 1825, d. Dec. 19, 1878, found material for his poems and narratives during his many travels throughout the world. His translation of Goethe's *Faust* (1870-71) gained him recognition as a scholar.

Taylor, Brook

The English mathematician Brook Taylor, b. Aug. 18, 1685, d. Dec. 29, 1731, formulated (1712) the famous theorem or process in the calculus for expanding functions into infinite series. He did not, however, grasp the fundamental importance that Lagrange later assigned to TAYLOR SERIES. In his *Methodus incrementorum directa et inversa* (Direct and Inverse Incremental Method, 1715) he invented integration by parts and founded the calculus of finite differences, and in *Linear Perspective* (1715) he developed a formal and rigorous theory of perspective.

R. CALINGER

Taylor, Cecil

The pianist and composer Cecil Percival Taylor, b. New York City, Mar. 15, 1933, a leader in the field of experimental jazz, has always had more influence than fame. Taylor's jazz style owes much to his admiration for Béla Bartók and Igor Stravinsky. His long, experimental works, moving away from accepted formal, melodic, and harmonic concepts, have pointed toward new paths for many other musicians and earned the admiration of the international jazz community; but his compositions, however, have proved too demanding for a wider audience. In addition to composing and performing, Taylor has taught at several universities.

Bibliography: Collier, James Lincoln, *The Making of Jazz* (1978); Jones, LeRoi, *Black Music* (1967).

Taylor, Edward

An outstanding poet of colonial America, Edward Taylor, b. near Coventry, England, 1642, d. June 24, 1729, went to New England in 1668 and, after graduation (1671) from Harvard, accepted what was to be a lifelong ministry at Westfield, Mass. There, despite arduous duties, he found time to write more than 200 "Preparatory Meditations" (1682-1725) and several longer poems, including the Calvinist "God's Determinations Touching His Elect" (c.1682). Taylor's books and manuscripts passed to the Yale library in 1883, but his poems were not published until 1939.

ROBERT D. ARNER

Bibliography: Grabo, Norman S., *Edward Taylor* (1962); Keller, Karl, *The Example of Edward Taylor* (1975); Scheick, William J., *The Will and the Word: The Poetry of Edward Taylor* (1973).

Taylor, Edward Thompson

The Methodist preacher Edward Thompson Taylor, b. Richmond, Va., Dec. 25, 1793, d. Apr. 5, 1871, spent more than 40 years as minister of Seamen's Bethel Church in Boston. A cabin boy at the age of 7, he preached sermons full of nautical imagery and language. The sermon of Father Mapple in Melville's *Moby-Dick* reflects Taylor's style.

Taylor, Elizabeth   (actress)

Elizabeth Taylor, in one of her finest performances, played Martha opposite Richard Burton's George in the film version of Who's Afraid of Virginia Woolf? *(1966). Taylor and Burton first appeared together in* Cleopatra *(1963), at that time the world's costliest film.*

A violet-eyed English beauty, film actress Elizabeth Taylor, b. London, Feb. 27, 1932, was catapulted to stardom while still a child by her fourth Hollywood movie, *National Velvet* (1944). Although subsequently as celebrated for her glamorous personal life and numerous marriages—most notably to actor Richard Burton—as for her acting ability, she gave creditable performances in *A Place in the Sun* (1951), *Cat on a Hot Tin Roof* (1958), *Suddenly, Last Summer* (1959), *Butterfield 8* (1960), and *Who's Afraid of Virginia Woolf?* (1966). For the last two she won Academy Awards. She has appeared on Broadway (1981; 1983), and also occasionally on television.

Bibliography: Kelley, Kitty, *Elizabeth Taylor: The Last Star* (1982); Sheppard, Dick, *Elizabeth* (1974).

Taylor, Elizabeth   (novelist)

An English writer whose novels and stories are comparable to Jane Austen's in their wit, delicate style, and lack of sentimentality, Elizabeth Taylor, b. July 3, 1912, d. Nov. 19, 1975, draws from her knowledge of ordinary middle-class life. *The Wedding Group* (1968) describes the results of a rather impulsive marriage; *Mrs. Palfrey at the Claremont* (1971) explores the practical realities of widowhood. Taylor's fiction typically involves the poignant loneliness that her characters endure.

Taylor, Frederick Winslow

The U.S. inventor and engineer Frederick Winslow Taylor, b. Philadelphia, Mar. 20, 1856, d. Mar. 21, 1915, is known as the "father of scientific management." He began working at the age of 18 as an apprentice pattern maker and machinist in Philadelphia. Three years later he joined Midvale Steel Company as a machine shop laborer and worked his way up to chief engineer. In 1881, Taylor began to study how individual tasks were being performed at the mill. He timed each task and then greatly increased individual productivity on the job by rearranging work stations and the flow of materials through the mill. Thus began the first time and motion studies that made Taylor famous. He applied his principles of efficiency engineering to many industries, especially steel mills, as a consulting engineer after graduating (1883) from Stevens Institute of Technology. His *Principles of Scientific Management* (1911) is a classic in industrial psychology.

Bibliography: Copley, Frank B., *Frederick W. Taylor, Father of Scientific Management* (1923); Kakar, Sudhir, *Frederick Taylor: A Study in Personality and Innovation* (1970).

Taylor, Jeremy

The English bishop and devotional writer Jeremy Taylor, b. Aug. 15, 1613, d. Aug. 13, 1667, was educated at Cambridge, where he later taught, as well as at Oxford. Favored by Archbishop William Laud, Taylor served various parishes, finally becoming chaplain to Charles I. After the royalist defeat in the civil war, he was deprived of his parish (1644) and became private chaplain to the 2d earl of Carbery in Wales. There Taylor produced his classic, *Rule and Exercises of Holy Living* (1650), and . . . *of Holy Dying* (1651). After the Restoration, Taylor became (1660) bishop of Down, Connor, and Dromore in Ireland and vice-chancellor of Trinity College, Dublin.

JAMES D. NELSON

Bibliography: Davies, Horton, *Worship and Theology in England*, vol. 2 (1975); Hughes, H. T., *The Piety of Jeremy Taylor* (1960); Stranks, C. J., *The Life and Writings of Jeremy Taylor* (1952; repr. 1973).

Taylor, John   (clergyman)

John Taylor, b. England, Nov. 1, 1808, d. July 25, 1887, was an effective missionary and propagandist for the Mormon faith. In 1838 he was chosen an apostle by Joseph Smith. He was seriously wounded by the mob in Carthage, Ill., that lynched Smith in 1844. Taylor supported the succession of Brigham Young to the leadership and played a major role in the colonizing of Utah. In 1880 he succeeded Young as president of the church. In 1884, as a result of federal legislation against the Mormon doctrine of polygamy, Taylor went into hiding.

Bibliography: Roberts, B. H., *The Life of John Taylor* (1892; repr. 1963); Taylor, S. W., *The Kingdom or Nothing* (1976).

Taylor, John   (poet)

John Taylor, b. Aug. 24, 1580, d. December 1653, is commonly called England's "Water Poet" because, in addition to writing verse, he was long employed as a waterman on the River Thames. His frequent journeys resulted in the recollections *Travels in Germany* (1617), *The Pennyless Pilgrimage* (1618), and *The Praise of Hemp-seed* (1620).

Taylor, Maxwell D.

The American general Maxwell Davenport Taylor, b. Keytesville, Mo., Aug. 26, 1901, d. Apr. 19, 1987, had a long and notable military career and served (1964–65) as U.S. ambassador to South Vietnam. During World War II he helped organize the 82d Division (the first U.S. airborne division). At considerable risk, he infiltrated Axis lines before the Allied invasion of Italy in 1943 to confer with Italian officials. In 1944, commanding the 101st Airborne Division, Taylor participated in the assault on Normandy in June and later, with his unit, landed from the air in the Netherlands. He led the UN Eighth Army near the end of the Korean War. As army chief of staff (1955–59) and chairman of the joint chiefs of staff (1962–64), Taylor pressed for greater stress on balanced conventional forces. While ambassador to South Vietnam he backed substantial escalation of U.S. involvement after initially resisting such action. Taylor wrote *The Uncertain Trumpet* (1960) and other books.

WARREN W. HASSLER, JR.

Taylor, Paul

The dancer and choreographer Paul Taylor, b. Pittsburgh, Pa., July 29, 1930, is one of the masters of modern American theater dance (see MODERN DANCE). After studying at the Juilliard School of Music in New York City, he performed with the companies of Pearl Lang and Merce Cunningham in 1953. From the mid-1950s to the early 1960s, Taylor danced many principal roles in the Martha Graham Company. At the same time he presented his experimental choreography in pieces like *Epic* (1957), in which he wore a business suit and performed everyday gestures to recorded time signals. In 1961, he began to devote himself entirely to his own company and presented *Insects and Heroes* to general acclaim. Since then, he has choreographed many such characteristic works, blending contemporary elements—broad humor and simplified movements—with traditional aspects of dance: the use of classical music accompaniment and a concern with form. *Esplanade* (1975) sets basic movements like running, walking, and falling in dance arrangements and is performed to Bach violin concertos. *Private Domain* (1987) is his autobiography.

JOHN HOWELL

Bibliography: Cohen, Selma Jeanne, *The Modern Dance* (1966).

Taylor, Peter

Peter Matthew Hillsman Taylor, b. Trenton, Tenn., Jan. 8, 1917, is a distinguished American fiction writer. A distinctly Southern author, Taylor chooses to express his ironic perception of social change through descriptions of small-town life in Tennessee. His writing is regional but far from parochial: his psychologically complex works delve beneath and beyond his literal settings to disclose the universal yearnings of the human heart. Though mostly a short-story writer—his collections include *Miss Leonora When Last Seen* (1963), *In the Miro District* (1977), *The Old Forest* (1985), and *The Collected Stories* (1986)—Taylor has also written novels and plays. His novel *A Summons to Memphis* (1986) won the Pulitzer Prize.

Taylor, Zachary

Zachary Taylor was a military leader and the 12th president of the United States (1849–50).

Early Life and Career. Taylor was born in Orange County, Va., on Nov. 24, 1784, into a prominent Virginia family—his father had served with George Washington during the American Revolution. Taylor was raised on the Kentucky frontier, however, and received little formal education. He joined the army in 1808 and distinguished himself in the defense of Fort Harrison against the Indians during the War of 1812, rising to the rank of major. In 1816, after a one-year hiatus, he reentered the army and for the next 16 years served at various frontier posts. Promoted (1832) to colonel, he led the First Infantry Regiment in the Black Hawk War. He participated (1837–38) in the Seminole Wars, winning promotion to brigadier general as well as the nickname Old Rough and Ready.

Following a tour (1841–44) at Fort Smith, Ark., Taylor was placed in command of the military department of the Southwest and established a permanent home in Baton Rouge, La. In 1845, President James K. Polk ordered him to occupy the Republic of Texas after its annexation to the United States was approved and to defend Texas against a threatened Mexican invasion. Taylor sailed from Louisiana to Corpus Christi on July 23, establishing a camp on the south bank of the Nueces River. The ensuing MEXICAN WAR raised him from relative obscurity to the presidency.

Mexican War. The government of Mexico was taken over in December 1845 by radical Mexican Centralists who regarded the annexation of Texas as an act of war and Taylor's military occupation of Texas as an invasion of Mexican territory. After the failure of a U.S. peace initiative, Polk ordered Taylor to move his forces south to the Rio Grande. The general did so in March 1846, amid increasing threats of hostility from the Mexican Centralists. The Mexican War began on April 25, after Mexican troops had crossed the Rio Grande and attacked an American detachment. Additional Mexican attacks followed at Palo Alto (May 8) and Resaca de la Palma (May 9), but Taylor won unexpected victories that were responsible, in part, for the overthrow of Mexico's Centralist government.

On May 13 the United States declared war; shortly thereafter, Taylor was voted a gold medal and promoted to major general (June 29, 1846). More important, perhaps, he captured the popular fancy and was mentioned as a possible 1848 presidential candidate. His military decisions for the rest of the Mexican campaign, however, have been criticized. Plagued by inefficient logistical support, raw and untrained recruits, and inadequate transportation, Taylor was slow to occupy Matamoros and thus gave the enemy a chance to withdraw. He did not pursue the fleeing Mexican army southward but began a movement up the Rio Grande. By August he had reached Camargo and besieged Monterrey, Mexico's largest

ZACHARY TAYLOR
12th President of the United States (1849–50)

Nickname: "Old Rough and Ready"
Born: Nov. 24, 1784, near Barboursville, Va.
Profession: Soldier
Religious Affiliation: Episcopalian
Marriage: June 21, 1810, to Margaret Mackall Smith (1788–1852)
Children: Ann Mackall Taylor (1811–75); Sarah Knox Taylor (1814–35); Octavia P. Taylor (1816–20); Margaret Smith Taylor (1819–20); Mary Elizabeth Taylor (1824–1909); Richard Taylor (1826–79)
Political Affiliation: Whig
Writings: *Letters of Zachary Taylor* (1908)
Died: July 9, 1850, Washington, D.C.
Buried: Zachary Taylor National Cemetery, near Louisville, Ky.

Vice-President and Cabinet Members
Vice-President: Millard Fillmore
Secretary of State: John M. Clayton
Secretary of the Treasury: William M. Meredith
Secretary of War: George W. Crawford
Attorney General: Reverdy Johnson
Postmaster General: Jacob Collamer
Secretary of the Navy: William B. Preston
Secretary of the Interior: Thomas Ewing

community, which fell on September 24, after 4 days of hard fighting. Lacking supplies, Taylor—in what may have been his greatest military blunder—granted an 8-week armistice to the Mexican commander, Gen. Pedro de Ampudia, allowing him to withdraw southward still in possession of most of his arms and ammunition.

Polk criticized Taylor severely, ordering him to release most of his troops to Gen. Winfield SCOTT and take a defensive position. Taylor, however, occupied Saltillo, the capital of Coahuila in northern Mexico. Polk, hoping to arrange an armistice, allowed Mexican dictator Antonio López de SANTA ANNA safe passage through the U.S. blockade at Veracruz. At Buena

Vista, Santa Anna attacked Taylor, who won a surprise victory.
Presidency. The victories brought Taylor widespread acclaim; his alleged blunders were largely overlooked. His popularity as a military hero enabled him to overtake Sen. Henry Clay of Kentucky and win the Whig nomination for the presidency, with Millard FILLMORE as his running mate. In the November election—a three-way contest in which he faced Democrat Lewis Cass and Free Soiler Martin Van Buren—Taylor won 15 of the then 30 states and a plurality of the popular vote.

During his brief term (Mar. 5, 1849–July 9, 1850), Taylor presided over the ratification of the CLAYTON-BULWER TREATY and the near secession of the South over the issue of slavery in the territory newly acquired from Mexico. A supporter of the WILMOT PROVISO (1846), which stipulated that the Mexican Cession should be closed to slavery, Taylor encouraged both New Mexico and California to apply for admission as free states. He further angered his Southern followers by ignoring the claims of Texas—a slave state—to territory assigned to New Mexico. The COMPROMISE OF 1850 prevented Southern secession for the time being, although it did not pass Congress until after Taylor's death. The president died on July 9 of cholera. Fillmore succeeded him.   SEYMOUR V. CONNOR

Bibliography: Bauer, K. Jack, *Zachary Taylor*, ed. by W. J. Cooper, Jr. (1985); Dyer, Brainerd, *Zachary Taylor* (1846; repr. 1967); Hamilton, Holman, *Zachary Taylor*, 2 vols. (1941, 1951; repr. 1966); McKinley, S. B., and Bent, Silas, *Old Rough and Ready* (1946).

Taylor series

A Taylor series is a means of expressing a mathematical function as an infinite sum. The function sin x can be represented as: $\sin x = b_0 + b_1 x + b_2 x^2 + b_3 x^3 + \ldots$, provided the sum reaches a limiting value. The problem of finding the coefficients b_0, b_1, b_2, . . . was solved by Brook Taylor (1685–1731) and Colin Maclaurin (1698–1746). Specifically, the series is called a Taylor series when the function is expressed in terms of $x - a$, where a is a constant (often selected to ensure that the series converges); if $a = 0$, the resulting series is usually called a Maclaurin series. Some important series (expansions of functions) are:

$$\sin x = x - \frac{x^3}{3!} + \frac{x^5}{5!} - \frac{x^7}{7!} + \ldots$$

$$\cos x = 1 - \frac{x^2}{2!} + \frac{x^4}{4!} - \frac{x^6}{6!} + \ldots$$

$$e^x 1 + x + \frac{x^2}{2!} + \frac{x^3}{3!} + \frac{x^4}{4!} + \ldots$$

For computational purposes, the Taylor and Maclaurin series provide a rapid and simple means of calculating the value of a transcendental function to any desired degree of accuracy.   STEPHEN FLEISHMAN

Bibliography: Leithold, Louis, *The Calculus with Analytic Geometry*, part 1 (1972).

tayra   [ty'-ruh]

The tayra, T. barbara, is a small, omnivorous mammal found in wooded areas of Central and South America. A member of the weasel family, it has a slim body, short legs, and a long tail. In feeding on fruit, tayras sometimes injure commercial crops, especially bananas.

The tayra, *Tayra barbara*, in the weasel family, Mustelidae, is a slender-bodied, agile animal found in forests from southern Mexico to Argentina. It is about 63 cm (25 in) long, plus a 45-cm (18-in) tail, and typically has a dark brownish coat and a lighter head and chest patch.   EVERETT SENTMAN

Tayside   [tay'-syd]

Tayside is an administrative region in east central Scotland, with an area of 7,501 km² (2,895 mi²) and a population of 394,400 (1984 est.). The region slopes from western hills to the North Sea coast in the east. The major cities are DUNDEE and PERTH. The economy is based on the manufacture of linens and woolens, distilling, sheep raising, shipbuilding, and tourism at the coastal resort towns.

Tayside was constituted during the 1975 reorganization of local government in Scotland from the former counties of ANGUS, KINROSS, and most of PERTH.

Tbilisi   [tuh-bil'-ee-see]

Tbilisi, formerly Tiflis, is the capital of the Georgian Soviet Socialist Republic of the USSR, located in Transcaucasia. The city's population is 1,158,000 (1985 est.). It is situated along both banks of the Kura River in an intermontane basin, at an elevation of 406 to 522 m (1,332 to 1,712 ft). The name *Tbilisi* derives from a Georgian word meaning "warm," reflecting the presence of hot sulfur springs.

Tbilisi is an important manufacturing and transportation center, at the junction of railroads and highways. It is the southern terminus of the Georgian Military Highway across the Caucasus Mountains. Tbilisi's diversified industries include the manufacture of electric locomotives, machine tools, and electrical engineering products. Textile, paper, and apparel manufacturing, liquor distilling, and food processing are also important. Energy is obtained from nearby hydroelectric stations and a gas-fired thermal power station.

The city's location on the Kura River, hemmed in by the Surami Range, has given Tbilisi an elongated shape, extending 27 km (17 mi) along the river. Formal gardens enhance the city's parks. Most of the major public buildings are on the Prospekt Rustaveli, the main thoroughfare, named for the classic Georgian poet Shota Rustaveli. Historical sites include the ruins of the ancient fortress Narikala, on a right-bank hill, and the 13th-century Metekhi castle and cathedral, across the river. Nearby is the 5th-century Sioni Cathedral and the 6th-century Anchikhati Cathedral.

Tbilisi is an important cultural and educational center, with the Georgian Academy of Sciences (founded in 1941), a university (1918), a conservatory, an art academy, and theaters. On Mtatsminda Hill is a pantheon, containing the graves of prominent Georgian cultural figures. The existence of a fortress on the site of Tbilisi was first reported in the 4th century. Georgia's capital since the 11th century, Tbilisi grew more rapidly after Georgia's union with Russia in the early 19th century.   THEODORE SHABAD

TBT: see TRIBUTYL TIN.

Tchaikovsky, Peter Ilich   [chy-kawf'-skee]

The eminent Russian composer Peter Ilich Tchaikovsky was born on May 7 (N.S.), 1840, in a settlement adjacent to the Kama-Votkinsk Metal Works (managed by his father) in the Ural Mountains. The first mention of his involvement with music appears in a letter of 1844 that reports him as having helped compose a song, "Mama's in Petersburg." At home he heard folk songs, popular arias, and romances sung by his mother, and pieces played by a mechanical organ, among them excerpts from Wolfgang Amadeus Mozart's *Don Giovanni*. (Mozart would remain Tchaikovsky's most beloved composer.) Piano lessons, started about the age of five, continued in Saint Petersburg, where he entered boarding school in 1848. From 1850 to 1859 he attended the School of Jurisprudence, where he assisted in a choir conducted by Gavriil Lomakin and studied piano with Rudolph Kündinger and har-

Peter Ilich Tchaikovsky, probably the most popular 19th-century Russian composer, was also the first to have a formal musical education. By 1874, when this photograph was taken, the composer was 34 years old and was teaching at the Moscow Conservatory of Music. He had already composed, among many other works, three of his ten operas, the first two of his six symphonies, and the Romeo and Juliet Overture-Fantasy, and he was completing his Piano Concerto no. 1.

mony with Kündinger's brother. Assigned on graduation to the Ministry of Justice, Tchaikovsky continued to be drawn to music, and in 1861 he began classes sponsored by the Russian Music Society. The year after, he left his job and entered the just-founded Saint Petersburg Conservatory. Working zealously under Anton Rubinstein and Nikolai Zaremba, he received a Silver Medal for his graduation cantata on Johann Schiller's An die Freude in December 1865.

At Nikolai Rubinstein's invitation, Tchaikovsky taught theory in Moscow, joining the faculty of the new Moscow Conservatory when it opened in September 1866. During his 11 years there, he composed his Piano Concerto no. 1 (1875), the ballet Swan Lake (1876), four operas, three symphonies, and many smaller works. He also established close ties with the composers of the nationalist group known as "The Five," especially Mily Balakirev and Nikolai Rimsky-Korsakov; the critic Vladimir Stasov called him the "sixth member of their circle."

Marriage in July 1877 to Antonina Miliukova triggered an emotional crisis, perhaps related to his homosexuality, that brought him near suicide. He fled Moscow in a state of turmoil but managed to finish three masterpieces—the Fourth Symphony, the Violin Concerto, and the opera Eugene Onegin—before May 1878, when his wife agreed to separation (they were never divorced). An annuity from Nadezhda von Meck, granted during his crisis, allowed him to quit (1878) teaching. His association with von Meck, begun in an exchange of letters about a commission in 1876, was sustained in voluminous correspondence over 13 years, although they never met. From 1878 to 1885, Tchaikovsky lived sometimes in Russia, sometimes in western Europe. His reputation grew with the Capriccio italien (1880), the 1812 overture (1880), two more operas the Liturgy (1878) and the Vespers (1881). During his last years he lived in or near Moscow. In 1888, Tsar Alexander III granted him a yearly pension.

Tchaikovsky's fame, as both conductor and composer, spread as the result of a series of international tours, which brought him to the United States in 1891. He continued to compose—the ballets Sleeping Beauty (1889) and Nutcracker (1892), the Fifth (1888), Sixth (1893), and Manfred (1885) symphonies, and three final operas. Younger composers emulated him, among them Sergei Taneyev, Anton Arensky, Mikhail Ippolitov-Ivanov, and, later, Sergei Rachmaninoff. A few days after conducting the premiere of his Sixth Symphony, he contracted cholera and died in Saint Petersburg on Nov. 6 (N.S.), 1893.

Tchaikovsky's lyric gift owes much to Russian folk song, which he quotes (First Piano Concerto, Second and Fourth symphonies) or imitates (First Symphony, Second String Quartet), and to the 19th-century Russian salon song, whose traits permeate his vocal melody (songs and romances, Eugene Onegin) and even infuse his instrumental themes (Fifth and Sixth symphonies). The expressive pathos of his themes depends on abundant use of suspensions and anticipations, which also pervade his rich harmonies.

MALCOLM HAMRICK BROWN

Bibliography: Abraham, Gerald, ed., Tchaikovsky: A Symposium (1945); Brown, David, The Early Years, 1840–1874, vol. 1 in Tchaikovsky: A Biographical and Critical Study (1978); Garden, Edward, Tchaikovsky (1973); Strutte, Wilson, Tchaikovsky: His Life and Times (1978); Volkoff, Vladimir, Tchaikovsky (1975); Warrack, John, Tchaikovsky (1973).

Tchelitchew, Pavel   [chay-lee'-chef]

The neoromantic artist Pavel Tchelitchew, b. Moscow, Sept. 21 (N.S.), 1898, d. July 31, 1957, is best known for his tormented metamorphic paintings and his imaginative ballet designs. He fled the USSR in 1921 and worked as a scenic designer in Berlin until he moved to Paris in 1923. Tchelitchew was soon a prominent member of Gertrude Stein's artistic circle. His paintings of the 1920s show strong surrealist elements, with fantastic distortions of everyday objects. He continued to design scenery and costumes for leading ballet companies. After his move to the United States in 1934, Tchelitchew began the sketches for his major painting, Hide-and-Seek (Cache-Cache) (1940–42; Museum of Modern Art, New York City), a nightmarish vision of infant heads and internal and external organs enmeshed in skeins of blood vessels.

Bibliography: Kirstein, Lincoln, Pavel Tchelitchew (1964) and Pavel Tchelitchew Drawings, rev. ed. (1970); Tyler, Parker, The Divine Comedy of Pavel Tchelitchew (1967).

Tcherepnin, Aleksandr Nikolayevich   [chir-ip-neen']

The Russian-born composer and pianist Aleksandr Nikolayevich Tcherepnin, b. Jan. 20 (N.S.), 1899, d. Sept. 29, 1977, was the son of the prominent composer and conductor Nikolay Tcherepnin (1873–1945). After piano studies with his mother, he wrote his first opera at the age of 12. He briefly attended (1917) Saint Petersburg Conservatory, then began touring as a pianist, arriving in 1921 in Paris, where he studied piano with Isador Philipp. He subsequently toured as pianist and composer in Europe, the United States, and—from 1934 to 1937—China and Japan and married the pianist Lee Hsien-Ming. He lived in Paris from 1938, resumed his international tours in 1947, and finally settled (1949) in Chicago, where he and his wife taught at De Paul University. In his compositions he experimented with Oriental scales and a nine-tone scale of his own devising and developed a method of polyphonic rhythm. His works include operas, ballets, cantatas, piano concertos, symphonies, chamber music, songs, and solo piano pieces.

Bibliography: Ewen, David, Composers Since 1900 (1969) and World of Twentieth Century Music (1968).

Tcherkassky, Marianna   [chir-kahs'-kee]

Marianna Tcherkassky, b. Glen Cove, N.Y., Oct. 28, 1952, is one of the most talented young ballerinas in American Ballet Theatre. She joined the company in 1970 and became a principal dancer in 1976. She created the role of Clara in Mikhail Baryshnikov's Nutcracker (1976) and has been acclaimed in Giselle and Le Spectre de la Rose.   MICHAEL ROBERTSON

Bibliography: Payne, Charles, American Ballet Theatre (1978).

Tchernichowsky, Saul   [chur-nuh-chawf'-skee]

A physician by training, Saul Tchernichowsky, b. Russia, Aug. 20 (N.S.), 1875, d. Oct. 14, 1943, achieved renown as an outstanding modern Hebrew poet. His poetry, inspired by the classics, dealt not only with national Jewish themes but also with such universal themes as love and nature. Heroism and beauty were among the Greek ideals that he extolled in such varied poetic forms as the idyll, the sonnet, and the ballad. Unsurpassed as a translator, Tchernichowsky translated into Hebrew from the literatures of half a dozen languages.

Bibliography: Silberschlag, Eisig, *Saul Tschernichowsky, Poet of Revolt* (1968).

Te Deum laudamus

The Latin hymn *Te Deum laudamus* (''we praise Thee, God'') is attributed to Nicetas, bishop of Remesiana in Dacia, who lived in the late 4th and early 5th centuries. Although this tripartite composition soon found a firm place in the liturgy for matins, it also came to be used for general festive occasions. It was infrequently set by composers of the pre-1600 period but later became popular in the middle baroque (Benevoli, Purcell) and subsequently in lavishly scored versions by Boyce, Graun, Handel (*Utrecht Te Deum*, 1713; *Dettingen Te Deum*, 1743), and others. The festive nature of the text inspired works by Berlioz (1855), Bruckner (1884), Dvořák (1896), and Verdi (1898), and in the 20th century by Vaughan Williams with the *Festival Te Deum*, written for the coronation of King George VI in 1937.   DENIS STEVENS

Te Kanawa, Kiri

Kiri Te Kanawa, b. Gisborne, New Zealand, Mar. 6, 1944, is an internationally renowned opera singer who in 1982 was made a Dame of the British Empire. A soprano, she won numerous singing competitions in New Zealand and Australia prior to becoming a student at the London Opera Centre. She began an association with the Royal Opera Company, Covent Garden, in 1970, achieving her first major success (1971) as the countess in Mozart's *Marriage of Figaro*. In 1974 she made her New York Metropolitan Opera debut in Verdi's *Otello*. She sang at the 1981 wedding of Britain's Prince of Wales.

tea

Tea is the beverage made when the processed leaves of the tea plant are infused with boiling water. Native to Southeast Asia, the tea plant, *Camellia sinensis*, is a small, shrublike, evergreen tree that belongs to the family Theaceae; its seeds contain a volatile oil, and its leaves have the chemicals CAFFEINE and tannin. The dark green leaves are elliptical in shape and have serrated edges, and the plant produces aromatic, white blossoms. Although second to coffee in commercial value, tea ranks first as the most popular beverage in the world. Many also use it medicinally as a stimulant.

History. The origins of tea culture and the brewing of dried tea leaves into a beverage are obscure; experts believe, however, that the tea plant originated in a region encompassing Tibet, western China, and northern India. According to ancient Chinese legend, the emperor Shen-Nung learned how to brew the beverage in 2737 BC when a few leaves from the plant accidentally fell into water he was boiling. Tea leaves began to be processed and were sold in cakes of steamed leaves or in powder or leaf form. Lu Yü's *The Classic of Tea*, published in China in AD 780, described the cultivation, processing, and use of tea. Tea was introduced by Chinese Buddhist monks into Japan. Tea culture then spread to Java, the Dutch East Indies, and other tropical and subtropical areas. British merchants formed the East India Company (1600–1858) and introduced teas into England and the American colonies.

Cultivation. Tea plants are grown on tea plantations, called gardens or estates, in areas that have a great amount of rainfall and rich, loamy soil. In certain areas, shade trees are planted throughout the gardens to protect the tea plants from too much sun and weed growth and to enrich the soil.

Tea-plant seeds are planted in a nursery and, when the young trees are between 6 and 18 months old, they are replanted in the garden. Nowadays, however, plants are frequently cloned. The tea plants are pruned periodically in order to maintain a height of about 1 m (3 ft) and to encourage the growth of new leaves. Plants grown at low altitudes produce leaves for commercial use after 2½ years, and those grown at high altitudes are ready in 5 years. The best teas are

Tea, C. sinensis, is a shrub with abundant foliage, camellialike flowers, and berries containing one to three seeds. The beverage made from leaves of the tea plant is among the world's most popular drinks.

produced at altitudes of 1,000 to 2,200 m (3,000 to 7,000 ft), because tea plants grow more slowly in cooler air and their leaves yield a better flavor. The tea produced on the lower slopes of the Himalayas near Darjeeling, India, is considered to be among the finest in the world.

Processing. The leaves are hand plucked by experienced workers. The smallest, youngest leaves only are used to produce tea. The three main types of tea being produced today are black (fermented), oolong (semifermented), and green (unfermented).

In order to make black tea, harvested leaves are spread on withering racks to dry. The leaves become soft and pliable and are then roller crushed to break the cell walls and release an enzyme. This process gives the tea its flavor. After rolling, the lumps of tea are broken and spread in a fermentation room to oxidize, which turns the leaves to a copper color. The leaves are finally hot-air dried in a process that stops fermentation and turns the leaves black. After the tea is processed, it is sieved to produce tea leaves of a uniform size and to facilitate blending and packing. Leaf-grade sizes run from pekoe, the coarsest size, to flowery orange pekoe, the smallest. Tippy golden flowery orange pekoe designates a tea hontaining the golden-colored tip, obtained from the bud during manufacture. The broken teas, having leaves broken during processing, are broken orange pekoe, broken pekoe, fan-

Tea leaves are harvested on a plantation in Darjeeling, India. Located in the Himalayan foothills, Darjeeling has a high altitude and rainfall conducive to tea cultivation. The crop from Darjeeling has made India a leading producer and exporter of tea.

nings, pekoe fannings, and dust, the last of which is the smallest-size leaf particle.

The tea plant found in Taiwan and south China appears to be most suitable for preparing oolong tea. The process begins in the same manner as that for black tea. The aroma, however, develops more quickly, and when the leaf is fired or dried, a coppery color forms around the edge of the leaf while the center remains green. The oolong flavor is fruity and pungent.

Green tea is produced much like the others, except that the leaf is heated before rolling in order to destroy the enzyme. The leaf then remains green throughout further manufacture and the aroma characteristic of black tea does not develop. Green tea is graded by age and style; for instance, gunpowder tea consists of balls of young or middle-aged leaves, and young hyson refers to slightly twisted or rolled young or middle-aged leaves.

Unblended and Blended Varieties. Various unblended and blended teas have achieved fame for their characteristic flavors. Among the unblended teas are Assam and Darjeeling, produced in India; the Ceylon teas, which have a smooth, flowery flavor; and Keemun, a dark China black tea also known as English Breakfast tea. Among the more popular blended teas are Irish Breakfast (high-grown Ceylon and Assam teas); Russian style, which is a China Congou sometimes containing other teas or scents; and Earl Grey, a black tea flavored with bergamot or lavender oil.

World Production. India, Sri Lanka (Ceylon), the People's Republic of China, Japan, Indonesia, Kenya, and the Transcaucasian regions of the USSR (Georgia and Azerbaijan) are the world's leading producers of tea. Of the estimated 1.8 billion metric tons (1981) produced worldwide annually, India accounts for more than one-third, China ranks second, and Sri Lanka ranks third.   ROBERT H. DICK

Bibliography: Eden, T., *Tea,* 3d ed. (1976); Harler, C. R., *Tea Growing* (1966) and *Tea Manufacture* (1963); Sarkar, Goutam K., *The World Tea Economy* (1972); Schafer, Charles and Violet, *Teacraft* (1975); Schapira, Joel, et al., *The Book of Coffee and Tea* (1982); Yü, Lu, *The Classic of Tea,* trans. by Francis Carpenter (1974).

tea ceremony

The Japanese tea ceremony, or *cha-no-yu,* is the ancient practice of serving tea according to a strict ritual that defines the manner in which tea is prepared and served. Rooted in ZEN BUDDHISM, the art of the tea ceremony symbolizes aesthetic simplicity through the elimination of the unnecessary.

The traditional ceremony, as practiced today, takes place in a tea room, or *cha-shitsu,* situated in a garden or a special room within a house. The simply constructed room is small, accommodating a host and five guests, and the floors are covered with straw (tatami) mats. The most formal ceremony takes four hours, and two types of green tea are served. A gong is sounded to signal the beginning of the ceremony. Following a prescribed pattern, the host prepares the tea with the utmost exactness. The principal guest is served first, after which the ritual is repeated. The accurate and delicate performance of each act is thought to represent the fundamental Zen principles of harmony, respect, purity, and tranquility.

The tea ceremony was originated in China by Buddhist monks who believed that tea had medicinal qualities. It was brought to Japan in the 13th century, but it was not until the 16th century that Zen monks had mastered, codified, and ennobled the drinking of tea. Once practiced only in Zen monasteries, the tea ceremony is now popular among the general public.   BETH F. SIMON

Bibliography: Hayashiya, T., et al., *Japanese Arts and the Tea Ceremony* (1975); Lee, Sherman E., *Tea Taste in Japanese Art* (1963; repr. 1979); Okakura, Kakuzo, *The Book of Tea* (1926; repr. 1978); Sadler, A., *Cha-No-Yu: The Japanese Tea Ceremony* (1977); Tanaka, S., *The Tea Ceremony* (1973; repr. 1983).

Teach, Edward: see BLACKBEARD.

teacher education: see TEACHING.

Teachers College, Columbia University

Established in 1887, Teachers College (enrollment: 4,200; library: 408,900 volumes) is the graduate school of education of Columbia University in New York City. Master's degrees and doctorates are granted in all programs, which are concerned with teacher education and education administration.

teaching

Teaching is the purposeful imparting of information or skills or both to another individual or to a group. Whereas an individual can learn without a teacher, a person cannot teach without a student. There is some debate as to whether teaching also implies learning. Does a student have to learn for teaching to have taken place? Historically, teaching has not been defined in this restrictive manner; the teacher was thought to be responsible for the quantity and quality of material covered and the way in which it was presented. Students have been held responsible for learning. Recent accountability movements, however, have placed a larger measure of the responsibility for student learning on the teacher. Some definitions of teaching now imply that students must learn in order for teaching to have taken place.

The concept of teaching can be greatly broadened to include computers, textbooks, or educational television. Generally speaking, however, the word *teacher* refers to human beings, whether they be parents, scout leaders, or classroom teachers. The teacher may use various technologies as aids in instruction, but it is nonetheless the human teacher who makes the decisions concerning the content and the means by which instruction is delivered.

The range of classroom teachers is broad, indeed. There are preschool teachers, elementary, secondary, and higher education teachers, as well as teachers in industry and teachers of teachers. Teaching can impart information about how to ride a bike, how to fill in an employment form, or how to interpret a passage from Shakespeare. The number of individuals involved in teaching far exceeds that in any other profession.

There are several essential requirements for teachers, whatever they are teaching: they must know the material they are to teach, they must be able to organize and articulate the material in a manner understandable to the student, and they must manage the students in order to maintain student attention on the learning task.

This article will focus on teaching as a human endeavor. Specifically, it will concentrate on the career and conditions of, preparation for, and practice of teaching.

CAREER CONDITIONS AND TEACHER EDUCATION

Complaints about the quality of teaching are not new, but they became especially loud in the late 1970s and during the 1980s. Many and consistently negative comments have been documented concerning U.S. teacher effectiveness and instructional methods during the 19th and the first half of the 20th centuries. Both urban and rural areas complained about the lack of effectiveness and commitment of teachers, although the rural districts had greater trouble than urban areas in retaining their teaching force. While teachers are now staying in the profession for longer periods than ever before, complaints about their quality persist. "Never before in the nation's history has the caliber of those entering the teaching profession been as low as it is today," wrote Emily Feistritzer in a major Carnegie Foundation report in 1983 on the conditions of teaching.

Two types of solutions aimed at improving the quality of teaching have dominated 19th- and 20th-century policy discussions. One concerns improving the conditions of teaching; the second, lengthening and improving the quality of teacher education.

Poor Conditions. While many articles decry the conditions of teaching today, in most parts of the world teaching has not traditionally been an occupation that receives adequate support. Salaries are low: in the United States, for example, beginning salaries of teachers, adjusted for 12 months, are lower than those for any other field requiring a bachelor's degree, and they top out sooner and at a lower level than other college-degree-level occupations. Classrooms are often crowded, materials and supplies outdated or nonexistent, and in certain schools and locales teachers are threatened with physical violence. Public esteem for teachers and schools is low, at least as it is reported in the media and various public surveys—although parents of children in school are happier with the schools than is the general public.

With few exceptions around the world (Japan being one), teaching has for some time been a female occupation. Some writers, including the pioneer U.S. feminist Susan B. Anthony, have suggested that the lower-than-deserved status and salaries of teachers are additional instances of discrimination against women. Teaching, consequently, was not an occupation that one stayed in year after year. Some women quit to get married and have children, and other teachers left teaching to pursue more lucrative occupations. At the present time, school districts are having especial difficulty attracting and retaining math and science teachers because the salaries in related occupations, such as computer programming, are luring prospective and practicing teachers away from education.

General U.S. teacher shortages were highlighted in 1985, when New York City and Georgia and other states recruited abroad for teachers, and Miami searched the northern states. It was estimated that 1.3 million new teachers would be needed in the United States by 1990. At the same time, some observers saw American teachers on the threshold of catching up on pay. New Jersey in 1985 became the first state to adopt a state-wide minimum for teachers' salaries.

Associations of and for Teachers. The low salaries and poor conditions of teaching created the ideal atmosphere for the formation of teachers' associations designed to provide a unified voice for the establishment and protection of employment rights for teachers, and to improve salaries and other conditions. In almost every country of the world, there is at least one dues-collecting teacher organization to which members belong, voluntarily or not.

Two rival organizations sprang up in the United States. The earlier one (1857), the NATIONAL EDUCATION ASSOCIATION (NEA), is a loosely organized group of local, state, and national organizations that includes both administrators and teachers in its membership. Many teachers viewed the involvement of both teachers and administrators in the NEA as conflict of interest; administrators who make decisions about teachers' salaries might not be willing to work for increased teachers' salaries. The AMERICAN FEDERATION OF TEACHERS (AFT), a teacher-only labor union formed in 1916, fought for the right to create bargaining units in school districts. The AFT unabashedly works to obtain higher teacher salaries and better conditions for teachers; it has called strikes. As administrators began forming their own associations (such as the American Association of School Administrators) and as teachers began to dominate the organizations, the NEA moved closer to the AFT in demanding higher salaries and better treatment of teachers in such matters as evaluations and tolerating strikes.

Numerous education associations in the United States lobby for their members' rights and best interests. Teacher educators, for example, have theirs—the American Association of Colleges for Teacher Education and the Association of Teacher Educators; vocational educators have several, as do speech and hearing therapists, teachers of mathematics, and school volunteers. College professors have the AMERICAN ASSOCIATION OF UNIVERSITY PROFESSORS. At times, these organizations press for policies that are not in the best interest of the AFT and NEA memberships. Due to the large membership of NEA and AFT, however, they are probably the most powerful of all education organizations. Recently, they both have become more involved in supporting politicians whose philosophies match their own.

Teacher Preparation. During the 19th century few state or local regulations existed concerning the education-level prerequisite to becoming a teacher. Often, when a student finished a grade level, she or he turned around and taught it the next year. Few teacher training institutions existed, and those which did were often associated with and at the level of sec-

ondary schools. From 1900 on, during the period of such influential theorists as John DEWEY and Edward L. THORNDIKE, teacher education was steadily lengthened and improved to the point that four-year, degree-granting programs, specializing in teaching, were established. These normal schools were initially designed for prospective secondary rather than elementary teachers; in the United States, as around the world, requirements for secondary teaching have, until recently, exceeded those of elementary teaching. In the United States, state legislation began to mandate the educational requirements for becoming a teacher. In 1946, 20 states mandated a bachelor's degree for elementary teaching; by the 1970s, all states required the degree. By the mid-1980s, about half of all U.S. elementary and secondary teachers held degrees beyond the bachelor's.

Most teacher-preparation programs consist of subject matter and general liberal arts courses, as well as specialized pedagogical courses. In some places, a student is expected to earn a B.A. degree before entering the teacher education program. More generally, however, the prospective teacher receives a B.A. in teaching. There is an inherent tension between the academic and pedagogical requirements. Some recent reform proposals, for example, suggest that teachers should take more subject-matter courses and skip the pedagogical courses. Others argue that prospective teachers should spend more time in practical application experiences before entering the profession.

Nonetheless, the pedagogical programs, broadly speaking, are remarkably similar around the world. Methods courses prepare students to teach specific subject-matter areas; courses in teaching and learning specialize in generic teaching skills and LEARNING THEORY and assessment theory; foundations courses prepare students for the intellectual, social, and cultural settings in which schooling has been and is taking place, and practice teaching provides students with supervised teaching experiences in classrooms.

In the United States approximately 40% of a prospective secondary school teacher's college preparation is devoted to general liberal arts education, 40% to the specific subject matter area she or he is going to teach, and 20% in professional studies. The figures for elementary education are: 40% general liberal arts, 15% in other liberal arts, and 45% in professional studies.

In most countries the national government controls the accreditation of the teacher-education institutions and the certification of the graduates. In the United States all the states control the certification of the graduates, but not all control accreditation. Instead, there is an independent, nongovern-

A prerecorded lecture is presented by videotape to a high school class in Utulei, in Western Samoa. The use of taped and broadcast educational television programs is central to education in many developing countries, where teaching facilities are limited.

mental national association that provides accreditation to those institutions which apply and pass the review. The National Council for Accreditation of Teacher Education (NCATE) cannot require an institution to submit itself to a review, but its member institutions graduate 87% of school personnel.

Recent concern with the quality of U.S. teacher education has spawned a number of reform suggestions. One harks back to the notion of a fifth or sixth year, or a master's degree in teacher education, in which students would enter the teacher education program only after receiving a bachelor's degree. Another is the notion of continuing supervisory support for teachers into the first several years of teaching, variously called internship or beginning teacher programs.

Changes in teacher education around the world precede, mirror, or follow the patterns within the United States. The patterns, however, are similar. For example, a committee report in 1897 in England called for teacher preparation for secondary school teachers to follow the receipt of a bachelor's degree. This reform was considered and much later implemented in California. In many places in the world, secondary school teachers are still receiving much more education than elementary. For example, in some countries in Africa, elementary school teachers require only one or two years of additional training following their own elementary education.

TEACHING METHODS AND AIDS

Teaching is a highly complex occupation. It has been described in terms of very different types of roles. For example, teachers are executives, supervising students and planning programs within the workplace. Teachers manage time, material, knowledge, and students. They are expert communicators with their students as well as with parents and other adults within the school, and they are decision makers, making numerous decisions in one class period, often simultaneously and "on their feet." They also have a series of lesser roles such as lunchroom and school-bus monitors, and file clerks.

In their basic role as instructors, teachers have a number of methods for involving their students in the content of the curriculum. The most popular, by far, is the lecture technique. Excluding lab periods, approximately 90% of college teaching is lecture technique. The figure is somewhat lower at the secondary level, and lower still in primary-school classrooms. Secondary teachers also rely extensively on seatwork, during which students work at their desks on an assignment, and teachers circulate to answer questions or sit at their own desks and correct the seatwork. Many teachers in secondary and sometimes postsecondary classes use discussion sessions to stimulate their students' interest, and to assess their grasp of the material. Discussion sessions go beyond the usual question-and-answer sequences that accompany lectures, because they are meant to help students extend their knowledge

Students in a language laboratory can listen to recorded lessons selected by the teacher at a central console or individually by each student. They can also record their own efforts to speak the language and receive individual instruction from the teacher at the console.

Computers are multiplying in the schools, although debate continues as to their most efficient use, especially for young children. Many programs simply review classroom learning. More ambitious is the "discovery learning" approach, encouraging active experimentation.

through higher-level thinking.

Grouping of students within the classroom occurs primarily at the elementary level. This organizational arrangement places students together in two or more groups in the classroom to improve the learning conditions for those students. For example, most early elementary reading teachers place their students in two to three groups. Grouping in reading places students of the same achievement level together to enable the teacher to more easily work with them. Grouping, however, is becoming more popular in other subjects, and for other purposes. Cooperative learning groups, for example, place students of different abilities in the same group, and the students within that group tutor each other on assignments. These programs have been shown to be effective in raising students' achievement as well as improving their social skills and attitudes toward one another.

Another method that is increasing in popularity is the use of simulations, particularly for adults learning different types of skills. Simulations attempt to create conditions as close to the real situation in which the individual will be performing the skill as possible. For example, some teacher-education programs include sequences in which one student will teach a lesson to his or her fellow students who are posing as elementary or secondary students. Airline pilots log many hours on flight simulators, and driver-education courses are beginning to involve simulation computer work. Simulations are not effective for general education, because the setting in which the skill or information will eventually be used is not known.

Until recently the use of technology in teaching has been minimal, indeed. Technological aids include the textbook, chalkboard, wall posters, and material for specialized courses such as science equipment for labs and sewing machines for domestic science courses. The overhead projector, an example of an audiovisual teaching aid, has increased somewhat in popularity, but it is not a standard item in most classrooms. Educational technology has not made great inroads into the classroom. Innovations such as educational television and TEACHING MACHINES have often found their way into dusty school closets. (See also PROGRAMMED LEARNING.)

One exception appears to be the computer, although it is not yet clear whether school computers will end up in a special room called a computer lab, in the classrooms, or elsewhere. It is certain that computers are in students' homes, and they are finding their way in ever-increasing numbers into the classrooms. Initially, computers were used to provide students with extra practice in subjects such as math. Called computer-assisted-instruction (CAI), these programs appeal to the students and do at least as well as teacher instruction in raising student achievement.

While CAI is still in practice, computers are also being used for other purposes. Teachers and principals use them to maintain information about their students. Computers are used as a tool in helping students learn a skill such as writing, and some computer programs actually teach students a new skill or piece of knowledge. Many of the programs are in the form of games to help motivate students. It is unclear, however, whether the students actually learn skills beyond performing the game, or the degree to which teachers need to be involved in the process to ensure that students learn what was intended.

The major problems with computers in the schools are: (1) extensive staff development is required to help teachers learn to use computers; (2) the software has not kept up with the capacity of the machines or the interests of the students. Many programs are simply electronic page-turners.

VIRGINIA RICHARDSON KOEHLER

Bibliography: Cuban, Larry, *How Teachers Taught: Constancy and Change in American Classrooms, 1890–1980* (1983); Feistritzer, Emily, *The Condition of Teaching: A State by State Analysis* (1983); Hopkins, David, and Reid, Ken, eds., *Rethinking Teacher Education* (1984); Howey, Kenneth, and Gardner, William, eds., *The Education of Teachers: A Look Ahead* (1982); Lortie, Dan C., *The Schoolteacher: A Sociological Study* (1975); National Educational Association, *Prices, Budgets, Salaries and Income* (1983); Sarason, Seymour, *The Culture of the School and the Problem of Change*, 2d ed. (1982); Shulman, Lee, and Sykes, Gary, eds., *Handbook of Teaching and Policy* (1983); Whitrock, Merle, ed., *Handbook of Research on Teaching*, 3d ed. (1985).

See also: CURRICULUM; EDUCATION; PRESCHOOL EDUCATION; PRIMARY EDUCATION; SECONDARY EDUCATION; UNITED STATES, EDUCATION IN THE.

teaching machines

This McDonnell Douglas flight simulator, used to train pilots on the ground, is a computer-controlled teaching machine that also uses manipulated objects. Cockpit controls and instrumentation respond to the pilot's control movements, flight motion is simulated, and a visual representation is projected in front of the cockpit window.

Teaching machines, which are used in PROGRAMMED LEARNING, are devices that are able to store instructional information, present displays selected from this information, receive responses from a learner, and act on those responses in order to select additional displays or to calculate and generate new data and displays.

Sidney L. Pressey is usually given credit for developing in the 1920s the first teaching machine, a device that stored test questions and presented them one at a time to a student, who responded by pressing a lever. The student was able to move on to the next question only if the answer was correct.

Teaching machines received major impetus during the 1950s from the work of B. F. SKINNER. Self-instruction programs written according to Skinner's methods were often administered by means of a machine that presented a graded series of questions, each requiring a written response. The machine kept the correct answer hidden until after the student had written his or her answer.

Teaching machines may be divided into four classes—print media, audiovisual media, manipulated objects, and computer-based machines. A variety of devices are based on print media. Whereas programmed books are not considered teaching machines, many mechanical devices based on paper displays have been developed.

Audiovisual media include audio tapes, filmstrips, color slides, motion pictures, and videotapes. To be considered a teaching machine, audiovisual devices must present different displays depending on responses from a learner. A cockpit simulator in which a pilot trainee can move the controls and observe simulated displays on instruments is an example of a teaching machine employing manipulated objects.

A computer-based teaching machine is a computer-controlled television display on which color images, some accompanied by audio and some in motion, can be displayed depending on choices made by a student. The student uses a typewriterlike keyboard to enter his or her responses.

Unless controlled by a computer, teaching machines based on print media and audiovisual media are for the most part extremely limited in the kinds of responses they can receive and the kinds of contingent actions they can take. These devices, however, are the most widely available and at the lowest prices, and good programs are available.

C. VICTOR BUNDERSON

Bibliography: Andreae, John H., *Thinking with the Teachable Machine* (1978); Dorsett, Loyd G., *Audio-Visual Teaching Machines* (1971); Hunter, Beverly, et al., *Learning Alternatives in U.S. Education* (1975); Jackson, Philip W., *The Teacher and the Machine* (1968).

Teague, Walter D. [teeg]

Walter Dorwin Teague, b. Decatur, Ind., Dec. 18, 1883, d. Dec. 5, 1960, was one of the earliest industrial designers who, along with Henry Dreyfuss and Raymond Loewy, helped establish INDUSTRIAL DESIGN as a separate discipline and a recognized profession. Teague studied at the Art Students League of New York from 1903 to 1907, then worked as an artist and designer and, in 1926, designed the Kodak Baby Brownie, a simple, functional, and highly successful camera that established Teague's reputation as an industrial designer. The design assignments that followed included automobiles, service stations, railway equipment, airplane interiors, household and heating appliances, business machines, machine tools, offices, showrooms, department stores, furniture, and magazines. Teague wrote *Design This Day—The Technique of Order in the Machine Age* (1940), *Land of Plenty, A Summary of Possibilities* (1947), and, with John Storok, *Flour for Man's Bread: A History of Milling* (1952).

teak

Teak is the common name for *Tectona grandis* of the family Verbenaceae. Native to India, Burma, and Thailand, the tree grows to a height of 46 m (150 ft) and has a straight, often buttressed trunk and a spreading crown. The large, drooping leaves, opposite or occasionally whorled on the four-sided branches, grow to 30 cm (1 ft) in length and 5–30 cm (2–12 in) in width. The foliage is covered with hairs beneath and generally resembles tobacco leaves, although it is harder and rougher. The white flowers are small and numerous, and the fruit is a drupe. Trees have gray bark, white sapwood, and a yellow to brown aromatic heartwood that retains its fragrance for years.

Since ancient times teak has been one of the world's most valuable timber trees. The wood is easily worked and well noted for its resistance to decay. Intact pieces more than 200 years old have been found in India. Teakwood is used for ships, wharves, and bridges as well as for fine furniture, venetian blinds, and veneer. Teak also refers specifically to the wood and its characteristic color, which ranges from olive to yellowish gray or moderate brown.

Rhodesian teak comes from *Baikiaea plurijuga* of the family Leguminosae. Native to Angola and North and South Rhodesia, its lumber, also valuable, is used especially for flooring.

NATALIE UHL

Bibliography: Hill, Albert F., *Economic Botany*, 2d ed. (1952); Bramwell, Martyn, and Palmer, Jeanette, eds., *International Book of Wood* (1976); Schery, Robert W., *Plants for Man*, 2d ed. (1972); Schuler, Stanley, ed., *Simon and Schuster's Guide to Trees* (1978).

Teamsters, Chauffeurs, Warehousemen, and Helpers of America, International Brotherhood of

The International Brotherhood of Teamsters, Chauffeurs, Warehousemen, and Helpers of America (1903) is a labor union that represents truck drivers and workers in a variety of industries. Team drivers were organized as an American Federation of Labor affiliate in 1899. Troubled from the start by corruption and alleged links to organized crime, the Teamsters nevertheless grew to become the largest union in the United States, with 1.7 million members by 1988. The investigations of the McClellan Committee in 1957 led to the conviction of Teamsters president Dave Beck and the expulsion of the Teamsters from the AFL-CIO. Beck was replaced by James R. HOFFA, who was imprisoned in 1967 for jury tampering and fraud. Other presidents were Frank FITZSIMMONS (1971–81), Roy Williams (1981–83), and Jackie Presser (1983–88). During their presidencies, Williams was convicted of bribery and Presser was under indictment on racketeering charges. William J. McCarthy became president in 1988, following Presser's death. In 1987 the Teamsters rejoined the AFL-CIO.

Bibliography: Brill, Steven, *The Teamsters* (1978); Dobbs, Farrell, *Teamster Bureaucracy* (1977); Friedman, Samuel, *Teamster Rank and File* (1982).

Teapot Dome

Teapot Dome, near Caspar, Wyo., was a federally owned oil reserve involved, with the reserve at Elk Hills, Calif., in a scandal associated with the administration of U.S. president Warren G. HARDING. Teapot Dome subsequently became a symbol of scandal in the 1920s.

Although they had been set aside (1915) to provide the navy with emergency fuel reserves, the oil fields—by order of Harding—were placed (1921) under jurisdiction of the Department of the Interior. In 1922, Secretary of the Interior Albert B. Fall arranged for the lease of the fields to private developers, without competitive bidding, in exchange for the construction of naval oil-storage depots. A public scandal resulted in 1924 when a congressional investigative committee heard testimony of suspicious dealings involving politicians. The private developers had made large profits as a result of the arrangements with Fall, who was convicted of receiving a bribe, fired, and sentenced to one year in prison. In 1927 the oil reserves reverted to U.S. government control through a Supreme Court decision.   K. AUSTIN KERR

Bibliography: Bates, J. Leonard, *Origins of Teapot Dome* (1963; repr. 1978); Noggle, Burl, *Teapot Dome: Oil and Politics in the 1920's* (1962); Werner, M. R., and Starr, John, *Teapot Dome* (1959).

tear gas

Chemical substances that produce severe irritation of the lachrymal (tear) glands are known as lachrymatory agents or tear gases. The term *gas* is misleading, because many irritant chemicals are disseminated in solid (tiny particles) or liquid form. One of the most common tear gases used today, chloroacetophenone (code named CN), was developed during World War I for one of the first large-scale chemical-warfare actions. The irritant produces tearing very quickly. If the concentration is high enough or if the time of exposure is prolonged, irritation of the mucous membranes of the nose and throat may also occur. High exposures in a confined space may produce some edema or fluid accumulation in the lungs, and in a few cases the chemical may have been the cause of death. A more recent "tearing" or irritant agent, which received extensive use by U.S. forces in Vietnam, is the chemical agent known as CS (2-chlorobenzylidenemalononitrile). In very mild exposures, CS almost instantly produces copious tearing and an irritation of the nose, mouth, and throat. At higher concentrations, the effects are almost unbearable. Recovery from CS exposure takes longer than that from CN.

Law enforcement agents worldwide often use tear gas in order to control mobs or riots. Tear gas is also useful in evic-

ting armed persons from barricaded positions or hiding places. MACE, a form of tear gas used primarily to subdue individuals in close-encounter situations, is sprayed from a hand-held can.   JAMES M. McCULLOUGH

Bibliography: Swearengen, Thomas F., *Tear Gas Munitions* (1966).

tears

Tears, which are secreted by the two lachrimal glands, bathe and cleanse the cornea of the EYE. They are salty and contain lysozyme, an enzyme that kills bacteria and therefore minimizes eye infections. Tears flow over the conjunctiva, the moist membrane that covers each eyeball, and are collected by lachrimal canals located at the inner angle of each eye. From the canals, tears pass by way of the nasal lachrimal ducts into the nasal cavities.   ROY HARTENSTEIN

Teasdale, Sara   [teez'-dayl]

Sara Teasdale, b. St. Louis, Mo., Aug. 8, 1884, d. Jan. 29, 1933, was one of the finest American lyric poets of her generation. Marked by great simplicity, clarity, and a recurring sense of loss, her love lyrics, as in *Love Songs* (1917), which won a special poetry award, show the influence of Christina Rossetti. She published several additional volumes, including *Flame and Shadow* (1920), and edited a poetry anthology for young people, *Rainbow Gold* (1922). The poetry of her later collections, *Dark of the Moon* (1926) and *Strange Victory* (1933), is increasingly subtle and haunted by suffering. She died a suicide.

Bibliography: Carpenter, Margaret H., *Sara Teasdale: A Biography* (1977); Drake, William, *Sara Teasdale: Woman and Poet* (1979).

teasel   [tee'-zul]

The common teasel, *D. fullonum, is an herb native to southern Eurasia and northern Africa. Its burrlike heads have often been used by weavers to comb the nap of wool textiles; its seeds are used for bird feed.*

Teasel refers to any of about 15 species of biennial or perennial plants of the genus *Dipsacus* in the family Dipsacaceae. They are native to the temperate regions of Europe, western Asia, and North Africa. The plants are spiny, with opposite leaves, and bear cone-shaped heads of small purple flowers encased in prickly bracts. A few species of teasel are cultivated as ornamentals, some of which make an attractive addition to dried flower arrangements. Root infusions of teasel plants have been used medicinally as ointments and for stomach relief.

The most commercially important teasel is the biennial species Fuller's teasel, *D. sativus,* whose flower head has curved bracts that have long been used to raise (to "tease") the napped surfaces on wool and other fabrics. The term *teasel* may also refer to any implement used for raising the nap on fabrics. The value of the teasel flower head as a comb is that its curved bracts will yield to any real obstruction and not tear the fabric as metallic combs might.   NATALIE UHL

Teatro Olimpico   [tay-ah'-troh oh-leem'-pee-koh]

The oldest surviving theater of the Renaissance, the Teatro Olimpico in Vicenza, Italy, was designed in 1580 by Andrea PALLADIO for the Olympic Academy and completed by Vincenzo Scamozzi in 1585. The theater introduced several innovations. The semielliptical seating area held about 3,000 people. A shallow orchestra and a narrow 25-m-long (82-ft) stage were backed by an elaborate facade modeled after the Roman *scaena frons* (see THEATER ARCHITECTURE AND STAGING). Scamozzi's five vanishing-perspective alleys built behind the three doors in the facade were a unique feature of the theater. The current ceiling and fresco date from the 19th century.   ARNOLD ARONSON

Bibliography: Heydenreich, Ludwig, and Lotz, Wolfgang, *Architecture in Italy 1400-1600* (1974).

Tebaldi, Renata   [tay-bahl'-dee]

Noted for her sumptuous voice as well as her affecting portrayals of such operatic heroines as Desdemona in Verdi's *Otello*, Renata Tebaldi, b. Feb. 1, 1922, was one of the most popular and lauded Italian sopranos of the 1950s and '60s. She studied with Carmen Melis and made her debut as Elena in Boito's *Mefistofele* in 1944. Encouraged by Arturo Toscanini, she became a principal singer at La Scala, Covent Garden, and, finally, the Metropolitan Opera, where she first appeared as Desdemona in 1955. There she revealed her dramatic skills in numerous leading roles: in Puccini's *La Bohème* and *Tosca*, in Verdi's *Aïda* and *La Traviata*, and in Ponchielli's *La Gioconda*.

Bibliography: Harris, Kenn, *Renata Tebaldi* (1974); Seroff, V. I., *Renata Tebaldi: The Woman and the Diva* (1961; repr. 1970).

technetium   [tek-nee'-shee-uhm]

The chemical element technetium is a radioactive metal. Its symbol is Tc; its atomic number, 43; and its atomic weight, 99 (stablest isotope). In 1937, C. Perrier and Emilio Segrè bombarded molybdenum with deuterons and produced the isotope ^{97}Tc. They named the new element technetium, from the Greek for "artificial," because technetium was the first element produced artificially. The chemical behavior of technetium resembles that of rhenium. In medicine, technetium is used in brain, thyroid, and other organ scanning.

technical education

Technical education prepares individuals for entry into occupations that lie between the skilled crafts and the engineering and scientific professions. These occupations usually involve the use of scientific apparatus and machinery, often in laboratories. Programs in technical education stress the understanding and application of the basic principles of science and mathematics. Because of this emphasis, technical education differs from vocational-education programs, which aim to develop manual and technical skills generally related to a single occupation.

Technical education in the United States was influenced by similar programs in Europe. The Technical High School in Germany and the Central School of Trades and Industries in France were especially important because they included mathematics and science in manual-trades training. Such programs generally corresponded to post-high-school grade levels. The Russian trade-analysis system was also a significant influence.

The Industrial Revolution in the United States in the 19th century was the single most important factor in signaling the need for technical education. Because apprentice-training programs could no longer meet the demand for a pool of technically trained talent, a number of mechanics schools or institutes were founded. Important among these were the General Society of Mechanics and Tradesmen in New York City (1820), the Rensselaer School (later Rensselaer Polytechnic Institute) in Troy, N.Y. (1824), and the Ohio Mechanics Institute in Cincinnati, Ohio (1828). Federal support for such programs came later with the passage of the MORRILL ACTS in 1862, which promoted public agricultural and mechanical colleges. The SMITH-HUGHES ACT of 1917 funded public vocational-technical programs at the secondary school level and adult education programs in public schools.

A wide and often confusing variation exists among the education and training requirements for the technical occupations. Although all such training takes place at the post-high-school level, the scope and length of the program differs with the training institution and the job requirements. This postsecondary training is offered in community colleges, vocational-technical schools, technical institutes, military service schools, and universities. The offerings range from training in health services, applied engineering, and science to industrial production, transportation, and communications. Further confusion exists among the titles attached to different levels of jobs. The words *technician* and *technologist* are frequently interchanged, and the length of the training programs differs according to the sponsoring institution. The following explanations may serve to clarify this situation.

A technologist, who usually has a 4-year baccalaureate degree from a technical institute or college, is a person qualified for a technical-supervisory or management position. Some jobs for technologists require only from 2 to 4 years of study. The technologist must have an appropriate background in science and mathematics, shop or laboratory courses, management and administration, general education, and frequently a specialized internship.

A technician is a person qualified for positions requiring applied technical skill and knowledge. Such work is narrower in scope than that of a technologist, and the qualifications generally include completion of a 2-year associate degree program from a community college or technical institute and often on-the-job training. This training stresses applications of science and mathematics to laboratory operations and processes.

A technical assistant is a person qualified to operate complex machines, instruments, and equipment. The tasks of such people as a dental assistant who cleans teeth and uses X-ray equipment are highly specialized. Such people become qualified through on-the-job training or in a community college or technical school through 3- to 12-month programs that combine class work with field experience.   JOHN R. LINDBECK

Bibliography: Barlow, Melvin L., *History of Industrial Education in the United States* (1967); Drake, Sandra L., ed., *Community, Junior, and Technical College Directory* (1977); Ferrin, Richard I., and Arbeiter, Solomon, *Bridging the Gap: A Study of Education-to-Work Linkages* (1975); Harper, William A., *Community, Junior, and Technical Colleges* (1977); Powers, Thomas F., ed., *Educating for Careers: Policy Issues in a Time of Change* (1977); Stratton, Julius A., *Science and the Educated Man* (1971).

technology

Technology is a major cultural determinant, no less important in shaping human lives than philosophy, religion, social organization, or political systems. In the broadest sense, these forces are also aspects of technology. The French sociologist Jacques Ellul has defined *la technique* as the totality of all rational methods in every field of human activity, so that, for example, education, law, sports, propaganda, and the social sciences are all technologies in that sense. At the other end of the scale, common parlance limits the term's meaning to specific industrial arts.

The terms *science* and *technology* are often confounded. The confusion arises because so much of contemporary technology is based on the natural sciences—such disciplines as physics, chemistry, biology, and other branches of knowledge that deal with the study, measurement, and understanding of natural phenomena. The achievements of the electronics, pharmaceutical, and plastics industries are based on a huge body of scientific investigation.

In simplest terms, the concern of science is "why," and of technology, "how." The relationship between the two is actually much more complex, however, and varies from industry to industry: some technologies are science intensive, whereas the manufacture of such items as cigarettes or furniture depends much less on science. In fact, much of modern technology developed without any scientific input whatever, and there are many examples of entire sciences arising from earlier technologies or developing in an effort to explain findings made by scientifically naive artisans. For instance, gunnery led to ballistics; the steam engine, to thermodynamics; powered flight, to aerodynamics; primitive metalworking, to metallurgy; and communications, to radio astronomy.

TECHNOLOGICAL INNOVATION

Industrial Revolutions. During certain periods in history innovations in technology have grown at such a rapid pace that they have produced what have become known as industrial revolutions. The term INDUSTRIAL REVOLUTION originally referred to the developments that transformed Great Britain, between 1750 and 1830, from a largely rural population making a living almost entirely from agriculture to a town-centered society engaged increasingly in factory manufacture. Other lands bordering on the North Atlantic underwent the same process soon thereafter, followed by other nations in Europe and elsewhere during the 19th century, and still others (such as Russia and Japan) in the first half of the 20th century. In some countries this transformation is only now taking place or still lies in the future.

The Industrial Revolution—based initially on waterpower and later on steam engines and other energy converters—had the effect of replacing human and animal muscle as the principal source of power with machines. This change put much vaster resources at society's disposal and substantially raised living standards in all societies capable of taking advantage of technological innovations. To be sure, these triumphs have also had their darker side, such as the misery that attended the initial displacements of industrialization and the pollution and despoliation of the environment.

A transformation of comparable significance began in the middle of the 20th century with the emergence of science-intensive industries, which were based on chemistry, modern physics, and especially mathematics. The electronic computer was the most prominent technological development of the time; another was the amazing proliferation of artificial materials, many of which were developed for specific purposes. This transformation has been called the Second Industrial Revolution, in which many of the functions performed by the senses and the human mind have begun to be replaced by machines, some of which greatly extend the range of possible achievements. It is sometimes also called the Scientific and Technical Revolution. As examples of this transformation, approaching aircraft are guided safely to a fogged-in airport by means of radar and radio, and the exact dimensions and quality of metal products are maintained during mass production by means of electronic sensors and controls. The near-instantaneous corrections needed to launch a space vehicle into a prescribed orbit require a computer to process the requisite information. In the 1970s new techniques were developed in the field of genetics to revolutionize medicine, the chemical industry, and agriculture.

Research and Development. In the 20th century technological innovation has been to a large degree institutionalized by organized research and development (R & D). This phenomenon paralleled, and to some extent antedated, the Second Industrial Revolution. Some large firms in science-intensive industries, such as communications, petroleum, and drugs, maintain R & D laboratories employing thousands of people. Also, independent organizations provide R & D, consulting, and other services under contract to specific clients, most often manufacturers who lack the staff and facilities to provide their own. R & D organizations operated or largely sponsored by national governments are another source of technological innovation, as are the engineering and science departments and research institutes of universities.

Under these circumstances private inventors are likely to play a progressively smaller role in bringing about innovation, although they are not likely to disappear altogether. That smaller role is especially evident in the stages of innovation that follow INVENTION—development, testing, design, production, marketing, and distribution—that now often require financial and managerial resources that are beyond the capabilities of the inventor-entrepreneur.

TECHNOLOGY AND SOCIETY

Examples abound of the ways technology cuts across vastly different political and economic systems. The sociologist Reinhard Bendix compared the American, British, and Soviet experience in his *Work and Authority in Industry* (1956) and found that the managerial concerns about the attitudes of workers and productivity were similar in all three countries. Even earlier, James Burnham in *The Managerial Revolution* (1941) put the case for a convergence toward similar patterns of industrial organization in democratic, fascist, and communist societies. More recently, such critics as Jacques Ellul have concluded even more sweepingly that technology has its own dynamic that not only reaches across political ideologies but also represents a monstrous force that must be contained with the utmost vigilance if it is not to enslave people. This negative view finds expression in various ways, from calls for a complete halt in further technological development to suggestions of milder forms of controlling or taming technology.

Technology Assessment. Some observers insist that the real dangers from technology, such as irreversible ecological damage and temporary unemployment, can be dealt with by self-imposed administrative restraints. This approach was institutionalized in 1973 when the Office of Technology Assessment was established to advise the U.S. Congress on the effects and impacts of new technologies.

Any major development is now attended by proponents and opponents with conflicting interests, such as business, labor, the administrative and technical elite, politicians, environmentalists, economists, and public advocates. The promise of technology assessment is that an impartial body can lay aside all vested interests and provide decision makers with rational advice as to which developments are truly in the public interest. This promise is still far from being fulfilled because the methods of technology assessment are relatively primitive at present. Its critics say that it may never rise above a sort of guesswork shored up by informed judgment; supporters predict its triumph, especially in fields in which conditions are highly complex and events proceed along paths that defy intuition.

Technology Transfer. Because the rate of technological development is uneven across the globe, technology is sometimes charged with contributing to the gap between rich and poor nations and thus increasing international tensions. The opposite view holds that only through technology can the less-developed countries improve their lot, provided the more advanced nations use technology to help the less-developed countries rather than to hold them in thrall. Supplying the products of technology is one way of providing help, especially if these products are appropriate to the recipients' needs. Giant tractors and crops requiring expensive fertilizers are of little use in a region in which intensive agriculture at a bare subsistence level prevails; hand tools, small motors, and other implements of intermediate technology are more welcome in such an environment.

Even more effective is transfer of the technology itself, by the provision of blueprints, models, designs, patents, and other know-how and by the establishment of workshops, factories, training programs, and agricultural and engineering colleges. Less obvious but equally important is the need for basic science curricula, professional organizations, and publications. These and other intellectual underpinnings of technology are taken for granted in developed countries but are in short supply in most less-developed countries. Technology transfer is supported by the governments of most developed nations, some of which may hope to gain not only a relaxation of tensions but an enlargement of their own economic, political, and cultural spheres of influence. Technology transfer is also the province of several technical and specialized agencies of the United Nations (such as the World Bank) and other international organizations.

Effects on the Individual. There can be no doubt that modern technology greatly affects the lives of individuals. The life of a moderately affluent city dweller in a developed country is vastly different from that of a moderately affluent villager in a less-developed country, and substantial differences often exist among citizens of the same country. These differences in the standards of living are to a considerable extent determined by technology. Even what at a first glance may seem to be nontechnical amenities—well-lit art galleries, nondrafty churches, safe schools, efficient distribution of food and clothing, humane prisons, accessible medical care, inexpensive books—all depend to a large degree on technology.   CHARLES SÜSSKIND

Bibliography: Ballard, Edward Goodwin, *Man and Technology* (1978); David, Paul A., *Technical Choice, Innovation and Economic Growth* (1975); Dunn, P. D., *Appropriate Technology: Technology with a Human Face* (1979); Ellul, Jacques, *The Technological Society* (1967); Ferkis, Victor C., *Technological Man* (1969); Hickman, Larry, and Al-Hibri, Azizah, *Technology and Human Affairs* (1980); Kasson, John F., *Civilizing the Machine* (1976); Morison, Elting E., *From Know-how to Nowhere* (1975); Mumford, Lewis, *The Myth of the Machine* (1967) and *Technics and Civilization* (1934; repr. 1963); Rosenberg, Nathan, *Perspectives in Technology* (1976); Skolnikoff, Eugene B., *Science, Technology and American Foreign Policy* (1967); Süsskind, Charles, *Understanding Technology* (1973).

technology, history of

The history of technology is the study of the changes through which economic, cultural, and military techniques have evolved and of the social, economic, and political consequences those changes have produced. To reach a full understanding of the history of technology, historians cannot confine their attention to instruments and techniques alone but must consider as well a large domain of events, some of them seemingly remote, that have had a bearing on the evolution of technology: the role of the technologist and engineer and their status and training; geography and climate; division of labor; the processes of invention and innovation; the diffusion of knowledge; the technical consequences of research; the relationship between technology and science; traditions of art; and the development of crafts.

The history of technology begins with the use of stone tools by the earliest humans—and perhaps even by their prehuman ancestors. The field of study may be divided into four major periods: the Paleolithic (Old Stone Age), beginning about 2.5 million years ago; the Neolithic (New Stone Age) transition, dating from about 9000 BC; agricultural civilization, which originated with the invention of the plow in the 4th millennium BC; and industrial civilization, which covers the past 250 years. These divisions are approximate, schematic, and sometimes extensively overlapping; even today, with agricultural and industrial civilizations existing side by side and each incorporating technology that is characteristic of the other, there also exist isolated groups of people who still employ Stone Age technology. Similarly, rudimentary forms of agriculture (or at least horticulture) may have been practiced occasionally during the Paleolithic, which was characterized by hunting and gathering.

The Paleolithic era and the Neolithic transition, which jointly constitute more than 99% of the time span of technological history, lie properly in the domain of the prehistorian—mainly the archaeologist, anthropologist, and paleontologist. Although this article is concerned primarily with the historical era (agricultural and industrial civilizations), a summary of Paleolithic and Neolithic technology will serve to highlight the origins of agriculture.

PALEOLITHIC AND NEOLITHIC PRELUDE

Paleolithic technology (see PALEOLITHIC PERIOD) was the creation of both modern humans (*Homo sapiens*) and at least one extinct species, *Homo erectus*. Hunting of animals and gathering of eggs, insects, and edible plants were the dominant economic activities. On the evidence of surviving hunting-gathering societies, it may be supposed that a dual economy existed in which men hunted and women gathered. By the end of the Paleolithic, humanity's technological repertoire included stone tools, the use of fire, spears and spear throwers, the bow and arrow, simple oil lamps, pigments, mortars and pestles, and bone sewing needles.

The Neolithic transition (see NEOLITHIC PERIOD) is characterized by the origins of food production through the development of animal and plant husbandry. There is indirect evidence that the sheep was domesticated in the Middle East about 9000 BC. Over the next three millennia wild cereal plants were domesticated, animal and plant husbandry were further developed, and small farming communities were formed (often in upland areas, where rainfall was adequate). Cultivation was accomplished with the use of the digging stick and the wood hoe. The Paleolithic division of labor persisted into the Neolithic Period, with men tending herds of animals and women managing garden plots. Late Neolithic stone tools were improved by polishing, and polished stone axes were used to prepare forest clearings for cultivation. Modern tests with Neolithic axes have demonstrated their remarkable effectiveness in the felling of trees.

Neolithic crafts included pottery, spinning and weaving, basketmaking, and house building. The discovery of Neolithic artifacts on islands in the Mediterranean also testified to the early use of boats.

AGRICULTURAL CIVILIZATION

The invention that marked the beginning of agricultural civilization was the ox-drawn plow. It originated in the Middle East in the 4th millennium BC. Although the circumstances of its invention are unknown, the early scratch plow (or ard)

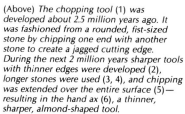

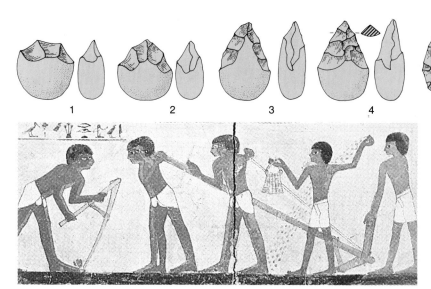

(Above) *The chopping tool* (1) *was developed about 2.5 million years ago. It was fashioned from a rounded, fist-sized stone by chipping one end with another stone to create a jagged cutting edge. During the next 2 million years sharper tools with thinner edges were developed* (2), *longer stones were used* (3, 4), *and chipping was extended over the entire surface* (5)— *resulting in the hand ax* (6), *a thinner, sharper, almond-shaped tool.*

(Left) *The primitive wooden scratch plow seen in this Egyptian tomb painting (c.1600 BC) was developed from the digging stick.*

Cuneiform writing, one of the oldest forms of written communication, was used in Mesopotamia as early as 3000 BC. A wooden stylus pressed characters into these clay tablets while they were still soft, and the tablets were then dried in the sunlight until hard.

was probably derived through modifications of the Neolithic adze and the hoe. Because traction was supplied by oxen, the provinces of animal husbandry and plant cultivation were merged, and the dual economy that had originated in the Paleolithic was now replaced by an economy of field cultivation. Combined with the techniques of fallowing, irrigation, and flood control that date from the same period, plow agriculture was successfully established in the rain-sparse river valleys of Mesopotamia, Egypt, and India, and the breakthrough to civilization was accomplished.

Plow agriculture was accompanied by an array of momentous developments. Writing evolved; the political state came into being (possibly through the conflicting pressures of expanding population and limited fertile land in the river valleys); chronic warfare set in; and copper and bronze metallurgy was devised.

Bronze Age. The earliest phase of agricultural civilization is commonly known as the BRONZE AGE. The use of copper and bronze (an alloy of copper and tin) gave rise to a variety of techniques and devices and to a complex of skilled artisans. Copper ores had to be mined and tin ores collected, often from distant sources, thereby encouraging commerce, cultural intercourse, and sometimes conquest; furnaces, crucibles, and fuels had to be provided for the smelting of the ores; and intricate molds, often made of several pieces, had to be prepared for the casting of the metal.

Copper and bronze hand weapons came into use, but by far the most important innovation in military technology during the Bronze Age was the horse-drawn two-wheeled chariot. Although cumbersome two- and four-wheeled carts had been invented earlier, the highly mobile war chariot carrying an archer armed with the short, compound bow revolutionized military tactics after 1700 BC.

Capable of fast strikes and quick retreats, the light two-wheeled chariot revolutionized early military technology. This Greek chariot from about 500 BC had two four-spoked wheels attached to a fixed axle. It was used both on the battlefield and for racing.

Building technology also developed rapidly during the Bronze Age and, in the form of pyramidal structures, reached monumental proportions. In Mesopotamia molded, kiln-dried bricks were the favored building material for large structures, whereas in Egypt the famous pyramids were commonly built of limestone blocks. After this limestone was quarried with wooden, stone, and copper tools, the blocks were transported to the building site by barges and sledges. Methods of construction and the achievement of structural stability, however (rather than the quarrying and transportation of materials), presented the most formidable problems that Bronze Age builders succeeded in solving.

The substantial technical and cultural progress of these early civilizations, the emergence of crafts whose practitioners were relieved of the need to participate in food production, the increase in population, and the rise of many urban societies centered in impressively wealthy cities were entirely based on the productivity, and hence on the food surpluses, of plow agriculture. At first, surpluses adequate to sustain civilization were possible only on irrigated land, so that the earliest civilizations were confined to alluvial river valleys. As the technology of plow agriculture improved, civilization spread to rain-fed lands away from the river valleys.

Iron Age. By the end of the 2d millennium BC iron metallurgy was developed, and a new technical era began. About 1000 BC an IRON AGE civilization arose in Greece that was based on rain-watered agriculture and used the implements of the new metallurgy. The production of wrought iron called for a technology fundamentally different from that of either copper or bronze. Higher furnace temperatures were required, and the iron emerged from the furnace as a red-hot, pasty ball that had to be worked by hammering, rather than as liquid metal that could be poured from crucibles into molds.

Bronze and iron found their widest use in the paraphernalia of war. Hoplites (from the Greek *hoplon,* a round shield)—ranks of drilled infantry armored with helmets, corselets, greaves, and shields and armed with iron-tipped spears—became the backbone of Greek military power. The geographical position of Greece in the Mediterranean encouraged the development of ocean-borne commerce, and the Greeks built and maintained a large fleet of merchant ships and men-of-war.

Greek building technology provided the technical basis for a notable architecture (see GREEK ARCHITECTURE). Although the arch had been invented long before, Greek builders, using stone as their material, confined themselves to the post-and-lintel (column-and-beam) structural mode. To enable stone beams to resist cracking at their lower surfaces (where they are stretched), they were necessarily of massive size, with short spans, and rested on many columns. On occasion the Greek builders embedded wrought-iron bars in grooves formed in the beams to keep the tension in the stone within an acceptable range.

The Greeks coined the term *architekton* to describe the practitioners of the fields encompassed in modern times by the disciplines of engineering and architecture—building, tunneling, mining, and hydraulic projects. Later, during the period of Greek imperialism (336–323 BC) under Alexander the Great, the *architekton* was engaged in the design and construction of the catapult, with which Alexander supplied his armies.

In general, Greek technology remained independent of the scientific tradition that Greek natural philosophers were creating. Between 250 BC and AD 100, however, a school of scientist-engineers flourished at Alexandria and produced treatises on mechanical and pneumatic devices that display an interest both in the philosophy of nature and in the application of empirical formulas to engineering design.

Roman and Medieval Innovations. The skill of Roman engineers is legendary. In the art of building they mastered the technique of the stone arch and its variations in the vault and the dome (see ARCH AND VAULT; ROMAN ART AND ARCHITECTURE). In contrast to the post-and-lintel method, buildings employing arches primarily produce compressive forces and thereby

For thousands of years human muscles were the only source of power for building construction. King Sennacherib of Assyria used slave laborers—the most common labor force for large-scale projects—to build (c.700 BC) his palace at Nineveh. More than 40 laborers were needed to pull this sledge with its 2-ton stone block (center), while another gang used a long lever at the rear of the sledge to reduce friction.

Classical Greek architecture was based on the post-and-lintel system of construction. The Temple of Poseidon (c.460 BC), Paestum, Italy, is an example of the Doric order, by which the Greeks first established the refined proportions later used in the Ionic and Corinthian orders.

improve the efficiency of stone, which is desperately weak under tension. Characteristically, the stone arch is composed of wedge-shaped blocks that must be supported during the construction process, generally by a temporary wooden scaffold, until the arch is complete. Once the arch is complete, the wedges are in equilibrium, provided that the horizontal thrust is resisted either externally by buttresses or internally by a tie-bar across the opening. The same principle was adapted to the construction of vaults and domes. The accomplishments of Roman engineers are best illustrated by their refinement of AQUEDUCT design, in which they combine elements of bridge building, road making, tunneling, pressure piping, and reservoir construction.

The flowering of agricultural civilization in Europe north of Rome during the Middle Ages was foreshadowed by Roman technical innovations. Roman engineers were familiar with the principle of the WATERWHEEL and its associated gearing as early as the 1st century BC, and they occasionally employed it in the construction of MILLS. Even more important was the development of a heavy PLOW capable of turning the clay soils of northern Europe. The ancient light plow drawn by a pair of oxen was effective in the dry climates of the Middle East and the Mediterranean world, where the soils were light and friable. In northern Italy and in transalpine Europe the light plow permitted tillage only on well-drained upland soils, whereas the wet, cohesive soils of the vast lowlands and the north European plain could not be cultivated. The heavy plow with its vertical coulter, horizontal plowshare, and moldboard to turn the soil, mounted on wheels and drawn by teams of four, six, or eight animals yoked in pairs, made pos-

The Pont du Gard, a Roman aqueduct near Remoulins, France, is an impressive example of Roman engineering genius. Part of a 41-km (25.5-mi) water-supply system, it has three tiers of arches that support a water channel running 49 m (160 ft) above the Gard River valley.

The vertical water mill, which uses a waterwheel that rotates in a vertical plane to harness the energy of flowing water, was designed by Roman engineers as early as the 1st century BC. Here the stream turns the waterwheel, which drives gears that convert the energy into a rotary motion used to grind corn.

The development of heavy plows equipped with moldboards made it possible for farmers to cultivate the clay soils of northern Europe. The moldboard—a curved plate that lifts and turns the soil—helped to improve drainage, aerate the soil, and uproot and bury weeds.

The introduction of the flying buttress by 12th-century builders made possible the construction of the great medieval cathedrals. As seen in this cross section of a Gothic cathedral, the flying buttress (A) is a masonry arch or half-arch that supports the roof vault by displacing the thrust of the ceiling from the upper portion of the wall onto exterior supports. This innovation enabled builders to construct thin walls of great height, complete with vast windows of stained glass.

sible the civilization of northern Europe. During Roman times a coulter was sometimes used, and the light plow was occasionally mounted on wheels; development was slow, however, and it was only in the 9th and 10th centuries that the fully developed heavy plow came widely into use and began to transform Europe. Extensive tracts of fertile land were opened to cultivation. The depth of the cut made by the heavy plow and the overturning of the sod increased fertility, and elimination of the need for cross-plowing increased productivity.

As the heavy plow began to transform European agriculture, property relations and social patterns also began to change. The square tracts characteristic of light-plow cultivation (because the fields were cross-plowed) gave way to elongated tracts (the "long acre"), on which the heavy plow would not have to be turned around as often. Peasants found it necessary to pool their resources in order to form the teams of oxen required to pull a heavy plow. The heavy plow and communal tillage became the basis of the manorial system, which provided medieval Europe with food surpluses, an increasing number of skilled artisans removed from the web of food production, and a growing population. About the same time, the introduction of the HORSESHOE and the horse collar permitted the substitution of the horse, with its greater speed and endurance, for the ox, completing the agricultural revolution that the heavy plow had initiated.

The Middle Ages in Europe were in general prodigiously innovative. In the 8th century iron became widely available and once again was adapted to military needs. Heavy cavalry, its lance-bearing riders armored with wrought iron and stabilized by SADDLE and STIRRUPS, became the shock troops of medieval Europe. In the 12th century water mills, which had not been widely used until then, and windmills, the concept of which was only then reaching Europe from the East, brought a revolution in the production of power (see WINDMILLS AND WIND POWER). At first both devices were used mainly in corn mills, but the windmill soon acquired its characteristic role as a water-pumping engine, and the waterwheel was adapted to a variety of enterprises including sawmills, hammer mills, and stamping mills. The application of waterpower to the bellows of the blast furnace made possible for the first time the production of large quantities of cast iron.

The technical and cultural progress of the late Middle Ages is most vividly exemplified by GOTHIC ARCHITECTURE. The urbanization of Europe was accompanied by waves of CATHEDRAL building, and in the 12th century builders introduced a series of innovations that enabled them to achieve structural lightness while carrying their vaults to extreme heights and admitting substantially more light through large expanses of

(Below) By the 15th century the carrack, a full-rigged, three- or four-masted sailing ship, had appeared. Capable of long ocean voyages, such ships rapidly opened the world to commercial exploration. Their maneuverability transformed the nature of sea warfare.

glass windows. The flying BUTTRESS, calculated to resist the thrust of the central vaults, became a hallmark of these lofty structures, which, within a century, achieved vault heights of 49 m (160 ft). The master masons who designed these remarkable buildings proceeded without the insights of science, basing their specifications only on experience, rules of thumb, intuition, and daring.

Medieval Europe's inventive impulse contained the seeds of both the reformation of medieval society and the achievement of European influence throughout the world. During the 14th century FIREARMS appeared in Europe. Early guns were made either of wrought-iron strips hooped together to form the barrel or of cast brass or bronze. Ironically, the bell-founders, who had refined their technique in the casting of church BELLS, now turned to the casting of CANNONS. The craft of the gunsmith came into being, and national arsenals were established. Before the middle of the 16th century, English founders had perfected the casting of iron, instead of bronze, guns, thereby sharply reducing the cost of ordnance.

The medieval castle was an easy target for the new WEAPONS, and, along with large catapults, the castle passed from the scene. New FORTIFICATIONS were now required—polygonal and star-shaped—to increase the length of ramparts on which guns could be mounted and to present unfavorable shot-deflection angles to attacking gunners. Hand guns were also rapidly developed, and by the end of the 16th century they had swept the long-bow from the field. The MUSKET in particular made infantry once again the most decisive force on the battlefield.

Parallel with these developments in land warfare, the sailing SHIP was being transformed into a formidable instrument of naval power, world exploration, and commerce. In the 15th century the carrack appeared—full-rigged, more manageable than earlier sailing ships, and capable of ocean voyaging. Armed with hundreds of iron and brass guns, carracks of more than 1,000 tons served as both merchantmen and men-of-war. In the second half of the 16th century the galleon was developed primarily as a fighting ship. The GALLEON showed most of its guns through ports cut in the hull, and its handling was improved over that of earlier ships by increasing the length-to-breadth ratio of the hull and by reducing the size of the forecastle and the afterdeck.

The Renaissance. From the 15th through the 17th century, the period designated by cultural historians as the Renaissance, the new warfare employing guns and armed ships changed Europe from a provincial region to a center of world power. The New World was explored and conquered, and commerce with the East—carried on by armed merchantmen—grew increasingly profitable. European cultural life flourished, abetted by the appearance of the printed book (see PRINTING) during the 15th century. Additionally, in turn, the widening interest

in technology and industry was reflected in the publication of richly illustrated technical treatises.

The new technology produced new problems, partly as a result of the increased use of iron in the making of cast-iron ordnance. Because the blast furnace was charged with ore and fuel in intimate contact, attempts to use coal as the fuel invariably failed because the impurities that it contained were absorbed by the iron. It was thus necessary to charge the blast furnace with charcoal (derived from wood) as the fuel, and by the end of the 16th century the iron industry was consuming timber at a prodigious rate. Combined with the demands of SHIPBUILDING (the largest ships of the time each required several thousand trees in their construction), the iron industry was rapidly deforesting Europe. The "timber famine" was most severely evident in the British Isles, where the making of both guns and ships was booming.

Shortly afterward a second problem arose, this one in the mining industry. As mines were sunk to ever greater depths in search of minerals, the shafts filled with groundwater and had to be constantly pumped. A variety of devices were employed, including the suction pump, which was powered by the draft of animals at the pit-head. By the end of the 17th century, however, it became evident that more-powerful engines would be needed.

INDUSTRIAL CIVILIZATION: EIGHTEENTH CENTURY
Both the problem of high consumption of timber in the smelting of iron ore and the problem of flooding in deep mines received technical solutions early in the 18th century. These solutions, both of which were reached in Great Britain, where the problems were most sharply felt, set the stage for the Industrial Revolution.

In 1709 the ironmaster Abraham DARBY I succeeded in producing sound cast iron in a blast furnace charged with iron ore and coal (and soon afterward with coke, derived from coal). In 1712 another Englishman engaged in the iron trade, Thomas NEWCOMEN, invented the STEAM ENGINE for the purpose of driving the pumps used in clearing groundwater from mine shafts. By the end of the 18th century the British iron industry had largely replaced charcoal with coke. Within a short time, too, Newcomen engines were serving most of the larger collieries in Great Britain, making possible the opening of new mines that otherwise would have been unworkable.

These two innovations, the steam engine and the making of iron with coal, not only broke critical bottlenecks that were constraining economic progress, but also produced an interlocked complex of industrial development: the steam engine promoted coal production by clearing flooded mine shafts; coal (in the form of coke) revived the iron industry, which had begun to slump as a result of the timber famine; iron was used in the further production of steam engines, and this in turn demanded improved metalworking techniques.

In the 1760s, James WATT increased the efficiency of the Newcomen engine by providing it with a separate condenser, thereby obviating the need alternately to heat and cool the cylinder and piston. Watt followed this important invention with a remarkable series of additional contributions: "sun-and-planet" gearing to translate the reciprocating motion of the steam engine into rotary motion for operating mills; the double-acting steam engine and the "parallel motion" used to connect its rigid piston rods to the overhead beam without causing the rods to wobble; the principle of steam cutoff, whereby Watt recognized that because of its expansive power steam need not be admitted into the cylinder during the entire stroke; and an indicator for determining the pressure in the cylinder during the cycle. John WILKINSON designed a boring machine that radically improved the accuracy with which steam-engine cylinders could be bored; the steam engine was combined with cast-iron blowing cylinders to produce a more powerful draft in the blast furnace than the older bellows could provide; and by the beginning of the 19th century the compact, high-pressure steam engine (in contrast with the Newcomen and Watt engines, which relied on atmospheric pressure) was invented, opening the way to the construction of steamboats and steam locomotives.

This 1507 woodcut depicts two workers manipulating a printing press while a third (right) sets words into type. The Gutenberg press, developed during the 15th century, made possible the widespread, rapid diffusion of culture and knowledge.

Clifton Suspension Bridge at Bristol, England, completed in 1861 after a long delay, exemplified the daring modes of construction that 19th-century technology made possible. This print, dating from before 1861, shows the bridge towers as they had been originally planned.

Abraham Darby's Coalbrookdale ironworks in Shropshire, England, used another major technological development leading to the Industrial Revolution: in 1709, Darby learned how to smelt iron with coke instead of with increasingly scarce wood-derived charcoal.

This web of technical innovation is characteristic of the Industrial Revolution. It may be seen as well in the TEXTILE INDUSTRIES, where SPINNING and WEAVING machinery were alternately improved in a pattern of reciprocating challenge and response. The application of steam power further stimulated the concentration of industry in mills and factories and, where it replaced the waterwheel, steam power released industry from its need to be near rural waterpower sites. Cities became the hubs of industrial growth and the centers to which waves of agrarian population migrated as industrial civilization took hold.

Agriculture, too, was changing (see AGRICULTURE, HISTORY OF), and some of the changes furthered the exodus of farmers from the land. The tradition of communal pastures increasingly gave way to enclosed fields, which promoted agriculture by permitting continuous cropping and by improving stock-raising: more fodder could be produced, and the promiscuous breeding of livestock could be prevented. Moreover, during the century following 1750, industry directly affected agriculture by manufacturing new implements and new machines. Many wooden and wrought-iron tools fashioned by local artisans were replaced by cast-iron tools produced in

James Watt's reciprocating steam engine, developed during the late 18th century, was a major stimulus to the Industrial Revolution. The motion of the steam-driven rocking beam (top) was converted into the rotary motion of the flywheel (right) for driving factory engines.

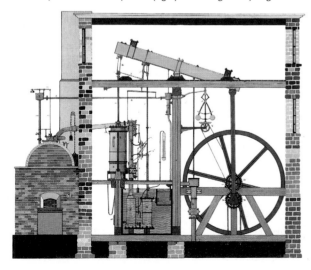

factories. Mechanical devices, some even steam-powered, were introduced for reaping, threshing, and plowing.

Iron also changed the landscape as the introduction of structural iron altered the mode of building. Stone had been a hallmark of monumental building throughout the time of agricultural civilization. Public buildings were generally made of stone, and stone-arch bridges dotted the landscape. In the last quarter of the 18th century, however, British ironmasters found a new use for cast iron (which, like stone, is strong in compression and weak in tension) when they succeeded in casting the components of the arch bridge. Early in the 19th century the introduction of structural WROUGHT IRON made possible the large suspension bridge, and by 1850 the wrought-iron tubular bridge for carrying railroads made its appearance.

If the engineer was instrumental in making the Industrial Revolution, it can equally be said that the Industrial Revolution gave rise to the ENGINEERING profession as it is recognized today. Where previously engineers had risen through the ranks of craftsmen, in the 18th century it was becoming apparent that the act of design could be codified in the form of technical training, and the military services began to seek such training for their officer corps. In the 1740s the British government established a military academy at Woolwich at which cadets were instructed in the application of elementary mathematics and statics to gunnery and the design of fortifications.

Later in the century John SMEATON coined the term "civil engineer" to distinguish civilian engineers from the increasing number of military engineers being graduated from Woolwich. A short-lived fraternity that called itself the Society of Civil Engineers (the "Smeatonians") formed around Smeaton; the first true professional organization in the field of engineering, however, was the Institution of Civil Engineers, founded in London in 1818.

Technical studies penetrated the established universities slowly, and it was in new institutions—such as the École Polytechnique in Paris and the University of London—that engineering first took root in university education.

HAROLD DORN

INDUSTRIAL CIVILIZATION: NINETEENTH CENTURY
Power. The basic source of converting energy into power during the 19th century was James Watt's double-acting STEAM ENGINE. High-pressure steam for steam-run, or "horseless," carriages was developed by Richard TREVITHICK in England (1802) and Oliver EVANS in the United States (1805). Through most of the 19th century waterpower was the principal competitor of steam, and its use was markedly stimulated by the water turbine, developed (1827) in France by Benoît Fourneyron. By the end of the century the steam TURBINE was introduced by Carl Gustav de Laval in Sweden (1882) and Sir Charles Algernon PARSONS in Great Britain (1884), but its application was delayed until the 20th century.

Experiments with the INTERNAL-COMBUSTION ENGINE began

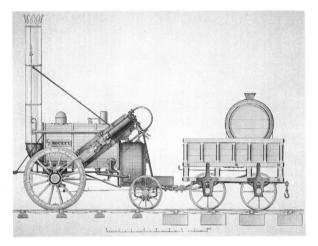

(Above) *The American inventor John Fitch tried to apply steam to water travel; his first model, seen here, was demonstrated at Philadelphia in 1787. It met with disappointment, and the first successful steamboat was not launched until 1807, by Robert Fulton.*

(Left) *The modern era of rapid land transportation was initiated by such steam locomotives as the English engineer George Stephenson's* Rocket *(1829). It had a tubular boiler, and wheels driven directly by the pistons. Rail networks spread quickly across Europe and America.*

early in the century but without success until Jean Joseph Étienne LENOIR built an operational if inefficient two-cycle engine (1860) and the first AUTOMOBILE with this type of engine in 1862. The critical breakthrough in designing an efficient internal-combustion engine came in 1876, when Nikolaus August OTTO marketed the "Silent Otto" gas engine, having four cycles: intake, compression, stroke, and exhaust. In the 1880s the engine was adopted by Karl BENZ and Gottlieb DAIMLER to power motor vehicles. Rudolf DIESEL's engine, in which combustion is produced by high pressure in the cylinder, was exhibited in 1897.

Electric power became possible with the nearly simultaneous discovery (1831) of electromagnetic induction by Michael Faraday (England) and Joseph Henry (United States), but its application required the development of a practical dynamo and electric motor. The dynamo evolved in a series of steps, beginning with the first one built (1855 patent), by Søren Hjorth of Denmark. Simultaneously, experiments in electric lighting (see LIGHTING DEVICES) culminated with Thomas A. EDISON's invention of the incandescent lamp in 1879. Edison opened (1882) the first direct-current central generating station, on Pearl Street in New York City. Frank J. SPRAGUE produced a successful direct-current electric motor in 1884 and applied it in 1887 to a street-trolley railway in Richmond, Va. Immediately afterward Nikola TESLA, a Hungarian immigrant to the United States, developed (1888) the first successful alternating-current induction motor.

Industry. The INDUSTRIAL REVOLUTION, which began in Great Britain in the 18th century, spread to the rest of western Europe and North America during the 19th century. The pattern of diffusion was quite uniform, beginning with textiles, coal, and iron. In textiles such improvements as the Jacquard LOOM (France, 1801) were developed, which allowed fabrics with woven patterns to be produced cheaply. The SEWING MACHINE was invented (1846) in the United States by Elias HOWE and mass-marketed (1851) by Isaac Merritt SINGER. Iron was the basic metal of industry until after the discovery by Henry BESSEMER (British patent, 1856) and William Kelly (U.S. patent, 1847) of a process for making large amounts of steel cheaply (see IRON AND STEEL INDUSTRY). The superior Siemens-Martin openhearth process for making high-quality steel was first demonstrated in France in 1863.

Once steel was more readily available, it became an important material for construction (see BUILDING CONSTRUCTION), notably in the American SKYSCRAPER and in bridges (see BRIDGE, engineering). It made possible heavier railroad equipment and replaced iron in shipbuilding—iron ships themselves were an innovation of the mid-19th century. Steel also influenced warfare by permitting high-powered, long-range weapons and more-efficient armor to be designed.

An equally important development was increased mechanization. In 1807, Robert FULTON designed the first practical steamboat, the CLERMONT, using James Watt's steam engine. STEAMBOATS were restricted at first to inland coastal waters—

(Above) *Thomas Edison's commercial power station for incandescent lighting opened in New York City on Sept. 4, 1882, shortly after he directed the opening of the world's first such station in London. The advent of electric lighting in the home had a great impact on everyday life.*

(Left) *Henry Ford's assembly-line process—shown at the Ford Motor Co. plant at Highland Park, Mich.—further transformed society by putting the public on wheels and was adopted for the mass production of many other goods. The auto, however, also created pollution and energy problems.*

until more fuel-efficient engines were designed in order to make ocean voyages practical. The steam railway is considered to have begun (1825) in England with the Stockton and Darlington Railway, but the first convincing demonstration of the steam LOCOMOTIVE was George Stephenson's ROCKET on the Liverpool and Manchester Railway in 1829 (see RAILROAD). Rail transportation spread rapidly, competing with the elaborate CANAL systems, built during the same time, as an economical method of inland transportation. The mechanization of agriculture began with Cyrus McCORMICK's REAPER (1831) in the United States.

New industries also appeared. The CHEMICAL INDUSTRY was revolutionized by the SOLVAY PROCESS for making alkalis (Belgium, 1872) and the development of the first plastic celluloid (United States, 1861) and of coal-tar dyes (England, 1856). Charles GOODYEAR made RUBBER (United States, 1839) usable, and ALUMINUM came into industrial use with the Hall-Heroult electrolytic process (United States–France, 1886).

The PETROLEUM INDUSTRY was born in 1859, when Edwin L. DRAKE sank an oil well in Titusville, Pa. The industry's major product during the 19th century was kerosene for illumination. The TELEGRAPH, perfected (United States, 1837) by Samuel F. B. MORSE and his assistant Alfred Vail, and the TELEPHONE, invented (United States, 1876) by Alexander Graham BELL, fostered communications industries based on electricity.

INDUSTRIAL CIVILIZATION: TWENTIETH CENTURY

Before 1945. The technological and industrial expansion of the 19th century continued unabated during the 20th century. Geographically, industrialization spread into eastern Europe, specifically Russia, and into Japan. Motor-vehicle manufacturing grew to an enormous scale (see AUTOMOTIVE INDUSTRY), especially after Henry FORD's adoption (1913) of MASS PRODUCTION by the moving ASSEMBLY LINE. Mass production and the proliferating use of automobiles created a demand for gasoline that stimulated worldwide exploration for oil as well as research in oil-refining techniques. In addition, oil to a great degree replaced coal as a fuel. Another effect of the automobile was extensive highway construction (see ROADS AND HIGHWAYS).

AVIATION is a 20th-century phenomenon, beginning with the invention (1903) of the airplane by the Wright brothers (see WRIGHT, ORVILLE AND WILBUR). Constant improvements in airframe design and engines made military aviation (see AIRCRAFT, MILITARY) a dominant feature of warfare by 1945, and commercial aviation had AIRCRAFT capable of transatlantic travel by the same year. Lighter-than-air craft (see AIRSHIP) were developed by the German Ferdinand, Graf von ZEPPELIN, and had potential for both military and commercial use, but a series of disasters—notably the burning (1937) of the HINDENBURG—destroyed confidence in them.

Communications was transformed by Guglielmo MARCONI's invention of RADIO in 1896 and by the subsequent discovery of the vacuum tube. Radio quickly became indispensable for maritime and military communication and it also generated an extensive entertainment industry during the 1920s. The

The rapid development of computers in the mid-20th century has revolutionized technology to a degree unsurpassed by previous advances. In this production line for automobiles, robots programmed by computers have replaced a human labor force.

moving-picture industry also developed at that time (see FILM, HISTORY OF). Experiments with TELEVISION achieved success in the 1930s, but commercial application was delayed until after World War II.

In the chemical industry further developments occurred in PLASTICS and SYNTHETIC FIBERS. NYLON was discovered by Wallace H. Carothers at Du Pont in 1927 and was manufactured by 1939.

In agricultural technology, farm mechanization progressed with the adoption both of steam power and then of the internal-combustion engine for farm machinery. Research in genetics and soil chemistry led to the development of hybrid corn and other disease-resistant crops. Other innovations included the introduction of the Rust cotton picker in 1939 and chemical FERTILIZERS and PESTICIDES.

Technological advance influenced and was influenced by the wars of the 20th century. During World War I there occurred the first general use of long-range ARTILLERY, MACHINE GUNS, POISON GAS, SUBMARINES, TORPEDOES, tanks (see ARMORED VECHICLE), aircraft, and radio. World War II introduced AIRCRAFT CARRIERS, RADAR, SONAR, ballistic missiles, and, above all, the ATOMIC BOMB. The jet engine (see JET PROPULSION) had been experimented with before World War II by Sir Frank Whittle (Great Britain, 1930) and Hans von Ohain (Germany, 1935); the Germans had a few jet fighters in operation toward the end of the war.

Since 1945. In the years since World War II, technological advance accelerated. NUCLEAR ENERGY has been used successfully in large warships. More important, nuclear power permits

(Right) *From the first powered flight of 12 seconds by the Wright brothers at Kitty Hawk, N.C., on Dec. 17, 1903, to the current exploration of space by piloted and automated vehicles, the 20th century has seen an explosive development of new technologies in unforeseen directions.*

submarines to stay submerged for long periods. Commercially, nuclear energy is being used in several countries to generate electric power, although it also presents problems of reactor accidents and radioactive waste disposal.

Not only the ELECTRONICS INDUSTRY but almost every field of technology was revolutionized by the invention (1947) of the TRANSISTOR by John BARDEEN, Walter BRATTAIN, and William SHOCKLEY. Although the first electronic COMPUTER, named ENIAC, had already been placed in operation in 1946, for example, the transistor made possible far more sophisticated computer circuitry in increasingly small spaces—especially with the development of INTEGRATED CIRCUITS in the 1950s. Electronic miniaturization has made practical the computerization of such ordinary devices as automobiles, kitchen appliances, and toys as well as the automation of large industrial processes, and powerful MINICOMPUTERS and MICROCOMPUTERS have become available at affordable costs to small businesses and to individuals.

The inventions of the MASER (1954) and LASER (1960) have also led to revolutionary advancements in technology. Lasers, in particular, have found wide applications in information storage, audiovisual devices, communications, and surgery as well as in physics and FUSION ENERGY research.

In medicine, ANTIBIOTICS were first used extensively during World War II, and many new families of DRUGS as well as new drug-delivery techniques have been developed since then. Advanced RADIOLOGY techniques such as NUCLEAR MAGNETIC RESONANCE IMAGING and PETT are now in use, and a range of organ-transplant operations has become almost routine (see TRANSPLANTATION, ORGAN). In 1982 the first artificial heart was placed in a human being (see HEART, ARTIFICIAL). By the 1980s, GENETIC ENGINEERING techniques had become basic to biomedical research and were in commercial use.

The field of SPACE EXPLORATION advanced spectacularly in the modern era. Beginning with rocket and missile experiments in World War II (see ROCKETS AND MISSILES), it opened up with the launching (1957) of the first artificial Earth satellite, the Soviet Union's *Sputnik 1* (see SPUTNIK). After extensive preparation the United States achieved a manned Moon landing in 1969 (see APOLLO PROGRAM); in the 1980s, manned space efforts focused on the Soviet SALYUT and Mir programs and the U.S. SPACE SHUTTLE but also included a number of long-range SPACE STATION plans. Space probes have observed at close range the planets Mercury, Venus, Mars, Jupiter, Saturn, and Uranus, and a small fleet of automated craft met Halley's comet during its most recent visit in 1986. Finally, a wide range of Earth satellites are routinely being launched to provide a wealth of services and data (see SATELLITE, ARTIFICIAL).

Technological advancements are now rapid and widely applied, and they can cause immediate and profound effects in such areas as global economics, national health, and national security. For these reasons the guarding of technologies and technological secrets has become an important concern of nations. The guarding of technological secrets is also a major concern of large, technology-dependent corporations, whose economic survival can be affected by the disclosure to competitors of even a single strategic technological secret.

JOHN B. RAE

Bibliography: Black, G. W., Jr., *American Science and Technology: A Bicentennial Bibliography* (1979); Bugliarello, George, and Doner, D. B., eds., *History and Philosophy of Technology* (1979); Ferguson, E. S., *Bibliography of the History of Technology* (1968); Forbes, R. J., *Studies in Ancient Technology*, 9 vols., 2d ed. (1964–72); Hall, A. R., and Smith, Norman, *History of Technology*, 8th ed. (1983); Hindle, Brooke, *Technology in Early America* (1968) and *America's Wooden Age* (1985); Hodges, Henry, *Technology in the Ancient World* (1970); Kranzberg, Melvin, and Pursell, C. W., Jr., eds., *Technology in Western Civilization*, 2 vols. (1967); Needham, Joseph, *Science and Civilisation in China*, 6 vols. (1954–); Pursell, C. W., Jr., ed., *Technology in America* (1981); Singer, Charles, et al., eds., *A History of Technology*, 5 vols. (1954–58); White, Lynn, *Medieval Technology and Social Change* (1962); Williams, T. I., *A Short History of Twentieth Century Technology*, 1900–1950 (1982); Yarwood, Doreen, *Five Hundred Years of Technology in the Home* (1983).

See also: separate entries on the industries and technologies discussed.

tectonism: see DIASTROPHISM.

Tecumseh [tuh-kuhm'-suh]

Tecumseh, a Shawnee chief, united midwestern Indian tribes under the common goal of resisting encroachment on Indian lands. After his supporters were routed in 1811 by Gen. William Henry Harrison at the Battle of Tippecanoe, Tecumseh joined forces with the British. Two years later the Indian leader was slain in Upper Canada at the Battle of the Thames. (Field Museum of Natural History, Chicago.)

Tecumseh, b. 1768, d. Oct. 5, 1813, was a SHAWNEE warrior chief who with his brother, the SHAWNEE PROPHET, attempted to stop the advance of white settlement in the Old Northwest. Tecumseh believed that Indians must return to a state of purity; that they must forget intertribal rivalries and confederate; and that individual tribes must not sell land that all Indians held in common. In 1809 tribes in the Indiana Territory ceded much of their land to the United States. Tecumseh protested to Gov. William Henry HARRISON, but in vain. In the fall of 1811 he determined to carry his message to the CHICKASAW, CHOCTAW, and CREEK. He went south, leaving his brother in charge at Prophet's Town, near Tippecanoe Creek, a utopian village where the Indians were to practice Tecumseh's principles; before going, Tecumseh warned his brother not to attack Harrison's nearby forces. The Prophet ignored the warning and attacked. The Battle of Tippecanoe (see TIPPECANOE, BATTLE OF) was not decisive, but Prophet's Town was destroyed and Indian resistance broken. After Tecumseh's return, he joined the British against the Americans in the WAR OF 1812. As a brigadier general, Tecumseh led 2,000 warriors. He fought at Frenchtown, Raisin River, Fort Meigs, and Fort Stephenson. His last battle was the Battle of the Thames at Chatham, Ontario, where, clothed in Indian deerskin garments, he was killed leading his warriors.

DANIEL JACOBSON

Bibliography: Drake, Benjamin, *Life of Tecumseh and of His Brother* (1841; repr. 1969); Edmunds, R. D., *Tecumseh and the Quest for Indian Leadership* (1984); Icenhower, Joseph B., *Tecumseh and the Indian Confederation* (1975); Sugden, John, *Tecumseh's Last Stand* (1985).

Tedder, Arthur William Tedder, 1st Baron
[ted'-ur]

Arthur William Tedder, b. July 11, 1890, d. June 3, 1967, was a British air marshal during World War II. As British air commander in the Middle East (1941–43), he played a key role in the North African campaigns and the Allied landings in Italy. Deputy Allied commander (1943–45) under Dwight D. Eisenhower, he gave air support for the invasion of Normandy and the last Allied advances. He was made 1st Baron Tedder of Glenguin in 1946.

teenagers: see ADOLESCENCE; YOUNG PEOPLE.

teeth

Teeth are numerous, hard tissue structures in the mouths of animals—vertebrate and invertebrate—used to tear, crush, and grind food. Among other purposes, they are used for defense (biting). The shape of teeth, their structure, their number, and the means of their attachment to the jaws vary con-

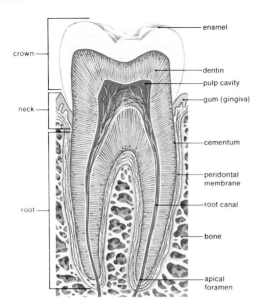

A human tooth consists of three regions: an exposed portion, the crown; a root, which embeds in the jawbone; and a slightly constricted neck at the gum level. The three layers of a tooth are the dentin, which makes up most of the tooth; a hard enamel, which covers the dentin of the crown; and the pulp, composed of connective tissue rich in nerves and blood vessels. These vessels and nerves enter and leave the tooth through the apical foramen. The periodontal membrane lines the tooth socket and secretes the bony cementum that holds the tooth in place.

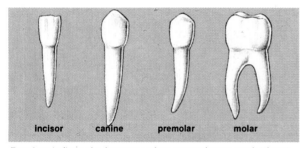

Drawings indicate the four types of permanent human teeth (above) and their arrangement in the jaws (below; broken lines represent roots). Chisel-shaped incisors have sharp edges for cutting. The more pointed canine teeth, or cuspids, are used for tearing food. Premolars, or bicuspids, and molars possess broad crowns with cusps, or elevations, for grinding. Normally, molars each have two or three roots, first upper premolars have two, and the other teeth have one.

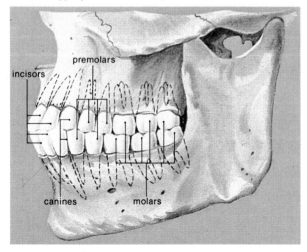

siderably. All true teeth typically have three layers.

Human Teeth. In humans the teeth are composed of an inner layer of dentin that, above the gum line, is covered by a layer of enamel. Called the crown, this part of the tooth is extremely hard. The root portion of the tooth is covered with a bonelike substance called cementum. The root is embedded in the jawbone and lies in a socket, where the cementum is attached to the adjacent bone by a periodontal membrane, consisting of fine connective tissue fibers. The tooth is also attached to the gum tissue (gingiva); at this connection there is a slight depression called the gingival crevice. The first of the two sets of human teeth, called the primary dentition, emerges in steps between the ages of 6 months and 2 years. Between the ages of 6 and 13 years a second (and permanent) set of teeth sequentially replaces the first. Between the ages of 18 and 21 years, 4 molars called wisdom teeth emerge.

The 20 primary teeth—4 central incisors, 4 lateral incisors, 4 canines (cuspids), and 8 molars—begin to develop prior to birth. They are eventually replaced—beginning around the age of 6—by 32 permanent teeth: 4 central incisors, 4 lateral incisors, 4 cuspids, 8 bicuspids (premolars), and 12 molars. The 4 wisdom teeth develop after the other 8 molars, as the jaws increase in size. If this increase is insufficient, the wisdom teeth may become impacted, that is, wedged between the jawbone and other teeth, sometimes resulting in pain and inflammation.

The upper teeth, called maxillary, and the lower teeth, called mandibular, are shaped in such a manner that they interdigitate (fit together) when the jaws are closed. This fit is essential for the teeth to function properly when biting food with the incisors (front teeth) and when chewing and grinding food with the back teeth (molars and premolars). The molars and premolars have large surfaces with points (called cusps) and grooves so that they fit together extremely well.

Human teeth are derived from both the mesoderm (middle layer) and the ectoderm (outer layer) of the embryo. The enamel is formed by special cells called ameloblasts, which are part of enamel-making organs that bud off from the surface tissue (epithelium) of the mouth. Each organ initially looks like a sphere with an indentation that gradually assumes the shape of the tooth to be formed. The enamel of the crown consists of calcified enamel rods or prisms pointed toward the tooth surface. The enamel rods have a crystalline hydroxylapatite structure, like that found in bone, which makes the enamel extremely hard and strong. Dentin is formed by special cells called odontoblasts and consists of tubules that contain fibrils of odontoblast protoplasm. Enamel and dentin are held tightly together at their junction by a meshwork of organic material. Pain-mediating nerves are present at the enamel-dentin junction and within the dentin tubules. The central portion of the tooth, called the dental pulp, is composed of loose connective tissue and contains nerves and blood vessels that are extensions of those within the jawbone. The pulp is lined with odontoblasts, which, in the event of tooth decay (dental caries) or an injury, are capable of producing reparative dentin throughout the life of the tooth.

Other Vertebrates. The teeth of mammals differ in dental formula and in shape. The primates have teeth resembling those of humans, but the canine teeth tend to be larger and more pointed, especially in the males. The baboon has two premolars and three molars in each quadrant of the dentition, as do the Old World monkeys. The New World monkeys have three premolars and three molars. Among the carnivores the dog has four premolars and two molars, as well as three incisors and large canines, which are separated from the incisor and posterior teeth. The members of the cat family have two or three premolars and only one molar. Ungulates have premolars and molars with flattened surfaces, necessary for the chewing of grass or hay. Rodents have one incisor and three molars in each quadrant, but the incisors are unusual in that they are constantly developing and erupting as the incisal edges are worn down.

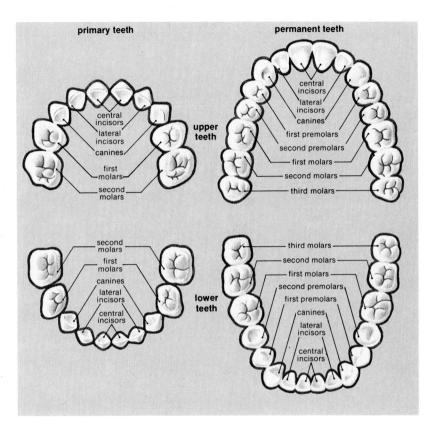

primary teeth

central incisors
lateral incisors
canines
first molars
second molars

upper teeth

permanent teeth

central incisors
lateral incisors
canines
first premolars
second premolars
first molars
second molars
third molars

second molars
first molars
canines
lateral incisors
central incisors

lower teeth

third molars
second molars
first molars
second premolars
first premolars
canines
lateral incisors
central incisors

Humans normally develop 20 primary, or deciduous, teeth and 32 permanent teeth. The primary teeth, which begin to form before a child is born, usually push through the gums between the ages of 6 months and 2 years. Central incisors commonly appear when the child is 6 to 8 months old, followed by the lateral incisors at about 7 to 9 months of age, first molars at about 12 to 14 months, canines at from 16 to 20 months, and second molars at roughly 20 to 24 months. The permanent dentition begins to erupt at about 6 or 7 years of age and, by the age of 13 years, has usually replaced all of the primary teeth. The first molars are the first permanent teeth to appear, followed by the central incisors at 6 to 8 years, lateral incisors at 7 to 9 years, canines and premolars at from 9 to 12 years, and second molars at about 11 to 13 years. The third molars, or wisdom teeth, which erupt at approximately 18 to 21 years of age, complete the dentition. The times of eruption may vary widely from one individual to another.

Fish have multiple similar teeth (homodont dentition), which are, essentially, modified scales composed of cornified material and consisting of crowns only. Amphibians tend to have fewer teeth than fish, but reptiles have unusual dental patterns ranging from an absence of teeth in turtles and one or two rows of sharp teeth ankylosed to bone in snakes to the thecodont (teeth in sockets) arrangement in crocodiles. Vertebrates without teeth include all modern birds and some bony fishes in addition to turtles.

Evolution of Teeth. Because of their high degree of calcification, teeth have been well preserved over thousands of years, and they have been used extensively in studies on the evolution of humans from hominidlike primates. Archaeologists have outlined the size, shape, and orientation of grooves and ridges for the teeth of the various precursors of humans, and these observations can often help to establish the type of

hominid unearthed in excavations of prehistoric sites. The evolution of teeth has also been postulated by paleontologists, beginning with the study of fossils of long-extinct animals. Primitive toothlike, conical, noncalcified structures are found in lampreys. Cartilaginous fish such as sharks have toothlike structures that are composed of solid osteodentin and that are formed at the bony surface of the jaws rather than developing within sockets. The teeth of more advanced fish are variable in structure but are usually composed of osteodentin. Large reptiles such as alligators have developed a regular dentition with teeth suspended in sockets rather than fused to bone, and some specialization of teeth occurs, with several teeth in each quadrant being larger than the others. The specialization continues in mammals, with variations in dentition related to food requirements.

Diseases. Teeth can be affected by a variety of diseases as

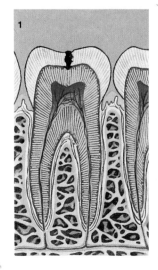
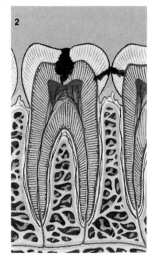
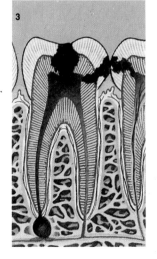

1
2
3

Tooth decay, also called dental caries, is a complex disease that involves bacteria, food particles, saliva, and poor oral hygiene. It is believed that certain bacteria produce acids that dissolve the tooth enamel (1), causing a cavity. If untreated, the decay spreads to the dentin and, sometimes, to an adjacent tooth (2). If the cavity is still untreated, the decay extends into the pulp (3), causing a toothache; an abscess, or sac of pus, may form at the base of the root. In this illustration the pulp of the next tooth has also been attacked.

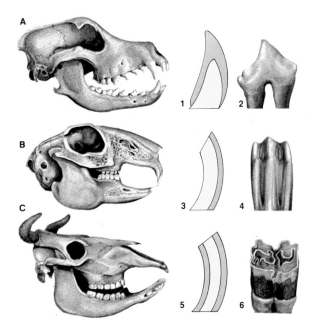

The dog (A), a carnivore, has large, sharp canine teeth (1) and certain cheek teeth (2) specialized for shearing. Rodents (B) are herbivores with chisellike, continuously growing incisors (3) for gnawing and cheek teeth (4) adapted for grinding; they lack canine teeth. The cow (C), a grazing ruminant, cuts vegetation with its lower incisors (5)—it lacks upper incisors—and chews it with broad, flat cheek teeth (6). Enamel (green) and dentine (yellow) are shown.

well as by developmental malformations. The common diseases of human dentition are dental caries, periodontal disease, and malocclusion.

Dental caries is a bacterially caused resorption or destruction of the enamel and dentin of the tooth, leading eventually, if untreated, to an infection of the dental pulp and an abscess of the apex of the tooth. The caries-causing bacteria proliferate within a protective covering, called plaque, on the tooth surfaces and produce both acid and enzymes to break down the calcified substances of the tooth. Sweets and other foods that stick to the tooth surface increase the activity of the caries-producing bacteria. Saliva, containing immunoglobulins and other antibacterial substances, tends to protect against caries, and decreased flow of saliva usually results in increased caries. Tooth shape and hereditary factors also determine a person's susceptibility to the disease.

Periodontal disease is a chronic or low-grade infection of the tissues supporting the tooth and can result in tooth loss by recession or loss of the supporting tissues. Malocclusion, or significant inability to close the teeth properly because of abnormal alignment, results in difficulty in chewing and can eventually lead to increased caries and periodontal disease risk. Preventive measures against the development of periodontal disease and caries include proper oral hygiene procedures to remove bacterial plaque from the surfaces of teeth, and public health procedures such as the addition of fluoride to drinking water.

Dental diseases also occur in animals, and many species are used for studies in the experimental pathology of caries and periodontal disease.   GERALD SHKLAR

Bibliography: Besford, John, *Good Mouthkeeping* (1984); Cormier, P. P., and Levy, J. I., *Community Oral Hygiene* (1981); Garner, L. P., *Essentials of Oral Histology and Embryology* (1982); Guinta, J. D., *Oral Pathology*, 2d ed. (1984); Himber, Jacob, *The Complete Family Guide to Dental Health* (1978); Kurten, Bjorn, ed., *Teeth: Form, Function and Evolution* (1982); Moss, Stephen J., *Your Children's Teeth* (1977); Murray, J. J., *The Prevention of Oral Disease* (1984); Pollack, R. L., ed., *Nutrition in Oral Health and Disease* (1985); Renner, Robert, *An Introduction to Dental Anatomy* (1985); Scott, J. H., and Sy-

mons, Norman, *Introduction to Dental Anatomy,* 9th ed. (1983); Tyldesley, W. R., *Oral Medicine,* 2d ed. (1981).

See also: DENTISTRY; DENTURES.

Teflon

Teflon, one of the earlier PLASTICS to be developed (1938), is a Du Pont trade name for the white, soft, waxy, and nonadhesive polymer of tetrafluoroethylene. Teflon has a useful temperature range exceeding 250° C (about 500° F), is inert to all chemicals except molten alkali metals and fluorine gas, and does not burn. Its electrical insulating properties and low friction are outstanding. The chemical industry uses Teflon in tubing, stopcocks, gaskets, and chemical-resistant work surfaces. It is also used for low-friction bearings and rollers and as a coating on saw blades. Cooking utensils may be coated with Teflon to prevent food from sticking.   W. J. PATTON

See also: FLUORINE; FLUOROCARBON.

Tegea [tee'-jee-uh]

Tegea (modern Alea), 12 km (7.5 mi) southeast of modern Tripolis, Greece, was one of the largest, most powerful cities of ancient Arcadia, known for its beautiful Temple of Athena Alea. After the archaic-period temple burned (395 BC), SCOPAS of Paros designed its replacement, which has a portico of Doric columns and, inside, Ionic and Corinthian orders. The pediments bore distinctive sculptures from Scopas's workshop; these are now at the local museum and in Athens. Tegea was sacked (AD c.395) by Alaric, but the town continued to flourish until it was supplanted by Tripolis in the 14th century.   JEAN MACINTOSH TURFA

Tegnér, Esaias [teng-nair']

The Swedish romantic poet Esaias Tegnér, b. Nov. 13, 1782, d. Nov. 2, 1846, became professor of Greek at Lund University in 1810, bishop of Växjö in 1824, and later a member of parliament. His poetry was first influenced by Swedish classicism and later by German philosophy. The patriotic poem *Sweden* (1811; Eng. trans., 1930) strengthened Tegnér's initial popularity as a poet, and his work culminated with what was to be the Swedish national epic, *Frithiofs Saga* (1825; Eng. trans., 1833), based on an Icelandic theme. The pessimistic *Mjältsjukan* (Ode to Melancholy, c.1826) marks the beginning of Tegnér's decline, which involved a period of mental illness.

Tegucigalpa [tay-goo-see-gahl'-pah]

Tegucigalpa, the capital of Honduras, lies in a small basin in the south central part of the country, about 975 m (3,200 ft) above sea level. It has a population of 509,000 (1983 est.). With no railroad, the city depends on a road linking it with the PAN-AMERICAN HIGHWAY and on the international airport at Toncontín, 6 km (4 mi) outside the city. The manufactures, mostly for local consumption, include textiles, sugar, and tobacco products. An 18th-century cathedral and the University of Honduras (1847) are located there. The city consists of two parts. Old Tegucigalpa, on the slopes of Mount Picacho, was founded during the 1570s as a silver- and gold-mining camp; in 1880 it became the capital of Honduras. Comayaguela, which lies across the Choluteca River, merged with the older settlement in 1938.

Tehran [tair-ahn']

Tehran (also Teheran) is the capital and largest city of Iran. The city is located at an elevation of 1,200 m (3,940 ft) at the southern foot of the Elburz Mountains, and snowcapped Mount DEMAVEND is nearby. The population of the city is 5,734,199 (1982 est.), and that of the 282-km^2 (109-mi^2) metropolitan area is 6,300,000. The name is derived from old Persian roots and means "warm place."

Contemporary City. Since the overthrow (1979) of MUHAMMAD REZA SHAH PAHLAVI and the establishment of an Islamic republic in Iran, Tehran has been a city in transition. At the start of Englab Avenue (formerly Reza Shah Avenue) is the

Shahyad Monument (1971). Built by the former shah to celebrate 2,500 years of Persian history, it is now called Freedom (*Azadai*) Monument. Hosseineh Mosque, closed down by the former regime, has been reopened as an Islamic training center with an extensive Islamic library. The Reza Shah Pahlavi Mausoleum has been renamed the Center for Islamic Studies and converted to religious use. Gulestan, Marble (Marmar), and Saadabad palaces are now maintained by the new regime to illustrate the opulence in which the former royal family lived. Old Shanhashani Park on Mosaddeq Street (formerly Pahlavi Street) has been renamed Melaat Park. In this same area of the lower city, in a labyrinth of narrow, covered alleys, are the famous bazaars of Tehran, a myriad of small shops and stalls grouped according to wares sold. The city's two major universities are the University of Tehran (1934) and the National University (1960).

The majority of the people are both Muslim and Persian, although Jewish, Christian Armenian, and other minorities also live there. Persian is the predominant language. The educated classes generally also speak English or French.

Before the revolution Tehran was the focus of Iran's industrial-modernization program. The city continues to produce about half of the country's manufactured goods. Numerous banks and insurance companies are located in the city. A petroleum refinery and an auto assembly plant are nearby.

History. The city of Tehran stands near the site of the former Iranian capital of Rey, which was destroyed by Mongols in 1220. The nearby village of Tehran was fortified in the 16th century, and since 1788 it has served as the capital of Iran. During the 19th century Tehran had a population of 120,000 and an area of 5 km² (2 mi²).

Tehran's vast modern expansion began under REZA SHAH PAHLAVI (r. 1925–41). By 1939 the population of the city had reached 500,000, and by 1960 it was 2,000,000. The results of this phenomenal growth have been the inevitable problems of air pollution and of perennial traffic jams that are among the world's worst.

In November 1979 militant Iranian students took the U.S. embassy and held the diplomatic personnel hostage, demanding that the deposed shah and his financial assets be returned to Iran. This precipitated a prolonged international crisis.

ARTHUR CAMPBELL TURNER

Tehran Conference

The Tehran Conference, which took place in the Iranian capital from Nov. 28 to Dec. 1, 1943, decided and coordinated the Allies' European strategy in World War II and gave guarantees for Iran's independence. U.S. president Franklin D. Roosevelt, British prime minister Winston Churchill, and Soviet premier Joseph Stalin attended.

The British and American leaders were anxious to ensure that a Russian offensive would coincide with the invasion of German-occupied France, and they also discussed other strategic issues.

ROBIN BUSS

Tehuacán Valley [tay-wah-kahn']

Large-scale archaeological investigations conducted during the 1960s and '70s in the Tehuacán Valley, in the semiarid highlands of Puebla, Mexico, have revealed a continuous cultural sequence extending from before 7000 BC until after the Spanish conquest. The 456 known sites range from tiny early camps to Coxcatlán, the large town that dominated the valley during AZTEC times. Tehuacán's dryness has favored the preservation of plant remains and other normally perishable materials, which provide unique evidence concerning the processes by which village farming developed in MESOAMERICA. The first inhabitants of Tehuacán were small, roving bands of food collectors. After 7000 BC plants were cultivated, gradually increasing in number and in the importance of their contribution to the diet. By 1000 BC the people of Tehuacán occupied settled village communities. Maize, beans, squash, and a variety of other crops supplied the bulk of their food.

JOHN S. HENDERSON

Bibliography: Adams, R. E. W., *Prehistoric Mesoamerica* (1977).

Tehuantepec, Isthmus of [tay-wahn-tay-pek', is'-muhs]

The Isthmus of Tehuantepec is the narrowest part of Mexico, between the Gulf of Mexico and the Pacific Ocean. About 220 km (140 mi) wide, it is crossed by a railroad. The northern half, part of the state of Veracruz, is swampy and tropically humid. The drier southern half, part of the state of Oaxaca, produces sugarcane, sorghum, and corn.

Tehuelche [tuh-wel'-chee]

The Tehuelche Indians, whose language was related to the ARAUCANIAN linguistic family, formerly roamed the grasslands of Patagonia in pursuit of guanaco and smaller game, moving from one water hole to another and living in small patrilineal bands of about 100 members each. They lived in *toldos*, animal-hide lean-tos, which they carried with them. They did not practice agriculture and had no domesticated animals except dogs. Shamanistic religious practice prevailed, along with a belief in bush spirits and some conceptualization of a supreme, otiose deity. The Tehuelche population probably never exceeded several thousand.

The simple organization of the Tehuelche changed radically after the arrival of the Spaniards (from 1520 on) introduced horses into Patagonia. The Tehuelche first hunted horses, then learned to ride them, after which they were able to increase their hunting territory. This led them into conflict with Indians of the Gran Chaco, who had also acquired horses and had begun to extend their territories. Military chieftainship developed, whereas there had been no chiefs before, and predatory raiding supplanted hunting. By the late 19th century traditional life had waned, and the Tehuelche were gradually absorbed into the gaucho population of Argentina.

LOUIS C. FARON

Bibliography: Steward, Julian H., ed., *Handbook of South American Indians*, vol. 1 (1946), and, with Faron, Louis, *Native Peoples of South America* (1959).

teiid [tee'-id]

Teiids are lizards found only in the New World, mostly in warm areas. About 200 species, classified in 40 genera, make up the family Teiidae, thought to be the counterpart of the Old World LACERTIDS. Teiids, which characteristically have deeply forked tongues and conical front teeth, and lack osteoderms, or bony skin plates, are a very diverse group. Some—the microteiids (subfamily Gymnophthalminae)—are generally small and have the anterior nasal scales separated by frontonasal scales. Some of these species, such as members of the South American genus *Bachia,* are burrowers with degenerate limbs. Other teiids—the macroteiids (subfamily Teiinae)—are generally medium-to-large lizards and have the anterior nasal scales intact. These species are mostly terrestrial (*Cnemidophorus*) or semiaquatic (*Dracaena*) and have well-developed limbs. The RACE RUNNERS (*Cnemidophorus*), ranging from the southern United States through South America, are known for their long, whiplike tails, speed, and, in some cases, unusual reproductive behavior, with all-female populations reproducing through PARTHENOGENESIS.

JONATHAN CAMPBELL

Teilhard de Chardin, Pierre [tay-ahr' duh shahr-dan']

The theologian and paleontologist Pierre Marie Joseph Teilhard de Chardin, b. May 1, 1881, d. Apr. 10, 1955, was a French Roman Catholic priest who developed a religiously oriented doctrine of cosmic evolution. Although Teilhard became a Jesuit at the age of 18 and remained faithful to the order for the rest of his life, a reading of Henri Bergson coupled with an interest in the sciences made him into a convinced evolutionist, and he spent his life attempting to show that the acceptance of evolution does not involve the rejection of Christianity. His efforts to convince the church that it should accept the implications of the Darwinian revolution

Pierre Teilhard de Chardin was a French Roman Catholic priest whose doctrine of cosmic evolution stirred much controversy. Teilhard argued that as evolution becomes more complex, it converges into one unified end point, Jesus Christ. Because of the debate that arose from his work, the Roman Catholic church banned the publication of his religious writings until after his death.

met such powerful resistance that in 1926 he was removed by his superiors from the Institut Catholique in Paris, where he had been a lecturer.

For the next 20 years he lived in China, where he was involved in paleontological research that led to the discovery of PEKING MAN, and also completed his major work, *The Phenomenon of Man* (1955; Eng. trans., 1959). Despite numerous applications to Rome, he was not allowed to publish writings other than scientific studies, with the result that none of his religious works appeared until after his death.

Bergson, one of Teilhard's points of departure, had denied that nonliving matter evolves and had affirmed that evolution is divergent, resulting in increasingly diverse life forms. Teilhard denied both these opinions. Nonliving matter, he held, is profoundly historical. Long before the emergence of living things it was subject to a law of complexification, resulting in a continuing, irreversible drift toward increasingly complex organization. The latest creature to emerge from this process is humankind, with its capacity for self-conscious thought.

Humans as they are now known are not the end of the process, he asserted. Everything that arises converges. Widely different human cultures around the Earth are now converging toward an omega point, identified by Teilhard as Christ, at which consciousness can find a new unity. Already humankind has covered the Earth's surface with a noosphere, a sort of collective human consciousness superimposed on the already-existing biosphere, and which Teilhard believed is evident in the present worldwide complex of transportation and communication. The result of human evolution on this planet, he held, will be an integration of personal consciousness in a divine milieu—the spirit of Christ at work in the world. Attacked by both scientists and believers, Teilhard's thought has nevertheless inspired and broadened the thought of theologians, philosophers, and scientists. Among his other works are *The Divine Milieu* (1957; Eng. trans., 1960), *The Future of Man* (1959; Eng. trans., 1964), *Hymn of the Universe* (1964; Eng. trans., 1965), and *Christianity and Evolution* (1969; Eng. trans., 1971). PETE A. Y. GUNTER

Bibliography: Browning, G. O., et al., eds., *Teilhard de Chardin: In Quest of the Perfection of Man* (1973); Cuénot, Claude, *Teilhard de Chardin: A Biographical Study* (1965); De Lubac, Henri, *Teilhard de Chardin: The Man and His Meaning* (1965); Lukas, Mary and Ellen, *Teilhard* (1977); Speaight, Robert, *Teilhard de Chardin: A Biography* (1967).

Teirlinck, Herman [tayr'-link]

The Flemish novelist and playwright Herman Teirlinck, b. Feb. 24, 1879, d. Feb. 4, 1967, began his career by writing naturalistic regional novels but soon became a writer of aesthetically refined, fin-de-siècle prose about city life. In the 1920s and '30s he championed socially committed community art, expressionist and experimental drama, and plays for outside theaters and mass audiences. With *Maria Speermalie* (1940) and *Het Gevecht met de Engel* (Fight with the Angel, 1952),

Teirlinck returned to the regional novel. *The Man in the Mirror* (1956; Eng. trans., 1963) is a refined exercise in prose that is strongly autobiographical in character. THEO D'HAEN

teju [tuh-zhoo']

The tejus, or tegus, genus *Tupinambis*, are large, fast-moving lizards of the family Teiidae. They inhabit tropical and subtropical regions of South America, where they feed on insects and small vertebrates, soft fruits, leaves, and birds' eggs. They measure 60 to 90 cm (2 to 3 ft) long and have powerful legs and long tails. The teju lays its eggs, usually six to eight in a clutch, in termite mounds, which serve as perfect incubators with well-regulated temperature and humidity. STEVEN C. ANDERSON

The common teju, T. teguixin, *a lizard native to eastern South America, lives in forests with dense undergrowth.*

Tekakwitha, Kateri [tek-ahk-with'-uh]

The first North American Indian proposed for canonization by the Roman Catholic church, Kateri Tekakwitha, b. near Auriesville, N.Y., 1656, d. Apr. 17, 1680, was the daughter of a Mohawk chief. Her Algonquin mother and her father died in a smallpox epidemic when she was 4 years old, and she was later instructed and baptized by a Jesuit missionary, who gave her the name Kateri, or Katherine. To escape persecution in her village, she fled to the Christian mission at Sault Saint Louis, near Montreal, where she lived until her death at the age of 24. She was revered for her kindness, faith, and endurance of suffering. Documentation for her canonization was introduced in 1932.

Bibliography: Buehrle, M. C., *Kateri of the Mohawks* (1954); Sargent, Daniel, *Catherine Tekakwitha* (1936).

tektites

Tektites are black or green, spheroidal, pear-shaped, or button-shaped natural glass objects containing 70% to 80% silicon dioxide (SiO_2). They generally weigh several grams, but specimens weighing several hundred grams are common. Found in strewnfields in Australia, Indonesia, Southeast Asia, the Philippines, Czechoslovakia, West Africa, Texas, and Georgia, tektites were deposited 700,000 to 32 million years ago, based on the ages of the rocks in or upon which they rest. Microtektites, glass beads less than a millimeter in diameter, are found in cores of young marine sediments near some strewnfields.

The origin of tektites is highly controversial. The shapes, surface pits, and grooves of tektites indicate that they were once molten and their outer surfaces were aerodynamically molded by hypersonic flight through the Earth's atmosphere. Although this interpretation suggests an extraterrestrial source, their cosmic-ray exposure ages are too short for tektites to have come from outside the Earth-Moon system. Furthermore, their chemical compositions are unlike most analyzed lunar rocks but similar to some terrestrial igneous and sedimentary ones. Most experts, therefore, favor an origin by melting during terrestrial meteorite impacts, followed by the quenching of ejected droplets and remelting during high-speed atmospheric flight. Some strewnfields are close to known impact craters of similar age, although most are not.

Another theory is that tektites are volcanic rather than impact glasses, a product of lunar volcanism.   LAWRENCE GROSSMAN

Bibliography: O'Keefe, John Aloysius, *Tektites and Their Origin* (1976).

See also: METEORITE CRATERS.

Tel Aviv   [tel uh-veev']

Tel Aviv, Israel's second largest city, is located on the Mediterranean coast of Israel about 55 km (35 mi) northwest of Jerusalem. The municipality, covering 52 km² (20 mi²), has a population of 334,900 (1981 est.); the larger metropolitan area (the Tel Aviv District), spreading over 171 km² (66 m²), contains 995,900 people (1979 est.). Tel Aviv enjoys a mild Mediterranean climate throughout the year, with January temperatures averaging 13° C (56° F) and an August mean of 27° C (80° F). Rain, concentrated in the winter months, amounts to 560 mm (22 in) annually.

Contemporary City. A predominantly modern city, Tel Aviv presents a skyscraper facade along Ha-Yarkon Street, which fronts the coast and contains the city's major hotels. The leading commercial enterprises are located to the east. By contrast, the ancient port city of JAFFA, incorporated into Tel Aviv in 1949, is medieval in appearance.

The economic, financial, commercial, and cultural center of Israel, Tel Aviv is also a transportation hub and the main center of the nation's tourist trade. Easy access to all points of interest within the country is provided by rail connections to Jerusalem, Haifa, and Beersheba and by an extensive bus network operating out of the city. Tel Aviv—and Israel—are connected to the rest of the world via the international airport at Lod, 14 km (9 mi) southeast of the city; the port of Ashdod, 31 km (19 mi) to the south; and the port of Haifa, 80 km (50 mi) to the northeast.

The location of more than 50% of Israel's industrial plants in Tel Aviv makes it the country's principal manufacturing

Tel Aviv, the second largest city and industrial center of Israel, lies along the eastern shore of the Mediterranean Sea. The southwestern section of the city, Jaffa, was a predominantly Arab settlement before it was incorporated into Tel Aviv in 1949.

center. Industries include textiles; metals and engineering products; vehicles; electric and electronic equipment; furniture and wood products; food and tobacco processing; diamond polishing; and printing and publishing. The Tel Aviv stock exchange is Israel's only such institution, and most banks, insurance companies, and other large corporations are headquartered there.

Tel Aviv is the home of Bar-Ilan University (1953) and Tel Aviv University (1953), as well as of the Israeli national theater, Habimah, and the Israel Philharmonic. The Tel Aviv Museum, the Ha'aretz Museum, the Museum of the Diaspora, and a zoo add to the cultural life of the city.

History. The growth of the city, after its founding in 1909 as a Jewish suburb of the largely Arab town of Jaffa, was sparked by the issuance of the Balfour Declaration (1917); by the anti-Jewish rioting in Jaffa (1921); and by the rise of Nazism in Germany. The independence of Israel in 1948 was followed by a population increase in Tel Aviv of more than 60% within the next 4 years, as well as by the departure of virtually all the 65,000 Arab residents of Jaffa.

Tel Aviv served (1948–49) as the temporary headquarters for the provisional government of Israel. It remains the headquarters of Histadrut, the Israeli Ministry of Defense, some foreign embassies, and several political parties. Tel Aviv is governed by a 31-member council elected for a 4-year term.

IRA M. SHESKIN

Bibliography: Kohansky, M., *Tel Aviv and Environs* (1973).

Tel Aviv University

Founded in 1953 and incorporating an early school of law and economics (1935), Institute of Natural Sciences, and the Institute of Jewish Studies, Tel Aviv University (enrollment: 18,500; library: 460,000 volumes) is a coeducational municipal institution in Tel Aviv, Israel. It has faculties of humanities, sciences, medicine, law, music, social work, and social science. Many research institutes are attached to the university.

Telanthropus: see HOMO ERECTUS.

telecommunications

Telecommunications refers to long-distance communication (the Greek *tele* means "far off"). At present, such communication is carried out with the aid of electronic equipment such as the RADIO, TELEGRAPH, TELEPHONE, and TELEVISION. In earlier times, however, smoke signals, drums, light beacons, and various forms of SEMAPHORE were used for the same purpose (see SIGNALING). The information that is transmitted can be in the form of voice, symbols, pictures, or data, or a combination of these. Data communication is a rapidly growing part of telecommunications. The physical equipment for a telecommunications system includes a TRANSMITTER, one or more RECEIVERS, and a channel or means of communication such as the air, wire, CABLE, COMMUNICATIONS SATELLITE, or some combination of these.

In general, a steady carrier-signal of some sort of ELECTROMAGNETIC RADIATION is generated by the transmitter, and the information to be transmitted is superimposed on the carrier signal. This process is called MODULATION, and the carrier is said to be modulated by the information. RADIO AND TELEVISION BROADCASTING make use of AMPLITUDE MODULATION (AM) and FREQUENCY MODULATION (FM). The receiver picks up the signals and demodulates, or decodes, them, converting them back into a form that can convey the original information. By a process called multiplexing, several different signals can be transmitted over a single channel (see MULTIPLEXER). The carrier signal is divided into separate subcarriers, each of which can be modulated by a different signal. At the receiving end of the system, these signals can be separated from the carrier and distributed as needed.

For a long time it seemed that there was some inherent and unbridgeable gap between the kinds of signals used in the telegraph and the telephone. Telegraph signals are digital, or numeric, in nature, and each letter of the alphabet is represented by a specific combination of dots and dashes (or on-off signals). The speech transmitted by telephone, in contrast, is ordinarily represented by a wave form—a wave that continuously varies in shape. The height, or amplitude, of the wave at any moment represents the strength or voltage of the signal at that time. This type of information is called analog, because the wave shape is physically related to, or is analogous to, the speech signal. In digital transmission, on the other hand, the information is transmitted via signals representing a series of ones and zeroes (see DIGITAL TECHNOLOGY).

Today it is possible to mix together different forms of information—speech, music, video signals, business data—and send them over the same carrier signal. Using a method known as pulse-code modulation (PCM), for example, the information is sent as a series of on-off pulses. Because the transmission is digital in form, greater accuracy is maintained. A long-distance analog signal is subject to a loss of quality; a digital signal, however, is likely to be interpreted correctly, because it is simply a series of on-off signals. Another advantage of PCM is that pulse signals can be compressed to a remarkable degree, thus increasing transmission capacity.

Another way of increasing channel capacity is to use for the carrier wave electromagnetic radiation of higher frequency than radio frequencies. Microwaves have greater carrier capacity than radio waves. FIBER OPTICS makes use of light waves, which have even greater capacity. Light provides carrier waves having a frequency of 10^{14} hertz (cycles per second), which is 10,000 (10^4) times higher than microwaves and 10^8 times higher than radio waves. A single glass fiber measuring 0.013 cm (0.005 in) in diameter can replace 10,000 telephone wires. Fiber-optic transmission of telephone conversations is now used in many U.S. telephone systems.

Engineers and planners in telecommunications look forward to a time in the near future when telephone, computer, facsimile (FAX), television, and even mail will be linked together in a single electronic system, which has been named the Integrated Services Digital Network (ISDN). ISDN is an evolving system of international standards that will eventually provide high-speed digital voice and data transmission over existing telephone wiring.

The first vital step toward the actualization of an ISDN system is the digitization of telephone systems, beginning with telephone switching circuits, the units at central exchanges that connect telephone lines, routing incoming calls from line to line or from a line to a link with another central exchange. Although the job of converting to digital switching was begun as early as the 1960s in some large central exchanges in the United States, most exchanges still use electromechanical switching devices. In addition, the telephone itself will have to be adapted to receive and send digitally, rather than in the analog mode it uses today.

With a digitized telephone service, the telecommunications possibilities are enormous. They range from a continuation of conventional telephoning (although digitization should reproduce spoken messages with a sound quality much closer to the actual voice) to countrywide and worldwide transmission systems capable of communicating almost instantly.

An ISDN interface with a single user begins with a digitized telephone and includes a computer, television monitor and controls, and a FAX—all connected by a single telephone wire to an ISDN central exchange. In place of the MODEM now used to convert digital to analog signals, a terminal adapter will connect the computer with the telephone system. With the adapter, multiple simultaneous connections become possible: computers can run several tasks at the same time, while the user exchanges voice and computer data with other users and other computers.

ISDN capabilities should eventually include the interconnection through the public telephone system of Local Area Networks (LANs)—the private, interoffice systems that already exist to link together electronics within an office or within a building. It will provide information and database services, electronic mail, video services, interactive services such as catalog shopping, FAX systems, building and home security systems, and other electronic marvels, such as real-time video, the long-awaited videophone that transmits live video images via telephone. HAL HELLMAN

Bibliography: Alisoukas, V., and Tomasi, W., *Digital and Data Communications* (1985); Arterton, C., *Teledemocracy: Telecommunications and Democratic Participation* (1987); Ettinger, J. E., *Communication Networks: Private Networks within the Public Domain* (1985); Heilborn, J., *Using Telecommunications* (1988); Hellman, H., *Communications in the World of the Future*, 2d ed. (1975); Kincaid, P., and Ouverson, M., *Through the Micromaze: Visual Guide to Telecommunications* (1985); Maynard, J., *Computer and Telecommunications Handbook* (1984); Murphy, B., *The World Wired Up* (1984); Rosen, A., *Telecommunications* (1987).

telegraph

For most of human existence, only visual and acoustic methods of signaling were available, as in the use of beacon fires or the sounds from church bells. By the early years of the 19th century, however, the understanding of electric and magnetic phenomena had so progressed that using an electric current to communicate between two separated stations became possible, and the age of the telegraph had arrived.

HISTORY

During the early 19th century the transmission of a message by telegraph was simple: a switch, or key, could be used by the operator to supply short pulses of electric current to the wire (line) from a battery; the circuit was completed through

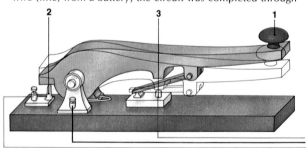

(Above) *A Morse two-pole telegraph key is essentially a switch for opening and closing an electric circuit between two telegraph stations. When the transmission line (red) is not in use, current flows from the power line (black) through a bypass line (blue). Depressing the key (1) breaks the bypass contact (2), and a current pulse is sent through the transmission-line contact (3).*

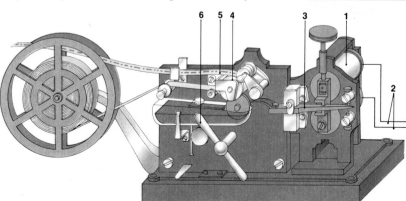

(Left) *In an early Morse receiver-printer, electromagnetic coils (1) were energized by a current pulse transmitted through a telegraph line (2). The coils attracted a lever (3) that pressed an inked roller (4) against a moving paper strip (5) driven by a clockwork motor wound by a handle (6).*

the earth. The pulses could be dispatched in time patterns forming codes representing the letters and numbers that formed the message. The problem of how to detect the current pulses at the remote receiving station was solved in 1819, when Hans C. OERSTED discovered that a wire carrying an electric current deflected a magnetic needle, the sense of the deflection being reversed with reversal of the direction of flow of the current. Deflecting needle telegraphs, also known as electric telegraphs, were investigated by such famous scientists as André Marie Ampère, Carl F. Gauss, and Wilhelm E. Weber, but the most successful instrument was that of William F. Cooke and Charles Wheatstone, who installed the first railway telegraph in England in 1837.

The invention of the electromagnet by William Sturgeon in 1825 and the researches of Michael Faraday and Joseph Henry on electromagnetic phenomena about 1831 stimulated Samuel F. B. MORSE to devise a telegraph receiver. In the receiver an electromagnet, energized by the pulse of current from the line, attracted a soft iron armature; this action produced deflection in the straight line being scribed on a moving strip of paper by a pencil carried by the armature. Morse, along with Alfred Vail, greatly improved this receiver and adapted it to print the dot and dash symbols of MORSE CODE, which Morse had invented for the representation of alphanumeric characters. The two symbols corresponded to pulses of short and long duration, respectively. In 1844, Morse successfully demonstrated this magnetic telegraph by sending the message "What hath God wrought" from Baltimore to Washington. Morse's receiver was widely adopted; because the dot and dash signals could easily be determined from the sound of the clicking armature, however, the recording of messages on paper was abandoned for many years.

Signaling distances were greatly improved by the use of a relay, an electromagnet receiver that used the feeble current from the line to operate a switch that provided local battery power to key a further length of telegraph line. The relay was the only form of amplifier available to telegraph engineers until the invention of the thermionic triode tube by Lee De Forest in 1907. Utilization of the early telegraph lines was also increased by the invention of devices to permit duplex working—transmission of signals in opposite directions simultaneously over the same line. Diplexing, the transmission of two signals simultaneously in the same direction, was also invented. The combination of diplex with duplex by Thomas Alva Edison in 1874 created quadruplex, which allowed the transmission of two messages in each direction, a total of four messages transmitted simultaneously.

The rapid growth of commercial telegraph traffic stimulated the development of other methods to increase the speed of handling of signals. One solution was the development of a tape-reader machine, which transmitted Morse signals at high

rate in accordance with a message that was expressed as a sequence of holes in a perforated tape. Wheatstone produced such a system in 1858, which operated in association with a Morse inker to print the received signals on a moving tape. Improvements to this machine included the development of perforators to prepare the transmitter tape on a keyboard instrument. The received Morse signals were inscribed by an undulator and had to be read by an operator, who typed or wrote the message. By these improvements speeds of up to 400 words per minute were achieved by 1900. Many of these devices also found application in radio telegraphy, which was introduced by Guglielmo MARCONI in 1897, and in submarine telegraphy, which was in use as early as 1851.

MULTIPLEX SYSTEM

The time division, or multiplex, system of telegraphy, perfected by Émile Baudot in 1874, increased the traffic capacity of a line permitting up to six operators to share it on a cyclic basis. Instead of Morse code, a five-unit code was used in which every character contained five symbol elements, each being of equal duration and designated as a mark or a space according to the provisions of the code and corresponding to current on and current off, respectively. Five keys were available to the operators, who set up the units of the character to be transmitted. A modified form of Baudot's five-unit code was ultimately adopted as the International Telegraph Alphabet No. 2. In this alphabet, the letter *P*, for example, is represented as three perforations on a transmission tape located in this way: □ · □ · □ —a 01101 in binary characters. Baudot's system continued in use, particularly in Europe, until well into the 20th century, and its extension was halted only by the increasing popularity of the telephone after World War I.

CARRIER TELEGRAPHY

The versatility of thermionic tubes as generators, amplifiers, and detectors of signals ultimately led to the abandonment of all electromechanical multiplex systems and achieved the virtual coincidence between the techniques employed in the telegraph and telephone systems. The telephone was invented by Alexander Graham Bell in 1876, after which telephone service developed rapidly in the United States and in most of the countries of Europe. Although the telephone at first posed a commercial threat to the telegraph, the fact that the two instruments fulfilled complementary rather than competing functions was soon recognized. The growth of telephone networks in fact, stimulated the development of new techniques in telegraphy, such as voice-frequency telegraph channeling systems that carried up to 24 telegraphy channels in a single telephone channel.

The signaling element of the simple telegraph is a direct-current (DC) pulse corresponding to the dot or dash of the Morse code or the signals of the five-unit code. In the carrier system, a voice-frequency, alternating current (tone) is modulated by the sequence of DC pulses that constitute the message. One such tone provides a single telegraph channel; a number of tones, however, are employed equally spaced in frequency to fill a voice-frequency channel covering approximately 350 to 3,200 Hz. This band of telegraph carriers, in association with a number of similar telegraph bands as well as telephone channels, are impressed on a single high-frequency carrier that is carried by a single transmission line. The channels are separated at the receiver through a sequence of filters, and the telegraph signal from a particular carrier is extracted by the usual detection process for application to a teletypewriter.

THE TELETYPEWRITER

The increase in traffic that the carrier telegraph system stimulated caused a great increase in the number of terminal stations and therefore led to the development of the teletypewriter for the transmission and reception of telegraph messages. A teletypewriter possesses a typewriter keyboard; the depression of a key supplies the correct sequence of impulses directly to the telegraph line in accordance with the five-unit code. In addition, the pulses, both outgoing and incoming, activate the machine to print the messages in typescript. The combination of carrier telegraphy and teletypewriter terminals has resulted in enormous growth in the

Morse code is used in manual telegraphy. Letters of the alphabet are transmitted as combinations of long and short pulses of electric current according to an internationally accepted system of dots and dashes. Automatic operation of teletypewriters or other machines requires the use of a special binary Murray code in which groups of five signals are sent (dots) or not sent (spaces).

letter	Morse code	Morse-code electrical signals	five-unit code	five-unit-code electrical signals
A	· —			
E	·			
O	— — —			
Y	— · — —			

national and international telegraphy networks and in the associated telegraph switching centers that form the modern Telex system. The interchange of data between the massive data banks created by modern electronic data-processing systems is expected to create the demand for channels of communication that have much higher transmission rates than have been used in the past. Modern solid-state repeaters are used in telephone- and submarine-cable systems and by television coaxial cables, microwave, optical fiber, and satellite links. The development of solid-state integrated circuits has completed the transition from the simple telegraph of 1837 to modern digital data-transmission systems.   SIR ERIC EASTWOOD

Bibliography: Freebody, J. W., *Telegraphy* (1959); Jolley, E. H., *Introduction to Telephony and Telegraphy* (1970); Smith, Sydney F., *Telephony and Telegraphy*, 3d ed. (1978); Sterling, Christopher M., *An Original Anthology: Eyewitness to Early American Telegraphy* (1974); Thompson, Robert L., *Wiring a Continent* (1947; repr. 1972); Wiesner, *Telegraph and Data Transmission over Shortwave Radio Links* (1984).

telekinesis: see PSYCHOKINESIS.

Telemann, Georg Philipp   [tel'-uh-mahn]

The German composer and organist Georg Philipp Telemann, b. Mar. 14, 1681, d. June 25, 1767, was regarded during his lifetime as one of Germany's greatest musicians. He was so prolific that he was never able to count the number of his compositions. Self-taught in music, he studied languages and science at the University of Leipzig. He held a series of important musical positions, culminating in that of music director of the five largest churches in Hamburg, from 1720 until his death. Telemann traveled widely, absorbing various musical styles and incorporating them into his own compositions. He was a friend of Johann Sebastian Bach and godfather to Bach's son Carl Philipp Emanuel. Handel, also his friend, was quoted as saying that Telemann could write an 8-part motet as easily as anybody else could write a letter. Telemann's contrapuntal skill, melodic facility in the Italian style, French elegance, and fertile imagination resulted in music that was fluent but often lacking in depth. His reputation and influence on German musicians have been minimal, but since the mid-20th century his music has been increasingly performed and recorded. Telemann's amazing productivity resulted in 12 cycles of cantatas for the entire church year. He also composed huge quantities of chamber music; many concertos, and solo harpsichord and organ works; about 600 orchestral suites; and 40 operas.   FARLEY K. HUTCHINS

Bibliography: Bukofzer, M., *Music in the Baroque Era* (1947); Petzholdt, R., *Georg Philipp Telemann*, trans. by H. Fitzpatrick (1974).

telemetry   [tuh-lem'-uh-tree]

The word *telemetry* refers to communications systems that make measurements at remote or inaccessible points and transmit these measurements to receiving equipment where they are monitored, recorded, and displayed. Telemetry's major uses include monitoring electric generating stations, gathering meteorological and oceanographic data, and monitoring spaceflights and body conditions.

Telemetric systems consist of a measuring-transmitting instrument, a medium of transmission, a receiver, and recording or display equipment. The measuring-transmitting instrument is usually a TRANSDUCER, which converts physical stimuli into electrical signals. Transducers take many forms and can be designed to respond to pressure, mechanical stress, or acceleration. Temperature-sensing transducers may be of the THERMISTOR type, which rapidly lose electrical resistance as temperature rises, or of the THERMOCOUPLE type, which are wire junctions of metals that produce a current when heated.

A line is employed in short-distance telemetry or where radio transmission is expensive or impractical, such as in a large city. For aerospace applications and transmission over long distances, radio is used. The radio signal may carry at one time several types of information, which are combined into a single signal by a process called multiplexing. Sonic-

and light-telemetry-transmission systems are still in the experimental stage. Telemetry-receiving equipment extracts the data from the signal and presents it in usable form. Data may be displayed on a screen, recorded on magnetic tape, or automatically typed and printed out on a sheet of paper.

Bibliography: Gruenberg, E., *Handbook of Telemetry and Remote Control* (1967); Mackay, R., *Bio-Medical Telemetry*, 2d ed. (1970).

teleology   [tee-lee-ahl'-uh-jee]

Teleology is the study of things or events in terms of their purposes or ends. From ancient times to the present, many philosophers and scientists have thought that various natural processes could be explained only in terms of the purposes that they were achieving or in terms of the ends or goals that they were reaching. In ARISTOTLE's physics, four types of explanation were offered, but the most important one was in terms of the purpose (Greek: *telos*), or final goal, of physical change. For Aristotle all processes of change were purposeful. From the examination of the world in terms of purpose and the discovery of such apparent purposes, a teleological argument for the existence of God was worked out, claiming that the purposes found in nature required a purposeful Designer.

In the development of modern science, one of the first contentions of Galileo Galilei and René Descartes was that purposes could neither be known nor discovered. Although scientists have progressively removed teleological inquiry from one branch of the study of nature after another, the central issue remains: whether teleological explanation is necessary to account for the behavior of living or conscious beings or whether all of their behavior can be explained without it.   RICHARD H. POPKIN

Bibliography: Collins, James, *Interpreting Modern Philosophy* (1972); Hull, David, *Philosophy of Biological Science* (1974); McFarland, J. D., *Kant's Concept of Teleology* (1969); Taylor, Charles, *The Explanation of Behaviour* (1964); Woodfield, Andrew, *Teleology* (1976); Wright, Larry, *Teleological Explanations* (1976).

teleost   [tel'-ee-ahst]

A teleost, subclass Teleostei, is a bony FISH with rayed fins. The vast majority of familiar fishes are teleosts, with between 18,000 and 25,000 species now recognized and new species being identified each year. The several major groups include the Osteoglossomorpha, a primitive freshwater group that includes bonytongues and MOONEYES; the Elopomorpha, a primarily marine group including true BONEFISHES, EELS, and TARPONS; the Clupeomorpha, or herringlike fishes (see HERRING); and the Euteleostei, or higher teleosts, including the CARP, CATFISH, CHARACIN, COD, PIKE, SALMON, TROUT, and many perchlike species (see PERCH).   E. O. WILEY

telepathy: see EXTRASENSORY PERCEPTION.

telephone

The telephone is a device for reproducing sound at a distance from its source by means of the transmission of an electrical signal. The word refers both to the familiar handset and to the huge telephone system that makes possible person-to-person communications throughout most of the world. There are more than 400 million telephones worldwide, with over 155 million in the United States alone. Americans make more than 800 million phone calls every day.

Basic Principles. The telephone now in use is similar to the original device patented by Alexander Graham BELL in 1876 and 1877. Because sound waves do not travel very far (or very fast), there were many attempts to devise systems like the telephone, in which the sound waves are converted into electrical oscillations, which can be sent long distances and travel about 900,000 times faster than sound; these oscillations are then converted back into sound waves at the receiving end. Bell had theorized (1875) that if he could find a way to make an electric current vary in intensity precisely as air varies in density during the production of sound, he could

In 1877, Alexander Graham Bell, the Scottish-American inventor of the telephone, lectured about his invention to an audience in Lyceum Hall, Salem, Mass. During his lecture he demonstrated that he could converse by telephone with his assistant, Thomas A. Watson, 29 km (18 mi) away in Boston.

made only through the carbon, which is a reasonably good conductor of electricity. Vibration of the membrane/piston causes the electrical resistance of the carbon grains to vary: a sound wave, which is compressional, will force the grains closer together, decreasing the resistance. Changes in resistance result in variations in the amount of electricity passing through the circuit, and hence the connecting line.

At the receiving end (the earpiece), a second membrane is made to perform vibrations similar to the ones induced in the first one. This is accomplished by causing it to be variably attracted by a wire-wound iron core, or electromagnet, where the wire is part of the circuit. As the current in the circuit varies, the membrane vibrates with the same wave pattern as the transmitter membrane. As the receiving diaphragm vibrates, it pushes against the air, setting the air molecules into vibration at the same rate, and thus it reproduces the original sound.

The telephone must operate as part of a complete electric circuit, and so it needs a power source, a conductor, and a switch. The power source is electricity; the conductor in the basic system is the pair of wires that lead from the transmitting and receiving telephones to the central office; and the switch is the cradle or pair of buttons that moves when the user picks up the handpiece. Lifting the handpiece closes an electric circuit to produce a dial tone, which indicates that the system is ready for a call to be made. The dial (or, in a touch-tone phone, the panel of buttons) sends out an electrical code that establishes the correct connections needed to single out the other telephone that is dialed from the many millions connected to the system.

Switching Systems. In the first commercial system the receiver and transmitter were one and the same. This worked well enough for a primitive device. Manual connections were made in central switching offices by operators at manual switchboards. Today the vast majority of switching is done

transmit speech. Aided by Thomas A. Watson, Bell succeeded in developing a practical telephone. Although a vast number of improvements have been made in Bell's original system, the basic principles—using voice vibrations to control a larger source of power and creating a variable resistance in an electrical circuit—remain the same. In a modern telephone the speaker talks into the mouthpiece, behind which is a transmitter. Vibrating air molecules produced by the speech generate vibrations in a thin aluminum diaphragm. These vibrations are transmitted to a small piston, which is the cover for a metallic box filled with small granules of carbon. Electrical contact is

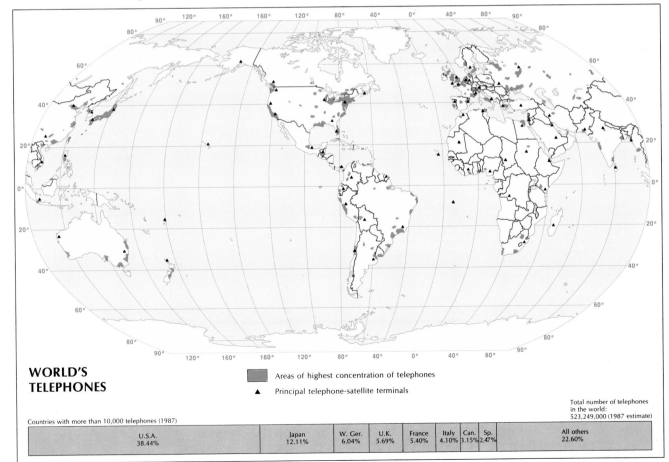

WORLD'S TELEPHONES

Areas of highest concentration of telephones

▲ Principal telephone-satellite terminals

Total number of telephones in the world: 523,249,000 (1987 estimate)

Countries with more than 10,000 telephones (1987)

| U.S.A. 38.44% | Japan 12.11% | W. Ger. 6.04% | U.K. 5.69% | France 5.40% | Italy 4.10% | Can. 3.15% | Sp. 2.47% | All others 22.60% |

automatically, at least in the technologically advanced countries. Through a system called Direct Distance Dialing, it is possible for almost all Americans to dial almost anywhere in the country. From most exchanges it is even possible to dial overseas calls. Automatic switching began in 1892 with the introduction of the first dial exchange, in La Porte, Ind. For each call a series of electromechanical selector switches, called relays, automatically move into the correct positions. The round telephone dial was deliberately designed to require a moment's wait after each digit is dialed, so as to give the switches time to make the necessary connections. With electronic switching systems, however, this delay is not needed, and push-button telephones can be used. Modern switching equipment makes the needed connections in a few seconds and also routes the signal around crowded exchanges.

In many cities, CELLULAR RADIO networks are set up to provide automatic switching for portable telephones carried by automobiles. In such a system, a phone on the move is repeatedly transferred to the transmitter of the next local "cell," thereby maintaining a constant service.

Electronic switching systems using computers can be set up to provide additional services; for example, such systems can automatically forward calls, add a third party to a call, alert a caller when another call is waiting, and identify frequently called numbers by the use of only two digits.

Carrier Systems. Telephone messages are sent bunched together over trunk lines, increasing the number of conversations that can be carried by any one conductor. The signals that contain the information being transmitted are carried by high-frequency waves. Generally, the wider the bands of frequency that are used as carriers, the more information they can handle.

Telephone signals are transmitted by copper telephone wire—the most common transmission form—or by cable, radio relay, microwaves, and, most recently, optical fiber lines (see FIBER OPTICS). The advantages of fiber transmission include greater data capacities and higher transmission speeds. The fibers are lighter than copper wire and are not easily affected by stray magnetic fields. COMMUNICATIONS SATELLITES transmit overseas, ship-to-shore, and plane-to-shore telephone messages. Mobile cellular phones make use of radio waves.

Digital Systems. As telephones have become more and more central to the transmission of messages and data from such digital devices as computers, and as the use of telephones themselves has increased, it has become necessary to find better, faster methods of transmission than the analog systems presently used. (In analog systems, the shape of the electrical signal carried by the telephone wire is directly analogous to the sound waves produced by voice.) Digital telephone systems take rapid samplings of sound and translate them into signal pulses carrying digital one/zero codes. With digitized systems, computer messages can be transmitted directly, without digital-to-analog translation by a MODEM. Digitizing will permit the creation of digital networks, allowing communications between computers, for instance, and between digital systems within and among businesses, factories, and other organizations. A complete nationwide and worldwide TELECOMMUNICATION system—the high-speed delivery of voice and data messages—is dependent on digitized phone systems.

In order to digitize telephone systems, the electromagnetic or electronic switches in central exchanges must be replaced by digital switches, a process that has already been begun by many telephone companies. Digital switches are solid-state semiconductors. They provide faster switching, more accurate transmission of sound, and such features as the automatic transfer of calls and itemized customer bills, in addition to being able to transmit both voice and data on the same line.

Extended Uses. During the 1920s, news associations began to send pictures over specially built telephone lines. In 1924, telephone wires carried the first coast-to-coast radio broadcast, and in 1927 the first experimental long-distance television transmission was demonstrated at Bell Laboratories, the central research facility of the telephone industry at that time. Teletypewriter-exchange service, wherein typed messages are sent between machines interconnected through switching centers, like telephones, was introduced in 1931. Today, the virtues of all-digital telephone systems are illustrated by, for example, the phenomenon of COMPUTER NETWORKING and by the existence of Local Area Networks (LANs), private systems set up in offices, or throughout a building or a locality, which can connect and provide intercommunication between such devices as computers, facsimile machines, video machines, and telephones.

Research in telephones has produced sound motion pictures, solar batteries, the artificial larynx, the transistor (originally developed to provide improved amplification for repeaters on long-distance lines), electrical recording of phonograph records, radio astronomy, and optical communications. Still to come, perhaps, are inexpensive picturephones (in existence but not yet economically practical) and the wrist telephone.

The Telephone Industry. The American Telephone & Telegraph Company (AT&T) was formed in Boston on July 9, 1877, as the Bell Telephone Company by the inventor Alexander Graham Bell and two financial backers. For two years the company had to compete with the Western Union Telegraph Company, which had hired Thomas Alva Edison to develop a different form of telephone transmitter so that it would not have to use Bell's invention. The competition ended in 1879 when Bell Telephone brought a successful suit against Western Union for infringement of its patents. The company moved to New York City in 1885 and was reorganized as AT&T, with the Bell System as one of its subsidiaries.

Although the Bell patents expired in 1894, AT&T soon bought up most prospective competitors, won control of about 85 percent of the U.S. telephone market, and became linked with corporate and government telephone systems around the world. After 1934 its activities were regulated by the Federal Communications Commission (FCC).

From 1974 to 1982, AT&T was involved in an antitrust suit brought against it by the U.S. Department of Justice. Presided over by Judge Harold H. Greene, the case resulted in a massive reorganization of the U.S. telephone industry. AT&T was forced to relinquish its 22 Bell System companies, as well as the Bell name. The 22 operating companies were reorganized under the control of 7 regional telephone companies and continued to offer local telephone service. AT&T was allowed to maintain its long-distance telephone business, and it was also allowed to enter into businesses from which it had been previously excluded by court decree. These include data processing and computer communications. While AT&T is now becoming a diversified, high-technology business, it is finding itself in serious competition both with other long-distance telephone companies and with makers of telephone equipment. Newer long-distance companies include MCI Communications and GTE Corporation.　　　　HAL HELLMAN

Bibliography: Boettinger, H. M., *The Telephone Book: Bell, Watson, Vail and American Life, 1876–1976*, rev. ed. (1983); Chorofas, D. N., *Telephony* (1984); Crump, S., *Cellular Telephones* (1985); De Sola Pool, I., *The Social Impact of the Telephone* (1977); Fike, J. L., and Friend, G. E., *Understanding Telephone Electronics*, 2d ed. (1984); Shooshan, H. M., III, ed., *Disconnecting Bell* (1984).

telescope, optical

An optical astronomical telescope is an instrument that is used to collect light from a celestial object, to bring the light to focus and produce an image, and to magnify that image. The two main types of telescopes are refractors, which use lenses, and reflectors, which use mirrors. The main lens or mirror that focuses the light is called the objective. Both telescopes have an eyepiece, or combination of small lenses, to magnify the image formed by the objective. In addition, the reflector telescope uses a small secondary mirror to reflect the light from the main, or primary, mirror to a convenient position for placement of the eyepiece or of auxiliary equipment, such as a photometer or spectrograph. In general, refractor telescopes are used for lunar and planetary studies, as well as for astrometric work involving precision measurements of

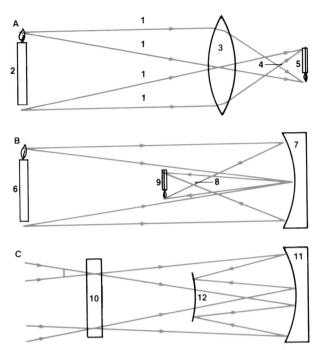

In a refracting telescope, or refractor (A), light rays (1) from an object (2) pass through a lens (3), are bent, or refracted, to a focal point (4), and form an inverted image (5). In a reflector (B), light rays from the object (6) are reflected by a concave mirror (7) to a common focus (8) and form an inverted image (9). In a Schmidt telescope, or camera (C)—because it is used only for photographic work—an aberration-free wide field of view is obtained by use of a spherical mirror and a correcting lens. Light from an object passes through a thin lens, or corrector plate (10), and is reflected from the spherical mirror (11) to a curved focal surface (12), which holds the photographic film.

double stars and stellar proper motions. Reflector telescopes are preferred for extragalactic studies, photography of faint objects, photometry, and spectrographic work.

A third type of telescope—a catadioptric telescope—uses a combination of lenses and mirrors to obtain the advantages of both the refractor and the reflector. The most famous of this type is the SCHMIDT TELESCOPE, developed (1934) by the German optician Bernhard Schmidt. It uses a concave spherical mirror in combination with a thin glass corrector plate; the plate is precisely ground to obtain a very wide, uniform field of view. The Schmidt telescope, however, cannot be used for optical viewing; it is used instead as a large camera by exposing a photographic plate at the focus of the mirror. Smaller catadioptric instruments use secondary mirrors at the focus of the primary mirror to permit viewing.

The optical instruments described in this article are used to observe and photograph objects in the visible region of the electromagnetic spectrum, ranging into the near-infrared and ultraviolet regions as well. For work in other regions of the spectrum, different forms of devices are used to perform equivalent functions, such as the parabolic antennas of RADIO ASTRONOMY (see GAMMA-RAY ASTRONOMY; INFRARED ASTRONOMY; ULTRAVIOLET ASTRONOMY; X-RAY ASTRONOMY).

HISTORY

Tradition attributes the invention of the telescope to the accidental alignment of two lenses of opposite curvature and diverse focal length by Hans Lippershey in Holland in 1608. The principle, however, may have been known to Roger Bacon in the 13th century and to the early spectacle makers of Italy.

Refractors. GALILEO GALILEI constructed (1609) the first lens, or refracting, telescope for astronomical purposes. Using several versions, he discovered the four brightest Jovian satellites, lunar mountains, sunspots, the starry nature of the Milky Way, and the apparent elongation of Saturn, now known to be its rings. Galileo's simple lenses suffered from a variety of

aberrations, or defects of image formation: chromatic aberration, or the variation of focal length (see LENS) with color; spherical aberration, the variation of focal length with distance of parallel rays from the lens axis; coma, the increasing blur of a point image as the angle of the rays to the axis increases; and distortion, the imaging of straight lines in the object as curves (see ABERRATION, CHROMATIC; ABERRATION, SPHERICAL; COMA, optics). These aberrations were minimized in a variety of ways. Christiaan HUYGENS constructed extremely long aerial telescopes in which the objective lens was mounted on a pole and connected to the eyepiece by only a taut wire. Despite extraordinary difficulties, such instruments achieved useful results, especially in lunar mapping.

The 18th-century London optician John DOLLOND combined (1757) a convex crown glass and a concave dense flint to make a compound lens that compensated for the chromatic aberrations at two wavelengths. Two-component lenses of increasing sophistication have since been developed, and today computer programs exist for the design of lens systems with multiple components. Two-component objectives are the rule for refractors, which have been used for charting the sky, determining stellar parallaxes and proper motions, making photometric plates for analysis by diaphragm photometers, and undertaking double-star astrometry.

The largest visual refractors are at LICK OBSERVATORY (36 in/91 cm) and YERKES OBSERVATORY (40 in/102 cm). The size of refractors is limited by the difficulty of making large defect-free glass blanks and by the distortion caused by the sagging of the lens under its own weight. Refractors with lenses cut diametrically in two (Repsold heliometers) and sliding with respect to each other were used by Friedrich Bessel and Sir David Gill in the 19th century to measure angular separations for determination of solar and even stellar parallaxes. Triplet lenses have been used for wide-field sky mapping and observing asteroids.

Reflectors. In England in the 17th century, attention turned to mirror, or reflecting, telescopes, which usually consisted of two mirrors because of the mistaken belief that lens aberrations were irreparable. James GREGORY proposed (1663) a configuration in which a primary concave parabolic mirror converges the light to one focus of a concave ellipsoidal mirror. Reflection of light rays at its surface causes convergence to the ellipsoid's second focus, located behind the main mirror and reached through a central hole in it. The tube length is thus less than the sum of the focal lengths of the two mirrors. Because of construction difficulties, only a few Gregorians have been made; the largest, 50 in (130 cm) in diameter, is at Canberra, Australia.

Isaac NEWTON proposed (1668) a telescope in which a primary parabolic mirror reflects light rays to an inclined flat (in small instruments, a totally reflecting prism) placed centrally in the tube; this flat in turn reflects the rays to an observer located at the side of the upper end of the tube. An original instrument built by Newton still exists, at the Royal Society of London. Many large- and medium-sized reflectors are Newtonian in design, although for diameters less than 1 m (3.3 ft) the weights of instrumentation capable of being carried far from the support axes are small, and for larger-diameter instruments elaborate carriages are needed to give an observer access to the focus. For large Newtonians the focal ratio—the ratio of aperture size to focal length—is typically near f/4. In some cases—the Hale 200-in (5.1-m) telescope at PALOMAR OBSERVATORY and the 120-in (3.0-m) telescope at Lick Observatory, for instance—only a single mirror is used, and access to the prime focus is from a central cage containing the observer. Some large telescopes, such as the 156-in (4-m) KITT PEAK NATIONAL OBSERVATORY and the 153-in (3.9-m) ANGLO-AUSTRALIAN TELESCOPE, carry observers at the Cassegrain focus. Except for work done at the prime focus, both old and recently built large telescopes use television viewing systems and electronic devices instead of human observers at the focus.

Early reflectors had mirrors made of speculum metal—a brittle alloy consisting of copper and tin—which required repolishing and refiguring when it became tarnished. Sir William HERSCHEL used such mirrors for making telescopes, including one 48 in (1.2 m) in diameter. The Herschelian con-

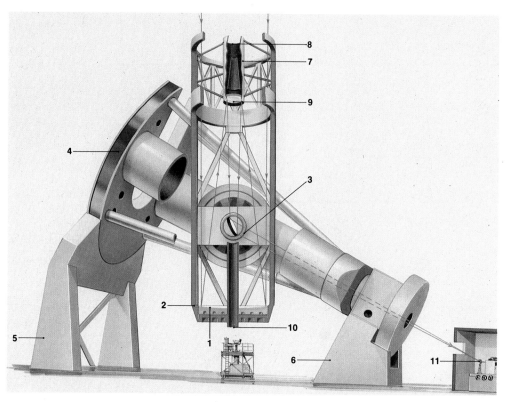

The Hale reflector is located on California's Palomar Mountain. The 455,000-kg (500-ton) telescope has a 200-in-diameter (508-cm) aluminized Pyrex glass mirror (1) with a focal length of 16.8 m (55 ft). The mirror is mounted in a tube (2) that moves about the declination axis (3) within a yoke (4). The yoke, which forms the polar axis, turns on oil-pad bearings on the northern (5) and southern (6) piers. A 1.5-m (5-ft) cage (7) provides space for an observer at the prime focus (8) and contains the coudé and Cassegrain secondary mirrors (9). The focal lengths are 80.2 m (263 ft) at the Cassegrain focus (10) and 150 m (492 ft) at the coudé focus (11). The telescope is housed in a 42-m-diameter (137-ft) dome with a shutter opening of 9 m (30 ft) and is operated from a main control panel.

THE WORLD'S LARGEST REFLECTING TELESCOPES

Diameter in	m	Observatory	Approximate Location	Went into Operation
236	6.0	Special Astrophysical (BTA telescope)	Zelenchukskaya, USSR	1976
200	5.1	Palomar (Hale telescope)	Palomar Mountain, Calif.	1948
176*	4.5	Mount Hopkins (Multiple Mirror telescope)	Amado, Ariz.	1979
158	4.0	Cerro Tololo Inter-American	La Serena, Chile	1975
158	4.0	Kitt Peak National (Mayall telescope)	Tucson, Ariz.	1973
153	3.9	Siding Spring (Anglo-Australian telescope)	Coonabarabran, New South Wales, Australia	1974
150	3.8	Mauna Kea (United Kingdom infrared telescope)	Mauna Kea, Hawaii	1978
144	3.6	Mauna Kea (Canada-France-Hawaii telescope)	Mauna Kea, Hawaii	1979
142	3.6	European Southern	La Silla, Chile	1977
120	3.0	Mauna Kea (NASA–University of Hawaii infrared telescope)	Mauna Kea, Hawaii	1979
120	3.0	Lick (Shane telescope)	Mt. Hamilton, Calif.	1959
107	2.7	McDonald	Mt. Locke, Texas	1968
102	2.6	Crimean Astrophysical (Shajn telescope)	Partizanskoye, USSR	1960
102	2.6	Byurakan Astrophysical	Yerevan, Armenian SSR	1976
100	2.5	Las Campanas (Irénée du Pont telescope)	Las Campanas, Chile	1977
100	2.5	Mount Wilson (Hooker telescope)	Mount Wilson, Calif.	1917

*The six 72-in (1.8-m) mirrors of the Multiple Mirror telescope used in concert have the light-gathering equivalent of a single mirror of this size.

figuration has the main mirror slightly tilted to feed an eyepiece mounted at one side of the upper end of the tube.

William Parsons, 3d earl of Rosse (1800–67), built (1845) at Birr Castle in Ireland a 72-in (180-cm) reflector with a speculum-metal mirror and used it to observe galaxies. Glass was first used for the manufacture of telescope mirrors in 1856, by Carl August von Steinheil and Jean FOUCAULT; such optical surfaces were silvered by chemical processes developed by Justus von LIEBIG and John A. Brashear. A silver coating on glass is now superseded by vacuum-deposited aluminum and sometimes other metals by means of a technique developed in 1934. Between the world wars, glass with a low coefficient of thermal expansion (Pyrex) came into use, but since World War II such glass has largely been replaced by quartz (fused or vapor-condensed) and in some cases by special ceramics noted for their low thermal expansion.

During the 20th century several large reflecting telescopes were built on mountain sites in clear-air regions. Since World War II, telescope sizes have escalated, and instruments larger than 100 in (2.5 m) in diameter are now common.

OPTICS AND MECHANICS

Visual telescopes perform the functions of light gathering, magnifying, and increasing resolving power.

Light Gathering. The light-gathering power of a telescope is its ability to see faint objects as compared to the ability of the dark-adapted human eye. It is directly proportional to the square of the diameter of the telescope objective. For example, a star viewed by the giant Hale telescope at Palomar Observatory appears approximately one million times as bright as it does to the naked eye.

Magnification. Magnification is the increase in apparent angular size of an object when viewed through a telescope, as compared to the object's apparent size when viewed by the naked eye. Telescope magnification is computable as the ratio of the objective's focal length to the focal length of the telescope's eyepiece. Usually a telescope has several eyepieces for varying the magnification as desired.

Resolving Power. A telescope's resolving power is defined as the minimum angular distance it can determine between two stars of moderate brightness under ideal viewing conditions.

The Multiple Mirror Telescope on Mount Hopkins, Ariz., is housed in a four-story building. As the telescope scans the sky, the entire structure with its support facilities rotates on a circular track.

This minimum distance, measured in RADIANS, is equal to the ratio of the wavelength of the light to the diameter of the telescope's objective. Magnification must be sufficiently substantial to compress the emerging rays to the size of the pupil of the eye, but not so large that the apparent scale greatly exceeds the angular resolution.

Lenses. Simple telescopes of the Galilean type produce erect images, whereas astronomical-type telescopes produce inverted images. Terrestrial eyepieces containing several lenses also produce erect images. Two-lens eyepieces, such as those made by Christiaan Huygens, the British optician Jesse Ramsden, and the German manufacturer Carl ZEISS, improve the correction of aberrations and increase the field of view; a Ramsden eyepiece with an achromatic lens is known as a Kellner eyepiece. The Ramsden eyepiece also allows for the insertion of a glass grid or of cross hairs in the plane of the primary telescope image. Barlow lenses, developed by British physicist Peter Barlow, yield increased magnification. In photographic telescopes the plate is inserted in the plane or curved focal surface of the optical system.

Mountings. Astronomical telescopes are mounted on two perpendicular axes in order to give access to any point in the sky. Telescopes are driven by electric motors to compensate for Earth rotation, so that the telescope continues to point toward a particular celestial object. Most telescopes use the equatorial system of mounting, in which one axis is parallel to the Earth's polar axis and the other axis is used for adjustments in declination. The development of computer-controlled drive along both axes, however, has made altazimuth mountings—mountings on vertical and horizontal axes—desirable, because they are simpler and more economical. Several large telescopes have such mountings, including the Multiple Mirror Telescope (MMT) on Mount Hopkins, Ariz., which operates in the visible and near-ultraviolet spectral regions and performs as an INTERFEROMETER in the infrared.

DESIGN INNOVATIONS

The MMT represents one of several design innovations that have been adopted by telescope makers in the late 20th century to avoid the extreme technical problems of producing very large single mirrors and keeping them from sagging or being otherwise distorted by environmental effects. The MMT, which began operating in 1979, consists of six telescopes, each 72 in (1.8 m) in diameter, that are computer-guided to perform as a single light-gathering mirror 176 in (4.5 m) in diameter. The resolving power is limited to that of the individual mirrors, but when the MMT functions as an interferometer the resolving power is significantly increased.

Other projects adopting the MMT approach include the proposed Columbus project, a joint effort of the University of Arizona, the University of Chicago, Ohio State University, and Italy's Arcetri Astrophysical Observatory. Employing two 316-in (8-m) mirrors, its binocular telescope (to be constructed on Mount Graham, Ariz., by the mid-1990s) will have a light-gathering capacity comparable to a telescope with a single 444-in (11.3-m) mirror. Similarly, the planned Very Large Telescope (VLT) of the European Southern Observatory is designed to consist of four 316-in telescopes that are aligned so as to function as a telescope twice as wide.

Mirrors of a size larger than 200 in (5.1 m) still present major design problems, and one innovative approach to their construction is being used by an American astronomer, Roger Angel. His team, working at the University of Arizona, has developed a technique for spin-casting mirrors rather than starting with giant slabs of cooled glass. Molten borosilicate glass is placed in a mold that creates a lightweight honeycomb backing to the paraboloidal surface produced by spinning the mold. The cooled mirror surface thus produced requires only a fraction of the polishing that was needed for mirrors produced in the traditional way.

The liquid-mirror concept is not new, in the sense that a mirror made of spinning liquid mercury was built and used to view the Moon as early as 1909; and, although liquid-mercury mirrors must remain fixed, they are attracting renewed interest as a low-cost approach to telescope design. Another innovation is the "active optics" proposed for the VLT; hundreds of servomotor-driven mounting points will support the VLT's 4 thin mirrors and counterbalance any warping caused by temperature change or gravity.

(Above) *A telescope mirror is spin-cast at the University of Arizona, using the so-called "spinning oven" developed by a research team led by American astronomer Roger Angel.* (Right) *Standing beside the finished mirror, a technician exhibits its ability to come to a focal point even before it is cleaned. The white filling seen in the honeycomb sections consists of ceramic fibers that are washed away with a pressure sprayer.*

The Keck Telescope being built on Mauna Kea in Hawaii is to have a primary mirror made of 36 hexagonal segments, each with its separate control. Together, they will function as a single parabolic mirror. In this scale model the secondary mirror positioned above the primary is not shown. It will reflect the collected light back through a hole in the center of the primary to optical devices below.

Another innovation is seen in the segmented-mirror design of the Keck Telescope being built on Mauna Kea by the California Institute of Technology and the University of California. The mirror, 400 in (10 m) wide, will consist of 36 hexagonal mirrors each about 72 in (1.8 m) wide and weighing 635 kg (1,400 lb). The mirrors are to be placed under stress and then ground and polished to a spherical shape; when the stress is relieved, the mirrors will assume their desired curvatures for the final, computer-controlled array.

Computerization is, in fact, assuming a leading role in many modern telescope functions. For example, the Advanced Technology Telescope at Australia's Mount Stromlo and Siding Spring Observatories has a fully computerized control system, and a photoelectric telescope at Fairborn Observatory in Arizona is programmed to function completely automatically for up to several years, if desired.

DAVID S. EVANS

Bibliography: Asimov, Isaac, *Eyes on the Universe: A History of the Telescope* (1975); Bell, Louis, *The Telescope* (1981); Cohen, Martin, *In Quest of Telescopes* (1980); Cornell, James, and Carr, John, eds., *Infinite Vistas* (1985); Mammana, D. L., "The Incredible Spinning Oven," *Sky & Telescope*, July 1985; Muirden, James, *How to Use an Astronomical Telescope* (1985); Robinson, L. J., "Update: Telescopes of the Future," *Sky & Telescope*, July 1986; Texereau, Jean, *How to Make a Telescope*, 2d ed. (1984).

See also: OBSERVATORY, ASTRONOMICAL.

Telesio, Bernardino   [tay-lay'-zee-oh]

Bernardino Telesio, b. 1509, d. Oct. 1, 1588, was an Italian philosopher and scientist who reacted against 16th-century Aristotelianism. After early studies in Milan and Rome, he received a doctorate in medicine at Padua in 1535. He taught at Naples and at Cosenza, where with others he formed an academy (today the Accademia Telesiana) dedicated to the pursuit of natural science.

In his work, *De rerum natura* (On the Nature of Things, 1586), Telesio portrays the universe as a closed, determinate system always operating in the same way. From sense data the individual can come to understand and to control the universe. All things arise through the interaction of three principles, heat, cold, and matter, which have been created by God, who exercises a general providence over the universe. Because all nature is governed by these principles, the difference between animate and inanimate existence is a question of degree. Animate beings possess a subtle, or rarified, spirit; they derive knowledge through sensation. Intellection is an inferior form of sensation. Pleasure and pain are sensations produced by health and decay, and behavior accords with the instinct of self-preservation. Unlike other animals, human beings are endowed by God with a higher soul.   JOHN P. DOYLE

Bibliography: Abbagnano, Nicola, *Bernardino Telesio* (1941); Cassirer, Ernst, *The Individual and the Cosmos in Renaissance Philosophy* (1963); Fallico, A. B., and Shapiro, H., eds., *The Italian Philosophers* (1967), vol. 1 in *Renaissance Philosophy*; Kristeller, Paul O., *Eight Philosophers of the Italian Renaissance* (1964); Van Deusen, N. C., *Telesio, the First of the Moderns* (1932).

teletext

Teletext is the generic name for electronic systems that transmit data via broadcast or cable TV signals to specially equipped television receivers. Teletext services generally provide about 100 "pages," or frames, of text and graphic information, usually timely material such as news headlines, sports scores, weather, and traffic or financial reports. Information is grouped by subject "menus," and viewers can request that frames be displayed on demand, usually by keying numbers into a hand-held, remote-control device. Entertainment information (such as TV program listings) and TV program captions (for hearing-impaired viewers or foreign-language subtitles) can also be transmitted via teletext.

Teletext systems use the "vertical blanking interval" (VBI) of the TV signal. The VBI is a thick black bar that may be seen when the video signal rolls on a TV screen; it carries 21 scanning lines, 8 of which have been allocated by the Federal Communications Commission (FCC) for teletext and data transmission. Teletext data is encoded within a standard TV signal, but users must have a special decoder to retrieve and view the text and graphic content. Such decoders may be built into a TV set or cable TV decoder, or may be installed as an external device.

National networks and local stations may develop and transmit teletext material. CBS-TV has offered "Extravision" teletext on a limited basis since 1983. At about the same time, Taft Broadcasting began transmitting "Electra" teletext on its TV station in Cincinnati, Ohio and nationally to cable TV viewers. A paucity of decoders has severely limited the number of U.S. teletext viewers. By 1986 fewer than 5,000 U.S. homes had regular access to teletext. This low usage encouraged broadcasters to explore other uses of the VBI for data transmission to business or institutional customers rather than to home viewers.

Teletext has been offered widely in Europe since the late 1970s. In Great Britain more than 3.5 million homes are equipped with decoders to watch "Ceefax" (the British Broadcasting Corporation's teletext service) and "Oracle" (Independent TV's teletext).   GARY ARLEN

Bibliography: Veith, Richard, *Television's Teletext* (1983).

television

Television is the electronic transmission of moving images with accompanying sound, sent—usually in color—from a central source or sources to home television screens.

From the 1950s, when television viewing first became common in the United States, until the mid-1970s the technology available to the television audience was relatively simple and consisted essentially of a TV set. The last decade, however, has seen an explosion of new devices for home entertainment, all of them outgrowths of basic television technology. The entire field, including television itself, is now referred to as *video*, a word that includes in its meaning almost all the systems devoted to electronically creating images.

The article VIDEO introduces the field with a discussion of its history, the industries involved in producing video devices, and the effect of various branches of video on education, business, and communications. VIDEO TECHNOLOGY describes the basic science underlying video techniques and devices and outlines the various technologies involved. VIDEO ART, VIDEO GAMES, and VIDEO MUSIC are outgrowths of the technology that are both entertaining and offer practical and artistic possibilities. The PAINTBOX is a basic tool of the video artist.

VIDEOTEX and TELETEXT are methods of providing two-way interaction between the television viewer and the broadcaster or cable system. VIDEO CAMERA and VIDEO RECORDING describe the methods used to record images and sound electronically.

TELEVISION PRODUCTION describes how a TV program is made. TELEVISION TRANSMISSION outlines the various types of image transmission, including CABLE TV and COMMUNICATIONS SATELLITES. TELEVISION, NONCOMMERCIAL discusses the history and functions of educational and public television. RADIO AND TELEVISION BROADCASTING examines the development of each industry and their relationship to one another.

television, noncommercial

Noncommercial television is a system of broadcasting that is financed by means other than advertising revenues. In noncommercial television, stations supply programs directly to the audience, whereas, it might be said, commercial television supplies audiences to advertisers. That, rather than diverging programming philosophies, is the essential difference between the two systems. Broadcast television, in all its forms, is *the* mass medium of our time, with a reach greater than that of any other means of communication. Historically, commercialism has been criticized for inhibiting the free expression of television's vast potential. Much of television's best programming, however, has been that which recognizes and builds on the reality of broadcasting's mass appeal, rather than that which fights against it.

The United States. As U.S. television broadcasting blossomed in the 1940s and '50s, it reflected well-established patterns of radio broadcasting with regard to financing as well as to regulation. Commercial television broadcasting came to derive its economic power from the existence of three networks whose coordination of broadcast schedules allows the airing of advertisements on a nationwide basis. Ironically, the controlling power of the networks has no recognition in U.S. broadcasting law. As the broadcasting scholar Erik Barnouw has observed, the Communications Act of 1934 (a slightly modified reenactment of a 1927 law and the basis for all U.S. radio and television broadcasting regulations) was based on a notion that was out of date in 1927 and completely without foundation in 1934: "that American broadcasting was a local responsibility exercised by individual station licensees." Thus, government assumed no responsibility for encouraging noncommercial (or commercial) broadcasting.

The development of future noncommercial television broadcasting was also thwarted in 1934, with the defeat of the Wagner-Hatfield bill, which would have allocated 25 percent of U.S. broadcasting frequencies for educational purposes. Although schools and colleges had been among the most active of radio broadcasting's pioneers (72 educational stations were on the air by 1923), the absence of a protected portion of the spectrum for these stations caused a decline throughout the 1930s and '40s. Commercial broadcasters aired a certain amount of nonprofit, "sustaining" programming; how much (and how good) depended mostly on their public-relations needs, which fluctuated widely.

Noncommercial television broadcasting languished until 1952, when Frieda Hennock, a member of the Federal Communications Commission appointed by President Harry S. Truman, spearheaded a drive to reserve as-yet unlicensed television channels for education. Set aside were 242 channels, but most of them were in the hard-to-tune ultra-high-frequency (UHF) band—and no funds were allocated to pay for programs or administration. Nonetheless, a loosely knit chain of educational television stations emerged in the 1950s and early 1960s, funded at first by the Ford Foundation and after 1962 by grants from the federal government.

In 1967, Congress passed the Public Broadcasting Act, and noncommercial television and radio in the United States had a national mandate for the first time. Great care was taken, however, that Public Broadcasting not become a "fourth network." Authority to run the system was divided between competing local stations (303 by 1984) and two overlapping Washington bureaucracies: the Public Broadcasting Service (PBS) and the Corporation for Public Broadcasting (CPB). Chronically underfunded, PBS is financed principally from viewer donations, private sponsoring underwriters, and congressional appropriations (which were reduced markedly in 1982). Thus

hampered, public television was subjected to open manipulation by Presidents Lyndon B. Johnson and Richard M. Nixon, as well as more subtle pressures by subsequent administrations. It has evolved into a generally noncontroversial and noncompetitive supplement to the commercial networks.

The strongest area of public broadcasting's schedule is in cultural programming—science documentaries, concerts, operas, plays (especially historical costume dramas), and children's programs. Many of the best children's programs—including, notably, SESAME STREET—have been products of the Children's Television Workshop, an independent, nonprofit organization. Public television's weakest area is in public affairs, a fact underscored by the 1984 cancellation of "Inside Story," one of PBS's few regularly scheduled news-documentary series, because of discontinued funding.

Although public television provides entertaining and well-produced programs for America's upscale professionals, it has most often been the commercial networks that have pioneered new forms, bold topics, and unorthodox concepts. Public television has been too poor, too divided against itself, and too uncertain of its goals to play it anything but safe.

Other Countries. Probably the best-known noncommercial television system is the British Broadcasting Corporation (BBC), created by royal charter in 1927. Its founder, Lord Reith, was a Scotsman with a deeply religious sense of public duty. The BBC was established to "educate and enlighten" as well as to entertain, and a deep sense of mission has always pervaded the organization. This philosophy is diametrically opposed to the American system, in which commercial broadcasters attempt to anticipate and fulfill viewer preferences. In one classic definition, "the 'public interest' means that which interests the public." The BBC's dedication to quality programming has made it "the least bad broadcasting company in the world," according to its friends, but stuffy and paternalistic to those who are less enthusiastic about its virtues.

The BBC, and many similar broadcasting organizations in Western Europe and Japan, are funded on an entirely different basis from American public television. An annual license fee on every television set in the country ensures not only adequate operating revenues, but also financial stability, political insulation, and room for long-range planning. Since 1954, Britain has had a "mixed" broadcasting system, with the profit-oriented Independent Broadcasting Authority now running two of Britain's four television channels.

Canada also has a dual system. The Canadian Broadcasting Corporation (CBC), a public body created in 1936, is financed by the government, with supplementary advertising revenue. Canada's commercial network is CTV.

In recent years various Western countries have tried to retain BBC-like quality while increasing decentralization as well as access by a wide range of constituents. Dutch television, perhaps because it was so frequently a target of illegal "pirate" stations operating just outside Dutch territorial waters, provides airtime to groups ranging from political dissidents to radical homosexuals. Italy has a de-facto two-tiered system, with the government operating the noncommercial Radio-televisione Italiana (RAI) on a nationwide basis, and a plethora of small, local stations broadcasting "alternative" services.

The best-financed (and perhaps technically most advanced) noncommercial broadcasting system is the Japanese NHK, which exists side-by-side with commercial stations.

Government-controlled Soviet and Communist-bloc broadcasters do not have the political independence that is so fundamental to Western systems, but in order to maintain acceptable levels of viewership, both technical quality and programming sophistication have improved in recent years. The most stringently controlled systems are those in authoritarian developing countries, where television and radio are frequently used for personal propaganda by the chief of state.

Perhaps, as the media analyst Anthony Smith has observed, the way a country organizes its broadcasting system reveals "a strange coded version of that country's entire political culture." International systems have seldom followed the lead of U.S. commercial television operations. It is the BBC that is most frequently admired.

PAUL MARETH

Bibliography: Barnouw, Erik, *Tube of Plenty* (1975; repr. 1982); British Broadcasting Corporation, *Annual Report* (1984); Carnegie Commission on Educational Television, *Public Television: A Program for Action* (1967) and *A Public Trust* (1979); Frank, Ronald E., and Greenberg, Marshall G., *Audiences for Public TV* (1982); Head, Sydney, and Sterling, Christopher, *Broadcasting in America,* 4th ed. (1982); Lesser, Gerald, *Children and Television: Lessons from Sesame Street* (1974); Smith, Anthony, *The Shadow in the Cave: The Broadcaster, His Audience and the State* (1973).

television production

A television production is the creation of a television show. In a broader sense, TV production also involves pre- and post-production activities such as scriptwriting, set design, and videotape editing.

Television production is loosely divided into broadcast and nonbroadcast. Broadcast television is generally produced by the commercial TV stations and professional production companies that make the dramas, comedy series, newscasts, documentaries, game shows, and advertisements familiar to television viewers. Nonbroadcast television is produced for a much narrower audience. Businesses, private production companies, and some college TV studios specialize in creating educational and industrial programming used in schools or for on-the-job training. Much of today's TV production is performed on a small scale in hospitals, churches, and schools for demonstration or training purposes, for recording speeches, or for documenting events. Some of these shows may appear on the public channels made available to communities by their cable-system operators.

The Production Staff. In small educational, cable, and industrial TV studios, all phases of a TV production might be handled by one or two people. In larger commercial studios and broadcast TV stations, teleproduction activities are assigned to a number of specialists. They include the executive producer, who manages budget and coordinates advertising and other financial support. He or she is often in charge of several programs or series. The producer hires personnel for an individual production and coordinates production elements. The director directs talent during production, selects shots, and coordinates the production crew, transforming the script into the final TV production. TV writers range from those who create dramas and other staged fiction to the staff people who script news reports and other verbal material. A TV script usually includes rough visual and sound directions. "Talent" includes actors, reporters, hosts, guests, off-camera narrators—anyone who appears before the camera, or whose voice is heard.

The camera operator aims and moves the camera and composes shots. The audio engineer mixes sound from the studio microphones with recorded music and sound effects to produce the final sound that will be broadcast or recorded. The technical director operates the camera switcher, switching from camera to camera upon command from the director. The lighting director aims and balances the brightness of the studio lights. The video engineer adjusts electronic camera controls for optimal TV picture, and may also operate the videotape recorders. The floor manager supervises studio activities, relays the director's cues to the talent, handles cue cards, and coordinates the work of the stagehands who set up and move sets, props, and equipment.

Finally, the editor takes the original tapes, which contain both video and audio tracks, and melds all the segments together using editing videocassette recorders and other electronic instruments.

Video Equipment Systems. In a TV studio the cameras send their pictures (video) into the control room, where the signals are passed to a switcher/special effects generator and to a bank of control-room monitors. The director chooses the desired shot from these camera monitors and calls it out to the technical director. The technical director then pushes the corresponding button on the switcher, selecting that particular shot to be recorded or broadcast. Switching instantly from one picture to another is called a cut. Other controls on the switcher permit pictures to be mixed together in various ways,

resembling the basic effects used in movie editing: fade in, fade out, dissolve, split screen. In the wipe, a border moves across the screen, replacing one picture with another. In the key, text, graphics, or parts of another scene appear to be laid over the original TV image. For the chroma key, a performer or prop is shown before a blue background, which is then electronically removed from the picture and replaced with another camera's picture—a weather map, for example.

The more elaborate digital video effects whereby a picture can be bent, rotated, wrapped into a cylinder, or molded into a ball require digital frame store devices, which divide the picture into thousands of picture elements (pixels) and convert these elements into numbers. These numbers are algebraically manipulated by computer and then converted back into a modified picture. For instance, doubling all the horizontal pixels would create a picture stretched to twice its normal width.

Electronically generated titles and graphics, video from another videotape, or a signal received from a satellite or from a portable microwave transmitter several miles away may provide other visual elements that can be mixed with the camera shots. Photographic slides and films can also be mixed, once they have been translated into video images in a machine called a telecine.

Sound (audio) is picked up by microphones in the studio and is routed to an audio mixing console, where the sound engineer and the director select which mikes are to be heard and their sound levels. Recorded music, sound effects, or the sound from other videotapes or movies can also be mixed with the microphone sound. The final audio and video signals are then recorded on a videotape recorder or are sent to a transmission facility to be broadcast "live."

TV cameras must have their electronic signals synchronized with one another, in order for their pictures to be mixable by the switcher. This task is performed by a master sync generator. The sync generator may also be used to create test signals like color bars, which are used by the video engineer to calibrate and adjust the color video signals in the system.

The most important video test equipment is the waveform monitor and the vectorscope. The waveform monitor graphically displays the video signal's intensity. The strengths of the various components of this signal are compared and matched to a standard marked on the waveform monitor's screen. The vectorscope measures the phase of color video test signals, and displays this information as dots on the vectorscope screen. When the color is adjusted correctly, the dots fall exactly within little boxes etched on its screen.

Portable TV systems may have only one camera connected to one video tape recorder; or they may have several cameras controlled from a miniature control room in a van or trailer.

The central device in a television control booth is the switcher, which cuts between two or more video sources (camera and videotape, for example), adding effects and superimposing titles and other graphics.

Both the newscaster and the cameramen in the studio at Cable News Network wear headphones to hear directions from the control booth. The newscaster's is an almost invisible speaker lodged in one ear.

The Cosby family at home on TV. The interior of their house has been built in "sets," realistic sections of kitchen, living room, and other spaces that are large enough for both cast and cameras to move easily.

The camera signals can be monitored for quality, switched or mixed, and recorded; or they can be transmitted via microwave back to the main studio to be combined with other elements of the TV show.

In postproduction, videotape is edited, and special effects, titles or graphics, and sound effects may be added. Most complex TV productions are assembled in postproduction because it is nearly impossible to coordinate live the many shots, decisions, and details that go into such productions.

The Making of a TV Series. The process begins with a concept proposal, usually submitted by a film company or independent producer. If the proposal is accepted the producer prepares a budget for a pilot episode and selects a TV director. During the following weeks, location scouts, casting directors, and wardrobe, makeup, set-design, special-effects, and music personnel are hired, along with production crews and talent. The pilot may be produced on a sound stage before a live audience or shot on location. The network entertainment president may then decide to cancel the project or—after test-marketing—schedule the program for broadcast.

The Production of a News Program. An evening network newscast begins to take shape at the noon rundown meeting between the executive producer and the production staff, where 25 or so stories are chosen to pursue. Also in attendance, via a conference phone call, will be news bureau chiefs, both foreign and domestic, offering stories that are being followed by their reporters. Each bureau then begins writing, recording, and editing the videotape for its particular story. The bureaus generally produce several, different-length versions of a story, and—via courier or satellite—transmit the stories back to the head office at around 5:00 PM Eastern time.

As the stories come in, the executive producer begins to organize the final rundown of stories, selecting the 14 to 20 stories that will air that evening. The associate director calculates the timing and duration of the stories so that the newscast lasts exactly 22½ minutes out of a 30-minute program that includes commercials. The associate director also arranges for names, titles, and graphics to be prepared to accompany the live parts of the newscast or to introduce taped segments. Meanwhile, staff writers prepare the newscasters' scripts, which include lead-ins to each story. Late-breaking stories may be filed only minutes before air time, and some appear live, making it necessary to constantly juggle the remaining stories before and during the newscast.

During the production the TV director selects the camera shots and calls for the videotapes to be played on cue. Meanwhile, the entire broadcast is being recorded for delayed playback to the West Coast one-half hour later. Often, late-breaking news events or technical difficulties make it necessary to perform the newscast live a second time rather than use the recorded newscast.

Foresight is the virtue that makes it possible for a news team to produce such complicated shows on a daily basis. Background information and video segments are collected days in advance for stories that *may* occur. ENG (Electronic News Gathering) crews are sent to locations where a newsworthy event may take place. Reporters will often follow numerous quiet stories, anticipating that when one erupts into a solid news story, they will be ready with background facts, contacts, and sources to interview.

Local news is produced mostly live, with prerecorded segments played during the newscast. The news content is under more local control, with newscasters writing much of their own scripts, reporting some of the events directly, and editing the videotape for their own feature stories.

Sportscasting. Sportscasts are usually performed live with multiple cameras positioned to provide different views of the action. A temporary control room, usually in a van or trailer, houses the TV monitors, switcher, audio, and other production equipment. The director sits in the control room, selecting the camera shots and calling for titles, graphic inserts, or prerecorded segments. An announcing booth houses the sports commentators, who are supplied with one or more TV monitors, allowing them to comment on replays or sideline shots.

Although most cameras are wired directly to the van's control room, some cameras are totally portable, transmitting their pictures via microwave to nearby repeaters, which boost the signal and beam it back to the control room.

Several cameras may send their signals directly to videotape recorders, making it possible for the director to call for an instant replay from one of them.

Preparations for major events, such as the Olympics, begin months before their occurrence. Miles of trenches may be dug to hold TV and power cables. Camera platforms are built at strategic lookout points. Independent power supplies and back-up supplies are built to assure uninterrupted power. A complex telephone and intercom system is constructed to enable instructions or reports to reach every point in the production area.   PETER UTZ

Bibliography: Gianakos, Larry, J., *Television Drama Series Programming: A Comprehensive Chronicle* (1980); Hilliard, Robert, *Television Broadcasting: An Introduction,* 2d ed. (1978); Hunter, Julius, and Gross, Lynne S., *Broadcast News: The Inside Out* (1980); Litman, Barry R., *Vertical Structure of the Television Broadcasting Industry* (1979); Long, Stewart, *The Development of the Television Network Oligopoly* (1979); Matusow, Barbara, *The Evening Stars: The Making of a Network News Anchor* (1984); Rader, Benjamin G., *In Its Own Image: How Television Has Transformed Sports* (1984); Stephens, Mitchell, *Broadcast News: Radio Journalism and an Introduction to Television* (1980); Utz, Peter, *Video User's Handbook,* 2d ed. (1982); Wurtzel, Alan, *Television Production,* 2d ed. (1983); Zettl, Herbert, *Television Production Handbook,* 4th ed. (1984).

television transmission

Television images can be relayed from one point to another by a variety of transmission systems, which include the following: (1) Over-the-air propagation of ELECTROMAGNETIC RADIATION, or waves, such as those used for ordinary TV broadcasting. These are normally radiated in an omnidirectional pattern, and over 85 million TV households in the United States receive such transmissions. (2) The use of dedicated lines (cables laid underground or strung on existing power or telephone poles) with either metallic or fiber-optic cores that carry the signals and connect the program source (the head end) with the subscriber. Cable television serves 43% of all TV households. (3) Geosynchronous or orbiting satellites receiving TV signals from a ground station (uplink) and relaying them back to Earth over an antenna that covers a specified terrestrial area. Receiving dishes (TVROs, for Television Receive Only) can be fairly small for home use, or large and powerful, like those used in "Earth stations" by cable companies and TV networks.

The Television Channel. Television signals are transmitted over internationally allocated blocks of frequencies referred to as channels. These channels are situated in various noncontiguous frequency ranges of the electromagnetic spectrum (see RADIO). These ranges are: (1) Very High Frequency (VHF): 54–72 MHz (channels 2–4), 76–88 MHz (channels 5–6), and 174–216 MHz (channels 7–13); (2) Ultra High Frequency (UHF): 470–806 MHz (channels 14–69); and (3) Super High Frequency (SHF): 0.9–40 GHz for terrestrial and satellite services.

Television transmission systems around the world are not uniform, and various countries use both different image-scanning rates and different channel bandwidths. Consequently, there is no compatibility between television broadcasts in North America and Europe. This means a standard American TV set will not work properly in most European countries.

Television image scanning consists of horizontal lines that are sequentially displaced in a vertical direction until the whole image area is covered (see VIDEO TECHNOLOGY). When no picture information is present, the full set of scanning lines is called a raster. The scanning of a single image is called a field, and the horizontal and vertical scan rates are normally synchronous with the local power-line frequency. Because the world is generally divided into 50-Hz and 60-Hz electrical power frequencies, television systems use either 50-field or 60-field image-scanning rates.

The television broadcasting standards now in use include 525 lines, 60 fields in North America, Japan, and other U.S.-oriented countries, and 625 lines, 50 fields in Europe, Australia, most of Asia, Africa, and a few South American countries.

RF (Radio Frequency) spectra and channel allocations also vary outside of North America. VHF frequencies extend from 45.0 MHz to 229.75 MHz, and UHF from 471.25 MHz to 860.75 MHz. The normal North American channel bandwidth (the width of frequencies required to carry the channel) is 6.0 MHz, with the video and sound carriers displaced, or separated, by 4.5 MHz. Other areas use a variety of channel bandwidths and video-to-sound carrier displacement.

The assignment of television channels in the electromagnetic frequency spectrum is not only for normal home television services, but also for a variety of broadcast-related services that transmit images and sound between various points. VHF and UHF are, of course, purely home-viewer-oriented frequency bands, but the SHF bands cater to the multiple distribution services (MDS) of pay-per-view TV systems in the 2.15-GHz range. Some 2.0–4.0–GHz channel allocations are for television studios to send news stories back over terrestrial or satellite links from their Electronic News Gathering (ENG) mobile vehicles, and the 4.0–6.0–GHz band is used by cable TV companies to distribute primary program material to their head-end (studio) facilities. The KU band, 12.0–14.0 GHz, is also used for internal network distribution of programs and data by the national networks, such as NBC and PBS.

Terrestrial Broadcast Systems. These systems include both omnidirectional broadcasting and point-to-point broadcasting

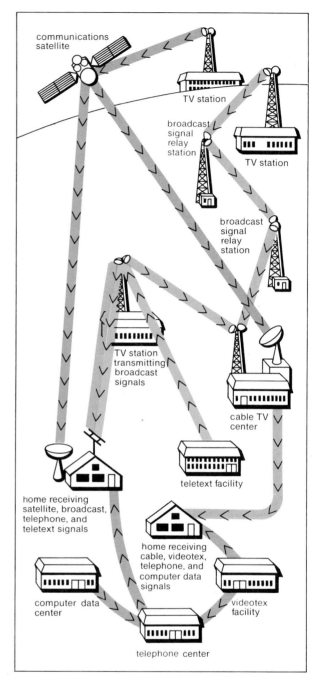

In this schematic view of the different modes of television transmission, the blue represents the most basic and the oldest system: broadcast transmission, where a TV station sends its signal out from a tower, and it is picked up and retransmitted in areas—such as valleys—where the signal often fades. The red lines are communications satellite signals, which are received by the satellite from TV networks, cable, TV production, and other companies, and are returned to "earth stations," large, commercially operated dish antennas. To prevent unpaid use of satellite signals by home dish owners, many signals are now scrambled, and all dish owners must use decoders in order to receive them. Brown is the cable wire, which carries satellite and broadcast signals to home subscribers. The green represents videotex and computer transmissions via telephone, as well as ordinary telephone signals. The orange is the teletext signal— actually part of the TV signal, but receivable only by those with special teletext decoders.

using line-of-sight propagation. The omnidirectional systems can include both high- and low-power TV stations that radiate their programs over a given service area using an antenna placed at the highest altitude possible overlooking that area. Local topography, including hills, valleys, or high-rise buildings, will interfere with the reception of the TV signals if they are adjacent to, or between, the transmitting antenna and the home receiver. The interference will appear as a multipath signal or "ghost" displaced to the right of the principal image, and be either negative or positive. Ghosting is due to reflections from these nearby surfaces, which create a secondary TV signal that arrives at the home receiver antenna a little later than the direct signal.

Unlike lower-frequency radio waves, which travel around terrestrial obstacles, television signals radiate in straight lines, and in hilly or mountainous terrain the signal shadows in the valleys prohibit good TV reception. To overcome this, TV stations have low-power satellite repeaters that pick up the original signal at a point above the valley, then retransmit it into the shadow area.

Low-power television (LPTV) is also used for limited coverage of a primary service area by broadcasters catering to a particular group of viewers with some specific commonality, such as religion, ethnic background, business interests, and so on.

Point-to-point broadcast systems usually use SHF links to provide transmission of TV images from the studio to the transmitter, or from a news event to the studio. These transmissions are made over parabolic (dish) antennas ranging in diameter from 0.3 to 1.8 m (1 to 6 ft) and are set up to "look" at each other over the distance to be covered. The same principle is used in the distribution of some subscriber entertainment, although in this case the transmitting antenna may cover a wider angle, while the small receiving rooftop dishes are aimed at the transmitter.

All omnidirectional TV broadcast systems are limited in radiating their electromagnetic signals to the geographic horizon, and these signals decay in strength as the square of the distance. Therefore home viewers in the primary signal area, or within a 48-km (30-mi) radius, get an acceptable picture, but beyond that radius, "fringe area" reception will have a "snowy" appearance due to noise mixed with the TV signal.

Nonbroadcast Systems. There are two additional methods of bringing television signals to the home: cable television and satellite transmission. Cable first developed to serve shadow areas, by putting up a community antenna and distributing the signals by coaxial cable to the homes in the valley. These were called CATV systems and were often simply cooperative ventures among neighbors.

Eventually it became obvious that picking up a variety of clear channel signals and redistributing them, to viewers willing to pay both for better picture quality and for a greater range of programming, was a viable business. Cable companies today pick up local and distant channels with high-quality receiving dishes to bring in special programming such as HBO, ESPN, or the Disney channel. All of these channels are processed at the cable-TV facility (head end) and are then redistributed to subscribers on the same or newly allocated channels.

Cable television is most easily installed in areas where there are no problems with stringing or trenching wires, and where population density can support the capital outlay needed to implement a system. City-center urban areas impose high installation complexity and cost, while remote areas do not have the potential subscribership to warrant the expense. Cable's greatest advantage is its ability to bring a large number of channels to the subscriber and to provide some interactivity between the viewer and the head end.

COMMUNICATIONS SATELLITES for television use are launched by such private companies as RCA or Western Union, as well as by Intelsat (International Telecommunications Satellite Consortium). The U.S. satellites beam TV signals to Earth from geostationary equatorial orbits, 35,900 km (22,300 mi) above Earth's surface. They are positioned between 75° and 145° west latitudes, at 3° (2,202 km/1,377 mi) or 2° (1,468 km/918 mi)

A solar-powered satellite maintains its geosynchronous orbit over the Earth's equator. Its main dish antenna casts a "footprint"—the area where its signals are received—over the continental United States, while a spot antenna covers the islands of Hawaii.

spacing, to cover the North American continent. Their transmitting antennas are positioned to create a "footprint"—a particular area on the continent that is covered by their signal. Each satellite has many transponders, devices that receive signals from Earth, amplify, change signal frequency, and retransmit them. Each transponder can transmit one color-TV channel, or relay a large number of audio or data signals in channels within its frequency spectrum. Transponder capacity may increase in the future, as will the number of transponders per satellite, which may grow from the present 24 to as many as 40.

Satellite transmissions are used to efficiently distribute TV and radio programs from one geographic location to another by networks, cable companies, individual broadcasters, program providers, and industrial, educational, and other organizations. Programs intended for specific subscribers are scrambled so that only the intended recipients, with appropriate decoders, can receive the program. Satellites are also used to relay long-distance telephone service for subscribers, and to transmit high-density business data between banks and other large computer data users.

Direct broadcast satellites (DBS) are another means of giving viewers access to TV programming, although at this time operational plans exist only in Europe and Japan. When they come, DBS systems in North America will operate in the KU band (12.0–19.0 GHz). Their signals will be picked up by

This small home dish antenna receives signals from a powerful direct broadcast satellite (DBS), amplifies them with a low-noise amplifier, and converts them to a lower frequency for display by a TV receiver.

home satellite receivers, small-dish TVROs that are aimed at the specific satellite carrying the desired programs. DBS home systems consist of the receiving dish antenna and a low-noise amplifier that boosts the antenna signal level and feeds it to a coaxial cable. The cable converts the SHF signals to lower frequencies and puts them on channels that the home TV set can display.

DBS satellites must have the capacity to beam very powerful signals back to the small dishes (some may be only 0.3m/1 ft in diameter) that will be used by homeowners, and they will therefore cost almost twice as much as ordinary satellites. Japan has already launched an experimental DBS satellite for home use, and France is planning to launch two.

Ancillary TV Services. The television channel may be used in part, or totally, to provide ancillary information to the viewer that is not primarily intended for home entertainment. These services may be program related, such as closed captioning for the hearing impaired, or nonprogram related, such as teletext, or videotex. Another potential is high-definition television (HDTV), which would be transmitted in a nonstandard method.

Closed captioning uses a blank line (number 21) in the vertical interval of the TV signal to transmit digital data carrying subtitles for the program material. A special decoder in the home TV receiver converts this data into captions on the TV screen.

TELETEXT uses a number of blank lines (lines 11–18) in the vertical interval to provide high-speed digital data containing ''pages'' of information that the viewer can select and display by using a numeric keypad that controls a special teletext decoder. This information covers topics such as news, weather, sports, shopping, and so on and includes a sophisticated closed-captioning service.

VIDEOTEX transmissions use high-speed data signals in a full TV channel that is designated solely as an information source. It provides viewers with a wide variety of high-density information from data bands that have access to stock-market quotations (such as Dow Jones), news wires (UPI), airline, train, or bus schedules, product catalogs, encyclopedia articles, business information from financial data bases, and so forth. The viewer uses a keyboard attached to the TV set, with a videotex decoder, to find the desired information.

High-definition television uses more lines and a much wider bandwidth to generate images of exceptionally higher quality than normal television. Because of this, special-broadcast transmission systems and HDTV receivers are needed. Different HDTV systems use more than 1,000 horizontal lines and 50 to 100 fields to scan and display these high-quality television images.

TV Broadcast Industry Status. Cable and satellite services have had a great effect on the television industry in both North America and Europe. In North America, especially in Canada and the United States where cable penetration is high and where satellite reception is widespread, there has been a downward trend in network viewership that has caused some curtailment of network services. New, smaller network associations are forming that challenge the traditional national networks, because satellite linkups are cost effective and easily established. Intercontinental TV program distribution is now so commonplace that multinational networks can also form, if there are no political restraints.

In Europe, where technological innovations are slower to impact home TV services and because television in European countries is under much tighter government control, the effect of cable and satellite services will be felt only after these services become operational at the end of the 1980s, and into the 1990s.

For the home viewer in the United States, these additional services, coupled with VCR and VIDEODISC developments, continue to provide a much broader range of programming and a much more convenient way of obtaining entertainment and information than any ever offered before.   JOSEPH ROIZEN

Bibliography: Knowledge Industry Publ., eds., *Video Age: TV Technology and Applications in the 1980s* (1982); Martin, James, *The Wired Society* (1978).

telex: see TELEGRAPH.

Telford, Thomas

Thomas Telford, b. Aug. 9, 1757, d. Sept. 2, 1834, was an innovative British engineer renowned for his construction of roads, bridges, and canals. In Scotland alone, Telford built more than 1,450 km (900 mi) of roads, 120 bridges, and the Caledonian canal and built or improved harbors at Aberdeen and Dundee. The famous suspension bridges over the Menai Strait (1819–25) and the Conway estuary (1826) were built by Telford, who also developed improved road-building techniques.

Bibliography: Pearce, R. M., *Thomas Telford* (1973); Penfold, Alastair, ed., *Thomas Telford, Engineer* (1980).

tell

A tell (or tepe), in Middle Eastern archaeology, is a mound formed by the successive buildup of mud-brick construction and other cultural debris of ancient ruins. The superposition of cultural layers in a tell provides the archaeologist with a chronological sequence of its human habitation.

PHILIP KOHL

Tell, William

William Tell is a legendary hero of Switzerland and a universal symbol of resistance to oppression. He was supposedly a native of Bürglen in the area of Uri, which was under the tyrannical control of the bailiffs of Austrian overlords.

In 1307, Tell is supposed to have refused to obey the commands of Bailiff Gessler. He was then forced to shoot an apple placed on the head of his son (a familiar folklore motif); he succeeded and went on to lead a victorious uprising. The German dramatist J. C. Friedrich von SCHILLER wrote *William Tell* (1804), a play that Gioacchino ROSSINI made into an opera.

Tell el-Sultan: see JERICHO.

Tell Hariri: see MARI.

Tell-Tale Heart, The

A short story by Edgar Allan POE, ''The Tell-Tale Heart'' (1843) concerns premeditated murder and compulsive confession. The narrator must kill because his victim has a vulturelike eye. Hiding the dismembered corpse under the floor, the narrator confidently welcomes the police but soon hears a pulsation that intensifies; he attempts to stop it by screaming out the truth. The tale has rising dramatic tension, and the reader wonders, Whose heart did the narrator really hear?

ROBERT L. GALE

Teller, Edward

Edward Teller, b. Jan. 15, 1908, is a Hungarian-born American physicist known for his work on the hydrogen bomb. During World War II he was a member of the MANHATTAN PROJECT for the development of the atomic bomb. At that time he also began formulating the theoretical foundations for a hydrogen fusion bomb and was a major proponent of its development. He received (1962) the Atomic Energy Commission's Fermi Award and has received other honors and awards for his contributions to chemical and nuclear physics.   JAMES A. BOOTH

Bibliography: Blumberg, Stanley A., and Owens, Gwinn, *Energy and Conflict: The Life and Times of Edward Teller* (1976); Teller, Edward, *The Reluctant Revolutionary* (1964); York, Herbert, *The Advisors: Oppenheimer, Teller, and the Superbomb* (1976).

Teller, Henry Moore

Henry Moore Teller, b. Allegany County, N.Y., May 23, 1830, d. Feb. 23, 1914, a U.S. senator (1876–82, 1885–1909) from

Colorado, was known mainly for the Teller Resolution (1898); attached to the declaration of war against Spain, it committed the United States to an independent Cuba. Teller was also secretary of the interior (1882–85). He broke with the Republicans in 1896 over the free-silver issue and became a founder of the Silver Republican party. In 1900 he became a Democrat. Despite his sponsorship of the Teller Resolution, he voted against a similar independence pledge for the Philippines.

Bibliography: Ellis, Elmer, *Henry Moore Teller, Defender of the West* (1941).

Téllez, Gabriel: see TIRSO DE MOLINA.

Telloh: see LAGASH.

telluride minerals [tel'-yuh-ryd]

The telluride minerals are natural metallic compounds, tellurium based but mineralogically similar to the SULFIDE MINERALS. They occur mainly in veins associated with gold, silver, nickel, and copper ore deposits. The principal species are CALAVERITE, KRENNERITE, and SYLVANITE, which are tellurides of gold and silver; muthmannite is similar to and intimately associated with these minerals. Other tellurides include tetradymite, a metallic steel-gray bismuth telluride (hardness, 1½ to 2; specific gravity, 7.3); hessite and petzite, metallic-gray silver tellurides (hardness, 2 to 3; specific gravity, 8.2 to 9.0); and melonite, a metallic reddish white nickel telluride (hardness, 1 to 1½; specific gravity, 7.4).

tellurium [tel-ur'-ee-uhm]

The chemical element tellurium, located in Group VIA of the periodic table, is a grayish white, brittle, lustrous solid. Its symbol is Te, its atomic number 52, and its atomic weight 127.6 (average weight of its 8 naturally occurring isotopes). Although it exhibits some metallic characteristics, tellurium is classed as a nonmetal. Its chemical properties resemble those of selenium. Tellurium was first extracted by F. J. M. von Reichenstein in 1782. M. H. Klaproth suggested (1798) that the new element be named for the Latin word for earth, *tellus*. Tellurium is used to increase ductility in steel and copper alloys and to color glass and ceramics.

Tellus: see GAEA.

Telstar

Telstar was the first commercial experiment in the use of active-repeater communications satellites in low, elliptical orbits. *Telstar 1* was launched by a Delta rocket from Cape Canaveral on July 10, 1962. It went into an orbit with an apogee of 5,636 km (3,503 mi) and a perigee of 954 km (593 mi) at an angle of 44.8° to the equator and with a period of 158 min. *Telstar 2* was similarly launched on May 7, 1963, with an apogee of 10,801 km (6,713 mi) and a perigee of 972 km (604 mi) at an angle of 42.7° to the equator and with a period of 225 min.

The satellites were multifaceted aluminum spheroids with magnesium frames 87 cm (34.5 in) in diameter and weighed 79 kg (175 lb). They were manufactured by the Bell Telephone Laboratories for the American Telephone and Telegraph Company, which paid NASA to launch them. Unlike later communications satellites, *Telstar 1* had only a single transponder to receive and retransmit signals. It was powered by 3,600 solar cells on the outside structure, and interior nickel-cadmium batteries. The satellite transmitted the first direct television pictures from the United States to Europe on July 10, 1962. *Telstar 1* ceased operation on Feb. 21, 1963, after some of its transistors were damaged by radiation from a high-altitude explosion of an atomic bomb detonated in 1962. *Telstar 2* was designed to withstand the radiation encountered by the earlier satellite. Also, like the earlier satellite, it

The telecommunications satellite Telstar 2 relayed transmissions between the United States and Europe from 1963 to 1965. It measured 87 cm (34.5 in) in diameter and weighed 79 kg (175 lb). Solar cells, arranged in rectangular panels on its surface, kept its batteries charged while in orbit. The tiny rods visible around its circumference are microwave antennas.

could process either six simultaneous two-way telephone calls or a single television channel. On its tenth orbit, *Telstar 2* transmitted the first transatlantic color-television program. *Telstar 2* continued to operate satisfactorily until it was shut off in May 1965.

Both of the satellites also carried sensors to determine the effects of space radiation on various components of communications satellites, such as solar cells and transistors. Much valuable information in these areas was obtained from the Telstars.   MITCHELL SHARPE

Bibliography: Clarke, Arthur C., *Voice across the Sea*, rev. ed. (1975); Pierce, J. R., *The Beginnings of Satellite Communications* (1968); Pratt, Timothy, and Postian, C. W., *Satellite Communications* (1986).

See also: COMMUNICATIONS SATELLITE.

Temin, Howard Martin [tem'-in]

Howard Martin Temin, b. Philadelphia, Dec. 10, 1934, an American oncologist and geneticist, shared the 1975 Nobel Prize for physiology or medicine for "discoveries concerning the interaction between tumor viruses and the genetic material of the cell." He demonstrated (1970) the existence of the enzyme known as reverse transcriptase (see RETROVIRUS).

Temne [tem'-nee]

The Temne are an African people of northwest Sierra Leone, who migrated there from Sudanic states by the 12th century. Their language is in the Western Atlantic subdivision of the Niger-Congo language family (see AFRICAN LANGUAGES). They numbered approximately 1,200,000 in the mid-1980s. An agricultural people, the Temne grow rice, groundnuts, cassava, cotton, and millet as well as palm products and kola nuts as cash crops. They keep cattle and goats, which they trade with neighboring Sudanic peoples. Fishing, carried out by women, is of secondary importance. Individual villages and groups of villages composed of circular mud and wattle houses are headed by the eldest competent male member of the founding father's descent group. These villages, in turn, make up chiefdoms, political units headed by chiefs who are elected. All leaders gain supernatural sanction through association with secret societies (*poro*).

Patrilineal clans form corporate groups that provide mutual aid and regulate the distribution of property. Bride-price and polygamy are practiced. Traditional religious beliefs centering on a supreme deity, nature deities, and ancestor worship are gradually being supplanted by the Islamic and Christian religions, especially in the northwestern chiefdoms.

                                                    JAMES W. HERRICK

Bibliography: Thomas, Northcote W., *Anthropological Report on Sierra Leone* (1970); Winterbottom, Thomas, *Account of the Native Africans in the Neighborhood of Sierra Leone*, 2 vols., 2d ed. (1969); Wylie, Kenneth, *The Political Kingdoms of the Temne* (1977).

tempera   [tem'-pur-uh]

Tempera is a painting technique in which water-soluble paints are mixed with (or "tempered" by) an emulsifying agent with binding and adhesive properties. The emulsifier may be a synthetic agent or a natural substance such as animal glue, milk, fig sap, or egg yolk (historically the most commonly used substance). Tempera can be applied to paper, canvas, primed wood, or plaster surfaces. When used on dried plaster it is known as *fresco secco* (see FRESCO PAINTING). One of the oldest PAINTING TECHNIQUES, tempera was widely used by the Egyptians, Greeks, and Romans. The Byzantines were among the first to use an egg binder. Tempera continued to be the most widely used painting technique through the 15th century.

Tempera dries quickly, becoming insoluble in water so that several layers of paint can be applied. The resulting overlay of semiopaque paints gives tempera paintings a luminous quality, but such a gradual buildup requires patient, methodical work and discourages spontaneous inventiveness and fluid forms. The image must be well worked out in advance using some sort of preparatory drawings—a necessity that dictates a painstaking and crisply linear style. Tempera, however, offers a wider color range and allows for the inclusion of many finer details than true fresco, or *buon fresco*. Tempera was ideally suited to the cooperative workshop practices by which paintings were produced from early Christian times through the 15th century.

Tempera continued to enjoy widespread popularity in southern Europe until at least 1500, but northern artists began to experiment with tempera and oils during the early 15th century. Jan van EYCK is thought to have invented oil paint by using emulsions of oil and egg with his pigment. After having been almost entirely supplanted by oil painting during the early 16th century, tempera was not revived until postimpressionist artists rediscovered its unique properties. Several 20th-century artists, including Ben SHAHN and Andrew WYETH, have experimented with this medium.   ADELHEID M. GEALT

Bibliography: Mayer, Ralph, *The Artist's Handbook of Materials and Techniques*, 3d rev. ed. (1970), and *The Painter's Craft*, rev. ed. (1966); Thompson, Daniel V., *The Practice of Tempera Painting* (1936; repr. 1962); Vickrey, Robert, and Cochrane, Diane, *New Techniques in Egg Tempera* (1973).

temperance movement

The temperance movement in the United States during the 19th and 20th centuries was largely a nonurban, Protestant-led drive to promote, by both persuasion and law, abstinence from alcoholic beverages. Although moderate drinking was

Women of the temperance movement present an antiliquor petition to the New York State legislature in this 19th-century engraving. The movement sought to mitigate what it saw to be the evils of alcohol by encouraging abstinence and curtailing the liquor supply.

generally accepted during the 18th century, by the early 19th century, many observers began to perceive an increase in the use—and abuse—of drink. With the immigration of ethnic groups whose culture accepted the use of these beverages, the growth of cities, and the concentration of industrial workers in them, reformers became increasingly aware of and concerned about excesses in the consumption of alcohol. The American Temperance Society, founded in 1826, began gathering pledges of abstinence. In the 1840s the Washington Temperance Societies conducted revival-style meetings to encourage similar pledges. Reformer Neal Dow persuaded Maine to approve (1846) the first statewide prohibition law and then led attempts to secure such laws elsewhere; the Civil War interrupted this effort. The Prohibition party, formed in 1869, ran presidential candidates, including Dow. The Woman's Christian Temperance Union (see WCTU), in 1874, and the politically potent Anti-Saloon League, established on a national scale in 1895, also favored banning the liquor traffic. Despite this intense activity and the passage of many liquor laws, the sale and use of alcohol remained widespread. Then during World War I, the temperance movement was unexpectedly aided by the need to conserve grain. In 1917, Congress passed the 18TH AMENDMENT (see PROHIBITION), ratified in January 1919; however, it proved unenforceable and was repealed by the 21ST AMENDMENT, ratified in 1933. Thereafter, the temperance movement waned. With the founding of ALCOHOLICS ANONYMOUS in 1935, attention began to shift to the treatment of alcoholism.

Bibliography: Asbury, Herbert, *The Great Illusion* (1950); Gusfield, Joseph R., *Symbolic Crusade: Status Politics and the American Temperance Movement* (1963); Kobler, John, *Ardent Spirits* (1973); Krout, John A., *The Origins of Prohibition* (1925; repr. 1967).

temperate climate

The term *temperate* is used to refer to any climate that has moderate temperatures, or to all climates of the middle latitudes. As a climatological concept, it implies an absence of great seasonal extremes of temperature in regions that are also neither continuously hot nor continuously cold throughout the year.

The ancient Greeks recognized latitude as the primary control of temperature and divided the world into torrid, temperate, and frigid zones. The North Temperate Zone extends from the Tropic of Cancer to the Arctic Circle, and the South Temperate Zone, from the Tropic of Capricorn to the Antarctic Circle.

Air masses and storms traveling in the mid-latitude westerly wind belts of each hemisphere combine with land and water effects to create a wide variety of climates within the temperate zones. In the Northern Hemisphere the west coasts of continents have a temperate maritime climate. In contrast, the continental interiors have greater annual ranges of mean and extreme temperatures. Broad expanses of water in the Southern Hemisphere also limit the annual temperature range. Both the North and South Temperate zones are belts of frequent storms, especially in winter.

HOWARD J. CRITCHFIELD

Bibliography: Haurwitz, Bernhard, and Austin, James M., *Climatology* (1944); Trewartha, Glenn T., *Introduction to Climate*, 4th ed. (1968).

temperature

Temperature is a measure of the escaping tendency of heat and an index of an object's thermal condition. Heat always flows of itself from high to lower temperatures. Two objects are in mutual thermal equilibrium, regardless of shape, color, chemical composition, or any other property, only if they have the same temperature.

Temperature is related to molecular motion. The greater the variety and disorder in the random motions of an object's molecules, the higher its temperature. At ABSOLUTE ZERO, random motions vanish.

Temperature Measurement. Temperature may be registered by any property that depends on a substance's thermal state: volume (at constant pressure), electrical resistance, and perhaps even visible color for extremely hot objects such as stars.

Most substances expand when heated. When confined in glass tubes, columns of mercury and alcohol increase in length as they get hotter, although not at the same rates or even, over a range of thermal states, at the same relative rates. John Dalton and Joseph Louis Gay-Lussac discovered, however, that all dilute gases expand in precisely the same way: 36.61% of their initial volumes in going from the normal freezing point (fp) to the normal boiling point (bp) of pure water. A temperature scale based upon that fact, the ideal gas temperature scale, T, is established by setting T proportional to the gas volume V: $T = kV$. Thus, for water,

$$\frac{T_{bp} - T_{fp}}{T_{fp}} = \frac{V_{bp} - V_{fp}}{V_{fp}} = 0.3661$$

If one desires to have for water $T_{bp} - T_{fp} = 100$ degrees, as on the Celsius scale, then one must take $T_{fp} = 100/0.3661 = 273.15$. If on the other hand one desires to have for water $T_{bp} - T_{fp} = 180$ degrees, as on the Fahrenheit scale ($212 - 32 = 180$), then one must take $T_{fp} = 180/0.3661 = 491.67$. The first scale corresponds to the Kelvin scale (degrees the same size as the Celsius degree), the second to the Rankine scale (degrees the same size as the Fahrenheit degree). On the Celsius scale, absolute zero lies 273.15 degrees below the freezing point of water: that is, at $0 - 273.15 = -273.15$. On the Fahrenheit scale, absolute zero lies 491.67 degrees below the freezing point of water: that is, at $32 - 491.67 = -459.67$.

Absolute zero has been closely approached but can never be attained. Between, for example, 0.000001 and 1 degree Kelvin, changes in some physical properties are as pronounced as between 1 and 1,000,000 degrees Kelvin for other properties.   HENRY A. BENT

Bibliography: Belcher, W. E., et al., *Temperature Measurement* (1956); King, Allen L., *Thermophysics* (1962); Kutz, Myer, *Temperature Control* (1968); Wolfe, Hugh C., ed., *Temperature: Its Measurement and Control in Science and Industry* (1955); Zemansky, Mark W., *Temperatures Very Low and Very High* (1964).

See also: GAS LAWS; HEAT AND HEAT TRANSFER; THERMODYNAMICS; THERMOMETER.

temperature, body: see BODY TEMPERATURE.

temperature inversion: see INVERSION.

tempering

Tempering is the process of toughening glass and metals, particularly steel. During its manufacture, steel is heated to a high temperature and quenched or cooled quickly. This rapid cooling creates a buildup of internal stresses that cause the metal to become brittle. The tempering of steel involves the subsequent reheating of the metal to a temperature below the point to which it was first heated. It is then allowed to cool slowly. This reheating and cooling process softens the steel, relieving the internal stresses set up by the original heating and quenching operations. The softening is accompanied by an important increase in toughness that is a direct result of the alleviation of brittleness of the steel. Temperature and rate of cooling will vary depending on the type of steel used, the desired properties, and the intended use of the steel. Generally, steel is tempered at temperatures ranging from 200° to 600° C (400° to 1,100° F).

Tempering glass involves first heating it until it becomes pliable and then cooling it by air blasts or by immersion into liquids. Tempering can increase the hardness of glass up to five times its normal hardness.

See also: ANNEALING.

Tempest, The

Probably the last play that William SHAKESPEARE wrote before he retired from the theater, *The Tempest* (c.1610–11) is a ro-

mantic comedy that puts strong emphasis on magical and wonderful effects. Thus Miranda, who has never seen a human being other than her father, Prospero, is moved when she first sees other men: "How beauteous mankind is! O brave new world/ That has such people in't!" Shakespeare endows the wooing of Ferdinand and Miranda with an earnestness that is never undercut. Caliban, also a natural creature but a born monster, evil, deformed, and ineducable, stands in sharp contrast to Miranda. The play has no direct literary source but is related to Renaissance travel literature and especially to some contemporary pamphlets about Bermuda.   MAURICE CHARNEY

Tempietto   [tem-piet'-toh]

The Tempietto ("small temple") at the church of San Pietro in Montorio, Rome, was built in 1502 by Donato BRAMANTE to mark the traditional site of the martyrdom of Saint Peter. Like many earlier Christian memorial buildings (martyria), it is a circular structure; at the time it was built, however, it was not this feature but the rich and explicitly classical detail on the building—the dome, columns, and balustrade—that seemed remarkable. The Tempietto is now set in a square courtyard to the side of the church. Its planned setting—a circular cloister of 16 columns—was never carried out.   DAVID CAST

Bibliography: Heydenreich, L. H., and Lotz, Wolfgang, *Architecture in Italy: 1400–1600* (1974).

Templars   [temp'-lurz]

An illustration (c.1470–83) from Boccaccio's Lives of Illustrious Men portrays Philip IV of France attending the execution (1314) of Jacques de Molay, grand master of the Knights Templar. Philip's persecution of the Knights led to the suppression of the order and the dispersal of their substantial properties.

The Poor Fellow-Soldiers of Christ and the Temple of Solomon, or Knights Templar, were a military and religious order founded in Jerusalem during the CRUSADES. The founders were Hugh de Payns and Geoffroy de Saint-Omer, knights who established (1118) a religious community to protect pilgrims in the Holy Land. Baldwin II, Latin king of Jerusalem, gave them a dwelling on the ancient site of the Temple. Saint BERNARD OF CLAIRVAUX drew up the order's rules, which included the notion of fighting the enemies of God under vows of poverty, chastity, and obedience. The Templars, divided into knights, chaplains, sergeants, and craftsmen, were organized under a grand master and general council and were responsible only to the pope and not to secular rulers. Wearing a white cloak with a red cross, they attracted many nobles and soon became an expert military force and a powerful, wealthy order. In Europe their churches were often round, and their commanderies served as banks. After 1291, when the crusading forces were driven from Palestine, the Templars' main activity became banking—the lending of money (even to kings)—and their enormous landholdings and financial strength aroused great hostility among rulers and clergy alike.

PHILIP IV of France, sorely in need of money, charged the Templars with heresy and immorality (1307). They were arrested and put on trial, and confessions were extracted by torture. Similar attacks were mounted against the order in Spain and England, and Pope Clement V, after initially opposing the trials, suppressed the Knights Templar by papal bull at the Council of Vienne in 1312. When the Grand Master, Jacques de Molay, and other leaders of the Templars retracted their forced confessions and declared their innocence and the innocence of the order, Philip had them burned at the stake at Paris on Mar. 18, 1314.

The Templars' holdings were dispersed, some going to the Knights Hospitalers and some to secular rulers, although Philip received none. The guilt of the Templars was hotly debated down to the 20th century. Most modern scholars, however, believe that the charges against them were fabricated.

CYPRIAN DAVIS, O.S.B.

Bibliography: Barber, Malcolm, *Trial of the Templars* (1978); Legman, George, *The Guilt of the Templars* (1966); Parker, T. W., *The Knights Templars in England* (1963); Seward, Desmond, *The Monks of War* (1972); Simon, Edith, *The Piebald Standard: A Biography of the Knights Templars* (1959; repr. 1977).

temple

A temple is a building or enclosed space set aside for worship. Temple architecture in general can be divided into three categories: the open-air sanctuary; the cave, or rock-cut, temple (a secret place of worship); and the house for the deity or cult object, also called the freestanding temple. Not considered temples are the Christian CHURCH, the Jewish SYNAGOGUE, and the Muslim MOSQUE, although their forms and functions often resemble those of temples.

PREHISTORIC TEMPLES

The Magdalenian societies (15,000-9000 BC) of the Paleolithic period used natural caves such as those found at ALTAMIRA in Spain and LASCAUX in France. Elaborately decorated with paintings, and occasionally with sculpture, these caves provided a sacred space for hunting rites (see PREHISTORIC ART).

The oldest (c.6000-5650 BC) artificial temples extant are those discovered at ÇATAL HÜYÜK, Turkey. Constructed of mud brick on a timber framework, these cavelike enclosures have plastered walls covered with paintings and molded sculpture dedicated to a MOTHER GODDESS cult. Other types of Neolithic temples include the open-air sanctuary of STONE-HENGE (c.2100-1900 BC), which probably served a calendrical function, and the rock-cut, domed temples of Malta (c.3000-2000 BC), dedicated to a mother goddess cult.

MESOPOTAMIA

The Mesopotamian temples of the period 3000-500 BC were intended to serve as houses for deities—the house's existence ensured the deity's presence and, under the proper circumstances, its protective influence. Mesopotamian temples were almost invariably rectangular in layout and built of mud brick. The worshiper entered through a doorway in one of the long sides of the building; the cult statue stood to the left, and the altar for offerings to the right. Surrounding the main room were storage rooms.

Early Mesopotamian temples were the first raised structures of their kind—for example, the so-called White Temple at URUK (c.3000 BC), dedicated to the god ANU, was elevated by a 12.2-m-high (40-ft) artificial mound and approached by a ramp. True ZIGGURATS—stepped, pyramidal structures rising from a rectangular or square base—were built first by the Sumerian civilization. In the ziggurat at UR, built (c.2100 BC) by UR-NAMMU, the temple is placed atop a series of concentric mud-brick terraces piled one on top of the other to a height of more than 30.5 m (100 ft). Ur-type ziggurats were approached by three steep stairways and guarded by a gatehouse to bar the unauthorized from entering. The Babylonians, under Hammurabi, continued traditional Sumerian forms, but the KASSITES reoriented their temples to face east and added sculpture in molded bricks, as can be seen in the Temple of Karaindash (c.1440 BC) at Uruk, dedicated to the mother goddess Innana.

The earliest Assyrian temples, such as that of Ishtar, built between 1241 and 1205 BC by Tikulti-Ninurta I, had an off-axis doorway to the cult room and two flights of interior stairs

Mnajdra, a megalithic temple on the southern coast of Malta, dates from the early Copper Age (c.2800 BC). This rock-cut temple is typical of the prehistoric Maltese sanctuaries, around which a religious cult associated with the mother goddess flourished.

leading to a niche for the cult statue. These internalized ziggurats gave way in late Assyrian architecture to true ziggurats that contained as many as seven different levels connected by a continuous ramp. Some of these structures rose to heights of 90 m (300 ft) or more, and many, such as that at KHORSA-BAD (c.706 BC), had steps made of colored brick. The Neo-Babylonians produced NEBUCHADNEZZAR II's ziggurat (c.612-539 BC) at BABYLON, which had white, black, red, blue, orange, silver, and gold levels. The sacred rooms atop these later ziggurats were used for astronomical observation as well as for devotional rites.

EGYPT

Temples in ancient Egypt were of two main types: freestanding temples for deities and temples attached to funerary structures. Rock-cut temples of both types also were used. The purpose of freestanding temples was to house a cult statue, whereas the funerary shrines were built to receive the offerings for the dead.

Freestanding temples of the Old Kingdom period (2680-2258 BC) generally followed the layout of the Temple of Khentiamentiw (c.3000 BC) at ABYDOS, which is about 15.25 m (50 ft) long, trapezoidal in shape, and composed of successive rooms that culminate in a niche for the cult statue. Funerary temples such as that of Khafre (c.2600 BC) at GIZA, which were attached to PYRAMIDS by causeways, housed statues of the king, in which his spirit was thought to be present to receive offerings.

In the Middle Kingdom period (2134-1786 BC) freestanding temples were built at Karnak, Luxor, Medamud, and Tod, but all have disappeared beneath their New Kingdom successors. The most remarkable extant structure of this age is the combined mortuary temple and tomb of the 11th dynasty at DEIR EL-BAHRI begun (c.2050 BC) by King Mentuhotep II. The tomb's central core—recently proved to have had a flat roof—was surrounded by a sculptured and painted colonnade and was approached by a ramp leading to the structure through a garden.

The greatest proliferation of Egyptian temple building took place during the New Kingdom period (1570-1080 BC). Three typical examples of freestanding temples are the Temple of Amon at KARNAK, the Temple of Amon at LUXOR, and the Temple of the Aten at Karnak, all of which were constructed between 2060 and 1200 BC. Basically similar in organization, all three temples had monumental gateways, or pylons, leading to a succession of courtyards and halls laid out along a central axis. As the worshiper moved along the axis, the interior gradually grew dim until almost total darkness shrouded the cult statue standing at the end of the axis. The plan of the impressive New Kingdom temple of Re Harakte at ABU SIMBEL, constructed (c.1250 BC) under King RAMSES II, is similar to that of Egyptian freestanding temples except that the structure is carved out of a cliff face and colossal statues of the king replaced the pylons.

The vast rock-cut mortuary temple (c.1480 BC) of Queen HATSHEPSUT is perhaps the outstanding structure surviving from the New Kingdom. Built at Deir el-Bahri just north of the temple of Mentuhotep, it is composed of two terraces surrounded by decorated colonnades; the entire edifice was fronted with lush gardens.

MEDITERRANEAN PERIPHERY

Hittite temples present an unmistakably different aspect from that of Mesopotamian temples, although the two temple types display some similarities (see HITTITE ART AND ARCHITECTURE). Common features of Hittite structures are central courtyards open to the sky, entrances on the axes, pillared halls on at least one side, and subsidiary rooms. The cult

This drawing depicts Etemenaki, a ziggurat dedicated to the god Marduk, built during the reign of the Neo-Babylonian king Nebuchadnezzar II (6th century BC). Located in the royal city of Babylon, the ziggurat, a temple tower form that originated with the Sumerians, was renowned in the ancient world as the Tower of Babel.

chamber usually is located off-axis and is lighted by outside windows. Typical examples (c.1400-1250 BC) can be found at BOĞAZKÖY, Turkey.

Solomon's Temple. The most renowned temple of this age was the Temple of Solomon in Jerusalem. Completed (c.952 BC) with the aid of Phoenician artisans, it was destroyed in 586 BC; most of the knowledge about it comes from the Bible and from the evidence supplied by other Palestinian temples. Apparently the temple faced east and had three main rooms disposed axially with the entrance. The anteroom, or *Ulam*, was a rectangular space entered through one of the short sides; flanking the *Ulam* were square rooms that led to the small storage rooms, or *Yasiya*, that surrounded the temple on the other three sides. Beyond the *Ulam* was the main sanctuary, or *Hekal*, and beyond that, a flight of stairs that led to the Holy of Holies, or *Debir*, where the Ark of the Covenant was kept. The temple was built out of stone and had a flat wooden roof made from imported cypresses and cedar. Bronze pillars known as *Yakhin* and *Boaz*, which may have symbolized the relationship between the monarchy and the temple, stood in front of the edifice.

MINOAN CRETE AND MYCENAEAN GREECE

So far as is known, no monumental freestanding temples were built by the Minoan civilization of Crete (fl. 2200-1500 BC; see MINOAN ART) except possibly Arkhanes. The west wings of Minoan palaces did contain shrines and associated rooms, and the palaces at KNOSSOS and Zakro (c.1600-1450 BC) had public altars situated in their central courts.

Minoan culture greatly influenced roughly contemporary Mycenaean civilization of Greece (see AEGEAN CIVILIZATION; MYCENAE), whose shrines are known primarily through representations on seal rings. The most significant feature of Mycenaean structures was their use of the megaron, or HOUSE form, which influenced much of early GREEK ARCHITECTURE.

GREEK TEMPLES

Archaic Period. The earliest Greek temples date from the end of the Orientalizing period (7th century BC). Along with small funerary temples dedicated to heroes, buildings erected to house large cult statues were the principal form of temple at this time. The Mycenaean megaron plan seems to have provided the model for these early structures, which had two-columned porches and hipped or gabled roofs. The Temple of Apollo at Thermon (c.620 BC) in Aetolia was a true temple of the Doric order, made of wood; wooden pillars gradually gave way to stone pillars, as in the Temple of Hera (c.600 BC and later) at OLYMPIA.

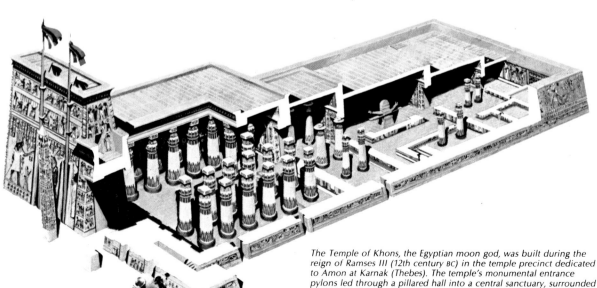

The Temple of Khons, the Egyptian moon god, was built during the reign of Ramses III (12th century BC) in the temple precinct dedicated to Amon at Karnak (Thebes). The temple's monumental entrance pylons led through a pillared hall into a central sanctuary, surrounded by subsidiary chapels and courts. An inner sanctuary, reserved for the holiest of religious ceremonies, was located at the far end of the temple. It is characteristic of the temple architecture developed during the New Kingdom period (1570-1085 BC).

(Left) *The court of the women is seen in this view of Herod's Temple, as reconstructed in a model of ancient Jerusalem by the archaeologist Michael Avi-Yonah. The actual temple, constructed by Herod the Great in the 1st century BC, was destroyed by the Romans in AD 70.*

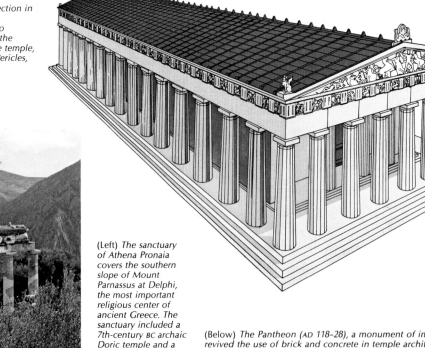

(Right) *The design of the Parthenon (c.447–432 BC) embodies technical perfection in classical Greek temple architecture. Dedicated to Athena and symbolizing the supremacy of Athens, the temple, built during the rule of Pericles, dominates the Athenian Acropolis.*

(Left) *The sanctuary of Athena Pronaia covers the southern slope of Mount Parnassus at Delphi, the most important religious center of ancient Greece. The sanctuary included a 7th-century BC archaic Doric temple and a 5th-century BC temple dedicated to Athena.*

(Below) *The Pantheon (AD 118–28), a monument of imperial Rome, revived the use of brick and concrete in temple architecture. Its symmetry is enhanced by its hemispherical dome, in which a single, circular opening (oculus) was cut as a source of interior lighting.*

Initially, the cult room, or cella, of Greek temples was a long, dark space with a row of columns down the center. Because this plan obscured the statue, the temple builders gradually adopted a shorter cella with two rows of columns, one on either side of the statue. At about the same time, the Ionic order began to appear in Greek colonies in Anatolia, particularly in the Temple of Hera (c.575 BC) at Samos. The Samos temple apparently inspired the Temple of Artemis (c.560–546 BC) at Ephesus, which featured a double colonnade influenced by Egyptian temple halls. Doric and Ionic temples of the archaic period (600–480 BC) display tendencies toward larger scale, more harmonious proportions, and greater use of marble and decorative sculpture.

Classical Period. After the Persian Wars ended (479 BC), Greek culture entered its classical era, which was marked by a tremendous growth in building activity in Greece, Sicily, and southern Italy. The greatest Doric temples of classical Greece are the Temple of Zeus (designed c.460 BC) at Olympia and the Parthenon (447–432 BC) on the Athens ACROPOLIS, whose principal builders were ICTINUS and CALLICRATES. A century of refinement and experimentation produced in these buildings a harmonious blend of geometric proportions, optical effects, and sculptural decoration that have remained unmatched. Also reaching its apogee at this time was the Ionic order, whose delicate, graceful decorative effects were used to great advantage on the Acropolis in both the Erechtheum (421–405 BC) and the Temple of Athena Nike (c.427 BC).

In the temple architecture of the late classical period, which was inaugurated by Ictinus's Temple of Apollo (c.420 BC) at Bassae, the interior space was transformed into an area for public assembly—a development that forced a return to the long cella. More prolix decoration began to appear on temple exteriors, where the newly designed Corinthian capitals made their initial appearance. Finally, a round temple form emerged for the first time in the Tholos (c.420 BC) at Delphi.

Hellenistic Period. During the Hellenistic period the Ionic order prospered, the Corinthian order became more popular, and the Doric order declined. Among the huge Ionic temples that were erected during the 4th century BC in Anatolia, particularly striking are the Temple of Artemis (rebuilt 356 BC) at Ephesus, the Temple of Apollo (c.330 BC) at Didyma, and the Temple of Artemis (c.325 BC) at SARDIS. All of these buildings are noteworthy for their complicated interiors. Sardis has a double cella, and Didyma a temple within a temple. On the Greek mainland the elongated, pedimented Hellenistic Doric temple largely was abandoned after 200 BC in favor of Corinthian structures such as the Temple of Olympian Zeus (completed AD 131) at Athens.

ROME

Republican Era. Temples in republican Rome generally followed the Etruscan pattern of small structures that stood atop high podiums (see ROMAN ART AND ARCHITECTURE). They were made of a volcanic stone called tufa and featured a deep, columned porch and a narrow cella. An early example of this type is the Temple of Jupiter (c.510 BC) on the Capitoline; representative of later republican shrines are three tufa temples (c.100 BC) in the Forum Holitorium. Toward the end of the republican era, temple building passed through a transitional phase that engendered both traditional buildings such as the Temple of Fortuna Virilis (c.80 BC) in Rome and radically new structures such as the Sanctuary of Fortuna Primigenia (c.80 BC) in Palestrina. Built on a steep mountainside at the order of the dictator Sulla, the Palestrina temple is an elaborate, symmetrically laid out, molded-concrete complex, in which the shrine itself seems lost amid the magnificent staircases, terraces, and fountains.

Imperial Rome. The victory (29 BC) of Emperor Augustus inaugurated an attempt to turn Rome from a city of brick into one of marble. Augustus chose to follow the Hellenistic and classical models of Greece, using concrete only in concealed parts of buildings. Many older temples were refaced with marble, and new shrines such as the Temple of Mars Ultor (2 BC) in the Forum Augusti were erected at the focal points of forum complexes. Sharing in this building boom were many of the Roman provinces, which were graced with new temples such as the MAISON CARRÉE (c.16 BC) in Nîmes.

The next great period in Imperial architecture was initiated by Emperor Hadrian, who built (AD c.118) the Temple of Trajan in Trajan's Forum. Hadrian's crowning achievement was the domed PANTHEON (c.118–28) in Rome, which reintroduced molded concrete into temple architecture. A tribute to both Roman engineering genius and Greek aesthetics, the Pantheon is a harmonious, balanced structure surmounted by an enormous hemispherical dome that symbolized the universe. The design of Byzantine churches and Muslim mosques was influenced greatly by the Pantheon.

The Antonine emperors (r. 138–80) were more traditional builders, as the Temple of Antoninus and Faustina (c.141) in the Roman Forum attests, but the Severans (r. 193–235) introduced colossal temples dedicated to exotic foreign deities. Especially notable was the Temple of SERAPIS, built (c.215) by Caracalla, which had 12 columns across its 25-m-high (81-ft) facade. Emperor Aurelian's enormous Temple of the Invincible Sun (c.275), a round structure set within a rectangular enclosure, was the last important temple built in Rome.

INDIA

Buddhist Temples. The Maurya emperors (r. 322–185 BC) are the earliest-known temple builders in India (see INDIAN ART AND ARCHITECTURE). Emperor ASOKA, the most renowned patron of early Buddhism, sponsored the construction of thousands of STUPAS—brick-faced, domical mounds containing the relics of the Buddha. During the Sunga period (185–172 BC), stupas became more and more elaborate structures, whose form symbolically represented the Buddhist universe.

Asoka's reign also witnessed the appearance of rock-cut basilical temples known as chaityas. As they evolved, chaityas developed into colonnaded halls of worship housing the Buddha's image, which had become an integral part of the Buddhist temple. The chaitya at Karli (c.80 BC) is representative of this phase of chaitya building.

An interregnum era (AD 1st–3d century), characterized by weak governments and few great monuments, was followed by the brilliant Gupta period (320–647), which is notable both for the climax of Buddhist art and the revival of Hinduism throughout the country. At this time, the Buddhist temple form culminated in elaborate, freestanding brick chaitya halls

This chaitya (vaulted hall; AD 600–42) is one of 29 Buddhist cave sanctuaries carved into a cliff at Ajanta, India, dating from the 2d century BC to the 7th century AD. At the end of the naved hall is a stupa commemorating the Buddha in his achievement of nirvana.

The shrine (AD c.800) at Borobudur in central Java is a unique example of Buddhist temple architecture. The pyramidal monument is surmounted by a circular stupa consisting of nine levels and is noted for its relief friezes illustrating scenes from the life of Buddha.

such as that at Chezarla (4th-5th century). In addition, unprecedented square-plan temples, apparently derived from civil meeting-halls, appeared at Ladh Khan (c.450) and elsewhere.

Hindu Temples. Although the 5th-century brick temple at Bhitargaon established the prototype for Hindu temples throughout Southeast Asia and in Indonesia, Hindu temple building did not make a significant impact in India until the ascension (647) of the Hindu dynasties. The Hindu temple was not a place of public assembly but a shelter for the deity's image; the temple's form often symbolized the world mountain. Of the three main types of Hindu temple—*nagara, dravida,* and *vesara*—the *nagara* is the oldest and the most important. Conical or convex in shape, the *nagara* is crowned with a spire known as a *sikhara;* a representative example is that at Galanganatha (7th century). The *dravida,* on the other hand, consisted of a series of ascending terraces, or *bhumis,* representing the hierarchy of the divinities; on each terrace is a *stupika,* or "little stupa." Typical *vesaras,* such as Bhima's Rath (625-74) in MAHABALIPURAM, were barrel-vaulted halls derived from Buddhist chaitya halls. The peak of Hindu temple building occurred in about 1000, when the opulently embellished *nagara* temples of KHAJURAHO were erected. Echoing the ornate sculptural decoration of later Hindu shrines were the fantastic white-marble temples of the Jain religion built at Mount Abu from the 10th to the 13th century.

SOUTHEAST ASIA

Cambodia. Under the Khmer Empire, centered in modern-day Kampuchia, temple architecture reached new heights in the period between AD 800 and 1450. At the Khmer capital of ANGKOR two great temple complexes dedicated to Vishnu, but reflecting Hindu influences, were built in the 12th century. Angkor Wat, built (1st half of the 12th century) by Emperor Suryavarman II, has been called the world's largest religious structure. The temple proper, a stupa-based stepped pyramid topped by 4 conical towers surrounding a 63-m (202-ft) central tower, rises from an immense 305-m (1000-ft) platform that, in turn, is set within a moated rectangular enclosure, whose perimeter measures nearly 4 km (2.5 mi). Surrounding the entire structure are three series of corbeled galleries. Perhaps the most stunning aspect of this huge complex is the magnificent low-relief sculptural decoration that covers its miles of walls. At the nearby temple complex of the Bayon (late 12th-early 13th century) in Angkor Thom, erected by Emperor Jayavarman VII, even more elaborate sculptural decoration adorns the architecture.

Indonesia. Hindu and Buddhist temples vied for dominance in 9th-century Java and Sumatra. Indian influence is apparent in the greatest Javanese monument, the enormous temple of BOROBUDUR (8th century), which is located atop a hill and approached by a rising series of stairways. The 9-level circular stupa, which surmounts a square stepped pyramid and is crowned with a lofty spire, is decorated with reliefs that illustrate in successive stages the process of Buddhist enlightenment.

CHINA

Chinese temples, unlike those of India or Southeast Asia, traditionally were made of wood—a fact that accounts for the relatively small number of structures that have survived (see CHINESE ART AND ARCHITECTURE). Temple construction dates back at least to the Chou dynasty (1027-256 BC). Poems of the *Shih Ching* (6th century BC) mention ancestor-cult temples containing pillared halls of pine and cypress, and Confucius mentions that certain types of architecture were appropriate to certain social ranks.

Monumental shrines built during the Han dynasty (202 BC–AD 220) are comparable in stylistic development to the Roman development of Greek temple types. From this time, almost all Chinese temple complexes, regardless of the religion represented, follow the same basic plan of an open courtyard flanked on three sides by identical buildings and on the fourth side by a ceremonial gate. Many Taoist shrines were erected by Han emperors, but the greatest stimulus for temple building under the Han occurred when Buddhism was introduced (1st century AD) from India. Along with Buddhism

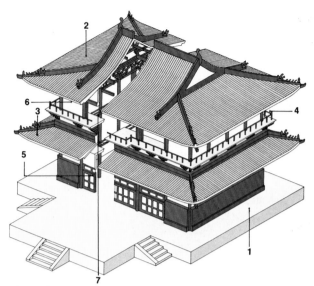

The pavilion dedicated to Kuan-yin, the Chinese bodhisattva of compassion, is one of the few remaining shrines at Tu-lo-ssu, a temple complex in Hopei, China. The upper two floor levels of the three-story hall surround a well, where a colossal clay statue of Kuan-yin is enclosed. The pavilion consists of a stone podium (1); a hipped roof (2); overhanging eaves (3); support brackets (4); a three-door entrance (5); open bays (6); and galleries facing the interior (7).

came a variation of the Indian stupa form, on which the PAGODA—a tower composed of superimposed stories with overhanging roofs—was based.

Buddhism flourished under the Six Dynasties (221-589). There were 42 pagodas in Lo-yang under the Chin (265-316); by the time of the Northern Wei (386-535) there were more than 500 in Lo-yang alone and about 30,000 throughout Northern China, although most of these were destroyed in the reaction against Buddhism under the Northern Chou (557-81). As they proliferated, pagodas grew taller, and some stone structures began to appear. The usual number of stories increased from 3 in the 4th century to 5 in the 6th century, and Wu Ti of Liang built (535) a 12-story pagoda that reputedly was about 122 m (400 ft) tall. These pagodas are imitated in the surviving rock-cut temples of YUN-KANG (late 6th century).

Under the Sui (589-618) and T'ang dynasties (618-906) imperial-scale building became the rule. The major temple form of this era was a complex consisting of two pagodas for relics and a central worship hall for the images of Buddha. Although other buildings in the temple complexes remained wooden, the use of masonry in pagodas became common.

Toward the end of the T'ang dynasty, Taoism regained preeminence, and Buddhist architecture declined. In the Five Dynasties (906-60) and Sung (960-1279) periods, temple building prospered, particularly in the 11th century, then declined as the emperors embraced the ascetic Ch'an Buddhist sect. Sung pagodas tend to be hexagonal or octagonal structures made of brick, as exemplified by the 13-story T'ieh-t'a (c.1044) at K'AI-FENG. The succeeding Yüan dynasty (1279-1368) further developed the Sung temple-types into a three-stage division: a high base, a shaft, and a crown. Bases are octagonal and decorated with sculpture, as are the shafts, and crowns generally are composed of 13 close-set roofs. Under the Ming and Ch'ing (1368-1912) dynasties, temple construction, along with Chinese architecture in general, gradually declined into mere repetition of Sung formulas. Among the few notable buildings erected were the T'ai-miao, or Grand Ancestral Shrine (15th century), in Peking—a long, narrow assembly building that recalls early Chinese palaces—and the Chih-hua-ssu (completed c.1444), a Ming version of a traditional Buddhist structure.

JAPAN

The earliest-known Japanese temples were wooden Shinto

The Zu Shi Miao temple in Canton, China, possesses the same overall plan of other Taoist temples, which are simpler and comprise fewer buildings than Buddhist temples. The temple is designed with an open courtyard, flanked on three sides by identical buildings and on the fourth side by a ceremonial gate. In keeping with traditional Taoist beliefs, temple architects strove to complement the natural setting and environment.

the primacy of the *kondo* and the removal of the pagodas from the sanctuary proper.

The Heian period (784-1185), however, marked a revival of Japanese, as opposed to Chinese, forms. Reform elements in Buddhism reacted against the scale and luxury of Nara-style temples, and ritual-centered Tantric Buddhism became pre-eminent. The greatest sanctuary built in this era was the Hoshoji (1077) of Heian (now Kyoto), whose octagonal, 9-story pagoda was located on an island on axis with the *kondo*. The planning of the *kondo* received special attention at Hoshoji and other Tantric temples, at which rites had to be performed in secret but with the congregation present. This requirement led to the development of forehalls in Tantric *kondos*, such as that at Koryuji (c.818).

During the Kamakura period (1185-1333), four styles of temple architecture coexisted: an archaic native style, two imported Chinese styles, and a progressive native style. Of the two Chinese styles, the Karayo, an imitation of Sung architecture, was by far the most popular; the Tenjikuyo, introduced by Chinese architects, proved to be unsuited to Japanese taste. Because it was closely associated with the Zen sect, which gained many adherents in Japan in the 13th century, the Karayo flourished throughout the country. Its principal innovation was an elevated shrine in the *kondo*. Also

The Hoodo, or Phoenix Hall, part of the Byodoin temple in Uji, near Kyoto, Japan, dates from the late Heian period. The temple complex was originally a family villa and was converted into a temple sanctuary by Fujiwara Yorimichi in 1052. The Hoodo has a central pavilion, connecting galleries, and corner pavilions. It houses a statue of the Buddha of the West, Amida, carved by the sculptor Jocho.

shrines—largely unornamented and gabled-roofed sanctuaries that looked like granaries or houses (see JAPANESE ART AND ARCHITECTURE). Some, such as the Izumo Shrine (AD c.1st century) at Ise, were elevated structures approached by a flight of stairs. The interior generally contained an off-axis sacred chamber and a central pillar that symbolized the pillar of heaven. Each temple stood within an enclosure entered through elaborately decorated gateways, or *torii*.

The first Buddhist temple in Japan was built (552) to house a gilded bronze statue of the Buddha presented to Emperor Kimmei by the Korean king of Paekche. Under the patronage of Prince Shotoku Taishi, who built (588) the Shitennoji Temple at OSAKA, Buddhism became firmly established, and many pagodas were built. Unlike Chinese examples, Japanese Buddhist shrines were relatively simple sanctuaries consisting of the pagoda to shelter relics, and an assembly hall, or *kondo*, for worship of the Buddha's image. The difficulty of reconciling a large pagoda with the traditionally small Japanese monastery took centuries to resolve, and eventually pagodas were discarded or built outside the enclosure walls.

An important innovation occurred when the Golden Hall of the Horyuji, at Nara, was created (c.607) as the shrine for two important images associated with Emperor Shotoku. After the Golden Hall, temples became larger and even more magnificent complexes. In the monastery at Yakushiji (c.720), the *kondo* resembled a Chinese throne hall, and the two pagodas were situated far from the center of the complex. During the Nara period (710-84) temple foundations grew even larger, rivaling those of T'ang China. Particularly impressive was the huge monastery of Todaiji (begun 745), which demonstrated

widespread was a progressive Japanese style, the Wayo, which developed further the Heian style. Typical examples were Kanshinii (14th century) and Saimyoji (c.1250).

The later Japanese periods (1333-present)—Muromachi, Momoyama, and Edo—displayed eclecticism and modesty of scale. Southward orientation, frequent in earlier periods, gave way, with the emergence of the Shin sect, to eastern orientation—the direction the Amida Buddha faced. Only the *kondo* received monumental treatment, and interiors tended to imitate palace architecture. Representative of this later style was the Honganji Temple (1585) at Kyoto, a shrine of the Shin sect.

JOHN STEPHENS CRAWFORD

Bibliography: Boethius, Axel, and Ward-Perkins, John, *Etruscan and Early Roman Architecture* (1970); Brandon, S. G. F., *Man and God in Art and Ritual* (1975); Dinsmoor, William, *The Architecture of Ancient Greece*, 3d ed. (1975); Frankfort, Henri, *The Art and Architecture of the Ancient Orient*, 4th ed. (1969); Mellaart, James, *Earliest Civilizations of the Near East* (1965); Michell, George, *The Hindu Temple* (1978); Murray, Margaret A., *Egyptian Temples* (1931; repr. 1976); Paine, Robert, and Soper, Alexander, *The Art and Architecture of Japan*, rev. ed. (1975); Rowland, Benjamin, *The Art and Architecture of India*, rev. ed. (1977); Sickman, Laurence, and Soper, Alexander, *The Art and Architecture of China*, 3d ed. (1968); Sitwell, Sacheverell, *Great Temples of the East* (1962); Smith, William, *The Art and Architecture of Ancient Egypt* (1965); Tomlinson, R. A., *Greek Sanctuaries* (1977).

Temple, Shirley

A phenomenal child sensation in movies of the 1930s, Shirley Temple, b. Santa Monica, Calif., Apr. 23, 1928, became better known in the 1970s for her political activism on behalf of the Republican party. During the Depression, however, her curls,

Shirley Temple, America's most popular child star of the 1930s, curtsies in this publicity photograph. After retiring from films, Temple became active in politics. She has been appointed as a representative to the United Nations General Assembly (1969), ambassador to Ghana (1974), and chief of protocol of the Department of State (1976).

her dimples, and her undoubted talent in such films as *Little Miss Marker* (1934), *The Little Colonel* (1935), *Captain January* (1936), *Wee Willie Winkie* (1937), *Heidi* (1937), *Rebecca of Sunnybrook Farm* (1938), and *The Little Princess* (1939) completely captivated America. She retired from films in 1949 after a series of unremarkable teenage and adult roles. As Mrs. Shirley Temple Black, the former star served as a delegate to the United Nations (1969), as U.S. Ambassador to Ghana (1974), and as U.S. Chief of Protocol (1976) in the Ford administration.

Bibliography: Windeler, Robert, *Shirley Temple* (1976).

Temple, William   (archbishop)

William Temple, b. Oct. 15, 1881, d. Oct. 26, 1944, archbishop of Canterbury (1942–44), was a noted theologian and leader of the ecumenical movement. The son of Frederick Temple, archbishop of Canterbury (1896–1902), he was educated at Balliol College, Oxford, and ordained in the Church of England in 1909. Temple was headmaster of Repton School (1910–14) and then became rector of Saint James's, Piccadilly, London. In 1917 he left Saint James's to devote his time to church renewal through the Life and Liberty movement. Temple was consecrated bishop of Manchester in 1921, archbishop of York in 1929, and archbishop of Canterbury in 1942.

Noted as a champion of social and economic justice, Temple was first president of the Workers' Educational Association. His influential writings include *Nature, Man, and God* (1934) and *Christianity and the Social Order* (1942).

JOHN E. BOOTY

Bibliography: Carmichael, John D., and Goodwin, Harold S., *William Temple's Political Legacy* (1963); Iremonger, F. A., *William Temple, Archbishop of Canterbury: His Life and Letters* (1948); Thomas, Owen C., *William Temple's Philosophy of Religion* (1961).

Temple, Sir William   (essayist)

An English diplomat and essayist whose prose style was greatly admired, Sir William Temple, b. Apr. 6, 1628, d. Jan. 27, 1699, played a leading part in negotiating the anti-French TRIPLE ALLIANCE (1668) with the Netherlands and in 1677 helped to arrange the marriage of William of Orange and Mary, the niece of Charles II. During his retirement, when Jonathan Swift served briefly as his secretary, Temple published long works on history and politics and shorter essays on literature and antiquity. With *Upon Ancient and Modern Learning* (1690), Temple introduced to England the French debate on the virtues of classical as opposed to "modern" literature, later satirized by Swift in *The Battle of the Books*.

ROBIN BUSS

Bibliography: Woodbridge, Homer E., *Sir William Temple* (1940; repr. 1973).

tempo

The tempo, or rate of speed, of a piece of music is determined by its character, the physical conditions of performance, and the instructions transmitted by the composer. Before the 17th century, performers knew the correct tempo from the notation, for note values were related to tempo. The adoption of time signatures and tempo marks made possible a variety of durations for any note. The time signature ¾ gave a quarter note one pulse; ½ gave it half a pulse; ⁴⁄₈ gave it two pulses. The rate at which these pulses occurred could be modified by the use of tempo markings, such as allegro or andante. A high degree of accuracy in tempo indications was made possible by the invention of the METRONOME, a device that shows the number of beats per minute. Composers have been inconsistent in their use of it, however, and conductors have often modified a composer's indications, either because of a different interpretation of the composition or because of the conditions under which it is performed.

ELWYN A. WIENANDT

Bibliography: Apel, Willi, *The Notation of Polyphonic Music, 900–1600*, 5th ed. (1961); Donington, Robert, *The Interpretation of Early Music* (1974).

Ten Commandments

A basic set of divine laws in the Bible, also called the Decalogue (from the Greek *deka,* "ten," and *logos,* "word"), the Ten Commandments form the fundamental ethical code of Judaism, Christianity, and Islam. According to the biblical narrative, God gave the commandments to MOSES on Mount Sinai and inscribed them on two stone tablets. Moses broke the tablets in anger when he found his people worshiping the GOLDEN CALF, but eventually he replaced them and enshrined them in the ARK OF THE COVENANT. Two slightly different versions of the commandments are found in Exod. 20:1–17 and Deut. 5:6–21.

Two traditions are also adhered to for listing the commandments. Lutherans and Roman Catholics consider the opening prohibitions against false worship as one commandment, whereas most other Protestants and the Eastern Orthodox follow the Hebrew tradition of dividing them into two. The latter maintain the number at ten by combining the final prohibitions against covetousness.

The opening commandments concern reverence for the one God, who will tolerate no rivals; the making and worship of graven images is forbidden, as is taking God's name in vain; observance of the Sabbath is enjoined. The other commandments regulate human relationships: the injunctions to honor one's parents and the bans on killing, adultery, stealing, false witness, and covetousness. The New Testament summarizes the Decalogue in the two great commandments (Mark 12:28–31).

Bibliography: Goldman, Solomon, *Ten Commandments,* ed. by Maurice Samuel (1963); Nielsen, Eduard, *Ten Commandments in New Perspective* (1968).

Ten Lost Tribes of Israel

Old Testament tradition traces the origin of the Jewish people to 12 tribes. At the death (c.920) of King Solomon, the tribes split into two kingdoms: the tribes of Judah and Benjamin formed the southern kingdom of Judah, and the remaining ten constituted the northern kingdom of Israel. When Israel was conquered by the Assyrians in 722–21 BC, the ten tribes as organized entities disappeared from the stage of history.

Many of the members of the ten tribes were apparently deported to Assyria and eventually became part of the worldwide Jewish Diaspora. Others probably merged into the Gentile population of the empire. Various fanciful theories have claimed certain peoples, for example, the American Indians, as the lost tribes.

Bibliography: Brough, R. Clayton, *The Last Tribes* (1979); Heaton, E. W., *The Hebrew Kingdoms* (1968); Noth, Martin, *The Old Testament World,* 4th ed. (1966).

Ten Years' War

The Ten Years' War (1868–78), an unsuccessful guerrilla campaign against Spanish rule in Cuba, laid the groundwork for the eventual freedom of Cuba (1898). Native Cubans had long resented Spain's arbitrary treatment of the colony, the taxes and censorship, the refusal to emancipate slaves, and the overall government corruption. Taking advantage of revolutionary ferment in Spain, Carlos Manuel de CÉSPEDES and his followers declared Cuban independence at Yara in October 1868. The provisional government soon controlled the eastern half of the island and attracted widespread support.

The bloody war dragged on for nearly 10 years. Guerrilla tactics were used against the Spanish army that arrived in 1876, but no decisive battles were fought. Cuban efforts to secure U.S. intervention failed. The war ended in 1878, when Spain, at the Pact of El Zanjón, promised amnesty and political reform. Complete emancipation was eventually granted, but many other promises were broken. Cuban rebels once again took up arms in 1895 and achieved independence 3 years later.

Bibliography: Lee, Fitzhugh, and Wheeler, Joseph, *Cuba's Struggle against Spain* (1976); Thomas, Hugh, *Cuba* (1971).

tenant

A tenant is a person who holds lands or tenements (buildings or dwellings) by any kind of TITLE or right, whether permanently or temporarily. More commonly, a tenant is one who has the temporary use of a house or apartment owned by another person (the landlord), with a LEASE usually spelling out the duration and terms of the lessee's tenancy.

Legally, the idea of tenancy is used in different ways, such as tenancy for a fixed period, tenancy at will, and tenancy at sufferance (or hold-over tenancy). Tenancy for a fixed period means that the tenant (or lessee) can, upon the payment of rent, occupy a house or apartment for a stated period of time, according to the terms of the lease. Tenancy at will is a rental agreement in which the tenant can occupy a house or apartment for an indefinite period. Either party can end the agreement at any time but usually only upon proper written notice. Most states have statutes governing the time necessary for notice of termination to be given. Tenancy at sufferance (hold-over tenancy) takes effect if a tenant occupies a house or apartment beyond the time period specified in the lease. A tenant at sufferance is not a trespasser, because he or she originally occupied the premises with the landlord's permission. Upon entering the premises and demanding possession, however, the landlord can sue the tenant for trespass and evict the tenant. If the landlord allows the tenant to remain, the landlord also has the right to extend the tenant's lease.

A tenant usually cannot sublease a house or apartment to another person (a subtenant) without the written permission of the landlord (see ASSIGNMENT). If a tenant sublets by permission, he or she still remains responsible for the subtenant's obligations to the landlord, unless the landlord has signed an agreement releasing the tenant from responsibility.

Bibliography: Faber, Stuart J., *Handbook of Landlord-Tenant Law* (1982); Hill, David S., *Landlord and Tenant Law in a Nutshell,* 2d ed. (1986).

Tender Is the Night

F. Scott FITZGERALD's most ambitious novel, *Tender Is the Night* (1934), is flawed by problems of organization that arise mainly from the author's shifting conceptions of the novel. One of the earliest versions was to be called *The Boy Who Killed His Mother*; a later version, *The Drunkard's Holiday*. As published, the novel draws heavily upon Zelda Fitzgerald's mental illness and Fitzgerald's alcoholism and self-destructive tendencies. The story is that of Dick Diver, a young psychiatrist, and his marriage to a schizophrenic patient, Nicole Warren. In effecting her cure, he loses her to another man and then experiences a pathetic decline. Fitzgerald's powers of language and characterization help the novel rise above its unconvincing story line. He continued revising the novel after its publication.   KENNETH EBLE

Bibliography: Bruccoli, Matthew J., *The Composition of "Tender Is the Night"* (1963); Fitzgerald, Zelda, *Save Me the Waltz* (1972).

tendon

Tendons are bands of tough, ropelike connective tissue joining muscles to bones or cartilage and transmitting the force of MUSCLE CONTRACTION to move skeletal parts. Consisting of closely packed, parallel bundles of white collagen fibers, tendons are resistant to extension but quite flexible and strong. They therefore can be angulated around bone to change the final direction of the pull during the muscle contraction.

Like an arm in a sleeve, tendons slide up and down within a sheath of fibrous material called the vagina fibrosa. Inside this sheath is a fine network of lymphatic vessels and a small amount of fluid to facilitate tendon movement by reducing friction. The entire structure is bound in place by small projections of connective tissue. Tendons vary in shape and size; they are attached either directly to the bone by projecting fibrils or to the periosteum.   JANET VAUGHAN

tendonitis

Tendonitis, or tendinitis, is an inflammation of the lining of a tendon's sheath and the enclosed tendon. In calcific tendonitis, a common cause of shoulder pain, calcium deposits in tendons near the shoulder joint cause secondary inflammation of a nearby fluid-filled sac, called a bursa. The bursa may rupture and be invaded by an inflammatory fluid containing insoluble calcium salts, a condition known as BURSITIS. Surgery for removal of large calcium deposits is required in only a few cases. Drugs are often prescribed for the relief of pain and inflammation of tendonitis.   PETER L. PETRAKIS

tendril

A tendril is a slender, modified plant stem, leaf, or stipule that aids in plant support. Once the tendril makes contact with a solid object, growth increases on the uncontacted side, causing the tendril to coil around the object—a process called thigmotropism. Tendrils are found in climbing plants such as the pea and the grape and may also contain adhesive disks, as with Boston ivy.

Tenerife: see SANTA CRUZ DE TENERIFE.

Teng Hsiao-p'ing   (Deng Xiaoping)   [duhng shee-ow'-ping]

Teng Hsiao-p'ing, b. Szechwan (Sichuan) province, 1904, is one of the towering figures of the Chinese Communist party (CCP). He joined the Communist Youth League in 1922 and the CCP in 1924 and studied in France and the Soviet Union in the 1920s. A veteran of the LONG MARCH, Teng was a senior political officer in the Red Army from 1927 to 1949 and became a member of the party Central Committee in 1945.

Teng Hsiao-p'ing is China's ultimate survivor. Twice purged by Mao Tse-tung, Teng became China's foremost leader by skillfully dominating three key hierarchies—army, government, and Communist party. The driving force behind China's rapid economic modernization and the transfer of power to a younger generation, Teng played a key role in raising modern China to the ranks of the great powers.

From 1949, when the People's Republic of China was established, Teng was among the most senior officials in southwest China. In 1952 he was transferred to Peking, where he advanced to become a vice-premier of the State Council (1952), a politburo member (1955), and party general secretary (1956) and served as a key negotiator in the troubled relationship with the USSR. In the early stages of the CULTURAL REVOLUTION, however, Teng was denounced as a "capitalist roader" and dismissed from all his posts. He returned to a top political role in 1973, was again purged in 1976, and was brought back to senior government, party, and military posts in mid-1977, after MAO TSE-TUNG's death.

In the period from 1977 to 1980, Teng outmaneuvered party leader HUA KUO-FENG to become China's paramount leader, although he did not assume the seemingly most senior posts in the party or the government. After 1978 he was the man chiefly responsible for China's rapid economic modernization, which included extensive contacts with the United States, Japan, and Western Europe. He was also credited with orchestrating an orderly transfer of power to a younger generation of leaders. At the 13th party congress in 1987, Teng resigned from the politburo, although he remained head of the Central Military Commission.   DONALD W. KLEIN

tengu   [tayng-goo]

In Japanese folklore, the tengu are mischievous goblins who inhabit the mountains or the air and cause storms and volcanic eruptions. Birdlike creatures with wings and long beaks, they flock in cryptomeria trees, or evergreens. Their chief is Sojobo. The tengu are said to be reincarnations of proud or vindictive persons, especially priests or warriors.

Teniers, David, the Younger   [tuh-neerz' or ten'-yurz]

The Flemish painter and engraver David Teniers the Younger, b. December 1610, d. Apr. 25, 1690, was a master of genre subjects and the most distinguished member of a large family of painters. He studied with his father, David Teniers the Elder, and his early works, such as *The Five Senses* (1635; Musée des Beaux-Arts, Brussels), owe much to Frans Francken II and Jan Breughel the Elder, whose daughter he married in 1637. Until 1638, however, he was principally influenced by the sometimes violent peasant scenes of Adriaen Brouwer—as in *The Barn* (1634; Staatliche Kunsthalle, Karlsruhe, West Germany)—and maintained a close connection with Dutch art. Teniers's genre scenes are usually more detached and genteel, with a greater refinement and delicacy of color. He was skilled at the depiction of everyday rural events, as in *Village Fête* (1646; Hermitage, Leningrad), but he also painted religious and mythological subjects. About 1651, Teniers moved to Brussels, where he served as court painter, tapestry designer, and curator of paintings to the Spanish regent, Archduke Leopold William.   MARCUS B. BURKE

Bibliography: Gerson, Horst, and Ter Kuile, E. H., *Art and Architecture in Belgium, 1600 to 1800* (1960); Liedtke, W., *Flemish Paintings in the Metropolitan Museum of Art*, 2 vols. (1984); Wilenski, R. H., *Flemish Painters, 1430–1830*, 2 vols. (1960).

Tennant, Smithson   [ten'-uhnt]

The English chemist Smithson Tennant, b. Nov. 30, 1761, d. Feb. 22, 1815, discovered (1804) the elements iridium and osmium in platinum ore and investigated (1796) the chemical nature of diamond, showing that it is a form of pure carbon. He was a professor of chemistry at Cambridge University.
          RALPH GABLE

Tennent, Gilbert

Gilbert Tennent, b. Ireland, Feb. 5, 1703, d. July 23, 1764, the son of William Tennent, was a Presbyterian leader of America's first widespread religious revival, the GREAT AWAKENING. While a minister in New Brunswick, N.J. (from 1726), Tennent came under the influence of a neighboring Dutch Reformed minister, Theodore Frelinghuysen, who taught that religion was to be a matter of the heart as well as the mind. With George Whitefield and others, Tennent traveled extensively on evangelistic missions during 1740 and 1741. His sermon "The Dangers of an Unconverted Ministry" (1740) was one of the factors leading to a rupture of colonial Presbyterianism into the New Side, prorevival, and the Old Side, traditionalist, factions. Tennent, who moved to Philadelphia's Second Presbyterian Church in 1743, eventually moderated his views and was instrumental in the reuniting of the Presbyterians in 1758.   MARK A. NOLL

Bibliography: Maxson, C. H., *The Great Awakening in the Middle Colonies* (1920); Trinterud, Leonard J., *The Forming of an American Tradition: A Re-examination of Colonial Presbyterianism* (1949).

Tennent, William

A Presbyterian minister and founder of the Log College, William Tennent, b. Ireland, 1673, d. May 6, 1746, served his denomination for nearly 30 years. Ordained (1706) an Anglican priest, he joined the Presbyterian ministry after emigrating to Pennsylvania about 1718. Near his church in Neshaminy, Pa., Tennent founded a school, the Log College, to train evangelical ministers. His students became a dynamic force in developing American Presbyterianism and extending the GREAT AWAKENING, and his school was the forerunner of other institutions, notably the College of New Jersey (1746; now Princeton University). William was the father of Gilbert Tennent.

Bibliography: Alexander, Archibald, *Biographical Sketches of the Founder and Principal Alumni of the Log College* (1845; repr. 1968); Tennent, Mary A., *Light in Darkness* (1971).

Tennessee

Tennessee, a southeastern state, stretches about 770 km (480 mi) from the Appalachian Mountains in the east to the Mississippi River in the west. It is bounded by Kentucky and Virginia on the north; North Carolina on the east; Georgia, Alabama, and Mississippi on the south; and Arkansas and Missouri on the west. Tennessee was named for the great river that cuts through the state, although the meaning of the word *Tennessee* is unknown. From its rough frontier origins Tennessee played an important role in the nation's history even before statehood in 1796. Tennessee gained its nickname, The Volunteer State, from the large numbers of soldiers it sent to the Revolutionary War, the War of 1812, the Mexican War, and the Civil War. Today Tennessee is a prosperous state, with much industrial and agricultural potential.

LAND AND RESOURCES

The state's land surface rolls and tumbles under a variety of climates and vegetation, which mark the three traditional divisions of its territory into East, Middle, and West Tennessee. East Tennessee extends from the GREAT SMOKY MOUNTAINS across a series of elongated ridges and valleys into the CUMBERLAND PLATEAU. In Middle Tennessee the Nashville Basin is rimmed by a heavily carved upland, and West Tennessee contains the Coastal Plain and the Mississippi Bottoms.

The physical environment is extremely varied. The Great Smoky Mountains rise to elevations exceeding 1,830 m (6,000 ft), and the range is among the oldest on Earth. Clingmans Dome at 2,025 m (6,643 ft), the highest point in Tennessee, is the second highest point east of the Mississippi River. Eastward from the mountains the Ridge and Valley Province consists of layers of limestone, sandstone, dolomite, and shale, which were crumpled into elongated mountains 400 to 350 million years ago. The mountains' erosional remnants are the present northeast-southwest trending ridges and intervening valleys. The ridges reach 799 m (2,620 ft) in elevation, and the valleys descend to 195 m (640 ft). Westward of the Ridge and Valley, the Cumberland Plateau varies in width from 80 to 113 km (50 to 70 mi) and in height from 610 to 1,067 m (2,000 to 3,500 ft). Its limestone and sandstone rocks have been deeply cut by streams, and most of the surface is steeply sloped. A spectacular entrenchment about 7 km (4.5 mi) wide and 113 to 129 km (70 to 80 mi) long called the Sequatchie valley occupies the southeastern margin of the plateau.

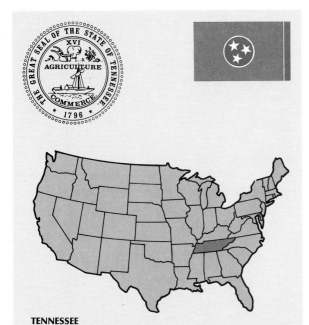

TENNESSEE

LAND. Area: 109,152 km² (42,144 mi²); rank: 34th. Capital: Nashville-Davidson (1986 est. pop., 473,670). Largest city: Memphis (1986 est. pop., 652,640). Counties: 95. Elevations: highest—2,025 m (6,643 ft), at Clingmans Dome; lowest—55 m (182 ft), at the Mississippi River.

PEOPLE. Population (1987 est.): 4,855,000; rank: 16th; density: 45.5 persons per km² (118 per mi²). Distribution (1986): 66.8% metropolitan, 33.2% nonmetropolitan. Average annual change (1980–87): +0.8%.

EDUCATION. Public enrollment (1986): elementary—577,045; secondary—241,028; higher—149,443. Nonpublic enrollment (1980): elementary—22,700; secondary—12,600; combined—32,700; higher (1986)—47,626. Institutions of higher education (1985): 80.

ECONOMY. State personal income (1986): $57.7 billion; rank: 21st. Median family income (1979): $16,564; rank: 44th. Nonagricultural labor distribution (1986): manufacturing—492,000 persons; wholesale and retail trade—450,000; government—314,000; services—385,000; transportation and public utilities—97,000; finance, insurance, and real estate—94,000; construction—90,000. Agriculture: income (1986)—$1.9 billion. Forestry: sawtimber volume (1987 prelim.)—43.46 billion board feet. Mining: value (1985)—$715 million. Manufacturing: value added (1985)—$22.2 billion. Services: value (1982)—$7.1 billion.

GOVERNMENT (1989). Governor: Ned McWherter, Democrat. U.S. Congress: Senate—2 Democrats; House—6 Democrats, 3 Republicans. Electoral college votes: 11. State legislature: 33 senators, 99 representatives.

STATE SYMBOLS. Statehood: June 1, 1796; the 16th state. Nickname: Volunteer State; bird: mockingbird; flower: iris; tree: tulip poplar; motto: Agriculture and Commerce; songs: "The Tennessee Waltz," "When It's Iris Time in Tennessee," "My Tennessee," "My Homeland, Tennessee," "Rocky Top."

The plateau drops off sharply to the west into the Nashville Basin. The basin, a rolling, rocky, oval-shaped lowland, averages about 183 m (600 ft) in elevation. It extends approximately 129 km (80 mi) north-south and 80 km (50 mi) east-west. It is surrounded by the Highland Rim, which, with the basin, was eroded from the plateau surface. The Highland Rim stands about 61 to 122 m (200 to 400 ft) higher than the basin and is 32 to 97 km (20 to 60 mi) wide. Most of the surface is gently to steeply sloping.

Farther west is the coastal lowland of West Tennessee. The rocks there are younger, and the surface more level, than any other region in the state. In the northwestern part of Tennessee is Reelfoot Lake, a shallow water body created in 1811–12 by the New Madrid earthquake.

Soils. Most of Tennessee's soils are thin and rocky, with deeper deposits occurring in the plains of West Tennessee and in eastern valleys. The steeply sloping areas are subject to heavy erosion and have low natural fertility. Near the Mississippi River are thick deposits of loess.

Climate. Tennessee's climate is transitional between the long, hot summers and mild winters farther south and the more severe winters and shorter summers of the Middle West. January temperatures normally average 5° C (41° F) in the west and 3° C (37° F) in the east. July temperatures average 26° C (79° F) in the west and 22° C (71° F) in the east. The eastern mountains receive more precipitation (1,270–1,525 mm/50–60 in) than any part of the continental United States except the Pacific Northwest. Statewide precipitation averages 1,270 mm (50 in).

Rivers and Lakes. Drainage in much of the state is partially below the surface, because the limestone rock layers are easily soluble and pocketed with underground caverns. The Tennessee River and the Cumberland River both make wide loops from Kentucky into Tennessee and back again, emptying into the Ohio River. The rivers of West Tennessee drain directly into the Mississippi River.

Vegetation and Resources. More than half of Tennessee is forested. East Tennessee contains a mix of hardwoods and softwoods, whereas most other areas are dominated by hardwoods. Cedar trees are prominent in the Nashville Basin. The once-abundant wildlife is now strictly protected.

Stone, coal, zinc, sand, gravel, phosphate rock, copper, and clays are the leading minerals by value. Barite, sulfur, and lime are also important, but water is Tennessee's most highly developed resource. The Tennessee Valley Authority changed the Tennessee River and its major tributaries from flood-prone streams into a series of quiet reservoirs behind concrete and steel dams.

PEOPLE

Tennessee's overall population density (1987 est.) is 45.5 persons per km² (118 per mi²), and approximately 60% of the population is urban. Nashville-Davidson is the capital, and Memphis is the state's largest city. Other major cities are Knoxville and Chattanooga.

Although Tennessee has traditionally been a state of high birthrates and substantial out-migration, that trend has been reversed since 1973. More people migrate into than out of the state. Birth and death rates are slightly higher than the national average.

Blacks account for almost 19% of the population (1980), with heaviest concentrations in the greater Memphis area. Most Tennesseans are predominantly of German, English, or Italian extraction. The religious denomination with the largest membership is the Baptist church, followed by the Churches

Nashville is the capital of Tennessee, and government buildings, including the state capitol (left), are clustered around War Memorial Plaza in the city center. Nearby are the many bank and insurance buildings that make Nashville a major regional financial center.

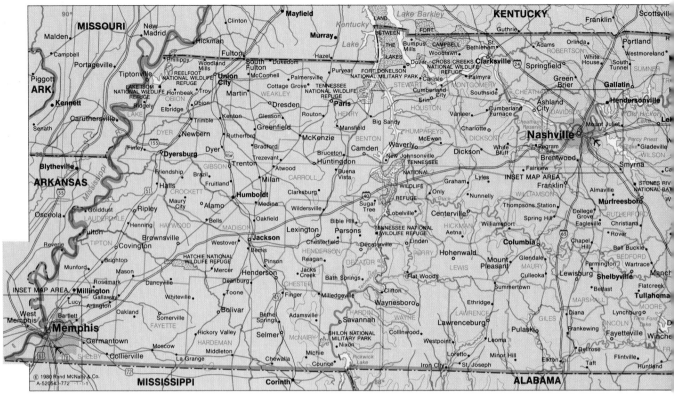

of Christ, Methodist and Presbyterian churches, and Church of the Nazarene.

Education. A statewide tax-supported school system was established in Tennessee in 1873. Not until 1909, however, was the program effectively funded. Prior to 1873, education was provided by privately owned schools, usually controlled by churches. The public school system is administered by a commissioner of education, appointed by the governor to a four-year term, who heads the state department of education and makes recommendations to a 10-member state board of edu-

The observation tower atop Clingmans Dome (2,025 m/6,643 ft), the highest point in Tennessee, affords a spectacular view of the surrounding Great Smoky Mountains National Park. The park, situated along the Tennessee-North Carolina border, was authorized in 1926.

cation. Institutions of higher education include numerous public and private colleges and universities. The University of Tennessee and its various branches (see TENNESSEE, STATE UNIVERSITIES OF) operate under a single board of trustees. Other state universities and community colleges operate under a Board of Regents. The Tennessee Higher Education Commission coordinates all higher education in the state. Prominent private universities are VANDERBILT UNIVERSITY in Nashville and the University of the South (see SOUTH, UNIVERSITY OF THE) in Sewanee.

The largest book collection in Tennessee is housed in the Joint Universities Libraries (a pooling of collections from Vanderbilt University, Peabody College, and Scarritt College) in Nashville. The second largest collection is that of the University of Tennessee Libraries in Knoxville. The state's public libraries house several million volumes.

Cultural Attractions and Historic Sites. Tennessee's state museum is housed in the War Memorial Building in Nashville. The American Museum of Science and Energy in Oak Ridge contains a major collection of technology, and smaller museums are found in nearly every city. Live theater is presented at the universities and in most large towns. Nashville, home of the GRAND OLE OPRY, is the nation's center for country and western music. The Parthenon in Nashville is an exact replica of the Greek Parthenon in Athens and was built in 1897 for the Tennessee Centennial.

The Hermitage (Andrew Jackson's home near Nashville), the Andrew Johnson National Historic Site near Greeneville, the several Civil War battlefields at Lookout Mountain, Shiloh, Chickamauga, and Murfreesboro, and the CUMBERLAND GAP National Historical Park are among the major historical sites. Knoxville's Blount Mansion (1792) and the Memphis home of Elvis Presley are also favorite attractions for visitors.

Great Smoky Mountains National Park draws millions of visitors each year. Pinson Mounds, near Jackson, has outstanding archaeological sites and the remains of an Indian city. The state also maintains state parks and recreation areas.

Communications. Tennessee has a number of daily newspapers. The *Memphis Commercial Appeal* has the largest circulation, followed by the *Nashville Tennessean*. Numerous peri-

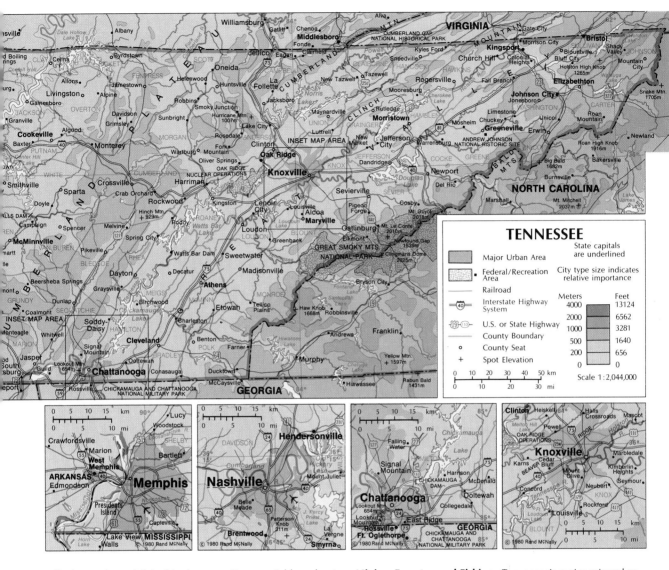

odicals are also published in the state. Commercial broadcasting is conducted through many radio and television stations.

ECONOMIC ACTIVITY

From its agricultural beginnings, Tennessee has become increasingly industrialized. As the economy diversifies, median incomes and standards of living rise, although the per capita income has remained below the national average.

Manufacturing. A significant percentage of the state's labor force is employed in manufacturing, which accounts for about one-quarter of the gross state product. The major industries in the state are those producing chemicals, electrical equipment, processed foods, nonelectrical machinery, fabricated metals, transportation equipment, rubber and plastic products, furniture, and textiles. Manufacturing centers are in Memphis, Nashville, Knoxville, and Chattanooga.

Agriculture. Tennessee's best agricultural lands are in the coastal lowlands near the Mississippi River where the surface is level and soils are relatively deep and fertile. Agriculture employs only a small percentage of the state's labor force. Farm sizes average only about 55 ha (135 acres), compared to the national average of 184 ha (455 acres). Livestock products account for about half of all farm income, and cattle is the leading commodity. Tennessee is also a leading dairy state in the south. The major crops are soybeans, tobacco, cotton, and corn. Horses are also raised, primarily in Middle and West Tennessee.

Mining, Forestry, and Fishing. Tennessee's major mineral resources are bituminous coal, stone, and zinc. Tennessee ranks first among U.S. states in the production of zinc. The state's commercial timberland is 90% privately owned. Commercial fishing is of negligible importance, but sport fishing is popular.

Energy. The giant Tennessee Valley Authority (TVA), an agency of the federal government, is the nation's largest power-generation system and generates almost all of Tennessee's electrical power. Most of that power is generated from coal-burning plants; the remainder comes from hydroelectric plants.

Transportation. Memphis, Nashville, Knoxville, and Chattanooga are major junction points for the interstate highway network as well as rail-, water-, and air-transportation centers. The Mississippi River forms Tennessee's western border and is a major navigational route, as is the Tennessee-Tombigbee Waterway, linking Tennessee cities with ports on the Gulf of Mexico. Memphis International Airport is the state's major air terminal.

GOVERNMENT

Government in Tennessee operates under a constitution adopted in 1870 and amended several times. The governor is elected to a 4-year term and may serve only two consecutive terms. The General Assembly consists of a house of representatives with 99 members elected to 2-year terms and a

(Above) *Corn, the third most valuable crop harvested in Tennessee, matures on a farm in the northeastern portion of the state.*

(Left) *Houseboats float on the lake created behind Norris Dam, the first dam constructed by the Tennessee Valley Authority (TVA).*

senate with 33 members elected to 4-year terms. Each of Tennessee's 95 counties is governed by a county court composed of a county judge and several magistrates. The 5 Supreme Court justices, although theoretically elected, usually serve until death or retirement. Most cities and towns have a mayor-council form of government. Some cities have opted for home rule rather than being under the state legislature. A metropolitan government has been adopted by Nashville-Davidson County.

Tennessee has always been divided politically—as well as socially and economically—between east and west. East Tennessee is a Republican bastion, and West and Middle Tennessee are strongly Democratic. From Reconstruction through the mid-1960s, Republicans usually won statewide elections only when their Democratic rivals were split over an issue. Since the mid-1960s, however, this pattern has begun to change. Republicans are regularly elected to some of the 9 congressional seats. Sen. Howard H. BAKER, Jr., served as the U.S. Senate majority (Republican) leader from 1981 until his retirement in 1985. Three Tennesseans have served as U.S. president: Andrew Jackson, James K. Polk, and Andrew Johnson.

HISTORY

The earliest-known inhabitants of Tennessee were MOUND BUILDERS, and when Europeans penetrated the area they found that these Indian groups were still present. The Spanish explorer Hernando DE SOTO was the first European to enter what is now Tennessee. He crossed the state and discovered (1541) the Mississippi River near present-day Memphis. At that time the CHEROKEE Indians inhabited East Tennessee; the SHAWNEE, Middle Tennessee—apparently on Cherokee sufferance; and the CHICKASAW, West Tennessee. The Chickasaw did not cede West Tennessee until 1818.

Both France and England claimed parts of the territory during the 17th and 18th centuries, but in 1763 the French relinquished all lands east of the Mississippi to England, and permanent European settlement began. In 1772 the settlers in a few isolated centers organized themselves into the WATAUGA ASSOCIATION for protection and administration of justice. Two leaders of this association were John SEVIER and James ROBERTSON, who founded (1779) a community near present-day Nashville.

The Tennessee pioneers joined in the American Revolution, and forces led by Sevier and Isaac SHELBY were instrumental in winning the important Battle of Kings Mountain (Oct. 7, 1780). The victory prevented the joining of two British forces and hastened the surrender of Cornwallis at Yorktown.

Following the Revolution and numerous skirmishes with the Cherokees for control of the territory, the State of FRANKLIN was formed (1784) in eastern Tennessee out of land ceded by

North Carolina to the federal government. North Carolina refused to recognize the new state, however, and Sevier, Franklin's governor, was arrested in 1788 and the new state collapsed. North Carolina again ceded its western territory in 1789, and President Washington commissioned (1790) William BLOUNT governor of all U.S. territory south of the Ohio River. On June 1, 1796, Tennessee became the 16th state; Sevier was its first governor.

In the War of 1812, Tennessee supplied 28,000 troops and had more soldiers than any other state in the Battle of New Orleans, won by native son Andrew JACKSON. Tennessee furnished most of the men and the commanders for the ensuing Indian wars east of the Mississippi. Among the state's famous Volunteers were Davy CROCKETT, who died at the Alamo, and Gen. Sam HOUSTON, who became the first president of the Republic of Texas.

At the outbreak of the Civil War, Tennessee was torn between the nearly unanimous support of the Union in the abolitionist east and equally strong support of the Confederacy in the slave-holding middle and west. As a result Tennessee was the last Southern state to secede. Because of its position as a border state, more battles of the Civil War were fought on Tennessee territory than any other state except Virginia. After the Union victories at Fort Donelson and Fort Pillow, Tennessee was placed under military rule, with Andrew JOHNSON as military governor. After the war Tennessee was the first Confederate state to be readmitted to the Union, but Reconstruction proved to be a difficult period in the state's history. With the election of Democrat John C. Brown as governor in 1870, Reconstruction ended, and nearly a century of Democratic domination of state politics began.

After the Civil War, agriculture made only a slow revival as the state's economic mainstay, and the ongoing process of industrialization began. In addition to the losses of the war, the population of Memphis was nearly wiped out by a yellow fever epidemic in 1878.

The tiny town of Dayton became the center of national attention in 1925 when the famous SCOPES TRIAL brought together William Jennings Bryan and Clarence S. Darrow in a bitter lawsuit concerning the teaching of Darwin's theory of evolution. The case was a test of a Tennessee statute (1925) prohibiting the teaching of evolution (which offended religious fundamentalists) in the state's public school system. The challenge was unsuccessful, and the law remained on the books until 1967.

Tennessean Cordell HULL served as secretary of state under President Franklin Roosevelt and received the Nobel Peace Prize. Estes KEFAUVER, elected from Tennessee to the U.S. Senate in 1948, became a leader in struggles for civil rights and gainst organized crime. Desegregation of public schools proceeded slowly but without serious incident in Tennessee. On Apr. 4, 1968, the Rev. Martin Luther King, Jr., was assassinated in Memphis.

Today Tennessee still has its traditional contrasts between the industrialized east and the more agricultural west. These distinctions are now more a source of strength than conflict, however. In-migration to the state is increasing; Tennessee should, therefore, be able to profit from its location in the Sun Belt and gain new industry and a better standard of living for its citizens.   SIDNEY R. JUMPER

Bibliography:
HISTORY: Bergeron, Paul H., *Paths of the Past: Tennessee, Seventeen Seventy–Nineteen Seventy* (1979); Corlew, Robert E., *Tennessee: A Short History* (1981); Dykeman, Wilma, *Tennessee* (1975); Williams, Samuel C., *Tennessee during the Revolutionary War* (1975).
LAND AND PEOPLE: Clark, Joe, *Tennessee Hill Folk* (1972); Fullerton, Ralph O., and Ray, John B., *Tennessee: Geographical Patterns and Regions* (1977); Luther, Edward T., *Our Restless Earth: The Geologic Regions of Tennessee* (1977); Matthews, Elmora M., *Neighbor and Kin: Life in a Tennessee Ridge Community* (1966).
POLITICS AND GOVERNMENT: Abernethy, Thomas P., *From Frontier to Plantation in Tennessee* (1932; repr. 1979); Greene, Lee S., et al., *Government in Tennessee*, 4th ed. (1982).

Tennessee, state universities of

All the state universities of Tennessee are coeducational and grant undergraduate and graduate degrees. The **University of Tennessee** (1794), a land-grant institution that offers a wide variety of courses in the humanities and the sciences, has its main campus at Knoxville (enrollment: 27,000; library: 1,400,000 volumes). Other campuses are at Chattanooga (1886; enrollment: 7,800; library: 316,000 volumes), with the graduate engineering center; Martin (1927; enrollment: 5,700; library: 300,000 volumes), with schools of agriculture, education, home economics, and liberal arts; and Memphis (1911; enrollment: 2,000; library: 125,000 volumes), where the schools of medical science are located. At Kingsport is a graduate center; at Tullahoma, a space institute; and at Oak Ridge, a school of biomedical science that grants graduate degrees.

Other state universities are **Tennessee State** (1912; enrollment: 8,100; library: 420,000 volumes), a land-grant school at Nashville; **Austin Peay State** (1927; enrollment: 5,400; library: 213,000 volumes), at Clarksville; **East Tennessee State** (1911; enrollment: 9,800; library: 616,000 volumes), at Johnson City; **Memphis State** (1912; enrollment: 22,000; library: 900,000 volumes), at Memphis; **Middle Tennessee State** (1911; enrollment: 11,000; library: 453,000 volumes), at Murfreesboro; and **Tennessee Technological** (1915; enrollment: 7,900; library: 519,000 volumes), at Cookeville.

Tennessee River

The Tennessee River, one of the principal rivers of the southeastern United States and a major tributary of the OHIO RIVER, flows in a half circle through the states of Tennessee, Alabama, and Kentucky. Formed by the Holston and French Broad rivers near Knoxville, Tenn., it empties into the Ohio at Paducah, Ky., after a course of 1,049 km (652 mi); it drains an area of about 105,150 km² (40,600 mi²). Principal tributaries include the Little Tennessee, Hiwassee, Paint Rock, Duck, Clinch, Flint, and Elk. The river was an important route for the invasion of Confederate territory by Union forces during the Civil War (see FORT HENRY AND FORT DONELSON). When the Tennessee Valley Authority was established in 1933 the river was accessible only to flatboats. The resulting series of dams, reservoirs, and locks has harnessed the river for power, flood control, and navigation. Late in 1984 the $2-billion Tennessee-Tombigbee Waterway was completed. It connects the Tennessee, in northeast Mississippi, with the Gulf of Mexico at Mobile, Ala., via a 377-km-long (234-mi) system of canals and locks along the Tombigbee River.

Tennessee Valley Authority

The Tennessee Valley Authority (TVA) is an agency of the United States designed to foster development in the Tennessee River Valley and certain adjacent territories. The TVA extends over large areas in seven states: Tennessee, North Carolina, Virginia, Georgia, Alabama, Mississippi, and Kentucky. It was created by the Congress in May 1933 as a major feature in the New Deal administration of Franklin D. Roosevelt. Its creation grew from the need to use the World War I hydroelectric and related facilities in north Alabama as well as to provide navigation and flood control on the Tennessee River.

In 1933 interest in regional planning was high and an agency independent of cabinet departments offered a new approach. Although similar agencies were later considered, the TVA remains unique. Proposals to create other such agencies have been opposed by states and by federal departments because of the fear that TVA-type agencies would remove some of their authority and functions. Private power companies were also opposed to what they considered unfair competition by the government.

The authority's tasks include flood control, the promotion of navigation from the river mouth to Knoxville (about 1,050 km/650 mi), and the production and sale of electric power. The TVA has also improved farm and forestry practices, produced and distributed fertilizer, and fostered recreational facilities, including the Land Between the Lakes National Recreation Area, 69,000 ha (170,000 acres) of parkland between the Kentucky and Barkley reservoirs.

Although opposition to the TVA was expressed by private power companies and by conservatives who opposed government involvement in general, the production and sale of hydroelectric power was justified legally as a by-product of flood-control and navigation dams. Nevertheless, hydroelectric production is no longer the major source of the power produced by the TVA. By 1982, of a total system capacity of 32,164 megawatts (MW), hydro capacity was 3,302 MW (10.3% of total capacity); coal-fired, 17,648 (54.9%); combustion turbine, 2,510 (7.8%); and nuclear, 5,897 (18.3%). The system capacity owned by ALCOA, Inc., and the Army Corps of Engineers was 1,277 MW (4% of total capacity), and the pumped-storage capacity was 1,530 MW (4.7%).

The TVA's dams form an integrated system that aids flood control on the Tennessee, Ohio, and Mississippi rivers. The agency inherited the existing Wilson Dam at Muscle Shoals and some smaller privately built structures. The Army Corps of Engineers had already started Norris Dam in east Tennessee. As of 1984, the TVA system was operating 49 dams that it has built or acquired since 1933. Forty of these dams are located in the Tennessee River Basin (36 owned by TVA and 4 by ALCOA, Inc., but operated by TVA). Nine are located in the Cumberland River Basin (1 owned by TVA and 8 by the Army Corps of Engineers). The Columbia Dam is under construction. High dams, designed for flood control, are found on tributaries. The highest, Fontana, reaches 146 m (480 ft) above its foundation. Run-of-the-river dams, which are not so high, are still sizable enough to form great lakes, the longest being Kentucky Lake; these structures include navigation locks.

The TVA is governed by a three-member board appointed by the president with consent of the Senate; the president designates one member to chair the authority. Board appointments have generally been free from outright political manipulation. The TVA was given considerable freedom from bureaucratic procedures, particularly in personnel and fiscal administration. Personnel management takes no account of political patronage, and accounting follows corporate practice. Some cabinet officers, most notably Harold L. ICKES, when he was secretary of the interior, contemplated adding the TVA to their own domains, but the authority has resisted such absorption.

The TVA made cooperation with the states and localities a major feature of its policy, particularly in agriculture. In its power operations it has paid little attention to states; power is distributed to large industries and to municipalities and rural cooperatives. In contract negotiations the TVA dominates municipalities and cooperatives. It seeks to enlarge power usage at the lowest feasible rates. At first the authority had some impact on the formation of planning commissions, but its influence on urban land-use planning has not been great.

The TVA is financed by appropriations, earnings, and borrowing. Flood-control and navigation operations and similar functions are supported by appropriations in accordance with practice elsewhere. Prior to 1959 most of the money for dams and steam plants was provided by appropriations; proceeds from bonds up to that time were used to buy properties from other systems. The TVA is now authorized to borrow funds for the purpose of constructing power facilities. Revenues from power operation pay power-operating expenses. Since 1933 the TVA has secured about $22.5 billion for all programs, of which about $18 billion has been used for power. Beginning with fiscal year 1961 the TVA was required to make a return to the U.S. Treasury on its investment in power facilities. Through 1987 more than $2.2 billion had been returned, including some nonpower proceeds. The TVA divides among the states in its area an amount equal to 5 percent of its gross power revenues of the preceding year, and it makes payments to states and counties equal to their former property taxes on TVA property.

Long opposed by conservatives favoring private development, the TVA came under fire from a new quarter during the 1970s. Environmentalists opposed the TVA's use of strip-mined and polluting coal and its operation of nuclear power plants. They charged that the federal government was generally insensitive to environmental needs in its commitment to growth and development and that the TVA had promoted energy-intensive industry in a time of incipient energy shortage. The Tellico Dam, held up for several years because of environmental issues, embroiled the TVA in national controversy. During the 1980s safety problems beset TVA's nuclear power facilities. The two operational plants were shut down.

The TVA's achievements are not easy to assess. It has certainly helped to transform agricultural practice in the area, and it has contributed greatly to flood control and the prevention of soil erosion. It has also aided Southern industrial growth. It has not, however, proved a model of regional development or a yardstick against which other utilities can be measured, as had once been hoped.   LEE S. GREENE

Bibliography: Chandler, William U., *Myth of TVA* (1984); Hargrove, Erwin, and Conkin, P. K., eds., *TVA: Fifty Years of Grass-Roots Bureaucracy* (1983); Hobday, V. C., *Sparks at the Grassroots* (1969); Hubbard, P. J., *Origins of the TVA* (1968); Lilienthal, D. E., *The TVA Years, 1939–45* (1964); McDonald, M. J., and Muldowny, John, *TVA and the Dispossessed* (1982); McGraw, T. K., *TVA and the Power Fight* (1971); Morgan, A. E., *The Making of TVA* (1974).

Tennessee walking horse

The Tennessee walking horse is a popular riding horse and also a show horse. Sometimes known as the plantation walking horse, it was developed during the late 18th century by

The Tennessee walking horse is named for its natural gait—a distinctive running walk. It was developed in Tennessee in the late 1800s from the Standardbred, Thoroughbred, and American saddle horse.

Tennessee plantation owners from breeds then present in their area to provide a comfortable-riding utility horse to use for inspecting crops. Larger, more powerful, and less elegant than the American saddle horse, the Tennessee walking horse averages 15 hands (155 cm/61 in) high and weighs from 454 to 636 kg (1,000 to 1,400 lb). It has three gaits—flat walk, canter, and a running walk of up to 10–13 km/h (6–8 mph).

EVERETT SENTMAN

Tenniel, Sir John   [ten'-ee-uhl]

Alice's encounter with Tweedledum and Tweedledee is one of the illustrations Sir John Tenniel created for the first edition of Lewis Carroll's Through the Looking-Glass *(1872).*

The British artist and cartoonist Sir John Tenniel, b. Feb. 28, 1820, d. Feb. 25, 1914, is best known as the illustrator of Lewis Carroll's ALICE'S ADVENTURES IN WONDERLAND (1865) and *Through the Looking-Glass* (1872). Educated at the Royal Academy schools, he won a competition in 1845 for a mural at the House of Lords in the Palace of Westminster. In 1850, Tenniel joined the staff of the satirical periodical *Punch*. From 1851 until his retirement in 1901, he produced more than 2,000 drawings, caricatures, and political cartoons for that magazine, including the noted "Dropping the Pilot" (1890), about the dismissal of Otto von Bismarck. Tenniel illustrated numerous books, including *Aesop's Fables* (1848) and Richard Harris Barnham's *Ingoldsby Legends* (1864). Tenniel was knighted in 1893.

tennis

Tennis, also known as lawn tennis, is probably the most popular and universal of the racquet-and-ball sports. The basic object of the game is to use a racquet to hit the ball over a net but within the boundaries of the opposite half of the court. The game is one of the great international pastimes. It is played both competitively and informally by more than 20 million Americans and perhaps twice that many people worldwide. For most participants tennis provides a few hours of exercise several times a month. With the proliferation of indoor courts, most notably in the United States, the sport is played all year round. Organized competition in the United States is governed by the United States Tennis Association (USTA), and international matches are regulated by the International Tennis Federation (ITF). Other variations include BADMINTON, PADDLE TENNIS, PLATFORM TENNIS, RACQUETBALL, SQUASH, and TABLE TENNIS.

HISTORY

The word *tennis* is derived from the Old French name for the game, *tenetz*. A tennislike game was played in late-13th-century France, primarily in Paris among the upper classes. Some authorities believe that the French learned about the game from the Italians and the Greeks, who were known to play a similar game during that period. The French game was called *jeu de paume*, "game of the palm," because the players used the palms of their hands to strike the ball. Later, racquets were used to allow the players greater reach. Approximately 100 years later, the British aristocracy started to play the

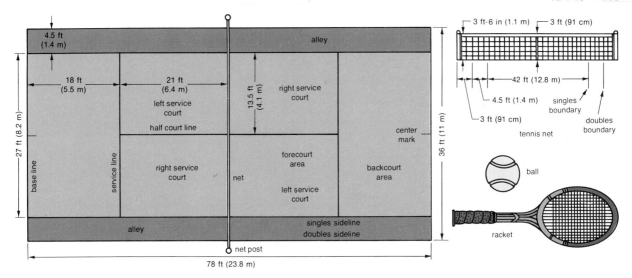

Tennis is a sport played on a 78-by-36-ft (23.8-by-11-m) court bisected by a net 3.5 ft (1.1 m) high (top right). Players hit a ball back and forth across the net with a strung racket (bottom right). Points are scored when a player fails to return the ball over the net or hits it out of bounds.

game. The game was played indoors with a cumbersome racquet and a confusing set of rules. This game, somewhat similar to badminton, is still played today and is called court tennis in the United States and real tennis in Great Britain.

It was not until 1873, however, that Maj. Walter Clopton Wingfield, making use of his knowledge of real tennis, invented lawn tennis. In December 1873, Wingfield announced a set of rules for his new racquet game. The game was played outdoors on grass on an hourglass-shaped court, and the net was much higher than it is today. Wingfield patented the sport in February 1874. Lawn tennis grew rapidly in popularity in Great Britain, and before long the game spread to the United States.

Mary Ewing Outerbridge, a wealthy woman from Staten Island, was on vacation in Bermuda in early 1874 and noticed some British men playing the game Wingfield had recently invented. She returned to Staten Island in the spring of 1874 and brought tennis equipment with her. The game was soon disseminated to other parts of the United States. Courts were built in Nahant, Mass., Newport, R.I., and Philadelphia.

Tennis continued to flourish in the United States, and the first U.S. tennis championship was held in 1881 at the Newport Casino in Newport, R.I. The U.S. championship moved to Forest Hills, N.Y., and was held there from 1915 to 1920. From 1921 to 1923 the championship was held at the Germantown

This 1880 woodcut shows a scene from an early U.S. tennis tournament, held in New Brighton on Staten Island, N.Y. Tennis costume has developed from the cumbersome formality that was characteristic of the early decades of tennis to the utilitarian and sometimes colorful dress of contemporary players.

Cricket Club in Philadelphia. The tournament moved back to Forest Hills in 1924 and was played there through 1977. In 1978 the event moved to the U.S. Tennis Association National Tennis Center in Flushing Meadow, N.Y.

International interest in tennis paralleled the interest shown within the United States. Wimbledon, the first of the major international championships, was played in 1877. The French championship was first played in 1891, and the Australian championship, in 1905. Along with the U.S. championship these tournaments soon became known as the Big Four, and they constitute the so-called Grand Slam of tennis. National teams have been competing for the Davis Cup, symbol of international tennis supremacy, since 1900. A series of zonal and interzonal matches is held annually to select a challenger. The defending nation also participates in the qualifying rounds.

EQUIPMENT AND COURT

The standard tennis court is 78 ft (23.8 m) long. For singles play, the court is 27 ft (8.2 m) wide; for doubles, the width is extended to 36 ft (11 m). A net 3.5 ft (1.1 m) high at the ends and 3 ft (91 cm) high at the center divides the length of the court in half. Toward the backline, or baseline, and 21 ft (6.4 m) from the net, is the service line. The service line, the net, and the singles sidelines form the service area. The area is divided by a center line to form two service courts, each 13.5 ft (4.1 m) wide.

The ball, traditionally white, although now often high-visibility yellow, is hollow rubber and has a wool and artificial fiber covering. For informal play, racquets may be of almost any size, weight, shape, or construction. Most racquets are 27 in (68.6 cm) long with faces 9 in (22.9 cm) wide; weight is usually 13–15 oz (368.5–425.2 g). Racquet handles are covered with leather, cloth, or plastic to ensure a good grip. Strings may be made of nylon, gut, or plastic. Although wood is the most frequently used frame material, steel, aluminum, boron, and graphite are also used.

PLAY

Serve is determined by flipping a racquet. Players serve for one complete game. The serve used most often is the overhead serve. This is accomplished by tossing the ball into the air and, with a throwing motion of the racquet hand, hitting the ball with the face of the racquet. The server must stand behind the baseline and on the first serve of the game must stay to the right of the center of the court. A proper serve will pass over the net into the service court diagonally opposite. On each serve the server has two opportunities to make a legal serve. Missing both serves results in a "double fault" and the loss of a point. After the scoring of the first point in any individual game, the server moves to the left of the cen-

BRITISH (WIMBLEDON) CHAMPIONS

Year	Winner (Country)	Year	Winner (Country)	Year	Winner (Country)
MEN'S SINGLES		1953	E. Victor Seixas (U.S.)	1912	Ethel W. Larcombe (U.K.)
1877	Spencer W. Gore (U.K.)	1954	Jaroslav Drobny (Czech.)	1913–14	Dorothy D. Chambers (U.K.)
1878	P. Frank Hadow (U.K.)	1955	Tony Trabert (U.S.)	1915–18	No competition
1879–80	J. T. Hartley (U.K.)	1956–57	Lewis Hoad (Austr.)	1919–23	Suzanne Lenglen (Fr.)
1881–86	William Renshaw (U.K.)	1958	Ashley Cooper (Austr.)	1924	Kathleen McKane (U.K.)
1887	Herbert F. Lawford (U.K.)	1959	Alejandro Olmedo (Peru)	1925	Suzanne Lenglen (Fr.)
1888	Ernest Renshaw (U.K.)	1960	Neale Frazer (Austr.)	1926	Kathleen McKane Godfree (U.K.)
1889	William Renshaw (U.K.)	1961–62	Rodney Laver (Austr.)	1927–29	Helen N. Wills (U.S.)
1890	Willoughby J. Hamilton (U.K.)	1963	Charles McKinley (U.S.)	1930	Helen Wills Moody (U.S.)
1891–92	Wilfred Baddeley (U.K.)	1964–65	Roy Emerson (Austr.)	1931	Cecil Aussem (Ger.)
1893–94	Joshua L. Pim (U.K.)	1966	Manuel Santana (Spain)	1932–33	Helen Wills Moody (U.S.)
1895	Wilfred Baddeley (U.K.)	1967	John Newcombe (Austr.)	1934	Dorothy E. Round (U.K.)
1896	Harold S. Mahony (U.K.)	1968–69	Rodney Laver (Austr.)	1935	Helen Wills Moody (U.S.)
1897–1900	Reginald Doherty (U.K.)	1970–71	John Newcombe (Austr.)	1936	Helen H. Jacobs (U.S.)
1901	Arthur W. Gore (U.K.)	1972	Stanley Smith (U.S.)	1937	Dorothy E. Round (U.K.)
1902–06	Hugh L. Doherty (U.K.)	1973	Jan Kodes (Czech.)	1938	Helen Wills Moody (U.S.)
1907	Norman Brookes (Austr.)	1974	James Connors (U.S.)	1939	Alice Marble (U.S.)
1908–09	Arthur W. Gore (U.K.)	1975	Arthur Ashe (U.S.)	1940–45	No competition
1910–13	Anthony F. Wilding (N.Z.)	1976–80	Björn Borg (Sweden)	1946	Pauline Betz (U.S.)
1914	Norman Brookes (Austr.)	1981	John McEnroe (U.S.)	1947	Margaret Osborne (U.S.)
1915–18	No competition	1982	James Connors (U.S.)	1948–50	Louise Brough (U.S.)
1919	Gerald Patterson (Austr.)	1983–84	John McEnroe (U.S.)	1951	Doris J. Hart (U.S.)
1920–21	William T. Tilden (U.S.)	1985–86	Boris Becker (W.Ger.)	1952–54	Maureen Connolly (U.S.)
1922	Gerald Patterson (Austr.)	1987	Pat Cash (Austr.)	1955	Louise Brough (U.S.)
1923	William Johnston (U.S.)	1988	Stefan Edberg (Sweden)	1956	Shirley J. Fry (U.S.)
1924	Jean Borotra (Fr.)	**WOMEN'S SINGLES**		1957–58	Althea Gibson (U.S.)
1925	René Lacoste (Fr.)	1884–85	Maud Watson (U.K.)	1959–60	Maria Bueno (Brazil)
1926	Jean Borotra (Fr.)	1886	Blanche Bingley (U.K.)	1961	Angela Mortimer (U.K.)
1927	Henri Cochet (Fr.)	1887–88	Lottie Dod (U.K.)	1962	Karen H. Susman (U.S.)
1928	René Lacoste (Fr.)	1889	Blanche Bingley Hillyard (U.K.)	1963	Margaret Smith (Austr.)
1929	Henri Cochet (Fr.)	1890	L. Rice (U.K.)	1964	Maria Bueno (Brazil)
1930	William T. Tilden (U.S.)	1891–93	Lottie Dod (U.K.)	1965	Margaret Smith (Austr.)
1931	Sidney B. Wood (U.S.)	1894	Blanche Bingley Hillyard (U.K.)	1966–68	Billie Jean King (U.S.)
1932	Ellsworth Vines (U.S.)	1895–96	Charlotte Cooper (U.K.)	1969	Ann Haydon Jones (U.K.)
1933	John Crawford (Austr.)	1897	Blanche Bingley Hillyard (U.K.)	1970	Margaret Smith Court (Austr.)
1934–36	Fred J. Perry (U.K.)	1898	Charlotte Cooper (U.K.)	1971	Evonne Goolagong (Austr.)
1937–38	J. Donald Budge (U.S.)	1899–1900	Blanche Bingley Hillyard (U.K.)	1972–73	Billie Jean King (U.S.)
1939	Robert L. Riggs (U.S.)	1901	Charlotte Cooper Sterry (U.K.)	1974	Chris Evert (U.S.)
1940–45	No competition	1902	M. E. Robb (U.K.)	1975	Billie Jean King (U.S.)
1946	Yvon Petra (Fr.)	1903–04	Dorothy K. Douglass (U.K.)	1976	Chris Evert (U.S.)
1947	John A. Kramer (U.S.)	1905	May G. Sutton (U.S.)	1977	Virginia Wade (U.K.)
1948	Robert Falkenburg (U.S.)	1906	Dorothy K. Douglass (U.K.)	1978–79	Martina Navratilova (Czech.)
1949	Fred R. Schroeder (U.S.)	1907	May G. Sutton (U.S.)	1980	Evonne Goolagong (Austr.)
1950	J. Edward Patty (U.S.)	1908	Charlotte Cooper Sterry (U.K.)	1981	Chris Evert Lloyd (U.S.)
1951	Richard Savitt (U.S.)	1909	Dorothea P. Boothby (U.K.)	1982–87	Martina Navratilova (U.S.)
1952	Frank Sedgman (Austr.)	1910–11	Dorothy D. Chambers (U.K.)	1988	Steffi Graf (W.Ger.)

ter of the court and serves to the other service area. After each point this change of service court is repeated. In doubles, as in singles, one person serves for the entire game, but the serve is directed first to one member of the opposing team and then to the other. Should a serve touch the net and then fall into the appropriate service court, the ball is termed a *let*, and the server is permitted to try that serve again. A foot fault is called if the server's foot touches or crosses the baseline before the ball is struck, resulting in the loss of a point.

After the serve the players attempt to hit the ball back and forth over the net until one player commits an error or is unable to return the ball. A point is lost when a player fails to hit the ball before the second bounce, hits the ball into the net, hits the ball out of bounds, touches the net with the racquet or with the body, hits the ball twice, is hit by the ball, or hits the ball before it crosses the net. Players switch court sides after the first game and after each odd-numbered game.

SCORING

A unique system is used to keep score in tennis. Games, which consist of four points, are scored as follows: "love" indicates no score, "15" indicates one point scored, "30" indicates two points, "40" indicates three points, and "game" indicates four points. If a tie of 40-all occurs, the situation is called *deuce,* and to win one player must score two points more than the opponent in that game.

Tennis matches are usually won by winning the best out of three or the best out of five "sets." In most cases, a set is

Martina Navratilova leaps for a forehand volley at the 1984 Wimbledon tournament, whose singles title she won for the third consecutive year. After her 1987 victory, she had won eight times overall (1978–79, 1982–87). Navratilova's phenomenal singles and doubles performances in the 1980s assure her place as one of the greatest women players of all time. She has won more prize money than any tennis player—man or woman—in history.

U.S. OPEN CHAMPIONS

Year	Winner (Country)	Year	Winner (Country)	Year	Winner (Country)
MEN'S SINGLES		1958	Ashley Cooper (Austr.)	1909–11	Hazel V. Hotchkiss (U.S.)
1881–87	Richard D. Sears (U.S.)	1959–60	Neale Fraser (Austr.)	1912–14	Mary K. Browne (U.S.)
1888–89	Henry W. Slocum, Jr. (U.S.)	1961	Roy Emerson (Austr.)	1915–18	Molla Bjurstedt (U.S.)
1890–92	Oliver S. Campbell (U.S.)	1962	Rodney Laver (Austr.)	1919	Hazel H. Wightman (U.S.)
1893–94	Robert D. Wrenn (U.S.)	1963	Rafael Osuna (Mex.)	1920–22	Molla B. Mallory (U.S.)
1895	Fred H. Hovey (U.S.)	1964	Roy Emerson (Austr.)	1923–25	Helen N. Wills (U.S.)
1896–97	Robert D. Wrenn (U.S.)	1965	Manuel Santana (Spain)	1926	Molla B. Mallory (U.S.)
1898–1900	Malcolm D. Whitman (U.S.)	1966	Fred S. Stolle (Austr.)	1927–29	Helen N. Wills (U.S.)
1901–02	William A. Larned (U.S.)	1967	John Newcombe (Austr.)	1930	Betty Nuthall (U.K.)
1903	Hugh L. Doherty (U.K.)	1968	Arthur Ashe (U.S.)	1931	Helen Wills Moody (U.S.)
1904	Holcombe Ward (U.S.)	1969	Rodney Laver (Austr.)	1932–35	Helen H. Jacobs (U.S.)
1905	Beals C. Wright (U.S.)	1970	Kenneth Rosewall (Austr.)	1936	Alice Marble (U.S.)
1906	William J. Clothier (U.S.)	1971	Stanley Smith (U.S.)	1937	Anita Lizana (Chile)
1907–11	William A. Larned (U.S.)	1972	Ilie Nastase (Rom.)	1938–40	Alice Marble (U.S.)
1912–13	Maurice E. McLoughlin (U.S.)	1973	John Newcombe (Austr.)	1941	Sarah Palfrey Cooke (U.S.)
1914	R. Norris Williams (U.S.)	1974	James Connors (U.S.)	1942–44	Pauline M. Betz (U.S.)
1915	William M. Johnston (U.S.)	1975	Manuel Orantes (Spain)	1945	Sarah Palfrey Cooke (U.S.)
1916	R. Norris Williams (U.S.)	1976	James Connors (U.S.)	1946	Pauline M. Betz (U.S.)
1917–18	R. Lindley Murray (U.S.)	1977	Guillermo Vilas (Argent.)	1947	Louise Brough (U.S.)
1919	William M. Johnston (U.S.)	1978	James Connors (U.S.)	1948–50	Margaret O. du Pont (U.S.)
1920–25	William T. Tilden (U.S.)	1979–81	John McEnroe (U.S.)	1951–53	Maureen Connolly (U.S.)
1926–27	René Lacoste (Fr.)	1982–83	James Connors (U.S.)	1954–55	Doris Hart (U.S.)
1928	Henri Cochet (Fr.)	1984	John McEnroe (U.S.)	1956	Shirley J. Fry (U.S.)
1929	William T. Tilden (U.S.)	1985–87	Ivan Lendl (Czech.)	1957–58	Althea Gibson (U.S.)
1930	John H. Doeg (U.S.)	1988	Mats Wilander (Sweden)	1959	Maria Bueno (Brazil)
1931–32	H. Ellsworth Vines, Jr. (U.S.)	**WOMEN'S SINGLES**		1960–61	Darlene Hard (U.S.)
1933–34	Frederick J. Perry (U.K.)	1887	Ellen F. Hansell (U.S.)	1962	Margaret Smith (Austr.)
1935	Wilmer L. Allison (U.S.)	1888–89	Bertha L. Townsend (U.S.)	1963–64	Maria Bueno (Brazil)
1936	Frederick J. Perry (U.K.)	1890	Ellen C. Roosevelt (U.S.)	1965	Margaret Smith (Austr.)
1937–38	J. Donald Budge (U.S.)	1891–92	Mabel E. Cahill (U.S.)	1966	Maria Bueno (Brazil)
1939	Robert L. Riggs (U.S.)	1893	Aline M. Terry (U.S.)	1967	Billie Jean King (U.S.)
1940	W. Donald McNeill (U.S.)	1894	Helen R. Helwig (U.S.)	1968	Virginia Wade (U.K.)
1941	Robert L. Riggs (U.S.)	1895	Juliette P. Atkinson (U.S.)	1969–70	Margaret Smith Court (Austr.)
1942	Frederick R. Schroeder (U.S.)	1896	Elisabeth H. Moore (U.S.)	1971–72	Billie Jean King (U.S.)
1943	Joseph E. Hunt (U.S.)	1897–98	Juliette P. Atkinson (U.S.)	1973	Margaret Smith Court (Austr.)
1944–45	Frank A. Parker (U.S.)	1899	Marion Jones (U.S.)	1974	Billie Jean King (U.S.)
1946–47	John A. Kramer (U.S.)	1900	Myrtle McAteer (U.S.)	1975–78	Chris Evert (U.S.)
1948–49	Richard A. Gonzales (U.S.)	1901	Elisabeth H. Moore (U.S.)	1979	Tracy Austin (U.S.)
1950	Arthur D. Larsen (U.S.)	1902	Marion Jones (U.S.)	1980	Chris Evert Lloyd (U.S.)
1951–52	Frank Sedgman (Austr.)	1903	Elisabeth H. Moore (U.S.)	1981	Tracy Austin (U.S.)
1953	Tony Trabert (U.S.)	1904	May G. Sutton (U.S.)	1982	Chris Evert Lloyd (U.S.)
1954	E. Victor Seixas, Jr. (U.S.)	1905	Elisabeth H. Moore (U.S.)	1983–84	Martina Navratilova (U.S.)
1955	Tony Trabert (U.S.)	1906	Helen Homans (U.S.)	1985	Hana Mandlikova (Czech.)
1956	Kenneth Rosewall (Austr.)	1907	Evelyn Sears (U.S.)	1986–87	Martina Navratilova (U.S.)
1957	Malcolm Anderson (Austr.)	1908	Maud Bargar-Wallach (U.S.)	1988	Steffi Graf (W.Ger.)

awarded to the player who wins six games before the opponent has won more than four. Formerly, if a set was tied at five games apiece, the method used to resolve it was similar to the deuce arrangement in the individual games. Thus, set scores of 7–5, 10–8, or 15–13 were not uncommon. A recent innovation called a tie breaker is now generally used to terminate quickly what might turn into an extended set. Whenever a set is tied at six games apiece, the tie breaker is invoked. There are two tie-breaking systems. In one the first player to score five out of nine individual points wins the set; in the other the first player to score seven individual points wins, provided the margin of victory is two points or more.

THE OPEN-TOURNAMENT MOVEMENT

For the first 90 years of organized competition professionals were not allowed to compete against amateurs. Most tennis historians agree that the growth of tennis was stunted considerably by keeping the professionals out of the major tournaments, thus depriving the public of the opportunity to watch all the best players in action against each other.

In March 1968, however, led by the British Lawn Tennis Association, the International Lawn Tennis Federation (now the International Tennis Federation) voted unanimously to approve and sanction "open" tennis. They approved about a dozen open tournaments for 1968. With most of the best amateur and professional players battling in the most prestigious tournaments, interest in tennis on both the spectator and the player levels grew dramatically. Professionals have come to dominate the sport, playing for huge sums of money—the

men's tour offered $25 million in prize money in 1988, and the women's circuit, about $15 million.   STEVE FLINK

Bibliography: Anthony, Julie, and Bolletieri, Nick, *A Winning Combination* (1980); Collins, Bud, and Hollander, Zander, eds., *Modern Encyclopedia of Tennis* (1980); Gallwey, W. Timothy, *The Inner Game of Tennis* (1974) and *Inner Tennis* (1976); Hopman, Harry, *Better Tennis* (1976); Laver, Rod, *The Education of a Tennis Player* (1973); Navratilova, Martina, and Carillo, Mary, *Tennis My Way: A Complete Guide to Training and Playing* (1984); Tilden, Bill, *How to Play Better Tennis* (1962); Tingay, Lance, *Tennis: A Pictorial History* (1977); U.S. Professional Tennis Association, *Tennis: A Professional Guide* (1984).

Tennyson, Alfred, Lord   [ten'-i-suhn]

The preeminent English poet of his time, Alfred, Lord Tennyson, b. Somersby, Lincolnshire, Aug. 6, 1809, d. Oct. 6, 1892, began writing poetry as a child and, with two of his brothers, Frederick and Charles, published a volume of poems before he entered Cambridge University in 1827. There he formed a close friendship with Arthur Hallam, whose death (1833), combined with the poor reception of his own *Poems* (1832), plunged Tennyson into a decade-long silence during which he wrote much but published little. Reemerging as a mature poet in 1842 with a two-volume collection of new and revised poems that included "Locksley Hall," "Ulysses," "Morte d'Arthur," "Mariana," and "The Lady of Shalott," he then established his eminence with *In Memoriam* (1850), his elegy for Hallam. Later the same year he was named poet laureate, and in 1859 he began publishing his version of a national epic

Alfred, Lord Tennyson, portrayed (1891) by Witt Maugetson, epitomized the moral and philosophical concerns of the Victorian age in his work. His appointment as England's poet laureate followed the publication of In Memoriam (1850), one of the finest elegies in English literature. His poetry is now acclaimed for its great lyricism and technical virtuosity. (National Portrait Gallery, London.)

in IDYLLS OF THE KING, retellings of Arthurian legends.

As laureate, Tennyson composed a number of poems on national occasions, notably The CHARGE OF THE LIGHT BRIGADE. In the exquisite lyrics of "Maud" (1855), he used as the nucleus for an extended psychological monodrama some verses he had written almost 20 years before. After the success of *Enoch Arden and Other Poems* (1864), which sold 40,000 copies, and by the time the immensely popular *Idylls of the King* had reached completion (1885), Tennyson had become both a celebrity and a sage. He accepted a baron and a seat in the House of Lords in 1884.

One of Tennyson's important concerns was to involve his poetry in the public life of the time without sacrificing personal feeling and perception. During the early 1830s reviewers had attacked the moody introspection of his lyrics and their artful images and melodious sound as too remote from common experience. So *In Memoriam* first enlarges the poet's personal sorrow into doubts about the order of the universe, then concludes with assurances that the loss of individual lives will be made good both in eternity and in the advance of human history. Similarly, during the last decade of his life, Tennyson complemented his analyses of Greek figures—*Tiresias, and Other Poems* (1885) and *The Death of Oenone* (1892)—with reflections on death and the meaning of life—*Locksley Hall Sixty Years After* (1886) and "Crossing the Bar" (1889)—and with historical plays such as the highly successful *Becket* (1884).   Reviewed by EDGAR F. SHANNON, JR.

Bibliography: Albright, Daniel, *Tennyson: The Muses' Tug-of-War* (1987); Buckley, Jerome H., *Tennyson: The Growth of a Poet* (1960); Culler, A. Dwight, *The Poetry of Tennyson* (1977); Jump, John D., ed., *Tennyson: The Critical Heritage* (1967); Kincaid, James R., *Tennyson's Major Poems* (1975); Martin, Robert B., *Tennyson: The Unquiet Heart* (1980); Pitt, Valerie, *Tennyson Laureate* (1962); Richardson, Joanna, *The Pre-Eminent Victorian: A Study of Tennyson* (1962; repr. 1973); Ricks, Christopher B., *Tennyson* (1972); Tucker, Herbert F., Jr., *Tennyson and the Doom of Romanticism* (1988).

Tenochtitlán   [tay-nohch-teet-lahn']

The Aztec capital of Tenochtitlán (at modern Mexico City) was founded in AD 1345 (or 1325, according to some chronicles) on a muddy island in the lake that at that time filled the Basin of Mexico. A second group of Aztec settled the nearby island of Tlatelolco in 1358. Both sites began as small collections of reed huts but, with the growth of Aztec power, developed into cities, eventually fusing into a single great conurbation.

By 1519, the year the Spaniards arrived, Tenochtitlán-Tlatelolco had a population of more than 150,000. It was laid out on a grid plan and covered more than 12 km² (4.6 mi²), much of this consisting of reclaimed swampland that formed a zone of fertile garden plots around the edge of the city. At the center of Tenochtitlán was a large walled precinct, the focus of religious activity, containing the main temples (dedicated to Huitzilopochtli, Tlaloc the Rain God, and Quetzalcóatl); also

found here were schools and priests' quarters, a court for the ritual ballgame, a wooden rack holding the skulls of sacrificial victims, and many commemorative sculptures. Just outside the precinct walls were the palaces of MONTEZUMA II and earlier rulers. A 16-km (10-mi) dike sealed off part of the lake and controlled flooding, so that Tenochtitlán, like a Mexican Venice, stood on an island in an artificial lagoon. Causeways linked the island to the lakeshore, and canals reached to all parts of the city.

Between 1519 and 1521, Tenochtitlán was besieged by the Spaniards under Hernán CORTÉS. To create space for their cavalry to maneuver, the invaders pulled down most of the city's buildings, later constructing colonial Mexico City on the same spot. Because of these activities and the gradual expansion of the modern national capital, only a few mutilated Aztec buildings can be seen today.   WARWICK BRAY

Bibliography: Bray, Warwick, *Everyday Life of the Aztecs* (1968; repr. 1987); Broda, Johanna, et al., *The Great Temple of Tenochtitlán* (1987).

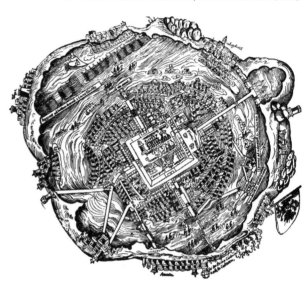

At the center of this map of the Aztec capital Tenochtitlán, from the letters of Hernán Cortés (published 1524), lies the enclosed sacred precinct, which was dominated by a great pyramid with two temples, dedicated to the gods Huitzilopochtli and Tlaloc, built on top.

tenor

The highest adult male voice, excepting falsetto and COUNTERTENOR, is the tenor, with a range roughly from C below middle C upward for about two octaves. The name is derived from the lowest part sung in 12th-century polyphony, where it was the responsibility of the tenor to hold (*tenere*) the cantus firmus in lengthened notes. As choral voices divided into tenor and bass, the term took on its present meaning. The distinction between lyric and dramatic tenors is one of quality rather than range, the two being akin to their soprano counterparts.

A heldentenor, one with exceptional qualities of endurance, is required for certain roles in the German romantic opera literature, particularly Wagnerian roles. Tenor also signifies instruments next higher than the bass of the same family, as in tenor saxophone and tenor trombone.   ELWYN A. WIENANDT

tenpounder

The tenpounder, or ladyfish, *Elops saurus*, is one of the most primitive of bony fishes. Closely related to the tarpon, it is found in tropical and subtropical seas around the world. Reaching a length of about 90 cm (3 ft) and a weight up to 4.7 kg (10 lb), it has a bony plate under the mouth, many small sharp teeth in the mouth, a single soft-rayed dorsal fin, and a long, deeply forked tail. It feeds on small fishes and crustaceans, and its larval form is transparent and ribbonlike. The tenpounder is not highly regarded as food but is a popular game fish because it makes exciting leaps when hooked.

C. P. IDYLL

tenrec   [ten'-rek]

The tenrec, Tenrec ecaudatus, is a small mammal native to Madagascar. One of the largest of the insectivores, it uses its snout to dig for worms and insects.

The 20 or more species of tenrecs are a group of essentially primitive, earthworm- and insect-eating mammals indigenous to Madagascar that form the family Tenrecidae. Nocturnal animals with poor vision, the sharply muzzled tenrecs grow to about 37 cm (15 in). They have compact bodies and short legs and nest in burrows. Extremely prolific, tenrecs bear litters of up to 25; the female has up to 12 pairs of mammary glands. The spring tenrec, or Madagascar hedgehog, erects its stiff, spiny hairs and curls into a ball when threatened, thus resembling a true hedgehog. Some tenrecs hibernate through the hot, dry season.

EVERETT SENTMAN

Tenskwatawa: see SHAWNEE PROPHET.

tent caterpillar

Tent caterpillar is the common name for the larval, or caterpillar, stage of certain moths (genus *Malacosoma*) of the family Lasiocampidae. The larva are economically important because they often seriously damage tree foliage. Adult females lay egg clusters on tree twigs. The hatched caterpillars construct a tentlike shelter of silk to which they return at night after feeding on foliage. Mature larvae are about 7.5 cm (3 in) long, with bright spots or streaks on a dark, hairy body.

STEPHEN C. REINGOLD

10th Amendment

The 10th Amendment (1791) is the final amendment in the BILL OF RIGHTS of the U.S. Constitution. It provides that those powers not delegated to the federal government by the Constitution nor prohibited to the states are reserved to the states or to the people. The main purpose of the amendment was to counter fears that the new national government would trespass on the authority of the states.

Although the amendment does not enumerate these reserved powers, traditionally they have included internal matters such as local government, education, and regulation of commerce, labor, and business within the state, as well as such matters as marriage, divorce, inheritance, and related family concerns. The states also share certain powers with the federal government, such as establishing courts, chartering banks, imposing taxes, and protecting the public health. The 10th Amendment is not seen today as limiting the authority of the federal government where the exercise of its powers might interfere with those of the states. The reverse was the case, however, from the time that Roger Brooke Taney became (1836) chief justice of the Supreme Court until a century later (see NATIONAL LABOR RELATIONS BOARD V. JONES & LAUGHLIN STEEL CORPORATION, 1937, and UNITED STATES V. DARBY, 1941). During that time, in famous cases such as *Collector v. Day* (1871), HAMMER V. DAGENHART (1918), and SCHECHTER POULTRY CORPORATION V. UNITED STATES (1935), the 10th Amendment had been cited to curtail powers of Congress.

See also: STATE RIGHTS.

tenure: see ACADEMIC FREEDOM.

Tenure of Office Act

The Tenure of Office Act, passed by the U.S. Congress over President Andrew JOHNSON's veto on Mar. 2, 1867, stipulated that a president could not, without Senate approval, remove any officeholder appointed with the Senate's consent.

The act was adopted in part to keep in office appointees sympathetic to Radical RECONSTRUCTION, particularly Secretary of War Edwin M. STANTON. Johnson defied the act with his dismissal of Stanton on Feb. 21, 1868, spurring the House of Representatives to impeach the chief executive three days later. The act was amended in 1869, repealed in 1887, and declared to have been unconstitutional by the U.S. Supreme Court in 1926.

Teotihuacán   [tay-oh-tee-wah-kahn']

The Pyramid of the Sun at Teotihuacán, one of the earliest commercial and religious centers of pre-Columbian central Mexico, is famed for its monumental size and impressive architecture. Teotihuacán flourished during the early part of the 1st millennium AD.

Teotihuacán, located just northeast of Mexico City, dominated central Mexico and much of the rest of MESOAMERICA during the early part of the 1st millennium AD. Although still a small settlement in about 200 BC, by AD 100 it had become a large center with a population of 50,000 or more. Known for its enormous expanse of monumental architecture, Teotihuacán was the first true city in Mesoamerica and one of its largest. At its peak (AD c.600) it housed more than 100,000 people and was the capital of a powerful state or empire. Its direct political influence reached EL TAJÍN and a number of other Gulf Coast centers. KAMINALJUYÚ, in the highlands of Guatemala, was another Teotihuacán outpost and a center for economic interaction with the MAYA.

Farmers formed the backbone of Teotihuacán society, and political officials, priests, merchants, and military leaders made up the elite. Craft specialists—stoneworkers, potters, sculptors, painters, and the like—lived in their own neighborhoods, as did foreign residents. After 600, Teotihuacán influence began to shrink, probably because of internal stresses, including agricultural problems. By 650 it had lost its dominance, and shortly thereafter it was looted and burned. Although Teotihuacán was never again the seat of great power, a small population lived on in its valley. The Aztec believed that the ruins had been built by the gods, and they sometimes made pilgrimages there.

Mexican and foreign archaeologists have undertaken extensive excavation and reconstruction at Teotihuacán throughout the 20th century. A large-scale mapping project during the 1960s produced the first accurate plan of the city.

At its peak Teotihuacán covered about 20 km² (8 mi²), with temples, palaces, markets, reservoirs, and more than 2,000 multiroomed apartment compounds. The streets and buildings were laid out on a grid plan, and even streams within the city were channeled to conform to the pattern. At the intersection of the principal avenues were the main temple-palace complex (the Citadel) and the chief marketplace (the Great Compound). The so-called Street of the Dead, lined with palaces and temples, ran north past the enormous Pyramid of the Sun to the slightly smaller Pyramid of the Moon, both of which also supported temples. Polychrome murals adorned the walls of major buildings, many depicting gods later worshiped by the AZTEC. JOHN S. HENDERSON

Bibliography: Adams, R. E. W., *Prehistoric Mesoamerica* (1977); Millon, R. F., et al., *Pyramid of the Sun at Teotihuacán* (1965) and *Urbanization at Teotihuacán* (1973).

Tepe Gawra [te'-pe gow-rah']

At the ancient site of Tepe Gawra, 24 km (15 mi) northeast of Mosul, Iraq, archaeologists discovered remains covering a sequence of settlements dating from the Neolithic period to the middle of the 2d millennium BC. The temple at Tepe Gawra, among the earliest known in northern Mesopotamia, contains a number of features basic to Mesopotamian temples in later periods. It is entered through a stairway leading to a platform; its center is a cella, along one side of which is placed an altar and offering table. Subsidiary rooms in the corner bastions are set off from the central area. The temple's walls are buttressed both inside and out, an architectural feature that continued to distinguish Mesopotamian temples from secular buildings until the Hellenistic period. Tepe Gawra was first discovered by Austen Henry Layard; excavations were conducted at the site in the 1920s and '30s. PHILIP KOHL

Bibliography: Speiser, E. A., et al., *Excavations at Tepe Gawra*, 2 vols. (1935, 1950).

Tepe Yahya [te'-pe yah-yah']

The archaeological site of Tepe Yahya, in Iran, 225 km (140 mi) south of Kerman, spans several millennia of intermittent occupation from 4500 BC to AD 500. Throughout this time the settlement maintained its position as a political center of the Iranian Plateau. Once thought to have been a cultural backwater, this region has emerged as part of a complex pattern of interaction that linked several diverse cultures, including those of Mesopotamia and of the Indus Valley. The most spectacular periods at Tepe Yahya were 3100–2900 BC and 2600–2500 BC, when it appears to have served as a thriving center of commerce and overland trade, including the export of chlorite. Discovered (1967) by a team of Harvard University archaeologists, Tepe Yahya was excavated from 1968 to 1977. PHILIP KOHL

Bibliography: Sabloff, J. A., and Lamberg-Karlovsky, C. C., eds., *Ancient Civilization and Trade* (1975).

tepee [tee'-pee]

Tepee, or *tipi*, is a Sioux Indian word for a portable dwelling composed of a framework of long wooden poles pointed together and fastened at the top and spread out on the ground in a circle at the butt ends, with a tent cover of skins being drawn around the frame and fastened on the ground with pegs or weighted with stones. Most tepees have a central fireplace over which a smokehole is formed by drawing the cover apart at the apex. A tepee may be as large as 4.5 m (15 ft) high and 7 to 9 m (23 to 30 ft) in diameter and can be assembled or disassembled by an expert within a few minutes. Tepees traditionally were used principally by the bison hunters of the Great Plains of North America, notably the BLACKFOOT, CHEYENNE, CROW, and SIOUX. GENE WELTFISH

Bibliography: Laubin, Reginald and Gladys, *The Indian Tipi: Its History, Construction and Use*, 2d ed. (1977).

Tepic [tay-peek']

Tepic (1982 est. pop., 177,007), capital city of Nayarit state in western Mexico, lies about 32 km (20 mi) from the Pacific Ocean. It is a food-processing and commercial center for the surrounding agricultural area, which produces corn, sugarcane, rice, coffee, and tobacco. Founded in 1531, Tepic remained isolated until the arrival of the railroad in 1912.

tequila [tuh-kee'-luh]

Tequila is an alcoholic beverage made of the fermented and distilled sap taken from the base of AGAVE plants, especially those cultivated in the Mexican state of Jalisco. The liquor, which is usually distilled twice to achieve the desired purity and potency, is colorless and is not aged. (A few tequilas, however, may be put up to age in oak vats, and they take on a pale yellow color.) Alcohol content ranges from 80 to 100 proof (40% to 50%). Mescal and pulque, both similar to tequila but heavier in flavor, are distilled from sap taken from the roots, stalk, and leaves of wild agave plants.

Ter Borch, Gerard [tur-bork']

In A Boy Ridding His Dog of Fleas (c.1665), a typically charming genre scene by Gerard Ter Borch, the boy has cast aside his lesson book to attend to the dog, which endures his ministrations with a look of watchful calm. (Bayerische Staatsgemäldesammlungen, Munich.)

With Jan Vermeer and Pieter de Hooch, Gerard Ter Borch, b. 1617, d. Dec. 8, 1681, was one of the principal creators of the high genre style of the 1650s and '60s that was the climax of the long tradition of Dutch realism. Ter Borch revealed a world in which the writing of a letter, the playing of a guitar, or the peeling of an apple could be a major event. Ter Borch came from a family of artists, and by his late teens his paintings of soldiers and their women quietly drinking and playing cards or backgammon had become well known. Throughout his career he was a sensitive portrait painter who portrayed his well-dressed subjects with a vulnerability unusual in commissioned portraits.

He did the official painting (1648; National Gallery, London) of the signatories of the Treaty of Westphalia, which ended the Thirty Years' War and confirmed the independence of the

Netherlands from Spain. In the 1650s and '60s, Ter Borch did his greatest work, paintings of women in boudoirs looking in the mirror, arranging their hair, or reading love letters. His brilliant painting of satins, oriental carpets, and jewels was partly a response to the extraordinary affluence in Dutch society after 1650; it also arose from a love of the textures and the materials themselves. Above all, his subjects seem to live in a world that is gentle, safe, and civilized.

FRANKLIN W. ROBINSON

Bibliography: Rosenberg, Jakob, et al., *Dutch Art and Architecture, 1600-1800*, 2d ed. (1972).

terbium   [tur'-bee-uhm]

Terbium is a chemical element, a very rare silver-gray metal of the LANTHANIDE SERIES. Its symbol is Tb, its atomic number 65, and its atomic weight 158.9254. Terbium was discovered in 1843 by C. G. Mosander; it was first extracted in fairly pure form by G. Urbain in 1905. It is not used in industry but is studied because of its complex magnetic behavior.

Terbrugghen, Hendrick   [tair-brug'-huhn]

Hendrick Terbrugghen, b. 1588, d. Nov. 1, 1629, was the most influential of the Utrecht school of Dutch painters who followed the example of Michelangelo Merisi da Caravaggio. After studying with Abraham Bloemaert, Terbrugghen lived in Rome from about 1604 to 1614. There he probably met Caravaggio, whose naturalism he was to adopt so faithfully. Northern Renaissance artists such as Albrecht Dürer, Lucas van Leyden, Quentin Massys, and Marinus van Reymerswaele also inspired him. His earliest-dated extant painting is *Christ Mocked* (1620; Statens Museum for Kunst, Copenhagen). The *Calling of Saint Matthew* (1621; Centraal Museum, Utrecht) relies for inspiration on Caravaggio's picture of the same subject in San Luigi dei Francesi, Rome. Terbrugghen also painted numerous half-length drinking or music-making figures derived from the early work of Caravaggio and his followers, such as Bartolomeo Manfredi. In a later work, *Saint Sebastian Tended by Saint Irene and Her Maid* (1625; Allen Memorial Art Museum, Oberlin, Ohio), there is a tender solemnity to the figures and a luminous yellow lighting that was later to influence Jan Vermeer. The *Crucifixion* (c.1625; Metropolitan Museum of Art, New York City) combines realistic figure types with reminiscences of the art of Matthias Grünewald and northern Gothic sculpture.   EDWARD J. SULLIVAN

Bibliography: Dayton Institute of Arts, *Hendrick Terbrugghen in America* (1965); Nicolson, Benedict, *Hendrick Terbrugghen* (1958) and "Second Thoughts about Terbrugghen," *Burlington Magazine*, November 1960; Stechow, Wolfgang, "Terbrugghen's *Saint Sebastian*," *Burlington Magazine*, March 1954.

Terence   [tair'-uhns]

The Roman playwright Terence, the anglicized name of Publius Terentius Afer, c.185-c.159 BC, was born in Carthage and came to Rome as the young slave of a senator who gave him a good education and set him free. SCIPIO AFRICANUS MINOR became his patron, encouraging him to adapt Greek plays of the so-called New Comedy—especially the plays of MENANDER—for the Roman stage.

Between 166 and 160 BC, Terence had six plays produced, some of them with great success: *Andria* (The Girl from Andros), *Heautontimorumenos* (The Self-Torturer), *Eunuchus* (The Eunuch), *Phormio* (the name of the principal character, an ingratiating parasite), *Adelphi* (The Brothers), and *Hecyra* (The Mother-in-Law). The character portrayal, gentle humor, warmth of feeling, and elegance of Terence's dialogue all reflect the exquisite good manners and high culture of upperclass society in postclassical Athens and 2d-century BC Rome. More refined but less original than Rome's other preeminent comic dramatist, PLAUTUS, with whom he is often compared, Terence nevertheless excelled at suspenseful plots and familiarized his Roman audiences with the stock characters that have become part of the staple fare of Western romantic comedy.   GEORG LUCK

Bibliography: Norwood, Gilbert, *The Art of Terence* (1923; repr. 1965).

Teresa, Mother   [tuh-ray'-suh]

Mother Teresa, winner of the 1979 Nobel Peace Prize, dedicated her life to the service of Calcutta's homeless poor and founded (1950) a Roman Catholic order to expand her work. Her compassionate service includes the establishment of leper colonies and homes for the dying.

Internationally respected for her work to relieve the sufferings of the poor and dying, Mother Teresa of Calcutta, b. Aug. 27, 1910, was awarded the 1979 Nobel Peace Prize. An Albanian originally named Agnes Gonxha Bejaxhiu, she entered the order of the Sisters of Our Lady of Loreto at the age of 18. She taught in the order's school in Calcutta until 1946, when she experienced what she described as a "call within a call" to aid the desperately poor of India in a way that required she leave her convent. She received permission from Rome to do this and began her work by bringing dying persons from the streets into a home where they could die in peace and dignity. She also established an orphanage. Gradually other women joined her, and in 1950 she received official approval for a congregation of sisters, the Missionaries of Charity, whose members are dedicated to serving the poorest of the poor. The community at present includes 700 sisters of various nationalities who work on five continents.

JOAN A. RANGE

Bibliography: Doig, Desmond, *Mother Theresa: Her People and Her Work* (1976); Gorrée, Georges, and Barbier, Jean, *For the Love of God: Mother Teresa of Calcutta*, trans. by Paula Speakman (1974); Mosteller, Sue, *My Brother, My Sister* (1973); Muggeridge, Malcolm, *Something Beautiful for God* (1971).

Teresa of Ávila, Saint   [ah'-vee-lah]

Saint Teresa of Ávila, b. Mar. 28, 1515, d. Oct. 4, 1582, was a Spanish Carmelite and mystic who was declared a doctor of the church in 1970. The daughter of a noble Spanish family, she was originally named Teresa de Cespeda y Ahumada. In 1535 she entered the Carmelite monastery of the Incarnation at Ávila, where the nuns observed the rules of the order in a relaxed ("mitigated") way. After a serious illness and a prolonged period of spiritual apathy Teresa experienced (1555) a spiritual reawakening that convinced her of the need for strict observance of the austere Carmelite rule. Despite strong opposition, she succeeded (1562) in opening the Convent of Saint Joseph in Ávila, the first of the reformed Carmelite houses. Until her death she led the way in reforming both the male and female branches of the Carmelite order. Along with Saint John of the Cross, she is considered the founder of the Discalced ("shoeless") Carmelites.

Besides her activity in directing the reform of her order, which involved extensive travel and communication with nobility and church officials, Teresa wrote many works, among which are some of the greatest classics of mystical literature. A mystic of great stature who achieved the rare state of union referred to as mystical marriage, she wrote advice and direction for others, especially her nuns, with unusual beauty and equally unusual practical wisdom. She is considered an authority on spirituality in the Western world, and her writings are read and studied today as much as ever. Teresa's best-known works are *The Way of Perfection* (1583), *The Interior Castle* (1588), *The Book of Foundations* (1610), and her *Life* (1611). Feast day: Oct. 15.   JOAN A. RANGE

Bibliography: Beevers, John, *Storm of Glory* (1977); Hatzfeld, H. A., *Santa Teresa di Ávila* (1969).

Tereshkova, Valentina Vladimirovna Nikolayeva   [te-ruhsh-koh'-vuh]

Valentina Tereshkova, the first woman to travel in space, was a textile-factory worker and an amateur parachutist when she was selected to participate in the Soviet Union's cosmonaut program shortly after the successful spaceflight of Yuri Gagarin. Tereshkova's Vostok 6 spacecraft was launched on June 16, 1963, and completed 48 orbits in 70 hr 50 min before returning to Earth.

The Soviet cosmonaut Valentina Vladimirovna Nikolayeva Tereshkova, b. Mar. 6, 1937, was the first woman in space. She was a textile-factory assembly worker and amateur parachutist at the time she was recruited (1961) into a special cosmonaut program under the direction of Soviet premier Nikita Khrushchev. Four women were trained to make a one-time woman-in-space flight, after which the program was to be disbanded. Tereshkova received a commission in the Soviet Air Force and took part in an 18-month orientation program before being selected as the prime pilot for the flight of *Vostok 6*. She was launched on June 16, 1963, and spent nearly 3 days in space at the same time as cosmonaut Valery Bykovsky in *Vostok 5* (the spaceships were in separate orbits).

Tereshkova, whose space radio call sign was *Chaika* (seagull), was an effective goodwill ambassador on the world tours that followed her flight and removal from flight status. On Nov. 3, 1963, she married cosmonaut Andrian Nikolayev; their first child, a daughter named Yelena Andrianovna Nikolayeva, b. June 8, 1964, has been a subject of medical interest because of the exposure to space of both her parents. Tereshkova later served on political organizations, including committees connected with the international women's movement, and was elected to the Soviet parliament as a delegate from her home town of Yaroslavl.   JAMES E. OBERG

Bibliography: Sharpe, Mitchell R., *"It Is I, Sea Gull": Valentina Tereshkova, First Woman in Space* (1975).

Terhune, Albert Payson   [tur-hoon']

Famous as a writer of novels about dogs, Albert Payson Terhune, b. Newark, N.J., Dec. 21, 1872, d. Feb. 18, 1942, was also an internationally known collie dog breeder. He achieved an international reputation with *Lad: A Dog* (1919). His other novels include *Lad of Sunnybank* (1928) and *The Way of a Dog* (1932).   F. M. PAULSEN

Terkel, Studs   [tur'-kul]

The writer and journalist Studs Louis Terkel, b. New York City, May 16, 1912, has given Americans an extensive view of themselves through his nationally syndicated broadcasts and penetrating oral histories. Terkel has also been a stage actor, sports columnist, lecturer, reporter, playwright (*Amazing*

Grace, 1959), and host of music festivals. He has demonstrated uncanny ability as an interviewer, both in his radio ("Wax Museum") and television ("Studs' Place") shows and in his books, which include *Division Street, America* (1966); about urban unrest; *Hard Times: An Oral History of the Great Depression* (1970); *Working* (1974); *The Good War: An Oral History of World War II* (1984; Pulitzer Prize, 1985); and *Chicago* (1986).   ERNEST C. HYNDS

Terman, Lewis   [tur'-muhn]

The pioneer of intelligence tests in the United States, Lewis Madison Terman, b. Johnson County, Ind., Jan. 15, 1877, d. Dec. 21, 1956, was an educational psychologist known for his long-term study of highly intelligent individuals. Terman obtained his Ph.D. at Clark University (1905) with an investigation of differences between groups of very bright and very dull children on a wide range of tests. He joined the faculty of Stanford University in 1910 and worked there until his retirement (1942). In 1916 he adapted the Binet intelligence test (see STANFORD-BINET TEST) and introduced the term *intelligence quotient* (IQ). The Stanford-Binet scale and its subsequent revisions by Terman and Maud A. Merrill became the most widely used of all mental tests for children. Terman was largely responsible for producing Alpha and Beta group tests for U.S. Army recruits in 1917. In the 1920s he began his studies of approximately 1,500 of the brightest children in California, with IQs of 135 and up, and traced their careers in four volumes of *Genetic Studies of Genius* (1925–59), documenting their high accomplishments and generally superior social adjustment.   PHILIP E. VERNON

Bibliography: Seagoe, May V., *Terman and the Gifted* (1975).

See also: INTELLIGENCE.

termite

Termites (order Isoptera) are mainly tropical and subtropical insects, comprising nearly 1,800 species in about 200 genera. Common to warm and humid climates, they are also found in North America and southern Europe. Termites evolved from roachlike ancestors. They are the only insects other than bees, ants, and wasps (order Hymenoptera) to form true societies.

Known primarily for their destruction of wooden structures, termites can also be agricultural pests. A common method of termite control has entailed the use of CHLORDANE. In 1987, however, in light of the determination that this pesticide can cause cancer, the United States Environmental Protection Agency banned almost all of its uses, including above-ground antitermite applications; it may only be injected into the ground beneath homes.

Feeding Habits. All termites are herbivorous, and many feed on decaying wood. Termites are able to digest cellulose, a carbohydrate found in plants, because of bacteria in their intestines. Some species also have symbiotic protozoa in the gut. Many subterranean or mound-building species cultivate fungi that help to break down plant material that has been incorporated into "fungus gardens."

Life Cycle. In many ways the life cycle and habits of termites are similar to those of ants. (This is the reason termites are also referred to as "white ants," although termites and ants differ in a number of important aspects.) The individuals of the society are divided into castes: the primary reproductives (king and queen), the supplementary reproductives, the workers, and the soldiers. The king and queen stay together after mating. Commonly the queen's ovaries grow enormously so that her abdomen becomes greatly distended, and she is able to lay eggs continuously at a rapid rate. This activity restricts her mobility, and in some species she is confined with the king in a thick-walled "queen cell." The eggs hatch into young brood, which resemble small workers and, in more primitive kinds of termites, behave like them. In other species the young are fairly helpless and are fed by the workers. After several molts they develop into workers or soldiers. Some develop into reproductives, which become winged only when they fly together in a swarm, mate, and found new colonies.

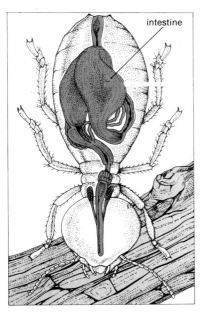

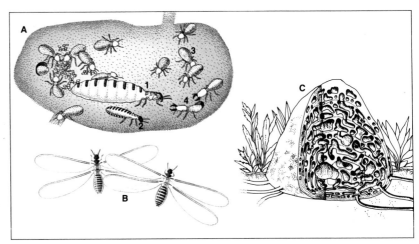

(Left) Termites contain numerous symbiotic protozoa (minute organisms) within their intestine, which break down wood cellulose to digestible glucose. (Below) Termite colonies (A) consist of specialized forms, such as the reproductive queen (1) and king (2), worker (3), and soldier (4). Winged reproductive termites (B) mate and form new colonies once a year. Termite mounds (C) contain interconnected cavities, and tunnels lead to food.

Structure. Primary reproductives have two pairs of wings on the thorax. They range from 5 to 22 mm (0.2 to 0.8 in) in length and are brown to black in color, and the head is round. The mouthparts bite, the antennae are many-segmented, and the eyes are compound. Two small claws are borne at the end of each leg. No external genital organs are present. Workers are usually smaller than the reproductives and in most species lack eyes. They never have wings. The soldiers, which form 5 percent of the total colony, are the defensive elements. Their heads are generally so extremely modified for this function that they are unable to feed themselves. Their weapons are their powerful jaws, chemical secretions, or both. Some of the damp-wood termite species have soldiers with very large, heavily armored head capsules and powerful cutting jaws. Those of other species have scissorlike mandibles. Some soldiers, the so-called nasute soldiers, have a frontal gland that opens through a pore on the top of the head. When the soldier bites, a droplet of toxic or sticky secretion squirts out of this gland through the head, which is drawn forward in the shape of a nozzle. The jet of liquid dries when in the air and forms a sticky thread that entangles the adversary.

Defense and Nest Structure. The defenses of soldiers are directed against ants, the main predators of termites in most parts of the world. The nest structure is also a defensive fortress, adapted to withstand the incursions of other insects and effects of climate. It also provides a milieu for the development of the brood and fungus gardens, which are tended by the workers.

The most primitive nests are simple burrows in wood. Nests on trees or mound nests on the ground comprise chewed vegetable material mixed with clay or fecal material. The mounds of certain species of *Macrotermes* rise as high as 6 m (20 ft) in savanna regions of West Africa. The hive of the nest is near ground level and contains the queen cell, brood chambers, and fungus gardens. Workers leave the nest through subterranean tunnels and forage for vegetable material, which is stored in the upper part before being incorporated into the fungus gardens. The hot and humid air that results from the activity of the nest rises by convection into air spaces and passes to ducts near the surface for both exchange and cooling. As the air becomes denser, it sinks and passes to ducts leading to the base, thus ensuring a continuous circulation during the day.   HOWARD GALER

Bibliography: Howse, P. E., *Termites* (1970); Krishna, K., and Weesner, F. M., eds., *Biology of Termites*, 2 vols. (1969–70); Watson, J. A., ed., *Caste Differentiation in Social Insects* (1985).

tern

The common tern, S. hirundo, a pigeon-sized seabird related to the gull, is the most frequently seen tern in North America. The black tern, C. nigra (in flight), builds its nest in shallow water. Unlike most terns, it searches for food on land as well as in the water.

A tern is a slender seabird with a pointed, straight bill; long, pointed wings; relatively short legs with webbed or partially webbed feet; and often a forked tail. Sometimes known as sea swallows, terns are most common along coastal regions but are also found in midocean and along marshes and rivers. About 40 species, closely related to gulls, skuas, and skimmers, make up the subfamily Sterninae of the family Laridae. Many species are highly migratory, the most spectacular being the Arctic tern, *Sterna paradisaea*, which nests within the Arctic Circle and winters in Antarctica—an annual round trip of more than 17,500 km (11,000 mi).

Terns vary in size from the 20-cm (8-in) little, or least, tern, *S. albifrons*, to the Caspian tern, *S. caspia*, often more than 50 cm (20 in) long. Most terns are typically white with a grayish back and a black cap. However, some species, particularly marsh terns (genus *Chlidonias*), have blackish plumage; some, including many noddies (genus *Anous*), are brownish or sooty-colored; and one, the fairy tern, *Gygis alba*, is entirely white.

Most terns dive into the water to capture prey. Fish is the main food item, but insects and various aquatic organisms are also taken. Some terns eat crustaceans or small lizards. Most terns nest in large colonies. Nests are built on the ground or sometimes in low bushes. The one to three eggs and the young are usually cryptically colored.   GARY D. SCHNELL

Bibliography: Bent, Arthur C., *Life Histories of North American Gulls and Terns* (1921); Delacorte, Peter, and Witte, Michael C., *The Book of Terns* (1978).

Terni   [tayr′-nee]

Terni (1983 est. pop., 111,347), capital of Terni province in the Umbria region of central Italy, lies on the Nera River about 100 km (60 mi) north of Rome. Industries, powered by hydroelectric plants on the Nera and its tributaries, include the production of steel, armaments, electrochemicals, textiles, and foodstuffs. Although the city was severely damaged during World War II, several medieval churches have survived, as well as a waterfall created by the Romans in 271 BC.

Founded in the 7th century BC on the site of a Neolithic village, the settlement flourished under the Romans as Interamna Nahors. Terni came under the rule of the papacy in the 14th century.

Ternifine man   [tair-nee-feen′]

The skeletal and cultural remains of Ternifine man were discovered by the French paleontologist Camille Arambourg (1885–1969) at the site of Ternifine on the Agris Plain near Oran, Algeria, in 1954 and 1955. The specimens, three adult lower jaws, some milk teeth, and a skull bone of a young child, represent the remains of four individuals. The large, chinless mandibles are similar to the HOMO ERECTUS specimens from CHOU-K′OU-TIEN in China. The lakeside deposit, Middle Pleistocene in age, also contained stone flake tools belonging to the Lower Paleolithic ACHEULEAN tradition, commonly associated with the skeletal remains of *Homo erectus* in Europe and Africa.   ALAN MANN AND NANCY MINUGH

Bibliography: White, Edmund, and Brown, Dale, *The First Men* (1973).

terpene   [tur′-peen]

A terpene is a naturally occurring organic compound with the general formula $(C_5H_8)_n$. Until recently this definition was used rather strictly. The term *terpenoid*, referring to related compounds containing oxygen, has fallen into disuse, and both classes are now known as terpenes.

The terpenes share a common general formula and often have structures related to the diene isoprene:

isoprene
(2-methyl-1, 3-butadiene)

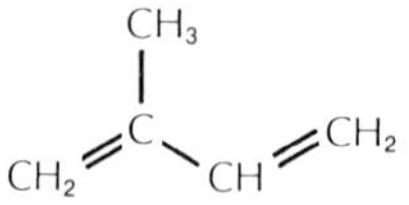

The number of isoprene units serves as the most common classification system for the large number of known terpenes. The German chemist Otto Wallach received the Nobel Prize for chemistry in 1910 for his extensive studies of terpene chemistry.

The formulas by which the terpenes are represented often show only the bonds and oxygen groups. In the structure below it is assumed that a carbon atom with the required number of hydrogen atoms (to total four bonds) exists at each intersection or line end. The isoprene units in each example are

shown by dashed lines.
Monoterpenes $(C_{10}H_{16})$

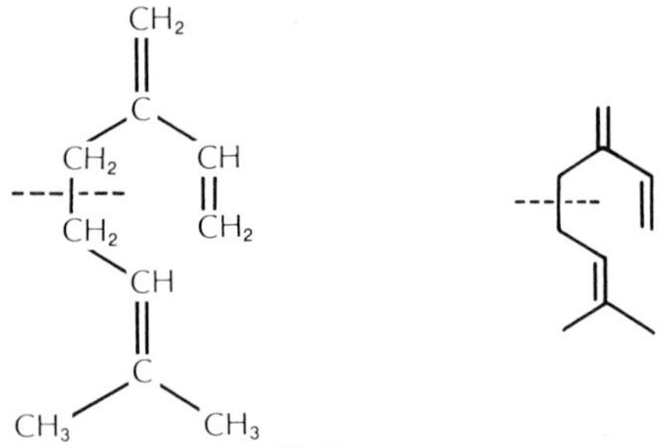

myrcene
(bayberry wax)

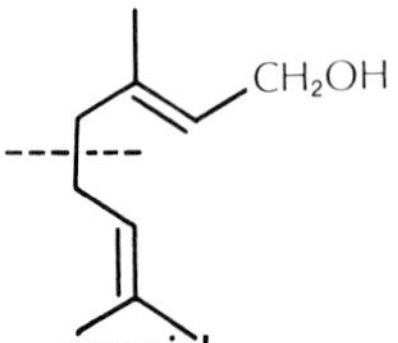

geraniol
(rose perfumes)

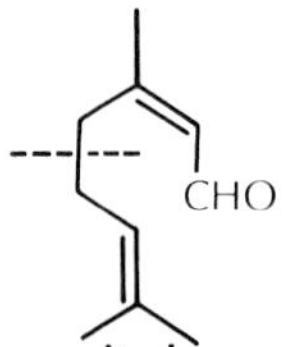

citral
(lemon-grass oil)

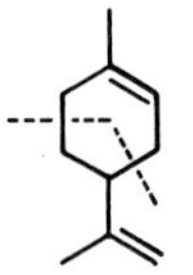

limonene
(orange and lemon oils)

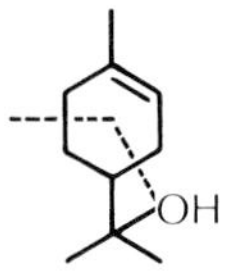

α-terpineol
(cardamon and marjoram oils)

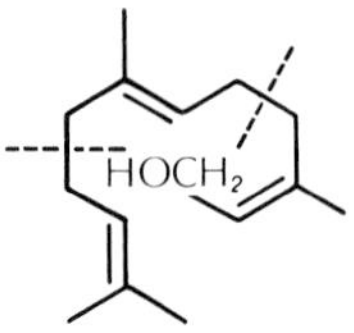

farnesol
(insect hormone)

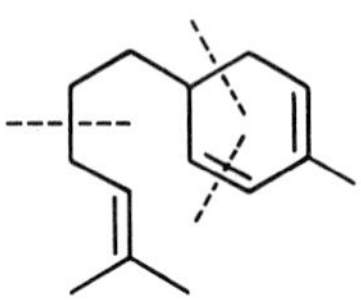

zingiberene
(ginger oil)

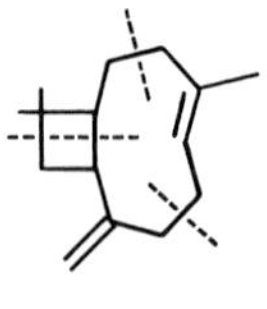

caryophyllene
(clove oil)

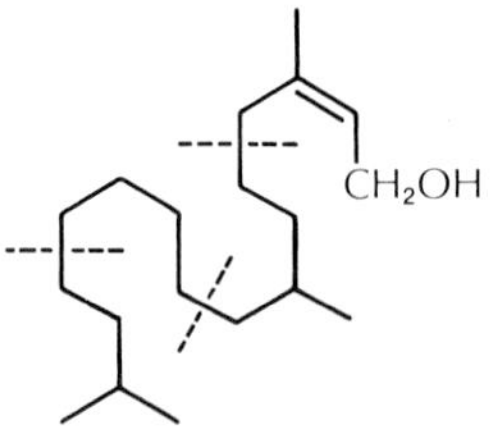

vitamin A

phytol
(from chlorophyll)

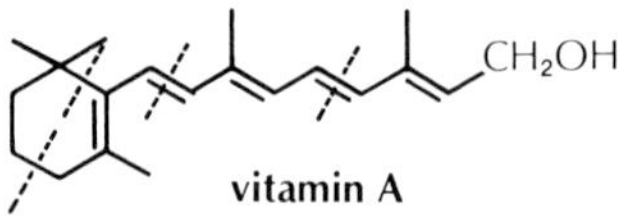

Many terpenes are commercially valuable. For example, the mono- and sesquiterpenes are major constituents of many essential oils prized as perfumes and flavors. There are important relationships between the higher terpenes and the steroids, carotenoids, and vitamins. The carotenoid β-carotene (a tetraterpene) is related to vitamin A (a diterpene). A spectacular example of biogenesis involves the conversion of the triterpene squalene $(C_{30}H_{48})$ found in shark-liver oil into the steroid cholesterol. Natural and synthetic RUBBERS, both examples of the polyterpenes, contain 4,000 to 5,000 isoprene units. The arrangement of these units is important:

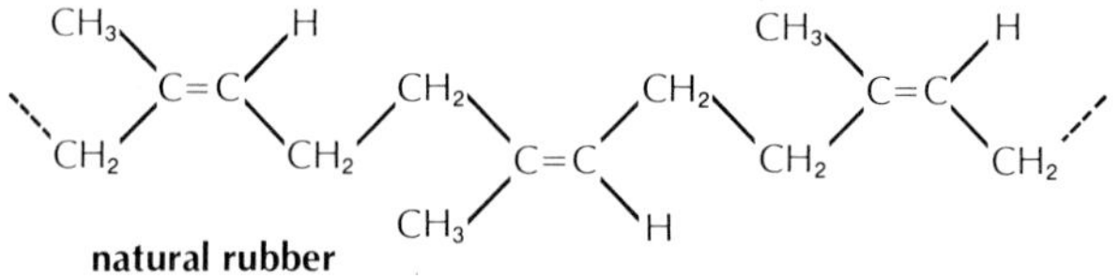

natural rubber

Until the relationship of the isoprenes to each other was appreciated (1955), good synthetic rubber could not be produced.

K. THOMAS FINLEY

Bibliography: Newman, A. A., ed., *Chemistry of Terpenes and Terpenoids* (1972); Richards, J. H., and Hendrickson, J. B., *The Biosynthesis of Steroids, Terpenes, and Acetongenins* (1964); Simonsen, J. L., ed., *Terpenes,* 5 vols. (1953-57).

Terra: see GAEA.

Terra, Gabriel   [tay'-rah]

Gabriel Terra, b. Aug. 1, 1873, d. Sept. 15, 1942, was president of Uruguay from 1931 to 1938. He was a member of the Colorado party, whose leader, José BATLLE Y ORDÓÑEZ, had, in the second decade of the 1900s, initiated programs that turned Uruguay into a welfare state. In 1933, Terra, in collaboration with Blanco party leader Luis Alberto de Herrera, suspended congress, abolished the constitution, and created a dictatorship, discarding the collegial executive system. After the new constitution of 1934 formalized a Blanco–Colorado patronage-sharing arrangement and enhanced executive power, Terra was reelected. He extended Batlle's welfare policies, but despite Uruguay's democratic reputation, he repressed dissent and governed largely by decree. Terra was succeeded by an elected president, Alfredo Baldomir, his brother-in-law.

Bibliography: Taylor, Philip B., *Government and Politics of Uruguay* (1962).

Terra Amata   [te'-rah uh-mah'-tuh]

Terra Amata, near Nice on the French Mediterranean coast, is an Early Pleistocene archaeological site that was excavated (1966) by the French archaeologist Henry de Lumley. Dating from about 400,000 years ago, it has revealed a remarkable succession of short, seasonal occupations on beach and dune deposits. Repeated constructions of oval huts made out of skins and branches weighed down by rings of stones and supported by posts and stakes were recorded. These huts, which measure 7-15 by 4-6 m (23-49 by 13-20 ft), contained hearths and quantities of artifacts and animal bone fragments. Cervids, elephants, and boars were hunted; the presence of shells and fish bones suggests that sea resources were also exploited. Finds of specialized stone tools dating from the Lower Paleolithic Period included unifacially flaked pebble tools, flake scrapers, notches, and denticulates, as well as a few coarse bifaces and cleavers indicating an early ACHEULEAN industry. A human footprint and coprolites were also found, the pollen recovered from the latter reflecting a spring or early summer occupation.

JACQUES BORDAZ

Bibliography: Lumley, Henry de, "A Paleolithic Camp at Nice," *Scientific American,* May 1969.

terra-cotta   [te'-rah kot'-tuh]

Terra-cotta (Italian for "baked earth") is a type of hard-baked clay, or earthenware, produced by means of a single firing. Usually rendered brownish red in color after firing, terra-cotta may be either glazed (covered with a layer of molten glass) or left in its natural state, in which it is sometimes referred to as "biscuit."

Ancient Traditions. Terra-cotta objects unearthed at sites in widely separated regions provide clear evidence of the manifold uses that prehistoric and ancient peoples found for this earthenware. Despite its porous nature, terra-cotta from earliest times served a general purpose in the making of domestic pots; at a later stage of development, glaze was lightly applied to the interior of terra-cotta vessels to render them watertight (see POTTERY AND PORCELAIN). Terra-cotta art flourished simultaneously in a wide range of early cultures. Among the many types of terra-cotta sculpture produced in the ancient world were votive figures associated with the fertility cults practiced by the inhabitants of the Indus Valley (3d-2d millennia BC); Japanese figures dating from the Jomon (3d-2d millennium BC) and Haniwa periods (AD 300-645); finely mod-

(Above) *This terra-cotta statuette (14th-13th century BC) exemplifies a type of fertility image common in Aegean Bronze Age art.*

(Left) *This terra-cotta figurine dates from Hellenistic times. (Louvre, Paris.)*

eled figures executed by the artisans of the ancient Aegean, Egyptian, and Greek civilizations; pre-Columbian American figurines dating from c.2000 BC; and large freestanding statuary executed (from the 5th century BC) by artists of the prehistoric Nok culture of present-day northern Nigeria.

Mesopotamian tombs of the 3d-2d millennia BC have been found to contain singular, shoe-shaped coffins made of terra-cotta coated with a vitreous saline glaze, as well as terra-cotta toys, votive offerings, and various utilitarian and ornamental objects. By about 2000 BC the Assyrians and Babylonians had discovered how to use copper to obtain a rich turquoise blue coloring that could be applied to decorative terra-cotta tiles. These tiles, used for the embellishment of interior and exterior walls and the decoration of buildings generally, were

This finely modeled terra-cotta head of a woman (11th-15th century) exemplifies the naturalistic techniques used by the Yoruba artists of Ife, Nigeria. Ife, believed to be the oldest Yoruban town, flourished as a religious center for several centuries. The terra-cotta pieces from Ife, discovered in the early part of this century, reflect the Yoruban assimilation of Egyptian and Mediterranean artistic traditions. (Museum für Völkerkunde, Berlin.)

This bodhisattva (7th-8th century), sculpted from coarse terra-cotta, was discovered in a Buddhist monastery in Fodukistan, Afghanistan. The execution of the sculpture combines traditional Indo-Iranian influences with the distinctive artistic traditions of indigenous artists. Statues sculpted in this manner were supported by a wooden core and were often painted and gilded. (Musée Guimet, Paris.)

greatly admired both for the quality of the ware itself and for the striking geometrical patterns in which the tiles were arranged.

Among all the civilizations of the ancient world, the Greeks used terra-cotta in the most varied ways, producing all kinds of domestic wares, ornaments, and sculptures. In Greek architecture its uses ranged from bricks and roof tiles to sculpture, pavements, and ornamental work. Terra-cotta also was favored for making pots, lamps, jars, and spindle whorls, as well as for large-scale objects such as sarcophagi. Some surviving amphorae, the beautifully shaped Greek jars used to hold wine and food, are of superior quality, but the majority are made from a coarse, buff-colored paste incorporating a glaze that, after firing, gives a slight sheen to the ware. Greek sculptors used terra-cotta to produce models for bronze statues.

They also crafted enormous numbers of terra-cotta figures. From early, small statuettes that served religious or funerary functions, Greek terra-cotta figures evolved (c.7th century BC)

Luca della Robbia's highly naturalistic and graceful Madonna in the Rose Garden (1450-60) is representative of the enameled terra-cotta pieces created by Luca's workshop in Florence, Italy. This type of terra-cotta work, known as majolica, was white-glazed and then hand-painted. Through the della Robbia family's influence, the popularity of enameled terra-cottas spread throughout Europe during the Renaissance. (Museo Nazionale, Florence.)

into highly artistic creations that displayed exquisite artistry. During Greece's Classical period (6th–5th centuries BC), Tanagra, in Boeotia, became the leading center of production of terra-cotta figurines, although fine examples of terra-cotta figure art have been recovered from archaeological sites throughout the Greek domains in the eastern and central Mediterranean. Etruscan sculptors and potters learned terra-cotta work from Greek artists, as did Roman sculptors.

Renaissance to the Present. With the end of the Roman Empire (5th century), the artistic use of terra-cotta largely ceased in Europe until the late 14th century, when molded terra-cotta details began to appear on buildings in Germany and Italy. During the Early Renaissance period (c.1415–1500) in Italy, such sculptors as DONATELLO, Jacopo della QUERCIA, and Andrea del VERROCHIO executed both freestanding and relief sculptures in terra-cotta. Luca Della Robbia (see DELLA ROBBIA family), a Florentine sculptor, produced brilliantly enameled plaques and medallions in MAJOLICA (terra-cotta highly decorated with enamels and luster pigments)—an immensely popular decorative medium that was developed further by his nephew Andrea and the latter's sons, Luca II, Giovanni, and Girolamo.

The use of terra-cotta for decorative work in architecture spread (16th century) from Italy to the rest of Europe and remained popular until the 18th century, by which time it had been superseded almost completely by marble. In the late 19th and early 20th centuries, however, the use of molded terra-cotta ornaments and decorative fittings was revived by several American architectural firms, most notably Adler and Sullivan of Chicago. The most prominent American designers included the architects Thomas Hastings (see CARRÈRE AND HASTINGS), Bernard MAYBECK, James RENWICK, and Louis SULLIVAN.

Meanwhile, terra-cotta experienced two waves of popularity in Great Britain. Josiah WEDGWOOD revived interest in terra-cotta in the late 1760s, when he introduced his improved earthenware, a harder and less brittle terra-cotta body produced by adding a proportion of calcined flint and pulverized potash to iron-free potter's clay. Then, in the mid-19th-century Victorian era, a passion for bright-hued terra-cotta statuary, garden ornaments, plaques, medallions, fountains, and figures on pedestals swept across the country. Although these works were executed in various colors, red terra-cotta was by far the most popular.

In the 20th century, terra-cotta has been used extensively as both a building material and a decorative medium, and such major sculptors as Aristide MAILLOL and Pablo PICASSO have produced significant works in terra-cotta.

CHARLES PLATTEN WOODHOUSE

Bibliography: Allan, J. W., *Mediaeval Middle Eastern Pottery* (1971); Chesterman, James, *Classical Terracotta Figures* (1974); Fagg, William, *The Art of Western Africa: Tribal Masks and Sculptures* (1967); Gonen, Ribkah, *Ancient Pottery* (1973); Green, David, *Pottery: Materials and Techniques* (1967); Higgins, Reynold, *Greek Terracottas* (1967); Marquand, Allan, *Robbia Heraldry* (1919; repr. 1972); Nicholson, Felicity, *Greek, Etruscan and Roman Pottery and Small Terracottas* (1965); Strommenger, Eva, *5000 Years of the Art of Mesopotamia*, trans. by Christina Haglund (1964); Woodhouse, C. P., *The World's Master Potters* (1974).

Terramycin: see ANTIBIOTICS.

terrarium

A terrarium is a closed container housing a collection of miniature trees, shrubs, or cacti (and occasionally even small animals such as snails, frogs, or snakes) and forming a living, almost self-sustaining environment. The terrarium's scenic quality and the fact that the plants and animals used can be found growing in the wild have made the creation of terraria a popular horticultural hobby. Any lidded glass or plastic container may be used. Its bottom is covered with an inch or two of sand or gravel over which a layer of a growing medium is spread. The field and woods terraria, which nurture forest- and field-growing plants, will have rich, damp earth or sphagnum moss as the growing medium; moisture from the soil and from plant respiration remains inside. A dryer environment, with a minimum of topsoil, is used for desert terraria containing cacti or succulents.

Terre Haute   [tair'-uh hoht]

Terre Haute (1980 pop., 61,125), a city in western Indiana and the seat of Vigo County, is situated on the Wabash River about 110 km (70 mi) west of Indianapolis. A commercial center in a coal-mining and agricultural area, the city manufactures bricks, tiles, bottles, steel products, and foodstuffs. Indiana State College is located there.

Laid out in 1816, Terre Haute began to grow after the construction of the NATIONAL ROAD (1838), the Wabash and Erie Canal (1849), and the Richmond Railroad (1852). Discovery of coal in 1875 prompted industrial development. The birthplace of the labor organizer and founder of the U.S. Socialist party, Eugene V. Debs, Terre Haute was known for its militant union activity.

territorial waters

Territorial waters are considered by international law those waters which fall within the jurisdiction of sovereign states. These waters include waters immediately adjacent to a nation's shoreline. In the 18th century the extent of shoreline territorial waters was fixed at 3 mi (4.8 km) from the low watermark or straight coastal baseline, a distance determined on the basis of cannon-firing range at that time. As with inland territorial waters, the seabed and its subsoil, as well as the airspace above them, come under the exclusive jurisdiction of a sovereign state, except in the case of innocent passage—the peacetime transit of merchant ships. Innocent passage does not include the right to fish or the traffic of submerged submarines. Lakes or rivers on national boundaries are under national control to the middle of navigable channels.

With the adoption (1982) of the United Nations Convention on the Law of the Sea, rules for all parts and uses of the sea have been established. Key features of the international treaty that pertain to coastal nations include a 12-naut-mi (22.2-km) sovereignty limit with the right of innocent passage of foreign vessels; exclusive economic rights with respect to fish and other marine life extending 200 naut mi (370.4 km); and sovereign rights over the continental shelf for the purpose of exploration and exploitation of oil and minerals extending 200–350 naut mi (370.4–648.2 km) with part of the revenue derived from the shelf beyond 200 naut mi to be shared with the international community. The United States remained opposed to the part of the convention on deep-seabed exploration and exploitation. Israel, Turkey, and Venezuela also voted against the treaty in the United Nations.

Bibliography: Anand, R. P., *Origin and Development of the Law of the Sea* (1983); ''Sea Law,'' in *UN Chronicle,* June 1982.

See also: SEA, LAW OF THE; SEAS, FREEDOM OF THE.

territoriality

Territoriality is broadly defined as the defense of space; in particular, territorial behavior among many animals serves to exclude other individuals of the same species from areas of mating and breeding. For example, a male robin announces his claim to a patch of land in the spring by repeatedly singing his species' song. An intruder male that enters this patch will usually be quickly chased away, but occasionally the two males will fight for the territory, which in rare cases will change hands. The territorial competition among male robins eventually results in the subdivision of a woodlot into a mosaic of plots, each of which is held by one male (see BIRD). A female is attracted to and mates with a male who holds a territory, and the pair then raises a clutch of young on the plot.

Territoriality is not the sole province of vertebrates or male animals, nor is it restricted to the defense of a general breeding area. Certain limpets (marine mollusks), using their hat-shaped shells to push opponents away, defend small areas on tidal-zone rocks that have the thick algal patches on which they feed. Among the many territorial insects are the huge cicada-killer wasps, which engage in aerial aggression against one another to establish territories near areas where females are emerging from underground cells.

The key to the modern analysis of territoriality is the recognition that this behavior has reproductive benefits (exclusive use of the resources in an area) and reproductive costs (the time and energy and risks taken to exclude others from the territory). Territoriality evolved in some species because it was reproductively advantageous to individuals. In general, the scarcer the resource, the more valuable its possession and the greater the gain from territoriality. Animals will be territorial only when their living space contains or attracts a limited resource that enhances individual reproductive success. Territorial songbirds defend woodlot areas best suited for rearing a brood; these areas contain above-average supplies of food and good nesting sites. The aggressive limpet defends a local concentration of food as well as a secure resting site that protects it from waves. The cicada-killer male defends a site that it judges will produce more or better food than other sites.

In a number of species, the territory itself does not contain useful food, shelter, egg-laying sites, or concentrations of mates; rather, the territory is important because ownership of it is a precondition for acceptance by a female. For example, in sage grouse, certain African antelope, and some tropical hummingbirds, males gather in groups and compete for ownership of a small patch of ground or areas about a perch. Females come to the group display area, known as a lek, not to secure food or a nest site but to select as mates those males which hold certain territories. These males, because they have been able to exclude all others from the prime sites, have demonstrated their competitive superiority and are therefore consistently chosen by visiting females. In lek species, territoriality gives a male a chance to attract a limited resource, namely, receptive females.

The costs, as well as the benefits, greatly influence the occurrence and form of territorial behavior. Territories generally tend to be relatively small compared to the undefended home ranges of many animal species. The larger the territory, the greater the area from which intruders need to be expelled; more time and energy are required, therefore, to enjoy the benefits of sole ownership of the resources contained in the area. As a result animals tend to defend resources that are concentrated in a small, defensible site and not resources that are scattered over a broad area. Territories, moreover, shrink in size as the number of competitors increases and may even be abandoned if the intruder rate passes a certain point. For example, African sunbirds defend feeding territories that contain nectar-producing flowers only if some patches are much more productive than others and only if intruders are relatively few; because of this particular territorial behavior the costs of defense are minimal. If the density of cicada-killer males is very high, individuals simply stop trying to defend an area and instead devote all their time and energy to attempting to be the first to reach a freshly emerged female. These observations show that animals can be sensitive to the costs and benefits of territorial behavior and can adjust their aggressive responses in biologically adaptive ways.   JOHN ALCOCK

Bibliography: Alcock, John, *Animal Behavior: An Evolutionary Approach,* 3d ed. (1983); Andrewartha, H. G., *Introduction to the Study of Animal Populations* (1961); Barnard, C. J., *Animal Behavior: Ecology and Evolution* (1983); Klopfer, Peter H., *Habitats and Territories* (1969); Stokes, Allen W., ed., *Territory* (1974).

territory

In government a territory is that part of a country which has not been admitted to full and equal status within the larger union or federation. In the United States the Ordinance of 1787 set out a plan for administering the Northwest Territory, an area lying between the Ohio and Mississippi rivers. It included provisions for basic civil and political rights and eventual admission—if self-government seemed secure—as a state. The Northwest Ordinance served as the model for the regulation of later territories such as the Louisiana and the Oregon territories, and 31 states were territories or parts of territories before being admitted to the Union. The U.S. Constitution (Article IV, Section 3) empowered Congress to control territories.

All of the territories contiguous to the United States had been admitted as states by 1912, and Alaska and Hawaii by 1959. (Australia and Canada still have contiguous territories.) Puerto Rico, a U.S. territory since the Spanish-American War, secured commonwealth status in 1952, becoming the most autonomous of all U.S. territories. All U.S. territories are administered by the Office of Territorial and International Affairs of the Department of the Interior. Included are the territories of Guam, American Samoa, the Virgin Islands, the Commonwealth of the Northern Mariana Islands, and the Trust Territory of the Pacific Islands, which includes the Marshall Islands, Palau, and Micronesia. Although administered by the United States, the Trust Territory islands are under UN trusteeship.

terrorism

Terrorism is the sustained, clandestine use of violence—murder, kidnapping, bombings—to achieve a political purpose. Definitions in the U.S. Intelligence and Surveillance Act of 1979 and the United Kingdom Prevention of Terrorism Act of 1976 stress the use of violence to coerce or intimidate the civilian population with a view to affecting governmental policy. In popular usage, however, as influenced by politicians and the media, *terrorism* is now increasingly used as a generic term for all kinds of political violence, especially as manifested in revolutionary and guerrilla warfare.

Nevertheless, not all political violence short of conventional war is terrorism. Political assassination may or may not be a terrorist act, depending on the degree of commitment to a sustained program of terror. Assassinations of Tsar Alexander II and other prominent figures in imperial Russia by nihilists and social revolutionaries were part of a sustained program of violence aimed at bringing down the tsarist regime and as such were terrorist acts. On the other hand, the assassinations of Presidents Abraham Lincoln and John F. Kennedy, while undoubtedly political in motive, were not part of a sustained program and hence cannot properly be called terrorism. The term is inappropriately applied to the suicide attacks of religious fanatics on military personnel in a war zone, as in the case of the bombings of U.S. Marine and French Foreign Legion bunkers in Lebanon in 1983, although not to the bombings of the U.S. Embassy (1983–84).

The deliberate killing of civilians to intimidate the civilian population or government is one of the worst features of contemporary terrorism and can clearly be distinguished from the type of clandestine warfare waged by resistance groups or insurgency movements against official and military targets. By their actions, the PALESTINE LIBERATION ORGANIZATION (PLO) and the Provisional Wing of the IRISH REPUBLICAN ARMY (IRA) are terrorist organizations. But one would not use the term to describe the Polish and French underground resistance movements of World War II. When governments engage in illegal and clandestine kidnapping and murder to intimidate their people—as in the case of the Nazis in Germany and the Argentine military junta in power from 1976 to 1983—the term *state terrorism* is appropriate.

One key characteristic of modern terrorism is its quest for spectacular horror effects in order to attract media coverage. Terrorist atrocities like the PLO's murder of helpless athletes at the 1972 Olympics are perpetrated to publicize a cause. Most of the victims of the Italian Red Brigades and the German Baader-Meinhof gang were selected for symbolic reasons.

Another characteristic of modern terrorism is its international dimension—the ability of terrorists to slip across national frontiers, the support given to certain terrorist groups by a few countries dedicated to revolutionary change, and logistical ties that exist between terrorist groups of widely divergent ideologies and objectives. The 1985 hijacking by Palestinians of the Italian cruise ship *Achille Lauro* off Egypt, and the murder of a U.S. passenger, dramatized the international ramifications of terrorism.

Whereas prevention of domestic terrorism is in general the province of local law-enforcement agencies or security forces, at the international level effective counterterrorist action runs into obstacles raised by traditional concepts of national sovereignty. In theory, perpetrators of crimes in one country can, if apprehended in another country, be extradited for trial, and there is hardly a terrorist crime imaginable that is not well covered by criminal statutes. In practice, however, law-enforcement officials tend to give foreign fugitives from justice a low priority. Moreover, a well-established exception for political offenses may protect from extradition all but the most flagrant offenders.

In recent years international efforts to counter terrorism have led to the Tokyo and Montreal Conventions (1963 and 1971) on hijacking and sabotage of civilian aircraft; the Hague Convention of 1979 on hostage-taking; and the 1973 convention on crimes against diplomats. These conventions established categories of international crimes that are punishable by any state regardless of the nationality of criminal or victim or locality of the offense.

In democracies, the need to protect civil liberties, the difficulty of proving conspiracy, and the devastating nature of terrorist outrages have shifted the emphasis from deterrence to prevention. Today, by general consensus the most effective means of frustrating terrorist activity is through detailed intelligence obtained primarily by penetration of terrorist networks.   CHARLES MAECHLING, JR.

Bibliography: Alexander, Yonah, *International Terrorism*, rev. ed. (1981); Alexander, Yonah, and Myers, Kenneth, eds., *Terrorism in Europe* (1982); Crenshaw, Martha, ed., *Terrorism, Legitimacy, and Power* (1982); Dobson, Christopher, and Payne, Ronald, *The Terrorists*, rev. ed. (1982); Laqueur, Walter, *Terrorism* (1977).

Terry, Dame Ellen Alice

The most celebrated English actress of her day, Ellen Terry, b. Feb. 27, 1847, d. July 21, 1928, played with Sir Henry IRVING in Shakespeare and romantic melodrama at London's Lyceum Theatre from 1878 to 1902 and remained a great theatrical personality until the 1920s. George Bernard Shaw wrote *Captain Brassbound's Conversion* especially for her, and her published correspondence (1931) with the great playwright reveals her own considerable literary talent. Terry was the mother of the set designer Gordon Craig. She was made a Dame of the British Empire in 1925.   ROGER MANVELL

Bibliography: Manvell, Roger, *Ellen Terry* (1968); Terry, Ellen, *The Story of My Life* (1908; repr. 1933 as *Memoirs*).

Terry, Walter

Walter Terry, b. Brooklyn, N.Y., May 14, 1913, d. Oct. 4, 1982, was a dance critic who helped pioneer the profession in the United States. Terry was dance critic for the *Boston Herald* (1936–39) and for the respected and influential *New York Herald Tribune* (1939–42; 1945–66), with an interval of air force service during World War II. He wrote for the *World Journal Tribune* (1966–67) and was dance critic for *Saturday Review* (1976–82). Terry was educated at the University of North Carolina and studied both modern dance and ballet with several famous teachers. He was a frequent lecturer in the United States and abroad and wrote 17 books on dance, including *The Dance in America*, rev. ed. (1971).   ROBERT J. PIERCE

Tertiary Period   [tur'-shee-air-ee]

The Tertiary Period is the older of two subdivisions of the Cenozoic Era and represents some 63 million years of geologic time, commencing about 65 million years ago. The remainder of the Cenozoic Era is the Quaternary Period, representing the most recent period of geologic time. The term *Tertiary* is a remnant of an 18th-century classification that attempted to group the age of all rocks into four divisions. The Tertiary comprises five epochs of unequal duration—Paleocene, Eocene, Oligocene, Miocene, and Pliocene.

CRUSTAL MOVEMENT: PALEOGEOGRAPHY

Paleocene-Eocene. During the Eocene Epoch significant paleogeographic changes occurred in the world. The formation of the Norwegian-Greenland Sea, as a result of separation of Greenland and Scandinavia along a northern exten-

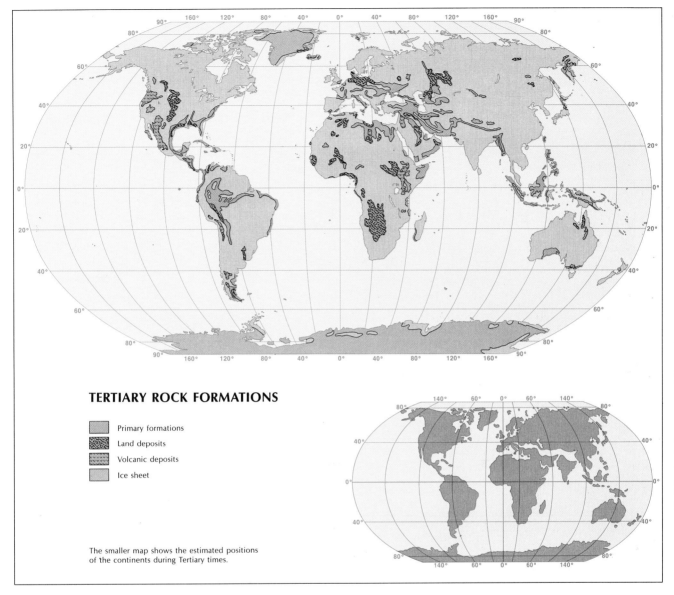

TERTIARY ROCK FORMATIONS

- ▨ Primary formations
- ▨ Land deposits
- ▨ Volcanic deposits
- ▨ Ice sheet

The smaller map shows the estimated positions of the continents during Tertiary times.

sion of the Mid-Atlantic Ridge (Reykjanes Ridge), led to a marine connection between the Atlantic and polar regions. A significant cooling of several degrees of the water below 1,000 m (3,300 ft) occurred at the end of the Eocene Epoch (about 38 million years ago), essentially forming the thermal structure of the oceans as it is known today.

During the Middle and Late Eocene the Pyreneean orogeny led to the formation of the east-west mountain range, the Pyrenees, between Spain and France. In Asia the junction of India, Tibet, and Iran with the Asian landmass essentially closed the eastern Tethys Sea and unified the Asian landmass in its modern form.

Oligocene-Miocene. The closure of the north-south interior Uralian Seaway during the Early Oligocene resulted in a unification of the Eurasian landmass, allowing extensive faunal migrations. Communication between North America and Eurasia occurred sporadically across the Bering Land Bridge.

The establishment of the world Circumantarctic Current, the largest oceanic current system on the planet, occurred between 30 and 25 million years ago, during the Late Oligocene. The circumglobal current system thermally isolated Antarctica (in its polar location) from the rest of the world and led to the development of a major continental ice sheet by at

least Middle Miocene time (about 12 to 10 million years ago). In the Early Miocene, about 18 million years ago, the junction of Eurasia and Africa resulted in the isolation of the western part of the Tethys Sea from the Indo-Pacific faunal province, resulting in the spread into Eurasia (and later, western Europe) of African ancestral mammals (including ancestral hominoids).

Pliocene. Approximately 3½ million years ago, during the Pliocene Epoch, the uplift of the Isthmus of Panama terminated the exchange between Atlantic and Pacific marine faunas that had occurred for more than 125 million years and at the same time initiated major, mostly southward migration of North and South American mammals.

The Northern Hemisphere polar ice cap formed about 3 million years ago, and since that time its growth and retreat has resulted in a cyclical series of glacial and interglacial periods.

Major orogenic, or mountain-forming, activity during the Pliocene was centered on the west coast of North America where the coastal ranges (Cascade, Olympic, and California coast ranges) were uplifted. Continuation of the uplift of the Andes and Himalayas took place during the Pliocene Epoch. In the Mediterranean Basin significant subsidence of the sea-

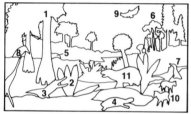

Warm, humid climates characterized the Lower Eocene Epoch, about 50 million years ago. In southeastern England a tropical or subtropical lowland met the sea along a coastal area that supported swamps of bald cypress, Taxodium (1), and the trunkless nipa palm, Nypa (2). Crocodiles, Crocodylus (3), and river turtles, Podocnemis (4), were common in shallow water. Drier land supported forests of Magnolia (5) and sabal palm, Sabal (6), as well as a fauna of early birds and mammals. Odontopteryx (7), a gannetlike bird, had unusual toothlike outgrowths of bone along its jaws. A kingfisherlike bird (8) and the vulture Lithornis (9) are usually assigned to Oligocene and Paleocene faunas, respectively. The fox-sized eohippus, or dawn horse, Hyracotherium (10), browsed in Lower Eocene forests. The hippopotamuslike Coryphodon (11) belongs to an extinct group of hoofed mammals, the pantodonts.

floor occurred—particularly in the Tyrrhenian Sea—with the reestablishment of normal marine connections with the Atlantic Ocean.

CLIMATE

Tertiary climates in North America were generally warmer and more humid than those of today. Tropical and subtropical conditions prevailed as far north as the Canadian border during the Early Tertiary, and arid conditions were later developed in the Great Plains. Toward the end of the Tertiary Period, the climate across the globe grew steadily colder, leading to the establishment of the first Pliocene Ice Age.

EVOLUTION

Mammals. The Tertiary Period—the Age of Mammals—witnessed a complex and extremely successful invasion by these animals of the various ecologic niches made available by the demise of the reptiles at the end of the Cretaceous Period. Placentals quickly achieved dominance over the marsupials in the Early Tertiary Period. Early radiation of primitive forms occurred during the Paleocene and Eocene, followed by their replacement with essentially modern forms during later epochs of the Tertiary and Quaternary periods.

Migration of mammals between Europe and North America

EPOCHS OF THE TERTIARY PERIOD

Epoch	Approximate Duration (millions of years)	Approximate Beginning (millions of years ago)
Pliocene	9	12
Miocene	14	26
Oligocene	12	38
Eocene	16	54
Paleocene	11	65

by way of a land bridge route (Iceland-Faeroe Ridge) throughout the Paleocene Epoch was abruptly terminated near the lower-middle Eocene boundary (50 million years ago). After this time, European and North American mammalian faunas evolved separately from each other.

Marine Fauna. Throughout the Tertiary Period, microscopic foraminifera dominated the marine environment. A rapid radiation of calcareous plankton was initiated during the Paleocene Epoch, following their virtual extinction at the close of the Cretaceous Period.

The period of planktonic flora and fauna diversification in the Eocene Epoch was followed by gradual declines and extinctions and then a stasis period of transition in the Oligocene. Toward the end of this epoch, a new period of radiation commenced, leading to the establishment of precursors of modern planktonic forms in the Miocene. The marked deterioration in climate during the Pliocene resulted in the extinction of numerous marine plankton.

Plants. Tertiary plant fossils tend to be strikingly modern in appearance. The period marks the development of the grasses, which influenced mammalian evolution from mainly browsers to grazers. The Late Tertiary cooling to which the Earth was subjected also resulted in the distinct zonal distribution of plant life.

TERTIARY DEPOSITS

Tertiary rocks consist mostly of loosely consolidated continental and marine sediments, many of which are extremely fossiliferous. Evidence of pronounced igneous activity is prevalent in several areas as well. The major sedimentary rock divisions were first established in Europe, where they are particularly well developed, especially in the structural basins of London, Paris, and Vienna.

Tertiary sediments are prevalent in northern Africa and

By the Miocene Epoch, climates had moderated and grassland habitats became extensive. Herds of mammals roamed the savannalike plains of North America. Many animal remains have been found in deposits from the Lower Miocene, about 20 million years ago. Moropus (1), a relative of the horses, measured about 2.7 m (9 ft) in length and had claws rather than hooves. Dinohyus (2) was a giant piglike animal about 3.2 m (10.5 ft) long. Stenomylus (3) was a small, graceful, long-necked camel. Diceratherium (4), a small, three-toed rhinoceros, possessed a pair of short horns on the end of its nose. Parahippus (5) was the first horse with high-crowned teeth, an adaptation to grazing; although it had three toes on each foot, the side toes were reduced and it walked mainly on the middle toes. Numerous corkscrew-shaped burrows (6) were presumably inhabited by a form of rodent that has been named Daemonelix.

southern South America and are coupled with volcanic activity in New Zealand, Australia, and India.

In North America, Tertiary sediments are prevalent along the length of the Atlantic and Gulf coastal plains, in the Great Plains region of the United States and Canada, and in the Great Basin region of the western United States. Tertiary volcanic activity is pronounced in the Columbia and Snake River region of Oregon, Washington, Idaho, and Nevada, where immense basaltic plateaus were formed from numerous, successive lava flows. Mounts Shasta, Hood, and Rainier and Lassen Peak are also the result of Tertiary volcanism.

Much of the world's oil supply is produced from Tertiary rocks in South America, the East Indies, the Middle East, the USSR, and California and the Gulf Coast region. Salt is mined from the salt domes of the Gulf Coast. Coal, lignite, oil shale, and several precious metals are also mined from Tertiary deposits.

W. A. BERGGREN

Bibliography: Davies, Arthur Morley, *Tertiary Faunas*, 2d ed. (1975); Dott, Robert H., Jr., and Batten, Roger L., *Evolution of the Earth*, 2d ed. (1976); Harbaugh, John W., *Stratigraphy and the Geologic Time Scale*, 2d ed. (1974); Pearson, Ronald, *Animals and Plants of the Cenozoic Era* (1964); Petersen, Morris S., et al., *Historical Geology of North America* (1973); Seyfert, Carl K., and Sirkin, Leslie A., *Earth History and Plate Tectonics: An Introduction to Historical Geology* (1973).

Tertullian [tur-tul'-ee-uhn]

Quintus Septimius Florens Tertullianus, b. Carthage, c.155, d. after 220, was one of the greatest Western theologians and writers of Christian antiquity. Through his writings a witness to the doctrine and discipline of the early church in belief and worship is preserved.

An advocate in the law courts in Rome, Tertullian converted (c.193) to Christianity. About 207 he broke with the church and joined the Montanists (see MONTANISM) in Africa. Soon after, however, he broke with them and formed his own party, known as the Tertullianists.

An extremist by nature, he had gone through a period of licentiousness during his early years, but later he advocated a severe asceticism and discipline that his followers found hard to emulate.

Tertullian was a man of fiery temperament, great talent, and unrelenting purpose. He wrote with brilliant rhetoric and biting satire. His passion for truth led him into polemics with his enemies: in turn pagans, Jews, heretics, and Catholics. His admiration for Christian heroism under persecution seems to have been the strongest factor in his conversion.

Tertullian's writings, notably *Apologeticum, De praescriptione haereticorum*, and *De carne Christi*, had a lasting effect on Christian thought, especially through those who, like CYPRIAN of Carthage, always regarded him as a "master." He also greatly influenced the development of Western thought and the creation of Christian ecclesiastical Latin.

AGNES CUNNINGHAM

Bibliography: Barnes, T. D., *Tertullian: A Historical and Literary Study* (1971); Sider, R. D., *Ancient Rhetoric and the Art of Tertullian* (1971).

Terzaghi, Karl [tair-tsah'-gee]

The Austrian-born American civil engineer Karl Anton Terzaghi, b. Oct. 2, 1883, d. Oct. 25, 1963, was known as the father of modern soil mechanics; his treatise *Erdbaumechanik auf Bodenphysikalischer Grundlage* (Soil Mechanics Based on Soil Physics, 1925) pioneered this field. A consulting engineer of worldwide scope and reputation, Terzaghi developed concepts concerning the relationship between strain, frictional resistance, and the stress state of a soil mass.

Teschen   [tesh'-en]

Teschen, a historic region in central Europe, straddles the Czechoslovak-Polish border. Part of Silesia since the 11th century, Teschen became one of the most industrialized regions of Austria-Hungary in the 19th century. Subject of a border dispute, the area was divided between Poland and Czechoslovakia in 1920. Germany occupied Teschen in 1939, but in 1945 the 1920 boundaries were restored.

BRUCE L. LaROSE

Tesla, Nikola   [tes'-luh]

The Croatian-American electrician and inventor Nikola Tesla, b. July 9, 1856, d. Jan. 7, 1943, made practical the use of alternating current. After emigrating (1884) to the United States, he worked briefly for Thomas Edison. In 1888 he demonstrated how a magnetic field could be made to rotate if two coils at right angles were supplied with alternating current of different phases (90 degrees out of phase with each other). Tesla patented his alternating-current motor, which was purchased by George WESTINGHOUSE and made the basis for the Westinghouse power system.

After 1903, Tesla did noteworthy research on high-voltage electricity, transformers, telephone and telegraph systems, and plants for power transmission without wires.

Bibliography: Hunt, Inez, and Draper, W. W., *Lightning in His Hands* (1977; repr. 1986); O'Neill, John J., *Prodigal Genius: The Life of Nikola Tesla* (1944; repr. 1986).

Tess of the D'Urbervilles

Generally considered one of Thomas HARDY's greatest novels, *Tess of the D'Urbervilles* (1891) explores the tragic consequences of the seduction of the peasant girl Tess Durbeyfield by Alec D'Urberville. Tess's seduction does not affect her essential purity. Her undoing is precipitated, rather, by the rigidly conventional attitudes of Angel Clare, the man she marries, but who abandons her on learning of her misfortune. Tess is forced to seek the protection of her seducer, whom she eventually murders in order to free herself. She is arrested and hanged, but Hardy's account of her life questions the justice of her fate and society's treatment of her.

Bibliography: McLauchlan, Juliet, *Tess of the D'Urbervilles* (1971).

Tessai   [tay-sy]

Tomioka Tessai, 1836–1924, was a Japanese artist who carried the Nanga school of Japanese painting into the modern era. Born in Kyoto, he was educated in Shinto, Confucianism, Buddhism, and Japanese literature. As a Shinto priest Tessai allied himself with the forces seeking a restoration of imperial rule and was forced to flee to Nagasaki, where he studied the Chinese-derived literati style known as Nanga. Tessai produced more than 20,000 paintings of traditional Chinese and Japanese subjects.

BARBARA BRENNAN FORD

Bibliography: Cahill, James, *Scholar Painters of Japan* (1972).

Tessin   (family)   [te-seen']

The Swedish Tessin family, originally from Pomerania, included two distinguished architects and an influential statesman.

Count **Nicodemus Tessin the Elder**, b. Dec. 7, 1615, d. May 24, 1681, made his most important contributions after travels through Germany, Italy, France, and Holland (1651–53); these visits helped to shape the French–Dutch classicism seen in his secular works and the Italian baroque style typical of his ecclesiastical designs. Among his many achievements are the Borgholm (1654–60), Skokloster (1653), and Drottningholm (1662–86) palaces and the cathedral at Kalmar (1660).

Count **Nicodemus Tessin the Younger**, b. May 23, 1654, d. Apr. 10, 1728, was influenced by Giovanni Lorenzo Bernini, Carlo Fontana, and André Le Nôtre during wide-ranging travels in Germany, France, and Italy. He is best known for his role in rebuilding, in the baroque style, the Swedish Royal Palace (begun 1697) in Stockholm.

Count **Carl Gustaf Tessin**, b. Sept. 5, 1695, d. Jan. 7, 1770,

the son of Tessin the Younger, became a shaper of Sweden's foreign policy, a parliamentary leader, and tutor to the future king Gustav III. He played an important role in promoting artistic contacts between Sweden and the rest of Europe.

Bibliography: Laurin, Carl, et al., *Scandinavian Art* (1922; repr. 1970); Paulson, Thomas, *Scandinavian Architecture* (1958).

test: see EDUCATIONAL MEASUREMENT AND TESTING; PSYCHOLOGICAL TESTING.

Test Acts

Test acts were laws passed in post-Reformation England, Scotland, and Ireland to limit office holding to those professing the established religion. In England the Test Act of 1673 was passed by Parliament to exclude from public office all persons refusing to take oaths of allegiance and supremacy to the crown or to receive the sacraments according to the rites of the Church of England. The legislators feared that King CHARLES II's alliance with France and his Declaration of Indulgence (1672), suspending the penal laws against Roman Catholics, would lead to the revival of Roman Catholicism as the national religion. The act was extended in 1678 to members of Parliament. Thus non-Anglicans were formally excluded from public life. Roman Catholic King JAMES II (r. 1685–88) was unable to secure repeal. After 1689, however, it became customary to pass bills of indemnity legalizing the acts of nonconforming magistrates. The Test Act remained law until 1828, a year before CATHOLIC EMANCIPATION restored other civil rights to Roman Catholics. Test acts were abolished in 1871 in Ireland and in 1889 in Scotland.

MAURICE ASHLEY

Bibliography: Aveling, J. C. H., *The Handle and the Axe* (1976); Mensing, R. C., *Toleration and Parliament 1660–1719* (1979); Miller, John, *Popery and Politics in England, 1660–1688* (1973); Ogg, David, *England in the Reign of Charles II*, 2 vols. (1956; repr. 1984).

testicle   see REPRODUCTIVE SYSTEM, HUMAN.

testosterone: see SEX HORMONES.

tetanus   [tet'-nuhs]

Tetanus, or lockjaw, an acute and often fatal infectious disease of the human nervous system, is characterized by severe spasms of the voluntary muscles and convulsions. The symptoms are caused by a toxin produced by *Clostridium tetani*, an anaerobic bacterium that can infect deep wounds where oxygen is unavailable; its spores can be found in soil and in animal feces. The incubation period is usually five to ten days, and the most frequently occurring symptom is jaw stiffness, which progresses to trismus—difficulty in opening the jaws. Other symptoms include difficulty in swallowing, stiffness of the arms or legs, fever, headache, and sore throat. Convulsions can result in death through suffocation. The prognosis is poor if symptoms progress rapidly or treatment is delayed. Treatment includes tetanus antitoxin, and the disease can be prevented by immunization with toxoid.

tetany   [tet'-uh-nee]

Tetany is an abnormal condition characterized by convulsions and intermittent attacks of sustained, painful muscular contraction and flexing of wrists and ankles, apprehension, and difficult inhalation. Tetany generally results from low blood calcium, which causes hyperexcitability of the muscles. The condition resembles but is unrelated to epilepsy.

PETER L. PETRAKIS

Tethys Sea

Tethys is the name that geologists have given to the primarily east-west seaway that lay between Eurasian and African crustal plates (see PLATE TECTONICS) during the later PALEOZOIC

ERA and the MESOZOIC ERA. The sea occupied a zone of crustal weakness that was a major GEOSYNCLINE during that stretch of geologic time. Layers of sediment began accumulating in the subsiding seafloor depression of Tethys toward the end of the Paleozoic; by the end of the Mesozoic, they had attained thicknesses of a few thousand meters. Beginning in the CRETACEOUS PERIOD, the geosynclinal sediments of the western Tethys were squeezed together and buckled upward by the collision of the northward-drifting African plate with Eurasia. This uplift created the Alpine ranges of Europe, the Taurus Mountains of Turkey, and the Zagros Mountains of Iran, and it left in place of the western Tethys a greatly shrunken remnant now known as the Mediterranean Sea. Somewhat later, during the Oligocene Epoch of the TERTIARY PERIOD, northward-drifting India collided with Eurasia, closing the eastern Tethys and crumpling the sediments that had accumulated there. Uplift of these eastern sediments created the Himalayan ranges, marking the final phase of a geosynclinal cycle that had begun more than 200 million years earlier.   PETER MARGOLIN

Tetley, Glen   [tet'-lee]

Glen Tetley, b. Cleveland, Ohio, Feb. 3, 1926, is an American choreographer whose major work has been done in Europe. Tetley came to New York City to study modern dance with Hanya Holm in 1946 and performed with her until 1951. During the 1950s he performed with such diverse groups as New York City Opera, American Ballet Theatre (ABT), and the companies of Robert Joffrey, Martha Graham, and John Butler. Tetley's first program of choreography, presented in 1962, included his still-popular *Pierrot Lunaire.*

He went to Netherlands Dance Theater as guest artist in 1962 and was its joint artistic director (1969–70) with Hans van Manen. From 1974 to 1976, Tetley was director of Stuttgart Ballet, and he choreographed *Voluntaries* (1974) as a tribute to its late director John Cranko. He has staged ballets for ABT, Ballet Rambert, the Royal Ballet, and the Batsheva Dance Company of Israel. His recent ballets include the full-length *The Tempest, Summer's End,* and *Firebird.*
          MICHAEL ROBERTSON

Teton Dam   [tee'-tuhn]

The Teton Dam and Reservoir were the principal features of the Teton Basin Project on the Teton River in southeastern Idaho. This multipurpose project was designed to provide irrigation, power production, flood control, and recreation. The project was begun in 1972, despite controversy over the safety of the dam site. Reservoir filling began in October, 1975 when the river outlet was closed. On June 5, 1976, the earth embankment dam collapsed as a result of the internal erosion of the core material. The wall of water released by the collapse killed 11 people, left more than 25,000 homeless, and flooded a 780-km^2 (300-mi^2) area.   THOMAS J. CONCANNON

Teton Range

The Teton Range, a chain of the ROCKY MOUNTAINS, extends immediately south of Yellowstone National Park in northwestern Wyoming and eastern Idaho. About 65 km (40 mi) long, it lies partly within Grand Teton National Park and Bridger-Teton and Targhee national forests. The highest peak, Grand Teton (4,199 m/13,776 ft), was first scaled by Nathaniel P. Langford and James Stevenson in 1872. Jackson, Wyo., a popular tourist center, is to the south. John Colter was the first white person to explore (1807–08) the range.

tetra   [tet'-ruh]

Tetras are any of a number of small, active, attractively colored or marked freshwater fishes of the family Characidae (the CHARACINS). Native primarily to tropical America, many of these fishes were once classified in the genus *Tetragonopterus,* from which the common name is derived. Tetras are popular aquarium fishes and are bred on a large scale.

tetracycline: see ANTIBIOTICS.

tetragonal system

CRYSTALS that can be referred to three mutually perpendicular axes, two of which are of equal length, belong to the tetragonal system. This system contains seven classes. The symmetry element that distinguishes tetragonal crystals from crystals of other systems is a unique fourfold symmetry axis coincident with the *c* crystallographic axis. Common minerals belonging to the tetragonal system include CHALCOPYRITE, IDOCRASE, RUTILE, SCAPOLITE, and ZIRCON. Crystals in the highest-order class in this system can possess as many elements as one fourfold symmetry axis, four twofold symmetry axes, and five planes of symmetry. Crystals of the lowest-order class possess only a unique fourfold inversion axis.

Tetragonal crystals are optically uniaxial, and, as in the hexagonal system, the optical axis coincides with the *c* (fourfold) crystallographic axis. Extinction is always parallel in crystals belonging to this system.   JOAN FITZPATRICK

tetrahedrite

The widely distributed copper and iron antimony SULFIDE MINERAL tetrahedrite [(Cu, Fe)$_{12}$Sb$_4$S$_{13}$], a copper ore, usually contains some arsenic and thus grades into the associated mineral tennantite. These minerals form gray to black tetrahedral crystals (isometric system), crystal groups, and granular masses. Hardness is 3 to 4½ and specific gravity is 4.4 to 5.1. Occurrences are in medium- to low-temperature ore veins, commonly with CHALCOPYRITE. Major deposits occur in Montana, Bohemia, Hungary, Chile, Peru, and Bolivia.

Tetrazzini, Luisa   [tay-trah-tsee'-nee]

Luisa Tetrazzini, an operatic soprano, b. Florence, Italy, June 8, 1871, d. April 28, 1940, made her debut at age 19 in Meyerbeer's *L'Africaine* at the Teatro Pagliano (now Teatro Verdi) in Florence. She spent several years in Argentina and Brazil and was first heard in New York at the Manhattan Opera House, as Violetta in Verdi's *La Traviata.* She made her last public appearance at the Paramount Theater, New York City, in 1931, and retired to teach in Milan. Her voice was noted for its fluency in coloratura coupled with unusual fullness and richness.   RAYMOND GRAUNKE

Bibliography: Tetrazzini, Luisa, *My Life of Song* (1921).

tetrode: see ELECTRON TUBE.

Tetzel, Johann   [tet'-sul]

A German Dominican friar, Johann Tetzel, b. *c.*1465, d. Aug. 11, 1519, was a preacher of INDULGENCES. His promotion of the indulgence issued for the rebuilding of Saint Peter's, Rome, aroused the anger of Martin LUTHER, who partly in reaction issued his 95 Theses (1517).

Teutonic Knights   [too-tahn'-ik]

Founded in 1190 by German merchants to serve a hospital during the siege of Acre in the Third Crusade, the Teutonic Knights were originally called the Brothers of the Hospital of Saint Mary of the Teutons in Jerusalem. By 1198 they had become a military order similar to the Templars and Knights Hospitalers. The members, who were nobles, took vows of poverty, chastity, and obedience. During the 13th century the order moved to eastern Europe and began its principal work—crusading against the pagan peoples in the east. Under the leadership of Hermann von Salza, grand master from 1210 to 1239, the order began to carve out for itself the military-monastic state of PRUSSIA. By its administration and colonization it played a central role in the eastward expansion of German culture and power—the DRANG NACH OSTEN.

In 1237 the Teutonic Knights merged with the Livonian Knights, who had created a similar domain for themselves in the Baltic lands (see LIVONIA). Their eastward expansion was halted (1240) by defeat at the hands of ALEXANDER NEVSKY. The order made repeated and unsuccessful attempts to conquer Lithuania, which it continued to threaten even after Lithuania entered into (1386) a personal union with Poland and converted to Latin Christianity. In 1410, Polish-Lithuanian forces defeated the Knights in the Battle of TANNENBERG. After further fighting the Teutonic Knights were forced (1466; Treaty of Torun) to cede Pomerelia and West Prussia to Poland, retaining East Prussia only as a fief of the Polish crown.

During the 16th century the order's grand master, Albert of Brandenburg, converted (1525) to Lutheranism and declared Prussia a secular duchy (see ALBERT, FIRST DUKE OF PRUSSIA). At this point the Livonian Knights resumed their independence until they were dissolved in 1561. A remaining branch of the order retained lands in central and southern Germany until 1809. Today the order is reorganized as a clerical order engaged in pastoral work and health care. Its headquarters is in Vienna.   CYPRIAN DAVIS, O.S.B.

Bibliography: Burleigh, Michael, *Prussian Society and the German Order* (1984); Seward, Desmond, *The Monks of War* (1972); Urban, William, *The Livonian Crusade* (1981); Zajaczkowski, S., *Rise and Fall of the Teutonic Order in Prussia* (1935).

Tevfik Fikret   [tev-feek' feek-ret']

Tevfik Fikret was the pseudonym of the Turkish poet Mehmed Tevfik, b. Dec. 24, 1867, d. Aug. 19, 1915, remembered for his tender romantic lyrics as well as stirring poems of social protest. His major collection, *Rübab-I Şikeste* (The Broken Lute, 1896), introduced many stanzaic and stylistic innovations. *Haluk'un Defteri* (Haluk's Notebook, 1911), addressed to his only son, laments oppression and social injustice.
                                                TALAT SAIT HALMAN

Texarkana   [tek-sar-kan'-uh]

Texarkana is a city bisected by the Texas-Arkansas border, about 260 km (160 mi) northeast of Dallas, Tex. The Arkansas section, which is the seat of Miller County, has a population of 21,459 (1980); the Texas section has 31,271 residents. The industry of the dual municipality, which has separate governments, includes processing and distribution of cotton and lumber and manufacture of clay products, tires, furniture, and mobile homes. The city is a railroad junction and has several U.S. Army installations. It was settled in 1874.

Texas

Stretching 1,244 km (773 mi) from east to west and 1,289 km (801 mi) from north to south, Texas, the Lone Star State, occupies almost 7.5% of the nation's total land area—a region as large as all of New England, New York, Pennsylvania, Ohio, and Illinois combined. With its 16,789,000 inhabitants (1987 est.), Texas is the third most populous state in the country. It derives its name from the Spanish and Indian words *tejas* and *techas,* meaning "friends" or "allies."

Texas shows the influence of both the Indians and the Spanish, French, and other European explorers and missionaries. In 1820, Moses and Stephen F. Austin started the Anglo-American colonization that culminated in the organization of a provisional government at San Felipe on Nov. 3, 1835, and in independence from Mexico on Mar. 2, 1836. After almost 10 years as an independent republic, Texas became a U.S. state on Dec. 29, 1845.

The modern economic development of Texas started in January 1901 with the eruption of an oil well drilled at Spindletop, near Beaumont. The rapid discovery of oil in various other parts of the state led to a boom that has never really stopped. The economy of Texas has become highly diversified, and its population has more than quadrupled during this century.

LAND AND RESOURCES
Topography and Soils. Four major physiographic subdivisions of North America are found in Texas: the Gulf Coastal Plain

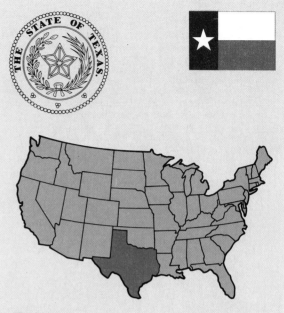

TEXAS

LAND. Area: 691,027 km² (266,807 mi²); rank: 2d. Capital: Austin (1986 est. pop., 466,550). Largest city: Houston (1986 est. pop., 1,728,910). Counties: 254. Elevations: highest—2,667 m (8,749 ft), at Guadalupe Peak; lowest—sea level, at the Gulf of Mexico.
PEOPLE. Population (1987 est.): 16,789,000; rank: 3d; density: 24.7 persons per km² (64 per mi²). Distribution (1986): 80.7% metropolitan, 19.3% nonmetropolitan. Average annual change (1980–87): +2.6%.
EDUCATION. Public enrollment (1986): elementary—2,317,454; secondary—892,061; higher—685,542. Nonpublic enrollment (1980): elementary—94,200; secondary—20,200; combined—30,700; higher (1986)—90,477. Institutions of higher education (1985): 155.
ECONOMY. State personal income (1986): $224.9 billion; rank: 3d. Median family income (1979): $19,618; rank: 27th. Nonagricultural labor distribution (1986): manufacturing—960,000 persons; wholesale and retail trade—1,685,000; government—1,119,000; services—1,372,000; transportation and public utilities—375,000; finance, insurance, and real estate—448,000; construction—414,000. Agriculture: income (1986)—$8.4 billion. Fishing: value (1986)—$246 million. Forestry: sawtimber volume (1987 prelim.)—52 billion board feet. Mining: value (1985)—$40.2 billion. Manufacturing: value added (1985)—$55.2 billion. Services: value (1982)—$34.6 billion.
GOVERNMENT (1989). Governor: William P. Clements, Republican. U.S. Congress: Senate—1 Democrat, 1 Republican; House—19 Democrats, 8 Republicans. Electoral college votes: 29. State legislature: 31 senators, 150 representatives.
STATE SYMBOLS. Statehood: Dec. 29, 1845; the 28th state. Nickname: Lone Star State; bird: mockingbird; flower: bluebonnet; tree: pecan; motto: Friendship; song: "Texas, Our Texas."

in the east and southeast, the North Central Plains running north to southeastward in the center of the state, the Great High Plains in the northwest, and the Trans-Pecos Mountains to the extreme west and southwest. The topography of Texas rises gradually from east to west, reaching its highest point in Guadalupe Peak (2,667 m/8,749 ft) in the Trans-Pecos.

The Gulf Coastal Plain, extending about 80 to 100 km (50 to 60 mi) inland from the Gulf of Mexico, from sea level to an altitude of about 150 m (500 ft), has a rolling-to-hilly surface. Its western part consists of a fertile belt of land of irregular width known as the Blackland Prairie.

Inland from the Coastal Plain, the North Central Plains of Texas are the southern extension of the GREAT PLAINS and reach southwestward across the entire state to the Rio Grande. The plains' southern portion is known as the Ed-

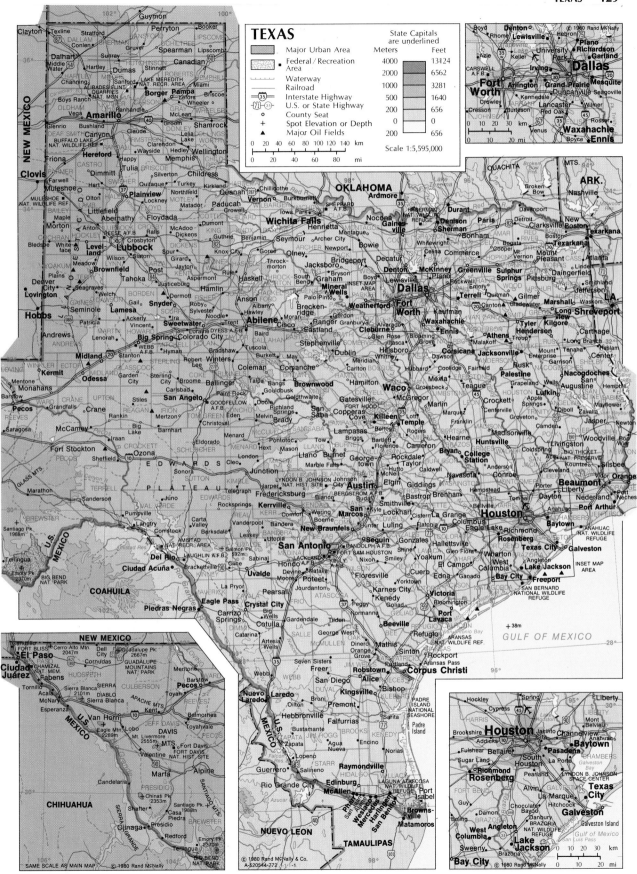

TEXAS

- Major Urban Area
- Federal / Recreation Area
- Waterway
- Railroad
- Interstate Highway
- U.S. or State Highway
- ○ County Seat
- + Spot Elevation or Depth
- ▲ Major Oil Fields

State Capitals are underlined

Meters	Feet
4000	13124
2000	6562
1000	3281
500	1640
200	656
0	0
200	656

Scale 1:5,595,000

© 1980 Rand McNally & Co.
A-520544-772

wards Plateau. The border of the North Central Plains on the west is the Staked Plain, or *Llano Estacado* in Spanish. It consists of a flat-topped tableland with an elevation of about 1,200 m (4,000 ft). Lying between Mexico and New Mexico, the barren Trans-Pecos region in southwestern Texas alternates between rolling hills in the Pecos River valley and the isolated high ridges of the Guadalupe and Davis mountains.

Texas is divided into 14 land resource areas that have similar or related soils, vegetation, topography, and climate. The soils vary greatly in depth from one region to another and show different physical properties; all need fertilizing, however, and some need irrigating to make them productive.

Rivers and Lakes. Texas has two sources of water: aquifers, found under more than half the state, and streams with their reservoirs. Water from the former has traditionally been an essential source of municipal supplies; because of falling water tables, however, cities more and more must now depend on surface reservoirs.

The state's 3,700 streams have a combined length of approximately 130,000 km (80,000 mi). Among the major rivers are the RIO GRANDE, which drops about 3,650 m (12,000 ft) from source to mouth and constitutes the border with Mexico; the RED RIVER, which partly separates Texas from Oklahoma and Arkansas; the COLORADO RIVER of Texas (965 km/600 mi), which is the longest river entirely within the state; and the Sabine, which forms the southern half of the boundary between Texas and Louisiana. Other rivers include the PECOS and the Devils, both tributaries of the Rio Grande; the Nueces; and the Guadalupe.

Texas has relatively few natural lakes but hundreds of artificial ones. These were developed to provide hydroelectricity, to store water, or to irrigate farmland. Among the largest are Lake Texoma (partly in Oklahoma) on the Red River, the Falcon and Amistad reservoirs on the Rio Grande, Sam Rayburn Reservoir on the Angelina River in eastern Texas, Lake Texarkana on the Sulphur River, Toledo Bend Reservoir on the Sabine, Lake Travis on the Colorado, and Lake Livingston on the Trinity River north of Houston.

Climate. The climates of Texas range from the hot subhumid found in the Rio Grande valley to the cold semiarid of the northern part of the Panhandle, and from the warm humid in the east to the arid of the Trans-Pecos. Rainfall varies from 1,400 mm (55 in) in the east to less than 250 mm (10 in) in the west. The average number of days with some precipitation ranges from 44 in El Paso to 110 in Houston. Drought can be a serious problem, especially in the Great High Plains, where an average of seven droughts occur in a 10-year period. Temperatures, too, vary greatly, ranging from 49° C (120° F) to −31° C (−23° F). Each year about 100 tornadoes occur, most frequently in the Red River valley.

Vegetation and Animal Life. The dense pine forests of eastern Texas contrast with the deserts of the western part of the state, and the grassy plains of the north contrast with the semiarid brushes of southern Texas. Eastern Texas vegetation is characterized by dense pine forests and a variety of hardwoods including oak, hickory, ash, and magnolia. The central region is dominated by oak, elm, and pecan, as well as, on the Edwards Plateau, by cedar and mesquite. Shrubs of the grasslands of the lower altitudes of the west include acacia, mesquite, and mimosa; the Trans-Pecos Mountains have pine, fir, and spruce. The Rio Grande valley is mostly covered by brush, mesquite, cedar, post oak, and in places a dense growth of prickly pear. In the southwest are found cactus, agave, and yucca.

Texas is the temporary home every year for many migratory birds. Aransas Wildlife Refuge, for example, on the Gulf above Corpus Christi, provides the winter quarters for the almost extinct whooping crane. The state's indigenous animals include the mule and white-tailed deer, black bear, mountain lion, antelope, and bighorn, but the American bison, or buffalo, is found only in zoos and on a few ranches. Among the smaller mammals are the muskrat, raccoon, opossum, jackrabbit, fox, mink, coyote, and armadillo.

Resources. Minerals represent a very significant part of the state's natural wealth. The known petroleum deposits of Tex-

as—about 8 billion barrels—make up approximately one-third of the known U.S. supply. The Texas Panhandle is one of the world's great natural-gas reservoirs. Mineral fuels generally account for over 90% of the value of all minerals produced in the state, although Texas is also a leading producer of natural graphite, magnesium, sulfur, and cement and has considerable reserves of lignite (low-grade coal). Uranium was discovered in 1954 in the Coastal Plain, and additional deposits have been found in various other parts of the state. The state's great variety of soils must also be numbered in the list of its resources.

PEOPLE

Although surpassed in population only by California and New York, Texas is still considerably less crowded than the nation as a whole; the huge area of Texas means that the state's population density is less than that of the nation as a whole. Yet the state's population increased by 42% between 1970 and 1985—well above the national average (16.8%)—partly as a result of in-migration. Most of the population increase since World War II has been within the state's 28 Standard Metropolitan Statistical Areas (SMSAs), especially the suburbs. Rural areas, however, which had a stable or decreasing population until the mid-1960s, have begun to show a moderate to rapid growth, as have many nonmetropolitan areas adjacent to the SMSAs. But the population of Texas remains unequally distributed. In 1980 the state's seven largest metropolitan areas accounted for nearly 61% of its population; by 1985 all the SMSAs accounted for 80.5% of the total population.

Racially, Texas is made up of whites, who constitute about 80% of the population; blacks, 12%; and other nonwhites, 8%. Persons of Spanish origin account for 21% of the population. European settlers during the 19th and early 20th centuries included Germans, Swedes, and Czechs.

Counties and Cities. Texas has 254 counties ranging in population from 91 (Loving County, 1980) to 2,409,547 (Harris, 1980), and in size from Rockwall's 386 km² (149 mi²) to Brewster's 16,035 km² (6,191 mi²), nearly equal to the combined areas of Connecticut and Rhode Island. Major cities include the capital, AUSTIN; the state's largest city, HOUSTON; and DALLAS and FORT WORTH, only about 50 km (30 mi) apart. SAN ANTONIO is a fast-growing shipping center for oil and agricultural products; other important commercial centers are ABILENE, AMARILLO, BEAUMONT, BROWNSVILLE, CORPUS CHRISTI, EL PASO, GALVESTON, LAREDO, LUBBOCK, MIDLAND, PORT ARTHUR, WACO, and WICHITA FALLS.

Education. In 1839, Texas president Mirabeau B. LAMAR set aside land in each county for public schools and for a state university. Today the average daily attendance in Texas public schools exceeds 2 million, and higher education in the state includes almost 100 public institutions (see TEXAS, STATE UNIVERSITIES OF). Additional thousands of elementary and secondary students attend private schools, and Texas has several dozen private institutions of higher education (including BAYLOR, RICE, and Southern Methodist universities).

Culture and Historical Sites. Texas has several hundred public libraries—the largest being those in Dallas and Houston; the libraries of the University of Texas at Austin have the state's largest collections. There are more than 300 museums (up from 82 in 1964), and there are 3 major symphony orchestras—in Dallas, Houston, and San Antonio. Among the outstanding museums are the Dallas and Fort Worth museums of fine arts, the McNay Art Institute and Witte Museum in San Antonio, the Museum of Fine Arts, the Contemporary Arts Museum, and the Menil Collection in Houston, and the Amon Carter Museum of Western Art in Fort Worth. Well-known symphony orchestras are also in Amarillo, Fort Worth, and Austin. The Dallas and Austin ballets and the Alley Theatre in Houston have national reputations. The Dallas Civic, Houston Grand, and San Antonio operas are the state's major opera companies.

The ALAMO in San Antonio is the most famous historical site; others are San Antonio Missions National Historic Park, San Jacinto Monument east of Houston, Fort Davis National Historic Site, and the Lyndon Baines Johnson Presidential Library—part of the University of Texas in Austin.

(Right) *Oil-rich Houston, the largest city in Texas, has become a showcase of contemporary architecture. At the center of this view of the downtown area is the RepublicBank Center (1983). Its red granite and stepped gables contrast strikingly with the more traditional skyscrapers surrounding it.*

(Below) *A fishing boat from Corpus Christi moves across Corpus Christi Bay. Protected by Padre and Mustang islands, the bay is rich in both fin and shellfish species.*

Communications. The first newspaper in Texas, the *Gaceta de Texas* (Texas Gazette), was published in Spanish in 1813 at Nacogdoches. Among the oldest English newspapers are the *Galveston News* (1842) and the *Dallas Morning News* (1885). There are numerous other morning and evening dailies, and Texas is well supplied with radio stations, both AM and FM, as well as with television stations.

ECONOMIC ACTIVITY

For decades oil influenced every aspect of the economic development of Texas. This included the tax structure, since a high percentage of the state's tax revenues was derived from oil and gas. This changed in the mid-1980s when oil prices collapsed devastatingly, greatly diminishing tax revenues and adversely affecting not only oil-related industries but also many others, such as real estate and banking. Slow economic recovery began in 1987, however, helped by the industrial diversification that had already begun in Texas and that was now intensified. The service industries, notably retail and wholesale trade, contribute well over half of the gross state product of Texas.

Agriculture. Texas is a leading agricultural state, frequently ranking third (after California and Iowa) in gross farm income. Agricultural statistics in Texas have been affected by modern technology, which increases productivity: in consequence, the number of persons living on farms has markedly decreased in recent decades. Another trend has been a decline in the total number of farms and ranches.

(Right) *Galveston, on a Gulf of Mexico barrier island, is today a port and resort for nearby Houston. In 1528 the first Spaniard to visit present-day Texas landed nearby. From 1817 to 1821 the privateer Jean Lafitte made the site his base until, under pressure from the U.S. government, he burned the settlement and sailed away.*

(Right) *Cattle are herded across rangeland in Texas. Because of the mild climate, beef cattle can graze outdoors throughout the year, and Texas leads the nation in their output.*

(Below) *Texas leads the nation in the production of cotton, although its yield per hectare is much lower than that of the other major cotton-producing states. Cultivation of this valuable cash crop, begun during the 1820s in the fertile river valleys, now occurs throughout most of the state.*

The largest share of agricultural income is derived from beef cattle; Texas leads the nation in the number of beef cattle, which usually exceed 14 million head. Cotton is the leading crop and the state's second-most-valuable farm product. Texas also leads in national production of grain sorghum, watermelons, cabbages, and spinach. Wheat, corn, and other grains are also important. There is good farmland located in most parts of the state, some of it made more productive by use of irrigation and of dry-farming techniques (used in the Panhandle, for example, for wheat production).

Forestry and Fishing. Production of timber—more softwoods than hardwoods—represents a small share of the gross state product of Texas, but shipments of lumber and wood products and of paper and allied products are worth many times that share. As for fishing, shrimp accounts for over 90% of Texas's total commercial catch. Other species caught include crabs, oysters, flounder, and red snapper.

Mining. Texas is the nation's most important producer of minerals. It leads the nation in the production of mineral fuels, with petroleum the most valuable and natural gas the second most valuable. Texas in recent years (excepting the downturn of the mid-1980s) has supplied about one-third of the U.S. production of both oil and natural gas. A foremost state in nonfuel minerals, Texas is a leading producer of natural graphite, magnesium, sulfur, and cement. The eastern part of the state has lignite coal mines. Metals mined in Texas include iron, uranium, magnesium, and sodium.

Manufacturing. Before World War II, manufacturing in Texas centered on processing the raw materials, notably petroleum and agricultural products, available in the state. The decades since the war have seen an emphasis on diversification in manufacturing, however, as well as significant industrial expansion. In the late 1980s, in the wake of the disastrous oil slump, state leaders were attempting to attract more high-tech industries to Texas.

Manufactures include a wide range of petroleum and coal products, nonelectrical machinery, chemicals, and food products. Other broad categories of Texan manufactures include electrical machinery and equipment, fabricated metals, primary metals, and transportation equipment. Specific manufactures include such diverse items as wristwatches, radios, cosmetics and drugs, leather goods, recreational boats, and mobile homes. A large number of the approximately 15% of the labor force employed in manufacturing in Texas work in the Dallas–Fort Worth and Houston metropolitan areas.

Tourism. Texas attracts millions of out-of-state visitors annually; its tourist-related businesses compete with those of California and Florida for the U.S. travel market. Many visitors explore Dallas, San Antonio, Houston, Fort Worth, El Paso, Austin, and other cities. Sites of special interest range from Nacogdoches in East Texas, one of the state's oldest cities, to the Lyndon B. Johnson Space Center near Houston. Texas's two national parks, BIG BEND and Guadalupe Mountains, are also popular, as are the numerous and varied state recreation areas. Hunting and fishing are popular pastimes for visitors and Texans alike, as are professional and college sports events.

Transportation and Foreign Trade. As befits its hugeness, Texas ranks first nationally in total highway and railroad mileage. It also has the most airports (about 1,200). There are 12 deepwater ports along the Gulf of Mexico, with Houston the busiest (and ranking among the most active of all U.S. ports). The year 1988 commemorated the 135th anniversary of the first railroad operation in Texas; railway mileage reached its peak in 1922 (approximately 27,500 km/17,000 mi), but the volume of rail freight started to increase again after World War II.

Texas is a major U.S. exporter of manufactured goods, including chemicals and allied products. Also exported are agricultural products—especially cotton and food grains. Texas is habitually the nation's leading exporter of sulfur; additionally, its exports of iron and steel scrap also rank high. Other exports

Big Bend National Park, named for the 90° curve the Rio Grande takes there at Mariscal Canyon, is located in southwestern Texas along the U.S.-Mexican border. The park's diverse scenery ranges from mountain peaks to canyons carved by the river.

include natural gas and fishery products, especially shrimp.

Energy. Texas consumes more energy than any other state—more than 60% of its natural gas and about 40% of its oil never leave its borders. About 90% of the energy consumed in Texas comes from petroleum and natural gas.

GOVERNMENT AND POLITICS

The present Texas constitution was adopted on Feb. 15, 1876, but has been amended many times. The chief executive is the governor, who since 1975 serves for 4 years. Legislative authority is exercised by the senate, with 31 members elected for 4-year terms, and the house of representatives, with 150 members elected for 2-year terms. The legislature meets biennially in odd-numbered years. The highest courts of Texas include the nine-member supreme court and the five-member court of criminal appeals. Judges of the two courts are elected to 6-year overlapping terms. The state delegation to the U.S. House of Representatives was enlarged from 24 to 27 in the reapportionment after the 1980 census.

In 1978 the state elected its first Republican governor (William P. Clements, Jr.) since 1870, and Republican John Tower served in the U.S. Senate from 1961 until his retirement in 1985. Despite the popularity of some individual Republicans, including Ronald Reagan, Democrats have dominated state-level politics since Reconstruction; competition occurs chiefly between the liberal and conservative wings of the Democratic party. Many Texans, such as former U.S. House Speaker Sam RAYBURN, have played influential roles in national affairs. Henry Cisneros attracted national attention after he became (1981) the first Mexican-American mayor of a major U.S. city (San Antonio), although minority groups have generally been underrepresented in Texas politics.

HISTORY

Evidence of a meeting in eastern Texas between Middle American prehistoric cultures and temple MOUND BUILDERS from the eastern part of what is now the United States has been discovered in an Indian mound on the Neches River, and many tribal groups—including the APACHE, CADDO, and Comanche—inhabited what is now Texas.

Conquest and Colonization. The first European explorers were the Spaniards Álvar Núñez CABEZA DE VACA (1528) and Francisco CORONADO (1541). Other Spanish expeditions followed during the next century, and in 1682, Ysleta, near El Paso, became the first European settlement in Texas. Three years later Robert Cavalier, sieur de LA SALLE, brought the second flag (French) to Texas. He landed at the head of Lavaca Bay and established Fort Saint Louis.

La Salle was killed by one of his own men in 1687, and his fort was destroyed by disease and the Indians. About 1714, however, the Spanish felt threatened by another Frenchman,

the explorer and trader Louis Juchereau de Saint Denis. Although he claimed that his intention was simply to establish trade, he was arrested and sent to Mexico City. The Spanish then redoubled their efforts to settle Texas, and by the middle of the 18th century they had mounted more than 100 expeditions to the area.

American Interest in Texas. The sale (1803) of Louisiana to the United States increased interest in Texas from the east. Augustus Magee, a U.S. army officer in Louisiana, befriended the Mexican patriot Bernardo Gutiérrez, who had been fighting for his country's independence from Spain. Together they led an expedition into Texas and captured Nacogdoches, Goliad, and San Antonio before Magee died mysteriously in Goliad.

In 1819, Dr. James Long of Natchez, Miss., led another expedition to Texas, hoping to make the region an independent state. He captured Nacogdoches but his forces were soon defeated. A year later, Moses Austin visited San Antonio and sought permission to settle Americans in Texas. Upon returning to Missouri, his dying request was that his son, Stephen AUSTIN, carry out his plans, which the Spanish had approved.

McKittrick Canyon is situated in Guadalupe Mountains National Park. The park covers 308 km² (119 mi²) in western Texas and contains a vast limestone fossil reef and unusual vegetation and wildlife.

In 1821 the white population of Texas was 7,000, with Goliad, San Antonio, and Nacogdoches the only towns of any size. During this period Mexico secured its independence from Spain, and, in 1823, Stephen Austin went to Mexico City to seek confirmation of his father's grant. A new law required that agents introduce at least 200 families of colonists, so Austin made an agreement with the Mexican governor to settle 300 American families. Colonization was so successful, however, that by 1836 the population of Texas had grown to 50,000.

Revolution and Republic. Differences in language, culture, and religion soon led to difficulties between the new Anglo-American settlers and the Mexican government. Because of the great distance between Texas and Mexico City, cultural and commercial ties grew stronger with the United States, and some settlers hoped that U.S. boundaries would be extended to include Texas.

In 1830 the Mexican congress enacted a law to limit immigration to Texas. But this only increased dissatisfaction, for neither the Mexican national constitution nor the constitution of 1827 for the state of Coahuila–Texas granted rights that Anglo-Americans considered inalienable, such as trial by jury and the right of bail. Most settlers also found unacceptable the requirement that they become Roman Catholics because most of them were Protestants.

War broke out between the American settlers and the Mexican government in 1835, and the Texans won the first battle at Gonzales on Oct. 2, 1835. The same year the Texans captured San Antonio after a devastating siege; a provisional government was set up on Mar. 2, 1836, and Sam Houston was named commander in chief of the Texas armies, Stephen Austin having gone to Washington to solicit aid from the U.S. government.

In March and April 1836 one of the most heroic battles in history occurred at the Alamo. The besieged Texas forces commanded by William B. Travis had been reduced to 157. He appealed for help, and about 30 additional men from Gonzales broke through the lines of the Mexican general, Antonio Santa Anna. The 187 defenders, commanded by Travis, James Bowie, and Davy Crockett, then held the Alamo for another 5 days before it fell. March also saw a massacre at Goliad, in which the outnumbered Texans, having surrendered after a battle on Coleto Creek, returned to Goliad only to be killed on the orders of Santa Anna.

Despite reverses, the Texans declared their independence in a great spirit of resistance, and on Mar. 2, 1836, David Burnet was named provisional president. Thinking the war was over, Santa Anna moved eastward with his army. Sam Houston's troops—half the number of the Mexicans—occupied a position at the junction of the San Jacinto River and Buffalo Bayou, opposite Santa Anna's camp. On the afternoon of April 21 the Texans attacked while Santa Anna was having his siesta. Their battle cry was "Remember the Alamo; Remember Goliad." Santa Anna fled but was taken the next day and held prisoner for 6 months. (See Texas Revolution.)

Statehood and the Mexican War. The Texas republic, whose independence had been recognized by the United States, Great Britain, France, Holland, and Belgium, was soon struggling with Indian wars, raids by Mexican forces, and financial problems. In September 1836, Texans voted for annexation by the United States; approval by the U.S. Congress was delayed until 1845, however, because of the northern states' opposition to the extension of slavery. On Dec. 29, 1845, the U.S. Congress accepted the Texas state constitution, and Texas became the 28th state, with legal slavery.

The Mexican War between the United States and Mexico followed, and the first battle took place on the very day of statehood. The U.S. victory in that war established the Rio Grande as the border between Mexico and the United States. Texas, however, claimed all the territory from the mouth of the Rio Grande to its source in southern Colorado, a claim vigorously opposed by those who wished to exclude slavery from the territories newly acquired from Mexico. In 1850, as part of the Compromise of 1850, Texas relinquished its claim to half of what today is New Mexico and portions of Colorado, Wyoming, Oklahoma, and Kansas in exchange for the sum of $10 million.

Texas withdrew from the Union on Feb. 1, 1861. Little fighting took place on Texas soil during the Civil War, the most important engagements being the capture and recapture of Galveston, the principal port. A battle took place at Palmito Ranch near Brownsville, after General Lee had already surrendered at Appomattox.

Military rule following the Civil War was short-lived, but the state was inundated with carpetbaggers. On Mar. 30, 1870, Texas was readmitted to the Union after ratifying the 13th, 14th, and 15th amendments to the U.S. Constitution. Following the Civil War cattle ranching became increasingly important to the economy, and vast herds were driven to the railroad in Kansas over the Chisholm Trail.

Modern Era. When the 20th century began, about 3 million people lived in Texas, and agriculture dominated the economy. Then in 1901, Spindletop, the state's first great oil gusher, was discovered. Soon oil was found in virtually every part of the state, and the great east Texas oil field, discovered in 1930, helped lessen the impact of the Depression.

Racial segregation was a continuing issue throughout most of the 1950s and '60s, but by 1966, Texas ranked first among southern states in integrating its schools. The poll tax was abolished by court action in 1966. Another court decision led to redistricting the Texas legislature to conform to the Supreme Court policy of one person, one vote.

Politically prominent Texans in the 1960s, '70s, and '80s included President Lyndon B. Johnson, Congresswoman Barbara Jordan, and Vice-President George Bush. In 1987 the Texas legislature approved a landmark $5.7 billion tax increase, the largest by any state in U.S. history. Some critics claimed that it did not completely correct Texas's past reliance on oil-industry taxes at a time when the state was becoming more dependent on service industries.　　GEORGE W. HOFFMAN

Bibliography:
GENERAL: Federal Writers' Project, *Texas: A Guide to the Lone Star State*, rev. ed. (1969); Holmes, William, *The Encyclopedia of Texas* (1984); McDonald, Archie P., ed., *The Texas Experience* (1986); Richardson, Rupert N., et al., *Texas: The Lone Star State*, 4th ed. (1981).
LAND AND PEOPLE: Dobie, J. Frank, ed., *Legends of Texas* (1924; repr. 1976); Duke, Cordia Sloan and Frantz, Joe B., *6000 Miles of Fence: Life on the XIT Ranch of Texas* (1981); Jordan, Terry G., *Immigration to Texas* (1981); Nevin, David, *The Texans* (1976).
HISTORY: Buenger, Walter L., ed., *Texas History* (1983); Fehrenbach, T. R., *Lone Star: A History of Texas and the Texans* (1983); Rosenbaum, Robert J., ed., *Readings in Texas History* (1982); Siegel, Stanley E., *A History of Texas to 1865* (1981); Smyrl, Frank H., ed., *Texas History* (1985); Wintz, Cary D., ed., *A History of Texas* (1983).
ECONOMICS, POLITICS, AND GOVERNMENT: Anderson, James E., et al., *Texas Politics: An Introduction*, 4th ed. (1984); Kraemer, Richard H., and Newell, Charldean, *Essentials of Texas Politics*, 3d ed. (1986); Maxwell, Robert S., *Texas Economic Growth, 1890 to World War II* (1982); Pettus, Beryl E., and Bland, Randall W., *Texas Government Today*, 4th ed. (1986); Spratt, John S., *The Road to Spindletop: Economic Change in Texas, 1875–1901* (1983).

Texas, state universities of

All the state universities of Texas are coeducational and most grant both undergraduate and graduate degrees. The **University of Texas** (1881) has seven campuses. A chancellor heads the entire university system. Austin (enrollment: 48,000; library: 5,057,600 volumes), the first and main campus, has schools of arts and sciences, law, architecture, social work, and library science and the Lyndon Baines Johnson School of Public Affairs. Other academic centers are in Arlington (1895; enrollment: 23,400; library: 794,800 volumes), Dallas (1969; enrollment, 7,750; library: 441,600 volumes), El Paso (1913; enrollment: 15,300; library: 644,600 volumes), San Antonio (1969; enrollment: 12,600; library: 364,800 volumes), and Tyler (1971; enrollment: 3,540; library: 169,000 volumes). The campus of the University of Texas of the Permian Basin (1969; enrollment: 2,000; library: 205,300 volumes) is at Odessa. Medical schools are at San Antonio, Dallas, Houston, and Galveston. An observatory at Mount Locke and a marine science institute at Port Aransas are part of the university.

Texas Agricultural and Mechanical University (1876; enrollment: 36,800; library: 2,400,000 volumes), a land-grant and sea-grant school at College Station, offers students the option of a military regulation of their nonacademic life and an opportunity to obtain a commission in the U.S. Army or Air Force. The academic program includes liberal arts and stresses agriculture, technology, and sciences. This emphasis is found also at the other institutions in the Texas A & M system: **Prairie View Agricultural and Mechanical University** (1876; enrollment: 4,400; library: 250,000 volumes), a predominantly black land-grant school at Prairie View; **Tarleton State University** (1899; enrollment: 4,600; library: 210,000 volumes), at Stephenville; **Texas A & M** (1971; enrollment: 600; library: 40,000 volumes) at Galveston, offering degrees in marine science, marine engineering, and marine transportation.

Other state universities are **Angelo State** (1928; enrollment: 6,160; library: 330,500 volumes), at San Angelo; **Corpus Christi State** (1971; enrollment: 3,590; library: 220,780 volumes), at Corpus Christi; the main campus of **East Texas State** (1889; enrollment: 7,100; library: 940,000 volumes), at Commerce; **Lamar** (1923; enrollment: 15,835; library: 791,150 volumes), at Beaumont; **Laredo State** (1969; enrollment: 920; library: 139,800 volumes), at Laredo; **Midwestern State** (1922; enrollment: 4,850; library: 375,000 volumes), at Wichita Falls; **North Texas State** (1890; enrollment: 21,400; library: 1,637,100 volumes), at Denton; **Pan American** (1927; enrollment: 10,000; library: 549,250 volumes), at Edinburg; **Sam Houston State** (1879; enrollment: 10,470; library: 725,800 volumes), at Huntsville; **Southwest Texas State** (1899; enrollment: 19,200; library: 726,100 volumes), at San Marcos; **Stephen F. Austin State** (1923; enrollment: 12,550; library: 433,400 volumes), at Nacogdoches; **Sul Ross State** (1917; enrollment: 2,240; library: 222,870 volumes), at Alpine; **Texas Arts and Industries** (1917; enrollment: 5,500; library: 748,000 volumes), at Kingsville; **Texas Southern** (1947; enrollment: 8,900; library: 573,000 volumes), at Houston; **Texas Tech** (1923; enrollment: 23,400; library: 2,500,000 volumes), at Lubbock; **Texas Woman's** (1901; enrollment: 8,250; library: 718,400 volumes), at Denton; the main campus of the **University of Houston** (1927; enrollment: 32,000; library: 1,300,000 volumes), at Houston; and **West Texas State** (1909; enrollment: 6,475; library: 575,000 volumes), at Canyon.

Texas Rangers

The Texas Rangers originated in the 1820s as a volunteer corps to prevent Indian attacks and later became lawmen; their exploits have become legendary. In 1835, the year before the Republic of Texas was born, the rangers became an official, full-time corps that was paid to defend the frontier. The United States annexed Texas in 1845 and protection of the frontier became a federal responsibility; the rangers then reverted to a volunteer, militia-type organization. Under John Coffee (Jack) Hays, they fought in federal service during the Mexican War, winning national attention for their skill and bravery. Reorganized in 1874, the rangers—with the gradual end of the Indian wars—became a statewide law-enforcement agency responsible for suppressing feuds and riots, controlling cattle thefts, and capturing train robbers. Since 1935 they have operated as a branch of the Texas Department of Public Safety. SEYMOUR V. CONNOR

Bibliography: Durham, George, *Taming the Nueces Strip* (1962); Gillett, James B., *Six Years with the Texas Rangers, 1875 to 1881* (1976); Greer, James K., ed., *Buck Barry, Texas Ranger and Frontiersman* (1984); Webb, Walter P., *Texas Rangers*, rev. ed. (1965).

Texas Revolution

In the Texas Revolution of 1835–36, American colonists in Texas secured the independence of that area from Mexico and subsequently established a republic. Since the 1820s many settlers from the United States had colonized Texas; by the 1830s they far outnumbered the Texas Mexicans. Mexican dictator Antonio López de SANTA ANNA attempted to reverse this trend by such measures as abolishing slavery and enforcing the collection of customs duties. The settlers rebelled

A Mexican army begins its assault of the Alamo, a former Spanish mission in San Antonio that was defended by a force of fewer than 200 Texas volunteers for 13 days in 1836. The numerically superior Mexicans eventually stormed the Alamo, killing the defenders.

(originally as part of a general federalist resistance to Santa Anna's Centralist government, which had overthrown the Mexican Constitution of 1824). Hostilities began at Gonzales on Oct. 2, 1835; the Texans repelled a Mexican force sent to disarm them and won subsequent victories.

In February 1836, Santa Anna, undiscouraged, led a large army across the Rio Grande; he was delayed, however, by the unexpectedly determined defense of the ALAMO. Meanwhile, the Texans declared their independence from Mexico on Mar. 2, 1836, and organized a provisional government. Sam HOUSTON led a successful retreat, but other insurgents were defeated and massacred in late March. Santa Anna pursued the rebels, overstretching his supply line and thus isolating his forces on San Jacinto Prairie. There, on April 21, he was routed by Houston and taken prisoner. Mexican troops then withdrew from Texas. The Republic of Texas (with its Lone Star flag) remained independent until 1845, when it became part of the United States. SEYMOUR V. CONNOR

Bibliography: Connor, Seymour V., *Texas, A History* (1971); Jenkins, J. H., ed., *Papers of the Texas Revolution*, 10 vols. (1973); Santos, R. G., *Santa Anna's Campaign against Texas, 1835–1836* (1982).

textile industry

The word *textile* (from the Latin *texere*, "to weave") originally meant a fabric made from woven fibers. Today the term signifies any of a vast number of fabrics produced by weaving, knitting, felting, and other techniques; it also refers to the enterprises that spin yarn from fiber or from synthetic materials and to the finishers and dyers of fabrics. This article summarizes the development of the industry. Particular aspects are treated in greater depth in articles for which cross-references are provided throughout. In addition, the articles RUGS AND CARPETS and TAPESTRY discuss the development of important textile styles and techniques.

The Use of Natural Fibers. Until the 20th century all of the fibrous raw materials available for textile use were based on animal hair, plant or seed fibers, or the product of the silkworm. These are all organic fibers and are rapidly degraded by weathering or are destroyed by decomposing agents in the soil. Only a few samples of textile products have remained from prehistoric eras. COTTON, FLAX, SILK, and WOOL probably represent the major fibers available to ancient civilizations, although other fibrous materials may also have been used—especially the bast fibers from HEMP, JUTE, and sisal.

The earliest known samples of yarn and fabric of any kind were found near Robenhausen, Switzerland, where excavations unearthed bundles of flax fibers and yarns and fragments of plain-weave linen fabric, estimated to be about 7,000 years old. Woven wool fabrics may have been used as

Two women weave cloth, working from the top of the loom downward, in this detail from a Greek vase painting (c.560 BC). Their warp-weighted hand loom was used to weave wool, cotton, or linen, the most common fabrics used in ancient Greece.

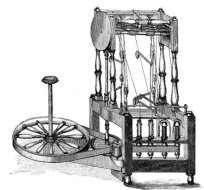

The water-powered spinning machine patented in 1769 by Sir Richard Arkwright made it possible to produce an inexpensive all-cotton cloth for the first time. Arkwright's invention stimulated the development of the great English textile factories of the 18th and 19th centuries.

early as 4000 BC in Mesopotamia, and wool spinning and weaving became cottage industries wherever sheep (or, in the New World, the members of the llama family) were raised.

The cotton plant is indigenous to India, Egypt, and the warmer regions of the Americas; it was in these regions that the fiber was first used to make textiles. Cotton did not achieve commercial importance in Europe until after the colonization of the New World. Silk culture remained a specialty of the Chinese from its beginnings (c.2600 BC) until the 6th century AD, when silkworms were first raised in the Byzantine Empire. (See also FIBER, TEXTILE.)

Synthetic Fibers. The desire to invent a fiber that resembled silk spurred the development of RAYON (1891), the first SYNTHETIC FIBER, and of its successors, NYLON (1939) and the various forms of polyester. Most synthetics are made by forcing a thick solution of polymerized chemicals through "spinneret" nozzles and hardening the resulting filament in a chemical bath (see PLASTICS).

Synthetic fibers have changed the textile industry radically. Their development has reduced world demand for natural fibers, and they have significantly broadened the area in which fibers are used—for example, as reinforcement in automobile tires.

Yarn Production. Silk is the only natural filament fiber, and it usually requires only the twisting together of several filaments to make a yarn. The other natural fibers must first be straightened and laid parallel by combing; then they must be drawn out into a continuous yarn by SPINNING. The spindle is the earliest spinning tool, and the spinning wheel (which first appeared in Europe about 1400) is its earliest mechanization. It was only during the late 18th century, with the invention

(1767) of the spinning jenny, a machine that operated a number of spindles at one time, that yarn could be produced in appreciable volume. Richard Arkwright's spinning frame (1769) and Samuel Crompton's "mule" (1779) increased yarn production to the point at which one worker could operate 1,000 spindles at one time. Modern spinning machines are based on early-19th-century innovations, primarily the ring-spinning frame invented by the American John Sharp in 1828.

Fabric Production. The hand LOOM, in many variations, was for many centuries the basic WEAVING instrument. Mechanical improvements began to be developed in ancient times: the heddle, to which alternate warp threads are tied, was probably the first major innovation; the foot treadle, which could operate one or a series of heddles, followed shortly. Foot-powered looms with several sets of heddles appeared in Europe during the 13th century. Combined with the frame-mounted batten which was used to beat the weft, or filling yarns, into place, such looms were the principal types used in Europe for many years.

The first step in the creation of the modern loom was the invention by John Kay in 1733 of the flying shuttle, which allowed the weaver to send the shuttle across the width of the loom automatically. Edmund Cartwright devised the first steam-powered loom and, with James Watt, built (1785) the first steam-driven textile mill in England. Since that year innumerable improvements have been made in the power loom, beginning with the Jacquard (see JACQUARD, JOSEPH MARIE) punched-card system (1801), which provided the first successfully automated pattern weaving. Most modern looms are essentially high-speed versions of the early power looms, now made of steel instead of wood and operating almost entirely automatically.

Chinese women prepare silk threads for weaving on a loom in this 17th-century woodcut. Sericulture, the raising of silkworms and the production of cloth from the fibers of their cocoons, has traditionally been a vital economic activity throughout the Orient.

Workers operate a spinning mule in a large English factory. The first of these machines was built in 1779 by Samuel Crompton. Because it was capable of simultaneously producing many fine threads, the spinning mule had superseded the slower spinning jenny by the 1830s.

A printer aligns unfinished cloth under a mechanical silk-screen printer. Each screen acts as a stencil, applying a thick paint of a single color to form a portion of the final pattern.

The development of textile printing machines during the first half of the 19th century greatly increased production and reduced costs over the previous method of pattern weaving. Designs were applied as fabric passed between rollers into which patterns have been engraved.

Dyeing, Printing, and Finishing. Techniques of yarn and fabric dyeing have increased in complexity, especially since the 19th-century discovery of coal-tar DYES and the 20th-century development of synthetic fibers. Fabric printing came late to Europe (18th century) and was at first confined principally to BLOCK PRINTING. (The SILK-SCREEN PRINTING process was developed for fabrics only during the mid-1800s.) Roller printing, using engraved copper rolls, was used first in England in 1785, followed in the same year by improvements that allowed roller printing in six colors, all in perfect register. Modern roller printing can produce in 1 minute 183 m (200 yd) of fabric printed in 16 or more colors.

Modern finishing processes go far beyond the early processes, which were largely confined to shearing or brushing the nap of the fabric, to filling, or sizing, the cloth, and to passing it through calendar rolls to produce a glazed effect. Finishing today includes the preshrinking of cotton, wool, and rayon fabrics; mercerizing—treating cotton yarns and fabrics with caustic solutions to improve their strength and luster; and applying a number of different finishes that increase, among other things, crease resistance and water, flame, or mildew repellency. The properties of wash-and-wear fabrics often are obtained through finishing.

The Industry. Until the latter years of the 18th century the production of textiles was a handcraft, practiced in small units by skilled artisans and by cottage spinners and weavers. Large and economically vital cloth industries had emerged in

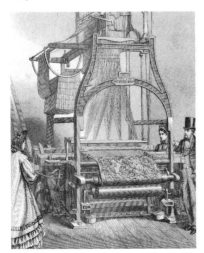

The Jacquard loom, which was developed in France in 1801, was the first machine capable of weaving figured patterns. The loom's weaving pattern was regulated by a chain of punched cards, a control mechanism similar to that used in early computers.

Britain, Belgium, and other European countries. With the exception of the GOBELIN tapestry works in Paris, however, few factories in the contemporary sense existed.

The technical advances achieved during the 1700s, particularly in Britain, were the impetus not only for the establishment of the modern textile industry, but for the FACTORY SYSTEM and the INDUSTRIAL REVOLUTION as a whole.

Cloth had been made by American colonists since the building of a cloth "mill" in Massachusetts in 1638. The era of powered textile manufacturing, however, was inaugurated by an Englishman. Samuel SLATER, a former mill supervisor in England, rebuilt from memory a spinning frame in Providence, R.I., in 1790 and later founded several other mills.

Three years later Eli WHITNEY introduced his cotton gin, and the speed with which it could clean harvested cotton created a new demand for cotton fabrics. Factories sprang up throughout the eastern United States, particularly in New England. The perfection of a practical SEWING MACHINE during the mid-19th century increased the consumption of fabrics, and the American industry reached competitive status with its European counterparts.

After World War II the textile industry underwent significant changes throughout the world. Continuing a trend that had begun years earlier, much of the U.S. industry moved south from New England. New factories for the production of synthetic fiber were built almost exclusively in the southeastern and mid-Atlantic states. The cotton-spinning and weaving mills that had populated factory towns in Massachusetts and New Hampshire during the 19th and early 20th centuries closed one after another as the industry moved closer to energy sources and to lower-cost labor.

At the same time, textile manufacturing expanded overseas. Large textile establishments in China, Taiwan, Japan, and South Korea became competitive with American and European industry. Restrictive quotas and tariffs frequently have been imposed by countries that deem their industries threatened by foreign production. To counter the lower price of foreign textiles, the U.S. industry is becoming almost entirely automated. Computer-controlled technology has reduced labor needs and improved quality, as well as allowing manufacturers to make quick changes in the types of textiles they produce, in response to changing consumer preferences.

Reviewed by FRED FORTRESS

Bibliography: Addy, J., The Textile Revolution (1976); Andrews, M. G., The Men and the Mills: A History of the Southern Textile Industry (1988); Burnham, D. W., Warp and Weft: A Dictionary of Textile Terms (1982); Celikiz, G., and Kuehni, R. G., eds., Color Technology in the Textile Industry (1983); Corbman, B., Textiles: Fiber to Fabric, 6th ed. (1982); Gentille, T., Printed Textiles (1987); Grayson, M., ed., Encyclopedia of Textiles, Fibers, and Non-Woven Fabrics (1984); Grossbart, J., et al., An Introductory Textile Manual (1982); Hollen, N., and Saddler, J., Textiles, 6th ed. (1988); Kulik, G., et al., eds., The New England Mill Village, 1790–1860 (1982); Lyle, D. S., Modern Textiles, 2d ed. (1982); Thomas, M., Textiles: History of an Art (1985); Tortora, P. G., Understanding Textiles, 3d ed. (1987).

Textile Workers Union: see AMALGAMATED CLOTHING AND TEXTILE WORKERS UNION.

Tey, Josephine [tay]

Josephine Tey was the pseudonym used by the Scottish writer Elizabeth Mackintosh, b. 1896, d. Feb. 13, 1952, to sign her eight well-known mystery novels, most of which feature Inspector Alan Grant. Mackintosh also wrote biographies, plays, and a novel, usually signing these works "Gordon Daviot"; but her Josephine Tey detective books provide the foundation for her continuing popularity. Alfred Hitchcock filmed *A Shilling for Candles* (1936) under the title *Young and Innocent* (1937). Other outstanding Tey works include *Miss Pym Disposes* (1946), *Brat Farrar* (1949), *The Daughter of Time* (1951), and *The Singing Sands* (1952).

Tezcatlipoca [tes-kaht-lee-poh′-kah]

Tezcatlipoca was one of the most powerful gods worshiped in Aztec Mexico. He was among the creators of the Universe, ever young and virile, all-powerful and all-knowing. In his mirror of black volcanic glass he could see everything that happened in the world. He could transform himself at will into a jaguar or other animal. He was the god of darkness, the night sky, sorcery, and warfare, and the protector of the schools where young warriors were trained. His rivalry with QUETZALCÓATL and the struggles between these two gods are the subject of many Aztec myths.   WARWICK BRAY

Bibliography: Spence, Lewis, *The Gods of Mexico* (1922).

Thackeray, William Makepeace [thak′-uh-ree]

William Makepeace Thackeray, one of the most prominent British novelists of the Victorian age, is best known as the author of Vanity Fair (1847-48). A successful lecturer, Thackeray published much of his work in contemporary periodicals, receiving acclaim for such satiric, perceptive essays as those collected in Roundabout Papers (1860-63). He is seen here in a portrait by Samuel Laurence. (National Portrait Gallery, London.)

A master of urbane irony, William Makepeace Thackeray, b. July 18, 1811, d. Dec. 24, 1863, explored the moral and social pretensions of the Victorian age in his fiction.

Born in Calcutta, India, Thackeray went to school in England and then traveled widely on the Continent. When he returned to London he began to write satirical magazine pieces. These include *The Yellowplush Correspondence* (1837-38), a view of high society through the eyes of a servant; *A Shabby Genteel Story* (1840); and *The Book of Snobs* (1846-48). *The Luck of Barry Lyndon* (1844), Thackeray's novel of this period, employs the 18th-century picaresque mode to chronicle the downfall of a handsome, socially ambitious rogue.

Thackeray's masterpiece, *Vanity Fair* (1847-48)—a panoramic novel ranging from the drawing rooms of London to the Battle of Waterloo—grew from his early works. Subtitled "a Novel without a Hero," *Vanity Fair* contains no character who exemplifies moral heroism. Instead, in concentrating on the amoral maneuvers of Becky Sharp in her drive for social position, Thackeray portrays an entire society that is, in his words, "living without God in the world," occupied only with the vanities of worldly advancement. This realistic, satiric

novel was followed by *Pendennis* (1848-50), an account of a young man growing up that draws heavily upon the author's own life. Thackeray subsequently turned to the historical novel with *Henry Esmond* (1852), a tale of political and religious intrigue in 18th-century England. Its sequel, *The Virginians* (1857-59), continues the adventures of this family in America. Thackeray's interest in the 18th century also appears in his popular lectures on *The English Humourists of the Eighteenth Century* (1851) and *The Four Georges* (1855-60), both delivered during tours of the United States. Thackeray also possessed artistic talent; he illustrated many of his own works, including *Vanity Fair*. His last major work was *The Newcomes* (1853-55), a rambling, often sentimental family saga. He died before he could finish his last novel, *Denis Duval*.

Although Thackeray's reputation declined in the early 20th century because of his use of such Victorian literary conventions as overt and intrusive authorial commentary, modern critics find his comic mode the sophisticated expression of a darkly moral vision that portrays a secular world in which ethical and social controls have dissolved and self-interest is the primary motive for human behavior.   HERBERT L. SUSSMAN

Bibliography: Ray, Gordon, *Thackeray: The Age of Wisdom, 1847-1863* (1958) and *Thackeray: The Uses of Adversity, 1811-1846* (1955); McMaster, Juliet, *Thackeray: The Major Novels* (1971); Hardy, Barbara, *The Exposure of Luxury: Radical Themes in Thackeray* (1972); Tillotson, Geoffrey, *Thackeray the Novelist* (1954).

Thaddaeus, Saint [thad′-ee-uhs]

Thaddaeus is mentioned in Mark 3:18 and Matt. 10:3 as one of Jesus Christ's original 12 apostles. He is often identified with the Jude, or Judas, son of James, in Luke 6:16. Although this identification helps reconcile the biblical lists of apostles, little is known of this minor figure. Feast day: October 28 (Western); June 19 (Eastern).

See also: JUDE, EPISTLE OF.

Thai [ty]

The Thai, or Siamese, are the dominant ethnic group of Thailand, in Southeast Asia. Their language, which is tonal and largely monosyllabic, has not been affiliated with any other Asian linguistic family. The Thai are descendants of groups that moved southward from China as early as the 8th century. The first Thai kingdom (Sukhothai) was founded in the 13th century. Unlike other Southeast Asian countries, Thailand was never a European colony; in fact, Thai means "free." About 75% of the population of Thailand is ethnic Thai. Most Thai are rural people, although an increasing number live in towns and cities. They are predominantly rice farmers, although they also raise yams, chilies, rubber, coconuts, and cotton. Genealogical descent is traced through both parents. The family is the most important social and economic unit. Social class differences are based on age, occupation, education, and wealth. Most Thai are Buddhists; a tiny minority are Christians. The Thai, however, also traditionally believe in spirits and ghosts that influence their lives in many ways. Thai art forms—music and dance, lacquerware, wood carving, and silverwork—are highly developed.   DONN V. HART

Bibliography: Anuman, Rajadhon, *Life and Ritual in Old Siam*, ed. by William J. Gedney (1961; repr. 1979); De Young, John E., *Village Life in Modern Thailand* (1955); Skinner, G. William, ed., *Change and Persistence in Thai Society* (1975).

Thai language: see SINO-TIBETAN LANGUAGES.

Thailand

The Kingdom of Thailand, located in Southeast Asia on the Gulf of Thailand and the Andaman Sea, shares boundaries with Burma on the west and northwest, Laos on the east and northeast, Kampuchea (Cambodia) on the southeast, and Malaysia on the south. Known also as Siam (before 1939 and from 1945 to 1949), the country was named Thailand, meaning "land of the free," in 1939. Thailand, although rich in rub-

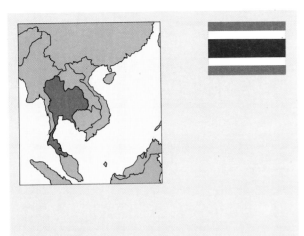

PRATHET THAI

LAND. Area: 514,000 km² (198,456 mi²). Capital and largest city: Bangkok (1984 est. pop., 5,018,327).
PEOPLE. Population (1988 est.): 54,700,000; density: 106 persons per km² (276 per mi²). Distribution (1988): 17% urban, 83% rural. Annual growth (1979–86): 2.1%. Official language: Thai. Major religions: Buddhism, Islam.
EDUCATION AND HEALTH. Literacy (1984): 91% of adult population. Universities (1986): 12. Hospital beds (1984): 80,620. Physicians (1984): 8,058. Life expectancy (1986): women—67.3; men—61.3. Infant mortality (1988): 52 per 1,000 live births.
ECONOMY. GNP (1986): $40.18 billion; $612 per capita. Labor distribution (1987): agriculture and fishing—61%; commerce and services—19%; manufacturing—8%; government and public authorities—5%; construction—2%. Foreign trade (1986): imports—$9.4 billion; exports—$8.7 billion; principal trade partners—Japan, United States, Singapore, Malaysia. Currency: 1 baht = 100 satangs.
GOVERNMENT. Type: constitutional monarchy. Legislature: National Assembly. Political subdivisions: 72 provinces.
COMMUNICATIONS. Railroads (1986): 3,735 km (2,321 mi) total. Roads (1985): 36,325 km (22,515 mi) total. Major ports: 3. Major airfields: 3.

ber and in mineral resources, was never colonized by Europeans and has existed as a unified monarchy since 1350. The capital, BANGKOK, was established in 1782.

LAND AND RESOURCES
Thailand consists of a compact heartland, or mainland, and a long southern peninsular extension of the MALAY PENINSULA. It has a maximum north-south extent of about 1,700 km (1,100 mi) and a maximum east-west extent of about 800 km (500 mi). Forests occupy approximately 30% of the land area and farmland approximately 38%.

Four topographical regions are usually distinguished. Of these, the most important is the central region, which occupies almost one-third of the nation and includes the fertile alluvial lowlands of the Chao Phraya, Thailand's "rice bowl." The central region is the historical core of Thailand, and all but one of the former capitals have been located on the banks of the Chao Phraya or its distributary to the west. Thailand's three other distinct topographical areas are the northern region, a mountainous, forested section that rises to Doi Inthanon (2,595 m/8,514 ft), the nation's highest peak; the northeastern, or Khorat Plateau, region, an area extremely poor in resources with unproductive lateritic soils; and the southern, or peninsular, region on the Malay Peninsula, rich in rubber and tin.

The principal rivers are the MEKONG, which follows much of the border with Laos; the Chao Phraya in the central region; and the Mun, a tributary of the Mekong in northeastern Thailand. The flow of the rivers varies considerably because of the nation's tropical monsoon climate. A distinct dry season occurs from October to February, and a wet season from March to September. Rain is heaviest along the border with Burma, where about 5,590 mm (220 in) falls annually, diminishing to

less than 1,522 mm (60 in) over most of the Chao Phraya basin and the Khorat Plateau. Temperatures range between 24° and 30° C (75° and 86° F) throughout the year.

Thailand's richest natural resource lies in its agricultural potential. The country's fertile central plain regularly produces more rice than the nation requires. Other important crops include maize, cassava, and kenaf. Thailand is one of the world's largest producers of rubber. Extensive rain forests also provide teak and other valuable hardwoods. Thailand has long been one of the world's most important producers of tin. Other minerals include tungsten, lead, fluorite, and lignite. Large deposits of natural gas are being developed offshore in the Gulf of Thailand.

PEOPLE
Today Thailand has a population more than twice the 26,258,000 recorded in 1960; it continues to grow at more than 2% a year. Improvements in health care have reduced the death rate, but the birthrate remains high.

Ethnic Thai make up about 75% of the population; ethnic Chinese, the largest minority, about 14%; and Malays, living mainly on the peninsula, about 4%. Scattered MON communities occur in the central region and KHMER and other "hill people" in the northeast and along the border with Burma. Thai is spoken by approximately 97% of the population and is the official language; Malay, Chinese, Lao, and other languages are spoken by the minorities. English is used in government and commerce. Theravada Buddhism, considered the national religion, is professed by about 95%; Malays, who are predominantly Muslim, form the largest religious minority.

About 30% of the population live in the Chao Phraya basin, but even in the basin's densely settled delta region population densities are generally lower than in other Asian rice-growing nations. More than 82% of the total population live in rural areas. Bangkok is the largest urban area, followed by CHIANG MAI in the northern region.

Education has been compulsory for many years, and all children between the ages of 7 and 14 are now required to attend school. An estimated 82% of the adult population are considered literate. Thai culture has its roots in Hinduism and Buddhism, which reached Thailand from India after the 3d century by way of the Three Pagodas Pass in the Bilauktaung Range west of the central region. Thailand's written literature dates from the 13th century, when the modern system of Thai writing was introduced. The golden age in Thai arts occurred during the 13th and 14th centuries and is reflected at its best in the many temples (wats) surviving from that period.

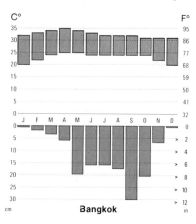

Bars indicate monthly ranges of temperatures (red) and precipitation (blue) in Bangkok, the capital of Thailand. This city, situated on the banks of the Chao Phraya River a short distance north of the Gulf of Thailand, has a tropical wet-dry climate.

ECONOMIC ACTIVITY

National economic planning was introduced into Thailand in 1961. Removal of regional economic disparities, diversification of the economy, industrialization, and general economic development were conceived as the goals of this program.

Agriculture accounts for one-fourth of the gross national product and employs, along with fishing, 63.2% of the labor force. Rice is the principal crop, the basis for all Thai meals, and the leading export. It is grown mainly in the Chao Phraya basin, and irrigation during the dry season allows production of two crops a year.

Rubber, the second most important export, is produced in the southern peninsula. Plantation estates are generally small, and rubber production in Thailand competes at somewhat of a disadvantage with that of Malaysia.

Manufacturing accounts for about one-fifth of the country's gross national product and employs about 10.4% of the labor force. The major industries are rice milling, tapioca clipping, and tin and petroleum refining, as well as the production of jute sacking, cotton textiles, clothing, footwear, refined sugar, cement, and tobacco. In addition, silk articles, jewelry, carved wood items, and cigarettes are produced in many homes, both in cities and villages, and are marketed. Imported petroleum is the primary energy source.

Most traffic moves by water or along the nation's 3,855-km-long (2,395-mi) rail system radiating from Bangkok. Many roads are passable only in the dry season. The chief port is Bangkok, which handles more than 90% of Thailand's foreign trade. The principal exports are rice, rubber, and tin. Petroleum, machinery, and chemicals are the leading imports. The major trading partners are Japan and the United States. In 1981, with a gross national product of $34.2 billion ($711 per capita), Thailand had exports of $6.9 billion and imports of $10.0 billion.

GOVERNMENT

Thailand is a constitutional monarchy, with the king exercising little power. The present monarch is King Bhumibol Adulyadej, who ascended the throne after his brother's death in 1946 and was crowned king in 1950. Constitutionally, power rests with the prime minister, a cabinet, and a bicameral legislature (National Assembly) composed of an appointed senate and elected house of representatives. In practice, however, the military has exerted great influence on civilian affairs, ruling the country intermittently after constitutional government began in 1932. The present constitution, promulgated in 1978 following the 1977 military overthrow of the government of Thanin Kravichien, is Thailand's 12th since 1932.

Bangkok, the capital and principal metropolitan area of Thailand, has an attractive blend of Western and Thai architecture. The city is especially noted for its more than 400 temples, or wats, of which Wat Arun (Temple of Dawn; right) is a famous example.

Marshal Sarit Thanarat. Sarit died in 1963, and his successor, Gen. (later Field Marshal) Thanom Kittikachorn, initiated a brief return to politically fractionalized civilian rule in 1968 but replaced it with martial rule in 1971 as unrest mounted. In 1973 an interim civilian government led by Sanya Dharmasakti was installed. Elections held in 1975 failed to produce a majority, and coalition governments led by Seni Pramoj and Kukrit Pramoj, respectively, both failed to unite the divided nation. Seni was reelected to office in 1976 but later that year was ousted in a military coup led by Admiral Saangad Chaloryoo. Thanin Kraivichien was named prime minister, but he was replaced in 1977 in a bloodless coup that brought Gen. Kriangsak Chomanan to power. Elections in 1979 returned Kriangsak to office as prime minister of an elected government, but he resigned in 1980. Gen. Prem Tinsulanonda, the new prime minister, survived an attempted coup in 1981 and remained prime minister following elections in 1981 and 1986. Invited to remain in office after elections in 1988, Prem unexpectedly refused. He was succeeded by deputy premier Chatichai Choonhaven. ASHOK K. DUTT

Bibliography:
GENERAL: Basche, James, *Thailand* (1971); Bunge, F. M., ed., *Thailand: A Country Study* (1981); Duncan, William, *Thailand* (1976); Keyes, Charles F., *Thailand* (1987).
PEOPLE AND CULTURE: Lewis, Paul and Elaine, *Peoples of the Golden Triangle* (1984); Moore, Frank J., *Thailand: Its People, Its Society, Its Culture* (1974); Sharp, Lauriston, and Hanks, Lucien M., *Bang Chan: Social History of a Rural Community in Thailand* (1978); Skinner, G. William, ed., *Change and Persistence in Thai Society* (1975).
ECONOMICS: Donner, Wolf, *The Five Faces of Thailand* (1978); Foster, Brian, *Commerce and Ethnic Differences* (1982); Ingram, James C., *Economic Change in Thailand, 1850–1970,* rev. ed. (1971); Rozenthal, A. A., *Finance and Development in Thailand* (1970).
POLITICS AND GOVERNMENT: Bates, B. A., *The End of the Absolute Monarchy in Thailand* (1985); Girling, John L., *Thailand* (1985); Neher, Clark D., ed., *Modern Thai Politics* (1976); Riggs, Fred W., *Thailand: The Modernization of a Bureaucratic Polity* (1966); Samudavanija, Chai-Anan: *The Thai Young Turks* (1982).
HISTORY: Landon, K. P., *The Chinese in Thailand* (1941; repr. 1973); Nakahara, J., and Witton, R. A., *Development and Conflict in Thailand* (1971); Syamananda, R., *A History of Thailand* (1971); Terwiel, B. J., *A History of Modern Thailand* (1984); Vella, W. F., *Chaiyo! King Vajiravudh and the Development of Thai Nationalism* (1978); Wales, H., *Dvaravati* (1969); Wyatt D. K., *Thailand* (1985).

A rural Thai home is usually raised on stilts to keep it above the seasonal flood level. This village is near Chiang Mai, in northern Thailand, where the government has settled many of the hill people who once practiced shifting agriculture into permanent communities.

HISTORY

The history of Thailand before settlement by the Thais remains in dispute. Northeastern Thailand may have been the site of the earliest rice cultivation in Asia, and excavations in this region indicate that the metalsmiths of BAN CHIANG were working in bronze by the 2d millennium BC and possibly much earlier. The Funan Empire dominated after the 3d century, and the Mon kingdom of Dvaravati (c.550–1253), with the capital at Nakom Pathom, after c.675. Dvaravati became (11th century) a viceroyalty under the KHMER EMPIRE.

The Thais, who cultivated wet rice and who were attracted by the agricultural potential of the watery Chao Phraya basin, began migrating into the region from south China in the 11th century and established the kingdoms of Sukhothai and Chiang Mai. Sukhothai (1238–1419) overpowered Dvaravati by 1238 and, maintaining friendly relations with Chiang Mai, gained control by absorbing the Khmers. In the 14th century the Thai kingdom of Ayutthaya (1350–1767) subdued Sukhothai and other small kingdoms and became a regional center of wealth and power. Portuguese envoys arrived in 1511—the first Europeans to visit Siam—but, unlike the rest of Southeast Asia, Thailand never became a European colony.

Burmans destroyed the capital at Ayutthaya (AYUTHIA) in 1767, and a new era, the Bangkok Period (1767–1932), began with the establishment of a new capital at Thon Buri, across the Chao Phraya from modern Bangkok. The present royal house is descended from General Chakkri, the second king of this period. In the 19th century King MONGKUT, or Rama IV (r. 1851–68), who ruled as an absolute monarch, began to modernize Thailand. His son CHULALONGKORN, or Rama V (r. 1868–1910), intensified the process by abolishing slavery and introducing railroads, telegraph services, and scientific education. This exposure to Western ideas culminated in a bloodless revolution by the Thai elite in 1932, who demanded a constitutional government limiting the powers of the king.

The revolution also began the struggle between military and civilian groups for control of the government, a continuing feature of Thai political life today. A civilian government under Seni Pramoj led the nation between 1945 and 1946 after the end of Japanese control in World War II. In 1947 a bloodless military coup brought Field Marshal Phibul Songgram to power, and a similar coup in 1957 replaced him with Field

When monsoon rains flood the rice fields, farmers travel by boat. Rice remains the leading crop and chief export of Thailand, although other cash crops such as cassava, corn, sugarcane, and kenaf have become increasingly important to the economy.

Thailand, Gulf of

The Gulf of Thailand (formerly the Gulf of Siam) is a shallow arm of the South China Sea with an area of about 238,000 km² (92,000 mi²). The gulf is bordered by Thailand on the west and north and Kampuchea and Vietnam on the east. The gulf is an important fishing ground and has many islands. Thailand's major port, Bangkok, is on the Chao Phraya River, about 50 km (30 mi) north of its mouth on the gulf.

Thales of Miletus   [thay'-leez, my-lee'-tuhs]

Thales of Miletus, c.636–c.546 BC, was the first known Greek philosopher and scientist. Because none of his writing survives, it is difficult to separate fact from legend in the accounts of his views. He achieved renown as a military advisor and engineer and was evidently a shrewd man of affairs. Stories of his travels to Egypt and Babylon rest on dubious inferences. He is said to have predicted an eclipse of the Sun in 585 BC. Although he probably knew some practical techniques of angle measurement, stories that he proved geometrical theorems have no basis.

Thales apparently held that the Earth floats on water; all things come to be from water; and all things somehow consist of water. He manifests the tendencies, characteristic of early Greek philosophy, to treat questions of material composition and questions of material origin as the same question and to seek the explanation of natural events by pointing to an underlying material element. Explanations for his choice of water as that element point to its evident importance in the growth and nutrition of living things and its central role in daily life. Thales is traditionally considered the teacher of ANAXIMANDER and the first figure in the MILESIAN SCHOOL of PRE-SOCRATIC PHILOSOPHY.   MARTHA C. NUSSBAUM

Bibliography: Guthrie, W. K. C., *The Earlier Presocratics and the Pythagoreans*, vol. 1 in *A History of Greek Philosophy* (1962); Hussey, Edward, *The Presocratics* (1972); Kirk, G. S., and Raven, J. E., *The Presocratic Philosophers* (1957).

thalidomide   [thuh-lid'-uh-myd]

In 1961 the drug thalidomide, widely used to treat nausea and vomiting during pregnancy, was found to be associated with a syndrome of congenital malformations, particularly a severe handicapping abnormality of the arms. About 10,000 such children were born worldwide, with 5,000 in Germany alone. (Doubts concerning the drug's safety had prevented its sale in the United States.) The tragedy led to stringent governmental regulations for testing new drugs for teratogenic (malformation-inducing) hazards.   HAROLD KALTER

Bibliography: Mellin, G. W., and Katzenstein, M., "The Saga of Thalidomide," *The New England Journal of Medicine* 267 (1962); McBride, W. G., "Thalidomide Embryopathy," *Teratology* 16 (1977); Swinyard, C. A., ed., *Limb Development and Deformity* (1969).

thallium   [thal'-ee-uhm]

Thallium is a heavy metal with a physical resemblance to lead and a chemical resemblance to potassium. It is a member of group IIIA. Its chemical symbol is Tl, atomic number 81, and atomic weight 204.37. Sir William Crookes of Great Britain first detected it spectroscopically in 1861 from the bright green color it imparts to flames. (The name derives somewhat obscurely from the Greek root *thallos*, meaning green or young twig.) The metal was isolated the following year by Crookes and independently by the French chemist Claude-Auguste Lamy. Thallium is more abundant in the Earth's crust than mercury but is more widely dispersed. It is found principally in potash minerals and in zinc and lead sulfide ores.

Thallium is a soft, gray white metal (m.p. 303° C, b.p. 1453° C, density 11.8 g/cm³). It forms compounds in two oxidation states, the more stable thallous (+1), which resembles potassium, and the strongly oxidizing thallic (+3), which behaves as aluminum. The metal dissolves in warm dilute mineral acids, forming thallous salts and liberating hydrogen gas. Because of their extreme toxicity, thallium compounds are restricted to unique applications: specialized photocells, certain optical glasses, and low-freezing liquid mercury-thallium alloys for stratospheric and arctic thermometers. At one time thallous sulfate was widely used as a rat and insect poison, but this use has largely been abandoned.   PHILIP C. KELLER

Bibliography: Korenman, I. M., *Analytical Chemistry of Thallium* (1972); Lee, A. G., *Chemistry of Thallium* (1971); Smith, Ivan C., and Carson, Bonnie L., *Thallium* (1977).

Thames, River   [temz]

The Thames is a river in southern England, rising in the Cotswold Hills of Gloucestershire and flowing east, through London, to its estuary on the North Sea. The river is 248 km (154 mi) long from its source at Thameshead to London Bridge, from which it flows an additional 90 km (56 mi) to the open sea. The Goring Gap near Reading divides the upper river basin from the lower. The upper basin, centered on Oxford, is composed of limestone. Below the Goring Gap is the London Basin, ringed by chalk hills but floored with gravel and clay. London lies at the lowest bridging point on the river. The Thames, England's principal river, has many tributaries: the Churn, Coln, Windrush, Evenlode, Cherwell, Ock, Thame, Kennet, Loddon, Colne, Wey, Mole, and finally the Medway, which flows into the Thames estuary.

The river's flow varies with the seasons and is greatest in winter, when the land along its banks is subject to flooding. The tide ascends to Teddington Lock, about 30 km (20 mi) upstream from London Bridge. Due to the danger of inundation by sea surges along the lower river, a 0.52-km-wide (0.32-mi) movable flood barrier was constructed at Woolwich. It became operational in 1982 and was dedicated in 1984. The freshwater Thames serves as the chief water supply for London, its western suburbs, and areas around Oxford. The heavy traffic of seagoing ships docks below London Bridge, while passenger steamers, pleasure boats, and barges navigate above London. Rowing regattas, such as the internationally famous Henley Regatta, are also held on the Thames.   NORMAN J. G. POUNDS

Thanatos   [than'-uh-tahs]

In Greek mythology, Thanatos was the god of death. He dwelt with his brother Sleep in the underworld and is portrayed as winged, bearded, and holding a sword. He was said to be the only god who shunned sacrificial offerings.

Thanksgiving Day

Thanksgiving is an annual holiday celebrated in the United States on the fourth Thursday in November. The first Thanksgiving, three days of prayer and feasting, was celebrated by the Plymouth colonists in 1621 to give thanks for their first harvest and for surviving the first terrible Massachusetts winter. The first national Thanksgiving Day, proclaimed by President George Washington, was celebrated on Nov. 26, 1789. In 1863, President Abraham Lincoln made Thanksgiving an annual holiday to be commemorated on the last Thursday in November. For 3 years (1939–41) under President Franklin D. Roosevelt, the day was celebrated on the third Thursday in November, primarily to extend the Christmas shopping season, which traditionally began after Thanksgiving. The holiday was returned to the fourth November Thursday by Congress in 1941.

In Canada, Thanksgiving, first observed in November 1879, is officially celebrated on the second Monday in October.

Thant, U   [thahnt, oo]

The Burmese educator-diplomat U Thant, b. Jan. 22, 1909, d. Nov. 25, 1974, was the first Asian secretary general of the United Nations. Born in Pantanaw during British rule of Burma, Thant was educated at the University of Rangoon and became headmaster of the politically oriented National High School in his native township. Thant served (1953–57) as secretary to U Nu, a fellow Pantanaw educator who became (1948) the first premier of independent Burma. A devout Buddhist and fervent anticommunist, Thant is generally credited with having influenced U Nu to recognize the People's Republic of China in 1949; Burma was the first noncommunist country to do so.

In 1957, Thant was named Burma's permanent representative to the United Nations (UN). Four years later, when Dag Hammarskjöld was killed in a plane crash, Thant became acting UN secretary general. Elected to the position in 1962, he continued in office until his retirement in 1971. Thant was involved in the settlement of many international crises, including the Cuban Missile Crisis (1962), the Congo Crisis (1963), the civil war in Cyprus (1964), and the India-Pakistan War (1965).   RICHARD BUTWELL

Bibliography: Abreu, Terence, *Under the Third Roof* (1987); Bingham, June, *U Thant: The Search for Peace* (1966); Thant, U, *View from the U.N.* (1978).

Thar Desert   [tahr]

The Thar, or Great Indian, Desert is located in northwestern India and southeastern Pakistan. The desert has an approximate area of 250,000 km² (97,000 mi²). It is bordered on the west by the Indus River, on the east by the Aravalli Range, on the north by the Punjab plain and the Sutlej River, and on the south by the Rann of Kutch. The desert's aridity is caused by the dry prevailing monsoon winds. The annual rainfall varies between 100 mm (4 in) in the west and 500 mm (20 in) in the east. Much of the Thar consists of shifting dunes as high as about 150 m (500 ft) and exposed resistant sandstone. Wheat and cotton are grown on the irrigated Indus plain in the northeast, but most areas support only grass, scrub, jujube, and acacia. The great bustard, black buck, francolin (a genus of partridge), and quail are indigenous to the Thar. Nomads raise sheep, cattle, and camels. Coal, gypsum, and limestone are mined, and salt is taken from saline lakes. Irrigation has made some population of the desert possible since the 1930s.

Tharp, Twyla   [thahrp, twy'-luh]

Twyla Tharp, b. Portland, Ind., July 1, 1941, is a provocative and controversial choreographer who, since the early 1970s, has developed a uniquely original movement style based on ballet, tap, black-jazz, and social dance forms. Her style is at once both casual and rigorous, pop and high art. Tharp danced (1963–65) with the Paul Taylor Dance Company before forming her own group. Her *Deuce Coupe*, created for the Joffrey Ballet in 1973, brought her nationwide attention. For American Ballet Theatre (ABT), she choreographed both *Push Comes to Shove* (1976), the first American work created for Mikhail BARYSHNIKOV, and *Bach Partita* (1983), her first full-scale classical ballet. Tharp joined ABT as a resident choreographer in 1988, bringing along six dancers from her former troupe. She also has choreographed several films, most notably *Amadeus* (1984), and in 1985 she choreographed and directed the Broadway version of *Singin' in the Rain*.

ROBERT J. PIERCE

Thatcher, Margaret   [thach'-ur]

Margaret Hilda Thatcher, b. Oct. 13, 1925, Britain's first woman prime minister and the longest-serving British prime minister of the 20th century, has reshaped the image of her country's Conservative party. Born Margaret Roberts in Grantham, Lincolnshire, where her father was mayor, she studied chemistry at Oxford and worked as a research chemist before marrying Denis Thatcher, a businessman, in 1951. A Conservative party activist since her school days, she was elected to the House of Commons in 1959 and entered Edward Heath's shadow cabinet in 1967. Thatcher served under Heath as secretary of state for education and science from 1970 to 1974; then challenged him for the party leadership in 1975 and won, becoming the first woman to lead a major British party.

Vigorously attacking the Labour government of James Callaghan and profiting from public dissatisfaction with labor unrest, she led the Conservatives to a 44-seat majority in the general election of May 1979 and formed her first government. She won a second electoral victory with a majority of 144 in 1983, and a third with a 101-seat majority in 1987. Al-

Margaret Thatcher waves to reporters while campaigning prior to Britain's 1979 general elections. Speaking out against Britain's "slither and slide toward the socialist state," Thatcher led her Conservative party to a decisive victory. Her government was reelected, winning a substantial majority in Parliament, in the elections of 1983 and 1987, making her the first British premier to win three successive elections in more than 150 years.

though her parliamentary majorities in 1983 and 1987 were of landslide proportions, the percentage of the popular vote— 42% in 1983 and 43% in 1987—was actually lower than the 44% the Tories won in 1979. Thatcher's party benefited from the fact that its opposition was divided three ways (among Labour, Liberals, and Social Democrats) and from divisions within the Labour party.

Proud of her middle-class, NONCONFORMIST, small-town background, Thatcher extolls the virtues of freedom, hard work, thrift, and personal responsibility, and has a strong dislike for socialism. As prime minister she has rejected the welfare-state policies followed for decades by both Labourites and Conservatives, promoting a free-enterprise economy, tight monetary policies to control inflation, lower taxes, reduced government spending, PRIVATIZATION of nationalized industries and public housing, and restrictions on trade unions. Firmly committed to the Western alliance, she has strengthened British defenses and successfully pursued (1982) a war with Argentina over the FALKLAND ISLANDS. She accepts British membership in the European Economic Community (EEC) but has resisted EEC measures that she regards as infringements on Britain's sovereignty.

Thatcher's policies have contributed to reducing inflation, reversing the decline of British productivity, and increasing the percentage of British homeowners; they have not reduced unemployment, however, and have contributed to a growing disparity between the prosperous south and an economically deprived north, Wales, and Scotland.   JOHN J. GORDON, JR.

Bibliography: Harris, Kenneth, *Thatcher* (1988); Kavanaugh, Dennis, *Thatcherism and British Politics* (1987).

Thayer, Abbott   [thay'-ur]

The American neo-Renaissance artist Abbott Handerson Thayer, b. Boston, Aug. 12, 1849, d. May 29, 1921, began his career as an animal painter. After studying the human figure with J. L. Gérôme in Paris, he returned to America to paint portraits and idealized studies of women in religious and allegorical works. *Florence Protecting the Arts* (1894; Bowdoin College Museum, Brunswick, Maine) is a well-known Thayer mural. Thayer's natural history research contributed to the development of military camouflage.   JOAN C. SIEGFRIED

Bibliography: White, Nelson, *Abbott H. Thayer* (1951; repr. 1969).

theater, history of the

Theater (from the Greek verb *theasthai*, "to view" or "to see," whence *theatron*, or "seeing place") may be defined not only as a structure in which dramatic performances are given, but as the sum of all the arts required for the production of a dramatic, or imitative, action. These include ACTING, theater COSTUME AND MAKEUP, DIRECTING, STAGE LIGHTING, theater architecture (see THEATER ARCHITECTURE AND STAGING), machin-

A 1st-century AD relief from a private house in Pompeii depicts masked actors performing in a comedy. The theatrical traditions of ancient Greece, widely adopted by the Romans, included the wearing of masks to identify the actors and, possibly, to amplify the voice. (Museo Nazionale, Naples.)

ery and special effects, and dramaturgy or playwriting (see DRAMA). Theater is an eclectic art form that often employs music and dance in its productions as well as the talents of leading artists from outside the theater. Other mimetic performing arts, such as OPERA and BALLET, are closely related to the theater, the principal distinctions being that opera consists of song and musical dialogue throughout, whereas ballet is an art of rhythmic movement precisely timed to music. With these reservations, the following essay focuses on the evolution of the theater in different periods and cultures.

Origins of the Theater. The theater originated in the cultures of primitive societies, whose members, it is thought, used imitative dances to propitiate the supernatural powers that were believed to control events crucial to their survival. A shaman, priest, or medicine man (in effect, the first director) taught complicated dance steps and led these ritual dance-dramas—to persuade or compel supernatural forces to regulate the seasons and elements, to ensure the Earth's fertility, and to grant the tribe success in hunting and warfare. Other ritual dances were believed to expel evil spirits that caused disease and to force the souls of the newly dead to depart the world of the living. The priests and performers in these dance-dramas wore MASKS, which sometimes represented the spirits invoked, and costumes made of skins, rushes, and bark. As knowledge of natural phenomena increased, drama ceased to be exclusively ritualistic and also became an educational tool, especially in initiation ceremonies that acquainted the young with tribal culture. A later development, more germane to the evolution of the theater and drama of today, was the enactment of legends of gods and tribal heroes. Such dramas were also performed in early civilized societies. In Egypt, for example, dramas dealing with the god Osiris continued to be produced until at least as late as the 5th century BC.

Classical Greek and Roman Theater. The history of European theater begins with the Greeks, whose annual festivals in honor of the god Dionysus included competitions in TRAGEDY and COMEDY. According to tradition, the first of these dramatic forms evolved from choral songs (choric dithyrambs) concerning the death and resurrection of Dionysus. This occurred about the middle of the 6th century BC, when THESPIS of Icaria, in a drama of his own composition, impersonated a character and engaged the chorus in dialogue, thereby becoming both the first playwright and the first actor. Thespis won first prize in the initial tragedy competition held at Athens in 534 BC and is also credited with the introduction of masks, which were thereafter a conventional feature of Greek and Roman theater. The tragedians AESCHYLUS and SOPHOCLES later added a second and a third actor to tragedy, and about the beginning of the 5th century BC comedy was given written form by Epicharmus

of Syracuse and was also admitted to the festivals. The ancient chorus was retained as an integral part of Greek drama and eventually consisted of a standard number of members: 15 in tragedy and 24 in comedy. In a SATYR PLAY, a short burlesque that dramatists were expected to submit along with their tragedies, the chorus comprised either 12 or 15 members. All of the roles were played by men; women were not allowed to perform in the Greek theater.

The early Greek playwrights not only wrote and frequently acted in their plays but also served as directors and choreographers; some may also have composed their own music (Greek tragedy was intensely musical). Sophocles is said to have been a scene designer and Aeschylus to have invented the tragic costume. Tragic actors wore a tight-sleeved, belted, patterned tunic called a chiton; a variety of cloaks over the chiton; the cothurnus, or tragedian's boot, which in later periods became exaggeratedly elevated by the addition of a wooden platform to the sole; and the helmetlike mask with attached wig, in which the forehead elevation was proportional to the social status of the character represented. Characters in Old Comedy were usually costumed in short chitons heavily padded in front and behind and wore grotesque masks and stuffed phalluses. With the arrival of New Comedy in the later 4th century BC these features were discarded and comic characters became more respectably dressed.

The original Greek theater at Athens was simply a large circle known as the orchēstra ("dancing place"). Here the choric dithyrambs and early plays of Thespis and Aeschylus were staged, while spectators sat on seats set into the southern slope of the Acropolis. The only scenery consisted of a few set pieces such as tombs and rocks, and it was not until about 460 BC that a skené, or stage building, originally of wood, was added at the rear of the orchestra. The actors then made their entrances and exits through this structure, although the chorus continued to enter from the sides and the acting was still confined to the flat orchestra. A limited amount of scenery, painted on panels attached to the skené, may have been used at this time, and several special effects and machines were available. The last included the eccyclema, or "wheeling out" machine, a wagon or perhaps a turntable on which bloody tableaux were displayed after a murder had occurred in the palace, represented by the skené, and a crane by which actors representing gods could be flown above the stage. The playwright EURIPIDES was fond of both these devices, and his contemporary ARISTOPHANES ridiculed his use of them in several of his comedies.

By the 4th century BC the playwright no longer controlled all aspects of production. The Greek theater had become a professional institution with specialists responsible for the var-

The Roman theater in Orange, France, is typical of the theaters built during the Imperial era. Many of its features would later be copied by Italian Renaissance architects, especially the low raised stage and the scaenae frons, the grandiose, permanent architectural facade.

A 1547 miniature of the Valenciennes passion play shows the small sets, or mansions, in front of which scenes from the life of Christ were acted out. The mansions include Paradise, the Temple, Jerusalem, and the fire-breathing Mouth of Hell. (Bibliothèque Nationale, Paris.)

ious aspects of theatrical art. In the next two centuries, during the Hellenistic Age, the physical structure of the theater continued to evolve, the most notable innovation being the addition of a raised stage (*logeion* or "speaking place") to the building, where most of the acting took place. The Romans, whose capital did not possess a permanent theater until 55 BC, also staged their productions on a raised stage before an elaborately decorated stage building and reduced the orchestra, as well as the auditorium, to a semicircle. Unlike the Greeks, however, they rarely set their theaters into hillsides but built freestanding structures that could be covered by huge awnings and are reputed to have seated as many as 40,000 spectators. Within these magnificent buildings both tragedy and comedy—almost entirely derived from Greek models—were performed, as well as a Roman innovation, pantomime (see MIME AND PANTOMIME), in which a single actor, frequently changing masks and accompanied by a large chorus and orchestra, mimed and danced all the roles in the drama.

Although early Roman actors were often slaves owned by managers who offered their performers and plays to the magistrates in charge of the *ludi*, or games, at which drama was presented, later actors like Claudius Aesopus, Roscius, and the pantomimists Pylades and Bathyllus—all of whom flourished in the 1st century BC—were citizens and attained considerable fame and fortune. Far more opportunities existed for dramatic performances in Rome and its territories than in Greece; therefore, Roman actors were able to work a good part of the year.

Medieval Theater. Unfortunately, later Roman actors did not find favor with the early Christians, who denounced the theater as the "shrine of Venus" (an allusion to the prostitutes who frequented the Roman theater, as well as to its pagan origins) and objected to its parodies of Christian sacraments. Consequently, a barrage of church decrees was directed against the theater and anyone patronizing it, and by the end of the 7th century theatrical entertainments had been extinguished in both the western and eastern Roman Empire. Yet, paradoxically, the church was also responsible for the rebirth of the theater during the Middle Ages, when dramatic performances based on the story of the Resurrection were introduced into the Easter service (see MEDIEVAL DRAMA). From these little tropes, originally performed by monks and priests, arose the great cycles of mystery plays that dramatized virtually every phase of biblical history. Produced by the various guilds and lay religious brotherhoods, and sometimes by entire communities, these vast cycles occasionally took as many as 25 or even 40 days to perform. They were given outdoors—in town squares, Roman amphitheaters, and sometimes on wagon stages that moved through city streets—and typically made use of a neutral playing area, the *platea*, on which all of the set pieces and scenic buildings, called "mansions," were arranged in advance. The acting, primarily by amateurs, was realistic, as were the theatrical tricks that included such spectacular effects as flames and smoke belching from Hellmouth,

floods of water, massacres with flowing blood, and hangings and crucifixions that often posed serious hazards for the actors. The directors were also usually amateurs, although a few were professionals who traveled from city to city.

The Renaissance. By the mid-16th century the medieval religious theater was in decline, to be shortly succeeded by a revival of secular drama performed by professional acting companies. In England such troupes had been attached to the households of noblemen and the king since the 15th century. At first they performed in halls and inns but eventually in theaters of their own, the first of which—named "The Theatre"—was erected on the outskirts of London in 1576. Other ELIZABETHAN PLAYHOUSES, including the Curtain, the Rose, and the famous GLOBE THEATER, followed soon after. In general these theaters were circular or polygonal structures, consisting of a three-story "frame" surrounding an open-air yard. Spectators sat in boxes or galleries within the frame or stood below in the yard, a large portion of which was occupied by a platform stage that was partially protected by a "shadow" or roof. At the rear of the stage was the "tiring house," where the actors dressed and stored their properties. There were two or more entrances to the stage from this building, which also possessed a gallery or upper acting area and, perhaps, an alcove or inner stage, on a level with the platform stage, that could be closed off by a curtain. At the top of the tiring house was the hut, from which a limited amount of machinery was operated. The staging practices in these playhouses were indebted to the medieval theater, with set pieces and mansions continuing in use. The actors' costumes, mainly contemporary and only rarely attempting historical accuracy, were often sumptuous and represented an investment second only to the expense of the playhouse.

Elizabethan actors—all of whom were male—were organized under the guild system of masters, journeymen, and apprentices. These troupes were known by the titles of the noblemen or members of the royal family who were their patrons. Thus William SHAKESPEARE and the actor Richard BURBAGE, the original interpreter of Hamlet, Othello, and Richard III, were both members of the Lord CHAMBERLAIN's MEN, who in 1603 came under the patronage of the king and thereafter were known as the King's Men; while their contemporary Edward ALLEYN, who performed the leading roles in the plays of Christopher MARLOWE, was a member of the rival Lord ADMIRAL's MEN, later Prince Henry's Men. Those master actors who pooled their resources to erect the theaters and purchase the costumes and properties required by their companies were also known as "sharers." This was the system adopted by the Lord Chamberlain's Men, in which Shakespeare was both a master actor and sharer, although other companies sometimes played in theaters owned by nonactors, like the enterprising Philip Henslowe, the father-in-law of Alleyn, who built and managed no less than three theaters. The sharers or managers also bought plays outright from dramatists, who were not entitled to royalties or any additional payments if their works

A contemporary copy of Johann de Witt's sketch (c.1596) of the Swan Theatre shows a typical Elizabethan playhouse. The yard, or pit, surrounded the stage, and it was here that most of the audience stood. To the rear of the stage was the tiring house, surmounted by the hut, from which special effects were produced.

were published. Besides performing in the large public playhouses, Elizabethan actors frequently took their productions to court and, during the winter months, appeared in smaller indoor houses known as ''private'' theaters.

In Spain, where professional actors, led by such legendary figures as Lope de RUEDA, also came into their own in the 16th century, the public theaters were owned by religious brotherhoods and municipal governments. Set up in *corrales,* or large yards between houses, such theaters were similar to those in England. Again there was a platform stage, behind which was a two-story building with both upper and inner acting areas. Spectators, however, occupied rooms (*aposentos,* or ''boxes'') in the adjacent houses in addition to sitting on benches or in boxes or standing in the yard. These theaters, originally open to the weather, remained in use until the mid-18th century.

In Spain, as in England, all roles were portrayed by males, a convention that persisted until 1587. The actors were under contract to managers, known as *autores de comedias,* who purchased costumes and plays and hired out their troupes to the lessees of the *corrales.* The companies were also engaged to perform at annual religious festivals and, especially during the 17th century, at the Spanish court, where productions were heavily influenced by Italian staging practices. During this period, too, Spanish drama experienced its golden age, with such prolific playwrights as Lope de VEGA and Pedro CALDERÓN DE LA BARCA writing hundreds of secular and religious plays.

It was in Renaissance Italy, however, that the theater first broke definitively with the medieval tradition. Inspired by descriptions of the ancient Roman theater in the writings of VI-

The Royal Theater in Turin, designed by architect Benedetto Alfieri, was built in 1738. The theater was renowned for its acoustics and for its commodious orchestra pit (which is nevertheless not large enough to hold all the musicians in this portrait). Like most European theaters of the time, it presented operas as often as dramas. (Museo Civico, Turin.)

TRUVIUS and other Latin authors, the Italian humanists (see HUMANISM) deliberately set out to re-create its structure, an endeavor that culminated in the TEATRO OLIMPICO at Vicenza, designed by the architect Andrea PALLADIO and opened in 1585.

From their reading, the humanists also learned that the Greeks and Romans had occasionally used illusionistic paintings on their stages and had devised three-sided revolving prisms (*periaktoi*) to change such scenery—descriptions which led, as early as 1508, to the use of unified, perspective settings and, shortly afterward, to experiments with *periaktoi* and other methods of changing scenery before the eyes of the audience. A proscenium frame and front curtain then came into use, as did a variety of flying machines and special effects. Because the majority of Renaissance theaters were indoor structures, lighting—supplied by candles and oil lamps—also became an important consideration.

The actors in the early Italian theater were usually amateurs. By the mid-16th century, however, they had been supplanted to a great extent by the professional players of the COMMEDIA DELL'ARTE who, in addition to the improvised comedies for which they were famous, were equally at home in literary and musical drama. In improvised comedy, the actors appeared as stock characters—Pantalone, Arlecchino, Pulcinella, the Dottore—in standardized costumes and wearing masks, although actors impersonating female servants such as Columbine and the characters of young lovers usually dispensed with the last convention. A notable feature of these companies is that from their inception some seem to have included women. The beautiful Isabella Andreini (1562–1604), who belonged to the troupe known as the Gelosi, was the most celebrated actress of her day and was also a gifted dramatist and poet.

Because the *commedia* players traveled widely and were extremely popular outside Italy, they exerted considerable influence on the theaters of other nations. Their appearance in 16th-century Spain, for example, led to the admission of women to the Spanish companies, and in Paris, where they were known as La COMÉDIE ITALIENNE, they were even given a theater of their own.

Baroque and 18th-Century Theater. By the early 17th century the Italian theater had given rise to the architectural structure and staging conventions that, with minor variations, have remained in use to the present day. The auditorium itself, as evidenced in opera houses built at Venice and elsewhere, had evolved into a bench-filled ''orchestra,'' or parterre area, before the stage and a series of galleries divided into boxes at the sides and rear of the house. The stage, separated from the auditorium by the familiar proscenium, or ''picture frame,'' was decorated with perspective settings painted on flats, which could easily be changed either by hand or, through a later invention of the designer Giacomo Torelli (1608–78), by an ingenious mechanical system of chariots, ropes, and counterweights. Similar architectural structures and scenic practices were soon adopted throughout Europe, although a few countries, such as England and France, retained vestiges of their earlier platform stages in the shape of ''aprons,'' or forestages, in front of the proscenium.

A peculiarity of the early English and American theaters was the presence of two or more doors opening onto the apron. The actors often made their entrances and exits through these—a convention that persisted, as did the apron, until well into the 19th century. It was also customary for more ostentatious spectators to sit on these forestages, often to the annoyance of both the actors, who had to move among them, and the other spectators.

The admission of women to both French and English acting companies began during the 17th century. In England, following the accession of Charles II in 1660, the earlier convention of using boy apprentices for female roles was abandoned, and such actresses as Elizabeth Barry and Anne Bracegirdle appeared in the plays of Thomas Otway and William Congreve. In France the former acrobat Thérèse du Parc, after starting with MOLIÈRE's troupe, became a leading tragedienne in the plays of Jean RACINE and was followed by the actress known as La Champmeslé, who in 1677 created the title role in Ra-

Two figures from the commedia dell'arte cavort in a painted copy of an etching by the engraver Jacques Callot. His commedia sketches (1621) convey perfectly the zany, bawdy, dance-and-mime character of this early theatrical genre. (Museo Teatrale, Milan.)

cine's *Phèdre* and later became the first leading tragedienne at La Comédie Française. These actresses were complemented by such male actors as Thomas Betterton, famed for his naturalness in both tragedy and comedy, and Michel Baron, who was personally trained by Molière. In addition to salaries or, in some cases, shares in the companies' profits, actors were granted "benefits"—performances from which they were entitled to the profits after the house expenses had been deducted. English playwrights also received benefits after their plays had run a certain number of nights and, like their French colleagues, retained the right to publish their works. As yet there was no professional director, the duties of this office usually falling to one of the principal actors and sometimes to the dramatist. Molière, who was an actor as well as a playwright, directed the members of his company, and Racine coached the actors in his plays.

By the early 18th century a few individuals, like the English playwright Aaron Hill, were urging reform in costume and scenic practices. David GARRICK, possibly the finest actor of the century, attempted historically accurate productions while managing the DRURY LANE THEATRE in London from 1747 to 1776. The playwright and actor Charles Macklin, whose career spanned most of the century, experimented with realistic costumes in his roles of Shylock and Macbeth. In France, actors such as Hippolyte Clairon and the director of the Opéra Comique, Charles Simon Favart, initiated similar reforms at their theaters. In general, however, there was no consistent attention paid to such details, settings were mainly of stock types used repeatedly in different plays, and it was not until the 19th century that it became customary to create historically accurate costumes and settings for individual productions.

Meanwhile, the American colonial theater—supplied with English actors, English plays, and following English stage practices—had taken its first tentative steps, and in Germany, where English and French influences had dominated during the 16th and 17th centuries, native actors and playwrights had at last come into their own. Spurred on by such figures as Konrad Ekhof (1720–78), known as the father of German acting, and Gotthold Ephraim LESSING, the first German playwright of distinction, both court and municipal theaters experienced a period of unprecedented growth and support by the aristocracy and the emerging middle class. There shortly followed such versatile artists as the actor Friedrich L. Schröder (1744–1816), who directed the Hamburg National Theater during the last third of the century—where he encouraged the young German playwrights who formed the revolutionary STURM UND DRANG school of drama and was famous for his productions of Shakespeare—and the actor, playwright, and director August Wilhelm Iffland (1759–1814), who worked at Mannheim and Berlin. At the court theater of Weimar, under

the artistic management of Johann Wolfgang von GOETHE during the period 1791–1817, a distinctive style of ensemble acting and unified production known as Weimar Classicism evolved. The actors (and sometimes even the audiences) were carefully disciplined by the autocratic director; costumes and settings were based on historical research; and the plays of Goethe and of his friend Johann Friedrich von SCHILLER were splendidly produced. The 18th century was also the last great age of aristocratic theater, particularly in France and the Germanic countries where ballet and opera were supported on a lavish scale. At the court theaters of Vienna, Dresden, Berlin, Saint Petersburg, and Bologna, the beautiful settings of the Bibienas (see GALLI DA BIBIENA family) and their followers often enhanced such productions.

Oriental Theater. Although it exerted relatively little influence on Western theater, the theater of the Orient has an equally long and illustrious history. Its origins also appear to have been in ritualistic dance-dramas, and to this day dance and music play an important role in the Oriental theater. In the West the theater has most often followed a realistic style of presentation, but the theater of the East remains intensely symbolic, requiring considerable sophistication on the part of its viewers. The actors appear in masks or wear highly artificial, masklike makeup whose appearance and colors indicate the characters' social status and qualities. The design and colors of costumes are equally symbolic; movements and gestures, each of which carries a precise meaning, are carefully choreographed and codified; speech is artificial and often musical; and scenery and stage properties are usually minimal. Indeed, scenery is frequently omitted altogether, and properties are often used to represent a startling variety of locales. In the Chinese theater, for example, a few chairs and a table may be variously arranged to indicate a bridge, a boat, or even a mountain; an actor with a small whip in his hand represents a man on horseback.

The earliest Oriental theaters are believed to have been in India, where Sanskrit dramas were produced in temples and at court several centuries before the birth of Christ. The acting area seems to have been a raised platform before a curtain; in place of scenery the actors or a narrator set the stage with dialogue and pantomime. In China, where the distinctive form of theater known as Peking Opera evolved at the end of the 18th century, the stage was originally a roofed platform with two doors at the rear. Stagehands, dressed in black and by convention understood to be invisible, manipulated properties while the drama was in progress. Female roles, at least until recently, were undertaken by males; the actor MEI LAN-FANG, who also performed in the West, was the outstanding interpreter of women in the 20th century.

More familiar to contemporary Western audiences, however, is the theater of Japan, where three indigenous forms—No DRAMA, BUNRAKU, and KABUKI—are still produced and have occasionally been seen in Europe and the United States. The No theater originated in the 14th century and was initially given before aristocratic and priestly audiences. The masked actors are exclusively male and traditionally make their entrances onto the roofed platform stage along a "bridge" or runway at the rear. In Bunraku, all of the actors are puppets, each of whose complicated movements require no less than three expert handlers. It was for this theater that CHIKAMATSU MONZAEMON, the most famous of Japanese playwrights, wrote many of his later dramas.

Chikamatsu also wrote for the popular Kabuki theater, which began in the 17th century and borrowed many elements from No and Bunraku. This form of theater, in which dance plays a prominent role and the actors appear in exaggerated makeup, is more realistic in its scenic practices. Traps are used to raise and lower actors and scenery, and in the 18th century rapid shifts of setting became possible with the introduction of the revolving stage—a feature eventually adopted by Western theater. A runway (*hanamichi*) over which the actors make their entrances is another characteristic feature of the Kabuki playhouse. Unlike the runway in the No theater, however, this connects with the front of the stage and runs through the auditorium from the rear of the house.

The design of the Japanese Kabuki theater encourages an intimacy between actors and audience, who are in close contact as the actors move along the hanamichi, or walkway, that connects the stage with the rear of the theater. The walkway is used for entrances and exits, and as an auxiliary stage when scenery on the main stage is shifted.

Another well-known form of Oriental theater, the shadow puppet plays still performed in Indonesia, may have originated in India or China. Toward the end of the 18th century, when they were known as *ombres chinoises* (see SHADOW PLAY), these plays were introduced to Paris and later, in the 1790s, were shown in London by Philip ASTLEY, the famous circus proprietor.

19th-Century Theater. At the close of the 18th century a number of social and political events wrought profound changes in the European theater. The turmoil of the French Revolution foretold the end of the aristocratic tradition, and the cities, as a result of the Industrial Revolution, now experienced a tremendous swelling of their populations as laborers poured in from the countryside. New forms of drama evolved that reflected these changes, and in London, Paris, and other major cities a host of new theaters appeared to cater to the tastes of working-class audiences who delighted in pantomimes, spectacles, vaudevilles (see MUSIC HALL, VAUDEVILLE, AND BURLESQUE), and—an invention of the playwrights August von KOTZEBUE and Guilbert de Pixérécourt—melodrama. On a somewhat higher plane romantic drama and revivals of the classics, produced at the major theaters, were performed by such notable actors as François Joseph TALMA, Mademoiselles Mars and Duchenois, and Rachel, the famous interpreter of Racine's *Phèdre*, in France; John Philip Kemble (see KEMBLE family) and his sister Sarah SIDDONS, Edmund Kean (see KEAN family), and William Charles MACREADY were the reigning stars in England. In the United States, which continued to be

heavily dependent on Europe for its drama and theater practices during most of the 19th century, the first native actors to achieve international reputations now appeared: the Negro tragedian Ira ALDRIDGE, the brawny Edwin FORREST, Charlotte Saunders CUSHMAN, whose repertoire of roles included Hamlet and Romeo, and Edwin Booth (see BOOTH family), who also managed his own theater in New York City.

Few innovations in theater architecture were achieved during the 19th century, although lighting and scenic practices experienced numerous changes. By the 1820s gas had replaced candles and oil lamps in many theaters; limelight and the carbon arc for spotlighting effects were in common use by the mid-century; and in 1881, with the opening of the Savoy Theatre in London, the stage was first lit by electricity. Stages became fully trapped (a few, like Booth's New York theater, had hydraulic lifts), and scenery could be raised from below or "flown in" from above the stage. Settings, properties, and costumes attained maximum realism and historical accuracy. The old flats on which scenery had formerly been painted in perspective gave way to elaborate practical settings (changes of setting often required long waits between scenes); the completely enclosed or "box" set came into use for comedies; moving PANORAMAS facilitated spectacular travel effects; even the plays of Shakespeare were now performed with meticu-

France's great actress Sarah Bernhardt found the equal to her exotic flamboyance in the art of Alfons Mucha. His first Bernhardt poster, for the play Gismonda (1894), made his name in Paris, and he continued to produce not only posters but also costume and jewelry designs for the Divine Sarah— including this advertisement for the actress as the anguished, revenge-seeking heroine of Corneille's Médeé.

Edwin Booth, the most popular U.S. actor of the last half of the 19th century, is shown here costumed as Hamlet, his most famous role. The 1848 playbill for a St. Louis theater advertises his father, the English actor Junius Brutus Booth, Sr., in the same role. Edwin's versions of Shakespeare were as close as 19th-century audiences came to hearing the original plays—most Shakespeare productions of the time were bowdlerized and vulgarized.

The first production of Chekhov's Uncle Vanya *(shown here, a scene from act 4) was staged at the Moscow Art Theater in October 1899, directed by Konstantin Stanislavsky and Vladimir Nemirovich-Danchenko. Their theatrical goal—in Stanislavsky's words, to convey "the inner truth, the truth of feeling and experience"—was achieved by their actors through intense study and many long rehearsals. Their productions were notable as well for the scrupulous realism of settings and effects. Nemirovich-Danchenko's contributions to the Moscow Art Theater are often ignored, yet as literary director he established the reputation of the theater by reviving Chekhov's* The Seagull *(1898) after its disastrous debut production in Saint Petersburg; and it was he who persuaded Chekhov to continue his career as a playwright.*

lous attention to historical accuracy. Libraries and archives were ransacked to provide authentic sources for designers and costumers; real animals, including dogs, horses, and even elephants, joined the actors; volcanoes erupted, hurricanes toppled mock trees, and ships—as in Shakespeare's *Tempest*— sank on cue. The "long run" became increasingly common, and the older repertory system—under which theaters had changed their bills almost nightly and a single house might present dozens of new and old plays in a single season—was gradually abandoned.

Concurrent with the rise of these elaborately planned productions was the arrival of the modern director, who might still be a leading actor, but was responsible for overseeing every aspect of production and for imposing a unity on the whole. This arrangement also encouraged an ensemble style of acting, in which the actors blended their talents and none starred at the expense of others—or of the play itself. Among the earliest of this new breed in England were the actress, dancer, and singer Madame VESTRIS, who produced comedies and extravaganzas at her elegant little theater, the Olympic, in the 1830s, and in the 1850s Charles Kean, son of Edmund, who was celebrated for his Shakespearean productions at the Princess's Theatre. Kean was especially noted for his skillful handling of crowd scenes and exerted a profound influence on George II, duke of SAXE-MEININGEN, whose own company of German actors toured throughout Europe in the 1870s and 1880s and in turn directly influenced such later directors as André ANTOINE and Konstantin STANISLAVSKY. The principles of this style of production—sometimes referred to as the "theater of the *régisseur* (director)"—are still widely followed, although most present-day directors do not act in their productions. The status of the playwright also improved during the 19th century. At the urging of dramatists such as Dion BOUCICAULT, who also directed and acted in his popular plays on both sides of the Atlantic, COPYRIGHT laws were enacted to protect authors' rights, and dramatists now became entitled to royalties.

By the final decades of the 19th century a number of playwrights had tired of the romantic claptrap and artificial dramas of their predecessors. Seeking to give a truer depiction of life, these authors—Émile ZOLA, Henrik IBSEN, and Gerhardt HAUPTMANN among them—founded the naturalistic school of drama. Because their controversial works were forbidden in the commercial theaters of most countries, it became necessary to establish subscription theaters, which were nominally private and thus beyond the control of official censors. From this necessity sprang the Independent Theater movement, the first of whose theaters, the Théâtre Libre in Paris, was founded by André Antoine in 1887. Die FREIE BÜHNE in Berlin and the Independent Theater (1891) in London followed a few years later. As even newer schools of drama appeared on the scene, playwrights continued to find outlets for their works in theaters that pursued artistic rather than commercial objectives. In 1898 the MOSCOW ART THEATER—famous above all for

its productions of Anton CHEKHOV—was founded by Konstantin Stanislavsky and Vladimir Ivanovich NEMIROVICH-DANCHENKO, and in 1907 the expressionist author August STRINDBERG opened the Intima Teatern in Stockholm, where he presented his own plays. Meanwhile, even the classical repertory was undergoing an intensive reevaluation. In 1894 the English director William Poel founded the Elizabethan Stage Society, whose productions of Shakespeare and other Elizabethan dramatists broke with the 19th-century tradition of realistic staging and attempted to re-create the conventions and architectural arrangements of Shakespeare's day—an approach that is still followed at numerous Shakespeare festival theaters.

20th-Century Theater. At the turn of the 19th century a number of designers were also calling for a break with older traditions. Both Gordon CRAIG and Adolphe APPIA argued for settings and lighting that were suggestive and expressive of the mood of the drama rather than realistic. Their ideas have influenced many later theater artists—in the United States the most eminent has been Robert Edmond JONES—although no particular school of design can be said to predominate at the present day. Indeed, 20th-century stage designs have included both the most elaborately detailed naturalistic settings and stages devoid of anything but a few essential properties, not to mention the bizarre constructivist (see CONSTRUCTIVISM) settings created in the 1920s for the Russian director Vsevolod Emilievich MEYERHOLD, who expected his actors to physicalize their emotions and to perform within playgroundlike settings as gymnasts and acrobats. The Italianate proscenium-frame stage—an object of scorn to avant-garde directors—remains entrenched in the majority of theaters, but the Renaissance acting platform has reemerged as the "thrust stage," and a few experimental theaters have used arena staging or THEATER IN THE ROUND—an innovation whose antecedents can be traced to the theaters of prehistory.

The eclecticism that pervades the 20th-century theater is perhaps best summarized in the international career of the Austrian director Max REINHARDT, who worked in an amazing variety of locales that included large and small theaters with and without proscenium frames, cabarets, churches, royal palaces and riding schools, the converted Circus Schumann in Berlin, and even outdoor settings such as the Hollywood Bowl and the square before the cathedral in Salzburg, Austria. (In the 1930s, Reinhardt also directed a few films in Hollywood.) The playwrights whose works he produced ranged from Sophocles through Shakespeare and Calderon to such modern writers as Frank Wedekind and Luigi Pirandello. Each production received its own unique style and scenic treatment, with the latter often incorporating the latest technical developments, including the revolving stage and plaster domes or cycloramas behind and above the stage.

As with design, architecture, and theatrical direction, there is no dominant style of acting in the 20th century. METHOD ACTING, derived from Stanislavsky's teachings, has been found useful by many directors and actors in naturalistic productions (see ACTORS STUDIO, and Lee STRASBERG), but it is also recognized that deliberately artificial styles are more appropriate to the works of dramatists outside the realistic tradition. Bertolt BRECHT—whose theories of production have perhaps been more influential than those of anyone else in the second half of the century—always insisted that actors in his plays remain aware of the fact that they were acting and that they not surrender their personalities to the characters they were impersonating. The play itself and the social message it contained were to be of paramount interest; the spectators were to be continually reminded that they were viewing a theatrical event so that they would not sympathize with the characters as real-life figures and thereby allow their critical judgment to be clouded by emotion. Lest the actors themselves prove incapable of such detachment, Brecht employed a number of devices to ''alienate'' his audiences from any illusions of reality that might endanger their objectivity. His plays were presented as historical rather than as immediate events; projected captions were used to inform spectators in advance what they were to witness in a forthcoming scene; musical numbers and humorous episodes were inserted to undercut serious ones; lighting and sets were nonrealistic; even the stagehands' activities were visible.

Both realistic and nonrealistic traditions of production flour-ish in the contemporary theater. While the former appears to be favored by the majority of Western playgoers, the latter has nevertheless become increasingly acceptable as 20th-century spectators have gained greater sophistication through exposure to the plays and production styles of other nations and periods. Although audiences may not approve, neither are they apt to be surprised when such revolutionary groups as the LIVING THEATRE, taking their cue from the theories of Brecht, not only seek to arouse their audiences to some social action but deliberately go out of their way to embarrass and insult them, or when a director such as Peter BROOK, in a variation of the Chinese theater, introduces acrobatics and juggling into a production of Shakespeare's *A Midsummer Night's Dream.* The theater, as these experiments serve to remind us, continues to be an evolving institution—as viable, as exciting, and sometimes as controversial as it was in the days of Aeschylus, Shakespeare, and Ibsen.   A. H. SAXON

Bibliography: Arnott, Peter, *The Theater in Its Time* (1981); Berthold, Margot, *A History of World Theater,* trans. by Edith Simmons (1972); Bogard, Travis, *American Drama* (1978); Braun, Edward, *The Director and the Stage: From Naturalism to Grotowski* (1982); Brockett, Oscar G., *History of the Theatre,* 4th ed. (1981); Gascoigne, Bamber, *World Theatre: An Illustrated History* (1968); Kernodle, George R., *From Art to Theatre: Form and Convention in the Renaissance* (1944); Macgo-

(Left) *The original production of Arthur Miller's Pulitzer Prize–winning play,* Death of a Salesman, *starred Mildred Dunnock and Lee J. Cobb. The play galvanized the 1949 New York theater world, not only for its drama—which overturned classical notions of tragedy by portraying the life of an ordinary man in tragic terms—but also for its setting, created by stage designer Jo Mielziner. A single unit, it gave the illusion of a multiplicity of settings with an ingenious use of lighting and props.* (Right) *The 1982 Broadway production of* Cats *also received acclamation for its setting, a junkyard filled with gigantic litter appropriately sized for the cats who live in it. Critics claimed, however, that the plot, based on T. S. Eliot's verses* Old Possum's Book of Practical Cats *(1939), was too small for the outsize production.*

(Below) *Modern directors of Shakespeare are no longer inhibited by earlier requirements for realistic settings, and stage design has become one of the many elements they utilize to transmit their ideas about the plays.* (Left) *A 1976 production of* As You Like It *at the American Shakespeare Theater in Stratford, Conn., was described by director Michael Kahn as ''a kind of chamber production,'' intimate and small scale, an Arcadian vision of love set in an idealized forest of Arden.* (Right) *The open-air Delacorte Theater in New York City's Central Park was the site for this 1984* Henry V, *starring Kevin Kline. Director Wilford Leach mounted a traditional production with opulent costumes and a single set: a small but elegant castle that split in two at act 4, scene 4, to reveal the smoke and carnage of the battlefield at Agincourt.*

wan, Kenneth, and Melnitz, William, *The Living Stage: A History of the World Theatre* (1955); Nagler, A. M., *A Source Book in Theatrical History (Sources of Theatrical History)* (1952); Nicoll, Allardyce, *The Development of the Theatre: A Study of Theatrical Art from the Beginnings to the Present Day*, 5th ed. (1966); Oenslager, Donald, *Stage Design: Four Centuries of Scenic Invention* (1975); Roberts, Vera M., *On Stage: A History of Theatre*, 2d ed. (1974); *The Oxford Companion to the Theatre*, ed. by Phyllis Hartnoll, 4th ed. (1983); Simonson, Lee, *The Stage Is Set*, rev. ed. (1963); Wickham, Glynne, *The Medieval Theatre* (1974).

theater architecture and staging

Theater architecture and staging is the arrangement of space for a theatrical performance and its audience. Periods in theater history may be distinguished by the shape and size of the stage and auditorium, the type and amount of scenery, and the function of the scenery in relation to the performers. Techniques of staging have always been determined by convention—a theatrical shorthand accepted by spectators. Scenery re-creating the outside world, or dialogue delivered as if it were everyday speech, for instance, would have seemed alien to many cultures and is not common in most non-Western theaters today. The development of Western theater does, however, show a tendency toward the illusion of reality.

Greek Theater. Little is known of the origins of theater, but it is generally assumed that the ancient Greek theater grew out of religious rituals that were probably performed in a roughly circular space. During the 6th century BC the Athenians built the first Theater of Dionysus by constructing a dancing circle, or orchestra, at the base of a hillside, thus forming a natural amphitheater. The seating area, which surrounded the orchestra on three sides, held as many as 17,000 spectators by the 4th century BC.

At first the main performers were the chorus, but the increasing prominence of the individual actor led to modifications in the performing area that took place over a period of several hundred years. A stage house, or *skené*, was placed at the rear of the orchestra, opposite the audience. In addition to its functions as dressing room, storage area, and architectural background, it concealed the actors, who entered the stage through its three doors. A raised stage called the proscenium was added to the front of the *skené* and gradually encroached on the orchestra until, by the 2d century BC, the orchestra was little more than a semicircle.

Scenery in the Greek theater was limited and stylized. Painted scenery of some kind may have been used as early as the 5th century BC. Panels representing the general location of the dramatic action may have been painted on *periaktoi*—prisms set vertically in the facade of the *skené* that could be pivoted to display different scenes. Various mechanical devices were used, consisting mostly of rolling platforms and an apparatus that enabled actors portraying gods to "fly."

Roman Theater. Roman theater existed at least as early as the 2d century BC, but the first permanent Roman playhouse was Pompey's Theater, built in 55 BC. Although Roman theater architecture was based on Greek models, the use of the arch enabled the Romans to build immense, freestanding, open-air theaters, many of which seated more than 15,000 spectators.

The auditorium, or *cavea*, of a typical Roman theater was a semicircle around a smaller semicircular orchestra. The orchestra was often used for additional seating or sometimes flooded for aquatic spectacles. The stage, between 6 and 12 m (20 and 40 ft) deep and as much as 60 m (200 ft) long, was backed by an elaborate facade, the *scaena frons*, often three stories high. The *scaena frons* had between three and five doors and numerous niches, statues, frescoes, and pediments. The stage was often roofed, and an awning could be stretched across the *cavea* to shelter the spectators.

Medieval Theater. The last recorded Roman performance took place in AD 533, and Western theater was not reborn until the liturgical dramas of the church developed in the 10th century. At first these plays were performed in churches, and as the plays became more elaborate the entire church was used. Small booths called mansions represented the various settings—such as Jerusalem, Hell, and Heaven—and the per-

Edward Gordon Craig's 1903 stage setting for Henrik Ibsen's historical drama The Vikings at Helgeland *(1858)* was created in association with his mother, the renowned British actress Ellen Terry. Craig, one of the most influential pioneers of stage design and dramatic theory, united subtle lighting effects with simple settings to evoke rather than re-create the desired atmosphere. Craig also introduced abstract scenery.

formers and spectators moved from one to the other as the performance took place in an acting area called the *platea*.

By the early 13th century most performances took place outside the church in churchyards or market squares on both fixed and mobile stages. Some fixed stages imitated the mansion and *platea* arrangement of the church, whereas others employed a long, raised, rectangular stage with mansions abutting the rear and sides. The scene of the action was suggested by the mansion from which an actor entered. Moving stages were more common in England; pageant wagons were used for mystery plays and the Corpus Christi cycle (see MEDIEVAL DRAMA). Evidence suggests that some medieval performances took place in theaters in the round. Little attempt was made to create the illusion of reality—a piece of red cloth represented the Red Sea, for example—but scenery was elaborate and technically sophisticated. The mansion representing Hell, especially, was a tour de force of fireworks, machinery, and special effects.

Italian Theater. Renaissance Italian theater developed in the courts of the nobility in settings that differed radically from those of the past. The invention of perspective painting in the 14th and 15th centuries led to painted scenery that attempted to create the illusion of reality. The most influential theatrical work of the Renaissance was Sebastiano SERLIO's *Second Book of Architecture* (1545; Eng. trans., 1611), which proposed three basic perspective scenes—tragic, comic, and satiric—to correspond with the work performed. The scenes consisted of a painted backdrop and three pairs of angled side-wings—freestanding units that masked the space on either side of the stage.

Serlio's scenes were permanent, but as court productions became more elaborate it became necessary to change scenery during a performance. Movable scenery evolved over a 200-year period and was a major innovation of the Renaissance theater.

The first practical system was introduced about 1600. Known as flat-wing and groove, it consisted of a series of flats—canvas-covered frames on which scenery was painted—set in grooves on the stage floor. Flats could be pulled off-stage to reveal a second set. The major disadvantages of this arrangement were the number of stagehands required and the difficulty of coordinating changes. This problem was solved in 1645 by Giacomo Torelli (1608–78) with the chariot-and-pole system. Flats were mounted on poles that passed through slots in the floor to rolling wagons, or "chariots," beneath the stage. These, in turn, were attached to winches by a system of ropes and pulleys. Changes of scenery became so fascinating that they were frequently made during a performance for no dramatic reason.

Monumental scenic design was made possible in the 17th century by the use of multiple perspective. Although sets still fostered the illusion of reality, they created the illusion that the world of the stage was of a larger scale than that of the audience, thereby reinforcing the sense of distance between

A contemporary engraving shows the lavishly decorated New Park Theater, opened in New York City in 1821 to replace the original Park Theater (1798), which had burned down. Both the Park and the New Park were important institutions. The Park—in its time the city's sole theater—maintained a repertory company until it initiated the financially rewarding practice of importing celebrated English stars.

stage and auditorium. The mythical and allegorical content of the plays was aided by complex machinery, especially flying apparatus such as chariots and "cloud machines." Grandiose Italianate design reached its peak with the Bibiena family (see GALLI DA BIBIENA family), whose designs were popular throughout 18th-century Europe.

Renaissance architects attempted to re-create Greek and Roman theaters, but because their information was often ambiguous or incomplete, the result was a new style of theater architecture. Serlio adapted the Roman form to rectangular palace halls, but no building specifically designed as a theater was constructed until the 1530s. The oldest surviving Renaissance theater is Andrea Palladio's TEATRO OLIMPICO.

The major development in Renaissance theater architecture was the proscenium arch—a curved or rectangular frame enclosing the stage—which is found in many modern theaters. The first theater to use the proscenium arch was the Teatro Farnese (1619) in Parma, Italy, designed by Giovanni Battista

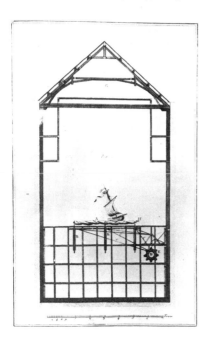

The Palais Royal Theater in Paris, built by Cardinal Richelieu in 1641, was equipped with devices for producing many kinds of movements, sounds, and transformations on stage. Most of the machines were copies of Italian designs. A contemporary drawing shows a cutaway view of stage and substage, with the device that produces the waves that rock the wooden model of a ship.

Aleotti (1546–1636). The proscenium arch masks the offstage space and aids scenic illusion by separating the stage and auditorium; the audience must look through the opening onto the stage. The U-shaped seating area for the audience in the Teatro Farnese also influenced theater design and is now a common feature of European theaters and OPERA HOUSES. The Teatro Farnese was the first theater designed for the use of moveable scenery, and one of the first to use a curtain in front of the proscenium arch. Its steeply banked seating tiers held an audience of 3,500, who came to see the fabulous spectacles that only a theater of this size and complexity could mount: not only opera, ballet, and drama, but—on the spacious orchestra floor separating the audience from the stage—extravaganzas and ceremonials of all kinds.

English Theater. The English ELIZABETHAN PLAYHOUSE evolved independently and took two distinct forms: private, indoor theaters, and public, outdoor theaters. The first permanent public theater in London was The Theatre, erected in 1576 by James Burbage; the first private theater, The Blackfriars, was opened the same year. The public theaters were round or rectangular open-air structures, with a roofed, three-tiered gallery for spectators that nearly surrounded the raised rectangular stage. The stage extended into an area known as the pit or yard that provided standing room for spectators. Behind the roofed stage was the tiring house, a backstage space for dressing rooms and property storage and sometimes a musicians' gallery. Two or three doors opened onto the stage from the facade of the tiring house, and there were probably trapdoors in the stage floor. Scenery was limited to a few props, but the spectacle was enhanced by elaborate costumes. Open-air performances took place in daylight, but torches or candles indicated a nocturnal scene. The most elaborate private theatrical entertainments of this period were court MASQUES employing Italian design concepts.

The theater was suppressed by the Puritan government between 1642 and 1660, but after the restoration of the monarchy theatrical activity resumed. Like the French theaters of the time, the first new English theaters were built in converted tennis courts. These theaters combined the Elizabethan platform stage with the Italian proscenium. Changeable scenery was placed behind the proscenium arch while the actors performed on a forestage in front of it. In virtually all Western theaters until the 19th century, scenery merely provided a background; actors performed in front of the scenery rather than in the midst of it. During the following century, however, the forestage decreased in size, and the space for the audience increased until the entire production took place behind the proscenium arch.

19th-Century Theater. By the 19th century almost all European and American theaters were variations on the Italian baroque opera-house style exemplified by the Paris Opéra (1874). During this period scenery and techniques of staging changed considerably. The Meiningen Players, the court troupe of George II, duke of SAXE-MEININGEN, encouraged the use of historically accurate sets, and the rising popularity of MELODRAMA led to spectacles that employed the latest advances in STAGE LIGHTING and machinery.

As plays became more realistic in style the box set, an interior setting depicting three walls of a room, became prevalent. Scene changes were no longer made in full view of the audience, and new methods of scene shifting were developed using elevator stages, revolving platforms, and hydraulic machinery. A more naturalistic arrangement of freestanding scenic elements was made possible by the invention of the stage brace.

The major architectural advance of the 19th century was achieved in 1876 by Richard WAGNER at the Bayreuth Festspielhaus, where private boxes were eliminated and a wedge-shaped amphitheater provided all spectators with equal visibility. Wagner concealed the orchestra and darkened the auditorium during performances to minimize distractions and enhance illusion. Wagner's staging techniques, however, offered few innovations, and stages in general have not changed significantly since the mid-19th century, except in the types and amount of mechanical apparatus.

20th-Century Theater. The so-called new stagecraft of the 20th century, strongly influenced by the designs and theories of Adolphe APPIA and Gordon CRAIG, was the outcome of increased awareness of Oriental stagecraft (see BUNRAKU; KABUKI; NO DRAMA) and of several European antinaturalistic theatrical movements. The stage designer Josef SVOBODA has even dispensed with three-dimensional scenery by using projected images. Since the mid-19th century several attempts have been made to re-create the open stage of the ancient Greeks and the Elizabethans by removing the proscenium arch. Popular alternatives to the proscenium design include the thrust stage—a platform surrounded by the audience on three sides—and the arena stage (see THEATER IN THE ROUND) which is completely surrounded by the audience. Some experiments have also been made with environmental staging, in which the stage surrounds the audience or several stages are interspersed through an audience area, thus creating a playing space like that of certain medieval performances.

Whereas most commercial theaters have retained the traditional proscenium, the modern theater as a whole is eclectic and offers opportunities to witness virtually every kind of staging technique. Scenery tends to follow the specific needs of a play rather than any particular style. If a contemporary style of theater architecture exists, then it is the multipurpose auditorium, a flexible, adaptable space designed to suit all needs and all types of performance.   ARNOLD ARONSON

Bibliography: Aronson, Arnold, *The History and Theory of Environmental Scenography* (1981); Bieber, Margarete, *The History of Greek and Roman Theatre* (1961); Burian, Jarka, *The Scenography of Josef Svoboda* (1971); Craig, Edward G., *Scene* (1928; repr. 1968); Hewitt, Barnard, ed., *The Renaissance Stage* (1958); Izenour, George, *Theater Design* (1977); Leacroft, Richard, *The Development of the English Playhouse* (1973); Moynet, Jean-Pierre, *French Theatrical Production in the 19th Century* (1976); Nicoll, Allardyce, *The Development of the Theatre* (1966); Scholz, Janos, *Baroque and Romantic Stage Design* (1950); Southern, Richard, *The Seven Ages of the Theatre* (1961); Weil, Mark, *Baroque Theater and Stage Design* (1983).

theater festivals

Arising out of fertility and harvest ceremonies, early drama was intimately connected with seasonal feasts, or festivals. The plays performed at regular intervals in ancient Athens to honor the god Dionysus suggest the theater's originally sacred and occasional character. This character was preserved in medieval Europe by the mystery and miracle plays: performed by acting guilds on designated holy days (originally Easter, then Christmas and Corpus Christi), the plays retained the drama's communal, ritual aspect within the context of a new calendar and new faith.

Since the Renaissance, theater festivals have become gradually more secularized. Beginning with the princely *trionfi* of 17th-century Italy, court and public drama in the baroque era became increasingly devoted to municipal and national celebrations, and spectacle replaced ritual as the dominant mode of performance. Amateur groups, however, continued to perform medieval passion plays; one group in OBERAMMERGAU, Germany, began performing a 15th-century passion text in 1634; its decennial productions continue today.

At the SALZBURG FESTIVAL, noted for Mozart performances, outdoor productions of another 15th-century play, EVERYMAN, have taken place since 1920. Most modern festivals focus on more recent plays. In the 19th century, the revived idea of regular theatrical celebrations led to the founding of the BAYREUTH WAGNER FESTIVAL (1876) and the Shakespeare Memorial Theatre in Stratford-on-Avon (1879). Both continue their seasonal activities, and the latter has inspired numerous other Shakespeare festivals (more than 25 in the United States alone), including major events in Stratford, Ontario; Stratford, Conn.; San Diego, Calif.; Burlington, Vt.; and Lakewood, Ohio.

Festivals in the 20th century are international and eclectic. Those at Venice (the Beinnale, 1934), Avignon (1947), Dubrovnik (1950), Bergen (1953), Spoleto (1958; see SPOLETO FESTIVAL), and Chichester (1962) regularly invite troupes from abroad, some of which feature dance and music as well as drama. The Edinburgh International Festival of Music and Drama (1947) has hosted the Royal Shakespeare Company and the Comédie Française along with other important theatrical companies from France, Italy, and the United States, and numerous repertory groups. The Parisian Théâtre des Nations festival (1954), like its short-lived but brilliant contemporary, London's World Theatre Season (1964–73), has also concentrated on presenting foreign troupes, including the Berliner Ensemble and the Moscow Art Theater, but is now turning to the efforts of Third World countries. This is true also of Brazil's Fete Mambembao.

Of about 500 festivals now held regularly, only a few—such as the Bernard Shaw Festival in Niagara-on-the-Lake, Ontario—focus on single dramatists. A few others—like those at Athens and Epidaurus—have revived classical plays. Most attempt to unite nations in a celebration of the communal, if no longer sacred, dimension of drama.

Bibliography: Loney, Glenn, and MacKay, Patricia, *The Shakespeare Complex* (1975); Merin, Jennifer, with Elizabeth B. Burdick, *International Directory of Theater, Dance and Folklore Festivals* (1979); Meyer, Nancy, *Festivals of the West* (1975).

theater in the round

A performing space surrounded on all sides by the audience, usually in raked or tiered seats, theater in the round creates an intimacy not possible with proscenium staging and makes the audience more aware of itself. Glenn Hughes's Penthouse Theatre at the University of Washington (1940) was the first modern theater totally devoted to this form; Margo JONES's Theatre '50 in Dallas (1950) became the first professional arena stage. Modern contributions to this form of staging include the productions of Vsevolod E. MEYERHOLD, Nikolai P. Okhlopkov, and Max REINHARDT in Europe, Norman BEL GEDDES and Robert Edmond JONES in the United States, and Robert Atkins and Stephen Joseph in England.

ARNOLD ARONSON

Bibliography: Jones, Margo, *Theatre-in-the-Round* (1951); Joseph, Stephen, *Theatre in the Round* (1968).

theater of cruelty: see ARTAUD, ANTONIN.

theater of fact

The type of political drama known as theater of fact, or documentary theater, was made famous by Erwin PISCATOR in his productions of Rolf HOCHHUTH's *The Deputy* (1963; Eng. trans., 1964), Heinar Kipphardt's *In the Matter of J. R. Oppenheimer* (1964; Eng. trans., 1967), and Peter WEISS's *The Investigation* (1965; Eng. trans., 1966). The staging of a documentary play characteristically employs factual material—such as reports, conference minutes, journals, newspaper articles, photos, films, or tape recordings—to relate the course of an important historical incident from a new critical perspective. The audience is led to question the authenticity of the accepted or official version of an event by the very framework of the play, which assumes the general form of a trial. This dramatic structure allows for a new hearing of the events that often leads to a new verdict. The facts themselves are tendentious, selected with a view toward agitating the audience and thereby raising its political consciousness.

A few years after the theater of fact made an impression in Germany, the United States witnessed a spate of documentary productions that included Howard Sackler's *The Great White Hope* (1968), Arthur Kopit's *Indians* (1968), N. R. Davidson's *El Hajj Malik: A Play about Malcolm X* (1968); Conor Cruise O'Brien's *Murderous Angels* (1970), and Donald Freed's *The United States vs. Julius and Ethel Rosenberg* (1969). Although in the more conservative climate of the 1970s documentary drama lost some of its explosive potential, it continues to provide a forum for re-creating historical and political events within a critical framework.   JACK ZIPES

Bibliography: Berthold, Margot, *A History of World Theater*, trans. by Edith Simmons (1972); Willett, John, *The Theater of Erwin Piscator* (1979).

theater of the absurd

The theater of the absurd refers to tendencies in dramatic literature that emerged in Paris during the late 1940s and early '50s in the plays of Arthur ADAMOV, Fernando ARRABAL, Samuel BECKETT, Jean GENET, Eugène IONESCO, and Jean TARDIEU. Its roots can be found in the allegorical morality plays of the Middle Ages and the *autos sacramentales* (allegorical religious dramas) of baroque Spain; the nonsense literature of writers like Lewis Carroll; the dream plays of Strindberg and the dream novels of James Joyce and Franz Kafka; the grotesque drama of Alfred JARRY; and the frantic farces of Georges FEYDEAU. Its direct forerunners were the DADA movement and the SURREALISM of the 1920s and '30s. One of its most potent theoretical sources was *The Theater and its Double* (1938; Eng. trans., 1958) by Antonin ARTAUD.

The term *theater of the absurd* derives from the philosophical use of the word *absurd* by such existentialist thinkers as Albert CAMUS and Jean Paul SARTRE. Camus, particularly, argued that humanity had to resign itself to recognizing that a fully satisfying rational explanation of the universe was beyond its reach; in that sense, the world must ultimately be seen as absurd.

The playwrights loosely grouped under the label of the absurd endeavor to convey their sense of bewilderment, anxiety, and wonder in the face of an inexplicable universe. They rely heavily on poetic metaphor as a means of projecting outward their innermost states of mind. Hence, the images of the theater of the absurd tend to assume the quality of fantasy, dream, and nightmare; they do not so much portray the outward appearance of reality as the playwright's emotional perception of an inner reality. Thus Beckett's *Happy Days* (1961) expresses a generalized human anxiety about the approach of death through the concrete image of a woman sunk waist-deep in the ground in the first act and neck-deep in the second; and Ionesco's *Rhinoceros* (1960; Eng. trans., 1960) demonstrates the playwright's anxiety about the spread of inhuman totalitarian tendencies in society by showing the population of a city turning into savage pachyderms.

Writers outside France who in the 1950s and '60s showed the influence of the theater of the absurd include Harold PINTER and Tom STOPPARD in England, Günter GRASS and Peter WEISS in Germany, Edward ALBEE, Israel HOROVITZ, and Sam SHEPARD in the United States, and Václav HAVEL in Czechoslovakia.   MARTIN ESSLIN

Bibliography: Esslin, Martin, *The Theatre of the Absurd*, 2d ed. (1968); Gassner, John, *Directions in Modern Theatre and Drama* (1965); Gilman, Richard, *The Making of Modern Drama* (1974); Grossvogel, David I., *Four Playwrights and a Postscript: Brecht, Ionesco, Beckett, Genet* (1962; repr. 1976).

(Left to right) Peter Bull, Paul Daneman, Peter Woodthorpe, and Timothy Bateson are seen in Peter Hall's 1955 production of Samuel Beckett's absurdist play Waiting for Godot *(1952).* Waiting for Godot *defines humanity as hapless characters endlessly and futilely awaiting the arrival of an unknown but presumably beneficent authority.*

Théâtre Français: see COMÉDIE FRANÇAISE, LA.

Theatre Guild

The Theatre Guild was an American theater society founded in New York City in 1919 to promote excellence in theatrical productions on a noncommercial basis.

In its heyday in the 1920s the Guild produced plays by O'Neill, Shaw, and Chekhov and featured such established stars as Helen Hayes and Lunt and Fontanne. In 1935 it produced Gershwin's *Porgy and Bess* and in 1943, Rodgers and Hammerstein's *Oklahoma!*

Théâtre Libre: see ANTOINE, ANDRÉ.

Théâtre National Populaire   (TNP)

Bringing quality theater at low prices to a mass audience, the government-subsidized Théâtre National Populaire, established by Firman Gémier in 1920, became a major force in contemporary French theater under the directorship (1951–63) of Jean VILAR.

Experimental in set design and lighting, Vilar's company produced both classic and modern drama in the provinces and in its Paris home, the Palais de Chaillot. Georges Wilson succeeded Vilar as director.

theatricalism

Used to describe the stylized work of many directors and avant-garde theater troupes, theatricalism most often refers to the antirealist trend in world theater between 1905 and 1940. While never united in a movement as such, practitioners of theatricalism were shaped by similar influences and shared common notions about the theater's unique function. To realize their goals, they radically altered classical plays and often relied on stylized modes of performance.

Reacting against the widespread acceptance of NATURALISM and REALISM in the commercial theater and the growth of the feature-length silent film after the turn of the century, the first theatricalists sought inspiration in Japanese NO DRAMA and the COMMEDIA DELL'ARTE tradition.

Declaring that "the theater's place is in the theater," producers like Gordon CRAIG, working throughout Europe, Max REINHARDT in Germany, and Jacques COPEAU in France began to create dynamic performance styles that emphasized each play's own nonrealistic qualities. Frequently they borrowed from traditional and popular genres, such as mime and puppet theater.

A typical theatricalist production was mounted in a monumental fashion with spectacular musical, lighting, and costuming effects; a poetic text often served as its foundation. Some performances were staged in unusual environments, such as circus arenas or cathedrals, that highlighted the play's larger-than-life aspects; masks and elaborate makeup were sometimes used.

The most famous individual examples of theatricalism are undoubtedly Reinhardt's productions of *Oedipus Rex* in Berlin in 1910 and his annual outdoor staging of *Everyman* in Salzburg, starting in 1920.   MEL GORDON

Bibliography: Gassner, John, *Directions in Modern Theatre and Drama* (1965).

Thebes   (Egypt)   [theebz]

A capital of ancient Egypt, Thebes rose in importance as the home of several royal families from the 11th dynasty (established c.2133 BC). Kings of the 12th dynasty lived near Memphis but honored the Theban god Amon, and under the 17th and 18th dynasties Thebes became the capital of the Egyptian empire. Kings of the 19th and 20th dynasties lived in the north but lavished attention on Thebes. As the empire began to decline (c.1200 BC), Thebes was controlled by militaristic high priests; in 661 the city was sacked by the Assyrians. Thebes continued to be an important center during Ptolemaic

Ruins of the temple of Amon-Re, a major Egyptian deity, are on the east bank of the Nile River at the ancient Egyptian capital of Thebes. The complex of palaces, temples, and funerary structures at Thebes was built over a period of more than two millennia.

times (304–30 BC), but it declined thereafter and now consists of the villages of Luxor and Karnak.

Some Theban monuments are very well preserved. On the east bank of the Nile the principal ancient town site is covered by modern settlements, but two great temple complexes remain. Amon's temple at KARNAK is the larger, covering more than 54 ha (133 acres) and representing almost 2,000 years of building activity (from 2000 BC). The other temple, at LUXOR, was begun in 1417 BC. On the west bank are tombs of 11th- and 17th- to 20th-dynasty royalty. The New Kingdom burial grounds are in the remote valley where TUTANKHAMEN's tomb was found. Several large royal funerary temples survive at the edge of the river, and the desert foothills are filled with tombs of nobles who lived during the New Kingdom and later. Many of the temples are decorated with paintings that are masterpieces of Egyptian art. Several west-bank towns were important, particularly the palace-city of Amenhotep III at Malkata and the town of Medinet Habu.

DAVID O'CONNOR

Bibliography: Kamil, Jill, *Luxor: A Guide to Ancient Thebes,* 2d ed. (1976); Nims, Charles, *Thebes of the Pharaohs* (1965); Riefstahl, Elizabeth, *Thebes in the Time of Amunhotep Third* (1971); Winlock, H. E., *The Rise and Fall of the Middle Kingdom in Thebes* (1947).

Thebes (Greece)

Thebes, modern Thívai, was the principal city of BOEOTIA, a region of ancient Greece to the northwest of Athens. It existed in Mycenaean times and retained its importance after the Dorian invasion, although it was unable to unite Boeotia as, for example, Athens had united Attica. In 480–479 BC, Thebes sided with Persia during the PERSIAN WARS but escaped destruction when the Persians were defeated (479) at Plataea, a nearby Boeotian city. A dispute about the control of Plataea sparked the enmity between Thebes and Athens, which continued throughout the 5th century. Thebes was a Spartan ally in the PELOPONNESIAN WAR (431–404).

Thebes's great but brief moment of power came in the 4th century, primarily because of the military genius of EPAMINONDAS. After a period of unsuccessful conflict with Sparta, then the leading power of Greece, Thebes won a great victory at Leuctra in 371, driving the Spartans out of central Greece and invading the Peloponnesus itself. Theban predominance ended soon after Epaminondas's death in the Battle of Mantinea (362). PHILIP II of Macedonia defeated Thebes and Athens in 338 at Chaeronea; a Theban revolt led ALEXANDER THE GREAT to destroy Thebes in 336 BC. The rebuilt city continued undistinguished but tranquil through Roman times.

CHARLES W. FORNARA

Bibliography: Bury, J. B., and Meiggs, Russell, *History of Greece,* 4th ed. (1975).

theft: see LARCENY.

theism [thee'-izm]

Theism is a philosophically or theologically reasoned understanding of reality that affirms that the source and continuing ground of all things is in God; that the meaning and fulfillment of all things lie in their relation to God; and that God intends to realize that meaning and fulfillment. Thus theism is distinguished from AGNOSTICISM in claiming it to be possible to know of God, or of ultimate reality. It is distinguished from PANTHEISM in affirming that God is in some sense "personal" and so transcends the world even as a totality and is distinct from the world and its parts. Finally, it is distinguished from DEISM, which denies God's active, present participation in the world's being and the world's history. Historically, theism so understood represents a reasoned articulation of the understanding of God characteristic of the Jewish, Christian, and, to some extent, Islamic faiths.

LANGDON GILKEY

Bibliography: Fenn, William W., *Theism: The Implication of Experience* (1969); Hall, James, *Knowledge, Belief, and Transcendence; Philosophical Problems in Religion* (1975); Mascall, E. L., *He Who Is: A Study in Traditional Theism* (1966; repr. 1970); Monson, Charles H., ed., *Great Issues Concerning Theism* (1965).

Themistocles [thuh-mis'-tuh-kleez]

Themistocles, c.524–c.460 BC, one of the greatest statesmen of Athens, was the creator of the Athenian navy and, through it, of the Athenian empire. In 483 he persuaded Athens to build a fleet with revenue from newly discovered silver mines. This fleet and Themistocles' brilliant strategies crushed Persian king XERXES I's hopes of conquest at the Battle of SALAMIS (480). Soon thereafter Athens became the dominant power of the DELIAN LEAGUE.

After this personal triumph, little is known of Themistocles until about 472, when he was ostracized or banished on suspicion of plotting with the Persians. Retiring to Argos, he instigated trouble for Sparta, which he regarded as the natural opponent of Athens. These dealings and his alleged association with the discredited Spartan regent PAUSANIAS led to a charge of treason. Condemned to death, Themistocles made a sensational escape to the Persian court. After learning Persian, he met with Xerxes' son and successor, Artaxerxes I, and was granted fiefs by the king in exchange for his loyalty. Some reports alleged that Themistocles committed suicide when called upon to take part in a naval war against the Athenians.

CHARLES W. FORNARA

Bibliography: Podlecki, Anthony J., *The Life of Themistocles* (1975).

Thénard, Louis Jacques, Baron [tay-nahr']

Louis Jacques Thénard, b. May 4, 1777, d. June 21, 1857, a French chemist, discovered (1801) sebacic acid and (1818) hydrogen peroxide, and he investigated fatty acids and esters. With his friend Joseph Louis Gay-Lussac he investigated chlorine, iodine, and potassium and—after Humphry Davy—isolated boron. He taught in Paris and was (1845–52) Chancellor of the University of France.

Theocritus [thee-ahk'-ri-tuhs]

The Greek poet Theocritus, c.310 BC–c.250 BC, wrote 30 short poems, the *Idylls,* on pastoral and mythical subjects, love, and scenes of contemporary society. His bucolic poems strongly influenced Vergil's *Eclogues* and thereafter the development of PASTORAL LITERATURE.

CHARLES SEGAL

theodolite [thee-ahd'-uh-lyt]

A theodolite is an optical instrument used in surveying to measure horizontal and vertical angles. It is designed on the same general principles as the transit; generally, the traditional- or American-style instrument with exposed controls and verniers is called a transit, and the more modern European model a theodolite.

The theodolite is smaller than a transit and has a telescope that is less than 15 cm (6 in) long, compared to about 26 cm (10 in) for the transit. The theodolite telescope uses prisms in order to enlarge the image and has three leveling screws; the transit, on the other hand, uses lenses and has four leveling screws.

Because adjusting and measuring devices are enclosed in a theodolite, its appearance is smooth and streamlined compared to the transit. It has optical micrometers that allow angles to be read more accurately with a single measurement than can be read by repetition with a transit.

CHARLES A. HERUBIN

Theodora, Byzantine Empress

Theodora, b. AD c.500, d. June 548, was the celebrated wife of the Byzantine emperor JUSTINIAN I. In his *Secret History*, Procopius of Caesarea alleges that before her marriage (525) she had been an actress and prostitute. Her charms and personality undeniably exerted great influence over Justinian. During the Nika Riot (532) her vigorous encouragement prevented him from fleeing the capital and thereby probably saved his crown. Her influence on public policy and the fate of ministers could be decisive. She strove, with partial success, to win her husband's tolerance of MONOPHYSITISM. After her death Justinian's rule lost intensity and purpose. C. M. BRAND

Bibliography: Browning, Robert, *Justinian and Theodora* (1971); Diehl, Charles, *Theodora: Empress of Byzantium,* trans. by Samuel R. Rosenbaum (1972).

Theodorakis, Mikis   [thay-oh-doh-rah'-kees]

The Greek composer Mikis Michael George Theodorakis, b. July 29, 1925, first attained international renown with his score for the film *Zorba the Greek* (1965). Concurrently a political activist, he was elected (1964) as a Communist member of the Greek Parliament. He was arrested in 1967 after a military coup and while in detention composed the music for *Z*, a film about political repression. International acclaim and concern won his release, after which he went into exile in Paris. KAREN MONSON

Theodore of Mopsuestia   [mahp-soo-es'-chuh]

A biblical commentator and bishop of Mopsuestia in Cilicia, Theodore, c.350–428, was a representative of the Christology of the Antiochene school. He was born at Antioch and there studied rhetoric, literature, and biblical exegesis with his friend Saint John CHRYSOSTOM. Ordained a priest about 383, he was consecrated bishop of Mopsuestia in 392.

In his interpretation of Scripture, Theodore employed a critical and scientific approach, taking a historical rather than an allegorical approach to Genesis and the Psalms. Theodore's Christology, although it contributed to NESTORIANISM, anticipated the formula adopted at the Council of CHALCEDON (451) on the dual but united natures of Christ. His views were nevertheless condemned at the Councils of Ephesus and Constantinople (553). ROSS MACKENZIE

Bibliography: Greer, R. A., *Theodore of Mopsuestia* (1961); Norris, R. A., *Manhood and Christ* (1963).

Theodoret   [thee-ahd'-uh-ret]

A theologian of the Antiochene school, Theodoret, b. Antioch, c.393, d. c.458, was a monk of Apamea and bishop of Cyrus, Syria (423). A friend of Nestorius (see NESTORIANISM), he became embroiled in the controversy with Saint CYRIL OF ALEXANDRIA, whose views, he held, implied a confusion of the divine and human natures of Christ. Cyril's successor, the powerful Dioscorus, accused (448) Theodoret of dividing Christ into two natures, and although Theodoret insisted on the unity, he was anathematized. The Robber Synod of Ephesus (449), defending Cyril's theology, deposed Theodoret and forced him into exile for a year. At the Council of CHALCEDON (451), Theodoret was identified with the Nestorian opposition, but he was persuaded to renounce Nestorius and was recognized as orthodox.

Theodoret's surviving writings are fine expressions of the Antiochene school of interpretation. ROSS MACKENZIE

Bibliography: Delaney, John J., and Tobin, James E., *Dictionary of Catholic Biography* (1961); Quasten, Johannes, *Patrology* (1950).

Theodoric the Great, King of the Ostrogoths
[thee-ahd'-ur-ik]

Theodoric, b. c.455, d. Aug. 30, 526, was king (471–526) of the Ostrogoths (see GOTHS) and ruler (493–526) of Italy. Theodoric spent much of his youth as a hostage in Constantinople, where he learned that the crumbling Roman Empire had much of value to offer his people. Succeeding his father, Theodemir, he established his followers in what is today Bulgaria. In 488 the emperor Zeno sent Theodoric to drive the Germanic chieftain Odoacer out of Italy. Theodoric slew Odoacer and took control of Italy. He employed able Roman administrators, such as Cassiodorus and Liberius, patronized the arts, and sought the support of influential Romans, including the philosopher and statesman Boethius. Theodoric's plans to establish harmony between Goths and Romans failed, however, in part because his people adhered to Arianism, and the Romans, to orthodox Catholic Christianity. In addition, leadership rivalries and other factors nullified his goal of uniting the Germanic dynasties of the West through a matrix of marriage alliances. A few years after Theodoric's death Justinian I dispatched an invasion force that destroyed the Ostrogothic state. BERNARD S. BACHRACH

Bibliography: Hodgkin, Thomas, *Theodoric the Goth* (1900; repr. 1973).

Theodosius I, Roman Emperor   (Theodosius the Great)   [thee-oh-dohz'-ee-uhs]

Theodosius I, b. northwest Spain, Jan. 11, 347, d. Jan. 17, 395, reigned from 379 over the eastern part of the later Roman Empire (the Byzantine Empire) and from 392 over the western portion as well; he was the last ruler of the whole empire. He was given a military education by his father, a general, and was selected by Gratian, ruler of the western half of the empire, to succeed Valens in the East and to control the incursions of the GOTHS. In 382, to end the Visigoths' ravages, he concluded a treaty that granted them territory north of the Balkan Mountains; they agreed to furnish troops to the Roman army. Theodosius found his realm divided between Catholic and Arian Christians (see ARIANISM). He therefore convened the First Ecumenical Council of Constantinople in 381 (see CONSTANTINOPLE, COUNCILS OF). The council produced new theological formulas that convinced most Arians to convert to Catholicism.

Twice Theodosius intervened in the West. After Gratian's death, he recovered the western part of the empire (388) from the usurper Maximus and remained in Italy until 391, supporting Valentinian II. During this stay, Saint Ambrose, bishop of Milan, scored a long-remembered triumph over Theodosius. In 390, angered at the people of Thessalonica, the emperor ordered a general massacre there. Ambrose ex-

Theodosius I (the Great), the last ruler of the whole Roman Empire, combated Arianism and paganism within the empire. He convened (381) the First Council of Constantinople, which established the orthodox Christian teaching on the Trinity.

communicated him, and only public penance won the emperor forgiveness. Valentinian died in 392, and Theodosius soon began to assert his authority over the West. In 394, to suppress the pagan pretender Eugenius, he again invaded Italy and briefly reunified the empire. He died at Milan soon after, leaving the East to his elder son Arcadius and the West to his son Honorius. C. M. BRAND

Bibliography: Jones, A. H. M., *The Later Roman Empire, 284–602,* 2 vols. (1964); King, Noel Q., *The Emperor Theodosius and the Establishment of Christianity* (1961).

Theodosius II, Roman Emperor in the East

Ruler (408-50) of the eastern Roman Empire, Theodosius II, b. Apr. 10, 401, d. July 28, 450, was the son and successor of Arcadius. Theodosius, basically a scholar, tended to let others—including his sister Pulcheria (399-453) and his wife, Eudocia (d. 460)—influence state decisions. Despite this weakness, he inspired his generals to repel invading Persians in 421, 422, and 441. His administration was highlighted by the Council of Ephesus (431; see EPHESUS, COUNCIL OF) and publication of the Theodosian Code of laws (438). Theodosius was succeeded by Marcian (r. 450-57).

Theognis [thee-ahg'-nis]

Theognis of Megara, a Greek poet of the mid-6th century BC, is credited with about 1,400 lines in the elegiac meter. Conservative and pessimistic in tone, his poems lament the loss of aristocratic values and reflect on wealth, marriage, and the vicissitudes of friendship and poverty. CHARLES SEGAL

Bibliography: Allen, T. W., *Theognis* (1934); Bowra, C. M., *Early Greek Elegists* (1938; repr. 1969).

Theogony [thee-ahg'-uh-nee]

The *Theogony* (c.800 BC), by the poet HESIOD, is a genealogical account of the Greek divinities from the beginning of time and is the earliest Greek religious work. Without any plot, the poem moves chronologically through various generations, beginning with Chaos, Earth, and Eros. It then proceeds from the Titans, Cyclops, and Giants to the rule of Cronus, who swallows all his children out of fear; yet Zeus survives, and supplants him. The poem finally describes the creation of the other Olympian deities and the human offspring of divine parentage, such as Hercules, Achilles, and Aeneas. JAMES J. WILHELM

theological seminaries

A theological seminary is a professional school that trains Protestant ministers, Roman Catholic and Orthodox priests, and rabbis. Seminaries accept people who hold at least a bachelor's degree. Seminary curricula generally consist of history, theology, scripture, ethics, biblical languages, and subjects related to pastoral duties.

PROTESTANT SEMINARIES

Protestant seminaries, as separate professional schools, are largely a product of the 19th century, their greatest period of growth corresponding to the rise of denominationalism, from about 1820 to 1880. Prior to that time education for the ministry consisted of the usual collegiate curriculum followed by a brief apprenticeship with a clergyman.

Of the 109 accredited, predominantly Protestant seminaries in the United States and Canada, 20 are interdenominational schools. Seventeen of these seminaries are integral parts of universities. Since 1965 there has been a rapid growth in the cluster, or consortium-based, seminary, in which the member seminaries, sometimes both Protestant and Roman Catholic, share curricula, libraries, and other resources. The average Protestant seminary has an enrollment of about 250 men and women; a few have as many as 1,000 or more students. Student enrollment increased about 44 percent in the mid–1970s to a total of approximately 38,000, of which about 7,500 are women. The number of specialized courses for women and for blacks is increasing. A small number of seminaries currently have student bodies drawn from ethnic minorities.

Although most seminary students plan to be ordained, many enter a seminary in order to investigate such a life's work or to earn a degree in theological studies. After 3 to 4 years of study the degrees of B.D., Th.M., and D.Min. are awarded.

ROMAN CATHOLIC SEMINARIES

Although the first Roman Catholic seminaries in the United States were founded at the beginning of the 19th century, the period of most rapid expansion occurred from 1880 to 1910, with many dioceses establishing parish-oriented seminaries and with religious orders founding their own seminaries. There are 38 accredited Roman Catholic seminaries, some of which are associated with Protestant seminaries in cluster arrangements. Admission requires a degree from an accredited college, university, or collegiate seminary, plus sponsorship by the appropriate Ordinary. Although women are not eligible for ordination, about 750 women are enrolled in seminary degree programs. The 4-year course of study leads to the M.Div. or M.A. degree.

JEWISH SEMINARIES

Since the late 19th century each of the major traditions of Judaism has maintained a seminary. The seminary for Orthodox Judaism is part of Yeshiva University in New York City. About 75 students are enrolled in the 3-year course. The seminary for Conservative Judaism is The Jewish Theological Seminary, also in New York City, with about 100 students in a 6-year course of study. The seminary for Reformed Judaism is The Hebrew Union College–Jewish Institute of Religion in Cincinnati, Ohio, with about 200 students. At ordination all the seminaries confer the title of rabbi on the candidates, with an M.A. or a D.H.L. being conferred after 2 or 3 years of further study.

The largest professional association of seminaries is the Association of Theological Schools of the United States and Canada, which is composed of about 150 accredited and 50 associate institutions, for which it publishes a directory and factbook at regular intervals. WALTER WAGONER

Bibliography: Allen, Yorke, *A Seminary Survey* (1960); Niebuhr, H. Richard, and Williams, Daniel D., eds., *The Ministry in Historical Perspectives* (1956); Niebuhr, H. Richard, et al., *The Advancement of Theological Education* (1957); Pilch, Judah, ed., *A History of Jewish Education in America* (1969); Wagoner, Walter D., *The Seminary* (1966).

theology

The term *theology* is a compound of the Greek words *theos* ("god") and *logos* ("word," "discourse," "thought," "reason"). Theology may therefore be defined as reasoned discourse about God. In a strict sense theology considers only the existence and nature of divine being. In its wider and more usual sense, however, it may encompass the full range of the divine's relationships to the world and to humanity as well as the full variety of human responses to the divine. Although used more commonly of Western religions, the term may be applied to the systematic study and presentation of any religion.

The first to use the term was apparently the Greek philosopher Plato, for whom theology meant a rational conception of the divine as opposed to poetic myths about the gods. The subsequent Greek tradition of rational theology survived well into Christian times, and aspects of it have been influential in shaping various Jewish, Christian, and Islamic theologies.

In early Christianity, theology had a number of meanings. It referred, for instance, to the whole mystery of God, to particular teachings about God (for example, the doctrine of the Trinity), or to a stage in the mystical knowledge of God. In general, however, theology implied an understanding of God over and above simple belief in God. Only in the medieval period did theology become an academic field, or "science," in somewhat the modern sense. With the rise of medieval universities, theological faculties began to emerge, and theology itself came to be defined as a science like other sciences in the medieval curriculum. It proceeded from its own first principles, followed accepted canons of rational inquiry, and produced an organized body of knowledge in its own right.

Since the Middle Ages theology has included both academic and nonacademic forms of religious inquiry, often in tension with each other.

In the course of its history theology has been subdivided according to various patterns. One typical pattern distinguishes between historical, systematic, and philosophical theology. The first studies the content of a religious tradition; the second attempts comprehensive explanations and expositions of its doctrines; and the third investigates the philosophical presuppositions and implications of religious belief. Also important are moral theology, or ethics, which explores the moral dimensions of the religious life, and practical theology, which interprets the forms of worship, styles of organization, and modes of interpersonal relationship within religious communities.

Although different questions have preoccupied theologians at different times, certain topics have established themselves as basic to theological study. These include the basis for humans' knowledge of God, the being and attributes of God, the relation of God to the world and of the world to God, the modes of divine governance of human affairs, the source and character of human alienation from the divine, the manner of humanity's restoration to God, and the ultimate destiny of humankind. Such themes have been central throughout theology's history and continue to dominate theological reflection today.　　　　　　　WILLIAM S. BABCOCK

Bibliography: Ferre, Frederick, *Language, Logic, and God* (1961; repr. 1977); Harvey, Van, *A Handbook of Theological Terms* (1964); Schleiermacher, Friedrich, *Brief Outline on the Study of Theology*, trans. by Terrence N. Tice (1966); Smart, Ninian, *Reasons and Faiths* (1958).

Theophanes the Greek　[thee-ah'-fuh-neez]

Theophanes the Greek, a Byzantine painter active c.1340–c.1405, decorated churches, painted icons, and illuminated books with religious and secular scenes. In Constantinople alone, he painted 40 churches. Of these paintings and others in Galata and Chalcedon none survive, although their style is typified by works (c.1315) in the Church of SAINT SAVIOR IN THE CHORA. Theophanes was also highly active and influential in Russia, especially through his pupil Andrei RUBLEV. Theophanes was in Russia by at least 1378, when he painted the Church of the Transfiguration at Novgorod. A number of icons are attributed to him, but authorities disagree on which. Most agree, however, that the late-14th-century *Dormition of the Virgin* (Tretyakov Gallery, Moscow) is his work.　　　　　　　JOHN STEPHENS CRAWFORD

Bibliography: Talbot-Rice, David, *Byzantine Painting: The Last Phase* (1968); Talbot-Rice, Tamara, *A Concise History of Russian Art* (1967).

Theophrastus　[thee-oh-fras'-tuhs]

A Greek philosopher and scientist and Aristotle's most famous pupil, Theophrastus, c.371–c.286 BC, headed the PERIPATETICS following Aristotle. Although he criticized some basic Aristotelian positions, Theophrastus's works—few of which are extant—were primarily developments of those of Aristotle, with the emphasis on the empirical and scientific. Theophrastus's own scientific works, particularly those in botany, were highly influential. Theophrastus is also known for his *Doctrines of the Natural Philosophers*; for *Characters*, a satirical study of ethical types; and for his contributions to logic.

Bibliography: Ross, W. D., and Forbes, F. H., eds., *Theophrastus: Metaphysics* (1978).

theorbo　[thee-ohr'-boh]

An obsolete stringed instrument, the theorbo was the smaller of the archlutes, the other being the CHITARRONE. The theorbo was used from the late 16th century until the end of the 18th century and served principally as an accompanying instrument. Its strings were longer than those of the LUTE, often by as much as 35.5 cm (14 in), resulting in such widely spaced frets on the fingerboard that rapid performance was not possible. A second set of strings, parallel to the fingerboard, pro-

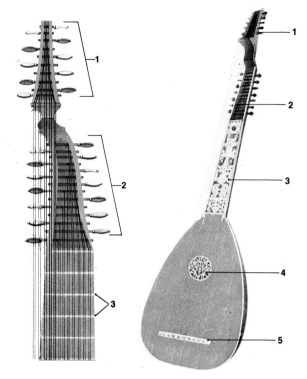

The theorbo, a bass lute popular from the 16th to 18th centuries, had an extra pegbox (1) with five pairs of bass strings and a main pegbox (2) with seven pairs of strings, all attached to a bridge (5). It had widely spaced frets (3) and a sound hole (4) in the form of a rose.

vided additional bass notes. These strings were strung from an offset pegbox and were beyond the reach of the player's left hand; consequently, each string could produce only a single pitch.　　　　　　　ELWYN A. WIENANDT

theoretical physics

Theoretical physics seeks to understand and describe, in the simplest way possible, the fundamental aspects of the observed physical world. It encompasses all attempts at a theoretical understanding of matter and its interactions, in the small and in the large, from the most minute constructs of quarks and gluons to the properties of massive stars and entire galaxies. The subject is vast and points in many directions, but there are common threads of understanding and technique that run through all its subdivisions.

Properly speaking, theoretical physics cannot exist without its twin discipline, experimental physics; theories become valid and observations become laws (see LAW, PHYSICAL) only when the conclusions drawn from them are repeatedly verified experimentally. This has been the custom in recent centuries, and as a result there now exists an extraordinary situation: it is possible to give fairly precise descriptions of almost all observed physical phenomena in terms of four FUNDAMENTAL INTERACTIONS and a few empirical conservation laws (see CONSERVATION, LAWS OF).

The natural language of physics, as of the other natural sciences, is mathematics, but mathematics considered as a tool rather than as an end in itself. Because physics is frequently concerned with the interaction of systems containing many subsystems—called systems with "many degrees of freedom"—much mathematical analysis is directed toward the approximate solution of a few basic relevant equations made complicated by their many degrees of freedom. Even relatively simple systems can interact in complicated ways, and approximations must be used in the mathematical description of them. In fact, one of the marks of a successful theory is that in effect it treats exactly, or to a very good approximation, the one or two degrees of freedom most important to the problem and approximates all the rest. Exact mathematical solutions are rare and are usually important as guideposts, suggesting the correct road for further development, rather than for any intrinsic value.

Idealization. Before the known laws and symmetries can be applied to a system, there must be a working definition of what constitutes that system. This is an important point, because physical systems are generally complex, comprising huge numbers of atoms or many degrees of freedom, or both. One must first specify the system by deciding which of its features are relevant to the problem at hand. For example, in studying the acceleration of gravity on freely falling objects the simplest system to consider is composed of the Earth, the objects, and the interaction between them. As velocities increase, the damping effects of air resistance must be included, giving a more complicated system but one that is necessary for this physical problem. If still more accuracy is desired, more complicated Coriolis forces could be included, together with the slight variation of gravitational acceleration with altitude.

Another example concerns the energy levels of atoms, which may be treated as isolated in situations of low density, so that the system becomes a single atom in possible interaction with the electromagnetic field. For high densities, the effect of neighboring atoms on the energy levels of each cannot be neglected, in which case the system must include the possibility that outer-shell electrons can skip from atom to atom. In each case, a certain idealization is necessary in order to define the appropriate system; part of the art of theoretical physics is to choose that idealization which most simply expresses the essential physics.

Laws and Symmetries. Experimentally, a few grand conservation laws have been found to hold for all systems, although these laws take different forms in different branches of physics. Conservation means that certain quantities such as electric charge, energy, mass, momentum, and angular momentum must remain unchanged during the motion of all components of the system. (Relativistically, mass and energy are related and need not obey separate conservation laws.) In the presence of "external potentials," these laws apparently can be violated, but if the system is enlarged to include the motion of those objects which define the external fields, the total quantities are again found to be rigorously conserved. In addition, there are certain conservation laws that need be only approximately conserved, such as isotopic spin in nuclear or particle physics, where there is conservation of a "strong" interaction current as long as weaker, electromagnetic effects are ignored.

In any problem, one must specify the applicable laws of motion, which form the expression of the essential physics. In classical systems (excluding general relativity), the relevant law is typically Newton's second law: force equals mass times acceleration. This statement takes different forms for discrete and continuous systems, and it may be formulated in a way that bears little resemblance to Newton's original statement. Classical electromagnetism is governed by MAXWELL'S EQUATIONS, again regardless of the form of this expression (which may be written so as to resemble a mechanical system). For quantum systems there is another and crucial addition—the UNCERTAINTY PRINCIPLE—that must be built into the basic method of description and computation.

Deduction and Inference. Although the language of physics is mathematics, which can profitably be used to describe classical and quantum systems, there is a deeper sense to the variety of description that lies at the heart of theoretical physics. The scientist searches for the quantities that contain the essence of the physical laws and are capable of reproducing a particular experimental result but that are also sufficiently general to be independent of that special experiment and applicable to many other situations. For example, the electrostatic flux passing through any closed surface (the product of electric field times area, summed over all points on the surface) is, experimentally, always proportional to the total charge enclosed by that surface; it makes no difference

whether the surface is a sphere or a cube or whether it is large or small. That experimental fact can be transformed into a statement that describes the generation of an electrostatic field **E** by a specified charge density (electric charge per unit volume) ρ: $\nabla \cdot \mathbf{E} = 4\pi\rho$. This relation is known as Gauss's Law and can be applied to many other situations involving charges and electrostatic fields. The scientist seeks to deduce from the particular experiment the most fundamental expression relating the physical quantities involved.

Not only is such deduction at the root of theoretical descriptions, but there is a rarer and more highly prized activity that might be termed inference. The mathematical expression of physical laws typically has, or should have, a certain symmetry or elegance; and there have been a few great occasions when aesthetic arguments have pointed the way toward a more correct version of a theory. Examples are Maxwell's inclusion of the electromagnetic "displacement current" on the grounds of symmetry rather than hard experiment and Einstein's formulation of his special and general theories of relativity. Out of these successful theoretical assumptions have come so many experimentally verified predictions that these theories are necessarily considered to be physically true. Needless to say, the number of such successful, aesthetically based or completed theories is very small.

The urge to theorize in this way has not slackened in recent years; it is currently almost a full-time occupation in unification attempts in elementary particle theory. One of the most persistent theoretical suggestions concerns the introduction of isolated magnetic poles, or monopoles, as would be suggested by analogy with electrostatics (see MONOPOLE, MAGNETIC). Another example concerns the introduction of a "local theory of gauge invariance" for the strong interactions by Chen Ning YANG and Robert L. Mills in 1954. It was written mainly for aesthetic reasons and lay virtually untouched for more than a decade, until it was invoked in attempts to understand the fundamental interactions, including the ELECTROWEAK THEORY. A final example is the theory of strings, developed in the 1960s, which treats fundamental particles as one-dimensional entities. SUPERSTRING THEORIES are very recent versions that attempt to reconcile all fundamental forces and particles.

H. M. FRIED

Bibliography: Constant, F. W., *Theoretical Physics: Mechanics* (1979); De Shalit, Amos, and Feshback, Herman, *Theoretical Nuclear Physics* (1974); Harris, Edward G., *Introduction to Modern Theoretical Physics*, 2 vols. (1975); Kompaneyets, Alexander, *Theoretical Physics* (1975); Landau, L. D., *A Shorter Course of Theoretical Physics* (1974); Slater, John C., and Frank, Nathaniel H., *Introduction to Theoretical Physics* (1933).

theosophy

The term *theosophy* is derived from the Greek *theos* ("god") and *sophia* ("wisdom") and means wisdom of or about God. In a general sense, theosophy refers to a broad spectrum of occult or mystical philosophies, often pantheistic in nature. The Western theosophical tradition may be said to be derived from the hermetic tradition of the Renaissance and post-Renaissance and is characterized by an emphasis on the hidden tradition passed down in a succession from the ancients. This tradition is thought to provide a universal key to nature and to humanity's role therein.

More specifically, the term refers to the Theosophical Society, its offshoots, and the doctrines held by its members. The most important early figure in the movement was Helena Petrovna BLAVATSKY, who, along with H. S. Olcott (1832–1907) and W. Q. Judge (1851-96), founded the society in 1875. In numerous works, including *Isis Unveiled* (2 vols., 1877) and *The Secret Doctrine* (2 vols., 1888), Blavatsky elaborated an amalgamation of previous theories that were claimed to be derived from the mahatmas of ancient India. The Theosophical Society grew rapidly in Europe and the United States, its two most influential adherents being Annie BESANT and Rudolf STEINER.

According to Madame Blavatsky, the doctrines of theosophy rest on three fundamental propositions. The first postulates an omnipresent, boundless, and immutable principle

Annie Besant, president (1907–33) of the Theosophical Society in Asia and Europe, was photographed (1923) in Bombay with Indian political leaders. Besant became involved with Indian nationalist politics while directing the society's activities at its Indian headquarters.

that transcends human understanding. It is the one unchanging reality, or infinite potentiality, inherent in all life and covers all that humans have tried to say about God. The second deals with the universality of the law of periodicity recorded by science as found in all nature. As morning, noon, and night are succeeded by morning again, so birth, youth, adulthood, and death are succeeded by rebirth. Reincarnation is the process of human development, in which all growth is governed by the law of justice or KARMA. The third proposition declares the fundamental identity of all souls with the universal Over-Soul, suggesting that brotherhood is a fact in nature, and the obligatory pilgrimage for every soul through numerous cycles of incarnation (see TRANSMIGRATION OF SOULS). Theosophy admits of no privileges or special gifts in humans except those won by their own effort and merit. Perfected individuals and great teachers, such as Buddha, Jesus, and the mahatmas, are universal beings, the flower of evolution.

After the death (1891) of Madame Blavatsky a battle for leadership of the society ensued, from which Annie Besant emerged as leader in Europe and Asia, whereas W. Q. Judge led a secessionist movement in the United States. Under Besant, the society flourished. In 1911 she put forward Jiddu KRISHNAMURTI as a World Teacher, around whom she founded the Order of the Star of India. This action seems to have provoked Steiner, who, with a large number of followers, left to found the Anthroposophical Society.

The various divisions and subdivisions have continued since that time and have influenced numerous literary and intellectual figures. The groups continue to carry on active meetings and publishing programs.

Bibliography: Ellwood, R., *Theosophy* (1986) and, as ed., *Eastern Spirituality in America* (1987); Moore, R. L., *In Search of White Crows: Spiritualism, Parapsychology, and American Culture* (1977); Webb, J., *The Occult Underground* (1974) and *The Occult Establishment* (1976).

Thera   [thee'-ruh]

Thera is the ancient name of the Cycladic island of Thíra (also called Santorini) in the southern Aegean; it has an active volcano. In the middle of the 2d millennium BC an eruption of the explosive type, like that which overwhelmed Pompeii, buried Thera's flourishing Bronze Age settlements beneath meters of pumice. Subsequent collapse of the magma chamber formed the impressive sea-filled caldera and left three small islands in place of the previous large one. The main island (present-day Thíra) was resettled before the end of the Bronze Age and was later (9th century BC) occupied by Dorian Greeks, who built their city on a limestone height to the east of the modern village of Akrotiri.

Thera's Bronze Age ruins were first explored in the 1860s and 1870s, while pumice was being quarried for use in building the Suez Canal. In 1967 excavation was resumed at the site of the chief Bronze Age town near Akrotiri. Many of the remarkably preserved buildings were adorned with spectacular wall paintings in a Cretan style, and great quantities of Minoan-style pottery have been found. Comparing the artifacts and ruins of Thera with those found at other Bronze Age sites, archaeologists have traditionally dated the destruction of Thera at about 1500 BC. But evidence from radiocarbon dating of plant remains on Thera, anomalies in the world dendrochronological (tree ring) record, and volcanic deposits buried in Greenland's ice sheets suggest that 1628 BC is a more accurate date. Due to the new evidence, archaeologists may have to redate some events relevant to Minoan culture. Considerable controversy also surrounds the speculations that the Greek legend of ATLANTIS may be linked to the cataclysmic destruction of Thera.   SINCLAIR HOOD

Bibliography: Doumas, C., ed., *Thera and the Aegean World* (1978; repr. 1982); Marinatos, Spyridon N., *Some Words about the Legend of Atlantis*, 2d ed. (1972), and *Excavations at Thera*, 7 vols. (1968–72); Page, Denys L., *The Santorini Volcano* (1970).

Theramenes   [thuh-ram'-uh-neez]

Theramenes, d. 404 BC, an Athenian politician active in the final stage of the Peloponnesian War, was a founding member of the Four Hundred, a conservative or oligarchic group that seized power in 411 BC. Breaking with it four months later, he helped to establish a more moderate group, the Five Thousand, but then endorsed the restoration of full democracy. He was active in the naval war against Sparta. After the Battle of Aegospotami, Theramenes negotiated peace in 404, became one of the Thirty Tyrants—a reactionary group then installed as the government—and shortly thereafter was condemned to death in a dispute with Critias, the most radical of the Thirty.
CHARLES W. FORNARA

therapsid: see MAMMAL; TRIASSIC PERIOD.

Theravada Buddhism: see BUDDHISM.

theremin   [thair'-uh-min]

The theremin, one of the first successful electronic musical instruments, was invented about 1924 by the Russian Leon Theremin. Pitches are controlled by the proximity of the player's right hand to the instrument; the left hand controls the volume. It is capable of playing only melodies. The theremin fell into disuse about the middle of the century, when the attention of composers was captured by the invention of more sophisticated electronic instruments (see ELECTRONIC MUSIC).
ELWYN A. WIENANDT

Thérèse, Saint   [tay-rez']

Saint Thérèse of Lisieux, b. Alençon, France, Jan. 2, 1873, d. Sept. 30, 1897, is one of the most popular saints of the Roman Catholic church. Born Thérèse Martin, one of nine children of a devout Catholic family, she entered the Carmelite convent at the age of 15. Nine years later she died of tuberculosis.

Her life was marked by its simplicity and goodness, and after her death her spiritual autobiography, *The Story of a Soul* (1898; Eng. trans., 1958), aroused great interest. Known as the "Little Flower of Jesus," she was canonized on May 17, 1925, and her shrine at Lisieux has become a major place of pilgrimage. Saint Thérèse is the patron of foreign missions—with Saint Francis Xavier—and of aviators. Feast day: Oct. 3.
JOAN A. RANGE

Bibliography: Clarke, John, *Saint Thérèse of Lisieux: General Correspondence* (1982); Ulanov, Barry, *The Making of a Modern Saint: A Biographical Study of Thérèse of Lisieux* (1966).

Thériault, Yves   [tay-ree-oh']

Yves Thériault, b. Quebec City, Nov. 28, 1915, is one of the most versatile of contemporary French Canadian authors. His first book (1944), a collection of short stories, has been followed by novels—notably *Agaguk* (1958), which won the Prix de la Province de Quebec and the Prix France-Canada—plays, a prose poem (1963), and children's stories.

thermal imaging: see NIGHT SIGHTS.

thermal pollution: see POLLUTION, ENVIRONMENTAL.

thermionic emission

Thermionic emission is the phenomenon by which electrons are emitted into a vacuum as a result of the thermal excitation of a metal or oxide-coated conductor. The cathode of an electron tube, for instance, is a thermionic emitter. Although thermionic emission can be observed in all metals, tungsten and tantalum are particularly efficient thermionic emitters. Rare-earth oxides of barium and strontium are also used.

Practical thermionic emitters may be heated directly or indirectly. A directly heated emitter may resemble the filament of an incandescent lamp; in fact, such a filament is itself a thermionic emitter. Indirectly heated thermionic emitters generally consist of an oxide-coated substrate placed in close proximity to a heater element. Thermionic emission may also be achieved by directing a beam of electrons against a suitable target.

Thermionic emission requires the presence of a vacuum. Efficient thermionic emitters should be sufficiently robust to withstand mechanical vibration and the effects of any residual gases in the evacuated envelope in which the emitter is contained. These constraints are more easily met by metal emitters, but oxide-coated emitters are more efficient at lower temperatures.

Thermionic emission is also known as the Edison effect, because Thomas A. Edison discovered (1883) the phenomenon while developing filaments for the electric light bulb.

FORRESTT M. MIMS III

Bibliography: Jenkins, R. O., and Trodden, W. C., *Electron and Ion Emission from Solids* (1965).

thermistor [thur'-mis-tur]

A thermistor is a small electronic component, made from a SEMICONDUCTOR (often manganese and nickel oxides), that changes its electrical resistance in response to temperature. Used to measure temperature electronically, it also serves to compensate for excessive power consumption by an electronic circuit by sensing the accompanying temperature increase and applying negative feedback; this feedback returns the circuit to a safe operating level (see RESISTOR).

FORRESTT M. MIMS III

Bibliography: Driscoll, Frederich F., and Coughlin, Robert F., *Solid State Devices and Applications* (1975).

thermochemistry

Thermochemistry is a branch of physical science that studies the energy changes that take place when a chemical reaction or phase change occurs. The energy change is usually caused by the breaking or forming of a chemical bond in a reaction, and the energy change is called the heat of the reaction. When a chemical bond is broken, energy is absorbed, and when a chemical bond forms, energy is given off. When a reaction liberates energy in the form of heat it is exothermic, and when it absorbs heat it is endothermic.

When the relationship between work and heat was investigated, it was shown that they were both forms of energy. The most important studies were conducted from 1840 to 1850 by James Prescott JOULE, who discovered that mechanical work could be converted to heat. Heat was measured in calories (a calorie, abbreviated cal, is defined as the amount of heat required to raise the temperature of one gram of water one Celsius degree), and the unit of work, formerly the newton-meter, has been renamed in Joule's honor. The two units are related in this way: 1 calorie = 4.184 joules. Joule also discovered that when energy apparently disappears it is actually converted to another form of energy. His work led to the law of conservation of energy, which states that energy can be neither created nor destroyed, but may be transformed from one form to another. This law is one way of stating the first law of thermodynamics and is the basis for the fundamental concepts of thermochemistry.

Heat of Reaction. The quantity of heat liberated or absorbed by substances undergoing reaction is called the heat of reaction. Experimental measurements can be done directly in a calorimeter. The change in heat is symbolized by ΔH and is given a negative sign if the reaction liberates energy (exothermic) or a positive sign if energy is absorbed (endothermic). For example, hydrogen burns in air to form water: $H_2(g) + \frac{1}{2}O_2(g) \rightarrow H_2O(l)$ $\Delta H = -68.32$ kcal.

The reaction is exothermic, yielding 68.32 kcal of heat per mole of hydrogen (or water). If the water were electrolyzed back into its elements, 68.32 kcal per mole would be absorbed.

Heat of Formation. When a compound is formed from its elements, the heat of reaction when one mole is formed is the molar heat of formation, ΔH_f. This quantity is a useful indicator of the stability of the compound. Most compounds have negative heats of formation, because energy was released in their formation.

Compounds with a high negative heat of formation are very stable. Those with a small heat of formation, positive or negative, are generally unstable. They often are easily decomposed or will react readily. If a compound has a large positive heat of formation, it may react violently or decompose explosively because of the large amounts of energy stored within it.

Heat of Combustion. The heat of combustion, ΔH_c, of a substance is the heat of reaction released by the complete combustion of one mole of a substance. The heat of combustion of hydrogen, for example, is the same as the heat of formation of water, -68.32 kcal. Combustion data for various fuels are important to engineers developing heat/energy systems.

HEAT OF FORMATION OF VARIOUS SUBSTANCES
(kilocalories per mole at 25° C)

Substance	Formula	ΔH_f
acetylene	C_2H_2	+54.19
ammonia	NH_3	−11.04
barium nitrate	$Ba(NO_3)_2$	−237.06
benzene	C_6H_6	+11.72
carbon (diamond)*	C	+0.45
copper sulfate	$CuSO_4$	−184.00
ethyl alcohol	C_2H_5OH	−66.36
hydrogen chloride	HCl	−22.06
mercury fulminate	$HgC_2N_2O_3$	+64.00
nitric acid	HNO_3	−41.40
ozone*	O_3	+34.00
sodium chloride	NaCl	−70.96
water	H_2O	−68.32

* The heat of formation of an element in its stablest form is 0.00. For carbon and oxygen these forms are graphite and O_2, respectively.

HEAT OF COMBUSTION OF VARIOUS SUBSTANCES
(kilocalories per mole at 25° C)

Substance	Formula	ΔH_c
hydrogen	H_2	−68.32
carbon (graphite)	C	−94.05
carbon monoxide	CO	−67.64
methyl alcohol	CH_3OH	−173.64
ethyl alcohol	C_2H_5OH	−326.68
propane	C_3H_8	−530.60
butane	C_4H_{10}	−678.98
octane	C_8H_{18}	−1,307.53
acetylene	C_2H_2	−310.62
propylene	C_3H_6	−491.99
benzene	C_6H_6	−780.98
toluene	$C_6H_5CH_3$	−934.50

Determination of Heat of Reaction. In order to calculate the heat of a reaction, or the change in enthalpy ΔH, the heat content of the reactants is determined and subtracted from the heat content of the products. Consider propane (C_3H_8) being burned in air to form water and carbon dioxide; the heat content of the substances are their heats of formation multiplied by the number of moles of each substance in the reaction

$$C_3H_8(g) + 5O_2(g) \rightarrow 3CO_2(g) + 4H_2O(1)$$

ΔH_f, kcal: -24.82 O -94.05 -68.32

$$\Delta H = 3(-94.05) + 4(-68.32) - (-24.82) = -530.61 \text{ kcal}$$

Other Thermochemical Values. The change in entropy, ΔS, for a reaction is equal to the entropy of the products minus the entropy of the reactants. For the above reaction, the values for the entropy of each substance can be found from thermodynamic tables and are, in cal/mole-degree: propane, 64.50; oxygen, 49.00; carbon dioxide, 51.06; and water, 16.72. Thus, ΔS for the combustion of propane is -89.44 cal/mole-degree.

Another property that can be determined for this reaction is the free-energy change. This quantity was first defined in 1875 by the American physicist Josiah Willard Gibbs as the amount of energy in a system that can be converted to useful work (at constant temperature and pressure). This amount may be calculated from the differences in the final and initial free energy of the substances or from $\Delta G = H - T\Delta S$, where T is the absolute temperature (25° C = 298K). In the example using propane, $\Delta G -530.61 - 298(-.08744) = -503.96$ kcal/mole. The significance of this result is that a large amount of work can be derived from the combustion of propane. In general, reactions that have a large, negative change in free energy are spontaneous; that is, they tend to occur without the addition of external CHEMICAL ENERGY.   WILLIAM H. NYCE

Bibliography: Cox, J. D., and Pilcher, G., *Thermochemistry of Organic and Organometallic Compounds* (1970); Ellis, A. J., and Mahon, W. A., eds., *Chemistry and Geothermal Systems* (1977); Ives, D. J., *Chemical Thermodynamics* (1971); Klotz, Irving M., and Rosenberg, R. M., *Chemical Thermodynamics*, 3d ed. (1972); Mortimer, C. T., and Ashcroft, S. J., *Thermochemistry of Transition Metal Complexes* (1970); Skinner, H. A., *Thermochemistry and Thermodynamics* (1976); Stull, Daniel R., and Sinke, Gerard C., eds., *Thermodynamic Properties of the Elements* (1956).

thermocline

A thermocline is a permanent or temporary boundary layer formed in oceans and lakes between warm and cold water masses. Little or no water moves through the thermocline, because water density changes with water temperature. The thickness of the thermocline varies with the season and with the latitude, and its permanence in any given body of water depends on these and other factors such as mixing processes within the water and meteorological processes affecting the water surface. Generally, during the fall (during monsoon season in tropical climates), deeper lakes undergo a mixing process that temporarily destroys the thermocline. The deepest thermocline in the world ocean is more or less symmetrical about the equator, with its upper surface from 100 to 700 m (300 to 2,300 ft) below the ocean surface, and ending about 55° N or S latitude. This thermocline is permanent in the sense that its changes do not depend on seasonal or shorter-period changes.

Bibliography: Strahler, Arthur N. and Alan H., *Environmental Geosciences: Interaction between Natural Systems and Man* (1973).

thermocouple

A thermocouple is a small electrical device used for measuring temperature. It consists of two wires of dissimilar metals joined together at their ends, forming two junctions. If the junctions are at different temperatures, a voltage will be produced that is approximately proportional to the temperature difference, a phenomenon discovered by the German physicist Thomas Seebeck (1770–1831). The voltage produced can be measured and used to determine the temperature at one junction if the other junction is kept at a known temperature (usually 0° C [32° F]).

Thermocouples can be made from various combinations of materials, depending on the temperature range that is to be measured. Plantinum and a platinum-rhodium alloy, chromel and alumel, and iron and constantan are some of the combinations commonly used. Some thermocouples can measure temperatures down to $-200°$ C ($-330°$ F), whereas others can operate at values as high as 1,800° C (3,200° F). Small temperature differences can be measured more accurately by using a thermopile, a device consisting of several thermocouples arranged in series. In a thermopile, the small voltage outputs of each element are added, thus permitting a greater response to a given temperature change than available with a thermocouple.   FRANK J. OLIVER

Bibliography: Kinzie, P. A., *Thermocouple Temperature Measurement* (1973).

See also: THERMOELECTRICITY.

thermodynamics

Thermodynamics is the branch of the physical sciences that studies the transfer of heat and the interconversion of heat and work in various physical and chemical processes. The word *thermodynamics* is derived from the Greek words *thermos* (heat) and *dynamis* (power). The study of thermodynamics is central to both chemistry and physics and is becoming increasingly important in understanding biological and geological processes.

There are several subdisciplines within this blend of chemistry and physics. These include: *classical thermodynamics*, which considers the transfer of energy and work in macroscopic systems—that is, without any consideration of the nature of the forces and interactions between individual (microscopic) particles; *statistical thermodynamics*, which considers microscopic behavior, describing energy relationships on the statistical behavior of large groups of individual atoms or molecules and relying heavily on the mathematical implications of quantum theory; and *chemical thermodynamics*, which focuses on energy transfer during chemical reactions and the work done by chemical systems (see PHYSICAL CHEMISTRY).

Thermodynamics is limited in its scope. It emphasizes the initial and the final state of a system (the system being all of the components that interact) and the path, or manner, by which the change takes place, but it provides no information concerning either the speed of the change or what occurs at the atomic and molecular levels during the course of the change.

DEVELOPMENT OF THERMODYNAMICS

The early studies of thermodynamics were motivated by the desire to derive useful work from heat energy. The first reaction turbine was described by Hero (or Heron) of Alexandria (AD c.120); it consisted of a pivoted copper sphere fitted with two bent nozzles and partially filled with water. When the sphere was heated over a fire, steam would escape from the nozzles and the sphere would rotate. The device was not designed to do useful work but was instead a curiosity, and the nature of HEAT AND HEAT TRANSFER at that time remained mere speculation.

The changes that occur when substances burn were initially accounted for, in the late 17th century, by proposing the existence of an invisible material substance called PHLOGISTON, which was supposedly lost when combustion took place.

In 1789, Antoine LAVOISIER prepared oxygen from mercuric oxide; in doing so he demonstrated the law of conservation of mass and thus overthrew the phlogiston theory. Lavoisier proposed that heat, which he called *caloric*, was an element, probably a weightless fluid surrounding the atoms of substances, and that this fluid could be removed during the course of a reaction. The observation that heat flowed from warmer to colder bodies when such bodies were placed in thermal contact was explained by proposing that particles of caloric repelled one another.

Somewhat simultaneous to these chemical advances, the

actual conversion of heat to useful work was progressing as well. At the end of the 17th century Thomas Savery invented a machine to pump water from a well, using steam and a system of tanks and hand-operated valves. Savery's pump is generally hailed as the first practical application of steam power. Thomas Newcomen developed Savery's invention into the first piston engine in 1712. The design of the steam-powered piston engine was further refined by James WATT during the last quarter of the 18th century.

Mechanical Equivalent of Heat. The downfall of the caloric theory was initiated by Sir Benjamin Thompson, Count Rumford. After spending his early years in America and England, Thompson became a minister of war and minister of police in Bavaria. In 1798, while overseeing the boring of cannon at the Munich Arsenal, Thompson noted that an apparently inexhaustible amount of heat was produced during the procedure. By having the cannon bored underwater, he found that a given quantity of water always required the same amount of time to come to a boil. If the caloric theory were correct, there would come a time when all of the caloric had been removed from the atoms of the cannon and no more heat would appear. Instead, Thompson interpreted his results as a demonstration that work was being converted into heat, just as the steam engines of his time converted heat into work. In 1799, Sir Humphry DAVY demonstrated that pieces of ice melt more rapidly when rubbed together, even in a vacuum. This provided additional support to the idea that work could be converted into heat.

A precise determination of the mechanical equivalent of heat was reported in 1849 by James JOULE. With the use of very precise homemade thermometers, Joule found that by stirring water (mechanical work input), its temperature was increased (heat output). His conversion factor of 0.241 calories of heat energy equaling one joule of work was based on the observation that to generate one calorie of heat, a 1-kg weight must fall through a distance of 42.4 cm (the work performed by the falling weight was used to mechanically stir the water).

Joule also electrically heated gases and measured the resulting pressure changes; he found similar results here on the interconversion of work and heat.

The First Law of Thermodynamics. The findings of Joule and others led Rudolf CLAUSIUS, a German physicist, to state in 1850 that "In any process, energy can be changed from one form to another (including heat and work), but it is never created or destroyed." This is the first law of thermodynamics. An adequate mathematical statement of this first law is $\Delta E = q - w$, where ΔE is the change (Δ) in internal energy (E) of the system, q is the heat added to the system (a negative value if heat is taken away), and w is work done by the system. In thermodynamic terms, a system is defined as a part of the total universe that is isolated from the rest of the universe by definite boundaries, such as the coffee in a covered Styrofoam cup; a closed room; a cylinder in an engine; or the human body. The internal energy, E, of such a system is a state function; this means that E is dependent only on the state of the system at a given time, and not on how the state was achieved.

If the system considered is a chemical system of fixed volume—for example, a substance in a sealed bulb—the system cannot do work (w) in the traditional sense, as could a piston expanding against an external pressure. If no other type of work (such as electrical) is done on or by the system, then $\Delta E = q_v$, which means that an increase in internal energy is equal to the amount of heat absorbed at constant volume (the subscript v indicates that the volume of the system remains constant throughout the process). If the heat is absorbed at constant pressure instead of constant volume (which can occur to any unenclosed system), the increase in the energy of the system is represented by the state function, H, which is closely related to the internal energy. Changes in H (heat content) are called changes in ENTHALPY, and $\Delta H = q_p$, where the subscript p indicates constant pressure.

In 1840, before Joule had made his determinations of the mechanical equivalent of heat, Germain Henri Hess reported the results of experiments that indicated that the heat evolved or absorbed in a given chemical reaction (ΔH) is independent of the particular manner (or path) in which the reaction takes place. This generalization is now known as HESS'S LAW and is one of the basic postulates of THERMOCHEMISTRY.

The Second Law of Thermodynamics. The steam engine developed by James Watt in 1769 was a type of heat engine, a device that withdraws heat from a heat source, converts some of this heat into useful work, and transfers the remainder of the heat to a cooler reservoir. A major advance in the understanding of the heat engine was provided in 1824 by N. L. Sadi Carnot, a French engineer, in his discussion of the cyclic nature of the heat engine. This theoretical approach is known as the CARNOT CYCLE.

A result of the analysis of the heat engine in terms of the Carnot cycle is the second law of thermodynamics, which may be stated in a variety of ways. According to Rudolf Clausius, "It is impossible for a self-acting machine, unaided by external agency, to convey heat from a body at one temperature to another body at a higher temperature." William Thomson (Lord KELVIN), a British thermodynamicist, proposed that "it is impossible by a cyclic process to take heat from a reservoir and convert it into work without, in the same operation, transferring heat from a hot to a cold reservoir."

Entropy. The second law of thermodynamics leads to a new state function S, the ENTROPY of a system. The increase in the entropy of a system when heat is added to it must be at least q/T, where q is the added heat and T is the absolute temperature. If the heat is added in an idealized (reversible) process, $\Delta S = q/T$, but for real (irreversible) processes, the entropy change is always greater than this value.

Ludwig BOLTZMANN, an Austrian physicist, demonstrated the significance of entropy on the molecular level in 1877, relating entropy to disorder. J. Willard GIBBS, an American mathematical physicist, referred to entropy as a measure of the "mixed-upedness" of the system.

The second law of thermodynamics may also be stated in terms of entropy: in a spontaneous irreversible process, the total entropy of the system and its surroundings always increases; for any process, the total entropy of a system and its surroundings never decreases.

The Third Law of Thermodynamics. Entropy as a measure of disorder is a function of temperature, increasing temperature resulting in an increase in entropy (positive ΔS). The third law of thermodynamics considers perfect order, and it states that the entropy of a perfect crystal is zero only at ABSOLUTE ZERO. This reference point allows absolute entropy values to be expressed for compounds at temperatures above absolute zero.

EQUILIBRIUM AND FREE ENERGY

While thermodynamics does not deal with the speed of a chemical reaction, the driving force (or spontaneity) of a chemical reaction is a thermodynamic consideration. A reaction is said to be spontaneous if the reactants and the products of a chemical reaction are mixed together under carefully specified conditions and the quantity of the products increases while the quantity of reactants decreases.

The spontaneity (or, less precisely, the direction) of a chemical reaction may be predicted by an evaluation of thermodynamic functions. Marcellin Berthelot, a French thermodynamicist, and Julius Thomsen, a Danish thermodynamicist, proposed in 1878 that every chemical change proceeds in such a direction that it will produce the most heat; in other words, all spontaneous reactions are those that result in a decrease in enthalpy, H, and are thus exothermic. This statement is incorrect, for many exceptions are known in which chemical reactions are spontaneous (proceed to more products than reactants) even though they are endothermic reactions (result in an increase in enthalpy).

The Gibbs Free Energy Function. Chemical reactions always occur in a direction (at constant temperature and pressure) that results in a decrease in the free energy of the system. The free energy of the system, G, is also a state function. (Several years ago free energy was designated by the symbol

F, but it is now called Gibbs free energy for its discoverer, J. Willard Gibbs, and is given the symbol *G*.) The free energy is defined by $G = H - TS$; and, at constant temperature, $\Delta G = \Delta H - T\Delta S$. A reaction is spontaneous if ΔG is negative, that is, if the reaction proceeds to a state of lower free energy. A negative ΔG may be the result of a negative ΔH (an exothermic reaction) and/or a positive $T\Delta S$ (the absolute temperature multiplied by a positive ΔS), indicative of an increase in entropy (or disorder) of the system. Spontaneous chemical reactions will continue until the minimum of free energy for the system is reached, so that, with reference to further reaction, $\Delta G = 0$. At this point a dynamic equilibrium is reached in the system (see CHEMICAL KINETICS AND EQUILIBRIUM). As long as the reaction conditions remain unchanged, no macroscopic change will be noted in the system; there will be no further change in the amounts of reactants and products even though, microscopically, the chemical reactions continue, because the reactants are being formed at the same rate as the products. Equilibrium, in a thermodynamic sense, is defined by $\Delta G = 0$.

Oxidation-Reduction Reactions. An efficient conversion of energy into work is accomplished by electrochemical cells (see ELECTROCHEMISTRY). An oxidation-reduction reaction takes place spontaneously in such an arrangement that the free energy released is converted into electrical energy. Nonspontaneous oxidation-reduction reactions (reactions with a positive value of ΔG) can be caused to occur by doing work on the system by means of an external energy source (usually a DC electrical power supply). This process, which causes oxidation-reduction reactions to proceed in the reverse direction from that which would have been spontaneous, is called ELECTROLYSIS and was developed by Michael FARADAY in 1833.

CHANGES IN STATE

Thermodynamics also studies changes in physical state, such as solid ice becoming liquid water. At temperatures above 0° C and at atmospheric pressure, ice spontaneously melts, an endothermic reaction (positive ΔH) that is driven by a positive ΔS; that is, liquid water is much more disordered than solid water. At 0° C and atmospheric pressure, solid ice and liquid water exist in PHASE EQUILIBRIUM ($\Delta G = 0$). In 1876, Gibbs established a relationship between the number of phases present in a system, the number of components, and the number of degrees of freedom (the number of variables such as temperature and pressure), the values of which must be specified in order to characterize the system.

A phase may be considered a homogeneous region of matter separated from other homogeneous regions by phase boundaries. For a pure substance, three phases are generally considered: solid, liquid, and vapor. Other types of phases exist, such as the two solid crystalline forms of carbon (graphite and diamond), and the ionized gaseous phase of matter known as plasma (see PLASMA PHYSICS).

If a sample of a pure substance is a solid, and heat (*q*) is added to the substance, the temperature (*T*) will increase, indicating an increase in the heat content (*H*). The temperature of the solid will continue to increase until the solid begins to melt, at which point the two phases, solid and liquid, coexist in equilibrium ($\Delta G = 0$). This is the melting point and is reported at atmospheric pressure. The heat necessary to convert one mole of a solid substance into one mole of its liquid form is the molar heat of fusion (ΔH_f).

After the solid has been converted to liquid, additional input of heat into the system will cause an increase in temperature until the liquid and the gaseous form of the substance coexist in equilibrium at atmospheric pressure. This temperature is called the boiling point. The heat necessary to convert one mole of a liquid substance into one mole of its gaseous form is the molar heat of vaporization (ΔH_v). The one set of conditions (temperature and pressure, in the above example) at which the solid, liquid, and gas may coexist in equilibrium is called the *triple point*. (See also CRITICAL CONSTANTS.)

A liquid-gas equilibrium may exist at a number of different temperatures. In 1834 the French engineer B. P. E. Clapeyron carried out studies on liquids and gases, later refined by Clausius. The relationship between the equilibrium vapor pressures of a liquid, its temperature, and its molar heat of vaporization is now called the Clausius-Clapeyron equation.

EQUATION OF STATE

Experimental measurements on solids, liquids, and gases have indicated that the volume (*V*) occupied by a substance is dependent on the absolute temperature (*T*), the pressure (*P*), and the amount of the substance, usually expressed in moles (*n*). If three of these properties are known, the fourth is fixed by a relationship called an equation of state. The equation of state for a gas is $PV = nRT$, where *R* is a proportionality constant in appropriate units (see GAS LAWS). Gases that obey this equation are called ideal gases. The equation is obeyed by real systems when the distances between the particles of the gas are large (high *V* and *T*, low *P* and *n*). Under this condition the volume occupied by the gas molecules or atoms is small compared to the total volume, and the attractive and repulsive forces between the atoms and molecules are negligible. Real gases (as opposed to ideal gases) frequently show deviations from ideal behavior; in 1873, Johannes D. van der Waals proposed a modification of this equation to correct for nonideal behavior. An extreme would be that the product of the gas's pressure and volume is predicted to be zero at absolute zero. In fact any gas will liquefy at low temperature, and the equation of state of a gas would no longer apply.

The nonideal behavior of gases has an important thermodynamic consequence. If an ideal gas is allowed to pass through an orifice from a region of higher pressure to one of lower pressure, no heat is evolved or absorbed, no change in internal energy has taken place, and therefore there is no change in temperature. Real gases, however, behave differently. All real gases, except for hydrogen and helium, cool when expanded in this fashion. If no heat is transferred (an ADIABATIC PROCESS, or one in which $q = 0$), the internal energy of the system decreases because of the work done by the system in decreasing the attractive forces between the gas molecules. This phenomenon is called the Joule-Thomson effect and has significance in such areas as refrigeration, the liquefaction of gases, and artificial snow production.

THE ULTIMATE SOURCE OF ENERGY

The first law of thermodynamics has been called the law of conservation of energy. Lavoisier stated also the law of conservation of mass at the end of the 18th century. Relativity physics has demonstrated that the real conservation law is one combined of these two, and that matter and energy may be interconverted according to Einstein's equation $E = mc^2$, where *E* is energy in ergs, *m* is the mass in grams, and *c* is the speed of light in centimeters per second. All energy ultimately originates from the conversion of mass into energy. In the burning of gasoline, the mass of the combustion products is slightly less than the mass of the reactants by an amount precisely proportional to the amount of energy (heat) produced. Some of this heat may be converted into useful work and some must be lost. Nuclear power uses nuclear reactions as a source of heat to power heat engines (turbines), which convert this heat energy into other energy forms (for example, electricity). In nuclear reactions, substantially more mass is converted into energy; thus, far less fuel is required to provide an equivalent amount of energy. As always, the goal is the efficient conversion of this heat into work.

STATISTICAL THERMODYNAMICS

The major concern of thermodynamics is the state functions and the properties of the macroscopic system. Statistical thermodynamics deals with the distribution of the various atoms and molecules that make up the system and with the energy levels of these particles. The second law of thermodynamics on the atomic and molecular level is a statistical law; it expresses a tendency toward randomness and disorder in a system having a large number of particles. Statistical thermodynamics uses probability functions and complex mathematical methods to express thermodynamic functions in accord with the KINETIC THEORY OF MATTER.   NORMAN V. DUFFY

Bibliography: Adkins, Clement J., *Equilibrium Thermodynamics*, 3d ed. (1984); Andrews, Frank C., *Thermodynamics: Principles and Applications* (1971); Dickerson, Richard E., et al., *Chemical Principles* (1974); Fermi, Enrico, *Thermodynamics* (1937); Hatsopoulos, George

N., and Keenan, Joseph H., *Principles of General Thermodynamics* (1965; repr. 1981); Moore, Walter J., *Basic Physical Chemistry* (1983); Mott-Smith, Morton, *The Concept of Energy Simply Explained* (1934); Sonntag, Richard E., and Van Wylen, Gordon J., *Introduction to Thermodynamics: Classical and Statistical*, 2d ed. (1982); Sussman, M. V., *Elementary General Thermodynamics* (1972); Zemansky, M. W., and Dittman, Richard, *Heat and Thermodynamics,* 6th ed. (1981).

thermoelectricity

Thermoelectricity is electricity generated by the direct action of heat. The subject also includes the study of heat generated by electricity, but not in the usual manner (Joule heating); the effects are the result of interactions between mobile electric charges and thermal conditions. Thermoelectric effects occur in liquids and solids, which may be metals, semimetals, semiconductors, or ionic conductors. None of the major thermoelectric effects have been found in insulators or superconductors. The three major thermoelectric effects are the Seebeck effect, the Peltier effect, and the Thomson effect.

Seebeck Effect. If a homogeneous material having mobile charges has temperature T_1 at one end and T_2 at the other end while it is in an open circuit, then a difference in electric voltage will occur between the two ends. This voltage is directly proportional to the temperature difference $T_1 - T_2$. If the material is homogeneous, the voltage will depend only on T_1 and T_2 and will be independent of the detailed temperature conditions between the two ends (law of Magnus).

The existence of a voltage difference caused by a temperature difference was first reported to the Prussian Academy of Sciences by Thomas Seebeck in 1822. Seebeck failed to understand the basic nature of his discovery, because in subsequent experiments he used closed circuits of two dissimilar materials and claimed that the resulting deflections of nearby magnetic-compass needles proved that heat currents produce the same effect as electric currents. OHM'S LAW, stated in 1827, showed that Seebeck's use of closed circuits had inadvertently produced electric currents.

Peltier Effect. Unlike the Seebeck effect, which occurs in a single material in the presence of a temperature difference without an electric current, the Peltier effect only occurs at the junction of two dissimilar materials when electric current flows. Heat, called the Peltier heat, is either emitted or absorbed at the junction, depending on the direction of current flow. This effect was discovered by the French physicist Jean C. A. Peltier in 1834. Once again the basic nature of the effect was misunderstood; Peltier believed that he had discovered a violation of Ohm's law. In 1838, Heinrich Lenz demonstrated the true nature of this effect when he used a bismuth-antimony junction and froze a drop of water when passing electric current in one direction (absorbing heat) and then melted the drop by reversing the current (emitting heat).

Thomson Effect. In 1854, William Thomson (later to become Lord KELVIN for his contributions in laying the first transatlantic cable) used thermodynamic arguments to relate the Peltier and Seebeck effects. In the process he predicted a third effect—namely, that an electric current flowing through a homogeneous material that also has a temperature difference will cause the emission or absorption of heat in the body of the material. The direction of the electric current relative to the sense of the temperature difference (that is, flowing toward higher or lower temperature) determines whether heat is emitted or absorbed. This effect was subsequently discovered and called the Thomson effect.

Principle. The Seebeck and Peltier effects readily lend themselves to qualitative description. Temperature differences produce a force of diffusion that causes the mobile charges to deviate from a uniform distribution. This redistribution causes electric forces. The final result is a steady-state situation where diffusive and electric forces balance each other and thus cause no net motion (no electric current) but have effected a nonuniform distribution of the mobile charges. This distribution is related to the temperature difference and causes the Seebeck voltage. In the Peltier effect a net motion exists, and thus the charges transport energy. The energy associated with each charge differs in the two materials. When a charge moves from one material to the other, at the junction it emits or absorbs this difference in energy and causes the Peltier effect. The Thomson effect is too subtle for such a qualitative description.

Uses. Thermoelectricity is practically applied in two general areas—the use of thermal energy to generate electric energy, and the use of electric energy for heating or refrigeration.

Electrical generation is based on the Seebeck effect. Metals show small Seebeck effects, but material properties dictate their use in thermometers. The thermocouple, an open circuit using two dissimilar metals, is a widely used thermometer.

Semiconductors show much larger Seebeck effects, and they are commonly used to generate electric power. Because any source of the heat energy is acceptable, a variety of methods are in use: heat from kerosene lamps and firewood (in remote areas of the Soviet Union), heat from nuclear decays (in space and in floating weather stations), and heat from direct sunlight (in space) have all been combined with semiconductors to generate electric power ranging from a few watts up to several hundred watts.

The Peltier effect is used in refrigeration and heating; a modern single-stage Peltier cooler can reduce temperatures to nearly 70 C degrees (125 F degrees) below room temperature. In comparison to more conventional systems, Peltier coolers have the advantages of very local heat transfer (occurring only at the junction) and no moving parts; they also have the disadvantages of lower efficiencies and higher costs.

Numerous special circumstances have justified the use of a Peltier cooler. Important factors are its durability, resulting from the absence of moving parts, and its versatility—by reversing the current direction, it can be changed from a cooling to a heating system. A number of electronic systems require very local cooling or heating to obtain optimum performance; Peltier systems are ideal in these instances and have been used with transistors, lasers, microwave amplifiers, and light detectors. Peltier coolers have also been used to maintain biological samples during periods of storage and transfer. The largest Peltier-effect systems built so far are air conditioners used on U.S. Navy submarines. C. L. FOILES

Bibliography: Barnard, R. D., *Thermoelectricity in Metals and Alloys* (1973); Blatt, Frank J., et al., *Thermoelectric Power of Metals* (1976); Goldsmid, H. J., *Applications of Thermoelectricity* (1960); Harman, T. C., and Honig, H. M., *Thermoelectric and Thermomagnetic Effects and Applications* (1967).

thermography (medicine)

Thermography, in medicine, is the measurement of thermal radiation, or heat, given off by the human body. The amount emitted depends on several factors, including state of health; in addition, some body areas have a larger blood supply than others and therefore emit more heat. The devices used to measure these temperature differences produce electronic signals on an oscilloscope, which can then be photographed on special film or projected onto a television monitor. The image produced is called a thermogram.

Inflammatory diseases can be diagnosed with thermography, because arthritic conditions, bone tumors and bone infections such as osteomyelitis, and muscle and tendon diseases resulting from inflammation produce heat radiation. Blockages of blood vessels also can be detected, because areas of reduced blood flow produce "cold spots" on a thermogram. Disorders such as atherosclerosis, which causes decreased circulation to the hands and feet, can therefore be detected in this way. (Interestingly, cigarette smoking also lowers heat emission from the fingers; circulation does not return to normal for about 1½ hours after a single cigarette, as revealed on a thermogram.) Nerve injury produces cold spots as well, and thermography has proved useful in diagnosing some spine injuries that produce pain and disability but that appear normal according to other tests. Thermography, however, is no longer considered useful for detecting BREAST cancer, because benign conditions such as cysts also produce extra heat and because many women with no breast disease at all have also given false positive readings. WILLIAM A. CHECK

thermography (printing)

Thermography (meaning "heated printing"), a means of raised-letter printing that simulates engraved printing at considerably less cost, is used to create special effects for printing letterheads, invitations, greeting cards, and other such purposes. In thermography, special oily, slow-drying inks are used for printing conventionally by letterpress or lithography; the wet inks are then dusted with a fusible powdered compound, and excess powder is removed from the nonprinting areas by suction. The sheet is then passed under a heater that fuses the ink and powder. Another type of ink contains an agent that expands when exposed to heat. This process is not to be confused with a copying process of the same name (see COPYING MACHINE).   MICHAEL H. BRUNO

thermoluminescence: see LUMINESCENCE.

thermometer

The thermometer, a device for measuring TEMPERATURE, is used in many forms, basically divided into mechanical and electri-

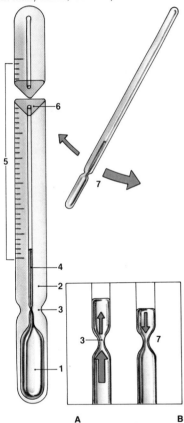

(Left) *A clinical, or fever, thermometer consists of a bulb of mercury (1) in a glass stem (2). Body heat causes the mercury to expand through a constriction (3) into a capillary tube (4), where it is measured against a scale (5). The shape of the glass (6) acts as a magnifying lens to facilitate reading. Surface tension at the constriction keeps the mercury at its highest reading until shaken down by hand (7). (Below) A minimum and maximum thermometer (A) utilizes changes in the volume of a liquid (1) inside a U-shaped tube. When the temperature falls (B), the liquid contracts, displacing a column of mercury (2) upward. A rise in temperature (C) causes expansion of the liquid and upward displacement of the mercury at right. Steel indicators (3) pushed by the mercury mark the readings.*

cal types. The best-known mechanical type is the liquid-in-glass thermometer, and an important electrical type is the resistance thermometer. To cover the full range of temperature measurement, from near absolute zero to thousands of degrees, other instruments are also used, such as the BOLOMETER, PYROMETER, thermocouple, and thermopile.

The liquid-in-glass thermometer consists of a small bulb reservoir and a calibrated fine-bore capillary tube. The liquid in the bulb rises or falls in the tube as it expands or contracts in response to temperature changes. The height of the column is measured against the markings on the tube. Mercury is the preferred liquid in quality thermometers; it freezes at $-38.9°$ C $(-38°$ F) and boils at $357°$ C $(675°$ F). The accuracy of industrial mercury thermometers is 1% of the column. Other liquids used are dye-colored alcohol, toluene, and pentane, the last with a freezing point of $-200°$ C $(-328°$ F).

A second type of liquid-expansion thermometer consists of a liquid-filled metal bulb and capillary tube attached to either a spiral tube or a bellows. As the temperature of the bulb changes, the pressure or the volume of the liquid changes, moving an indicator across a scale.

A typical gas or vapor thermometer similarly consists of a bulb and a capillary tube connected to a pressure-measuring device. The gas thermometer is simple, rugged, and accurate and has a wide response. Vapor-pressure thermometers respond to the pressure exerted by saturated vapor in equilibrium with a volatile liquid. It is similar to the gas thermometer in construction. The principal advantage of the vapor-pressure type is the large change in pressure obtained for small temperature changes, resulting in high sensitivity.

Electrical resistance thermometers operate on the principle that the resistivity of most metals increases with increased temperature. This principle was discovered in 1821 by Sir Humphry Davy, but this phenomenon was not used until the construction of a platinum resistance thermometer in 1861 by the German engineer Ernst W. von Siemens. In 1886 the British physicist Hugh L. Callendar proposed this thermometer as a new standard of accuracy in temperature measurement. Today the U.S. National Bureau of Standards uses high-precision platinum resistance thermometers, accurate to $0.001°$ C, to define the key points on the International Practical Temperature Scale, established in 1968. Both copper-wire and nickel-wire resistance thermometers are much lower in cost than platinum and have a precision of $0.05°$ C. In the range of $10°$ to $2°$ above absolute zero, impurity-doped germanium resistance thermometers are used, calibrated against the temperature of liquid helium.   FRANK J. OLIVER

A bimetallic strip thermometer (A) registers temperature changes based on the difference in expansion rates of two metals. The thermometer's indicator (1) is connected to a coiled metal helix (2) consisting of two lengths of copper and invar, which is a nickel-iron alloy, bonded together. As the temperature rises (B), the copper expands more rapidly than the invar. The helix then unwinds (3), which causes the indicator to move along the scale.

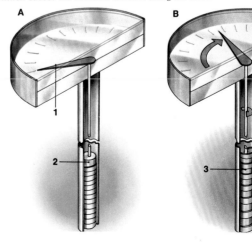

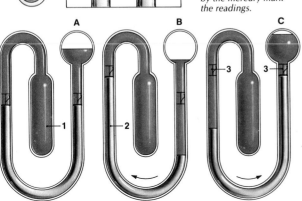

THESEUS 167

Bibliography: Benedict, Robert P., *Fundamentals of Temperature, Pressure, and Flow Measurements*, 2d ed. (1977); Doyle, F. E., and Byrom, G. T., *Instrumentation: Temperature* (1970); Middleton, W. E. Knowles, *A History of the Thermometer and Its Use in Meteorology* (1966).

thermonuclear reaction: see FUSION, NUCLEAR; FUSION ENERGY; HYDROGEN BOMB.

Thermopylae   [thur-mahp'-uh-lee]

Thermopylae is a pass in Greece lying between Mount Oeta and the Gulf of Malia's southern shore. Because of its strategic importance on the route from Thessaly to Locris, it was the site of three notable ancient battles. In 480 BC the Spartans under LEONIDAS heroically defended Thermopylae against Xerxes' Persians; in 279 BC the Greeks blocked the Gauls under Brennus for months; and in 191 BC, ANTIOCHUS III of Syria tried in vain to hold the pass against the Romans.

thermosphere

The thermosphere is the highest and largest of the four atmospheric layers (see ATMOSPHERE). It extends from the mesopause (about 80 km/50 mi above sea level), where the average temperature is a low of about −80° C (−112° F), to the thermopause (about 600 km/375 mi above sea level), where the temperature may reach highs of 225° C (440° F) at night during a period of minimum solar activity, and 1,475° C (2,690° F) in the daytime during a period of maximum solar activity. The upper part of the thermosphere is warm, because it readily absorbs solar ultraviolet radiation. The thermosphere is the only heterogeneous atmospheric layer. Vertical mixing takes place in the homosphere, the lowest 80 km (50 mi) of the thermosphere. Above the homosphere, however, position changes drastically, with gravity pulling the heavier gases (oxygen and nitrogen) toward the bottom of the thermosphere and consequently making helium and hydrogen the predominant particles in the top.   WILLEM VAN DER BIJL

thermostat

A thermostat is an electromechanical on/off switch that is activated by temperature changes. It is typically used to control a heating or cooling system. The sensing element is usually a spiral bimetallic strip that coils and uncoils in response to temperature changes because of differential expansion of the two bonded metals. The switch element is either a set of electrical contacts or a glass-encapsulated mercury switch that controls a low-voltage relay. The relay can actuate a motor starter and igniter for an oil burner, a heavy-duty switch for

The thermostat in an electric air conditioner (A) is operated by a bimetallic strip (1) that responds to changes in room temperature. The strip is welded from two metals that have different coefficients of thermal expansion. When the temperature rises (B), the outer metal expands faster than the inner one, causing the strip to bend toward a fixed contact (2). The connection completes an electric circuit that starts the air conditioner's motor. The distance between the contacts can be adjusted (C) to change the minimum operational temperature.

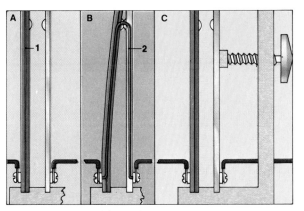

electrical units, or a solenoid-operated valve on a gas furnace. The thermostat may also control a house-type air conditioner or heat pump.   FRANK J. OLIVER

Theroux, Paul

Among the most popular of contemporary writers, Paul Theroux, b. Medford, Mass., Apr. 10, 1941, is also one of the most prolific, basing much of his work on his long experience as an expatriate and traveler. Theroux's early career as a teacher in Malawi, Uganda, and Singapore gave him the background for many of his early novels—*Girls At Play* (1969), *Jungle Lovers* (1971), *Saint Jack* (1973; film, 1979), among others. The highly successful *Mosquito Coast* (1982; film, 1986) focuses on the American self-help tradition gone berserk in a tropical jungle. *O-Zone* (1986) is an apocalyptic novel of an A-bombed future. Theroux's nonfiction includes several books based on railroad expeditions (such as *The Great Railway Bazaar: By Train through Asia*, 1975). *The Kingdom by the Sea* (1985) is a rather bitter account of his journey on foot around Great Britain.

Theroux's older brother, Alexander, b. Aug. 17, 1939, is also a talented writer who has published novels (*Three Wogs*, 1972; *Darconville's Cat*, 1981) and several books for children.

thesaurus   [thuh-saw'-ruhs]

A thesaurus, from the Greek for "storehouse" or "treasure," is a catalog of words and phrases designed to facilitate literary composition. Like a dictionary of synonyms, it groups related words together, but unlike such a dictionary it is arranged conceptually, with entries organized without regard to spelling. These headings are further divided according to meaning and parts of speech, so that the word *biased*, for example, might be found under the category "obliquity" (grouped with the related adjectives *leaning, beveled,* and *sloped*) and also under "narrow-mindedness" (along with *prejudiced, one-sided,* and *partial*). An alphabetical index lists entries.

The British cleric John Wilkins brought out a "conceptual dictionary," with tables, as early as 1668. The first successful example, however, was devised by Peter Mark Roget (1779–1869), a British physician who produced his *Thesaurus of English Words and Phrases* in 1852. Today, revised editions of *Roget's International Thesaurus* remain the standard by which other thesauri are judged.

Theseus   [thee'-see-uhs]

In Greek mythology Theseus was usually regarded as the hero who organized Athens into a city, became its first true king, and set it upon the path of civilization. The son of either Aegeus, king of Athens, or Poseidon and Aethra, Theseus was born and grew up in Troezen, in Argolis. On his way to Athens to claim his patrimony, he performed six labors; all but one involved killing robbers and murderers by their own methods. At last, Theseus arrived in Athens and was greeted by his father Aegeus and his stepmother MEDEA. Jealous of his influence over Aegeus, Medea tried to kill Theseus by sending him to rid the plain of Marathon of a wild bull; once Theseus had sacrificed the bull to Apollo, Medea tried to poison him. Aegeus saw through her plot, and Medea escaped to Asia.

Further adventures of Theseus were killing the MINOTAUR in Crete with the aid of ARIADNE, whom he loved and later deserted at Naxos; becoming king of Athens upon the death of Aegeus and uniting the Attic communities into a single state; assisting OEDIPUS in his last, blind days; warring against the AMAZONS and abducting their queen, Hippolyta (or Antiope), by whom he had a son HIPPOLYTUS; trying to kidnap PERSEPHONE from the underworld, for which Hades punished him by chaining him to a bench (Theseus was eventually rescued by Hercules); and marrying Phaedra, Ariadne's sister, who made improper advances toward Hippolytus and who, after falsely accusing Hippolytus, hanged herself. Banished from Athens after a descendant of an old king of Athens stirred up a conspiracy against him, Theseus went to Skyros, where King Lycomedes pushed him off a cliff to his death.

Later, Cimon of Athens recovered the body of Theseus and reburied it in Athens. Many other deeds were ascribed to Theseus, several of them paralleling feats of Hercules, such as participating in the voyage of the Argonauts and the Calydonian boar hunt. Theseus was also credited with founding the Isthmian Games, held every 2 years in Corinth, in honor of the god Poseidon.   ROBERT E. WOLVERTON

Thespis   [thes'-pis]

Thespis (fl. 6th century BC) was an Attic poet traditionally regarded as the founder of Greek tragedy. Hardly anything is known of him, but he is believed to have introduced the role of an actor—separate from those of the chorus and chorus leader, which modified dithyrambic performance (exchanges between chorus and leader) by instituting spoken dialogue and thus inventing the drama. The word *thespian* (actor) is derived from his name.

Thessalonians, Epistles to the   [thes-uh-loh'-nee-uhnz]

The two Epistles to the Thessalonians, books of the New Testament of the BIBLE, are the first of Saint PAUL's letters, written about AD 50 from Corinth to his recently founded community of Christians at Thessalonika. Paul reviews his stay with them, expresses concern for their welfare, and encourages them in suffering. Paul also instructs them on the Second Coming of Jesus, which he expected imminently at this early stage in his career, and reassures them that those already dead will rise and that certain signs will precede the end. Some scholars hold that 2 Thessalonians is by a later disciple of Paul.
                                    ANTHONY J. SALDARINI

Bibliography: Best, Ernest, *A Commentary on the First and Second Epistles to the Thessalonians* (1972); Giblin, G. H., *The Threat to Faith* (1967).

Thessaloníki: see SALONIKA.

Thessaly   [thes'-uh-lee]

Thessaly is a historic region of Greece. It occupies the northeastern part of the Greek peninsula and is bounded by Macedonia to the north, the Aegean Sea to the east, ancient Aetolia to the south, and the upland Epirus to the west. The major city is Lárisa. Thessaly encompasses the two largest plains of Greece, where fertile soils support grain, tobacco, and vegetable crops.

Thessaly's name comes from the Thessali, a Dorian people from Epirus who conquered the region before 1000 BC and ruled through powerful military families. From the 6th century BC these families joined in a loose military confederation. Philip II of Macedonia entered Thessaly in 353 BC and gradually subjugated the region. Thessaly became a Roman protectorate in 197 BC and part of the province of Macedonia in 146 BC. Slavs, Arabs, Bulgarians, Normans, and Walachians invaded and settled Byzantine Thessaly between the 7th and 13th centuries. The region was ruled by the Turks from the end of the 14th century to 1881, when most of it was ceded to Greece. Thessaly roughly corresponds to the modern Greek departments of Kardítsa, Lárisa, Magnisía, and Tríkala.

Bibliography: Hansen, Hazel D., *Early Civilization in Thessaly* (1933).

theta wave: see BRAIN.

Thetis   [thee'-tis]

In Greek mythology Thetis, mother of ACHILLES, was a sea goddess attended by the Nereids and beloved by both Zeus and Poseidon. Neither would marry her, however, because an oracle had decreed that she would bear a son mightier than his father. Thetis married King Peleus and, according to Homer, when Achilles was born, she resolved to make him invulnerable by dipping him into the River Styx. Only his heel, by which she held him, could thereafter be pierced successfully by a weapon.

Thibault, Jacques Anatole François: see FRANCE, ANATOLE.

thickhead

Thickhead is the common name for a group of shrikelike birds constituting the subfamily Pachycephalinae in the Old World flycatcher family, Muscicapidae. Thickheads inhabit scrublands and forests from Australia east to Polynesia. From 12 to 28 cm (5 to 11 in) long, they have large heads and heavy, hooked bills and feed mainly on insects. Most are brownish or greenish gray above and lighter below, often with a white throat. Many species are called *whistlers* because of their melodious calls.   ROBERT J. RAIKOW

Thiebaud, Wayne   [tee'-boh]

Wayne Morton Thiebaud, b. Mesa, Ariz., Nov. 15, 1920, is a figurative painter who became prominent during the mid-1950s for his thick, impasto paintings of subjects such as mass-produced food and household and workshop objects. Because of his use of such commercial subjects, Thiebaud has been mistakenly identified as a pop artist, but his naturalistic, varied images are more personal than the true pop style. In his more recent works Thiebaud concentrates on lushly painted figures of familiar American types dressed in typical department-store clothing.   BARBARA CAVALIERE

Bibliography: Coplans, John, *Wayne Thiebaud* (1968).

Thiers, Adolphe   [tee-air']

Louis Adolphe Thiers helped found the Third Republic in France following the collapse of Napoleon III's regime during the Franco-Prussian War. As head of the provisional government he negotiated peace with the Prussians and ordered suppression of the Paris Commune (1871). He then served (1871-73) as first president of the republic.

The French statesman and writer Louis Adolphe Thiers, b. Apr. 18, 1797, d. Sept. 3, 1877, was a founder and the first president of France's Third Republic. Trained for the law, he began his career as a journalist and then wrote his celebrated *History of the French Revolution* (10 vols., 1823-27; Eng. trans., 5 vols., 1895). In 1830 he helped start the liberal daily *Le National*, which helped foment the July Revolution (1830) that overthrew Charles X and brought Louis Philippe to the throne. Thiers served the new government in various positions, including foreign minister, through the 1830s. Unable to convince Louis Philippe to adopt an anti-English policy, he resigned in 1840 (although remaining a deputy) and again wrote history, beginning a 20-volume study of Napoleon I, *History of the Consulate and the Empire* (1845-62; Eng. trans., 1845-62).

In the revolutionary year 1848, Thiers was a member of both the constituent and legislative assemblies. Once classified as a liberal monarchist, he was now known as a conservative—and chauvinistic—republican. He was banished in 1851 after NAPOLEON III's coup d'état but returned in less than a year. In 1863 he returned to politics as a deputy. A leader of the antiimperialists in the chamber, he repeatedly warned Napoleon III of the Prussian threat. Before the FRANCO-PRUSSIAN WAR (1870–71) he vainly tried to make mutual-defense agreements with other European countries.

After the Prussian victory and the collapse of the Napoleonic government in 1871, Thiers was chosen leader of the National Assembly. He made peace with the Prussians in March, in May he crushed the radical uprising of the Paris Commune, and in August he became president of the new Republic. His prestige, ability, and will aided France's recovery, but his inflexibility made him many enemies. A monarchist majority gained power in the 1873 by-elections, forcing his resignation; a monarchist, Patrice MacMahon, became the second president. Thiers then led the republican opposition until his death.   P. M. EWY

Bibliography: Albrecht-Carrie, René, *Adolphe Thiers* (1977); Bury, J. P., and Tombs, R. P., *Thiers, 1797–1877* (1986).

Thieu, Nguyen Van: see NGUYEN VAN THIEU.

Thimbu   [thim-boo']

Thimbu (or Thimphu), the capital of Bhutan since 1962, lies in the Himalayas in the west central part of the country at an altitude of 2,425 m (7,950 ft). The population is 20,000 (1985 est.). A modern city, Thimbu developed around Bhutan's largest monastery, the red-roofed, fortified Tashichhodzong, which also serves as the meeting hall of the National Assembly. Rice, corn, and wheat grow in the surrounding area. The city is linked to Phuntsholing on the Indian border by a 195-km-long (120-mi) road through the mountains; an east-west highway was completed in 1975.

thin-film technology

Thin-film technology makes it possible to deposit a very thin layer of material—down to a few atoms in thickness—upon a substrate. This can be achieved in many ways. In the various methods of EPITAXY, a crystalline layer of molecules is artificially grown on the substrate; the added layer mimics the geometric structure of the substrate. In the sputtering method of deposition, materials are bombarded with an inert gas, such as argon, and the resultant element beams deposit the materials on glass, plastic, metal, or other surfaces. In the Langmuir-Blodgett technique, long-chain organic molecules called amphiphiles are suspended on a water surface, and are then transferred to a substrate, such as glass, that has been submerged in the water.

Thin films are important in MICROELECTRONICS fabrication, in which ever-larger numbers of components are fitted onto the microchip. Protective plastic coatings can also be placed on microcircuits through thin-film deposition. Likewise, SUPERCONDUCTING materials can be deposited on a substrate and, because of their unique electronic behavior, may eventually account for a tremendous speedup in the amount of time it takes microchips to process information.

Thin-film technology has been used in the fabrication of more-efficient solar cells. Compact thin-film chemical sensors have been developed that can instantaneously detect substances, such as poison gases in air or impurities in blood, in concentrations of a few parts per billion. In the future, thin-film technology will be integral to the development of solid-state lasers and microchips that process information optically. Thin-film diamond layers may have many uses both as an abrasive and as a protective coating.

Bibliography: Eckertova, L., *Physics of Thin Films*, 2d rev. ed. (1986); Klabunde, J., ed., *Thin Films* (1986).

think tanks

Think tank (or, less commonly, *think factory*) is an informal but widely recognized term used to refer to a particular type of research institution that began to proliferate in the United States after World War II. A think tank differs from other research institutions in that it concentrates its research on issues that relate to policy making.

A popular term to describe the work of think tanks is *policy research,* which consists of research that produces ideas analysis and alternatives relative to people who make policy. Think tanks are often employed by government agencies to work on military, social, technical, and economic problems.

Several other characteristics typify the work of a think tank. Generally, its approach is future-directed in that it is interested in long-range planning, and it is apt to use scientific methodologies. Because of the nature of the problems it tackles and the techniques it employs, a think tank is invariably multidisciplinary—it is seldom limited to professionals from one field while working on any given project, and on large projects it will almost always use a team of experts from a number of fields. Finally, a think tank usually works with a relatively large degree of freedom both in defining the problem it is investigating and in making its formulations and recommendations. (See also FUTUROLOGY.)

Although they are not generally well known to the public at large, think tanks, beginning in the mid-1950s, were employed to work on and had an impact on most of the major—and many of the minor—policy issues in the United States. These issues include such diverse matters as pollution control, the closing of military bases, new weapons systems, the reorganization of the Post Office, and the future of solar energy.

In the private sector, think tanks supported by various political and religious groups research problems and strive to make their recommendations known to the government, the news media, and the general public.   PAUL DICKSON

Bibliography: Dickson, Paul, *Think Tanks* (1971); VanGundy, A. B., *Managing Group Creativity* (1984).

thinking: see CONCEPT FORMATION AND ATTAINMENT; PROBLEM SOLVING; REASONING.

3d Amendment

The 3d Amendment (1791) to the U.S. Constitution requires that the military have the consent of the owner to the housing of soldiers in private homes during peacetime; in the event of war the matter must be resolved "in a manner to be prescribed by law." This amendment arose from the resentment of the American colonists over the commandeering of their homes at will by British authorities as soldiers' quarters. The issue of quartering soldiers in private homes is not relevant to the modern conduct of military affairs, nor has it ever been the subject of a judicial decision. Nevertheless, the principle underlying the 3d Amendment remains significant in that it implies the supremacy of civilian authority over the military, a principle that is more fully expressed in the constitutional delegation of such authority to the president and Congress.

Third Reich   [ryk]

Adolf Hitler's National Socialist (Nazi) regime in Germany (1933–45) called itself the Third Reich, a designation chosen to identify the Nazi Reich, or empire, as third in succession to the Holy Roman Empire and German Empire of 1871–1918.

Third Republic: see FRANCE, HISTORY OF.

Third World

In its most general sense, the term *Third World* refers collectively to more than 100 countries of Africa, Asia, and Latin America. The term emerged in Europe during the late 1940s, referring to a "third force," not aligned with either the Communist or Western blocs. In the 1950s it was occasionally used to describe the newly independent states of Asia and Africa. Latin American countries were not encompassed by the term at first because of their more distant colonial past and their close ties to the United States. By the early 1960s, when threats to U.S. hegemony were emerging in Latin America and European decolonization was accelerating in Africa, Third World acquired its present meaning. It also came to refer primarily to economic characteristics and was frequently adopted in preference to such words as *undeveloped, backward, traditional, nonwestern,* or *underdeveloped,* which had derogatory or misleading connotations. Third World countries were generally distinguished from those of the first world (industrialized free-market economies) and second world (industrialized centrally planned economies) on the basis of indicators of industrial development, poverty, vulnerability to international economic conditions, and quality of life. Recently, economic differences among Third World countries have been increasing. Some are on the verge of industrial status, but others (sometimes called "fourth world" nations) are experiencing little economic growth, industrial or otherwise. With the rise of oil prices in the 1970s, the petroleum-exporting countries emerged as a new group of nonindustrial but nonetheless high-income Third World nations. *Third World* has also been used to refer to people of African, Asian, or Latin American extraction living in the United States. Debate has emerged over the utility of such an all-inclusive term.

In most Third World countries, gross national product and per capita income levels are distinctly lower than those of industrialized countries, and income is often very unevenly distributed. Third World economies are often dependent on the export of primary products or simple manufactured goods that are highly vulnerable to fluctuations in international prices and to industrialized country trade restrictions. Third World countries tend to have low to modest life expectancy and modest to high rates of infant mortality and illiteracy. Indices of health and nutrition range from extremely low to modest, and access to social services such as education, health care, potable water, and sanitation is usually constricted for the majority of the population. Political characteristics vary widely, although governmental instability is common, and the military and foreign interests frequently play active roles in domestic politics.

Internationally, Third World countries tend to be seen and to identify themselves in opposition to industrialized countries, acting collectively (in the Group of 77, for example) to redress their generally subordinate relationship to older centers of economic and political power. This is particularly true of their relationship to the international capitalist economy, which, they frequently contend, systematically discriminates against the Third World by foreclosing opportunities for economic development. Their collective demand for modification of this relationship, formalized in wide-ranging proposals in the 1970s and 1980s to create a new international economic order, led to an ambitious but generally inconclusive "North-South" dialogue, in which the Third World nations of the South, including the newly powerful oil exporting nations, challenged the still preponderant policies and institutions of the industrialized nations of the North.   MERILEE S. GRINDLE

Bibliography: Critchfield, Richard, *Villages* (1981); Feinberg, Richard, *Intemperate Zone* (1983); Gillis, Malcolm, et al., *The Economics of Development* (1983); Harrison, Paul, *Inside the Third World* (1982).

See also: NONALIGNED NATIONS MOVEMENT.

13th Amendment

The 13th Amendment to the U.S. Constitution states that "neither slavery nor involuntary servitude" shall exist in the United States and gives Congress the power to enforce this article by legislation. Although this amendment, which was ratified in 1865, had been preceded by a federal restriction on the importation of slaves in 1808, by the EMANCIPATION PROCLAMATION of 1863, and by legislative bans against slavery in many of the states prior to 1865, the 13th Amendment was the first unconditional constitutional action to terminate the institution of slavery and the first of the amendments to protect the equal status of black people (others are the 14th, 15th, and 24th Amendments). The 13th Amendment has recently been interpreted by the Supreme Court to include prohibition of public or private racial discrimination in the disposal of property, in

the making and enforcement of contracts, and in private employment.

Although specifically directed against slavery, the ban against involuntary servitude ("except as a punishment for crime") has been viewed by the federal courts as applicable to other conditions of forced labor.

Bibliography: Aptheker, Herbert, *And Why Not Every Man? The Story of the Fight against Negro Slavery* (1961); Berry, Mary Frances, *Military Necessity and Civil Rights Policy: Black Citizenship and the Constitution, 1861–1868* (1977).

Thirty-nine Articles

The basic summary of belief of the Church of England (see ENGLAND, CHURCH OF), the Thirty-nine Articles of Religion were drawn up by the church in convocation in 1563 on the basis of the earlier Forty-two Articles of 1553. Subscription to them by the clergy was ordered by act of Parliament in 1571. Devised to exclude Roman Catholics and Anabaptists, but not to provide a dogmatic definition of faith—in many instances, they are ambiguously phrased—the articles were influenced by the confessions of Augsburg and Württemberg (earlier statements of Protestant belief). They concern fundamental Christian truths (Articles 1–5), the rule of faith (Articles 6–8), individual religion (Articles 9–18), corporate religion (Articles 19–36), and national religion (Articles 37–39). Retained in use by the various churches of the ANGLICAN COMMUNION, the Articles have been changed only as circumstances require. Thus the Protestant EPISCOPAL CHURCH OF the United States has retained them, without requiring assent, changing only those articles affected by the independence of the United States from England (Articles 36 and 37).   JOHN E. BOOTY

Bibliography: Bicknell, Edward J., *A Theological Introduction to the Thirty-nine Articles of the Church of England* (1947); Fuhrmann, P. T., *Introduction to the Great Creeds of the Church* (1960); Ross, Kenneth N., *The Thirty-nine Articles* (1957).

Thirty Years' War

The Thirty Years' War (1618–48) was the last major European war of religion and the first all-European struggle for power. It was, in fact, a series of wars fought mainly on German soil and was only part of a larger struggle to alter the European balance of power.

The religious wars that had divided Germany and the Holy Roman Empire as a result of the Protestant REFORMATION ended in compromise with the Peace of Augsburg (1555), and there was peace between the Protestant and Roman Catholic states of the empire for the next 50 years. In the early 17th century, however, tensions between the rival faiths revived.

The Bohemian War. Hostilities broke out on May 23, 1618, when a number of Protestant Bohemian noblemen threw two royal governors of their country out of the windows of the Hradčany Palace in Prague (an event known as the Defenestration of Prague). It was a rebellion typical of this period by men of great privilege and power who saw a threat in the advance of royal power: in this case in the absolutist and Catholic policies of their king, Ferdinand of HABSBURG, soon to be elected Holy Roman Emperor FERDINAND II. Both sides were convinced that they were fighting for a holy cause, and both feared not only political defeat but annihilation if the other won. Therefore, both sides looked for allies and widened the conflict, entangling it with the religious and political struggles of their neighbors.

The Bohemians appealed to Gábor BETHLEN, Protestant prince of Transylvania, who, with the encouragement of his overlord, the Ottoman sultan of Turkey, was hoping to win the crown of Hungary from the Habsburgs. They also elected FREDERICK V of the Palatinate as their new king. They hoped that Frederick's father-in-law, JAMES I of England, and his uncle, MAURICE OF NASSAU, virtual ruler of the United Provinces of the Netherlands, would lend him support.

Ferdinand called on Poland but especially on his cousins MAXIMILIAN, duke of Bavaria (leader of the Catholic League of German princes), and on the Habsburg king of Spain, PHILIP

III. On Nov. 8, 1620, Maximilian's general, Graf von TILLY, defeated the Bohemians at White Mountain near Prague, and Frederick—the Winter King—lost his crown as suddenly as he had won it. He continued to fight, employing various mercenary leaders, including Ernst, Graf von MANSFELD, and relying on some English and a great deal of Dutch help. In 1623, however, the Palatinate was overrun by Spanish and Bavarian troops, and Frederick's electoral vote was transferred to Maximilian of Bavaria.

Expansion of the War. In 1621 the Dutch and Spanish had renewed the war that had started two generations previously with the revolt of the Netherlands (see DUTCH REVOLT). This struggle remained an important factor in the Thirty Years' War. It ranged to the Caribbean, the South Atlantic, and the Indian Ocean. The Dutch captured the Gold Coast, parts of Angola, and half of Brazil from the Portuguese, only to lose Angola and Brazil to Portugal, after that kingdom reasserted its independence from Spain, in 1640.

In Europe, Dutch and Spanish money and military expertise fueled the fighting. Spanish troops fought in Germany, Italy, and France. The Dutch, with a much smaller population, preferred to finance military allies. After Frederick's generals these allies included, first, CHRISTIAN IV of Denmark, who feared the continued victories of Tilly's armies. In April 1626, Mansfeld met defeat at Dessau Bridge by a new imperial army raised by a wealthy and ambitious former Protestant Bohemian, Albrecht von WALLENSTEIN. Four months later Christian was routed by Tilly at Lutter am Barenberge. With victory apparently in hand, Emperor Ferdinand issued (Mar. 29, 1629) the Edict of Restitution, which restored to the Catholic church all property taken by the Protestants since 1552.

After Denmark's withdrawal (May 1629) from the war, however, another Scandinavian power joined the fray. Encouraged by France, Sweden concluded a truce with its Baltic rival Poland, and in July 1630 the Swedish king GUSTAV II ADOLF landed in Pomerania to begin a series of victorious campaigns against the imperial armies. At Breitenfeld (Sept. 17, 1631) and at the Lech River (Apr. 15, 1632) he defeated Tilly, and at Lützen (Nov. 16, 1632) the Swedes defeated Wallenstein, although Gustav Adolf was killed.

Throughout these years, the Catholic King LOUIS XIII of France, the traditional rival of the house of Habsburg for preeminence in Europe, had observed Tilly's and Wallenstein's victories with increasing concern, although he had waged several civil wars against his own Protestant subjects, the Huguenots. Despite some help from England, the Huguenots were defeated, and France turned to fight Spain, with only partial success, in northern Italy. After Gustav Adolf's death and after the Swedes suffered a severe defeat at Nördlingen

The Peace of Westphalia, concluded in 1648 after 5 years of negotiations, ended the Thirty Years' War and effectively destroyed the Holy Roman Empire. The signing of the treaties was painted (1648) by the Dutch painter Gerard Ter Borch. (National Gallery, London.)

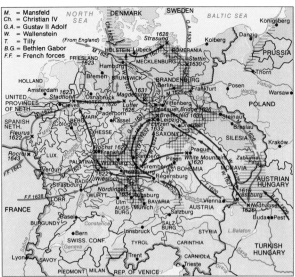

THE THIRTY YEARS' WAR, 1618-48

M. = Mansfeld
Ch. = Christian IV
G.A. = Gustav II Adolf
W. = Wallenstein
T. = Tilly
B.G. = Bethlen Gabor
F.F. = French forces

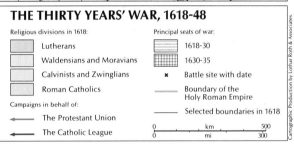

Religious divisions in 1618:

Lutherans

Waldensians and Moravians

Calvinists and Zwinglians

Roman Catholics

Campaigns in behalf of:

⟵ The Protestant Union

⟵ The Catholic League

Principal seats of war:

1618-30

1630-35

× Battle site with date

Boundary of the Holy Roman Empire

Selected boundaries in 1618

0 km 500
0 mi 300

Cartographic Production by Lothar Roth & Associates.

(Sept. 6, 1634), France openly declared (1635) war on Spain, in alliance with the United Provinces, Sweden, and some German Protestant princes.

The ring of alliances was virtually complete; no treaty between any two states, or even group of states, could now end the war. The intervention of France on the "Protestant" side cut across the religious alignments of the combatants. More and more, religious motivation and aims dropped into the background. In 1640 both Catalonia and Portugal rebelled against Spain, although all three were Catholic. In 1643 the Protestant Christian of Denmark, fearing the increasing power of Protestant Sweden, restarted the old Danish-Swedish rivalry for the control of the Sound (Öresund), the northwestern entrance to the Baltic. Once more the Danes were heavily defeated and lost their monopoly control over the Sound.

Peace Settlements. From 1643 the ambassadors of the combatants met in peace congresses in the Westphalian cities of Münster and Osnabrück. Because there was no truce, the relative position of parties continued to change; all wanted to negotiate from strength. It therefore took 5 years to conclude peace—in January 1648 between Spain and the United Provinces and in October 1648 between France, Sweden, the Holy Roman emperor, and the German princes (see WESTPHALIA, PEACE OF). The war between France and Spain continued until 1659 (Peace of the Pyrenees), with Britain joining France against Spain in 1656; the wars between Sweden and Poland and between Sweden and Denmark flared up again and were not settled until 1660 (Peace of Oliva and Peace of Copenhagen).

The Peace of Westphalia solved some problems. The Habsburgs had failed to reassert imperial power, and the German princes were left with virtual political independence and with the right to choose their religion. Their subjects were given no such choice but were allowed to emigrate. In European power politics, religion no longer determined alliances, nor did it lead countries into war. Sweden had become the dominant power in the Baltic, and France had displaced Spain as the dominant power in western Europe.

The common people bore the real cost of the war. Historians disagree on precise figures, but in Brandenburg, Mecklenburg, Pomerania, the Palatinate, Württemberg, and parts of Bavaria, civilian population losses may have been 50 percent or more. The horrors of the Thirty Years' War lived on in popular memory as those of no other war in Europe before the 20th century.

H. G. KOENIGSBERGER

Bibliography: Bireley, Robert S., *Religion and Politics in the Age of the Counterreformation* (1981); Israel, Jonathan I., *The Dutch Republic and the Hispanic World, 1606–1661* (1982); Koenigsberger, H. G., *The Habsburgs and Europe 1516–1660* (1971); Pagès, Georges, *The Thirty Years War, 1618–1648,* trans. by David Maland and John Hooper (1970); Polišenský, J. V., *The Thirty Years War,* trans. by Robert Evans (1971); Wedgwood, C. V., *The Thirty Years War* (1938; repr. 1981).

thistle

The creeping Canada thistle, C. arvense, *is a noxious, ubiquitous, prickly perennial weed. It is able to reproduce itself from root fragments, and plowing it under spreads rather than kills it. At times the thistle is grown for display because of its stark natural beauty.*

Thistle is the common name used to refer to several genera (notably *Cirsium*) of the family Compositae. These spiny herbaceous plants, native to the Northern Hemisphere, are characterized by dense heads of small white, yellow, red, or purple flowers.

Canadian thistle, *C. arvense,* is a troublesome weed in North America, but species such as the Scotch, or cotton, thistle, *Onopordum acanthium,* can make attractive garden plants.

FRANK B. SALISBURY

Thom, René [tohm]

The French mathematician René Thom, b. Sept. 2, 1923, is known for his development of CATASTROPHE THEORY, a mathematical treatment of sudden transformations and unpredictable discontinuities and divergences in nature. That is, Thom's theory is an attempt to describe satisfactorily—as differential calculus cannot—those situations in which gradually changing forces lead to so-called catastrophes, or abrupt changes, whether in the physical and biological world or in the social sciences. Presented in *Structural Stability and Morphogenesis* (1972; Eng. trans., 1975), the theory is still being evaluated for its actual usefulness.

Thomas, Saint

One of the original 12 apostles of Jesus Christ, Thomas, called Didymus, refused to believe in the testimony of the other apostles concerning the resurrection of Jesus until he saw the wounds of the resurrected Christ himself (John 20:24, 25, 26–29). From this comes the expression "doubting Thomas."

Thomas earlier had expressed great devotion (John 11:16) and a questioning mind (John 14:5).

Eusebius of Caesarea records that Thomas became a missionary to Parthia. The *Acts of Thomas* (3d century), however, states that he was martyred in India. The MALABAR CHRISTIANS claim that their church was founded by him. This tradition can neither be substantiated nor denied on the basis of current evidence. Saint Thomas' Mount in Madras is the traditional site of his martyrdom. Feast day: July 3 (Western and Syrian); Oct. 6 (Eastern).

DOUGLAS EZELL

Bibliography: Griffith, Leonard, *Gospel Characters* (1976); Perumalil, Hormice C., and Hambye, E. R., eds., *Christianity in India* (1973).

Thomas, Ambroise

The French composer Charles Louis Ambroise Thomas, b. Aug. 5, 1811, d. Feb. 12, 1896, is best known for his opera *Mignon,* first performed in Paris in 1866. He studied at the Paris Conservatory, won the Prix de Rome (1832) and, after a 3-year stay in Italy, returned to Paris to compose operas. In 1852 he was appointed teacher of composition at the conservatory, becoming its director in 1871. His other operas include *Raymond* (1851), *Le Carnaval de Venise* (1857), the very successful *Hamlet* (1868), and *Françoise de Rimini* (1882). Thomas's graceful and melodious style has been compared to that of Gounod. His other works include sacred music, ballets, chamber music, and songs.

Bibliography: Bacharach, Alfred L., ed., *The Music Makers* (1957); Hervey, Arthur, *Masters of French Music* (1894; repr. 1977).

Thomas, Augustus

The American dramatist Augustus Thomas, b. St. Louis, Mo., Jan. 8, 1857, d. Aug. 12, 1934, wrote plays on native themes, the most popular of which was *The Witching Hour* (1907), a melodrama that thrilled audiences with its portrayal of hypnotism. Thomas also wrote romantic and racy "local color" plays such as *Alabama* (1891), *In Mizzoura* (1893), and *Arizona* (1899).

MYRON MATLAW

Thomas, Dylan

Dylan Thomas, a 20th-century Welsh poet, expressed a resilient innocence and a strenuous love of life in such poems as "Fern Hill" and "Do Not Go Gentle into That Good Night." Widely known for his powerful poetry readings over BBC radio, he became a popular, if controversial, figure. He died at the age of 39, the author of a lyrical and poignant body of verse.

One of the best-known British poets of the mid-20th century, Dylan Marlais Thomas, b. Swansea, Wales, Oct. 27, 1914, d. Nov. 9, 1953, is remembered for his highly original, obscure poems, his amusing prose tales and plays, and his turbulent, well-publicized personal life. His most popular works include the radio play UNDER MILK WOOD (posthumously published, 1954) and the sketch "A Child's Christmas in Wales" (1955), but his more ambitious work consists of the complex poems in which he expressed a deeply romantic vision.

Thomas's first book of verse, *18 Poems* (1934), was praised by a few discriminating critics in spite of its obscurity, and in 1936 a second volume, *Twenty-Five Poems,* followed. Thomas married in 1937 and lived with his wife, Caitlin, in poverty in England and Wales. During this period he began to write short stories. His main prose works include *Portrait of the*

Artist as a Young Dog (1940), a collection of autobiographical short stories; *Adventures in the Skin Trade* (1955); and *Quite Early One Morning* (1954), a collection of radio talks.

Rejected for military service during World War II, Thomas became relatively prosperous as a writer of radio scripts and films. He also published *The Map of Love* (1939), a volume of poems and fantastic short stories, and *Deaths and Entrances* (1946), another book of verse. Beginning in 1949, Thomas visited the United States several times, touring college campuses to read his poetry. His erratic behavior, however, showed that he suffered from mental disturbances, and he died in New York City after a period of depression and heavy drinking.

JACOB KORG

Bibliography: Ackerman, John, *Dylan Thomas: His Life and Work* (1964); Ferris, Paul, *Dylan Thomas: A Biography* (1977); FitzGibbon, Constantine, *The Life of Dylan Thomas* (1965); Moynihan, William T., *The Craft and Art of Dylan Thomas* (1966).

Thomas, George Henry

Union general George Henry Thomas, b. Southampton County, Va., July 31, 1816, d. Mar. 28, 1870, achieved fame for his victories in the western campaigns during the U.S. Civil War. After graduating (1840) from the U.S. Military Academy, he served in the Mexican War and taught (1851–54) at West Point. Thomas earned the epithet the Rock of Chickamauga after his strong defenses at the Battle of CHICKAMAUGA, in Tennessee, held the Confederates at bay (Sept. 19–20, 1863) until reinforcements arrived permitting the Federals an orderly withdrawal. Promoted to brigadier general and given command of the Army of the Cumberland, he played a key role in the Union victory at Chattanooga (November 1863; see CHATTANOOGA, BATTLES OF). At Nashville (Dec. 15–16, 1864) Thomas halted Confederate forces under Gen. John B. HOOD that threatened to cut the Federals' communications lines. Thomas later commanded military governments in Kentucky and Tennessee and the Division of the Pacific.

Bibliography: Cleaves, Freeman, *Rock of Chickamauga: The Life of General George H. Thomas* (1948; repr. 1974); Palumbo, F. A., *Major General George Henry Thomas, the Dependable General* (1983).

Thomas, Isaiah

The leading printer of his day, Isaiah Thomas, b. Boston, Jan. 19, 1749, d. Apr. 4, 1831, was also an early patriot. His paper *The Massachusetts Spy* (founded 1770) so angered the Tories that he moved it to Worcester, Mass., during the American Revolution. Thomas opened a bookstore with several branches, published *The Massachusetts Magazine* (1789–96), and in 1812 founded The American Antiquarian Society, to which he left land, a building, a large library, and substantial funds. His *History of Printing in America* (1810) contains accurate records of prices, processes, paper, and equipment.

Bibliography: Nichols, Charles L., *Isaiah Thomas* (1912; repr. 1971); Shipton, Clifford K., *Isaiah Thomas* (1948).

Thomas, Lewis

American medical administrator and author Lewis Thomas, b. Flushing, N.Y., Nov. 25, 1913, is best known for his philosophical essays on biology and human society. Thomas earned an M.D. from Harvard Medical School (1937) and held posts at Bellevue Medical Center, Yale University, and elsewhere. From 1973 to 1980 he served as president at Sloan-Kettering Cancer Center in New York City. His *The Lives of a Cell* (1974) won the National Book Award; other collected essays include *Medusa and the Snail* (1979) and *Late Night Thoughts while Listening to Mahler's Ninth Symphony* (1983).

Thomas, Lowell

A radio news broadcaster for 46 years, Lowell Thomas, b. Woodington, Ohio, Apr. 6, 1892, d. Aug. 29, 1981, also wrote more than 50 books about his worldwide travels and adventures. He grew up in the gold-mining community of Cripple Creek, Colo., and began his career as a newspaper reporter

Lowell Thomas, an American newscaster and journalist, studies wire-service reports prior to his nightly radio program. Thomas's distinguished career, spanning six decades, included such achievements as the exclusive coverage of T. E. Lawrence's Middle East campaign and the narration of innumerable wartime newsreels.

after graduating from the University of Denver. During World War I he reported from Europe and the Near East and did much to establish the legend of T. E. Lawrence—Lawrence of Arabia. After his news broadcasting career (1930–76), Thomas narrated the series "Lowell Thomas Remembers" until his death. He told the story of his life in *Good Evening Everybody* (1976) and *So Long until Tomorrow* (1977).

Thomas, Martha Carey

Martha Carey Thomas, b. Baltimore, Md., Jan. 2, 1857, d. Dec. 2, 1935, was an educator and early feminist. She became president of Bryn Mawr College in 1894, led the movement for women's admissions to The Johns Hopkins University in 1889, and participated in the movement for women's suffrage and educational equality.

MILDRED NAVARETTA

Bibliography: Finch, Edith, *Carey Thomas of Bryn Mawr* (1947).

Thomas, Michael Tilson

American conductor Michael Tilson Thomas, b. Hollywood, Calif., Dec. 21, 1944, in 1969 became Boston Symphony Orchestra's youngest associate conductor. From 1971 to 1979 served as music director of the Buffalo Philharmonic; he has since held guest-conducting posts. Thomas led the first American performances (1979) of the three-act version of Alban Berg's opera *Lulu* at the Santa Fe Opera.

KAREN MONSON

Bibliography: Ewen, David, ed., *Musicians since 1900* (1978).

Thomas, Norman

Norman Thomas, leader of the U.S. Socialist party from 1926 to 1955, was six times (1928, 1932, 1936, 1940, 1944, and 1948) an unsuccessful candidate for the presidency of the United States. A moderate socialist, Thomas was widely respected for his idealism and persistence.

Norman Mattoon Thomas, b. Marion, Ohio, Nov. 20, 1884, d. Dec. 19, 1968, was six times an unsuccessful SOCIALIST PARTY candidate for president of the United States between 1928 and 1948. A Presbyterian minister in East Harlem's slums, he became a pacifist and opposed American entry into World War I. In 1917 he helped found what became the American Civil Liberties Union. Thomas joined the Socialist party in 1918 and became its leader in 1926. Espousing a moderate, non-Marxist brand of socialism, he failed (except in the 1932 election) to halt the decline of his party.

Thomas worked against U.S. support for the Allies in World War II, but after Pearl Harbor, he gave the war effort critical support. He protested the internment of Japanese Americans and the postwar political prosecution of Communists. Thomas backed the Korean War in the early 1950s but opposed U.S. intervention in Indochina in the 1960s. His socialism became diluted by his advocacy of a mixed economy, and in his later years Thomas was a respected dissenter without any organizational base of support.   FRED GREENBAUM

Bibliography: Johnpoll, B. K., *Pacifist's Progress* (1970; repr. 1987); Swanberg, W. A., *Norman Thomas: The Last Idealist* (1976).

Thomas, Ross

Ross Thomas, b. Oklahoma City, Okla., Feb. 19, 1926, since 1966 has produced two successful series of mystery novels, both marked by urbane prose and hard realism about U.S. politics and character. *The Cold War Swap* (1966) won the 1967 Edgar Allan Poe Award. Other books include *The Porkchoppers* (1972), on labor union politics; *If You Can't Be Good* (1973), on congressional corruption; and *The Money Harvest* (1975), on the commodities market. Thomas has published several novels under the pseudonym Oliver Bleeck.

Thomas, Seth

Seth Thomas, b. Wolcott, Conn., Aug. 19, 1785, d. Jan. 29, 1859, was a U.S. manufacturer who pioneered in the mass production of clocks. In 1807, Thomas, an apprentice carpenter, joined Eli Terry and Silas Hoadley, two Connecticut clockmakers, in founding a manufacturing firm that in 3 years had produced 4,000 clocks. In 1812, Thomas launched his own factory, and 2 years later he began to produce shelf clocks with wooden works, inexpensively and in large quantities. He then built (1838) a mill to roll brass and make wire in order to manufacture brass clock movements. The Seth Thomas Clock Company was formally organized in 1853.

Thomas, Sidney Gilchrist

English metallurgist Sidney Gilchrist Thomas, b. Apr. 16, 1850, d. Feb. 1, 1885, invented (1875) a method, known as the basic Bessemer process, for the removal of phosphorus from iron. He and his cousin Percy Gilchrist refined this method and patented it in 1877. Thomas's method enabled the steel industry to use the abundant supply of phosphoric pig iron; the phosphorus content otherwise made steel brittle.

Thomas, William I.

The American sociologist and psychologist William Isaac Thomas, b. Russell County, Va., Aug. 13, 1863, d. Dec. 5, 1947, pioneered the study of interrelationships between biological and cultural factors in human behavior. Thomas, who taught (1895–1918) at the University of Chicago, stressed a "situational" approach to behavior and saw the interaction between social values and individual attitudes as the basic concern of social theory. Among his major works are *Sex and Society* (1907) and, with Florian Znaniecki, *The Polish Peasant in Europe and America* (5 vols., 1918–21).

Bibliography: Janowitz, Morris, *W. I. Thomas on Social Organization and Social Personality* (1966).

Thomas A. Edison State College

Established in 1972, Thomas A. Edison State College (enrollment: 5,300) in Trenton, N.J., is the first college in the United States granting the opportunity of gaining associate or bachelor's degrees to adults who have knowledge equivalent to that normally offered in a classroom. Degree credits are obtained by transferring them from another college and through college-equivalency examinations, prior-learning assessment, and correspondence courses. The college has no faculty and no instruction except a guided-study program based on the British open-university system and akin to correspondence study. Examinations are supervised by an academic council consisting of professors from colleges in New Jersey.

Thomas à Kempis

The probable author of the devotional treatise *The Imitation of Christ,* Thomas à Kempis, b. Kempen, Germany, c.1380, d. Aug. 8, 1471, was influenced by the tradition of Gerhard GROOTE and the BRETHREN OF THE COMMON LIFE. Thomas entered a monastery of the Augustinian canons and was ordained in 1413. He spent most of his life at this monastery, where he wrote many works of devotion and copied manuscripts. *The Imitation of Christ* embodies many of the key ideas of the *devotio moderna:* stress on being faithful to the movements of grace, on poverty and humility, and on guarding against temptations. The success of *Imitation* overshadows his other writings.   THOMAS E. MORRISSEY

Bibliography: De Montmorency, J. E., *Thomas A. Kempis: His Age and Book* (1906; repr. 1970); Hyma, A., *Brethren of the Common Life* (1950).

Thompson, Daley

Great Britain's Francis Morgan "Daley" Thompson, b. July 30, 1958, is only the second man in Olympic history to win two decathlons (1980, 1984; American Bob Mathias won in 1948 and 1952). Unbeaten in his event from 1978 to 1987, Thompson set the world record—8,847 points—in 1984. His bid for an unprecedented third Olympic gold medal in Seoul in 1988 was unsuccessful.

Thompson, David

David Thompson, b. London, Apr. 30, 1770, d. Feb. 10, 1857, the greatest 19th-century surveyor in North America, explored vast areas that later became part of western Canada and the northwestern United States. Apprenticed to the HUDSON'S BAY COMPANY at age 14, he spent several years at various company posts and learned surveying. In 1796 he blazed a new route to Lake Athabasca, traveling from York Factory by way of the Nelson, Burntwood, and Churchill rivers and Reindeer Lake to Fond du Lac. Dissatisfied with his employers, he joined the NORTH WEST COMPANY in 1797, becoming a partner in 1804.

For the North West Company, Thompson surveyed (1797–98) the Mississippi's headwaters, crossed (1807) the Canadian Rockies by the Howse Pass to the source of the Columbia, explored (1808–10) Washington, Idaho, and Montana, and became the first white person to travel (1811) the Columbia's entire length. Everywhere, he made observations that, after retirement in 1812, enabled him to complete a map (1813–14) that became the basis for all subsequent maps of western Canada. He surveyed (1816–26) the Canada-U.S. boundary between the St. Lawrence River and Lake of the Woods for the International Boundary Commission.   GEORGE F. G. STANLEY

Bibliography: Smith, James K., *David Thompson: Fur Trader, Explorer, Geographer* (1971); Thompson, David, *David Thompson's Narrative, 1784–1812,* ed. by Richard Glover (1962).

Thompson, Dorothy

The American journalist Dorothy Thompson, b. Lancaster, N.Y., July 9, 1894, d. Jan. 31, 1961, went to Europe in 1920 with no job and little money; her ingenuity and a knack for being where the news was gained her a position as foreign correspondent with the *Philadelphia Public Ledger* and *New York Evening Post.* She became head of the *Ledger* and *Evening Post*'s Berlin office in 1925 but was expelled from the country in 1934 for speaking out against Hitler. Her column "On the Record" ran from 1936 until 1958; selections from it appeared in *Let the Record Speak* (1939).

Bibliography: Sanders, M. K., *Dorothy Thompson: A Legend in Her Time* (1973); Sheean, Vincent, *Dorothy and Red* (1963).

Thompson, Edward Herbert

The American archaeologist Edward Herbert Thompson, b. Worcester, Mass., Sept. 28, 1856, d. May 11, 1935, directed important early explorations of the city of CHICHÉN ITZÁ, in Yucatán. While American consul in Yucatán (1885–1909) he conducted extensive archaeological fieldwork. Among his most significant projects was the dredging of the Sacred Well of Chichén Itzá, into which human sacrifices, gold, and precious stones had been thrown to appease the rain god thought to live at its bottom. He wrote of his explorations in *People of the Serpent* (1932).

Thompson, J. Eric

J. Eric Thompson, b. Dec. 31, 1898, d. Sept. 9, 1975, an English archaeologist with the Carnegie Institution of Washington, D.C., from 1935 to 1958, was one of the world's foremost authorities in deciphering Maya hieroglyphs. His correlation between the Maya and Christian calendars is used extensively by archaeologists to date Maya events. Thompson helped excavate and restore the famous Maya site of CHICHÉN ITZÁ. He was knighted in 1975. Among his many books are *The Civilization of the Mayas* (1927) and *Maya Hieroglyphic Writing: Introduction* (1950).

Thompson, Sir John Sparrow David

Sir John S. D. Thompson was Conservative prime minister of Canada from 1892 until his death in 1894. He had previously held the positions of prime minister of Nova Scotia and minister of justice for Canada.

The lawyer and politician Sir John Sparrow David Thompson, b. Nova Scotia, Nov. 10, 1844, d. Dec. 12, 1894, was prime minister of Canada in 1892–94. A Liberal-Conservative, he became Nova Scotia's prime minister (1882) before sitting on the provincial Supreme Court (1882–85). He was minister of justice (1885–91) in John A. Macdonald's federal administration and won the position of prime minister despite his Roman Catholicism.

Bibliography: Hutchison, Bruce, *Mr. Prime Minister* (1964).

Thompson, Randall

The composer and educator Randall Thompson, b. New York City, Apr. 21, 1899, d. July 9, 1984, is best known for his choral works, particularly *The Testament of Freedom* (1943) for men's voices and orchestra (or piano), and *Alleluia* (1940) for unaccompanied chorus. He studied at Harvard and then privately with Ernest Bloch. He was a Fellow (1922–25) of the American Academy in Rome and a director (1939–41) of the Curtis Institute in Philadelphia, and he taught at various universities, including Harvard (1948–65). His other choral works include *Requiem* (1958), *The Passion According to St. Luke* (1965), and *The Place of the Blest* (1969). He also wrote orchestral works (including three symphonies) and chamber music (including two string quartets).

Bibliography: Chase, Gilbert, *America's Music*, 2d ed. (1966); Howard, J. T., *Our Contemporary Composers*, 4th ed. (1965).

Thompson, William Hale

William Hale Thompson, called "Big Bill," b. Boston, May 14, 1867, d. Mar. 19, 1944, was a colorful Republican machine leader who served three terms (1915–23, 1927–31) as mayor of Chicago. His political career was marked by both his rabid anti-British sentiments and his inability or unwillingness to prevent the open operation of criminal gangs. He lost a race for governor in 1936.

Bibliography: Wendt, L., and Kogan, H., *Big Bill of Chicago* (1953).

Thomsen, Christian Jürgensen

Christian Jürgensen Thomsen, b. Dec. 29, 1788, d. May 21, 1865, was the Danish archaeologist who evolved the Stone, Bronze, and Iron three-age system of PREHISTORY. He served (1816–65) as the first curator of the Museum of Northern Antiquities, later the National Museum in Copenhagen. His arrangement of the antiquities in the collection showed a practical example of this system, and this method was recognized to be of great value in interpreting the prehistoric past.

Thomson, Benjamin: see RUMFORD, BENJAMIN THOMSON, COUNT.

Thomson, Charles

Charles Thomson, b. County Derry, Ireland, Nov. 29, 1729, d. Aug. 16, 1824, was a Pennsylvania patriot leader in the era of the American Revolution and secretary of the Continental Congress (1774–89). He arrived in America as an orphan in 1739 and became a prosperous Philadelphia merchant. His strong opposition to British policies led John Adams to call him "the Sam Adams of Philadelphia." Thomson helped secure Pennsylvania's approval for the meeting of the First Continental Congress in 1774. Although the colony's conservatives blocked his election as a delegate, he was able to participate because the Congress chose him as its secretary.

Bibliography: Hendricks, J. Edwin, *Charles Thomson and the Making of a New Nation* (1979).

Thomson, Sir Charles Wyville

The Scottish naturalist Sir Charles Wyville Thomson, b. Mar. 5, 1830, d. Mar. 10, 1882, established the existence of life at great ocean depths. Director of the round-the-world voyage (1872–76) of the H.M.S. *Challenger,* he made discoveries about the ocean waters and ocean floor that provided a basis for modern oceanography.   JEAN SILVERMAN

Bibliography: Deacon, Margaret, *Scientists at Sea, 1650–1900* (1971).

Thomson, Sir George Paget

Sir George Paget Thomson, b. May 3, 1892, d. Sept. 10, 1975, a British physicist, shared the Nobel Prize for physics in 1937 for his work on electron diffraction through gold foil, which confirmed Louis de Broglie's theory that free electrons behave both like waves and like particles. The son of J. J. Thomson, George Thomson did important work on nuclear fusion, was knighted in 1943, and served (1952–62) as Master of Corpus Christi College, Cambridge.   JAMES A. BOOTH

Bibliography: Thomson, Sir George, *The Inspiration of Science* (1961).

Thomson, James   (1700–48)

The Scottish poet James Thomson, b. Sept. 11, 1700, d. Aug. 27, 1748, best known as author of the immensely popular blank-verse poem *The Seasons* (1730), also wrote tragedies and the Spenserian epic *The Castle of Indolence* (1748). He traveled to London in 1725 and a year later published *Winter,* the first of his four season poems. As the initiator of a new descriptive mode in poetry, Thomson anticipated a key feature of 19th-century romanticism.   ROBIN BUSS

Bibliography: Agrawal, R. R., *Tradition and Experiment in the Poetry of James Thomson* (1981); Cohen, R., *Unfolding of the Seasons* (1970).

Thomson, James (1834-82)

The Scottish poet James Thomson, b. Nov. 23, 1834, d. June 3, 1882, foreshadowed in *The City of Dreadful Night* (1874) the despair and isolation characteristic of 20th-century poetry. To distinguish himself from the James Thomson of *The Seasons*, he adopted the pen name Bysshe Volanis, in tribute to Percy Bysshe Shelley and Novalis.   ROBIN BUSS

Bibliography: Walker, Imogene B., *James Thomson (B.V.): A Critical Study* (1950; repr. 1976).

Thomson, John

A Scottish explorer and photographer, John Thomson, 1837-1921, spent 10 years in the 1860s and '70s in the Far East and published several ethnographic and archaeological works on the region, among them the four-volume *Illustrations of China and Its People* (1873-74). He also illustrated *Street Life in London* (1877), one of the earliest uses of photography for purposes of social documentation.

Thomson, Joseph

Joseph Thomson, b. Feb. 14, 1858, d. Aug. 2, 1895, was a Scottish explorer of Africa. Having studied geology at the University of Edinburgh, he led an expedition for the Royal Geographical Society to Lakes Tanganyika and Rukwa in 1879-80. In 1883-84 he became the first white to cross modern Kenya, visiting Lake Baringo and seeing Mount Kenya before reaching Lake Victoria.

In 1885, Thomson was in northern Nigeria, where he concluded commercial treaties with some of the leaders of the emirates. In 1890, Cecil RHODES sent him to win Katanga for the British South Africa Company, but instead he gained mining and administrative rights for Britain in what is now Zambia. He described his travels in *To the Central African Lakes and Back* (2 vols., 1881), *Through Masai Land* (1883), and other works.   Reviewed by ROBERT I. ROTBERG

Bibliography: Rotberg, Robert I., *Joseph Thomson and the Exploration of Africa* (1971).

Thomson, Sir Joseph John

Sir Joseph John Thomson, a pioneer in modern physics, discovered the electron in 1895, revolutionizing existing theories of atomic structure. Thomson is also recognized for his investigations into the conduction of electricity through gases—which earned him the 1906 Nobel Prize for physics—and for his work on the mathematics of the electromagnetic-field theory proposed by James Maxwell.

Sir Joseph John Thomson, b. Dec. 18, 1856, d. Aug. 30, 1940, is universally recognized as the British scientist who discovered and identified the electron. At the age of 27 he succeeded (1884) Lord Rayleigh as professor of physics at Trinity College, Cambridge, and was named director of its Cavendish Laboratory in the same year, continuing in that position until 1919. Thomson demonstrated (1897) that CATHODE RAYS were actually units of electrical current made up of negatively charged particles of subatomic size. He believed them to be an inte-

gral part of all matter and theorized a model of atomic structure in which a quantity of negatively charged electrons was embedded in a sphere of positive electricity, the two charges neutralizing each other. For these investigations he won (1906) the Nobel Prize for physics; in 1908 he was knighted.

Subsequently, Thomson turned his attention to positively charged ions. His research showed that neon gas was made up of a combination of two different types of ions, each with a different charge, or mass, or both. He did this by using magnetic and electric fields to deflect the stream of positive ions of neon gas onto two different parts of a photographic plate. This demonstration clearly pointed to the possibility that ordinary elements might exist as isotopes (varieties of atoms of the same element, which have the same atomic number but differ in mass).

Thomson was a highly gifted teacher—seven of his research assistants as well as his son, George, won Nobel Prizes for physics—and he led Great Britain to dominance in the field of subatomic particles in the early decades of the 20th century. He was accorded the honor of burial in Westminster Abbey.   JAMES A. BOOTH

Bibliography: Rayleigh, Robert J., *The Life of Sir J. J. Thomson* (1942; repr. 1969); Thomson, George Paget, *J. J. Thomson and the Cavendish Laboratory in His Day* (1965).

Thomson, Tom

The bold forms and vivid colors of Tom Thomson's The West Wind (1916-17) are characteristic of his style. The theme of the beauty, grandeur, and isolation of the northern Canadian wilderness pervades Thomson's landscapes, many of which were inspired by the vistas of Algonquin Park, Ontario. (Art Gallery of Ontario, Toronto.)

The best-known Canadian landscape painter of his time, Tom Thomson, b. Claremont, Ontario, Aug. 4, 1877, made his first trip to the untouched forests and lakes of Algonquin Park in northern Ontario in 1912. This region provided him with his major themes, expressed in his most famous work, *The West Wind* (1916-17; Art Gallery of Ontario, Toronto), in which humanity's struggle with nature is symbolized by a lone pine bent fiercely against a gale. Also evident is Thomson's lively, expressive brushwork and vibrant coloration, which often led him close to abstraction. His wilderness subjects had great influence on later Canadian landscape painters, especially the GROUP OF SEVEN. Although Thomson's career was cut short by his tragic drowning in July 1917, he has since become a legendary figure in Canadian painting.   DAVID WISTOW

Bibliography: Mellen, Peter, *The Group of Seven* (1970); Murray, Joan, *The Art of Tom Thomson* (1973); Reid, Dennis, *The Jack Pine* (1975); Town, Harold, and Silcox, David, *Tom Thomson* (1977).

Thomson, Virgil

The prominent American composer and critic Virgil Thomson, b. Kansas City, Mo., Nov. 25, 1896, attended Harvard University, and while an undergraduate he obtained a traveling fellowship (1921–22) to study with Nadia Boulanger in Paris. Study with Boulanger was a fruitful experience for many American composers of his generation and for Thomson prompted a return to Paris (1925–32). During these Parisian sojourns he associated with Erik Satie, the group of French composers known as Les Six, and with the writers Jean Cocteau and Gertrude Stein, all of whom influenced his work. Thomson's first opera, *Four Saints in Three Acts* (1928; libretto by Gertrude Stein), and many of his other works show aspects akin to the Dada movement in French art of the 1920s. A number of his works were inspired by the theater. His other works include the opera *The Mother of Us All* (1947), *Symphony on a Hymn Tune* (1928), choral works, chamber music, songs, and piano and organ pieces.

Early in the 1920s, Thomson's work as a music critic began with contributions to *Vanity Fair* and *The Boston Transcript.* When he settled permanently in New York in 1940 he became music critic (until 1954) for the *New York Herald Tribune.* His books include *The State of Music* (1939), *The Musical Scene* (1945), *The Art of Judging Music* (1948), *Virgil Thomson on Virgil Thomson* (1966; repr. 1985), and *American Music since 1910* (1971).   QUENTIN W. QUEREAU

Bibliography: Hoover, K., and Cage, J., *Virgil Thomson* (1959; repr. 1970); Tommasini, A., ed., *Virgil Thomson's Musical Portraits* (1986).

Thomson, William: see KELVIN, WILLIAM THOMSON, 1ST BARON.

Thonga   [tahng'-guh]

The Thonga (or Tsonga) are a BANTU-speaking people who live in southern Mozambique and in parts of Swaziland and the Republic of South Africa. Their culture is closely related to that of the SHONA, and their language has affinities with both NGUNI and SOTHO. Primarily agriculturists who raise maize, millet, and sorghum, the Thonga also depend for their subsistence on animal husbandry, trading, fishing, and hunting. A characteristic feature of Thonga social life is that soon after weaning, children are sent to live for several years in the domestic group of their mothers' brothers. Although in most southern African societies priestly functions are carried out by senior male paternal relatives, Thonga men rely on their maternal uncles to perform sacrifices to their ancestors, an essential feature of their traditional religion.

For centuries the indigenous peoples of Mozambique were dominated by the Portuguese until independence was granted in 1975. Owing to poor industrial development in their homeland, many Thonga continue to work as migrant laborers in South Africa, Zimbabwe, Zambia, and Malawi. In the mid-1980s the Thonga population numbered more than 3 million.   PETER CARSTENS

Bibliography: Colson, Elizabeth, *Marriage and Family among the Plateau Thonga* (1958) and *Plateau Thonga of Northern Rhodesia* (1970); Goldman, Irving, "The Bathonga of South Africa," in *Cooperation and Competition among Primitive Peoples,* ed. by Margaret Mead (1937); Junod, Herrie, *The Life of a South African Tribe,* 2 vols., 2d ed. (1926; repr. 1984); Radcliff-Brown, A. R., *Structure and Function in Primitive Society* (1952).

Thor   (mythology)   [thohr]

In Norse mythology Thor was the personification of thunder and the principal war god. Son of the chief god, ODIN, and second only to him in importance, Thor was particularly popular among the lower classes of society. He was armed with a hammer (Mjolnir) that returned to his hand after he hurled it at enemies, a belt that doubled his strength when he wore it, and iron gloves that helped him use the Mjolnir effectively. Most of his battles were fought against giants, and he was benevolent to humankind. Thor was noted for his ability to drink vast amounts; he is generally portrayed as a crude, red-bearded, middle-aged warrior who relied on his immense strength rather than on his wits.

According to one popular legend, the giant who constructed the residence of the gods was rewarded with the Mjolnir. When it fell into the giant Thrym's possession, Thor retrieved it by pretending to be the goddess FREYA, whom Thrym demanded as his wife in exchange for the hammer.

Thor, also known as Atli, is identified with Donar, the thunder god of Teutonic mythology. His name survives in the English weekday name *Thursday* and in its German counterpart, *Donnerstag.*   C. SCOTT LITTLETON

Thor   (rocket)

This American Thor-Delta rocket was used to boost the European HEOS 1 satellite into orbit in 1968. The Thor-Delta, a three-stage solid-propellant rocket, was first launched in 1960 and is a variation of the earlier Thor, a liquid-fuel intermediate-range ballistic missile.

Thor was an intermediate-range ballistic missile (IRBM) developed by the United States in the mid-1950s to provide the first element of a nuclear deterrent against the Soviet missile challenge (see ROCKETS AND MISSILES). It was later adapted for use as a space rocket. The prime contract for the Thor was awarded by the U.S. Air Force Ballistic Missile Division to the Douglas Aircraft Company of Santa Monica, Calif., on Dec. 27, 1955.

The Thor missile stood 19.8 m (65 ft) tall and was fueled with liquid oxygen and kerosene. The lift-off weight was about 49,900 kg (110,000 lb). A single, gimbal-mounted rocket engine delivered a thrust of about 667,000 newtons (68,040 kg/150,000 lb) at sea level. A blunt heat shield protected a thermonuclear warhead. Guidance depended on a preset inertial system. Range was 2,780 km (1,725 mi).

After a series of four unsuccessful launches in 1957, the first satisfactory flight of the Thor occurred on September 20 of that year; it first flew with its guidance system in December. Sixty Thor IRBMs were based at four sites in eastern England under RAF Bomber Command between 1958 and 1963. The missiles were withdrawn when ICBMs became operational in the United States.

In conjunction with upper stages such as AGENA, DELTA, and Able, the modified Thor has been used to launch many U.S. satellites and space probes. The thrust-augmented Thor (TAT) boosted thrust to 1,470,000 newtons (150,000 kg/330,000 lb).   KENNETH GATLAND

thorax: see CHEST.

Thórdarson, Agnar   [tohr'-dahr-suhn, ahng'-nahr]

Agnar Thórdarson, b. Sept. 11, 1917, is an Icelandic playwright and novelist known for his analytical depictions of contemporary society. Among his works are *The Sword* (1953; Eng. trans., 1970), a novel of post–World War II Reykjavik, and the plays *Atoms and Madams* (1956; Eng. trans., 1967), *Gauksklukkan* (The Cuckoo Clock, 1958), *Sannleikur í gifsi* (Truth in Plaster, 1965), and *Lausnargjaldid* (The Ransom, 1973). He has also written short stories, serial plays for radio, and television plays.   HALLBERG HALLMUNDSSON

Thoreau, Henry David   [thohr'-oh or thuh-roh']

Henry David Thoreau expressed his principles through symbolic action as well as the written word, seeking the simplicity of nature at Walden Pond and affirming the primacy of the individual conscience by refusing to pay his taxes. His accounts of these actions in Walden (1854) and "Civil Disobedience" (1849) are only part of his corpus of reflections, nature and travel writings, and poetry.

The writer and naturalist Henry David Thoreau, b. Concord, Mass., July 12, 1817, d. May 6, 1862, is best known for WALDEN, an account of his experiment in simple living, and for the essay "Civil Disobedience" (1849), whose doctrine of passive resistance influenced Mahatma Gandhi and Martin Luther King, Jr. Essentially a philosopher of individualism, Thoreau placed nature above materialism in private life and ethics above conformity in politics.

The Journal. Raised in genteel poverty, Thoreau graduated from Harvard in 1837 and returned to Concord, there becoming a close friend of Ralph Waldo EMERSON and other transcendentalists. With Emerson's encouragement, Thoreau continued with a journal that he had begun in 1834. It was conceived as a literary notebook, but it gradually developed into a work of art in its own right, serving as a record of the author's thoughts and discoveries about nature and containing his comments on the culture of his time. Eventually reaching more than 2 million words, it ran to 14 volumes when published in 1906.

Having worked briefly as a teacher in Concord and as a tutor to the children of Emerson's brother in New York, Thoreau much preferred the literary career urged on him by Emerson. He published essays, poems, and reviews in various magazines, including Emerson's *The Dial,* whose editorship Thoreau assumed briefly in 1843 when Emerson was away.

Walden. Now permanently established in the neighborhood of Concord, Thoreau built a small cabin in 1845 on Emerson's land near Walden Pond and lived there for 2 years. His purpose in going to the pond was to simplify his life, reduce his expenses, and devote his time to writing and observing nature. Out of his experiment came two books, *A Week on the Concord and Merrimack Rivers* (1849), the description of a rowboat excursion he had taken with his brother in 1839, and *Walden* (1854). The former was a complete failure, selling only 219 copies in 4 years; but the latter, received more favorably, laid the foundation for Thoreau's reputation.

In July 1846, a year after moving into his cabin, Thoreau refused to pay his poll tax as a protest against American slavery and went to jail. Freed the next morning when an aunt, over his objections, paid the tax, he wrote "Resistance to Civil Government," later better known as "Civil Disobedience." In it he emphasized personal ethics and responsibility, urging the individual to follow the dictates of conscience in any con-

flict between it and the civil law and to violate unjust laws to effect their repeal. Thoreau continued his protests against slavery by lecturing, by aiding escaped slaves in their flight to freedom in Canada, and by publicly defending John Brown when he attacked Harpers Ferry in 1859.

Travels and Nature Study. Unable to support himself through his writing, Thoreau worked for a time as a laborer, including a stint in his family's pencil factory, and as a surveyor. During this period in the latter 1850s, he traveled extensively, recounting his excursions in essays on Cape Cod (1865), Quebec (1866), and the Maine wilderness (1864).

For most of his adult life Thoreau spent a large part of each day examining the flora and fauna of Concord. The journal records of his observations are among the most complete for any American locale, and his essay *Succession of Forest Trees* (1860) is a major contribution to natural history. At the time of his death he was engaged in a massive study of native fruits and seeds.

Place in American Thought. Long ill with tuberculosis, Thoreau died after a futile journey (1861) to Minnesota in search of better health. He is buried in Sleepy Hollow Cemetery in Concord, near the graves of his friends Emerson, Nathaniel Hawthorne, and Bronson Alcott.

In his lifetime often dismissed as an imitator of Emerson, Thoreau has slowly won an independent reputation as one of America's greatest prose stylists; as a naturalist, pioneer ecologist, and conservationist; as an advocate of the simple life; and as a proponent of democratic individualism. A visionary humanist, he gave perhaps the best summary of his thought in *Walden*'s succinct and yet profound injunction, "Simplify, simplify."   WALTER HARDING

Bibliography: Cavell, Stanley, *The Senses of Walden* (1972); Harding, Walter, *A Thoreau Handbook* (1959) and *The Days of Henry Thoreau* (1965); Lebeaux, Richard, *Young Man Thoreau* (1977); Paul, Sherman, *The Shores of America: Thoreau's Inward Exploration* (1958).

Thorfinn Karlsefni   [thohr'-fin kahrl'-sev-nee]

Thorfinn Karlsefni, an Icelandic explorer, attempted (c.1010) to found a settlement in North America soon after LEIF ERIKSSON's voyage there. According to two Icelandic sagas, Thorfinn was a wealthy trader who led a Viking expedition to the territory called VINLAND, in North America, and wintered there. The Scandinavians, both men and women, traded and then fought with the native Skraelings (roughly, "savages"). The descriptions of Skraeling culture in the sagas are consistent with American Indian life. Because of Skraeling attacks, the settlement was abandoned after three winters. Its location, like that of the earlier Viking settlements, is a matter of scholarly debate; L'ANSE AUX MEADOWS is one possible site. Thorfinn eventually settled in Iceland.

Bibliography: Ingstad, A. S., *Norse Discovery of America* (1977); Reman, E., *The Norse Discoveries and Explorations in America* (1949).

thorium   [thohr'-ee-uhm]

The element thorium is a radioactive metal of the ACTINIDE SERIES. Its symbol is Th, its atomic number 90, and the atomic weight of its stablest isotope 232.038. Thorium was discovered in 1828 by J. J. Berzelius. Because it can be converted into fissionable uranium-233 in a BREEDER REACTOR, it may become an important source of atomic fuel. Thorium is also used in one type of RADIOMETRIC AGE-DATING technique.

Thorn, Gaston   [tohrn]

A Luxembourgian politician, Gaston Thorn, b. Sept. 3, 1928, became president of the Commission of the European Communities in January 1981. Thorn began (1957) his political career as a member of the Luxembourg town council. In 1959 he was elected to the Chamber of Deputies, and in 1961 he became president of the Democratic party. Thorn went on to become prime minister (1974–79) and foreign minister (1979–80). He was also elected president of the Federation of Liberal and Democratic Parties of the European Community and of the 30th session of the UN General Assembly.

Thorn-Prikker, Johan   [tohrn-prik'-ur]

Johan Thorn-Prikker, b. June 5, 1868, d. Mar. 5, 1932, was a painter, designer, and decorator of the Dutch Jugendstil. His early style showed the influence of Paul Gauguin and the French symbolists (the Nabis), Japanese prints, and the Flemish primitives. Paintings of this period are in the Kröller-Müller Museum in Otterlo, Belgium. Thorn-Prikker later turned toward the linear idiom of Art Nouveau. After 1895 his work became more austere and, from 1902 on, gradually more angular and geometric.   MAGDALENA DABROWSKI

Thorndike, Edward L.

Edward Lee Thorndike, b. Williamsburg, Mass., Aug. 31, 1874, d. Aug. 9, 1949, was a major figure in several fields of psychology: learning theory, applied psychology, and mental measurement. First influenced by William James at Harvard, he then went to Columbia University where he earned his Ph.D. with James McK. CATTEL and taught there from 1909 to 1940. His learning theory, applied to animals and human beings, added the principle of effect (success, pleasure, satisfaction) to Hermann Ebbinghaus's principle of exercise. Thorndike rid his theories of the mentalism of earlier psychologists and paved the way for the behaviorism of B. F. SKINNER and John B. WATSON. He published about 500 books and articles, including his thesis *Animal Intelligence* (1898), *Educational Psychology* (1903, later in three volumes), and *Mental and Social Measurements* (1904), and was president of the American Psychological Association.   E. B. PAGE

Bibliography: Jonçich, Geraldine M., *The Sane Positivist: A Biography of Edward Lee Thorndike* (1968).

Thorndike, Dame Sybil

One of England's foremost actresses, Sybil Thorndike, b. Oct. 24, 1882, d. June 9, 1976, had an immense range that allowed her to perform equally well in tragic or comic parts, in Shakespearean or in modern drama. Her most acclaimed performances were in *The Trojan Women* (1920), *Saint Joan* (1924), and *The Family Reunion* (1956).

Thornhill, Sir James

Sir James Thornhill, b. 1675 or 1676, d. May 4, 1734, was an English painter in the baroque tradition. Although his early training remains obscure, he clearly had a knowledge of architecture and may have mastered the painting techniques of the Italian and French artists then working in England. He excelled in large-scale decoration of palace interiors in the grand manner—that is, grandiose compositions of figures in animated or rhetorical postures. His first major commission was the ceiling decoration (1707-14) of the Painted Hall at Greenwich, and it was followed by commissions at Hampton Court (1714-15) and Blenheim (1716).   PHILIP GOULD

Bibliography: Brocklebank, Joan, *Sir James Thornhill of Dorset 1675-1734* (1975); Waterhouse, Ellis K., *Painting in Britain, 1530-1790*, 2d ed. (1962).

Thornthwaite climatic classification   [thohrn'-thwayt]

In 1948 the American climatologist C. W. Thornthwaite (1899-1963) introduced an empirical climatic classification based on the climatic water budget. The classification involves a thermal efficiency index, which is equivalent to the potential evapotranspiration—the amount of moisture that would be evaporated from soil and transpired by plants if the supply were unlimited—and a moisture index, which is the difference between precipitation and potential evapotranspiration. An earlier system (1931) proposed by Thornthwaite was based on five distinct humidity provinces characterized by distinct vegetation. The problem of estimating potential evapotranspiration has restricted the use of this system.   WALTRAUD A. R. BRINKMANN

Bibliography: Oliver, J. E., *Climate and Man's Environment* (1973).

Thoroddsen, Jón   [toh'-rawt-sen]

Author of the first modern novel of Icelandic literature, Jón Thoroddsen, 1818-68, studied law in Copenhagen and on returning to Iceland became a magistrate. Nature poems and patriotic songs were his first literary works. Soon after fighting in the Danish-German war (1848-50), he published a novel, *Lad and Lass* (1850; Eng. trans., 1890). His principal work, *Maður og kona* (Man and Wife, published posthumously, 1876), remained unfinished but is considered an important innovation in Icelandic fiction. A realistic portrayal of rural life, it is enriched by picturesque scenes of folk life and comic subordinate characters.   AAGE JØRGENSEN

Thoroughbred

The Thoroughbred is a light horse of superior speed and stamina used for flat racing, the steeplechase, hunting, and polo.

The Thoroughbred is a breed of horse developed for speed and elegance in racing. Some Thoroughbreds are also used for hunting and polo. About 16 hands (1.6 m/64 in) tall, the animals weigh from about 455 to 680 kg (1,000 to 1,500 lb) and have short, slim bodies with long muscles and long, strong legs. The head is delicate, somewhat like that of an Arabian horse. A Thoroughbred's speed depends on its individual ability, track conditions, weight carried, and distance run. The horses are high-spirited and nervous, and some tend to develop unsoundness of wind and limb. In the United States, Thoroughbreds are often bay colored but may also be chestnut, gray, roan, brown, or black.

All Thoroughbreds are descended from three Oriental stallions—Godolphin Barb, Darley Arabian, and Byerly Turk—imported into England between 1689 and 1724. They were bred with English mares having a strong mixture of Arabian, Turk, and Barb blood and soon produced progeny that grew to be as much as 20 cm (8 in) taller than their sires. A son of Darley Arabian, Bulle Rock, was imported into Virginia in 1730; soon other Thoroughbreds were brought to America. The most famous U.S. Thoroughbred was Man O'War (1917-47), who had only one defeat in 21 races.   EVERETT SENTMAN

Bibliography: Hollingsworth, Kent, *The Kentucky Thoroughbred* (1976); Napier, Miles, *Blood Will Tell* (1976).

Thorpe, Jeremy   [thohrp]

British politician John Jeremy Thorpe, b. Apr. 29, 1929, educated at Eton and Oxford, started (1954) his career as a barrister and became (1959) a Liberal member of Parliament for North Devon. He energetically served (1967–76) as leader of the Liberal party, which was able to poll a postwar high of 19.3 percent of the votes cast in the general election in the spring of 1974. Thorpe's seemingly brilliant political future was shattered when a scandal erupted in 1976, involving a charge that he conspired to murder an alleged homosexual lover, Norman Scott. Thorpe resigned as leader of the Liberal party and was arrested in 1978. Acquitted in 1979, Thorpe ran unsuccessfully to regain his parliamentary seat.

Thorpe, Jim

James Francis Thorpe, b. Prague, Okla., May 28, 1888, d. Mar. 28, 1953, was an American athlete who was selected by sportswriters as the greatest athlete of the first half of the 20th century. Thorpe, who was of American Indian, Irish, and French descent, played football at the Carlisle (Pa.) Indian School and was an All-American in 1911 and 1912. While at Carlisle, he also played lacrosse and baseball and ran track. In the 1912 Olympic Games, Thorpe set records in winning the decathlon and the pentathlon. In 1913 he was stripped of his gold medals when it was learned that he had earned money playing baseball. Thorpe started playing professional football in 1915 for the Canton Bulldogs, and in ensuing years he played for Marion, Toledo, Rock Island, and New York. He also played professional baseball from 1913 to 1919. In 1963 he was made a charter member of the Pro Football Hall of Fame. In 1982 the International Olympic Committee voted to restore the medals it had rescinded nearly 70 years before.

Bibliography: Newcombe, Jack, *Best of the Athletic Boys* (1975); Wheeler, Robert W., *Jim Thorpe* (1975; repr. 1978).

Thorvaldsen, Bertel   [tohr'-vahl-sen]

The sculptural precision and clarity of Bertel Thorvaldsen's Hebe (1806) is characteristic of his neoclassical style, derived from Greek and Roman artistic traditions. The 19th-century Danish sculptor worked in Rome for most of his life and used themes from classical antiquity as the principal subjects for his sculptures. The Thorvaldsen Museum (1839–48), which houses his tomb and much of his artwork, is in Copenhagen. (National Museet, Copenhagen.)

Bertel Thorvaldsen, one of Denmark's most famous sculptors and a leading figure in European NEOCLASSICISM, was born in Copenhagen on Nov. 19, 1770, and died on Mar. 24, 1844. The son of a wood-carver, he entered the Copenhagen Royal Academy of Fine Art in 1781, studying with the neoclassical sculptor N. A. Abildgaard and winning a prize to study in Rome in 1796. In Rome he studied the artworks of classical antiquity, which reinforced his already developing style. He remained in Rome throughout his working career except for a brief stay (1819) in Copenhagen and his final return (1838) to that city.

Between 1800 and his death Thorvaldsen executed important commissions throughout Europe, including his monumental *Triumphal Entry of Alexander the Great into Babylon* (1812; Quirinale Palace, Rome), which celebrated a visit to Rome by Napoleon I. After the death (1822) of Antonio Canova, Thorvaldsen became the principal spokesman for neoclassical art and Europe's most influential sculptor. Although he is still admired for his modeling and draftsmanship, Thorvaldsen's reputation has diminished somewhat over the years, his highly finished works being generally regarded by modern critics as cold and lifeless when compared with the more baroque forms of Canova or of John Flaxman. Among his most successful works are carved reliefs such as *Cupid Received by Anacreon* (1823; Thorvaldsen Museum, Copenhagen), which exemplifies the clarity, intensity, and simplicity of his interpretation of classical sources.   ALVIN R. MARTIN

Bibliography: Arts Council of Great Britain, *The Age of Neo-Classicism* (1972); Hawley, Henry, *Neo-Classicism: Style and Motif* (1964); Thorvaldsen Museum, *Catalogue of Thorvaldsen's Museum* (1961).

Thoth   [thahth]

Thoth was the Greek name for the Egyptian deity Djhowtey, god of learning, wisdom, and magic. In late Egyptian mythology he was the creator and orderer of the universe and the inventor of writing, arithmetic, and astronomy. Thoth was depicted as an ibis-headed man carrying a pen and an ink holder or as a dog-headed baboon. In the Hellenistic period he was identified with the Greek god HERMES and in later European lore with Hermes Trismegistus, patron of magicians. "The Book of Thoth" is a traditional name for tarot cards.

Thousand Islands

The Thousand Islands are more than 1,500 densely wooded islands in the ST. LAWRENCE RIVER reaching from Prince Edward Point on Lake Ontario downstream for 130 km (80 mi) to Brockville, Ontario. Several are included in Canada's St. Lawrence Islands National Park, and others are part of New York State.

Thousand and One Nights: see ARABIAN NIGHTS.

Thrace   [thrays]

Thrace is a historic region in the southeastern Balkans, corresponding to the northeastern Greek province of Thrace (Thráki), European Turkey, and southern Bulgaria. The region is bounded by the Black Sea in the east and the Aegean and Sea of Marmara in the south. To the ancient Greeks Thrace extended as far north as the Danube and as far west as the Vardar River. The Roman province of Thrace, however, was bounded by the Balkan Mountains in the north and the Nestos River in the west, and this smaller area is the one to which the name *Thrace* is now applied. The terrain is mountainous, dominated by the Balkan, Rhodope, and Pangaeus ranges, but the fertile Thracian plain or Maritsa River valley accounts for the region's largely agricultural economy. Important products are tobacco, grain, cotton, olive oil, and fruit. EDIRNE, ISTANBUL, and SOFIA are the region's principal cities.

Thrace was originally settled by the Thracians, a people of Indo-European stock who were famous in the ancient world as warriors. The Greeks began colonizing the region's coasts in the 7th century BC. BYZANTIUM, site of Istanbul, was the most important Greek colony. Thrace was dominated in turn by the Persians, Greeks, and Romans. In AD 46, Emperor Claudius reduced Thrace to a Roman province. Beginning in the 3d century AD, Roman, and later Byzantine, control was challenged by repeated Germanic and Slavic invasions. A Bulgarian state was established in the 7th century and, apart from one period of eclipse (1081–1186), dominated the area until the Ottoman Turks overran Thrace between 1361 and 1453. As the Ottoman Empire disintegrated in the late 19th and early 20th centuries, Thrace was divided, fought over, and redivided among the successor states, Bulgaria, Greece, and Turkey. The present-day political boundaries were created by 1923.

thrasher

The brown thrasher, T. rufum (left), is the only thrasher found east of the Rockies. The California thrasher, T. redivivum, has short wings and often runs on the ground instead of flying. Both feed on the ground, using their curved bills to search for food.

Thrashers are medium-sized songbirds found in North and Central America. About 17 species, related to catbirds and mockingbirds, are classified in the mimic thrush family, Mimidae. Thrashers range from 20 to 30 cm (8 to 12 in) in length, are slim and long-tailed, and typically have long, more-or-less decurved bills. Most are brown or gray above and spotted or streaked below. The brown thrasher, *Toxostoma rufum,* of the eastern United States, breeds as far north as southern Canada. Reddish brown above, white and heavily striped below, it has two white wing bars. It feeds on insects and fruit and, like other thrashers, vocalizes a variety of sounds as well as a lengthy song. Both parents typically incubate the four pale green, spotted eggs and care for the chicks. The sage thrasher, *Oreoscoptes montanus,* of the western United States, is somewhat smaller and darker and has a shorter tail.

WILLIAM SANDFORD

Thrasybulus   [thras-uh-bue'-luhs]

The Athenian general Thrasybulus, d. c.389 BC, became a popular hero because of his opposition to the Thirty Tyrants, who had suppressed democracy in Athens. In 411 and 410 BC he won naval victories over the Spartans during the Peloponnesian War. Exiled by the Thirty, he returned (403) with a small army and helped to restore democracy. With Athens again at war with Sparta, from 395, Thrasybulus led a fleet toward Rhodes and was murdered at Aspendus.   ROBIN BUSS

thread

Thread is a tightly twisted strand of fiber that is spun from silk, cotton, wool, or synthetic material. Thread is generally more tightly twisted, and of thinner diameter, than yarn (see SPINNING). Cotton thread was first commercially manufactured in Paisley, Scotland, in 1806, when the Napoleonic blockade of Britain cut off the supply of silk thread. Cotton quickly surpassed silk in popularity because it was strong and low in price. To make thread, cotton fibers are cleaned, combed, and rolled into firm coils. The coils are stretched on a drawing frame and flattened by heavy rollers. These fiber ribbons are then folded, pressed, and drawn out on doubling frames. Finished thread is dyed or bleached and wound on spools or bobbins. Cotton thread is often mercerized, or immersed in a caustic soda solution, which increases strength and luster and gives the thread a greater affinity for dye.

Thread is numbered according to thickness, the lower numbers representing the thicker threads. Buttonhole twist, a strong lustrous silk thread, is three times the diameter of fine sewing silk and is used for handworked buttonholes. Synthetic thread withstands high-speed machine sewing and offers great resistance to seam failure and abrasion.

threadfin

A threadfin is a marine, mostly inshore, tropical fish with separate, filamentous rays on the lower part of the pectoral fin. More than 30 species of threadfin, which are also often known as tasselfish, make up the family Polynemidae. Most are 60 cm (2 ft) or less in length and have an anchovylike overhung snout. An Indo-Pacific threadfin, *Eleutheroma tetradactylum,* reaches 1.8 m (6 ft) in length.

three-body problem

A classic, unsolved problem is to describe and predict the motions of three objects (or "point masses") whose movement is subject only to their mutual gravitational attractions. The situation is approximated in many instances in nature. For example, a number of triple-star systems have been observed; a good approximation for the motion of an asteroid is found by considering only the Sun, Jupiter, and the asteroid; and to specify the motion of the Moon, the primary problem to be solved is that in which only the Earth, Moon, and Sun are taken into account. The laws governing the motion of the three bodies are Newton's laws of motion and the law of gravitation. The corresponding two-body problem was completely solved by Isaac Newton, but the three-body problem has been solved for only a few special cases. The most famous of these were discovered by Leonhard EULER and Joseph Louis de LAGRANGE.

Colinear Case. Euler showed (1767) that three bodies can lie permanently on a straight line that will usually rotate in space in a plane. The colinear solutions are unstable because a small disturbance will lead to a large departure from colinearity. For a system consisting of the Earth, Moon, and a space vehicle, the colinear points, especially the one between the Earth and the Moon, are considered as possible "parking" points for the vehicle because only a small amount of guidance would be needed to keep it there.

Triangular Case. Lagrange showed (1772) that three bodies can lie at the apexes of an equilateral triangle, which in general rotates in its plane and pulsates. If one of the bodies is sufficiently massive compared with the other two, then the triangular configuration is apparently stable, but this theory has not been rigorously proved. Two groups of asteroids in the solar system, called the TROJANS, are so located that, on the average, they, the Sun, and Jupiter form equilateral triangles.

General Case. Almost any particular orbit can be followed by numerical calculation, but it can be followed only for a limited time because of the errors that inevitably accumulate in such a computation. Also, approximate formulas can be found for orbits, but these are useful only over a limited period. Instead of asking for detailed quantitative information, the following qualitative questions might be asked: Can motion such as that presently followed by the system Earth, Moon, and Sun remain similar for all time? Can two bodies capture a third to form a permanently bound triple system? What can be said about the permanence or stability of a triple-star system? In general, such questions cannot be answered, but scientists do know that capture is at least extremely unlikely and that if three bodies are put together in a random way, one will almost certainly escape.

The Restricted Problem of Three Bodies. A simplified version of the problem is the restricted problem of three bodies. In this case, one of the bodies is assumed to be "massless"—in other words, to have mass so insignificant as not to affect the motion of the other two, which move around each other in circular orbits, while the massless body (which is affected, of course, by the other two) moves in the common orbital plane. The motion of a space vehicle in the Earth-Moon system is an approximation to this problem. This is one of the most famous problems in mathematics and remains unsolved despite intensive work by many mathematicians.

J. M. A. DANBY

A massless body (such as a space vehicle) of sufficiently low energy is confined permanently within the so-called Hill regions, named for the American mathematician George William Hill. As the energy of the body increases (from Figures A to F), the Hill regions (white) expand and the forbidden regions (shaded) contract. With sufficient energy a space vehicle can escape the Earth and approach the Moon, and with still more energy it can escape from the Earth-Moon system.

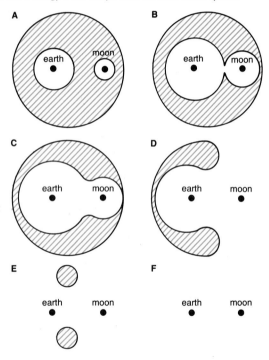

Bibliography: Danby, J., *Fundamentals of Celestial Mechanics* (1962).

Three Marias, The

The Three Marias are the three Portuguese writers **Maria Isabel Barreno**, b. July 10, 1939, **Maria Teresa Horta**, b. May 20, 1937, and **Maria Fátima Velho de Costa**, b. June 26, 1938, who collaborated on the controversial *New Portuguese Letters* (1972; Eng. trans., 1975), an anthology of poems, fictitious letters, and some of the authors' own correspondence. Based on the classic *Letters of a Portuguese Nun* (1669; Eng. trans., 1678) supposedly written by Sister Mariana Alcoforado (1640–1723) to her faithless lover, the anthology was promptly banned in Portugal because of its sexual frankness and open criticism of the country's repressive government. Put on trial, the authors were held by the authorities until the 1974 revolution ended the old regime.

NORWOOD ANDREWS, JR.

Three Musketeers, The

A historical novel by Alexandre DUMAS père, *The Three Musketeers* (1844) is set during the reign of LOUIS XIII (1610–43) and based on actual events. Three musketeers, loyal servants

of the king, are joined by the dashing D'Artagnan; the four together take on Louis's enemies, in particular the soldiers of Cardinal Richelieu. Influenced by Sir Walter Scott, Dumas's narrative is dramatic and abounds in local color. It was so successful that Dumas wrote two sequels: *Twenty Years After* (1845; Eng. trans., 1846) and *The Vicomte of Bragelonne* (1850; Eng. trans., 1857).

JOSEPH A. REITER

Three Sisters, The

The Three Sisters (1901; Eng. trans., 1926), a four-act play by Anton CHEKHOV, is a study of shattered illusions. It depicts three women, Irina, Masha, and Olga, who fail to realize their much-advertised ambition to leave the provinces and return to Moscow. Instead, they experience disappointment both in love and work, as does their brother Andrey. In keeping with Chekhov's unobtrusively original method as a playwright, *The Three Sisters* is characterized by little action and much inconsequential dialogue. The characters' inner world is expertly delineated, however, and Chekhov characteristically distills drama out of the undramatic, making the trivialities of everyday life seem simultaneously ridiculous and profoundly moving.

RONALD HINGLEY

Threepenny Opera, The

The Threepenny Opera is a popular play by Bertolt BRECHT, with music by Kurt WEILL, that was first produced in 1928. An adaptation of John Gay's THE BEGGAR'S OPERA (1728), it is an anticapitalistic satire that caustically portrays European culture between the two world wars. The robber, Macheath, marries Polly Peachum, and her father, furious at the marriage, has Macheath arrested in a brothel with his favorite, Jenny. In prison, Macheath captures the heart of Lucy, the police chief's daughter, who engineers his escape. Rearrested and about to be hanged, Macheath is saved by a royal pardon.

MYRON MATLAW

thrift

Thrift is the common name for some species of perennial herbs of the genus *Armeria* in the family Plumbaginaceae. They are small plants with basal rosettes of narrow evergreen leaves and bear pink or white flowers. Native to a cool climate, they are commonly found in well-drained soils on sea cliffs and high mountains in western Europe. The most cultivated species is *A. maritima*, which is generally planted on borders, along walks, and in rock gardens.

thrips

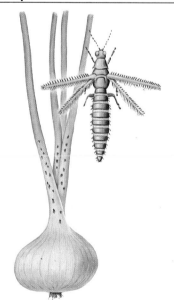

An onion thrip, Thrips tabaci, is an agricultural pest throughout the world. The adult lays eggs on a cultivated plant, such as an onion, cabbage, or tobacco; the hatched nymph (not shown) sucks juices from the plant.

Numbering about 4,000 species worldwide, thrips are common insects comprising the order Thysanoptera. Rarely longer than 3 mm (⅛ in), thrips can be serious pests of cultivated plants. Feeding on flowers, leaves, and even twigs with their conical, sucking mouthparts, thrips cause severe injury to plant epidermal cells. Prolific breeders, thrips can spawn several generations each year. Males are rare or unknown in some species, and parthenogenesis—the development of new individuals from unfertilized eggs—is common. Generally black or brownish, most species have two pairs of narrow wings fringed with long hairs.   DONALD J. BORROR

thrombophlebitis: see PHLEBITIS.

thrombosis [thrahm-boh'-sis]

Thrombosis is the formation of a blood clot (thrombus) in a blood vessel. It can occur when a blood vessel is injured by infection or trauma. If the injury is caused by bacteria, they may eventually disintegrate the clot, causing infectious particles to be carried through the bloodstream to establish secondary infections (metastases) at other sites. Alternatively, the entire clot can break loose, especially in the absence of infection, and be carried through the circulatory system until it reaches a blood vessel too narrow to pass. There it lodges and instantly blocks circulation, a condition called *embolism*. Tissues normally supplied by the obstructed vessel disintegrate and die unless their needs can be met by other nearby blood vessels called *collaterals*. The clinical consequences of an embolism depend on where it occurs. If it occurs in the brain, it can cause a stroke. If it occurs in a coronary artery, it can cause a heart attack.   PETER L. PETRAKIS

Through the Looking-Glass

A fantasy written for older children, Lewis CARROLL's *Through the Looking-Glass, and What Alice Found There* (1872) is a sequel to ALICE'S ADVENTURES IN WONDERLAND (1865). The book recounts a dream in which Alice moves across the landscape of a chessboard until she is crowned queen. The plot is elaborated as a game of chess, and in characters such as Humpty Dumpty and poems such as "Jabberwocky" Carroll has sophisticated fun with the conventions of logic and language. Even more than its predecessor, the book is permeated by a sense of the sadness of growing up, especially in the character of the White Knight.   DONALD J. GRAY

thrush (bird)

Thrushes, family Turdidae, comprise more than 300 species of SONGBIRDS, including some of the world's best-known birds: the American robin, *Turdus migratorius;* the European blackbird, *T. merula;* bluebirds, genus *Sialia;* and the nightingale, *Luscinia megarhynchos.* A number of other birds not in the thrush family also have the word *thrush* as part of their common name. Thrushes are found throughout the world, except in New Zealand and Antarctica, but are most numerous in the Old World. Many species are migratory.

Thrushes are from 10 to 33 cm (4 to 13 in) long and have stout legs—with a characteristic scale arrangement called a booted tarsus—and stout feet. Many of the adults are brownish and often spotted; the young are at least partially spotted. The birds feed mainly on insects, but they also eat fruit. The female alone usually builds an open, cup-shaped nest of grass, leaves, and moss and incubates the two to six pale-colored, often spotted eggs.

The wood thrush, *Hylocichla mustelina,* is a familiar North American thrush. It has cinnamon upper parts, a spotted white breast and sides, and is known for its flutelike song.   GARY D. SCHNELL

Bibliography: Bent, Arthur C., *Life Histories of North American Thrushes, Kinglets and Their Allies* (1949).

thrush (infection): see CANDIDIASIS.

thrust fault: see FAULT.

Thucydides [thoo-sid'-i-deez]

Thucydides, c.460–c.400 BC, the Athenian historian of the PELOPONNESIAN WAR, is considered by many to be the greatest of the ancient Greek historians. His work had a profound influence on the development of historical writing. Although he was a relative of the great soldier and statesman CIMON, Thucydides was also an admirer of Cimon's political opponent, PERICLES. Thucydides served as general in 424 but was banished from Athens in that year for his failure to protect Amphipolis from the Spartans. He returned from exile after the war ended in 404.

Thucydides began writing his HISTORY OF THE PELOPONNESIAN WAR in 431 when the great war broke out. He believed that the war would prove epochal and that his account would possess permanent value because such significant conflicts were bound to occur in future epochs "so long as human nature remained the same." The speeches he inserted into his history, brilliantly conceived and written, probe deeply into human motivation and explain the policy of states in terms of human psychology.

The song of the varied thrush, Ixoreus naevius (female and male, left), *is a series of long notes on different pitches. Songs of the Swainson's thrush,* Hylocichla ustulata (center), *and the wood thrush,* H. mustelina (right), *have patterns of flutelike phrases.*

Thucydides, the first Greek to write contemporary history, was deeply indebted to HERODOTUS for his conception of the fundamental importance of historical writing. Unlike Herodotus, however, who considered it his duty to repeat what people said without necessarily subscribing to it, Thucydides made every effort to authenticate the facts he reported, and he shows unusual sophistication in his awareness of the way that witnesses often misremember what they have seen.

Although an admirer of Periclean democracy, Thucydides was not a democratic ideologue. He approved of the curtailment of the democracy in 411 and even found the oligarchic constitution of Chios admirable. In statesmen he valued above all intelligence and foresight, qualities possessed by his heroes Themistocles and Pericles. Generally, his *History* is remarkable for its objectivity, although his treatment of Sparta and Athens shows that he greatly admired the qualities attributed to the Athenians—inventiveness, daring, and aggressiveness. The *History* is incomplete, ending abruptly with Thucydides' narrative of the events of 411 BC.

CHARLES W. FORNARA

Bibliography: Abbott, George F., *Thucydides: A Study in Historical Reality* (1970); Adcock, Sir Frank Ezra, *Thucydides and His History* (1963; repr. 1973); Cochran, C. N., *Thucydides and the Science of History* (1929; repr. 1965); Connor, W. Robert, *Thucydides* (1984); Cornford, F. M., *Thucydides Mythhistoricus* (1907); Gomme, Arnold Wycombe, et al., *A Historical Commentary on Thucydides,* 5 vols. (1945–81); Woodhead, Arthur Geoffrey, *Thucydides on the Nature of Power* (1970).

Thucydides, a 5th-century-BC Greek historian and member of the Athenian aristocracy, is remembered for his History of the Peloponnesian War, *a record of the decline of Athenian power. Thucydides' importance as a historian lies in his emphasis on individual action rather than fate in controlling the course of events.*

Thugs   [thuhgz]

The Thugs (from Sanskrit, "to conceal") were organized gangs of murderers who for more than 600 years wandered India robbing and killing wayfarers by ritual methods (strangling with scarves) and with sacrificial rites accompanying the burial. Devoted to Kali, the terrible form of Shiva's consort, the Thugs had their own jargon and signs of recognition and functioned as a subcaste within the Indian social structure (they were so reported in surveys during the 19th century). In the 1830s the British administration, in cooperation with some of the princely states, rounded up most of the Thugs. After 1840 the gangs disappeared.   KARL H. POTTER

Bibliography: Bruce, George L., *The Stranglers: The Cult of Thuggee and Its Overthrow in British India* (1968).

A mid-19th-century painting portrays the method used by the Thugs in their ritual murders. Three Thugs were usually assigned to each victim, who was chosen according to a divinatory ritual. The victim was strangled with a scarf or handkerchief, the traditional murder weapon. Before burial the body was ritually mutilated.

thulium   [thoo'-lee-uhm]

Thulium is a lustrous metallic element of the rare earth LATHANIDE SERIES, group IIIB of the periodic table. Its symbol is Tm, its atomic number 69, its atomic weight 168.934, and its valence 3. It was discovered by the Swedish chemist Per Teodor Cleve in 1879. The synthetic isotope ^{170}Tm is radioactive and used as a source of gamma rays in portable X-ray machines.

Thumb   (family)

Originally a family of stonemasons from the Voralberg district of western Austria, the Thumb family and their close relations the Beer family, as well as such other Voralberger masons as the Moosbruggers, became leading architects from the mid-17th to the mid-18th century. In southern Germany, Switzerland, and Austria, they worked first in the baroque style and later in the rococo style as well.

The principal Thumb architects were **Peter I**, his sons **Michael** (*c.*1640–90) and **Christian** (*c.*1640–1726), and Michael's son **Peter II** (b. Dec. 18, 1681, d. May 4, 1766), who was probably the most distinguished of all. Among their major works are the abbey churches at Obermarchthal (1686–92), Saint Peter in the Black Forest (1724–27), and Saint Gallen (1755–65), as well as the pilgrimage church at Birnau (1746–50) and libraries at the monasteries of Saint Peter (1737–50) and Saint Gallen (1757–67).

Bibliography: Hitchcock, Henry-Russell, *Rococo Architecture in Southern Germany* (1968).

Thunder Bay

Thunder Bay, one of Canada's largest ports and the western terminus of the ST. LAWRENCE SEAWAY, was formed in 1970 by the merger of Fort William and Port Arthur. Located in west central Ontario on Lake Superior's Thunder Bay, it has a population of 112,272 (1986). The city is a major grain shipping center; other economic activities include mining, paper and pulp milling, food processing, lumbering, and shipbuilding. Lakehead University (1965) is located there.

The inhabitants of the area when the first Europeans came were Ojibwa Indians. Probably first settled by the French in the 1670s, the site was permanently settled in the early 19th century when the North West Company built the fur-trading port of Fort William. Port Arthur developed as a silver-mining city after the 1870s. In the 1880s the Canadian Pacific Railway boosted the area's growth, and in 1906 the two cities merged their harbors.

thunderstorm

Heating of the Earth's land surface often causes thermals, or parcels of warm air, to rise to the level of condensation. If the thermals contain sufficient moisture and the atmosphere is conditionally unstable, towering cumulus clouds may form. Under suitable conditions the cumulus towers may merge to form CUMULONIMBUS CLOUDS, which have the distinctive feature of an anvil-shaped top. Cumulonimbus clouds in turn produce thunderstorms, which are local storms accompanied always by LIGHTNING and thunder, often by strong gusts of wind and heavy rainfall (see PRECIPITATION, weather), and occasionally by TORNADOES and hail.

Thunderstorms play an important role in the Earth's hydrologic cycle and general circulation by vertically transporting a large part of the heat and water vapor that enters the atmosphere from the Earth's surface in response to solar heating. Thunderstorms produce a large fraction of the annual rainfall in many areas of the world, especially the semiarid and tropical equatorial regions. In most areas of the world, especially those regions in the United States, Canada, and the Ukraine where corn and wheat are the major crops, rainfall during the peak growing season is supplied by thunderstorms. Thunderstorms are also the engines of tropical disturbances that bring a large fraction of the annual rainfall to tropical coastal regions.

FORMATION AND CIRCULATION

During the cumulus stage, the growing cloud is characterized by the initial formation of small precipitation elements and the presence of generally active updrafts throughout its vertical extent. Updraft velocities may exceed 10 m/sec (33 ft/sec) in the interior of the cloud. In the mature stage the cloud has expanded laterally and grown to greater heights in the atmosphere. A strong updraft over a broad area exists in the cloud's upper levels. In a less intense thunderstorm a downdraft originating at heights of 3 to 5 km (2 to 3 mi) above the cloud base often pinches off the updraft air at low levels, leading to the eventual demise of the cloud. New clouds frequently form along an advancing air mass that is chilled by the evaporation of rain and that emanates from the downdraft spreading laterally beneath the cloud. Thunderstorms often contain precipitation in the form of raindrops, graupel, and small hail in the interior of the cloud and snowflakes in the outflow levels and the cirrus anvil. Moderate to heavy rainfall occurs over broad regions below the cloud base. Eventually the updraft weakens and a downdraft spreads throughout the cloud, weakening the rainfall and dissipating the cloud.

Isolated thunderstorms occasionally form over small hot spots above flat terrain or by the lifting of moist air over ridges or mountaintops. Generally, however, thunderstorms consume so much moisture that they require a well-organized field of low-level moisture convergence for their sustenance. Thunderstorms thus typically form in conditionally unstable air masses in conjunction with a larger-scale circulation such as that produced by a MONSOON, a sea breeze (see WIND), or a mid-latitude or tropical cyclonic disturbance (see CYCLONE AND ANTICYCLONE).

DESTRUCTIVE POTENTIAL

A small fraction of the total number of thunderstorms develops into exceptionally large and intense severe local storms that produce violent windstorms, tornadoes, large hailstones, heavy rainfall, and intense lightning. Severe local storms typically form in air masses that exhibit high conditional instability, have a well-organized source of low-level moisture convergence, and exhibit substantial shear, or change in speed and direction of the horizontal wind per unit of height, through a deep layer of the atmosphere.

Thunderstorms are notorious for their destructive potential. Thunderstorm-associated lightning causes 100 to 200 deaths and several hundred million dollars worth of property damage and ignites approximately 10,000 forest fires each year in the United States alone. Hail annually causes several hundred million dollars worth of crop loss in the United States. Downbursts, the outflow from intense downdrafts, can produce maximum surface wind speeds in excess of 80 m/sec (180 mph), causing considerable structural damage and creating a potential hazard for aircraft landing or departing from airports. FLASH FLOODS, generally caused by relatively stationary and persistent thunderstorms forming over watersheds feeding deep valleys and canyons, are rapidly becoming one of the highest-ranking forms of storm-related killers because of the continued expansion of urban areas into flood-prone areas.   WILLIAM R. COTTON

Bibliography: Battan, L. J., *The Nature of Violent Storms* (1961) and *The Thunderstorm* (1964); Byers, H. R., and Braham, R. R., *The Thunderstorm* (1949); Mason, B. J., *The Physics of Clouds* (1971); Schonland, Basil, *The Flight of Thunderbolts*, 2d ed. (1964).

Thünen, Johann Heinrich von   [tue'-nen]

Johann Heinrich von Thünen, b. June 24, 1783, d. Sept. 22, 1850, was a German agriculturist. In 1826 he wrote *Der isolierte Staat* (The Isolated State), in which he proposed his theoretical model showing concentric belts of agricultural production surrounding a market center and demonstrating the relationship of commodity transportation costs to production location. Thünen laid the foundations of contemporary spatial theory.   GEOFFREY JOHN MARTIN

See also: CENTRAL PLACE THEORY.

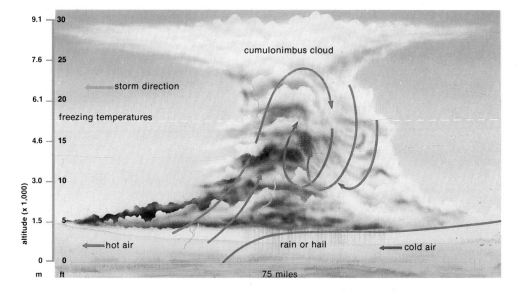

Thunderstorms are short-lived, intense local storms that are normally accompanied by thunder, lightning, and heavy rainfall or hail. Such storms occur when a rapidly moving mass of cold air overtakes and lifts a large mass of warm, humid air. The result is a strong updraft of air and the formation of a huge cumulonimbus cloud. Raindrops form in the warm air at low altitudes, whereas ice crystals and snow form in the upper cold regions of the cloud. Subsequent strong downdrafts produce the heavy rain or hail.

cumulonimbus cloud

storm direction

freezing temperatures

altitude (x 1,000)

9.1 — 30
7.6 — 25
6.1 — 20
4.6 — 15
3.0 — 10
1.5 — 5
0 — 0
m   ft

hot air

rain or hail

cold air

75 miles

Thurber, James [thur'-bur]

James Thurber has amused readers with his sketches and fables since the publication of his first work, My Life and Hard Times, *in 1933. Thurber's short stories often portray human beings in the modern age as virtually impotent in the face of simple everyday events.*

Highly regarded as an American humorist, James Grover Thurber, b. Columbus, Ohio, Dec. 8, 1894, d. Nov. 2, 1961, is remembered for his *New Yorker* essays and cartoons, for such short stories as "The Catbird Seat" and "The Secret Life of Walter Mitty," for children's books including *The Thirteen Clocks* (1950), and, as coauthor with Elliot Nugent, for the witty Broadway play *The Male Animal* (1940). Thurber portrayed the modern world in all its confusions and frustrations, most successfully in two books illustrated by himself—*Fables for Our Time* (1940) and *Further Fables for Our Time* (1956). About animals who talk and act like Thurber's fellow Americans, the fables present such morals as "It is better to have the ring of freedom in your ears than in your nose."

JAMES K. ROBINSON

Bibliography: Arner, Robert, *James Thurber: An Introduction* (1979); Kenney, Catherine, *Thurber's Anatomy of Confusion* (1984); Morsberger, Robert E., *James Thurber* (1964).

Thuringia [thur-in'-jee-uh]

Thuringia (German: Thüringen) is a historic region in the southwestern corner of East Germany. Important cities include GERA, GOTHA, JENA, and WEIMAR. The Thuringian Basin, where most of the inhabitants live, has most of the arable land. Thuringia has numerous rivers, many of them harnessed for hydroelectric power. The forested hills have many spas.

The region's name is derived from the Thuringians, a Germanic tribe that arrived after AD 350. Thuringia was under Frankish rule from about 634 to 814. The house of Wettin controlled the region from 1265 to the 15th century. Thuringia was successively a part of the duchy—and then kingdom—of SAXONY (1485–1918), a state under the Weimar Republic (1919–34), a part of Saxony (1934–45), and a part of East Germany (since 1945).

BRUCE LA ROSE

Thurmond, Strom [thur'-muhnd, strahm]

James Strom Thurmond, b. Edgeville, S.C., Dec. 5, 1902, has served as U.S. senator from South Carolina since 1954. In 1946, Thurmond was elected governor of South Carolina, and in 1948 he ran for president as the candidate of the Southern, antiintegration States' Rights Democrats, who opposed President Harry S. Truman's liberal civil rights policies. Thurmond carried four states. A Republican from 1964, he was chairman of the Senate Judiciary Committee from 1981 to 1987.

Bibliography: Lachiotte, Alberta, *Rebel Senator* (1966).

Thurnwald, Richard [toorn'-vahlt]

Richard Thurnwald, b. Sept. 18, 1869, d. Jan. 19, 1954, was a German anthropologist noted for his comparative study of economic systems and social organization in primitive societies and for his ethnographic research in New Guinea and East Africa. His writings include *Banaro Society: Social Organization and Kinship* (1916), *Economics in Primitive Communities* (1932), and *Die Menschliche Gesellschaft* (Human Society, 1935).

JAMES W. HERRICK

Thurstone, L. L. [thur'-stuhn]

Louis Leon Thurstone, b. Chicago, May 29, 1887, d. Sept. 29, 1955, was a pioneer in the field of psychological measurement. Thurstone's contributions to psychological test theory provide the foundation for today's aptitude and achievement tests and for modern methods of assessing attitudes and opinions. He is best known for having developed multiple-factor analysis, a procedure widely adopted in the social sciences for analyzing relations among sets of variables. He was a dedicated teacher, and many of his students have become distinguished psychologists.

Educated both in Sweden and in the United States, Thurstone graduated in 1912 from Cornell University's College of Engineering. Following brief periods as a laboratory assistant to Thomas A. Edison and as an instructor of engineering at the University of Minnesota, he received (1917) a doctorate in psychology from the University of Chicago. At the Carnegie Institute of Technology (1915–23), he rose to the rank of professor and chairman of the Department of Psychology. At the University of Chicago (1924–52), he served from 1938 as Charles F. Grey Distinguished Service Professor. From 1952 until his death, he was research professor and director of the Psychometric Laboratory that he established at the University of North Carolina.

LYLE V. JONES

Bibliography: Fredericksen, Norman, ed., *Leon Thurstone's Contributions to Mathematical Psychology* (1964); Guilford, J. P., *Louis Leon Thurstone, 1887–1955* (1957); Wood, Dorothy A., *Louis Leon Thurstone* (1962).

Thus Spake Zarathustra

Friedrich W. NIETZSCHE's most profound work, *Thus Spake Zarathustra* (1883–85; Eng. trans., 1954) expresses the philosopher's mature thought in rhapsodic verse and prose form. Zarathustra, the ancient Persian prophet and Nietzsche's spokesman, comments and sermonizes on human existence. Modern civilization, God, Christianity, Western morality, and democracy are all denounced on the grounds that they inhibit the creation of the human ideal, the "Superman," who is strong and self-sufficient. The problems of death and nothingness are also investigated. Pivotal in Western thought, *Thus Spake Zarathustra* has influenced or caused violent reactions in countless 20th-century writers and thinkers.

JOSEPH A. REITER

Thutmose I, King of Egypt [thut'-mohz]

Thutmose I, d. *c.*1512 BC, 18th-dynasty king of Egypt (r. *c.*1525–*c.*1512), successor to his father, Amenhotep I, extended his empire southward deeper into Nubia; later, during his Asian campaigns, he reached the Euphrates. He was the first king to be buried in the Valley of the Kings at Thebes. Thutmose II, his son, succeeded him.

ROBIN BUSS

Thutmose II, King of Egypt

Thutmose II (r. *c.*1512–*c.*1504 BC) was an Egyptian king of the 18th dynasty. He married his half sister HATSHEPSUT and succeeded his father, Thutmose I. During his reign Thutmose put down rebellions in Nubia and Palestine and continued temple construction at KARNAK. He was succeeded by his son Thutmose III, under regency of Hatshepsut.

Thutmose III, King of Egypt

Thutmose III, d. 1450 BC, 18th-dynasty ruler of Egypt (*c.*1504–1450 BC), the greatest of ancient Egypt's warrior kings, expanded and consolidated Egyptian control over an empire of unprecedented extent in western Asia and Africa. Thutmose was young when his predecessor and father, Thutmose II, died; he had to serve as junior partner in a co-kingship with his aunt HATSHEPSUT until 1482. Between 1482 and 1462, he personally led many victorious campaigns in Syria, Palestine, and Phoenicia. In a battle on the east bank of the Euphrates he defeated the powerful kingdom of MITANNI, his chief rival for control of the Near East. Meanwhile, his armies in Nubia pushed beyond the Nile's 4th cataract. Thutmose set up an efficient administration in the conquered territories, in which vassal kings and chiefs were forced to pay heavy tribute to Egypt. Much of this tribute Thutmose used to build new temples in gratitude to the Egyptian gods. His son Amenhotep II succeeded him.   DAVID O'CONNOR

Bibliography: Gardiner, A. H., *Egypt of the Pharaohs* (1961).

thyme   [tym]

Thyme, T. vulgaris, *a perennial herb, is an ingredient of* bouquet garni *("herb bundle"), used to season meats, soups, sauces, and vegetables. It grows easily in a garden or planted in a pot by a kitchen window.*

Thyme is the common name applied to about 300 to 400 species of the genus *Thymus,* family Labiatae, that are native to temperate Eurasia. French thyme (also called German or English thyme), *T. vulgaris,* is a perennial herb whose leaves provide the common thyme of the spice shelf. Native to southern Europe, French thyme is cultivated in France, Spain, and the United States. The oil extracted from the plant is used in perfumes and medicines. Many other species and varieties of thyme exist, some scented with such distinct odors as caraway, lemon, or oregano. Wild or creeping thyme, *T. serpyllum,* is a popular rock-garden evergreen.
                                                     ARTHUR O. TUCKER

thymus   [thy'-muhs]

The thymus is a vascular organ of the lymphatic system situated just behind the breastbone. The human thymus continues to grow for about a year after birth, reaching a weight of about 42 grams (1.8 oz); this size is maintained until puberty. After puberty the lymphatic tissue is replaced by fat, but the thymus remains functional throughout life.

   The main function of the thymus is to process lymphocytes received from the blood-producing bone marrow and fetal liver. These cells proliferate and differentiate in the thymus into thymic lymphoid cells called T cells, each one programmed for the number of antigens to which it will react. In humans the cellular immune system requires the presence of the thymus at birth; this system allows the body to recognize foreign—that is, "nonself"—tissue and to attack malignant cells, viral infection, fungal infection, and some bacteria (see also IMMUNITY, biology). Little is known of the factors and processes of thymic function. The importance of the thymus to the human immune system, however, is readily demonstrated in some patients with congenital thymic deficiency states by the restoration of immunological responsiveness after fetal thymus grafts.   ROBERT A. JOYCE

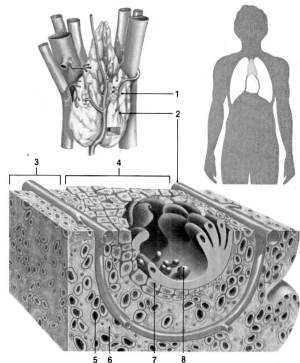

The thymus gland (1) is an organ of the lymphatic system, which protects the body against infection. Located behind the sternum, near the heart and lungs, it is well supplied with blood vessels (2). Its two main lobes are each subdivided into numerous lobules; a network of delicate connective tissue holds the lobes and lobules together. Within each lobule are two zones of tissue: an inner zone called the cortex (3) and an outer zone called the medulla (4). The cortex is composed of lymphocytes (5), white blood cells that produce antibodies and attack bacteria; these lymphocytes are packed into a fiber structure called a reticulum (6). The medulla has a more cellular reticulum (7) and contains thymic corpuscles (Hassall's corpuscles) (8), which are concentric clusters of epithelial cells enclosing a core of granular cells. The function of these corpuscles is not yet understood. The thymus is most active during fetal and childhood growth, its main functions appearing to be the production of lymphocytes and the destruction of defective lymphocytes. The thymus may also secrete a hormone that influences the response of lymphocytes to foreign tissue. After puberty the thymus slowly degenerates—the cortex becomes thinner, and the lymphocytes are replaced by deposits of fat.

Bibliography: Biggar, W. D., et al., *Thymus Involvement in Immunity and Disease,* new ed. (1973); Goldstein, Gideon, and Mackay, Ian R., *Human Thymus* (1970); Van Bekkum, D. W., ed., *The Biological Activity of Thymic Hormones* (1975).

thyratron   [thy'-ruh-trahn]

A thyratron is a gas-filled ELECTRON TUBE that can rapidly switch large electrical currents. Normally the gas in the tube has a high electrical resistance, and no current flows between the tube's cathode and plate. A small electrical current applied to one or more control electrodes, however, ionizes the gas in the tube. The electrical resistance of the gas then becomes negligible, and current can flow through the tube. Thyratrons are used to control motors, generators, and welders and in other applications where large electrical currents must be switched.   FORREST M. MIMS III

Bibliography: Geppert, Donovan V., *Basic Electron Tubes* (1951).

thyroid function test   [thy'-royd]

A thyroid function test measures the efficiency of THYROXINE and triiodothyronine production by the thyroid gland. These two thyroid hormones, which contain iodine, regulate body metabolism. If the hormones are deficient, as in the condition called myxedema, metabolism is slowed down. If they are in excess, as in exophthalmic GOITER, metabolism is accelerated. The oldest method of measuring thyroid function is the determination of the basal metabolic rate, or BMR. The test involves measurement of the body's oxygen requirement during a condition of absolute rest, called the basal state. The amount of oxygen is related to the amount of thyroid hormone present. The relationship of the BMR to thyroid hormone levels, however, is indirect and inexact. The BMR test has thus been superseded by such tests as the radiation method, which measures the rate at which injected radioactive iodine becomes concentrated in the thyroid gland. This rate is directly related to the rate of thyroid hormone synthesis. Other tests include measurement of the competitive protein-binding of thyroxine, serum thyroxine, the level of thyroid-stimulating hormone (TSH), free thyroxine in blood and urine, and triiodothyronine estimations.   PETER L. PETRAKIS

Bibliography: Sterling, K., *Diagnosis and Treatment of Thyroid Diseases* (1975); Thomson, John A., *Clinical Tests of Thyroid Function* (1974).

thyroid gland

The thyroid, an endocrine gland, synthesizes, stores, and secretes two hormones—thyroxine, or tetraiodothyronine (T_4), and triiodothyronine (T_3)—that are chemically related and important to human growth and metabolism. Located below the larynx (voice box), the thyroid's two lobes occur on either side of the windpipe, connected by an isthmus (band of tissue). The gland is composed of many hollow sacs (follicles) filled with colloid (a gelatin material), which contains thyroglobulin, the storage form of the hormones. Essential to the synthesis of the hormones is inorganic iodide, which diffuses from the blood into the follicle cells. A third hormone, thyrocalcitonin or calcitonin, acts against excessive levels of calcium in the blood and against the effects of parathyroid hormone on bone resorption. The manufacture and transport of

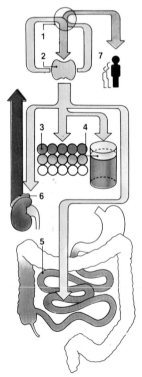 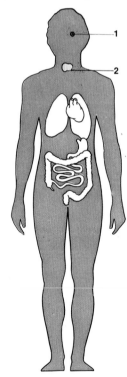

The thyroid gland regulates the body's use of energy. When signaled by the pituitary (1), the thyroid (2) releases hormones into the bloodstream; the hormones are transported to the body's cells (3) and stimulate them to burn more fuel. These hormones affect blood cholesterol levels (4), intestinal absorption of sugars (5), the adrenal medulla (6), which influences the brain, and growth hormone (7).

this hormone is not fully understood. It is believed to be secreted by the C cells found between the follicles.

Thyroid hormone secretion is controlled by thyroid-stimulating hormone (TSH), or thyrotropin, from the anterior pituitary. In turn, the resultant increase in the level of thyroid hormone in the blood serves to signal the pituitary to stop releasing the thyrotropin (negative feedback). This homeostatic mechanism keeps the level of thyroid hormone in the circulatory system within a constant range. A lack of thyroid function in infants causes cretinism, whereas a loss or low levels of the thyroid hormones later in life result in hypothyroidism, or myxedema, and possibly GOITER. Overproduction of the hormones, or hyperthyroidism, also may result in goiter.

Bibliography: Hershman, Jerome M., and Bray, G. A., eds., *The Thyroid: Physiology and Treatment of Disease* (1978); Werner, Sidney C., and Ingbar, Sidney H., eds., *The Thyroid*, 4th ed. (1978).

See also: ENDOCRINE SYSTEM, DISEASES OF THE.

thyroxine   [thy-rahk'-seen]

Thyroxine, or tetraiodothyronine, is the major hormone secreted by the thyroid gland. The other thyroid hormone, triiodothyronine, has a similar metabolic action. Both hormones are iodinated derivatives of the amino acid tyrosine and are released into the bloodstream as a complex with plasma globulin, a protein. Their synthesis and secretion regulates and is regulated by a hormone called the thyroid-stimulating hormone (TSH), secreted by the hypophysis, or pituitary gland. The function of thyroxine and triiodothyronine is to accelerate cellular metabolism, but the exact mechanisms of their action are not clear. Their effects include increased carbohydrate metabolism rate and increased protein synthesis and breakdown rates. Synthetic preparations of thyroxine are used to treat thyroid-deficiency diseases in adults and cretinism in children.   PETER L. PETRAKIS

Thysanoptera: see THRIPS.

Thysanura: see BRISTLETAIL.

ti   [tee]

Ti, Hawaiian good luck plant, and tree of kings are common names for *Cordyline terminalis* of the family Agavaceae. Native to tropical Asia, ti plants grow to 3 m (10 ft) with dark glossy leaves 30 to 75 cm (12 to 30 in) long and 5 to 12 cm (2 to 5 in) wide. Many cultivars of ti have been grown for their foliage and are sometimes placed under the genus *Dracaena*. These plants have attractive white, rose, pink, or yellow leaf margins, strips, or spots and make excellent houseplants.

Tiahuanaco . [tee-ah-wah-nah'-koh]

The important pre-Columbian site of Tiahuanaco (also Tiahuanacu), near the eastern margin of Lake Titicaca on the Bolivian altiplano at an altitude of about 4,000 m (13,125 ft), was occupied from about AD 100 to perhaps 1000. Within Tiahuanaco's extensive fine-cut masonry ruins archaeologists have defined six architectural complexes, all of which were probably used primarily for religious ceremonies. The most important structure, the Kalasasaya, is near the center of the site; the so-called Subterranean Temple lies to the east, and the enclosures of Putuni, Laka Kollu, and Q'eri Kala are on the west. Still farther west, near the lake, is a sizable cemetery.

The Kalasasaya, a large but low enclosed platform, is the site of the famous Gate of the Sun, which is topped by a relief-work frieze, at the center of which is a figure wearing a radiating headdress and carrying a staff in each hand. At the center of the Subterranean Temple stood the 7.3-m-tall (22-ft) Bennett Stele (named for its discoverer), which shows a figure in headdress carrying a large beaker in one hand and a *strombus* shell in the other.

The motifs and art styles of Tiahuanaco heavily influenced

large areas of highland Bolivia, southern Peru, northern Chile, and northwest Argentina during the period 500–1000. Little is known of the sociopolitical organization that underlay this pervasive influence, although Tiahuanaco was probably able to export elements of its religion and may have established important economic links with far-flung areas. Recent evidence suggests that the site may have been much larger than its core zone of elaborate structures and thus have had a sizable resident population.   CRAIG MORRIS

Bibliography: Bennett, Wendell C., *Andean Culture History*, 2d ed. (1964); Lumbreras, Luis G., *The Peoples and Cultures of Ancient Peru*, trans. by Betty Meggers (1974); Posnansky, Arthur, *Tiahuanacu: The Cradle of American Man*, 4 vols. (1945–58).

See also: PRE-COLUMBIAN ART AND ARCHITECTURE.

tiara: see CROWNS AND CORONETS.

Tibbett, Lawrence

Lawrence Tibbett, operatic and concert baritone, b. Bakersfield, Calif., Nov. 16, 1896, d. New York City, July 15, 1960, made his Metropolitan Opera debut as a monk in Mussorgsky's *Boris Godunov*. He spent 2 years in a succession of small roles before winning sensational success as Ford in Verdi's *Falstaff* on Jan. 2, 1925. He created an impressive list of roles in new operas, notably the title parts in Deems Taylor's *Peter Ibbetson* (1931) and Louis Gruenberg's *Emperor Jones* (1933) and the leading baritone role in Howard Hanson's *Merry Mount* (1934). He was often heard on radio and in recitals and appeared in several films.   RAYMOND GRAUNKE

Bibliography: Ewen, David, ed., *Men and Women Who Make Music* (1949) and *Musicians since 1900* (1978).

Tiber River   [ty'-bur]

The 406-km-long (252-mi) Tiber River, the second longest in Italy, rises in the Etruscan Apennines, about 65 km (40 mi) east of Florence, and flows south past Perugia to Rome, 26 km (16 mi) from its mouth on the Tyrrhenian Sea. Navigable only near Rome, the Tiber is not commercially important. In ancient times it served as a boundary between Latin tribes in the south and Etruscans in the north.

Tiberias   [ty-bir'-ee-uhs]

Tiberias (Teverya in Hebrew), one of the four holy cities of Judaism, is a port on the western shore of the Sea of Galilee in northeastern Israel. It has a population of 29,000 (1982 est.). A commercial and transportation center, Tiberias is a popular resort because of its warm climate, beautiful scenery, and hot mineral springs. The tomb of the philosopher Maimonides is a notable landmark.

Founded by Herod Antipas in AD c.20 and named for the Roman emperor Tiberius, the city became the center of Jewish scholarship in the 2d century. The Mishnah and the Jerusalem Talmud were edited there. In 636 the city was taken by the Arabs, and it was destroyed during the 12th century. Tiberias was reestablished during the 18th century.

Tiberias, Lake: see GALILEE, SEA OF.

Tiberius, Roman Emperor

Tiberius Julius Caesar Augustus, b. Nov. 16, 42 BC, d. Mar. 16, AD 37, was the second emperor (r. AD 14–37) of Rome. He was the son of Tiberius Claudius Nero and LIVIA DRUSILLA, who later married Octavian (see AUGUSTUS, ROMAN EMPEROR). In 12 BC, Tiberius was forced to marry Augustus's daughter, Julia. In the event of Augustus's death he was to act as tutor of Augustus's grandsons by Julia's previous marriage. Tiberius resented his role, and from 6 BC to AD 2 he lived in retirement in Rhodes. After the premature deaths of the grandsons, Augustus adopted (AD 4) Tiberius and recognized him as his successor.

Tiberius was an accomplished general. He quelled revolts in the Danubian provinces (12–9 BC), fought in Germany (9–7

BC, AD 4–6) and elsewhere, and won the allegiance of his soldiers. When Augustus died, Tiberius was already in possession of the chief military command; after a show of reluctance, he let the Senate proclaim him emperor. A scheming and suspicious ruler, Tiberius instituted a reign of terror, especially after 23, when Sejanus, prefect of the Praetorian guard, became his chief advisor. Numerous senators, and also members of the family of his nephew GERMANICUS CAESAR, were accused of treason and executed; in 31 Sejanus met the same fate. Tiberius ruled from AD 26 until his death in seclusion on Capri; he was succeeded by Caligula.   J. LINDERSKI

Bibliography: Levick, Barbara M., *Tiberius the Politician* (1976; repr. 1986); Seager, Robin, *Tiberius* (1972).

Tibesti Massif   [tee-bes'-tee]

The Tibesti Massif is a mountainous region in the central Sahara. Located mainly in northern Chad but extending into southern Libya, it has a total east-west length of about 485 km (300 mi) and a maximum north-south width of about 280 km (175 mi). The highest peak, the extinct volcano Emi Koussi, rises to 3,415 m (11,204 ft). Of volcanic origin, these extremely rugged mountains arose when the Sahara's climate was more humid. The sandstone-covered rocks have been shaped by water and wind erosion into complicated shapes. Vegetation is sparse, although dates, vegetables, watermelons, tobacco, and grains are grown in oases. Seminomadic tribes raise camels, sheep, and goats. The first European to explore (c.1870) the range was Gustav Nachtigal.

Tibet   (Xizang)   [ti-bet']

Tibet, since 1965 the Tibetan Autonomous Region of the People's Republic of China, forms the southwestern part of China. Tibet has an area of 1,221,700 km² (471,700 mi²) and has about 1,930,000 inhabitants (1983 est.). The awesome Himalayas form Tibet's southern boundaries with India, Nepal, Bhutan, Burma, and Pakistan.

Land and People. Much of Tibet consists of the largest and highest plateau on Earth (average elevation: 4,600 m/15,000 ft). The plateau is ringed by mountains, including the KUNLUN MOUNTAINS in the north. In the south the HIMALAYAS contain the world's highest peaks, including Mount EVEREST (8,848 m/29,028 ft), and are the source of the great rivers of east and south Asia, including the HWANG HO and INDUS. Tibet's climate varies little with the seasons. Lhasa's daily temperature ranges from a maximum of 7° C (45° F) to a minimum of −8° C (18° F). Because the monsoons are blocked by the mountains, Tibet receives only 255 mm (10 in) of rain annually.

Cultivable land is limited to valleys, mainly in the east and southeast, where the plateau dips below 3,650 m (12,000 ft) and where most of Tibet's inhabitants live. The principal cities and towns are LHASA, the capital; Jih-k'a-tse (Shigatse); Chiang-tzu (Gyangtse); and Ch'ang-tu. The main crop is barley, cultivated with the aid of the native yak, or the dzo, a cross between a cow and a yak. Butter made from the milk of these animals, mixed with ground barley in tea, makes tsampa, the staple of the Tibetan diet.

History. The plateau's harsh environment, its physical isolation, a strong isolationist policy by its leaders, and the independence of its people kept Tibet free of direct foreign control for much of its history. The Tibetans developed the distinctive form of Buddhism called Lamaism (see TIBETAN BUDDHISM). The monks (*lamas*) who headed the many great monasteries and Buddhist sects held political power and owned the land. The DALAI LAMA, the temporal and spiritual leader, was believed to be the reincarnation of the ancestor of all Tibetans. The Panchen Lama, the head of Tibet's most important monastery, was considered the secondary spiritual leader.

By the 7th century the independent kingdom of Tibet was flourishing. In 1207, Tibet paid tribute to Genghis Khan, the Mongol emperor. From 1279 to 1368, Tibet was under the control of the YÜAN (Mongol) dynasty of China, but subsequently regained its independence. Tibet came under the

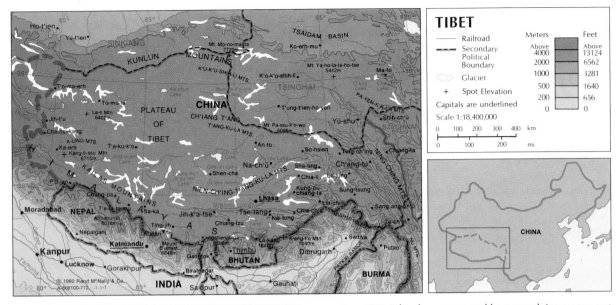

TIBET

		Meters	Feet
——	Railroad		
- - -	Secondary Political Boundary	Above 4000	Above 13124
⌒	Glacier	2000	6562
+	Spot Elevation	1000	3281
		500	1640
		200	656
		0	0

Capitals are underlined

Scale 1:18,400,000

The Potala palace (begun 1643), the former residence of the Dalai Lamas, towers over the Tibetan capital of Lhasa. Tibet's Chinese rulers converted the palace into a museum after the Dalai Lama fled (1959) to India, where he established a government-in-exile.

nominal protection of the Chinese Ch'ing dynasty (established 1644), although for the most part the country retained control over internal affairs. During the early 20th century the British cast their eye toward Tibet; in 1903, Col. Francis YOUNGHUS-BAND led a military expedition to Lhasa to establish trading posts. Treaties (1906, 1907) between China and Great Britain recognized China's sovereignty over Tibet.

With the downfall (1911) of the Ch'ing, Tibet declared its independence, which it maintained until 1950. In that year Chinese forces invaded to gain control of what was considered a strategic border area, and in 1951 a defeated Tibet signed a treaty making it part of China. In 1959 resentment of Chinese domination erupted into an uprising, which was violently crushed by Chinese forces. The Dalai Lama and many of his followers escaped to India, and the Panchen Lama was installed (1959–64) as nominal head of government. In 1965, Tibet was officially constituted an autonomous region of Chi-

na; since 1980 it has been governed by a people's government whose leader also heads the Tibetan Communist party.

After 1959 the Chinese abolished serfdom and built roads to improve access to Lhasa. Particularly during the Cultural Revolution (1966–69), they collectivized agriculture and tried forcibly to assimilate the Tibetans. Religious worship was banned, Chinese was declared the official language, and almost all monasteries and other religious monuments were destroyed. In 1980 the Chinese government tacitly admitted that its policies had caused economic hardship and failed to eradicate the Tibetan identity. Holy sites were reopened to Tibetan pilgrims, and Tibetan language and culture were no longer rigidly suppressed. Per capita income remained well below the national average, however, and Han Chinese settlement continued. Renewed Tibetan protests against Chinese rule erupted in October 1987.   JOHN E. MACDONALD

Bibliography: Avedon, J. F., *In Exile from the Land of Snows* (1984); Bell, C. T., *Tibet, Past and Present* (1924; repr. 1971); Burman, B. R., *Religion and Politics in Tibet* (1979); Richardson, H. E., *Tibet and Its History*, 2d rev. ed. (1984); Snellgrove, D. L., and Richardson, H. E., *The Cultural History of Tibet* (1968; repr. 1986); Stein, R. A., *Tibetan Civilization*, rev. ed. (1972); Tung, R. J., *A Portrait of Lost Tibet* (1980).

Tibetan art: see LAMAIST ART AND ARCHITECTURE.

Tibetan Buddhism

Tibetan Buddhism, also called Lamaism, is a distinctive form of BUDDHISM that arose (7th century) in Tibet and later spread throughout the Himalayan region, including neighboring Bhutan, Nepal, and Sikkim. The history of Tibetan Buddhism can be divided into three periods. During the 7th–9th century AD Buddhism was first introduced from India and was slowly accepted under Buddhist kings in the face of opposition by adherents of the indigenous shamanistic religion of Tibet, Bon. Instrumental in this process were the Indian Mahayana Buddhist masters Padmasambhava and Shantarakshita. During the 9th century, however, King gLang Dar Ma persecuted the new faith and effectively eclipsed it for some time.

The second period began with the reintroduction of Buddhism from India and its successive reform in the 11th century. Powerful ecclesiastical organizations were established and soon began to rule the countryside in alliance with clans of nobles or the distant Mongol rulers. During this period the Tibetan Buddhist canon (notable for its accurate translations of now-lost Sanskrit texts and its helpful commentaries) was compiled, and some of the sects that have persisted to the present were formed. These include the Sa-skya-pa, the rNy-ing-ma-pa (who traced their roots back to Padmasambhava),

This child is a 17th incarnate lama of the Yellow Hat (dGe-lugs-pa) sect, at the Kye monastery in Spiti, Himachal Pradesh state, India. In Tibetan Buddhism, lamaist succession is based on direct reincarnation. It is believed that when a lama dies his soul passes into a newly born infant, who is then sought out by members of the religious community. Through a series of divinations and tasks, the incarnate lama is identified and revered for life.

and the bKa'rgyud-pa (to which belonged the famous yogi MI-LAREPA, or Mi-la ras-pa, 1040–1123).

The third period began with the great reformer Tsong-kha-pa (1357–1419), who founded the dGe-lugs-pa sect—the so-called Yellow Hats—to which the line of the DALAI LAMAS belongs. Each of these lamas was thought to be the reincarnation of his predecessor (as well as that of the bodhisattva Avalokitesvara) and became, at least nominally, the religious and secular ruler of the country. In 1959 the present, or 14th, Dalai Lama fled Tibet along with thousands of his followers. Since then they have all been living in exile, primarily in India.

Among the characteristic features of Tibetan Buddhism are its ready acceptance of the Buddhist TANTRAS as an integral and culminating part of the Buddhist way; its emphasis on the importance of the master-disciple relationship for both religious scholarship and meditation; its recognition of a huge pantheon of Buddhas, bodhisattvas, saints, demons, and deities; its sectarianism, which resulted less from religious disputes than from the great secular powers of the rival monastic organizations; and, finally, the marked piety of both monastic and lay Tibetan Buddhists, which receives expression in their spinning of prayer wheels, their pilgrimages to and circumambulation of holy sites, prostrations and offerings, recitation of texts, and chanting of MANTRAS, especially the famous invocation to Avalokitesvara *Om Mani Padme Hum.*

JOSEPH M. KITAGAWA AND JOHN S. STRONG

Bibliography: Bell, C. T., *The Religion of Tibet* (1931; repr. 1968); Beyer, Stephan, *The Cult of Tara* (1973); Michael, Franz, *Rule by Incarnation* (1982); Tucci, Giuseppe, *The Religions of Tibet* (1980).

Tibetan language: see SINO-TIBETAN LANGUAGES.

Tibetan spaniel

The Tibetan spaniel, long raised as a watchdog and companion in the monasteries of Tibet, is not a true spaniel breed. It looks something like the related PEKINGESE but has a slightly longer muzzle, longer and straighter legs, and a softer, silkier, and less profuse coat. Tibetan spaniels come in many colors and weigh about 4 to 7 kg (9 to 15 lb). The breed became popular in Britain after World War II and was officially recognized by the American Kennel Club in 1984.

Bibliography: Braund, Kathryn, *The Uncommon Dog Breeds* (1975).

Tibetan terrier

The shaggy Tibetan terriers—which are not a true terrier breed of dogs—were originally bred in Tibetan monasteries. Closely

resembling the Old English sheepdog and the Lhasa apso, the dogs stand 35 to 40 cm (14 to 16 in) high at the shoulder and weigh 8.2 to 13.6 kg (18 to 30 lb). They have fine, profuse double coats, well-feathered tails curled up over their backs, and loose-hanging ears. They come in many colors, either solid or mottled with white.   JOHN MANDEVILLE

Bibliography: Marvin, John T., *Book of All Terriers*, 2d ed. (1976).

The Tibetan terrier is a medium-sized nonsporting dog with a long, full coat. Native to Tibet, it was known as "luck bringer" or "holy dog" and kept as a companion. According to legend, the breed was kept pure for many centuries to avoid ill fortune that might result from mating these esteemed pets with other breeds.

Tibullus   [ti-bul'-uhs]

Ranked foremost among Roman elegiac poets by Quintilian, Albius Tibullus, *c.*48–19 BC, wrote mostly on the subject of love in a style that was simple but elegantly refined. Unlike his contemporaries Horace and Ovid, Tibullus seems to have remained aloof from Roman public affairs; his preference for a life of rural seclusion, often praised in his bucolic poems, was probably genuine. In the two books of poetry that can definitely be attributed to him, he addresses his mistresses Delia and—later—Nemesis, as well as the young man Marathus.

Bibliography: Putnam, Michael, *Tibullus: A Commentary* (1973).

tic

Two forms of a muscular disorder known as tic occur: nervous tic and tic douloureux. Nervous tic is a recurrent, spasmodic, involuntary reaction that is apt to develop in certain muscles during emotional stress and sometimes accompanies psychoneurotic disorders. Repeated shrugging, blinking, and clearing of the throat are examples of nervous tics. Children are prone to the malady but generally outgrow it. Tic douloureux (trigeminal neuralgia), on the other hand, mainly strikes the elderly. It is a reflex contraction of the facial muscles in response to sharp pain affecting the trigeminal nerve, a cranial nerve serving the entire face; the cause of the nerve damage is generally unknown. The condition can be relieved with drugs such as carbamazepine and phenytoin; surgery is considered only as a last resort.

tick

Ticks are small-to-microscopic, eight-legged, often brightly colored bloodsucking parasites that feed on reptiles, birds, and mammals, including humans. Together with closely related mites, they make up the order Acarina of the class Arachnida, phylum Arthropoda. Ticks are found worldwide but are most abundant in tropical and subtropical areas. They

The Rocky Mountain wood tick, Dermacentor andersoni, is a major transmitter of the diseases known in the United States as Rocky Mountain spotted fever and tularemia, or rabbit fever.

attach themselves to their host by means of specially adapted mouthparts. Two basic kinds exist: hard ticks, family Ixodidae—with mouthparts visible from above and hard scutes covering all or part of the body—and soft ticks, family Argasidae—with leathery bodies and the mouthparts hidden by the back.

In the typical life cycle, the female lays several thousand eggs that hatch into active six-legged larvae. The larvae feed on a host and develop into eight-legged nymphs, which, in turn, feed and develop into adults. A few tick species stay on one host for the entire cycle, but most have a new host or hosts in some or every developmental stage. Some can survive for several years as adults while waiting for a host.

Hard ticks secrete nerve poisons that sometimes cause paralysis or death. Ticks can also harm their hosts by causing excessive blood loss or by transmitting diseases among animals, including humans. Among such diseases are Q FEVER, RELAPSING FEVER, ROCKY MOUNTAIN SPOTTED FEVER, TULAREMIA, Lyme disease (a disorder involving recurrent inflammation of the joints), and some forms of encephalitis and spirochetosis.

Bibliography: McDaniel, B., *How to Know the Mites and Ticks* (1979); Meyer, M. C., and Olsen, O. W., *Essentials of Parasitology,* 3d ed. (1980); Obenchain, F., and Galun, R., eds., *The Physiology of Ticks* (1982).

tickseed

Tickseed is the common name for any of about 100 species of annual or perennial herbs of the genus *Coreopsis,* the family Compositae. These summer-blooming ornamental flowers have flower heads that are solitary or in branched clusters, each with yellow disk flowers and yellow, pink, white, or variegated ray flowers. Golden coreopsis, *C. tinctoria,* is a popular garden annual.   FRANK B. SALISBURY

Ticonderoga   [ty-kahn-dur-oh'-guh]

Ticonderoga, a stone fort between Lake Champlain and Lake George in what is now northern New York State, was an object of contention during the French and Indian War of 1754–63 and the American Revolution. The French built it in 1755

as an outpost of Fort Saint Frederic (Crown Point) and named it Carillon. In 1758 the marquis de Montcalm repulsed a British assault led by Maj. Gen. James Abercrombie in one of the bloodiest battles of the colonial wars. Jeffrey Amherst succeeded in taking it from the French the following year. At the beginning of the Revolutionary War, Ethan Allen and his Green Mountain Boys seized (May 1775) Ticonderoga from the British. Gen. John Burgoyne recaptured it in 1777, but the British abandoned it later in the year. Restored in the early 20th century, it stands today as a historic monument.

Bibliography: Hamilton, E. P., *Fort Ticonderoga* (1964).

tidal bore

A tidal bore consists of a breaking tidal wave that travels up some rivers about two or three times as fast as the incoming tide. It is formed on those rivers where the mass and momentum of the incoming tide are concentrated into a narrow front by the gradual narrowing of the river channel, by a rise in the river bed, or by both. A tidal bore is highest near the river banks. The largest tidal bores occur on the Amazon River in Brazil (5 m/16.4 ft) and the Chien Tang Kiang River in China (7.5 m/24.6 ft). Canada's Bay of Fundy is also known for its tidal bore.

Bibliography: Komar, P., *Beach Processes and Sedimentation* (1976).

tidal energy

At more than 100 coastal locations around the world the TIDES rise and fall far enough within an estuary or a partially enclosed basin to make the generation of electricity by tidal force economically feasible. Two tidal-energy plants are currently in use: a 240-MW (1 megawatt = 1,000 kilowatts) facility at the mouth of the Rance River, near Normandy, France, and a 400-kW experimental generator at Kislaya Guba, on the White Sea, north of Murmansk, USSR. A 1,500-kW plant is under construction at Mezen, also in the USSR.

Tidal energy is harnessed by building a barrier across the mouth of an estuary or inlet and by installing turbines in the barrier that are turned by the inflow and outflow of water (see HYDROELECTRIC POWER). At the Rance River plant, where the

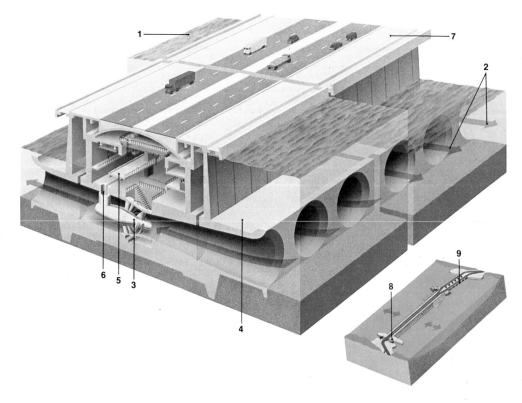

This 240-MW tidal-power station is located on an estuary of the Rance River in France. Tides at the station reach a height of 13.5 m (44 ft). As the tide rises (1), water is channeled through 24 tunnels (2) containing turbine-generator bulbs (3), which convert the force of the flowing water to electricity. At low tide, seawater held in the storage basin (4) is channeled back through the turbines to produce additional energy. A service chamber (5) contains operating equipment and offers access (6) to the turbines. The roof (7) serves as a bridge over the estuary. An aerial view of the station (inset) shows a lock for passage of ships (8) and movable dam gates (9).

maximum tidal range is 13.5 m (44 ft), twenty-four 10-MW turbine-generators are in place; the turbines have blades of adjustable pitch to handle varying flow speeds and are reversible so that power can be produced during both the rise and fall of the tides. Tidal-power plants are best used as a contributing element in a utility grid, because the level of power available from them fluctuates.

The world potential of electricity production from the tides may be as high as 60 million kW, an amount equal to 5% of the world's present generating capacity, with a potential of more than 500 billion kW h per year, or greater than 7% of annual world demand. Tidal energy could be economically harnessed at two locations in North America; at Turnagain Bay in Cook Inlet, Alaska, and in the Bay of Fundy, which is made up of nine smaller bays that lie mostly in Canadian territory between New Brunswick, Nova Scotia, and the state of Maine. The total potential capacity of the Bay of Fundy is nearly 30,000 MW—the equivalent of about 30 conventional power plants. The three most promising sites on the Bay of Fundy have a combined potential of 9,000 MW. This represents about 3.5% of current U.S. generating capacity; the amount of power that could be produced by these three sites in one year is about 79 billion kW h. Passamaquoddy Bay, the only portion of the Bay of Fundy that lies along the coast of the United States, has a potential capacity of 1,800 MW and might produce as much as 16 billion kW h per year. The idea of harnessing the tides in Passamaquoddy Bay has been controversial, however, since it was first suggested in the 1930s.

GEORGE ELLIS

Bibliography: Gray, T. K., and Gashus, O. J., eds., *Tidal Power* (1972); Severn, R. T., et al., eds., *Tidal Power and Estuary Management* (1979); Stephens, H. S., *Wave and Tidal Energy International Symposium* (1979).

tide

Tides are the periodic rise and fall of the sea surface, occurring once or twice a day. They are to be distinguished from tidal surges, which are fluctuations of sea level caused by persistent winds and changes in barometric pressure. Tides may be regarded as surface waves of very long wavelength, whose motions are driven by the gravitational attraction of the Sun and Moon and by the Earth's rotation (see WATER WAVE). Their periods are therefore determined by the periods of these same astronomical forces.

Although it appears that the Moon simply circles the Earth, actually both the Earth and the Moon revolve around a common center of mass located between their centers. A particle of water on the Earth's surface is thus subjected, in addition to the Earth's own gravitational pull, to the gravitational attraction of the Moon and the centrifugal force due to the rotation of the Earth-Moon system. For the system as a whole the latter two forces are in balance. The centrifugal force is the same for all points on the Earth's surface. The Moon's gravitational pull, however, is stronger for those points on the side of the Earth nearer the Moon and weaker for points on the side farther from the Moon. Therefore the gravitational attraction and the centrifugal force are out of balance everywhere on the Earth's surface; the difference between them is the tide-producing force, which has a component parallel to the surface and thus produces tidal currents that cause sea level to rise and fall periodically. The Moon's gravitation pulls the water into a bulge on the side of the Earth under the Moon, and the centrifugal force produces a similar bulge on the opposite side of the Earth.

The gravitational pull of the Sun produces tides in exactly the same way; because the Sun and Earth are much farther apart, however, the tidal forces due to the Sun are only 0.46 of those due to the Moon.

The maximum tides, called spring tides, occur when the Sun, Moon, and Earth all lie approximately in a straight line, so that the tidal forces of the Sun and Moon reinforce each other. Minimum tides, called neap tides, occur when the Sun and Moon are about 90° apart as viewed from the Earth, so that their gravitational attractions partially cancel each other.

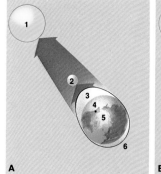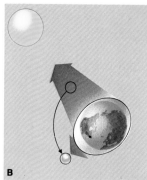
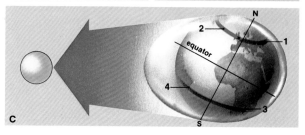

Two ocean tides occur on Earth every 24 hr 50 min. (A) During spring tides, a large tidal bulge (3) is produced on Earth (5) by the combined effects of the Sun (1) and the Moon (2). A smaller and opposite tidal bulge (6) is caused simultaneously by centrifugal forces resulting from the Earth's rotation about the common center of gravity (4) of the Earth-Moon system. (B) Smaller neap tides occur when the Sun and Moon partially neutralize each other's effects. (C) Because the axis of the tidal bulges is inclined to the Earth's equator, any particular location on the Earth's surface will experience different tidal heights (1, 2 and 3, 4) during each daily rotation.

The levels of spring and neap tides are about 20 percent above and below the average tidal limits.

Equilibrium Tide. A useful concept for examining the response of the ocean to tide-producing forces is that of the equilibrium tide. This is a simplification based on the assumptions that there are no continents to impede the flow of water on the Earth's surface and that the water is at all times in static equilibrium. The equilibrium tide forced by the Moon consists of high-water bulges directly under the Moon and on the opposite side of the Earth and of two low-water troughs in the other quadrants. As the Earth rotates, an observer who remains in one location will see two high waters and two low waters per day (the semidiurnal tide) as the bulges and troughs pass by. The equilibrium tide forced by the Sun is similar but smaller; its highs and lows do not necessarily occur at the same times as those due to the Moon. If the declination, or inclination of the Moon's orbit to the plane of the Earth's equator, is appreciable (the maximum is 28.5°), the two high-water bulges of the equilibrium tide will no longer be centered on the equator. An observer located anywhere other than the equator will therefore see two high waters of unequal height during a day.

The equilibrium tide-producing forces can be broken down into various constituents related to the components of the motions of the Earth, Moon, and Sun, such as declinations and periods of rotation (see table). The principal lunar and solar semidiurnal (twice-daily) constituents, for example, are called M_2 and S_2. The tides due to these constituents recur at intervals of 12.42 and 12.00 solar hours, respectively. The O_1 and K_1 constituents, on the other hand, produce tides that recur at intervals of 25.82 and 23.93 hours, respectively, and thus are called diurnal (daily) constituents. The relative importance of diurnal and semidiurnal tides at a particular place is expressed by the ratio $(K_1 + O_1)/(M_2 + S_2)$. Tides are predominantly semidiurnal for values of this ratio less than 1 and predominantly diurnal for values greater than 1.

Complications to the Equilibrium Tide. The simple equilib-

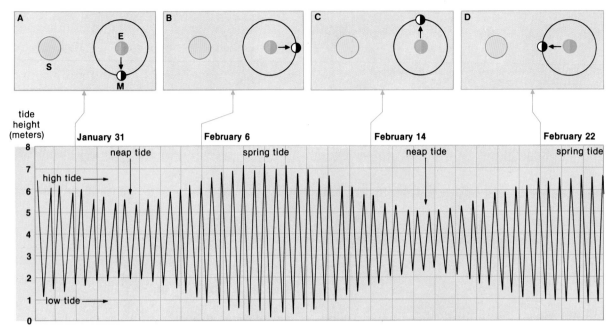

tide height (meters)

January 31   **February 6**   **February 14**   **February 22**

neap tide   spring tide   neap tide   spring tide

high tide ⟶

low tide ⟶

When the Sun (S), Moon (M), and Earth (E) are in line at full moon (B) and at new moon (D), the gravitational forces of the Sun and the Moon combine to give spring tides, or higher tides than normal. When the Sun and Moon are at right angles to each other with respect to the Earth at first quarter (A) and at last quarter (C), the Moon's tidal forces are partially canceled by the Sun's tidal forces, and the resulting neap tides are lower than usual. A graph of tide heights versus time reveals a 2-day lag of the tides behind the Moon's phases.

THE MOST IMPORTANT TIDE-GENERATING CONSTITUENTS

	Symbol	Period (solar hr)	Amplitude ($M_2 = 100$)	Description
Semidiurnal tides	M_2	12.42	100.0	Main lunar semidiurnal constituent
(two tides per day)	S_2	12.00	46.6	Main solar semidiurnal constituent
	N_2	12.66	19.1	Lunar constituent due to monthly variation in Moon's distance
	K_2	11.97	12.7	Solar-lunar constituent due to changes in declination of Sun and Moon throughout their orbital cycle
Diurnal tides	K_1	23.93	58.4	Solar-lunar constituent
(one tide per day)	O_1	25.82	41.5	Main lunar diurnal constituent
	P_1	24.07	19.3	Main solar diurnal constituent
Long-period tides	M_f	327.86	17.2	Moon's fortnightly constituent

SOURCE: Defant, A., Ebb and Flow (Ann Arbor: University of Michigan Press, 1958). Reprinted by permission of University of Michigan Press.

rium-tide concept is complicated in practice by such factors as the varying depth of the ocean, the existence and complex shapes of continents, and the Coriolis effect. Because the tides are waves of very long wavelength, their motions are strongly affected by their interaction with the seafloor. In the deep ocean the tidal range rarely exceeds 0.5 m (1.6 ft), but in shallow coastal waters the tidal range increases, just as surf grows when it approaches a beach. This effect is reinforced in bays and estuaries whose natural period of oscillation is close to the tidal period. Tides in the Bay of Fundy, for example, have a range of 13.6 m (44.6 ft).

Friction with the seafloor is also important. The Earth rotates on its axis faster than the Moon revolves around it, and friction therefore drags the high-water bulge ahead of its equilibrium position directly beneath the Moon.

Tidal currents are also constrained by the continents surrounding the ocean basins. The CORIOLIS EFFECT deflects currents to the right in the Northern Hemisphere and to the left in the Southern Hemisphere (see OCEAN CURRENTS); tidal currents therefore tend to move counterclockwise around ocean basins in the Northern Hemisphere and clockwise in the Southern Hemisphere. High water thus occurs at different times in different locations in an ocean basin. High-water information is commonly plotted on maps—called cotidal charts—that show lines connecting locations at which high water occurs at the same time.

Detailed predictions of tidal ranges and high-water times for a particular location can be made by carefully analyzing local sea-level records. The theoretical problem of predicting the tides for large regions of the ocean, however, has not yet been completely solved. Current research involves computer simulation of tides and tidal currents in complex coastal areas and simulation of the response of ocean basins to tide-producing forces.

Bibliography: Clancy, E. P., The Tides (1968); Defant, A., Ebb and Flow (1958); Goldreich, Peter, "Tides and the Earth-Moon System," Scientific American, April 1972; Knauss, J. A., Introduction to Physical Oceanography (1978); Macmillan, D. H., Tides (1966); Tricker, R. A. R., Bores, Breakers, Waves and Wakes (1964); Wylie, F. E., Tides and the Pull of the Moon (1979).

Tieck, Ludwig   [teek]

Johann Ludwig Tieck, b. May 31, 1773, d. Apr. 28, 1853, was the most prolific and versatile writer of German ROMANTICISM. He wrote novels, plays, and stories and was active as an editor and translator. Along with Novalis and the brothers Schlegel, Tieck belonged to the first German romantic group in Jena.

Tieck's novels William Lovell (1795–96) and Franz Sternbalds Wanderungen (The Wanderings of Franz Sternbald, 1798) are after the manner of Goethe's Wilhelm Meister and deal with youth's search for an identity and social role. His plays range from such historicomythological works as *Karl von Berneck* (1793–95), *Genoveva* (1799), and *Kaiser Oktavianus* (1804) to the satirical comedies for which he first gained fame: *Puss-in-Boots* (1797; Eng. trans., 1974), *The Land of Upside Down* (1798; Eng. trans., 1978), and *Prinz Zerbino* (1799). Tieck also collaborated with August Wilhelm von Schlegel on the excellent translation of Shakespeare that remains in use in Germany today.

Tieck's reputation rests ultimately on his stories. Some are based on medieval legends; others—like *Blond Eckbert* (1797; Eng. trans., 1974) and *Der Runenberg* (1804)—are free inventions that explore the incursion of the supernatural into ordinary life, foreshadowing the horror tales of Hoffmann and Poe.   LILIAN R. FURST

Bibliography: Paulin, R., *Ludwig Tieck* (1985); Zeydel, E. H., *Ludwig Tieck, the German Romanticist* (1935; repr. 1971).

Tien Shan   [tee-en shahn]

A mountain range located in Central Asia, the Tien Shan (Chinese, "celestial mountains") extend 3,000 km (1,800 mi) from the Kirghiz Soviet Socialist Republic northeast through the Sinkiang region of western China to the Mongolian frontier. The Gissar-Alai, Chu-Ili, Karatau, K'a-erh-li-k'o, and Dzhungarian Alatau mountains all belong to the Tien Shan, whose highest point, Pobeda Peak on the Kirghiz–Sinkiang border, reaches 7,444 m (24,406 ft). Principal rivers of the range include the Chu, Ili, Naryn, Sarydzhaz, and Zeravshan. Temperatures in the foothills vary from −4° to 27° C (25° to 81° F) and at higher altitudes from −23° to 5° C (−9° to 41° F). The KIRGHIZ, UIGHUR, and Chinese who inhabit the mountains maintain an economy based on agriculture and the herding of horses, sheep, and cattle. Copper, lead, zinc, mercury, antimony, and tungsten are mined.

Tientsin   (Tianjin)   [tin-tsin]

Tientsin, a city in northeastern China in Hopei province, is one of the leading industrial centers of the country. China's third largest city, Tientsin has a population of 5,220,000 (1983 est.). It is located on the Grand Canal about 130 km (80 mi) southeast of Peking, at the confluence of the five major tributaries of the Hai Ho near the Po Hai (gulf) of the Yellow Sea.

Tientsin is known for its chemical and textile industries as well as handicraft products, such as carpets, rugs, clay objects, and woodblock prints. The city has a wide range of manufacturing industries, producing iron and steel, machinery, electronics equipment, paper, and processed food. Salt production and fishing are important along the Po Hai. Tientsin is also one of China's leading trading ports.

A transport center since the 10th century, Tientsin was opened to urban and commercial development by concessions made to European nations in the 19th century. It was the capital of Hopei province (1955–67) but is now under the direct administration of the national government. Some two-thirds of the city was destroyed or damaged by a 1976 earthquake; there has since been substantial rebuilding.
                                                              JAMES CHAN

Tientsin, Treaties of

The Treaties of Tientsin (1858), imposed on China by Britain, France, Russia, and the United States, were among many unequal treaties that opened that country to Western penetration and deprived it of territory. The treaties followed China's effective defeat by Britain and France in the second OPIUM WAR (1856–60).

The treaties opened new ports to foreign trade, permitted foreigners to travel in the interior and navigate the Yangtze River, allowed Christian missionary activity, sanctioned the establishment of foreign legations in Peking, and legalized the opium trade.

When the Chinese resisted implementation of the treaties an Anglo-French force occupied (1860) Peking and burned the famous Summer Palace.

Tiepolo   (family)   [tee-ay'-poh-loh]

Giambattista Tiepolo's Meeting of Anthony and Cleopatra *(c.1745–50) is a detail from a series of sumptuous monumental frescoes in the Palazzo Labia, Venice. His effortless handling of light, color, and illusionistic effects made him Italy's greatest rococo painter.*

Giambattista Tiepolo, b. Mar. 5, 1696, d. Mar. 27, 1770, was the last great Italian painter in the Renaissance tradition. He created a style that combines flawless draftsmanship, total command of perspective, and monumental compositional structure with brilliant color and silvery light—a style so dazzling as to be equaled only by that of Paolo Veronese in the history of Italian art. Tiepolo's reputation for technical virtuosity in painting, drawing, and printmaking was so great that he was said to be capable of completing a picture in less time than it took others to prepare their paints. His output was enormous and he never lacked patrons; he was most appreciated in northern Italy, Germany (where he worked from 1750 to 1753), and Spain (1762–70), where he died.

Tiepolo studied painting with Gregorio Lazzarini, but the major influence on his early work was the dark and dramatic style of Giovanni Battista Piazzetta. In the late 1720s, inspired by the revival of 16th-century Venetian colorism pioneered by Sebastiano Ricci, Tiepolo lightened his palette and, in the course of the 1730s, completed a series of major fresco decorations infused with luminous color, derived from the style of Veronese. By 1740, Tiepolo had acquired the final element of his mature style, a complete mastery of spatial illusion, which culminated in the *Transport of the Holy House of Loreto* (1743–44), the spectacular ceiling fresco painted for the Venetian Church of the Scalzi. Tragically, this masterpiece was destroyed in 1915, but Tiepolo's beautiful and freely painted oil sketch has been preserved (1743; Accademia, Venice). It records the bold foreshortening and spacious, asymmetrical design of the lost ceiling.

His prodigious inventiveness made Tiepolo the greatest monumental decorator of the century in secular as well as ecclesiastical commissions. In the Palazzo Labia in Venice, Tiepolo and Girolamo Mengozzi-Colonna, his frequent collaborator, envisioned *The Banquet of Cleopatra* (c.1745–50) as a theatrical event taking place behind a pierced screen of illusionistic architecture; this idea is rendered so convincingly that real and fictive space are virtually indistinguishable. At Würzburg, Tiepolo created costumes and a setting of such ravishing beauty that he transformed the depiction of an insignificant event in medieval German history, the *Marriage of Frederick Barbarossa* (1752; Resìdenz, Würzburg), into one of the greatest masterworks of the 18th century.

Tiepolo exercised his genius for spectacle even in his altarpieces and has therefore been accused of religious insincerity. But the tender pathos conveyed in the *Martyrdom of Saint Agatha* (1750; Staatliche Museen, Berlin) attests to the depth and truth of his faith.

Tiepolo trained his sons **Giandomenico Tiepolo,** b. Aug. 30, 1727, d. Mar. 3, 1804, and **Lorenzo Tiepolo,** b. Aug. 8, 1736, d. Aug. 8?, 1776, as painters; they continued his style. Domenico, a distinguished painter in his own right, assisted his father ably in Würzburg and Madrid but showed a special gift for genre painting, as revealed in his charming scenes of rural peasant life that decorate the Guest House of the Villa Valmarana (1757; Vicenza, Italy). Lorenzo, far less gifted, chose to remain in Spain after Giambattista's death and is best represented by his numerous pastel portraits, today in the Prado.

LESLIE JONES

Bibliography: Levey, Michael, *Painting in XVIIIth Century Venice* (1959); Morrassi, Antonio, *G. B. Tiepolo: His Life and Work* (1955); Rizzi, Aldo, *The Etchings of the Tiepolos* (1971); Von Hadeln, Detlev, *The Drawings of G. B. Tiepolo,* 2 vols. (1970).

Tierra del Fuego   [tee-air'-uh del fway'-goh]

Tierra del Fuego is a group of islands separated from the southern tip of the South American mainland by the Strait of MAGELLAN. The eastern third of the archipelago belongs to Argentina (1980 pop., 29,451); the western two-thirds is Chilean (pop. unavailable). The islands are sparsely populated by three Indian tribes as well as by Chilean and Argentinian settlers. The total land mass of the archipelago is about 73,740 km² (28,470 mi²). Isla Grande de Tierra del Fuego, the archipelago's largest island, accounts for about two-thirds of the land area. On Isla Grande is the principal settlement, the Argentine city of USHUAIA. Mount Sarmiento, the islands' highest point at about 2,300 m (7,550 ft), is located to the west, where the mountains are an extension of the Andes range. Chief economic activities are petroleum extraction and sheep raising. The climate is moderately cold, with high winds and variable rain.

Ferdinand Magellan came upon the area in 1520; he named it "Land of Fire" (in Spanish, Tierra del Fuego) because he observed inhabitants carrying fires. In 1578, Sir Francis Drake sighted Cape HORN, the southernmost point of South America. The Argentine-Chilean boundary was fixed in 1881.

Tiffany, Charles Lewis

American jeweler Charles Lewis Tiffany, b. Killingly, Conn., Feb. 15, 1812, d. Feb. 18, 1902, founded the prestigious New York City jewelry store that bears his name. In 1837, Tiffany opened a stationery store in that city and then added glassware, china, and jewelry, mostly imported from Europe, to his stock. Tiffany's soon became one of the leading jewelry trading houses in the United States. In 1848, Tiffany's began manufacturing its own jewelry. Tiffany and Company, incorporated in 1868, became famous for improving and setting styles of silverware and other fine jewelry.

Tiffany, Louis Comfort

The plant forms and drooping shape of this bronze-base stained-glass table lamp, produced (c.1900) in the Tiffany Studios, epitomize Art Nouveau style. One of the leading American exponents of Art Nouveau, Louis Comfort Tiffany made major contributions to the decorative arts of the late 19th and the early 20th century. Tiffany's work reflects the exotic decorative traditions of the Orient and the Near East. (Metropolitan Museum of Art, New York City.)

Louis Comfort Tiffany, b. New York City, Jan. 17, 1848, d. Feb. 18, 1933, was the most notable American contributor to the ART NOUVEAU style. Although he was renowned for his work in stained and iridescent glass, his accomplishments ranged from painting, architecture, and interior design to such crafts as mosaic and jewelry. He was the eldest son of Charles L. Tiffany, founder of Tiffany and Company. Louis took up painting and became a pupil of the landscapist George Inness. In 1868, Tiffany journeyed to Paris and to North Africa, where he acquired a love for Islamic art that was to influence his work.

Tiffany's interest in the Arts and Crafts movement and in the writings of its mentor William Morris led him to found the decorating firm of Louis C. Tiffany and Associated Artists in 1881; within a year it was enormously successful. Tiffany designed interiors for New York City theaters, clubs, and private homes. His Veterans' Room (1880) in the Seventh Regiment Armory in New York City remains unchanged, as does his immense stained-glass curtain (completed 1911) in Mexico City's Art Nouveau Palacio de Bellas Artes.

Greatly impressed by French art glass, Tiffany began producing glassware in 1893, for which he hired American and European artisans. His term for the vases, lampshades, and decorative household objects that were made was *Favrile,* derived from the early French word for "handcrafted." In their asymmetrical shapes, floral patterns, and vivid, iridescent colors, these pieces are the epitome of Art Nouveau.

In 1904, Tiffany built a palatial summer home, Laurelton Hall, on Long Island, N.Y. The style was Islamic-inspired Art Nouveau; the villa's steel-frame construction and glass-paneled walls were architectural innovations.

By the time of his death, in 1933, Tiffany's works and Art Nouveau in general were out of style. Beginning in the 1950s, however, interest in Tiffany's contribution to American culture has steadily increased.   EDWARD M. PLUNKETT

Bibliography: Koch, Robert, *Louis C. Tiffany's Art Glass* (1977); McKean, Hugh F., *The Lost Treasures of Louis Comfort Tiffany* (1980) and *The Treasures of Tiffany* (1982).

Tiflis: see TBILISI.

tiger

The tiger, P. tigris, with its strong legs and claws, is an able hunter but needs sufficient cover to attack fleet prey before they have time to escape. The tiger hunts by sight and hearing rather than smell.

The tiger, *Panthera tigris,* is the largest and most powerful of the cat family, Felidae. Tigers prefer forests but are adaptable and range from the cold wastelands of Manchuria and Siberia to the thornbush of India and the hot bamboo jungles and rain forests of Malaysia. They were once found throughout southern Asia, but hunting and forest clearing have restricted their range and limited their numbers. Several subspecies, such as the Siberian and the Sumatran tigers, are near extinction. The male tiger may stand 1 m (40 in) at the shoulder, have a head and body length of 2.7 m (9 ft) and a tail of about 90 cm (3 ft), and weigh from 180 to 270 kg (about 400 to 600 lb). Tigresses are smaller. The upper coat is usually reddish yellow to tawny, marked with blackish stripes; the underparts are whitish.

Tigers typically come out at night to stalk prey. They prefer large prey, bringing it down with their claws after a brief fast rush, but they also eat small animals. The males are usually solitary hunters. From 1 to 6 but usually 2 or 3 helpless cubs, weighing only about 1.3 to 1.8 kg (3 to 4 lb), are born after a gestation period of 98 to 109 days. They become independent at about 2 to 3 years. The average life span is 15 years.

Bibliography: Thapar, V., *Tiger* (1986).

tiger's-eye

Tiger's-eye is a silky appearing, fibrous variety of quartz, ranging from golden yellow to brown, that is used extensively as an ornamental stone.

Tiger's-eye, a variety of rich golden yellow to brownish QUARTZ, is polished as a semiprecious ornamental stone to display its characteristic chatoyancy—a band of pearly luminescence resulting from reflection of light from parallel inclusions. The quartz originally contained fibers of crocidolite, a bluish asbestos; their alteration to iron oxides produced color banding. Silica subsequently replaced the iron oxides. In the similar blue-colored gem hawk's-eye, the crocidolite fibers were replaced by silica before alteration. The best examples have been found at Griqualand West in South Africa.

Tiglath-Pileser III, King of Assyria   [tig-lath-pil-ee'-zur]

Tiglath-Pileser III, d. 727 BC, king of Assyria (r. 745–727 BC), restored Assyria's imperial power after the chaos resulting from a plague, the evil omen of a solar eclipse (763), and the weakness of a royal family overthrown by a revolution in 745. As a result of the upheaval, Tiglath-Pileser replaced Ashurni-rari (r. *c.*754–*c.*745). He campaigned successfully in 743 against the Armenian kingdom of Urartu, which had menaced the frontier. Defeating various coalitions of western states in Syria, his forces sacked Damascus in 732. Israel was made a vassal state. After an anti-Assyrian faction took over Babylonia in 734, Tiglath-Pileser seized (729) the Babylonian throne. As king there he was called Pul or Pulu. He was succeeded by his son, Shalmaneser V.   TOM B. JONES

Bibliography: Anspacher, A. S., *Tiglath Pileser III* (1912; repr. 1966).

Tigranes I, King of Armenia   [ty-gray'-neez]

Tigranes I, also known as Tigranes the Great, *c.*140–*c.*55 BC, king of Armenia from 95, became one of the most powerful rulers in the Near East. He conquered large areas in Media, Syria, and Mesopotamia and built a new capital named Tigranocerta. The Romans, concerned by the threat from Tigranes' empire, sent an army against him in 69, defeating him in 66 with the help of his own son. Tigranes was permitted to keep his throne, but he was required to pay tribute to Rome.

Tigré   [ti-gray']

The Tigré are two groups of people of northern Ethiopia. The southern Tigré, for whom Tigré province is named, are closely related to the AMHARA. Their language, Tigrinya, is directly descended from Ge'ez, the sacred liturgical language of the Orthodox church of Ethiopia. Together with the Amhara, they consider themselves to be the only true Christians; they follow the doctrine of MONOPHYSITISM. Although they are distinguished from the Amhara in little except what results from their geographical isolation from each other, this isolation has led to political rivalry, including demands for a separate Tigré state. In the mid-1980s there were nearly 4 million southern Tigré.

The culturally distinct northern Tigré, who numbered about 2 million in the mid-1980s, are mostly nomadic Muslim herders living in ERITREA province. Their language, Tigré, is related to Tigrinya.   BRIAN SPOONER

Bibliography: Leslau, W., *Ethiopians Speak* (1965); Levine, D. N., *Greater Ethiopia* (1960; repr. 1977); Lipsky, G. A., *Ethiopia* (1962).

Tigris River   [ty'-gris]

The Tigris River flows 1,900 km (1,180 mi) through southeastern Turkey and Iraq, draining an area of 373,000 km^2 (144,000 mi^2). With the EUPHRATES RIVER, the Tigris supplies water to the dry plain formerly called Mesopotamia.

Navigable only between Baghdad and al-Qurnah, the Tigris begins at Lake Golcuk in east central Turkey and flows southeast past the Turkish agricultural center of Diyarbakir and through petroleum fields to Mosul in Iraq. The river continues south past a large irrigation barrage at Samarra to Baghdad, then southeast to al-Qurnah, where it joins the Euphrates to form the SHATT-AL-ARAB, which empties into the Persian Gulf. The Tigris provides irrigation waters for the cultivation of wheat, barley, millet, and rice. The Sumerians dug canals along the Tigris as early as 2400 BC, and the ruins of such ancient cities as CTESIPHON, NINEVEH, and SELEUCIA line its banks.

Tijou, Jean   [tee-zhoo']

An ironworker of French origin, Jean Tijou, active in England *c.*1689–*c.*1712, revolutionized the design and practice of decorative ironwork in England. He worked at Hampton Court Palace from about 1689 to 1700, executing the balustrades for the King's and Queen's staircases, the gates, and the great screen for the Fountain Garden, all in a new flamboyant baroque style of repoussé acanthus and scrolled ornaments. Tijou also worked for Sir Christopher Wren at Saint Paul's Cathedral (Sanctuary Screen, 1696) and for fashionable patrons at Chatsworth, Burghley, Drayton, and Stoneyhurst. In 1693, Tijou published *A New Booke of Drawings,* the first English book of designs for ironwork, based in many cases on engravings by the French designer Daniel Marot. When he left England about 1712, Tijou had established a strong tradition of ironwork that was carried on by the English smiths.

Reviewed by KATHRYN B. HIESINGER

Bibliography: Ayrton, Maxwele, and Silcock, Arnold, *Wrought Iron and Its Decorative Use* (1929); Lister, Raymond, *Decorative Ironwork in Great Britain* (1970).

Tijuana   [tee-hwah'-nah]

Tijuana (1980 pop., 461,257) is a large city in northwestern Baja California, Mexico, about 20 km (12 mi) south of San Diego, Calif. An industrial center that produces textiles, electronics, and foodstuffs, Tijuana is a principal point of entry into Mexico for U.S. tourists. The city is a shipping center for wheat, barley, and wine grapes. Founded in the mid-19th century, Tijuana was notorious during the U.S. prohibition era for its gambling casinos and numerous bars.

Tikal   [tee-kahl']

Tikal, in northeastern Guatemala, was the largest and most powerful of all ancient MAYA centers. By the 1st century AD it had grown from a village into a substantial ceremonial-civic center. Early art indicates connections with the IZAPA civilization to the south. In AD 292, Tikal erected the first dated monument in the Maya lowlands. Public construction flourished—notably, tall temple-pyramids and elaborate palaces—and Tikal, as the capital of a large regional state, quickly became the most powerful lowland center. Art and architecture point to ties with TEOTIHUACÁN, the powerful central Mexican city, probably by way of KAMINALJUYÚ, its outpost in highland Guatemala. By 800, Tikal had passed its peak, and the center ceased to function before the end of the century, although squatter groups lived on amid the ruins.

The University of Pennsylvania, in cooperation with the Guatemalan government, conducted extensive excavation and restoration at Tikal in the 1950s and '60s. The city's hub was the Great Plaza, flanked by two enormous temple-pyramids, a cluster of smaller temples, and a large palace complex. Other temples and palaces, along with ball courts, reservoirs, and causeways, occupied the surrounding zone. Greater Tikal, limited by defensive earthworks on the north and south, covered more than 100 km² (40 mi²); its peak population was nearly 50,000.

JOHN S. HENDERSON

Bibliography: Coe, W. R., *Tikal: A Handbook of the Ancient Maya Ruins* (1967).

Tikhonov, Nikolai A.   [tee'-kuh-nahf]

Nikolai Aleksandrovich Tikhonov, b. May 1905, served as premier of the USSR from 1980 to 1985. A veteran Communist party bureaucrat, he was elected deputy to the Supreme Soviet (1958) and deputy premier (1976) and became (1979) a member of the ruling politburo. He was succeeded as premier by Nikolai Ryzhkov.

Tilak, Bal Gangadhar   [tee'-lahk]

Bal Gangadhar Tilak, b. July 23, 1856, d. Aug. 1, 1920, was an Indian scholar, religious philosopher, and nationalist, who defended Hindu traditionalism and became the leader of extremist opposition to British rule. He often came into conflict with more moderate nationalists, most notably Gopal Krishna Gokhale. Tilak was jailed by the British for sedition in 1897 and 1908. He advocated the boycott of British goods (1905) and passive resistance (1906) as weapons of the nationalist movement. In 1907 he left the Indian National Congress because of its moderate policies. In 1916 he founded the Home Rule League and rejoined the Congress.

Bibliography: Wolpert, S. A., *Tilak and Gokhale* (1962).

Tilden, Bill

Bill Tilden, one of the most gifted and popular tennis players of the 1920s and '30s, won seven U.S., three Wimbledon, and two professional singles championships during his career. His cannonball serve, powerful ground strokes, and flair for the dramatic made his appeal widespread in Europe as well as in the United States. Tilden also acted on Broadway several times, once in a play that he wrote.

William Tatem Tilden, Jr., b. Germantown, Pa., Feb. 10, 1893, d. June 5, 1953, an American tennis star of extraordinary versatility and guile, was the world's dominant player during the 1920s. He won 10 Grand Slam singles titles in his career: 7 U.S. titles (1920–25, 1929) and 3 at Wimbledon (1920–21, 1930). He led the United States to 7 Davis Cup victories (1920–26) by winning 34 of 41 matches and after turning professional won two singles titles (1931, 1935), the last at an age (42) when most players have retired. Tilden was a superb all-around competitor and a brilliant tactician.

Bibliography: Deford, Frank, *Big Bill Tilden: The Triumphs and the Tragedy* (1976); Tilden, William T., *My Story* (1948).

Tilden, Samuel J.

A leading corporation lawyer and Democratic politician, Samuel Jones Tilden, b. New Lebanon, N.Y., Feb. 9, 1814, d. Aug. 4, 1886, was governor of New York (1874–76) and the Democratic candidate for president of the United States in the contested election of 1876. He attended law school in New York, was admitted to the bar in 1841, and became corporation counsel for New York City in 1843. In 1846 he served in the New York state legislature and was a member of the state constitutional convention.

Tilden was a leader of the Free-Soil Barnburner Democrats in New York. Because the trend of the state's politics from the

Samuel J. Tilden was governor of New York from 1874 to 1876. As state chairman of the Democratic party, he helped engineer the downfall of the corrupt Tweed Ring at Tammany Hall. He won a majority of the popular vote in the 1876 presidential election but was denied office on the basis of a dispute over electoral votes.

mid-1840s through the 1850s favored the rival pro-southern or Hunker Democrats (see HUNKERS AND BARNBURNERS), Tilden concentrated on his legal practice. Specializing in railroad reorganization cases, he built a large personal fortune. Politically inactive during the Civil War, he urged Democrats to act as a loyal opposition. Tilden gained political prominence while chairman of the New York State Democratic Committee (1866–74). He actively supported the Democratic presidential tickets in 1868 and 1872. Late in 1871 he moved to the forefront of the campaign to drive William M. TWEED's corrupt New York City political machine from power. Tilden's anti-Tweed activities established his credentials as a reformer, although his critics noted that he had initially been reluctant to join the anti-Tweed cause.

In 1874, campaigning under a reform banner, Tilden was elected governor of New York. He attacked corruption in state politics and sought to bring about a general reduction of state expenditures. On national issues, he criticized Radical Reconstruction policy and advocated a hard-money policy. As the Democratic presidential nominee in 1876, Tilden won a 250,000-vote plurality but lost the election when the disputed electoral votes of four states were awarded by a special commission to Republican candidate Rutherford B. HAYES. Although Tilden believed he had been cheated out of the presidency, he acquiesced in the result, largely withdrawing from active political life thereafter. He left most of his $6 million estate to New York City for the establishment of a free public library.   GERALD W. McFARLAND

Bibliography: Bigelow, John, *The Life of Samuel J. Tilden*, 2 vols. (1895) and, as ed., *Letters and Literary Memorials of Samuel J. Tilden*, 2 vols. (1908; repr. 1971); Flick, Alexander C., and Lobrano, Gustav S., *Samuel Jones Tilden: A Study in Political Sagacity* (1939; repr. 1973).

tilefish

Found from the Nova Scotia coast to the Gulf of Mexico, the perchlike tilefish, *Lopholatilus chamaeleonticeps*, is most abundant at depths of 80 to 360 m (260 to 1200 ft). Tilefish may weigh up to about 22 kg (50 lb) and are bottom feeders with strong grasping teeth. The back and sides of the adult fish are bluish grey, with yellow spots, and the face and underside are rose.   ALFRED PERLMUTTER

till and tillite   [til, til'-yt]

Till is a sedimentary deposit named by Scottish farmers before geologists understood its origin. Deposition of tills occurred during the four major ICE AGES of the Pleistocene Epoch, from about 2 million years ago to the present. Advancing glaciers (see GLACIER AND GLACIATION) incorporated particles of rock and soil ranging in size from rock flour to boulders. The glacial advances acted like conveyer belts, bringing the particles to the terminus and depositing them as MORAINES. The resultant piles of glacial debris are known as drift, and till can be defined as nonsorted, unstratified drift deposited directly from glaciers. Examples of till deposition include the Bunker Hill and Breeds Hill DRUMLINS in Boston.

Till is distinguished from CONGLOMERATES by the surface texture of the component rocks. The rock surfaces of till have facets caused by the abrasion of the rocks in the bottom layer of ice. Conglomerates, on the other hand, consist of rocks that have been rounded by water transportation. Till that is converted to solid rock, is known as tillite. Almost all rock types are contained in tillite, the largest percentage being igneous and metamorphic rock. The weathering of tillite produces an excellent tillable soil.   KENNETH W. KILMER

Tillamook   [til'-uh-muk]

The Tillamook were a North American Indian tribe of the northwest coastal region of what is now the state of Oregon. The southernmost of the Coast SALISH-speakers, they traditionally relied on salmon and other fish and shellfish for their subsistence. Their well-developed fishing technology included nets, weirs, fishhooks, and harpoons. Hunting and gathering from temporary homes was carried out during the summer.

Like other Northwest Coast tribes, they built permanent winter homes of wood planks and beams. The most important social unit was the extended patrilocal family; tribal identities were vague. Family headmen existed, but there were no village chiefs or councils of elders, nor was there a rigid concept of land ownership. Small fishing sites were passed on to family clusters, but river rights were freely loaned. Reportedly the most powerful tribe on the Oregon coast before contact with Europeans, the Tillamook population was reduced from an estimated 2,200 at the time they were visited (1805) by the Lewis and Clark Expedition to only 200 members by 1850. The last full-blooded Tillamook died in the 1950s.   JAMES W. HERRICK

Bibliography: Harr, David, ed., *Oregon Indians I* (1974); Sauter, John, and Johnson, Bruce, *Tillamook Indians of the Oregon Coast* (1974).

Tilley, Sir Samuel Leonard   [til'-ee]

Sir Samuel Leonard Tilley, b. Gagetown, New Brunswick, May 8, 1818, d. June 25, 1896, a prominent Canadian politician, helped form the Canadian Confederation. He entered New Brunswick's Legislative Assembly as a Reformer in 1850. As provincial premier (1861–65), Tilley was New Brunswick's leading advocate of Confederation. In 1864 and 1866–67 he attended the conferences that produced Confederation, and he helped bring his province into the union. Tilley was minister of customs (1867–73) and minister of finance (1873) in the first Canadian cabinet. Minister of finance again (1878–85), he introduced the protective tariff plan called the National Policy.   D. M. L. FARR

Bibliography: Hannay, James, *Sir Leonard Tilley* (1926); Morton, William L., *The Critical Years: The Union of British North America* (1964).

Tillich, Paul   [til'-ik]

Paul Tillich, b. Starzeddel, Germany, Aug. 20, 1886, d. Oct. 22, 1965, is considered one of the most creative and influential philosopher-theologians of the 20th century. Through his many writings and lectures on culture—including art, science, technology, psychotherapy, medicine, politics, and social history—Tillich almost alone took on the classical philosopher's task of providing a profound, unifying, and original interpretation of the entire scope of human existence. True to the central theme of his own thought, Tillich's lifework presents a religious interpretation of all culture that remains quite unsurpassed.

Raised in a learned, sedate, patriarchal Lutheran pastor's home, Tillich represented in his early training a union of traditional Lutheran piety and liberal German idealistic culture. As a chaplain in the German army during World War I, Tillich experienced both the reality and the universality of conflict and death and also the destruction of that same cultural unity. He became, in his subsequent career as a university professor in Germany, the intellectual leader of a group devoted to "religious socialism" and wrote several important pieces on politics, society, and history, including *The Socialist Decision* (1932). When the National Socialists came to power in 1933, Tillich's clear opposition to their ideology and policies and, above all, to their early persecution of Jews led to his dismissal (1933) from his professorship at the University of Frankfurt and his subsequent emigration to the United States. He taught first at Union Theological Seminary (1933–55) in New York, then at Harvard University (1955–62), and finally as Nuveen Professor of Theology at the University of Chicago Divinity School (1962–65). In the second half of his life Tillich became the leading philosophical and theological figure in the United States. In his teaching and in such works as *The Courage to Be* (1952), *Theology of Culture* (1959), and *The Eternal Now* (1963), he fostered a new sense of depth, a new recognition and understanding of the tragic, and a new confidence in an ultimate, meaningful unity to life.

Tillich's two central concepts in his theology and cultural analyses are on the one hand the idea of the "unconditional"—the divine ground or power of being and meaning—and on the other hand the idea of "ultimate concern." In *Dy-*

namics of Faith (1957) and in his most important work, Systematic Theology (3 vols., 1951–63), he argues that the holy, sacred, and ultimate ground or source of all life is the direct concern of religious faith; in the language of religion, the ultimate is God. Indirectly, then, God is the object of the quest of philosophy—that unity of subject and object, of thought and being, which philosophical inquiry both presupposes and seeks (that is, "Being-Itself") but cannot, without the help of religion, find. Again, indirectly, it is the "substance" of culture—it is the unconditional meaning and deep concern that makes the human quest for and creation of truth, beauty, and the good possible. For Tillich religion was the "substance" of culture. Thus, although cultural life and history itself evidenced a distorted, self-destructive character, the "unexpected" has happened and will continue to happen. The living God, the creative power of being and meaning, has manifested itself in the new Being, centered in Jesus as the Christ, accepting the unacceptable, overcoming separation and thereby destruction and despair, and providing the conditions with which the anxieties and the terrors of the human state are conquered and the creative possibilities of the human being are opened.   LANGDON GILKEY

Bibliography: Kegley, C. W., ed., The Theology of Paul Tillich, rev. ed. (1982) Kelsey, D. H., The Fabric of Paul Tillich's Theology (1967); Lyons, J. R., ed., The Intellectual Legacy of Paul Tillich (1969); Pauck, Wilhelm and Marion, Paul Tillich: His Life and Thought, 2 vols., (1976); Rowe, W. L., Religious Symbols and God: A Philosophical Study of Paul Tillich's Theology (1968); Thatcher, Adrian, The Ontology of Paul Tillich (1978); Tillich, Hannah, From Place to Place (1976) and From Time to Time (1974).

Tillman, Benjamin Ryan   [til'-muhn]

Benjamin Ryan Tillman, b. Edgefield County, S.C., Aug. 11, 1847, d. July 3, 1918, a South Carolina governor (1890–94) and U.S. senator (1895–1918), was a spokesman for southern agrarianism and a vitriolic racist. He became prominent politically in 1885, when he began organizing South Carolina farmers to overthrow the old-guard Democrats who controlled state politics. Tillman's angry attacks on the Bourbon Democrats helped him win two terms as governor. His accomplishments included tax reform, expansion of the state railroad commission's powers, and establishment of Clemson College—an agricultural school—and Winthrop College for women. Tillman's influence also meant that the new state constitution of 1895 included a number of JIM CROW LAWS and virtually disenfranchised blacks.

In the Senate, "Pitchfork Ben" soon won national notoriety for his agrarian radicalism and his racism. In 1906 he helped secure passage of the Hepburn Act regulating railroad rates. Ill health and disagreements with allies gradually weakened his influence from about 1902.   GERALD W. McFARLAND

Bibliography: Simkins, Francis B., Pitchfork Ben Tillman, South Carolinian (1944; repr. 1964), and The Tillman Movement in South Carolina (1926; repr. 1964).

Tilly, Johann Tserclaes, Graf von   [til'-ee, tsair-klahs']

Johann Tserclaes, Graf von Tilly, b. February 1559, d. 1632, fought in the service of Bavaria and the Holy Roman emperor during the THIRTY YEARS' WAR. Tilly began his army career in a Spanish regiment and served under Alessandro FARNESE during the Dutch Revolt. Commanding the armies of Bavaria and the Catholic League at the beginning of the Thirty Years' War, he defeated (1620) the Bohemians at the White Mountain, conquered the Palatinate, and defeated (1626) CHRISTIAN IV of Denmark at Lutter. In 1631, commanding the combined Bavarian and imperial armies, Tilly was defeated by GUSTAV II ADOLF of Sweden at Breitenfeld. Thereafter he could not prevent the Swedish advance into Bavaria. Mortally wounded at the Battle of the Lech, he died on Apr. 30, 1632. Tilly introduced modern methods of warfare from the Netherlands into Germany and was, technically, among the best commanders of his age. His reputation suffered, somewhat unjustly, from the sacking and burning of Magdeburg by his troops in 1631,

acts that resulted in the loss of an estimated 20 to 25 thousand lives.   H. G. KOENIGSBERGER

Bibliography: Wedgwood, Cicely V., The Thirty Years' War (1938; repr. 1969).

Tilsit, Treaties of   [til'-zit]

During the NAPOLEONIC WARS the Treaties of Tilsit ended the War of the Third Coalition—in which Russia, Prussia, and Austria were allied against Napoleonic France—and gave NAPOLEON I almost total control over Europe. Having defeated the Russians at Friedland on June 14, 1807, Napoleon opened negotiations with Emperor ALEXANDER I on June 25 on a raft in the Neman River near the East Prussian town of Tilsit (now Sovetsk, in the USSR); later, King FREDERICK WILLIAM III of Prussia also took part.

Under the treaty signed on July 7, France made peace with Russia, which, in turn, promised (covertly) to mediate between France and Britain and to ally with the French if the British refused mediation. By the treaty of July 9 most of Prussia's territory west of the Elbe River became part of the French-controlled Kingdom of Westphalia, and its Polish provinces were ceded to the newly created Duchy of Warsaw. Prussia was also obliged to reduce the size of its army, to negotiate arrangements for French troops, to garrison some of its fortresses, and to join the Continental System against Britain. The peace of Tilsit was abruptly shattered when Napoleon invaded Russia in 1812.

Timbuktu   [tim-buhk-too']

Timbuktu (French: Tombouctou), an administrative city in central Mali and a historic trading center, lies at the junction of trade routes on the southern edge of the Sahara Desert just north of the Niger River. The population of 20,483 (1976) consists largely of merchants. Salt trading is the principal commercial activity.

Timbuktu was founded in the 11th century by TUAREGS and became part of the Mali kingdom in the 13th century. From 1468 to 1591, Timbuktu developed under SONGHAI rule into an important intellectual and cultural center, as well as a commercial hub where gold, slaves, and salt were traded. Morocco conquered the city in 1591, and Timbuktu declined under its rule because little protection was provided against Fulani and Tuareg invasions. The French established an outpost at Timbuktu in the 1890s, but the city never regained its past glory. The city became part of Mali in 1960.

Time

The first modern weekly newsmagazine, Time remains the leader in its field with a circulation of nearly 4.5 million. Started in 1923 by Henry R. LUCE and Briton Hadden, Time sought to attract the busy reader by organizing news into compartments and presenting and analyzing it in a distinctive narrative style. It has come to epitomize group journalism, in which teams of researchers, writers, and editors prepare articles. Long noted for its Republican and pro-Chiang China biases, Time adopted (1964) a more liberal stance under its second editor in chief, Hedley Donovan.   THEODORE PETERSON

Bibliography: Halberstam, David, The Powers That Be (1979); Mott, F. L., A History of American Magazines, vol. 5 (1968); Tebbel, John, The American Magazine: A Compact History (1969).

time

The experience of time, or of time duration, has received great attention in literature and philosophy. The experience varies among individuals and, because of its subjective nature, may appear to be inconsistent even in one individual. In scientific work, a numerical measure is used to order observations of events. If "now" is assigned the numerical value zero, then it is usual to assign earlier times negative values and later times positive values. To obtain a time scale, some periodic phenomenon that has repetitions occurring at a uniform rate that may be subdivided and counted must be used.

Modern Concept of Time. Before the 20th century it was assumed as self-evident that a single, universal, uniform time scale existed. For two events that are widely separated in space, it had been assumed that there is no difficulty in defining the meaning of the concept of simultaneity—namely, if to one observer the events appeared to occur simultaneously, then all other observers would agree that the events were indeed simultaneous. Albert Einstein, however, early in the 20th century, recognized that because of the universal constancy of the speed of light the measurement of time depends on the motion of the observer.

Consider events A and B separated in space, which appear simultaneous to one observer; to another observer, then, who is in motion relative to the first, the event A may occur before or after B, depending on the direction of the relative motion between the two observers. Thus, in the modern view, time is no longer absolute, but dependent on the relative motion of observers making the time measurements. According to the theory of RELATIVITY, time is but one aspect of a more general four-dimensional SPACE-TIME CONTINUUM, in which events occur in the universe. Time and space are different aspects of this underlying four-dimensional continuum. Frequently time is described as a fourth dimension.

Time Scales. From earliest times the rotation of the Earth (or the apparent location of the Sun in the sky) has been used to establish a uniform time scale. In order to specify a date, using the apparent motion of the Sun as a time scale, days must be counted from some reference date (see CALENDAR). In addition, a clock is used to measure fractions of a day.

Time derived from the apparent position of the Sun in the sky is called apparent solar time. Because of the eccentricity of the Earth's orbit around the Sun and the inclination of the Earth's rotation axis to the orbital plane, apparent solar time is not a uniform time scale. These effects can, however, be calculated and corrections applied to obtain a more uniform time scale called mean solar time. Universal Time (UT0) is equivalent to mean solar time at the Greenwich Meridian (GREENWICH MEAN TIME, or GMT). Observations of the apparent motion of a distant star may be used to obtain yet another time scale used in astronomy, called sidereal time.

Additional small deviations from uniformity of UT0 may be traced to small effects, such as the wandering of the Earth's polar axis and other periodic fluctuations of the Earth's rotation; accounting for these effects leads to additional, even more uniform, time scales (UT1 and UT2).

Ephemeris time is determined by the orbital motion of the Earth about the Sun and is not affected by fluctuations in the Earth's rotation. Astronomical observations may be used to determine ephemeris time to an accuracy of roughly 0.05 seconds, averaged over a nine-year period.

Atomic Timekeeping. The invention of the quartz crystal oscillator and of the ATOMIC CLOCK makes possible the measurement of time and frequency more accurately than any other physical quantity. Thus, in addition to astronomical time scales, there are other time scales such as atomic time (AT), based on the microwave resonances of certain atoms in a magnetic field. Counting the cycles of an electromagnetic signal in resonance with cesium atoms provides an accuracy of a few billionths of a second over short intervals of a minute or less.

Since about 1960 a number of laboratories around the world have cooperated in comparing their atomic time scales, leading to the formation of a weighted average of the various atomic time scales, which is now disseminated to the public as *Universal Coordinated Time* (UTC). In order to keep UTC in agreement with the length of the day, seconds are occasionally added to or deleted from the atomic time scale (a "leap second"). By international agreement, UTC is maintained within 0.7 seconds of the navigator's time scale, UT1.

Defining the Second. The advancement of precision in time measurement has resulted in redefinitions of the second. Prior to 1956, one second was defined as the fraction 1/86,400 of the mean solar day. From 1956 to 1967, it was the ephemeris second, defined as the fraction 1/31556925.9747 of the tropical year at 00h 00m 00s 31 December 1899. The second is cur-

rently defined as the duration of 9,192,631,770 periods of the radiation corresponding to the transition between the two hyperfine levels of the ground state of the cesium-133 atom.

W. E. BRITTIN AND N. ASHBY

Bibliography: Blair, Byron E., *Time and Frequency* (1974); Cowan, Harrison J., *Time and Its Measurement: From the Stone Age to the Nuclear Age* (1958); Elton, Lewis R. B., *Time and Man* (1978); Gold, Thomas, and Schumacher, D. L., eds., *The Nature of Time* (1967); Howse, Derek, *Greenwich Time and the Discovery of the Longitude* (1980); Reichenbach, Hans, *The Philosophy of Space and Time* (1957); Schlegel, Richard, *Time and the Physical World* (1961); Toulmin, Stephen V., and Goodfield, June, *The Discovery of Time* (1976); Ward, F. A. B., *Time Measurement* (1967); Whitrow, G. J., *The Natural Philosophy of Time*, 2d ed. (1981); Zwart, P. J., *About Time: A Philosophical Inquiry Into the Origin and Nature of Time* (1976).

See also: CLOCKS AND WATCHES; TIME REVERSAL INVARIANCE.

time and motion study

A time and motion study systematically investigates work activities in order to determine the preferred method of doing work and the standard time required to perform a specific task. This type of study is also known as work design or methods design. Its objective is to combine methods, materials, tools, equipment, and working conditions so that jobs may be accomplished efficiently and effectively.

The concept of a time study was first proposed by Frederick Winslow TAYLOR in 1881. Pioneering work was done by Frank and Lillian GILBRETH. They developed (1911) an approach that makes possible the analysis of the elementary motions of a manual operation, and the assignment of time values to each. The most common approach is to time a task with a stopwatch; adjustments are then made for such factors as the ability of the particular individual being studied, fatigue, and delays. Once the preferred method of doing work has been established, a standard time may be determined for each task. The standard time may be used for planning and scheduling work, for cost estimating and labor-cost control, or as the basis for a wage-incentive plan.

JAMES S. DYER

Bibliography: Barnes, Ralph M., *Motion and Time Study: Design and Measurement of Work*, 7th ed. (1980); Nadler, Gerald, *Work Design: A Systems Concept* (1972); Niebel, Benjamin W., *Motion and Time Study*, 7th ed. (1982).

See also: INDUSTRIAL PSYCHOLOGY.

Time of Troubles

In Russian history, the Time of Troubles was the period that followed the death (1598) of Tsar Fyodor I, the last ruler of the Rurik dynasty, and lasted until the crowning (1613) of the first Romanov. During Fyodor's reign (1584–98) real power lay in the hands of his brother-in-law, BORIS GODUNOV. Fyodor's half brother, Dmitry, was killed in 1591, possibly by order of Godunov, who became tsar when Fyodor died.

In 1604 a pretender who claimed to be Dmitry and who had the support of King SIGISMUND III of Poland appeared. This "false Dmitry" became tsar upon the assassination of Godunov's son and successor, Fyodor II (r. 1605). Dmitry's close ties with Poland, however, angered the Russian boyars. Led by Prince Vasily Shuisky, they provoked an uprising in which Dmitry was killed; Shuisky became tsar as Vasily IV (r. 1606–10). In 1607 another pretender named Dmitry appeared, again with Polish support. Polish troops entered Moscow in 1610 in his defense, but he was killed. Sigismund attempted to place his own son Władysław on the Russian throne but then decided that he wanted to rule there himself; he succeeded only in uniting the Russians against the Polish invaders. Two more pretenders sought the Russian throne, but Russian forces under Prince Dmitry Pozharsky finally retook Moscow in 1612, and in 1613 a *zemsky sobor* (national council dominated by the boyars) unanimously elected as tsar 17-year-old Michael Romanov (see MICHAEL, TSAR OF RUSSIA).

Bibliography: Khuchevskii, V. O., *A Course in Russian History: The Seventeenth Century*, trans. by A. J. Rieber (1972); Niven, Alexander C., *A Brief History of Russia to 1689* (1978); Platonov, S. F., *The Time of Troubles*, trans. by John T. Alexander (1970).

time reversal invariance

A motion in which events appear in reverse order is said to be time reversed with respect to the original motion. If some motion is possible according to known physical laws, then the time-reversed motion is almost always possible. This possibility is true for motions caused by gravitational and electromagnetic forces, and it is said that these laws exhibit time reversal invariance or have time reversal as a basic symmetry. For example, it would be unusual to observe a real process in which an egg broken on the floor collects itself and flies up whole into a person's hand, as in a movie run backward. Nevertheless, according to known physical law such a process is not impossible, although it is too unlikely to expect it actually to happen. Movies of simpler processes, however, such as a spinning top or a vibrating bell, appear nearly normal when run backward.

The basic natural laws governing most elementary processes are invariant under time reversal; however, most natural processes themselves do not appear to be symmetric under time reversal. This result is because of the complexity of macroscopic systems containing many particles. For example, consider a vessel divided into two parts by an airtight partition, one part containing air and the other evacuated. If the partition is removed, air will expand until both parts of the vessel are filled. To obtain the time-reversed motion in which all the air filling the vessel streams to one side, the velocities of all the molecules would have to be reversed, an impossible task. The complexity of this system results in an extremely small likelihood that the time-reversed motion could occur. Complex systems generally develop in time toward a more probable state; this increase in likelihood is related to an increase of ENTROPY of the system.

On the subatomic level there are additional forces to consider with respect to time reversal invariance—the strong nuclear force responsible for binding atomic nuclei and the weak force responsible for the radioactive decay of such particles as the neutron. The neutron decays into a proton, an electron, and an antineutrino and is represented symbolically by: $n \rightarrow p + e + \bar{\nu}$. The motion that is time reversed with respect to the neutron decay is represented by: $\bar{\nu} + e + p \rightarrow n$, in which an antineutrino, an electron, and a proton come together to form a neutron. In order for the time-reversed reaction to correspond to the original decay, the energies of the incoming particles must be the same as those of the previous outgoing particles, and the velocities and spins of the particles must be reversed. This process is possible, although unlikely.

Experiments with elementary particles test time reversal invariance by observing processes in which elementary particles are produced, interact, and decay. Time reversal invariance appears to be a valid symmetry for all processes except in the weak decay of K mesons (kaons).   W. BRITTIN AND N. ASHBY

Bibliography: Davies, P. C. W., *The Physics of Time Asymmetry,* 2d ed. (1977).

time-sharing

Time-sharing is the simultaneous use of a central COMPUTER by independent access stations. Because of high processing speeds, modern computers are often idle; in the time taken by a user to type a command, a computer can make thousands and even millions of computations. Time-sharing therefore makes use of this available time, by means of a central program that schedules the access of individual terminals into the main unit (see OPERATING SYSTEMS). Time-sharing may take place within a single business organization but is also practiced on much wider scales, with geographically dispersed terminals connected via cable or telephone lines to the central unit. Such access is often obtained by firms that do not wish to purchase their own computer systems.

time zones

A time zone is a longitudinal strip of the Earth's surface, stretching from pole to pole and sharing the same time of

International time zones to the west of the Prime Meridian (0° longitude) are progressively earlier; to the east they are later. The date moves one day forward for persons crossing the International Date Line from east to west, and one day backward from west to east.

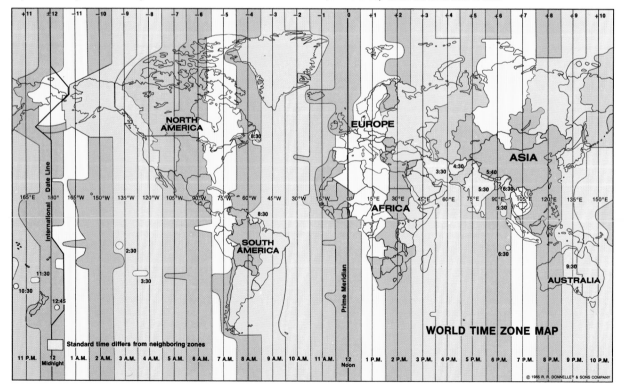

WORLD TIME ZONE MAP

day or night. The Earth requires 24 hours to make one complete rotation on its axis; thus the direct rays of the Sun pass through one degree of longitude every 4 minutes. To allow for time changes on an hourly basis, each time zone covers 15° of longitude in width. In practice, however, the zone boundary lines are drawn to accommodate political units. In addition, for various reasons a number of countries differ considerably from international practice in their time designations.

ROBERT S. WEINER

See also: GREENWICH MEAN TIME; INTERNATIONAL DATE LINE; UNIVERSAL TIME.

Times, The

The Times of London, a newspaper founded in 1785 by John Walter (see WALTER family) as the *Daily Universal Register*, received its present name in 1788. During the 19th century the paper became the unofficial voice of the government regardless of the party in power. A continuing emphasis on book reviews led to the establishment in 1902 of the weekly *Times Literary Supplement*. Purchased by Lord Thomson of Fleet (Roy Thomson) in 1966, *The Times* had a circulation of 350,000 in late 1978 when publication was suspended for a year by disputes over the introduction of a labor-saving computer-typesetting process that caused a reduction in the work force. Publication resumed in late 1979, and in 1981 *The Times* was purchased by the publisher Rupert MURDOCH. Circulation had risen to about 500,000 by 1985.

Timgad   [tim'-gad]

The ruins of Timgad (ancient Thamugadi), in northeastern Algeria about 350 km (220 mi) southeast of Algiers, are the most complete of all the Roman centers in North Africa. Excavation (begun by a French team in 1881) has laid bare the entire plan of the colony, founded (AD 100) by the Emperor Trajan in rich farmland as a settlement for army veterans. Thamugadi prospered through commerce and agriculture; by 150 it had grown beyond its walls into the surrounding countryside. In the 4th century the city became the center of the heretical DONATIST sect. Saharan raiders sacked it in the 5th century.

The site's remarkably regular plan resembles a military camp but was designed for civilian occupation: the walls enclose a square area, 355 m (1,165 ft) per side, divided into quadrants by two colonnaded avenues and subdivided by a grid of streets. The crowding of temples, baths, markets, offices, a theater, and houses within the walls forced many of the larger structures, especially baths, outside. Almost no sculpture has been preserved, but the remains of mosaic floors are notable.

JOHN P. OLESON

Bibliography: Barton, I. R., *Africa in the Roman Empire* (1972); Raven, Susan, *Rome in Africa* (1969).

Timişoara   [tee-meesh-wah'-rah]

Timişoara (Hungarian: Temesvár) is a city in western Romania with a population of 261,950 (1983). Linked with the Danube in Yugoslavia via the Bega Canal, the city produces both industrial and consumer goods. Timişoara University (1962) is there, and landmarks include a 14th-century palace and two 18th-century cathedrals. First documented in 1212, Timişoara was a Hungarian border fortress until it was taken (1552) by the Turks. The Austrians captured the city in 1716, and it became part of Romania in 1920.

Timmermans, Felix   [tim'-ur-mahns]

The Flemish author Felix Timmermans, b. Lier, Belgium, July 5, 1886, d. Jan. 24, 1947, is best known for his depictions of small-town life. The main character of his novel *Pallieter* (1916; Eng. trans., 1924) was a rustic hero with enormous natural appetites, and *Boerenpsalm* (Peasant Psalm, 1935) elaborated the type still further. Timmermans also wrote biographies of Saint Francis (1932; Eng. trans., 1974) and the painter Pieter Bruegel the Elder (1928; Eng. trans., 1930).

Timoleon   [tim-oh'-lee-uhn]

A Corinthian general, Timoleon, d. *c.*334 BC, rid Greek Sicily of tyrants and earned the appellation "the scourge of tyrants." Citizens of the Corinthian-colonized city of Syracuse in Sicily appealed to Corinth, a Greek city, for assistance in overthrowing the tyrant DIONYSIUS THE YOUNGER; in response Corinth sent Timoleon to Sicily with an army in 344 BC. He defeated Dionysius and established a modified democratic government in Syracuse. He subsequently defeated a Carthaginian invasion in 341 and Hicetas, the tyrant of Leontini, in 340. By 337, Timoleon had deposed the remaining tyrants of Greek Sicily; he retired soon thereafter.

Bibliography: Westlake, H. D., *Timoleon and His Relations with Tyrants* (1952).

Timor   [tee'-mohr]

Timor, an island in Indonesia, is the largest and easternmost of the Lesser Sunda Islands in the Malay Archipelago. The island covers 33,850 km² (13,070 mi²). The people are Indonesian Malays. The island's interior is mountainous, rimmed by narrow coastal plains and swamplands. Timor is divided into two provinces: West Timor is administered as part of Nusa Tenggara Timur, which includes nearby islands, and East Timor is administered separately as Timor Timur. The cities of Kupang and Dili serve as provincial capitals and as the principal commercial centers of West and East Timor, respectively. Most Timorese practice subsistence agriculture on small farm plots, but coffee, tea, rubber, coconuts, and sandalwood are exported. Christianity is the leading religion.

Portugal began trading with Timor in 1520, and treaties (1860, 1914) between the Portuguese and the Dutch divided the island in half. Dutch-controlled West Timor joined recently independent Indonesia in 1950, and East Timor remained a Portuguese colony. After the Portuguese departed in 1975, Indonesia intervened to prevent Fretelin, the independence movement, from gaining control of the area. The ensuing struggle caused widespread economic hardship, and the United Nations passed several resolutions condemning the Indonesian government's formal incorporation of East Timor as the 27th province of Indonesia in July 1976. By the 1980s conditions had improved somewhat, although sporadic fighting continued in the mountainous interior.

Bibliography: Jolliffe, Jill, *East Timor: Nationalism and Colonialism* (1978).

timothy

Timothy is the common name for about ten species of perennial plants of the genus *Phleum* in the grass family, Gramineae. These grasses are native to the cool and temperate regions of Europe and Asia, although they became naturalized in North America after being introduced by the colonists. The stalk grows to a height of 1.5 m (5 ft), with leaves 40 cm (1 ft) long, and terminates in dense spikes of bearded spikelets, which may grow to 15 cm (6 in). Commercially this grass has been widely grown for hay, but it does not make a good permanent pasture grass.

Timothy, Epistles to

The two Epistles to Timothy, in the New Testament of the Bible, are classified with the Epistle to Titus as the Pastoral Epistles. They are addressed by Saint Paul to his companion, Timothy, leader of the church at Ephesus (I Tim. 1:3), who is known from Acts and other epistles. The letters are pastoral in that they urge Timothy to combat false teaching and guide his people in preserving the truth; they also give detailed instructions concerning the duties of bishops, deacons, widows, and other Christians. Many scholars think that these letters were written about AD 100 in Paul's name, rather than by Paul himself, because the language differs from that of the other epistles. They carry a heavy emphasis on tradition being handed on, and church structures seem more developed than in Paul's day.

ANTHONY J. SALDARINI

Bibliography: Brown, Raymond, *Timothy-James* (1983); Dibelius, Martin, and Conzelmann, Hans, *The Pastoral Epistles* (Eng. trans., 1972); Johnson, Luke T., *First and Second Timothy* (1987).

Timothy, Saint

Saint Timothy was a young assistant and disciple of Saint PAUL in the missionary activities described in the New Testament. Born of a pagan father and a Jewish mother, Timothy was already a member of the Christian church at Lystra when Paul met him. His name appears with Paul's in the greetings of seven of the Pauline epistles. According to tradition, he was made bishop of Ephesus, where he was martyred (AD 97) when he protested orgies accompanying the worship of Artemis. Feast day: Jan. 26 (formerly Jan. 24; Western); Jan. 22 (Eastern).

timpani: see KETTLEDRUM.

Timrod, Henry   [tim'-rahd]

Called the "laureate of the Confederacy," Henry Timrod, b. Charleston, S.C., Dec. 8, 1828, d. Oct. 6, 1867, is best known for his "Magnolia Cemetery Ode." Prevented from serving in the Confederate army by poor health, he wrote inspirational, patriotic verse that predicted great victories and future glory for the Confederacy. Several of his poems were used as marching songs. His most ambitious work, "Ethnogenesis" (1861), was an epic of the birth of the new nation.

CHARLOTTE SOLOMON

Timur   [tee-moor']

Timur, or Tamerlane, enters his capital city of Samarkand in this 14th-century Persian miniature. This conqueror, who acclaimed descent from Genghis Khan, led his Turko-Mongol armies in brilliant military campaigns against India, Persia, and the Ottoman Empire. Timur's vast empire collapsed shortly after his death in 1405.

Timur, or Tamerlane, b. Apr. 8, 1336, d. February 1405, a Mongol conqueror, was widely regarded as the military equal of the earlier Genghis Khan, whom Timur—probably falsely—claimed as a direct ancestor. Timur, however, was a different kind of military tactician, striking quickly and often without plan, whereas Genghis usually organized his campaigns carefully and moved with deliberation. Timur, moreover, made no contribution to the governance or legal systems of the peoples he conquered. His cruelty went beyond that of any other Mongol khan or ruler—he was responsible for the deaths of hundreds of thousands of people. His name also appears as Tamburlaine or Timur Lenk (Timur the Lame; he was wounded in battle as a young man and walked with a limp).

Timur belonged to an Islamic, Turkized Mongol tribe living in the area of Transoxiana (today's Uzbek SSR). By 1370 he had established himself as the ruler of this region, making Samarkand his capital. From there he launched his career of expansion.

Having conquered (by 1381) Khorezm and Herat, Timur began a successful onslaught against the rulers and peoples of the Middle East and Transcaucasia, although he was diverted several times by military threats from Tokhtamysh, his former ally and khan of the GOLDEN HORDE. During the 5-year campaign of 1392–96, he completed his conquest of Iran, occupied Baghdad, and routed the Golden Horde. In 1398 he invaded India and occupied Delhi. In 1400, Timur began a campaign in which he invaded Syria and Anatolia and inflicted (1402) a devastating defeat on the Ottoman sultan Bayezid I at Ankara.

Timur died during a vain attempt to conquer China. Turko-Mongol influence subsequently declined, although the brief rule of Timur's descendants, the Timurids, brought a period of cultural grandeur.   RICHARD BUTWELL

Bibliography: Hookham, Hilda, *Tamburlaine, the Conqueror* (1962); Wepaman, Dennis, *Tamerlane* (1986).

Timurids   (dynasty)   [tim-oor'-idz]

The Timurids, descendants of the Turko-Mongol conqueror Timur (Tamerlane), established a short-lived but culturally significant reign in Persia and central Asia following Timur's death (1405).

Timur's empire was divided after he died. His fourth son, **Shah Rokh** (1377–1447), had by 1407 gained power over most of Persia, however; in contrast to the violence of his father, he established peace and a stable economy and patronized the arts and religion. Shah Rokh's son, **Ulugh Beg** (1394–1449), served as viceroy in adjacent Transoxiania, where the arts were also supported.

The rule of the Timurids, one of the most culturally brilliant of the medieval period, was brief. In 1452, the last important Timurid ruler, **Abu Said**, established control over Persia from Mesopotamia to Transoxiania. His defeat and execution by Turkoman invaders in 1469 ended Timurid governance of western and southern Persia. **Husayn Baygarah** (1478–1506), another Timurid, ruled eastern Persia from 1469 until his death; this area experienced its own cultural flowering during these years, but it fell to the Uzbeks in 1507. BABUR, a member of the Timurid line, founded the Mogul dynasty in India in 1526.   RICHARD BUTWELL

Bibliography: Grousset, René, *The Empire of the Steppes,* trans. by Naomi Walford (1970).

tin

Tin, a solid, rather unreactive metal, in group IVA of the periodic table, has an atomic number of 50 and an atomic weight of 118.69. Its chemical symbol, Sn, is derived from *stannum,* the Latin word for tin. Tin has ten naturally occurring isotopes; the most abundant is $^{120}_{50}Sn$ (32.85%). BRONZE, an alloy of copper and tin, has been known since 2500–2000 BC (the BRONZE AGE). The first inclusion of tin in bronze was probably an accidental result of tin ore being found in copper ore; pure tin was probably obtained at a later date.

Tin is relatively rare (about 0.001% in the Earth's crust) and is obtained from its chief ore, cassiterite (SnO_2), a naturally occurring tin oxide, by various refining methods, including carbon reduction. Important ore deposits are found in Malaysia, Indonesia, Zaire, Nigeria, and Bolivia.
Physical Properties. White tin, the element's familiar allotropic form (see ALLOTROPE), is a silvery white, soft, ductile metal that melts at 232° C and boils at 2,270° C. Below 13.2° C (55.8° F), pure metallic tin slowly converts to gray tin, a different crystalline form that is less dense and lacks the metallic properties of white tin. The white form is normally used; gray tin has few, if any, uses.
Chemical Properties. In its chemical compounds, tin exhibits two common oxidation states, +2 and +4. Tin dissolves in hydrochloric acid, reacting to yield stannous chloride, $SnCl_2$, and hydrogen gas. Concentrated nitric acid oxidizes tin to the +4 oxidation state, forming stannic oxide, SnO_2. A strong

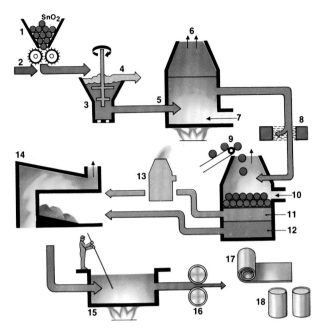

Tin, a soft silvery white metal of low melting point, is obtained from cassiterite, a heavy oxide ore. The ore is crushed (1) and mixed with oil and water (2) in a flotation tank (3). The light parts of the ore rise and are skimmed off (4). The heavy tin oxide, whch sinks to the bottom, is dried and placed in a roasting oven (5), where it is heated in air (7) to remove arsenic and sulfur as volatile oxides (6). Other impurities are removed by a chemical leaching process (8). The purified ore is heated with coke (9) and air (10) in a reverberatory oven. The tin oxide is reduced to tin (12), and the impurities collect in a floating layer (11) of molten slag. This crude tin and additional tin recovered (13) from the slag are first refined by a controlled melting process (14) and then by a poling process (15), in which the remaining metal impurities are removed. The refined tin is then rolled (16) into sheets for processing into tinplate (17) and tin cans (18).

base, such as sodium hydroxide, dissolves tin to form a stannate, a chemical SALT.

When exposed to the atmosphere and moisture, tin forms a protective oxide coating that resists further corrosion. When tin reacts with excess chlorine gas, stannous chloride, $SnCl_2$, a colorless liquid and electrical conductor, is formed. The reaction of tin with hydrofluoric acid yields stannous fluoride, SnF_2, a white, water-soluble compound that is added to toothpaste to help prevent tooth decay.

Alloys. Tin is a major component in many useful ALLOYS. When mixed with tin to form bronze, copper is easier to cast and has superior mechanical properties. Pewter is an alloy of tin hardened with antimony and copper. Tin alloys are also used in solder, bearings, and type metals. Commonly used solders are alloys of tin and lead.

Tinplate. Because of its resistance to corrosion, tin is used as a protective coating for other metals that corrode easily. Most of the tin imported into the United States is used for plating steel. Tin cans are actually steel cans with a thin coating of metallic tin. Once a portion of the tin coating is removed and steel is exposed to the atmosphere and moisture, rapid corrosion begins. The tinplate also prevents the organic acids contained in many foods from reacting with the steel can. The plating of the steel with tin is accomplished either by ELECTROLYSIS or by dipping the steel into molten tin.

Production. More than 200,000 metric tons (220,462 U.S. tons) of tin are produced annually worldwide. The major tin-producing countries are Malaysia, Indonesia, Bolivia, Thailand, the USSR, China, and Brazil.   NORMAN V. DUFFY

Bibliography: Baldwin, William L., *The World Tin Market: Political Pricing and Economic Competition* (1983); Barry, B. T., and Thwaites, C. G., *Tin and Its Alloys and Compounds* (1983); Rahn, A., *Tin in Organic Synthesis* (1987).

Tin Drum, The

The Tin Drum (1959; Eng. trans., 1962; film, 1980), by Günter GRASS, won international acclaim for its author and established him as one of postwar Germany's major novelists. Reflecting Grass's life from his childhood in Danzig to his wartime experiences, the novel takes the form of a first-person narrative by a dwarf, Oskar Matzerath, who is in a mental asylum. This provides the springboard for a scathing attack on the religious, moral, and political values of the German middle classes and a bold analysis of the charged subject of nazism. It is also a richly comic novel that brilliantly exploits the resources of language.   R. M. FORD

Tin Pan Alley

Originally, *Tin Pan Alley* referred to the popular songwriting trade centered in New York City, but eventually the phrase came to include the entire American pop-music industry from the 1880s to the 1950s. At its worst, Tin Pan Alley connotes the mass production of artless music; at its best, it represents America's most original and characteristic musical expression. According to legend the term was coined between 1900 and 1903 by songwriter-journalist Monroe Rosenfeld, who was inspired by the clashing sounds of pianos and singing voices from countless open windows on New York City's West 28th Street, once the site of dozens of music publishing companies.

Aggressive marketing of popular sheet music began in the 1880s, and by the 1890s sales of hit songs had reached the millions. At first, most popular songs were introduced on the musical stage, but in the 1930s radio and sound movies began playing an increasing role, and phonograph records replaced sheet music as the measure of sales success. Despite the lessened importance of sheet music, control of America's mainstream popular music remained with a few major corporations. This control was lost, signaling the end of Tin Pan Alley in the 1950s with the advent of ROCK MUSIC.

EDWARD A. BERLIN

Bibliography: DeLong, T. A., *The Mighty Music Box: The Golden Age of American Musical Radio* (1980); Goldberg, I., *Tin Pan Alley* (1930); Hamm, C., *Yesterdays: Popular Song in America* (1979); Marcuse, M. F., *Tin Pan Alley in Gaslight* (1959); Meyer, H., *The Gold in Tin Pan Alley* (1958; repr. 1977); Shepherd, J., *Tin Pan Alley* (1982); Wilder, Alec, *American Popular Song* (1972); Wilk, M., *They're Playing Our Song* (1974; repr. 1986).

See also: MUSIC HALL; VAUDEVILLE, AND BURLESQUE; MUSICAL COMEDY.

tinamou   [tin'-uh-moo]

The variegated tinamou, Crypturellus variegatus, found in tropical and subtropical forests and thickets, feeds exclusively on vegetation.

A tinamou is a ground-dwelling game bird found from southern Mexico to southern Argentina in diverse habitats from lowland jungles to treeless Andean slopes. The more than 30 species, related to flightless rheas, make up the family Tinamidae, the sole family of the order Tinamiformes. Quail-sized to chicken-sized, tinamous generally have small heads, thin necks, short, rounded wings, short tails, and thick legs with three, short front toes and sometimes a fourth, elevated hind toe. The plumage—usually gray or brown and often streaked and spotted—provides excellent camouflage. Tinamous feed chiefly on vegetable matter, especially berries, and on insects. Tinamou eggs are large, glossy, and beautifully colored. Although considerable variety exists in pair bonding, males usually build the nest, incubate the eggs—up to 12 in a clutch—for about 3 weeks, and then care for the young.

Tinbergen, Jan   [tin'-bair-guhn]

The Dutch economist Jan Tinbergen, b. Apr. 12, 1903, shared (1969) the first Nobel Prize for economics with Ragnar Frisch. Tinbergen, a graduate (1929) of Leiden University, received the award for constructing econometric systems—developing and using mathematical models to analyze and structure behavior. As a result of his work (1936-38) with the League of Nations, he developed the first econometric model of a national economy.

A professor (1933-73) at the Netherlands School of Economics, Tinbergen served (1945-55) as director of the Dutch central planning bureau. In 1965 he was appointed chairman of the UN Committee for Development Planning. His books include *Shaping the World Economy* (1962) and *Development Planning* (1967).

Tinbergen, Nikolaas

The Dutch zoologist and ethologist Nikolaas Tinbergen, b. Apr. 15, 1907, was a pioneer in the study of animal behavior under natural conditions and shared with Konrad Lorenz and Karl von Frisch the 1973 Nobel Prize for physiology or medicine. Tinbergen analyzed specific stimuli that elicit specific animal responses. His works include *The Study of Instinct* (1951), *Social Behavior in Animals* (1953), *The Herring Gull's World* (1960), and *Animal Behavior* (1965).

Bibliography: Cohen, David, *Psychologists on Psychology* (1977).

Tindemans, Leo   [tin'-de-mahns]

The Belgian statesman Leo Tindemans, b. Apr. 16, 1922, served (1974-79) as prime minister of Belgium. In 1961 he was elected to the Chamber of Deputies. On Oct. 10, 1979, Tindemans submitted the resignation of his government after a dispute with members of his coalition on restructuring Belgium into a federal state that could allow separate assemblies for its different linguistic regions.

Ting, Samuel Chao Chung

The American physicist Samuel Chao Chung Ting, b. Ann Arbor, Mich., Jan. 27, 1936, made (1974) a major discovery in the field of elementary particle physics by detecting the existence of a new, relatively stable heavy particle called *J* (or *psi*, as the identical particle detected contemporaneously by Burton Richter is called). Elementary particles had been hypothesized to be made up of three species of even smaller units called QUARKS, but to understand the inner structure of the new particle required the hypothesis of a fourth species of quark with a new quality called charm. A professor of physics at the Massachusetts Institute of Technology, Ting was awarded (1975) the Nobel Prize for physics.

See also: FUNDAMENTAL PARTICLES.

Tinguely, Jean   [tan-glee']

Jean Tinguely, b. May 22, 1925, is an internationally known kinetic sculptor. He was educated at the School of Fine Arts in Basel, Switzerland, and moved to Paris in 1952. Since 1959 he has lived in Düsseldorf, Germany, although the development of his sculpture has taken him throughout Europe and the United States. Salvaging discarded machine parts, Tinguely recycles them in elaborate, sometimes immense works of art. They are powered by electric motors, and their moving parts make satirical comment on the complexity and dehumanization of the machine age. Art itself is one of Tinguely's targets—some of his machines employ pencil and paper to produce "drawings" of an abstract sort. He designed his large *Homage to New York* (1960) to destroy itself in the garden of New York City's Museum of Modern Art, which it did, although only partially. Tinguely is considered to be a contemporary exponent of the disruptive, "antiart" spirit of Dada.

CARTER RATCLIFF

Bibliography: Hulten, Karl G., *Jean Tinguely: Me'ta* (1976); Rubin, William Stanley, *Dada, Surrealism and Their Heritage* (1968); Schwartz, R. Waldo, *The Hand and the Eye of the Sculptor* (1969); Tomkins, Calvin, *The Bride and the Bachelors* (1968).

tinnitus   [tin'-uh-tuhs]

Tinnitus is a ringing, buzzing, or roaring sensation in the ears. Objective tinnitus, which is audible by another person through a stethoscope, is usually caused by disturbed blood circulation or by muscular spasms in the middle ear or soft palate.

Subjective tinnitus, which is heard only by the person experiencing it, stems from irritated nerve endings in the inner ear and often accompanies hearing loss.

PETER L. PETRAKIS

Tintoretto   [teen-toh-ret'-toh]

Nicknamed Tintoretto—"Little Dyer"—in reference to his father's trade, Jacopo Robusti, b. c.1518, d. May 31, 1594, produced some of the greatest glories of 16th-century Venetian painting. His art has been said to combine the color of his Venetian predecessor, Titian, with the drawing of Michelangelo. He would have known the latter's work at least through drawings, casts, or models; he may also have seen sculpture and paintings by Michelangelo in Florence and Rome, although it is uncertain whether he visited those cities. Even in his earliest known works, however, Tintoretto displayed a new and unique vigor. Some of his characteristics have been called Mannerist; these include his weaving together of figures into an elaborate pattern, his tendency to direct the viewer's eye rapidly through the space of a picture to a high and off-center vanishing point, and his dramatic counterpoint of light and dark (chiaroscuro). Tintoretto rarely, however,

Susanna and the Elders (c. 1550), by the prolific Venetian painter Tintoretto, is judged to be the finest of his three versions of the Old Testament episode. Set in a Renaissance garden, it depicts the moment when Susanna becomes aware of the prying elder peering around the sheltering arbor. (Kunsthistorissches Museum, Vienna.)

used these devices merely as demonstrations of his virtuosity in producing the clever, graceful, and startling effects often associated with Mannerism. In planning compositions, he arranged small, draped figures on a miniature stage so that he could manipulate both lighting and perspective. The use of a wide, square-ended brush enabled him to produce an extremely large number of paintings with unprecedented speed. In carrying out large commissions he was aided also by numerous assistants and pupils, among them his sons Domenico and Marco and his daughter Marietta.

Tintoretto's most extensive cycles of paintings were made for the Scuola of the Confraternity of San Rocco and for the DUCAL PALACE, both in Venice. His work at the Scuola, which began in 1565 and continued, intermittently, to 1587, included, in one room, an enormous *Crucifixion* and other scenes of Christ's Passion. On the ceiling of another room he painted 13 Old Testament events, among which *Moses Striking Water from the Rock* is especially notable for its illusionism. On the walls of the same room he depicted 10 complementary occurrences from the New Testament. In yet another room he painted a history of the Virgin. In the Ducal Palace, Tintoretto depicted a huge battle scene, the *Siege of Zara* (1584–87); a vast *Paradise* (1588); and many other paintings on religious, historical, mythological, and allegorical themes. Three of his most famous paintings deal with the patron saint of Venice, Mark the Evangelist: *Miracle of the Slave* (1548), *Transport of St. Mark's Body* (1562–66)—both at the Accademia, Venice—and *Discovery of St. Mark's Body* (1562–66; Brera, Milan).

EDITH W. KIRSCH

Bibliography: Newton, Eric, *Tintoretto* (1952); Pignatti, T., and Valcanover, F., *Tintoretto* (1985); Ridolfi, C., *The Life of Tintoretto*, trans. by C. and R. Enggass (1984); Tietze, Hans, *Tintoretto: The Paintings and Drawings* (1948).

Tippecanoe, Battle of [tip-uh-kuh-noo']

In the Battle of Tippecanoe (Nov. 7, 1811), Indiana territorial governor William Henry HARRISON, with 1,000 U.S. regulars and militiamen, defeated the Shawnee Indians on the Tippecanoe River near present Lafayette, Ind. The Indians were led by the SHAWNEE PROPHET, brother of their chief, Tecumseh. Harrison's men burned the Indians' chief village, the Prophet's Town, and then withdrew. Although it was indecisive, the battle made Harrison a national hero.

Tipperary (county)

Tipperary, a hilly inland county in southern Ireland in the province of Munster, has an area of 4,293 km² (1,658 mi²) and a population of 135,261 (1981). Clonmel (1971 pop., 11,622) and Tipperary are the major towns.

Dairying is the main economic activity, but the cultivation of oats and potatoes, cattle raising, food processing, slate quarrying, and coal mining are also important. The Rock of Cashel, a one-time seat of the kings of Munster, is the most notable landmark.

Tipperary was dominated by the Butler family from 1185 to 1715. Today it is divided administratively into North Riding and South Riding.

Tipperary (town)

Tipperary (Irish: Tiobraid Árann) is a town of County Tipperary in south central Ireland. The population is 4,984 (1981). Tipperary is the marketing and processing center for the surrounding agricultural and dairying region. The town grew around an Augustinian priory founded in the 13th century, the ruins of which remain.

Tippett, Michael [tip'-it]

The English composer Michael Kemp Tippett, b. Jan. 2, 1905, creates music with a strong humanist message, in a style that is contemporary and yet firmly in the symphonic mainstream. Although some consider his pacifism and his philosophy naive, his texts and librettos—which Tippett writes himself—are usually presented with structural sophistication and a sure

sense of the theater. His four operas—*The Midsummer Marriage* (1955), *King Priam* (1962), *The Knot Garden* (1970), and *The Ice Break* (1977)—are among the most important of the late 20th century and have received increased international attention. Tippett's Third Symphony (1972) makes references to Beethoven's Ninth Symphony; his Fourth Symphony (1977) is a virtuoso piece composed for the Chicago Symphony. Among his other important works are the oratorio *A Child of Our Time* (1944) and the Concerto for Double String Orchestra (1939), as well as string quartets and piano sonatas. Tippett was knighted in 1966. He is the author of a collection of essays, *Moving into Aquarius* (1966), and *Music of the Angels* (1980).

KAREN MONSON

Bibliography: Matthews, David, *Michael Tippett* (1980); White, E. W., *Tippett and His Operas* (1979).

Tippu Sultan, Sultan of Mysore [tip'-oo, my-sohr']

Tippu Sultan (also Tippoo Sahib and Tibu Sahib), b. c.1750, d. May 4, 1799, sultan of Mysore (1782–99) in southern India, successfully resisted British conquest for many years. Having studied Western military operations, Tippu commanded the troops of his father, HYDER ALI, in numerous battles against neighboring states. He defeated the British in the Second Mysore War (1780–84) and preserved his empire. Clashing again with the British (1789–92), he scored impressive initial successes but finally was forced to give up half his holdings. Trying to oust the British in the Fourth Mysore War (1799), he died in battle against a superior force, and his empire was destroyed.

Bibliography: Khan, Mohibbul Hasan, *History of Tipu Sultan* (1951); Spear, Percival, *India: A Modern History* (1961).

Tiradentes [tee-rah-then'-tuhs]

Joaquim José da Silva Xavier, or "Tiradentes," b. Nov. 12, 1748, d. Apr. 21, 1792, is considered one of Brazil's greatest martyrs and a forerunner of independence. A sometime merchant and militia officer, he earned his nickname, which means "tooth puller," by working as an amateur physician and dentist. An admirer of republican ideas, he became (1788) a leader of the Inconfidência Mineira, an abortive revolt against Portuguese rule, but was imprisoned in 1789. Tiradentes was hanged and quartered in Rio de Janeiro.

Bibliography: Maxwell, Kenneth, *Conflicts and Conspiracies: Brazil and Portugal 1750–1808* (1973).

Tiranë [tee-rah'-nuh]

Tiranë, the capital and largest city of Albania, lies in the west central part of the country, about 30 km (20 mi) from the Adriatic coast. The population is 206,100 (1983 est.). A major industrial center, the city produces textiles, wood items, cigarettes, shoes, and dairy products; coal is mined nearby. Tiranë is linked by rail with Durrës, the chief port of Albania. The city's historic center, surrounded by government buildings, consists of Skanderbeg Square, where the Etehem Bey Mosque (1819) is located. Most of the city, however, has a modern appearance, with broad streets and boulevards. Cultural institutions include the state university (1957) and several museums. Founded in the 17th century by a Turkish general, Tiranë became the capital of Albania in 1920.

tire

Tires are rubber-and-fabric devices that, when attached to the wheels of a vehicle, provide the contact between the vehicle and the surface over which it travels. Tires may be either solid or pneumatic (air-filled) in structure, with the latter by far the most prevalent today. Each modern automotive tire supports 50 times its own weight. Compressed air within the tire carries 90 percent of the load, with the tire's complex structure of rubber and fabric carrying the remaining 10 percent.

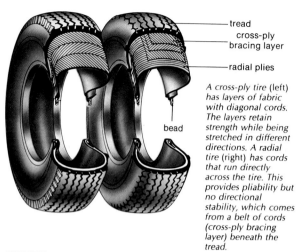

tread
cross-ply
bracing layer
radial plies
bead

A cross-ply tire (left) has layers of fabric with diagonal cords. The layers retain strength while being stretched in different directions. A radial tire (right) has cords that run directly across the tire. This provides pliability but no directional stability, which comes from a belt of cords (cross-ply bracing layer) beneath the tread.

HISTORY

The first pneumatic tire was patented in 1845 by Robert W. THOMSON. His "elastic bearings" for carriages were made from several layers of rubber-saturated canvas. John DUNLOP patented (1888) a pneumatic tire for bicycles and formed a company for manufacturing tires for bicycles and automobiles. By 1900 and the dawn of the automobile age, tires had round cross sections, separate inner tubes inflated to a pressure of 70 lb/in^2 (5 kg/cm^2), and rubber-coated, cotton-cloth covers, but they still had no tread patterns. Treads, which alleviated the danger of sideslip, were introduced 10 years later. Layers of reinforcing cord date from the 1920s; whitewalls followed in 1929. These so-called balloon tires ran at a lower inflation pressure and gave a smoother ride than their earlier counterparts. The 1930s saw the introduction of synthetic materials in tire construction. The last major change—elimination of separate inner tubes—came in 1954.

Many refinements have occurred in tire geometry, materials, and construction over the years. Frequent roadside patching, which was a problem with early tires, is no longer necessary with modern tubeless tires.

CONSTRUCTION

The most visible parts of a tire are the tread, which grips the road surface, and the supporting sidewalls, which run from tread to wheel rim. Tread patterns are especially important when the road is wet. The forward portion of a tire's contact patch wipes away water so that the rest of the patch grips a drier surface. Continuous channels from the center to the edge of the tread direct the water outward. Without a carefully designed tread, water would form a wedge and cause the tire to lift off the road. This so-called aquaplaning phenomenon is one reason that smooth tires (whether they are intentionally smooth racing slicks or regular tires that have been worn bald) are dangerous in wet conditions. Snow tires and off-highway tires have deeper treads or separate cleats that bite through snow, slush, or dirt to grip the firmer surface beneath.

A tire's sidewalls have two conflicting purposes: they flex up and down, helping cushion the vehicle from road irregularities, yet they must be relatively rigid horizontally in order to transfer loads of steering, braking, and acceleration. At their innermost edges, sidewalls meet the tire's beads (hoops of steel wire covered with hard rubber). Each bead reinforces the interface between the tire and wheel-rim and fixes the tire's inner diameter.

Reinforcing cords, which give the tire its strength, are arranged beneath the tire's surface. The three classes of modern tires can be distinguished by the direction of the cords. A bias-ply tire, the earliest, has two or more plies of cord running across the tire at an angle, or bias, from the tire's centerline; the cords thus form a crisscross pattern from bead to bead. In a belted-bias tire, reinforcing belts are placed between the plies. A radial tire has reinforcing cords running

hoop-fashion from bead to bead. Like a bias-belted tire, a radial has reinforcing belts under its tread, but radial belt cords are angled closer to the tire's centerline. The lack of bias sidewall reinforcement makes a radial's sidewalls more flexible. This gives the tread a better grip and longer life; it also gives the radial tire its characteristic underinflated look.

Tire construction begins with the sidewall. The different rubber compounds necessitated by the different requirements of each part of the tire are brought together to form sidewall-tread-sidewall strips. Beads are formed from wound and rubber-coated steel wires. Steel or synthetic-fiber fabric is rubber-coated and cut either at an angle or straight across, depending on tire type. All these materials are assembled for hand lay-up on a rotating, collapsible drum. The operator carefully aligns reinforcing fabric over a rubber liner. An error of 1° in cord angle is noticeable; a 2° error can cause a tire to be scrapped. Next, the beads and tread-sidewall strip are added, and the result is an uncured, or green, tire. A heated press molds the tread pattern and vulcanizes the rubber.

DESIGNATIONS

Tires come in many sizes, each described by a coded sequence. For example, the designation FR78–14 means that the tire is a radial (R), designed for a 14-in.-diameter wheel, of medium (F) width (A is the narrowest width and B, C, D, and so on are progressively wider). The number 78 describes the tire's cross-sectional profile: its height is 78 percent of its width; the cross-section of FR60 would be somewhat more squat. International Standards Organization dimensions are also common: a P165/75R13 tire is a passenger-car (P) radial (R), 165-mm-wide tire, with a 75 percent profile, for a 13-in. wheel. Because of different handling characteristics, tires of differing size or type should not be mixed.

DENNIS SIMANAITIS

Bibliography: Day, John, *The Bosch Book of the Motor Car* (1976); Hays, Donald F., and Browne, Alan L., eds., *The Physics of Tire Traction* (1974); Shuldinger, Herbert, "Grading Tire Quality," *Popular Science*, April 1980.

Tiresias [ty-ree'-see-uhs]

In Greek mythology Tiresias was a blind Theban soothsayer. According to one legend Athena blinded him when he accidentally came upon her bathing. His mother, the nymph Chariclo, begged for mercy; so Athena gave him the power of prophecy, as well as a golden staff to guide him in walking. Another tale relates how Tiresias, who had been changed into a woman and then back into a man, was asked to settle a quarrel between Zeus and Hera about which sex enjoyed love more. He said woman, angering Hera, who then blinded him. Zeus compensated him by giving him long life and the gift of prophecy, but Hera decreed that no one would believe his predictions.

Tirol: see TYROL.

TIROS

The original TIROS (Television and Infrared Observation Satellite) series of ten weather satellites, launched by the National Aeronautics and Space Administration (NASA) between 1960 and 1965, was developed to test television cameras and Sun-angle and horizon scanners for use in meteorology (see SATELLITE, ARTIFICIAL). Although begun on an experimental basis, the program soon became semioperational. Each of the satellites carried two television cameras, one with a wide-angle lens and the other providing a narrower field of view in greater detail. Other instruments included several infrared sensors, a horizon seeker, a tape recorder for storing images, and three radios for transmitting images and other data to Earth. Power was provided by solar cells and, within the craft, by nickel-cadmium batteries.

The next generation of satellites in the program, a series of nine ESSA (Environmental Science Service Administration) craft launched between 1966 and 1969, formed the Tiros Operational System (TOS), relaying cloud-cover images to simple stations located in several countries. The ESSA satellites used advanced cameras that had been tested on early entries in NASA's NIMBUS program, a series designed for more wide-ranging scientific studies in meteorology.

ESSA was followed by the ITOS/NOAA series, initiated by the launching of *Tiros-M* in 1970. Once in orbit, the satellite was renamed *ITOS-1* (Improved Tiros Operational Satellite-1). The five satellites that followed it into orbit from 1970 to 1976 were named NOAA, for the National Oceanic and Atmospheric Administration, ESSA's successor. Each craft provided day-and-night global coverage every 12 hours and could either relay images and radiometric data automatically or store them for later playback. Each also carried advanced instruments, such as radiometers for obtaining vertical temperature profiles of the atmosphere.

The third generation of satellites in the program began operation with the launching of *TIROS-N* in 1978, the first in a series of eight planned polar-orbit meteorological satellites. Succeeding entries in the series have continued the NOAA numbering sequence, beginning with *NOAA-6* in 1979. These satellites are equipped with more sophisticated cameras and radiometers as well as infrared, stratospheric, and microwave sounders. In addition, they can provide readings of sea-surface temperatures, identify snow cover and ice at sea, and measure particle densities in the upper atmosphere in order to predict the onset of solar disturbances. Operated by the National Oceanic and Atmospheric Administration, they and the Nimbus and Geostationary Operational Environmental Satellites (see GOES) are essential units within the U.S. National Operational Meteorological System (see METEOROLOGY).

Bibliography: Committee on Atmospheric Sciences, National Academy of Sciences, *The Atmospheric Sciences* (1977); Gatland, Kenneth, *The Illustrated Encyclopedia of Space Technology* (1981); Taggart, Ralph, *New Weather Satellite Handbook* (1981).

Tirpitz, Alfred von [tir'-pits]

Alfred von Tirpitz, b. Mar. 19, 1849, d. Mar. 6, 1930, created the German High Seas Fleet and was one of the most powerful figures in the imperial government of WILLIAM II. Entering the Prussian navy in 1865, he supervised the development of torpedoes for the German fleet in the 1870s and '80s. Later, as head of the Imperial Naval Office (from 1897) and grand admiral (from 1911), he skillfully built a battleship fleet second only to Britain's. Despite Tirpitz's efforts and his initially strong official and public backing, the German government decided to limit its buildup, which had succeeded in alienating the British and in coopting resources needed to maintain the strength of the army. The German navy was thus unprepared for World War I. Frustrated also in his support of unrestricted submarine warfare, Tirpitz resigned in 1916 and helped to organize a new ultranationalistic party. He wrote a personal defense, *My Memoirs* (1919; Eng. trans., 2 vols., 1919). From 1924 to 1928 he represented an extreme right-wing party in the Reichstag.   FREDERIC B. M. HOLLYDAY

Bibliography: Herwig, H.H., *Luxury Fleet: The Imperial German Navy, 1888–1918* (1980); Kehr, Eckart, *Battleship Building and Party Politics in Germany, 1894–1901* (1973); Steinberg, Jonathan, *Yesterday's Deterrent: Tirpitz and the Birth of the German Battle Fleet* (1965).

Tirso de Molina [teer'-soh day moh-lee'-nah]

Tirso de Molina was the pseudonym of the Spanish playwright Gabriel Téllez, b. Madrid, c.1584, d. 1648. Notable among his hundreds of plays is *The Love Rogue* (1630; Eng. trans., 1924), which created the character of Don Juan. A disciple of Lope de VEGA, Tirso de Molina also wrote Boccaccio-like stories, published in *Los Cigarrales de Toledo* (The Orchards of Toledo, 1621). He became a Mercedarian monk in 1601 and compiled (1637–39) a history of his order.

Bibliography: Bushee, Alice H., *Three Centuries of Tirso de Molina* (1939); McClelland, Ivy L., *Tirso de Molina* (1948); Williamsen, Vern G., *An Annotated, Analytical Bibliography of Tirso de Molina Studies, 1673–1977* (1979).

Tiryns [ty'-rinz]

Late Bronze Age Tiryns—in the northeast corner of Greece's Peloponnesus near modern Argos—was a massive fortress whose great walls, like those of neighboring MYCENAE, were said to have been built by the legendary Cyclopes. The low hill on which the fortress stood had been occupied by an important settlement in the Early and the Middle Bronze Age, from c.2500 BC on. The first defenses were built c.1400 BC, but the fortifications were greatly strengthened about a century later. In the middle of the 13th century BC they were extended to include the lower part of the hill to the north. At the height of its prominence the town evidently bordered on the sea, although it is now some distance inland. In 1884–85, the archaeologists Heinrich Schliemann and Wilhelm Dörpfeld excavated the Late Bronze Age (Mycenaean) palace, which had been destroyed by fire and abandoned in about 1200 BC. A Greek Doric temple was later erected on its ruins. German archaeologists have continued to excavate at Tiryns periodically since 1905.   SINCLAIR HOOD

Bibliography: Mylonas, George E., *Mycenae and the Mycenaean Age* (1966); Schliemann, Heinrich, *Tiryns* (1885; repr. 1968); Simpson, R. H., *A Gazetteer and Atlas of Mycenaean Sites* (1981); Voigtlaender, W., *Tiryns*, trans. by S. C. D. Slenczka (1972).

Tischbein (family) [tish'-byn]

The German Tischbein family included several artists; at least 26 members of the family were recorded during the 18th and early 19th centuries. Among the most significant of these were the painter **Johann Valentin Tischbein**, b. Dec. 11, 1715, d. Apr. 24, 1768, and his son **Johann Friedrich August Tischbein**, b. Mar. 9, 1750, d. June 21, 1812, a painter known as the "Leipzig" Tischbein. The painter and etcher **Johann Heinrich Tischbein the Elder**, b. Oct. 14, 1722, d. Aug. 22, 1789, was known as the "Kassel" Tischbein. His nephew **Johann Heinrich Wilhelm Tischbein**, b. Feb. 15, 1751, d. June 26, 1829, was known as the "Goethe" Tischbein; his portrait *Goethe in the Campagna* (1786–87; Städelsches Kunstinstitut, Frankfurt) is a monument of the classical revival.   JEFFERY HOWE

Bibliography: Novotny, Fritz, *Painting and Sculpture in Europe, 1780–1880* (1971).

Tiselius, Arne Wilhelm Kaurin [tee-sayl'-yuhs]

The Swedish biochemist Arne Wilhelm Kaurin Tiselius, b. Aug. 10, 1902, d. Oct. 29, 1976, won (1948) the Nobel Prize for chemistry for isolating and defining the four different types of proteins in blood serum and for developing ELECTROPHORESIS and adsorption chromatography as analytical tools. He also devised other highly refined methods of separating and analyzing biological systems and pioneered in the development of blood substitutes for use in transfusions.

Tissaphernes, Persian Satrap [tis-uh-fur'-neez]

Tissaphernes, d. 395 BC, was a Persian governor (satrap) and general in Anatolia. As governor of Lydia and Caria and general of the Achaemenid forces he allied (413 BC) with Sparta against Athens and recaptured most of Ionia. CYRUS THE YOUNGER was made governor of Lydia and commander of the army in 407, however, and Tissaphernes' command was limited to Caria. When Cyrus revolted against his brother ARTAXERXES II, Tissaphernes helped defeat Cyrus at the Battle of Cunaxa (401) and regained the governorship of Lydia. Defeated by the Spartans in 395, however, he was soon assassinated at the order of Artaxerxes.   RICHARD N. FRYE

Tissot, James [tee-soh']

The French painter James Joseph Jacques Tissot, b. Oct. 15, 1836, d. Aug. 8, 1902, is known especially for his charming illustrations of Victorian life. After studying at the École des Beaux-Arts in Paris, he fought in the Franco-Prussian War and then settled in England. As a caricaturist for *Vanity Fair*, he met London's social elite and became a fashionable portrait painter, especially of elegantly dressed women. In 1886, moved by a religious impulse, he made his first trip to Palestine and then devoted the next 10 years to illustrating the Bible in watercolor paintings. His research for these works, many of which belong to the Brooklyn Museum in Brooklyn, N.Y., was painstaking and often included visits to the sites of the biblical incidents.   PEARL GORDON

Bibliography: Laver, James, "*Vulgar Society*" (1936); Zerner, Henri, et al., *James Joseph Jacques Tissot, 1836-1902* (1968).

tissue, animal

Tissues are structured groupings of cells specialized to perform a common function necessary to the survival of the multicellular animal. Different tissues are needed so that the many abilities of the single-celled organism can be variously assigned to cells differentiated for that purpose. The process of tissue formation (histogenesis) evolves from the earlier process of cell differentiation. The fertilized ovum, a single cell, divides to form the blastula, in which tissues are not yet defined. As growth continues, the cells of the blastula begin to form the three germ layers—ectoderm, mesoderm, and endoderm—through the process of gastrulation. Cell differentiation during gastrulation begins the process of histogenesis and continues into the formation of organs. The cells in a tissue look more or less alike and contribute the same type of service, distinguishing five general classifications.

Epithelial Tissue. Epithelial tissue consists of a layer of cells covering the surfaces of an animal and lining its tubes for digestion, respiration, circulation, reproduction, and excretion. This layer controls what is absorbed into and lost from the organism. The epithelium is composed of continuous sheets of adjacent cells: outgrowths and ingrowths of epithelium form the sensitive surfaces of sensory organs, glands, hair and nails, and other structures.

Muscle Tissues. The ability to contract and relax and thus provide movement is characteristic of muscle tissue. There are three types. Smooth muscle is activated by the autonomic nervous system. Skeletal muscle is controlled by the central nervous system and, to a certain extent, by the will. Cardiac muscle is characterized by its ability to contract rhythmically.

Nerve Tissues. Nerve tissues consist of extraordinarily complex cells called neurons, which respond in a specific way to a variety of stimuli so as to transfer information from one part of the body to another.

Connective Tissues. Varied in structure to permit them to support the entire body and to connect its parts, connective tissues contain large amounts of extracellular matter modified into different types. Fibrous tissue is found in tendons and ligaments; elastic tissue in ligaments between the vertebrae, arterial walls, and trachea; and cartilaginous tissue in joints and present during the development of bone. Adipose tissue, with its fat deposits, cushions and supports vital organs and stores excess food.

Fluid Tissues. Fluid tissues are the blood and lymph, whose specialized functions include the distribution of food and oxygen to other tissues, carrying waste products from the tissues to the kidneys and lungs, and carrying defensive cells and other substances to destroy disease-producing agents.

W. A. BERESFORD

Bibliography: Borysenko, Myrin, et al., *Functional Histology* (1979); Gourne, Geoffrey H., *An Introduction to Functional Histology*, 2d ed. (1960); Ham, Arthur, *Histology*, 7th ed. (1974); Humason, Gretchen L., *Animal Tissue Techniques*, 4th ed. (1979); Munger, B., *Animal Diversity* (1974); Windle, W. F., *Textbook of Histology*, 5th ed. (1976).

tissue culture

As a major advancement in biological research, tissue cultures have allowed investigators to maintain animal and plant cells or parts of an organ outside the donor's body. Cultured cells may grow by increasing in size and number, or they may either perform specialized functions or change into cells with special functions not present in the original cells. Normal mammalian cells in culture divide about once every 24 hours. Tissue-culture methodology has given researchers the oppor-

tunity to study specific cells and their interactions; to study cancer cells; to produce viral vaccines and hormones; to identify genetic defects; to classify malignant tumors; and to determine tissue compatibility in transplantation (tissue typing). Plant cells are also cultured to yield information on growth, metabolism, and cancers.

The cells are maintained in an incubating nutrient medium designed to closely approximate the serum or extracellular fluid of the donor—sap in the case of plants. Natural fluids or synthetic mixtures are used, or a combination of the two, called a semidefined medium. Some of the essential constituents of a medium are major ions, such as sodium; sugar, such as glucose for energy; enzymes; hormones; amino acids; respiratory gases; and water. The cells are usually grown as a single layer on a glass or plastic surface, unless they are suspended in a fluid medium under constant agitation. Sterile techniques and equipment are necessary, but antibiotics have reduced the need for absolute sterility. The cells are examined using light microscopy and other optical systems.

Bibliography: Kruse, Paul, and Patterson, M. K., eds., *Tissue Culture: Methods and Applications* (1973); White, Philip R., *The Cultivation of Animal and Plant Cells*, 2d ed. (1963).

Tisza, István, Count [tis'-ah]

A Hungarian statesman, Count István (Stephen) Tisza, b. Apr. 22, 1861, entered the Hungarian parliament in 1886 and became leader of the Liberal party, prime minister (1903-05), and a champion of the Habsburg Dual Monarchy that guaranteed Hungarian domination of the eastern half of Austria-Hungary. Again prime minister (1913–17), Tisza reluctantly supported World War I but resigned when the new emperor, CHARLES I, sought to reform the franchise. Tisza was assassinated on Oct. 31, 1918, at the outbreak of the revolt for total Hungarian independence.

Tisza River

The Tisza River, 997 km (619 mi) long and with a drainage area of about 157,000 km² (60,600 mi²), rises in two headstreams in the western Ukraine; it then flows south and west through eastern Hungary and northeasten Yugoslavia to join the DANUBE RIVER 45 km (28 mi) north of Belgrade. Navigable for 725 km (450 mi), the Tisza often floods.

Titan (astronomy) [ty'-tuhn]

Titan, the largest satellite of the planet SATURN, was discovered in 1655 by Christiaan Huygens. The *Voyager 1* spacecraft determined Titan's diameter to be 5,140 km (3,194 mi) and its density to be about 1.92 g/cm³ (120 lb/ft³), indicating a rocky core with a thick ice mantle. The surface, obscured by a dense, opaque reddish brown haze, has a temperature of about −178° C (−288° F). According to *Voyager 1*, Titan's unique atmosphere—about 1.6 times denser than Earth's—consists mostly of nitrogen with about 6% methane, a trace of hydrogen, and possibly 12% argon.

Titan (rocket)

Titan, the largest U.S. intercontinental ballistic missile (ICBM), is also used as a launcher (see ROCKETS AND MISSILES). The two-stage Titan II ICBM stands 31.4 m (103 ft) tall and has a diameter of 3.05 m (10 ft). The lift-off weight is about 149,690 kg (330,000 lb). Operationally, the single reentry vehicle usually carries a thermonuclear warhead of 5 to 10 megatons yield. The top range is 15,000 km (9,300 mi). Titan II has been in service since 1963, with 3 wings of 18 missiles each, stored in underground silos at Davis-Monthan AFB, Ariz., McConnell AFB, Kans., and Little Rock AFB, Ark.

Each of the two first-stage Titan II engines develops a thrust of 956,000 newtons (98,000 kg/215,000 lb). The single second-stage engine develops 445,000 newtons (45,500 kg/100,000 lb) of thrust. Both stages use storable N_2O_4 and aerozine-50 propellants, in contrast to Titan I, an earlier version that employed nonstorable liquid oxygen and kerosene propellants. Guidance is obtained by an inertial system acting on the engines, gimbal-mounted for thrust vector control. Modified Titan IIs were used in the GEMINI PROGRAM, and other modified Titans are used to launch Earth satellites and space probes. Heavy payloads are launched by the Titan IIID, consisting of two Titan core stages and two strap-on solid-propellant boosters. Titan 34D, used for unmanned military launches, is still more powerful; the explosion of a 34D in April 1986 while launching a photoreconnaissance satellite from Vandenberg Air Force Base, however, caused severe damage to its launch pad. The Titan IIIC consists of a Titan II core, a restartable transstage with a thrust exceeding 70,000 newtons (7,257 kg/16,000 lb), and two strap-on boosters. The Titan IIIE, which launched two VIKING probes to Mars and two VOYAGER probes to Jupiter, Saturn, and Uranus, combined the technology of Titan IIIC with the high-performance CENTAUR stage.

KENNETH GATLAND

Bibliography: Gatland, Kenneth, *The Illustrated Encyclopedia of Space Technology* (1981).

Titanic   [ty-tan'-ik]

The *Titanic*, a British passenger liner, struck an iceberg off Newfoundland on the night of Apr. 14–15, 1912, and sank. The ship, the largest and most luxurious built up to that time, was on its maiden voyage from Southampton to New York, carrying more than 2,200 people; about 1,500 drowned.

Official inquiries determined that the *Titanic* was traveling too fast for the known icy conditions; it rammed the iceberg at a speed of 22 knots (41 km/h; 25 mph). The large loss of life was partly because of the failure of a nearby ship, the *Californian*, to respond to the distress signals, and the insufficient number of lifeboats on the *Titanic*. The shipwreck, considered by contemporaries the worst in history, prompted international agreements to improve safety procedures at sea. The sunken vessel was located by a team of U.S. and French researchers, using a remote-control submarine, in 1985.

Bibliography: Lord, Walter, *A Night to Remember* (1955), and *The Night Lives On* (1986); Wade, Wyn, *The Titanic: End of a Dream* (1979).

titanium   [ty-tay'-nee-uhm]

Titanium is a silvery gray metal resembling polished steel. A transition element in Group IVB of the periodic table, its symbol is Ti, its atomic number 22, and its atomic weight 47.90. Titanium was first discovered as its oxygen compound in 1791 by William Gregor and named in 1795 by Martin H. Klaproth after the Titans of Greek mythology. The pure metal, obtained in 1910, remained a curiosity until an economical purification process was discovered in 1946.

Occurrence. Titanium is the ninth most abundant element, constituting about 0.63% of the Earth's crust. Rock samples from the Moon indicate titanium is far more abundant there. The most important titanium minerals are anatase, brookite, and rutile, all forms of titanium dioxide (TiO_2).

Uses. Because titanium is as strong as steel and 45% lighter, it is especially suitable for use in aviation and astronautics. About 50% of titanium production is used for jet engine components (rotors, fins, and compressor parts). Titanium alloys readily with other metals such as aluminum and tin. The alloy composition Ti + 2.5% tin + 5% aluminum is used when high strength at high temperatures is required; and the alloy Ti + 8% aluminum + molybdenum + vanadium is used in applications at low temperatures. Each supersonic transport (SST) contains about 270,000 kg (600,000 lb) of titanium.

Compounds. Not many titanium compounds are used commercially. Titanium tetrachloride ($TiCl_4$) is a colorless liquid that fumes in moist air; it is used in the manufacture of artificial pearls and iridescent glass and, by the military, to create smokescreens. The most important titanium oxide is TiO_2, which is a white substance with a high reflective power. It is used extensively in both house paint and artist's paint, replacing the poisonous lead white. Titanium dioxide is processed at very high temperatures into artificial rutile, which is used as a semiprecious stone (titania). Titania has a light yellow color and a higher index of refraction than diamond but is rather soft.

STEPHEN FLEISHMAN

Bibliography: Clark, Robin, et al., *The Chemistry of Titanium, Zirconium and Hafnium* (1975); Donachie, Matthew, Jr., *Titanium and Titanium Alloys* (1982); Seagel, S. R., and Bannon, B. P., "Titanium: Its Properties and Uses," *Chemical Engineering,* Mar. 8, 1982.

titanothere   [ty-tan'-uh-thir]

The Brontotherium, a member of the Titanothere family that flourished more than 30 million years ago, was a giant herbivore.

Titanotheres are extinct rhinoceroslike mammals related to the horse. They first appeared in North America during the early Eocene, about 54 million years ago. The earliest forms, such as *Lambdotherium* and *Eotitanops*, were small and hornless. By the lower Oligocene, about 38 million years ago, the titanotheres had reached Asia and eastern Europe and had grown to be giants. *Brontotherium*, of North America, stood 2.4 m (8 ft) high at the shoulders, was 4.5 m (15 ft) long, and weighed about 5 tons. Many titanotheres had also developed horns, often Y- or U-shaped, on the ends of their snouts. The animals became extinct after the Middle Oligocene, about 32 million years ago.

Bibliography: U.S. Geological Survey, *Titanotheres of Ancient Wyoming, Dakota, and Nebraska* (1929; repr. 1980).

Titans   [ty'-tuhnz]

In Greek mythology, the Titans were the 12 offspring of URANUS (Heaven) and GAEA (Earth). In Hesiod's *Theogony* their names are given as Oceanus, the stream surrounding the world; Coius; Crius; Hyperion, sometimes regarded as a sun god; Iapetus, known as the father of Prometheus and Atlas in some myths; Thea, who was apparently associated with the sky; Rhea, who married CRONUS and mothered the original Olympian gods; Themis, sometimes listed as an earth goddess and an early wife of Zeus, who bore him the Hours and the Fates; MNEMOSYNE ("Memory"), mother, by Zeus, of the nine Muses; Phoebe, later identified with the moon; Tethys, sometimes associated with water; and Cronus, the most famous of the group, who castrated and killed his father and later led the Titans in their losing war against Zeus and the Olympians. Several authors, including Vergil, pictured the Titans in the section of the underworld called Tartarus, where they underwent lasting torment because of their sins against the gods.

ROBERT E. WOLVERTON

Titchener, Edward B.   [tich'-nur]

Edward Bradford Titchener, b. England, Jan. 11, 1867, d. Aug. 3, 1927, was the principal advocate in the United States of controlled introspection as the best investigative technique for psychology. Titchener found controlled introspection the only adequate means for describing and classifying the contents of consciousness, which Titchener felt were the main legitimate enterprises of experimental psychology.

After receiving his B.A. from Oxford in 1890, Titchener went to Leipzig to study with Wilhelm Wundt, founder of the first experimental psychology laboratory. In 1892, Titchener moved to Cornell University, where he taught for the remainder of his career.

Titchener's adherence to Wundt's theory and method made him the principal target of new American movements in psychology. Functionalists, behaviorists, and Gestalt psychologists alike tended to formulate their positions against the so-called structuralism of Titchener. His works include a 4-volume *Experimental Psychology* (1901-05) and *Experimental Psychology of the Thought Processes* (1909).

BERNARD KAPLAN

Bibliography: Boring, Edwin G., *A History of Experimental Psychology*, 2d ed. (1950), and *Psychologist at Large* (1961).

tithe   [tyth]

A tithe is one-tenth of income or produce usually paid—whether levied as an official tax or offered as a voluntary contribution—to support a church and its charitable activities (although occasionally tithing has been used for secular purposes). Ancient peoples, such as early Hebrews, commonly levied tithes. Tithing was a common practice of the Roman Catholic church in western Europe beginning in the 6th century. About 200 years later it became compulsory by law in the Carolingian empire. Laws prescribing tithes were introduced in England during the 10th century. Tithing was abolished in France after the revolution of 1789. Some Protestant bodies (the Mormon church, for example) consider the tithe mandatory.

Bibliography: Constable, Giles, *Monastic Tithes from Their Origins to the Twelfth Century* (1964); Evans, Eric J., *The Contentious Tithe: The Tithe Problem and English Agriculture, 1750-1850* (1976).

Titian   [tish'-uhn]

Tiziano Vecellio, or Titian, b. *c.*1488, d. Aug. 27, 1576, was the greatest painter of the Renaissance in Venice and ranks as one of the most brilliant and influential masters in the entire development of European art. About 400 surviving paintings can be attributed to Titian with confidence, and many other now-lost works are known to have been produced during his extremely long and prolific career.

Born in Pieve di Cadore in the Dolomite region of Italy, Ti-

For his Venus of Urbino *(1538) the Venetian master Titian chose an indoor setting, a richly furbished palace bedroom, instead of the conventional pastoral landscape used for mythological scenes. The goddess is thus transformed into a courtesan reclining on her bed and gazing at the observer with an inviting glance. (Uffizi, Florence.)*

tian went as a young man to study painting in Venice, and, with the exception of a number of short sojourns in other cities, he was to work there throughout his life. Little is known of Titian's early training and practice in Venice. Although he studied under the famous painters Gentile and Giovanni Bellini, the tutelage of Giorgione in the early years of the 16th century gave the first great impetus to his style. So completely did the young Titian absorb Giorgione's use of color and brush technique and the sublime, poetic vision of his landscape and figure paintings that debate continues over the attribution of works considered either collaborations between the elder Giorgione and the young Titian or works wholly by one or the other. By 1508, Titian was working as an independent painter alongside Giorgione on a project for frescoes, now mostly destroyed, for the Fondaco dei Tedeschi in Venice.

By the middle of the second decade of the 16th century Titian was painting such works as *Sacred and Profane Love* (*c.*1515, Galleria Borghese, Rome), which gives a full sense of the harmony and rich tonality of his sensuous classical style. His painting of the *Assumption* (completed 1518; Church of the Frari, Venice) displays the full extent of his powers in a work that is at once monumental in scale, intensely energetic, and vibrant in coloring.

Titian's personal development over an exceptionally long career was far ranging. The works of early maturity and others, such as *Bacchanal* and *The Worship of Venus* (both *c.*1519; Prado, Madrid), were succeeded in Titian's middle period (after *c.*1520) by a long series of exuberant, powerfully modeled compositions such as *Bacchus and Ariadne* (1523; National Gallery, London), *The Entombment* (*c.*1525; Louvre, Paris), and *Venus of Urbino* (1538; Uffizi, Florence).

With the arrival (1527) in Venice of the writer and courtier Pietro ARETINO, Titian discovered a lifelong friend who was to broadcast his fame far and wide. In part because of Aretino's introduction Titian met Holy Roman Emperor Charles V in Bologna in 1529 and executed his portrait. A remarkably close relationship was subsequently established between the emperor and the painter.

In 1533, Titian executed a second portrait, was named court painter to the emperor, and was granted, along with his family, patents of nobility. Titian also became a favorite of, and executed many works for, Charles V's son, Philip II of Spain.

Titian, in great demand for his portraits as well as for his altarpieces and classical subjects, portrayed many of the most prominent European princes and sovereigns as well as notable personalities within his immediate circle. A rapid worker, Titian had the gift of penetrating the character of his sitters and was able to convey these insights, together with an air of dignity and an astonishing sense of physical vitality.

Titian, who had refused an invitation in 1513 to become painter to the papal court, traveled to Rome in 1545, where he was received as a great celebrity and made a citizen of the city. A work prompted by this visit is *Pope Paul III and his Grandsons, Cardinals Alessandro and Ottavio Farnese* (1546; Museo di Capodimonte, Naples).

In 1548, Titian went to Augsburg in Bavaria at the invitation of Charles V. There he executed, among many other portraits of illustrious personages assembled for the Diet of Augsburg, *Emperor Charles V on Horseback* (Prado), one of his most distinguished works, and the prototype for equestrian portraits by later artists.

The extremely rich effects of color, atmosphere, and light, always a remarkable feature of Titian's painting style, became even more pronounced in the works of his late period (after *c.*1545). In his control of rapidly applied and thickly brushed paint, Titian was capable of producing an astonishingly tangible fusion of physical substance and light-filled atmosphere, as in *The Entombment* (1559; Prado), *Venus and Adonis* (*c.*1560; versions in Metropolitan Museum of Art, New York City, and National Gallery of Art, Washington, D.C.), and *The Rape of Europa* (1562; Gardner Museum, Boston).

In his final works, *The Crown of Thorns* (*c.*1570; Bayerische Staatsgemaldesammlung, Munich) and *The Deposition* (1576; unfinished; Accademia, Venice), Titian became even more simplified and bold in his technique, endowing his works with an emotional impact that is mystical and haunting in its power.   Reviewed by ULRICH HIESINGER

Bibliography: Cecchi, Dario, *Titian,* trans. by N. Wydenbruck (1958; repr. 1977); Morassi, Antonio, *Titian* (1964); Panofsky, Erwin, *Problems in Titian, Mostly Iconographic* (1969); Rosand, David, *Titian* (1978); Wethey, H. E., *The Paintings of Titian,* 3 vols. (1969-75); Williams, Jay, *The World of Titian* (1968).

See also: ITALIAN ART AND ARCHITECTURE; PAINTING; RENAISSANCE ART AND ARCHITECTURE.

Titicaca, Lake   [tee-tee-kah′-kah]

Lake Titicaca lies in the Andes Mountains on the border of Bolivia and Peru at an altitude of 3,810 m (12,500 ft). It is the world's highest lake that can be navigated by large vessels. Covering an area of about 8,300 km² (3,200 mi²), it is fed by more than 25 tributaries and drained by the small Río Desaguadero. A small southeastern basin called Uinamarca is linked with the northwestern part, Chucuito, by the narrow Strait of Tiquina. Chucuito has a maximum depth of about 280 m (920 ft), which keeps the waters at an annual average temperature of 11° C (51° F). This in turn moderates the local climate to allow cultivation of crops not usually grown at such high altitudes—corn, barley, quinoa, and potatoes. Only two indigenous species of fish, killifish and catfish, inhabit the lake. Trout were introduced in 1939.

Settled since prehistoric times by AYMARA Indians, the shores of the lake remain densely populated. Modern steamboats and traditional reed boats (balsas) connect the lakeside settlements.

Titius-Bode law   [tee′-tee-us-boh′-de]

The Titius-Bode "law," proposed (1766) by Johann Daniel Titius and popularized (1772) by Johann Elert BODE, was an attempt to explain the various mean distances of the planets from the Sun. The "law," which has never been explained by any physical argument, is expressed by the empirical formula $a = (n+4)/10$, where a is the calculated mean distance expressed in ASTRONOMICAL UNITS of a planet from the Sun and n is the progression of numbers 0, 3, 6, 12, 24, 48, 96, 192, and

TITIUS-BODE LAW

Titius-Bode Progression	Planet	Planet's Actual Mean Distance (AU)
(0 + 4)/10 = 0.4	Mercury	0.387
(3 + 4)/10 = 0.7	Venus	0.723
(6 + 4)/10 = 1.0	Earth	1.000
(12 + 4)/10 = 1.6	Mars	1.524
(24 + 4)/10 = 2.8	(Asteroids)	—
(48 + 4)/10 = 5.2	Jupiter	5.203
(96 + 4)/10 = 10.0	Saturn	9.539
(192 + 4)/10 = 19.6	Uranus	19.191
—	Neptune	30.071
(384 + 4)/10 = 38.8	Pluto	39.158

384. The "law" approximates fairly well the mean distances of the planets (Mercury through Saturn) known at the time it was proposed and gives close values for the distances of Uranus, discovered in 1781, and some of the asteroids (between Mars and Jupiter), which began to be discovered in 1801. The distance of Neptune, however, does not fit within the "law."
                                              CRAIG B. WAFF

Bibliography: Nieto, M., *The Titius-Bode Law of Planetary Distance* (1972).

title

A title, as used in PROPERTY law, is the means by which an owner of property has just and legal possession of that property. Titles can be acquired through purchase or inheritance. Different types of title to one property can be held—for example, a MORTGAGE held by a bank on property owned by a

person with a legal title to that property is an equitable title that expires on final payment. A DEED to a title is legal evidence of that title and thus of the holder's right to possess such property. The term *clear title* or *good title* means that the land is free of any or all encumbrances, such as an EASEMENT that could allow a neighbor the right to cross a property to reach a highway. A good title is one that the courts recognize as valid and thus free from doubts. Such a title is unflawed by LIENS (debt-claims) or by competing titles and ensures that the holder is the sole, legitimate possessor, without fear of any challenge being made to ownership. Once full claim to the property is established, a prospective buyer will be more willing to buy because no encumbrances can weaken an owner's clear title to the property. The danger, however, that a title to property could be successfully challenged led to the development of title insurance.

See also: TORRENS SYSTEM.

titles of nobility and honor

Titles of nobility and honor are the terms used to categorize those persons holding high rank in a nation socially organized along aristocratic lines. Modern European titles originated in feudal times, largely during the early Holy Roman Empire. Titles were formerly widespread, but today only a few nations recognize a formal peerage, Great Britain being the preeminent example. A provision of Article I, Section 9 of the U.S. Constitution prohibits the granting of titles of nobility by the United States.

Ruling Titles. In the traditional aristocratic society the monarch represents the apex of the hierarchy. The commonest titles of rulers are emperor (empress) and king (queen). Rulers of smaller nations often hold lesser titles: prince (princess), grand duke, or duke. Nonruling members of royal families also generally hold titles of nobility: prince or princess, duke or duchess, and sometimes lesser titles. In Britain, for example, the children of the sovereign are princes and princesses; the sons are often also created royal dukes. Prince Philip, the husband of Queen Elizabeth II, is also a royal duke: the duke of Edinburgh.

Duke. The duke (from the Latin *dux,* "leader") is the highest title in the peerage. The first nonruling duke was created in England by Edward III, who made his oldest son, Edward, the Black Prince, duke of Cornwall in 1337. The title, however, had a checkered career. It vanished altogether during the reign of Elizabeth I (who had her cousin, the duke of Norfolk, beheaded for treason). Elizabeth's successor, James I, reinstated the title. Great victors in battle have been raised to dukedoms (for example, Marlborough and Wellington), but mostly the title went hand in hand with the great landholding magnates. Many of these were concentrated in mid-England, which became known as the Dukeries. No new nonroyal dukedoms have been created in the 20th century; the last created duke without royal connections was the duke of Westminster in 1874.

Marquess. This title dates from the Norman period. Originally the title applied to lords guarding the border areas, or marches. In Germany the comparable title was *Markgraf* (margrave), granted to counts who stood on border guard for the ruler; margraves could be further distinguished by the type of territory over which they ruled (*Landgraf* or *Pfalzgraf*).

Earl. The title of earl—third in precedence and the oldest title and rank of English nobles—is of Saxon-Danish origin (meaning "chieftain"). The earl was originally one who administered a shire or province. The equivalent Continental title is count (from the Latin *comes,* "companion"). In more recent times earldoms in Britain were conferred on retiring prime ministers but this practice has fallen into disuse, the last being Sir Anthony Eden, who became the earl of Avon in 1961.

Viscount. This title, which means vice-count, deputy, or lieutenant of a count, is an office that was well established in the Holy Roman Empire of Frederick I Barbarossa. Leading British soldiers of World War II (for example, Field Marshal Montgomery) were raised to the title of viscount.

EUROPEAN TITLES OF NOBILITY

British		French		German		Italian		Spanish	
Masculine	**Feminine**	**Masculine**	**Feminine**	**Masculine**	**Feminine**	**Masculine**	**Feminine**	**Masculine**	**Feminine**
duke	duchess	duc	duchesse	Herzog	Herzogin	duca	duchesa	duque	duquesa
*		prince	princesse	Fürst	Fürstin	Principe	principessa	principe	principesa
				Prinz†	Prinzessin				
marquess	marchioness	marquis	marquise	Markgraf	Markgräfin	marchese	marchesa	marqués	marquesa
				Pfalzgraf	Pfalzgräfin				
				Landgraf	Landgräfin				
earl	countess	comte	comtesse	Graf	Gräfin	conte	contessa	conde	condesa
viscount	viscountess	vicomte	vicomtesse			visconte	viscontessa	visconde	viscondesa
baron	baroness	baron	baronne	Baron	Baronin	barone	baronessa	barón	baronesa
				Freiherr	Freiherrin				
				Freier	Freierin				

* British prince or princess is a royal title, not one of nobility.
† Courtesy title for son/daughter of kings or dukes.

Baron. Finally, the lowest on the ladder of peerage are the barons. They too came to England with the Norman invasion, and on the Continent barons remain the most numerous relics of a bygone age. The name meant an individual holding land directly from the sovereign.

Baronets and Knights. Members of these ranks are not members of the peerage; that is, they do not sit in the House of Lords. Baronets and KNIGHTS are both titled "Sir," but baronetcies are hereditary, and knighthoods are not. The term *baronet* was first applied to nobles who had lost the right of individual summons to Parliament in the 14th century. The hereditary order of baronets was introduced by King James I in 1611, and the title was sold to gentlemen prepared to establish plantations in Ireland. Nova Scotia was accorded a similar status for newly created baronets in 1624. The baronet is styled "Sir Thomas Beecham, Bart."

British knighthood has two forms: (1) the oldest and simplest is the Knight (derived from the saxon *cnyt*, signifying "attendant") Bachelor, and (2) the knight enrolled in one of the 8 orders of chivalry: the Order of the Garter—the oldest existing honor—for England, the Order of the Thistle for Scotland, the Order of the Bath, the Order of Saint Patrick, the Order of Saint Michael and Saint George, the Order of the Star of India, the Royal Victorian Order, and the Order of the British Empire.

French and German equivalents of the British knight are *chevaliers* and *ritters*. Both terms mean "horseman," which indicates that the title was connected with mounted warriors and reflects the fact that from the days of the Roman Empire, mounted warriors enjoyed high social status.

Titles and Honors in the Modern Age. Active nobility has practically died out on the European continent with the extinction of the principal dynasties—Russian, French, Austrian, German, and Italian. Even in Britain, a considerable adaptation has been made. The creation of peers had always been a political act. This fact was apparent, for example, in 1832 when Lord Grey, the prime minister, forced the House of Lords to pass the Reform Bill by threatening to have King William IV create enough new Whig peers to pack the House of Lords with his supporters. In 1911, Herbert Asquith's Liberal government used the same threat to force the House of Lords to accept the Parliament Bill that effectively ended its political powers. The Life Peerages Act of 1958 allows nonhereditary barons and baronesses to be created. No new hereditary peers were created between 1964 and 1983, when the practice was revived. The Peerage Act of 1963 was passed to permit individuals to disclaim peerages and remain commoners—thus, for example, qualifying them to remain members of the House of Commons where real political power lies. The value of the modern honors system to Britain is that political or other services may be acknowledged by titles rather than by gold. Some observers see the system as a symbolic and inexpensive way of rewarding those who have performed some noteworthy service.

Almost all other nations have orders of honor, although the United States is extremely sparing and has just one, the Legion of Merit, which is for foreigners. In contrast Panama, for example, has 2 and the USSR, 17.   JAMES McMILLAN

Bibliography: *Burke's Peerage and Baronetage* (quadrennial); *Debrett's Peerage, Baronetage and Companionage*, 104th ed. (1980); McMillan, James, *The Honours Game* (1969); Perrott, Roy, *The Aristocrats* (1968); Pine, L. G., *The Story of Titles* (1969).

titmouse

The bridled titmouse, P. wollweberi, a small, gregarious bird, is found in mountainous regions of the southwestern United States and northern Mexico.

Titmouse is the common name for birds of the cosmopolitan family Paridae and, more specifically, for four small (12 to 15 cm/4.5 to 6 in) species of the genus *Parus* that are crested, mostly gray and white, and native to the United States and Mexico. In nonbreeding seasons titmice are gregarious, often joining the closely related chickadees and other winter birds in small, roving bands. The tufted titmouse, with a prominent crest and chestnut sides, is common in the eastern United States, the plain titmouse in the West, and the bridled titmouse in Mexico and the southwestern United States. Like chickadees, titmice tend to be tamed.   WILLIAM SANDFORD

Tito   [tee'-toh]

Marshal Tito (Josip Brož), b. May 25, 1892, d. May 4, 1980, became Yugoslavia's political leader in 1943 as president of the National Liberation Committee. A soldier in the Austro-Hungarian army in World War I, he was imprisoned in Russia but fought there for the revolution. He returned to Croatia, became (1927–28) a trade unionist, and then joined the illegal Communist party, acquiring the code name "Tito" when he became a member of the politburo in 1934. A recruiter (1936–38) for the International Brigade in Spain's Civil War, and an organizer of Yugoslavia's partisan forces after Germany's invasion during World War II, Tito led the highly effective Partisan Resistance Movement against Axis occupation of Yugoslavia. With the support of the USSR, the United States, and Great Britain, Tito officially became (1945) head of the new federal government. Although his regime was essentially a communist dictatorship, Tito's resistance to Soviet control

Marshal Tito, Yugoslavia's head of state from 1945 until his death in 1980, established a communist state notable for its policies of economic decentralization and increased worker participation in government. A staunch defender of Yugoslav independence, Tito broke with the USSR in 1948 and maintained a foreign policy of nonalignment.

led to a major split between himself and Stalin, and in 1948, Yugoslavia was expelled from the Soviet bloc. Tito then followed an independent course in foreign affairs—maintaining good relations with the East European socialist states, while establishing ties with the Western powers and nonaligned nations. Made marshal of Yugoslavia and elected president in 1953, Tito became president for life in 1974.

Bibliography: Auty, Phyllis, *Tito: A Biography*, rev. ed. (1974); Dedijer, Vladimir, *Tito* (1972); Djilas, Milovan, *Tito* (1980); Maclean, Fitzroy, *The Heretic: The Life and Times of Josip Broz-Tito* (1957); Roberts, Walter R., *Tito, Mihailovic and the Allies, 1941–1945* (1973).

Titograd   [tee'-toh-grahd]

Titograd (1981 pop., 132,290), the capital of Yugoslavia's republic of Montenegro, lies about 300 km (185 mi) southwest of Belgrade. The city manufactures tobacco, furniture, and food products. Only a few landmarks survived the World War II destruction, among them an 18th-century Turkish tower and a mosque. Known as Podgorica since the 1320s, the city was under the Turks from 1474 to 1878, and in 1921 it became part of Yugoslavia. It was renamed Titograd in 1946.

Titov, Gherman S.   [tee-tawf']

The Soviet cosmonaut Gherman Stepanovich Titov, b. Sept. 11, 1935, was the second person to orbit the Earth. Titov was a Soviet Air Force jet pilot who was picked in the first group of cosmonauts in March 1960. He was backup pilot for the first manned spaceflight, *Vostok 1*, in April 1961, and on Aug. 6–7, 1961, he was pilot of the 25-hr 18-min *Vostok 2* flight. Apparent medical problems on the flight may have removed him from flight status, but in the early 1970s he was reported working as a test pilot on the Soviet Backfire long-range bomber program and as a specialist in long-range space communication. Titov is also a deputy editor of the Soviet journal *Aviatsiya i Kosmonavtika* (Aviation and Cosmonautics).

JAMES E. OBERG

Bibliography: Burchett, W., and Purdy, C. A., *Gherman Titov's Flight into Space* (1962); Titov, Gherman S., *700,000 Kilometers through Space* (1962) and, with Martin Caidan, *I am Eagle!* (1962).

titration   [ty-tray'-shuhn]

In chemistry a titration is a procedure for analyzing a sample solution by gradually adding another solution and measuring the minimum volume required to react with all of the analyte (constituent of interest) in the sample. The titrant (the solution that is added) contains a reagent whose concentration is accurately known (standard solution); it is added to the sample solution using a calibrated volumetric burette to measure accurately the volume delivered.

When a precisely sufficient volume of titrant has been added, the equivalence point, or endpoint, is reached. An endpoint can be located either visually, using a suitable chemical INDICATOR, or instrumentally, using an instrument to monitor some appropriate physical property of the solution, such as pH or optical absorbance, that changes during the titration. Ideally, the experimental endpoint coincides with the true equivalence point, where an exactly equivalent amount of the titrant has been added, but in practice some discrepancy (titration error) exists. Proper choice of endpoint location system minimizes this error.

A visual (indicator) titration is usually carried out by placing the measured sample solution and indicator in a flask or beaker. The solution is stirred, either continuously or after each added increment of titrant, to ensure thorough mixing of the reactants; otherwise, premature indication of the endpoint may occur. Initially, the titrant may be added rapidly, or in large increments, but near the endpoint it must be added slowly and finally in very small increments to avoid accidental overrun of the endpoint. Addition of titrant is stopped when the indicator changes color.

An instrumental titration requires that the titrant be added beyond the endpoint and that instrument readings be taken both before and after the endpoint to provide data to calculate the endpoint. A graph of the instrument response plotted against the volume of added titrant reveals either an abrupt change or a change of slope at the endpoint, depending on the nature of the solution property measured.

Once the concentration of an analyte in a solution is accurately known, the solution may be used as a titrant itself for other analyses. If the titration is part of a QUANTITATIVE CHEMICAL ANALYSIS, the data may be used to enable a chemist to determine the composition of an unknown sample. Titrations can also be used to determine the number of acidic, basic, or other reactive groups of a compound. In such cases there may be more than one equivalence point. Titration data of acids and bases is used to determine the dissociation constant (see CHEMICAL EQUILIBRIUM AND KINETICS) of molecules containing these groups.   LAURANCE A. KNECHT

Bibliography: Barthel, Josef, *Thermometric Titrations* (1975); Fritz, James S., *Acid-Base Titration in Non-Aqueous Solvents* (1973); Huber, Walter, *Titrations in Nonaqueous Solvents* (1967); Lambert, J., et al., *The Essentials of Volumetric Analysis,* 2d ed. (1971); Stock, J. T., *Amperometric Titrations: Chemical Analysis* (1965; repr. 1975).

Titus, Epistle to   [ty'-tuhs]

The Epistle to Titus, in the New Testament of the BIBLE, is one of the Pastoral Epistles (the others being the two Epistles to Timothy). It is addressed by Saint PAUL to his companion Titus, who has been left in charge in Crete to correct errors and appoint church leaders. Titus is urged to promote sound doctrine, sober behavior, and appropriate submission to those in authority. Many scholars think that the epistle was written in AD 100 in Paul's name rather than by Paul himself, because of differences in language, teaching, and church structure.

ANTHONY J. SALDARINI

Bibliography: Dibelius, Martin, and Conzelmann, Hans, *The Pastoral Epistles* (Eng. trans., 1972); Harrison, Percy N., *The Problem of the Pastoral Epistles* (1921; repr. 1972).

Titus, Roman Emperor

Titus Flavius Vespasianus, b. Dec. 30, AD 39, d. Sept. 13, 81, spent most of his life in military service before succeeding (79) his father, VESPASIAN, as Roman emperor. In 70, Titus was entrusted with the command against the Jewish rebels. He captured Jerusalem and in 71 returned to Rome, where his father made him commander of the Praetorian guard. Later historians regarded Titus as an ideal emperor, in part because he spent great sums on games and monuments, including the COLOSSEUM. To the victims of the famous eruption (79) of Vesuvius and the plague and fire (80) in Rome he dispensed generous aid. The "era of good feeling" ended when he was succeeded by his brother Domitian.   JOHN W. EADIE

Bibliography: Grant, Michael, *Twelve Caesars* (1975); Henderson, B. W., *Five Roman Emperors* (1927).

tityra

The tityras comprise four species of compact, medium-sized birds in the family *Cotingidae* found in Central and South America. All have hooked bills and a pearly gray plumage with black masks, crown patches, wings, and tail. Shy birds with far-reaching calls, tityras nest in high trees and feed on insects and fruit.   GEORGE J. WALLACE

Tiv   [tiv]

The Tiv, speakers of the Nyanza or Benue-Congo subgroup of the Niger-Congo language family (see AFRICAN LANGUAGES), live in the vicinity of the Benue River in northern Nigeria. Their population numbered 1,393,649 in 1982. Prosperous sub-sistence farmers and traders, the Tiv grow yams, millet, and sorghum and keep small livestock (goats and sheep), along with some cattle. Their villages are composed of compounds consisting of sleeping huts, reception huts, and granaries. The marketplace is the hub of social activity.

Tiv political organization—and the possibility of conflict or alliance among territorial kin groups—is traditionally based on the relative closeness of patrilineal descent members to an apical male ancestor. Nonetheless, all Tiv have united against neighboring enemy tribes because of their common ancestry. Traditionally, lineage elders settled political disputes, and the Tiv had no paramount chiefs, although one was established by the British administration in 1948. Polygamy, separate mother-child households for multiple wives, and BRIDE-PRICE characterize Tiv family formation and structure. Their religious system involves a complex set of beliefs centered on su-pernatural forces (*akombo*), derived from a creator god, and on witchcraft.   JAMES W. HERRICK

Bibliography: Abraham, R. C., *Tiv People*, 2d ed. (1968); Akiga, Akighirga Sai, *Akiga's Story: The Tiv Tribe as Seen by One of Its Members*, trans. by Rupert East (1939; repr. 1965); Bohannan, Laura and Paul, *The Tiv of Central Nigeria* (1969).

Tlaxcala   (city)   [tlahs-kah'-lah]

Tlaxcala, the capital of Tlaxcala state in east central Mexico, lies 100 km (60 mi) east of Mexico City; it has a population of 35,384 (1980). The city has textile industries; it is the site of the first Roman Catholic church (1521) on the American main-land. Once the capital of Tlaxcalan Indians, it was conquered by Hernán Cortés in 1519.

Tlaxcala   (state)

Tlaxcala (meaning "rocky place" in Nahuatl), a state on the central plateau of Mexico, has an area of 3,914 km² (1,511 mi²) and a population of 556,597 (1980). The capital is the city of Tlaxcala. The smallest and most densely populated state in the country, Tlaxcala is primarily agricultural. The present Tlaxcala corresponds to the preconquest Tlaxcala kingdom, which was never subjugated by the Aztecs but was conquered by the Spanish under Hernán Cortés in 1519. Afterward, the Tlaxcalans became Cortés's allies and helped him destroy the Aztec empire.   LEON YACHER

Tlaxcalan   [tlahs-kah-lahn']

The Tlaxcalan are Nahuatl-speaking Indians of North America descended from the Chichimec, who in preconquest times in-habited the Tlaxcala-Puebla region, an area roughly equiva-lent to the modern Mexican state of Tlaxcala. The Tlaxcalan population, estimated to number more than 500,000 in 1980, is distributed in 44 independent *municípios*, most of which are in rural areas.

Living in what is probably the most ethnically and racially homogeneous area of the central Mexican highlands, the rural Tlaxcalan have maintained a strong identification with their cultural heritage. Their economy is based on cultivation, es-pecially of maize, beans, and maguey. A key feature of Tlax-calan social organization is a system of localized, patrilineal kinship units. The communities' sacred-oriented world view—the *mayordomía* (cargo) system, the *ayuntamiento religioso*

(local religious government), barrio organization, elements of kinship and *compadrazgo*, and a folk religion containing a mesh of Christian and pagan beliefs—has not succumbed to westernization.   LOUIS C. FARON

Bibliography: *Handbook of Middle American Indians*, vol. 2 (1967); Nutini, Hugo G., *San Bernardino Contla* (1968).

Tlingit   [tling'-git]

The 13 Tlingit tribes are a group of North American Indians of the Nadene linguistic stock who formerly occupied the Alas-kan Panhandle from Yakutat Bay southward, except for part of Prince of Wales Island. Their population numbered an esti-mated 10,000 in the mid-18th century but had dwindled to about 4,500 around the turn of the 19th century. Culturally adapted to rugged, forested coasts, they depended primarily on fish, sea mammals, mollusks, and berries for their subsis-tence. They built huge wooden dugout canoes, multifamily plank houses, and wooden storage boxes and dishes, made masks and woven spruce-root baskets, and twined robes of mountain-goat wool. Matrilineal exogamous MOIETIES (com-plementary divisions) functioned on socioceremonial occa-sions, such as those celebrating life crises, house building, memorial rites, or POTLATCHES—ceremonial feasts involving property distribution. Each moiety consisted of about 20 named groups.

Conflict between the Russians and the Tlingit was frequent. In 1799 the Russians built a fort on an island in the southeast archipelago, but in 1802 the Tlingit drove them out. Later, Russian trader Aleksandr Andreyevich BARANOV recaptured the fort and turned it into a trading post, which grew into the present-day city of Sitka. The Tlingit now number approxi-mately 14,000 to 15,000 (1980 est.) and live principally in Alaska.   PHILIP DRUCKER

Bibliography: Jones, L., *A Study of the Tlingits of Alaska* (1914; repr. 1970); Krause, A., *The Tlingit Indians* (1956; repr. 1970); Olsen, R. L., *Social Structure and Social Life of the Tlingit in Alaska* (1967).

TMJ syndrome

Temporomandibular joint (TMJ) syndrome, also known as myofacial pain dysfunction, is a disorder in the joint between the mandible (lower jaw bone) and the temporal bone of the skull. Symptoms include blurred vision, sinus problems, and pain in the jaw, head, neck, shoulders, and ears. Possible causes are arthritis, malocclusion (bad bite), bruxism (grind-ing or clenching of teeth), muscle tension, and psychological stress. Treatment ranges from jaw exercises and drug therapy to dental procedures and, in severe cases, surgery. It is esti-mated that nearly 25 percent of the U.S. population suffers from some form of TMJ syndrome, although most cases are not treated.

TNP: see THÉÂTRE NATIONAL POPULAIRE.

TNT

TNT (trinitrotoluene) is one of the most commonly used high EXPLOSIVES in the world. Discovered in 1863 for use in the dye industry, TNT was not used as an explosive until 1904, but it achieved widespread use during World War I. By World War II it was the standard military high explosive. TNT is produced by reacting toluene with nitric acid in the presence of sulfuric acid. The three-step nitration first produces mono-, then di-, and finally trinitrotoluene.

The explosive is extremely insensitive to physical shock, can be burned in small quantities without danger of detona-tion, and is virtually insoluble in water. Its low melting point, 80.5° C (177° F), makes it ideal for cast-loading munitions, which are prepared by melting the TNT with steam and pour-ing the liquid directly into the shell.   DAVID N. BUCKNER

To Kill a Mockingbird

To Kill a Mockingbird (1960), Harper Lee's first novel, won the Pulitzer Prize for fiction. Set in a small Alabama town and narrated by a young girl, Scout Finch, the novel relates the impact of a rape trial on the community. A young black man, accused of rape, is defended by Scout's father, a lawyer. Although the narrator's angle of vision is limited, it becomes clear that the trial has aroused all the latent tensions of the community.   CHARLOTTE D. SOLOMON

To the Lighthouse

To the Lighthouse (1927), regarded as one of Virginia WOOLF's finest novels, uses a carefully patterned STREAM OF CONSCIOUSNESS technique that attempts to echo the scattered conversations and random thoughts that occur in the minds of several of the characters. Usually the narrators are observing Mr. and Mrs. Ramsay, an upper-middle-class British couple on vacation with a houseful of children and guests. Mrs. Ramsay, the heart of the group, devotes her life completely to her family—a fact realized by them only after her death.
CHARLOTTE D. SOLOMON

toad

The American toad, B. americanus, burrows about 1 m (3 ft) deep in loose soil in the fall and hibernates until spring.

Toads are rough-skinned, generally land-dwelling, tailless amphibians closely related to frogs. True toads make up the family Bufonidae. More than 200 species, classified in the genus *Bufo*, are found in North and South America, Europe, Asia, and Africa from sea level to more than 4,500 m (15,000 ft) in the Himalayas. Members of other genera are also found throughout the world except in Australia and Antarctica—some (the *Atelopus*, *Dendrophryniscus*, and *Oreophrynella* species) only in tropical areas.

The name *toad* is, however, also used to refer to members of certain frog families. These include the Mexican burrowing toad, *Rhinophrynus dorsalis*, in the family Rhinophrynidae; the Surinam toads, genus *Pipa*, in the family Pipidae; the fire-bellied toads, *Bombina*, and the midwife toad, *Alytes obstetricans*, of the family Discoglossidae; and the spadefoot toads, *Scaphiopus*, of the family Pelobatidae.

Toads generally have squat bodies and short legs. Most are moderate-sized, about 5 to 8 cm (2 to 3 in) long; some, however, such as the oak toad, *Bufo quercus*, of the southeastern United States and some tropical species may be only 20 to 30 mm (0.8 to 1.2 in); others, such as Blomberg's toad, *B. blombergi*, may reach 150 mm (6 in) or more. Most are drab, with shades of brown, tan, gray, or black serving to conceal the animal.

A few genera of toad are brightly colored or spotted. Malaysian tree toads, *Pedostibes*, for example, are green with yellow and blue spots, and male Costa Rican toads, *B. periglenes*, are bright gold.

A toad's thick, warty skin allows it to inhabit drier regions than does a frog. Toads are found in fields, gardens, woodlands, and meadows as well as moister areas. They frequently use horny projections on their hind feet to dig shallow burrows in which to hide. As cold weather approaches, they find a secluded spot and hibernate for several months. Toads do not jump as frogs do, but make short hops or even walk. They are carnivorous, feeding mostly on insects. Toads are the prey of many animals. When provoked or injured, toads secrete a poison from their skin. In most species poison glands are scattered over the body, but they may be concentrated on the side of the neck. The poison is a thick, white alkaloid that may kill a predator or merely taste unpleasant.

Toads also defend themselves by inflating their bodies, a tactic that increases their bulk and makes them harder to swallow.

Toads typically breed in water. The eggs are laid in strings, the male fertilizing them as they are extruded. Toads are remarkably prolific, most laying 20,000 eggs in a single clutch, with the giant toad producing as many as 100,000 eggs at a time. The eggs hatch into tailed aquatic larvae, known as tadpoles, that metamorphose into the adult form in a few weeks. Several toads depart from this mode of reproduction. Some species (*Nectophryne* species) lay eggs on land and lack a free-swimming tadpole stage, whereas in others (*Nectophrynoides*) fertilization is internal and birth is given to fully formed toadlets.   JONATHAN CAMPBELL

Bibliography: Cochran, Doris M., *Living Amphibians of the World* (1961); Goin, Coleman J. T., et al., *Introduction to Herpetology*, 3d ed. (1978); Porter, George, *The World of the Frog and the Toad* (1967); Wright, Albert H. and Anna A., *Handbook of Frogs and Toads in the United States and Canada*, 3d ed. (1949).

toadfish

The toadfish is a wide-bodied, usually drab-colored, often pugnacious fish found mostly in warm coastal regions. The more than 30 species constitute the family Batrachoididae. Toadfish are usually less than 38 cm (15 in) long, are often slime-covered, and have a large head with upward-directed eyes and a large mouth. Some species (genus *Thalassophryne*) have venom glands attached to fanglike dorsal-fin spines. Other species (genus *Porichthys*), often known as midshipmen, have light organs on the belly. Mostly bottom dwelling and slow moving, toadfish feed on crustaceans, mollusks, and small fishes. One common species in the western Atlantic is the 25-cm-long (10-in), shallow-water oyster toadfish, *Opsanus*. When caught by an angler, it grunts, erects spines, and may inflict a painful wound. The male guards the adhesive eggs, often laid in buried litter, for about 3 weeks before they hatch.   ALFRED PERLMUTTER

The oyster toadfish, O. tau, a carnivorous fish whose name is derived from its warty skin, lives in coastal waters of the western Atlantic.

toadflax

Common toadflax, L. vulgaris, a flaxlike weed, has flowers the color of butter and egg yolks, giving the plant its common name, butter-and-eggs.

Toadflax refers to any of 100 species in the genus *Linaria* of the family Scrophulariaceae. These annual or perennial herbs are widely distributed in the temperate Northern Hemisphere, mainly in the Mediterranean region. The common toadflax, *L. vulgaris*, is a vigorous perennial often regarded as a weed.

FRANK B. SALISBURY

toadstool

Toadstool is a common term for fleshy and umbrella–shaped poisonous fungi. MUSHROOM is the term usually applied to edible species of fungi. Scientists who study fungi, however, make no such distinction between toadstools and mushrooms. Many of the poisonous types belong to the genus *Amanita*. Some species in this genus have a volva, or cup, often nearly hidden in the ground, into which the stem usually fits. Because this cup, termed the *death cup*, can be present or absent in either edible or poisonous mushrooms of the genus, it is inaccurate to try to identify a poisonous mushroom simply through the presence of a volva. The specific species must be identified using other characteristics. The commonly encountered poisonous fungi include the death cup, *A. phalloides*, the destroying angel, *A. verna*, and the fly amanita, *A. muscaria*.

tobacco

Tobacco is a tall, herbaceous plant the leaves of which are harvested, cured, and rolled into cigars, shredded for use in cigarettes and pipes, and processed for chewing or snuff. Tobacco is an important crop in almost all tropical countries as well as in many temperate ones. The main source of commercial tobacco is *Nicotiana tabacum*, although *Nicotiana rustica* is also grown and is used in oriental tobaccos. Growers have developed a wide range of morphologically different types, from the small-leaved aromatic tobaccos to the large, broad-leaved cigar tobaccos. The most practical means of classifying them is by the method used for curing or drying the leaf.

HISTORY

Tobacco is native to the Americas, and the practice of inhaling the smoke of the dried plant material has been documented in the Mayan culture more than 2,000 years ago. The Mayans moved northward from Central America through the Aztec Empire and eventually took their customs to North American Indian tribes. The Arawak Indians of the Caribbean smoked tobacco; Christopher Columbus, during his 1492 voyage, found them smoking loosely rolled cigars. The Spanish took tobacco seeds to Europe, where Jean Nicot gave the

The tobacco plant N. tabacum *develops the large fragrant leaves that have been smoked in many forms for at least 2,000 years. Leaves are harvested after carefully controlled growth, sewn or strung together* (right), *and dried in a variety of ways.*

plant its generic name, *Nicotiana*. Sir Walter Raleigh began the popularization of pipe smoking in Great Britain in 1586, and the cultivation and consumption of tobacco spread with each voyage of discovery from Europe.

Two kinds of tobacco were traded between Europe and America: Spanish, from the West Indies and South America, and Virginia, from what is now the state of Virginia. The Spaniards were the first Europeans to cultivate substantial amounts of tobacco. Despite its popularity in England, James I—who vehemently disapproved of tobacco—forbade its production there.

Europeans at first smoked their tobacco in PIPES, and later in cigars. Cigarettes spread in popularity only after the Crimean War (1854–56); their spread was aided by the development in the United States of the first cigarette-making machine in 1881 (see DUKE, JAMES BUCHANAN).

CULTIVATION

Unlike most other annual agricultural crops, tobacco has a small seed (1 oz = 300,000 seeds), which cannot be sown directly in the field. Seedlings are raised in carefully selected and tended seedbeds where protection is given against heavy rain and excess sun. Young seedlings are planted out by hand or mechanical transplanter, and spacing between seedlings and rows varies with the kind of tobacco and with the location. The crop needs a minimum of 120 frost-free days and can be grown in a variety of soils.

Producing disease-resistant tobacco of acceptable quality is difficult, because the plant is susceptible to many diseases. Chemical control is now widely practiced, although the choice of chemicals is limited by the need to ensure that they do not taint the tobacco when it is smoked.

In the United States and Canada tobacco is often stalk-cut by machine, but in many parts of the world, it is still harvested leaf by leaf. Only a fully ripe leaf is used. After harvesting, leaves are tied together in pairs on curing sticks or strings.

CURING

Flue Curing. Used mainly in the manufacture of cigarettes, flue-cured tobacco is lemon, orange, or mahogany in color, with a high sugar content and a medium-to-high nicotine content. Flue curing requires a closed building equipped with a system of ventilation and a source of heat. When heat and humidity are controlled, leaf color changes, moisture is quickly removed, and the leaf and stems dry.

Air Curing. This group includes the original air-cured tobaccos of South and Central America, the cigar tobaccos (subdivided into wrappers, binders, and fillers, depending on their use), and the burley tobaccos, an important component of American cigarettes. These have a low sugar content but vary in nicotine content. Air curing requires an open framework in which sticks of leaves (or whole plants) are hung, protected from wind and sun. Leaf color changes from green to yellow, as leaves and stems dry slowly.

Fire Curing. Fire-cured tobacco, generally dark brown, is used mostly for pipe tobacco mixtures, snuff, and chewing tobacco and has a low sugar but high nicotine content. Fire curing employs an enclosed barn similar to that used for flue curing. Small fires are built on the floor, and the leaves cure in a smoke-laden atmosphere. Whereas flue curing takes 6 to 8 days, fire curing, using far lower temperatures, may take up to 4 weeks.

Sun Curing. Sun curing is the drying of uncovered sticks or strings of leaf in the sun. Of all sun-cured tobaccos, the best known are the so-called oriental tobaccos of Turkey, Greece, Yugoslavia, and nearby countries. These are used in cigarettes and have characteristic aromas. They are low in both sugar and nicotine.

GRADING AND AGING

After curing, the moisture content is standardized (the process is called redrying) to maintain the characteristics of the tobacco for the 12 to 18 months it is held prior to being used. (Oriental tobaccos are not redried; instead they are stored in small bales and allowed to ferment.) After storage, moisture is added and tobacco is blended to achieve the differing qualities needed for cigarettes, cigars, pipe tobaccos, snuff, or chewing tobacco.

SOME MAJOR TOBACCO TYPES

Name	Where Grown	Curing Method	Characteristics	Uses
Virginia, or "Bright"	United States: North Carolina, South Carolina, Virginia, Georgia, Florida	Flue-cured	Bright yellowish color, sweet flavor	Cigarette and pipe tobacco
Burley	United States: Tennessee, Kentucky, Ohio	Air-cured	Low nicotine content, mild flavor	Cigarette and pipe tobacco
Perique	United States: Louisiana	Pressed and allowed to soak in its own juices	Black color, strong-flavored	Snuff, chewing, and pipe tobacco
Turkish	Turkey, Greece, Yugoslavia	Sun-cured, fermented	Highly aromatic	Cigar and pipe tobacco
Latakia	Syria	Entire plant, including flower, smoke-cured	Aromatic, smoky flavor	Primarily pipe tobacco
Shiraz (Nicotina persica)	Iran	Sun-cured	Aromatic	Pipe tobacco
Cuban, or Havana	Cuba	Air-cured	Aromatic, rich-flavored	Cigars
Sumatra	Sumatra	Air-cured	Elastic, stretchable leaf	Cigar wrappers
Shade-grown	United States: Connecticut River Valley, Florida, Georgia	Air-cured	Grown under netting to produce perfect leaves	Cigar wrappers

In the mid 1980s, the leading tobacco producers were China, with almost double the crop of the United States, the next largest producer, India, Brazil, the USSR, and Turkey.

THE U.S. TOBACCO INDUSTRY

Some 180,000 farms in six southern states grow tobacco, often as the only crop. In many hundreds of small towns, it provides the farmer with the sole source of cash to buy equipment and supplies from his local merchants. The U.S. Department of Agriculture includes tobacco in its price-support system, both because of its economic significance to the South and because, for many years, it has been an important export crop. American cigarette manufacturers also play a major part in the U.S. economy, earning millions from their domestic and their foreign sales.

Fears of the health effects of long-term use of tobacco (see NICOTINE and SMOKING) have cut per capita cigarette consumption in the United States by almost 20 percent in the past two decades. In addition, the U.S. share of the world tobacco market fell from 30% to 18% in the same period, while imports of low-cost Brazilian and African tobaccos have cut into its domestic tobacco sales.

The cigarette industry continues to deny that there is a direct connection between the ingestion of tobacco smoke and the development of respiratory diseases. Although there have been several suits, claims of injury caused by cigarette consumption have not yet been accepted in a court of law.

Despite antismoking campaigns and health warnings on cigarette packets, there are still about 55 million U.S. smokers. Tobacco products such as snuff and chewing tobacco attract the young, who apparently believe that "smokeless" tobacco is safer than cigarettes. In 1986 the Federal Trade Commission began to require warnings on packages of these products, indicating that they are not safe alternatives to cigarettes and may cause mouth cancer and gum disease.

Tobacco companies nevertheless continue to promote their products (except on television, where tobacco advertising is now banned). The companies flourish on the domestic sale of tobacco products, and on tobacco exports to Third World countries, especially in Asia.

Bibliography: Axton, William F., *Tobacco and Kentucky* (1975); Finger, William R., ed., *The Tobacco Industry in Transition* (1981); Fisher, Robert L., *The Odyssey of Tobacco* (1939); Main, G. L., *Tobacco Colony: Life in Early Maryland, 1650–1720* (1982); Morton, Louis, *Robert Carter of Nomini Hall: A Virginia Planter of the 18th Century* (1941; repr. 1983); Robiscsek, Francis, *The Smoking Gods: Tobacco in Maya Art, History, and Religion* (1978); Seig, Louis, *Tobacco, Peacepipes, and Indians* (1971); Taylor, Peter, *The Smoke Ring: Tobacco, Money, and International Politics* (1984); Tilley, Nannie M., *The R. T. Reynolds Tobacco Company* (1985); Tucker, David, *Tobacco: An International Perspective* (1985).

Tobacco Road

Tobacco Road (1932), a novel by Erskine CALDWELL, deals half-humorously, half-seriously, with an amoral family of Georgia sharecroppers. Living in a rickety cabin are Jeeter Lester, the impoverished patriarch, his mother, wife, children, and as-

sorted relatives. They marry at very young ages and play a slightly mad game of sexual musical chairs until Jeeter and his wife perish in a fire. Jack Kirkland dramatized the novel in 1933, and the play ran for more than 3,000 performances.

CHARLOTTE D. SOLOMON

Tobago: see TRINIDAD AND TOBAGO.

Tobey, Mark [toh'-bee]

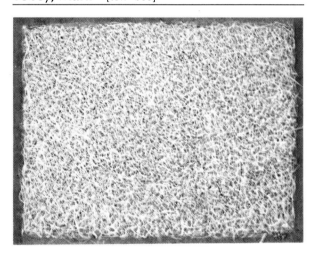

Mark Tobey's Microcosmos *(1959), painted in what the artist called "white writing," suggests a self-contained web of tense energy. Tobey, working in isolation, evolved his distinctive abstract style in the 1930s from the study of Oriental calligraphy. (Private collection.)*

Mark Tobey, b. Centerville, Wis., Dec. 11, 1890, d. Apr. 24, 1976, was more than 40 years old when he developed the unique calligraphic painting style for which he is known. He viewed this "white writing," characterized by meshed, light lines set against a darker background, as a means of evoking the chaotic energy of cities and of humanity itself. The Oriental affinities of Tobey's art are often cited, and both Chinese and Japanese art clearly influenced his linear expression. It was his Baha'i faith, however, which stresses the oneness of humankind, that gave Tobey's lines their symbolic meaning. His evocative spirituality is exemplified by *Early Light* (1970; collection of the artist's estate, Basel, Switzerland).

HARRY RAND

Bibliography: Dahl, Arthur L., *Mark Tobey: Art and Belief* (1984); Russell, John, *Tobey* (n.d.); Seitz, William C., *Mark Tobey* (1962); *Tobey's 80: A Retrospective* (1970).

Tobit, Book of [toh'-bit]

Tobit, or Tobias, is a book in the Old Testament APOCRYPHA, written (c.200–170 BC) in Hebrew or Aramaic and constructed as a didactic romance. It became popular among Hellenistic Jews and Christians in its Greek translation. The book relates how Tobit, a devout Jew in exile in Assyria, and his son Tobias were rewarded for their piety and good deeds. Tobit buried the bodies of executed Jews in Nineveh. Despite this and other good works, he was blinded. As he prayed for God to end his life, Sarah, a widow whose seven husbands have each been killed by the demon Asmodeus on their wedding night, also entreats God to end her misery. In answer to these prayers, God sends the angel Raphael to Earth to help them. Tobias marries Sarah and, with Raphael's help, overcomes the demon and restores his father's sight. The demonology, magic, and folklore motifs in the story show affinities with ancient Near Eastern stories from 500 BC on.   NORMAN K. GOTTWALD

Bibliography: Brockington, L. H., *A Critical Introduction to the Apocrypha* (1961); Zeitlin, Solomon, et al., eds., *Jewish Apocryphal Literature* (1958).

tobogganing

Tobogganing is a winter sport in which a runnerless sled is used to slide down an incline or course of snow or ice. It is primarily a recreational sport whose popularity peaked in the northern United States and Canada in the 1930s. Although its popularity has declined, it remains attractive primarily because great strength or skill is not required.

American Indians built the first toboggans about 5,000 years ago to transport goods over long distances in the snow. Tobogganing developed as a sport in the 1880s among Americans and Englishmen vacationing at Saint Moritz, Switzerland, and thrived until the 1930s ascent of skiing.

Originally, the Indians made their toboggans out of animal skins stretched tightly over wooden frames. A modern toboggan is made of several long, thin boards curled up and backward in front to form a prow. Crosspieces—to secure the individual boards—and low side railings with rope holds prevent the passengers or cargo from shifting position. Most toboggans are about 46 cm (18 in) wide and 1.2–2.7 m (4–9 ft) long and can reach speeds of 100 km/h (62.1 mph) with four to six people riding in a sitting position.

In Europe the various kinds of sledding, especially Cresta racing and luging (see LUGE), are also called tobogganing. Sledding, a form of transportation also of ancient origin, developed as a sport in 19th-century mountain resorts. Cresta tobogganing, in which the rider lies down on a "skeleton," a light wooden body with steel runners, has been practiced for a century on the treacherous 1,212-m-long (1,325-yd) run in the Cresta Valley at Saint Moritz.

Tobruk   [toh-bruk']

Tobruk is a port city in northeastern Libya on the Mediterranean Sea with a population of 71,800 (1981 est.). Food processing is the major industry. The principal export is petroleum, transported by pipeline from the Sarir oil field 515 km (320 mi) to the south. Originally a Greek agricultural colony, Tobruk later became a Roman fortress and an important city on the caravan routes. The Italians occupied it in 1911 and used it as a military base. During World War II, Tobruk was taken by the Allies in 1941, lost to the Germans in June 1942, and retaken by the British within a few months.

Tocantins River   [tohk-uh-teens']

The Tocantins River, 2,700 km (1,678 mi) long, is a Brazilian river rising in south central Goiás state, north of Brasília. It flows north and northwest to the Pará River, an arm of the Amazon delta, draining an area of about 836,570 km² (323,000 mi²). Navigation is impeded by numerous rapids and cascades along its length. In the river's lower course Brazil nuts are gathered from the surrounding tropical rain forest.

toccata   [tuh-kah'-tuh]

The term *toccata* (derived from the Italian *toccare*, "to touch") is a title for keyboard pieces in free style—generally with much elaborate passage work in rapid tempo—that exhibit the player's touch, or dexterity. The term's significance is imprecise, however, when applied to such works as the harpsichord toccatas of J. S. Bach, which are divided into several contrasting movements. Rhapsodic and virtuoso elements are generally characteristic of the genre.

As it originated in the 16th century, the toccata consisted of alternating chordal and scale passages, but by the end of the century fugal passages also had been introduced. The toccata tended to become a brilliant showpiece, but examples for the organ by Giralomo Frescobaldi are in a restrained style and were sometimes performed during mass. The genre was further developed by such 17th-century organists as Dietrich Buxtehude, Johann Pachelbel, and Jan Sweelinck, culminating in the great toccatas and fugues for organ by Bach. The toccatas of later composers—Robert Schumann and Sergei Prokofiev, for example—are usually in a fast tempo with the same figuration and continuous rhythm throughout.

Tocqueville, Alexis de   [tohk-veel']

Alexis de Tocqueville, b. July 19, 1805, d. Apr. 16, 1859, was a French politician and writer best known for his classic study of the United States, *Democracy in America* (2 vols., 1835, 1840; Eng. trans., 2 vols., 1835–40). A member of an aristocratic family, Tocqueville joined the government service as a lawyer and went (1831) to the United States to study the American penal system. Profoundly affected by his experience, he returned (1832) to France and while serving in the Chamber of Deputies completed *Democracy in America*. In 1849, Tocqueville served as minister of foreign affairs. He later wrote *The Old Regime and the French Revolution* (1856; Eng. trans., 1856), an introductory volume to a planned history of the French Revolution. In *Democracy in America*, Tocqueville affirmed his commitment to human freedoms and helped establish the European view of the United States as a land of liberty, equality, and political wisdom. The book appraises the American experience from the viewpoint of an enlightened European whose own society was still constricted by aristocratic privilege. Tocqueville felt that the old aristocratic institutions of Europe would inevitably give way to democracy and social equality, and he held up the American system as a successful model. Tocqueville's praise for the young country's ideals was not unqualified, however. He felt that democracy was an inevitable political force; at the same time, however, he feared that virtues he valued—freedom, civic participation, taste, creativity—would be imperiled by "the tyranny of the majority," individualism, and other democratic despotisms. Tocqueville believed that America's egalitarian spirit and democratic institutions "awaken and foster a passion for equality which they can never entirely satisfy."
                    Reviewed by JAMES T. SCHLEIFER

Bibliography: Boesche, R., *The Strange Liberalism of Alexis de Tocqueville* (1987) and, as ed., *Alexis de Tocqueville: Selected Letters on Politics and Society* (1985); Drescher, Seymour I., *Dilemmas of Democracy* (1968) and *Tocqueville and England* (1964); Hereth, M., *Alexis de Tocqueville*, trans. by G. F. Bogardus (1986); Lerner, Max, *Tocqueville and American Civilization* (1966); Schleifer, J. T., *The Making of Tocqueville's "Democracy in America"* (1980); Zetterbaum, Marvin, *Tocqueville and the Problem of Democracy* (1967).

Todd, Alexander R.

The British chemist Alexander Robertus Todd, Baron Todd of Trumpington, b. Oct. 2, 1907, received the 1957 Nobel Prize for chemistry for synthesizing coenzymes and all the naturally occurring nucleotides—the building blocks of the nucleic acids. Two of them, adenosine diphosphate (ADP) and triphosphate (ATP), are essential to the storage of energy in the body. Todd's work on nucleic acid structure was essential to the later definitive description of DNA by James Watson and Francis Crick. His autobiography, *Time to Remember*, was published in 1983.   HENRY M. LEICESTER

Bibliography: Farber, Eduard, *Nobel Prize Winners in Chemistry, 1901–1961* (1963).

tody   [toh'-dee]

The five species of todies are the sole living members of the bird genus *Todus* and the family Todidae. Tiny, bright to pale green birds with bright red bibs, they inhabit a few islands in the West Indies. Persistent chatterers, todies have flattened, serrate bills surrounded by facial bristles, and short tails. They catch insects in rapid, whirring flight, and they nest in burrows.

Togliatti   [toh-lee-aht'-tee]

A major center of the Soviet automobile and chemicals industries, Togliatti (1985 est. pop., 594,000) is located on the Volga River about 100 km (60 mi) upstream from Kuibyshev near the Kuibyshev Dam. Once known as Stavropol, the small town was transplanted from the river's banks following the dam's construction in the 1950s and renamed in honor of the Italian Communist leader Palmiro Togliatti when a Fiat car plant was built there in 1964.

Togliatti, Palmiro

Palmiro Togliatti, b. Mar. 26, 1893, led the Italian Communist party from 1926 until his death on Aug. 21, 1964. Working steadily for the party since its creation in 1921, Togliatti was jailed (1925) by the Fascist regime of Benito Mussolini, but was released under a general amnesty. In exile from 1926, he became party leader and worked principally from Paris. He served as chief of Comintern operations in Spain during the civil war (1936–39) there and spent most of World War II in the USSR. Togliatti returned to Italy in 1944 and served in a number of wartime coalition governments. After the war he molded Italy's Communists into one of Western Europe's strongest Communist parties and increasingly advocated the independence of national Communist parties from the Soviet party line.

Bibliography: Swearingen, Roger, ed., *Leaders of the Communist World* (1971).

Togo   [toh'-goh]

The Republic of Togo is located on the Gulf of Guinea in western Africa immediately north of the equator. It is a long, narrow country, lying between Benin on the east and Ghana on the west, with Burkina Faso bordering the north. Once a German colony, Togo gained its independence from a French-administered United Nations trusteeship in 1960.

LAND AND RESOURCES

Beyond the 48 km (30 mi) of coastal plain lies an ancient plateau, 60–460 m (200–1,500 ft) in elevation, which covers more than half of the country. A small mountain chain interrupts the plateau, with the highest elevation at Pic Baumann (986 m/3,235 ft). In the north the plateau gives way to the alluvial plain of the Oti River. To the east is the Plain of Mono.

Togo has three distinct climatic regions. The south has a drier tropical climate with its rainy season occurring during October and November. Rainfall averages 711 mm (28 in) per year in the south and 1,600 mm (63 in) per year in the plateau region. In the north a rainy season from April to July deposits about 1,143 mm (45 in) of precipitation. Temperatures throughout the country average about 26° C (78° F).

The southern half of the country is drained by the Mono River and its tributaries, while the north is drained by the Oti, an affluent of the VOLTA River. Along the sandy coastline is a fringe of cocoa palms and mangroves, whereas savanna covers most areas of the interior. Togo has deposits of iron ore in the north and phosphates in the southeast.

PEOPLE

Togo has 37 different ethnic groups. In the south, the largest groups are the EWE and the Mina; in the north, the chief ethnic group is the Cabrais.

French is the official language, and Ewe is the lingua franca of half the population. Dagomba and Kabie are also widely spoken in the north, although the many Hamitic peoples speak a multitude of different languages. The population is

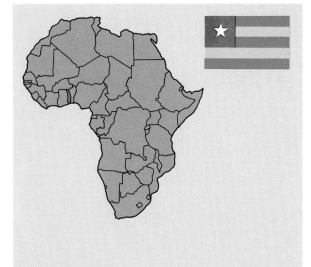

TOGOLESE REPUBLIC

LAND. Area: 56,785 km² (21,925 mi²). Capital and largest city: Lomé (1983 est. pop., 366,476).
PEOPLE. Population (1988 est.): 3,300,000; density (1988 est.): 58.1 persons per km² (150.5 per mi²). Distribution (1987): 22% urban, 78% rural. Annual growth (1987): 3.3%. Official language: French. Major religions: traditional religions, Christianity, Islam.
EDUCATION AND HEALTH. Literacy (1985): 41% of adult population. Universities (1987): 1. Hospital beds (1982): 3,655. Physicians (1985): 230. Life expectancy (1980–85): women—50.2; men—46.9. Infant mortality (1987): 117 per 1,000 live births.
ECONOMY. GNP (1986): $780 million; $250 per capita. Labor distribution (1985): agriculture—71%; other—29%. Foreign trade (1984): imports—$233 million; exports—$191 million; principal trade partners—France, the Netherlands, Ivory Coast, Yugoslavia. Currency: 1 C.F.A. franc = 100 centimes.
GOVERNMENT. Type: one-party state. Legislature: National Assembly. Political subdivisions: 5 regions.
COMMUNICATIONS. Railroads (1985): 525 km (326 mi) total. Roads (1986 est.): 7,000 km (4,350 mi) total. Major ports: 1. Major airfields: 1.

about 37% Christian and 18% Muslim. The remaining inhabitants practice traditional African religions. LOMÉ, the capital, is the largest town and chief port.

Six years of primary education is compulsory, but only about two-thirds of all children attend primary school and only about one-fifth continue on to secondary school. The university at Lomé was founded in 1965. Health services are poor, and life expectancy is low.

ECONOMIC ACTIVITY

About two-thirds of the working population are engaged in agriculture, primarily at the subsistence level. Yams, cassava, corn, beans, rice, millet, and sorghum are grown for food; coffee, cacao, and cotton are the main cash crops. The country has been generally self-sufficient in food since 1982. Fish provide an important source of protein, and livestock is raised in both the north and the south.

Phosphates, the chief source of foreign exchange, comprise about 50% of exports. Phosphate mining began in 1961; since 1976 the national economy has been adversely affected by low world prices for phosphates. Industries other than phosphate processing, including cotton ginning, food processing, and handicrafts, generally produce for the domestic market.

Togo is burdened by a large foreign debt. In 1983 the government introduced a stringent economic austerity program and began to privatize many inefficient state-owned industries. Development efforts in the 1980s focused primarily on increasing productivity in the agricultural sector and developing mineral resources other than phosphates.

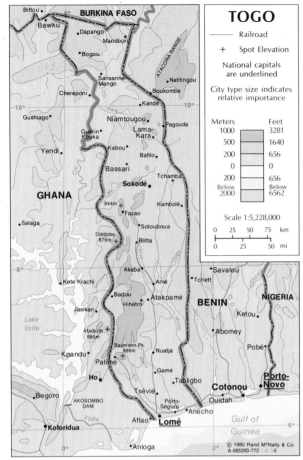

TOGO

— Railroad

+ Spot Elevation

National capitals are underlined

City type size indicates relative importance

Meters	Feet
1000	3281
500	1640
200	656
0	0
200	656
Below 2000	Below 6562

Scale 1:5,228,000

0   25   50   75   km
0   25   50 mi

© 1980 Rand McNally & Co.
A-585200-772 -1- -1-3

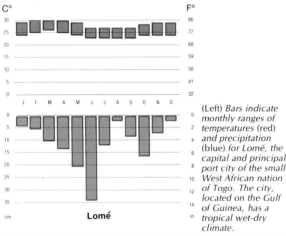

(Left) Bars indicate monthly ranges of temperatures (red) and precipitation (blue) for Lomé, the capital and principal port city of the small West African nation of Togo. The city, located on the Gulf of Guinea, has a tropical wet-dry climate.

HISTORY AND GOVERNMENT

The Ewe and related peoples moved into what is now Togo from the east between the 12th and 18th centuries. The area was part of the German colony of TOGOLAND (1884–1914). It was then administered by France as a League of Nations mandate and later as a UN trust territory until it gained independence on Apr. 27, 1960. Sylvanus Olympio, the first president of independent Togo, was assassinated in a 1963 coup. His successor, Nicolas Grunitzy, fled after a coup in January 1967 and was replaced by Gnassingbe Eyadema, the head of the armed forces. Eyadema appointed a civilian cabinet and established (1969) the Togolese People's Assembly, the sole political party. In 1979 voters approved a new constitution cre-

ating a directly elected legislature. Eyadema, reelected in 1979 and 1986, has survived several coup attempts.

JOHN W. SNADEN

Bibliography: Crowder, M., West Africa (1977); Hargreaves, J. D., West Africa Partitioned (1985); Knoll, A., Togo under Imperial Germany (1978).

Togo Heihachiro   [toh'-goh hay-hah'-chee-roh]

The Japanese admiral Togo Heihachiro, b. 1846, d. May 30, 1934, was a hero in the RUSSO-JAPANESE WAR (1904–05). After studying naval science in England, he served with distinction in the Sino-Japanese War (1894–95). As Japanese naval commander, Togo attacked Port Arthur in 1904, and in 1905 he won a decisive victory at the Battle of TSUSHIMA.

Togoland

The German colony of Togoland, in West Africa, was founded in 1884. After World War I it was made a League of Nations mandate, with the western half under British administration and the eastern half administered by France. In 1948 it became a United Nations trust territory. British Togoland chose (1956) to merge with the Gold Coast (now Ghana); the French zone became the independent nation of Togo in 1960.

Tohaku   [toh-hah'-koo]

The Japanese painter Hasegawa Tohaku, 1539–1610, was the only artist of the Momoyama period to compete successfully with Kano EITOKU for the patronage of the shogun Hideyoshi. Connections with the tea master at Daitoku-ji, Sen no Rikyu, enabled him to study the Chinese paintings held at that monastery, and his work is greatly influenced by that of the Chinese painter Mu-ch'i. In his masterpiece, the set of screens titled Pines in Mist (National Museum, Tokyo), he combined Mu-ch'i's ink-wash technique with the lyric mood of a Japanese scene.

BARBARA BRENNAN FORD

toilet

The toilet, or water closet, is a bathroom fixture for the disposal of human waste, using a bowl that can be flushed with water. Latrines were sometimes water-flushed in ancient times and the Middle Ages, utilizing either diverted streams or buckets. The modern water closet, pioneered (1775) by London watchmaker Alexander Cumming and improved (1778) by inventor Joseph Bramah, originally consisted of a cast-iron bowl with a flap valve (a hinged valve permitting flow in only one direction); the bowl emptied directly into the drains. Later a trap—a curved section of pipe that contained standing water—was added to prevent sewer gas from entering the house. In the mid-19th century, ceramic toilet bowls were introduced for easier cleaning, and traps were made more effective by venting. In 1890 the modern "washdown closet" form was developed; the elevated water-tank was lowered to its present position about 1915. Public toilets have long used flush valves rather than tanks.

FRANCES GIES

Bibliography: Reyburn, Wallace, Flushed with Pride (1871); Wright, Laurence, Clean and Decent (1960).

Tojo Hideki   [toh'-joh hee-day'-kee]

Tojo Hideki, b. Dec. 30, 1884, d. Dec. 23, 1948, prime minister (1941–44) of Japan during World War II, was a leading advocate of Japanese military conquest. After graduating (c.1915) from the Military Staff College, he gained rank steadily and by 1937 was commander in Manchuria.

Japan's prime minister KONOE FUMINARO made Tojo minister of war in 1940. After becoming prime minister as well in October 1941, Tojo approved the attack against the United States at Pearl Harbor. His initial successes against the United States and in Southeast Asia made him highly respected, but with Allied forces on the offensive, Tojo was forced to resign in July 1944. Arrested in 1945 as a war criminal, he was found guilty by the International Military Tribunal and was hanged.

Bibliography: Browne, Courtney, Tojo: The Last Banzai (1967).

tokamak

The tokamak is one of the more promising devices intended to release nuclear FUSION ENERGY. By means of strong magnetic fields it can contain a plasma consisting of electrically charged particles at high temperature. In such a plasma the fusion of nuclei of hydrogen isotopes (deuterium and tritium) provides great quantities of heat energy, which can be converted into useful electrical energy. At present, however, more energy is required to achieve fusion than is released.

The tokamak apparatus represents one of several approaches to nuclear fusion that have been studied since the early 1950s. Its relative and predecessor, the Stellarator, was developed at Princeton University. The tokamak design, conceived by Soviet scientists Andrei SAKHAROV and Igor Tamm, began to draw interest in the early 1960s. (The word *tokamak* is an acronym for Russian words meaning "toroidal magnetic chamber.") Tokamaks also have been and are being built in the United States, Japan, the United Kingdom, and some nations of Western Europe.

The main components of a tokamak are (1) a doughnut-shaped vacuum chamber (torus) in which the plasma is produced; (2) current-carrying, superconducting magnetic coils wrapped around the torus to produce a magnetic field that restrains charges from moving outward (magnetic confinement); (3) additional coils to produce a changing magnetic field that induces a current in the plasma and thus provides ohmic heating toward the temperature—50 million K—at which nuclear fusion occurs (these currents along the axis of the torus produce another field that helps confine the plasma); and (4) a "blanket" material, such as liquid lithium, surrounding the plasma to take up the energy of neutrons produced in the fusion reaction, to capture slow neutrons to produce fresh tritium fuel, and to provide protective shielding for the magnet coils. Other features include a neutral beam injector, as a source of auxiliary plasma heating; divertor coils that remove impurities and unburned fuel; a deuterium-tritium fuel-pellet generator; and electrical energy transfer equipment (a steam generator and a turbine generator).

The goal of tokamak research is to reach the "break-even" condition, in which as much fusion energy is released as is supplied externally to the tokamak. Fusion scientists are trying to achieve this goal at various large tokamak projects around the world. These include the Tokamak Fusion Test Reactor (TFTR) at Princeton, which was put into operation in 1982; the Joint European Torus (JET), a tokamak constructed in England by the European Economic Commission and put into operation in 1983; the Japanese Tokamak (JT-60) in Japan, which began operating in 1985; and the Soviet Union's T-15, which was scheduled to start up in the later 1980s. The facilities are all taking somewhat different approaches to solving the problem of sustained nuclear fusion. By 1986 the JET had achieved high-confinement mode, or H-mode, a necessary step toward the break-even condition. The TFTR aims to achieve that condition by 1989. If successful, the tokamak could contribute greatly to relieving the world's energy problems by using hydrogen isotopes as fuel, since such isotopes occur naturally in water. RAYMOND L. MURRAY

Bibliography: Bromberg, J. L., *Fusion* (1982); Gross, R. A., *Fusion Energy* (1984); Furth, H. P., "Reaching Ignition in the Tokamak," *Physics Today*, March 1985; Heppenheimer, T. A., *The Man-Made Sun* (1984); Johnstone, Bob, "Japan's Rising Man-Made Sun," *New Scientist*, Feb. 26, 1987; Roth, J. R., *Introduction to Fusion Energy* (1986); Stacey, W. M., Jr., *Fusion and Technology* (1984).

Tokelau [tohk-uh-low']

Tokelau, a non-self-governing territory of New Zealand, is made up of three atolls—Atafu, Fakaofo, and Nukunono—located in Polynesia in the south central Pacific Ocean. Although each atoll has its own center for administering village affairs, Tokelau's official administrative base is in Apia, Western Samoa. The territory's total land area is about 10 km² (4 mi²); the population, mostly POLYNESIAN, is 1,627 (1984). Agriculture and fishing are the economic mainstays; coconuts are the principal crop. Weaving is also important.

British explorer John Byron discovered the islands in 1765. Britain annexed them in 1877 and made the Tokelaus (then known as the Union Islands) part of the crown colony of the Gilbert and Ellice Islands (see KIRIBATI; TUVALU) in 1916. Assigned to New Zealand in 1925, they became a territory of that country in 1948.

Tokugawa (family) [toh-koo-gah'-wah]

The Tokugawa house, founded by Tokugawa IEYASU, dominated Japanese politics from 1603 to 1867 (the Tokugawa period). Ieyasu emerged from the Battle of Sekigahara (1600) as the most powerful military leader in Japan. Appointed shogun by the emperor in 1603, he established the capital at his castle town of Edo (Tokyo) and constructed a political system with the shogun as national authority and the daimyo (lords) as local rulers. **Hidetada** (1579–1632; r. 1605–23) succeeded his father as shogun, while Ieyasu retired to consolidate Tokugawa power. The third shogun, **Iemitsu** (1604–51; r. 1623–51), barred trade with the West and suppressed Christianity. His insular policies were perpetuated for two centuries.

The Tokugawa monopolized foreign trade, mining, and the major cities of Edo, Kyoto, Osaka, and Nagasaki. Only vassals of the ruling house were appointed to powerful positions; the clergy and nobility were placed under Tokugawa control, as was the emperor. All the daimyo had to reside at Edo for part of the year, and when elsewhere, they left family members at Edo as hostages. The Tokugawa controlled one-fourth of the rice lands, certified daimyo succession and land titles, and regulated the actions of their vassals. **Yoshinobu** (or Keiki; 1827–1913, r. 1866–67), the 15th and last Tokugawa, was overthrown amid rising dissatisfaction over the dynasty's inability to prevent Western penetration. The subsequent MEIJI RESTORATION marked the emergence of modern Japan.
WILLIAM B. HAUSER

Bibliography: Sansom, George, *A History of Japan 1615–1867* (1963); Totman, Conrad D., *Japan before Perry* (1981); Wigmore, John H., ed., *Law and Justice in Tokugawa Japan* (1986).

Tokugawa Ieyasu: see IEYASU, SHOGUN OF JAPAN.

Tokyo

Tokyo is the capital and most important city of Japan. Lying at the southeastern elbow of Honshu, the largest Japanese island, it is one of the world's leading financial and commercial centers. The Tokyo prefecture, made up of 23 central wards, 2 counties, and several islands south of Tokyo Bay, has a population of 11,780,500 (1985), nearly 10% of the population of all Japan. The inner wards, which made up the original city, have a population of 8,386,000 (1986 est.). From Tokyo, at the head of Tokyo Bay, through Kawasaki and Yokohama, on the western shore, extends a conurbation within which more than 25,000,000 people live.

Contemporary City. Twice during the 20th century Tokyo was nearly destroyed, once after the tragic earthquake and fire of 1923 and a second time after the incendiary-bomb air raids of World War II. Although each reconstruction resulted in a more modern city, Tokyo today presents a random pattern of the ancient and the ultramodern. At the center of the city is the Imperial Palace, set amid beautiful gardens and encircled by inner and outer moats. Nearby is the National Diet building (1936), for many years the tallest building in Japan. Toward the bay is the world-famous Ginza district. The area's surroundings range from bazaarlike at its southwest end to opulent at its northeastern limits. The Marunouchi district, the most Westernized in Tokyo, is home to many of Japan's multinational corporations. Komazawa Olympic Park contains structures designed by Kenzo TANGE for the 1964 Games.

Urban Character. Increasingly cosmopolitan in character, Tokyo is a city of two alphabets. Most public signs tell their story in both the ideogrammatic *kangi* (characters) of classical Japanese and Roman-lettered phonetic spellings. As a modern city grafted onto an older one, Tokyo suffers severe housing problems, and until recently 40% of inner-city residences did not have indoor plumbing. Housing projects, such as the

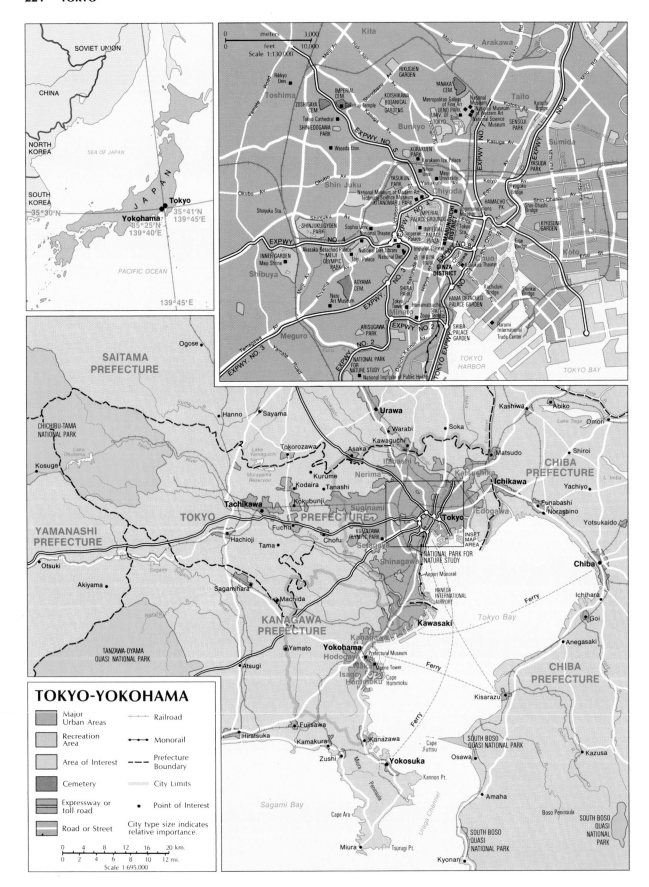

SOVIET UNION

CHINA

NORTH KOREA

SOUTH KOREA

SEA OF JAPAN

J A P A N

PACIFIC OCEAN

Tokyo
35°41'N
139°45'E

Yokohama
35°25'N
139°40'E

35°30'N

139°45'E

Kita

Arakawa

Toshima

Taito

Bunkyo

Sumida

Shin Juku

Chiyoda

Chuo

Koto

Shibuya

Minato

Meguro

TOKYO HARBOR

TOKYO BAY

SAITAMA PREFECTURE

CHICHIBU-TAMA NATIONAL PARK

Ogose

Hanno

Sayama

Urawa

Warabi

Soka

Kashiwa

Abiko

Omori

Tokorozawa

Kawaguchi

Matsudo

Shiroi

CHIBA PREFECTURE

Yachiyo

Kosuge

Asaka

Ichikawa

Funabashi

Norasbino

Kurume

Nerima

Katsusbika

YAMANASHI PREFECTURE

Kodaira

Tanashi

Itabashi

Edogawa

Yotsukaido

Tachikawa

Kokubunji

Suginami

Tokyo

TOKYO   PREFECTURE

Fuchu

Chofu

INSET MAP AREA

Otsuki

Hachioji

Tama

Selagaya

Shinagawa

NATIONAL PARK FOR NATURE STUDY

Chiba

Akiyama

Sagamihara

Machida

Airport Monorail

Ichihara

Goi

KANAGAWA PREFECTURE

Yamato

HANEDA INTERNATIONAL AIRPORT

Kawasaki

Anegasaki

TANZAWA-OYAMA QUASI NATIONAL PARK

Atsugi

Kanagawa

Tokyo Bay

CHIBA PREFECTURE

Yokohama

Hodogaya

Prefectural Museum

Naka

Marine Tower

Isago

Cape Hommoku

Hommoku

Kisarazu

Kazusa

Fujisawa

Ferry

Hiratsuka

Kanazawa

SOUTH BOSO QUASI NATIONAL PARK

Kamakura

Cape Futtsu

Osawa

Zushi

Yokosuka

Kannon Pt.

Amaha

Miura Peninsula

Cape Ara

Boso Peninsula

SOUTH BOSO QUASI NATIONAL PARK

Sagami Bay

Uraga Channel

Miura

Tsurugi Pt.

Kyonan

TOKYO-YOKOHAMA

Major Urban Areas

Recreation Area

Area of Interest

Cemetery

Expressway or toll road

Road or Street

Railroad

Monorail

Prefecture Boundary

City Limits

Point of Interest

City type size indicates relative importance.

0   4   8   12   16   20 km.
0   2   4   6   8 10 12 mi.
Scale 1:695,000

(Right) *Tokyo, the capital of Japan and one of the great industrial cities of the world, is located on the eastern coast of Honshu, the largest of the Japanese islands. Tokyo formally became the nation's capital in 1868, when Japan's emperor assumed residency in the city.*

(Below) *The Niju-bashi (Double Bridge) spans a moat surrounding the grounds of the Imperial Palace, residence of Japan's Emperor Hirohito. The Imperial Palace, formerly a warlord's castle, is located in the Chiyoda district of central Tokyo.*

Tama New Town Project (1965–72), have been built in the outlying areas to encourage population dispersal; the daytime population of the 3 central wards of the city is 5 times the nighttime population. The narrow streets of the older districts add to traffic congestion; roadway makes up only 10% of Tokyo's surface, compared to the 20–40% in most modern cities. A well-engineered but overworked mass transit system includes a monorail line between downtown Tokyo and Haneda Airport to the south. Tokyo prefecture has an elected governor and assembly, but the wards exercise a great deal of autonomy through their own elected councils.

Economy. Tokyo is the commercial and industrial heart of Japan. It is also the nerve center of the country's international corporate activity. Tokyo-based multinational companies employ workers in branches throughout the world. Within the city are manufactured many of the consumer products for

which Japan is now famous: for example, electronic equipment, cameras, and automobiles. Tokyo is the hub of an extensive national railroad system. A computerized, all-electric, standard-gauge line links Tokyo at the eastern end of the Tokaido Megalopolis with Fukuoka at its western end. A high-speed interurban express links Tokyo and Osaka, the country's second city. Dentsu, the largest advertising agency outside the United States, is in Tokyo. The harbors of Tokyo and Yokohama have been combined to form one administration named Keihin. Tokyo now handles primarily domestic trade.

Religion and Culture. Tokyo is a city of many shrines, with religious fervor directed toward honoring the cultural heritage. The Meiji Shrine, dedicated to the Emperor Meiji (r. 1867–1912), maintained in a beautiful garden setting, attracts millions of visitors each year. Within Tokyo's many parks, museums adjoin shrines and pagodas. The National Museum, the National Science Museum, the National Museum of Western Art, and the Metropolitan Gallery of Fine Art are in Ueno Park. The Technical Science Museum and the National Museum of Modern Art are located in Kitanomaru Park. Within Tokyo and its suburbs are more than 100 universities, including the University of Tokyo.

History. The city of Edo was established in the 12th century. In the 1590s, the local ruler Tokugawa IEYASU established control over the entire country and made himself (1603) shogun (military governor). Although the imperial capital remained in Kyoto, the real seat of government was Edo under the TOKUGAWA family. In 1853, Commodore Matthew PERRY directed U.S. warships into the bay to force the shogun to open Japan to Western commerce. In 1868 the shogunate surrendered power to the emperor, who moved the imperial court to Edo, renamed the city Tokyo ("Eastern capital"), and restored direct imperial rule (see MEIJI RESTORATION). By the time of the great earthquake of 1923, the population of Tokyo had exceeded 7 million. After the second destruction of Tokyo during World War II, the city became the administrative center of the U.S. occupation forces (1945–52). Since then Tokyo has had the highest rate of industrial growth among the world's major cities.

JAMES CHAN

Bibliography: Allinson, Gary D., *Suburban Tokyo* (1979); Azumi, Atsushi, *Tokyo* (1972); Kirkup, James, *Tokyo* (1966); Maraini, Fosco, *Tokyo* (1976); Yazaki, Takeo, *Socioeconomic Structure of the Tokyo Metropolitan Complex*, trans. by Mitsugu Matsuda (1970).

Tokyo, University of

Established in 1877, the University of Tokyo (enrollment: 19,000; library: 4,500,000 volumes), Japan's first national university, is a coeducational institution in Tokyo. It offers undergraduate and graduate degrees in its schools of humanities, sciences, law, and education. Many cultural and scientific institutes and an astronomical observatory are associated with the university.

Tokyo Rose

Tokyo Rose was the nickname given by U.S. troops in the Pacific to at least a dozen women who broadcast enemy propaganda and music to them from Japan during World War II. One of these women, Iva Ikuki Toguri D'Aquino, a U.S. citizen, was convicted of treason in 1949. Imprisoned until 1956, she steadfastly claimed to have worked under duress. On Jan. 19, 1977, President Gerald R. Ford granted her a pardon.

Toland, John   [toh'-luhnd]

The British deistic apologist John Toland, b. 1670, d. Mar. 11, 1722, was prosecuted for his controversial *Christianity Not Mysterious* (1696), in which he contended that neither God nor revelation was beyond the comprehension of human reason. Toland's books contributed to later discussions concerning the nature of reason and revelation and the genuineness of the New Testament.

Bibliography: Cragg, G. R., *From Puritanism to the Age of Reason* (1966); Daniel, S. H., *John Toland* (1984).

Tolbert, William R., Jr.   [tahl'-burt]

The Liberian political leader William Richard Tolbert, Jr., b. May 13, 1913, served as president of his country from July 23, 1971, until his death in a military coup on Apr. 12, 1980. He was previously the Liberian treasury's disbursing officer (1936–43), a member of Liberia's House of Representatives (1943–51), and vice-president (1951–71).

Bibliography: Sankwulo, W., *Tolbert of Liberia* (1979); Smith, Robert A., *His Challenge Is Mankind: William R. Tolbert: A Political Portrait* (1972).

Toledo   (Ohio) [tuh-lee'-doh]

Toledo is a city in northwestern Ohio near the Michigan line, where the Maumee River empties into Lake Erie. The seat of Lucas County, Toledo has a population of 354,635 (1980), with 791,599 persons in the 5-county metropolitan area. Toledo is one of the major Great Lakes shipping ports, handling grain, coal, and iron ore. It is also an important petroleum-refining and industrial center and a leading producer of automotive parts and glass. The University of Toledo (1872) is located there, as are the Toledo Museum of Art, the Toledo Zoological Gardens, and an extensive park system.

The Battle of Fallen Timbers (1794), which hastened the collapse of Indian resistance in the area, was fought nearby. Soon afterward, Fort Industry was built in what is now downtown Toledo. In 1817, Port Lawrence was founded on the site. A dispute between Michigan Territory and the state of Ohio over inclusion of the Toledo area in Ohio's canal system led to the "Toledo War" of 1835. President Andrew Jackson decided the question in Ohio's favor. In return, Michigan was awarded the Upper Peninsula and granted statehood.

Toledo   (Spain) [toh-lay'-doh]

Toledo, a city in central Spain and the capital of the province of Toledo, lies on the Tagus River, about 70 km (40 mi) southwest of Madrid. Its population is 57,769 (1981). The old city is a maze of narrow streets built on steep bluffs above the river and dominated by the Alcázar.

Although the traditional industries of sword manufacturing and engraved metalworking survive, Toledo's economy depends on tourists attracted to its wealth of religious and secular architecture. The city's principal landmarks are the Gothic cathedral (begun 1227), the Franciscan friary of San Juan de los Reyes (1476), and the Alcázar, a fortress (rebuilt 1538). Also of historic significance are several medieval mosques and synagogues, two bridges over the Tagus River, a variety of 10th-to-16th-century gateways, and the city's me-

dieval walls. Its museums and churches contain paintings by El Greco, Velázquez, Murillo, and other Spanish masters. Toledo is the seat of the archbishop primate of Spain.

Toledo was well established before it was conquered by the Romans in 192 BC. Roman Toletum was the provincial capital of Carpentia. The city served as capital of the Visigothic kingdom from the middle of the 6th century until it was captured by the Moors in 712. Its cultural and economic preeminence under Muslim rule did not end when Alfonso VI of León and Castile reconquered it in 1085. Christian, Arab, and Jewish culture blended in medieval Toledo and aided in the transmission of classical learning to western Europe. Toledo declined after Madrid became the Spanish capital in 1560. The city was a battleground during the War of the Spanish Succession (1701–14), the Peninsular War (1808–14), and the Spanish Civil War (1936), when the Alcázar was defended by the Nationalists.   NORMAN J. G. POUNDS

Toledo, Francisco de

Francisco de Toledo y Figueroa, b. July 10, 1515, d. Apr. 21, 1582, Spanish viceroy of Peru (1569–81), instituted administrative reforms that remained in force until the end of the colonial period. Following a 5-year tour of Peru, Toledo reformed local government and finance, revitalized the University of San Marcos at Lima, and regularized the *mita*, a system of forced native labor. He suppressed the last remnants of Inca power and was responsible for the execution (1572) of the Inca leader Tupac Amaru.

Bibliography: Zimmerman, Arthur F., *Francisco de Toledo* (1938).

Tolkien, J. R. R.   [tohl'-keen]

J. R. R. Tolkien is best known as the creator of Middle Earth, the world of his fantasy trilogy The Lord of the Rings. *A professor of Old English language and literature at Oxford University, Tolkien drew upon his scholarly interest in Nordic heritage to create the languages and myths of elves, dwarfs, and the homey creatures he called "hobbits." His work portrays the struggle of peaceful creatures against evil powers.*

The English writer and scholar John Ronald Reuel Tolkien, b. Bloemfontein, South Africa, Jan. 3, 1892, d. Sept. 2, 1973, reestablished fantasy as a serious form in modern English literature. As professor of medieval English literature at Oxford University, he presented (1936) the influential lecture "Beowulf: The Monsters and the Critics," an aesthetic justification of the presence of the mythological creatures—Grendel and the dragon—in the medieval poem; he then went on to publish his own fantasy, The HOBBIT (1937). There followed his critical theory of fantasy, "On Fairy-Stories" (1939), and his masterpieces, the mythological romances *The Lord of the Rings* (1954–55) and *The Silmarillion* (1977).

Brought to England as a child upon the death of his father

in 1896, Tolkien was educated at King Edward's School in Birmingham and at Oxford. He enlisted in 1915 in the Lancashire Fusiliers; before leaving for France, he married his longtime sweetheart, Edith Bratt. Tolkien saw action in the Battle of the Somme, but trench fever kept him frequently hospitalized during 1917. He held academic posts in philology and in English language and literature from 1920 until his retirement in 1959.

Inclination and profession moved Tolkien to study the heroic literature of northern Europe—*Beowulf*, the *Edda*, the *Kalevala*. The spirit of these poems and their languages underlies his humorous and whimsical writings, such as *Farmer Giles of Ham* (1949) and *The Adventures of Tom Bombadil* (1962), as well as his more substantial works.   RANDEL HELMS

Bibliography: Carpenter, Humphrey, *Tolkien: A Biography* (1977); Helms, Randel, *Tolkien's World* (1974).

Toller, Ernst   [tohl'-ur]

Ernst Toller, b. Dec. 1, 1893, d. May 22, 1939, was the most politically engaged representative of German left-wing expressionism. Besides being an active dramatist, he participated in the Bavarian Communist revolution of 1919 and served a 5-year prison sentence when it failed. A prime target of the Nazis, Toller left Germany even before Hitler's takeover. Estranged from his wife and despondent over the German invasion of Czechoslovakia, he committed suicide in New York.

Toller's most famous writings are the plays *Transfiguration* (1919; Eng. trans., 1935), about a soldier who after the war becomes a revolutionary; *The Machine-Wreckers* (1922; Eng. trans., 1923), which concerns the insurrection of the English weavers in 1812; and *Brokenbow* (1923; Eng. trans., 1926), about society's rejection of a returning soldier. While living in American exile, he became well known for the autobiographical *I Was a German* (1933; Eng. trans., 1934), a moving and tragic account of a man without a country.   SOL GITTLEMAN

Bibliography: Ossar, Michael, *Anarchism in the Dramas of Ernst Toller* (1976); Spalek, John M., *Ernst Toller and His Critics* (1968); Willibrand, W. A., *Ernst Toller and His Ideology* (1945).

Tollund man   [toh'-lund]

Tollund man, the best preserved and most famous of the prehistoric corpses found in Scandinavian bogs, was unearthed in the Tollund peat bog of central Jutland, Denmark. The well-preserved corpse of this Iron Age man was clothed only

Tollund man, discovered (1950) in Tollund Fen in Jutland, Denmark, was one of the best-preserved corpses found in the Scandinavian peat bogs. Peat-bog burials, often associated with ritual sacrifices, were common during the period from c.100 BC to AD 500. (National Museet, Copenhagen.)

in a cap, belt, and cloak. Because he had been hanged with a leather rope, it is presumed that he was a sacrificial victim. His stomach contents were sufficiently well preserved to show that his last meal had consisted of a gruel made of barley, linseed, knotweed, and other cultivated weeds; this evidence of a vegetarian diet has since been confirmed by other peat-bog burials. Bog burials of the Tollund type have been found in Denmark, Schleswig-Holstein, and Lower Saxony and span the period from around 100 BC to AD 500. Tollund man is now on display in the National Museum, Copenhagen.
      LLOYD LAING

Bibliography: Glob, P. V., *The Bog People* (1969).

Tolman, Edward C.   [tohl'-muhn]

The American psychologist Edward Chase Tolman, b. West Newton, Mass., Apr. 14, 1886, d. Nov. 19, 1959, was the principal exponent of a cognitive learning theory that attempted to unite the methods of behaviorism with the concept of mentalism. Tolman attended Harvard University, where he was strongly influenced by Ralph Barton Perry. Shortly after receiving (1915) his doctorate from Harvard, Tolman began teaching (1918) at the University of California at Berkeley, an association he maintained until his death.

Following Perry's theories, Tolman insisted on viewing organisms as intrinsically goal directed, as "experiencing" environmental stimuli as signs, as forming "cognitive maps" of their environments, and as behaving in ways relevant to the attainment of goals. Tolman's behaviorism was "molar" (working with large units of behavior) rather than "molecular" (working with small units of behavior), purposive rather than mechanistic.

In his later academic life Tolman was strongly influenced both by the ideas of Kurt Lewin and of Egon Brunswik and by psychoanalysis. Tolman collaborated with Talcott Parsons, Edward Shils, and others in advancing a general theory of action integrating psychology, psychoanalysis, economics, and sociology. His major writings include *Purposive Behavior in Animals and Men* (1932) and *Drives toward War* (1942).
      BERNARD KAPLAN

Bibliography: Tolman, E. C., "Autobiography," in *A History of Psychology in Autobiography*, vol. 4, ed. by E. G. Boring (1952).

Tolson, M. B.

The American poet, playwright, and teacher Melvin Beaunorus Tolson, b. Moberly, Mo., Feb. 6, 1900, d. Aug. 29, 1966, has won more recognition in Liberia, where he was named poet laureate in 1947, than in his own country. His first volume of poems, *Rendezvous with America* (1944), was received with enthusiasm for its complex view of life and its wide sympathies, and his *Libretto for the Republic of Liberia* (1953) was hailed as worthy of comparison with *The Waste Land* and *Paterson*. His last book, *Harlem Gallery: Book I, The Curator* (1965), exemplifies his compact, metaphoric language and tragicomic vision of man in society.

Bibliography: Flasch, Joy, *Melvin B. Tolson* (1972).

Tolstoi, Count Aleksei Konstantinovich
[tohl'-stoy or tuhl-stoy']

A distant cousin of Leo Tolstoi, Count Aleksei Konstantinovich Tolstoi, b. Sept. 5 (N.S.), 1817, d. Oct. 10 (N.S.), 1875, was an outstanding Russian poet, novelist, and playwright. Although he spent much of his life in tsarist circles, serving in the Russian foreign ministry and numbering among his friends Tsar Alexander II himself, Tolstoi's love of liberty led him to give up his court career to preserve his freedom of expression. The satirical poems that he published under the name Kozma Prutkov ridiculing Russian bureaucratic officiousness and pretentiousness, are masterpieces of humor and parody. Tolstoi's three historical plays in blank verse, *The Death of Ivan the Terrible* (1866; Eng. trans., 1869), *Tsar Fyodor Ivanovitch* (1868; Eng. trans., 1923), and *Tsar Boris* (1870), were set in 16th-century Russia, as was his novel, *Prince Sere-*

bryani (1862; Eng. trans., 1874); all concern the conflict in Russia with autocratic repression. Many of his lyrics were set to music by such composers as Tchaikovsky, Mussorgsky, and Rimsky-Korsakov.

Bibliography: Dalton, Margaret, *A. K. Tolstoy* (1972).

Tolstoi, Aleksei Nikolayevich

Soviet novelist Count Aleksei Nikolayevich Tolstoi, b. Jan. 10 (N.S.), 1883, d. Feb. 23, 1945, emigrated after the Bolshevik revolution of 1917 but in 1923 renounced his title and returned to the USSR. His early stories and novels portray the decaying gentry, as does his masterful fictionalized autobiography, *Nikita's Childhood* (1921; Eng. trans., 1945). Both *Aelita* (1922) and *The Death Box* (1925; Eng. trans., 1936) combine science fiction and ideology, the latter novel depicting a totalitarian order that the inventor of a death ray tries to impose on the world. Tolstoi's two most influential works were the historical trilogy *The Road to Calvary* (1922–41; Eng. trans., 1945) and the unfinished *Peter the First* (1929–45; Eng. trans., 1956). The former gives a panoramic view of the years before World War I, capturing the atmosphere of gloom and futility that pervaded Russia's artistic Bohemia, and the latter recounts the turmoil of Russia's westernization during the early 18th century. Critics have taxed Tolstoi with intellectual shallowness and intrusive philosophizing but recognize his thematic and stylistic verve.   RALPH E. MATLAW

Tolstoi, Count Leo

Count Leo Tolstoi, considered one of the greatest figures of world literature, was a major influence on late-19th-century Russian philosophical thought. Although moral and religious didacticism pervade much of his later work, Tolstoi's descriptive genius and psychological acuity, best displayed in War and Peace *(1862–69)* and Anna Karenina *(1873–76), remain the* vital force in all his writings, ensuring his position as one of Russia's finest novelists.

Count Leo Tolstoi, b. Sept. 9 (N.S.), 1828, d. Nov. 22 (N.S.), 1910, was Russia's greatest novelist and one of its most influential moral philosophers. He was born near Moscow at Yasnaya Polyana, or "Clear Glade," the estate where he was to spend most of his life. At the age of nine he became an orphan, and thereafter he was raised by aunts. In 1847 he left the University of Kazan to reform his estate, but he was unprepared for the task and moved to Moscow. Five years later, Tolstoi volunteered for the army in the Caucasus; he participated in the defense of Sevastopol and was hailed as a rising literary star for his fictionalized *Childhood* (1852; Eng. trans., 1862), *Youth* (1857; Eng. trans., 1862), and *Sevastopol Sketches* (1855–56; Eng. trans., 1888), which already contained some of the main features of his mature work—psychological analysis of unprecedented detail, and a description of war that seeks to replace romanticized glory with a realistic view of battle as unglamorous actions performed by ordinary men.

Philosophy. Tolstoi retired from the army in 1856, traveled in Europe, and returned to his estate, where he founded a school for peasant children that anticipated several modern educational practices. He was married in 1862 and a year later published a novel he had begun much earlier, *The Cossacks*

(1863; Eng. trans., 1878). It was during this period that he wrote the novels upon which most of his fame rests: WAR AND PEACE and ANNA KARENINA. A deep-seated dissatisfaction with himself and a long-frustrated search for meaning in life, however, led to the crisis Tolstoi described in his *Confession* (1879; Eng. trans., 1921) and *Memoirs of a Madman* (1884; Eng. trans., 1943). In these works he also formulated a doctrine to live by, based on nonresistance to evil, renunciation of wealth, self-improvement through physical work, and nonparticipation in such social phenomena as war, juries, and the like.

The doctrine had an enormous vogue, profoundly influencing Mahatma Gandhi, among others. Yasnaya Polyana became a place of pilgrimage, and Tolstoi was revered and emulated throughout the world. Constant strife, however, existed between Tolstoi's wife and his followers; finally, after many scenes, Tolstoi left the estate in October 1910, became ill, and died at nearby Astapovo a few weeks later.

War and Peace, and Anna Karenina. In *War and Peace,* Tolstoi chronicled the histories of several families against the backdrop of the Napoleonic Wars. The leading characters—Prince Andrei, Pierre, and Natasha—develop and grow into maturity and are finally integrated into the process of life, which they accept as the answer to their personal searches for meaning. Critics have objected to the lack of traditional plot, and to the author's philosophical and historical reflections; these things are essential, however, to Tolstoi's conception of art.

Anna Karenina also weaves together several plots. Anna gives up family and social position to live with her lover, Vronsky, and her brother's less consuming adulterous passions lead to marital strife. The courtship and rewarding marriage of Levin and Kitty, based on Tolstoi's own experience, provide a contrast. Although the novel's scope is smaller than that of *War and Peace,* and its techniques differ, it also presents an extensive picture of Russia. The end of the novel depicts the crisis the author was undergoing himself.

Later Works. After arriving at his doctrine of nonresistance and nonparticipation, Tolstoi at first refrained from writing fiction. He expounded his philosophy in a series of tracts, including *What Is Art?* (1897; Eng. trans., 1898), which renounced much of his earlier work as too complex and not morally uplifting. He returned to imaginative literature, however. The theme of death, already vital in his early writings, is reexamined in his most influential study, *The Death of Ivan Ilych* (1886; Eng. trans., 1888), a ruthless and appalling depiction of a life void of meaning, and in *Master and Man* (1895; Eng. trans., 1895). Tolstoi had once described sexual desire naturally and vividly, but now he preached sexual abstinence and wrote on the conflict of passion and morality in *The Devil* (1889; Eng. trans. 1926), *The Kreutzer Sonata* (1890; Eng. trans., 1890), and *Father Sergius* (1898; Eng. trans., 1912). His last novel, *Resurrection* (1899; Eng. trans., 1899), published to aid a dissident sect, includes memorable scenes in the courts and jails of Moscow, but is flawed by didactic intrusions. He returned to earlier themes and techniques in the novella *Hadji Murad* (1904; Eng. trans., 1912).   RALPH E. MATLAW

Bibliography: Bayley, John, *Tolstoy and the Novel* (1966); Berlin, Isaiah, *The Hedgehog and the Fox: An Essay on Tolstoy's View of History* (1953); Duffield, Holly G., *Literature and Aesthetics: Tolstoy and the Critics* (1965); Gifford, Henry, ed., *Leo Tolstoy: A Critical Anthology* (1972); Hecht, Leo, *Tolstoy the Rebel* (1975); Jones, Malcolm, ed., *New Essays on Tolstoy* (1978); Matlaw, Ralph E., ed., *Tolstoy: A Collection of Critical Essays* (1967); Maude, Aylmer, *The Life of Tolstoy,* 2 vols. (1908–10; repr. 1953); Redpath, Theodore, *Tolstoy* (1960); Simmons, Ernest J., *Introduction to Tolstoy's Writings* (1968) and *Leo Tolstoy,* 2 vols. (1945; repr. 1973); Tolstoy, Leo, *Tolstoy's Letters,* ed. and trans. by R. F. Christian, 2 vols. (1978); Tolstoy, Tatyana, *Tolstoy Remembered,* trans. by Derek Coltman (1977); Troyat, Henri, *Tolstoy* (1960).

Toltec [tahl'-tek]

The Toltecs, an ancient people of MESOAMERICA, dominated central Mexico from the late 10th until the mid-12th century AD. Many of the area's later peoples, notably the AZTECS, claimed descent from the Toltecs.

Immigrants from the north, the Toltecs moved into the Valley of Mexico after the collapse of TEOTIHUACÁN late in the 7th century AD. In the mid-10th century they moved northwest, establishing themselves at TULA, which quickly became the capital of a powerful Toltec state. The area under the direct political control of the rulers at Tula was centered north of the Valley of Mexico. Toltec commercial ties and cultural influence stretched north beyond the frontiers of Mesoamerica into the southwestern United States. Late in the 10th century, Toltecs penetrated Yucatán and established a Toltec-MAYA state with its capital at CHICHÉN ITZÁ. Toltec traders also maintained ties with Guatemala, Nicaragua, and Costa Rica.

In the 12th century, Toltec power waned, as droughts disrupted agriculture and Tula came under heavy pressure from displaced peoples. About 1150, Tula was abandoned and savagely razed, and many Toltecs moved south and east. In the Valley of Mexico, their descendants were prime participants in the ensuing period of political conflict that ended with the rise of the Aztec state. JOHN S. HENDERSON

Bibliography: Adams, R. E. W., *Prehistoric Mesoamerica* (1977).

Toluca [toh-loo'-kah]

Toluca (1980 pop., 357,071), the capital of the state of Mexico in central Mexico, lies about 65 km (40 mi) southeast of Mexico City. The city is an agricultural and manufacturing center as well as a summer resort. It was founded by the Spanish in 1530 and was long the fiefdom of the Cortés family.

Tom Jones

Tom Jones (1749; film, 1963) is the finest novel of Henry FIELDING. By humorously deploying the devices of mock epic and romance and by giving his narrative a wide social range, Fielding opened the way for the novels of Dickens, George Eliot, and Thackeray. *Tom Jones* recounts the adventures of the foundling Tom, a generous but hot-blooded young man who is temporarily banished by his benefactor, Squire Allworthy, through the deviousness of the odious Blifil, his rival for the hand of Sophia. The explosive Squire Western, saintly schoolmaster Partridge, and amorous Lady Bellaston are among the memorable characters of the novel, which Fielding infused with a morality of relaxed Christian benevolence.

Bibliography: Battestin, Martin C., ed., *Twentieth Century Interpretations of Tom Jones* (1968); Harrison, Bernard, *Henry Fielding's Tom Jones: The Novelist as Moral Philosopher* (1975); Miller, Henry Knight, *Henry Fielding's Tom Jones and the Romance Tradition* (1976).

Tom Sawyer

One of Mark TWAIN's most popular novels, *The Adventures of Tom Sawyer* (1876) captures the spirit of boyhood as it was experienced in a small Mississippi River town in mid-19th-century Missouri. Being out of favor with his Aunt Polly and his sweetheart Becky Thatcher, Tom is plunged into a series of adventures, which begin in a graveyard when he and Huck Finn witness a murder committed by the half-breed Injun Joe. They continue through the boys' escape to a nearby island, their attendance at their own funeral when the townspeople believe them dead, Tom's crucial testimony at the murder trial of an innocent man, his reconciliation with his aunt, and Tom and Becky's disappearance in a cave in which Injun Joe is lurking. *Tom Sawyer* inspired three sequels, of which HUCKLEBERRY FINN alone is of major significance.

Bibliography: Norton, Charles A., *Writing Tom Sawyer* (1983).

Tom Thumb (entertainer)

General Tom Thumb was the stage name of Charles Sherwood Stratton, b. Bridgeport, Conn., Jan. 4, 1838, d. July 15, 1883, the 63.5-cm (25 in) midget discovered in 1842 by the showman P. T. BARNUM. Growing to 101.5 cm (40 in) at maturity, Tom Thumb performed at the American Museum and toured extensively. A. H. SAXON

Bibliography: Desmond, Alice Curtis, *Barnum Presents: General Tom Thumb* (1954); Saxon, A. H., ed., *The Autobiography of Mrs. Tom Thumb* (1978).

Tom Thumb (locomotive)

Tom Thumb, an experimental locomotive, was built by Peter Cooper of New York, who was anxious for the newly formed Baltimore & Ohio (B & O) Railroad to use locomotives instead of horses for motive power. In building the first locomotive in the United States, Cooper used old musket barrels for boiler tubing. The engine weighed only a ton and produced about 1.5 hp. On Aug. 28, 1830, the Tom Thumb was tested on a double track outside of Baltimore, Md. It pulled a wagonload of company dignitaries one way, and on the return trip it lost its famous race with a gray horse when it lost a pulley belt. The B & O officials were convinced, however, to convert to steam power. JOHN F. STOVER

Bibliography: Bruce, Alfred W., *The Steam Locomotive in America* (1952).

tomahawk

Tomahawk is an Algonquian term for a type of striking or throwing weapon. Originally the tomahawk consisted of a carved wooden club about 60 cm (2 ft) long with a 15-cm (6-in) ball of sculptured wood, beryl, or bone attached at its striking end by thongs. The head was sometimes covered with leather. Some tomahawks also had a tobacco pipe attached. Regional structural variations included curved heads of sharpened bone or stone and the addition of decorative and symbolic materials such as feathers or hair where the head was attached to an ornately inlaid handle. These weapons were widely used in hunting and warfare by the aboriginal inhabitants of the northeastern United States, the Great Lakes, and the upper Saint Lawrence region of Canada. With the coming of European trade goods, a knife was sometimes inserted into the ball of the war club. Eventually, commercial tomahawks, in which a metal ax blade replaced the ball, were imported for sale to the Indians. At the end of hostilities among Indians the tomahawk was frequently buried as part of the peace ceremony, giving rise to the expression "bury the hatchet" to indicate the end of a disagreement. JAMES W. HERRICK

Bibliography: Peterson, H. L., *American Indian Tomahawks* (1965).

Tomasson, Helgi [too'-mah-son]

Classical ballet dancer Helgi Tomasson, b. Reykjavik, Iceland, Oct. 8, 1942, made his debut with the Copenhagen Tivoli Ballet (1958). Encouraged by American choreographer Jerome Robbins, he attended the School of American Ballet in New York City. He danced with the Joffrey Ballet (1961–64), the Harkness Ballet (1964–70), and New York City Ballet (1970–85), where he created central roles in works by George Balanchine and Robbins and choreographed such ballets as *Menuetto* (1984). In 1985 he retired as a performer and became director of the San Francisco Ballet. TOBI TOBIAS

Bibliography: Kirstein, Lincoln, *The New York City Ballet* (1973).

tomato

Tomato is the common name for a perennial herb, *Lycopersicon lycopersicum,* of the NIGHTSHADE family, Solanaceae, and for its edible fruit. Like the potato and the green pepper, to which it is closely related, the tomato originated in Central America. Spanish explorers introduced tomato seeds to Europe and to North America, but the "love apple" did not become popular in either area until the 19th century.

Botanically, the tomato is a fruit, but for purposes of trade it is classified as a vegetable. Because tomatoes are warm-season plants and sensitive to frosts, they are grown as annuals in temperate climates. Rich in potassium and vitamins A and C, varieties range in size from 2 cm (less than 1 in) in diameter to over 15 cm (6 in); in color from white to yellow to orange to deep red; in shape from ovals to oblongs to teardrops; and in flavor from highly acidic to very sweet. They are cultivated commercially in every U.S. state except Alaska.

Tomatoes are the most widely used canned vegetable in the United States. About 75 percent of the total tomato crop

The tomato, L. esculentum, *became popular in the United States only in the 19th century. Illustrated are* (left) *a plant with large-fruited red tomatoes in various stages of ripeness;* (upper left) *flowers and newly set fruit;* (upper middle) *the large-fruited red tomato, which is the most common variety;* (lower middle) *yellow large-fruited and pear tomatoes;* (upper right) *cherry tomatoes; and* (lower right) *the Italian plum tomato, used in Italian sauces and pastes.*

is processed into juice, canned tomatoes, sauces, pastes, and catsup. New varieties have been developed with qualities that make them harvestable by machine; they all ripen simultaneously and have tough skins and a squarish shape. In the United States, California, Michigan, and Ohio lead in growing processing tomatoes. Florida is the leading producer of fresh tomatoes, although some of the fresh produce available in winter is imported from Mexico and Israel, or from Dutch greenhouses. Yearly U.S. production averages about 7.7 million metric tons (8.5 million U.S. tons), grown on 158,000 hectares (390,000 acres).   O. A. LORENZ

Bibliography: DuBose, F., *The Total Tomato* (1985); Gould, W., *Tomato Production, Processing and Quality Evaluation,* 2d ed. (1983).

tomb

A tomb is a place of BURIAL, in the form of a SARCOPHAGUS, crypt, vault, or chamber, located either above or below ground. The term *tomb* also refers to monuments erected over graves to commemorate the dead. Chamber tombs built of huge boulders or smaller stones were constructed in many parts of prehistoric Europe from about 4000 to 1000 BC (see EUROPEAN PREHISTORY). They were often used for collective burials and were usually covered with a mound of earth or piled-up stones. The most common types of stone-built chamber tombs are the gallery grave, a single axial chamber, and the passage grave, a round, square, or irregularly shaped chamber entered through a narrow, stone-faced passage (see MEGALITH).

In ancient Egypt the earliest monumental tomb was the MASTABA of the Predynastic Period (c.3500–3100 BC), a rectangular structure with a flat top and either stepped or sloping sides. By about 3000 BC the PYRAMIDS came into use as tomb monuments, the most spectacular being those of the Old Kingdom rulers Khufu, Khafre, and Menkaure, at Giza. During the New Kingdom (1570–1085 BC), royal dead often were buried in rock-cut tombs excavated deep into the sides of mountains. A notable example is the tomb of Queen Hatshepsut at DEIR EL-BAHRI, with elaborate colonnades and processional ramps at the entrance (see EGYPTIAN ART AND ARCHITECTURE).

The most impressive tombs associated with ancient AEGEAN CIVILIZATION are beehive-shaped stone chambers called *tholoi.* The largest and best preserved of these corbel-roofed structures, the so-called Treasury of Atreus (late 14th century BC), at MYCENAE, rises to a height of about 13.5 m (45 ft). Classical Greek tombs dating from the 5th century BC often were marked by a STELE, an upright stone slab usually bearing a commemorative inscription and sometimes also fine relief decoration. Among the most magnificent tombs of ancient times was the structure built (c.350 BC) at Halicarnassus (mod-

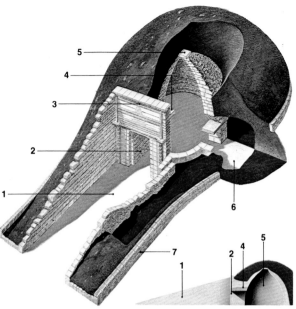

This cutaway diagram illustrates the construction of the Treasury of Atreus (14th century BC), the largest Mycenaean domed tomb. The dromos (1), a long, narrow, uncovered passage, leads to an entrance (2) with a facade (3), supported by a double lintel (4) and once embellished with colored stone pilasters. The tholos (5) is adjoined by a side chamber (6) that was the actual burial crypt. A retaining wall (7) surrounded the base of the mound covering the tomb.

ern Bodrum, Turkey) for Mausolus, the ruler of Caria, and his spouse, Artemisia. The colonnaded edifice, now almost totally destroyed, was about 50 m (165 ft) high and was surmounted by a truncated pyramid supporting a four-horse chariot. Considered one of the SEVEN WONDERS OF THE WORLD, the Mausoleum of Halicarnassus is the origin of the term *mausoleum,* which may be applied to any aboveground architectural funerary monument.

In the ancient Mediterranean world the large underground

The Tomb of the Reliefs (3d century BC) from the Etruscan necropolis at Caere, Italy, is an underground chamber built to resemble the interior of an Etruscan home. The rock-cut tomb is decorated with fine painted stucco reliefs of household utensils and weapons.

placed on top of the tomb was an effigy sculpture of the deceased, represented kneeling in prayer or as a gisant (a reclining figure usually shown lying in repose or in the form of a decaying corpse). A splendid example of late-16th-century sepulchral sculpture is Germain Pilon's monumental tomb of Henry II and Catherine de Médicis (1565–72; Abbey of Saint-Denis, Paris), in which appear two pairs of idealized statues of the couple—one pair as living and one as dead.

During the baroque and neoclassical periods tomb monuments often displayed a complex tableau of sculptures intended as a dramatic allegorical statement about life and death, as in François Girardon's tomb of Richelieu (begun 1675; Church of the Sorbonne, Paris). With the work of Antonio CANOVA and other neoclassical sculptors religious symbols began to disappear almost entirely from tomb monuments. After the 18th century fewer and fewer tombs were placed inside churches. Important personages were buried mainly in churchyards, such as the famous Père Lachaise in Paris, or in specially erected mausoleums. Notable 19th- and 20th-century tombs include that of Napoleon, in the Dome des Invalides in Paris; Ulysses S. Grant's tomb, in New York City; and the Lenin Mausoleum, in Red Square, Moscow. Several countries honor their war dead with tombs for the UNKNOWN SOLDIER.

Bibliography: Ariès, Philippe, *Images of Man and Death* (Eng. trans., 1985); Grinsell, Leslie V., *Barrow, Pyramid and Tomb* (1975); Hertling L., and Kirschbaum, E., *The Roman Catacombs and Their Martyrs*, rev. ed. (1960); Paludan, Ann, *The Imperial Ming Tombs* (1981); Panofsky, Erwin, *Tomb Sculpture* (1964); Rush, Alfred C., *Death and Burial in Christian Antiquity* (1941).

Tombalbaye, N'Garta [tahm-bul-bah'-yay, uhn-gahr'-tah]

N'Garta (originally François) Tombalbaye, b. June 15, 1918, d. Apr. 13, 1975, was prime minister (1959–60) and first president (1960–75) of Chad. Initially a teacher, he later became a trade unionist and a member of the Parti Progressiste Tchadien (PPT). When Chad gained independence from France in 1960, Tombalbaye became head of state. Attempting to control endemic conflict between the ethnically diverse Muslims of the north and the dominant black peoples of the south, Tombalbaye, a Christian, banned all opposition parties (1962), called in French troops (1968), and instituted internal reforms. He was slain during a military coup.   L. H. GANN

Tombaugh, Clyde William [tahm'-baw]

The American astronomer Clyde W. Tombaugh, b. Streator, Ill., Feb. 4, 1906, is known for his discovery of the planet PLUTO. As an assistant at Lowell Observatory, Tombaugh continued Percival Lowell's search for a planet beyond Neptune. Using a blink microscope to compare the positions of star images on photographic plates, Tombaugh detected Pluto on Feb. 18, 1930. He subsequently obtained degrees from the University of Kansas (1936, 1939) and Arizona State University (1960) and has been a member of the astronomy department at New Mexico State University since 1955.   STEVEN J. DICK

Tombigbee River [tahm-big'-bee]

The Tombigbee River, about 845 km (525 mi) long, is a tributary of the MOBILE RIVER in Alabama. From Mississippi the Tombigbee flows southeast into Alabama, joining the Alabama River to form the Mobile River. The Tennessee-Tombigbee Waterway, opened in 1985, utilizes a stretch of the Tombigbee to connect the Tennessee River with the Gulf of Mexico.

Tombouctou: see TIMBUKTU.

Tombstone

Tombstone (1980 pop., 1,632), a city in southeastern Arizona, about 105 km (65 mi) southeast of Tucson, is famous for its past as a lawless silver-mining center of the 1880s. The Bird

The formality and elegant simplicity of the funerary monument (finished 1810) of the Italian tragic poet Vittorio Alfieri by Antonio Canova, a principal exponent of neoclassical sculpture, reflects the influence of ancient Roman art. (Santa Croce, Florence.)

chamber tombs of the ETRUSCANS often were furnished with rich fresco-type wall paintings illustrating mythological themes as well as scenes from daily life. Notable Roman tombs include the remarkable sepulcher of the baker Eurysaces and his wife, built (c.60 BC) in the shape of an enormous baker's oven, and the marble-sheathed mausoleum of Hadrian (now called the CASTEL SANT'ANGELO; see ROMAN ART AND ARCHITECTURE). Niches in the walls of the narrow subterranean passages of Rome's CATACOMBS served as a place of Christian burial from the 2d to the 5th century. A parallel tradition of ornate aristocratic tomb memorials also existed in Early Christian times, exemplified in the beautiful SANTA COSTANZA in Rome, a circular, domed structure erected (c.350) as a mausoleum for the daughter of Constantine the Great (see EARLY CHRISTIAN ART AND ARCHITECTURE).

Among cultures of the East, the most elaborate Chinese tombs date from the Ch'in (221–206 BC) and Han (202 BC–AD 220) dynasties, when vaulted underground burial chambers often were richly furnished with mural paintings and relief work and with great quantities of funerary sculpture (see CHINESE ART AND ARCHITECTURE). In Japan, during the protohistoric Tumulus period (AD 250–500), royal tombs were surmounted by immense artificial mounds (tumuli) up to about 2,500 m (8,202 ft) in circumference and 20 m (66 ft) in height (see JAPANESE ART AND ARCHITECTURE).

In the Islamic world, large, often lavish tomb monuments were built, beginning in the 10th century, for rulers and members of their families. An early masterpiece in central Asia is the brick-walled royal mausoleum of the Samanids (c.940; Bukhara, Uzbek SSR). The most famous Muslim tomb monument is the 17th-century TAJ MAHAL, in Agra, India, built for the favorite wife of the Mogul ruler Shah Jahan (see MOGUL ART AND ARCHITECTURE).

Throughout the Middle Ages and the Renaissance period in Europe, important persons commonly were entombed in a sarcophagus, crypt, or shrine within a church. Frequently

Cage Theater, the O.K. Corral, and Boothill Graveyard are the main tourist attractions. The city was declared a national historic landmark in 1962.

tombstone

Stephen Fisk, who died at 23 years of age by falling down a well in 1785, is commemorated by this elaborately carved tombstone from Wales, Mass. The verses beneath the young man's image are a grim reminder of mortality.

Tombstones are markers erected at the head or, less often, the foot of a grave for the purposes of commemorating the individual buried there. Most are vertical, although in recent years some cemeteries have required that they be set flush with the ground. Wood and metal markers are not uncommon, but most tombstones are made of stone and decorated with incised words and designs that generally convey both visual and verbal information about the deceased as well as about the meaning of death.

Tombstones have been used in various cultures for centuries. In Europe, only the upper classes had grave markers and commemorative devices until the 16th century, when the economic power of the middle classes increased and a new Protestant theology emerged that emphasized the worth of the individual. Because tombs, murals, and other monuments were too expensive for all but the rich, tombstones became the most popular form of marker for the middle class. Of particular interest because of their elaborate carvings and unusual epitaphs (inscriptions) are the tombstones of England and New England dating from the late 17th to the early 19th century. Among the many different motifs used on these markers, the three most common were the skull-faced death's head (17th to early 18th century), the cherubic-faced winged angel (mid-18th century), and the urn-and-willow (late 18th to early 19th century) (see FOLK ART).

The nature of tombstone art changed markedly with the development (mid-19th century) of the romanticized and landscaped CEMETERY. During this period, tombstone iconography began to emphasize themes of eternity and rebirth and to reflect the personal experience of the individual (as in the increasing use of symbols denoting occupations of fraternal organizations). The material used for the stones changed as well, as marble or limestone replaced slate and sandstone. Contemporary tombstones generally continue the traditions of the 19th century. Usually carved in granite by mechanical means, modern stones rarely include more than the name and dates of the deceased.

PATRICK H. BUTLER III

Bibliography: Benes, Peters, The Masks of Orthodoxy: Folk Gravestone Carving in Plymouth County, Massachusetts, 1689–1805 (1977); Burgess, Frederick, English Churchyard Memorials (1963); Deetz, James, In Small Things Forgotten (1977); Ludwig, A. I., Graven Images: New England Stonecarving and Its Symbols, 1650–1815 (1966); Stannard, D. E., The Puritan Way of Death (1977).

Tomkins, Thomas

Thomas Tomkins, b. 1572, d. June 1656, was the most famous member of a large family of English musicians. He was well known for his long period of service as organist of the Chapel Royal and Worcester Cathedral and for his numerous compositions, many of which were published in Songs or Madrigals (1622) and Musica Deo Sacra (1668). The latter contains 5 services and 95 anthems, ranging from small-scale works for men's voices to elaborate verse anthems for soloists, choir, and organ. Much of his church music remained in manuscript, however, as did his keyboard music (for virginals or organ) and his numerous compositions for consort of viols. He was a pupil of William Byrd's, whose influence is apparent in his earlier works.   DENIS STEVENS

Bibliography: Stevens, Denis, Thomas Tomkins (1957).

Tomlin, Bradley Walker

The American painter Bradley Walker Tomlin, b. Syracuse, N.Y., Aug. 19, 1899, d. May 11, 1953, worked in a number of different styles ranging from realism through cubism and surrealism and, finally, abstraction. The paintings from the last years of Tomlin's life established his reputation as one of the first exponents of abstract expressionism.

During the 1920s, Tomlin studied painting in Europe; later, he designed magazine covers for Vogue and House and Garden and also painted portraits. In 1937, impressed by surrealism and cubism, Tomlin adopted a more abstract style which, during the 1950s, evolved into geometric patterns interwoven with calligraphic markings.   VALENTIN TATRANSKY

Bibliography: Bauer, John H., Bradley Walker Tomlin (1957).

Tomonaga, Sin-itiro   [toh-moh-nah'-gah, seen-ee-chee'-roh]

The Japanese theoretical physicist Sin-itiro Tomonaga, b. Mar. 31, 1906, d. July 8, 1979, shared the 1965 Nobel Prize for physics with R. P. Feynman and J. S. Schwinger for his achievement (independent from the others) in making the mathematical predictions of quantum electrodynamics consistent with the observed physical phenomena of the special theory of relativity. A student of Werner Heisenberg's in Germany, Tomonaga joined the faculty of the Tokyo University of Education in 1941, serving as its president from 1956 to 1962.

Tompkins, Daniel D.

Daniel D. Tompkins, b. Scarsdale, N.Y., June 21, 1774, d. June 11, 1825, was vice-president of the United States (1817–25) under James MONROE. He was a New York supreme court justice (1804–07) and subsequently promoted democratic reforms as the state's governor (1807–17).

Throughout the War of 1812 he had to contend with a recalcitrant Federalist contingent in the legislature and with the threat of a British invasion from Canada. During his vice-presidency Tompkins was occupied with a long controversy arising out of charges that he had mishandled funds while serving as governor.

tonality

In its broadest sense, tonality in music means a sense of tonal gravity by which the listener consciously or subconsciously perceives that the main musical impulses arise from and flow toward one or a limited number of tone centers, the most important of these being the point of ultimate repose. In its more commonly used meaning, however, tonality is synonymous with KEY and refers to the use of the melodic and harmonic vocabulary of the major and minor system prevalent in music since the 17th century (see also ATONALITY). The main tonal center is established by the triad based on the tonic, or key note, which is the first step of the scale. The second important tonal center is the dominant, or fifth step of the scale; a possible third center is the subdominant, the fourth scale step. Chords based on these tonal centers perform specific functions and ultimately serve to strengthen the tonic (key note).

tone

The term *tone* has several distinct meanings in music: (1) a sound of definite pitch, referred to in English usage as a *note;* (2) the quality of sound produced by an instrument or voice (see MUSIC); (3) the interval consisting of two semitones, or half-steps—for example, from C to D, an interval of a major second; and (4) one of the plainsong formulas used for singing psalms and other parts of the Western liturgy.

Tone, Wolfe   [tohn]

An Irish patriot, Theobald Wolfe Tone, b. June 20, 1763, d. Nov. 19, 1798, was the most colorful leader of the Society of UNITED IRISHMEN. In 1791 he turned from an undistinguished legal career to help found the society, which eventually came to advocate Irish independence from Britain. Tone left Ireland in 1795 to avoid prosecution, and he began soliciting military assistance from revolutionary France for the United Irish cause. He accompanied an abortive French expedition to the Irish coast in December 1796. During the Irish rebellion of 1798, Tone was captured with the crew of a French vessel off Donegal. He committed suicide while awaiting execution for treason. He wrote an autobiography.   DAVID W. MILLER

Bibliography: Baylan, Henry, *Theobald Wolfe Tone* (1981); Cronin, Sean, and Roche, Richard, *Freedom the Wolfe Tone Way* (1973); Mac-Dermot, Frank, *Theobald Wolfe Tone: A Biographical Study* (1939).

tone poem: see SYMPHONIC POEM.

tong

A tong is a community or fraternal organization of Chinese in the United States. The first tongs were founded in the 1850s; they functioned as secret societies for immigrants, primarily those from the Canton region. The term is derived from the Chinese word for "hall" or "reception room." In such meeting places, family elders and village officials in China traditionally gathered to make decisions and set community policies; the word could also mean "court of justice."

When the Chinese first arrived in North America they discovered that their new environment was harsh, with many economic, political, and social restrictions. To aid and protect themselves many Chinese banded together in communal groups based on former village structures and ties. In time, competition between the various tongs resulted in much-publicized violence. These internecine wars grew to such proportions that in 1933 the U.S. government intervened and deported large numbers of their members. With changing conditions, the tongs changed. Today their role is reduced and their power curtailed, and they are only one of the many community organizations of the Chinese-Americans.

See also: ORIENTAL AMERICANS.

Tonga   [tahng'-guh]

The Kingdom of Tonga is a former British protectorate that gained independence within the Commonwealth of Nations on June 4, 1970. The kingdom is composed of an archipelago of more than 150 islands about 640 km (400 mi) east of Fiji in the South Pacific Ocean. NUKUALOFA is the capital and principal town.

LAND, PEOPLE, AND ECONOMY

Two parallel island chains extend in a north-south direction. Those to the west are volcanic and those to the east, limestone. They are divided into three major groups: Vavau in the north, Haapai in the center, and Tongatapu to the south. The limestone islands have fertile soils partially derived from volcanic ash. Average temperatures range from 24° C (75° F) in the north to 23° C (73° F) in the south, and rainfall varies from 2,286 mm (90 in) in Vavau to 1,702 mm (67 in) in Tongatapu.

KINGDOM OF TONGA

LAND. Area: 699 km² (270 mi²). Capital and largest city: Nukualofa (1984 pop., 27,740).
PEOPLE. Population (1986 est.): 104,000; density (1986 est.): 149 persons per km² (385 per mi²). Distribution (1980): 32% urban, 68% rural. Annual growth (1984): 2.8%. Official languages: Tongan, English. Major religion: Christianity.
EDUCATION AND HEALTH. Literacy (1986 est.): 90–95% of adult population. Universities (1987): none. Hospital beds (1985): 307. Physicians (1985): 53. Life expectancy (1980–85): women—64.8; men—61.0. Infant mortality (1983): 6.4 per 1,000 live births.
ECONOMY. GNP (1985): $70 million; $730 per capita. Labor distribution (1986): agriculture and fishing—75%; other—25%. Foreign trade (1985): imports—$86.4 million; exports—$10.5 million; principal trade partners—New Zealand, Australia, Japan. Currency: 1 pa'anga (Tongan dollar) = 100 seniti.
GOVERNMENT. Type: constitutional monarchy. Legislature: Legislative Assembly. Political subdivisions: 3 main island groups.
COMMUNICATIONS. Railroads (1987): none. Roads (1984): 433 km (269 mi) total. Major ports: 1. Major airfields: 1.

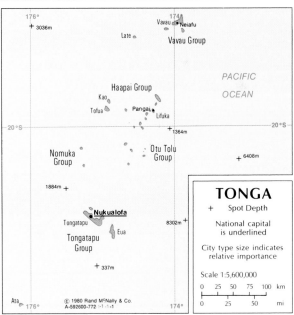

The Tongans are Polynesians and speak a language derived from Samoan. The majority of the population is Christian. Education and health care are free, and literacy is high.

Tonga is an agricultural country with copra, bananas, and vanilla the principal exports. Small-scale manufacturing and the fishing industry have expanded steadily, and tourism and remittances from Tongan workers abroad help to offset the country's large trade deficit. Tonga also receives substantial foreign aid.

GOVERNMENT AND HISTORY

The monarch and his or her privy council (including the prime minister) form the executive branch of government.

The legislative assembly is composed of 23 members, of whom 7 are popularly elected.

Capt. James Cook arrived there in 1773 and named the archipelago the "Friendly Islands." A constitutional monarchy was established by King George Tupou I in 1875, and Tonga became a British protectorate in 1900. The present monarch is King Taufa'ahau Tupou IV, who succeeded his mother, Queen Salote, in 1965.   JOHN W. SNADEN

Bibliography: Latukefu, Sione, *Church and State in Tonga* (1974); Rutherford, Noel, ed., *Friendly Islands: A History of Tonga* (1978); Wood, A. J., *A History and Geography of Tonga*, rev. ed. (1963).

Tonga Trench: see OCEANIC TRENCHES.

tongue

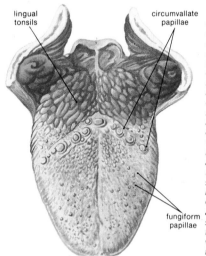

lingual tonsils

circumvallate papillae

fungiform papillae

The human tongue is a mass of skeletal muscle covered by a mucous membrane. It is the primary site of the taste buds, is an essential part of speech production, and is used in chewing and swallowing. The anterior section contains papillae, which house the taste buds. Filiform papillae are long and thin, and fungiform papillae are shaped like mushroom caps. Circumvallate papillae are flattened structures found in front of the root, which is covered by the lingual tonsils.

The tongue, a muscular organ on the floor of the mouth, provides the sense of taste and assists in chewing, swallowing, and speaking. It is firmly anchored by connective tissues to the front and side walls of the pharynx, or throat, and to the hyoid bone in the neck. The front two-thirds of the tongue, called the body, is demarcated from the back one-third, called the root, by a V-shaped boundary. The upper surface of the body of the tongue has numerous raised projections called papillae. The upper surface of the sides of the root of the tongue exhibits irregular bulgings called the lingual TONSILS.

Three types of papillae are prominent in adult humans. A fourth type, foliate papillae, is rudimentary in humans but is well developed along the dorsolateral aspect of the rear, or posterior, part of the tongue in many animals. The most numerous type, filiform, appears under the microscope as inverted V-shaped structures. They do not contain taste buds and function mainly to provide friction to help in the movement of food. Scattered among them are the second most abundant type, the fungiform papillae. These knoblike projections, located mostly on the upper central area of the tongue, contain the taste buds. The third type, the vallate, or circumvallate, papillae, is the largest and also contains taste buds. About 13 in number, they occur in the V-shaped row which demarcates the body from the root of the tongue.   ROY HARTENSTEIN

tongue-tie

Tongue-tie is a birth deformity in which the mobility of the tongue is restricted by an abnormally short frenum, the vertical fold of mucous membrane that anchors the tongue to the floor of the mouth. The condition affects pronunciation but is easily corrected by surgically cutting the frenum.   PETER L. PETRAKIS

tongue worm

Tongue worms, bloodsucking parasites in the phylum Pentastomida, are found in the respiratory systems of several animals, including humans. They require two hosts in the life cycle. The adult *Linguatula serrata* lives in carnivores. Herbivores act as hosts for the nymphs, which encapsulate in visceral organs. Carnivores become infected when they feed on dead intermediate hosts. Symptoms, although not always present, include coughing and difficulty in breathing. No effective treatment has been found.

tongues, speaking in

Speaking in tongues (glossolalia) is a Christian religious phenomenon in which the believer, in an ecstatic state, speaks in a foreign language or utters unintelligible sounds that are taken to contain a divine message. Many Christians believe the genuine gift of tongues to have been confined to earliest Christianity, at PENTECOST, and during conversion experiences. Modern revivalist movements such as the Pentacostalists and Charismatics believe it to be given in our time as a testimony to the special presence of the HOLY SPIRIT. Many psychologists explain the phenomenon as a hypnotic trance that results from religious excitement.   PAUL MERRITT BASSETT

Bibliography: Goodman, F. D., *Speaking in Tongues* (1972); Kelsey, Morton T., *Tongue-Speaking* (1964); Samarin, W. J., *Tongues of Men and Angels* (1972).

Tonkin   [tahng'-kin]

Tonkin, the northernmost portion of Vietnam, was constituted as a protectorate during the period of French colonial rule in INDOCHINA. The area is centered on the RED RIVER delta and extends on the north to the Chinese border. HANOI and HAIPHONG are the major cities.

Tonkin was the first home in Southeast Asia of the Vietnamese, who moved into the area from their original location in southeastern coastal China under pressure from the expanding Chinese. From the 2d century BC to the 10th century AD the Chinese ruled Tonkin (and adjacent northern ANNAM). France intervened militarily in Tonkin in 1873–74 and again in 1882. In 1883, Tonkin became a French protectorate as part of Indochina.

China's historical interest in Tonkin was reflected anew in the immediate post–World War II occupation by Nationalist Chinese troops. The French negotiated a Chinese evacuation in 1946, but France was unable to regain its control over Tonkin's countryside. Although Hanoi and Haiphong remained in French hands until 1954, rural Tonkin was increasingly dominated by the insurgent VIET MINH, led by HO CHI MINH.   RICHARD BUTWELL

Tonkin, Gulf of

The Gulf of Tonkin is a shallow, irregularly shaped extension of the South China Sea, about 500 km (300 mi) long and 250 km (150 mi) wide. It is bordered on the north and east by China and on the west by Vietnam. The main port is HAIPHONG in Vietnam.

In 1964 the gulf was the scene of a reported North Vietnamese attack on two U.S. destroyers. The resultant Tonkin Gulf Resolution was used to justify an increased U.S. military presence in Vietnam.   WILLIAM WITHINGTON

Tonkin Gulf Resolution

On Aug. 5, 1964, U.S. president Lyndon B. Johnson placed before Congress a measure, known as the Tonkin Gulf Resolution, that gave the president broad powers in responding to attacks on American forces and that served as the basis for the subsequent increasing involvement of the United States in the VIETNAM WAR. The resolution, passed 2 days later by both houses of Congress with only two "no" votes (by senators Wayne Morse and Ernest Gruening), was a response to alleged attacks earlier in August by North Vietnamese torpedo boats on the U.S. destroyers *Maddox* and *C. Turner Joy,* which were operating in the Gulf of Tonkin. Although the American ships were not damaged, retaliation against the North Vietnamese was carried out quickly and on a large scale. As disaffection with the role of the United States in Vietnam grew, many members of Congress questioned the wisdom of the measure, and in 1967 the Senate Foreign Relations Committee conducted an investigation into the matter. Congress repealed the Tonkin Gulf Resolution on Dec. 31, 1970.

Bibliography: Galloway, John, *The Gulf of Tonkin Resolution* (1970).

tonsillitis

Tonsillitis is an acute or chronic inflammation of the tonsils, located near the back of the tongue. (The adenoids, lymph glands located behind the nose, are often simultaneously inflamed.) Tonsillitis, which usually develops suddenly as a result of a streptococcal infection but may also be caused by a viral infection, is characterized by sore throat, fever, chills, headache, poor appetite, and weakness. The tonsils become swollen and red, with streaks of pus often visible on their surface. Acute tonsillitis usually clears up in about a week, but antibiotics are often administered to prevent complications such as middle-ear and sinus infections, formation of deep abscesses, spread of infection to other organs, and chronic tonsillitis. In chronic tonsillitis the tonsils tend to flare up in episodes of acute infection; the usual treatment is surgical removal. Tonsillitis is more common in children than in adults.   PETER L. PETRAKIS

Bibliography: Adams, George L., et al., *Boies's Fundamentals of Otolaryngology,* 5th ed. (1978); Parkinson, Roy H., *Tonsil and Allied Problems* (1951).

tonsils

Tonsils are spongy lymphoid tissues at the back of the throat, composed mainly of lymphocytic cells held together by fibrous connective tissue. There are three types. The palatine tonsils, usually referred to as "the tonsils," are visible between the arches that extend from the uvula (bell-shaped structure) to the floor of the mouth. The pharyngeal tonsils, usually referred to as the adenoids, lie at the back of the throat. The lingual tonsils are on the upper surface of each side of the back of the TONGUE. The tonsils function to protect the pharynx and the remainder of the body from infectious organisms. Chronic or acute inflammation of the tonsils, called tonsillitis, may serve as a source of infection elsewhere in the body.

Bibliography: Antoni, Franz, and Staub, Maria, eds., *Tonsils: Structure, Immunology, and Chemistry* (1978).

tonsure [tahn'-shur]

Tonsure (from Latin, "to shave") is the ritual practice found in many cultures of clipping hair from the head to mark a transition in life, usually in a religious context. In Buddhism, Hinduism, Jainism, and Christianity it is part of the initiation into monastic life or the priesthood. Christian tonsure is found as early as the 4th century. In the Eastern church the whole head was traditionally shaved, although more recently the hair is merely cut close. In the West a dispute arose (6th and 7th century) between the Roman church, which shaved the crown of the head leaving a fringe of hair around the outer portion of the head, and the Celtic church, which shaved the front of the head. The Roman practice dominated. Tonsure was abolished by the Roman Catholic church in 1972.

Tonty, Henri de [tahn-tee']

Henri de Tonty (or Tonti), b. probably in Paris, c.1650, d. September 1704, fur trader and explorer, tirelessly promoted French interests in the interior of North America. He went to Canada from France in 1687, after 10 years' military service in Europe. As lieutenant of Robert Cavelier, sieur de LA SALLE, Tonty supervised (1679–80) the construction of Fort Conti below Niagara Falls, of the ship the *Griffon* on Lake Erie, and of Fort Crévecoeur on the Illinois River. In 1682, Tonty and La Salle followed the Mississippi to its mouth, returning north to build Fort Saint Louis on the Illinois and to persuade the tribes of the region to move close to the fort. In 1684, he helped to hold off a strong Iroquois attack on the Illinois country; but in 1687 he could mobilize only 80 Illinois warriors to assist New France's governor in an offensive against the Iroquois. Having been unable to find La Salle at the mouth of the Mississippi in 1686, Tonty learned only 3 years later of his superior's death. From 1690 to 1700 he traded aggressively in the Illinois country and then helped Pierre Le Moyne, sieur d'IBERVILLE, establish a post at the mouth of the

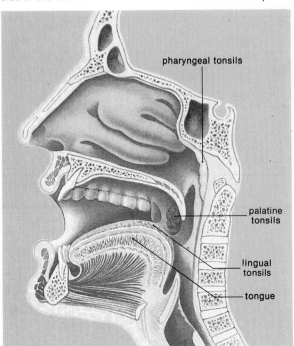

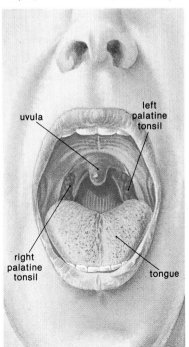

Tonsils are located at the back of the mouth and in the throat. Composed of lymphoid tissue, they help defend the body against disease organisms, such as bacteria and viruses, that are carried in the air. The tonsils form lymphocytes—white blood cells that produce antibodies—which combat harmful organisms that become trapped in the mucous membrane lining the mouth, nose, and throat. The palatine tonsils (side and front view) are located on both sides of the back of the mouth. The pharyngeal tonsils, or adenoids (side view), are found in the throat at the back of the nasal cavity. The lingual tonsils (side view) are located on the back of the tongue.

Mississippi. He subsequently worked to keep the allegiance of the Indians of that region to French interests.

F. J. THORPE

Bibliography: Brebner, J. B., *The Explorers of North America* (1933); Murphy, E. R., *Henry de Tonti, Fur Trader of the Mississippi* (1941); Osler, E. B., *La Salle* (1967).

Tony Awards

The Tony Awards, the most prestigious of American stage awards, honor distinguished achievement in 27 categories of theater production. Winners receive medallions from the League of New York Theatres and Producers on behalf of the American Theatre Wing, which established the annual presentations in 1947 to honor its former chairwoman, the actress, director, and producer Antoinette Perry (1888-1946).

Bibliography: Stevenson, Isabella, ed., *The Tony Award* (1975).

Tooker, George

George Tooker, b. Brooklyn, N.Y., Aug. 5, 1920, is an American realist painter whose work has a strongly surrealist quality. Set in anonymous contemporary architectural vistas, Tooker's subject is the paranoiac feelings of the contemporary city dweller.

In *The Subway* (1950; Whitney Museum of American Art, New York), one sees a woman becoming aware of her isolation and the menace of an aseptic subway station peopled with ominous, threatening figures. Most of Tooker's work is executed in egg tempera, which allows him to achieve the greatest possible realism in his work.

ROWLAND ELZEA

tool and die making

Tool and die making is a very highly skilled trade in which a machinist uses machine tools, hand tools, and grinding and polishing equipment to make such tools as jigs, fixtures, and dies. The enormous quantities of metal products that are consumed in modern times—kitchen utensils, refrigerators, and automobiles, for instance—are the direct result of the expertise of machinists in the tool and die maker's trade.

The term *die* in metalworking usually refers to a production device used to produce piece parts from sheet metal by punching, shearing, bending, or drawing. Forging dies are also used for forming hot metals under pressure. Thread-cutting tools, used to make external threads on bolts, are also called dies. Tooling includes holding fixtures for workpieces and jigs, which are used to guide cutting tools into the workpiece.

A die set consists of two die plates, the upper of which is called a punch holder and the lower of which is called a die plate. The punch of a press tool enters into an opening or cavity, which is part of the die. A punch press is a machine that forces the two halves of the die together to rapidly produce identical parts from sheet metal. Dies are made from special tool steels that are often hardened and tempered after machining, and they are subsequently ground and finished to very close tolerances and smooth finishes.

The tool and die maker removes stock from the tool steel blank by band sawing, milling, and drilling and by using other metal-cutting machines such as a die sinker. Nontraditional machining methods are rapidly displacing the use of machine tools for die making because of their versatility and speed, especially in machining previously hardened metals. Among these new processes is the electrical discharge machine (EDM), in which an electrode made of metal or graphite is made to pass into or through a metal die plate. In this way, the machining of the die cavity is accomplished by gradual erosion from a pulsed spark discharge while the die part is submerged in oil. Metals as hard as tungsten carbide are easily formed into die plates by this method. Electrochemical milling (ECM), electrochemical grinding (ECG), and ultrasonic machining are also used for die making.

JOHN E. NEELY

Bibliography: Arnett, Harold E., and Smith, Donald N., *The Tool and Die Industry* (1975).

Toombs, Robert

An American congressman and senator, Robert Augustus Toombs, b. near Washington, Ga., July 2, 1810, d. Dec. 15, 1885, was a Confederate leader during the U.S. Civil War. Toombs practiced law and served in the Georgia legislature (1837-40, 1841-44) and the U.S. House of Representatives (1845-53) before entering (1853) the Senate. A Whig until 1850, he became a Democrat and a leading defender of Southern rights.

In 1861, realizing that the Republicans would never permit the expansion of slavery, Toombs became a secessionist and withdrew from the Senate. He hoped to become president of the Confederacy but served instead as Jefferson DAVIS's secretary of state. Unhappy in that post, Toombs resigned in July 1861 and was made a general. Not receiving a promotion after playing a prominent role in the Battle of Antietam (1862), he resigned from the army and became an outspoken critic of the Davis administration. In 1865, Toombs fled to Cuba and then to Europe. He returned to Georgia in 1867 and resumed the practice of law.

RICHARD M. MCMURRY

Bibliography: Thompson, William Y., *Robert Toombs of Georgia* (1966).

Toomer, Jean

The writer Jean Toomer, b. Washington, D.C., Dec. 26, 1894, d. Mar. 30, 1967, is best known for his experimental novel, *Cane* (1923), a thematically unified collection of short fiction, poetry, and drama that juxtaposes the lives of Southern rural blacks with those of their Northern urban counterparts. A prominent figure in the HARLEM RENAISSANCE, Toomer abandoned writing after *Cane*'s initial lukewarm reception and retreated with his wife to southeastern Pennsylvania.

tooth decay: see TEETH.

toothwort

Toothwort (pepperroot) is the common name for about 10 species of perennial European, Asian, and North American herbs of the genus *Dentaria*, mustard family, Cruciferae. The name refers to the toothed or scaly root stock, which is often pleasant tasting. The four-petaled, white or pale purple flowers form a terminal cluster that is valued in wild or rock gardens.

FRANK B. SALISBURY

topaz

Topaz (left) is a transparent aluminum fluorosilicate mineral that occurs as hard prismatic crystals of various colors. Long prized as a gemstone, the golden variety in particular is cut into brilliant faceted jewels (right).

Topaz, an aluminum SILICATE MINERAL [$Al_2(F, OH)_2SiO_4$], is a highly valued gemstone and the birthstone for November. It forms colorless to straw yellow, bluish or brown, transparent to subtranslucent prismatic crystals (orthorhombic system). Topaz occurs in high-temperature veins, in pegmatites, and in granites and rhyolites, where it is one of the last minerals to form. Hardness is 8, luster is vitreous, and specific gravity is

3.4 to 3.6; it has one highly perfect cleavage. Common topaz is widespread, and fine gem material comes from Saxony, the Ural Mountains, Brazil, Japan, Mexico, and the Cairngorm Mountains in Scotland.

Topchiyev, Aleksandr Vasilievich [tohp'-chee-ef]

Aleksandr Vasilievich Topchiyev, b. Aug. 9 (N.S.), 1907, d. Dec. 27, 1962, was a Russian chemist known for his work on the reactions and synthesis of petroleum hydrocarbons, in particular the nitration of hydrocarbons and the use of boron trifluoride as a catalyst. This work greatly advanced the development of the petrochemical industry in the post–World War II USSR.   O. BERTRAND RAMSAY

Topeka [tuh-pee'-kuh]

Topeka is the capital and third largest city of Kansas. Located in the northeastern part of the state and bisected by the Kansas River, the city is the seat of Shawnee County and has a population of 115,266 (1980). Topeka is a rail hub and an important shipping and marketing center for the farm products of the surrounding rich agricultural region. The city has varied industries, including flour, tire, and pharmaceutical manufacturing and meat-packing plants. Topeka is the site of Washburn University (1865) and of the Menninger Clinic.

Topeka was founded in 1854 by antislavery colonists led by Charles Robinson and Cyrus Holliday. Holliday later chose the city as the terminus for his railroad—the Atchison, Topeka, and Santa Fe. The city was a center of conflict between free-soil and proslavery factions in Kansas Territory in the mid-19th century. Topeka became the state capital in 1861.

Topkapi Palace Museum [tohp-kah'-pee]

The Topkapi Palace Museum in Istanbul, Turkey, housed in the former sultans' palace, contains extensive art collections and royal treasures. Construction of the sprawling Ottoman palace complex with its many courtyards was begun in 1454. Most of the buildings date from the reign of Suleiman the Magnificent (1520–66), but additions were made through the 19th century. Stonework, woodcarving, ceramic tile, and colored glass are sumptuously combined in the interior decorations. Within the palace is kept the collection of imperial jewels, including an 86-carat diamond and a magnificent 17th-century emerald- and diamond-studded dagger. Also on display are rare swords and jewel-encrusted thrones of the sultans; Islamic calligraphy, miniatures, and textiles; and one of the largest collections of European and Oriental porcelains in the world.

topography

Topography is the description or mapping of the physical features of any given area on the Earth's surface. The graphic symbols used to display the features include hachures (parallel lines indicating land-surface variations), contour lines, plastic shading, and color layers. (See MAPS AND MAPMAKING.)
                                                ROBERT S. WEINER

topology

Topology is a branch of pure mathematics that deals with abstract spaces, which may be thought of as generalizations of ordinary three-dimensional space. That is, whereas classical geometry is concerned with measurable quantities of position, such as angle, area, and so forth, topology is concerned with abstract, unmeasurable properties of relative position and space. It also considers functions that map one abstract space into another. Topology began to evolve from algebra and analysis as a separate branch at the beginning of the 20th century. One aspect of topology deals with geometric figures that can be deformed into one another without tearing the figures or attaching points of them together. Because deformations of this type can be carried out by stretching a rubber sheet, topology is sometimes known as rubber-sheet geome-

try. Modern topology, however, extends beyond this introductory aspect of the subject. Some particular structures and problems of topology are treated in the articles FOUR-COLOR THEOREM, KLEIN BOTTLE, KÖNIGSBERG BRIDGE PROBLEM, and MÖBIUS STRIP.

METRIC SPACES

The accurate mathematical definition of an abstract topological space—a set with no structure but the relative position of its elements—is beyond the scope of this article. Here attention is restricted to spaces that are situated in some Euclidean space, described as follows. Euclidean 1-space, called R^1, is the line. Euclidean 2-space, R^2, is the plane; that is, R^2 consists of all ordered pairs (x,y) of real numbers—x and y may be thought of as the coordinates of the point (x,y). Similarly, 3-space, R^3, consists of ordered triples (x,y,z) of real numbers, R^4 is all quadruples (x,y,z,w), and so on. Thus a Euclidean n-space, R^n, can be defined for each positive integer n.

In each of these spaces there is a means of measuring distance, which is called a *metric*. If a,b are in R^1, the distance $d(a,b)$ from a to b is defined as $d(a,b) = \sqrt{(a-b)^2}$. If $a = (x_1,y_1)$ and $b = (x_2,y_2)$ are in R^2, the distance between them is defined as $d(a,b) = \sqrt{(x_1 - x_2)^2 + (y_1 - y_2)^2}$. Distances can be defined similarly for higher spaces.

If A is some subset of R^n, the metric of R^n can also be used to measure the distance between any two points of A because any points of A are also points of R^n. In this way any subset of some Euclidean space becomes a metric space, and this is what will be meant by the word *space* in this article.

GRAPHS

A reasonably simple, yet interesting, class of spaces is the finite graphs. A finite graph G consists of a finite set of points, $v_1, \ldots, v_m$ in R^3, and some straight line segments $e^1, \ldots, e^k$ joining some of these points. The v's are called the vertices, and the e's are called edges. The vertices are to be situated so that no two edges intersect except at vertices. It is not difficult to prove that this can always be done.

On the other hand, this cannot always be done if the graphs are constructed in R^2 instead of R^3. In particular, the following two graphs cannot be put in the plane (without having edges intersect), even if bending of the edges is allowed.

g_1
(5 vertices, 5 edges)

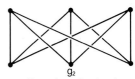

g_2
(6 vertices, 9 edges)

If G_1 and G_2 cannot be put in R^2, then no larger graph that contains G_1 or G_2 as a part can be put in R^2 either. In 1930, C. Kuratowski proved that any graph G that contains neither G_1 nor G_2 can be put in R^2.

Even though graphs have been studied for a long time, many significant questions about graphs still remain unanswered and are studied in graph theory.

CLOSED SURFACES

Closed surfaces are an important class of spaces. These are spaces that, near any one point, look like a (possibly bent) piece of a plane. For example, in space R^3, S^2 is to be considered the set of all points (x,y,z) whose distance from $(0,0,0)$ equals 1; that is, all (x,y,z) such that $\sqrt{x^2 + y^2 + z^2} = 1$. The set S^2 is called the 2-sphere and is just like the surface of a ball. It is a closed surface because any point of S^2 has a small neighborhood that is a bent disk.

In space R^2 the unit square S, that is, all (x,y) such that $0 \leq x \leq 1$ and $0 \leq y \leq 1$, is not a closed surface because a point with x or y equal to 0 or 1 will not have a disk neighborhood—some points have only half-disk neighborhoods, and the four corners have only quarter-disk neighborhoods. But suppose the square is bent until its top and bottom edges come in contact and are glued together to produce a cylinder.

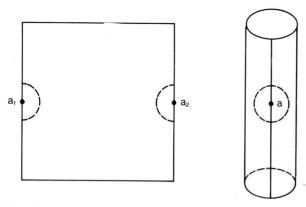

Then the points a_1 and a_2 become the single point a, which now has a disk neighborhood. The points on the two ends of the cylinder, however, still have only half-disk neighborhoods. The surface can be made closed by gluing these two ends together. Actually, two different ways exist for doing this. First, the cylinder can be bent around until the two ends come together, giving a closed surface called a TORUS.

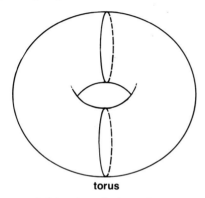

torus

The other way of gluing the cylinder ends together is more difficult to visualize because it cannot be done in 3-space (R^3). But in 4-space (R^4), the ends can be attached as indicated schematically

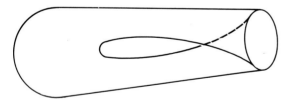

without causing any self-intersections of the surface. The resulting closed surface is called a Klein bottle. It cannot be put in the space R^3.

Another important closed surface that cannot be put in R^3 is the projective plane, which can be described as follows. The two ends of a strip of paper are attached after putting in a half twist, producing the Möbius strip M.

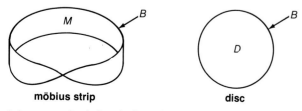

möbius strip   disc

It is easy to check that the boundary B of M is connected—that is, no natural way to break the boundary into two parts

exists. Thus it is the same as the boundary of the disk D. The projective plane is the closed surface obtained by gluing these two boundaries together.

HOMEOMORPHISMS

It has been implicit in the discussion up to now that a space can be bent and still be considered the same space. But if parts of it are glued together, it must then be considered a new space. This distinction can be made precise by introducing the concepts of the CONTINUITY of a function and the homeomorphism of functions and figures.

The idea of continuity is that the function "does not tear" the space or that "nearby points go to nearby points." This concept is defined as follows. Let f be a function sending points of a space X to points of a space Y. The notation here is that a point x in X is sent by f into a point in Y denoted by $f(x)$. Then f is to be continuous

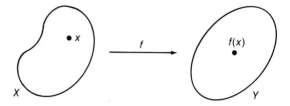

at a point x_0 if points near x_0 go to points near $f(x_0)$. A function is a one-to-one correspondence if for every point y in Y there is exactly one point x in X such that $f(x) = y$. If f is one-to-one, the result is a function f^{-1} (the inverse of f) mapping Y to X by letting $f^{-1}(y)$ be the unique value of x for which $f(x) = y$. A function f from X to Y is a homeomorphism if it is one-to-one and if both f and f^{-1} are continuous. Figures are called homeomorphic if one can be deformed into the other without tearing or attaching points together. Thus a sphere, a cube, and a pyramid are homeomorphic figures.

Two spaces are topologically equivalent if a homeomorphism from one to the other exists. A property is a topological property if it is unchanged by a homeomorphism. It can sometimes be difficult to decide if two spaces are homeomorphic. Two very specific and simply described 5-dimensional spaces X and Y exist; for 25 years topologists tried to decide whether or not X and Y were homeomorphic, but only during the late 1970s was it finally proved that they are.

MORTON L. CURTIS

Bibliography: Barr, Stephen, *Experiments in Topology* (1972); Chinn, William G., and Steenrod, Norman E., *First Concepts of Topology* (1966); Christie, Dan E., *Basic Topology* (1976); Pedoe, Dan, *The Gentle Art of Mathematics* (1958; new ed., 1973); Wallace, Andrew H., *An Introduction to Algebraic Topology* (1957).

Torah   [tohr'-uh]

Torah (a Hebrew word meaning "instruction"), in its broadest sense, refers to the entire body of Jewish teaching incorporated in the Old Testament and the Talmud and in later rabbinical commentaries. In early biblical times, the term meant the oral instruction of the priests on ritual, legal, or moral questions. Gradually the name was applied to written collections of the priestly decisions, most specifically to the written Mosaic law contained in the first five books of the Bible—Genesis, Exodus, Leviticus, Numbers, and Deuteronomy—also called the Pentateuch. The Torah, in the latter sense, is preserved on scrolls kept in the ark of every synagogue; reading of the Torah is central to the synagogue service.

Bibliography: Noth, Martin, *A History of Pentateuchal Traditions*, trans. by Bernhard W. Anderson (1972); Sanders, James A., *Torah and Canon* (1972).

Tordesillas, Treaty of   [tohr-day-seel'-yahs]

The Treaty of Tordesillas, concluded on June 7, 1494, decided the rival claims of Spain and Portugal to lands in the New World. After the first voyage of Columbus, Spain secured papal confirmation of its claims to non-Christian lands discovered west of a line of demarcation 100 leagues west of the

Cape Verde Islands. Portugal received the lands to the east of this line. JOHN II of Portugal, however, was dissatisfied with the plan and negotiated a treaty with the Spanish, signed at Tordesillas, Spain, moving the line 270 leagues farther west. The shift made possible the successful Portuguese claim to Brazil, discovered in 1500 by Pedro Cabral.   ROBIN BUSS

Torelli, Giuseppe   [toh-rel'-lee]

The Italian violinist and composer Giuseppe Torelli, b. Apr. 22, 1658, d. Feb. 8, 1709, was a pioneer in the development of the concerto grosso and perhaps the originator of the solo violin concerto. He was active in Bologna (1686–95, 1701–09), Ansbach (1697–99), and Vienna (1699–1701). His *concerti grossi* (published 1709)—together with those of Arcangelo Corelli—represent, in balance and nobility, the classical ideal of the form. His other works include sinfonias, trio sonatas, and other chamber music for strings.

Tories: see LOYALISTS.

Torii Kiyomasu: see KIYOMASU.

Torii Kiyonaga: see KIYONAGA.

Torii Kiyonobu: see KIYONOBU.

tornado

The word *tornado* is probably derived from the Spanish *tronada* ("thunderstorm"). Tornadoes are also popularly called twisters or cyclones and are characterized by rapidly rotating columns of air hanging from cumulonimbus clouds. They are generally observed as tube- or funnel-shaped clouds. At ground level they are usually small in diameter (generally 0.8 km/0.5 mi or less) and travel an average of only about 8 to 24 km (5 to 15 mi). Ground contact is often of an intermittent nature—lasting usually less than a couple of minutes in any particular area—because the funnel skips along.

CAUSES AND CLASSIFICATION

Tornadoes are the result of great instability in the atmosphere and are often associated with severe THUNDERSTORMS. The full details of the formation of tornadoes are not known; the existence of a strong updraft, such as that generated by a severe thunderstorm, and the conservation of angular (rotational) momentum, however, are fundamental considerations. Recent theories suggest that the falling of rain or hail drags air from aloft, and the resultant inrush of air tightens the rotational motion. The tornado proper is inside the tornado cyclone, an area of low pressure about 8 to 24 km (5 to 15 mi) in diameter with wind speeds of approximately 240 km/h (150 mph) or less. The tornado center is an area of exceedingly low pressure. This extreme pressure gradient causes buildings to explode as the tornado effect is felt, if they are not sufficiently ventilated for rapid adjustment to the change in pressure. Wind speeds of approximately 800 km/h (500 mph) have been inferred from the resultant damage.

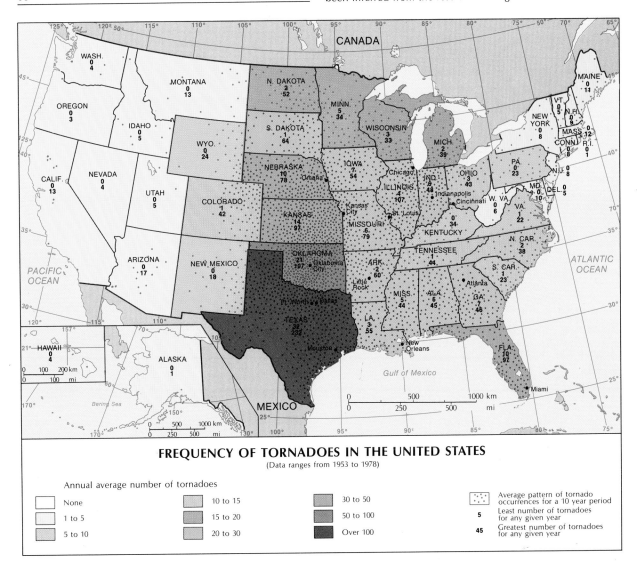

FREQUENCY OF TORNADOES IN THE UNITED STATES
(Data ranges from 1953 to 1978)

Annual average number of tornadoes

None	10 to 15	30 to 50
1 to 5	15 to 20	50 to 100
5 to 10	20 to 30	Over 100

Average pattern of tornado occurrences for a 10 year period

5 Least number of tornadoes for any given year

45 Greatest number of tornadoes for any given year

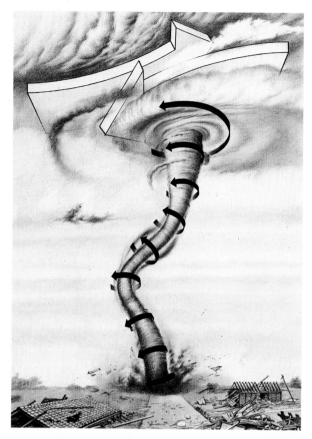

Tornadoes are dark, rapidly rotating funnel-shaped columns of air, water droplets, and dust projecting down from cumulonimbus clouds. The smallest but the most violent of all storms, they usually originate where cold and warm air masses interact and are always associated with severe thunderstorms. High wind speeds, ranging up to 800 km/h (500 mph), and areas of exceedingly low pressure within the tornado's vortex can cause destruction of everything in its ground path.

In the United States, tornadoes are most often associated with conditions in advance of cold fronts, and weather forecasts include tornado alerts when these conditions arise. Tornadoes can occur, however, ahead of warm fronts or even behind cold fronts. Tornadoes also occur frequently with hurricanes; the record number is the 115 spawned by Hurricane Beulah, which hit Brownsville, Tex., in September 1967. A WATERSPOUT that builds downward from heavy clouds is simply a tornado over water, but it is usually smaller in size and intensity than its land counterpart.

Tornadoes are now classified on the Fujita-Pearson scale, which links maximum wind speed, path length, and path width. A 0,0,0 tornado would have maximum wind speeds of below 117 km/h (73 mph), a path length of less than 1.6 km (1 mi), and a path width of no greater than 16 m (53 ft); a 5,5,5 tornado would have values of 420 to 512 km/h (261 to 318 mph), 161 to 507 km (100 to 315 mi), and 1.6 to 5.0 km (1.0 to 3.1 mi), respectively. The Fujita scale for damaging winds uses only the first digit of the Fujita-Pearson scale.

FUJITA SCALE FOR DAMAGING WINDS

Scale	Wind Speed		Damage
	km/h	mph	
0	64–116	40–72	Light
1	117–180	73–112	Moderate
2	181–253	113–157	Considerable
3	254–332	158–206	Severe
4	333–419	207–260	Devastating
5	420–512	261–318	Incredible

OCCURRENCE

One of the largest and strongest tornadoes on record is the Tri-State tornado of Mar. 18, 1925. This twister traveled about 352 km (219 mi)—mostly in Missouri and in parts of Kansas and Illinois—and killed 689 people. The most outstanding incidence of tornadoes is the superoutbreak of 148 that occurred between 1:10 PM on Apr. 3, 1974, and 5:20 AM on Apr. 4, 1974, in an area of the midwestern United States from the Canadian border to Alabama and mainly between 83° and 87° west longitude. More than 300 persons were killed and more than 6,000 injured. The city of Xenia, Ohio, was the hardest hit, with 34 fatalities, and some towns were visited by two tornadoes. One tornado left a path 8 km (5 mi) wide; another followed a trajectory 195 km (121 mi) long.

The greatest incidence of tornadoes is generally assumed to be in North America, and especially in the Mississippi Valley. On an equal area basis, however, other countries, such as Italy, New Zealand, and the United Kingdom, exceed or at least challenge the incidence rate of the United States. In actual numbers observed, Australia, with about 20 annually, ranks second to the United States. The United States is notable for the incidence of severe tornadoes of scale 4 or 5. Tornadoes occurring in the tropics are usually extremely weak and often begin as waterspouts. The Stockholm and Leningrad areas appear to be the northernmost regions that experience tornadoes.

Within the United States, Texas records the greatest number, usually about 15 to 20 percent of the nation's annual total of about 1,000. On an area basis, however, Texas ranks ninth, far behind Oklahoma, Kansas, and Massachusetts. A rather steady increase in the annual total has been observed, probably as a result of the improving reporting system. The seasonal maximum occurs in the spring and early summer, although tornadoes have been reported in all months. The height of the tornado activity is in early spring in the southern United States, later across the more northerly regions, and in July in western Canada. Tornadoes most frequently occur during the middle and late afternoon. There is a large interannual variation; for instance, Texas reported only 77 twisters in 1966 but 232 the following year. A record 794 people were killed by tornadoes in the United States in 1925, but fewer than 30 were killed in 1937 and 1962.   JOHN F. GRIFFITHS

Bibliography: Battan, L. J., *The Nature of Violent Storms* (1961); Smith, Roger, "Untwisting the Mysteries of Tornadoes," *New Scientist*, Feb. 28, 1980; Stanford, John L., *Tornado* (1977); Weems, John Edward, *The Tornado* (1977); Wolford, Laura V., *Tornado Occurrences in the United States* (1960).

Toronto

Toronto City Hall, designed (1958) by the Finnish architect Viljo Revell and dedicated in 1965, is located in the city's downtown area. The two semicircular buildings, rising 20 and 27 stories above a smaller central rotunda, stand on Nathan Phillips Square, the site of numerous recreational activities.

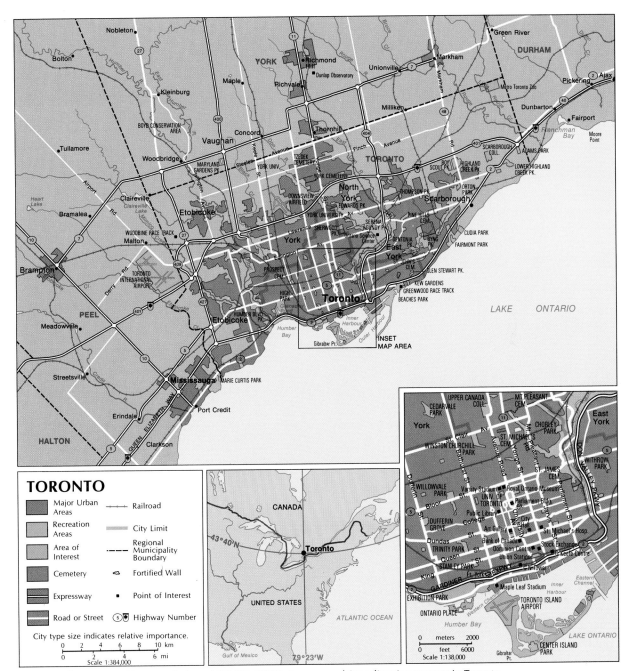

TORONTO

Major Urban Areas	┼┼┼┼ Railroad
Recreation Areas	▨▨▨ City Limit
Area of Interest	Regional Municipality Boundary
Cemetery	◁ Fortified Wall
Expressway	▪ Point of Interest
Road or Street	⑤◉ Highway Number

City type size indicates relative importance.

0 2 4 6 8 10 km
0 2 4 6 mi
Scale 1:384,000

Scale 1:138,000

The City of Toronto, with a population of 612,289 (1986), is the core segment of the Municipality of Metropolitan Toronto, created in 1953. The latter, consisting of five cities and one suburban borough, has a population of 2,192,721 (1986). Located on the shore of Lake Ontario, Toronto is the capital of Ontario and a leading financial, industrial, and cultural center.

Contemporary City. For most of its history Toronto's population was homogenous, composed principally of persons of British descent. After World War II a dramatic influx of immigrants from both continental Europe and Asia began. Since then the city has absorbed approximately 30% of all the post-war immigrants to Canada, making it one of the most cosmopolitan cities on the North American continent. The largest single ethnic group in metropolitan Toronto is still composed of persons of British origin, but there are also sizable numbers of Italian, German, French, Asian, Ukrainian, Polish, Dutch, and Scandinavian persons in Toronto.

Toronto's economic development has benefited from the city's location on the Great Lakes, and its role as an inland port greatly increased with completion (1959) of the St. Lawrence Seaway. The city is also the focus of Canada's major railroad lines. With a highly diversified manufacturing base, the city is considered Canada's industrial hub. Its principal products are textiles; wood products; fabricated metals, machinery, and electrical apparatus; transportation equipment; and chemicals. Food processing, particularly meat packing, is a growing industry. Most of Canada's leading book and magazine publishers, as well as the country's two largest daily newspapers—the *Toronto Globe and Mail* and *Toronto Star*—are located there. The city ranks behind Hollywood and New York City in television program production. As a financial center Toronto is considered to have surpassed Montreal, and its stock exchange is one of North America's most active.

The skyline of central Toronto, near the shore of Lake Ontario, is dominated by the CN Tower (left), *the world's tallest self-supporting structure. Because of its location the city has served as a major commercial center since it was founded by the British during the 18th century.*

Much of the retail activity is concentrated on Yonge Street.

While many North American cities have suffered varying degrees of deterioration at their cores, Toronto's downtown area has experienced massive and rapid new construction. Among the buildings of major architectural distinction are Viljo Revell's new City Hall, Mies van der Rohe's Dominion Centre, and I. M. Pei's Commerce Court West. The 553-m-high (1,815-ft) CN Tower is the world's tallest freestanding structure. Ontario Place, a complex of artificial islands next to the waterfront—adjacent to the grounds of the Canadian National Exhibition—provides theaters, as well as restaurants and marinas. The professional sports teams are the Maple Leafs (hockey), Blue Jays (baseball), and Argonauts (football).

Although Toronto supports a growing number of small legitimate theaters, the largest and most modern are the O'Keefe Centre for the Performing Arts—home of the National Ballet of Canada—and the St. Lawrence Centre for the Performing Arts. The Toronto Symphony performs in the striking Roy Thomson Hall, opened in 1982. The University of Toronto (1827) and YORK UNIVERSITY (1959) are major institutions. The Royal Ontario Museum is part of the University of Toronto.

History. The first white man to visit (1615) the site of the future city of Toronto was the French explorer Etienne Brûlé. In 1720 the French established a small trading post there and called it Fort Toronto. (The name *Toronto* is said to have been derived from an Indian term meaning "place of meeting.") In 1750 a new and larger Fort Rouillé was built. In 1759, however, the French burned Fort Rouillé to prevent it from falling into the hands of the British, who had just captured Fort Niagara. So ended the French regime at Toronto. In 1793 the British established a settlement there named York, which became the capital of Upper Canada (Ontario). Only in 1834, when it was incorporated as a city, did Toronto regain its original name. The first mayor of the city was William Lyon MACKENZIE. In 1837, after he had lost office, he led an unsuccessful rebellion against the government of Upper Canada. With the arrival of railroads (1850s), Toronto experienced rapid economic growth.

In 1953 the creation of the Metropolitan Toronto Corporation introduced regional government. Today, although each unit of Metropolitan Toronto has its own mayor and council, overall matters, such as police and fire protection, come under a separate Metropolitan Council.   BRUCE WEST

Bibliography: Glazebrook, G. P., *Story of Toronto* (1971); West, Bruce, *Toronto* (1979).

Toronto, University of

Established in 1827, the University of Toronto (enrollment: 51,500; libraries: 5,646,000 volumes) is a coeducational provincial institution in Toronto, Ontario, Canada. It has faculties of arts and sciences, music, education, architecture, medicine, dentistry, nursing, engineering, forestry, and library science, all with undergraduate and graduate programs. Federated universities are the University of Trinity College (1851), Victoria University (1890), and the University of Saint Michael's College (1852), with an undergraduate arts and sciences program, a Roman Catholic theological school, and the Pontifical Institute of Medieval Studies. The last publishes texts and translations of works of medieval literature. Liberal arts colleges of the University of Toronto are Erindale (1964), Innis (1964), New (1962), Scarborough (1964), University (1853), and Woodsworth (1974). Federated theological colleges are Emmanuel (1928, United Church of Canada), Knox (1844, Presbyterian), and Wycliffe (1877, Anglican). Among the university's facilities are the Centre for Russian and East European Studies and the Institute for Aerospace Studies. The university is the controlling body of the Royal Conservatory of Music and the ROYAL ONTARIO MUSEUM.

torpedo (fish): see RAY.

torpedo (projectile)

A modern torpedo is a large, cigar-shaped, self-propelled, underwater projectile that can be launched from aircraft and both surface and subsurface ships (see NAVAL VESSELS) against surface and submersible targets. Until the post–Civil War era, the term *torpedo* was used to designate many forms of moored or fixed mines. One naval version, the spar torpedo, consisted of a charge fixed to the end of a pole (spar), which detonated on contact with the target.

The father of the modern torpedo was the British engineer Robert WHITEHEAD, who demonstrated the first self-propelled torpedo in 1866. In 1895, an Austrian, Ludwig Obry, adapted the gyroscope to provide the torpedo with reliable directional control, a development that permitted ships to fire their torpedoes at targets not in line with the direction of launch. More modern developments include steam power, electric drive, a complex family of homing devices, and missile-delivered torpedoes.

The first torpedo-carrying class of ship, the torpedo boat (see PT BOAT) came into being during the late 19th century. The threat of these small, fast ships led to the development of the torpedo-boat DESTROYER (or, simply, destroyer), which was larger, about as fast, and armed with both torpedoes and guns. The torpedo-firing SUBMARINE achieved its status as a true weapon during World War I, and the postwar period witnessed the development of the torpedo airplane. Since World War II, rocket-assisted and missile-launched torpedoes have become standard equipment in the world's navies.

Contemporary torpedoes consist of four major components,

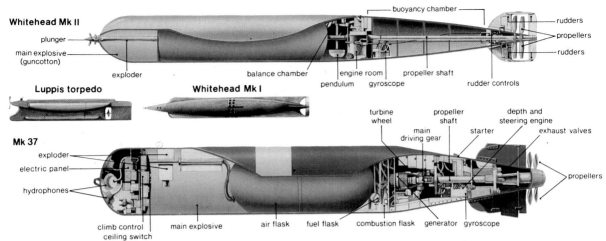

Whitehead Mk II
- plunger
- main explosive (guncotton)
- exploder
- balance chamber
- buoyancy chamber
- rudders
- propellers
- rudders
- engine room
- pendulum
- gyroscope
- propeller shaft
- rudder controls

Luppis torpedo

Whitehead Mk I

Mk 37
- exploder
- electric panel
- hydrophones
- climb control ceiling switch
- main explosive
- air flask
- fuel flask
- combustion flask
- generator
- gyroscope
- turbine wheel
- main driving gear
- propeller shaft
- starter
- depth and steering engine
- exhaust valves
- propellers

In 1864 the British engineer Robert Whitehead began to develop a clockwork-driven torpedo designed by Captain Luppis of the Austrian navy but later rejected the idea in favor of his own design—a self-propelled torpedo powered by compressed air. The basic Mk I was then modified and improved and by the mid-1890s had evolved into the more sophisticated Mk II, which carried a 45- to 180-kg (100- to 400-lb) charge of guncotton and a steering mechanism controlled by a gyroscope. The modern Mk 37, used by the U.S. Navy since 1957, carries 150 kg (330 lb) of high explosives in its warhead and an automatic homing system that employs hydrophones to detect sounds made by the target ship.

which are, from front to rear, a warhead, a fuel section, an afterbody, and a tail section. The warhead includes the explosive charge, an exploding mechanism, and, in the case of homing torpedoes, the homing device, which is normally mounted forward of the actual warhead. The fuel section contains the batteries of an electric torpedo or compressed air, water, and fuel for steam torpedoes. The afterbody encloses the propulsion motor, its gear box, the gyroscope, and the depth-regulating mechanism. The tail section encloses the propeller shaft and supports the external tail blades and their individual rudders and elevators. The propeller or propellers are mounted at the extreme end of the torpedo, immediately behind the rudders and elevators.

Torpedo guidance systems now in use include wire guidance, programmed search, acoustic, and active and passive sonar. Wire guidance is used for short ranges and allows control commands to be transmitted from the launcher by way of wires to the torpedo during its run. Programmed search is the result of commands initiated by systems within the torpedo. Acoustic torpedoes are guided to the target by the noise (cavitation) of the target's screws. SONAR signals can be generated from the torpedo (active) or triggered by the target's noise (passive). Modern torpedo guidance systems are often combinations of several systems.

The world's major torpedo manufacturers today are France, West Germany, Italy, Sweden, the United Kingdom, the United States, and the USSR.   RUSSELL J. PARKINSON

Bibliography: Fulton, Robert, *Torpedo War and Submarine Explosions* (1810; repr. 1971); Grey, Edwyn, *A Damned Un-English Weapon* (1971) and *The Devil's Device* (1975); Pretty, Ronald T., ed., *Jane's Weapon Systems* (annual).

torque   [tohrk]

Torque in rotational motion corresponds to force in linear motion. It is the product of the force tending to rotate an object, multiplied by the perpendicular radius arm through which the force acts (see STATICS). The net torque on an object is proportional to the resulting change in angular momentum. Torque is a vector directed along the rotational axis. If the fingers of the right hand curl in the direction of the change of rotation, the extended thumb points in the direction of the torque.   C. E. SWARTZ

Torquemada, Tomás de   [tohr-kay-mah'-dah]

Tomás de Torquemada, b. 1420, d. Sept. 16, 1498, grand inquisitor of the Spanish INQUISITION, has come to symbolize religious fanaticism and persecution. He studied in Valladolid, joined (1434) the Dominicans, served (1452-74) as prior of the Monastery of Santa Cruz in Segovia, and became (1474) confessor and advisor to the "Catholic kings"—Isabella I and Ferdinand II. Although he was probably of Jewish descent, Torquemada instigated attacks on orthodox Jews and Marranos (Jews who had nominally converted to Christianity). An inquisition was established to deal with this matter in 1478, and in 1483, Torquemada was made grand inquisitor.

Torquemada pushed vigorously the prosecution of Jews, apostates, witches, crypto-Jews, and other spiritual "offenders." Two thousand died and many more were tortured under his authorization. Under his influence, Ferdinand and Isabella expelled (1492) from Spain all Jews who had not converted—more than 160,000 people.   THOMAS E. MORRISSEY

Bibliography: Hope, Thomas, *Torquemada: Scourge of the Jews* (1939); Longhurst, John E., *The Age of Torquemada*, 2d ed. (1962); Walsh, William T., *Characters of the Inquisition* (1969).

Torralba and Ambrona

Torralba and Ambrona, two open-air archaeological sites about 150 km (90 mi) northeast of Madrid, Spain, are prehistoric killing and butchering areas that have yielded rich data on the practices of Middle Pleistocene hunters sometime between 700,000 and 300,000 years ago. The excavations, directed (1961-63) by the American anthropologist F. C. Howell, indicate that large mammals, especially elephants, were probably driven into swamps by fire-wielding prehistoric hunters who then stoned and speared their prey. The specialized Lower Paleolithic stone tools used in the butchering include mainly scrapers, denticulates, and ACHEULEAN bifaces (notably cleavers) similar to those found at sites in northwestern Morocco. The composition of the faunal remains indicates that the fleshiest parts of the larger animals were carried to the base camps, not one of which has yet been found.   JACQUES BORDAZ

Bibliography: Butzer, Karl W., and Isaac, Glyn, eds., *After the Australopithecines* (1975).

Torrence, Ridgely   [tohr'-ens]

The writer Frederick Ridgely Torrence, b. Xenia, Ohio, Nov. 27, 1874, d. Dec. 25, 1950, is best remembered for his trilogy, *Plays for a Negro Theatre* (1917). He also served (1920-33) as poetry editor of *The New Republic*, edited the *Selected Letters* (1940) of Edwin Arlington Robinson, and published a collection of his own verse, *Poems* (1941), which won the Shelley Memorial Prize.   JAMES HART

Bibliography: Clum, John M., *Ridgely Torrence* (1972).

Torrens, Sir Robert [tohr'-uhnz]

Sir Robert Richard Torrens, b. 1814, d. Aug. 31, 1884, was an Australian politician and land-titles reformer whose new, simplified method of land transfer, the Torrens system, was eventually adopted in much of the world. In 1839, Torrens emigrated from Ireland to South Australia, where his father, Col. Robert Torrens, was a founding colonist. He served in the legislative council (1851–55) and in 1857 was premier for one month. In 1858, Parliament passed his land-transfer bill. After returning to England in 1863, Torrens served in Parliament (1868–74); he was knighted in 1872.   E. J. TAPP

Bibliography: Pike, D., *Paradise of Dissent: South Australia, 1829–1857* (1957).

Torrens system

The Torrens system, which was invented in 1858 by the Australian statesman Sir Robert Torrens, is a system guaranteeing land TITLES and assuring owners that their rights to property will not be challenged. The Torrens system was first used in Australia and was also introduced into other parts of the British Commonwealth. In the rapidly growing United States of the 19th century, hundreds of thousands of deeds, mortgages, and land contracts were deposited in public record offices, which were little more than storehouses with indexes. Late in the century, private U.S. title companies began charging fees to check land titles, but their searches were not exhaustive, and the courts were crowded with cases involving title disputes. To clear up the title tangle, Illinois, Ohio, Massachusetts, and California passed title-registration statutes in the late 1890s, and the Torrens system went into effect in an optional form in Illinois in 1897.

Under the Torrens system a land title is traced back to the original grant (from an English or Spanish king or from the federal or state government), and all questions as to its validity are cleared up. After this exhaustive scrutiny, the title is, in effect, insured by the state. Unfortunately, the high cost of a Torrens search has limited its use and effectiveness.

Bibliography: Friedman, L. M., *A History of American Law* (1973); Shick, B. C., and Plotkin, I. H., *Torrens in the United States* (1978).

Torreón [toh-ray-ohn']

Torreón (1980 pop., 328,086), a city in southwestern Coahuila state, north central Mexico, lies 315 km (195 mi) west of Monterrey. Torreón is a milling center for the cotton and wheat grown nearby. In addition, the city has a smelter for silver, zinc, copper, and lead mined in the vicinity.

One of the newest Mexican cities, Torreón was founded in 1893 as a railroad junction. It remained underdeveloped until the formation (1936) of Laguna District, a large, state-sponsored agricultural irrigation cooperative for cotton growing.

Torres Bodet, Jaime [taw'-rahs boh-day']

An avant-garde Mexican poet and novelist, Jaime Torres Bodet, b. Mexico City, Apr. 17, 1902, was influenced by French symbolism and surrealism in his earlier verse and later wrote hermetic poetry that is characteristic rich in complex imagery. His evolution as a poet can be traced in the volumes *Fervor* (1918), *Poemas* (1924), *Destierro* (Exile, 1930), *Cripta* (Crypt, 1937), *Sonetos* (1949), and *Fronteras* (Frontiers, 1954). His fiction, including the experimental novel *Margarita de Niebla* (Margarita of the Mist, 1927), *Primero de enero* (The First of January, 1935), and *Sombras* (Shadows, 1937), is considered both Proustian and prophetic of the new novel of postwar France. Torres Bodet was a diplomat and government minister for much of his life, as well as UNESCO's director general (1948–52). He took his own life on May 13, 1974.

Bibliography: Karsen, Sonja, *Jaime Torres Bodet* (1971).

Torres Strait [tohr'-uhs]

The Torres Strait separates Australia from New Guinea and links the Coral and Arafura seas. About 150 km (95 mi) wide and dotted with volcanic islands and coral reefs, the strait is used for local shipping and pearl diving. The first European to sail through it was the Spaniard Luis Vaez de Torres in 1606.

Torreya [tohr'-ee-yuh]

The California torreya, T. californica, is an evergreen tree that bears minute buds, which develop into nuts that externally resemble pecans.

Torreya is a genus representing six species of trees and shrubs in the yew family, Taxaceae. Native to localized areas of China, Japan, and North America, these plants are handsome evergreens but little known in cultivation. Leaves are flattened needles arranged in two ranks with two sunken waxy-appearing bands paralleling the midrib. Stinking cedar, *T. taxifolia*, which may be found in Florida, emits a putrid or fetid odor when bruised.   FRANK B. SALISBURY

Torricelli, Evangelista [tohr-ee-chel'-lee]

The Italian mathematician and physicist Evangelista Torricelli, b. Oct. 15, 1608, d. Oct. 25, 1647, proposed (1643) an experiment—later performed by his colleague Vincenzo Vivian—that demonstrated that atmospheric pressure determines the height to which a fluid will rise in a tube inverted over a saucer of the same liquid. This concept led to the development of the barometer. Torricelli, who served (1641–42) as Galileo's secretary and succeeded him as the court mathematician and philosopher to Grand Duke Ferdinando II of Tuscany, also proved that the flow of liquid through an opening is proportional to the square root of the height of the liquid (Torricelli's theorem).

Bibliography: Middleton, W. E. K., *The History of the Barometer* (1964).

Torrijos Herrera, Omar [tohr-ee'-hohs hay-ray'-rah]

Brig. Gen. Omar Torrijos Herrera, b. Feb. 13, 1929, dominated Panama from 1968 until his death in a plane crash on July 31, 1981. A career soldier, he led the coup that overthrew President Arnulfo Arias in 1968 and became formal chief of state in 1972. He successfully negotiated the Panama Canal treaties of 1978 with U.S. president Jimmy Carter. In 1978, Torrijos resigned as chief of state, and Aristides Royo, a close political ally, was elected president. As head of the National Guard, Torrijos remained the most powerful person in the country.

Bibliography: Greene, Graham, *Getting to Know the General* (1984).

Torstenson, Lennart [tohr'-stuhn-sohn']

The Swedish field marshal Lennart Torstenson, b. Aug. 17, 1603, d. Apr. 7, 1651, was the greatest artillery officer of the

THIRTY YEARS' WAR. He became commander of the Swedish field artillery in 1630 and shared in the great victories of King GUSTAV II ADOLF. He became chief of staff under Johan Banér in 1635 and then commander of the Swedish army in 1641. Torstenson won a major victory over the imperial army at the second Battle of Breitenfeld (1642), and his lightning attacks on Moravia (1642, 1643), Denmark (1643–44), and Bohemia (1645) became legendary. After retiring in 1646, Torstenson was a supporter of Queen CHRISTINA's policies and was made count of Ortala in 1647.   J. R. CHRISTIANSON

Bibliography: Lisk, Jill, *The Struggle for Supremacy in the Baltic: 1600–1725* (1967); Wedgwood, C. V., *The Thirty Years War* (1938; repr. 1969).

tort [tohrt]

Torts are a group of civil wrongs that in some way bring injury to persons or property and for which the law provides a remedy in the form of an award of a sum of money (money damages). The term *civil wrong* refers to the fact that a suit based on tort is not prosecuted by the state in a criminal proceeding but rather is initiated by a private party acting as the plaintiff. Tort suits are distinguished from those in CONTRACT, in that a contract is based on an agreement of the parties, whereas a tort is inflicted without the consent and over the objection of the complaining party. Torts are a diverse group of wrongful acts; some of the more important are ASSAULT AND BATTERY, libel and slander (see DEFAMATION), NEGLIGENCE, TRESPASS, false imprisonment, and malicious prosecution.

The origins of tort go back nearly 700 years, almost to the dawn of the English COMMON LAW. Originally the functions of CRIMINAL LAW—which today provide for a government's punishing for wrongful conduct—and of tort law—which provide for a private party securing reimbursement for certain wrongs—were not distinguished from one another. These have gradually become two clearly separate areas of law, but even today some laypersons may find them confusing because the same act—striking another for example—may give rise to suits both in criminal law and in tort. The government has a duty to maintain public order and may therefore prosecute and punish wrongful conduct; yet a party injured by the wrongful act is not compensated for the wrong by the criminal prosecution and may therefore sue in tort to recover money damages for the same act.

In earlier times torts were divided according to injury direct (termed *trespass*) or indirect (termed *trespass on the case*). Within the past 150 years this distinction has been abandoned, and the primary line of distinction is now based on whether the tort is intentional (for instance, battery, assault, false imprisonment, and malicious prosecution) or negligent (the tort of negligence). These torts will be discussed below, along with torts that are not classified according to the presence or absence of intent (for instance, defamation, trespass, and CONVERSION).

INTENTIONAL TORTS

Battery. Battery consists of any intentional, unpermitted contact inflicted upon another. For intent to be found, it is sufficient if the defendant should have realized the act would probably cause an unpermitted contact, as when he or she throws a brick out the window into the midst of a crowd. The actual contact is ordinarily obvious, as when a person strikes another with fists or a club, but could include shooting, administering poison secretly, or any other form of contact not consented to by the victim. Injuries in athletic contests that result from a violation of rules intended for the protection of players may also constitute battery.

Certain unpermitted contacts are privileged, meaning that the perpetrator has a right to engage in such conduct. Parents have a privilege to discipline their children within reason; police have a privilege to use force in enforcing the law, and citizens have a privilege to defend themselves, their families, or their homes, as long as the force used is necessary and within reason.

Assault. An assault is essentially an offer, attempt, or threat to commit battery. The tort arises only when the perpetrator has the present apparent ability to carry out the battery. Making a threatening phone call would not constitute an assault because the *present* apparent ability to carry out the battery is lacking. In fact, mere words do not constitute an assault. Some motion or gesture must be made suggesting that a battery is actually about to take place. Assault, like battery, requires an intent. No matter how frightening, conduct that is merely careless (such as mishandling firearms) will not constitute an assault.

False Imprisonment. Any intentional, unlawful total restraint will constitute false imprisonment. Intent to restrain is essential, but restraint need not amount to a physical confinement. A party ordered to remain in a store, under threat of physical abuse, while a clerk sends for police, is being restrained. Whether this act amounts to false imprisonment depends on whether the restraint was legally justified under the circumstances. Although intent to restrain is essential to this tort, motive is irrelevant. Locking a drunk in a closet to prevent him or her from driving home would constitute false imprisonment, regardless of the laudable motive.

False arrest is a subcategory of false imprisonment. The term *false arrest* is applied when the restraint is imposed under pretense of legal authority that is actually lacking. Police may be held liable for false arrest when they arrest without the necessary legal authority. Merely arresting a party who subsequently is found not guilty of the crime does not constitute false arrest.

Malicious Prosecution. Malicious prosecution is the remedy for instituting—with the intent to injure or harm—criminal proceedings against the plaintiff. To prove a case in malicious prosecution, the plaintiff must show that he or she was charged with a crime at the malicious instigation of the defendant, was tried, and found not guilty.

Malicious prosecution differs from false imprisonment in that the key element in malicious prosecution is being wrongfully brought to trial, whereas that of false imprisonment is being wrongfully confined.

NEGLIGENCE

The rationale behind the tort of negligence is that even though an injury may not have been intentional, it nonetheless may be blameworthy because the defendant did not use reasonable care under the circumstances. On the other hand, before negligence may be found, some wrongful act or omission on the part of the defendant has to have been made. Unavoidable injuries do occur, and even though a plaintiff is injured, if the defendant is in no way at fault, he or she is not liable.

In terms of the frequency of suits brought, negligence is not only the most important tort, but it is, with the exception of divorce, the most frequent suit of any kind brought in courts of record. Automobile accidents are a source of a great deal of this litigation, but negligence suits may arise from a variety of causes, including airplane and railway accidents, physical injury to customers on business premises, the failure of physicians or other professionals to meet the standards of their calling, and many other situations in which careless conduct of one party might cause injury to another.

The technical requirements for a suit in negligence are a duty to exercise care, a breach of that duty, and a proximate cause between the breach of the duty and an injury to the plaintiff.

Usually a duty exists to avoid injuring others, but exceptions occur. An individual is usually not under a legal duty to maintain land and buildings so that unexpected trespassers will be safe. In some instances courts have found no duty on the basis that the defendant could not possibly have foreseen that his or her act would endanger the plaintiff. In most negligence cases, however, the duty of the defendant to avoid injuring the plaintiff is reasonably clear.

The defendant fails to perform his or her duty when he or she does not conduct himself or herself as a reasonably prudent person in avoiding injury to others. Whether or not the defendant has done so is largely a jury question, and the jury, in turn, will apply community standards to determine what is reasonable conduct.

Even though the defendant is found not to have acted as a reasonably prudent person, he or she is liable for the tort of negligence only if a fairly close cause-and-effect relationship exists between the careless conduct and the subsequent injury. This cause-and-effect relationship is what is meant by the term *proximate cause.* In most cases, the defendant's act was clearly a cause of the plaintiff's injury, and only rarely does the outcome of a negligence case depend on a question of whether or not a cause was sufficiently immediate.

The final requirement for a negligence suit is that the plaintiff be injured. The injury may be to person or property, but if to person, the injury must be caused by at least some impact. Most cases do not allow damages for purely mental distress. (A new tort category of intentional infliction of mental suffering, however, has gained increasing recognition in recent years.) After concluding that the defendant was liable for the plaintiff's injury, the jury determines a specific sum that will fairly compensate the plaintiff and awards this as money damages.

Even though a case in negligence may be established as outlined above, the defendant may still defend on the basis of contributory negligence or, in some states, comparative negligence. Contributory negligence means that the plaintiff's own negligence was partly the cause of the injury. If this can be shown, the defendant will win, even though he or she was much more at fault than the plaintiff.

Because of the harshness of the contributory negligence doctrine in offering a defense in cases where the defendant was more negligent than the plaintiff, about half the states have substituted in its place the defense of comparative negligence. Under this defense, instead of negligence on the part of plaintiff completely barring his or her claim, the award to plaintiff is diminished in proportion to the amount of his or her own negligence, as determined by the jury.

OTHER TORTS

Defamation. Injury to reputation is protected by the tort of defamation, which is really two closely related torts, libel and slander. Libel consists of written or permanently recorded injuries to reputation; slander consists of oral injuries.

The first requirement of defamation is an injurious statement, usually in writing in the case of libel and oral in the case of slander. The statement must be one that would expose the plaintiff to hatred, contempt, or ridicule; that is, it must seriously affect reputation. The statement must be transmitted to at least one person other than the defamer and the defamed, and the statement must be false. In cases in which the truth of the statement is contested, the defendant may be found liable unless he or she can prove truth.

A number of instances occur in which a party is given a legal right to make statements that would otherwise be defamation. This right to be exempted from libel or slander suits is called privilege. Legislators, high executive officials, and judges have an absolute, or unlimited, privilege when conducting official business. The same holds true of communications between husband and wife. A number of other instances exist in which privilege is available, as long as the statement was not made with malice (that is, knowing it to be false or in reckless disregard to whether it is true or false). This is termed qualified privilege. Qualified privilege is available in commenting on public officials, on the work of public figures such as entertainers, and in a number of other instances of minor importance (see NEW YORK TIMES COMPANY V. SULLIVAN).

Trespass. Trespass provides protection for interests in real property (land or buildings) and will offer a remedy for any entry of a thing or person upon the real property possessed by another. Although the traditional rule was that trespass would be found even in the case of accidental or unintended entry onto the land of another, the more modern rule is that liability will be found only in the event of intentional or negligent entry or while carrying on especially hazardous activities, such as dynamiting, which might damage the property of another. Common types of trespass are felling timber, cultivating fields, or simply moving into structures on the property of another. Because of the impracticality of bringing suit for minor trespass, such as walking across the land of another, many states have enacted statutes making such acts subject to minor criminal penalties.

Conversion. Conversion provides a remedy for interference in rights to personal property (in other words, any movable property, as distinguished from real property). Acts such as wrongfully acquiring possession, transferring, withholding, or damaging the personal property of another constitutes conversion. The remedy for conversion is a forced sale; that is, the defendant is required to pay the plaintiff the value of the converted property (see TROVER), and the defendant then is given the property.   JON P. McCONNELL

Bibliography: Dias, R. W., and Markesinis, B. S., *Tort Law* (1984); Fleming, J. G., *An Introduction to the Law of Torts,* 2d ed. (1985); Green, Leon, *The Litigation Process in Tort Law,* 2d ed. (1977); Hall, K. L., ed., *Tort Law in American History* (1987); Henderson, J. A., and Pearson, R. N., *The Torts Process,* 2d ed. (1981); Landes, W. M., and Posner, R. A., *The Economic Structure of Tort Law* (1987); Rabin, Robert, *Perspectives on Tort Law,* 2d ed. (1983); White, G. E., *Tort Law in America: An Intellectual History* (1980).

tortoise

The radiated tortoise, T. radiata, of Madagascar bears radiating patterns on its shell. It has been overexploited for its edible meat.

Tortoises are terrestrial TURTLES having short, elephantlike feet with unwebbed toes. They are found primarily in dry areas. Sometimes called "land turtles," the more than 40 species of tortoises, classified in several genera making up the family Testudinidae, are found in all temperate and tropical areas except Australia and Polynesia. They range in size from about 15 cm (6 in) to more than 90 cm (3 ft), usually have a high-domed shell, and can draw their heads completely in under their shells. They are generally slow-moving, plant-eating, and long-lived. The largest and best known species, some reaching 230 kg (500 lb)—genus *Testudo*—are found on the Galapagos Islands off Ecuador in the Pacific and on some Indian Ocean islands. Four species of gopher tortoises (genus *Gopherus*), found in the southern United States and northern Mexico, are known for their burrowing habits. Other species, genera *Testudo* and *Geochelone*, are found across southern Europe and Asia and in South America, and occur in a wide variety of forms. Some species (genus *Kinixys*) have hinged upper shells and others (genus *Malacochersus*) possess flat and pancakelike shells. The latter are found in Africa and on Madagascar and other nearby islands.   JONATHAN CAMPBELL

Bibliography: Noel-Hume, Ivor and Audrey, *Tortoises* (1973).

torture

Torture is the deliberate infliction of pain by one person on another. Universal methods of physical torture include beatings, electric shocks, and prolonged hanging by the arms or the feet; the injection of drugs can cause psychic as well as physical pain. These are the essential features of torture: at least two persons are involved, a perpetrator and a victim; the perpetrator has physical control over the victim; and torture is purposeful and systematic. Its purpose is to break the will of the victim and to dehumanize him or her; the intent may be

A medieval heretic is broken on the wheel. This method of torture, which stretched and dislocated joints of the body, was one of the devices used by the Inquisition to extract confessions of heresy or witchcraft or to obtain accusations against others suspected of such practices.

to punish, to obtain information, to extract a confession from the victim or a third party, or to intimidate the victim or others.

Torture has been used for at least 2,000 years and has been widespread. It was part of the legal process in both ancient Greece and Rome. Early Greek and Roman laws specified that only slaves might be tortured, but later freemen could be tortured in cases of treason. It was the right of a master to offer his slaves for torture in order to prove his own innocence or to discipline them. In the Middle Ages, torture was included in proceedings of the Catholic INQUISITION. In colonial America, "witches" were tortured by dunkings and other punishments to prove their guilt or make them recant their beliefs.

A movement in Europe to abolish torture began in about 1750 and continued through the 19th century. During the Age of Enlightenment, opposition to torture was based on both humanitarianism and the legal theory that torture is not necessary to produce evidence for conviction.

The first European countries to abolish torture entirely, such as Sweden and Prussia, had only recently incorporated torture into their law codes. In France the NAPOLEONIC CODE forbade torture as part of the legal process and served as a model of statutory reform throughout Europe. The 5th Amendment to the U.S. Constitution (prohibiting self-incrimination) and the 8th Amendment (prohibiting cruel and unusual punishment) effectively outlaw torture in the United States.

Torture has been resurgent in the 20th century. Germany's Third Reich brought back torture vengefully in its concentration and death camps, as did Soviet dictator Joseph Stalin in the GULAG system and, more recently, the Pol Pot regime in Kampuchea (Cambodia). In Nazi Germany, physicians became intimately involved in the development of the instruments of torture and in carrying out torture, transforming it into a medical specialty. Psychiatry, notably in the Soviet Union, has also been adapted to this purpose, including abuse of psychoactive drugs and forced commitment of dissidents.

In the 1980s, torture was officially sanctioned in approximately 70 nations, though it was not legal anywhere. The most notable systematic users of torture include authoritarian countries and police states in which power is concentrated in few persons or only one. Examples include Chile, where under the state of emergency (1973–88) there was large-scale detention, torture, and murder of suspected opponents of government; and South Africa, where detained and tortured persons are almost exclusively black, and many are children.

The United Nations in 1984 adopted the Convention against Torture and Other Cruel, Inhuman, or Degrading Treatment or Punishment, which obliges states to make torture a punishable offense and provides for the extradition of torturers and the compensation of victims. The largest private organization committed to the elimination of torture around the world is AMNESTY INTERNATIONAL. Various groups have established centers to aid and treat the victims of torture, both in their native lands and in the countries to which refugees have fled.

ELENA O. NIGHTINGALE

Bibliography: Amnesty International, *Torture in the Eighties* (1984); Nightingale, E. O., and Stover, Eric, eds., *The Breaking of Bodies and Minds: Torture, Psychiatric Abuse and the Health Professions* (1985); Peters, Edward, *Torture* (1985).

torus   [tohr'-us]

A *torus,* or *anchor ring,* is the mathematical name for the shape of such common objects as doughnuts, hoops, rings, and tires (see TOPOLOGY). It is defined as the solid generated by the revolution of a circle about an axis that is in the plane of the circle but does not intersect the circle itself. If the radius of the circle is r and the center of the circle is a distance k from the axis, then the torus will have surface area $4\pi^2 kr$ and volume $2\pi^2 kr^2$.

Tory party

The Tory party of England, which dates from 1679, consisted originally of people who gave loyal support to the Church of England and to the king and who preferred, at most, only gradual constitutional and social reforms. When King CHARLES II was asked by petitioners to call a Parliament in 1679 to exclude his Roman Catholic brother (later King JAMES II) from the succession, the supporters of the king and of hereditary succession were nicknamed Tories, a name for Irish outlaws. Their opponents, who favored exclusion, were called Whigs.

The Tory party had a checkered history between 1679 and 1714. It gave its support to Charles II and James II, was generally favored by King WILLIAM III, and was responsible for obtaining the Peace of Utrecht (see UTRECHT, PEACE OF) under Queen Anne. The party then split between the Whimsical Tories, who favored a Protestant successor to the queen, and the Jacobite Tories (see JACOBITES), who wanted to put James II's eldest son, a Roman Catholic, on the throne.

For a long time during the 18th century, party labels were meaningless, but a second Tory party came into existence under William Pitt the Younger, who was prime minister for 19 years between 1783 and 1806. After the Napoleonic Wars the conservative duke of WELLINGTON led the party, but its opposition to the first parliamentary Reform Bill proved disastrous. In the 1830s the Tory leader Sir Robert PEEL urged a more moderate party stance of working for reform "without infringing on established rights." When he repealed (1846) the protectionist Corn Laws, however, he was considered to have betrayed Tory principles. His followers, the Peelites, subsequently coalesced with the Whigs (who were evolving into the Liberal party), and it was left to Benjamin Disraeli, who opposed Peel, to transform the Tories into the CONSERVATIVE PARTY envisaged by Peel. The word *Tory* is commonly used today in a derogatory sense to describe the Conservative party of Britain. In American usage the term was applied to Loyalists during the American Revolution.

MAURICE ASHLEY

Bibliography: Colley, Linda, *In Defiance of Oligarchy: The Tory Party 1714–1760* (1982); Feiling, Keith G., *A History of the Tory Party, 1640–1714* (1924; repr. 1959) and *The Second Tory Party, 1714–1832* (1938; repr. 1959).

Tosca   [tohs'-kah]

The opera *Tosca,* which received its first performance at the Teatro Costanzi in Rome on Jan. 14, 1900, is one of Giacomo PUCCINI's most popular works. The libretto, by Giuseppe Giacosa and Luigi Illica, is based on a play by Victorien Sardou set in Rome in the early 19th century.

Bibliography: Ashbrook, William, *The Operas of Puccini* (1968); Hughes, Spike, *Famous Puccini Operas,* rev. ed. (1972).

Toscanini, Arturo   [tohs-kah-nee'-nee]

The Italian conductor Arturo Toscanini, b. Mar. 25, 1867, d. Jan. 16, 1957, was among the finest and most admired musicians of his time. After graduating (1885) with honors from the conservatory in his native Parma, he was engaged as cellist and coach by an opera company bound for Brazil. When, in Rio, the troupe's conductor walked out, Toscanini stepped

Arturo Toscanini, one of the world's greatest conductors, demonstrated his remarkable abilities when he substituted in a performance of Verdi's Aïda, conducting from memory at the age of 19. As director of many of the world's great orchestras, he elicited exhilarating virtuoso performances. His fidelity to the composer's scores has become a standard for modern interpretation.

in, leading Verdi's *Aïda* without a score (1886). (In later life he was able to overcome the disadvantage of nearsightedness with his prodigious memory.) Returning to Italy, he was in the orchestra for the first performance of Verdi's *Otello* (1887) and led the premieres of Leoncavallo's *Pagliacci* (1892) and Puccini's *La Bohème* (1896). In 1898 he became chief conductor at La Scala, Milan. Toscanini's career in the United States began in 1908, when he commenced a 7-year tenure at the Metropolitan Opera. Subsequently, he was principal conductor of the New York Philharmonic (1928–36) and of the NBC Symphony, created for him in 1937 and disbanded on his retirement in 1954. He was a welcome visitor to London and was acclaimed at the Bayreuth and Salzburg festivals, where later, in protest against nazism, he refused to appear.

Although Toscanini conducted some 20th-century works, including those of Stravinsky, his repertoire was drawn primarily from the period bounded by Haydn at one extreme and Debussy at the other. He was devoted to the operas of Verdi and Wagner and to the symphonies of Beethoven and Brahms. His rehearsal tantrums were legendary, but he won the affection of his musicians, from whom he could command playing of astonishing unanimity, energy, and clarity.

One of the great cult figures of his time, Toscanini became the incarnation of music for a vast audience. Because he was famous for an absolutely faithful interpretation of a composer's intentions as they appeared on the printed score, few listeners questioned the authority of his performances. Today, when freer readings of scores are accepted, and often expected, Toscanini's adherence to the score seems evidence of a certain rigidity. Yet there is no doubt about his genius, which is still obvious in the many recorded performances that he left behind.

Bibliography: Haggin, B. H., *Conversations with Toscanini*, 2d ed. (1980), and *The Musician I Knew* (1980); Horowitz, J., *Understanding Toscanini* (1987); Sachs, Harvey, *Toscanini* (1978; repr. 1988); Taubman, H. H., *The Maestro: The Life of Arturo Toscanini* (1951; repr. 1977).

Toshusai Sharaku: see SHARAKU.

totalitarianism

Totalitarianism is a form of government in which all societal resources are monopolized by the state in an effort to penetrate and control all aspects of public and private life. This control is facilitated by propaganda and by advances in technology.

Both in theory and practice, totalitarianism is of relatively recent origin. First used to describe the organizational principles of the National Socialist (Nazi) party in Germany, the term gained currency in political analysis after World War II. Older concepts, such as DICTATORSHIP and DESPOTISM, were deemed inadequate by Western social scientists to describe this modern phenomenon.

Principal Features. Totalitarian regimes are characterized by distinctive types of ideology and organization. Totalitarian ideologies reject existing society as corrupt, immoral, and beyond reform, project an alternative society in which these wrongs are to be redressed, and provide plans and programs for realizing the alternative order. These ideologies, supported by propaganda campaigns, demand total conformity on the part of the people.

Totalitarian forms of organization enforce this demand for conformity. Totalitarian societies are rigid hierarchies dominated by one political party and usually by a single leader. The party penetrates the entire country through regional, provincial, local, and "primary" (party-cell) organization. Youth, professional, cultural, and sports groups supplement the party's political control. A paramilitary secret police ensures compliance. Information and ideas are effectively organized through the control of television, radio, the press, and education at all levels.

In short, totalitarian regimes seek to dominate all aspects of national life. In this respect totalitarianism differs from older concepts of dictatorship or tyranny, which seek limited—typically political—control. In addition, totalitarian regimes mobilize and make use of mass political participation, whereas dictatorships seek only pacified and submissive populations. Finally, totalitarian regimes seek the complete reconstruction of the individual and society; dictatorships attempt simply to rule over the individual and society.

Types of Totalitarianism. Two types of totalitarianism may be distinguished: NAZISM and FASCISM on the right and COMMUNISM on the left. While sharing the ideological and organizational features discussed above, the two differ in important respects. Right totalitarian movements, such as the Nazi party in Germany and the Fascists in Italy, have drawn their popular support mainly from middle classes seeking to maintain the status quo and advance their own social position. Left totalitarianism, such as that of the USSR, relies instead on a lower or working class seeking to eliminate, not preserve, class distinctions. Right totalitarianism has been outspokenly racist and elitist, whereas, in theory, left totalitarianism has not. Right totalitarianism, unlike its leftist counterpart, rests on a cult of the hero, although in practice the cults of Joseph Stalin and Mao Tse-tung have been as pronounced as those of Adolf Hitler and Benito Mussolini. Moreover, right totalitarianism has supported and enforced the private ownership of industrial wealth. A distinguishing feature of communism, by contrast, is the collective ownership of such capital.

A final difference lies in the role of terror and violence in the two types of totalitarian societies. Left totalitarianism has arisen in relatively undeveloped countries through the unleashing of massive revolutionary violence and terror and the elimination of all opponents—political, social, military, economic—in short order. Terror and violence have tended to level off or decline after these regimes have consolidated their power. By contrast, right totalitarian regimes (particularly the Nazis), arising in relatively advanced societies, have relied on the support of traditional elites to attain power. The old elites, coexisting in a subordinate role with the new, have continued to pose a challenge and threat. Escalating levels of terror and violence resulting from such struggles contributed to the eventual collapse of the two major right totalitarian regimes, Nazi Germany and Fascist Italy. The Communist governments in the USSR and China, by contrast, have survived to the present day, and similar regimes have arisen elsewhere.

MOSTAFA REJAI

Bibliography: Arendt, Hannah, *The Origins of Totalitarianism*, rev. ed. (1966; repr. 1983); Bracher, Karl Dietrich, *The German Dictatorship: The Origin, Structure and Effects of National Socialism*, trans. by Jean Steinberg (1970); Friedrich, Carl J., ed., *Totalitarianism* (1954); Friedrich, Carl J., and Brzezinski, Zbigniew, *Totalitarian Dictatorship and Autocracy*, 2d ed. (1965); Germino, D. L., *The Italian Fascist Party in Power: A Study of Totalitarian Rule* (1959; repr. 1971); Gregor, J. A., *The Ideology of Fascism* (1969); Hough, Jerry F., and Fainsod, Merle, *How the Soviet Union Is Governed* (1979); Radel, Lucien, *Roots of Totalitarianism* (1975); Soper, Steven P., *Totalitarianism: A Conceptual Approach* (1985); Talmon, J. A., *The Origins of Totalitarian Democracy*, rev. ed. (1960; repr. 1985).

totem

A totem is an animal, plant, object, or natural phenomenon associated with a social or kinship group and toward which that group may adopt a ritual attitude. The term *totemism* has been applied to a great diversity of beliefs and practices found among various preliterate cultures. The classic example of totemism would be a society in which there are a number of subgroups, such as CLANS, each one of which has a special relationship with a particular kind of animal. Often the clan has the totem's name, and its members are conceived of as being related to the totem through mythical ancestry. If the totem is an animal, clan members typically will abstain from eating it, and the well-being and increase of the totem animal will be the purpose of clan rituals. The features of clan-type social organization, special ritual relations with animals or plants, and naming of groups for natural species do not necessarily accompany one another, however. Among variations are sexual totemism, in which the totem is identified collectively with

Carved and painted totem poles, such as these in an Indian village near Vancouver, British Columbia, are created by a number of North American Indian peoples of the Pacific Northwest. The plant and animal totems, depicted in familiar, standardized forms, have traditionally symbolized ancestral spirits and are often associated with particular legends documenting each clan or tribe's lineage and social position.

the members of either sex, and individual totemism, in which a sorcerer is thought to have gained the assistance of an animal species. Both traditionally occur among Australian Aborigines of southeastern Australia. Polynesian totemism usually involves relations with spirit beings that can manifest themselves in animals. The Ojibwa Indians of North America, from whose language the word *totem* is derived, have clans named for fish, mammals, and birds but without connected dietary restrictions and with little ritual.

Many interpretations of totemism have been offered. The sociologist Émile Durkheim saw in the relation to the totem a symbolic expression of the sentiments of attachment to the group; he interpreted this as an elementary form of religion (see PRIMITIVE RELIGION). In examining the connection between totemism and the incest taboo, Sigmund Freud sought an explanation in the anxieties of basic human psychology. More recently, the anthropologist Claude Lévi-Strauss has suggested that totemism reflects a kind of logic in which the differences between species and kinds in the natural world are used to express the categorization of society.

The massive carved posts—the so-called totem poles—of such Northwest Coast Indians as the Haida, Tlingit, and Tsimshian were traditionally erected to memorialize important events, to mark land ownership, or as monuments to the

dead. Their carvings concern family histories and show ancestors along with the spirits—in animal or human form—that aided them (see INDIANS OF NORTH AMERICA, ART OF THE).

CHRISTIAN CLERK

Bibliography: Durkheim, Émile, *The Elementary Forms of the Religious Life* (1915; repr. 1971); Freud, Sigmund, *Totem and Taboo* (1918; repr. 1960); Leach, Edmund, ed., *The Structural Study of Myth and Totemism* (1967); Lévi-Strauss, Claude, *Totemism*, trans. by Rodney Needham (1969).

toucan   [too'-kan]

The toco toucan, Ramphastos toco, found in rain forests from Guyana to Bolivia and south to Argentina, is rather tame and makes an amusing pet.

Toucans are boldly marked arboreal birds that have very large, serrated, and often multicolored bills that may exceed the birds' body length. About 37 species, making up the family Ramphastidae, are found from sea level to about 3,000 m (10,000 ft) in woody regions of Central America and tropical South America (see JUNGLE AND RAIN FOREST). Toucans usually have a body length of 30 to 60 cm (1 to 2 ft), short and rounded wings, and strong legs with two toes oriented forward and two backward. The tongue has a featherlike fringe along each edge. The beak and plumage are usually brightly colored. Toucans are often gregarious and noisy. Most feed mainly on small fruits, but some eat insects, small lizards, and bird nestlings and eggs. They typically nest in tree cavities, where both parents incubate the one to four glossy white eggs and care for the young. The largest toucans and those with the largest bills—genus *Ramphastos*—typically have black plumage offset by brightly colored throats, breast spots, and feathers above and below the tail. The 11 species of aracaris, genus *Pteroglossus*, are black or dark green above and lighter below, often with scarlet patches. Other species include the high-altitude green toucanets, *Aulacorhynchus*, the hill toucans, *Andigena*, and the lowland-forest short-billed toucans, *Selenidera*.

GARY D. SCHNELL

touch: see SENSES AND SENSATION.

Toulmin, Stephen   [tool'-min]

Stephen Edelston Toulmin, b. London, Mar. 25, 1922, professor of philosophy at Northwestern University, has written and lectured on ethics, epistemology, and the philosophy of science. He sees rationality in science and philosophy as having less to do with logical systems than with the "preparedness to respond to novel situations with open minds." His writings include *The Uses of Argument* (1958), *Knowing and Acting* (1976), *The Return to Cosmology* (1982), and *The Place of Reason in Ethics* (1986).

Toulon   [too-lohn']

Toulon, a commercial and industrial city in southeastern France, lies on the Mediterranean Sea about 50 km (30 mi) east of Marseille. The population is 179,423 (1982). Toulon's harbor serves as the primary naval base of the French Mediterranean fleet. The city's economy is based on shipbuilding, engineering industries, petroleum refining, wine making, food processing, tanning, and the production of chemicals and furniture. In recent years tourism has become increasingly important. A modern resort area with a beautiful beach and hotels has developed at Le Mourillon, just west of Toulon. Extensively damaged during World War II, much of the city has been reconstructed, but the charm of the old section north of the harbor still remains.

Toulon, or Telo Martius as it was then known, served as a naval station for the Romans. Acquired by the French crown in 1481, Toulon was developed as a port by Henry IV (r. 1589–1610) and enlarged and fortified by Cardinal Richelieu and Sébastien Le Prestre de Vauban in the 17th century. The English captured Toulon in 1793, but the French recaptured it a year later in a battle in which Napoléon Bonaparte became a hero. During World War II much of the French fleet was scuttled in Toulon's harbor in November 1942 to prevent its seizure by the Germans. A submarine base during the period of German occupation, Toulon suffered heavy Allied bombing in 1943 and 1944. It was retaken by the French in August 1944.

LAWRENCE M. SOMMERS

Toulouse [too-looz']

Toulouse is a major city in southern France, on the east bank of the Garonne River, about 600 km (370 mi) south of Paris. The population is 347,995 (1982). Canals (including the 17th-century Canal du Midi) connect Toulouse to the Atlantic and the Mediterranean.

Since the end of World War II, Toulouse has become a center of the French aerospace industry and associated production of electronics and chemicals. The older established manufactures are leather, shoes, textiles, stained glass, and machinery. The city serves as the agricultural market center

for the surrounding Aquitaine Basin. Historic landmarks include the Romanesque Basilica of Saint-Sernin (11th–12th century) and the Gothic Cathedral of Saint-Étienne, begun during the 11th century. The University of Toulouse (1229) is the second oldest university in France.

Toulouse, known as Tolosa, was an important Gallic city when it was taken by the Romans in 106 BC. Later it was the capital (AD 419–507) of the Visigothic kingdom of Toulouse. From the 9th century Toulouse was the seat of a powerful county and the center of the distinctive LANGUEDOC culture. In the 13th century, after the crusade against the ALBIGENSES, a sect widespread in the area, the county was annexed to the French crown. The city, however, enjoyed virtual autonomy until 1790. The British defeated the French at Toulouse in 1814. During World War II, Toulouse was occupied by the Germans from 1942 to 1944 and suffered considerable damage.

LAWRENCE M. SOMMERS

Toulouse-Lautrec, Henri de [too-looz'-loh-trek']

Henri Marie Raymond de Toulouse-Lautrec, b. Albi, France, Nov. 24, 1864, was a leading postimpressionist artist whose paintings, lithography, and posters contributed much to the development of ART NOUVEAU in the 1890s. He was also a harsh and witty chronicler of the gaudy nightlife and the sordid elements of late-19th-century Parisian society.

A sickly and sheltered child of an aristocratic family, Toulouse-Lautrec from an early age concentrated on observing and drawing, rather than participating in, social activities. This tendency toward dispassionate observation was reinforced tragically when two falls (1878–79), abetted by bone disease, resulted in crippling injuries to his legs, which thereafter remained stunted. A grotesque-looking cripple, with the legs of a boy and the torso of a young man, he concentrated

At the Salon of the Rue des Moulins (1894) is one of a series of Parisian brothel scenes painted by Henri de Toulouse-Lautrec beginning in 1892. Typical of his mature style is the angular, off-center composition, abruptly cut off at the frame. Bathed in harsh, theatrical light, the prim madam sits bolt upright, surrounded by the casually dressed women lounging on sofas as they wait for customers. Lautrec, unrelentingly honest in his portrayal of their masklike faces and tawdry surroundings, also conveys without sentimentality a sense of their life's meaningless boredom. (Musée Toulouse-Lautrec, Albi, France.)

more than ever on developing his career as an artist.

After failing his first baccalaureate examinations and receiving his parents' consent to study art, Toulouse-Lautrec studied (1882) with the academic painter Léon Bonnat and then entered (1883) the atelier of Fernand Cormon, where he befriended such other avant-garde artists as Vincent van Gogh. Dating from this time are several psychologically penetrating portraits, especially of his mother, that show in their color and brushwork his absorption of impressionism. In the later 1880s he was influenced by Japanese prints, whose large areas of a single color and strong contours and patterning he emulated. An even more formative influence on the young artist was the work of Edgar Degas, whose concern with movement and expression Toulouse-Lautrec began to interpret in a way that stressed angular protrusions of the body and outlandish behavior.

He was by this time haunting the dance halls and nightclubs of Montmartre, taking his subjects from his observations of what occurred on stage and among the patrons. To convey the frenetic and artificial atmosphere of these pleasure spots in such works as *At the Moulin Rouge* (1892; Art Institute of Chicago) and *La Goulue at the Moulin Rouge* (1892; Museum of Modern Art, New York City), he chose acid and garish colors and adopted a drawing style that is almost grotesque in its exaggerations. He applied the same techniques to the striking posters he designed (1890s) to advertise night spots and to immortalize the style and mannerisms of their most celebrated performers, including the dancers Jane Avril and Loie Fuller and the singers Aristide Bruant and Yvette Guilbert. In creating these famous works he greatly advanced the art of color lithography. His surviving drawings and sketches for the posters give the effect of speed and casualness, but in fact they represent a painstaking discipline and mastery in their extended use of line and reduction to essentials. The linear and uncluttered appearance of these works, as well as their flat, almost two-dimensional quality, owed much to Japanese art.

Alcoholism led to the failure of his health in 1899, and for the last few years of his life he confined his efforts to painting or drawing circus and jockey scenes from memory. After paralysis struck, Toulouse-Lautrec died at Malromé on Sept. 9, 1901.   MARK ROSKILL

Bibliography: Adhémar, Jean, ed., *Henri de Toulouse-Lautrec: His Complete Lithographs and Drawings,* trans. by Marianne Alexandre (1965); Bouret, Jean, *The Life and Work of Toulouse-Lautrec,* trans. by Daphne Woodward (1966); Cooper, Douglas, *Henri de Toulouse-Lautrec* (1955); Huisman, Philippe, and Dortu, M. G., *Lautrec by Lautrec,* trans. by Corinne Bellow (1964); Lucie-Smith, Edward, *Toulouse-Lautrec* (1977); Muller, Joseph-Emile, *Toulouse-Lautrec,* trans. by Wade Stevenson (1975); Perruchot, Henri, *Toulouse-Lautrec: A Definitive Biography,* trans. by Humphrey Hare (1961).

touraco   [toor'-uh-koh]

The great blue touraco, Corythaeola cristata, *is native to the dense forests of West Africa. The largest of all touracos, it reaches 70 cm (28 in) in length.*

Touracos are arboreal, often exotically colored African birds, the 21 species of which constitute the family Musophagidae. Usually seen in pairs, touracos have loud, distinctive calls. Ranging from 38 to 70 cm (15 to 28 in) in length, they have long tails and a reversible fourth toe and are often colored in combinations of blue and green. Most species have a distinctive crimson color on their rounded wings as a result of a unique pigment, turacin. Some also have a unique green pigment, turacoverdin. Touracos feed mainly on fruits, insects, and snails.   ROBERT J. RAIKOW

Touraine   [too-ren']

Touraine is a historic region in the Loire valley of west central France, largely corresponding with the department of Indre-et-Loire. TOURS, the medieval capital, is the region's industrial and commercial center. The Loire valley's fertile soil supports nursery gardens, meadows, orchards, and vineyards. The region's tourist industry is connected with its renowned Renaissance châteaux, such as Amboise, Chinon, Azay-le-Rideau, Chenonceaux, and Valençay, which were built during the 15th and 16th centuries. The name *Touraine* is derived from the Turones, a Gallic people conquered by the Romans. After centuries of rule by the counts of Blois and Anjou, Touraine came under English control in 1154 but was conquered (1203–05) by Philip II of France.   TIMOTHY J. RICKARD

Touré, Sékou   [too-ray', say-koo']

Ahmed Sékou Touré, b. Jan. 9, 1922, d. Mar. 27, 1984, a son of peasant farmers, was the first president of Guinea and black Africa's longest-ruling modern head of state (1958–84). The charismatic Touré, a pan-Africanist and a socialist, began his public career in labor-union activities. He helped to found (1946) an African nationalist party, served (1950s) as mayor of Conakry and deputy from Guinea to the French National Assembly, and became president when Guinea voted to become fully independent rather than join the French Community. Touré, who also served as prime minister (1958–72) and head of Guinea's only party, silenced all internal dissent. His relations with other countries were inconsistent.

Bibliography: Adamolekun, 'Ladipo, *Sékou Touré's Guinea: An Experiment in Nation Building* (1976); Davidson, Basil, *The Liberation of Guinée* (1969); Fuller, Hoyt W., *Journey to Africa* (1971).

Tourette's syndrome

Gilles de la Tourette's disease, commonly known as Tourette's syndrome, is a rare neurological disorder characterized by involuntary utterances (sometimes including vulgarities) and body movements and by tics. The disease is usually manifested during early childhood and often worsens through adolescence. The syndrome's obvious and attention-getting symptoms add to the emotional stress of its victims, which can exacerbate their condition. Males are afflicted three to four times more often than females, although familial patterns are more prevalent in female patients. The cause is not known, and there is no known cure. Symptomatic treatment has been successful in a large percentage of cases, however, with carefully controlled dosages of butyrophenones (major tranquilizers), particularly haloperidol. The disease is named for the French physician Gilles de la Tourette, who first described the syndrome in 1885.

Bibliography: Shapiro, Arthur K., et al., eds., *Gilles de la Tourette's Syndrome* (1978).

tourism

The term *tourism* refers both to travel undertaken for pleasure and to the modern multimillion-dollar business that caters to the tourist's need for transportation, accommodation, food, entertainment, recreation, health, souvenirs, and social contact.

TOURISM FROM ANCIENT TIMES THROUGH THE 18TH CENTURY
Mass tourism is a relatively modern phenomenon, but travelers have reacted as tourists, regardless of the purpose of their

journeys, since the beginning of recorded history. To write his history of the war between the Greeks and the Persians, Herodotus personally visited many of the areas making up the Persian Empire. Like many present cultural chauvinists, Herodotus reacted with shock to the foreign ways of Egypt, where, he found, nothing was done as it was in Greece.

Probably the most famous traveler of all time was Marco POLO, who recorded his adventures at the court of Kublai Khan; his travels by land through Central Asia, the Gobi Desert, and the Mongol Empire from Tibet to Burma and southern India; and his 3½-year sea voyage home after an extended stay of 17 years (1275–92). After 700 years tourists can still profitably read the observations of that Venetian trader when contemplating their own trips to China and the Far East. Few travelers of any age have ventured so widely or written so authoritatively as IBN BATTUTA (c.1304–c.1377), who, beginning with a pilgrimage to Mecca in 1326, over the next 30 years covered most of the Islamic world. For equally vivid descriptions of the Muslim holy cities, Africa, and the mysterious East, armchair travelers would have to await the narratives of such 19th-century scholar-explorer-eccentrics as Sir Richard Burton and Charles Montagu Doughty. During the 20th century T. E. Lawrence, Lowell Thomas, Freya Stark, and H. V. Morton helped answer this need for vicarious adventure in out-of-the-way places by their knowledgeable accounts.

If more people did not take to the road, it was because throughout most of recorded history travel was no pleasure. Roads were poor or nonexistent, inns uncomfortable, and transportation expensive and inconvenient. Only the favored few even tried to escape the congestion of the city for mountain or seaside retreats in summer, or for curative thermal spas if they suffered from ill health. The country estate and the watering place of Roman times and the religious pilgrimage popular in the Middle Ages, however, represented the small beginnings of what would one day become a tidal wave of tourism. From the start some of the spas frequented by the Romans were also centers of luxury, gambling, and high living and thus attracted those who sought nothing but pleasure—in other words, tourists. The prestige of Athens as a cultural center even after it had lost its political importance also made it a tourist attraction among Romans with pretensions to learning.

By the 18th century the leisure time available to Europe's aristocracy led to a fashion for travel among the sons of the wealthier classes. On the Continent university students were encouraged to spend a year at a foreign institution, while in Great Britain was born the idea of the Grand Tour, an educational journey that comprised a year or two of travel and learning in the major cities of western Europe. One such privileged youth was the Scotsman James Boswell, who between 1763 and 1766 toured Holland, Germany and Switzerland, Italy, Corsica, and France. He was as zealous a journal keeper as he was a traveler, a habit that served him and English letters particularly well when later he recorded *The Journal of a Tour to the Hebrides with Samuel Johnson* (1785).

An equally great boon to tourism was the revolution in aesthetic consciousness that transformed attitudes toward nature. Mountains, forests, and seas, which for centuries had seemed forbidding and malignant, were now endowed with majesty, glamour, and even divinity. The rediscovery of the beauties of untamed nature coincided with the newfound love bestowed upon ancient times and all the ruins and remnants of the distant past that were strewn about the European landscape, especially in Italy. This romantic sensibility created the appetite for viewing and sightseeing without which tourism as it exists today could never have evolved.

THE TECHNOLOGICAL UNDERPINNINGS OF TOURISM
For all but the young and hearty, however, more than an aesthetic revolution was necessary to make tourism a practical proposition, even among the wealthy. For long-distance travel to become comfortable and attractive, the Industrial Revolution had to provide transport that was both safer and faster than the horse and carriage and the sailing vessel. This was accomplished by the rapid proliferation of railroads in Great Britain and Western Europe starting in the 1840s and by the advent of the steel-built, oceangoing steamship in the 1880s.

With these two technological advances the great age of luxury travel dawned.

By Victorian times, tourism had become an industry, an economic fact quickly exploited by Karl BAEDEKER and his son, who provided travelers with solidly researched guidebooks in several languages, and by Thomas Cook (1808–92), whose London-based travel agency was offering, by the 1850s, guided tours of Europe and, a decade later, of the United States.

American tourism had begun with annual local migrations to mountain and seashore summer homes; longer trips to such fashionable spas as Saratoga Springs, N.Y., White Sulphur Springs, W.Va., and Hot Springs, Ark.; and leisurely trips up and down the Mississippi and Ohio rivers on the floating hotels known as paddlewheel steamers. The development of the sleeping car by George M. PULLMAN in the 1860s opened the way to comfortable, even palatial, long-distance travel and did much to popularize the idea of cross-country trips and interest in North America's growing number of national parks. The first-class accommodations offered by more than a dozen competing transatlantic steamship companies provided wealthy Americans with a sybaritic experience that made traveling as enjoyable as arriving. Enthusiasm for this luxury trade did not peak until the 1920s, when more than 140 luxury liners regularly plied the Atlantic. Simultaneously, Americans had at their daily disposal about 20,000 scheduled trains.

Meanwhile, the development of an American automobile industry based on mass-production methods—and the road system this inspired—opened tourism to the middle classes for the first time. The widespread ownership of cars revolutionized resort travel by making it possible to situate hotel and recreational sites far from both cities and railroad stations. On the other hand, the proliferation of automobiles and road travel beginning in the 1920s signaled the steady decline of passenger-train service and the bankruptcy of many of the remaining U.S. railroads by the 1960s. The luxury liner would also succumb, in its turn, to the relentless march of technology.

TOURISM AS A MAJOR INTERNATIONAL INDUSTRY
Both world wars contributed to the American taste for foreign travel by exposing millions of service personnel to the excitement of faraway places. International tourism as a giant industry did not get under way until the 1950s, however. Of the many factors contributing to this boom, the two most important were U.S. prosperity relative to other countries' faltering economies in the postwar world, which gave the U.S. dollar unusual purchasing power abroad, and the advent of jet travel in 1958, which made it possible to cross the Atlantic in seven to eight hours, half the time taken by propeller aircraft and about one-eighteenth that required by surface transport—all for approximately the same price. Jet speeds not only made accessible places that were previously considered remote, such as the South Pacific, the Far East, South America, and Africa, but also opened up the world of international travel to ordinary working people with only a short annual vacation.

Adding to the convenience and attractiveness of long-distance tourism were the availability of traveler's checks, which reduced the risks of travel; the incentive of reduced fares by way of Eurail passes, issued by Europe's state-owned railway systems; the growth in the United States of reduced-fare charter flights for groups; deferred payment plans; travel packages that combined several different kinds of transportation options in addition to meeting the tourist's preferences in hotel accommodations and guided tours; and a wide variety of specialized group tours.

Since the 1960s the nationals of most European countries, once again prosperous after a postwar economic struggle of 15 to 20 years, and of Japan have also shared in these travel trends. Tourism, in fact, plays a substantial role in the economies of many European countries—Austria, Greece, Italy, Spain, and Switzerland, for instance—where revenues from the tourist industry make an essential contribution toward reducing unfavorable balances of trade. It plays an even larger economic role in developing African and Caribbean nations.

Statistically, Europe as a geographic area remains the international favorite among tourists (many of European origin themselves). In 1983 over 5 million Americans visited Europe and the Mediterranean, spending almost $4.5 billion. Overall, 10 million U.S. travelers abroad spent about $14 billion in 1983, while foreign visitors to the United States, numbering almost 8 million, spent over $11 billion. Americans spend more money in Western Europe than in any other single area. Among European countries, the United Kingdom is still the uncontested front-runner with American tourists; France, West Germany, and Italy are the next most frequently traveled European countries. The most popular destinations for U.S. tourists after Europe are Mexico and Canada.

Tourism in the United States and its possessions is also big business. It is the most important industry in Hawaii, for instance, and accounts for 75 percent of the economy of the American Virgin Islands. In fact, according to the American Society of Travel Agents, tourism constitutes the first, second, or third most important industry in 46 of the 50 states.

Tourism in the future may be affected by circumstances difficult to predict, as it has been in the past—the gasoline shortage of the 1970s and periodic weakness of the dollar relative to the harder currencies of some other countries. No doubt, like the stately passenger liners that were converted into hotels or year-round cruise ships once the days of their transatlantic runs had ended, Americans will adjust their travel plans to whatever circumstances exist. One thing seemed certain: by 1980, with more than half of all Americans taking at least one trip per year of 200 miles or more requiring a flight or hotel stay, tourism had become an essential feature of the American way of life, no longer a pasture reserved for the privileged few.   ELEANOR M. GATES

Bibliography: Burkart, A. J., *Tourism: Past, Present and Future* (1975; repr. 1981); Gorman, Michael, and Height, Frank, eds., *Design for Tourism* (1977); Gunn, Clare A., *Tourism Planning* (1979); Lundberg, Donald E., *The Tourist Business*, 4th rev. ed. (1980); McIntosh, Robert W., and Goeldner, Charles R., *Tourism: Principles, Practices, Philosophies*, 4th ed. (1984); Milne, Robert Scott, *Opportunities in Travel Careers*, 2d ed. (1980); Smith, Valene L., ed., *Hosts and Guests: The Anthropology of Tourism* (1977); Turner, Louise, and Ash, John, *The Golden Hordes: International Tourism and the Pleasure Periphery* (1977).

tourmaline   [tur'-muh-leen]

Tourmalines are widespread and abundant complex boron and aluminum SILICATE MINERALS having the general formula $(Na,Ca)(Mg, Fe^{+2}, Fe^{+3}, Al, Li)_3Al_6(BO_3)_3Si_6O_{18}(OH)_4$. Tourmalines form slender, three-, six-, or nine-sided prismatic crystals (hexagonal system) in parallel or radiating groups. Hardness is 7 to 7½, luster is vitreous to resinous, streak is uncolored, and specific gravity is 3.0 to 3.2. The alkali tourmalines, which contain sodium, potassium, or lithium, are pink (rubellite), green (Brazilian emerald), or colorless (achroite), whereas magnesium tourmaline is yellow brown to brownish black (dravite), and iron tourmaline is deep black (schorl). Color gradation along the lengths of crystals is common, with pink usually found at one end grading into green at

Tourmaline, a common, highly complex boron and aluminum silicate, is a popular gemstone because it is found in almost every conceivable color. Some crystals may change color from one end to the other or may show concentric bands of pink and green.

the other. Tourmalines develop an electrical charge when heated or deformed, and slabs cut perpendicular to the long axis can polarize light.

The best developed tourmaline crystals are most commonly found in pegmatites. Crystals are also found in limestones altered by granitic intrusions and, because of high resistance to weathering, in detrital deposits and sedimentary rocks. Transparent colored stones and opaque black crystals are faceted as gemstones. Most gem material comes from Ceylon gem gravels and from pegmatites found in Madagascar, the Ural Mountains, and Maine. Tourmaline is the birthstone for October.

Tournachon, Gaspard Félix: see NADAR.

Tournai   [toor-nay']

Tournai (Flemish: Doornik) is a city in southwestern Belgium, located on the Scheldt River, 75 km (47 mi) southwest of Brussels. It has a population of 67,291 (1983 est.). During the Middle Ages, Tournai was a center for artisans and became famous for tapestry weaving and copperware. Other industries include quarrying and the manufacture of steel and leather goods. Among the buildings of historic interest are the Cathedral of Notre Dame (11th–12th century), the Belfry (1188), the Pont des Trous (13th century), and the Tower of Henry VIII (1513–16).

Originally a Roman city, Tournai became a Merovingian capital in the 6th century. Subsequently it belonged to Flanders, France, England, and the Netherlands; since 1830 it has been a part of Belgium.

Tourneur, Cyril   [tur'-nur]

The English dramatist Cyril Tourneur, b. *c.*1575, d. Feb. 28, 1626, is thought to have written *The Revenger's Tragedy* (1607), the outstanding example of a revenge tragedy and one of the supreme achievements of Jacobean drama. In the only play certainly by Tourneur, *The Atheist's Tragedy* (1611), also a revenge tragedy, religious prohibitions are set against the blood-revenger's duty, with God finally intervening directly to take vengeance.

Tours   [toor]

Tours, a city in west central France with a population of 132,209 (1982), lies about 210 km (130 mi) southwest of Paris on the Loire River. The principal manufactures are silk, processed foods, building materials, footwear, chemicals, and electrical equipment. Tours also serves as the trading center for wine and dried fruit from the surrounding countryside. Historic landmarks include the Gothic Cathedral of Saint-Gatien and the remains of the Basilica of Saint-Martin, both begun in the 12th century. Near Tours are many of the famous châteaus of the Loire Valley.

The Roman Tours was known as Caesarodunum from about AD 150 and as Civitas Turonum from the 5th century. Two of its bishops, Saint Martin (d. 397) and Gregory of Tours (d. 594), made the city famous. Following the introduction of the silk industry in the 15th century, Tours prospered, but its Huguenot population was dispersed after the revocation (1685) of the Edict of Nantes. From September to December 1870, Tours was the seat of the French government during the siege of Paris in the Franco-Prussian War.

Toussaint L'Ouverture, François Dominique
[too-san' loo-vair-tuer']

More than any other individual, François Dominique Toussaint L'Ouverture, b. 1743, d. Apr. 7, 1803, was the liberator of Haiti, the first independent nation in Latin America. Although born in Haiti to African slave parents, Toussaint was said to be the grandson of an African king and was literate in French and Latin. Trained as a veterinarian, he worked in his plantation's stables and participated in the Haitian slave uprising of the 1790s. Serving with the black rebel forces, he often switched sides between rival factions. In 1793 he joined the Spanish army that had attacked the French in Haiti, but in 1794 he allied himself with the French, who had promised to abolish slavery, and was promoted to the rank of general.

Toussaint's efforts in preventing a Spanish-English invasion and in defending the French against the rebel force of André Rigaud earned him the titles of lieutenant governor and commander in chief of the Haitian forces. He proved to be an excellent administrator and strategist: the mulatto-held south was reincorporated into the black-dominated north; the British withdrew in 1798; and the Spanish were pushed out of the eastern part of the island.

By 1801, Toussaint ruled all of the island of Hispaniola with only nominal deference to France, and he assumed the title of governor general for life. Napoleon I, however, anxious to reestablish French authority, dispatched his brother-in-law, Gen. Charles Leclerc, with 20,000 troops to the colony in January 1802. Forced to surrender a few months later, Toussaint was imprisoned in France, where he died. The French invasion proved unsuccessful, and Haiti achieved its independence in 1804.

Bibliography: James, Cyril L., *Black Jacobins: Toussaint L'Ouverture and the San Domingo Revolution* (1963); Korngold, Ralph, *Citizen Toussaint* (1949; repr. 1979); Scherman, Katharine, *Slave Who Freed Haiti: The Story of Toussaint L'Ouverture* (1964); Tyson, George F., ed., *Toussaint L'Ouverture* (1973).

Tovey, Sir Donald Francis   [toh'-vee]

The English musician Donald Francis Tovey, b. July 17, 1875, d. July 10, 1940, after private study of piano and composition, read classics at Balliol College, Oxford (B.A., 1898). He soon became known as a pianist, giving a series of chamber music concerts in London, Berlin, and Vienna, and later organized and conducted the Reid Symphony Orchestra in Edinburgh, where he was Reid Professor of Music at the university from 1914. His compositions, which include a symphony (1913), an opera (1932), and a cello concerto (1934) written for his friend Pablo Casals, were generally well received. But it is as an engaging, highly original writer of music that Tovey is best remembered: his program notes, collected in *Essays in Musical Analysis* (7 vols., 1935–44), combine illuminating description and penetrating formal analysis, and his lectures, essays, and articles are crowded with insights and suggestive comparisons. Notwithstanding his enormous erudition, Tovey wrote essentially for a broad musical public; he published "companions" to Bach's *Art of Fugue* and Beethoven's piano sonatas (both 1931) and left unfinished an important study of Beethoven (1944). He was knighted in 1935.

Bibliography: Grierson, Mary, *Donald Francis Tovey: A Biography Based on Letters* (1952; repr. 1970).

Tower of Babel: see BABEL, TOWER OF.

Tower of London

The Tower of London is an ancient building complex at the edge of the City of London on the north bank of the Thames. Now a well-known monument, the first section—the White Tower—was begun by William I (r. 1066–87) in 1078, shortly after the Norman Conquest. The outer walls were once surrounded by a moat, which was drained in the 19th century. The structure is actually made up of concentric fortifications—extended in the 12th and 13th centuries—that include 13 towers, including the Bloody Tower. The Beauchamp Tower, which probably dates from the 13th century, is named for Thomas de Beauchamp, earl of Warwick, who was imprisoned there by Richard II in 1397.

Many famous people were imprisoned in the Tower, and some of them, including Lady Jane Grey, Thomas More, Anne Boleyn, and Walter Raleigh, were executed there. Henry VI was murdered there, as—almost certainly—were the so-called Princes in the Tower, Edward V and his brother. A royal residence until the reign (1603–25) of James I, the Tower has also served as a storehouse for ordnance, records, and animals; at

The concentric fortifications of the Tower of London surround the White Tower, built by William the Conqueror. The Traitors' Gate (left), facing the Thames, was once the main entrance. Immediately behind it are the square Bloody Tower, where, allegedly, the Princes in the Tower were murdered in 1485, and the round Wakefield Tower.

one time it was also the mint. The Crown Jewels are displayed at the Tower of London in an underground vault under the parade ground in front of Waterloo Barracks. The yeoman warders who guard the tower are called BEEFEATERS and still wear a picturesque Tudor uniform.

Bibliography: Hibbert, Christopher, *The Tower of London* (1971); Minney, R. J., *The Tower of London* (1971); Wilson, Derek, *The Tower: The Tumultuous History of the Tower of London from 1078* (1979).

towhee   [toh'-ee]

The rufous-sided towhee, P. erythrophthalmus (top), and the brown towhee, P. fuscus (bottom), are ground feeders of the finch family.

Named for their calls, towhees are the seven species of North American songbirds constituting the genus *Pipilo* in the finch family, Fringillidae. The migratory rufous-sided towhee, *P. erythrophthalmus*, is chestnut flanked and grows to about 23 cm (9 in). The other towhees, predominantly found in the western United States, have widely varying plumages. Ground feeders that scratch about for seeds and insects, towhees can be beneficial to agriculture by consuming the seeds of weeds.

WILLIAM F. SANDFORD

Town, Ithiel

The American architect and engineer Ithiel Town, b. Thompson, Conn., Oct. 3, 1784, d. June 13, 1844, began work as a carpenter and later studied with the architect Asher Benjamin. Town's first major building is the Georgian-style Center Congregational Church (1812–14) in New Haven, Conn., where two of his finest residences—the Hillhouse estate (1828) and his own villa (1830)—still stand. He also built more than 50 bridges in New England and patented (1820) the Town lattice truss, a significant bridge-building development.

Town moved his practice to New York City in 1827 and established (1829), with Alexander Jackson Davis, an influential architectural firm. Their most important surviving buildings are the New York Custom House (1832–42; now Federal Hall National Memorial); the Old State Capitol (1837; reconstructed 1966–68) in Springfield, Ill.; and the Wadsworth Athenaeum (1842) in Hartford, Conn.

Bibliography: Hamlin, Talbot, *Greek Revival Architecture in America* (1944); Middleton, Robin, and Watkin, David, *Neoclassical and 19th Century Architecture* (1980); Newton, Roger, *Town and Davis* (1942).

town meeting

A town meeting is an assembly of the qualified voters of a community for the purpose of attending to public business. The institution originated with the first settlers of the Massachusetts Bay Colony, who stipulated church membership as the major qualification. In colonial times the meetings were generally held weekly, but nowadays the voters are summoned, usually in the spring, by a warrant that sets forth the agenda to be discussed. Although the town meeting exists outside New England, it flourishes most vigorously there. It is often cited as the purest form of direct democracy because every citizen has the right to speak in debate and vote on legislation. The decisions of the people are executed by their elected officials, the selectmen, who, in effect, govern during the intervals between meetings. Unfortunately, the town meeting can function well only in small rural towns; it is unwieldy, inefficient, and inadequate for the needs of modern cities.   MARTIN TORODASH

Bibliography: Daniels, Bruce C., ed., *Town and County: Essays on the Structure of Local Government in the American Colonies* (1978); Sly, John F., *Town Government in Massachusetts 1620–1930* (1930; repr. 1967); Zuckerman, Michael, *Peaceable Kingdoms: New England Towns in the Eighteenth Century* (1970; repr. 1983).

Townes, Charles Hard   [townz]

The American physicist Charles Hard Townes, b. Greenville, S.C., July 28, 1915, shared the 1964 Nobel Prize for physics for his investigations into quantum electronics and his invention (1953) of the MASER, a device that generates a powerful pulse of microwaves. During the late 1950s, Townes developed solid-state masers that amplified ultra-weak signals with great efficiency, and in 1958 he developed the concept of the LASER. After earning (1939) his Ph.D. degree from the California Institute of Technology, Townes worked (1939–47) at Bell Telephone Laboratories and taught at Columbia University (1948–61), the Massachusetts Institute of Technology (1961–66), and the University of California at Berkeley (1967–   ).

Bibliography: National Geographic Society, *Those Inventive Americans* (1971); Thomas, Shirley, *Men of Space*, vol. 5 (1965).

Townsend, Francis Everett

Francis Everett Townsend, b. Livingston County, Ill., Jan. 13, 1867, d. Sept. 1, 1960, an American physician, proposed and helped publicize a controversial old-age assistance plan during the Depression of the 1930s. Townsend suggested (1933) that all retirees over the age of 60 should receive $200 a month (in scrip) to be spent within the month, the funds to come from a national sales tax. In 1934 he established Old Age Revolving Pensions, Ltd., a loose organization of local clubs that within 2 years numbered 7,000—with a total membership of about 1.5 million. The popularity of Townsend's proposals was a factor leading to the passage of the Social Security Act in 1935.   RICHARD POLENBERG

Bibliography: Holtzman, Abraham, *The Townsend Movement* (1973); Townsend, Francis E., *New Horizons* (1943).

Townshend, Charles Townshend, 2d Viscount

Charles Townshend, 2d Viscount Townshend, b. Apr. 18, 1674, d. June 21, 1738, was a British Whig statesman and agricultural innovator whose political career was closely involved with that of Sir Robert WALPOLE, his brother-in-law. Townshend was secretary of state for the northern department from 1714 to 1716 and again held that post (1721–30) during the period of Walpole's ministry. He seemed to be the senior partner, until his adventurous foreign policy brought the two into conflict during the late 1720s. Walpole's growing strength at court enabled him to force Townshend's resignation in 1730. In retirement Townshend devised improvements in farming, particularly in crop rotation, that made him an important figure in the history of agricultural science.   PAUL LANGFORD

Bibliography: Namier, Lewis B., and Brooks, John, *Charles Townshend* (1964).

Townshend Acts

The Townshend Acts, British legislation intended to raise revenue, tighten customs enforcement, and assert imperial authority in America, were sponsored by Chancellor of the Exchequer Charles Townshend (1725–67) and enacted on June 29, 1767. The key statute levied import duties on glass, lead, paint, paper, and tea. Other bills authorized blank search warrants called WRITS OF ASSISTANCE, created three additional vice-admiralty courts, which operated without juries, established a board of customs commissioners headquartered in Boston, and suspended the New York assembly for not complying with the Quartering Act of 1765.

Americans protested the Townshend duties, as they had the earlier STAMP ACT, with constitutional petitions, boycotts, and violence. They now rejected all forms of parliamentary taxation, whether external duties on imports or internal taxes like the stamp levies. The protests ended with the repeal (1770) of the duties except for the ultimately explosive Tea Tax.

LARRY R. GERLACH

Bibliography: Forster, C. P., *The Uncontrolled Chancellor* (1978); Jensen, Merrill, *The Founding of a Nation* (1968).

township

A township, in the United States—as distinguished from a town, which is mainly a population center—is a geographical and political division of a county. In the Middle Atlantic states the township is often the basic unit of local government, assuming many of the functions carried out by county governments in other parts of the country. Townships can choose their own officers and committees—frequently at township meetings patterned after the New England town meeting. There is often a local police force, fire protection company, tax assessor, clerk, treasurer, health official, sheriff, and mayor. The township is also a basic survey unit of measurement—set by the Ordinance of 1787 for western lands—for U.S. public lands; a public-land township measures 6 mi^2 (9.7 km^2) and contains 36 sections.

toxic shock syndrome

Toxic shock syndrome (TSS) is a relatively rare disease associated with infections by varieties of the common bacterium *Staphylococcus aureus*. It is apparently caused by absorption of a bacterial toxin into the bloodstream of persons lacking antibodies against the toxin. Symptoms include sudden onset of high fever, vomiting, diarrhea, low blood pressure, and a sunburnlike skin rash. About 75% of the cases affect menstruating women, but TSS also occurs in children, men, and non-menstruating women; 30% of the patients experience more than one attack, and 10% of all cases are fatal.

In menstruating women, TSS has been associated with use of superabsorbing tampons containing fibers that strongly absorb magnesium, which seems to enhance toxin production. In other persons, TSS has been linked with various infections and the use of some contraceptive devices. Preventive measures for menstruating women include not using tampons or using them intermittently with external pads. Treatment includes antibiotic and supportive therapy and short-term use of corticosteroids. PHILIP S. BRACHMAN, M.D.

toxic wastes: see POLLUTANTS, CHEMICAL.

toxicology

Toxicology is the science of POISONS, including not only their physical and chemical effects but also their detection and antidotes. Toxicity is the ability of a substance to produce injury upon reaching a susceptible site in or on the body.

Substances are ranked according to a system of toxicity ratings used to indicate their relative hazard: *unknown,* for substances for which insufficient toxicity data are available; *no toxicity,* for materials that cause no harm under conditions of normal use or that produce toxic effects only because of overwhelming dosages or unusual conditions; *slight toxicity,* for materials that produce only slight effects on the skin or other organs of the body from either a single (acute) or repeated (chronic) exposure; *moderate toxicity,* for materials producing moderate effects on the skin or other organs of the body from either acute or chronic exposure; and *severe toxicity,* for materials that threaten life or cause permanent physical impairment or disfigurement from such exposure.

The dosage level and the period of time over which the dosage occurs determine the effect of a substance on an organism. Normally safe substances, such as salt and water, can cause illness or even death if consumed in sufficient amounts. Recognized poisons can differ from each other in toxicity by factors as great as 10 billion. The study of toxic effects within the body is aided by the study of the biochemicals called porphyrins (see HEMOGLOBIN), whose ratios can serve as markers for some kinds of toxic metals and chemicals.

LD_{50} is a notation describing toxic level: a statistical estimate of the dosage required to kill 50% of an indefinite population of test animals. ED_{50}, a more general notation, describes the median effective dosage required to produce a specified effect in 50% of the population; such an effect, for example, may be tumor production or inhibition of enzyme production. Other factors in determining toxicity include exposure route, physical nature of the toxicant, temperature, humidity, and condition of the subject. The determination of the toxicity and dosage of a substance involves exposing isolated living tissues, cells, and various animals to the substance. Normally, no testing is performed on human volunteers until animal studies are completed.

A tremendous number of substances can act as poisons, and an organism can be exposed to these substances by various routes. As a result, toxicology has branched into several specialized areas, including economic toxicology, concerned with chemicals used in drugs, food additives, pesticides, and cosmetics; forensic toxicology, involving the medical and legal aspects of poisonous materials when death or severe injury is the result of their use; industrial toxicology, in which the effects of pollutants in the working environment are evaluated (see POLLUTANTS, CHEMICAL); and environmental toxicology, which is the evaluation of the synergistic effects of chemicals in the environment (see ENVIRONMENTAL HEALTH).

The chemical and pharmaceutical industry has developed a vast number of compounds that are capable of both potential injury and benefit. Many beneficial drugs are poisonous if abused. In general, however, their usefulness outweighs the results of improper use. Government regulations of the pharmaceutical and chemical industry are based on the results of toxicological investigations. THOMAS CONCANNON

Bibliography: Chambers, P. L., et al., eds., *Toxicology in the Use and Misuse of Foods, Drugs, and Chemicals* (1983); Hodgson, E., and Levi, P. E., *A Textbook of Modern Toxicology* (1987); Lu, F. C., *Basic Toxicology* (1985); Moriarty, F., ed., *Ectoxicology* (1983).

toxoplasmosis

Toxoplasmosis is a disease caused by the protozoan *Toxoplasma gondii,* which lives in muscle and brain cells of a host animal and is acquired when uncooked, infected tissue is eaten. In cats, the parasite can live in intestinal cells, and people risk infection by contact with the cat's feces. Toxoplasmosis damages the brain, eyes, muscle, heart, liver, or lungs. If acquired during pregnancy, the parasite can severely damage the fetus. Certain phases of the disease respond to sulfonamides used with pyrimethamine. France and Austria require prenatal testing for toxoplasmosis, and treat infected women with the antibiotic spiramycin to reduce the risk of transmission of the parasite to the fetus. The United States does not require such testing. PETER L. PETRAKIS

toy

Sixteenth-century toys were handmade and therefore not as abundant as their modern counterparts, but toys like those pictured in Pieter Brueghel's Children's Games *(1560) can be seen in any playground today. They include hoops, jacks, balls, rattles, tops, and two sizes of stilts. The painting, however, does not represent quite what its title suggests. Most of the figures that seem so soberly absorbed in childish amusements are grownups, Brueghel's message being the vacuity of adult life. (Kunsthistorisches Museum, Vienna.)*

Toys are play objects used primarily by children. Natural objects, such as sticks, fir cones, seed pods, bones, and smooth round stones, may well have been the first toys. DOLLS, balls, spin-tops, and pull-toys made of a wide variety of materials are the fundamental toys of nearly every culture. The ball seems to be the oldest toy shape; it is made, even today, of diverse materials—deer hide, animal bladders, split cane, wood, and tissue paper as well as rubber and plastic. The development of the spin-top may have been contemporary with that of the ball, and both ball and top apparently derived from the gourds and seed pods that provided the original forms.

The animal was another early and fundamental toy shape. Although some of the animal figures found at ancient sites were used as ornaments or as miniature representations of objects intended to accompany the dead into the afterlife, a few animal shapes have been found that seem to have been intended for use only in play. Wheeled pull- or push-toys carved in the shapes of animals in white limestone date from Persia of the 12th century BC, for example. Clues to the nature of many old toys have been found on ancient vases and reliefs, which often depict hobbyhorses, carts, hoops, balls, tops, and musical instruments.

Little is known about the types of toys used by European children prior to the 13th century AD, when woodcuts and the decorations in illuminated manuscripts began to include illustrations of hobbyhorses, toy windmills, bubble pipes, puppets, balls, kites, and other toys. Renaissance paintings of children often depict them with hobbyhorses or drums.

Toys had been almost entirely handcrafted until late in the 18th century, when mass-produced toys began to appear for the first time. Metal rapidly replaced wood in many toys, and mechanical toys—windup animals, clockwork dolls, and inexpensive music boxes—became a standard toy type. (Music boxes had once been available only to adults as a costly curiosity.) Optical toys then made their mass appearance. A favorite was the cylindrical zoetrope, through which one could see a picture "move" as one turned the cylinder. In the 19th century dollhouses reflected the Victorian penchant for cluttered opulence, and some had working lifts and other ingenious mechanical devices.

In the 20th century, toys have proliferated along with other items of mass production. New materials have increased the range of possible toy shapes and functions. Replacing the tin soldier, a new population of detailed plastic fighting figures, from GI Joe to highly advanced and aggressive creatures from outer space, have made their way out of Saturday-morning television cartoons to the shelves of toy retailers—over the objections of many parent groups, who fear the hostile and sexist attitudes of this new generation of "war" toys. New "robots" range from small, unwired creatures whose shapes can be transformed into cars or planes, to electronic objects capable of obeying control-box commands. Toy supermarket chains have become big business and contribute to the enormous success of whole toy genres, such as the phenomenal Cabbage Patch Dolls. In reaction to the vast numbers of look-alike toys on toy-store shelves, many seek out simple wooden and cloth toys, often handcrafted, usually reproductions of the more innocent playthings of earlier childhoods. Nostalgia may also be responsible for the reborn enthusiasm for the teddy bear, a toy dear to many adults as well as to children.

Bibliography: Fraser, Antonia, *A History of Toys* (1966); Hertz, Louis, *The Toy Collector* (1969); Ketchum, William C., Jr., *Toys and Games* (1981); King, Constance E., *The Encyclopedia of Toys* (1978); Moran, Brian, *Battery Toys* (1984); O'Brien, Richard, *Collecting Toys* (1984); Parkison, Ralph F., *Wooden Toys and Games* (1984); Pressland, David, *The Art of the Tin Toy* (1976); Remise, Jac, and Fondlin, Jean, *The Golden Age of Toys* (1967); White, Gwen, *Antique Toys and Their Background* (1971); Whitton, Blair, *American Clockwork Toys* (1981).

See also: GAMES; PLAY.

Toynbee, Arnold   [toyn'-bee]

Arnold Joseph Toynbee, b. Apr. 14, 1889, d. Oct. 22, 1975, a British historian and philosopher, searched for patterns in the growth and decay of civilizations. From 1925 to 1955 he was

Arnold Toynbee is considered one of the 20th century's most eminent philosophers of history. His nontraditional approach to a comprehensive exploration of the cyclical patterns of civilization, manifested in his 12-volume Study of History, *has elicited both acclaim and controversy.*

director of studies at the Royal Institute of International Affairs and research professor of international history at the University of London.

In his monumental *Study of History* (12 vols., 1934–61), the best known of his many works, Toynbee stated that the breakdown of a civilization occurs when creative minorities fail to respond successfully to challenges and give way to dominant minorities ruling merely by force over masses turned into proletariats. In the early volumes, published in the 1930s, Toynbee contended that the West would not escape this fate. Later, however, he predicted the development of a universal religion combining the best in Western and Eastern traditions and leading to the founding of a new order. Criticized by professional historians as speculative, Toynbee's work nevertheless remains significant as a challenge to the narrow Europocentric approach of traditional historical scholarship.

GEORG G. IGGERS

Bibliography: Gargan, Edward T., ed., *The Intent of Toynbee's "History"* (1961); Stromberg, Ronald N., *Arnold J. Toynbee: Historian for an Age in Crisis* (1972); Winetrout, Kenneth, *Arnold J. Toynbee* (1975).

Toyotomi Hideyoshi: see HIDEYOSHI.

Tozzi, Federigo   [taht'-tsee, fay-day-ree'-goh]

Federigo Tozzi, b. Jan. 1, 1883, d. Mar. 21, 1920, was an Italian writer most of whose work consists of somber analyses of his own morbid and mystical temperament. His novels—which include *Con gli occhi chiusi* (With Closed Eyes, 1918), *Three Crosses* (1920; Eng. trans., 1921), and *Il podere* (The Farm, 1921)—were published only at the end of his life or posthumously.   LOUIS KIBLER

TR-1:   see U-2.

Trabzon   [trab-zohn']

Trabzon (Trebizond) is a Black Sea port in northeastern Turkey, with a population of 107,412 (1980). Exports include locally produced filberts and other nuts, beans, tobacco, hides, and minerals. Founded as Trapezus by Greeks in 756 BC, it became an important Roman outpost in the 1st century AD. When the Fourth Crusade seized the Byzantine capital, Constantinople, in 1204, Byzantine refugees established the empire of Trebizond. It continued as a separate state after the Byzantines recovered (1261) control of Constantinople and became a major commercial center. It held out against Ottoman Turkish conquest until 1461.

tracer: see NUCLEAR MEDICINE.

trachea [tray'-kee-uh]

The trachea, or windpipe, is a cylindrical air tube extending from the lower part of the larynx, or voicebox, downward approximately 11 cm (4.4 in) in adults to branch into two air tubes, called the bronchi. The walls of the trachea are composed of two layers. The innermost layer, the mucosa, is a moist membrane whose free surface is lined with epithelial tissue containing a few mucus-producing cells and numerous ciliated cells. The mucus serves to lubricate the passageway. The cilia, small hairlike processes extending from the free surface of the cells, beat back and forth rapidly, driving the mucus, and any particles that the mucus entraps, toward the throat. Most of this mucus is secreted by glands within the mucosa into the lumen of the trachea.

The outermost layer of the tracheal wall is the cartilaginous layer. This layer is composed of 16 to 20 incomplete cartilaginous rings whose open ends are directed backward. These rings are embedded in connective tissue containing smooth muscle fibers and are formed into complete rings by a strip of ligament called the annular ligament. These rings keep the trachea open. The tracheal wall is covered with connective tissue that supports blood vessels, lymph vessels, and nerve fibers from the autonomic nervous system.   ROY HARTENSTEIN

tracheophyte [tray'-kee-oh-fyt]

Tracheophytes are plants of the phylum Tracheophyta that, with the BRYOPHYTES, comprise the terrestrial plants. The term *tracheophyte* literally means "windpipe plant," a reference to the water-conducting cells, or xylem, of these plants. Xylem cells are empty and have wall thickenings, thereby resembling the trachea of an animal. The tracheophytes are the dominant land plants and include all trees.

Both bryophytes and tracheophytes have an ALTERNATION OF GENERATIONS in their reproductive cycles. The gametophyte, or gamete (sperm and egg)-producing plant, is succeeded by the sporophyte, or spore-producing plant. Tracheophytes may be either homosporous or heterosporous. Almost all ferns, horsetails, and some club mosses are homosporous. Following meiosis, they produce spores that give rise to gametophytes bearing both male and female organs. A few ferns, some club mosses, and all seed plants are heterosporous. They produce two types of spores: the microspores, which give rise to male gametophytes, and the megaspores, which give rise to female gametophytes. The recognizable form of the bryophytes is the gametophyte, and the sporophyte is the familiar form of the tracheophytes. The more evolved the tracheophyte, the smaller the gametophyte stage. The most commonly known male gamete of tracheophytes is the pollen of GYMNOSPERMS and ANGIOSPERMS. The female gamete of these members is a microscopic ovule, the embryo sac. Ovules mature into SEEDS following fertilization. The organ systems evolve in the sporophyte generation, accompanied by the development of vascular systems: xylem (dead cells) and phloem (live cells).

The most primitive tracheophyte, genus *Psilotum*, lacks true roots and leaves. Club mosses have all organ systems, but their leaves are primitive, and the leaves of horsetails are degenerate. Ferns have advanced leaf form, and seeds first appear in the gymnosperms. Angiosperms are the most advanced group. Terrestrial adaptations characteristic of angiosperms are the presence of a vascular system; floral organs (stamens and pistils) and pollination; fruit and seed; broad leaves (deciduous in temperate climates); perennial roots with annual shoots; and complete life-cycle developments, seed to fruit, in a single growing season. Fruits take many different forms and textures, from fleshy, like the berry of the tomato, to the stony outer coverings of nuts and drupes.   CARL D. FINSTAD

Trachodon [trak'-uh-dahn]

Trachodon is the name applied to one of the duckbilled DINOSAURS of the family Hadrosauridae (suborder Ornithopoda, order Ornithischia). The name was proposed for a single fossil tooth, about 65 million years old, found in the Up-

The Anatosaurus, *one of the most recent* Trachodons, *lived about 70 million years ago. It was about 5.5 m (18 ft) tall and weighed 5-6 tons.*

per Cretaceous Judith River Formation of Montana—the first fossil remains of a duckbilled dinosaur to be found. More completely known members of the family Hadrosauridae are *Anatosaurus, Corythosaurus,* and *Lambeosaurus. Anatosaurus,* commonly believed to be identical to *Trachodon,* stood 5.5 m (18 ft) high on its hind legs, attained a total length of 12 m (40 ft), and weighed 6 tons or more. The duckbills, or hadrosaurs, were bipedal herbivores with broad, flat, toothless beaks, behind which was a bank, or battery, of hundreds of teeth used for crushing and grinding plant material. *Anatosaurus,* with its webbed front feet and crocodilelike tail, is often depicted as an amphibious animal, but the structure of its teeth and the finding of conifer needles in the stomach of one specimen indicate that it and other hadrosaurs may have been terrestrial browsers.   JOHN H. OSTROM

trachoma [truh-koh'-muh]

Trachoma, a contagious bacterial disease of the conjunctiva, lids, and cornea of the eye, results in a chronic inflammation that may eventually lead to corneal scarring and blindness. Caused by a strain of *Chlamydia trachomatis,* it is an extremely important problem because it affects more than 400 million people, particularly in the underdeveloped countries of Asia and Africa. Although rare in the United States, it is found in American Indians of the Southwest. Because antibiotics are effective treatment for this disease, the World Health Organization in association with local health agencies has mounted a worldwide offensive against trachoma.
     THOMAS P. MATTINGLY AND MELVIN L. RUBIN

trachyte [trak'-yt]

Trachytes are volcanic rocks of intermediate silica and high alkali content. The lava flows from which they originate are usually quite viscous, and consequently they occur as short, thick flows, as tuffs, or as small dikes and sills. Feldspars are the major minerals found in trachytes. Either quartz or feldspathoids, but never both, may also occur, along with alkalirich mafic minerals such as aegirine, augite, hornblende, and biotite. The lath-shaped feldspar crystals are often aligned with the flow direction of the magma, giving rise to the typical trachytic texture. Trachytes are mineralogically and chemically similar to the coarser-grained syenites.   JAMES A. WHITNEY

track and field

Track and field, or athletics as it is called in many countries, is the designation given to contests for men and women that involve running, jumping for height and distance, and throwing for distance using implements of standardized design. Competitions in track and field are called meets and are usually held outdoors, with the running events taking place on a portion of or around a 400-m (437.4-yd) or 440-yd (402.3-m) oval made out of cinders, clay, or synthetic compounds.

The field events—those disciplines involving jumping and throwing—generally take place at the same time as the running events, on the area within the track's circumference, or nearby.

Meets are held indoors during the winter months on smaller ovals, which vary from 5 to 12 laps to the mile in size. Races of differing lengths from those held outdoors are often run, and several of the field events that require a large space are not held. Indoor tracks are generally made of wood and are often banked to offset the sharp turns of the smaller ovals.

Separate but related sports are often considered to be part of the track-and-field family. Cross-country is a fall and winter activity for distance runners, with races of 3.2–19.3 km (2–12 mi) being run over pastoral terrain—often golf courses in the United States and rugged farmland in other countries. Road running, especially of the MARATHON distance (26 mi 385 yd/42.2 km) is an increasingly popular activity, with races taking place over a measured course on city streets or country roads. Road races may be of any length, up to and beyond 160 m (99.4 mi). Long-distance walking events are usually held on road courses as well.

The outdoor track season is usually March to June in the United States and through September in Europe and Asia. The cross-country season is generally from September until early December in the United States, although in Europe meets are often held throughout the winter until the start of the outdoor track season. Indoor meets are held in the winter months, December through March. Road races are held throughout the year, regardless of weather conditions.

HISTORY

Track and field is one of the oldest of sports. Athletic contests were often held in conjunction with religious festivals, as with the OLYMPIC GAMES of ancient Greece. For 11 centuries, starting in 776 BC, these affairs—for men only—were enormously popular and prestigious events. The Romans continued the Olympic tradition until the time of the Christian emperor Theodosius, who banned the Games in AD 394. During the Middle Ages, except for a short-lived revival in 12th-century England, organized track and field all but disappeared. The true development of track and field as a modern sport started in England during the 19th century. English public school and university students gave the sport impetus through their interclass meets, or meetings as they are still called in Britain, and in 1849 the Royal Military Academy held the first organized track and field meet of modern times.

Not until the 1860s, however, did the sport flourish. In 1866 the first English championships were held by the newly formed Amateur Athletic Club, which opened the competition to all "gentlemen amateurs"—specifically, athletes who received no financial compensation for their efforts. This code has lasted to the present day and is the basis of the rules governing the sport. The Amateur Athletic Club gave way to the Amateur Athletic Association in 1880, which has conducted the annual national championships since that date. Although meets were held on the North American continent as early as 1839, track and field first gained popularity in the late 1860s, after the formation of the New York Athletic Club in 1868. The AMATEUR ATHLETIC UNION OF THE UNITED STATES (AAU), an association of track and field clubs, was formed in 1887 and has governed the sport in the United States since then.

In 1896 the first modern Olympic Games were staged. Although initially of limited appeal, the Olympics captured the imagination of athletes and grew steadily, making track and

field an international sport for the first time. In 1913 the International Amateur Athletic Federation (IAAF) was formed by representatives from 16 countries. The IAAF was charged with establishing standard rules for the sport, approving world records, and ensuring that the amateur code was adhered to; it continues to carry out these duties today.

The participation of women in track and field is a relatively recent development. In 1921 representatives from six countries formed an athletic federation for women, which merged with the IAAF in 1936. Participation by women has grown rapidly in many countries in recent years, particularly in the United States, where many schools have added women's track and field to their athletic programs.

RULES AND SCORING.

All races are started by the firing of a gun by an official at the starting line. For races up to and including one lap of an outdoor track, the runners must stay for the entire distance within lanes marked on the track. There may be six to eight lanes, with each lane usually measuring 1.2 m (4 ft) in width. The winner in each race is the runner whose torso first breaks the vertical plane of the finish line. Races are timed either by mechanical watches or by more sophisticated, electronic photo-timers that can measure finishes to the hundredth of a second. Sometimes, owing to the number of contestants in a competition, qualifying rounds, or heats, are held to narrow the contestants down to the fastest runners.

Athletes in the field events also have qualifying rounds. In the horizontal jumps and throws, athletes are allowed three preliminary attempts if the field numbers more than eight participants. Then the best performers are allowed three more attempts. In the vertical jumps—the high jump and pole vault—the participants are allowed to continue until they have three successive failures. If two or more contestants tie, the competitor with the fewest failures at the last height cleared is the winner; if still tied, the total number of failures is the deciding factor; if a tie remains, the total number of jumps is considered. Scoring systems differ according to the meet. Many national competitions are scored on the basis of 10 points for first place, 8 for second, on down to 1 point for sixth. In international meets, the scoring is 5 for first place, 3 for second, 2 for third, and 1 for fourth. The team with the highest total wins.

For road races, cross-country meets, and walking competitions, the winner is given 1 point, the second-place finisher 2 points, and so on; the finish positions are totaled, and the team with the lowest score is the winner.

TRACK EVENTS

The sprints are all-out efforts over the entire distance run. Outdoors the sprints are 100–440 yd (91.4–402.3 m) or the metric distances of 100, 200, and 400 m (109.3, 218.6, and 437.2 yd). Indoor sprints are often as short as 50 yd (45.7 m), or as long as 500 m (546.8 yd).

Sprinters use a crouch start in which, after being commanded to get "on your marks" by the starter, the contestant kneels with one knee on the ground and both hands resting behind the starting line. On the "get set" command, the sprinter raises the knee from the ground in anticipation of the gun. When it fires, the runner will accelerate as quickly as possible from the starting line. To facilitate a quick start by giving the runner something to push off against, devices known as starting blocks are used.

In the longer sprints—200 m (218.6 yd) and 220 yd (201.1 m), 400 m (437.2 yd) and 440 yd (402.3 m)—the races are run in assigned lanes for the entire circumference of the track. To ensure fairness for all participants, the start is staggered so that runners farther out from the inside lane start farther ahead of the contestants to their left, who have a smaller circumference to run around; as a result, all runners travel the same distance.

The middle distance races range from 800 to 2,000 m (874.4 to 2,187.2 yd), although by far the most popular of these events has been the mile (1.6 km); top runners often complete the mile in less than four minutes. Such is the popularity of the mile that it is the only event of English measure still recognized by the IAAF for record purposes. While the 880-yd

American sprinter Florence Griffith Joyner rounds the curve in the 200-meter final at the 1988 Olympic Games in Seoul, South Korea. During 1988, Griffith Joyner emerged as the world's fastest woman, running a world record 10.49-sec 100 m in July and a world record 21.34-sec 200 m in Seoul. "Flo-Jo" earned gold medals in both of those events, as well as in the 4 × 100-m relay.

(804.7-m), 2-mi (3.2-km), and other English distances are still run, only metric marks are now ratifiable as world records. In the middle distances, fatigue becomes an increasingly important factor, requiring the competitors to pace themselves so that they can finish the race in the shortest possible time; or, if the race is a tactical one, to be able to summon a sprint at the end in order to defeat the other contestants.

The long distances range from 3,000 to 30,000 m (1.9 to 18.6 mi) and the marathon. Also recognized by the IAAF is the one-hour run, in which the participants run as far as they can within one hour's time. As with the middle distances, the longer the race, the less decisive is the inherent speed of the various competitors. Rather, the endurance fitness of the athletes and their use of various strategies play a more important role. A distance runner with less natural speed than his or her rivals may speed up the pace in the middle of a race in order to break away from and thus disconcert the other runners.

Besides the distance races on the track, which usually are no farther than 10,000 m (6.2 mi), many of the longer races are run on the roads. Because of the varying venues and conditions, no world records are kept by the IAAF for these road races. Similarly, no records are kept for cross-country races, which, at the international level, are often 12,000 m (7.4 mi). Perhaps the most unusual of the distance track events is the 3,000-m (1.9-mi) STEEPLECHASE, in which the contestants must negotiate 28 sturdy wooden barriers and 7 water jumps. Race walking, on the other hand, is fast walking with the stipulation that the walker must maintain unbroken contact with the ground and lock the knee for an instant while the foot is on the ground.

The hurdle races require an athlete to possess the speed of a sprinter and the ability to clear 10 barriers 106.7 cm (42 in) high in the men's 110-m (120.3-yd) hurdles, and 10 barriers of 91.4 cm (36 in) in the 400-m hurdles. In the United States, equivalent distances of 120 yd (109.7 m) and 440 yd (402.3 m) are sometimes run. Women race over 100 m and 8 barriers 84 cm (33 in) high. In both men's and women's races, no penalty is assessed for knocking down hurdles, unless done deliberately with the hand. The rear leg or foot may not trail alongside the hurdle, but must be drawn over the top.

In the relay races teams of four athletes run separate distances, or legs. They exchange a hollow tube called a baton within designated exchange zones. The most common relay events are the 4 × 100-m (109.3-yd) relay and the 4 × 400-m (437.2-yd) relay. Relay meets are particularly popular in the United States, owing in part to the American school system, which has traditionally placed emphasis on interscholastic team competition.

FIELD EVENTS
Competitors in the high jump attempt to clear a crossbar. The contestant may make the takeoff for the high jump using only one foot, not two. Over the past half-century, jumping styles

have changed dramatically, from the "scissors" technique, to the "straddle," to the now-predominant "Fosbury flop." In the scissors the competitor kept the body upright over the bar. In the straddle, still used by some, the athlete approaches the bar and kicks the lead leg upward, then contours the body over the bar, facedown. The flop was popularized by Dick Fosbury, an American who developed the style and used it to win the 1968 Olympic gold medal. The athlete approaches the bar almost straight on, then twists his or her body so that the back is facing the bar before landing in the pit. These landing areas, which at one time were recesses filled with sawdust, are now well-padded foam-rubber mats.

In the pole vault, as in the high jump, the object is for the athlete to pass over a bar without knocking it off, in this case with the aid of a pole. In the vault, too, a foam-rubber pit is employed to break the athlete's fall. Because the IAAF rules place no restrictions on the composition of the pole, it has undergone dramatic changes as new materials have become available. Bamboo and heavy metal models have given way to the fiberglass pole, which has a high degree of flexibility and allows the athlete adept in its use to catapult over the bar. Most vaulters use an approach run of approximately 40 m (131 ft) while carrying the pole nearly parallel to the ground. The athlete then plants the pole in a sunken box, which is positioned immediately in front of the pit, and rides the pole during the catapulting phase, before twisting the body facedown to the bar and arcing over while releasing the pole.

In the long jump, or broad jump as it was once called, the contestants run at full speed down a cinder or synthetic runway to a takeoff board. This board marks the point where the athlete must leave the ground. He or she may step on the board but must not allow any portion of the foot to go over it; otherwise, he or she is charged with a foul and the jump is invalidated. After a legal jump, the contestant's mark is measured from the front edge of the takeoff board to the nearest point of contact in the sand-filled pit.

The triple jump requires its contestants to hop, step, and jump into the pit. When the athlete reaches the board, he or

(Above) Jackie Joyner-Kersee of the United States competes in the long jump at the 1988 Olympics. In the mid- to late 1980s, Joyner-Kersee was hailed as the world's greatest woman athlete because of her domination in the heptathlon, for which she set several world records. She won an Olympic gold medal in that event, and another in the long jump. She also holds the American record in the 100-m hurdles. (Below) Soviet pole vaulter Sergei Bubka, seen here clearing the bar by an extraordinary margin, was virtually unbeatable in his event from the mid-1980s, raising the world standard many times. He won the 1988 Olympic gold medal, two and a half months after vaulting 6.06 m (19 ft 10½ in).

MEN'S WORLD TRACK AND FIELD RECORDS

Event	Record	Record Holder	Date
100 m	9.83 sec	Ben Johnson (Canada)	Aug. 30, 1987
200 m	19.72 sec	Pietro Mennea (Italy)	Sept. 12, 1979
400 m	43.29 sec	Butch Reynolds (USA)	Aug. 17, 1988
800 m	1 min 41.73 sec	Sebastian Coe (Gr. Br.)	June 10, 1981
1,000 m	2 min 12.18 sec	Sebastian Coe (Gr. Br.)	July 11,1981
1,500 m	3 min 29.46 sec	Said Aouita (Mor.)	Aug. 23, 1985
Mile	3 min 46.32 sec	Steve Cram (Gr. Br.)	July 27, 1985
2,000 m	4 min 50.81 sec	Said Aouita (Mor.)	July 16, 1987
3,000 m	7 min 32.1 sec	Henry Rono (Kenya)	June 27, 1978
Steeplechase	8 min 5.4 sec	Henry Rono (Kenya)	May 14, 1978
5,000 m	12 min 58.39 sec	Said Aouita (Mor.)	July 22, 1987
10,000 m	27 min 13.81 sec	Fernando Mamede (Port.)	July 2, 1984
20,000 m	57 min 24.2 sec	Jos Hermens (Neth.)	May 1, 1976
25,000 m	1 hr 13 min 55.8 sec	Toshihiko Seko (Japan)	Mar. 22, 1981
30,000 m	1 hr 29 min 18.8 sec	Toshihiko Seko (Japan)	Mar. 22, 1981
Marathon	2 hr 6 min 50 sec	Belaine Densimo (Eth.)	Apr. 17, 1988
110-m hurdles	12.93	Renaldo Nehemiah (USA)	July 19, 1981
400-m hurdles	47.02 sec	Edwin Moses (USA)	Aug. 31, 1983
High jump	2.43 m (7 ft 11½ in)	Javier Sotomayor (Cuba)	Sept. 8, 1988
Pole vault	6.06 m (19 ft 10½ in)	Sergei Bubka (USSR)	July 10, 1988
Long jump	8.90 m (29 ft 2.5 in)	Bob Beamon (USA)	Oct. 18, 1968
Triple jump	17.97 m (58 ft 11½ in)	Willie Banks (USA)	June 16, 1985
Shot put	23.06 m (75 ft 8 in)	Ulf Timmermann (E.Ger.)	May 22, 1988
Discus throw	74.08 m (243 ft)	Jurgen Schult (E.Ger.)	June 6, 1986
Hammer throw	86.74 m (284 ft 7 in)	Yuri Sedykh (USSR)	Aug. 30, 1986
Javelin throw	87.66 m (287 ft 7 in)	Jan Zelezny (Czech.)	May 31, 1987
Decathlon	8,847 points	Daley Thompson (Gr. Br.)	Aug. 8–9, 1984
20-km walk	1 hr 18 min 40 sec	Ernesto Canto (Mex.)	May 5, 1984
30-km walk	2 hr 7 min 59.8 sec	José Marin (Spain)	Aug. 4, 1979
50-km walk	3 hr 41 min 39 sec	Raul Gonzales (Mex.)	May 25, 1979
4 × 100-m relay	37.83 sec	USA (S. Graddy, R. Brown, C. Smith, C. Lewis)	Aug. 11, 1984
4 × 200-m relay	1 min 20.26 sec	Univ. of So. Calif. (J. Andres, J. Sanford, B. Mullins, C. Edwards)	May 27, 1978
4 × 400-m relay	2 min 56.16 sec	USA (V. Matthews, R. Freeman, L. James, L. Evans/D. Everett, S. Lewis, K. Robinzine, B. Reynolds)	Oct. 20, 1968/Oct. 10, 1988
4 × 800-m relay	7 min 3.89 sec	Gr. Br. (P. Elliott, G. Cook, S. Cram, S. Coe)	Aug. 30, 1982
4 × 1,500-m relay	14 min 38.8 sec	W.Ger. (T. Wessinghage, H. Hudak, M. Lederer, K. Fleschen)	Aug. 17, 1977

she takes off and lands on the same foot; then, while attempting to maintain momentum, the athlete takes an exaggerated step, landing on the opposite foot and then continues into the pit with a third jump, landing with both feet.

In the shot put, as in the other throwing events in track and field, the competitors perform from a circular base constructed of concrete or synthetic material. The shot circle is 7 ft (2.1 m) in diameter and has a toeboard at the front of it. In the ''O'Brien'' technique, the most popular style, the athlete is positioned at the back of the ring, with the 16-lb (7.2-kg) metal ball—8 lb 13 oz (4 kg) for women—tucked under the chin. The contestant then crouches low on one foot and with his or her back to the toeboard thrusts to the front of the ring. As the shotputter reaches the toeboard, his or her body must be torqued in order to provide the impulse to shove the shot forward. The athlete may touch the toeboard but not go beyond it or touch the top of it.

The discus throw employs a platelike implement weighing 2 kg (4 lb 6.55 oz) for men and 1 kg (2 lb 3.27 oz) for women. It is one of the oldest of events; it was popular in the ancient Greek Olympics. The thrower enters a ring 2.5 m (8 ft 2.5 in) in diameter and takes up a position at the back. The athlete rests the discus—usually made of wood, with a metal rim—in the throwing hand. He or she then makes one and one-half quick turns and releases the discus at shoulder level.

The implement used in the hammer throw is actually a metal ball similar to the shot. It is attached by a 3 ft 11.75-in-long (1.21-m) steel wire and handle, and the entire implement weighs 16 lb (7.26 kg). The athlete turns several times in the circle, gripping the handle of the hammer with both hands, and attempts to release at the moment of maximum centrifugal force. Indoors, a shorthandled version of the hammer, weighing 35 lb (15.9 kg), is used.

The javelin is a spearlike shaft of wood or metal at least 260 cm (8 ft 6.62 in) long for men and 220 cm (7 ft 2.61 in) for women, with a metal tip at one end and a grip bound around

WOMEN'S WORLD TRACK AND FIELD RECORDS

Event	Record	Record Holder	Date
100 m	10.49 sec	Florence Griffith Joyner (USA)	July 16, 1988
200 m	21.34 sec	Florence Griffith Joyner (USA)	Sept. 29, 1988
400 m	47.60 sec	Marita Koch (E.Ger.)	Oct. 6, 1985
800 m	1 min 53.28 sec	Jarmila Kratochvilova (Czech.)	July 26, 1983
1,500 m	3 min 52.47 sec	Tatyana Kazankina (USSR)	Aug. 13, 1980
Mile	4 min 16.71 sec	Mary Decker (USA)	Aug. 21, 1985
3,000 m	8 min 22.62 sec	Tatyana Kazankina (USSR)	Aug. 26, 1984
5,000 m	14 min 37.33 sec	Ingrid Kristiansen (Nor.)	Aug. 5, 1986
10,000 m	30 min 13.74 sec	Ingrid Kristiansen (Nor.)	July 5, 1986
Marathon	2 hr 21 min 6 sec	Ingrid Kristiansen (Nor.)	Apr. 21, 1985
100-m hurdles	12.21 sec	Yordanka Donkova (Bulg.)	Aug. 21, 1988
400-m hurdles	52.94 sec	Marina Stepanova (USSR)	Sept. 17, 1986
High jump	2.09 m (6 ft 10¼ in)	Stefka Kostadinova (Bulg.)	Aug. 30, 1987
Long jump	7.52 m (24 ft 8¼ in)	Galina Chistyakova (USSR)	June 11, 1988
Shot put	22.63 m (74 ft 3 in)	Natalya Lisovskaya (USSR)	June 7, 1987
Discus throw	76.80 m (252 ft)	Gabriele Reinsch (E.Ger.)	July 9, 1988
Javelin throw	80.00 m (262 ft 5 in)	Petra Felke (E.Ger.)	Sept. 9, 1988
Heptathlon	7,291 points	Jackie Joyner-Kersee (USA)	Sept. 23–24, 1988
4 × 100-m relay	41.37 sec	E.Ger. (S. Gladisch, S. Rieger, I. Auerswald, M. Gohr)	Oct. 6, 1985
4 × 200-m relay	1 min 28.15 sec	E.Ger. (K. Müller, B. Wockei, M. Koch, M. Gohr)	Aug. 9, 1980
4 × 400-m relay	3 min 15.18 sec	USSR (T. Ledovskaya, O. Nazarova, M. Pinigina, O. Bryzgina)	Oct. 10, 1988
4 × 800-m relay	7 min 50.17 sec	USSR (N. Olizarenko, L. Gurina, L. Borisova, I. Podyalova)	Aug. 5, 1984

the shaft at the approximate center of gravity. After a short but rapid approach run, the 800-g (1 lb 12.2-oz) javelin—600 g (1 lb 5.16 oz) for women—is thrown overhand. The javelin point must come down first for the throw to be legal.

Often held at major track meets are the DECATHLON for men and the heptathlon for women (see PENTATHLON), events that test all-around capabilities.   TOM JORDAN

Bibliography: Anthony, Don, *Field Athletics* (1982); Archdeacon, H. C., and Ellsworth, Ken, eds., *Track Cyclopedia*, 10th ed. (1985); Doherty, Ken, *Track and Field Omnibook,* 4th ed. (1985); Foreman, Ken, *Track and Field*, 2d ed. (1983); Matthews, Peter, *Track and Field Athletics: The Records* (1986); Payne, Howard and Rosemary, *The Science of Track and Field Athletics* (1984).

tracking station

Tracking stations are optical, radar, and radio facilities used to collect data from spacecraft and rockets. Tracking stations are usually ground based but have been placed aboard ships, aircraft, and satellites. Optical tracking is used mainly for orbit determination of inactive spacecraft or of satellites equipped with optical ranging devices. Radio tracking is used extensively to acquire data from spacecraft and to transmit commands. Communications ranges can be as short as hundreds of meters at launch or as long as billions of kilometers.

In the early years of the space program, spacecraft were optically tracked by special cameras. By triangulating images against a star background, a satellite's orbit could be accurately determined. Radio tracking can provide accuracies comparable to optical tracking when receivers are operated as an INTERFEROMETER. Radar can also be used if the signal is strong enough or the target carries a transponder (transmitting responder). Orbit determination, however, is only a relatively small part of the tracking process. Its main objective is to take data collected by a spacecraft, transmit it in a uniform manner to a receiver, and then disseminate it to the users.

Manned space missions place the greatest demand on tracking networks, which must monitor spacecraft systems, crew health, and science equipment and transmit voice and video as well. Project Apollo, which placed men on the Moon, monitored the missions with tracking stations extending down the Atlantic Ocean from Cape Canaveral. They were joined by other stations for Earth-orbit tracking and supplemented by tracking ships and modified Boeing 707 jets. Deep-space communications were maintained by 26-m and 64-m-wide (85- and 210-ft) paraboloid antennas at Madrid, Spain; Honeysuckle Creek, Australia; and Goldstone, Calif. For use by the SPACE SHUTTLE program and other projects, NASA planned to augment its facilities with several Tracking and Data Relay Satellites (TDRS) that would collect data and transmit them to ground facilities through a station at White Sands, N.Mex. The second TDRS was aboard the Shuttle *Challenger* when it was destroyed during launch in 1986, but a replacement was orbited by the Shuttle *Discovery* in 1988.

A number of systems have been developed for tracking unmanned satellites and detecting missiles. These include the radar stations of the Ballistic Missile Early Warning System (see BMEWS) and the air force's Pave Paws system for detecting submarine-launched missiles. The SPADATS system includes the air force's worldwide network of cameras and radars, called Spacetrack; the navy's Space Surveillance System, a series of radio transmitters and receivers; and Canada's Satellite Tracking Unit. The North American Defense Command (Norad) routinely tracks satellites, releasing warnings through the air force's Satellite Control Facility if a collision between satellites seems imminent. The latter facility is being supplanted by the worldwide Ground-based Electro-Optical Deep Space Surveillance system (GEODSS). All of these systems are being united into a Consolidated Space Operations Center (CSOC), but its completion depends on deployment of the TDRS series.   DAVID DOOLING

Bibliography: Banke, Jim, "STS-26: A Mission Overview," *Space World,* September 1988; Gatland, Kenneth, ed., *The Illustrated Encyclopedia of Space Technology* (1981); Yuen, J. H., *Deep Space Telecommunications Systems Engineering* (1983).

tractor

The term *tractor* generally refers to a self-propelled pulling, pushing, and powering machine used in construction, mining, and agriculture. The word is also used for the tractor cab, the hauling end of a trucking rig. Historically, the word seems to have been first applied to a steam-powered machine that was developed in the mid-19th century to pull plows and other farm equipment; a cumbersome device, it required a large operating crew. The introduction of the gasoline engine in the 1890s reduced the weight of tractors and increased their mobility and versatility. Larger tractors were developed in the 1930s, using diesel engines that were more efficient and economical than gasoline engines. In later years, kerosene and liquefied petroleum gas have also been used to power some tractors.

The work tractor is a multipurpose machine that is mounted on crawler tracks or rubber tires; it provides low-speed tractive power on its own, and it may also be used as a mount and power source for machines such as pipe-laying equipment, front-end loaders, and bulldozers. The truck tractor is a powerful vehicle that is used to haul an unpowered trailer, forming a tractor-trailer rig. Many such tractors are diesel-powered, but gas turbines may be used on especially large vehicles. Designed solely for road-speed operation, truck tractors may have two or more axles. Loads can be changed quickly by switching trailers, which can then be loaded and unloaded without restricting the use of the tractor (see TRUCKING INDUSTRY).   R. L. PEURIFOY

Bibliography: Baldwin, Nick, *Classic American Farm Tractors* (1985); Jones, F. R., and Aldred, W. H., *Farm Power and Tractors*, 5th ed. (1980); Liljedahl, J. B., et al., *Tractors and Their Power Units*, 3d ed. (1984); Mills, R. K., *Implement and Tractor* (1986).

Tracy, Spencer

Spencer Tracy, an American actor of great range and virtuosity, remained one of Hollywood's most important personalities for more than 40 years. A compelling dramatic performer known for his sensitive character portrayals, Tracy is also remembered for the light comedic roles he played opposite Katharine Hepburn.

The actor Spencer Tracy, b. Milwaukee, Wis., Apr. 5, 1900, d. June 10, 1967, was a top screen star for 40 years and is especially remembered for his film partnership with Katharine HEPBURN. Among the nine movies they made together are *Woman of the Year* (1942), *Adam's Rib* (1949), and *Guess Who's Coming to Dinner?* (1967), Tracy's last. He won Academy Awards for his performances as a fisherman in *Captains Courageous* (1937) and Father Flanagan in *Boys Town* (1938).

Bibliography: Deschner, Donald, *The Complete Films of Spencer Tracy* (1987); Tozzi, Romano, *Spencer Tracy* (1973).

trade associations

A trade association is a nonprofit organization of business enterprises that are engaged in a particular industry or trade. Business firms voluntarily join a trade association to gain benefits for their industry or trade group that will also benefit them individually. By acting collectively, firms can often bring about results that they could not achieve on their own. Some trade associations represent huge industries and have many members: for example, the National Automobile Dealers Association numbers about 20,000. Small or specialty industries may have only a few members; the Gold-filled Manufacturers Association has 6. Trade associations usually represent a trade group or industry within a single country.

Trade associations have a variety of functions. They help promote trade for the industry as a whole through such means as advertising. They also facilitate the exchange of relevant information within a particular industry. Other trade association functions include the provision of a forum for the discussion and resolution of common problems; the promulgation of codes of ethics and procedures regulating business practices within the industry; the standardization of products; and the sponsoring of industry-related research.

Most activities of modern trade associations tend to foster competition. For example, providing individual firms with technical, price, and other information affecting their industry may enable them to limit their costs or to improve their operating efficiency. Trade associations have sometimes acted in ways that have suppressed competition, however. In the late 19th century especially, some trade associations acted as cartels, and the individual firms operating within a particular industry collaborated to fix prices or limit output or divide sales territory to increase their profits by restricting competition. Such restraints of trade were forbidden by the Sherman Anti-Trust Act, which was passed by Congress in 1890 and upheld as constitutional by the U.S. Supreme Court in 1911. Nearly all modern trade associations carefully adhere to the laws that cover the activities of trade associations. Nevertheless, certain practices, such as agreements to make public detailed information on the prices charged by individual firms, may limit competition by revealing price-cutters because these firms may then raise their prices to a more uniform level.

The beginnings of trade associations can be traced back to the guild system of the Middle Ages. Modern U.S. trade associations had their origins in the formation of the National Association of Cotton Manufacturers (1854) and other manufacturing associations prior to the Civil War.   JACK MURRAY

trade fairs

Trade fairs are exhibitions designed to display new products for the purpose of promoting their sale and utilization. They have developed from a long tradition of bazaars, caravans, and fairs dating back to ancient times. Throughout history fairs have been held to facilitate buying, selling, and bartering. The European fair—the ones held in various towns of the French region of Champagne were particularly notable—reached its peak in the 13th and 14th centuries but began to decline as an institution when goods became more easily available through the introduction of modern merchandising methods, particularly permanent shops. In the United States the fair developed as an exhibition, mainly of agricultural and horticultural products. The first permanent fair was initiated by Elkanah Watson in Pittsfield, Mass., in 1810, and the enthusiastic response to it led to the development of annual state and county fairs eventually across the entire country. The first of the WORLD'S FAIRS, the CRYSTAL PALACE exposition in London in 1851, was essentially an elaborate trade show. (See also CARNIVALS AND FAIRS.)

In recent years the business, or trade, fair has become a staple of commercial life. Exhibitions are held, for the most part, on a regular basis to promote almost all phases of manufacture. Governments use international trade fairs as a way of implementing cooperative ventures.

trade union: see LABOR UNION.

trade winds

The trade winds, or trades, which are a major component of the general circulation of the atmosphere, are the winds that occupy the lowest kilometer (0.6 mi) of the atmosphere over most of the tropical oceans. The pressure difference between the subtropical highs (semipermanent high-pressure centers located near 30° north and 30° south latitudes in the Atlantic and Pacific oceans) and the equatorial trough (a band of low pressure extending around the Earth near the equator) produces an equatorially directed force that opposes the Coriolis force (arising from the rotation of the Earth) and frictional drag at the air-sea interface. The trade winds, which result from the balance among these three forces, blow from the northeast over areas north of the equatorial trough and from the southeast over areas south of the equatorial trough. Because these winds have consistent direction and velocity, they became known in the days of sailing ships as the northeast and southeast trades.

Until recently the northeast and southeast trades were thought to be separated by a broad equatorial band of calm winds called the DOLDRUMS. Evidence from satellites shows, however, that the transition between the northeast and southeast trades occurs generally in a narrow band several degrees north of the equator; this region is called the intertropical convergence zone, or ITCZ (see TROPICAL CLIMATE).

JAMES R. HOLTON

Bibliography: Kals, William S., *The Riddle of the Winds* (1977); Riehl, Herbert, *Introduction to the Atmosphere*, 3d ed. (1978).

trademark

A trademark is a word or words, name, symbol, label, device, or picture applied or attached to a manufacturer's or merchant's product to identify it and distinguish it from similar products sold by others. Its most common form is the brand name. A trademark is different from both a COPYRIGHT and a PATENT. In a trademark the protection is in the symbol that distinguishes the product, not in the product itself.

A trademark in the United States comes into being as soon as and for as long as it is used. Trademarks that are not properly protected, however, may become generic terms and available to all manufacturers. Registering trademarks helps protect them. In the United States, trademark registration provisions were first enacted by Congress in 1870 and modified in 1881 and 1905. Federal registration under the Lanham Trademark Act of 1946 is made by filing an application, labels confirming trademark use, and a fee with the U.S. Patent and Trademark Office. Most Western countries, the USSR, and Japan have similar trademark requirements, although many countries do not require use prior to registration.

Trademarks fall into a number of categories: (1) A technical mark is one that indicates the source or origin of the product, and it has two categories: coined terms, which comprise "nonsense" syllables that do not exist as words in the English language, and English-language words that are completely arbitrary. Thus, *Xas* would be a coined or fanciful mark; a word such as *Car* would be an arbitrary mark as applied to ice cream. A technical mark is regarded as a "strong" mark that can be protected easily against infringement. (2) Descriptive marks are terms that describe a characteristic or feature of the goods and are generally difficult to protect as others may use similar terms to describe competitive products. (3) Suggestive marks are an intermediate category: not as "strong" as coined or arbitrary terms, and not descriptive marks. *Happy* for birthday candles is a valid mark but its scope of protection would be less than that of a "strong" mark. In addition to trademarks for products, there are other types of marks such as (1) service marks, which are used in the sale or advertising of services; (2) certification marks, which are used in connection with the products or services of one other than the owner of the mark to certify its origin, quality, or other characteristics (the U.S. Department of Agriculture—USDA—"seal of approval" and the USDA Shield Design for butter, eggs, poultry, and other goods comes within this classification); (3) collective marks, which are trademarks or service marks used by the members of a cooperative, an association, a union, or another collective group or organization. *Better Business Bureau* is an example.   MARTIN J. BERAN

Bibliography: Frankenstein, George and Diane, *Brandnames*, rev. ed. (1986); Hambleton, R., *Branding of America* (1987); Hurst, W. E., and Woessner, F., *How to Register a Trademark* (1983); Kamekura, Y., *Trademark Designs of the World* (1981); Mainhardt, P., and Havelock, K., *Concise Trademark Law and Practice* (1983); Room, Adrian, *Dictionary of Trade Name Origins* (1984); Samuels, Jeffrey M., ed., *Patent, Trademark, and Copyright Laws* (1985).

Trades Union Congress

The Trades Union Congress (TUC) in Great Britain is the organization that represents the collective interests of labor unions on a wide range of issues, from domestic labor laws to foreign policy. Founded at Manchester in 1868, the TUC, after reorganization as a loose federation in 1871, pressed for improved labor legislation. Originally an umbrella organization for unions of skilled craftsmen, the TUC acquired a socialist orientation at the turn of the century influenced by the syndicalist (see SYNDICALISM) concept of one union for all workers. The TUC operates as a lobbying group, not as a governing body, and the 91 member unions each retain the right of independent action to advance the economic interests of its members, who total about 9.8 million.

trading stamps

Trading stamps are a promotional device offered by some retail stores to increase sales, to attract customers with bonuses for their purchases, and as an alternative to advertising. The stamps are issued according to the amount spent. They are collected in special stamp books that can then be redeemed for merchandise—by selecting goods either from the store that issued the stamps or from special redemption centers that offer a catalog of merchandise available. Although stores that offer trading stamps sometimes charge slightly more for their goods, the practice of stamp giving has generally been popular with the public. Trading stamps were first issued in 1892.

Bibliography: Fulop, Christina, *The Role of Trading Stamps in Retail Competition*, 2d ed. (1973).

Trafalgar, Battle of   [truh-fal'-gur]

The Battle of Trafalgar (Oct. 21, 1805), a decisive sea clash of the NAPOLEONIC WARS, destroyed NAPOLEON I's plans for an invasion of England. Adm. Horatio NELSON, commanding a British fleet of 27 ships, defeated a combined French-Spanish fleet of 33 ships under Admiral Villeneuve off Spain's southwest coast by breaking through the French battle line and capturing 17 ships. Nelson's words before the battle, "England expects that every man will do his duty," have become immortal. He died in the battle.

Bibliography: Bennet, Geoffrey, *The Battle of Trafalgar* (1977).

traffic control

The term *traffic control* refers not only to road, rail, sea, and air transportation but also the traffic of shoppers in a supermarket, the flow of papers in large offices, and the movement of components on an assembly line. This article discusses only transportation traffic. For the other types, see OPERATIONS RESEARCH; SYSTEMS ENGINEERING.

The primary aims of all traffic-control systems are to speed the traveler and to save fuel, but almost everywhere the crisis of congested systems has supervened. Thus the most urgent objective of present-day control systems is to increase capacity, unblock problem points, and maintain safety. Contemporary transportation systems are so large that available funds cannot pay for new facilities needed, such as automated computer-controlled highways and the automatic programming of every automobile to its destination—an improvement for which the technology has already been devised.

Railroads. The first fully controlled transportation mode in the West was the early railroad, which for the first time introduced a complete control system under central management. Gauge of the track (distance between the rails) was unified, a system of visual SIGNALING was introduced to warn of obstruc-

tions ahead, and telegraphic communication (later telephone and radio) was used throughout the system and gradually extended to the national and international level. In recent years fully automatic train control has been introduced, including, for example, conductive cable systems laid between the rails to sense train speed, transmit instructions, and, if necessary, cause trains to change speed or stop. In the 1920s automated trains ran in Chicago and on London's Post Office railway, and today urban rapid-transit systems are generally operated by computer. Especially comprehensive automatic control may be found at large switching yards.

Roads. On ROADS AND HIGHWAYS, progress has been slower and except for general road improvement has been confined to the cities. Some forms of traffic control are simple and relatively inexpensive; these include SPEED LIMITS, one-way streets, prohibition of turning across oncoming traffic, tidal-flow schemes where lanes are reversed at peak hours, and—above all—clear signs indicating that these controls are in effect. Some improvements, however, require more money. Electric traffic signals were introduced in 1928; today visual control systems are linked to pneumatic vehicle detectors and electronic queue detectors, and signals and television pictures are fed to a central computer control room with human managers, who can take charge in emergency. Basic QUEUEING THEORY, formulated in 1908 by A. K. Erlang in a study of Copenhagen's telephone system, has assisted in speeding traffic flow of all kinds.

Aviation. The mode of transportation subject to the most advanced and costly control is AVIATION. Much of the world's airspace over land areas is controlled and is divided into air corridors linking large terminal airspaces. All areas are divided into Flight Information Regions, each with a traffic control center and radio communications. Most advanced aircraft have precision navigation systems, either self-contained systems such as the inertial and Doppler systems or systems that rely on external help: VOR (Very high frequency Omnidirectional Radio), radar navigation, and global systems using satellites or the Omega network. (See GUIDANCE AND CONTROL SYSTEMS.) Thus aircraft can maintain their position on fixed routes accurately, usually flying at known and reported flight levels (height above ground), and in the neighborhood of airports can be controlled with the utmost precision by traffic controllers (see AIRPORT). Rules in force depend on the weather and type of aircraft. Under VFR (Visual Flight Rules) small or simple aircraft may proceed without radio; but under IFR (Instrument Flight Rules) conditions, only radio-equipped aircraft may fly, and no VFR-only airplane is allowed to penetrate controlled airspace. Special rules govern separation of traffic on different routes, military airplanes, and such low fliers as agricultural crop dusters.

Shipping. Sea traffic has been greatly assisted by RADAR and the development of precision navigation aids and collision-warning systems. Despite this assistance, accidents and collisions at sea continue to occur, and sea traffic is more in need of proper control than any other mode of transportation. Even in dense traffic areas the only rule is to avoid other ships, and for many years the introduction of a proper sea-traffic control system has been urged. The dangers have magnified with increasing size of the vessels, and the threat (and actual occurrence) of collisions between large tankers is especially serious.

BILL GUNSTON

Bibliography: Carter, E., and Hamburger, W., *Introduction to Transportation Engineering: Highways and Transit* (1978); Clearnman, Brian, *Transportation Markings: A Study in Communications* (1981); Flood, Kenneth U., *Traffic Management*, 3d ed. (1975); Institute of Transportation Engineers, *Transportation and Traffic Engineering Handbook*, 2d ed. (1982); Garrison, Paul, *How the Air Traffic Control System Works* (1979); Hand, Bruce, et al., *Traffic Investigation and Control*, 2d ed. (1980); O'Flaherty, C. A., ed., *Highways: Traffic Planning and Engineering*, vol. 1, 3d ed. (1986); Oglesby, C., *Highway Engineering*, 3d ed. (1986).

tragacanth   [trag'-uh-kanth]

Tragacanth is a gum exuded by a small shrub of the pea family, *Astragalus gummifera*, and related leguminous plants. The plants grow in areas of southeastern Europe and southwestern Asia, and the gum is used in food as an emulsifier and thickening agent. Although no longer as important commercially as other gums, tragacanth is one of the oldest drugs known and is still used in medicine as a soothing agent and as an adhesive in pill manufacture. In textile printing the gum is used as a sizing material. Much of the tragacanth used in the United States comes from Iran.   FRANCES GIES

See also: GUM.

tragedy

As a literary term, *tragedy* refers to a drama in which a heroic protagonist meets an unhappy or calamitous end, brought about by some fatal flaw of character, by circumstances outside his or her control, or simply by destiny. Invented and developed in ancient Greece (see GREEK LITERATURE, ANCIENT), tragic drama has had a long but sporadic history in Western literature. Yet the great tragedies of the Greeks and of the Renaissance rank among the most compelling and most fascinating of all the works of literature.
Greek Tragedy. It is believed that Greek tragedy emerged from the cult of DIONYSUS, god of fertility, wine, and poetry. At first, chants and dances were performed in honor of the god and his attendants by a chorus whose leader, the coryphaeus, engaged in chanted dialogue with the group. In the middle of the 6th century BC, the Athenian poet THESPIS replaced the coryphaeus by a distinct actor, the protagonist, who, being masked, could actually play several roles if he withdrew to the wings whenever the chorus performed alone. The great innovation of AESCHYLUS was to introduce a second actor, so that now a dialogue could take place between two individuals in addition to the dialogue between actor and chorus. SOPHOCLES and EURIPIDES used a third actor, and with this the formal evolution of Greek tragedy came to an end.
Roman, Renaissance, and Early Modern Tragedy. Of Roman tragedy—closely modeled on that of Greece—only the works of Lucius Annaeus SENECA influenced later epochs. The short duration of the brilliant phase of creation in Greece is matched by the brevity of other great periods of tragic drama in Western civilization: Elizabethan England—a few decades on either side of 1600; the Spanish Golden Age—roughly the same period; France—from the 1630s to the 1690s; Germany—approximately three decades on either side of 1800. It may be argued, however, that during the 19th century such novelists as Dostoyevsky, Melville, and Hardy successfully transferred the tragic vision from the drama to the novel. At the same time, they and many other writers removed the concerns of tragedy from gods, rulers, and aristocrats to the middle and lower classes.
The Tragic Vision. The first and still the most influential definition of tragic drama was sketched out in the POETICS OF ARISTOTLE. For Aristotle tragedy is a unified action; it is serious, complete, plausible; it has action of substantial magnitude; most important, it concerns the fall of a hero whose misfortune is brought about not by vice or depravity but by some error or frailty—the tragic flaw; its incidents arouse "the pleasure of pity and fear" and by so doing accomplish the purgation or catharsis of these emotions in the audience.

In the Renaissance such rules as the unities of time, place, and action were derived from Aristotle. Thus the great so-called classical tragedies of the French playwrights Pierre CORNEILLE and Jean RACINE restricted their actions to a single place, such as a room in a palace, and to a single day, while subordinate actions—especially comic ones—and low or vulgar words were rigorously excluded. By contrast, William SHAKESPEARE in England and Lope de VEGA in Spain disregarded many of these rules and wrote tragedies that ignore many of the classical prescriptions. Both the classical and the romantic approach bore fruit in the tragedies of GOETHE and SCHILLER.
Contemporary Tragedy. Today a tragedy is still taken to be a work of high seriousness arousing the audience's deepest emotions. A protagonist is required for whom the audience can feel a fundamental sympathy. His or her downfall is the inevitable result of some major enterprise or decision; it is not caused by chance events. The downfall must shake the audience deeply and be felt as important.

A recurring issue during the 20th century has been whether truly tragic literature is still possible. Traditionally, tragedy had attached a terrifying importance to the destiny of humanity. Now it is asked whether in a debunking and unheroic age such a vision of human stature can be sustained. A play such as T. S. Eliot's *Murder in the Cathedral* or Jean Anouilh's *Antigone* (1944; Eng. trans., 1946) is cast in the old heroic mold; but are works such as Eugene O'NEILL's *Long Day's Journey into Night* or Arthur Miller's DEATH OF A SALESMAN tragic, or—because their protagonists are "nobodies"—merely pathetic? If such works are indeed modern tragedies, it must be granted that the concept of tragedy has changed significantly, although essential points, such as sympathy for the protagonist and the inevitability of his or her downfall, firmly bind 20th-century tragedy to the tradition.   OSCAR MANDEL

Bibliography: Albrecht, W. P., *The Sublime Pleasures of Tragedy* (1975); Belsey, C., *The Subject of Tragedy* (1985); Bradley, A. C., *Shakespearean Tragedy* (1904; repr. 1985); Brereton, G., *Principles of Tragedy* (1968); Kaufmann, W., *Tragedy and Philosophy* (1979); Lesky, A., *Greek Tragedy* (1967); Mandel, O., *A Definition of Tragedy* (1961; repr. 1982); Nietzsche, F., *The Birth of Tragedy*, trans. by W. Kaufmann (1967); Poole, A., *Tragedy and the Greek Example* (1987); Sewall, R. B., *The Vision of Tragedy*, rev., enl. ed. (1979); Steiner, G., *The Death of Tragedy* (1961); Williams, R., *Modern Tragedy* (1966).

tragicomedy

Tragicomedy is a sophisticated and deliberately ambiguous genre of drama that combines and somehow fuses the mutually opposed patterns and responses of TRAGEDY and COMEDY. Unlike comedy, tragicomedy stirs deep emotions and directly confronts human suffering, mortality, and death. Unlike tragedy, tragicomedy rejects absolutes, the inevitability of catastrophe, and the need for heroism and sacrifice. The tragic impasse is avoided, but the carefree release of comedy is denied.

As a mixed mode, tragicomedy follows no single set of conventions and often contradicts normal expectations. The Roman dramatist PLAUTUS first used the term *tragicomedy* in the prologue to *Amphitryon,* a play that violated decorum by dealing with both gods and slaves and by mixing the heroic and the farcical. The genre flourished during the Renaissance, producing in Italy two pastoral tragicomedies, Tasso's *Aminta* (1573) and Guarini's *Il Pastor fido* (The Faithful Shepherd, 1590). Shakespeare's late tragicomic romances, The TEMPEST and *Cymbeline,* followed a precedent established by the tragicomedies of Francis BEAUMONT and John FLETCHER.

In the modern era, starting with Ibsen's The WILD DUCK and continuing to the plays of Beckett, Ionesco, and Pinter, tragicomedy has again become an important dramatic form for presenting the unresolved dualities of existence. Characterized by jarring discontinuity of tone and action, contemporary tragicomedy leaves the spectator bewildered and uncertain whether to laugh or cry. As in Beckett's WAITING FOR GODOT, the tragicomic mode often self-consciously calls attention to itself as theater.

Bibliography: Guthke, Karl S., *Modern Tragicomedy* (1966); Herrick, Marvin T., *Tragicomedy: Its Origins and Development in Italy, France, and England* (1955); Hirst, David L., *Tragicomedy* (1984); Maguire, Nancy K., ed., *Renaissance Tragicomedy* (1986); Ristine, Frank H., *English Tragicomedy: Its Origin and History* (1910); Styan, J. L., *The Dark Comedy: The Development of Modern Comic Tragedy*, 2d ed. (1968).

See also: THEATER OF THE ABSURD.

trailer: see MOBILE HOME; TRUCKING INDUSTRY.

trailing arbutus

Trailing arbutus is the common name for *Epigaea repens,* a creeping evergreen shrub of the family Ericaceae. Native to North America, it grows particularly well in the shade of pine trees in the eastern United States. The tubular white or pink flower cluster is the state flower of Massachusetts.

Traini, Francesco   [trah-ee'-nee]

Francesco Traini, a Pisan painter active between 1321 and 1347, is the subject of much controversy because scholars disagree over which works may justly be attributed to him. His one signed and dated work is the Saint Dominic polyptych (1344–45; Santa Catherina, Pisa). His disputed paintings include the well-known frescoes entitled *Triumph of Death* and *Last Judgment* (c.1350; Campo Santo, Pisa). These are superb but provincial reflections on the panoramas by Ambrogio Lorenzetti in Siena.   ALAN P. DARR

Trajan, Roman Emperor   [tray'-juhn]

The Roman emperor Trajan (r. 98–117) extended the boundaries of the empire to include Dacia and part of the eastern kingdom of Parthia. In addition to his military achievements, Trajan implemented highly successful civil, economic, and social programs.

Trajan (Marcus Ulpius Traianus), b. Sept. 18, AD 53, d. August 117, Roman emperor (AD 98–117), pursued an aggressive, expansionist policy and gained a reputation for his benevolence. Born in Roman Spain, he distinguished himself early on in military and political posts and in AD 97 received from the emperor Nerva (r. 96–98) the rank of caesar and a share of imperial power. Supported by the military, Trajan became sole emperor at Nerva's death. An effective administrator, Trajan reduced taxes and sponsored subsidies for the poor, a massive building program, and the admission of provincials to prominent positions. He became best known, however, for his campaigns against the Dacians (101–02, 105–06), which led to the creation of a Roman province north of the Danube, and for his war with the Parthians (113–17), Rome's principal adversary in the East. Trajan captured the Parthian capital, Ctesiphon, and marched to the Persian Gulf but could not eliminate resistance. By Trajan's death the Parthians were again in control of most of the overrun territory. Hadrian, his successor, retained the province of Dacia but renounced most of Trajan's eastern "conquests."   JOHN W. EADIE

Bibliography: Henderson, B. W., *Five Roman Emperors* (1927); Lepper, F. A., *Trajan's Parthian War* (1948; repr. 1979); Rossi, Lino, *Trajan's Column and the Dacian Wars*, trans. by J. M. C. Toynbee (1971).

Trakl, Georg   [trah'-kul]

The Austrian poet Georg Trakl, b. Salzburg, Feb. 3, 1887, d. Nov. 3, 1914, was preoccupied with images of death, decay, and the misery of civilization. His first collection, *Gedichte* (Poems, 1913), includes some of the best expressionist poetry written in the German language; other important poems were published posthumously in *Der Herbst der Einsamen* (The Autumn of the Lonely, 1920) and *Gesang des Abgeschiedenen* (Song of the Departed, 1933). Trakl died from an overdose of drugs while serving as a pharmacist in the army.

trampoline: see GYMNASTICS.

trance

A trance is a sleeplike condition in which a person's responses to stimuli and knowledge of what is happening are minimal. Trances are common in HYPNOSIS and HYSTERIA.

tranquilizer

Tranquilizers are a group of drugs prescribed to relieve ANXIETY, tension, and agitation while having comparatively few adverse effects. Because they act as mild depressants on the central nervous system, however, they can lead to drowsiness and some degree of mental confusion. Also known as ataractics or anxiolytics, they are sometimes grouped as the "mild" tranquilizers, in contrast with stronger SEDATIVES such as barbiturates, the PSYCHOTROPIC DRUGS used in the treatment of mental disorders, and ALCOHOL.

As a group, tranquilizers are the most commonly used prescription drugs in the United States. They include the benzodiazepines (such as VALIUM and LIBRIUM), the dephenylmethanes (Vistaril and Atarax), and the propanedios (tybamate and meprobamate, also called Equanil and Miltown). Physicians choose between the various tranquilizers on the basis of their appropriateness to meet a specific need.

Anxiety is a normal response to STRESS and requires treatment only when the degree of physiological disturbance of the sympathetic nervous system interferes with the patient's overall functioning. Such disturbances may include accelerated heart rate, palpitations, involuntary movements, insomnia or other sleep disorders, diarrhea, bandlike headaches, increased rate of urination, and gastric discomfort. Tranquilizers provide temporary relief in such instances, although the mere masking of symptoms in this way is potentially hazardous. With continuous use the tranquilizers also decrease in effectiveness, and dependency can occur (see DRUG ABUSE). Buspirone hydrochloride (BuSpar), which was approved by the U.S. Food and Drug Administration in 1986, appears to avoid these problems of drowsiness and possible dependency associated with other tranquilizers.

Bibliography: Gabe, Jonathan, and Williams, Paul, eds., *Tranquillisers* (1986); Winger, Gail, *Valium: The Tranquil Trap* (1986).

Trans-Alaska Pipeline

The Trans-Alaska Pipeline is an oil pipeline that runs from Prudhoe Bay, an arm of the Arctic Ocean, 1,285 km (800 mi) south to Valdez, an ice-free port on the Gulf of Alaska. The 1.2-m-diameter (48-in) pipeline is designed to carry more than two million barrels of crude oil per day from the Alaskan North Slopes, located some 400 km (250 mi) north of the Arctic Circle. (The North Slopes contain estimated reserves of nearly 10 billion barrels.)

The project, which received congressional approval in 1973, was opposed by environmentalists, who feared the harmful effects of the construction on the land, wildlife, and people of Alaska; some studies have shown that oil drilling in northern Alaska has indeed caused significant environmental damage. The pipeline was built by the Alyeska Pipeline Service Company, a consortium of 8 oil corporations, and was completed in 1977 at a cost of almost $8 billion. In addition to the pipeline, the project included a tanker terminal at Valdez, 12 pumping stations, and the Yukon River Bridge, a joint venture of Alyeska and the state of Alaska.

Refinery and transport problems have reduced the potential contribution of Alaskan oil to the U.S. oil supply. West Coast oil-refinery capacity has proved to be insufficient to handle the Alaskan crude, and much of the oil is carried by tanker to Japan or to refineries on the Gulf Coast and in the East. Proposals for a new pipeline to transport the oil from Washington State to Minnesota (over the so-called Northern Tier states) and from there to the East Coast were dropped in 1983 because of opposition from the Washington State government. A 1986 U.S. Department of the Interior recommendation that the Arctic National Wildlife Refuge, located east of Prudhoe Bay, be opened to oil exploration has not yet been approved by Congress.   FRANK RAGLAND

Bibliography: Berry, Mary C., *Alaska Pipeline: The Politics of Oil and Native Land Claims* (1975); Laycock, George, "Wilderness by the Barrel," *Audubon* 90 (May 1988); Mead, Robert D., *Journeys down the Line* (1978); Roscow, James P., *800 Miles to Valdez* (1977).

Trans-Amazonian Highway

The Trans-Amazonian Highway is a series of roads in Brazil built to spur the development of the Amazon River basin. The major arteries are an east-west route from the Atlantic coast to the Peruvian border, a north-south Rio de Janeiro-Brasília-Belém route, and a south-north route from São Paulo to Santarém. A network of feeder roads has opened a huge region to settlement.

Trans-Andine Railroad

The Trans-Andine Railroad, a railroad between Chile and Argentina, is one of several lines built across the high Andes of South America. An east-west road, the line was constructed in the early 20th century from Santiago, Chile, across the Andes to Mendoza, where it connected with the rail system of Argentina. When the line was completed in 1910 it helped provide rail service between the capitals of the two republics. The line was fully electrified by the 1950s.   JOHN F. STOVER

Trans-Canada Highway

The Trans-Canada Highway—begun in 1949, opened in 1962, and completed in 1965—is a 7,825-km-long (4,860-mi) road across southern Canada, from St. John's, Newfoundland, to Victoria on Vancouver Island, British Columbia. It is the longest national highway in the world. The paved, occasionally divided road, passing through all Canadian provinces, was jointly financed by the federal and provincial governments.

Trans-Caspian Railroad

The Trans-Caspian Railroad is a Russian railway that links the Caspian Sea to Tashkent. Begun in 1880, by 1888 the railroad had reached Samarkand, nearly 1,600 km (1,000 mi) east of the Caspian Sea. Russia's aims in building the railroad were imperialistic rather than economic, and it was several years before connections were made with the rest of the Russian rail network.   JOHN F. STOVER

Bibliography: Stephenson, Graham, *Russia from 1812 to 1945* (1969).

Trans-Siberian Railroad

The Trans-Siberian Railroad is a Russian railroad connecting Moscow with Vladivostok. Completed in 1916, it is the longest continuous rail line in the world. During the 1880s, a line had been built as far east as Chelyabinsk, 1,700 km (1,054 mi) from Moscow. The major portion of the Siberian sectors were finished between 1891 and 1900. The completion of the Chinese Eastern Railway in Manchuria, and a short water connection across Lake Baikal, gave Russia a new transportation route across Asia by 1903. In 1904 a rail loop around the foot of Lake Baikal was opened, and in 1916 the Amur sector (located north of the Amur River) was finished.

Since 1916 several branch lines have been added, and recently much of the route has been electrified. In the 1970s a passenger train, the *Russia*, made the 9,250-km (5,750-mi) trip in less than 8 days. The 1984 completion of a 3,200-km (2,000-mi) parallel rail line, the Baikal-Amur Mainline (BAM), 160 to 320 km (100 to 200 mi) north of the Trans-Siberian Railroad in eastern Siberia, opened mineral-rich areas of Siberia to exploitation.   JOHN F. STOVER

Bibliography: Meakin, A., *Ribbon of Iron* (1901; repr. 1970); Niven, A., *From Moscow to Vladivostok* (1985).

transactional analysis

Transactional analysis, originated by Eric Berne and popularized by Thomas A. Harris, is a psychological theory that analyzes the structure of social interactions. In such interactions individuals assume three alternate personality states—"adult," "parent," and "child"—analogous to Freud's ego, superego, and id. Relationships are balanced if complementary states are presented; for instance, a husband's "child" balances a wife's "parent." Relationships are unbalanced and disruptive if nonreciprocal states are presented—an employee's "adult" does not balance an employer's "parent."

There are also four basic life positions that individuals take in interactions with others. These are stated as "I'm OK, you're OK"; "I'm OK, you're not OK"; "I'm not OK, you're OK"; "I'm not OK, you're not OK." People's lives are structured as "scripts" or life plans for obtaining certain "payoffs" or goals. People have a need for a minimum level of social gratification, or "strokes." In relationships, individuals repeatedly play out certain "games," eliciting psychological payoffs.

Psychotherapy from a transactional-analysis approach consists of identifying and analyzing the patient's styles and positions of interaction. It is oriented to the immediate present, and "games" within therapy are analyzed. The therapist plays a consultative and directive role.   LYNN REHM

Bibliography: Berne, Eric, *Games People Play* (1964); Harris, Thomas, *I'm OK, You're OK* (1969).

transcendence, divine

The concept of divine transcendence states that God is elevated above and extrinsic to the universe that he created. In the Judeo-Christian tradition, God is viewed as combining the apparent opposites of transcendence and immanence (see IMMANENCE, DIVINE) in that he both transcends the universe and is active in it. Traditional Christian philosophy, exemplified particularly in the works of Thomas Aquinas, treats God as transcendent in the sense that he created the world; that he has perfect knowledge of all earthly things, which indeed derive from him; that he is infinite and eternal; and that, unlike humans, he is identical with his own essence.

transcendental function

A transcendental function is a function that is not a root of a polynomial equation. Such functions arise frequently in mathematics and science. A function that is a root of a polynomial equation is an algebraic function; all other functions are called transcendental. The importance of transcendental functions stems from the fact that most of the functions that describe natural phenomena turn out to be transcendental functions. The six trigonometric functions (see TRIGONOMETRY)—sine, cosine, tangent, cotangent, secant, and cosecant—are all transcendental, for example, as are the logarithmic, exponential, and hyperbolic functions.   WILLIAM W. ADAMS

transcendental number

A transcendental number is an IRRATIONAL NUMBER—meaning a number that cannot be represented as the quotient of two integers—that is also not a root of any polynomial equation with integer coefficients (see NUMBER). It was not established until 1851 (by Joseph Liouville) that transcendental numbers exist. In 1882, Ferdinand Lindemann proved that the number π (pi) is transcendental. One consequence of this result is that it demonstrated the impossibility of constructing by ruler and compass a circle and square of the same area. Today the theory of transcendental numbers is an active area of research and it has major applications in NUMBER THEORY.   WILLIAM W. ADAMS

Bibliography: Courant, Richard, and Robbins, Herbert, *What Is Mathematics? An Elementary Approach to Ideas and Methods* (1978).

transcendentalism

Transcendentalism was an American movement that flourished from the mid-1830s until the mid-1840s. The transcendentalists generally believed in an intuitive idealism, the idea of an organic universe suffused by an immanent God, the divinity of humankind, and the importance of the individual's own moral insight as opposed to the rule of the many. Although the movement was short-lived, it helped change the direction of American literature, religion, and social thought.

The origins of transcendentalism are literary, philosophical, and religious. The transcendentalists championed such English and continental writers as Thomas Carlyle and Goethe, who broke with the literary formalism of the 18th century. They followed the philosophy of Immanuel KANT in believing that humans had an innate ability to perceive that their existence transcended mere sensory experience, as opposed to the then-prevailing *tabula rasa* beliefs of John Locke. Primarily, most scholars agree, the transcendental movement was a direct result of a search for a religious intuitionism and excitement lacking in the conventional religion of the day. Thus the transcendentalists spurned contemporary organized religion by demanding a return to the spirit and the teachings of Christ that they felt gave Christianity its validity.

Nearly all the major participants in the transcendental movement were men educated at Harvard College who went on to become Unitarian ministers living in the vicinity of Boston. In September 1836, Ralph Waldo EMERSON and three friends met in Boston for, in Emerson's words, "the free discussion of theological & moral subjects." From this group was formed the Transcendental Club, which met nearly 30 times over the next four years.

The most important member of the club—and of the movement—was Emerson. During the transcendental period he published five works that established his reputation: *Nature* (1836), the first book to state the basic principles of transcendentalism; the "American Scholar Address" (1837), which called for an original literature based on American themes; the "Divinity School Address" (1838), which called for a religion of inspiration to replace the formalism of the day; and *Essays* (1841) and *Essays: Second Series* (1844), which included such pieces as "Self-Reliance" and "The Poet." Through these works and well-attended public lectures, Emerson conveyed the group's concerns to a wide, interested audience.

Other transcendentalists tended to deal with specific areas within the large framework that Emerson had laid out. Bronson ALCOTT's inductive and Socratic philosophies of education were expressed in *Record of a School* (1835) and *Conversations with Children on the Gospels* (1836–37); Margaret FULLER's *Woman in the Nineteenth Century* (1845) decried the traditional stereotyped roles for men and women; and Theodore PARKER, in *A Discourse on the Transient and Permanent in Christianity* (1841) and *A Discourse of Matters Pertaining to Religion* (1842), argued for the permanent traits of intuitive religion as opposed to the passing doctrines, rites, and creeds of existing institutions. Finally, all the transcendentalists were involved in the antislavery movement.

Two periodicals were associated with the movement. The *Western Messenger* (1835–41)—edited for three years by Unitarian minister James Freeman CLARKE—was published in the Ohio Valley and supported the transcendentalists when most conservative journals opposed them. The DIAL (1840–44), edited by Fuller and Emerson, featured numerous contributions by Parker, Henry David THOREAU, and the editors, and was the most visible gathering point for the group.

The transcendentalists also participated in two utopian communal efforts. Fruitlands (June 1843–January 1844), at Harvard, Mass., involved Alcott's family and a ragtag band of about a dozen. It failed through a combination of lack of funds, incompetent management, and internal bickering about its aims and methods. The BROOK FARM community (April 1841–September 1847), at West Roxbury, Mass., was one of America's most famous communal experiments and the best example of the social aspect of transcendentalism. Founded by George RIPLEY and his wife, Sophia, as a community in which everyone shared in the work and the profits yet had time for contemplation and artistic endeavors, it briefly included Nathaniel Hawthorne (and formed the basis for his novel *The Blithedale Romance*) and had many transcendentalists as visitors. In March 1845, influenced by the French utopian thinker Charles Fourier, the members reorganized as Brook Farm Phalanx, but Fourier's strictly regimented plans clashed with the transcendental concept of personal freedom, their finances—never solid to begin with—worsened, and a disas-

trous fire in 1846 assured Brook Farm's collapse.

Although transcendentalism as an organized movement died out in the 1840s, the ideas of its participants have influenced American life and letters down to the present day. The challenges to the Unitarian establishment by Parker and others resulted in significant changes in that religion's organization. Alcott's educational reforms helped to accelerate acceptance of a belief that children should learn by thinking and not just by rote memorization. Emerson's eloquent expressions of organicism in art (everything proceeds from a natural order, followed by but not imposed upon man) did much to counteract the poetic conservatism of his day and helped lead to the experimental verse of Walt Whitman. Thoreau's belief in the importance of simple living in accordance with nature (*Walden*, 1854) has become part of the American canon. And Emerson's concept of self-reliance and Thoreau's idea of civil disobedience both lie behind the American belief that an individual must oppose laws thought to be unjust. Indeed, Martin Luther King, Jr., acknowledged his debt to Thoreau as a major influence in forming his own social thought. Transcendentalism has not died—it has been absorbed and revivified in the fabric of American society.

JOEL MYERSON

Bibliography: Buell, L., *Literary Transcendentalism: Style and Vision in the American Renaissance* (1973); Frothingham, Octavius Brooks, *Transcendentalism in New England* (1876); Hutchison, W. R., *The Transcendentalist Ministers* (1959); Miller, Perry, ed., *The Transcendentalists: An Anthology* (1950); Myerson, Joel, *The New England Transcendentalists and the "Dial"* (1980); Swift, L., *Brook Farm* (1900).

transcontinental railroad

The transcontinental railroad in North America became a reality on May 10, 1869, when the tracks of the Union Pacific joined those of the Central Pacific at Promontory Point, Utah. The event fulfilled dreams of spanning the continent that were spurred by settlement of the American West and that dated back to at least 1845. Interest in a transcontinental railroad was heightened by the acquisition of Oregon (1846) and California (1848) and the subsequent gold rush. In 1853, Congress appropriated $150,000 to defray expenses of surveying feasible routes, but the question of the best one quickly became a matter of sectional controversy.

TRANSCONTINENTAL RAILROADS, 1850-90

1 Northern Pacific
2 Central Pacific
3 Union Pacific
4 Kansas Pacific
5 Atchison, Topeka, and Santa Fe
6 Southern Pacific
7 Atlantic & Pacific (until 1880)
8 Texas & Pacific

Cartographic Production by Lothar Roth & Associates

Once the South left the Union, Congress pushed through the Pacific Railroad Act (July 1, 1862), which authorized the Central Pacific to build eastward from San Francisco and the Union Pacific to build westward from Omaha, Nebr., via South Pass; the two were to join at the California-Nevada line. Each company was to receive 400 ft (122 m) of right-of-way through public (or 100 ft/31 m—through private) lands and 10 alternate square-mile sections of public land for each mile of tract laid. Loans of $16,000 to $48,000 per mile—depending on the grade of the terrain—were also available as a first mortgage on the railroad. In 1864, Congress doubled the land grant and made the financial subsidy a second lien on the property. It again amended the original legislation in 1866 to allow the Central Pacific to advance eastward until it met the Union Pacific, thereby turning the project into a construction race.

Chinese workers were employed by the Central Pacific, and the Union Pacific hired Irish immigrants and Civil War veterans. During the winter of 1868-69 the two railroads employed about 25,000 laborers.

Both lines experienced many problems. The Central Pacific had to ship in steel rails from the East Coast by sea, whereas the Union Pacific had to transport ballast and lumber for crossties from Wisconsin. The latter company experienced difficulty with the Plains Indians, primarily because railroad crews were slaughtering the Indians' buffalo herds for meat. The Central Pacific had to tunnel through the High Sierras, bridge deep gorges, and construct 40 mi (64 km) of snowsheds to protect against snow and avalanches. Ultimately, the Union Pacific laid 1,086 mi (1,747 km) of track and the Central Pacific, 689 mi (1,109 km).

A number of scandals accompanied the transcontinental project. The most famous involved CRÉDIT MOBILIER OF AMERICA, the Union Pacific's construction company, through which some of the railroad's directors and various politicians pocketed enormous profits.

While the first transcontinental line was opening the Great Plains, three other railroads were pushing toward the West Coast. By 1883 the Southern Pacific connected New Orleans and Los Angeles, the Santa Fe ran between Chicago and Southern California via Albuquerque, and the Northern Pacific extended from Duluth to Portland.

Construction of the CANADIAN PACIFIC RAILWAY was also attended by scandal (see PACIFIC SCANDAL), but the main line between Montreal and the Pacific coast was completed in 1885.

W. EUGENE HOLLON

Bibliography: Athearn, Robert G., *Union Pacific Country* (1971); Galloway, John D., *The First Transcontinental Railroad: Central Pacific, Union Pacific* (1930); Howard, Robert W., *The Story of the First Transcontinental Railroad* (1962); Riegal, Robert E., *The Story of the Western Railroads* (1926); Winther, Oscar O., *The Transportation Frontier: Trans-Mississippi West, 1865-1890* (1964).

transducer [tranz-doo'-sur]

A transducer is a device that transforms input energy into output energy; the forms of the input and output energy may be identical or different. The electric conversion transducer, for example, changes electricity from one frequency to another, and some of the most common transducers change energy from one form into another. Among these are the electroacoustic transducer (sound into electricity), the piezoelectric (electricity into motion, or vice versa), and the ultrasonic (electricity into ultrasound). In the microphone, a familiar electroacoustic transducer, the sound wave first impinges upon a diaphragm inside the microphone, causing it to move. The diaphragm's movement then causes a change in some property of an electric current.

Piezoelectric transducers are crystals that can generate an electric charge when they are deformed by pressure or torque. A common example is the phonograph needle, in which the motion of the stylus twists a piezoelectric crystal in order to produce an electric current that drives the amplifier. Other piezoelectric transducers, which vibrate on frequency, are used widely in radio and television broadcasting.

Ultrasonic transducers produce ultrasonic energy (sound waves above the range of human hearing) by converting input electrical, mechanical, or hydraulic energy. Ultrasound is used in materials testing and as an alternative to X rays in medicine.

transept [tran'-sept]

In a cross-shaped church, the transepts are the transverse arms of the building and are placed at the crossing, the juncture of the NAVE and the choir. Transepts were added to provide additional space at each side of the ALTAR. Several English Gothic cathedrals, such as SALISBURY CATHEDRAL, have double transepts; the second set, with shorter arms, is placed east of the first set and is closer to the APSE.

See also: CATHEDRALS AND CHURCHES.

transference

In PSYCHOANALYSIS, transference is the shift by a patient undergoing analysis of his or her emotions associated with past figures, such as parents, to the analyst. Transference is considered a necessary therapeutic development.

Transfiguration

The Gospels according to Matthew (17:1-13), Mark (9:2-13), and Luke (9:28-36) describe an occasion on which Jesus took his disciples Peter, James, and John to a mountaintop (traditionally Mount Tabor, although Mount Hermon is preferred by many scholars) and there appeared "transfigured" (manifesting glory) with Moses and Elijah. The Transfiguration is understood by Christians as a testimony that Jesus fulfilled the Old Testament prophecies of the Messiah. The Feast of the Transfiguration is observed on Aug. 6.

transform fault

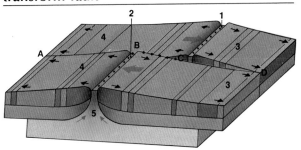

A transform fault (BC) is found between two mid-oceanic ridges (1, 2) that separate two receding crustal plates (3, 4). As hot magma rises (5) from the mantle and cools, new ocean crust forms on either side of the fault and moves away (black arrows) from the ridges at identical speeds but in opposite directions. These motions are the reverse of those (green arrows) which would result if the ridges were moving away from each other. No relative movement occurs along AB and CD, where the material moves at the same speed and in the same direction.

Transform faults are the shear boundaries of the Earth's segmented crustal plates (see PLATE TECTONICS). The faults are located perpendicular to mid-oceanic ridges and are occasionally marked by scarps. In contrast to the mid-oceanic ridges, where new ocean crust is generated, and trenches (subduction zones), where crust is consumed, crust along transform faults is conserved as the adjacent crustal plates simply slide past one another. Most transform faults, like the other two types of plate boundaries, lie beneath the ocean, but the SAN ANDREAS FAULT in California is a prime example located on land. Strike-slip faulting along a transform fault is a major cause of EARTHQUAKES, but these are generally less intense than those associated with subduction zones.

The name *transform fault* is derived from the displacement, or transformation, of a fault into a different type of plate boundary at the ends of the fault shear zone. This boundary is either a mid-oceanic ridge, a trench, or a triple junction (point intersection of three crustal plates). Both ends of the San Andreas Fault, northwest of San Francisco and south of the Gulf of California, intersect triple junctions.

CRAIG AMERIGIAN AND MICHAEL T. LEDBETTER

Bibliography: Press, Frank, and Siever, Raymond, *Earth* (1974).

transformation

In mathematics, a transformation is a rule by which a given mathematical object may be changed into another one of the same kind. The idea of a transformation has its roots in the fact that the same object or event can be observed from different points of view, with its appearance depending on the viewpoint. For instance, a circle looks like a circle when viewed straight on but like an ellipse when viewed obliquely. There is a transformation law that indicates how to predict the apparent shape from the new viewpoint, given the shape from the old point of view. (Special mention should be made of the identity transformation, which leaves everything unchanged.) This idea has been most fruitful in mathematics and physics, where it has led to a number of theories, including Einstein's theory of relativity.

A transformation that undoes the work of another transformation is called the inverse transformation to the latter. For instance, the inverse of a clockwise rotation by 90° is a counterclockwise rotation by the same amount.

Most mathematical transformations may be classified as geometric or algebraic transformations. A geometric transformation is a mapping of a geometrical object into itself. For example, a Euclidean transformation of the plane into itself is one that transforms geometric figures into congruent figures. Rotations and translations (shifts) are examples of Euclidean transformations, because a square or any other geometric figure can be rotated or translated without changing its size and shape. Under a linear transformation, the image of a square will always be a parallelogram, but it need neither retain its right angles nor maintain the same area.

Algebraic transformations are rules for obtaining new algebraic expressions from old ones by making a substitution in the variables. For example, the substitution $x' = x + y$, $y' = 2x - y$ transforms the expression $x'^2 + y'^2$ into $(x + y)^2 + (2x - y)^2$, which equals $5x^2 - 2xy + 2y^2$. This algebraic transformation and the geometric transformation are related through analytic geometry: if the geometrical points are given coordinates, then geometric transformations can be expressed in terms of algebraic transformations of the coordinates and vice versa.

AVNER ASH

Bibliography: Pettofrezzo, A. J., *Matrices and Transformations* (1978).

transformer

A transformer is an electrical device that transfers electric energy from one coil, or winding, to another by electromagnetic induction. The transferred energy may be at a higher or lower voltage. Transformers can only operate on alternating current (AC) or on direct current with a superimposed AC component (pulsating DC).

Transformers are generally classed as step-up or step-down transformers. A step-up transformer increases the voltage, and a step-down transformer reduces it. At electric generating plants, step-up transformers (called generator transformers) increase the generator voltage to a higher voltage, which is then transmitted through power lines over long distances with little loss. In the locality where the electricity will be used, step-down transformers then lower the voltage. A distribution transformer makes the final step-down in voltage for homes and businesses. Consumers may use additional step-down transformers to operate such devices as doorbells and toy electric trains.

The operation of the transformer is based on the principle discovered in 1830 by Joseph Henry that electrical energy can be transferred efficiently by mutual ELECTROMAGNETIC INDUCTION from one winding to another. When the primary winding is energized by an AC source, an alternating magnetic flux is

established in the transformer core. This flux links the turns of both primary and secondary, thereby inducing voltages in them. Because the same flux cuts both windings, the same voltage is induced in each turn of both windings. The total induced voltage in each winding is therefore proportional to the number of turns in that winding. This proportion is known as the turns ratio, which, when multiplied by the applied voltage, determines the secondary voltage. Transformers have no moving parts. The typical transformer has two windings, insulated electrically from each other, wound on a common magnetic circuit of laminated sheet steel (the core). The core provides a circuit of low reluctance for the magnetic flux. The primary is always connected to the source of power, and the secondary winding receives the electrical energy by mutual induction from the primary winding and delivers it to the connected electric load. In some transformer windings, taps are provided so that less than the full number of turns may be used. This allows a transformer with a single pair of coils to provide more than one voltage or current.

Two types of transformer construction are the core type and the shell type. In the core-type transformer, the windings surround the laminated metal core. In the shell-type transformer, the metal core surrounds the windings. Distribution transformers are generally of the core type, whereas some of the largest high-voltage power transformers are of the shell type. Small transformers are air cooled, and larger transformers usually are oil cooled.

Transformers are built in single-phase and polyphase units. Most power and distribution systems use three-phase lines. A three-phase transformer consists of separate insulated windings for the different phases. The windings are wound on a three-legged core capable of establishing three magnetic fluxes displaced by 120° in time phase. Transformers also may be classed according to the frequency range for which they are designed, such as audio frequency, power frequency, and radio frequency.

Transformers require little care and maintenance because of their simple, rugged, and durable construction. The efficiency of transformers is high. In some transformers efficiency

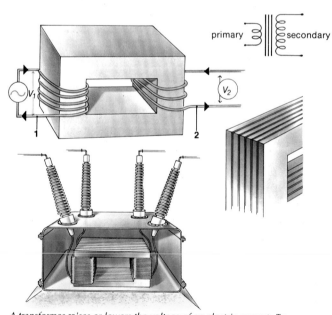

A transformer raises or lowers the voltage of an electric current. To construct a transformer (upper left), wire is coiled around each leg of a laminated metal core (detail, lower right). When alternating current enters the first coil (1) a magnetic field travels through the core and induces current in the second coil (2). The ratio between the number of windings in each coil determines whether the voltage (V1, V2) will be stepped up or stepped down. The standard diagram for a step-up transformer is seen at upper right. Large transformers require cooling and are usually submerged in a tank of oil (lower left).

is 99 percent. Because of this efficiency and their ability to vary voltage easily, transformers are largely responsible for the more extensive use of alternating current than direct current.
DONALD L. ANGLIN

Bibliography: American Institute of Physics, *The Transformer* (1976); Pansini, Anthony J., *Basic Electrical Power Transformers* (1976).

transgression, marine

A marine transgression, or covering of land area by the sea, can be caused by the melting of polar ice masses (eustatic), the downwarping of land as a result of crustal stresses (tectonic), or the depression of crustal blocks of varying density (isostatic). A marine transgression successively deposits nonmarine, littoral, shallow-marine, and deep-marine sediments as the sea floods a particular region. Transgressive deposits display progressively younger ages as they are traced in the direction of shoreline migration. (See REGRESSION, MARINE.)

transistor

The transistor is a solid-state electronic component that is able to control a relatively large electrical current flowing between two regions of a SEMICONDUCTOR crystal by a very small current or voltage applied to an intermediate region. This electronic analogy of the mechanical valve permits the transistor to act as a proportional amplifier or electronic switch, applications that formerly could be accomplished only with the ELECTRON TUBE.

Because the transistor is mechanically robust, produces relatively little heat, and is exceptionally small, its invention in 1948 by Walter H. Brattain, John Bardeen, and William Shockley at Bell Laboratories ushered in a new era of miniaturized electronics. The INTEGRATED CIRCUIT and other MICROELECTRONIC devices are among the most significant by-products of the transistor.

The first transistors were called point-contact devices because two of the three electrodes that made electrical contact to the component were tiny wires pressed against the surface of a small semiconductor crystal to form a closely spaced pair of rectifying regions—regions in which current can flow in one desired direction only. Point-contact transistors were inherently fragile, and their characteristics were difficult to predict. In 1952, Shockley invented a vastly improved form of transistor in which the rectifying contacts were replaced by a pair of internal pn junctions similar to the *pn* junction of a semiconductor junction diode. (A pn junction is the dividing surface between two semiconductor regions, n and p, of different conductivity.) All transistors can be classified as either bipolar or field-effect devices.

THE BIPOLAR TRANSISTOR

The bipolar transistor is a small chip of semiconductor, ordinarily silicon or germanium, with an internal structure resembling two back-to-back junction diodes. This structure is achieved by transforming both ends of a bar of n-type semiconductor into p-type material. The result is a pair of pn junctions within a single semiconductor chip, and the transistor is called a pnp device. A second way to achieve the desired pair of junctions is to transform both ends of a p-type bar into n-type material to give an npn device.

Whether pnp or npn, the central region of the transistor, which is called the base, controls the current flowing between the two outer regions, which are called the emitter and collector.

Operation. In the operation of, for example, the npn transistor, electrons from an external source are injected into the emitter, where they readily cross over into the p-type base. The holes ("missing" electrons) in the base are quickly filled by the incoming electrons, and the resulting negative charge acts to repel further electrons that would otherwise arrive from the emitter.

A comparatively small positive current applied to the base can produce additional holes that will, in turn, permit more electrons to be injected into the base from the emitter. The base region purposefully contains significantly fewer holes than the emitter and collector contain free electrons, so a

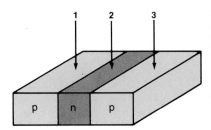

A pnp junction transistor consists of an n-type, or negative (n), material between two p-type, or positive (p), bars. This transistor has three electrodes: an emitter (1), base (2), and collector (3).

substantial percentage of the injected electrons pass through the base and enter the collector before the holes in the base are filled. The application of additional holes into the base encourages more or less emitter-collector current flow, much as a throttle controls the speed of an engine.

Emitter current passes from the base to the collector even though the base is more positive than the collector (reverse bias). If the base-collector junction were fabricated like the pn junction in a conventional diode, only a tiny reverse current would flow.

In a transistor, however, the base is lightly doped and exceedingly thin. The light dopant concentration means many electrons must enter the base before all the holes are filled, and the thin geometry means many electrons are immediately adjacent to the base-collector junction. Consequently, as many as 99% of the free electrons injected into the base wander into the base-collector junction region and are swept into the collector.

Applications. Because the emitter-collector current is up to several hundred times greater than the emitter-base current, the transistor qualifies as an efficient current amplifier. In a typical application, a small current generated by a voice directed toward a microphone is applied to the base of a transistor. This small base current controls the much larger emitter-collector current that is applied to the terminals of a loudspeaker, which emits a greatly amplified sound.

A junction transistor may also be used as an electronic switch. Below a point known as saturation, or cutoff, the ratio of the base current to the emitter-collector current is constant. At saturation the transistor reaches its highest possible conductivity, and further increases in base current fail to increase the emitter-collector current. A comparatively small base current easily saturates a transistor into full conduction and causes it to act as a solid-state on-off switch. This mode of operation has many uses, particularly in digital electronic circuits.

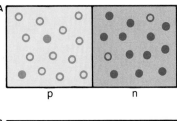

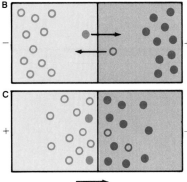

A pn junction (A) has an excess of electrons (dark circles) on the n side and of positive holes (light circles) on the p side. No current flows across the junction. (B) When the negative pole (−) of a battery is connected to the p material, the positive holes on that side are drawn away from the junction. On the other hand, the positive pole (+) on th n side pulls its electrons away. Only a few electrons and holes (arrows) are then left on opposite sides to carry a weak current. (C) If the connections are reversed, the junction becomes a conductor because both electrons and holes can then flow.

Virtually identical action occurs in pnp units, the single exception being that holes rather than electrons are the principal carriers of current. Consequently, the polarity of current applied to a pnp transistor is opposite that applied to an npn device. Both types are used in electronic circuits.

THE FIELD EFFECT TRANSISTOR

The field effect transistor, or FET, was first conceived by J. E. Lilienfeld in 1925, but it was not until 1952 that Shockley, one of the coinventors of the bipolar transistor, proposed the detailed theory of FET operation. FETs may be classified according to their structure as junction or metal-oxide-semiconductor (MOS) devices. Both have certain characteristics that make them superior to bipolar (pnp and npn) transistors in several applications.

JFET. The junction FET, or JFET, consists of a silicon bar containing a narrow region of n- or p-type material, called the channel, that passes between two facing regions having an opposite polarity and called the gate regions. The FET is designated according to the polarity of its channel as either n-channel or p-channel. Electrical terminals called the source and drain are attached to either end of the channel. A terminal is also attached to the gate regions.

In the case of the n-channel FET, an electrical current can flow into the channel through the source, pass with relative ease through the channel, and exit via the drain. The current flow can be decreased by applying a negative voltage to the gate. This action depletes the number of free electrons in the channel, which would otherwise act as current carriers. More gate voltage expands the depletion regions on either side of the channel until they eventually merge and block the flow of current. The channel resistance is then very high, and pinch-off is said to have occurred.

A very small change in gate voltage is enough to alter a comparatively large current flow. Therefore the FET is a voltage amplifier. In this respect, a FET resembles a TRIODE electron tube more than a current amplifier such as the bipolar transistor. The gate corresponds to the grid, whereas the source and drain correspond to the cathode and anode, or plate, respectively.

Like the grid of the electron tube, the gate of the FET is characterized by a very high input impedance because the gate-channel junction is a reverse-biased pn junction diode. This characteristic means the gate will draw only a minuscule current from an input signal source.

MOSFETs. The metal-oxide-semiconductor field effect transistor, or MOSFET, has an even higher input impedance than the JFET because its gate is a film of metal separated from the upper surface of the silicon channel by an insulating layer of silicon dioxide.

Two principal kinds of MOSFETs exist. In the depletion type a current is able to flow between the source and drain terminals connected to either an n-type or p-type channel. A voltage applied to the gate increases the channel resistance by attracting current carriers to the region adjacent to the metal gate. As with the JFET, sufficient gate voltage will cause pinch-off to occur. In the enhancement MOSFET the channel resistance is normally high. Applying a voltage to the gate causes current carriers to be drawn into the channel, thus lowering its resistance.

Both kinds of MOSFETs provide proportional control over the channel current by means of a voltage applied to the gate

and therefore qualify as voltage amplifiers. Both kinds also have a significantly higher input impedance than the JFET as a result of the glasslike silicon dioxide insulating layer between the metal gate and the silicon channel.

This enhanced impedance is accompanied by a potential disadvantage, however, because the MOSFET is highly susceptible to permanent damage from the effects of static electricity. A high-voltage static charge from a fingertip or even a plastic bag used to package the MOSFET can easily puncture the oxide layer separating the gate from the channel. For this reason the leads of a MOSFET are electrically connected to each other prior to installation in a circuit to drain away any unwanted static electricity.

The internal structure of the MOSFET is much simpler than that of the bipolar transistor. Furthermore, electronic logic circuits using MOSFETs are simpler, smaller, and use fewer components than those using bipolar transistors. For these reasons MOSFET technology has been emphasized in the production of numerous kinds of highly complex, large-scale integrated circuits, including those used in digital wristwatches, pocket calculators, and computers. Tiny arrays of thousands of parallel-connected MOSFETs, called power MOSFETs, have very low resistance and can switch hundreds of amperes.

The highly complex network of thousands of MOSFET transistors on a single silicon chip consumes much less power than an equivalent circuit made with bipolar transistors. It also operates over a wider voltage range and includes up to several times more transistors on the same size chip. The only significant drawbacks are vulnerability to static electricity and somewhat slower operating speed.

NEW DEVELOPMENTS

Complementary metal-oxide-semiconductor circuitry, or CMOS, comprises pairs of n- and p-channel transistors that are controlled at the same time by a single circuit. This makes more efficient use of the chip and cuts down on both power need and heat production. For these reasons, CMOS technology is gaining wide acceptance despite its slower operating speeds. Emitted coupling logic, ECL, is a bipolar technology that is extremely fast but also expensive and not compatible with other technologies. Other areas of research include the development of gallium-arsenide chips, superconducting materials, and electron tunneling through junctions.

FORREST M. MIMS III

Bibliography: Getrew, I. E., *Modeling the Bipolar Transistor* (1978); Kiver, Milton S., *Transistor and Integrated Electronics*, 4th ed. (1972); Pollack, Harvey, *Transistor Theory and Circuits Made Simple* (1982); Rutkowski, George B., *Solid-State Electronics* (1972).

Transit

Transit was a series of U.S. experimental satellites launched between 1959 and 1964 to prove that satellites could be used for navigational purposes. The primary instrumentation of a Transit satellite consisted of two ultrastable oscillators for use with a Doppler-shift navigation experiment, and a transmitter for sending data from a sensor that measured Earth's albedo in the infrared region and engineering information on the internal operation of the satellite. Power for the earlier satellites was supplied by external solar cells that charged internal nickel-cadmium batteries. A SNAP 3 nuclear generator was the primary power supply beginning with *Transit 4A*, the first American satellite to be so powered. Beginning with *Transit 2A* (1960), smaller, scientific satellites were launched with the primary satellite and released by means of springs. Information about the launches of Transit satellites and their piggyback subsatellites began to be classified by the Department of Defense beginning in 1963. The system proved the usefulness of satellites as extremely accurate navigation aids for ships, locating their positions to within less than 100 m (330 ft). The Transit system became fully operational in 1964 and was followed by similar satellites under such names as Navy Navigation Satellite and Transit Improvement Program.

MITCHELL R. SHARPE

Bibliography: Richards, Geoff, "Transit—The First Navigational Satellite System," *Spaceflight*, February 1979.

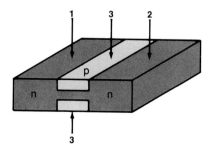

In a junction field effect transistor with an n-channel, two p-type layers are joined to a grooved n-type bar, or channel. External connections include: a source (1), a drain (2), and a gate, or control electrode (3).

transit, surveying

A transit is an optical instrument used in SURVEYING to measure horizontal and vertical angles; it is also used to extend straight lines and to produce level lines for determining elevations. A telescope with cross hairs is fixed to a horizontal axle on a frame. The axle rotates in a vertical circle and the frame in a horizontal circle so that the line of sight can be directed to any point; the angle of rotation thus consists of vertical and horizontal components. Vertical angles are read on a calibrated circle that rotates with the telescope past a stationary index and vernier on the frame, and horizontal angles are read with an index and vernier that rotate with the frame past a calibrated circle. The transit also has vials containing leveling bubbles as well as leveling screws; it requires a tripod for support and a plumb line for centering over a point. A compass is often built in to determine a reference direction.
                                        CHARLES A. HERUBIN

See also: THEODOLITE.

transit circle

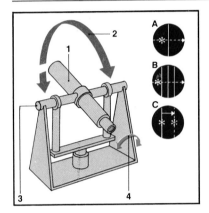

The transit circle is a refracting telescope (1) that can only be used in a north-south direction along the plane of an observer's celestial meridian (2). A grid of vertical wires enables the observer to track and time passages (A, B, C) of stars across the meridian. The shaft (3) can be reversed 180° to compensate for instrument errors. The mounting adjusts (4) to correct for east-west deviations.

A transit circle is an instrument designed to determine accurately the exact time at which a celestial object transits, or passes, an observer's celestial meridian, which is a fundamental reference circle from which star positions are measured. The instrument was invented by the Danish astronomer Ole Roemer in 1689. It consists of a telescope, generally 15 to 25 cm (6 to 10 in) in diameter, mounted so that it can rotate only in a north and south direction along the meridian. The telescope eyepiece contains a fine, movable vertical wire and a stationary grid of vertical wires, the central one of which coincides exactly with the meridian. The movable wire is kept centered on the observed star, planet, Sun, Moon, or other object by means of a micrometer screw, and the exact moment of meridian transit is recorded; in modern times such recordings are made electronically. The data obtained with transit circles are used to determine the right ascension of a celestial object, to make corrections to clocks used in observatories, and to determine the longitude of an observer's location. The declination, or angular distance of the object above the celestial equator, can also be read from a calibrated circle attached to the horizontal axis. More accurate positional data are obtained, however, with a meridian circle—a variant of the transit telescope—which contains a larger and more accurate declination circle.
                                        ARTHUR F. CACELLA

Bibliography: Motz, Lloyd, and Duncan, Anneta, *Essentials of Astronomy* (1978); Stoy, R. H., ed., *Everyman's Astronomy* (1974).

transition elements

The chemical elements are arranged in the PERIODIC TABLE in such a way that each element progressively adds an electron to the configuration of the previous element, filling subshells and shells of lowest energy (see ATOM). The transition elements are those that add electrons to an inner subshell after some electrons have taken positions in an outer shell. This is possible because the energy levels of the shells overlap. Thus the transition elements fill *d* or *f* subshells, while the representative elements fill *s* or *p* subshells. This article is restricted to the *d* transition elements; the *f* transition elements are discussed in LANTHANIDE SERIES and ACTINIDE SERIES (actually transition series within a transition series).

General Properties. The transition elements are all METALS, a feature related to the presence of one or two electrons in the outermost shell of their atoms. They are generally hard, strong metals with high melting and boiling points; they are also usually electropositive—that is, they react by tending to lose, rather than gain, electrons. Certain unique properties of the transition elements are related to their *d* subshell electrons. These properties include variable oxidation states, formation of brightly colored compounds, tendency to form many complexes, and ferromagnetism and paramagnetism.

Oxidation States. The oxidation states of transition elements are usually written as Roman numerals; thus, Fe(III) describes the oxidation of the Fe^{3+} ion. The early elements of each transition series have their highest oxidation states equal to their group number in the periodic table; examples are Ti (IV), V(V), Cr(VI), and Mn(VII). In highly ionic compounds atoms in these highest oxidation states have the electronic configurations of the noble gases; all of the examples above

ELECTRON STRUCTURE OF THE FOURTH SERIES OF ELEMENTS

	Element	Symbol	Atomic Number	1s	2s	2p	3s	3p	3d	4s	4p
Representative Elements	potassium	K	19	2	2	6	2	6		1	
	calcium	Ca	20	2	2	6	2	6		2	
1st Transition Series	scandium	Sc	21	2	2	6	2	6	1	2	
	titanium	Ti	22	2	2	6	2	6	2	2	
	vanadium	V	23	2	2	6	2	6	3	2	
	chromium	Cr	24	2	2	6	2	6	5	1	
	manganese	Mn	25	2	2	6	2	6	5	2	
	iron	Fe	26	2	2	6	2	6	6	2	
	cobalt	Co	27	2	2	6	2	6	7	2	
	nickel	Ni	28	2	2	6	2	6	8	2	
	copper	Cu	29	2	2	6	2	6	10	1	
	zinc	Zn	30	2	2	6	2	6	10	2	
Representative Elements	gallium	Ga	31	2	2	6	2	6	10	2	1
	germanium	Ge	32	2	2	6	2	6	10	2	2
	arsenic	As	33	2	2	6	2	6	10	2	3
	selenium	Se	34	2	2	6	2	6	10	2	4
	bromine	Br	35	2	2	6	2	6	10	2	5
	krypton	Kr	36	2	2	6	2	6	10	2	6

may be symbolized by the ELECTRON CONFIGURATION of argon, which would immediately precede potassium in the accompanying table by lacking a 4s electron. The transition elements show a wide variety of oxidation states by easily sharing their d electrons with other elements in covalent bonds or by allowing electrons from other elements to enter their unfilled d orbitals. Manganese (VII) is usually covalently bonded as permanganate, MnO_4^-, sharing its 4s and 3d electrons with oxygen atoms. Manganese is an extreme example of a transition element displaying many oxidation states; every state from Mn(−III) to Mn(VII) is known.

Complexes. The formation and structures of tightly bonded complexes of many transition elements were first elucidated by Alfred WERNER, the founder of coordination chemistry, between 1892 and 1911. He explained why the two compounds $CoCl_3\cdot6NH_3$ and $CoCl_3\cdot5NH_3$ have strikingly different physical and chemical properties; they are COORDINATION COMPOUNDS in which six LIGANDS surround each metal ion—six ammonia molecules in the former compound, correctly written as $[Co(NH_3)_6]Cl_3$, and five ammonia molecules and one chloride in the second, $[Co(NH_3)_5Cl]Cl_2$. Each transition-metal ion is found to display characteristic coordination numbers; cobalt (III) always has the coordination number 6, with six tightly bound ligands at the corners of a regular octahedron.

Biological Occurrence. Transition metals form complexes with a wide variety of organic molecules, including many that have vital biological functions. For example, hemoglobin (oxygen transport) contains iron, and vitamin B_{12} (oxygen transfer) contains cobalt.

LESTER R. MORSS

Bibliography: Basolo, Fred, et al., eds., *Transition Metal Chemistry*, 2 vols. (1973); Cotton, F. A., and Wilkinson, G., *Advanced Inorganic Chemistry*, 4th ed. (1980); Larsen, E. M., *Transition Elements* (1965); Mueller, A., and Diemann, E., *Transition Metal Chemistry* (1981).

Transjordan: see JORDAN.

Transkei [tran-sky']

The Republic of Transkei, located on the east coast of South Africa, was declared independent on Oct. 26, 1976. Under South Africa's APARTHEID policy, the 1959 Promotion of Self-Government Act called for the gradual creation of ten independent African homelands, of which Transkei was the first. Transkei's independence, however, is not recognized by the United Nations or by any country other than South Africa. The territory covers 41,002 km² (15,831 mi²).

LAND, PEOPLE, AND ECONOMY

Transkei comprises three separate blocks of land bounded by the Indian Ocean on the east, the Drakensberg on the west, the Great Kei River on the south, Lesotho on the northwest, and Natal on the north. Much of Transkei is a grass-covered plateau deeply dissected by fast-flowing perennial rivers (Umzimvubu and Bashee). Coastal regions have a frost-free, humid, subtropical climate. The interior is drier and more temperate and sometimes experiences winter frosts and snow. Soils are severely eroded because of poor farming practices, overgrazing, and heavy summer rains.

The resident population of 2,517,000 (1984 est.) belongs primarily to the XHOSA ethnic group but includes several thousand whites and persons of mixed racial origin. Additional Xhosa reside in South Africa and in the Ciskei homeland, which was declared independent on Dec. 4, 1981. Transkei's population is primarily rural. The capital and largest city, Umtata, is linked by rail to East London.

The Xhosa are primarily subsistence cultivators and pastoralists. Because population pressure is high and industrial opportunities are limited, about 327,000 Xhosa (mainly men) are migrant workers in South Africa; labor is Transkei's main export. Some light industry is centered in Umtata and Butterworth, but most manufactured goods and half the territory's food requirements must be imported from South Africa. It is heavily dependent on South Africa for financial aid.

HISTORY AND GOVERNMENT

In 1848, Transkei was annexed by Britain, and in 1865 it was joined to Cape Province. In 1959 it became the first South Af-

rican bantustan, and subsequently it was the first bantustan to achieve self-government (1963) and then full independence (1976). At independence, persons classified as Transkei nationals lost their South African citizenship. Transkei has a single-chamber parliament. The president, elected by parliament to a 7-year term, appoints a council of ministers headed by a prime minister.

ALAN C. G. BEST

Bibliography: Laurence, Patrick, *The Transkei: South Africa's Politics of Partition* (1976); Southall, Roger, *South Africa's Transkei* (1983); Stultz, Newell M., *Transkei's Half Loaf* (1979).

translation (linguistics): see APPLIED LINGUISTICS.

translation (mathematics)

A Cartesian COORDINATE SYSTEM contains two intersecting lines called coordinate axes; their point of intersection is called the origin of the system. A translation of the coordinate axes involves the shifting of the origin from one point to another point without changing the direction of the coordinate axes. A common reason for translating axes is to simplify the equation under consideration. For example, the equation of the circle $x^2 + y^2 − 4x − 6y + 9 = 0$ takes the form $x^2 + y^2 = 4$ if the origin is moved to the point (2, 3). In mechanics a motion in which all points of a system have identical displacements is called a translation. The translation is called rectilinear if each point moves in a line. The motion of a rigid body is a combination of translation and rotation.

V. K. BALAKRISHNAN

Bibliography: Leithold, Louis, *The Calculus with Analytic Geometry*, vol. 1, 4th ed. (1982).

transmigration of souls

Transmigration of souls, sometimes called metempsychosis, is based on the idea that a soul may pass out of one body and reside in another (human or animal) or in an inanimate object. The idea appears in various forms in tribal cultures in many parts of the world (for example, Africa, Madagascar, Oceania, and South America). The notion was familiar in ancient Greece, notably in Orphism (see ORPHEUS), and was adopted in a philosophical form by PLATO and the PYTHAGOREANS. The belief gained some currency in gnostic and occult forms of Christianity and Judaism and was introduced into Renaissance thought by the recovery of the Hermetic books.

The most fully articulated doctrine of transmigration is found in HINDUISM. It does not appear in the earliest Hindu scriptures (the Rig Veda) but was developed at a later period in the UPANISHADS (c.600 BC). Central to the conception of human destiny after death was the belief that human beings are born and die many times. Souls are regarded as emanations of the divine spirit. Each soul passes from one body to another in a continuous cycle of births and deaths, their condition in each existence being determined by their actions in previous births. Thus, transmigration is closely interwoven with the concept of KARMA (action), which involves the inevitable working out, for good or ill, of all action in a future existence. The whole experience of life, whether of happiness or sorrow, is a just reward for deeds (good or bad) done in earlier existences. The cycle of karma and transmigration may extend through innumerable lives; the ultimate goal is the reabsorption of the soul into the ocean of divinity from whence it came. This union occurs when the individual realizes the truth about the soul and the Absolute (Brahman) and the soul becomes one with Brahman. The Buddhist concept of *samsara* (a cycle of rebirth) often appears similar. The classical Buddhist doctrine of anatta ("no soul"), however, specifically rejects the Hindu view. The Buddhist position on the workings of karma is exceedingly complex.

The idea of transmigration has been propagated in the Western world by movements such as THEOSOPHY and by the more recent proliferation of Oriental religious cults. Most of these Westernized versions appear to lack the intellectual rigor and philosophical content of the classical Hindu doctrine.

CHARLES W. RANSON

transmission, automotive

An automotive transmission is a device for transmitting power from the engine to the drive shaft, from which it is eventually carried to the wheels. The device must convert the power from the relatively fixed high angular velocity and low torque (turning force) of the engine crankshaft to the variable, usually lower speeds and higher torques needed at the wheels. The crankshaft is the part of the engine that converts the back-and-forth (reciprocating) motion of the engine pistons into rotary motion.

Generally, the transmission converts the engine power by means of a system of gears, providing a variety of gear ratios between the engine and the wheels. When the vehicle is starting from rest, the transmission is placed in first, or low, gear in order to produce a high torque at a low wheel speed. As the car speeds up, the driver shifts or the automatic transmission is shifted into a higher gear. With each higher gear, the drive shaft turns faster but with less power and torque. As an example, consider a simple three-speed transmission. When the car starts from rest in first gear, the gear ratio might be 3 to 1 (3:1). This means that the crankshaft turns three times to turn the drive shaft once. After the car gains some speed, the transmission is shifted into second gear, with a gear ratio of, say, 2:1. After a further increase in wheel

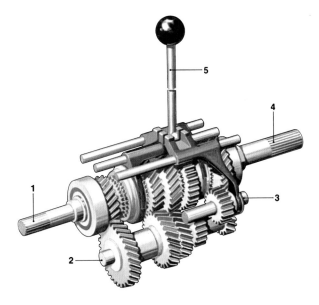

(Below) *The various gear positions transmit engine power* (indicated by red arrows). *Engine power on the spinning input shaft moves to the layshaft and from there to the output shaft (and the road wheels) by way of the output shaft's locked gear. In first gear (A), the largest gear is engaged for low-speed driving. Second (B) and third (C) gears use wheels of smaller size (closer gear ratios). The highest gear (D) is attained by directly coupling the input and output shafts. In reverse (E), the idler shaft (1) meshes the reverse gears on the layshaft and output shaft, whose direction then is reversed.*

(Above) *The gearbox is the part of the transmission that houses the gears. A modern gearbox has an input shaft (1) from the engine, a layshaft (2), an idler (3), and an output shaft (4). All the gears are constantly in mesh with the exception of the idler gear, which is used for reverse. The gear wheels spin freely about the output shaft, but the wheels on the layshaft are fixed to it. A gear is engaged when the gearshift lever (5) locks a gear wheel on the output shaft into place. (Note that although the input and the output shafts are in a direct line, they are not connected.)*

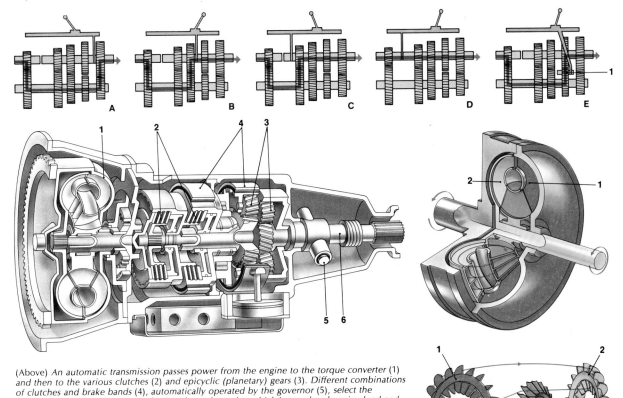

(Above) *An automatic transmission passes power from the engine to the torque converter (1) and then to the various clutches (2) and epicyclic (planetary) gears (3). Different combinations of clutches and brake bands (4), automatically operated by the governor (5), select the appropriate driving gear. Gear selection depends on the vehicle's speed and engine load and on the position of the accelerator pedal, which is linked to the governor on the output shaft (6). (Right) A torque converter, which couples the engine and the gearbox, works much like two fans facing each other: if the blades of one fan are turning, the air current created will turn the blades of the other fan. Similarly, when the torque converter's engine-driven impeller (1) turns, with oil (instead of air) as the medium (red arrows show direction of motion), the turbine blades (2) will turn.*

speed, a shift is made into high, or third, gear. This is also called direct drive, because there is no gear reduction in the transmission: the gear ratio is 1:1, and the drive shaft turns at the same speed as the crankshaft.

The two basic types of transmission are the manual type, in which the gears are selected by the driver, and the automatic transmission, in which the gear ratios are selected automatically by the device.

Manual Transmission. Early transmissions were all manually operated. There were two shafts, each with several gears of different sizes. One shaft could be moved, or shifted, with respect to the other in order to mesh, or engage, a gear on one shaft with a gear on the other. Several combinations of gearing were available. The first such sliding-gear transmission is generally credited to a Frenchman, Émile Levassor (1890).

For most cars a transmission with three forward gears and one reverse gear is adequate. In some smaller cars with small engines, four- or five-speed transmissions are used to compensate for the lower torque available from the engine. Trucks designed to haul heavy loads may have as many as 20 forward speeds and four speeds in reverse. The part of the transmission that houses the gears is called the gearbox. A manual transmission has a clutch to disconnect the engine crankshaft from the gearbox while shifting gears. The driver shifts gears by manipulating a shift lever, which is connected to the transmission by a mechanical linkage. There is, therefore, some choice in the location of the shift lever, which may be on the steering column or on the floor.

The older, sliding-gear transmission has largely been replaced by synchromesh transmission, in which synchronizers allow the gear teeth to be in constant mesh, turning freely on their shafts. The selected combination of gears is first synchronized (the teeth on the two gears are brought to the same speed of rotation) and then locked together so that power is transmitted to the drive shaft and then to the DIFFERENTIAL.

A clutch consists of a flywheel (1), which is fixed to the engine shaft and rotates with it, a driven plate (2), which is attached to the gearbox shaft, and a pressure plate (3), which clamps the driven plate to the flywheel by means of powerful springs (4).

(Left) When shifting gears the clutch is disengaged (A) by pushing in the pedal and allowing the flywheel to rotate independently of the driven plate. When the pedal is released (B) the springs clamp the plates together, and power is transmitted from the flywheel to the driven plate.

Automatic Transmission. Automatic transmissions use a torque converter—to couple the engine and the gearbox. It is a form of fluid coupling in which one rotating member causes the transmission fluid to rotate; the fluid, in turn, imparts a rotating motion to another rotating member on another shaft that is connected to the gearbox. The coupling of the torque converter is flexible, allowing slippage, for example, when the car is starting from rest and the wheels are not moving. As the car gains speed, slippage is reduced, and at cruising speeds the driven member turns almost as fast as the driving member. The gearbox contains a set of planetary gears, with clutches and brake bands for engaging the desired gears.

WILLIAM H. CROUSE

Bibliography: Crouse, William H., and Anglin, Donald L., *Automotive Transmissions and Power Trains*, 5th ed. (1976); Giles, J. G., et al., *Gears and Transmissions* (1971); Schofield, Miles, ed., *Petersen's Basic Clutches and Transmissions* (1971); Stockel, Martin W., *Auto Mechanics Fundamentals*, 3d ed. (1974).

transmitter

A transmitter, in radio communications, is a device used to impress information, such as voice or music, on a carrier wave and then to broadcast that wave through space in the form of electromagnetic radiation. The carrier wave, which has a definite frequency, is generated by an electrical OSCILLATOR and is a simple, repetitive sine wave. The oscillator is usually a crystalline material chosen for frequency stability. Information is superimposed on the carrier wave by altering one of the wave's basic characteristics in a process called MODULATION. The most common methods are AMPLITUDE MODULATION (AM) and FREQUENCY MODULATION (FM), in which, respectively, the amplitude and frequency of the carrier wave are altered. In AM the audio frequency, varying as the sound to be transmitted, is mixed with the carrier frequency in a manner that causes the carrier amplitude to vary at the same rate while the carrier frequency remains unchanged. In FM the frequency varies while the amplitude stays the same. Pulse-code modulation is a useful form of modulation for radio relay, for example, in a telephone network. In this system a series of identical pulses is used rather than a sine wave, and modulation is achieved by varying the pulse position or timing; with this method each repeater station can transmit noise-free pulses, even if the incoming signal has been degraded by static and other electrical noise.

In the transmitter the carrier is first generated and modulated at low power, say, a few watts. After modulation, the carrier signal is amplifed to the desired level of power, sometimes many kilowatts, depending on how great a coverage is involved, and then radiated from the transmitting ANTENNA. The signal is subsequently picked up by a RECEIVER and converted back to its original form.

HAL HELLMAN

Bibliography: Finnegan, Patrick, *Broadcast Engineering and Maintenance Handbook* (1976); Marcus, Abraham and W., *Elements of Radio*, 6th ed. (1973); Noll, Edward M., *Radio Transmitter Principles and Projects* (1973).

transmutation of elements

Transmutation, the conversion of one element into another, is associated with the attempts of the alchemists to change base metals to gold. Because an element is defined as a substance that cannot be changed into, or produced from, simpler forms of matter, transmutation cannot be accomplished by any chemical reaction. A transmutation entails a change in the atomic nucleus and thus may be effected by a nuclear reaction or may occur spontaneously by radioactive decay.

The first artificial transmutation of a nonradioactive element was achieved in 1919 by Ernest Rutherford. He found that on collision with an alpha particle (from a natural emitter), an atom of nitrogen was converted to an ion of oxygen and a hydrogen nucleus. In 1932, John D. Cockcroft and Ernest Walton achieved the first entirely artificial transmutation of an element by bombarding lithium with electrically accelerated protons. Attempts were made in the 1930s to produce a TRANSURANIUM ELEMENT by bombarding uranium with free neutrons; the unexpected result was the discovery of nuclear fission in 1938. Eventually, in 1940, E. M. McMillan and P. H. Abelson first positively produced and identified a transuranium element, which they named neptunium.

Transmutation is now a common process because of the availability of powerful particle accelerators and nuclear reactors, and virtually every element has been prepared artificially. More than 1,500 radioisotopes have been synthesized, many of which have valuable medical and industrial uses. The alchemists' dream is possible today: base metals can be transmuted to gold. The cost of the required energy, however, exceeds the value of the product. STEPHEN FLEISHMAN

See also: HALF-LIFE; NUCLEAR PHYSICS; RADIOACTIVITY.

transplantation, organ

Organ transplantation has a short history, having originated in the mid-1950s with the work of researchers at the Peter Bent Brigham Hospital in Boston. They showed that dogs could survive in good health with one kidney that had been transplanted from the loin to another part of the body, an operation termed an *autotransplant*. This required skillful and expeditious surgery, but because the organ remained in the same individual there could be no rejection. These workers felt that a patient dying of kidney failure who was fortunate enough to have an identical twin might benefit from kidney transplantation, because identical twins arise from a single egg and thence may be regarded in a biological sense as being the same individual.

Rejection. Unfortunately, grafts between individuals who are not identical twins are usually destroyed within a matter of days or weeks. The mechanism of this destruction was discovered by Peter Brian MEDAWAR and his colleagues in the early 1940s to be an immune reaction of the body's lymphoid organs (lymph nodes, spleen, and bone marrow), similar in principle to the IMMUNITY resulting from exposure to the measles virus. A foreign graft, following recognition by the recipient's body, triggers a complicated response leading to rapid destruction of the graft. Cells produced from lymphoid organs produce antibodies that circulate in the blood and act specifically against the foreign organ. Other cells directly infiltrate the organ and proceed to damage its blood vessels and substance.

Tissue Typing. Research in the following years was directed at understanding and overcoming this rejection process. The aggressiveness of the immune response depends on the genetic gap between the donor and the recipient, and there is now much information on so-called tissue types, which are identified on white blood cells. These are analogous to the red-blood-cell groups important in blood transfusion. An important series of tissue antigens was discovered; in humans it resides on the sixth chromosome. Various components of this major histocompatibility complex (MHC) can be matched between donor and recipient. The Mendelian inheritance of the MHC means that there is a one-in-four chance of a given individual's having an MHC identical to that of his sibling. Transplants between MHC-matched siblings have excellent results, nearly as good as those between identical twins. A person inherits one MHC-containing chromosome from each parent, so that if a parent gives his or her child a kidney there will be expected at least a 50% matching of the MHC, and results are quite good; some 70% of grafts will be functioning after one year and 50% at five years. Grafts from unrelated donors do less well, even when taking into account matching for the MHC. This would suggest that other important antigens active in vivo are not covered by the current matching techniques.

Immunosuppression. Attempts to impair the activity of the lymphoid organs eventually led to the use of a combination of corticosteroid drugs with the antileukemia drug azathioprine (Imuran). These drugs became the central immunosuppressive regimen in patients in the early 1960s and have been responsible for the results mentioned above. The addition of antilymphocyte globulin has been reported by some workers to be beneficial, but others have found little advantage. This agent is produced in animals by the injection of human lymphoid tissues. It has been difficult to obtain consistently effective preparations.

Another group of drugs, the CYCLOSPORINE family, has also become a major importance for immunosuppression. The drugs, first derived from a fungus, *Tolypocladium inflatum,* were found to block the activity of the lymphocytes called T-helper cells, which initiate the function of the cells that attack foreign tissues. Following their discovery in the early 1970s, the cyclosporines were used to advantage in numerous experimental transplant operations, and in the early 1980s they became available for clinical use. Cyclosporines also have the potential of harmful side effects such as kidney damage or, in heart-transplant operations, increase of hypertension, and they impair the immune system's ability to fight off infectious organisms. Nevertheless, since their introduction, they have dramatically increased survival rates in a variety of operations. For example, the average one-year survival rate for liver transplants in the early 1980s was 70%, as compared to the average of 33% between 1963 and 1979.

Present Status and Future Outlook. All organ grafts require a careful vascular junction between the blood vessels of the donor organ and those of the recipient. The kidney and liver require additional connections for drainage of urine and bile. Kidney grafting has been the most successful organ transplant thus far, because patients with kidney failure can be kept in good health by regular hemodialysis (see KIDNEY, ARTIFICIAL). For other organs no such equivalent luxury exists. Nevertheless, numerous kinds of transplant operations are performed, including heart, heart-lung, single-lung, bone-marrow, skin, and pancreas transferrals. With the advent of cyclosporine the success rate for many of these operations has increased as it did in the case of liver transplants, but some others remain notably difficult—as, for example, pancreas operations. (The use of cyclosporine for the transplantation of entire limbs is also being explored, using laboratory animals. For example, entire legs have been transplanted from one rat to another without being rejected; in some cases the legs were even restored to partial function.)

Interestingly, in some transplant patients exceptionally good results have been obtained when the tissue match was poor. This may be the result of some specific desensitization that allows the recipient to accept the graft despite a strong biological difference, and it raises the possibility of deliberately inducing such acceptance. One route being explored in the 1980s is that of producing monoclonal antibodies (see ANTIBODY; GENETIC ENGINEERING) that attack specific T cells of the immune system without impairing the other T cells needed to fight infections. Another route would be to strip a donor organ completely of the immune cells called macrophages before transplantation. In the meantime, physicians are continuing to rely on the use of immunosuppressive drugs. R. Y. CALNE

Bibliography: Calne, R. Y., *Organ Grafts* (1975) and, as ed., *Transplantation Immunology* (1984); Fox, R. C., and Swazey, J. P., *The Courage to Fail: A Social View of Organ Transplants and Dialysis,* 2d ed. (1979); Gabriel, Roger, *A Patient's Guide to Dialysis and Transplantation* (1982); White, Kristin, "Marrow Transplants," *Medical World News,* Aug. 22, 1983.

Transport and General Workers' Union

The Transport and General Workers' Union (TGWU) is the largest and most complex of the British labor (trade) unions. It represents a core of dock and road-transport workers and includes affiliated sections that represent flour millers, tin-platers, bakery, construction, textile, and electrical workers. A dock strike in 1889 gave impetus to organization efforts among unskilled laborers, and the Dock, Wharf, Riverside, and General Workers' Union, the TGWU's predecessor, was created. In 1922 the Dock Workers' Union absorbed numerous other unions and was reorganized as the TGWU. The TGWU grew rapidly after World War II as it organized white-collar workers. In 1983 it had a membership of approximately 1.63 million.

Bibliography: Gard, Elizabeth, *The British Trade Unions* (1983); Pelling, Henry, *A History of British Trade Unionism,* 3d ed. (1976).

transportation

Transportation is the movement or conveying of persons and goods from one location to another. As human beings, from ancient times to the 20th century, sought to make their transport facilities more efficient, they have always endeavored to move people and property with the least expenditure of time, effort, and cost. Improved transportation has helped make possible progress toward better living, the modern systems of manufacturing and commerce, and the complex, interdependent urban economy present in much of the world today.

This article will cover: (1) the history of transportation, with an emphasis on that in the United States; (2) the political, economic, and social effects of transportation; and (3) the future of transportation. The military aspects of transportation are covered in AIRCRAFT, MILITARY; ARMORED VEHICLES; and NAVAL VESSELS.

EARLY HISTORY

Land Transportation. Primitive human beings soon supplemented their own carrying of goods and possessions by starting to domesticate animals—training them to bear small loads and pull crude sleds (see ANIMAL HUSBANDRY). The first animals so domesticated included asses, camels, dogs, elephants, goats, horses, and oxen. The invention of the WHEEL, probably in western Asia, was a great step forward in transport. As the wheel was perfected, crude carts and WAGONS began to appear in the Tigris-Euphrates valley about 3500 BC, and later in Crete, Egypt, and China. Wheeled vehicles could not use the narrow paths and trails used by pack animals, and early roads were soon being built by the Assyrians and the Persians. The Romans, however, were the major builders of roads (see ROADS AND HIGHWAYS; ROMAN ROADS) in the ancient world, and at the peak of their power their well-constructed roads led from Rome to most parts of the expanding empire. Travelers could move at speeds of nearly 10 km/h (6 mph), a rate that was not materially bettered until the early 19th century.

After the fall of Rome in the 5th century land haulage generally declined because the highways suffered from inadequate maintenance. Such improvements, however, as the horse collar (10th century), the addition of springs to coaches (mid-17th century; see COACH AND CARRIAGE), new methods of road construction, and the introduction of toll roads, or TURNPIKES (18th century), all continued to ease and speed land travel.

Water Transportation. Water transportation also began early in human history. No doubt the first watercraft, the simple raft and the crude CANOE, both evolved from floating logs. Along the Tigris and Euphrates rivers the first BOATS were either hide-covered wicker baskets or dugout canoes, and in Egypt bundles of papyrus rushes were built into crude watercraft. Later the Cretans and Phoenicians built wooden SHIPS—oar-propelled GALLEYS with a single sail—that dominated trade on the Mediterranean. Water itself was moved via AQUEDUCTS, possibly as early as the 10th century BC.

The next major improvements in water transportation (see SHIPBUILDING) did not appear until late medieval times. The introduction of the compass (see COMPASS, NAVIGATIONAL) and RUDDER into Europe by 1300, and later the square sail, did much to improve ocean transportation. By the 15th century the nation-states of England, France, Portugal, and Spain were beginning to build three-masted ships, a vast improvement over earlier craft. Soon these countries were leaders in the Age of Exploration, which expanded ocean commerce well beyond the confines of the Mediterranean. Larger and more numerous sailing vessels improved commerce with the New World during the 17th and 18th centuries, and for a brief period in the 19th century U.S.-built clipper ships were actually faster than the early steamships.

CANALS were another important form of water transportation. The invention of the lock, which was in use in Europe before 1500, stimulated the construction of more and larger canals, such as the Canal du Midi in France, the extensive English canal system in the 18th century, and the U.S. network of the mid-19th century.

(Above) *This drawing by Hans Holbein the Younger depicts a caravel, a small merchant ship often used for exploration during the 15th and 16th centuries.*

(Left) *Supertankers, or very large crude carriers, such as the Universe Island, carry large volumes of liquid cargo, especially oil. Economic factors have dictated the construction of these vehicles—the largest mobile objects ever built—but serious concern has been expressed about the environmental problems they can · cause if wrecked.*

MOTORIZED TRANSPORTATION

The greatest improvements in transportation have appeared in the last two centuries, a period during which the INDUSTRIAL REVOLUTION has vastly changed the economic life of the entire world.

Steamships. James Watt's STEAM ENGINE, perfected in the 1760s, was to do much more than provide power for many factories in England. By the end of the 18th century, French, Scottish, and American inventors were trying to apply the steam engine to navigation. In 1775 a Frenchman, Jacques Périer, built an early STEAMBOAT, and in 1807, Robert FULTON launched the steamboat CLERMONT on the Hudson River. In 1819 the steamer SAVANNAH crossed the Atlantic, and by the middle of the 19th century steam navigation was replacing the sailing vessel, with many of the new ships built of iron rather than wood.

This new form of water transportation was particularly important in the broad Mississippi River valley of the United States. Hundreds of flat-hulled, tall-stacked western steamboats served the triangular territory reaching from Pittsburgh and Montana down to New Orleans. Until the 1850s the expansion of the western frontier was vitally tied to the side-wheelers and stern-wheelers serving the 25,700 km (16,000 mi) of navigable streams in the inland Mississippi River basin. The western steamboat gave way to the railroad only with the coming of the Civil War.

The first locomotive to haul paying passengers was the Catch-me-who-can, *which was built by the Cornish engineer Richard Trevithick and operated by him on a circular track in London in 1808. It pulled a single carriage at a speed of 19 km/h (12 mph).*

Horse-drawn stagecoaches, introduced into England in 1640 and into North America in the 1750s, provided a means of long-distance, overland, public transportation before the railroads. Horses were changed at stages, or stopping points, about every 32 km (20 mi).

Railroads. Crude railways—horse-drawn wagons with wooden wheels and rails—had been used in English and European mines during the 17th century. Between 1797 and 1813, Richard TREVITHICK and other early inventors adapted primitive steam locomotives to the mine railway. In 1825, George STEPHENSON built and equipped the 32-km (20-mi) Stockton and Darlington Railway, the first public railway in the world to be powered by a steam locomotive, and a fever of RAILROAD building began in England.

Although it first appeared in England, the railroad had its most dramatic growth in the United States. By 1840 more than 4,800 km (3,000 mi) of railroad were already operating in the eastern states, a figure 40% greater than the total railroad mileage of Europe. By the eve of the Civil War the iron network in the United States was more than 48,000 km (30,000 mi) long, and the railroads of the western lines had nearly caught up with the ever-moving western frontier. By 1860 the railroad had clearly shown its superiority over turnpikes, canals, and steamboats.

Following the Civil War several railroad lines were extended all the way to the Pacific coast (see TRANSCONTINENTAL RAILROAD), the first being the Union Pacific–Central Pacific, completed in 1869. Railroad construction in general was very rapid in the postwar decades; by 1890 the length of the U.S. rail system was 262,000 km (163,000 mi), and by 1916 it had reached an all-time high of 409,000 km (254,000 mi). Since World War I, however, the U.S. railroads have been in a decline, due partly to the rapid development of private automobiles, trucks, buses, pipelines, and airlines.

Motor Vehicles. The first new mode of transportation to challenge the railroad was the motor vehicle, which was made possible by the invention, in the 1860s and '70s, of the INTERNAL COMBUSTION ENGINE. The AUTOMOBILE found its greatest popularity in the United States, where the first "horseless carriages" appeared in the 1890s. In 1908, Henry Ford introduced the MODEL T, which proved so popular that by 1914, Ford had adopted MASS PRODUCTION methods to meet the demand. The Federal Highway Act of 1921 provided for primary highway routes across the length and breadth of the nation. The typical American family purchased its first car during the 1920s, and by 1930 there were 23 million passenger cars registered in the United States. Two hundred million motor vehicles had been produced in the nation within 70 years of their first appearance. The automobile thus became in many ways as important to the 20th century as the railroads had been to the 19th.

During the same period intercity BUSES took over a large

The introduction of mass-production methods enabled a large part of the American public to purchase their own automobiles and gave them an unprecedented amount of mobility. This development, however, led quickly to increasing problems of traffic flow, as can be seen in this view of a 1917 traffic jam along 42d Street in New York City.

Multilevel intersections enable vehicles on intersecting roads to pass each other without hindrance. Interchanges enable vehicles to travel from one road to another. Such intersections and interchanges are built on expressways or at severe congestion points.

portion of commercial passenger travel, and trucks (see TRUCKING INDUSTRY) began carrying much of the nation's freight.

Pipelines. The first small pipelines (see PIPE AND PIPELINE) in the United States appeared in the oil fields of Pennsylvania just after the Civil War, and by 1900, John D. Rockefeller controlled a network of about 64,000 km (40,000 mi). By 1980, pipelines were carrying 23% of the nation's intercity freight traffic. In most years since World War II pipelines have moved as much freight as highway trucks.

Aviation. At the turn of the century most people thought it preposterous that they would ever travel through the air in a machine heavier than the air itself. The airplane proved its potential in World War I, however, and in 1918 regular AIRMAIL service was started between Washington, D.C., and New York City. Air passenger traffic expanded quickly in the 1930s, and by 1939 air travel accounted for 2% of all commercial intercity travel. Air travel grew rapidly after World War II and in 1957 exceeded rail passenger travel for the first time. In 1980 nearly 83% of all commercial travel in the United States was by air (see AIRCRAFT; AVIATION).

POLITICAL, ECONOMIC, AND SOCIAL EFFECTS

A nation's political development and success, both in peace and war, are rather directly tied to the transportation facilities available in that nation. Throughout history a nation's political unity and power to govern have varied with its success or failure in providing some measure of transportation. In the ancient world the broad Nile River made possible the centralized government as well as the prosperity of early Egypt. Several centuries later the power and wealth of the Roman Empire was in great measure due to its success in road building plus the wealth and variety of its waterborne Mediterranean trades. In the same way, the dominance of British sea power helped make possible the extent and wealth of the British Empire in the 18th and 19th centuries. In the 19th century the varied internal improvements, especially the railroad, also helped bring the distant western American frontier firmly under the political control of the United States. Transportation facilities have also had political significance as modern nations have provided their citizens with postal systems.

Government Aid, Regulation, and Ownership. Many governments in recent decades have provided aid for their transportation facilities, have regulated or placed legal restrictions upon their operation, and in many cases have taken full control through the process of nationalization. Both European nations and the United States aided the new modes of transport that appeared in the 19th and 20th centuries. Early in the 19th century the U.S. government gave modest land grants to some canal projects in the Northwest Territory and also subscribed to the stock of a few other canal companies. In the decades after 1850 many western railroads in the United States received federal land grants to help with their construction—grants that would finally reach a total of 53 million ha (131 million acres). In return the land-grant railroads gave special rates—often a reduction of 50%—for the shipment of the federal government's freight and troops. In the 20th century both federal and state governments have supplied much money, in addition to that collected from state and federal gasoline taxes, for highway construction. During the same period federal money has aided water transportation on the Great Lakes, the major rivers, and the coastal WATERWAYS of the nation. Since World War I air transportation in the United States has received substantial federal grants for weather, navigational, and AIRPORT facilities.

GOVERNMENT REGULATION of construction standards appeared in many nations in the early years of railroad development. As the railroad monopoly of transportation increased in the United States during the late 19th century, an insistent public demand for more government regulation developed. Federal legislation in 1887 established the INTERSTATE COMMERCE COMMISSION, which had some power to restrain freight rates. Much more stringent federal railroad regulation developed early in the 20th century during the Progressive movement. In the 1920s and '30s federal regulation over highway and air transportation was adopted. Most of the regulatory

Before the historic 1903 flight of their self-propelled airplane, Orville and Wilbur Wright conducted several hundred glider flights off of Kill Devil Hill near Kitty Hawk, N.C. These flights enabled them to solve the problems of controlling a plane's motion while in the air.

agencies concerned with transportation were transferred (1966) to the newly established Department of Transportation (see TRANSPORTATION, U.S. DEPARTMENT OF). In 1971 the creation of the federally subsidized AMTRAK passenger service relieved most U.S. railroads of the annual passenger-service deficits they had known for many years. In 1976 the federal government set up the Consolidated Rail Corporation (Conrail) to take over the freight operations of the Penn Central and several other bankrupt lines in the northeastern United States. During 1979 and 1980 federal legislation generally reduced much of the governmental regulation of transportation in the United States.

For centuries most highways and roads have been publicly owned or managed. In the past century other forms of transport have also been taken over by the government. By the middle decades of the 20th century nearly all the railroads outside of North America were government owned and operated. The rail system of the United States, which amounts to about one-fourth of the total world rail mileage, is one of the few in which private ownership and operation still prevails. In Canada rail operation and ownership is roughly half private and half nationalized. Most of the airlines and some of the ocean-shipping lines in Europe have also become government owned and operated.

Economic Effects. The economic impact of transportation has also been great. Many experts estimate that in modern industrial nations today the total costs of freight and travel (both commercial and private) amount to about one-fifth of the nation's gross national product. In the United States in the 1970s the AUTOMOTIVE INDUSTRY, directly or indirectly, was supporting one worker in seven among the gainfully employed. These relatively high costs of transportation have resulted in an interdependent economy that has greatly increased the standard of living for the industrialized world. In such an economy efficient transportation makes possible a greater division of labor, provides mass production with cheaper costs, and creates national and even worldwide markets. Today's developing countries, which have little industry and a low standard of living, rarely possess modern facilities of transportation.

In the early 19th century a CONESTOGA wagon on a poor road could economically carry only light, fairly high-value goods over short distances. In the modern United States the railroad freight car, the truck on a paved highway, the river barge, and the pipeline economically carry over long distances freight that is bulky, heavy, and relatively low in value. Corn from Iowa, wheat from Kansas, fruit and vegetables from Florida and California, coal from Wyoming, iron ore from Minnesota, automobiles from Detroit, furniture from

Supersonic transports, such as the Concorde, which was built by the British and French governments, provide the fastest commercial means of transportation. The Concorde can carry up to 130 passengers at twice the speed of sound (2,125 km/h; 1,320 mph).

five hours. By the late 1970s the CONCORDE, a SUPERSONIC TRANSPORT aircraft built by the British and French governments, was carrying passengers across the Atlantic Ocean at twice the speed of sound. Airline travel around the world has become so commonplace that the oceangoing passenger liners of the mid-20th century have almost disappeared.

Social Effects. The social effects of transportation have also been important. Improved transportation increases a people's mobility, which in turn allows a greater interchange of ideas and cultural accomplishments. More efficient transportation reduces isolation and makes educational and recreational facilities more available.

Both the location and the growth of cities are dependent on transportation. Before the Industrial Revolution most large cities either were major seaports or were located on important navigable rivers. With the coming of railroads, towns that failed to obtain a railroad often became villages, whereas cities with a future were those which were becoming railroad terminals. In the mid-19th century, St. Louis, Mo., a river town, was soon surpassed in economic importance by Chicago, a growing rail terminal. In the last century the major industrial cities of the world have had their expanding populations served in turn by horsecars, electric streetcars, buses, ELEVATED RAILROADS, and SUBWAYS.

Increased urban transportation, resulting from increased commercial traffic and increased commuter travel to and from cities, has caused such problems as increased congestion, air pollution, and damage to road surfaces; the pollutants from road surfaces are also major contaminants of the water systems (see ENVIRONMENTAL HEALTH). The problems of urban transportation in the United States were relieved to some degree by the Urban Mass Transportation Act of 1964, which promoted the development of mass-transit facilities, such as rapid rail systems and better commuter bus and rail services,

North Carolina, and oil from Alaska all can be transported thousands of kilometers to distant markets.

The same kind of change occurred in passenger travel between the time of the Concord STAGECOACH and today's jet airliner. Travel that once took months now takes days or even hours. Travel from New York City to San Francisco in 1848 could take four months; in the 1920s a fast train made the trip in three days; and today a jet makes the trip in four or

Most of the principal airline and shipping transportation routes follow great circles, or paths of shortest distance along the curvature of the Earth. Such factors as the presence of land or convenient stopover points, however, may force indirect routes.

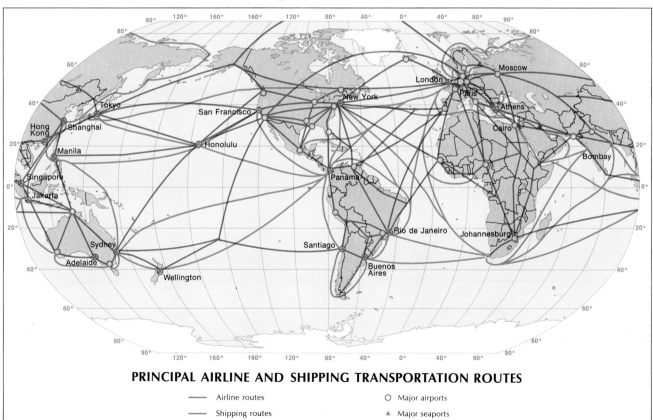

PRINCIPAL AIRLINE AND SHIPPING TRANSPORTATION ROUTES

——— Airline routes   O Major airports

——— Shipping routes   ▲ Major seaports

The world's fastest train, France's TGV (an acronym from words that mean "train of great speed"), began operating in 1981. The train, powered by overhead electric lines, is capable of speeds of 370 km/h (236 mph). Its eight cars form a single unit, and it moves on rails that are continuously welded. France hopes that such high-speed trains will eventually form a network across Europe, signaling a new era in surface transportation.

and encouraged a program of car pooling. The Highway Safety Acts of 1966 and 1970 and the Clean Air Amendment of 1970 are among several legislative attempts to decrease accidents, noise, and pollution and to facilitate travel on heavily used roads (see TRAFFIC CONTROL). The transport of hazardous materials—dangerous because of possible leakage en route—has also been increasingly regulated since 1970.

In the 20th century the automobile created few new major cities but instead caused a major suburban expansion. Other social effects of the automobile constituted a virtual revolution in American life. In 1956 the Interstate Highway Act provided federal aid for a system of four-lane superhighways (see INTERSTATE HIGHWAY SYSTEM) that vastly improved the nation's 4.8 million-km (3 million-mi) road network.

THE FUTURE

The current emphasis on energy conservation and the environment represents both an opportunity and a challenge for tomorrow's transportation. In future decades railroads may well return to more efficient locomotives fueled by coal rather than oil, because petroleum reserves are more limited. The recent growth of suburbs may be reversed, with new emphasis being placed on mass transit for all major cities. Commercial transportation through space (from one point to another on the Earth) is unlikely to be developed in the remaining years of this century. The U.S. SPACE SHUTTLE, however, which began operations in the early 1980s, was designed to reduce the launching costs of, and to enable the in-orbit repair of, Earth satellites.   JOHN F. STOVER

Bibliography: Adams, John, *Transport Planning* (1981); Altschuler, Donald, *Transportation in America* (1982); Bray, P., and Brown, B., *Transport through the Ages* (1971); Coyle, John J., and Bardi, E. J., *Transportation* (1982); DuJonchay, Yvon, *Handbook of World Transport* (1981); Glaister, S., *Fundamentals of Transport Economics* (1981); Hutchins, G. B., *Transportation and the Environment* (1977); Money, Lloyd J., *Transportation Energy and the Future* (1984); Young, A. P., and Cresswell, R. W., *The Urban Transport Future* (1982).

Transportation, U.S. Department of

The U.S. Department of Transportation (DOT), established (Oct. 15, 1966) by act of Congress, is that part of the executive branch responsible for policies aimed at environmental safety and an efficient national transportation system that can also facilitate matters in national defense. The secretary of transportation, who is a member of the president's cabinet, and the secretary's staff are responsible for overseeing more than 30 agencies. The major divisions of the DOT are the U.S. COAST GUARD, FEDERAL AVIATION ADMINISTRATION, the Federal Highway Administration, the Federal Railroad Administration, Urban Mass Transportation Administration, Maritime Administration, St. Lawrence Seaway Development Corp., and the National Highway Traffic Safety Administration. In 1983 the department had a budget authority of $21.1 billion.

Bibliography: Davis, G. M., *The Department of Transportation* (1970); Guandolo, John, *Transportation Law*, 4th ed. (1983).

transposing instruments: see WIND INSTRUMENTS.

transposon

Transposons are segments of DNA that can change locations among the chromosomes and extrachromosomal DNA molecules of bacteria and higher organisms (see GENETIC CODE). A transposon is replicated along with the rest of the chromosome in its new location, and it is transmitted to all daughter cells during subsequent cell divisions. Each transposon contains a gene for the enzyme transposase, which permits it to move successfully from one location to another. In addition, both ends of a transposon terminate in a special sequence of DNA bases, called an insertion sequence, that facilitates its incorporation into its new location.

A number of genetic effects can accompany the insertion of a transposon within or near a gene. The transposon may prevent the gene from functioning, thereby acting as the equivalent of a mutation. On the other hand, insertion of a transposon into a chromosome may result in the deletion or rearrangement of part of the chromosome. In bacteria, transposons have been found to carry genes for drug resistance, toxin production, and the breakdown of certain compounds. These transposons are usually located in self-replicating extrachromosomal DNA molecules called PLASMIDS.   LOUIS LEVINE

Bibliography: Cohen, S. N., and Shapiro, J. A., "Transposable Genetic Elements," *Scientific American*, February 1980.

transsexual: see SEX REASSIGNMENT.

transubstantiation: see EUCHARIST.

transuranium elements   [trans-yur-ay'-nee-uhm]

The transuranium ELEMENTS are the chemical elements (see PERIODIC TABLE) that have atomic numbers greater than uranium (93 and higher). The transuranium elements have only radioactive ISOTOPES because their large nuclei are unstable. All have half-lives much shorter than the age of the Earth and (with the exception of trace amounts of NEPTUNIUM and PLUTONIUM) are not found in nature (see ELEMENT 107; ELEMENT 108; ELEMENT 109). Synthesis of these elements began in 1940 (see TRANSMUTATION OF ELEMENTS). Elements 93–103 are members of the ACTINIDE SERIES, and those with an atomic number of 104 and higher are called SUPERHEAVY ELEMENTS. By international agreement, the latter are no longer being named for scientists but are instead called simply by the Latin form of their individual atomic numbers.

A claim for the discovery of a transuranium element requires a valid nuclear reaction and a means of chemical identification. Because the half-lives of the heaviest isotopes are no more than a few minutes or seconds, ingenious methods of rapid synthesis, isolation, and identification have had to be developed. The chemical identification of these short-lived isotopes is often based on the discovery of just a few atoms. MENDELEVIUM, for example, was identified by the separation of five atoms, using an ion-exchange column and assuming properties analogous to those of fermium (the nearest actinide element) and thulium (the lanthanide homologue of mendelevium).   LESTER R. MORSS

Bibliography: Keller, C., *The Chemistry of the Transuranium Elements* (1971); Seaborg, Glenn T., ed., *Transuranium Elements: Products of Modern Alchemy* (1978).

Transvaal   [tranz-vahl']

Transvaal, the northernmost, mineral-rich province of South Africa, has an area of 283,917 km² (109,625 mi²). Of its population of 8,351,000 (1980), about 75% is black and 25% is white. PRETORIA is the capital, JOHANNESBURG the largest city. The economy is based on agriculture, diversified industry, and the region's vast mineral resources, which include gold, diamonds, coal, uranium, platinum, and chromite. The WIT-

WATERSRAND region contains the world's richest gold field. KRUGER NATIONAL PARK is in the northeast.

Originally inhabited by BANTU tribes, Transvaal was settled in 1838 by AFRIKANERS, who founded the South African Republic in 1856. Britain annexed the region in 1877, which led to disputes over the Afrikaners' sovereignty and eventually to the SOUTH AFRICAN WAR (1899–1900). Transvaal became a province of the Union of South Africa in 1910.

transverse wave: see WAVES AND WAVE MOTION.

transvestism

Transvestism, also known as cross-dressing, is a sexual variance wherein the individual, usually male, experiences sexual satisfaction from dressing in clothing generally worn by the opposite sex. Most transvestites are heterosexual and are not interested in changing, by way of sex-transformation surgical procedures, into the opposite sex.

The incidence of transvestism in the population is probably less than one percent. Apart from their cross-dressing, which may be only occasional, transvestites tend to be conventional in their sexual habits and often marry. The causes of transvestism are not definitely known. Psychological theories frequently suggest that faulty or abnormal parent-child interactions are at the root of this variance. Psychotherapy, including behavior modification techniques, can be effective in treating transvestism.   STEPHEN P. MCCARY

Bibliography: Brierley, Harry, *Transvestism* (1979); Green, Richard, *Sexual Identity Conflict in Children and Adults* (1974); Mahoney, E. R., *Human Sexuality* (1983); Talamini, John T., *Boys Will Be Girls: The Hidden World of the Heterosexual Male Transvestite* (1980).

Transylvania   [tran-sul-vay'-nee-uh]

Romania's historic region of Transylvania, sheltered by the Carpathians and Transylvanian Alps, has long been home to diverse peoples— including Magyars, Szeklers, and Germans, in addition to Romanians.

Transylvania (Romanian: Transilvania; Hungarian: Erdély) is a hilly region in northwestern Romania, enclosed on the east and south by the Carpathian Mountains and Transylvanian Alps and on the west by the Bihor Mountains. The main cities are CLUJ, BRAŞOV, and Sibiu, but the population is mostly rural and agricultural. Cereal grains, potatoes, sugar beets, and flax are grown there. Forestry is also important. Minerals include lignite, iron, copper, and natural gas, and steel and chemicals are manufactured.

Ethnic Romanians form the majority of the population; significant minorities include Hungarians (Magyars) and, to a lesser extent, Germans, both of which are especially numerous in the towns. The SZEKLERS, or Szekelys, are a Magyarized people of disputed origin.

Transylvania was at the center of the Roman province of Dacia after AD 106. From the 11th to the 16th century Transylvania was ruled by Hungary; it then became an autonomous principality of the Ottoman Empire. In 1699 it came under the Habsburgs as part of Hungary. A Romanian national revival took place there in the second part of the 19th century, and in 1920 the historic Transylvania was incorporated into Romania. Northern Transylvania was transfered to Hungary in 1940 and restored to Romania in 1945. In the late 1980s a conflict arose between Romania and Hungary over alleged Romanian mistreatment of its Hungarian population.

NORMAN J. G. POUNDS

Bibliography: Cadzow, John, and Ludanyi, Andrew, eds., *Transylvania: The Roots of Ethnic Conflict* (1984); Pascu, Ştefan, *A History of Transylvania,* trans. by Robert Ladd (1982); Verdery, Katherine, *Transylvanian Villagers* (1983).

Transylvania Company

The Transylvania Company, first organized as the Louisa Company in 1774, was an association of North Carolina land speculators who proposed to colonize and exploit a huge area illegally obtained from the Cherokee Indians—the land mass between the Kentucky River and the highlands south of the Cumberland (now part of Kentucky and Tennessee). Richard HENDERSON, a leader of the company, dispatched Daniel BOONE to blaze a trail (the WILDERNESS ROAD) and followed him to the Kentucky fort that was later called Boonesborough. Henderson's attempt to establish a proprietary colony in Boonesborough was resisted by many of the settlers and thwarted by the states of Virginia and North Carolina, whose chartered limits encompassed Transylvania. In compensation for this loss and for the labor of opening the frontier, Henderson was given 200,000-acre (about 81,000-ha) tracts in both Kentucky (by Virginia) and Tennessee (by North Carolina).

REGINALD HORSMAN

Bibliography: Lester, W. S., *The Transylvania Colony* (1935).

trap door spider

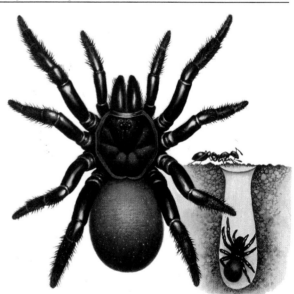

The predatory trap door spider, family Ctenizidae, is well equipped for digging, having, in addition to its interior fangs, a row of exterior teeth under its jaw to assist in soil removal. The silk-lined walls of its burrow may extend downward as far as 25 cm (10 in), providing it with a secure burrow from which to ambush its prey.

Trap door spiders construct burrows lined by their silk and closed by a hinged door of silk, moss, and soil. There they lie in wait for passing prey, usually an insect; when the prey touches silken threads radiating out on the ground near the door, the spiders quickly open the door and seize it. Closely related to tarantulas, trap door spiders make up the family Ctenizidae. They are generally small, are harmless to humans, and are found in many warm climates. They also use their burrows for protection and as nest sites, the female spinning her egg sac for about 300 eggs in the burrow.

trapezoid   [trap'-uh-zoyd]

A trapezoid is a four-sided plane figure that has two parallel sides. The parallel sides are called the bases, and the nonparallel sides are called legs. If the legs are of equal length, the trapezoid is an isosceles trapezoid. The perpendicular distance between the bases is called the altitude; the area of a trapezoid is equal to half the sum of the bases times the altitude.

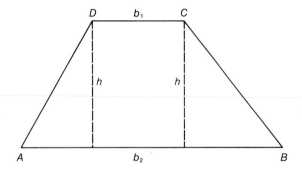

Trappists [trap'-ists]

Trappists is the popular name for members of the Roman Catholic order of CISTERCIANS of the Strict Observance (O.C.S.O. or O.C.R.), which traces its beginnings back to the reforms introduced (1664) by Armand Jean le Bouthillier de Rancé (1626–1700) at the monastery of La Trappe near Séez, France. He stressed the penitential aspect of monasticism—little food, no meat, hard manual labor, and strict silence. Eventually these measures were adopted by other Cistercian monasteries. Expelled from France during the French Revolution, the La Trappe community survived as exiles under Dom Augustine de Lestrange. They returned to La Trappe in 1815.

In the mid-20th century the Trappists increased in membership, particularly in the United States. One influential member was the writer Thomas Merton. The Trappist monks and nuns, who wear a white habit with black scapular, now have about 70 abbeys worldwide.   CYPRIAN DAVIS, O.S.B.

Bibliography: Krailsheimer, Alban J., *Armand-Jean de Rancé: Abbot of La Trappe* (1974); Lekai, Louis, *Cistercians: Ideals and Reality* (1977); Merton, Thomas, *The Silent Life* (1957).

Traubel, Helen [trow'-bul]

Helen Traubel, operatic and concert soprano, b. St. Louis, Mo., June 20, 1899, d. July 28, 1972, was the first American-born and -trained artist to sing the Wagnerian roles of Isolde and Brünnhilde at the Metropolitan Opera. After her 1939 Metropolitan debut as Sieglinde in *Die Walküre*, she alternated with Kirsten Flagstad in Wagnerian roles until the latter's departure in 1941. Traubel made her London debut in 1953. A series of nightclub engagements led to a dispute with and her resignation from the Metropolitan Opera, but she continued to perform actively on radio and in films.
                                                    RAYMOND GRAUNKE

traveler's check

Traveler's checks were devised by the American Express Company in 1891 to protect travelers who might otherwise carry large amounts of cash that could be lost or stolen. These checks are sold, usually for a small handling fee, by banks or express agencies in different denominations and in most of the world's major currencies. Traveler's checks are accepted as payment almost everywhere in the world; they can also be converted into cash and are redeemable in foreign currencies according to the prevailing rate of exchange. Each check is signed by the purchaser when it is issued and again when it is cashed, and the number on each check is recorded to guarantee reimbursement if the checks are lost or stolen.

traveler's-tree

Traveler's-tree, *Ravenala madagascariensis,* a member of the family Strelitziaceae, has a palmlike trunk and grows to a

height of 10 to 20 m (30 to 70 ft). Its large leaves are about 4 m (13 ft) long and form a fanlike arrangement; the large flower clusters are white. Each leaf sheath holds about a liter (1 qt) of water; this has served as a refreshing drink for travelers, accounting for the tree's common name. The tree is grown in southern California and Florida.   FRANK B. SALISBURY

traveling-wave tube

The traveling-wave tube is a specialized ELECTRON TUBE capable of amplifying a MICROWAVE signal. An electron gun at one end of the cylindrical tube generates electrons that are confined into a narrow beam by an electromagnetic coil wound around the circumference of the tube. Microwave energy entering the tube near the electron gun travels by means of a waveguide along the path of the electron beam, where it modulates the beam by forcing the electrons in the beam to group into bunches. The amplified microwave energy then passes out the far end of the tube. The electron beam leaves the tube through a collector.

Traveling-wave tubes are efficient and can amplify signals over a wide range of frequencies. They are used in microwave transmitters and receivers for radar systems, in spacecraft, and in other applications. Other important microwave tubes are the KLYSTRON and the MAGNETRON.
                                                    FORREST M. MIMS III

Bibliography: Gewartowski, J. W., and Watson, H. A., *Principles of Electron Tubes* (1965).

Traven, B. [trah'-ven]

B. Traven, or Ben Traven, was the pseudonym of Berick Traven Torsvan, b. Chicago, Mar. 5, 1890, d. Mar. 27, 1969. Among his dozen novels, written in German, *The Treasure of the Sierra Madre* (1927; Eng. trans., 1934)—a grimly ironic story of human greed that was made into a classic film by John Huston in 1948—is easily the most famous. Traven guarded his privacy so closely that even his identity remained a mystery until after his death. He resided in Germany for the duration of World War I and subsequently moved to Mexico.

Bibliography: Baumann, Michael, *B. Traven: An Introduction* (1976); Chankin, Donald, *Anonymity and Death: The Fiction of B. Traven* (1975).

Travers, Morris William [trav'-urz]

The English physical chemist Morris William Travers, b. Jan. 24, 1872, d. Aug. 25, 1961, discovered (with William Ramsay) the inert gases neon, krypton, argon, and xenon. Travers and Ramsay discovered these gases by evaporating liquid air and collecting fractions, which were then analyzed spectroscopically. In his later career Travers worked in glass technology, high temperatures (furnaces and fuels), and low temperatures (cryogenics). He published a biography of Ramsay in 1956.
                                                    ROBERT J. PARDOWSKI

travertine [trav'-ur-teen]

Water flowing down the walls of a cave can form sheets of calcite; such sheets, called travertine, or flowstone, are composed of crystals of calcium carbonate that sparkle when light shines on them. Mud or minerals dissolved in the water give travertine a color other than the normal white. Travertine often forms rimstone dams as high as 1 m (3.3 ft) on cave floors; such dams impound water in crescent-shaped pools. Travertine occasionally forms along surface streams and lakes with high calcium-carbonate content.
                                                    BROTHER G. NICHOLAS

Bibliography: Moore, George, and Brother G. Nicholas, *Speleology: the Study of Caves* (1978).

travesty: see BURLESQUE AND TRAVESTY.

Traviata, La [trah-vee-ah'-tah, lah]

A celebrated play by Alexandre Dumas the Younger, *La Dame aux Camélias*—known on the English-speaking stage as *Ca-*

mille—formed the basis of Giuseppe VERDI's opera *La Traviata* (The Transgressor), first performed in Venice on Mar. 6, 1853. The story is based on the life of the Parisian cocotte Marie Duplessis, who died of consumption at the age of 23. The libretto is by F. M. Piave.

Travis, William B.   [trav'-is]

Both lawyer and soldier, William Barrett Travis, b. Edgefield, S.C., Aug. 9, 1809, d. Mar. 6, 1836, was a hero of the TEXAS REVOLUTION. He took part in the capture of San Antonio in December 1835 and led the defense of the ALAMO against Mexican seige from Feb. 23 to Mar. 6, 1836. Travis died when the entire garrison was massacred.

travois   [trav-oy']

A travois is a drag frame consisting of two long poles, the front tips tied together on the back of a dog, the stub ends splayed out and dragging on the ground, connected in mid-length with a piece of netting or skin. It was used among the Plains Indians to carry a load of up to 27 kg (60 lb) across the Plains in the course of their migrations. The load might consist of a quarter of a bison, firewood, or a baby or child. When the Indians acquired the horse, they used a much larger version of the travois with long TEPEE poles, which could carry an injured person or other larger loads.   GENE WELTFISH

Bibliography: Lowie, Robert H., *Indians of the Plains* (1963).

trawler: see FISHING INDUSTRY.

treadmill

A treadmill is a machine in which a wheel oriented with a horizontal axis of rotation is turned by persons or animals walking, or treading, on boards arranged about the periphery of the wheel. This arrangement permits the multiplication of the applied force, as in a lever. Various types of treadmills were used in ancient times, both to lift water and to grind grain.

Treadmills attached to cranes were used to lift heavy objects from Roman times, and perhaps earlier, through the late Middle Ages in Europe. Treadmills came to be used as instruments of prison discipline, especially during the 16th and 17th centuries. Similar types of mechanisms have been developed for operation by different types of animals in sideshows, at the circus, and as novelty items. Because of the monotonous and dulling nature of working a treadmill, the name of this device has been adapted for the description of undesirable situations and chores.

treason

Treason, a crime against the state to which allegiance is owed, consists of attempting to overthrow the government or betraying it into the hands of its enemies. Under English law *high treason* was once so broad a term that it was used until the 19th century to justify punishing all sorts of persons who were judged as enemies of the monarch. The U.S. Constitution narrowly defines treason and specifically declares: "No Person shall be convicted of Treason unless on the Testimony of two Witnesses to the same overt Act, or on Confession in open Court." This constitutional statement was strictly followed by Chief Justice John Marshall in the 1807 trial of Aaron BURR, who was charged with treason for allegedly plotting to establish an independent republic in the Louisiana Territory but who was acquitted because the prosecution could not prove Burr guilty of "an overt act of levying war." Less than 40 federal prosecutions for treason have occurred, and only once in its history has the U.S. Supreme Court sustained a conviction for treason (*Haupt* v. *United States*, 1947). Many state constitutions have treason provisions, but only two persons have been successfully prosecuted by states: Thomas Dorr (see DORR'S REBELLION) and John BROWN.

Bibliography: Chapin, Bradley, *The American Law of Treason: Revolutionary and Early National Origins* (1964); Hurst, James W., *The Law of Treason in the United States: Collected Essays* (1971); West, Rebecca, *The New Meaning of Treason* (1964).

Treasure Island

Treasure Island (1883) is a classic adventure story by Robert Louis STEVENSON. The narrator, young Jim Hawkins, describes a hunt for buried treasure, which involves a voyage on the schooner *Hispaniola* and a clash with pirates led by the notorious one-legged Long John Silver. Other memorable characters include the blind villain, Pew, and the marooned seaman, Ben Gunn.   R. M. FORD

Treasury, U.S. Department of the

The U.S. Department of the Treasury is the department of the executive branch of government that oversees the nation's finances. The department was created in 1789, and its first secretary was Alexander Hamilton.

The secretary of the treasury is the second-ranking officer (after the secretary of state) in the president's cabinet. He or she is the president's chief advisor on fiscal affairs and is responsible for managing the public debt. The law requires the secretary to report each year to the Congress on the government's fiscal operations and its financial condition. The secretary is also involved in financial dealings with other nations. The secretary has special staffs dealing with such matters as defense lending, debt analysis, financial analysis, international finance, international tax affairs, and law-enforcement coordination.

The Treasury Department's operating bureaus include the COMPTROLLER OF THE CURRENCY, who supervises national banks; the U.S. Customs Service, which collects taxes on goods brought into the country from abroad; the Bureau of Engraving and Printing, which produces currency, bonds, Federal Reserve notes, and postage stamps; the Bureau of Government Financial Operations, which is responsible for money management; the INTERNAL REVENUE SERVICE, which collects taxes; the United States Mint, which manufactures coinage; the Bureau of Alcohol, Tobacco and Firearms, which is a law enforcement agency; and the SECRET SERVICE, which protects top U.S. officials and presidential candidates and enforces laws against counterfeiting.

Bibliography: Gaines, Tilford C., *Techniques of Treasury Debt Management* (1962); Gurney, Gene and Clare, *The United States Treasury: A Pictorial History* (1977); Taus, Esther R., *Central Banking Functions of the United States Treasury, 1789–1941* (1943; repr. 1966).

treaty

A treaty is a formal agreement that regulates relations between two or more sovereign states. Treaties are known to have existed since before 3000 BC. They are mentioned in the Old Testament and in Greek and Roman literature. Treaties may pertain to political matters, such as alliances or the cessation of armed conflict; commerce, such as tariffs or navigation; legal issues, such as extradition or copyright agreements; and matters of confederation and integration, as in the setting up of international and supranational organizations.

In republics the power to negotiate treaties usually lies within the province of the chief executive. In the United States, the Department of State, under the authority of the president, usually assumes the task of formulating a treaty. A treaty goes into effect only after it has been ratified in accordance with each nation's requirements. Ratification in the United States requires approval by two-thirds of the Senate. (The president, however, may make executive agreements that do not need Senate approval.) In Britain ratification depends on acceptance by Parliament and the crown. In other countries as well, ratification is usually the responsibility of the head of state or the national legislature, or both.

A treaty may be terminated either by the consent of all parties concerned or if a clause in a treaty provides an expiration date or permits cancellation by either party after due notice.

Treaties can be—but are not necessarily—terminated or suspended by the outbreak of war between warring parties, except for treaties regulating the conduct of war. Failure of one party to observe the terms of a treaty, moreover, entitles the other party to abrogate it.

In the United States, states may not make treaties, and treaties constitute part of the supreme law of the land, taking precedence over all laws and state constitutions. Early in its history, the United States made many treaties with the American Indians. These treaties dealt with the Indian tribes as foreign governments and are legally binding. Congress declared, however, in 1871 that the Indians were no longer to be regarded as independent nations; thereafter treaties were no longer necessary to regulate relations with the Indians.

Bibliography: McNair, Lord, *The Law of Treaties* (1986); Millar, T. B., and Ward, R., *Current International Treaties* (1984).

Trebizond: see TRABZON.

treble

Treble is a term usually used to refer to children's voices of high range, whereas the equivalent high voice of an adult woman is called a SOPRANO. It is also a name given to certain high-pitched instruments such as the treble recorder and treble viol as well as to the uppermost part of a musical composition, or to the highest pitches as opposed to the lower, BASS, parts and the name of a CLEF, also called the G clef. The term, however, is often loosely used to characterize women's voices and high-pitched instruments in general.

Treblinka   [treb-link'-uh]

Treblinka was a concentration camp 80 km (50 mi) from Warsaw, Poland, used by the German Nazis in their program of exterminating the Jews. First established by the Germans as a slave labor camp in 1941, Treblinka was turned into a death camp early in 1942. From July to September 1942, 300,000 Jews

were deported from Warsaw to Treblinka. In mid-May 1943, the entire population of the Warsaw ghetto was dispersed and transported to Treblinka and some of the other death camps. By July 11, 1945, when the armies of the USSR entered Warsaw, 800,000 Jewish men, women, and children had been put to death at Treblinka.   MILDRED NAVARETTA

Bibliography: Arad, Yitzhak, *Belzec, Sobibor, Treblinka* (1987); Hyams, Joseph, *A Field of Buttercups* (1968); Steiner, Jean François, *Treblinka*, trans. by Helen Weaver (1967; repr. 1979).

tree

A tree is generally defined as an erect PLANT with a single woody stem capable of reaching heights of at least 6–8 m (20–25 ft) at maturity. Depending on environmental conditions and age, however, some tree species may exhibit growth forms characteristic of SHRUBS and VINES. Trees dominate the ecosystem because they grow to large sizes and live for many years. For example, the coast redwood, *Sequoia sempervirens,* attains the greatest height (112 m/368 ft) of any tree species. The Sierran redwood, *Sequoiadendron giganteum,* has the largest diameter, reaching 9 m (30 ft). Although relatively short, the bristlecone pine, *Pinus aristata,* is one of the oldest trees known, attaining the age of about 4,600 years, which far exceeds the life span of 100 to 250 years of most trees.

CLASSIFICATION

Trees are classified in a variety of ways but are most commonly divided into two groups on the basis of their reproductive structures. The GYMNOSPERMS (meaning naked seeds), evolutionarily the more primitive group, bear seeds on modified leaf structures called scales, which are often aggregated into cones. They include such well-known trees as the pines (*Pinus*), firs (*Abies*), spruces (*Picea*), and hemlocks (*Tsuga*). The gymnosperms are often referred to as CONIFERS, EVERGREENS, needle-bearing trees, or softwoods. These designations may be misleading, however. Cycads (*Cycas, Zamia*) are classified as gymnosperms but have conelike reproductive structures, not true cones, and hence are not conifers. Some gymno-

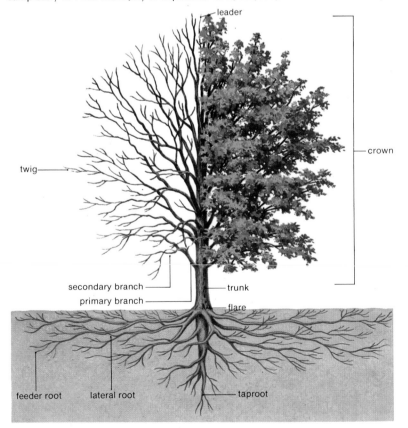

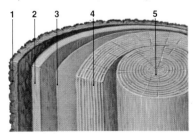

(Left) *A white oak,* Quercus alba, *with its roots and half of its branches exposed, illustrates the external anatomy of a tree. The root system anchors the tree and supplies it with water and nutrients from the soil. The trunk, typically braced by a swelling, or flare, at its base, tapers to its highest branch, the leader, and supports the branches, twigs, and leaves. The leaves, exposed to sunlight, produce food for the entire tree by means of photosynthesis.*

(Below) *A cross section of a tree trunk reveals several concentric layers. Outer bark (1), composed of dead cells, protects the inner layers. Phloem (2), or inner bark, conducts food from the leaves to the rest of the tree. Cells of the cambium (3) divide to produce phloem and, on the inner side, wood (xylem). Sapwood (4), a mixture of living and dead cells, carries water and nutrients up the trunk. Heartwood (5), composed of dead cells, adds strength.*

Labels on tree diagram: leader, crown, twig, secondary branch, primary branch, trunk, flare, feeder root, lateral root, taproot

sperms, such as the ginko, *Ginkgo biloba,* have broad leaves, instead of needles. Not all gymnosperms are evergreens; the larches, *Larix,* for instance, shed their leaves during the winter. Also, some gymnosperms have WOOD of considerable hardness.

The other major group of trees, the ANGIOSPERMS, the most highly evolved land plants, have flowers and bear their seeds enclosed in a FRUIT, which is the ripened ovary of a FLOWER. Representative flowering trees include the oaks (*Quercus*), beeches (*Fagus*), poplars (*Populus*), birches (*Betula*), cherries (*Prunus*), tulip trees (*Liriodendron*), elms (*Ulmus*), ashes (*Fraxinus*), and maples (*Acer*). Angiospermous trees are sometimes referred to as deciduous trees (those which lose their leaves for part of the year) or hardwoods. Not all angiospermous trees are deciduous, however; many species in the genus *Eucalyptus* are evergreen. Some flowering trees have wood that is relatively soft.

While the scientific classification of trees is based upon the evolutionary relationships between species, genera, and families, relying heavily on the characteristics of the reproductive structures described above, leaf, fruit, bud, and bark characteristics are also useful in tree identification.

STRUCTURE AND FUNCTION

Trees have four major structural components, the stem, or trunk, including branches and twigs; leaves; roots; and reproductive structures.

Stem. The stem supports the tree and provides pathways for the upward transport of water and nutrients and the downward movement of carbohydrates. Very little of the stem actually consists of elements of living cells. Elements of the stem are arranged concentrically in cross-section. The outer BARK consists mostly of dead cells and protects the living tissue of the stem. The inner bark, or phloem, is composed of living cells through which various organic materials are transported throughout the stem and root system. A thin cambial layer, which consists of meristematic tissue, or undifferentiated cells that are capable of reproducing themselves, is located at the interface of the bark and woody stem. This layer, called the cambium, generates phloem to the outside and xylem (wood) to the inside. The xylem is differentiated into SAPWOOD and heartwood. The sapwood, located next to the cambium, consists primarily of dead cells that are used to transport water and nutrients up through the stem to the crown, or the upper portion of the stem, branches, and leaves. In older trees the inner core of wood consists of heartwood, which is composed of dead cells that contain deposits of various organic and inorganic chemicals and is no longer functional in the movement of water.

Leaves. Leaves are the sites of food production in most trees. Chlorophyll makes the leaves appear green in color. Leaves come in a wide variety of sizes and shapes, from large compound structures (as in walnuts, *Juglans,* and hickories, *Carya*) to needles (as in pines) and tiny scales (as in junipers, *Juniperus*). The life span of leaves also varies greatly from less than one year to over 20 years in some species. Leaves are important as sites for gaseous exchanges such as the absorption of carbon dioxide (CO_2), which is the gas used to produce carbohydrates in PHOTOSYNTHESIS, and transpiration (loss of water vapor), which is an important process in maintaining the flow of water from the root system to the crown of the tree. Leaves have small openings or pores, called STOMATA, which are the sites for most of these exchanges. Many tree species have a high degree of control over the size of the stomatal openings and can reduce water losses during times of moisture stress within the plant. Waxy coatings on the surfaces of some leaves are one example of an adaptation that reduces generalized moisture loss.

Roots. The root system consists of one or more large, woody roots and an extensive network of fine roots. The large roots anchor the tree, and the fine roots carry out the critical function of absorbing water and nutrients from the soil. Water absorbed by the fine root system moves through the coarse roots, stem, and branches to the leaves. The fine root system typically consists of both small, nonwoody root hairs and MYCORRHIZAE. Mycorrhizae are complex structures that incorpo-

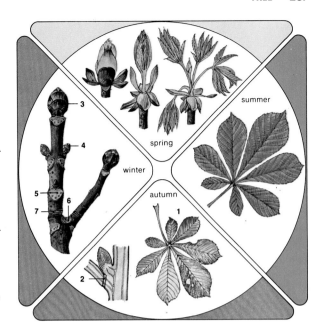

(Above) *Deciduous trees of the temperate zones undergo an annual growth cycle that depends largely on temperature and day length. In spring, leaves emerge from the buds and begin photosynthesis; the shoot elongates; and the bud scales fall, leaving a set of scars. The leaves continue photosynthesis throughout the summer. In autumn, depletion of chlorophyll and the presence of other pigments cause the leaves to change color (1); an abscission zone (2) forms at the base of the leaf, and the leaf falls. Buds protect partly formed leaves during winter dormancy; a winter twig shows a newly formed terminal bud (3), lateral bud (4), leaf scar (5), flower scar (6), and bud scale scar of the previous year's terminal bud (7).*

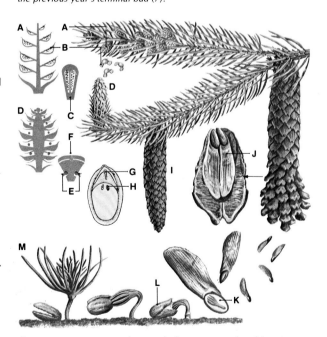

Gymnospermous trees produce seeds that are not enclosed in an ovary. Male cones (A) of the Norway spruce, Picea abies, shed pollen grains (B) from two sacs under each cone scale (C). Female cones (D) have two unfertilized eggs (E) per scale (F). After a pollen grain lands on a female cone, the nucleus of the grain grows down a pollen tube (G) and fuses with an egg (H) to form a seed. At maturity, the female cone (I) hangs from the branch, allowing winged seeds (J) on each scale to be dispersed by the wind. On a suitable site, the seed embryo (K) germinates (L) and becomes a spruce seedling (M).

rate both fungal strands, or hyphae, and root hairs. These structures greatly increase the absorptive capabilities of the tree's root system, and the fungus receives carbohydrates and other complex organic molecules manufactured by the tree. Many fungal species form this symbiotic relationship with trees, and, in turn, most tree species benefit by having mycorrhizae (see SYMBIOSIS). Symbiotic nitrogen-fixing bacteria living in the roots of some trees, such as alder, *Alnus,* and some legumes provide usable nitrogen compounds to the host plant; the bacteria obtain food from the tree in return. The absorptive portion of the tree's root system typically must have a high rate of turnover (growth and mortality) in order to exploit the moisture and nutrient resources of the soil; hence, much photosynthate is required for maintenance of the roots.

Reproductive Structures. In most gymnosperms the seed-bearing structure is the conelike strobilus. Male, or pollen-producing, and female, or ovuliferous, strobili are borne on different branches of the same tree. In angiospermous trees, the ovary of the flower contains the ovules that become seeds following pollination and fertilization. Perfect flowers have both male and female parts; imperfect flowers are either male or female. Many trees, such as beeches, which have male and female flowers on the same plant, are monoecious. Dioecious trees, such as willows, *Salix,* have male and female flowers on separate individuals.

GROWTH AND DEVELOPMENT
Growth of a tree occurs from division of cells in the meristematic tissue in the cambium and the tips of the branches and roots. Cambial cell division results in an increase in tree diameter. The xylem cells added to the stem usually differentiate into thin-walled springwood and thick-walled summerwood that produce the annual rings visible in cross-sections of most tree trunks from temperate areas. The meristems associated with the crown produce elongation of the branches, resulting in increases in tree height. Trees elongate only at these growing tips; hence, a point on a tree trunk, such as a forking of branches, will always remain at the same height above the ground.

The life cycle of a tree begins with the development of a seed that may have been dispersed by wind or animals. When the seed begins to germinate, or grow, it becomes a seedling. Trees are most vulnerable to environmental stresses at the seedling stage, and many tree seedlings are eaten at this stage of development or die because of excessive heat or drought. Those which survive and grow larger will, in turn, begin to produce seed, typically after 10 to 30 years.

Trees are potentially immortal since meristematic tissues are retained throughout the life of the tree. Death usually results from some environmental agent, such as fire, wind, lightning, drought, or human cutting, or from a biological cause, such as disease or insect attack. As a tree ages it may become more susceptible to insect pests or diseases, such as bark beetles or fungal root rots, which contribute directly or indirectly to its death. Most trees actually die of several causes. Insects or diseases introduced from outside of a species' natural range can cause very high levels of mortality, as exemplified by the white pine blister rust, chestnut blight, balsam woolly aphid, and Dutch elm disease; all of these diseases were introduced into North America from Eurasia by humans and have caused catastrophic death of affected tree species. Environmental pollution in the form of ACID RAIN can also seriously weaken or kill trees.

ECOLOGY AND DISTRIBUTION
Moisture, temperature, and nutrient conditions are the most important environmental factors affecting the establishment and growth of tree species. Forests are widely distributed in the temperate and tropical regions of the world and are a reflection of favorable moisture and temperature regimes in these areas (see FORESTS AND FORESTRY). Some notable forest regions in North America are the pine forests of the southeastern states, the deciduous hardwood forests of the northeastern and Great Lakes region, the mixed coniferous forests of the Rocky Mountains and Sierra Nevada, and the dense coniferous forests of the Pacific Coast. Two of the most widespread forest formations in the world are the taiga, a coniferous, primarily evergreen, forest of boreal and subarctic regions, and the pine-juniper savannas of warm regions with seasonal drought (see TAIGA CLIMATE; SAVANNA LIFE). Africa, South and Central America, and Southeast Asia are sites of extensive tropical rain forests that are being rapidly logged, partially for agriculture (see JUNGLE AND RAIN FOREST).

Tree species tolerate different environmental conditions. Trees grow more slowly, attain smaller dimensions, and are often more widely spaced in cold or arid regions. Cold temperatures, short growing seasons, and heavy snows prevent the growth of trees at high elevations and high latitudes. Moisture stress typically limits tree growth at lower timberlines, such as those adjacent to grasslands or deserts. Ecological differences among trees result in changes in forest composition across a landscape.

IMPORTANCE
Trees are valuable to humankind for many products and amenities. Many trees are major sources of food, primarily as fruits and NUTS; also, sugar is derived from the sap of some trees. Wood is a major source of fuel for heating and cooking, particularly in developing countries. Construction materials from wood include LUMBER, PLYWOOD, and particle board. Wood is the major source of fiber for the production of pulp and PAPER. Trees are a primary or secondary source for many chemical products. Some fibers, such as RAYON, are produced from wood pulp. The bark of some tree species is the major source of tannins. Other chemicals are harvested directly from living trees, such as RUBBER and various resins, which are then refined to such products as TURPENTINE.

Trees also provide numerous services. They protect soils from erosion and help maintain high-quality water supplies. Tree root systems make a major contribution to soil stability. Living trees create valuable wildlife habitats. Standing dead trees, often called snags, also serve as animal habitats. Downed trees are important in conserving and cycling nutrients, in reducing soil erosion, as wildlife habitats, and as nursing sites for the establishment of other plants. Trees create shelterbelts in agricultural regions and attractive and effective barriers in urban areas, and also contribute aesthetically to many natural and domesticated landscapes.

JERRY F. FRANKLIN

Bibliography: Archer, R. R., *Growth Stresses and Strains in Trees* (1986); Clapham, A. R., *The Oxford Book of Trees* (1975); Davis, B., *The Gardener's Illustrated Encyclopedia of Trees and Shrubs* (1987); Harlow, W. M., *Textbook of Dendrology,* 6th ed. (1979); Kozlowski, T. T., *Tree Growth and Environmental Stresses* (1979); Mitchell, A., *The Trees of North America* (1987); Sinclair, W. A., et al., *Diseases of Trees and Shrubs* (1986); Walker, L. C., *Trees: An Introduction to Trees and Forest Ecology for the Amateur Naturalist* (1984); Zimmerman, M. H., and Brown, C. L., *Trees: Structure and Function* (1975).

Tree, Ellen: see KEAN (family).

Tree, Sir Herbert Beerbohm

Sir Herbert Draper Beerbohm Tree, b. Dec. 17, 1853, d. July 2, 1917, half brother of Sir Max Beerbohm, was an English actor-manager whose Shakespearean productions rivaled those of his more famous rival, Sir Henry IRVING. Tree assumed management of London's Haymarket Theatre in 1887, and his subsequent success enabled him to build His Majesty's Theatre in 1897. Tree was considered a great character actor, especially famous for his portrayals of Falstaff, Shylock, Svengali, and Malvolio.   COLETTE BROOKS

Bibliography: Bingham, Madeleine, *Great Lover: The Life and Art of Herbert Beerbohm Tree* (1979).

tree diagram

A tree diagram, or dendrogram, is a pictorial method used in statistics to list all possible outcomes of a sequence of trials. It takes its name from the similarity of its shape to that of a tree, with "branches" growing out of a central "trunk." Tree diagrams are most common in PROBABILITY theory as an aid to computing the probabilities of occurrence of a sequence of events. When each branch is labeled with the probability of obtaining that particular outcome on that trial, the probability of an entire sequence of outcomes is represented by the product of the probabilities on the corresponding path through the tree. Tree diagrams also help a person to count the number of ways in which various final outcomes can arise. They are primarily an aid to learning; once the concept and technique involved have been mastered, tree diagrams need no longer be used by the student.

DAVID S. MOORE

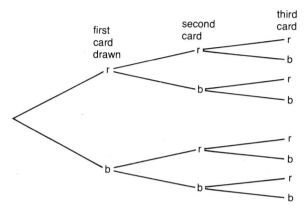

The experiment of drawing three cards from a shuffled deck and recording whether each card is red (r) or black (b) can be represented by a tree diagram, which indicates eight different paths through the tree from its root to its tip, corresponding to the eight possible results of the three draws.

tree frog

Tree frogs are members of the family Hylidae, which consists of more than 450 species, including true tree frogs and peepers (*Hyla*), cricket frogs (*Acris*), and chorus frogs (*Pseudacris*). Tree frogs are found on all temperate and tropical continents except Australia. They range in size from diminutive (less than 2.5 cm/1 in long) to large frogs. Most are good jumpers and are arboreal (living in trees), with climbing aided by toe discs and cartilages between the ultimate and penultimate phalanges. A few genera (*Acris, Pseudacris,* and *Limnaoedus*), however, have reduced toe discs and tend to be terrestrial. Most tree frogs lay eggs in water, but some, such as *Gastrotheca* and *Hemiphractus,* carry their eggs on their backs; a few (for example, *H. rosenbergi* and *H. faber*) build mud nests near water, and still others (phyllomedusines) deposit their eggs on overhanging leaves, the tadpoles later falling into the water.

JONATHAN CAMPBELL

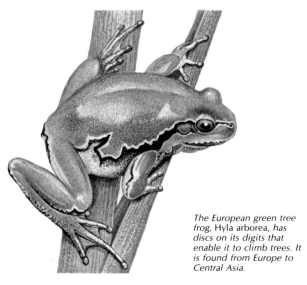

The European green tree frog, Hyla arborea, has discs on its digits that enable it to climb trees. It is found from Europe to Central Asia.

tree of heaven: see AILANTHUS.

tree-ring dating: see DENDROCHRONOLOGY.

tree shrew

The common tree shrew, T. glis, has a squirrellike body approximately 20 cm (8 in) long and a bushy tail of about the same length. It is primarily a ground dweller that nests in tree roots or in fallen trees.

A tree shrew is a small, squirrel-shaped mammal found in forested areas of India, southern China, southeastern Asia, Indonesia, and parts of the Philippines. About 15 species—10 typical tree shrews of the genus *Tupaia;* the Indian tree shrew, *Anathana;* the smooth-tailed tree shrews, *Dendrogale;* the Philippine tree shrew, *Urogale;* and the small, pen-tailed tree shrew, *Ptilocercus*—make up the family Tupaiidae. Some zoologists classify tree shrews as primates because of their relatively large brains, eyes in orbits surrounded by bone, and other features; others classify them with shrews and moles as insectivores. Tree shrews are usually less than 45 cm (18 in) in length—approximately half of which is the long tail—and weigh less than 0.5 kg (1 lb). They have long snouts, squirrel-like ears, and five fingers and five toes, each with sharp, slightly curved claws. The fur is usually brownish, often with shadings of other colors. Swift runners and good climbers, tree shrews feed mainly on fruits and insects. They like water for both drinking and bathing. Their gestation period is 45 to 56 days; a litter usually consists of only one or two.

treehopper

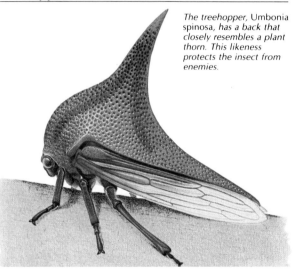

The treehopper, Umbonia spinosa, has a back that closely resembles a plant thorn. This likeness protects the insect from enemies.

Often bizarrely shaped, the treehoppers are small jumping insects of the family Membracidae and are related to leafhoppers and spittlebugs. Rarely longer than 10 mm (0.4 in), they usually appear humpbacked; the pronotum (the body part just behind the head) extends back over the body, sometimes assuming a thornlike shape. Common in vegetation, treehoppers can damage crops by sucking the juice out of young seedlings. The buffalo treehopper damages apple trees by laying its eggs in the bark.   DONALD J. BORROR

Treitschke, Heinrich von   [trych'-keh]

The German historian Heinrich von Treitschke, b. Sept. 15, 1834, d. Apr. 28, 1896, an eloquent and influential nationalist, strongly supported German unification under Prussian auspices, an authoritarian state, and German imperial expansion. He held several university professorships and was also a Reichstag member (1871–84). Treitschke's greatest work, the *History of Germany in the 19th Century* (1879–94; Eng. trans., 7 vols., 1915–19), reflects both his literary skill and his strong prejudices.

Trelleborg   [trel-uh-borg']

The ancient fortified settlement at Trelleborg, situated on the west coast of the Danish island of Zealand, was a major Viking military and naval base of the late 10th and the 11th century. Trelleborg's regular and measured layout reveals a remarkable degree of sophistication in planning and construction. The main inner enclosure is circular in plan. The four gateways set into its timber-laced defenses conform to the primary compass points and were linked by timber roadways that divided the interior into four equal segments. Each quadrant contained four timber buildings of bow-sided plan grouped into squares, each building being subdivided internally around a central, principal room. The outer enclosure contained 13 more boat-shaped houses set radially within the defensive rampart, and two additional buildings flanked the road to the outer entrance. To the east lay the camp cemetery, in which about 150 graves, including communal burials, have been discovered.   D. W. HARDING

Bibliography: Glob, P. V., *Denmark: An Archaeological History from the Stone Age to the Vikings,* trans. by Joan Bulman (1971); Munksgaard, Elisabeth, *Denmark: An Archaeological Guide* (1974).

tremolite: see AMPHIBOLE.

trench fever

Trench fever, an acute infectious disease caused by the microorganism *Rickettsia quintana,* is transmitted from person to person by the bite of the body louse. Outbreaks may occur in wartime armies. Symptoms include the sudden onset of fever, headache, weakness, sore muscles, and a rash. Recovery occurs in most cases but may be delayed for several months, and relapses sometimes happen. Treatment with tetracycline is effective.   J. MICHAEL S. DIXON

Trent, Council of

The Council of Trent, the 19th ecumenical council of the Roman Catholic church, was held at Trent in northern Italy between 1545 and 1563. It marked a major turning point in the efforts of the Catholic church to respond to the challenge of the Protestant REFORMATION and formed a key part of the COUNTER-REFORMATION. The need for such a council had long been perceived by certain church leaders, but initial attempts to organize it were opposed by FRANCIS I of France, who feared it would strengthen Holy Roman Emperor CHARLES V, and by the popes themselves, who feared a revival of CONCILI-ARISM. The council eventually met during three separate periods (1545–47, 1551–52, 1562–63) under the leadership of three different popes (PAUL III, Julius III, PIUS IV). All of its decrees were formally confirmed by Pope Pius IV in 1564.

In the area of religious doctrine, the council refused any concessions to the Protestants and, in the process, crystallized and codified Catholic dogma far more than ever before. It directly opposed Protestantism by reaffirming the existence of seven sacraments, transubstantiation, purgatory, the necessity of the priesthood, and justification by works as well as by faith. Clerical celibacy and monasticism were maintained, and decrees were issued in favor of the efficacy of relics, indulgences, and the veneration of the Virgin Mary and the saints.

This engraving, after a painting by Titian, portrays a session of the Council of Trent in 1555. A response to the Protestant Reformation, the Council articulated Roman Catholic doctrines and produced reform measures that were fundamental to the Counter-Reformation.

Tradition was declared coequal to Scripture as a source of spiritual knowledge, and the sole right of the church to interpret the Bible was asserted.

At the same time, the council took steps to reform many of the major abuses within the church that had partly incited the Reformation: decrees were issued requiring episcopal residence and a limitation on the plurality of benefices, and movements were instigated to reform certain monastic orders and to provide for the education of the clergy through the creation of a seminary in every diocese.

Attendance at the council was often relatively meager, and it was dominated by Italian and Spanish prelates. Several European monarchs kept their distance from the council's decrees, only partially enforcing them or, in the case of the French kings, never officially accepting them at all. The Council of Trent helped, however, to catalyze a movement within the Catholic clergy and laity for widespread religious renewal and reform, a movement that yielded substantial results in the 17th century.   T. TACKETT

Bibliography: Jedin, Hubert, *A History of the Council of Trent,* trans. by Ernest Graf, 2 vols. (1957–61); McNally, Robert E., *Council of Trent, The Spiritual Exercises and the Catholic Reform* (1970); O'Donohoe, J. A., *Tridentine Seminary Legislation* (1957); Schroeder, H. J., *Canons and Decrees of the Council of Trent* (1950).

Trent, River

The River Trent, 274 km (170 mi) long, rises in central England, just north of Stoke-on-Trent in northern Staffordshire and flows southeast, then northeast past Nottingham, and north to the Humber estuary, which enters the North Sea near Grimsby. The river is used for barge traffic below Nottingham and for water supply and recreation.

Trent Affair

The Trent Affair was a diplomatic crisis between Great Britain and the United States during the U.S. Civil War involving freedom of the seas. It began on Nov. 8, 1861, when Captain Charles WILKES of the U.S. warship *San Jacinto* forcibly removed Confederate diplomats James M. MASON and John SLIDELL from the British mail steamer *Trent* near Havana and took them to Boston, where they were imprisoned. Although this action seemed, to many Northerners, a triumph for the Union, it went against both international law and longstanding American claims for the rights of neutral vessels. The British government became incensed and sent 8,000 troops to Canada. For a short time President Abraham Lincoln's administration was unwilling to yield. Once enthusiasm had subsided, however, Secretary of State William H. Seward repudiated the seizure and announced (Dec. 26, 1861) that the prisoners would soon be released.   ROBERT H. FERRELL

Bibliography: Ferris, Norman B., *The Trent Affair* (1977); John, Evan, *Atlantic Impact, 1861* (1952).

Trentino-Alto Adige   [trayn-tee'-noh-ahl-toh ah'-dee-jay]

Trentino-Alto Adige is an autonomous region of northern Italy bordered by Switzerland to the northwest and Austria to the north. With its capital at Trent (Italian: Trento), the region has an area of 13,613 km² (5,256 mi²) and a population of 876,249 (1980 est.). The Tyrolean Alps in the north and the Dolomites in the east give most of Trentino-Alto Adige an average elevation of more than 900 m (3,000 ft) and support timber and tourist industries. The region supplies Italy with hydroelectric power and minerals, and fertile river valleys of the south provide grain, fruit, wine, and livestock. Formerly known as Venezia Tridentina, the region was annexed to Austria in 1814 as part of the Tyrol and was ceded to Italy in 1919. Most of the inhabitants of the northern province, with its capital at BOLZANO, speak German, whereas a majority of those in the southern province of Trento speak Italian.   DANIEL R. LESNICK

Trenton   [tren'-tuhn]

Trenton, the capital of New Jersey since 1790 and the seat of Mercer County, lies at the head of navigation on the Delaware River, about 48 km (30 mi) north of Philadelphia. The city's population is 92,124 (1980). A port and transportation hub in the New York-Philadelphia corridor, the city is also a major industrial center. Ceramics, rubber, cables, plastics, textiles, plumbing and bathroom fixtures, linoleum, pumps, and paper products are manufactured there. The state museum, Rider College (1865), and a planetarium are located in Trenton. The gilt dome of the state house (1792) is a city landmark.

In 1679, Mahlon Stacy, an English Quaker, built a log mill and a house on the site of the modern city. The settlement was first known as The Falls, then as Stacy's Mills, and finally, in 1721, it was named Trenton for William Trent, a Philadelphia merchant who laid out the town. The city was the scene of a December 1776 battle between George Washington's soldiers and Hessian mercenaries during the American Revolution. In 1784 and again in 1799, Trenton served as the capital of the United States. The construction of the Delaware and Raritan Canal and the arrival of the railroad in the 1830s stimulated the city's growth.

Trenton, Battle of

The Battle of Trenton (Dec. 26, 1776) was a crucial early victory for the American forces in the American Revolution. On Christmas night 1776, Gen. George Washington and about 2,500 Continental soldiers crossed the ice-clogged Delaware River from Pennsylvania. Early the next morning they surprised Hessian mercenaries in the British service encamped at Trenton, N.J. American casualties were light, but the Hessian commander was mortally wounded in the ensuing battle, and more than 900 of his men were captured. Washington also came away with badly needed arms and stores. After their earlier defeats in New York, the Trenton victory restored the Americans' flagging morale.

Bibliography: Bill, Alfred Hoyt, *The Campaign of Princeton, 1776–1777* (1948; repr. 1975); Ketchum, Richard M., *The Winter Soldiers* (1973); Smith, Samuel S., *The Battle of Trenton* (1965).

Treponema   [trep-uh-nee'-muh]

Treponema is a genus of parasitic spirochetes; they are unicellular, spiral-shaped microorganisms that are found in the oral cavity, intestinal tract, and genital regions of humans and animals. Some spirochetal species are pathogenic; for instance, *T. pallidum* causes human venereal and congenital syphilis, and *T. pertenue* causes yaws.   WAYBURN S. JETER

trespass   [tres'-pas]

Trespass is entry into or use of real or personal property without the consent of the one who possesses (owns or controls) that property. Such illegal entry is punishable even if no loss of property or damage results, if the entry was unintentional or accidental, and whether the trespass took the form of invasion by a human being or by some object (for example, a tree cut down that may have fallen on someone else's land). Unless trespass involves force or intimidation that leads to a breach of the peace (see ASSAULT AND BATTERY), trespass is not considered a criminal matter, but a TORT, a civil injury.

Trevelyan, G. M.   [truh-vel'-yuhn]

The English historian George Macaulay Trevelyan, b. Feb. 16, 1876, d. July 21, 1962, wrote in the liberal tradition, principally on 18th- and 19th-century England. Trevelyan, who stressed the development of literary style, was professor of modern history at Cambridge University (1927–40), master of Trinity College, Cambridge (1940–51), and chancellor of Durham University (1949–57). He wrote many books, including studies of the 2d Earl Grey (1920); his father, the historian Sir George Otto Trevelyan (1932); *Garibaldi* (1907, 1909, 1911); *A History of England* (1926); and *English Social History* (1942).

Bibliography: Moorman, Mary, *George Macaulay Trevelyan* (1980); Plumb, J. H., *Trevelyan* (1951; repr. 1969).

Trevi Fountain   [tray'-vee]

The Trevi Fountain in Rome, an enormous structure about 20 m (66 ft) wide, was erected (1732–62) as an imposing entranceway at the point where water from an ancient aqueduct reaches the city. Designed by Nicola SALVI, this spectacular baroque monument is an imaginative fusion of architecture and sculpture with the natural elements of rocks and gushing water. According to popular tradition, any foreigner who throws a coin into the fountain's vast basin is assured of returning to Rome.   MARK J. ZUCKER

Bibliography: Cooke, Hereward Lester, "The Documents Relating to the Fountain of Trevi," *Art Bulletin,* September 1956.

Trevino, Lee   [truh-vee'-noh]

The highly successful American professional golfer Lee Buck Trevino, b. Dallas, Tex., Dec. 1, 1939, competed in Far Eastern tournaments while serving in the U.S. Marines. He worked as a golf instructor after his discharge and won (1965) the Texas State Open. Trevino has twice won the U.S. Open (1968, 1971), the British Open (1971–72), and the Professional Golfers' Association (PGA) title (1974, 1984). He was also the Canadian Open champion three times (1971, 1977, 1979). Trevino has earned the Vardon Trophy, awarded annually to the PGA player with the best average score per round, five times. His career winnings exceed $3 million, third after Jack Nicklaus and Tom Watson.   HOWARD LISS

Trevithick, Richard   [trev'-i-thik]

The English engineer and inventor Richard Trevithick, b. Apr. 13, 1771, d. Apr. 22, 1833, built the first high-pressure steam engine and the first steam-powered carriage to transport passengers. In the 1790s, Trevithick constructed improved versions of existing engines and in 1801 built a steam carriage that transported several passengers for a short distance. In 1804 he constructed the first steam locomotive to travel on tracks, proving that an engine pulling carriages on iron wheels running on smooth rails could provide enough traction to transport 5 wagons, 10 tons of ore, and 70 passengers. Trevithick was also the inventor of a steam threshing machine and the first mechanical rock-boring machine.

Bibliography: Dickinson, Henry W., and Titley, Arthur, *Richard Trevithick* (1934); Rolt, L. T. C., *The Cornish Giant* (1960).

trial

A trial is a formal legal examination before a COURT of civil or criminal issues between two parties, the plaintiff and the defendant. A civil trial is initiated when the plaintiff files a complaint against the defending party to obtain legal redress. A criminal trial usually begins with service of a WARRANT OF ARREST by the state (plaintiff) on a suspected criminal (defendant) and INDICTMENT of the latter by a GRAND JURY. Article III, Section 2, and the 6TH AMENDMENT of the U.S. Constitution require the federal government to grant a JURY trial in criminal cases. The 6th Amendment also guarantees, among other things, the right to a "speedy and public trial," and "impartial jury," and the "assistance of counsel." A federal jury must be composed of 12 persons, and its verdict must be unanimous. A judge, the presiding officer of the trial court, usually rules on matters of LEGAL PROCEDURE and sentencing. The 7TH AMENDMENT requires the federal government to guarantee a jury trial in certain kinds of civil cases, but a jury trial often is waived by the parties when small sums of money are involved.

Although state laws on judicial procedure may vary, in 1968 the U.S. Supreme Court applied the 6th Amendment guarantee of a jury trial in criminal cases to the states through the 14TH AMENDMENT. In 1970 the Supreme Court upheld a state criminal trial by a jury of less than 12 persons, but in a 1978 case it commanded that a jury must have at least 6 persons. In two 1972 cases the Supreme Court upheld nonunanimous jury verdicts for some types of criminal offenses. In 1979 controversy arose over the Supreme Court's ruling that the public trial guarantee is a right of the accused—which that person can waive—and not necessarily a constitutional right of the public or the press.

Bibliography: Blom-Cooper, Louis, *The Language of the Law* (1965); Cushman, Robert F., ed., *Cases in Constitutional Law*, 4th ed. (1975); Swindler, William F., *Court and Constitution in the 20th Century: The Modern Interpretation* (1974).

See also: CIVIL LAW; COMMON LAW; CRIMINAL LAW; DUE PROCESS; EQUITY (law); EVIDENCE; WITNESS.

Trial, The

The Trial (1925), one of Franz KAFKA's major novels, was published posthumously without being completed or prepared for publication by the author. Its hero, Joseph K., is arrested without knowing his crime and subsequently is examined and tried. He finds himself in a situation in which conventional human assumptions have no validity. The language of the novel is concise and deceptively lucid, but the reader must remain uncertain as to whether the events depicted are those of real life or a nightmare.

trial by combat

Trial by combat, of which dueling is a form, was revived (501) by Gundobad, king of Burgundy, as a "dint of sword" solution to justice and became in Europe an acceptable legal practice that for centuries was served by special ceremonies and codes of honor. Victory or defeat in the contest signified the "judgment of God" as to a participant's innocence or guilt. Introduced into England by William the Conqueror in the late 11th century, trial by combat, or "Trial by Battel," continued as a legal alternative to trial by jury until 1819. Judicial duels were at first fought only in person by the contestants, but later proxy fighters were allowed to wage battle. Such champions received minor punishment if they lost, but the principals who sponsored them were hanged. Death in battle, when it happened, was its own punishment in the case of both losers—champion or principal.

triangle   (mathematics)

A triangle is a plane geometrical figure formed by three line segments connecting three points not lying on the same line. Each line segment is called a side, and the points they connect are called vertices. The altitude of a triangle is the perpendicular distance from any vertex to the opposite side, this side then being designated as the base. The area of a triangle is one-half the product of the base and the corresponding altitude. The angles inside the triangle total 180° and are called interior angles.

Variations in interior angles and in relative lengths of the sides permit six different triangles to be distinguished. On the basis of the angles, an acute triangle is one whose interior angles are each less than 90°, whereas an obtuse triangle has one interior angle that is greater than 90° but (by definition) less than 180°. A right triangle contains one interior angle that is equal to 90°, the side opposite this right angle being called the hypotenuse and the other two sides the legs. On the basis of the sides, a scalene triangle has three unequal sides, an isosceles triangle has two equal sides, and an equilateral triangle has three equal sides.

EUCLID proved that the sum of the three interior angles equals the sum of two right angles (180°). To PYTHAGORAS OF SAMOS is ascribed the theorem stating that in a right triangle the square of the hypotenuse equals the sum of the squares of the legs (see PYTHAGORAS, THEOREM OF).

Special lines can be drawn in a triangle. A line joining a vertex to the middle point of the opposite side is called a median; the three medians of a triangle intersect in one point, called the centroid. A line through a vertex that divides the interior angle into two equal angles is a bisector; the three bisectors intersect in one point, which is the center of a circle inscribed within the triangle—that is, the three sides of the triangle are tangent to the inscribed circle.

Bibliography: Banks, J. Houston, et al., *Geometry: Its Elements and Structure* (1972); Jacobs, Harold R., *Geometry* (1974); Konkle, Gail, *Shapes and Perceptions: An Intuitive Approach to Geometry* (1974).

triangle   (music)

The percussion instrument called the triangle is made from a steel rod bent into a triangle with one corner open. It is suspended from a cord and struck with a metal rod. The triangle first entered European music as part of the "Turkish" music that intrigued 18th-century composers and audiences. The combination of triangle, cymbals, and bass drum was used by Franz Josef Haydn, Wolfgang Amadeus Mozart, and Ludwig van Beethoven; later, the instrument was used separately. Some of its most effective moments consist of single, isolated strokes, as in Richard Wagner's overture to *Die Meistersinger*. The instrument is relatively small, each side being about 18 cm (7 in) to 25 cm (10 in) long.   ELWYN A. WIENANDT

See also: PERCUSSION INSTRUMENTS.

Triassic Period   [try-as'-ik]

The Triassic Period is the lowest (oldest) division of the Mesozoic Era and covers geological time from about 225 to 190 million years ago. The Latin term *trias* (meaning "three," later modified to Triassic) was proposed in 1834 for a striking three-unit sequence of strata in central Germany, lying above the Permian and below the Jurassic strata. These strata consist of an upper and lower unit of nonmarine RED BEDS (red sedimentary rock) separated by a marine limestone, shale, and sandstone unit. In contrast to this predominantly continental, central European sequence, the Alpine and Mediterranean regions exhibit a complete marine fossiliferous sequence. Stratigraphic zonation of the marine strata is based primarily on the fossil record of several invertebrates: ammonites and, to a lesser extent, certain bivalves.

TRIASSIC DEPOSITION

Economic resources of Tertiary sediments are relatively limited. Salt and gypsum have been mined, however, in central Europe and in the western United States. Minor coal deposits are found in North Carolina and Virginia, and Triassic sandstone (brownstone) has been quarried in the eastern United States for use as building material.

Geosyncline and Shelf Deposits. The Triassic Period was a time of great continentality; that is, vast areas of land were above sea level, and seas were almost entirely confined to ocean basins and geosynclinal belts that bordered some of the continental areas such as the Tethys zone and the circum-Pacific region. Shelf seas transgressed onto the margins of the land areas facing the Arctic Ocean.

The Tethys was an extremely complex geosynclinal belt extending from Spain through the Alpine-Himalayan region to

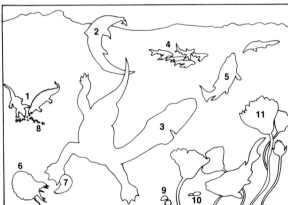

During the Triassic Period much of Europe was covered by a shallow, limy sea. This contained a variety of reptiles, fishes, ammonites, brachiopods, bivalve mollusks, and crinoids. The stout-bodied reptile Placodus (1), about 2 m (6.5 ft) in length, had protruding front teeth for picking shellfish from the seafloor and large, flat side teeth for crushing them. Mixosaurus (2), a primitive, fish-eating ichtyosaur, probably resembled a porpoise; it possessed paddlelike limbs and a long beak. Nothosaurus (3), up to 3 m (10 ft) in length, had webbed feet, a long, slender neck, and jaws with numerous sharp teeth adapted for catching fish. Fish included Thoracopterus (4), with large pectoral fins like those of a modern flying fish, and Semionotus (5). Ammonites, cephalopod mollusks with coiled, chambered shells, flourished during the Triassic; these included Trachyceras (6), with a shell marked by transverse ridges, and Cladiscites (7), whose shell was ribbed lengthwise. Brachiopods, or lamp shells, such as Coenothyris (8) and Tetractinella (9), and bivalve mollusks, including Myophoria (10), lived on the seafloor. Stalked crinoids, or sea lilies, such as Encrinites (11), were locally abundant. Remains of these animals were preserved in the mud of the seafloor, which eventually solidified into limestone and was later raised to form the Alps.

the Pacific Ocean. The marginal regions of this geosynclinal belt have detrital facies, often interbedded with continental red-bed deposits. The dominant sediments in the central area of the geosyncline are carbonate rocks.

In the circum-Pacific geosynclinal belt, GRAYWACKE, shale, siliceous sediments, and volcanics are the predominant facies, often of great thickness. The shelf deposits of the circum-Arctic region are all sandstone, siltstone, and shale. Marine Triassic sediment is also present in northern Madagascar; coastal Western Australia; the coastal belt of Queensland, Australia; and near the tip end of the Antarctic peninsula.

Continental Deposits. Continental sediments, especially red-bed facies, are particularly widespread and characteristic of the Triassic Period. Red beds consist of sedimentary deposits (sandstone, siltstone, and shale) formed under arid conditions and associated with evaporite deposits. Their color results from the oxidation of hematite (ferric oxide) contained within the rock structure.

CRUSTAL MOVEMENT

Igneous Activity. Extrusive and intrusive igneous activity was not particularly intense during the Triassic Period. In some areas, however, such as the PALISADES, notable landforms have resulted from resistant igneous flows within the red-bed deposits.

Orogenic Activity. Orogenic activity, or the formation of mountains, was not particularly intense during most of the Triassic Period. By the Late Triassic Period, new rifts were forming within Pangea (the supercontinent formed during the Permian Period), and it began to split apart, eventually moving North America westward and opening the Atlantic Ocean basin.

In Late Triassic time the Crimea and Caucasus (Black Sea area) as well as a zone east of the Zagros Mountains (Iran) began to be affected. Much of China underwent varying degrees of diastrophism, and in Japan a pronounced orogeny occurred in late Middle Triassic time.

CLIMATE

The climate throughout the Triassic Period was remarkably similar throughout the world. The worldwide conditions of aridity that prevailed are believed to reflect the environment of the massive Pangean supercontinent.

LIFE FORMS

Because a great extinction of marine invertebrate life took place toward the close of the Permian, the fossil record of the Lower Triassic Period has an impoverished aspect.

Marine Fauna. The predominant invertebrate fossils are the ubiquitous ammonites, which evolved into many varieties from a single group that survived the mass extinctions of the Permian Period.

Bivalves and brachiopods are also present in the fossil record but are much less prevalent. In some cases, however, bivalve remains form thick beds comprised entirely of fossil material. All other major invertebrate groups tend to be rare or absent in the Lower Triassic fossil record. During Middle and Upper Triassic time, the ammonites maintained their predominance, but the other groups became more diverse and conspicuous in the fossil record.

Terrestrial Fauna. Unlike many of the invertebrates, vertebrate animals, which in the Lower Triassic consisted only of amphibians and reptiles, showed no significant changes in evolutionary tempo and mode in the passage from the Permian to the Triassic. The thecodonts, one of the important reptilian groups of the Triassic, gave rise to the dinosaurs, flying reptiles, and icthyosaurs, plus several short-lived groups including a crocodilelike reptile group called phytosaurs. Another important Triassic reptilian group was the mammallike reptiles, the therapsids, believed to represent precursors of the first true mammals (therians), which appear in Late Triassic deposits.

Plants. Triassic floras are distinctive because they are dominated by GYMNOSPERMS, with ferns, conifers, cycads, and ginkgoes being the most common forms. The fossil floral record

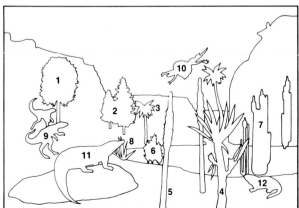

The Midlands of Triassic England consisted of desert plains dotted with temporary salt lakes and bordered by an area of limestone cliffs. This environment supported a flora of conifers, cycadlike plants, ferns, and horsetails and a fauna dominated by reptiles. Triassic conifers included Araucarites (1), which resembled the modern monkey puzzle tree, and Voltzia (2). Pterophyllum (3) and other cycadlike plants (4) were seed-bearing plants with pinnately compound leaves. The lycopsid Pleuromeia (5), about 1.2 m (4 ft) tall, is related to the modern club mosses. Other plants included the horsetails Equisetites (6) and Neocalamites (7) and the fern Dictyophyllum (8). Reptiles diversified, especially in the Late Triassic. Scleromochlus (9), now regarded as a primitive dinosaur, was about 1 m (3.3 ft) long and bipedal, with reduced front limbs. The early lizard Kuehneosaurus (10), about 50 cm (20 in) long, had spreading ribs that probably supported "wings" for gliding. Stagonolepis (11) was a heavily armored herbivorous reptile, about 3 m (10 ft) long, with a blunt, piglike snout. Rhynchocephalians (12), which resemble lizards, flourished in the Triassic; they are represented today by only one species, the tuatara, Sphenodon punctatus, of New Zealand. The earliest known mammals (not shown) appear in Late Triassic rocks.

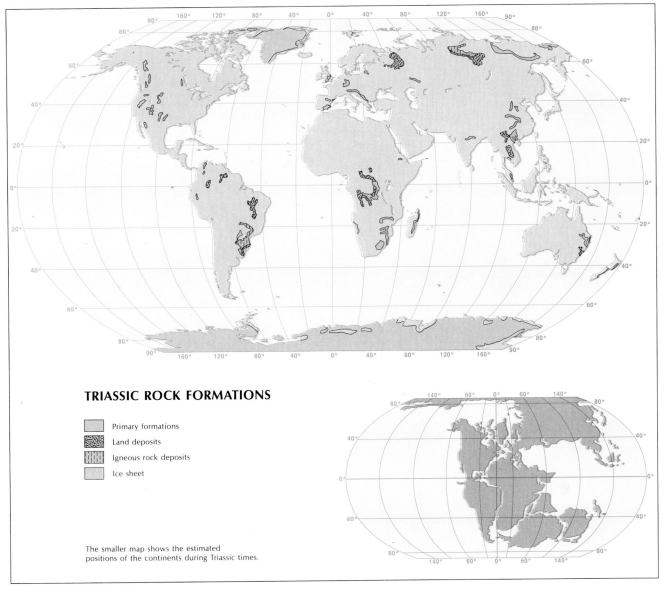

TRIASSIC ROCK FORMATIONS

- Primary formations
- Land deposits
- Igneous rock deposits
- Ice sheet

The smaller map shows the estimated
positions of the continents during Triassic times.

for the Triassic is not well documented, probably because of
the widespread aridity of the period.   BERNHARD KUMMEL

Bibliography: Kummel, Bernhard, *History of the Earth*, 2d ed. (1970);
Logan, Alan, and Hills, L. V., eds., *The Permian and Triassic Systems
and Their Mutual Boundary* (1973); Walker, J. C., *Earth History* (1986).

tribe

In anthropology, the term *tribe* has been used to indicate a
group of people sharing common values, general customs,
language, and usually contiguous territory. The term commonly refers to groups within which kin relations are important, but it can be extended to groups numbering several million people. The importance of KINSHIP is reflected in the tradition—common in tribal societies—that every member is descended from a real or supposed common ancestor. Tribes
may be genetically heterogeneous, however, because of absorption of people of other cultural or genetic backgrounds
through adoption, marriage, conquest, or political alliance.
The term *tribe* is falling out of favor because it has connotations of backwardness, because areas covered by individual
features used as criteria may not coincide with each other or
with the political boundaries associated with a tribe, and because large tribes are internally differentiated into distinct
groups. In current usage, the terms *ethnic group* and *ethnicity*
are commonly preferred to the terms *tribe* and *tribalism*.

JAMES LOWELL GIBBS, JR.

Bibliography: Davis, Kingsley, *A Structural Analysis of Kinship* (1980);
Fried, M. H., *The Notion of Tribe* (1975); Gluckman, Max, *Politics, Law
and Ritual in Tribal Society* (1977); Sahlins, M. D., *Tribesmen* (1968).

tribunes

Tribunes were officials in ancient Rome. Of the various kinds
of military and civil tribunates, the most important was the tribune of the plebs. From the early 5th century BC, these tribunes were elected annually by plebeian assemblies; by 449,
they numbered 10. Protectors of the PLEBEIANS, the tribunes acquired over the next 200 years the right to veto the actions of
the magistrates and to offer legislation. In the 2d century BC,
the GRACCHUS family used the office to pursue radical social
ends. Lucius Cornelius SULLA repressed the tribunate in the
following century, but it was restored after his death. The office's powers were later assumed by the emperor, although
the office itself remained in existence into the 5th century AD.

Bibliography: Adcock, F. E., *Roman Political Ideas and Practice*
(1964); Levick, Barbara, *The Government of the Roman Empire* (1985).

tributyl tin

Tributyl tin (TBT) is an organic compound widely used as an additive in paints for ship hulls because it inhibits the growth of barnacles and algae. Commercially introduced in the 1960s for this purpose, TBT is long-lasting and reduces the need for ship maintenance. It also lowers fuel costs by decreasing the drag caused by hull growths. The use of TBT has come under increasing attack since the 1970s, however, when its toxic and mutation-causing effects on indigenous life forms and commercially grown oysters began to be observed in coastal waters. A paint from which TBT leaches less readily has been developed, but U.S. environmental groups still urge that the use of TBT be severely restricted as it has been in France (1982) and Great Britain (1986).

Bibliography: Goldberg, E. D., "TBT," *Environment,* October 1986.

Triceratops   [try-sair'-uh-tahps]

Triceratops, a herbivorous ceratopsid dinosaur of the Late Cretaceous Period, was about 6 m (20 ft) long and probably weighed about 7 tons. Ceratopsids were the last group of dinosaurs to become extinct.

Triceratops was one of the last of the highly successful horned dinosaurs (suborder Ceratopsia, order Ornithischia). It is known from perhaps hundreds of partial to complete fossil skeletons collected in western North America from Late Cretaceous rocks about 70 million years old. The name *Triceratops* means "three horn face" and derives from the prominent horns on the skull: one on the snout and one above each eye. There can be little doubt that these horns were used in aggressive behavior, whether for defense against contemporaneous predators, such as *Tyrannosaurus* and *Gorgosaurus,* or in sparring matches with others of its own kind.

Triceratops averaged less than 6 m (20 ft) long but attained a length of 9 m (30 ft) and a weight of 7 tons. It was large-bodied and stocky-legged, with an expansive bony shield, or frill, extending back over the neck and shoulders. Even without this frill the head was huge; with the frill included, the skull was more than half as long as the body. This frill, formed by the rearward flaring of the parietal and squamosal bones of the skull, was the distinctive feature of all horned dinosaurs and may have protected the vulnerable neck region against attack. It also provided for the attachment of large neck muscles required for turning and maneuvering the horn-bearing head during combat and provided enlarged areas for attachment of powerful jaw muscles. *Triceratops* possessed a strong, turtlelike beak for plucking plants and long tooth rows in the cheeks for slicing that food—an unusual system among herbivores.   JOHN H. OSTROM

Bibliography: Colbert, E. H., *Dinosaurs: An Illustrated History* (1983); Glut, Donald E., *The New Dinosaur Dictionary* (1982).

trichinosis   [trik-uh-noh'-sis]

Trichinosis (or trichiniasis), a parasitic disease caused by the roundworm *Trichinella spiralis,* usually results from eating infected pork products that are raw or undercooked. Worldwide in occurrence, it is most prevalent in much of Europe and throughout the United States. Adult worms live in the lining of the small intestines of pigs, leaving encysted larvae (trichinae) in the intestinal wall. When ingested by humans, the larvae encyst in the stomach, burrow into the intestinal wall, and mature and mate within 3 or 4 days. One adult female worm can produce 1,000 living larvae in 6 weeks. Larvae are carried by the bloodstream to all parts of the body, but the only survivors are those reaching skeletal muscle, particularly the tongue, diaphragm, and pectoral and eye muscles. They invade individual fibers, coil up, and encyst. Encysted larvae may survive for up to 30 years. Gastrointestinal symptoms develop within 1 or 2 days after pork ingestion; fever, nausea, muscular soreness, edema, and eosinophilia occur in 1 to 2 weeks. Symptoms subside in 3 months, after encystment. Trichinosis is prevented through proper cooking and by not feeding hogs infected pork wastes.   DAVID F. METTRICK

Bibliography: Campbell, W. C., ed., *Trichinella and Trichinosis* (1983).

Trichomonas   [trik-uh-mahn'-uhs]

Trichomonas is a genus of zooflagellate protozoa in the order Trichomonadida that are common parasites in the digestive system of animals. The cells are pear-shaped and have three to five flagella. The stiff portion of the cytoplasm, called the oxostyle, gives support. Three species are found in humans. *T. vaginalis* can cause irritation to the vaginal mucosa. *T. buccalisa,* found in the mouth, and *T. hominis,* found in the intestine, are not pathogenic forms.

trichomoniasis   [trik-uh-muh-ny'-uh-sis]

Trichomoniasis is a genitourinary infection by a parasitic protozoan *Trichomonas vaginalis.* The infection, usually transmitted by sexual intercourse, generally occurs in the vagina but may also be found in the urethra and bladder in either sex and in the prostate gland in males, who can serve as carriers. To avoid reinfection, both partners therefore must be treated simultaneously. Vaginal symptoms include itching, burning, and an irritative discharge; urethral symptoms are painful urination and a mild discharge. Some females have no symptoms.   PETER L. PETRAKIS

triclinic system   [try-klin'-ik]

CRYSTALS that can be referred to three mutually oblique axes of unequal lengths are classified in the triclinic system. This is the system of lowest symmetry, and it contains only two classes. The first class possesses only one center of symmetry, and the second class has no symmetry at all. Triclinic crystals can generally be identified by a lack of any twofold symmetry element and by the oblique axial inclination. Triclinic minerals are in all cases optically biaxial. None of the three optical directions coincide with the three crystallographic directions, and extinction is always inclined. Minerals crystallizing in this system include microline (see FELDSPAR), TURQUOISE, and the plagioclase feldspars.   JOAN FITZPATRICK

Trident   [try'-dent]

Trident 1 (C-4) is a submarine-launched ballistic missile (SLBM) developed for the U.S. Navy Fleet Ballistic Missile Force (see ROCKETS AND MISSILES). It has three stages; is 10.4 m (34 ft) long, 188 cm (74 in) in diameter, and weighs 29,500 kg (65,047 lb) at lift-off; uses solid fuel; and has a range of about 7,400 km (4,600 mi), approximately 70 percent greater than that of the navy's POSEIDON missile. The Trident's guidance system is lighter than the Poseidon's all-inertial system, and its ability to sight on stars enables the Trident to meet the earlier missile's accuracy objectives at greater ranges. The post-boost control system permits corrections for errors in launch-position data while ensuring a high level of terminal maneuverability. Trident's nuclear payload is a multiple independently targeted reentry vehicle, or MIRV (see MIRV MISSILE), that carries eight nuclear warheads of 100-kiloton yield each. By 1987, 8 Ohio-class Trident submarines and 12 refitted Lafayette-class Poseidon submarines each carried 16 Trident missiles. The Trident 2 (D-5) carries a heavier payload and is scheduled for operational status before 1990.

RONALD T. PRETTY

Trier   [treer]

Trier (French: Trèves), a city in southwestern West Germany, lies on the Moselle (Mosel) River just east of Luxembourg and 110 km (70 mi) southwest of Bonn. With a population of 94,683 (1982 est.), the city is an important railroad junction and serves as a center for the Moselle wine region. Manufactures include machinery, textiles, beer, and metal and tobacco products. Trier has a theological seminary (1773) and a university (1970). Among its historical sites are the house where Karl Marx was born and many Roman ruins, notably the Porta Nigra (a fortified gate), baths (4th century AD), and an amphitheater (AD c.100).

Founded by the Roman emperor Augustus in 15 BC as Augusta Treverorum and named for the Treveri, an eastern Gallic people, Trier became capital of the Roman province of Belgica in the 2d century AD and served as an imperial capital and residence from about 295. Trier later became the seat of a bishopric (4th century), archbishopric (9th century), and imperial electorate (12th century). The city was secularized in 1797 and its university (founded 1473) closed. Ceded in turn to France (1801) and Prussia (1815), and occupied by the French after World War I, Trier suffered heavy damage during World War II.

Trieste   [tree-es'-tay]

Trieste (German: Triest; Slovenian: Trst), a city in northeastern Italy and capital of the Friuli-Venezia Giulia region, lies along the Gulf of Trieste at the head of the Adriatic Sea about 110 km (70 mi) northeast of Venice. Situated on the northwestern side of Istria on the Yugoslav border, Trieste has been contested between Italy and Yugoslavia. The city has a population of 246,305 (1983 est.), most of whom are Italian but with significant Slovenian, Croatian, and German-speaking minorities. Trieste fans out from its deepwater port with a small, picturesque medieval section closer to the port and a newer commercial and industrial complex farther out.

Shipbuilding and cargo handling are Trieste's key industries. The city has also become a major international scientific center. Historic sites include Roman ruins, the Romanesque Cathedral of San Giusto (built in the 14th century from two older churches), a medieval castle (1470–1680) housing a museum, and Miramare Castle (1854–56), built for Archduke Maximilian of Austria (later emperor of Mexico). The University of Trieste was founded in 1938.

The ancient city, called Tergeste, fell to the Romans c.177 BC; harbor facilities were constructed (33 BC) under the super-

vision of Emperor Augustus. The Ostrogoths ruled Trieste from AD 493 to 539, followed by the Byzantines (539–752), the Lombards (752–c.790), the bishops of Trieste—first as barons (c.850–933), then as imperial princes (948–1202)—and finally by Austria for most of the period from 1382 to 1918. Trieste served as an imperial free port from 1719 to 1891, and on the eve of World War I was the Austro–Hungarian empire's principal harbor. Italy occupied the city in 1918 and acquired it formally a year later by the Treaty of Saint Germain. Trieste fell to the Germans in 1943 and to the Yugoslavs in 1945. From 1947 to 1954 the city and its environs were administered as the Free Territory of Trieste, divided into two zones under Yugoslav and U.S.–British control. In 1954 the city and a small part of the territory went to Italy, the rest to Yugoslavia.

DANIEL R. LESNICK

triforium   [try-fohr'-ee-uhm]

In church architecture, the triforium is the second of three stories in the NAVE walls; it is a galleried walkway above the ARCADE of the side aisles and below the CLERESTORY. It seems to have been introduced in Romanesque churches in Italy and France (see ROMANESQUE ART AND ARCHITECTURE) and was a regular feature in Gothic churches (see GOTHIC ART AND ARCHITECTURE) until the Late Gothic period (16th century). The triforium was windowless except in some Early Romanesque and Middle Gothic churches. The blind triforium in Chartres Cathedral is typical.

triggerfish

Triggerfish are shallow-water fishes found in oceans around the world but are most common in tropical seas. They are named for the unusual triggering or locking mechanism of their spinous top fin. When the first large spine is erected, the second small spine moves forward, locking the first into an upright position and becoming itself erect. The third spine, if present, then also erects and locks the second spine into an upright position. The locking mechanism can be released only by depressing spines in reverse order: depressing the third spine releases the second from the upright position; depressing the second releases the first. When threatened by a predator or angler, a frightened triggerfish dashes into a crevice or small hole in a coral reef, locks its spinous top fin in an upright position, and presses down the lower part of its body. It thus wedges itself tightly into the opening and becomes difficult to dislodge. Triggerfish are less than 60 cm (2 ft) long and have variously colored bony scales. They have small mouths with strong teeth and can rotate each eye independently. About 30 species, related to puffers and ocean sunfishes, make up the family Balistidae. The queen triggerfish, *Balistes vetula*, grows to a length of 30 cm (12 in) and has brilliant colors. Found on both sides of the Atlantic, it is common on Caribbean reefs, where it is considered an excellent food.

ALFRED PERLMUTTER

Bibliography: Nelson, J. S., *Fishes of the World*, 2d ed. (1984).

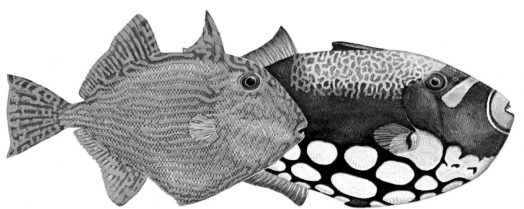

The triggerfish, family Balistidae, has a triggerlike top fin that can be locked in a vertical position. If alarmed, a fish may retreat to a coral cavity, erect its fin, and jam itself in place. The decorated triggerfish, Pseudobalistes fuscus (left), has its fin erect (locked). The clown triggerfish, Balistoides niger (right), has its fin folded.

trigonal system: see HEXAGONAL SYSTEM.

trigonometry

Trigonometry is a branch of mathematics that developed from simple mensuration (measurement of geometric quantities), geometry, and surveying. In its modern form it makes use of concepts from algebra and analysis. Initially it involved the mathematics of practical problems, such as construction and land measurement; it has since been extended to the geometry of three-dimensional spaces in the form of SPHERICAL TRIGONOMETRY. This article, however, will deal only with plane trigonometry.

Land survey makes use of the process of triangulation, in which a chosen network of triangles is measured. In pure triangulation, a base line to one triangle is measured, and the rest of the survey involves measuring angles only; in mixed triangulation, certain sides and angles are measured; in chain triangulation, only sides are measured.

Basic Concepts. Trigonometric concepts are used to minimize the amount of measuring involved. These concepts depend on the concepts of enlargement and similarity. Equiangular triangles have the same shape, but only in the special case of congruency do they have the same size. Any set of similar triangles has the invariant property of proportionality; that is, ratios of pairs of corresponding sides are in the same proportion. In the language of transformation geometry, for similar triangles, one triangle is an enlargement of another, or any triangle can be transformed into another by applying the same scale factor to each part of the triangle. In the case of a fractional scale factor the enlargement is, in fact, a reduction.

Ratios. Trigonometry uses the fact that ratios of pairs of sides of triangles are functions of the angles. The basis for mensuration of triangles is the right-angled triangle. The term *trigonometry* means literally the measurement of trigons (triangles). This mensuration approach defines the six trigonometric ratios in terms of ratios of lengths of sides of a right triangle. The analytic approach defines the ratios in terms of the coordinates of a point on the circumference of a unit circle, $x^2 + y^2 = 1$. These ratios define the trigonometric functions.

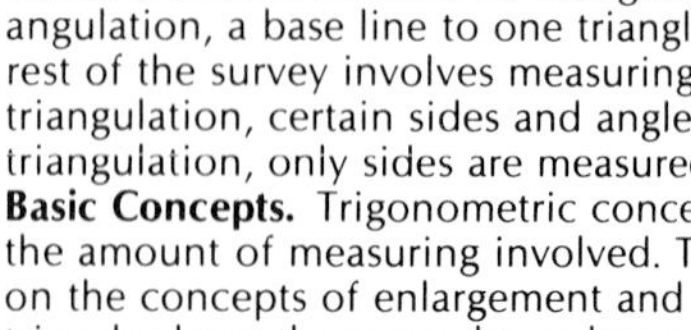

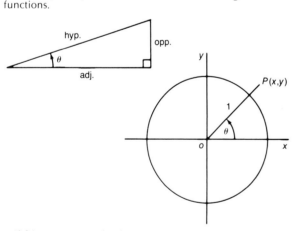

If θ is an acute angle, the trigonometric ratios of θ are conveniently defined as ratios of different lengths of the corresponding right triangle: the hypotenuse, the side adjacent to the angle θ, and the side opposite to θ.

sine (sin) θ = opp/hyp
tangent (tan) θ = opp/adj
secant (sec) θ = hyp/adj
cosine (cos) θ = adj/hyp
cotangent (cot, ctn) θ = adj/opp
cosecant (cosec, csc) θ = hyp/opp

The coratios are the ratios of complementary angles (angles whose sum is 90°); for example, $\cos \theta = \sin (90° - \theta)$. Every ratio has a reciprocal ratio.

Trigonometric Functions. Trigonometric functions, often known as the circular functions, are defined in terms of the trigonometric ratios. If point $P(x,y)$ lies on the circumference of a unit circle $x^2 + y^2 = 1$, then the trigonometric functions of θ, where θ is the angle that the line OP makes with the positive direction of the x-axis, are defined as:

$\sin \theta = y$ $\sec \theta = 1/x$ $\cot \theta = x/y$
$\tan \theta = y/x$ $\cos \theta = x$ $\csc \theta = 1/y$

The signs of the coordinates determine the signs of the ratios. If θ is acute, all ratios are positive; these values of θ are fully tabulated in standard trigonometric tables. The ratios of angles greater than a right angle (90°) can be converted to ratios of acute angles by appropriate reduction formulas. The reduction formulas are trigonometric identities that express the trigonometric ratios of an angle of any size in terms of the trigonometric ratios of an acute angle.

If $y = \sin x$, then the inverse statement, that x is the angle whose sine is y, is written x = inverse sin y, or arc sin y, or more commonly $\sin^{-1} y$. Hence $x = \sin^{-1} y$ is the inverse function of $y = \sin x$. Similar notation is used for other trigonometric functions. The -1 in the notation is not an exponent, and $\sin^{-1} y$ is different from $(\sin y)^{-1}$; the latter is the reciprocal of sin y.

Trigonometric functions have many applications in algebra. They are used in rationalizing quadratic surds (square roots). For example, the algebraic function $y = (a^2 + x^2)^{1/2}$ can be transformed into the rational trigonometric function $y = a \sec u$ using the identity $1 + \tan^2 u = \sec^2 u$ and substitution $x = a \tan u$. Similarly, $y = (a^2 - x^2)^{1/2}$ and $y = (x^2 - a^2)^{1/2}$ can be rationalized by suitable use of identities and substitutions. Substitutions have various uses in facilitating processes in the calculus.

Trigonometric functions also have value in applied mathematics. For example, all oscillations can be represented as PERIODIC FUNCTIONS, that is, functions that repeat their values at equal intervals of the independent variable. Any periodic function can be represented by an infinite trigonometric series. A Fourier series is an example (see FOURIER ANALYSIS).

Polar Coordinates. Trigonometric functions are used in polar coordinates, the system in which the position of a point P is determined by its distance OP from a fixed point O and by the angle that OP makes with an initial line OX (see COORDINATE SYSTEMS, mathematics). The analytic definition of trigonometric functions above uses the special case of polar coordinates when the distance OP is unity. In the general application to points in a plane, point O is the pole; OP is the radius vector of P; OX is the polar axis; angle XOP or θ, measured counterclockwise, is called the polar angle, vectorial angle, azimuth, or amplitude of P. The Cartesian coordinates (x,y) of P, when O is the origin and OX is the x-axis, are related by the equations $x = r \cos \theta$, $y = r \sin \theta$ and $r = (x^2 + y^2)^{1/2}$, $\theta = \tan^{-1}(y/x)$. This system can be extended to form spherical coordinates in space.

Identity. If a trigonometric equation is true for all values of its variables, it is an identity. Some trigonometric identities state relations between various combinations of the six trigonometric functions determined by their definitions. Others are trigonometric forms of classical geometric theorems.

The theorem of Pythagoras, $a^2 = b^2 + c^2$, for a right triangle ABC with angle A being the right angle, can be transformed by replacing b and c by $a \sin B$ and $a \cos B$, respectively. The simplified identity is then, for any angle Θ, $\sin^2 \Theta + \cos^2 \Theta = 1$. By using the identity $\tan \Theta = \sin \Theta / \cos \Theta$, alternative forms can be derived: $\tan^2 \Theta + 1 = \sec^2 \Theta$ and $\cot^2 \Theta + 1 = \csc^2 \Theta$. The extension of the theorem of Pythagoras can be written as the cosine formula (cosine rule) $a^2 = b^2 + c^2 - 2bc \cos A$, with similar versions for cos B and cos C that are obtained by changing the letters in cyclic order.

The six trigonometric ratios for single angles can be used to form the addition and subtraction formulas.

$\sin (A \pm B) = \sin A \cos B \pm \cos A \sin B$
$\cos (A + B) = \cos A \cos B \mp \sin A \sin B$
$\tan (A \pm B) = (\tan A \pm \tan B)/(1 \mp \tan A \tan B)$

If B is set equal to A in the above addition formulas, the following double-angle formulas are obtained:

$$\sin 2A = 2 \sin A \cos A$$
$$\cos 2A = \cos^2 A - \sin^2 A$$
$$\tan 2A = (2 \tan A)/(1 - \tan^2 A)$$

By setting $B = 2A$, triple-angle formulas can be obtained for $\sin 3A$, $\cos 3A$, and $\tan 3A$. The sine formula (sine rule), which applies to any triangle ABC with sides a, b, and c, is $a/\sin A = b/\sin B = c/\sin C = 2R$ where R is the radius of the circumscribing circle. These formulas are useful in the solution of triangles, that is, the determination of measurements of a triangle from given data. The reduction formulas in trigonometry are identities that express trigonometric ratios of any angle in terms of ratios of acute angles. For example, $\cos (180° + A) = -\cos A$, where A is an acute angle.

Apart from their use in simplifying trigonometric problems, trigonometric identities are often used in algebra and calculus. ALARIC MILLINGTON

Bibliography: Drooyan, Irving, et al., *Essentials of Trigonometry*, 4th ed. (1986); Keedy, Mervin L., and Bittinger, Marvin L., *Trigonometry: Triangles and Functions*, 4th ed. (1986); Swokowski, Earl W., *Fundamentals of Trigonometry*, 6th ed. (1986).

triiodothyronine: see HORMONES; THYROID GLAND.

trill

The trill—often called a shake in British usage—is a musical ornament produced by rapidly alternating a written note with its upper neighbor. It was introduced in the 16th century to enliven cadential patterns, becoming most popular in keyboard and vocal music, although it was adopted generally. By the 17th century, signs and abbreviations (such as t, tr, +, and w) were used to indicate the points at which a trill should be executed. ELWYN A. WIENANDT

Bibliography: Crocker, R. L., *A History of Musical Styles* (1966; repr. 1986); Donington, Robert, *The Interpretation of Early Music* (1974).

Trilling, Lionel [tril'-ing]

The distinguished critic, teacher, and novelist Lionel Trilling, b. New York City, July 4, 1905, d. Nov. 7, 1975, combined an elegant and passionate response to literature with shrewd analysis of society, politics, and culture. Both qualities are found in his first book, *Matthew Arnold* (1939), and in subsequent collections of essays, the most important being *The Liberal Imagination* (1950). His novel *The Middle of the Journey* (1947) is notable for its play of moral and political ideas; he also wrote such fine short stories as "Of This Time, Of That Place" and "The Other Margaret." Trilling taught English for more than 40 years at Columbia University, and his Norton Lectures delivered at Harvard were published as *Sincerity and Authenticity* (1972). WILLIAM H. PRITCHARD

Bibliography: Boyers, R., *Lionel Trilling* (1977); Chace, W. M., *Lionel Trilling* (1980); Krupnick, M., *Lionel Trilling and Cultural Criticism in America* (1986).

trilobite [try'-luh-byt]

Trilobites are extinct marine arthropods whose fossils date from the early Cambrian to the end of the Permian Period, or about 600 million to 225 million years ago, although it is believed that the animals originated at least 100 million years earlier. Comprising about 1,500 genera and more than 2,500 species, they are classified as the Trilobita, which is variously recognized as either a subphylum or a class of the phylum Arthropoda. They may be closely related to living crustaceans, spiders, and horseshoe crabs.

The trilobite body consisted of few to many segments, most of which bore jointed, branched or unbranched, leglike appendages. The upper body covering, or shell, was typically divided into three longitudinal lobes: a prominent central, or axial, lobe extending from head to tail, and one less prominent, pleural lobe on each side. Most trilobites were also differentiated into three transverse sections: the head, or cepha-

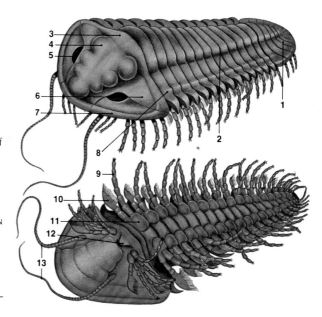

Trilobites, now extinct, were segmented, hard-shelled marine animals with bodies that consisted of a tailpiece, or pygidium (1), a thorax (2), and a head shield, or cephalon (3). The cephalon of a typical Calymene trilobite comprised a bulbous glabella (4), eyes (5), fixed cheeks (6), and weakly attached free cheeks (7). The thorax contained jointed segments, or pleurons (8). The animal had numerous legs for walking (9), legs with feathery gills for breathing and swimming (10), masticating organs (11) that picked up food and passed it to the mouth (12), and two antennae with taste and smell organs (13).

lon, commonly bore eyes and antennae, and it consisted of fused segments more or less formed into a rigid shield; the middle section, or thorax, was flexible, and some trilobites were capable of curling their bodies like modern sow bugs; and the tail, or pygidium, was fused and rigid. The covering of the underbody is thought to have been fleshy. The mouth was located at the bottom rear of the head, and the stomach was situated in front of the mouth, in the upper part of the head; the digestive tract, therefore, formed a J-shaped loop inside the head, from the mouth to the stomach. Most trilobites were between 2 and 7 cm (¾ and 2¾ in) long, but sizes could range from 6 mm (¼ in) to almost 75 cm (30 in). The animals molted as they grew.

Trilobites were distributed worldwide in diverse marine environments. Many dug shallow burrows; others probably scurried about on the seafloor, feeding as predators or scavengers. A few seem to have been part of the drifting plankton, and some may have been swimmers. Trilobites declined markedly about 500 million years ago, at the close of the Cambrian, but underwent renewed development early in the Ordovician, about 490 million years ago. Their fossils are used by paleontologists to make time correlations of rocks and to reconstruct marine environments.

Bibliography: Bergstrom, Jan, *Organization, Life and Systematics of Trilobites* (1973); Eldredge, Niles, "An Extravagance of Species," *Natural History*, July 1980; Levi-Setti, Riccardo, *Trilobites* (1975); Tasch, Paul, *Paleobiology of the Invertebrates*, 2d ed. (1980); Whittington, H. B., *The Burgess Shale* (1985).

Trincomalee [tring-kuh-muh-lee']

The seaport of Trincomalee lies on a peninsula in Trincomalee Bay on the northeastern coast of Sri Lanka about 230 km (145 mi) northeast of Colombo. The city's population is 46,000 (1982 est.). The town has good rail and road connections with the rest of the country and one of the world's best natural harbors. Tea is the main export.

Since ancient times the town has been inhabited by Tamil people. The Portuguese arrived in 1622, to be succeeded by the Dutch (1639), French (1673), and British (1795). The British held the port until 1957, even though Sri Lanka became independent in 1948.

Trinidad and Tobago   [trin'-i-dad, tuh-bay'-goh]

Trinidad and Tobago is an independent nation in the Caribbean Sea, 11 km (7 mi) from Venezuela. The country, a member of the Commonwealth of Nations, is composed of two islands—Trinidad (4,828 km²/1,864 mi²) and Tobago (300 km²/116 mi²), which is 31 km (19 mi) to the northeast. The capital and largest city is PORT OF SPAIN.

LAND, PEOPLE, and ECONOMY

Trinidad's main physical feature is the Northern Range, running east to west at an average elevation of 457 m (1,500 ft). It includes the nation's highest point, El Cerro del Aripo (940 m/3,084 ft). The Central and Southern ranges run parallel to, but are not as high as, the Northern Range. Tobago's Main Range follows the island's northeast-southwest trend. The climate is tropical, with a mean annual temperature of 27° C (80° F). Rainfall totals about 1,780 mm (70 in) annually.

The people of Trinidad and Tobago are mostly of African (43%) and Asian Indian (40%) descent. Free secondary education was introduced in 1960. Health services are free.

Petroleum and gas production dominates the Trinidad and Tobago economy, and petroleum and petroleum products accounted for over 80% of exports until the worldwide oil glut of the mid-1980s. At that point the nation's economy plunged. Pitch Lake on Trinidad is the world's largest natural source of asphalt. Major industries in addition to petrochemicals include food processing and cement production. Tourists—attracted by the beaches and by the annual carnival, featuring CALYPSO and STEEL BAND music—are an important source of revenue. Although agricultural production is economically important—sugar, cocoa, coffee, and citrus are exported—the nation is largely dependent on food imports.

HISTORY AND GOVERNMENT

Trinidad, discovered by Christopher Columbus in 1498, was first a Spanish and then (1797) a British colony. The first British settlers (1616) on Tobago were driven out by the Carib

REPUBLIC OF TRINIDAD AND TOBAGO

LAND. Area: 5,130 km² (1,981 mi²). Capital and largest city: Port of Spain (1986 est. pop., 57,400).
PEOPLE. Population (1988 est.): 1,300,000; density: 253 persons per km² (656 per mi²). Distribution (1988): 29% urban, 71% rural. Annual growth (1987): 2.4%. Official language: English. Major religions: Roman Catholicism, Hinduism, Protestantism, Islam.
EDUCATION AND HEALTH. Literacy (1987): 89% of adult population. Universities (1988): 1. Hospital beds (1985): 4,087. Physicians (1985): 1,103. Life expectancy (1987): women—72; men—67. Infant mortality (1984): 20 per 1,000 live births.
ECONOMY. GDP (1986 est.): $7.83 billion; $6,390 per capita. Labor distribution (1985): agriculture—10.9%; manufacturing, mining, quarrying—14.8%; construction and utilities—18.1%; services—47.9%; unemployed—15.4%. Foreign trade (1987): imports—$1.2 billion; exports—$1.5 billion; principal trade partners (1985)—United States, United Kingdom, Caribbean nations, Japan. Currency: 1 Trinidad and Tobago dollar = 100 cents.
GOVERNMENT. Type: republic. Legislature: House of Representatives, Senate. Political subdivisions: 8 counties.
COMMUNICATIONS. Railroads (1987): none. Roads (1987): 4,000 km (2,485 mi) paved; 4,000 km (2,485 mi) unpaved. Major ports: 1. Major airfields: 1.

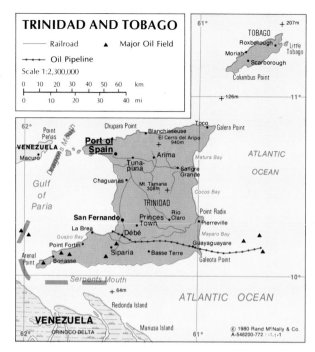

TRINIDAD AND TOBAGO

——— Railroad   ▲ Major Oil Field
⊷•⊷• Oil Pipeline
Scale 1:2,300,000

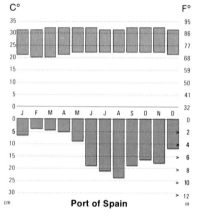

C°   F°

Port of Spain

Bars indicate monthly ranges of temperatures (red) and precipitation (blue) of Port of Spain, the capital of Trinidad and Tobago. Located on the west coast of Trinidad, Port of Spain has the tropical wet climate typical of both islands.

Indians. The island subsequently came under Dutch and French control before the British acquired it in 1814. Trinidad and Tobago were politically united in 1888 and in 1962 became an independent nation. Tobago Island was given full internal self-government in 1987.   THOMAS MATHEWS

Bibliography: Black, Jan Knipper, et al., *Area Handbook for Trinidad and Tobago* (1976); Carmichael, Gertrude, *The History of the West Indian Islands of Trinidad and Tobago, 1498–1900* (1961); Evans, F. C., *A First Geography of Trinidad and Tobago* (1968); Magid, Alvin, *Urban Nationalism* (1988); Niddrie, David L., *Tobago* (1982); Ryan, Selwyn, *Race and Nationalism in Trinidad and Tobago* (1972).

Trinity

The Trinity refers to the Christian understanding of GOD as a unity of three persons: Father, Son, and Holy Spirit. All are equally God and so one, each sharing in the divine attributes of ultimacy, eternity, and changelessness; yet they are distinguishable in their relations to each other and in their roles within creaturely and human life and destiny.

The doctrine of the Trinity is a postscriptural attempt to bring to coherent expression diverse affirmations about God, all of which seemed necessary to a full statement of Christian experience and belief. First, from the Hebrew Scriptures and the clear tradition of Jesus' teaching, the church affirmed that not only is God one, but he is also the creative and sovereign

Father and thus, by implication, transcendent of finite limits, time, and change—all of which characterize God's creatures. Second, it was affirmed that JESUS CHRIST was more than a great prophet adopted by God; rather he was "the Son of God," "the Word made flesh," the divine LOGOS itself incarnate in a man. Third, the HOLY SPIRIT, from whose presence the community of believers received their faith, their confidence in the truth of that faith, their holiness, and, above all, the efficacy of both baptism and the Eucharist, was necessarily also God—God's presence in their midst. For Christians, then, the one God appeared in what they called a threefold "economy," in, so to speak, three forms or modes.

Difficulties soon emerged in formulating and understanding this threefold "economy." Divergent views led early to numerous Trinitarian controversies such as those over subordinationism (the teaching that the Son is subordinate to the Father and the Holy Spirit to both; see ARIANISM) and modalism (the view that the three modes are transitory; see MONARCHIANISM and SABELLIANISM). The Councils of Nicaea (325) and Constantinople (381) outlined the dogma of the Trinity in express rejection of these teachings.

The Nicene, or Niceno-Constantinopolitan, CREED has defined through the ages, for both Catholic (Roman and Orthodox) and Reformation (Lutheran, Reformed, and Anglican) churches, the basic doctrine of the Trinity. Catholic and Protestant theology has sought in various ways to make the doctrine stated at Nicaea comprehensible. Saint Augustine's lucid analogies of the divine Trinity in our experience of ourselves as memory, understanding, and will, and in our experience of our own existence as characterized by being, truth, and love, have been the point of departure for most subsequent study. In the religious thought of the Enlightenment (17th and 18th centuries), there was a strong reaction against Trinitarianism as an "orthodox" mystery without basis in either experience or reason—this was the view of UNITARIANISM and DEISM and of much 19th-century liberal theology. The great figures of 20th-century theology—Karl BARTH, Paul TILLICH, and, most recently, Karl RAHNER—despite their diversity of outlook, have again found the Trinity a central, in fact an unavoidable, structure for expressing the Christian understanding of God.

LANGDON GILKEY

Bibliography: Fortman, Edmund J., The Triune God: A Historical Study of the Doctrine of the Trinity (1972); Lonergan, Bernard J. F., The Way to Nicaea: The Dialectical Development of Trinitarian Theology (1976); Richardson, C. C., The Doctrine of the Trinity (1958); Welch, Claude, In This Name: The Doctrine of the Trinity in Contemporary Theology (1952).

Trinity College, Dublin

Founded in 1592, Trinity College (enrollment: 4,890; library: 2,000,000 volumes) in Dublin, Ireland, is the sole constituent college of Dublin University. The coeducational school offers undergraduate and graduate degrees in arts, mathematics, engineering, medicine, veterinary medicine, dentistry, natural sciences, and social studies. The library has many manuscripts, including the Book of Durrow and the Book of Kells.

Trinity College (Hartford, Conn.)

Established in 1823 by the Prostestant Episcopal Church, Trinity College (enrollment: 1,840; library: 590,000 volumes) is now an independent nonsectarian liberal arts school for men and women in Hartford, Conn. Undergraduate and graduate degrees are granted.

Trinity College (Washington, D.C.)

Established in 1897, Trinity College (enrollment: 800; library: 170,000 volumes) in Washington, D.C., is a liberal arts school for women and is conducted by the Sisters of Notre Dame de Namur. Bachelor's and master's degrees are granted.

triode [try'-ohd]

A triode is a three-terminal ELECTRON TUBE that can control the flow of current between its cathode and its anode by means of a voltage applied to a third element, the grid. The triode is used to amplify weak alternating current (AC) signals (see AMPLIFIER). If the tube is gas-filled, it is known as a thyratron, which is essentially a controlled RECTIFIER rather than an amplifier. A triode can also be used in an OSCILLATOR circuit.

The triode evolved from the DIODE when in 1907 the American inventor Lee De Forest added the grid between the cathode and the anode. Initially known as the audion, the triode was a giant step forward in electronics because it made possible the process of amplification.

Operation. The triode is a thermionic device; that is, heat is required to make the cathode emit electrons. This may be done either by means of a separate heater placed close to the cathode or by using a filament that is both the heater and the cathode. The indirectly heated cathode is used in AC equipment, and the directly heated cathode is preferred in battery-operated equipment because it is more efficient and causes less drain on the battery. The anode is usually held at some positive voltage, perhaps 200 or 300 V, so the negatively charged electrons move toward the anode and a direct current (DC) flows in the external circuit. The grid between the cathode and the plate is maintained at some average negative voltage (bias), which tends to repel some electrons and reduces the current. If a small AC signal voltage, however, is applied to the grid, superimposed on the DC voltage, the electrons flowing through the tube will alternately increase and decrease from the previous average level. This variation in current flowing through a resistor in the external anode circuit develops the output signal, which is now an enlarged version of the input signal. The amount of amplification, or voltage gain, depends on three things: the amplification factor of the tube, or its μ (mu—typically 20 to 100); the plate resistance of the tube; and the amount of external resistance.

Types and Applications. There are five different basic types of construction that may be used in triode tubes. A glass miniature tube is typically 2 cm (0.8 in) in diameter and 5 cm (2 in) long. An example of such a tube is the 12AE7 triode, developed specifically to operate at 12.6 V for automobile radios. A 6K4 tube is a metal subminiature triode, 1 cm (0.4 in) in diameter and 3.8 cm (1.5 in) long. Its anode voltage must be 200 V. Other types are the compactron, nuvistor, and planar ceramic triodes. An example of the last type is the 7720, a VHF triode suitable for operation at 500 MHz. It is only 0.85 cm (0.3 in) in diameter and 1.25 cm (0.5 in) high, rivaling some transistors for small size.

Triodes have been almost completely replaced by the generally smaller, cooler, and more reliable transistor in most new audio, radio, television, and computer applications, although many remain in existing equipment. A few triode applications exist at high frequencies (the low end of the microwave region), where large amounts of power are required, particularly in communications equipment.

ALLEN MOTTERSHEAD

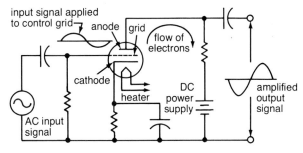

input signal applied to control grid — anode — grid — flow of electrons — cathode — heater — DC power supply — AC input signal — amplified output signal

Bibliography: Kloeffler, R. G., Electron Tubes (1966); Mottershead, Allen, Electronic Devices and Circuits (1973).

Tripitaka: see BUDDHIST SACRED LITERATURE.

Triple Alliance

The name Triple Alliance has been applied to several separate coalitions of European powers. The Triple Alliance of 1668, formed by England, Sweden, and the Dutch Republic, was aimed at halting encroachment into the Low Countries by France's Louis XIV. The Triple Alliance of 1717, made up of France, Britain, and the Dutch Republic, was directed against Spanish aspirations to Italian territory. The Holy Roman emperor's adherence to the pact in 1718 made it a Quadruple Alliance. The Triple Alliance of 1788, consisting of Britain, the Dutch Republic, and Prussia, sought to check French influence in the Netherlands and Russia's ambitions in the Middle East.

The most famous Triple Alliance was that of 1882, composed of Germany, Austria-Hungary, and Italy. Its terms provided that if any of the parties were attacked by two or more powers, its allies would come to its aid. Orchestrated by German chancellor Otto von BISMARCK, it originated with the Dual Alliance of 1879, between Germany and Austria-Hungary, to which Italy was added in 1882. Germany was motivated by a desire to isolate France; Austria-Hungary sought support against Russia, its rival in the Balkans; and Italy, although fearful of Austro-Hungarian expansion, wanted help in pursuing its North African territorial ambitions. The alliance was renewed periodically.

Meanwhile, a series of bilateral agreements produced the TRIPLE ENTENTE (1907) among Britain, France, and Russia. Europe was thus divided into the two camps that fought each other in WORLD WAR I, except that Italy renounced the alliance and joined the Entente powers in 1915.

Bibliography: Bullen, Roger, and Bridge, Roy, *The Great Powers and the European States System, 1815–1914* (1980); Langer, W. L., *European Alliances and Alignments, 1871–1890*, 2d ed. (1950; repr. 1964).

Triple Alliance, War of the

In the War of the Triple Alliance (1865–70), also known as the Paraguayan War, Paraguay confronted an alliance of Argentina, Brazil, and Uruguay. Hostilities began when Uruguayan conservatives convinced the dictator of Paraguay, Francisco Solano LÓPEZ, that Brazil and Argentina were about to invade Paraguay. López declared war (January 1865) on Brazil and then on Argentina when Argentine president Bartolomé Mitre refused him permission to cross Argentine territory. Uruguay, which had made a secret alliance with Brazil and Argentina, declared war on May 1, 1865. Alliance armies defeated the vastly outnumbered Paraguayan forces on land and sea and then blockaded all river traffic, but the Paraguayans fought back, subduing the alliance at Curupayty (September 1866). In 1868, Brazilian troops took river fortresses, and at the beginning of 1869, alliance forces sacked the Paraguayan capital at Asunción. López was shot (Mar. 1, 1870) by the allies, and the bloody war ended shortly thereafter. Paraguay, whose population was severely reduced, took decades to recover.

Bibliography: Kolinski, C. J., *Independence or Death* (1965); Williams, J. H., *The Rise and Fall of the Paraguayan Republic* (1979).

Triple Entente

The Triple Entente—an alignment of Britain, France, and Russia that led to their alliance in WORLD WAR I—resulted from a series of bilateral diplomatic agreements among them between 1894 and 1907. The Franco-Russian Alliance of 1894 stemmed from France's fear of isolation at the hands of Germany, which had formed the TRIPLE ALLIANCE with Austria-Hungary and Italy in 1882. Russia wanted support against Austria-Hungary, its rival in the Balkans. In 1904, Britain, fearing growing German naval power, entered into the Entente Cordiale with France. Thus, the two longtime antagonists terminated their colonial rivalry in Africa. Britain also sought reconciliation with its inveterate enemy Russia, which was amenable following a humiliating defeat in the Russo-Japanese War (1904–05). The Anglo-Russian Convention of 1907 settled their differences by establishing separate spheres of influence in Persia. With this agreement, the Triple Entente, an understanding rather than an alliance, was complete. In World War I the Triple Entente faced the Triple Alliance minus Italy, which defected to the Entente.   ROBIN BUSS

Bibliography: Schmitt, Bernadotte E., *Triple Alliance and Triple Entente* (1934); Taylor, A. J. P., *The Struggle for Mastery in Europe, 1848–1918* (1954; repr. 1971).

triple point

A triple point, in chemistry, is the set of physical conditions (temperature and pressure) at which three phases of a substance—usually gas, liquid, and solid—coexist in equilibrium. In PHASE EQUILIBRIUM diagrams, the triple point occurs at the intersection of the pressure-temperature curves for the three phase pairs. Some triple points are useful as calibration points for pressure and temperature. For example, the triple point of water at 4.58 mm Hg and 273.16 K specifies 0.01° on the Celsius scale. Another useful triple point is that of hydrogen at 52.8 mm Hg and 13.81 K.   E. R. GRILLY AND A. F. SCHUCH

Bibliography: Moore, Walter J., *Physical Chemistry*, 4th ed. (1972).

Tripoli   (Lebanon)   [trip'-uh-lee]

Tripoli (Arabic: Tarabulus) is a city in northwestern Lebanon located north of Beirut on the Mediterranean Sea. Lebanon's second largest city, it is a major commercial port with a population of 198,000 (1982 est.). The inhabitants are mainly Muslims. Petroleum refining, sponge fishing, fruit and tobacco processing, and citrus fruit exporting dominate the economy. Of historical interest are the Great Mosque (1294), the Teynal Mosque (1336), and the 15th-century Tower of the Lions, which protected the port and is located in the old city.

Founded in the 7th century BC, Tripoli was in 300 BC the capital of Tripolis, a Phoenician federation including Sidon, Tyre, and Aradus. Tripoli was ruled by the Seleucids (198–64 BC), Romans and Byzantines (64 BC–AD 638), and Arabs (from AD 638). The city and its famous library were destroyed in the early 12th century during the First Crusade. Crusaders rebuilt the city and made it a bishopric, but it was destroyed in 1289 by Mamelukes, who ruled until 1516. Tripoli became part of Lebanon in 1920.

Tripoli   (Libya)

Tripoli, the capital of Libya, is located in the northwestern part of the country on the Mediterranean Sea. Its population is 858,500 (1981 est.). Tripoli is Libya's main port and has major road and air connections. The city lies in an oasis and receives the products (olives, citrus fruits, and tobacco) of the surrounding agricultural region. Industries include fishing, carpet weaving, tanning, and shipping (fruit, oil, and fish). Historic landmarks include the marble Marcus Aurelius Triumphal Arch (AD 163), the Karamanli Mosque (1736), and the Mosque of Gurgi (1883). The modern city lies to the southwest of the ancient quarter and houses cultural and government buildings.

Tripoli (known in ancient times as Oea) was founded by the Phoenicians in the 7th century BC. It was later taken by the Romans (146 BC), the Vandals (AD c.450), the Byzantines (6th century), and the Arabs (7th century). Apart from a brief period of Norman rule (1146–58), Tripoli remained under Arab control until 1510, when it fell to the Spanish. Conquered by the Turks in 1551, it became a provincial capital of the Ottoman Empire and a major center of the Barbary pirates (see BARBARY STATES). Italy seized Tripoli in the Italo-Libyan War of 1911–12. The British held the city from 1943 until Libya's independence in 1951.

Tripolitan War   [trih-pahl'-i-tuhn]

The Tripolitan War (1801–05) between the United States and Tripoli was an effort by the United States to end extortion payments to Barbary Coast pirates.

Prior to 1801 the United States, along with the European powers, routinely negotiated extortionate treaties and paid tribute to the North African BARBARY STATES (Tripoli, Algiers, Morocco, and Tunis) in exchange for the safe passage of merchant vessels through the Mediterranean. In 1801 the pasha of Tripoli repudiated his treaty with the United States and declared war. President Thomas Jefferson dispatched the navy's Mediterranean squadron, and the initial American show of

Barbary pirates raid a U.S. ship in the Mediterranean in 1801. The United States had previously followed the European practice of paying tribute to the Barbary rulers to protect its shipping from piracy. A breakdown of this system led to the Tripolitan War (1801–05).

force discouraged the other Barbary States from backing Tripoli. Between 1803 and 1805, Commodore Edward PREBLE bombarded and blockaded Tripoli, Lieutenant Stephen DECATUR entered Tripoli harbor and burned the captured frigate *Philadelphia*, and William Eaton launched an overland campaign. In 1805 the pasha signed a treaty requiring ransom for American prisoners plus occasional presents but ending annual tribute.

A final resolution of the problems with the Barbary States came in 1815 when Congress, responding to piratical attacks on U.S. commerce, declared war on Algiers. Decatur rushed a squadron to the Mediterranean, where he dictated peace on American terms to Algiers and then to Tunis and Tripoli. The American payment of tribute and the intermittent wars with the Barbary States ended, but the United States established a permanent naval squadron in the Mediterranean.

KENNETH J. HAGAN

Bibliography: Chidsey, Donald B., *The Wars in Barbary* (1971); Irwin, Ray W., *The Diplomatic Relations of the United States with the Barbary Powers, 1776–1816* (1931); Tucker, Glenn, *Dawn Like Thunder: Barbary Wars and Birth of the U.S. Navy* (1963); Wright, Louis B., and McLeod, Julia H., *The First Americans in North Africa: William Eaton's Struggle for a Vigorous Policy against the Barbary Pirates, 1779-1805* (1945).

Tripura   [trip'-oo-rah]

Tripura, a state in northeastern India formerly called Hill Tippera, has an area of 10,477 km² (4,045 mi²) and a population of 2,053,058 (1981). The capital and only urban center is Agartala (1981 pop., 131,513). Bordered on the north, west, and south by Bangladesh, the state is primarily agricultural. Crops include rice, jute, cotton, tea, and fruit.

Tripura is a remnant of a large independent Hindu kingdom, dating from the 7th century AD. It was conquered by the Moguls in 1733 and passed under British control in 1808. Tripura became a union territory of India in 1956 and a state in 1972.

trireme: see GALLEY.

Trissino, Giangiorgio   [trees-see'-noh, jahn-johr'-joh]

The Italian poet and humanist Giangiorgio Trissino, b. July 8, 1478, d. Dec. 8, 1550, is best remembered for *Sofonisba* (1515; first produced in 1524), the first tragedy in the Greek style in modern literature. His treatise on poetics, *Sei divisioni della poetica* (The Six Kinds of Poetry, 1529), is based on that of Aristotle. With *L'Italia liberata dai Goti* (Italy Liberated from the Goths, 1547–48), written in 11-syllable rhymeless lines, Trissino attempted to revive the Italian tradition of heroic poetry.

Tristan and Isolde   [tris'-tuhn, i-sohl'-duh]

Tristan and Isolde, or Tristram and Iseult, are famous lovers in Celtic and Arthurian legend (see ARTHUR AND ARTHURIAN LEGEND). Tristan, nephew of King Mark of Cornwall, and Isolde, Mark's wife, drink a love potion and become tragically enmeshed in an adulterous passion that involves them in secrecy and intrigue. Their story was told in the Middle Ages by the Anglo-Norman poet Thomas (*c*.1170), by GOTTFRIED VON STRASSBURG (*c*.1210), who inspired Richard Wagner's opera, and by Sir Thomas Malory, in his MORTE DARTHUR, and in the 19th century by Tennyson (in IDYLLS OF THE KING), Matthew Arnold ("Tristram and Iseult," 1852), and Swinburne (*Tristram of Lyonesse*, 1882).   DAVID M. ZESMER

Tristan and Isolde   (opera)

Written between 1857–59, the three-act opera *Tristan and Isolde*, with both text and music by Richard WAGNER, is a watershed in the history of music. The fatal love of the Irish princess Isolde and the Cornish knight Tristan had been recounted by poets since the 12th century. Wagner, compressing the ancient tale, fashioned from it a new kind of music drama, a drama of inwardness rather than incident, more audible in the orchestra than visible on the stage. Voices are treated as instruments, threads in a symphonic tapestry of unprecedented sensuousness. The work is filled with a desperate longing given sustained musical expression in a new harmonic idiom, itself the fount of later chromaticism and, eventually, of ATONALITY.

The composer waited 6 years for the first performance (Munich, June 10, 1865), finally accomplished through the patronage of the king of Bavaria, Ludwig II. Twice, at Karlsruhe and Vienna, the work had been put into rehearsal, and twice it had been given up as unstageable. Its leading roles are among the most taxing in all opera: tenors, especially, cannot forget that the first Tristan, Ludwig Schnorr von Carolsfeld, died shortly after the premiere.

Biographers of Wagner have heard in *Tristan* the echoes of his life, and a myriad of influences, particularly the philosophy of Arthur Schopenhauer, have been identified and explored. But these, however interesting, are not the ultimate sources of the opera's power, which can be felt at its fullest in the prelude to act 1, the great love duet of act 2, and the monologue of the delirious Tristan in act 3. The work received its Metropolitan Opera debut on Dec. 1, 1886, with Lili Lehmann and Albert Niemann in the principal roles.

Bibliography: Barzun, Jacques, *Darwin, Marx, Wagner*, 2d ed. (1958); Newman, Ernest, *The Wagner Operas* (1949; repr. 1983); Wagner, Richard, *Tristan und Isolde*, trans. and intro. by Stewart Robb (1965); Zuckerman, E., *The First Hundred Years of Wagner's Tristan* (1964).

Tristan da Cunha Islands   [tris'-tan duh koo'-nuh]

The Tristan da Cunha Islands are a group of small volcanic islands in the south Atlantic Ocean. The islands are a dependency of the British colony of Saint Helena. The largest and northernmost island, also called Tristan da Cunha, is the only one that is inhabited. Others include Inaccessible, Nightingale, and Gough. The total area is about 117 km² (45 mi²). Circular, Tristan da Cunha island has an area of 104 km² (40 mi²) and a circumference of about 34 km (21 mi). A volcano 2,060 m (6,760 ft) high is in the center of the island. The population of 323 (1981) speaks a 19th-century English dialect. Edinburgh is the island's main village. Fishing, particularly for crayfish, is the principal occupation. Some crops are farmed on the mountainous plateaus. A weather station operates on Gough, and a radio base is located on Tristan.

The islands were discovered in 1506 by the Portuguese Tristao da CUNHA, for whom they were named. The first inhabitants, originally from Saint Helena, were shipwrecked on Tristan during the 19th century. The British took formal control in 1816. Tristan's volcano erupted in 1961, and the inhabitants were evacuated to England. Most of them returned to the island by 1963.

Tristram Shandy   [tris'-truhm shan'-dee]

The Life and Opinions of Tristram Shandy, Gentleman (1759–67), by Laurence STERNE, is ostensibly an autobiography, with the narrator beginning with the circumstances of his conception. Actually, the book consists almost entirely of character sketches and anecdotes in which Tristram describes his family and friends, notably his father, Walter, his uncle Toby, and Parson Yorick. The result is a parody of the order and coherence of novels. Sterne was influenced by satirists like Rabelais and Swift, but the book is loosely based on John Locke's theory of the association of ideas, and much of its comedy comes from the special associations that define each character.   JOHN RICHETTI

Bibliography: Holtz, William V., *Image and Immortality: A Study of Tristram Shandy* (1970); Traugott, John, *Tristram Shandy's World: Sterne's Philosophical Rhetoric* (1954; repr. 1970).

tritium   [trit'-ee-uhm]

Tritium, ^3H or T, is the heaviest hydrogen isotope and the only radioactive form of HYDROGEN. Its nucleus contains 2 neutrons and 1 proton, and its atomic weight is 3.016. Tritium has a half-life of 12.26 years. Before 1954 rainwater contained between 1 and 10 tritium atoms to every 10^{18} hydrogen atoms, but because tritium is used in nuclear weapons, thermonuclear tests sharply raised this proportion. Tritium is also used in the luminous dials of watches and other permanent light sources. In biological research it is used as an isotopic tracer (see NUCLEAR MEDICINE), especially in DNA and RNA studies.

See also: DEUTERIUM.

tritium dating: see RADIOMETRIC AGE-DATING.

Triton   [try'-tahn]

In Greek mythology, Triton, a gigantic sea god, part man and part fish, was the son of Amphitrite and POSEIDON. He raised rocks from the sea and created islands with his trident, and he blew on a trumpet made from a conch shell. Triton freed AENEAS's ships when they were grounded in a storm, but when Misenus, Aeneas's main trumpeter, challenged Triton to a musical contest, Triton drowned him.

triumphal arch

The triumphal arch, which dates back to the Roman Empire, is a freestanding ceremonial gateway erected in honor of a military triumph or, in more recent times, as a civic monument or urban landmark. The earliest known triumphal arch was built in Rome in 196 BC (destroyed). Another, the Fornix Fabianus, was erected in the Roman Forum in 121 BC (destroyed). Such arches later spread throughout Italy, Gaul, Africa, and the other provinces of the Roman Empire. The best known and most elaborate are the arches of Titus (AD 81), Septimius Severus (203), and Constantine (c.315), all in Rome.

Because the arch signified, among other things, the temporary or permanent deification of the triumphal hero, it was incorporated into the early Christian basilica, where it covered the altar and later evolved into the chancel. It is therefore related to the medieval ciborium.

triumvirate   [try-uhm'-vur-uht]

The triumvirates of ancient Rome, boards made up of three men, were used in various kinds of administration. In one famous triumvirate, sometimes called the First Triumvirate (60–53 BC), Julius Caesar, Marcus Licinius Crassus, and Pompey the Great joined together unofficially to rule Rome and its dominions. The so-called Second Triumvirate, an official arrangement created in 43 BC to establish order following Caesar's assassination, consisted of Mark Antony, Octavian (later Augustus), and Marcus Aemilius Lepidus. Octavian eventually became sole ruler.

Trobriand Islanders   [troh'-bree-and]

The Trobriand Islanders are MELANESIANS who occupy a group of small coral islands north of New Guinea in the Pacific Ocean. They are primarily garden horticulturists, with particular villages specializing in fishing, carving, and woodwork. A traditional Trobriand village consisted of two concentric circles, an outer ring of dwellings and an inner ring of storehouses for yams. Each subclan lived in a separate section of the circle and had its own land and resources. The subclan was based on matrilineal descent. On reaching maturity a youth joined his mother's brother and other members of that subclan. At the annual harvest, a man gave the larger part of his share to his sister's household. A chief acquired wealth through multiple marriages to women who were sisters of local village headmen. In this way, he could have authority over a number of villages that were his allies in war. The Trobriand Islanders live at the center of the KULA RING, a highly systematized circular pattern of trade among the island groups east and north of New Guinea. The islanders have long had contact with missionaries and administrators and, more recently, with tourists. Since World War II radical changes have occurred in traditional living patterns, but the Kula Ring still functions. Trobriand Islanders numbered about 12,700 in the early 1970s.   RONALD M. BERNDT

Bibliography: Malinowski, Bronislaw, *Argonauts of the Western Pacific* (1922; repr. 1961), *Coral Gardens and Their Magic,* 2 vols. (1935; repr. 1978), and *The Ethnography of Malinowski: The Trobriand Islands, 1915–1918,* ed. by Michael Young (1979).

trochee: see VERSIFICATION.

Troeltsch, Ernst   [trurlch]

Ernest Troeltsch, b. Feb. 17, 1865, d. Feb. 1, 1923, a German Protestant theologian, sociologist, and philosopher, made significant contributions to the sociology of religion and the philosophy of history through a lifelong effort to reconcile the absolute claims of theology and ethics with the relative facts of historical and social change. Troeltsch gave up a career as a Lutheran minister to serve as a professor at the universities of Göttingen, Bonn, Heidelberg, and, ultimately, Berlin.

Two contrasting assumptions governed Troeltsch's inquiries: (1) The laws of morality are, as Immanuel Kant held, universal and necessary, and (2) studies in history and sociology reveal the growth and change of moral consciousness over time and across cultures. These two assumptions can be unified, he held, only through the belief that absolute morality must realize itself through persons in history, not in value systems. Kant's ethics are thus fulfilled in an "ontology of personality." Troeltsch developed his interactive approach at length in *The Social Teachings of the Christian Churches* (1912; Eng. trans., 1931). After World War I he attacked the German glorification of the state and urged a return to the philosophy of the Enlightenment.   PETE A. Y. GUNTER

Bibliography: Clayton, J. P., ed., *Ernst Troeltsch and the Future of Theology* (1976); Reist, Benjamin A., *Toward a Theology of Involvement: The Thought of Ernst Troeltsch* (1966).

trogon   [troh'-gahn]

Trogons are small or medium-sized tropical birds with beautifully colored, often iridescent plumage. Approximately 34 species of trogons, including the QUETZAL, make up the family Trogonidae. They are believed to be related to bee eaters and kingfishers.

Trogons are found in tropical Africa and Asia, the Philippines and Malaysia, and from South America north through Mexico; one species—the elegant, or coppery-tailed, trogon, *Trogon elegans,* a metallic, golden green bird less than 30 cm (1 ft) long—ranges into Texas and Arizona. Trogons typically have a short, broad, and sometimes serrate bill and a long tail. The small feet are unique, with the first and second toes directed backward and the third and fourth directed forward. Alone or in pairs, they perch on branches, often with the feet covered by feathers. They feed on insects, other small prey, and fruit, and lay two to five whitish eggs.

ROBERT J. RAIKOW

troika [troy'-kuh]

The troika is a type of SLED used almost exclusively in the USSR and Hungary and distinguished by the fact that it is drawn by three horses harnessed abreast. (Most sled harnessing uses one horse or a pair of horses.) Occasionally, the horses are harnessed as a "unicorn team," with one horse in front and two behind. The troika has become a distinctively Russian object, often used as a symbol of Russia in paintings and literature of the 19th century.

Troilus and Cressida [troy'-luhs, kres'-i-duh]

Troilus and Cressida, probably performed in 1602 and published in 1609, is one of William SHAKESPEARE's later, so-called bitter comedies. Drawing on material from Geoffrey Chaucer and John Lydgate, but using neither as a direct source, the play portrays a flawed Cressida, condemned as heartless and faithless for her practical acceptance of the situation when she is arbitrarily returned from Troy to the Greek camp in exchange for a Trojan prisoner. The abandoned Troilus, her lover, also loses Hector, his brother, as the play ends with Hector's death at the hands of Achilles.　　MARJORIE COLLINS

Trois Frères, Les [twah frair, lay]

The cave of Les Trois Frères, discovered (1912) at Montesquieu-Avantès in the department of Ariège, southern France, contains the finest group of Paleolithic (Middle and Late Magdalenian) engravings known to date. The representations include bison, reindeer, ibex, and the famous "sorcerer"—a masked human being wearing antlers and a reindeer tail.　　LYA DAMS

Trois-Rivières [twah-ree-vee-air']

Trois-Rivières, a port city in Quebec, midway between the cities of Montreal and Quebec, lies on the northern shore of the St. Lawrence River at the mouth of the Saint Maurice River. It has a population of 50,122 (1986). The city's industries produce pulp, textiles, and paper, particularly newsprint. It is the site of an Ursuline convent (1697), the University of Quebec at Trois-Rivières (1969), a museum, and many historic buildings, including the ruins of Les Forges Saint Maurice, an iron foundry dating from about 1730.

One of the oldest settlements of Canada, Trois-Rivières was founded in 1634 by Samuel de Champlain and named for the three channels of the Saint Maurice River at this point.

Trojan War [troh'-juhn]

In Greek mythology the Trojan War pitted a coalition of Greek principalities against TROY, a city located on the coast of what is now Anatolia, just south of the entrance to the Dardanelles. The war was the subject of HOMER's *Iliad* and *Odyssey.*

According to Homer and other Greek epic poets, King PRIAM's son PARIS brought HELEN, wife of King MENELAUS of Sparta, back to Troy with him. To recover Helen, the Greeks sent an expedition to Troy under AGAMEMNON, brother of Menelaus. The war lasted 10 years, although the first 9 years seem to have been indecisive. Only in the tenth year, after ACHILLES had killed HECTOR, the greatest of the Trojan warriors, were the Greeks assured of victory.

Using a stratagem devised by ODYSSEUS, the Greeks feigned retreat; the Greek fleet sailed out of sight, leaving behind as a "gift" the Trojan Horse. Inside the large wooden horse was concealed a squad of Greek soldiers who, after the horse had been dragged into the unsuspecting city and under the cover of darkness, emerged and opened the gates. After the Greek fleet quietly returned, the soldiers entered Troy and great slaughter followed. Many Trojan women, including members of the royal family, were carried off into captivity.

The work of the 19th-century archaeologist Heinrich SCHLIEMANN showed that the story of the war was probably based on historical events of the early 12th century BC. Some scholars believe that the Trojans were a Luwian-speaking people who came into conflict with the Mycenaean Greeks.

Bibliography: Boston Museum of Fine Arts, *The Trojan War in Greek Art* (1965); Clarke, Howard, *Homer's Readers: A Historical Introduction to the Iliad and the Odyssey* (1980); Wood, Michael, *In Search of the Trojan War* (1986).

Trojan Women, The

First produced in 415 BC, *The Trojan Women,* by the Greek tragic dramatist EURIPIDES, is one of the most compelling antiwar plays ever written. Opening just after Troy has fallen to the Greeks, it tells how the Trojan queen, Hecuba, suffers as her daughter Polyxena is sacrificed to the dead Achilles and as another daughter, Cassandra, is made the concubine of Agamemnon. Then her grandson Astyanax, the child of Hector and Andromache, is thrown from a tower to his death on the advice of Odysseus. The pathos culminates as Hecuba is led away as the slave of Odysseus.　　JAMES J. WILHELM

Trojans

The Trojans are two groups of ASTEROIDS that have accumulated at the two stable positions (LIBRATION points) in Jupiter's orbit. In 1772 the French mathematician Joseph Louis de Lagrange calculated that three bodies rotating as an equilateral triangle have stable orbits. Thus, if the Sun and Jupiter are taken as two vertices of a triangle, then positions 60° ahead and behind Jupiter in its orbit are stable. The first Trojan asteroid was found on Feb. 12, 1906. Now more than 1,000 are known, twice as many ahead of Jupiter as behind.

See also: THREE-BODY PROBLEM.

troll:　see FAIRY.

trolley car:　see STREETCAR.

Trollope, Anthony [trahl'-uhp]

The prolific and popular novelist Anthony Trollope, b. Apr. 24, 1815, d. Dec. 6, 1882, left in his many works a rich record of the manners of clerical and political life in Victorian England. The son of Frances Trollope, a popular woman writer who published more than 100 works including *The Domestic Manners of the Americans* (1832), Trollope became a clerk in the Post Office as a young man. He continued this career throughout his life, ultimately becoming an important official.

His first novel, *MacDermots of Bally Coran* (1845), was unsuccessful, but in 1855 he established his reputation with *The Warden,* the first of the chronicles of Barsetshire, a series of novels dealing with clerical life in the imaginary cathedral city of Barchester. In later works of this group, such as *Barchester Towers* (1857), *Doctor Thorne* (1858), and *The Last Chronicle of Barset* (1867), he concentrated less upon religious issues than upon personal relationships.

Anthony Trollope, portrayed (1865) by Samuel Laurence, was one of the most popular novelists of the Victorian age. Initially famous for his Barsetshire novels, today Trollope is acclaimed also for the Palliser series of novels and for The Way We Live Now (1875), a more penetrating and disillusioned account of 19th-century English life than are his previous works. (National Portrait Gallery, London.)

After an unsuccessful campaign for Parliament, Trollope's interest in political life found expression in the series of parliamentary novels that follow the fortunes of the aristocratic Palliser family and the newly rich Phineas Finn. In such novels as *Phineas Finn: The Irish Member* (1869), *The Eustace Diamonds* (1873), and *The Prime Minister* (1876), Trollope is more concerned with the relations between the sexes than with the political conflicts of his day. A prolific writer, he also published such social satires as *The Way We Live Now* (1875) and a romance of the future, *The Fixed Period* (1882).

Although the posthumous publication of Trollope's *Autobiography* (1883)—which records his journeyman writing of a quota of words each day while working as a civil servant—temporarily dimmed his reputation, modern readers find satisfaction in his portrayal of a satisfied, prosperous society that has long since disappeared. Recent critics see his mild irony as a sophisticated means of engaging serious moral issues.

HERBERT L. SUSSMAN

Bibliography: Bareham, T., ed., *Anthony Trollope* (1980); Sadleir, Michael, *Trollope: A Commentary* (1927; repr. 1975); Snow, C. P., *Trollope: His Life and Art* (1975); Wright, A., *Anthony Trollope* (1983).

Trollope, Frances

Frances Milton Trollope, b. Stapleton, Somerset, Mar. 10, 1780, d. Oct. 6, 1863, the mother of the English novelist Anthony Trollope, was the author of many novels and travel books. Her novels include the popular *Vicar of Wrexhill* (1837) and *Widow Barnaby* (1839), but her best-known work is *Domestic Manners of the Americans* (1832), a violent attack on American life written after the author's unsuccessful attempt to establish a business in Cincinnati. ROBIN BUSS

trombone

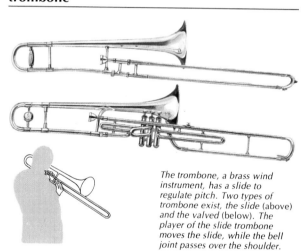

The trombone, a brass wind instrument, has a slide to regulate pitch. Two types of trombone exist, the slide (above) and the valved (below). The player of the slide trombone moves the slide, while the bell joint passes over the shoulder.

The trombone emerged as a variation of the medieval TRUMPET when the slide, in the form of a U-bend, was created (mid-15th century), immediately producing an efficient and unique low brass instrument capable of playing all chromatics. From that time to the present, the instrument has consisted fundamentally of a bell section including attached inner slides, outer slides, and mouthpiece, the tube being cylindrical up to a gradual expansion toward the bell.

The early trombone (sackbut) differs from its modern counterpart primarily by its narrow tube of heavier metal, its small expansion at the end, and its funnel-shaped mouthpiece similar to the horn, the result being a mellow tone with command of soft through moderately loud dynamics, eminently suitable for combining with voices, soft woodwinds, or strings. It was soon characterized as a solemn instrument to be used at court, church, and civic functions.

By the end of the 18th century, the trombone had acquired a flared bell and tubular stays. It had also lost popularity temporarily. Its revival was sparked by the need of the develop-

ing military bands for a brighter sound with louder dynamics. Makers responded to this demand, thinning the metal, enlarging the bore, and changing the mouthpiece to a hemispherical shape with a sharp edge at the throat. Opera, having used trombones sporadically, now exploited their brilliant tone, and by the mid-19th century German orchestras had adopted three as a standard: the E-flat alto, B-flat tenor, and F bass.

The French, however, used three tenors. Eventually, the French usage prevailed, and the alto became obsolete. The third tenor was combined, by means of a left-hand thumb valve, with tubing to extend the horn to the bass range.

Experiments were made during the 19th century, including the production of valved trombones, which sacrificed the unique chromatic accuracy of the slide without contributing compensating advantages. Lasting changes included the addition of a tuning slide with a weighted balancer, a water valve, additional stays, a receiver pipe for the mouthpiece, and metal alloys and overlays, especially applied to prevent wear in the slide and to reduce friction in movement. Changed in function, but little in design, from their Renaissance origins, trombones together with trumpets provide a magnificent choir of brilliant brass tone for both orchestra and band.

ROBERT A. WARNER

Bibliography: Bate, Philip, *The Trumpet and the Trombone: An Outline of Their History, Development and Construction*, rev. ed. (1978); Dempster, Stuart, *The Modern Trombone* (1979); Gregory, Robin, *The Trombone: The Instrument and Its Music* (1973).

Tromp (family) [trohmp]

The Dutch admirals **Maarten Tromp**, b. Apr. 23, 1598, d. Aug. 10, 1653, and **Cornelius Tromp**, b. Sept. 9, 1629, d. May 29, 1691, father and son, commanded Dutch fleets in decisive battles against Spain, England, and France. In 1639, Maarten defeated pirates operating from Dunkirk (Dunkerque) and destroyed a Spanish-Portuguese armada in the Battle of the Downs. In the first of the ANGLO-DUTCH WARS (1652–54), he fought with mixed success against British fleets and was killed in battle. His son Cornelius, an impulsive and reckless commander, was dismissed during the second Anglo-Dutch War (1665–67) but fought brilliantly against England and France in the third (1672–74). He then defeated Swedish forces at the head of a Dutch-Danish fleet (1676–78). HERBERT H. ROWEN

Bibliography: Boxer, Charles R., *The Anglo-Dutch Wars of the 17th Century, 1652–1674* (1974).

trompe l'oeil: see ILLUSIONISM.

Trondheim [trohn'-haym]

Trondheim, a city on the west central coast of Norway, is situated about 400 km (250 mi) north of Oslo. An important transportation hub and seaport, it has a population of 134,100 (1984 est.). Shipbuilding and manufacturing of hardware, building materials, and fish products are the main industries. The city is the site of the Technical University of Norway (1900) and the Royal Norwegian Society of Sciences (1760). Historical landmarks include Nidaros Cathedral (1075), where several Norse kings and Norway's King Haakon VII (r. 1905–57) were crowned. The cathedral, built from Norwegian blue soapstone and white marble, contains the tomb of St. King Olaf II (Saint Olaf).

Founded as Kaupangr by King Olaf I in 997, Trondheim was an archbishopric from 1152 until the Reformation (1537). The city was an important commercial center during the 12th and 13th centuries, but its importance later diminished.

trope: see FIGURES OF SPEECH.

trophic level: see ECOLOGY.

tropic bird

Tropic birds are seabirds that have the middle tail feathers extremely elongated—up to 53 cm (21 in) long. The three spe-

The red-billed tropic bird, P. aethereus, *is a strong-winged bird of tropical Pacific, Atlantic, and Indian seas. Including its characteristically long tail feathers, it is about 75 cm (30 in) in length.*

cies, which make up the genus *Phaethon,* family Phaethontidae, are found in all warm oceans. Excluding the tail feathers, tropic birds are about 40–48 cm (16–19 in) long and have stout, pointed bills, large, powerful wings, and very short legs with webbed toes. The plumage is white with some black on the head and wings. Clumsy on land, they are graceful in the air, often making long flights far out to sea. They also occasionally hover over fishing grounds, diving for their prey—mainly fish and squid. A single pale, often spotted, oval egg is laid on a ledge, often within a small hole or rock crevice or under vegetation. Both parents incubate the eggs and care for the young, which, after 2 or 3 months, plunge into the water and begin attempts at flying. JOEL CRACRAFT

Tropic of Cancer

Despite its literary merit, *Tropic of Cancer* (1934), a novel by Henry MILLER first published in Paris, was banned by U.S. officials for its obscenity and was not published in the United States until 1961. Based on Miller's long stay in Paris during the 1930s, the novel records the "descent to the very bowels of the earth" of a young poet. After reaching a state of complete physical and spiritual degradation, he achieves the peak of his creative powers and experiences a newly found joy and intensity in living. CHARLOTTE D. SOLOMON

tropic of Cancer

The tropic of Cancer corresponds approximately to the 23°30′ north latitude. Considered the boundary between the torrid zone of the tropics and the temperate zone of the middle latitudes, it defines the northern extent of the perpendicular rays of the Sun, which reach it about June 21, to mark the Northern Hemisphere's summer solstice. ROBERT S. WEINER

tropic of Capricorn

The tropic of Capricorn corresponds approximately to the 23°30′ south latitude. It marks the southern extent of the perpendicular rays of the Sun and the artificial boundary between the tropics and the southern temperate zone. The Northern Hemisphere's winter solstice occurs when the perpendicular rays of the Sun reach the tropic of Capricorn, about December 21. ROBERT S. WEINER

tropical climate

The tropics, the region of the Earth between the latitudes 30° north and 30° south, encompasses a wide variety of climate regimes; these regimes range from deserts with virtually no rainfall to mountainous jungles with rainfall exceeding 1,000 cm (400 in) per year. Tropical climates, however, can be broadly classified into three types: the oceanic trade-wind regime, the equatorial regime, and the continental monsoon regime.

The trade-wind belt, which extends across most of the tropical Atlantic and Pacific oceans, is a region characterized by rather steady winds and relatively small seasonal variations in rainfall and temperature. Trade-wind climates vary from very dry conditions in the eastern oceans to very wet conditions in the western oceans.

The equatorial climate regime is characterized by a broad band of low pressure centered near the intertropical convergence zone (ITCZ; a narrow zone of rising air and intense precipitation that marks the transition between the northeast and southeast trade-wind regimes). The ITCZ generally lies several degrees latitude north of the equator. In most longitudes it undergoes a seasonal migration from about 15° north to 5° south, with the maximum northward displacement occurring during the Northern Hemisphere summer. Locations close to the equator tend to have two rainy seasons corresponding to the passages of the ITCZ during its northward and southward migration.

The continental tropics have climates characterized by monsoons (from the Arabic *mausin,* a "season"). Monsoon circulations are driven by the seasonally reversing temperature difference between the land surface and the adjacent ocean. In the summer, when the land surface is warmer than the sea surface, the low-level winds are directed from sea to land, whereas in the winter the winds are reversed. The most important example is the Southeast Asian monsoon, which in summer is characterized by moist southwest winds blowing from the Indian Ocean and heavy rainfall over the continent, and in winter by dry northeast winds blowing from the interior of the continent. JAMES R. HOLTON

Bibliography: Riehl, Herbert, *Introduction to the Atmosphere,* 3d ed. (1978).

tropical easterlies: see TRADE WINDS.

tropical fish

Tropical fish are small fishes that have become popular as pets in aquariums because of their beauty and their interesting behavior. Most aquarium fishes are in fact from the tropics or warm temperate areas, but the term is also used for some species from cooler waters. Several hundred species of fish, most of them freshwater species, have become adapted to aquarium life. The most popular belong to the families Poeciliidae (the live-bearing GUPPIES and PLATYS), Characidae (the TETRAS), Cyprinidae (the MINNOWS, CARPS, and barbs), Cichlidae (the ANGELFISHES and jewelfishes), and the Anabantidae (the labyrinth fishes). In recent years saltwater aquariums have become more popular, and a large number of marine fishes are now raised, many from the family Chaetodontidae.

Raising aquarium fish is believed to be the second most popular hobby in the United States (after photography), with 20 to 26 million households possessing aquariums. Estimates of the number of aquarium fishes sold annually range up to 350 million. In the past most tropical fish were imported, with South America—especially the Amazon basin and Guyana—supplying the greatest number. Africa is the place of origin of many cichlids and catfishes, and southern Asia supplies gouramis, danios, and barbs. In recent years most of the tropical fish sold in the United States have been raised domestically, especially in Florida. The substantial imports that still enter the country (about 20 percent of sales) come principally through Miami.

Freshwater Fish. The live-bearers (family Poeciliidae) are among the most fascinating and popular of aquarium fishes. These are all small fishes—SWORDTAILS, guppies, and platys—from the warmer parts of North and South America. Fertilization is internal, and the young are born alive. The anal fin of the male is modified into an elongated gonopodium used to insert the sperm. The young are retained in the oviducts of the female but derive no nourishment from her body.

The guppy, *Poecilia reticulata,* named for the Reverend Robert Guppy, an Anglican clergyman who brought back the first of these from Trinidad in the 19th century, is perhaps the most popular of the tropical fishes. Guppies have been selectively bred to produce a wide variety of colors and characters. The platys, which are small, stockily built fishes from southern

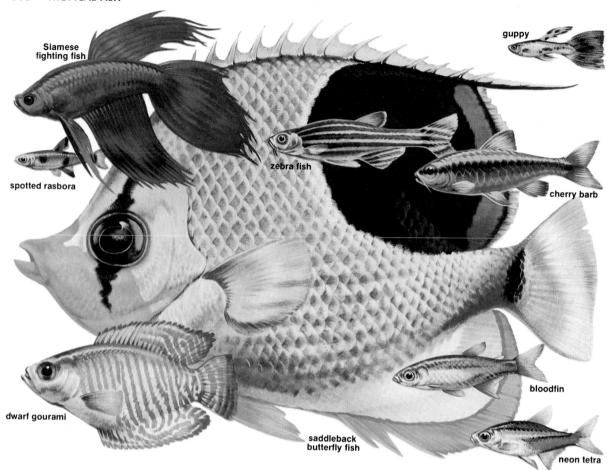

Diversity in coloration and body form have contributed to the popularity of tropical fish. The guppy, Poecilia reticulata, *is a prolific live-bearer. The danio family includes the blue-striped zebra fish,* Brachydanio rerio, *and the spotted rasbora,* Rasbora maculatta. *The bloodfin,* Aphyocharax rubripinnis, *and the neon tetra,* Hyphessobrycon innessi, *are named for their striking coloration, as is the cherry barb,* Barbus titteya. *A laterally compressed body and long dorsal and anal fins characterize the dwarf gourami,* Colissa lalia. *Male Siamese fighting fish,* Betta splendens, *have been selectively bred for flamboyant colors. The saddleback butterfly fish,* Chaetodon ephippium, *is a popular marine aquarium fish.*

Mexico, exhibit brilliant color variants and modified forms. Swordtails from Central America and Mexico are vividly and variously colored.

Tetras and other members of the family Characidae are among the most brilliantly colored of fishes; they are popular also for their graceful movements, small size, and liveliness. The young of CHARACINS receive no care from the parents, who may in fact feed on them. The glowing neon tetra, *Hyphessobrycon innesi,* from South America was once extremely rare. The head-and-tail-light fish, *Hemigrammus ocellifer,* is dazzling; seen in overhead light, the upper part of the eye and the top of the tail shine as though made of glowing copper. The bloodfin, *Aphyocharax rubripinnis,* has flaming fins that contrast with a silvery to purplish body.

GOLDFISH (family Cyprinidae) are perhaps the original aquarium fishes and are still very popular. They have been bred for centuries to produce striking colors and astonishing varieties. The danios are brightly colored cyprinids from Southeast Asia. The barbs are small, strikingly attractive fishes from Asia and Africa.

Members of the family Anabantidae are often highly colored, but perhaps their main attraction is their breeding behavior. These fishes have accessory air chambers, and they use oxygen directly from the air as well as through gills; air is also used in nest building. The SIAMESE FIGHTING FISH, *Betta splendens,* is the best known of the anabantids. The male builds the nest, gulping air at the surface and releasing it in bubbles coated with mucus. These float to the surface to form a raft. The eggs are extruded and fertilized, and the male takes them in his mouth, encloses each in a bubble, and

attaches it to the underside of the nest. If the young fall the male collects them, encloses them in a bubble, and returns them to the nest. He guards them for a week, but after that he may eat the brood he has taken so much care to protect. Fighting fish are bred in Thailand for combat; many encounters end in death. The paradise fish, *Macropodus opercularis,* and the gouramis, genus *Colisa,* are other popular anabantids.

Saltwater Fish. Saltwater tropical fishes are more difficult to raise than those from freshwater, but recent advances, including the development of artificial seawater and subsand filters, have made it possible for many more people to maintain these fishes. Perhaps the most popular saltwater tropicals are the angelfishes and the BUTTERFLY FISHES (family Chaetodontidae). Common on coral reefs of the Caribbean and Hawaii, these are the most colorful of all marine fishes. Another popular saltwater aquarium fish is the SEA HORSE. It swims upright in a slow and stately manner by the propeller action of its dorsal fin. In an aquarium it must have weeds or other objects around which to fasten its prehensile tail.   C. P. IDYLL

Bibliography: Axelrod, Herbert R., and Vorderwinkler, William, *Encyclopedia of Tropical Fish,* rev. ed. (1975); Cust, George, and Bird, Peter, *Tropical Freshwater Aquaria* (1971); Julian, T. W., *The Dell Encyclopedia of Tropical Fish* (1974); Madsen, J. M., *Aquarium Fishes in Color* (1975); Pitcher, Frederick W., *Identification Guide to Marine Tropical Aquarium Fish* (1977); Randall, John E., *Caribbean Reef Fishes* (1976).

tropical fruit

Tropical fruits represent a major group within a classification scheme of fruits by temperature zone; temperate fruits constitute the other major group. There are, in general, more varieties of fruit in the tropical zones, but a larger number in the temperate zones are of economic importance. More than 100 species of tropical fruits serve as foods, but only about 20 of these are of commercial importance. These include the AVOCADO, BANANA, CITRUS FRUITS, COCONUT, GUAVA, MANGO, PAPAYA, and PINEAPPLE. Most of the remaining species are dicotyledonous trees that are grown and valued only locally.

Some tropical fruit species are still very near to the wild state, and it is hard to determine where a list of tropical cultivated fruits should begin and end. Approximately 55% are American in origin, 35% Asian, and 10% African. Conservatism—an unwillingness to eat untried foods—is probably mainly responsible for the limited geographical spread of many species, but some are ecologically demanding, for reasons yet largely unknown; the mangosteen, rambutan, and akee, for example, often grow poorly outside their native areas. Collectively, tropical fruits offer a great range of characteristics: sweet or sour; dry or juicy; odorless, fragrant, or stinking; and smooth, rough, fibrous, or sticky in texture. A few of the more exotic tropical fruits are: (1) from tropical America, the soursop and its relatives (*Annona*), the star apple (*Chrysophyllum*), the tree tomato (*Cyphomandra*), the several passion fruits (*Passiflora*), and the hog plum (*Spondias*); (2) from Africa, the TAMARIND (*Tamarindus*) and the akee (*Blighia*, also cultivated in Jamaica); and (3) from tropical Asia, the DURIAN (*Durio*, famous for its smell, repulsive or delightful, according to taste), the rose apple (*Eugenia*), the MANGOSTEEN (*Garcinia*), the LITCHI (*Litchi*), and the rambutan (*Nephelium*).

N. W. SIMMONDS

Bibliography: Jagtiani, Jethro, et al., *Tropical Fruit Processing* (1987); Morton, J. F., *Fruits of Warm Climates* (1987); Norman, M. J., *The Ecology of Tropical Food Crops* (1984); Popenoe, Wilson, *Manual of Tropical and Subtropical Fruits: Excluding the Banana, Coconut, Pineapple, Citrus Fruits, Olive and Fig* (1974); Sampson, J. A., *Tropical Fruits*, 2d ed. (1986).

tropical year

The tropical YEAR is the period of time of one revolution of the Earth around the Sun measured between successive vernal EQUINOXES. It equals 365.24220 mean solar days, or 365 days, 5 hours, 48 minutes, 46 seconds. Also called the solar year or the year of the seasons, the tropical year is the basis of the calendar.

tropism   [trohp'-izm]

In botany the orientation, or directed movement, of plants in response to a nonuniform, or directional, external stimulus is called a tropism. The term was formerly applied also to orientation in animals, such as amoebas and flatworms, that respond to stimuli in a similar-appearing way, but these responses are now properly called taxes and kineses. It is convenient to classify tropisms according to the nature of the stimulus: a response to light is called phototropism; to gravity, gravitropism (formerly called geotropism); to water, hydrotropism; to chemical stimulus, chemotropism; and to touch, thigmotropism. Tropisms are very important in determining the orientation of plants in space. Plant stems have a strong tendency to turn toward the light (positive phototropism) and away from gravity (negative gravitropism). Most

roots grow toward gravity (positive gravitropism); if roots respond to light, they turn away from it (negative phototropism).

Phototropism was first rigorously studied in canary grass and oat seedlings as early as 1880 by Charles Darwin and his son Francis. The Darwins found that it was the actively growing tip of the coleoptile, the sheath surrounding the young shoot, that perceived the phototropically active light, even though curvature was observed in the cells below the tip. They thus concluded that "some influence is transmitted from the upper to the lower part, causing the latter to bend."

About 30 years later (1910–13) the Danish scientist P. Boysen-Jensen found that if a thin layer of gelatin was placed between the tip and the rest of an oat coleoptile, the coleoptile would still respond by bending toward the light. These results suggested that a diffusible chemical, passing through the gelatin, was involved.

A few years later, in Hungary, A. Paál demonstrated that coleoptiles could be made to bend even in complete darkness if the tip was cut off and then replaced but offset to one side. The coleoptile always bent away from the side on which the tip was placed. Apparently that side of the coleoptile underneath the offset tip grew more rapidly than the side not under it. These results suggested that phototropism might be explained as a differential growth response to some chemical stimulus emanating from the very tip of the coleoptile and under the control of light.

The conclusive experiments were performed in Holland by F. W. Went in the late 1920s. Drawing on the experiences of his predecessors, Went showed that if the cutoff tips were allowed to stand on small, gelatinous agar blocks for a period of time in darkness, and the blocks were then placed offset on coleoptile stumps, the stumps would bend away from the blocks. Apparently a growth-stimulating substance was manufactured in the tips of the coleoptiles and collected by diffusion into agar blocks.

This hormonelike substance, called auxin, was subsequently identified as β-indoleacetic acid (IAA) (see HORMONE, PLANT). Auxin is produced in the tips of coleoptiles (or stems) and, moving downward, stimulates the cells below the tip to elongate. In darkness or under uniform illumination, the movement of auxin from the tip is uniform: all cells are stimulated to grow about the same amount, and the coleoptile (or stem) grows vertically. Nonuniform illumination clearly establishes a differential in auxin flow out of the tip, with more auxin flowing down the shaded side of the coleoptile (or stem). The cells on the shaded side thus elongate more rapidly than those on the lighted side, overshooting them and forcing the coleoptile to bend toward the light.

One possible mechanism for controlling the amount of auxin flow on each side could be the destruction or inactivation of auxin by light on the brighter side—this theory was popular for several years. If this was the case, however, and because auxin is a general growth-stimulating hormone in plants, it is difficult to imagine how plants would be able to grow at all in strong light.

An alternative mechanism was proposed by N. Cholodny and demonstrated experimentally by Went. The Cholodny-Went theory states that unilateral, or one-sided, illumination interacts with the system transporting the auxin, causing it to divert, or laterally translocate, the auxin toward the shaded side as it moves out of the tip. Went's experiments in support

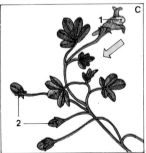

The involuntary response of plants to light is called phototropism. Plant shoots grow toward the light (positive) when cell growth is accelerated on the shady side. Roots and seed pods often grow away from light (negative). (A) A seedling exposed to light on all sides grows straight. (B) Light on only one side results in growth in that direction. (C) Whereas a flower (1) grows toward light, a seed pod (2) may grow away from it.

of this theory were amply confirmed and extended in an elegant series of experiments by W. R. Briggs during the 1960s.

Several important questions, however, remain to be answered if phototropism is to be completely understood. Because it is a response to light, there must be a pigment present to absorb the effective light. In the case of phototropism, the effective light is from the blue region of the spectrum. A comparison of the action spectrum of phototropism with absorption spectra of probable pigments indicates that both β-carotene and riboflavin may be involved. The mechanism by which absorbed light induces the lateral translocation of auxin is unknown. The significance of phototropism to the plant is clearly to assist in orienting the plant toward light that it requires for photosynthesis.

Growth movements in response to gravity are called gravitropism. Roots are positively gravitropic, growing in the direction of the Earth's gravitational field. Primary roots are more positively gravitropic than secondary roots. Shoots are negatively gravitropic, growing away from the gravitational field. Gravitropism has received increasing attention in recent years because of an interest in growing plants in the gravity-free environment of outer space.

Many branches, leaves, and other structures grow at various intermediate angles to the gravitational field. Such behavior is called plagiotropism. A plagiotropic movement is shown by the creeping stems called rhizomes, which respond both gravitropically and phototropically and grow at right angles to gravity. Experiments have demonstrated that gravitropism is caused by differential auxin concentration, with more auxin collecting on the lower side of the shoot or root. How higher concentrations on the lower sides of both shoots and roots produce opposite effects is not clearly understood, nor is gravity's effect on auxin distribution known with certainty.

In roots, where gravitropism has been studied most extensively, scientists believe that heavy starch-containing organelles called amyloplasts respond to gravity by settling in cells in the root tip. The pressure generated by the accumulation of amyloplasts triggers an increased auxin concentration in cells in the lower side of the root. Gravitropism helps the plant to best fill available space, sending the shoot upward for maximum absorption of carbon dioxide and light, and the root system downward into the soil for absorption of water and essential mineral elements. The gravitropic response of roots can be modified under conditions of highly unequal moisture distribution, when hydrotropism causes the roots to deviate from their normal downward path.

An excellent example of chemotropism is seen following pollination of flowers. Growth of the pollen tube down through the style toward the ovary is a chemotropic response, apparently to a gradient in calcium concentration. Thigmotropism is most readily seen in the tendrils of climbing vines or pea seedlings. The tendrils are stimulated to grow in the direction of physical contact with a solid object, and they tend to wrap around whatever structures they contact. This response obviously assists the plant in obtaining necessary support. Although many theories have been advanced to explain

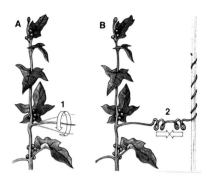

Thigmotropism is plant growth in response to touch. (A) Growing tendrils of climbers search for a support with circular movements (1). (B) When a support is found, the tendril coils around it. The unattached portion also coils, drawing the plant closer to the support. The coils change direction at the inversion point (2).

these phenomena, their mechanisms remain unknown.

Plant movements that are independent of the direction of the stimulus or that are caused by nondirectional stimuli are called nastic movements, or nasties. These include the closing or opening of flowers in daylight or darkness, actions believed to be influenced by light and temperature.

W. G. HOPKINS

Bibliography: Barlow, P. W., and Carr, D. J., eds., *Positional Controls in Plant Development* (1984); Bopp, M., ed., *Plant Growth Substances* (1985); Davies, P. J., ed., *Plant Hormones and Their Role in Plant Growth and Development* (1987); Evans, M. L., et al., "How Roots Respond to Gravity," *Scientific American*, December 1986; Gordon, S. A., and Cohen, M. J., eds., *Gravity and the Organism* (1971); Pandey, S. N., and Sinha, B. K., *Plant Physiology*, rev. ed. (1986); Salisbury, F. B., and Ross, C., *Plant Physiology*, 3d ed. (1985).

tropopause   [troh'-poh-pawz]

The tropopause is the boundary between the troposphere and STRATOSPHERE. In the troposphere the temperature generally decreases with height; above the tropopause, about 15 to 20 km (9 to 12 mi) in the tropics and about 10 km (6 mi) in polar areas, the temperature no longer decreases. In some instances it remains constant, and at other times or places it increases with height. The tropopause is relatively cold because it is situated far from the two nearest good partial absorbers of parts of sunlight: the Earth's surface and the ozonosphere, or OZONE LAYER.   WILLEM VAN DER BIJL

troposphere   [troh'-puhs-feer]

The troposphere, the lowest layer of the Earth's ATMOSPHERE, has for its upper boundary the tropopause and for its lower boundary the Earth's surface, where important heat and water-vapor fluxes occur (usually upward during the day and downward during the night). Virtually all weather, or short-term variation in the atmosphere, occurs in the troposphere, as well as considerable turning to turbulence—hence its name, derived from the Greek words *tropos*, "a turn," and *sphaira*, "ball." The troposphere contains 99% of the atmosphere's water vapor and 90% of the air. Air temperature decreases with increasing height, except when inversions occur.   WILLEM VAN DER BIJL

Trotsky, Leon   [traht'-skee]

Leon Trotsky, b. as Lev Davidovich Bronstein, Nov. 7 (N.S.), 1879, d. Aug. 21, 1940, was second only to Vladimir Ilich LENIN as polemicist and organizer of the Bolshevik phase of the RUSSIAN REVOLUTIONS OF 1917. A charismatic orator and superb tactician, he was also a brilliant theorist whose writings greatly influenced socialist movements worldwide. His practical skills enabled him to plan the Petrograd uprising in November 1917 and to create the Red Army that saved the Bolshevik regime in the ensuing Civil War (1918–20). But his fierce independence and aloofness prevented him from gaining broad party support after Lenin's death, in his unsuccessful struggle for power with Joseph STALIN.

Early Life and Revolutionary Activity. Trotsky, the son of a relatively prosperous Jewish farmer in Yanovka, in the Ukraine, was sent at the age of 9 to school in Odessa. Rebel-

Gravitropism is a plant's response to gravity, where (A) shoots grow upward (negative) and roots downward (positive). These responses also occur when the plant is placed in an abnormal position (B), such as on its side. Auxins are assumed to be the cause.

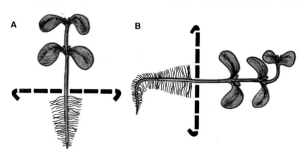

Leon Trotsky, one of the leaders and major theoreticians of the Russian Revolution, organized the Red Army and served as Soviet commissar of foreign affairs and of war under Lenin. Trotsky advanced the idea of "permanent revolution" and opposed the rise of a dictatorial bureaucracy. Exiled by Stalin, he was later assassinated.

lious and outspoken, he became at the age of 18 a professional revolutionary. He was arrested in 1898 and was later exiled to Siberia, where he joined the Social Democratic party. In 1902 he escaped abroad, met Lenin, and began his troubled relationship with the Bolshevik party (see BOLSHEVIKS AND MENSHEVIKS).

Trotsky admired Lenin's pragmatism, but after the Social Democratic split in 1903 he sided with the Mensheviks because he feared that Lenin's "elitist" organizational methods would lead to dictatorship. An independent-minded leftwinger, Trotsky wrote extensively in the radical press, and during the Russian Revolution of 1905 he returned to take a leading role in the Saint Petersburg (later Petrograd) Workers' Soviet. Arrested, tried, and again exiled to Siberia, he escaped abroad again in 1907 and wrote extensively until he returned to Russia in 1917.

Trotsky's major writings centered on the question of revolutionary development. Recognizing the weakness of Russia's bourgeoisie, he argued that the first, "bourgeois" stage of revolution could be carried out only with the help of Russia's organized workers, and that this stage would lead to a condition of "permanent revolution." The proletariat, who would have brought the bourgeoisie to power, would then gradually assume political control. As the revolution passed into worker hands in backward Russia, workers' revolts would spread to the more advanced capitalist societies of Europe and would establish socialist regimes to aid and protect the weak Russian revolutionary government.

Revolutionary Leader and Soviet Official. This outlook, soon to affect much Third World revolutionary thinking, structured Trotsky's activism in 1917. Returning to Russia independently of Lenin after the March 1917 revolution, he called on the workers to overthrow the liberal provisional government. In August he joined the Bolshevik party, whose long-time loyalists (including Stalin) regarded him as an interloper. However, Trotsky rapidly won a leading role with his spellbinding speeches and organizational energy. In September he was elected chairman of the Petrograd Soviet, and from that post he organized the Bolshevik forces that overthrew the regime of Aleksandr Kerensky.

Appointed commissar of foreign affairs (1917–18), Trotsky unsuccessfully opposed the annexationist Brest-Litovsk treaty with Germany, but he retained Lenin's confidence and became commissar of war (1918–25). From the demoralized remnants of tsarist forces he managed to organize an efficient Red Army, a truly remarkable feat; but his brusque style, his impatience with criticism and incompetence, and his decision to rely on "military specialists" won him few friends. Rank-and-file party comrades saw him as aloof and remote.

Known as a "left Bolshevik" and an advocate of both rapid, planned industrialization and party democracy, Trotsky watched impatiently after 1921 as the party course seemed to support neither. In a series of essays labeled "The New Course" (1923), he bitterly criticized the growing bureaucratization of the party and argued for greater centralized planning. Much of his hostility was directed against Stalin, whom he loathed. In response, Stalin stated his own position, both by his activities within the party organization and in his advocacy of "socialism in one country" (the antithesis of Trotsky's advocacy of world revolution). With Lenin's death in January 1924, Trotsky proved either too self-confident or too impatient to work carefully at practical politics. Within weeks he was censured for "factionalism," and within three years he was stripped of all posts and expelled from the party.

Exile. Condemned to internal exile in 1928, he was banished from the USSR the following year. Trotsky then lived in Turkey (1929–33), France (1933–35), Norway (1935–36), and Mexico (1936–40). He continued to write on a wide range of issues: culture, literature, politics, international affairs, revolutionary theory, and women. He completed his massive *History of the Russian Revolution* (3 vols., 1931–33; Eng. trans., 1932–33), also working energetically to expose Stalin—most notably in *The Revolution Betrayed* (1937). At the treason trials held (1936–38) in Moscow, Trotsky was denounced in absentia as the archconspirator against the Soviet regime. He was finally axed to death by a Stalinist agent at his home in a suburb of Mexico City. Many of Trotsky's writings have appeared in English translation, including *Literature and Revolution* (1925), *Terrorism and Communism* (1921; rev. ed., 1935), and *Diary in Exile, 1935* (1958). Trotsky's correspondence during his years in exile was made public by Harvard University in January 1980.

WILLIAM G. ROSENBERG

Bibliography: Carmichael, Joel, *Trotsky: An Appreciation of His Life* (1975); Deutscher, Isaac, *The Prophet Armed* (1954), *The Prophet Unarmed* (1959), and *The Prophet Outcast* (1963); Eastman, Max, *Leon Trotsky: Portait of a Youth* (1925); Howe, Irving, *Leon Trotsky* (1978) and, as ed., *The Basic Writings of Trotsky* (1963); Segal, Ronald, *Leon Trotsky: A Biography* (1979); Serge, Victor, and Trotsky, Natalia Sedova, *Life and Death of Leon Trotsky*, trans. by Arnold J. Pomerans (1975); Warth, Robert D., *Leon Trotsky* (1977); Wolfe, Bertram D., *Three Who Made a Revolution* (1948).

trotter

Trotters, the horses used in harness racing, are able to trot at speeds up to about 48 km/h (30 mph) over short distances. Trotting is a gait, or sequence of foot movements, in which the diagonally opposite feet (for example, the left front and right rear) move in synchrony. Several breeds have been developed to race at a trot, an unnatural gait for a horse moving at high speed. The American standardbred is considered by many to be the premier breed of racing trotters. It is of the thoroughbred type but sturdier, with shorter legs.

troubadour: see MINSTRELS, MINNESINGERS, AND TROUBADOURS.

trout

Strongly colored, active fish of cold or temperate lakes and rapid streams, the approximately 15 species of trout are grouped with the SALMON in the family Salmonidae. All but two of the genus *Salmo* are regarded as trout. Once limited to the Northern Hemisphere, they are valued as game and food fish and have been introduced into a number of areas in the Southern Hemisphere. Although predominantly a freshwater fish, some species migrate to the ocean after spawning upriver. Trout generally thrive in water temperatures below 10°–18° C (50°–65° F).

The trout has a moderately long, unspecialized body that is laterally compressed, smooth, and muscular. Axial and paired fins are without spines. The softer, fleshy adipose fin, between the dorsal and caudal fin, is an indicator that the trout is a salmonid. All scales are small except for the elongated axial scale at the base of each pelvic fin.

The trout's diet changes with age. Fry, or newly hatched fish, feed on aquatic insect larvae for the most part. They progress to eating winged insects. As adults, small fishes, shrimp, and winged insects constitute the bulk of their diet.

Many male and female trout return after maturing (3 to 4 years) to the same place they were hatched in order to spawn. Most trout breed in early spring in running water. The female lays her eggs in a depression she makes by vigorously vibrating her tail in the gravelly shallows. The nearby male discharges his sperm fertilizing approximately 200 eggs, which hatch in about 40 days. As many as 10,000 eggs may be laid per season by a single female. More than 90% of fry are killed during the first 3 or 4 months of life by predators such as the water shrew, mink, and larger trout.

One of the best-known trout is the brown trout, or sea trout, *S. trutta,* of Europe. They keep to the deeper pools and overhanging shelter of mountain streams. In the Terek and Kura rivers, brown trout support a commercial fishery.

The Seven lake trout, *S. ischchan,* and the cutthroat trout, *S. clarkii,* have both been able to adapt to special environments. Their genetic plasticity has enabled them to invade new and changing mountain drainages and occupy ephemeral lakes. Both species have been subjected to severe recent modifications of habitat and reduction of population by dams and other human constructions.

One of the most popular gamefish is the rainbow trout, *S. gairdneri,* the several forms of which are native to American Pacific Coast streams. The rainbow trout gets its name from the broad band of red along its side.

For most trout populations, measures for control and conservation have been established through government agencies and associations. Artificially propagated fish are planted in order to provide extra catches for more anglers. Trout fishing is very popular, and in some countries, including the United States, a tax is placed on fishing products (equipment, boats, clothing) to help fund research and management aimed at improving the sport.   RICHARD G. MILLER

The rainbow trout, S. gairdneri (top), *native to the North American Pacific coast, is stocked in lakes throughout the world as a game fish. The lake trout,* S. lasustris (bottom), *also popular among anglers, thrives in cold, deep lakes of the United States and Canada.*

Bibliography: Bergman, Ray, and Janes, Edward C., *Trout* (1976); Brooks, Charles E., *The Trout and the Stream* (1974); Van Gytenbeek, G. P., *The Way of a Trout* (1972).

trout-perch

Trout-perch (family Percopsidae) comprise two species of small sandy-colored, nearly transparent fish found throughout most of southern Canada and the northern United States. Trout-perch are easily recognized by the combination of coarse ctenoid scales, spines in the dorsal and anal fins, and the presence of an adipose fin. Although typically lake dwelling, they are sometimes found in turbid, cool streams. In lakes, trout-perch migrate at night from deep water into shal-

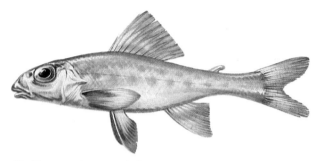

The blunt-nosed trout-perch, Percopsis omiscomaycus, *like the trout and salmon, has a small, fleshy adipose fin behind its dorsal fin. Also called the sandroller, it reaches a maximum size of 15 cm (6 in).*

low to feed and are themselves important forage fish for the larger, commercially important species such as walleye, trout, and pike. Trout-perch spawn in the spring in streams and on shallow, gravelly lake bottoms.   ALAN R. EMERY

Trova, Ernest   [troh'-vuh]

One of the most widely exhibited American sculptors, Ernest Trova, b. St. Louis, Mo., Feb. 19, 1927, is known for his image of the "falling man," a streamlined, anonymous symbol of the individual in the mechanical age. Since the early 1960s, Trova's work has featured variants on this theme, which he has expressed in both large and small works, in single figures and groups, and in a variety of materials—from chrome-plated steel to Plexiglas. The falling man is more a homage to machine-age culture than a detached comment on it. Thus, Trova is less ironic than the pop artists, with whom he has often been compared.   CARTER RATCLIFF

Bibliography: Kultermann, Udo, *Trova* (1978).

Trovatore, Il   [troh-vah-tohr'-ay, eel]

Giuseppe VERDI's *Il Trovatore* (The Troubadour), with libretto by Salvatore Cammarano (completed by L. E. Bardare), had its premiere in Rome on Jan. 19, 1853. The plot was based on a drama by the Spanish playwright, Antonio García Gutiérrez. The rather ludicrous complications of the libretto have often been criticized, but the opera has remained popular for the lyrical ardor of its music and the powerful roles of Manrico and his gypsy mother, Azucena.

trover   [troh'-vur]

Trover is an action in law to recover damages from a person who has wrongfully withheld and used another's property. It differs from a writ of REPLEVIN, which is aimed only at the recovery of the property itself. Trover is the legal action against the TORT of conversion.

Troy   (archaeological site)

The name *Troy* refers both to the remains of a Bronze Age fortress and city at Hissarlik in modern Turkey, near the entrance to the Dardanelles, and to the legendary city of King Priam that was destroyed by ancient Greeks in the TROJAN WAR. There are reasons to believe that the physical remains in Turkey correspond, in part at least, to the city in Greek literature. Troy was once known also as Ilios or Ilion; this is reflected in the name of Homer's epic poem the *Iliad,* a work that claims to relate the story of Troy's fall.

In modern times Troy was rediscovered and excavated by Heinrich SCHLIEMANN (1870–90) and, after his death, by his colleague Wilhelm Dörpfeld (1893–94). Within the mound of archaeological layers (strata) at the site, which reaches a depth of more than 15 m (50 ft), Schliemann and Dörpfeld distinguished nine major divisions (Troy I-IX). The strata at Troy were reexamined (1932–38) by an archaeological expedition from the University of Cincinnati, directed by Carl W. Blegen.

From the evidence recovered by Schliemann, Dörpfeld, and Blegen, the long history of Troy can be reconstructed. Its first settlers arrived about 3000 BC, and its earlier phases (Troy I–VII, 3000–1100 BC), when it existed as a powerful fortress, are more interesting than its later life as a city (Troy VIII and IX, 700 BC–AD c.400). The earliest settlement, Troy I, lasted about 500 years (3000–2500 BC); it was a small fortress enclosed by a strong wall. Houses were built with foundations of stone and walls of clay brick. The settlers knew of copper but normally used bone and stone for tools and weapons. Most of their surviving possessions are of earthenware pottery. Troy I, like many other ancient settlements, came to its end in a devastating fire.

Troy II (2500–2200 BC), although only 122 m (400 ft) across, was slightly larger than the preceding settlement and had more massive walls and larger buildings. It was wealthier than Troy I; it possessed much gold and silver and made much more use of copper. Its artisans were more advanced; the potter's wheel, for example, appeared at Troy during phase II, when the Trojans were in contact with both the Aegean world to the west and central Anatolia to the east. Troy's power and wealth were probably derived from its strategic position, controlling important trade routes between Asia and Europe. The ruler, his family, and their most trusted retainers probably lived in the fortress, whereas the majority of the Trojan people lived in the surrounding countryside, grew grain and other crops, tended livestock, and provided troops when required.

Troy II, like Troy I, suffered catastrophic devastation by fire. Although the character of the fortress was preserved throughout periods III–V (2200–1800 BC), this era was undistinguished. The high point of Troy's history was Troy VI (1800–1300 BC). The area enclosed by the citadel was then about 230 m (750 ft) across, with finely crafted stone walls and stoutly fortified gates. Once again, the rulers of Troy occupied a position of power and importance in relation to the neighboring peoples of the Aegean and Anatolia.

Troy VI was destroyed by earthquake. Troy VIIa (1300–1200 BC), resettled by the survivors of Troy VI, depended on the same fortifications. Its houses were crowded together; many had large storage jars sunk beneath the floors. The impression is that of a community under stress, possibly like Priam's citadel, the siege of which figures in the *Iliad* and other stories of the Trojan War. According to Greek tradition, Troy fell in 1184 BC. The archaeological evidence supports a date of about 1200 BC for the destruction of Troy VIIa. Resettlement followed on a small scale during Troy VIIb (1200–1100 BC).

Thereafter, the site seems to have been deserted for about four centuries. About 700 BC new settlers appeared, and a city

Excavations of the ancient city of Troy, in Hissarlik, Turkey, were begun (1870) by Heinrich Schliemann and were continued in this century under the direction of Carl Blegen. Stratigraphical research has revealed nine levels at Troy, the earliest dated at 3000 BC.

of modest size grew up over and around the ruins of the Bronze Age fortress. During the Hellenistic and Roman eras, efforts were made to rehabilitate the ancient site, which became important mainly as a tourist attraction. It is not known to have survived beyond the 4th century AD, but its memory remained influential on the Western imagination.

CEDRIC BOULTER

Bibliography: Blegen, Carl W., *Troy and Trojans* (1963); Page, Denys L., *History and the Homeric Iliad* (1959); Rapp, G., and Gifford, J. A., eds., *Troy: The Archaeological Geology* (1982); Scherer, Margaret R., *The Legends of Troy in Art and Literature* (1963); Schliemann, Heinrich, *Ilios* (1880; repr. 1977); Wood, M., *In Search of the Trojan War* (1986); Young, Arthur M., *Troy and Her Legend* (1948; repr. 1971).

Troy (New York)

Situated in eastern New York on the east bank of the Hudson River, almost across from Albany, Troy is the seat of Rensselaer County. It has a population of 56,638 (1980). Once a prominent industrial center, the city has experienced a decline in manufacturing. Rensselaer Polytechnic Institute (1824) and Russell Sage College (1916) are there. The area near Troy was explored by Henry Hudson in 1609, and the site itself was included in a patroonship granted to Kiliaen Van Rensselaer by the Dutch West India Company in 1629. The city was laid out in 1786. Samuel Wilson of Troy, who supplied meat stamped "U.S." to the army in the War of 1812, is believed to have been the original "Uncle Sam."

troy weight: see WEIGHTS AND MEASURES.

Troyes [twah]

The French city of Troyes (1982 pop., 63,581) lies on the Seine River about 150 km (95 mi) southeast of Paris. It is a road and rail junction and the home of the French hosiery industry. Landmarks include the Gothic Cathedral of Saint-Pierre et Saint-Paul (begun 13th century). Dating from pre-Roman times, the city was a prosperous medieval commercial center. It was the seat of the counts of Champagne from the early 11th century and the site of the Champagne fairs (12th–13th centuries). A stronghold of Protestantism, Troyes declined after the revocation of the Edict of Nantes in 1685 drove away many of its commercial leaders.

Troyon, Constant [twah-yohn']

A French artist specializing in landscapes and animal subjects, Constant Troyon, b. Aug. 28, 1810, d. Mar. 20, 1865, began his career as a painter of Sèvres porcelain. His interest in landscape painting brought him into contact with such artists of the Barbizon school as Théodore Rousseau, Paul Huet, and Jules Dupré, who extolled and practiced the direct study of nature. Troyon was also influenced by 17th-century Dutch painting. After 1833 he frequently exhibited in the French Academy's annual Salon.

PHILIP GOULD

Trübner, Wilhelm [troob'-nur]

The German painter Wilhelm Trübner, b. Feb. 3, 1851, d. Dec. 21, 1917, was a follower of the 19th-century realist Wilhelm Liebl, whose work he encountered as a student at the academy of art in Munich. In 1870 he joined the "Liebl circle," whose members chose to paint scenes of everyday life in preference to the historical subjects emphasized by academicians. Trübner showed a particular interest in landscape.

ELIZABETH PUTZ

Bibliography: Finke, Ulrich, *German Painting from Romanticism to Expressionism* (1974).

Trucial States: see UNITED ARAB EMIRATES.

trucking industry

The trucking industry is made up of those persons and firms engaged in the business of owning and operating motor trucks for hire to transport products over roads. Such companies are known as carriers.

CLASSIFICATION OF CARRIERS

The three principal categories of carriers are: private carriers, who use trucks to transport only their own products from farm to market, or raw materials from source to processing or manufacturing plants, or finished products to their markets, or for interplant movements; contract carriers, who enter into contractual agreements, usually long-term in nature, with business establishments to transport materials and products for those firms; and common carriers, who serve the general public on any and all commodities. A contract carrier may contract with several firms; however, shipments from different firms cannot be mixed together. Common carriers are granted operating certificates by the INTERSTATE COMMERCE COMMISSION (ICC) as either irregular-route carriers or regular-route carriers.

Irregular-route carriers serve the public on "call and demand." They usually operate from a central office or terminal, shipping either specified commodities (such as textile products) or general commodities from specified points or areas to other specified areas.

Regular-route common carriers are granted authority by the ICC to operate over specified highway routes on a regular basis, using terminals located strategically to consolidate and distribute freight in a surrounding area. Commodities handled by regular-route carriers may be specified, or the carrier may have authority to handle general commodities, usually with some exceptions for which special and specific authority must be granted by the ICC. Such special goods include small-package express, armored express (for transporting items of unusual value), household goods, automobiles, explosives, liquids carried in tank trucks, dry bulk goods, logs, and cement.

Agricultural produce (unprocessed farm products) is not subject to ICC regulation and may be handled by what are known as unregulated motor carriers. The ability of a truck to pick up produce from several farms and bring it quickly to market makes trucking well suited for this purpose.

HISTORY

The first load-carrying, self-propelled road vehicles were vans hauled by steam engines. These vehicles, which were experimented with throughout the 19th century, first appeared in discernible number in Great Britain in the 1870s. In 1892 the Frenchman Maurice Le Blanc introduced steam-powered cartage vehicles for commercial users (Paris department stores). Karil BENZ's invention (1885) of the gasoline-powered internal-combustion automobile spurred the development of a similarly powered load-carrying vehicle, the first example of which probably was produced (1896) by the German engineer Gottlieb DAIMLER.

Early trucks were relatively heavy and had crude mechanisms. They were confined to city deliveries and hauling, because they could not manage the mud and potholes of outlying roads. In 1903 the Automobile Club of America staged the first U.S. commercial-vehicle contest to test the economy, reliability, durability, speed, and carrying capacity of the truck—the newest mode of freight transportation. Stimulated by the results of that contest, the manufacture and use of motor trucks flourished. By 1908, 4,000 trucks were in use in the United States, transporting goods of every type wherever streets and roads were passable. By the start (1914) of World War I, 300,000 trucks were in use, and by the war's end (1918) there were more than a million.

By 1915 most manufacturers had settled on a conventional construction in which the engine was located ahead of the front wall of the cab. Early trucks resembled horse-drawn wagons of the 19th century. They lacked roofs, doors, and windshields; nothing protected the driver from the elements. The vehicle was driven on the right side. TIRES were of solid rubber. The ride was uncomfortable but bearable because the top speed was only 2 km/h (20 mph). Then came roofs, roll-down curtains, windshields, doors, and side windows. By 1930 most truck cabs were fully enclosed.

Few modern (as opposed to steam-engine-hauled) trailers were built before 1915. The first type of modern trailer used was the full trailer, defined as a towed trailer whose entire weight rests on its own axles. By 1920 the semitrailer, whose front end rests on the rear portion of the hauling truck tractor, was gaining in popularity. In a semitrailer the truck tractor usually has a disk, known popularly as a fifth wheel, located on a horizontal platform over its rear wheels; a pin located under the front of the trailer locks into this disk, thus attaching the trailer to the tractor and furnishing support for the front end of the trailer. A semitrailer can therefore quickly be detached from a tractor, so that the tractor can be used to haul a second semitrailer at the same time that the first is being unloaded.

All early trucks were powered by either steam engines or internal-combustion engines. The first tractors powered by diesel engines were built in the early 1930s. Diesel engines burned fuel oil instead of gasoline and ranged in power from 125 to 500 hp. Following World War II the diesel gradually became accepted in most heavy trucks and in some smaller trucks as well.

The first modern tilt-cab, or cab-over, truck was built in 1935; in this truck type, the cab is placed over the engine and can be tilted up and forward to gain access to the engine. This allows a great savings in the length of the tractor, so that trailers can be longer and hence carry larger payloads.

Trucks were used extensively by the military during World War I, which gave a major boost to the trucking industry. The U.S. Army had a fleet of 2,400 trucks in 1917 and added another 230,000 vehicles in 1918. Trucks also made a major contribution to the transportation of supplies during World War II.

In the late 1920s and early 1930s the trucking industry, which was dominated by large numbers of itinerant owner-operators, was considered by many to be unstable, chaotic, and in need of economic regulation. The National Industrial Recovery Act (NRA) of 1933 brought together two organized groups of trucking officials to develop a code of fair competition and led to the formation of the American Trucking Associations. The organization submitted its code to the NRA in 1934. Every for-hire carrier was required to observe maximum hours of labor and minimum wages for all employees. The Motor Carrier Act of 1935 provided for safety regulation of interstate carriers, as well as economic regulation of for-hire carriers under the authority of the Interstate Commerce Commission (ICC).

REGULATION AND DEREGULATION

Under ICC regulation, operators with for-hire trucks who wished to carry freight into interstate markets had to apply to the ICC for a license to do so. Licenses were granted only if the need for additional truck capacity could be proved, and permission often also included the obligation to serve less profitable markets within the license region. In addition, the types of freight that could be carried by any one ICC-licensed truck were limited, with some commodities—such as food—under severe regulatory restrictions. Exemptions from ICC regulation were extended only to certain independent owner-operators, farmer cooperative truckers, and private carriers serving only their parent companies.

The setting of trucking rates, which had been a matter between the individual trucker and the customer, gave way to the establishment of rate bureaus, which are owned and supported by all participating carriers. The bureaus researched and analyzed costs in order to establish competitive rates for the industry. Such an arrangement was made possible by a Justice Department antitrust exemption giving regulated trucking firms the power to collectively set rates subject to approval by the ICC.

In 1980, however, Congress passed a trucking deregulation bill in the hope of increasing competition within the industry—and therefore saving consumers about $5 billion annually by reducing shipping costs. By removing many of the ICC regulations, the bill made entrance into the industry easier for new trucking firms, gave individual truckers greater rate-setting powers, and ended some types of collective rate making. It loosened ICC powers over route setting and over the categories of commodities that may be hauled by individual trucking firms, particularly easing restrictions on food hauling.

Since deregulation the ICC has granted licenses to about 3,000 new carriers and approved 35,000 requests for expansion of routes—a vast increase over its approvals before deregulation. The large, established carriers find deregulation cutting into their business; smaller truckers and most shippers, however, generally approve lessened ICC control. Its effects on consumer costs are still undetermined.

European countries differ in their approaches to regulating the trucking industry. Great Britain, for example, has largely eschewed regulation, whereas the Netherlands partially regulates trucking, and West Germany has full regulation of the type practiced in the United States before 1980.

Truck weight and size limits on interstate highways are regulated by the states, although they may not exceed the maxima set by the federal government: a gross weight of 36,000 kg (80,000 lb) and 18.3 m (60 ft) in length and 2.4 m (8 ft) in width. If maxima are increased—as many in the industry would like—road and excise taxes on trucks will no doubt increase also, to compensate for wear and tear that heavier trucks impose on highways. Trucks pay about 50% of all federal and state road user taxes.

TYPES

Today's truck is the result of engineering and technological advances of the 20th century, with economy, environmental impact, safety, and driver comfort as much a part of design as the load factor. A number of special types of trucks are built to perform specific functions.

The pickup truck has a carrying capacity of 0.5 to 5 U.S. tons. Smaller types usually have a conventional design, whereas larger sizes have the cab situated over the engine. The loading area is designed for the particular job to be performed. It may have a flat bed, open bed, stake body, or closed van.

The panel truck is a completely enclosed van having a capacity of about 0.5 U.S. tons. The straight truck may have a conventional or cab-over-engine design. The body length is designed for the job function. Where double- and triple-trailers are used, the straight truck may be used as the tractor, with the trailer or trailers coupled behind.

The tractor may have a conventional or cab-over-engine design. It has a so-called fifth wheel and may have rear dual wheels mounted on a single axle, or tandem axles, depending on the usage.

The semitrailer is a vehicle designed to be pulled by a tractor. It has either single or tandem axles on the rear. A steel plate with a welded or molded pin that is located on the bottom front slips and locks into the fifth wheel of the tractor. A "semi" may be an open flatbed, stake body, or fully enclosed van box.

The full trailer is similar to the semitrailer except that it has front wheels as well as rear wheels and has a tongue for hooking it to a tractor or another trailer. A tandem unit consists of two trailers pulled behind a single tractor. They are generally not allowed on small or congested roads.

Trucks that are even more specialized—for performing special and unusual jobs—include FIRE ENGINES, refrigerated vans, mobile cranes, EARTH-MOVING MACHINERY, dump trucks, concrete mixers, garbage and trash trucks, and tank trucks for both dry- and liquid-bulk hauling.

PARTS AND SYSTEMS

The basic difference between trucks and automobiles is that automobiles are people carriers whereas trucks are freight haulers; thus, each has its own characteristics geared to what is required. Trucks are larger, the ultimate limiting factor being the length, width, and weight permitted on the highways. Some trucks used exclusively in off-highway work, such as open-pit mining and earth-moving construction, are huge vehicles capable of carrying more than 50 tons.

Gasoline or diesel internal-combustion engines requiring electrical ignition systems are commonly used as power units, with the horsepower ranging from 35 in light pickup trucks and vans to 250–300 in line-haul (long-distance) tractors, and even higher in special equipment. Whereas fuel consumption

in light trucks may be comparable to that of heavier automobiles, the large trucks obtain only an average of 13 km (8 mi) per gallon of fuel. With the introduction of the diesel engine to trucking and the availability of refined diesel fuel, operating efficiency was greatly improved.

Transmissions and drive-axle assemblies for trucks are larger, tougher, and far more intricate than those in automobiles. Automatic transmissions are available for some smaller trucks. Larger trucks, however, have manual transmissions, often with from four to ten forward speeds. Except for the front steering wheels, which are single wheels, larger trucks and tractors usually utilize dual-wheels, often in tandem, allowing as many as five axles on a tractor semitrailer with 18 tires. On smaller pickup trucks, the brakes are hydraulic, like those used in automobiles. Larger trucks and tractors, however, are equipped with a sophisticated system of air brakes with a greater stopping ability. Special devices are also used to prevent jackknifing while braking. Steering systems for trucks often have a hydraulic power-assist unit to reduce the steering effort. Truck cabs are designed and built to be comfortable and to prevent fatigue. Line-haul trucks and tractors are usually air-conditioned, are equipped with radios, and have a driver's seat that adjusts to a number of positions. Some tractors used for long-distance runs have a sleeping compartment, allowing one driver to rest while another operates the vehicle.

Because of the rapid increase in the price of fuel in recent years, much research has been conducted on improved fuel economy. Recent advances include aerodynamic drag reduction, demand-actuated fan drive systems, steel radial tires, synthetic lubricants, and engine and drive train modifications. Drag can be dramatically reduced by an air deflector. This device, which comes in various shapes, improves the streamlining by deflecting air over the top of the trailer. The new fan systems—used also in some automobiles—turn the fan on and off as needed, either by a temperature-sensing device or by a centrifugal clutch that disconnects the fan when the engine, and hence vehicle, speed is high enough to provide

TRUCK AND BUS REGISTRATION BY CONTINENT AND IN SELECTED COUNTRIES (1985)

Africa	4,057,500	South America	4,917,000
Central African Rep.	3,800	Argentina	1,427,500
Egypt	292,800	Chile	291,300
Ivory Coast	52,400	Ecuador	37,300
Kenya	39,500	Guyana	30,000
Libya	275,000	Paraguay	27,000
Morocco	218,100	Peru	209,300
Nigeria	640,000	Uruguay	100,000
South Africa	1,233,900	Venezuela	682,000
Uganda	8,800		
Zimbabwe	80,000	**Europe**	**25,475,000**
		Austria	622,300
Asia	**30,369,000**	Belgium	356,000
Arab Emirates	51,000	Bulgaria	27,400
Bangladesh	35,000	Czechoslovakia	425,100
China, People's		Denmark	267,400
Republic of	2,374,000	Finland	200,500
India	2,237,000	France	2,765,500
Israel	125,050	Germany, East	656,800
Japan	18,312,600	Germany, West	1,722,600
Pakistan	127,400	Greece	620,700
Philippines	108,600	Hungary	176,000
Saudi Arabia	1,966,100	Ireland	109,800
Taiwan	429,400	Italy	1,824,000
Turkey	553,000	Netherlands	428,200
		Norway	249,600
North and Central		Poland	862,800
America	**45,681,000**	Portugal	356,000
Canada	3,148,500	Spain	1,610,000
Costa Rica	72,800	USSR	9,613,000
Haiti	11,600	United Kingdom	727,800
Mexico	1,978,000	Yugoslavia	644,000
Nicaragua	42,200	**Oceania**	**2,523,000**
Trinidad/Tobago	80,000	Australia	2,131,000
United States	39,790,000	New Zealand	302,300

SOURCE: Motor Vehicles Manufacturers Association of the U.S., Inc.

adequate cooling. Having the fan disconnected when not needed can save a considerable amount of energy.

THE INDUSTRY TODAY

In the late 1980s there were over 40 million trucks of all sizes registered in the United States. Only about one million were combination tractor-semitrailers, the standard vehicles used by the trucking industry. Compact pickups, station wagons on truck chassis, and minibuses represented the largest increase in numbers, as car owners discovered the advantages of owning small trucklike vehicles. Truck industry revenues totaled over $200 billion annually, the product of over 600 billion ton miles of freight carried. The industry employed about 8 million people, making it the largest private industrial employer.

The Motor Vehicle Manufacturers Association projects the following for 1995: the demand for truck haulage will double; alternative forms of energy will be used by trucks; and line-haul trucks of 50 U.S. tons (45,360 kg/100,000 lb) will become standard.   WILBERT M. HITE

Bibliography: Button, K. J., and Pearman, A. D., *The Economics of Urban Freight Transport* (1981); Childs, W. R., *Trucking and the Public Interest* (1985); Educational Research Council of America, *Truck Driver*, rev. ed. (1976); Harper, D. V., *Trucking in America* (1978); J. J. Keller and Assoc., Inc., *Federal Motor Carrier Safety Regulations Pocket Book*, rev. ed. (1987); Jaskiewicz, L., and Kiley, E. J., *Free Wheeling? A Reference for Economic Deregulation of the Motor Carrier Industry* (1987); Loup-Nory, J., *The Long Haul: Trucking in America* (1980); Madsen, A., *The Open Road* (1982); Society of Automotive Engineers, *Truck Safety* (1986).

Trudeau, Garry   [troo'-doh]

Garry Beekman Trudeau, b. New York City, 1948, creator of the popular "Doonesbury" cartoon, became the first comic-strip artist to win (1975) the Pulitzer Prize for editorial cartooning. Satirizing public figures and politics, "Doonesbury" appeals mostly to young adults. Trudeau suspended the strip from Jan. 1, 1983, to Sept. 30, 1984; upon its return, it appeared in some 775 newspapers. The strip has often been collected and published in book form. With Elizabeth Swados as composer, Trudeau wrote the Broadway musical *Doonesbury* in 1983.   ROY PAUL NELSON

Trudeau, Pierre Elliott

Pierre Elliott Trudeau, b. Montreal, Oct. 18, 1919, served as prime minister of Canada from 1968 to 1979, and again from 1980 to 1984. Educated in law at the University of Montreal (1943) and in political economy at Harvard University (M.A., 1945), Trudeau then practiced and taught law, specializing in civil liberties. He was first elected to the House of Commons in 1965. After serving (1967–68) as minister of justice and attorney general of Canada he succeeded (1968) Lester Pearson as prime minister and Liberal party leader.

Trudeau won a landslide electoral victory in 1968 and began a program to effect greater independence from the United States. He greatly expanded Canada's contacts with the USSR and with developing countries, recognized (1970) China, increased Sino-Canadian trade, and withdrew half of Canada's NATO troops from Europe. Trudeau also established (1973) the Federal Investment Review Agency to oversee foreign investments in Canada.

A confirmed federalist, Trudeau—aided somewhat by his French background—attempted to blunt the separatist movement in Quebec by sponsoring the Official Languages Act (1969), making French-language services available in all federal government operations. In 1970, to counter separatist terrorism, Trudeau briefly imposed martial law, a move in which he was widely supported. He was beset, however, by political and economic problems. His party lost its parliamentary majority in 1972, and Trudeau's government survived only through a shaky coalition with the New Democratic party. The Liberals again achieved a majority in 1974, but Trudeau's popularity continued to decline, and the Liberal government was defeated in May 1979.

After announcing his resignation as Liberal leader, Trudeau

Pierre Elliott Trudeau served as Canada's prime minister for a second time (1980–84), returning to the post he had previously occupied for more than a decade (1968–79). Trudeau, leader of the nation's Liberal party, promoted Canadian control of its own economy and struggled to quell the secessionist movement in French-speaking Quebec.

was persuaded to lead the party in new elections in February 1980. He returned as prime minister after the Liberals won an overall majority. He soon faced strong provincial challenges to federal authority. A proposal of autonomy for Quebec was defeated in a referendum in May 1980, but Alberta, in turn, challenged government policy on oil pricing. Trudeau's formula for revising the federal constitution was opposed by most provincial premiers until a compromise was reached—with only Quebec dissenting—in November 1981. The new Constitution Act became law in April 1982. Trudeau resigned as prime minister on June 30, 1984.   Reviewed by P. B. WAITE

Bibliography: Butson, T., *Pierre Trudeau* (1986); Gwyn, Richard, *The Northern Magus* (1980); Radwanski, G., *Trudeau* (1978).

Truffaut, François   [troo-foh']

The French film director François Truffaut appears with Jacqueline Bisset on the set of Day for Night *(1973), a film about the making of a film in which Truffaut himself played the part of a director beset by the emotional difficulties of his actors.*

An important force in French filmmaking for more than 25 years, François Truffaut, b. Feb. 6, 1932, d. Oct. 21, 1984, began his cinematic career as a critic (1951–59) for the film journal *Cahiers du Cinéma*. Encouraged by its editor, film theorist André Bazin, he started directing in the mid-1950s, most notably the short film *Les Mistons* (The Mischief Makers, 1958). His first full-length film, *The 400 Blows* (1959), featuring his cinematic alter ego Antoine Doinel, immediately established him as a leader of French NEW WAVE cinema. Later films in the continuing Doinel series include *Love at Twenty* (1962),

Stolen Kisses (1968), *Bed and Board* (1970), and *Love on the Run* (1978).

Influenced by Jean Renoir, Jean Vigo, Alfred Hitchcock, and, not least, by Hollywood films of the 1930s and '40s, Truffaut explored a variety of film genres in *Shoot the Piano Player* (1960) and *The Bride Wore Black* (1967), takeoffs on FILM NOIR; *Mississippi Mermaid* (1969), in which Truffaut superimposes his own romantic stamp on a conventional mystery framework; and the science-fictional *Fahrenheit 451* (1966). *Jules and Jim* (1961), with its successful blend of narrative and structural approaches, is considered his masterpiece.

In his later work Truffaut was drawn into studies of human motivation and excessive passion, as exemplified by *The Wild Child* (1970), in which he appeared as Dr. Itard, and the hauntingly beautiful *The Story of Adèle H.* (1975), which traces the pathological career of Victor Hugo's daughter. Sometimes sentimental, Truffaut perhaps best expressed his elegance and irony in the Pirandellian *Day for Night* (1973). His last films include *The Last Métro* (1980) and *Confidentially Yours* (1984).   GAUTAM DASGUPTA

Bibliography: Crisp, C. G., *François Truffaut* (1972); Insdorf, Annette, *François Truffaut* (1978); Petrie, G., *The Cinema of François Truffaut* (1970); Truffaut, François, *The Films of My Life* (1975; Eng. trans., 1978).

truffle   [truhf'-uhl]

The truffle is a pungent wild fungus, highly prized as a food delicacy. The name is popularly used to describe both the fungus and its fruiting bodies. The truffle fungus is believed to have a symbiotic relationship with the roots of trees, particularly oak and beech trees. Agronomists have not been successful in cultivating truffles, but the fungus has often appeared where groves of oak and beech trees are planted. The edible part of the truffle is a spore-producing fruiting body that grows about 0.3 m (1 ft) underground. Most culinary truffles belong to the genus *Tuber* and are found in western Europe, although North Africa also produces a truffle in some quantity. (Truffles are occasionally found along the Pacific coast in the United States.) Depending on the species, their color varies from white to brown or black, and their size ranges from 2 to 15 cm (0.75 to 6 in). *T. melanosporum* is the famed black Périgord truffle of France. Trained dogs or pigs are used to sniff out the truffles, and 300 to 500 tons are harvested annually. An even more pungent and odoriferous white truffle, *T. magnatum*, grows in the Italian Piedmont area.

Bibliography: Gray, William D., *The Use of Fungi as Food and in Food Processing* (1971).

Trujillo, Rafael   [troo-hee'-oh]

Rafael Leonidas Trujillo Molina, b. Oct. 24, 1891, d. May 30, 1961, was dictator of the Dominican Republic. He joined the army in 1919, rose through the ranks, and became a general by 1927. A participant in the coup against President Horacio Vásquez in 1930, Trujillo ran unopposed for president of the republic later that year. By keeping a firm grip on the army, he dominated the government completely for the rest of his life. He was president until 1938 and then again from 1942 to 1952. After 1952 he gave the position to his brother, Hector, although he retained power behind the scenes.

Trujillo's reign was despotic and cruel. Civil liberties were almost nonexistent, and the secret police made arrests practically at will. He did, however, bring public order and economic stability to the island. Opposition grew, especially among Trujillo's Caribbean neighbors, and the Organization of American States finally voted to ostracize and censure him. He was assassinated by army leaders.

Bibliography: Crassweller, Robert D., *Trujillo: The Life and Times of a Caribbean Dictator* (1966); Diederich, Bernard, *Trujillo: The Death of the Goat* (1978); Galindez, Jesus de, *The Era of Trujillo, Dominican Dictator*, ed. by Russell H. Fitzgibbon (1973).

Truman, Harry S.

Harry S. Truman, 33d president of the United States (1945–53), carried on the New Deal reform tradition and committed the nation to the containment of Soviet power. His policies shaped American politics and diplomacy for a generation.

Early Life and Career. Truman was born on May 8, 1884, in Lamar, Mo. and spent his early life in Independence, Mo., near Kansas City. After graduating from high school, he worked at various jobs and then, in 1906, took over the family farm. He became active in Democratic politics, the Farm Bureau Federation, the Masonic Lodge, and the National Guard. After serving in France during World War I, he left the farm and became a partner in a men's clothing store in Kansas City, but the business failed in 1921.

Going into politics as an ally of Thomas J. PENDERGAST's Kansas City Democratic machine, Truman won election to the Jackson County Court (county commission) in 1922. Defeated in 1924, he was elected presiding judge in 1926 and held the office for 8 years.

In 1934, Truman was elected to the U.S. Senate, where he supported Franklin D. ROOSEVELT's New Deal. He barely won reelection in 1940. In 1941, however, Truman became chairman of a special Senate committee investigating inefficiency and corruption in World War II military spending programs. Widely praised for his committee work and liked throughout the Democratic party, he was chosen for the Democratic vice-presidential nomination in 1944, replacing Henry A. WALLACE. Vice-president for only 82 days, Truman became president when Roosevelt died on Apr. 12, 1945, and immediately faced serious foreign and domestic problems.

Presidency: First Term (1945–49). With Germany's surrender (May 8, 1945), differences with the USSR began to come into the open. Determined to dominate Eastern Europe and control at least a portion of Germany, the Soviet government claimed the prerogative of establishing spheres of influence in violation of the principles of democracy and self-determination that had justified the war for most Americans. In July the POTSDAM CONFERENCE, Truman's only personal meeting with Joseph Stalin, provided no settlement. While at Potsdam, Truman authorized the use of the just-perfected atomic bomb against Japan. After the bombing of Hiroshima (August 6) and Nagasaki (August 9), Japan surrendered unconditionally on Aug. 14, 1945.

When the war ended, relations with the USSR degenerated into COLD WAR. The United States protested Soviet behavior in Eastern Europe with no effect. The USSR also supported a Communist-led insurrection in Greece, pressured Turkey for control of the straits between the Black Sea and the Mediterranean, refused to withdraw wartime troops from northwestern Iran, and rejected an American proposal for United Nations control of atomic energy.

Truman countered with a policy of containment. In March 1946, reacting in part to American demands, the USSR pulled out of Iran. In March 1947, Truman asked Congress to vote heavy military and economic aid to Greece and Turkey and proclaimed the policy that became known as the Truman Doctrine—a program of assistance to countries resisting outside domination. The administration in 1947 also formulated the MARSHALL PLAN, an expensive, comprehensive program for the reconstruction of Western Europe. Partly in response the Russians staged a coup d'etat in Czechoslovakia in February 1948; they also blockaded the Western sector of Berlin (June 1948–May 1949) but were unable to force American withdrawal. Instead, the United States and the major non-Communist European nations negotiated the North Atlantic Treaty, forming NATO (see NORTH ATLANTIC TREATY ORGANIZATION), in 1949. Also in 1949, Truman introduced in Congress the POINT FOUR PROGRAM of technical aid for backward areas, intended to check the spread of communism.

Truman's domestic proposals, known as the FAIR DEAL, were built upon Roosevelt's New Deal and included broad social-welfare reforms. Willing to intervene extensively in the economy, Truman supported economic controls in times of emergency and backed legislation to underwrite full employment. He ordered (1948) the desegregation of the armed forces, let the Justice Department support blacks in civil rights cases, and was the first president since Reconstruction to have a legislative civil rights program.

HARRY S. TRUMAN
33d President of the United States (1945–53)

Nickname: "Give 'Em Hell Harry"
Born: May 8, 1884, Lamar, Mo.
Education: University of Kansas City Law School
Profession: Farmer, Public Official
Religious Affiliation: Baptist
Marriage: June 28, 1919, to Elizabeth Virginia Wallace
(1885–1982)
Children: Mary Margaret Truman (1924–   )
Political Affiliation: Democrat
Writings: *Memoirs* (2 vols., 1955–56)
Died: Dec. 26, 1972, Kansas City, Mo.
Buried: Independence, Mo.

Vice-President and Cabinet Members
Vice-President: Alben W. Barkley (1949–53)
Secretary of State: Edward R. Stettinius (1945); James
   F. Byrnes (1945–47); George C. Marshall (1947–49);
   Dean G. Acheson (1949–53)
Secretary of the Treasury: Henry Morgenthau, Jr.
   (1945); Frederick M. Vinson (1945–46); John W.
   Snyder (1946–53)
Secretary of War: Henry L. Stimson (1945); Robert P.
   Patterson (1945–47); Kenneth C. Royall (1947)
Secretary of Defense: James V. Forrestal (1947–49);
   Louis A. Johnson (1949–50); George C. Marshall
   (1950–51); Robert A. Lovett (1951–53)
Attorney General: Francis B. Biddle (1945); Thomas
   C. Clark (1945–49); J. Howard McGrath (1949–52)
Postmaster General: Frank C. Walker (1945); Robert
   E. Hannegan (1945–47); Jesse M. Donaldson
   (1947–53)
Secretary of the Navy: James V. Forrestal (1945–47)
Secretary of the Interior: Harold L. Ickes (1945–46);
   Julius A. Krug (1946–49); Oscar L. Chapman
   (1950–53)
Secretary of Agriculture: Claude R. Wickard (1945);
   Clinton P. Anderson (1945–48); Charles F. Brannan
   (1948–53)
Secretary of Commerce: Henry A. Wallace (1945–46);
   William Averell Harriman (1946–48); Charles Saw-
   yer (1948–53)
Secretary of Labor: Frances Perkins (1945); Lewis B.
   Schwellenbach (1945–48); Maurice J. Tobin
   (1949–53)

Although he attempted to maintain the New Deal political coalition, Truman's political position was nevertheless precarious during his first term. A poor speaker with little personal appeal, he seemed a weak leader by comparison with the charismatic Roosevelt. Although his foreign policy initiatives won assent on Capitol Hill, his domestic legislation fared poorly. A Democratic Congress rejected most of his proposals in 1945–46; its most important accomplishment, the Employment Act of 1946, established the Council of Economic Advisers but failed to guarantee full employment. During the period of severe postwar inflation, Truman's attempts to prevent major strikes, including seizure of the coal mines during a 1946 walkout, alienated labor unions, while his efforts to maintain price controls angered business and agricultural interests. In September 1946, Truman dismissed Secretary of Commerce Henry WALLACE for criticizing the administration's tough line toward the USSR. The result was further division in a Democratic party already divided by Southerners' anger over Truman's civil rights program. Consequently, the Democrats lost the congressional elections of 1946. In 1947–48, Truman regained labor support with his unsuccessful veto of the Taft-Hartley Act (or LABOR-MANAGEMENT RELATIONS ACT), and he spiritedly denounced as reactionary a Republican Congress that would not pass his domestic programs. Truman seemed certain, however, to be a one-term president.

In the election of 1948 he faced opposition not only from Republican Thomas E. DEWEY but also from left-wing and southern factions of his own party that backed the Progressive candidate, Wallace, and States Righter (Dixiecrat) Strom THURMOND. Barnstorming the country, Truman pleased crowds with his peppery "give 'em hell" style and successfully presented himself as a scrappy underdog champion of the common people against the privileged. He won a narrow but startling upset victory with 49.5 percent of the vote to Dewey's 45.1 percent. The Democrats, moreover, regained control of Congress.

Presidency: Second Term (1949–52). During his second term, Truman continued to work for domestic reforms but with limited success. He obtained increases in several ongoing New Deal programs, such as social security. He also secured passage of the Housing Act of 1949, which provided extensive federal subsidies for low- and middle-income housing. The other elements of his program all died in Congress.

By the end of 1949 reverses in the cold war had made communism the nation's major domestic issue. In mid-1949 the Chinese Nationalist government of CHIANG KAI-SHEK retreated to Taiwan, abandoning the mainland to the Communists. The Truman administration had sharply reduced American aid to the corrupt and inefficient Nationalists, and now, in the eyes of many, was responsible for the loss of China. Almost at the same time, moreover, the administration announced that the USSR had tested its first atomic bomb. Shortly thereafter came a stunning series of Communist espionage cases, including those of Alger HISS and Julius and Ethel ROSENBERG, that involved U.S. atomic secrets and possible penetration of sensitive government offices. Although Truman had authorized a stringent program of loyalty investigations of federal employees in 1947, he now came under wide attack for having been soft on Communist subversion. In early 1950, Republican Sen. Joseph R. MCCARTHY assumed leadership of the assault with repeated charges of Communist infiltration of the State Department and other key government agencies. With McCarthyism flourishing, Congress passed (1950), over Truman's veto, the MCCARRAN ACT, which restricted the civil rights of Communists.

Truman's prompt intervention in response to the invasion of South Korea by the Communist North in June 1950 brought him only more difficulties. By early 1951 the KOREAN WAR was at a frustrating stalemate. The president dismissed Gen. Douglas MACARTHUR for advocating drastic military measures against the Communists and, as a result, faced widespread disapproval. When Truman seized the steel industry in 1952 to avoid a strike and maintain defense production, the U.S. Supreme Court declared the seizure unconstitutional. Further weakened by discoveries of corruption in his administration, Truman announced in March 1952 that he would not run for reelection. Adlai E. Stevenson, his choice for the Democratic presidential nomination, lost the election to Dwight D. Eisenhower. In retirement, Truman remained active in politics, wrote his *Memoirs* (2 vols., 1955–56) and *Mr. Citizen* (1960), lectured extensively, and helped establish the Truman Library. In the final years of his life he became almost a folk hero. Truman died on Dec. 26, 1972.   ALONZO L. HAMBY

Bibliography: Bernstein, Barton J., ed., *Politics and Policies of the Truman Administration* (1970); Donovan, Robert J., *Conflict and Crisis: The Presidency of Harry S. Truman, 1945-1948* (1977); Hamby, Alonzo L., *Beyond the New Deal: Harry S. Truman and American Liberalism* (1973) and, as ed., *Harry S. Truman and the Fair Deal* (1974); Hillman, William, ed., *Mr. President* (1952); Miller, Merle, *Plain Speaking* (1974); Phillips, Cabell, *The Truman Presidency* (1966); Truman, Margaret, *Harry S. Truman* (1972).

Trumbull, John

An American painter whose works record the people and events connected with the nation's founding, John Trumbull, b. Lebanon, Conn., June 6, 1756, d. Nov. 10, 1843, was the son of Connecticut's governor and among the first educated, native-born Americans to dedicate themselves to painting. Hoping to ennoble art through his pictorial documentation of the American Revolution, Trumbull took part in the war as an aide-de-camp to George Washington and personally knew the patriots and leaders of the period.

Trumbull studied with Benjamin West in London and while abroad produced some of his best paintings—a series of small-scale portraits of Americans and several historical scenes. One of these, *The Battle of Bunker's Hill* (1786; Yale University Art Gallery, New Haven, Conn.), composed of many figures in close combat, is organized along a sweeping diagonal; the dramatic contrasts of light and shadow culminate in the highlighted soldier dying in the arms of a comrade.

Trumbull's hopes of becoming his nation's official history painter were frustrated until 1817, when Congress commissioned him to paint four scenes from the war for the Rotunda of the Capitol—a project Trumbull had conceived about 30 years earlier. Unfortunately his talents were no longer equal to the task. One of these scenes, *The Declaration of Independence* (1818), is an example of the rather dry and mechanically executed work of his later career. In 1817 he was ap-

pointed director of the American Academy of the Fine Arts in New York City, from which he retired in 1836. In 1831, Trumbull gave his art collection to Yale University.   PHILIP GOULD

Bibliography: Jaffe, Irma B., *John Trumbull, Patriot-Artist of the American Revolution* (1975); Sizer, Theodore, *The Works of Colonel John Trumbull: Artist of the American Revolution*, rev. ed. (1967); Trumbull, John, *The Autobiography of Colonel John Trumbull*, ed. by Theodore Sizer, rev. ed. (1953).

Trumbull, Jonathan

Jonathan Trumbull, b. Lebanon, Conn., Oct. 12, 1710, d. Aug. 17, 1785, a merchant and governor of Connecticut (1796-84) during the American Revolution, was the only colonial governor who supported the independence movement. With Trumbull's leadership, Connecticut provided important supplies for the Continental Army.

Bibliography: Roth, David Morris, *Connecticut's War Governor, Jonathan Trumbull* (1974); Weaver, Glenn, *Jonathan Trumbull, Connecticut's Merchant Magistrate, 1710-1785* (1956).

Trumbull, Lyman

Lyman Trumbull, b. Colchester, Conn., Oct. 12, 1813, d. June 25, 1896, was a leading Republican politician during the Civil War and Reconstruction era. Settling in Illinois as a young man, he was elected to the U.S. Senate in 1854.

Trumbull was known as an able constitutionalist and a man of conscience. Originally a Democrat, he became a Free-Soil Republican. A strong supporter of the Union war effort, he nevertheless criticized Abraham Lincoln's wartime use of executive power. Although opposed to Andrew Johnson's Reconstruction policies, Trumbull was one of seven Republicans who voted against convicting Johnson during the Senate impeachment trial. Dismayed by Republican corruption under the Grant regime, he joined the Liberal Republican bolt in 1872, subsequently returning to the Democratic party. He remained politically active after leaving the Senate in 1873 but never again held elective office.   GERALD W. MCFARLAND

Bibliography: Krug, Mark M., *Lyman Trumbull, Conservative Radical* (1965).

trumpet

A trumpet is a tube whose enclosed air column is vibrated by buzzing the lips on a mouth hole or mouthpiece. This tube

John Trumbull's The Battle of Bunker's Hill (1786) is typical of his representations of scenes from the American Revolution in its emotional intensity and nationalistic subject. Dramatic lighting, careful composition, and forceful movement emphasize the focal point, the death of a soldier. (Yale University Art Gallery, New Haven, Conn.)

The modern trumpet emits clear, ringing tones when air in its brass bore is set in vibration. The three valves direct air through the instrument's tubing, varying the pitch by altering the length of the air column. Playing position is shown (left).

originally was a hollow log or bone, then a cane, and ultimately a metal or ivory instrument. The loud blasts of these primitive instruments banished evil spirits and summoned gods. In later periods the trumpet was used in ritual and war.

By 1400 the unwieldy Western straight trumpet was often bent into an S shape. By 1500 the S shape was condensed to the contemporary single-form loop, which resembles the trumpet of Claudio Monteverdi and J. S. Bach. The 7-ft (2.1-m) tube pitched in D (with attachable C-loop) was designed to produce well-articulated pitches through the fourth octave of the harmonic series. The natural trumpet, although difficult to master, could be used with brilliant and impressive melodic effect in its highest (clarino) range. Trumpets were traditionally reserved for royalty, who created restrictive guilds to guard the privilege and prestige of clarino trumpeters.

In the classic period (late 18th century), the demanding clarino technique became outmoded. Trumpets were shortened, which placed the five remaining usable partials in the treble range, first to F with crooks from E to C, then to the presently standard B-flat with A-slide. Partially successful attempts to adopt a slide extension were made. Valves, first applied in 1824, were considered unnecessary and made little impression before the mid-19th century; their use did not achieve full melodic potential until later.

Recently a 4-ft (1.2-m) trumpet in high C has been adopted by many orchestral musicians, and trumpets in high D, F, and piccolo B-flat are used for performances of baroque music. Richard Wagner made use of a bass trumpet in C in *The Ring of the Nibelung*. A cone of wood or fiber, called a mute, is often used with the trumpet to produce special effects.

ROBERT A. WARNER

Bibliography: Johnson, Keith, *The Art of Trumpet Playing* (1981); Menke, Werner, *History of the Trumpet of Bach and Handel*, rev. ed. trans. by Gerald Abraham (1960; repr. 1986); Sherman, Roger C., *The Trumpeter's Handbook* (1979).

trumpet creeper

Trumpet creeper is the common name for two species of the genus *Campsis* in the Bignoniaceae family. These deciduous shrubs use aerial roots for climbing. They produce dark, shining pinnate leaves and trumpet-shaped scarlet or orange flowers 6 to 8 cm (3 in) long.

trumpet tree

The name trumpet tree is applied to approximately 100 species of woody plants in the genus *Tabebuia,* family Bignoniaceae, that are native to tropical America. Several species of *Tabebuia* produce excellent timber, including *T. rosea* and *T. serratifolia*. Some trumpet trees have large, colorful flowers and are often planted as street trees.

trumpeter

Trumpeters are three species of large, mostly black birds known for their deep, loud, trumpetlike cry. They are classified in the genus *Psophia*, family Psophiidae, and are found in tropical forests of South America. They are thought to be related to cranes and rails and are placed with them in the order Gruiformes. Trumpeters are pheasant-sized—43 to 53 cm (17 to 21 in) long—with a moderately long neck, rounded wings, long legs, and short tail. The head is small and rounded and the bill stout and slightly downcurved. The plumage is soft and has a velvety appearance on the head and neck. The common trumpeter, *Psophia crepitans*, has gray on the wings and back; the white-winged trumpeter, *P. leucoptera*, is white on the wings, and the green-winged trumpeter, *P. viridis*, is green on the wings and brown on the back. Highly gregarious, trumpeters gather in flocks of up to 20 birds on the forest floor. They are reluctant to fly and sometimes escape enemies by running. They roost in trees and nest in tree holes.

ROBERT J. RAIKOW

Trumpler, Robert Julius

The Swiss-born American astronomer Robert Julius Trumpler, b. Oct. 2, 1886, d. Sept. 10, 1956, demonstrated (1930) that interstellar dust dimmed and reddened the light from distant stars, making them appear much farther away than they actually are. His discovery that massive blue stars predominate in some galactic clusters, whereas yellow and red giants predominate in others, led to current theories of stellar evolution. After immigrating (1915) to the United States, Trumpler worked (1919–51) at Lick Observatory.

truss

A truss is a term used in engineering or architecture to refer to a structure formed by connecting the ends of straight pieces of metal or wood to form a series of triangles lying in a single plane. The design of a truss is based on the principle that a triangle is a rigid configuration that cannot collapse or change its shape unless the length of one of the sides is changed. A truss consists of several triangular structures, each exerting pressure against the other, capable of supporting considerable weight over a large span.

The first trusses were most likely made of wood and used for building homes and roofs. During the 18th and early 19th centuries cast and wrought iron were used, and later in the 19th century steel became the preferred truss material.

Trusses are used for the construction of railroad bridges and iron-frame buildings and in roof and floor systems. They are also used in the construction of certain industrial machines and in the design of aircraft and automobile frames.

The truss, a rigid construction framework consisting of triangles, can bear greater loads than a nontriangular counterpart. Various types of trusses have been designed for roofs, such as the Fink and Pratt, and for suspension bridges, such as the Pratt and Warren. The vertical and diagonal members of a truss are called the web.

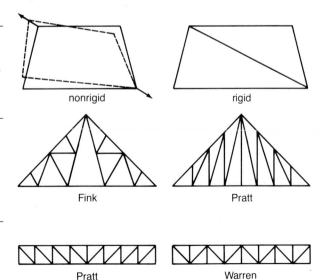

nonrigid   rigid

Fink   Pratt

Pratt   Warren

trust

In law, a trust is a form of property ownership in which one person agrees to hold property for the benefit of another. The person holding the property is called the trustee, and the person who benefits is called the beneficiary. (For information on the trust as an entity in business and industry, see CARTEL; MONOPOLY AND COMPETITION.)

Fiduciary Relationship. The duty of the trustee is to manage the property solely in the interest of the beneficiary. This is called a fiduciary relationship because the trustee is expected to act in good faith and to work loyally for the interest of the beneficiary. The beneficiary has no power or right to tell the trustee how to perform his or her tasks—for example, what stocks or bonds to buy or sell. The trustee is regarded as the legal owner of the property, the beneficiary as the equitable owner. Thus, in the eyes of the law the trust involves dual ownership: the trustee has the right to administer the property, and the beneficiary has the right to enjoy its benefits. If the beneficiary believes that the trustee is not acting in his or her best interests, the only recourse is to file a law suit against the trustee.

Origin of the Trust Concept. The trust institution exists only in Great Britain, the United States, and other countries whose legal systems are derived from British COMMON LAW. The origin of the trust concept lies in the dual system of courts that grew up in England. In addition to the traditional judicial system, a separate and somewhat competing entity, the court of chancery or EQUITY, also developed. The traditional law courts treated the trustee as the owner of the property. If a beneficiary claimed that the trustee had not fulfilled his duty to hold the property in trust for the beneficiary, the latter could get no relief in the law courts. The court of equity, however, was willing to step in and prevent the trustee from handling the property in any way other than for the advantage of the beneficiary. Thus the rights of the beneficiary came to be called those of equitable ownership, because only the equity court would protect them.

The Testamentary Trust. A trust created in a WILL is called a testamentary trust. Such a trust is most commonly used in family situations. For example, a father who is a successful businessman may have several small children. He wishes to leave his property to his wife and the children if he should die, but his wife does not want the responsibility of managing the property, and the children are too young to do so. The father, in his will, can leave his property to a trustee, such as a bank. The bank will be instructed to invest and reinvest the property as it deems best. It will pay out the income from the property to the man's wife for her life, and then to the children until they reach a certain age, such as 25. After that it will turn the property over to the children, and the trust will terminate.

The Inter Vivos Trust. In the foregoing example the father created the trust in his will, to take effect upon his death. Trusts also may be created *inter vivos*, a Latin phrase used by lawyers that means "between the living." Thus the father could have transferred his property to the bank in trust while he was still alive. The bank would have paid the income to him until he died, and then, to the wife and children.

The creator, or settlor, of an *inter vivos* trust may retain the right to revoke the trust at any time. If the creator does retain that right it is called a revocable trust. A revocable trust is, in effect, a conditional gift to the beneficiaries, because it may be revoked at any time by the settlor. This feature of a revocable trust contrasts with the normal rule of law relating to gifts, which is that a gift once given cannot be revoked.

The trust arrangement is also used in a variety of situations in which it seems desirable to separate the management and control of property from the beneficiaries. A trust may be established for charitable purposes, such as providing scholarships for needy students. Pension trusts are established by business firms to provide retirement benefits for their employees. Insurance trusts can be used to hold insurance policies and to dispose of the proceeds upon the death of the insured. Another reason trusts are instituted is to prevent estate shrink-

age through debts, taxes, and expenses.

Trustees. Because of the broad powers given to the trustee, selection of the trustee is done with great care. Commercial institutions have arisen that engage specifically in the business of acting as trustees. They are paid a fee out of the income of the trust. Usually such commercial trustees are also engaged in the banking business. They often have the word *trust* in their bank name and maintain a trust department that is separate from their banking activities. In the United States approximately 3,000 institutions—banking and nonbanking—act as trustees.   JOHN M. STEADMAN

Bibliography: Haskell, Paul G., *Preface to the Law of Trust* (1975); Lehrman, A. M., *The Complete Book of Wills and Trusts* (1978); Starchild, A., *Building Wealth: A Layman's Guide to Trust Planning* (1981).

trust territory

A trust territory is a territory that is administered by another country under supervision of the United Nations Trusteeship Council. The council is composed of member nations that administer trust territories and permanent nonadministering Security Council members. Each trust territory has been governed by the provisions of a trusteeship agreement. Such an agreement usually gave the administering state full legislative, administrative, and judicial powers over the territory.

The 11 trust territories established after World War II were former German colonies in Africa and the Pacific that had been administered by various countries under the mandate system of the League of Nations between World Wars I and II (with the exception of former Italian Somaliland, returned to Italian administration as a trust territory in 1950). Unlike the mandate system, the system of trust territories was intended to advance the indigenous inhabitants toward self-government. By 1975, ten of the trust territories had gained independence or chosen to become part of other nations. The British-administered trust territory of TOGOLAND merged with the Gold Coast (now Ghana) in 1956, while French-administered Togoland became the independent nation of Togo in 1960. Also in 1960, Italian-administered Somaliland merged with the British protectorate of Somaliland to form independent Somalia, and French-administered Cameroons became the independent nation of Cameroon. In 1961 the southern part of British-administered Cameroons voted to unite with Cameroon; the northern part voted for union with Nigeria. Tanganyika, also administered by Great Britain, gained independence that same year (see TANZANIA). Belgian-administered RUANDA-URUNDI divided into the nations of Rwanda and Burundi in 1962. Western Samoa, administered by New Zealand, gained independence in 1962; independence came in 1968 for Nauru, administered by Australia and on behalf of New Zealand and Great Britain. Australian-administered New Guinea was united administratively with the Australian dependency of Papua in 1949; the two gained independence as Papua New Guinea in 1975.

The sole remaining trust territory is the U.S.-administered Trust Territory of the Pacific Islands (see PACIFIC ISLANDS, TRUST TERRITORY OF THE). It has been divided into the Commonwealth of the Northern Marianas, the Marshall Islands, the Federated States of Micronesia, and the Republic of Palau (Belau). All four entities are internally self-governing but will remain technically part of the trust territory until the trusteeship is formally terminated by the United Nations. Due to U.S. security requirements, this is the only trust territory designated a "strategic area" under the UN Charter; trusteeship functions are exercised by the Security Council.

Bibliography: Mezerik, A. G., ed., *Colonialism and the United Nations* (1964); Murray, J. N., *The United Nations Trusteeship System* (1957); Toussaint, C. E., *The Trusteeship System of the United Nations* (1957).

trustee

A trustee is a person who has been given legal title to property (the TRUST) bequeathed or deeded (by the trustor or settlor) for the benefit of another (the equitable owner, or beneficiary). In drawing up a WILL, the trustor may put property in trust by designating a trustee to manage it.

In the United States the use of trustees became significant in the 1820s as wealthy individuals began drawing up wills that created property trusts and named trustee managers. Until 1830, however, the responsibilities of the trustees were somewhat restricted. The trustee was, for example, allowed to invest a trust's money only in government bonds or first mortgages on land. Then a Massachusetts court handed down a decision containing the "prudent investor" rule, allowing the trustee to make other investments, such as in sound corporate stocks. By the middle of the 19th century corporations had learned to create monopolies by having voting shares of competing firms controlled by the same trustees. This led to the passage of antitrust laws (see MONOPOLY AND COMPETITION).

Bibliography: Dukeminier, Jesse, and Johanson, Stanley, *Wills, Trusts and Estates*, 3d ed. (1984).

Truth, Sojourner

Sojourner Truth was a charismatic evangelist who traveled through the United States during the 19th century preaching on behalf of abolition of slavery and women's rights. Born into slavery and unable to read or write, she acted in obedience to visions and voices she claimed to receive. After the Civil War she helped in the resettlement of emancipated slaves.

Sojourner Truth, b. Hurley, N.Y., c.1797, d. Nov. 26, 1883, was an American preacher, abolitionist, and feminist. Born into slavery and given the name Isabella Baumfree, she ran away when her master refused to acknowledge New York's emancipation act of 1827. After settling in New York City, she became involved with a religious cult but, disillusioned, broke with it in 1843, adopting her new name as symbolic of her spiritual mission. Thereafter, Sojourner Truth took up the struggle for black emancipation and women's suffrage, becoming the leading black woman orator. After the U.S. Civil War she continued to work on behalf of both blacks and women.   RONALD L. LEWIS

Bibliography: Bernard, Jacqueline, *Journey Toward Freedom: The Story of Sojourner Truth* (1967); Gilbert, Olive, *Narrative of Sojourner Truth* (1878; repr. 1968); Ortiz, Victoria, *Sojourner Truth, a Self-made Woman* (1974).

trypanosomiasis   [truh-pan-uh-soh-my'-uh-sis]

Trypanosomiasis is a disease caused by parasitic protozoa of the family Trypanosomidae, which also contains the protozoa that cause LEISHMANIASIS. In humans, two variations of *Trypanosoma brucei*—*T. b. gambiense* and *T. b. rhodesiense*—cause African sleeping sickness, while *T. cruzi* causes Chagas's disease, or South American trypanosomiasis. Both *T. brucei* and *T. vivax*, which cause animal trypanosomiasis in Africa, have spread to South America.

African sleeping sickness is transmitted by the bite of an infected TSETSE FLY. In humans the first symptom is a local inflammation (trypanosomal chancre) at the site of the bite. Systemic symptoms follow, such as fever and chills, headache, edema of the extremities, and enlargement of the lymph glands. Damage to the central nervous system may take years to develop, but it is manifested by sleepiness, lethargy, headache, and eventually motor disturbances, convulsions, and

coma; without treatment, the disease is fatal. Antimicrobial agents have been found effective against trypanosomiasis if given early in the disease. Vaccine research is being conducted, but it is complicated by the parasite's ability to alter its antigens once inside a host.

Chagas's disease is transmitted to humans by a predatory bug, *Triatoma;* the bite wound is contaminated by the insect's feces, which contain the parasite. *T. cruzi* is carried by both wild and domesticated animals. The disease is characterized by fever, spleen and liver enlargement, and nervous-system and heart-muscle damage. The acute form of the disease is usually confined to children and can be fatal. No universally effective treatment exists.   PETER L. PETRAKIS

Bibliography: Ford, John, *Role of the Trypanosomiases in African Ecology* (1971); Kolata, Gina, "Scrutinizing Sleeping Sickness," *Science*, Nov. 23, 1984; McKelvey, John H., *Man against Tsetse* (1973).

Ts'ao Chih   (Cao Zhi)   [tsow ji]

The Chinese poet and essayist Ts'ao Chih, 192–232, was the third son of Ts'ao Ts'ao and younger brother of Ts'ao P'ei, who became Emperor Wen of the Wei dynasty. Ts'ao Chih's precocious literary talent won the admiration of his father, who had once considered him for the throne. This aroused the jealousy of his brother, the emperor, who made his life miserable and sent him into exile, where he died. Ts'ao Chih excelled in lyrical poetry, especially in the five-syllable verse form. His poems are charged with intense mental anguish and pessimism.   ANGELA JUNG PALANDRI

Ts'ao Hsüeh-Ch'in   (Cao Xueqin)   [tsow shwe-chin]

Ts'ao Hsüeh-Ch'in, b. c.1717, d. Feb. 12, 1763, is best remembered as the author of The DREAM OF THE RED CHAMBER, one of the greatest Chinese novels. Born into a wealthy and powerful family, Ts'ao died in poverty, the wrongdoings of a relative having led to the family's downfall in 1728. His novel—said to be inspired by the vicissitudes of his own life—first appeared in 80 chapters, but in later editions 40 more were added by the editor Kao O, who claimed to have found them among the author's papers.   ANGELA JUNG PALANDRI

Ts'ao Yü   (Cao Yu)   [tsow yoo]

The Chinese writer Ts'ao Yü, also known as Wan Chia-pao, b. 1910, introduced Western-style drama to China. The most notable of his six early plays, *The Thunderstorm* (1934; Eng. trans., 1958), was inspired by Ibsen and sets the disintegration of a family against the backdrop of an approaching storm. Ts'ao Yü studied Western literature at Ch'ing-hua University in Peking and after a lapse of 15 years began writing plays again in 1956.

Tsedenbal, Yumzhagiyen   [sed-uhn-bahl', yuhm-zah-gyuhn]

The Mongolian Communist leader Yumzhagiyen Tsedenbal, b. Sept. 17, 1916, served as secretary-general of the Central Committee of the Mongolian People's Republic from 1940 to 1954 and headed the party from 1958 to 1984. He was head of state from 1974 until his retirement in 1984.

Tseng Kuo-fan   (Zeng Guofan)   [dzung gwah-fahn]

A loyal official of the CH'ING dynasty, Tseng Kuo-fan, b. Nov. 26, 1811, d. Mar. 12, 1872, was a Chinese scholar in the traditional mold. Admitted at the age of 28 to the Hanlin Academy, Tseng thereafter rose rapidly in Ch'ing court circles, partly due to the sponsorship of the powerful grand councillor Mu-chang-a. The Hsiang army, raised (1853) by Tseng in his native Hunan province by order of the Ch'ing, became the model for the armies of his protégés LI HUNG-CHANG and TSO TSUNG-T'ANG. Tseng coordinated the campaign by these provincial armies that finally suppressed the TAIPING REBELLION

(1850–64). He was also the chief architect of the T'ung-chih Restoration (1862–74), an attempt to buttress Ch'ing rule.

Bibliography: Hail, William James, *Tseng Kuo-fan and the Taiping Rebellion* (1927; repr. 1964).

tsetse fly   [tset'-see]

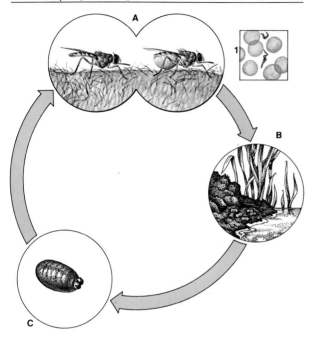

Tsetse flies, genus Glossina, are African insects that transmit deadly sleeping sickness to humans and the pernicious disease nagana to cattle. An adult fly, G. palpalis, sucks blood from a human arm (A; before and after feeding). Trypanosomes (1), parasitic flagellate protozoans, injected into the blood cause sleeping sickness. The female tsetse fly hatches her eggs internally and lays living larvae on soil near water (B). The larvae burrow into the soil within an hour and become pupae. In 4 weeks the pupa (C) becomes an adult.

Found only in Africa, primarily south of the Tropic of Cancer, tsetse flies are two-winged flies that carry parasites that cause serious illness in humans and domesticated animals. About 22 species make up the genus *Glossina*, family Glossinidae. Tsetse flies are about 0.6 to 1.2 cm (0.25 to 0.5 in) long and usually hold the wings flat against the body. They vary from light yellow brown to dark brown, some with black abdominal bands. Adults depend on blood for survival and are equipped with piercing mouthparts with which they bite and suck blood from their victims. As they suck they transmit parasites of the genus *Trypanosoma* (see TRYPANOSOMIASIS), some of which cause African sleeping sickness in humans and others of which cause nagana, an animal disease. Full-grown larvae, born singly at intervals of about 10 to 15 days, are deposited in mangrove roots and in the shade of other vegetation where soils are moist and loose. International research programs are attempting to deal with the tsetse problem. ROBERT NOVAK AND GEORGE CRAIG

Bibliography: McKelvey, John H., Jr., *Man Against Tsetse* (1973).

Tshombe, Moise Kapenda   [chohm'-bay, moh-ees' kuh-pen'-dah]

The Congolese politician Moise Kapenda Tshombe, b. Nov. 19, 1919, d. June 28, 1969, led the province of Katanga (now SHABA) in its period (1960–63) of secession from the newly independent Republic of the Congo (now Zaire). Tshombe was educated in mission schools and subsequently served as a member of the Katanga Provincial Council (1951–53). In 1959 he became president of the Rassemblement Katangais (CONAKAT; Confédération des Associations Tribales du Ka-

tanga), a party supported mainly by members of the Lunda tribe. At the Belgo-African Conference, held at Brussels in 1960 to prepare the Belgian Congo for independence, Tshombe called for a loose federation of provinces, closely tied to Belgium. The conference rejected his proposal, and when the Congo achieved its independence that year as a centralized republic, Tshombe was elected provincial president of Katanga. Shortly afterward he declared Katanga to be independent, but the insurgent province, rich in copper and other resources, was crushed by the central government with the aid of United Nations troops. In 1963, Tshombe agreed to give up his secessionist plans and fled to Spain. In 1964, President Joseph KASAVUBU of the Congo asked him to form a government, but in 1965, Tshombe was dismissed from the premiership—partly because he used white mercenaries to put down a rebellion. He returned to Spain but was later kidnapped—to prevent his return to the Congo—and taken to Algeria, where he remained under house arrest until his death. He wrote *My Fifteen Months in Government* (Eng. trans., 1967). L. H. GANN

The controversial Zairian political figure Moise Kapenda Tshombe declared the independence of the mineral-rich Katanga (now Shaba) province of the Congo (now Zaire) in 1960. His secession plan failed when UN troops defeated his mercenary army after a 3-year struggle.

Bibliography: Colvin, Ian Goodhope, *The Rise and Fall of Moise Tshombe: A Biography* (1968).

Tsimshian   [tsim'-shee-uhn]

Tsimshian, a North American Indian tribe of the Northwest Coast area, traditionally included a loose confederacy of nine tribes, with salmon-fishing and berrying grounds on the lower Skeena River and winter villages along Metlakatla Pass west of modern Prince Rupert. Two more Tsimshian tribes had villages just below the Skeena canyon, and three more lived on Douglas Channel and on Porcher and Swindle islands. The term also refers to the language that was spoken by the Gitksan and Niska.

Each tribe had four divisions, one for each major matrilineal kin group. All were salmon fishers; coastal tribes were also deep-sea fishers and sea hunters. Men of riverine tribes excelled as land hunters. The nine Coast tribes and the Niska held exclusive rights to separate olachon fishing grounds at the mouth of the Nass River. Oil rendered from these fish harvested in enormous quantities was an important food and a valuable barter item. The Tsimshian traded it to the HAIDA for huge canoes, carved boxes, and dried halibut, and to the TLINGIT for plaques of copper and mountain-goat wool robes.

The Tsimshian, Gitksan, and Niska carvers of memorial poles, masks, and elegant raven rattles were often hired by chiefs of other groups. Within each tribe each matriclan had its chief, who inherited the position from his mother's eldest brother. Close kin were considered lesser chiefs or nobles. Other clan members were commoners. A chief might have one or more slaves, or chattels, not considered members of society. Chiefs gave POTLATCHES to commemorate predecessors and honor heirs. Many chiefs held rights to ceremonies of KWAKIUTL origin.

After 1834 the nine confederated tribes built winter houses near Hudson Bay Company's Fort (now Port) Simpson. The missionary William Duncan worked among the Tsimshian beginning in 1857. Eventually he moved his converts to build a model community at Metlakatla, where they adopted white lifeways and abandoned their Indian past. Duncan later quarreled with his bishop and moved with most of his congregation to Alaska, where the U.S. Congress gave them the right to settle on Annette Island at "New Metlakatla." Today the Tsimshian number about 12,000 and live on reservations in British Columbia and Alaska.   PHILIP DRUCKER

Bibliography: Boas, Franz, *Tsimshian Mythology* (1916; repr. 1970); Durlach, Theresa, *The Relationship Systems of the Tlingit, Haida, and Tsimshian* (1928; repr. 1974); Garfield, Viola E., and Wingert, Paul S., *Tsimshian Indians and Their Arts* (1966); Miller, Jay, and Eastman, Carol, eds., *The Tsimshian and Other Peoples of the Northwest Coast* (1984).

Tsin: see CHIN (dynasties).

Tsinan (Jinan) [jee'-nahn]

Tsinan, the capital of Shantung (Shandong) province in eastern China, lies just south of the Hwang Ho (Yellow River), 370 km (230 mi) south of Peking. The city (1983 est. pop., 1,360,000) is a commercial, educational, and transportation center for the province. Industries include food processing, textiles, iron and steel, electrical parts, machine tools, paper, and chemicals. Archaeological remains indicate that Tsinan was settled during the Shang dynasty (c.1600–c.1027 BC). The Venetian traveler Marco Polo visited the city in the 13th century. Occupied by the Japanese from 1937 to 1945, it was taken by the Communists after a major battle in 1948.

Tsinghai (Qinghai) [ching'-hy]

Tsinghai is a mountainous province in west central China, with an area of 721,000 km² (278,400 mi²) and a population of 3,930,000 (1983 est.) composed of Tibetans, Han Chinese, Mongols, and other ethnic groups. The capital is Hsi-ning (Xining; 1982 pop., 364,000). The province forms the northeastern section of the Tibetan plateau. The two largest Chinese rivers, the Hwang Ho and the Yangtze, have their headwaters there. The economy is based on the cultivation of spring wheat, barley, potatoes, and fruits and on sheep raising and horse breeding. Petroleum fields in the Tsaidam (Qaidam) Basin in the northwest have been worked since the late 1950s, and coal is mined in the northeast.

Because of its remote location, Tsinghai came under Chinese control as late as the 3d century BC. It has been a province of China since 1928.

Tsingtao (Qingdao) [ching'-dao]

Tsingtao, a city in northern China, is the largest industrial center in Shantung (Shandong) province and is located on a hilly promontory on the southeast shore of Chiao-chou (Jiazhou) Bay, an inlet of the Yellow Sea. Its population is 1,210,000 (1983 est.). Tsingtao is essentially an industrial port city. Cotton and silk fabrics, textile machinery, diesel locomotives, and railroad cars are among its manufactures. The city has an excellent natural harbor and is able to accommodate large oceangoing vessels. It also has an important naval base. Tsingtao is a popular health and summer resort. The city is the home of Shantung University (1926). Originally a small fishing village, Tsingtao became a trade center during the Ch'ing dynasty (1644–1911). Its history as a modern city dates from 1898, when it became a German leased territory. Japan occupied the city in 1914–22 and 1938–45.   JAMES CHAN

Tsiolkovsky, Konstantin [tsee-ohl-kahv'-skee]

Konstantin Tsiolkovsky conducted pioneering research in the field of astronautics. A self-taught scientist, he worked on many theoretical aspects of rocketry and reactive thrust, including the use of liquid fuels and multistage rockets, human spaceflight, and space colonization. Among the young engineers whose rocket-building efforts he encouraged was Sergei Korolev, the chief designer of Soviet spacecraft in the 1950s and 1960s.

Konstantin Eduardovich Tsiolkovsky (also Ziolkowsky), b. Sept. 17 (N.S.), 1857, d. Sept. 19, 1935, was a visionary Russian theorist and writer on space travel who, decades ahead of his time, forecast many of the features of modern astronautics. Although nearly deaf from a childhood bout with scarlet fever, Tsiolkovsky educated himself and became a high school teacher of mathematics. Among his articles, which attracted little notice outside Russia, was "Research into Interplanetary Space by Means of Rocket Power" (1903); it described the motion of a rocket in vacuum and weightlessness. He also wrote science-fiction accounts of space adventures in which he accurately described artificial satellites, spacesuits, space colonies, and asteroid mining. These books include *On the Moon* (1895), *Dreams of the Earth and Sky* (1895), and *Beyond the Earth* (1920).

Following the publication of the works of astronautics pioneer Hermann Oberth in 1923, Tsiolkovsky's earlier articles were republished, enjoying great popularity in Russia and finally earning him a measure of international recognition. There is a museum honoring Tsiolkovsky's achievements in Kaluga, where he taught, and a prominent crater on the back of the Moon is named for him.   JAMES E. OBERG

Bibliography: Blagonravov, A. A., ed., *K. E. Tsiolkovsky: Selected Works* (1968); Ley, Willy, *Rockets, Missiles and Men in Space*, rev. ed. (1968); Oberg, James E., "The Why of Sputnik," *Space World*, December 1977.

Tso Tsung-t'ang (Zuo Zongtang) [dzoh dzoong-tahng]

The Chinese general and statesman Tso Tsung-t'ang, b. Nov. 10, 1812, d. Sept. 5, 1885, helped revitalize the foundering CH'ING dynasty (1644–1911). With LI HUNG-CHANG and TSENG KUO-FAN he quelled the TAIPING REBELLION, subsequently becoming governor of his native Hunan province, governor general of Fukien and Chekiang provinces, military commander in campaigns against the Nien and Chinese Muslim rebellions, and court advisor on a wide range of subjects. An advocate of modernization for the Chinese military, Tso arranged for the foreign purchase as well as the domestic manufacture of modern arms; in 1866 he founded an arsenal, navy yard, and technical school at Foochow.

Bibliography: Bales, W. L., *Tso Tsung-t'ang: Soldier and Statesman of Old China* (1937); Chen, Gideon, *Tso Tsung-t'ang: Pioneer Promoter of the Modern Dockyard and the Woolen Mill in China* (1961).

Tsubouchi Shoyo [tsoo-boh-oo-chee shoh'-yoh]

Tsubouchi Shoyo, b. June 22, 1859, d. Feb. 28, 1935, was a Japanese critic, novelist, playwright, and translator. In his pioneering essay, "The Essence of the Novel" (1885; partial Eng. trans., 1956), he urged writers to treat fiction as a serious art form and championed psychological realism and the vernacular style. Although himself unsuccessful in putting his theories into practice, Tsubouchi spurred others to create a truly modern idiom.   EDWARD B. FOWLER

Tsukuba   [tsu'-ku-bah]

Tsukuba (Science City), a city in Japan about 60 km (37 mi) northeast of Tokyo, was founded in 1963 by the Japanese government to serve as headquarters for the country's basic scientific and engineering research. Built in what was once an area of forests and farms, Tsukuba has a campuslike atmosphere designed to encourage original research. Its modern laboratories and other facilities house a large number of government and private research institutes and the University of Tsukuba (formerly Tokyo University of Education). The city, whose population of 143,000 (1984 est.) includes a scientific community of about 34,000, attracted attention as the site of a science and technology fair, Expo '85.

tsunami   [tsoo-nah'-mee]

Tsunamis, or seismic sea waves, potentially the most catastrophic of all ocean waves, are generated by tectonic displacements—for example, volcanism, landslides, or earthquakes—of the seafloor, which in turn cause a sudden displacement of the water above and the formation of a small group of WATER WAVES having wavelength equal to the water depth (up to several thousand meters) at the point of origin. These waves can travel radially outward for thousands of kilometers while retaining substantial energy. Their speed—characteristic of gravity waves in shallow water and thus equal to $\sqrt{gD}$, where g is the gravitational constant and D is the depth—is generally about 500 km/h (300 mph), and their periods range from 5 to 60 minutes. In the open ocean their amplitude is usually less than 1 m (3.3 ft); thus tsunamis often go unnoticed by ships at sea. In very shallow water, however, they undergo the same type of increase in amplitude as swell approaching a beach. The resultant waves can be devastating to coastal areas; the 37-m (120-ft) waves from the 1883 Krakatoa eruption, for example, killed 36,000 people.

The characteristics of tsunamis as they approach shore are greatly affected by wave refraction over the local bathymetry. Tsunami-producing earthquakes usually exceed 6.5 on the Richter scale, and most tsumanis occur in the Pacific Ocean because of the seismic activity around its perimeter. A tsunami warning system for the Pacific Ocean has been established; it consists of strategically placed seismic stations and a communications network.   ROBERT E. WILSON

Bibliography: Adams, W. M., ed., *Tsunamis in the Pacific Ocean* (1970); Iwasaki, T., and Iida, K., eds., *Tsunamis* (1983); Russell, R. C., *Waves and Tides* (1953); Shepard, F. P., *Submarine Geology*, 3d ed. (1973).

Tsushima, Battle of   [tsoo'-shee-mah]

The principal naval battle of the RUSSO-JAPANESE WAR, the Battle of Tsushima (May 27–28, 1905), fought in Tsushima Strait, south of the Sea of Japan, ended with the annihilation of the Russian fleet by the Japanese. Russia thus became the first modern European power to succumb to an Asiatic force.

Tswana   [tswah'-nuh]

The Tswana (also known as Bechuana or Botswana) are a Bantu-speaking people of the SOTHO group of southern Africa. Of an estimated population of 3,000,000 in the 1980s, about one-third (976,000) were living in Botswana (formerly the Bechuanaland Protectorate) and the remainder in the Republic of South Africa. The Tswana comprise a number of separate tribal groupings, each of which, according to oral tradition, is descended from a common ancestral stock. Although the Tswana traditionally are a cattle-keeping people, subsistence farming of maize and sorghum is an important component of their economy. Traditional economic practices have been seriously disrupted by the periodic migration of large numbers of Tswana men to work as wage laborers in the industrial and mining centers of South Africa.

Important aspects of Tswana society are an elaborate system of stratification based on wealth and a clearcut dichotomy between the nobility (descendants of ruling lineages) and the rest of the population—divided into commoners, foreigners, hereditary household servants, and serfs, the latter consisting of the SAN (Bushmen). Politically, every category with the exception of servants and serfs is represented through a network of district headmen and their local councils.

                                                          PETER CARSTENS

Bibliography: Schapera, Isaac, *Tribal Innovators: Tswana Chiefs and Social Change, 1795–1940* (1970) and *The Tswana* (1953; repr. 1968).

Tu Fu   (Du Fu)   [doo-foo]

Tu Fu, 712–70, considered China's greatest poet by many critics, traced his ancestry back to the 3d-century Confucian scholar Tu Yü. A precocious child and the son of a scholar-official, Tu Fu nonetheless failed his government examinations in 736. After a second unsuccessful attempt to secure a career as a scholar-official, he was able to obtain a minor post before being caught up in the An Lu-shan rebellion in 755. He was captured by the rebels but escaped and joined the imperial court. After a period of retirement (760–65) at his hut near Ch'eng-tu, he spent the last years of his life traveling.

Tu Fu had met the older poet LI PO in 744 and was deeply influenced by him. The greater part of Tu Fu's 1,457 surviving poems were written during the last 12 years of his life. He was a master of *Lü Shih*, or "regulated verse," which requires lines of five or seven words arranged into eight-line stanzas according to a strict rhyme-scheme.

Bibliography: Cooper, Arthur, ed. and trans., *Li Po and Tu Fu* (1973); Davis, A. R., *Tu Fu* (1971); Hung, W., *Tu Fu*, 2 vols. (1952; repr. 1969).

Tuareg   [twah'-reg]

The Tuareg, a Berber subgroup, traditionally have led a nomadic lifestyle, traveling in migratory bands in the south central mountains of the Sahara. The Tuareg have long subsisted by raising camels, goats, and cattle and acting as trans-Saharan guides for travelers. The reduction of herds by severe droughts in 1968–74 and in the early 1980s forced many Tuareg to abandon their nomadic way of life.

The Tuareg, the most celebrated of the tribal populations of the Sahara Desert in Africa, for centuries controlled the valuable trans-Saharan caravan trade in slaves, gold, and ivory. They speak a BERBER language and have a rich oral literature. They also have their own alphabet, which is descended from ancient Phoenician script. Their population, an estimated 300,000–400,000 during the 1970s, is divided into federations occupying isolated mountains and high country. Tuareg society is highly stratified, with as many as half of the people being serfs and slaves. The noble classes are all nomadic pastoralists. Patron-client relationships bridge the classes, and each federation is ruled by a chief, hereditary through the female line. In religion the Tuareg are Muslims. Unlike other Muslims, however, not only do they reckon descent matrilineally for certain purposes, as in the succession of chiefs, but also their women enjoy considerable freedom. Tuareg men, not women, wear a veil. Although this practice probably originated to protect men against sun, wind, and sand in their desert exposure, it has been highly ritualized, and the veil is seldom removed, even in camp.

The Tuareg are now divided politically under the various jurisdictions of Algeria, Tunisia, Mali, Libya, and Burkina Faso. The closing of national boundaries from about 1960, as these countries became independent, reduced the pastoralists' mobility, resulting in severe hardship from the long droughts of 1968–74 and the 1980s. As a result, nomadic Tuareg populations were greatly reduced by starvation and as a result of migration to urban centers, and the future of the nomadic Tuareg is now unclear. BRIAN SPOONER

Bibliography: Clarke, Thurston, *The Last Caravan* (1978); Fuchs, Peter, *The Land of Veiled Men* (1956); Keenan, Jeremy, *The Tuareg: People of Ahagar* (1978); Norris, H. T., *The Tuareg: Their Islamic Legacy and Its Diffusion in the Sahel* (1976); Rennel, F. J., *The People of the Veil* (1926; repr. 1966).

tuatara   [too-uh-tar'-uh]

Tuatara, S. punctatus, is a rare "living fossil" now restricted to government-protected habitats on islands off New Zealand.

The tuatara is a lizardlike reptile found only on a few small islands off New Zealand. Often called a "living fossil," the tuatara, *Sphenodon punctatus*, is the only living member of an otherwise extinct order of reptiles—the Rhynochocephalia. Fossils found in Eurasia, South America, and Africa indicate that the order flourished in the Triassic and Jurassic periods, about 225 million to 135 million years ago.

Tuataras are about 50 to 80 cm (20 to 31 in) long and have loose, scaly, drab brownish-green skin and a crest of spines along the back and tail. They are distinguished from lizards by an extra arch in the skull, by a firmly anchored quadrate bone, and by the lack of a copulatory organ in the male. Nocturnal and more active at lower temperatures than other reptiles, they emerge from their burrow homes, often shared with petrels, to feed on insects and other small animals. The eggs are laid in a hole and require 13 months to hatch.

JONATHAN CAMPBELL

tuba

Tuba refers to a family of lip-vibrated, upright, valved, metal wind instruments with a folded tube of wide, conical bore. It was designed to fill an urgent need in brass bands for a satisfactory bass to the valved bugle. Although the tuba was soon built in sizes ranging from an unsatisfactory B-flat soprano to various enormous double basses, only the baritone in B-flat (along with the wider-bored euphonium) and the basses in F, E-flat, CC, and BB-flat survive.

The orchestral tuba is the double bass of the brass section of the orchestra. It is often used to play quick staccato solos but can also play sustained melodies. The tuba used in military bands may have a fiberglass bell to lessen its weight when carried in marches.

In 1835, Berlin instrument maker Johann Gottfried Moritz, working with bandmaster Wilhelm Wieprecht, patented the first bass-tuba, completely distinct from the valved OPHICLEIDE, for use in German bands. In 1845, Adolfe Sax, working in Paris, patented a homogenous family of tubas under the name Sax-horn; these were subsequently adopted by French bands. Sax and other makers patented slightly different models under other names; the result was a confusing array of tuba instruments in all sizes. Among them the Viennese helicon bass (1849), with its circular coil formed to rest on the player's shoulder, provided an appropriate bass for the marching band and inspired the American sousaphone (1898). Also noteworthy are the 9-foot and 12-foot Wagner tubas in B-flat and F respectively; made with left-hand valves and relatively narrow bore and played with deep conical mouthpieces by French hornists, these instruments provide a new color midway between the mellow horn and the more aggressive tuba. Since the composition of Wagner's *Ring*, these instruments have been used in other large orchestral scores.

Tuba is also the Roman name for the Etruscan-Grecian *salpinx*, a straight, wide-bored, conical, usually bronze trumpet, ending in a slight flare and played with a detachable ivory mouthpiece. ROBERT A. WARNER

Bibliography: Baines, Anthony, *Brass Instruments* (1939; repr. 1981); Barbour, J. Murray, *Trumpets, Horns, and Music* (1964); Bevan, Clifford, *The Tuba Family* (1978); Dundas, Richard J., *Twentieth Century Brass Musical Instruments in the United States* (1986).

tuber

Tuber is a Latin term for a lump or swelling and refers to the bulky terminal portion of an underground stem or rhizome of a plant with modified nodes, buds, and leaves. The functions of tubers are food storage and vegetative reproduction; the most commonly stored food is starch. Under natural conditions the attached thin part of the stem or rhizome dies in the autumn or winter, whereas the remaining tuber is able to produce shoots from its buds the following growing season. The most well-known example of this modified stem structure is the potato. JOSEPH F. BECKER

tuberculosis

An acute or chronic infectious disease of humans and various animals, tuberculosis is caused by bacteria of the genus *Mycobacterium*, often called tubercle bacilli. One of the oldest diseases, it was known as consumption or the great white plague. Human infection with *M. tuberculosis* was one of the

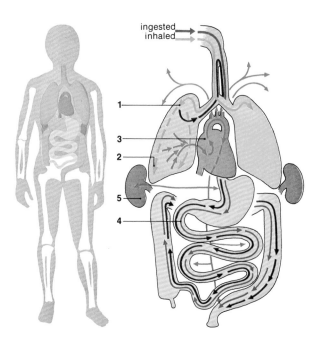

Tuberculosis, a contagious disease caused by tubercle bacilli, genus Mycobacterium, *is most often contracted by inhalation but can also result from ingesting unpasteurized milk. In most active cases the bacteria produce lesions, known as tubercles, in the lungs (1). Occasionally, the bacteria infect the lymph nodes (2) that drain the lungs, enter the bloodstream (3), and spread to such organs as the kidneys (5), bones and joints, brain, or genital organs. Ingested tubercle bacteria may infect the throat or the intestines (4).*

Infection of the lungs accounts for perhaps 90 percent of all tuberculosis cases. Inhaled bacteria enter the lungs and cause inflammation in small areas called primary foci (1). These enlarge and form tubercles, which consist of a center (2) of cells that have been destroyed by bacteria (3), plus a surrounding ring of phagocytic, or bacteria-engulfing, cells (4). Usually, the tubercles heal and leave small scars, but in some serious cases the tubercles grow and large cavities (5) result from the detachment of lung tissue.

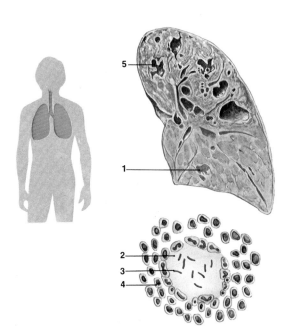

leading causes of death until antituberculous drugs were introduced in the 1940s. The bacillus infects the lungs by inhalation of infected droplets formed during coughing of an individual with the active form of the disease. In the vast majority of cases the infection is localized and symptomless, but it may progress to cause chronic pulmonary tuberculosis (active form). The infection can be detected in those who do not develop the disease through a positive tuberculin skin test consisting of a skin injection of a purified protein derived from the bacillus; swelling at the site indicates the presence of infection. The bacilli can remain dormant for years before becoming active. Their widespread presence helps to account for the observed and most likely AIDS-related resurgence of tuberculosis in the United States in the mid-1980s, particularly in prison populations.

Typical symptoms include fatigue, loss of weight and appetite, night sweats and fever, and persistent cough. Sputum is often streaked with blood; sometimes massive hemorrhages occur as the lung tissue is destroyed by the disease. Fluid may collect in the pleural cavity. Gradual deterioration occurs and, if the disease is untreated, death is common. Tuberculosis may spread from the lungs to any part of the body. Other forms of infection include tuberculous meningitis and miliary tuberculosis, a rapidly fatal form causing disease in many organs. Tuberculosis may also affect lymph nodes, bones, joints, genital organs, kidneys, and skin.

Treatment is with combinations of antituberculous drugs such as isoniazid, rifampin, and streptomycin given for long periods. Tuberculosis may also be acquired from animals, as by drinking their unpasteurized milk. A vaccine known as BCG (Bacille Calmette-Guérin), prepared from a living but weakened strain of tubercle bacilli, confers some protection against tuberculosis.   J. MICHAEL S. DIXON

Bibliography: Caldwell, Mark, *The Last Crusade: The War on Consumption 1862–1954* (1988); Keers, Robert, *Pulmonary Tuberculosis* (1979); Mooney, Elizabeth, *In the Shadow of the White Plague* (1979); Waksman, S. A., *The Conquest of Tuberculosis* (1964).

tuberose   [toob'-rohz]

The tuberose, P. tuberosa, is one of the most fragrant of cultivated plants. It is native to southwestern North America and is grown throughout the world in greenhouses and gardens.

Tuberose is the common name for *Polianthes tuberosa,* a perennial garden plant of the family Agavaceae. It is native to southwestern North America but is known only from cultivation. Tuberose plants have tuberous roots and bear clusters of fragrant, waxy, white flowers, which are used in perfumes.

Tubman, Harriet

Harriet Tubman, b. Dorchester County, Md., c.1821, d. Mar. 10, 1913, was a fugitive slave and abolitionist who became a legendary figure of the UNDERGROUND RAILROAD. Born to slave parents, she escaped (c.1849) to freedom by following the north star. Throughout the 1850s she made repeated journeys

Harriet Tubman, who escaped from slavery in Maryland c.1849, returned repeatedly to the South to lead about 300 other fugitive slaves to freedom. At one point a reward of $40,000 was posted for her capture, but she always eluded pursuit and reportedly never lost a charge. Tubman continued her dangerous exploits during the Civil War, serving as a Union spy and scout. She was known as "the Moses of her people."

into slave territory, leading about 300 other fugitives, including her parents, to freedom. Maintaining martial discipline on flights north, Tubman often forced panicky or exhausted "passengers" ahead by threatening them with a loaded pistol. She was aided by Quakers and other abolitionists, and John Brown sought her counsel for the Harpers Ferry raid in 1859. When the Civil War began she served as an army cook and nurse and became a spy and guide for Union forays into Maryland and Virginia. After the war she managed a home in Auburn, N.Y., for indigent and elderly blacks until her death; she was buried with full military honors.   RONALD L. LEWIS

Bibliography: Bradford, Sarah Elizabeth, *Harriet Tubman* (1886; rev. ed. 1961); Conrad, Earl, *Harriet Tubman* (1942; repr. 1970).

Tubman, William V. S.

William Vacanarat Shadrach Tubman, b. Nov. 29, 1895, d. July 23, 1971, was one of Liberia's most effective presidents. A descendant of black American settlers, he studied to be a lay Methodist preacher and subsequently entered public service. During the 1920s and '30s, after taking a law degree, he served in the Liberian Senate, where he championed the cause of the tribes of the interior against the established oligarchy. He was appointed to the Supreme Court in 1937 and served as Liberia's president from 1944 until his death. Tubman encouraged foreign capital investments, granted the franchise to women, encouraged tribespeople to participate in government, built up public schools, and expanded revenues, public services, and the army. He insisted that customary tribal laws be maintained insofar as they were "humane and reasonable" but also tried to encourage the immigration of westernized blacks from the United States, the West Indies, and the British West African colonies.   L. H. GANN

Bibliography: Liebnow, Gus, *Liberia: The Evolution of Privilege* (1969); Lowenkopf, Martin, *Politics in Liberia: The Conservative Road to Development* (1976); Wreh, Tuan, *The Love of Liberty: The Rule of President William V. S. Tubman in Liberia, 1944–1971* (1976).

Tubulidentata   [toob'-yuh-luh-den-tah'-tuh]

Tubulidentata is an order of mammals that contains only one family, Orycteropodidae, with one living genus, *Orycteropus*, and a single species—the AARDVARK, *Orycteropus afer*. The name of the order refers to tubules radiating from a central pulp cavity in the teeth of the aardvark. Fossils of order members have been found in North America, Europe, and western Asia.   EVERETT SENTMAN

Tucker, Richard

Richard Tucker, b. New York City, Aug. 28, 1914, d. Jan. 8, 1975, was one of the greatest operatic tenors of his generation. In early childhood he attracted attention with his liturgical singing in synagogue but received no operatic training until he was in his mid-20s. He made his debut (1945) at the

Metropolitan Opera as Enzo in Ponchielli's *La Gioconda* and remained with the company for his entire 30-year career, specializing in the Italian repertory.

Bibliography: Drake, James A., *Richard Tucker* (1984).

Tucson   [too'-sahn]

Tucson, the second largest city in Arizona, is located about 110 km (68 mi) north of Mexico. The seat of Pima County, Tucson has a population of 330,537 (1980), and metropolitan Pima County, 531,263. In a valley surrounded by the Santa Catalina Mountains, the city is a distribution center for vegetables, citrus fruits, cotton, livestock, and dairy products. Copper mining is important. Tucson produces guided missiles, electronic equipment, steel, paints, soap, and clothing. Because of its warm, dry climate, it is a tourist and resort center. Tucson has historical museums and a symphony orchestra; nearby are located Saguaro National Monument, Coronado National Forest, and Tucson Mountain Park. The University of Arizona (1885) is located in Tucson.

An Indian settlement, Stjukshon, occupied the site when the Jesuit Eusebio Kino arrived in the late 17th century and established the mission of San Xavier del Bac. By 1776 a Spanish army post was there. The area passed to the United States in the Gadsden Purchase (1853), and from 1867 to 1877, Tucson was the capital of Arizona Territory. The arrival of the Southern Pacific Railroad in 1880 and discovery of nearby silver and copper deposits assured its prosperity.

Tucumán   [too-koo-mahn']

Tucumán, or San Miguel de Tucumán (1980 pop., 498,579), is a city and provincial capital located in northwestern Argentina. Sugar refining is the major industry, but processing of grain, meat, and milk is also important. Tucumán is becoming a popular tourist resort because of its warm climate.

Founded (1565) by Diego de Villaroel, a Spanish conquistador, Tucumán was relocated to its present site in 1668 after frequent Indian raids. Argentina's declaration of independence and first constitution were written at the Congress of Tucumán (1816–20). The introduction of sugarcane cultivation in the early 19th century spurred Tucumán's economic growth.

Tudor   (dynasty)

The Tudors, a family of Welsh origin, ruled England from 1485 to 1603. The first family member of note was **Owen Tudor**, *c.*1400–1461, who married (*c.*1429) Catherine of Valois, the widow of the Lancastrian king Henry V. Owen fought on the Lancastrian side during the Wars of the Roses (1455–85; see ROSES, WARS OF THE). His eldest son, **Edmund Tudor**, *c.*1430–1456, married Margaret Beaufort (see BEAUFORT family), a descendant of King Edward III. Edmund's posthumous son became the first Tudor monarch as HENRY VII, winning the throne when he defeated (1485) the Yorkist king Richard III at Bosworth Field and thereby ended the Wars of the Roses. Henry VII's son succeeded him as HENRY VIII and was succeeded in turn by his children, EDWARD VI, MARY I, and ELIZABETH I. Queen Elizabeth had no direct heirs; thus on her death (1603) the throne passed to James VI, king of Scotland, a descendant of **Margaret Tudor**, 1489–1541, daughter of Henry VII. As James I, he was the first of the Stuart family to rule England. Although the reign of the Tudors was a period of great religious strife, the English monarchy consolidated its power, English nationalism and naval strength grew, and literature and scholarship flourished.   STANFORD E. LEHMBERG

Bibliography: Elton, G. R., *England under the Tudors,* 2d ed. (1974); Morris, Christopher, *The Tudors,* rev. ed. (1976); Plowden, Alison, *The House of Tudor* (1976; repr. 1982).

Tudor, Antony

Antony Tudor (William Cook), b. London, Apr. 4, 1908, d. Apr. 19, 1987, was a British choreographer who first explored the depths of human psychology in ballet. At the age of 20 he began to study ballet with Marie RAMBERT, who encouraged him to try choreography. For her company he made such masterpieces as *Jardin aux lilas* (Lilac Garden; 1936) and *Dark Elegies* (1937). In 1938, together with Hugh Laing and other dancers who left Rambert, he formed the London Ballet. After the outbreak of World War II this company was absorbed back into Ballet Rambert.

Tudor and Laing, meanwhile, had accepted an invitation to join the newly founded (American) Ballet Theatre (ABT) in New York City. For this company, Tudor revived some of the works he had made in Britain, then in 1942 choreographed *Pillar of Fire*. Characteristically, it was completed only after long and detailed rehearsal; it made the reputation of both Tudor and Nora Kaye, who created the leading role of a repressed spinster. This work was followed by *Dim Lustre* (1943), *Romeo and Juliet* (1943), and *Undertow* (1945).

In 1950, Tudor left ABT to head the·Metropolitan Opera Ballet School and briefly worked with the Royal Swedish Ballet and New York City Ballet, but for many years he produced no major work. In 1967, however, he was invited by Sir Frederick Ashton to choreograph *Shadowplay* for the Royal Ballet. In 1974 he rejoined ABT as associate director and choreographed *The Leaves Are Fading* (1975) and *The Tiller in the Fields* (1979). He became choreographer emeritus of ABT in 1980.

DAVID VAUGHAN

Bibliography: Gruen, John, *Private World of Ballet* (1976); Hunt, Marilyn, "Antony Tudor: Master Provocateur," *Dance Magazine*, May 1987.

Tudor style

The term *Tudor style* describes the forms of English architecture during the reign of the first Tudors, Henry VII and Henry VIII—that is, from about 1480 to about 1540. It is, in essence, a Gothic architecture that retains asymmetrical plans, pointed windows, and ribbed vaulting; this is clear in such buildings as Eltham Palace, London (c.1475); the Gatehouse, Saint Osyth's Priory, Essex (c.1475); Magdalen College, Oxford (1474–90); and the chapel of Henry VII, Westminster Abbey (1503–19). The last of these is the masterpiece of the English PERPENDICULAR GOTHIC STYLE, a form characterized by a very rich and detailed yet orderly articulation of forms. In time, especially after 1500, the Tudor style began to reflect European influences. In the most general terms, plans became more symmetrical and designs were increasingly seen in terms of small, individual units rather than the linear patterning that is so marked in the English Gothic. More specifically, new forms came into use and more and more exotic detailing, often carried out by European artisans, was introduced, including simple octagonal towers, polychrome brick, niches, plaques, decorated chimneys, and—inside the buildings—the most elaborate fireplaces. Such detailing and planning changed the character of this architecture without altering its fundamental form; this is seen, for example, in the still predominantly Gothic form of such buildings as the Tower, Eton College (1515); Barrington Court, Somerset (1515–48); the Hall, Layer Marney, Essex (c.1520); Compton Wynyates, Warwickshire (c.1520); Sutton Place, Surrey (1523–27); Hengrave Hall, Suffolk (1525–38); and the Quadrangle, Christ Church, Oxford (1525–29). These forms could only be succeeded by a fundamentally different architecture, which was to become known as the ELIZABETHAN STYLE.   DAVID CAST

Bibliography: Harvey, John, *An Introduction to Tudor Architecture* (1949); Lees-Milne, James, *Tudor Renaissance* (1951); Smith, Roger T., *Gothic Architecture in England* (1983).

tufa: see SINTER.

tuff

The igneous rock tuff is composed of fragmental material blown out of a volcano. The volcanic fragments may be vitric (glass), crystalline, or lithic (rock). Tuff erupted in a hot gas cloud (*nuée ardente*) may be hot enough upon deposition to deform the glass shards within it and to form a hard, massive rock known as a welded tuff, or ignimbrite.

JAMES A. WHITNEY

Tufts University

Established in 1852, Tufts University (enrollment: 7,507; library; 638,000 volumes) is a private coeducational institution in Medford, Mass. Jackson College is its college for women. Tufts includes schools of dentistry, medicine, and engineering and the Fletcher School of Law and Diplomacy.

tugboat

The tugboat is a small, powerful craft used to move barges, to berth large ocean-going ships, and to tow disabled vessels. Paddlewheel-propelled tugboats made their appearance around 1800 with the beginning of the age of steam. Screws replaced paddlewheels about 1850, and by 1900 diesel engines had supplanted steam. In the past century the size of tugs has remained fairly constant, ranging from 21 to 64 m (70 to 210 ft), but their engines are now about ten times more powerful, with some generating more than 3,000 hp. Berthing tugs have resilient wooden hulls that prevent damage to both ship and tug during the docking operation. On inland waterways tugs are used with dumb (nonpowered) barges. In the United States tugs usually push a line of barges, whereas in Europe they pull the barges by a towline. A single tugboat may power 10 to 20 barges.

JOSEPH GIES

Bibliography: Rosenblum, Richard, *Tugboats* (1976).

Tugwell, Rexford G.

Rexford Guy Tugwell, b. Sinclairville, N.Y., July 10, 1891, d. July 21, 1979, was an American economist, political scientist, and public official. In 1932 he joined Franklin D. Roosevelt's campaign staff as part of what came to be called the BRAIN TRUST, a group of leading political and social thinkers recruited to advise the president-to-be. During Roosevelt's first two terms, Tugwell—as assistant secretary and then under secretary of agriculture—headed the Rural Resettlement Administration, where he worked on moving farmers to more productive land. An active voice in U.S. politics for nearly 60 years, he later served as governor of Puerto Rico (1941–46) and director of the University of Chicago's Institute of Planning (1946–52). Among his many books are his autobiography, *The Light of Other Days* (1962), and *The Brain Trust* (1968).

THOMAS K. WAGNER

Bibliography: Mitchell, Broadus, "Rexford Guy Tugwell," in *Challenge*, July 1978; Sternsher, B., *Rexford Tugwell and the New Deal* (1964).

Tuileries   [twee'-lur-eez]

The name *Tuileries* designates both the gardens in Paris lying along the right bank of the Seine from the Palace of the LOUVRE to the Place de la Concorde and the palace formerly situated there. The word is derived from the tile factories, or *tuileries*, that were established there in the 13th century. Although modified, the garden still follows the overall plan (1664) of André Le Nôtre. The Palace of the Tuileries was begun in 1564 for Catherine de Médicis by the architect Philibert DELORME; it was occupied only intermittently by French royalty until Louis XVI and his family were compelled to reside there during the French Revolution. Thereafter, several of France's rulers made it their personal headquarters. After 1792 the palace became the target of popular uprisings and in 1871 was burned during the Commune of Paris.   ROBERT NEUMANN

Tula   [too'-luh]

Tula, about 60 km (37 mi) northwest of Mexico City, was the dominant center in north central Mexico between the 10th and 12th centuries AD. After the arrival of the Toltecs in the mid-10th century, Tula, formerly a modest outpost of TEOTIHUACÁN, quickly grew into the capital of the powerful TOLTEC state. Commercial ties stretched north into the southwestern United States and southeast to Guatemala and beyond. Shortly before 1000, a deposed ruler named for the god Quetzalcóatl led a group of Toltecs to Yucatán, where they established themselves as overlords. The old MAYA center of CHICHÉN ITZÁ, rebuilt in the image of Tula, became a hybrid

Toltec-Maya capital. About 1150, Toltec power came to an end. Tula was razed, and the refugees fled south to the Valley of Mexico and beyond.

At its peak, Tula covered about 11 km² (4.2 mi²), with a population in the tens of thousands. The main civic center was a terraced acropolis complex supporting several hundred temples, palaces, colonnades, ball courts, altars, and other platforms. The most prominent building was a temple-pyramid sacred to Quetzalcóatl, the Feathered Serpent. Painted reliefs emphasizing military themes along with representations of Quetzalcóatl adorned the principal structures. *Chacmools*, reclining human figures that served as receptacles for offerings, stood before most temples. Several smaller civic groups were interspersed among outlying residential areas. Mexican and foreign archaeologists have conducted extensive excavations at Tula since 1940.   JOHN S. HENDERSON

Bibliography: Adams, R. E. W., *Prehistoric Mesoamerica* (1977).

Tulane University   [too-layn']

Established in 1834, Tulane University (enrollment: 9,200; library: 1,500,000 volumes) is a private coeducational institution in New Orleans, La. Newcomb College (1886) is its college for women. Tulane has schools of law, medicine, public health and tropical medicine, and social work.

tularemia   [too-luh-ree'-mee-uh]

An acute, infectious, sometimes fatal disease to humans, tularemia, or "rabbit fever," mainly occurs in rodents and wild rabbits. Caused by a bacterium (*Francisella tularensis*), the disease is named after Tulare County, Calif., where it was first identified in ground squirrels in 1911. Humans can contract tularemia through direct contact with infected animals, such as when skinning cottontail rabbits, or indirectly from bites by infected ticks or deerflies, the primary transmitters. Following a 2-day to 10-day incubation period, symptoms develop that include an ulcer at the site of entry, swollen lymph nodes, and intermittent high fever and headaches for several weeks. From 5 to 30 percent of untreated patients may die; treatment involves the use of the antibiotics streptomycin or tetracycline.   J. MICHAEL S. DIXON

tulip

The tulip T. gesnerana *has been a favorite garden and greenhouse flower for centuries. The breeder tulip (left)* is the most familiar variety. Two other types are the small, wild tulip (center) *and the* parrot tulip (right), *which is popular for its elaborate petals.*

Tulip is the common name for between 50 and 150 species of the genus *Tulipa* in the lily family, Liliaceae. These prize garden flowers, native to Asia, historically have been associated with one major producer, the Netherlands, although they are now grown throughout the temperate regions of the world. Tulips are hardy perennial herbs grown from bulbs, which produce long, broad leaves from the base or stem. Cup-shaped or bell-shaped flowers are borne on a single scape and come in a variety of solitary or variegated colors except blue. Bulbs should be planted in rich, well-drained soils during the fall for flowering the following spring. Extensive horticultural breeding has produced numerous cultivars and hybrids used in modern gardens.

tulip tree

The tulip tree, or yellow poplar, L. tulipifera, *native to the eastern United States, grows up to 61 m (200 ft) tall. Its leaves are squarish in shape, and it produces flowers that resemble tulips.*

The tulip tree, or yellow poplar, *Liriodendron tulipifera,* is a deciduous forest tree of the eastern United States and southern Ontario. It is not a poplar, but rather a member of the magnolia family, Magnoliaceae. This tree is used as an ornamental, having showy, tulip-shaped, yellow-green flowers with a broad orange band at the base and distinctive four-lobed, notch-tipped leaves. The cone-shaped fruits contain many overlapping winged seeds. Tulip trees are resistant to disease and grow quickly, attaining heights up to 60 m (190 ft), taller than any other eastern forest tree. The light, soft, easily worked wood is commercially valued for plywood, furniture, boxes, and interior trim, and the flower is a source of nectar for honeybees.

Tull, Jethro

Jethro Tull, b. 1674, d. Feb. 21, 1741, was an English agriculturalist and inventor who had an important influence on English agricultural methods. Educated in law at Oxford University, Tull inherited his father's farm and in the early 1700s began to study farming practices and devise new agricultural systems. Convinced that crops would grow better if planted in rows—with between-row cultivation to keep weeds down—Tull devised the first successful mechanical seed drill and a horse-drawn row cultivator. He published *The Horse-hoeing Husbandry, or an Essay on the Principles of Tillage and Vegetation* in 1733.

Bibliography: Fussell, G. E., *Jethro Tull: His Influence On Mechanized Agriculture* (1973).

See also: AGRICULTURE, HISTORY OF.

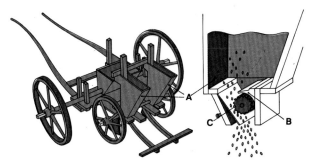

Jethro Tull's seed drill (c.1701) made it possible to plant crop seed in regular rows that would require no subsequent thinning. Seed was placed in two hoppers (A), the openings of which were operated by a spring-loaded tongue (B). As the mechanism was drawn forward by a draft animal, a wooden cog (C) spun, permitting seed to flow downward into furrows at regular intervals.

Tulsa   [tuhl'-suh]

Tulsa, a city on the Arkansas River in northeastern Oklahoma, is the seat of Tulsa County and the financial and commercial center of a major oil-producing region. The state's second largest city, Tulsa has a population of 360,919 (1980), with 689,628 persons in the 6-county metropolitan area.

Hundreds of petroleum concerns maintain plants and offices in Tulsa. The aviation-aerospace industry, wholesale distribution, mining, metal processing, and manufacture of machinery contribute to the city's economy. With major airlines, trucklines, and railroads, as well as barge traffic along the McClellan-Kerr Waterway, Tulsa is a transportation center. The city supports a symphony orchestra, ballet, opera, theater, and museums. The University of Tulsa (1894) and Oral Roberts University (1963) are there.

Settlement in the Tulsa area began in 1836, when Creek Indians moved there from Alabama. Arrival of the St. Louis–San Francisco Railway in 1882 brought settlers, and the town's principal industry became cattle shipping. The city's phenomenal economic and population growth began in 1901 with the discovery of vast petroleum deposits nearby.

tumbleweed

Tumbleweed gets its name because winds break off the plant from its roots and then tumble it along meadows and roads, thus dispersing the seeds. A rolling tumbleweed, with its many curving branches that form a rounded basket, is a familiar sight in the American West.

The name tumbleweed applies to several plants that are dislodged and rolled along by the wind when mature or dead. The most common in western North America is the Russian thistle, *Salsola kali*, family Chenopodiaceae; it has reddish, spine-tipped leaves and small flowers. Others include *Amaranthus albus,* family Amaranthaceae, and *Sisymbriamum altiassiamum,* family Cruciferae.   FRANK B. SALISBURY

tumor

A tumor is a mass of new tissue growth (neoplasm) that is unresponsive to normal controls or the organizing influence of adjacent tissues; it has no useful physiological function. This definition applies to both malignant and benign tumors. Malignant, or cancerous, tumors, however, are additionally defined by their invasion of local tissue and their ability to spread, or metastasize, in other parts of the body (see CANCER).

A benign tumor generally grows slowly and kills the host only if it interferes in some way with a critical function. It is usually encapsulated within a membrane. The cells of benign tumors closely resemble the cells of the tissue of origin. Superficial benign tumors include warts and moles.

A malignant tumor, by definition, always kills (unless treated) because of its invasive and metastatic characteristics. The tumor grows locally by encroachment into surrounding normal tissues; from these crablike processes cancer gets its name. The tumor spreads to distant sites by the breaking off of malignant cells, which move through the blood and lymphatic systems, attach themselves, and begin to grow as new colonies. Malignant tumors are diagnosed by examination of their vascularity, shape, form of cell division, and differentiation. More than a hundred different types of malignant tumors have been identified in humans. In general, if the tumor is derived from epithelial tissue, it is a carcinoma, and if it arises from connective tissue, it is a sarcoma.

The factors controlling tumor growth are as poorly understood as those which control normal tissue growth, which stops at maturity (except to repair or replace). Tumors in laboratory animals may be transplanted to a second host using only a single tumor cell. This suggests that only one normal cell need become transformed (cancerous) for tumor growth to begin. It is thought, however, that many transformed cells die or remain latent or dormant for extended periods before successful tumor growth is established. Tumors have been experimentally induced in animals by chemical, physical, and viral agents, and by radiation and chronic irritation.

Tumor necrosis factor (TNF) is a powerful protein produced by the body's own immune system that cancer researchers have found can kill tumors. A similar protein, called cachectin, that had been identified as a major cause of weight loss in individuals with cancer or serious infections, was later indicated to be the same as TNF. The substances play a dual role in the immune system. Currently, TNF is being tested in humans as an anticancer agent. Since it has severe side effects, such as weight loss, fever, blood-pressure reduction, and shock, TNF will likely be used in combination with other drugs.   DANIEL P. GRISWOLD

Bibliography: Louis, C. J., *Tumours: Basic Principles and Clinical Aspects* (1978); Pitot, H. C., *Fundamentals of Oncology,* rev. ed. (1985).

Tun-huang   (Dunhuang)   [doon-hwang]

The Chinese oasis town of Tun-huang, in the extreme northwest of Kansu province, was the ancient entryway to China for merchants and Buddhist missionaries traveling the SILK ROAD across central Asia. It was fortified by the Chinese in the Han period (202 BC–AD 220) and flourished as a trading center until the mid-8th century, when it fell under Tibetan rule and the caravan route shifted northward. Tun-huang was a major Buddhist monastic and pilgrimage site, known for its Caves of the Thousand Buddhas (Chien-fo-tung), a series of richly ornamented rock-cut sanctuaries whose construction began in the 4th century. A valuable collection of Buddhist objects enclosed since the 11th century was discovered (1907–08) among the caves by Sir Aurel STEIN. The finds included painted silk banners, sculptures, and a large library of Buddhist and secular manuscripts, many of which are now in the Musée Guimet, Paris, and the British Museum, London.

tuna

Tunas are among the largest, most specialized, and most commercially important of all fishes. Seven species, making up the genus *Thunnus* of the tuna-and-mackerel family,

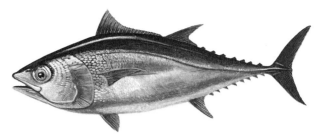

The bluefin tuna, T. thynnus, *found worldwide, mostly in temperate and subtropical waters, is an important food fish.*

Scombridae, are found in temperate and tropical oceans around the world and account for a major proportion of the U.S. fish catch and U.S. fish imports.

Tunas typically have cigar-shaped, streamlined bodies with two dorsal fins—the first spiny, the second soft-rayed and followed by finlets—a narrow tail region, and a large, deeply forked tail. They vary extensively in size, color, and fin length. Along with the mackerel sharks, tunas are unique among fishes in having a body temperature higher than that of the surrounding water—a result of a complex circulatory system and continuous sustained activity. Fast swimmers, traveling at more than 48 km/h (30 mph), they typically migrate long distances and appear only seasonally in any one location. Tunas occur both in surface waters and at great depths, where their large eyes help them to see in the dark. They feed on other fishes and on squid.

The largest species, a highly prized sport fish, is the bluefin, *Thunnus thynnus,* found worldwide. Some specimens exceed 4.2 m (14 ft) and weigh more than 680 kg (1,500 lb). Other important species include the albacore, *T. alalunga,* a small fish, often less than 18 kg (40 lb), which is famed for its tasty white meat; the large yellowfin, *T. albacares;* and the deep-water bigeye, *T. obesus.*

The tuna fishery is controlled by international agreements limiting how much fishers may take and where they may fish—limits that are not always observed. Another major problem is created by the method used to harvest tuna (as well as salmon and squid): huge nets are stretched across kilometers of ocean, capturing sea birds, seals, porpoises, and dolphins along with the tuna. In some parts of the Pacific, the porpoise and dolphin kill has been huge, constituting a threat to their populations.   CAMM SWIFT

Bibliography: Nakamura, H., *Tuna Distribution and Migration* (1978).

tundra   [tuhn'-druh]

Derived from a Finnish word for "barren land," the term *tundra* refers to the treeless area found circling the North Pole. Similar conditions found at high elevations on mountain slopes are called Alpine tundra.

The equatorward limits of the tundra coincide approximately with the warmest isotherm of 10° C (50° F), which in the Northern Hemisphere marks a boundary between the tundra and the TAIGA CLIMATE. Some climatologists define the southern boundary of the Arctic tundra at the southern limit of permafrost, or permanently frozen subsoil. In the Alpine tundra, permafrost is seldom found.

The tundra is characterized by lakes, bogs, and streams. Vegetation consists of mosses, lichens, grasses, and dwarf shrubs. The regrowth of vegetation is slow, and severe erosion can cause scarring of the landscape. The tundra differs from the polar region and the evergreen forest belt by two features: alternate freezing and thawing of the topsoil, and permafrost.

Although few in number, tundra animals sometimes achieve large populations, as, for example, the lemmings.

Some animals remain in the tundra (musk ox and polar bear), whereas others range to the taiga (ptarmigan, caribou, and snowy owl). The sizable numbers of birds include ducks, geese, and plovers.

Tundra winters are long and cold, whereas summers are short and cool. Average annual temperatures are generally below 0° C (32° F), and the annual range is large except in areas that are favored by ice-free waters offshore. Barrow, Alaska, has a February average of −28° C (−18° F) and a July average of 4° C (39° F). Western tundra coasts of Alaska and Europe experience more moderate temperatures due to maritime influences. Low sun angle and sea ice cause low temperatures even during the long days of summer. Frost may occur in any month.

The low temperatures and poor drainage characteristic of the Arctic tundra result in acidic soils and lead to accumulation of organic debris. The lower part of the soil profile typically becomes waterlogged and has a gley clay soil horizon. Soils are characteristically boggy and rocky; permafrost is another characteristic of these soils.

Annual precipitation is less than 350 mm (14 in) over most of the tundra; the precipitation falls mainly during the warmer half of the year.

Average winter snow depths are small, but strong winds cause blizzards and drifting. Ice fog may form under clear skies in winter, whereas coastal fogs or low stratus clouds are common in summer.

Certain high mountains situated in the middle and low latitudes have climates similar to those of the Arctic tundra. Although sometimes described as having a tundra climate, these areas are properly distinguished as alpine or highland. Alpine tundra regions are characterized by greater amounts of precipitation and rocky, boggy soil similar to that of the Arctic tundra.

Bibliography: Critchfield, Howard J., *General Climatology*, 3d ed. (1974); Trewartha, Glenn T., *An Introduction to Climate*, 4th ed. (1968).

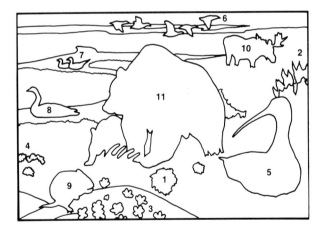

During the short, cool tundra summers, water from melted snow collects above the permafrost to form marshy areas. Although most plants reproduce by asexual means, many flower during the brief growing season. North American tundra vegetation includes cotton grass, Eriophorum (1), a perennial sedge with cottony flower clusters; fireweed, Epilobium (2), a common herb; saxifrage, Saxifraga (3), often found on rock outcrops; and forget-me-not, Myosotis (4), which bears small, showy flowers. Lichens and mosses are also common. Many birds nest on the tundra during summer; most, including the four species shown, migrate south to avoid the long, harsh winter. The whimbrel, or Hudsonian curlew, Numenius phaeopus (5), nests in a grass-lined depression in the ground. Common eider ducks, Somateria mollissima (6; males shown), nest along the seacoast. The pintail duck, Anas acuta (7), and Canada goose, Branta canadensis (8), have wide breeding ranges in North America. Most land mammals do not migrate. Meadow voles, Microtus (9), winter in runways between the snow and ground, where they feed on vegetation. Moose, Alces alces (10), and brown bear, Ursus arctos (11; shown with cub), which usually inhabit northern forests, sometimes venture onto the tundra.

tuner

A tuner is an electronic device that receives the signals broadcast from a RADIO station and converts them into a form that can drive an AMPLIFIER. To do this, the tuner must first strengthen, or amplify, the weak signal it receives from the ANTENNA and then isolate the desired signal by filtering out all other signals and electrical NOISE. The tuner may be built on a separate chassis and be a separate component of a high-fidelity sound system, or the tuner section may be part of a RECEIVER, which houses amplifiers as well as the tuner.

ARTHUR BIDERMAN

Tung Ch'i-ch'ang (Dong Qichang) [doon chee-chang]

Tung Ch'i-ch'ang, b. Feb. 10, 1555, d. 1636, was an important Chinese scholar-painter and the most influential writer on the theory of painting in the late Ming period. Tung's painting opened up a new direction for such later artists as the Four Wangs (see WANGS, FOUR) of the Ch'ing dynasty. Instead of the naturalism preferred by his contemporaries, Tung was interested in the formal structure of the picture and stressed the importance of studying the ancient models and calligraphy. As an art theorist, he divided previous Chinese painters into two groups, which he called the Northern and Southern schools. His advocacy of the Southern school, and particularly the four Yüan masters, had a long-lasting influence on later aestheticians.

LOUISA SHEN TING

Bibliography: Bush, Susan, *The Chinese Literati on Painting* (1971); Hummel, Arthur, *Eminent Chinese of the Ch'ing Period (1644-1912)* (1943); Sirén, Osvald, *Chinese Painting: Leading Masters and Principles*, vol. 5 (1958).

tung oil [tuhng]

Tung oil is an inedible oil obtained from tung nuts, the seeds of the tung-oil tree, *Aleurites fordii*, of the spurge family, Euphorbiaceae. Seeds are roasted, ground, and pressed to produce the oil, which is used principally as a drying agent in paints and varnishes and as a waterproofing material in the manufacture of linoleum. The tree is native to East Asia, and China is the major oil producer. Tung-oil tree culture, however, has also been introduced in other warm areas, and some of the oil is now obtained from crops produced in the southern United States.

tungsten [tuhng'-stuhn]

Tungsten is a heavy metallic element, a member of the third series of transition metals. It has the symbol W, its atomic number is 74, and its atomic weight is 183.85. The name is derived from the Swedish *tung sten*, meaning "heavy stone." Tungsten is also known as wolfram, from wolframite, the mineral from which the element was first recognized by Peter Woulfe in 1779. The metal was first isolated in 1783 by the de Elhuyar brothers by the charcoal reduction of an acid in wolframite.

Tungsten occurs principally in the minerals scheelite ($CaWO_4$), wolframite ([Fe,Mn]WO_4), huebnerite ($MnWO_4$), and ferberite ($FeWO_4$), which are found in California, North Carolina, South Korea, Bolivia, the USSR, and Portugal. Unconfirmed reports of very large deposits of tungsten ores have come from China. The metal is obtained commercially by the reduction of tungstic oxide with hydrogen or carbon. Pure tungsten is steel gray to tin white in color. Its physical properties include the highest melting point of all metals, 3410° C, a boiling point of 5660° C, and a density of 19.3 g/cm³.

The outer electronic configuration of tungsten is $5s^25p^65d^46s^2$, and in keeping with the other transition metals it displays a range of oxidation states—0, +1, +2, +3, +4, +5, and +6—as exemplified by the formation of many complex ions and coordination complexes.

Pure tungsten is easily forged, spun, drawn, and extruded, whereas the impure metal is brittle and can be fabricated only with difficulty. Tungsten oxidizes in air, especially at higher temperatures, but is resistant to corrosion and is only slightly attacked by most mineral acids.

Because heat causes tungsten to expand at about the same rate as glass, the metal is widely used to make glass-to-metal seals. Tungsten or its alloys are used for filaments for electric lamps, electron and television tubes, electrical contact points for automobile distributors, heating elements for electrical furnaces, and many space, missile, and high-temperature applications.

Tungsten carbide is an important compound in the metalworking, mining, and petroleum industries. Alloys such as high-speed steel, cristite, and stellite, used in high-speed tools, contain tungsten. Other important tungsten compounds are calcium and magnesium tungstates, which are used in fluorescent lighting, and tungsten disulfide, which is used as a high-temperature lubricant at temperatures up to 500° C. Tungsten compounds also find uses in the chemical, paint, and tanning industries.

J. ALISTAIR KERR

Bibliography: Cotton, F. A., and Wilkinson, G., *Advanced Inorganic Chemistry*, 4th ed. (1980); Elwell, W. T., and Wood, D. F., *Analytical Chemistry of Molybdenum and Tungsten* (1971); Rieck, G. D., *Tungsten and Its Compounds* (1967); Yih, S. H., and Wang, T. C., *Tungsten: Sources, Metallurgy, Properties, and Applications* (1979).

Tungus   [tuhn-guhs']

The Tungus (Evenk) are a people who originated in the Amur River valley and spread into northeastern Asia. They live mainly in Siberia, with some populations in Mongolia and China, and they speak dialects of the Tungus-Manchu subdivision of the URAL-ALTAIC language family. Subgroups of the Tungus are the Evenk, Even, Orochon, and Negedal. The Tungus are closely related to the Manchu, and perhaps to MONGOLS and TURKS; part of the population of Japan may be of Tungus ancestry. Baykal Mongoloid in physical type, the Tungus are distinguished by light skin, a weak inner-eyelid skin fold, and sparse facial hair. Their economy is based on reindeer breeding, augmented by hunting and fishing. Reindeer are bred as pack animals and also as pack-and-saddle animals. Reindeer milk, meat, broth, and bone marrow are dietary staples; raw reindeer liver and a jelled reindeer-blood sausage are considered delicacies. Reindeer hide is used to make clothing and boots. Traditionally, Tungus camps were open to any kinship unit and tribe; marriage partners were chosen from outside the kin group. Before the Tungus came under Soviet administration, clan cults and shamanism (see SHAMAN) were important religious elements. In the 1980s about 30,000 Tungus lived on collective farms, and their children were educated in boarding schools.

VICTOR L. MOTE

Bibliography: Friend, Morton, *The Vanishing Tungus* (1973); Levin, M. G., *Ethnic Origins of the Peoples of Northeastern Asia* (1972).

Tunguska fireball

At sunrise on June 30, 1908, the area near the Tunguska River in Siberia was the site of a tremendous explosion that had the force of a modern H-bomb and took place at an altitude of several kilometers. Although the explosion flattened trees for kilometers in all directions, no crater was formed, and aside from some microscopic nodules extracted from the soil, no recognizable fragments of an extraterrestrial object remain. Space scientists generally believe that the explosion was caused by a small comet that disintegrated in midair; several smaller events of a similar nature have since been observed. Various UFO enthusiasts in the USSR and elsewhere, however, have suggested that the blast was atomic and was created artificially—a fanciful idea that depends in the main on misinterpretation, exaggeration, and falsification of the relevant data, according to many observers.

JAMES E. OBERG

Bibliography: Chaikin, Andrew, "Target: Tunguska," *Sky & Telescope*, January 1984; Meadows, Jack, *Space Garbage* (1985); Stonely, Jack, *Cauldron of Hell*, ed. by A. T. Lawton (1978).

tunicate   [too'-nuh-kayt]

Tunicates are solitary or colonial marine animals encased in an often thick covering called a tunic. They are primitive chordates, the larval forms possessing a notochord and nerve cord, and as such are forerunners of the vertebrates. The

more than 1,300 species, making up the chordate subphylum Tunicata, or Urochordata, are classified in three classes: the usually sessile SEA SQUIRTS (Ascidiacea); the free-swimming, cask-shaped chain tunicates and salps (Thaliacea); and the surface-dwelling tadpolelike larvaceans (Larvacea). Adult tunicates, often transparent, range in size from microscopic to a diameter of 30 cm (1 ft) or more. Cilia associated with a perforated pharynx are used for feeding. The life cycle of most forms includes a remarkable metamorphosis from a pelagic larval stage resembling a miniature tadpole to an often nondescript adult that essentially lacks the chordate characteristics.

J. H. BUSHNELL

tuning fork

A tuning fork, a slender, pocket-sized metal device consisting of a stem with two prongs, is used to provide a standard for the judging of pitch accuracy in voices and musical instruments. When gently tapped it is set in vibration, producing a pure tone (without overtones) that remains—because it is made of chromium-nickel-steel alloy—virtually the same in all weathers. Tuning forks are usually set at the standard "international A" pitch (440 vibrations per second).

Tunis   [too'-nis]

Tunis, the capital and largest city of Tunisia, is situated about 10 km (6 mi) inland from the southern shore of the Gulf of Tunis (an inlet of the Mediterranean Sea), on an isthmus separating the shallow Lake of Tunis from the Sedjoumi salt marsh. The lake is connected by canal (built 1893) to the adjacent port of Halq al-Wadi (formerly La Goulette). The city's population is 596,654 (1984 est.), but an estimated 950,000 people live in the greater metropolitan area.

The commercial and industrial center of the country, Tunis is served by two airports and is the hub of the nation's road and rail networks. The nucleus of Tunis is the densely populated medina (old city), an oval-shaped district consisting of low white buildings, inner courtyards, and narrow streets clinging to the side of the western hills, which slope down from the site of the old fort, or Casbah (demolished 1956). The modern city, centering on the Avenue Habi Bourguiba, is on low-lying land and between the medina and the lake.

The main industries of Tunis are the processing of olive oil and other foodstuffs and the manufacture of textiles, carpets, chemicals, and cement. Tourism is also important. Two thermonuclear plants are located at Halq al-Wadi. The city's cultural centers are the University of Tunis (1960); the Bardo Museum, which houses an important archaeological collection; and the Kouba Museum of Islamic Art. Points of interest include Zitouna Mosque (732), remnants of the city's medieval walls, and the Roman aqueduct connecting Zaghouan and CARTHAGE, located 14 km (9 mi) to the northeast.

Colonized by Phoenicians in the 9th century BC, the city was a dependency of Carthage until that city's destruction in 146 BC. Tunis flourished as part of the Roman Empire, and following the Arab conquest in the 7th century the city served as the seat of several Muslim dynasties. Under the administration of Turkish beys from the late 16th century, Tunis became a center of Barbary Coast piracy (see BARBARY STATES). The city, along with the rest of Tunisia, was brought under French rule in 1881. Following the French withdrawal (1956), the once-large European population greatly declined, as did the Jewish population; today Tunis is largely composed of Arabic-speaking Muslims.

GARY L. FOWLER

Tunisia   [too-nee'-zhuh]

The Republic of Tunisia, smallest of the four countries in the North African MAGHRIB, borders Algeria on the west and Libya on the southeast. On the east and north it has nearly 1,300 km (800 mi) of Mediterranean coastline. Agriculture is the mainstay of the economy, but minerals and tourism are also important sources of revenue. Tunisia became independent in 1956 after more than 70 years as a French protectorate. Tunis is its capital.

Drainage. Intermittent streams form after heavy rains but eventually fan out as they cross the steppes, and the water evaporates in salt flats, or sebkhas. The only perennial stream in Tunisia is the Medjerda, which flows through the north. Two large intermittent salt lakes occupy a vast depression south of the steppes. The larger, Shatt Djerid, extends from the west near Gabès to the Algerian border and lies 16 m (52 ft) below sea level.

Resources. Petroleum, calcium phosphates, and iron ore are the most important mineral resources. Beaches and historical sites attract many visitors, and tourism is very important.

PEOPLE

Arabization of the native BERBER population proceeded rapidly after the ARAB conquest in the 7th century. Large numbers of Spanish Arabs settled in northern Tunisia in the 16th century, and Italian and French colonists arrived there after 1850. The Jewish community in Tunisia was one of the oldest and

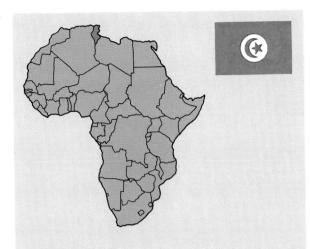

REPUBLIC OF TUNISIA

LAND. Area: 163,610 km² (63,170 mi²). Capital and largest city: Tunis (1984 pop., 556,654).

PEOPLE. Population (1986 est.): 7,424,000; density (1986 est.): 45 persons per km² (118 per mi²). Distribution (1984): 49% urban, 51% rural. Annual growth (1973–85): 2.4%. Official language: Arabic. Major religion: Islam.

EDUCATION AND HEALTH. Literacy (1984): 46% of adult population. Universities (1984): 1. Hospital beds (1983): 14,727. Physicians (1982): 1,732. Life expectancy (1980–85): women—61.1; men—60.1. Infant mortality (1984): 12 per 1,000 live births.

ECONOMY. GNP (1985): $8.73 billion; $1,220 per capita. Labor distribution (1984): agriculture—27%; manufacturing—19%; government and services—17%; construction—13%; trade—9%; transportation and communications—5%. Foreign trade (1985): imports—$2.9 billion; exports—$1.8 billion; principal trade partners—France, Italy, West Germany, United States. Currency: 1 dinar = 1,000 millimes.

GOVERNMENT. Type: republic. Legislature: National Assembly. Political subdivisions: 23 governorates.

COMMUNICATIONS. Railroads (1985): 2,118 km (1,316 mi) total. Roads (1982): 25,352 km (15,752 mi) total. Major ports: 5. Major airfields: 5.

LAND AND RESOURCES

Tunisia has three distinct physical regions: the northern mountains, the central steppe, and the southern desert. The ATLAS MOUNTAINS extend into northern Tunisia where they form two chains, the Northern Tell and the High Tell. The highest peaks are Mount Chambi, which rises to 1,544 m (5,066 ft) near the Algerian border, and Mount Mrhila, at 1,378 m (4,521 ft), southwest of Tunis. The Medjerda Valley, which separates the two chains, is a series of basins with rich alluvial soils. Cork oak and evergreen forests cover the northern mountains.

The steppe plateau of central Tunisia slopes eastward toward the coastal plain of the Sahel, which extends into Libya. The High Steppe, which has an average elevation of 457 m (1,500 ft), is composed of alluvial basins surrounded by low, barren mountains. The Low Steppe, with an average elevation of 183 m (600 ft), is a flat, gravel-covered plateau. The northernmost section of the SAHARA Desert lies in the extreme south of Tunisia.

Climate. Tunisia has a Mediterranean climate in the north, with mild, rainy winters and hot, dry summers. Winter rainfall ranges from an average 406 mm (16 in) a year in the northeast to less than 152 mm (6 in) in the south. Precipitation is irregular, and prolonged periods of drought are common in central and southern Tunisia. Temperatures along the coast are moderated by the sea, averaging 7° C (45° F) in January and 32° C (90° F) in August. Daily and annual ranges are greater elsewhere. Southern Tunisia has an arid climate, and hot, dry SIROCCO winds from the Sahara are common in summer.

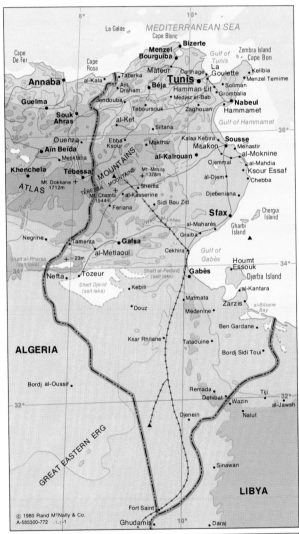

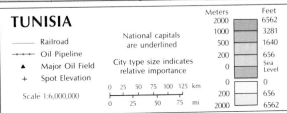

TUNISIA

⸺ Railroad	National capitals are underlined
⊶⊶⊶ Oil Pipeline	
▲ Major Oil Field	City type size indicates relative importance
+ Spot Elevation	

Scale 1:6,000,000

Meters	Feet
2000	6562
1000	3281
500	1640
200	656
0	Sea Level
0	0
200	656
2000	6562

0 25 50 75 100 125 km
0 25 50 75 mi

© 1980 Rand McNally & Co.
A-585300-772 -1-1-1

C° / F° chart

Bars indicate monthly ranges of temperature (red) and precipitation (blue) in Tunis, the capital of Tunisia, which has a Mediterranean climate. Southern Tunisia, which has the desert climate of the Sahara, is much drier.

Tunis

most important in North Africa, but most of the non-Muslim minorities have now emigrated.

Arabic is the official language and Islam the official religion of Tunisia. However, French remains a dominant language in the press, in education, and in government. Berber-speaking people, who form less than 1% of the population, live in small isolated villages in southern Tunisia.

Demography. About 16% of Tunisians live in cities of 50,000 persons or more. TUNIS and SFAX are the largest cities. The coastal city of BIZERTE is a major port. Tunisia has a serious unemployment problem aggravated by a high rate of population growth; three of every five Tunisians are less than 25 years of age.

Education and Health. Primary education is mandatory; higher education is pursued primarily at the University of Tunis (1960). Medical care is provided through a social security system to all wage earners.

The Arts. Tunisian arts are a mixture of the traditional and modern, with strong European influences, especially French. French is the language of science but Arabic that of literature, and the government has encouraged the creation of a national literature. Traditional crafts have had a revival; textiles, pottery, and woodwork are especially important. A movement has begun to develop a national music. In general, the government has made a major effort to encourage the arts and to diffuse cultural benefits to the entire population.

ECONOMIC ACTIVITY

The Tunisian nation has worked diligently to gain control of its resources, and the government plays an active role in development planning. In most sectors, however, growth faces difficulties.

The economy is based on agriculture and mining, although the proportion of the labor force engaged in agriculture has steadily declined. Cereals and wheat are the main crops, and citrus fruits, olive oil, dates, and wine are also important. Livestock includes sheep, goats, and cattle; forestry is confined to cork and oak. Phosphates and petroleum are the major mineral resources.

The tourist and fishing industries are of increasing importance, and foreign companies have been encouraged to establish factories in Tunisia for the manufacture of export-oriented goods. Manufactured goods include textiles and clothing, paper, steel products, construction materials, household articles, cement, and fertilizers. Projects such as the iron smelter and petroleum refinery at Bizerte and a chemical complex at Gabès are attempts at large-scale development.

Tunisia's road and rail network centers on Tunis, which is served by several airports and linked by canal to the port of Halq al-Wadi on the Gulf of Tunis. Telecommunications are relatively well developed.

Crude petroleum accounts for 41% of exports. Textiles account for another 21%, and phosphates and chemicals, 17%. Imports consist chiefly of raw materials, machinery, foodstuffs, and consumer goods. Remittances from workers abroad, long an important source of income, have declined in recent years. The country suffers from a recurrent trade deficit, which is partially covered by tourist receipts and foreign aid and loans.

(Above) Livestock graze on an arid hillside in Matmata, a village in eastern Tunisia. Although the raising of livestock is an important economic activity, the nation's most valuable agricultural products are the wheat, olive oil, and fruits grown farther north.

(Right) Tunis, the capital of Tunisia, is situated along a coastal lagoon that opens into the Mediterranean Sea. The city lies near the ruins of ancient Carthage, a city-state that controlled a maritime trade empire before being destroyed by Rome.

GOVERNMENT

The 1959 Tunisian constitution vests legislative power in the National Assembly, elected by universal suffrage. The president is the chief executive of the republic; a cabinet, headed by a prime minister, is responsible to him. Judicial independence is constitutionally guaranteed. Habib BOURGUIBA, who ruled Tunisia from 1957 to 1987, was elected president for life in 1975. The Democratic Constitutional Assembly (formerly the Destour Socialist party) controls political life, although opposition parties have been legal since 1983.

HISTORY

Tunisia was part of the ancient city-state of CARTHAGE, which fell to the Romans in 146 BC. It was an important part of the Roman Empire's Africa province because it was agriculturally rich, and its fisheries, mines, and quarries were productive.

The Arabs gained control in the 7th century and moved the capital from Carthage to al-Kaiouan. The Arabic language and Islam replaced Latin and Christianity, and the native Berbers supported the new Arab empire. Successive invasions by Bedouins from Arabia, Normans from Sicily, and Moroccans followed. The Ottoman Empire conquered Tunisia in 1574.

As one of the so-called BARBARY STATES, Tunisia became a center of piracy, on which the public treasury depended until about 1817. As the country fell into political and economic chaos, Great Britain, Italy, and France vied for influence. France finally gained a free hand at the 1878 Congress of Berlin and established a protectorate in 1881.

The protectorate lasted until 1956. In 1957 a republic was proclaimed with Habib Bourguiba as its president. Bourguiba subsequently consolidated his political power in Tunisia and strengthened relations with France and the Arab states. Palestinian leader Yasir ARAFAT had his headquarters in Tunis from 1982 to 1986. In 1983, Tunisia signed a cooperation agreement with Algeria and Mauritania. Economic problems sparked antigovernment riots in 1984 and contributed to a rise in Islamic fundamentalism and the seizure of power in November 1987 by Prime Minister Zine el-Abidine Ben Ali, who praised the ailing Bourguiba but said he was no longer fit to govern. Ben Ali released many political prisoners and improved ties with Libya.

GARY L. FOWLER

Bibliography: American University, *Tunisia: A Country Study*, 2d ed. (1979); Anderson, L., *The State and Social Transformation in Tunisia and Libya, 1830–1980* (1986); Knapp, W., *Tunisia* (1970); Moore, C. H., *Tunisia since Independence* (1965; repr. 1982); Perkins, K. J., *Tunisia* (1986); Rudebeck, L., *Party and People* (1969); Salem, N., *Habib Bourguiba, Islam, and the Creation of Tunisia* (1984); Simmons, J., and Stone, R. A., eds., *Change in Tunisia* (1976).

tunnel

A tunnel is a primarily horizontal passageway produced by excavation and used for transportation, mining, conducting water and sewerage, or housing underground facilities. Modern tunneling techniques include drilling and blasting, soft-ground tunneling by shield, use of prefabricated tubes, and, most recently, mechanical excavation.

HISTORY

Constituting one of the earliest engineering techniques, tunnels were built in Paleolithic times in order to extend natural caves. The Babylonians dug tunnels for irrigation, and the ancient Egyptians and Indians dug them for tombs and temple rooms. The ancient Greeks, who used tunnels for draining marshes and for AQUEDUCTS, built (6th century BC) such tunnels as that on the island of Samos, constructed by Eupalinus of Megara; it was 1,000 m (3,300 ft) long.

The Romans built tunnels from shafts that also provided ventilation; they also developed (probably from Etruscan origins) the fire-quenching method of hard-rock tunneling, in which rock was heated by fire and suddenly cooled by water thrown against it, causing it to scale or crack. The Roman Pausilippo Tunnel was built (36 BC) to connect Pozzuoli with Naples; cut through volcanic rock, it was 1,500 m (4,800 ft) long, 7.5 m (25 ft) wide, and 9 m (30 ft) high.

Canal builders enlarged the art of tunneling in the 17th and 18th centuries. Pierre Riquet first used (1666–81) blasting with gunpowder in building the Malpas Tunnel near Béziers for the Languedoc Canal. Notable canal-tunnels were built in England in the 18th century by self-taught engineer James Brindley.

The coming of the railroad brought a tremendous demand for tunnels. The first steam-railway tunnel, the Wapping, under Liverpool, was built by George STEPHENSON in 1826–27. Great strides in tunnel technology were made in digging railroad tunnels through mountain rock, beginning with the first Alpine tunnel, the Mont Cenis Tunnel (14 km/8.5 mi long) between Italy and France (1857–71). Although the Mont Cenis Tunnel was begun using manual drilling, engineer Germain Sommeiller later employed many revolutionary techniques, including rail-mounted drill carriages, compressed-air drills, and hydraulic compressors.

At the same time in the United States, the 7.2-km (4.5-mi) Hoosac Tunnel was being built (1855–76) through the Berkshires. Important advances in its construction included one of the first uses of dynamite, electric detonation of explosives, and the use of steam and compressed-air drills.

Subsequent major Alpine tunnels included the 15-km (9.3-mi) SAINT GOTTHARD TUNNEL (1872–82); the 20-km (12-mi) First Simplon Tunnel (1898–1906), between Italy and Switzerland, for many years the longest transportation tunnel in the world; and the 14-km (9-mi) Lötschberg Tunnel (1906–11).

Paralleling the development of rock tunneling in the 19th century was that of subaqueous tunneling, made possible by the invention of the tunneling shield (a metal shell the size of the tunnel) by engineer Marc Brunel (see BRUNEL family), a French émigré, in London. Brunel's first shield, designed to tunnel under the River Thames between Rotherhithe and Wapping (begun 1825), was a rectangular box made up of 12 parallel cast-iron segments divided into three stories, so that 36 sandhogs could work in individual cells, removing material through windows. The shield was advanced by screw jacks and was followed by a team of bricklayers who lined the tunnel, while the excavated material was collected and removed

NOTABLE TUNNELS OF THE WORLD

Name	Date Completed	Location	Length	Type
Canal du Midi (Languedoc)	1681	Béziers, France	157 m (515 ft)	Canal
Rotherhithe and Wapping	1843	London	370 m (1,200 ft)	Pedestrian*
Mont Cenis (Fréjus)	1871	Alps (France-Italy)	14 km (8.5 mi)	Railroad
Hoosac	1876	Massachusetts	7 km (4.5 mi)	Railroad
Saint Gotthard	1882	Alps (Switzerland)	15 km (9.3 mi)	Railroad
Simplon I	1906	Alps (Italy-Switzerland)	20 km (12 mi)	Railroad
Holland	1927	New York City	2.6 km (1.6 mi)	Automobile
Queensway	1934	Liverpool, England	4.6 km (2.9 mi)	Automobile
Tanna	1934	Japan	8 km (5 mi)	Railroad
Lincoln	1937, 1954, 1957†	New York City	2.5 km (1.6 mi)	Automobile
Mont Blanc	1965	Alps (France-Italy)	11.7 km (7.2 mi)	Automobile
Dai-Shimizu	1982	Japan	22.2 km (13.8 mi)	Railroad
Saint Gotthard	1980	Alps (Switzerland)	16.3 km (10.1 mi)	Automobile
Seelisberg	1980	Alps (Switzerland)	9.3 km (5.8 mi)	Automobile
Seikan	1988	Japan (undersea)	54 km (33 mi)	Railroad
Fort McHenry	1985	Baltimore	2.2 km (1.4 mi)	Automobile

*Now part of London Underground.
†Three tubes.

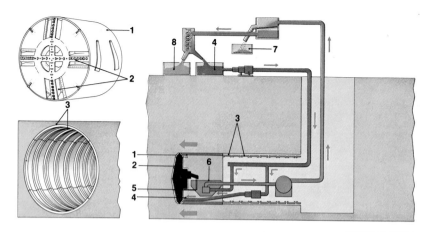

(Below) In tunneling through hard rocks, holes (1) are first drilled, then filled with dynamite, and exploded in a set sequence. The blasts are timed so that the center sections are blasted first. After the debris is taken away in cars on tracks (2), the tunnel is usually lined with reinforced concrete (3).

to the rear. Financial problems and a severe water influx that killed six workers halted progress for 7 years, but a new shield was built and the tunnel was finally completed in 1843.

The Rotherhithe Tunnel, today part of the London Underground but originally designed for pedestrians, was followed (1869–70) by a small-diameter, 402-m (1,320-ft) pedestrian tunnel at Tower Hill, driven in 1 year by Peter Barlow and James Henry Greathead using a cylindrical shield designed by Greathead. The Greathead technique, employing compressed air to keep water out of the heading (the tunnel face in front of the shield), became the accepted method for tunneling soft ground.

In the United States, De Witt Haskins pioneered (1874) the use of compressed air and the airlock in an enterprise under the Hudson River at New York City. Haskins did not use a shield, and two serious blowouts killed 20 workers, forcing temporary abandonment of the project. The East River Gas Tunnel, excavated by Charles M. Jacobs in 1892–94, finally brought together the shield, compressed air, and airlock (see CAISSON), and the same technique was used (1904) to complete Haskins's Hudson project (today part of the Hudson Tubes) and other Hudson tunnels.

The automobile created a new problem, that of ventilating lethal carbon monoxide fumes. Clifford Holland solved this problem in the HOLLAND TUNNEL (1927), under the Hudson River, by using a system of fans and air ducts.

CONSTRUCTION
Even though engineers today employ a wide variety of new technological devices (lasers to provide tracings of ground formations, for example; new explosives; specially designed tunnel-boring machinery), they continue to use many of the established techniques.

Soft-Ground Tunneling. The basic tool for tunneling through soft ground, especially in water-bearing strata, remains the shield. In its modern form the shield has a circular cross section with a cutting edge driven forward by powered jacks. Material excavated through working pockets in the face is removed by conveyor or cars on rails. In tunneling under rivers, the use of compressed air is often necessary; workers enter and leave through an airlock, with a decompression chamber used to prevent the BENDS.

A subaqueous tunneling technique perfected (1906–10) by W. J. Wilgus for a railroad tunnel under the Detroit River, called the build-and-sink, or immersed-tube, method, has become steadily more popular for large vehicular tunnels under rivers. A trench is first excavated and leveled in the river bottom. Sections of concrete-lined steel tube or prestressed concrete are sealed at both ends with temporary bulkheads and towed into place over the trench. The sections are then ballasted, sunk in the trench, and coupled together by divers. When the tunnel is complete, it is covered over for protection. For SUBWAYS, a widely used technique is the cut-and-cover method, which limits disruption by excavating a short section from the surface and immediately covering it over.

Rock Tunneling. Tunneling through hard rock with explosive

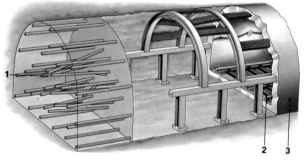

charges follows the long-established cycle of drilling, planting the charges, blasting, ventilating, and mucking (clearing the tunnel of debris); the process has been greatly accelerated, however, by high-speed drilling machinery. Full-diameter drilling and blasting was pioneered (1958–65) in the 11.7-km (7.2-mi) Mont Blanc vehicular tunnel between France and Italy. To reinforce the rock where cracks have developed, steel bolts are used. The tunnel's rock face is also strengthened by blowing layers of concrete on the prepared rock surface.

The most important modern development in rock tunneling is full-face boring, a technique pioneered in 1882, when Col. Frederick Beaumont invented a machine to bore through chalk for the English Channel Tunnel project. The Channel Tunnel, or "Chunnel," a cooperative Anglo-French project, has been begun twice within the past century. It was stopped once, in 1883, because of British fears of invasion, and again in 1974, because the binational supersonic CONCORDE proved a more attractive project. In 1986 a 3-tunnel scheme

In the immersed-tube method of tunnel construction, an underwater trench (1) is first dredged and leveled with a sand-aggregate foundation (2). Prefabricated steel or prestressed-concrete tunnel sections are sealed with temporary bulkheads, floated into position between pontoons (3), and sunk end to end into the trench by filling the ballast tanks (4) with water. Divers bolt or weld (5) the sections together. The completed tunnel segments are then covered with earth (6), and the bulkheads are removed to permit fitting out.

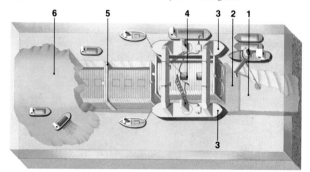

was agreed on by the two countries, and work was begun in early 1988. Adaptations of Beaumont's machine, called moles, have been used since the 1950s. Their round heads—some more than 9.1 m (30 ft) in diameter—have rotating cutters that bite away and toss soil or rock to bucket conveyors on the head edge. Mole machines are used in the Chunnel, as they are used on land, especially in mountains where blasting often weakens the rock surrounding the tunnel.

Undersea Tunneling. The first tunnels built under the ocean floor were the 10-km (6.2-mi) Japanese Kanmon railroad tunnels (1936–44), for which both rock and soft-ground techniques were used. The Seikan Tunnel, completed in 1988, links the Japanese islands of Honshu and Hokkaido. It is the world's deepest underwater tunnel and the longest transportation (railroad) tunnel, with a length of 54 km (33 mi).

JOSEPH GIES

Bibliography: Beaver, Patrick, *A History of Tunnels* (1973); Bonavia, M. R., *Channel Tunnel* (1987); Gies, Joseph, *Adventure Underground* (1962); Jones, M. J., ed., *Tunnelling '82* (1982); Megaw, T. M., and Bartlett, J., *Tunnels: Planning, Design, Construction*, 2 vols. (1981–82); Stack, Barbara, *Handbook of Mining and Tunnelling Machinery* (1982).

See also: COAL AND COAL MINING.

tunnel effect

In physics, the tunnel effect, or tunneling, is a phenomenon in which electrons or other elementary particles move through sufficiently thin potential barriers. Theoretically, it is explained by QUANTUM MECHANICS and application of the Schrödinger wave equation. Treated as waves, electrons and other small particles can be described by wave equations, the solutions of which predict a small probability for the tunneling of particles through thin layers of solid or vacuum. The tunnel effect is exploited in a number of scientific applications, including semiconductors, sensitive electronic measuring instruments, and molecular-level microscopy.

Tunney, Gene   [tuhn'-ee]

James Joseph "Gene" Tunney, b. New York City, May 25, 1898, d. Nov. 7, 1978, was an American boxer who retired as the undefeated heavyweight boxing champion after two memorable victories over Jack Dempsey. Tunney lost only one fight in his career, to Harry Greb, as a light-heavyweight, whom he later beat, before becoming the heavyweight champion. Tunney, a masterful boxer, easily gained a 10-round decision over the champion Dempsey, previously considered unbeatable, on Sept. 23, 1926, in Philadelphia. He defended the title against Dempsey on Sept. 22, 1927, in Chicago—the famous "long count" fight in which Tunney was knocked down for about 13 seconds in the 7th round. The referee refused to start the count, however, because Dempsey at first did not go to a neutral corner. Tunney went on to score a convincing decision. For the fight he received $990,445, then a record purse. Tunney retired in 1928 with a record of 56 victories (41 by knockout), 1 loss, 1 draw, 17 no decisions, and 1 no contest. He was elected to the Boxing Hall of Fame in 1955. Tunney's son, John Varick Tunney, b. New York City, June 26, 1934, served as Democratic congressional representative (1965–70) and U.S. senator (1971–77) from California.

Bibliography: Heimer, Melvin L., *The Long Count* (1969).

Tupí   [too-pee']

Tupí, or Tupí-Guaraní, is one of the most widespread native American languages in tropical South America. Traditionally, cultural variations were great among Tupian-speaking peoples, although tropical forest horticulture with manioc as the principal crop and hunting and fishing were important activities for all groups. Religion was shamanistically oriented (see SHAMAN), and the extended family formed the basic social unit. Many Tupian groups on the lower Amazon were exceedingly warlike; some are alleged to have practiced cannibalism.

From a center of origin probably south of the Amazon, various Tupian-speaking groups migrated in several directions until the late 16th century. The Tupinambarana, for example, journeyed along the Amazon to the Madeira until they reached its headwaters in Bolivia; they then returned downstream to the island of Tupinambarana in the Amazon. The Omagua reached the mouth of the Juruá River, and the Cocama traveled still farther to the Ucayalí in Peru. The Tupinambá crossed eastern Brazil to the Atlantic and also migrated south to Porto Allegre, a distance of 3,200 km (2,000 mi). Tupians who moved inland were called the Guaraní of Paraguay; those who reached the frontier of the Inca empire were known as the Chiriguano. Tupian-speakers comprised one of the largest native populations at the time of the Spanish conquest.

LOUIS C. FARON

Bibliography: Key, M. R., *The Grouping of South American Indian Languages* (1979); Klein, H. E., and Stark, L. R., eds., *South American Indian Languages* (1985); Steward, J. H., and Faron, L., *Native Peoples of South America* (1959).

Tupper, Sir Charles   [tuhp'-ur]

Sir Charles Tupper, b. Amherst, Nova Scotia, July 2, 1821, d. Oct. 30, 1915, premier (1864–67) of Nova Scotia and prime minister (1896) of Canada, led Nova Scotia into the Canadian Confederation in 1867 over great opposition. Tupper, a physician, sat in the Nova Scotia assembly as a Conservative (1855–67). After serving as provincial premier, he won election to the Canadian House of Commons in 1867 and served there until 1884. He was a cabinet member (1870–73, 1878–84) during both of the administrations of Sir John A. Macdonald. Tupper served as high commissioner to London (1884–87, 1888–96), returning to Canada to become prime minister. After a few months in office he was forced to resign when the Conservatives were defeated at the polls. He led the opposition (1886–1901) until his retirement.

P. B. WAITE

Bibliography: Longley, James W., *Sir Charles Tupper* (1926).

Tura, Cosimo   [too'-rah]

Cosimo Tura, b. c.1430, d. April 1495, was the most important 15th-century painter from Ferrara, Italy, seat of the Este family and one of the most cultivated courts in Renaissance Italy. Tura's birthdate and Ferrara's location near Venice suggest the general outlines of his training. His aesthetic was grounded in the illusionistic, antiquarian style of the Paduan artist Francesco Squarcione, who also influenced Tura's contemporary Andrea Mantegna. Netherlandish painters, such as Rogier van der Weyden, who visited Ferrara in 1449, left their mark on Tura, as can be seen in the characteristic tense linearism of his manner. Among his most exemplary paintings are the frescoes (1469–71) in the Palazzo Schifanoia in Ferrara and the *Roverella Madonna* (c.1474; National Gallery, London).

WILLIAM HOOD

Bibliography: Hartt, Frederick, *History of Italian Renaissance Art*, 2d ed. (1980); Ruhmer, Eberhard, *Tura: Paintings and Drawings* (1958).

turbidimeter   [tur-buh-dim'-uh-tur]

A turbidimeter is an instrument that measures the concentration of suspended particles in solutions, a very important factor in water and environmental control systems. Sir John Tyndall observed (1860) that particles that are invisible are easily discernible when directly in the path of a strong light beam and viewed from the side; these particles become visible because they reflect some of the incident light. The measurement of the reflected light is directly related to the number of particles in suspension and is the basis of the turbidimeter. A PHOTOMETER may be calibrated in units of turbidity. A dual-beam turbidimeter can compare unknown samples directly against a standard solution. Typical uses of this instrument include control of beverage clarity, tanning operations, water and waste treatment, and determination of bacterial growth rates.

DOUGLAS M. CONSIDINE

turbidity current: see DENSITY CURRENT.

turbine [tur'-buhn]

A turbine is a rotary machine that converts the kinetic energy in a stream of fluid (gas or liquid) into mechanical energy. The stream of fluid is guided to a rotor, a wheel that is mounted to a shaft from which power is taken. The fluid strikes a series of buckets, fins, or blades on the rotor, and the energy in the fluid makes the rotor spin. Turbines are an example of Newton's third law of motion, which states that for every action there is an equal and opposite reaction. The earliest known turbine was built (AD c.75) by the Greek inventor Hero of Alexandria. His device was a hollow ball that spun in reaction to jets of escaping steam. Although only a toy, this early reaction turbine demonstrated the principle later used in the aircraft jet engine.

Turbines may be classed as impulse turbines or reaction turbines, depending on the force that causes the rotor to revolve. An impulse turbine is driven by the force of a fluid striking it. In a reaction turbine, such as Hero's toy, nozzles are mounted on the rotor and revolve with it.

The three main types of turbines are classified on the basis of the fluid that supplies the driving force: the gas turbine, the steam turbine, and the water, or hydraulic, turbine (see WATERWHEEL; HYDROELECTRIC POWER).

Gas Turbine. The gas turbine is a rotary engine that converts heat energy into mechanical energy by a continuous process that compresses, heats, and expands a gas. The basic gas turbine was patented in England in 1791 by John Barber. In 1930, Frank WHITTLE in England was granted the first of his many patents for aircraft jet engines, which are essentially gas turbines.

A typical gas turbine has an axial or centrifugal air COMPRESSOR that furnishes a continuous supply of air to a combustion chamber; the compressor and combustion chamber constitute the gasifier section of the turbine. In the combustion chamber, fuel is added to the air and then ignited. When the fuel burns, it produces a hot, high-pressure gas. As the gas leaves the combustion chamber, it spins the power-turbine rotor (the power section), which provides power and also drives the air

The rotor of a steam turbine is lowered into its casing during assembly. Its components include (from left) the large blades of the low-pressure stage; the medium-sized and small blades of the reaction stage; the Curtis wheel; and the drive-shaft mechanism.

compressor. The net power available for work from a gas turbine is the power available from the gases minus the power required to turn the compressor.

Generally, if power is taken mechanically from the shaft of the power-turbine rotor, the engine is called a gas turbine. In a jet engine, however, propulsion is provided by a powerful stream of exhaust gas (see JET PROPULSION).

Steam Turbine. A steam turbine is a rotary machine that converts the heat energy of steam into mechanical energy. Steam turbines developed little from the time of Hero to the end of the 19th century, at which time Carl Gustaf de Laval, a Swede, built several successful single-stage turbines ranging in size from five to several hundred horsepower. Sir Charles PARSONS in England and Charles G. Curtis in the United States applied (1884 and 1895, respectively) for patents on a turbine design in which several bladed rotors were connected to the same shaft. In this design, the energy of the steam was put to work in small stages, one after the other. Each stage of the turbine was larger than the one that preceded it, because the steam must be expanded to maintain its energy. Using stages, turbines could run more efficiently at low speeds and could be built in large sizes.

In a typical steam turbine, steam strikes against curved or angular blades fastened to the movable rotor and causes it to spin. The steam then meets another set of blades that are fastened to the casing, or stationary shell, of the turbine; these blades redirect the steam so it can effectively push against the next set of rotor blades. This process is repeated as the steam travels the length of the turbine through the various stages.

Steam turbines provide more than 80 percent of the electricity generated in the world and power most of the world's largest ships.

DONALD L. ANGLIN

Bibliography: Balje, O. E., *Turbo-Mechanics* (1981); Hawthorne, W. R., ed., *Aerodynamics of Turbines and Compressors* (1964); Mironer, Alan, *Engineering Fluid Mechanics* (1979); Shepherd, Dennis G., *Introduction to the Gas Turbine*, 2d ed. (1960), and *Principles of Turbomachinery* (1956); Staniar, William, ed., *Prime Movers*, 3d ed. (1966); Streeter, Victor L., and Wylie, E. Benjamin, *Fluid Mechanics*, 7th ed. (1979).

See also: POWER, GENERATION AND TRANSMISSION OF.

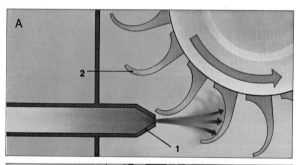

An impulse turbine, such as the Pelton wheel (A), has a stationary nozzle (1) that converts a fluid's pressure energy into kinetic energy. This kinetic energy is then directed against buckets (2) mounted on a wheel, which produces rotation. In the other basic type of turbine, called a reaction turbine (B), a set of stationary nozzles (3) injects pressurized fluid between a set of blades that are mounted on a rotating wheel (4). The fluid moves the blades, and as they move they accelerate the fluid still further, creating the reaction that drives the wheel.

turbot [tur'-buht]

Turbot is the common name for several species of FLATFISHES (flounders). The true turbot, *Scophthalmus maximus*, a popular food in Europe, is found in the Mediterranean and along the Atlantic coast of Europe. Brownish and almost circular, it has both eyes on one side and lies buried on the bottom on its blind side. Several American flounders of the family Pleuronectidae are also sometimes called turbots: for example, the spotted turbots, genus *Pleuromichthys*, of the Pacific, and the Greenland halibut or turbot, *Reinhardtius hippoglossoides*, of the Atlantic.   E. O. WILEY

Turenne, Henri de La Tour d'Auvergne, Vicomte de   [too-ren']

Marshal Henri de La Tour d'Auvergne, vicomte de Turenne, b. Sept. 11, 1611, d. July 27, 1675, was one of the greatest military officers in French history. He served his military apprenticeship under his uncles, the princes of Orange, Frederick Henry and Maurice of Nassau, fighting in support of the Dutch revolt against Spain. From 1630 to 1642 he fought in nearly every theater of the conflict directed by Cardinal Richelieu, the French minister, against the Spaniards in the THIRTY YEARS' WAR. Although the duc de Bouillon, Turenne's brother, was involved in plots against the cardinal, Richelieu always trusted Turenne. Cardinal Mazarin, who succeeded Richelieu in 1643, accorded the vicomte less confidence, however. Until the Peace of Westphalia (1648), Turenne and his colleague and rival Louis II, prince de Condé, campaigned against the Habsburgs in Germany. Condé's impetuosity was matched by Turenne's reserve and careful planning.

During the civil wars of the FRONDE (1648–52), Turenne was induced by Condé's sister, the duchesse de Longueville, to side with the rebels. In 1651, however, Turenne became reconciled with the crown; he served Mazarin and defeated Condé at the Battle of Saint-Antoine (1652), outside Paris. From 1653 until the Peace of the Pyrenees in 1659, Turenne campaigned against Spain in Flanders, while Condé served the enemy. The Battle of the Dunes (June 14, 1658), near Dunkerque, was Turenne's greatest victory over his rival. He campaigned for Louis XIV against the Spanish (1667–68) and the Dutch and the Germans (1672–75) and was killed in battle in Germany.   J. H. M. SALMON

Bibliography: Goubert, Pierre, *Louis XIV and Twenty Million Frenchmen*, trans. by Anne Carter (1970); Weygand, Maxime, *Turenne, Marshall of France*, trans. by G. B. Ives (1930).

Turgenev, Ivan   [toor-gayn'-yif]

Turgenev, a 19th-century Russian writer, is believed to have hastened the abolition of serfdom through his stories of peasant life. His masterpiece, Fathers and Sons (1862), polarized Russian society along radical-conservative lines. In addition to writing plays, novels, and essays, Turgenev helped popularize Russian literature in western Europe.

Ivan Sergeyevich Turgenev, b. Orel province, Nov. 9 (N.S.), 1818, d. Sept. 3 (N.S.), 1883, was one of Russia's greatest writers. Educated in Moscow and Saint Petersburg, and having studied philosophy in Berlin, he was sympathetic to liberal Western opinions and a friend of Mikhail Bakunin, Aleksandr Herzen, and Vissarion Belinsky. Turgenev wrote some poetry in the 1840s but soon discovered that prose fiction was his proper domain. Among his plays—all written early in his career—*A Month in the Country* (1855; Eng. trans., 1933) anticipates Anton Chekhov.

Turgenev's fame was established by *A Sportsman's Sketches* (1847–52; Eng. trans., 1855), a cycle of stories about the landowners and serfs of central Russia. Most of the stories are naturalistic and are given structure by a subtle synchronization of nature imagery and human experience. They are unified by an ever-present tension between images of death, decay, and stagnation and evocations of natural resilience, vigor, and beauty. Because the former are usually attributes of the masters, and the latter of the serfs, *Sketches* became associated with Russian social reform, and it may have hastened the emancipation of the serfs.

Beginning with *Rudin* (1856; Eng. trans., 1873), Turgenev produced a series of novels and stories in which he explored social problems such as the ideological split between the generation of the 1840s and the new, radical generation that followed. *On the Eve* (1859; Eng. trans., 1871) has a young emancipated Russian woman marry a Bulgarian freedom fighter; the love story is played out against the backdrop of Russia's national aspirations. FATHERS AND SONS, Turgenev's most famous work, features the nihilist Bazarov, who would like to destroy the entire structure of society and build a new order based on rational scientific principles. *Virgin Soil* (1877; Eng. trans., 1877) examines the collapse of the populist movement of the 1870s.

After 1858, Turgenev lived mostly abroad. Some of his later stories, notably "The Torrents of Spring" (1871; Eng. trans., 1874), are set in the West and are apolitical. In his best work, Turgenev constantly came back to a theme he had formulated in his essay "Hamlet and Don Quixote" (1860; Eng. trans., 1930)—a Hamlet, paralyzed by his thoughts and despair, and wandering through a godless world in which blind nature is the only reality, meets a Don Quixote who is enthusiastically following a transcendent ideal.   VICTOR TERRAS

Bibliography: Freeborn, Richard, *Turgenev: The Novelist's Novelist* (1960); Garnett, Edward, *Turgenev* (1974); Ledovsky, Marina, *The Other Turgenev* (1973); Moser, Charles A., *Ivan Turgenev* (1972); Pritchett, Victor S., *The Gentle Barbarian: The Life and Work of Turgenev* (1977); Yarmolinsky, Avrahm, *Turgenev: The Man, His Art, and His Age* (1959).

Turgot, Anne Robert Jacques   [tuer-goh']

Anne Robert Jacques Turgot, b. May 10, 1727, d. Mar. 18, 1781, was a French economic theorist, provincial administrator, and controller general of finances (1774–76) whose bold reforms of the nearly collapsed financial structure of France were blocked by the forces of privilege. Having abandoned theological studies in 1751 to become a royal magistrate, he held various administrative posts until his appointment as intendant (1761–74) of impoverished Limoges; there he vigorously pursued road building, scientific farming, town planning, and equitable taxation. A friend of the Enlightenment and a disciple of the PHYSIOCRATS, he wrote *Réflexions sur la formation et la distribution des richesses* (Reflections on the Function and Distribution of Wealth, 1766), articles in Diderot's *Encyclopédie*, and other works advocating national prosperity by freeing landed wealth from governmental controls.

At the outset of LOUIS XVI's reign, Turgot took over (1774) the controller generalship and reduced the government's massive debt by curbing court and military costs; his conservative slogan was "No bankruptcy, no new taxes, no loans." But his bold freeing of the grain trade from internal tariffs in 1775 was ill-timed because a crop failure drove prices too high and triggered riots. The military was used to restore order, and in 1776, Turgot introduced the even bolder Six Edicts, abolishing guilds and replacing forced peasant road work (the *corvée*) with a tax on all landowners. Opposition by the privileged clergy and nobility and the Parlement of Paris brought about his project's collapse and his own dismissal.

A. LLOYD MOOTE

Bibliography: Dakin, D., *Turgot and the Ancien Regime in France* (1939; repr. 1965); Groenewegen, P. D., *The Economics of A. R. J. Turgot* (1977); Lodge, E., *Sully, Colbert, Turgot* (1931); Meek, R. L., ed. and trans., *Turgot on Progress, Sociology and Economics* (1973).

Turin   [tur'-in]

Turin (Italian: Torino), a city in northwestern Italy and capital of the Piedmont region, occupies the left bank of the Po River 515 km (320 mi) northwest of Rome. Turin's population of 1,035,565 (1987 est.) places it fourth among Italian cities after Rome, Milan, and Naples. Accounting for 80% of Italian automobile production, Turin ranks second after Milan as an industrial city. Other products include textiles, aircraft, ball bearings, rubber and tires, leather goods, paper, metal goods, plastics, radios and televisions, pharmaceuticals, chocolate, wines, and clothing. A major commercial and transportation hub, Turin has a military base and international airport and is a leading fashion center. The city also has a university (1404), an art academy (1652), a musical conservatory (1867), and many museums and libraries. Historic buildings include the Renaissance Cathedral of San Giovanni Battista (1492–98), the basilica of Superga (1717–31) with its burial chapel of the house of Savoy, and the Palazzo Madama (begun 13th century), Palazzo Reale (1648–58), and Palazzo Carignano (1680), the meeting place of the first Italian parliament in 1861.

Founded by the Taurini (hence at first called Taurasia) and subsequently destroyed by Hannibal in 218 BC, the city became a Roman military colony during the 1st century BC. After rule by Lombards (568–774) and Franks (774–888), Turin passed to the house of Savoy in 1046 and became the capital first of the duchy of Savoy (1563) and then of the kingdom of Sardinia (1720). Following a period of French control (1798–1814), the city became the center of the Savoy-led Risorgimento, or Italian unification movement, and served as the first capital of a united kingdom of Italy (1861–65). Heavily damaged by Allied bombing during World War II, Turin now has a modern appearance, with wide piazzas and regularly spaced streets and parks.   DANIEL R. LESNICK

Turina, Joaquin   [too-ree'-nah]

Joaquin Turina, b. Dec. 9, 1882, d. Jan. 14, 1949, was a Spanish composer, pianist, and conductor. Emulating the example of Isaac Albéniz and Manuel de Falla, he wrote a large number of works for piano, orchestra, and voice evoking Spanish scenes, often those of his native city, Seville. Typical orchestral works include *La Procesión del rocío* (Procession of the Virgin, 1912), evoking a popular religious procession, *Sinfonía Sevillana* (Sevillian Symphony, 1920), and *Canto a Sevilla* (Song to Seville, 1924, with soprano solo). One of his best-known pieces is *La Oración del torero* (The Toreador's Prayer, 1925) for strings.   MARTIN COOPER

Turing, Alan

Alan Mathison Turing, b. June 23, 1912, d. June 7, 1954, was a British mathematician who is best remembered for theoretical computing devices that bear his name and are based on his ideas (Turing machines). While a graduate student at Princeton University in 1936, Turing published "On Computable Numbers," a paper in which he conceived of a machine that could move from one state to another by following a rigorous set of rules. This led to a computing scheme that foreshadowed the logic of digital computers. During World War II, Turing worked in the British Foreign Office, where he played a leading role in efforts to break enemy codes. He later worked on the development of an electronic computer, on theories of artificial intelligence, and on the application of mathematical theory to biological forms. In later years Turing was professionally hindered by personal attributes, particularly following his arrest for violation of British homosexuality statutes in 1952. He committed suicide at the age of 41. *Breaking the Code* (1987), a play by Hugh Whitemore, is based on his life.

Bibliography: Hodges, Andrew, *Alan Turing: The Enigma* (1983).

Turkana   [tur-kah'-nuh]

The Turkana are an African people who speak an Eastern Nilotic language within the Nilo-Saharan linguistic family (see AFRICAN LANGUAGES). They inhabit a hot, low region in north-

west Kenya and northeast Uganda. In the mid-1700s they moved into northwest Kenya and adopted camel herding from local tribespeople. Turkana migrations southward in the late 19th century were halted (c.1900) by the British.

Relatively isolated, the Turkana are a seminomadic pastoral people who practice shifting cultivation of cereal grains part of the year. Livestock (cattle, goats, and sheep) and milk products form the basis of their subsistence, although hunting and gathering are also practiced. Leatherworking, carried out by women, is highly developed. Political leadership is vested in the heads of small, extended patrilineal families. Age sets play a significant role in their social organization. Clans exist and polygamy with BRIDE-PRICE is practiced. Plural wives live in separate mother-child households. A high god is worshiped, with rites and ceremonies revolving around health and subsistence.   JAMES W. HERRICK

Bibliography: Gulliver, P. H., *The Family Herds* (1955; repr. 1979); Hendriksen, G., *Economic Growth and Ecological Balance* (1985).

Turkana, Lake: see RUDOLF, LAKE.

Turkana man: see SKULL 1470.

Turkestan: see TURKISTAN.

Turkey

Turkey is an independent republic occupying a region, partly in Europe and partly in Asia, that has played a major role in

REPUBLIC OF TURKEY

LAND. Area: 780,576 km² (301,382 mi²). Capital: Ankara (1987 est. pop., 3,462,880). Largest city: Istanbul (1987 est. pop., 5,858,558).

PEOPLE. Population (1988 est.): 52,900,000; density: 67.7 persons per km² (175.5 per mi²). Distribution (1988): 53% urban, 47% rural. Annual growth (1987–88): 2.2%. Official language: Turkish. Major religion: Islam.

EDUCATION AND HEALTH. Literacy (1987): 70–80% of adult population. Universities (1987): 22. Hospital beds (1985): 103,918. Physicians (1985): 36,427. Life expectancy (1988): 63. Infant mortality (1988): 95 per 1,000 live births.

ECONOMY. GNP (1987): $58.7 billion; $1,110 per capita. Labor distribution (1986): agriculture—58.3%; services—28.7%; industry and energy—13%. Foreign trade (1987): imports—$14.2 billion; exports—$10.2 billion; principal trade partners (1987)—West Germany, United States, Iraq, Italy, Iran, Saudi Arabia. Currency: 1 Turkish lira = 100 kurus.

GOVERNMENT. Type: republic. Legislature: Grand National Assembly. Political subdivisions: 67 provinces.

COMMUNICATIONS. Railroads (1987): 10,328 km (6,418 mi) total. Roads (1987): 125,400 km (77,920 mi) total; about half are paved. Major ports: 4. Major airfields: 6.

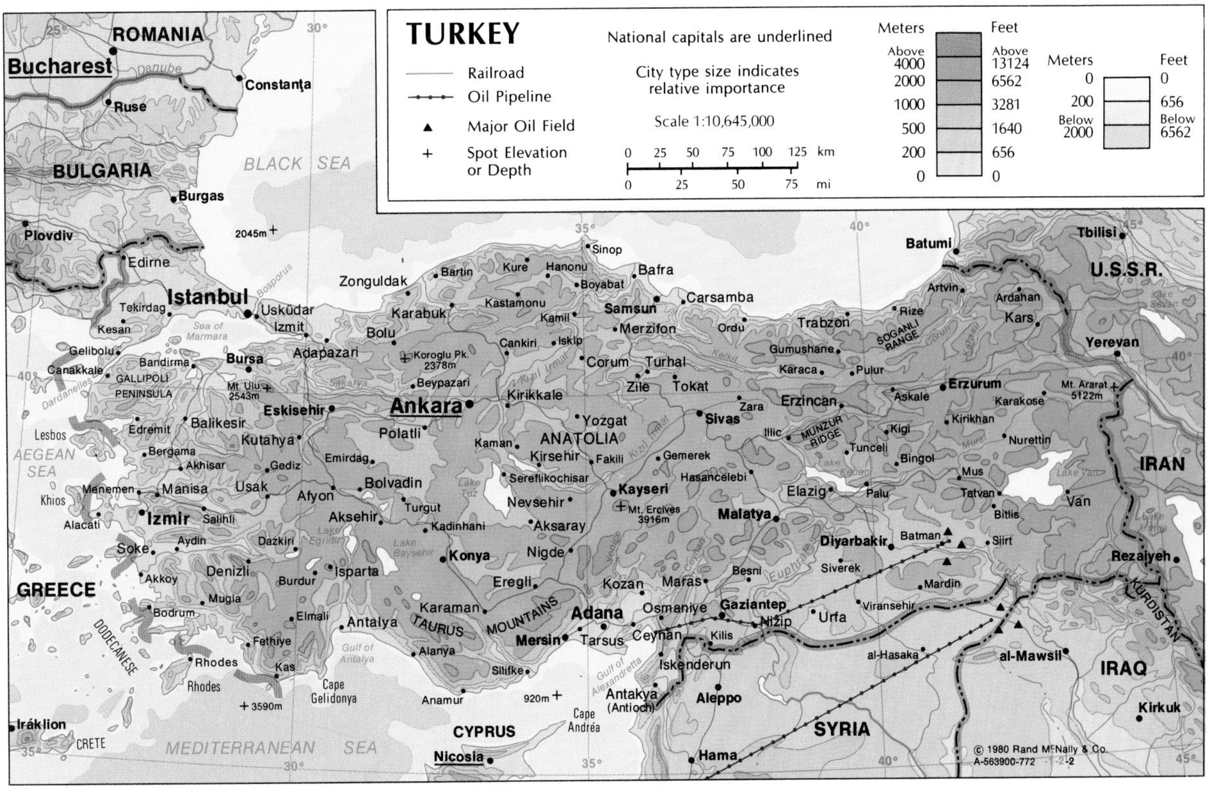

TURKEY

National capitals are underlined

City type size indicates relative importance

Scale 1:10,645,000

	Railroad
	Oil Pipeline
▲	Major Oil Field
+	Spot Elevation or Depth

Meters	Feet
Above 4000	Above 13124
2000	6562
1000	3281
500	1640
200	656
0	0

Meters	Feet
0	0
200	656
Below 2000	Below 6562

0 25 50 75 100 125 km
0 25 50 75 mi

ROMANIA
Bucharest
Constanța
Ruse
BULGARIA
Burgas
BLACK SEA
Plovdiv
Edirne
Istanbul
Tekirdag
Üsküdar
Kesan
Izmit
Gelibolu
Canakkale
Bandirma
Bursa
GALLIPOLI PENINSULA
Lesbos
Edremit
Balikesir
Eskisehir
AEGEAN SEA
Bergama
Akhisar
Gediz
Kutahya
Khios
Manisa
Usak
Izmir
Salihli
Afyon
Aksehir
Soke
Aydin
Dazkiri
Denizli
Isparta
GREECE
Akkoy
Burdur
Mugla
DODECANESE
Bodrum
Elmali
Antalya
Fethiye
TAURUS MOUNTAINS
Rhodes
Kas
Cape Gelidonya
Anamur
Rhodes
CRETE
Iráklion
MEDITERRANEAN SEA
Zonguldak
Bartin
Kastamonu
Karabuk
Kamil
Bolu
Koroglu Pk. 2378m
Cankiri
Beypazari
Adapazari
Ankara
Polatli
Kirikkale
Kaman
ANATOLIA
Kirsehir
Emirdag
Bolvadin
Turgut
Kadinhani
Kaman
Nevsehir
Konya
Nigde
Aksaray
Eregli
Kozan
Karaman
Adana
Mersin
Tarsus
Ceyhan
Silifke
Antakya (Antioch)
CYPRUS
Nicosia
Sinop
Bafra
Samsun
Carsamba
Merzifon
Ordu
Corum
Turhal
Zile
Tokat
Yozgat
Sivas
Gemerek
Hasancelebi
Kayseri
Mt. Erciyes 3916m
Maras
Osmaniye
Gaziantep
Nizip
Kilis
Aleppo
Hama
SYRIA
Trabzon
Rize
Gumushane
Karaca
Pulur
Erzincan
Illic
MUNZUR RIDGE
Tunceli
Bingol
Elazig
Malatya
Diyarbakir
Batman
Siverek
Besni
Urfa
Viransehir
Mardin
al-Hasaka
IRAQ
al-Mawsil
Kirkuk
USSR
Batumi
Tbilisi
Artvin
Ardahan
Kars
Yerevan
Erzurum
Karakose
Mt. Ararat 5122m
Askale
Kigi
Kirikhan
Nurettin
Mus
Tatvan
Van
Bitlis
IRAN
Rezaiyeh
KURDISTAN
Iskenderun

© 1980 Rand McNally & Co. A-563900-772

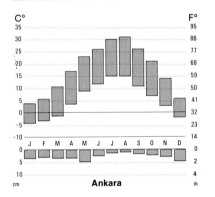

Ankara

Annual climate charts for two cities in Turkey illustrate distinct climate zones in that country. Bars indicate the monthly ranges of temperatures (red) and precipitation (blue). Ankara, on the Anatolian Plateau, has a steppe climate, and Istanbul, situated on the Bosporus, the strait separating Asia and Europe, has a Mediterranean climate.

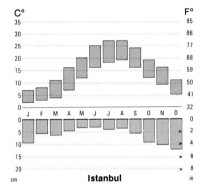

Istanbul

world history as a bridge connecting East and West. European Turkey, known as eastern THRACE, is bounded on the north by the BLACK SEA and Bulgaria and on the west by the AEGEAN SEA and Greece. It is separated from Asian Turkey (ANATOLIA or Asia Minor) by the BOSPORUS, the Sea of MARMARA, and the DARDANELLES Strait. Anatolia is bounded on the north by the Black Sea; on the east by the USSR and Iran; on the south by Iraq, Syria, and the Mediterranean Sea; and on the west by the Aegean Sea.

Turkey is one of the more developed Middle Eastern countries, and industrialization is in progress. Tourism, stimulated by the fine climate and the abundance of historic sites, such as TROY, PERGAMUM, and EPHESUS, is beginning to gain importance. Modern Turkey was founded on Oct. 29, 1923, as the successor of the Ottoman Empire.

LAND AND RESOURCES

Turkey lies within the Alpine-Himalayan mountain belt. More than 75% of the land lies at elevations above 500 m (1,640 ft), and the average elevation is 1,100 m (3,600 ft). Turkey is one of the most active earthquake regions in the world. The Arabian, African, Eurasian Aegean, and Turkish plates all converge in Turkish territory, resulting in severe seismic and volcanic activity.

The country may be divided into four physical regions: the central Anatolian plateau and surrounding mountains, the eastern highlands, the Aegean coastland, and Thrace. The central Anatolian plateau is separated from the coastal lowlands by the Pontic Mountains in the north and the TAURUS MOUNTAINS in the south. The Pontic (Northern Anatolian) Mountains increase in height toward the east, where their highest peak, Kaçkar Dağı (3,937 m/12,917 ft), is found. The Taurus Mountains rise to 3,734 m (12,251 ft) in the Ala Dağ chain. Composed mainly of limestone, they have caves, underground streams, and potholes. Small glaciers are found in the eastern sections of both the Taurus and Pontic ranges. The central plateau is composed of uplifted blocks and downfolded troughs. Shallow salt lakes—Lake Tuz is the largest—and geologically young volcanic features characterize the landscape.

The eastern highlands are dotted with peaks reaching elevations of 3,000–4,500 m (10,000–15,000 ft) and surrounded by high lava-covered plateaus. The highest of the peaks is Mount ARARAT (Ağri Dağı; 5,122 m/16,804 ft), in the extreme east. Vast stretches of the highlands consist of barren waste. Lake VAN is a large salt lake with underground connections to the Tigris and Euphrates rivers, whose headwaters rise in the nearby mountains.

(Below) *These natural conical structures were formed from the limestone of the Anatolian plateau by wind erosion over centuries. The formations have been hollowed out by some of the inhabitants of this region in south central Turkey to provide additional housing.*

(Above) *Ankara, the capital and second largest city of Turkey, is located in the central portion of the country, on the Anatolian plateau. The seat of Turkey's government was transferred from Istanbul to Ankara in 1923, when the nation became an independent republic.*

The Aegean coastland is an area of elongated mountain ridges cut by steep valleys. Thrace comprises a central plain of rolling terrain surrounded by mountains of moderate height.

Soils. Turkey has numerous soil types. About 40% of the land, including the Black Sea coast and most of the northeast, is covered by red and gray brown podzols and by brown forest soils. The Aegean and Mediterranean coasts are characterized by mountain soils (brown forest, terra rossa, rendzina). Chestnut and desert soils are found in central Anatolia. The southeast has rich chernozems and chestnut-type soils.

Climate. Because of the mountainous terrain and maritime influence, climates vary greatly. The Aegean and Mediterranean coasts enjoy a 29° C (84° F) mean temperature in July and a 9° C (48° F) mean in January. Rainfall is concentrated in the winter; Antalya on the southern coast receives an annual average of 991 mm (39 in). The Black Sea coast is somewhat cooler, and the rainfall is heavier, averaging 2,438 mm (96 in). The northeast has warm summers but severe winters averaging −9° C (16° F). Precipitation occurs more evenly throughout the year, and the snow cover lasts 120 days. The central plateau has hot, dry summers averaging 23° C (73° F) and cold, moist winters, when temperatures average below 0° C (32° F).

Drainage. The TIGRIS RIVER and the EUPHRATES RIVER originate in eastern Turkey before flowing to the Persian Gulf. The Araks and Kuruçay rivers flow to the Caspian Sea; the Kizil and Sakarya to the Black Sea; the Macestus to the Sea of Marmara; and the Gediz and the Büyükmenderes to the Aegean. The Göksu, Seyhan, and Ceyhan rivers flow to the Mediterranean. Most Turkish rivers are not navigable, having irregular, shallow beds and seasonal depth changes.

Vegetation and Animal Life. The Black Sea coast is the most densely forested region in Turkey, with both coniferous and deciduous trees. Much of the south, west, and northwest is covered by Mediterranean vegetation of thick, scrubby underbrush. The dry central plateau is steppe land, with short grasses, bushes, and stunted willow trees. Wild animals include the wolf, fox, bear, and wildcat. The water buffalo, camel, and Angora goat are domesticated.

Mineral Resources. Production and transport costs limit the importance of many minerals. Copper from Ergani in the Diyarbakir region and chrome from Fethiye are mined for export. The presence of coal near Eregli on the Black Sea and in Thrace and of iron ore in the Sivas region has been important to the industrialization effort. Petroleum, boron minerals, mercury, and manganese are also found.

PEOPLE

The people of Turkey are overwhelmingly TURKS (about 90%) and Sunni Muslim (98%). About 3 million KURDS live in the eastern provinces, and several hundred thousand Arabs inhabit the Hatay enclave adjacent to Syria. The number of Greeks was dramatically reduced by the population exchange between Greece and Turkey following the Treaty of Lausanne (1923). About 25,000 Jews live primarily in Istanbul, Ankara, and İzmir. The Greek Orthodox community is the largest Christian denomination, followed by the Gregorian church. Most of the population speak Turkish (see URAL-ALTAIC LANGUAGES), although minorities speak Arabic and Kurdish.

More than half the population live in urban areas. ISTANBUL is the cultural, industrial, and commercial center; ANKARA is the capital. Other major cities are İZMIR, ADANA, Antakya (or ANTIOCH), KONYA, EDIRNE, TRABZON, and BURSA. Large-scale migration to the cities since mid-century has led to overcrowding. The birthrate and average life expectancy are closer to the norm for a Middle Eastern country than for a European country. The population density is highest in the coastal regions, especially along the Black Sea.

Education and Health. The educational system of Turkey was modernized after the founding of the republic as part of an effort to westernize Turkish society. Today education is mostly public and free, and about three-fourths of the population are literate. Funds, teachers, and facilities are scant in remote areas of the country. The University of Istanbul (1453), the Aegean University (1955) at İzmir, and the Middle East Technical University (1956) at Ankara are Turkey's largest institutions of higher learning.

Medical services are free to the poor. Although health service is improving, rural areas suffer shortages of physicians and facilities; the infant mortality rate is close to the average for an Asian country. Trachoma and tuberculosis are the most prevalent communicable diseases.

The Arts. Although Islam dominated artistic expression under the Ottomans (see ISLAMIC ART AND ARCHITECTURE), Turkish culture since 1923 has been imbued with the spirit of nationalism. Turkish literature has been affected from both the East (chiefly Persia) and the West (mainly France). Many writers focus on life in Turkish villages. Modern painting and sculpture are of limited appeal; the people prefer folk art and decorative crafts. Traditional Ottoman music continues to be popular, although Western-style music is making inroads.

ECONOMIC ACTIVITY

Turkey's economic development began in the mid-1920s under Kemal Atatürk, first president of the Turkish republic, who attempted to westernize and industrialize the economy. After World War II the Marshall Plan and Turkish membership in the Organization for Economic Cooperation and Development (OECD) further encouraged development. The per capita income, however, remained lower than in most industrialized countries. Turkey receives significant financial aid from the European Economic Community (EEC), to which it applied for membership in 1987. The inflation rate has fluctuated during the 1980s but remains high, as does the unemployment rate. Many Turks work abroad, which helps to keep unemployment under control; remittances from these workers provide a major source of foreign exchange.

Manufacturing and Energy. Manufacturing provides about 20% of the nation's GNP but employs only a small percentage of the labor force. Food processing accounts for one-third of all manufacturing, textiles and clothing for about 20%. Steel production, particularly at Eregli and İskenderun, is also important. Other major industrial products include machinery and metal goods, vehicles, petrochemicals, fertilizers, and pulp and paper. İskenderun is the terminus of an important oil pipeline from Iraq, and petroleum-based industries are being developed in the region. Energy needs remain low on a per capita basis despite a remarkable increase in total national energy consumption. Nevertheless, the cost of imported petroleum is a heavy burden, and an effort is being made to develop other sources of power generation, especially by building hydroelectric plants on the Euphrates River. The construction of the country's first nuclear power station was postponed following the Chernobyl accident in 1986.

Agriculture, Forestry, and Fishing. Agriculture accounts for less than 20% of the GNP, although it employs well over half of the labor force. Just over a third of the land is under cultivation, and productivity is low. Cereals are the principal crop. Vegetables, grapes, sugar beets, potatoes, and oilseeds are also grown, and cattle, sheep, goats, and poultry are raised. Overgrazing is a problem in many parts of the country. Forests, covering more than 25% of the land, are protected by the state, but exploitation has been slow. Much of the wood harvest is used for energy. The commercial fishing industry is being developed.

Transportation. Domestic transportation, chiefly by road, is difficult in many areas because of the rough terrain. Turkey is an important transit route from Europe to the Middle East, and long stretches of railroads were built by foreign powers through Turkish territory. The first bridge across the Bosporus was completed in 1973; a second is under construction. Istanbul has the nation's major international airport and is one of the world's major ports.

Trade. Principal exports include cotton, fruits, nuts, tobacco, metals, cereals, textiles and clothing, and livestock. Imports include machinery, chemicals, crude oil, base metals, fertilizers, mineral products, and vehicles. Middle Eastern nations are beginning to rival Western European countries and the United States as Turkey's trading partners.

GOVERNMENT

From 1973 to 1980 the country had a series of weak coalition governments that were unable to handle increasingly serious economic problems and political violence. The prime ministership alternated between Süleyman Demirel of the moderate right Justice party and Bülent Ecevit, leader of the moderate left Republican People's party. With the government unable to resolve Turkey's difficulties, the military intervened in 1980 for the third time since the proclamation of the Turkish republic, deposing Demirel in a bloodless coup led by Gen. Kenan EVREN. (Turkey previously was under military control from 1960 to 1961 and from 1971 to 1973.) In 1982 the voters approved a new constitution, which established an authoritarian presidential system and installed Evren as president for a seven-year period. Demirel, Ecevit, and other former political leaders were excluded from participation in politics for ten years. Elections for a unicameral national assembly were held in November 1983. The ruling National Security Council was then dissolved and Turgut Ozal, head of the newly formed conservative Motherland party, became prime minister. Martial law was gradually lifted, although a number of restrictions on civil liberties remained.

Turkey is divided into 67 provinces (ils), administered by governors (valis). Local governments have the right to collect taxes for local use.

HISTORY

Anatolia is one of the oldest continually inhabited regions in the world, and it has repeatedly served as a battleground for foreign powers. The earliest major empire in the area was that of the HITTITES, from the 18th through the 13th century BC. Subsequently, the Phrygians (see PHRYGIA), an Indo-European people, achieved ascendancy until their kingdom was destroyed by the CIMMERIANS in the 7th century BC. The most powerful of Phrygia's successor states was LYDIA. Coastal Anatolia meanwhile was settled by Greeks. The entire area was overrun by the Persians during the 6th and 5th centuries and fell to Alexander the Great in 334 BC. Anatolia was subsequently divided into a number of small Hellenistic kingdoms (including BITHYNIA, CAPPADOCIA, PERGAMUM, and PONTUS), all of which had succumbed to Rome by the mid-1st century BC. In AD 324 the Roman emperor CONSTANTINE I chose Constantinople, now Istanbul, as the capital of the Roman Empire. It subsequently became the capital of the Eastern Roman or BYZANTINE EMPIRE.

In 1055 a group of Central Asiatic Turks, the SELJUKS, con-

Istanbul (formerly Constantinople), Turkey's largest and commercially most important city, was the capital of the Byzantine and Ottoman empires. The city's oldest section, Stamboul, is linked to the mainland across the Golden Horn by the Galata Bridge (left). The Bosporus is visible beyond the Yeni Mosque (right).

quered Baghdad and established a Middle Eastern and Anatolian empire. When this empire was broken up by the Mongol invasion, one of the remaining local powers became known as the Ottoman dynasty, after its leader OSMAN I. The OTTOMAN EMPIRE spread from northwestern Anatolia and captured Constantinople in 1453. At the peak of their power the Ottomans controlled much of the eastern Mediterranean. The Ottomans had a sophisticated system of internal administration and also organized the first standing army in Europe, the JANISSARIES, a highly trained corps of war captives and Christians who were converted to Islam.

As the Ottoman Empire began to collapse under its own weight in the 18th and 19th centuries, it became a battleground for rival European powers, wedged as it was between the Russian and Austrian empires (see EASTERN QUESTION). These rivalries led to the RUSSO-TURKISH WARS, the CRIMEAN WAR, and the BALKAN WARS. By the outbreak of World War I the Ottoman Empire had essentially been divided into spheres of influence by the great European powers, but a reform movement was active within the Ottoman Empire itself. The YOUNG TURKS brought about a revolution in 1908 and were successful in introducing civil and social reforms.

The Ottomans were drawn into World War I on the German side. At the end of the war the empire was formally dissolved, and the Allies divided it among themselves. The straits into the Black Sea were neutralized, and a Greek occupation army landed at Smyrna, now Izmir. In 1922, however, the Turks, led by Mustafa Kemal (later known as Kemal ATATÜRK) and İsmet İNÖNÜ, defeated the armies occupying Anatolia. İnönü then won what has been called "the greatest diplomatic victory in history" when the Treaty of Lausanne (see LAUSANNE, TREATY OF) recognized the Republic of Turkey.

The republic was declared on Oct. 29, 1923, and Atatürk was elected its first president. Ruling as a benevolent dictator, Atatürk aimed to transform the nation into a modern Western state. Religion and state were separated; women were emancipated and given the right to vote; Western law, Hindu-Arabic numerals, and the Roman alphabet were adopted. The state supported the development of critical industries and businesses. Although theoretically head of a constitutional democracy, President Atatürk ruled as a virtual dictator until his death in 1938.

Turkey remained neutral in World War II until it joined the Allies in February 1945. Turkey joined the North Atlantic Treaty Organization (NATO) in 1952.

Atatürk had been succeeded as president by İnönü. Control of the government was then gained by Prime Minister Adnan MENDERES of the Democrat party, who won a landslide victory over İnönü in 1950. The excesses of his administration led to a coup in 1960 by Gen. Cemal Gürsel and to Menderes's execution in 1961. A new constitution was adopted in 1961, and İnönü became prime minister.

In 1964 the age-old enmity between Greece and Turkey was inflamed by fighting on Cyprus between the Greek and Turkish sections of the population. Ten years later, after Cypriot president Makarios had been overthrown and Greece appeared ready to annex Cyprus, Turkish troops invaded the island, occupying the northern portion of it. Cyprus was subsequently partitioned, and a separate Turkish Republic of Northern Cyprus was created in 1983. Meanwhile, the seizure of power by Turkish military leaders in September 1980 and the imposition of martial law drew criticism from the European Community, which Turkey hoped to join. Civilian government was restored in 1983, martial law was ended in 1985, and parliamentary elections in 1987 gave a majority to Prime Minister Turgut Ozal's Motherland party. In 1988, Ozal held a series of talks with Greek leader Andreas Papandreou in an attempt to reconcile differences between Greece and Turkey over Cyprus and other issues.   IRA M. SHESKIN

Bibliography: Bianchi, Robert, *Interest Groups and Political Development in Turkey* (1984); Dewdney, John C., *Turkey: An Introductory Geography* (1971); Geyikdaqi, Mehmet, *Political Parties in Turkey* (1984); Hale, William, *The Political and Economic Development of Modern Turkey* (1981); Kagitcibagi, Cigdem, and Sunar, Diane, eds., *Sex Roles, Family, and Community in Turkey* (1982); Kopits, George,

Structural Reform, Stabilization, and Growth in Turkey (1987); Lewis, Bernard, *The Emergence of Modern Turkey*, 2d ed. (1968); Mango, Andrew, *Discovering Turkey* (1972); Nyrop, Richard F., et al., *Area Handbook for the Republic of Turkey*, 2d ed. (1973); Ozbudun, Ergun, *Social Change and Political Participation in Turkey* (1976); Pierce, Joe, *Life in a Turkish Village* (1983); Schick, Irvin, and Tonak, E. Ahmet, eds., *Turkey in Transition* (1986); Shaw, S. J., *History of the Ottoman Empire and Modern Turkey*, 2 vols. (1977); Stark, Freya, *Gateways and Caravans: A Portrait of Turkey* (1971); Tachau, Frank, *Turkey* (1984); Váli, F. A., *Bridge across the Bosporus: The Foreign Policy of Turkey* (1971); Weiker, Walter, *The Modernization of Turkey* (1981).

turkey

The male wild turkey, M. gallopavo, generally has iridescent green and brown plumage, a red snood over the bill, and a red wattle and caruncles on the throat. During courtship (background) it fans its tail feathers, struts, and gobbles to attract a group of females.

The turkey is a large game bird native to North American forested areas and now raised commercially for food in most parts of the world. Two species—the wild turkey, *Meleagris gallopavo*, of the eastern and central United States and Mexico, and the ocellated turkey, *Agriocharis ocellata*, of Mexico's Yucatán Peninsula and adjacent areas—make up the family Meleagrididae, which is classified with pheasants in the order Galliformes. An adult male wild turkey is about 1.2 m (4 ft) long and has metallic greenish, bronze, or brownish plumage, broad rounded wings and tail, and long, slim, spurred legs. A tuft of hairlike feathers hangs from the breast, a fleshy growth called a snood adorns the front of the head, and brightly colored growths called caruncles and a pouchlike area called a wattle mark the throat region. The smaller ocellated turkey lacks the tuft of breast feathers, is more brilliantly colored, and has bright eyespots on the tail coverts. Turkeys feed on acorns, seeds, berries, and insects. The hen alone incubates the 11 to 20 pale spotted eggs for approximately 28 days; the young are called poults.

Domestication of the turkey probably began in Mexico. The Spanish carried the bird to Europe in the 16th century, and the English colonists brought domesticated turkeys with them to America in the 17th century. Several varieties have been developed, including the popular family-sized table bird, the Beltsville white.   GARY D. SCHNELL

Bibliography: Williams, L. E., Jr., *The Book of the Wild Turkey* (1981).

See also: POULTRY.

Turkic languages: see URAL-ALTAIC LANGUAGES.

Turkish language: see URAL-ALTAIC LANGUAGES.

Turkistan   [turk'-is-tan]

Turkistan (or Turkestan) is the historical name of a vast Central Asian region inhabited by peoples of the USSR and China who speak URAL-ALTAIC LANGUAGES. Turkistan covers an area of about 5,450,000 km² (2,100,000 mi²), with a population of nearly 54 million (1985 est.). It is bounded on the west by the CASPIAN SEA, on the north by Siberia and Mongolia, on the south by Iran, Afghanistan, and Tibet, and on the east by China proper.

The area's average annual precipitation totals less than 254 mm (10 in). The region consists of dry steppe in the north and desert in the south. Among the great deserts of Turkistan are the KARA KUM, the KYZYL KUM, and the TAKLA MAKAN. Most of the region is drained by rivers that flow into inland seas and lakes. The AMU DARYA and the SYR DARYA flow into the ARAL SEA; the Ili River flows into Lake BALKHASH; and the TARIM RIVER flows into a depression occupied by the salt lake LOP NOR. The TIEN SHAN mountain system, on the Soviet-Chinese border, divides Turkistan into a western, or Soviet, portion and an eastern, or Chinese, portion.

Politically, the Soviet portion consists of four constituent republics of the USSR. They are the Kazakh Soviet Socialist Republic in the north, and three Soviet Central Asian republics—the Kirghiz, Turkmen, and Uzbek SSRs. Although it is a Soviet Central Asian republic, the Tadzhik SSR is inhabited by the Iranian-language TADZHIK and is not considered part of Turkistan. The Chinese portion of Turkistan, known as Sinkiang (Xinjiang), is inhabited by Han Chinese and Turkic-speaking Uighur peoples and forms the Sinkiang Uighur Autonomous Region of China.   THEODORE SHABAD

Turkmen   [turk'-men]

The Turkmen, or Turkoman, are a Central Asian ethnic group related to Anatolian TURKS. They are Mediterranean Caucasoid in physical type and speak an Oguz-Turkic language. Oguz Turks arrived on the Kazakh Upland in AD 600. After the Arab conquest the Oguz expanded across Turkmenia into the Middle East, and the Seljuk and Ottoman empires developed. The Turkmen appeared as an ethnic group about AD 1000. Militarily skillful, they frustrated Russian and British expansion until 1885 and were the last Central Asian group to fall. In the 1980s two-thirds of the nearly 4,000,000 Turkmen lived in the Turkmen Soviet Socialist Republic. The remaining third were distributed among Afghanistan, Iran, Iraq, Syria, and Turkey.

Although traditionally nomadic, most Turkmen today are settled people; those in the USSR are collectivized cotton farmers. As nomads they lived in lightweight felt tents (YURTS), which enabled them mobility serving both economic and military purposes. Slaving and livestock raids supplemented income from pastoralism. In their highly stratified, male-dominated, extended families, descent was reckoned through the father's line. Males did not leave their fathers' households until the age of 30 to 40, after as many as 20 years of marriage. As SUNNITE Muslims, Turkmen strictly enforced female subordination and BRIDE-PRICE. Women traditionally lived in seclusion, weaving Bukharan carpets.   VICTOR L. MOTE

Bibliography: Coon, Carleton S., *Caravan: Story of the Middle East* (1969); Rywkin, M., *Moscow's Muslim Challenge* (1982); Wimbush, E., *Soviet Nationalities in Strategic Perspective* (1985); Wixman, R., *The Peoples of the USSR* (1984).

Turkmen Soviet Socialist Republic

The Turkmen Soviet Socialist Republic, in Central Asia, is one of the 15 constituent republics of the USSR. It lies on the east shore of the Caspian Sea and is bordered on the south by Iran and Afghanistan. Its area is about 488,100 km² (188,450 mi²), and its population is 3,123,000 (1984 est.). Its capital is Ashkhabad (1985 est. pop., 356,000).

More than 80% of Turkmenia is desert, consisting of the KARA KUM (black sands). Along the boundary with Iran lies the Kopet Dagh, a mountain range that rises to 2,941 m (9,650 ft). The climate is arid and has mean temperatures ranging

from 0° C (32° F) in January to 32° C (90° F) in July.

The population is concentrated in oases along the AMU DARYA river, which flows near the republic's eastern border with Uzbekistan; along the foot of the Kopet Dagh in the south; and in oases watered by the Murgab and Tedzhen rivers. The Turkmen people, who comprise two-thirds of the population, are Muslim in religion and speak a Turkic language. About two-thirds of the Turkmen still live in rural areas. Ethnic Russians, who account for 15% of the population, live almost exclusively in cities. About 8% are UZBEKS. Major cities—in addition to Ashkhabad—are Chardzhou (1984 est. pop., 155,000), Tashauz (99,000), Mary (83,000), Nebit-Dag (79,000), and Krasnovodsk (56,000).

The leading economic activities are petroleum and natural-gas extraction, sheep raising, and cotton farming. Turkmenia's share in the Soviet cotton crop has risen from 9% to 13% since the 1960s as a result of the construction of the Kara Kum irrigation canal.

The region that is now Turkmenia was conquered by tsarist Russia in the 1870s and 1880s. After the Bolshevik Revolution of 1917, the Soviet regime gained control only in 1923 and established the Turkmen republic in 1924.   THEODORE SHABAD

Turkoman: see TURKMEN.

Turks

Turks, or Turkic peoples, are the principal descendants of large bands of nomads who roamed in the Altai Mountains (and thus are also called the Altaic peoples) in northern Mongolia and on the steppes of Central Asia during the early centuries of the Christian era. Their language is a branch of the URAL-ALTAIC family, characterized by the attachment of prepositions, inflections, and other grammatical forms as suffixes to nouns, by vowel harmony, and by clarity of structure. Physically, most of the Turkic peoples resemble the Mongols, although those of the west have been so mixed with conquered native peoples that they cannot be distinguished from other Mediterranean ethnic groups.

6th to 9th Centuries. The original Central Asian Turkic nomads established their first great empire in the 6th century AD, a nomadic confederation that they called Gök Türk (Sky Turk) and that the Chinese called Tu Kiu. This empire stretched across the steppes from Transoxiania to northern China and the Pacific Ocean and developed some of the characteristic features of subsequent Turkish culture: military organization, tactics, and weapons and political and social structure and titles. Shamanistic in religion and tribal in organization, Gök Türk broke up in the 7th century. The eastern part of the confederation became assimilated with Chinese civilization and gave rise to the MONGOLS. The western part contracted and ultimately was strongly influenced by the Islamic civilization of the Middle East.

In the 8th century the Karluk settled in the I-li and Chu river valleys between the Issik-Kul and Balkhash lakes. The UIGHUR remained in northern Mongolia, and the KIRGHIZ wandered in the steppes to the north. The Oghuz (or Ghuz) Turks, called the TURKMEN (Turkoman) in Europe, dominated the area between Mongolia and Transoxiania, where contacts with Muslim missionaries, merchants, and warriors led to further assimilation. At the same time, many other Turks in Central Asia were converted to the Christian Nestorian church, Buddhism, and Zoroastrianism, resulting in a great deal of mutual interaction.

9th to Mid-13th Centuries. Under the leadership of the SELJUK warrior family, the Oghuz tribes entered Iran and then other parts of the Middle East, as raiders and mercenaries in the service of the weakening ABBASID caliphs and also of many towns that hired them to provide defenses against the anarchical conditions of the time. The Seljuks soon emerged (1055) as secular rulers, or sultans, of the entire Islamic Middle East with the exception of Egypt and Syria, which remained under Shiite FATIMID rule. The Abbasid caliphs remained only as religious leaders, with no real power. The Seljuks developed the madrasahs, or Islamic colleges; these

The 16th-century Turkish sultan Suleiman the Magnificent (also called the Lawgiver), whose conquests expanded the Ottoman Empire in both Europe and Asia, brought the empire to the height of its political and cultural influence. (University Library, Istanbul.)

were centers of a religious and bureaucratic revival, whereas the sultanate became the legal basis for administrative reorganization and codification. As they gained control of the settled state, they developed a slave army of MAMELUKES and in the late 11th century drove the nomad mercenaries into the lands of their enemies, primarily the Christian Byzantines, Armenians, and Georgians of Anatolia and the Caucasus, precipitating an overwhelming Turkish conquest and transformation of Anatolia into the homeland of the Turks.

The Seljuk empire of Rum, or Roum (1063–1300), with its capital at Konya (Iconium), dominated most of Anatolia except for the west, where feudatory Byzantine lords held out, and the southeast, in Cilicia, where the Armenians built a new kingdom. In addition, after 1150, Seljuk weakness enabled various Turkmen leaders to establish their own principalities along the fringes of the empire of Rum. There they acted as ghazis, or fighters for the faith of Islam against the infidels. The Great Seljuks defended Syria and Palestine against incursions during the CRUSADES, limiting the domination of the Crusaders to coastal areas at most; contact between Islam and the crusading representatives of Christianity was largely limited to military matters and trade.

In the meantime, in Central Asia the Kirghiz pushed the Uighur out of Mongolia in the late 9th century. The Uighur moved south into Sinkiang, in northern China, and west into Transoxiania. The Kirghiz also moved, finally settling in the mountains of what is now the USSR, where they remain today. The Mongols of north China were formed into a powerful military confederation under the leadership of GENGHIS KHAN about 1200. They conquered China and the Asian steppes between north China and Transoxiania and by the middle of the

13th century had invaded and conquered the Seljuk-Abbasid Middle East as well as Anatolia. The Mongols brought substantial devastation; at the same time, however, they introduced Christian and Buddhist elements from Central Asia and established trade and cultural relations between the Middle East and China.

Mid-13th to 20th Centuries. When the great Mongol Empire was broken up among the sons of Genghis Khan, the Mongol dynasty of the Ilkhans, founded by Hulagü, took control of the Middle East from 1256 to 1353. Subsequent Ilkhanid decline led to new anarchy and the threat of a renewed Mongol invasion of the Middle East by the GOLDEN HORDE, which ruled southern Russia, and later by forces under the powerful conqueror TIMUR. Ultimately, however, one of the Turkmen principalities in northeastern Anatolia, that of the Ottomans, built a new empire (see OTTOMAN EMPIRE) starting in the 14th century. Using an army of Oghuz nomads and Christian mercenaries, the Ottomans first conquered southeastern Europe as far as the Danube in the 15th century. Then, after taking Byzantine Constantinople in 1453, they went on to overrun Egypt, Syria, and Arabia in the early years of the 16th century and Iraq, western Iran, and the Caucasus in the east and Hungary in the west in the middle of the century. The Ottoman Empire then began a long decline that finally led to its breakup after World War I.

The Turkish conquest of Anatolia had caused a substantial displacement of the native Christian population there, where most moved to the cities. Little ethnic change resulted in southeastern Europe, however, except for areas of Serbia, Albania, and Greece, where the Turkish tribes settled, and in Bosnia, where the indigenous Slavic BOGOMILS converted to Islam because of previous Christian persecution. Muslims and Christians alike were allowed to retain their religious and national traditions within autonomous settlements. These ultimately became the centers for national movements and independent states that rose on the ruins of the Ottoman Empire in the 19th and 20th centuries.

Present Distribution. In 1980 an estimated 42 million Turks were living in Turkey. Most of the Turkish inhabitants of the independent states of southeastern Europe had been massacred or driven out, but about 1.3 million still survived in Greece, Bulgaria, Cyprus, Albania, Romania, and southern Yugoslavia. About 29 million modern descendants of the Oghuz and their Turkic relatives lived in the USSR: 1 million Turkmen, concentrated in the deserts east of the Caspian Sea and north of Iran; 9 million Kirghiz, in northeastern Central Asia bordering China; 4.5 million KAZAKH; 1 million Crimean TATAR; 5.2 million Kazan Tatar, who live in the central Volga River valley along with an unknown number of Bashkir; 4 million Azeri Turks, who live in the Azerbaijan SSR in the Caucasus, as well as another 4 million in the northwest Iranian province of Azerbaijan; the KARAKALPAK, related to the Kazakh; the Kipchak (called Polovtsy by the CUMANS), who settled in southern Russia and the Caucasus starting in the 12th century; and 300,000 YAKUT, who were pushed by the Mongols into Siberia, along the Lena River. The Gagauz of BESSARABIA and the DOBRUJA Turks have been largely destroyed as communities, although many survive in Turkey and in European states.   STANFORD J. SHAW

Bibliography: Barthold, W., *Turkistan Down to the Mongol Invasion,* 3d ed. (1968); Czaplicka, M. A., *The Turks of Central Asia in History and at the Present Day* (1918; repr. 1973); Esin, E. A., *A History of Pre-Islamic and Early Islamic Turkish Culture* (1980); Grousset, René, *The Empire of the Steppes* (1970); Hostler, C. W., *Turkism and the Soviets* (1957); Hotham, D., *The Turks* (1972); Kushner, David, *The Rise of Turkish Nationalism* (1977); Poppe, N., *Introduction to Altaic Linguistics* (1965).

Turks and Caicos Islands

The Turks and Caicos Islands are a group of about 30 islands in the British West Indies that form the southeast continuation of the Bahamas. The total area is 430 km² (166 mi²), and the population is 7,436 (1980). Only seven of the islands are inhabited, including Grand Turk (1980 pop., 3,146), where the seat of government is located; Salt Cay; Grand Caicos, the largest island; and South Caicos, site of Cockburn Harbor. Grand Turk also serves as a U.S. guided missile tracking station. The economy is based on fishing, tourism, and financial services. The islands, sighted by Juan Ponce de León in 1512, were later claimed by Britain but were not permanently settled until 1776. At various times they were ruled from other British colonies in the area—Bermuda, the Bahamas, and Jamaica. Negotiations for full independence began in the early 1980s.

Turku   [toor'-koo]

Turku (Swedish: Åbo), a port city in southwestern Finland, lies at the mouth of the Aurajoki River on the Gulf of Bothnia, about 160 km (100 mi) northwest of Helsinki. With a population of 163,665 (1982 est.), Turku ranks as Finland's third largest city. An industrial city with shipyards, food processing plants, steel and textile mills, and pottery works, Turku also has several important libraries, museums, and theaters. The Swedish University of Åbo (1917) and the University of Turku (1920) serve, respectively, the Swedish and Finnish populations of this bilingual city.

Turku began as a trading center just north of its present location. During the 13th century the city moved south and began to grow around its cathedral (1290) and castle. Before the Russian takeover in 1812, Turku was Finland's largest city and served as its capital. The city was heavily damaged during the Russo-Finnish War (1939–40) and World War II.

turmeric   [tur'-muh-rik]

Turmeric, C. longa, is commercially grown in tropical regions throughout the world for use as a spice and for the dye made from its dried rhizomes.

Turmeric is the common name for a perennial herb, *Curcuma longa*, of the ginger family, Zingiberacea, and for the dye and spice made from its tuberous roots. Turmeric is native to southern Asia and has been cultivated since ancient times in China and Indonesia; it is also cultivated in India, Jamaica, Haiti, and Peru. The plant grows about 1 m (3 ft) tall and has large, bright green leaves and yellow flowers. After the rhizomes, or roots, have been cleaned and oven dried, they are ground into a peppery-flavored orange yellow powder that is a basic ingredient of curry and is used in prepared mustard.

Turnbull, William, Jr.

The architect William Turnbull, Jr., b. New York City, Apr. 1, 1935, a founding member of the San Francisco firm of Moore Lyndon Turnbull Whittaker, first achieved national recognition as a codesigner of the Sea Ranch condominiums, Calif. (1965). With Charles Moore, he also helped to design the Faculty Club (1968) at the University of California, Santa Barbara. After graduating from Princeton University (M. Arch., 1959), Turnbull became known for designs that often involve a witty

blending of illusion and reality. The Zimmerman house (1976) in Virginia, for example, answered the client's wish to have both sunlit interiors and shady porches. Turnbull has demonstrated, most recently in the library and city museum (1974–77) for Biloxi, Miss., a remarkable ability to combine the picturesque with historical references and postmodern forms.

J. MEREDITH NEIL

Bibliography: Jencks, Charles A., *The Language of Post-Modern Architecture* (1977).

Turner, Frederick Jackson

Frederick Jackson Turner, a Wisconsin-born historian, produced a landmark of American scholarship in "The Significance of the Frontier in American History," a paper presented to the American Historical Association in 1893. Turner's explanation of the frontier's effect on democracy in the United States had a profound impact on American historiography.

Frederick Jackson Turner, b. Portage, Wis., Nov. 14, 1861, d. Mar. 14, 1932, was an American historian whose "FRONTIER thesis," also known as the "Turner thesis," strongly influenced the writing of U.S. history. He received (1890) his Ph.D. at The Johns Hopkins University and taught at the University of Wisconsin (1889–1910) and at Harvard (1910–24). In 1927, Turner became senior research associate at the Henry E. Huntington Library in San Marino, Calif.

At a meeting of the American Historical Association in 1893, Turner presented his famous thesis in a paper entitled "The Significance of the Frontier in American History," which altered the course of American scholarship and is still recognized as the most influential single piece of historical writing produced in the United States. Turner argued that the existence of free land and the advance of settlement westward had exerted a crucial influence on the development of American institutions and character. Democracy, individualism, practicality, inquisitiveness, mobility, optimism, materialism, and wastefulness, he contended, were rooted in the pioneer experience. With the closing of the frontier, Turner stated, the first period of American history ended, and a major shift in the national psychology began. After decades of debate, scholars gradually accepted the frontier thesis as a suggestive interpretation rather than a theory to be proved or disproved. The thesis induced historians to look more to the American environment in seeking to explain the course of U.S. history.

An outstanding teacher who helped build an excellent graduate history program at Wisconsin, Turner published only a few works, including *The Frontier in American History* (1920). *The Significance of Sections in American History* (1932), a posthumously published collection of his essays, won a Pulitzer Prize in 1933.

W. EUGENE HOLLON

Bibliography: Bennett, J. D., *Frederick Jackson Turner* (1975); Billington, R. A., *Frederick Jackson Turner* (1973); Carpenter, R. H., *The Eloquence of Frederick Jackson Turner* (1983); Jacobs, W. R., ed., *Frederick Jackson Turner's Legacy* (1965; repr. 1977).

Turner, John N.

The short-term Canadian prime minister John Napier Turner, b. Richmond, England, June 7, 1929, went to Canada with his

John N. Turner was the prime minister of Canada for less than three months in 1984. Turner had easily succeeded the retiring Pierre Trudeau as Liberal party leader and prime minister, but in the September 1984 election he and the Liberals were beaten by the Progressive Conservatives under Brian Mulroney. They were defeated again in November 1988.

family in 1932. He was educated in Ottawa and later received degrees in political science (1949) from the University of British Columbia and in law (1952) from Oxford, where he held a Rhodes Scholarship. He also studied at the University of Paris; fluent in French, he practiced at the Quebec bar early in his legal career.

A Liberal, Turner was elected to the House of Commons in 1962. He first joined the cabinet as minister without portfolio under Prime Minister Lester Pearson; in July 1968, Pierre Trudeau appointed him minister of justice. Turner became finance minister in 1972, but in 1976 he retired to return to private law practice. In the minds of many Canadians, however, Turner remained heir to the Liberal party leadership. When Trudeau announced his retirement, Turner easily won the party leadership and, on June 30, 1984, was sworn in as prime minister. He called an election for September 4. On that day the Liberals were overwhelmingly defeated by the Progressive Conservatives, led by Brian Mulroney. Surviving the criticism that followed, Turner again led the Liberals in the election of Nov. 21, 1988. Campaigning vigorously in opposition to the free trade treaty with the United States, he mounted a strong challenge to Mulroney, but the Liberals were defeated.

P. B. WAITE

Turner, Joseph Mallord William

The British artist Joseph Mallord William Turner, b. Apr. 23, 1775, d. Dec. 19, 1851, is often regarded as the greatest of all landscape painters and an artist of uniquely varied ability. He drew as a child and began his studies at the Royal Academy schools (1789–93) in his early teens. He also copied the watercolors of others and learned from the example of his friend Thomas Girtin. The steady demand for drawings of picturesque architecture prompted the young Turner to travel throughout Britain, Wales, Yorkshire, and Scotland as well as the southern counties. These journeys made him aware of natural scenery and atmosphere and suggested the use of the oil medium. In 1796 he began to exhibit oils at the Royal Academy. The splendidly poetic *Buttermere Lake* (1798; Tate Gallery, London) was finished, as was Turner's habit, from notations made in one of the sketchbooks he always carried.

Turner was elected to the Royal Academy in 1802 and in the same year left for a visit to France that marks the beginning of a new phase in his career. His *Calais Pier* (1803; Tate Gallery) magnificently recalls the stormy crossing. He recorded his first view of the Alps in watercolors, and a visit to the Louvre opened his eyes to the richness of European artistic tradition. When the Napoleonic wars ended, he began to alternate tours on the Continent with expeditions in Britain, and his work became wonderfully varied. He liked to paint epic scenes of catastrophe in which the fury of the elements underlines humanity's insignificance within nature's scheme; an example is *The Wreck of a Transport Ship* (c.1805–10; Gulbenkian Foundation, Lisbon). Other works in this vein include *Burning of the Houses of Parliament* (1835; Philadelphia Museum of Art) and *Snow Storm at Sea* (1842; Tate Gallery). A number of his earlier oils show him refining his own ideas by working after the manner of such masters as Claude Lorrain and Aelbert Cuyp. The mezzotinted plates of his *Liber Studiorum* (1807–19) review the variety of his themes: *Historical, Mountainous, Pastoral, Marine,* and *Architectural.* Turner's visits to Italy from 1819 on made him increasingly conscious of the effects of light and color, an interest reflected in both his watercolors and his oils. These increasingly experimental and abstract productions culminated in the gorgeous Swiss watercolors of

The "Fighting Téméraire" Tugged to Her Last Berth To Be Broken Up, *painted by the English romanticist Joseph Mallord William Turner in 1838, is a classic example of his art, embodying allegory, the glorification of nature, and consummate handling of light and color. The three-masted battleship, with a glorious history well known to Turner's audience, becomes a spectral image of the obsolete past; the steam-powered tugboat, its black smoke smudging the radiant sky, symbolizes the advent of the new industrial age. The artist has set their voyage on a glassy sea against a fiery sunset, suggesting to the viewer the passing of a heroic age. (National Gallery, London.)*

1840–46. The well-known *Fighting Téméraire* (1838; National Gallery, London) was rivaled, some years later, by *Rain, Steam and Speed* (1844; National Gallery).

After Turner's death approximately 280 paintings and 19,000 drawings and watercolors were cataloged by John Ruskin. A new building at the Tate Gallery in London—the Clore Gallery for the Turner Collection—designed by the Scottish architect James STIRLING opened in 1987. It is devoted entirely to the nearly 300 oil paintings and the 19,000 works on paper that comprise the national collection of Turner's work.

WILLIAM GAUNT

Bibliography: Butlin, Martin, *Turner Watercolors*, 2 vols. (1962, 1968); Butlin, Martin, and Joll, Evelyn, *The Paintings of J. M. W. Turner*, 2 vols., rev. ed. (1984); Finberg, A. J., *The Life of J. M. W. Turner, R. A.,* 2d ed. (1961); Gaunt, William, *Turner* (1983); Lindsay, Jack, *J. M. W. Turner: His Life and Works* (1966); Reynolds, Graham, *Turner* (1969; repr. 1985); Rothstein, John K., and Butlin, Martin, *Turner* (1964); Wilton, Andrew, *J. M. W. Turner* (1982).

Turner, Nat

Nat Turner, b. Southampton County, Va., Oct. 2, 1800, d. Nov. 11, 1831, led the deadliest black slave revolt in U.S. history. Turner, born a slave, became a skilled carpenter as well as a preacher. He believed that he was the chosen instrument of a vengeful God; through violence he hoped to achieve retribution and freedom for his race. Interpreting a solar eclipse as the signal for action, Turner launched his insurrection on Aug. 21, 1831. His following grew to about 70, and at least 57 whites were killed before the revolt was quashed 4 days later. Turner, captured on October 30, was tried and executed. The insurrection prompted the vengeful killing of many innocent slaves and led to the enactment of stricter slave codes. It effectively ended any Southern sympathy for abolitionism.

RONALD L. LEWIS

Bibliography: Aptheker, Herbert, *Nat Turner's Slave Rebellion* (1966); Tragle, Henry I., *The Southampton Slave Revolt of 1831* (1971).

Turner, Roscoe

The pioneer U.S. aviator Roscoe Turner, b. Corinth, Miss., Sept. 29, 1895, d. June 23, 1970, is best known for his many feats as a racer and stunt flyer during the 1920s. Turner won distinction as a flyer in World War I. (He was belatedly [1952] awarded the Distinguished Flying Cross for his war service.) For 8 years after his discharge in 1919, he made his living as a barnstorming stunt flyer. In 1933, Turner set a record by flying from New York to Los Angeles in 11 hours, 30 minutes.

Bibliography: Hood, Joseph F., *The Skyracers: Speed Kings of Aviation's Golden Age* (1969); Rutherford, Roy, *Colonel Roscoe Turner, Knight-Errant of the Air* (1947).

Turner, Ted

The U.S. entrepreneur and sportsman Robert Edward Turner III, b. Cincinnati, Ohio, Nov. 19, 1938, rebuilt his father's ailing billboard-advertising business and bought (1970) an Atlanta TV station that became satellite/cable "superstation" WTBS, the cornerstone of the Turner Broadcasting System (TBS). TBS launched the Cable News Network (CNN) in 1980. Turner bought the Atlanta Braves baseball team in 1976; an avid yachtsman, he won the America's Cup races in 1977.

Turner's syndrome: see GENETIC DISEASES.

turnip

The turnip, *Brassica rapa*, of the mustard family, Crucifereae, is a biennial herb grown as an annual. Its white-fleshed roots are eaten as a vegetable, and its leaves, which are rich in minerals and vitamins A and C, are used as greens. Turnips differ from RUTABAGA, or Swedish turnip, in their more globular root form and their lighter-colored flesh. Grown best in cool climates, turnip roots can be stored for several months at cool temperatures.

O. A. LORENZ

The turnip, B. rapa, has been cultivated for centuries for its nutritious roots and edible greens.

turnpike

A turnpike is a road whose construction or maintenance costs are defrayed by fees collected from the road's users. In 1663 the justices of the counties of Hertford, Huntingdon, and Cambridge in England obtained powers to levy tolls to improve the London-York road. The barriers erected for this purpose were originally pivoted bars shaped like pikes; hence the name. During the 18th century, all the major roads in Britain were improved by turnpike trusts.

In the United States, Virginia built a turnpike in 1785, and this example was followed in other states, the funds usually being provided by private subscribers. As the development of railroads undermined the finances of the turnpike trusts, the roads were taken over by the public authorities, and the word *turnpike* fell into disuse until it was revived for the Pennsylvania Turnpike (1940). Later, turnpikes were created as a source of funds for highway construction.

CHARLES S. DUNBAR

Bibliography: Albert, W., *Turnpike Road Systems, 1663–1840* (1972).

turnstone

The turnstones, medium-sized, ploverlike, migratory shorebirds of the sandpiper family, are named for their habit of turning over small stones to feed on the animal life beneath. Found almost worldwide, the ruddy turnstone, *Arenaria interpres*, is harlequin-patterned in chestnut, black, and white; the black turnstone, *A. melanocephala*, is chiefly confined to the North American Pacific coast.

turntable

A mechanism for playing phonograph records, the turntable consists of a platter driven by a motor at a constant speed, and a tone arm, with a STEREO CARTRIDGE and stylus (needle) attached. As the record turns on the platter, the stylus moves over the record grooves, "reading" the two stereo channels engraved in the groove walls. The mechanical motion imparted to the stylus is transformed in the cartridge into electrical signals, and carried by wires in the tone arm to the AMPLIFIER. Here the signals are strengthened before reaching the LOUDSPEAKERS, where they are converted into sound (see SOUND RECORDING AND REPRODUCTION).

Most turntables are driven either by a motor that is directly connected to the platter by a shaft, or by a belt that circles both the motor shaft and the underside of the platter. In order to keep the stylus at the correct angle in relation to the grooves, the tone arm pivots slightly as it tracks across the record. But because pivoted arms may create a slight distortion in sound, a linear-tracking system has been developed where the entire arm moves across the record, maintaining the correct angle at all times.

turnverein [toorn'-fair-yn]

Turnvereins are social and athletic clubs of German origin that were established in the United States and other countries by German immigrants. The educator Friedrich Ludwig JAHN organized the first turnverein in 1811; its purpose was to offer German youth rigorous physical training and to inculcate moral strength. The first turnverein in the United States was founded in Cincinnati, Ohio, in 1848.

turpentine

Turpentine is a clear, volatile, water-immiscible hydrocarbon fluid obtained from both the exudate of living and the heartwood of dead coniferous trees. The southeast United States, with its extensive pine forests, has been the world's prime source since the early 1700s. The Greek island of Chios, however, is probably the oldest commercial source of turpentine.

Turpentine is collected by four basic methods. Gum turpentine is steam-distilled from pine exudate collected in cups. Wood turpentine is solvent-extracted from the heartwood of stumps and taproots that have aged in the ground for 10 to 15 years. Distilled turpentine is also derived from deadwood. Sulfate turpentine is made from the resinous portion of wood pulp. ROSIN is a by-product of some turpentine manufacturing processes. Turpentine was used mainly as a solvent of oil-based paints and varnishes until low-cost gasoline-derived solvents became available. Today it is used primarily for clean-up work. JOHN J. OBERLE

turpentine tree

Turpentine tree is the common name for *Syncarpia glomulifera* of the myrtle family, Myrtaceae. This evergreen shade tree, native to Australia, may grow as high as 60 m (200 ft), with elliptic to oblong leaves as much as 7 cm (3 in) long, and with white flowers and fibrous bark. The wood is valued for its durability and fire resistance and is used in shipbuilding, flooring, and cabinetwork. The name *turpentine tree* also refers to trees in the pine family, Pinaceae, that yield turpentine, notably the longleaf pine, *Pinus palustris*, and the slash pine, *P. elliotti*, of the southeastern United States.

turquoise

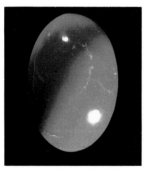

Turquoise (left) is an opaque, blue to blue green copper-aluminum phosphate mineral that has been used as a gemstone since at least 3400 BC. A turquoise gem (right) is most often cut in a dome-shaped, or cabochon, form.

Turquoise, the birthstone for December, is a hydrated copper and aluminum PHOSPHATE MINERAL ($CuAl_6(PO_4)_4(OH)_8 \cdot 4H_2O$) that displays a blue to greenish blue, apple green, or grayish color; the most highly prized variety is sky blue or robin's-egg blue. Hardness is 5 to 6, streak is white to pale green, luster is waxy, and specific gravity is 2.6 to 2.8.

Turquoise commonly occurs in veinlets penetrating weathered, aluminum-rich, sedimentary or volcanic rocks (where it has been deposited from circulating phosphatic waters) in arid climates, and in small, fine-grained, rounded masses.

Turquoise has been mined from Serabit el Khad-im on the Sinai Peninsula since about 3400 BC at what may be one of the world's first hard-rock mining operations. The bracelets of Egypt's Queen Zer contain carved Sinai turquoise and are possibly the world's oldest jewelry. The name (French for "Turkish") refers to the trade of the material from the famous, still-active mines at Neyshabur, Iran, through Turkey to Europe. The deposits in the arid American Southwest have been worked since before the Spanish conquest; some jewelry has been found dating from perhaps AD 900.

Bibliography: Branson, Oscar T., *Turquoise* (1975).

Turtle

The *Turtle*, the first combat submarine, was designed by David Bushnell and was launched during the American Revolution. A wooden craft shaped like a wide-bellied barrel, the *Turtle* had a one-man crew and was driven by two hand-cranked screw propellers, one for forward and one for vertical movement. It had a complex system of valves, air vents, and ballast pumps to control submergence and was armed with a mine equipped with a time fuse. Although the *Turtle's* attack on the British flagship *Eagle* off New York on the night of Sept. 6, 1776, failed, many of the principles embodied in the *Turtle* were used again by Robert Fulton in his submarine, the NAUTILUS. JOHN F. GUILMARTIN, JR.

Bibliography: Burgess, Robert F., *Ships beneath the Sea* (1975).

turtle

Turtles are reptiles of the order Chelonia, also called the Testudines or Testudinata, characterized by a body-encasing shell of usually fused, bony plates covered by large, horny scales. Turtles occur worldwide from the tropics to temperate regions in terrestrial, freshwater, and marine habitats. In contrast to other reptiles, whose greater diversity and abundance center in tropical regions, turtle species are most numerous in southeastern North America and southeastern Asia.

Turtle size is conventionally measured by the length of the upper shell (carapace) or the lower shell (plastron) in a straight line from front to rear. Turtles range in size from about 7.5 cm (3 in) in some specimens of the striped mud turtle, *Kinosternon baurii*, to 2.4 m (8 ft) and 725 kg (1,600 lb) in the leatherback, *Dermochelys coriacea*. The extinct sea turtle *Archelon ischyros* reached 6 m (19.5 ft) in length, as did the fossil tortoise *Colossochelys atlas*.

The earliest fossil remains of shelled vertebrates recognized as turtles are from the Triassic Period, approximately 200 million years ago. Turtles have gone essentially unchanged in anatomical appearance since that time. The pre-Triassic ancestors of turtles are unknown, but a traceable ancestry as far back as the Triassic is impressive: the direct ancestors of three entire classes of vertebrates—modern mammals, birds, and amphibians—can be reliably traced back to the Jurassic Period, or about 160 million years.

CHARACTERISTICS

Although the earliest-known extinct turtle had teeth on the roof of its mouth, all living turtles are toothless. The edges of the jaws are covered with a hard, sharp-edged, horny sheath, which may be smooth or have toothlike serrations.

Turtles have no external ear openings, but an ear covering (tympanum) is sometimes visible. Although their internal ear structures are well developed and able to detect low-frequency vibrations, turtles are unresponsive to airborne sounds. Their sense of smell, however, is good.

The Shell. The turtle's upper shell, or carapace, is commonly constructed of about 50 bones. These bones are believed to have evolved as new structures (dermal plates formed in embryonic connective tissue) rather than as modifications of previously existing parts of the skeleton. Unique among backboned animals, the turtle's skeletal limb-support systems—the shoulder and hip girdles—are inside the rib cage, the shoulder girdle partly adding to the formation and strength of the shell. The turtle's backbone is also incorporated into the shell for an increased degree of solidity; shortened by the loss of vertebral bones, it contains only two sacral (pelvic) and ten trunk vertebrae. The three lengthwise rows of bony plates in the upper shell are fused to the backbone and ribs beneath. The plates of the middle row are fused to the neural arches of the trunk vertebrae and are known as neural plates. On each side of this middle row is a row of costal plates, fused to the ribs (costae) of these vertebrae. The three longitudinal rows of bony plates are surrounded by a border of smaller bony plates called peripherals.

The lower shell, or plastron, typically contains nine bones: a small, single plate in front and four pairs of bony plates behind. The single plate and the first pair of plates were derived from bones of the shoulder girdle; the remaining three pairs of plates may have arisen as new structures or may have been derived, at least in part, from skeletal elements called abdominal ribs.

The bridge, formed by the upward-curving outer edges of the plastron, is usually present, connecting the plastron to the carapace.

The outer surface of both the upper and lower bony shell is covered by an extremely thin layer of skin, the epidermis, which contains both nerves and blood vessels. Covering this skin is a thick layer composed of large, horny scales called scutes, shields, or laminae. These scutes form the exterior shell seen on living turtles. Pressure on these scutes can be detected by nerves in the skin below. The number, position, size, and shape of the scutes are not identical to those of the bony plates beneath; indeed, it is common for the scutes to lie across the junction of two bony plates, thus lending additional strength to the shell. Although marked variations do occur and certain scutes are given specific names, the scutes of the carapace can be divided broadly into three main longitudinal rows—the vertebral scutes in the middle and a row of pleural scutes on each side—and a surrounding border of smaller scutes called marginals. Similarly, the scutes of the plastron can be broadly regarded as consisting of six pairs arranged in a double row from front to rear, plus a small scute at each leg opening. The soft-shelled turtles, family Trionychidae, however, lack the horny scutes and instead have their somewhat reduced bony shells covered by a thick, fleshy layer of skin. The leatherback turtle also has a thick, leathery skin, but it is ridged and embedded with small bony plates.

Respiration. Because of the rigid shell, turtles are unable to expand their "chests" to breathe. Consequently, inflation of the lungs, located just beneath the upper shell, is made possible only by altering the volume of space within the shell. Two sets of muscles at the rear of the body form the primary breathing mechanism. Broadly speaking, when these muscles are effectively contracted, they pull the internal organs up against the lungs, forcing out the air; the process is reversed in inhaling. Muscles associated with the front limbs also contribute to the breathing action: when contracted, they rotate the shoulder girdle outward, adding to the expanding space; when relaxed, they allow the shoulder girdle to return inward, reducing the space.

Many turtles can also obtain oxygen by other means. All aquatic turtles are believed able to use the tissues lining the insides of their mouths to absorb oxygen from the water. Soft-shelled turtles are able to obtain oxygen from water through the skin overlaying their shells, and marine turtles have sacs in the cloaca (rectum) that are also thought capable of extracting oxygen from water.

Dormancy. Turtles in temperate regions hibernate during colder periods of the year. The ability to respire through tissues of the cloaca, throat, and skin while underwater permits some species to go for long, cold periods (weeks or months) without breathing air directly. Turtles in tropical regions and some temperate areas may aestivate during hot, dry periods. An ability to shut down metabolism during unfavorable periods appears to be an adaptive trait among turtles in both aquatic and terrestrial forms throughout the world.

Feeding. Turtles as a group are omnivorous, eating both plant and animal matter, living or dead. A few species, however, are specialized feeders. Food is not chewed. The sharp cutting beak and strong throat muscles are used to force bite-sized pieces down the esophagus to the stomach.

Reproduction. Turtles mate after a period of courtship which may include the male chasing the female and vibrating its long claws in front of her. The females of some species, such as the box turtle, *Terrapene carolina*, and the diamondback terrapin, *Malaclemys terrapin*, are known to be able to store sperm for up to 4 years, producing fertile eggs for several seasons without additional matings.

All turtles are egg layers and all deposit their white eggs on land. The small mud and musk turtles, family Kinosternidae, lay tiny, oblong eggs about 1 to 2 cm (0.5 to 0.75 in) long, with a strong calcareous shell. The largest eggs, laid by the sea turtles, are round with a tough, leathery shell and can be up to 6 cm (2.5 in) in diameter. The time between ovulation and egg deposition is usually only a few days. Egg incubation time may be as short as 45 days for some species or more than 100 days for others. Females of some species characteristically lay only one or two eggs, whereas the sea turtles average more than 100 eggs per clutch.

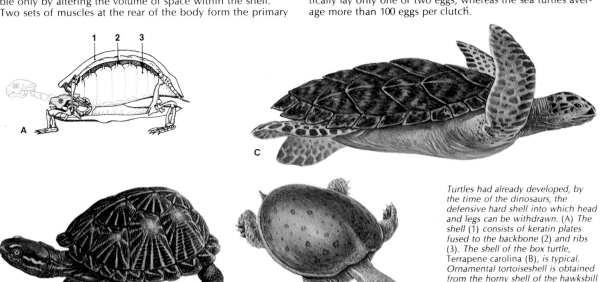

Turtles had already developed, by the time of the dinosaurs, the defensive hard shell into which head and legs can be withdrawn. (A) The shell (1) consists of keratin plates fused to the backbone (2) and ribs (3). The shell of the box turtle, Terrapene carolina (B), is typical. Ornamental tortoiseshell is obtained from the horny shell of the hawksbill turtle, Dermochelys imbricata (C). Shells of aquatic turtles such as the Florida soft-shelled turtle, Trionyx ferox (D), have evolved to contain no keratin.

Longevity. Growth rates of juvenile turtles are relatively rapid compared to those of adults. Nonetheless, individuals of some species take as long as 10 years to reach maturity. Many species display sexual dimorphism as adults, with the female sometimes being more than twice as large as the male. A unique feature of some species is the development of annual growth rings on each shell scute. Thus, the ages of young individuals can be determined before the rings begin wearing off.

Turtles live much longer than most other animals. Evidence exists for captive specimens of several species that have lived for 50 years in captivity. Even in natural populations, small forms such as box turtles, *Terrapene,* and painted turtles, *Chrysemys,* of the United States have average adult ages that have been reliably estimated at 30 to 50 years.

IMPORTANCE OF TURTLES

The eggs and meat of turtles are of economic importance as a food source. Turtle meat and soups range from staples to delicacies, depending on the time, the place, and the culture. Millions of eggs of marine turtles are collected each year as food. The eggs of some freshwater species are also intensively harvested. The most dramatic example is perhaps the South American river turtle, *Podocnemis,* from which more than 40 million eggs are taken annually to be used as food or as a source of oil. The once highly fashionable "tortoiseshell" of the hawksbill turtle, *Eretmochelys imbricata,* is still in demand, even with the expanding use of plastics. Aquatic turtles are often significant scavengers in natural or artificial lakes. In addition, a major pet trade has thrived on the sale of untold thousands of baby turtles of a dozen species across the world. The sale of pet turtles has greatly diminished in recent years because of the discovery of transmissible *Salmonella* disease in many of the specimens. Efforts are now being made to sell "sterilized" and rather inhumanely, individually packaged baby turtles.

Conservation. Despite their protective shells, some turtle species are in grave danger. The sea turtles' plight has been widely publicized. Thousands of nests are destroyed by humans each year. Habitat change, however, is perhaps the major threat to most turtles. At this time more than 30 species of turtles are officially recognized as in potential danger of extinction. In addition, some species are recognized by particular countries or states as being threatened.

TAXONOMY AND CLASSIFICATION

Because there are not native land turtles in Britain, the British traditionally refer only to the sea turtles as *turtles,* and to all other members of this reptile group as *tortoises,* even if the latter are aquatic forms. In the United States, however, *turtle* refers to all members of the order Chelonia, whereas *tortoise* has a more restricted usage, referring only to the land-dwelling forms. *Terrapin,* derived from an American Indian word, commonly refers to the diamondback terrapin, *Malaclemys terrapin,* a brackish-water inhabitant of the U.S. Atlantic and Gulf coasts.

Approximately 250 species of turtles exist in the world today. Living species are assigned to one of two suborders. Members of the suborder Pleurodira, the side-necked turtles, are characterized by the withdrawal of their heads into their shells by a sideways bending of the neck. This suborder contains two families, four genera, and about 50 species. The suborder Cryptodira, whose members withdraw their heads into their shells by a vertical bending of the neck into an S-shaped curve, consists of about 12 families, 60 genera, and 200 species.

Families Pelomedusidae and Chelidae. The side-necked turtles are restricted predominantly to the Southern Hemisphere. With the one rare exception of the pitted-shell turtle, *Carettochelys,* the sole member of its family, the only turtles occurring in Australia are species in the family Chelidae. *Podocnemis,* of the family Pelomedusidae, occurs in South America and Madagascar but not in Africa.

Family Chelydridae. The common snapper, *Chelydra,* and alligator snapper, *Macroclemys,* are the only genera in this family. Common snappers are found throughout eastern North America and range to northern South America. Alligator snap-

pers are confined to southeastern North America.

Family Emydidae. More than one-third of the world's turtle species are in this family. The heaviest concentrations are in North America and Asia, with few representatives in Europe, South America, or Africa and none in Australia. Most emydids are at least partially aquatic, but the North American box turtle, *Terrapene,* is terrestrial.

Family Testudinidae. The high-domed terrestrial tortoises have become almost legendary because of the famous giants of the Galapagos Islands, but desert regions are also successfully occupied by these tortoises, who can adjust to midday heat and aridity by retreating into deep burrows.

Family Trionychidae. The species in this family represent an extreme in shell shape and texture. The flattened, leathery carapace is adapted for fast swimming. The soft-shell turtles are almost exclusively aquatic; they go onto land only for nesting purposes.

Families Cheloniidae and Dermochelyidae. The SEA TURTLES are adapted to their marine environment by their generally large size, expert swimming abilities, and the physiological capacity to excrete salt through the lacrimal glands around their eyes. The six species of chelonids have the typical hard shells of other turtles, but the leatherback, *Dermochelys,* lacks the epidermal scutes.

Other Families. The Platysternidae, Dermatemydidae, and Carettochelydidae are each represented by a single species occurring, respectively, in Asia, Central America, and New Guinea and Australia. The family Kinosternidae includes some of the smallest turtles in the world, the mud and musk turtles. The two dozen species are confined to the Americas.

WHIT GIBBONS

Bibliography: Carr, A. F., *Handbook of Turtles* (1952); Ernst, C. H., and Barbour, R. W., *Turtles of the United States* (1972); Harless, Marion, and Morlock, Henry, *Turtles: Perspectives and Research* (1979); Nicholls, Richard E., *Book of Turtles* (1977); Pope, Clifford H., *Turtles of the United States and Canada* (1939); Pritchard, Peter C., *Encyclopedia of Turtles* (1979).

Tuscaloosa   [tuhs-kuh-loos'-uh]

Tuscaloosa is the seat of Tuscaloosa County in western Alabama on the Black Warrior River; it has a population of 75,211 (1980). The city's industries, which produce paper, fabricated metal products, chemicals, tires, and lumber, are based on its nearby coal, iron, and timber resources. Tuscaloosa is also a distribution center for cotton grown in the surrounding farmlands. The University of Alabama (1831) is in the city.

Tuscaloosa was settled in 1809 by Creek Indians, but after its destruction in an 1813 battle between the Creek and U.S. troops, the town was resettled in 1816 by white planters. Tuscaloosa served as state capital from 1826 to 1846.

Tuscany   [tuhs'-kuh-nee]

Tuscany (Italian: Toscana), a region in west central Italy with an area of 22,988 km² (8,876 mi²), is bounded by the Tyrrhenian and Ligurian seas to the west and the regions of Emilia-Romagna to the north, the Marche and Umbria to the east, and Rome to the south. With its capital at FLORENCE, and comprising the provinces of Arezzo, Florence, Grosseto, Livorno, Lucca, Massa-Carrara, Pisa, Pistoia, and Siena, as well as ELBA and other islands in the Tuscan Archipelago, the region has a population of 3,600,233 (1980 est.).

In spite of an often hilly or mountainous terrain with extensive mineral deposits (notably Carrara marble), Tuscany produces a wide array of agricultural products—grain, olives, tobacco, grapes (made into Chianti wine), and livestock. Tuscan manufactures include ships, textiles, chemicals, and steel. Tourists come to see the region's striking countryside and medieval and Renaissance towns and cities.

Successively ruled by Etruscans, Romans (4th century BC–6th century AD), Lombards (6th-8th centuries), and Franks (8th-12th centuries), Tuscany began in the 11th century to break up into numerous free communes. During the 14th through 16th centuries, however, Florence progressively brought the region's city-states under its domination, and in 1569 the MEDICI rulers of Florence were created grand dukes of Tuscany. In 1737 the grand duchy passed to the house of Habsburg-Lorraine, in whose possession it remained (except for a period of French rule, 1799–1814) until joining united Italy in 1860. DANIEL R. LESNICK

Tuscarora [tuhs-kuh-rohr'-uh]

The Tuscarora, an Iroquoian-speaking tribe of North American Indians, lived in numerous villages along the rivers of present-day North Carolina during the 17th century. They were hunters, farmers, fishers, and avid traders; in 1600 they numbered an estimated 5,000. The English settlers' encroachment on Indian territory soon led to conflict, however. The Tuscarora, seeking peace, sent a statement of their grievances and eight wampum belts, via the Susquehanna, to the governor of Pennsylvania, whose response was negative. Accordingly the Susquehanna brought the belts to the Five Nations Iroquois League and urged them to protect the Tuscarora.

After an unannounced expedition by white settlers through Tuscarora lands, the enraged Indians on Sept. 22, 1711, fell upon the colonists, killing 130 of them and thereby beginning the Tuscarora War (1711–13). With help from Virginia and South Carolina, the North Carolinians defeated the Tuscarora. The Iroquois then honored the wampum belts and invited the Tuscarora north. They settled in northern Pennsylvania and New York and in 1722 became the sixth nation of the Iroquois. After the American Revolution those Tuscarora who had sided with the British fled to Canada, where they were granted lands on Grand River in Ontario. In 1797 the American Tuscarora were granted a reservation in Niagara County, N.Y. The Tuscarora now number about 660 (1987 est.).

DANIEL JACOBSON

Bibliography: Graymont, Barbara, ed., *Fighting Tuscarora: The Autobiography of Chief Clinton Richard* (1973); Johnson, F. Roy, *Tuscaroras*, 2 vols. (1968); Wallace, Anthony F. C., *The Modal Personality Structure of the Tuscarora Indians* (1952).

tusk shell

Tusk, or tooth, shells are about 200 species of marine mollusks making up the class Scaphopoda. Their small, curved, tapered shells resemble teeth or elephant tusks. Only the larger open end of the shell, from which the muscular burrowing foot is extended, is embedded in sand. Water exchange occurs through the smaller end. J. H. BUSHNELL

Tuskegee Institute [tuhs-kee'-gee]

Established in 1881 by Booker T. Washington as a training school for black teachers, Tuskegee Institute (enrollment: 3,275; library: 240,000 volumes) is now a private coeducational university and technical institute in Tuskegee Institute, Ala. Among the schools that offer both bachelor's and master's degrees are those of arts and sciences; engineering and architecture; education; agriculture and home economics; and veterinary medicine, which also offers a D.V.M.

Tussaud, Madame [too-soh']

The noted wax modeler and museum proprietress Madame Tussaud was born Marie Grosholtz in Switzerland on Dec. 7, 1761. After learning her craft from her uncle, a Parisian waxworker, she was imprisoned during France's Reign of Terror but escaped the guillotine by making death masks from the severed heads of its victims. In 1802, after separating from her husband, Madame Tussaud left for England. With her collection of modeled likenesses, she toured the country until 1835 when she established her famous wax museum in London, which she managed until her death, on Apr. 15, 1850. The museum's collection of historical figures, which reflects its founder's interest in the macabre, was partially destroyed by fire in 1925; restored in 1928, it remains a tourist attraction.

Bibliography: Cottrell, Leonard, *Madame Tussaud* (1951); Leslie, Anita, and Chapman, Pauline, *Madame Tussaud: Waxmaker Extraordinary* (1979).

Tutankhamen, King of Egypt [toot-ahng-kah'-men]

The gold funerary mask of the Egyptian pharaoh Tutankhamen is one of thousands of opulent art objects found in the king's tomb at Thebes. Hidden by rock cuttings from a later tomb, Tutankhamen's burial chamber was not discovered until 1922. It proved to be a magnificent storehouse of ancient Egyptian artifacts. (Egyptian Museum, Cairo.)

Tutankhamen, a pharaoh (r. 1361–1352 BC) of the 18th dynasty, is one of the most famous Egyptian kings because his tomb was the richest of the few royal burial chambers that survived comparatively intact. The son-in-law of AKHENATEN, he was only 9 years old when he succeeded his brother Smenkhkare (r. 1364–1361 BC), and for much of his reign Egypt was actually governed by his senior officials. The vizier Ay skillfully replaced Akhenaten's monotheistic cult of Aten (Aton) with the traditional polytheistic religion. Tell el-Amarna, the monotheistic center, was abandoned, the capital was returned to Thebes, and the cults of the state god Amen (Amon) and other gods were revived. The king himself changed his name from *Tutankhaten* ("living image of Aten") to *Tutankhamen* ("living image of Amen"). His general, Horemheb, fought Hittite attacks on the Egyptian empire in northern Syria. Tutankhamen died at the age of 18 and was succeeded by Ay (r. 1352–1348), who married Tutankhamen's widow and appropriated the king's tomb for himself. Although all the other tombs in the VALLEY OF THE KINGS at Thebes were later plundered, the tomb in which Tutankhamen was ultimately buried was hidden by rock chips dumped from cutting the tomb of a later king. In 1922, Howard CARTER discovered the tomb, which was filled with extraordinary treasure, including a solid gold coffin, a gold mask, jewelry, and other artifacts.

DAVID O'CONNOR

Bibliography: Burton, Harry, *Wonderful Things: The Discovery of Tutankhamun's Tomb*, ed. by Polly Cone (1976); Carter, Howard, and Mace, A. C., *Tomb of Tutankhamen*, 3 vols. (1954); Desroches-Noblecourt, Christiane, *Tutankhamen* (1963); Edwards, I. E. S., *Tutankhamun: The Tomb and Its Treasures* (1977); Hoving, Thomas, *Tutankhamun: The Untold Story* (1978; repr. 1984); Magnusson, Magnus, *Tutankhamun* (1972).

Tutsi [toot'-see]

The Tutsi, or Watutsi, are a central African people who controlled the former kingdoms of Ruanda and Urundi, to which they came, probably from Ethiopia, in the 1500s. They constitute about 9% (1983 est.) of Rwanda's and 14.4% (1980) of Burundi's population. An aristocratic people, the Tutsi live partly by keeping cattle and partly by the agricultural tribute that they extract from a lower class of peasant cultivators, the

Hutu. The tribute obligation puts the Hutu at great risk of starvation during the frequent famines in the region.

The Tutsi are a gigantic people, often 2.1 m (7 ft) tall. They built their state, traditionally ruled by a mwami (king), by subjugating the indigenous Hutu, who had at first welcomed them as guests. Although the Tutsi state was based on exaction and inequality, it had an elaborate system of checks against exploitation beyond certain limits. Nevertheless, few rulers in postcolonial Africa have provoked their subjects to such violent revolution as the Tutsi kings.   RICHARD WERBNER

Bibliography: Maquet, Jacques, *Power and Society in Africa* (1971) and *The Premise of Inequality in Ruanda* (1961).

Tutu, Desmond

In 1984 the Rt. Rev. Desmond Mpilo Tutu, b. Oct. 7, 1931, an Anglican bishop, became the second South African opponent of APARTHEID to be awarded the Nobel Peace Prize (after Albert John LUTHULI in 1960). Ordained in 1960, he served as Anglican dean of Johannesburg (1975–76) and bishop of Lesotho (1976–78) before becoming (1979) the first black general-secretary of the South African Council of Churches. In 1984 he was elected the first black bishop of Johannesburg, and in 1986 he was elected archbishop of Cape Town, thus becoming titular head of the Anglican church in South Africa. Tutu, an advocate of nonviolence, has called for outside economic pressure to force South Africa's white authorities to end apartheid. His views have been published in two volumes of sermons and addresses—*Crying in the Wilderness* (1982) and *Hope and Suffering* (1983).

Tutuola, Amos   [too-too-oh'-luh]

Amos Tutuola, b. Abeokuta, Nigeria, June 1920, was the first African writer to achieve international fame. Although his native language is Yoruba and his formal education never extended beyond elementary school, he has written all his novels in English. His distinctive style is thus shaped by effective use of a limited vocabulary and by the grammar of West African vernacular English. He submitted his first manuscript to a missionary press, which forwarded it to the British firm that eventually published it in 1952. The novel, *The Palm-Wine Drinkard,* is a romance built out of elements from Yoruba folklore and mythology. Tutuola's other novels include *Simbi and the Satyr of the Dark Jungle* (1955), *Feather Woman of the Jungle* (1962), *Ajaiyi and His Inherited Poverty* (1967), and *The Witch Herbalist of the Remote Town* (1980).

RICHARD K. PRIEBE

Bibliography: Collins, Harold R., *Amos Tutuola* (1969); Lindfors, Bernth, ed., *Critical Perspectives on Amos Tutuola* (1975).

Tuva   [too'-vuh]

Tuva, or the Tuvinian Autonomous Soviet Socialist Republic of the Russian SFSR, in the USSR, lies adjacent to Mongolia in central Siberia. It has an area of about 170,500 km² (65,800 mi²) and a population of 276,000 (1984 est.). Most inhabitants are TUVAN. The capital is Kyzyl. The economy is based on pastoral farming, lumbering, and mining. Part of China from 1757 until 1911, the region became an independent republic, Tannu Tuva, in 1921. It was incorporated into the USSR in 1944 and became an autonomous republic in 1961.

Tuvalu   [too-vuh-loo']

Tuvalu, formerly known as the Ellice Islands, is an independent state in the Commonwealth of Nations. The nine-island cluster is located in the Pacific Ocean just south of Kiribati (formerly the Gilbert Islands) near the intersection of the equator and the international date line. Tuvalu's population is principally Polynesian. The capital is Funafuti atoll. The economy is based on subsistence agriculture and fishing, and a small amount of copra is exported. Population growth has severely strained Tuvalu's limited resources; remittances from Tuvaluans working abroad, revenues from a trust fund established by aid donors in 1987, foreign aid, and the sale of postage stamps are important sources of income.

TUVALU

LAND. Area: 26 km² (10 mi²). Capital: Funafuti atoll (1985 pop., 2,810).
PEOPLE. Population (1987 est.): 8,329; density: 359 persons per km² (824 per mi²). Distribution (1985): 34% urban, 66% rural. Annual growth (1985): 1.3%. Official language: English. Major religion: Protestantism.
EDUCATION AND HEALTH. Literacy (1983): 95.5% of adult population. Universities (1988): none. Hospital beds (1984): 36. Physicians (1985): 4. Life expectancy (1979): women—60.1; men—59.6. Infant mortality (1985): 35 per 1,000 live births.
ECONOMY. GNP (1984): $4 million; $500 per capita. Labor distribution (1979): industry—12%; fishing—22%; government and services—50%. Foreign trade (1983 est.): imports—$2.8 million; exports—$1.0 million; principal trade partners—Australia, New Zealand, Fiji. Currency: 1 Australian dollar = 100 cents.
GOVERNMENT. Type: constitutional monarchy. Legislature: Parliament. Political subdivisions: none.
COMMUNICATIONS. Railroads (1988): none. Roads (1985): 8 km (5 mi) total. Major ports: 1. Major airfields: 1.

According to tradition, Tuvalu was first settled by Samoans and Tongans. Visited by the Spanish navigator Alvaro de Mendaña in 1568, the islands became a British protectorate in 1892 and part of the Gilbert and Ellice Islands Colony in 1916. They became a separate self-governing colony in 1975 and gained independence in 1978. In 1983 the United States formally renounced its claim to four Tuvaluan islands.

Bibliography: Geddes, W. H., and Chambers, A., *Atoll Economy* (1982).

Tuvan

The Tuvan are a Mongoloid people speaking a northeast Turkic branch of the URAL-ALTAIC LANGUAGES. Tuvan are fine-featured, with yellowish skin, high cheekbones, and distinct inner-eyelid skin folds. Originally NOMADS, they traveled cross-country on fur-wrapped skis in the region of the snow-capped Sayan Mountains. Lowland Tuvan herded horses, cattle, and sheep; moving onto higher ground, they raised camels, yaks, and reindeer. They carried with them lightweight felt tents, called yurts. Highland Tuvan dwelled in birch-bark teepees.

First mentioned early in the 1st millennium in Chinese chronicles, the Mongol-dominated Tuvan have been a conquered people for almost all of their history. Traditionally, they were organized into clans based on the father's line; women were treated as chattel. In the early 1980s about 166,000 Tuvan lived as collective farmers and stock breeders in Tuva. The remaining 25,000 lived in Mongolia.

VICTOR L. MOTE

Bibliography: Jochelson, Vladimir, *Peoples of Asiatic Russia* (1928; repr. 1970); Levin, M. G., and Potapov, L. P., eds., *The Peoples of Siberia* (1964); Symmons-Symonolewicz, Konstantin, *The Non-Slavic Peoples of the Soviet Union* (1972).

Tuxtla Gutiérrez   [toos'-tlah goot-yay'-rays]

Tuxtla Gutiérrez (1980 pop., 166,476), the capital city of Chiapas state, is located in southeastern Mexico. A commercial center located on the Pan American Highway, the city has industries that process locally grown coffee, tobacco, cotton, and corn. The Mayan ruins of BONAMPAK are nearby. Originally an Indian settlement, it was first visited by Spaniards in 1546.

Twachtman, John Henry   [twahk'-muhn]

John Henry Twachtman, b. Cincinnati, Ohio, Aug. 4, 1853, d. Aug. 8, 1902, was a founding member of The Ten, a group of American painters who drew from both impressionism and the tonalism of James McNeill Whistler to create a variety of highly individual styles. Having studied with Frank Duveneck, Twachtman attended the Royal Academy in Munich, visited Venice, and studied in Paris before returning to America in 1885. By then he had developed his distinctive, lyrical approach to landscape in which forms abstracted from nature are painted in subtle but strongly brushed colors, as in *Snowbound* (c.1890-1900; Art Institute of Chicago).   DAVID TATHAM

Bibliography: Corn, Wanda, *The Color of Mood* (1972); Young, Mahroni S., *American Impressionists* (1975).

Twain, Mark

Mark Twain, who was immensely popular during his lifetime as a humorous writer and lecturer, is often heralded today as the first fiction writer to achieve a uniquely American voice. His shrewd insight into character, his ironic humor, and his free use of the vernacular have placed such works as Adventures of Huckleberry Finn (1884) and A Connecticut Yankee in King Arthur's Court (1889) among the best-loved works of American fiction.

Mark Twain was the pseudonym of Samuel Langhorne Clemens, b. Florida, Mo., Nov. 30, 1835, d. Apr. 21, 1910, who achieved worldwide fame during his lifetime as an author, lecturer, satirist, and humorist. Since his death his literary stature has further increased, with such writers as Ernest Hemingway and William Faulkner declaring his works—particularly HUCKLEBERRY FINN—a major influence on 20th-century American fiction.

Twain was raised in Hannibal, Mo., on the Mississippi River. His writing career began shortly after the death of his father in 1847. Apprenticed first to a printer, he soon joined his brother Orion's *Hannibal Journal*, supplying copy and becoming familiar with much of the frontier humor of the time, such as George W. Harris's Sut Lovingood yarns and other works of the so-called Southwestern Humorists.

From 1853 to 1857, Twain visited and periodically worked as a printer in New York, Philadelphia, St. Louis, and Cincinnati, corresponding with his brother's newspapers under various pseudonyms. After a visit to New Orleans in 1857, he learned the difficult art of steamboat piloting, an occupation that he followed until the Civil War closed the river, and that furnished the background for "Old Times on the Mississippi" (1875), later included in the expanded *Life on the Mississippi* (1883).

In 1861, Twain traveled by stagecoach to Carson City, Nev., with his brother Orion, who had been appointed territorial

secretary. After unsuccessful attempts at silver and gold mining, he returned to writing as a correspondent for the *Virginia City Territorial Enterprise*. At first he signed his humorous and imaginative sketches "Josh," but early in 1863 he adopted the now-famous name Mark Twain, borrowed from the Mississippi leadsman's call meaning "two fathoms" deep—safe water for a steamboat.

Twain went to San Francisco in 1864. Dubbed the "Wild Humorist of the Pacific Slope," he achieved a measure of national fame with his story "The Celebrated Jumping Frog of Calaveras County" (1865). A trip to Hawaii in 1866 furnished articles for the *Sacramento Union* and materials for the first lecture, on his return, in a long and successful career as a public speaker. The following year he traveled to the Mediterranean and the Holy Land, providing letters to the *San Francisco Alta California* that, in their revised form as *The Innocents Abroad* (1869), won immediate international attention.

In 1870, Twain married Olivia Langdon of Elmira, N.Y. After serving briefly as editor and part-owner of the *Buffalo Express*, he moved to Hartford, Conn., in 1871, abandoning journalism in order to devote his full attention to serious literature. There, and during summers in Elmira, he produced *Roughing It* (1872), an account of his Western years; *The Gilded Age* (1873, with Charles Dudley Warner), a satire of get-rich-quick schemes and political chicanery; the new pieces for *Sketches, New and Old* (1875); and TOM SAWYER (1875), his classic tale of boyhood.

A European sojourn in 1878-79 inspired *A Tramp Abroad* (1880), soon followed by *The Prince and the Pauper* (1882), Twain's first historical novel. He later turned to history again in the allegorical satire *A Connecticut Yankee in King Arthur's Court* (1889), his most powerful fictional indictment of political and social injustice. Meanwhile, he completed *Life on the Mississippi* (1883) and, after establishing his own firm, Charles L. Webster and Co., published his masterpiece, *Adventures of Huckleberry Finn*, in 1884.

Increasingly involved financial problems prompted Twain to move to Europe in 1891, just after finishing *The American Claimant* (1892). In 1894, following the failure of his publishing company and of the Paige typesetting machine in which he had invested heavily, Twain was forced to declare bankruptcy. During this period he turned out a number of works, generally inferior to his best: *The Tragedy of Pudd'nhead Wilson* (1894), *Tom Sawyer Abroad* (1894), *Personal Recollections of Joan of Arc* (1896), and *Tom Sawyer, Detective* (1896). In 1895, to help recoup his losses, he embarked on a world lecture tour, later described in *Following the Equator* (1897).

Although his financial situation rapidly improved, additional stress and sorrow came with the deaths of Twain's daughter Susy in 1896 and of his wife in 1904. His writings of the late 1890s and 1900s became more pessimistic than ever; "The Man That Corrupted Hadleyburg" (1898) and *What Is Man?* (1906) are particularly scathing examinations of human nature. Yet, these works also imply that proper understanding of human motivations can result in progress. Moreover, recent volumes in the Mark Twain Papers series—*Which Was the Dream?, and Other Symbolic Writings of the Later Years* (1967), *Mark Twain's Mysterious Stranger Manuscripts* (1969), and *Mark Twain's Fables of Man* (1972)—suggest that the period was not the wasteland described by some critics.

H. G. BAETZHOLD

Bibliography: Anderson, Frederick, and Sanderson, K. M., eds., *Mark Twain: The Critical Heritage* (1972); Blair, Walter, *Mark Twain and Huck Finn* (1960); Branch, Edgar M., *The Literary Apprenticeship of Mark Twain* (1950); Brooks, Van Wyck, *Ordeal of Mark Twain*, rev. ed. (1933; repr. 1977); Budd, Louis J., *Mark Twain: Social Philosopher* (1962); De Voto, Bernard, *Mark Twain's America* (1932); Fatout, Paul, *Mark Twain on the Lecture Circuit* (1960); Hill, Hamlin, *Mark Twain, God's Fool* (1973); Howells, William Dean, *My Mark Twain* (1910); Kaplan, Justin, *Mark Twain and His World* (1974) and *Mr. Clemens and Mark Twain* (1966); Lynn, Kenneth, *Mark Twain and Southwestern Humor* (1959); Paine, Albert B., *Mark Twain: A Biography*, 3 vols., new ed. (1935); Sanderlin, George, *Mark Twain as Others Saw Him* (1978); Smith, Henry Nash, *Mark Twain: The Development of a Writer* (1962); Wecter, Dixon, *Sam Clemens of Hannibal* (1952).

twayblade   [tway'-blayd]

Twayblade is a common name used for two genera of the orchid family, Orchidaceae. *Liparis* has about 250 species worldwide, whereas *Listera* has about 30 north-temperate species. Twayblades grow from a corm or pseudobulb and do not typically flower until the 10th year. In *Listera*, pollen grains are freed when the plant is disturbed by a visitor.

FRANK B. SALISBURY

tweed

Tweed is a somewhat hairy, textured woolen fabric originally hand-woven by country people who lived near the River Tweed between England and Scotland. It is now often spun and woven by machine, but Harris tweed, exported from the islands of the Outer Hebrides off the northern coast of Scotland, is still hand-woven. Vegetable dyes are used for the wool yarns and, in the best tweeds, produce the muted, subtle colors that give the fabric its distinctive look. Tweed patterns are usually traditional twills, checks, and herringbones.

ISABEL B. WINGATE

Tweed, River

The River Tweed rises in the southern uplands of Scotland and flows for 156 km (97 mi), entering the North Sea near Berwick-on-Tweed, England. For 27 km (17 mi) it follows the Scottish-English border. Tweed cloth is a major product of the river valley communities.

Tweed, William M.

A battered William M. Tweed appears in a Harper's Weekly cartoon by Thomas Nast following the 1871 elections. In those elections "Boss" Tweed himself was returned to the state senate, but many of his Tammany Hall candidates were defeated by reformers.

The Democratic boss of New York City in the 1860s, William Marcy (or Magear) Tweed, b. New York City, Apr. 3, 1823, d. Apr. 12, 1878, spent his last years in jail because of his corrupt conduct of public business. A bookkeeper for many years, he increasingly devoted himself to politics. In the early 1850s he became foreman of a volunteer fire company, which he allied with TAMMANY HALL; he also served as an alderman (1851-55) and U.S. representative (1853-55). In 1856 he became a member of the county board of supervisors and a school commissioner. Over the next 5 years Tweed and his allies won many key city and county offices; by the end of 1861 they thoroughly dominated both Tammany Hall and local government.

In 1868, Tweed became a state senator; John T. Hoffman, a protégé of his, was elected governor in 1869. His ring began applying its methods to state politics. Penniless in 1861, Tweed had acquired a fortune of at least $2.5 million by 1871, largely through influence peddling and kickbacks from the sale of city contracts and franchises. Altogether the ring stole from $40 million to $200 million of public funds.

Revelations in 1870 regarding the ring's thievery and the formation (1871) of a citizens' committee headed by Samuel J. TILDEN led in 1873 to Tweed's conviction for fraud. Escaping custody, in 1875, Tweed fled to Spain. Recognized in 1876 through a Thomas Nast cartoon, he was returned to New York, where he died in jail.

GERALD W. McFARLAND

Bibliography: Callow, Alexander B., *The Tweed Ring* (1966); Hershkowitz, Leo, *Tweed's New York* (1977); Lynch, D. T., *Boss Tweed* (1927); Mandelbaum, Seymour J., *Boss Tweed's New York* (1965).

12th Amendment

The 12th Amendment (1804) to the U.S. Constitution provides for the reform of the method by which the ELECTORAL COLLEGE elects the president and vice-president. Under the terms of Article II, Section 1 of the Constitution, the electors were to cast their votes for both offices on a single ballot without specifying which of the two candidates on their ballot was preferred as president and which as vice-president. The candidate receiving the highest number of electoral votes would then become president, and the runner-up would become vice-president.

The unforeseen formation of political parties, however, resulted in the electoral college's choosing in 1796 a president and vice-president from different parties under the old procedure. In 1800 party-pledged electors were chosen. The casting of two ballots for the same ticket resulted in a tie between presidential candidate Thomas Jefferson and his own running mate, Aaron Burr. The House of Representatives eventually voted for Jefferson after a protracted deadlock. This event triggered the demand for the 12th Amendment.

The 12th Amendment provides the following: (1) separate ballots are used for each office; (2) persons with the greatest number of votes for each office will be elected if that number constitutes a majority of the total electors; (3) if no such majority is met for either or both of the two highest offices, the House of Representatives will then vote for the president from among the three highest candidates and the Senate will vote for the vice-president from among the two highest candidates; (4) no person constitutionally ineligible to be president can be vice-president.

Twelfth Night

Shakespeare's *Twelfth Night, or, What You Will,* possibly first performed for the Queen of England on the twelfth night after Christmas in 1601, depends on many of the conventions of romance—mistaken identity, shipwreck, disguise, fortuitous meetings— especially as these were developed by Italian Renaissance writers. Through the force of love (Viola's and Sebastian's), Orsino and Olivia are cured of their self-love, but the puritanical steward Malvolio cannot be drawn into the magic circle of comedy, and he exits from the play with threats of revenge on all the comic manipulators. The play contains some of Shakespeare's funniest low comedy, much of it supplied by Sir Toby Belch and Sir Andrew Aguecheek.

twelve-tone system

The twelve-tone system is a method of musical composition invented by Arnold Schoenberg about 1920 and adopted by his followers. Through its use music is released from the limitations of tonality (see ATONALITY) because none of the 12 notes of the chromatic scale is given more importance than the others. In place of traditional scale systems, the composer establishes for each composition a row using all 12 notes and usually avoiding any hint of chordal or key dependence. In the strict application of the technique, each note is sounded in serial order, and no note is repeated until the other 11 have been used. The row and its parts may be used also in inversion, retrograde, and retrograde inversion (see SERIAL MUSIC). The result is a complex variation technique of a contrapuntal nature. Before mid-century, Alban Berg and Anton Webern had become prominent in twelve-tone composition, and the method has been widely practiced. Later composers have applied aspects of serial technique to rhythm, dynamics, accents, and other musical elements as well.

ELWYN A. WIENANDT

Bibliography: Perle, George, *Serial Composition and Atonality*, 3d ed. (1972); Rufer, Joseph, *Composition with Twelve Notes* (1952).

20th Amendment

The 20th Amendment (1933) to the U.S. Constitution provides for the orderly installation of the president, vice-president, and members of Congress, shortens their LAME DUCK status, and clarifies the status of the president-elect and vice-president-elect in regard to presidential succession. Prior to this amendment the old Congress had met for a 4-month session, and the new Congress did not convene until the following December; the presidential term had lasted until March 4 following the November elections; no provisions were made for the possibility of the inability to serve of the president-elect and vice-president-elect.

The four major provisions of the amendment are as follows: (1) The terms of the president and vice-president will end on January 20 of the year following an election, and new terms will begin on that date; senators and representatives will end and begin their terms on January 3. (2) Congress will assemble at least once a year, and this meeting will begin on January 3 unless Congress selects another day. (3) If the president-elect dies, the vice-president-elect becomes president; or, if the president has not been chosen (under the 12TH AMENDMENT) or if the president-elect does not qualify, the vice-president-elect serves as president until a president does qualify; or, if neither qualifies, Congress will declare how to appoint an acting president until a president or vice-president is qualified. (4) If it becomes the duty of Congress to choose a president or vice-president, Congress will also provide by law for the orderly succession to these offices in the event that a person who has been so designated dies or is disqualified.

25th Amendment

The 25th Amendment (1967) to the U.S. Constitution provides procedures for fulfilling the duties of the presidency in the event of the removal, death, or resignation of a president; it is also concerned with the prompt filling of a vice-presidential vacancy.

The amendment has four provisions stating that: (1) in the event of removal, death, or resignation of a president, the vice-president becomes president; (2) in the event of a vacancy in the vice-presidential office, the president nominates a vice-president who must be confirmed by a majority vote in the Senate and House of Representatives; (3) when a president declares himself or herself unable to serve in office, his or her duties will be taken over by the vice-president as acting president until the president declares himself or herself able to serve again; (4) when the vice-president and either a majority of the heads of the executive departments or a specific congressionally determined body considers a president unable to fulfill his or her duties, the vice-president becomes acting president; when the president then declares that he or she is again able to fulfill the office, he or she resumes those duties unless the vice-president and either a majority of the heads of the executive departments or a specific congressionally determined group declare within 4 days that the president is unfit. At that point Congress is required to assemble to decide the issue within 21 days. A two-thirds vote is required to declare the president unfit, in which case the vice-president continues to be acting president.

Bibliography: Feerick, John D., *The Twenty-fifth Amendment: Its Complete History and Earliest Applications* (1976).

21st Amendment

The 21st Amendment (1933) to the U.S. Constitution repeals the 18TH AMENDMENT, which prohibited the making of and trafficking in intoxicating liquors. The 21st Amendment thus became the only amendment to date that was adopted to repeal an earlier amendment. Despite efforts of federal government agencies to enforce the antiliquor laws empowered by the 18th Amendment (1919–33), prohibition was unpopular and a failure both legally and as a moral experiment. The repeal of the 18th Amendment, however, did not revoke other laws in effect on the regulation of licenses and on taxes related to the liquor industry. The primary intent of the 21st Amendment was to end federal bans against the manufacture, sale, transportation, importation, and exportation of intoxicating beverages.

Bibliography: Brown, Everett S., ed., *Ratification of the Twenty-first Amendment to the Constitution of the United States* (1938; repr. 1970).

24th Amendment

The 24th Amendment to the U.S. Constitution, proposed by Congress on Aug. 27, 1962, and ratified Jan. 23, 1964, bans the use of POLL TAXES in federal elections (a device imposed by some states to circumvent the 15TH AMENDMENT's guarantee of equal voting rights). Intended to alleviate the burdens of black and poor citizens, it states that in any presidential or congressional election, no citizen can be denied, by the state or federal government, the right to vote because of failure to pay either a poll tax or any other tax. Moreover, it gives Congress the power to enforce such a right. Although 45 states—all but Alabama, Arkansas, Mississippi, Texas, and Virginia—did not use a poll tax as a prerequisite to vote, an amendment was needed to eliminate the practice altogether.

Although the 24th Amendment prohibited the poll tax only in federal elections, the Supreme Court declared in *Harper* v. *Virginia State Board of Elections* (1966) that the poll tax was unconstitutional in state elections on the grounds that it violated the clause of the 14th Amendment guaranteeing EQUAL PROTECTION OF THE LAWS. The amendment led to the Voting Rights Act of 1965.

twenty-one: see BLACKJACK.

22d Amendment

The 22d Amendment (1951) to the U.S. Constitution limits the presidential tenure to two terms of office. It further states that if a vice-president succeeds to the presidency with two years or less of the former president's term remaining, then the new president may be elected for two more terms; otherwise, the new president may be elected for only one more term.

This amendment was proposed by a Republican Congress in reaction to the four-term presidency of Franklin D. Roosevelt, who broke the two-term tradition begun by George Washington. It also reflected national concern with the prolonged domination of any one president in that office and the growth of executive power. Critics of the amendment have felt that it weakens a second-term president and could present a hazard in a time of crisis.

26th Amendment

The 26th Amendment (1971) to the U.S. Constitution is the fourth of the amendments to clarify voting rights (others are the 15TH AMENDMENT, the 19TH AMENDMENT, and the 23d Amendment). This amendment states that the right of citizens who are 18 years or older to vote "shall not be denied or abridged by the United States or by any state on account of age."

The passage of this amendment was spurred by the massive protests in the 1960s of students and other young people regarding the war in Vietnam. In response to the argument, "If we're old enough to fight, we're old enough to vote," this amendment was adopted; it reduced the voting age from 21 years to 18 years and provided the opportunity for younger people to participate in the political process and to have a voting voice in the affairs of government. The amendment followed the Voting Rights Act of 1970, which as a result of a Supreme Court decision, lowered the voting age only in national elections.

23d Amendment

The 23d Amendment to the U.S. Constitution, proposed by Congress on June 16, 1960, and ratified Mar. 29, 1961, granted citizens of the District of Columbia the right to vote in presidential elections—a right denied since the founding of the District from portions of Maryland and Virginia in 1802. The amendment states that the number of electors, appointed by the District government, for president and vice-president cannot exceed those of the least-populated state—or 3 votes in the electoral college; furthermore, they must be subject—as are all electors from every state in the United States—to rules of procedure set forth in the 12TH AMENDMENT. Congress, furthermore, was given power to legislate for the District government in order to implement the amendment. Among the provisions subsequently adopted by Congress is a 1-year residence requirement.

Twenty Thousand Leagues Under the Sea

Twenty Thousand Leagues Under the Sea (1870), a futuristic adventure novel by Jules VERNE, was one of the most successful early attempts to exploit the growing contemporary interest in science. It demonstrated Verne's genius for utilizing his own scientific interests and prophetic talents to produce exciting and occasionally didactic romantic science fiction. The story describes the adventures of Professor Aronnax (the narrator), Conseil (his manservant), and Ned (a harpoonist), on board the submarine *Nautilus*, commanded by the mysterious and vengeful Captain Nemo, who has great appeal as a romantic hero. R. M. FORD

twilight

Scattered and reflected light from the sunlit portion of the atmosphere enables inhabitants within a 2,000-km-wide (1,250-mi) band just outside the lighted half of the Earth to move about fairly well without artificial illumination; such periods of twilight occur just before sunrise and just after sunset. Duration of twilight varies with the time of year and latitudinal position. At the equator, twilight throughout the year lasts approximately one hour each morning and evening; at latitudes greater than 67½°, twilight lasts 24 hours near the time of the winter solstice and is nonexistent near the time of the summer solstice; at these times the Sun is, respectively, continuously below and continuously above the horizon.
ROBERT C. FITE

twill

The term *twill* designates both a textile weave characterized by diagonal structural designs and the cloth made from that weave. The weave may be varied to produce broken or intertwining effects. Twill fabrics are usually firm and are used especially in suits and in sport and work clothes. Twill-weave fabrics are also used for linings, pockets, and mattress ticking. Serge, gabardine, and cheviot are major types of twill.
ISABEL B. WINGATE

twinflower

Twinflower, *Linnaea borealis,* is the common name for a half-woody subshrub in the family Caprifoliaceae. It has trailing stems, roundish evergreen leaves, and pinkish or nearly white, bell-shaped, twin flowers. The plant is distributed in North America from Labrador to Alaska and in the mountains south to Maryland and California. Twinflower was the favorite flower of the great Swedish botanist, Carolus Linnaeus, who named the genus for himself. FRANK B. SALISBURY

Twining v. New Jersey

The case of *Twining* v. *New Jersey* (1908) dealt with the applicability of the SELF-INCRIMINATION clause of the 5th Amend-

ment to the states through the 14th Amendment. Albert Twining had been convicted of knowingly showing a state bank examiner a false document. At his trial Twining had refused to take the witness stand, and under New Jersey law the jury had been instructed that it might draw an unfavorable inference against him for his failure to testify in his own behalf. The question before the Supreme Court was "whether the New Jersey law violated the 14th Amendment either by abridging his privileges and immunities as a citizen of the United States or by depriving him of due process of law."

With Justice William H. Moody as its spokesman, the Court held that the right against self-incrimination was neither a privilege of federal citizenship nor specifically a part of DUE PROCESS of law. The privilege against self-incrimination, said Moody, had never been regarded as a part of due process in English law but rather as a "wise and beneficent rule of evidence developed in the course of judicial decision." Although applicable to the national government under the Bill of Rights, Moody concluded, it was not a guarantee in state judicial proceedings. The decision was reversed by *Malloy* v. *Hogan* (1964), which incorporated the self-incrimination clause of the 5th Amendment into the due process clause of the 14th and therefore made it applicable to the states.
ROBERT J. STEAMER

twinleaf

Twinleaf is the common name for a hardy, perennial plant, *Jeffersonia diphylla,* in the family Berberidaceae. Native to eastern North America, it is found from Ontario to as far south as Alabama. Each leaf stalk grows directly from the rootstock, with the leaf split into two kidney-shaped divisions.

two-body problem

A classic physics problem is that of describing the resultant motion of two objects when they are subjected only to their mutually attractive force. The theoretical problem was completely solved by Isaac Newton and published in his *Principia Mathematica* (book 3, 1687). The motion is called Keplerian motion because it was summarized by Johannes Kepler before Newton; in fact, Newton could have derived the law of gravitation from KEPLER'S LAWS. For the case of two astronomical bodies, which are mutually attracted by gravitation, Newton showed that the motion is confined to a plane and that the motion of one body with regard to the other follows a curve of the various CONIC SECTIONS, that is, either an ellipse (of which a circle is a special case), a parabola, or a hyperbola. Electrically charged particles, which also obey an INVERSE SQUARE LAW of attraction (or repulsion) similar to gravitation, also have conic-section motions.

This solution, however, has only limited application in practice because of the presence of other bodies. The determination of the motion of the Earth-Moon system, for example, requires the inclusion of the effects caused by the Sun, the planets Jupiter and Saturn, the equatorial bulge of the Earth, and even the effects of the Earth's tides. The problem of exactly determining the relative motions of three bodies has not yet been solved. STEPHEN FLEISHMAN

Bibliography: Skinner, Ray, *Mechanics* (1969); Van De Kamp, Peter, *Elements of Astromechanics* (1964).

See also: THREE-BODY PROBLEM.

Two Sicilies, Kingdom of the

The Two Sicilies was a name intermittently used for the kingdoms of Sicily and Naples when the two were jointly ruled. First used (1443) by ALFONSO V, king of Aragon, Sicily, and Naples, it was an official name from 1815 to 1861.

Tworkov, Jack   [twohr'-kawv]

First recognized in the 1950s as an exponent of the abstract expressionism of the New York school, the American painter Jack Tworkov, b. Biala, Poland, Aug. 15, 1900, d. Sept. 4, 1982, began working in a new geometric style during the 1960s. His

brightly colored abstract works involve a type of gestural, calligraphic brushwork that creates exciting tensions. Tworkov's
painting style changed after 1965 from apparent spontaneity
to conscious planning within imposed limits. Rigidly geometric compositions based on a grid structure are softened by an
overlay of muted, toned brushwork reminiscent of his earlier
work. Shapes often seem to project or recede, creating a
strong sense of movement.   LISA M. MESSINGER

Bibliography: Bryant, Edward, *Jack Tworkov* (1964).

Tyler, Anne

The American novelist and short-story writer Anne Tyler, b.
Minneapolis, Minn., Oct. 25, 1941, writes mainly of life in
small Southern towns, although her themes concern the human condition in general. From her first novel, *If Morning
Ever Comes* (1964), to the recent *Morgan's Passing* (1980) and
Dinner at the Homesick Restaurant (1982), she has observed
human isolation and praised those who have the courage to
overcome it. Tyler writes in a clear, graceful style, revealing
her characters through the use of crisp dialogue and an
imaginative handling of the clutter and detail of ordinary life.
Her short stories have appeared in many magazines, including
Seventeen and the *New Yorker*.

Tyler, John

The tenth president of the United States (1841–45), John Tyler
was the first to succeed to office on the death of an incumbent president. Born in Charles City County, Va., on Mar. 29,
1790, he was the son of John Tyler, who was to be governor
of Virginia (1808–11). The young Tyler was educated as a
member of the Tidewater plantation aristocracy and graduated from the College of William and Mary in 1807. He then
studied law and in 1811, at the age of 21, was elected to the
Virginia legislature.

Early Political Career. Throughout his career Tyler displayed a
political independence and a commitment to state rights that
was tenacious even by Virginia standards. He upheld the view
that federal powers must be limited to those specified in the
Constitution and consistently opposed the idea of a national
bank with state branches, seeing this as an unwarranted federal infringement upon the constitutional rights of the states.
Serving in the U.S. House of Representatives (1817–21), he rejected the national economic program advocated by Henry
Clay and John C. Calhoun, voting against protective tariffs,
federal aid for internal improvements, and the successful bill
to charter a second Bank of the United States. Tyler also opposed the Missouri Compromise of 1820 as an unconstitutional limitation of the rights of slaveholders. Retiring from
Congress in 1821, he served as Virginia's governor (1825–27).

Tyler returned to Washington in 1827 as a senator, supporting parties and measures strictly by the standard of their fidelity to his strict constitutional views. He endorsed Andrew
Jackson's presidential candidacy and supported Jackson's
stand against internal improvements and the second Bank of
the United States. Tyler opposed the tariffs of 1828 and 1832
but condemned South Carolina's nullification of those laws in
1832. He also, however, opposed the Jackson-sponsored
Force Bill of 1833 authorizing the use of military force to suppress nullification—Tyler cast the only Senate vote against the
measure. In 1834 he censured the president's removal of federal funds from the National Bank. In February 1836 the Jack-
sonian-controlled Virginia legislature instructed Tyler to vote
to expunge the Senate censure resolution against the president on this matter. He refused, resigned his seat, and severed his Democratic party ties.

The Whig party, united only in opposition to Jackson,
chose Tyler in 1836 as the vice-presidential candidate on one
of its sectional tickets. In 1839 the Whig national convention
chose westerner William Henry Harrison as its presidential
candidate and unanimously nominated Tyler as vice-president
to balance the ticket. The party issued no platform and won
the 1840 race with mass rallies, songs, and slogans such as
"Tippecanoe and Tyler, too."

JOHN TYLER
10th President of the United States (1841–45)·

Nickname: "Accidental President"; "His Accidency"
Born: Mar. 29, 1790, Charles City County, Va.
Education: College of William and Mary (graduated
1807)
Profession: Lawyer
Religious Affiliation: Episcopalian
Marriage: Mar. 29, 1813, to Letitia Christian
(1790–1842); June 26, 1844, to Julia Gardiner
(1820–89)
Children: Mary Tyler (1815–48); Robert Tyler (1816–77);
John Tyler (1819–96); Letitia Tyler (1821–1907); Eliza-
beth Tyler (1823–50); Anne Contesse Tyler (1825); Al-
ice Tyler (1827–54); Tazewell Tyler (1830–74); David
Gardiner Tyler (1846–1927); John Alexander Tyler
(1848–83); Julia Gardiner Tyler (1849–71); Lachlan Ty-
ler (1851–1902); Lyon Gardiner Tyler (1853–1935);
Robert Fitzwalter Tyler (1856–1927); Pearl Tyler
(1860–1947)
Political Affiliation: Democrat; Whig
Died: Jan. 18, 1862, Richmond, Va.
Buried: Hollywood Cemetery, Richmond, Va.

Vice-President and Cabinet Members
Vice-President: None
Secretary of State: Daniel Webster (1841–43); Abel P.
Upshur (1843–44); John C. Calhoun (1844–45)
Secretary of the Treasury: Thomas Ewing (1841);
Walter Forward (1841–43); John C. Spencer
(1843–44); George M. Bibb (1844–45)
Secretary of War: John Bell (1841); John C. Spencer
(1841–43); James M. Porter (1843–44); William Wil-
kins (1844–45)
Attorney General: John J. Crittenden (1841); Hugh S.
Legaré (1841–43); John Nelson (1843–45)
Postmaster General: Francis Granger (1841); Charles
A. Wickliffe (1841–45)
Secretary of the Navy: George E. Badger (1841); Abel
P. Upshur (1841–43); David Henshaw (1843–44);
Thomas W. Gilmer (1844); John Y. Mason (1844–45)

Presidency. The 69-year-old Harrison died after a month as president, and on Apr. 6, 1841, Tyler took the oath of office. Tyler asserted and by resolution Congress affirmed that he had the full powers of office and not merely those of an acting president. His constitutional scruples, however, placed him on a collision course with the nationalist-minded Whig congressional caucus and its leader, Henry Clay. Tyler vetoed two Whig bills to create a new national bank. In retaliation, the Whig cabinet—with the exception of Secretary of State Daniel Webster—resigned in September 1841, and soon after the caucus expelled the president from his party. Tyler ultimately vetoed more bills than Jackson and in 1845 became the first president to have Congress override his veto.

Tyler's greatest successes came in the realm of foreign policy. He supported Webster in the talks leading to the WEB-STER-ASHBURTON TREATY (1842), which settled the Maine boundary dispute. He ended the Seminole War, extended the Monroe Doctrine to Hawaii, and opened the first American trade mission to China.

After Webster resigned in May 1843, Tyler vigorously pursued the annexation of the slaveholding Republic of Texas. To avoid the delicate slavery issue, both parties had carefully sidestepped the Texas question. Politically independent, Tyler negotiated a treaty with Texas. Although the Senate rejected the treaty in June 1844, Tyler had forced the issue of annexation into national politics. A man without a party, he did not run for reelection in 1844, but Democrat James K. Polk won the presidency (over Henry Clay) on an annexationist platform, and in March 1845, Tyler signed a joint resolution of Congress annexing Texas.

Later Life. Tyler retired to his Virginia plantation in 1845. In February 1861 he reentered public life to sponsor and chair the Washington peace convention, which sought to devise a compromise to avert civil war. When the Senate rejected his plan, Tyler urged Virginia's immediate secession. Having served in the provisional Confederate Congress in 1861, he was elected to the Confederate House of Representatives but died before he could take office.   SIDNEY NATHANS

Bibliography: Chidsey, Donald B., *And Tyler Too* (1978); Chitwood, Oliver Perry, *John Tyler* (1939; repr. 1964); Fraser, Hugh R., *Democracy in the Making: The Jackson-Tyler Era* (1938; repr. 1969); Lambert, Oscar D., *Presidential Politics in the United States, 1841-1844* (1956); Merk, Frederick and Lois B., *Fruits of Propaganda in the Tyler Administration* (1971); Morgan, Robert J., *A Whig Embattled: The Presidency under John Tyler* (1954; repr. 1974); Seager, Robert, *And Tyler Too: A Biography of John and Julia Gardiner Tyler* (1963).

Tyler, Ralph Winfred

Ralph Winfred Tyler, b. Chicago, Apr. 22, 1902, pioneered in education evaluation, wrote extensively on curriculum design, worked with Robert M. HUTCHINS to restructure the University of Chicago, served as a founder and director (for 13 years) of the CENTER FOR ADVANCED STUDY IN THE BEHAVIORAL SCIENCES, in Stanford, Calif., and founded the NATIONAL ASSESSMENT OF EDUCATIONAL PROGRESS. His *Basic Principles of Curriculum and Instruction* (1950) is a widely used text.

Tyler, Royall

The American writer and jurist Royall Tyler, b. Boston, July 18, 1757, d. Aug. 26, 1826, wrote *The Contrast* (1787), the first American comedy on a native theme. Inspired by Sheridan's *School for Scandal, The Contrast* caricatures contemporary American society and features Jonathan, a shrewd but unsophisticated bumpkin, the first of many stage Yankees. Tyler also wrote four other plays, poetry, a novel, and a comic opera. He was chief justice (1807-13) of the Vermont Supreme Court and professor of jurisprudence (1811-14) at the University of Vermont.   MYRON MATLAW

Bibliography: Tanselle, George T., *Royall Tyler* (1967).

Tylor, Sir Edward B.

Sir Edward Burnett Tylor, b. Oct. 2, 1832, d. Jan. 2, 1917, is considered the founder of anthropology in Great Britain. He is known for his research on culture, cultural evolution, and the origin and development of religion. Tylor was born into a well-to-do British Quaker family. When he was 24 years of age, concern for his health led him to travel to the United States, and while on a crowded omnibus in Havana he chanced to meet a virtuoso traveler, Henry Christy. The two went to Mexico, and by then Tylor's fascination with ethnology and archaeology had taken permanent hold. He returned to Great Britain and soon published his first book, *Anahuac: Mexico and the Mexicans, Ancient and Modern* (1861).

In developing his view of progressive cultural evolution, Tylor held that earlier stages of development could be known by what he termed *survivals,* ancient traits that lingered on in more advanced cultures. Also noteworthy is Tylor's theory of ANIMISM, that primitive religions endow natural objects with a soul. Tylor never earned a university degree, but his research and writing established his position. He became keeper of the University Museum at Oxford in 1883, where he was a professor of anthropology from 1896 to 1909. His major works include *Primitive Culture* (1871) and *Anthropology* (1881).

Bibliography: Burrow, John W., *Evolution and Society: A Study in Victorian Social Theory* (1966); Marett, R. R., *Tylor* (1936).

tympanum   [tim'-puh-nuhm]

In classical architecture the tympanum is the triangular area enclosed by the pediment above a doorway, window, or portico. In Romanesque and Gothic churches the tympana—areas above doors and windows or within decorative arcades—are enclosed in round or pointed arches. Classical tympana were filled with sculpture in-the-round of mythical beings; medieval tympana, with stone bas-reliefs of either abstract designs, such as representations of flora, fauna, or imaginary creatures, or illustrations of biblical themes, such as the Last Judgment or the life of the Virgin Mary.

Tynan, Kenneth   [ty'-nuhn]

The British drama critic Kenneth Tynan, b. Apr. 2, 1927, d. July 26, 1980, was celebrated for his acerbic, witty reviews and for his interest in drama as a medium of social criticism. During the 1950s he was drama critic of the *Evening Standard,* the *Observer,* and the *New Yorker* and from 1963 to 1973 served as literary manager of the National Theatre, London. Tynan's satirical revue *Oh! Calcutta!* (1969) ran for many years on Broadway. A collection of his biographical sketches, *Show People,* was published in 1980.

Tyndale, William   [tin'-duhl]

William Tyndale, b. *c.*1494, d. Oct. 6, 1536, was an early English Protestant reformer most famous for his English translation of the Bible. After education at Oxford and Cambridge he began his life work of biblical study. In 1524, after failing to find patronage in England for his translation project, he moved to Germany. At Cologne he began printing his translation of the New Testament, but he was interrupted by legal injunction and completed the work in Worms in 1526. When copies arrived in England, the work was denounced by the church hierarchy and others, such as Sir Thomas More, who demanded his death as a heretic. Thereafter, Tyndale lived most of the time in Antwerp, where he revised his New Testament and printed translations of the Pentateuch and of Jonah. He also wrote Protestant tracts. In 1535 he was arrested and imprisoned at Vilvorde, near Brussels. He was condemned for heresy and executed.

Tyndale's work shows the influence of Martin Luther, whom he knew in Germany and who was probably responsible for his conversion to Protestantism. Unlike earlier English translators, he was a master of Greek and Hebrew and was able to benefit from Erasmus's Greek version of the New Testament. Lively and full of Anglo-Saxon terms, Tyndale's revised version (1534) is the principal source for the language of the King James version.   FREDERICK A. NORWOOD

Bibliography: Duffield, Gervase E., ed., *The Work of William Tyndale* (1965); Mozley, J. F., *William Tyndale* (1937; repr. 1971); Williams, Charles H., *William Tyndale* (1969).

Tyndall, John   [tin'-dul]

Long associated with London's Royal Institution, the Irishman John Tyndall, b. Aug. 2, 1820, d. Dec. 4, 1893, was a physicist of wide-ranging interests and a popularizer of science. His original contributions, embodied in more than 180 research papers, cover topics ranging from diamagnetism and sound transmission to glacial movements and mountaineering. He is best known for his study of light scattering (the Tyndall effect), his work on heat conduction, and his opposition to the doctrine of the spontaneous generation of life. In numerous books, articles, and addresses he explained science to the layperson, urged public support for research, and advocated the philosophy of scientific naturalism.   ROBERT SILLIMAN

Bibliography: Crowther, James G., *Scientific Types* (1970); Hall, Marie B., *All Scientists Now* (1985).

type and typesetting

In PRINTING, *type* is the term used to describe the full range of alphabetic and numeric characters and punctuation marks necessary for the composition of text. Typesetting is the craft of arranging type—either by hand or machine—into readable form. Typography involves the choice of type and the design of pages for a book or other printed piece.

TYPEFOUNDING AND HAND SETTING

The German Johann Gutenberg is credited with developing the first successful technology for the rapid and accurate manufacture of type, a process known as typefounding. In Gutenberg's method, a character was engraved in relief on the end of a hard metal punch, which was then driven into a softer piece of metal known as a matrix. The matrix was placed in an adjustable type mold, and molten metal was poured into the mold, hardening almost instantaneously. After a few finishing operations, the new piece of type, its relief image identical to that on the punch, was ready to be used. The essential elements of Gutenburg's process, invented about the middle of the 15th century, were so simple and reliable that they remained virtually unchanged until well into the 19th century.

Type terminology, dating from the days when all type was set by hand and printed almost exclusively by LETTERPRESS, also remains the same. A font of type comprises all the uppercase and lowercase letters of the alphabet (the term *case* derives from the printer's case, a hinged double box in which all

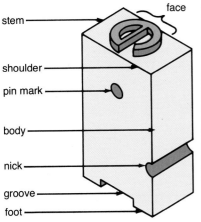

A piece of modern movable type differs little from the type used by Johann Gutenberg. Type is made of an alloy of lead, antimony, and tin and cast as a rectangular block. The letter to be printed is raised and is known as the face. The nick, groove, and pin mark on the body of the type help align it on a composing stick during the process of typesetting.

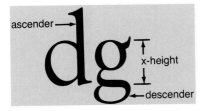

The length of lowercase type is given in terms of the x-height, the ascender, and the descender. The total length of the type from ascender to descender determines the point size.

the capital letters are kept in the upper case), as well as numbers, punctuation marks, ligatures (characters made of two letters joined together—œ, for example), and special characters in a particular design and size. Points constitute an important category of size. One point is equivalent to 0.01383 inches (0.35128 mm), and all type is designated in point size. There are 12 points to a pica, and approximately 72 points to the inch (25.4 mm).

To set type, the compositor uses a composing stick that is calibrated in picas and adjusted to whatever line length is specified in the typographer's design. Divisions between words and sentences are made with assorted metal space units; the widths of these spaces are based on the em, a unit of measurement that is a square of the typeface's point size: that is, a 10 point em is 10 points wide and 10 points high. One-half of an em is an en. When space is needed between lines of composed type, thin strips of metal called leads (2 points thick) or slugs (6 points thick) are inserted.

When the compositor nears the end of the line, he inserts spacing material between the words to make the line of type fit tightly, a process called justification. When the composing stick is full of lines, the justified type is removed and laid on metal galley trays. The lines of type are "leaded out" on the galleys, and proofs—single sheets printed by hand—are pulled and corrections made. Page makeup includes breaking up the galleys into page-long sections of text, making space for illustrations, and adding running heads, chapter titles, folios (page numbers), and the like. After page proofs have been made and approved, the type is locked into a form and made ready for printing.

THE DEVELOPMENT OF TYPEFACES

Early typeface designs were based on the pen-drawn letters of the scribes who, before Gutenberg, had produced books by hand. Gutenberg's typefaces were modeled on the formal black-letter styles popular in Germany at the time. As the art of printing spread, less formal black-letter type designs made their appearance, each based on a different popular handwriting style. The scribal hands favored in Italy by humanist scholars were of an entirely different nature. Lowercase letters were modeled on 9th-century Carolingian scripts, while the uppercase letters were derived from first- and second-century Roman capitals inscribed in stone. The great beauty and legibility of these Italian humanist scripts inspired type designers to make faithful copies in metal, variations of which are used to this day and are called "romans." Influential early roman faces were designed in Venice by the French printer Nicolas Jenson during the 1470s. Aldus MANUTIUS, a Venetian printer, also designed a celebrated romans and was the first to introduce (1501) an italic typeface, which was based on Italian cursive hand.

By the middle of the 16th century, type designers had begun to integrate Renaissance ideals of proportion into their types, many of which were formed according to geometric principles. An increasing French design influence was obvious in the work of Claude Garamond and Robert Granjon, whose designs were not slavish copies of pen-drawn letter forms, but new forms, made possible because both were expert cutters on steel. French types dominated book printing throughout Europe for over 100 years, finally giving way in the 17th century to the fresh but somewhat crude types of Dutch foundries. The chief features of Dutch types were the high contrast between thick and thin lines, a stress on the vertical rather than the slightly angled position of older types, and large capitals. The sturdy vigor of these types particularly appealed to English printers who imported them in large quantities. In the 1720s, however, the great English typefounder William CASLON issued his first types. Though they showed an unmistakable Dutch influence, his designs were less harsh and quite readable, soon becoming great favorites with printers.

The typefaces discussed so far are classified by historians as old-style romans. So-called transitional faces began to appear in the 18th century, characterized by increased contrast between thick and thin lines, lighter serifs, and a strong vertical stress. (A serif is the short, angled line at the ends of a letter's

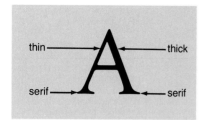

A modern Roman typeface is characterized by thin and thick lines as well as by the presence of serifs—short-stroke lines at the base of the letter.

regular
italic
light
medium
bold
condensed

Type families, such as the Helvetica typefaces illustrated, have in common the absence or presence of serifs and the thickness of lines in a letter. Within families type can vary from regular, perpendicular letters to slanted, italic letters and can range from light to bold and also to condensed letters.

HAUS movement during the 1920s, and Paul Renner's 1927 sans serif, Futura, enjoyed great commercial success.

Typographers today enjoy the fruits of five centuries of type design. Typefaces based on old-style, transitional, and modern styles continue to be popular for bookwork, while sans serifs predominate in advertising and magazines. During the last three decades or so, a class of typefaces that combines serif and sans-serif features has been used with great versatility, a notable example being Hermann Zapf's Optima, in which this encyclopedia is set.

TWENTIETH-CENTURY DEVELOPMENTS IN TYPESETTING

Throughout the 19th century, various attempts were made to develop reliable mechanical typesetting machines. The chief defects of these early machines lay in their inability to provide automatic justification. With the invention of the LINOTYPE machine by Ottmar Mergenthaler during the 1880s, and later the development of the MONOTYPE, the mechanical problems were solved. Ambitious type-design programs were initiated by both the linotype and monotype companies; along with entirely new designs, fresh interpretations of historic faces were commissioned.

Letter forms are classified in groups. Humanist typefaces, typified by Jenson, have little contrast between stroke lines, whereas the Garalde group, represented by Garamond, have stressed and unstressed strokes. Baskerville, one of the Reale group, combines characteristics of both. Bodoni, one of the Didone group, and Clarendon, a slab-serif type, illustrate the uses of the serif. In a sans-serif type, such as Universe, the serif is omitted. Glyphic typefaces, such as Chisel, are used for display. The Script group, which includes Palace, and Graphic types, such as Space Age, have a hand-drawn appearance.

upper and lower strokes.) The types of the English printer John BASKERVILLE, first used in 1757, are often described as the first true transitionals.

Toward the end of the 18th century, neoclassical, or modern romans, began to appear, marked by thin, graceful serifs, their most significant feature. The types of Parisian printer-founder Firmin Didot and his counterpart in Italy, Giambattista BODONI, were prototypical examples of the style.

The 19th century was an extremely active period in type design. Most printers bought their types from intensely competitive commercial type foundries whose rate of production, spurred by new technologies, had increased dramatically. With no copyright protection for typeface designs, typefounders were ruthless in their practice of copying the products of their competitors.

Among the more important developments were the introduction of square-serif designs in 1815 by the English founder Vincent Figgins and, a year later, the first sans-serif—a type without serif strokes—by William Caslon IV. All-cap, heavily weighted, square-serif (known also as slab serif) designs were rugged types that became popular with printers handling advertising. With the incorporation of a lowercase alphabet, square serifs evolved by mid-century into a popular family of types known as Clarendons.

Except for a few durable romans, 19th-century American typefaces for use in books tended to be fairly mundane. There were, however, a huge variety of display and ornamental faces that were featured in newspaper headlines and text, in advertising, catalogs, and the like.

By the end of the 19th century, the speed of printing presses had increased; hard, machine-made paper was commonplace, and the economies of the printing industry precluded typographical niceties. On the printed page, type looked weak and ineffectual. By way of protest, in 1888 the English craftsman William MORRIS designed a typeface based on 15th-century Jensonian models. Called Golden, it influenced the type designs of other private presses, as well as attracting the attention of commercial foundries who admired its dense, old-style characteristics. Sparking a revival of interest in old-style designs, it was quickly copied; Jenson was the name given to the American version of the Morris design.

Although the vigorous types of Morris and others were much admired, less emphatic designs prevailed in the early 20th century. One of the more important was Cheltenham, an old-style type designed by the architect Bertram Goodhue. Sans-serif designs by Herbert Bayer emerged from the BAU-

ABCDEFGHIJKLMNOPQRSTU
abcdefghijklmnopqrstuvwxyzabcdefg
HUMANIST   JENSON OLD STYLE

ABCDEFGHIJKLMNOPQRSTUVA
abcdefghijklmnopqrstuvwxyzabcdefg
GARALDE   GARAMOND BOOK

ABCDEFGHIJKLMNOPQRSTUVWXYZ
abcdefghijklmnopqrstuvwxyzabcdefgh
REALE   BASKERVILLE

ABCDEFGHIJKLMNOPQRSTUVWXY
abcdefghijklmnopqrstuvwxyzabcdefghij
DIDONE   BODONI

ABCDEFGHIJKLMNOPQRSTUVW
abcdefghijklmnopqrstuvwxyzabcd
SLAB SERIF   CLARENDON

ABCDEFGHIJKLMNOPQRSTUVWXY
abcdefghijklmnopqrstuvwxyzabcdef
LINEALE   UNIVERSE

ABCDEFGHIJKLMNOPQRSTUV
abcdefghijklmnopqrstuvwxyza
GLYPHIC   CHISEL

ABCDEFGHIJKLMNOPQR
abcdefghijklmnoopqrstuvwxyzabcdefghij
SCRIPT   PALACE

ABCCDEEFFGGHHIJKLM
GRAPHIC   SPACE AGE OUTLINE

 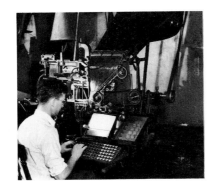 

(Left) *In typesetting by hand, letters are placed one by one in a composing stick.* (Center) *Linotype uses a keyboard to assemble a line of matrices—metal blocks with engraved letters—on a spaceboard; the line is then cast, using molten type metal.* (Right) *In phototypesetting a cathode-ray tube (CRT) machine composes a text by computer; a video display terminal (VDT) is used to change copy before printing on film.*

Like the earlier handcasting of type, both the linotype and the monotype used molten, or "hot," metal. The decline of letterpress relief printing and an increase in the use of offset spurred research into the development of composition systems dispensing with metal typecasting altogether. In 1946 an Intertype Fotosetter was tested at the U.S. Government Printing Office. The Fotosetter was a line-casting machine containing brass matrices that had film negatives of characters inserted into their sides. Light was focused through the negatives onto photosensitized paper and produced images of type from which printing plates could be made.

Second-generation phototypesetters made their debut in 1954 with the introduction of the Photon 200 machine. Here, a spinning film matrix contained all of the characters in a font, with a stroboscopic light source, and a system of lenses for focusing images of type in the desired sizes onto sensitized paper. The next generation of phototypesetters stored fonts digitally on a magnetic core. Typesetting code was sent to a character generator, which produced bright images on a cathode ray tube. These in turn were focused through lenses onto sensitized paper.

Fourth-generation systems have been introduced that feature digitally stored fonts and very-high-resolution laser-driven imaging devices. An added advantage of these latest machines is their ability to produce line and half-tone images, as well as type.

TYPE AS AN ELEMENT IN BOOK DESIGN

The choice of an appropriate typeface is a crucial element in the design of a book. Conscientious typographers consider many factors before selecting a typeface, including length of text, type and quality of paper, the printing process to be used, and the subject of the book itself. Types that are weak or light in appearance are tiring to read when used as text faces, while bold or unusual faces call attention to themselves. Publications directed at a mass readership, like newspapers and magazines, require types of a special nature. During the late 19th and early 20th centuries, a number of so-called legibility faces were designed specifically for high-speed, high-quality printing applications. They had, typically, sturdy serifs and large x-heights (basically, a measure of readability). Two celebrated types in this class are Century and Times Roman.

While the ideal text face should be readable and well-balanced, display types are meant to be visible. In addition to large, bold versions of text faces, printers have at their disposal a vast arsenal of display types that are ornate, decorated, or otherwise embellished to make them stand out. Such display types have been produced mainly for use by advertising typographers and are a phenomenon of the 19th and 20th centuries.

Changes in the way books are produced have influenced the appearance of type on the printed page. While letterpress was the dominant printing process, type designers had to take into account factors that were peculiar to that process, including the slight three-dimensional effect obtained when metal type is pressed into paper. Though that effect is much cherished by book lovers, the offset printing process dominates today, and designers must consider its unique characteristics.

The manner in which letters are now produced has also affected their design. As each new electronic typesetting system is readied for market, font libraries compatible with the system's hardware must be prepared. Information about each character's shape is stored in computer memory as a bit-map; the simpler a design, the less memory is required. Thus in the copying of old faces for phototypesetting (or "cold type"), there is a tendency to eliminate many of the quirks that gave these types life and individuality. The best modern designs, therefore, are not so much adaptations of old faces as new ones, specifically created with the limitations of computer storage and electronic output devices in mind.

DAVID PANKOW

Bibliography: Axel-Nilsson, Christian, *Type Studies* (1985); Burns, Aaron, ed., *The ITC Typeface Collection* (1982); Carter, Sebastian, *20th Century Type Designers* (1987); Goudy, Frederick W., *Alphabet and Elements of Lettering* (1922); Jaspert, W. Pincus, et al., *Encyclopedia of Type Faces*, 5th, rev. ed. (1984); Knuth, Donald, *Computers and Typesetting*, 5 vols. (1986); Lawson, Alexander, *Printing Types: An Introduction* (1971); La Buz, Robert, *Typesetting and Typography* (1987); McSherry, James E., *Computer Typesetting* (1984); Swann, Cal, *Techniques of Typography* (1982); Updike, D. B., *Printing Types: Their History, Forms, and Use*, 2d ed. (1937).

See also: BOOK; PUBLISHING, DESKTOP.

typewriter

A typewriter is a machine that can reproduce printed characters on paper. It has a keyboard containing the letters of the alphabet, numbers, common punctuation marks, and various controls. Until the 1970s, most typewriters were virtually identical, differing only in their source of power, manual or electric. Today's newest machines are the result of the electronic revolution and differ in almost every respect from older models.

The first practical typewriter was developed by Christopher Latham SHOLES and was patented in 1868. Six years later, Eliphalet Remington and Sons, a firm of gunsmiths, placed the first commercial typewriter on the market. This early model, called the Remington, had a cylinder, or carriage, to hold the paper, along with line-spacing and carriage-return mechanisms; a device called an escapement that moved the carriage after each letter was struck; type-holding rods arranged in a semicircle, so that when the keys were depressed each rod struck at the proper point on the paper; an inked ribbon against which the raised letters on the rods struck, transferring their images to the paper; and a keyboard similar to that of present-day typewriters.

Subsequent refinements to the early typewriter included the addition of a shift bar, permitting the user to type both capital and lowercase letters, and an improved rod arrangement that allowed the typist to see what was being typed. (In early models, the type was printed on top of the cylinder.)

These three typewriters illustrate three basic ways of producing typewritten characters. (Right) A manual typewriter operates through the pressure of fingers on the keys. When a key (1) is struck, a key lever (2) and linkage (3) force the end of the type bar (4) against the ink ribbon (5), and the raised typeslug (6) impresses its image on the paper. Other components include the movable carriage (7) and the platen (8). In both of the electrically powered machines seen below, the carriage is stationary; instead, the carrier (9), holding a type element and ink ribbon, moves along the platen. (Below left) The surface of the golf-ball element (10) is studded with raised characters. It rotates and stationary strikes to press the appropriate character against the paper. (Below right) The daisy-wheel element (11), with type slugs at the ends of flexible strips, spins to place the proper strip where a hammer mechanism (12) strikes it against the paper.

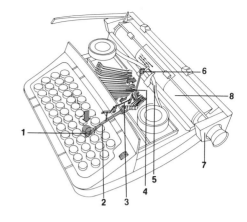

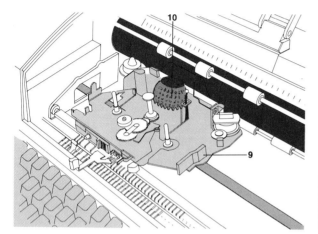

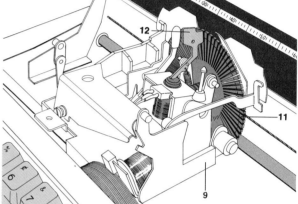

Electric typewriters, which power the operations of the machine with an electric motor, were introduced by 1920. In the 1920s, small portable typewriters become commercially successful.

The first basic change in typewriter operation appeared in 1961: a machine that eliminated the letter rods, using instead a small, rotating ball with the type symbols covering it in relief. Instead of a moving carriage and stationary letters, this new typewriter used a stationary carriage over which the ball moved and printed with great speed. The ball has been replaced on newer typewriters by a daisy-wheel printer—a plastic disk about 10 cm (4 in) in diameter, with flexible spokes each of which ends in a character. The wheel rotates rapidly to bring a particular character into printing position, the spoke is struck against a carbon-backed plastic ribbon, and its impression appears on the paper. Both ball and wheel are made in a variety of typefaces and can easily be changed.

Electronic typewriters approach WORD PROCESSORS in many of the things they are able to do: they can move text around, check spelling, store documents in a memory. Some incorporate calculators. A few are designed in such a way that they can serve as printers when attached to computers. Some have attachments for a screen and a memory device, making them true word processors.

Despite the revolutionary advances in typewriter capabilities, one essential element has remained unchanged since the first Remington. The keyboard arrangement, nicknamed QWERTY for the top line of letters, was designed to make it easier for salesmen to sell the machines. All the letters in the word "typewriter" are in the top line. A much more efficient arrangement was devised in 1936 by August Dvořák, cousin of the composer. With the Dvořák keyboard, the right hand does equal work with the left, the strongest fingers do the most work, and 70% of the typing takes place on the "home row," where the fingers naturally rest.

Bibliography: Cassingham, R. C., *The Dvořák Keyboard* (1986); Mares, George C., *The History of the Typewriter* (1985).

typhoid fever [ty'-foid]

A severe, generalized human disease, typhoid fever is caused by the bacterium *Salmonella typhi*, which enters the body in water or food contaminated with the feces or urine of a carrier of the disease. Chronic carriers—2% to 5% of patients who have recovered—are the main source of infection. After an incubation period of 7 to 21 days, the illness begins with fever, lethargy, headache, and loss of appetite. Increasing weakness and abdominal discomfort develop during the second week, when a rose-colored rash may appear. Intestinal bleeding or perforation may occur in the second or third week and can be fatal.

Treatment with chloramphenicol or ampicillin has reduced the mortality rate from 30% to 2%. In untreated patients, recovery may begin after about 4 weeks. In urban areas, transmission of typhoid fever may occur through food contaminated by polluted water or by food handlers who are carriers. Typhoid fever can be prevented by sanitary disposal of human excreta and by chlorination of drinking water. Injection of a vaccine prepared from killed typhoid bacilli affords moderate short-term protection from the disease.   J. MICHAEL S. DIXON

typhoon: see HURRICANE AND TYPHOON.

typhus [ty'-fuhs]

Typhus is any of several infectious diseases, each caused by a different rickettsia microorganism. Louse, or epidemic, typhus is the most serious form; the infectious organism, *Rickettsia prowazekii*, lives only in humans and in body lice. The louse's infected feces reach the human bloodstream through scratches in the skin or settlement of the feces in the mucus membranes of the eye or the respiratory tract. The major symptoms are intractable headache, extensive skin rash, and high fever. The mortality rate is significant in untreated persons over 50 years of age. Antibiotic therapy is effective if started early. Louse typhus can be prevented through vaccination. Endemic murine typhus, or flea typhus, caused by *R. mooseri* and transmitted from rats to humans by fleas, is much milder and causes fewer fatalities.   PETER L. PETRAKIS

Typographical Union, International: see

INTERNATIONAL TYPOGRAPHICAL UNION.

Tyrannosaurus   [tuh-ran'-uh-sohr'-uhs]

Tarbosaurus, *a close Asian relative of* Tyrannosaurus, *was a meat-eating dinosaur that lived about 70 million years ago. The fiercest and last of the now-extinct carnivorous dinosaurs, it was 15 m (50 ft) long and 5.5 m (18 ft) high and had a huge head armed with dozens of sharp, flesh-tearing teeth that were up to 20 cm (8 in) long.*

The best known of all dinosaurs, *Tyrannosaurus* was the largest and the last of the meat-eating carnosaurs (infraorder Carnosauria, suborder Theropoda, order Saurischia); it is known from a few skeletons and numerous fossil fragments from the latest Cretaceous strata of western North America, about 65 million years old. A close relative, *Tarbosaurus,* has been collected in greater abundance from Asian deposits of similar age.

Tyrannosaurus walked on its hind legs and stood about 5.5 m (18 ft) high; its total length was almost 15 m (50 ft), and it may have exceeded 8 tons in weight. Its huge head, up to 1.5 m (5 ft) long, was carried on a short, sturdy neck. The jaws were long and powerful and bore dozens of curved, serrated teeth up to 20 cm (8 in) long. The massive hind legs, armed with large claws, were about 3 m (10 ft) in length, but the front limbs were very small—only about 75 cm (30 in) long. The front limbs, consequently, have been generally described as useless, but the presence of sizable claws on the two fingers of each hand and the large dimensions of the internal skeletal supports (the pectoral girdle) for the front limbs, which suggest the presence of strong muscles, indicate that these limbs served some purpose. One suggestion has been that the arms helped to anchor the massive body and prevent forward slippage when *Tyrannosaurus* arose from a resting position. *Tyrannosaurus*'s long, heavy tail provided counterbalance for its front-heavy body. Its bulky body and heavy legs imply that *Tyrannosaurus* stalked its prey rather than pursued it; possibly it lived by scavenging as well. Either way, *Ty-*

rannosaurus was obviously well designed for feeding on the other large dinosaurs.   JOHN H. OSTROM

Bibliography: DeCamp, Lyon S., *The Day of the Dinosaur* (1968); Tweedie, Michael, *The World of Dinosaurs* (1977).

tyrant flycatcher

Tyrant flycatchers are small- to medium-sized birds known for their boldness and pugnacity and for their habit of darting from an exposed perch to catch insects in midair. More than 300 species, including phoebes and kingbirds, make up the family Tyrannidae. Found throughout the Western Hemisphere, they are most abundant in the tropics. Most have broad, flattened bills, generally surrounded by bristles, and subdued plumage, but some are brightly colored. Nesting behavior varies among the species.   ROBERT J. RAIKOW

Tyre   [tyr]

Tyre was a great trading port of ancient PHOENICIA, located on the Mediterranean Sea about 40 km (25 mi) south of Sidon. The city gave its name to the dye known as Tyrian purple. Today Tyre survives as the small southern Lebanese town of Sur (1982 est. pop., 23,000).

Founded on an island, perhaps as a colony of Sidon, Tyre possessed one of the best harbors on the coast. Until the 4th century BC the city was almost impregnable against siege, but Alexander the Great reduced Tyre in 332 BC by building a causeway that joined the island to the mainland.

Already long established, Tyre entered history as a vassal of the 18th dynasty of Egypt (1570–1320 BC). Following the disruption of Egypt and other Near Eastern powers in the age of the Sea Peoples, the city not only had attained an independent position but seems to have dominated Sidon. During the 10th century BC, Tyre supplied cedars, carpenters, masons, and bronzesmiths for King David (r. *c.*1000–*c.*960 BC) and King Solomon (r. *c.*960–*c.*921 BC), and Tyrian sailors were available for Solomon's Red Sea fleet. In the Mediterranean, under Hiram (r. 969–936 BC) and earlier rulers Tyre developed trade with Cyprus and Spain and founded such colonies as Utica and Carthage.

Subject to Assyria during the 8th and 7th centuries BC, Tyre was dominated by the Persians from 538 to 332 BC. After its capture by Alexander the Great, Tyre was ruled by the Ptolemies, Seleucids, Romans, and Muslim Arabs (AD 638–1124). It was part of the Latin kingdom of Jerusalem in the 12th and 13th centuries but fell to the Mamelukes and was destroyed in 1291.   LOUIS L. ORLIN

Bibliography: Harden, Donald, *The Phoenicians,* 2d ed. (1963).

Tyrian purple   [tir'-ee-uhn]

Tyrian purple is a strong dye—ranging in color from blue to crimson—made from the crushed shells of certain mussels and whelks. The ancient Mediterranean cities of Sidon and Tyre were the focus of this dye industry, but some experts claim the dye was produced elsewhere as early as 1500 BC. Only a small portion of the shell could be used, making the dyed cloth very costly and limiting its use to the wealthy. Tyrian purple garments became a mark of the Roman aristocracy.

Tyrol   [tir-ohl']

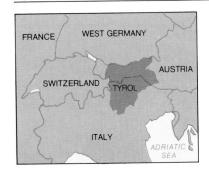

The shaded area of the map indicates the location of Tyrol, which is now divided between the Austrian province of the same name and the Italian region of Trentino-Alto Adige.

Tyrol is a historic region mainly corresponding to the western Austrian province of Tyrol and the northern Italian administrative region of TRENTINO-ALTO ADIGE. The Alps dominate the area, with the highest peak, Wildspitze, reaching 3,774 m (12,382 ft). The economy is based on farming, mining, copper smelting, the pharmaceutical and chemical industries, and the production of hardware, textiles, glass, and skiing equipment. Tourism is important to the entire region. The best known resorts are INNSBRUCK, Kitzbühel, Seefeld, and the Ziller Valley.

Medieval Tyrol became a Habsburg possession in 1363, and in 1803 it was expanded to include the mostly Italian-speaking Trentino. In 1809, Tyrol became part of Bavaria, but it reverted to Austria in 1815. The entire South Tyrol (Trentino and German-speaking Bolzano) was given to Italy in 1919.

BRUCE L. LaROSE

Bibliography: Proctor, Alan, *The Tyrol* (1986).

Tyrone [tir-ohn']

Tyrone, a former county of Ulster province, is in west central Northern Ireland. With an area of 3,265 km² (1,260 mi²), it was the largest county in Northern Ireland. Omagh was the county town. Mountains are found in the north and southwest. Extensive moorlands occur in the center, where Lough NEAGH is situated. Potatoes, barley growing, and livestock raising are important. Tourism, whiskey distilling, and the manufacture of crystal and linen complement the economy. Tyrone became a county in the early 17th century after the English defeated the O'Neill family, which had ruled the region since the 5th century. The county was abolished as an administrative unit in 1973.

Tyrone, Hugh O'Neill, 2d Earl of

Hugh O'Neill, 2d earl of Tyrone, b. c.1540, d. July 20, 1616, was an Ulster chieftain who led the last stand of the old Gaelic social order against English rule from 1595 to 1603. Originating in the north, his provincial rebellion spread throughout the country following initial victories and became a struggle to separate Catholic Ireland from England. Four years after his defeat and submission in 1603, O'Neill and other Irish tribal chiefs, restive in the role of mere English-style landlords, sailed to the Continent. The crown used this so-called Flight of the Earls as an excuse to confiscate their vast lands for Protestant settlement.

DAVID W. MILLER

Bibliography: Falls, Cyril, *Elizabeth's Irish Wars* (1950); Gainsford, Thomas, *The History of the Earle of Tirone* (1968).

Tyrrell, George [tir'-ul]

The English theologian George Tyrrell, b. Feb. 6, 1861, d. July 15, 1909, was a leading modernist (see MODERNISM) in the Roman Catholic church. Originally an Anglican, he converted (1879) to Roman Catholicism, entered (1880) the Jesuit order, and was ordained (1891) into the priesthood.

After teaching philosophy, writing, and counseling, Tyrrell became disenchanted with Roman Catholic orthodoxy, stressing, rather, the importance of internal religious experience. His critical writings caused his expulsion (1906) from the Jesuits, and, after his criticism (1907) of Pope Pius X's condemnation of modernism, he was refused the sacraments. His writings include *Lex Orandi* (1904), *Lex Credendi* (1906), *A Much Abused Letter* (1906), and *Through Scylla and Charybdis* (1907).

Bibliography: Leonard, Ellen, *George Tyrrell and the Catholic Tradition* (1982); Ratté, John, *Three Modernists: Alfred Loisy, George Tyrrell, William L. Sullivan* (1967); Sagovsky, Nicholas, *Between Two Worlds: George Tyrrell's Relationship to the Thought of Matthew Arnold* (1982); Weaver, M. J., ed., *Letters from a "Modernist"* (1981).

Tyrrhenian Sea [tir-een'-ee-uhn]

The Tyrrhenian Sea, part of the MEDITERRANEAN SEA, lies between the Italian mainland and the islands of Sicily, Sardinia, and Corsica. It adjoins the Ionian Sea on the south and the Ligurian Sea on the north. Naples, Salerno, and Palermo are the major ports.

Tyrtaeus [tur-tee'-uhs]

A Greek elegiac poet of the 7th century BC, Tyrtaeus was probably from Sparta. Only fragments of his poems survive, but he was celebrated for his martial songs stressing courage and love of country. Most of his elegies are associated with the Spartan campaign during the second Messenian War, in which he served as a general.

Tyuratam Cosmodrome: see BAIKONUR COSMODROME.

Tyutchev, Fyodor [tee-oo'-chif]

Fyodor Ivanovich Tyutchev, b. Dec. 5 (N.S.), 1803, d. July 27 (N.S.), 1873, wrote some of the most moving love poems and nature lyrics in the Russian language. A diplomat, he lived in Munich for many years, befriending Heine and coming under the influence of Schelling and German romantic idealism. His 300 poems are all short lyrics and frequently reflect his dualistic view of the world as both orderly and chaotic. He also wrote (in French) brilliant political articles of a conservative cast.

RALPH E. MATLAW

Bibliography: Conant, R., *The Political Poetry and Ideology of F. I. Tiutchev* (1983); Gregg, R. A., *Fedor Tiutchev* (1965).

Tzara, Tristan [tsah'-rah]

A Romanian by birth, poet and playwright Tristan Tzara, b. Apr. 4, 1896, d. Dec. 25, 1963, is known principally as the founder of the DADA movement, which, together with Richard Hülsenbeck and Hugo Ball, he organized in Zurich in 1916. Tzara moved to Paris in 1919. He broke with André Breton, Louis Aragon, and other members of the movement in 1923 when they turned to surrealism; after the mid-1930s, when Tzara joined the French Communist party, the tone of his own writing changed noticeably. At his death, however, Tzara left essays on art in which he claimed that he had always been a Dadaist. His early works—including the plays *La première aventure celeste de M. Antipyrine* (The First Celestial Adventure of Mr. Aspirin, 1916) and *La coeur a gaz* (The Gas Heart, 1923) and the epic poem *The Approximate Man* (1931; Eng. trans., 1973)—indicate by their titles something of the irrational playfulness of Dadaism.

Bibliography: Peterson, Elmer, *Tristan Tzara: Dada and Surrational Theorist* (1971).

Tz'u-hsi, Dowager Empress of China (Cixi) [tsoo-shee]

Commonly known among Western historians as "The Old Buddha," the Empress Dowager Tz'u-hsi, b. Nov. 29, 1835, d. Nov. 15, 1908, used a series of "regencies" to rule de facto for the final 5 decades of the CH'ING dynasty in China. As concubine to the Hsien-feng emperor, Tz'u-hsi bore his only son. In 1861, when the 5-year-old boy became the T'ung-chih emperor, Tz'u-hsi contrived to become coregent with the empress, Hsien-feng's former senior consort Tz'u-an. On the death of the T'ung-chih emperor in 1875, Tz'u-hsi maintained herself in power by manipulating the succession to put her infant nephew on the throne as the Kuang-hsü emperor.

Her rule was autocratic, ruthless, and extravagant. In 1898, Tz'u-hsi nullified the decrees issued by the Kuang-hsü emperor in collaboration with K'ANG YU-WEI to modernize China (since called the Hundred Days of Reform) by seizing the emperor in a coup d'etat to begin her third regency. In 1900 the BOXER UPRISING, an antiforeign rebellion, won her support less for reasons of state than because of her belief that the foreign powers intended to demand her retirement. The day before her death Tz'u-hsi appointed the 2-year-old Henry Pu-yi to succeed his uncle, the Kuang-hsü emperor, who had suddenly and mysteriously died.

Bibliography: Haldane, Charlotte, *Last Great Empress of China* (1965); Hummel, A. W., ed., *Eminent Chinese of the Ch'ing Period, 1644–1912*, 2 vols. (1943–44); Warner, Marina, *Dragon Empress: The Life and Times of Tz'u-hsi, Empress Dowager of China: 1835–1908* (1972; repr. 1986).

Y	PHOENICIAN		ETRUSCAN	Y
Y	EARLY HEBREW		EARLY LATIN	V
4	EARLY ARAMAIC		CLASSICAL LATIN	V
Y	EARLY GREEK		RUSSIAN-CYRILLIC	У
Y	CLASSICAL GREEK	**Uu** MODERN LATIN	GERMAN-GOTHIC	𝔘

U

U/u is the twenty-first letter of the English alphabet. The letter is actually a variant of the next letter in the alphabet, *V/v*. The Latin alphabet used *V/v* for both consonantal *w* and vocalic *u*, but in late Latin the sound of *w* became *v*. Although the rounded form of *V/v*—*U/u*—was used in late-Latin inscriptions, the sounds *u*, *v*, and *w* were generally indistinguishable in writing. The two forms of the letter continued in use, but the differentiation of vocalic *u* from consonantal *v* by use of the letters *U/u* and *V/v* was not fully established in English writing until the 17th century.

Like all English vowels, *U/u* has a wide variety of sounds depending on the accent and the sounds surrounding it. Short *u* is usually pronounced as in *sun* or *hum*, and long *u* is normally the sound found in *rule*. In some instances there is a *y* sound before *u*, as in *use* or *mule*.

I. J. GELB AND R. M. WHITING

U-boat: see SUBMARINE.

U Thant: see THANT, U.

U-2

With the advent in the 1950s of the advanced and graceful U.S. single-seat reconnaissance aircraft, the Lockheed U-2, the technique of aerial reconnaissance underwent a significant and dramatic transformation. Conceived in 1954, the U-2 was designed, constructed, and operated under conditions of the utmost secrecy; its intended role was concealed by allocation of the official designation U-2 to indicate a utility airplane.

Virtually a powered glider, the U-2 was able to attain and cruise at great heights by virtue of its unusually wide wing-

The U-2, a high-altitude reconnaissance aircraft introduced by Lockheed in 1955, is capable of speeds to 795 km/h (494 mph) and an altitude of 27,400 m (90,000 ft). It was a U-2 that took the aerial photographs revealing concealed Soviet missile bases in Cuba in 1962.

span, 24.4 m (80 ft), almost twice the length of its body. The prototype U-2 was first flown in 1955. The U-2A production version was powered by a Pratt and Whitney J57-P-37A turbojet engine with 5,040 kg (11,200 lb) of static thrust, a range of approximately 4,200 km (2,600 mi), an initial climb rate of 2,286 m/min (7,500 ft/min), and a maximum altitude of about 22,900 m (75,000 ft). The U-2A entered service with the United States Air Force (USAF) and the National Aeronautics and Space Administration (NASA) in 1956.

Substantially increased performance was provided in the U-2B, introduced in 1959, which utilized the Pratt and Whitney J75-P-13 engine (7,650 kg/17,000 lb of static thrust) and wing tanks that enabled it to approach a ceiling of approximately 27,400 m (90,000 ft) and a range of about 6,400 km (4,000 mi). The plane carried a comprehensive array of cameras as well as sensitive electronic equipment designed to record and monitor radio and radar transmissions.

On May 1, 1960, a U-2B flown by Francis Gary Powers was shot down near Sverdlovsk in the USSR by a Soviet surface-to-air missile. This incident occurred only days before President Dwight D. Eisenhower and Soviet Chairman Nikita Khrushchev met at a summit conference in Paris. The United States at first denied that it had any planes spying on the USSR. After the Russians produced the captured pilot and parts of the plane, however, the United States admitted to the spying. Powers was released on Feb. 10, 1962, in a prisoner exchange.

Although direct overflights of the USSR ended with the Powers incident, the U-2 continued to be used elsewhere in the world. In October 1962, U-2 surveillance found evidence of Soviet missiles in Cuba, which led to the CUBAN MISSILE CRISIS. The U-2's performance also made it an excellent high-altitude research aircraft. Many of the reconnaissance duties formerly carried out by U-2s are currently handled by satellites.

PETER M. H. LEWIS

Bibliography: Taylor, J., and Mondey, D., *Spies in the Sky* (1972).

Uaxactún [wah-hahk-toon']

Uaxactún, in the lowlands of northeastern Guatemala, was a modest civic-ceremonial center of the ancient MAYA. First occupied before 500 BC, Uaxactún began to erect public buildings early in the 1st century AD. The most famous is a temple-platform decorated with plaster masks in the Izapan (see IZAPA) style. Although always dominated by TIKAL, 24 km (15 mi) to the south, Uaxactún flourished from the 4th to the 8th century AD, building a series of temple-palace complexes. Shortly after 800, Uaxactún began to decline and was virtually abandoned by the end of the century. Explorations of the site by the Carnegie Institution of Washington in the 1930s laid the groundwork for modern investigations of Classic Maya civilization.

JOHN S. HENDERSON

Bibliography: Coe, M. D., *The Maya* (1966).

Ubangi River [oo-bahng'-gee]

The Ubangi River, a 2,255-km-long (1,400-mi) tributary of the CONGO RIVER in central Africa, drains an area of about 771,800 km² (298,000 mi²). Rising as the Uele River just north of Lake Albert, in northeastern Zaire, it flows west across northern Zaire and joins the Bomu river at Yakoma, forming the Ubangi proper. It continues west, marking the Zaire–Central African Republic boundary, and then turns south, following the Congo–Zaire boundary. The river is navigable for barges as far as Bangui, the capital of the Central African Republic. The upper reaches of the river were explored by Georg Schweinfurth in 1870, and the link with the Congo was established by Wilhelm Junker in 1882–83.

Uccello, Paolo   [oot-chel'-loh]

Paolo Uccello, b. Paolo di Dono c.1397, d. Dec. 10, 1475, was one of the most ingenious practitioners of the art of perspective in Italian Renaissance painting. Throughout his career he was preoccupied with the effects of foreshortening and the mechanics of rendering architectural space. He accentuated these characteristics to such a degree, however, that his paintings—as opposed, for example, to those of his contemporary Masaccio—never appear to be extensions of reality.

Documents record Uccello's presence in Florence between 1407 and 1424; he is also known to have visited Venice in 1425. Having been commissioned to paint an equestrian monument of the English mercenary soldier Sir John Hawkwood, he created an extraordinary fresco (1436; Florence Cathedral) depicting a monumental stone statue; the pedestal is seen from below, but the horse and rider are seen from the side. In the late 1440s he painted frescoes of the Flood in the Green Cloister of Santa Maria Novella, manipulating the effects of perspective to the extreme.

Among Uccello's most famous paintings are three battle scenes (1455–60) now in the Uffizi in Florence, the Louvre in Paris, and the National Gallery in London. In these, brightly and irrationally colored equestrian figures battle before a tapestrylike backdrop; fallen horses, riders, and broken lances are carefully arranged along horizontal and diagonal lines that establish a gridlike perspective system. His last major commission was the predella for the altar of the Confraternity of the Holy Sacrament at Urbino (1465–69; Palazzo Ducale, Urbino), for which Joos van Ghent was to provide the main panel. Uccello also executed many careful drawings of objects rendered in perspective. Despite his genius, however, he died poor and neglected.

R. G. CALKINS

Bibliography: Carli, Enzo, *All the Paintings of Paolo Uccello*, trans. by Marion Fitzallan (1963); Pope-Hennessy, John, *The Complete Works of Paolo Uccello* (1950).

Udall   (family)   [yoo'-dawl]

The U.S. congressman **Morris King Udall**, b. Saint Johns, Ariz., June 15, 1922, was an unsuccessful candidate for the Democratic presidential nomination in 1976. He received his LL.B. from the University of Arizona in 1949 and practiced law until 1961, when he was elected to the U.S. House of Representatives. He was regularly reelected. His brother **Stewart Lee Udall**, b. Saint Johns, Ariz., Jan. 31, 1920, was U.S. secretary of the interior from 1961 to 1969. He also received his law degree from the University of Arizona (1948), practiced law, and represented Arizona (1955–61) as a Democrat in the U.S. House of Representatives.

Udall, Nicholas   [yoo'-duhl]

Nicholas Udall, b. c.1505, d. Dec. 23, 1556, wrote the earliest extant English comedy, *Ralph Roister Doister*, first produced at Windsor Castle in 1552. The play borrows from Plautus and Terence, but the incidents and dialogue are original, and Udall added songs and elements of farce.

Udine   [oo'-dee-nay]

Udine is the capital of Udine province in the Friuli-Venezia Giulia administrative region of northeastern Italy. Located about 65 km (40 mi) northwest of Trieste, Udine has a population of 101,264 (1981). The city's industries manufacture textiles, machinery, and food products. Its arcaded central square is considered one of the loveliest in Italy. An imposing 16th-century Venetian castle overlooks the city.

Udine was laid out on a mound allegedly built by Attila the

In The Rout of San Romano, *the Florentine artist Paolo Uccello reconstructed an actual battle of 1432 as a brilliant display of perspective by placing splendidly caparisoned figures on a grid of lances, swords, and banners. (1455–60; National Gallery, London.)*

Hun in 452. It came under Venetian control in 1420 and passed to Austria in 1797. In 1866, Udine became part of Italy; from 1915 to 1917 it was the headquarters of the Italian army.

Ueberroth, Peter   [yoo'-bur-awth]

Self-made millionaire Peter Victor Ueberroth, b. Evanston, Ill., Sept. 2, 1937, achieved fame as president of the Los Angeles Olympic Organizing Committee (LAOOC) in 1984. He masterminded a financial plan that allowed the Games to turn a profit while costing Los Angeles taxpayers nothing. After the Olympics, Ueberroth became commissioner of baseball.

Ueda Akinari   [oo-ay'-dah ah-kee-nah'-ree]

The Japanese writer Ueda Akinari, b. June 25, 1734, d. June 27, 1809, is known chiefly as the author of a famous collection of supernatural tales, *Ugetsu monogatari* (1768; trans. as *Tales of Moonlight and Rain*, 1972). As a young man he managed the family business while writing short fiction and haiku. After the publication of his masterpiece brought him popular acclaim, he turned to the study of medicine, philology, and history. He later produced a second group of stories, *Harusame monogatari* (1808; trans. as *Tales of the Spring Rain*, 1975). He was a respected authority on ancient Japanese writing, but it was his stories—mingling a scholarly, allusive style with conventional ghostly elements—that secured his fame. *Ugetsu monogatari* was filmed (1953) by Kenji Mizoguchi.

Bibliography: Putzar, Edward D., trans., *Japanese Literature* (1973).

Uelsmann, Jerry N.   [ools'-muhn]

The American photographer Jerry Norman Uelsmann, b. Detroit, June 11, 1934, employs innovative darkroom techniques to create PHOTOMONTAGES that juxtapose disparate elements, some in combinations of negative and positive images. His work, which he calls postvisualization, has influenced many contemporary photographers. Widely exhibited, Uelsmann has taught at the University of Florida since 1960.

Ufa   [oo-fah']

Ufa is the capital of the Bashkir Autonomous Republic within the Russian republic of the USSR. The city has a population of 1,064,000 (1985 est.). Ufa is situated on the Belaya River, a tributary of the Kama, in the western Urals. The city dates from the 16th century, when it was founded by the Russians as a fortified eastern outpost. In the Soviet period it became one of the country's largest petroleum-refining and petrochemical centers.   THEODORE SHABAD

Uffizi   [oof-eet'-see]

The Uffizi Palace in Florence, Italy, consists of two long, connected parallel buildings by the Arno River near the Palazzo Vecchio. Commissioned (1560) as a civic structure by Cosimo I de'Medici, it was designed and in part built by Giorgio VASARI. Today the Uffizi serves as a museum that houses one of the world's major art collections.

The first room beyond the entrance holds three large Madonnas by Cimabue, Duccio, and Giotto. Subsequent rooms hold important Sienese paintings by Simone Martini and Pietro Lorenzetti. The next gallery is occupied by the works of 14th- and early-15th-century Florentine painters, including Bernardo Daddi, Lorenzo Monaco, and Gentile da Fabriano. Additional galleries display works by Paolo Uccello, Fra Angelico, Alesso Baldovinetti, Fra Filippo Lippi, Antonio Pollaiuolo, Sandro Botticelli, Piero della Francesca, Leonardo da Vinci, Andrea del Verrocchio, Michelangelo, Raphael, Andrea del Sarto, and Jacopo Pontormo. The German school is represented by Albrecht Dürer, Lucas Cranach the Elder, and Albrecht Altdorfer; Flemish-school works by Rogier van der Weyden and Hugo van der Goes are also there. The later 16th century in Italy is represented by Bronzino, Rosso Fiorentino, Parmigianino, Titian, and Paolo Veronese.

Works from the 17th and 18th centuries include paintings by Caravaggio, Rembrandt, Claude Lorrain, and Jean Baptiste Chardin. An extensive collection of antique sculpture is displayed along the corridors, where it is exhibited with a superb collection of Belgian and Florentine tapestries. The Uffizi's *Gabinetto dei Disegni e Stampe* holds more than 100,000 prints and drawings.   ADELHEID M. GEALT

Bibliography: Becherucci, L., *Uffizi, Florence* (1968); Berti, L., *Uffizi* (1981); Micheletti, M., and Lenzini, M., *The Uffizi* (1984).

UFO: see UNIDENTIFIED FLYING OBJECT.

Uganda   [yoo-gahn'-dah]

Uganda, a small landlocked state located on the equator in East Africa, is bordered by Sudan to the north, Zaire to the west, Rwanda and Tanzania to the south, and Kenya to the east. Uganda's international borders and the basis of its economic system were created (1893–1926) as British rule supplanted older and much smaller political economies, which remained a focus for cultural, economic, and political competition.

Independent since 1962, Uganda has, until recently, earned the reputation of a state unable to create a political and economic order that either protects or serves its citizens. Before the National Resistance Movement (NRM) took control of the government in January 1986, each postindependence govern-

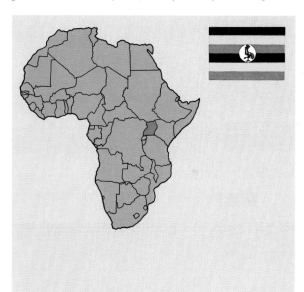

REPUBLIC OF UGANDA

LAND. Area: 236,036 km² (91,134 mi²). Capital and largest city: Kampala (1980 pop., 458,503). Co-capital: Entebbe (1980 pop., 21,289).

PEOPLE. Population (1986 est.): 15,000,000. Density (1986 est.): 63.5 persons per km² (164.6 per mi²). Distribution (1980): 8% urban, 92% rural. Annual growth (1980): 2.8%. Official language: English. Major religions: Roman Catholicism, Protestantism, Islam.

EDUCATION AND HEALTH. Literacy (1980): 50% of adult population. Universities (1986): 1. Hospital beds (1981): 19,782. Physicians (1981): 611. Life expectancy (1983): women—50; men—48. Infant mortality (1986): 112 per 1,000 live births.

ECONOMY. GNP (1983): $3.06 billion; $205 per capita. Labor force (1981): agriculture—83%; services—11%; industry—6%. Foreign trade (1983): imports—$114 million; exports—$366 million; principal trade partners—Kenya, United Kingdom, United States. Currency: 1 Uganda shilling = 100 cents.

GOVERNMENT. Type: republic. Legislature: National Resistance Council (interim). Political subdivisions: 33 districts, 1 municipality.

COMMUNICATIONS. Railroads (1982): 1,286 km (799 mi) total. Roads (1984): 27,824 km (17,289 mi) total. Major ports: none. Major airfields: 1.

UGANDA

		National capitals are underlined		
———	Railroad	City type size indicates relative importance		
+	Spot Elevation			

	Meters	Feet
	Above 4000	Above 13124
	2000	6562
	1000	3281
	500	1640

Scale 1:8,400,000

0 50 100 150 200 km
0   50   100 mi

LAND AND RESOURCES

Uganda occupies part of a high plateau that averages 915 m (3,000 ft) in the less hilly and lower north and rises to 1,340 m (4,400 ft) near Kampala. On the southwestern border near the equator are the volcanic Virunga Mountains and the permanently snowcapped peaks of the RUWENZORI Range, including Mount Stanley (5,110 m/16,763 ft), Uganda's highest point. These mountains form part of the western branch of the EAST AFRICAN RIFT SYSTEM. On the eastern border are several extinct volcanoes, including Mount ELGON. Lakes cover almost one-fifth of Uganda's area. Rivers in the south drain into Lake Victoria (see VICTORIA, LAKE), the third largest lake in the world, from which the Victoria Nile flows into Lake Albert (Lake Mobutu; see ALBERT, LAKE).

Most of Uganda has relatively reliable rainfall in two distinct wet seasons (March–May and October–November). The semiarid northeast receives 625 to 1,000 mm (25 to 39 in) of rainfall between April and August, while annual rainfall near Lake Victoria averages 1,500 mm (59 in). Temperatures, which are moderated by altitude, reach 35° C (95° F) on the Rift floor near Lake George and along the Sudanese border. In the southwestern highlands they drop to 5° C (40° F).

Copper (the most valuable of Uganda's minerals) and small amounts of gold, tungsten, tin, lead, and wolfram have been extracted, primarily in the southwest. Salt deposits near Kasese have long been mined on a small scale, and brick clay supports a brick-making industry in the south.

Uganda has four national parks, the newest of which was established in 1984. Tourism, formerly a leading foreign-exchange earner, has virtually disappeared since 1972, and some once-numerous wildlife species have almost disappeared due to poaching and wanton slaughter by soldiers.

PEOPLE

While ethnic identification seldom matches cultural practices or adequately explains political action, it is regarded as important by most Ugandans. Some groups, such as the Nyoro east of Lake Albert and the GANDA north and west of Lake Victoria, have long histories. Others, such as the Gisu of Mount Elgon and the widely scattered Nubians, were created for political reasons during the colonial period. Additional groups include the Acholi and Langi of north-central Uganda and the Karamojong of the northeast. Almost all the 74,308 Indians and 9,533 Europeans listed in the 1969 census have since left.

English is the official language, but SWAHILI is widely spo-

ment in turn left the country in worse shape than it found it. Some 300,000 Ugandans may have been slaughtered during the rule (1971–79) of Idi AMIN DADA, and mass killings resumed in the early 1980s under Milton OBOTE. Two wars against the central government—one (1979) involving the Tanzanian army assisted by Ugandan exiles, the other (1981–86) by the NRM's guerrilla army, composed solely of Ugandans—further damaged the economic and social order.

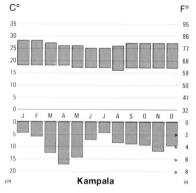

Kampala

(Above) Bars indicate monthly ranges of temperatures (red) and precipitation (blue) of Kampala, the capital and largest city of Uganda. Located only 32 km (20 mi) north of the equator at an altitude of approximately 1,200 m (4,000 ft), Kampala has a tropical wet-dry climate moderated considerably by its highland location.

Owen Falls Dam spans the Victoria Nile as it flows from its outlet at Lake Victoria near the town of Jinja, Uganda. This dam is an important source of hydroelectric power. After its completion in 1954, new industries developed in the vicinity of Jinja.

ken, and Luganda is a common language in the south. Christians probably account for more than 70% of the population, with Catholics outnumbering Protestants. Islam claims perhaps 5% of the population and is probably expanding.

Rapid population growth has led to serious pressures on arable land, particularly in the southwest. Only a small percentage of the population is urban, and insecurity and the high cost of food have reduced net migration from the countryside to towns. KAMPALA, the capital (with ENTEBBE) and only large urban center, contains ten times as many people as Jinja, the second-largest city. Health care has deteriorated dramatically, and the percentage of children enrolled in primary (but not secondary) school has dropped since the early 1970s.

ECONOMIC ACTIVITY

During the colonial period an economy based on supplying raw materials for British industries and markets for European manufactured goods supplanted indigenous trade and technologies. The first source of colonial exports, cotton, was later overtaken by coffee. A tiny manufacturing sector was stimulated by the construction of a hydroelectric station at Owen Falls, but it remained dependent on imported machinery. The new colonial economy developed unevenly, so production and opportunities for wealth were unequally distributed—an important reason for later political difficulties.

Fundamental change occurred in 1972 when Amin expelled the Indians, who had controlled much of Uganda's credit and trade. Government failure to pay realistic prices for cotton, coffee, and other crops eventually caused severe declines in official sales of all crops, and the looting that accompanied both the 1979 and 1981–86 wars crippled production. Since 1979, Uganda has depended almost entirely on coffee for foreign-exchange earnings. Because cotton was grown primarily in the north and east, while coffee is produced in the center and southwest, this change severely exacerbates the existing uneven development.

Severe inflation and low real wages, particularly for officials, led to widespread corruption, a black market, and banditry—but also to growing sophistication in trade. Some farmland was shifted from export crops to food crops that could be sold in the cities, causing a modest redistribution of income from the urban to the rural sector.

Uganda exports its goods primarily through the Kenyan port of Mombasa. Its railroad extends from Kenya to Kilembe in the west and Pakwach in the north. The country's once excellent road system has deteriorated badly since 1971.

HISTORY AND GOVERNMENT

The indigenous inhabitants of what is now Uganda ranged from the ancient centralized and rival kingdoms of Buganda and Bunyoro to the decentralized Acholi and Amba. Extensive migration and trade relations previously existing among peoples throughout Uganda have been obscured by identifications reflecting the moment when British rule tended to freeze groups into their present places.

British explorer John Hanning SPEKE reached Buganda in 1862 during his successful search for the source of the Nile. Missionaries followed, and shortly after there were rivalries at the court of the Ganda kabaka (king), which led to religious persecution and then to religious wars. By siding with one faction, Capt. Frederick D. Lugard (later 1st Baron LUGARD) established a military presence that committed a reluctant British government to make Uganda a protectorate (1894). In 1900, Buganda's leading chiefs signed an agreement accepting British protection in return for freehold rights in land for themselves. This provided Britain with a base from which to consolidate colonial rule over the rest of Uganda and created the opportunity for Buganda to reinforce its cultural separation from and more rapid economic growth than its neighbors.

The intricate federal constitution under which Uganda received formal independence on Oct. 9, 1962, recognized four kingdoms, ten ordinary districts, and one "special" district. Milton Obote, a Langi, became prime minister in an uneasy coalition with Kabaka Yekka, the Ganda party, following two sharply contested national elections. The coalition soon broke down, and a battle between the national and Buganda governments led to the exile of the kabaka, the elimination of

Kampala, the capital of independent Uganda, was once the capital of the kingdom of Buganda. It also served as the administrative and commercial center of Uganda during British colonial rule.

federalism, and a direct role for the army in national politics. After further intrigue, Obote was overthrown on Jan. 25, 1971, in a military coup led by Idi Amin Dada, a Nubian who had been Obote's choice for army chief of staff.

Amin, who assumed dictatorial powers, was eventually condemned by the international community for his excesses. He was not dislodged from power, however, until he invaded northern Tanzania in 1978. The Tanzanian military response, supported originally by about 1,000 Ugandan soldiers in exile, led to the liberation of Kampala in April 1979 and the ouster of Amin's forces from the country in June.

After an unstable 18-month interim, Obote emerged the victor in December 1980 elections widely considered fraudulent. Yoweri Museveni, defense minister during part of the interim period, soon fled into the bush northwest of Kampala to launch a guerrilla movement (later called the NRM) to oppose Obote. Hundreds of thousands of Ganda were uprooted from their homes, tortured, and killed as undisciplined government soldiers made a brutal but vain effort to end the insurgency. The NRM created a disciplined army, established popular councils, and carried out political education in the areas it controlled. In April 1985 it opened a second front in the west. Meanwhile, corruption, theft, and coercion by government officials reduced their credibility.

On July 27, 1985, Obote was again overthrown in a military coup by a faction within his army, which then named Lt.-Gen. Tito Okello head of state. The new government made overtures to the NRM, but when it invited former Amin soldiers to join it, the NRM continued to fight. The NRM set up an interim government over western and part of central Uganda and shifted from guerrilla to conventional war. Peace negotiations between the Kampala government and the NRM, organized by Kenyan president Daniel arap Moi, resulted in an agreement on Dec. 18, 1985. Each side accused the other of violating the accord, however, and the NRM marched on Kampala, ousting Okello's government on Jan. 26, 1986, and taking full control of the country two months later.

During its first year in power the NRM concentrated on restoring order, rehabilitating the economy, and laying the groundwork for a new social order. Day-to-day policy-making was overseen by the cabinet, headed by President Museveni and including representatives from all the old political parties. The supreme political body, the National Resistance Council, met infrequently. The NRM declared itself an interim government, with a four-year term that was to end with the election of a constituent assembly to prepare a new constitution for Uganda.

NELSON KASFIR

Bibliography: Avirgan, T., and Honey, M., *War in Uganda: The Legacy of Idi Amin* (1982); Fallers, L., ed., *The King's Men* (1964); Hansen, H. B., *Mission, Church and State in a Colonial Setting: Uganda 1890–*

1925 (1984); Jorgensen, J., *Uganda: A Modern History* (1980); Kabwegyere, T. B., *The Politics of State Formation: The Nature and Effects of Colonialism in Uganda* (1974); Kasfir, N., *The Shrinking Political Arena* (1976); Low, D. A., *Buganda in Modern History* (1971); Mamdani, M., *Politics and Class Formation in Uganda* (1976); Nabudere, D. W., *Imperialism and Revolution in Uganda* (1980); Steinhart, E. I., *Conflict and Collaboration: The Kingdoms of Western Uganda* (1977); Uganda Government, *Atlas of Uganda*, 2d ed. (1967); Uzoigwe, G. N., ed., *Uganda: The Dilemma of Nationhood* (1982).

Ugarit   [oo-guh-reet']

The ancient city of Ugarit and its port have been identified with the mound of the present-day village of Ras Shamra and the small harbor of Minet-el-Beida, 10 km (6 mi) north of Latakia, in northwestern Syria. Excavated since 1929 by the French Archaeological Mission, the site is of immense importance for the understanding of Canaanite civilization.

Although efforts in the field have been concentrated principally on the Late Bronze Age city, a deep sounding has demonstrated that the site was occupied as far back as the 7th millennium BC. A text discovered at MARI has shown that from the 2d millennium BC the city bore the name Ugarit. Because the kingdom of Ugarit was under Egypt's political control, many of its rulers are known from the written records of Egypt, Mesopotamia, and Hittite Anatolia. From the time of Niqmadu II of Ugarit (c.1360–1330 BC), tablets discovered at Ras Shamra itself provide valuable evidence concerning the customs, institutions, and culture of the city. The texts have shown that Ugarit's influence extended over a considerable area and that its port was an important commercial center for trade with Egypt, Anatolia, and the Aegean world.

Excavations have revealed the vast palace of Niqmadu covering about 10,000 m² (107,600 ft²) and containing 90 rooms, 5 large courtyards, an interior garden, and 12 staircases. Several archives have been found bearing tablets written in various languages: Babylonian, Hurrian, Cypro-Minoan, Sumerian, and Hittite cuneiform and Egyptian and Hittite hieroglyphic. Of greatest interest were those written in a previously unknown language, now called Ugaritic. Composed of the Babylonian system of cuneiform (wedge-shaped) signs, this language was West Semitic and alphabetic, showing similarities to later Hebrew, unlike the syllabic Babylonian system. Apart from their economic texts, the archives also contain writings that have shed light on Canaanite religion and mythology.

In addition to a second, smaller palace, a large part of the residential area has been exposed, revealing spacious private houses. Many of these were equipped with burial vaults that have yielded rich finds. Two temples, dedicated to Baal and to Dagon, have been excavated. In the harbor district, large storehouses with numerous jars still in position were found. The cosmopolitan nature of the city, the result of its extensive trading, is reflected in its art objects, which show influences from many areas. An ivory plaque found at Minet-el-Beida depicts a goddess in an Aegean posture wearing a Syrian costume combined with Egyptian and Hittite motifs.

The city-state survived beyond Niqmadu's reign, despite the troubled political climate. With the ever increasing power of Hittite Anatolia, Ugarit was obliged to play a double game, nominally subject to Egypt yet at times receiving even military aid from the Hittites. Nevertheless, the end of Ugarit eventually came from a different direction when, in the late 13th century BC, the city was destroyed by the SEA PEOPLES. Occupation was not resumed, and the site lay abandoned until the 6th or 5th century BC, when a small Greek settlement was established there.   JONATHAN N. TUBB

Bibliography: Gordon, Cyrus H., *Ugarit and Minoan Crete* (1966); Heltzer, Michael, *The Rural Community in Ancient Ugarit* (1976).

Uhland, Johann Ludwig   [oo'-lahnt]

The German poet Johann Ludwig Uhland, b. Apr. 26, 1787, d. Nov. 13, 1862, saw 50 editions of his *Gedichte* (Poems, 1815) published, each containing new works. Vigorous, marked by brevity and a folktalelike simplicity, many of his poems were set to music by Schubert, Schumann, Brahms, and Liszt. A lawyer, politician, and scholar, Uhland also published (1822)

a study of the 13th-century minnesinger Walther von der Vogelweide.   CARL R. MUELLER

Uhle, Max   [oo'-le]

Max Uhle, b. Mar. 3, 1856, d. May 11, 1944, is considered the father of Peruvian archaeology. His explorations included archaeological expeditions in the valleys of Chinca and Ica, where he discovered the source of NAZCA pottery. He also worked in Chile and Ecuador.

Bibliography: Menzel, Dorothy, *The Archaeology of Ancient Peru and the Work of Max Uhle* (1977).

Uhuru   [oo-hoo'-roo]

Uhuru (also known as *Small Astronomy Satellite 1*, *SAS 1*, and *Explorer 42*), the first in a series of three Explorer satellites developed for NASA to investigate X-ray and gamma-ray sources both inside and outside the Galaxy, was launched atop a Scout rocket from the Italian San Marcos platform off the coast of Kenya on Kenya's Independence Day (Dec. 12, 1970).

The main structure of the satellite was a 143-kg (315-lb) aluminum cylindrical drum 61 cm (2 ft) in diameter and 61 cm (2 ft) high. Four panels of solar-energy cells hinged around the circumference of the cylinder provided 27 W of electrical power. Star and Sun sensors permitted the locations of specific sources to be determined. Two X-ray detectors with mechanical collimators were located atop the drum.

Uhuru and its two subsequent (1972 and 1975) companions—*Explorers 48* (*SAS 2*) and *53*—were all highly successful and laid the groundwork for more advanced satellites. *Uhuru* produced data that led astronomers to argue the existence of superclusters of galaxies bound together by a hot but thin gas with a mass many times that of the galaxies themselves (see X-RAY ASTRONOMY).   MITCHELL R. SHARPE

Bibliography: Watts, Raymond N., "The First X-Ray Astronomy Satellite," *Sky and Telescope*, January 1971.

Uighur   [wee'-gur]

The Uighur are the major ethnic group of the Chinese province of Sinkiang. Speakers of a southeast Turkic variety of the URAL-ALTAIC LANGUAGE family, they are light-skinned, relatively tall people with brown hair, brown or lighter eye-color, and aquiline noses. Basically of Mongoloid racial stock, they tend to resemble more closely Central Asian TURKS than the Chinese Mongolian physical type. In the mid-1980s the Uighur numbered nearly 6,000,000 in Sinkiang and more than 211,000 in the USSR, chiefly in the Uzbek and Kirghiz republics.

The Uighur originated on the Mongol steppes during the 6th century AD, and by 744 they were absolute rulers of their realm (see MONGOLS). Defeated (840) by the Yenisey KIRGHIZ, they fled into Sinkiang. Originally NOMADS, the Uighur shifted early to settled agriculture. For 11 centuries they lived on irrigated oases of the Tarim River basin and also in cities, where they have worked as merchants, shopowners, and innkeepers. Their indigenous religion combined shamanistic and Buddhist traditions, but they converted to Islam about 900. SUNNITE Muslims, the Uighur have been variously described by scholars as extremely devout, indolent, and pleasure-loving. From the time of Marco Polo, they were noted for casual relationships between the sexes. Divorce was easy, leading to family instability. Yet, in what seems a contradiction, the Uighur were strongly influenced by the ascetic philosophy of SUFISM, and some Uighur were monklike DERVISHES.

The name *Uighur* passed out of usage from the period of the Mongol conquests (1200s) to the 1920s, when it was revived by the Soviets and the Chinese. Uighur undoubtedly is related to the Chinese term *Hui*, meaning Muslims.   VICTOR L. MOTE

Bibliography: Mackerras, Colin, ed., *The Uighur Empire According to the T'ang Dynastic Histories* (1968; repr. 1973).

Ukiyo-e   [oo'-kee-yoh-ay]

Ukiyo-e (literally, "pictures of the floating world") was a school of art that flourished in Japan from the mid-17th to the mid-19th century. The rough equivalent of lower-class genre art in the West, Ukiyo-e encompassed paintings, wood-block prints, and illustrated books that reflected the delight of the Edo (modern Tokyo) middle classes in the sensuous pleasures of the commoner's world. (See JAPANESE ART AND ARCHITECTURE.)

Beginning with the monochrome prints of Hishikawa MO-RONOBU, the school's nominal founder, and the erotic album illustrations of his contemporary Sugimura Jihei (fl. 1680–98), Ukiyo-e artists took as their primary subjects the beautiful and licentious courtesans of Edo's demimonde. Ukiyo-e art was expanded and revitalized significantly when the Torii masters KIYONOBU I and KIYOMASU began dominating (c.1700) the print world of Edo with their hand-colored broadsheets depicting actors of the kabuki, or popular theater. Matinee idols of the popular stage and courtesans of the pleasure districts contin-

Courtesan (18th century) epitomizes the subtle emotional rendering and elegance of the artwork of Suzuki Harunobu, an artist preeminent in the Japanese Ukiyo-e school. Ukiyo-e, an art form using colored wood-block prints to portray popular scenes, reached its height during the 18th century. The reduplicative element of Ukiyo-e made it widely available to the masses and increased its popularity. (Musée Guimet, Paris.)

ued to dominate the Ukiyo-e world until the emergence of landscapists in the 19th century.

In the 1740s publishers perfected a registration process for multiple printing with colors, an innovation generally credited to the artist Okumura MASANOBU (1686–1764). This phase of Ukiyo-e art culminated in the spectacular polychrome prints of the six great masters of the period 1750–1850: Suzuki HARU-NOBU, Torii KIYONAGA, Kitagawa UTAMARO, Toshusai SHARAKU, and the landscapists Katsushika HOKUSAI and Ando HIROSHIGE. In their best works, these artists produced lively and brilliant-ly conceived masterpieces in alliance with publishers of taste and with craftsmen who skillfully translated their designs into the wood-block medium. Their broadsheet prints, whether of fashion-plate courtesans, kabuki actors, or poetic landscapes, vividly evoke the spirit of the age.

Ukiyo-e prints gained wide popularity among Western collectors during the late 19th century and exerted a significant influence on several impressionist and postimpressionist artists. A contemporary reappraisal by the Japanese critics has elevated Ukiyo-e to the status of the most universally known and appreciated of all the Japanese arts.   HOWARD LINK

Bibliography: Benyon, Lawrence, *Japanese Colour Prints*, 2d ed. (1960); Michener, James A., *Japanese Prints: From the Early Masters to the Modern* (1959); Narazaki, Muneshige, *The Japanese Print: Its Evolution and Essence*, trans. by C. H. Mitchell (1966); Stanley-Barker, Joan, *Japanese Art* (1984); Yoshida, Susugu, *Ukiyo-E: Two Hundred Fifty Years of Japanese Art* (1979).

Ukrainian language: see SLAVIC LANGUAGES.

Ukrainian Soviet Socialist Republic   [yoo-krayn'-ee-uhn]

The Ukrainian Soviet Socialist Republic is one of the 15 constituent republics of the USSR. It occupies the north shore of the Black Sea and the Sea of Azov and borders in the west on Romania, Hungary, Czechoslovakia, and Poland. The area is about 603,677 km² (233,089 mi²), and the population is 50,840,000 (1985 est.). The republic's capital is KIEV. The name *Ukraine*, which arose in the 11th century, means "border territory," reflecting its position on the Polish frontier.

Most of the Ukraine is physically part of the Russian, or East European, plain; the only uplands are the Ukrainian segment of the CARPATHIAN MOUNTAINS in the southwest, and the Crimean Mountains along the southern coast of the CRIMEA. The principal rivers, all trending northwest-southeast, are the DNEPR, the DNESTR, the DONETS, and the Southern Bug. The climate is moderately continental, with mean monthly temperatures ranging from −7° C (19° F) in January to 23° C (73° F) in July. Precipitation ranges from about 710 mm (28 in) in the northwest to about 300 mm (12 in) in the southeast. Most of the republic is covered with fertile chernozem soils; forests occupy less than 10% of the area, in the northwest.

The Ukrainian people, who represent 75% of the population, are a Slavic group of Russian Orthodox religion whose language is related to Russian and Polish (see SLAVIC LANGUAGES). Russians represent less than 20% of the population and live mainly in cities, whereas the ethnic Ukrainians are only 45% urban. Jews are an important urban minority. The principal cities in addition to Kiev are DNEPROPETROVSK, DONETSK, KHARKOV, LVOV, ODESSA, and ZAPOROZHYE.

Economically, the Ukraine is the USSR's second most important republic, after the Russian republic. Rich in mineral resources, it has the nation's largest coal-producing district, the DONETS BASIN, and the biggest iron-ore mining area, at KRIVOI ROG. The republic accounts for more than 40% of the Soviet steel output. The Ukraine also mines most of the USSR's manganese and titanium ores. Manufacturing is highly developed and diversified, producing a wide range of machinery and industrial equipment and chemicals. The Ukraine is also a key agricultural region, contributing as much as 25% of the grain in some years and an average 60% of the sugar. Irrigation is being expanded to increase yields in dry areas.

In 1986 a serious accident at the CHERNOBYL nuclear power plant north of Kiev spread harmful radiation across the Ukraine and into neighboring countries, forcing the evacuation of 135,000 people from the immediate area.

The medieval Russian state known as Kievan Rus' was centered at Kiev and included portions of what later became Russia and the Ukraine. An independent state, the Kingdom of Galicia and Volhynia, existed in the western Ukraine in the 13th and 14th centuries. By the beginning of the 15th century, most of the Ukraine had been absorbed by the Kingdom of Poland-Lithuania (after 1569, the Kingdom of Poland). The eastern Ukraine became independent in 1654 but quickly fell under Russian control, becoming known as "Little Russia." The western Ukraine remained Polish until the partitions of Poland (1772–95), when most of it was also annexed by Russia. After the Russian Revolutions (1917), a portion of the western area was restored to Poland; in the remainder of the Ukraine the Bolsheviks defeated nationalists who wanted independence, forming the Ukrainian SSR, which became part of the Soviet Union in 1922.

Ukrainian separatism was suppressed during the Stalin era, and millions of Ukrainians died of famine during the agricultural collectivization of the early 1930s. During World War II some Ukrainians sided with Germany against the Soviet Union, and in the Polish Ukraine (seized by the USSR in 1939) nationalist guerrillas resisted Soviet rule until the early 1950s. The territory of the Ukrainian SSR was completed by the addition of the Carpathian Ukraine (RUTHENIA), taken from Hungary in 1945. In the post-Stalin era an effort was made to integrate the Ukraine into the mainstream of Soviet life; the Soviet leaders Nikita Khrushchev and Leonid Brezhnev were both of Ukrainian origin.

Bibliography: Bilinsky, Yaroslav, *The Second Soviet Republic: The Ukraine after World War II* (1964); Conquest, Robert, *Harvest of Sorrow* (1986); Koropeckyj, I. S., ed., *The Ukraine within the USSR: An Economic Balance Sheet* (1977); Reshetar, John, *The Ukrainian Revolution, 1917–1920* (1952).

ukulele [yoo-kuh-lay'-lee]

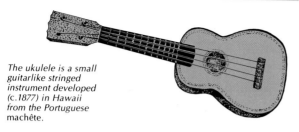

The ukulele is a small guitarlike stringed instrument developed (c.1877) in Hawaii from the Portuguese machête.

The ukulele is a small, guitar-shaped instrument with four strings, a fretted fingerboard, little resonance, and more harmonic than melodic capabilities. Its music is notated in simple TABLATURE that shows finger placement on the strings. The instrument originated in Hawaii and had a vogue in American collegiate life and amateur music in the 1920s and '30s.

ELWYN A. WIENANDT

Ulan Bator [oo'-lahn bah'-tor]

Ulan Bator, the capital and the largest city of Mongolia, lies in the north central part of the country. The city's population is 457,000 (1981 est.). An economic and transportation center, Ulan Bator has textile, leather, lumber, cement, meat-packing, and pharmaceutical plants. Ulan Bator is the seat of the National Choibalsan University (1942) and the Academy of Sciences.

The site of Ulan Bator, along the caravan route between Russia and China, was settled in 1639 as a Lamaist monastery and named Da Khure. Mongolian autonomy was proclaimed there in 1911. The Soviet Red Army occupied the city in 1921, and in 1924, when Mongolia became a people's republic, it was given its present name, which means ''Red Hero.''

Ulanova, Galina Sergeyevna [oo-lah'-noh-vah]

Galina Sergeyevna Ulanova, b. Saint Petersburg (now Leningrad), Jan. 10 (N.S.), 1910, whose name has become a symbol for Soviet ballet, was trained in the celebrated Maryinsky School on Theater Street, first under her mother, Maria Romanova, then with Agrippina Vaganova. She graduated into the Leningrad Kirov Ballet in 1928; in 1944 she was transferred to Moscow's Bolshoi Ballet. Ulanova was celebrated for her incomparable interpretations of the touchstone ballets of the international repertoire, and was equally identified with such peculiarly Russian classics as *The Humpbacked Horse.* Although Ulanova did not appear outside the Soviet Union until 1951, when she was past her physical prime, her artistry was given tumultuous recognition in the West. Her dancing, characterized by the sustained flow of movement known as the cantilena style, had a profound purity and simplicity. This was fused with the wholehearted emotional conviction she brought to her portrayal of a role.

TOBI TOBIAS

Bibliography: Kahn, Albert E., *Days With Ulanova* (1962); Ulanova, Galina, *The Making of a Ballerina* (1955).

Ulbricht, Walter [ool'-brikt]

Walter Ulbricht, b. June 30, 1893, d. Aug. 1, 1973, was dictator of East Germany. A cabinetmaker by trade and an active socialist by 1912, he joined the German Communist party when it was established in 1918. Trained at the Lenin School in Moscow in the early 1920s, he was a member of the German parliament, the Reichstag, from 1928 to 1933. When Adolf Hitler came to power in 1933, Ulbricht left Germany, serving as a Comintern agent and working with the Republicans during the Spanish Civil War and with the Russians during World War II. At the end of the war, he laid the foundations in the Soviet zone of occupation for the East German satellite state formally established in 1949 as the German Democratic Republic. Ulbricht became deputy prime minister in 1949 and secretary of the Socialist Unity (Communist) party

in 1950. His harsh regime provoked an open rebellion in 1953 and a stream of refugees to West Germany, stopped only by the Berlin Wall, built in 1961. As the result of strikingly successful economic reforms introduced during the last decade of Ulbricht's rule, East Germany achieved the highest standard of living in the Communist world. Ulbricht relinquished the powerful party secretaryship in 1971 but remained chairman of the Council of State, retaining, until his death, the titular dignity of German head of state.

DONALD S. DETWILER

Bibliography: Stern, Carola, *Ulbricht,* trans. by Abe Farbstein (1965).

ulcer

An ulcer is a pitting of a mucous or skin surface that results from an erosion or disintegration of the tissues. Ulcers of the gastrointestinal tract, called peptic ulcers, are relatively common and are thought to occur in 1 to 20 percent of the population in developed countries.

Peptic Ulcers. Peptic ulcers occur most commonly in the duodenum near the junction with the stomach, and in the stomach wall. They usually occur singly as round or oval lesions. The erosions are usually shallow but can penetrate the entire wall, leading to hemorrhage and possibly death. Pain, the predominant symptom, occurs one to three hours after a meal and is usually relieved with alkalis. The cause of such ulcers is not established, although Australian researchers in 1984 suggestively linked the presence of a newly observed form of *Campylobacter* bacteria with their development. At any rate, when gastric juices (consisting of hydrochloric acid, mucus, and a digestive enzyme called pepsin) act upon the walls of the digestive tract, a peptic ulcer results. The fact that ulcers of the duodenum are frequently associated with excess secretion of gastric acid and that ulcers of the stomach are not suggests that the two lesions may be separate disease entities. Entry of acid-peptic contents from the stomach into the lower esophagus can also cause ulcers in that area. Peptic ulcers tend to become chronic; after healing, they may recur.

Stress Ulcers. Another type of ulcer, the so-called stress ulcer, differs from peptic ulcers in its cause and characteristics. Stress ulcers usually occur in the stomach and are seen as multiple, shallow, bleeding erosions. Although they tend to heal rapidly because of their shallowness, they can perforate and cause severe bleeding. They tend to cause less pain than the chronic peptic ulcer. The term *stress* has led to misconceptions about the role of psychological factors in their development, because they occur most often in patients who have been subjected to marked physical injury such as severe trauma, burns (resulting in Curling's ulcer), or major surgery, and are more common in elderly or debilitated patients. Stress ulcers that occur because of central nervous system disease are called Cushing's ulcers. The ''chronic peptic ulcer'' seems in fact to be more related to psychological factors than are ''stress ulcers,'' but no identifiable psychological injuries have been reported, and they are not more common in ''executive types.'' The chronic peptic ulcer develops when there is imbalance between the normal ''aggressive'' factors, the acid-peptic secretions, and the normal ''resistance'' factors such as mucous secretions and rapid cellular replacement. Psychological influences may alter these factors through cerebral reactions altering lower brainstem function, with the resultant vagal nervous stimulation directly affecting the stomach and duodenum.

Treatment. Peptic ulcers, whether chronic or stress, can usually be treated by medical therapy alone. The drugs most commonly used are alkaline buffering agents and a special class of antihistamine called cimetidine, which blocks the histamine-2 receptors in the stomach that regulate gastric secretion. Newer drugs and drugs under development include sucrasulfate, prostaglandin compounds, and anticholinergic agents that inhibit acid secretion; such agents include pirenzepine, which exerts antipepsin and antigastrin activity as well. Carbenoxolone, which increases mucus secretion, and colloidal bismuth, which is antipeptic, have also been used. When drug therapy alone fails, however, surgical therapy is attempted. This approach may include removal of the distal part of the stomach, which produces the gastric stimulant hormone called gastrin, combined with a vagotomy (severing of the vagus nerves) to remove stimulation from the central nervous system.

Skin Ulcers. Ulcerations of the skin may occur as a result of the actions of bacterial toxins, as in anthrax ulcerations and chancres of syphilis. In diseases such as tuberculosis the toxins may enter the bloodstream and ulcerate the linings of the bladder, lungs, or other organs. Decubitus ulcers, or bedsores, result from the pressures exerted by prolonged bed rest. Ulcers also may occur on legs and feet because of the poor or blocked circulation that can result from, for example, arteriosclerosis, emboli, and infarctions. Diabetes tends to increase their incidence. Therapy of skin ulcers is based upon their cause and may involve topical treatment—using drug-containing ointments, pastes, or powders—or systemic drug administration. Specific antibiotics, zinc oxide, or other agents may be used.   CARL J. PFEIFFER

Bibliography: Pfeiffer, Carl J., *Peptic Ulcer* (1971) and *Drugs and Peptic Ulcer* (1982).

ulexite: see BORATE MINERALS.

Ullmann, Liv   [ool'-mahn]

A Norwegian dramatic actress, Liv Ullmann, b. Tokyo, Dec. 16, 1938, is best known for the films she has made with Ingmar BERGMAN. Most striking in *Persona* (1966), she has also given fine performances in *Shame* (1968), *Cries and Whispers* (1972), *Scenes from a Marriage* (1974), *Face to Face* (1976), *Autumn Sonata* (1978), and in Jan Troell's *The Emigrants* (1972). She appeared (1979) on Broadway in *I Remember Mama.*

Bibliography: Ullmann, Liv, *Changing* (1977).

Ulothrix   [yoo'-luh-thriks]

Ulothrix is a genus of unbranched, filamentous green ALGAE, phylum Chlorophyta, with bandlike CHLOROPLASTS that nearly encircle the perimeter of each cell. In the sea the algae occur in the intertidal zone, often growing on other algae. In fresh water they are commonly found attached to rocks or plants in clear, cool streams by means of a specialized holdfast cell. In asexual reproduction, the parent plant releases zoospores with four flagella that germinate to form new filaments. In sexual reproduction, *Ulothrix* releases biflagellate gametes that unite with other gametes to reproduce a zygospore that germinates into zoospores, which form new filaments.

Ulster   [uhl'-stur]

Ulster, the northernmost of the four ancient Irish kingdoms, encompasses NORTHERN IRELAND and three counties of Ireland. Ulster was dominated by the earls of Tyrone (O'Neill clan) and the earls of Tyrconnell (O'Donnell clan) from the 5th century until the 12th-century Anglo-Norman invasion. Ulster's clans (see TYRONE, HUGH O'NEILL, 2D EARL OF) unsuccessfully rebelled against England from 1594 to 1601. King James I of England colonized the area with Scottish Presbyterians. Descendants of these Protestants led the opposition to Irish home rule during the late 19th and early 20th centuries, and in 1920 they forced the partition of Ireland, with most of Ulster remaining under British rule (see IRELAND, HISTORY OF).

ultramarine

Ultramarine is both a blue green color and the pigment that is used to produce that color. The pigment was made during the Middle Ages by reducing the semiprecious stone lapis lazuli to a powder and mixing it with oil. The name *ultramarine*, which means "beyond the sea," was coined because the stone was imported from Asia by ship. Lapis lazuli was too rare for ultramarine to come into general use by artists until the early 19th century, when a method for producing the pigment using a powdered, roasted mixture of kaolin clay, sodium sulfate, and charcoal was developed.

ultramontanism   [uhl-truh-mahn'-tuh-nizm]

Ultramontanism (from Latin, meaning "beyond the mountains"; specifically, beyond the Alps, in Rome) refers to the position of those Roman Catholics who historically have emphasized the importance of centralized papal authority over the authority of kings and regional ecclesiastical hierarchies. It was often used in opposition to such nationalist positions as GALLICANISM (France), Josephinism (Austria), or Febronianism (Germany), which favored strong national churches, and to CONCILIARISM, which subordinated the pope's authority to that of a council of bishops. From the 17th century, ultramontanism became closely associated with the attitude of the Society of Jesus as elucidated by theologians such as Francisco SUÁREZ. Among the basic tenets of ultramontanism were the superiority of popes over councils and kings, even in temporal questions, the primacy of the popes over all other bishops, and, in some cases, papal infallibility in matters of faith and morals. The ultramontanists attained their greatest triumph in the late 19th century with the formal proclamation (1870) of papal primacy and INFALLIBILITY.   T. TACKETT

ultrasonics

Ultrasonics is the term used to describe the study of all sound-like waves whose frequency is above the range of normal human hearing. Audible sound frequencies (see SOUND AND ACOUSTICS) extend from about 30 to 20,000 hertz (1 Hz = 1 cycle per second). The actual waves and the vibrations producing them are called ultrasound. As late as 1900 ultrasound was still a novelty, and by 1930 it was a small area of physics research. In the 1960s and '70s, however, it became a research tool in physics, an instrument for flaw detection in engineering, a rival to the X ray in medicine, and a reliable method of underwater sound-signaling. The range of frequencies available has been extended to millions and even billions of hertz (megahertz and gigahertz).

Generation. The principal modern sources of ultrasound are specially cut crystals of materials such as quartz or ceramics such as barium titanate and lead zirconate. The application of an alternating electrical voltage across the opposite faces of a plate made of such a material produces an alternating expansion and contraction of the plate at the impressed frequency. This phenomenon in crystals, known as PIEZOELECTRICITY, was first discovered in the 1880s by Paul-Jacques and Pierre Curie. If the frequency of alternation f is such that $f = c/2l$, where c is the speed of sound in the material and l is the thickness of the plate, the expansions and contractions become very large, and the plate is said to exhibit RESONANCE.

Similar effects are observed in ceramics. Ceramic objects have the added advantage of being able to be cast in special shapes that are convenient for engineering applications. In addition, some materials, such as cadmium sulfide, can be deposited in thin films on a solid medium. Such material can then serve as a transducer. Still other ultrasonic transducers are produced in ferromagnetic materials by varying the magnetic-field intensity in the material.

Wave Properties. Ultrasonic waves travel through matter with virtually the same speed as sound waves—hundreds of meters per second in air, thousands of meters per second in solids, and 1,500 m/sec (5,000 ft/sec) in water. Most of the properties of sound waves (reflection, refraction, and so forth) are also characteristic of ultrasound. The attenuation of sound waves increases with the frequency, however, so that ultrasonic waves are damped far more rapidly than those of ordinary sound. For example, an ultrasonic wave of 1 MHz frequency passing through water will lose half of its intensity over a distance of 20 m (66 ft) through absorption of the energy by the water; in air, the distance over which the intensity falls by half would be a few centimeters. At the audio frequency of 20,000 Hz, the corresponding distances for water and for air would be about 50 km (30 mi) and 5 m (16.5 ft).

In addition to waves that travel through the bulk of a material, it is also possible to send waves along the surface of a solid. These waves, called Rayleigh waves, can be produced and detected by minute metallic "fingers" deposited on the surface of a piezoelectric substrate. Techniques utilizing surface waves have been widely exploited in signal processing.

Applications. Perhaps the most widespread use of ultrasound has been in the detection of obstacles in materials that do not transmit light (optically opaque materials). Thus, ultrasound is used in underwater signaling because a low-frequency ultrasonic beam can penetrate many kilometers of the ocean and be reflected back from any obstacle. This is the principle of SONAR, which can be used to identify submarines and map the ocean bottom. Sonar can even be used to measure the thickness of ice packs by submarines traveling under the polar ice caps.

If a short pulse of ultrasound is sent into a metal, it will be reflected from any cracks or minute defects such as blowholes. A system generating such pulses is widely used in flaw detection in solids (nondestructive testing). Because different solids and liquids reflect at different rates, the reflection of an ultrasonic pulse can also be used in medical examinations, especially of unborn fetuses in difficult pregnancies, and in the detection of brain tumors and breast cancers. Echocardiography, the study of heart motions by ultrasonic means, is another medical application (see RADIOLOGY).

An important physical property of ultrasound is the vigorous small-scale vibration of the medium that it represents. This property has led to many industrial applications. The vibrations can be used to shake dirt or other deposits off metals (ultrasonic cleaning). Such vibrations can also be used in soldering or welding. The ultrasonic transducer serves to remove oxide from the outer surface of the material, making more efficient the use of heat in the joining process. Plastic powders can be molded into small cylinders by similar techniques. Ultrasound is used today in the atomization of liquids and even metals, and also in the precipitation of smoke particles. In addition, the vibrations of the transducer can be conveyed to a cutting edge in ultrasonic drills and saws, which are used in dentistry and surgery. Pulses of ultrasound are also used to shatter kidney stones.

The dissipation of the sound energy in a medium results in local heating and motion of any fluid present. Both these phenomena are medically useful in ultrasonic therapy or massage. Highly concentrated (focused) beams of ultrasound can also be used to destroy cells and have had some medical application, as in treatment of secondary glaucoma.

Another developing field of research is the interaction of light and sound known as acoustic HOLOGRAPHY. In this meth-

The ultrasonic pulse-echo technique of finding cracks and other flaws in various materials makes use of the reflection properties of sound waves. A probe (1) transmits a pulsed beam (2) of ultrasound waves with frquencies above 20,000 Hz into the material. The transmitted and reflected waves from the bottom surface (3) and from flaws (4) are converted into electrical signals and displayed on an oscilloscope.

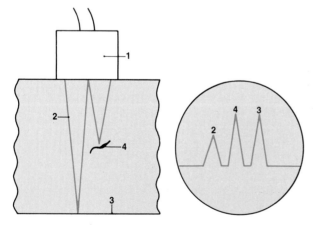

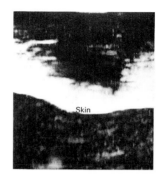
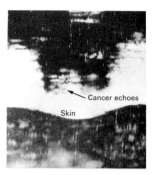

(Above) *The ultrasonic pulse-echo technique of medical diagnosis was first used by doctors in 1950 to detect tumors in a human body. A woman's breast was scanned with a beam of ultrasound, and the reflections of sound from different regions of the breast were displayed on a cathode-ray tube. The scan of a normal breast (shown at left) was found to differ from that of a tumorous breast (right). (Below) Ultrasound scans have since become a common diagnostic tool. Holding the scanner above the kidneys of a patient, the technician observes the resulting image on the screen at the side of the bed.*

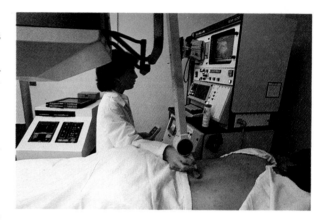

od the surface of a water-air interface is deformed by an incident ultrasonic beam originating in the water. A light beam is then reflected from the water surface, becoming spatially modulated. This modulated light beam can be used to reconstruct the original sound beam. If the ultrasound is directed through a human body or an industrial sample, it is possible to construct images of the interior of the object.

ROBERT T. BEYER

Bibliography: Berry, Michael V., *The Diffraction of Light by Ultrasound* (1966); Blitz, Jack, *Fundamentals of Ultrasonics* (1967); Cracknell, A. P., and Clark, J. L., *Ultrasonics* (1979); Greguss, P., *Ultrasonic Imaging* (1980); Hagen-Amsart, Sandra L., *Textbook of Diagnostic Ultrasonography*, 2d ed. (1983); Wicks, J. D., *Fundamentals of Ultrasonographic Techniques* (1983).

ultraviolet astronomy

Ultraviolet astronomy relates to celestial observations made in the ultraviolet region of the electromagnetic spectrum, ranging from wavelengths of about 4000 Å down to about 100 Å. The ozone layer in the Earth's upper atmosphere, as well as atmospheric oxygen and nitrogen, effectively keep all ultraviolet radiation with wavelengths shorter than 2900 Å from reaching the Earth's surface. The development of the field of ultraviolet astronomy began with the orbiting of space observatories in the 1960s. Observing celestial objects in ultraviolet light allows astronomers to obtain valuable information about the nature of such peculiar objects as quasars, Seyfert galaxies, and unusual radio galaxies. The presence and amounts of most elements in interstellar space can be determined only by ultraviolet studies. The properties of hot stars, white dwarfs, planetary nebulae, and even the atmospheres

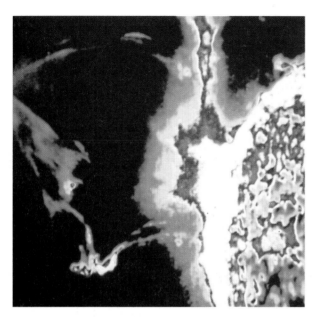

This photograph of a solar prominence, or an eruption of gas from the Sun's visible surface, was taken in ultraviolet (UV) light. The image has been color coded to reveal areas of similar UV intensity. The variations in intensity reflect differences in gas density.

of stars and planets can be obtained more directly from ultraviolet than from visible-light observations.

The Sun's chromosphere and corona have been intensively studied in ultraviolet light since Mar. 7, 1962, when the first of a series of eight Orbiting Solar Observatories (see OSO) was launched. The *Copernicus* satellite, the second of two Orbiting Astronomical Observatories (see OAO) to operate successfully in orbit, was launched on Aug. 21, 1972, and functioned until early 1981. Among the more important results obtained from *Copernicus* were the discovery of huge clouds of hydrogen surrounding the heads of comets; hot, rapidly moving clouds of interstellar gas made up of numerous elements; ultraviolet emission from hot, young stars that is higher than expected; large amounts of matter being ejected into space at high speeds from hot O- and B-type stars; and bright blue stars in old globular clusters. In addition, *Copernicus* indicated that clouds of cold interstellar gas are not uniformly distributed throughout space but tend to occur in isolated clumps. A more puzzling observation revealed that in gas clouds the concentration of elements heavier than helium is considerably lower than expected. Astronomers theorize that the missing mass is probably in the form of dust grains.

The most advanced ultraviolet satellite—the *International Ultraviolet Explorer*—was placed in geosynchronous orbit on Jan. 26, 1978. This satellite has recorded spectra from quasars, peculiar galaxies, collapsed stars, planetary nebulae, interstellar gas clouds, and thousands of stars.   ARTHUR F. CACELLA

Bibliography: Chapman, R. D., ed., *The Universe at Ultraviolet Wavelengths: The First Two Years of IUE* (1980); Espesnek, Fred, "The New Era in Ultraviolet Astronomy," *Astronomy*, October 1978; Goldberg, Leo, "Ultraviolet Astronomy," *Scientific American*, June 1969; Snow, Theodore P., "Ultraviolet Spectroscopy with Copernicus," *Sky & Telescope*, November 1977; Wampler, E. J., "Ultraviolet, Optical and Infrared Astronomy," *Physics Today*, November 1982.

ultraviolet light

Electromagnetic radiation having wavelengths shorter than visible light but longer than X rays is called ultraviolet light, or ultraviolet radiation. This light is invisible to human eyes and is also known as black light. The ultraviolet region of the spectrum was discovered in 1801 by John Ritter in the course of photochemical experiments.

Ultraviolet light is generally divided into the near (4000 to 3000 Å), the far (3000 to 2000 Å), and the vacuum (2000 to 40 Å) ultraviolet regions. The last wavelengths, which are particularly harmful to life, are strongly absorbed by the Earth's atmosphere.

Ultraviolet light is created by the same processes that generate visible light—transitions in atoms in which an electron in a high-energy state returns to a less energetic state. Fluorescent and mercury-vapor lamps produce large amounts of ultraviolet light, which is filtered out when the lamps are intended for optical use; the reverse procedure—that is, filtering out the visible light—is used to achieve black-light effects.

The biological effects of ultraviolet light include sunburn and tanning. Excessive exposure can be harmful, especially to the eyes. Far ultraviolet light has the capacity to destroy certain kinds of bacteria and is used for the sterilization of foodstuffs and medicinal equipment.   STEPHEN FLEISHMAN

Bibliography: Koller, L. R., *Ultraviolet Radiation*, 2d ed. (1965); Summer, W., *Ultra-Violet and Infra-Red Engineering* (1962).

Ulysses   (mythology):   see ODYSSEUS.

Ulysses   (novel)   [yoo-lis'-eez]

Arguably the single most influential novel of the 20th century, James JOYCE's *Ulysses* (1922) is a modern epic whose structure loosely parallels that of Homer's *Odyssey*. Set in Dublin, the novel deals with one day (June 16, 1904) in the lives of Leopold Bloom, a wandering Jew whose sense of estrangement from society makes him a universal symbol of humanity, Stephen Dedalus, and Leopold's sensuous wife, Molly, whose final affirmation of life is given in the lengthy interior monologue that concludes the book. *Ulysses* is noted for its erudite allusions to theology, mythology, history, and language; its stylistic virtuosity; its masterful use of the interior monologue and other innovative STREAM OF CONSCIOUSNESS techniques; its encyclopedic breadth of detail; and, above all, its richly comic portrayal of life. Banned from the United States as obscene until 1933, *Ulysses* is today generally considered one of the highest achievements of modern literature. A new edition of *Ulysses*—the result of seven years' work by an international team of scholars assisted by a computer—correcting about 5,000 printer's errors, was published on Bloomsday 1984.

Bibliography: Adams, Robert M., *Surface and Symbol: The Consistency of James Joyce's "Ulysses"* (1962); Ellmann, Richard, *Ulysses on the Liffey* (1972); Gilbert, Stuart, *James Joyce's "Ulysses": A Study*, 2d ed. (1955); Groden, Michael, *"Ulysses" in Progress* (1977).

Umar I   [oo-mahr']

The second Muslim caliph (r. 634–44), Umar I, b. *c.*581, d. Nov. 3, 644, did much to extend and consolidate the empire of Islam. A father-in-law of the prophet Muhammad, he was named by Abu Bakr, the first caliph, to be his successor. Umar spread Islam by conquest into the Byzantine lands of Palestine, Syria, and Egypt, and into the Sassanian Persian Empire, establishing the principles of Islamic law in the conquered areas. He was killed by a Persian slave.   ROBIN BUSS

Umar, al-Hajj

Al-Hajj Umar, b. *c.*1794, d. Feb. 12, 1864, was a major intellectual and political figure in the 19th-century Islamic revolutions in West Africa. A member of the Tokolor tribe of Senegal, he studied for many years in Muslim schools in both West Africa and Arabia. In Mecca he was appointed caliph for West Africa by the reformist Tijaniyya brotherhood. Beginning in the 1840s, Umar and his armed followers overthrew many West African rulers and established a new, militarily strong Tokolor empire centered on the mid-Niger Valley (present-day Mali). Al-Hajj Umar was killed during an uprising by the Muslim FULANI of Maçina and other peoples. But his son and successor, Ahmadu Tijani, maintained the Tokolor state until French conquest in 1893.   ROBERT R. GRIFFETH

Bibliography: Martin, B. G., *Muslim Brotherhoods in 19th-Century Africa* (1976).

Umayyads   [oo-mah'-yahdz]

The Umayyads were an Islamic dynasty established by the ca-liph MUAWIYAH I in 661. An earlier caliph, Uthman (r. 644–56), had been a member of the powerful Umayyad clan, but he was murdered and replaced by ALI. When Muawiyah, previ-ously governor of Syria, seized the caliphate, he made the succession hereditary and thus inaugurated dynastic rule. From their capital at Damascus, the Umayyad caliphs ruled a vast empire, extending from Europe to India, until 750. There-after the line continued in Spain until 1031.

In place of the theocratic government of the early caliphs, Muawiyah created a more autocratic and secular regime, which sought to maintain the privileges of the Arabs and the fruits of their conquests. Islam was reserved as a privilege of the Arabs and was not forced upon the conquered peoples, whose society was preserved and strongly influenced the gov-ernment, art, and economy of the dynasty. In government, Muawiyah adopted the bureaucratic structure of the former Byzantine state as well as hereditary succession. In art and ar-chitecture a similar adaptation was made; the most important innovation was the mosque.

A policy of continuous expansion, reaching its maximum extent under al-Walid I (r. 705–15), brought northwest Africa, Spain, western India, and portions of Central Asia into the Is-lamic empire and added greatly to Umayyad wealth. This ex-pansion was the result of an efficient Syrian army and a pow-erful navy. The Umayyad period was characterized by Arabi-zation—the spread and intermarriage of Arabs with native peoples and the adoption of Arabic as the common language within the empire. The dynasty collapsed because of internal tribal and geographical rivalries and a return to the principles of Islam as the foundation of the state. It was overthrown by the ABBASIDS, who massacred most members of the family. The Umayyad dynasty survived only in Spain, where ABD AL-RAHMAN I founded (756) the Umayyad emirate (later caliphate) of Córdoba.   MICHAEL W. DOLS

Bibliography: Hawting, G. R., *The First Dynasty of Islam* (1986); Sha-ban, M. A., *Islamic History A.D. 600–750* (1971).

Umberto: for Italian kings of this name, see HUMBERT.

umbilical cord   [uhm-bil'-i-kul]

The umbilical cord, which occurs in placental mammals, arises from the abdomen of a developing fetus and attaches to the placenta. It is the tissue through which the fetus obtains its food and oxygen from and expels its waste products into the mother's circulatory system. About 0.6 m (2 ft) long and 1.2 cm (0.5 in) in diameter in humans, the umbilical cord contains two arteries and a single vein. Just after birth, when it is no longer needed, the umbilical cord is cut, and the former site of attachment is known as the umbilicus, or navel.

See also: DEVELOPMENT; PREGNANCY AND BIRTH.

umbrella

The umbrella (from the Latin, *umbra*, "shade"), used for pro-tection against rain or sun, is usually a small, round canopy of fabric, paper, or plastic that is held open or can be col-lapsed by means of hinged ribs that radiate from a central shaft. The bottom of the shaft serves as a handle. Used in the Orient and in Mediterranean civilizations since ancient times, and often associated with high rank, the umbrella vanished from Europe after the collapse of the Roman Empire. It was reintroduced during the late 16th century and, particularly as a sunshade or parasol, rapidly became an elegant fashion, often made with shades of silk and shafts of ebony or ivory. Umbrella manufacture grew in importance until, by the end of the 1800s, the making of English steel-wire umbrella frames had become a major industry.

umbrella bird

Umbrella birds are glossy black, crow-sized birds of the ge-nus *Cephalopterus*, family Cotingidae, found in the treetops of

tropical forests of Central and South America. They feed on fruits and large insects. During courtship displays, males spread their crests, which curve over the bill in an umbrella-like fashion, and inflate their throat wattles—in two forms feathered, in one bare and brightly colored—while uttering loud calls. Brownish, spotted eggs are laid in a loose stick nest.   WILLIAM A. LUNK

umbrella pine

Umbrella pine is the common name for the tree species *Sciad-opitys verticillata* of the family Taxodiaceae. This evergreen conifer, native to forests in central Japan, bears double nee-dles arranged in whorls like an umbrella. *S. verticillata* thrives in fertile, moist, shady sites. The tree is popular as an orna-mental in many countries because of its unique appearance.

umbrella plant

Umbrella plant is the common name for several species in the genera *Cyperus* and *Peltiphyllum* of the families Cyperaceae and Saxifragaceae, respectively. The name refers to the plant's flower cluster or drooping leaves extending from a sin-gle stock, which has the appearance of an umbrella. *P. pelta-tum* is a popular California garden plant.

FRANK B. SALISBURY

Umbria   [oom'-bree-ah]

Umbria is a region in the Apennine mountains of central Italy, northeast of Rome, covering about 8,460 km^2 (3,270 mi^2) in area. Its population is 813,507 (1983 est.). Umbria encom-passes the two provinces of Perugia and Terni. The regional capital is PERUGIA. Umbria is largely agricultural, producing grapes, sugar beets, and olives. Cattle and hogs are also raised. Chemicals, iron and steel, processed foods, and tex-tiles are manufactured. Terni has a large hydroelectric power plant. Umbria's beautiful countryside and medieval cities, in-cluding ASSISI, Orvieto, Perugia, and Spoleto, are tourist at-tractions.

Umbria fell to Rome in the 3d century BC. Various warring tribes controlled the region in the early Middle Ages. Largely an area of independent fiefdoms from the 12th century, Um-bria was part of the PAPAL STATES from the 16th century until 1860, when it joined newly united Italy. The region was occu-pied by Allied troops in June and July of 1944 during World War II.   DANIEL R. LESNICK

Un-American Activities, House Committee on

The House Un-American Activities Committee (HUAC) was established (1938) as a special committee by the U.S. House of Representatives. Under the chairmanship of Texas Demo-cratic representative Martin Dies, Jr., it investigated fascist, communist, and other so-called extremist or subversive politi-cal organizations. In January 1945 it became a standing com-mittee. The Dies Committee, as it was first called, investigat-ed the German-American Bund and the Silver Shirt Legion, both pro-Nazi organizations, and the U.S. Communist party's infiltration of the Federal Theatre Project and the Federal Writers Project. Its original intent was to halt Axis propaganda in the United States, but much of its attention was eventually centered on New Deal liberals, artists and intellectuals, and labor leaders.

After World War II and over the next 30 years, HUAC con-centrated its efforts primarily on communist and left-wing or-ganizations. In October 1947 it presented evidence that ten Hollywood writers and directors had communist affiliations. The HOLLYWOOD TEN, as they were called, refused to affirm or deny the charges made against them and were jailed for con-tempt. In 1948, HUAC's investigation of communists in the higher levels of the State Department led to its famous hear-ings on Alger HISS. In 1950 the committee, responding to the red-scare tactics of Sen. Joseph P. McCarthy, Republican of Wisconsin, sponsored a bill requiring U.S. communists to reg-ister as foreign agents, denying them passports, and excluding

Robert Stripling (left), *chief investigator for HUAC, and Rep. Richard M. Nixon examine the microfilm of State Department documents used as evidence in the 1948 hearings involving Alger Hiss and Whittaker Chambers. The film had been hidden in a pumpkin on Chambers's farm.*

them from government and defense-industry employment. This bill became law as the McCarran Act, but the registration provision and travel ban were eventually overturned by the courts. Dissent and public protest resulted in the decline of McCarthyism and the power of the committee. In 1969, HUAC was renamed the Internal Security Committee and in 1975 it was abolished; its functions were transferred to the House Judiciary Committee.

Bibliography: Beck, Carl, *Contempt of Congress: A Study of the Prosecutions Initiated by the Committee on Un-American Activities, 1945-1957* (1959; repr. 1974); Goodman, Walter, *The Committee: The Extraordinary Career of the House Committee on Un-American Activities* (1968); Trumbo, Dalton, *The Time of the Toad: A Study of Inquisition in America* (1972).

Unamuno, Miguel de   [oo-nah-moo'-noh]

An important Spanish philosopher whose writings defined modern existentialist issues, Miguel de Unamuno y Jugo, b. Sept. 29, 1864, d. Dec. 31, 1936, was also an innovative novelist, playwright, and poet. A Basque and self-styled provincial who lived in Madrid only long enough to obtain his doctorate (1884), Unamuno spent the rest of his life at the University of Salamanca, where he was professor of ancient Greek, or in exile (1924-30). Although at first a socialist, his political ideas were peculiarly his own. He supported the Allies during World War I when Spain was neutral. In the 1920s he waged a campaign against Spain's Alfonso XIII and the dictator Primo de Rivera. After a republic was declared in Spain in 1931, Unamuno at first defended, then attacked it.

His philosophical and literary writings are also difficult to categorize. Raised a devout Catholic, Unamuno experienced a religious crisis in 1897. Afterwards he stressed the struggle to believe rather than faith itself, which he had apparently lost. Although his first novel *Paz en la guerra* (Peace in War, 1897) was realistic, his later works were either experimental after the manner of Pirandello or confessional. His most famous novels are *Mist* (1914; Eng. trans., 1928) and *San Manuel Bueno, mártir* (1933; Eng. trans., 1957). Although also an original poet, Unamuno is best known for his essays: *Life of Don Quixote and Sancho* (1905; Eng. trans., 1927), *The Tragic Sense of Life* (1913; Eng. trans., 1921), and *The Agony of Christianity* (1924; Eng. trans., 1928). His style is unique in modern Spanish letters.   PHILIP W. SILVER

Bibliography: Ilie, Paul, *Unamuno: An Existential View of Self and Society* (1967); Mora, José Ferrater, *Unamuno: A Philosophy of Tragedy*, trans. by Philip Silver (1962); Nozick, Martin, *Miguel de Unamuno* (1971).

Uncas   [ung'-kuhs]

The MOHEGAN chief Uncas, b. *c.*1606, d. *c.*1683, was the leader of the pro-English, accommodationist faction of his tribe. He married the daughter of the tribe's anti-English paramount chief, Sassacus, and led a rebellion against him. When Sassacus was deposed and the PEQUOT defeated (1637), the ambitious Uncas gained control of the reunited Pequot-Mohegan tribe.

With English support Uncas launched a campaign of conquest against other New England tribes, which made his people the most powerful Indians in New England. In 1643 he ordered the murder of the NARRAGANSETT chief Miantonomo, and in 1675 he sided with the English during KING PHILIP'S WAR.   JAMES A. CLIFTON

Bibliography: Dockstader, Frederick J.,, *Great North American Indians* (1977); Peale, A. J., *Uncas and the Mohegan-Pequot* (1939).

uncertainty principle

Developed by Werner Heisenberg in 1927, the uncertainty principle states that there are absolute limits on the accuracy to which *pairs* of physical quantities can be measured. Classical physics sets no limit on the accuracy of the measurement of the position and the momentum of a particle. In contrast, one of the postulates of QUANTUM MECHANICS is that the process of measurement itself disturbs the system being measured. For example, the process of measuring the position x of a particle disturbs the particle's momentum p, and vice versa, so that $\Delta x\, \Delta p \geq h/2\pi$, where Δx is the uncertainty of the position and Δp the uncertainty of the momentum. Planck's constant h defines the size of the uncertainty. Because of the minuteness of h, the uncertainty is significant only when extremely small quantities are measured.

Heisenberg provided a number of physical illustrations of the uncertainty principle, for example, attempting to measure accurately the position of an atom by viewing it with an ideal microscope. After the light interacts with the atom it can be analyzed to determine the atom's position. The light, however, also imparts momentum to the atom by the COMPTON EFFECT, which introduces uncertainty in the determination of that property.

The uncertainty principle, in its statement of the limits of observation, is a part of the present scientific view of the nature of physical reality, with implications for philosophy in general.   HERBERT L. STRAUSS

Bibliography: Bohm, David, *Causality and Chance in Modern Physics* (1971); Bohr, Niels, *Atomic Physics and Human Knowledge* (1961); Heisenberg, Werner, *The Physical Principles of the Quantum Theory*, trans. by Carl Eckart and Frank Hoyt (1949).

Uncle Remus

Uncle Remus is the fictional narrator of a series of animal fables created by the Georgia journalist Joel Chandler HARRIS. Speaking in a southern black dialect, Uncle Remus narrates encounters between Brer Rabbit, Brer Fox, and Brer Bear in which Brer Rabbit continually outwits his foes. In a typical story, Brer Rabbit begs his captors to throw him anywhere but in the briar patch, using psychology to effect his escape.

Uncle Sam

Uncle Sam is a symbolic character who is commonly employed in cartoons as the personification of the United States. He is depicted as a tall, slender figure with long white hair and beard who is usually dressed in a swallow-tailed coat decorated with stars, a pair of striped trousers, and a top hat with stars and stripes on it. The name was first used in conjunction with the United States in a derogatory sense, by those opposing the War of 1812. Later in the 19th century cartoonists created figures called Uncle Sam and his nephew Brother Jonathan, a rural Yankee wit dating from the 18th century, and for a time the two were used interchangeably as symbols for the country. It was cartoonist Thomas Nast who, in the 1870s, drew the figure commonly associated with Uncle Sam today. The most familiar depictions of Uncle Sam,

Uncle Sam is the widely recognized symbol for the United States. First created by cartoonists in the 1800s, Uncle Sam changed from a character of derision to one of respectability. In World Wars I and II, Uncle Sam was known as the patriotic figure of J. M. Flagg's army recruitment posters.

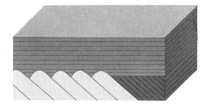

A disconformity is recognized by the parallel structure of the rock layers above and below the unconformity, or break in the strata.

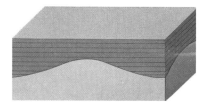

In an angular unconformity the older rock layers below the unconformity are deformed and tilted with respect to the younger layers above.

In a nonconformity the more recent sedimentary layers are laid down on a nonlayered surface of either igneous or metamorphic rocks.

however, are those appearing on the recruiting posters that were used during World Wars I and II. These were drawn by James Montgomery Flagg, who served as his own model. Although the precise origins of the name are uncertain, in 1961 Congress recognized Uncle Sam as the namesake of Samuel Wilson (1766–1854), a Troy, N.Y., inspector of army supplies during the War of 1812.

Bibliography: Jordan, P. D., *Uncle Sam of America* (1953); Ketchum, Alton, *Uncle Sam: The Man and the Legend* (1959).

Uncle Tom's Cabin

Harriet Beecher STOWE's best-known novel, *Uncle Tom's Cabin; or, Life Among the Lowly*, first published serially in 1851–52, was an enormously popular tale of the injustices of slavery. Uncle Tom, an almost Christlike model of goodness and charity, is a house slave who is reluctantly sold by his first owners. He is ultimately beaten to death by Simon Legree, a tyrannical overseer, after many heartrending examples of generosity and heroism. Little Eva and Topsy are other memorable characters in the novel. Once believed to be a major cause of the Civil War, the novel did popularize the abolitionist movement. The term *Uncle Tom* is today used pejoratively to describe a black American who is too deferential to whites.　　　　　　　CHARLOTTE D. SOLOMON

Uncle Vanya

Subtitled *Scenes from Country Life,* the play *Uncle Vanya* (1897) is one of the most expertly crafted of the works of the Russian author Anton CHEKHOV. It was first performed at the Moscow Art Theater in 1899. As in other Chekhov dramas, the plot is minimal, the interaction of the characters all-important. The play is set in a country manor house, where Uncle Vanya and his niece, Sonya, have for years been caring for an elderly professor and his second wife, with whom Vanya is in love. The professor is a brother-in-law of Vanya and the father of Sonya by his first wife. By the play's end, the professor is exposed as a fraud, but Vanya and Sonya discover that their devotion has been its own reward.　　WILLIAM B. CUMMINGS

unconformity

A substantial break in the sequence of deposition, which interrupts the geologic record, is called an unconformity. American usage now recognizes four types: (1) nonconformity is an unconformity that has sedimentary strata overlying nonlayered igneous or metamorphic rocks; (2) angular unconformity is eroded folded or tilted strata upon which discordant layers of sediment have been deposited; (3) disconformity is an erosion surface of substantial relief, with the strata above the surface parallel to those below; and (4) paracon-

formity is an almost planar surface of nondeposition between essentially parallel strata. Paraconformity may be difficult to recognize in the field but nonetheless represents unrecorded geologic time as indicated by the fossils found above and below the break.

The importance of unconformities was first recognized in 1788 by the Scottish geologist James Hutton, who correctly interpreted an angular unconformity between Silurian and Devonian rocks at Siccar Point, Scotland. Charles Darwin, in *The Origin of Species* (1859), emphasized the incompleteness of the geologic record as evidenced by numerous unconformities and argued that more geologic time is represented by breaks than by continuous deposits. This fact is certainly true for any single area on the continents. The task of the geologist, therefore, involves piecing together fragmentary local records to compile a more or less complete history of the Earth. The modern gathering of deep-ocean sediment cores makes available complete, almost continuous geologic records; deep-sea sediments, however, are seldom found older than about 200 million years.　　　　　　　PAUL BOYER

Bibliography: Dunbar, C. O., and Rodgers, J., *Principles of Stratigraphy* (1957).

unconscious

Although thinkers and poets of many cultures and historical periods have understood the importance of an irrational realm of mental life essentially alien and unknown to the rational, conscious intellect, Sigmund FREUD is generally credited with having made the unconscious a cornerstone of modern clinical psychology and psychiatry. Freud created a model of the mind divided into conscious, preconscious, and unconscious regions or systems. The conscious system was said to contain those ideas of which the person was immediately aware. The preconscious system contained ideas of which the person was not immediately aware, but could easily become so by simply turning attention to them. In contrast, the unconscious contained ideas of which the person could never become aware because their emergence into consciousness was prevented through a process termed repression.

Freud portrayed the unconscious system as a subterranean world of primitive urges and desires, repressed during childhood and relentlessly clamoring for expression and fulfillment through dreams, mistakes, and symptoms. Carl JUNG expanded this theory further by subdividing the unconscious into a personal unconscious, which was similar to Freud's concept, and a collective or transpersonal unconscious. Jung pictured the latter as a storehouse of unconscious memories not from a person's individual past but from his or her ancestral past.

ROBERT D. STOLOROW

Bibliography: Bowers, K. S., and Meichenbaum, Donald, *The Unconscious Reconsidered* (1984); Ellenberger, Henri F., *The Discovery of the Unconscious* (1970; repr. 1981); Freud, Sigmund, *The Interpretation of Dreams,* trans. and ed. by James Strachey (1955); Jung, Carl G., *Two Essays on Analytical Psychology,* 2d ed. (1972), in his *Collected Works,* ed. by Herbert Read et al., trans. by R. F. C. Hull.

See also: PSYCHOANALYSIS.

UNCTAD: see UNITED NATIONS CONFERENCE ON TRADE AND DEVELOPMENT.

Under Milk Wood

In his radio play *Under Milk Wood* (1954), Dylan THOMAS attempted to create a new form of poetry for a mass audience. The play chronicles the events of one day in a small Welsh fishing village. Various speakers tell their stories, while two voices serve as commentators. The play depends on the supercharged, rhythmic, evocative quality of the language rather than on action or characterization. Beneath a veneer of social propriety, represented by the prim Mrs. Grundy, a web of sexual attractions and intrigues is revealed.

underemployment

Underemployment occurs when a worker's abilities and education are not being fully used in a job position. Until the 1970s, in most industrialized countries, technical progress had created more skilled jobs than it eliminated. An increase in the educational level of the work force, combined with a general slowing of economic growth (which slows the upgrading of jobs), however, has begun to create underemployment in some industrialized societies. In developing countries underemployment is the common term for "disguised unemployment"—when employed resources are not used with maximum efficiency.

Bibliography: Sullivan, T. A., *Marginal Workers, Marginal Jobs* (1978).

Underground Railroad

The term *Underground Railroad* arose as a colloquialism during America's pre–Civil War decades; it referred to secret, organized efforts by Northerners to help escaped slaves find safe shelter in the free states or Canada. Such assistance was necessary because the Fugitive Slave Act of 1793 and the stricter Fugitive Slave Act of 1850 (see FUGITIVE SLAVE LAWS) allowed slaveowners to recapture their escaped slaves.

Despite Harriet TUBMAN's well-known forays into the deep South to spirit slaves to freedom, the great majority of escaped slaves acted on their own. They made the most dangerous part of their trip—across the slave states to free territory—without organized help. Many of them, however, once they reached the free states, were guided along prearranged Underground Railroad routes, receiving shelter, food, and clothing at various "stations," as the homes of the Railroad's supporters were known.

In general, it was northern free blacks, not white abolitionists, who played the most important role in the planning, communication, and decision making within the network of escape. The railroad was most active in Ohio, Indiana, and Pennsylvania, but it existed throughout the North. Most estimates of the number of slaves aided by the railroad fall between 50,000 and 100,000.

JAMES BREWER STEWART

Bibliography: Gara, Larry, *The Liberty Line: The Legend of the Underground Railroad* (1961).

Underhill, Evelyn

English writer and mystic Evelyn Underhill, b. Dec. 6, 1875, d. June 15, 1941, underwent a religious experience in 1907 that turned her to the lifelong study of mysticism. The first of her many books, *Mysticism* (1911), became a standard work on the subject.

Bibliography: Cropper, M. B., *Evelyn Underhill* (1958).

underwater archaeology

Underwater archaeology is the study of human artifacts from the past that lie beneath bodies of water. The lure of these lost remains has fascinated people since ancient times. Classical authors described a statue of the Greek god Poseidon and other underwater remains visible at Helice, a town that disappeared under the Gulf of Corinth during an earthquake in the 4th century BC. In the 15th century an ancient statue was raised from Lake Nemi in Italy during an attempt to salvage a pair of Roman ships. In the early 19th century another statue—the Piombino Apollo, now in the Louvre—was netted near Elba by Italian fishermen. Even today, surviving Greek bronze statues come mostly from the sea, usually the chance finds of fishermen, swimmers, or sponge divers.

Although a primitive diving suit was used in later, 16th-century explorations of Lake Nemi, two English brothers, John and Charles Deane, developed a more practical one early in the 19th century, using it to salvage artifacts from the *Mary Rose,* an English vessel that sank near Portsmouth in 1545. Similar equipment made possible the raising of art objects from Roman shipwrecks in the Mediterranean early in the 20th century, the salvage of the American Revolutionary War vessel *Philadelphia* from Lake Champlain, and the recovery of Maya artifacts from a cenote (well) at Chichén Itzá, Mexico. True archaeological excavation, however, became possible only with the diving mobility provided by the aqualung, or scuba, which was developed in France in 1943.

Amateur and professional scuba divers pioneered underwater excavations in the Mediterranean, introducing air lifts (suction pipes) for digging, air-filled lifting bags for raising heavy artifacts, and grids for making accurate site plans. The first complete excavation of an ancient wreck on the seabed by a diving archaeologist was that of a Bronze Age ship off Cape Gelidonya, Turkey, in 1960. The raising of the 17th-century Swedish warship *Vasa* from Stockholm harbor followed in 1961. The *Asherah,* a submarine designed for archaeological exploration, was launched in 1964. Using sonar and magnetometers for surveys, divers have made many further discoveries since that time. In 1985 the wreck of the ocean liner *Titanic,* which sank in 1912, was located at a depth of 2 miles by a remote-control submarine.

At first underwater archaeology was seen mainly as a way of collecting well-preserved artifacts. Dated wrecks have yielded the largest known assemblages of medieval Islamic glass, English Tudor longbows, dated Byzantine pottery, Chinese celadons, and implements from the Aegean Bronze Age.

Beginning in the 1960s, however, improved mapping methods and conservation techniques permitted fragmentary wooden hulls to be accurately recorded, conserved, and restored for study and museum display. Underwater archaeology thus developed a subdiscipline, nautical archaeology, devoted to the history of seafaring.

In the early years, most underwater archaeological work was done in the Mediterranean. More recently, serious research has spread around the globe: Spanish Armada wrecks off Ireland, Viking and Renaissance ships in northern Europe, early Spanish galleons in the Caribbean, a medieval Chinese junk off Korea, and a 17th-century Portuguese merchant ship on the coast of Kenya, have all been excavated; the *Mary Rose* was raised in 1982.

Underwater archaeology is not limited to the study of ships. Drowned habitation sites are also being explored, including a prehistoric site off Israel, lake dwellings in Switzerland, and the city of Port Royal, Jamaica, which sank in an earthquake in 1692.

GEORGE F. BASS

Bibliography: Bass, George F., *Archaeology beneath the Sea* (1975); Muckelroy, Keith, ed., *Archeology under Water* (1980).

See also: SALVAGE, MARINE.

Underwood, Oscar W.

Oscar Wilder Underwood, b. Louisville, Ky., May 6, 1862, d. Jan. 25, 1929, was a U.S. representative (1895–96, 1897–1915) and senator (1915–27) who cosponsored an important tariff act. An Alabama Democrat, Underwood was the chairman of the House Ways and Means Committee, in which capacity he sponsored and helped write the Underwood Tariff Act of 1913, a law that greatly reduced tariffs. In the Senate he was a supporter of President Woodrow Wilson's foreign policy and served as Democratic floor leader (1921–23). Underwood was an unsuccessful candidate for the Democratic presidential nomination in 1912 and 1924.

Underwriters' Laboratories

Underwriters' Laboratories, Inc. (UL), is a private U.S. company that attempts to determine the fire, electrical-shock, and casualty hazards of various products submitted to it by manufacturers. The company was founded in 1894 by William H. Merrill, an engineer who wanted to test light bulbs suspected of causing fires. The products it tests today range from machinery, appliances, and electrical equipment of all kinds to medical and dental equipment, robots, and other high-technology devices.

Undset, Sigrid   [un'-set]

A celebrated Norwegian novelist, Sigrid Undset, b. May 20, 1882, d. June 10, 1949, gained international fame as the author of historical novels and in 1928 received the Nobel Prize for literature. Although her father, an archaeologist, had introduced her to Norwegian medieval history at an early age, her first novels were set in contemporary Norway. *Fru Marta Oulie* (1907), *Jenny* (1911; Eng. trans., 1921), and *Images in a Mirror* (1917; Eng. trans., 1938) all deal with the role of modern women, caught between traditional duties and a new need for freedom.

The historical trilogy *Kristin Lavransdatter* (1920–22; Eng. trans., 1923–27) ranks as one of the great works of Norwegian literature. It portrays the triumphs and tragedies of its protagonist, Kristin, from age seven to her death in the plague 40 years later. Set in 14th-century Norway, the trilogy offers a penetrating analysis of a woman's development from childhood to maturity and a picture of the life and culture of medieval Norway.

Undset converted to Catholicism in 1925, and her next historical novel, the tetralogy *The Master of Hestviken* (1925–27; Eng. trans., 1928–30), also set in medieval Norway, shows her increasing preoccupation with religious questions. From the 1930s on, she dealt with more contemporary issues, expressing in her novels a concern for religious and racial tolerance. An early and forceful critic of Nazism, Undset fled to Sweden and then to the United States after the German invasion of Norway in 1940. She returned to Norway in 1945.

KJETIL A. FLATIN

Bibliography: Bayerschmidt, Carl Frank, *Sigrid Undset* (1970); Winsnes, A. H., *Sigrid Undset: A Study in Christian Realism* (1949; Eng. trans., 1953).

undulant fever: see BRUCELLOSIS.

unemployment: see EMPLOYMENT AND UNEMPLOYMENT.

unemployment insurance

Unemployment insurance is insurance against loss of pay when an employee loses his or her job. It is designed to provide unemployed workers with income for a limited period of time while they look for other jobs. In the United States federal law sets down guidelines and minimum standards for the program, to be financed by a payroll tax on employers with four or more employees. The individual states administer the program in cooperation with the federal government. Some states exceed the minimum federal requirements. A great many states have extended coverage to employers with fewer than four employees. Some states have also elected to give insurance to workers excluded by the federal law, such as farm and domestic workers. The program covers more than 85% of the entire labor force.

The amount of the benefits paid differs in the various states. The rates generally take into account the applicant's previous level of earnings. (Ordinarily, the amount is one-half the applicant's previous salary up to a maximum that varies from state to state; in 1982 the average weekly payment was $119.) Another factor taken into consideration may be the number of the applicant's dependents. The length of the pay period also varies and is generally tied to the overall employment picture. The normal length is 26 weeks with 13-week increments in effect when the unemployment in a given area rises above a stated percentage.

To be eligible for unemployment insurance, persons must usually have worked a minimum period in a job—20 weeks in many states—have earned a certain amount of money, or both. A worker can, however, be denied benefits if he or she quits a job without good cause or is fired because of misconduct. Unemployment benefits may also be denied if a worker is involved in a labor dispute that has brought about a work stoppage or if he or she refuses a suitable job without good cause.

Unemployment insurance was introduced in Western Europe early in the 20th century, the first such program being adopted by Great Britain in 1911. The U.S. program was an important element of the New Deal program of President Franklin D. Roosevelt. It was introduced in 1935 as part of the Social Security Act (see SOCIAL SECURITY).

Bibliography: Blaustein, Saul J., *Job and Income Security for Unemployed Workers* (1981); Blaustein, Saul J., and Craig, Isabel, *An International Review of Unemployment Insurance Schemes* (1977); Hammermesh, Daniel S., *Jobless Pay and the Economy* (1977); Murray, M. G., *Income for the Unemployed* (1971).

UNESCO: see UNITED NATIONS EDUCATIONAL, SCIENTIFIC, AND CULTURAL ORGANIZATION.

Ungaretti, Giuseppe   [oon-gah-ret'-tee]

Giuseppe Ungaretti, b. Feb. 10, 1888, d. June 1, 1970, was, with Eugenio Montale and Salvatore Quasimodo, one of the chief architects of a new Italian poetry, distinguished by its simplicity and its lack of conventional rhyme schemes or punctuation. Born in Alexandria, Egypt, and educated at the Sorbonne (Paris), Ungaretti wrote mostly autobiographical poems inspired by his memories of Egypt, his experiences in World War I, and the death of his young son Antonietto. A lyric tension and evocative power characterize his poetry, which is collected in *The Life of a Man* (1947; Eng. trans., 1958), which incorporates *The Buried Harbor* (1916) and *The Joy* (1919).

SERGIO PACIFICI

Ungava   [ung-gah'-vuh]

Ungava, a peninsular region of northeastern Canada, is bordered by Hudson Bay on the west and by the Labrador Sea on the east. Iron ore is the principal resource. Originally part of the Northwest Territories, Ungava was annexed to Quebec in 1912. In 1927 the eastern section of the peninsula became part of Newfoundland, and the name Ungava has since been used for the Quebec part of the region.

ungulate   [uhng'-gue-luht]

An ungulate is a mammal whose toes end in hooves made up of hardened skin tissue. Four orders of mammals can be classed as ungulates: the Artiodactyla, or even-toed ungulates, including deer, camels, cattle, pigs, giraffes, and sheep; the Perissodactyla, or odd-toed ungulates, including horses, donkeys, zebras, tapirs, and rhinoceroses; the Proboscidea, or elephants; and the Hyracoidea, or hyraxes.

EVERETT SENTMAN

UNICEF: see UNITED NATIONS CHILDREN'S FUND.

unicorn

One of the six panels from the Lady with the Unicorn *tapestry (c.1490–1500) portrays a maiden with a docile unicorn, a legendary creature variously represented throughout history as a fantastic animal resembling a horse with a single horn projecting from its forehead. It has been conjectured that ancient accounts of the unicorn were based on descriptions of the Indian rhinoceros. (Musée de Cluny, Paris.)*

In both Western and Eastern mythology, the unicorn is a fabulous animal resembling a horse but with a single long horn growing out of its forehead. Those who drank out of its horn were protected from poisoning, stomach trouble, and epilepsy. According to medieval European folklore and art, the unicorn could be captured only by a virgin, thus symbolizing the power of spiritual love over fierceness. The medieval Christian church elaborated this story into an allegory of the incarnation and death of Christ. In Chinese mythology, the unicorn presides over literature.

unicorn plant

Unicorn plant is the common name for *Proboscidea louisiana* of the family Martyniaceae. This North American herb is grown for its ornamental hanging pods. The woody pods have thick bodies about 10 to 15 cm (4 to 6 in) long, ending in a curved beak that splits into two clawlike appendages.

FRANK B. SALISBURY

unidentified flying object

An unidentified flying object (UFO) is an unusual aerial or potentially airborne object that cannot be readily identified. Approximately 90% of raw UFO reports are interpreted as misperceptions of conventional objects, hoaxes, or hallucinations. The remaining 10% constitute the UFO enigma.

The date of the earliest UFO sighting is unknown. Some UFO researchers believe that there were UFO sightings in ancient times. The evidence for such sightings, however, is scanty and therefore purely speculative. Most UFO researchers date the beginning of the UFO phenomenon with the sighting of dirigiblelike "mystery airships" over the United States during 1896–97. The next significant group of reports came during World War II from Allied and Axis pilots who reported seeing strange metallike objects, which they called "foo fighters," in controlled flight around their planes. In 1946 people in Europe, particularly Scandinavia, reported large-scale sightings of silent "ghost rockets." None of these phenomena has been satisfactorily explained.

The UFO phenomenon entered public consciousness on June 24, 1947, when private pilot Kenneth Arnold reported sighting nine circular objects flying across his airplane's path in the skies over the state of Washington. He described their movements as being like "saucers skipping over water" and the term *flying saucer* was born.

Since 1947 there have been UFO sightings in nearly every country. Occasionally the number of sightings rapidly in-

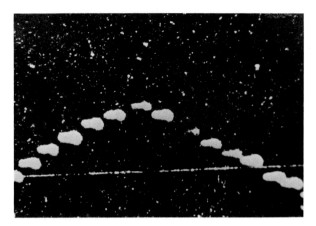

This photo of the "Lubbock Lights"—seen over Lubbock, Tex., on at least 14 occasions during late 1951—is one of several analyzed by the U.S. Air Force, which concluded that the photos were not a hoax. Reanalysis indicated that the lights were reflections from birds.

creases and a UFO wave ensues. For instance, UFO waves occurred in France and Italy in 1954, in New Guinea in 1958, and in the USSR in 1967. In the United States, waves occurred in 1947, 1952, 1957, 1965–67, and 1973. UFO researchers have been unable to predict or explain UFO waves. Attempts to link them to media publicity about UFOs, hysterical contagion, or "societal stress" have proved unsuccessful. Although intensive publicity has prompted people to report sightings they had previously made, such publicity is not considered responsible for new reports.

A study of reports suggests that UFO sightings are random, and no pattern of UFO witnesses has been found. Witnesses cut across economic, class, racial, and educational lines. A greater percentage of reports, however, have come from people living in rural areas than from those living in urban areas. The reasons for this disparity are unknown.

Witnesses report a great variety of sizes and shapes of UFOs, including amorphous and changing-shape objects. The classic "two bowls joined at the rim" shape is reported often, but reports of objects shaped like cigars, squares, balls, triangles, rings, and hats are also common.

The U.S. Air Force attempted to study the UFO phenomenon from 1948 to 1969 through its Project Blue Book. After collecting reports for 21 years, it concluded that UFOs did not represent a threat to the national security, and it could find no evidence that UFOs were of extraterrestrial origin. In 1953, however, the Central Intelligence Agency suggested that the USSR might be able to use "flying-saucer hysteria" as a psychological warfare weapon against the United States. Therefore, from 1953 to 1969, the U.S. Air Force was concerned mainly with the incidence of UFO reports and never seriously considered the idea that UFOs per se might represent anomalous or unique phenomena.

DAVID M. JACOBS

Bibliography: Hendry, Allan, *The UFO Handbook* (1979); Jacobs, David M., *The UFO Controversy in America* (1975); Sagan, Carl, and Page, Thornton, eds., *UFOs: A Scientific Debate* (1973); Shaeffer, Robert, *The UFO Verdict: Examining the Evidence* (1981).

unified field theory

In the early years of the 20th century classical attempts were made, principally by Albert Einstein, to unify two of the fundamental forces of nature, gravitation and electromagnetism. After presenting his theory of gravitation (the general theory of RELATIVITY), Einstein set out to reconcile his results with the description of electromagnetism given by MAXWELL'S EQUATIONS. Maxwell had described electromagnetism in terms of an antisymmetric tensor, whereas Einstein's theory of gravitation was based on the concept of a symmetric metric tensor (see SYMMETRY, PHYSICS). Einstein's failure to form a successful unified field theory must be judged in light of the fact that two of the fundamental forces, the weak and strong nuclear forces, had not been discovered.

Einstein's idea was to combine both descriptions into a single, nonsymmetric tensor, thereby treating both subjects from an essentially geometric point of view. Other attempts to incorporate electromagnetism into the basically geometric formalism of general relativity were made by Hermann Weyl (1918) and more recently by John Wheeler; although some theories are more aesthetic than others, all lack the connection with quantum phenomena that is so important for interactions other than gravitation.

More-recent attempts at unification have been made from the quite different point of view of merging the quantum field theories that describe (or are supposed to describe) the four fundamental interactions of gravity, electromagnetism, and the weak and the strong nuclear interactions. The most successful unification so far has been given by Steven Weinberg, Abdus Salam, and Sheldon Glashow, joining electromagnetism and the weak interactions (see ELECTROWEAK THEORY). In the simplest version of this type of unified gauge theory, forces are transmitted by the exchange of four different types of particles called bosons, which are assumed to be massless. By means of a "broken symmetry" an effective generation of masses occurs, with three bosons, W^+, W^-, and Z^0 particles, having masses on the order of 50 to 100 times the mass of the proton, and a 4th boson, the photon, remaining massless. The W and Z bosons were detected by high-energy experiments at the CERN laboratories in 1983. Weinberg, Salam, and Glashow shared the 1979 Nobel Prize for physics for their model.

Many other unified theories, involving the strong interaction (GRAND UNIFICATION THEORIES) and even gravitation (supersymmetry theories) have recently been proposed. Such schemes to date have unavoidable and questionable consequences, such as the removal of the separate conservation of baryon and lepton number; they predict that a proton could decay into a lepton plus pions—an improbable event that is being searched for at the present.   H. M. FRIED

Bibliography: Bergmann, Peter G., *Introduction to the Theory of Relativity* (1942; repr. 1976); Einstein, Albert, *The Meaning of Relativity*, 5th ed. (1956); Hadlock, Charles, *Field Theory and Its Classical Problems* (1979); Tonnelat, Marie A., *Einstein's Theory of Unified Fields* (1966).

uniformitarianism

The concept that "the present is the key to the past" was developed by the Scottish geologist James HUTTON (1788); the concept consists of the principle that geological processes in the past operated according to the same natural laws that apply today and was given the name *uniformitarianism* by Sir Charles LYELL (1830).

At the end of the 18th century, geology was in its infancy. CATASTROPHISM—the concept that the Earth was shaped by unique, violent events—was rampant, and some philosophical underpinning was needed to curb the wild fantasies of unbridled speculation. Because geology is primarily an observational science, it inherently lacks some of the discipline of the experimental sciences such as chemistry, where simple, repeatable laboratory tests can in many instances settle disputed theories. In Hutton's day, therefore, geology needed a standard for testing theories. Hutton asserted that "the past history of our globe must be explained by what can be seen to be happening now." Past geologic events were to be explained by processes that could be tested by observation somewhere in the modern world. This approach had the effect of stimulating investigation into contemporary geologic processes, and it simplified investigations of Earth history by eliminating from immediate consideration the more extreme catastrophist explanations. At base, Hutton's principle (which is often called *actualism*) is rooted in the sine qua non of modern science, the belief in the unchanging natural law of an orderly universe.

The subsequent writings of Sir Charles Lyell, particularly the many editions of his *Principles of Geology*, popularized the uniformitarian idea among English-speaking geologists.

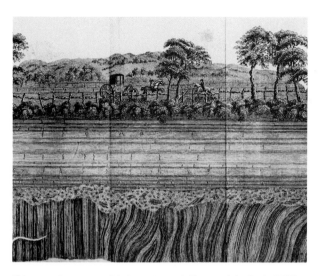

This engraving appeared in James Hutton's Theory of the Earth *(1795), in which he advanced the concept of uniformitarianism as a geological principle. It shows horizontal rock strata resting on inclined strata. Hutton attributed such unconformities between strata to gradual geological processes rather than to sudden catastrophic events.*

Lyell's work extended the meaning of the concept to include the assertion that past geologic processes have operated at a more or less constant rate equivalent to the rates seen today, and that the most important geologic processes are slow. Whereas many important geologic processes—such as erosion or the uplift of folded mountains—are slow, however, some large results also are not necessarily evidences of slow changes; furthermore, changes in rates of processes and probably in conditions, such as atmospheric composition, have occurred. Thus, strict "Lyellian" uniformitarianism (gradualism) is maintained by few geologists today. Actualism, on the other hand, is almost universally accepted.

One of the most important influences of uniformitarianism was on the development of the theory of evolution. Charles Darwin obtained a copy of Lyell's *Principles of Geology* shortly before boarding the *Beagle* for the voyage that led to his theory. Darwin and Lyell were close friends and correspondents, and although Lyell was slow to accept the transmutation of species, he strongly urged his colleague to publish his ideas and eventually become a convert. In Darwin's *Origin of Species* the emphasis is on slow, gradual process operating over eons of time, which is the hallmark of Lyellian uniformitarianism. The extended period of time available for evolution is now indisputably documented by radioisotope dating of ancient rocks; whether evolution is an essentially uniform and gradual process or one punctuated by rapid bursts of change is still a subject of debate.   PAUL BOYER

Bibliography: Albritton, Claude C., ed., *History of Geology* (1978); Berggren, W. A., and Van Couvering, John, eds., *Catastrophes and Earth History: The New Uniformitarianism* (1983); Fenton, Carroll L. and Mildred A., *Giants of Geology*, rev. ed. (1952).

union: see SET THEORY.

union, labor: see LABOR UNION.

Union College

Established in 1795, Union College (enrollment: 3,400; library: 350,000 volumes) was made part of Union University in 1873, along with Albany Medical College (1839), Albany Law School (1951), Dudley Observatory (1852), and Albany College of Pharmacy (1881). A private coeducational liberal arts school in Schenectady, N.Y., Union College was the first liberal arts college to have an engineering program.

Union Islands: see TOKELAU ISLANDS.

Union Jack

The Union Jack is the flag of the United Kingdom of Great Britain and Northern Ireland. It combines the crosses of Saint George of England, Saint Andrew of Scotland, and Saint Patrick of Ireland. The Union Jack's origin is nautical; a jack is a small identifying flag usually flown on the bow of a ship. The flag in its present form has been in use since 1801, when Ireland joined the Union. Its colors are red, white, and blue, and variations of it are the official flags of many former British dependencies.

union label

The union label is an emblem affixed to finished products such as clothing or machinery to show that they were made by members of specific trade unions. The purpose of the label is to encourage purchasers to seek out items that have been made by U.S. union labor, especially in preference to foreign-made items. The Label and Service Trade Department of the AFL-CIO supervises the union label program.

Union Leagues

The Union Leagues were formed during the U.S. Civil War to foster allegiance to the U.S. government. The first units appeared throughout the North in 1862, and in May 1863 a Washington-based national council was created. The Union Leagues distributed patriotic literature, promoted interracial recruiting, and raised funds for soldier relief.

After the Civil War the Union Leagues survived primarily as social clubs in the North. In the South, however, they served for a time to establish Republican party organizations. At first, some antisecessionist southern whites joined, but most of them resigned when the clubs, controlled by radical Republicans, began admitting blacks in 1867. The Ku Klux Klan strongly opposed the Union Leagues. By 1870, they had lost their influence.

Union Pacific Railroad: see TRANSCONTINENTAL RAILROAD.

Union party

The Union party was organized in the United States in 1936 by right-wing critics of President Franklin D. Roosevelt. Its major founders were Father Charles E. COUGHLIN, popular anti-Semitic radio priest; fascist sympathizer Gerald L. K. Smith, head of the late Huey Long's Share the Wealth Movement; and Dr. Francis E. TOWNSEND, old-age pension advocate. It nominated Congressman William Lemke, Republican of North Dakota, for president and Thomas C. O'Brien for vice-president. Because of poor campaign strategy, indifferent press coverage, and gross miscalculation of popular support, the party polled a disappointing 892,378 votes and disintegrated soon after the election.

The name *Union party* was also briefly adopted by the Republicans in 1864, when they renominated Abraham Lincoln for presidency and adopted War Democrat Andrew Johnson as his running mate. The name was soon dropped.

Bibliography: Bennett, David H., *Demagogues in the Depression: American Radicals and the Union Party, 1932–36* (1969); Blackorby, Edward C., *Prairie Rebel: William Lemke* (1963).

union shop

A place of employment where all workers must belong to a union is called a union shop. Anyone may be employed but within a stated time must join the union. This specified time period varies within each industry and according to the contractual agreement between management and labor. The union shop differs from the CLOSED SHOP, where all persons hired must already be union members, and from the OPEN SHOP, where employees need not join a union. Union shops are banned in states where RIGHT-TO-WORK LAWS prescribe an open-shop arrangement.   J. DONALD WEINRAUCH

Bibliography: Hanson, Charles, et al., *The Closed Shop* (1982); Northrup, Herbert, *Open Shop Construction Revisited* (1984).

Union of South Africa: see SOUTH AFRICA.

Union of Soviet Socialist Republics

The Union of Soviet Socialist Republics (usually known as the USSR or the Soviet Union) is the world's largest country, comprising one-sixth of the Earth's land surface. Its 22,402,200 km² (8,649,512 mi²) take up the eastern half of Europe and the northern third of Asia. The USSR includes 11 of the world's 24 time zones. No other country is bounded by so many nations. Along its western borders lie Norway, Finland, Poland, Czechoslovakia, Hungary, and Romania; to its south are Turkey, Iran, Afghanistan, China, Mongolia, and North Korea. The Arctic Ocean forms the northern boundary; to the east lies the Pacific. Neither these coasts nor the Baltic and Black Seas afford the USSR direct access to the world's major shipping lanes.

As the world's first and most militarily powerful socialist state, the USSR commands a preeminent position in international affairs, matched only by that of the United States. Formed on Dec. 30, 1922, the USSR now consists of 15 union republics, 20 autonomous republics, 8 autonomous regions, 10 autonomous districts, 6 territories, and 123 regions. As described in the 1977 constitution, the Soviet Union is governed

UNION OF SOVIET SOCIALIST REPUBLICS

LAND. Area: 22,402,200 km² (8,649,512 mi²). Capital and largest city: Moscow (1986 est. pop., 8,714,000).

PEOPLE. Population (1988 est.): 286,000,000; density: 12.7 persons per km² (33.1 per mi²). Distribution (1988): 65% urban, 35% rural. Annual growth (1987–88): 1.0%. Official language: Russian. Major religions: Eastern Orthodoxy and other Christian churches, Islam, Judaism.

EDUCATION AND HEALTH. Literacy (1988): 99% of adult population. Universities (1987): 69. Hospital beds (1987): 3,669,000. Physicians (1987): 1,202,000. Life expectancy (1988): 69. Infant mortality (1987): 25 per 1,000 live births.

ECONOMY. GNP (1987): $2,116 billion; $7,400 per capita. Labor distribution (1986): agriculture—23%; industry and other nonagricultural fields—77%. Foreign trade (1986): imports— $88.87 billion; exports—$97.05 billion; principal trade partners—East Germany, Czechoslovakia, Bulgaria, Poland, Hungary, Cuba. Currency: 1 ruble = 100 kopeks.

GOVERNMENT. Type: single-party Communist state. Legislature: Supreme Soviet. Political subdivisions: 15 union republics.

COMMUNICATIONS. Railroads (1986): 145,600 km (90,472 mi). Roads (1986): 971,500 km (604,000 mi) total, 84% paved. Major ports: 53. Airfields: 4,530.

ATLANTIC OCEAN

UNITED KINGDOM

●London

NORTH SEA

●Paris
FRANCE
BELG.
LUX.
NETH.
●Amsterdam
●Bonn
●Hamburg
DENMARK
●Copenhagen

SVALBARD
(Norway)

NORWEGIAN SEA

Arctic Circle

BARENTS SEA

Franz Jose

NORWAY
●Bergen
●Oslo

SWEDEN
●Stockholm

Gulf of Bothnia

FINLAND
●Turku
●Helsinki

Baltic Sea

North Cape

NOVAYA ZEMLYA

KARA SEA

WEST GERMANY
EAST GERMANY
●Berlin

SWITZ.
AUSTRIA
●Vienna
CZECHOSLOVAKIA
POLAND
●Warsaw
●Kaliningrad
R.S.F.R.
LITHUANIAN S.S.R.
●Vilna
●Riga
ESTONIAN S.S.R.
Gulf of Finland
●Tallinn
L. Peipus

●Murmansk
●Kirovsk
KOLA PEN.
White Sea
L. Ladoga
●Leningrad
●Petrozavodsk
Lake Onega
●Arkhangelsk
Kolguev Island
Vaygach I.
YAMAL PEN.

YUGOSLAVIA
●Budapest
HUNGARY
ROMANIA
●Bucharest
BULGARIA

●Belgrade

CARPATHIAN MTS.
●Lvov
●Brest
BYELORUSSIAN S.S.R.
●Minsk
●Gomel
UKRAINIAN S.S.R.
●Kiev
●Vinnitsa
●Kishinev
Dnester
Prut
Dnepr
●Smolensk
●Kalinin
●Novgorod
L. Ilmen
Rybinsk Res.
Volga
●Vologda
●Andropov
●Yaroslavl
●Kotlas
N. Dvina
Pechora
●Vorkuta
●Salekhard
Ob. Bay
●Dudinka

Mt. Narodnaya 1894m
RUSSIAN S.F.S.R.
URAL MOUNTAINS
●Sergin
WEST SIBERIAN LOWLAND

●Bryansk
●Orel
●Kursk
●Voronezh
●Moscow (Moskva)
●Ivanovo
●Tula
Oka
Gorki Res.
●Gorky
●Kirov
●Bereznik
●Kazan
●Izhevsk
Kama
●Perm
●Serov
●Khanty-Mansiysk
Ob

●Kharkov
●Odessa
●Krivoy Rog
●Dnepropetrovsk
●Zaporozhye
CRIMEA
●Sevastopol
●Yalta
●Zhdanov
●Donetsk
●Voroshilovgrad
●Rostov-on-Don
Sea of Azov
●Kerch
BLACK SEA
●Ankara
TURKEY
●Ulyanovsk
●Penza
●Saratov
Kuybyshev Res.
●Naberezhnyye Chelny
●Nizhniy Tagil
●Sverdlovsk
●Chelyabinsk
SIBER
Chulym

●Kuibyshev
Belaya
Ufa
URAL
●Magnitogorsk
●Kurgan
●Petropavlovsk
●Omsk
●Tomsk
Yeniseys
●Achins
●Krasnoya

●Krasnodar
●Stavropol
Volgograd Reservoir
Don
●Volgograd
●Orenburg
●Orsk
Tobol
Chany
Irtysh
Novosibirsk Res.
●Novosibirsk
●Kemerovo
●Novo-Kuznetsk

Mt. Elbrus 5642m
CAUCASUS MTS.
●Batumi
●Tbilisi
●Erzurum
ARMENIAN
Mt. Ararat 5165m
●Yerevan
AZERBAIJAN S.S.R.
●Baku
CASPIAN DEPRESSION
●Astrakhan
●Guryev
Emba
KIRGHIZ STEPPE
●Tselinograd
●Pavlodar
●Barnaul
●Biysk
SAYAN
ALTAI MTS.
Mt. Belukha 4506m

●Grozny
●Makhachkala
●Shevchenko
Ural
UST-URT PLATEAU
CASPIAN SEA
●Aralsk
KAZAKH S.S.R.
●Karaganda
KAZAKH STEPPE
●Semipalatinsk
●Ust-Kamenogorsk
Zaysan
Lake Zaysan
L. Alakol

LEB.
SYRIA
Euphrates
IRAQ
●Baghdad
Kara-Bogaz Gulf
●Krasnovodsk
●Kungrad
TURKMEN S.S.R.
TURAN LOWLAND
Amu Darya
Aral Sea
Syr Darya
KYZYL KUM
UZBEK S.S.R.
KARA KUM
Lake Balkhash
●Balkhash
L. Issyk Kul
●Druzba
●Alma-Ata
●Frunze
●Kulja
●Urumchi
TIEN SHAN

NEUTRAL ZONE
SAUDI ARABIA
KUWAIT
●Kuwait
●Abadan
Persian Gulf
ZAGROS MTS.
ELBURZ MTS.
Mt. Demavend 5604m
●Tehran
IRAN
●Ashkhabad
●Mashhad
●Bukhara
●Samarkand
●Tashkent
●Andizhan
KIRGHIZ S.S.R.
●Dushanbe
TADZHIK
Pobedy Pk. 7439m
TURFAN DEPRESSION -154m

●Termez
●Kushka
●Herat
AFGHANISTAN
HINDU KUSH
PAKISTAN
●Kabul
Communism Peak 7495m
PAMIRS
●Kashgar
TAKLA MAKAN DESERT
Lop Nor

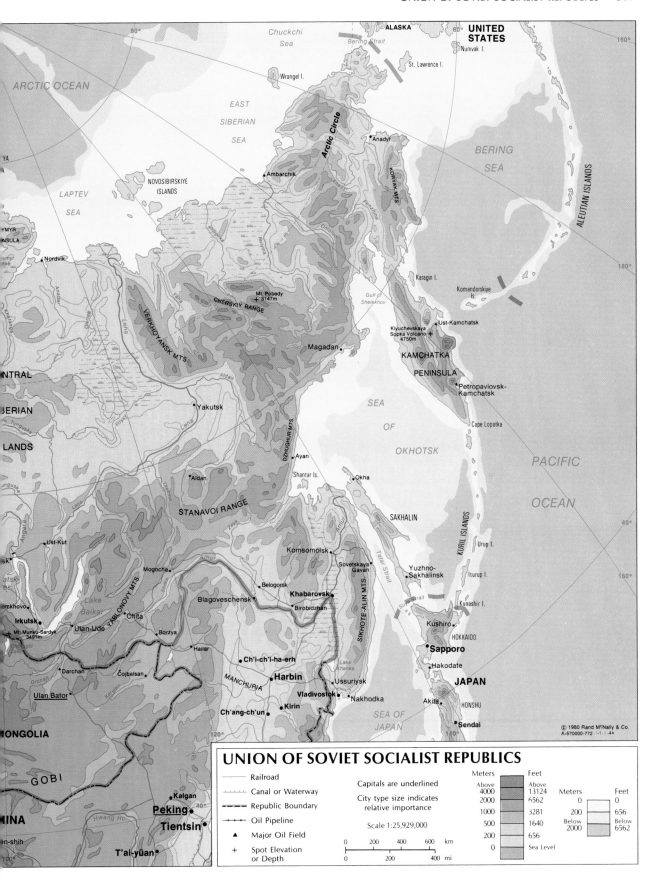

UNION OF SOVIET SOCIALIST REPUBLICS

———	Railroad
⊢⊢⊢⊢	Canal or Waterway
—·—·—	Republic Boundary
+·+·+·	Oil Pipeline
▲	Major Oil Field
+	Spot Elevation or Depth

Capitals are underlined

City type size indicates relative importance

Scale 1:25,929,000

0	200	400	600	km
0		200	400	mi

Meters	Feet
Above 4000	Above 13124
2000	6562
1000	3281
500	1640
200	656
0	Sea Level

Meters	Feet
0	0
200	656
Below 2000	Below 6562

© 1980 Rand McNally & Co.
A-570000-772 -1-1-46

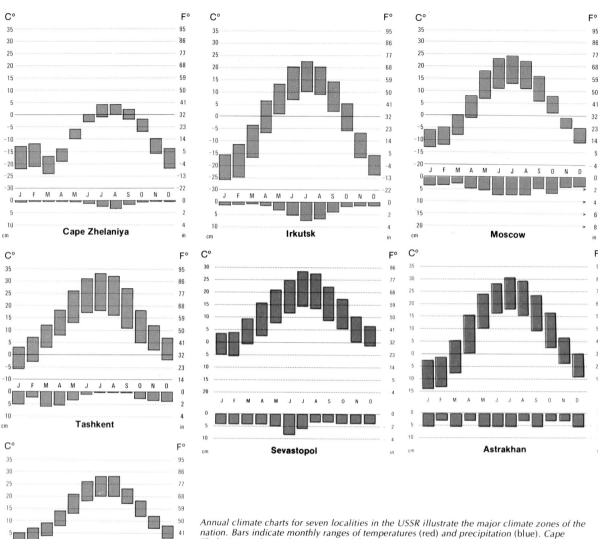

Annual climate charts for seven localities in the USSR illustrate the major climate zones of the nation. Bars indicate monthly ranges of temperatures (red) and precipitation (blue). Cape Zhelaniya, at the northern extreme of the Arctic islands of Novaya Zemlya, has the severe temperatures and low precipitation of the tundra. Irkutsk, an industrial center located 48 km (30 mi) northwest of Lake Baikal in southern Siberia, has a subarctic climate of extreme temperature variation. The capital and largest city of the USSR, Moscow has the continental humid climate characteristic of its central continental location. Tashkent, a commercial center at an oasis of the Central Asian desert, has a steppe climate. The port and naval base Sevastopol, located on the Black Sea coast of the Crimean Peninsula, has a temperate Mediterranean climate, whereas Astrakhan, a port on the Caspian Sea at the mouth of the Volga River, has the minimal precipitation and high temperatures of the surrounding desert region. Lenkoran, a Caspian Sea port near the Iranian border, has the mild temperatures and high precipitation of a subtropical humid climate.

by Soviets ("councils") of People's Deputies, with the Communist party of the Soviet Union (CPSU) constituting "the leading and directing force of Soviet society and the nucleus of its political system." The party in turn is said to be guided by the principles of Marxism-Leninism, according to which the USSR has achieved socialism, but not yet communism, considered the highest stage of human existence.

Thanks to its immense size, the USSR contains an abundance of raw material, fuel, and power resources. These began to be extensively exploited with the advent of full industrialization in the 1930s. At that time and well into the period after World War II, Soviet policy emphasized heavy industry. Virtually all substantial industrial enterprises are state owned, though provisions for small-scale producer and service cooperatives and joint ownership of industrial enterprises with foreign firms now exist.

Despite prodigious advances in certain fields, most notably education and space exploration, the USSR has lagged con-

siderably in the development of computer technology and the availability and quality of housing and consumer goods. In agriculture the USSR is the world's largest producer of wheat, potatoes, cotton, and sugar. These and other crops are produced primarily on state farms (sovkhozy) and collective farms (kolkhozy). Private garden plots, which constitute less than 4% of arable land, account for a much larger proportion of certain vegetable and dairy products.

The Soviet Union is more or less coextensive with the Russian Empire, which was overthrown by the RUSSIAN REVOLUTIONS OF 1917. A civil war followed in which the BOLSHEVIKS (Communists), led by V. I. LENIN, prevailed. Lenin is revered today as the founding father of the Soviet Union. After his death (1924), Joseph STALIN seized power, defeating in turn the Left Opposition under Leon TROTSKY and the Right Oppositionists including Nikolai BUKHARIN. Stalin launched campaigns to collectivize agriculture and develop heavy industry; he provided the country with a modern industrial base, but at

This small village in the USSR's central Urals clings to the heavily forested hillside. With coniferous and deciduous forests covering approximately one-third of its land area, the USSR produces vast quantities of paper, paper products, and sawed timber.

the cost of massive social dislocation, violence, and loss of life. No less traumatic was the GREAT PURGE of 1936–38, a reign of terror in which millions perished. This was followed by the devastation of World War II, remembered with pride because of the Soviet victory over the German invaders.

The death of Stalin in 1953 was followed by a "thaw" in cultural policy and a period of economic and political reform under Nikita S. KHRUSHCHEV. In October 1964, however, Khrushchev was forced to resign as general secretary owing to the failure of his agricultural policies, his shake-up of the party structure, and a series of diplomatic defeats. His successor, Leonid I. BREZHNEV, presided over a period of unprecedented political stability and economic prosperity. He also pursued an improvement in relations with the West, which had been so bad since the late 1940s that they were characterized as a COLD WAR.

Stability, however, proved detrimental to innovation, and in Brezhnev's last years economic stagnation and social malaise set in. At the same time, détente gave way to renewed East-West tensions, particularly after the Soviet intervention in Afghanistan in 1979. Yuri V. ANDROPOV, former chairman of the State Security Committee (KGB) and a stern disciplinarian, succeeded Brezhnev upon the latter's death in 1982. Andropov's agenda for sweeping changes in personnel and social policy was cut short by his death in 1984. The pace of reform temporarily slowed under Konstantin U. CHERNENKO (1984–85), a protégé of Brezhnev. But since March 1985 the position of general secretary has been occupied by the much younger and more vigorous Mikhail S. GORBACHEV. Under the watchwords GLASNOST ("openness") and *perestroika* ("restructuring"), Gorbachev has encouraged public debate about the Soviet model of socialism, its past failings and successes, and future course. In September 1988 Gorbachev strengthened his position by a thorough reorganization of party and government structures in which he himself assumed the presidency.

LAND AND RESOURCES

The broad Russian (or East European) plain, covering most of the European part of the country, extends from the Baltic Sea to the URAL MOUNTAINS and from the shores of the Arctic Ocean to the northern coast of the Black Sea. The plain has an average altitude of 170 m (560 ft) above sea level. Hills with an elevation of about 300–400 m (1,000–1,300 ft) separate a series of lowland depressions. The plain is bordered in the extreme northwest by the uplands of KARELIA and the mountains of the Kola Peninsula; in the southwest and south by the moderately high CARPATHIAN and Crimean mountain ranges; in the southeast by the much higher CAUCASUS MOUNTAINS; and in the east by the less formidable Ural Mountains, which run for some 2,000 km (1,240 mi) from north to south and constitute the traditional boundary between Europe and Asia.

To the east of the Urals lies the enormous expanse of SIBERIA. This is divided into a flat and largely swampy West Siberian Plain, which is connected in the south to the Turan Lowland; the Central Siberian Plateau, which is bounded by the YENISEI RIVER on the west and the LENA RIVER on the east; and a series of mountain ranges running in arclike fashion between the Lena and the Pacific Ocean. Jutting out from eastern Siberia for nearly 1,300 km (800 mi) is the KAMCHATKA PENINSULA, which along with the KURIL ISLANDS lying to its south forms part of the East Asian volcanic arc.

The highest mountain ranges in the Soviet Union lie along its southern border. In addition to the Caucasus, which rise to a maximum height of 5,642 m (18,510 ft) at Mount ELBRUS, they include the PAMIRS on the border with Afghanistan, the TIEN SHAN on the Chinese frontier, and farther to the east, the ALTAI MOUNTAINS on the border of Mongolia. The highest mountain in the USSR is COMMUNISM PEAK, with an elevation of 7,495 m (24,590 ft), located in the Pamirs in the TADZHIK SSR. The lowest elevation is 132 m (433 ft) below sea level, recorded in the Mangyshliak Peninsula, which abuts the eastern shore of the CASPIAN SEA.

Soviet territory includes a number of large islands and island groups. In the Pacific, these include the Kuril Islands, SAKHALIN, which runs north-south for more than 900 km (560 mi), and the easternmost extension of the Aleutian chain. Arctic islands include FRANZ JOSEF LAND, NOVAYA ZEMLYA, the Novosibirskye Islands, Severnaya Zemlya, and WRANGEL ISLAND.

Soils. The Soviet plains reveal a series of distinct soil belts, or zones. Along the Arctic coast, covering about 8% of Soviet territory, is a band of infertile tundra soil that is more or less permanently frozen. South of the tundra lies the gray brown belt of taiga soils roughly corresponding to the coniferous forest zone and constituting a third of the country.

Farther still to the south stretches the black-earth (CHERNOZEM) zone, occupying about 9% of the country and nearly half the world's area of this soil type. The black earth lies under the grassy vegetation of the steppe and forest steppe. Rich in humus, it is the most fertile zone and the area in which most of the country's grain crops are grown. To the east and beyond the Caspian Sea to the south, the soil contains less moisture and humus, and its color is more that of chestnut. In the semidesert and desert areas of Central Asia, these soils give way to gray-earth soils (serozems), high in salt content.

Red-earth soils are present in parts of the Caucasus and the foothills of the Central Asian ranges. Elsewhere in the 31% of Soviet territory consisting of mountainous terrain, vertical bands of soil, generally thin and stony, can be found.

Climate. With the exception of the southern Far Eastern coast, which has a foggy monsoonal climate and the Baltic and Black Sea littorals, the climate almost everywhere in the Soviet Union is markedly continental. Continentality increases from west to east and is particularly evident in Central Asia and eastern Siberia, where the temperature range is greatest and precipitation the least.

Four latitudinal climatic belts can be discerned. The far north displays an Arctic climate. Mean temperatures in summer hover around the freezing point and in January reach −50° C (−58° F) at Verkhoiansk in eastern Siberia, where the world's lowest temperature outside of Antarctica has been recorded. Northern European Russia and Siberia above 60°

The peaks of Mount Elbrus, the highest mountain in the Caucasus Mountains, rise to an elevation of 5,642 m (18,510 ft) from the surrounding steppelands. Both the broad plains and small river valleys of the region are cultivated to produce important grain crops.

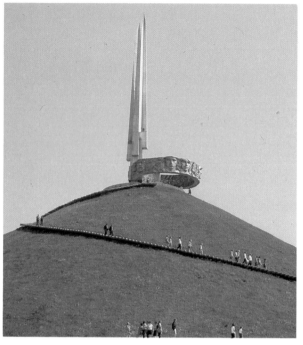

The Kurgan Slabi, a memorial to the Soviet war dead of World War II, is situated near Minsk. The capital and largest city of the Belorussian S.S.R., Minsk was virtually destroyed when it was recaptured from the Germans during the Soviet offensive in 1944.

north latitude are in a subarctic belt; the remainder of European Russia and Siberia as well as most of Central Asia are in the temperate belt; and parts of Transcaucasia and the southernmost areas of Central Asia are subtropical.

In winter a cold continental air mass situated over eastern Siberia spreads cold dry air throughout much of the rest of the country. Mean temperatures for January reach a high of 6° C (43° F) at Batumi on the Black Sea but in most places are below freezing. Precipitation is greatest in the west, where 200 to 300 mm (8 to 12 in) are recorded between October and March, and least in Central Asia and eastern Siberia, where only 50 to 100 mm (2 to 4 in) fall. Winter precipitation is mostly in the form of snow.

In summer a system of low pressure covers Soviet territory, except the southern Russian plain. Winds are predominantly westerly, bringing moisture-laiden air from the Atlantic. Consequently, most precipitation falls during the warm half of the year, averaging 500 mm (20 in) in the west but only 150–200 mm (6–8 in) in eastern Siberia. The heaviest rainfall—up to 1,200 mm (47 in)—is in the western Caucasus, the least on the southern Turan plain in the Uzbek and Turkmen republics.

Drainage.   About half of all rivers in the USSR drain into the Arctic Ocean. The largest of these are the Northern DVINA and PECHORA in European Russia and the OB, Yenisei, Lena, and Kolyma of Siberia. The Pacific Ocean's Bering Sea, Sea of Japan, and Sea of Okhotsk drain all the Far Eastern rivers, the largest of which is the AMUR. The Atlantic Ocean ultimately receives the waters of rivers that empty into the Black Sea (the Danube, DNEPR, and DNESTR), the Sea of Azov (DON and Kuban) and the Baltic Sea (the NEVA and Western DVINA). The internal Caspian-Aral drainage basin covers the eastern Caucasus, the southeastern part of the Russian plain, the desert and semidesert areas of the Turan plain, and the Pamir and Tien Shan ranges. The VOLGA River, the longest in Europe, and the Ural flow into the Caspian; the AMU DARYA and SYR DARYA drain into the ARAL Sea. Most rivers are covered with ice for part of the year—up to 8 or 9 months in the extreme north.

The USSR contains approximately 270,000 lakes, including five of the world's largest: the Caspian and Aral Seas, Lake

BAIKAL, whose depth of 1,620 m (5,315 ft) makes it the world's deepest, Lake BALKHASH, and Lake LADOGA. Unevenly distributed throughout Soviet territory, the lakes vary considerably in mineral-salt and sulfate content. Diversion of the flow of the Amu Darya and Syr Darya has significantly increased the salinity and lowered the level of the Aral Sea. Marshlands cover nearly 10% of Soviet territory, primarily in the tundra and forest zones where precipitation exceeds evaporation.

Vegetation and Animal Life.   As with soils and climate, natural vegetation follows a latitudinally based zonal pattern. In the far north is the TUNDRA zone, where vegetation is restricted to mosses, lichens, and scrub; animal life includes the Arctic fox, reindeer, lemmings, and in summer, migratory geese, ducks, and swans. The largest vegetational zone is the TAIGA, in which coniferous forests of fir, pine, and larch harbor elk, deer, brown bear, lynx, sable, squirrels, and foxes. Toward the south, broad-leaved trees such as birch, oak, maple, lime, and ash are interspersed with the conifers and in this area are found such representative fauna as deer, wild pig, and mink. A transition zone of forest-steppe gives way farther south to the mixed-grass and grassy steppe, which is now almost entirely under the plow. Trees exist only along river banks or flood plains. The most common animals are burrowing rodents (marmot, jerboa, hamster) and such birds as the kestrel, lark, and eagle. Finally, the southernmost zone consists of semidesert and desert vegetation such as dry grasses, wormwood, and saltwort that support the jackel, lizards, spiders, ravens, and bustards. Vegetation and fauna along parts of the Black Sea coast are of the Mediterranean type.

Natural Resources.   The Soviet Union has a wide variety of mineral resources. Coal reserves are widely scattered, and large quantities are exported. Oil, which has been produced since the 1880s, is found mainly in the Volga-Urals area as well as in the North Caucasus, western Siberia, and the older fields at BAKU in AZERBAIJAN. Natural gas, the production of which has greatly increased in recent years, is extracted principally from the Volga-Urals, the Ukraine, and western Siberia. Soviet iron-ore reserves account for approximately 40% of the world's total. Among the nonferrous ores, manganese, copper, chromium, and magnesium are produced in large quantities, as are nickel and tungsten. Soviet gold production is thought to rank second in the world.

Arable land constitutes only 10% of Soviet territory, while another 17% consists of meadows and pastures. The agricultural belt stretches from the western border of the country into Siberia south of Omsk and Novosibirsk and north of the Turan Lowland. Some 40% of the country is forested.

Water resources are abundant but unevenly distributed. The most water-deprived part of the country are the Central Asian republics, while the soggiest area is the north.

PEOPLE

Although the number of distinct ethnic or nationality groups in the USSR has been steadily declining, more than 100 still exist, most of which are associated with a particular republic or lesser political entity. Of the 15 union republics, the largest and most populous is the RUSSIAN SOVIET FEDERATED SOCIALIST REPUBLIC (RSFSR), in which Great Russians predominate. Two other Slavic nationalities inhabit the UKRAINIAN and BELORUSSIAN republics. The MOLDAVIAN republic in the southwest is inhabited mainly by a people related to Romanians, and the LITHUANIAN, LATVIAN, and ESTONIAN republics by those three Baltic peoples, although Russians constitute a sizable minority, particularly in Latvia and Estonia (see BALTIC STATES). The 3 Transcaucasian republics—the ARMENIAN, GEORGIAN, and AZERBAIJAN—are based on the largest nationality groups in that region. The remaining 5 republics, constituting Soviet Central Asia, are the KAZAKH, UZBEK, TADZHIK, TURKMEN, and KIRGHIZ republics. The Uzbeks are the most numerous of the Central Asian peoples. Among the larger ethnic groups living either in autonomous republics of their own or scattered among different administrative areas are the Tatars, Bashkirs, Germans, Jews, and Poles. Indigenous Siberian peoples are widely scattered and in some cases number only a few thousand.

Languages. Russian is the official language of the USSR and also is the native tongue of the largest nationality group. Ukrainian and Belorussian are closely related to Russian and

This shopping district is in Irkutsk, an administrative capital in southeastern Siberia. A river port and industrial center, Irkutsk produces heavy machinery and a variety of consumer goods.

together with it, make up the main Slavic languages spoken within the country. Other Indo-European languages are the two Baltic languages, Latvian and Lithuanian; the Romance language of the Moldavians (Romanians); Armenian; and the Iranian language of the Tadzhiks and Ossetes. Four subfamilies of Ural-Altaic languages exist in the Soviet Union. The Turkic subfamily is represented by Azerbaijani, Kazakh, Kirghiz, Turkmen, Uzbek, and Tatar; the Finno-Ugric subfamily is represented primarily by Estonian; Kalmyk and Buryat are the main Mongolic languages; and the Tungusic subfamily is spoken by a variety of Siberian peoples.

Ethnic groups use their indigenous language as a second official language within their particular ethnic territory.

Religion. Since 1918, church and state have been officially separated, as have the school and the church. This is in contrast to—and was in reaction against—the prerevolutionary period, when Russian Orthodoxy was closely integrated into the structure of the tsarist state. According to Article 52 of the 1977 constitution, citizens of the USSR are guaranteed "the right to profess or not to profess any religion, and to conduct religious worship or atheistic propaganda." The state has reserved the right to distinguish between the profession and propagation of religion, and those accused of the latter have been severely repressed on occasion.

It is impossible to accurately determine the number of religious believers or church members, but it has been estimated that some 40% of the population could be included in the former category. The Russian Orthodox church, which celebrated 1,000 years of Christianity in 1988, commands the membership of the dominant Slavic groups (except for sizable numbers of Ukrainians who are affiliated with a branch of Catholicism that was banned by Soviet authorities in the late 1940s) as well as Moldavians and some Finno-Ugric peoples. Western Christianity is represented by Catholicism (primarily among the Lithuanians), as well as by Lutheranism (among Latvians and Estonians) and other Protestant groups. Both the Georgians and the Armenians have their own national Christian churches.

The Turkic-speaking peoples of the USSR are mainly Muslims, making Islam the second most important religious faith in the USSR. Buddhism, the predominant religion among the Mongolic-language groups, and Judaism have smaller, though still significant, numbers of believers.

Demography. Like other developed societies, the USSR has exhibited a long-term decline in both birthrates and death rates, although the rate of decline in the birthrate has been greater in European Russia than in areas such as Central Asia. Since emigration and immigration are statistically negligible, population growth has occurred almost entirely as a result of the excess of births over deaths.

Soviet history has been marked by several demographic catastrophes. The civil war was accompanied by widespread epidemics and a process of deurbanization, followed by a severe famine in 1921–22. Famine struck again in 1932–33 in connection with the dislocations caused by collectivization, particularly in the Ukraine and the north Caucasus. The greatest catastrophe of all was World War II, which cost the USSR some 20 million lives.

Roughly two-thirds of the Soviet population live in what are classified as urban areas. This is in marked contrast to 1928, when more than four-fifths of the population was rural based. Twenty-two cities have populations in excess of one million. They are: MOSCOW, LENINGRAD, GORKY, KIUBYSHEV, and KAZAN in European Russia; SVERDLOVSK, CHELYABINSK, PERM, and UFA in the Urals; NOVOSIBIRSK and OMSK in Siberia; KIEV, KHARKOV, DNEPROPETROVSK, ODESSA, and DONETSK in the Ukraine; MINSK in Belorussia; BAKU, TBILISI, and YEREVAN in Transcaucasia; and TASHKENT and ALMA-ATA in Central Asia.

Health and Health Care. The medical and dental professions are socialized in the USSR. Medical care is essentially free to patients, who may be treated either in clinics attached to their places of work or at district and city hospitals and clinics. Private practice is permitted by law but is restricted and rare.

Medical practitioners consist of doctors, who receive six years of specialized training, and paramedics, known as feldshers, who have four years of training. Public health is a sphere in which female employment is predominant; about two-thirds of all doctors are women. Salaries are on average below manual workers' wages.

The quality of medical care is the source of much complaint. It tends to be poorest in small towns and rural areas. The USSR has one of the world's highest physician-patient ratios, although there is considerable regional variation. The ratio is highest in the Georgian republic and lowest in the Tadzhik republic.

Science. State support for scientific research is extensive, and much emphasis is placed on the transformation of scientific knowledge into technology, a process known in the USSR as the scientific-technical revolution. Research is conducted in thousands of institutes throughout the country, mostly under the authority of the ACADEMY OF SCIENCES OF THE USSR and its affiliates. Government ministries and higher educational establishments also sponsor research, as do the All-Union Lenin Academy of Agricultural Sciences and the USSR Academy of Medical Sciences. (For information on schools, see SOVIET EDUCATION.)

The fate of science and scientists has varied considerably under successive Soviet administrations. In the Stalin era, scientists were forced to conform to official scientific doctrines laid down by the party, and scientific progress suffered as a result. In more recent decades, Soviet science has made great strides in certain fields, but it has lagged behind the United States and other western nations in terms of the application of theoretical work. This has been the case particularly in the medical sciences, chemistry, and biology, where the application of advanced technology has been increasingly important. The computer revolution is slowly penetrating Soviet society, and this is one area where the Gorbachev administration is committed to investing heavily.

Arts. From the classical refinement of the ballet and impassioned poetry readings to the acrobatics of the Moiseyev dance troupe and the broad, slapstick humor of the circus, the arts occupy an especially important place in Soviet life. State support of the arts, through such agencies as Glavlit, Goskontsert, and Goskino, and the Communist party's ideologically informed cultural policy have circumscribed the range and themes of artistic expression. But even within those limits, which have fluctuated from time to time, Soviet artists have made major contributions to modern culture.

The arts were swept by several competing movements during the first decade of Soviet power, as rival schools sought to translate the revolutionary dynamism in politics into a new vision of culture. While poets such as Anna AKHMATOVA, Osip MANDELSTAM, and Boris PASTERNAK stood aloof from these developments, others, most notably Vladimir MAYAKOVSKY and Sergei YESENIN, were profoundly affected by them, although in different ways. Prose writers, such as Boris PILNYAK, Isaac BABEL, Mikhail BULGAKOV, and Mikhail ZOSHCHENKO, vividly and often humorously captured the contradictions of the times in their short stories. Also noteworthy were the films of Sergei EISENSTEIN and Dziga VERTOV and the graphics of El LISSITSKY.

All this came to an end during the First Five-Year Plan, when writers and other artists were under heavy pressure from the Communist party to portray the "passion for construction." Construction novels, such as Valentin KATAYEV's *Time Forward!* (1932; Eng. trans., 1933) and Nikolai Ostrovsky's *How the Steel Was Tempered* (1934; Eng. trans., n.d.) fulfilled this demand and served as prototypes for the officially prescribed doctrine of SOCIALIST REALISM. Fine arts, music, and architecture felt the impact of socialist realism as well. In painting and sculpture, depictions of muscle-bound workers and smiling collective farmers crowded out other themes, and abstractionism was deemed decadent; in music, the romantic tradition was extolled; and in architecture, neoromantic monumentality prevailed.

Even in the context of such limitations, some Soviet writers and artists managed to enrich Soviet and world culture. Mikhail SHOLOKHOV was awarded (1965) a Nobel prize, largely on the strength of his novel *And Quiet Flows the Don* (4 vols., 1928–40; Eng. trans. in 2 vols., 1934–40); Sergei PROKOFIEV, Dmitry SHOSTAKOVICH, and Aram KHATCHATURIAN each composed a large body of music that has entered the classical repertoire; Soviet ballet also maintained its high standards.

Upon the death of Stalin, literary controls were relaxed. A new generation of poets emerged, among whom Yevgeny YEVTUSHENKO and Andrei VOZNESENSKY were most prominent. Still, restrictions on what could be published persisted. Pasternak's novel *Doctor Zhivago* (1958) had to be published abroad, setting a precedent that was followed by other authors, including Aleksandr SOLZHENITSYN, who was stripped of his Soviet citizenship in 1973. In addition to *tamizdat* (works published abroad), many authors resorted to circulating their works in the form of *samizdat* ("self-publishing").

In the meantime, the canons of socialist realism were stretched almost to the point of meaninglessness, and censorship appeared increasingly arbitrary and ineffective. Novelists such as Yuri Trifonov, Fedor Abramov, Valerii Rasputin, Sergei Zalygin, Anatoli Rybakov, Fazil Iskander, and Chinghiz Aitmatov have been able to explore a wide range of themes, not all of which affirm the Soviet way of life. Under the policy of *glasnost*, literature, the cinema, and the theater have been enlivened, and the range of cultural discourse has expanded to unprecedented proportions.

ECONOMIC ACTIVITY

The chief characteristic of the Soviet economic system has been the administration of all industry, transportation, construction, wholesale and most retail trade, as well as a substantial part of agricultural production by central state institutions. The only economic activities not directly administered by the state have been the collective farms, the family plots belonging to collective farmers, and the collective-farm-market sector of retail trade.

Since the First Five-Year Plan of 1928–32, when this system took shape, the entire economy, including the price structure, has been tied to five-year plans that are adjusted annually and even quarterly to take account of and correct imbalances. Prior to 1928, the New Economic Policy (NEP) prevailed, under which state ownership was limited to the "commanding heights" of the economy (large-scale industry, banking, and foreign commerce). Full-scale industrialization and forced collectivization ensued, driving millions of peasants to con-

The Bolshoi Ballet, the premier company of Moscow, performs the Stone Flower, *one of the more colorful ballets of its repertoire, based on Russian folktales and danced to music by Sergei Prokofiev. This world-renowned company traces its origins to a ballet school for orphans founded in 1773. Ballet is an extremely popular art form in the USSR.*

struction sites or into towns and setting back productivity on the land for at least a decade. The emphasis in industry was on developing means of production and armaments rather than consumer goods or housing, and this emphasis continued until after Stalin's death.

While the USSR enjoyed considerable economic growth in the 1950s and 1960s, the failure of the party and state to effectively administer more complex economic processes and the poor performance of the agricultural and service sectors kept growth rates low in the 1970s and early 1980s. Since 1985 the Soviet government has embarked on an ambitious program of acceleration of economic mechanisms. This program has included the reintroduction of limited private enterprise, and more flexible price structure, decentralization of economic decision-making down to the enterprise level, and other reforms as well.

Manufacturing. The USSR is the world's leading producer of a number of important industrial goods including pig iron, cement, and steel. In recent decades, the chemical industry, aided by the rapid growth of oil and natural-gas extraction, has expanded. Industrial plants are typically large, though not nearly as sophisticated in design or automation as in the industrialized West. The greatest concentration of manufacturing is in the Ukraine, near traditional sources of fuel, and in the Central Industrial Region, which stretches from Moscow east to Gorky.

Mining. The Soviet Union remains essentially self-sufficient in industrial raw materials and fuels. The KRIVOI ROG area in the eastern Ukraine has long been a center of iron-ore mining. Coal is produced in widely scattered areas, from the DONETS BASIN in the Ukraine and the Pechora River region in the northern RSFSR, to the KUZNETSK BASIN of western Siberia and the Karaganda Basin in Kazakhstan. The Urals are the source for most nonferrous minerals, except for gold, which is mined in the Lena River basin, in the far northeast of Siberia, and in the Tien Shan mountains of Central Asia.

The Baku oil fields, for many decades the major petroleum-producing area in the country, are all but depleted. Newer areas, however, particularly in the Volga-Urals region and in the Tiumen district of western Siberia, have more than compensated. The USSR thus remains one of the world's largest petroleum producers, exporting large quantities to Eastern Europe. Finally, natural-gas production has expanded rapidly, and in recent years the USSR has become a major supplier to Western Europe.

Energy. The essential problem for Soviet planners with respect to energy sources is how to tap the potentially unlimited reserves that lie to the east of the Urals without making it prohibitively expensive to do so. Two strategies have been pursued simultaneously. One has been to develop means of transportation that will convey large quantities of energy from the more remote regions of the east to the more populated and industrialized areas of the country. The other has been to locate new industry in Siberia and encourage migration to the area. While monetary and other benefits have attracted many to work in the relatively inhospitable climate of Siberia, turnover has been high.

Coal was once the principal energy source, but its use has declined considerably since the 1950s. Petroleum, gas, hydroelectric, and nuclear power have all been developed rapidly since 1960. Gigantic dams built across the ANGARA RIVER at Bratsk and on the Kama River provide abundant electricity for nearby industrial plants built in the 1960s and '70s. Nuclear power has been generated, especially in the European part of the country, to offset that area's deficiency of mineral fuels. According to the Twelfth Five-Year Plan (1986–90), 20% of all power is to be derived from nuclear power stations. However, the nuclear power program suffered a major setback in April 1986, when several explosions occurred at the CHERNOBYL plant north of Kiev. The radiation released into the atmosphere caused the evacuation of several hundred thousand people in the surrounding area and the contamination of much of the Ukraine and several neighboring countries. This was the worst accident in the history of nuclear power generation.

Magnitogorsk, one of the principal metallurgic centers of the USSR, is located on the Ural River in the Russian republic. The construction of this planned city, on the site of both iron and magnetite deposits, was the focus of the USSR's first Five-Year Plan (1928–32).

Agriculture. Soviet agriculture comprises three distinct institutional arrangements: state farms, which operate more or less as industrial enterprises, paying wages and salaries to their work force; collective farms, cooperative units that sell a fixed quota of their output to the state at predetermined prices and remunerate their members on the basis of a complex system of labor inputs; and private plots belonging to collective farmers and workers in industry and the state-farm sector. Although representing only a tiny part of total crop acreage, the private plots account for a significant proportion of the USSR's vegetables, meat, and dairy products.

Flax and dairy farming are prominent in the far north. South of this zone, potatoes, rye, and hemp are cultivated and livestock production is carried out extensively. Farther to the south, in the broad steppe region, wheat, barley, and corn are the principal crops, though in the western Ukraine, sugar beets are the main crop. The dryer, eastern part of the steppe supports sheep grazing and cotton production. Fruit and vegetables are abundant in the small subtropical areas of the Crimea, the southern Caucasus, and Central Asia.

In the opinion of most western experts, agriculture is the Achilles' heel of the Soviet economy. Lack of motivation among state farm workers, whose income is not usually tied to their performance, and collective farmers, who have suffered because of the relatively low prices paid by the state for their produce, is certainly a major factor inhibiting productivity. Others include the low prestige attached to agricultural work and the relative lack of cultural amenities in the countryside, both of which have contributed to the out-migration of talented and skilled youths; inefficient utilization of agricultural machinery and its poor quality; the inadequacy of infrastructure such as paved roads, medical care, and storage facilities; the campaign style of administration—whereby great attention would be devoted to a particular crop or technique for a short period of time—which led to several disasters in the 1960s; and the vagaries of weather.

(Left) *The small village of Listvenitshnoie is located along the shore of Lake Baikal, in southeastern Siberia. This body of water is Eurasia's largest, and the world's deepest, freshwater lake.*

(Below) *Dessert wine is produced from grapes grown on the foothills of the Caucasus Mountains in the Georgian republic. Because this region is sheltered by the mountains, it enjoys a warm climate suitable for grape cultivation.*

As a result of the shift in the Soviet diet toward meat consumption and the inability of agriculture to meet the need for high-grade fodder, the USSR has had to import cereal crops from several western countries. Self-sufficiency in cereals is one of the key aims of current agricultural policy.

Forestry. The USSR ranks as the world's leading producer of timber. The locus of the industry has shifted from the depleted forests of central European Russia northward and, more recently, eastward into Siberia. The processing of the timber into pulp, paper, particle board, and plywood has benefited in recent decades from the expansion of the electricity grid and the chemicals industry, but has been a major source of water pollution, particularly in Lake Baikal. As in the case of energy and mineral resources, supplies of timber are abundant, but most are located in regions that are remote and can only be tapped at great economic and human costs.

Fishing. The USSR along with Japan has one of the world's largest fishing industries. Soviet trawlers and factory ships ply the fishing grounds off the North American and African Atlantic coasts as well as the Pacific. Dried and salted fish have long been a feature of the Russian diet, and the USSR is the leading producer of caviar—the processed salted roe of sturgeon—culled mainly from the Caspian Sea.

As in agriculture and the fur and timber industries, fishing in the USSR is organized along state and cooperative lines.

Transportation. The USSR's immense overland expanses and the spread of its principal production area across several thousand kilometers have placed a premium on the development of a national transportation network. The need for transporting large quantities of bulk items over long distances and the predominant flatness of the terrain have contributed to making railroads the principal mode of transport.

The TRANS-SIBERIAN RAILROAD, completed in the early years of this century, opened up Siberia and the Russian Far East to settlement and food and mineral production. During the 1920s the Turksib line was constructed, linking the Central Asian cities of Tashkent and Alma-Ata to the rest of the nation's rail network. Not until the construction of the Baikal-Amur Mainline (BAM) in the 1970s and early 1980s was another project of these dimensions undertaken. The main purpose of the railroad, which runs north of the Trans-Siberian, is to tap hitherto inaccessible resources, although its military value in case of a war with China is thought to have played a role in its location as well. The reconstruction of many lines and the introduction of diesel and electrical traction have greatly enhanced the efficiency of Soviet railroads. Electrical systems, including both tram and trolley bus services, play a crucial role in urban and suburban passenger conveyance. Underground rail, or subway, systems serve all the largest Soviet cities.

Next to railroads, the USSR's extensive pipeline network is the most important in economic terms. Carrying oil and natural gas from the Volga-Urals region and western Siberia, the network traverses Siberia and extends westward to the main exporting ports on the Baltic and Black seas, the industrial centers of the USSR, and across land to the rest of Europe.

Road transport is limited mainly to short-haul movements, connecting farms with railheads. The highway system, densest in the European part of the country, generally has kept pace with increases in automobile and truck production. However, there is much room for improvement in road maintenance and amenities for vehicular traffic. Inland water transport constitutes only a small proportion of overall freight movement. The Volga system is the main artery, linking Moscow with the Caspian Sea and the Urals and, via the Volga-Don canal, the Ukraine and the Black Sea ports. The Soviet merchant marine has expanded to become one of the world's largest. In addition to carrying most of the freight destined for export, it connects the Soviet Far East and northern Siberia with the rest of the country through the northern sea route.

Air transport is used mostly for passenger travel. Serving more than 3,500 localities within the USSR and linking it to

Ruins of the 14th-century Gediminas Castle overlook the confluence of the Neris and Vilna rivers, with the city of Vilna in the distance. Settled during the 10th century, Vilna is today the capital of the Lithuanian republic and is a major industrial and cultural center.

countries in Europe, Africa, Asia, and North America, Soviet air transport accounts for approximately one-quarter of the world total by volume of traffic.

Trade. Goods are distributed in four different ways in the USSR. First in terms of total sales are state outlets, which sell items at uniform prices throughout the country. These prices are fixed by the State Committee on Prices, and in most cases they have remained stable for several decades, irrespective of steadily rising production costs in agriculture and falling costs in industry. Second, there are consumer cooperatives, which primarily serve rural regions. Prices charged by the cooperatives are generally higher than in state stores, but the quality and variety of produce are greater. The third type of retail trade consists of collective farm markets, where prices are essentially determined by supply and demand. Finally, retail sales occur informally either by barter arrangement or through the private sale of used or contraband goods.

Foreign trade has played a relatively minor role in Soviet economic activity, partly because of the country's rich and diverse economic base and partly because self-sufficiency has been a cardinal principle of economic policy. Until World

War II the USSR exported raw materials to various European countries in exchange for capital goods. After the war the Eastern European states and China became its main trading partners. Beginning in 1960, trade with Western Europe and the developing countries increased at a faster rate. However, economic ties with Eastern Europe—as well as Cuba—have remained strong. Comecon (the Council for Mutual Economic Assistance), which includes the USSR, Hungary, Poland, Czechoslovakia, East Germany, Romania, Bulgaria, Mongolia, and Cuba, has promoted economic integration among these countries via joint investment projects and the specialization of production.

The composition of Soviet exports and imports reflects the intermediate level of the country's development. Earnings from the export of raw materials such as oil, timber, coal, and natural gas are used to purchase capital equipment and some consumer goods. Trade with Eastern Europe is roughly balanced. Exchanges with the developing countries show an excess of exports over imports, while the Soviet Union's need for advanced technology from the industrialized West has exceeded its ability to find markets there for its own goods.

Until recently, foreign trade was conducted as a state monopoly under the Ministry of Foreign Trade. It is now possible, however, for some state enterprises to enter into direct relations with foreign firms and conclude trade agreements.

Communications. The Soviet mass media are essentially organs of the party and state for the dissemination of information, viewpoints, and entertainment that are intended to encourage identification with and participation in officially approved activities. Newspapers with national circulation are Pravda, the Communist party's national daily; Izvestia, the government newspaper; *Komsomolskaya Pravda*, published by the central committee of the Komsomol; *Trud*, the organ of the All-Union Central Council of Trade Unions; and *Krasnaya Zvezda*, the organ of the Ministry of Defense. In addition, there are regional and city newspapers, published in the main language of the constituent republic, and organs of various ministries and trade unions. Among the weeklies, the Union of Soviet Writers' *Literaturnaya Gazeta* appeals mostly to the intelligentsia, while *Ogonek* has a broader readership. The monthly journal *Novi Mir* is devoted to serializations of novels, poetry, economic analysis, and political and social commentary.

Moscow is the nerve center of the broadcast media. By use of communications satellites, its programs are transmitted to all parts of the USSR and can be picked up in foreign lands as well. "Vremia," the main television news program, is said to have a nightly audience of some 200 million people.

The policy of *glasnost* has enlivened the Soviet media. Investigative reporting, accounts of accidents occurring within the Soviet Union, revelations about the past, and debates about current issues now appear regularly.

Forming a transitional zone between Siberia's taiga, which is heavily forested with conifers, and the steppe, or grassland, is the wooded steppe, a region characterized by deciduous trees. This broad east-west belt of the USSR is traversed by the Trans-Siberian Railroad.

GOVERNMENT

The USSR is nominally a federation of 15 equal republics, each of which has had the right, under the successive constitutions of 1923, 1936, and 1977, of secession. In practice, the USSR is a highly centralized state under the authority of the Communist party. According to Article 6 of the 1977 constitution, the party is "the leading and guiding force of Soviet society and the nucleus of its political system."

The Communist Party. Policy-making, personnel selection, and supervision of public activities are the main functions of the party. The party itself is a highly centralized body with its nucleus consisting of the Moscow-based Central Committee, POLITBURO, and Secretariat. Since 1961, all-union party congresses, consisting of delegates from republic and regional party organizations, have met every five years. Their main purpose is to assess the party's performance and focus the energy of the party toward fulfillment of its goals.

The Central Committee of the party consists of several hundred members who are elected by the all-union congress from a single slate drawn up by the Politburo and Secretariat. Members occupy key positions in party and state organs at the union republic and regional levels, the economic ministries, the armed forces and police, the national trade union council, and other major public organizations. Plenary sessions of the Central Committee are held twice or three times a year in Moscow, essentially to ratify policy decisions taken at the Politburo level.

The Politburo, a much smaller body, is composed of both full and candidate members, chosen from within the Central Committee. The Politburo is a collegiate body whose decisions are collective, though not necessarily unanimous. The general secretary of the party traditionally has presided over its meetings and speaks in the name of the Politburo. The role of the Secretariat is to implement party policies and control all lower branches of the party through its full-time staff of secretaries and special departments.

All lower territorial branches of the party replicate the central organs in their organizational structure. The lowest level of the party consists of primary party organizations (PPOs), which exist at places of work. Convened to discuss party assignments and the implementation of decisions reached at higher levels, the PPOs selectively recruit new members who must pass through a probationary period.

All important positions in the party and government are filled by party members who have been cleared by higher party bodies. Through this power, called *nomenklatura* in Russian, the party apparatus has ensured itself of direct access to and control over all state institutions, production enterprises, and public organizations. The other way in which the central apparatus has exercised control over lower party organizations and their members is through the principle of "democratic centralism." According to this principle, all issues arising before the membership are open for debate, but all decisions of the central organs of the party must be implemented and publicly defended.

The internal workings of the party and its monopolistic exercise of political power have been characteristic features of the Soviet political system since the early 1920s. The party structure has undergone modification from time to time, most notably under Khrushchev in the early 1960s, but the political culture of Soviet communism militated against radical changes. However, as lack of public accountability, careerism, and corruption became increasingly evident under Brezhnev, the prestige of the party fell. Seeking to return the party to "Leninist norms," Mikhail Gorbachev has called for a number of reforms, including limited tenure for all party officials, multiple candidates, secret-ballot elections, and "socialist pluralism."

National and Local Government. Soviet government represents a vast pyramidal structure, with local village, city, and county SOVIETS (councils) at the base and the two-chamber Supreme Soviet at the apex. Each soviet consists of delegates nominated by trade unions, collective farms, party organizations, and a number of other groups and elected by universal suffrage. The soviet in turn chooses an executive committee, which is the functioning organ of government at the local,

(Left) *Red banners led the 1967 Moscow parade celebrating the 50th anniversary of the Soviet October Revolution. Like the annual May Day celebration, the parade marched through the city's Red Square, with the domes of Saint Basil's Church in the background.*

(Right) *Tree-lined streets of Kiev approach the steep right bank of the Dnepr River, where the city's ancient churches and historic monuments stand. Founded during the 5th century, Kiev is one of Europe's oldest cities and is the capital of the USSR's Ukrainian Republic.*

district (*raion* or *okrug*), territorial (*krai*), and regional (*oblast*) levels. Within each of the 15 republics, executive functions of government are exercised by councils of ministers, nominally chosen by republic soviets.

The same pattern prevails at the all-union level, except that the Supreme Soviet contains two chambers with equal powers. The Soviet of the Union, with approximately 800 members, is elected at large from districts with 300,000 inhabitants; the Soviet of Nationalities consists of 32 delegates from union republics, 11 from autonomous republics, 5 from autonomous *oblasts*, and 1 from autonomous *okrugs*. The full Supreme Soviet meets twice a year to approve party-initiated legislation. In between sessions, a 39-member Presidium exercises legislative power. The chairman of the Presidium is the nominal head of state. The executive organ of government at the national level is the Council of Ministers, presided over by a chairman or prime minister. Attached to the Council of Ministers are a number of standing commissions and committees such as the State Planning Committee (Gosplan), the State Committee on Prices, the State Committee for Science and Technology, and the Committee of State Security (KGB).

Altogether, approximately 2 million people serve as soviet deputies, over half of whom are replaced at elections that are held every two and a half years. Representation tends to parallel that of the entire Soviet population in terms of ethnicity, sex, and vocation. Participation in the soviets has been largely honorific, since they have functioned as rubber stamps for legislation initiated by central party organs and approved by higher state bodies. As in the case of the party, though, this tradition has been called into question under Gorbachev. In 1988 a campaign was launched to enhance the autonomous power and prestige of the soviets.

Law and the Judiciary. The Supreme Court of the USSR, whose members are appointed by the Supreme Soviet, is the highest judicial body in the land. It has both original and appellate jurisdiction over civil, criminal, and military cases. Republic and regional-level courts are elected by respective soviets every five years. Like the USSR Supreme Court, they may initiate cases or hear them on appeal from lower courts.

The vast majority of cases are handled by People's Courts, in which a professional judge is assisted by two lay assessors. The judge, nominated by the party, is formally elected by the constituents of the district. Assessors, the Soviet equivalent of a jury, usually concur with the decision of the judge.

The Procuracy enjoys broad powers of supervision over governmental employees, initiates criminal investigations, acts as the prosecutional attorney, and appeals decisions of lower courts to higher courts. The procurator general is appointed by the Supreme Soviet of the USSR for a seven-year term. Republic procurators are appointed by the procurator general, and they in turn appoint procurators to regional and district courts, subject to confirmation by the procurator general. Soviet citizens have the right to legal defense by attorneys who receive fees for their services.

Completing the court system are military tribunals, which hear cases of espionage, and a separate hierarchy of state arbitration (*Gosarbitrazh*) tribunals. These handle contract disputes between state enterprises and may award damages.

Soviet criminal law embraces crimes against the state, which include slandering the Soviet system and negligence or abuse of office. The role of the courts is intended to be educational, instilling an awareness of citizens' socialist obligations to the community. The maximum term of deprivation of freedom is 15 years. Certain kinds of murder, sabotage, treason, and espionage are punishable by death.

Armed Forces. The USSR's immense size and limited access to oceans have favored the development of a large land army supported by a tactical air force. Acquisition of nuclear weapons and long-range and medium-range missiles greatly enhanced the army's strategic capabilities, and by the 1970s, parity with the nuclear forces of the NATO countries was achieved. Since the 1960s the Soviet navy has expanded from what previously had been a coastal patrol force, and today has a significant presence in the northern Pacific, Atlantic, and Indian oceans as well as the Mediterranean Sea. The So-

viet armed forces conduct joint maneuvers and plan military strategy with the Communist countries of Eastern Europe that belong to the WARSAW TREATY ORGANIZATION.

The Soviet armed forces are under the direction of the Ministry of Defense, headed by a marshal of the Soviet Union. His deputies preside over the five major service branches: the army, the navy, the strategic rocket forces, the air force, and the air defense forces. There is also a sizable paramilitary force consisting of border guards and security troops under the direction of the KGB. The Communist party maintains close control of the armed forces through its political officers, attached to units down to the battalion level. Senior members of the high command sit on the party's Central Committee. Military service in the USSR is mandatory for all males and consists of two years in the army or three in the navy.

LEWIS SIEGELBAUM

Bibliography:
GENERAL: Brown, Archie, et al., eds., *The Cambridge Encyclopedia of Russia and the Soviet Union* (1982); Kerblay, Basile, *Modern Soviet Society* (1983); Shipler, David, *Russia: Broken Idols, Solemn Dreams* (1983); Smith, Hedrick, *The Russians* (1983); Walker, Martin, *The Waking Giant* (1987).
GEOGRAPHY: Gregory, James S., *Russian Land, Soviet People* (1968); Lydolph, Paul E., *Geography of the U.S.S.R.* (1980); Mathieson, R. S., *The Soviet Union: An Economic Geography* (1975).
ECONOMICS: Aganbegyan, Abel, *The Economic Challenge of Perestroika* (1988); Gregory, Paul R., and Stuart, Robert C., *Soviet Economic Structure and Performance*, 3d ed. (1986); Nove, Alec, *The Soviet Economic System* (1977); Shabad, Theodore, and Dienes, Leslie, *The Soviet Energy System* (1979).
FOREIGN RELATIONS: Gartoff, Raymond L., *Détente and Confrontation* (1985); Jelavich, Barbara, *St. Petersburg and Moscow: Tsarist and Soviet Foreign Policy, 1814–1974* (1974); Korbonski, Andrej, and Fukuyama, Francis, eds., *The Soviet Union and the Third World* (1987).
POLITICS AND GOVERNMENT: Gorbachev, Mikhail, *Perestroika: New Thinking for Our Country and the World* (1987); Hough, Jerry F., and Fainsod, Merle, *How the Soviet Union Is Governed* (1979); Lewin, Moshe, *The Gorbachev Phenomenon* (1988) and *Political Undercurrents in Soviet Economic Debates* (1975); McCauley, Mary, *Politics and the Soviet Union* (1977).
SOCIAL LIFE AND CUSTOMS: Atkinson, Dorothy, Dallin, Alexander, and Lapidus, Gail, eds., *Women in Russia* (1977); Katz, Zev, ed., *Handbook of Major Soviet Nationalities* (1975); Millar, James, *Politics, Work and Daily Life in the USSR* (1987); Riordan, James, *Sport in Soviet Society* (1977).

See also: COMMUNISM; RUSSIA/UNION OF SOVIET SOCIALIST REPUBLICS, HISTORY OF; RUSSIAN ART AND ARCHITECTURE; RUSSIAN LITERATURE; RUSSIAN MUSIC; and articles on individual republics.

Union Theological Seminary

Founded in 1836, Union (enrollment: 450; library: 650,000 volumes) is a private interdenominational Protestant theological seminary for men and women in New York City. It grants degrees in religious education and music and in theology.

Unitarian Universalist Association

Th Unitarian Universalist Association was formed in 1961 by consolidation of the American Unitarian Association (1825) and the Universalist Church of America (1793). At continental headquarters in Boston, the association carries on common activities, such as church extension, ministerial settlement, and preparation of educational materials, but it does not exercise hierarchical control. Humanitarian concerns are entrusted to a related organization, the Unitarian Universalist Service Committee. The denomination is connected with similar groups abroad through the International Association for Religious Freedom. It has 956 churches and lay-led fellowships in North America, with 173,167 adult members and 1,069 ordained clergy (1988).

See also: UNITARIANISM; UNIVERSALISM.

Unitarianism

Unitarianism is a form of Christianity that asserts that God is one person, the Father, rather than three persons in one, as the doctrine of the Trinity holds. A number of religious groups in Transylvania, Poland, Great Britain, and North

America have been designated as unitarian because of this belief. It has not been their only distinguishing mark, however, and at times not even the most important one. As significant has been their confidence in the reasoning and moral abilities of people—in contrast to traditions that emphasize original sin and human depravity—as well as an avoidance of dogma.

Modern Unitarianism dates to the period of the Protestant Reformation. A Unitarian movement has existed in Transylvania since the 1560s, when the leader was Francis David (1510–79). In Poland, Unitarianism flourished for a hundred years as the Minor Reformed Church until persecution forced (1660) its adherents into exile. The key figure in the Polish movement was Faustus Socinus (1539–1604; see SOCINIANISM). Isolated individual unitarians lived in England in the 1600s, most notably John BIDDLE, but Unitarianism developed as a formal movement in the 1700s, partly within the Church of England but mainly in dissenting circles.

In America the religious liberalism that came to be known as Unitarianism appeared within the congregational churches in Massachusetts as a reaction against the revivalism of the GREAT AWAKENING (1740–43). The election (1805) of Henry Ware as Hollis Professor of Divinity at Harvard University touched off a controversy, as a result of which the liberals became a separate denomination. William Ellery CHANNING's sermon entitled "Unitarian Christianity" (1819) was an influential statement of their beliefs.

In 1838, Ralph Waldo EMERSON's divinity school address declared that religious truth should be based on the authority of inner consciousness, not on external historical proofs. More conservative Unitarians were critical of Emerson and his followers, known as transcendentalists, fearing that such subjectivism would destroy the claim of Christianity to be a divinely revealed religion. Since the controversy over TRANSCENDENTALISM, some within the denomination have always felt it important to maintain continuity with the Christian tradition, whereas others have found Christianity to be intellectually limited and emotionally restrictive.

In 1961 the Unitarians merged with the Universalists in the Unitarian Universalist Association, uniting two denominations with roughly parallel histories and a similar tradition of religious liberalism.

Bibliography: Ahlstrom, S. E., and Carey, J. S., eds., *An American Reformation* (1984); Howe, D. W., *The Unitarian Conscience* (1970); Wilbur, Earl Morse, *A History of Unitarianism*, 2 vols. (1945, 1952); Wright, Conrad, *The Beginnings of Unitarianism in America* (1955; repr. 1976) and, as ed., *A Stream of Light* (1975).

Unitas, Johnny   [yoo-ny'-tuhs]

John Unitas, b. Pittsburgh, Pa., May 7, 1933, an American professional football player, was considered by many to be the greatest quarterback of his era. After a college career at the University of Louisville, he was drafted by the Pittsburgh Steelers of the National Football League (NFL) but did not qualify for the team in the 1955 season. Unitas earned a living that year playing semiprofessional football for $6 per game. The next year he joined the Baltimore Colts, and in 17 seasons as their quarterback he led them to 4 NFL championships. During his career Unitas threw touchdown passes in 47 consecutive games, and in 23 games he passed for more than 300 yd, marks that are both NFL records. He completed 2,830 passes (out of 5,186 attempts) for 40,239 yd and 290 touchdowns—all NFL career records when he retired. Unitas was the Player of the Year in 1959, 1964, and 1967, and he made 10 All Star game appearances. Traded to the San Diego Chargers in 1973, he played there for 1 year before retiring. In 1979 he was elected to the Pro Football Hall of Fame.

Bibliography: Chass, M., *Power Football* (1973); Duroska, L., ed., *Great Pro Quarterbacks* (1972); Morse, C. and A., *Johnny Unitas* (1974).

United Arab Emirates

The United Arab Emirates (UAE)—composed of the sheikhdoms of Abu Dhabi, Dubai, Sharjah, Ras al-Khaimah, Umm al-Qaiwain, Ajman, and Fujairah—is located on a flat coastal plain of the Arabian Peninsula, along the Persian Gulf. The borders with Qatar on the northwest, Saudi Arabia on the south and west, and Oman on the east are undefined, as are the borders between the individual sheikhdoms. Two neutral zones are shared by several sheikhdoms.

LAND, PEOPLE, AND ECONOMY

About 80% of the UAE's area is in Abu Dhabi. The climate is hot and dry, with mean January temperatures of 18° C (65° F) and mean July temperatures of 33° C (92° F). Rainfall averages 152 mm (6 in) annually. The major resource is petroleum.

Only 42% of the inhabitants are Arabs because the petroleum boom has brought in a flood of foreign workers. About 50% of the population are South Asian. The native population is overwhelmingly Muslim (95%). ABU DHABI, the capital, and DUBAI are the chief cities. Six years of primary education are free and compulsory. Health services are good because of extensive social services provided by petroleum wealth.

Petroleum, first exported in 1962, dominates the economy of the UAE. By 1985 this once-underdeveloped region had the world's highest per capita income—$19,120—even though its petroleum revenues declined in the 1980s due to a world oil glut. The new wealth has been invested in capital improvements and social services in all the emirates, although petroleum production is concentrated in Abu Dhabi and Dubai. Industrial development is primarily petroleum related and is hampered by a lack of trained personnel and other raw materials. The desert environment supports limited irrigated agriculture; fishing, poultry raising, and sheep herding also provide domestic food sources. Petroleum exports have given the UAE a large trade surplus.

HISTORY AND GOVERNMENT

At one time this area was known as the "Pirate Coast," reflecting the major occupation of the inhabitants. To protect its ships, Great Britain, beginning in 1820, made several treaties with the Arab leaders outlawing sea battles. Britain handled foreign relations for the area, then known as Trucial Oman or

UNITED ARAB EMIRATES

LAND. Area: 83,600 km² (32,278 mi²). Capital and largest city: Abu Dhabi (1981 pop., 243,000).

PEOPLE. Population (1987 est.): 1,400,000; density (1987 est.): 16.7 persons per km² (43.3 per mi²). Distribution (1987 est.): 81% urban, 19% rural. Annual growth (1987 est.): 2.6%. Official language: Arabic. Major religion: Islam.

EDUCATION AND HEALTH. Literacy (1984): 71% of adult population. Universities (1987): 1. Hospital beds (1984): 4,853. Physicians (1984): 1,840. Life expectancy (1980–85): women—65.6; men—61.6. Infant mortality (1987 est.): 35 per 1,000 live births.

ECONOMY. GNP (1985): $26.4 billion; $19,120 per capita. Labor distribution (1984): services—35%; construction—25%; trade—14%; manufacturing—6%; agriculture—5%; mining—2%. Foreign trade (1984): imports—$6.9 billion; exports—$14.1 billion; principal trade partners—Japan, United States, France, Italy, West Germany. Currency: 1 UAE dirham = 100 fils.

GOVERNMENT. Type: federation of emirates. Legislature: Federal National Council. Political subdivisions: 7 emirates.

COMMUNICATIONS. Railroads (1987): none. Roads (1981): 1,300 km (800 mi) total. Major ports: 3. Major airfields: 5.

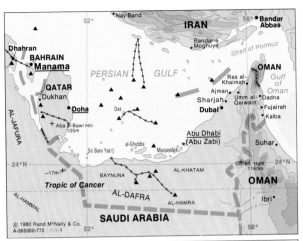

UNITED ARAB EMIRATES

——— Railroad

+--+--+ Oil Pipeline

▲ Major Oil Field

+ Spot Elevation

National capitals
are underlined

City type size indicates
relative importance

Meters	Feet
2000	6562
1000	3281
500	1640
200	656
0	Sea Level
0	0
200	656
2000	3281

0   50   100   150   200 km
0   50   100 mi

Scale 1:8,880,000

© 1980 Rand McNally & Co.
A-565000-772

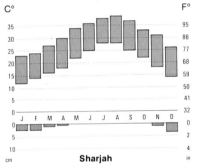

Bars indicate monthly ranges of temperatures (red) and precipitation (blue) in Sharjah, one of the seven members of the United Arab Emirates. Sharjah, bordering the Persian Gulf, has a desert climate.

Sharjah

the Trucial States. The United Arab Emirates gained full independence on Dec. 2, 1971, although Ras al-Khaimah did not join until 1972. There are no elections or legal political parties; authority rests with the seven hereditary sheikhs, who control their own domains and choose a president from among their number. Zaid bin Sultan al-Nahayan, of Abu Dhabi, has been president since 1971.   IRA M. SHESKIN

Bibliography: Anthony, J. D., *Arab States of the Lower Gulf* (1975); Cottrell, A. J., ed., *The Persian Gulf States* (1980); El Mallakh, R., *The Economic Development of the United Arab Emirates* (1981); Hawley, D., *The Trucial States* (1971); Niblock, T., ed., *Social and Economic Development in the Arab Gulf* (1980).

United Arab Republic

The United Arab Republic (UAR) was a short-lived federation of Egypt and Syria formed in February 1958 with President Gamal Abdel Nasser of Egypt as head of state. The founders hoped that the federation might lead to the ultimate unification of all Arab peoples. Syria, however, became disenchanted by Egypt's domination of the federation and left the union in September 1961. Yemen (Sana), which had joined the UAR in a trade pact known as the United Arab States, left the association shortly thereafter. Egypt retained United Arab Republic as its official name until 1971.

United Auto Workers

The International Union, United Automobile, Aerospace and Agricultural Implement Workers of America (UAW) is an industrial union for workers, engineers, and technicians, involved in the manufacturing of automobiles, aircraft, and farm equipment. The UAW was formed in 1935 as an American Federation of Labor affiliate but left the AFL the following year to join the newly formed Congress of Industrial Organizations (CIO). After a hard-fought struggle that included a nationwide sit-down strike in General Motors plants in 1937, the UAW won recognition by the automobile industry. In 1969, under the leadership of Walter P. REUTHER, the union withdrew from the AFL-CIO and became independent; it reaffiliated in 1981. In 1984 its membership was 1,151,086, and the UAW had 1,517 locals. In March 1985 the Canadian council of the UAW, with about 10% of the total UAW membership, voted to form a separate union.

Bibliography: Babson, Steve, *Working Detroit: The Making of a Union Town* (1984); Howe, Irving, and Widick, B. J., *The UAW and Walter Reuther* (1949; repr. 1973).

United Church of Christ

The United Church of Christ was established in 1957 as a union of the Congregational Christian Churches and the Evangelical and Reformed Church. With a current membership of nearly 1.7 million communicants located in about 6,500 congregations in 39 conferences (state and regional organizations), the United Church of Christ is the "youngest" of the major Protestant denominations in the United States. Its roots lie in the teachings of such 16th-century reformers as Martin Luther and Ulrich Zwingli and in CONGREGATIONALISM.

The basic unit of the United Church is the local church, which is guaranteed autonomy, or freedom, in the decisions it makes. That freedom is the "freedom of the gospel," however, and every corporate body within the church, whether a local church or a conference or the General Synod, is supposed to make its decisions in the light of the gospel and out of a sense of responsibility to the whole fellowship.

The General Synod of the United Church of Christ, which meets biennially, is the representative, deliberative body composed of 675–725 delegates elected by the conferences. The officers of the church and the General Synod are the president, secretary, and director of finance and treasurer. The national program agencies include the United Church Board for World Ministries, United Church Board for Homeland Ministries, Office for Church in Society, Office of Communication, Stewardship Council, United Church Foundation Pension Boards, and Commission for Racial Justice. The United Church of Christ is a member of the National Council of Churches, the World Council of Churches, and the World Alliance of Reformed Churches.   AVERY D. POST

Bibliography: Gunnemann, Louis H., *The Shaping of the United Church of Christ* (1977); Keiling, Hanns P., and Battles, Ford L., eds., *The Formation of the United Church of Christ* (1977); Zikmund, Barbara B., *Hidden Histories in the United Church of Christ* (1984).

United Empire Loyalists: see LOYALISTS.

United Farm Workers of America: see CHAVEZ, CESAR.

United Irishmen, Society of

The Society of United Irishmen, inspired by the French Revolution, was founded in 1791 to seek parliamentary reform and legal equality for all Irish. Its leaders included Belfast Presbyterian merchants and such Dublin intellectuals as Wolfe TONE. They found support among rural Presbyterians in Ulster and among Roman Catholic peasants. After war broke out (1793) between Great Britain and France the society began advocating violent revolution and was harshly suppressed by the British. Spurred by promises of French support, the movement planned a rebellion in 1798, resulting only in three isolated local revolts that were quickly put down.   DAVID W. MILLER

Bibliography: Pakenham, Thomas, *The Year of Liberty* (1969).

United Kingdom

The United Kingdom of Great Britain and Northern Ireland lies at the northwestern edge of Europe, separated from the European mainland by the ENGLISH CHANNEL, the NORTH SEA, and the narrow Strait of Dover (see DOVER, STRAIT OF). It consists of the formerly separate kingdoms of ENGLAND and SCOTLAND, the principality of WALES—which are collectively referred to as GREAT BRITAIN—and six counties of NORTHERN IRELAND, which elected to remain within the United Kingdom in 1921 when southern Ireland withdrew to form the Irish Free State (after 1949, the Republic of Ireland, or Eire). The loss of Ireland and its withdrawal from the COMMONWEALTH OF NATIONS in 1949 rendered politically obsolete the use of the collective term British Isles. Other integral parts of the United Kingdom are the outlying HEBRIDES, ORKNEY ISLANDS, and SHETLAND ISLANDS, off the coast of Scotland; Anglesey (see GWYNEDD), off the coast of Wales; and the ISLE OF WIGHT and the SCILLY ISLANDS, off the southwest coast of England. Separate from the kingdom but administered by the crown, each with its own laws and systems of taxation, are the ISLE OF MAN, located in the Irish Sea; and the CHANNEL ISLANDS, located off the northwest coast of France.

England is the largest and most populous unit in the kingdom, with an area of 130,439 km² (50,363 mi²) and a population (1986 est.) of 47,254,500. Wales, located to the west and separated from England by a boundary dating back to the Middle Ages, has an area of 20,768 km² (8,018 mi²) and

2,821,000 inhabitants; it became part of the English kingdom in 1282 but continues to maintain a separate language and national identity. Scotland—with an area of 78,772 km² (30,414 mi²) and 5,121,000 inhabitants—lies to the north, separated from England by a boundary that extends from Solway Firth (estuary) on the west, across the sparsely populated Cheviot Hills, to north of Berwick upon Tweed. Scotland and England were ruled by the same monarchs after 1603 and were united in 1707 to form the kingdom of Great Britain. Ireland was made an integral part of the kingdom in 1801, changing the official name to the United Kingdom of Great Britain and Ireland. The present name was adopted after the partition of Ireland in 1921. Northern Ireland has an area of 14,121 km² (5,452 mi²) and a population of 1,566,800.

Commonly described as "in Europe but not of it," Great Britain and Ireland remained relatively isolated from world events until the 15th century when the Age of Discovery placed them on the world's newly charted sea-lanes and trading routes. Increasingly, the island nation looked away from Europe in later centuries and across the seas to the Americas, India, the Far East, southern and interior Africa, Australia, and New Zealand. Overseas colonies were established, forming an enormous BRITISH EMPIRE. Many of these colonies chose to retain trade and other ties to Britain when granted independence and are today part of the Commonwealth; because of these ties, however, the United Kingdom's entry into the EUROPEAN ECONOMIC COMMUNITY (EEC) in 1973 was preceded by lengthy negotiations and dispute.

The INDUSTRIAL REVOLUTION began in the United Kingdom, which in the 19th century became the preeminent industrial and trading nation in the world. In the 20th century, however, competition from more recently industrialized countries as well as the loss of its colonies (which had provided raw materials for Britain's industries and markets for their finished products) brought an economic decline. In the 1960s and '70s se-

UNITED KINGDOM OF GREAT BRITAIN AND NORTHERN IRELAND

LAND. Area: 244,100 km² (94,247 mi²). Capital and largest city: London (1986 est. pop., 6,775,200).

PEOPLE. Population (1988 est.): 57,100,000; density: 233.9 persons per km² (605.9 per mi²). Distribution (1988): 91% urban, 9% rural. Annual growth (1987–88): 0.2%. Official language: English. Major religions: Anglicanism (Church of England), Roman Catholicism, Presbyterianism (Church of Scotland).

EDUCATION AND HEALTH. Literacy (1987): 100% of adult population. Universities (1988): 43. Hospital beds (1985): 419,000. Physicians (1985): 84,700. Life expectancy (1988): 75. Infant mortality (1987): 9.5 per 1,000 live births.

ECONOMY. GNP (1986): $504.9 billion; $8,430 per capita. Labor distribution (1986): agriculture, forestry, and fishing—1.2%; mining, manufacturing, and construction—23.3%; services—53.2%; self-employed, unemployed, other—22.3%. Foreign trade (1986): imports—$127.5 billion; exports—$108.2 billion; principal trade partners—West Germany, United States, France, Netherlands. Currency: 1 pound sterling = 100 new pence.

GOVERNMENT. Type: constitutional monarchy. Legislature: Parliament. Political subdivisions: England (45 counties and Greater London); Scotland (9 regions and 3 "island districts"); Wales (8 counties); Northern Ireland (6 counties or 26 districts).

COMMUNICATIONS. Railroads (1987): 17,628 km (10,953 mi) total. Roads (1985): 339,483 km (210,944 mi) paved; 23,499 km (14,601 mi) unpaved. Major ports: 11. Airfields (international, 1988): 7.

One of Britain's great historic landmarks is the Tower of London, a medieval fortress dating back to the time of William the Conqueror (late 11th century). Once famous as a prison and place of execution, the Tower is now a museum and the repository of the crown jewels.

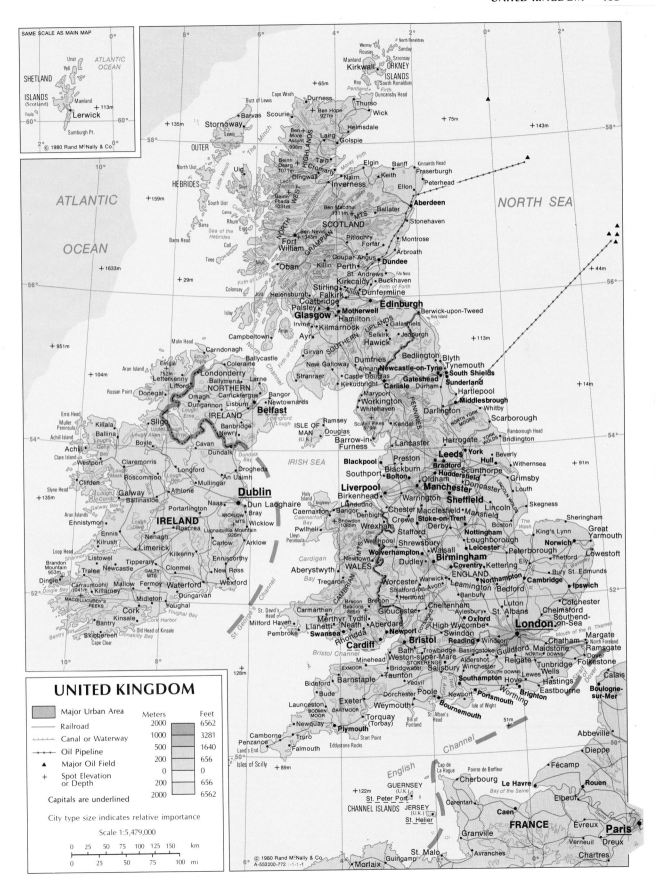

UNITED KINGDOM

Major Urban Area
Railroad
Canal or Waterway
Oil Pipeline
▲ Major Oil Field
+ Spot Elevation or Depth

Meters	Feet
2000	6562
1000	3281
500	1640
200	656
0	0
200	656
2000	6562

Capitals are underlined

City type size indicates relative importance

Scale 1:5,479,000

0 25 50 75 100 125 150 km
0 25 50 75 100 mi

© 1980 Rand McNally & Co.
A-553200-772 -1-1-1

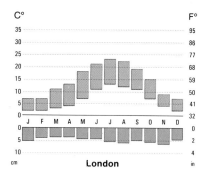

C° / F° chart axes: 35/95, 30/86, 25/77, 20/68, 15/59, 10/50, 5/41, 0/32

J F M A M J J A S O N D

0 / 0
5 / 2
10 / 4

cm **London** in

(Above) *Bars indicate monthly ranges of temperatures (red) and precipitation (blue) for the city of London, which is the capital of the United Kingdom. London has a marine west-coast climate.*

(Right) *Stow-on-the-Wold is one of the most picturesque villages of the Cotswold Hills, an area in Gloucestershire and Avon known for its beautiful old market towns built of the distinctive, honey-colored local limestone.*

(Below) *Dedicated in 1984, the Thames Flood Barrier at Woolwich protects London from being flooded by high tides from the North Sea. The visible portion consists of a line of concrete piers with rounded steel tops. Attached to the piers are gates on the riverbed that can be raised to form a barrier against a rising tide.*

vere labor disputes, unprecedented inflation, and declining exports contributed to a series of economic crises.

During the Industrial Revolution the country became rapidly urbanized, and today more than 70% of the total population is concentrated in cities occupying 10% of the total land area.

To protect the remaining countryside, national planning legislation has established ten national parks in the most scenic areas, including Dartmoor, the Lake District, the Pennines, the Snowdonia, the Pembrokeshire coast, North York Moors, Yorkshire Dales, Northumbria, Exmoor, and the Brecon Beacons. Other areas are also protected as Areas of Outstanding Natural Beauty.

LAND AND RESOURCES

Despite its small size, variety of scene is the main characteristic of the United Kingdom.

Lowland England. The largest area of flat plain occurs in The Fens, located on the east coast around The Wash. Before they were drained to produce a rich agricultural landscape similar to the polders in the Netherlands, The Fens were an area of marshland. Smaller flat areas are found along the Humber Riv-

ER estuary farther north on the east coast; along the Thames below London; and in Romney Marsh, in the southeastern county of Kent. Elsewhere, lowland England in the south and east is rolling country with a variety of landforms reflecting differences in underlying rock types. Especially prominent are the low hills and scarps developed on chalk rocks of Cretaceous age (135 million to 65 million years ago). They occur in the North and South Downs to the south of London, where the scarps face south and north, respectively, into The Weald; in Salisbury Plain, where the downs converge at their western end; and in the low hills that continue westward through the southern counties of Wiltshire and Dorset and swing eastward through the Isle of Wight. Northwestward from Salisbury Plain, the chalk hills form the prominent Chiltern Hills to the northwest of London; fall to lower elevations in the hills of East Anglia (Norfolk and Suffolk counties); and farther north form the Lincoln and York Wolds on either side of the Humber estuary.

To the west, separated from the chalk hills by an intervening lowland developed mainly on clays, rise a northeast-trending series of uplands developed on limestones of Jurassic age (190 million to 135 million years ago). They extend from the southern county of Dorset to the North York moors on England's northeast coast, and include the Cotswolds, which form a scarped edge overlooking the River Severn valley and rise to a high point of 314 m (1,031 ft) in Cleeve Cloud, near Cheltenham.

Also prominent in lowland England are the Mendip Hills, which rise to 326 m (1,068 ft) in Black Down, in the southwest near Bristol; Exmoor, which rises to 520 m (1,707 ft) in Dunkery Beacon farther west; Dartmoor, a granite-formed upland that rises to 621 m (2,039 ft) in High Willhays in the southwestern peninsula; and the Malvern Hills, which exceed 300 m (1,000 ft) between Gloucester and Worcester. Glacial deposits greatly modify topography and landforms north of an irregular line joining the River Thames and the Bristol Channel; often burying the underlying rock to considerable depths, the mantle of glacial deposits creates differing soil conditions as well as different drainage conditions from field to field.

Upland England. Uplands predominate in northern and western England. The most extensive uplands are the PENNINES, which rise to 893 m (2,930 ft) in Cross Fell. Underlain mainly by limestones and grits of Carboniferous age (345 million to 280 million years ago), the Pennines are bordered on both sides by discontinuous coalfields, and the open moorlands of the Pennines contrast starkly with the sprawling industrial cities near the coal deposits. Numerous broad river valleys, known locally as dales, drain eastward across the mountains into the Vale of York, a north-south extension of lowland England that serves as the main route northward into Scotland. West of the Pennines are the Lancashire and Cheshire Plains and farther north England's scenic Lake District, which rises to 978 m (3,210 ft) in Scafell Pike, England's highest peak.

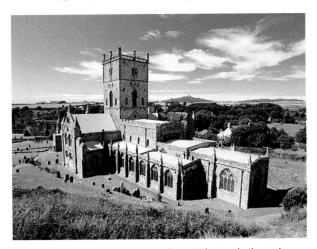

The Anglican cathedral of Saint David's in Wales was built mostly between the late 12th and the late 14th centuries on the site of a monastery founded by Saint David, the patron saint of Wales. It was a popular place of pilgrimage in medieval times.

Wales and Scotland. Unlike England, the topography of Wales and Scotland is dominated more by mountains and uplands than by lowlands. The highest mountain in Wales is Snowdon, which rises to 1,085 m (3,560 ft) in the northwest. In South Wales the Brecon Beacons rise to 886 m (2,907 ft) and, as in the Pennines, the barren, windswept uplands contrast with the deep and generally narrow coal-mining valleys farther south. The principal lowlands in Wales are on the island of Anglesey and along the western coasts of Caernarvon and Cardigan bays. Southern Scotland is dominated by low ranges of the Southern Uplands, which rise to elevations exceeding 610 m (2,000 ft) in parts of the Tweedsmuir Hills. To

the north of the Southern Uplands are the geologically complex, down-faulted Scottish Central Lowlands that extend northeastward across the country from the Firth of Clyde on the west coast to the firths (estuaries) of Tay and Forth on the east coast. The lowlands are interpenetrated by uplands, including the Pentlands, Campsies, Ochils, and Sidlaws; all rise over 300 m (1,000 ft), with peaks reaching over 610 m (2,000 ft) in the Ochils. North and west of the Central Lowlands are the HIGHLANDS, a large upland region divided by the Glen More (Great Glen), a deep depression that extends from Fort William to Inverness and is occupied in part by Loch (lake) NESS. Narrow lowlands border the Highlands in the east. The western Highlands are rugged and mountainous and include BEN NEVIS, the highest point in the United Kingdom. Numerous other peaks reach over 1,200 m (4,000 ft) in the Cairngorm Mountains, the most extensive area of mountainous terrain in the Highlands. On the western island of SKYE, the scenic Cuillin Hills rise to more than 900 m (3,000 ft) in places, with lower, moorland-covered peaks common on the other islands of the Inner and Outer Hebrides.

Northern Ireland. The structural depression forming the Scottish Central Lowlands extends southwestward across the Irish Sea to form the area of lowlands surrounding Lough (lake) NEAGH, which is situated to the west of Belfast in Northern Ireland. Scenic mountains of low elevation border the lowlands area on all sides. To the northeast rise the Antrim Mountains, which reach a high point of 554 m (1,817 ft); formed on basaltic rocks of Eocene age (54 million to 38 million years ago), the mountains reach the sea on the north coast in the famous steps of the GIANT'S CAUSEWAY. The Sperrin Mountains form the northwestern edge of the depression and reach a high point of 683 m (2,240 ft) in Mount Sawel. Forming parts of the southern edge of the depression in part are the Mourne Mountains, which are located south of Belfast and which rise to 852 m (2,796 ft) in Slieve Donard, the highest point in Northern Ireland.

Soils. The richest soils include the reclaimed alluvial deposits in The Fens, alluvial soils along the Mersey River and west coast, and brick earths and other deep soils used for fruit and vegetable cultivation in the London basin. Elsewhere, soil fertility varies greatly because of underlying rock differences, but modern methods of fertilization make natural fertility less important than such other conditions as soil texture, drainage, climate, and slope. In general terms, soils in the drier east and south are used mainly for crops, and soils in the more humid west and north and in some clay areas are used mainly for dairying. Sheep are grazed generally on poorer soils in moorland and upland areas.

Climate. The United Kingdom has a highly variable temperate marine west-coast type of climate. Relatively few periods of continuously dry weather occur; they are usually caused by anticyclonic systems and are associated with unusually warm days in summer and cold periods in winter. Much more com-

The ruins of the 14th-century fortress Dunluce Castle overlook basaltic cliffs in County Antrim, the northeasternmost portion of Northern Ireland. Ramore Head, where the castle is located, extends into the North Channel, which separates Northern Ireland from Scotland.

mon is the variable weather that occurs as cyclonic depressions sweep in from the Atlantic Ocean, bringing high winds and abundant rainfall to the west in winter and lower amounts of rainfall in summer. Mountainous west coast areas generally receive more than 2,540 mm (100 in) of rain a year, but rainfall amounts diminish rapidly eastward; the Cairngorm Mountains receive only about 1,000–1,270 mm (40–50 in) a year, and most lowlands in the west, between approximately 500 and 750 mm (20 and 30 in). The driest areas surround the Thames estuary in southeastern England, where less than 500 mm (20 in) of rain falls each year. In the wetter western areas, 2 out of 3 days are usually rainy; in the drier east, rain falls on almost one out of every two days. No permanent snows exist, but snow may lie on the ground for 2 months or more in the Cairngorm Mountains and other parts of the Highlands. In winter, temperatures are colder in the east than in the west; snow covers the ground for about 18 days in Aberdeen, an average of 6 days in London, and hardly at all along the entire southern coast or the west coast as far north as Glasgow. In summer, a more normal decrease in temperature from south to north occurs; average July temperatures range from about 17° C (63° F) on the southern coast and in London, to 12° C (54° F) in the north of Scotland.

Drainage. The SEVERN and THAMES are the longest rivers. Other major rivers are the AVON, CLYDE, FORTH, MERSEY, TAY, TRENT, TWEED, Ouse, Tees, and Tyne. These and other rivers are all used either for shipping, water supplies, or hydroelectric power; their flow is, accordingly, highly regulated. Many of the rivers are canalized and are linked with other river systems in an intricate, and now largely abandoned, canal system dating from the early Industrial Revolution. Drinking water is derived from subsurface supplies and from numerous reservoirs in the Pennines, in the Welsh mountains, and in Scotland. Untreated sewage effluent no longer enters the major rivers, and even the Irwell—which runs through Manchester and was once described as the "hardest-worked river in the world" (and certainly the filthiest)—is now clean enough for fishing.

Vegetation and Animal Life. Although forests cover only 7% of the land area, the British landscape presents a characteristically wooded appearance. This impression stems mainly from the presence of many trees in hedgerows and pastures, coverts planted for game birds, shelter belts planted beside farmhouses and exposed fields, and ornamental plantings on great estates. Little remains of the original oak and birch forest cover, and most of today's forests consist of pines and other conifers planted in reforestation programs in depopu-

lated areas of Scotland and Wales. The largest forests in England occur in the Breckland to the northeast of Cambridge; in Kielder Forest in Northumberland; and as the remnants of the historic Forest of Dean (in Gloucestershire) and Sherwood Forest (in Nottinghamshire); and the New Forest (in Hampshire), a former royal hunting preserve. More extensive than forests are the expanses of treeless moorland that cover much of the Pennines, Highlands, and other exposed upland areas; on the drier moors heather predominates, and on the wetter moors, various grasses and mosses. Extensive areas of alpine flora occur at high elevations in the Cairngorms and other parts of the Highlands. Game birds include grouse, on the moors, and pheasants. Deer are hunted with horses and hounds on Exmoor; deer stalking (on foot) is preferred in the Scottish Highlands. Foxes are hunted in rural areas.

Resources. The United Kingdom has long been rich in energy resources but deficient in food and industrial raw materials. Extensive coal deposits occur around the eastern and western edges of the Pennines, in South Wales, in the western MIDLANDS (Birmingham area), and in the Scottish Central Lowland. Easily accessible coal seams are, however, largely exhausted. Fortunately for the energy-hungry British economy, large deposits of petroleum and natural gas under the North Sea came into commercial production in 1975; by the end of the 1980s the United Kingdom is expected to be self-sufficient in petroleum.

Other mineral deposits are of small importance. They include tin, mined in small amounts in Cornwall; low-grade iron ores in the Jurassic rocks of Lincolnshire and Northamptonshire in the eastern Midlands, used in steel mills at Scun-

(Above) *Loweswater, located in West Cumberland, is one of the smaller of the 15 lakes in England's Lake District. This mountainous region of northwestern England, which includes the country's highest peaks, has enjoyed a long history as an artistic retreat.*

(Left) *Edinburgh Castle, located in the oldest part of the city, serves as the background for a performance given at the Edinburgh International Festival of Music and Drama, which has been held annually since 1947. As Scotland's capital, Edinburgh is an important cultural and administrative center.*

(Above) *The town of Worsley, in northwestern England, is noted for its historic houses and landmarks. The Bridgewater Canal, constructed during the 18th century, helped change the character of Worsley from an agricultural community to a coal-mining and textile center.*

(Left) *This workers' community is located near textile factories in Lancashire, in the moorlands of northwestern England, where textile manufacture is most concentrated. Since the 1600s the region has been engaged in textile production.*

thorpe and Corby; kaolinite (china clay), mined in parts of Cornwall; and sands and gravels, quarried for road-building materials. Of the total land area about 30% is used for crops and 50% for pasture; agricultural productivity has been greatly improved since World War II, and only half of all food needs are now imported, compared with two-thirds before the war.

PEOPLE

Except in the case of recent immigrants, the British population tends to classify itself more in terms of national and regional origins than by racial or ethnic criteria. About 83% of the total population live in England, 9% in Scotland, 5% in Wales, and 3% in Northern Ireland. More than 2% are non-Caucasian immigrants who arrived in recent decades from the British West Indies, Pakistan, India, and other Commonwealth or former Commonwealth countries.

Earlier efforts to recognize in the nonimmigrant population various Nordic, Alpine, and Mediterranean racial strains are now questioned, and the most that can be said with authority is that the population is primarily descended from a mixture of Europeans that have at different times invaded and occupied the islands. Traces of early settlement go back to the Paleolithic era, but the first main occupation was by CELTS, who came by direct migration from continental Europe and also as travelers along the western sea routes linking Brittany to Cornwall, Ireland, Scotland, and the Orkney and Shetland islands. The Roman occupation began in AD 43. Most of the English Lowland was eventually romanized, but outlying areas of Wales, the Pennines, the Lake District, and Scotland remained a nonpacified zone from which Celtic marauders might unexpectedly attack. ANGLO-SAXONS came after the decline of Roman Britain and colonized most of the English lowland after the 5th century; they failed, like the Romans, to colonize the north and west, and the division between an Anglo-Saxon south and east and a predominantly Celtic north and west has persisted to this day. Danes settled alongside the English in the 9th century and briefly controlled northeastern and central parts of the English lowland as the DANELAW. The Danish invasions were part of large-scale VIKING movements from the 9th to 11th centuries. Other Vikings (Norse) sailed the western sea routes and settled in the Orkney and Shetland islands, along the west coasts of Scotland, in Ireland, in the Lake District, and in western coastal areas as far south as the Isle of Man. NORMANS conquered England in 1066. Anglo-Nor-

mans had conquered Wales by 1284 but did not anglicize the population much beyond the towns and castles they established along the lowland fringes of North and South Wales; they were also unable to subdue the Scots. Added to this early ethnic mixture were later refugees from continental Europe, such as the French HUGUENOTS; many Irish migrants in the 18th and 19th centuries; Poles and other displaced persons during and after World War II; and since the 1960s more than 1.3 million Asian, West Indian, and other nonwhite immigrants. Historically, most immigrants have in time been absorbed into British society following an initial period of tension.

Languages. The official language is English. Other languages include the CELTIC LANGUAGES Welsh, the national language of Wales, and Scottish Gaelic, so named to distinguish it from Irish Gaelic, the national language of Ireland. According to the 1981 census, Welsh was spoken by about 520,000 people, or about 19% of the total Welsh population, down from 715,000 in 1951. Most Welsh speakers are concentrated in the rural northern and western counties of Wales, where they constitute about 75% of the total population; all but a few are also recorded as English speaking. Welsh nationalism has been strongly linked with encouraging the wider use of Welsh, and since the Welsh Language Act of 1967, the language has enjoyed parity with English in governmental and legal matters throughout Wales. Scottish Gaelic was spoken by some 80,000 people in 1981, down from 95,500 in 1951; it is used primarily in the western Highlands and on the islands. The Scottish nationalist movement is less concerned with promoting Gaelic as a national language for Scotland than with improving economic and social conditions by diverting a greater share of North Sea oil profits to Scotland in the future. Cornish, once used in the southwestern peninsula, and Manx, used on the Isle of Man, are virtually extinct.

Religion. The Anglican Church of England (see ENGLAND, CHURCH OF) and the Presbyterian Church of Scotland (see SCOTLAND, CHURCH OF) are established national churches, but neither is subsidized by the state. Wales has no established church, nor has Northern Ireland, which is approximately two-thirds Protestant and one-third Roman Catholic. The Church of England has the nominal, if not the practical, support of about 60% of the English; about 40% of all Scots support the Church of Scotland. Roman Catholicism is heavily represented in Liverpool, Manchester, Glasgow, and other large industrial cities with large numbers of Irish and continental European immigrant workers. Methodist, Baptist, and United Reform (Presbyterian and Congregational) churches are found almost everywhere in England and Wales; in Scotland the Episcopal (Anglican) church has small numbers of adherents in most towns and a few villages. Other Christian groups include the Society of Friends (Quakers) and the Salvation Army. About 450,000 Jews live in the United Kingdom, mainly in the London area. In addition, recent immigrants have established Islamic mosques and Hindu and Sikh temples in some of the major cities.

Demography. The birthrate is 13.1 (1981) per 1,000 inhabitants and the death rate 11.8. This is a marked change from the mid-1970s, when birth and death rates were virtually balanced at 11.7 per 1,000 inhabitants, giving the nation a near-zero rate of population growth. It is not yet clear whether the change represents a permanent trend.

The population is highly urbanized, and the United Kingdom is the fourth most densely populated nation in Europe (after the Netherlands, Belgium, and West Germany). The most densely populated part of the United Kingdom is England, with 354 persons per km² (918 per mi²); Scotland has a density of 65 per km² (168 per mi²); Wales, 134 per km² (347 per mi²); and Northern Ireland, 110 per km² (284 per mi²). About 35% of the total population is concentrated in the Greater London area and seven other conurbations (continuously built-up urban areas)—Central Clydeside (based on GLASGOW), Tyne and Wear (based on the central cities of NEWCASTLE UPON TYNE and Sunderland), Merseyside (LIVERPOOL and

(Left) *Eton College, the largest English public school for boys, is located in the village of Eton, across the River Thames from Windsor. It was founded in 1440 by Henry VI.*

Tom Tower, Christ Church, designed by Sir Christopher Wren, stands on Tom Quad, the largest quadrangle of Oxford University, England's oldest and most distinguished university. One of Oxford's 35 colleges, Christ Church was founded by Cardinal Wolsey in 1524.

environs), Greater MANCHESTER, West Yorkshire (based on LEEDS and BRADFORD), South Yorkshire (based on SHEFFIELD), and the West Midlands (BIRMINGHAM and the Black Country). Another substantial portion of the population is urbanized in smaller towns with more than 50,000 inhabitants, including the environs of BELFAST and CARDIFF. The most sparsely populated areas are the Highlands of Scotland, upland areas of Wales, and the Pennines.

Areas of most rapid population growth are in outer London, where several of the post-1945 NEW TOWNS (designed to relieve urban congestion) are located, such as Crawley, Bracknell, Hemel Hempstead, Stevenage, Harlow, and Basildon; in the western Midlands; and in the eastern Midlands around DERBY and NOTTINGHAM. By contrast, the old textile and other industrial towns of the Pennines—such as BOLTON, Oldham, Burnley, Blackburn, and Manchester for cotton and Bradford, Halifax and Huddersfield for woolens—are declining, and stagnation is also seen in the industrialized northeast of England and in most of Scotland. The greatest losses of population are occurring in the mining valleys of South Wales and in inner-city areas of Liverpool, Manchester, and Glasgow. Government planning is a major influence in the redistribution of population as the economy changes and in the creation of communities providing higher standards of urban life for the working class as well as for the more affluent.

Education and Health. Education is free and compulsory for all children between the ages of 5 and 16. Nursery schools are also provided for children under 5, but the supply of such schools does not meet the demand. In most cases children in the BRITISH EDUCATION system move from a junior to a senior school at age 11, with some local authorities choosing to transfer children at age 12 or 13. Current educational policy is for comprehensive schools to educate all children up to age 16. A minority stay on in school until 18 or 19 and join a sixth form (upper class level) in the school that prepares them for entrance to university or other forms of higher education. In some areas special sixth form colleges are provided. The majority of the school population, however, leave school at 16 and either go to work or continue education in colleges of further education, technical schools, or colleges offering vocational training on either a full-time, part-time, or evening basis. Evening school classes enroll large numbers of adults in a wide range of academic and recreational classes.

The old grammar schools are now almost completely merged into the comprehensive system of education, although some have chosen to become independent. As independent schools, they, like such prestigious "public" (private) schools as ETON COLLEGE, RUGBY SCHOOL, and WINCHESTER COLLEGE, no longer receive state aid but are required to maintain the same standards of staffing and equipment as the state schools; like them, too, they are subject to periodic inspection. Higher education is provided at 34 universities in England and Wales, including the prestigious universities of CAMBRIDGE, LONDON, and OXFORD; at 8 in Scotland; and at 2 in Northern Ireland. In addition, 7 university colleges and medical and technological institutions are allied with the University of Wales, and the OPEN UNIVERSITY provides instruction and degrees for home-based students via national television channels.

Medical care is provided free or for a small charge to most of the population through the National Health Service. In addition, a small minority financially able to do so choose to remain outside the system and be private, fee-paying patients of hospitals, physicians, and dentists. Under the National Health Service, small charges are made for prescriptions (except for children and senior citizens), for dental treatment, and for optical and other special services. Normally, no costs are incurred by the patient for routine medical care, including visits to the doctor's office, house calls, or hospitalization as a patient or outpatient. Life expectancy is 69 years for men and 75 for women. The principal causes of death are heart and circulatory diseases and cancer. Infant mortality is 12.9 per 1,000 live births.

The Arts. More than 35,000 books are published annually in the United Kingdom, including paperback editions. The best-known university presses are at Oxford and Cambridge, but

(Left) *During Glasgow's growth as a major port, extensive shipyards and dock installations were constructed along both banks of the Clyde River. By the early 1800s, Glasgow—Scotland's largest city—had established itself as a shipbuilding and industrial center.*

(Below) *The town of Mevagissy is a small fishing port and tourist resort along Saint Austell Bay in southwestern Cornwall. The area is also an important source of kaolin for the production of china.*

most other publishers maintain their headquarters in London and, for the Scottish presses, in Edinburgh and Glasgow. For the nation's vast literary heritage see separate entries on ENGLISH LITERATURE, SCOTTISH LITERATURE, and WELSH LITERATURE. Foremost painters include William HOGARTH, Thomas GAINSBOROUGH, Joseph Mallord William TURNER, John CONSTABLE, and William BLAKE (see ENGLISH ART AND ARCHITECTURE). The works of these and other painters are maintained in London at the NATIONAL GALLERY, TATE GALLERY, and other galleries and in some larger cities outside London. Special art exhibitions by the Royal Academy in London attract large crowds every year. Leading composers of ENGLISH MUSIC include Henry PURCELL, Edward ELGAR, Ralph VAUGHN WILLIAMS, and Benjamin BRITTEN. The Albert Hall and Royal Festival Hall are important concert centers in London, and first-class orchestras are maintained in London, Liverpool, Manchester, and Birmingham and by the BBC (British Broadcasting Corporation). The GLYNDEBOURNE OPERA FESTIVAL, ROYAL BALLET, Royal Opera, and English National Opera (formerly Sadler's Wells Opera) are all internationally famous. In Wales *eisteddfods*, festivals of music (especially choral music) and art, are held throughout the year, the most famous being the Royal National Eisteddfod. In Scotland the major event in the arts is the 3-week annual Edinburgh International Festival of Music, Drama, and Art at the end of the summer. Other important cultural events in Britain are the Chichester Festival, the Shakespearean plays at the Royal Shakespeare Theatre in Stratford-on-Avon, and local music and drama festivals. The main source of government support for music and drama is the Arts Council.

ECONOMIC ACTIVITY
In the 14th and 15th centuries, England developed a flourishing wool trade with the Continent and a cottage-based textile industry in sheep-raising areas of the Cotswolds, Pennines, East Anglia (Norwich area), and the southwest. In the 18th century the invention of power-driven textile machinery revolutionized this earlier industry, and spinning and weaving operations moved out of the home and into factories. Early factories were powered by running water, and the abundance of this waterpower (and of soft water for the wool-washing processes) concentrated the early textile industry in the Pennines. Steam engines, fueled by coal, replaced water power after the 1780s, and the coalfields developed as major industrial centers. Lancashire (west Pennines) developed as a cotton textile center; Yorkshire (east Pennines), as the center of woolen

manufactures; Birmingham and the Black Country (West Midlands), as a center for the manufacture of machinery and precision equipment; and the Glasgow area, as a shipbuilding and metallurgical center. By 1851 the United Kingdom was the world's leading industrial nation. It lost this industrial preeminence after the 1920s as other nations began to industrialize. It experimented with nationalization of steel and other key industries in the 1940s and, despite widespread opposition, joined the EEC in 1973.

Manufacturing. Workers directly engaged in manufacturing number approximately 6 million, or about 23% of the total labor force. Of these, about 29% are engaged in the metallurgical and engineering industries, about 5% in chemical industries, about 10% in food processing, and 6% in textile manufacturing. About 10% work in vehicle manufacture, and 8% work in the paper, printing, and publishing industries. Increasing efficiency of production and elimination of uneconomic plants continue to reduce the numbers working in manufacturing. The main centers of industry are on the coalfields of northern England and Scotland, in the western Midlands, and around the major ports, including London.

Queen Elizabeth II, on horseback, reviews a parade of Guards at the entrance to Buckingham Palace in London. The palace, designed (1825) by John Nash, is the principal residence of the British monarch.

(Below) Among Liverpool's Pier Head group of office buildings is the Royal Liver Building (1908–10). Located on the Mersey River in northwestern England, Liverpool has been a major port since the 1700s. From the harbor there are ferry and tunnel connections to Birkenhead.

Mining. Only about 1.2% of the labor force is engaged in mining. Petroleum is the principal mineral produced, with production rapidly approaching the self-sufficiency level of 2 million barrels a day in the early 1980s and proven reserves under the North Sea estimated at 14.8 billion barrels in 1982. Natural gas is produced in association with petroleum. Coal is also mined, but employment in the coal industry has dropped from more than 1 million in 1913 to about 275,000 in the early 1980s, mainly because of loss of export markets, increasing use of petroleum and other fuels, and exhaustion of easily worked coal seams in the coalfields. Coal production has also declined by about half from a peak of about 291 million metric tons (321 million U.S. tons) in 1913 to 130 million metric tons (143 million U.S. tons) in 1980. Sands and gravels are of considerable economic significance; iron ores, tin, and kaolinite (china clay) are of lesser importance.

Power. In 1980 the United Kingdom ranked second in Europe, after West Germany, in electricity production, with an output of about 281 billion kW h. About 65% of all coal mined is used to generate electricity; in addition, large oil-powered generating stations are located near London, Southampton, and other ports. Hydroelectricity contributed about 5.2 billion kW h of the total; most of it is produced in the Scottish Highlands and in southwestern Scotland, with smaller amounts produced in northwestern Wales. Approximately 12% of all electricity is derived from nuclear power. An estimated 21.5% of the nation's total fuel supply is derived from natural gas, which is mined in increasing amounts from under the North Sea; over half of the gas is used for industrial and commercial purposes. Coal and oil each supply about 37%.

Agriculture. Approximately three-fourths of all the land area of England and Wales is used for farming, excluding moorlands used for grazing; in Scotland less than one-fourth of the total area is farmed. The main crops are wheat, barley, oats, peas, beans, vegetables, sugar beets, and green fodder crops; most are grown in the east and south of England, on the east coast of Scotland, and on the Lancashire and Cheshire plains. Livestock farming, mainly for beef and dairy products, prevails in lowland areas elsewhere, with sheep farming predominant on higher ground. Truck farming (called market gardening in the United Kingdom) is important near London and other large cities and on the south coast. Flowers and early potatoes are a specialty in mild and sheltered areas of Cornwall and the Scilly Islands. Less than 2% of the total labor force is engaged in agriculture, and the number of people working the land has declined steadily since 1945 in the face of increased mechanization and greater agricultural efficiency.

Forestry and Fishing. Forestry is of minor national importance but has given useful employment in remote districts that have

been reforested. In some areas the state-owned forests are also open for visitors and have become economically important as tourist attractions; in other areas, including the Lake District, reforestation is opposed for fear that it would spoil open mountain views and thereby damage a thriving tourist industry. Fishing has long been a major activity, and large fishing ports include Lerwick (in the Shetland Islands), Aberdeen, Grimsby, Hull, Lowestoft, North Shields, and Yarmouth on the east coast, and Fleetwood and Milford Haven on the west coast. Major fish-processing industries are located in Aberdeen, Grimsby, Hull, and Yarmouth. In 1980, 710,500 metric tons (783,192 U.S. tons) of fish were landed, but international tensions over access to fishing grounds in the North Atlantic and Arctic threaten the industry.

Transportation. More than 2,400 km (1,490 mi) of high-speed-motorway supplement the United Kingdom's older and slower highway system based on 13,161 km (8,178 mi) of trunk roads radiating out from London with "bypasses" around major cities to lessen congestion. Railroads were nationalized in 1947, and service was reduced and modernized by British Railways (BR), which operates about 18,000 km (11,200 mi) of track in England, Scotland, and Wales. More than 320 km (200 mi) of wide-gauge track is operated by Northern Ireland Railways (NIR). Many rail lines are currently or are scheduled to be electrified, including a number of commuter routes into London and the well-traveled routes between London and Birmingham, Manchester, Liverpool, and Glasgow. Except for the Manchester Ship Canal, canals and canalized rivers carry little freight today. The busiest ports—some brought to recent prominence by North Sea oil—are London, Milford Haven, Tees and Hartlepool, Forth, Grimsby and Immingham, Southampton, Shetland (Sullom Voe), Medway, Orkney (Flotta), Liverpool, and Manchester.

Trade. Imports generally exceed exports by value, but the difference is usually balanced by income from worldwide financial, insurance, and transport services and from an increasingly successful tourist industry. More than half of all exports consist of electrical equipment, aircraft and aircraft engines, road vehicles and tractors, scientific instruments, and other metallurgical and engineering products. Other leading exports are chemical products, which have increased in recent years, and textiles, which have declined. The four main groups of imports are semimanufactured goods; manufactured articles; petroleum and other raw materials; and food, drink, and tobacco. Britain's main trading partners are countries of the European Community.

GOVERNMENT

The United Kingdom is a constitutional monarchy with a parliamentary form of government. The ruling sovereign (since 1952) is Queen ELIZABETH II; the heir apparent is Prince CHARLES, who by tradition as the eldest son of the monarch is Prince of Wales. As head of state the sovereign ceremonially opens each new session of Parliament and entrusts executive authority to the prime minister (since 1979, Margaret THATCHER) and the cabinet. Legislative authority rests with a bicameral Parliament, but effective power lies more with the directly elected House of Commons (lower house) than with the House of Lords (upper house), consisting of hereditary and life peers. The prime minister is appointed by the sovereign as the leader of the majority party or coalition of parties in the House of Commons. The maximum term of Parliament is 5 years, but elections may be called earlier if the government loses the support of the Commons or if it chooses.

The principal political parties are the CONSERVATIVE PARTY, led by Margaret Thatcher, and the LABOUR PARTY, led by Neil Kinnock. Other parties include the LIBERAL PARTY, led by David Steel; the Social Democratic party, which broke away from the Labour party in 1981; the Communist party; and the locally important Ulster Unionist party, the Scottish National party, and the Plaid Cymru (Welsh Nationalist party).

Of the 650 members in the Commons, 523 represent England, 38 represent Wales, 72 represent Scotland, and 17 represent Northern Ireland. The Isle of Man and the Channel Islands have separate local assemblies and are self-governing.

Plans to provide devolution (home rule) to Scotland and Wales ended in 1979, when voters in Wales rejected a plan to establish a Welsh assembly in Cardiff, and voters in Scotland approved, but with less than the necessary majority, establishment of a separate assembly for Scotland in Edinburgh. Home rule had been in effect for Northern Ireland (since 1921) but was ended in 1972 because of continuing Protestant-Catholic hostilities. Government of Northern Ireland now rests with the secretary of state for Northern Ireland, who is answerable to the Parliament in London. By a 1985 Anglo-Irish agreement, the government of the Republic of Ireland was given a consultative role in the affairs of Northern Ireland.

Local government in England underwent major reorganization in 1974. Local administration is now managed through 6 metropolitan counties; 39 nonmetropolitan counties; and Greater London, which has a central council for overall planning and local councils for the administration of the 32 boroughs and the City of London. The 6 metropolitan counties are the conurbations of Tyne and Wear, Merseyside, Greater Manchester, West Yorkshire, South Yorkshire, and the West Midlands. The 39 nonmetropolitan counties are subdivided into 296 districts. Wales is divided into 8 counties, subdivided into 37 districts; Scotland is divided into 9 regions and 3 "island districts"—Shetland, Orkney, and the Western Isles—and subdivided into 53 districts.

British dependencies overseas include Gibraltar, Bermuda, British Virgin Islands, Falkland Islands, Turks and Caicos Islands, Cayman Islands, Montserrat, Hong Kong, the British Indian Ocean Territory, Saint Helena, Ascension, Tristan da Cunha, and the Pitcairn Islands.   THOMAS W. FREEMAN

Bibliography: GENERAL: Blythe, Ronald, *Akenfield: Portrait of an English Village* (1969); Churchill, Winston L. S., *The Island Race* (1964); Derry, T. K., *United Kingdom Today* (1970); Fawcett, Charles B., *Political Geography of the British Empire* (1933); Fleure, Herbert J., and Davies, M., *A Natural History of Man in Britain*, rev. ed. (1970); Freeman, Thomas W., *Geography and Planning*, 4th ed. (1974), and *Geography and Regional Administration: England and Wales: 1830–1968* (1968); Graves, Norman, and White, John, *Geography of the British Isles* (1971); Halsey, Albert H., *Change in British Society* (1978); Irwin, John, *Modern Britain: An Introduction* (1976); Mauger, Peter, and Smith, Leslie, *The British People, 1902–1968* (1972); Sampson, Anthony, *The Changing Anatomy of Britain* (1983); Theroux, Paul, *The Kingdom by the Sea* (1983).

CULTURE: Betts, Ernest, *The Film Business: A History of British Cinema, 1896–1972* (1973); Cox, C. B., and Dyson, A. E., eds., *The Twentieth Century Mind: History, Ideas, and Literature in Britain*, 3 vols. (1972); Maxwell, Robert, *New British Architecture* (1972); Sunderland, J., *Painting in Britain, 1525–1975* (1976); Young, P. M., *A History of British Music* (1967).

ECONOMY: Allen, George C., *The Structure of Industry in Britain* (1970); Alt, James E., *The Politics of Economic Decline* (1979); Anthony, Vivian S., *British Overseas Trade*, 3d ed. (1976); Brittan, Samuel, *The Economic Consequences of Democracy* (1979); Morris, Derek, ed., *The Economic System of the United Kingdom* (1977); Murphy, Brian, *A History of the British Economy*, 2 vols. (1973); Stamp, Laurence Dudley, and Beaver, Stanley H., *The British Isles: A Geographic and Economic Survey*, 6th ed. (1971).

GOVERNMENT AND POLITICS: Bromhead, Peter, *Britain's Developing Constitution* (1974); Carter, Gwendolen M., *Government of the United Kingdom*, 3d ed. (1972); Cook, Chris, and Ramsden, John, eds., *Trends in British Politics since 1945* (1978); Osmond, John, *Creative Conflict: The Politics of Welsh Devolution* (1978).

HISTORY: Childs, David, *Britain since 1945* (1980); Gamble, Andrew, *Britain in Decline* (1983); Lloyd, T. O., *The British Empire, 1558 to 1983* (1984); Mowat, C. F., *Great Britain since 1914* (1971); Riley, P. W., *The Union of England and Scotland* (1979).

See also: GREAT BRITAIN, HISTORY OF; separate articles on all counties and major cities and land features in the United Kingdom.

United Methodist Church: see METHODISM.

United Mine Workers of America

The United Mine Workers of America (UMW) is an independent labor union, organized on an industrial basis, comprising workers in the coal industry. It was founded in 1890 through the merger of several earlier organizations.

Always militant, it almost disintegrated several times from economic depression, employer hostility, and periodic unemployment. In 1897 it initiated a successful organization drive; in 1898 it achieved an 8-hour work day in the important areas of western Pennsylvania, Indiana, Ohio, and Illinois. John L. Lewis headed the union from 1920 to 1960. During that period the UMW was at the center of the militant labor movement. When the National Industrial Recovery Act (NIRA) of 1933 guaranteed a union's right to bargain and organize, Lewis fought to organize other industrial unions, but the American Federation of Labor (AFL) refused to support him. He then created the Committee for Industrial Organization, which became (1938) the Congress of Industrial Organizations (CIO), for which the UMW provided support until it withdrew in 1942. Following World War II the UMW's agreement to automation in mining cost many miners their jobs but brought greater benefits to those remaining; the union's pioneering work in the development of welfare funds continues to this day. It rejoined the AFL in 1946 but again became independent in 1947.

Lewis was succeeded (1960) as president by Thomas Kennedy, after whose death (1963) W. A. "Tony" Boyle assumed leadership. Boyle's opponent Joseph Yablonski was murdered in 1969; Boyle was subsequently forced out (1972) of the presidency and convicted (1974) of the murder. Arnold Miller then became president. He was succeeded by Samuel Church in 1979, who was defeated in 1982 UMW elections by Richard

Trumka. In 1983 the UMW had 161,745 members and 54,862 retired members. The union had assets of $53.5 million in 1981.

Bibliography: Armbrister, Trevor, *Act of Vengeance: The Yablonski Murders and Their Solution* (1975); Dobofsky, Melvin, and Van Tine, Warren, *John L. Lewis: A Biography* (1977); Levy, Elizabeth, and Richards, Tad, *Struggle and Lose, Struggle and Win: The United Mine Workers* (1977).

United Nations

The United Nations (UN) is a general international organization established at the end of World War II to promote international peace and security. It is the second such organization, having replaced the LEAGUE OF NATIONS, which was founded in the aftermath of World War I.

ORIGINS AND PURPOSE

The United Nations officially came into existence on Oct. 24, 1945, when 51 original members ratified its charter. The main purposes of the organization were to "save succeeding generations from the scourge of war"; develop friendly relations among states; cooperate in solving international economic, social, cultural, and humanitarian problems; and promote respect for human rights and fundamental freedoms.

To enable it to work toward its goals, the UN was equipped with six major organs: the Security Council, General Assembly, Economic and Social Council, Trusteeship Council, INTERNATIONAL COURT OF JUSTICE, and the Secretariat. In addition, a number of specialized agencies were attached to the UN system to deal with specific international problems. The primary responsibility for the maintenance of international peace and security was assigned to the Security Council. Based on the assumption that the five major military contributors to victory in World War II—the United States, the USSR, Great Britain, France, and China—could reach unanimity on the question of peace in the postwar world, the Security Council was to be the international guardian of peace. The second major UN organ, the General Assembly, was to operate as a forum for debating world issues. The underlying assumption in creating the General Assembly was that the airing of disputes among nations could contribute to the pacific settlement of those disputes as well as to peaceful changes in the international system.

A third principal organ, the Economic and Social Council, was created in the belief that a great deal of international strife was rooted in poverty and misery and that therefore the UN should do its utmost to help raise standards of living and improve economic conditions throughout the world. Because, moreover, the founders of the UN saw colonialism as another frequent source of war, they felt it necessary also to employ the new world organization to mitigate the anger of dependent peoples against their colonial masters. To devise a technique whereby independence could be gained with as little

bloodshed as possible, they provided a fourth major organ, the Trusteeship Council. Yet another cause of war was believed by the founders of the UN to lie in the absence of common legal standards among nations. For this reason they included within the UN framework a world court—the International Court of Justice. Finally, the founders of the UN were convinced that the maintenance of peace required a nucleus of men and women whose loyalty was first and foremost not to any particular nation but to the entire international community. To form such an international civil service, they established a sixth major organ of the United Nations, the Secretariat, headed by the secretary-general.

STRUCTURE AND POWERS

The Security Council.   The organ with the primary responsibility for maintaining peace and security is the Security Council. Originally the Security Council had 11 members, but now it has 15. Five of these—China, France, the USSR, Great Britain, and the United States—are permanent members. The other ten members are elected by the General Assembly for 2-year terms. Each member of the council has one vote. Decisions on matters of procedure must carry by an affirmative vote of at least 9 of the 15 members. Decisions on substantive matters also require nine votes, with no negative vote from any of the five permanent members. This is the so-called Great Power unanimity rule, often referred to as the "veto." All five permanent members have exercised the veto right at one time or another. If a permanent member does not support a decision but has no desire to block it through a veto, it may abstain; an abstention is not regarded as a veto.

Under the charter, all members of the UN agree to accept and carry out the decisions of the council. While other organs of the UN make recommendations to governments, the council alone has the power to make decisions which member states are obligated under the charter to carry out. When a dispute leads to open warfare, the council may decide on cease-fire directives, enforcement measures, or collective military action. Sometimes it sends UN observers or peacekeeping forces to help reduce tensions in troubled areas.

A state that is not a member of the UN or is a member of the UN but not of the Security Council may participate, without vote, in its discussions when the council considers that the country's interests are specially affected.

The General Assembly.   The General Assembly is composed of all member states of the UN. It is the main deliberative organ of the UN and has the right to discuss and make recommendations on all matters within the scope of the charter. It has no power to compel action by any government, but its recommendations carry moral weight as an expression of world opinion. As new problems arise, the General Assembly initiates activities to deal with them. The General Assembly, consequently, has encouraged humanitarian relief efforts, devel-

The United Nations Security Council, comprising five permanent and ten temporary members, was conceived as the principal peacekeeping body of the UN. Unlike other organs of the UN, the Security Council is able to make decisions binding on all members of the organization.

opment programs, campaigns against colonialism and racism, and the negotiation of treaties and other agreements on matters of global concern, such as the Law of the Sea.

The General Assembly expanded its role during the Korean War. Under the Uniting for Peace resolution, adopted by the General Assembly in November 1950, the assembly gave itself the power to take action if the Security Council, because of the lack of unanimity of its permanent members, fails to act in a case where there appears to be a threat to the peace, a breach of the peace, or an act of aggression.

Each member of the General Assembly has one vote. Decisions on important questions—such as recommendations on peace and security; admission, suspension, and expulsion of members; and budgetary matters—need a two-thirds majority. Decisions on other questions are by simple majority. The regular session begins each year on the third Tuesday in September and continues usually until mid-December.

The Economic and Social Council. The Economic and Social Council, under the authority of the General Assembly, coordinates the economic and social work of the UN and the specialized agencies and institutions. The council makes recommendations and initiates activities relating to development, world trade, natural resources, human rights, population, social welfare, science and technology, and many other economic and social questions.

The council has 54 members. One-third of its members are elected each year by the General Assembly for a 3-year term of office. Voting in the Economic and Social Council is by simple majority; each member has one vote.

Trusteeship Council. The Trusteeship Council was established to deal with nonindependent territories previously held under League of Nations mandate, territories taken from the defeated World War II powers, and such other territories as might be handed over to it by their possessors. It operates under the authority of the General Assembly.

The Trusteeship Council consists of representatives of those states which administer trust territories, representatives of permanent members of the Security Council that do not administer trust territories, and enough others to assure that membership is divided equally between administering and nonadministering states. The principal activities of the Trusteeship Council have included receiving annual reports from the administering states and periodically visiting the territories. Since its establishment the Trusteeship Council has seen the 11 trust territories originally under its control transformed into other entities.

International Court of Justice. The International Court of Justice receives cases from states and international organizations. The court is also empowered to give advisory opinions when requested to do so by organs of the UN and specialized agencies. Generally, states have preferred to resolve their disputes outside of the jurisdiction of the court.

Secretariat. The first secretary-general of the United Nations was Trygve LIE of Norway, who served until 1953. Dag HAMMARSKJÖLD, of Sweden, served from 1953 until his death in a plane crash in Africa in 1961, when he was succeeded by U THANT of Burma. Kurt WALDHEIM of Austria served two consecutive terms from January 1972 to December 1981. In January 1982, Javier PÉREZ DE CUÉLLAR of Peru began a five-year term, which was extended, in October 1986, through 1991.

The Secretariat, an international staff working at UN headquarters and in the field, carries out the day-to-day work of the UN. Each staff member takes an oath not to seek or receive instructions from any outside authority; under the UN Charter, each member state undertakes not to seek to influence the Secretariat in the discharge of its duties. In practice, however, this provision has been violated.

The work of the secretary-general and the staff is varied and includes providing mediation in resolving international disputes; administering peacekeeping operations; preparing surveys of world economic trends and problems; studying human rights and natural resources; organizing international conferences; compiling statistics; and interpreting speeches, translating documents, and servicing the communications media of the world with information about the UN.

Specialized Agencies. The specialized agencies attached to the United Nations system can be divided roughly into two groups. The first group, the major purpose of which is to broaden and facilitate communications among nations, includes the Universal Postal Union (UPU; see POSTAL UNION, UNIVERSAL), the INTERNATIONAL CIVIL AVIATION ORGANIZATION (ICAO), the WORLD METEOROLOGICAL ORGANIZATION (WMO), the International Telecommunication Union (ITU), and the Inter-Governmental Maritime Consultative Organization (IMCO). The second group may be called the "welfare" agencies, in the sense that each is intended to improve world economic, social, and cultural conditions and thus build defenses for peace. The oldest of these is the INTERNATIONAL LABOR ORGANIZATION (ILO). Other agencies in this group include the FOOD AND AGRICULTURE ORGANIZATION (FAO), the WORLD HEALTH ORGANIZATION (WHO), the UNITED NATIONS EDUCATIONAL, SCIENTIFIC, AND CULTURAL ORGANIZATION (UNESCO), the WORLD BANK, the INTERNATIONAL DEVELOPMENT ASSOCIATION (IDA), the INTERNATIONAL FINANCE CORPORATION (IFC), the INTERNATIONAL MONETARY FUND (IMF), the INTERNATIONAL ATOMIC ENERGY AGENCY (IAEA), the GENERAL AGREEMENT ON TARIFFS AND TRADE (GATT), the Office of the United Nations High Commissioner for Refugees (UNHCR; see REFUGEES, OFFICE OF THE UNITED NATIONS HIGH COMMISSIONER FOR), and the United Nations Relief and Works Agency for Palestine Refugees (UNRWA).

DEVELOPMENTS SINCE 1945

The UN has experienced many changes since 1945 when the United States was the most dominant of the 51 states in the organization. Today the organization has about three times (159 in 1987) as many member states, the representatives from Africa, Asia, and Latin America play major roles in its affairs, and the USSR and its allies are much more influential in the UN today than they were in 1945.

The cold war between the United States and the USSR had a serious impact on the UN, as did the rise of the colonial world to self-government and the increased interdependence among nations. One effect of the cold war was the opposition from 1949 until 1971 by the United States to the admission of the People's Republic of China to the UN. When Communist China was finally admitted in 1971, the Republic of China (Taiwan) lost its seat.

Militarily, the UN reflected the rising international tensions both between the USSR and the United States and also among emerging nations. When Soviet-supported North Korea invaded American-supported South Korea in June 1950, the Security Council—with the USSR absent—called upon all members to "repel the armed attack." Because almost 90 percent of the non-Korean forces fighting under the UN flag were U.S. forces, the UN unified command was primarily a U.S. operation.

The United Nations has since engaged in other military activities, but these have not been on the scale of the Korean War, nor were the military forces of the United States directly involved. The UN established several major peacekeeping forces in the Middle East, Africa, and Cyprus.

The UN military action in the Middle East was considerably less dramatic than the Korean campaign. The first United Nations Emergency Force (UNEF) that was dispatched to the troubled area in 1956 never exceeded 6,000 troops. UNEF was not meant to be a fighting army; its purpose was to serve as a symbol of the UN's involvement, which, it was hoped, would succeed in bringing about the neutralization of the disputed areas. It constituted for the first time a genuine international police force not dominated by any single power. In fact, all the great powers were specifically excluded from it.

The second United Nations Emergency Force (UNEF II) was established immediately after the conclusion of the war between Israel and its Arab neighbors in late October 1973. The force was deployed by the Security Council along the disengagement line that had been negotiated between Israel and Egypt by U.S. secretary of state Henry Kissinger. In May 1974, in the wake of the disengagement arrangement that had been worked out by Secretary Kissinger between Israel and Syria, the Security Council established a small (1,250-person) UN

MEMBERSHIP OF THE UNITED NATIONS
(As of September 1984)

Member	Date of Admission	Member	Date of Admission	Member	Date of Admission
Afghanistan	Nov. 19, 1946	Greece*	Oct. 25, 1945	Philippines*	Oct. 24, 1945
Albania	Dec. 14, 1955	Grenada	Sept. 17, 1974	Poland*	Oct. 24, 1945
Algeria	Oct. 8, 1962	Guatemala*	Nov. 21, 1945	Portugal	Dec. 14, 1955
Angola	Dec. 1, 1976	Guinea	Dec. 12, 1958	Qatar	Sept. 21, 1971
Antigua and Barbuda	Nov. 11, 1981	Guinea-Bissau	Sept. 17, 1974	Romania	Dec. 14, 1955
Argentina*	Oct. 24, 1945	Guyana	Sept. 20, 1966	Rwanda	Sept. 18, 1962
Australia*	Nov. 1, 1945	Haiti*	Oct. 24, 1945	Saint Christopher and	
Austria	Dec. 14, 1955	Honduras*	Dec. 17, 1945	Nevis	Sept. 23 1983
Bahamas	Sept. 18, 1973	Hungary	Dec. 14, 1955	Saint Lucia	Sept. 21, 1979
Bahrain	Sept. 21, 1971	Iceland	Dec. 19, 1946	Saint Vincent and the	
Bangladesh	Sept. 17, 1974	India*	Oct. 30, 1945	Grenadines	Sept. 16, 1980
Barbados	Dec. 9, 1966	Indonesia	Sept. 28, 1950	Sao Tomé and Príncipe	Sept. 16, 1975
Belgium*	Dec. 27, 1945	Iran*	Oct. 24, 1945	Saudi Arabia*	Oct. 24, 1945
Belize	Sept. 25, 1981	Iraq*	Dec. 21, 1945	Senegal	Sept. 28, 1960
Belorussian Soviet		Ireland	Dec. 14, 1955	Seychelles	Sept. 21, 1976
Socialist Republic*	Oct. 24, 1945	Israel	May 11, 1949	Sierra Leone	Sept. 27, 1961
Benin (formerly Dahomey)	Sept. 20, 1960	Italy	Dec. 14, 1955	Singapore	Sept. 21, 1965
Bhutan	Sept. 21, 1971	Ivory Coast	Sept. 20, 1960	Solomon Islands	Sept. 19, 1978
Bolivia*	Nov. 14, 1945	Jamaica	Sept. 18, 1962	Somalia	Sept. 20, 1960
Botswana	Oct. 17, 1966	Japan	Dec. 18, 1956	South Africa*	Nov. 7, 1945
Brazil*	Oct. 24, 1945	Jordan	Dec. 14, 1955	Spain	Dec. 14, 1955
Brunei	Sept. 21, 1984	Kampuchea	Dec. 14, 1955	Sri Lanka	Dec. 14, 1955
Bulgaria	Dec. 14, 1955	Kenya	Dec. 16, 1963	Sudan	Nov. 12, 1956
Burma	Apr. 19, 1948	Kuwait	May 14, 1963	Suriname	Dec. 4, 1975
Burundi	Sept. 18, 1962	Laos	Dec. 14, 1955	Swaziland	Sept. 24, 1968
Cameroon	Sept. 20, 1960	Lebanon*	Oct. 24, 1945	Sweden	Nov. 19, 1946
Canada*	Nov. 9, 1945	Lesotho	Oct. 17, 1966	Syrian Arab Republic*	Oct. 24, 1945
Cape Verde	Sept. 16, 1975	Liberia*	Nov. 2, 1945	Tanzania	Dec. 14, 1961
Central African Republic	Sept. 20, 1960	Libya	Dec. 14, 1955	Thailand	Dec. 16, 1946
Chad	Sept. 20, 1960	Luxembourg*	Oct. 24, 1945	Togo	Sept. 20, 1960
Chile*	Oct. 24, 1945	Madagascar (Malagasy		Trinidad and Tobago	Sept. 18, 1962
China†	Oct. 24, 1945	Republic)	Sept. 20, 1960	Tunisia	Nov. 12, 1956
Colombia*	Nov. 5, 1945	Malawi	Dec. 1, 1964	Turkey*	Oct. 24, 1945
Comoros	Nov. 12, 1975	Malaysia	Sept. 17, 1957	Uganda	Oct. 25, 1962
Congo	Sept. 20, 1960	Maldives	Sept. 21, 1965	Ukrainian Soviet Socialist	
Costa Rica*	Nov. 2, 1945	Mali	Sept. 28, 1960	Republic*	Oct. 24, 1945
Cuba*	Oct. 24, 1945	Malta	Dec. 1, 1964	Union of Soviet Socialist	
Cyprus	Sept. 20, 1960	Mauritania	Oct. 27, 1961	Republics*	Oct. 24, 1945
Czechoslovakia*	Oct. 24, 1945	Mauritius	Apr. 24, 1968	United Arab Emirates	Dec. 9, 1971
Denmark*	Oct. 24, 1945	Mexico*	Nov. 7, 1945	United Kingdom of Great	
Djibouti	Sept. 20, 1977	Mongolia	Oct. 27, 1961	Britain and Northern	
Dominica	Sept. 18, 1979	Morocco	Nov. 12, 1956	Ireland*	Oct. 24, 1945
Dominican Republic*	Oct. 24, 1945	Mozambique	Sept. 16, 1975	United States of America*	Oct. 24, 1945
Ecuador*	Dec. 21, 1945	Nepal	Dec. 14, 1955	Upper Volta	Sept. 20, 1960
Egypt*	Oct. 24, 1945	Netherlands*	Dec. 10, 1945	Uruguay*	Dec. 18, 1945
El Salvador*	Oct. 24, 1945	New Zealand*	Oct. 24, 1945	Vanuatu	Sept. 15, 1981
Equatorial Guinea	Nov. 12, 1968	Nicaragua*	Oct. 24, 1945	Venezuela*	Nov. 15, 1945
Ethiopia*	Nov. 13, 1945	Niger	Sept. 20, 1960	Vietnam	Sept. 20, 1977
Fiji	Oct. 13, 1970	Nigeria	Oct. 7, 1960	Western Samoa	Dec. 15, 1976
Finland	Dec. 14, 1955	Norway*	Nov. 27, 1945	Yemen Arab Republic	Sept. 30, 1947
France*	Oct. 24, 1945	Oman	Oct. 7, 1971	Yemen, People's	
Gabon	Sept. 20, 1960	Pakistan	Sept. 30, 1947	Democratic Republic of	Dec. 14, 1967
Gambia	Sept. 21, 1965	Panama*	Nov. 13, 1945	Yugoslavia*	Oct. 24, 1945
Germany, East	Sept. 18, 1973	Papua New Guinea	Oct. 10, 1975	Zaire	Sept. 20, 1960
Germany, West	Sept. 18, 1973	Paraguay*	Oct. 24, 1945	Zambia	Dec. 1, 1964
Ghana	Mar. 8, 1957	Peru*	Oct. 31, 1945	Zimbabwe	Aug. 25, 1980

*Original member.
†The Republic of China (Taiwan) represented China until 1971, when the UN voted to have China represented by the People's Republic of China.

Disengagement Observer Force drawn from UNEF. They were transferred for patrol duty to the Golan Heights. In an attempt to separate Israelis and Palestinian guerrillas, the UN Interim Forces in Lebanon (UNIFIL) was established in 1978. By mid-1982, 7,000 troops had been deployed to southern Lebanon, they were brushed aside when Israel occupied west Beirut in September 1982, but they stayed on.

Perhaps the most complex military challenge to confront the United Nations was the one that occurred in the Congo between 1960 and 1964. The UN force of 20,000 mostly African troops had to attempt to keep brutal tribal warfare to a minimum, assume some governmental functions, and forestall great power intervention.

In March 1964 yet another peacekeeping experiment was launched, this time in Cyprus. When the Greek and Turkish communities on that island found themselves unable to resolve their differences and civil war became an increasingly ominous threat, the Security Council met in emergency session and authorized a peace force. Three thousand British troops already on the island were deputized as UN policemen, and in addition Canada, Sweden, Ireland, and Finland contributed troops, bringing the total to 7,000.

Along with its peacekeeping operations, the UN has also been responsible for a number of important treaties in the area of arms control. Most significant among these are the treaties demilitarizing outer space (1967), prohibiting the spread of nuclear weapons (1968), prohibiting the emplacement of nuclear weapons on the ocean floors (1971), imposing a ban on biochemical warfare (1975), and establishing a ban on environmental warfare (1976).

The 1970s witnessed an integrated approach by the United Nations to deal with some of the world's most critical nonmilitary problems. A series of global conferences was organized under UN auspices to address the main challenges facing the world. The first of these was a World Conference on the Human Environment held in Stockholm in 1972. The year 1974 saw a number of global conferences concerned with such matters as raw materials and development, the law of the sea, world population, and world food. All these conferences emphasized the need to respond to global challenges with global initiatives. This "planetary management" movement continued to gather momentum throughout the 1970s and during the 1980s, with more international conferences. These dealt with the status of women, urban growth, the spread of deserts, and, once more, the law of the sea and population.

In recent years the United Nations has been the object of considerable criticism in many quarters. Its seeming inability to deal with political crises is often blamed for its declining reputation. The total powerlessness of the UN during the Vietnam War added especially to the criticism. This kind of criticism overlooks the fact that many disputes are brought to the UN only when the participants in the crisis have already failed to resolve it and it has become acute, even violent. Another criticism has been aimed at the voting rules of the General Assembly, which stipulate that each member has one vote, regardless of its size. Thus China, with a population of over 1 billion has the same vote as the Seychelles, with a population of about 65,000.

Whatever the criticisms, however, nations have felt it useful to remain in the organization rather than leave it. For that reason, the United Nations is an institution that continues to play a role in the international political arena.

JOHN G. STOESSINGER

Bibliography: Bailey, Sydney D., *The Procedure of the UN Security Council* (1975); Barros, James, ed., *The United Nations: Past, Present, and Future* (1972); Claude, Inis L., *Swords into Plowshares*, 4th ed. (1971); Eichelberger, C. M., *The UN: The First Twenty-Five Years*, 4th ed. (1970); Elmandjra, Mahdi, *The United Nations System: An Analysis* (1973); Finley, Blanche, *The Structure of the United Nations General Assembly*, 3 vols. (1977); Goodrich, Leland M., *The United Nations in a Changing World* (1974); Goodrich, Leland M., et al., *Charter of the United Nations: Commentary and Documents*, 3d ed. (1969); Gordenker, Leon, ed., *The United Nations in International Politics* (1971); Hajnal, Peter I., *Guide to United Nations Organization, Documentation and Publishing for Students, Researchers, Librarians* (1978); Kaufman, J., *United Nations Decision Making* (1980); Kim, Samuel S., *China, the United Nations, and World Order* (1979); Murphy, John F., *The United Nations and the Control of International Violence* (1983); United Nations, *Everyone's United Nations*, 9th ed. (1979), and *Basic Facts about the United Nations* (1980); Yeselson, Abraham, *A Dangerous Place: The United Nations as a Weapon in World Politics* (1974).

United Nations Children's Fund

The United Nations Children's Fund (UNICEF) was established as the United Nations International Children's Emergency Fund in 1946 at the General Assembly's first session. Originally it was responsible for assisting child welfare programs in countries devastated by World War II, but after 1950 its scope expanded to developing nations. UNICEF helps governments develop national nutrition programs and child health and welfare services and gives direct aid in the form of food and medical supplies to children in emergency situations.

UNICEF was awarded the Nobel Peace Prize (1965). It is governed by a 41-nation executive board elected by the UN Economic and Social Council and administered by an executive director headquartered in New York City. UNICEF is financed totally by voluntary contributions from governments, individuals, organizations, and activities such as the sale of UNICEF greeting cards.

JOHN G. STOESSINGER

Bibliography: Russell, Vivian, *The History of UNICEF* (1974).

United Nations Educational, Scientific, and Cultural Organization

The United Nations Educational, Scientific, and Cultural Organization, or UNESCO, was established at a London conference in November 1945. In 1946 it became a specialized agency of the United Nations. Its purpose was to further the cause of peace by increasing understanding among nations through education and research. Its founders, believing that nations' ignorance of one another cause distrust and can lead to war, wrote in the preamble of the UNESCO charter: "Since war begins in the minds of men, it is in the minds of men that the defenses of peace must be constructed."

The organization was the culmination of more than 25 years of attempts to establish international cooperation in education and culture and is a successor to the League of Nations International Committee on Intellectual Cooperation. UNESCO's activities fall into the following general categories: expanding and directing education so as to enable the people of every country to further their own development; helping to establish the scientific and technological foundations through which every country can make better use of its resources; encouraging national cultural values and the preservation of cultural heritage so as to derive maximum advantage from modernization without the loss of cultural identity and diversity; developing communication for the balanced flow of information and information systems for the universal pooling of knowledge; and promoting the social sciences as instruments for the realization of human rights, justice, and peace. UNESCO is geared to act even in crisis situations, as when, for example, it set up emergency schools for Arab refugee children in the Middle East.

Like other specialized organizations of the UN, UNESCO has its own budget, constitution, and separate organization. UNESCO is guided by the General Conference composed of one representative from each member country. It meets biennially to approve a program and budget. An Executive Board consisting of 45 members elected by the General Conference meets two or three times a year and is responsible for executing the program of the General Conference. The Secretariat carries out the program. It consists of a director-general and an international staff, headquartered in Paris. In 1986, UNESCO had 158 members.

In December 1984 the United States, having announced its intention a year earlier, withdrew from UNESCO because of the agency's inefficient administration and increased politicization, including attacks against Western press freedom. The United Kingdom and Singapore, following the U.S. example, withdrew at the end of 1985.

Bibliography: Evans, G. H., *The United States and UNESCO* (1971); Hajnal, Peter I., *Guide to UNESCO* (1983); Hoggart, Richard, *An Idea and Its Servants: UNESCO from Within* (1978); Sewell, James P., *UNESCO and World Politics* (1975).

United Negro College Fund

The United Negro College Fund, founded in 1944, is an association of 42 fully accredited private colleges, universities, and professional schools primarily for black students. Its primary purpose is fund raising, and it also advises its member schools and coordinates research on black higher education.

United Presbyterian Church: see PRESBYTERIANISM.

United Press International: see PRESS AGENCIES AND SYNDICATES.

United Service Organizations

The United Service Organizations (USO) were founded in 1941 to provide United States military personnel with clubs and centers that serve social, educational, and religious needs. A civilian federation, the USO is staffed largely by unpaid volunteers and funded by private contributions. The organizations operate service facilities and outreach programs in nearly 175 U.S. and overseas locations.

United States

The United States of America is located in the middle of the North American continent. The 48 states of the conterminous United States stretch from the Atlantic Ocean in the east, where the country has a 6,000-km-long (3,700-mi) coastline—including the Gulf of Mexico—to the Pacific, where the coast stretches for 2,100 km (1,300 mi). The United States shares borders with only 2 other countries. In the north the border extends across the width of both Canada and the United States and between Alaska (the 49th state) and Canada for 8,900 km (5,500 mi); in the south the shorter border with Mexico is 3,111 km (1,933 mi) long. Hawaii (the 50th state) is composed of a group of Pacific islands about 3,400 km (2,100 mi) southwest of San Francisco; Alaska occupies the northwestern extremity of North America, with a 10,700-km (6,700-mi) coastline on the Pacific and Arctic oceans.

The United States is the world's fourth largest country (after the USSR, Canada, and China) and the fourth most populous (after China, India, and the USSR). The 50 states are blessed with a variety of mineral, agricultural, water, and other land resources that provide the basis for a highly productive economy—in fact, the United States is the world's wealthiest nation. For most of the 20th century the country has enjoyed economic preeminence throughout the world, particularly during the post–World War II era. Yet within the United

UNITED STATES OF AMERICA

   LAND. Area: 9,372,575 km² (3,618,770 mi²). Capital: Washington, D.C. (1987 est. pop., 626,000). Largest city: New York (1986 est. pop., 7,262,700).
   PEOPLE. Population (1988 est.): 246,100,000; density (1988 est.): 26 persons per km² (68 per mi²). Distribution (1988): 74% urban, 26% rural. Annual growth (1987–88 est.): 0.94%. Official language: English. Major religions: Protestantism, Roman Catholicism, Judaism, Orthodoxy.
   EDUCATION AND HEALTH. Literacy (1987): 99% of adult population. Universities and colleges (1985): 3,340. Hospital beds (1985): 1,308,500. Physicians (1985): 577,000. Life expectancy (1987): women—76.3; men—71.6. Infant mortality (January–June 1987): 10.2 per 1,000 live births.
   ECONOMY. GNP (1986): $4.24 trillion; $17,528 per capita. Labor distribution (1986): agriculture—2.9%; mining—0.8%; construction—6.6%; manufacturing—19%; transportation, communication, and other public utilities—7%; wholesale and retail trade—21%; finance, insurance, real estate—6.8%; services—31.3%; public administration—4.6%; unemployed—7%. Foreign trade (1986): imports—$387.1 billion; exports—$206.4 billion; principal trade partners—Canada, Japan, Mexico, United Kingdom, West Germany. Currency: 1 dollar = 100 cents.
   GOVERNMENT. Type: federal republic. Legislature: Congress. Political subdivisions: 50 states, 1 federal district.
   COMMUNICATIONS. Railroads (1987): 270,312 km (167,964 mi) total. Roads (1986): 6,215,182 km (3,861,934 mi) total, 88% paved. Major ports: 44. Airfields: 16,582.

States, the population, per capita wealth, and general welfare are unevenly distributed, with areas of affluence often contiguous with areas of poverty. Some areas are well developed, whereas others are still developing. Beginning in the early 1970s the United States faced economic difficulties brought on by a high foreign trade deficit due mostly to the rapidly increasing cost of imported petroleum; the declining value of the U.S. dollar abroad; a high level of federal and state spending; and unprecedented inflation. Late in the 1980s inflation was under control and oil products were cheaper, but the trade deficit and huge national debt still stirred concern.

The United States plays a prominent role in world affairs and is an influential member of such multinational organizations as the United Nations (headquartered in New York City) and the World Bank (headquartered in Washington, D.C.). The United States, a capitalist nation, has frequently found itself in opposition to the USSR, the most powerful Communist country.

The United States came into existence as a result of the American Revolution (1775–83), during which the original thirteen states declared and won their independence from Great Britain. During the 19th century, while the European powers built worldwide empires, the young United States focused on expansion across the North American continent and on internal development. Nevertheless, the country gradually acquired some overseas territories, collectively known as the United States outlying territories, that it continues to administer. These include Guam and Puerto Rico (both acquired in 1899); American Samoa (acquired in 1900); the Panama Canal Zone (acquired in 1903 but scheduled for return to Panama by the year 2000); and the U.S. Virgin Islands (acquired in 1917). The Trust Territory of the Pacific Islands (see Pacific Islands, Trust Territory of the) was established in 1947 to govern the Caroline Islands, Mariana Islands, and Marshall Islands.

LAND AND RESOURCES
The United States covers 9,372,575 km² (3,618,770 mi²), which divide into several large natural regions, each with unique topography, geology, and resources.
Eastern United States. Along the coasts of the Gulf of Mexico and the Atlantic Ocean northward to Long Island is a coastal plain, almost all of it below 100 m (300 ft) in altitude and with an average width of 160–320 km (100–200 mi). This coastal plain covers about 10% of the country's total land areas. Except for the muddy delta of the Mississippi River, the shores of the plain are sandy, most of them with barrier beaches surmounted by dunes and backed by shallow, muddy estuaries of brackish or salt water. These include marshlands, so-called wetlands, that are biologically important because they breed tremendous quantities of the primitive plants and animals that provide the basic food supply for all higher organisms living there.

The coastal plain extends under the Gulf of Mexico and Atlantic Ocean, more than 320 km (200 mi) in places, where it forms the continental shelf. Long Island, Martha's Vineyard, Nantucket Island, and Block Island are actually tops of coastal plain hills projecting above sea level. The coastal plain is the subject of conflicting interests among its fishing, shipping, petroleum, mineral resources, seashore recreation, and residential uses.

Inland from the coastal plain, and almost parallel to the Atlantic coast, is the Appalachian Mountain system, which extends from Alabama and Georgia north to Canada; in New England the old rocks of the highlands extend to the coast and form rocky shores. The Appalachian Mountains divide into natural regions. To the east, bordering the Atlantic coastal plain, is a transitional zone, the Piedmont Plateau, which has elevations ranging from approximately 100 to 300 m (300 to 1,000 ft) above sea level. The boundary between the Piedmont and the coastal plain is an escarpment across which the rivers tumble in falls to the lower coastal plain. This Fall Line marks the head of navigation, and cities of the urban corridor—such as Trenton, N.J., Philadelphia, Wilmington, Del., Baltimore, Md., Washington, D.C., and Richmond, Va.—are located on the Fall Line.

The Nubble Lighthouse, built in 1879, is one of the many warning beacons posted along the perilously rocky coast of Maine. The nearby community of York, now restored as a colonial village, was the first English settlement in America to receive (1641) a city charter.

In NEW ENGLAND are found the GREEN MOUNTAINS, the WHITE MOUNTAINS, and the BERKSHIRE HILLS. Farther south the mountain ridges of the BLUE RIDGE reach 2,037 m (6,687 ft) at Mount MITCHELL in North Carolina, the highest point east of the Mississippi River. West of the Blue Ridge is a hilly region called the Ridge and Valley Province, about 40–120 km (25–75 mi) wide. Farther west are the coal-rich, roughly dissected and mountainous Appalachian Plateaus; the easternmost portion, ALLEGHENY MOUNTAINS (or Plateau), mostly between 300 and 1,000 m (1,000 and 3,300 ft) in altitude, rise up abruptly from the Ridge and Valley Province. Throughout the Appalachian Plateaus as a whole local relief commonly exceeds 500 m (1,600 ft). Moreover, the steep mountainsides are unstable, which makes coal mining difficult. To the west of the GREAT SMOKY MOUNTAINS, the Ridge and Valley Province separates them from the CUMBERLAND PLATEAU.

Midwest. The Appalachians give way to a central lowland and the GREAT PLAINS that extend 1,600 km (1,000 mi) west to the Rocky Mountains and reach from Canada south to the Gulf coastal plain. Some highland areas in the Midwest are the OZARK Mountains in Arkansas and Missouri, the Ouachita Mountains in Arkansas and Oklahoma, the MESABI RANGE in Minnesota, and the BLACK HILLS in South Dakota. The lowest part of the region is along the Mississippi River, at about 300 m (1,000 ft). West of the river the plains rise westward to the 1-mi-high (1.6-km) base of the Rocky Mountains. The northern section of the central lowlands has more irregular topography, partly because of its glacial debris.

Rockies and Great Basin. The ROCKY MOUNTAINS, extending northward from New Mexico into Canada, have many summit ridges higher than 3,000 m (10,000 ft), and many peaks reach above 4,250 m (14,000 ft). The highest point in the U.S. portion of the Rockies, Mount ELBERT, reaches 4,399 m (14,432 ft) in Colorado. The Rockies form a bold, east-facing mountain front—including the dramatic Front Range in Colorado—that was a major barrier to the westward expansion of the United States. In Wyoming the mountain ranges are isolated from one another by intermontane basins and plains. The Wyo-

(Above) The many restored mansions and historic town houses of Charleston, S.C., preserve the era of the seaport's prosperity during America's colonial period.

(Left) Denver, the capital of Colorado, is situated on a plateau at the base of the Front Range of the Rocky Mountains in the north central portion of the state. The dome of the capitol is gilded with 5.68 kg (12.5 lb) of gold extracted from Colorado's mines.

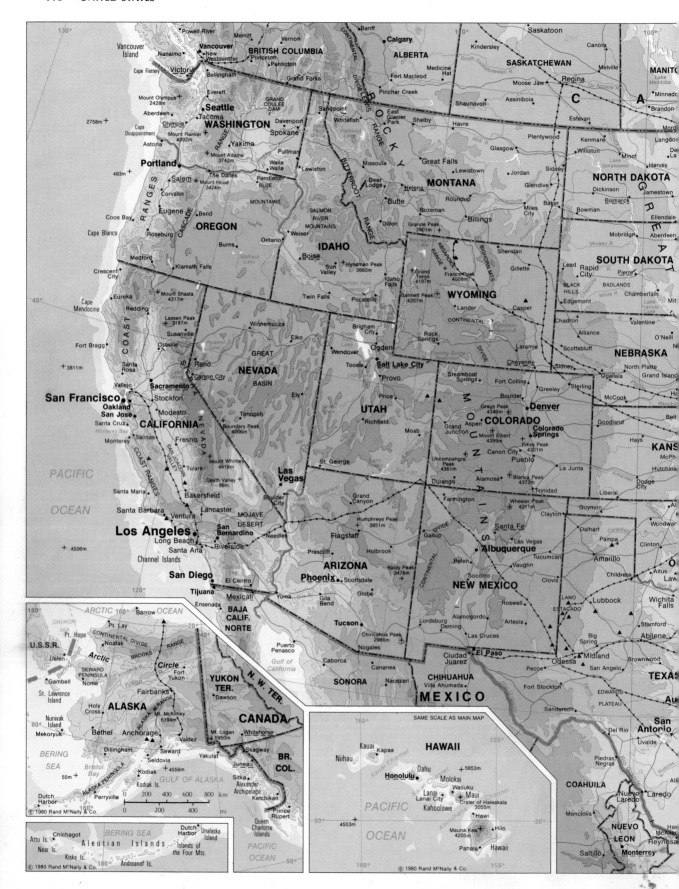

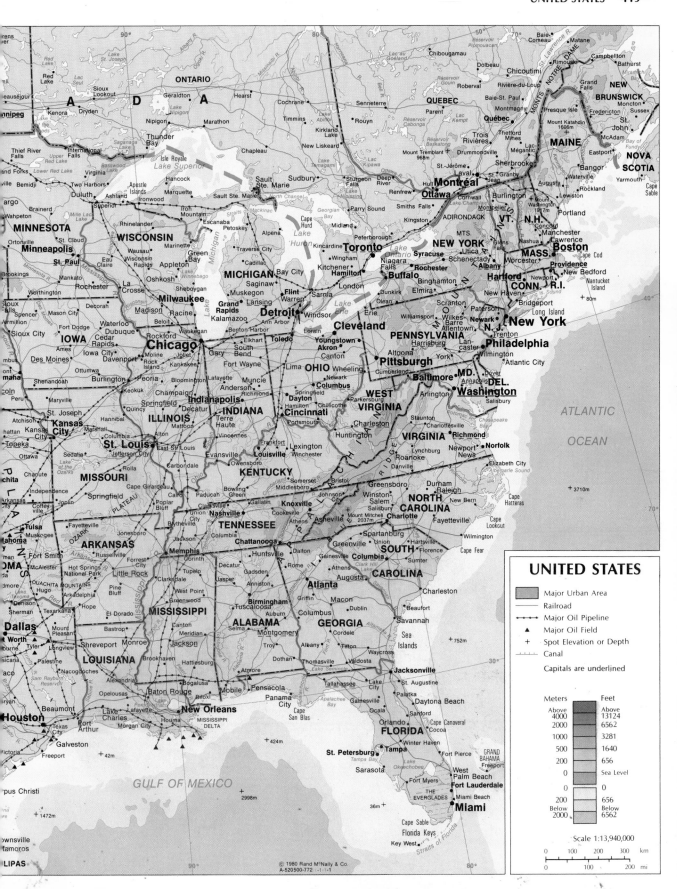

UNITED STATES

	Major Urban Area
	Railroad
	Major Oil Pipeline
▲	Major Oil Field
+	Spot Elevation or Depth
	Canal

Capitals are underlined

Meters	Feet
Above 4000	Above 13124
2000	6562
1000	3281
500	1640
200	656
0	Sea Level
0	0
200	656
Below 2000	Below 6562

Scale 1:13,940,000

0 100 200 300 km

0 100 200 mi

(Left) *The world's largest dormant volcanic crater, produced over eons by the eruptions of Haleakala (3,055 m/10,023 ft), covers 49 km² (19 mi²) of the Hawaiian island of Maui. The crater and surrounding area became part of a national park in 1916.*

(Below) *Juneau, the capital of Alaska, occupies a narrow coastal strip of the Panhandle region in the southeastern portion of the state. Like many Alaskan cities, Juneau was founded by prospectors seeking gold in the area during the late 19th century.*

(Above) *The lowest elevation in the Western Hemisphere—86 m (282 ft) below sea level—occurs in Death Valley, an arid basin in southeastern California. It is also one of the Earth's hottest regions, having reached a maximum temperature of 57° C (134° F) in 1913.*

ming Basin was the main passage through the Rockies used by wagon trains traveling west.

Beyond the Rockies are elevated plateaus. In the south is the COLORADO PLATEAU, averaging about 1,500 m (5,000 ft) above sea level. The plateau is cut by spectacular canyons, including the GRAND CANYON of the Colorado River. To the north are somewhat lower lava plateaus along the Snake and Columbia rivers.

West of the Colorado Plateau and south of the lava plateaus is the GREAT BASIN, part of the BASIN AND RANGE PROVINCE. It consists of scores of closed desert basins containing playa, or ephemeral lakes, and separated by equally numerous rocky and mountainous ridges, most of which trend north-south. Most of the basins range between 1,200 and 1,500 m (4,000 and 5,000 ft) in altitude. The mountain ranges separating the basins are mostly 500 to 2,000 m (1,500 to 6,000 ft) higher. South of the Great Basin is a lower area also without exterior drainage and including DEATH VALLEY and the SALTON SEA, both below sea level. East of the Colorado River, more desert basins and ranges extend east to the Great Plains. The RIO GRANDE, rising in southwestern Colorado and flowing south through New Mexico, connects several of these basins.

West Coast. Much larger basins and ranges form the Pacific Mountains. In California is the SIERRA NEVADA, mostly a granite block, about 725 km (450 mi) long and 125 km (75 mi) wide. The highest peak, Mount WHITNEY, reaches 4,418 m (14,494 ft). In northernmost California and in Oregon and Washington the Sierra gives way to the volcanic CASCADE RANGE. Mount RAINIER reaches 4,392 m (14,410 ft). West of these mountains are broad, long basins—the Great Valley in central California and the valley of the WILLAMETTE RIVER and Puget Trough in Oregon and Washington. The low parts of these basins are only a little higher than sea level. West of them are the COAST RANGES, which extend from California to Alaska. These ranges are only half as high as the Sierra and Cascades and form rocky headlands facing the Pacific Ocean. Sandy beaches are found mostly in coves between the headlands and at a few protected bays. Almost no continental shelf borders the Pacific coast.

Alaska and Hawaii. Alaska, whose area is equal to one-sixth of the area of the lower 48 states, consists of mountain ranges curving concentrically around the Gulf of Alaska and extending west in an arc forming the ALEUTIAN ISLANDS. North America's highest point, Mount MCKINLEY (6,194 m/20,320 ft), is in the Alaska Range. North of these mountains is a broad pla-

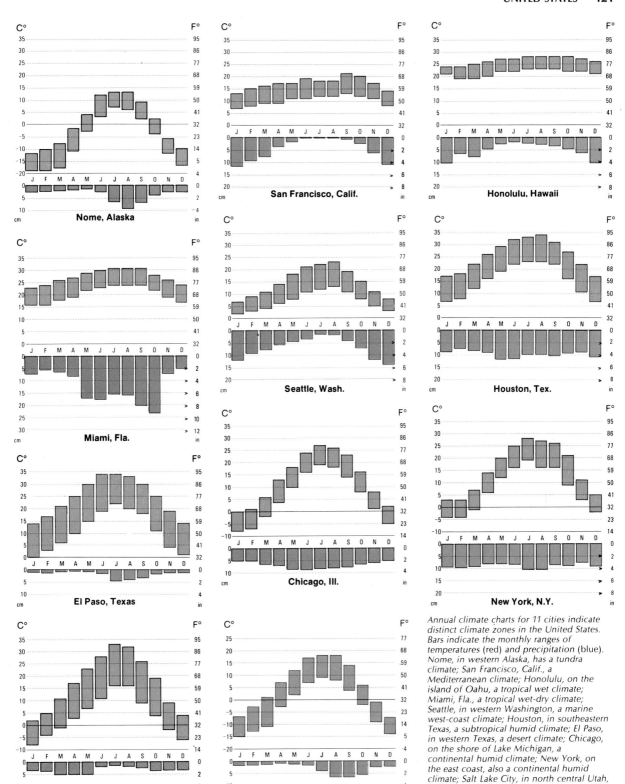

Annual climate charts for 11 cities indicate distinct climate zones in the United States. Bars indicate the monthly ranges of temperatures (red) and precipitation (blue). Nome, in western Alaska, has a tundra climate; San Francisco, Calif., a Mediterranean climate; Honolulu, on the island of Oahu, a tropical wet climate; Miami, Fla., a tropical wet-dry climate; Seattle, in western Washington, a marine west-coast climate; Houston, in southeastern Texas, a subtropical humid climate; El Paso, in western Texas, a desert climate; Chicago, on the shore of Lake Michigan, a continental humid climate; New York, on the east coast, also a continental humid climate; Salt Lake City, in north central Utah, a steppe climate; and Anchorage, in southern Alaska, a subarctic climate.

teau bisected by the Yukon River. North of it is the BROOKS RANGE, the northern base of which slopes to the Arctic Ocean, including the oil-rich PRUDHOE BAY area.

Hawaii, the 50th state, located near the center of the Pacific Ocean, consists of volcanic islands aligned in a north-westerly direction. The volcanism is older and the islands are lower northwestward. Either the ocean crust is moving northwest across a hot spot, or the hot spot is moving southeast under the crust. Active volcanoes, KILAUEA and MAUNA LOA, are located on Hawaii, the southeasternmost island.

Geologic Structure. Like other continents, North America has a central nucleus called a shield. The CANADIAN SHIELD, as it is termed, is mostly in Canada but extends southward into the United States at Lake Superior. Shield rocks are more than 1 billion years old, and some are 4 billion years old. In the central lowland and Appalachian region, surrounding the exposed shield, is a stable platform, underlain by shield rocks but overlain by younger sedimentary rocks, averaging about 1,700 to 3,000 m (5,600 to 10,000 ft) thick. These sedimentary rocks are 1 billion to 225 million years old (late Precambrian and Paleozoic). Overlying these in the western part of the stable platform are younger sedimentary formations 60 to 150 million years old (Mesozoic). All these sedimentary rocks are generally almost horizontal; mountains are few—the BLACK HILLS, the southern Rockies, and mountains in Oklahoma and Arkansas are exceptions.

The eastern and western edges of the stable platform were downwarped to form linear troughs thousands of kilometers long and hundreds of kilometers wide. These troughs (or geosynclines) were then flooded by seas. The trough along the eastern edge of the platform, the present-day site of the Appalachians, accumulated sediments approximately 12,000 m (40,000 ft) thick. West of the platform, at the site of the Great Basin, the geosynclines lasted longer and the sediments accumulated to thicknesses exceeding 30,500 m (100,000 ft). After formation of the troughs, the sides were squeezed together, and the sedimentary formations were folded, faulted, up-

lifted, and subsequently sculptured by erosion to form the mountains along the east and west sides of the continent.

During the last 60 million years (the Cenozoic Era), the Atlantic and Gulf coastal plains were submerged and the western United States was uplifted in a broad arch extending from the Mississippi River to the Pacific. The basins and ranges developed largely by faulting of the previously folded and arched rocks. These crustal movements were accompanied by extensive volcanic activity that formed the lava plateaus along the Snake and Columbia rivers; the Cascade Range; the Coast Ranges in Oregon; features around the southwestern and southern edges of the Colorado Plateau; and other isolated eruptions in the Great Basin.

Surface Deposits and Soils. In the southeastern United States the ground is clayey and thick, in places deeper than 30 m (100 ft). The clay formed as a result of weathering that altered the minerals in hard rocks, even granite, to clay minerals. Iron was disseminated through the clay, staining it red, the characteristic color of such ground. Similar soil formed along the very wet northwest coast of the United States. In less humid parts of the country, weathering is less intense, mostly less than a meter deep, and the ground contains little clay. In humid regions, such as the Appalachians, 95% of the mountainsides are covered with colluvium—loose, weathered rock debris. Even in the Rocky Mountains more than 80% of the ground is covered with colluvium, although the deposits are thinner than in humid regions.

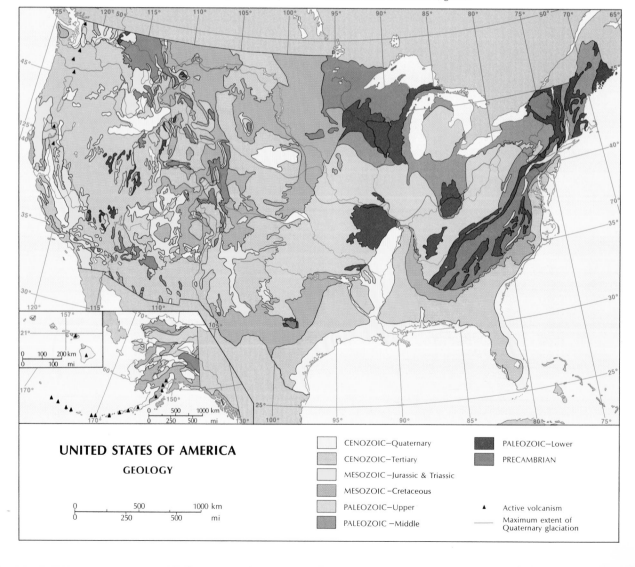

UNITED STATES OF AMERICA

GEOLOGY

0   500   1000 km
0   250   500   mi

CENOZOIC—Quaternary
CENOZOIC—Tertiary
MESOZOIC—Jurassic & Triassic
MESOZOIC—Cretaceous
PALEOZOIC—Upper
PALEOZOIC—Middle

PALEOZOIC—Lower
PRECAMBRIAN

▲ Active volcanism
       Maximum extent of
       Quaternary glaciation

Other extensive surface deposits include those of the Pleistocene glaciers that covered Canada and extended into the northern United States. They reached as far south as Long Island, northern Pennsylvania, the Ohio and Missouri rivers, and Puget Sound lowland. In hilly New England, the deposits are stony; on the plains, less so. Stones cleared from New England fields have been used to build the stone walls so characteristic of that region.

In the central United States the glacial deposits and much of the country to the south are covered by wind-laid silt (loess). These deposits form some of the best agricultural land in the United States. They were produced as the Pleistocene glaciers melted, discharging floods southward, and as the floods ebbed, west winds blew dust clouds eastward from the channels. The deposits become thinner and finer grained eastward from the rivers. Although highly productive, these soils are subject to wind erosion and gullying. Winds have also built sand dunes, not only in the western deserts but on many lake shores, including those of the Great Lakes.

Other surface deposits were laid down by streams, as alluvial floodplains in valley bottoms, and as fan-shaped deposits where valleys issue from mountains. Alluvial bottoms are fertile land and important sources of groundwater, although subject to pollution. They also are subject to flooding, as are alluvial fans.

Lake deposits are numerous in glaciated areas, but they are most extensive in the desert depressions of the Great Basin.

This seeming anomaly occurs because those basins collected meltwater from ice fields and glaciers in the mountains. Even Death Valley, where annual precipitation averages only about 38 mm (1.5 in), had a lake approximately 180 m (600 ft) deep. The east part of the Great Basin contained Pleistocene Lake Bonneville, which covered 52,000 km² (20,000 mi²) and had a maximum depth of 300 m (1,000 ft). GREAT SALT LAKE is a salt-brine remainder from that Pleistocene lake, as are the BONNEVILLE SALT FLATS. Death Valley is now without a lake but has a salt pan.

Despite 40 years of conservation education and other efforts, no more than 25% of U.S. farmlands are managed according to approved soil-conservation practices. The United States continues to deplete its soil resources by erosion and loss of organic matter.

Climate. Most of the United States has a continental climate, characterized by considerable annual variability. Coastal regions, moderated by the oceans, have less variable climates; Hawaii has slight variability, with most of the variation due to elevation. Alaska is partly cold-wet and partly cold-dry. Much of the northern half of the state is permanently frozen, in places to depths as great as 300 m (1,000 ft).

The eastern United States is humid, with annual precipitation averaging more than 500 mm (20 in). The western part of the country—beginning approximately at 100° west longitude—except for the mountains and the maritime Pacific coast, is mostly semiarid with annual precipitation averaging

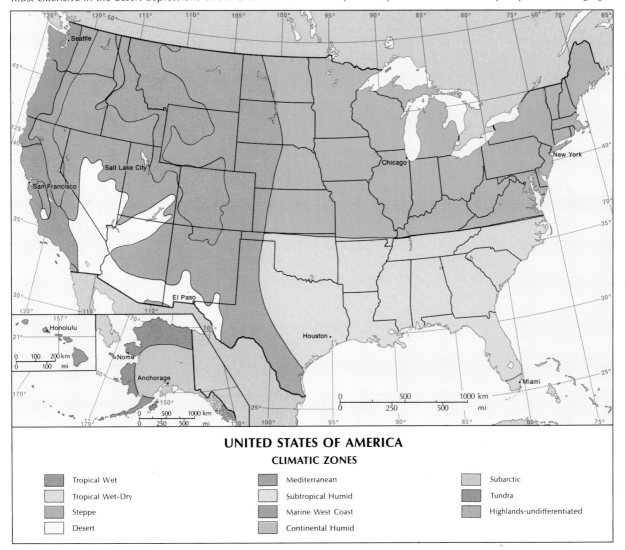

UNITED STATES OF AMERICA
CLIMATIC ZONES

Tropical Wet

Tropical Wet-Dry

Steppe

Desert

Mediterranean

Subtropical Humid

Marine West Coast

Continental Humid

Subarctic

Tundra

Highlands-undifferentiated

The Badlands, a portion of which was established as a national park in 1978, lies between the White and Cheyenne rivers in southwestern South Dakota. Areas of this arid, eroded region contain fossil beds bearing the remains of prehistoric reptiles and mammals.

between 250 and 500 mm (10 and 20 in), but parts are arid with annual precipitation averaging less than 250 mm (10 in). The western mountains receive about 500 mm (20 in) of precipitation yearly. The northwestern coast receives more than 2,500 mm (100 in) of precipitation each year.

A traverse eastward across the United States illustrates the importance of seasonal differences in precipitation. Along the Pacific coast precipitation occurs mostly during the winter. In the central United States it is greatest during the summer growing season, further contributing (along with the rich soils) to the agricultural productivity of that region. In eastern states precipitation is rather even throughout the year. The traverse also shows that precipitation is greatest at the mountains and least to the leeward of them.

The country's temperatures are as varied as precipitation and are heavily influenced by latitude, with longer and colder winters farther north. Temperatures are also influenced by proximity to the oceans. In the northeastern part of the country the average annual temperature in New York is 13° C (55° F). Farther south is a subtropical zone: Charleston, S.C., has an average annual temperature of 19° C (66° F). The only

The rocks of Bryce Canyon National Park, in southwest Utah, have been sculpted by wind and rain into a myriad of colorful shapes. The canyons of the park are about 300 m (1,000 ft) deep in places.

tropical zone of the United States occurs in southern Florida, and Miami experiences an average temperature of 24° C (75° F). In the central United States the continental climate is not moderated by the ocean, and seasonal differences are more extreme. In Minneapolis, Minn., the average temperature is 7° C (45° F), whereas in Tulsa, Okla., only about 2° farther west but 1,030 km (640 mi) south, the temperature averages 16° C (61° F). Along the west coast, temperatures, moderated by the ocean, are mild. Portland, Oreg., has an average annual temperature of 12° C (54° F); Los Angeles, in the Mediterranean climate zone, experiences a temperature of 17° C (63° F).

Climate hazards in the United States include hurricanes along the Gulf and Atlantic coasts, tornadoes in the southeast and central states, hail on the western plains, dry electric storms that cause forest fires on western mountains, floods in the central and eastern states and along the Pacific coast in winter, and droughts in most of the western states.

Rivers and Lakes. Inland water covers about 200,000 km² (78,500 mi²), or almost 2% of the total area of the United States. The MISSISSIPPI RIVER, flowing south across the eastern half of the conterminous United States, is major both in length (3,779 km/2,348 mi) and in annual discharge (18,200 m³ per sec/650,000 ft³ per sec). By contrast, the COLORADO RIVER (Colorado) is about one-third as long as the Mississippi River system, but its average annual discharge is only 2% as great.

(Above) The Mississippi River, the longest inland waterway in the United States, flows 3,779 km (2,348 mi) from its source, at Lake Itasca in north central Minnesota, to its mouth, on the Gulf of Mexico.

(Left) Olympic National Park is famous for its coniferous rain forest, which lies along the windward (western) slopes of the Olympic Mountains of northwestern Washington, the area receiving the greatest annual rainfall in the continental United States.

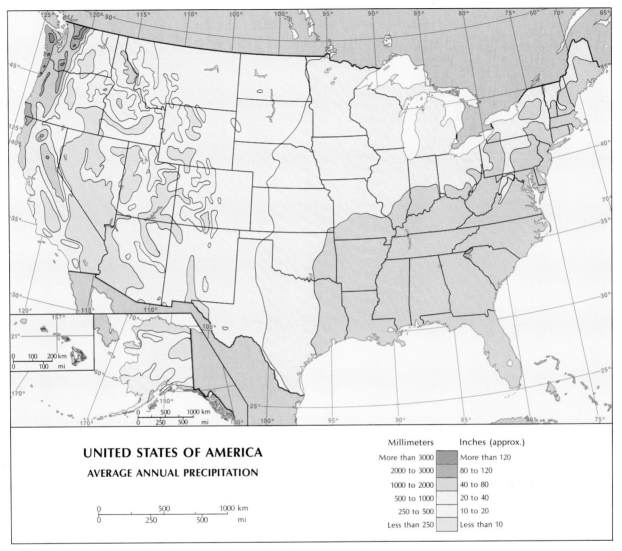

UNITED STATES OF AMERICA

AVERAGE ANNUAL PRECIPITATION

Millimeters		Inches (approx.)
More than 3000		More than 120
2000 to 3000		80 to 120
1000 to 2000		40 to 80
500 to 1000		20 to 40
250 to 500		10 to 20
Less than 250		Less than 10

An area along the Atlantic seaboard, only slightly larger than the Colorado River basin, has 20 rivers—including the CONNECTICUT RIVER, DELAWARE RIVER, HUDSON RIVER, and SUSQUEHANNA RIVER—each only one-third as long as the Colorado but together discharging 20 times as much as the Colorado.

In terms of discharge, the major rivers, in addition to the Mississippi, are the SAINT LAWRENCE RIVER, OHIO RIVER, MISSOURI RIVER, COLUMBIA RIVER, and SNAKE RIVER. The YUKON RIVER is Alaska's principal river. Where annual precipitation averages less than 500 mm (20 in), even main streams are mostly ephemeral, flowing only when there are wet seasons or local storms. Water supplies in those areas, to a considerable degree, must be obtained from groundwater, and in parts of the arid southwestern states withdrawals (mostly for irrigation) have caused groundwater levels to fall alarmingly in places, enough to cause localized subsidence of the land surface and even damage to buildings.

Lakes and peat bogs are numerous in the glaciated parts of the United States, especially in northern Minnesota. The lakes are small and used primarily for recreation, but the GREAT LAKES are important arteries of transportation. Florida has lakes and bogs at limestone sinks, including Lake OKEECHOBEE. The troughs of the Great Basin have ephemeral lakes. A few permanent ones are located at the eastern foot of the Sierra Nevada. The Salton Sea and Great Salt Lake are saline. Many of the lakes, especially in the west, have been created by dams; Lake MEAD has the greatest capacity.

Vegetation. With such varied climate and topography, it is hardly surprising that the vegetation of the United States is equally varied. In Florida the subtropical vegetation includes mangrove and palmetto. Farther north in the southeastern states, forests of loblolly and slash pines grade north near the Tennessee River to hardwood forest with oak and hickory. In the Great Lakes region a different pine forest—of white pine—appears, and north of this are fir and spruce. In Alaska, north of the spruce zone, is tundra. These differences northward reflect decreasing temperature, especially shortening of the growing season.

More striking differences occur between the humid east and the arid west. Hardwood forest extends westward beyond the Mississippi River, giving way to grassland on the plains. Rocky Mountain forests are chiefly coniferous, with pine and Douglas fir near the base and spruce and true fir extending upward to the timberline (3,500 m/11,500 ft in the Southern Rockies). Above that the growing season is too short for trees.

West of the Rockies, on the plateaus and in the Great Basin, desert shrubs occur, with patches of woodland or forest on the isolated mountain ranges. These western mountains have two timberlines, one at high altitude because of the cold and the other near the mountain base, below which trees cannot grow because of insufficient precipitation.

Forests rather like those in the Rockies grow on the eastern slopes of the Sierra Nevada and the Cascades; the western

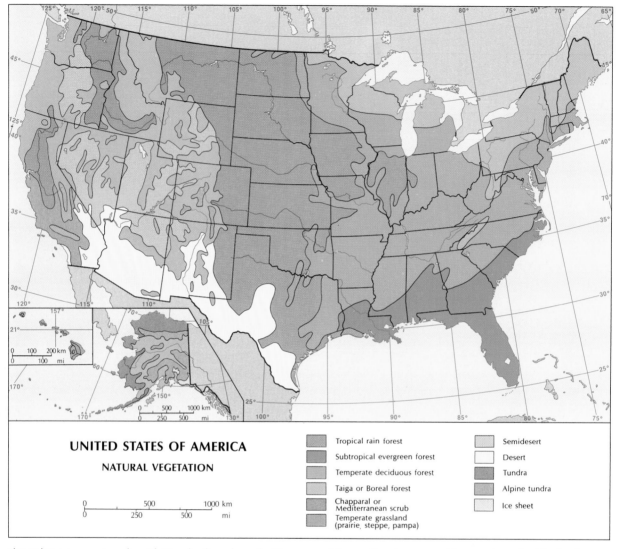

UNITED STATES OF AMERICA

NATURAL VEGETATION

Tropical rain forest	Semidesert
Subtropical evergreen forest	Desert
Temperate deciduous forest	Tundra
Taiga or Boreal forest	Alpine tundra
Chapparal or Mediterranean scrub	Ice sheet
Temperate grassland (prairie, steppe, pampa)	

slopes have evergreen oaks with Douglas fir and, on the Sierra Nevada, sequoia. The central Coast Ranges have redwood, grading north to Douglas fir and spruce, and grading south to a scrubby growth known as chapparal.

Resources. Agriculturally, the United States is richly productive, with many crops providing a surplus for export. Most of the eastern two-thirds of the conterminous United States is arable; the land of the western United States is used mostly for grazing but has considerable irrigated lands for crops. The principal U.S. crops are: fruit, truck farming products, and special crops (including rice and sugarcane) along the Gulf coast, in irrigated areas of the west, and near urban areas in the east; cotton in the southeastern states and on some irrigated lands in the west; tobacco, peanuts, fruit, and general farm products on the Atlantic coastal plain and in the eastern Appalachians; dairy products and hay in the northern states; and corn, wheat, and soybeans on the plains.

Livestock on farms habitually totals over 100 million cattle and additional millions of hogs and sheep and hundreds of millions of chickens and turkeys. The grazing capacity of the land is very unequal. The humid half of the country can support as many as 500 cows per year per mi² (193 per km²), whereas the semiarid and arid western half can support fewer than 100 per mi² (40 per km²) and some parts support only about 10 head per mi² (4 per km²).

Commercial forests cover more than 2,000,000 km² (800,000 mi²), especially in the northwestern, northern midwestern,

and the southeastern states. They produce, besides lumber, paper pulp, resins, and syrup. The annual forest cut and burn is less than the growth, but care is needed to minimize water and erosion losses due to grazing and lumbering. In recent years increased recycling of paper is reducing consumption of paper pulp.

Changing interests in water resources are reflected in the history of water management. First, the need for transportation led to the building of canals, such as the ERIE CANAL, in the eastern states in the early 19th century. Second came the great period of flood control, especially along the Mississippi River. Third came a period of large-scale development of irrigation systems in the west, beginning around the turn of the century. Fourth came a period of developing hydroelectricity, beginning during the 1930s. Today's principal concern is pollution control. In the future will come a stage when controls will be needed to prevent groundwater withdrawals from exceeding recharge.

Mineral production, although less than 5% of the gross national product (GNP), is vitally important. No nation is self-sufficient in minerals, and although the United States has more than its share, nevertheless domestic production of many minerals is less than demand, necessitating imports. Fossil-fuel shortages combined with high demand threatens the United States with severe economic problems. Alternate sources of energy such as solar, geothermal, and wind energy are in the early stages of development.

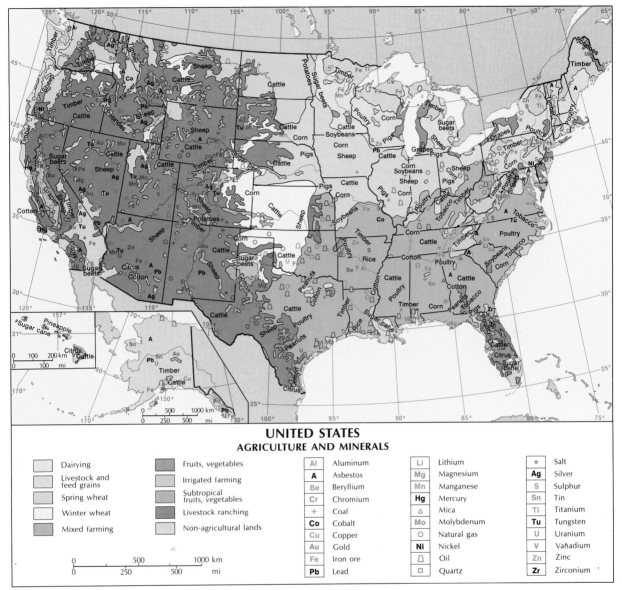

UNITED STATES
AGRICULTURE AND MINERALS

Dairying	
Livestock and feed grains	
Spring wheat	
Winter wheat	
Mixed farming	

Fruits, vegetables	
Irrigated farming	
Subtropical fruits, vegetables	
Livestock ranching	
Non-agricultural lands	

Al	Aluminum
A	Asbestos
Be	Beryllium
Cr	Chromium
+	Coal
Co	Cobalt
Cu	Copper
Au	Gold
Fe	Iron ore
Pb	Lead

Li	Lithium
Mg	Magnesium
Mn	Manganese
Hg	Mercury
△	Mica
Mo	Molybdenum
O	Natural gas
Ni	Nickel
▢	Oil
▭	Quartz

•	Salt
Ag	Silver
S	Sulphur
Sn	Tin
Ti	Titanium
Tu	Tungsten
U	Uranium
V	Vanadium
Zn	Zinc
Zr	Zirconium

Vast fields of wheat, such as these in Washington State, cover 23,002,000 ha (56,839,000 acres) of the nation's land surface, yielding a harvest of 1,799 million bushels of the grain (1978). Wheat is the fourth most valuable crop cultivated in the United States, ranking behind corn, soybeans, and hay.

PEOPLE

Prior to the discovery (1492) of the New World by Christopher Columbus the area of the United States had an Indian population averaging only about 1 person per 13 to 26 km² (roughly 1 person per 5 to 10 mi²). When George Washington was president in 1790 the population had grown to almost 4,000,000; only 5 cities had populations exceeding 10,000. During the next 100 years the population doubled 4 times—to about 8 million in 1815, to 16 million in 1840, to 32 million in 1861–62, and to 64 million in 1890. Demographers believe that in the late 1980s the population will probably reach about 250 million.

Ethnic Composition. In 1980 the native American population (see INDIANS, AMERICAN; ESKIMO; and ALEUT) totaled more than 1.4 million. Of the Indians, who constitute the overwhelming majority, approximately half live on some 275 reservations. There they engage in farming and sheepherding and excel in such crafts as pottery making, rug and basket weaving, silversmithing, and beadwork. Most reservation land is located in Arizona, New Mexico, Utah, South Dakota, Washington, and Montana. The half of the Indian population off reservations live mostly in cities, especially in the north, central, and western states and in Alaska.

About 11.7% of the total population—26,500,000 persons (1980)—are black, almost all descendants of slaves. Somewhat more than half are concentrated in the southern and southeastern states, the remainder in urban centers of the northeast, north central, and Pacific states. Migration continues from the southern and southeastern states to the urban areas (see BLACK AMERICANS). The vast majority of Americans, however, are descended from Europeans who were attracted to the United States by religious and political freedom and economic opportunities. During the colonial period most settlers came from the British Isles and settled along the eastern seaboard; the French settled the St. Lawrence River valley. The first great IMMIGRATION wave—from 1820 to 1860—saw the arrival of more than 5 million new Americans. Of these, 90% were from England, Ireland, and Germany. By the middle of the 19th century the culture and customs of western Europe dominated the United States from coast to coast.

After the Civil War, immigration increased dramatically; between 1860 and 1920, about 29 million persons arrived. The composition of the immigrant population had shifted, and most came from eastern and southern Europe—Russia, Poland, the Balkans, and Italy. Unlike many earlier immigrants, they remained in the eastern states and industrial midwestern states such as Michigan and Illinois, usually settling in the cities, rather than continuing west. During the same period increasing numbers of Asians, especially Chinese and Japa-

Taos, N.Mex., is the site of a community of Pueblo Indians. The two communal structures there, one four stories and the other five stories high, are the home of about 1,800 people. The Pueblo continue to maintain much of their traditional culture.

nese, migrated to the Pacific coast and to Hawaii. These immigrants tended to form ethnic enclaves within the predominantly western European communities (see ORIENTAL AMERICANS). The white immigrants, on the other hand, mixed to a considerable degree with the earlier western European stocks, beginning the so-called American melting pot. The mixing process was facilitated by the public school system. In the southern part of the country, where most blacks lived, however, the races were segregated until the middle of the 20th century, and although diminishing, de facto segregation remains a national problem.

The total population of Spanish origin in the United States is probably about 22 million. Of that number, about 14.6 million are legal Hispanic residents and the others are illegal aliens. In southern Texas, New Mexico, Arizona, and southern California, a considerable percentage of the population is of Mexican-American origin (see CHICANO). Each year thousands more enter the United States, most illegally, because of overpopulation in Mexico and greater opportunities in the United States. The new arrivals do not settle near the border where employment is limited but migrate to the interior of the United States, especially to urban areas. The eastern states have also experienced an influx of Spanish-speaking immigrants from Central America and the Caribbean, especially Puerto Rico and Cuba. Most live in the cities, especially New York and Miami. (See also HISPANIC AMERICANS.)

The skyline of Chicago features several of the world's tallest buildings. From the observation deck of the twin-spired John Hancock Center visitors can see portions of four states—Illinois, Indiana, Michigan, and Wisconsin. Lake Michigan appears in the background.

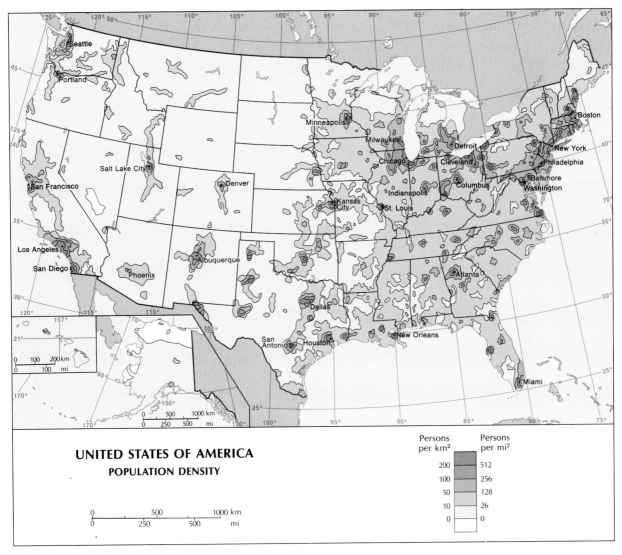

UNITED STATES OF AMERICA
POPULATION DENSITY

Persons per km²		Persons per mi²
200		512
100		256
50		128
10		26
0		0

Religion. More than half of all Americans are practicing Protestants, with Baptists outnumbering members of other individual denominations, including those of the Methodists, Lutherans, Presbyterians, Episcopalians, Latter-day Saints, Pentacostalists, Churches of Christ, and United Church of Christ. Nearly 22% of the U.S. population are Roman Catholic. About 1.5% belong to Eastern Orthodox churches, and another 2.6% are Jewish. Other major world religions—Buddhism, Hinduism, Islam, and the many tribal religions, notably from Africa—are lightly represented in the United States.

Demography. The annual rate of population increase in the United States is 1.14% (1970-80). In 1980, 73.7% of the total population lived in urban, including metropolitan, areas. Thirty-nine cities had more than 1 million inhabitants in the metropolitan areas, and 22 cities had more than 500,000 residents in the city center: BALTIMORE, BOSTON, CHICAGO, CLEVELAND, COLUMBUS (Ohio), DALLAS, DETROIT, HOUSTON, INDIANAPOLIS, JACKSONVILLE, LOS ANGELES, MEMPHIS, MILWAUKEE, NEW ORLEANS, NEW YORK, PHILADELPHIA, PHOENIX, SAN ANTONIO, SAN DIEGO, SAN FRANCISCO, SAN JOSE, and WASHINGTON, D.C.

Urban problems have developed in many U.S. cities be-

Miami Beach, one of the nation's outstanding resort centers, occupies a narrow island bordered by Biscayne Bay and Miami on the west and the Atlantic Ocean on the east. The island on which the city developed is largely artificial, having been created as part of a major land-reclamation project during the early decades of the 20th century.

(Left) *The Statue of Liberty, the famous landmark in New York Harbor, was presented as a gift from France to the United States in 1886. The massive sculpture, the island on which it rests, and nearby Ellis Island—formerly a major immigration port—are maintained as a national monument.*

(Below) *Hundreds of thousands of visitors travel to New Orleans each year to enjoy the festivities of Mardi Gras. This city-wide celebration, which marks the beginning of the Lenten season, dates from the French colonial era.*

cause large numbers of the more affluent whites have moved out of the city centers to the suburbs. Much light industry and other businesses have followed them. Thus many large cities are faced with decaying downtown and residential areas—often primarily the home of blacks and Hispanics. As a consequence the tax base of many cities has been eroded, and almost every major city faces financial difficulties.

In 1985 the country's overall population density was 25.8 persons per km² (67 per mi²), but great regional variations exist: New Jersey, with 391 persons per km² (1,013 per mi²), has the highest density; the lightest density in the lower 48 states is in Wyoming (1.9 per km²/5 per mi²), although Alaska has only 0.38 per km² (1 per mi²). Through the 1970s and well into the 1980s some areas, mostly the northeastern and the north central states, experienced a decline in population, whereas other states, such as Arizona, Florida, Nevada, and Texas—in the Sunbelt—experienced higher-than-average increases due to in-migration. The birthrate in the United States is 16 per 1,000 inhabitants (1987), a figure about equal to Canada's but higher than that of most of Western Europe. The death rate, 9 per 1,000 inhabitants, is about equal to, or a bit lower than, that of the other industrialized nations.

Health and Education. In 1984 the United States had almost 7,000 hospitals, and an average of 5.7 hospital beds for every 1,000 inhabitants. About 542,000 physicians were practicing. Female residents of the United States have a life expectancy of about 76 years at birth, whereas for males it is 72 years. The average life expectancy at birth for all whites is 75.3 years; for blacks, however, it is 69.7 years, although it has increased from 45 years in 1920. The nation's infant mortality rate is 10.5 per 1,000 live births. Although this is one of the world's lowest rates, it is surpassed by that of several European nations, especially Scandinavian countries.

Illiteracy has been almost eliminated in the United States. The median school years completed by U.S. citizens 25 years and older in 1985 was 12.9 years. Approximately 20% of all Americans have received associate, bachelor's, or higher degrees.

Education is required between the ages of 5 and 16. Public primary and secondary education is mostly locally funded. In 1985, 44.9 million pupils attended public schools; 9 million students attended private schools. Of the nation's 3,331 institutions of higher education (1984), 2,025 are 4-year institutions, and the remainder are 2-year schools. Privately operated institutions constitute 56% of the total, including many of the nation's most prestigious universities and colleges. Public institutions, although representing 44% of the total, enroll almost 80% of the students; each state operates a university sys-

tem. Beginning in the 1960s, 2-year institutions grew most rapidly; many of these community colleges are operated by counties and municipalities. For a more detailed description of the country's educational system, see UNITED STATES, EDUCATION IN THE.

Communications. In 1721 the *New England Courant* began publication in Boston. By 1985 there were 1,676 daily newspapers published in the United States, more than 50 of them in languages other than English. The English-language papers had a total circulation of 62,800,000. Among the best-known of the dailies with circulations exceeding 500,000 are the CHICAGO TRIBUNE, NEW YORK TIMES, WASHINGTON POST, and the *Los Angeles Times;* the ST. LOUIS POST-DISPATCH, *Atlanta Constitution, Miami Herald,* and *Toledo Blade* are also important. The CHRISTIAN SCIENCE MONITOR, WALL STREET JOURNAL, and *USA Today* are the principal nationally circulated dailies.

The country is served by 4,718 AM and 3,875 FM radio stations (1985). There are more than 295 million television sets in the United States and more than 900 commercial stations. In addition, cable television and public television are becoming popular alternatives to commercial television, which has been dominated by 3 networks; in 1986, 316 public stations and 7,600 cable systems operated.

ECONOMIC ACTIVITY

Economic Development. During the colonial period, after establishing subsistence farms along the Atlantic seaboard, the pioneer settlers developed a maritime and shipbuilding industry. Forests provided the timbers needed for ships and homes. Until after the middle of the 19th century wood also was the nation's principal source for fuel, and wood ashes produced potash.

The submerged part of the coastal plain off the New England coast at Georges Bank was and remains one of the world's great fishing areas, especially for herring, mackerel, and cod, and the shores yielded lobsters, crabs, and shellfish. Whaling was important during colonial times but declined after the mid-19th century. Other economic activities in the eastern United States related to water navigation included development of steamboats and construction of canals around waterfalls and rapids to permit access by water to the Appalachians and the Ohio River. During the early 19th century the falls were also used to develop power for mills in the early stage of the Industrial Revolution.

Mineral resources along the Eastern Seaboard were meager. Salt was produced from seawater at evaporating pans. Iron ore was obtained from bogs. Coal was produced from early Mesozoic formations near Richmond, Va. Manufacturing and other industries became increasingly important when coal became plentiful because of improved roads, canals, and newly built railroads that followed the westward migration. Where iron and coal could be economically joined, the giant steel industry developed, as at Pittsburgh and west to Chicago.

Political and social changes affected the economy too. The Civil War freed the slaves, but high prices for cotton led to borrowing to hire labor. Collapse of the market brought ruin to the old plantation system and led to an era of small farms.

As settlements and transportation lines spread across the central states, copper and iron were produced in the Lake Superior region. The great asset of the central United States, however, was and remains agricultural. The mechanized plow and harvester were invented to reap the produce of the vast fields there, as was barbed wire (1873) for fencing the plains farther west where trees are scarce. In the 1860s the railroads developed refrigerator cars. Agricultural products from the Midwest provided the basis of food-processing industries, such as flour milling in Minneapolis and Milwaukee.

The Rocky Mountain states were first explored and exploited by fur traders during the two decades preceding the Civil War. Gathering furs had started in New England and spread westward across the Great Lakes region—first by the French, later by the HUDSON'S BAY COMPANY for England, and then by American trappers and traders farther west and south, some working for companies such as John Jacob Astor's AMERICAN FUR COMPANY (see also FUR TRADE). When gold was

A flock of sheep graze in a farm pasture in an Appalachian valley of West Virginia. The Appalachian Mountains, the most extensive mountain system in the eastern portion of the United States and Canada, stretch from southern Newfoundland into central Alabama.

discovered (1848) in California, trappers already had blazed the way. The extensive and varied mineral deposits of the Rocky Mountains were discovered following the California GOLD RUSH.

The economy of the western United States today is based on livestock; irrigated farming; lumbering; metal mining (especially copper and molybdenum); energy resources (including oil, gas, coal, uranium, and hydroelectricity); transportation by railroad, highways, air, and pipelines and by shipping along the Pacific coast; manufacturing; offshore fisheries; and outstanding recreational attractions. More than two-thirds of the country's national parks are in the West.

Alaska's economy depends chiefly on fisheries, oil, and recreation. Hawaii produces pineapples, sugarcane, and nuts but depends primarily on income from the large military and naval bases there and from tourism.

Contemporary Economy. In 1981 the gross national product (GNP) of the United States reached $2.9 trillion, the highest in the world. The per-capita income of $9,521 (1980) is also among the world's highest.

Agriculture, fishing, and forestry together employ less than 4% of the total labor force, and contribute about 3% of the GNP. The leading crops, in order of value, are corn, soybeans, wheat, hay, cotton, tobacco, sorghum, rice, and potatoes. Most livestock is produced in the West and Midwest. The

This massive oil refining complex is situated near Perth Amboy, in northeastern New Jersey. This portion of the state has been one of the nation's centers of oil refining since the 1870s, when Bayonne became the terminus of an oil pipeline operated by John D. Rockefeller.

United States is the world's leading producer of meat, soybeans, and corn, and the second largest producer of wheat, tobacco, hogs, and cattle.

Forests cover about 3,000,000 km² (1,200,000 mi²), but of that total only about one-third is commercial timberland. Forests yield an annual income of several hundred million dollars. Income from the U.S. fishing industry was $2.3 billion in 1985. The Pacific states—especially Alaska and California—lead the nation in the value of their catch; Louisiana, on the Gulf coast, is also a leading producer.

Almost one-fifth of the labor force is engaged in manufacturing, and industry contributes about the same proportion to the GNP. In 1985 the value added by manufacturing was $795 billion. The leading industries, in order of value, are nonelectrical machinery, transportation equipment, chemicals, primary metals (including steel), processed foods, paper and allied products, refined petroleum and petroleum products, electrical and electronic equipment, and fabricated metal products. The large corporation dominates manufacturing in the United States, and in 1985 the 100 largest industrial concerns held about 70% of manufacturing assets. The country is a world leader in production and export in heavy industry, especially primary metals (steel, aluminum, copper); in transportation equipment, such as automobiles; and in printing and publishing.

In 1985 the United States produced 2.5 trillion kW h of electricity, the highest in the world—and about double that of the USSR, the second highest producer. Of that total, 57% was derived from coal, 4% from petroleum, 12% from natural gas, 16% from nuclear power, and 11% from hydroelectricity. Of the petroleum used for energy production, about one-third or more is imported. The country's total installed capacity is 698.1 million kW (1985).

Mining accounts for only about 3.1% of the GNP but produced $122.8 billion in 1985, 92% of which was derived from mineral fuels—coal, natural gas, and petroleum. The principal minerals, in order of value, are petroleum, natural gas, coal, portland cement, stone, copper, iron ore, sand and gravel, phosphates, lime, clay, salt, uranium, molybdenum, zinc, sulfur, lead, silver, and gold.

As in the other highly developed countries—the so-called postindustrial nations—the service sector, widely defined, in the United States employs the great bulk of the labor force (70% in 1985) and produces the largest percentage of the GNP (also 70% in 1985). Over 75 million persons work (1985) in transportation and public utilities; wholesale and retail trade; finance, insurance, and real estate; and services such as hotels, communications, and health care, as well as government. Together they produced $2.8 trillion.

Tourism is also an important industry. In 1985, 7.5 million foreign tourists visited the country. Among foreigners and Americans alike, the National Park Service sites, including 49 national parks and 77 national monuments, are the favorite destinations. Major cities—including New York, Los Angeles, and Miami—are also important tourist magnets.

As recently as 1975, U.S. exports were 10% greater than imports. Almost 20% of this international trade was with Canada; 17% was with other Western Hemisphere nations; about 25% was with Western European countries; and trade with Japan aggregated less than 10% of the total. In the 1980s, however, the U.S. trade balance reversed, sparked by large increases in the cost of petroleum imports; the value of imports of petroleum and petroleum products increased from $1.3 billion in 1970 to $62 billion in 1980. In 1985 the U.S. trade deficit was nearly $150 billion.

In addition to petroleum, principal imports are automobiles, nonelectrical machinery, electrical equipment, and chemicals. The principal industrial exports are machinery, transportation equipment, and chemicals; soybeans and corn are the leading agricultural exports.

In 1987 the United States had 6,365,590 km (3,955,393 mi) of highways, including 88,641 km (55,079 mi) of expressways. Rail tracks totaled 270,312 km (167,964 mi). Of all passenger traffic in 1985, 82% was by private automobile, 16% by air, and only 0.6% by rail. During the same year, however, 37% of freight was carried by rail and 25% by motor vehicles. Leading U.S. seaports include New York, New Orleans, Houston, and Baton Rouge, La. St. Louis is the nation's leading inland port.

GOVERNMENT

The United States has a democratic government, meaning that it is "elected by the people and for the people." Every adult (aged 18 and over) can vote, yet only about 55% of the eligible voters exercise this right. Voters usually choose between the two political parties that dominate U.S. politics—the DEMOCRATIC PARTY and the REPUBLICAN PARTY.

The country has a federal system of government in which power is divided between the national, or federal, government and the governments of the 50 states. A third level of government is provided at the local level by municipal and county authorities. Theoretically, the responsibilities of the different levels are delineated in the federal (see CONSTITUTION OF THE UNITED STATES) and state constitutions, although actually the responsibilities overlap.

The federal government and each of the 50 state governments are divided into three branches—executive, legislative, and judicial. Municipal and county governments are more varied but to a considerable degree are patterned after the

Trading on the New York Stock Exchange—like other financial and business transactions—is now accomplished largely through computers. This has facilitated the development of a global market in financial securities. When the New York Market crashed on Oct. 19, 1987, the panic spread instantly to other financial centers. The severity of the plunge—a record 22.6% in New York—was attributed by some observers to massive computerized selling.

Washington, D.C., the nation's capital, is a federal territory occupying 179 km² (69 mi²) along the Potomac River between Maryland and Virginia. The city, which was built to the plan of the French military engineer Pierre Charles L'Enfant, became the seat of the national government in 1800.

federal and state models. The executive branch of the federal government is headed by the president (see PRESIDENT OF THE UNITED STATES) and vice-president, elected every 4 years. The administrative duties of the executive branch are divided among 13 departments: State, Treasury, Defense, Justice, Interior, Agriculture, Commerce, Labor, Health and Human Services, Housing and Urban Development, Transportation, Energy, and Education. Numerous federal agencies, including those for regulation of the private sector (see GOVERNMENT REGULATION) supplement the activities of these departments. The secretary of each department sits on the cabinet, the president's principal advisory body.

The legislative branch of the federal government—the CONGRESS OF THE UNITED STATES—consists of a 100-member SENATE, with 2 senators elected from each state, and a HOUSE OF REPRESENTATIVES, with 435 elected members, one for approximately every 560,000 persons. Reapportionment for the latter occurs every 10 years. Senators serve 6-year terms and representatives serve for 2 years. All budget appropriations originate in the House of Representatives, but the Senate must concur. Presidential appointees are confirmed by the Senate. The Senate also has the responsibility of approving treaties with foreign governments. Similarly, most states have 2 legislative bodies, although Nebraska has a unicameral body of 49 members. The chief executive of each state is the GOVERNOR.

The federal judicial branch consists of the SUPREME COURT OF THE UNITED STATES—the nation's highest judicial body—with a chief justice and eight other members appointed by the president with the advice and consent of the Senate; and 90 district courts, at least one in each state. They consider violations of federal law and certain civil cases involving persons in different states. Decisions may be appealed to the 12 U.S. appellate courts. Each state has a system of courts paralleling the federal system.

State and local governments have responsibility for such local services as water supply, waste disposal, police and fire protection, hospitals and health, parks and recreation, schools, and libraries, but to a considerable degree each of these activities is shared by all levels of government including the federal government. The federal government alone has responsibility for national defense, but even this responsibility is shared with the states to the degree that each state has a national guard or militia.   CHARLES B. HUNT

Bibliography:

DESCRIPTION, GEOGRAPHY, AND PHYSIOGRAPHY: Birnbaum, Stephen, ed., *United States, 1987* (1986); Callison, Charles, ed., *America's Natural Resources*, rev. ed. (1967); Hunt, Charles B., *Natural Regions of the United States and Canada* (1974); Paterson, J. H., *North America: A Geography of Canada and the United States*, 7th ed. (1984); Pirkle,

E. C., and Yoho, W. H., *Natural Landscapes of the United States*, 3d ed. (1982); Ruffner, James, ed., *Climates of the States*, 2 vols. (1976); U.S. Geological Survey, *The National Atlas of the United States of America* (1970); Watson, J. Wreford, *The United States* (1983); White, C. L., et al., *Regional Geography of Anglo-America*, 6th ed. (1985).

PEOPLE AND CULTURE: Boorstin, Daniel, *The Americans*, 3 vols. (1958–73; repr. 1984–85); Cohen, Wilbur J., and Westoff, Charles F., *Demographic Dynamics in America* (1977); Commager, Henry Steele, *The Empire of Reason: How Europe Imagined and America Realized the Enlightenment* (1977; repr. 1984); Dinnerstein, Leonard, *Ethnic Americans: A History of Immigration and Assimilation* (1975); Douglas, Ann, *The Feminization of American Culture* (1977); Gordon, Milton, *Assimilation in American Life: The Role of Race, Religion and National Origins* (1964); Highan, John, and Conkin, Paul K., eds., *New Directions in American Intellectual History* (1980); Hodgson, Godfrey, *America in Our Time* (1976); Lasch, Christopher, *The Culture of Narcissism: American Life in an Age of Diminishing Expectations* (1979); Mulder, John M., and Wilson, John F., *Religion in American History* (1978); Pells, Richard H., *The Liberal Mind in a Conservative Age* (1985); Roueché, Berton, *Sea to Shining Sea* (1986); U.S. Bureau of the Census, *Statistical Abstract of the United States* (annual).

ECONOMICS: Adams, Walter, *The Structure of American Industry*, 7th ed. (1985); Duffy, James H., *Domestic Affairs: American Programs and Priorities* (1979); Hacker, L. M., *The Course of American Economic Growth and Development* (1970); Handlin, Oscar and Mary, *The Wealth of the American People: A History of American Affluence* (1975); Kirkland, Edward C., *A History of American Economic Life*, 4th ed. (1969); Porter, Glenn, *Encyclopedia of American Economic History*, 3 vols. (1980); Rodgers, Harrell R., *Poor Women, Poor Families* (1986); Sampson, R. J., *The American Economy* (1983); Tufte, Edward R., *Political Control of the Economy* (1978; repr. 1980).

FOREIGN POLICY: Belfiglio, Valente J., *American Foreign Policy*, 2d ed. (1983); Combs, Gerald, *Brief U.S. Foreign Policy* (1986); DeConde, Alexander, ed., *Encyclopedia of American Foreign Policy*, 3 vols. (1978); Hughes, Barry B., et al., *Energy in the Global Arena* (1985); Isaak, R. A., *American Democracy and World Power* (1977).

POLITICS AND GOVERNMENT: Adrian, Charles R., *Governing Our Fifty States and Their Communities*, 4th ed. (1978); Armbruster, M. E., *The Presidents of the United States and Their Administrations from Washington to the Present*, 7th ed. (1981); Council of State Governments, *The Book of the States* (biennial); Domhoff, G. William, *The Powers That Be: Processes of Ruling-Class Domination in America* (1979); Freeman, Roger A., *The Growth of the American Government* (1975); Janowitz, Morris, *The Last Half-Century: Societal Change and Politics in America* (1978); Johnson, Donald B., comp., *National Party Platforms*, 2 vols. (1978); Lawler, Peter A., ed., *American Political Rhetoric* (1983); Lees, John D., *The Political System of the United States*, rev. ed. (1983); Office of the Federal Register, *United States Government Manual* (annual); Sohner, Charles P., and Martin, Helen P., *American Government and Politics Today*, 4th ed. (1984); Vidich, Arthur, and Bensman, Joseph, *American Society: The Welfare State and Beyond*, rev. ed. (1986).

See also: AMERICAN ART AND ARCHITECTURE; AMERICAN LITERATURE; AMERICAN MUSIC; NORTH AMERICA; and separate articles on each U.S. state, important cities, and major land features.

United States, education in the

Public education in the United States takes place in more than 85,000 elementary and secondary schools (see PRIMARY EDUCATION; MIDDLE SCHOOLS AND JUNIOR HIGH SCHOOLS; SECONDARY EDUCATION), on which over $110 billion a year is spent. More than 3,200 private and public colleges, COMMUNITY AND JUNIOR COLLEGES, and UNIVERSITIES exist (including GRADUATE EDUCATION), on which more than $70 billion a year is spent. In addition, PRIVATE SCHOOLS, PRESCHOOL EDUCATION PROGRAMS, ADULT EDUCATION programs, federal INDIAN SCHOOLS, and schools on federal installations abroad are components of the U.S. educational system. Almost 88% of the regular day-school students and almost 73% of the students in higher education are enrolled in public institutions.

BASIC STATISTICS

Enrollment. Although enrollments were low early in the 20th century, by the 1980s almost all 5- to 13-year-olds and more than 90% of the 5- to 17-year-olds were enrolled in school. The proportion of 17-year-olds with high school diplomas has increased from 7% in 1901 to almost 74% in 1981; another 10% earn diplomas by the time they are 29 years of age. The educational attainment of 70% of all persons over 25 years of age includes four years of high school or more.

Between 1971 and 1981, public school enrollment dropped by 6 million students, or almost 13%. A gradual climb in elementary school enrollments is expected to regain by 1990 the 33.5 million student enrollment (from kindergarten to grade 8) recorded in the early 1970s.

Significant changes in school enrollments are also resulting from regional differences in population growth. The areas of major growth include southern and western states; the areas of decline or stable growth include urbanized northeastern and central states. In all regions, however, enrollments in large cities are declining more rapidly than the national average. Despite these changes, urban systems remain large and unwieldy. More than one-third of the elementary and secondary students in Arizona are in Phoenix, and the New York City school system, with almost a million students, is larger than that of every state west of the Mississippi except California and Texas. Population shifts from these urban schools are resulting in an increasing proportion of low-income racial and ethnic minority students.

Costs. Public-school costs in 1981–82 were $112.4 billion, of which 9% came from federal sources, 48% from state sources, and 43% from local sources. Until the 1970s more than 50% came from local sources. The 1980 expenditures per pupil amounted to about $2,500, ranging from lows of $1,741 (Alabama) and $1,788 (Mississippi) to $3,681 (New York) and $5,146 (Alaska). Dramatic variation occurs among districts within a state, tending to reflect local wealth.

LOCAL AUTHORITY

School Districts. The United States has about 15,600 school districts, a number that is dropping as small districts merge. More than 50% of the districts enroll fewer than 1,000 students. Elementary districts, which may also include junior high or middle schools, and high school districts are often distinct, and neither necessarily conforms to political boundaries.

History of Powers and Responsibilities. American public education began in the late 18th century as a local endeavor, with citizens taking the initiative to clear land, build schools, hire teachers, raise funds, and determine who would supervise the operation. This early tradition explains the longstanding American conviction that public schools are primarily the responsibility of the communities they serve. During the late 19th century the emphasis of schools at the postprimary level shifted from a common basic learning for all students to a differentiated curriculum to prepare young people for varied social roles. From about the 1860s on, professionally trained teachers and administrators were common. At this time, schools became increasingly secular. By the 1920s the responsibility for supervision had largely been assumed by professional staff, and the size of school boards was reduced. Compulsory attendance laws became widespread before the 1920s.

Now school board powers include hiring and reviewing the performance of the superintendent, setting policy guidelines, and approving administrative actions and recommendations. Some districts have the power to levy taxes within state-imposed limits. In these instances school boards tend to be involved in budget making and district finances. The extent of board involvement varies with the interests of their members. In some large districts local advisory councils, with no formal authority, have on occasion influenced the selection of teachers, principals, and textbooks. Their involvement also depends on the interests of their members.

STATE AUTHORITY

Primary Authority. Formal control of American public schools is held by state government. The powers of local school boards are, in all states, derived from state powers by the delegation of state governments. In general, states reserve powers to legislate and enforce policy guidelines, academic standards, and accreditation review procedures. State legislation determines the system of school finance, criteria for licensing school personnel, and the ages of compulsory attendance. State agencies are responsible for curriculum review, quality control, and general supervision of the educational institutions. States cannot bar private education but can exercise indirect control over private institutions through CURRICULUM requirements, ACCREDITATION standards, and criteria for the licensing of professional staff.

History of Powers and Responsibilities. State influence on education was encouraged by the common-school movement (from about 1830 to 1860), an educational campaign particularly strong in the northern and Midwestern states. Advocates of common schools sought to establish more schools and to organize systems of comparable schools within the states. The effort focused on elementary education, but growing support for public high schools was being generated as well. Horace MANN, perhaps the major leader in the movement, argued that common schools would be the "new enabling institutions" that would produce the quality of citizens needed to guarantee national survival through industrialization and urban growth. They would, it was thought, educate voters for civic responsibility, Americanize recent immigrants, and teach young people to avoid vice and crime. To realize such goals, it was argued, schools must be inclusive, comparable, and accessible. They could not be left to local whim. By 1861 most Union states had active state school offices, and by 1900 about half of the states had them. At first they merely collected data, recommended improvements, and inspected and compared schools. The wider powers already mentioned developed in the 20th century.

FEDERAL INTERVENTION

History of Powers and Responsibilities. The U.S. Constitution does not explicitly mention education. Until after the Civil War both houses of Congress refused to establish standing committees on education on the grounds that the subject fell within state prerogatives. Nevertheless, new states were required to reserve land for the support of schools, and in the late 1830s surplus federal funds were returned to states to be used for a number of purposes, including education. It was at this time that the common-school movement grew. Education programs for Indian tribes began before 1820. When the Department of Agriculture was established (1862), educational services constituted one of its major assignments. Among the services offered by the FREEDMEN'S BUREAU (1865) after the Civil War were educational services. A U.S. Department of Education was approved in 1867 but later was reorganized as a bureau in the Department of the Interior, where it played only a minor role for almost a century.

The major federal educational enactment of the 19th century was the MORRILL ACT, enacted in 1862. It offered land grants to the states for endowing and maintaining at least one college that would promote scientific, agricultural, industrial, and military studies and agricultural experimentation. A second act (1890) provided continuing federal support for LAND-GRANT COLLEGES. These annual appropriations were to be withheld from states practicing segregation unless separate agricultural and mechanical BLACK COLLEGES were provided. The law led to the creation of 17 land-grant institutions for blacks. Among the land-grant colleges are such distinguished institutions as Cornell and Rutgers universities, the Michigan State University, the University of Illinois, and Texas Agricultural and Mechanical University. In the first half of the 20th century, Congress approved aid for VOCATIONAL EDUCATION, education-related public works during the Depression, veterans education, and school districts "impacted" by the children of federal employees. (See G.I. BILL OF RIGHTS.)

Developments in 1958 and Following. The NATIONAL DEFENSE EDUCATION ACT (NDEA) of 1958 approved the use of federal funds to support science and mathematics education and modern foreign-language instruction. Funds from the NDEA were employed to strengthen secondary-school and college programs and to underwrite low-interest loans to students in higher education. The ELEMENTARY AND SECONDARY EDUCATION ACT OF 1965 (ESEA) represented the most direct federal intervention in education in U.S. history. In making funds available to local and state education agencies offering programs for economically and educationally disadvantaged children, ESEA committed the federal government to enhancing equal educational opportunity. Major infusions of federal funds to support education followed throughout the 1960s. By 1978 the cost of federal education programs exceeded $25 billion. The Education Consolidation and Improvement Act of 1981 altered the mode of distributing a large portion of federal education funds by consolidating 42 programs into 7 programs fundable through block grants to the states.

Federal intervention has neither augmented local and state operating budgets nor exercised direct control of education. Rather, it has been problem focused, targeted for particular populations, and limited in duration. Although many programs exist scattered among about 40 agencies, the principal agency is the U.S. Department of Education.

Supreme Court Decisions. During the 1960s, '70s, and '80s the U.S. Supreme Court established major precedents in the areas of student rights, school finance, and access to education. *Tinker* v. *Des Moines Independent Community School District* (1969) upheld the constitutional rights to freedom of speech and expression of public-school students and teachers. The ruling has been applied to decisions involving underground newspapers, demonstrations, and refusal to participate in patriotic exercises. *Goss* v. *Lopez* (1975) guaranteed due process to students in cases involving suspension and expulsion. In *Ingraham* v. *Wright* (1977) the Court concluded that corporal punishment is not prohibited by the constitutional prohibition of cruel and unusual punishment. *San Antonio Independent School District* v. *Rodriguez* (1973) held that school finance reform is a matter to be resolved by state lawmakers and not a constitutional issue. *Mueller et al.* v. *Allen et al.* (1983) upheld a Minnesota law allowing tax deductions for the costs of public and private education.

BROWN V. BOARD OF EDUCATION OF TOPEKA, KANSAS (1954) barred the de jure segregation of students by race, ruling that separate schools were inherently unequal. It was the first of a series of decisions directly promoting school desegregation. UNIVERSITY OF CALIFORNIA V. BAKKE (1978) approved admissions policies that seek to promote the inclusion of certain groups but barred the use of group quotas.

CURRENT ISSUES

Among the issues facing American education are the declining enrollment—which will require the curtailing of programs, the abandonment of facilities, and reductions in the staff—and the question of whether there should be bilingual education and, if so, in what form. Both issues will be intensified by changes in the nation's demography. The school-age population represents a decreasing proportion of the total population. Fewer taxpayers directly concerned as parents with the quality of schools may result in further reductions in educational spending. Absolute and proportional increases in the Spanish-speaking population affect the controversy over BILINGUAL EDUCATION. Several other major issues must be faced in the early 1980s.

Student Achievement. Recent studies have indicated significant declines in student achievement in reading, mathemat-

ics, science, and social studies. Hope exists, however, that the scores have "bottomed out." Students in inner-city schools, especially those from low-income and minority-group families, generally test lower than their suburban, middle-class counterparts. In 1983 several critical reports recommended sweeping curriculum and policy changes to raise student achievement, including a longer school day and academic year, additional high school graduation requirements in the sciences and mathematics, competency testing in basic areas of study, and higher admissions requirements for colleges and universities. The lack of fresh resources will require the reallocation of existing funds to support the new emphasis on measured achievement.

Teacher Shortages and Merit Pay. The lack of qualified teachers, especially in science and mathematics, will be a major concern throughout the 1980s. The problem has resulted from a combination of factors. Women, historically the major source of school personnel, are moving into different professions. Relative to others with similar levels of education preparation, teachers are underpaid. Recent studies indicate strong dissatisfaction among teachers with their working conditions. As a consequence, the number and quality of teacher candidates have fallen. Merit pay for teachers and creation of a new career path for outstanding teachers, the master teacher, have been proposed as ways to attract more able people into the profession. The proposals offer long-term career incentives, but teacher organizations fear that the proposals would supplant efforts to correct the salary inequities of teachers generally.   DONALD WARREN

Bibliography: Boyer, Ernest, *High School* (1983); Butts, R. Freeman, *Public Education in the United States: From Revolution to Reform, 1776–1976* (1978); Cremin, Lawrence A., *Traditions of American Education* (1977); Goodlad, John I., *A Place Called School* (1983); Gumbert, Edgar B., and Spring, Joel H., *The Superschool and the Superstate: American Education in the Twentieth Century, 1918–1970* (1974); Tesconi, Charles A., Jr., *Schooling in America* (1975); Tyack, David B., *The One Best System: A History of American Urban Education* (1974); Warren, Donald R., *To Enforce Education: A History of the Founding Years of the U.S. Office of Education* (1974).

United States, history of the

Many peoples have contributed to the development of the United States of America, a vast nation that arose from a scattering of British colonial outposts in the New World. The first humans to inhabit the North American continent were migrants from northeast Asia who established settlements in North America as early as 8000 BC and possibly much earlier (see NORTH AMERICAN ARCHAEOLOGY). By about AD 1500 the native peoples of the areas north of the Rio Grande had developed a variety of different cultures (see INDIANS, AMERICAN). The vast region stretching eastward from the Rocky Mountains to the Atlantic Ocean was relatively sparsely populated by tribes whose economies were generally based on hunting and gathering, fishing, and farming.

VIKINGS explored the North American mainland in the 10th and 11th centuries and settled there briefly (see VINLAND). Of more lasting importance, however, was the first voyage (1492–93) of Christopher COLUMBUS, which inaugurated an age of great European EXPLORATION of the Western Hemisphere. Various European states (including Spain, France, England, the Netherlands, and Portugal) and their trading companies sent out expeditions to explore the New World during the century and a half that followed.

The Spanish claimed vast areas including Florida, Mexico, and the region west of the Mississippi River although they concentrated their settlement south of the Rio Grande. The French explored much of the area that became Canada and established several settlements there. Of most significance, however, for the subsequent development of the United States, was the English colonization of the region along the Atlantic coast.

BRITISH COLONIES IN NORTH AMERICA

At the end of the period of turmoil associated with the Protestant Reformation in England, the English people became free to turn their attention to some other matters and to seek new

(Left) *Christopher Columbus, portrayed (1519) by the Italian painter Sebastiano del Piombo, initiated the exploration and colonization of the New World when he discovered the lands of the Western Hemisphere. Columbus himself began efforts to colonize the West Indies during his four voyages. (Metropolitan Museum of Art, New York City.)*

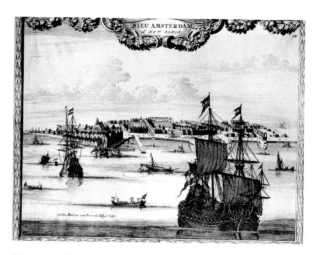

New Amsterdam, renamed New York when the English claimed (1664) the area from the Dutch, became the second largest port in the colonies by the late 1700s. The harbor is portrayed in this early-18th-century engraving. (New York Public Library.)

opportunities outside their tiny island. Internal stability under Elizabeth I (r. 1558–1603) and an expanding economy combined with a bold intellectual ferment to produce a soaring self-confidence. Ireland experienced the first impact: by the beginning of the 17th century it had been wholly subjugated by the English. Scottish and English Protestants were dispatched to "colonize" where the savage Irish, as they were called, had been expelled, especially in the northern provinces. Then, entrepreneurs began to look to North America, claimed by England on the basis of John CABOT's voyages of discovery (1497–99).

The Chesapeake Colonies. The English had failed in their attempts in the 1580s to found a colony at ROANOKE on the Virginia coast. In 1606, however, the LONDON COMPANY, established to exploit North American resources, sent settlers to what in 1607 became JAMESTOWN, the first permanent English colony in the New World. The colonists suffered extreme hardships, and by 1622, of the more than 10,000 who had immigrated, only 2,000 remained alive. In 1624 control of the failing company passed to the crown, making Virginia a royal colony. Soon the tobacco trade was flourishing, the death rate had fallen, and with a legislature (the House of Burgesses, established in 1619) and an abundance of land, the colony entered a period of prosperity. Individual farms, available at low cost, were worked primarily by white indentured servants (laborers who were bound to work for a number of

A map (c.1606–08) of North America, drawn for the Virginia Company of London (or London Company), shows the area claimed by England (Virginia) sandwiched between the French (Nova Francia) and Spanish (Florida) areas. Jamestown, Va., was the first permanent English colony.

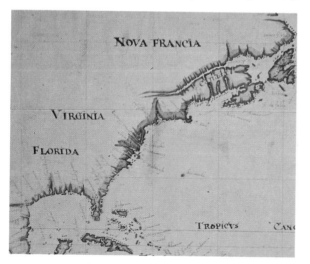

years to pay for their passage before receiving full freedom). The Chesapeake Bay area became a land of opportunity for poor English people.

In 1632, Maryland was granted to the CALVERT family as a personal possession, to serve as a refuge for Roman Catholics. Protestants, as well, flooded into the colony, and in 1649 the Toleration Act was issued, guaranteeing freedom of worship in Maryland to all Trinitarian Christians.

The New England Colonies. In 1620, Puritan Separatists, later called PILGRIMS, sailed on the MAYFLOWER to New England, establishing PLYMOUTH COLONY, the first permanent settlement there. They were followed in 1629 by other Puritans (see PURITANISM), under the auspices of the MASSACHUSETTS BAY COMPANY, who settled the area around Boston. During the Great Puritan Migration that followed (1629–42), about 16,000 settlers arrived in the Massachusetts Bay Colony. The Puritans set out to build a "city on a hill" intended to provide a model of godly living for the world. Strict Calvinists, strongly communal, and living in closely bound villages, they envisioned a God angered at human transgressions, who chose, purely according to his inscrutable will, a mere "righteous fragment" for salvation. Dissidents of a Baptist orientation founded Rhode Island (chartered 1644). In 1639, Puritans on what was then the frontier established the Fundamental Orders of Connecticut, the first written constitution in North America; the colony was chartered in 1662. The settlements in New Hampshire that sprang up in the 1620s were finally proclaimed a separate royal colony in 1679. Plymouth later became (1691) part of the royal colony of Massachusetts.

The Restoration Colonies. A long era (1642–60) of turmoil in England, which included the Civil War, Oliver Cromwell's republican Commonwealth, and the Protectorate, ended with the restoration of the Stuarts in the person of Charles II. An amazing period ensued, during which colonies were founded and other acquisitions were made. In 1663, Carolina was chartered; settlement began in 1670, and from the start the colony flourished. The territory later came under royal control as South Carolina (1721) and North Carolina (1729).

In 1664 an English fleet arrived to claim by right of prior discovery the land along the Hudson and Delaware rivers that had been settled and occupied by the Dutch since 1624. Most of NEW NETHERLAND now became New York colony and its principal settlement, New Amsterdam, became the city of New York. New York colony, already multiethnic and strongly commercial in spirit, came under control of the crown in 1685. New Jersey, sparsely settled by the Dutch, Swedes, and others, was also part of this English claim. Its proprietors divided it into East and West Jersey in 1676, but the colony was reunited as a royal province in 1702.

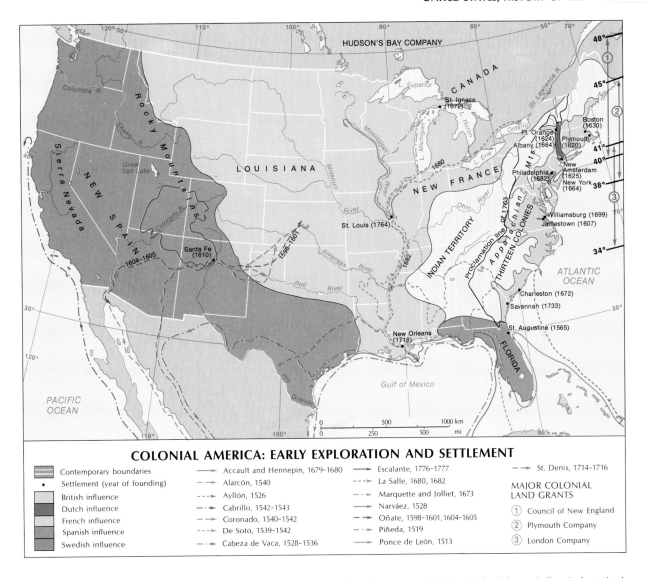

COLONIAL AMERICA: EARLY EXPLORATION AND SETTLEMENT

Contemporary boundaries	→ Accault and Hennepin, 1679–1680	→ Escalante, 1776–1777
• Settlement (year of founding)	–→ Alarcón, 1540	--→ La Salle, 1680, 1682
British influence	--→ Ayllón, 1526	–·→ Marquette and Jolliet, 1673
Dutch influence	–·→ Cabrillo, 1542–1543	–→ Narváez, 1528
French influence	–→ Coronado, 1540–1542	–→ Oñate, 1598–1601, 1604–1605
Spanish influence	--→ De Soto, 1539–1542	–·→ Piñeda, 1519
Swedish influence	–·→ Cabeza de Vaca, 1528–1536	→ Ponce de León, 1513

– – → St. Denis, 1714–1716

MAJOR COLONIAL
LAND GRANTS

① Council of New England
② Plymouth Company
③ London Company

Early exploration of the territories later forming the United States was conducted primarily by the Spanish and French, while the British, and for a time the Dutch and Swedes, concentrated on settlement. The latitudinal boundaries of the early English land grants appear at right.

William Penn's treaty (c.1682) with the Delaware Indians is dramatized in this Quaker painting. Penn's liberal policies, including payment for Indian lands, made Pennsylvania one of the most prosperous colonies. (Abby Aldrich Rockefeller Folk Art Collection, Williamsburg, Va.)

In 1681, Pennsylvania, and in 1682, what eventually became (1776) Delaware, were granted to William PENN, who founded a great Quaker settlement in and around Philadelphia. Quaker theology differed widely from that of the New England Puritans. Believing in a loving God who speaks directly to each penitent soul and offers salvation freely, Quakers found elaborate church organizations and ordained clerics unnecessary.

Indian Wars. In 1675 disease-ridden and poverty-stricken Indians in New England set off KING PHILIP'S WAR against the whites. Almost every Massachusetts town experienced the horror of Indian warfare; thousands on both sides were slaughtered before King Philip, the Wampanoag chief, was killed in 1676 and the war ended. Virginians, appalled at this event, in 1676 began attacking the Occaneechees despite the disapproval of the royal governor, Sir William BERKELEY. Then, under Nathaniel Bacon, dissatisfied and angry colonists expelled Berkeley from Jamestown and proclaimed Bacon's Laws, which gave the right to vote to all freedmen. Royal troops soon arrived to put down the uprising, known as BACON'S REBELLION.

Along the Mohawk River in New York, the Five Nations of

the IROQUOIS LEAGUE maintained their powerful confederacy with its sophisticated governing structure and strong religious faith. Allies of the English against the French along the Saint Lawrence River, they dominated a vast region westward to Lake Superior with their powerful and well-organized armies. The FRENCH AND INDIAN WARS, a series of great wars between the two European powers and their Indian allies, ended in 1763 when French rule was eradicated from North America and Canada was placed under the British crown.

18th-Century Social and Economic Developments. In the 1700s the British colonies grew rapidly in population and wealth. A formerly crude society acquired a polished and numerous elite. Trade and cities flourished. The 250,000 settlers who had lived in the mainland colonies to the south of Canada in 1700 became 2,250,000 by 1775 and would grow to 5,300,000 by 1800. Settlement expanded widely from the coastal beachheads of the 17th century into back-country regions with profoundly divergent ways of life.

Several non-English ethnic groups migrated to the British colonies in large numbers during the 18th century. By 1775, Germans, who settled primarily in the Middle Colonies but also in the back-country South, numbered about 250,000. They were members of the Lutheran and German Reformed (Calvinist) churches or of pietist sects (Moravians, Mennonites, Amish, and the like); the pietists, in particular, tended to live separately, avoiding English-speaking peoples. From the 1730s waves of Scots-Irish immigrants, numbering perhaps 250,000 by the time of the Revolution, swelled the ranks of the non-English group. Forming dense settlements in Pennsylvania, as well as in New York's Hudson Valley and in the back-country South, they brought with them the Presbyterian church, which was to become widely prominent in American life. Many of these immigrants were indentured servants; a small percentage were criminals, transported from the jails of England, where they had been imprisoned for debt or for more serious crimes. The colony of Georgia was granted in 1732 to reformers, led by James OGLETHORPE, who envisioned it as an asylum for English debtors, as well as a buffer against Spanish Florida. Georgia, too, was colonized by many non-English people.

The Growth of Slavery. Slaves from Africa were used in small numbers in the colonies from about 1619 (see BLACK AMERICANS; SLAVERY). After British merchants joined the Dutch in the slave trade later in the 17th century, prices tumbled and increasing numbers of black people were transported into the southern colonies to be used for plantation labor. Slaves were also used in the northern colonies, but in far fewer numbers. The survival rates as well as birthrates tended to be high for slaves brought to the North American mainland colonies—in contrast to those transported to the West Indies or to South America.

The expansion of slavery was the most fateful event of the pre-Revolutionary years. Virginia had only about 16,000 slaves in 1700; by 1770 it held more than 187,000, or almost half the population of the colony. In low country South Carolina, with its rice and indigo plantations, only 25,000 out of a total population of 100,000 were white in 1775. Fearful whites mounted slave patrols and exacted savage penalties upon transgression in order to maintain black passivity.

Meanwhile, on the basis of abundant slave labor, the world of great plantations emerged, creating sharp distinctions in wealth among whites. Southern society was dominated by the aristocracy; however, whites of all classes were united in their fear of blacks. Miscegenation was common, especially where slaves were most numerous, and mulattos were regarded as black, not white. An almost total absence of government in this sparsely settled, rural southern environment resulted in complete license on the part of owners in the treatment of their slaves. Paradoxically, the ideal of liberty— of freedom from all restraints—was powerful in the southern white mind.

Religious Trends. As transatlantic trade increased, communication between the colonies and England became closer, and English customs and institutions exerted a stronger influence on the Americans. The aristocracy aped London fashions, and colonials participated in British cultural movements. The Church of England, the established church in the southern colonies and in the four counties in and around New York City, grew in status and influence. At the same time, in both Britain and America, an increasingly rationalistic and scientific outlook, born in the science of Sir Isaac NEWTON and the philosophy of John LOCKE, made religious observance more logical and of this world. Deism and so-called natural religion scoffed at Christianity and the Bible as a collection of ancient superstitions.

Then from England came an upsurge of evangelical Protestantism, led by John Wesley (the eventual founder of the Methodist church; see WESLEY family) and George WHITEFIELD. It sought to combat the new rationalism and foster a revival of enthusiasm in Christian faith and worship. Beginning in 1738, with Whitefield's arrival in the colonies, a movement known as the GREAT AWAKENING swept the colonials, gaining strength from an earlier outbreak of revivalism in Massachusetts (1734–35) led by Jonathan EDWARDS. Intensely democratic in spirit, the Great Awakening was the first intercolonial cultural movement. It vastly reenergized a Puritanism that, since the mid-1600s, had lost its vigor. All churches were electrified by its power—either in support or in opposition. The movement also revived the earlier Puritan notion that America was to be a "city on a hill," a special place of God's work, to stand in sharp contrast to what was regarded as corrupt and irreligious England.

A German engraving (1732) portrays Lutherans from Salzburg, Austria, departing for the New World. During the 18th century many German Protestants emigrated to North America to escape religious persecution. More than 70 percent settled in the Middle Colonies.

This engraving depicts worshipers flocking to a revival meeting during the so-called Great Awakening of the 1730s and 1740s. The individualistic focus of its preaching and its attack on established religious authority gave this movement a strongly democratic appeal.

British forces under Gen. James Wolfe scaled the bluffs above Quebec to capture the city from the French on Sept. 13, 1759. This battle marked the turning point of the French and Indian War (1754-63), the last of several conflicts that eliminated French rule in North America.

An American cartoon portrays a procession of British dignitaries mourning the demise of the Stamp Act of 1765. This tax legislation was repealed (1766) when the colonists boycotted British goods, but Parliament imposed the Townshend Duties only 15 months later.

THE AMERICAN REVOLUTION

By the middle of the 18th century the wave of American expansion was beginning to top the Appalachian rise and move into the valley of the Ohio. Colonial land companies looked covetously to that frontier. The French, foreseeing a serious threat to their fur trade with the Indians, acted decisively. In 1749 they sent an expedition to reinforce their claim to the Ohio Valley and subsequently established a string of forts there. The British and the colonists were forced to respond to the move or suffer the loss of the vast interior, long claimed by both British and French. The French and Indian War (1754-63) that resulted became a worldwide conflict, called the SEVEN YEARS' WAR in Europe. At its end, the British had taken over most of France's colonial empire as well as Spanish Florida and had become dominant in North America except for Spain's possessions west of the Mississippi River.

Rising Tensions. A delirious pride over the victory swept the colonies and equaled that of the British at home. Outbursts of patriotic celebration and cries of loyalty to the crown infused the Americans. The tremendous cost of the war itself and the huge responsibility accompanying the new possessions, however, left Britain with an immense war debt and heavy administrative costs. At the same time the elimination of French rule in North America lifted the burden of fear of that power from the colonists, inducing them to be more independent-minded. The war effort itself had contributed to a new sense of pride and confidence in their own military prowess. In addition, the rapid growth rate of the mid-18th century had compelled colonial governments to become far more active than that of old, established England. Because most male colonists possessed property and the right to vote, the result was the emergence of a turbulent world of democratic politics.

London authorities attempted to meet the costs of imperial administration by levying a tax on the colonials; the STAMP ACT of 1765 required a tax on all public documents, newspapers, notes and bonds, and almost every other printed paper. A raging controversy that brought business practically to a standstill erupted in the colonies. A Stamp Act Congress, a gathering of representatives from nine colonies, met in New York in October 1765 to issue a solemn protest. It held that the colonials possessed the same rights and liberties as did the British at home, among which was the principle that "no taxes be imposed on them but with their own consent, given personally or by their representatives." In March 1766, Parliament repealed the Stamp Act; it passed the Declaratory Act, asserting its complete sovereignty over the colonies.

Thereafter the transatlantic controversy was rarely quiet. The colonists regarded the standing army of about 6,000 troops maintained by London in the colonies after 1763 with great suspicion—such a peacetime force had never been pre-

sent before. British authorities defended the force as necessary to preserve peace on the frontier, especially after PONTIAC'S REBELLION (1763-65), which had been launched by the brilliant Indian leader Pontiac to expel the British from the interior and restore French rule. In another attempt to quell Indian unrest, London established the Proclamation Line of 1763. Set along the crest of the Appalachians, the line represented a limit imposed on colonial movement west until a more effective Indian program could be developed. The colonists were much angered by the prohibition. Historical memories of the use of standing armies by European kings to override liberty caused widespread suspicion among the colonists that the soldiers stationed on the Line of 1763 were to be employed not against the Indians, but against the colonials themselves should they prove difficult to govern.

Indeed, for many years colonists had been reading the radical British press, which argued the existence of a Tory plot in England to crush liberty throughout the empire. Surviving from the English Civil War of the previous century was a profound distrust of monarchy among a small fringe of radical members of Britain's Whig party, primarily Scots and Irish and English Dissenters—that is, Protestants who were not members of the Church of England. As members of the minority out-groups in British life, they had suffered many political and economic disadvantages. Radical Whigs insisted that a corrupt network of Church of England bishops, great landlords, and financiers had combined with the royal government to exploit the community at large, and that—frightened of criticism—this Tory conspiracy sought to destroy liberty and freedom.

In the cultural politics of the British Empire, American colonists were also an out-group; they bitterly resented the disdain and derision shown them by the metropolitan English. Furthermore, most free colonists were either Dissenters (the Congregationalists in New England and the Presbyterians and Baptists in New York and the South); or non-English peoples with ancient reasons for hating the English (the Scots-Irish); or outsiders in a British-dominated society (Germans and Dutch); or slaveowners sharply conscious of the distaste with which they were regarded by the British at home.

A divisive controversy racked the colonies in the mid-18th century concerning the privileges of the Church of England. Many believed in the existence of an Anglican plot against religious liberty. In New England it was widely asserted that the colonial tie to immoral, affluent, Anglican-dominated Britain was endangering the soul of America. Many southerners also disapproved of the ostentatious plantation living that grew out of the tobacco trade—as well as the widespread bankruptcies resulting from dropping tobacco prices—and urged separation from Britain.

The current ideology among many colonists was that of re-

The Boston Massacre (Mar. 5, 1770), in which British troops fired on a rioting crowd and killed five men, is depicted in an engraving by the Boston silversmith Paul Revere. The incident was a factor in the repeal of the Townshend Duties. (New York Public Library.)

publicanism. The radicalism of the 18th century, it called for grounding government in the people, giving them the vote, holding frequent elections, abolishing established churches, and separating the powers of government to guard against tyranny. Republicans also advocated that most offices be elective and that government be kept simple, limited, and respectful of the rights of citizens.

Deterioration of Imperial Ties. In this prickly atmosphere London's heavy-handedness caused angry reactions on the part of Americans. The Quartering Act of 1765 ordered colonial assemblies to house the standing army; to override the resulting protests in America, London suspended the New York assembly until it capitulated. In 1767 the TOWNSHEND ACTS levied tariffs on many articles imported into the colonies. These imports were designed to raise funds to pay wages to the army as well as to the royal governors and judges, who had formerly been dependent on colonial assemblies for their salaries. Nonimportation associations immediately sprang up in the colonies to boycott British goods. When mob attacks prevented commissioners from enforcing the revenue laws, part of the army was placed (1768) in Boston to protect the commissioners. This action confirmed the colonists' suspicion that the troops were maintained in the colonies to deprive them of their liberty. In March 1770 a group of soldiers fired into a crowd that was harassing them, killing five persons; news of the BOSTON MASSACRE spread through the colonies.

The chastened ministry in London now repealed all the Townshend duties except for that on tea. Nonetheless, the economic centralization long reflected in the NAVIGATION ACTS—which compelled much of the colonial trade to pass through Britain on its way to the European continent—served to remind colonials of the heavy price exacted from them for membership in the empire. The Sugar Act of 1764, latest in a long line of such restrictive measures, produced by its taxes a huge revenue for the crown. By 1776 it drained from the colonies about £600,000, an enormous sum. The colonial balance of trade with England was always unfavorable for the Americans, who found it difficult to retain enough cash to purchase necessary goods.

In 1772 the crown, having earlier declared its right to dismiss colonial judges at its pleasure, stated its intention to pay directly the salaries of governors and judges in Massachusetts.

Samuel ADAMS, for many years a passionate republican, immediately created the intercolonial Committee of Correspondence. Revolutionary sentiment mounted. In December 1773 swarms of colonials disguised as Mohawks boarded recently arrived tea ships in Boston harbor, flinging their cargo into the water. The furious royal government responded to this BOSTON TEA PARTY by the so-called INTOLERABLE ACTS of 1774, practically eliminating self-government in Massachusetts and closing Boston's port.

Virginia moved to support Massachusetts by convening the First CONTINENTAL CONGRESS in Philadelphia in the fall of 1774. It drew up declarations of rights and grievances and called for nonimportation of British goods. Colonial militia began drilling in the Massachusetts countryside. New Englanders were convinced that they were soon to have their churches placed under the jurisdiction of Anglican bishops. They believed, as well, that the landowning British aristocracy was determined, through the levying of ruinous taxes, to reduce the freeholding yeomanry of New England to the status of tenants. The word "slavery" was constantly on their lips.

The War for Independence. In April 1775, Gen. Thomas GAGE in Boston was instructed to take the offensive against the Massachusetts troublemakers, now declared traitors to the crown. Charged with bringing an end to the training of militia and gathering up all arms and ammunition in colonial hands, on April 19, Gage sent a body of 800 soldiers to Concord to commandeer arms. On that day, the Battles of LEXINGTON AND CONCORD took place, royal troops fled back to Boston, and American campfires began burning around the city. The war of the AMERICAN REVOLUTION had begun.

It soon became a world war, with England's European enemies gladly joining in opposing England in order to gain revenge for past humiliations. British forces were engaged in battle from the Caribbean and the American colonies to the coasts of India. Furthermore, the United Colonies, as the Continental Congress called the rebelling 13 colonies, were widely scattered in a huge wilderness and were occupied by a people most of whom were in arms. The dispersion of the American population meant that the small (by modern standards) cities of New York, Boston, and Philadelphia could be taken and held for long periods without affecting the outcome.

LOYALISTS numbered about 60,000, living predominantly along the coast where people of English ethnic background and anglicized culture were most numerous, but they were widely separated and weak. Pennsylvania's Quakers had looked to the crown as their protector against the Scots-Irish and other militant groups in Pennsylvania. The Quakers were appalled at the rebellion, aggressively led in the Middle Colonies by the Presbyterian Scots-Irish, and refused to lend it support. London deluded itself, however, with the belief that

Thomas Jefferson, with other members of the drafting committee, present the Declaration of Independence to the Continental Congress, meeting in Philadelphia. This document, approved on July 4, 1776, asserted the fundamental ideals of American government.

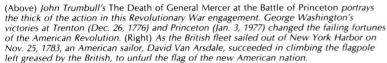

(Above) *John Trumbull's* The Death of General Mercer at the Battle of Princeton *portrays the thick of the action in this Revolutionary War engagement. George Washington's victories at Trenton (Dec. 26, 1776) and Princeton (Jan. 3, 1977) changed the failing fortunes of the American Revolution.* (Right) *As the British fleet sailed out of New York Harbor on Nov. 25, 1783, an American sailor, David Van Arsdale, succeeded in climbing the flagpole left greased by the British, to unfurl the flag of the new American nation.*

the Loyalists represented a majority that would soon resume control and end the conflict.

Within a brief period after the Battle of Concord, practically all royal authority disappeared from the 13 colonies. Rebel governments were established in each colony, and the Continental Congress in Philadelphia provided a rudimentary national government. The task now before the British was to fight their way back onto the continent, reestablish royal governments in each colony, and defeat the colonial army. By March 1776 the British evacuated Boston, moving to take and hold New York City. Within days of the British arrival in New York, however, the Congress in Philadelphia issued (July 4) the DECLARATION OF INDEPENDENCE. In December 1776, Gen. George WASHINGTON reversed the early trend of American defeats by a stunning victory at Trenton, N.J. (see TRENTON, BATTLE OF). Thereafter, as the fighting wore on and the cause survived, Washington became in America and abroad a symbol of strength and great bravery.

In February 1778 the French joined the conflict by signing an alliance with the Continental Congress. With the aid of the French fleet the British army in the north was reduced to a bridgehead at New York City. Shifting its efforts to the south, the royal army campaigned through Georgia and the Carolinas between 1778 and 1780, marching to the James Peninsula, in Virginia, in 1781. Here, in the YORKTOWN CAMPAIGN, by the combined efforts of Washington's troops and the French army and navy, Lord CORNWALLIS was forced to surrender on Oct. 19, 1781. The fighting, effectively, was over. In September 1783 the Treaty of Paris secured American independence on generous terms. The new nation was given an immense domain that ran westward to the Mississippi River (except for Britain's Canadian colonies and East and West Florida, which reverted to Spanish rule).

A NEW NATION

The first federal constitution of the new American republic was the ARTICLES OF CONFEDERATION. With ratification of that document in 1781, the nation had adopted its formal name, the United States of America.

Government under the Articles of Confederation. Under the Articles the only national institution was the Confederation Congress, with limited powers not unlike those of the United Nations. The states retained their sovereignty, with each state government selecting representatives to sit in the Congress. No national executive or judiciary had been established. Each state delegation received an equal vote on all issues. Congress was charged with carrying on the foreign relations of the United States, but because it had no taxing powers (it could only request funds from the states), it had no strength

to back up its diplomacy. In addition, it had no jurisdiction over interstate commerce; each state could erect tariffs against its neighbors.

The Confederation Congress, however, achieved one great victory: it succeeded in bringing all 13 of the states to agree on a plan for organizing and governing the western territories (the "public lands") beyond the Appalachians. Each state ceded its western claims to the Congress, which in three ordinances dealing with the Northwest (1784, 1785, and 1787) provided that new states established in the western regions would be equal in status to the older ones. After a territorial stage of quasi self-government, they would pass to full statehood. The land in the NORTHWEST TERRITORY (the Old Northwest, that is, the area north of the Ohio River) would be surveyed in square parcels, 6 mi (9.7 km) on a side, divided into 36 sections, and sold to settlers at low cost; one plot would be reserved for the support of public schools. Furthermore, slavery was declared illegal in the Northwest Territory. (The Southwest Territory, below the Ohio, was organized by the later federal Congress in 1790 as slave country.)

The Confederation Congress, however, did not survive. Because of its lack of taxing power, its currency was of little value; widespread social turbulence in the separate states led many Americans to despair of the new nation. The republic—regarded as a highly precarious form of government in a world of monarchies—was founded with the conviction that the people would exercise the virtue and self-denial required under self-government. Soon, however, that assumption seemed widely discredited. SHAYS'S REBELLION in Massachusetts (1786–87) was an attempt to aid debtors by forcibly closing the court system; mobs terrorized legislators and judges to achieve this end. The new state legislatures, which had assumed all powers when royal governors were expelled, confiscated property, overturned judicial decisions, issued floods of unsecured paper money, and enacted torrents of legislation, some of it ex post facto (effective retroactively).

The established social and political elite (as distinct from the rough new antiauthoritarian politicians who had begun to invade the state legislatures, talking aggressively about "democracy" and "liberty") urgently asserted the need for a strong national government. The influence that the London authorities had formerly provided as a balance to local government was absent. Minorities that had been protected by the crown, such as the Baptists in Massachusetts and the Quakers in Pennsylvania, were now defenseless. The wealthy classes maintained that they were at the mercy of the masses. The new United States was so weak that it was regarded contemptuously all over the world and its diplomats ignored.

We the People *of the United States, in order to form a more perfect Union, establish Justice, insure domestic Tranquility, provide for the common defence, promote the general Welfare, and secure the Blessings of Liberty to ourselves and our Posterity, do ordain and establish this Constitution for the United States of America.*

Article I

Section 1. All legislative Powers herein granted shall be vested in a Congress of the United States, which shall consist of a Senate and House of Representatives.

Section 2. The House of Representatives shall be composed of Members chosen every second Year by the People of the several States, and the Electors in each State shall have Qualifications requisite for Electors of the most numerous Branch of the State Legislature.

The Constitution of the United States was drawn up in Philadelphia in 1787 and ratified by the required nine states by June 21, 1788. It superseded the Articles of Confederation and laid the foundations of the federal system of government that has remained in force since 1789.

The Constitutional Convention of 1787. A chain of meetings, beginning with one between Virginia and Maryland in 1786 to solve mutual commercial problems and including the larger ANNAPOLIS CONVENTION later that year, led to the CONSTITUTIONAL CONVENTION in Philadelphia in 1787. Deciding to start afresh and fashion a new national government independent of, and superior to, the states, the delegates made a crucial decision: the nation's source of sovereignty was to lie in the people directly, not in the existing states. Using the British Parliament as a model, they provided for a CONGRESS OF THE UNITED STATES that would have two houses to check and balance one another. One house would be elected directly by the people of each state, with representation proportionate to population; the other would provide equal representation for each state (two senators each), to be chosen by the state legislatures.

The powers of the national government were to be those previously exercised by London: regulation of interstate and foreign commerce, foreign affairs and defense, and Indian affairs; control of the national domain; and promotion of "the general Welfare." Most important, the Congress was empowered to levy "taxes, duties, imposts, and excises." The states were prohibited from carrying on foreign relations, coining money, passing ex post facto laws, impairing the obligations of contracts, and establishing tariffs. Furthermore, if social turbulence within a state became serious, the federal government, following invitation by the legislature or the executive of that state, could bring in troops to insure "a republican form of government."

A PRESIDENT OF THE UNITED STATES with powers much like those of the British king, except that the office would be elective, was created. Chosen by a special body (an ELECTORAL COLLEGE), the president would be an independent and powerful national leader, effectively in command of the government. Recalling the assaults on judicial power that had been

rampant in the states, the Constitutional Convention also created a fully independent SUPREME COURT OF THE UNITED STATES, members of which could be removed only if they committed a crime. Then, most important, the document that was drawn up at Philadelphia stated that the Constitution, as well as laws and treaties made under the authority of the U.S. government, "shall be the supreme Law of the Land."

The proposed constitution was to be ratified by specially elected ratifying conventions in each state and to become operative after nine states had ratified it. In the national debate that arose over ratification, ANTI-FEDERALISTS opposed the concentration of power in the national government under the document; a key question was the absence of a BILL OF RIGHTS. Many Americans thought that a bill of rights was necessary to preserve individual liberties, and to accommodate this view proponents of the Constitution promised to add such a bill to the document after ratification. With the clear understanding that amendments would be added, ratification by nine states was completed (1788) and the CONSTITUTION OF THE UNITED STATES became operative. The Bill of Rights was then drafted by the first Congress and became the first ten amendments to the Constitution.

Diverging Visions of the American Republic. In the first elections for the new federal Congress (1789), those favoring the new system won a huge majority. George Washington was unanimously elected to be chief executive, the only president so honored. He was inaugurated in the temporary capital, New York City, on Apr. 30, 1789. The American experiment in republican self-government now began again. The unanimity expressed in Washington's election would prove short-lived.

Under the leadership of Secretary of the Treasury Alexander HAMILTON, Congress pledged (1790) the revenues of the federal government to pay off all the outstanding debt of the old Articles of Confederation government as well as the state debts. Much of the domestic debt was in currency that had

(Left) *An engraving shows President George Washington (left) with members of his first cabinet— (from left) Gen. Henry Knox, secretary of war; Alexander Hamilton, secretary of the treasury; Thomas Jefferson, secretary of state; and Edmund Randolph, the first attorney general.*

(Right) *Washington's death is memorialized in this Chinese export painting (c.1800), executed on glass. (Winterthur Museum, Delaware.)*

badly depreciated in value, but Congress agreed to fund it at its higher face value; at one stroke, the financial credit of the new government was assured. Southerners, however, mistrusted the plan, claiming that it served only to enrich northern speculators because the southern states had largely paid off their debts. Many southerners feared, too, that the new nation would be dominated by New Englanders, whose criticism of southern slavery and living styles offended them. Before assenting to the funding proposal, the southerners had obtained agreement that the national capital (after 10 years in Philadelphia) would be placed in the South, on the Potomac River.

In 1791, Hamilton persuaded Congress to charter the BANK OF THE UNITED STATES, modeled after the Bank of England. Primarily private (some of its trustees would be federally appointed), it would receive and hold the government's revenues, issue currency and regulate that of state-chartered banks, and be free to invest as it saw fit the federal tax moneys in its vaults. Because it would control the largest pool of capital in the country, it could shape the growth of the national economy. Hamilton also proposed (with limited success) that protective tariffs be established to exclude foreign goods and thus stimulate the development of U.S. factories. In short, he laid out the economic philosophy of what became the FEDERALIST PARTY: that the government should actively encourage economic growth by providing aid to capitalists. Flourishing cities and a vigorous industrial order: this was the American future he envisioned. His strongly nationalist position gained the support of the elites in New York City and Philadelphia as well as broad-based support among the Yankees of New England.

On the other hand, southerners, a rural and widely dispersed people, feared the cities and the power of remote bankers. With Thomas JEFFERSON they worked to counteract the Federalists' anglicized vision of the United States. Southerners rejected the concept of an active government, preferring one committed to laissez-faire (that is, allowing people to act without government interference) in all areas—economic and cultural. Jefferson declared that close ties between government and capitalists would inevitably lead to corruption and exploitation. In his view, behind-the-scene schemers would use graft to secure special advantages (tariffs, bounties, and the like) that would allow them to profiteer at the community's expense.

The Middle Atlantic states at first supported the nationalistic Federalists, who won a second term for Washington in 1792 and elected John ADAMS to the presidency in 1796. However, many of the Scots-Irish, Germans, and Dutch in these states disliked Yankees and distrusted financiers and business proprietors. The growing working class in Philadelphia and New York City turned against the Federalists' elitism. By 1800 the ethnic minorities of the Middle Atlantic states helped swing that region behind Jefferson, a Virginian, and his Democratic-Republican party, giving the presidency to Jefferson. Thereafter, until 1860, with few intermissions, the South and the Middle Atlantic states together dominated the federal government. Although the U.S. Constitution had made no mention of POLITICAL PARTIES, it had taken only a decade for the development of a party system that roughly reflected two diverging visions for the new republic. Political parties would remain an integral part of the American system of government.

During the 1790s, however, foreign affairs became dominant, and dreams of republican simplicity and quietude were dashed. A long series of wars between Britain and Revolutionary France began in that decade, and the Americans were inevitably pulled into the fray. By JAY'S TREATY (1794) the United States reluctantly agreed to British wartime confiscation of U.S. ship cargoes, alleged to be contraband, in return for British evacuation of western forts on American soil and the opening of the British West Indies to U.S. vessels. Under John Adams, similar depredations by the French navy against American trading ships led to the Quasi-War (1798–1801) on the high seas. Federalist hysteria over alleged French-inspired subversion produced the ALIEN AND SEDITION ACTS (1798),

The Franco-American convention ending the Quasi-War was signed at Mortefontaine, France, in 1800 and ratified in 1801. U.S. fears of French imperial ambitions in the New World were finally allayed when Napoleon sold the vast Louisiana Territory to the United States in 1803.

which sought to crush all criticism of the government.

The Democratic Republic. As president, Jefferson attempted to implement the Democratic-Republican vision of America; he cut back the central government's activities, reducing the size of the court system, letting excise taxes lapse, and contracting the military forces. Paradoxically, in what was perhaps Jefferson's greatest achievement as president, he vastly increased the scope of U.S. power: the securing of the LOUISIANA PURCHASE (1803) from France practically doubled American territory, placing the western boundary of the United States along the base of the Rocky Mountains.

In 1811, under Jefferson's successor, James MADISON, the 20-year charter of the Bank of the United States was allowed to lapse, further eroding the Federalists' nationalist program. Renewed warfare between Britain and France, during which American foreign trade was progressively throttled down almost to nothing, led eventually to the WAR OF 1812. The British insisted on the right freely to commandeer U.S. cargoes as contraband and to impress American sailors into their navy. To many Americans the republic seemed in grave peril.

With reluctance and against unanimous Federalist opposition, Congress made the decision to go to war against Britain. Except for some initial naval victories, the war went badly for the Americans. Western Indians, under the gifted TECUMSEH, fought on the British side. In 1814, however, an invading army

U.S. troops under Gen. William Henry Harrison defeated the British and their Indian allies in the Battle of the Thames (Oct. 5, 1813) during the War of 1812. This battle, in which the Indian leader Tecumseh was killed, secured U.S. control of the Northwest.

(Right) *Thousands of Americans crossed the plains in covered wagons during the westward migration of 1815-50. Quicksand along river crossings in Nebraska's Platte valley was one of many obstacles they encountered.*

(Below) *Miners sought gold in and near riverbeds during the California gold rush (1848-49), an event that stimulated an era of rapid economic, agricultural, and industrial growths in the Far West. (Museum of Fine Arts, Boston.)*

from Canada was repelled. Then, just as a peace treaty was being concluded in Ghent (Belgium), Andrew JACKSON crushed another invading British army as it sought to take New Orleans. The war thus ended on a triumphant note, and the republic was confirmed. The Federalists, who in the HART-FORD CONVENTION (in Connecticut, 1814) had capped their opposition to the war with demands for major changes in the Constitution, now were regarded as disloyal, and their party dwindled down to a base in New England and in the 1820s dissolved. Robbed of their enemy, Jeffersonian Democratic-Republicans broke into factions, effectively disappearing as a national party.

AN AGE OF BOUNDLESSNESS: 1815-50
The volatile and expansive years from 1815 to 1850 were, in many ways, an age of boundlessness when limits that had previously curbed human aspirations seemed to disappear.

Economic and Cultural Ferment. After 1815 the American economy began to expand rapidly. The cotton boom in the South spread settlement swiftly across the Gulf Plains: the Deep South was born. Farmers also moved into the Lake Plains north of the Ohio River, their migration greatly accelerating after the completion of the ERIE CANAL in 1825. Practically all Indians east of the Mississippi were placed on small reservations or forced to move to the Great Plains beyond the Missouri River. Canals and railroads opened the interior to swift expansion, of both settlement and trade. In the Midwest many new cities, such as Chicago, appeared, as enormous empires of wheat and livestock farms came into being. From 1815 to 1850 a new western state entered the Union, on the average, every 2½ years.

The westward movement of the FRONTIER was matched in the Northeast by rapid economic development. National pro-

ductivity surged during the 1820s; prices spurted to a peak during the 1830s and dropped for a time during the 1840s; both prices and productivity soared upward again during the 1850s, reaching new heights. A business cycle had appeared, producing periods of boom and bust, and the factory system became well developed. After the GOLD RUSH that began in California in 1848-49, industrial development was further stimulated during the 1850s by the arrival of $500 million in gold and silver from the Sierra Nevada and other western regions. A willingness to take risks formerly thought wildly imprudent became a national virtue. Land values rose, and hundreds of new communities appeared in the western states.

Meanwhile, property tests for voting were disappearing, white manhood suffrage became the rule, and most offices were made elective. A communications revolution centering in the inexpensive newspaper and in a national fascination with mass education (except in the South) sent literacy rates soaring. The Second Great Awakening (1787-1825), a new religious revival that originated in New England, spread an evangelical excitement across the country. In its wake a ferment of social reform swept the northern states. The slave system of the South spread westward as rapidly as the free labor system of the North, and during the 1830s ABOLITIONISTS mounted a crusade to hammer at the evils of slavery.

Expansion of the American Domain. The years 1815-50 brought further expansion of the national domain. In the Anglo-American Convention of 1818, the 49th parallel was established as the border between Canada and the United States from the Lake of the Woods to the Rockies, and in the Adams-Onís Treaty of 1819, Spain ceded Florida and its claims in the Oregon Country to the United States. During the 1840s a sense of MANIFEST DESTINY seized the American mind (although many individuals, especially in New England, were more restrained in their thinking). Continent-wide expansion seemed inevitable. Texas, which had declared its independence from Mexico in 1835-36 (see TEXAS REVOLUTION), was annexed in 1845. Then a dispute with Mexico concerning the Rio Grande as the border of Texas led to the MEXICAN WAR (1846-48). While U.S. armies invaded the heartland of Mexico to gain victory, other forces sliced off the northern half of that country—the provinces of New Mexico and Alta California. In the Treaty of GUADALUPE HIDALGO (1848), $15 million was paid for the Mexican cession of those provinces, more than 3 million km² (roughly 1 million m²).

In 1846, Britain and the United States settled the OREGON QUESTION, concluding a treaty that divided the Oregon Country at the 49th parallel and bringing the Pacific Northwest into the American nation. In addition, by the GADSDEN PURCHASE of 1853 the United States acquired (for $10 million) the southern portions of the present states of New Mexico and Arizona. By 1860 the Union comprised 33 states, packed solid through the first rank beyond the Mississippi and reaching

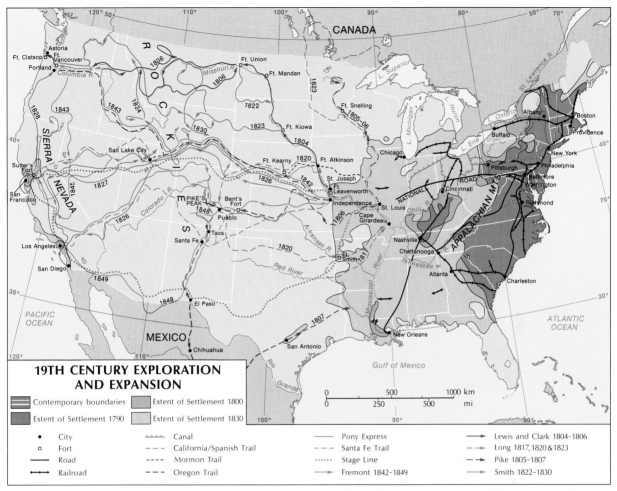

19TH CENTURY EXPLORATION AND EXPANSION

▓ Contemporary boundaries	▓ Extent of Settlement 1800
▓ Extent of Settlement 1790	░ Extent of Settlement 1830

● City	┴┴┴ Canal	── Pony Express	➡ Lewis and Clark 1804–1806
□ Fort	─ ─ ─ California/Spanish Trail	─ ─ ─ Santa Fe Trail	➡ Long 1817, 1820 & 1823
── Road	---- Mormon Trail	⋯⋯⋯ Stage Line	➡ Pike 1805–1807
⟷ Railroad	─ ─ ─ Oregon Trail	➡ Fremont 1842–1849	➡ Smith 1822–1830

westward to include Texas, as well as California and Oregon on the Pacific Coast. Fed by a high birthrate and by the heavy immigration from Ireland and Germany that surged dramatically during the 1840s, the nation's population was leaping upward: from 9.6 million in 1820 to 23 million in 1850 and 31.5 million in 1860.

Domestic Politics: 1815–46. In a nationalist frame of mind at the end of the War of 1812, Congress chartered the Second Bank of the United States in 1816, erected the first protective tariff (see TARIFF ACTS), and supported internal improvements (roads and bridges) to open the interior. President James MONROE presided (1817–25) over the so-called Era of Good Feelings, followed by John Quincy ADAMS (1825–29).

Chief Justice John MARSHALL led the Supreme Court in a crucial series of decisions, beginning in 1819. He declared that within its powers the federal government could not be interfered with by the states (McCULLOCH v. MARYLAND) and that regulation of interstate and international commerce was solely a federal preserve (GIBBONS v. OGDEN and BROWN v. MARYLAND). In 1820, in the MISSOURI COMPROMISE, Congress took charge of the question of slavery in the territories by declaring it illegal above 36°30' in the huge region acquired by the Louisiana Purchase. Witnessing the Latin American revolutions against Spanish rule, the American government in 1823 asserted its paramountcy in the Western Hemisphere by issuing the MONROE DOCTRINE. In diplomatic but clear language it stated that the United States would fight to exclude further European extensions of sovereignty into its hemisphere.

During Andrew JACKSON's presidency (1829–37) a sharp bipolarization occurred again in the nation's politics. Of Scots-Irish descent, Jackson hated the English, and he was, in

Acquisition of the Louisiana Territory in 1803 spurred exploration across the continent both by government-sponsored expeditions and by independent parties, particularly fur trappers and traders. They blazed westward routes later used by the wagon trains of emigrants.

Gen. Winfield Scott's troops land (1847) at Veracruz on their way to the occupation of Mexico City, the final U.S. triumph in the Mexican War. U.S. "manifest destiny" was greatly furthered by the terms of the Treaty of Guadelupe Hidalgo (1848), dictated by the United States.

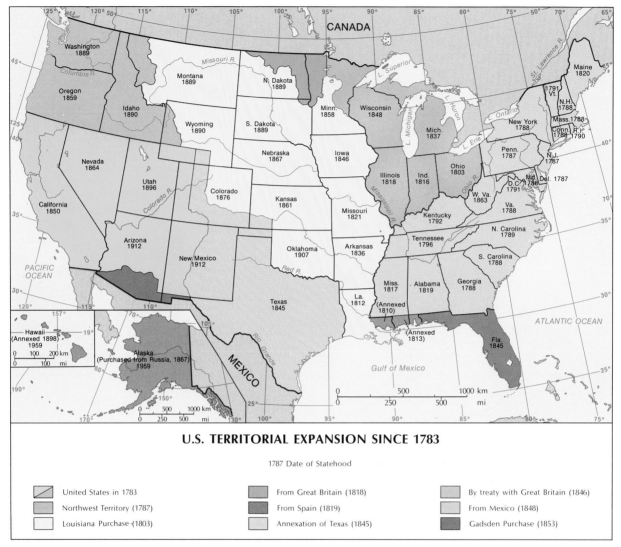

U.S. TERRITORIAL EXPANSION SINCE 1783

1787 Date of Statehood

United States in 1783	From Great Britain (1818)	By treaty with Great Britain (1846)
Northwest Territory (1787)	From Spain (1819)	From Mexico (1848)
Louisiana Purchase (1803)	Annexation of Texas (1845)	Gadsden Purchase (1853)

Between 1783, when the western boundary of the United States was set at the Mississippi River, and 1853, the year of the Gadsden Purchase, the country expanded threefold to its present continental limits. Alaska and Hawaii were acquired in 1867 and 1898, respectively.

turn, as thoroughly disliked by New Englanders, who thought him violent and barbaric. He made enemies in the South, as well, when in 1832 South Carolina, asserting superior STATE RIGHTS, attempted to declare null and void within its borders the tariff of 1828 (see NULLIFICATION). In his Nullification Proclamation (1832), Jackson declared that the federal government was supreme according to the Constitution. He skillfully outmaneuvered the South Carolinians, forcing them to relent. In 1832 he vetoed the rechartering of the Second Bank of the United States on the grounds that it caused the booms and busts that so alarmed the country and that it served the wealthy while exploiting the farmers and working people. To oppose him, the old Federalist coalition was reborn in the form of the American WHIG PARTY. With a DEMOCRATIC PARTY emerging behind Jackson and embodying the old Jeffersonian Democratic-Republican coalition, two-party rivalries appeared in every state. By the 1840s modern mass political parties, organized down into every ward and precinct, had appeared.

Led by Henry CLAY and Daniel WEBSTER, the Whigs called for protective tariffs, a national bank, and internal improvements to stimulate the economy. Moralists in politics, they also demanded active intervention by state governments to maintain the sanctity of the Sabbath, put down alcoholic bev-

erages, and "Americanize" the immigrants in the public schools. Yankees, who by now had migrated in great numbers into the Midwest, leaned strongly toward the Whigs. Many southerners admired Yankee ways and tended to vote for Whig candidates, too.

Democrats continued to condemn banks and tariffs as sources of corruption and exploitation, and in Jefferson's tradition insisted on cultural laissez-faire, the freedom of people to live as they desired. The minority out-groups—Irish Catholics and Germans—concurred, voting strongly Democratic in order to ward off the imposition of Yankee morals. During Martin VAN BUREN's presidency (1837-41) Democrats succeeded in entirely separating banking and government in the INDEPENDENT TREASURY SYSTEM, by which the government stored and controlled its own funds. A brief Whig interlude under William Henry HARRISON (1841) and John TYLER (1841-45) was followed by the presidency of the Democrat James K. POLK (1845-49), who in the Walker Tariff (1846) brought the United States closer to a free-trade basis.

Growing Sectional Conflicts. President Polk's war with Mexico ripped open the slavery question again. Was it to be allowed in the new territories? The WILMOT PROVISO (1846), which would have excluded slavery, became a rallying point for both sides, being voted on again and again in Congress and successfully held off by southerners. Abolitionism, led by William Lloyd GARRISON and others and now strong in many northern circles, called for the immediate emancipation of slaves with no compensation to slaveowners. Most northern whites disliked blacks and did not support abolition; they did want to disallow slavery in the territories so they could be preserved for white settlement based on northern ideals: free labor, dignity of work, and economic progress.

In 1848 northerners impatient with both of the existing parties formed the FREE-SOIL PARTY. By polling 300,000 votes for their candidate, Martin Van Buren, they denied victory to the Democrats and put the Whig Zachary TAYLOR in the White House (1849-50; on his death Millard FILLMORE became president, 1850-53). The COMPROMISE OF 1850 seemed to settle the slavery expansion issue by the principle of POPULAR SOVEREIGNTY, allowing the people who lived in the Mexican cession to decide for themselves. A strong FUGITIVE SLAVE LAW was also passed in 1850, giving new powers to slaveowners to reach into northern states to recapture escaped slaves.

THE CIVIL WAR ERA

As the 1850s began, it seemed for a time that the issue of slavery and other sectional differences between North and South might eventually be reconciled. But with the westward thrust of the American nation, all attempts at compromise were thwarted, and diverging economic, political, and philosophical interests became more apparent. The resulting civil war transformed the American nation.

Political Fragmentation. In 1854 the KANSAS-NEBRASKA ACT threw open the huge unorganized lands of the Louisiana Purchase to popular sovereignty, repealing the Missouri Compromise line of 1820. The North exploded in rage. Thousands defected from the Whig party to establish a new and much more antisouthern body (and one wholly limited to the northern states), the REPUBLICAN PARTY. The Republicans were aided by an enormous anti-Catholic outburst under way at the same time, aimed at the large wave of Irish Catholic immigration. Anti-Catholicism was already draining away Whigs to a new organization, the American party, soon known as the KNOW-NOTHING PARTY. When in 1856 it proved unable to hold together its members, north and south, because of disagreements over slavery, the anti-Catholics joined the Republicans.

In Kansas civil war broke out between pro-slavery and anti-slavery advocates, as settlers attempted to formalize their position on the institution prior to the territory's admission as a state. The Democratic presidents Franklin PIERCE (1853-57) and James BUCHANAN (1857-61) appeared to favor the pro-slavery group in Kansas despite its use of fraud and violence. In 1857 the Supreme Court, southern dominated, intensified northern alarm in its decision in the case of DRED SCOTT V. SANDFORD. The Court ruled that Congress had no authority to exclude slavery from the territories and thus, that the Missouri Compromise line had been unconstitutional all along. Thousands of northerners now became convinced that a "slave conspiracy" had infiltrated the national government

(Left) *A painting by Thomas Moran depicts slaves escaping through a swamp. The Fugitive Slave Law of 1850, which provided for the return of runaway slaves across state lines, was a major cause of conflict between North and South. (Philbrook Art Center, Tulsa, Okla.)*

(Below) *On the eve of the Civil War the nation was polarized between the states prohibiting slavery and those permitting it. The territories had been opened to slavery by the popular-sovereignty provision in the Kansas-Nebraska Act (1854).*

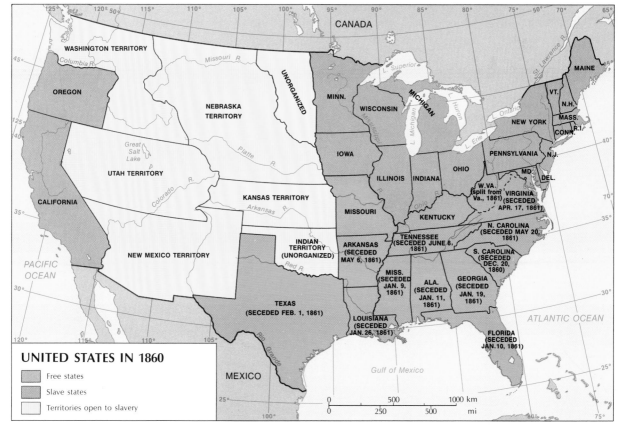

UNITED STATES IN 1860

- Free states
- Slave states
- Territories open to slavery

and that it intended to make slavery a nationwide institution.

In 1860 the political system became completely fragmented. The Democrats split into northern and southern wings, presenting two different candidates for the presidency; the small CONSTITUTIONAL UNION PARTY attempted to rally the former Whigs behind a third. The Republicans, however, were able to secure the election of Abraham LINCOLN to the White House.

Southerners had viewed the rise of the Yankee-dominated Republican party with great alarm. They were convinced that the party was secretly controlled by abolitionists (although most northerners detested the abolitionists) and that Yankees believed in using government to enforce their moralistic crusades. In 1859, John BROWN led a raid on the federal arsenal at Harpers Ferry, Va., hoping to incite a slave insurrection. His action—and his subsequent deification by some northerners—helped persuade southerners that emancipation of the slaves, if northerners obtained control of the country, was sooner or later inevitable.

Secession. Southern leaders had threatened to leave the Union if Lincoln won the election of 1860. Many South Carolinians, in particular, were convinced that Republican-sponsored emancipation would lead to bloody massacres as blacks sought vengeance against whites. In order to prevent this horror South Carolina seceded in December 1860, soon after the victory of Lincoln, an undeniably sectional candidate; it was optimistic about the eventual outcome of its action. Before Lincoln's inauguration (March 1861) six more states followed (Mississippi, Florida, Alabama, Georgia, Louisiana, and Texas). In February their representatives gathered in Montgomery, Ala., to form the CONFEDERATE STATES OF AMERICA. On Apr. 12, 1861, when President Lincoln moved to reprovision the federal troops at FORT SUMTER, in Charleston Harbor, Confederate shore batteries launched a 34-hour battering of the installation, forcing its surrender. The U.S. CIVIL WAR had begun.

The War between the States. Lincoln moved swiftly. On April 15 he called the remaining states to provide 75,000 troops to put down the Confederacy; Virginia, Arkansas, North Carolina, and Tennessee reluctantly seceded. The capital of the Confederacy moved to Richmond. On July 21, 1861, the first major battle between Union and Confederate forces occurred—at Bull Run (see BULL RUN, BATTLES OF), south of Washington, D.C.—resulting in a dramatic southern victory. Thereafter, both sides settled down to a long conflict.

It became an immense struggle. With a total U.S. population of fewer than 32 million, the number of dead reached 620,000 (360,000 northerners out of an army of about 1.5 million and 260,000 southerners in an army of about 1 million). In contrast, during World War II, when the American population was 135 million and its military forces fought for 4 years throughout the world, the total dead reached 400,000. In 1861 about 22 million people lived in the North, as against some 9 million people in the South, of whom 3.5 million were black. Although the North possessed a vigorous system of industry and a well-developed railroad network, Europeans were highly skeptical of a northern victory because the Confederacy was practically as large as Western Europe and fought with a determined passion for its independence. The North had to invade and defeat the opposition in order to win; the South had only to defend its borders. The conflict was not so uneven as it seemed.

Lincoln launched an all-out effort: he declared a naval blockade of the Confederacy; worked hard to maintain the loyalty of the slaveholding border states (Delaware, Maryland, Kentucky, and Missouri); invaded Tennessee to gain a base of power in the heart of the Confederacy; cut the South in two by taking the Mississippi River; and looked for a general who could win. This last task took him 2 years. Gen. George B. MCCLELLAN proved disappointingly conservative, and his successors were bumblers. After Gen. Ulysses S. GRANT won major victories in the western theater, Lincoln brought him to Washington in 1864 to face the brilliant Confederate commander, Robert E. LEE.

By mid-1863 the South was in desperate straits, lacking

(Above) *At the First Battle of Bull Run, on July 21, 1861, Gen. Thomas J. Jackson earned his nickname, Stonewall, in holding the Confederate line against a Union advance. The South's victory in the first major battle of the Civil War shattered Northern complacency.*

(Opposite page) *Even early in the Civil War the Union foot soldier (right) was more formally equipped than his Confederate counterpart. As the war disrupted the already limited industrial capacity of the South, Confederate supplies became so scarce that some men marched barefoot.*

both food and supplies. A great northward thrust was turned back at Gettysburg, Pa., in July of that year (see GETTYSBURG, BATTLE OF). Thereafter, Grant mounted a relentless campaign that hammered down toward Richmond, at hideous cost in casualties. Union Gen. William T. SHERMAN, meanwhile, was slashing through Georgia to the sea, leaving a wide swath of total destruction, and then turning northward through the Carolinas. By April 1865, Grant had finally rounded Lee's flank, and on the 9th of that month, Lee surrendered at APPOMATTOX COURT HOUSE. Confederate president Jefferson DAVIS intended to fight on, but it was hopeless. The Civil War was over.•

A Nation Transformed: The North. The war had transformed both North and South. On Jan. 1, 1863, Lincoln had issued his EMANCIPATION PROCLAMATION, declaring slavery dead wherever rebellion existed (in the border states, it was terminated by later local action). In addition, the enormous war effort taught the North lessons in modern organization and the use of large corporations. In Washington the Republican majority

Gen. William T. Sherman, Gen. Ulysses S. Grant, and Rear Adm. David D. Porter advise a pensive President Abraham Lincoln on the conduct of the latter months of the Civil War in this painting, The Peace-Makers, *by G.P.A. Healy. (1894; White House Collection.)*

enacted a classically Hamiltonian program: high protective tariffs, lavish aid to capitalists to build railroads and exploit natural resources, free homestead grants for settlers, and banking and currency legislation that created one national system of paper money. The MORRILL ACT of 1862 provided grants of land for the establishment of land-grant universities in each state to train the agriculturalists, engineers, and other professionals needed to run an industrialized economy.

The two-party system survived in the North despite the war. Democrats never sank below 40 percent of the vote because many northerners opposed the conflict, or at least Republican policies. In the DRAFT RIOTS of 1863, Irish Catholics and other New Yorkers fiercely protested the new conscription law, which seemed a special hardship to poor people. The rioters, as well as many other northerners, were hostile toward abolition; they feared that Republican policies would send hordes of freed slaves northward to compete for jobs. Democrats also opposed the powerful centralizing tendencies of the programs pushed by the Republicans, as well as their aid to capitalists.

Reconstruction. A week after Appomattox, Lincoln was assassinated. Now Andrew JOHNSON assumed office and moved quickly to establish a plan for RECONSTRUCTION. He asked southern whites only to repudiate debts owed by the Confederacy, declare secession null and void, and ratify the 13TH AMENDMENT (which declared slavery illegal). When Congress convened in December 1865, newly elected southerners were already on the scene waiting to be admitted to their seats. Many of them had been elected on the basis of BLACK CODES, established in the southern states in 1865–66 to restore a form of quasi-slavery. To the shocked and angered North, it seemed that the sufferings endured in the war had been in vain: politics as before the war—only now with a powerful southern Democratic bloc in Congress—would resume.

The Republican majority in Congress refused to admit southern legislators to their seats until a congressional committee reexamined the entire question of Reconstruction. Soon, Radical Republicans (those who wished to use the victory as an opportunity to remake the South in the Yankee image) were in open conflict with Johnson. He attempted to terminate the FREEDMEN'S BUREAU (an agency established in 1865 to aid refugees) and to veto legislation aimed at protecting the civil rights of former slaves (see CIVIL RIGHTS ACTS). In the congressional election of 1866 a huge majority of Repub-

licans was elected, and the Radicals gained a precarious ascendancy. Senator Charles SUMNER of Massachusetts and Representative Thaddeus STEVENS (New England-born) of Pennsylvania were among the leaders of the Radical cause.

The 14TH AMENDMENT (enacted in 1866; ratified in 1868) made all persons born or naturalized in the country U.S. citizens and forbade any state to interfere with their fundamental civil rights. In March 1867 all state governments in the South were terminated and military occupation established. Federal commanders were charged with reconstructing southern governments through constitutional conventions, to which delegates were to be elected by universal male suffrage. After a new state government was in operation and had ratified the 14th Amendment, its representatives would be admitted to Congress. In February 1868 an impeachment effort sought unsuccessfully to remove President Johnson from office.

The Republican majority in Congress made no significant effort to create social equality for blacks, but only to give them the vote and to ensure them equal protection under the law (trial by jury, freedom of movement, the right to hold office and any employment, and the like). This political equality would give blacks an equal start, Republicans insisted, and they would then carry the burden of proving themselves equal in other ways. Yet Republicans well knew that anti-black attitudes persisted in the North as well as in the South. Until ratification (1870) of the 15TH AMENDMENT, which made it illegal to deny the vote on the grounds of race, most northern states refused blacks the vote.

A Nation Transformed: The South. Like the North, the South was transformed by the Civil War and its aftermath. Southerners had learned lessons in the effectiveness of a strong central government and realized the impossibility of continuing the old ways of the antebellum period. Former Whigs in the South, often called Conservatives, pushed eagerly to build industry and commerce in the Yankee style. Meanwhile, reconstructed southern state governments enacted many reforms, establishing free public schools for all, popular election of all officials, more equitable taxes, and more humane penal laws.

Republican Ulysses S. Grant was elected president in 1868 with electoral votes gained in occupied southern states. Democrats alleged that Radical Reconstruction was not genuinely concerned with aiding black people, but with using southern black votes to keep the Republicans in power in Congress and to retain their protective tariffs and other aids to industrialists. When evidence of corruption surfaced during the Grant administration, Democrats declared that it proved that the outcome of Republican friendliness to capitalists was graft and plunder.

By 1870 the antisouthern mood that had supported Radical Reconstruction had faded, as had the surge of concern for southern blacks. New domestic problems were pushing to the fore. A resurgence of white voting in the South, together with

Reconstruction, identified in this 1880 cartoon with a Napoleonic President Grant, the "Bayonet Rule" of federal occupation troops, and carpetbag Republican governments, helped create a "Solid South" for the Democratic party.

Locomotives of the Union Pacific and Central Pacific railways meet at Promontory Point, Utah, marking the completion of the first transcontinental railroad. The event occurred on May 10, 1869, after a gold spike was drive into the last rail linking the two lines.

the use of violence to intimidate blacks and their white sympathizers, brought southern states back into Democratic hands. Northerners, awakened to economic questions by the great depression that began in 1873 and lasted for 5 years, tacitly agreed to return the race issue to the control of southern whites.

After the disputed election of 1876, amid evidence of electoral corruption, the Republican presidential candidate promised to withdraw the last federal occupation troops from the South. The election was decided by a congressional electoral commission, and Rutherford B. Hayes became president. As promised, he withdrew (1877) the troops; Reconstruction was over.

THE GILDED AGE
The era known as the Gilded Age (1870s to 1890s) was a time of vigorous, exploitative individualism. Despite widespread suffering by industrial workers, southern sharecroppers, displaced American Indians, and other groups, a mood of optimism possessed the United States. The theories of the English biologist Charles Darwin—expounded in The Origin of Species (1859)—concerning the natural selection of organisms best suited to survive in their environment began to influence American opinion. Some intellectuals in the United States applied the idea of the survival of the fittest to human societies (Social Darwinism) and arrived at the belief that government aid to the unfortunate was wrong.

Industrialization and Large-Scale Exploitation of Natural Resources. During the Gilded Age ambitious and imaginative

capitalists ranged the continent looking for new opportunities. Business lurched erratically from upswings to slumps, while the country's industrial base grew rapidly. Factories and mines labored heavily through these years to provide the raw materials and finished products needed for expansion of the railroad system. In 1865 (as construction of the first TRANSCONTINENTAL RAILROAD was underway; completed 1869) approximately 56,000 km (35,000 mi) of track stretched across the United States; by 1910 the total reached about 386,000 km (240,000 mi) of interconnected uniform-gauge track. By 1890 the United States contained one-third of the world's railroad trackage.

After new gold and silver discoveries in the late 1850s, until about 1875, individual prospectors explored the western country and desert basins in search of mineral riches. Then mining corporations took over, using hired laborers and eastern-trained engineers. Indians were either brutally exterminated or placed on small reservations. Warfare with the Great Plains Indians broke out in 1864; these INDIAN WARS did not entirely subside until after the slaughtering of the buffalo herds, the basis of Indian life, which had occurred by the mid-1880s. Through the DAWES ACT of 1887, which forced most Indians to choose 160-acre (65-ha) allotments within their reservations, reformers hoped to break down tribal bonds and induce Indians to take up sedentary agriculture. Unallocated reservation lands were declared surplus and sold to whites.

Cattle ranching was the first large-scale enterprise to invade the Great Plains beginning in the late 1860s. By the 1880s, however, the open range began to give way to fenced pastureland and to agriculture, made possible by the newly invented barbed-wire fence and by "dry farming," a technique of preserving soil moisture by frequent plowing. Millions of farmers moved into the high plains west of the 100th meridian. So huge was their grain output that slumping world

(Below) An engraving of the Dupont mills near Wilmington, Del., illustrates burgeoning American industry about 1880.

(Left) Nineteenth-century American inventors in Christian Schussele's Men of Progress are (from left) William Morton (ether anesthesia), James Bogardus (cast-iron construction), Samuel Colt (revolver), Cyrus McCormick (reaper), Joseph Saxton (fountain pen), Charles Goodyear (vulcanized rubber), Peter Cooper (locomotive), Jordan Mott (coal stove), Joseph Henry (physics), Eliphalet Nott (coal stove), John Ericsson (screw propeller), Frederick Sickells (steam engine), Samuel Morse (telegraph), Henry Burden (machinery), Robert Hoe (printing), Erastus Bigelow (power loom), Isaiah Jennings (dental tools), and Thomas Blanchard (machine tools).

A peace parley between Gen. George Crook (2d from right) and Geronimo (2d from left) is recorded in this photograph taken shortly before the Apache leader's final surrender (1886). Geronimo waged a 10-year struggle against removal to the reservation.

prices beginning in the mid-1880s put them into severe financial straits. Meanwhile, the vast continental sweep between Kansas and California became filled with new states.

By the early 1900s the nation's economy, tied together by the railroads into a single market, was no longer composed primarily of thousands of small producers who sold to local markets. Rather, it was dominated by a small number of large firms that sold nationwide and to the world at large. With great size, however, came large and complex problems. In 1887, Congress created the INTERSTATE COMMERCE COMMISSION to curb cutthroat competition among the railroads and to ensure that railroad rates were "reasonable and just." In 1890, on the other hand, Congress attempted to restore competition through passage of the SHERMAN ANTI-TRUST ACT, which declared illegal trusts and other combinations that restrained trade. The U.S. Supreme Court favored laissez-faire and consistently blocked both federal and state efforts to regulate private business. The so-called robber barons and their immense fortunes were practically unscathed as they exploited the nation's natural resources and dominated its economic life.

New Social Groupings: Immigrants, Urbanites, and Union Members. In 1890 the American people numbered 63 million, double the 1860 population. During these years the nation's

cities underwent tremendous growth. Many new urbanites came from the American countryside, but many others came from abroad. From 1860 to 1890 more than 10 million immigrants arrived in the United States; from 1890 to 1920, 15 million more arrived (see IMMIGRATION). Most were concentrated in northern cities: by 1910, 75 percent of immigrants lived in urban areas, while less than 50 percent of native-born Americans did so. In the 1880s the so-called new immigration began: in addition to the Germans, Scandinavians, Irish, and others of the older immigrant groups, there came such peoples as Italians, Poles, Hungarians, Bohemians, Greeks, and Jews (from central and eastern Europe, especially Russia). Roman Catholics grew in number from 1.6 million in 1850 to 12 million in 1900, producing a renewed outburst of bitter anti-Catholic nativism in the 1880s. The large cities, with their saloons, theaters, dance halls, and immigrant slums, were feared by many native American Protestants, who lived primarily in small cities and the rural countryside.

The outbreak of labor protests from the 1870s on, often characterized by immigrant workers opposing native-born employers, intensified the hostility. In 1878 the KNIGHTS OF LABOR formed, opening its ranks to all working people, skilled or unskilled. The Knights called for sweeping social and economic reforms, and their numbers rose to 700,000 in 1886. Then, as the organization broke apart because of internal stresses, the American Federation of Labor, under Samuel GOMPERS, formed to take its place. Concentrating on skilled craftworkers and tight organization, it endured.

Domestic Politics. Gilded Age politics became a contest between evenly balanced Republicans and Democrats. Winning elections by small margins, they alternated in their control of Congress and the White House. Five men served as Republican presidents: Hayes; James A. GARFIELD (1881); Chester A. ARTHUR (1881–85), who succeeded Garfield on his assassination; Benjamin HARRISON (1889–93); and William McKINLEY (1897–1901). Their party regarded industrial growth and capitalist leadership with approval, believing that they led to an ever-widening opening of opportunity for all.

Grover CLEVELAND rose from obscurity to become Democratic governor of New York in the early 1880s and then U.S. president (1885–89; 1893–97; although he won a popular-vote plurality in the election of 1888, he lost to Harrison in the electoral college). Reared a Jacksonian Democrat, he believed that society is always in danger of exploitation by the wealthy and powerful. A vigorous president, he labored to clean up government by making civil service effective; took back huge land grants given out fraudulently in the West; and battled to lower the protective tariff.

In the Great Plains and the South, grain and cotton farmers,

Joseph Keppler's The Bosses of the Senate *satirizes the power of the trusts, corporations holding monopoly control within their industries, on the eve of the passage (1890) of the Sherman Anti-Trust Act. Standard Oil, the first of such trusts, was broken up in 1911.*

Immigrants crowd the decks of a ship bound for New York in 1893. More than 25 million Europeans immigrated to the United States between 1860 and 1920. Many flocked to the urban centers along the eastern seaboard; others helped to settle the West.

suffering from falling crop prices, demanded currency inflation to raise prices. By 1892 a POPULIST PARTY had appeared, to
call for free coinage of silver to achieve this goal. Cleveland
resisted, stating that such a monetary policy would destroy
confidence, prolong the great depression that began in 1893,
and injure city consumers. In 1896 the Democrats, taken over
by southern and western inflationists, ran William Jennings
BRYAN on a FREE SILVER platform. Ethnic voters surged into the
Republican ranks—for the depression was a disastrous one
and the Republican party had always urged active government intervention to stimulate the economy. In addition, as
city dwellers they feared inflation. William McKinley's election began a long period of one-party (Republican) domination in the northern states and in Washington.

THE PROGRESSIVE ERA

During the period known as the Progressive Era (1890s to
about 1920) the U.S. government became increasingly activist
in both domestic and foreign policy. Progressive, that is, reform-minded, political leaders sought to extend their vision
of a just and rational order to all areas of society and some,
indeed, to all reaches of the globe.

America Looks Outward. During the 1890s, U.S. foreign policy became aggressively activist. As American industrial productivity grew, many reformers urged the need for foreign
markets. Others held that the United States had a mission to
carry Anglo-Saxon culture to all of humankind, to spread law
and order and American civilization. In 1895 the United States
intervened bluntly in the VENEZUELA BOUNDARY DISPUTE between Venezuela and imperial Britain, warning that, under
the Monroe Doctrine, American force might be used if Venezuela were not treated equitably. A Cuban revolution against
Spain, begun in 1895, finally led to the SPANISH-AMERICAN WAR
(1898), undertaken to free Cuba. From that war the United
States emerged with a protectorate over Cuba and an island
empire consisting of the Philippines, Puerto Rico, and Guam.
The United States also annexed the Hawaiian Islands in 1898,
completing a bridge to the markets of the Far East. In 1900
the American government announced the OPEN DOOR POLICY,
pledging to support continued Chinese independence as well
as equal access for all nations to China's markets.

William McKinley's assassination brought Theodore ROOSE-
VELT to the presidency in 1901. A proud patriot, he sought to
make the United States a great power in the world. In 1903
he aided Panama in becoming independent of Colombia,
then secured from Panama the right for the United States to
build and control a canal through the isthmus. In 1904, in the
Roosevelt Corollary to the Monroe Doctrine, he asserted the
right of the United States to intervene in the internal affairs
of Western Hemisphere nations to prevent "chronic wrong-

doing." The following year his good offices helped end the
Russo-Japanese War. Having much strengthened the navy,
Roosevelt sent (1907) the Great White Fleet on a spectacular
round-the-world cruise to display American power.

Progressivism at Home. Meanwhile, the Progressive Era was
also underway in domestic politics. City governments were
transformed, becoming relatively honest and efficient; social
workers labored to improve slum housing, health, and education; and in many states reform movements democratized,
purified, and humanized government. Under Roosevelt the
national government strengthened or created regulatory
agencies that exerted increasing influence over business enterprise: the Hepburn Act (1906) reinforced the Interstate
Commerce Commission; the Forest Service, under Gifford
PINCHOT from 1898 to 1910, guided lumbering companies in
the conservation of—and more rational and efficient exploitation of—woodland resources; the Pure Food and Drug Act
(1906; see PURE FOOD AND DRUG LAWS) attempted to protect
consumers from fraudulent labeling and adulteration of products. Beginning in 1902, Roosevelt also used the Justice Department and lawsuits (or the threat of them) to mount a revived assault on monopoly under the Sherman Anti-Trust
Law. William Howard TAFT, his successor as president
(1909–13), drew back in his policies, continuing only the anti-
trust campaign. He approved passage of the 16TH AMENDMENT
(the income tax amendment, 1913), however; in time it would
transform the federal government by giving it access to enormous revenues.

Republicans were split in the election of 1912. The regular
nomination went to Taft, and a short-lived PROGRESSIVE PARTY
was formed to run Theodore Roosevelt. Democrat Woodrow
WILSON (1913-21) was therefore able to win the presidency.
Attacking corporate power, he won a drastic lowering of the
tariff (1913) and establishment of a Tariff Commission (1916);
creation of the FEDERAL RESERVE SYSTEM (1913) to supervise
banking and currency; a broadened antimonopoly program
under the CLAYTON ANTI-TRUST ACT (1914); control over the
hours of labor on the railroads (Adamson Act, 1916); and creation of a body to ensure fair and open competition in business (Fair Trade Commission, 1914).

During the Progressive Era, southern governments imposed
a wide range of JIM CROW LAWS on black people, using the
rationale that such legalization of segregation resulted in a
more orderly, systematic electoral system and society. Many
of the steps that had been taken toward racial equality during
the Reconstruction period were thus reversed. The federal
government upheld the principle of racial segregation in the
U.S. Supreme Court case PLESSY V. FERGUSON (1896), as long as
blacks were provided with "separate but equal" facilities. In
the face of the rigidly segregated society that confronted
them, blacks themselves were divided concerning the appropriate course of action. Since 1895, Booker T. WASHINGTON
had urged that blacks should not actively agitate for equality,
but should acquire craft skills, work industriously, and convince whites of their abilities. W. E. B. Du BOIS insisted instead (in The Souls of Black Folk, 1903) that black people
ceaselessly protest Jim Crow laws, demand education in the
highest professions as well as in crafts, and work for complete social integration. In 1910 the NATIONAL ASSOCIATION FOR
THE ADVANCEMENT OF COLORED PEOPLE (NAACP) was founded
to advance these ideals.

Intervention and World War. President Taft continued to
stress the economic aspects of Roosevelt's interventionist
spirit. Under Taft's foreign policy (called dollar diplomacy)
U.S. firms were encouraged to increase investments in countries bordering the Caribbean in the hope that the American
economic presence would ensure political stability there.
President Wilson went a step further, seeking not simply to
maintain order, but to advance democracy and self-rule. In
1915 he sent troops into Haiti to put an end to the chaos of
revolution—and to protect U.S. investments there—and in
1916 he did the same in the Dominican Republic; the two
countries were made virtual protectorates of the United
States. With Nicaragua he achieved the same end by diplomacy. In hope of tumbling the Mexican dictator Victoriano

U.S. warships steam into San Francisco Bay in The Fleet Entering the
Golden Gate, *by Henry Reuterdahl. The ships were part of the Great
White Fleet, 16 battleships that sailed (1907-09) around the world to
demonstrate that the United States was now second only to Britain as
a naval power. (U.S. Naval Academy Museum, Annapolis, Md.)*

Army recruits march out of an armory en route to training camp during World War I. The United States entered the war on Apr. 6, 1917, with an army of 200,000 men. By the end of the conflict this number had expanded to 4 million.

Members of the Equal Suffrage League of St. Louis, Mo., demonstrate for their cause. Although the suffrage movement had begun more than half a century earlier, nationwide suffrage for women did not become a reality until 1920, when the 19th Amendment was ratified.

Huerta, Wilson at first denied him diplomatic recognition, then in April 1914 sent troops to occupy the Mexican port city of Veracruz and keep from Huerta its import revenues. The Mexicans were deeply offended, and in November 1914, Wilson withdrew American forces. The bloody civil war that racked Mexico until 1920 sent the first large migration of Mexicans, perhaps a million people, into the United States (see CHICANO).

After the outbreak of World War I in August 1914, Wilson sought vainly to bring peace. In early 1917, however, Germany's unrestricted use of submarine attacks against neutral as well as Allied shipping inflamed American opinion for war (see LUSITANIA). Wilson decided that if the United States was to have any hope of influencing world affairs, it was imperative that it enter the war and fight to protect democracy against what he called German autocracy.

America's entry into the war (April 1917) was the climax of the Progressive Era: Wilson's aim was the extension of democracy and the creation of a just world order. In January 1918 he issued his FOURTEEN POINTS as a proposed basis for peace: freedom of the seas and removal of all barriers to trade; an end to secret diplomacy; general disarmament; self-government for the submerged nationalities in the German and Austro-Hungarian empires; and a league of nations. The addition of more than a million American troops to the Allied armies turned the balance against the Germans in 1918, and an armistice on November 11 ended the war. At the PARIS PEACE CONFERENCE, however, Wilson failed in much of his program, for the other Allies were not interested in a "peace without victory." The British would not agree to freedom of the seas; tariffs did not tumble; self-determination was often violated; key negotiations were kept secret; but in the end Wilson obtained his greatest objective, establishment of the League of Nations to provide collective security against future aggression. Many at home, however, preferred to return to America's traditional isolation from world affairs. When Wilson tried imperiously to force the Senate to accept the entire treaty, he failed. The United States never became a member of the League of Nations.

THE UNITED STATES TURNS INWARD: THE 1920S AND 1930S

After its participation in the conflagration then known as the Great War, the American nation was ready to turn inward and concentrate on domestic affairs (a "return to normalcy," as 1920 presidential candidate Warren Harding called it). Private concerns preoccupied most Americans during the 1920s until the Great Depression of the next decade, when increasing numbers turned, in their collective misfortune, to government for solutions to economic problems that challenged the very basis of U.S. capitalistic society.

The 1920s: Decade of Optimism. By the 1920s innovative forces thrusting into American life were creating a new way of living. The automobile and the hard-surfaced road produced mobility and a blurring of the traditional rural-urban split. The radio and motion pictures inaugurated a national culture, one built on new, urban values. The 19TH AMENDMENT (1920) gave women the vote in national politics and symbolized their persistence in efforts to break out of old patterns of domesticity. The war had accelerated their entrance into business, industry, and the professions and their adoption of practices, such as drinking and smoking, traditionally considered masculine. So, too, young people turned to new leaders and values and sought unorthodox dress, recreations, and morals.

Traditional WASP (white, Anglo-Saxon Protestant) America fought the new ways. The adoption of PROHIBITION in 1919 (with ratification of the 18TH AMENDMENT) had been a victory of Yankee moral values over those of immigrants, but now many of the great cities practically ignored the measure. The Russian Revolution of 1917 sent a Red Scare shivering through the country in 1919-20; suspicion centered on labor unions as alleged instruments of Moscow. The KU KLUX KLAN, stronger in the northern Republican countryside than in the South, attacked the so-called New Negro, who returned from the fighting in France with a new sense of personal dignity (the HARLEM RENAISSANCE expressed this spirit through the arts), and the millions of Roman Catholics and Jews who had been flooding into the country since the 1890s. The Immigra-

During a rustic outing Thomas Edison (left) poses with three other notable Americans, naturalist John Burroughs and Henry Ford, the automobile manufacturer (seated on water wheel), and Harvey Firestone (right), founder of the world's largest rubber company.

(Left) *A painting (c.1934) by Ben Shahn lampoons the actions of bootleggers who defied the 18th Amendment, which prohibited the sale of alcoholic beverages in the United States. (Museum of the City of New York.)*

(Below) *Margaret Bourke-White captured some of the irony of American life during the late 1930s in her photograph of black flood victims in a breadline beneath a patriotically idyllic billboard.*

tion Law of 1924 established a quota system that discriminated against all groups except northern and western Europeans. In 1925 the spectacular SCOPES TRIAL in Dayton, Tenn., convicted a high school science teacher of presenting Darwinian theories of evolution, which fundamentalist Protestants bitterly opposed.

New ideas, however, continued to inundate the country, and optimism remained high. The U.S. population delighted in the "miracles" that new inventions had brought them—electric lights, airplanes, new communication systems. Charles LINDBERGH's solo flight to Paris in 1927 seemed to capture the spirit of the age. The business community was praised for its values and productivity. Henry Ford (see FORD family) and his system of cheap mass production of automobiles for people of modest incomes was regarded as symbolic of the new era.

Three Republican presidents occupied the White House during the 1920s. Warren HARDING, a conservative, was swept into office by a landslide victory in 1920. He proved an inept president, and his administration was racked by scandals, including that of TEAPOT DOME. Calvin COOLIDGE, who succeeded to the office on Harding's death (1923), worshiped business as much as he detested government. Herbert HOOVER, an engineer, brought to the presidency (1929–33) a deep faith in the essential soundness of capitalism, which to him represented the fullest expression of individualism. In 1920 the U.S. census showed, for the first time, that a majority of Americans lived in cities of 2,500 people or more.

The 1930s: Decade of Depression. The stock market crash of October 1929 initiated a long economic decline that accelerated into a world catastrophe, the DEPRESSION OF THE 1930s. By 1933, 14 million Americans were unemployed, industrial production was down to one-third of its 1929 level, and national income had dropped by more than half. In the presence of deep national despair, Democratic challenger Franklin D.

ROOSEVELT easily defeated Hoover in the 1932 presidential election. After his inauguration, the NEW DEAL exploded in a whirlwind of legislation.

A new era commenced in American history, one in which a social democratic order similar to that of Western European countries appeared. The federal government under Roosevelt (and the presidency itself) experienced a vast expansion in its authority, especially over the economy. Roosevelt had a strong sense of community; he distrusted unchecked individualism and sympathized with suffering people. He nourished, however, no brooding rancor against the U.S. system. He sought to save capitalism, not supplant it.

Recovery was Roosevelt's first task. In the First New Deal (1933–35) he attempted to muster a spirit of emergency and rally all interests behind a common effort in which something was provided for everyone. Excessive competition and production were blamed for the collapse. Therefore, business proprietors and farmers were allowed to cooperate in establishing prices that would provide them with a profitable return and induce an upward turn (under the NATIONAL RECOVERY ADMINISTRATION and the AGRICULTURAL ADJUSTMENT ADMINISTRATION). By 1935, however, 10 million were still unemployed, the economy seemed lodged at a new plateau, and the U.S. Supreme Court was ruling such agencies unconstitutional.

The Second New Deal (1935–38) was more antibusiness and proconsumer. Roosevelt turned to vastly increased relief spending (under the WORKS PROGRESS ADMINISTRATION) to pump up consumer buying power. In 1933 he had decided to take the nation off the gold standard, except in international trade. Setting the price at which the government would buy gold at $35 an ounce, he induced so massive a flow of gold into the country that its basic stock of precious metal increased by one-third by 1940 (expanding by much more the currency available in the economy). This monetary policy and the spending to aid the unemployed succeeded in moving the economy toward recovery before 1940, when the impact of war-induced buying from Europe accelerated such movement.

The impact of the New Deal was perhaps strongest and most lasting in its basic reform measures, which profoundly altered the American system. Farm prices were supported and farm plantings centrally planned; the money supply became a federal, not private, responsibility under a strengthened Federal Reserve Board; and stock exchanges were put under regulation of the SECURITIES AND EXCHANGE COMMISSION. The FEDERAL DEPOSIT INSURANCE CORPORATION insured bank deposits, and banking practices were closely supervised under the Banking Act of 1933; the NATIONAL LABOR RELATIONS ACT made relations between employers and employees a matter of public concern and control; and under the direction of agencies such as the TENNESSEE VALLEY AUTHORITY government facilities supplied electrical power to entire regions, providing a standard for private utilities. Private utility monopolies were broken apart and placed under public regulation; antitrust efforts were reenergized; and economic recessions, then and afterward, were monitored by the federal government, which was ready to increase public spending to provide employment and ward off the onset of another depression.

For the majority of the population, New Deal legislation defined minimum standards of living: the Fair Labor Standards Act set MINIMUM WAGE and maximum hour limitations and included a prohibition on child labor in interstate commerce; the Social Security Act (see SOCIAL SECURITY) made provisions for old-age and disability pensions, unemployment insurance, monthly payments to mothers living alone with dependent children, and direct assistance to the blind and crippled.

In addition, the New Deal helped make it possible for organized unions to gain higher wages; in 1938 the Congress of Industrial Organizations (CIO) was formed; members were organized by industry rather than by craft. The New Deal also provided a sense of confidence that in a time of disaster the federal government would take positive action.

Meanwhile, totalitarian movements abroad were inducing

Oily fumes from burning battleships fill the air after Japan's attack (Dec. 7, 1941) on the U.S. naval base at Pearl Harbor, Hawaii. The raid, which crippled the U.S. Pacific fleet, precipitated U.S. entry into World War II.

U.S. troops wade ashore in a dramatic photograph taken during the Allied landings on the Normandy beaches on June 6, 1944. Under the overall command of General Eisenhower, this invasion of German-held France constituted the largest amphibious operation in history.

world crisis. Congress, mirroring public opinion, had grown disenchanted with the U.S. entry into World War I. This spirit of isolationism led to the passage (1935–37) of a series of neutrality acts. They required an arms embargo that would deny the sale of munitions to belligerents during a time of international war and prohibited loans to belligerents and the travel of Americans on ships owned by belligerents. Congress thus hoped to prevent involvements like those of 1914–17.

A WORLD POWER
The spirit of isolationism eroded steadily as Americans watched the aggressive moves of Adolf Hitler and his allies. President Roosevelt and the American people finally concluded that the United States could not survive as a nation, nor could Western civilization endure, if Hitler and fascism gained dominance over Europe. During the world war that followed, the American nation rose to the status of a major world power, a position that was not abandoned but confirmed in the cold-war years of the late 1940s and the 1950s.

Total War: 1941–45. In September 1940, Congress established the first peacetime draft in American history, and 6 months later it authorized Roosevelt to transfer munitions to Great Britain, now standing practically alone against Hitler, by a procedure called LEND-LEASE. On Dec. 7, 1941, the Japanese reacted to stiffening American diplomacy against its expansion into Southeast Asia by attacking the U.S. fleet at PEARL HARBOR in the Hawaiian Islands. This thrust was aimed at immobilizing American power long enough to allow the establishment of a wide imperial Japanese perimeter including all of the western Pacific and China, henceforth to be defended against all comers. Japan, however, in one stroke had succeeded in scuttling American isolationist sentiment, forcing the United States into World War II, and unifying the American people as never before in total war.

The first American military decision was to concentrate on defeating Hitler while fighting a holding action in the Pacific. The next was to form an alliance with Great Britain so close that even military commands were jointly staffed. The year 1942 was devoted to halting, after many defeats, the outward spread of Japanese power and to keeping Hitler's forces from overwhelming America's British and Soviet allies. Large shipments of munitions went to both allies. In November an American force invaded North Africa; it joined the British in defeating the German armies in that region by May 1943.

In 2 months the Allies were fighting the Germans in Sicily and Italy; at the same time U.S. forces in the Pacific were pushing in toward the Japanese home islands by means of an island-hopping offensive. On the long Russian front, German armies were being defeated and pushed back toward their borders. In June 1944 a huge Allied force landed on the French coast, an invasion preceded by 2 years of intense day-and-night bombing of Germany by British and American aircraft. By August 1944, Paris was recaptured. Hitler's empire was crumbling; clouds of bombers were raining destruction on German cities; and on Apr. 30, 1945, with the Soviet troops just a few miles from Berlin, Hitler committed suicide. Peace in Europe followed shortly.

The Pacific war continued, the Japanese home islands being rendered practically defenseless by July 1945. American aerial attacks burned out city after city. In April, Harry S. TRUMAN had succeeded to the presidency on Roosevelt's death. Now, advised that the alternative would be an invasion in which multitudes would perish, including many thousands of young Americans, he authorized use of the recently tested atomic bomb. On Aug. 6, the city of Hiroshima was obliterated; on Aug. 9, the same fate came to Nagasaki. Within a week, a cease-fire (which later research suggests was reachable without atomic attack) was achieved.

The political shape of the postwar world was set at the YALTA CONFERENCE (February 1945) between Roosevelt, Joseph Stalin, and Winston Churchill. Soviet occupation of Eastern European countries overrun by the Red Army was accepted, in return for a pledge to allow democratic governments to

Allied leaders (seated, left to right) Churchill, Roosevelt, and Stalin pose for an official portrait during their consultations at Yalta (February 1945). The decisions reached at the Yalta Conference largely shaped the geopolitical climate of the postwar era.

Berliners await the landing of an Allied cargo transport during the Berlin Airlift of 1948-49. The relief operation, a joint mission undertaken by the United States, Britain, and France, was a response to the Soviet blockade of all land and water routes into West Berlin.

United Nations troops were sent to South Korea in 1950 to aid in repelling an invasion by the Sino-Soviet supplied forces of North Korea. Although 16 allied countries were involved, the United States provided the bulk of the troops and supplies for the UN war effort.

rise within them. Soviet and Allied occupation zones in Germany were established, with Berlin, deep in the Soviet zone, to be jointly administered. In return for Soviet assistance in the invasion of Japan (which was eventually not needed), it was agreed that certain possessions in the Far East and rights in Manchuria, lost to the Japanese long before, would be restored to the USSR. Soon it was clear that the kind of democratic government envisioned by the Americans was not going to be allowed in the East European countries under Soviet control. Nor, as the Soviets pointed out, was the United States ready to admit the Soviets to any role in the occupation and government of Japan, whose internal constitution and economy were rearranged to fit American desires under Gen. Douglas MacArthur.

Cold-War Years. The breach widened steadily. Charges and countercharges were directed back and forth, the Soviets and Americans interpreting each other's actions in the worst possible light. Americans became convinced that the Soviets were thrusting out in every direction, seeking to communize not only the Soviet-occupied countries, but also Turkey, Greece, and Western Europe. In February 1946, Stalin declared in Moscow that there could never be a lasting peace with capitalism. Shortly thereafter, Churchill warned of the "iron curtain" that had descended across the middle of Europe. The COLD WAR had begun.

In March 1947, Truman asked Congress for funds to shore up Turkey and Greece, both under Soviet pressure, and announced the Truman Doctrine: that "it must be the policy of the United States to support free peoples who are resisting attempted subjugation by armed minorities or by outside pressures." Then the MARSHALL PLAN (named for George C. MARSHALL, U.S. chief of staff during the war and at this time secretary of state), approved by Congress in April 1948, sent $12 billion to the devastated countries of Europe to help them rebuild and fend off the despair on which communism was believed to feed.

True to its Democratic tradition, the Truman administration stressed multilateral diplomacy; that is, the building of an international order based on joint decision making. Nationalism, it was believed, must be tamed. The United Nations received strong American support. Meanwhile, the United States continued the drive toward a lowering of world tariffs (begun in the 1930s). During the war, all recipients of Lend-Lease had been required to commit themselves to lowered tariffs. These commitments were internationally formalized in 1947 in the GENERAL AGREEMENT ON TARIFFS AND TRADE, when 23 nations participated in an extensive mutual lowering of trade barriers. In 1948, at American initiative, the ORGANIZATION OF AMERICAN STATES was established to provide a regional multi-

lateral consultative body in the Western Hemisphere. Within Europe, the Marshall Plan required the formation of Europe-wide organizations, leading eventually to the Common Market.

Toward the USSR, the basic American policy was that known as containment: building "situations of strength" around its vast perimeter to prevent the outward spread of communism. Angered Americans blamed the USSR for world disorder and came to regard the peace of the entire world as a U.S. responsibility. After their immense war effort, many Americans believed that the United States could accomplish whatever it desired to do. Also, having defeated one form of tyranny, fascism, and now being engaged in resisting another, Stalinist communism, the American people assumed with few questions that, since their cause was just, whatever they did in its name was right. Critics of national policy were harshly condemned.

A series of East-West crises, most dramatically the Berlin Blockade of 1948-49, led to the creation (April 1949) of the NORTH ATLANTIC TREATY ORGANIZATION. The NATO alliance sought to link the United States militarily to Western Europe (including Greece and Turkey) by making an attack against one member an attack against all. As Europe recovered its prosperity, the focus of East-West confrontation shifted to Asia, where the British, French, and Dutch empires were collapsing and the Communist revolution in China was moving toward its victory (October 1949). In June 1950 the North Korean army invaded South Korea. The United Nations Security Council (which the Soviets were then boycotting) called on UN members jointly to repel this attack. Shortly afterward, a multinational force under Gen. Douglas MacArthur was battling to turn back North Korean forces in the KOREAN WAR. As the UN army swept northward to the Manchurian border, Chinese forces flooded southward to resist them, and a long, bloody seesaw war ensued. An armistice was not signed until July 1953, following 150,000 American casualties and millions of deaths among the Koreans and Chinese.

Domestic Developments during the Truman Years. In 1945, President Truman called on Congress to launch another program of domestic reform, but the nation was indifferent. It was riding a wave of affluence such as it had never dreamed of in the past. Tens of millions of people found themselves moving upward into a middle-class way of life. The cold war, and the pervasive fear of an atomic war, induced a trend toward national unity and a downplaying of social criticism. The Atomic Energy Act of 1946 nationalized nuclear power, putting it under civilian control, but no other bold departures were made. What fascinated Americans was the so-called baby boom—a huge increase in the birthrate (the population was at 150 million by 1950 and 179 million by 1960)—and the need to house new families and teach their children.

In the presence of rapidly rising inflation, labor unions called thousands of strikes, leading in 1948 to passage of the Taft-Hartley Act (see LABOR-MANAGEMENT RELATIONS ACT), which limited the powers of unions, declared certain of their tactics "unfair labor practices," and gave the president power to secure 80-day "cooling off periods" by court injunction. As union benefits increased nationwide, however, industrial warfare quieted. In 1948 the United Automobile Workers won automatic "cost of living" pay increases in their contracts and in 1955 the guaranteed annual wage. In 1955 merger negotiations were completed for the formation of the AMERICAN FEDERATION OF LABOR AND CONGRESS OF INDUSTRIAL ORGANIZATIONS (AFL-CIO); more than 85 percent of all union members were now in one organization.

Fears that Russian communism was taking over the entire world were pervasive during the Truman years. Soviet spy rings were discovered in the United States, Canada, and Great Britain. In 1948–50 a sensational trial for perjury led to the conviction of a former State Department official, Alger HISS, on the grounds that while in the department he had been part of a Communist cell and had passed secrets to the Soviets. In 1950 a Soviet spy ring was uncovered in the Los Alamos atomic installation. These events, together with the explosion (1949) of a Soviet atomic bomb and the victory (1949) of the Communists in China, prompted a widespread conviction that subversive conspiracies within the American government were leading toward Soviet triumph.

In February 1950, Republican Sen. Joseph R. MCCARTHY of Wisconsin began a 4-year national crisis, during which he insisted repeatedly that he had direct evidence of such conspiracies in the federal government, even in the army. The entire country seemed swept up in a hysteria in which anyone left of center was attacked as a subversive. A program to root out alleged security risks in the national government led to a massive collapse in morale in its departments; it destroyed the State Department's corps of experts on Far Eastern and Soviet affairs. The Truman administration's practice of foreign policy was brought practically to a halt. In 1952, Dwight D. EISENHOWER, nationally revered supreme commander in Europe during World War II, was elected president (1953–61) on the Republican ticket, but soon McCarthy was attacking him as well for running a "weak, immoral, and cowardly" foreign policy. In 1954 a long and dramatic series of congressional hearings, the first to be nationally televised, destroyed McCarthy's credibility. He was censured by the Senate, and a measure of national stability returned.

The Eisenhower Years. Eisenhower declared himself uninterested in repealing the New Deal, but he was socially and economically conservative and his presidency saw the enactment of few reforms. His appointment of Earl WARREN as chief justice of the United States, however, led to a Supreme Court that suddenly seized so bold and active a role in national life that many called it revolutionary. During Warren's

Sen. Joseph R. McCarthy, who vaulted into prominence through his unscrupulous crusade against alleged Communists in government, appears during the Army-McCarthy hearings in 1954. These nationally televised hearings led to McCarthy's condemnation by the U.S. Senate.

long tenure (1953–69), the Court swept away the legal basis for racial discrimination; ruled that every person must be represented equally in state legislatures and in the U.S. House of Representatives; changed criminal-justice procedures by ensuring crucial rights to the accused; broadened the artist's right to publish works shocking to the general public; and in major ways limited the government's ability to penalize individuals for their beliefs or associations.

No decision of the Warren Court was more historic than that in BROWN V. BOARD OF EDUCATION OF TOPEKA, KANSAS (1954), which ruled unanimously that racial segregation in the public schools was unconstitutional. This great decision—followed by others that struck down segregation in all public facilities and in elections and marriage laws—sparked a revolution in race-relations law. The separate-but-equal principle was cast aside, and the Second Reconstruction could get underway. Now black Americans could charge that the statutory discrimination that tied them down and kept them in a secondary caste was illegal, a fact that added enormous moral weight to their cause. Resistance by southern whites to desegregated public education would make the advance of that cause frustratingly slow, however. By 1965 black children had been admitted to white schools in fewer than 25 percent of southern school districts. The fight for racial equality was not limited to the South, for by 1960 only 60 percent of black Americans remained there; 73 percent of them also lived in cities: they were no longer simply a scattered, powerless rural labor force in the South.

In 1957 the Soviet government launched its first orbiting

Four men who served as presidents of the United States (left to right) John F. Kennedy, Lyndon B. Johnson, Dwight D. Eisenhower and Harry S. Truman, occupied the front pew during the funeral services for former Speaker of the House Sam Rayburn (November 1961), who served in that position longer than any other person in the nation's history.

satellite, Sputnik, and a national controversy erupted. Why are we so far behind in the crucial area of rocketry? Americans asked. Many critics replied that weaknesses in public education, especially in science and technology, were the root cause. In 1958, Congress enacted the first general education law since the Morrill Act of 1862—the NATIONAL DEFENSE EDUCATION ACT. It authorized $1 billion for education from primary level through university graduate training, inaugurating a national policy that became permanent thereafter and that resulted in the spending of huge sums and the transformation of American public education.

Eisenhower's foreign policy, under Secretary of State John Foster DULLES, was more nationalist and unilateral than Truman's. American-dominated alliances ringed the Soviet and Chinese perimeters. Little consultation with Western European allies preceded major American initiatives, and in consequence the United States and Western Europe began drifting apart. Persistent recessions in the American economy hobbled the national growth rate while the Soviet and Western European economies surged dramatically. An aggressive Nikita Khrushchev, Soviet premier, trumpeted that communism would bury capitalism and boasted of Moscow's powerful intercontinental missiles while encouraging so-called wars of liberation in Southeast Asia and elsewhere.

THE UNITED STATES SINCE 1960: NEW CHALLENGES TO THE AMERICAN SYSTEM

During the 1960s and 1970s cold-war concerns gave way as attention focused on social and cultural rebellions at home. Involvement in a long and indecisive war in Asia and scandals that reached into the White House eroded the confidence of many Americans in their country's values and system of government. The United States survived such challenges, however, and emerged from the 1970s subdued but intact.

The Exuberant Kennedy Years.   The Democratic senator John F. KENNEDY, asserting that he wanted to "get the country moving again," won the presidency in a narrow victory over Vice-President Richard M. NIXON in 1960. The charismatic Kennedy stimulated a startling burst of national enthusiasm and aroused high hopes among the young and the disadvantaged. Within 3 years his Peace Corps (see ACTION) sent about 10,000 Americans (mostly young people) abroad to work in 46 countries. Kennedy's ALLIANCE FOR PROGRESS proposed a 10-year plan to transform the economies of the Latin American nations (partially successful, it sunk out of sight during the Vietnam War). He also proposed massive tariff cuts between the increasingly protectionist European Common Market and the world at large. (The so-called Kennedy Round of tariff negotiations concluded in 1967 with the largest and widest tariff

Standing to attention as well as his suit permits, astronaut Edwin "Buzz" Aldrin salutes the U.S. flag as it waves over the lunar surface. Aldrin, copilot of the lunar lander on the epochal Apollo 11 mission (July 1969), became the second man to set foot on the Moon.

cuts in modern history.) In June 1961, Kennedy pulled together the disparate, disorganized space effort by giving it a common goal: placing an American on the moon. Responding enthusiastically, Congress poured out billions of dollars to finance the project. (After the APOLLO PROGRAM succeeded, on July 20, 1969, in landing astronauts on the moon, the space effort remained in motion, if at a reduced pace.)

Kennedy blundered into a major defeat within 3 months of entering the White House. He kept in motion a plan sponsored by the CENTRAL INTELLIGENCE AGENCY (CIA) and begun by the Eisenhower administration to land an invasion force in Cuba, which under Fidel Castro had become a communist state and a Soviet state. The BAY OF PIGS INVASION failed, utterly and completely. The force was quickly smashed when it struggled onto the beaches of the Bay of Pigs in April 1961. During the succeeding 2 years, Kennedy labored to break the rigid cold-war relationship with the USSR. In October 1962, however, he discovered that the Soviets were rapidly building missile emplacements in Cuba. Surrounding the island with a naval blockade, he induced the Soviets to desist, and the sites were eventually dismantled. The relieved world discovered that, when pushed to the crisis point, the two major powers could stop short of nuclear war. This CUBAN MISSILE CRISIS effectively ended the cold war.

The atomic bomb now seemed defused, and Moscow seemed ready to negotiate on crucial issues (perhaps, it was suggested 15 years later, to give the Soviets time to build a far more powerful armaments system). A new and more relaxed relationship developed slowly into the U.S.-Soviet DÉTENTE that emerged in the late 1960s and persisted through the 1970s. A test-ban treaty, the Moscow Agreement (see ARMS CONTROL), signed in October 1963 symbolized the opening of the new relationship. Three of the world's nuclear powers (Great Britain, the United States, and the USSR—the fourth, France, did not sign) agreed to end the detonation of atomic explosions in the atmosphere.

In this new environment of security, American culture, long restrained by the sense of team spirit and conformity that the crises of depression, war, and cold war had induced, broke loose into multiplying swift changes. People now began talking excitedly of "doing their own thing." The media were filled with discussions of the rapidly changing styles of dress and behavior among the young; of the "new woman" (or the "liberated woman," as she became known); of new sexual practices and attitudes and new styles of living. The sense of community faded. Romanticism shaped the new mood, with its emphasis on instinct and impulse rather than reason, ecstatic release rather than restraint, individualism and self-gratification rather than group discipline.

Assassination and Cultural Rebellion.   The excitement of Kennedy's presidency and his calls to youth to serve the nation had inspired the young, both black and white. His assassination in November 1963 shocked and dismayed Americans of all ages, and the psychological links he had fashioned between "the system" and young people began to dissolve. His successor, Lyndon B. JOHNSON, later shouldering the onus of an unpopular war, was unable to build a reservoir of trust among the young. As the large demographic group that had constituted the "baby boom" of the post-World War II years reached college age, it became the "wild generation" of student radicals and "hippies" who rebelled against political and cultural authority.

Styles of life changed swiftly. Effective oral contraceptives, *Playboy* magazine, and crucial Supreme Court decisions helped make the United States, long one of the world's most prudish nations in sexual matters, one of its most liberated. The drug culture mushroomed. Communal living groups of "dropouts" who rejected mass culture received widespread attention. People more than 30 years old reacted angrily against the flamboyant youth (always a small minority of the young generation) who flouted traditional standards, glorified self-indulgence, and scorned discipline.

In the second half of the 1960s this generation gap widened as many of the young (along with large numbers of older people) questioned U.S. involvement in Vietnam.

During the March on the Pentagon, a demonstration against the Vietnam War in 1967, protesters staged a "sit-down" when confronted by troops. Antiwar activism steadily increased in intensity until U.S. combat forces were finally withdrawn from Vietnam in 1973.

Martin Luther King, Jr. (front row, second from right) leads his supporters on the "freedom march" from Selma to Montgomery, Ala., in 1965. The march was staged as part of a drive to register black voters, specifically in Alabama and generally throughout the South.

Peaceful protests led to violent confrontations, and differences concerning styles of life blurred with disagreements about the degree of allegiance that individuals owed to the American system. In 1968 the assassinations of the Rev. Martin Luther KING, Jr., and President Kennedy's brother Robert F. KENNEDY seemed to confirm suspicions that dark currents of violence underlay many elements in American society.

Race Relations during the 1960s and 1970s. Race relations was one area with great potential for violence, although many black leaders stressed nonviolence. Since the mid-1950s, King and others had been leading disciplined mass protests of black Americans in the South against segregation, emphasizing appeals to the conscience of the white majority. The appeals of these leaders and judicial rulings on the illegality of segregationist practices were vital parts of the Second Reconstruction, which transformed the role and status of black Americans, energizing every other cultural movement as well. At the same time, southern white resistance to the ending of segregation, with its attendant violence, stimulated a northern-dominated Congress to enact (1957) the first civil rights law since 1875, creating the Commission on Civil Rights and prohibiting interference with the right to vote (blacks were still massively disenfranchised in many southern states). A second enactment (1960) provided federal referees to aid blacks in registering for and voting in federal elections. In 1962, President Kennedy dispatched troops to force the University of Mississippi (a state institution) to admit James Meredith, a black student. At the same time, he forbade racial or religious discrimination in federally financed housing.

Kennedy then asked Congress to enact a law to guarantee equal access to all public accommodations, forbid discrimination in any state program receiving federal aid, and outlaw discrimination in employment and voting. After Kennedy's death, President Johnson prodded Congress into enacting (August 1965) a voting-rights bill that eliminated all qualifying tests for registration that had as their objective limiting the right to vote to whites. Thereafter, massive voter registration drives in the South sent the proportion of registered blacks spurting upward from less than 30 to over 53 percent in 1966.

The civil rights phase of the black revolution had reached its legislative and judicial summit. Then, from 1964 to 1968, more than a hundred American cities were swept by RACE RI-OTS, which included dynamitings, guerrilla warfare, and huge conflagrations, as the anger of the northern black community at its relatively low income, high unemployment, and social exclusion exploded. At this violent expression of hopelessness the northern white community drew back rapidly from its reformist stance on the race issue (the so-called white backlash). In 1968, swinging rightward in its politics, the nation chose as president Richard M. Nixon, who was not in favor of using federal power to aid the disadvantaged. Individual advancement, he believed, had to come by individual effort.

Nonetheless, fundamental changes continued in relations between white and black. Although the economic disparity in income did not disappear—indeed, it widened, as unemployment within black ghettos and among black youths remained at a high level in the 1970s—white-dominated American culture opened itself significantly toward black people. Entrance requirements for schools and colleges were changed; hundreds of communities sought to work out equitable arrangements to end de facto segregation in the schools (usually with limited success, and to the accompaniment of a white flight to different school districts); graduate programs searched for black applicants; and integration in jobs and in the professions expanded. Blacks moved into the mainstream of the party system, for the voting-rights enactments transformed national politics. The daily impact of television helped make blacks, seen in shows and commercial advertisements, seem an integral part of a pluralistic nation.

Mexican Americans and Puerto Ricans were also becoming more prominent in American life. Reaching the level of 9 million by the 1960s, Spanish-surnamed Americans had become the second largest ethnic minority; they, too, were asserting their right to equitable treatment in politics, in culture, and in economic affairs.

Kennedy-Johnson Legislative Accomplishments. In his first 3 months of office, Kennedy sent 39 messages and letters to Congress asking for reform legislation—messages dealing with health care, education, housing and community development, civil rights, transportation, and many other areas. His narrow margin of victory in 1960, however, had not seemed a mandate for change, and an entrenched coalition of Republicans and conservative southern Democrats in Congress had prevented the achievement of many of Kennedy's legislative goals by the time of his death. Johnson, who in 1964 won an enormous victory over the Republican presidential candidate, Barry GOLDWATER, and carried on his coattails a large Democratic congressional majority, proceeded with consummate political skill to enact this broad program.

Johnson launched his WAR ON POVERTY, which focused on children and young people, providing them with better education and remedial training, and Congress created a domestic Peace Corps (VISTA). Huge sums went to the states for education. MEDICARE was enacted in 1965, providing millions of elderly Americans a kind of security from the costs of illness that they had never known before. Following Kennedy's Clean Air Act of 1963, the Water Quality Act of 1965 broadened the effort to combat pollution. New national parks were established, and a Wilderness Act to protect primeval regions was passed. The Economic Development Administration moved into depressed areas, such as Appalachia. Billions were appropriated for urban redevelopment and public housing.

At War in Vietnam. The VIETNAM WAR, however, destroyed the Johnson presidency. The United States had been the protector of South Vietnam since 1954, when the Geneva Conference had divided Vietnam into a communist North and a pro-Western South. By 1961 an internal revolution had brought the South Vietnamese regime to the point of toppling. President Kennedy, deciding that South Vietnam was salvageable and that he could not allow another communist victory, sent in 15,000 military advisors and large supplies of munitions. By 1964 it was clear that a collapse was again impending (the CIA warned that the reason was the regime's harshness and corruption), and Johnson decided to escalate American involvement. After his electoral victory that year, he began aerial bombardment of North Vietnam, which persisted almost continuously for 3 years to no apparent result other than the destruction of large parts of the North and heavy loss of life. Meanwhile, the world at large (and many Americans) condemned the U.S. military actions.

In April 1965, Johnson began sending American ground troops to Vietnam, the total reaching nearly 550,000 in early 1969. (In that year alone, with a full-scale naval, aerial, and ground war being waged in Vietnam, total expenditures there reached $100 billion.) Huge regions in the South were laid waste by American troops in search of hostile forces. Still victory eluded. Responding to mass public protests that went on year after year and put the United States in a state of near-insurrection—and in recognition of fruitless American casualties, which in 1967 passed 100,000—Johnson decided in March 1968 to halt the bombing of the North and to begin deescalation. At the same time he announced that he would not run for reelection. From being an immensely popular president, he had descended to a position as one of the most hated and reviled occupants of that office.

Foreign Policy under Nixon. When Richard M. Nixon became president in 1969, he profoundly changed U.S. foreign policy. The new theme was withdrawal from commitments around the globe. Nixon revived the kind of nationalist, unilateral foreign policy that, since Theodore Roosevelt, presidents of his political tradition had preferred. With Henry KISSINGER as an advisor and later as secretary of state, he began a kind of balance-of-power diplomacy. He preferred to keep the United States free of lasting commitments (even to former allies) so that it could move back and forth between the other four power centers—Europe, the USSR, China, and Japan—and maintain world equilibrium.

Nixon soon announced his "Vietnamization" policy, which meant a slow withdrawal of American forces and a heavy building up of the South Vietnam army. Nonetheless, in the 3 years 1969-71, 15,000 more Americans died fighting in Vietnam. In April 1970, Nixon launched a huge invasion of Cambodia in a vain attempt to clear out communist "sanctuaries."

A U.S. soldier looks on as a Vietnamese mother cradles her child after learning of her husband's death. The Vietnam War, which took the lives of about 1.7 million people, including 50,000 Americans, and devastated Vietnam, deeply divided the people of the United States.

On Apr. 29, 1974, President Nixon announced his release to the House Judiciary Committee of edited transcripts of his taped conversations relating to the Watergate scandal. Three months later he was forced to surrender the tapes themselves, and on Aug. 9, 1974, he resigned.

Then, most dramatically, he deflected world attention by ending the long American quarantine of Communist China, visiting Peking in February 1972 for general discussions on all matters of mutual concern—a move that led to the establishment (1979) of diplomatic relations. At the same time, he continued the heavy bombing attacks on North Vietnam that he had reinstituted in late 1971. He brushed aside as "without binding force or effect" the congressional attempt to halt American fighting in Vietnam by repealing the TONKIN GULF RESOLUTION of 1964, which had authorized Johnson to begin military operations. Nixon asserted that as commander in chief he could do anything he deemed necessary to protect the lives of American troops still in Vietnam.

In May 1972, Nixon became the first American president to consult with Soviet leaders in Moscow, leaving with major agreements relating to trade, cooperation in space programs and other fields of technology, cultural exchanges, and many other areas. He became more popular as prosperity waxed and as negotiations with the North Vietnamese in Paris seemed to be bringing the Vietnam War to a halt. In 1972 the Democrats nominated for the presidency Sen. George McGovern of South Dakota, a man who for years had advocated women's rights, black equality, and greater power for the young. With the nation's increasingly conservative cultural mood and the trend in Vietnam, Nixon won a massive landslide victory. In January 1973, Nixon announced a successful end to the Vietnamese negotiations: a cease-fire was established and an exchange of prisoners provided for.

Watergate. Few presidents could ever have been more confident of a successful second term than Richard Nixon at this point. But before the year 1973 was out, his administration had fallen into the gravest scandal in American history. By March 1974 the stunning events of the WATERGATE crisis and associated villainies had led to the resignation of more than a dozen high officials—including the vice-president (for the acceptance of graft)—and the indictment or conviction of many others. Their criminal acts included burglary, forgery, illegal wiretapping and electronic surveillance, perjury, obstruction of justice, bribery, and many other offenses.

These scandalous events had their roots in the long Democratic years beginning with Roosevelt, when the American presidency had risen in a kind of solitary majesty to become overwhelmingly the most powerful agency of government. All that was needed for grave events to occur was the appearance in the White House of individuals who would put this immense power to its full use. Lyndon Johnson was such a man, for he was driven by gargantuan dreams. One result was America's disastrous war in Vietnam. Richard Nixon, too, believed in the imperial authority of the presidency. He envi-

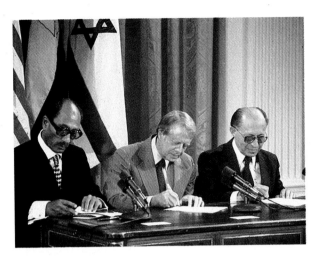

In March 1979, President Jimmy Carter was flanked by President Anwar al-Sadat (left) of Egypt and Prime Minister Menachem Begin of Israel at the signing of the "Camp David" peace treaty in Washington, D.C. The treaty ended a 31-year state of war between Egypt and Israel.

sioned politics as an arena in which he represented true Americanism and his critics the forces of subversion.

At least from 1969, Nixon operated on the principle that, at his direction, federal officials could violate the law. On June 17, 1972, members of his Special Investigations Unit (created without congressional authorization) were arrested while burglarizing the national Democratic party offices in the Watergate office-and-apartment complex in Washington, D.C.

A frantic effort then began, urged on by the president, to cover up links between the Watergate burglars and the executive branch. This cover-up constituted an obstruction of justice, a felony. This fact, however, was kept hidden through many months of congressional hearings (begun in May 1973) into the burglaries. Televised, they were watched by multitudes. The American people learned of millions of dollars jammed into office safes and sluiced about from hand to hand to finance shady dealings; of elaborate procedures for covering tracks and destroying papers; and of tapes recording the president's conversations with his aides.

With Watergate eroding Nixon's prestige, Congress finally halted American fighting in Indochina by cutting off funds (after Aug. 15, 1973) to finance the bombing of Cambodia, which had continued after the Vietnam Peace Agreement. Thus, America's longest war was finally concluded. In November 1973, Congress passed, over the president's veto, the War Powers Act, sharply limiting the executive's freedom of action in initiating foreign wars. When Vice-President Spiro T. AGNEW resigned his office on Oct. 10, 1973, Nixon, with Senate ratification, appointed Gerald R. Ford to replace him.

On July 24, 1974, the Supreme Court ordered Nixon to deliver his Oval Office tapes to Congress. This order, in turn, led to the revelation that he had directly approved the cover-up. Informed by Republican congressional leaders of his certain conviction in forthcoming impeachment proceedings, Richard Nixon resigned the presidency on Aug. 9, 1974.

The Third Century Begins. As the nation approached its bicentennial anniversary under President Gerald R. FORD (1974–77), it was reassured that the Constitution had worked: a president guilty of grave offenses had been made peacefully to leave his office. The American people had become aware, however, in the Vietnam conflict, of the limits to their nation's strength and of questions as to the moral legitimacy of its purposes. They had also learned, in the Watergate scandal, of the danger of corruption of the republic's democratic values. The nation's cities were in grave difficulties; its nonwhite peoples still lagged far behind the whites in income and opportunity; unemployment seemed fixed at a level of more than 6 percent, which, for minorities and the young, translat-

ed into much higher figures, and inflation threatened to erode the buying power of everyone in the country.

Most of these problems continued to plague the American nation during the presidency (1977–81) of Jimmy CARTER, Democrat of Georgia, who defeated Ford in the 1976 election. Carter brought to the presidency an informality and sense of piety. He arranged negotiations for an Egyptian-Israeli peace treaty (signed in 1979) and guided the Panama Canal treaty through narrow Senate approval (1978). Carter also had to deal with shortages of petroleum that threatened to bring the energy-hungry U.S. economy to a standstill, with soaring inflation rates, with the taking (1979) of U.S. hostages by Iranian militants (see IRANIAN HOSTAGE CRISIS), and with an international crisis precipitated by Soviet intervention (1979) in Afghanistan. His popularity waned as problems remained unsolved, and in 1980 the voters turned overwhelmingly to the conservative Republican candidate, Ronald REAGAN.

ROBERT KELLEY

The Reagan Era. Ronald Reagan entered the presidency on a wave of personal popularity. Hailed as the "great communicator," he established a remarkable rapport with the electorate that for the most part held through his two terms.

In domestic affairs, the Reagan presidency started with strong accomplishments in 1981, when the "Reagan revolution" was enacted. Reagan's goal was to cut back big government, to release free enterprise to be the productive heart of the country, and to stimulate the economy by drastic tax cuts. This program was intended to push productivity upward, create jobs for the unemployed, and cut inflation. (The Federal Reserve Board also attacked inflation by continuing a sharp restriction of the money supply it had begun under Jimmy Carter.) In August 1981 the Economic Recovery Tax Act and an Omnibus Budget and Reconciliation Act reduced taxes by 25 percent over a three-year period (about $280 billion, in total) and cut social-welfare spending across a broad front.

Part of the Reagan plan for economic revitalization involved cutting back on business and social regulation. Federal regulatory agencies eliminated many regulations on business, and were unaggressive enforcers thereafter, particularly in such areas as environmental regulation and industrial health and safety for workers. The federal government also pulled back sharply from an interventionist role in racial relations.

The passionately anti-Communist Reagan pushed military spending much higher than the increased rate achieved under Carter. Basically, recent Soviet emplacements of hundreds of medium-range nuclear missiles, aimed at the heart of Western Europe, and a vast increase in the Soviet navy had created alarm over military security. Consequently, Reagan got a $90-billion increase in already high arms spending. He allocated the money to new and very costly weapons, such as the MX

An inactive steel mill in Youngstown, Ohio, exemplifies the decline of the smokestack industries, particularly in the old industrial belt, or "Rust Bowl." The United States has made the transition to a "postindustrial" economy, one based increasingly on the service sectors and dependent on technological advances.

The invasion of the Caribbean island of Grenada by U.S. forces in October 1983 in order to overthrow the anti-American dictatorship there reflected a principal emphasis of President Ronald Reagan's foreign policy—resisting Communist influence in the hemisphere.

MISSILE; a strategic bomber, the B-1; new tanks; and a greatly expanded naval fleet and missile submarine force. Military expenditures reached 6.1 percent of the gross national product in 1982–83.

The result was a large revenue shortfall and a burgeoning national budget deficit that reached toward $200 billion annually. During his presidency, Reagan would borrow more money to make up his budget deficits than all earlier presidents combined. During his second administration the United States passed a historic point: it became for the first time since before World War I a debtor nation, and soon the nation with the largest debt owed to foreigners. In 1981 the deepest recession since 1940 had begun, lasting until 1983 and reducing tax revenues further. The inflation rate did drop to 4 percent in 1982, where it essentially remained thereafter, but the unemployment rate was notably high in 1982.

In time, Reagan's deficit spending and a loosening of the money supply by the Federal Reserve Board poured immense sums into the economy. A strong upward surge began in 1983; there was a highly encouraging growth in gross national product in 1984 of 6.7 percent. Despite a stunning stock-market collapse of 1929 proportions in October 1987 (the market later recovered strongly), the boom was still running vigorously in late 1988, Reagan's last year in office, with unemployment at 5.4 percent, lower than the 8 percent of 1981.

In September 1985 the Reagan administration led a concerted international effort to cut the large unfavorable balance in U.S. trade of imports over exports. This reduced considerably the international value of the U.S. dollar, though a large import surplus remained. There was national alarm over the towering twin deficits. In 1980 interest annually on the national debt was $52 billion; in 1988, it was about $151 billion.

In foreign policy the president held off on negotiations over arms reductions. His basic thesis was not to negotiate seriously until U.S. armed strength was greatly increased. In December 1983 he began the actual emplacement in Europe of hundreds of Pershing II intermediate-range missiles and hundreds more land-based cruise missiles, to which Carter and the NATO allies had agreed in 1979.

Also in 1983, reflecting the administration's concern about Communist influence to the south, U.S. forces invaded Grenada in the Caribbean to dislodge a pro-Communist government. Meanwhile, in Central America, Reagan supported so-called covert efforts by the Central Intelligence Agency (CIA) to overturn the Marxist-leaning Sandinista regime in Nicaragua. He considered Nicaragua a virtual Soviet satellite, saying that it was exporting arms to a bloody Marxist insurgency in El Salvador. He labeled the anti-Sandinista (or "contra") insurgency the "freedom fighters" of Nicaragua, though opponents of aid criticized them as being essentially the followers of Nicaragua's former dictator, Anastasio Somoza. Reagan strug-

gled with Congress to provide funds for military and general support to the contras, winning some victories, but Congress was reluctant. In 1984–85 that body declared military aid to the contras illegal.

In November 1984, Ronald Reagan won a triumphant runaway reelection victory over the Democratic nominee, Walter F. MONDALE, the electoral vote standing at 525-13. This victory apparently encouraged a group in the White House, composed principally of Vice Adm. John M. Poindexter, a national security advisor; a National Security Council deputy, Marine Lt. Col. Oliver North; and CIA director William J. Casey, to believe that the Reagan administration was now free to do as it wished in foreign policy, even if that required breaking the law.

This spawned the IRAN-CONTRA AFFAIR, a great national scandal that essentially immobilized President Reagan during his last two years in office, except for arms-control negotiations. Its origin lay in a secret early 1985 decision, approved by the president, to sell antitank and antiaircraft missiles to Iran in hope that that nation would secure the release of Americans held hostage by pro-Iranian forces in Lebanon. This violated the president's often reiterated pledge never to deal with terrorists or with nations supporting terrorism. Then, though Congress had declared further military aid to the contras illegal, Poindexter and North secretly diverted some of the profits received from Iran into arms purchases for the contras, without consulting the president. When these events were publicly revealed by a pro-Syrian magazine in Lebanon in November 1986 (just when the Democrats, a majority in the House, were winning back control of the Senate), a national uproar sprang up. This led to lengthy, nationally televised congressional hearings that exposed the wrongdoing and gravely sapped the president's moral authority. An earlier White House–appointed review board studying the crisis concluded that, through his passive administrative style, President Reagan had lost control of his government. By late 1988 the contra insurrection, its aid limited by an angered Congress to "humanitarian" needs (food, clothing, and medical supplies), appeared increasingly far from victory.

Many observers felt that a liberalizing shift in the Soviet regime, which brought Mikhail Gorbachev to leadership, in part made historic U.S.-Soviet arms agreements possible. Determined to turn the USSR toward economic revitalization, and prompted, too, the Reagan administration maintained, by the fact that the United States was now much more powerful,

The Iran-contra affair, involving secret arms sales to Iran and the diversion of profits to Nicaraguan "contra" rebels, led to joint televised hearings by U.S. House and Senate committees during the summer of 1987. A chief witness was Lt. Col. Oliver North (left).

President Ronald Reagan (left) greets Soviet leader Mikhail Gorbachev at the White House in December 1987. The two leaders signed a historic arms-control measure that eliminated an entire class of nuclear weapons, intermediate-range missiles. They also agreed to permit each other's inspectors into their factories and military facilities to ensure compliance with the disarmament accords.

Gorbachev in summit meetings with Reagan in November 1985 (Geneva) and October 1986 (Reykjavik, Iceland) changed the USSR's hard-line position. One problem persisted: despite Soviet (and domestic American as well as international) criticism, Reagan held to his controversial belief that a missile-proof defense shield—termed the STRATEGIC DEFENSE INITIATIVE—could be placed in space, and this put negotiations in doubt. On Dec. 8, 1987, however, the two leaders signed the Intermediate Nuclear Forces Treaty, which banned medium-range nuclear missiles in Europe. In consequence, the USSR would destroy over 650 missiles, and the United States more than 350. This, the first step ever taken to significantly reduce the number of nuclear weapons threatening the world, together with a decision to pursue negotiations for a 50-percent reduction in long-range strategic weapons, seemed finally to reverse the nuclear arms race, and open the possibility of a nuclear peace.

In 1988, Vice-President George Bush, the Republican nominee, swept 40 of the 50 states in the presidential election, easily defeating the Democrat, Gov. Michael Dukakis of Massachusetts. A booming economy, eased U.S.-Soviet relations, and overwhelming support from white Southerners led to this choice of continuity over change.

Bibliography: GENERAL: Ahlstrom, Sydney E., *A Religious History of the American People* (1972); Bailyn, Bernard, et al., *The Great Republic: A History of the American People,* 2d ed. (1981); Banner, Lois W., *Women in Modern America,* 2d ed. (1984); Curti, Merle Eugene, *The Growth of American Thought,* 3d ed. (1964; repr. 1981); Ferrell, Robert H., *American Diplomacy,* 3d ed. (1975); Heilbroner, R. L., and Singer, Aaron, *The Economic Transformation of America: 1600 to Present,* 2d ed. (1984); Hofstadter, Richard, *The American Political Tradition and the Men Who Made It,* 2d ed. (1973); Huckshorn, R. J., *Political Parties in America,* 2d ed. (1983); Kelley, Robert, *The Shaping of the American Past,* 2 vols., 4th ed. (1986); Meier, A., and Rudwick, E., *From Plantation to Ghetto,* 3d ed. (1976); Morison, S. E., and Commager, H. S., *The Growth of the American Republic,* 2 vols., 7th ed. (1980); Rayback, Joseph G., *A History of American Labor,* rev. ed. (1966).

To c.1860: Bailyn, Bernard, *Ideological Origins of the American Revolution* (1967) and *The Peopling of British North America* (1986); Boorstin, Daniel Joseph, *The Americans: The National Experience* (1965; repr. 1985); Genovese, Eugene, *Roll, Jordan, Roll: The World the Slaves Made* (1974); Jordan, Winthrop, *White over Black: American Attitudes toward the Negro, 1550–1812* (1968; repr. 1977); Meyers, Marvin, *The Jacksonian Persuasion* (1960); Ver Steeg, Clarence Lester, *The Formative Years, 1607–1763* (1964); Wood, Gordon S., *The Creation of the American Republic, 1776–1787* (1969).

FROM c.1860: Foner, Eric, *Reconstruction* (1988); Handlin, Oscar, *The Uprooted,* 2d ed. (1973); Higham, John, *Strangers in the Land: Patterns of American Nativism, 1860–1925,* 2d ed. (1965; repr. 1981); Hofstadter, Richard, *The Age of Reform: From Bryan to F. D. R.* (1955); Leuchtenburg, William E., *Franklin D. Roosevelt and the New Deal, 1932–1940* (1963) and *In the Shadow of FDR: From Harry Truman to Ronald Reagan* (1985); McPherson, James M., *Battle Cry of Freedom: The Civil War Era* (1988); Mayer, Jane, and McManus, Doyle, *Landslide: The Unmaking of the President, 1984–88* (1988); Mowry, G. E., *The Urban Nation, 1920–1980,* rev. ed. (1981); Nevins, Allan, *Ordeal of the Union,* 8 vols. (1947–71); O'Neill, William L., *Coming Apart: An Informal History of America in the 1960's* (1971); Randall, J. G., and Donald, David, *The Civil War and Reconstruction,* 2d ed. (1969); Webb, Walter P., *The Great Plains* (1959; repr. 1981); Wiebe, R. H., *The Search for Order, 1877–1920* (1967; repr. 1980); Williams, William A., *The Tragedy of American Diplomacy,* rev. 2d ed. (1986).

See also: AMERICAN ART AND ARCHITECTURE; AMERICAN LITERATURE; AMERICAN MUSIC; UNITED STATES.

United States Air Force Academy

The United States Air Force Academy educates and trains men and women for service in the U.S. Air Force. Founded in 1954, the academy is near Colorado Springs, Colo. The approximately 4,500 students are admitted by congressional appointment; the library has 583,000 bound volumes. Graduates receive the bachelor of science degree and commissions as second lieutenants in the U.S. Air Force. The government pays for a student's tuition and room and board and also pays him or her a basic salary.

Bibliography: Heise, J. Arthur, *The Brass Factories: A Frank Appraisal of West Point, Annapolis, and the Air Force Academy* (1969).

United States Coast Guard Academy

The United States Coast Guard Academy educates and trains men and women for duty in the U.S. Coast Guard, a service within the Department of Transportation and, in wartime, a highly specialized part of the U.S. Navy. The academy, founded in 1876, is in New London, Conn., and has 775 students and a library of 137,000 volumes. Admission to the academy is by competition and not by congressional appointment. Graduates receive the bachelor of science degree and appointments as ensigns in the U.S. Coast Guard. They must serve at least 5 years in the Coast Guard, whose functions include port safety, marine environmental protection, icebreaking, and enforcement of maritime laws.

United States Geological Survey

The United States Geological Survey is a federal agency charged with the classification of public lands, the examination of geologic structures, and the investigation of mineral resources in the United States. The Geological Survey is within the Department of the Interior and is primarily a research and fact-finding agency.

Early in the 19th century geology was incidental to federal expeditions because federally sponsored science, a form of public works, raised constitutional questions. Congress eventually followed foreign and state examples, however, and authorized (beginning in 1867) four western surveys with geology as their main purpose. The federal surveys, supervised by the War and Interior departments, were Clarence King's Geological Exploration of the 40th Parallel, Ferdinand HAYDEN's Geological and Geographical Survey of the Territories, John Wesley POWELL's Geographical and Geological Survey of the Rocky Mountain Region, and George M. Wheeler's Geographical Survey West of the 100th Meridian.

After rivalry developed among the civilian directors of the western surveys, Congress accepted the recommendation of the National Academy of Sciences that the functions of the several surveys be consolidated into one permanent agency. President Rutherford B. Hayes signed the bill establishing (1879) the Geological Survey. A legal interpretation of the enabling act restricted the agency to the West until 1882, when Congress extended the scope of its work to the eastern states. Over the years the Geological Survey has increasingly concentrated its activities on Earth resources. In 1962, Congress extended the Geological Survey's investigations to areas outside the United States.   ANNE MILLBROOKE

Bibliography: Brookings Institution, Washington, D.C., *The U.S. Geological Survey* (1918); Dupree, A. Hunter, *Science in the Federal Government* (1957; repr. 1986); Manning, Thomas G., *Government in Science: The U.S. Geological Survey 1867–1894* (1967).

United States Merchant Marine Academy

The United States Merchant Marine Academy, at Kings Point, N.Y., educates and trains men and women to serve in the U.S. Merchant Marine industry and for inactive duty as ensigns in the U.S. Naval Reserve. The academy, founded in 1943 and operated by the Maritime Administration, which is regulated by the Department of Transportation, requires its 900 students (midshipmen) to be nominated for admittance. The government provides tuition, room and board, and a basic salary to students, who spend some time at sea. Naval science courses are prescribed by the Department of the Navy. Graduates earn the bachelor of science degree and the Merchant Marine license as a third mate or a third assistant engineer and must serve in the naval reserve for 6 years. The academy has a library of 150,000 volumes.

United States Military Academy

The United States Military Academy, at West Point, N.Y., trains and educates the future officers of the regular U.S. Army. Since 1976, women have been admitted to the academy, and the first women cadets graduated in 1980. Admission to the academy, known as West Point, is by nomination by specified official sources (the vice president, senators, and U.S. representatives), who are entitled to nominate more candidates than will ultimately be accepted. Students from the U.S. dependencies and the District of Columbia may be nominated. Children of deceased or disabled veterans and of career military personnel of any of the armed forces are also eligible for appointment to West Point. Limited numbers of cadets may be from the other American republics and the Philippines. They may not, however, receive a commission in the U.S. Army upon graduation.

The 4-year program of study leads to the bachelor of science degree. Graduates, who receive commissions as second lieutenants, must serve in the U.S. Army for 5 years. The government provides tuition, room, and board. Cadets also receive one-half of a second lieutenant's basic pay.

The academy was established in 1802 in a Hudson River fortress, dating from the American Revolution. The entire post is now a national monument. The school was established to free American soldiers from wartime reliance on foreign military engineers, artillerymen, and drillmasters. Colonel Sylvanus Thayer, superintendent from 1817 to 1833, established West Point's tradition of academic excellence by insisting on regular study habits and a well-qualified faculty and by requiring every cadet to pass every course or make up his failure. During the first half of the 19th century, West Point emphasized civil engineering. For its first few decades it was the best civil engineering school in the country. Required courses in mathematics and engineering are still part of the curriculum.

Since 1900 and especially since the end of World War II, more emphasis has been placed on a balanced curriculum that includes the social sciences, the humanities, and ethics and on military leadership and management. Although the corps of cadets was increased from 2,529 to 4,417 in 1964, the U.S. Military Academy is still considered to be a small school with small classes and with an intensive academic, physical, and military training curriculum. It has a library of 500,000 volumes.

Partly because it was the first federal military academy to represent in an increasingly democratic society a profession generally considered to be conservative, and partly because part-time militia and reserve officers were constitutionally and politically powerful in the ground forces, West Point and its graduates have been thought politically and socially too conservative and have been said to spend too much time on military drill. Because the academy prepares officers for a practical professional career, its curriculum is broad and does not try to develop research scholars or scientists. Many West Point graduates continue their education at civilian graduate schools. In 1977 the academy's honor code was changed after a cheating incident in 1976 involving 150 cadets.

Bibliography: Ambrose, Stephen E., *Duty, Honor, Country: A History of West Point* (1966); Ellis, Joseph J.-M., and Moore, Robert, *School for Soldiers: West Point and the Profession of Arms* (1974); Galloway, K. Bruce, *West Point: America's Power Fraternity* (1973); Heise, J. Arthur, *The Brass Factories: A Frank Appraisal of West Point, Annapolis, and the Air Force Academy* (1969).

United States National Arboretum

The United States National Arboretum is a federally owned institution noted for its research on woody plants, particularly ornamentals such as camellias, hollies, magnolias, rhododendrons, and clematises. Located in Washington, D.C., it was founded in 1927 and covers 172 ha (425 acres).

United States Naval Academy

The United States Naval Academy, at Annapolis, Md., educates and trains men and women for service in the U.S. Navy or Marine Corps. Admission to the academy, known as Annapolis, is by nomination by the president, vice president, senators, U.S. representatives, and the secretary of the navy. Students from the U.S. dependencies and the District of Columbia may be nominated. Children of deceased or disabled veterans, of military personnel missing in action, and of prisoners of war are eligible for nomination to Annapolis. Qualified children of Medal of Honor recipients are admitted. Up to 40 cadets from foreign countries may be designated by the U.S. secretary of defense. The list of eligible countries changes annually. These cadets may not receive a commission in the U.S. Navy or Marine Corps.

The 4-year program of study leads to the bachelor of science degree. Graduates, who receive commissions as second lieutenants in the marine corps or as ensigns in the navy, must serve for 5 years. The government provides tuition and room and board. Cadets also receive a basic pay out of which other needs are paid. The academy, a U.S. National Historic Site, was founded as the Naval School in 1845 at Fort Severn in Annapolis to replace training by naval schoolmasters and other officers on warships on active service. Its founder was Secretary of the Navy George BANCROFT, a noted historian. The course sandwiched 3 years of sea duty between an entering and a final year on shore. Since 1850, when the school was reorganized and given its present name, it has had a 4-year curriculum similar to that of the U.S. Military Academy, with two summer cruises for intensive practical training. The curriculum includes practical engineering, science, and leadership courses of particular concern to the U.S. Navy and required and elective courses in the sciences and liberal arts.

Cadets at the U.S. Military Academy practice drill techniques on the parade grounds. The academy is noted for its rigorous standards in conduct and education. It is located at West Point, a military post on the Hudson River in New York State that dates back to 1778.

Assembled midshipmen (students) stand at parade rest during an awards ceremony at the U.S. Naval Academy in Annapolis, Md. Upon graduation, midshipment receive a bachelor of science degree and are commissioned into the U.S. Navy or the U.S. Marine Corps.

Unlike the military and air force academies, Annapolis has both a tenured civilian and a military faculty.

U.S. Naval Academy graduates play roles similar to those of the other federal academies. The curriculum, which prepares the 4,500 cadets for professional careers, is practically oriented and physically demanding. Like the curricula at the other academies, that at Annapolis has been frequently criticized as being crowded, superficial, and mechanized. But the academy must develop competent, motivated junior officers, prepared for immediate service before they enter other naval training or civilian educational institutions, where many cadets do graduate work.

Although Annapolis is a major source of higher commanders and professional expertise for an officers' corps drawn from many educational institutions, historians and social scientists have not analyzed the influence of Annapolis on these officers' military attitudes, career patterns, and mutual advancement and protection practices as closely or as critically as has been the case with West Point. The academy has a library of 515,000 volumes.

Bibliography: Banning, Kenneth, *Annapolis Today*, 6th ed. (1963); Crane, John, and Kiely, J. F., *The United States Naval Academy: The First Hundred Years* (1945); Edsall, Margaret H., *A Place Called the Yard: A Guide to the United States Naval Academy* (1976); Ilyinsky, Paul, et al., *The Annapolis Story: The Blue and Gold* (1974).

United States Naval Observatory

The United States Naval Observatory, established in 1842 at Washington, D.C., as an outgrowth of the Navy Department's Depot of Charts and Instruments, has responsibilities in the broad areas of navigation, time, and fundamental celestial reference systems. Because of these duties, it is one of the few institutions in the world to undertake astrometry—the determination, through continual observations, of the positions and motions of the Sun, the Moon, the planets, and principal stars. The data collected form the basis of the NAUTICAL ALMANAC and ephemeris time.

At the Washington site, 6-in (15-cm) and 7-in (18-cm) transit circles, specially designed telescopes that make observations only as an object crosses the meridian, are used to measure accurate positions of celestial bodies. Two photographic

zenith tubes determine mean solar time, and many atomic clocks determine atomic time. The observatory's master clock establishes standard time for the United States. A 61-in (155-cm) astrometric reflector in Flagstaff, Ariz., measures distances of faint nearby stars, and a 40-in (102-cm) Ritchey Chretien reflector, also at Flagstaff, observes comets and minor planets. The 26-in (66-cm) refractor, still in operation in Washington, was the instrument Asaph Hall used to discover the two moons of Mars in 1877.

United States outlying territories

The United States exercises sovereignty over 12 outlying territories. Each has a political status based on the degree of federal jurisdiction. Since 1959, when Alaska and Hawaii achieved statehood, the United States has had no incorporated territories—those in which the U.S. Constitution applies. Unincorporated territories, or possessions, can be either organized or unorganized. Organized territories are governed by congressional legislation functioning much as a state constitution. Unorganized territories have no such bodies of legislation. GUAM and the U.S. VIRGIN ISLANDS are organized territories. Unorganized territories are AMERICAN SAMOA; MIDWAY Island; WAKE ISLAND; Howland, Baker, and Jarvis islands; Johnston Atoll; Kingman Reef; Navassa Island; and Palmyra Island.

U.S. commonwealth status offers more local autonomy than that afforded a possession. The government functions under a constitution adopted by local residents following U.S. congressional enabling legislation. PUERTO RICO and the Northern MARIANA ISLANDS are U.S. commonwealths.

The United States also administered the Trust Territory of the PACIFIC ISLANDS under trusteeship granted by the United Nations (see TRUST TERRITORY). These islands were formerly under the MANDATE SYSTEM of the League of Nations. In 1986 the Northern Mariana Islands became a U.S. commonwealth, and the MARSHALL ISLANDS and the Federated States of MICRONESIA (YAP, Kosrae, Ponape, and Truk islands) gained limited independence in free association with the United States, which provides economic assistance and remains responsible for their defense. The UN Trusteeship Council approved a similar compact of free association for PALAU in 1988, despite a continuing dispute between Palau and the United States over the compact's interpretation.

Of the U.S. territories, Baker and Howland islands, Johnston Atoll, and Navassa Island were claimed under the Guano Islands Act of 1856. The act enables the United States to assume possession of an unoccupied, unclaimed area to extract GUANO deposits for fertilizer. American Samoa was acquired through agreements with the islands' residents. Uninhabited Kingman Reef was annexed, as were Midway and Wake islands. Palmyra Island was annexed with Hawaii; Puerto Rico was ceded to the United States by Spain; and the U.S. Virgin Islands were purchased from Denmark.   MARJORIE JOYCE

Bibliography: Dulles, F. R., *America in the Pacific* (1932; repr. 1969); Haas, W. H., ed., *American Empire* (1940); U.S. Department of State, *Trust Territory of the Pacific Islands* (1986).

United States Student Association

The United States Student Association, formed in 1978 by the merger of the U.S. National Student Association (1947) and the National Student Lobby (1971), is a confederation of 425 American college student governments. It is a lobbying organization for students, giving them a voice in the Department of Education, and acts as a clearinghouse for information on student concerns. Its headquarters is in Washington, D.C.

United States Trust Territory of the Pacific Islands: see PACIFIC ISLANDS, TRUST TERRITORY OF THE.

United States v. Butler

In the case of *United States* v. *Butler* (1936) the U.S. Supreme Court declared the Agricultural Adjustment Act of 1933 unconstitutional. The legislation had been an attempt to eliminate the chronic overproduction of agricultural products and thus to raise farm incomes. In return for reducing their production, farmers were to receive a subsidy from the government, financed through a tax levied on food processors. Butler, the receiver for Hoosac Mills, a cotton processor that refused to pay the tax, was sued by the government and ordered to pay.

Speaking for the majority of the Court, Justice Owen Roberts declared the law unconstitutional on the ground that Congress was levying a tax not for the general welfare but for local regulation. According to Roberts, the power granted in the Constitution to collect taxes extended only to national as distinguished from local matters, whereas agricultural production was essentially under control of the states. Roberts also cited the 10th Amendment as a limit on Congress's delegated powers in that it prohibits Congress from invading the reserved powers of the states. This doctrine was known as that of "dual federalism" and had been used sporadically to check the growth of national power throughout U.S. history. This case was among the last of the anti–New Deal decisions, and the subsequent Agricultural Adjustment Act of 1938—based as it was on the power of Congress to regulate interstate commerce—was upheld by the court in *Mulford* v. *Smith* (1939).

ROBERT J. STEAMER

United States v. Curtiss-Wright Export Corporation

In the case of *United States* v. *Curtiss-Wright Export Corporation* (1936), the U.S. Supreme Court gave strong support to the use of presidential power in foreign affairs. In May 1934, Congress, in hope of containing the fighting between Paraguay and Bolivia in the Chaco War, empowered the president to forbid the sale of munitions to both countries. President Franklin D. Roosevelt proclaimed an embargo on the sale of arms for approximately a year and a half. During the embargo the Curtiss-Wright Company was indicted for selling machine guns to Bolivia but argued that Congress had invalidly delegated legislative power to the president.

Upholding the president, the Court, in an opinion by Justice George Sutherland, observed that had the power been delegated in internal affairs, it would have been subject to challenge. In external affairs, however, Sutherland continued, the powers of the federal government differed significantly from those it possessed over domestic affairs, and the president particularly had "a degree of discretion and freedom from statutory restriction which would not be admissible where domestic affairs alone involved." In this vast external realm "the president alone has the power to speak or listen as a representative of the nation."

ROBERT J. STEAMER

United States v. Darby

In the case of *United States* v. *Darby* (1941), the U.S. Supreme Court unanimously upheld the Fair Labor Standards Act of 1938. The purpose of the law was to provide for minimum wages and maximum hours of work and to prohibit child labor in industrial firms across the nation. Because Congress must legislate under powers enumerated in the Constitution, it did so by prohibiting the shipment in interstate commerce of goods produced by employees who were paid less than 25 cents per hour or who worked more than 44 hours per week without pay. It also prohibited the use of interstate commerce for the products of any establishment that had employed child labor within the previous 30 days.

Justice Harlan F. Stone wrote the opinion that upheld the law, stating that Congress in regulating commerce might prohibit products absolutely. Otherwise, companies that manufactured goods under substandard labor conditions would be given an unfair economic advantage over enlightened companies. This opinion overruled the Court's position in HAMMER V. DAGENHART (1918). The doctrine of dual federalism (the idea that federal powers could not infringe on a reserved power of the states) was permanently laid to rest. *Darby* marks a return

to John Marshall's concept that commerce is to be regarded as an organic whole—that it does not and cannot stop at state lines.

ROBERT J. STEAMER

United States v. E. C. Knight Company

The case of *United States* v. *E. C. Knight Company* (1895), also called the Sugar Trust Case, was among the first in which the U.S. Supreme Court held that the SHERMAN ANTI-TRUST ACT of 1890 did not apply to manufacturing because no transaction across the state lines had occurred. Under the law, which forbade monopolies or restraint of trade, the government had brought suit against five sugar manufacturing companies after one of them, the American Sugar Refining Company, had purchased the other four, including the E. C. Knight Company, thus controlling over 98 percent of the nation's sugar-refining business.

The Court, with Chief Justice Melville W. Fuller as its spokesman, held that the combination had not violated the Sherman Act. Fuller's opinion distinguished between commerce and manufacturing, declaring that the latter was not commerce in the constitutional sense. "Doubtless the power to control the manufacture of a given thing," said Fuller, "involves . . . the control of its disposition, but this is a secondary, and not the primary sense. . . . Commerce succeeds to manufacture and is not a part of it." This decision took the teeth out of the Sherman Act and postponed firm congressional control over the economy until a later day when a new Supreme Court perceived the commerce power in broader terms (see SWIFT AND COMPANY V. UNITED STATES).

ROBERT J. STEAMER

United States v. Richard M. Nixon

The case of the *United States* v. *Nixon* (1974) grew out of the WATERGATE affair that ended in the resignation of President Richard M. Nixon. A federal grand jury had returned indictments against former Attorney General John Mitchell and others, alleging obstruction of justice. Special Prosecutor Leon Jaworski had then obtained a subpoena ordering the president to produce tape recordings of conversations with his advisors that were believed relevant to the upcoming trial of those indicted. The president declined to release certain of the tapes, claiming EXECUTIVE PRIVILEGE.

In a unanimous opinion the U.S. Supreme Court ordered the president to obey the subpoena. Although admitting that a claim of executive privilege was legitimate, the Court held in the words of Chief Justice Warren Burger that "neither the doctrine of separation of powers, nor the confidentiality of high level communications . . . can sustain an absolute, unqualified presidential privilege of immunity from judicial process under all circumstances." Executive privilege, continued Burger, cannot "prevail over the fundamental demands of due process of law in the fair administration of criminal justice." The opinion reaffirmed public confidence in the independence and integrity of the Court because five of the sitting justices had been appointed by Nixon.

ROBERT J. STEAMER

United States Weather Bureau: see NATIONAL WEATHER SERVICE.

United Steelworkers of America

The United Steelworkers of America (USWA) is a labor union with a membership of 750,000 workers in the steel, aluminum, and other metal refining industries. Its affiliation with the American Federation of Labor and Congress of Industrial Organizations (AFL-CIO) dates back to its origin as the Steel Workers Organizing Committee (SWOC) of the Committee for Industrial Organization. Organized in 1936 as an industrial union, the SWOC was aided by the growth in the demand for steel before and during World War II. In 1942 the constitution was rewritten giving the union its present name. Under President Philip Murray the USWA absorbed unionized aluminum workers and later, under I. W. Abel, workers in other metal, smelting, mining, and technical industries.

United Steelworkers of America v. Weber

In the case of *United Steelworkers of America* v. *Weber* (1979), the U.S. Supreme Court held that private employers could voluntarily adopt plans designed to eliminate "conspicuous racial imbalance in traditionally segregated job categories." The case arose when Brian F. Weber sued Kaiser Aluminum & Chemical Corporation and the United Steelworkers of America for setting aside half of the positions in a training program for minority workers and passing over Weber in favor of two black workers with less seniority. Weber was upheld by two federal courts, which asserted that the defendants had violated Title VII of the Civil Rights Act of 1964 and that AFFIRMATIVE ACTION voluntarily undertaken, when no previous history of discrimination is present, discriminates unfairly against whites. The Supreme Court, in a 5–2 decision written by Justice William J. Brennan, Jr., overruled the lower court, holding that the Kaiser program did not violate Title VII despite the absence of proof that the company had discriminated against blacks in the past. The decision, like the one in UNIVERSITY OF CALIFORNIA V. BAKKE (1978), did not clearly delineate the permissible scope of race-conscious EQUAL OPPORTUNITY programs.

United Way of America: see FUND RAISING.

units, physical

Measurement systems have been developed as needed to describe and quantitate physical systems or experimental situations. Human civilizations early developed systems of measurement for areas of land, for amounts of water, food, and other materials, and for duration of time. In each case, the quantity to be measured is specified by giving its size in terms of a numerical relationship to another similar quantity. A reference quantity becomes a unit for this measurement when it is chosen to have a numerical value of unity, such as 1 year or 1 bushel.

Measurement systems, such as the metric system and the English system, can be based on a convenient and arbitrary selection of a limited number of independent units, chosen by convention. All other units can be related algebraically to this set of units. For example, there need not be a separate unit for speed; it can be expressed as distance divided by time. The International System of Units, or the SI (from the original *Système International d'Unités*; see METRIC SYSTEM), is based on seven fundamental units. It now forms the basis for both international commerce and communication in science and technology and is replacing the local system of measurement that had evolved within each country.

Base Units. All measurable physical quantities can be described in terms of a limited number of units, called base units. The metric system specifies seven quantities whose units of measurement are units of length, mass, time, electric current, thermodynamic temperature, amount of substance, and luminous intensity. Other units of measurement are called derived units and, in principle, can be formed by combining the base units. Certain of these derived units have been given names of their own. For example, the metric unit of force is the newton, derived from mass times acceleration (which itself is derived from distance divided by time squared).

Standards. To assure that measurements of identical objects would be the same wherever they are made, a set of physical standards is required. The unit of length, the meter, was defined in 1791 by the French National Assembly to be one ten-millionth of the length of the quadrant of the Earth's meridian, and its physical realization was the length of a sintered platinum-iridium bar maintained under standard atmospheric conditions in the Archives of the Republic in Paris. The meter has since been redefined in terms of the speed of light in vacuum. The unit of mass, the kilogram, is the mass of a cubic decimeter (0.001 cubic meter) of water at 4° C (39° F), the temperature of maximum density. It, too, is represented by a platinum-iridium body.

PRESENT DEFINITION OF THE BASE UNITS OF THE SI

Unit of Length (meter): The meter is the length of the path traveled by light in vacuum during a time interval of 1/299,792,458 of a second.

Unit of Mass (kilogram): The kilogram is equal to the mass of the international prototype of the kilogram.

Unit of Time (second): The second is the duration of 9,192,631,770 periods of the radiation corresponding to the transition between the two hyperfine levels of the ground state of the cesium-133 atom.

Unit of Electric Current (ampere): The ampere is that constant current which, if maintained in two straight parallel conductors of infinite lengths and of negligible circular cross section, placed 1 meter apart in vacuum, would produce between these conductors a force equal to 2×10^{-7} newton per meter of length.

Unit of Thermodynamic Temperature (kelvin): The kelvin is the fraction 1/273.16 of the thermodynamic temperature of the triple point of water.

Unit of Amount of Substance (mole): The mole is the amount of substance of a system that contains as many elementary entities as there are atoms in 0.012 kilogram of carbon-12.

Unit of Luminous Intensity (candela): The candela is the luminous intensity, in the perpendicular direction, of a surface of 1/600,000 square meter of a blackbody at the temperature of freezing platinum under a pressure of 101,325 newtons per square meter.

Customary Units. The system of units built around the common English units of pound, foot, and degree Fahrenheit for the units of mass, length, and temperature evolved in Europe through practical use over many centuries. In the United States, the modern system of English units is commonly called the customary units. Similar systems developed in different countries.

CGS Units. The CGS (centimeter-gram-second) system of units is the oldest of several extended versions of the metric system. It developed as an attempt to define a system that could be derived from a limited set of base units: the unit of length was the centimeter (cm), 1/100 of the length of the meter bar maintained in Paris; the unit of mass was the gram (g), 1/1000 of the kilogram; and the unit of time, the second (s), was determined from astronomical observations. The units for most other quantities were derived by using the systems of equations relating different quantities. Thus the unit of velocity would be cm/s, the unit of momentum g•cm/s, and the unit of force g•cm/s² (which later came to be called the dyne). New definitions, however, were needed for other units, particularly in the relatively new fields of electricity and magnetism. The unit of electric charge could be defined either from

TABLE 1: EXAMPLES OF SI DERIVED UNITS EXPRESSED IN TERMS OF BASE UNITS

Quantity	SI Unit	
	Name	Symbol
Area	Square meter	m^2
Volume	Cubic meter	m^3
Speed (velocity)	Meter per second	m/s
Acceleration	Meter per second squared	m/s^2
Wave number	Waves per meter	m^{-1}
Mass density	Kilogram per cubic meter	kg/m^3
Current density	Ampere per square meter	A/m^2
Magnetic field strength	Ampere per meter	A/m
Concentration (of amount of substance)	Mole per cubic meter	mol/m^3
Specific volume	Cubic meter per kilogram	m^3/kg
Luminance	Candela per square meter	cd/m^2

COULOMB'S LAW or from the electromagnetic force exerted by a flowing charge. Two different units, the statcoulomb and the abcoulomb, were thus defined and were shown to be related by a factor of 3×10^{10} cm/sec, the speed of light.

MKS Units. The size of the CGS units made it difficult to accept them as practical units, especially in the growing electrical industry. To get around this difficulty, a new fundamental unit of current was defined, based on the coulomb, the unit of charge, which was set at 1 coulomb = 0.10 abcoulomb. The MKS system was thus determined by four base units—the meter, the kilogram, the second, and the ampere (1 coulomb per second)—and is sometimes referred to as the MKSA system.

Gaussian Units. A hybrid CGS system of both electrostatic and electromagnetic units has been used in the solution of problems clearly either electrostatic or electromagnetic in nature. The system is called the gaussian system of units.

Gravitational Units. For certain engineering applications it was found convenient to use the unit of force as a base unit, instead of the unit of mass. In this system the unit of mass is defined as the unit of force divided by the unit of gravitational acceleration, hence the term gravitational unit. In the customary gravitational system, the pound-force (lb_f) is the unit of force that defines the slug, the unit of mass (1 lb_f = 1 slug-ft/sec^2). The work unit is the foot-pound force (ft-lb_f).

SI (International System of Units). The General Conference on Weights and Measures, which was established by the Treaty of the Meter (1875) and which normally meets every 6 years, has assumed the responsibility for establishing a rational system of units. To describe completely all independent physical measurements, three new base units were introduced. To the four base units of the MKS system (the meter, the kilogram, the second, and the ampere) were added the units for the quantities of temperature (the kelvin, K), amount of substance (the mole, mol), and luminous intensity (the candela, cd). In 1960 the General Conference laid down rules for prefixes and the derived and supplementary units.

ARTHUR O. McCOUBREY AND DAVID T. GOLDMAN

Bibliography: Davis, T. S., *Constant Processes* (1978); Dresner, Stephen, *Units of Measurement* (1971); Goldman, D. T., and Bell, R. J., eds., *International System of Units (SI)*, 5th ed. (1986); Johnstone, W. D., *For Good Measure* (1975); Le Maraic, A. L., and Ciaramella, J. P., eds., *The Complete Metric System with the International System of Units*, rev. ed. (1973); Massey, B. S., *Measures in Science and Engineering* (1986); Wildi, Theodore, *Units*, 2d ed. (1972).

See also: ATOMIC CONSTANTS; MEASUREMENT.

UNIVAC

UNIVAC (Universal Automatic Computer) is the trade name of a line of electronic digital COMPUTERS produced by the Remington-Rand Univac Division of the Sperry-Rand Corporation. The first of these, the UNIVAC I computer built by Remington-Rand and accepted by the U.S. Bureau of the Census in April 1951, is generally credited as being the first commercially available stored-program electronic digital computer. Its design was based on the EDVAC, a machine planned by John Presper ECKERT and John W. MAUCHLY in association with John VON NEUMANN at the Moore School of Electrical Engineering of the University of Pennsylvania in 1946.

UNIVAC I employed for memory a unique system based on binary acoustic signals. It had twin arithmetic units run in parallel for error detection and converted binary information from memory into "words," each consisting of 12 alphabetic or decimal quantities. Arithmetic was performed on these words at a rate of 2,000 additions or 450 multiplications per second. Internal memory capacity was 1,000 words. Provision was made for high rates of data exchange with an external magnetic tape memory of large capacity and with high-speed printers. UNIVAC I was intended for statistical usage. By 1958 nearly 50 of the computers had been produced, but all of them have subsequently been phased out of service. The current UNIVAC 1100 series of computer systems, which began in the early 1960s, comprises a number of medium to large general-purpose data-processing models.   JULIAN BIGELOW

Bibliography: Williams, M. R., *A History of Computing Technology* (1985).

universal joint: see TRANSMISSION, AUTOMOTIVE.

universal language: see LANGUAGES, ARTIFICIAL.

Universal Postal Union: see POSTAL UNION, UNIVERSAL.

universal time: see TIME.

TABLE 2: SI DERIVED UNITS WITH SPECIAL NAMES

Quantity	SI Unit Name	Symbol	Expression in Terms of Other Units	Expression in Terms of SI Base Units
Frequency	Hertz	Hz		s^{-1}
Force	Newton	N		$m \cdot kg \cdot s^{-2}$
Pressure	Pascal	Pa	N/m^2	$m^{-1} \cdot kg \cdot s^{-2}$
Energy, work, quantity of heat	Joule	J	$N \cdot m$	$m^2 \cdot kg \cdot s^{-2}$
Power, radiant flux	Watt	W	J/s	$m^2 \cdot kg \cdot s^{-3}$
Quantity of electricity, electric charge	Coulomb	C	$A \cdot s$	$s \cdot A$
Electric potential, potential difference, electromotive force	Volt	V	W/A	$m^2 \cdot kg \cdot s^{-3} \cdot A^{-1}$
Capacitance	Farad	F	C/V	$m^{-2} \cdot kg^{-1} \cdot s^4 \cdot A^2$
Electric resistance	Ohm	Ω	V/A	$m^2 \cdot kg \cdot s^{-3} \cdot A^{-2}$
Conductance	Siemens	s	a/v	$M^{-2} \cdot kg^{-1} \cdot s^3 \cdot A^2$
Magnetic flux	Weber	Wb	$V \cdot s$	$m^2 \cdot kg \cdot s^{-2} \cdot A^{-1}$
Magnetic flux density	Tesla	T	Wb/m^2	$kg \cdot s^{-2} \cdot A^{-1}$
Inductance	Henry	H	Wb/A	$m^2 \cdot kg \cdot s^{-2} \cdot A^{-2}$
Luminous flux	Lumen	lm		$cd \cdot sr^*$
Illuminance	Lux	lx		$m^{-2} \cdot cd \cdot sr^*$
Celsius temperature	Degree Celsius	°C		K

*In this expression the steradian (sr) is treated as a base unit.

TABLE 3: EXAMPLES OF SI DERIVED UNITS EXPRESSED BY MEANS OF SPECIAL NAMES

Quantity	SI Unit Name	Symbol	Expression in Terms of SI Base Units
Dynamic viscosity	Pascal second	Pa·s	$m^{-1} \cdot kg \cdot s^{-1}$
Moment of force	Meter newton	N·m	$m^2 kg \cdot s^{-2}$
Surface tension	Newton per meter	N/m	$kg \cdot s^{-2}$
Power density, heat flux density, irradiance	Watt per square meter	W/m^2	$kg \cdot s^{-2}$
Heat capacity, entropy	Joule per kelvin	J/K	$m^2 \cdot kg \cdot s^{-2} K^{-1}$
Specific heat capacity, specific entropy	Joule per kilogram kelvin	J/(kg·K)	$m^2 \cdot s^{-2} \cdot K^{-1}$
Specific energy	Juole per kilogram	J/kg	$m^2 \cdot s^{-2}$
Thermal conductivity	Watt per meter kelvin	W/(m·K)	$m \cdot kg \cdot s^{-3} \cdot K^{-1}$
Energy density	Joule per cubic meter	J/m^3	$m^{-1} \cdot kg \cdot s^{-2}$
Electric field strength	Volt per meter	V/m	$m \cdot kg \cdot s^{-3} \cdot A^{-1}$
Electric charge density	Coulomb per cubic meter	C/m^3	$m^{-3} \cdot s \cdot A^{-1}$
Electric flux density	Coulomb per square meter	C/m^2	$m^{-2} \cdot s \cdot A$
Permittivity	Farad per meter	F/m	$m^{-3} \cdot kg^{-1} \cdot s^4 \cdot A^2$

universalism

Universalism is the theological doctrine that all souls will ultimately be saved and that there are no torments of hell. Universalism has been asserted at various times in different contexts throughout the history of the Christian church, as for example by Origen in the 3d century. As an organized religious movement, however, universalism dates from the late 1700s in America, where its early leaders were Hosea BALLOU, John MURRAY, and Elhanan Winchester. As a form of religious liberalism, it has had close contacts with UNITARIANISM throughout its history. The Universalist Church of America and the American Unitarian Association merged in 1961 to form a single denomination—the UNITARIAN UNIVERSALIST ASSOCIATION—which currently has about 172,000 members.

Bibliography: Casara, Ernest, ed., *Universalism in America* (1984).

universals

In philosophy, universals are general terms or abstract concepts, of which there may be particular individual instances. For example, *red* is a universal, of which the red square is an instance. Universals are considered essential to thought and language, but differing views exist as to their origin and nature of existence. A realist (see REALISM, philosophy), such as Plato, maintains that universals are eternal objects existing independently of the mind, although not in space and time. Conceptualists, such as Saint Thomas Aquinas and Saint Augustine, hold that universals are ideas in the mind of God or abstractions of the human intellect, as opposed to independent objects. Nominalists (see NOMINALISM), such as the medieval William of Occam and the contemporary Nelson Goodman, argue that universals are merely words, used to refer to the similarity among objects considered collectively.

Bibliography: Aaron, R. I., *Our Knowledge of Universals* (1975); Miller, J. W., *The Midworld of Symbols and Functioning Objects* (1982).

universe

The term *universe,* in astronomy, refers to all known and inferred celestial materials, including the Earth, and to the SPACE-TIME CONTINUUM in which they exist. The study of the universe as a whole is called COSMOLOGY.

Mythology and religion provide many CREATION ACCOUNTS of the origin of the universe. Through the centuries people also learned increasingly more about its physical nature. By the late 20th century the most widely accepted scientific theory of the origin of the universe was the BIG BANG THEORY. In elaborations of this concept, the universe is described as having expanded extremely rapidly, some 14 to 20 billion years ago, from an initial singularity, or "point" of virtual nothingness (see INFLATIONARY THEORY). According to the conceptually difficult general RELATIVITY theory, the universe has neither boundary nor center but is self-contained within the curvature of space-time. The physical universe appears to consist of vast "bubbles" of seemingly empty space, the "surface" of these bubbles being a frothlike network of EXTRAGALACTIC SYSTEMS of stars such as our own Milky Way system (see GALAXY, THE).

Some versions of current inflationary theory suggest that an infinity of universes might be capable of forming as did the known universe. These universes, however, would forever lie beyond the possibility of contact with this one.

university

A university is an institution of higher education that teaches the most advanced learning of its time and place and usually also fosters research in the sciences, humanities, and social sciences.

Traditionally a university consists of several colleges or faculties, including an undergraduate school and graduate schools in such fields as the arts and sciences, law, medicine, theology, engineering, and other professions (see GRADUATE EDUCATION). In terms of this standard definition, a university is clearly distinct from a college, which is a single school usually devoted to the education of undergraduates and sometimes to the training of future members of a profession. However, in the United States the line between university and college has become blurred, as some colleges call themselves universities. Universities, however, generally place greater emphasis on research by members of the faculty.

U.S. Universities. Most universities throughout the world offer some combination of training in the arts and sciences and in the traditionally respected learned professions. In Europe, undergraduate students spend almost all their time studying a single subject or a small group of subjects, thus specializing at an earlier age than American students, who are expected to choose a wide number and range of courses to obtain a general education, usually focusing on a single major subject only halfway through their undergraduate career. The commonly stated reason for this contrast is that U.S. high schools are of relatively poor quality, requiring that much general training be received on the college and university level. In fact European students usually do not receive a broadly balanced liberal education of the kind known in the United States.

American university students are tested at frequent intervals, often several times in each lecture course they take. As a rule, however, European students take few tests but are given intensive examinations at the end of their entire span of study. Outside the United States, technical training for the less traditional professions, for instance those requiring new kinds of technological skill, is usually conducted in institutes outside the university. Only in the United States do universities routinely encompass practical vocational subjects in fields as diverse as business management, filmmaking, pharmacy, veterinary science, and education of handicapped children.

The U.S. university thus tends to be a much more inclusive institution than the European; it comprehends almost any kind of advanced education. Likewise, it enrolls a much larger share of the young adult population than is the case in Western Europe. In 1988, U.S. colleges and universities enrolled approximately 12.5 million students, or about 50 percent of the country's college-age population. Nowhere in Western Europe were more than 35 percent of young adults accommodated in institutions of higher education; in Britain, for example, the figure was 14 percent. Nonetheless, European universities have expanded a great deal since World War II and have enrolled increasingly larger proportions of their students from working-class backgrounds. In Italy the universities have been opened to anyone who applies, although university facilities are strained because of the large numbers of students.

The University and the Employment Market. Although the U.S. rate of attendance is remarkably high, about half of American youth do not attend college or university, but end their education with high school or in short-term vocational programs. One reason some young people do not go on to college or university is parental expectation, or the general environment in which the child has been reared. In the United States most children grow up in circumstances that impel them to choose a job at the age of 18, a job that requires less skill and offers the immediate reward of a regular paycheck.

These may be among the factors explaining why a large proportion—at some periods as many as half—of those who begin college or university in the United States fail to complete the bachelor's degree awarded at the end of it.

The rational argument for attending college has always been that it greatly enhances earning power over a lifetime, although the college student makes a short-term sacrifice in earnings. In recent decades pay differences between many skilled and less-skilled occupations have dropped, and it has been contended that college or university training therefore offers fewer practical advantages. This may be true, but the advantage is still substantial. Although the overall economic situation varies over time, studies have shown that males with bachelor of arts degrees earned an average of about one-third more than those with only high-school educations.

Over the same years, there was an overproduction of graduate degrees in many areas—for instance, in the arts and sciences related to teaching careers, and possibly in law. It became difficult to find jobs in many fields that are considered attractive, for several reasons. U.S. universities overexpanded during the 1960s. A greatly lowered birthrate then created far less demand for teachers, because the population included fewer young people. Meanwhile the economy slowed, and there was a desire to hold down taxes, which furnish the support both for the educational system and for government employment in many areas requiring skill. U.S. colleges and universities therefore experienced a static or declining period in terms of enrollment. In the late 1980s, however, the number of applications sharply rose—taking many institutions by surprise. When many students over time faced the question of how good were the prospects for bright professional careers, one area remained relatively unaffected, opportunities in business careers.

The Development of the U.S. University. U.S. colleges and universities take a number of distinct forms. The earliest colleges, the oldest of which is Harvard College, founded in 1636, were private and had liberal arts programs. These institutions were extremely small and primitive by present standards. The same course of study was prescribed for everyone. Greek, Latin, and mathematics dominated the curriculum, which was based on that of the universities of Oxford and Cambridge. Seniors were given lectures, often by the college president himself, in philosophy. Most learning was by rote, and the tone of instruction was that of a school rather than a modern university. Yet advanced learning of any kind was treasured in colonial times. A strong desire existed to maintain a learned clergy in that highly religious age. Yet the early colleges also produced doctors, lawyers, and merchants. Their graduates, not all of whom came from wealthy families, were a small elite in the colonies, although a self-made man like Benjamin Franklin, who had no college education, could rise to prominence. As time went on, the new scientific learning of the European Enlightenment was incorporated into the colleges, where it was harmonized with Christian theology. Nature was believed to testify to God's intrinsic design. The amount of science teaching in the colleges increased during the early 19th century, although the curriculum remained largely prescribed and the study of classic languages was still enforced. As the West opened, hundreds of small colleges were founded.

One of the earliest state universities was created by Thomas Jefferson in Virginia in 1819. State universities promised a more democratic and practical approach to higher education, but for a long time they, too, were small, insecure institutions enforcing a surprisingly conventional curriculum in the classics and maintaining compulsory religious services. In 1862 the U.S. Congress passed the MORRILL ACT, which gave federal lands to states that would establish colleges devoted to agriculture and the mechanical arts. Some states used the funds from the sale of these lands to build their state universities; others established special agricultural colleges, though most of these later became universities as well. The land-grant colleges, as these institutions were called, slowly expanded in a more scientific direction until in the 20th century they often became very large and comprehensive, although they were devoted especially to technical and vocational training.

After the U.S. Civil War a spirit of reform captured the older private colleges. Cornell University, founded in 1866 partly with land-grant funds, and Harvard University, under the presidency of Charles W. ELIOT after 1869, took the lead in creating modern university education for undergraduates in the United States. The elective system of studies was introduced, under which students could choose their own courses from a wide variety of increasingly specialized subjects. Each subject became an academic department, run by the faculty teaching that subject; this collective control, rather than control by a single all-powerful professor in each field, has remained a distinctive feature of U.S., in contrast to European, university education. Departments began to take form in the 1880s and were fully developed by 1900, when Greek and Latin were generally dropped as required studies.

Meanwhile, a second wave of university reform, inspired by German universities, created graduate education. The Johns Hopkins University, founded in 1875 in Baltimore, Md., was the first U.S. educational institution committed to the idea of

a university. Most of the prestigious existing private universities, most of which by this time no longer called themselves colleges, adopted the idea of graduate education. Toward the end of the 19th century, major private universities were founded, including Stanford University and the University of Chicago in 1891. Yale University (1701) and Princeton University (1746) long tried to remain conservative, but gradually they followed the tide of innovation. Some state universities, at first the universities of Michigan, Wisconsin, and California, imitated the reformed private universities to become major centers of learning.

By the first decade of the 20th century, the U.S. university, whether private or public, had assumed its characteristic shape. It had become an extremely diverse, bureaucratic institution, devoted to a combination of general training in the liberal arts, training for the professions, and advanced scholarship and research. Faculty members were now expected to have a Ph.D. and to engage in research and publication.

Some critics said that the U.S. university resembled a vast department store, in which the numbered course offerings were like highly varied wares for sale. They complained about the size and power of the academic administration that had emerged to run the undertaking, noting that European universities often managed without it. Yet the European pattern actually involved an entrenched faculty conservatism, unresponsive to new demands, and (outside of England) a great measure of governmental control.

The period from the 1890s through the 1960s was marked by an enormous expansion in enrollments in U.S. universities and colleges. In 1900 there were 237,592 undergraduates in the United States, and only 4 percent of the age group attended college or university. This rose to 14 percent by 1940 and increased greatly after World War II, when the G.I. BILL OF RIGHTS legislation permitted veterans to attend colleges and universities at government expense. In 1985 there were 11,118,000 undergraduates enrolled in bachelor's degree credit programs in U.S. institutions of higher education and 1,129,000 students in graduate programs. In 1985 there were 3,340 U.S. institutions of higher education, of which 2,029 offered a 4-year program and the remaining 1,311 a 2-year program.

Around 1900 the smaller liberal arts colleges were often surpassed by the new or reformed universities. After 1910 a number of them were upgraded while remaining exclusively devoted to liberal education without advanced graduate training. Some pioneered in curricular experiments, especially in the humanities and fine arts. A few institutes of technology specialized instead in science education. But most institutions offered courses of study in all the important fields of learning. By 1910 the elective system had been universally modified to enforce requirements in several fields and to institute the subject major, with its own series of often demanding requirements within a particular field. The subject major grew in importance at leading universities after World War II, when there came into being a new level of seriousness and specialization in undergraduate education. By 1960 three-quarters of American college seniors aspired to go to graduate school. The liberal arts ideal continued, but beginning in the 1970s it seemed to suffer, at least away from the eastern United States, not only from the emphasis on research that had come to dominate universities since the 1950s, but also from a new wave of student demand for a more practical preparation for careers.

After World War II two other types of institution appeared in great numbers. Former state-run normal schools (teacher-training colleges) sought to upgrade themselves to full-scale liberal arts colleges, frequently styling themselves as state universities. Also, at first in California, but spreading nationally, a vast group of 2-year community (or junior) colleges came into existence, offering basic liberal arts courses for students intending to transfer to 4-year colleges or universities, along with terminal vocational training for other high school graduates. Some of these institutions are of high quality, but won popularity by their easy availability to students who could afford only to study part-time. In 1985 about 37 percent of

SELECTED HISTORICAL UNIVERSITIES OF THE WORLD

University and Location	Date Founded	Enrollment
Al-Azhar University, Cairo, Egypt	970	90,000
University of Basel, Switzerland	1460	6,600
University of Bologna, Italy	11th century	59,000
University of Bombay, India	1857	162,000
Cambridge University, United Kingdom	13th century	11,600
Catholic University of Louvain, Belgium	1425	23,000 (Dutch lang.) 18,000 (French lang.)
College of William and Mary, Williamsburg, Va., U.S.A.	1693	7,000
University of Copenhagen, Denmark	1479	24,500
University of Edinburgh, United Kingdom	1583	11,600
Georg-August University of Göttingen, West Germany	1737	30,000
Hacettepe University, Ankara, Turkey	1206	21,300
Harvard University, Cambridge, Mass., U.S.A.	1636	24,000
Istanbul University, Turkey	1453	30,000
Jagiellonian University, Kraków, Poland	1364	10,200
Laval University, Quebec, Canada	1852	20,800
Leningrad A. A. Zhdanov State University, USSR	1819	20,000
University of Lisbon, Portugal	1288	17,200
Loránd Eötvös University, Budapest, Hungary	1635	8,000
Martin Luther University, Halle-Wittenburg, East Germany	1502	8,600
University of Melbourne, Australia	1853	16,000
University of Montreal, Canada	1878	47,900
Moscow M. V. Lomonosov State University, USSR	1755	28,000
National Autonomous University of Mexico, Mexico City	1551	327,000
National University of Córdoba, Argentina	1613	70,000
National University of San Marcos, Lima, Peru	1551	34,200
University of North Carolina, Chapel Hill, N.C., U.S.A.	1795	23,000
Oxford University, United Kingdom	13th century	13,000
University of Paris, France	12th century	245,000
Peking (Beijing) University, China	1898	19,000
University of Pennsylvania, Philadelphia, Pa., U.S.A.	1740	22,500
Quaraouyine University, Fez, Morocco	859	3,600
Royal and Pontifical University of San Francisco Xavier of Chuquisaca, Sucre, Bolivia	1624	10,150
University of St. Andrews, United Kingdom	1411	3,800
University of Salamanca, Spain	1218	22,000
University of San Carlos of Guatemala, Guatemala City	1676	50,000
University of Santo Domingo, Dominican Republic	1538	52,200
University of Santo Tomas, Manila, Philippines	1611	45,150
State University of Leiden, Netherlands	1575	17,900
University of Sydney, Australia	1850	18,400
Tartu State University, USSR	1632	7,360
University of Tokyo, Japan	1877	20,300
University of Toronto, Canada	1827	51,000
Trinity College, Dublin, Ireland	1592	7,800
University of Uppsala, Sweden	1477	18,000
University of Vienna, Austria	1375	72,000
Vilnius Kapsukas State University, USSR	1579	16,700
Xavier Pontifical University, Bogotá, Colombia	1622	12,500
University of Zagreb, Yugoslavia	1669	41,200

SOURCE: *The World of Learning 1988* (1987).

American undergraduates were attending community colleges. There are colleges operated by religious denominations to cater to their own memberships, and there are colleges that have predominantly black enrollments.

Women's colleges had existed in the East since the 19th century, despite the rapid spread of coeducation before 1900, but in the early 1970s women were admitted to men's colleges, and men were admitted to some colleges hitherto reserved for women. Women had been attending college in the United States in increasing numbers since the 1890s, but in the 1970s their enrollment grew to represent nearly their share of the population. In the 1980s the number of women enrolled consistently exceeded the number of men enrolled (1985: 6,429,000 females; 5,818,000 males).

In 1986 nonwhites (mostly blacks) accounted for 15 percent of the total U.S. degree credit enrollment; the black enrollment in 1976 was 8.4 percent. This trend marked a significant change since the 1930s, when blacks were sometimes barred from major private universities. During the 1980s there was at least as much intellectual freedom as at any earlier time, although the politicization of students and faculties, which had erupted suddenly during the Vietnam War, largely subsided during the 1970s. In nonpolitical ways students have always been prone to high-spirited behavior.

U.S. universities were beset with problems during the 1980s. Private universities faced rising costs, which in turn resulted in higher tuition fees, and feared the competition of high-quality but less-expensive state universities. On average, the inflation-adjusted cost of a bachelor of arts degree rose 26 percent from 1980 to 1988; during that period the median income of families with college-age children rose only 5 percent. Government-subsidized student loans were down 13 percent, compounding the problems connected with the ever-higher costs of higher education. The spurt in applications in 1988 suggested that the prolonged decline and stagnation in enrollment experienced by many universities might be ending—despite the burdensome fees.

Academic purposes seemed less clear. The liberal arts curriculum suffered from lack of common agreement as to what every educated person should know. One prominent dispute involved the study of present-day values and the sources of American culture; some educators wanted to shift the emphasis from traditional European foundations to include the contributions of blacks, Hispanics, Asians, and American Indians.

Despite the problems, however, the enormously expanded base of operation for U.S. higher education created in the period 1945–70 has essentially remained intact.

LAURENCE VEYSEY

Bibliography: Ben-David, Joseph, *Trends in American Higher Education* (1981); Blits, Jan H., ed., *The American University: Problems, Prospects and Trends* (1985); Boyer, Ernest, *College: The Undergraduate Experience in America* (1988); Chapman, John W., ed., *The Western University on Trial* (1983); Makdisi, George, *The Rise of Colleges: Institutions of Learning in Islam and the West* (1982); Portman, David, ed., *Early Reform in American Higher Education* (1972); Prange, W. Werner, and Jowett, David, *Tomorrow's Universities: A World Wide Look at Educational Change* (1982); Rudolph, Frederick, *Curriculum: A History of the American Undergraduate Course of Study since 1636* (1977); Veysey, Laurence R., *The Emergence of the American University* (1965; repr. 1970).

University of California v. Bakke

In the case of *University of California* v. *Bakke* (1978), the U.S. Supreme Court held that even though universities may consider race and ethnic origins as a factor in evaluating candidates for admission, universities may not establish fixed racial quotas. The case arose when the medical school of the University of California at Davis twice rejected Allan Bakke's application while admitting members of racial minorities who had lower test scores. Bakke charged that the medical school's policy of setting aside 16 of 100 positions for racial minorities was a violation of the equal protection clause of the 14th Amendment.

In a complex 5–4 decision the Supreme Court ordered that Bakke be admitted, but the majority justices gave different reasons for their decision. One—Justice Lewis Powell—based his opinion on 14th Amendment grounds. The other four, including Chief Justice Warren Burger, ruled against the university on the ground that it had violated the Civil Rights Act of

1964, which provided that no person might be excluded from any federally funded institution because of race. The decision was viewed by some as a setback for U.S. blacks in their struggle for equality. Others saw it as a vindication of an individual's right to be judged on the basis of merit rather than race.   ROBERT J. STEAMER

Bibliography: Wilkinson, J. H., *From Brown to Bakke: The Supreme Court and School Integration, 1954–1978* (1979).

See also: EQUAL OPPORTUNITY; UNITED STEELWORKERS OF AMERICA V. WEBER.

University Wits

The University Wits were a group of playwrights, well-versed in classical literature, who helped shape the course of Elizabethan drama and profoundly influenced Shakespeare. They combined their learning with a keen understanding of the tastes of their Elizabethan audiences. The group included such diverse talents as Robert GREENE, Thomas KYD, John LYLY, and Christopher MARLOWE.

Unkei   [oon'-kay]

Unkei, b. 1148, d. Dec. 21, 1223, was a leader among the Japanese sculptors commissioned to restore the Todaiji, the great Buddhist temple in Nara, on which he worked from 1199 until his death. Unkei established the Kamakura period style of Japanese Buddhist sculpture, in which classic Nara-period forms are combined with the immediacy and realism of Sung Chinese sculpture. Unkei's followers (the Kei school) dominated the sculptural production of the 13th and 14th centuries.
                                           BARBARA BRENNAN FORD

Bibliography: Mori, Hisashi, *Sculpture of the Kamakura Period,* trans. by Katherine Eickmann (1974).

unknown soldier

The unknown soldier is an unidentified wartime casualty who has, since World War I, been memorialized by various countries as a representative of all those who died in their nation's service. In Paris, France, the tomb for the unknown soldier lies under the Arc de Triomphe (Arch of Triumph). In London, England, the unknown soldier's tomb is in Westminster Abbey. In the United States, four unknown servicemen—one from each world war, one from the Korean War, and one from the Vietnam War—are now buried in the Tomb of the Unknowns at Arlington National Cemetery in Virginia.

Unruh, Fritz von   [uhn'-roo]

The German playwright and novelist Fritz von Unruh, b. May 10, 1885, d. Nov. 28, 1970, although the son of a Prussian general and himself an officer during World War I, took a consistently antiwar stand in his writings. *Offiziere* (Officers, 1911), *Louis Ferdinand, Prinz von Preussen* (Louis Ferdinand, Prince of Prussia, 1913), and the pacifist *Ein Geschlecht* (A Family, 1917) all exhibit the near hysteria of early expressionist theater. His novel *The Way of Sacrifice* (1918; Eng. trans., 1928) gives a firsthand account of the carnage at the Battle of Verdun. Alarmed by the rise of the Nazis during the 1920s, Unruh went into self-imposed exile in Italy, France, and, in 1940, the United States. He returned to Germany in 1948, left—again embittered—in 1955, but returned finally in 1962.

Bibliography: Kronacher, Alwin, *Fritz von Unruh* (1946).

Unser, Al   [uhn'-sur]

Al Unser, b. Albuquerque, N.Mex., May 29, 1939, is an American racing car driver whose success culminated in wins at the Indianapolis 500-mi (804.7-km) race in 1970, 1971, 1978, and 1987; he is only the second man to have won the race four times. Unser competed in numerous Pike's Peak Hill Climb races, finishing second in 1960 and 1962 and first in 1964 and 1965. In 1968, Unser finished third in the United States Auto Club (USAC) National Championship rankings; in 1969, 1977, and 1978 he was ranked second, and he achieved first-place ranking in 1970. During his career Unser won over 35 National Championship races.

Unser, Bobby

Robert William Unser, b. Albuquerque, N.Mex., Feb. 20, 1934, is an American racing car driver who won the Indianapolis 500-mi (804.7-km) race in 1968, 1975, and 1981. He comes from a family of racing car drivers—his father was a driver and Bobby has competed in numerous races against his younger brother, Al—and started racing in 1949. Unser gained early fame in the Pike's Peak Hill Climb, which he won 12 times. In 1963 he entered his first Indianapolis race, and in 1968, the year of his first victory there, he gained the United States Auto Club (USAC) National Championship. He was National Champion again in 1974. During his career Unser won more than 25 National Championship races.

Untermeyer, Louis   [uhn'-tur-my-ur]

Poets and readers owe a great debt to the American editor and anthologist Louis Untermeyer, b. New York City, Oct. 1, 1885, d. Dec. 18, 1977. His *Modern American Poetry* (originally titled *Modern American Verse,* 1919) and *Modern British Poetry* (1920) have gone through numerous editions with each serving as a barometer for measuring the changing reputation and appeal of poets. Despite his personal sympathy for poets like Frost, Untermeyer tried to be catholic in his selection, and included many avant-garde writers. In his own poetry he showed a delightful humor. His works include many other anthologies, *Collected Parodies* (1926), translations, children's books, a novel, biographies, and two autobiographies: *From Another World* (1939) and *Bygones* (1965).   JAMES HART

Untouchables

Untouchables, now called Harijans, have traditionally occupied the lowest place in the CASTE system of Hindu India; they were called untouchable because they were considered to be outside the confines of caste. Their impurity derived from their traditional occupations, which might involve the taking of life (fishermen), working with carcasses (leatherworkers), or touching bodily wastes (laundrymen, sweepers). Traditionally, they were banned from Hindu temples; in parts of South India even the sight of an Untouchable was sufficient to pollute a member of a higher caste. In 1949 the Indian government outlawed the use of the term *Untouchables*. The group has been reclassified as the "Scheduled Castes" and has been granted special educational and political privileges. Today it is illegal to discriminate against a Harijan, yet they remain generally at the bottom of the caste hierarchy, performing the most menial roles demanded by society. The scheduled castes numbered more than 1 million in the early 1980s.
                         HILARY STANDING AND R. L. STIRRAT

Bibliography: Aggarwal, P. C., *Halfway to Equality: The Harijans of India* (1983); Das, D. P., *The Untouchables Story* (1985); Freeman, J. M., *Untouchable: An Indian Life History* (1979); Juergensmeyer, M., *Religion as a Social Vision* (1982); Kshirsagar, R. K., *Untouchability in India* (1982); Mahar, J. M., ed., *Untouchables in Contemporary India* (1972).

Up from Slavery

Up from Slavery (1901), the autobiography of the noted black educator Booker T. WASHINGTON, chronicles his rise from slavery to founder of Tuskegee Institute (1881), a school designed to provide vocational training for young blacks. Washington's emphasis on economic gains as the best route to black advancement, and his exclusion of political and social agitation as untimely, eventually led to his break with W. E. B. Du BOIS and other founders of the NAACP.

Upanishads   [oo-pan'-i-shadz]

The Upanishads are chronologically the latest portions of the VEDAS, the sacred texts of Hinduism. The earliest Upanishads, probably dating from 900 to 600 BC, represent the first development of philosophical reflections in Sanskrit literature; later works have also been accepted from time to time as Upanishads. According to a widespread tradition the oldest Upanishads are the Isa, Kena, Katha, Prasna, Mundaka, Mandukya, Taittiriya, Aitareya, Chandogya, Brhadaranyaka, Svetasvatara, Kaushitaki, and Maitri Upanishads. The material they comprise is part poetry, part prose. They contain didactic stories, allegories, and passages for meditation, a number of which are repeated in more than one Upanishad or elsewhere in the Vedic corpus. The fundamental concern of the Upanishads is the nature of reality. They teach the identity of the individual soul (atman) with the universal essence soul (Brahman). Because they are the final portions of the Vedas, they are also known as VEDANTA, ''the end of the Vedas,'' and their thought, as interpreted in succeeding centuries, is likewise known as Vedanta.

KARL H. POTTER

Bibliography: Deussen, Paul, *The Philosophy of the Upanishads* (1960); Easwaren, E., *The Upanishads: A Selection* (1987); Nikam, N. A., *Ten Principal Upanishads: Some Fundamental Ideas* (1974); Sharma, S., *Life in the Upanishads* (1985).

upas tree   [yoo'-puhs]

Upas tree is the common name for *Antiaris toxicaria* in the family Moraceae. Native to the tropics of Africa and Asia, these trees may reach 76 m (250 ft) high. They bear oblong, deciduous leaves and small pear-shaped fruits (drupes). The latex of the upas is highly toxic and has been used for poisoning arrows. In some areas the tree was fabled to be so poisonous that humans or animals who came close to it died.

Updike, John   [uhp'-dyk]

Famous among contemporary writers for his rich, elegant prose and the craftsmanship of his short stories and his many novels, John Hoyer Updike, b. Shillington, Pa., Mar. 18, 1932, was trained as a graphic artist. As an English major at Harvard (1950–54), he contributed cartoons, verse, and parodies to the *Harvard Lampoon.* Following a Knox Fellowship at the Ruskin School of Drawing and Fine Arts at Oxford (1954–55), Updike became a staff writer for the *New Yorker.* In 1957 he moved to Massachusetts to devote himself to fiction.

Middle-class manners, examined from almost every possible perspective, are Updike's favorite subject. The novel *Rabbit Run* (1960) and the story collection *Pigeon Feathers* (1962) are representative works from Updike's early period. Like Rabbit, many of Updike's later characters confuse sexuality with spiritual ecstasy, notably in *Couples* (1968). Updike's fondness for writing books in series has produced three Rabbit novels (the third, *Rabbit is Rich,* 1981, won a Pulitzer Prize);

John Updike began his writing career in the mid-1950s with short stories in the New Yorker *and has since written novels, poems, and critical pieces noted for their brilliant use of the language. Although Updike often explores the conflict between mundane existence and the possibility of higher purpose, he is also capable of writing lighter fare, such as* The Witches of Eastwick *(1984).*

Photo Jill Krementz © 1978

two books about the misadventures of Henry Bech (*Bech: A Book,* 1970; *Bech is Back,* 1982); and three novels that, in different ways, refer to *The Scarlet Letter* of Nathaniel Hawthorne: *A Month of Sundays* (1975), *Roger's Version* (1986), and *S* (1988), in which the main character is a contemporary Hester Prynne.

Updike has also achieved a reputation as a perceptive book reviewer in his pieces for the *New Yorker,* and as a poet.

JEROME KLINKOWITZ

Bibliography: Greiner, D. T., *John Updike's Novels,* 2d ed. (1985); Macnaughton, W. R., *Critical Essays on John Updike* (1982).

upholstery: see FURNITURE.

UPI: see PRESS AGENCIES AND SYNDICATES.

Upjohn, Richard

The architect Richard Upjohn, b. England, Jan. 22, 1802, d. Feb. 17, 1878, a devout Episcopalian, came to the United States in 1829 and devoted most of his career to the design of churches. His Trinity Church in New York City (1839–46) became the paradigm of fastidiously composed and detailed GOTHIC REVIVAL churches in America; Upjohn himself produced many variations of it. Often more original and sympathetic were his small rural churches built of wood. These became so popular that he published a group of designs and instructions for building them in *Upjohn's Rural Architecture* (1852). Upjohn also designed houses in various revivalist styles.

ANN VAN ZANTEN

Bibliography: Upjohn, E. M., *Richard Upjohn* (1939; repr. 1968).

upper class: see CLASS, SOCIAL.

Upper Volta: see BURKINA FASO.

Uppsala   [uhp'-sah-lah]

The city of Uppsala, a major Swedish cultural center, lies about 70 km (45 mi) north of Stockholm and has a population of 154,859 (1986 est.). Uppsala's industries manufacture machinery, clothing, drugs, musical instruments, and food products. Printing and publishing are also important. The University of Uppsala (1477) is Sweden's oldest institution of higher learning.

Gamla Uppsala, now a suburb 5 km (3 mi) to the north of the modern city, was the religious and political capital of the Vikings. Uppsala became the seat of the archbishop of Sweden in 1164 and a royal residence in the next century. The philosopher Emanuel Swedenborg and the scientist Carolus Linnaeus are buried in the 15th-century cathedral.

Upward Bound

Upward Bound is an educational program that emerged from the War on Poverty, launched by the U.S. government in the mid-1960s. The program seeks to motivate educationally and socially deprived high school students with academic potential to acquire a college education and help them to develop positive personal and social goals.

upwelling, oceanic

Oceanic upwelling is the slow ascending motion of deep water toward the surface; upwelling is produced primarily by the action of surface winds. The water typically comes from depths of less than a few hundred meters, and it is usually lower in temperature and higher in nutrients than the surface water it replaces.

Upwelling along the coasts (usually western) of continents is associated with the north-south winds blowing along these coasts. These winds produce a movement of water within the uppermost layer of the sea (the Ekman layer; see OCEAN CURRENTS), to the right of the wind direction in the Northern

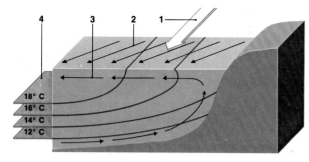

Along coastal areas a wind (1) blowing parallel to a shoreline may move the ocean surface current (2) and the resultant subsurface water mass (3) away from the coast as a result of the Coriolis effect. Upwelling, or upward flow of deep water, then occurs to replace the upper levels of water moving offshore. The flow can be monitored by checking water-temperature gradients (4), which decrease with depth.

Hemisphere and to the left in the Southern Hemisphere. When the movement in this layer (called Ekman transport) is directed offshore, deeper water will flow toward shore and will upwell near the coast. This process tends to intensify in low latitudes. The significant open-ocean upwelling in equatorial regions of both the Atlantic and the Pacific oceans is associated with a divergence in the surface Ekman transport produced by easterly winds near the equator. The process is generally strongest toward the eastern sides of the ocean basin.

Upwelling regions are marked by a depression in surface water temperature. Cold upwelled water along the west coasts of continents generally lowers air temperature, which increases the relative humidity and often produces fog. Upwelled water is often deficient in oxygen and rich in dissolved nutrients (phosphates, nitrates, silicates). The supply of nutrients to the surface layers leads to increased photosynthesis by phytoplankton; as a result, upwelling regions are some of the most biologically productive areas in the world's oceans. Along the Peruvian coast, for example, upwelling has produced one of the world's greatest anchovy fisheries. Upwelling around the Antarctic continent is responsible for huge blooms of phytoplankton, which form the basis of the marine food chain.   ROBERT E. WILSON

Bibliography: McLellan, H. J., *Elements of Physical Oceanography* (1966); Phillips, O. M., *The Dynamics of the Upper Ocean*, 2d ed. (1977); Pickard, G. L. *Descriptive Physical Oceanography*, 3d ed. (1979).

Ur

The ruins of Ur (modern Muqayyar), the ancient Sumerian capital and religious center that the Bible identifies as the early home of Abraham, lie about 300 km (187 mi) southeast of Baghdad, Iraq, and about 15 km (9.4 mi) southwest of the Euphrates River, which once flowed past the city. Modern studies have produced evidence that prehistoric occupation of the site (5th millennium BC) was interrupted by a flood that was formerly believed to have been the one described in Genesis. The city flourished during the 3d millennium BC, briefly serving (c.2500 BC) as the capital of SUMER under kings of the 1st dynasty of Ur. An extensive cemetery of approximately this period yielded several so-called Royal Tombs, which reflect the great wealth and unusual funerary customs of the city. Important persons were buried in these tombs, not only with magnificent treasures of gold, silver, and semiprecious stones, but also with their retinues of servants, ceremonial carts and animals, furniture, and utensils.

Following a period of Akkadian rule (c.2371–2230 BC), the city became the center of a Mesopotamian empire under the 3d dynasty of Ur, founded (c.2100 BC) by Ur-Nammu. Many of the important buildings on the site date from this period, although some were built on earlier ruins, and others were added to during later periods. Sacked (c.2000 BC) by the Elamites, Ur remained an important religious center maintained by

successive kings of Babylonia, in particular by the Neo-Babylonian kings Nebuchadnezzar II (r. 605–562 BC) and Nabonidus (d. c.538 BC). After the Achaemenid period (c.550 to 330 BC), the city declined, and its abandonment (4th century BC) may have resulted from a breakdown in the irrigation system after a change in the river's course.

The city walls, rebuilt (c.2100) by Ur-Nammu, enclose an oval area of about 33 ha (82 acres). Three main building complexes have been excavated: the raised ZIGGURAT and temple precinct surrounded by Nebuchadnezzar's retaining wall; the palace and temple of Nabonidus in the northeast section; and a residential quarter in the southeast part of the city. The ziggurat, whose lowest stage has been restored, was rebuilt by Nabonidus, incorporating Ur-Nammu's earlier building. Stairways on the northeastern side led to the summit, upon which stood a shrine to the moon-god Nannar, the patron deity of Ur. More temples stood within the walled precinct, including the Giparu, which was dedicated to Ningal, consort of Nannar. East of the Giparu stood Ehursag, possibly a royal palace used on ceremonial occasions. The royal mausoleums of the 3d dynasty and the Royal Tombs lie southeast of Ehursag. The residential quarter contains private houses of the early 2d millennium BC, the time at which Abraham is said to have lived at Ur. Cuneiform tablets from this area give information about the city's involvement in foreign trading during the late 3d and early 2d millennia BC, when Mesopotamian exports were transported to DILMUN (modern Bahrain) in the Persian Gulf, and there exchanged for copper and ivory from the East. Traces of two harbors have been found on the north and west sides of Ur.

The site of Ur was discovered in 1852, but not until the excavations carried out (1922–34) under the direction of Sir Leonard Woolley was detailed evidence of the city's history uncovered and present-day knowledge of early Mesopotamian culture substantially increased. Many objects from the Royal Tombs are now in the British Museum (London) and the Baghdad and University of Pennsylvania museums.

                                                    KATE FIELDEN

Bibliography: Lloyd, S., *Ruined Cities of Iraq* (1942); Woolley, C. L., *Excavations at Ur* (1964) and *Ur of the Chaldees* (1938).

The ziggurat at Ur, the religious and commercial center of Sumer from c.2120 to 2006 BC, was constructed during the reign of King Urnammu and rebuilt during the 6th century BC. The ziggurat was surmounted with a temple dedicated to the moon god Nannar.

Ur-Nammu, King of Ur   [ur-nah'-moo]

Ur-Nammu was the first king (r. c.2112–c.2095 BC) of the 3d dynasty of Sumerian kings at Ur in southern Mesopotamia. He was the author of the oldest known law code and built the lower part of the pyramidal temple (ziggurat) at Ur. His son Shulgi (r. c.2094–c.2047) succeeded him.   ROBIN BUSS

Uragami Gyokudo: see GYOKUDO.

Ural-Altaic languages   [yur'-ul-ahl-tay'-ik]

The many Ural-Altaic languages—constituting the Uralic and the Altaic languages—extend from Scandinavia, Hungary, and the Balkans in the west, to the easternmost reaches of the Amur and the island of Sakhalin, and from the Arctic Ocean to central Asia. According to some investigators, Japanese and Korean should also be considered Altaic languages (see JAPANESE LANGUAGE; KOREAN LANGUAGE).

Linguistic Features. All the Ural-Altaic languages share certain characteristics of syntax, morphology, and phonology. The languages use constructions of the type *the-by-me-hunted bear* rather than "the bear that I hunted," and *a-singing I went* rather than "I sang as I went." There are few if any conjunctions. Suffixation is the typical grammatical process—that is, meaningful elements are appended to stems, as in *house-my,* "my house," *go-(past)-I,* "I went," *house-from,* "from the house," *go-in-while,* "while (in the act of) going," and *house-(plural)-my-from,* "from my houses."

A great many Ural-Altaic languages require vowel harmony; the vowels that occur together in a given word must be of the same type. Thus *pöly,* "dust," is a possible word in Finnish because *ö* and *y* are both mid vowels and hence belong to the same phonetic class; likewise *polku,* "path," is possible because *o* and *u* are similar vowels. Words such as *pölu* or *poly* are not possible, because *ö* and *u,* or *o* and *y,* are too dissimilar. Stress generally falls on the first or last syllable.

Typically, the Ural-Altaic languages have no verb for "to have." Possession is expressed by constructions such as the Hungarian *nekem van,* "to-me there-is." Most of the languages do not express gender, do not have agreement between parts of speech (as in French *les bonnes filles,* "the good girls"), and do not permit consonant clusters, such as *pr-, spr-, -st,* or *-rst,* at the beginning or end of words.

Family Status. According to the standards set by linguists, languages that make up a family must show productive-predictive correspondences. The shape of a given word in one language should be predictable from the shape of the corresponding word, or cognate, in another language. Thus Hungarian *-d* at the end of stems, as in *ad,* "he gives," is known to correspond to the Finnish consonant sequence *-nt-* in the interior of words, as in Finnish *anta-,* "give."

All of the Uralic languages have been shown to be related—the vocabulary and grammar of each member language can be examined in the light of such correspondences—but Altaic is not a language family in the same sense that Uralic is, for similar laws of correspondence have yet to be discovered in Altaic. Altaic does have three branches, however—Turkic, Mongolian, and Manchu-Tungus—each of which forms a subfamily. Turkic and Mongolian on the one hand, and, to a lesser extent, Mongolian and Manchu-Tungus on the other, exhibit many striking resemblances. But the shared features may reflect only borrowing, and not a common origin.

URALIC LANGUAGES

The Uralic languages are traditionally divided into two major branches, Finno-Ugric and Samoyed. Finno-Ugric in turn contains two subgroups: Finnic and Ugric. The former is divided into the Baltic-Finnic, Volga-Finnic, and Permian languages; the latter comprises Hungarian and the Ob-Ugric languages.

Baltic-Finnic. Finnish and Estonian are the best known of the Baltic-Finnic languages. Others are Karelian, spoken in northwestern Russia and eastern Finland; Veps, spoken between the Dnepr and the Volga; Votian, spoken in the Udmurt Autonomous Republic of the USSR; and Livonian, spoken in the Livonia district of Latvia. Lapp is similar in structure to Finnish, but the various Lapp dialects—spoken in Norway, Sweden, Finland, and the Kola Peninsula of Russia—diverge greatly from each other in phonology and even to some extent in grammar.

Finnish has many cases, 12 of which are productive—that is, any Finnish noun can be followed by any of the 12 case suffixes. Another pervasive feature of the language is consonant gradation, such as the *t/d* alternation found in the declination of the Finnish word for "hundred": nominative *sata,* genitive *sadan,* ablative *sadalta,* partitive *sataa,* and so on. Finnish is also distinctive in having a verb that, translated roughly, means "not to."

Volga-Finnic and Permian. Mordvinian, spoken along the middle Volga, and Cheremis, spoken in the district where the Kama joins the Volga, constitute the Volga-Finnic language group. Both of them, but especially Mordvinian, are close to Finnish in grammar and vocabulary. Less like Finnish are the Permian languages—Zyrien and Votyak, spoken in northeastern European Russia. All of the Volga-Finnic and Permian languages have a negative verb and a large number of cases.

Ugric. The Finnic languages are more or less geographically contiguous, but the Ugric languages lie at opposite ends of the Finno-Ugric area—Hungarian occupying the extreme west, and the Ob-Ugric languages, Vogul and Ostyak, occupying the extreme east, in the Ob Valley beyond the Urals.

One of the most striking Ugric linguistic features is the so-called objective conjugation. In Hungarian, for instance, *adok* means "I give," and *adom* means "I give it" or "I give them." Thus the object of the verb—"it" or "them"—is incorporated in the verb form and does not need to be expressed separately. Vogul and Ostyak are still more precise. In these languages the objective conjugation has three distinct forms, to indicate whether the object is "it," "them" (plural), or "the two things" (dual). Furthermore, Vogul and Ostyak can also express the subject in the singular, plural, or dual.

Hungarian has more productive cases—upward of 20—than even Finnish has. Vogul and Ostyak, however, have only from four to seven cases, depending on dialect. The Ugric languages have no consonant gradation.

Samoyed. The Samoyed languages are the easternmost representatives of Uralic. Presumably they were the first to separate, as a group, from the original, proto-Uralic language. They are spoken in the northeastern corner of Europe, near Zyrian, and in north central Siberia. Yurak, Tavgi, and Yenisei form a North Samoyed group, and they can be distinguished from the South Samoyed language, Selkup. Other Samoyed languages are now extinct.

Loan Words and Early Records. In the course of their histories, the individual Uralic languages have come into contact with a great many languages from other families—Turkic, Germanic, Baltic (an earlier form of Latvian and Lithuanian), and Slavic. Finnish *kuningas,* "king," is an early loan from a Germanic language, hence its resemblance to English *king* and German *König.* Finnish *vapaa,* "free," was borrowed from a Slavic language—compare the Slavic root *svobod-.* The same Slavic root found its way, independently, into Hungarian, as evidenced by the word *szabad.*

The oldest significant text written in a Uralic language is a funeral sermon in Hungarian from about 1195. Finnish and Estonian texts survive from the Protestant Reformation, which swept over Scandinavia and much of the Baltic in the 16th century; the reformer of the Finns, Michael Agricola (1512–57), also translated the Bible into Finnish. Zyrien was recorded in the 15th century by Saint Stephen of Perm, apostle of the Zyriens, who fashioned its alphabet.

ALTAIC LANGUAGES

The Altaic languages are spread over an area that is even larger than that covered by Uralic. Of the three branches of Altaic, Turkic ranges from Anatolia to the Volga basin and central Asia; Mongolian extends from China and Mongolia as far west as the lower Volga and Afghanistan; and Manchu-Tungus occupies the northern coast of northeastern Siberia, and runs as far south as the Amur and as far west as the Yenisei, which divides Siberia into its eastern and western halves.

Turkic. Written evidence of the Turkic languages begins with the Orkhon inscriptions of the 8th century AD, found near the river Selenga in Mongolia, and continues wherever and whenever a Turkic population came into contact with one of the higher religions. Linguistically, the Turkic languages form a tightly knit group. Knowledge of one Turkic language usually enables an investigator to analyze words and simple sentences in any other Turkic language except Chuvash. To explain this, it is hypothesized that an original, proto-Turkic language split into two branches: West Turkic and East Turkic. West Turkic went its own way, both phonetically and in terms of contact with other languages, and eventually became Chuvash, spoken in the Volga Basin in the Chuvash Autonomous Republic of the USSR.

The early speakers of East Turkic must have remained together for a longer time and split up only comparatively recently into the many present-day languages. Still, the East Turkic languages are usually classed into five subdivisions: Oghuz, mainly represented by Turkish, the language of Turkey; Kipchak, which has over a dozen representative languages, including Kazan Tatar, Kazakh, Kirghiz, and Bashkir; Sayan Turkic, represented by Tuvin, Altai, Shor, and several other languages; Turki, represented primarily by Uighur and Uzbek; and Yakut, which comprises Yakut Proper, Khakas, and Dolgan.

Turkish, like Finnish, has vowel harmony. It also uses cases and possessive suffixes, which can combine as in *ev-ler-im-in*, "of my houses," made up of the word elements found in *ev-ler*, "houses," *ev-im*, "my house," and *ev-in*, "of the house." Such agglutination is also characteristic of Turkish verbs: compare *gel-mek*, "to come," *gel-ir-im*, "I come," *gel-iyor-um*, "I am coming," *gel-di-m*, "I came," *gel-me-mek*, "not to come," and *gel-me-d-in*, "I did not come."

Mongolian. Despite their considerable geographical dispersion, the present-day Mongolian languages or dialects are all closely related and all descend from a common proto-Mongolian parent language. The military conquests of Genghis Khan in the 13th century brought the Mongols well into Europe, and to this day traces of Mongolian may be discovered in a few provinces of Afghanistan, and among the Kalmyk-Mongols in the Kalmyk Autonomous Republic of the USSR.

Khalkha is the language of the Mongols of the Mongolian People's Republic, with its capital at Ulan Bator. Buriat is spoken in the Buriat Autonomous Republic of the USSR. Other Mongolian languages include Dagur, in northwestern Manchuria and the Chinese province of Sinkiang; Monguor, in Tsinghai province; Kalmyk; Oirat; Moghol; Santa; Paongan; and Yellow Uigur.

The grammatical processes encountered in the Mongolian languages are similar to those of Turkic. In the Khalkha word *bari-ld-aa-či-d-tə*, "to (the) wrestler," for instance, *bari-* is the stem, meaning "to seize"; *bari-ldə* means "to seize one another," hence, "to wrestle"; *bari-ld-aa* is the noun, "wrestling"; *bari-ld-aa-či* means "wrestler," and *bari-ld-aa-či-d*, "wrestlers"; and the final suffix, *-tə*, expresses the dative-locative case, "to" or "in." Khalkha has eight other cases, and in that respect—having many cases—the Mongolian languages resemble some of the Uralic representatives.

Manchu-Tungus. Just as the Turkic languages can be thought of as the western wing of Altaic, the Manchu-Tungus—also known simply as the Tungus—languages constitute the eastern wing. Most of these languages have been known only since the 19th century, but two of them, Manchu and Jurchen, are preserved in historical records that go back much further. Manchu, now spoken by only a few thousand people, was the original language of the tribe of horsemen that became the Ch'ing dynasty and occupied the Chinese throne from 1644 to 1912. Similarly, Jurchen, now extinct, was the language of the tribes that became the Chin dynasty, ruling from 1115 to 1234.

The Manchu-Tungus languages fall into two groups. South Tungus includes Manchu, Goldi, Olcha, Orok, Udihe, and Orochon. The North Tungus languages are Eveneki, or Tungus Proper, and Even, also known as Lamut.

THE RELATION BETWEEN URALIC AND ALTAIC
The grammatical structures of Uralic and Altaic are quite similar, and about 70 words in each group—like Finnish *käly*, "sister-in-law," and Uighur *kälin*, "bride" and "daughter-in-law"—appear to be cognates. But the correspondences between the two groups of languages are unsystematic; they could be the result of borrowing or chance. Alternatively, it is argued that the parallels between Uralic and Altaic are slight because the two groups split apart a long time ago.

In addition to the Ural-Altaic hypothesis, which is that Uralic and Altaic form a superfamily of languages, there is also an Indo-Uralic hypothesis, in which Uralic is linked with the INDO-EUROPEAN LANGUAGES; a Uralic-Yukagir hypothesis, linking Uralic and Yukagir, a Paleosiberian language; a Uralic-Luorawetlan (another Paleosiberian language or language family) hypothesis; a Uralic-Eskaleut (Eskimo and Aleut) hypothesis (see INDIAN LANGUAGES, AMERICAN); an Altaic-Korean

hypothesis; an Altaic-Japanese hypothesis; and an Altaic-Ainu hypothesis—Ainu being the language of the prehistoric inhabitants of the northern islands of Japan.

Bibliography: Benké, Loránd, and Imre, Samu, eds., *The Hungarian Language* (1972); Collinder, Björn, *An Introduction to the Uralic Languages* (1965) and *Survey of the Uralic Languages,* 2d ed. (1969); Hakulinen, Lauri, *The Structure and Development of the Finnish Language* (1953–55; Eng. trans., 1961); Matthews, W. K., *Languages of the U.S.S.R.* (1951); Menges, Karl H., *The Turkic Languages and People: An Introduction to Turkic Studies* (1968); Miller, Roy A., *Japanese and Other Altaic Languages* (1971); Poppe, Nicholas, *Introduction to Altaic Linguistics* (1965) and *Mongolian Language Handbook* (1970); Raun, Alo, *Essays in Finno-Ugric and Finnic Linguistics* (1971); Shirokogoroff, S. M., *Ethnological and Linguistical Aspects of the Ural-Altaic Hypothesis* (1970); Vago, R., *The Sound Pattern of Hungarian* (1980).

Ural Mountains [yur'-ul]

The Ural Mountains in the USSR extend from near the coast of the Arctic Ocean southward for more than 2,000 km (1,250 mi). Traditionally they form the boundary between Europe and Asia, but they do not constitute a significant boundary within the USSR. The tallest peak, Mount Narodnaya, reaches 1,894 m (6,214 ft), but much of the range is below 1,000 m (3,280 ft). The mountains are drained by the PECHORA, Ural, Kama, and Tobol rivers.

The Urals are built of parallel ridges trending north-south. They were formed in the course of the Hercynian Earth movements (about 250 million years ago). Toward the south the range broadens into a plateau, where Archaean rocks are to be found. Throughout its length the range has been intruded by granitic and other igneous rocks, which today give rise to the greatest relief. The Urals were glaciated, and the effects of glacial erosion are especially evident in the north.

The climate is characterized by winters of great length and severity: from −15° C to −21° C (5° F to −6° F) in January. Summers are short and cool. The annual rainfall varies from 254 mm (10 in) in the south to about 760 mm (30 in) in the north. Toward the arctic, the mountains are covered with low-growing tundra, but elsewhere a sparse coniferous forest dominates.

The central and southern Urals contain great mineral wealth, particularly iron ore, bauxite, copper, and zinc, as well as many rarer minerals. The southern Urals are flanked by coal and petroleum fields. These resources have given rise to smelting, metallurgical, and engineering industries, and to large industrial centers, including CHELYABINSK, MAGNITOGORSK, and SVERDLOVSK.

Exploration of the Urals began in the 11th century and continued into the 17th century. Industrialization of the region began in the 18th century with the exploitation of the area's vast mineral resources.

NORMAN J. G. POUNDS

Ural River

The Ural River is a 2,535-km-long (1,575-mi) river in the Russian and Kazakh republics of the USSR, with a drainage area of 231,000 km² (89,190 mi²). It rises in the Ural Mountains and flows south past the industrial city of Magnitogorsk, then west to Uralsk, where it turns south and continues through a semi-desert area to its delta at Guryev on the northern shore of the Caspian Sea. A source of hydroelectric power, the river is navigable to Uralsk during the ice-free season (mid-April to mid-November).

Uralic languages: see URAL-ALTAIC LANGUAGES.

Uraniborg Observatory   [oo-rah'-nee-bohrg]

Uraniborg Observatory, founded (1576) on the island of Hven, Denmark, by Tycho BRAHE, and disbanded in 1597, was the last observatory built before the invention of the telescope. It was considered modern because it was supported by the state and had organized data, a mural quadrant, and armillae. Brahe's accurate observations made at Uraniborg later enabled the German astronomer Johannes KEPLER to formulate his laws of planetary motion.

uranium

Uranium is a heavy, radioactive metal, the 92d element and a member of the ACTINIDE SERIES (Group IIIB) in the periodic table. Its atomic weight is 238.029; its name and chemical symbol, U, are derived from Uranus, because that planet was discovered a few years before the discovery of the element. A compound of uranium (uranium oxide) was discovered in the uranium ore pitchblende by the German chemist M. H. KLAPROTH in 1789. Klaproth believed that he had isolated the element, but this was not achieved until 1841, when the French chemist E. M. Péligot reduced uranium tetrachloride with potassium in a platinum crucible to obtain elementary uranium. It was in uranium-containing crystals that the French physicist A. H. BECQUEREL discovered RADIOACTIVITY in 1896.

Uranium is not as rare as was once believed. Widely distributed in the Earth's crust, uranium occurs to the extent of about 0.0004%, making the metal more plentiful than mercury, antimony, or silver. Before World War II, uranium was of interest as a source of RADIUM for medical use, and as a coloring agent in glass and ceramic glazes, in which it produces a yellow green color (vaseline glass). With the advent of the nuclear age, uranium now occupies a key position in nuclear weapons and NUCLEAR ENERGY.

Each individual neutral uranium atom consists of 92 protons in the nucleus and 92 electrons. Uranium has three naturally occurring isotopes: the most abundant is ^{238}U (99.276%), occurring with ^{235}U (0.718%) and ^{234}U (0.0056%). There are 14 isotopes in all, each radioactive. Except for traces of neptunium and plutonium, uranium is the heaviest atom found in nature.

Physical Properties. Pure uranium is a heavy, silvery white metal that melts at 1,132° C and boils at 3,818° C. Uranium has three different ALLOTROPES, or crystalline forms. The phase changes between these crystalline forms are important considerations in the design of metallic fuel rods for nuclear reactors. Uranium is a poor conductor of electricity, and it is soft, although it will harden when machined.

Chemical Properties. Uranium is a strongly electropositive element and is easily oxidized. When a massive sample of uranium is exposed to air, the surface is oxidized and protects the rest of the metal from oxidation near room temperature. The massive metal will burn in air at 700° C (1,292° F), and finely divided uranium is pyrophoric, igniting spontaneously in air.

In its chemical compounds uranium exhibits four common oxidation states: +3, +4, +5, and +6. Uranium reacts readily with most nonmetals and dissolves slowly in dilute mineral acids. The metal dissolves rapidly in oxidizing acids, such as nitric acid, yielding (in nitric acid) uranyl nitrate, $UO_2(NO_3)_2$. Much of the aqueous chemistry of uranium is dominated by the uranyl ion, UO_2^{2+}, and its derivatives. The metal is inert to basic solutions.

An important compound of uranium is the hexafluoride, UF_6. Uranium hexafluoride is volatile and, in the absence of water, chemically stable. Fractional diffusion of large volumes of this compound was used to separate ^{235}U from ^{238}U for use in the ATOMIC BOMB.

Radioactivity. Each of the naturally occurring isotopes of uranium are radioactive and decay by the following nuclear transformations:

$$^{238}_{92}U \rightarrow {}^{234}_{90}Th + {}^{4}_{2}He \qquad t_{1/2} = 4.5 \times 10^9 \text{ years}$$
$$^{235}_{92}U \rightarrow {}^{231}_{90}Th + {}^{4}_{2}He \qquad t_{1/2} = 7.1 \times 10^8 \text{ years}$$
$$^{234}_{92}U \rightarrow {}^{230}_{90}Th + {}^{4}_{2}He \qquad t_{1/2} = 2.5 \times 10^5 \text{ years}$$

The HALF-LIFE of each isotope is given by $t_{1/2}$. Each of the resulting thorium isotopes is also radioactive. The ^{238}U isotope decay begins a series of nuclear transformations, called the uranium series, that ends with the nonradioactive lead isotope, ^{206}Pb.

Mineralogy. Uranium is always found combined with other elements; its occurrence is controlled by its geochemical behavior. Thus, in igneous rocks, uranium exists in the +4 valence state. A large ion, it tends to be excluded from ferro-magnesian minerals that crystallize early in the geochemical process, instead becoming concentrated in residual liquids during the final stages of crystallization. In intermediate and granitic rocks, uranium typically substitutes for calcium in apatite and for zirconium in zircon. Uranium concentrations generally correlate with the silica content of igneous rocks; most uranium in igneous rocks, however, is believed to exist in amorphous intergranular films.

When exposed to more oxidizing conditions near the Earth's surface, primary uranium minerals are readily oxidized to the highly soluble +6 valence state. (Geologists theorize that in the oxygen-free atmosphere of early Precambrian time—more than 2.3 billion years ago—such oxidation did not occur, and grains of uranium minerals accumulated as detrital placer deposits in quartz-pebble conglomerates. Large deposits of this type, which may also contain gold, occur in Canada, South Africa, and Brazil.) Much of the oxidized uranium in solution ultimately reaches the oceans, where it may be selectively removed and incorporated into marine phosphorite deposits, adsorbed by clay minerals, or incorporated in the carbonate skeletons of organisms such as corals. Marine phosphorites constitute large uranium resources in Africa, the Soviet Union, Brazil, the Mediterranean region, and the United States. In Florida these low-grade deposits are extensively mined for their phosphate, which makes recovery of the uranium feasible. Some lignites and marine black shales also contain enough uranium to be considered resources.

Several important primary uranium ores exist, including uraninite (essentially UO_2), pitchblende (a massive form of uraninite, including more oxidized forms such as U_3O_8), and carnotite (a complex oxide that contains potassium and vanadium as well). Other complex oxides include brannerite and davidite; coffinite is a silicate mineral of uranium. The largest quantities of uranium ore are mined from the Blind River area in Ontario, Canada. Vein deposits have also been mined in Canada's Northwest Territories and Saskatchewan, in the Northern Territory of Australia, in Zaire, in France, and, in the United States, in Colorado, Utah, and Alaska. More than 99% of the uranium now being mined in the United States, however, comes from sedimentary deposits in New Mexico, Wyoming, Texas, Colorado, and Utah. These deposits apparently formed when uranium-bearing groundwater encountered chemically reducing conditions in sedimentary beds and precipitated minerals such as uraninite and coffinite.

Approximately 90% of the remaining uranium minerals are uranyl (UO_2^{++}) compounds. These minerals form mainly by alteration of primary ore minerals in pegmatites and veins or by precipitation from evaporating uranium-bearing groundwater. Almost half of the uranyl minerals are arsenates, phosphates, or vanadates; other such minerals include silicates, carbonates, and sulfates.

Production. No deposits of concentrated uranium ore have been discovered. As a result, uranium must be extracted from ores containing less than 0.1% uranium, so that substantial, complex processing of the ores is required. Usually it is necessary to preconcentrate the ore by grinding and by flotation or similar processes. The preconcentrated ore is then leached to bring the uranium compounds into solution. The resulting solution is filtered, absorbed onto an ion-exchange resin, eluted, precipitated, and purified to yield uranyl nitrate, which may be converted to other uranium compounds or reduced to yield the pure metal.

Nuclear Fission. In 1939 two German scientists, Otto HAHN and Fritz Strassman, reported that when ^{235}U absorbs slow neutrons, it forms ^{236}U, which then undergoes nuclear fission, splitting into two large fragments plus several neutrons. A typical fission reaction is

$$^{235}_{92}U + {}^{1}_{0}n \rightarrow {}^{236}_{92}U \rightarrow {}^{90}_{36}Kr + {}^{143}_{56}Ba + 3{}^{1}_{0}n$$

This reaction releases a tremendous amount of energy: the fission of a pound of ^{235}U produces about 2.5 million times as much energy as is produced by the burning of a pound of coal. The fission fragments include more neutrons that can cause fission of nearby ^{235}U atoms, thus setting up a nuclear

CHAIN REACTION. This and similar chain reactions are the source of energy for many nuclear reactors (also called atomic piles). The ^{238}U isotope absorbs high velocity neutrons to form, ultimately, ^{239}Pu, which is fissionable.

Uranium Reprocessing. Uranium oxide enriched with ^{235}U is used as fuel in nuclear reactors. Eventually, the accumulation of products of nuclear fission will stop the chain reaction. Before this point is reached the fuel assembly is removed and the fuel must either be disposed of or reprocessed to remove the radioactive fission products. It is estimated that if the spent nuclear fuel were reprocessed, 30% less uranium ore would need to be mined for a given amount of power.

Uranium depleted of its fissionable isotope, either from original processing or reprocessing, is used for a few nonnuclear purposes. Uranyl nitrate is used as a colored glaze for porcelain and glass and as an intensifier in photography. Uranyl acetate is used in dry copying inks and as a reagent in analytical chemistry. Because of its great density, the metal is used in inertial guidance systems, counterweights and ballast, and as a shielding material.   NORMAN V. DUFFY

Bibliography: Bailey, Robert, and Childers, Milton, *Applied Mineral Exploration with Special Reference to Uranium* (1977); Bickel, Lennard, *The Deadly Element* (1979); Capaldi, G., et al., eds., *Uranium Geochemistry, Mineralogy, Geology, Exploration and Resources* (1984); Cordfunke, E. H. P., *The Chemistry of Uranium* (1969); Merriman, J. R., and Benedict, M., eds., *Recent Developments in Uranium Enrichment* (1982); Moss, Norman, *The Politics of Uranium* (1982); Neff, T. L., *The International Uranium Market* (1984); Rich, R. A., et al., *Hydrothermal Uranium Deposits* (1977); Tatsch, J. H., *Uranium Deposits: Origin, Evolution and Present Characteristics* (1976).

Uranus   (astronomy)   [yoo-ray'-nuhs]

Uranus is the seventh PLANET from the Sun and was the first to be discovered since ancient times. Sir William HERSCHEL first observed the planet through a telescope on Mar. 13, 1781, seeing a featureless bluish green disk that he nevertheless recognized as a highly unusual object. Although Herschel wished to call the newly discovered planet Georgium Sidus (Georgian Star) for King George III of England, and although many French astronomers referred to it as Herschel, Johann Bode's proposal of the name *Uranus*—the mythological father of Saturn—was over the years accepted more and more widely and finally became universal in the mid-19th century.

The only spacecraft to encounter Uranus thus far, VOYAGER 2, collected data on the planet and its rings and satellites over a four-month period, between Nov. 4, 1985, and Feb. 25, 1986. *Voyager 2* passed within 107,000 km (66,500 mi) of the center of Uranus—about 81,450 km (50,625 mi) above its cloud tops—on Jan. 24, 1986.

Appearance. Although it was discovered with a telescope, Uranus reaches a maximum brightness of magnitude 5.5 and can be seen by the naked eye as a faint point of light in a clear, moonless sky. In *Voyager 2* photos, Uranus appears as a generally featureless disk, except for considerable darkening toward the edges. Faint banding is seen in contrast-enhanced images, as are transitory cloud plumes.

Orbit and Rotation. Uranus's average distance from the Sun is 2.875 billion km (1.786 billion mi), and the planet takes 84.013 years to make one complete revolution about the Sun. The orbit has an eccentricity of 0.0472 and an inclination of 0°46'. Its period of rotation was determined by *Voyager 2* to be 17.24 hours (±0.01 hours). One startling aspect of Uranus is that its rotation axis is inclined 97°54' from its orbital plane. This means that the poles of Uranus lie nearly in the plane of its orbit around the Sun.

Physical Characteristics. Uranus has an equatorial diameter of 51,100 km (31,750 mi), almost precisely four times that of the Earth, and a mass 14.58 times that of the Earth. The dark absorption bands discovered in 1869 in the red part of the spectrum of Uranus were identified in 1932 as being caused by methane gas in Uranus's atmosphere. This red absorption is the major cause of the blue green color of the planet; the methane absorbs much of the red light from the impinging white sunlight, leaving a bluish green color in the reflected sunlight. Measurements by *Voyager 2* verified that hydrogen is the main constituent of the visible atmosphere. Helium is the other major constituent, about 15% (±5%) in terms of molecular weight, which is a larger percentage than in the atmospheres of either Jupiter or Saturn. Together, hydrogen and helium make up more than 99% of Uranus's atmosphere, which extends to a depth of about 8,000 km (5,000 mi). A layer of methane ice clouds was detected by *Voyager 2* near a pressure level of about one atmosphere. Deep within Uranus exists a superheated water ocean, perhaps 10,000 km (6,000 mi) deep, which contains large concentrations of ionized chemicals. It is in this ocean that Uranus's magnetic field may originate. Beneath this ionic ocean, an Earth-sized core of molten rocky materials is believed to exist.

The magnetic field itself is tilted 60° to the rotation axis and is offset from the center of the planet, by about one third of Uranus's radius, toward the north pole. Because of the large offset, the surface magnetic field strength is not constant across Uranus, instead ranging from 0.1 to 1.1 Gauss. A well-developed magnetic tail extends away from the Sun; because of the tilt of the field, the tail has a large wobble whose period is the same as the rotation period of the planet.

Infrared measurements from *Voyager 2* indicate that Uranus has an effective temperature of -214° C (-353° F). Unlike the other giant planets, there is no evidence of any significant internal heat source. A very extended corona of atomic and molecular hydrogen encompasses all the known rings of the planet, perhaps heated by low-energy electrons. Sunlight fall-

(Left) *Uranus, seen as it would appear to human eyes from the vantage point of* Voyager 2, *is a featureless disk.* (Center) *A false-color view, however, reveals some details about the hood of smog covering the south polar area. The apparent small circles in these photos are actually image-processing defects.* (Right) *The innermost major moon, Miranda, has a chaotic surface in which old, heavily cratered terrain is interrupted by younger regions marked by scarps, ridges, and dark and bright bands. Giant cliffs are visible at the bottom, right.*

 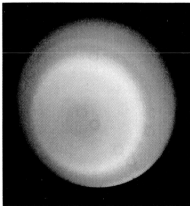 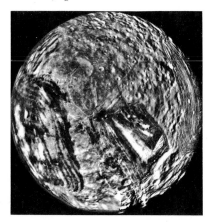

SATELLITES AND RINGS OF URANUS

Name	Average Distance from Center of Uranus km	mi	Period of Revolution (days)	Diameter or Ring Width km	mi	Orbital Inclination (degrees)	Orbital Eccentricity
1986U2R ring	38,000	24,000		2,500	1,500	0?	0?
6 ring	41,850	26,000		2	1	0.063	0.0010
5 ring	42,240	26,250		3	2	0.052	0.0019
4 ring	42,580	26,460		2	1	0.032	0.0011
Alpha ring	44,730	27,790		10	6	0.014	0.0008
Beta ring	45,670	28,380		9	6	0.005	0.0004
Eta ring	47,180	29,320		2	1	0.002	0.000
Gamma ring	47,630	29,600		3	2	0.011	0.000
Delta ring	48,310	30,020		6	4	0.004	0.000
Cordelia	49,700	30,900	0.33	40	25	0?	0?
1986U1R ring	50,040	31,090		2	1	0?	0?
Epsilon ring	51,160	31,790		58	36	0.001	0.0079
Ophelia	53,800	33,400	0.38	50	30	0?	0?
Bianca	59,200	36,800	0.43	50	30	0?	0?
Cressida	61,800	38,400	0.46	60	35	0?	0?
Desdemona	62,700	39,000	0.48	60	35	0?	0?
Juliet	64,600	40,100	0.49	80	50	0?	0?
Portia	66,100	41,100	0.51	80	50	0?	0?
Rosalind	69,900	43,400	0.56	60	35	0?	0?
Belinda	75,300	46,800	0.62	60	35	0?	0?
Puck	86,000	53,400	0.76	170	105	0?	0?
Miranda	129,900	80,700	1.41	484	301	4.2	0.0027
Ariel	190,900	118,600	2.52	1,160	720	0.3	0.0034
Umbriel	266,000	165,300	4.15	1,190	740	0.36	0.0050
Titania	436,300	271,100	8.70	1,610	1,000	0.14	0.0022
Oberon	583,400	362,500	13.46	1,550	960	0.10	0.0008

ing on this corona causes it to radiate ultraviolet light, a phenomenon that scientists have termed ELECTROGLOW.

Rings. The discovery on Mar. 10, 1977, that Uranus has rings was one of the most unexpected and exciting events of modern planetary astronomy. Subsequent observations have indicated the presence of 10 narrow rings of dark particles and one broad, diffuse ring, in addition to 100 or more possibly transient ringlets of dust-sized particles seen only in *Voyager 2* images of the backlighted rings.

The outermost ring (called the epsilon ring), in marked contrast to the rings of Saturn, has almost no particles smaller than about 20 cm (8 in). The other rings also seem to be deficient in small particles. Possibly the extended hydrogen corona exerts a drag on the orbiting ring particles that preferentially removes the smaller particles, causing them to fall into the planet. Because collisions between larger particles create smaller particles, atmospheric-drag forces could virtually destroy the rings in geologically short time periods. The rings are therefore relatively young or else are replenished by the breakup of small satellites.

Satellites. Uranus has five major satellites: MIRANDA, discovered by Gerard Kuiper in 1948; Ariel and Umbriel, discovered by William Lassell in 1851; and Titania and Oberon, discovered by William Herschel in 1787. Ten small satellites were also discovered in *Voyager 2* photographs, all of them orbiting Uranus well inside the orbit of Miranda. The five major satellites—and probably the ten smaller ones as well—appear to be in synchronous rotation; that is, they keep their same faces toward Uranus as they orbit the planet. Much like the ring particles, the smaller satellites appear to have surfaces as dark as coal. The major satellites have somewhat brighter surfaces, reflecting from 19% (Umbriel) to 40% (Ariel) of the sunlight that falls on them. In addition to being the darkest of the major satellites, Umbriel also has the fewest geological features. The other four satellites display increasingly complex geologies with decreasing distance from Uranus.

Oberon and Titania are remarkably similar in size, density color, and reflectivity. Titania, however, has a much larger fraction of small craters and more fractures across its surface, implying that Titania has a geologically younger surface. Oberon has one mountain that rises to an altitude of at least 20 km (12 mi) above the surrounding surface.

Although Umbriel and Ariel have similar diameters and densities, they differ dramatically in the appearance of their surfaces. Ariel's surface is literally covered with fractures and fault systems. Parallel fractures in several areas bound valleys that appear to have glacierlike flows along their floors. Water-ammonia ices become fluid at much lower temperatures than pure water ice and might form the observed glaciers.

Miranda is the innermost and smallest of the major moons. Its surface consists of an old, heavily cratered, rolling terrain with relatively uniform reflectivity, and a younger, complex terrain in three nearly rectangular regions characterized by parallel grooves, an abundance of vertical structures, and large brightness differences. The materials out of which Miranda was formed may not have melded together to form a uniform surface; its present bizarre appearance may be a frozen record of the late stages of the development of this satellite.

ELLIS D. MINER

Bibliography: Burgess, Eric, *Uranus and Neptune* (1988); Ingersoll, Andrew P., "Uranus," *Scientific American,* January 1987; Johnson, Torrence V., et al., "The Moons of Tartarus," *Scientific American,* April 1987; Laeser, Richard P., et al., "Engineering Voyager 2's Encounter with Uranus," *Scientific American,* November 1986; O'Meary, S. J., "A Visual History of Uranus," *Sky & Telescope,* November 1985; Stone, E. C., and Miner, E. D., "The Voyager 2 Encounter with the Uranian System," *Science,* July 4, 1986.

See also: SOLAR SYSTEM.

Uranus   (mythology)

In Greek mythology, Uranus represented the sky or heaven. He was both the son and husband of GAEA, the earth, by whom he fathered first the hundred-handed giants and the CYCLOPES, whom he banished to Tartarus, and later the TITANS. Gaea, angry because her children were imprisoned, set the Titans against Uranus. CRONUS, their leader, castrated Uranus and succeeded him as ruler of the universe. According to Hesiod's *Theogony,* APHRODITE was born of the foam of Uranus's discarded genitals as they fell in the sea. Blood falling from the wound on earth engendered the FURIES.

Urartu   [oor-ahr'-too]

The ancient kingdom of Urartu, centered in eastern Turkey, extended at the height of its prominence (8th century BC) into present-day northwestern Iran, Soviet Transcaucasia, and northern Syria. The mountain of Ararat where Noah's ark is said in the Old Testament to have struck land presumably lay within its borders. The Assyrians regarded Urartu as a threat by the 9th century BC, although references to Urartu already appear in Assyrian records dating from approximately 400 years earlier. Driven (late 8th century) from northern Syria, the Urartians subsequently were conquered by the Medes in the early 6th century BC, after years of hostilities with the Assyrians, Cimmerians, and Scythians.

After Urartu's rediscovery by early-19th-century travelers, related artifacts were uncovered (1877) at Toprakkale near Lake Van in Turkey. The site was reexamined by C. F. Lehmann-Haupt and his colleagues in 1898, but the citadel itself was properly documented only toward the mid-20th century. Excavations, notably those in Turkey and the Soviet Union, have vastly elucidated Urartian religious and secular architecture, figurative art, and impressive metalworking traditions.

LOUISE ALPERS BORDAZ

Bibliography: Azarpay, Guitty, *Urartian Art and Artifacts* (1968); Lloyd, Seton, *Early Highland Peoples of Anatolia* (1967); Metzger, Henri, *Anatolia II* (1969); Piotrovskii, Boris, *The Ancient Civilizations of Urartu*, trans. by James Hogarth (1969) and *Urartu: The Kingdom of Van and Its Art*, trans. by Peter S. Gelling (1967).

Urban, Joseph [ur'-buhn]

The architect and artist Joseph Urban, b. Vienna, May 26, 1872, d. July 10, 1933, emigrated to the United States in 1911 and there, as he had in Europe, distinguished himself by the amazingly wide range of his work. After graduating from the Art Academy and Polytechnicum in Vienna he worked as an architect, book illustrator, and set designer. His architectural projects included the interior of Vienna's Municipal Building (1903), a castle (1900) for Count Esterhazy in Hungary, the Tsar Bridge (1903) over the Neva River in Russia, and Austrian exhibition buildings at Paris (1900) and St. Louis (1904).

In the United States, Urban was best known as a scenic designer for the Metropolitan Opera Company (1918–33) and for the Ziegfeld Follies (beginning in 1914) in New York City. He also practiced architecture in New York—Ziegfeld Theater (1927; demolished) and New School for Social Research (1930)—and undertook interior decorating commissions—St. Regis Hotel (1927–33) and Central Park Casino (1929)—in New York as well as in Palm Beach, Fla. Urban's last completed work was with the 1933 Chicago World's Fair, where he served as director of color and consultant on lighting as well as designer of the panorama in the New York State Pavilion.

J. MEREDITH NEIL

Bibliography: Higham, Charles, *Ziegfeld* (1972); Robinson, Cervin, and Bletter, R. H., *Skyscraper Style: Art Deco New York* (1975).

urban anthropology

Urban anthropology is a relatively new but important subfield of cultural anthropology that focuses on the city as the locus of research. Traditionally, anthropologists have studied small, usually preliterate groups in remote areas. As complex industrial society penetrated into even isolated regions, however, many anthropologists began to redirect their field work toward the study of former hunter-gatherer groups and especially of farmers who migrated into the cities as laborers.

In transferring their skills to the city, urban anthropologists have retained many of the same research techniques used in more remote settings, including participant-observation, questionnaires, and surveys. Following their tradition of small-group research, many anthropologists have found it convenient to choose as the unit of analysis a particular ethnic or social group bounded by a particular locality or district. Some of these studies have neglected the relationship between the city and the group studied, and so have been referred to as "anthropology *in* the city." Other anthropologists, who follow the tradition of anthropological holism, focus on the city as a whole. This practice, sometimes called "anthropology *of the* city," seeks to understand the relationships of parts of a city to the whole as well as to compare development patterns of different cities. Among the questions that currently interest urban anthropologists are the causes and perpetuation of urban poverty (the so-called culture of poverty controversy); adap-

tive strategies of kin and nonkin networks, such as voluntary associations; and the relationship between ethnicity and social stratification.

ELAINE J. SCHECHTER

Bibliography: Collins, T. W., ed., *Cities in a Larger Context* (1980); Eames, Edwin, and Goode, J. G., *Anthropology of the City* (1977); Fox, R. G., *Urban Anthropology* (1977); Friedl, John, and Chrisman, N. J., eds., *City Ways: A Selective Reader in Urban Anthropology* (1975); Higgins, M. J., *Somos Tocayos: Anthropology of Urbanism and Poverty* (1983); Southall, Aidan, ed., *Urban Anthropology* (1973).

urban climate

Urban climates are special cases of MICROCLIMATES, the study of which is of great importance in the conservation of energy and in air-pollution control because of wind patterns created by heat and cold islands in cities. Urbanization has increasingly been responsible for the most radical of the climatic changes caused by humans. The city's compact mass of buildings and pavement constitutes a profound alteration of the natural landscape, resulting in an almost infinite number of microclimates. The urban-atmosphere system is reciprocally sustained by a complex web of feedbacks.

The city's microclimatic energy budget has been changed from that of rural areas in several basic ways. The large vertical surface areas of tall buildings expose a huge portion of the city to additional absorbed longwave and shortwave radiation. The surface materials are rocklike, with high conductivities, heat capacities, and reflectivities, and the surfaces are relatively impervious to moisture, which leads to rapid disposal of rain and snow. In addition, the city generates artificial heat and moisture because of its traffic, industries, and domestic heating and cooling. Last, the city also is a vast source of contaminants that are by-products of its daily activities. As a result, urban environments, in contrast to rural ones, have undergone decreases in incident solar radiation, visibility, and horizontal wind speed but have shown increases in contaminants, air temperature, fog, cloudiness, rainfall, snowfall, and the number of thunderstorms.

The existence of urban heat islands (and coexisting cold islands because of the shading effect of tall buildings) has long been recognized, and the study of them has become synonymous with urban climatology. The complex and constantly changing mosaic of heat and cold islands influences urban ecology in a variety of ways. In terms of air temperatures, the presence of heat islands is especially reflected in higher night minimum temperatures. Vertical temperature profiles indicate multiple inversions over cities that inhibit the escape of pollutants. As a result of heat islands, gradients of temperature and pressure induce local air circulation and increased convection. Also, the energy differential between city and country causes pollution emitted near the urban edge to drift in and concentrate near the city's core.

As urbanization increases, escaping heat plumes may combine to form larger regional heat islands; these can produce a stronger convection cell and feed the local heat islands with already polluted air. Such urban-induced changes, although intense at the megalopolis level, have not yet reached globally discernible magnitudes; however, they do seem close to producing regional changes.

WERNER H. TERJUNG

Bibliography: Landsberg, Helmut, *The Urban Climate* (1981); World Meteorological Organization, *Urban Climates* (1976).

Urban League, National

A U.S. interracial organization, the National Urban League was founded in 1910 to provide community services and to secure equal opportunities for black citizens. Initially the league was most concerned with providing new jobs for blacks in industry and in aiding southern migrants who had moved into northern cities. After World War II the organization became more directly involved in civil rights issues and in the improvement of employment and housing opportunities for American blacks. Its director from 1961 to 1971 was Whitney M. YOUNG, Jr. He was succeeded by Vernon JORDAN, who was subsequently replaced (1982) by John E. Jacob. The League's headquarters is in New York City.

urban planning

Urban planning can be defined variously as the formulation of alternative patterns of urban settlement, the rational use of resources to alleviate urban problems, and the provision of a city's physical and social infrastructure—transportation, utilities, housing, community facilities, and services. More simply, it is the art of building cities. Today planning is as much a part of the responsibility of urban government as the provision of services or the collection of taxes. Municipal governments prepare comprehensive or master plans to guide future development, capital budgets to program future expenditures for services, and zoning ordinances and subdivision regulations to control development.

Contemporary urban planning draws upon many disciplines. The social sciences quantify the size and characteristics of the future population, its needs, and its occupational structure and income distribution. ARCHITECTURE, ENGINEERING, LANDSCAPE ARCHITECTURE, and urban design provide the three-dimensional solutions that are the expression of broad development policy decisions. The science of ecology permits an increasingly accurate measurement of the environmental consequences of development and the control of their adverse effects. Law and political science provide the principal legislative and bureaucratic mechanisms that are used to implement planning decisions. Planning, however, is far from an exact science. Its prime area of concern is people and their relationship to the built environment. Although planning may anticipate the need for jobs, shelter, transportation, education, health, or recreation, its effectiveness is limited to putting restraints on private property rights and providing incentives to influence individual choices.

Planning is a repetitive or iterative process. It requires the formulation of social goals that can be translated into politically acceptable objectives that, in turn, can be detailed into specific programs and projects. Although social values and goals tend to evolve rather slowly, their transformation into operative programs tends to reflect immediate political objectives. The 2- to 4-year terms of city officials often dictate the periods over which the effectiveness of planning is measured and thus determine the scope of many local programs and projects. Planning is also a dynamic process. Population movements, economic fluctuations, technological innovations, or, more commonly, the obsolescence of the city's physical plant require periodic revisions of planning strategies.

HISTORY OF URBAN PLANNING

The human desire to shape the urban environment goes back to the earliest known cities that developed in the Fertile Crescent and in India between 5000 and 3500 BC. Even though ancient cities were small by modern standards, their populations were frequently crowded within a defensive wall. Developmental pressures within a restricted area almost certainly resulted in legal restrictions regarding private property rights. The city's rulers built and maintained works of public utility—defensive walls and citadels, bridges and roads, temples and markets—while laws protected public ways and private property from encroachments.

Urban Planning in the Ancient World. Ancient civilizations occasionally planned new cities or major additions to existing settlements. The most widespread plan was a rectangular or grid street pattern that allowed considerable flexibility in the size of blocks while maintaining a clear visual order. Noteworthy examples of this type of city plan include Kahun (Egypt, c.1890 BC), whose workers' quarter is separated by an internal wall from the wealthier districts; MILETUS (Anatolia, 479 BC), whose reconstruction, following its destruction (494 BC) by the Persians, was carried out in strict accord with the planning principles attributed to the Greek planner HIPPODAMUS OF MILETUS; and TIMGAD (Algeria, AD 100), one of a series of colonies for Roman veterans of Emperor Trajan's army that were built to protect the fertile coastal plain from nomadic raiders.

Vitruvius. By the 4th century BC a theory of urban planning already existed, as evidenced in the writings of Hippocrates, Plato, and Aristotle. It addressed issues of site selection and orientation, as influenced by natural features and climate; city form, including the optimal location for major buildings; the size and composition of the population; and urban government and laws. These theories were later modified and amplified into a veritable textbook on urban planning, VITRUVIUS's *De architectura* (after 27 BC; trans. as *Ten Books on Architecture*, 1826 and 1914). This work standardized the city plans that the Roman engineers used in the innumerable fortified settlements and provincial cities that they built throughout the empire. The typical Roman plan, vestiges of which are still clearly discernible in many cities of Europe, North Africa, and the Near East, consisted of two perpendicular main streets running north-south (*cardo*) and east-west (*decumanus*) with the city's main civic and mercantile square (*forum*) located at their intersection. Other uses were allocated in various ways among the four quadrants, whose streets ran parallel to the *cardo* and *decumanus*. Very large buildings, such as the amphitheater, were often relegated to the city's periphery, as were slaughterhouses and other unpleasant necessities.

Extensive public works were carried out in larger Roman cities, both of a utilitarian—aqueducts, sewers, harbor, markets—and of a social nature—public baths, gardens, library, amphitheater. In 3d-century Rome building regulations prescribed construction standards, maximum allowable building heights on public ways, and minimum setbacks from other buildings. At various times the imperial government interfered directly in housing, forcing owners to rebuild fire-damaged structures under penalty of confiscation (edict of Vespasian, AD c.70) and to repair dilapidated buildings (edict of Hadrian, AD c.129). Streets were widened to accommodate the growing number of heavy wagons, whose nighttime movement was banned (edict of Julius Caesar, 44 BC) as was the encroachment of stalls and shops on the public way (under Domitian, r. AD 81-96).

Medieval European Cities. Most of the Roman planning regulations fell into disuse during the protracted period of urban decadence that followed the dismembering (AD 476) of the empire, and they were not revived when European cities started flourishing again in the 10th and 11th centuries. They were replaced by a system of customary obligations that assigned to burgesses and guilds, or to work parties of residents, such traditional responsibilities of urban government as clearing refuse, maintaining highways, keeping the watch, and even repairing the city's walls. Even when a city's fortifications were extended to relieve overcrowding or to annex settlements beyond the walls, little effort was made to regulate the development of private property. Urban statutes, whether granted by charter or derived from local customs, were primarily concerned with collecting tolls and taxes, regulating the activities of the craft and merchant guilds, and ensuring an adequate supply in the town's markets.

Revival of the Rectangular Grid Plan. Occasionally, the establishment of a new settlement provided an opportunity to create a physical order in sharp contrast to the more or less tortuous pattern of most medieval cities. The simple geometry of the rectangular grid plan prevailed again, as in ancient times, in such late-medieval French *bastides* as Aigues-Mortes (1240) or Montpazier (1284)—new towns whose royal charters freed their inhabitants from feudal obligations and granted them advantageous trading privileges—and in the northern European trading cities of the Hanseatic League. Medieval theories of the city form were explicitly stated in Albrecht Dürer's idealized fortified capital of a kingdom in *Etliche Underricht zu Befestigung der Stett, Schlosz und Flecken* (1527; Guide to the Fortification of City, Castle, and Town), whose rigid spatial organization grouped classes by social status and segregated such noxious buildings as slaughterhouses, tanneries, and ironworks.

Renaissance Urban Planning. The shape of the city became more complicated as a result of improvements in the techniques of war and the reawakened interest in urban aesthetics in the Renaissance. The greater power of siege artillery required the replacement of vertical city walls with angular fortifications, whose sloping planes deflected the impact of iron cannonballs. Aesthetically, cities were embellished by widening streets and opening up squares within the dense medieval fabric and by building new churches, town halls, and palaces. Straight avenues culminating in a monumental square ornamented with symmetrical buildings in the classical style became fashionable in the more prosperous European cities.

Starting in the middle of the 15th century, Italian theorists created a voluminous body of literature on the theory of urban planning. Largely inspired by Vitruvius, it treated aesthetics as well as such pragmatic questions as the design of fortifications, construction techniques, the location of specific facilities, and the supply of water. The theories of Leon Battista ALBERTI in *De re aedificatoria* (c.1450; trans. as *On Architecture*, 1726) and of Andrea PALLADIO in *I quattro libri d'architettura* (1570; trans. as *The Four Books of Architecture*, 1716), among many others, established an urban style whose influence was felt throughout the Western World. The aesthetic principles of the time were given their full rein in the layout of new towns: Palmanova (Italy, 1593), Willemstad (The Netherlands, 1583), and Versailles (France, 1665) exemplify the symmetry, the use of broad avenues leading to main squares, and the clear street patterns advocated by the Italian theorists.

The creation of an orderly urban environment naturally led to the formulation of development controls to preserve it. The plan prepared for a fourfold extension of Amsterdam (The Netherlands, 1612) offers an exceptional example of a comprehensive effort to combine aesthetic and functional aspirations. Its three wide concentric canals, interconnected by smaller waterways radiating from the old town center, delineated a series of functional zones, with strict development controls governing the frontage of buildings on the canals, the use to which they could be put, their maximum height, and the general appearance of the building facade. These regulations were enforced through covenants between the Town Council, which had reclaimed the land and constructed canals and streets, and the purchaser of each lot. Similarly, the *Act for Rebuilding the City of London* (1667), following the great fire of 1666, not only provided for the widening of streets and the opening of new avenues but also specified the height, general appearance, and materials to be used in the new buildings.

The influence of Renaissance planning is also to be found in many of the new cities founded by Europeans in the Americas and in Asia. The Spanish colonial cities owed their rectangular plan and main square surrounded by the principal church and the government building to the Royal Ordinances of 1573 (*Leyes de las Indias*). William Penn's plan for Philadel-

phia (1682) and that for Montreal (1672) embodied the accepted planning principles of the time: straight streets and one or more public squares on which the principal buildings were located.

ORIGINS OF CONTEMPORARY PLANNING

Many of the problems that still plague our cities—slums, environmental pollution, social and economic segregation—came about during the Industrial Revolution. The incapacity of urban governments to enlarge their traditional responsibilities at a time when cities were developing rapidly led to the proliferation of substandard buildings, the intermingling of noisome industries and housing, and a density of development that overtaxed primitive water supplies and sewerage systems. Conditions in Manchester, England, in the 1830s were symptomatic of the urban deterioration that was taking place. The city's population had more than doubled in 30 years, and almost half of the housing units were slums. No less than 15% of the dwellings were damp cellars, and 20% had their only access to light and air through narrow passages, often less than 2 m (6 ft) wide; more than 80% of the dwellings had no running water, and 30 or more families commonly shared an outdoor privy; fewer than half of the streets were paved; refuse was collected only monthly in the poorer districts. At the end of the 19th century, almost 40% of the population of New York City, in large part newly arrived immigrants, lived in overcrowded tenements, many of whose rooms had no outside windows. Similar conditions prevailed in London, Berlin, Paris, Chicago, and other large cities. Infant mortality was high, and cholera epidemics broke out frequently.

19th-Century Urban Planning. Modern urban planning owes its origin to the necessity for creating a more sanitary urban environment by demolishing the worst slums and controlling the quality of new construction. In England the *Health of the Towns Act* (1868) empowered municipalities to prescribe sanitary standards for housing and to issue a "closing order" when a dwelling was "unfit for human habitation," whereas the *Public Health Act* (1875) allowed towns to regulate new buildings and mandated the construction of water and sewer systems and the removal of refuse. Elsewhere in Europe new districts were planned on the urban fringe, replacing the now-obsolete fortifications, as in Vienna (1856) and Copenhagen (1865). Slums were cleared and broad avenues pierced through older districts, as in Paris, where Baron Georges Eugène HAUSSMANN launched (1848) an ambitious plan in the course of which more than 40% of the city's houses were torn down and replaced with new buildings, while new districts were laid out on the periphery and an extensive system of parks was created.

In the United States, Pierre Charles L'ENFANT had laid out

(Below, left to right) *Six typical housing patterns are illustrated by these maps, based on aerial photographs of the United States, each representing 40 ha (100 acres). Three areas of single-family dwellings show both symmetrical construction on individual plots and houses clustered around cul-de-sacs in a wooded setting that provides the illusion of privacy. In cities, modern high-rise apartment blocks allow a*

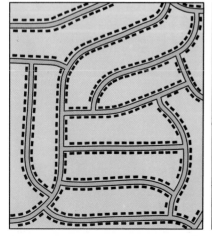
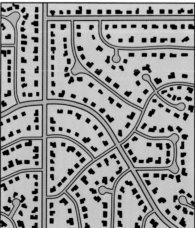
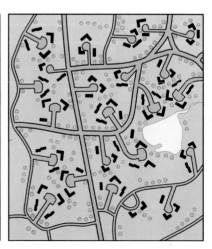

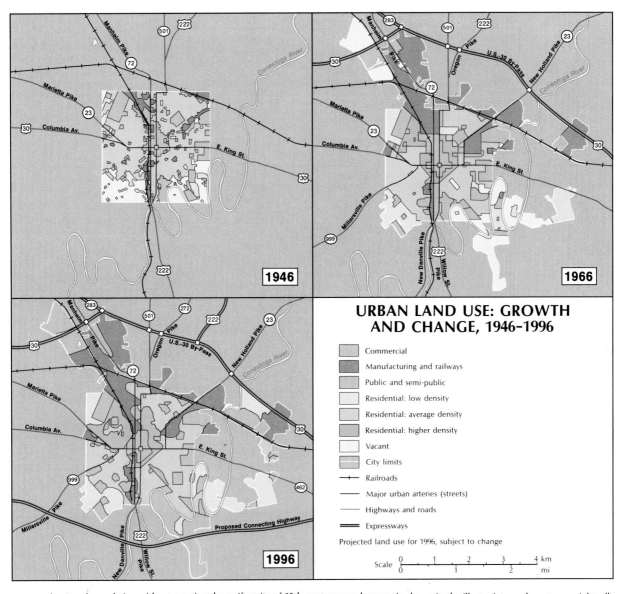

URBAN LAND USE: GROWTH AND CHANGE, 1946-1996

- ▉ Commercial
- ▉ Manufacturing and railways
- ▉ Public and semi-public
- ▉ Residential: low density
- ▉ Residential: average density
- ▉ Residential: higher density
- ▉ Vacant
- ▉ City limits
- —+— Railroads
- —— Major urban arteries (streets)
- —— Highways and roads
- ▬▬ Expressways

Projected land use for 1996, subject to change

Scale

greater density of population without creating the uniformity of 19th-century row-houses. As shown in the illustration on the extreme right, all these patterns are sometimes mixed in the same area. (Above) Three maps of an American city show the gradual spread of construction along railway lines and major highways and the growth of suburbs outside the former city limits.

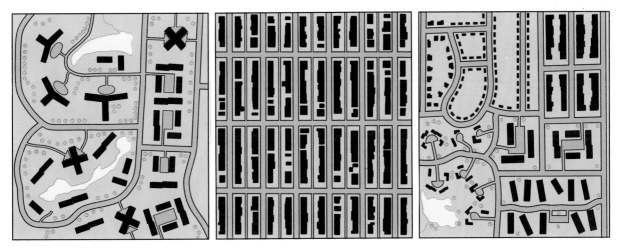

(1791) the new capital of Washington, D.C., on an enormous scale, with a rectangular street grid laid over a plan of radial avenues, with squares and circles at major intersections. Urban improvements had been limited to parks in the 19th century, but the European approach was popularized by Chicago's WORLD'S COLUMBIAN EXPOSITION OF 1893 whose dazzling white plaster buildings lining landscaped avenues fired the imagination of visitors with a vision of a more aesthetic and efficient urban environment. Plans, largely inspired by Haussmann's work in Paris, were prepared for a formal grouping of federal buildings in Washington, D.C. (1900), for San Francisco (1905), and for Chicago (1909). Many cities undertook to improve their water and sewer systems. Yet, despite improvements generated by the "City Beautiful" movement, city governments found imposing even minimal controls on private property politically difficult. The construction of unhealthy "old law" tenements was not outlawed in New York until 1901, and the new standards, prescribing an air shaft to ventilate inside rooms, were only marginally better. Only 22 cities had adopted height-restriction regulations by 1913; the first comprehensive zoning ordinance, specifying permitted uses as well as density of development, was not adopted in New York City until 1916.

CONTEMPORARY URBAN PLANNING

Effective urban planning comprises clear development objectives as well as the means to carry them out. Development objectives can vary greatly according to local conditions and the consensus that can be achieved on community goals. A city may choose to develop its unbuilt land, revitalize its downtown area, demolish its slums and replace them with new buildings, or any combination of these objectives. Its development objectives, usually combining social and physical aspects, are set forth in a comprehensive plan, which documents existing conditions, analyzes the causes of various shortcomings, and explores alternative solutions. By comparing the social, economic, and political costs and advantages of possible solutions, a preferred alternative can be selected and detailed into specific projects and programs.

The implementation of a plan occurs over many years; its progress is a function of the city's ability to finance it as well as of the plan's political viability. The means at the city's disposal may range from the use of its normal regulatory powers to legislate for the health, safety, and general welfare of the population to direct intervention in the private market through tax incentives, the purchase of land and buildings by eminent domain, demolition of unsafe structures, and new construction.

Zoning and Subdivision. Zoning and subdivision regulations are the powers most commonly used to regulate private development. Zoning separates land uses that are deemed incompatible by dividing the city into districts where only structures for specified uses, such as single-family homes, apartments, retail, or industry, can be built. Minimum lot sizes, maximum building heights, and setbacks from property lines are commonly part of zoning. Subdivision regulations prescribe the site-planning standards to be used in housing developments. They specify road widths and turning radii, sidewalk dimensions, utilities and drainage, street lighting, and landscaping. Together with building and health codes, zoning and subdivision regulations can effectively control the quality of new construction. They have little influence on urban social problems, however, except insofar as they help determine the cost of new housing by specifying the amount of land required by a dwelling and the standard to which it is to be improved. Because the cost of improved land in a suburban subdivision typically accounts for 25% to 28% of the cost of the dwelling, variations in this amount will affect the cost of housing. Zoning has thus tended to result in socio-economic stratification. In recent years large-lot suburban zoning ordinances have at times been declared unconstitutional by the courts as barriers to the mobility of lower-income families.

Urban Renewal in the United States. In the United States direct government intervention was the keystone of urban renewal. Intended in part to eliminate substandard housing,

which was estimated to account for 19% of dwellings in cities of 100,000 or more population, the urban-renewal legislation that was adopted as part of the 1949 Housing Act postulated a cooperative process between the public and private sectors. Local governments purchased land containing a specified percentage of substandard structures, prepared a reuse plan, undertook necessary demolition, provided new streets and utilities, and sold the improved parcels to private developers willing to build in accordance with the renewal plan. The difference between the public costs of the project and the resale value of the land was shared between the federal and local governments, the federal share amounting to two-thirds of the net cost. More than 2,000 projects with an average area of 72 acres were initiated under this controversial program; its major shortcomings were the displacement of low-income families and a failure to construct as many low- and moderate-income housing units as had been demolished.

New Towns. Direct government intervention also takes place in the planning of NEW TOWNS, whose origins go back to Ebenezer HOWARD who, in his book *Garden Cities of Tomorrow* (1898), proposed to relieve the congestion of London by building self-contained communities (see GARDEN CITY) on its periphery. In the United States, Howard's ideas were developed by Clarence Stein (1882–1975) and Henry WRIGHT in Radburn, N.J. (1928), and in the new towns, such as Greenbelt, Md. (1937), sponsored by the U.S. Resettlement Administration, which demonstrated the advantages of clustering housing in superblocks containing communal landscaped areas and of providing pedestrian and bicycle ways separate from vehicular traffic.

Howard's ideas became most influential in England and continental Europe. After World War II the British government, through its newly created Ministry of Town and Country Planning, undertook an ambitious program of planned decentralization. Twenty-eight new towns, with target populations varying from 25,000 to 300,000, were built near congested industrial cities. In Europe new towns of similar magnitude are an integral part of the regional plans of Copenhagen, Helsinki, Stockholm, and Paris and have been used as well to promote the growth of underdeveloped regions. In Third World countries new towns have been constructed to promote economic development and to provide new capital cities.

In the United States the magnitude of necessary public intervention has prevented the establishment of new towns from becoming official policy. The experience of other countries has shown that a large public investment was required to purchase the land and create the physical and social infrastructure. In addition, substantial financial incentives had to be offered to both housing developers and private industrial and commercial firms to induce them to locate in new towns, although some of these costs eventually could be recovered from land sales and taxes. The almost exclusively residential "new towns" that were privately developed in the United States starting in the 1960s—Reston, Va. (begun 1963), Columbia, Md. (begun 1962), Irvine, Calif. (begun 1960s)—are more akin to well-planned housing developments than to the self-contained European new towns.

URBAN PLANNING SINCE 1960

Urban planning has evolved rapidly since the 1960s, extending its historical concern with the built environment to social and economic issues. The question is no longer whether planning is necessary, but rather how extensive planning should be. In the United States and in most Western industrialized countries, urban planning is now commonly understood to include the delivery of social services, the development of employment opportunities for the economically disadvantaged, the search for housing solutions that avoid the stigma of public housing projects, and the protection of the environment. More attention is also being paid to the participation of those affected by planning decisions through mandatory public hearings and community discussion of development alternatives.

In the developing countries of the Third World a lack of investment capital and rates of urbanization two to three times higher than in the West, resulting from rapid population growth and migration from rural areas, have created problems of unprecedented magnitude. Typical urban planning priorities in the Third World include provision of a minimum sanitary shelter, when the average per-capita gross national product is often less than one-seventh that of the industrialized countries; construction of sufficient educational facilities, when typically almost half of the population are children below the age of 15 and 50% or more of adults are illiterate; and creation of employment, when the rate of entry into the labor force is 2.5 times higher than in the West. In light of these conditions, planning has tended to be a centralized government function whose major preoccupation has been the allocation of scarce resources to projects furthering national economic development objectives. The protection of the environment and the aesthetic appearance of cities have understandably received less attention than in the wealthier nations.

FRANÇOIS C. D. VIGIER

Bibliography: Batty, M., and Hutchinson, B., eds., *Systems Analysis in Urban Policy-Making and Planning* (1983); Blair, T. L., ed., *Urban Innovation Abroad* (1984); Brotchie, J., ed., *The Future of Urban Form* (1985); Cercero, R., *Suburban Gridlock* (1986); Clawson, M., and Hall, P., *Planning and Urban Growth: An Anglo-American Comparison* (1973); Ghosh, P. K., ed., *Urban Development in the Third World* (1984); Goodman, Percival and Paul, *Communitas* (1947; 2d rev. ed., 1960); Hugo-Brunt, M., *The History of City Planning* (1972); Olmsted, F. L., *Public Parks and the Enlargement of Towns* (1870; repr. 1970); Osborn, F. J., and Whittick, A., *New Towns* (1977); Sarin, M., *Urban Planning in the Third World: The Chandigarh Experience* (1982); Tunnard, C., *A World with a View: An Inquiry into the Nature of Scenic Values* (1978).

urban renewal: see CITY.

Urban II, Pope

Urban II, b. *c.*1042, d. July 24, 1099, was pope from 1088 until his death. He was a Frenchman named Odo. His great achievement was the continuance into the last years of the century—and in the face of opposition from Holy Roman Emperor HENRY IV—of the far-ranging ecclesiastical reform begun by Pope GREGORY VII.

After studying at the cathedral schools of Soissons and Reims, and after a period of service as archdeacon in the latter diocese, he became first monk and then prior at the great reforming monastery of Cluny. Going to Rome in 1078, he was created cardinal by Gregory VII and remained in the papal service until his own election as pope, succeeding Victor III. As pope, Urban had to vindicate his own legitimacy against an antipope—Clement III—who was sponsored by Henry IV. He contrived nonetheless to vindicate the preeminence of the papacy in Latin Christendom, not only by leading the reform but also by launching the First CRUSADE in 1095. A cult developed around Urban soon after his death, and Leo XIII beatified him in 1881. Feast day: July 29.   FRANCIS OAKLEY

Bibliography: Barraclough, Geoffrey, *The Medieval Papacy* (1968); Gossman, Francis J., *Pope Urban II and Canon Law* (1960).

Urban VI, Pope

Urban VI, b. *c.*1318, d. Oct. 15, 1389, pope from 1378 until his death, precipitated the Great SCHISM of the Western church. Originally named Bartolomeo Prignano, he became archbishop of Acerenza (1363) and of Bari (1377) and served as papal chancellor under Pope Gregory XI. Upon Gregory's death Urban was chosen to succeed him by a papal conclave strongly influenced by the Roman populace's demand for a Roman or Italian pope. Although known previously as an able administrator, as pope Urban acted in such a high-handed manner that he alienated the cardinals, and questions were raised about his sanity. Within a few months the powerful French cardinals returned to Avignon, declared Urban's election invalid, and elected Robert of Geneva (Clement VII) as "antipope." Thus the Great Schism began. Clement's supporters included Queen JOAN I of Naples. Urban secured her overthrow (1381) by Charles of Durazzo (CHARLES III of Naples)

but later led an expedition against Charles during which Urban was captured (1383–84). On his release he had five cardinals executed for conspiracy against him.

Bibliography: John, Eric, ed., *The Popes: A Concise Biographical History* (1964); Ullmann, Walter, *The Origins of the Great Schism* (1948).

Urban VIII, Pope

Urban VIII, b. Apr. 5, 1568, d. July 29, 1644, was pope from 1623 until his death. A Florentine aristocrat named Maffeo Barberini, he was named a cardinal in 1606 and bishop of Spoleto. As pope he encouraged the religious life by canonizing a number of saints and approving new orders. He revised the breviary, the missal, and the pontifical, and fostered missionary work by founding (1627) the Urban College of Propaganda. Urban also sponsored extensive building of military fortifications in the Papal States.

Urban's fear of Habsburg domination in Europe led him to favor France in the Thirty Years' War, although he tried to prevent Cardinal Richelieu's alliance with Sweden. Within Italy he was defeated in a war (1642–44) with the Farnese duke of Parma.

Urban was a noted scholar and poet and a patron of Giovanni Lorenzo Bernini. Despite his earlier friendship with Galileo, in 1633 he allowed the scientist to be imprisoned and forced to recant.

Bibliography: John, Eric, ed., *The Popes: A Concise Biographical History* (1964).

Urdu language: see INDO-IRANIAN LANGUAGES.

urea [yur-ee'-uh]

The formation of urea and its excretion in the urine is the body's principal means of eliminating excess nitrogen derived from amino acids, which are the molecular components of protein. Urea is a simple organic molecule, $CO(NH_2)_2$, in which almost half of the molecular weight is accounted for by nitrogen. An average adult male excretes about 30 grams (1 ounce) of urea in 24 hours if the diet consists of animal protein.

Urea is formed in the liver as the product of a set of biochemical reactions called the urea cycle. Although the urea cycle is complex, its net effect is the formation of urea molecules by combining nitrogen from the amino groups of amino acids with carbon and oxygen from carbon dioxide. Urea is carried from the liver by the bloodstream, and in the kidneys it is removed from the blood and concentrated for excretion. If the kidneys fail, blood urea concentration may rise to high levels, a toxic condition known as uremia. Urea and other waste products must be removed from the blood during uremia by a clinical procedure called blood dialysis.

PETER L. PETRAKIS

Bibliography: Grisolia, Santiago, et al., *The Urea Cycle* (1976).

uremia [yur-ee'-mee-uh]

Uremia is the term used to describe the wide variety of symptoms and physical abnormalities that result from the kidneys' failure to remove nitrogenous waste products normally excreted in the urine. The toxic effects of uremia affect virtually all human organs. The most common symptoms are high blood pressure, swelling (edema) of the ankles, nausea, vomiting, and weight loss. Anemia is almost always present because high blood levels of urea, one of the nitrogenous substances, shorten the life span of red blood cells. Other symptoms may include irritation of the heart sac (pericarditis), bleeding, muscle twitches, and itching (pruritus). In the later stages uremia causes agitation alternating with stupor, convulsions, coma, and ultimately death. Analysis of blood chemistries shows elevated levels of urea, creatinine, uric acid, phosphorus, and hydrogen ion. The levels of other minerals, hormones, and vitamins are abnormal as well. Removal of the toxins and improvement of the body's overload of fluids and acid are possible with the artificial kidney (hemodialysis), and patients are usually restored to a reasonably good state of health (see KIDNEY, ARTIFICIAL).

Bibliography: Merrill, John P., and Hampers, Constantine L., *Uremia: Progress in Pathophysiology and Treatment* (1971).

ureter   [yur-ee'-tur]

The ureter is a tube that extends from each kidney to the urinary bladder in birds, mammals, and reptiles. The moist membrane (mucosa) bordering its canal is lined with a transitional epithelium that is easily distended when large amounts of urine pass to the bladder. A wall of smooth muscle produces peristaltic waves (involuntary pulselike movements) that propel the urine into the bladder.   ROY HARTENSTEIN

urethra   [yur-eeth'-ruh]

The urethra is a canal that extends from the urinary bladder in placental mammals and discharges URINE or sperm externally. In the human female this canal runs along the front wall of the vagina, opening into the vestibule of the vulva, behind the clitoris; it is separate from the genital tract. In the male the vas deferens empties sperm into the urethra so that both sperm and urine pass to an opening at the extremity of the penis. An internal and external sphincter at the junction of the urethra and urinary bladder controls the emptying of the bladder.   ROY HARTENSTEIN

Urey, Harold Clayton   [yur'-ee]

Harold Clayton Urey, b. Walkerton, Ind., Apr. 29, 1893, d. Jan. 5, 1981, was awarded the 1934 Nobel Prize for chemistry for the discovery and isolation of deuterium (heavy hydrogen). Because of this recognition as a Nobel laureate and his experience in isotope separation, Urey was brought into the wartime Manhattan Project as head of the gaseous-diffusion project for uranium separation. Soon after the war, however, he began to speak out against the misuse of nuclear energy. His later research involved such diverse fields as geochemistry, astrophysics, and the origin of LIFE.

Bibliography: Silverstein, Alvin and Virginia, *Harold Urey* (1971).

uric acid   [yur'-ik]

Uric acid, the main end product or purine metabolism in humans and other primates, is derived from adenine and guanine, two purines that are important constituents of nucleic acids (DNA and RNA). In birds and reptiles, uric acid, a nitrogen-rich compound, performs the same function as UREA in mammals—ridding the body of excess nitrogen derived from amino acids. Birds and reptiles do not produce urea.

Uric acid is only slightly soluble, a property that accounts for the symptoms of GOUT, a disease in which levels of uric acid in the blood are elevated either from excess uric acid formation or from impaired uric acid excretion by the kidneys. The limited solubility of uric acid also causes the development of kidney stones; excess deposits of uric acid in the joints result in a condition called gouty arthritis, in which movement of a joint is accompanied by severe pain.
          PETER L. PETRAKIS

urine

Urine is an aqueous solution, ranging from a liquid to a semisolid, formed by the EXCRETORY SYSTEM in animals and released from the body. It is composed of organic and inorganic substances, primarily metabolic waste products and water. Organisms have varying requirements for water, and this is reflected in their urine composition. Freshwater drinking animals, for example, may need to rid their bodies of excess water. As a consequence, their urine will be dilute. Desert and marine mammals need to avoid water loss, and their urine can be very highly concentrated.

Birds and reptiles produce a urine that is white and composed of uric acid crystals suspended in solution. It is mixed

with fecal matter before expulsion. Land insects expel a nearly solid urine, and in some species it is stored as a body pigment rather than expelled. Amphibians and fishes release a liquid solution of urea that tends to be very dilute. In humans as well as other mammals, urine formation takes place in the nephrons of the kidneys. It is essentially a filtration of blood plasma, excluding most large molecules (over 70,000 molecular weight) such as albumin. In the average person, about 120 ml (3.6 fl oz) of filtrate are derived from 650 ml (19.5 fl oz) of plasma each minute by both kidneys. About 99 percent of the sodium, chloride, and water of the filtrate is reabsorbed before the urine exits the kidneys, leaving only about 1 ml of urine per minute for excretion. In the average adult, about 1,200–2,000 ml (40–67 fl oz) of urine are formed each day.

Because the kidney is the only way to eliminate nonvolatile acids from the body, urine is usually acid. In addition, the kidney is the primary route for excretion of metabolic endproducts, such as urea and uric acid from protein metabolism. Human urine also contains creatinine, inorganic salts, and the pigmented products of blood breakdown, such as urochrome, which gives urine its characteristic yellowish color. If kidney function decreases sufficiently, the body retains toxic substances, which leads to the development of UREMIA.

The kidneys have the ability to rid the body of excess water by putting out a dilute urine or to conserve water by putting out a concentrated urine. This is controlled by ANTIDIURETIC HORMONE. The various regulatory and excretory mechanisms of the kidneys allow the urine composition to vary, and thus maintain the constancy and volume of the fluid compartments of the body while eliminating unwanted substances.

Because most kidney diseases and several systemic diseases cause abnormal findings during chemical and microscopic examination of the urine, urinalysis is an extremely important laboratory test in clinical medicine.   JOHN M. WELLER

Bibliography: Lippman, Richard W., *Urine and the Urinary Sediment: A Practical Manual and Atlas*, 2d ed. (1977); Ross, Doris, and Neely, A. E., *Textbook of Urinalysis and Body Fluids* (1982).

Uris, Leon   [yur'-is]

An American novelist and screenwriter, Leon Uris, b. Baltimore, Md., Aug. 3, 1924, is famous for his massive, best-selling adventure novels in which a fictitious protagonist is placed in a semifactual historical context, such as the founding of the Israeli state (*Exodus,* 1959; film, 1961), the Berlin airlift (*Armageddon,* 1964), the Cuban missile crisis (*Topaz,* 1967; film, 1969), or the 1916 Easter Rising in Ireland (*Trinity,* 1976). Several of his novels have been adapted for film and television, and Uris has also written original screenplays, such as *Gunfight at the OK Corral* (1957).
          CHARLOTTE SOLOMON

Urmia, Lake   [oor'-mee-uh]

Lake Urmia is a salt lake in north Iran, which has a maximum depth of 16 m (52 ft) and an area ranging from 3,885 to 5,955 km² (1,500 to 2,300 mi²), depending on the season. The largest lake in Iran, it forms an interior drainage basin that receives water from the mountains but has no outlet. Ferry service links Sharifkhaneh and Gelemkhaneh. Migrating flamingos and pelicans frequent the lake, and on the small volcanic islands, leopards are common.

Urnfield culture

Urnfield culture was a Late Bronze Age culture of Europe distinguished by the rite of cremation burial in cemeteries, the ashes being interred in pottery urns. Ancestors of the CELTS, the Urnfielders originated in eastern Europe, where their cemeteries in Hungary and Romania can be traced back to the early 2d millennium BC. By the 14th century BC the Urnfielders had spread across the Rhine, and by 750 BC they had reached southern France. Urnfield sites have also been found in northeastern Spain, northern Italy, Sicily, and the Lipari Islands.

The Urnfielders built hill forts with timber-laced ramparts, and they probably traded with the classical world for wine.

They are thought to have developed the sword from the rapiers they encountered through contacts with the east Mediterranean. Urnfield culture ended in the 7th century BC, when it was replaced by the iron-using culture of the HALLSTATT Celts.

LLOYD LAING

Bibliography: Coles, J. M., and Harding, A. F., *The Bronze Age in Europe* (1980); Piggott, Stuart, *Ancient Europe* (1965).

Urochordata: see TUNICATE.

urogenital diseases

Urogenital diseases include diseases of the urinary tract of the EXCRETORY SYSTEM—from the KIDNEY to the external opening of the URETHRA—and of the tract of the REPRODUCTIVE SYSTEM. These diseases are commonly grouped for convenience because in males the two tracts share the terminal end and in females the tracts, although separate, are contiguous. Thus in either sex a problem in one tract is likely to affect the other. The medical specialties most directly concerned with urogenital diseases are GYNECOLOGY and urology; both involve the urinary tract, but the former specializes in female and the latter in male genital-tract disorders. The illnesses studied include a wide range of INFECTIOUS DISEASES, tumors, congenital (inborn) disorders, allergy and immunity problems, and diseases of other body systems or of general metabolism that also affect the urinary and genital tracts, such as cardiovascular diseases and diabetes.

Urinary-Tract Diseases. Among the more serious KIDNEY DISEASES are glomerulonephritis, nephrosis, and pyelonephritis. Of the many observed forms of glomerulonephritis, most show evidence of deposits of antibody-antigen complexes in the glomeruli, the kidney's filtering units; thus one common form of the disease occurs two to three weeks after an infection of the throat or skin with streptococci. Most cases are temporary but a few become chronic, leading to kidney failure and UREMIA. Nephrosis, or nephrotic syndrome, is an outpouring of protein into the urine due to glomeruli damage. This condition is not itself a disease but a symptom observed at some time in the course of chronic glomerulonephritis, multiple myeloma, lupus erythematosus, or other serious diseases. Pyelonephritis is a serious infection of kidney tissue that can result in permanent damage if not treated promptly. It usually results from bacterial infections of the BLADDER (see CYSTITIS) or of the URETER, the tube ascending from the bladder to the kidney.

Infections of the urethra, the final portion of the urinary tract, are collectively known as urethritis. Such infections include CHLAMYDIA and GONORRHEA (see also VENEREAL DISEASES), among others, although in females gonorrhea tends to ascend the genital passage. The agents responsible for urethritis can also spread into adjacent tissues.

Another urinary-tract affliction is the development of KIDNEY STONES and bladder stones; such stones also commonly arise in conjunction with infections. Stones are caused by the precipitation of insoluble materials from the URINE; some persons with GOUT form uric-acid stones, and some persons with tumors of the parathyroid glands form calcium stones. Small stones become trapped as they descend from the kidney into the ureter, and the waves of contraction to move them along produce the extremely painful condition known as ureteral COLIC.

Male Genital-Tract Diseases. One site along the male genital tract that is a frequent source of problems in middle and older age is the PROSTATE GLAND. The gland surrounds the urethra just below the bladder; because of this location, the prostate compresses the posterior urethra when it is enlarged by infections (prostatitis) or by benign tumors. The compression obstructs urinary flow and, if severe enough and continued over a long period of time, results in urinary-tract infection, severe renal damage, and uremia. Cancer of the prostate is uncommon in men under the age of 60, but its incidence increases steadily thereafter; its development is stimulated by male hormones and retarded—to a variable extent—by female hormones (see SEX HORMONES).

Female Genital-Tract Diseases. The vagina, uterus, and associated glands of the female genital tract are all common sites of venereal diseases and of a number of nonvenereal infections due to other bacteria and yeasts. Bacteria that move upward from the vagina during menstruation are also responsible for major problems of the fallopian tubes; such infections result in abscess of the tubes and in localized PERITONITIS. This serious and painful condition is known as pelvic inflammatory disease (PID). The condition can also lead to scarring of the fallopian tubes, which blocks the passage of ova and is a major cause of infertility. A number of bacteria—particularly those which cause gonorrhea—have been implicated in PID, as well as some viruses.

A number of benign and malignant cysts and tumors can develop in the female genital tract. In fact, no other organ exhibits as many distinct types of malignant tumors as the ovary. The ovary is also the seat of several types of benign cysts and solid tumors, including endometriosis—a benign transplant of cells from the uterine lining (endometrium) cast off during menstruation. In the endometrium itself, malignancies occur with increasing frequency among the elderly; malignancies of the uterine muscle, called leiomyosarcomas, are seen more occasionally, but the benign tumors called leiomyomas are also fairly common.

The PAP TEST is routinely given in the United States to detect cancer of the neck of the uterus, or cervix, another common malignancy. The vagina and associated glands are not common sites for tumors, except for the increased frequency of vaginal carcinomas seen in daughters of women who had been treated with large doses of progestins (sex hormones) while pregnant.

AARON D. FREEDMAN, M.D.

Bibliography: Kunin, C. M., *Detection, Prevention and Management of Urinary Tract Infections*, 3d ed. (1979); Resnick, M. I., and Older, R. A., *Diagnosis of Genitourinary Disorders* (1982); Rickham, P. P., et al., *Genito-Urinary Problems in Childhood* (1983); Shephard, B. O. and C. A., *The Complete Guide to Women's Health* (1982); Smith, D. R., *General Urology*, 11th ed. (1984).

Urquiza, Justo José de [oor-kee'-sah]

Justo José de Urquiza, b. Oct. 18, 1801, d. Apr. 11, 1870, an Argentine statesman and soldier, helped lead his country toward unity and constitutional government. Urquiza entered politics in his home province of Entre Ríos and for a time served the dictator Juan Manuel de ROSAS as principal field commander. In 1841 he became governor of Entre Ríos, maintaining his position with a strong military force and introducing educational, fiscal, and administrative reforms.

In 1852, Urquiza and other governors, chafing under the domination of Buenos Aires, joined with liberals, exiles, and Brazilian forces to defeat Rosas at the Battle of Monte Caseros. Urquiza then became provisional dictator of the Argentine Confederation; he sanctioned a new constitution (1853) based on that of the United States. In 1854 he was inaugurated president, but his efforts to achieve unity were hindered by the secession of Buenos Aires. Urquiza lost decisive battles against Buenos Aires at Cepeda in 1859 and at Pavón in 1861. His position in Entre Ríos declined, and he and his sons were assassinated by a follower of a political rival.

Ursa Major: see BIG DIPPER.

Ursa Minor: see LITTLE DIPPER.

Ursúa, Pedro de [oor-soo'-ah]

Pedro de Ursúa, c.1510–1561, was a Spanish soldier and explorer of South America. He went to the New World in 1545 and spent several years conquering the Indians of New Granada. After serving (1546) as governor of Bogotá, in what is now Colombia, he founded (1549) Pamplona, which he governed from 1549 to 1550. In 1558, Ursúa went to Peru, and 2 years later he accompanied Lope de AGUIRRE in a search for gold and for the headwaters of the Amazon River. It is believed that while on that journey Aguirre murdered Ursúa.

Ursula, Saint   [ur'-suh-luh]

The subject of popular legend during the Middle Ages, Saint Ursula was a 4th-century British princess and martyr. Returning from a pilgrimage to Rome, she and her 11,000 virgin companions were massacred at Cologne by the Huns. She is the patron saint of the Ursuline nuns (founded 1544). Feast day: Oct. 21 (suppressed in 1969).

Uruguay   [yur'-uh-gway or oo-roo-gwy']

Uruguay, the second smallest country in South America, forms a wedge between Argentina on the west and Brazil on the north and east. On the south is the Atlantic and the RÍO DE LA PLATA estuary. The Uruguay River follows the country's western border, suggesting the name during the colonial period—Banda Oriental (east bank). Almost half of Uruguay's inhabitants live in MONTEVIDEO, the capital and only large city.

LAND AND RESOURCES

The countryside consists of rolling hills and prairies. An extension of the Brazilian Highlands lies in the northeast. The Cuchilla Grande (Grand Hills) runs from the northeast toward the south. Sandy beaches form a strip along the coast that is the basis for a large tourist industry. Punta del Este, an internationally popular resort, is located there. The southern plains extend from the rich alluvial soil at the Río de la Plata

ORIENTAL REPUBLIC OF URUGUAY

LAND. Area: 176,220 km² (68,039 mi²). Capital and largest city: Montevideo (1983 est. pop., 1,255,600).
PEOPLE. Population (1987 est.): 2,964,052; density (1987 est.): 16.8 persons per km² (43.6 per mi²). Distribution (1984 est.): 84.5% urban, 15.5% rural. Annual growth (1987 est.): 0.39%. Official language: Spanish. Major religion: Roman Catholicism.
EDUCATION AND HEALTH. Literacy (1987): 94.3% of adult population. Universities (1987): 1. Hospital beds (1981): 23,000. Physicians (1986): 5,756. Life expectancy (1985): 73 years. Infant mortality (1983): 32 per 1,000 live births.
ECONOMY. GDP (1986): $5.2 billion; $1,760 per capita. Labor distribution (1982): manufacturing—19%; government—19%; agriculture—16%; commerce—12%; utilities, construction, transport, and communication—12%; other services—22%; unemployment (1986 est.)—11%. Foreign trade (1986): imports—$708 million; exports—$960 million; principal trade partners—Brazil, Argentina, United States, European Community. Currency: 1 new Uruguayan peso = 100 centésimos.
GOVERNMENT. Type: republic. Legislature: National Congress. Political subdivisions: 19 departments.
COMMUNICATIONS. Railroads (1987): 3,000 km (1,864 mi) total. Roads (1985): 12,000 km (7,456 mi) motorways; 40,000 km (24,855 mi) provincial roads. Major ports: 1. Major airfields: 2.

estuary as far north as 160 km (100 mi) inland from Montevideo, and farther north along the Uruguay River to Salto.
Climate. Uruguay's climate is characterized by temperatures ranging from about 10° C (50° F) in July to 22° C (71° F) in February. Summer temperatures in Artigas, in the north, reach 27° C (81° F). Precipitation is adequate, with a mean annual rainfall of about 890 mm (35 in) increasing northward. No dry season occurs.
Drainage. The Río de la Plata drains eastward to the Atlantic Ocean and the Río Negro, westward into the Uruguay River. The Cuchilla Grande acts as a drainage divide. Lakes and lagoons are numerous, some reaching 180 km² (70 mi²) in size. The largest lake in South America is the artificial Embalse del Río Negro, covering about 10,400 km² (4,000 mi²).
Vegetation and Animal Life. Most of Uruguay is covered with grassland. Wildlife has greatly diminished with the growth of human and livestock populations. Jaguars and pumas have become rare, and capybaras, foxes, deer, armadillos, and alligators are also declining in numbers. The American ostrich, or rhea, is now found infrequently, but many other bird species inhabit the country.

PEOPLE

Of the almost 3 million Uruguayans, more than 85% are of European—predominantly Spanish and Italian—origin. A small number of mestizos and blacks have survived, whereas the original Charrúa Indian population has been totally absorbed. Spanish is the official language. Roman Catholicism is the religion of two-thirds of the population.

More than 90% of Uruguay's population are literate. A publicly financed program provides instruction at no cost to the student. The University of the Republic (1849) is located in Montevideo. Inadequate classroom space presents a major problem, as does the surplus of graduates in professional fields forced to seek jobs abroad.

The health-care system provides adequate medical services for everyone. Uruguay has 69 (1986) government-run hospi-

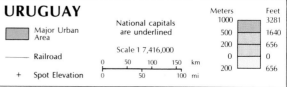

URUGUAY

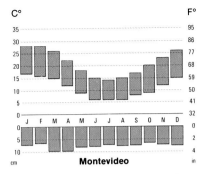

C° / F° chart — Montevideo

(Above) *Bars indicate monthly ranges of temperatures (red) and precipitation (blue) of Montevideo, the capital and largest city of Uruguay. Located in southern Uruguay on the alluvial plain of the Río de la Plata, the city has a subtropical humid climate.*

(Right) *Montevideo's Plaza de la Independencia, with its statue of the nationalist leader José Artigas, is one of the city's many expansive public squares. Montevideo has been the capital since Uruguay's independence in 1828 and is its major port on the Río de la Plata.*

tals, and the population's life expectancy is about 73 years.

Culture. A major representation in Uruguayan literature, drama, and music is the cowboylike gaucho. Foremost among 20th-century writers have been essayist José Enrique Rodó, short-story writer Horacio Quiroga, poet Juana de Ibarbourou, and novelists Mario Benedetti and Juan Carlos Onetti. Cultural activities are centered in Montevideo, where art and architecture have imitated European schools.

ECONOMIC ACTIVITY

Increased urbanization has forced the development of intensive agriculture, but in the interior, sheep and cattle grazing occupies more than 80% of the land. Uruguay, which has a minimum-wage law for agricultural workers, is largely self-sufficient in food production. It exploits its forest resources to a limited extent.

Public policy promotes industrialization in spite of the lack of minerals. No heavy industries have been developed. The government established Uruguay's largest meat-packing operation, encouraged the formation of dairy cooperatives, and created a publicly owned petroleum refinery.

The major industries continue to be agriculturally based. The deliberate development of the fishing industry was begun in the 1970s. The principal export items are wool, meat, and leather. Primary imports include petroleum, raw materials, chemicals, and machinery. Imports generally exceeded exports in value until the mid-1980s, when this trend was reversed.

GOVERNMENT AND HISTORY

Democracy in Uruguay collapsed in 1973 with a takeover by the armed forces. Labor unions and political parties were outlawed, and the independent judiciary was abolished. Each of the 19 departments was headed by an intendant designated by the central government.

On Mar. 1, 1985, Uruguay returned to its democratic tradition, after 12 years of military rule, when a centrist, Julio María Sanguinetti, took office as president. He had won the November 1984 election as the Colorado party candidate. The bicameral congress, dissolved in 1973, was restored, and a National Constituent Assembly was formed in 1985 to draw up a series of constitutional reforms.

Uruguay was the last colony settled by Spain in the Americas. Spain sent (1624) missionaries among the Charrúa Indians and founded (1726) Montevideo as a counter to Portuguese ambitions in the Río de la Plata estuary. In 1811 revolutionaries from the Banda Oriental, led by José Gervasio ARTIGAS, joined with the forces of the Buenos Aires junta in expelling the Spanish. An attempted federal union with Argentina failed because the latter sought to impose a centralized government on the Banda Oriental. Artigas, however, was unable to maintain Uruguayan independence against Brazil, which annexed the Banda Oriental in 1821.

A gaucho herds beef cattle in the rolling grasslands of central Uruguay. Livestock raising has long been a major economic activity in this South American nation. Today cattle and sheep continue to provide the meat, hides, and wool that are the nation's chief exports.

In 1825 the group called the Thirty-three Immortals, led by Juan Antonio LAVALLEJA, declared Uruguay's independence. War ensued, but both Argentina and Brazil recognized that independence in 1828.

Civil strife soon developed in the new country between two parties: the Blancos, led by Manuel Oribe, and the Colorados, led by Fructuoso RIVERA. Oribe was supported by Juan Manuel de ROSAS of Argentina, and war continued until the overthrow (1852) of Rosas. Renewed conflict between the Colorados and Blancos and intervention by Paraguay helped precipitate the War of the TRIPLE ALLIANCE (1865–70).

Peace and prosperity were finally achieved after 1903 under the leadership of President José BATLLE Y ORDÓÑEZ. Whereas few of his political and social reforms were adopted, the groundwork on which later reforms were built was his creation. In 1919 a new constitution was adopted, providing for a *colegiado,* a plural executive modeled on the Swiss pattern. The system was abolished in 1933, and for the next 10 years a mild dictatorship prevailed. A modified *colegiado* system was reintroduced in 1951.

After the mid-20th century, economic problems began to strain the political stability of the country. By the mid-1960s, strikes and riots had become prominent features of the sociopolitical scene. The 1967 return to presidential government did not alleviate the situation, and in the late 1960s, Marxist terrorist urban guerrillas called the Tupamaro National Liberation Front sought violent revolution. Between 1973 and 1976 the popularly elected government was eased out of office by the powerful armed forces. By the late 1970s the regime held thousands of political prisoners; civil rights violations continued into the 1980s. In 1984 the military permitted presidential elections, although several candidates were banned. The victor, Julio Sanguinetti, had joined in a pledge that there would be no purges for past abuses. He took office during a continuing economic crisis.   LARRY L. PIPPIN

Bibliography: Brannon, R. H., *The Agricultural Development of Uruguay* (1968); Dobler, Lavinia, *The Land and People of Uruguay,* rev. ed. (1972); Finch, M. H., *A Political Economy of Uruguay since 1870* (1981); Kaufman, Edy, *Uruguay in Transition: From Civilian to Military Rule* (1979); Ross, Gordon, *Argentina and Uruguay* (1976); Weil, Thomas E., et al., *Area Handbook for Uruguay* (1971).

Uruguay River

The Uruguay River, 1,610 km (1,000 mi) long, is a major South American river, draining approximately 307,000 km² (118,530 mi²). Its two main headstreams, the Pelotas and Canoas, rise about 65 km (40 mi) west of the Atlantic coast in southeastern Brazil and join near Piratuba. The river flows west and then turns southwest, flowing first along the Argentina-Brazil border and farther south along the Argentina-Uruguay border. Relatively silt-free, the Uruguay empties into the RÍO DE LA PLATA. It is navigable to Salto, 305 km (190 mi) upstream.

Uruk [oo'-ruk]

The ancient Sumerian city of Uruk (biblical Erech; modern Warka) lies 250 km (156 mi) southeast of Baghdad, Iraq. First settled (*c.*5000 BC) by the prehistoric inhabitants of Mesopotamia, the city developed (late 4th millennium BC) around the two sacred centers of Kullab and Eanna, which have yielded such evidence of early Sumerian civilization as monumental temples (at Eanna) decorated with cone mosaics, sophisticated sculpture, glyptic art, and some examples of the first, pictographic, writing. In the early 3d millennium BC, a 9.5-km-long (6-mi) city wall was built (according to tradition, by semimythological King Gilgamesh) to enclose an area of about 8.75 km² (3.4 mi²). Only intermittently independent, Uruk was subject to the Ur empire (*c.*2100–2000 BC) and to successive kings of Babylonia and Assyria, most of whom maintained its temples, as did the later Seleucids. Settlement declined during the Parthian period (247 BC–AD 226) and lay outside the city by Sassanian times (226–636).

Excavation is limited chiefly to the central sanctuaries. Eanna precinct, dedicated to the goddess Inanna, contains a ziggurat that was largely rebuilt (*c.*2100 BC) by Ur-Nammu of Ur.

To the west, at Kullab, ruins of the 4th-millennium BC White Temple stand on the Anu Ziggurat. The nearby Hellenistic Bit Resh (Principal Temple) was dedicated to Anu, the god of the heavens, and his consort. South of the Anu Ziggurat is the Seleucid temple of Irrigal, dedicated to the goddess Ishtar. Another Seleucid temple, the Bit Akitu, lies outside the northeastern city wall. The palace of Sinkashid (early 2d millennium BC) stands close to the western wall, and Parthian ruins, including the temple of Gareus, have been uncovered in the southern precincts of the city. Excavations at Uruk first were conducted in 1849–52; the ongoing German excavations were begun in 1913.   KATE FIELDEN

Bibliography: Hawkes, Jacquetta, ed., *Atlas of Ancient Archaeology* (1974); Mallowan, Sir Max, *Early Mesopotamia and Iran* (1965).

U.S. Information Agency

The U.S. Information Agency is an independent agency of the executive branch of the U.S. government founded in 1953. In 1977 it was merged with the Bureau of Educational and Cultural Affairs of the Department of State and was called for a few years the International Communications Agency. Its purpose is to spread information about the United States abroad, to inform the U.S. government about foreign opinion regarding the United States, and to arrange cultural and educational exchanges with foreign countries. The agency maintains libraries, reading rooms, and information centers in about 125 countries. Its largest component, the VOICE OF AMERICA, launched Radio Martí, to Cuba, in 1985.

U.S. News and World Report

A newsmagazine emphasizing the economic and social consequences of national and world affairs, *U.S. News and World Report* concentrates primarily on news of business, industry, finance, government, and the professions. David Lawrence (1888–1973), a newsman, founded the *United States News* as a weekly newspaper in 1933 and converted it to magazine format in 1940. In 1948 he merged it with *World Report,* begun 2 years earlier. Its circulation is over 2 million.

THEODORE PETERSON

U.S.A.

U.S.A. (1938), a novel by John DOS PASSOS, is an epic study from a radical-liberal point of view of the commercial vulgarization of American life from the beginning of the 20th century through the Depression of 1929–35. Divided into three books—*The 42nd Parallel* (1930), *1919* (1932), and *The Big Money* (1936)—*U.S.A.* is a collage of four kinds of materials: "Newsreels," recounting significant events through newspaper headlines, popular song lyrics, and other documentary sources; "Camera Eye," containing perceptions of such events through an anonymous stream-of-consciousness; poison-pen biographical sketches of the celebrities of the period; and long chapters from the linked histories of more than a dozen representative types of people.   WARREN FRENCH

Bibliography: Landsberg, Melvin, *Dos Passos Path to U.S.A.: A Political Biography, 1912–1936* (1973); Ludington, Townsend, *Twentieth Century Odyssey: The Life of John Dos Passos* (1980).

Ushuaia [oo-swy'-ah]

Ushuaia (1980 pop., 10,998), Argentina, founded as a Protestant mission in 1870, is the southernmost city in the world and the capital of Tierra del Fuego National Territory. Its port faces the Beagle Channel. Industries include sheep raising, lumbering, fishing, trapping, and tourism.

Usigli, Rodolfo [oo-seel'-yee]

The Mexican playwright and diplomat Rodolfo Usigli, b. Nov. 17, 1905, d. June 18, 1979, first won recognition as an author in 1936 with his comedy *Estado de secreto* (State of Secrecy). Influenced by the works of Shaw and Ibsen, Usigli's plays use sociopsychological problems as vehicles for an analysis of the Mexican character. His best play, *El gesticulador* (The Posturer, 1937), satirizes provincial politics, underscoring the betrayal of the Mexican revolution of 1910.   EDWARD MULLEN

Usman dan Fodio

Usman dan Fodio, 1754–1817, Islamic teacher and writer, led an Islamic reform movement that overthrew the Hausa city-state kingdoms of northern Nigeria and replaced them with a FULANI-dominated empire called the Sokoto caliphate. A native of the Hausa state of Gobir, he became a teacher and soon headed a community advocating the purification of Islam. Backed by the Fulani peoples, he directed the jihad (holy war) against the Hausa kingdoms that began in 1804. Within 4 years, his forces gained the upper hand. Usman acted as spiritual leader of the new Sokoto caliphate while others tended to its administration.   ROBERT R. GRIFFETH

Bibliography: Hiskett, Mervyn, *The Sword of Truth: The Life and Times of the Shehu Usuman dan Fodio* (1973); Last, Murray, *The Sokoto Caliphate* (1967).

USO: see UNITED SERVICE ORGANIZATIONS.

Ussher, James   [uhsh'-ur]

The Irish scholar and Anglican archbishop James Ussher, b. Jan. 4, 1581, d. Mar. 21, 1656, is best remembered for his long-accepted system of biblical chronology, which set the date of creation at 4004 BC. Ordained in 1601, he was professor of divinity at Trinity College, Dublin, before becoming bishop of Meath (1621) and archbishop of Armagh (1625). In England during the Irish revolt of 1641, he never returned to Ireland. He leaned toward Calvinism in theology, but he was royalist in politics. Ussher's scholarship was wide ranging and profound, and he made use of original manuscript sources. His greatest achievement was identifying the seven authentic letters of Ignatius of Antioch. He studied and wrote on Irish history, the creed, and church government. His library, including the magnificent Book of Kells, is preserved at Trinity College.   FREDERICK A. NORWOOD

USSR: see UNION OF SOVIET SOCIALIST REPUBLICS; RUSSIA/UNION OF SOVIET SOCIALIST REPUBLICS, HISTORY OF.

Ustinov, Peter   [yoo'-sti-nawf]

The actor, director, producer, playwright, and author Peter Ustinov, b. London, Apr. 16, 1921, has appeared in scores of plays and films, winning Academy Awards for his performances in *Spartacus* (1960) and *Topkapi* (1964) and three Emmy Awards for his television performances. A prolific author, he has written short stories (*Add a Dash of Pity,* 1966), a novel (*The Loser,* 1960), an autobiography (*Dear Me,* 1977), and plays for the stage and screen.

usury

Usury, the practice of charging an excessive rate of INTEREST on a loan, is regulated by many governments, and in the United States by state laws. The term originally meant any profit made from the loan of money. The Old Testament forbids the taking of interest. The medieval church also forbade usury, although as commercial societies developed in Europe, loaning money at interest became a necessity and the prohibition eventually disappeared. Islamic law, however, still forbids the practice.

In the United States the need for borrowed money was especially acute as the Western frontier advanced. The populist movement of the latter 1800s was fueled in part by Western demands for regulated, low-interest loans, and many state usury laws come out of this period. In recent years, most states have raised usury limits to conform with generally rising interest rates. A few states have eliminated usury laws entirely, counting on the resulting increased availability of funds and the competition between lenders to keep interest rates from soaring.

Bibliography: Arno Press and Silk, Leonard, eds., *Religious Attitudes toward Usury* (1972); Langholm, Odd, *The Aristotelian Analysis of Usury* (1985); Ryan, F. W., *Usury and Usury Laws* (1977).

Utagawa Kuniyoshi: see KUNIYOSHI.

Utah

Centrally located in the Rocky Mountain region, midway between Canada and Mexico, Utah is bordered by Wyoming on the northeast, Colorado on the east, Arizona on the south, Nevada on the west, and Idaho on the north. Utah is the 11th largest state and the 3d highest, with an average elevation of 1,859 m (6,100 ft). Except for a projection of Wyoming into its northeastern corner, Utah would be rectangular in shape, measuring 440 km (275 mi) from east to west and 555 km (345 mi) from north to south. Settled by Mormon pioneers

UTAH

    LAND. Area: 219,887 km² (84,899 mi²); rank: 11th. Capital and largest city: Salt Lake City (1986 est. pop., 158,440). Counties: 29. Elevations: highest—4,123 m (13,528 ft), at Kings Peak; lowest—610 m (2,000 ft), at Beaverdam Creek.
    PEOPLE. Population (1987 est.): 1,680,000; rank: 35th; density: 7.9 persons per km² (20.5 per mi²). Distribution (1986): 77% metropolitan, 23% nonmetropolitan. Average annual change (1980–87): +2.4%.
    EDUCATION. Public enrollment (1986): elementary—308,389; secondary—107,605; higher—73,067. Nonpublic enrollment (1980): elementary—2,800; secondary—2,100; combined—700; higher (1986)—33,146. Institutions of higher education (1985): 14.
    ECONOMY. State personal income (1986): $18.3 billion; rank: 35th. Median family income (1979): $20,024; rank: 22d. Nonagricultural labor distribution (1986): manufacturing—92,000 persons; wholesale and retail trade—153,000; government—141,000; services—138,000; transportation and public utilities—38,000; finance, insurance, and real estate—33,000; construction—33,000. Agriculture: income (1986)—$570 million. Forestry: sawtimber volume (1987 prelim.)—16.1 billion board feet. Mining: value (1985)—$1.9 billion. Manufacturing: value added (1985)—$4.8 billion. Services: value (1982)—$2.4 billion.
    GOVERNMENT (1989). Governor: Norman H. Bangerter, Republican. U.S. Congress: Senate—2 Republicans; House—1 Democrat, 2 Republicans. Electoral college votes: 5. State legislature: 29 senators, 75 representatives.
    STATE SYMBOLS. Statehood: Jan. 4, 1896; the 45th state. Nickname: Beehive State; bird: sea gull; flower: sego lily; tree: blue spruce; motto: Industry; song: "Utah, We Love Thee."

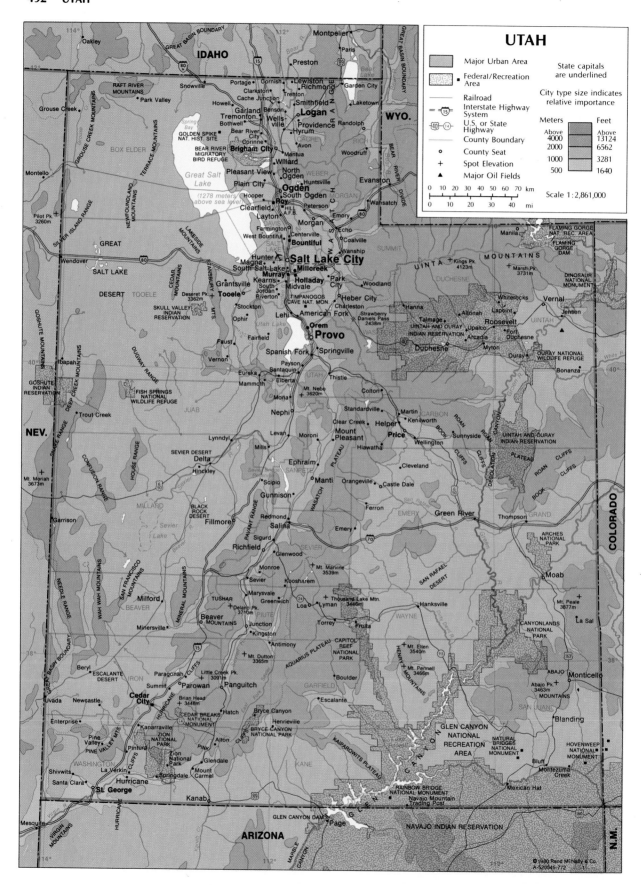

fleeing persecution in Illinois, Utah continues to have a large Mormon population. The state derives its name from the Ute Indians, who live in the Uinta Basin southeast of the capital, Salt Lake City.

LAND AND RESOURCES

The spine of the ROCKY MOUNTAINS runs down the middle of Utah, with the COLORADO PLATEAU to the east and the GREAT BASIN to the west. The part of the Rockies keeping to the main north-south axis is called the WASATCH RANGE. The Uinta Mountains, extending more than 160 km (100 mi) just below the Utah–Wyoming border, represent the longest east-west-trending range in the United States; Utah's highest point, Kings Peak, at 4,123 m (13,528 ft), lies within this range.

During its geologic history the Colorado Plateau gradually uplifted, causing the Colorado River and its tributaries to cut deep canyons and expose rock layers varying in color from white to orange, pink, and red. The Great Basin—the third largest region of interior drainage in the world—encompasses steep mountain ranges separated by broad desert flats.

Soils. Utah's soils range from the red and gray desert soils in the valleys to the alpine soils of the mountains. Most fertile are the alluvials and brown steppe—chestnut and chernozem loams formed along the bases of mountains. At higher elevations, gray brown podzolic soils underlie the state's forests.

Rivers and Lakes. Eastern Utah drains into the COLORADO RIVER and its branches; major tributaries of the Colorado include the GREEN RIVER and the San Juan. Streams in the western part of the state—such as the Jordan, Bear, Provo, Sevier, and Weber—flow into the Great Basin. The Virgin River in southwestern Utah empties into Lake Mead. In the extreme northwestern corner of the state, the Raft River drains into the Snake River.

In prehistoric times, Lake Bonneville, an inland sea, covered a large part of western Utah. Utah's most famous body of water, the GREAT SALT LAKE—the largest natural lake west of the Mississippi and the largest salt lake in the Western Hemisphere—is a remnant of Lake Bonneville, as are the BONNEVILLE SALT FLATS. Utah Lake, the state's largest natural freshwater lake, is dwarfed by the artificial Lake Powell—300 km (185 mi) from end to end, with an irregular shoreline.

Climate. Utah is the second driest state in the nation, with an average annual precipitation of 330 mm (13 in). Whereas the Great Salt Lake Desert receives only 127 mm (5 in) of precipitation per year, however, part of the Wasatch Range receives about 1,020 mm (40 in).

During the summer, average temperatures range between 18° C (65° F) and 28° C (83° F). Salt Lake City, for instance, has an average temperature in July of 25° C (77° F). In winter, temperatures fall below freezing, except in the southeastern corner of the state, where Saint George has an average January temperature of 4° C (39° F).

Vegetation and Animal Life. The vegetation of Utah's low-lying deserts includes the Joshua tree, creosote bush, mesquite, and several varieties of subtropical cacti. In the foothills piñon pine and gnarled juniper appear, and mountain flora include the blue spruce—the state tree—as well as the ponderosa pine, lodgepole pine, Douglas fir, Englemann spruce, and alpine fir. The nation's oldest trees, bristlecone pines, grow near the timberline, with some specimens dating back 3,000 years. The most common deciduous tree, the so-called quaking aspen, forms large stands at elevations well above 2,130 m (7,000 ft).

Although elk and a few moose inhabit the northern mountains, and pronghorn antelope and wild mustangs roam the western desert valleys, Utah's most prevalent big-game animal is the mule deer. Small buffalo herds can still be found in the Henry Mountains in the southeast and on Antelope Island in the Great Salt Lake, but desert bighorn sheep are limited to Zion and Canyonlands national parks. Cougars occupy the high mountain country. Smaller animals include the fur-bearing beaver, mink, marten, weasel, muskrat, badger, fox, and ringtail cat. The Great Basin rattlesnake is one of the most venomous creatures in North America.

The state's lakes and streams contain bass, catfish, Utah sucker, carp, yellow perch, and rainbow, brook, and brown trout. A unique subspecies, the Utah cutthroat trout, is found only in the Deep Creek Mountains of western Utah. Located in the middle of the Pacific flyway, Utah hosts hundreds of species of migratory birds. Game birds include the Hungarian and chukar partridge, ring-necked pheasant, sage grouse, and wild turkey; birds of prey include the bald and golden eagle, vultures, and several varieties of hawks. The sea gull earned its status as the state bird when in 1848 flocks of them devoured the millions of crickets that threatened to destroy the Mormon pioneers' first crops.

Resources. More than 200 commercially usable minerals are present in Utah, including rich deposits of copper, gold, molybdenum, and silver. Coal, natural gas, and oil are found in the Colorado Plateau, and deposits of oil and gas are found in the northwestern area of the state in what is called the Overthrust Belt. Almost 30% of Utah's total land area is forested; the forests are located in the state's mountainous areas. Divisions of the Department of Natural Resources oversee state lands and forests; wildlife, parks, and recreation areas; and water and mineral resources. Air pollution is an environmental problem along the populous Wasatch Front.

PEOPLE

During the 20th century, Utah's population has doubled almost every 40 years—from 276,749 in 1900, to 507,847 in 1930 and 1,059,273 in 1970. Between 1970 and 1980 the population increased by almost 40%, making Utah one of the fastest growing states in the country. The most densely populated area, the Wasatch Front, contains the state's three largest cities—SALT LAKE CITY, OGDEN (53 km/33 mi to the north), and PROVO (61 km/38 mi to the south). There metropolitan populations account for much of Utah's population.

Utah has by far the highest birthrate and one of the lowest death rates in the United States. Its infant mortality rate is lower than the national average, and the life expectancy of a state resident consistently runs above the national average. Because of the state's high birthrate, Utah residents tend to be younger than the U.S. population as a whole. Hispanic Americans constitute the largest ethnic minority in Utah. Utah also

Bryce Canyon National Park, in southern Utah, was named in honor of Ebenezer Bryce, who settled in the canyon in 1875. The region was initially designated Utah National Park in 1924 but was expanded and rededicated under its present name 4 years later.

(Above) *The copper-plated dome of Utah's state capitol (left), in Salt Lake City, rises to a height of 87 m (285 ft). Salt Lake City, the state's largest city, was founded in 1847 by Mormons fleeing religious persecution.*

(Right) *Sandstone monoliths formed through eons of erosion rise nearly 100 m (330 ft) above the desert floor along the Utah-Arizona border. This portion of the Navajo Indian Reservation is maintained for tourists as the Monument Valley Navajo Tribal Park.*

has small black and American Indian populations. Most Indians belong to the UTE, NAVAJO, PAIUTE, and SHOSHONI tribes. About 70% of the state's inhabitants are members of the Church of Jesus Christ of Latter-day Saints (see MORMONISM).

Education. One of the first acts of the Mormon settlers was to establish the University of Deseret in the parlor of an adobe cabin in Salt Lake City in 1850. This, the first public university west of the Mississippi, changed its name to the University of Utah in 1892. Today the state system includes three other 4-year institutions of higher education (see UTAH, STATE UNIVERSITIES AND COLLEGES OF). Utah's best-known private institution of higher learning, Mormon-supported BRIGHAM YOUNG UNIVERSITY, was established at Provo in 1875. Currently the state has one of the highest proportions in the nation of students attending college.

Culture. Salt Lake City's much-traveled Mormon Tabernacle Choir is world famous. Salt Lake City's new Bicentennial Arts Complex houses the internationally recognized Utah Symphony; the Ballet West, considered one of the best classical ballet companies in the nation; the Utah Repertory Dance Theatre and the Ririe-Woodbury Company, both noted for modern dance; and the Salt Lake Art Center. The Museums of Fine Arts and of Natural History on the University of Utah campus house the state's principal collections.

Historical Sites and Recreational Areas. The Golden Spike National Historic Site at Promontory, Utah, commemorates the joining on May 10, 1869, of the Union Pacific Railroad from the east and the Central Pacific from the west to complete the nation's first transcontinental railroad. The restored Beehive House, built in 1855 in Salt Lake City, was the home of Brigham Young; and on the capital's Temple Square stand the Salt Lake City Tabernacle and the Mormon Temple.

Each year several million tourists visit Utah. They are attracted by BRYCE CANYON NATIONAL PARK and Zion National Park as well as Arches, Canyonlands, and Capitol Reef national parks, various national monuments, and Utah's many state parks.

Communications. Of the state's daily newspapers, the two largest are in Salt Lake City—the *Tribune,* a morning paper, and the *Deseret News,* an evening daily. Other dailies include the *Ogden Standard-Examiner* and the *Provo Daily Herald,* both evening papers. Radio broadcasting is provided by a

number of AM and FM stations. The commercial television stations are supplemented by educational channels serving local areas. KSL Radio began broadcasting in 1922, making it one of the oldest stations in the country.

ECONOMIC ACTIVITY

Service industries account for about 75% of Utah's gross state product, and government in particular wields an important economic influence in the state. About 70% of Utah's lands are under federal control, and many civilian workers are on federal payrolls. Others are employed by the military or defense industries.

Agriculture. Of every 40 ha (100 acres) of land in Utah, only about 1.6 ha (4 acres) are suitable for cultivation. During the period of pioneering nearly everyone was engaged in farming. Recently, because of mechanization and improved farm management, only about 5% of Utah's labor force work in the agricultural sector. Livestock provides about 75% of the state's agricultural income, with beef cattle ranking first in value, followed by dairy products, turkeys, and hay. The most important crops are hay, wheat, and cherries. Other crops include alfalfa seed, apples, barley, onions, potatoes, sugar beets, and greenhouse products. Many fruits and vegetables are grown in north central Utah.

Forestry. About half of Utah's forestland is part of the national forest system. The national forests cover significant areas of Utah, but most of the land is not available for commercial timber enterprises. Among the trees that are harvested are the ponderosa pine, white fir, Douglas fir, Englemann spruce, subalpine fir, lodgepole pine, and aspen. The Dixie National Forest has large ponderosa pine stands. Panguitch, a town in southern Utah, is a sawmilling center.

Mining. Mineral production in Utah contributes about 3% to the state's gross product. Fuels account for the majority of Utah's mineral output, and petroleum is the state's leading mineral. Petroleum production was begun in 1948, and today major petroleum-producing areas are found in Duchesne, San Juan, and Uintah counties. Utah's second most valuable mineral is coal. Large and mostly undeveloped coal reserves are located in the Kaiparowits Plateau. Carbon, Emery, and Sevier counties are leading coal-producing areas. Utah also has reserves of natural gas. In 1980 there were additional natural-gas finds in northeastern Utah.

The most valuable nonfuel mineral found in the state is copper, and Utah ranks among the leading U.S. states in copper production. The mineral is taken mainly from a huge open-pit mine in Bingham Canyon in the Oquirrh Mountains southwest of Salt Lake City. Bingham Canyon also has rich deposits of gold, molybdenum, silver, lead, and zinc. The iron mines of Iron County have been worked since 1851, but it was the need for steel during World War II that expanded the iron mining operations into one of the largest in the western United States. Phosphate from the Uinta Mountains and potash from the Moab and Wendover regions are used for fertilizer. Utah is a leading producer of beryllium and Gilsonite and has significant reserves of uranium. Besides the sodium chloride obtained from evaporating beds along the southern and eastern shores of the Great Salt Lake, several minerals in solution are extracted from lake brines, including magnesium, chlorine, magnesium chloride, potassium sulfate, sodium sulfate, lithium, bromine, and boron.

Manufacturing. Utah's manufacturing is centered in the Salt Lake City area and in Cache, Utah, and Weber counties. Major state industries produce nonelectrical machinery (office machinery and construction and mining equipment); transportation equipment (aircraft equipment and systems for missiles and spacecraft); and food products. Other manufactures include electrical machinery and equipment; printing and publishing; petroleum and coal products; fabricated metals; chemical products; stone, clay, and glass products; and textiles.

Transportation. Utah is advantageously located on three interstate highways; I-15 crosses the state from north to south, and I-80 and I-70 are major east-west highways. Railroad service is provided by several rail freight lines. Major railroads are the Union Pacific and the Denver and Rio Grande Western. Amtrak provides passenger service. Utah's busiest airport is the Salt Lake City International Airport; every western city is within a 2-hour flight of Salt Lake City.

Energy. Most of Utah's electrical power comes from coal-fired steam units, but hydroelectric units produce some electricity. The coal-powered steam plants are located in Emery and Uintah counties; hydroelectricity comes from facilities at Flaming Gorge and Glen Canyon. Most electricity is supplied by the privately owned Utah Power and Light Company. Natural gas and oil are also energy sources in Utah.

The most important structures of Temple Square, around which Salt Lake City was laid out, include the 6-spired Temple, which only members of the Mormon faith may enter, and the tabernacle, which is internationally famous for its choir and 11,000-pipe organ.

GOVERNMENT AND POLITICS

Utah's constitution, written and proclaimed in 1895 shortly before statehood was granted on Jan. 4, 1896, included the provision—unusual at that time—that women were allowed to vote. The state's governor serves a 4-year term and may be reelected indefinitely; the legislature consists of the senate, whose 29 members (one from each county) serve 4-year terms, and the house of representatives, whose 75 members serve 2-year terms. Utah's highest court is the supreme court; it has 5 justices who serve 10-year terms. Other courts in the state are district courts, circuit courts, juvenile courts, and justice of the peace courts. Utah voters tend to be politically conservative and generally have voted Republican in presidential elections.

HISTORY

Prehistoric humans arrived in the Great Basin more than 10,000 years ago, practicing a hunting-and-gathering economy. The earliest ANASAZI, known as the Basket Makers, developed their culture on the Colorado Plateau over 2,000 years ago; they were followed by the PUEBLO Indian tribes, whose cliff dwellings and granaries can still be seen in southeastern Utah. More recent arrivals were the Ute, Paiute, Goshiute, and Navajo Indians, who inhabited the state when the first white settlers arrived.

Early European Explorers. In 1776 two Franciscan missionaries, Silvestre Vélez de ESCALANTE and Francisco Atanasio Domínguez, led an expedition into the "Northern Mystery" in order to establish a road from Santa Fe to the Spanish missions in California. By the mid-1820s, fur trappers and traders, including William Henry ASHLEY, James BRIDGER, and Jedediah Strong SMITH, had arrived; two other traders, Peter Skene Ogden and Etienne Provost, have given their names to Utah's second and third largest cities, Ogden and Provo.

In 1843–44, John C. FRÉMONT, of the U.S. Army Topographical Engineers, conducted the first scientific survey of the Great Basin. Also during the 1840s several parties of settlers traversed northern Utah on their way to California. The Bartleson-Bidwell party of emigrants made their journey in 1841, crossing the Great Basin on the famous Overland Trail. In 1846 the ill-fated DONNER PARTY blazed the first trail through Emigration Canyon—the same route followed a year later by the Mormon pioneers.

The salt flats of northwestern Utah are remnants of Lake Bonneville, a freshwater sea that covered the region during the Pleistocene Epoch. Great Salt Lake, a remainder of the sea, is the largest body of water between the Great Lakes and the Pacific coast.

The Mormons. The next chapter in Utah's history began at Carthage, Ill., on June 27, 1844, when Joseph SMITH, the founder of Mormonism, and his brother Hyrum were taken from jail and shot by a hostile mob. Persecution of Smith's followers—called Mormons—continued, and in the spring of 1847 most of them headed west, led by Brigham YOUNG. The first pioneers entered the Great Salt Lake valley in July 1847, and other companies arrived soon after.

When the Mormons came to Utah, it still belonged to Mexico. A year later, at the conclusion of the Mexican War, it became part of the United States, and in 1849 the Mormons established the State of Deseret (a name from the *Book of Mormon* meaning "honeybee" and signifying industriousness) and requested admission to the Union. Congress, however, refused to recognize Deseret—which stretched from Oregon to Mexico and as far west as the Sierra Nevada—and instead created the Territory of Utah, covering a much smaller area, with Brigham Young as governor.

Soon afterward, however, conflicts broke out between the Indians, especially the Ute, and the new settlers. Intermittent fighting continued until 1867, when the Ute settled on a reservation.

Before long, antagonisms developed between Utah and the federal government, which opposed the Mormon practice of polygamy. During the Utah War (1857–58), President James Buchanan sent troops to Utah, along with a new governor. During this period of tension and resentment, a party of Mormons led by John Doyle LEE attacked a group of non-Mormons traveling through the territory in the so-called MOUNTAIN MEADOWS MASSACRE (September 1857). The territory continued to make requests for statehood, but Congress always refused, until 1896, six years after the Mormons renounced their practice of polygamy.

Industrialization. The completion of the transcontinental railroad in 1869 brought new settlers—many of them non-Mormon—and a boom in both agriculture and industry. Silver, gold, lead, and zinc were discovered, and large-scale copper production began in 1907. Soon afterward several important new irrigation projects, notably that on Strawberry River (1913), brought thousands of acres of additional land under cultivation.

The two world wars stimulated mining and manufacturing, and by the early 1960s, Utah was no longer primarily an agricultural state. Hydroelectric projects such as those at Flaming Gorge and Glen Canyon dams (1964) have also encouraged industrial growth and urbanization.   ROBERT STARR WAITE

Bibliography: Arrington, L. J., and Alexander, T. G., *A Dependent Commonwealth: Utah's Economy from Statehood to the Great Depression* (1974); Buttle, F. J., *Utah Grows, Past and Present* (1970); Ellsworth, S. George, *Utah's Heritage* (1972); Emenhiser, Jedon A., *Utah's Governments* (1964); Federal Writers' Project, *Utah: A Guide to the State* (1941; repr. 1971); Larson, Gustave O., *The Americanization of Utah for Statehood* (1971); Long, E. B., *The Saints and the Union: Utah Territory during the Civil War* (1981); Papanikolas, Helen Z., ed., *The People of Utah* (1976); Peterson, Charles S., *Utah: A Bicentennial History* (1977); Poll, R. D., and Alexander, T. G., eds., *Utah's History* (1978); Stout, W. D., *History of Utah,* 3 vols. (1967–71).

Utah, state universities and colleges of

All the state-supported colleges and universities in Utah are coeducational. The **University of Utah** (1850; enrollment: 22,970; library: 1,990,000 volumes), at Salt Lake City, offers undergraduate and graduate degrees and has colleges of law, nursing, medicine, mines and mineral industries, pharmacy, engineering, fine arts, and humanities, and a school of social work. **Utah State University** (1888; enrollment: 9,940; library: 1,000,000 volumes), at Logan, is a land-grant institution offering undergraduate and graduate degrees. In addition to programs in the liberal arts and sciences, there are colleges of natural resources, agriculture, education, and engineering. State colleges offering undergraduate degrees in liberal arts and education are **Southern Utah State** (1897; enrollment: 2,100; library: 129,000 volumes), at Cedar City, and **Weber State** (1889; enrollment: 10,065; library: 315,000 volumes), at Ogden.

Utah War

The Utah War (1857–58) began as a result of religious tensions inspired by the Church of Jesus Christ of Latter-day Saints (see MORMONISM). Since the formation of the Utah Territory in 1850, some federal appointees and non-Mormon (Gentile) settlers had complained of political domination and abuse of Gentiles by the Mormon majority and Governor Brigham YOUNG. A Mormon religious revival—"the reformation"—and Gentile opposition to polygamy heightened tensions still more. Finally, President James Buchanan sent (May 1857) 2,500 troops of the U.S. Army to replace Young and enforce federal authority. In the hysteria that followed, Mormons participated in an attack—the MOUNTAIN MEADOWS MASSACRE of September 1857—in which 120 Gentiles were killed. Fearing reprisal, Mormon leaders sent out forces to destroy the army's supplies, thus delaying its arrival in Utah until the summer of 1858. By then, conciliation had prevented any clash of arms.   ELLIOTT WEST

Bibliography: Furniss, Norman F., *The Mormon Conflict, 1850–59* (1960); Hafen, L. R. and A. W., eds., *The Utah Expedition, 1857–58* (1958).

Utamaro   [oo-tah'-mah-roh]

Regarded as one of the greatest masters of UKIYO-E, the Japanese artist Utamaro, 1753–1806, dominated the art of the print in Edo (Tokyo) during the 1790s with his elegantly styled portraits of beautiful women. Little is known of his life. His family name was Kitagawa, originally Toriyama, but he used other names as well. A pupil (some say son) of Toriyama Sekien, Utamaro showed in his paintings and prints the influence of the Ukiyo-e masters Torii KIYONAGA and Kitao Masanobu. At its zenith in the early 1790s, Utamaro's art conveyed a sweetness and grace unmatched by his contemporaries. His intuitive grasp of feminine style enabled him to capture a certain erotic element in his half-length portraits, which were notable also for their clear, fresh color. Utamaro's work influenced not only his contemporaries but also Western artists, including Henri de Toulouse-Lautrec.   HOWARD LINK

Bibliography: Hillier, Jack R., *Utamaro: Color Prints and Paintings,* 2d ed. (1979); Kikuchi, Sadao, *Utamaro,* trans. by Myra Fraser and Massaki Tanaka (1976); Kondo, Ichitaro, *Kitagawa Utamaro, 1753–1806* (1956).

Ute   [yoot]

The Ute are a North American Indian tribe belonging to the Shoshonean division of the Uto-Aztecan linguistic stock. Their territory formerly extended from eastern Colorado into northern New Mexico, northeastern Arizona, and Utah. Before the introduction (c.1640) of the horse, the Ute lived in small groups. They harvested wild seeds and roots and organized rabbit and antelope drives. The extended family was the basic foraging unit.

By 1706 the Ute had turned to raiding the PUEBLO Indians and the Spanish in New Mexico for horses and livestock. Band leaders and war chiefs emerged to lead the migration to the bison hunting grounds and to conduct war raids. Ute culture took on a Plains overlay with the introduction of the tepee, eagle warbonnets, and the scalp dance. Mormon settlement of Utah further disrupted the Ute way of life. During the 1870s and '80s mining interests forced the Northern Ute from treaty lands, and they were eventually consolidated on the Uintah and Ouray reservations in northeastern Utah; the Southern Ute were confined (1877) to a small strip of southwestern Colorado. In 1981 the Ute population numbered about 4,500.   FRED W. VOGET

Bibliography: O'Neil, Floyd, and Sylvester, John D., eds., *Ute People: An Historical Study,* 3d ed. (1970); Rockwell, Wilson, *The Utes: A Forgotten People* (1956); Smith, Anne M., *Ethnography of the Northern Utes* (1974).

uterus

The uterus, or womb, is the female organ that holds and nourishes the developing mammal after fertilization until birth. In women this hollow, pear-shaped organ is about 8 cm

(3 in) long, weighs about 1.4 kg (3 lb), and has thick, muscular walls. It is suspended by ligaments between the bladder and the rectum. The uterus consists of a broad upper portion (fundus); a middle, narrower portion (body); and a neck (cervix) that protrudes into the vagina. The cervical canal links the vagina with the interior of the uterus (see REPRODUCTIVE SYSTEM, HUMAN).

The inner surface of the uterus is lined with a thick mucous membrane, the endometrium, in which the fertilized egg becomes implanted. In the absence of pregnancy, the outer cells of the endometrium are shed along with blood during MENSTRUATION. The uterine muscles contain elastic and collagenous fibers, which allow the uterus to expand during pregnancy and forcibly contract during labor prior to birth (see PREGNANCY AND BIRTH).   PETER L. PETRAKIS

Bibliography: Blandau, R. J., and Moghissi, Kamran, eds., *Biology of the Cervix* (1973); Wynn, R. M., ed., *Biology of the Uterus* (1977).

Utica   [yoo'-ti-kuh]

Utica, the seat of Oneida County, lies in central New York on the Mohawk River, 135 km (85 mi) west of Albany. It has a population of 75,632 (1980). Once a textile center, Utica is now dominated by the manufacture of electronic equipment, cutlery, paper and dairy products, and air conditioners. Settled in 1773 on the site of Fort Schuyler (1758), Utica was burned in an Indian and Loyalist attack in 1776 but was resettled after the American Revolution. The completion of the Erie Canal through Utica spurred the city's development.

utilitarianism

Utilitarianism is a theory in moral philosophy by which actions are judged to be right or wrong according to their consequences. A dictum made famous by the utilitarian Jeremy BENTHAM is that an individual should seek "the greatest happiness of the greatest number." Utilitarianism represents an extension into moral theory of an experimental, scientific mode of reasoning because it involves the calculation of causal consequences. Utilitarians must explain which kinds of consequences are to be sought or avoided. Utilitarians who equate happiness with pleasure are termed *hedonistic utilitarians;* those who regard happiness as incapable of reduction to any single notion such as pleasure are called *ideal* or *pluralistic utilitarians.*

Utilitarianism had its origins among the British philosophers of the 17th and 18th centuries. Its principal modern statements, however, come from Bentham, primarily in his *Introduction to the Principles of Morals and Legislation* (1789); from John Stuart MILL, primarily in *Utilitarianism* (1863); and from Henry SIDGWICK, in *The Methods of Ethics* (1874). The utilitarian tradition has been influential in the development of contemporary social, economic, and political thought.

Utilitarianism has an affinity with EMPIRICISM, the view that all knowledge arises from experience. By rejecting tradition, authority, or any supernatural basis for morality, utilitarianism makes human welfare the ultimate standard of right and wrong. It has thus often been associated with reform movements and causes.

Critics of utilitarianism usually argue that such actions as lying or cheating are wrong in themselves, apart from any ill consequences that might result. They point out that utilitarians must approve of lying and cheating if and when such actions promote positive consequences or the general welfare of society.

Utilitarianism has been the subject of continued discussion and refinement. Some utilitarians believe that the principle of utility should be applied to the evaluation of each individual act. Such a view is termed *act utilitarianism.* Others believe that the principle should be applied only to moral rules or general categories of actions. This view is labeled *rule utilitarianism.*   THOMAS K. HEARN, JR.

Bibliography: Capaldi, Nicholas, *Bentham, Mill, and the Utilitarians* (1965); Hearn, T. K., ed., *Studies in Utilitarianism* (1971); Regan, Donald, *Utilitarianism and Cooperation* (1980); Smart, J. J. C., *Utilitarianism: For and Against* (1973).

utility, public: see PUBLIC UTILITY.

Utopia   [yoo-toh'-pee-uh]

Utopia (1516; Eng. trans., 1551), by Saint Thomas MORE, is a Latin essay describing an ideal community, Utopia—literally, "no place." Divided into two parts, the work opens with a dialogue criticizing economic and social conditions in contemporary Europe, especially war, oppression of the poor, taxation, and unjust laws. Book 2, the narrative of Raphael Hythloday, describes the ideal community's religion, government, education, economics, wars, laws, and customs. Since its publication, *Utopia* has been interpreted variously as a satire against the corruption of the times, as a Christian humanist's view of a scholar's paradise, and as a blueprint for communism.   HERBERT M. LEVINE

Bibliography: Ames, Russell, *Citizen Thomas More and His Utopia* (1949; repr. 1969); Johnson, Robbin S., *More's Utopia: Ideal and Illusion* (1969); Nelson, William, ed., *Twentieth Century Interpretations of "Utopia"* (1968).

utopias

The imaginary island of Utopia, supposedly located somewhere in the Southern Hemisphere, was depicted on the title page of Thomas More's work of the same name, first published in 1516. One of the major humanist works of the Renaissance, Utopia consists of two books: the first, a scathing account of conditions in contemporary England, is designed to contrast sharply with the second, a delineation of More's conception of an ideal state ruled by reason. The adjective utopian was derived from this work.

Utopias are conceptions of ideal societies in which the social, political, and economic evils afflicting humankind have been eradicated and in which the state functions for the good and happiness of all. The use of the word *utopia* (which means "no place" in Greek) to designate a perfect society began with the publication in 1516 of Saint Thomas MORE's famous *Utopia,* depicting the way of life and social institutions on an imaginary island. More's *Utopia* gained a wide audience, and the term was subsequently applied to all such concepts advanced by social thinkers and visionaries. Although utopian literature does not usually dwell on the practical means by which perfect societies are created, its stated and implied criticisms of social ills and its presentation of alternative modes of existence have assured it a prominent place in the history of thought. Plato's REPUBLIC, written in the 4th century BC, is generally regarded as the earliest and greatest work in the genre, although the biblical Garden of Eden (see EDEN, GARDEN OF) might be described as a utopia. Other famous utopian works include Tommaso CAMPANELLA's *The City of the Sun* (1623; Eng. trans., 1937), Francis BACON's *New Atlantis* (1627), James Harrington's *Oceana* (1656), Samuel BUTLER's *Erewhon* (1872), Edward Bellamy's *Looking Backward* (1888), and William Morris's *News from Nowhere* (1891). Influential 20th-century examples of the genre include H. G. Wells's *Modern Utopia* (1905) and *Walden Two* (1948), by the behavioral psychologist B. F. Skinner.

During the 19th century numerous attempts were made actually to establish utopian communities. Most were experiments in utopian socialism, such as those advocated by the comte de SAINT-SIMON, Charles FOURIER, and Étienne CABET in France, Robert OWEN in Britain and the United States, and his son Robert Dale OWEN in the United States. Although they differed considerably in their specific views, these utopian thinkers concurred in the belief that ideal societies could be created without much difficulty, starting with the formation of small cooperative communities made up of their followers. Saint-Simon regarded technological progress and large-scale economic organization as being of utmost importance. Future happiness, he believed, was tied to industrial growth. Fourier, in contrast, repudiated industry. He favored agricultural communities in which people lived in small, self-sufficient "phalanxes" free from the restraints imposed by civilization. Experimental settlements based on the theories of the utopians were set up in Europe and the United States and included Robert Owen's famous cooperative communities in NEW HARMONY, Ind., and New Lanark, Scotland. Most did not long survive; one of the longest lasting was ONEIDA COMMUNITY, in New York State, which lasted from 1848 to 1881. By the middle of the 19th century the utopian socialists were beginning to be eclipsed by more militant radical movements, including anarchism and Marxism.

In modern times utopianism has frequently suggested a naive and impossibly impractical approach to reality. Nevertheless, the tradition of utopian literature has persisted as a device for exposing contemporary ills. Much recent writing has focused on scientific utopias in advanced technological societies. The publication of satiric antiutopias, sometimes called dystopias, has also continued. Prominent examples of this genre are Aldous Huxley's BRAVE NEW WORLD, George Orwell's NINETEEN EIGHTY-FOUR, and Kurt Vonnegut's *Player Piano* (1951).

Bibliography: Chianese, Robert L., *Peaceable Kingdoms: An Anthology of Utopian Writings* (1971); Elliot, Robert C., *The Shape of Utopia* (1970); Erasmus, Charles J., *In Search of the Common Good* (1977; repr. 1985); Ferguson, John, *Utopias of the Classical World* (1975); Goodwin, Barbara, and Taylor, Keith, *The Politics of Utopia* (1984); Manuel, Frank E., and Fritzi, P., *Utopian Thought in the Western World* (1979); Mumford, Lewis, *The Story of Utopias* (1941).

Utrecht   [yoo'-trekt or oo'-trekt]

Utrecht, a city in the central Netherlands and capital of Utrecht province, is located about 30 km (20 mi) southeast of Amsterdam. The city's population of 230,000 (1985 est.) is the fourth largest in the country. Crossed by canals, railroads, and branches of the Rhine River, Utrecht is a major transportation center. Metal, wood, chemical, and food products are manufactured there. Utrecht is a trade and financial center, with insurance companies and international industrial fairs. Historic landmarks include two sunken canals and the Gothic Dom tower (1321–83), which until 1674 was connected to Utrecht Cathedral (1254–1517). Utrecht is the site of a state university (1636), seat of the Roman Catholic archbishop of the Netherlands, and a center for Old Catholics (Jansenists).

Utrecht grew around a Roman fortress (AD c.48) and was called Trajectum ad Rhenum or Ultrajectum. Saint Willibrord became the city's first bishop (c.690) and converted the northern Netherlands to Christianity. Medieval Utrecht was a cloth-weaving town ruled, along with the surrounding province, by its bishops. The Habsburgs took control in 1527, but in 1579 seven provinces of the north formed the Union of Utrecht to drive out the Spanish (see DUTCH REVOLT). The city then became a Calvinist stronghold. In 1713 the War of Spanish Succession was concluded by the Treaty of Utrecht. The city was occupied by the French in 1795 and served as the residence of Louis Bonaparte during his reign (1806–10) as king of Holland.

JONATHAN E. HELMREICH

Utrecht, Peace of

The Peace of Utrecht, a series of international treaties (1713–14) ending the War of the SPANISH SUCCESSION in Europe, preserved the European balance of power by preventing either Bourbon France or Habsburg Austria from dominating the former Spanish Habsburg empire. PHILIP V, Bourbon grandson of Louis XIV of France, became king of Spain and its overseas colonies but renounced all claims to the French crown. From Spain, Austria received Milan, Naples, Sardinia, and the Spanish Netherlands, with a barrier of fortresses in the latter going to the Dutch United Provinces. Britain acquired from Spain a 30-year monopoly of the Spanish-American slave trade, Gibraltar, and Minorca and received Nova Scotia, Hudson's Bay, Newfoundland, and Saint Kitts from France, which agreed to stop backing the Jacobite claimant to the English throne. Prussia was given Upper Gelderland, Neuchâtel, and Valengin. The duke of Savoy obtained Sicily.

A. LLOYD MOOTE

Bibliography: Gerard, J. W., *The Peace of Utrecht* (1885).

Utrillo, Maurice   [oo-tree'-oh]

The French painter Maurice Utrillo, b. Dec. 26, 1883, d. Nov. 5, 1955, is known for his many uniquely personal interpretations of Parisian street scenes. A natural son of Suzanne VALADON, herself a painter and artists' model, he was legally adopted in 1891 by Miguel Utrillo, a Spanish writer and family friend. Maurice, who had no formal artistic training, began to paint in about 1901, while convalescing from the first of many breakdowns due to alcoholism. The streets of Montmartre, sometimes copied from postcards, were often his theme, and he captured the tawdry, dismal atmosphere of this humble quarter with striking authenticity.

Utrillo began with a somber palette, but he soon came under the influence of impressionism, which, from 1905 onward,

Sacré-Coeur (1924), by the 20th-century French artist Maurice Utrillo, is a colorful and imaginative view of the famed Parisian basilica on the summit of Montmartre. The church is decked with French flags to celebrate Bastille Day. (Mme. Jean Walther Collection, Paris.)

affected his brushwork and his use of color. The *Landscape at Pierrefitte* (1905; collection of Ailsa Mellon Bruce, New York City) is an example. His best pictures are those from the "white period" (1908–14), when he developed an interest in white buildings and his canvases began to show a rougher surface texture. His palette changed also, the impressionist scale being replaced by silky grays, delicate pinks, and strong blues—often contrasting with rich blacks and browns—as well as touches of rust and vermilion. During the final period, from 1914 onward, Utrillo's colors again became brighter and his paintings less somber in mood. Although he had begun to enjoy public acclaim, his output tended to decline in quality after 1923.   MAGDALENA DABROWSKI

Bibliography: DePolnay, Peter, *Enfant Terrible: The Life and World of Maurice Utrillo*, rev. ed. (1969); Georges, Waldemar, *Utrillo* (1960); Werner, Alfred, *Maurice Utrillo* (1969) and *Utrillo* (1985).

Uttar Pradesh   [u'-tahr prah'-dish]

Uttar Pradesh is a state of northern India, bounded by Tibet and Nepal. It has an area of 294,401 km² (113,673 mi²). Its population of 110,862,013 (1981) is the largest of any Indian state. The state capital is LUCKNOW. The greater portion of the state lies within the GANGES RIVER Plain. In the northwest are the HIMALAYAS. Nanda Devi is the tallest peak in Uttar Pradesh (7,817 m/25,645 ft). Summers are hot and dry, with mean temperatures of 32° C (90° F); winters are cool, with temperatures averaging 13° to 18° C (55° to 64° F). Rainfall is heaviest in the east, 1,000 mm to 2,000 mm (40 in to 80 in), but decreases westward to about 600 mm (24 in). The people are about 84% Hindu, and Hindi is the principal native language. KANPUR is the state's largest city and an important industrial center. VARANASI, Hardwar, and Mathura are major Hindu pilgrim centers. Other cities include Aligarh (a university town), Allahabad, and Bareilly.

Agriculture is the basis of the economy; the state is India's largest wheat producer. Other food crops are rice, sorghum, millet, barley, and corn. Cotton, peanuts, and sugarcane are raised for cash. Important industrial products are sugar, textiles, and leather; the main handicrafts are silk weaving, metal enameling, and ceramic manufacturing. The TAJ MAHAL in AGRA is a world-famous landmark.

Buddha is said to have preached his first sermon at SARNATH near Varanasi, where Emperor Asoka later installed a stupa (shrine). Muslim rulers were in control for most of the period from 1194 to 1724. During the Indian Mutiny (1857–58), Uttar Pradesh was the center of anti-British resistance.

                                          ASHOK K. DUTT

uvarovite: see GARNET.

Uxmal   [ooz-mahl']

Uxmal, in the low Puuc hills of northwestern Yucatán, Mexico, was one of the great regional capitals of ancient MAYA civilization. It was the center of the Puuc style of architecture, which features cement and rubble construction finished with thin stone veneers and elaborate stone mosaics. The most common decorative motifs are masks of the rain god, depicted with a long, curved projecting nose.

Uxmal flourished during the late Classic Period (AD 600 to 950), dominating a large part of northern Yucatán culturally, if not politically. Two great temple-pyramids, known as the Dwarf and the Magician, are the most prominent buildings in central Uxmal. The principal palace complexes (the so-called Nunnery Quadrangle and the Governor's Palace, Uxmal's finest building) are nearby. Additional monuments include a ball court and a variety of other temples and palaces.

Already in decline when the TOLTECS came to Yucatán late in the 10th century, Uxmal soon collapsed entirely. Spanish missionaries discovered the ruins of Uxmal before the end of the 16th century. Modern excavation and restoration work has been carried out by the Mexican government.

                                          JOHN S. HENDERSON

Bibliography: Coe, M. D., *The Maya* (1966); Schele, L., and Miller, M. E., *The Blood of Kings* (1986).

Uzbek   [ooz'-bek]

The Uzbek are an Asian people who speak a Turkic language of the URAL-ALTAIC linguistic family. After the TURKS, they represent the world's largest Turkic-speaking group. Descendants of an intermixture of Inner Asian Mongoloids and Central Asian Caucasoids, in physical type they are much less Mongoloid than the KAZAKH but more Mongoloid than the TURKMEN. During the early 1980s, 14,000,000 Uzbek lived in the Uzbek SSR and contiguous Soviet administrative regions, 1,300,000 lived in Afghanistan, and 25,000 lived in China.

Uzbek life-styles reflect their ancient history. The first inhabitants of Uzbekistan (since 1924, the Uzbek SSR) were nontribal, settled irrigationists. Other groups living there are descended from nomadic tribes of both Mongol and non-Mongol origin, whose waves of invasion occurred between the 6th and the 16th centuries. Most Uzbek today are cotton farmers, although in Afghanistan seminomadic traditions persist.

Society is stratified, male-dominated, and authoritative. Sunni Muslim (see SUNNITES) in religion, the Uzbek traditionally maintain BRIDE-PRICE, DOWRIES, and close kin LINEAGES. Kinship, diet, and clothing reflect ancient relations with the TADZHIK and regional dominance; if the Uzbek dominate, Uzbek men marry Tadzhik women, and if the Tadzhik dominate, their men marry Uzbek women.   VICTOR L. MOTE

Bibliography: Akramov, Z. M., et al., *Soviet Uzbekistan* (1973); Allworth, Edward, ed., *Central Asia* (1967); Dunn, Stephen P. and Ethel, eds., *Introduction to Soviet Ethnography* (1974); Weekes, Richard V., ed., *Muslim Peoples: A World Ethnographic Survey* (1978); Wixman, R., *The Peoples of the USSR* (1984).

Uzbek Soviet Socialist Republic

The Uzbek Soviet Socialist Republic is one of the 15 constituent republics of the USSR. It is located in Central Asia and extends from the TIEN SHAN mountain system to the ARAL SEA. The area is 449,583 km² (173,591 mi²), and the population is 17,496,000 (1984 est.). The capital is TASHKENT.

The topography of Uzbekistan is highly diverse. The southeast portion contains the foothills and valleys of the Tien Shan. The northwestern lowland portion is occupied by the KYZYL KUM desert, lying between the stream courses of the SYR DARYA and AMU DARYA. The climate is generally arid—annual precipitation may total as little as 100 mm (4 in)—with hot summers and cool winters.

The population is concentrated in oases and irrigated valleys. The Uzbek, who make up 65% of the total, are Sunni Muslims, speak a Turkic language, and are traditionally cotton farmers. About 75% of the Uzbek live in the countryside. Russians, who represent 13% of the population, are mainly city dwellers. Koreans, exiled to Uzbekistan in the 1930s from the Soviet Far East, are rice growers.

The province's most populous (1984) cities are, in addition to the capital, SAMARKAND (371,000), Andizhan (267,000), Namangan (265,000), Bukhara (204,000), Fergana (191,000), and Kokand (163,000).

Economic activities are centered in Tashkent and in the Tien Shan's Fergana Valley. Important mineral industries process natural gas; coal (Angren); steel (Bekabad); copper, zinc, and molybdenum (Almalyk); gold (Zarafshan); and uranium (Yangiabad).

Uzbekistan is the USSR's largest cotton producer, accounting for more than 60% of Soviet output; the cotton area is being expanded through irrigation. Other important agricultural products are alfalfa, dried fruit, and karakul, or Persian lamb skins.

Politically, the Uzbek republic includes a subsidiary ethnic area, the Kara-Kalpak Autonomous Soviet Socialist Republic, on the Aral Sea, with an area of 165,546 km² (63,920 mi²) and a Muslim, Turkic-speaking population of 1,075,000 (1985 est.). The Uzbek, who assumed a distinctive ethnic identity during the 16th century, were historically part of the khanates of Khiva, Bukhara, and Kokand. These khanates were conquered by Russia in the 1860s and '70s. The Uzbek were constituted as a Soviet republic in 1924.   THEODORE SHABAD

Y	PHOENICIAN		ETRUSCAN	V
Y	EARLY HEBREW	**Vv**	EARLY LATIN	V
4	EARLY ARAMAIC		CLASSICAL LATIN	V
Y	EARLY GREEK	MODERN LATIN	GERMAN-GOTHIC	𝖁
Y	CLASSICAL GREEK			

V

V/v is the twenty-second letter of the English alphabet. Both the letter and its position in the alphabet were derived from the Latin alphabet, which derived it from the Greek by way of the Etruscan. When the Greeks adapted a Semitic writing system to their own use, the Semitic sign *waw* was given two uses. One form of the sign was used as consonantal *w* and called *digamma;* although lost in the Greek alphabet, this sign eventually became the English letter *F/f.* A variant form of *waw* was used for vocalic *u,* called *upsilon,* and placed at the end of the alphabet after *tau,* which had been the last sign of the original Semitic writing system.

This sign was adopted in the Etruscan alphabet and thence came into the Latin alphabet as *V/v.* The Latin alphabet used *V/v* for both consonantal *w* and vocalic *u.* In late Latin, however, the sound of *w* became *v,* and the sounds *u, v,* and *w* were generally not distinguished in writing. Eventually the letters *U/u* and *W/w* were derived from Latin *V/v* as a device for differentiating the various sounds.

The sound of *V/v* is a voiced labiodental continuant—the voiced counterpart of *f*—made by expelling the voiced breath between the lower lip and the upper teeth as in *vice* or *love.*

I. J. GELB AND R. M. WHITING

V-1

The German V-1 flying bomb, or buzz bomb, known originally as the Fieseler Fi 103, was the first of the "weapons of vengeance," named in response to Allied air assaults on Germany during World War II. It emerged from proposals made in 1939, and the first flight test was made at PEENEMÜNDE in December 1941. The project was given high priority by the German High Command in 1942. The V-1 was used to attack London from sites near Calais, France, beginning in June 1944.

More than 8,000 were launched against London alone.

The V-1 was actually a small, pilotless plane, having an overall length of 7.9 m (25.9 ft) and a wingspan of 5.3 m (17.3 ft). It weighed 2,180 kg (4,806 lb), including gasoline fuel and an 850-kg (1,874-lb) warhead. Powered by a pulse-jet engine and ramp-launched, the V-1 flew a preset distance. Then it was put into a dive, and its engine cut out, giving the population below only a few seconds in which to take cover.

KENNETH GATLAND

V-2

The V-2, or Vengeance Weapon 2, was a liquid-propellant rocket developed at PEENEMÜNDE, Germany, between 1938 and 1942 under the technical direction of Wernher VON BRAUN. The rocket was part of a development series known as Aggregate, begun under the auspices of the German army at Kummersdorf in 1932. The V-2, fourth in the series, was also known as the A-4. Originally intended for battlefield use, it was eventually used to bomb Britain and other countries.

The V-2 stood over 14 m (46 ft) tall and at lift-off weighed 12,873 kg (28,380 lb), including a 998-kg (2,201-lb) warhead. It reached a maximum speed of about 5,705 km/h (3,545 mph) and had a range of about 320 km (200 mi).

Although the first successful V-2 test occurred on Oct. 3, 1942, it was not until July 27, 1943, that Adolf Hitler authorized full-scale development of the rocket. More than 4,300 were launched between Sept. 6, 1944, and Mar. 27, 1945, against London and southeastern England, Antwerp, and other targets. Many exploded before reaching their targets or were misdirected. Much postwar rocket technology was based on the V-2 (see ROCKETS AND MISSILES). KENNETH GATLAND

Bibliography: Kennedy, G. P., *Vengeance Weapon 2* (1983).

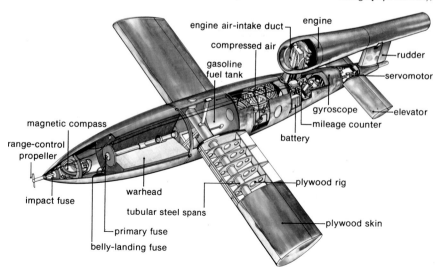

engine air-intake duct — engine
compressed air
gasoline fuel tank
— rudder
— servomotor
gyroscope
— elevator
— mileage counter
battery
magnetic compass
range-control propeller
— plywood rig
impact fuse
warhead
tubular steel spans
— plywood skin
— primary fuse
belly-landing fuse

The V-1, or buzz bomb, which was used by the Germans during World War II, was a simple mid-wing monoplane loaded with explosives, propelled by a pulse-jet engine, and guided by an automatic pilot along a preset path. On reaching its destination the plane crashed and detonated. The missile was launched from an inclined ramp pointed toward the target. During flight, steel flaps in front of the engine duct opened periodically, allowing air to enter and mix with gasoline and compressed air. Spark-plug ignition of the mixture furnished an intermittent thrust that accelerated the bomb to a speed of nearly 644 km/h (400 mph). The plane's course was maintained by a magnetically controlled gyroscope that directed a tail rudder. A mileage counter recorded the number of revolutions made by a nose propeller. When the predetermined distance was reached, a servomechanism depressed the elevators, sending the plane into a steep dive. Upon impact, any one of three fuses in the nose section could detonate the warhead.

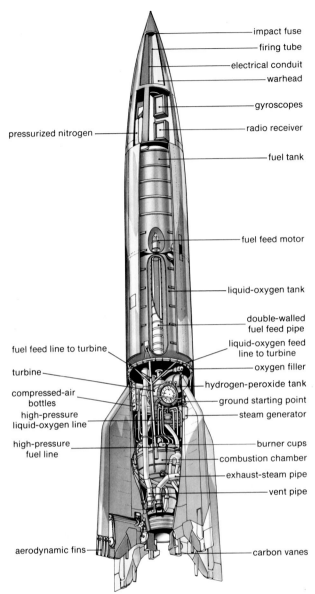

impact fuse
firing tube
electrical conduit
warhead
gyroscopes
radio receiver
pressurized nitrogen
fuel tank
fuel feed motor
liquid-oxygen tank
double-walled fuel feed pipe
liquid-oxygen feed line to turbine
fuel feed line to turbine
oxygen filler
turbine
hydrogen-peroxide tank
compressed-air bottles
ground starting point
high-pressure liquid-oxygen line
steam generator
high-pressure fuel line
burner cups
combustion chamber
exhaust-steam pipe
vent pipe
aerodynamic fins
carbon vanes

The V-2 supersonic rocket was launched vertically from a steel pad. The initial firing of its pyrotechnic igniter opened valves in the fuel lines, admitting liquid oxygen and alcohol-water into the combustion chamber. A turbine powered by steam from hydrogen peroxide and potassium permanganate pumped this fuel into 18 burner cups, where it was mixed with oxygen and ignited to produce a thrust exceeding 245,000 newtons, or 25,000 kg (55,116 lb). As the rocket gained altitude, its axis was tilted into the desired trajectory by a radio signal. Steering was supplied by an inertial-guidance system using 2 free gyroscopes. The rocket continued to fly on a straight path until burnout, when the impact of its fall detonated its explosive warhead.

V-E Day and V-J Day

V-E Day and V-J Day are the historic dates marking the end of WORLD WAR II (1939–45), a conflict fought on two main fronts—the European and Pacific theaters. V-E (Victory in Europe) Day was celebrated on May 8, 1945, following the surrender of Germany to the Allied forces. V-J (Victory over Japan) Day designates Sept. 2, 1945, the day on which Japan formally surrendered. It had sued for peace on August 10, following the Allied dropping of atomic bombs on the Japanese cities of Hiroshima (August 6) and Nagasaki (August 9).

Vaal River   [fahl]

The Vaal, a major river of South Africa, rises in the DRAKENSBERG range of the Transvaal, east of Johannesburg, and flows southwest for about 1,210 km (750 mi) to join the ORANGE RIVER. It forms part of the boundary between the provinces of Transvaal and Orange Free State.

Vaasa   [vah′-sah]

Vaasa (1985 pop., 54,472) is a port city in western Finland on the Gulf of Bothnia. Export items are mostly forest products; the principal manufactures are wood products, textiles, glass, and processed foods. The city was founded (1606) by the Swedish king Charles IX and named for Sweden's reigning house of Vasa. When Finland was controlled (1809–1917) by Russia the city was renamed Nikolainkau-Punki. Vaasa served (1918) as the national provisional capital for the White Guard during the Finnish war of independence.

vaccination

Vaccination is the inoculation of a person (or animal) in order to bring about IMMUNITY to an infectious (pathogenic) organism. The term (from the Latin *vacca*, "cow") originally meant immunization against SMALLPOX, because the procedure originated in 1796 when English physician Edward JENNER discovered that milkmaids who had contracted the mild disease cowpox (vaccinia) were immune to smallpox. The development of a cowpox vaccine against smallpox has since led to the production of vaccines against a wide range of diseases.

Vaccination is based on the ability of a person's immune system to respond much more effectively and rapidly to a microorganism the second or third time that the elements of the immune system encounter the invading organism. It was in this way, for example, that the milkmaids' immune systems were "primed" by the cowpox virus to respond effectively to the closely related smallpox virus.

A vaccine may consist of living organisms that are weakened, or attenuated, in a laboratory so that they create immunity but do not cause disease. It may also consist of related organisms that cause a similar but milder disease, of killed organisms, or of extracts of the organisms that can induce the desired immune response and subsequent immunity but do not cause the disease. Period booster immunization is recommended with most vaccines, because the immunity caused by the initial inoculation may decrease with time. The time interval before booster shots are required varies greatly with the type of vaccine.

Vaccination has occasional complications. Thus patients with a poorly functioning immune system have particular problems with certain vaccines. Immunodeficient patients may develop acute poliomyelitis from attenuated virus vaccine, for example, although they do not develop the disease from killed polio virus. Transient problems with mild fevers, muscle aches, and tenderness at the inoculation site are also common to many vaccines. Control of serious disease by vaccination, however, is usually worth such risks.

Most of the exceptionally effective vaccines are viral vaccines (see VIRUS), such as those for measles, mumps, and rubella. Influenza vaccines are recommended for individuals at high risk for serious infections of the lungs. Because influenza strains are different almost every year, vaccination should be carried out yearly in the susceptible population. Vaccination for yellow fever and certain types of hepatitis are also of proven efficacy. Also available and useful are vaccines for certain bacterial infections (see BACTERIA), such as typhoid fever, cholera, diphtheria, whooping cough, and tetanus. Among new viral vaccines being developed are vaccines against malaria, leprosy, and dengue fever. Researchers are also exploring the production of multipurpose vaccines through genetic engineering, using entities such as the vaccinia virus or the bacterium known as BCG to carry genes from several disease organisms.   DAVID S. GORDON, M.D.

Bibliography: Dreesman, G. R., et al., eds., *High-Technology Route to Virus Vaccines* (1985); National Research Council, *New Vaccine Development* (1985); Robbins, J. B., et al., eds., *Bacterial Vaccines* (1987).

vaccinia

Vaccinia, the COWPOX virus, is closely related to the variola, or SMALLPOX, virus. The term *vaccine* derives from vaccinia, because in the 18th century the English physician Edward JENNER used the vaccinia virus to develop the first successful preventive treatment for a communicable disease, smallpox; the treatment made possible the subsequent eradication of that disease. Vaccinia is currently of special interest in GENETIC ENGINEERING for several reasons. Adverse reactions to the virus are rare and well understood, so it is considered safe; it is more easily transportable than most viruses, because it can be freeze-dried and remain effective; its administration is simple; and it is a large virus, making possible the use of recombinant DNA techniques to create new vaccines. That is, genes from another virus can be spliced into vaccinia, creating a hybrid vaccine effective against both viruses. Research has focused especially on gene splicing with herpes simplex, hepatitis B, and influenza viruses. WILLIAM A. CHECK

vacuum

A vacuum may be defined most simply as a volume of space that contains no matter. On the Earth's surface this means, in practice, a volume from which as much matter has been removed as current technology makes possible, with the whole range of partial vacuums in between. In this sense, a perfect vacuum probably does not exist even in the depths of space, in the vast stretches between galaxies. Any given volume of space is likely to contain at least one or more particle of matter or one or more units of energy, which is the equivalent of matter (see RELATIVITY).

In physics the concept of a vacuum is more complex. According to QUANTUM MECHANICS and elementary particle theory (see FUNDAMENTAL PARTICLES), an ideal vacuum would be one that had a zero energy level besides lacking matter. Theory holds, however, that no such vacuum can exist. Even a vacuum with no measurable energy level is only a so-called "virtual" vacuum. Vacuum fluctuations are constantly producing "virtual" particles there that appear and disappear. The concept that a vacuum itself has structure is basic to modern physics and has been supported experimentally. It is also basic to current COSMOLOGY theories, according to which the entire universe arose from a virtual vacuum.

In the practical sense of a volume lacking as much matter as technology permits, a vacuum was first produced experimentally in the 17th century by the German physicist Otto von GUERICKE. Attempts to produce high vacuums were spurred in the later 19th century by the need to study such phenomena as electric discharges in gases. The electric light bulb, which had to be evacuated to prevent the filament from burning, emphasized the need for high-speed industrial vacuum pumps. Many such pumps were developed in the 20th century, including the rotary mercury pump, the molecular pump, and the cryogenic pump. Vacuums with PRESSURES as low as 10^{-15} mm of mercury have been attained (see BAROMETER). Besides their applications in science and advanced technology (see ELECTRON TUBE), vacuums are of use in practical ways. That is, the pressure differential between a vacuum and its surroundings is used to make vacuum cleaners, air and water pumps, and the carburetor, among other devices.

Bibliography: Abbott, Larry, "The Mystery of the Cosmological Constant," *Scientific American*, May 1988; Cole, K. C., "Much Ado about Nothing," *Discover*, June 1985; O'Hanlon, J. F., *A Users Guide to Vacuum Technology* (1980).

vacuum cleaner

The vacuum cleaner is an electrical appliance for removing dust and dirt from floors, walls, or furniture. An electric motor drives a high-speed fan, creating a vacuum that draws a current of air into a suction nozzle. Dirt is loosened by brushes or agitators attached to the nozzle and then drawn through a fabric or paper bag that allows air but not the dirt particles to escape. The bag must be emptied or discarded when full. The upright cleaner consists of a long-handled assembly contain-

A cutaway illustration indicates some major operational features of an upright vacuum cleaner. Dust and debris are loosened by the revolving action of a spiral brush-and-agitator bar (1). The bar is powered by an electric motor (2), which also operates the fan (3) that provides the cleaner's suction. A filter bag (4) collects the dust and cleans the exhaust air. The canister-type vacuum cleaner contrasts with the upright in that the debris enters the machine through a cleaning head attached to a flexible hose. It is less effective for carpet cleaning despite its superior suction power. Canisters having a power nozzle, however, combine the best qualities of both the upright and canister types.

ing motor, fan, brush, and agitator. Canister cleaners contain a motor and fan in a cylindrical or spherical housing to which a flexible hose with suction nozzle is connected. Other kinds of cleaners are hand and lightweight models and the wet vac, a canister type that sucks up liquid.

Suction carpet sweepers with mechanically operated fans or bellows were invented in the 1850s, but invention of the small electric motor was necessary before the vacuum cleaner could be successfully produced. The first electric vacuum cleaners were huge, stationary machines used to clean the floors of large buildings. One of the first portable electric cleaners was developed by James Murray Spangler, who sold his rights to the machine to William Henry Hoover, the first manufacturer to mass-produce vacuum cleaners successfully.

vacuum tube: see ELECTRON TUBE.

Vaduz [fah-doots']

Vaduz (1983 est. pop., 4,896) is the capital of the principality of Liechtenstein, located on the Swiss border 80 km (50 mi) southeast of Zurich, Switzerland. The ruling prince's residence, Vaduz castle, overlooks the town and the upper Rhine River valley. Vaduz dates from the 14th century and is a flourishing tourist center.

Vaganova, Agrippina [vah-gah'-nuh-vuh]

Agrippina Vaganova, b. Saint Petersburg (now Leningrad), June 24 (N.S.), 1879, d. Nov. 5, 1951, was the most influential Russian ballet teacher of modern times. Following the Russian Revolution, Vaganova fought successfully for the continued teaching of classical ballet. The curriculum she created at the Leningrad State Choreographic School—whose director she became in 1935 and that is now named for her—combined the best aspects of several training systems. Her method was designed to create virtuosos; her pupils included Marina Semyonova and Galina Ulanova. DALE HARRIS

Bibliography: Vaganova, Agrippina, *Fundamentals of the Classic Dance*, trans. by Anatole Chujoy (1946).

vagrancy

Vagrancy is a charge made against those who are perceived as drifters, loiterers, bums, streetwalkers or prostitutes, gamblers, beggars, destitute persons unable to find or keep employment, or persons who simply refuse regular employment. Vagrants are sometimes arrested, although they may not have committed crimes. From a legal standpoint vagrancy has been a controversial matter. It invites community disapproval and arrest; in the United States, however, many vagrancy ordinances have been deemed too vague and in violation of due process.

Vaiont Dam [vy-awnt']

The Vaiont Dam, the world's highest thin-arch DAM, located on the Vaiont River in the Italian Alps, was overtopped by a rock slide on Oct. 9, 1963, in the worst dam disaster since the Johnstown flood in 1889. Water and rocks thrown high above the crest of the dam destroyed everything in their path for several kilometers downstream, and about 3,000 lives were lost in the disaster. The slide was caused by adverse geological conditions in the dam area, a progressive weakening of the rock mass, and the effect of the impounded water on the stability of the steep rock slope.   THOMAS CONCANNON

Vakhtangov, Eugene [vahk-tahn'-gawf]

The Russian director Eugene Vakhtangov, b. Feb. 13 (N.S.), 1883, d. May 29, 1922, a protégé of Konstantin Stanislavsky and an admirer of Meyerhold, might have combined the realism of the one and the theatricalism of the other through his own gifts had he not died young. He played Tackleton in Dickens's *The Cricket on the Hearth* in the production by the First Studio of the MOSCOW ART THEATER. For the Habimah Theatre he directed *The Dybbuk* (1922) and, in his own studio, produced Maeterlinck's *The Miracle of Saint Anthony* (1921) and Gozzi's commedia dell'arte *Princess Turandot* (1922). He developed a grotesque style as a means of expressing the truth.   MARJORIE L. HOOVER

Bibliography: Simonov, Ruben, *Stanislavsky's Protégé: Eugene Vakhtangov,* trans. by Miriam Goldina (1969).

Valadon, Suzanne [vah-lah-dohn']

Suzanne Valadon, b. Marie Clémentine Valadon, Sept. 23, 1865, d. Apr. 19, 1938, was a versatile French painter of the human figure, landscape, and still life. Her earliest jobs were as a seamstress and a circus performer. While modeling for Pierre Auguste Renoir and Henri de Toulouse-Lautrec, she became acquainted with Edgar Degas, who was impressed with her artistic ability. Her paintings are characterized by strong outlines and bright colors. Having achieved success with her own work, she also inspired her son, Maurice UTRILLO, to become a painter.   ELEANOR TUFTS

Bibliography: Warnod Jeanine, *Suzanne Valadon* (1981).

Valdés Leal, Juan de [vahl-days' lay-ahl']

A Spanish painter who worked in both Córdoba and Seville, Juan de Valdés Leal, b. May 4, 1622, d. October 1690, is best known for his macabre interpretations of religious themes and his colorful, crowded compositions. He was influenced by Peter Paul Rubens and Francisco de Herrera the Younger. Valdés Leal's most famous paintings are the two *Hieroglyphs of Last Things* (1672; Hospital de la Caridad, Seville) in which skeletons and decomposing corpses remind the viewer of the ephemeral nature of earthly life.   EDWARD J. SULLIVAN

Bibliography: Kinkead, Duncan, *Juan de Valdés Leal (1622–1690); His Life and Work* (1977); Trapier, Elizabeth Du Gué, *Valdés Leal: Baroque Concept of Death and Suffering in his Paintings* (1956) and *Valdés Leal, Spanish Baroque Painter* (1960).

Valdez [val-deez']

Valdez (1980 pop., 3,079), a port city on Prince William Sound in south central Alaska, is the southern terminus of the petroleum pipeline from PRUDHOE BAY. The city is also a center for mining, hunting, and fishing. Founded in 1898, Valdez was devastated by an earthquake in 1964 and rebuilt on safer ground 7 km (4 mi) farther west.

Valdivia, Pedro de [vahl-dee'-vee-ah]

The Spanish conquistador and explorer Pedro de Valdivia, c.1500–1554, extended Spanish rule in Latin American south

from Peru into Chile. He entered military service in Spain, fought in Flanders and at Pavia, and participated in the conquest of Venezuela in 1535. Valdivia joined Francisco PIZARRO in Peru in 1538. With Pizarro's permission, he left Cuzco in 1540 with a small group of Spaniards and about 1,000 Indians, determined to establish a colony in Chile. After crossing the coastal desert, he founded (1541) the city of Santiago. Valdivia returned to Peru in 1547 and, as a reward for his support of the viceroy, Pedro de la Gasca, against the rebellion of Gonzalo Pizarro, was made governor of Chile in 1549. He founded Concepción the following year. Valdivia extended his conquests farther south and tried to secure his hold on Chile, but in 1554, while trying to suppress an uprising of the Araucanian Indians, he was taken prisoner and tortured to death.

Bibliography: Cunninghame Graham, R. B., *Pedro de Valdivia: Conqueror of Chile* (1926; repr. 1974); Pocock, H. S., *The Conquest of Chile* (1967); Vernon, Ida S. W., *Pedro de Valdivia* (1946).

valence [vay'-luhns]

The valence of an atom or RADICAL represents the number of CHEMICAL BONDS that the atom or radical may form. Valence is important because it determines how chemical formulas are written for various compounds. The idea of valence was first introduced in 1868, even though the principles of bonding were not understood. Valences were based on the number of atoms that could combine with one atom of hydrogen. For example, in the compound hydrogen chloride (HCl), one atom of chlorine is combined with one atom of hydrogen, so the chlorine atom was assigned a valence of one. This meant that hydrogen also had a valence of one. Electrochemical studies showed that elements formed positive or negative ions. Hydrogen formed H^+ and was assigned the valence of $+1$, and the valence of chlorine, which formed Cl^-, became -1. Water (H_2O) consists of two atoms of hydrogen combined with one atom of oxygen, so the valence of oxygen was determined to be -2, because the sum of the total valences of all the atoms in a compound must equal zero. Some compounds contain a group of atoms, called a radical, that react as a unit. In nitric acid (HNO_3), for example, a valence of -1 applies to the entire nitrate (NO_3) unit.

In 1916 the American chemist G. N. LEWIS discovered that in an organic compound the chemical bond consists of a pair of electrons between two atoms, each atom held together by the bond. Other discoveries and theories followed, explaining ionic bonding, covalent bonding, metallic bonding, and coordination bonds in metals, and the terms *oxidation state* and *oxidation number* replaced *valence.*

The oxidation number of an atom is the number of electrons the atom has gained, lost, or shared when it bonds with another atom. In the case of sodium chloride (NaCl), the sodium atom transfers one electron to the chlorine atom, so sodium has an oxidation number of $+1$ (sodium is in the $+1$ oxidation state) and chlorine an oxidation number of -1 (the -1 oxidation state).

An element may have several possible oxidation states by being able to bond in different ways. Nitrogen forms five compounds with oxygen: N_2O, NO, N_2O_3, NO_2 (= N_2O_4), and N_2O_5, with oxidation numbers $+1$, $+2$, $+3$, $+4$, and $+5$, respectively. In addition, the oxidation number of nitrogen in azides is $-1/3$, in hydroxylamine -1, in hydrazine -2, and in ammonia -3.   WILLIAM H. NYCE

Bibliography: Brady, James E., and Humiston, Gerard, *General Chemistry,* 3d ed. (1983); Petrucci, Ralph H., *General Chemistry,* 3d ed. (1982); Stranges, A. N., *Electrons and Valence* (1982).

Valencia (city in Spain) [vah-layn'-thee-ah]

Valencia, a city in eastern Spain and capital of Valencia province, is situated about 300 km (190 mi) southeast of Madrid. Its population is 770,277 (1982 est.). Valencia lies in a fertile and intensively cultivated plain, cut off from the rest of Spain by the mountainous rim of the Meseta. On the south bank of the Turia River, about 3 km (2 mi) from the Mediterranean

The main plaza in the center of Valencia is bordered by the town hall and other municipal buildings. An ancient city that once served as capital of an independent kingdom, Valencia is located on the Mediterranean coast at the mouth of the Turia River.

coast, the city is served by its seaport at El Grao. Its people mainly speak Spanish, although Valencia lies within the traditional Catalan region.

Oranges, rice, and vegetables, as well as wine and olive oil produced in the surrounding countryside, are exported through El Grao. Valencia's industries have grown rapidly to include food processing, distilling, shipbuilding, textile weaving, and metallurgy. Tourists are attracted by coastal resort facilities as well as the city's many historic sites, including two gates from the 14th-century city walls; the Gothic Cathedral of La Seo (13th–15th century); and the Gothic Lonja, or silk exchange (15th century). Valencia is the seat of an archdiocese and the site of a university (1500).

Valencia was settled by the Romans (138 BC) and called Valentia. It was captured by the Visigoths in AD 413 and by the Moors in 714. Valencia was the capital of the Moorish kingdom of Valencia (1021–1238), although the city was retaken and ruled by El CID from 1094 to his death 5 years later. It was reconquered by James I of Aragon in 1238. Valencia prospered commercially and culturally under the medieval kings of Aragon. The city suffered damage in the Peninsular War and Spanish Civil War, when it served as the Loyalist capital in 1936–37 and again in 1939.   NORMAN J. G. POUNDS

Valencia   (city in Venezuela)   [vah-layn'-see-ah]

Valencia (1981 est. pop., 616,200) is the third largest city in Venezuela and a leading industrial center. Located 120 km (75 mi) southwest of Caracas, in the agriculturally productive central highlands of northern Venezuela, it processes sugarcane, cotton, coffee, and tobacco and produces a wide variety of manufactured items including feeds, fertilizers, pharmaceuticals, plastics, tires, automobiles, and clothing. It is the capital of Carabobo state and the site of the state university (1852). The 18th-century cathedral is a major feature. Valencia was founded by the Spanish in 1555 and served briefly as the capital of Venezuela in 1812 and 1830.

Valencia   (region in Spain)

Valencia is a province located along the Mediterranean Sea in eastern Spain, covering an area of 10,760 km² (4,160 mi²). The population of 3,760,800 (1982 est.) is concentrated mainly in the coastal areas. The city of Valencia is the region's capital and principal urban center and Spain's third largest city. The region is crossed by mountain ranges in the interior and has

several fertile plains. Valencia's main agricultural products are citrus fruits, vegetables, dates, and rice. Olive oil is also an important product, and small-scale fishing is common. The main mineral deposits include marble and gypsum. Textile and chemical industries are well developed, especially in the city of Valencia. The region is well known for its coastal resorts and for the ruins of many old Iberian towns. Valencia was colonized by the Greeks and the Carthaginians, and in the 8th century the Moors invaded the area. The emirate of Valencia was established in 1021 and El CID ruled from 1094 to 1099. James I of Aragon conquered the region in 1238.

LEON YACHER

Valenciennes Passion Play: see PASSION PLAY.

Valens, Roman Emperor in the East
[vay'-luhnz]

Valens, b. c.328, ruled the eastern part of the Roman Empire after being appointed (364) coemperor by his brother, VALENTINIAN I, emperor in the West. An Arian Christian, Valens persecuted orthodox Christians. In 369 he defeated the Visigoths, but he was killed (Aug. 9, 378) in the Visigoths' great victory over the Romans at Adrianople. The next year Theodosius I was named to replace him as emperor in the East.

Bibliography: Jones, A. H. M., *The Later Roman Empire, 184–602: A Social, Economic, and Administrative Survey,* 2 vols. (1964).

Valentin de Boulogne   [vah-lahn-tan' duh boo-lohn'-yuh]

The painter Valentin de Boulogne, b. January 1594, d. Aug. 18, 1632, was an important French follower of Caravaggio and Bartolommeo Manfredi. In Rome by about 1612, Valentin had a brief but impressive career. The *Martyrdom of Saints Processus and Martinianus* (Vatican, Rome) was commissioned by Pope Urban VIII in 1631. Most of his paintings, however, depict the plebeian life of gamblers, drinkers, and gypsies. These people are generally shown in dark and dramatically lighted settings, often in close-up views that permit an emphasis on realistic detail. According to his 17th-century biographers, Valentin's bohemian existence helped to cause his early death.   NANETTE SALOMON

Bibliography: Blunt, Anthony, *Art and Architecture in France, 1500 to 1700,* 2d ed. (1970; repr. 1977); Wittkower, Rudolf, *Art and Architecture in Italy, 1600 to 1750,* 3d rev. ed. (1973; repr. 1978).

Valentine, Saint

The name Saint Valentine is given to two legendary Christian martyrs whose feasts were formerly observed on February 14. One, believed to be a Roman priest martyred c.269 during the persecution of Claudius the Goth, was buried on the Flaminian Way; the second was probably a bishop of Terni martyred in Rome. It is possible that these two legends were based on real people or, as some believe, one person. The association of Saint Valentine's Day with love and courtship may have arisen from the coincidence of the date with the Roman festival of LUPERCALIA. In 1969 the feast day was dropped from the Roman church calendar.

Valentinian I, Roman Emperor in the West
[val-uhn-tin'-ee-uhn]

Valentinian I, b. 321, d. Nov. 17, 375, was Roman emperor in the West (364–75); his brother VALENS commanded (364–78) in the East. Valentinian served ably under Emperors Julian and Jovian, and his troops proclaimed him emperor at Nicaea on Jovian's death. Valentinian fought the Alemanni successfully in Gaul and kept Roman power stable in Africa and Britain; he also built a system of frontier defenses in the north. Valentinian was notably tolerant of the Christians. He was succeeded by his sons Gratian and Valentinian II.

Bibliography: Alföldi, András, *A Conflict of Ideas in the Late Roman Empire: The Clash between the Senate and Valentinian I,* trans. by Harold Mattingly (1952).

Valentinian II, Roman Emperor in the West

Valentinian II, b. *c.*371, d. May 15, 392, Roman emperor in the West (375–92), succeeded his father, Valentinian I. He ruled with his brother GRATIAN, controlling Italy, Africa, and Illyricum during a period of religious strife between the Arian and Nicene Christians. Gratian was murdered by the usurper Maximus, who forced Valentinian to flee Italy (387). Restored to power by THEODOSIUS I in 388, Valentinian was later murdered, possibly by Arbogast of the Franks. He was succeeded by Eugenius (r. 392–94).

Valentinian III, Roman Emperor in the West

Valentinian III, b. July 2, 419, d. Mar. 16, 455, was Roman emperor in the West (425–55), following the usurper John (r. 423–25). During Valentinian's minority, his mother, Galla Placidia, served as regent, followed in 433 by the powerful general AETIUS, who was the actual ruler of the West while Valentinian remained the nominal emperor. Valentinian never took effective interest in affairs of state, although the empire was torn by barbarian invasions and religious discontinuity during his reign. In 444, he and Pope LEO I agreed that the bishop of Rome had authority over the provincial churches. Valentinian personally murdered (454) Aetius and was in turn murdered by Aetius's followers. He was succeeded by Maximus (r. 455).

Valentino: see FASHION DESIGN.

Valentino, Rudolph   [val-uhn-tee′-noh]

Rudolph Valentino, displaying the sultry charms and commanding presence that won him an international following, appears in Son of the Sheik *(1926), his last film. At his death, a few months later, mass hysteria marked the passing of the silent screen's greatest idol.*

The greatest Latin lover of the American silent screen, Rudolph Valentino, b. Rodolfo d'Antonguolla, Italy, May 6, 1895, d. Aug. 23, 1926, was catapulted to stardom by *The Four Horsemen of the Apocalypse* (1921) and remained an irresistible attraction until his death. His hypnotic eyes, flashing smile, and slicked-back hair added up to magic in such films as *The Sheik* (1921), *Blood and Sand* (1922), *Monsieur Beaucaire* (1924), *The Eagle* (1925), and *Son of the Sheik* (1926).

LESLIE HALLIWELL

Bibliography: Oberfirst, Robert, *Rudolph Valentino, the Man behind the Myth* (1962); Shulman, Irving, *Valentino* (1967); Walker, Alexander, *Rudolph Valentino* (1976).

Valentinus   [val-uhn-ty′-nuhs]

Valentinus, fl. 2d century AD, was a leading exponent of GNOSTICISM in both Alexandria and Rome. An Egyptian by birth, he spent many years (*c.*136–*c.*160) in Rome, where he aspired to become pope. When unsuccessful in this effort, he turned against the Roman church. He was excommunicated in Rome for his teachings.

Valentinus was the most intellectual of the Gnostic leaders and developed a gnosticism attractive enough to gain followers both in the East and West. Eastern Valentinianism was Docetist, claiming that Christ had a "pneumatic" body totally subject to the influence of the Spirit. Western (Italian) Valentinians taught a modified DOCETISM, attributing to Christ a "psychic" body, not fully "gnostic," but capable of salvation through perfect knowledge. Hippolytus of Rome, Irenaeus, and Tertullian all refuted Valentinian gnosticism.

AGNES CUNNINGHAM

Bibliography: Doresse, Jean, *The Secret Books of the Egyptian Gnostics* (1960); Jonas, Hans, *The Gnostic Religion* (1958); Pagels, Elaine, *The Gnostic Gospels* (1979).

Valera, Eamon de: see DE VALERA, EAMON.

Valera y Alcalá Galiano, Juan   [vah-lay′-rah ee ahl-kah-lah′ gah-lee-ah′-noh]

A master of the 19th-century Spanish novel, Don Juan Valera y Alcalá Galiano, b. Oct. 18, 1824, d. Apr. 18, 1905, is best known for his harmonious prose style. He combined a distinguished diplomatic career with the writing of novels, such as his acclaimed *Pepita Jiménez* (1874; Eng. trans., 1886), literary criticism, poetry, and translations.

Bibliography: De Coster, Cyrus Cole, *Juan Valera* (1974); Lott, Robert E., *Language and Psychology in "Pepita Jiménez"* (1970).

Valerian, Roman Emperor   [vuh-lair′-ee-uhn]

Valerian (Publius Licinius Valerianus), b. *c.*190, d. after 260, was Roman emperor from 253 to 260. Proclaimed emperor by his troops on the death of the emperor Gallus (r. 251–53), he named (253) his son GALLIENUS coemperor. During Valerian's reign the empire was continually ravaged by barbarian and Persian invaders, and the persecution of Christians was ordered (257). Valerian campaigned against the Persians but was defeated and captured at Edessa in 260. He presumably died in Persian captivity.

Valéry, Paul   [vah-lay-ree′]

Paul Ambroise Valéry, b. Sète, Oct. 30, 1871, d. Paris, July 20, 1945, was perhaps the greatest French poet of the 20th century. His reputation is based not only on his poetic output, but also on the critical power of his many books and essays dealing with philosophy, artistic creation, linguistics, education, science, and social and political questions. Evidence of his intellectual range is provided by the 5 volumes of essays entitled *Variety* (1924–44; Eng. trans., 1927, 1938) and by the 29 volumes of *Cahiers* (Notebooks, 1957–61). The latter were begun in 1894 when Valéry moved to Paris after studying law at Montpellier. In 1897 he became a civil servant in the French Ministry of War, and from 1900 to 1922 he acted as secretary to a paralyzed director of the Havas News Agency. He entered the Académie Française in 1925, traveled widely as a lecturer, and from 1937 occupied a specially created chair of poetics at the Collège de France.

Valéry's early poetry was influenced by symbolist aesthetics in general and by the work of Stéphane MALLARMÉ in particular. It was eventually collected in *Album de vers anciens, 1890–1900* (Album of Old Verses, 1920). His reputation during his first years in Paris also owed much to two prose works: *Introduction to the Method of Leonardo da Vinci* (1895; Eng. trans., 1929) showed his admiration for a fellow polymath, and *The Evening with Monsieur Teste* (1896; Eng. trans., 1925) examined a fictional monster with an entirely abstract intellect. Approximately 20 years of silence followed during which Valéry devoted himself to intense and wide-ranging philosophical reflection. Eventually, in 1917, he published one of his finest poems, *La Jeune Parque* (trans. as *The Young Fate*, 1970), a combination of enigmatic beauty and difficult, allusive SYMBOLISM. His poetic reputation was finally sealed by the

Paul Valéry, one of the foremost poets of the 20th century, applied an incisive analytical power to produce numerous poetical and critical works. His poetry reflects the influence of the French symbolists and is characterized by a fluid style and imagistic mastery. Valéry is portrayed (1925) by Jacques Émile Blanche. (Musée des Beaux Arts, Rouen.)

publication of *Charmes* (1922; rev. 1926), which collected such celebrated longer poems as *The Graveyard by the Sea* (1920; Eng. trans., 1932), and *Fragments du Narcisse, La Pythie, and Ébauche d'un serpent* (Sketch of a Serpent, 1922). This poetry is austere, controlled, and intensely intellectual, yet suggestive and evocative in its use of imagery and sound. Within the rules of traditional prosody, Valéry shows the mind exploring its own nature and processes.

Two much-admired prose works, *Eupalinos: or, The Architect* (Eng. trans., 1932) and *Dance and the Soul* (Eng. trans., 1951), were written in the form of Socratic dialogues and published together in 1923. The architect achieves dynamic repose; the dancer embodies controlled dynamism. Two later works in dialogue form are *Idée fixe* (1932; Eng. trans., 1965) and *Dialogue de l'arbre* (Dialogue of the Tree, 1943).

At the end of World War I, Valéry had written on the crisis of Western civilization. He continued to view the contemporary world with some asperity in *Reflections on the World Today* (1933; Eng. trans., 1948). These writings show his gift for aphorisms, also characteristic of *Rhumbs* (1926; Eng. trans., 1970). On his death he left an unfinished play, *My Faust* (Eng. trans., 1960), which was posthumously published in 1946.

JOHN CRUICKSHANK

Bibliography: Arnold, A. J., *Paul Valéry and His Critics* (1970; repr. 1972); Crow, Christine, *Paul Valéry: Consciousness and Nature* (1972); Mackay, Agnes E., *The Universal Self: A Study of Paul Valéry* (1982); Stimpson, Brian, *Paul Valéry and Music: A Study of the Techniques of Composition in Valéry's Poetry* (1984).

Valhalla   [val-hal'-uh]

In Norse mythology, Valhalla was the most beautiful mansion in ASGARD, where the heroes slain in battle feasted each night with ODIN on the boar Schrimnir and mead from the goat Heldrun. The heroes rode out each morning and fought one another until they were cut to pieces; they recovered from their wounds each evening.

Valium   [val'-ee-uhm]

Valium, a trade name for diazepam, is in the benzodiazepine group of drugs (as is LIBRIUM) and is the best known and most widely prescribed minor TRANQUILIZER. Introduced in 1963, it is used effectively for the relief of tension and anxiety and may be useful in the treatment of the symptoms of acute alcohol withdrawal. Valium is often used, with other measures, in the treatment of lower back pain, because it relieves skeletal-muscle spasms.

Excessive doses of Valium or doses in combination with alcohol or other nervous-system depressants may cause excessive sedation or decreased dexterity. Valium and other tranquilizers are frequently abused drugs, possibly habit-forming (see DRUG ABUSE).

Valkyries   [val-keer'-eez]

In Norse mythology the Valkyries were nine semidivine virgins—priestesses of the mother goddess FREYA—who rode armed on horseback to battlefields and decided who would live and who would die. They carried half of the dead heroes to VALHALLA, Odin's palace in Asgard, and waited on them at their feasts. Their leader was BRUNHILD.

Valladolid   [vahl-yah-doh-leed']

Valladolid, the capital of Valladolid province in north central Spain, is situated on the Pisuerga River, about 160 km (100 mi) northwest of Madrid. It has a population of 330,242 (1981). Valladolid's economy is based on processing the province's cereals, vegetables, and sugarcane. Chemicals, textiles, metal products, wine, and leather are produced. Historic sites include the 13th-century Church of San Pablo, the unfinished cathedral (begun 1580s), the Colegio de San Gregorio, the Rivadavia palace, and a monument to Christopher Columbus. Valladolid is the seat of the third oldest Spanish university, founded in 1346.

A city of obscure origins, Valladolid was liberated from the Moors in the 10th century and became part of the kingdom of León-Castile. It was the seat of the Castilian and later Spanish royal courts in the 14th and 15th centuries and during the reign (1600–06) of Philip III, after which the city declined. Valladolid was damaged in the Peninsular War and occupied by Nationalist forces in the Spanish Civil War (1936–39).

Vallandigham, Clement L.   [vuh-lan'-dig-ham]

The American politician Clement Laird Vallandigham, b. New Lisbon, Ohio, July 29, 1820, d. June 17, 1871, gained notoriety as a U.S. representative (1858–63) from Ohio during the U.S. Civil War, when he was the leading Northern critic of the government's policy toward the Confederacy. Vallandigham attended college in Pennsylvania but returned to Ohio to practice law; he also worked as a newspaperman and served in the state legislature (1845–47) as a Democrat.

An admirer of the South, Vallandigham vehemently attacked the war policies of President Abraham Lincoln. Greatly influenced by his legal training, by Calvinism, and by the ideas of Edmund Burke, he was essentially a conservative who feared the changes buffeting Civil War America. He opposed industry, centralization of government, and emancipation, while favoring peace, state rights, and white supremacy. These principles led him to support a negotiated peace on terms favorable to the South, to denounce military conscription, and to become the leader of the COPPERHEADS, or Peace Democrats.

In 1862, Vallandigham lost a bid for reelection. The next year he was convicted by a military commission of treasonable utterances and exiled to the Confederacy; he soon left the South for Canada. Running in absentia, he lost the 1863 Ohio gubernatorial election. Vallandigham returned to the United States in 1864 and thereafter made a number of further attempts, all unsuccessful, to win public office.

RICHARD M. McMURRY

Bibliography: Klement, Frank L., *The Limits of Dissent: Clement L. Vallandigham and the Civil War* (1970).

Vallayer-Coster, Anne   [vah-lay-yay'-kohs-tair']

The French painter Anne Vallayer-Coster, b. Dec. 21, 1744, d. Feb. 27, 1818, was most highly acclaimed for her still lifes and, in 1770, was admitted to the Académie Royale du Peintre et Sculpture. She was introduced to art at an early age, largely through her father, who was a goldsmith in the Gobelins factory. Her first recorded painting (1762) was a portrait; among her other paintings of people is *Woman Writing and Her Daughter* (1775; Bowes Museum, Barnard Castle, England). It was Vallayer-Coster's still lifes, however, that were most enthusiastically praised. Within this genre, her range of subject matter was vast, including musical instruments, military trophies, fruits and vegetables, flowers, lobsters, and dead game. She was also commissioned to design tapestries, and continued to exhibit in the Paris Salon until 1817.

ELEANOR TUFTS

Bibliography: Harris, A. S., and Nochlin, Linda, *Women Artists, 1550–1950* (1976).

Valle, Pietro della   [vahl'-lay]

Pietro della Valle, b. Apr. 11, 1586, d. Apr. 21, 1652, was an Italian traveler whose published letters contain important descriptions of his journeys in the Holy Land, Egypt, Syria, Persia, and India. After sailing (1614) from Venice, he spent a year in Istanbul, where he learned Turkish and Arabic before visiting the holy sites. Heading eastward, he attended (1617) the Persian court of Shah Abbas I in Isfahan and eventually reached (1623) India, where he remained for a year. In 1626, Valle returned to Rome. Pope Urban VIII appointed him a gentleman of the bedchamber.

Bibliography: Blunt, William, *Pietro's Pilgrimage* (1953).

Valle d'Aosta   [vahl'-lay dah-oh'-stah]

Valle d'Aosta is a region in the Alps of northwestern Italy, bordering France and Switzerland. Its area is 3,262 km² (1,260 mi²), and its population is 113,418 (1984 est.). The Italian slopes of Mont Blanc and the Matterhorn are located there. The capital is Aosta (1983 est. pop., 37,355). Tourism, farming, the manufacture of textiles, iron, and steel, and the production of hydroelectric power are important industries. Conquered by Rome about 25 BC, the region was later held by the Goths, Lombards, and dukes of Burgundy. It belonged to the house of Savoy (later the rulers of Sardinia-Piedmont) from 1238.

Valle Inclán, Ramón del   [vai'-ay een-klahn', rah-mohn' del]

A prolific and versatile member of the Generation of 1898, the Spanish novelist and playwright Ramón María del Valle Inclán, b. Oct. 28, 1866, d. Jan. 5, 1936, won notoriety with his four *Sonata* novels (1902–05; trans. as *The Pleasant Memoirs of the Marquis de Brandomín,* 1924). Fin-de-siècle in style, these show the influence of the modernist theory of Rubén Darío, whereas symbolism pervades the verse of *La Pipa de Kif* (The Marijuana Pipe, 1919). Valle Inclán is best known for his *esperpentos* ("grotesques"), in which he caricatured the corruption, superficiality, and brutality of the powerful; among these are the play *Luces de Bohemia* (Bohemian Lights, 1920) and the novel *The Tyrant* (1926; Eng. trans., 1929). His antipathy to the aristocracy is evident in the dramatic trilogy *Comedias bárbaras* (Barbaric Comedies, 1907–22) and in his unfinished novel sequence *El ruedo ibérico* (Iberian Tour, begun 1927).

Bibliography: Lyon, J., *The Theatre of Valle Inclán* (1984); Smith, Verity, *Ramón del Valle-Inclán* (1973); Zahareas, A. N., ed., *Ramón del Valle-Inclán: An Appraisal of His Life and Works* (1968).

Vallejo   [vuh-lay'-oh]

Vallejo (1980 pop., 80,303) is a port city on San Pablo Bay in California about 40 km (25 mi) northeast of San Francisco. Its industries include flour milling, food processing, petroleum refining, smelting, and port activities. Gen. Mariano G. Vallejo founded the city in 1850 as the new state capital, but the legislature met there only briefly in 1852–53.

Vallejo, Antonio Buero   [vah-lay'-oh]

The plays of the Spanish dramatist Antonio Buero Vallejo, b. Sept. 29, 1916, expose the oppressiveness of society, the difficulties of personal communication, and the plight of the poor. Imprisoned (1939–46) for his republican sentiments during the Spanish Civil War, he nevertheless earned a reputation with *Historia de una escalera* (Story of a Staircase, 1949), a study of tenement life. *La tejedora de sueños* (The Dream Weaver, 1952) recasts the myth of Ulysses. Both *En la ardiente oscuridad* (In the Burning Darkness, 1950) and *El concierto de San Ovidio* (The Concert at Saint Ovide, 1962) use blindness as a metaphor for human pain.

Bibliography: Halsey, M. T., *Antonio Buero Vallejo* (1973); Nicholas, R. L., *The Tragic Stages of Antonio Buero Vallejo* (1972); Vallejo, A. B., *Three Plays* (Eng. trans., 1985).

Vallejo, César

The Peruvian poet César Vallejo, b. Mar. 16, 1892, d. Apr. 15, 1938, focused on the theme of human suffering in the modernist poems of his first book, *Los heraldos negros* (The Black Heralds, 1918). In the more daring poems of *Trilce* (1922), with their unconventional grammar, dislocated syntax, and interior monologue, he related the impotence and isolation of people victimized by inexplicable forces. Born of Indian and white parentage in a rural section of Peru, Vallejo knew firsthand the plight of the underprivileged. In November 1920 he was imprisoned for 3 months for allegedly provoking a riot. After moving to Paris in 1923, he devoted much of his energy to supporting Marxism and, later, the Republican cause in the Spanish Civil War. Vallejo's *Human Poems* (1939; Eng. trans., 1968), his last book of poetry, expresses in more direct language than that of *Trilce* his solidarity with all victims of injustice.   KEITH ELLIS

Bibliography: Franco, Jean, *César Vallejo* (1976); Vallejo, César, *The Complete Posthumous Poetry* (1979).

Valletta   [vahl-let'-tah]

Valletta (1983 est. pop., 14,000) is the capital of Malta and a major Mediterranean port. The core of the city, founded in 1565, is located on a rocky promontory overlooking two deepwater harbors on the island's northwestern coast. British and NATO forces maintained bases there until 1979. Commercial shipping and tourism are the city's major activities.

Valley Forge

Valley Forge, 40 km (25 mi) west of Philadelphia, was the campground of 11,000 troops of George Washington's Continental Army from Dec. 19, 1777, to June 19, 1778. Because of the suffering endured there by the hungry, poorly clothed, and badly housed troops, 2,500 of whom died during the harsh winter, Valley Forge came to symbolize the heroism of the American revolutionaries. Despite adverse circumstances, Baron Friedrich von STEUBEN drilled the soldiers regularly and improved their discipline. Today the historic landmarks and monuments are preserved within Valley Forge National Historical Park (established 1976).

Bibliography: Bill, Alfred Hoyt, *Valley Forge* (1952); Reed, John F., *Valley Forge, Crucible of Victory* (1969); Stout, John J., *Ordeal at Valley Forge* (1963).

Valley of the Kings

The Valley of the Kings in western THEBES, Egypt, contains royal burial sites dating from the 18th dynasty (c.1570–1320 BC) and from the 19th dynasty (1320–1200 BC) of the New Kingdom. In the necropolis, the various chambers of the earlier tombs are built along a curving axis, whereas in the later examples chambers and corridors are arranged in parallel lines. More than 60 royal tombs are known, but many, such as that of Ramses II, are not yet accessible. Notable tombs include that of Ramses VI, containing a well-preserved painted relief of religious scenes. Directly beneath this tomb is that of TUTANKHAMEN, which was discovered (1922) by Howard CARTER. The tomb of SETI I, also known as Belzoni's Tomb after the Italian adventurer who first entered it in 1817, is noted for magnificent astronomical reliefs in its vaulted ceiling. At present the entire Valley of the Kings is being mapped, and a survey to determine the methods needed to prevent further damage to the tombs is being conducted by New York City's Brooklyn Museum.   ROBERT S. BIANCHI

Bibliography: Neubert, Otto, *The Valley of the Kings* (1957).

valley and ridge province

The valley-and-ridge type of topography consists of essentially parallel linear ridges of about equal elevation, and intervening valleys. Such a landscape is developed by the erosion of folded sedimentary layers; the valleys follow the softer materials (shale and limestone), and the ridges follow the outcrop of the more resistant sediments (sandstone and conglomerate).

The Valley and Ridge Physiographic Province of the United States, which extends from New York State to central Alabama, typifies such a landscape. The ridges there generally trend northeast to southwest. Streams generally follow the softer, more erodable materials. Exceptions include a few major rivers that cut across the structure and form narrow water gaps where they breach a ridge. The geologic history of the Valley and Ridge Province started with the deposition in the Paleozoic Era of a thick sequence of sediments; these sedimentary layers were crumpled into folds at the end of the era. Since then, weathering and erosion have reduced the area at least once to a peneplain, or fairly flat erosional surface. Most recently, the area has been arched up and the extensive valley system cut into the land.   JOHN A. SHIMER

Bibliography: Thornbury, W. D., *Regional Geomorphology* (1965).

Valley of Ten Thousand Smokes

The Valley of Ten Thousand Smokes is located in southern Alaska in the Aleutian Range, 40 km (25 mi) southwest of Anchorage. The valley, 150 km² (60 mi²) in area, is uninhabitable and marked by fissures spouting steam and gas. Formerly rich in plant and animal life, the valley was devastated in 1912 when a new volcano, Novarupta, emerged, covering the valley floor with sand and lava up to 200 m (700 ft) deep. Volcanic Mount KATMAI also erupted, creating a 5-km-wide (3-mi) crater and leaving a lake about 1,100 m (3,700 ft) below the rim. At the same time, fissures opened in the valley floor, all emitting steam heated to up to 648° C (1200° F). In 1918 the U.S. government moved to protect the valley, creating the Katmai National Monument, a 1,100,000-ha (2,791,000-acre) park. Fewer than 12 of the fissures are now active.

Vallonet Cave   [vahl'-oh-nay]

The archaeological cave site of Le Vallonet, on the Mediterranean coast near Roquebrune-Cap-Martin, 5 km (3 mi) west of Menton, France, is the earliest known habitation site in Europe and may have been used by some of the first hominids migrating into Europe from northern Africa. It has been dated to the end of the Lower Pleistocene, between 1,300,000 and 700,000 years ago. The site, which consists of a small inner chamber preceded by a narrow passage, was inhabited during a cold period (the Günz glaciation). No evidence for the use of fire exists, nor were human remains found. A few Lower Paleolithic pebble tools and flakes of limestone, quartzite, and flint were discovered, associated with many fragments of elephants, horses, deer, cattle, wild boar, and even parts of stranded whales. Some of the bones and antlers appear to have been cut or chipped for use as tools. The site was excavated (1959 and 1962) by the French archaeologist Henry de Lumley.   JACQUES BORDAZ

Bibliography: Coles, J. M., and Higgs, E. S., *The Archaeology of Early Man* (1969).

Vallotton, Félix   [vahl-uh-tohn']

A postimpressionist printmaker and painter as well as a critic and writer, Félix Édouard Vallotton, b. Dec. 28, 1865, d. Dec. 29, 1925, is known particularly for his revival of the woodcut as a graphic medium. Inspired by the Japanese Ukiyo-e woodcuts, Vallotton's widely published prints were distillations of Parisian life and its celebrities into bold, simplified patterns of black and white. He was an important member of the NABIS group in Paris, with whom he often exhibited his paintings.
                    STEPHANIE WINKELBAUER

Bibliography: St. James, Ashley, *Vallotton: Graphics* (1978).

Valois   (dynasty)   [vahl-wah']

The Valois dynasty produced the 13 kings who ruled France between 1328 and 1589. A branch of the CAPETIAN family, the Valois were descended from Charles of Valois (1270–1325), the younger brother of PHILIP IV. Charles was succeeded as

count of Valois by his son, who became King PHILIP VI in 1328. The Valois succession was challenged by the kings of England, descended from a daughter of Philip IV. This was a major factor contributing to the HUNDRED YEARS' WAR (1337–1453) and gave anti-Valois nobles an excuse to fight on the English side. For a time the English were also supported by the powerful dukes of BURGUNDY, a cadet line of the Valois. After CHARLES VII finally drove the English out of France in 1453, the Valois monarchs strengthened royal authority. On the death (1498) of CHARLES VIII the crown passed to the Orléans branch of the family in the person of LOUIS XII. He was succeeded (1515) by his cousin of the Angoulême branch, FRANCIS I. The last rulers of the dynasty were beset by the Wars of Religion (see RELIGION, WARS OF). The Valois dynasty ended with the assassination (1589) of HENRY III and was followed by the Bourbon dynasty.   JOHN B. HENNEMAN

Bibliography: Denieul-Cormier, Anne, *Wise and Foolish Kings* (1979); Vaughan, Richard, *Valois Burgundy* (1975).

Valois, Dame Ninette de

Through a combination of vision and singlemindedness, Ninette de Valois (Edris Stannus), b. June 6, 1898, in Baltiboys, Ireland, created Britain's national ballet. The company she founded in 1931 at Sadler's Wells Theatre in a working-class district of London is now the Royal Ballet, whose home is the Royal Opera House, Covent Garden. A student of Enrico Cecchetti, de Valois was a member of the Ballets Russes de Serge Diaghilev from 1923 to 1925. In 1926 she joined the London Old Vic Theatre to teach movement to its actors and to arrange dances for plays and operas at that theater. For some years she was a successful choreographer; *Job* (1931), *The Rake's Progress* (1935), and *Checkmate* (1937) are still performed in Great Britain. In 1963 she resigned as director of the Royal Ballet but has maintained a close connection with the company and its school. In 1951 she was created a Dame of the British Empire.   DALE HARRIS

Bibliography: de Valois, Ninette, *Invitation to the Ballet* (1937), *Come Dance with Me* (1957), and *Step by Step* (1977).

Valparaíso   [val-puh-ry'-zoh or vahl-pah-rah-ee'-soh]

Valparaíso, the capital of Valparaíso province, is the second largest city in Chile, with a population of 266,900 (1985 est.). Located on a bay of the Pacific Ocean in the central part of the country, it is also Chile's most important seaport. Elevators and cable railroads connect the waterfront and port with the hillside residential section of Los Cerros. Valparaíso's mild climate attracts many tourists each year. The city is an important producer of textiles, foodstuffs, chemicals, and leather goods. Two universities and the Chilean naval academy are also located there.

On his arrival in 1536, the Spanish conquistador Juan de Saavedra renamed the small Indian fishing village of Quintil and the surrounding bay Valparaíso (Valley of Paradise) for his birthplace in Spain. The city was sacked by English and Dutch pirates several times in the 16th century and was rocked by earthquakes in 1730, 1822, 1839, 1873, 1906–07, and 1971. After the 1906–07 earthquakes much of the city was rebuilt, but the 1971 earthquake destroyed many of the new buildings. Valparaíso's major period of growth began after Chilean independence (1818).   NEALE J. PEARSON

value-added tax

A value-added tax (VAT) is one levied on goods and services at each stage of production and distribution. For example, instead of a buyer's paying a 10 percent retail sales tax on a record player, VAT would be collected in bits and pieces at each stage of production—first from the makers of the record player's components, then from the firm that assembled it, then from the wholesaler, and finally from the retailer. Each firm involved in the chain of production would add the rate of the tax, 10 percent in this example, to the value of the goods it sells, bill its customers for the total including the tax, take a credit for whatever VAT it has paid on its raw materials, and then owe the difference, on the value it has added to the product, as tax. The entire tax is ultimately passed on to the consumer as a proportionately higher price.

VAT was introduced in France in 1954 and has been adopted by the Common Market members, including Great Britain. It has been proposed as an alternative to either the United States federal corporate-income tax or the Social Security tax. VAT's opponents consider it a regressive tax that hits low- and moderate-income people, who spend a large part of their incomes on consumption, harder than the rich. Its opponents, especially in Britain, have claimed that it is highly inflationary. Opponents also say that it is unnecessary in the United States, where compliance with the income-tax laws is excellent, compared with a country like France that has always had a high incidence of income-tax evasion.

Bibliography: Lindholm, Richard W., *Value-Added Tax and Other Tax Reforms* (1976); Shoup, Carl S., *Value-Added Tax* (1974); Wheatcroft, G. S., ed., *Value Added Tax in the Enlarged Common Market* (1973).

See also: INCOME TAX; TAXATION.

valve

A valve is a mechanical device serving to control the flow of gases or liquids through a pipe or other flow system. Incorporated in a vast range of mechanical equipment, from water faucets to nuclear reactor systems, valves are movable parts that can either completely permit or block flow, or partially block flow. They are usually made of brass, bronze, steel,

iron, or plastic, depending upon their function. They include gate, plug, globe, butterfly, check, safety, and spool valves.

A gate valve is basically a wedge-shaped disk that is lowered into a pipe to block flow. A plug valve, often found in the burets that are used for chemical titrations, is a plug that has a hole that can either be lined up with the pipe, permitting flow, or turned perpendicular to the pipe's opening in order to block flow. A globe valve, used to lessen or increase flow, is a plug or disk that fits in a seat; water faucets most frequently have globe valves to regulate flow. Such a valve is opened by turning a handwheel, which draws the plug away from the seat and allows increasing flow.

A butterfly valve is a circular disk, inside a pipe, that rotates on a hinge and allows alternating obstruction and passage of flow in rapid sequence. Gas is fed into an internal combustion engine by means of a butterfly valve in the carburetor. A check valve allows flow in only one direction; a simple example is the spherical plug of a snorkel, which permits a swimmer to breathe air but does not admit water to the tube.

Safety valves are designed to open when pressure within the flow system exceeds a maximum. The spool valve is a sliding valve with a complex system of inflow and outflow openings. Used in hydrostatic flow systems, the spool valve is powered to slide back and forth over the openings in such a manner that the flow of oil to various machine parts is regulated.   IAN BRADLEY

Bibliography: May, Kenneth D., *Advanced Valve Technology* (1965); Pearson, G. H., *Applications of Valves and Fittings* (1968) and *Valve Design* (1972); Schweitzer, Philip, *A Handbook of Valves* (1972).

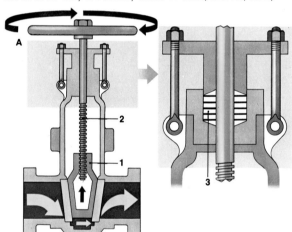

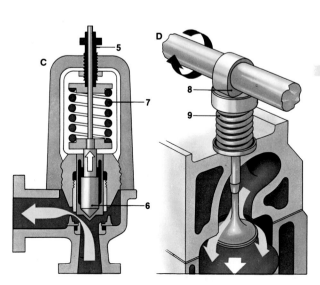

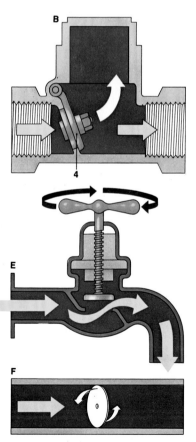

A valve employs a movable obstruction to regulate the movement of fluids in a passageway. In a gate valve (A) a gate (1) is raised by a handle-operated screw (2), which turns within a pressurized sealing chamber (see detail, 3). A swing-check valve (B), like the mitral valve in the human heart, permits movement in only one direction; any reverse flow causes automatic closing of the disk (4). In the safety valve of a steam boiler (C) an adjusting screw (5) holds down a plug (6) until pressure from accumulated steam forces the plug to rise against a spring (7). Similarly, the poppet valve (D), used in automobile engines, is depressed by a rotating cam (8) and returned by a spring (9). The disk in the globe valve of a domestic water tap (E) is raised from its circular seat by a screw thread. A butterfly valve (F) pivots between the open and closed positions on a central axis.

vampire

In Slavic folklore, a vampire is an evil spirit that takes possession of a corpse and, rising from its grave at night, sucks the blood of sleeping persons. The victims become vampires after death. Vampires are the ghosts of criminals, heretics, or suicides and can be put to rest only by having a wooden stake driven through their hearts.

Bibliography: Masters, Anthony, *The Natural History of the Vampire* (1972).

See also: DRACULA.

vampire bat: see BAT.

Van, Lake   [vahn]

Lake Van, the largest lake in Turkey, covers an area of about 3,800 km² (1,470 mi²) in the easternmost part of the country. It is extremely saline and has no outlet. The main economic activities of the area are extraction of sodium carbonate, fishing, and ferry service connecting cities onshore.

Van Allen radiation belts

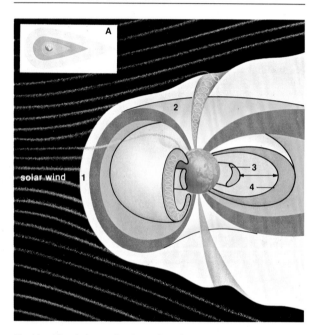

The Van Allen belts are doughnut-shaped zones of highly energetic charged particles within the Earth's magnetosphere, or magnetic-field region. The solar wind (yellow lines) distorts the magnetosphere, causing it to take the form of a teardrop with the tail pointing away from the Sun (A). Solar particles compress the Earth's magnetic field at the shock front (1) and flow around the field's boundary, or magnetopause (2). The most intense Van Allen belts include an inner zone of protons (3) and an outer zone of electrons (4).

The Van Allen radiation belts consist of concentric doughnut-shaped regions of energetically charged particles that encircle the Earth within the MAGNETOSPHERE. The belt nearest to the Earth, located within 1 Earth radius from the Earth's surface, was discovered by James A. Van Allen and his associates on the basis of data received from Geiger counters carried by the first U.S. satellites (*Explorers 1* and *3*) in January and March 1958, and by S. N. Vernov on the basis of similar data received from *Sputnik 2*. Readings from these initial satellites were puzzling, because no radiation was measured above about 1,000 km (620 mi). Investigators later discovered that these null readings occurred because the incident radiation was too intense to be measured by the Geiger counters. In December 1958 a second belt, at a distance of about 2 to 3 Earth radii from the Earth's surface, was discovered by Van

Allen's group. The first belt has been termed the *inner belt* and the second one the *classical outer belt*. In reality, no clear distinction separates the belts; the more energetically charged particles exist closer to the Earth, and belts of lower-energy particles extend outward to about 26,000 km (16,000 mi).

The energetically charged particles in these belts arise from various sources. Cosmic-ray particles (coming from interplanetary space), colliding with atmospheric atoms, produce neutrons that decay into energetic protons (10 million to 1,000 million electron-volts) and electrons. The resulting charged particles immediately get trapped by the Earth's magnetic field, because it constrains their motions perpendicular to the magnetic field vector. As a result, the particles spiral rapidly around the magnetic field lines, mirroring back and forth between the Northern and Southern hemispheres, with periods ranging from 0.1 to 3 seconds for the trip. Superimposed on this motion are a slow westward drift of protons and an eastward drift of electrons. These motions are relatively stable ones, and therefore the particles tend to remain trapped in the geomagnetic field for a very long time unless they are seriously disturbed by fluctuating electromagnetic fields. Some charged particles also penetrate from interplanetary space into the magnetosphere and diffuse slowly toward the Earth. The closer they approach the Earth, the more they are energized. Several artificial radiation belts were also created by the explosion of high-altitude nuclear bombs in 1958 and 1962, but they are currently decaying.

Additionally, a large belt of protons, with energies of the order of 50 thousand electron-volts, extends from about 3 to 9 Earth radii above the Earth's surface. This proton belt becomes greatly enhanced during a MAGNETIC STORM. Being positively charged, these protons drift westward and generate an intense westward electric current, reducing the magnetic field near the Earth's surface. This proton belt is often referred to as the ring current belt. During a magnetic storm, this belt contains the largest total amount of energy among the Van Allen belts. These protons are believed to be injected from the plasma sheet in the tail region of the magnetosphere during magnetospheric substorms.

A large belt of electrons, with energies of the order of 10 thousand to 50 thousand electron-volts and with an extent similar to that of the ring current belt, also surrounds the Earth. This belt is fed during auroral activity (see AURORAS). Being negatively charged, these electrons drift eastward. During this eastward drift motion, some of the electrons are freed by interaction with intense electromagnetic waves, descend into the polar upper atmosphere, and cause heavy ionization in the D region of the IONOSPHERE. Radio waves propagating through such a disturbed ionosphere are often completely absorbed, resulting in disruption of shortwave communications. When the Van Allen belts were first discovered, the belts were suggested as a source region of charged particles producing the aurora. Their contribution to auroral luminosity is now, however, considered to be subvisual.

S.-I. AKASOFU

Bibliography: Hess, W. N., *The Radiation Belt and Magnetosphere* (1968); Johnson, Francis S., ed., *Satellite Environment Handbook*, rev. ed. (1965); McCormac, B. M., *Earth's Particles and Fields* (1968) and *Radiation Trapped in the Earth's Magnetic Field* (1966); Roederer, J. G., *Dynamics of Geomagnetically Trapped Radiation* (1970).

Van Buren, Martin   [van buer'-en]

Martin Van Buren, eighth president of the United States (1837–41), governed during the Panic of 1837, America's worst economic crisis to that time. He played a key role in organizing the Democratic party and was the first president to be born a U.S. citizen.

Early Career. Of Dutch descent, Van Buren was born on Dec. 5, 1782, in Kinderhook, N.Y., the son of a farmer and tavern-keeper. He studied law and was admitted to the bar in 1803. Active in Democratic-Republican politics, he served as state senator (1812–20) and as attorney general of New York (1816–19). An opponent of Gov. DeWitt Clinton, Van Buren

MARTIN VAN BUREN
8th President of the United States (1837–41)

Nickname: "The Little Magician"; "The Red Fox of Kinderhook"
Born: Dec. 5, 1782, Kinderhook, N.Y.
Education: Kinderhook Academy (graduated 1796)
Profession: Lawyer
Religious Affiliation: Dutch Reformed
Marriage: Feb. 21, 1807, to Hannah Hoes (1783–1819)
Children: Abraham Van Buren (1807–73); John Van Buren (1810–66); Martin Van Buren (1812–55); Smith Thompson Van Buren (1817–76)
Political Affiliation: Democrat
Writings: *Inquiry into the Origin and Course of Political Parties in the United States* (1867); *The Autobiography of Martin Van Buren* (1920), ed. by John C. Fitzpatrick
Died: July 24, 1862, Kinderhook, N.Y.
Buried: Kinderhook Cemetery, Kinderhook, N.Y.

Vice-President and Cabinet Members
Vice-President: Richard M. Johnson
Secretary of State: John Forsyth
Secretary of the Treasury: Levi Woodbury
Secretary of War: Joel R. Poinsett
Attorney General: Benjamin F. Butler (1837–38); Felix Grundy (1838–39); Henry D. Gilpin (1840–41)
Postmaster General: Amos Kendall (1837–40); John M. Niles (1840–41)
Secretary of the Navy: Mahlon Dickerson (1837–38); James K. Paulding (1838–41)

led the Albany Regency, a political machine that challenged Clinton's control of state politics. His adroitness as a party boss earned Van Buren the nicknames "The Little Magician" and "The Fox of Kinderhook."

Elected to the U.S. Senate in 1821, Van Buren supported the unsuccessful presidential candidacy of William H. Crawford in 1824. During the administration of John Quincy Adams (1825–29), he led Senate opposition to the president and played a major role in organizing the political coalition that elected Andrew JACKSON president in 1828.

Jackson's Lieutenant. While in the Senate, Van Buren continued to dominate New York State politics through the Albany Regency and was elected governor in 1828; however, he resigned after only a few months in office to accept appointment as Jackson's secretary of state. Soon involved in a bitter power struggle with Vice-President John C. CALHOUN, Van Buren became a close companion and advisor to Jackson. Van Buren's position was strengthened by Jackson's disaffection with Calhoun, caused in part by the role of the vice-president's wife in snubbing the bride of Secretary of War John Henry EATON—the "Peggy Eaton Affair." Jackson also discovered that Calhoun had privately called for his censure in 1819 for his actions during the invasion of Florida, and was displeased with Calhoun's extreme state rights views. To enable Jackson to remove the pro-Calhoun element from his cabinet, Van Buren resigned. After calling for the resignation of all other cabinet members, Jackson appointed Van Buren minister to Great Britain. The Senate, with Calhoun casting the tie-breaking vote, refused to confirm the appointment. Enraged, Jackson supported Van Buren for the vice-presidency and then chose him as his successor.

In 1836, Van Buren easily won the Democratic presidential nomination as Jackson's protégé. The Whig party, declining to name a single candidate, sought to defeat Van Buren by running William Henry Harrison in the West and South and Daniel Webster in the Northeast. Although some southern Democrats defected, Van Buren won election with 170 electoral votes to 73 for runner-up Harrison.

Presidency. As president, Van Buren sought to hold southern Democrats in the party by adhering to a strict state rights policy on slavery. He opposed the abolition of the slave trade in the District of Columbia and favored guarantees that the federal government would not interfere with slavery in the states. Van Buren was opposed to the expansion of slavery, however, and his refusal to support the annexation of Texas offended many southerners. Meanwhile, his administration aroused further sectional opposition by conducting a protracted and costly war against the Seminole Indians (see SEMINOLE WARS) in Florida—a conflict that many northerners saw as a prelude to the admission of Florida as a slave state.

Van Buren's greatest political difficulties resulted from the nation's first major depression, the Panic of 1837, which began shortly after his inauguration. Committed to the Jeffersonian principle of limited government, he refused to yield to pressure for federal intervention to relieve economic distress. Restoration of full employment must come, he declared, from the efforts of private business. He saw his responsibility as limited to preventing the loss of federal funds as a result of the collapse of banks, whose alleged abuses he, like Jackson, had long criticized. Van Buren called for the establishment of an INDEPENDENT TREASURY SYSTEM that would divorce government and banking by placing all public monies in federally owned depositories. After much debate Congress finally established such a system in 1840.

Cautious and tactful in his foreign policy, Van Buren in 1838 sought to conciliate Great Britain in the CAROLINE AFFAIR, which arose over the sinking in American waters of a vessel supplying Canadian insurgents. In 1839 he intervened to prevent the so-called AROOSTOOK WAR, involving skirmishes over a boundary dispute between Maine and New Brunswick, from becoming a full-scale conflict.

Unsuccessful Presidential Bids. Despite his ability as chief executive, Van Buren gained a reputation as a devious political operator, and his failure to take decisive action to alleviate the hardships of the Panic of 1837 undermined his popularity. In 1840 he was defeated for reelection by the Whig candidate, William Henry Harrison, winning only 60 electoral votes to his opponent's 234.

Seeking the Democratic presidential nomination in 1844, Van Buren entered the nominating convention with the support of a majority of the delegates. His refusal, however, to support the annexation of Texas, which President John Tyler had made a burning national issue, cost him the support of the South, and he failed to receive the two-thirds vote necessary for nomination. The convention chose annexationist

James K. POLK of Tennessee, who subsequently won the presidential election.

In 1848, Van Buren was nominated for the presidency by the Barnburners (see HUNKERS AND BARNBURNERS), a faction of northern Democrats opposed to the extension of slavery. Despite his endorsement by the FREE-SOIL PARTY, Van Buren ran a poor third. Thereafter he took no further part in active politics. Van Buren died at Kinderhook on July 24, 1862. His memoirs, written in 1833, were published in 1920 as *The Autobiography of Martin Van Buren* (2 vols.).   ALFRED A. CAVE

Bibliography: Cole, Donald B., *Martin Van Buren and the American Political System* (1984; Curtis, James C., *The Fox at Bay: Martin Van Buren and the Presidency, 1837–1841* (1970); Lynch, Denis T., *Epoch and a Man: Martin Van Buren and His Times*, 2 vols. (1929; repr. 1971); Remini, Robert V., *Martin Van Buren and the Making of the Democratic Party* (1959; repr. 1970); Sloan, Irving J., ed., *Martin Van Buren, 1782–1862: Chronology, Documents, Bibliographical Aids* (1969); Wilson, Major L., *The Presidency of Martin Van Buren* (1984).

Van de Graaff, Robert Jemison   [van duh grahf]

The American physicist Robert Jemison Van de Graaff, b. Tuscaloosa, Ala., Dec. 20, 1901, d. Jan. 16, 1967, developed (1929) an electrostatic generator for the production of high voltages. He had conceived of the generator while studying at Oxford University (Ph.D., 1928). His apparatus was similar in action to the Wimshurst machine and formed the basis for later models used to transfer high energy to atomic particles. Van de Graaff was a professor at the Massachusetts Institute of Technology (1934–60), and in 1946 he helped to found the High Voltage Engineering Company.   RAYMOND J. SEEGER

Van de Graaff generator

The electrostatic device developed by Robert J. Van de Graaff was the first source of sufficiently high voltage to serve as a particle accelerator. It consists of a high-voltage terminal on an insulating stand, and a motor-driven silk belt that delivers an electric charge to the terminal. Charge is sprayed on the belt by a comb of sharp points and accumulates on the terminal, providing an electric potential of up to 10 million V. A

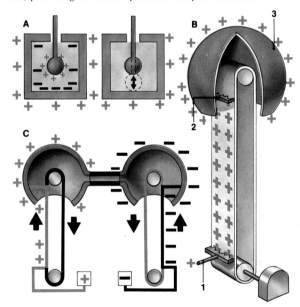

(A) *A positively charged sphere induces an equal, negative charge on the interior of a metal box and hence a positive charge on the exterior* (left). *If the sphere touches the interior, the charges cancel out and the exterior charge remains* (right). *Similarly, in a Van de Graaff generator* (B) *a charged comb* (1) *induces a charge on a belt of insulating material. Through another comb* (2) *inside the conducting sphere* (3) *the charge is transferred to the sphere's exterior. Two oppositely charged generators* (C) *yield a large electrical potential.*

particularly productive machine was built at the Carnegie Institution in Washington, D.C., where it was used for nuclear physics research during the 1930s; it is now on display at the Smithsonian Institution.

Higher voltages are achieved by enclosing the high-voltage apparatus in a pressurized tank. Several such machines have been built by the High Voltage Engineering Corporation founded by Van de Graaff and his associates. A more recent development is the tandem. Negative ions are accelerated from the ground to the terminal, where they are stripped of several electrons so that they become positive ions; as such they are accelerated back to the ground. If singly charged negative ions are accelerated to a terminal charged to 10 million V, they will gain 10 MeV of energy. If they are now stripped to a net positive charge of 6 electronic charges, they will gain another 60 MeV of energy on their way back to ground. Numerous tandems are in use; a tandem under construction by the National Electrostatics Corporation for installation at the Oak Ridge National Laboratory will be chargeable to 25 million V.   JOHN P. BLEWETT

Van de Velde, Henry

The Belgian Henry Van de Velde, b. Apr. 3, 1863, d. Oct. 25, 1957, began his career as a painter but in 1895 turned to decorative arts, design, and architecture. His own house (1894–96) at Uccle, Belgium, shows the influence of the English Arts and Crafts Movement. Van de Velde's early decorative work in Germany, where he moved in 1899, brought some of the extravagance of Belgian ART NOUVEAU to that country, but by 1902, in his interiors for the Folkwang (now Karl-Ernst Museum) at Hagen, the style's biomorphic forms are solidified and monumentalized. His numerous private houses with their thick walls, bulging bays, and heavy hipped roofs are preludes to his concrete Werkbund Theater (1914; demolished), Cologne, whose low, swelling forms and fleshy decoration are transitional between Art Nouveau and German expressionism. His other principal public building, the Rijksmuseum Kröller-Müller (1937–53), Otterloo, the Netherlands, turned to a graceful blend of contemporary influences, especially the International Style. Van de Velde was an influential writer and teacher as well; he founded (1902) in Weimar the Decorative Arts Seminar, the forerunner of the Bauhaus.

ANN VAN ZANTEN

Bibliography: Broeck, J. H. van den, *Guide to Dutch Architecture* (1955); Pevsner, Nikolaus, *Pioneers of Modern Design*, rev. ed. (1961).

van der Meer, Simon

Simon van der Meer, b. The Hague, Netherlands, Nov. 24, 1925, was awarded, along with Carlo RUBBIA, the 1984 Nobel Prize for physics for their work leading to discoveries of the W and Z FUNDAMENTAL PARTICLES. After obtaining an engineering degree from the Technical University in Delft, van der Meer joined, in 1956, the staff of CERN in Geneva (see EUROPEAN ORGANIZATION FOR NUCLEAR RESEARCH). Van der Meer's major contribution to the discovery of the W and Z particles was his design of a process, known as stochastic cooling, which was used to obtain large numbers of antiprotons.

van der Waals, Johannes Diderik

The Dutch physicist Johannes Diderik van der Waals, b. Nov. 23, 1837, d. Mar. 9, 1923, was known for his work in physical chemistry that led to the equation of state of gases and liquids. The van der Waals equation, presented in 1873 as a semitheoretical improvement over the ideal gas equation, resulted in his receiving the Nobel Prize for physics in 1910. The van der Waals force, the force between molecules, is named in his honor.   JAMES A. BOOTH

van der Waals equation

The van der Waals equation, derived by Johannes van der Waals, is an equation of state for gases and liquids that provides a reasonably good representation of the pressure-volume-temperature (*PVT*) data in the range of pressures and temperatures where the ideal gas law ($PV=nRT$) is invalid. The equation states: $(P + n^2a/V^2) (V - nb) = nRT$, where P = pressure, V = volume, T = temperature, n = moles of gas, R is the universal gas constant, and a and b are constants characteristic of the gas. The constants a and b are evaluated for each gas by fitting the equation to experimental measurements of PVT data. They may also be obtained by measurement of the critical temperature and critical pressure of the gas (see CRITICAL CONSTANTS). The constant a is then a measure of the attractive forces between the molecules, called van der Waals forces. The constant b is the approximate volume of a mole of the molecules in the liquid state.   GERALD C. ROPER

See also: GAS LAWS.

Van Devanter, Willis   [van duh-van'-tur]

Willis Van Devanter, b. Marion, Ind., Apr. 17, 1859, d. Feb. 8, 1941, served (1911-37) as associate justice on the U.S. Supreme Court. He practiced law before being elected (1890) chief justice of the Wyoming Supreme Court. Van Devanter then served (1903-10) on the U.S. Circuit Court; in 1911 President William H. Taft appointed him to the U.S. Supreme Court. Justice Van Devanter became one of the conservative majority on the Supreme Court that thwarted much of the New Deal legislation of President Franklin D. Roosevelt.

Van Diemen's Land: see TASMANIA.

Van Dine, S. S.   [van dyn]

S. S. Van Dine was the pseudonym of Willard Huntington Wright, b. Charlottesville, Va., 1888?, d. Apr. 11, 1939, an American scholar, editor, and art critic who turned to the writing of fiction after his health declined. He wrote a series of detective novels with an amateur sleuth as protagonist: Philo Vance, a languid purveyor of esoteric knowledge and icy logic, was a huge success. Between 1926 and 1938, 12 novels appeared, 11 of which were turned into movies, and, in the 1940s, Vance was also featured in a radio series. Among the best of the Van Dine novels are *The Greene Murder Case* (1928), *The Bishop Murder Case* (1929), and *The Scarab Murder Case* (1930).

van Dongen, Kees: see DONGEN, KEES VAN.

Van Doren, Carl

The writer, editor, and teacher Carl Clinton Van Doren, b. Hope, Ill., Sept. 10, 1885, d. July 18, 1950, was an early proponent of the serious study of American literature. Managing editor (1917-21) of the *Cambridge History of American Literature*, and literary editor of the *Nation* (1919-22) and *Century* (1922-25), he wrote such critical studies as *The American Novel* (1921; rev. ed., 1940) and *American Literature: An Introduction* (1933). He was also the author of a novel, *The Ninth Wave* (1926); a Pulitzer Prize–winning biography (1938) of Benjamin Franklin; and an autobiography, *Three Worlds* (1936).   C. CANTALUPO

Bibliography: Glicksberg, Charles Irving, *Carl Van Doren: Scholar and Skeptic* (1938); Van Doren, Dorothy Graffe, *The Professor and I* (1969).

Van Doren, Mark

A versatile man of letters, Mark Albert Van Doren, b. Hope, Ill., June 13, 1894, d. Dec. 10, 1972, a brother of Carl Van Doren, won a Pulitzer Prize for his *Collected Poems* (1940) and was an esteemed critic and university teacher. His numerous studies of authors—including Dryden, Hawthorne, and Shakespeare—his play *The Last Days of Lincoln* (1959), and his poetry, which explores the relationship between man and nature, are still admired. His later poetry includes the collections *Spring Birth* (1953) and *Morning Worship and Other Poems* (1960). He also wrote fiction and an autobiography (1958).

Van Druten, John   [van droo'-ten]

The American playwright John Van Druten, b. London, June 1, 1901, d. Dec. 19, 1957, wrote a series of popular stage comedies that were later filmed. These include *The Voice of the Turtle* (1943; film, 1948), *I Remember Mama* (1944; film, 1948), *Bell, Book and Candle* (1950; film, 1958), and *I Am a Camera* (1951; film, 1955), an adaptation of Christopher Isherwood's Berlin sketches.

Bibliography: Van Druten, John, *The Widening Circle* (1957).

van Dyck, Sir Anthony   [van dyk]

Charles I of England in Hunting Dress *(c.1634), one of several royal portraits by Sir Anthony van Dyck of his greatest patron, helped to establish a grandiose new tradition in English portraiture that was maintained by British artists through the 18th century. (Louvre, Paris.)*

The Flemish painter Sir Anthony (Anton) van Dyck, b. Mar. 22, 1599, d. Dec. 9, 1641, was noted primarily for his portraits and religious canvases. His gifts as an artist manifested themselves early in his life; he opened his own studio in Antwerp at the age of 16 and became a master of the city's artist's guild 2 years later. Between 1618 and 1620 he collaborated with Peter Paul Rubens, working with him as a younger colleague rather than as a student. He was later to attain a reputation second only to Rubens as the greatest painter in mid-17th-century Europe. Van Dyck owed much to Rubens and, like him, was strongly influenced by Titian's handling of color and composition.

Van Dyck's name is inextricably associated with the history of English painting; he made his first trip to London in 1620, where he was granted a court pension. With royal permission he left England in 1621 for Italy, where he studied, traveled, and painted until 1627. The full-length portrait *Marchesa Elena Grimaldi* (c.1625; National Gallery of Art, Washington, D.C.) exemplifies van Dyck's use of dark but harmonious color and an air of regal dignity bordering on arrogance that made his work so popular in the court of Charles I.

Van Dyck returned to Antwerp in 1627 and in 1630 became court painter to Archduchess Isabella, regent of the Netherlands. He settled in London in 1632 and was knighted and appointed principal painter to Charles I in the same year. He painted many portraits of the royal family as well as of court dignitaries and the nobility. His *Charles I on Horseback* (1638; National Gallery, London), one of several equestrian portraits he executed of the king, is a tour de force of dazzling brushwork and foreshortening, expressing the image of majesty and overwhelming power the king wished to project. Although much of van Dyck's work for the king had something of the flavor of image-building and propaganda about it, he was also capable of keen penetration and expression of character. His oval double portrait, *The Artist with Sir Endymion Porter* (c.1635, Prado, Madrid) reveals two worldly men, the painter and his patron, of sensitivity and intelligence.

Van Dyck also painted numerous religious and mythological subjects throughout his career. His debt to Italian Renaissance prototypes is, perhaps, clearer in these than in his portraits, as can be seen in *Cupid and Psyche* (c.1639; Royal Collections, Buckingham Palace, London).

Prior to van Dyck's arrival in England, English portraiture had tended to be formal and almost primitive in style, but he brought to it the full power of a completely articulated baroque style, and his influence extended through the 18th century. It is clearly visible in the work of Sir Peter Lely as well as in the portraits by Thomas Gainsborough and Sir Joshua Reynolds.   ROWLAND ELZEA

Bibliography: Martin, John R., and Feigenbaum, Gail, *Van Dyck as Religious Artist* (1979); Piper, David, *Van Dyck* (1968); Strong, Roy, *Charles I on Horseback* (1972).

van Eyck, Jan: see EYCK, JAN VAN.

Van Fleet, James Alward

James Alward Van Fleet, b. Coytesville, N.J., Mar. 19, 1892, commanded (1951–53) the U.S. 8th Army during the KOREAN WAR. A graduate (1915) of West Point, Van Fleet led a machine-gun battalion in World War I.

During World War II, Van Fleet commanded the regiment that made (1944) the initial assault on Utah Beach, in Normandy, and subsequently received rapid promotion. He was (1948–50) chief of the U.S. military mission to Greece, which helped fight Communist insurgents. Replacing Gen. Matthew B. Ridgway as 8th Army commander in Korea, Van Fleet was promoted (1951) to four-star general. He retired from active service in 1953.

van Gogh, Vincent   [van goh]

Although almost wholly unknown during his brief lifetime, the painter Vincent Willem van Gogh, b. Mar. 30, 1853, is today probably the most widely known and appreciated representative of POSTIMPRESSIONISM. His work became an important bridge between the 19th and 20th centuries; it was particu-

(Above) Self-Portrait with a Gray Hat *(1877) was painted by Vincent van Gogh during his 2-year stay in Paris; the pointillist technique (dots of color) is clear evidence of his new interest in the work of the impressionist painters whom he met there. (Rijksmuseum Vincent van Gogh, Amsterdam.)*

(Left) The Church at Auvers, *painted by Vincent van Gogh in June 1890, a month before his suicide, is in his high-keyed late style, with thick impasto, violent colors, strong contrasts, and deliberate distortion to achieve powerful expressive effects. The looming church silhouette is echoed by the pyramidal ground below it. (Louvre, Paris.)*

larly influential in the evolution of both FAUVISM and German EXPRESSIONISM.

Van Gogh clearly showed marked artistic talent even as a child, but neither he nor his family (his father was a Dutch clergyman) imagined that painting would become his career. Instead, at the age of 16, he went to work for Goupil and Company, an art gallery with which one of his uncles had long been associated; he was dismissed in 1876. Other false starts included a job in a Dordrecht bookstore during the spring of 1877, theological studies at the University of Amsterdam, and, from November 1878 to July 1879, service as a lay missionary in a coal-mining district in Belgium.

In 1880, Vincent chose art as a vocation and became dependent on his brother for money. Indeed, for the next 10 years Theo, who had also gone to work for Goupil, sent an allowance to Vincent, encouraged him to work, and wrote regularly. Vincent's thinking during his short but prolific career (approximately 750 paintings, 1,600 drawings, 9 lithographs, and 1 etching) is well documented in more than 700 letters that he wrote to Theo and others.

Van Gogh's early period includes all his work from 1879 through 1885. Between August 1879 and November 1885 he worked in Etten, The Hague—where he received some instruction from his cousin, Anton Mauve—and in Nuenen, among other places. In Nuenen he painted *The Potato Eaters* (1885; Rijksmuseum Vincent van Gogh, Amsterdam), his first important picture, which underscores his lifelong interest in peasant subjects.

During the winter of 1885–86 van Gogh studied at the academy in Antwerp, where he was forced to draw from plaster casts and to adopt academic principles that did not suit him. He moved to Paris, where he lived with Theo.

The Paris period (March 1886–February 1888) is extremely important because it enabled Vincent to see and to hear discussed the work of virtually every major artist there. Although van Gogh admired many members of the avant-garde, he also admired Eugène Delacroix, Jean François Millet, and the painters of the Barbizon and Hague schools. He respected painters as disparate as Adolphe Monticelli and J. L. E. Meissonier and such Japanese printmakers as Hiroshige, Hokusai, and Kesaï Yeisen. Numerous self-portraits, still lifes, and cityscapes date from this period, such as *Self-Portrait with a Straw Hat* (1887; Metropolitan Museum of Art, New York City), *A Pair of Shoes* (1886; Rijksmuseum Vincent van Gogh), and *Restaurant de la Sirène at Asnières* (1887; Louvre, Paris). During these years van Gogh's style shifted from the darker manner characteristic of his Nuenen period to a postimpressionist style heavily influenced by divisionism (also called pointillism; see SEURAT, GEORGES).

Van Gogh left Paris and moved to Arles in February 1888. His mature work and many of his most famous paintings date from the ensuing year. For example, he painted numerous blossoming orchards in the spring of 1888 (Rijksmuseum Vincent van Gogh), *The Night Café on the Place Lamartine, Arles* (1888; Yale University Art Gallery, New Haven, Conn.), *Still Life with Sunflowers* (several versions), and *The Bedroom at Arles* (1888; Rijksmuseum Vincent van Gogh).

In October 1888, Paul GAUGUIN came to live and work with van Gogh. After only 2 months, however, following the first of Vincent's attacks of dementia, in which he amputated his own earlobe, Gauguin left, having first summoned Theo from Paris. Thereafter, Vincent was hospitalized intermittently until the spring of 1890; he was voluntarily confined in the Asylum of Saint-Paul in Saint-Remy from May 1889 until May 1890. He continued to paint, however, and in June 1889 executed the *Starry Night* (Museum of Modern Art, New York City) and the extraordinary *Self-Portrait* (Louvre).

In the three months following his release from the hospital in May 1890, at the village of Auvers-sur-Oise outside Paris, Vincent produced many notable works including the *Portrait of Dr. Gachet* (private collection, New York City), *Field under Thunderclouds*, and the famous *Crows in the Wheatfields* (both Rijksmuseum Vincent van Gogh).

Although Vincent had finally begun to receive critical praise, he shot himself on July 27, 1890, and died two days

later. His grief-stricken brother died only six months thereafter.   CHARLES MOFFETT

Bibliography: de la Faille, J. B., *The Works of Vincent van Gogh,* trans. by James Brockway, rev. ed. (1970); Hammacher, Abraham M., *Genius and Disaster: The Ten Creative Years of Vincent van Gogh* (1968); Pollock, Griselda, and Orton, Fred, *Vincent van Gogh: Artist of his Time* (1978); Rewald, John, *Post-Impressionism from Van Gogh to Gauguin,* 2d ed. (1962); Schapiro, Meyer, *Van Gogh* (1950); Tralbaut, Marc Edo, *Vincent van Gogh,* trans. by Edita Lausanne (1969); van Gogh, Vincent, *The Complete Letters of Vincent van Gogh,* trans. by J. Van Gogh-Bonger and C. de Dood, 3 vols. (1958); Welsh-Ovcharov, Bogomila, ed., *Van Gogh in Perspective* (1974) and *Vincent van Gogh, His Paris Period, 1886–1888* (1976).

van Hamel, Martine   [van ham'-uhl]

Martine van Hamel, b. Brussels, Nov. 16, 1945, is a principal dancer with American Ballet Theatre (ABT). She joined National Ballet of Canada as soloist in 1963 and in 1965 won a gold medal in Varna, Bulgaria. She danced briefly with the Royal Swedish and Robert Joffrey ballet companies before joining ABT in 1970, where she has acquired a considerable following.   MICHAEL ROBERTSON

Bibliography: Payne, Charles, *American Ballet Theatre* (1978).

Van Itallie, Jean Claude   [van ee-tah-lee']

Formerly associated with the experimental Open Theatre, Belgian-born Jean Claude Van Itallie, b. May 25, 1936, is an American playwright whose works sharply criticize contemporary society. Using an experimental poetic dramatic form with the intention of breaking down traditional theatrical conventions, he has written *America Hurrah* (1966), *The Serpent* (1969), and *A Fable* (1975).   BONNIE MARRANCA

van Loo, Charles André   [vahn loh]

Charles André van Loo, b. Feb. 15, 1705, d. July 15, 1765, was prolific in the production of every category of painting, including portraiture and large decorative schemes. Denis Diderot acclaimed him as the first painter not only to the king but to the French nation as well. Unfortunately, van Loo's accomplishments, in all their diversity, are often prosaic. To modern judgment, it seems inexplicable that his timid style became synonymous with the excesses of the rococo and that his death was lamented as a national tragedy.

THOMAS WILLIAM SOKOLOWSKI

Bibliography: Kalnein, Wend Graf, and Levey, Michael, *Art and Architecture of the Eighteenth Century in France* (1972); Thuiller, J., and Chatelet, A., *French Painting from Le Nain to Fragonard* (1964).

Van Rensselaer   (family)   [van ren'-suh-lur]

The venerable Van Rensselaers of New York were noted for their wealth and social prominence. The family traces its origins to **Kiliaen Van Rensselaer**, 1595–1644, an Amsterdam jeweler and and stockholder of the Dutch colony of New Netherland, who in 1630 acquired a huge estate surrounding Fort Orange (Albany). Rensselaerswyck, the first, largest, and only successful patroonship (feudal estate; see PATROONS) in America became in 1685 an English manor, a kind of land grant that carried no civil authority and excluded the city of Albany. Kiliaen was an absentee proprietor, but his sons **Nicholas Van Rensselaer**, b. Amsterdam, September 1636, d. 1678, a Dutch Calvinist minister, and **Jeremias Van Rensselaer**, b. Amsterdam, c.1630, d. October 1674, established the family in America. **Stephen Van Rensselaer**, b. New York, Nov. 1, 1764, d. Jan. 26, 1839, the eighth and last of the patroons, was assemblyman, state senator, and lieutenant governor of New York as well as militia general in the War of 1812 and U.S. congressman (1822–29). Stephen contributed a great deal to the economic and educational development of New York State; in 1824 he founded Rensselaer Polytechnic Institute in Troy, the nation's first engineering school. The ANTIRENT WAR, a tenant uprising that prompted legislation ending perpetual leases and thus patroonships, began at Rensselaerswyck (1839–40).   LARRY R. GERLACH

Bibliography: Nissenson, Samuel G., *The Patroon's Domain* (1937); Van Rensselaer, Maunsell, *Annals of the Van Rensselaers in the U.S.* (1888); Van Rensselaer, May King, *The Van Rensselaers of the Manor of Rensselaerswyck* (1888).

Van Slyke, Helen   [van slyk]

Helen Van Slyke, b. Washington, D.C., July 9, 1919, d. July 3, 1979, wrote best-selling novels about the romantic and professional trials of modern women. Before publishing her first novel, *The Rich and the Righteous* (1971), she had a successful career in cosmetics, publishing, and advertising. Fashion editor (1938–43) of the *Washington Star* at the age of 18, she worked (1945–60) for *Glamour* magazine before becoming president (1963–68) of House of Fragrance, then vice-president of creative activities (1968–72) at Helena Rubenstein. Her first major book, *The Heart Listens* (1973), was followed by *Always Is Not Forever* (1977), *A Necessary Woman* (1979), and the posthumous *No Love Lost* (1980). Widely translated, her books sold more than 6 million copies in her lifetime.

Van Vechten, Carl   [van vek'-ten]

In a style that was the literary equivalent of Art Deco, Carl Van Vechten, b. Cedar Rapids, Iowa, June 17, 1880, d. Dec. 21, 1964, chronicled the smart, decadent New York society of the 1920s. His novels include *Peter Whiffle* (1922), *The Blind Bow-Boy* (1923), *Firecrackers* (1925), and *Parties* (1930). His best-known work, *Nigger Heaven* (1926), portrayed New York's black culture during the Harlem Renaissance, and *Spider Boy* (1928) satirized Hollywood. When the Great Depression came, Van Vechten abandoned fiction for photography.
                                                          WARREN FRENCH

Bibliography: Kellner, Bruce, *Carl Van Vechten and the Irreverent Decades* (1968); Lueders, Edward, *Carl Van Vechten* (1965); Van Vechten, Carl, *Sacred and Profane Memories* (1932).

Van Vleck, J. H.

The American mathematical physicist John Hasbrouck Van Vleck, b. Middleton, Conn., Mar. 13, 1899, d. Oct. 27, 1980, shared the 1977 Nobel Prize for physics for his fundamental work relating the quantum theory to magnetic phenomena. He taught at the University of Minnesota (1923–28), the University of Wisconsin (1928–34), and Harvard University (1934–69). While at Wisconsin, he showed (1930) that the quantum numbers of trivalent ions of rare-earth metals could be calculated accurately. He was one of the originators of the ligand field theory of molecular bonding.

Bibliography: Cohen, M. L., and Falicov, L. M., "1977 Nobel Prize in Physics," *Science*, Nov. 18, 1977.

Van Vogt, A. E.

The American writer Alfred Elton Van Vogt, b. Winnipeg, Manitoba, Apr. 26, 1912, a leading practitioner of science fiction, is known for his unfailing inventiveness, extraordinary plot constructions, and fast pace. He broke into the field by contributing stories to the magazine *Astounding* in 1939, and in 1946 was the guest of honor at the fourth World Science Fiction Convention. *Slan* (1946), which depicts the persecution of a superior mutant, is widely considered his best novel. His many other popular novels include *The Weapon Shops of Isher* (1951), *The World of Null-A* (1948), and its sequel, *The Pawns of Null-A* (1956).

Van Zeeland, Paul   [vahn zay'-lahnt]

Paul Van Zeeland, b. Nov. 11, 1893, d. Sept. 22, 1973, Belgian premier (1935–37), headed a coalition government that introduced a program similar to the New Deal in the United States and suppressed the fascist Rexist party. A Christian Democrat, he was later Belgium's foreign minister (1949–54).

vanadinite   [vuh-nay'-duh-nyt]

The uncommon lead vanadate mineral vanadinite $[Pb_5(VO_4)_3Cl]$ is an ore of vanadium and a minor source of lead. It forms brown, yellow, or red barrel-shaped prismatic crystals (hexagonal system) in oxidized zones of lead deposits. Hardness is 2¾ to 3, streak is white or pale yellow, and specific gravity is 6.88.

vanadium   [vuh-nay'-dee-uhm]

Vanadium is a bright white metal of group VB of the first series of TRANSITION ELEMENTS. It has the symbol V; its atomic number is 23, and its atomic weight is 50.9414. The element was discovered in 1801 by Andrés M. del Rio, but at the time the finding was dismissed as impure chromium. The element was rediscovered in 1830 by Nils G. Sefström, who named it in honor of the Scandinavian goddess Vanadis.

Among the 65 or so minerals in which vanadium occurs, the more important sources of the metal include carnotite, patronite, roscoelite, and vanadinite. Other sources of vanadium are in phosphate rock, certain iron ores, and some crude oils in the form of organic complexes. The extraction of vanadium from petroleum ash is a possible future source of the element. High-purity vanadium is obtained by reduction of vanadium trichloride (VCl_3) with magnesium or with magnesium-sodium mixtures. Because the major use of the metal is as an alloying agent for steel, pure vanadium is seldom extracted, and the bulk of the metal is currently made by the reduction of vanadium pentoxide (V_2O_5) with calcium.

Natural vanadium consists of two isotopes, ^{50}V and ^{51}V, the former being slightly radioactive. Seven other radioisotopes of the element have been synthesized. The pure metal is soft and ductile, with a melting point of 1,890° C, a boiling point of 3,380° C, and a density of 6.11 g/cm^3. This metal is resistant to corrosion by alkali, sulfuric and hydrochloric acids, and salt water but rapidly oxidizes in air above about 660° C. The outer electronic configuration of vanadium is $3d^2 4s^2$, and it exhibits oxidation states of −1, 0, +1, +2, +3, +4, and +5 in a wide variety of complex ions and coordination complexes.

Vanadium does not easily absorb neutrons released in nuclear-fission reactions and therefore is used as structural material in the nuclear industry. The metal is also used in forming high-speed tool steels; about 80% of the production of vanadium is used to make ferrovanadium or as a steel additive. Vanadium pentoxide is used in ceramics and as a catalyst. Vanadium and its compounds are toxic.

                                                          J. ALISTAIR KERR

Bibliography: Clark, R., and Brown, D., *The Chemistry of Vanadium, Niobium, and Tantalum* (1975).

Vanbrugh, Sir John   [van-bruh']

Sir John Vanbrugh, christened Jan. 24, 1664, d. Mar. 26, 1726, was an English playwright and architect whose most renowned works are BLENHEIM PALACE in Oxfordshire and Castle Howard in Yorkshire. Originally an officer in the English army, he resigned his commission after being imprisoned (1690–92) by the French for espionage. Vanbrugh turned to the theater, writing several popular comedies, including *The Relapse* (1696). After successfully devising (1699) plans for Castle Howard, however, he turned more and more to architectural work. Vanbrugh's design for Castle Howard, the palatial country home of his friend and associate the earl of Carlisle, successfully incorporated English baroque and French elements and was widely praised by contemporary observers. This success, combined with his social ties with the ruling Whig party, ensured his future employment as an architect and led directly to a succession of important government posts, including appointments as controller of the Board of Works (1702) and as a director of Greenwich Hospital (1703).

His most renowned—and most controversial—design was that of Blenheim Palace (begun 1705), a gift to John Churchill, 1st duke of Marlborough, from the nation. At Blenheim, Vanbrugh was able to work out the first entirely English version of baroque architecture, presenting an interplay of conflicting masses and idiosyncratic classical detailing, with Gothic and even Elizabethan elements in the skyline. This was a much-praised and much-criticized building. Throughout the early 1700s, while still working at Blenheim, he collaborated with Sir Christopher Wren and Nicholas Hawksmoor on several projects and executed numerous dramatic and original designs, including Vanbrugh Castle (c.1717) in Greenwich and the remodeling of Kimbolton Castle in Huntingdonshire (1707–10). He was also involved in planning gardens at Stowe in Buckinghamshire and Castle Howard, which established him as one of the founders of what was called the ''picturesque'' landscape. His work was always highly inventive but not imitable, and he had no followers.

DAVID CAST

Bibliography: Bingham, Madeleine, *Masks and Facades: Sir John Vanbrugh, the Man in His Setting* (1974); Downes, Kerry, *Vanbrugh* (1977); Harris, Bernard A., *Sir John Vanbrugh* (1967).

Vance, Cyrus R.   [vans]

Cyrus Vance, a U.S. secretary of state (1977–80), was the first cabinet member appointed by President-elect Jimmy Carter. Vance's diplomatic experience includes service as a presidential envoy to Greece and Turkey during their 1967 dispute over Cyprus and as a delegate to the Paris peace talks that took place during the Vietnam War.

Cyrus Roberts Vance, b. Clarksburg, W.Va., Mar. 27, 1917, was U.S. secretary of state from 1977 to 1980. A graduate of Yale Law School, he began his career in government as a special counsel for the Senate Armed Services Committee in 1957. He served as secretary of the army (1962–64) and deputy secretary of defense (1964–67). He later undertook a number of important diplomatic missions for President Lyndon Johnson. During the Cyprus crisis of 1967 he was credited by some observers with having averted a war between Greece and Turkey, and during the Paris peace conference on Vietnam he was deputy chief of the U.S. delegation (1968–69). As secretary of state in the Carter administration, Vance was involved in the Strategic Arms Limitation Talks (SALT), the negotiations leading to the Israeli-Egyptian peace treaty of 1979, and the prolonged efforts to secure release of the U.S. hostages in Iran. He resigned in protest against the commando attempt to rescue the hostages in April 1980.

vancomycin: see ANTIBIOTICS.

Vancouver   [van-koo'-vur]

Vancouver is a city in southwestern Canada opposite Vancouver Island in the province of British Columbia. Vancouver is Canada's third largest metropolis and recently has been one of the fastest growing. The city's population is 431,147, and that of the metropolitan area, 1,380,729 (1986). Occupying one of the world's most attractive city sites, Vancouver is surrounded by water and overlooked by mountains. The Strait of Georgia is to the west, Burrard Inlet is on the north, and the Fraser River delta is on the south. Just beyond Burrard Inlet the Coast Ranges rise abruptly to heights exceeding 1,500 m (5,000 ft). The climate of the area is perhaps the mildest in Canada, with temperatures averaging 3° C (37° F) in January and 18° C (64° F) in July. Vancouver's average annual precipitation is 1,018 mm (40 in). Most rainfall occurs in winter.

Vancouver is a major port of Canada and probably leads the world in grain exports. As the principal western terminus of Canada's transcontinental highway and rail routes, it is the primary city of western Canada as well as one of the nation's largest industrial centers. Major industries include the production of lumber and paper products, shipbuilding, food processing, petroleum refining, fish processing, and metal product manufacturing. A superport at Roberts Bank, 40 km (25 mi) to the south, is used for exporting coal and ores to Japan.

Vancouver is also a major destination of tourists. In addition to the city's scenic location, visitors enjoy beautiful gardens and world-famous Stanley Park, a combination of natural forest and parklands near the city center. The University of British Columbia was founded in Vancouver in 1908.

Vancouver was founded as a sawmill settlement called Granville on Burrard Inlet in the 1870s. The city was incorporated in 1886 and renamed for British naval captain George Vancouver, who had explored the area a century earlier. The first trans-Canada railway, the Canadian Pacific, arrived in

Vancouver, the leading city of western Canada, is situated along the Pacific coast of British Columbia, separated from Vancouver Island by the Strait of Georgia. The area was explored in 1792 by the British captain George Vancouver and first settled during the 1870s.

1887, and much of the city's early prosperity was based on the railroad. Other railways came soon after, and trans-Pacific ocean trade began to develop strongly in the late 19th century. Since World War II many immigrants from continental Europe and Asia and from the prairie provinces and eastern Canada have settled in Vancouver. In 1986 it was the site of a world's fair.   TOM McKNIGHT

Bibliography: Davis, Chuck, and Mooney, Shirley, *Vancouver: An Illustrated Chronology* (1986); Hull, R., et al., *Vancouver's Past* (1974).

Vancouver, George

George Vancouver, b. June 22, 1757, d. May 10, 1798, an English explorer, surveyed the west coast of North America from the San Francisco Bay area to British Columbia. He entered the Royal Navy in 1771 and sailed (1772–75, 1776–80) under Capt. James Cook. In 1791, Vancouver set out to explore the Pacific Northwest, obtain from the Spanish the return of Nootka (on what was later named Vancouver Island, in his honor), and search for a Northwest Passage. Sailing around the Cape of Good Hope, he surveyed portions of the Australian and New Zealand coasts. Between 1792 and 1794, he sailed along the North American coast as far south as San Luis Obispo, Calif., and as far north as Cook Inlet, Alaska. He was the first to circumnavigate Vancouver Island. Vancouver regained Nootka and reported that there was no Northwest Passage. Upon his return to England in 1795, he wrote *A Voyage of Discovery to the North Pacific Ocean and round the World*, 3 vols. and atlas (1798; repr. 1968).   GEORGE F. G. STANLEY

Bibliography: Anderson, Bern, *The Life and Voyages of Captain George Vancouver, Surveyor of the Sea* (1960; repr. 1966); Marshall, James S. and Carrie, *Vancouver's Voyage*, 2d ed. (1967).

Vancouver Island

Part of British Columbia, Canada, Vancouver is the largest island on the Pacific coast of North America. Covering 31,284 km² (12,079 mi²), it is 459 km (285 mi) long and averages 80 km (50 mi) in width. The population is 510,233 (1986). VICTORIA, the principal city, is the capital of British Columbia.

Mountainous and heavily forested, Vancouver Island has a rugged coastline with deep fjords and bays. The highest peak, Golden Hinde, rises 2,200 m (7,220 ft). The January average temperature is 3° C (37° F); the July average is 18° C (64° F). Yearly rainfall can total 3,800 mm (150 in). Economic activities include lumbering, paper manufacturing, fishing, and coal and iron-ore mining. Tourism is also important.

Originally inhabited by Nootka and Makah Indians, Vancouver Island was visited by James Cook in 1778 and subsequently settled by the Hudson's Bay Company. It became a British colony in 1849 and part of British Columbia in 1866.

Vandals   [van'-duhlz]

Among the barbarian peoples who attacked the Roman Empire in the 5th century AD were the Vandals, a Teutonic tribe that governed a North African kingdom from 439 to 534.

By the 4th century the Vandals were living in the area of the Tisza River (in what is now eastern Hungary). As the Huns moved west later in that century, they pushed the Vandals before them. In December 406 the Vandals crossed the Rhine and invaded Gaul. They ravaged Roman territory there and in 409 invaded Spain. Following a series of defeats inflicted in 417 by the Visigoths, who were fighting on behalf of the Romans, the Vandals moved south to Andalusia.

In 429 the new Vandal ruler GAISERIC abandoned Spain and invaded North Africa, which finally fell under his complete control in 439. Gaiseric, who ruled until 477, gained control of the western Mediterranean and sacked Rome in 455. It is to the latter act that the Vandals owe their name.

In North Africa the Vandals, who were Arian Christians, persecuted orthodox Christians (in a reversal of Roman practice). After Gaiseric's death his descendants had difficulty defending their frontiers, and in 533 the Byzantine general BELISARIUS invaded North Africa. By 534 the Vandal kingdom was in ruins.   BERNARD S. BACHRACH

Bibliography: Gordon, C. D., *The Age of Attila: Fifth Century Byzantium and the Barbarians* (1960); Wallace-Hadrill, J. M., *The Barbarian West, 400–1000*, 3d ed. (1967).

Vandenberg, Arthur H.   [van'-den-burg]

Arthur Hendrick Vandenberg, b. Grand Rapids, Mich., Mar. 22, 1884, d. Apr. 18, 1951, a leading Republican and U.S. senator from Michigan (1928–51), was a key figure in the establishment of a bipartisan foreign policy after World War II. After a year at the University of Michigan (1901–02), he worked on the *Grand Rapids Herald* and became its editor and publisher (1906–28). Having been active in state and local politics during this time, he was appointed to fill a vacant seat in the Senate (1928), to which he was elected soon after.

On domestic issues, Vandenberg was a moderate conservative. His real interest, however, was foreign policy. A leading opponent of President Franklin D. Roosevelt's internationalist policies before and during World War II, he reversed his views in the mid-1940s and strongly supported the containment policies of Harry S. Truman's administration. As ranking Republican and chairman of the Senate Foreign Relations Committee (1947–49), he was influential in developing bipartisan support for such efforts as aid to Greece and Turkey in 1947, the Marshall Plan in 1948, and the North Atlantic Treaty Organization in 1949.   JAMES T. PATTERSON

Bibliography: Tompkins, C. David, *Senator Arthur Vandenberg* (1970); Vandenberg, Arthur H., Jr., with Alex Morris, *The Private Papers of Senator Vandenberg* (1952).

Vandenberg Air Force Base

Vandenberg Air Force Base, located at Point Arguello, Calif., about 240 km (150 mi) north of Los Angeles, is the U.S. site for launching satellites southward over the Pacific Ocean into polar and near-polar orbits. (Missions requiring such orbits are not launched from Cape Canaveral, Fla., because they would involve overland flight.) The explosion of a Titan 34D booster at the base in 1986, however, also badly damaged the pad used for major polar-orbit launches.

Primarily an Air Force facility for test-launching intercontinental ballistic missiles, Vandenberg handles civilian launches through the Western Test Range office of the Kennedy Space Center. Established in 1958, it is named for Gen. Hoyt S. Vandenberg, a former Air Force chief of staff. Plans called for occasional SPACE SHUTTLE launches from the base to begin in the mid-1980s, but structural flaws found in the launch facility—plus delays resulting from the *Challenger* disaster in 1986—postponed these plans until the early 1990s.   DAVID DOOLING

Vanderbilt   (family)   [van'-dur-bilt]

The Vanderbilt family owes its prominence to its early association with rail and water transportation. **Cornelius Vanderbilt**, b. Staten Island, N.Y., May 27, 1794, d. Jan. 4, 1877, began a ferry service between New York City and Staten Island at the age of 16. In 1818 he entered the shipping company of Thomas Gibbons. As a result of the U.S. Supreme Court decision (GIBBONS V. OGDEN, 1824) nullifying the navigation monopoly that New York State had granted to Robert Fulton and Robert R. Livingston, Vanderbilt was able to gain control of much of the shipping business along the Hudson River. After leaving Gibbons's employ in 1829, he extended his own operations from New York to Boston by shrewdly entering into rate wars with his competitors. During the gold rush of 1849 he successfully opened a steamship route from New York to California that included an overland route across Nicaragua, thereby decreasing the time and cost of the journey significantly. In the 1850s, Vanderbilt entered into transatlantic competition with the Cunard and other lines. The 1860s marked his entry into the railroad field. By 1875, after he bought and consolidated many small holdings, his New York Central Railroad controlled the lucrative route between New York and Chicago. He founded Vanderbilt University in 1875.

At his death, Cornelius Vanderbilt's fortune was estimated

at $100 million. Of his 13 children, **William Henry Vanderbilt**, b. New Brunswick, N.J., May 8, 1821, d. Dec. 8, 1885, is notable for having expanded the family railroad holdings.

Bibliography: Andrews, Wayne, *The Vanderbilt Legend: The Story of the Vanderbilt Family: 1794-1940* (1941); Croffut, William A., *The Vanderbilts: And the Story of Their Fortune* (1886; repr. 1975); Hoyt, Edwin P., *The Vanderbilts and Their Fortunes* (1962); Lane, Wheaton J., *Commodore Vanderbilt: An Epic of the Steam Age* (1942; repr. 1973); Vidal, Gore, et al., *Great American Families* (1977).

Vanderbilt University

Established in 1873, Vanderbilt University (enrollment: 9,125; library: 1,450,000 volumes) is a private coeducational institution in Nashville, Tenn. Law, dentistry, nursing, medical, and engineering schools are part of the university. In 1979 the university absorbed George Peabody College for Teachers (1785).

Vanderlyn, John [van'-dur-lin]

John Vanderlyn's serenely idealized nude, Ariadne Asleep on the Island of Naxos *(1814), painted while the American artist was studying in Europe, reflects the clear color and line of the French neoclassical style. (Pennsylvania Academy of the Fine Arts, Philadelphia.)*

John Vanderlyn, b. Kingston, N.Y., Sept. 15, 1775, d. Aug. 23, 1852, was an American painter of landscapes and historical subjects. Aaron Burr recognized Vanderlyn's talent early in his career and supported his studies with the portraitist Gilbert Stuart in Philadelphia and his many years of study and work in Europe. In Paris and Rome, Vanderlyn thrived, perfecting a neoclassical style in the manner of Jacques Louis David and Jean Auguste Dominique Ingres that, in 1808, earned him a gold medal from Napoleon for his painting *Marius among the Ruins of Carthage* (1807; M. H. de Young Memorial Museum, San Francisco). After 1815, however, when Vanderlyn returned to the United States, his hopes for fame were never realized. He opened a rotunda in Manhattan to exhibit his panorama, *Palace and Gardens of Versailles* (1815; Metropolitan Museum of Art, New York City), but failed to prosper, and there was little demand for his paintings. Finally, in 1837, the government recognized him with a commission to paint *The Landing of Columbus* for the rotunda of the Capitol, but it was too late for the aging and disgruntled Vanderlyn. Although he spent the next 8 years in Paris working on the project, it could not measure up to the ambitious vision of his youth.

PHILIP GOULD

Bibliography: Lindsay, Kenneth C., *The Works of John Vanderlyn* (1970); Schoonmaker, Maurice, *John Vanderlyn, Artist, 1775-1852* (1950).

Vane, Sir Henry [vayn]

An English statesman, Sir Henry Vane the Younger, b. 1613, d. June 14, 1662, was a leading parliamentarian during the En-glish Civil War. A Puritan convert, he was colonial governor of Massachusetts (1636-37). Returning to England, Vane became a member of the Short and the Long Parliaments and negotiated (1643) the alliance bringing the Scots into the English Civil War on Parliament's side.

Although against the king's execution, Vane served on the Commonwealth's Council of State (1649-53), handling naval and foreign affairs. An advocate of parliamentary supremacy, he opposed the dissolution of the Rump Parliament by Oliver Cromwell in 1653 and was imprisoned (1656) for attacking Cromwell's Protectorate. In 1659 he supported the army's overthrow of Richard Cromwell. After the restoration of the monarchy, Vane was executed for high treason.

MAURICE ASHLEY

Bibliography: Adamson, J. H., and Folland, H. F., *Sir Harry Vane: His Life and Times* (1973); Rowe, Violet A., *Sir Henry Vane the Younger* (1970).

Vänern, Lake [ven'-urn]

Lake Vänern, the largest lake in Sweden, covers an area of 5,585 km² (2,156 mi²). Located in southwestern Sweden, Lake Vänern is a major link in the Göta Canal, linking the Kattegat to the Baltic Sea. Karlstad, Kristinehamn, Vänersborg, and Lidköping are major industrial centers along its shores.

vanga

Vangas are medium-sized birds found only in the forests of Madagascar. Twelve species, also known as vanga shrikes, make up the family Vangidae. They range from 12.5 to 30 cm (5 to 12 in) long and generally have heavy bills and black or white plumage sometimes tinged with brown or metallic blue. They feed on small animals, including tree frogs and lizards.

GEORGE J. WALLACE

Vanguard

The Vanguard program, begun in 1955, culminated in the successful launching of three scientific satellites. Initially a U.S. Navy project, the program was turned over to NASA in 1958. *Vanguard 1* was intended to be the first U.S. satellite (see SPACE EXPLORATION); troubles, however, with its launch vehicle, also named Vanguard, enabled the U.S. Army to orbit its *Explorer 1* first. *Vanguard 1* was successfully launched on Mar. 17, 1958, from Cape Canaveral, Fla. It went into orbit with an apogee of 3,961 km (2,462 mi) and a perigee of 652 km (405 mi) at an angle of 34.3° to the equator and had a period of 134 min. It transmitted data until May 1964. The satellite, a pressurized aluminum sphere, measured 16.5 cm (6.4 in) in diameter and weighed 1.5 kg (3.3 lb). Instrumentation consisted only of two radio transmitters for tracking the satellite. *Vanguard 2*, launched on Feb. 17, 1959, was a magnesium sphere 50.8 cm (20 in) in diameter. It weighed 10 kg (22 lb) and was instrumented with photocells and two optical telescopes to study Earth's cloud cover. *Vanguard 3* was also a magnesium sphere 50.8 cm in diameter, but it weighed 29 kg (64 lb). It was orbited on Sept. 18, 1959, and transmitted data through December 12 of that year. Its scientific instrumentation, provided by NASA's Goddard Space Flight Center, consisted of experiments to study Earth's magnetic field, the micrometeoroid flux in near-Earth space, and solar X rays.

Vanguard data resulted in a better understanding of the Earth's true shape; determined the location of the lower boundary of the Van Allen radiation belt, the density variations of the extreme upper atmosphere, and the extent of Earth's magnetic field in space; and gave early estimates of the micrometeoroid flux near Earth.

MITCHELL SHARPE

Bibliography: Buedeler, Werner, *Operation Vanguard* (1957); Caidin, Martin, *Vanguard!* (1957); Green, Constance McLaughlin, and Lomask, Milton, *Vanguard: A History* (NASA SP-4202; 1970); Stehling, Kurt R., *Project Vanguard* (1961).

vanilla

Vanilla is the name given to a genus of pantropical orchids (those which occur in tropical climates) and to the flavor extract obtained from the fruit pods of several of its species.

The vanilla V. planifolia, a member of the orchid family, is an epiphyte and obtains its food and water from air while anchored to another plant. This tropical American plant is cultivated for its seed pod (right), which is used to flavor food and beverages.

The best and most important commercial extract is obtained from *Vanilla planifolia,* which, like other members of the genus, is a climbing vine with aerial roots and fragrant, greenish yellow flowers. The Aztecs introduced (early 16th century) Spanish explorers to vanilla, and soon afterward it became popular in Europe.

In its native habitat vanilla is pollinated by bees and possibly hummingbirds; this yields a fruit set of only about 1 percent. When cultivated outside Central America, where its natural pollinators do not exist, vanilla normally does not set any fruit. Today vanilla beans are produced by hand pollination with a wooden needle; they are grown in Mexico, Indonesia, and Madagascar. The harvested, unripe, golden green beans are cured by alternating night-sweating with daily sun-drying, which produces the characteristic flavor and aroma. The curing process continues for 10 to 20 days, after which the beans are bundled for drying and development of the full aroma. This curing-and-drying procedure requires about 4 to 5 months. The resulting bean is wrinkled and chocolate colored.

The flavor and odor of the extract comes partially from a white crystal vanillin, which develops during the curing process. Vanilla beans, vanilla extracts and tinctures (alcoholic extracts), and vanilla resinoids (hydrocarbon solvent extracts) are the foremost food flavors for ice cream, puddings, cakes, chocolates, baked goods, syrups, candies, liqueurs, tobacco, and soft drinks. Vanilla tincture is also used in perfumes. Vanillin is now produced artificially from eugenol (derived from clove-stem oil) or acid hydrolysis of lignin (wood). Although the production of artificial vanilla flavoring has increased greatly over the years, natural vanilla extract remains the premium cooking standard.

Tahitian vanilla, a red brown vanilla bean derived from *V. tahitensis,* is cultivated in the South Pacific. Vanillon—West Indian, or Guadeloupe, vanilla—derived from *V. pompona,* has a more cherrylike odor, from heliotropine. It is used to flavor tobacco, soaps, perfumes, medicines, and liqueurs and is sometimes blended with true vanilla.   ARTHUR O. TUCKER

Bibliography: Rosengarten, F., *The Book of Spices,* rev. ed. (1981).

Vanity Fair

In *Vanity Fair, a Novel Without a Hero* (1848), William Makepeace THACKERAY describes the snobberies, hypocrisies, and foibles of 19th-century British society. The novel was first published in monthly installments in 1847–48. The title is taken from an episode in John Bunyan's *Pilgrim's Progress* in which Christian encounters worldly vanity. The novel remains popular for its portrait of the scheming adventuress Becky Sharp in the get-rich-quick London of the early 1800s. Against a setting that shifts between England and Brussels on the eve of the Battle of Waterloo, Thackeray shows the selfish pursuit of money and social position clashing with the virtues of honesty and fidelity represented by Becky's foil, Amelia Sedley, and Captain Dobbin.

van't Hoff, Jacobus Henricus   [vahn tawf]

The Dutch chemist Jacobus Henricus van't Hoff, b. Aug. 30, 1852, d. Mar. 1, 1911, received (1901) the first Nobel Prize for chemistry for the development of laws of chemical dynamics and of osmotic pressure in dilute solutions. Van't Hoff's pioneering work, especially in the discipline of PHYSICAL CHEMISTRY, had a significant influence on the chemical, physical, biological, and geological sciences. Independently and at the same time as Joseph Achille Le Bel, van't Hoff postulated (1874) that the carbon atom in organic compounds had a three-dimensional tetrahedral structure (see ORGANIC CHEMISTRY; STEREOCHEMISTRY) and that the possibility of asymmetry in certain compounds explained their OPTICAL ACTIVITY. He showed the analogy between gases and dissolved substances by applying thermodynamics to chemical reactions, and he developed laws that govern the relationship between temperature, molecular concentration, and the osmotic pressure of dilute solutions. He investigated the dynamic nature of chemical equilibria and the velocity of chemical reactions. During his later years he investigated the origin and formation of oceanic salt deposits, which became greatly important to the German potash industry.

Vantongerloo, Georges: see DE STIJL.

Vanuatu   [vah-noo-ah'-too]

REPUBLIC OF VANUATU

LAND. Area: 14,763 km² (5,700 mi²). Capital and largest city: Vila (1981 est. pop., 14,000).

PEOPLE. Population (1986 est.): 136,000; density (1986 est.): 9.2 persons per km² (23.9 per mi²). Distribution (1986): 18% urban, 82% rural. Annual growth (1984): 3.3%. Official languages: French, English, Bislama. Major religions: Presbyterianism, Roman Catholicism, Anglicanism.

EDUCATION AND HEALTH. Literacy: not available. Universities (1987): none. Hospital beds (1983): 437. Physicians (1984): 19. Life expectancy (1984): women—53.7; men—56.2. Infant mortality (1984): 94 per 1,000 live births.

ECONOMY. GNP (1984): $77 million; $575 (est.) per capita. Labor distribution (1979): agriculture—77%; government and services—11%; trade—4%. Foreign trade (1984): imports—$66 million; exports—$44 million; principal trade partners—Australia, Netherlands, Japan. Currency: 1 vatu = 100 centimes.

GOVERNMENT. Type: republic. Legislature: Parliament. Political subdivisions: none.

COMMUNICATIONS. Railroads (1987): none. Roads (1981): 1,062 km (660 mi) total. Major ports: 2. Major airfields: 2.

Vanuatu (formerly New Hebrides), a group of about 12 islands and about 60 islets extending for approximately 800 km (500 mi) in the southwestern Pacific, is located about 1,600 km (1,000 mi) northeast of Australia. More than half of the residents live on the islands of Efate (the site of Vila, the capital), Espiritu (the largest island), Malekula, and Tanna.

Most of the residents are Melanesian and speak Bislama, a pidgin.

Because the islands are mountainous in the interior, most inhabitants live on the coastal plains and practice subsistence agriculture. Commercial plantations produce copra, cocoa, and coffee for export, and fishing and meat production are also export oriented. Vanuatu has no direct taxation and is becoming a banking center. Tourism is also important to the economy, which was damaged by a severe hurricane in 1987.

In 1606 a short-lived Spanish settlement was established on Espiritu Santo. Capt. James Cook charted the islands and named them the New Hebrides in 1774. Soon British and French traders, planters, and missionaries arrived. Conflicts between Europeans and indigenous peoples, as well as between competing European interests, resulted (1887) in an agreement that led to joint British and French administration of the islands. In 1980, the year in which the islands were scheduled for independence, a rebellion on Espiritu Santo was put down by British and French troops. Independence was granted one week later, on July 30, 1980, and a parliamentary form of government was established. In 1987, Vanuatu signed a fishing agreement with the Soviet Union.

Bibliography: Carter, J., ed., *Pacific Islands Yearbook*, 15th ed. (1984); Douglas, N., *Vanuatu—A Guide* (1987).

Vanvitelli, Luigi   [vahn-vee-tel'-lee]

The Italian architect Luigi Vanvitelli, b. May 12, 1700, d. Mar. 1, 1773, is most famous for the palace he built (1752–74) at Caserta, 32 km (20 mi) north of Naples, for King Charles III. He worked in Loreto, Milan, Pesaro, and Rome—where he had been trained—there rebuilding Michelangelo's Santa Maria degli Angeli. The work at Caserta was finished (1774) by his son Carlo after Vanvitelli's death. The palace is immense, a huge rectangular block with four interior courtyards and about 1,200 rooms. Its design was influenced by the plans of Versailles and Inigo Jones's (unbuilt) scheme for Whitehall. In organizing Caserta, however, Vanvitelli was especially sensitive to scenographic interior effects: long vistas, seemingly endless sequences of rooms, and Piranesian glimpses of the courtyards seen from grand staircases that are always on a diagonal axis. In this sense, Caserta is clearly a late baroque work. Among Vanvitelli's other works in Naples are the church of the Annunciation (1761–82) and the Foro Carolino (1757–65), now the Piazza Dante.   DAVID CAST

Bibliography: Norberg-Schulz, Christian, *Late Baroque and Rococo Architecture* (1974); Wittkower, Rudolf, *Art and Architecture in Italy, 1600–1750*, 3d ed. (1973; repr. 1978).

Vanzetti, Bartolomeo: see SACCO AND VANZETTI CASE.

vapor pressure

The vapor pressure of a liquid is the pressure exerted by the gas when it is in equilibrium with the liquid state. The vapor pressure depends on temperature, increasing as the temperature increases.

When a liquid is introduced into an evacuated vessel, evaporation occurs until the pressure of the vapor reaches a definite maximum value and the two phases are in equilibrium. If the vapor is then compressed so that its pressure is momentarily greater than its equilibrium vapor pressure, some of it will condense to the liquid state to reestablish the equilibrium. A liquid boils (evaporates rapidly) when its vapor pressure equals the prevailing atmospheric pressure. The normal boiling point of any liquid is the temperature at which its vapor pressure equals one atmosphere (760 mm Hg).   GERALD C. ROPER

Varanasi   [vuh-rahn'-uh-see]

Varanasi (or Benares) is a sacred city for Hindus in Uttar Pradesh state, northern India, situated on the north bank of the Ganges River. Its population is 704,772 (1981). Jewelry, brasswork, lacquered toys, and gold-embroidered saris are impor-

tant handicraft products. The city's tourist industry caters to the many pilgrims who visit the holy city each year. Varanasi contains more than 1,500 temples and mosques. Almost all of the city's 5 km (3 mi) of river banks have been converted into ghats (brick steps), where worshipers bathe in the sacred Ganges. Benares Hindu University (1916) is one of India's most prominent seats of learning.

Originally known as Kasi, Varanasi is mentioned in late Vedic literature (c.8th century BC) and in the Hindu epics *Ramayana* and *Mahabharata*. The city encompasses SARNATH, where Buddha preached his first sermon in about 530 BC. From the 4th to the 6th century AD, Varanasi was a great cultural center, but the onset of Muslim occupation in 1193 resulted in the city's decline and the destruction of its ancient temples. (The major present-day temples date from the 18th and 19th centuries.) Varanasi was made a part of Uttar Pradesh in 1949.   ASHOK K. DUTT

Bibliography: Eck, Diana L., *Banaras: City of Light* (1982).

Varangians: see RURIK; VIKINGS.

Vardon, Harry   [vahr'-duhn]

The Briton Harry Vardon, b. May 9, 1870, d. Mar. 20, 1937, was the first of the great modern golfers. He won the British Open a record 6 times (1896, 1898–99, 1903, 1911, 1914) and entered the U.S. Open 3 times, winning once (1900) and twice finishing second, although he was 50 years of age at the time of his last appearance. Although he did not invent the overlapping grip, Vardon popularized it, and today it is called the Vardon grip. During a 12-year period he represented England 18 times in international competitions. An award, the Vardon Trophy, is given annually to the professional golfer with the lowest average number of strokes per round on the Professional Golfers' Association (PGA) tour.   HOWARD LISS

Bibliography: McDonnell, Michael, *Golf: The Great Ones* (1971).

Varèse, Edgar   [vah-rez']

Edgar Varèse is among the most original composers of the 20th century. One of the earliest exponents of electronic music, Varèse led the modern music movement in the United States, producing an experimental form of music he termed "organized sound." Varèse founded numerous organizations for the study and promotion of experimental music.

The French composer Edgar Varèse, b. Dec. 22, 1883, d. Nov. 6, 1965, was one of the greatest musical innovators of the 20th century. From 1904 he studied composition in Paris with Vincent d'Indy and Albert Roussel. Befriended by Claude Debussy and Romain Rolland, as well as by Ferruccio Busoni in Berlin and Richard Strauss in Vienna, he had the prospect of pursuing a successful career in Europe, but World War I intervened. Discharged from the army because of ill health, he went to New York in 1915 and played a leading role in the avant-garde movement of the 1920s and '30s. He was one of the founders of the International Composers' Guild (1921–27) and the Pan-American Association of Composers (1928–34), both dedicated to performing new music.

In his compositions, such as *Hyperprism* (1923), *Intégrales* (1925), *Arcana* (1925–27), and *Ionisation* (1930–33, for 13 percussion instruments), he rejected all traditional forms and melodic-harmonic procedures in favor of self-contained sound structures emphasizing percussion, including a wide array of noisemakers. In *Déserts* (1949–53) he alternated instruments with sections of taped electronic sound, and the *Poème électronique* (1957–58) was done entirely with tape, using 425 loudspeakers to project the sound throughout a moving spatial pattern.

GILBERT CHASE

Bibliography: Ouellette, Fernand, *Edgard Varèse*, trans. by Derek Coltman (1968); Varese, Louise, *Varèse: A Looking-Glass Diary* (1972).

Vargas, Getúlio Dornelles   [vahr'-gahs]

Getúlio Dornelles Vargas, b. Apr. 19, 1883, d. Aug. 24, 1954, Brazilian president (1930–45, 1951–54), promoted the modernization of Brazil. Having studied law, Vargas served his home state of Rio Grande do Sul as national congressman (1922–26) and governor (1928–30). From 1926 to 1927 he was finance minister in the national cabinet. Unsuccessful in his bid for the presidency in 1930, Vargas led a revolt that overthrew the government. Over the next 15 years, he effected massive transformations in the public and private sectors. His style was authoritarian and his appeal populist: unionization, industrialization, and social welfare programs gained him the working- and middle-class backing.

Vargas gave important support to the Allies during World War II, but his popularity declined sharply as democratic sentiment grew. In 1945 he was ousted by the army. Vargas won election as president in 1950, but his second tenure was beset with scandals and economic difficulties. Faced with growing opposition and expecting a coup, he resigned and then committed suicide.

Bibliography: Bourne, Richard, *Getúlio Vargas of Brazil, 1883–1954: Sphinx of the Pampas* (1974); Dulles, J. F., *Vargas of Brazil: A Political Biography* (1967); Levine, Robert M., *Vargas Regime and the Politics of Extremism in Brazil, 1934–1938* (1968); Loewenstein, Karl, *Brazil Under Vargas* (1942; repr. 1973).

Vargas Llosa, Mario   [vahr'-gahs yoh'-sah]

The novels of the major Peruvian writer Mario Vargas Llosa, b. Mar. 28, 1936, contain a mercilessly penetrating view of Peruvian society. Vargas's first collection of short stories, *Los jefes* (The Chiefs, 1958), won the Leopoldo Alas prize, but it was his technically innovative novels—*The Time of the Hero* (1962; Eng. trans., 1966), *The Green House* (1965; Eng. trans., 1968), *Conversation in the Cathedral* (1970; Eng. trans., 1975), and *Captain Pantoja and the Special Service* (1973; Eng. trans., 1978)—that brought him international recognition.

KEITH ELLIS

variable

A variable is a symbol that can be replaced by any element of some designated set of numbers (or other quantities) called the domain of the variable. Any member of the set is a value of the variable. If the set has only one member, the variable becomes a constant. If a mathematical sentence contains two variables related in such a way that when a replacement is made for the first variable the value of the second variable is determined, the first variable is called the independent variable, and the second is called the dependent variable.

JOE K. SMITH

Bibliography: Schaaf, William, *Basic Concepts of Elementary Mathematics,* 3d ed. (1969).

variable star

Variable stars are stars that vary in brightness, color, or magnetic field strength. A variable star may be either an eclipsing or a physical variable. An eclipsing variable is a binary star in which each of the orbiting components passes in front of the other, as seen from the Earth, giving periodic variations in the total brightness with the same period as the orbital period of the binary. Physical variables are single stars whose variations are caused by intrinsic pulsations or eruptions within the star itself. Eruptive physical variables are believed to be due to a

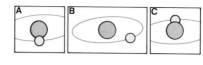

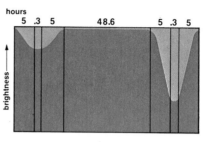

hours

5 .3 5   48.6   5 .3 5

brightness →

Algol, a double star system in the Perseus constellation, varies from maximum to minimum brightness every 69 hours. (A) When the bright star passes in front of the dim star, a slight drop in brightness is observed. (B) Maximum brightness results when neither star is eclipsed. (C) Minimum brightness occurs when the dim star covers the bright one.

sudden eruption inside the star; the more common pulsating variables are believed to represent intrinsic pulsations of the whole star. This article concerns only physical, or intrinsic, variables; see BINARY STARS for a discussion of eclipsing variables.

Variable-Star Designations. The first intrinsic variable star to be discovered (1596) was Mira Ceti. Only a few others were found until 1850. Later large numbers were discovered, at first by careful visual observations, and later primarily by photography or by photoelectric photometry. A few variable stars have special names, such as Mira Ceti. Most are designated by letters or by a number and the constellation name. The sequence of letters is R, S, T, . . . , Z; RR, RS, . . . , RZ; SS, ST, . . . , SZ; and so on to ZZ. Then AA, AB, . . . , AZ; BB, BC, . . . , BZ; and so on, until QZ is reached (the letter J is omitted). This takes care of the first 334 variable stars to be discovered in any constellation. Thereafter the letter V and a number, starting with V 335, are used. Examples are R Leonis, SZ Tauri, V 335 Sagittarii. In 1971 there were 4,018 eclipsing variables catalogued, about 1,600 eruptive variables, and about 13,800 pulsating variables.

Eruptive Variables. The light variations in eruptive variables may be large, as in NOVAE, or small, as in FLARE STARS and T TAURI STARS. Flare stars, also called UV Ceti stars, are cool, faint stars that brighten for only a few minutes. This phenomenon may be related to the solar flares found on the Sun. Only a few dozen such stars are known. T Tauri variables have no regular periods and are believed to be very young stars still in the contraction phase. There are also recurrent novae, R Corona Borealis stars, and other less-common types of eruptive variables.

Pulsating Variables. Pulsating variables may be divided into several broad groups. CEPHEIDS have periods between about 1 day and 50 days. Long-period variables have periods of several hundred days. RR LYRAE STARS have periods between a few hours and 1 day. W VIRGINIS STARS have periods of more than 1 day and are broadly similar to Cepheids, but with a smaller absolute magnitude. Several rarer kinds of stars are known, including RV Tauri stars and β Cephei stars. There are also many irregular variable stars known, plus others described as semiregular.

Of the 13,800 known pulsating variable stars, about 700 are classical Cepheids, 4,600 are long-period variables, 4,400 are RR Lyrae stars, and 3,900 are semiregular or irregular variables. Cepheids, RR Lyrae stars, and W Virginis stars have pulsation cycles that repeat with regularity. Long-period variables have cycles that essentially repeat, but with some differences from one cycle to the next: for example, one maximum may not be of the same brightness as the preceding maximum. In all these stars the whole star is successively expanding and contracting, accompanied by changes in surface temperature and total luminosity.

When a variable star is plotted in the HERTZSPRUNG-RUSSELL DIAGRAM, it is found that classical Cepheid variables occur in the giant-supergiant regions of the diagram for spectral types F to K. RR Lyrae stars occur in the middle of the Population II horizontal branch. Long-period variables occur in the bright-giant region, mostly for spectral type M (some are also of spectral type S and some are carbon stars).

Different classes of variable stars have different distributions in our galaxy. Classical Cepheids are all located quite close to the galactic plane. RR Lyrae stars occur at very large distances from the galactic plane. Long-period variables occur with a distribution in between the classical Cepheid and RR Lyrae distributions.

Several general relations apply to pulsating stars. The PERIOD-LUMINOSITY RELATION asserts that there is a relationship between the period of the variation of the brightness of a variable star and its absolute brightness. From the observed period one can immediately deduce the absolute brightness of the star, and thus its distance. The period-density relation states that the product of the period of a variable star and the square root of the mean density of the star is approximately constant. The value of the constant depends on the type of star. In general, stars with long periods have small densities and hence are likely to be large supergiant stars.

Other Types of Variables. Among less-common types of variable stars are the δ Scuti stars, which seem to be related to the classical Cepheids but are fainter, have spectral types A to F, have much smaller amplitudes of variation, and exhibit a curious double periodicity. Also showing a double periodicity are β Canis Majoris stars of spectral type B. A number of magnetic variable stars are known, in some of which the magnetic-field variations are periodic, and in others irregular. The prototype periodic magnetic variable is α Canum Venaticorum. Its magnetic field varies from −1,400 to +1,600 gauss with a period of 5.5 days. The intensities of many lines in the spectrum of the star vary with the same period. A good example of an irregular magnetic variable is γ Equulei. RR Lyrae has also been observed to possess a magnetic field.

PULSARS, when first discovered, were so named because it was thought that they were a new kind of pulsating star. Later work indicated that pulsars are rotating neutron stars, so that their name is a misnomer.   R. H. GARSTANG

Bibliography: Fitch, W. S., ed., *Multiple Periodic Variable Stars* (1976); Glasby, J. S., *Variable Stars* (1969); Manchester, R. N., and Taylor, J. H., *Pulsars* (1977); Strohmeier, W., *Variable Stars* (1972).

variance and covariance

Variance is the most common measure of scatter, or dispersion, in a statistical analysis. For large samples it equals the average of the squares of the deviations of each value from the MEAN. A small variance implies a small amount of scatter in the parameter under study. The variance in the heights of the police officers in Chicago is larger than the variance in the heights of their squad cars. The formula for finding the variance of N values of the variable X_i is $(X_1{}^2 + X_2{}^2 + \ldots X_N{}^2)/(N - 1)$. The square root of the variance equals the more familiar STANDARD DEVIATION.

Covariance is a measure of the tendency of two random variables to vary together. In a graph of one of the variables versus the other, a small covariance would produce points clustered tightly about a straight diagonal line. A large covariance might produce points centered about the same slanting line, but they would range further afield. Covariance and correlation are closely related concepts (see CORRELATION AND REGRESSION).   DONNA AND TOM LOGSDON

Bibliography: Taylor, J. R., *Error Analysis: The Study of Uncertainties in Physical Measurements* (1982).

variations

Variations is a general term applied to a compositional style, known and practiced in music of both the Western and non-Western worlds, whereby a melody or harmonic-rhythmic complex is subjected to varied treatment—usually in a series of organized repetitions, each of which forms a separate entity within the larger complex of a "theme and variations."

This term came into use in the 17th century, although the principle of varying a theme (whether invented by the composer, or folk song, or plainsong) had been known and developed under different names over the previous 500 years or

more. The theme and variations as now understood began its long and still active existence with the 16th-century lutenists, vihuelists, and writers for keyboard instruments. It was subsequently developed by such composers as Byrd, Froberger, Scheidt, and Sweelinck, then by Bach (*Goldberg Variations*) and Handel ("The Harmonious Blacksmith" from the Suite in E). In the melodic variations of Mozart's sonatas and Haydn's symphonies and late string quartets, peaks of classical perfection were often reached, although it was left for Beethoven, Schubert, Schumann, and Brahms to explore the possibilities of drama, character, and harmonic integration in such works as the *Diabelli Variations*, "Trout" Quintet, *Études Symphoniques*, and *Variations on a Theme of Haydn*. The orchestral repertoire was greatly enriched by such large-scale works as Dvořák's *Symphonic Variations*, a term used also for concertante compositions (as in Franck's work of that name for piano), and by such diverse pieces as Richard Strauss's *Don Quixote*.   DENIS STEVENS

Bibliography: Nelson, Robert U., *The Technique of Variation* (1948).

varicose vein

Varicose veins are abnormally dilated and tortuous veins. Although virtually any vein in the body can become varicose—HEMORRHOIDS, for example, are varicosities around the anus—most occur in the legs. In healthy veins, valves permit blood to flow toward the heart but not away from it. In varicose veins these valves do not work, perhaps because of patchy thinning of the vein walls. As a result the veins become inflated from the back pressure of blood.

Varicose veins occur more often in women than in men, especially during pregnancy, and some evidence exists that a predisposition to varicosity may be inherited. The condition is more likely to occur in people who stand for long periods of time or who do heavy lifting. Usually they cause no greater problems than an unsightly appearance, but sometimes they lead to a heavy feeling in the legs, especially by the end of the day; this sensation is often alleviated temporarily if the legs are elevated several times a day. They may also cause skin discoloration, itching, or inflammation (see PHLEBITIS). Varicose veins can be helped considerably by wearing support stockings. Occasionally they are treated by means of surgery.   JOHN KELTON, M.D.

Bibliography: Baron, H. C., and Gorin, Edward, *Varicose Veins: A Commonsense Approach to their Management* (1979); Ellis, Harold, *Varicose Veins* (1982).

Varley, Frederick [vahr'-lee]

Frederick Horseman Varley, b. Sheffield, England, Jan. 2, 1881, d. Sept. 8, 1969, was one of Canada's most distinguished portrait painters. Although he was among the landscapists known as the GROUP OF SEVEN, Varley devoted himself primarily to portraiture for many years. His expressive portraits have often been favorably compared with those of the Englishman Augustus John. In 1926, Varley moved to Vancouver; there he began to paint richly colored landscapes whose calm spirituality reflects his interest in Eastern philosophy.

DAVID WISTOW

Bibliography: Mellen, Peter, *The Group of Seven* (1970); National Gallery of Canada, Ottawa, *The Group of Seven* (1970).

Varna [vahr'-nah]

Varna is a major port on the Black Sea in northeastern Bulgaria, with a population of 295,038 (1982 est.). A major industrial center and naval base, Varna handles one-half of Bulgaria's waterborne cargo. Industries include shipbuilding, flour milling, food processing, and the manufacture of electrical equipment and textiles. Noted for its health spas and sandy beaches, Varna is a popular summer resort. It has a theater, an opera house, museums, a symphony orchestra, and art galleries. Nearby is the 6th-century Aladzha Monastery.

Founded in the 6th century BC by the Greeks and named Odessus, the city subsequently came under Thracian, Macedonian, and Roman rule. Known as Varna since AD 681, it was held by the Turks from 1444 to 1878, when it became part of independent Bulgaria. Between 1949 and 1956 the city was called Stalin.

varnish

A varnish is a solution of a hard RESIN, characteristically of natural origin; a drying oil; metallic compounds that act as driers; and solvent. Varnishes are intended to provide an essentially continuous, transparent film to protect or enhance the appearance of wood or other materials without altering the underlying texture or color. PIGMENTS used in varnishes are intended solely to regulate level of gloss; they have no hiding or masking abilities at the levels employed. This absence of opacifying pigment distinguishes a varnish from either a stain or PAINT, although varnishes are frequently employed as paint binders.

The name *varnish* is believed to be derived from *vernix*, the Latin word for "amber." A natural resin, amber was an ingredient used in varnishes as long ago as 250 BC. Even though varnishes based on natural products continue to be used, numerous synthetically based polymer solutions have been developed that often offer superior qualities, particularly with regard to lightness of color, adhesion, exterior durability, and flexibility. Alkyd resin solutions are the most widely used synthetic varnishes. Varnish is principally used on furniture and floors and over paint coatings; it also has various marine applications and is used as a sealing compound.

Drying Oils. Varnishes and other oil-containing resins are frequently classified as having short, medium, or long oil length according to the ratio of oil to resin. Most drying or semidrying oils have been satisfactorily employed in varnish formulations. Linseed, tung (chinawood oil), safflower, and soya are most frequently used. Chinawood oil is generally favored because of its ability to process quickly and provide excellent adhesion, flexibility, and durability, particularly when used on exterior surfaces.

Resins. Traditionally, such natural resins as Congo, Dammar, and Batu were used in quality varnishes. Political and economic factors, however, have limited the world supply and increased costs appreciably. A variety of substitutes, of both natural and synthetic origin, have successfully replaced these sources. Rosin and rosin derivatives, phenolics, petroleum resins, epoxy, and urethane resins all have achieved acceptance in varnishes.

JOHN J. OBERLE

Bibliography: Chatfield, Herbert W., ed., *Paint and Varnish Manufacture* (1955); Gaynes, Norman I., *Formulation of Organic Coatings* (1967); Martens, Charles R., *Technology of Paints, Varnishes, and Lacquers* (1968); Von Fischer, William, ed., *Paint and Varnish Technology* (1948; repr. 1964).

Varro

Marcus Terentius Varro, 116–c.27 BC, was the first universal scholar of the Roman civilization. In the first civil war he fought on the losing side, but Octavius forgave him and appointed him head of his planned public library. After being proscribed by Mark Antony in 43, he escaped, was pardoned by Octavius, and then devoted himself fully to research and writing.

From his reputed output of more than 600 volumes, the titles of only about 50 works are known. Of these, his treatise *De Re Rustica* (On Agriculture), which Vergil consulted when writing the *Georgics*, is preserved intact; approximately one-fourth remains from his important study *De Lingua Latina* (The Latin Language), long the basic source for Latin grammarians; and many fragments have survived from his *Menippean Satires*, as well as portions of *Antiquitates Rerum Humanarum et Divinarum* (History of Human and Divine Concerns), which the fathers of the Christian church used as a reference book on Roman religion.

varved deposit

Varved deposits are thinly bedded sediments formed as annual accumulations at the bottom of a lake and consisting of alternating coarse- and fine-grained layers. The basic unit of

Varved deposits are pairs of alternately light and dark layers of sediment in glacial lakes. Each varve, or pair, represents a year's deposit. The lower, thicker layer of light-colored, coarse-grained sand and silt is laid in the summer. The upper, thinner layer of fine-grained, dark clay and silt settles during the winter. Varves, like tree rings, are used to date the regions in which they are found.

such deposits is the varve, which is a couplet composed of a coarse-grained (sand or silt) layer and an overlying fine-grained (silt or clay) layer. Most varves are made up of mineral grains (quartz, illite, chlorite, and montmorillonite) or rock fragments; calcium carbonate precipitates or organic materials, however, occasionally predominate.

An individual varve may be as thin as a few millimeters (several hundredths of an inch) or more than 1 m (3 ft) thick; most, however, are from 1 to 5 cm (0.4 to 2 in) thick. Although color, grain size, and sedimentary structures can vary greatly in successive varves, an individual layer is usually distinct and may be traced great distances. This lateral continuity and the rhythmic alternation of sedimentary units are direct reflections of a lake origin.

Most varved deposits are formed in glacial lakes at or near the ice margin, and only a minor portion are attributed to tidal or hypersaline lakes. Features commonly found in varved deposits include dropstones (pebbles released from icebergs) and trace fossils (irregular markings thought to be caused by insect larvae foraging for organic matter on the lake bottom). The characteristic rhythmic alternation of layers is controlled by seasonal variations of sediment influx from the glacier into the lake. During the spring thaw, glacial melting releases sediment frozen in the ice. Supraglacial and subglacial streams draining the ice margin carry sediment to adjacent or nearby bodies of ponded meltwater (see LAKES, GLACIAL). Depending on the relative densities of the stream water and lake water, streams entering the lake flow onto the surface (hypopycnal flow), flow along the lake bottom as a density current (hyperpycnal flow), or mix with the lake water (homopycnal flow). On entering the lake, the larger sediment particles (sand and silt) quickly settle out, creating a thin lamination; the fine clay stays in suspension. In general the "summer layer" tends to thin away from the stream outlet. Fluctuations of stream discharge during the spring and summer months create a coarse-grained layer composed of several laminations. Occasionally, ripple cross-bedding is formed by fast-flowing density currents. Fine silt and clay brought in during summer runoff continue to settle out from the lake water column during the fall and winter, creating a uniformly thick layer over the entire lake bottom and completing the varve couplet.

The interpretation of a varve as an annual deposit is based on several different lines of evidence. First, the volume of sediment carried by a glacial stream to a lake during the summer has been shown to be approximately equal to the total volume of sediment making up the uppermost varve. Secondly, pollen grains found in successive horizons within the summer layer vary in number and type, reflecting expected seasonal changes in pollen production by local flora. Third, carbon-14 dating of extensive varved deposits in Sweden indicates that they were laid down during a period of more than 12,000 years. Most varved deposits exposed on the Earth's surface today were formed with the melting of the great continental glaciers during the recent Pleistocene Ice Age.

GAIL M. ASHLEY

See also: GLACIER AND GLACIATION.

Vasa (dynasty) [vah'-zuh]

The Vasa dynasty, which ruled Sweden (1523–1654) and Poland (1587–1668), rose to power as a great Swedish noble family in the days of Swedish autonomy under Danish kings. In 1521, Gustav Vasa led a successful rising against the Danes and subsequently ruled (1523–60) as King GUSTAV I. Three of his sons also ruled as Swedish kings. One of these sons, **John III**, 1537–92 (r. 1568–92), married the sister of the Polish king; their son, who represented the union of the Vasas with the Polish JAGELLO dynasty, was elected (1587) king of Poland as SIGISMUND III; he also served as king of Sweden. Sigismund was succeeded in Poland by two of his sons, **Władysław IV**, 1595–1648 (r. 1632–48), and JOHN II. John, who was childless, abdicated in 1668, marking the end of the Vasa dynasty on the Polish throne.

In Sweden, Vasa monarchs GUSTAV II ADOLF and his daughter CHRISTINA reigned during an age of greatness as Sweden gained superiority over Denmark and established an empire that dominated the western and northern Baltic. Christina, the last Vasa ruler of Sweden, abdicated (1654) in favor of a cousin, Charles X.   J. R. CHRISTIANSON

Bibliography: Roberts, Michael, *The Early Vasas: A History of Sweden 1523–1611* (1968).

Vasarely, Victor [vah-zah-ray-lee']

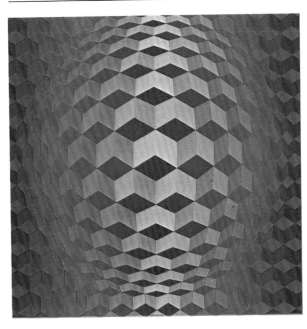

Cheyt-G *(1970), by the Hungarian-born artist Victor Vasarely, is an example of what is variously known as geometric, optical, or op art, in which the artist's intention is to bring about a striking, even dizzying, retinal effect in the beholder's eye. (Artist's collection.)*

The Hungarian artist Victor Vasarely, b. Apr. 9, 1908, is perhaps the best-known exponent of post–World War II geometric painting. He worked as a graphic designer until 1944; this experience may have helped to shape the complex black-and-white patterns of his earliest paintings. Soon after, he added intense contrasts of color. Typically, the artist arranges a large number of small, nearly identical geometric shapes in patterns that generate vivid illusions of depth and, in some cases, motion. A citizen of France since 1959, Vasarely had some 150 solo exhibitions in the half-century span 1930–80 and has won many international prizes.   CARTER RATCLIFF

Bibliography: Haftmann, Werner, *Painting in the Twentieth Century*, 2 vols. (1965); Spies, Werner, *Victor Vasarely* (1971); Vasarely, Victor, *Vasarely* (1965).

Vasari, Giorgio [vah-zah'-ree]

Giorgio Vasari, b. July 30, 1511, d. June 27, 1574, was an Italian writer, painter, and architect who is best known for his *Lives of the Most Eminent Painters, Sculptors, and Architects* (1550; rev. ed., 1568), which provides a thorough history of Italian Renaissance art through biographies of its principal practitioners. Modeled on the ancient Greek and Roman biographies of famous men, the *Lives* was the first book in Western history to concentrate exclusively on art and artists; its underlying thesis that art is an intellectual discipline practiced by individualistic geniuses, rather than a craft pursued by anonymous workers, ushered in the modern, as opposed to the medieval, view of artistic endeavor. Although it remains a primary source of information about Italian Renaissance and Mannerist artists, Vasari's work contains many lacunae and errors, particularly in the biographical data supplied, and its treatment of pre-15th-century artists is unreliable.

As a painter and architect Vasari displayed many of the tendencies associated with MANNERISM. His series of paintings (1570–72) in the Palazzo Vecchio of Florence celebrate the achievements of the Medici in highly stylized allegories replete with Manneristic exaggerations. Of his major architectural achievements, the Uffizi in Florence (1560–80), originally a governmental office building and now an art gallery and archive, is an important example of the Mannerist tendency to incorporate preexisting buildings in a new overall design. The influence of Michelangelo's architecture is reflected in its repetitive facade, which derives its visual effect from the duplication of ornamental elements. Vasari also designed (1573), although he did not oversee the construction of, the Loggia in Arezzo, a huge office block built as a speculative investment by a local guild. He also modernized and remodeled two important 13th-century churches in Florence, Santa Maria Novella (1565–72) and Santa Croce (1566–84).

Bibliography: Boase, T. S. R., *Giorgio Vasari: The Man and the Book* (1975); Rud, Einar, *Vasari's Life and Lives*, trans. by Reginald Spink (1963); Vasari, Giorgio, *Lives of the Most Eminent Painters, Sculptors, and Architects*, trans. by Gaston Du C. deVere, 3 vols. (1979).

Vasco da Gama: see GAMA, VASCO DA.

vascular plant: see TRACHEOPHYTE.

vasectomy

Vasectomy is the surgical sterilization of the male through the severing of the two sperm-carrying ducts, the vasa deferentia. This procedure prevents the sperm cells formed in the testes from reaching the storage structures called the ampullae. At the time of ejaculation, sperm cells in the ampullae are mixed with secretions of nearby glands to form the semen. Severing the vasa deferentia thus renders the semen sterile, that is, unable to fertilize an ovum.

Because the vasa deferentia lie almost entirely within the scrotum and thus outside the abdominal cavity, a vasectomy is a relatively simple procedure usually done under local anesthesia in a physician's office. Each vas deferens is exposed through a small incision, on the side of the upper part of the scrotum, and is severed; the severed ends of the vas deferens are then cauterized to seal them, and the incision is sutured. Sterility does not occur until residual sperm in the upper reproductive tract have left the body. Vasectomy has no effect on the production of the male hormone, testosterone.

Fertility may be restored by surgically rejoining the severed ends of the vasa deferentia; this operation has had a 40% success rate. Reversal of sterilization is an area of active research, and some clinicians have reported successful restoration in the majority of patients. Failures to reverse the procedure are due to such factors as infections and blood clots. By the mid-1980s vasectomy, along with tubal ligation in women, was the preferred method of birth control among U.S. couples who desired no further children.   PETER L. PETRAKIS

Bibliography: Goldstein, Marc, and Feldberg, Michael, *The Vasectomy Book* (1983); Mumford, S. T., *Vasectomy* (1978).

Vasily III, Grand Duke of Moscow [vuh-see'-lee]

Vasily III, b. 1479, d. Dec. 2, 1533, grand duke of Moscow (1505–33), succeeded his father, Ivan III. He annexed to Moscow the remaining independent Russian principalities (1510–23) and captured Smolensk from Lithuania (1514). He was succeeded by Ivan IV (the Terrible), his son.

vasopressin: see ANTIDIURETIC HORMONE.

Vassar College

Established in 1861, Vassar College (enrollment: 2,258; library: 600,000 volumes) is a private liberal arts institution in Poughkeepsie, N.Y. One of the Seven Sisters colleges, it became coeducational in 1969. Vassar is basically an undergraduate college but also offers master's degrees in some modern languages, biology, chemistry, and drama.

Västerås [ves'-tuh-rohs]

Västerås (1982 est. pop., 117,793), a city in east central Sweden on the northern shores of Lake Mälaren, lies about 105 km (65 mi) northwest of Stockholm. It is Sweden's leading inland port and a major center for the manufacture of electrical appliances, machinery, turbines, and glass. An important trading and cultural center since the Middle Ages, the city has a 12th-century castle and a 13th-century cathedral. The early Swedish parliament frequently convened in the city, and the Reformation in Sweden was launched there in 1527.

Vatican City

Vatican City is an independent state occupying 0.44 km² (0.17 mi²) on the west bank of the Tiber River, lying within the Italian capital city of Rome and almost completely surrounded by walls. Its population of 737 (1986 est.), only some of which

Vatican City, located in Rome on the west bank of the Tiber River (background), is bounded on the east by the keyhole-shaped piazza of Saint Peter's Basilica (center). The small city-state, which includes papal palaces and other structures, has been independent since 1929.

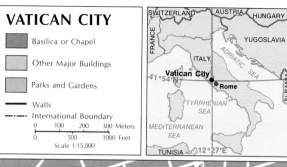

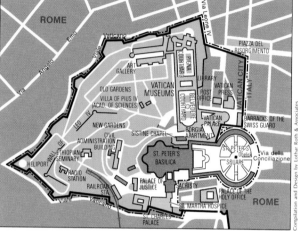

hold Vatican passports, consists primarily of employees of the Holy See, the central government of the Roman Catholic church. The Vatican also enjoys extraterritorial jurisdiction over Castel Gandolfo, the papal summer residence near Rome, and 13 churches and other buildings in Rome, including the Basilica of Saint John Lateran (Rome's cathedral) and the palace of San Callisto. Both the temporal and spiritual authority of the Vatican is vested in the pope as head of the Roman Catholic church. In practice the city's civil administration is managed by the Papal Commission for Vatican City, which delegates authority to a governor. The Vatican has its own newspaper (*L'Osservatore Romano*), railway station, postal service, police force, telephone system, radio, and bank with financial resources in Italy and abroad.

In addition to its role as the site of the Holy See, Vatican City is one of the world's great cultural resources. It is an important tourist center for Roman Catholics and those interested in art history (see VATICAN MUSEUMS AND GALLERIES). Visitors may enter Vatican City on the southeast through Giovanni Lorenzo Bernini's colonnade at Saint Peter's Square. SAINT PETER'S BASILICA is the largest and principal church of the Roman Catholic world. The Vatican Palace, constituting the Vatican proper, includes Michelangelo's frescoes on the ceilings of the SISTINE CHAPEL, Pintoricchio's frescoes in the Borgia Apartment, and Raphael's frescoes in the Raphael Rooms. The Vatican Library houses an extensive collection of manuscripts. Occupying a considerable portion of the city's land are the Vatican Gardens. The Pontifical Gregorian University was founded in 1553.

The Vatican's name derives from an isolated ridge of volcanic origin to the west of ancient Rome's low-lying hills. Saint Peter's Basilica was founded in the 4th century by the Emperor Constantine on the site tradition designates as Saint Peter's grave. The area became increasingly associated with the papacy, especially during the Renaissance. Between 1860 and 1870 the PAPAL STATES of central Italy, long ruled by the pope, were incorporated into the new Kingdom of Italy. The ensuing dispute between Italy and successive popes over church autonomy was settled by the LATERAN TREATY, which recognized the full and independent sovereignty of the Holy

See in Vatican City. Although not a permanent member, the Vatican has an observer at the United Nations.

DANIEL R. LESNICK

Bibliography: Letarouilly, Paul, *The Vatican and the Basilica of St. Peter* (1966); Neville, Robert, *The World of the Vatican* (1962); Pallenberg, Corrado, *Vatican Finances* (1971); Pucci, Eugenio, *The Vatican City* (1971); Wall, Bernard, *The Vatican Story* (1956).

Vatican Council, First

The First Vatican Council, the 20th ecumenical council of the Roman Catholic church, is best known for its decree affirming the doctrine of papal INFALLIBILITY. After a lengthy series of deliberations by preparatory commissions, it was opened by Pope PIUS IX in Saint Peter's Basilica on Dec. 8, 1869. Nearly 800 church leaders representing every continent attended, although the European members held a clear majority. Apparently the pope's primary purpose in convening the council was to obtain confirmation of the position he had taken in his *Syllabus of Errors* (1864), condemning a wide range of modern positions associated with the ideas of rationalism, liberalism, and materialism.

From the beginning, however, the question of infallibility dominated discussion. A vigorous minority opposed this doctrine both on theological and historical grounds and as being inopportune. Nonetheless, on July 18, 1870, the council solemnly accepted the proposition that when a pope speaks *ex cathedra* on faith or morals he does so with the supreme apostolic authority, which no Catholic may question or reject. About 60 members of the council effectively abstained by leaving Rome the day before the vote. Shortly after the vote on infallibility, the Franco-Prussian War and the successful invasion of the Roman state by the Italian army abruptly ended the council. The First Vatican Council marked the climax and triumph of the movement of ULTRAMONTANISM yet also helped stimulate a renewed wave of anticlericalism in several European states.

T. TACKETT

Bibliography: Butler, E. C., ed., *The Vatican Council*, 2 vols. (1930); Hennesey, J. J., *The First Council of the Vatican: The American Experience* (1963).

Vatican Council, Second

The Second Vatican Council, the 21st ecumenical council of the Roman Catholic church, was announced by Pope JOHN XXIII on Jan. 25, 1959. On Oct. 11, 1962, after four years of preparation, the council formally opened. Four sessions convened; the last three (1963–65) were presided over by Pope PAUL VI, who succeeded John as pontiff in June 1963. The council ended on Dec. 8, 1965.

Unlike previous ecumenical councils, the Second Vatican Council was not held to combat contemporary heresies or deal with awkward disciplinary questions but simply, in the words of Pope John's opening message, to renew "ourselves and the flocks committed to us, so that there may radiate before all men the lovable features of Jesus Christ, who shines in our hearts that God's splendor may be revealed."

The participants with full voting rights were all the bishops of the Roman Catholic church, of both the Western and Eastern rites, superiors-general of exempt religious orders, and prelates with their own special spheres of jurisdiction. Non-Catholic Christian churches and alliances and Catholic lay organizations were invited to send observers. These observers, however, had neither voice nor vote in the council deliberations.

The council produced 16 documents—all of which had to be approved by the pope before they became official—on such subjects as divine revelation, the sacred liturgy, the church in the modern world, the instruments of social communication, ecumenism, Eastern Catholic churches, renewal of religious life, the laity, the ministry and life of priests, missionary activity, Christian education, the relationship of the church to non-Christian religions, and religious freedom. Of these, the most important and influential for the subsequent life of the Roman Catholic church have been the Dogmatic Constitution on the Church, which gave renewed importance to the role of the bishops; the Constitution on the Sacred Liturgy, which authorized vernacularization of the liturgy and greater lay participation; the Pastoral Constitution on the Church in the Modern World, which acknowledged the need for the church to adapt itself to the contemporary world; the Decree on Ecumenism; and the Declaration on Religious Freedom. Together these documents present a church that is primarily a worshiping and serving community open to various points of view and religious traditions.

Although the Second Vatican Council had enormous impact, it cannot be isolated from prior and parallel liturgical, theological, biblical, and social developments. In few instances did the council initiate a new way of thinking for the church. It endorsed specific approaches, tentatively in some cases, and planted seeds for other, possibly more radical, changes in the future.

RICHARD P. MCBRIEN

Bibliography: Abbott, W. A., ed., *The Documents of Vatican II* (1966); Deretz, Jacques, and Nocent, Adrien, eds., *Dictionary of the Council* (1968); Miller, J. H., ed., *Vatican II: An Interfaith Appraisal* (1966); Vorgrimler, Herbert, ed., *Commentary on the Documents of Vatican II*, 5 vols. (1967–69).

Vatican museums and galleries

Set within the bastioned walls of VATICAN CITY are the Vatican Palaces, a large group of interconnecting buildings dating from the 14th to the 20th century, and SAINT PETER'S BASILICA. The palaces contain more than 1,400 rooms, most of which now house the museums, galleries, and libraries of the Vatican. Aside from the designated museums, a number of chapels and papal apartments are considered part of the museum collections and include the Stanze (rooms) of Julius II, frescoed by RAPHAEL and his school between 1508 and 1520; the Borgia Apartment of Alexander VI, with frescoes completed by PINTORICCHIO and his school in 1495; the Scala Regia (Royal Stairs), built during the 1660s for Urban VIII by Giovanni Lorenzo BERNINI; and the SISTINE CHAPEL, built by order of Sixtus IV in 1453, which contains, in addition to the monumental frescoes by MICHELANGELO, frescoes of scenes from the life of Moses by Sandro Botticelli, Perugino, and Luca Signorelli, among others. The collections of the seven major museums of the Vatican are among the largest, most important, and most valuable in the world.

The **Museo Pio-Clementino**, founded (late 18th century) by Clement XIV and Pius VI, is devoted entirely to Greek, Hellenistic, and Roman art. Among its many treasures are the Apollo Belvedere (Roman copy of a Greek 4th-century BC bronze) and the *Laocoön* (Hellenistic; c.100 BC).

The **Museo Chiaramonte**, founded (c.1820) by Pius VII, consists of the Galleria Chiaramonte, Galleria Lapidaria (Gallery

The Disputation of Saint Catherine *(1492–95), a brilliantly colored fresco by the Umbrian artist Pintoricchio, adorns a room of the Borgia Apartment in the Vatican Museum complex. The six-room suite is a grand display of Early Renaissance decorative art.*

of Inscriptions), and the huge Braccio Nuovo (New Wing; 1821). Its holdings are an extension of the Pio-Clementino classical collections and include the Augustus of the Prima Porta (c.20 BC), a collection of more than 5,000 stone inscriptions, and several hundred Roman portrait busts.

The **Museo Sacro** (Christian Museum), founded (1756) by Benedict XIV, displays a large collection of ecclesiastical decorative arts and two large Roman frescoes, the *Aldobrandini Wedding* and the *Odyssey Landscapes* (both 1st century BC). The **Museo Gregoriano Egiziano** (Egyptian Museum; founded 1839) has an extensive collection of Egyptian artifacts, as well as Eyptianized Roman sculptures from HADRIAN'S VILLA. The **Museo Gregoriano Etrusco** (Etruscan Museum; founded 1837) houses major collections of Etruscan bronzes and ceramics and a superb collection of Greek vases.

The **Pinacoteca** (Picture Gallery), founded (1932) by Pius XI, has a collection of approximately 500 paintings and tapestries by every Italian artist of consequence, as well as major works by other European artists of the first rank.

In 1973, Paul VI inaugurated the **Collection of Modern Religious Art**, a group of 540 contemporary paintings, sculptures, and stained glass on permanent exhibition in the refurbished Borgia Apartment and its adjacent rooms. Selections from the **Vatican Library**'s 60,000 manuscripts, 7,000 incunabula, and 950,000 printed books may be seen in the grandiose Sistine Hall and in adjoining exhibition rooms.

EDWARD T. McCLELLAN

Bibliography: Calvesi, Maurizio, *Treasures of the Vatican*, trans. by James Emmons (1962); Fellucci, Mario, *The Masterpieces of the Vatican* (1975); Matt, Leonard von, *Art in the Vatican* (1962); Ragghianti, Carlo L., *Vatican Museum* (1968).

Vättern, Lake   [vet'-urn]

Lake Vättern, located in southern Sweden and that nation's second largest lake, averages about 130 km (80 mi) long and 30 km (20 mi) wide and has an area of about 1,900 km² (735 mi²). The Göta Canal, connecting the Kattegat with the Baltic Sea, crosses the northern part of the lake. Jönkoping is at its southern end.

Vauban, Sébastien Le Prestre de   [voh-bahn']

The French military engineer Sébastien Le Prestre de Vauban, b. May 1, 1633, d. Mar. 30, 1707, was the renowned director of French siege-warfare during Louis XIV's wars. Born of minor nobility, Vauban became a royal engineer in 1655, won the king's favor by his spectacularly successful siege (1667) of Lille, and formed and headed the separate army engineering corps after 1672. His innovative line of eastern border fortresses during the Dutch War (1672-78) provided unprecedented protection against foreign invasion; he eventually built or improved about 300 fortresses, superb examples of early urban planning, and captured about 50 others. Vauban was a military innovator, introducing ricochet fire and the socket bayonet. He designed roads, bridges, canals, dikes, and aqueducts. Vauban became a marshal in 1703. A prolific and thoughtful writer on military engineering and many other subjects of public concern, he lost favor at court after publishing (1707) a proposal for a universal tax without exemption for nobility or clergy.   A. LLOYD MOOTE

Bibliography: Blomfield, Reginald, *Sébastien Le Prestre de Vauban, 1633-1707* (1938; repr. 1971).

vaudeville: see MUSIC HALL, VAUDEVILLE, AND BURLESQUE.

Vaughan, Henry   [vawn]

A Welsh poet who wrote in English, Henry Vaughan, b. Apr. 17, 1622, d. Apr. 23, 1695, influenced Wordsworth through his mystical concepts of childhood and nature. The two parts of his *Silex Scintillans* (1650, 1655) contain religious poetry marked by complex symbolism and intense although often colloquial language.   ROBIN BUSS

Bibliography: Friedenreich, K., *Henry Vaughan* (1978).

Vaughan, Sarah

Ranked as one of the foremost jazz song stylists, Sarah Lois Vaughan, b. Newark, N.J., Mar. 27, 1924, began by singing in her local Baptist church, then won (1943) a contest at Harlem's Apollo Theater and a job as vocalist with the Earl Hines band. Her best work has always been with small groups, however, and the influence of Dizzy GILLESPIE and Charlie PARKER is notable in Vaughan's complex bebop phrasing and in her impeccable scat singing. She has concertized extensively abroad and has appeared at the White House in performances for Presidents Johnson (1965) and Ford (1974).

Bibliography: Reisner, Robert, *The Jazz Titans* (1977).

Discography: *After Hours; Golden Hits; Sarah Vaughan Live; No Count Sarah; Sarah Vaughan* (3 vols.); *Swingin' Easy.*

Vaughan Williams, Ralph   [vawn wil'-yuhmz]

Ralph Vaughan Williams, a leading English composer of the 20th century, drew on English folk tradition and medieval and Tudor music to create a uniquely English compositional style. Beginning in 1910 and continuing through his wide variety of orchestral and choral forms, he combined traditional modes with progressive rhythms and harmonies.

Ralph Vaughan Williams, b. Oct. 12, 1872, d. Aug. 26, 1958, was an English composer, also active at various periods of his career as organist, conductor, lecturer, teacher, editor, and writer. His influence on the development of 20th-century music in England was immense. By reaching back into the music of Tudor times and delving into the treasury of folk music, he infused his own works with tradition, creating a truly contemporary idiom whose roots were solidly planted in the cultural soil of his country. He was music editor of the *English Hymnal*, edited two volumes of welcome odes for the Purcell Society, conducted the London Bach Choir, and collected folk songs on his travels through many parts of England. His nine symphonies range over the varying moods of *A Sea Symphony* (no. 1, 1910), the descriptive impressions of the *London* (no. 2, 1914), the serenity of the *Pastoral* (no. 3, 1930), the fury of the F minor (no. 4, 1935), the calm majesty of the D major (no. 5, 1943), and the atmospheric *Sinfonia antarctica* (no. 7, 1953). He also wrote concertos for violin (1925), piano (1933), oboe (1944), and bass tuba (1954); the richly orchestrated ballet *Job* (1930); and *Fantasia on a Theme of Thomas Tallis* (1910), a classic of its kind, for string quartet and double string orchestra. The quiet beauty of *The Lark Ascending* (1910) for violin and small orchestra was inspired by a poem of George Meredith. Works for the stage include the two-act ballad opera *Hugh the Drover* (1924); *The Pilgrim's Progress* (1951), based on John Bunyan's allegory; *Riders to the Sea* (1937), a one-act opera based on the play by J. M. Synge; and the four-act Shakespearean opera *Sir John in Love* (1929). Choral works form an important part of the composer's achievement, and the most outstanding are the Mass in G Minor (1923); the oratorio *Sancta Civitas* (1926) for two soloists, three choruses, and orchestra; a *Magnificat* (1932); the *Serenade to Music* (1938) for 16 solo voices and orchestra; and *Hodie* (1954), a Christmas cantata. Vaughan Williams was also a distinguished composer of songs, carols, and part-songs.   DENIS STEVENS

Bibliography: Kennedy, Michael, *The Works of Ralph Vaughan Williams* (1964); Lunn, John E., et al., *Ralph Vaughan Williams* (1971);

Vaughan Williams, Ralph, *National Music and Other Essays* (1972); Vaughan Williams, Ursula, *R. V. W.: A Biography of Ralph Vaughan Williams* (1964).

vault: see ARCH AND VAULT.

Vauquelin, Louis Nicolas   [voh-klan']

The French analytical and mineralogical chemist Louis Nicolas Vauquelin, b. May 16, 1763, d. Nov. 14, 1829, discovered the elements chromium (1797) and beryllium (1798), and from asparagus he isolated (1806) asparagine, the first amino acid to be discovered. He was an assistant (1784–92) to Antoine François, comte de Fourcroy.   GEORGE B. KAUFFMAN

Vauthier, Jean   [voh-tee-ay']

The French dramatist Jean Vauthier, b. Sept. 20, 1910, explores absurd situations in plays that highlight difficulties of communication and unfulfilled hopes for a divine revelation. By stressing gesture and movement as clues to a character's state of mind, Vauthier gives his plays a musical and rhythmic structure. His works include *Capitaine Bada* (Captain Bada, 1952), *Le Personnage Combattant* (The Fighting Person, 1956), *Les Prodiges* (The Wonders, 1959), *Le Rêveur* (The Dreamer, 1961), and *Le Sang* (Blood, 1970).   ROBIN BUSS

Vaux, Calvert   [vawks]

The English architect Calvert Vaux, b. London, Dec. 20, 1824, d. Nov. 19, 1895, came to the United States in 1850 to work with the landscape architect Andrew Jackson DOWNING. Together, they designed several picturesque villas in the Hudson River Valley. After Downing's death in 1852, Vaux completed a series of distinguished High Victorian designs. Notable among these were his bridges and pavilions for Central Park (1857; with Frederick Law OLMSTED), and his Jefferson Market Courthouse (1876; with Frederick Withers), both in New York City. His most extraordinary conceptions were his compositions of infinitely extendable bays for the Metropolitan Museum of Art (1874–80) and the American Museum of Natural History (finished 1877; both with Jacob Wrey Mould), both in New York City, and the vast, arcaded iron and glass building he proposed for the Philadelphia Centennial Exposition of 1876.   ANN VAN ZANTEN

Vaux-le-Vicomte, Château de   [voh-luh-vee-kohnt']

The Château de Vaux-le-Vicomte (1657–61), outside Paris, represents the crystallization of the French baroque château and was the model for the Palace of Versailles. It was built for Nicolas Fouquet, France's minister of finance, from designs by Louis LE VAU. The house has pronounced corner pavilions as well as a projecting oval central pavilion that is crowned by an ovoid, domed roof. The interiors were elaborately decorated under the supervision of Charles LE BRUN; the extensive formal gardens were the first important work of André LE NÔTRE. The grandeur of this entire complex led to an investigation of Fouquet's finances. Just as the building came to completion, he was arrested for embezzlement; the château and its gardens were confiscated by King Louis XIV.
   LELAND M. ROTH

Bibliography: Gebelin, François, *The Châteaux of France*, trans. by H. Eaton Hart (1964).

Vazov, Ivan   [vah'-zawf]

Ivan Vazov, b. June 27, 1850, d. Sept. 22, 1921, is the most famous figure in modern Bulgarian literature. His poems—especially *Izbavlenie* (Deliverance, 1878), *Epopeya na zabravenite* (Epic of the Forgotten, 1881–84), and *Slivnitsa* (Fusion, 1886)—recount the historical hardships and patriotic aspirations of his people. His internationally famous novel *Under the Yoke* (1894; Eng. trans., 1894) describes Bulgarian village life in the years before Bulgaria's liberation (1878) from Turkish rule. Vazov's involvement in nationalist politics twice forced him

into exile. After settling in Sofia in 1889, he was elected (1894) to the national assembly and served (1897–99) as minister of education while continuing to write poetry, drama, and fiction. Vazov's plays, especially the 1910 productions *Borislav* and *Kum propast* (Toward the Abyss), dominated the Sofia theater for a decade.

VCR: see VIDEO RECORDING.

VD: see VENEREAL DISEASE.

veal

Veal, the flesh of slaughtered calves less than 1 year old, is considered a by-product of the dairy industry. Male calves are uneconomic for dairy farmers to raise, because they reduce the volume of milk available for sale. Some calves are killed within a week of birth. Their flesh, which is soft and watery, is called bob veal. Some calves are fed milk replacers containing vitamins, minerals, and fat for 8 to 10 weeks before being slaughtered. This diet promotes rapid growth and prevents the flesh from becoming the red color of beef. These calves are anemic and weak, compared to normal calves, and must be raised in scrupulously clean quarters with controlled temperature and humidity. (True milk-fed veal is a European specialty and is rarely found in the United States.) Veal is usually dense and fine grained with a light pink color. It has little fat and a mild taste.   REX L. GILBREATH

Veblen, Oswald   [veb'-lin]

The American mathematician Oswald Veblen, b. Decorah, Iowa, June 24, 1880, d. Aug. 10, 1960, made important contributions to projective and differential geometry, and topology. His interest in the foundations of geometry led to his work on the axiom systems of projective geometry. Veblen's *Analysis Situs* (1922) provided the first systematic coverage of the basic ideas of topology. His major work in differential geometry led to important applications in relativity theory, and much of his work also found application in atomic physics. Veblen helped organize the Institute for Advanced Study, Princeton, N.J., and became a professor there in 1932.   HOWARD H. FRISINGER

Bibliography: MacLane, Saunders, *Oswald Veblen, 1880–1960: A Biographical Memoir* (1964).

Veblen, Thorstein B.

Thorstein Bunde Veblen, b. Valders, Wis., July 30, 1857, d. Aug. 3, 1929, is best known for his book *The Theory of the Leisure Class* (1899), a classic of social theory that introduced the concept of CONSPICUOUS CONSUMPTION. Veblen received a Ph.D. from Yale in 1884 and taught at the University of Chicago, Stanford University, the University of Wisconsin, and the New School for Social Research.

Veblen argued that a fundamental conflict exists between the making of goods and the making of money. In *The Theory of Business Enterprise* (1904), he argued that the entrepreneur is a reactionary predator whose perspective is diametrically opposed to that of the engineer or industrialist. Veblen's businessperson makes profits not by providing an outlet for the forces of industrialization and social evolution but by distorting them: by engaging in monetary manipulations, by restricting output to keep prices artificially high, and by interfering with the engineers who actually produce goods and services. The founder of the so-called institutionalist school, Veblen believed that economics must be studied as an aspect of a culture whose customs and habits constitute institutions that are rapidly changing.   RICHARD T. GILL

Bibliography: Daugert, Stanley M., *The Philosophy of Thorstein Veblen* (1950); Diggins, John P., *The Bard of Savagery: Thorstein Veblen and Modern Social Theory* (1978); Dowd, Douglas F., ed, *Thorstein Veblen* (1958; repro 1977); Qualey, Carlton C., ed., *Thorstein Veblen: The Carleton College Veblen Seminar Essays* (1968); Riesman, David, *Thorstein Veblen: A Critical Interpretation* (1975); Seckler, David W., *Thorstein Veblen and the Institutionalists* (1975).

Vecchietta   [vek-kee-et'-tah]

The Renaissance painter, sculptor, and architect Vecchietta, b. Lorenzo di Pietro, 1412, d. June 6, 1480, worked in a linear but naturalistic style that reflects Florentine influences. *The Assumption of the Virgin* (1461–62), an altarpiece for the cathedral at Pienza, is considered his masterwork. The influence of Donatello is noticeable in Vecchietta's marble and bronze sculpture, such as the relief *The Resurrection* (1472; Frick Collection, New York City).   ROSA MARIA LETTS

Bibliography: Hartt, Frederick, *History of Italian Renaissance Art* (1969).

vector analysis

A vector, in mathematics, is a quantity stating both a magnitude and a direction. Force, velocity (speed in a particular direction), acceleration, angular momentum, and torque, for example, are quantities that are vectors. By contrast, a quantity with a magnitude but not a direction—mass and volume, for example—is called a scalar. Because such physical quantities as velocity and force are vectors, vector analysis—the mathematical manipulation of vectors—plays an important role in physics and engineering.

Whereas scalars follow the ordinary arithmetical laws of addition, subtraction, and so on, vectors must be dealt with by geometrical techniques because they involve direction as well. The simplest example of this is the addition of two vectors, such as two forces acting on a body in two different directions. Vectors are commonly represented by directed line segments—whose direction and length represent the direction and magnitude of the quantity—and are written in boldface. Thus, in the example, two forces **A** and **B**, of different magnitudes, act on a body in different directions. The resultant force **A** + **B** is found by constructing a parallelogram and drawing a directed line segment as the diagonal of the parallelogram. The length and direction of the diagonal are the magnitude and direction of the resultant vector of force acting on the body.

Subtraction of vectors can be performed in the same manner simply by reversing the direction of the representative line segment to be subtracted and constructing the appropriate parallelogram. No limit exists to the number of vectors that can be handled graphically in this way. More-complex problems involving vectors, however, require the use of the calculus and other advanced mathematical operations.

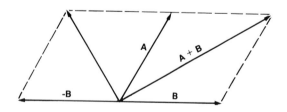

Bibliography: Campbell, Hugh G., *Introduction to Matrices, Vectors and Linear Programming*, 2d ed. (1977); Crowe, Michael J., *A History of Vector Analysis* (1967); Davis, Harry F., and Snider, Arthur D., *Introduction to Vector Analysis*, 4th ed. (1979); Thrall, R. M., and Tornheim, Leonard, *Vector Spaces and Matrices* (1957; repr. 1970).

vector of disease: see DISEASES, HUMAN.

Vedanta   [ve-dahn'-tuh]

Vedanta, a term meaning "the final portions of the VEDAS," refers to those philosophical systems of HINDUISM which take their inspiration from the UPANISHADS.

The principal texts of Vedanta are the early Upanishads, particularly the *Brihadaranyaka* and *Chandogya*; the *Brahma-sutras* (or *Vedantasutras*) of Baudarayana (dated between 100

BC and AD 100); and the BHAGAVAD GITA. Several distinct schools of interpretation emerged, the most notable of which are the Advaita (nondualist), Vishishtadvaita (qualified nondualist), and Dvaita (dualist) schools.

The earliest known exposition of Advaita Vedanta is in Gaudapada's *Karikas* on the Mandukya Upanishad (AD 600), but the school's most famous personage—and the most influential of classical Indian philosophers—was Shankara (early 8th century). A prolific writer, Shankara taught that there is only one reality, called either Brahman or Atman (the self); that all distinctions, all plurality is due to ignorance, or maya; and that liberation consists in eliminating ignorance and attaining that pure consciousness which is Brahman, or the Self. This theory, although not the only Vedanta doctrine, is so popular among intellectuals in India that it is frequently and uncritically identified with Vedanta or with Indian philosophy as a whole.

Ramanuja (1056–1137) developed the more theistically oriented Vishishtadvaita Vedanta, in which Brahman is a personal God, immanent in all souls and the world, but without obliterating the differences among them. He roundly criticizes Shankara's theories of maya and pure consciousness.

Madhva (1238–1317) founded Dvaita, or dualist, Vedanta, in which differences between God, world, and souls are fully recognized. Other important systems include the Dvaitadvaita of Nimbarka (13th century) and the Shuddhadvaita of Vallabha (1481–1533).

Scholars also speak of neo-Vedanta in characterizing the thought of certain 20th-century philosophers, such as Sarvepalli RADHAKRISHNAN, which represents a synthesis of classical Vedanta doctrines. Vedanta has sometimes been viewed as the essential philosophical core of Hinduism.

KARL H. POTTER

Bibliography: Deussen, Paul, *The System of the Vedanta*, trans. by Charles Johnston (1912; repr. 1973); Radhakrishnan, Sarvepalli, *The Brahma Sutra: The Philosophy of Spiritual Life* (1959).

Vedas   [vay'-duhz]

The Vedas (Sanskrit: "knowledge"), the most sacred books of HINDUISM and the oldest literature of India, represent the religious thought and activity of the Indo-European–speaking peoples who entered South Asia in the 2d millennium AD, although they probably also reflect the influence of the indigenous people of the area. The Vedic texts presumably date from between 1500 and 500 BC. This literature was preserved for centuries by an oral tradition in which particular families were entrusted with portions of the text for preservation. As a result, some parts of the texts are known by the names of the families they were assigned to.

In its narrowest sense, the term *Veda* applies to four collections of hymns (samhita): Rig Veda, Sama Veda, Yajur Veda, and Atharva Veda. These hymns and verses, addressed to various deities, were chanted during sacrificial rituals. In a wider sense, Veda refers to both these hymns and the materials that accreted around them to form four books with four parts. For each of the Rig, Sama, Yajur, and Atharva, there are not only hymns, but also Brahmanas—prose texts that explain and illustrate the significance of the ritual; Aranyakas, or forest-treatises—esoteric texts providing symbolic or magical interpretations of ritual formulae; and the commentaries called UPANISHADS—the beginnings of Hindu philosophy.

Vedic rituals essentially involved offerings to and with fire under precisely prescribed conditions by which the sacrificer hoped to communicate with the deities and thus to obtain desired results. The importance attached to the satisfaction of formal conditions required that a priest with knowledge of the proper forms officiate at the sacrifice. Many of the deities addressed by the sacrifice were identified or associated with natural objects of such forces as fire, water, and wind. Among the most important were Indra (thunder, war, and perhaps creator), Varuna (guardian of the cosmic order and moral law), Agni (fire, light), and Soma (a liquid used in the sacrifice). The form and functions of one god, however, were not strictly distinguished from those of others, and as the Vedic period progressed, thought developed from polytheism to monotheism and thence, in the Upanishads, to monism.

The relation of Vedism to the Hinduism of later centuries is complex and not well understood. The Vedas are preserved in traditional fashion in certain parts of India, and the tendency is widespread to look to them as expressions of the fundamental genius of Hindu thought and aspiration. The originals of the major Hindu gods—SHIVA and VISHNU—can be found among the minor deities of the Vedas. The sacrifice has, however, all but disappeared from India in its Vedic form, replaced by different rites, and the analogy, central to the Vedic ritual, between actions on Earth and events in the heavens is replaced in Hinduism by the goal of liberation from actions on Earth, from life itself. The concepts of KARMA and TRANSMIGRATION OF SOULS are not found in the Vedic corpus until the Upanishads.   KARL H. POTTER

Bibliography: Gonda, Jan, *Vedic Literature* (1975); Keith, A. B., *Religion and Philosophy of the Vedas and Upanishads*, 2 vols. (1926; repr. 1970); Raja, C. K., *The Vedas: A Critical Study* (1957).

Vedder, Elihu   [ved'-ur]

The American painter and illustrator Elihu Vedder, b. New York City, Feb. 26, 1836, d. Jan. 30, 1923, reveled in bizarre imagery. An expatriate, he lived in Rome from 1867 until his death. In *Questioner of the Sphinx* (1863; Museum of Fine Arts, Boston), the gigantic monument is being questioned by a wizened Arab. In *Memory* (c.1870; Los Angeles County Museum of Art), a disembodied head floats over a landscape. Vedder produced many book illustrations, the best known being the series (1884) of more than 50 in black and white for the *Rubaiyat of Omar Khayyam*.   ABRAHAM A. DAVIDSON

Bibliography: Soria, Regina, *Elihu Vedder (1971)*; Taylor, Joshua C., et al., *Perceptions and Evocations: The Art of Elihu Vedder* (1979).

Vedism: see HINDUISM; VEDAS.

Vega, Lope de   [vay'-gah]

Lope Félix de Vega Carpio, b. Nov. 25, 1562, d. Aug. 27, 1635, was, with his follower Calderón de la Barca, one of the two most important playwrights of the Spanish Golden Age. Traditionally considered the founder of the *comedia*, Lope was also its most influential early practitioner. Although little appreciated by the critics of his time, who felt that it was anti-Aristotelian, the *comedia* was extremely popular.

The plays of the *comedia* always have three acts, are in verse, and employ a variety of metrical forms. Typically, they are filled with movement and intrigue, and with vivid and dramatically convincing, though stereotypical, characters. The plays often include music and dance, and they mix scenes of the utmost gravity with those of comedy and farce.

Lope de Vega, Spain's foremost dramatist and poet of the Golden Age, wrote plays and poetry that celebrated Spanish traditions and extolled the customs of common people. Lope rejected the classical forms of drama, and instead introduced the comedia, which comprised both tragic and comic styles. He addressed his plays to a mass audience, rather than to the nobility.

Most of these traits are singled out in Lope's robust if playful defense of his own dramatic practice, *The New Art of Writing Plays* (1609; Eng. trans., 1914).

Called the Monster of Nature by his contemporaries because of his prodigious facility, Lope was an astonishingly prolific writer. He wrote about 800 plays, of which some 400–500 survive. In addition to his plays, however, Lope also wrote a bewildering variety of other works: hundreds of exquisite lyric poems, many long narrative poems on epic and mythological themes, numerous short stories and prose romances, and several didactic treatises in both verse and prose. Of all these nondramatic works, the single most important is *La Dorotea* (Dorothy, 1632), a long piece of fiction in dialogue form, based closely on Lope's own life.

Lope's enormous dramatic output is traditionally divided into various categories: *entremeses*—short comic interludes; *autos sacramentales*—allegorical works illustrating church doctrine; plays based on the Bible or on the lives of saints; plays dealing with historical episodes—for example, *Fuenteovejuna* (c.1611–18; Eng. trans., 1936) and *The Knight from Olmedo* (c.1615–26; Eng. trans., 1961); plays based on fictional sources—*Justice without Revenge* (1631; Eng. trans., 1961); cloak-and-dagger comedies—*The Dog in the Manger* (c.1613–15; Eng. trans., 1961); and so on.

Lope's plays all bear the distinctive marks of his artistry: lively characterization, supple versification, natural and flowing dialogue, great dramatic momentum, flashes of lyrical beauty. There is also the repeated celebration of certain cardinal virtues: love, honor, allegiance to the Catholic faith, loyalty to king and state. These constitute the ideological framework of Lope's theater and of the *comedia* in general.

Aptly, Lope's life was one of high personal drama. He was born in humble circumstances and rose to a position of great prominence and prestige. Along the way, he married twice; became embroiled in numerous love affairs, one of which led to a duel and subsequent banishment from Castile; served with the Spanish Armada; took orders in the church; and held the office of apostolic prothonotary.   DONALD R. LARSON

Bibliography: Flores, Angel, *Lope de Vega: Monster of Nature* (1930; repr. 1969); Larson, D. R., *The Honor Plays of Lope de Vega* (1977); Rennert, Hugo, *The Life of Lope de Vega* (1904; repr. 1968); Trueblood, A. S., *Experience and Artistic Expression in Lope de Vega: The Making of La Dorotea* (1974); Zuckerman-Ingber, Alix, *El Bien Mas Alto: A Reconsideration of Lope de Vega's Honor Plays* (1984).

vegetable

In horticulture, a vegetable is a herbaceous plant that is edible in whole or part. Parts usually eaten (and representative vegetables) include roots (beet); stems (asparagus); tubers (potato); leaf bases (onion); leaf petioles (celery); entire leaves (cabbage); flower parts (broccoli); immature fruit (cucumber); and mature fruit (tomato). Of great importance in the human diet, vegetables are rich in vitamins and minerals and supply fiber and bulk. Some are excellent protein sources when combined with other foods, such as beans with rice. They are usually low in calories.

Vegetables are cultured as annuals, with the exception of artichoke, asparagus, cardoon, chive, horseradish, and rhubarb, which are grown as perennials. Propagation is mostly by seed, but artichoke and rhubarb, for example, are propagated by divisions and Irish potato by tubers or tuber sections.
Growth Requirements. Vegetables are variable in climatic requirements. Temperature and, to a lesser extent, length of day are the climatic components most influential in determining yields. Cool-season crops grow best from 12° to 20° C (54° to 68° F) and include green peas, lettuce, cabbage, onions, and spinach. Warm-season crops grow best from 18° to 28° C (64° to 82° F) and include bean, eggplant, okra, pepper, sweet corn, and tomato.

The precise climatic requirements of many crops have resulted in much centralization of production in those areas with suitable climate. An excellent example is the Salinas Valley of California, which, because of ocean cooling, provides ideal conditions for the culture of such cool-season crops as lettuce, celery, and broccoli during the summer months.

cabbage

cauliflower

endive

broccoli

brussels sprouts

globe artichoke

spinach

kale

chicory

romaine lettuce

Greens commonly grown in temperate zones include varieties of cabbage—such as brussels sprouts, cauliflower, broccoli, and kale—and spinach, which is valued for its high iron and vitamin content. Lettuce varieties, such as romaine, as well as the herbs chicory and endive, are used as salad greens. Immature flower buds of the globe artichoke, when cooked, are considered a delicacy.

Rainfall during the growing season was formerly required for successful vegetable production. Today almost all commercially grown vegetables are raised under irrigated conditions or with supplemental irrigation. In some areas rainfall during the growing season is considered a detriment because it interferes with field operations and promotes plant disease infection.

Vegetables are grown on mineral or organic soils. Sandy loam and loam soils are the preferred types of mineral soils because of the desirable growth conditions and the ease of cultivation they provide. Heavier loams and clay soils are generally avoided. Organic soils, sometimes called peats or mucks, are important vegetable growing soils in parts of Florida, New York, Michigan, Wisconsin, and California. Because of their productive capacity, muck soils are often reserved for growing the crops of highest value.

Gourds that are eaten as vegetables include such New World varieties as vegetable marrow, pumpkin, and winter squash. Cucumber, an Asian variety of gourd, is often added to salads. Corn is a favorite food in North America but is used mostly for livestock feed in Europe.

vegetable marrow

corn

pumpkin

winter squash

cucumber

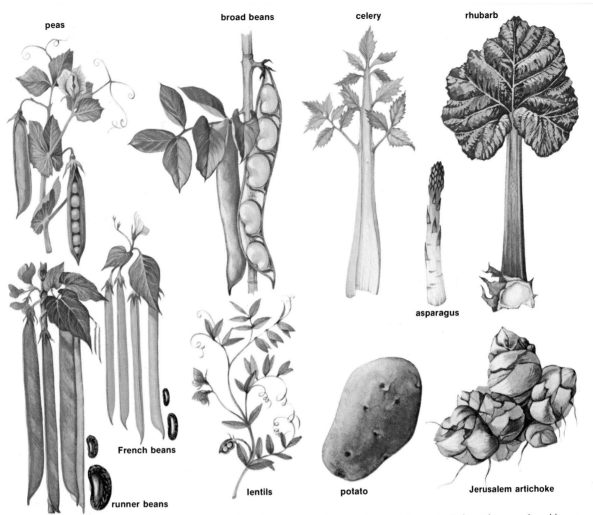

peas

broad beans

celery

rhubarb

asparagus

French beans

lentils

potato

Jerusalem artichoke

runner beans

A variety of plant parts are considered edible. Pulses — plants that have leguminous pods as their fruit — include garden peas, broad beans, runner beans, French beans, and lentils. Plants whose stems are eaten as vegetables include celery, asparagus, and rhubarb. Among tubers — enlarged underground stems of plants — are the potato and Jerusalem artichoke, the latter related to the sunflower.

Liberal use of fertilizers ensures the continuous and rapid growth that is necessary for high quality and yields.

Vegetable Production. The production of vegetables is highly intensive as compared with the production of such field crops as corn, wheat, and sugar beets. The potential crop value is great and justifies the use of comparatively high expenditure on labor, water, fertilizer, farm chemicals, mechanization, and other resources. Production for canning, freezing, or dehydration is usually distinct from fresh production. Greenhouse growing of vegetables is important in some areas, and significant quantities of tomatoes, cucumbers, and lettuce are grown in forcing structures. Mushroom production is a specialized part of the vegetable industry. Commercial production is supplemented by the produce from home gardens. About half of the families in the United States grow some of their own vegetables.

bell pepper

eggplant

tomato

The bell pepper, eggplant, and tomato are all members of the nightshade family. In earlier centuries the tomato, introduced into Europe from tropical America, was considered poisonous, but today it is one of the most valuable temperate-zone vegetable crops.

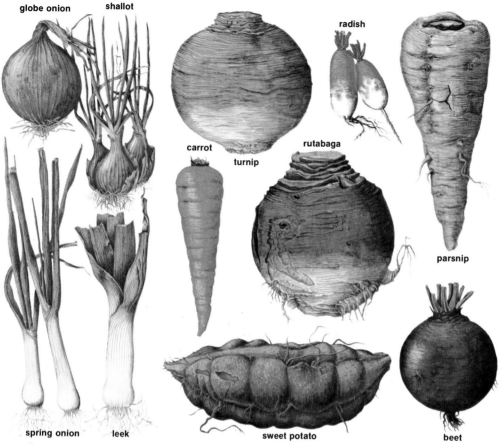

globe onion   shallot

radish

carrot

turnip

rutabaga

parsnip

spring onion   leek

sweet potato

beet

Onions are bulb vegetables used to season salads, soups, and cooked dishes. Common varieties include the globe onion, the shallot, the spring onion, and the leek. Such root vegetables as carrots, turnips, rutabagas, parsnips, and beets are harvested in autumn and winter; radishes are roots harvested in spring. The sweet potato, a tropical root vegetable, is related to the morning glory.

Vegetable production requires considerable hand labor because of the intensive nature of cropping, the variable maturities of plants in a field, and the perishable nature of the harvest. Horticulturists, geneticists, and engineers have developed more uniform plants and have designed intricate mechanical equipment for planting, cultivating, and harvesting vegetables. Perhaps the most notable example of this achievement has been the development of new tomato cultivars for processing, together with efficient field harvesters and a systematic approach to production. Virtually all processing tomatoes (those that will be canned or otherwise processed by the food industry) are now harvested mechanically.

Most vegetables are perishable and maintain peak quality for only a short period. A few, like potatoes and onions, will remain in excellent condition for many months with good storage.

The U.S. Industry. The vegetable industry produces a total farm income in excess of $5 billion annually. About one-half of the total vegetable crop is grown in California. Other major vegetable-producing states are Florida, Texas, New York, and Wisconsin. Some commercial vegetable farms are found in every state. Potatoes, tomatoes, lettuce, dried beans, and onions are the most commercially important vegetables grown in the United States.

Vegetable Consumption. Changes in dietary habits and consumption of meals away from home have influenced vegetable consumption. Overall per capita vegetable consumption is increasing, although the form in which vegetables are purchased is changing. Using 1947–49 as a base, total per capita vegetable consumption has increased about 11 kg (24 lb), and fresh consumption has declined about 9 kg (20 lb). During the same period per capita consumption of canned and frozen vegetables has increased 20 kg (44 lb).

Potatoes, tomatoes, lettuce, onions, and cabbage are the most widely eaten vegetables. Consumption of fresh cabbage, peas, spinach, beets, and cauliflower has declined, and fresh broccoli and lettuce consumption has increased. Canned snap beans, tomato products, pickles, frozen peas, broccoli, corn, and potato products have all increased in popularity. Consumption of other vegetables has remained fairly constant.

DONALD N. MAYNARD

Bibliography: Friedlander, Barbara, *The Secrets of the Seed—Vegetables, Fruits, and Nuts* (1974); Harrison, S. G., et al., *Oxford Book of Food Plants* (1969); Lovelock, Yann, *The Vegetable Book: An Unnatural History* (1972); Nelson, Kay S., *The Delectable Vegetable* (1976); Salunkhe, D. K., et al., eds., *Storage, Processing, and Nutritional Quality of Fruits and Vegetables* (1974); Thompson, Homer C., and Kelly, William C., *Vegetable Crops*, 5th ed. (1957); Ware, George W., and McCollum, J. P., *Producing Vegetable Crops*, 2d ed. (1975).

See also: articles on individual vegetables.

vegetable oils

Vegetable oils are oils obtained from certain field and tree crops. The field crops include soybeans, sunflowers, peanuts, rapeseed, safflower, sesame, cotton, corn, and flax. The most important tree crops are coconuts, palm, palm kernel, olives, castor, and tung.

The seven major vegetable oils—soybean, peanut, sunflower, coconut, palm, rapeseed, and cottonseed—are used primarily in food products. In the United States, salad and cooking oils, shortening, and margarine comprise a major share of the food-fat market; soybean oil is the primary vegetable oil used for these products. Other edible oil products include confectionary fats, toppings, frozen desserts, and other filled-milk products.

Demand in the food-fat market has shifted from solid fats to liquid oils and from animal fats to vegetable oils, stimulating technological developments in the processing of vegetable oils to yield stable products. Soybean oil requires special processing because of its unstable linolenic-acid component. Palm oil, which is a highly saturated oil, is used mainly for shortening; however, technological improvements in the frac-

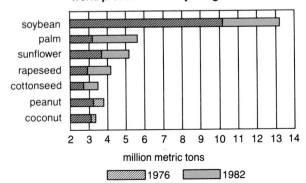

Vegetable oil, used mainly for cooking, although a small portion is utilized by industry, is a fatty oil obtained from seeds. The peanut, Arachis hypogaea (left), yields an oil content of 45–55%, second only to that of the soybean. The rape plant, genus Brassica (center), whose slender pods contain many coarse, dark seeds rich in oil, is cultivated primarily in the Far East. Oil from the seeds of the sunflower, Helianthus annuus (right), is especially beneficial to those minimizing cholesterol intake.

tionation of palm oil yield a liquid oil similar to peanut or olive, which is finding use as a cooking oil. Edible oils also have important nonfood uses, but such industrial oils as tung or castor have no food uses because of their toxic properties. Industrial vegetable oils are used in paints and varnishes, other drying oil products, fatty acids, feeds, resins, and plastics. Only about 7% of soybean oil utilization in the United States goes to nonfood or industrial uses.

The increasing world population and the global per capita consumption rate of fats and oils demand accelerated production of edible vegetable oils and technological innovation in their utilization. The worldwide production of vegetable oils in 1982 exceeded 41.5 million metric tons, comprising 70% of the total supply of fats and oils, which also includes animal fats and marine oils. Soybeans alone provided almost 20% of the world's fats and oils. The most rapidly expanding production of a vegetable oil has been that of palm oil, which tripled in the decade 1970–80. New tree plantings in Indonesia and western Malaysia have accounted for this rapid rise in production, which is expected to make palm oil a major competitor for soybean-oil markets.

Sunflower is another oilseed crop that has exhibited increased production. Although several factors account for the greater importance of sunflower oil, perhaps the most significant is the perceived health benefits of polyunsaturated oils. Sunflower oil contains more than 60% of the essential fatty acid linoleic acid, which is thought to play a beneficial role in reducing blood cholesterol. TIMOTHY L. MOUNTS

Bibliography: Bednarcyk, Norman E., *Edible Oils and Fats* (1969); Gillies, M. T., *Shortenings, Margarines, and Food Oils* (1974); Jeans, Helen, *About Vegetable Oils* (1973); Weiss, Theodore J., *Food Oils and Their Uses* (1970).

World production of major vegetable oils

	million metric tons
soybean	
palm	
sunflower	
rapeseed	
cottonseed	
peanut	
coconut	

2 3 4 5 6 7 8 9 10 11 12 13 14

million metric tons

▨ 1976   ▧ 1982

vegetarianism

Vegetarianism encompasses various philosophies and practices of not eating the flesh of animals, including red meat, poultry, and fish. The vegetarian diet consists mainly of cereal grains, legumes, nuts, seeds, vegetables, and fruits; soybeans, tofu (bean curd), and miso (fermented soybean paste) are popular sources of protein in many modern diets.

Vegetarians are classified according to which animal products they accept or eliminate from their diets. Vegans eat no dairy products or eggs. Lacto-vegetarians consume milk and cheese but not eggs. Ovo-vegetarians accept eggs but not dairy products. Lacto-ovo-vegetarians eat both dairy products and eggs. Some people abstain from eating meat for religious reasons, for example, Jains and most Buddhists and Hindus, for whom the killing and eating of animals violates the ethical precept of *ahimsa*, or nonviolence. Other, nonreligious people have embraced vegetarianism for similar ethical reasons. Still others believe that the vegetarian diet is healthier than a diet of meat and assert that flesh foods contain diseases and other substances that are harmful to humans. Some people have become vegetarians for ecological reasons because much less space and food outlay are needed to raise vegetables than livestock. They further argue that in a world of high population and scarce resources, vegetarianism is a practical method of averting world famine. People who eat a well-balanced vegetarian diet generally have lower blood pressure, less cholesterol in the blood, and less excess fat than those who eat meat. Some doctors claim vegetarians are less susceptible to heart disease and some forms of cancer than nonvegetarians. Vegetarians must take care, however, to eat the proper combinations of complementary foods in order to avoid protein and vitamin deficiencies.

Bibliography: Barkas, Janet, *The Vegetable Passion* (1975); Giehl, Dudley, *Vegetarianism: A Way of Life* (1979); Lappé, Frances M., *Diet for a Small Planet*, rev. ed. (1975).

vegetation: see BIOME; PLANT; PLANT DISTRIBUTION.

Veii [vay'-ee]

Veii, at the village of Isola Farnese, about 20 km (12 mi) northeast of Rome, is perhaps the most famous city of the ancient ETRUSCANS. It is known from Roman history, which describes Rome's wars with Veii, its close neighbor and rival. The historical account includes the slaughter of the noble family of the Fabii at the battle of the Cremera River (477 BC); the Roman general Camillus' capture of Veii and his *evocatio* (transfer) of the statue and cult of its patron goddess, Juno Regina, to Rome; and Rome's 10-year siege (modeled on the Trojan War) and subsequent annexation of Veii (396 BC). Roman literature also tells of Veiian art. In the later 6th century BC, Tarquinius, king of Rome, called in artists from Veii to make terra-cotta decorations for the temple of Jupiter Capitoline, and the sculptor Vulca modeled statues of Jupiter and Hercules. Numerous surviving *cuniculi* (drainage channels) show the Etruscans' skill in hydraulic engineering and may explain Roman tradition concerning Camillus' use of an underground passage to capture the city. Veii has also yielded some of the earliest Etruscan painted tombs, notably the Tomb of the Ducks (*c*.675–650 BC) and the Campana Tomb (*c*.600 BC).   LARISSA BONFANTE

Bibliography: Pallottino, Massimo, *The Etruscans* (1975).

Veil, Simone   [vay, see-muhn']

The French lawyer and governmental official Simone Veil, b. Simone Jacob on July 13, 1927, was president (1979–81) of the first directly elected European Parliament and in 1982 became chairman of that organization's legal affairs committee. Veil was incarcerated in the Auschwitz concentration camp from 1944 to 1945. After graduating from the Institut d'Études Politiques Paris she worked (1957–65) in the Ministry of Justice. She served (1970–74) as secretary-general of the Higher Council of Magistrates before becoming (1974–79) minister of health, family, and social security.

vein

A vein is a vessel that carries blood from the tissues toward or into the heart. A vein is not subjected to the high blood pressures found in ARTERIES; its walls do have three layers, but they are thinner and contain fewer muscle cells and elastic fibers. Many veins contain valves that prevent the backflow of blood, especially in the legs.

The venous system begins with small veins, called venules, that collect blood from the capillaries; these converge into successively larger veins and culminate in two major veins of the body, which conduct blood directly to the heart. One major vein, the superior vena cava, carries blood from the tissues of the head, neck, arms, and chest; the other, the inferior vena cava, returns blood to the heart from all parts of the body below chest level. The latter is the largest vein in the body. The portal vein conducts blood from the intestines toward the heart, but unlike other veins, the blood it carries enters the capillary system of the liver before passing into the inferior vena cava for return to the heart.

Disorders of veins include THROMBOSIS, involving a blood clot in a vein, and VARICOSE VEINS.   PETER L. PETRAKIS

Bibliography: Caro, C. G., et al., *The Mechanics of Circulation* (1979); Harcus, Alfred, and Adamson, Leslie, *Arteries and Veins* (1975).

See also: CIRCULATORY SYSTEM.

vein deposit

A vein is any tabular to sheetlike, quartz-rich body filling a fracture in rocks. The fractures may have been faults, joints, or other planar features. Nongeologists commonly use the term *vein* for any tabular body that is compositionally different from the surrounding rocks. A lode deposit consists of closely spaced, subparallel veins; a stockwork is a three-dimensional network of veinlets. Alteration minerals usually occur in rocks adjacent to mineralized veins, which generally originated in fractures across lower-grade mineralization. Veins continue to be important sources of gold, silver, uranium, and gems; the increased use of machinery, which ordinarily requires mining widths of 2 to 3 m (7 to 10 ft), has, however, rendered many veins uneconomic.

Vela

Vela was a series of 12 satellites developed for the U.S. Defense Advanced Projects Agency to detect nuclear detonations up to 160,000,000 km (100,000,000 mi) into deep space and, in the advanced models (*Vela 7* to *Vela 12*), in the Earth's atmosphere. The satellites have also provided data on solar flares and other solar radiation potentially hazardous to humans in space.

The satellites were launched (1963–70) in pairs from a single vehicle and placed 180° apart, by thrust from a solid-propellant motor inside the satellite, in circular orbits of about 111,000 km (69,000 mi) altitude. The advanced models are 26-sided polyhedrons with 28 detectors sensitive to X rays, gamma rays, neutrons, visible light, electromagnetic pulses, and energetic particles.

On Sept. 22, 1979, a Vela reported a brilliant flash between Africa and Antarctica. Some analysts have suggested the possibility of a clandestine nuclear test by South Africa or some other country; the satellite may have been hit by a micrometeoroid, however.   MITCHELL R. SHARPE

Velasco, José María   [vay-lahs'-koh]

José María Velasco, b. July 6, 1840, d. Aug. 25, 1912, was a Mexican landscape painter whose minutely detailed views of the Valley of Mexico won him an international reputation in the late 19th century. By supplementing his artistic training (from 1858) at the Academy of San Carlos in Mexico City with extensive study of the natural sciences, he was able to depict in naturalistic detail the plants and rocks strewn throughout the foreground of many of his paintings. Many of his works were painted near La Villa de Guadalupe Hidalgo, where Velasco lived from 1874 until his death. As a professor (1868–1902) at the Academy of San Carlos, he taught or influenced many 20th-century Mexican painters, including Diego Rivera.

DONALD AND MARTHA ROBERTSON

Bibliography: Helm, MacKinley, *Modern Mexican Painters* (1941); Philadelphia Museum of Art, *José María Velasco, 1840–1912,* exhibition catalog (1944).

Velasco, Luis de

Luis de Velasco, d. July 31, 1564, Spanish colonial administrator and second viceroy of New Spain (1550–64), became known for his honesty, wisdom, and eagerness to help and protect the natives of Mexico. He freed many Indian slaves, strengthened government supervision of Indians held in peonage, and attempted to remove Spaniards from Indian lands. The University of Mexico was founded (1553) during his administration.

Velasco unsuccessfully urged the crown to halt the importation of black slaves into New Spain. He expanded Spanish settlement northward, sent a colonizing expedition to Florida (1559), and equipped Miguel López de Legazpi's voyage to the Philippines (1564). His son, also called **Luis de Velasco,** b. 1534, d. Sept. 7, 1617, energetically continued his father's work by promoting the Indian economy as viceroy of New Spain (1590–95, 1607–11) and Peru (1595–1604). He later became president of the Council of the Indies.

Velasco Ibarra, José María

José María Velasco Ibarra, b. Mar. 19, 1893, d. Mar. 30, 1979, served as president of Ecuador five times. He was known more for his personal charisma than for a particular policy. In 1934 he was elected president as leader of the conservatives but was deposed the next year. In 1944, after a general strike, he regained the presidency by promising to break up the great estates. In 1947 he was deposed by conservatives who feared his assumption of dictatorial powers. After a 5-year exile, he again became president (1952–56). He was elected for the fourth time in 1960, but the austerity measures he imposed led to his ouster in 1961. In 1968, reelected for the fifth time, Velasco Ibarra quickly moved to establish a military dictatorship. He was deposed in 1972 when the army disapproved of his plan to return Ecuador to democratic rule.

Bibliography: Blankstein, G., *Ecuador: Constitution and Caudillos* (1951); Hurtado, O., *Political Power in Ecuador*, trans. by N. Mills, Jr. (1981).

Velázquez, Diego   [vay-lahth'-kayth]

Diego de Silva Velázquez was a 17th-century Spanish painter whose genius for composition and brilliant brushwork place him in the first rank of Western artists. He was baptized in Seville on June 6, 1599, and died on Aug. 6, 1660. Although his surviving works comprise only about 100 paintings and perhaps a few drawings, he has remained one of the most influential artists of all time.

Apprenticed at the age of 12 to Francisco Pacheco, Seville's leading teacher of painting, Velázquez became an independent master in 1617. His first mature productions, which were executed in a naturalistic style related to that of CARAVAGGIO,

Las Meninas (The Maids of Honor, *1656) is a puzzling masterpiece by the Spanish baroque master Diego Velázquez. One interpretation is that he is painting a portrait of the king and queen, whose reflections appear in the mirror on the rear wall. Watching them are their daughter, the Infanta Margarita, her ladies in waiting, the court dwarf, and, at rear, a courtier. (Prado, Madrid.)*

usually depicted closely studied, small groups of ordinary people strongly modeled in chiaroscuro (light and shadow). Even at this early stage of his career, Velázquez imbued his figure groups with a dignity and profound humanity that are characteristic of his art. Outstanding among the *bodegones,* or tavern scenes, in which he specialized in this period is *The Water Seller of Seville* (*c.*1619; Wellington Museum, London), whose solidly modeled figures are painted in a harmonious blend of greenish ocher and brown earth tones.

Shortly after moving (1623) to Madrid under the patronage of the Count-Duke of Olivares, he was named court painter to King Philip IV, whom Velázquez served for the rest of his life. Among the advantages of his official position was access to the royal art collections, and Velázquez's works henceforth demonstrate a debt to the free brushstrokes and vibrant color schemes of TITIAN.

These Italianate influences were strengthened by Velázquez's first visit (1629–31) to Italy. Contact with a wide variety of Italian works led him to experiment with increasingly fluid and loosely brushed paint, lighter colors, and multifigure compositions in interior settings, as in *The Forge of Vulcan* (1630; Prado, Madrid).

After his return to Madrid (January 1631), Velázquez created vivid portraits and other paintings for his royal employer, including *Philip IV in Brown and Silver* (*c.*1631; National Gallery, London) and a series of equestrian portraits.

Velázquez's masterpiece of the 1630s, *The Surrender of Breda* (1634–35; Prado), a sensitive group portrait, is set in a landscape representing the scene of a Spanish victory over the rebellious Dutch that had taken place a decade earlier; it exemplifies the virtue of magnanimity on the part of the victors.

From 1649 to 1651, Velázquez made a second tour of the cities of Italy, in order to select paintings and sculptures to decorate the newly remodeled Alcázar in Madrid, then the royal residence. His famous portraits *Juan de Pareja* (1649–50; Metropolitan Museum of Art, New York City) and *Pope Inno-*

cent X (1650; Galleria Doria Pamphili, Rome) were painted while he was in Rome and were greeted with great enthusiasm when they were displayed there.

Velázquez's achievements and aspirations are summed up in the celebrated painting known as *Las Meninas,* or *The Maids of Honor* (1656, Prado), in which he included a self-portrait as an ingenious claim to status for the painter and his art. Thanks to Velázquez's free brushstroke and mastery of tone and values, the figures and the atmosphere surrounding them seem to merge, with an effect of striking realism.

MADLYN MILLNER KAHR

Bibliography: De Salas, Xavier, *Velázquez* (1974); Justi, Carl, *Diego Velázquez and his Times* (1889; abridged English ed.); Kahr, M. M., *Velázquez: The Art of Painting* (1976); Lopez-Rey, José, *Velázquez: A Catalogue Raisonne of his Oeuvre* (1963) and *Velázquez' Work and World* (1968); Trapier, Elizabeth du Gue, *Velazquez* (1948).

Velázquez de Cuéllar, Diego   [vay-lahth'-kayth day kway'-ahr]

Diego Velázquez de Cuéllar, b. *c.*1465, d. June 12, 1524, a Spanish soldier, was the first governor of Cuba. He first saw the New World when he sailed with Christopher Columbus on the second voyage, to Hispaniola, in 1493. He returned to Spain and in 1511 received a commission to conquer Cuba. By 1514 the Spaniards controlled the whole island. Velázquez thereafter enjoyed considerable power as governor, founding Santiago (1514) and Havana (1515), and planning the conquest of Mexico. Two expeditions reached the coast in 1517 and in 1518. Velázquez put his brother-in-law, Hernán CORTÉS, in command of an expedition to the mainland in 1519, but, fearing Cortés as a rival, he sent Pánfilo de NARVÁEZ to countermand Cortés's orders. Cortés repulsed Velázquez's envoy, however, and proceeded to conquer the Aztec empire of Mexico. Velázquez was replaced as governor in 1521 but was reinstated in 1523.

Bibliography: Sauer, Carl O., *The Early Spanish Main* (1966).

Velikovsky, Immanuel   [vay-lee-kahf'-skee]

The controversial American physician and historian Immanuel Velikovsky, b. Vitebsk, Russia, June 10 (N.S.), 1895, d. Nov. 17, 1979, argued that the configuration of the solar system was changed in historical times and that this change caused cataclysmic upheavals on Earth. Macmillan, the original publisher of Velikovsky's *Worlds in Collision* (1950), transferred its rights to Doubleday after only 2 months of publication when Macmillan's sizable textbook business was endangered by a threatened boycott from many scientists who disapproved of Velikovsky's methodology.

In *Worlds in Collision*, Velikovsky claimed that a comet, after ejection from the planet Jupiter, had, over a period of

The controversial American historian Immanuel Velikovsky attempted to reconcile the development of the solar system with events described in ancient Hebrew and Egyptian writings. Although Velikovsky's theories are dismissed by most astronomers, his ideas have gained a popular following.

decades in the 15th century BC, during one of two encounters with the Earth, stopped the latter's rotation for a period of time, and had, in the 8th century BC, shifted the orbit of Mars after a near collision with that planet before settling into its present orbit as the planet Venus. These events and others, according to Velikovsky, caused many of the "miraculous" events described in Exodus and in Joshua 10 of the Bible and in other ancient writings and myths.

Although Velikovsky's theory led him to make certain claims, such as a relatively hot temperature for Venus, that were subsequently verified, many scientists have questioned the plausibility of the celestial events described by Velikovsky and the mechanisms that he proposed to account for them. Velikovsky's other works include *Ages in Chaos* (1952), *Earth in Upheaval* (1955), *Oedipus and Akhnaton* (1960), *Peoples of the Sea* (1977), and *Ramses II and His Time* (1978).

Bibliography: Bauer, H. H., *Beyond Velikovsky* (1984); de Grazia, A., ed., *The Velikovsky Affair* (1966); Goldsmith, D., ed., *Scientists Confront Velikovsky* (1977); Greenberg, L., et al., eds., *Velikovsky and Establishment Science* (1977) and *Scientists Confront Scientists Who Confront Velikovsky* (1978); Ransom, C., *The Age of Velikovsky* (1977).

vellum: see PARCHMENT.

velocity

Velocity is the distance an object travels in a specified direction during a unit of time (see MOTION, PLANAR). Velocity thus differs from SPEED, for which the direction is unspecified. Because velocity is a vector quantity, it has two components: a magnitude, or speed of motion, and a direction of motion. The velocity of an object may vary from one moment to the next if either the speed or the direction of motion changes, or if both change at the same time. Either variation is an ACCELERATION. For example, an object revolving in a circle (see MOTION, CIRCULAR) undergoes acceleration; it may have constant angular (rotative) speed, but its direction of motion constantly changes.   GARY S. SETTLES

velvet

Velvet is a fabric with a rich, soft texture produced by extra yarns in the warp that form a short pile. Originally made of silk, velvet may now be made of cotton or synthetic yarns. There are two methods of velvet manufacture. In one, the extra warp yarns are lifted over wires, and as the wires are withdrawn their knife-sharp ends cut the yarn. In the second method, two cloths are woven face-to-face, with the extra warp yarns interchanged between them, and are then cut apart to produce two pile fabrics.

Velvet has been used since the Middle Ages. Flattened or pressed velvet is called panne. Velvet with a high pile is called plush. Corduroy is a velvet whose pile has been cut in a striped pattern. Velveteen has pile made from extra fillings rather than from extra warp yarn.   ISABEL B. WINGATE

velvetleaf

Velvetleaf is the common name for the wildflower *Abutilon theophrasti*, of the mallow family, Malvaceae. This annual herb is velvety and thick-stemmed, with large heart-shaped leaves and simple yellow flowers. Native to India, it grows as a weed in some areas of the United States. In China it is used to make fiber for twine and rope.   OSWALD TIPPO

Venda

The diverse groups that became known as the Venda, a BANTU-speaking people, moved southward into northeastern South Africa in the early 1700s and came under control of the TRANSVAAL in 1898. The Venda are mostly farmers. Their religion centers on the worship of ancestral spirits, and the chiefs of the various tribal groups remain important. About two-thirds of all Venda live in the Venda homeland (1985 est. pop., 424,000), which was declared independent by the South African government in 1979. The homeland's area is 6,500 km² (2,510 mi²); Thonoyandou is the capital.

vending machine

The vending machine is a mechanical or electromechanical device that dispenses a product when a coin or paper currency is inserted in a slot. More than 6 million vending machines are in operation in the United States, not including coin-operated music and amusement game machines, storage lockers, and scales. Vended sales (chiefly soft drinks and cigarettes) passed $17 billion in the late 1980s.

The vending machine was probably invented about 200 BC when Hero of Alexandria described a coin-operated device designed to vend holy water in an Egyptian temple. In the 17th century, coin-operated honor boxes holding tobacco were common in English taverns. Machines vending postage stamps and chewing gum won public acceptance in the United States in the late 1880s, and machines offering candy bars and cigarettes were later marketed. Modern vending machines can provide refrigeration or heating for the sale of soft drinks, coffee, or sandwiches, and change-making devices enable one machine to be used for a variety of products selling for different prices.   ARTHUR E. YOHALEM

Bibliography: Colmer, Michael, *The Great Vending Machine Book* (1977); Rubin, Ken, *Drop Coin Here* (1978).

Vendôme, Louis Joseph, Duc de   [vahn-dohm']

Louis Joseph, duc de Vendôme, b. July 1, 1654, d. June 15, 1712, a French general under Louis XIV, fought for Philip V, French Bourbon heir to the Spanish throne, in the War of the SPANISH SUCCESSION (1701–14). He commanded the French forces defending Philip's Italian territories and defeated (1705) Prince Eugene of Savoy at Cassano. In Flanders, Vendôme was defeated (1708) by the duke of Marlborough at Oudenaarde. In Spain in 1710 he recaptured Madrid and defeated the Austrians at Villaviciosa.   A. LLOYD MOOTE

veneer

Veneer is a thin sheet of wood made from sliced or peeled logs. Veneer may be sliced longitudinally, by shaving thin layers of wood from a stationary log with a heavy knife. Peeled veneer results when a knife blade is pressed against a log so that a thin sheet of wood is peeled away as the log is turned. The veneer unwinds like cloth from a bolt. Peeled veneers, usually between 4.75 and 0.8 mm (0.19 and 0.03 in) thick and usually of softwood, are used to make packing crates and bushel baskets or are glued together to make plywood.

Sliced veneers have attractive grain patterns and can be as thin as 0.38 mm (0.015 in). Decorative plywood, made from sliced hardwood veneers, is used for paneling, doors, cabinets, and furniture. The inside layers may be made from peeled softwood, sliced hardwood, or particle board. Fine-grained veneers from decorative woods are often used as the surface layer on wood furniture.   ROBERT S. MANTHY

Venera

Venera, the Soviet program for the exploration of the planet Venus (see SPACE EXPLORATION), has employed various types of spacecraft to measure the composition and dynamics of the Venusian atmosphere and to analyze and radar-map the planet's surface. During the most recent passage of Halley's comet around the Sun, in 1985–86, two Soviet craft sent to observe the comet also released balloon probes into the Venusian atmosphere while on their way.

The relative movements of Earth and Venus around the Sun provide a periodic "launch window" opportunity during which probes can be launched (a few weeks every 18 months). Beginning in February 1961 the USSR repeatedly launched two or three probes during each launch window. After ten failures, the eleventh probe, *Venera 4*, was launched on June 12, 1967, and successfully relayed data from the Venusian atmosphere. The first probe to transmit data from the surface was the 15th attempt, *Venera 7*, in 1970. Three more probes resulted in one more successful landing, in 1972.

MAJOR SOVIET VENUS PROBES

Type	Date Launched	Mission	Results
Venera 1	Feb. 12, 1961	Flyby	Communications failed Feb. 27, 1964, at distance of 7.5 million km (4.7 million mi) from Earth; probe was launched from *Sputnik 8,* which was in Earth orbit
Zond 1	Apr. 2, 1964	Flyby	Communications failed about May 14, 1964
Venera 2	Nov. 12, 1965	Flyby	Communications failed just before flyby on Feb. 27, 1966
Venera 3	Nov. 16, 1965	Atmosphere probe	Communications failed just before entry into atmosphere on Mar. 1, 1966
Venera 4	June 12, 1967	Atmosphere probe	First return of data from within atmosphere on Oct. 18, 1967; crushed at altitude of 27 km (17 mi)
Venera 5	Jan. 5, 1969	Atmosphere probe	Entered atmosphere on May 16, 1969; returned data for 53 min down to an altitude of 24 to 26 km (15 to 16 mi)
Venera 6	Jan. 10, 1969	Atmosphere probe	Entered atmosphere on May 17, 1969; returned data for 51 min down to an altitude of 10 to 12 km (6 to 7 mi)
Venera 7	Aug. 17, 1970	Lander	First successful landing on Dec. 15, 1970; returned data for 23 min from surface
Venera 8	Mar. 27, 1972	Lander	Successful landing on July 22, 1972; returned data for 50 min from surface
Venera 9	June 8, 1975	Lander/orbiter	Became first spacecraft to orbit Venus on Oct. 22, 1975; lander returned first picture and data for 53 min from surface on same day
Venera 10	June 14, 1975	Lander/orbiter	Became second spacecraft to orbit Venus on Oct. 25, 1975; returned picture and data for 65 min from surface on same day
Venera 11	Sept. 9, 1978	Flyby/lander	Successful landing on Dec. 19, 1978; returned data for 110 min from surface
Venera 12	Sept. 14, 1978	Flyby/lander	Successful landing on Dec. 25, 1978; returned data for 95 min from surface
Venera 13	Oct. 30, 1981	Flyby/robot lander	Successful landing on Mar. 1, 1982; scooped up soil and transmitted data, including first color photos, for 127 min
Venera 14	Nov. 4, 1981	Flyby/robot lander	Successful landing on Mar. 5, 1982; transmitted soil data for nearly 60 min
Venera 15	June 2, 1983	Orbiter	Entered orbit around Venus on Oct. 10, 1983; began returning radar images of the surface 6 days later
Venera 16	June 7, 1983	Orbiter	Entered orbit around Venus on Oct. 14, 1983; began returning radar images of the surface 6 days later
Vega 1	Dec. 15, 1984	Balloon/lander	Balloon and lander entered atmosphere and separated on June 10, 1985
Vega 2	Dec. 21, 1984	Balloon/lander	Balloon and lander entered atmosphere and separated on June 15, 1985

SOURCE: Adapted from Nicholas L. Johnson, ''Soviet Atmospheric and Surface Venus Probes,'' *Spaceflight,* June 1978.

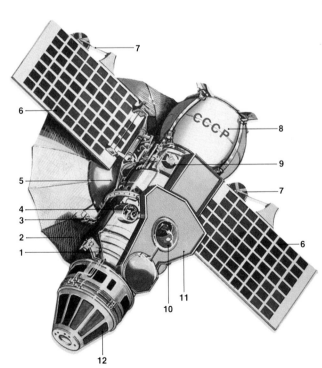

On Dec. 15, 1970, the Soviet *Venera 7* became the first artificial object to make a successful soft landing on Venus. Numbers indicate: pneumatic system (1) for operation of the nozzles of the orientation devices; high-gain umbrella antenna (2); cosmic-ray counter (3); sensor (4) for orienting spacecraft to the Sun; radiator cooler (5) for lowering vehicle temperature in Venus's atmosphere; solar panels (6); low-gain antennae (7); descent capsule (8); storage bottle (9) for compressed nitrogen; star-orientation sensor (10); protective panel (11); and housing (12) for course-correction engine.

The next Venus launch window was passed up in preparation for the launching of newer, heavier probes with the powerful Proton rocket in June 1975. *Venera 9* and *Venera 10* each dropped a probe into the Venusian atmosphere while maneuvering the main spacecraft into orbit around Venus. The probe relayed surface data and television pictures for 30 minutes each before losing contact with Earth. The Soviets launched two flyby-lander spacecraft, *Venera 11* and *Venera 12,* in 1978. The data transmission from the landing modules continued for 95 and 110 minutes after they landed.

In 1981 the Soviets launched the flyby-landers *Venera 13* and *Venera 14.* They made successful landings in March 1982. The landers transmitted the first color pictures of the surface of Venus, tested the electrical conductivity of the rocks, drilled through the Venusian surface to test lower strata, and scooped up soil samples for analyses. In 1983, *Venera 15* and *Venera 16* were launched, entering orbit around Venus in October of that year for extensive radar mapping of the planet.

In June 1985 four Soviet probes—two landers that analyzed soil, and two novel atmosphere balloons that briefly transmitted data from altitudes of 50–55 km (31–34 mi)—were dropped into the Venusian atmosphere by the Halley's-comet explorers, *Vega 1* and *Vega 2.*　　　　JAMES E. OBERG

Bibliography: Beatty, J. K., ''A Radar Tour of Venus,'' *Sky and Telescope,* June 1985; Eberhart, J., ''The Eyes of Venera 13 and 14: New Views of Venus,'' *Science News,* Mar. 20, 1982.

venereal disease

Gonorrhea, syphilis, and other venereal diseases are highly specific infections almost always acquired during sexual contact. Bacteria, protozoans, or fungi that cause venereal disease generally can attack only certain portions of the body, including the genital tract; they do not survive for long periods outside the human host, and so transmission by such objects as clothing or toilet seats is extremely rare. Venereal diseases range in effect from mild, annoying symptoms to life-threatening illnesses that spread from the reproductive tract to the entire body. The two most serious diseases are SYPHILIS and GONORRHEA; CHLAMYDIA, the most common venereal disease in the United States today, can also have serious effects. Less important infections include CHANCROID, simple warts, cold sores (see CANKER), and vaginitis. None of these diseases is acquired exclusively through sexual contact; the sexual partners of patients found to have a venereal disease, however, are likely infected. Therefore, people who have had sexual contact with infected patients should undergo examination and possibly therapy. People having sexual relations with more than one partner have a higher risk of acquiring a sexually transmitted disease. Patients who have one such disease may have contracted another at the same time.

COMMON SYNDROMES

Asymptomatic Carriage. People with a sexually transmitted disease may have no symptoms or symptoms that are so mild that they do not prompt the patient to seek medical attention. Almost half of the women with gonorrhea have no significant symptoms, and up to 5 percent of men acquiring gonococcal infection of the penis will feel perfectly well. Gonococcal infections in the throat or rectum are usually asymptomatic. As many as 25 percent of women and almost all men with trichomoniasis feel perfectly well, and the organisms associated with nonspecific urethritis are frequently carried asymptomatically in women.

Penile Discharge and Urethritis. Most men who acquire gonorrhea in the penis will within 1 week develop a puslike penile discharge and a burning sensation during urination. A more common cause of these symptoms is nonspecific urethritis, which can result from infection with a number of different organisms, especially *Chlamydia trachomatis*. Infection usually results in a milder mucous discharge than that of gonorrhea; the discharge may be accompanied by very mild feelings of discomfort on urination. Symptoms often appear 1 to 3 weeks after acquiring the infection. Untreated chlamydia may spread to the sperm-carrying canals and could cause sterility, so the condition should not be ignored. (In developing countries, chlamydia may also lead to TRACHOMA.) Women may experience burning during urination and have a mild vaginal discharge. If chlamydia is left untreated, however, inflammation of the fallopian tubes may occur, causing sterility, miscarriages, ectopic pregnancies, or possibly conjunctivitis in the newborn infant.

Vaginal Discharge. Many women note a vaginal discharge, which is a normal response to the action of female sex hormones. This normal discharge is usually free of odor and is not accompanied by vaginal irritation or soreness. Discharges associated with genital irritation or odor, however, may be symptoms of venereal disease. The most common venereal infection causing vaginal discharge is TRICHOMONIASIS. *Trichomonas vaginalis* is a protozoan that can infect the vagina and cause a thick, foul-smelling discharge to form. Infected women may have significant vaginal soreness and a burning sensation during urination. Men usually carry the parasite with no symptoms whatsoever. The bacterium *Corynebacterium vaginale* produces a milder form of vaginal irritation, which may be associated with a mild discharge and a distinctive fishlike odor. Once again, men often carry the organism without any symptoms at all. Vaginal discharge or irritation also can result from infection with the yeast *Candida albicans*. Oral contraceptives, antibiotics, and certain illnesses such as diabetes predispose to the development of vaginal CANDIDIASIS, and men having sexual contact with infected women may develop a superficial, itchy infection of the penis. The adult vagina is resistant to gonococcal infection, but the gonococcus can infect the mouth of the uterus and result in a cervical discharge that exits through the vagina and appears to be a vaginal discharge.

GENITAL SKIN LESIONS

Blisters. *Herpes simplex* (type 2), a virus closely related to the one causing cold sores or fever blisters, produces genital infections that appear 3 to 7 days after contact (see HERPES). The initial lesions are groups of tiny blisters that quickly rupture, leaving painful shallow sores, which may last for several weeks before healing with crusting. Although the lesions heal completely, the virus remains in the nerves of the genital tract, and the lesions may recur at irregular intervals. While the lesions are present, the disease is highly contagious, but between recurrences the risk of transmission to the sexual partner is quite low. Women may have herpetic involvement of the uterine cervix, which can occur in the absence of painful skin lesions and therefore go unnoticed.

Ulcers. Herpes simplex infections also are the most common cause of genital ulcers, affecting about ten times as many people as syphilis. Syphilis is another major cause of ulcers; one of the symptoms of syphilis is usually a single, relatively painless ulcer in the genital area. The sore, called a chancre, generally appears about 3 weeks after exposure at the site at which the infecting agent, *Treponema pallidum*, enters the body. Chancres have been found on the lips, mouth, and breasts and occasionally elsewhere. Even though the chancre always heals without treatment, the organisms are still present and may produce other manifestations of disease later in life. Somewhat larger, painful genital ulcers are symptomatic of a bacterial infection known as chancroid, common in Southeast Asia but rare in the United States.

Other Skin Lesions. Venereal warts, caused by the papilloma virus, resemble warts on other parts of the body, and appear on the external genitalia as rough-surfaced bumps. They may be single but are usually multiple and do not itch. Warts may appear up to 3 months following sexual contact. Small bumps or papules around the genitals or thighs may be molluscum contagiosum, a viral disease spread by contact; this infection is also acquired nonvenereally by young children. Itchy crusted lesions, or SCABIES, may result from infestation with the mite *Sarcoptes scabiei*. Scabies occurs when the mite burrows into the superficial layers of the skin. When skin temperature increases, the itching becomes worse and is characteristically severe at night or immediately following bathing. This disease is spread by skin-to-skin contact. Itching in the pubic-hair region may result from infestation with *Phthirus pubis*, the crab louse, which is spread by close contact and may be acquired during coitus.

OTHER INFECTIONS

Swelling of the lymph nodes in the groin may accompany many sexually transmitted infections and may be tender (herpes, chancroid) or painless (syphilis). Such swelling, called adenopathy, may be the only manifestation of a relatively rare sexually transmitted disease called lymphogranuloma venereum. Some forms of infectious hepatitis can be acquired by sexual contact, and gastrointestinal infections such as shigellosis and amebiasis have also been sexually transmitted.

Special Problems. Venereal disease can present certain problems in pregnant women and among homosexuals. If acquired during pregnancy, syphilis may be transmitted to the fetus before birth; such infections can result in miscarriage, stillbirth, congenital defects, or disorders that arise after the child is born. Sexually transmitted diseases are common in people with multiple sexual partners whether they are gay or straight. For instance, gay men may participate in receptive oral or anal sexual contact and may develop initial lesions of sexually transmitted diseases around the mouth or anus. They are also at risk of contracting the fatal disease called acquired immune deficiency syndrome (see AIDS). Many patients find it difficult to discuss their sexual practices with a physician, but information about the anatomic sites involved in sexual activity is crucial for appropriate diagnoses.

MANAGEMENT OF SEXUALLY TRANSMITTED DISEASES

Prevention. Any sexually active person runs the risk of acquiring a sexually transmitted disease, and the risk increases with the number of sexual partners and with the likelihood of infection among those sexual partners. A person having sex with a single individual but whose partner has multiple contacts is at high risk for acquiring a sexually transmitted infection. Because venereal diseases may be present without any symptoms, asking partners about symptoms does not assure good health. Mutual fidelity between sexual partners will keep the pair free of sexually transmitted infections; no other method provides complete protection against sexually transmitted diseases. The condom is partially effective if it is worn during all genital contact, but some of the genital area is still left uncovered. Washing the genitals or urinating immediately after intercourse also offers incomplete protection. Individuals with multiple sexual partners should probably be examined for sexually transmitted diseases at regular intervals.

Diagnosis and Treatment. Accurate diagnosis of venereal diseases can be made by a physician by taking a complete history of sexual practices and genital symptoms, carefully examining the entire genital area, and taking samples of discharge for microscopic examination and culture. At present, a blood test is useful only for the diagnosis of syphilis and tells nothing about the presence or absence of other venereal diseases. Effective, rapid treatment is available for almost all of the sexually transmitted infections. *Herpes simplex* infection has been a notable exception, but the drug acyclovir is proving useful in suppressing recurrent attacks.　　　MICHAEL F. REIN, M.D.

Bibliography: Brandt, Allan, *No Magic Bullet* (1985); Holmes, K. K., and Mardh, P.-A., *International Perspectives on Neglected Sexually Transmitted Diseases* (1982); Hyde, M. O., *VD*, 2d ed. (1982); Noble, R. C., *Sexually Transmitted Diseases* (1985); Richards, R. N., *Venereal Diseases and Their Avoidance* (1974); Spagna, V. A., and Prior, R. B., *Sexually Transmitted Diseases: A Clinical Approach* (1985); Stamm, W., and Handsfield, H., *Manual of Sexually Transmitted Diseases* (1983).

Veneto　[vay'-nay-toh]

Veneto is an administrative region of northeastern Italy, with an area of 18,363 km² (7,090 mi²) and a population of 4,361,527 (1984 est.). It borders Austria on the north and the Adriatic Sea on the east. The capital is VENICE. Other major cities are PADUA, VERONA, and VICENZA. The DOLOMITES form Veneto's northern rim, and the southern part of the region consists of the fertile plain of the ADIGE and PIAVE rivers. The PO RIVER marks the southern boundary. The main economic activity is agriculture, and the chief crops are wheat, corn, sugar beets, hemp, and fruits. Manufactures include textiles, chemicals, and paper; food processing and shipbuilding are also important.

Since the 15th century, Venice has dominated most of the region. After 1797, Veneto was held by Austria, and in 1866 it became part of unified Italy.　　　DANIEL R. LESNICK

Venezuela　[ven-ez-way'-luh or vay-nays-way'-lah]

Venezuela is located in northern South America, with the Caribbean Sea and the Atlantic Ocean to the north. The republic borders Colombia on the west and southwest, Brazil on the south, and Guyana on the east. *Venezuela* means "Little Venice," a name that early European explorers gave to the region of Lake Maracaibo, where Indian villages were built on pilings over the water. Venezuela's capital city is CARACAS, near the Caribbean coast. Venezuela has abundant natural resources; the country is plagued, however, by serious problems in the development of its human resources.

LAND AND RESOURCES

Venezuela is divided from north to south into three major regions: mountains, plains, and tropical forests. The Venezuelan ANDES stretch from the Colombian border northeastward for 322 km (200 mi) and contain Pico Bolívar, the nation's highest elevation, at 5,002 m (16,411 ft). The Cordillera del Norte runs east-west for 965 km (600 mi) in two parallel branches. Three heavily populated and fertile valleys dominate the intramontane basin. South of the mountain regions are the llanos (plains), an extensive area of sparsely populated savannas and scrub forests, cut by the northern tributaries of the Orinoco River. Tropical forests characterize the highlands to the south of the Orinoco. Extremely old rock formations in the Mount Roraima area have such great permeability that the high mesas found in La Gran Sabana (the Great Savanna) can absorb considerable amounts of condensed atmospheric humidity and underground water. They shed these waters from their perpendicular walls as waterfalls. ANGEL FALLS, cascading from Auyán-Tepui, is the world's highest cataract.

Soils. Venezuela's soils are generally low in fertility. Latosols cover most of the country, except for the highlands where mountain soils predominate.

Climate. The Venezuelan climate is mostly tropical. Average annual temperatures range from 20° C (69° F) in the Andes to

REPUBLIC OF VENEZUELA

　　LAND. Area: 912,050 km² (352,144 mi²). Capital and largest city: Caracas (1981 est. pop., 3,041,000).
　　PEOPLE. Population (1986 est.): 17,800,000. Density (1986 est.): 19.5 persons per km² (50.5 per mi²). Distribution (1985): 85.7% urban, 14.3% rural. Annual growth (1982–83): 3.1%. Official language: Spanish. Major religion: Roman Catholicism.
　　EDUCATION AND HEALTH. Literacy (1983): 85% of adult population. Universities (1985): 24. Hospital beds (1981): 42,061. Physicians (1980): 15,787. Life expectancy (1975–80): women—69; men—63.6. Infant mortality (1980): 31.0 per 1,000 live births.
　　ECONOMY. GNP (1983): $66.4 billion; $3,860 per capita. Labor distribution (1984): services—27%; commerce—22%; agriculture—16%; manufacturing—16%; construction—9%; transportation—7%; petroleum, utilities, and other—3%. Foreign trade (1984): imports—$7.5 billion; exports—$15.7 billion; principal trade partners—United States, Netherlands Antilles, Canada, Japan, Italy, West Germany. Currency: 1 bolívar = 100 céntimos.
　　GOVERNMENT. Type: republic. Legislature: National Congress. Political subdivisions: 20 states, 2 federal territories, 1 federal district.
　　COMMUNICATIONS. Railroads (1984): 502 km (312 mi) total. Roads (1981): 62,449 km (38,804 mi) total. Major ports: 6. Major airfields: 8.

28° C (82° F) in the Maracaibo Basin. Rainfall is abundant from May through December, averaging 533 mm (21 in) around Lake Maracaibo, 813 mm (32 in) in Caracas, 1,016 mm (40 in) in the llanos, and even larger amounts in the Andes.

Drainage. Lake MARACAIBO is the main feature of a depression north of the Andes. More than 130 rivers drain into this largest lake in South America. The ORINOCO RIVER, South America's second longest, drains 80% of the country. The extreme south is drained by the AMAZON RIVER.

Vegetation and Animal Life. The grasslands of the llanos give way to the southern tropical rain forest. Venezuela has a wide variety of animal life, including monkeys, jaguars, pumas, peccaries, manatees, sloths, anteaters, and armadillos. Tropical birds, such as parrots and macaws, are abundant.

Resources. Venezuela is a resource-rich nation. It is one of the world's largest petroleum producers, with proven reserves of about 24.5 billion barrels (excluding the rich heavy-oil belt in the Orinoco basin), although petroleum production has been declining steadily since 1970. The country also has substantial reserves of iron ore, bauxite, coal, diamonds, gold, and silver.

PEOPLE

Most people speak Spanish as their primary language and profess Roman Catholicism. About 67% of the people are mestizo, 21% white, 10% black, and 2% Indian. The largely urban population is concentrated in 17 cities with more than 100,000

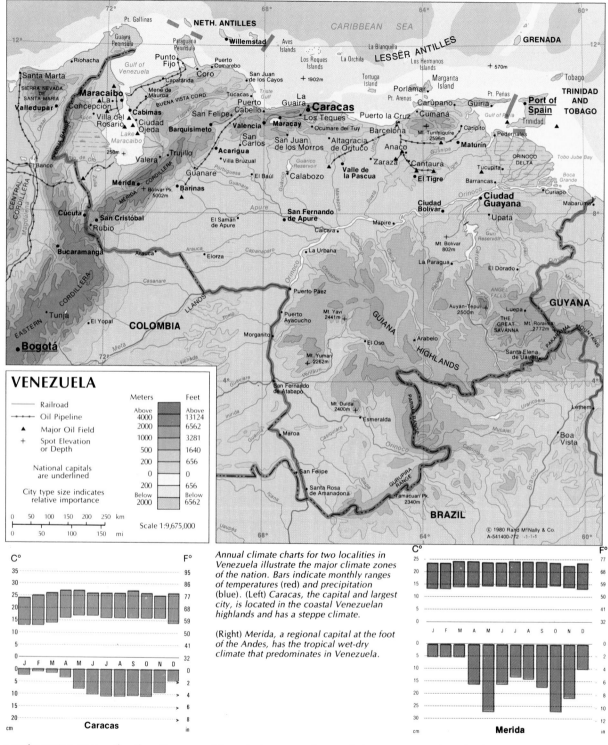

VENEZUELA

- —— Railroad
- •—•—• Oil Pipeline
- ▲ Major Oil Field
- + Spot Elevation or Depth

National capitals are underlined

City type size indicates relative importance

Meters	Feet
Above 4000	Above 13124
2000	6562
1000	3281
500	1640
200	656
0	0
200	656
Below 2000	Below 6562

0   50   100   150   200   250 km
0   50   100   150 mi

Scale 1:9,675,000

© 1980 Rand McNally & Co.
A-541400-772 -1-1-1

Annual climate charts for two localities in Venezuela illustrate the major climate zones of the nation. Bars indicate monthly ranges of temperatures (red) and precipitation (blue). (Left) Caracas, the capital and largest city, is located in the coastal Venezuelan highlands and has a steppe climate.

(Right) Merida, a regional capital at the foot of the Andes, has the tropical wet-dry climate that predominates in Venezuela.

Caracas

Merida

people. Major cities—other than Caracas and the petroleum center of MARACAIBO—are VALENCIA, Barquisimeto, and Maracay.

Life expectancy continues to rise, while the death and infant mortality rates have declined. Malnutrition is still common, however, and access to quality health care remains a problem.

Education. Since 1958 substantial improvements have been made in education, although approximately 10% to 13% of the population never enter the school system and only 50% complete their basic education. Public education is highly centralized and is free, and primary education is compulsory. Secondary education may include technical, teacher, or pre-university training. The autonomous National Council of Universities supervises higher education. The National Institute of Cooperative Education (INCE) trains adults and school dropouts. In 1982–83 total enrollment was estimated at 3.7 million, with about 280,000 in universities.

Caracas, the capital and most populous city of Venezuela, lies at an altitude of approximately 1,000 m (3,300 ft) in the nation's coastal mountains, The center of Venezuelan oil-refining and food-processing industries, the city has experienced rapid urban development.

The Arts. Venezuelan literature owes much to novelists Rómulo GALLEGOS, Arturo Uslar Pietri, Guillermo Meneses, Ramón Díaz Sánchez, and Salvador Garmendía. Acclaimed poets include Andres Eloy Blanco, Juan Liscano, Antonio Arraiz, and Vicente Gerbasi. Venezuelan philologist Angel Rosenblat is perhaps the finest of the Spanish language today. In the performing arts, Isaac Chocrón and Román Chalbaud are mainstays of the theater, whereas maestro Vicente Emilio Sojo revived interest in symphonic music. The National Department of Cinematography helps promising young directors.

Contemporary movements in the plastic arts are well represented: the kinetic school by Jesús Soto, Carlos Cruz-Diez, and Alejandro Otero; and the new figuration by Alirio Rodríguez. The National Institute of Culture and Fine Arts (INCIBA) promotes exhibits and performances and supports young talent.

ECONOMIC ACTIVITY

Once predominantly agricultural, the Venezuelan economy underwent a transformation during the 1970s based on petroleum wealth. The government's control of crucial natural resources resulted in tremendous profits from their exploitation and marketing. The revenue was used in ambitious projects such as those of the Fifth National Plan of 1976–80, which had as its main thrust the investment in basic industries such as steel, aluminum, and electric-power generation. As a result of heavy spending and heavy borrowing, however, the Venezuelan economy foundered in the early 1980s as oil prices fell.

Manufacturing. A need to adjust the economy to an anticipated annual oil-based income of $13 to $14 billion, down sharply from the peak years of Venezuela's affluence in the late 1970s, has made industrial diversification a government priority for the 1980s. The major development plan includes a steel complex, two aluminum plants, a tractor factory, and bauxite, gold, and timber production.

Agriculture. Only 3% of Venezuela's land area is cultivable; about 3% can be used for artificial pasture, and 17% is suitable for natural pasture. The main crops grown are sugarcane, bananas, rice, maize, coffee, cocoa, and cotton.

Fishing and Forestry. Venezuela's fish catch of 180,800 metric tons (1981) contributed substantially to export revenues. The timber wealth in the highlands has not been commercially developed.

Transportation. The main highway system, considered the best in Latin America, is being upgraded, and an inadequate national railroad network is to be increased to 4,020 km

(Above) *Angel Falls, the world's highest waterfall, descends 979 m (3,212 ft) from a massive plateau in Venezuela's remote Guiana Highlands. Discovered in 1935, the cataract is the most dramatic feature of a vast national park in Venezuela's southeast interior.*

(Left) *Petroleum from Venezuela's Lake Maracaibo region, which contains one of the world's richest petroleum deposits, has been Venezuela's chief export since 1918. Today petroleum revenues are being used to diversify Venezuelan industry and agriculture.*

(2,500 mi). Internal air transport is well developed.

Trade. A dramatic increase in imports reached a cost of $8.4 billion in 1977 and produced the first balance-of-payments deficit since 1967. Although the trade balance was favorable again by 1983, a great deal of food and manufactured goods must still be imported. Petroleum is by far the most important export, with aluminum second.

GOVERNMENT

The constitution of 1961 establishes a federal republic. The head of state, elected in December 1983, is President Jaime Lusinchi. The National Congress, made up of the Senate and the Chamber of Deputies, is the legislative branch. Magistrates of the supreme court are named by a joint session of Congress.

Governors of the 20 states are appointed by the president. General elections are held every 5 years under the supervision of the Supreme Electoral Council. Voting is universal and compulsory for those 18 years of age or older. The presidency is decided by simple majority, and the incumbent is ineligible for two consecutive terms.

HISTORY

Long inhabited by ARAWAK and CARIB Indians, Venezuela was visited by Columbus in 1498. Settlements were established by the Spanish in 1523 on the coast of Cumaná. In 1535, Nikolaus Federmann, working for the Weiser brothers (German bankers who were granted rights to Venezuela by Holy Roman Emperor Charles V), led an expedition in Venezuela and Colombia. Settlements were eventually established in the northwest part of Venezuela. In 1556, the Weisers' contract was terminated and Spain regained the region.

Venezuelan Creoles were active in the movement for independence from Spain. In 1806, Francisco de MIRANDA landed in Venezuela with a revolutionary force recruited in the United States. He captured Coro but was easily repulsed by loyalist troops. Venezuela's revolutionary congress declared its independence from Spain on July 5, 1811.

In 1821 the insurgent army of Simón BOLÍVAR defeated the Spaniards decisively at Carabobo, ending their domination over Colombia and Venezuela. In 1830, Venezuela withdrew from Bolívar's Gran Colombia federation and became a sovereign state. Political order and economic growth proved difficult to sustain simultaneously, except under José Antonio PÁEZ, Antonio GUZMÁN BLANCO, and Juan Vicente GÓMEZ. After the overthrow of dictator Guzmán in 1888, the brief progressive period was ended when dictator Cipriano CASTRO seized control in 1899. In 1908, when illness forced Castro to seek medical treatment in Europe, he left the government in the hands of Gómez. Gómez's successors were faced with the demands of an increasingly urban society and the democratic aspirations of the Generation of 1928. A democratic interlude (1945–48) was followed by a decade of military rule.

Since 1958, Venezuela has had democratic rule. Figures of the Generation of 1928, such as Rómulo BETANCOURT and Raúl Leoni of the Acción Democratica (AD) party, and younger men such as Rafael Caldera of the Christian Democratic party (COPEI), Carlos Andrés Pérez (AD), and Luis HERRERA CAMPÍNS (COPEI) have worked for democracy during their presidential administrations. Both AD and COPEI have acceded to the popular mandate as expressed in elections and have turned over control of the government without incident. After Jaime Lusinchi (AD) was sworn in as president in February 1984 he announced a wide-ranging austerity program to correct the ailing economy.

ENRIQUE A. BALOYRA

Bibliography:

GENERAL: Lieuwen, Edwin, *Venezuela*, 2d ed. (1965; repr. 1986); Lombardi, John V., *Venezuela* (1982).

ECONOMICS: Allen, L., *Venezuelan Economic Development* (1977); Coronel, G., *The Nationalization of the Venezuelan Oil Industry* (1983); Gilbert, Alan, and Healey, Patsy, *The Political Economy of the Land: The State and Urban Development in Venezuela* (1985).

POLITICS AND GOVERNMENT: Blank, David, *Venezuela: Politics in a Petroleum Republic* (1984); Levine, D. H., *Conflict and Political Change in Venezuela* (1973) and *Religion and Politics in Latin America* (1981); Powell, John D., *Political Mobilization of the Venezuelan Peasant* (1971); Tugwell, Franklin, *The Politics of Oil in Venezuela* (1975).

HISTORY AND ARCHAEOLOGY: Lombardi, John V., *People and Places in Colonial Venezuela* (1976); Marsland, William D. and Amy L., *Venezuela through Its History* (1954; repr. 1976); Morón, Guillermo, *A History of Venezuela* (1963); Rouse, Irving, and Cruxent, J. M., *Venezuelan Archaeology* (1963).

Venezuela Boundary Dispute

In 1895, U.S. Secretary of State Richard OLNEY invoked the MONROE DOCTRINE against Great Britain in Britain's dispute with Venezuela over the boundary between Venezuela and British Guiana. Contention over the boundary began in 1814, when the British took their part of Guiana from the Dutch, but it became serious only in the 1880s, after gold was discovered there. Upon appeal by Venezuela, Secretary Olney, in July 1895, sent a belligerent note to Lord Salisbury, the British prime minister and foreign secretary, warning against British pressure on Venezuela and asserting that "today the United States is practically sovereign on this continent, and its fiat is law upon the subjects to which it confines its interposition." After Salisbury denied the Monroe Doctrine's applicability, President Grover Cleveland, in December, backed Olney in a special message to Congress seeking funds for a boundary commission, its findings to be implemented by the United States. In 1896, Salisbury backed down and accepted arbitration. In 1899, an arbitral tribunal largely upheld Britain's pre-1880s claim; thereafter, diplomatic relations between Great Britain and Venezuela were renewed. After British Guiana gained independence as Guyana in 1966, Venezuela pressed its claim to more than half of the country.

ROBERT H. FERRELL

Bibliography: Hood, Miriam, *Gunboat Diplomacy, 1895–1905* (1975); Perkins, Dexter, *The Monroe Doctrine, 1867–1907* (1937).

Venice [ven'-is]

Venice (Italian: Venezia), the capital of Venezia province and of the Veneto region in northeastern Italy, lies on the Gulf of Venice at the north end of the Adriatic Sea. The political boundaries of the city were expanded in 1927 to include a mainland area around the Lagoon of Venice as well as the 118 small islands within the lagoon that comprise historic Venice. The city has a population of 340,873 (1983 est.).

The Historic City. The Grand Canal is historic Venice's main traffic artery, cutting a reverse S-shaped curve past outstanding Gothic, Romanesque, and Byzantine structures. Although a causeway connects the mainland to the historic city, road vehicles are garaged on the westernmost island, and travel about the city is by motorboats, water-buses, curved-prow gondolas, or on foot. The smaller canals, called *rii*, are crossed by more than 400 small footbridges, including the famous 16th-century Bridge of Sighs linking the ducal palace and the state prison. On the islands, narrow lanes lead to expansive squares. The largest of these is the Piazza San Marco, bordered on three sides by the Palazzo dei Procuratori (15th–16th century), and on the fourth by SAINT MARK'S BASILICA (9th century, rebuilt 11th–14th century). Between the church and the canal are the 99-m-high (325-ft) Campanile (a 1912 replica of the 12th-century original), and the DOGE'S PALACE. Nearby is the Libreria Vecchia, begun in 1536 by Jacopo SANSOVINO and completed after his death by Vincenzo SCAMOZZI. Across the Grand Canal is the Church of San Giorgio Maggiore, designed by Andrea PALLADIO. Among the city's many other notable churches is Santi Giovanni e Paolo (completed 1430), with a ceiling by Paolo VERONESE. The Church of Santa Maria dei Frari is the burial place of Titian. The Scuola Grande di San Rocco was originally decorated by TINTORETTO. Along the canal are the 15th-century Venetian-Gothic palace, Ca' d'Oro; the Palazzo Rezzonico, built in the 17th century by Baldassarre LONGHENA and the site of the death of Robert Browning; and the Palazzo Vendramin-Calergi, built in 1509 by Mauro CODUSSI in the Lombardesque style. The Accademia di Belle Arti (Venice Academy) contains a collection of masterpieces from the Venetian school of art, including those by Giorgione; Jacopo, Gentile, and Giovanni Bellini; Gentile da Fabriano; Vittore Carpaccio; Canaletto; Andrea Mantegna; and others. In recent years many of Venice's treasures have been repaired and restored. Modern Venice's commitment to the arts is also expressed in the Venice Biennale and in annual cinema, drama, and music festivals. Grand opera is still presented at the Teatro la Fenice, where works by Verdi, Rossini, Wagner, and Stravinsky were first performed.

Economy. Although tourism remains Venice's most important business, the modern city encompasses a newer, industrialized sector on the mainland, including Mestre and Marghera, the latter Venice's commercial port. Shipyards, petroleum refineries, and chemical and metallurgical industries contribute to the city's economy. Burano lace and Venetian glass are world-renowned. Lido Beach, on one of the seaward islands of the lagoon, is a famous bathing resort.

History. Mainlanders fleeing barbarians after the fall of Rome

The Palazzo Ducale, or Doge's Palace, served as the residence of Venice's elected rulers and contained its governmental offices during the Middle Ages, when the city was capital of a powerful maritime empire.

founded several settlements on the islands of the lagoon. In 697 authority was consolidated in Venice's first DOGE. Exploiting its natural maritime potential, Venice soon gained control of the Adriatic Sea, established outposts in the Levant, and became a staging area for the Crusades. The Venetian doge was instrumental in diverting the Fourth Crusade to conquer Constantinople in 1204. Thereafter, Venice was not only the unchallenged broker of most east-west commerce but also an interlocutor between the two cultures. In 1275 the Venetian Marco Polo reached Peking, opening a trade route between Europe and the Far East.

Venice continued to grow in power. In 1380 it defeated Genoa, its only European rival for mastery of the seas; at the Battle of Lepanto (1571), Venetian ships played an important role in the destruction of the Turkish fleet. Overshadowed as a mercantile center, however, first by the Portuguese discovery of an all-water route to the Far East around Africa and then by the growing importance of the Western Hemisphere, Venice went into decline. By the Treaty of Campo Formio (1797), the republic was dissolved and the city came under the rule of the Austrians. Venice fought against foreign domination throughout the Risorgimento and, in 1866, became part of the united Kingdom of Italy.

Industrialization in the 20th century has brought about economic prosperity and rapid population growth in greater Venice. At the same time, however, the city's delicate ecosystem is threatened. Air and water pollution continue to erode the facades of many ancient monuments. Dredging of the lagoon to facilitate entry of large tankers has altered the natural cleansing action of water movement. Severe flooding has damaged the foundations of many buildings, and the threat of future inundations appears certain. Efforts to save the historic city from physical collapse have come from private funds and from international organizations, especially the United Nations Educational, Scientific, and Cultural Organization.   DANIEL R. LESNICK

Bibliography: Bowdon, Maurice, *The Fall of Venice* (1970); Cole, Toby, ed., *Venice: A Portable Reader* (1979); Hale, John R., ed., *Renaissance Venice* (1973); Lane, Frederic C., *Venice, a Maritime Republic* (1973); Links, J. G., *Venice* (1977); McNeill, William H., *Venice: The Hinge of Europe, 1081–1797* (1974); Morris, James, *The World of Venice*, rev. ed. (1974); Ruskin, John, *The Stones of Venice*, 3 vols. (1851; repr. 1979); Tenenti, Alberto, *Piracy and the Decline of Venice, 1580–1615* (1967).

Venice Biennale

The Venice Biennale is the oldest and one of the most prestigious international art exhibitions. It is widely attended by artists, dealers, collectors, and critics. Celebrated for its enormous scope, it attracts artists from many countries and offers prizes awarded by an international panel of judges. The first exhibition, held in Venice in 1895, showed 516 art works. With few exceptions, it has since been held every other year and has grown in size to include more than 2,000 pieces. The Biennale was made an autonomous agency under Italian law in 1928; it receives funding from both the Italian government and the city of Venice and income from sales and admissions. The art selected has changed over the years depending on the political and social climate: from 1895 to 1914 excepted, salon-type art was shown; during the rise of fascism, from 1920 to 1942, Italian art was emphasized; since 1942 the Biennale has sought to reflect new, international trends in modern art.   LISA M. MESSINGER

Bibliography: Alloway, L., *The Venice Biennale 1895–1968* (1968).

Vening Meinesz, Felix   [myn-esh']

The Dutch geodesist and geophysicist Felix Andries Vening Meinesz, b. July 30, 1887, d. Aug. 10, 1966, was perhaps the 20th century's principal contributor to the measurement of gravity and to the understanding of the geodetic and geologic implications of large regional gravity anomalies. He first developed a three-pendulum apparatus for accurately measuring gravity at sea. He used this apparatus in submerged submarines for measuring gravity in most oceanic areas. The first measurements were made (1923–27) in a submarine traversing the Sundra arc-trench system, off Indonesia, where he observed a belt of large-amplitude negative anomalies along the trench axis. He proposed that such anomaly lineations are produced by the down-buckling of a rigid crust—an important forerunner of the concept of plate tectonics.

Vening Meinesz concluded that the shape of the Earth is approximated by an ellipsoid of revolution rather than a triaxial ellipsoid. He introduced the concept that the Earth's crust has strength because it is cool, and that it behaves like a rigid plate being flexed on a softer mantle. He was the first to show that the viscosity of the upper mantle is about 10^{22} poises and was an early advocate of a convecting mantle. He was elected president of the International Association of Geodesy (1933–55) and of the International Union of Geodesy and Geophysics (1948–51).   PETER DEHLINGER

Bibliography: Bomford, Guy, *Geodesy*, 2d ed. (1962); Heiskanen, Weikko A., and Moritz, Helmut, *Physical Geodesy* (1966).

venison [ven'-i-suhn]

Venison is the edible flesh of a wild animal, taken by hunting. Today the word refers specifically to the flesh of deer, but in England during the Middle Ages the flesh of boars, hares, bears, and other game animals was also called venison. In Norman times, large forests were set aside for the use of the king and his nobles; the possession of deer parks, and the eating of venison taken from them, were a proof of high social status. In North America, venison was a staple of the pioneer diet. It was often preserved by "jerking," or drying the meat over a campfire or in the sun.

Venizélos, Eleuthérios [ven-ee-zel'-aws, el-ef-thair'-ee-aws]

Eleuthérios Venizélos, b. Aug. 23, 1864, d. Mar. 18, 1936, several times prime minister of Greece, was one of the leading Greek politicians of his era. A native of Crete, he headed the liberal, nationalist movement on the island and participated in the 1897 revolt against Turkish rule. In 1905, Venizélos proclaimed the union of Crete with Greece, a goal not realized until 1913.

Venizélos went to Greece in 1909 to advise the Military League shortly after its coup d'etat. He was the Liberal party's leader and became prime minister in 1910. During the BALKAN WARS (1912–13), Venizélos helped defeat the Turks and almost doubled Greece's territory. Favoring Britain and France in World War I he resigned in 1915 because of conflicts with the pro-German king CONSTANTINE I, who advocated continuing neutrality. Venizélos formed a rival government in Salonika in 1916. He returned to Athens as prime minister in 1917, after Franco-British pressure forced Constantine to abdicate. Greece then entered the war on the Allied side.

After the war, Venizélos acquired substantial territory for Greece, particularly at Turkey's expense, but lost the elections in 1920. He served briefly as prime minister in 1924 and won the 1928 elections, but the worldwide depression led to his defeat in 1932. Implicated in the unsuccessful antimonarchist revolt of 1935, he fled Greece and died in exile in Paris.

S. VICTOR PAPACOSMA

Bibliography: Alastos, Doros, *Venizelos: Patriot, Statesman, Revolutionary* (1942; repr. 1978); Box, P. H., *Three Master Builders and Another* (1925).

Venn diagram

Venn diagrams are pictures that display simple relationships among sets. Generally a large set *U*, which represents the entire universe under consideration, is fixed and represented as a rectangular region. Subsets of *U* are drawn as circles inside the rectangle, and the overlapping of two such regions indicates the intersection of the corresponding sets. In this way simple propositions in set theory may be understood pictorially. The method is also used to clarify the logic used in the study of SYLLOGISMS. A Venn diagram, however, should never be considered to constitute proof of a statement in set theory. Proofs can only be performed rigorously by working logically from the axioms. Also, Venn diagrams are not much help when a person deals with four or more subsets of *U*.

AVNER ASH

venom

Venom is a poison secreted by certain snakes, insects, and other animals primarily for killing or paralyzing prey, and as digestive juices. The toxic components of snake venoms vary according to the species of snake and include neurotoxins and various enzymes, or hemotoxins. Neurotoxins interfere with nerve conduction and cause paralysis, including paralysis of the respiratory muscles. Hemotoxins hasten absorption of the venom, attack and destroy cells, or cause hemorrhage by interfering with blood coagulation.

Arachnid (scorpion and spider) venoms contain neurotoxins that in some species can cause death from respiratory paralysis. Although most spiders are venomous, in the United States only the brown spider and the black widow spider

have venom potent enough to cause occasional deaths. The venoms of stinging insects such as bees, wasps, and hornets generally produce local irritation and swelling by the action of histamine and other substances that increase vascular permeability.

PETER L. PETRAKIS

Bibliography: Minton, Sherman A., *Venom Diseases* (1974).

See also: POISONOUS PLANTS AND ANIMALS.

ventriloquism [ven-tril'-uh-kwizm]

Ventriloquism, from the Latin *venter,* meaning "belly," and *loquor,* meaning "to speak," is the ancient art of throwing the voice so that it seems to come from a source other than the speaker. The sounds are made with the lips motionless and the tongue drawn back so that only the tip of it moves. Entertainers such as Edgar Bergen (see BERGEN, EDGAR, AND MCCARTHY, CHARLIE) heighten the illusion by using puppets who seem to talk.

ROBERT C. TOLL

Bibliography: Detweiler, Clinton, *Ventriloquism in a Nutshell* (1974).

Ventris, Michael [ven'-tris]

Michael George Francis Ventris, b. July 12, 1922, d. Sept. 6, 1956, was a British architect and cryptographer who became famous for deciphering one part of the puzzling, ancient Mycenaean script known as LINEAR B, which he considered an early form of the Greek language. With John Chadwick, who collaborated on the decipherment, he published *Documents in Mycenaean Greek* (1956).

STEPHEN KOWALEWSKI

Bibliography: Chadwick, John, *The Decipherment of Linear B* (1958; repr. 1970); Daugherty, C. M., *Great Archaeologists* (1962).

Venturi, Robert [ven-tur'-ee]

The American architect Robert Venturi, b. Philadelphia, June 25, 1925, is one of the most provocative and influential theorists of the post-1960 reaction against the functionalist aesthetic of modern architecture usually called the INTERNATIONAL STYLE. As stated most fully in his *Complexity and Contradiction in American Architecture* (1966), Venturi's aesthetic is grounded in a rejection of the "prim dreams of pure order" espoused by modernist architects in favor of an architecture of eclecticism, ambiguity, and humor. Even more controversial was his proclamation of the vitality and intrinsic worth of American roadside-strip architecture in *Learning from Las Vegas* (1972). Together, these two works have become the gospel of POSTMODERN ARCHITECTURE.

Venturi's building designs have proven to be as unorthodox and provocative as his theories. Some, such as a residence he designed (1962) for his mother in Chestnut Hill, Pa., argue for a historical eclecticism that blends shapes and elements from a wide variety of styles. Others of his designs seem to echo the principles of pop art in their deliberate inclusion of commercial elements: his unexecuted design (1967) for the National Football Hall of Fame, for example, features a ballpark-scoreboard facade. Much of Venturi's later work has been undertaken in collaboration with his wife, Denise Scott Brown, and with John Rauch.

Bibliography: Jencks, Charles A., *The Language of Post-Modern Architecture* (1977).

Venus (astronomy)

Venus, the second PLANET from the Sun, is often called the Earth's sister planet because it so closely approximates our own world in diameter, mass, and density, and probably also in composition and internal structure. Venus, however, is shrouded in thick clouds that completely hide the surface of the planet. Because these bright clouds act like a mirror and reflect 75% of the sunlight, many believed that surface temperatures would be nearly the same on both planets. Descriptions written in the 1950s pictured global seas of frothy liquids, out of which rose mist-shrouded islands, or extensive rain forests through which dinosaurs roamed. The atmosphere and surface of Venus are now known to be very different

(Above) *Radar mapping of Venus by* Pioneer Venus 1, *which has been orbiting the planet since Dec. 4, 1978, revealed a surface that is mainly a rolling plain with isolated highlands. Shown here is the largest such region. About half the size of Africa, it is tentatively named Aphrodite. The surface also has fracture zones and volcanoes, possibly still active.*

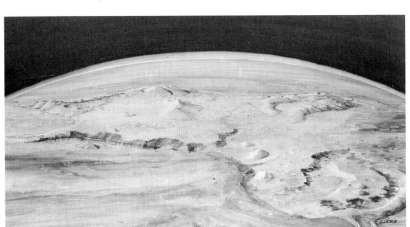

(Below) *Venus, the second planet from the Sun, is surrounded by an atmosphere of carbon dioxide. Infrared radiation from the planet's surface is absorbed and radiated back by this atmosphere, producing surface temperatures as high as 480°C (900°F). The atmospheric pressure is 88 times that found at sea level on Earth.*

from that of the Earth, making it by no means a sister planet in terms of conditions for life.

MISSIONS TO VENUS

The first successful flyby of Venus was made by the U.S. MAR-INER 2 craft on Dec. 14, 1962. This was followed by the *Mariner 5* flyby on Oct. 19, 1967, and the *Mariner 10* flyby on Feb. 5, 1974. The U.S. PIONEER *Venus 1* craft orbited Venus on Dec. 4, 1978, and this was accompanied by *Pioneer Venus 2*, which sent three probes through the Venusian atmosphere to the surface on Dec. 9, 1978.

The Soviet Union has had an even more ambitious Venus program, with 15 successful missions, including 10 landings. Between June 1967 and June 1983, 13 craft of the Soviet VE-NERA program flew by, orbited, or landed on Venus. In 1984 two Soviet craft, *Vega 1* and *Vega 2*—on their way to an encounter with Halley's Comet—deployed a pair of Venera-type landers and a pair of atmospheric balloons on Venus.

ORBIT AND ROTATION

Venus orbits at an average distance of 108.2 million km (67 million mi) from the Sun and completes one revolution in 224.7 days. In order to determine the rotation rate of the surface of the planet, radio waves sent from a radar station on Earth penetrate the clouds of Venus and are reflected from the surface of the planet back to Earth. Radio waves reflected from the side of Venus rotating toward the Earth are slightly decreased in wavelength, and those reflected from the receding sides are slightly increased in wavelength. The change in wavelength, called the Doppler shift, is a measure of the rate of rotation of the planet. Features such as high mountains are also tracked by radar across the surface. Both methods yield the same surprising result: Venus rotates backward compared to the Earth, and much more slowly—completing one rotation in 243 days. Tracking of weak features in the atmosphere reveals that the upper atmosphere also circulates backward once every 4 days. Ultraviolet images of the clouds taken by *Mariner 10* have confirmed this retrograde rotation.

The retrograde rotation of 243 days and the direct revolution about the Sun of 225 days combine to make the Venusian day—the time from one noon to the next—equal to 117 Earth days. The combined rotation and revolution also produce the unfortunate situation that every time Venus is closest to the Earth the same side of Venus is turned toward us. This unusual situation, including the slow backward rotation, may be caused by the gravitational force between the Earth and Venus.

The slow rotation may also be responsible for the apparent absence of a magnetic field on Venus. Like the Earth, our sister planet should have a large iron core, part of which, like the Earth's outer core, is expected to be molten. The slow spinning of Venus, however, apparently does not generate the kind of fluid motion within the core necessary to produce a magnetic field.

ATMOSPHERE

Earth-based telescopic studies of the reflected spectrum of Venus were able to show that its atmosphere is different from that of the Earth. Carbon dioxide, first detected in 1932, is now known to make up 98% of the Venusian atmosphere. By contrast, CO_2 makes up only 0.03% of the Earth's atmosphere, although a far greater amount, about equal to the total quantity in the Venusian atmosphere, is found in the rocks and oceans of the Earth. Nitrogen, the most abundant gas in the Earth's atmosphere, is less than 2% of the total on Venus.

In 1978, Pioneer Venus probes into the atmosphere revealed the presence of a few parts per million of helium, neon, and argon. Although in absolute terms the amounts of the latter two elements are small, nevertheless their abundances in the Venusian atmosphere are, respectively, 2,700 and 500 times greater than in the terrestrial atmosphere; the presence of such amounts indicates, according to present theories of the origin of the SOLAR SYSTEM, that the Sun may have begun to heat up only after the bulk of the planets had formed.

Within the clouds, liquid and solid sulfur particles and droplets of sulfuric acid are the major constituents. The Pioneer Venus probes revealed that below the clouds the atmosphere is composed of 0.1% to 0.4% water vapor and 60 parts per million of free oxygen—an indication that Venus at one time had abundant water but has since then lost it by various processes.

Not only is the Venusian atmosphere made principally of compounds rare in the Earth's atmosphere, but the total surface pressure is much higher than at sea level on Earth. Spacecraft observations have given a value of 88 atmospheres (1,300 lb/in^2), or 88 times atmospheric pressure at sea level on Earth. The enormous amounts of CO_2 in the atmosphere cause this high pressure.

Because of the phenomenon known as the greenhouse effect, the thick CO_2 atmosphere on Venus is primarily responsible for the planet's extremely high temperature. (The recently detected water vapor provides a second strong solar heat trap.) Sunlight filtering through the clouds strikes the surface, which heats up as it absorbs the visible light. When it becomes hot enough the surface radiates away the absorbed heat as infrared radiation. Infrared waves are longer than visible light waves and are readily absorbed by carbon dioxide in the lower atmosphere. Thus the heat is kept near ground level. When the CO_2 atoms radiate away the infrared, a large fraction goes back into the surface, causing the temperature to rise further. The same process operates on Earth: water vapor in the lower atmosphere traps some of the outgoing radiation and raises the Earth's temperature about 30 C degrees; otherwise the average temperature of the Earth would be about −20° C (−4° F). The huge reservoir of CO_2 gas in the atmosphere of Venus has increased the surface temperature there to about 480° C (900° F), about 280 C degrees more than what it would be if there were no greenhouse effect. Venus is actually hotter than MERCURY, as has been confirmed by Soviet spacecraft.

Although the clouds of Venus prevent much sunlight from ever reaching the surface, Soviet Venera spacecraft, equipped with searchlights for illuminating the surface, found no need for artificial lighting. Rocks near the spacecraft cast sharp shadows, indicating the lower atmosphere is clear. From about 31 to 48 km (19 to 30 mi) above the surface a haze made up of tiny particles of sulfuric acid exists. Above this haze is the densest of Venus's cloud layers; about 3 km (2 mi) thick, it consists mostly of large sulfur particles. A brief clear space is above this cloud layer; above this, between 52 and 58 km (32 and 35 mi), there is a second layer of clouds that contains a large number of liquid and solid sulfur particles as well as sulfuric acid droplets. A third layer of clouds, consisting of sulfuric acid droplets, is present between the altitudes of 65 and 70 km (40 and 43 mi). Another haze layer, possibly due to the presence of water vapor or ice crystals, extends about 10 km (6 mi) above the tops of the clouds.

Winds at the surface are relatively gentle—about 13 km/h (8 mph), based on Soviet lander data. Faster winds exist higher up, as would be expected from the 4-day rotation of the upper atmosphere as compared to the 243-day surface rotation. Spacecraft have recorded 175-km/h (110-mph) winds at 45 km (28 mi) above the surface. Strong vertical winds were discovered in 1985 by the Vega craft. *Venera 11* and *Venera 12* also detected what appears to be lightning activity.

SURFACE

Venera 8, which landed on Venus in July 1972, found a granitic composition of radioactive elements uranium, thorium, and potassium, suggesting a crust like the continents of Earth. *Venera 9* and *Venera 10,* which landed in separate locations in October 1975, found basalt, which is the same material that erupts from Hawaiian-type volcanoes and forms the floors of the ocean basins on Earth. The possibility of active volcanism on Venus is also strongly indicated by variations in the sulfur-dioxide content of the atmosphere.

In March 1982, *Venera 13* and *Venera 14* provided the first color photographs of the Venusian surface and a more detailed analysis of the crust. A robot lander measured the electrical conductivity of rocks, drilled a hole to study deeper rock layers, and scooped up soil samples. Preliminary studies indicate that the soil on Venus is much like that on Earth, particularly the basalt rock of volcanic origin on Earth. These studies also indicate that the two planets have had similar geological histories, including an early molten period and plate tectonics.

Radar observations from Earth, the U.S. Pioneer Venus probes, and *Venera 15* and *Venera 16* (which began orbiting the planet in October 1983), together with photographs taken by the Venera landers, have been used to map large parts of the surface terrain. It appears to be largely rolling plain interrupted by areas of highlands, craters, and regions of ridges and canyons that are evidence of extensive tectonic activity. What may be the largest volcano in the solar system appears as a conelike rise more than 700 km (435 mi) across. A troughlike depression running across 1,400 km (870 mi) of surface may be similar to the great rift valleys of Mars and may indicate rupturing of the crust.

There is no liquid water on the Venusian surface, and this "missing water" has long been a puzzle to scientists who generally believe that Earth and Venus started out as very similar twin planets. Data from the U.S. Pioneer Venus probes, however, indicates that Venus may once, billions of years ago, have been covered by an ocean of water. Scientists speculate that the planet lost its water, the hydrogen dissipating into the atmosphere, the oxygen into the interior, possibly because of the runaway greenhouse effect that kept heat trapped close to the surface. HERBERT FREY

Bibliography: Burgess, Eric, *Venus: An Errant Twin* (1985); Hunt, Garry, and Moore, Patrick, *The Planet Venus* (1983); Hunten, D. M., et al., eds., *Venus* (1983); Kerr, R. A., "Venusian Geology Coming into Focus," *Science,* May 18, 1984.

Venus (mythology)

An obscure deity of ancient Rome, by the 3d century BC Venus had become identified with the Greek goddess APHRODITE. Julius Caesar enshrined her as Venus Genetrix, the ancestor of his own family; in this aspect she was analogous to Mars, the paternal ancestor of the Romans. She was also worshiped in imperial Rome as Venus Felix, bringer of good luck; Venus Victrix, bringer of victory; Venus Verticordia, protector of female chastity; and Venus Libentina, patroness of sensual pleasure. In Vergil's *Aeneid*, she is the mother of Aeneas and aids him in his adventures.

Venus of Willendorf [vil'-en-dohrf]

The Venus of Willendorf is a Paleolithic statuette representing one of the earliest forms of statuary art. The exaggerated form of the limestone Venus figurine may have served to emphasize her power of fertility as the goddess of birth and mother of all living things. (Naturhistorisches Museum, Vienna.)

The carved limestone statuette known as the Venus of Willendorf was discovered (1908) at Willendorf, Austria, on the north bank of the Danube. Dating from the Aurignacian period (c.30,000–c.25,000 BC) of the Old Stone Age, the 10.2-cm (4-in) female figure, which still bears traces of red pigment, has exaggerated breasts and hips and precisely arranged braids encircling the faceless head. The heavy stress on the female anatomical features and the absence of facial expression emphasize the sexuality of the figure, which may have served as a symbol of fecundity. The Venus, now in the Naturhistorisches Museum, Vienna, is considered a masterpiece of PREHISTORIC ART. GIULIA BARTRUM

Venus's-flytrap: see CARNIVOROUS PLANTS.

Veracruz (city) [vay-rah-kroos']

Veracruz, a major port on the Gulf of Mexico and the largest city of the Mexican state of Veracruz, has a population of 340,500 (1983 est.). The city's inhabitants are known as *Jarochos.* Veracruz is Mexico's most important general cargo port, handling petroleum, fruits, molasses, and rum. The waterfront area has been rebuilt since a 1970 fire. The city is also a market center for a rich agricultural region. The hot, humid climate has fostered an important tourist industry, with fine beaches, such as Mocambo to the south, and many notable seafood restaurants. Many buildings dating from the colonial period have been preserved. The heart of Veracruz is the Plaza de la Constitución, the oldest Spanish plaza in North America. The Naval Academy and the Regional Technical Institute of Veracruz are located in the city.

Veracruz was established on Apr. 17, 1519, by Hernán

Cortés to serve as his base for the conquest of Mexico. U.S. troops landed in the city during the Mexican War in 1847 and again in 1914 during the Mexican Revolution. Both the 1857 and 1917 Mexican constitutions were proclaimed in Veracruz.

JAMES N. SNADEN

Veracruz (state)

Veracruz is a long and narrow state in east central Mexico, along the Gulf of Mexico, with an area of 72,815 km^2 (28,114 mi^2). The population is 6,171,000 (1984 est.); JALAPA is the capital, and the city of Veracruz is the largest urban center. Veracruz is primarily agricultural (coffee, sugarcane, bananas, and tobacco). Stock raising is concentrated on the lowlands; tropical forests yield dyewood, hardwoods, chicle, and rubber; and petroleum is produced. The Huastec and Totomac Indians live in Veracruz. Hernán Cortés landed there in 1519; Veracruz became a state in 1824.

LEON YACHER

verb: see PARTS OF SPEECH.

verbena [vur-bee'-nuh]

Verbena is the generic name for about 200 species of herbs and subshrubs in the vervain family, Verbenaceae. Native to the warmer regions of North and South America, these plants, often called vervains, are popular garden ornamentals. Verbena leaves are lance-shaped and toothed, and the flowers are borne in broad clusters. The garden verbena, *V. hybrida,* is one of the most common garden annuals.

Vercingetorix [vur-sin-jet'-uh-riks]

Vercingetorix, d. 46 BC, chieftain of the Averni of Gaul, united the Gallic tribes in 52 BC to resist subjugation by the Romans under Julius Caesar (see GALLIC WARS). After initial successes he was defeated by Caesar, brought to Rome, exhibited in Caesar's triumphal march, and executed.

Verde, Cape (country): see CAPE VERDE.

Verde, Cape (promontory) [vurd]

Cape Verde is a narrow promontory in Senegal extending 32 km (20 mi) into the Atlantic Ocean to form Africa's westernmost extremity at 170°32' west longitude. Its name refers to its distinctive green vegetation. Cape Almadies is at its westernmost tip. Dakar is on the southern shore.

Verdi, Giuseppe [vair'-dee]

Giuseppe Verdi, the foremost composer of Italian romantic opera, was born in the village of Le Roncole near Parma on

Giuseppe Verdi, one of the greatest Italian composers of the 19th century, created operas of dramatic intensity, soaring melody, and subtle characterization. La Traviata (1853), Aïda (1871), and Otello (1887) are three of his most highly acclaimed dramatic operas. His works are still among the most popular in the international operatic repertoire.

Oct. 10, 1813, the son of an innkeeper. His first formal musical studies were with the organist Ferdinando Provesi in the nearby town of Busseto, where he lived in the home of the merchant Antonio Barezzi, who supported him financially and whose daughter Margherita was to become his first wife. In 1832 he applied for admission to the Milan Conservatory, but he was refused because he was over the age limit and his piano playing was judged too weak. He pursued private studies in Milan with Vincenzo Lavigna until 1835, when he returned to the post of organist in Busseto. After 3 years his desire to write for the theater brought him back to Milan, where his first opera, *Oberto,* was performed in 1839.

A series of personal tragedies—the death of his wife and both his children in the space of 22 months (1838–40)—interrupted Verdi's career, but in 1842 he was induced by his Milan producer to write *Nabucco,* the opera that brought him his first great success. For a decade thereafter he was sought by all the great opera houses of Italy, and he produced 18 operas in 15 years, culminating in 3 of his best-known works—*Rigoletto* (1851), Il TROVATORE (The Troubador, 1853), and La TRAVIATA (The Wrongdoer, 1853).

By the early 1850s, Verdi had become an important international figure, and he began fulfilling commissions for theaters outside Italy—*Les Vêpres siciliennes* (Sicilian Vespers, 1855), *Don Carlos* (1867), and a revision (1865) of his earlier *Macbeth* (1847) for Paris; *La Forza del destino* (The Force of Destiny, 1862) for Saint Petersburg; and AÏDA (1871) for a new opera house in Cairo. During this period he was elected to a term in the first Italian parliament after the unification of the country (1861). His election was not merely a tribute to his great popularity; Verdi had introduced patriotic elements into his operas as early as *Nabucco,* and his name had become an acronym for "Vittorio Emanuele, Re D'Italia" ("Vittorio Emanuele, king of Italy"—the rallying cry of the political movement for the unification of Italy).

After *Aïda,* Verdi went into semiretirement with his second wife, the singer Giuseppina Strepponi. The only other major work of the 1870s was a Requiem Mass (1874) in memory of the novelist Alessandro Manzoni. He considered his operatic career finished, contenting himself with revisions of the earlier operas. But through the cajoling of his publisher Giulio Ricordi and the librettist Arrigo Boito, who had assisted (1881) with the revisions of *Simon Boccanegra* (1857), Verdi was induced to take up first *Otello* (1887) and then *Falstaff* (1893). These two Shakespearean operas, one tragic and the other comic, were the crowning achievements of his old age. Verdi died in Milan on Jan. 27, 1901.

Verdi was the most important figure in the succession of 19th-century composers of Italian opera, which began with Gioacchino Rossini and ended with Giacomo Puccini. His early operas adopt the basic procedures and style of his immediate predecessors, Vincenzo Bellini and Gaetano Donizetti. Emphasis is on the vocal line, accompaniments are simple, transitions from one piece to the next are mostly perfunctory, and scenes are constructed on a few conventional patterns, the most common comprising a pair of arias—a lyrical cantabile followed by an energetic cabaletta—for one of the principal singers. Verdi brought to these conventional procedures his own gift for memorable melody and a masculine vigor that was often lacking in his models. He favored compact librettos of a melodramatic sort, built around a few emotionally charged confrontations. The typical plot has a tenor and soprano as protagonists, opposed by a baritone who might be a romantic rival (as in *Il Trovatore*) or a father (as in *La Traviata*). These baritone roles have a special prominence in Verdi's operas.

The compact pattern of the early works is expanded somewhat in the operas that Verdi wrote for foreign theaters, especially in *Les Vêpres siciliennes, Don Carlos,* and the revised *Macbeth,* which incorporate the spectacle and ballet associated with French grand opera of the same period. In the works of the 1850s and '60s, Verdi relied less heavily on conventional methods: accompaniments are richer, musical transitions more interesting, and structures less predictable (in particular, the crowd-pleasing cabalettas grow less frequent).

As a result of this experimentation, perhaps, the operas of this period do not always make satisfactory wholes. No such problems exist in *Aida, Otello,* and *Falstaff,* however. In these the dramatic compression of the early works is achieved anew, and Verdi's technique, especially his control of the orchestral accompaniment, is at its most flexible.

Verdi's influence has been less decisive than that of his contemporary Richard Wagner. The new musical language that developed after 1900 owed more to Wagner's polyphony and chromatic harmony than to Verdi's lyricism, vigor, and clarity. As the more conservative (and popular) of the two, Verdi has also been regarded with suspicion by critics and academicians. His ready acceptance of conventional structures and his emphasis on the vocal line exaggerated the importance of melodic inspiration, and where the latter was uneven, inevitable lapses into banality occurred. As he matured, Verdi saw how to make his structures more flexible and his accompaniments more expressive, without sacrificing the power of his melodies. The musical achievement of the last operas and the quality of Verdi's dramatic insight in general have long been recognized.   DOUGLAS JOHNSON

Bibliography: Budden, Julian, *The Operas of Verdi,* 2 vols. (1973, 1978); Gatti, Carlo, *Verdi: The Man and His Music,* trans. by Elizabeth Abbott (1955); Godefroy, V., *The Dramatic Genius of Verdi,* 2 vols. (1975, 1978); Martin, George, *Verdi* (1963); Osborne, Charles, *The Complete Operas of Verdi* (1969); Walker, Frank, *The Man Verdi* (1962); Weaver, W., *Verdi: A Documentary Study* (1977).

verdin   [vur'-din]

The verdin, *Auriparus flaviceps,* is a small, slender, long-tailed member of the titmouse-and-chickadee family, Paridae, found in scrub-covered deserts of the southwestern United States and northwestern Mexico. It has a yellow head and chestnut shoulder patch and builds a globular nest for its four or five bluish green, spotted eggs.   GEORGE J. WALLACE

Verdun   [vair-duhn']

Verdun is a city on the Meuse River in northeastern France, in the department of Meuse. Its population is 21,516 (1982). The city manufactures metal products and furniture. Verdun has an 11th-century cathedral and a 17th-century town hall now housing a war museum.

Verdun's importance as a commercial center and military stronghold predated the Roman Empire. The Treaty of Verdun, signed there in 843, divided the Carolingian empire. Under French control since 1552, Verdun was a strategic fortress during the Franco-Prussian War (1870–71) and the site of a major World War I battle. It was captured by the Germans in World War II (1940) and liberated by the Americans in 1944. Verdun has been largely rebuilt.

Verdun, Battle of

The WORLD WAR I Battle of Verdun (Feb. 21–Nov. 26, 1916), an unsuccessful German effort to take the offensive in the west, was one of the longest and bloodiest encounters of the war. Total casualties have been estimated at about 542,000 French and about 434,000 Germans.

The German assault, directed by Gen. Erich von FALKEN-HAYN, began with a furious bombardment followed by an attack on the region surrounding Verdun, which lay in the middle of an Allied salient jutting into the German zone in northeastern France. Initially successful, the Germans captured Fort Douaumont (February 25).

Gen. Joseph JOFFRE, the French commander in chief, was determined to halt further retreat for reasons of morale as well as strategy. On February 25 he assigned Gen. Henri Philippe PÉTAIN to head the Verdun defense. Pétain, fighting under the famous motto *Ils ne passeront pas!* ("They shall not pass!"), reorganized his command and brought up reinforcements while the weary German troops paused. On March 6 the Germans attacked the western face of the salient; they were halted after initial advances, but the loss of life on both sides was enormous. A third offensive, from both east and west, began on April 9, but again the Germans were stopped.

German assaults continued into early July, and Pétain, who had been promoted and replaced as local commander by Gen. Robert NIVELLE, recommended withdrawal. During the summer, however, the Anglo-French Somme offensive (see SOMME, BATTLES OF THE) and the Russian Brusilov offensive drew off German manpower, and in the late summer the Germans adopted a defensive posture on the western front.

The French soon took the offensive. Under Gen. Charles Mangin they recaptured Fort Douaumont (October 24) and Fort Vaux (November 2). By the time the fighting at Verdun had ended in mid-December, the French had advanced almost to their February lines.   COL. T. N. DUPUY

Bibliography: Blend, Georges, *Verdun,* trans. by Frances Frenaye (1964); Horne, Alistair, *Death of a Generation* (1970) and *The Price of Glory: Verdun, 1916* (1962).

Verdun, Treaty of

The Treaty of Verdun (Aug. 10, 843) divided Charlemagne's Frankish Empire among the three sons of LOUIS I (Louis the Pious). The divisions coincided roughly with later national boundaries in Europe: CHARLES II (Charles the Bald) received lands corresponding to most of modern France; LOUIS THE GERMAN gained the lands east of the Rhine River (Germany); and LOTHAIR I, the eldest, took the imperial title and the Lombard kingdom (Italy) and lands to the north.   ROBIN BUSS

Verdy, Violette   [vair-dee']

The French ballerina and company director Violette Verdy (Nelly Guillerm), b. Dec. 1, 1933, made her debut with Roland Petit's Les Ballets des Champs-Elysées in 1945 and continued her association with Petit through the early 1950s in his Ballets de Paris. Her creation of the role of the Bride in Petit's *Le Loup* (The Wolf, 1953) made her an overnight sensation. She joined American Ballet Theatre in 1957. Between 1958 and 1977 she was a dancer with the New York City Ballet, and in 1984 she became a teacher there. Verdy also was director of the Paris Opera Ballet (1977–80) and associate director of the Boston Ballet (1980–84).   TOBI TOBIAS

Bibliography: Huckenpahler, Victoria, *Ballerina* (1978).

Verga, Giovanni   [vair'-gah]

The finest Italian novelist of the late 19th century, Giovanni Verga, b. Sept. 2, 1840, d. Jan. 27, 1922, wrote realistic novels that caused him to be compared with Flaubert and Zola. His mature works depicted—in a simple, naturalistic style that became associated with the term *verismo*—the life of impoverished Sicilian peasants. For example, his masterpiece, *The House by the Medlar Tree* (1881; Eng. trans., 1890), describes the futile efforts of a fishing family to better their lives. Italy's veristic theater was initiated by Verga's play *Rustic Chivalry* (1884; Eng. trans., 1955), on which Pietro Mascagni later based his opera *Cavalleria Rusticana* (1890).   LOUIS KIBLER

Bibliography: Alexander, Alfred, *Giovanni Verga: A Great Writer and His World* (1972); Cecchetti, Giovanni, *Giovanni Verga* (1978).

Vergil   [vur'-jil]

The great Roman poet Vergil (also spelled Virgil) was born Publius Vergilius Maro on Oct. 15, 70 BC in Andes, a village near Mantua in northern Italy. Vergil spent his childhood on his father's farm and was educated at Cremona, Milan, and then Rome, where he studied rhetoric. There he met poets and statesmen who were to play an important part in his life. When civil war broke out in 49 BC, he retired to Naples where he studied philosophy with the Epicurean Siro.

Beginning in 45 BC, encouraged by the statesman Pollio, Vergil spent eight or ten years composing the *Eclogues,* which were greatly admired in literary circles. They were adapted to the stage as mimes, and thus made him a popular, if elusive, figure. After the publication of the *Eclogues,* Vergil joined the literary circle of Gaius MAECENAS, which would later include the poets Horace and Propertius. Over a period of seven years he wrote the *Georgics,* a didactic poem on farming, described

A 14th-century manuscript illumination from Dante's epic The Divine Comedy portrays the Roman poet Vergil, Dante's guide, encouraging his poetic heir to begin his ascent of the Mount of Purgatory. Dante's 14th-century work is indebted to the structure and events of Vergil's Aeneid, the greatest epic of classical Rome. (Biblioteca Marciana, Venice.)

by the poet John Dryden as "the best Poem of the best Poet." The last years of Vergil's life were devoted to writing his epic poem, the *Aeneid*. He died in Brundisium on Sept. 21, 19 BC, after catching a fever on a trip to Greece and Asia, during which he had intended to complete the *Aeneid*. Before setting out on the voyage, Vergil had asked that the *Aeneid* be destroyed if anything should happen to him before the poem was complete, but the emperor Augustus overturned the request and had it published. (Also attributed to Vergil in his youth is a collection of poems known as the *Appendix Vergiliana*. The authenticity of most of these poems is now disputed or rejected.)

The *Eclogues,* written from 45 to 37 (or 35) BC, were praised for the quiet beauty and charm with which they captured the pastoral landscape. Vergil arranged these ten poems to fit the design of the book as a whole, a new development in poetry. Poems of Theocritus provide a model for some of Vergil's Eclogues, which depict an idyllic Arcadia, with Roman political concerns and real people in pastoral guise intruding on the peaceful setting. The fourth Eclogue prophesies a new golden age that will begin with the birth of an unnamed child. The sixth Eclogue is a unique blend of cosmology and myths.

The *Georgics,* written from 36 to 29 BC, is a didactic poem in four books purporting to teach farming. The poem's overall plan is summed up in the opening lines: what to plant and when, the cultivation of trees, especially the vine, and of livestock, and the art of beekeeping. The influence of Hesiod, Aratus, Callimachus, Varro, and Lucretius, as well as other poets in lesser degree, is evident in the poem. Vergil weaves together his diverse materials into a stunning creation that has been compared by many to a musical composition. Masterfully balancing the somber and the joyous, he evokes a love of the land that has seldom, if ever, been matched. Italy emerges as the "Saturnian land," fertile and varied in its produce, the beautiful land over which Saturnus ruled during the golden age. The horror of disease, embodied in the ravages of a plague, is relieved by the picture of the light and joyous bees, whose cultivation is said to have resulted from the tragedy of Orpheus and Eurydice. (Vergil's poem is the classic formulation of the details of this myth.) The poem ends with Aristaeus appeasing the offended deities and in the process discovering the art of beekeeping.

The AENEID ("the story of Aeneas"), written from 26 to 19 BC, became the national epic and established Vergil, with Homer, as one of the great epic poets. Roman poets before Vergil, including Naevius and Ennius, had already written of Aeneas's adventures. Vergil succeeded in unifying around the figure of Aeneas the theme of Homer's *Odyssey* (the search for a new home) in the first six books and that of the *Iliad* (the war and final reconciliation of the Trojans and the Latins) in the last six books, with multiple correspondences between the two halves.

Vergil's greatness was recognized in his own lifetime, soon after which the *Aeneid* was made a standard school text. In subsequent ages Vergil was viewed as the supreme poet, orator, philosopher, prophet, and theologian. Copies of the *Aeneid* were placed in temples for consultation. In 4th-century Rome the pagan opposition to the church used Vergil as its Bible, and Fulgentius turned the *Aeneid* into an allegory of the stages of human life. Dante made Vergil his guide in the *Divine Comedy.* More recent scholarship has emphasized the continuity of Vergil's work, his art of cumulative imagery, his use of language, and the music of his hexameters: "the stateliest measure ever moulded by the lips of man" (Tennyson).

PATRICIA A. JOHNSTON

Bibliography: Commager, S., ed., *Virgil* (1966); Comparetti, D., *Virgil in the Middle Ages* (1895); Johnson, W. R., *Darkness Visible* (1976); Johnston, P. A., *Vergil's Agricultural Golden Age* (1980); Leach, E. W., *Vergil's Eclogues* (1974); Miles, G. B., *Virgil's Georgics* (1980); Otis, B., *Virgil: A Study in Civilized Poetry* (1963); Putnam, M. C. J., *Virgil's Pastoral Art* (1979) and *Virgil's Poem of the Earth* (1970); Wilkinson, L. P., *The Georgics of Virgil* (1969).

Vergil, Polydore

Polydore Vergil, b. *c.*1470, d. Apr. 18, 1555, Italian cleric, historian, and writer, was a major transmitter of the new Renaissance scholarship to England. He lived in England for most of the time between 1502 and 1550; his *Anglica Historica* (26 vols., 1534), a history of England to 1537, influenced the Elizabethan chroniclers Edward Hall and Raphael Holinshed.

Verhaeren, Émile   [vair-ah-ren']

The Belgian symbolist poet Émile Verhaeren, b. May 21, 1855, d. Nov. 26, 1916, wrote visionary poetry, but is best remembered for three love poems he composed for his wife: "The Sunlit Hours" (1896; Eng. trans., 1916), "Afternoon" (1905; Eng. trans., 1917), and "The Evening Hours" (1911; Eng. trans., 1918).

verismo   [vair-ees'-moh]

Verismo (Italian for "realism"; sometimes Anglicized as *verism*), an artistic movement originating in the late 19th century, aimed at a realistic representation of contemporary life among ordinary people. The term is used for Italian opera of the period, which often featured violent plots and sordid surroundings resulting in melodrama that exploited individual moments of crisis at the expense of structural development and unity. The "pretty" tunes and virtuoso arias of operatic tradition were abandoned in favor of terser, less symmetrical melodies. Well-known examples of verismo operas include Mascagni's *Cavalleria Rusticana* (1890), Leoncavallo's *Pagliacci* (1892), and Charpentier's *Louise* (1900). Some of Puccini's operas also show the influence of verismo.

Veríssimo, Érico   [vuh-rees'-see-moh]

The modernist Brazilian writer Érico Veríssimo, b. Dec. 17, 1905, d. Nov. 28, 1975, chronicled the rise of his native state Rio Grande do Sul in his masterpiece, the trilogy *Time and the Wind,* comprising *The Continent* (1949; Eng. trans., 1951), *The Portrait* (1951; Eng. trans., 1951), and *O Arquipélago* (The Archipelago, 1961). He also wrote short stories, criticism, children's books, and travel essays.

Verlaine, Paul   [vair-len']

Paul Marie Verlaine, b. Metz, France, Mar. 30, 1844, d. Jan. 8, 1896, was one of France's finest symbolist poets, although he did not accept the designation himself. As a poet he was first associated with the PARNASSIANS, then with DECADENCE. In youth he was already troubled by the alcoholism and instability that were to torment his life. His marriage (1870) to the teenage Mathilde Mauté ended in separation after he began a homosexual relationship with the poet Arthur RIMBAUD and took to the road. For shooting his friend in the wrist in a moment of anger Verlaine was imprisoned (1873) for 18 months. Later he taught school in England and lived in the Ardennes. His last years in Paris, as he alternated between repentance

This portrait by Henri Flantin-Latour of the symbolist poet Paul Verlaine (left) was painted in 1872, when Verlaine was living with Arthur Rimbaud (right). Verlaine explored the musical qualities of the French language in Romances sans paroles (Songs without Words, 1874) and Sagesse (Wisdom, 1881). Later poems deal with his long conflict between carnality and piety. (Louvre, Paris.)

and backsliding, were years of suffering and dissipation during which he seemed to embody the contemporary decadence expressed in his sonnet ''Langueur.''

Yet this strangely bohemian figure was one of the most gifted writers of his age and, after his return to Catholicism in 1874, he wrote some of the century's most remarkable religious poetry, such as the sonnet sequence in Sagesse beginning ''Mon Dieu m'a dit: Mon fils, il faut m'aimer'' (''God said to me: My son, you must love me.''). He was welcomed as a lecturer at Oxford. His limpid lyricism makes him one of the major French poets of the modern period.

In his first volume of verse, Poèmes saturniens (Saturnine Poems, 1866), Verlaine's musical gift is already apparent. In Fêtes galantes (1869) he is inspired in part by French painting of the 18th century. His later volumes, La Bonne Chanson (The Good Song, 1870), Romances sans paroles (Songs without Words, 1874), and Sagesse (Wisdom, 1881) contain many of his most exquisite and best-known poems. Jadis et naguère (Once upon a Time and Not Long Ago, 1885) contains his ''Art poétique,'' which emphasizes the music of poetry, stresses nuance, and calls for the union of the vague with the precise. Verlaine's later collections of poems are of poorer quality. Among his prose writings are Les Poètes maudits (The Accursed Poets, 1884), Mémoires d'un veuf (Memoirs of a Widower, 1886), Mes hôpitaux (My Hospitals, 1891), Mes prisons (My Prisons, 1893), and Confessions (1895; Eng. trans., 1950). He died in a public infirmary and was buried in the Batignolles Cemetery in Paris.   Reviewed by PAUL A. MANKIN

Bibliography: Chadwick, Charles, Verlaine (1973); Coulon, Marcel, Poet under Saturn: The Tragedy of Verlaine (1970); Hanson, Lawrence and Elizabeth, Verlaine, Fool of God (1957); Stephan, Philip, Paul Verlaine and the Decadence, 1882–90 (1974).

See also: SYMBOLISM (literature).

Vermeer, Jan   [vur-mayr']

Jan or Johannes Vermeer van Delft, b. October 1632, d. December 1675, a Dutch genre painter who lived and worked in Delft, created some of the most exquisite paintings in Western art. His works are rare. Of the 35 or 36 paintings attributed to him, most portray figures in interiors. All his works are admired for the sensitivity with which he rendered effects of light and color and for the poetic quality of his images.

Little is known for certain about Vermeer's career. His teacher may have been Leonaert Bramer, a Delft artist who was a witness at Vermeer's marriage in 1653. His earliest signed and dated painting, The Procuress (1656; Gemäldegal-

erie Alte Meister, Dresden), is thematically related to a Dirck van Baburen painting that Vermeer owned and that appears in the background of two of his own paintings. Another possible influence was Hendrick Terbrugghen, whose style anticipated the light color tonalities of Vermeer's later works.

During the late 1650s, Vermeer, along with his colleague Pieter de Hooch, began to place a new emphasis on depicting figures within carefully composed interior spaces. Other Dutch painters, including Gerard Ter Borch and Gabriel Metsu, painted similar scenes, but they were less concerned with the articulation of the space than with the description of the figures and their actions. In early paintings such as The Milkmaid (c.1658; Rijksmuseum, Amsterdam), Vermeer struck a delicate balance between the compositional and figural elements, and he achieved highly sensuous surface effects by applying paint thickly and modeling his forms with firm strokes. Later he turned to thinner combinations of glazes to obtain the subtler and more transparent surfaces displayed in paintings such as Woman with a Water Jug (c.1664/5; Metropolitan Museum of Art, New York City).

A keen sensitivity to the effects of light and color and an interest in defining precise spatial relationships probably encouraged Vermeer to experiment with the camera obscura, an optical device that could project the image of objects placed before it. Although he may have sought to depict the camera's effects in his View of Delft (c.1660; Mauritshuis, The Hague), it is unlikely that Vermeer would have traced such an image, as some have charged. Moralizing references occur in several of Vermeer's works, although they tend to be obscured by the paintings' vibrant realism and their general lack of narrative elements. In his Love Letter (c.1670; Rijksmuseum, Amsterdam), a late painting in which the spatial environment becomes more complex and the figures appear more doll-like than in his earlier works, he includes on the back wall a painting of a boat at sea. Because this image was based on a contemporary emblem warning of the perils of love, it was clearly intended to add significance to the figures in the room.

After his death Vermeer was overlooked by all but the most discriminating collectors and art historians for more than 200

In Jan Vermeer's Young Woman Standing at a Virginal (c.1671) the artist has transformed a genre scene into a timeless, perfectly balanced composition through the meticulous placement of every object and a subtle distribution of color. (National Gallery, London.)

years. Only after 1866, when the French critic W. Thoré-Bürger ''rediscovered'' him, did Vermeer's works become widely known.   ARTHUR K. WHEELOCK

Bibliography: Blankert, Albert, *Vermeer of Delft* (1978); Goldscheider, Ludwig, *Johannes Vermeer: The Paintings* (1967); Gowing, Lawrence, *Vermeer*, rev. ed. (1975); Slatkes, Leonard J., *Vermeer and His Contemporaries* (1981); Swillens, P. T. A., *Johannes Vermeer, Painter of Delft 1632–1675* (1950); Wheelock, A. K., *Vermeer* (1981).

Vermeylen, August   [vair-my'-luhn]

The Belgian writer and educator August Vermeylen, b. May 12, 1872, d. Jan. 10, 1945, established the influential Flemish journal *Van-Nu-en-Straks* (From Now On, 1893–1903). He also furthered a Flemish literary revival through his essays and a novel, *De Wandelende Jood* (The Wandering Jew, 1906).

vermiculite: see MICA.

Vermigli, Pietro Martire   [vair-meel'-yee]

The Italian reformer and theologian Pietro Vermigli (Peter Martyr), b. May 8, 1500, d. Nov. 12, 1562, helped in the preparation of the English Book of Common Prayer. An abbot in the Augustinian order, he was influenced by Martin Bucer and Ulrich Zwingli and became active in the Reformation. When summoned for an inquiry by his order, he fled (1542) from Italy to Zurich and then Strasbourg, where he was appointed professor of theology. He moved to England in 1547 by invitation of Archbishop Thomas Cranmer and became professor of divinity at Oxford. In 1549 he took part in a famous disputation on the nature of the Eucharist. Imprisoned after the accession (1553) of the Catholic queen Mary, he was allowed to escape and return to Strasbourg and then to Zurich (1556), where he became a professor of Hebrew.
                                    FREDERICK A. NORWOOD

Bibliography: McLelland, J. C., *The Visible Words of God* (1957) and, as ed., *Peter Martyr Vermigli and Italian Reform* (1980).

Vermont

Vermont is the northwesternmost and second largest of the New England states. Its name is derived from the French phrase *monts verts,* ''green mountains,'' just as its capital, MONTPELIER, is named for the French city of Montpellier. Samuel de Champlain in 1609 was the first European to explore the region, and Lake Champlain in the northwestern part of the state bears his name. To the east the Connecticut River follows Vermont's 322-km (200-mi) border with New Hampshire. Vermont is bordered by Massachusetts on the south, New York on the west, and the Canadian province of Quebec on the north.

The only New England state without a seacoast, Vermont traditionally has been the region's most important agricultural state. Since World War II, however, Vermont's economy has become increasingly diversified, with recreation and manufacturing assuming greater importance.

The first European settlement in present-day Vermont was in 1666, when Pierre de St. Paul, sieur de la Motte, constructed a blockhouse on Isle la Motte in Lake Champlain. The settlement was temporary, however, and the first permanent settlement was by the English in 1724 at Fort Dummer (present-day Brattleboro). Vermont was admitted to the Union as the 14th state on Mar. 4, 1791, after having existed as an independent republic for 14 years.

LAND AND RESOURCES
Vermont's highest point, Mount Mansfield (1,339 m/4,393 ft), lies about 30 km (19 mi) almost due east of Burlington. The lowest elevation is along Lake Champlain, which lies at 29 m (95 ft) above sea level and drains northward into the St. Lawrence River. Vermont has 80 peaks exceeding 900 m (3,000 ft).

Occupying much of northwestern Vermont, the Champlain Valley lies quite flat close to the lake and was in fact at various times an old lake or seabed during the periods of higher water levels brought about by Pleistocene glaciation. Heavy clay soils mantle much of the area, often making drainage a

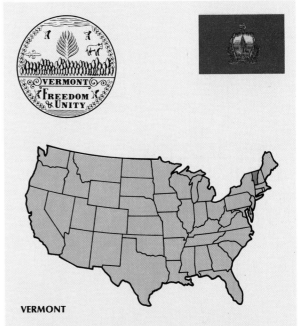

VERMONT

LAND. Area: 24,900 km² (9,614 mi²); rank: 43d. Capital: Montpelier (1980 pop., 8,241). Largest city: Burlington (1984 est. pop., 37,500). Counties: 14. Elevations: highest—1,339 m (4,393 ft), at Mount Mansfield; lowest—29 m (95 ft), at Lake Champlain.

PEOPLE. Population (1987 est.): 548,000; rank: 48th; density: 22.8 persons per km² (59 per mi²). Distribution (1986): 23.1% metropolitan, 76.9% nonmetropolitan. Average annual change (1980–87): +1.03%.

EDUCATION. Public enrollment (1986): elementary—63,392; secondary—28,720; higher—18,734. Nonpublic enrollment (1980): elementary—3,100; secondary—3,600; combined—200; higher (1986)—13,726. Institutions of higher education (1985): 22.

ECONOMY. State personal income (1986): $7.2 billion; rank: 47th. Median family income (1979): $17,205; rank: 40th. Nonagricultural labor distribution (1986): manufacturing—50,000 persons; wholesale and retail trade—53,000; government—38,000; services—57,000; transportation and public utilities—10,000; finance, insurance, and real estate—11,000; construction—15,000. Agriculture: income (1986)—$398 million. Forestry: sawtimber volume (1987 prelim.)—13.8 billion board feet. Mining: value (1985)—$50 million. Manufacturing: value added (1985)—$1.7 billion. Services: value (1982)—$806 million.

GOVERNMENT (1989). Governor: Madeleine Kunin, Democrat. U.S. Congress: Senate—1 Democrat, 1 Republican; House—1 Republican. Electoral college votes: 3. State legislature: 30 senators, 150 representatives.

STATE SYMBOLS. Statehood: Mar. 4, 1791; the 14th state. Nickname: Green Mountain State; bird: hermit thrush; flower: red clover; tree: sugar maple; motto: Freedom and Unity; song: ''Hail, Vermont!''

problem. Toward the mountains to the east, relief gradually increases, and dairy farming gives way to other land uses.

The narrow Valley of Vermont, located south of the Champlain Valley, is traversed by U.S. Route 7 extending from Bennington in the south to Brandon in the north. The valley was a major settlement route into Vermont, and marble is quarried in the north.

The Taconic Mountains extend along the border with New York west of the Valley of Vermont. The highest summit is Mount Equinox near Manchester (1,163 m/3,816 ft). Slate is quarried along the western side. To the east of the valleys and extending the entire length of the state, forming its backbone, are the GREEN MOUNTAINS. The mountains occasionally separate into two parallel ranges, and the western summits are higher.

The largest and also most diverse physical region in Ver-

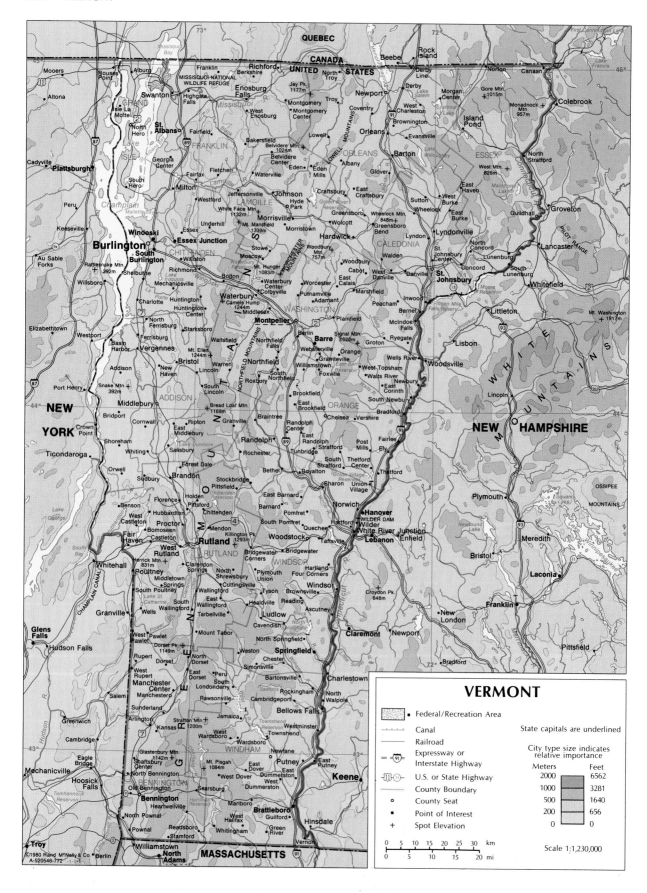

QUEBEC
CANADA
UNITED STATES

NEW
YORK

NEW HAMPSHIRE

MASSACHUSETTS

VERMONT

■ Federal/Recreation Area

Canal

Railroad

Expressway or
Interstate Highway

U.S. or State Highway

County Boundary

o County Seat

■ Point of Interest

+ Spot Elevation

State capitals are underlined

City type size indicates
relative importance

Meters	Feet
2000	6562
1000	3281
500	1640
200	656
0	0

Scale 1:1,230,000

0 5 10 15 20 25 30 km
0 5 10 15 20 mi

©1980 Rand McNally & Co.
A-520546-772

(Left) *Trees in their autumn colors add to the rustic charm of Weston, a small village in southern Vermont. Weston derives revenue from tourism by maintaining a water-powered grist mill, an authentic country store, and a market selling indigenous woodcraft products.*

(Below) *A sugar maple near Middlesex, a small town along the Winooski River, is tapped for its sap, which is collected in buckets, transferred to a horse-drawn tank (background), and boiled down into syrup. Vermont leads all states in the production of maple sugar and syrup.*

mont, the Vermont Piedmont, occupies most of the eastern portion of the state and includes the valleys of the White, West, and Black rivers, all of which drain into the Connecticut. With elevations less than 600 m (2,000 ft), the piedmont was an important area of early hill farming. Most farms have long been abandoned, and much of the land has reverted to forestry and recreational uses, although dairy farms still exist.

The Northeastern Highlands region, often referred to as the Northeast Kingdom, is a small, wild, and isolated mountainous area north of St. Johnsbury. It is geologically closely related to New Hampshire's nearby White Mountains. The highest summit is Gore Mountain (approximately 1,000 m/ 3,330 ft), and nearly all of the region lies above 600 m (2,000 ft).

Soils. Although Vermont soils generally are acid podzol and podzolic, local relief differences result in wide variations. At higher elevations glacial erosion has removed most surface material, and soils are thin or totally lacking. At the same time, substantial deposits of glacial gravels are found on the sides of lower valleys, and lake-bottom clays predominate in several larger basins such as the Champlain Valley and in the vicinities of Newport, Stowe, and Bennington. Nowhere are soils particularly fertile.

Rivers and Lakes. Streams originating in the uplands of the state drain in three directions. Much of the water from southwestern Vermont flows into the Hudson River; runoff in western Vermont drains into Lake Champlain (see CHAMPLAIN, LAKE), and thence into the St. Lawrence; and eastern Vermont lies within the CONNECTICUT RIVER drainage basin. The longest river in Vermont, Otter Creek in the Champlain Valley, extends only about 160 km (100 mi). Other larger streams are the Winooski, Lamoille, and Missisquoi rivers, all draining into Lake Champlain. After Lake Champlain (total area, 1,270 km²/490 mi²)—which is shared by New York State and Canada and is one of the largest freshwater lakes in the United States—Vermont's largest lake is Lake Memphremagog, partly in Canada.

Climate. Because of its inland location, Vermont receives little climatic impact from the Atlantic Ocean. An exception is the northeaster, which develops from low-pressure systems off the coast of Maine and generates moist northeastern airflow over the region, in the winter often bringing heavy snowfall to higher elevations. Also, because of its closer proximity to the Atlantic, southeastern Vermont tends to receive more precipitation than the sheltered Champlain Valley.

Precipitation patterns mostly reflect elevation. The Champlain Valley receives an average of 813 mm (32 in) annually,

whereas Somerset, at an elevation of 634 m (2,080 ft) in the Green Mountains of southern Vermont, receives more than 1,321 mm (52 in), and mountain summits even more, with snowfall totals of 3,810 mm (150 in) not uncommon.

Temperature is also influenced by elevation and inland location. The average January temperature for the state is −8° C (18° F), whereas the July temperature averages 19° C (67° F). Temperatures cooler than these persist at higher elevations, however, and somewhat warmer temperatures prevail in the valleys. Rutland, in the Champlain Valley, has an average temperature in January of −6° C (21° F) and in July of 21° C (70° F). Seasonal extremes prevail because of the lack of any significant marine influence. The record low temperature for Vermont is −46° C (−50° F); the record high of 41° C (105° F) occurred at Vernon on July 4, 1911. Growing seasons in the Champlain Valley are 150 days or more, but at higher elevations and in enclosed valleys some marginal farms have a growing season of only 90 days or even less.

Vegetation and Animal Life. Most of Vermont supports a natural vegetation of northern hardwoods, primarily birch, beech, and maple. Evergreens, especially balsam fir and spruce, predominate at higher elevations, often above 600 m (2,000 ft), and patches of alpine tundra are found on the summits of Mount Mansfield and Camels Hump. White cedar is found in the Champlain Valley, as are stands of oak and hickory. Currently about 70% of Vermont is forested, compared with only 30% a century ago, when farms were much more widespread. Subclimax white pine often covers pastures abandoned for 75 years or more.

Although the white-tailed deer is the primary sport animal in the state, weasels, shrews, red foxes, Canadian lynx, bobcats, beavers, porcupines, and snowshoe rabbits also abound. Fishers, a species of marten, are becoming common once again, as are coyotes. Moose occasionally enter the state. The last panther was shot about 1900, but sightings persist. About 300 black bears are shot annually.

Spruce grouse and partridge furnish good hunting in autumn, and wild turkeys have been established in the southwestern part of the state. Poisonous snakes are very rare, although the numerous places with names such as Snake Mountain and Rattlesnake Hill suggest that this was not always the case.

Environment. Because of its proximity to large urban areas of the Northeast, Vermont has been experiencing considerable pressure on its natural resources. In response, the legislature in 1970 passed one of the nation's most comprehensive environmental protection laws, Act 250 (Vermont Land Use and Development Law), putting Vermont, along with Oregon, to the fore in protecting its environment.

PEOPLE

In 1980 only about a third of Vermont's inhabitants were classed as urban; the remaining two-thirds, according to the U.S. Census Bureau, were rural dwellers. Thus Vermont was the most rural state in the country. A refinement of the rural figures, however, shows that of this population only a small minority were rural farm dwellers. Most of the state's population live in places with fewer than 2,500 inhabitants or in isolated rural dwellings—often former farms that are now nonfarm in function.

Only since 1960 has Vermont's population been growing in any significant way. In the 110 years between 1850 and 1960 the population went from 314,120 to 389,881, an increase of 24%. Since 1960 the rate of increase has been substantially greater. This recent growth, partly related to the ease of transportation by interstate highways, has been the result of net inmigration in addition to natural increase.

Vermont therefore is fast becoming an extension of the Atlantic coast urban region. Some residents even commute from the state to distant cities because no place in Vermont is more than 3 hours' drive from a large metropolitan area. The smaller towns and isolated rural areas, not the urban places, in Vermont are growing. Over all, by 1980 the population of those places in the state with fewer than 25,000 inhabitants had increased by about 15%, while several of Vermont's cities had declined in population.

The most significant ethnic minority are French Americans. In general, however, ethnic minorities are far less common in Vermont than in the more urbanized New England states. Welsh are uniquely concentrated in the slate districts in southwestern Vermont, and Italians are concentrated in the Barre granite area.

About 1% of the state's population are classed as black, Hispanic, Asian, or American Indian, and that small portion have a per capita income approximately on a par with the balance of the population.

BURLINGTON remains Vermont's largest city, followed by RUTLAND, BENNINGTON, Essex Town and Essex Junction, Colchester, Brattleboro, South Burlington, Springfield, BARRE, and St. Johnsbury.

Education. Vermont has a number of institutions of higher education: 6 publicly supported, the balance private. MIDDLEBURY COLLEGE and BENNINGTON COLLEGE are the best known of the latter. Other private institutions include Green Mountain College in Poultney, Norwich University in Northfield, St. Michael's College in Winooski, and Trinity College in Burlington. The University of Vermont, in Burlington, was founded in 1791.

Primary and secondary education is carried out by Vermont's public and private or parochial schools. Several of the latter, such as St. Johnsbury Academy and Bellows Free Academy in St. Albans, also serve as public schools for local children.

A pair of skiers follow a tree-lined trail along one of Vermont's slopes. Vermont offers many resorts and some of the finest skiing terrain in the eastern half of the United States, particularly in the northern portion of the Green Mountains.

Culture. Because of a long tradition of tourism, Vermont is dotted with museums catering to a variety of interests. Whereas many towns in the state have small historical society museums, the Shelburne Museum possesses one of the largest collections of Americana in the country and also boasts a fine research library and the sidewheel steamer *Ticonderoga*. The Fleming Museum at the University of Vermont specializes in art exhibits, and the Athenaeum in St. Johnsbury is famous for its collection of 19th-century paintings. Other art museums include the Brattleboro Museum and Art Center, the Southern Vermont Art Center in Manchester, and the Wood Art Gallery in Montpelier. The American Precision Museum at Windsor exhibits the development of machine tools; and St. Johnsbury has the Fairbanks Museum and Planetarium. The Vermont Museum, in Montpelier, operated by the Vermont Historical Society, features an outstanding library and collections of Vermontiana.

In addition to such amateur groups as the Lyric Theatre in Burlington, Vermont residents can see talented professional performers brought into the state by the Lane Series at the University of Vermont and by Middlebury and Bennington colleges. The state has three symphony orchestras—the Vermont Symphony, the Vermont Philharmonic, and the University of Vermont Symphony.

Historical Sites and Recreational Areas. Vermont highways are dotted with more than 1,200 historic site markers. The Bennington Battle Monument dominates the town's skyline, and at East Hubbardton are the Hubbardton Battlefield and Museum. Joseph Smith, the founder of Mormonism, was born in Sharon; Brigham Young, also a Mormon leader, was born in Whitingham. Windsor has the Old Constitution House, where Vermont's first constitution was written in 1777. The Revolutionary War fortifications on Mount Independence in Orwell, across from Fort Ticonderoga, N.Y., have been recently excavated.

Vermont has numerous state forests and state parks. In addition, the Green Mountain National Forest manages the thousands of hectares traversed by the APPALACHIAN TRAIL and the Long Trail. The Lye Brook and Bristol Cliffs wilderness areas also afford primitive solitude. Almost half the state's population participates in the annual deer-hunting season in November, and thousands of tourists visit the state's ski resorts.

Communications. Vermont has numerous AM and FM radio stations and several television broadcasting facilities. There are also cable television systems in operation in the state. Of the state's daily newspapers, the *Burlington Free Press* and the *Rutland Herald* (founded in 1794 as a weekly) have the largest circulations.

ECONOMIC ACTIVITY

Although Vermont once had a largely agricultural economy, since World War II manufacturing and tourism have replaced agriculture as the state's economic mainstays. Today, manufacturing accounts for about one-quarter of Vermont's gross state product, while agriculture accounts for only 5%. Tourism has become a major industry, principally because of the development of a modern transportation system and of the state's skiing and camping facilities.

Agriculture. Vermont is one of the nation's most rural states, yet it ranks near the bottom among U.S. states in terms of agricultural income. Although agriculture utilizes about 25% of the land, it provides only a small percentage of Vermont's gross state product. In terms of both land area under cultivation and value of products, however, Vermont is an important agricultural state in New England, particularly in the area of dairy farming. In terms of percentage of farm income derived from dairying, Vermont is a leading U.S. dairy state. Other valuable livestock products include beef cattle and calves, chickens, hogs, and turkeys.

Other agricultural products are derived from a few small truck farms, generally close to urban areas. Principal products include maple syrup, Christmas trees, and potatoes, and the raising of horses is becoming increasingly significant. Eggs are produced locally, and apple orchards are important along the Lake Champlain shoreline and also near Brattleboro and Bennington.

Manufacturing and Energy. Among Vermont's leading industry groups are electrical and electronic equipment, food and food products, nonelectrical machinery, fabricated metal products, paper and paper products, printing and publishing, and lumber and wood products. Computer equipment is processed in Essex Junction, and the Brattleboro area is important for printing and publishing. Springfield long has been a center for the machine-tool industry. About three-fourths of the state's industrial plants have fewer than 50 workers.

A problem facing the state is the high cost of energy. Because the state lacks fossil-fuel resources, electrical bills in Vermont are higher than in many other states. The bulk of Vermont's electrical power is generated by nuclear energy, coming from the lone nuclear power plant at Vernon, operated by Vermont Yankee Nuclear Power Corporation. The second greatest source of energy comes from hydroelectricity, with the remainder coming from coal and petroleum. Considerable attention has been given to alternate energy sources, especially wood-burning generators and hydroelectric sites. In 1940 electricity was produced commercially from the wind by a generator atop Grandpa's Knob near Rutland.

Forestry and Fishing. About three-fourths of Vermont is covered by forestland, much of it owned by lumber companies, and about one-quarter of the state's manufacturing enterprises depend on the lumber industry. Furniture plants and small paper mills, small and medium-sized sawmills, and woodenware manufacturing plants are scattered across the state, particularly in the northeast. Maple is the most valuable hardwood tree; softwoods of value include spruce and pine.

Vermont has almost no commercial fishing, but many out-of-state visitors come every year to fish the state's lakes and mountain streams.

Mining. At one time metals were an important source of state income, with copper being mined until 1958 in South Strafford. Today, however, mining in Vermont is limited to nonmetallic products, especially granite, marble, asbestos, slate, talc, and clay. Marble is quarried in the highly metamorphosed rocks running from Rutland south to Danby; the largest granite quarries in the United States are near Barre.

Transportation. Because Vermont industries generally do not involve bulky raw materials or products, most freight transportation within the state is by truck. The Central Vermont, the state's leading rail carrier, is an important through-freight link between eastern Canada and the Atlantic seaboard. Vermont's major export product, in tonnage, is milk—all transported in trucks. Lake Champlain provides barge transportation through canals to both the south and north, with fuel oil the major commodity coming into the

(Above) *Dairy cattle graze on a farm near Strafford, in the east central portion of the state. The majority of Vermont's farms are devoted to dairying and related operations.*

(Below) *Workers prepare to hoist a slab of granite at the Wells-Lamson quarry near Barre. Situated in Washington County in central Vermont, Barre is the center of an area with the largest granite quarries in the United States.*

state. The Connecticut River is not navigable, although the first canal in the United States, now a power canal, was built (1791–1802) at Bellows Falls.

GOVERNMENT AND POLITICS

Until recently, Vermont had one of the largest state legislatures in the country; its senate had 30 members and its house 246, representing every town and city in the state, even the 12 residents of Stratton. Under this system it was possible for 12% of Vermont's voters to elect a majority in the house. With reapportionment (1973–74) the senate still has its 30 members, from 13 senatorial districts, but the house has shrunk to 150 members. All state legislators are elected to 2-year terms, as is the governor.

Vermont has counties, cities, organized towns, unorganized towns, incorporated villages, and certain other areas called gores and grants. Local government is centered in towns, which function somewhat like townships; that is, the town may have several communities and rural districts under one government. Each town has its annual TOWN MEETING the first Tuesday in March, at which time the governing selectmen and other town officials are elected. Each of Vermont's cities also has a local government. The county courts provide about the only political identity for Vermont's counties.

In national politics Vermont became famous for its consistency in voting Republican. From the mid-19th to the mid-20th century, the state sent only Republican senators and representatives to Washington (and elected only Republican governors), and it always voted for the Republican presidential nominee. In 1964, however, Lyndon Johnson outpolled

Barry Goldwater by a margin of almost 2 to 1; and in 1974 the state elected Democrat Patrick J. Leahy to the Senate, where he joined Robert T. Stafford.

HISTORY

When Samuel de CHAMPLAIN traversed the lake that bears his name in 1609, Vermont was hunting territory for various AL-GONQUIN and Iroquois tribes (see IROQUOIS LEAGUE), and Algonquin groups such as the ABNAKI and MAHICAN were probably already permanent inhabitants of western parts of the state. In any event, most Vermont Indian place names are of Algonquin origin.

, The Champlain Valley was recognized early as the strategic lowland corridor between the French settlements to the north and the British ones to the south. The sieur de la Motte built a blockhouse on Isle la Motte in 1666, and Captain Jacobus de Warm from Albany constructed a trading post on Chimney Point in 1690. A French fort was built on the same site in 1730, and the ruins of its chimneys that stood for years gave the place its unusual name. Of the many later British, French, and American fortifications built throughout the valley, CROWN POINT and TICONDEROGA, both in New York State, are the largest and best known.

Claims of Massachusetts, New Hampshire, and New York.
Under the charter of the Massachusetts Bay Colony, Massachusetts had been granted the southern half of Vermont and southwestern New Hampshire, and to protect its settlements the colony erected a series of forts along the Connecticut River. Fort Dummer, the first permanent white settlement in what was to become Vermont, was built in 1724 near the present town of Brattleboro.

In 1741, however, George II ruled invalid Massachusetts's claims in Vermont and New Hampshire and fixed the northern boundary of Massachusetts at its present location. Gov. Benning Wentworth of New Hampshire saw this as an opportunity to grant lands west of the Connecticut River as far as a line about 30 km (20 mi) east of the Hudson River, the western boundary of both Massachusetts and Connecticut. In 1749 he granted the town of Bennington in southwestern Vermont, and subsequently, by 1764, he had granted a total of about 135 towns, making Vermont known as the "New Hampshire Grants."

But Wentworth's real-estate activities upset Gov. George Clinton of New York, who, citing early charters to the duke of York, claimed that New York extended eastward to the Connecticut River. The king was asked to render a decision in the dispute, but wartime activities (see FRENCH AND INDIAN WARS) postponed judgment until 1764, when George III and his council declared "the western banks of the river Connecticut to be the boundary line between the said two provinces of New Hampshire and New York." New York thereupon declared all of Wentworth's 135 grants null and void and began to make new grants to new grantees of lands already held and settled under New Hampshire title.

Independence and Statehood. Settlers were thunderstruck and angered, and most were fearful of losing their lands. Violent outbreaks against New York authority were common, especially in western Vermont, where the GREEN MOUNTAIN BOYS organized by Ethan ALLEN in 1770–71 harassed holders of Vermont land with New York titles. As the only organized military group in Vermont, the Boys later were able to support the cause of the colonies against the British, notably by helping Benedict Arnold capture the British fortress at Ticonderoga in 1775.

With the Declaration of Independence on July 4, 1776, Vermont settlers pondered their future. In a series of conventions the idea of independence was gradually accepted, and at Windsor on July 2–8, 1777, 70 delegates unanimously adopted a constitution that was almost an exact replica of Pennsylvania's. Vermont became the independent Republic of New Connecticut, alias Vermont, but the name *New Connecticut* was rarely used. After 14 years as an independent republic, Vermont was admitted to the Union as the 14th state on Mar. 4, 1791.

The 19th Century. Earliest industries in the new state included the production of potash and pear ash, largely for the

Canadian market because of the northward drainage of Lake Champlain. During the War of 1812, prosperous smuggling developed between Vermont and Canada, at the same time that America's first battleship, the *Saratoga*, built at Vergennes, was being sent into action under Commodore Thomas MACDONOUGH on Lake Champlain. The Battle of Plattsburgh in September 1814 gave Americans final control of the lake.

The Jefferson Embargo preceding the War of 1812, the war itself, and the opening (1823) of the Champlain Canal connecting Lake Champlain to the Hudson River all contributed to Vermont's growing orientation to the south and away from the north and Canada. The canal made it possible for Vermont farmers to ship goods to New York City, stimulating agriculture and wool production, until the 1860s when dairy farming began to dominate. During the Civil War the St. Albans Raid occurred (1864) when 22 Confederate soldiers based in Quebec robbed banks in St. Albans and fled to Canada. By the early 20th century, manufacturing replaced agriculture as the dominant economic activity.

A New Look. Today the southern orientation of Vermont has been reinforced dramatically by a changing population and socioeconomic character of the state. Retirees, second-home owners, and new resident commuters from Connecticut, New York, and Massachusetts are settling in the state. The population is growing fast through migration, tourism is booming, and the stability and quiet so characteristic of more than 175 years of statehood is rapidly disappearing from the Green Mountain State.

HAROLD A. MEEKS

Bibliography: Bearse, Ray, ed., *Vermont, A Guide to the Green Mountain State*, 2d ed. (1966); Fuller, Edmund, *Vermont, A History of the Green Mountain State* (1952); Hill, Ralph N., *Yankee Kingdom: Vermont and New Hampshire*, rev. ed. (1973); Hill, Ralph N., et al., *Vermont: A Special World* (1969); Jacobs, Elbridge C., *The Physical Features of Vermont* (1950); Jones, Matt B., *Vermont in the Making, 1750–1777* (1939; repr. 1968); Meeks, Harold A., *The Geographic Regions of Vermont* (1975); Merrill, Perry H., *Vermont under Four Flags* (1975).

Vermont, state university and colleges of

The **University of Vermont** (1791; enrollment: 8,950; library: 835,000 volumes) at Burlington is, like Vermont's state colleges, coeducational. In 1864 it joined the Vermont Agricultural College (1864), forming the University of Vermont and State Agricultural College, a land-grant school. The university, which offers bachelor's, master's, and doctor's degrees in many fields, has colleges of arts and sciences, agriculture, education, engineering, and medicine and schools of home economics, natural resources, and nursing.

Colleges offering liberal arts and teacher education programs on the undergraduate and graduate levels are **Castleton State** (1787; enrollment: 2,000; library: 100,000 volumes), at Castleton, and **Johnson State** (1828; enrollment: 1,100; library: 65,000 volumes), at Johnson. **Lyndon State** (1911; enrollment: 1,100; library: 65,000 volumes), at Lyndonville, is an undergraduate school.

vermouth

Vermouth is an alcoholic beverage with a white-wine base that is flavored with seeds, herbs, barks, flowers, and spices, according to each manufacturer's secret recipe. The drink is used primarily as an aperitif, or as an ingredient in martinis and manhattans. Sweet vermouth, also called Italian vermouth, is either *russo* (red) or *bianco* (white), whereas dry, or French, vermouth is white—pale amber, actually. Both kinds are produced in any part of the world in which grapes are grown.

Vermouth is made by adding sugar syrup or *mistelle* (unfermented grape juice stabilized with brandy) to ordinary white wine. The herbs and flavorings that give the drink its characteristic flavor are macerated and steeped in alcohol, which is combined with the wine. Herbs used include cinnamon, rhubarb, nutmeg, cloves, quinine, and anise; as many as 50 herbs and flavorings may be included in the recipe. The flavored alcohol is added to the wine, and this fortified wine is then blended, clarified, pasteurized, refrigerated, filtered, stored for a few months, and bottled. The name is thought to derive from *wermut*, the German name for "wormwood," because blossoms of the wormwood plant, *Artemisia absinthium*, have been the BITTERS traditionally used in vermouth.

Bibliography: Amerine, Maynard A., *Vermouth: An Annotated Bibliography* (1975); DeBlij, Harm Jan, *Wine* (1983); Hogg, Anthony, *Everybody's Wine Guide* (1986).

Verne, Jules [vurn]

Jules Verne, a French science-fiction writer, anticipated many aspects of 20th-century technology in his popular novels. The concept of a powered submarine was popularized by his Twenty Thousand Leagues Under the Sea *(1870), and several peculiarities of space travel, notably weightlessness, are first mentioned in* From the Earth to the Moon *(1865).*

The French novelist Jules Verne, b. Feb. 8, 1828, d. Mar. 24, 1905, almost single-handedly invented science fiction. He was educated in law but soon devoted himself to writing for the stage. The publication of *Five Weeks in a Balloon* (1863; Eng. trans., 1869) revealed his talent for stories of imaginary journeys. Verne had the ability to popularize science and created fantasies depicting journeys to the center of the earth, to the moon by rocketship, and through the ocean by submarine; some of these tales have proved remarkably prophetic.

His creations have inspired filmmakers: TWENTY THOUSAND LEAGUES UNDER THE SEA (1870; Eng. trans., 1873), the story of the diabolical Captain Nemo and his submarine, and *Around the World in Eighty Days* (1873; Eng. trans., 1873) became successful movies in 1954 and 1956 respectively. The second of these works concerns Phileas Fogg, who, with his servant Passepartout, wagers that he can make what seemed in 1873 an impossibly fast journey. Mixing humor, adventure, and scientific discovery, it is probably Verne's best-loved work.

ROBIN BUSS

Bibliography: Allott, Kenneth, *Jules Verne* (1940); Costello, Peter, *Jules Verne: Inventor of Science Fiction* (1978); Evans, I. O., *Jules Verne and His Work* (1965; repr. 1980); Jules-Verne, Jean, *Jules Verne: A Biography* (1976).

Verner, Karl Adolf [vair'-nur]

The Danish philologist Karl Adolf Verner, b. Mar. 7, 1846, d. Nov. 5, 1896, is best known as the formulator of Verner's law (1875), a hypothesis in HISTORICAL LINGUISTICS that explains why voiced fricatives instead of the voiceless ones predicted by GRIMM'S LAW are found in some Germanic words. Verner's theory that the voiced consonants preceded and the voiceless ones followed stressed syllables encouraged a group of linguists working in Leipzig to put forward the so-called neogrammarians' hypothesis that all sound changes are universal in their application.

DAVID YERKES

Vernet (family) [vair-nay']

The Vernet family gave rise to three generations of painters: **Claude Joseph**, b. Aug. 14, 1714, d. Dec. 3, 1789; his son **Carle**, b. July 14, 1758, d. Nov. 17, 1835; and Carle's son **Horace**, b. June 30, 1789, d. Jan. 17, 1863. Carle and Horace Vernet were primarily painters of military scenes, whereas Claude Joseph Vernet was one of the most popular landscape painters of the 18th century. His personal vision bridged the classical landscape style of Claude Lorrain and the 19th-century romantic landscapes; he spent 9 years (1754–63) painting views of 15 ports of France on a royal commission. One of his best-known works is the *Ponte Rotto* (1745; Louvre, Paris).

NANETTE SALOMON

Bibliography: Kalnein, W. G., and Levey, Michael, *Art and Architecture of the Eighteenth Century in France* (1972).

vernier [vur'-neer]

A vernier is an auxiliary scale, used for more accurately reading measurements of an instrument. The linear or circular format matches that of the main scale; the vernier slides along the main scale so that graduations of the two scales can be compared. The vernier scale is divided uniformly so that ten subdivisions of the vernier correspond to nine subdivisions of the main scale; thus each vernier subdivision is one-tenth shorter than a main-scale subdivision. The vernier is read by noting which subdivision most closely matches a main-scale subdivision. The word *vernier* also is used to designate equipment that incorporates a fine adjustment device, whether or not a vernier scale is used.

DOUGLAS M. CONSIDINE

Vernon, Edward

Edward Vernon, b. Nov. 12, 1684, d. Oct. 30, 1757, a British admiral, was known for his Caribbean exploits against the Spanish during the War of Jenkins's Ear (1739–41). Because he wore a coat of grogram (a coarse silk or silk-mix fabric), his men referred to him as "Old Grog." This nickname ("grog") was given to the rum-and-water mixture that he issued to them to control drunkenness. George Washington's family estate, Mount Vernon, was named for him.

Bibliography: Hartmann, Cyril, *Angry Admiral* (1953).

Verona [vay-roh'-nah]

Verona, a city in northeastern Italy, is situated on the Adige River about 100 km (60 mi) west of Venice and has a population of 261,947 (1983 est.). Located at a major highway junction and served by railroads, Verona is an agricultural market town. The city's industries manufacture paper, textiles, leather goods, pharmaceuticals, chemicals, and metal products. Verona is especially known for its Soave, Bardolino, and Valpolicella wines. Historic sites include a Roman amphitheater and ruins of two gateways (1st century AD), the Church of Santo Zeno Maggiore (rebuilt 12th–13th centuries), the cathedral (12th–15th centuries), the Castel Vecchio (1354), and the Loggia del Consiglio (15th century).

Verona became a Roman colony (89 BC) and prospered because of its key location. Ruled in the early Middle Ages by Ostrogoths, Lombards, and Franks, Verona became a free commune in the 12th century. Under the SCALA family (1260–1387), Verona grew prosperous and powerful. The city fell into decline and was ruled by Milan (1387–1405), Venice (1405–1797), and Austria (1797–1866), until it joined a united Italy.

DANIEL R. LESNICK

Veronese, Paolo [vay-roh-nay'-zay]

Together with Titian and Tintoretto, Paolo Caliari, c.1528–88, called Il Veronese for his birthplace of Verona, dominated Venetian painting of the 16th century. Trained in Verona, he was influenced initially by Giulio Romano, whose mastery of illusionistic devices and allegorical themes the young Veronese attempted to emulate in the elaborate frescoes he executed (early 1550s; now largely destroyed) with G. B. Zelotti

The Holy Family with Saint Barbara (c.1562-70) displays the rich colors and the air of opulence typical of Paolo Veronese's work in both sacred and secular subjects. He was one of the most prolific and popular Venetian artists of the 16th century. (Uffizi, Florence.)

for the interior of the Villa Soranza. By the time he moved (c.1553) to Venice, this love of illusionistic and fanciful effects had merged with an admiration for the sumptuous colors of Titian.

Although he was only 25 years of age at the time, Veronese immediately created a sensation in Venice with the brilliant color and illusionistic impact of the ceiling panels he painted (1553) for the Room of the Council of Ten and other chambers in the DOGE'S PALACE. In 1555 he undertook the decoration of the Church of San Sebastiano in Venice, which occupied him and his workshop intermittently for a decade. The San Sebastiano paintings exemplify Veronese's religious works and prove his ability to integrate painting and architecture, whether real or fictive, in a single decorative ensemble. This talent is best seen in his masterpiece, the interior of the Villa Barbaro (now Villa Volpi) at Maser, which had been designed by Andrea Palladio. Like other Venetian nobles, the Barbaro family established their country seat in a villa designed to revive the pleasures of country life as described by ancient Roman authors. Accordingly, the trompe l'oeil (illusionist) architecture, landscapes, and human figures with which Veronese covered the villa's interiors recall the similar decorations of ancient country houses. Typical of this colorful blend of classical quotation and inspired illusionism is the ceiling fresco called Abundance, Fortitude, and Envy (c.1561), an ingenious masterpiece of di sotto in su ("from below looking up") perspective.

The theatrical quality of much of Veronese's art is exemplified in the series of supper scenes he painted for various monastic refectories in Venice and outlying areas. The most famous of these is his Feast in the House of the Levi (1573; Accademia, Venice), in which dozens of life-size figures populate a loggia that stretches in three open bays across the painting's 13-m (42-ft) width. Behind the figures an elaborate perspective opens like a stage set onto a clear blue sky. Although Christ and other familiar New Testament characters occupy the center, the rest of the composition is crowded with exotic characters not mentioned in the biblical text. The inclusion of these unorthodox details caused Veronese to be called before the Inquisition to defend his painting against charges that it lacked the requisite seriousness and piety for a depiction of the Last Supper. Given 3 months to modify the composition, the painter chose to adopt the present title, which indicates a less elevated theme.

The very fact that Veronese's painting caused a stir indicates the power of his greatest work and the great reputation he had achieved. After his death his works remained popular

and eventually exerted a profound influence on baroque artists such as Pietro da Cortona and on such rococo artists as Giovanni Battista Tiepolo.   WILLIAM HOOD

Bibliography: Bell, Nancy, *Paolo Veronese* (1904; repr. 1971); Freedberg, S. J., *Painting in Italy: 1500 to 1600* (1970); Hartt, Frederick, *History of Italian Renaissance Art* (1974); Stearns, Frank P., *Four Great Venetians* (1901; repr. 1976).

Verrazano, Giovanni da   [vair-raht-sah'-noh]

An Italian navigator and explorer in France's service, Giovanni da Verrazano, c.1485-c.1528, sailed up the east coast of North America in 1524 and discovered New York and Narragansett bays. Commissioned by King Francis I that year to search for a western sea route to China, he explored from around Cape Fear, N.C., to at least the Maine coast and mistook either Delaware or Chesapeake Bay for the opening to the Pacific Ocean. In 1528, Verrazano crossed the Atlantic again, heading for Central America. He never returned. According to one report, Verrazano was killed by Indians.

Bibliography: Murphy, Henry C., *The Voyage of Verrazzano* (1970); Wroth, L. C., *The Voyages of Giovanni da Verrazzano, 1524-1528* (1970).

Verrazano-Narrows Bridge

The Verrazano-Narrows Bridge (1959-64), linking Long Island and Staten Island at the entrance to New York Harbor, has a span of 1,298 m (4,260 ft) and is a fitting tribute to its designer, Othmar H. AMMANN. Four main cables pass over the top of cellular steel towers, which soar 210 m (690 ft) above the water. These cables are designed to carry 12 lanes of traffic on two decks. Its towers were founded on huge monoliths sunk to depths of 32 m (105 ft) and 52 m (170 ft) by open dredging; the total weight of steel in the bridge is 135,000 metric tons (150,000 U.S. tons). The overall cost of the bridge, including extensive approaches, was $325 million.

SIR HUBERT SHIRLEY-SMITH

Bibliography: Talese, Gay, *The Bridge* (1964); Young, Edward M., *The Great Bridge: The Verrazano-Narrows Bridge* (1965).

Verres, Gaius   [vair'-eez]

Gaius Verres, c.120-43 BC, was a Roman politician who, as governor of Sicily (73-71), gained a reputation for oppression, exploitation, and corruption. Brought to trial, he was prosecuted with devastating success by CICERO. He lived in exile on the spoils of office until he was killed as a result of proscription by Mark Antony.

Verrocchio, Andrea del   [vair-rohk'-kee-oh]

Andrea di Michele di Francesco di Cioni, called Andrea del Verrocchio, b. 1435, d. Oct. 7, 1488, was one of the most accomplished Florentine sculptors of the Early Renaissance and the head of an important workshop that numbered among its assistants Leonardo da Vinci, Lorenzo di Credi, and probably Perugino. Verrocchio was trained as a goldsmith but successfully made the transition to sculpture on a monumental scale. An early-16th-century tradition associates him with the sculptor Desiderio da Settignano, which would help to explain his extraordinary technical facility. Another 16th-century tradition states that he trained under Donatello, with whom he had few stylistic affinities; Verrocchio did apparently succeed Donatello as the principal sculptor of the Medici family.

Verrocchio's first major work for them was the tomb of Piero and Giovanni de'Medici (completed 1472; San Lorenzo, Florence); during the 1460s and '70s he fulfilled commissions from Lorenzo de'Medici for a bronze *David* (Bargello, Florence), a bronze *Putto with a Dolphin* (Palazzo Vecchio, Florence), and the *Resurrection* (Palazzo Vecchio) in terra-cotta relief. The Medici tomb is a virtuoso work of bronze and marble, but the other three pieces all invite comparison with Donatello in both the choice and interpretation of subject matter. The studied characterization of the warriors' varied reactions in the *Resurrection*, for example, seems a deliberate commentary on Donatello's own dramatic reliefs. These early

Andrea del Verrocchio's bronze David (c.1475) stands in a classical contrapposto (twisted) pose over the severed head of Goliath. The statue was commissioned by Lorenzo de'Medici and sold (1476) to the Signoria of Florence. The elegant detail and finish of the bronze reveal Verrocchio's early training as a goldsmith. (Bargello, Florence.)

efforts also prefigure Verrocchio's later concern with precise detail, technical virtuosity, and dramatic effects.

In the large-scale works of his mature period, Verrocchio displays the mastery and sensitivity of Desiderio at his best. His major public work in Florence is the *Doubting of Thomas* (c.1465–83), a life-size group cast in bronze and placed in a niche at Or San Michele. While he was still working on this group Verrocchio was summoned (c.1483) to Venice to create an equestrian monument to the condottiere (mercenary captain) Bartolommeo Colleoni; a work of great dramatic power, it was completed (1495) after Verrocchio's death by the Venetian sculptor Alessandro Leopardi.

Although Verrocchio's workshop also produced a great number of paintings, only one, the Pistoia altarpiece (1478–85; Duomo, Pistoia), is clearly documented. The *Baptism of Christ* (c.1470; Uffizi, Florence) bears clear evidence of Verrocchio's hand and also that of the young Leonardo.

A. H. R. MARTINDALE

Bibliography: Passavant, Gunther, ed., *Verrocchio: Sculptures, Paintings, Drawings* (1969; repr. 1977); Seymour, Charles, Jr., *Sculpture in Italy 1400–1500* (1966) and *The Sculpture of Verrocchio* (1971).

Versailles [vair-sy']

Versailles, a city in north central France, is situated about 18 km (11 mi) southwest of Paris. The population is 91,494 (1982). Metal products, brandy, and footwear are manufactured locally. The city is an episcopal see as well as a local administrative and military center, and it has a national agricultural research station. Proximity to Paris makes Versailles a dormitory suburb. The economy, however, is chiefly based on tourists drawn by Louis XIV's world-renowned palace at Versailles, its grounds, and associated buildings.

Many historic events have taken place in Versailles. The declaration ending hostilities between the United States and Great Britain was signed there in 1783. The city served as headquarters of the German armies attacking Paris during the Franco-Prussian War (1870–71), and William I was crowned (1871) emperor of Germany in the palace. Versailles was the seat of the Allied War Council during World War I, and the Treaty of Versailles ending the war was signed in the Hall of Mirrors on June 28, 1919. The city was Allied General Headquarters (1944–45) in World War II. LAWRENCE M. SOMMERS

Bibliography: Barry, Joseph, *Passions and Politics: a Biography of Versailles* (1972); Hibbert, Christopher, *Versailles* (1972); Levron, Jacques, *Daily Life at Versailles in the Seventeenth and Eighteenth Centuries*, trans. by Claire E. Engel (1968).

Versailles, Palace of

The Palace of Versailles, for more than 100 years (1682–1790) the official residence of the kings of France, was in its heyday the most elegant and sumptuous palace in Europe, one that was envied and imitated by many foreign rulers. Originally a royal hunting lodge, the Versailles complex was rebuilt and greatly expanded (from 1669) by King Louis XIV, who commissioned Louis LE VAU to create a great palace that would provide a suitable setting for the ceremonies of the royal court. Le Vau's splendid monument to the French classical style of the mid-17th century is complemented by the extraordinary formal GARDENS laid out by André Le Nôtre, who arranged innumerable statues, vases, and fountains throughout the grounds. The gardens also contain subsidiary palaces, including the Grand Trianon (1687) and the PETIT TRIANON (1762–70). The classicist Charles LE BRUN supervised the decoration of the palace's interior, which retains its sumptuous and grandiose appearance despite the melting down (1689) of the original silver furniture to pay for Louis XIV's wars. Typical of the lavishness of the interior decoration is the dazzling and hugely expensive Hall of Mirrors (begun 1678).

Le Vau's original design was expanded by Jules HARDOUIN-MANSART, who, with Robert de COTTE, designed the impressive Royal Chapel (1689–1710) and added rooms in a lighter baroque style. During the 18th century many other interiors were redecorated in the rococo and Louis XVI styles. The last major addition (1757–70) to the palace was Ange Jacques Gabriel's (see GABRIEL family) enchanting opera house, which is famous for its illusionistic mirrors. After the French Revolution, during which the palace was stripped of most of its furnishings, Versailles gave way to the Tuileries in Paris as the royal residence. Louis Philippe designated Versailles a national museum, and intensive restoration work during this century has re-created some of the palace's former grandeur.

Bibliography: Arthaud, Gaston, *The Fully Illustrated Artistic Guide to the Treasures of Versailles* (1935; repr. 1984); Berger, Robert W., *Versailles* (1985).

See also: BAROQUE ART AND ARCHITECTURE; FURNITURE; ROCOCO STYLE; STYLES OF LOUIS XIII–XVI.

Versailles, Treaty of: see PARIS PEACE CONFERENCE.

verse, free: see VERSIFICATION.

versification

Versification is the art or practice of making verse. It is based on the principles of prosody, prosody being the theory of which versification is the practice. Discussion of either term leads to a consideration of those regular recurrences—RHYME, meter, stanza form—which distinguish verse from prose, and of those auxiliary recurrences and sound devices—alliteration, assonance, onomatopoeia (see FIGURES OF SPEECH)—found in both prose and verse but more frequently in verse. In the best verse such recurrences are functional as well as formal; they contribute to the meaning as well as to the sound.

All smooth-flowing language has rhythm; verse, or metrical language, only regularizes it. All metrical language is therefore rhythmical, but not all rhythmical language is metrical. Meter originally meant "measure"; verse is language in which the recurrent elements of rhythm exhibit patterns that can be identified and measured.

Accent or Stress. In English the basis of verse is accent or stress. In all words of more than a syllable, one syllable is pronounced with more emphasis than the others; in all sentences, some words receive more emphasis than others. This emphasis—a combination of pitch, loudness, duration, and timbre—is accent or stress. Although many degrees of stress occur in any utterance, most prosodists are content to recognize not more than four levels, which for purposes of scansion, or metrical analysis, may be reduced to two—stressed and unstressed.

Meter. English prosody commonly recognizes four principal meters—iambic, trochaic, anapestic, dactylic—and eight line lengths—monometer, dimeter, trimeter, tetrameter, pentameter, hexameter, heptameter, octameter. The meters are named after the four principal kinds of feet: the iamb, consisting of an unstressed followed by a stressed syllable (x /); the trochee (/ x); the anapest (x x /); and the dactyl (/ x x).

Metrical patterning is seldom completely regular, but it must be sufficiently constant so that beneath the actual rhythm an identifiable paradigm can be heard. If a poem is said to be written in iambic pentameter, all of its lines will consist of five feet, and a majority of the feet will be iambs. Yet variation is important, for perfect regularity soon becomes monotonous, and in good verse, deviations from regularity help convey meaning.

Of the numerous ways of giving variation to verse, the most obvious is the use of substitute feet—for instance, a trochee for an iamb, or a spondee (//) for any of the other types. Extra unaccented syllables may also be added at the ends or beginnings of lines, and the weights of stressed or unstressed feet may vary considerably. A pronounced difference of effect exists between verse that is heavily end-stopped and verse that is run-on or enjambed in which the sense of one line flows without interruption into the next. Considerable variation may also be obtained by the use and positioning of the internal pause, or CAESURA. Such pauses, commanded by the grammatical or rhetorical shape of the sentence, may or may not be indicated by punctuation, but they affect the rhythm without affecting the meter.

Blank Verse. The essential difference between verse and prose is meter; other, optional differences are rhyme and stanza form. Indeed, so much of the greatest English poetry has been written in unrhymed iambic pentameter that it has been given a special name, BLANK VERSE. This is the meter Shakespeare used in his tragedies, Milton in his two epics, and Wordsworth, Keats, Tennyson, and Robert Frost in some of their finest poems. It is a meter of great subtlety, variety, and dignity, capable both of rendering the humblest rhythms of colloquial speech and of rising to the heights of sublime eloquence.

Rhyme and Stanza Form. Rhyme is a feature of versification that by its recurrence at the ends of lines, regularly or irregularly arranged, further differentiates verse from prose; it can be used effectively to give musicality to the verse, to organize the lines, and to emphasize the words upon which the rhymes fall. Like meter, rhyme can be both a formal and an expressive feature of verse. In addition, it can be used in conjunction with meter to organize a poem into a third pattern of recurrence—the stanza.

A stanza is a group of lines of fixed number, meter, and rhyme pattern, repeated throughout a poem. Many traditional stanza forms have special names. For example, ballad meter consists of four alternating iambic tetrameter and trimeter lines with a rhyme scheme of *a b c b*, whereas a Spenserian stanza consists of eight lines of iambic pentameter plus a ninth line of iambic hexameter, the whole having a rhyme scheme of *a b a b b c b c c*. Elegiac stanzas, rhyme royal, and ottava rima involve only iambic pentameter, with four, seven, and eight lines, respectively, and rhyme schemes of *a b a b, a b a b b c c,* and *a b a b a b c c*. In addition, meter and rhyme may prescribe the pattern for a whole poem, such as the LIMERICK or English SONNET.

Free Verse. Free verse, the principal vehicle of contemporary poetry, is, by these standards, not verse at all: that is, it is nonmetrical. Its only distinction from rhythmical prose is its arrangement on the page in lines of unequal length, determined by the writer on aesthetic grounds of cadence, breath, sound, or meaning. In prose the lines are of an equal length determined by the printer; thus, free verse has one rhythmical feature that prose lacks, the extra brief pause that usually accompanies a line end. The difference, however, is slight. Yeats divided a passage from Pater's prose into cadenced lines of unequal length and included it in his *Oxford Book of Modern Verse* (1936). It is a poem, but it is not verse in the sense of having identifiable meter.

Poetry. POETRY may be composed in either prose or verse. "Thirty days hath September, / April, June, and November" is verse but not poetry; Melville's *Moby-Dick* is prose but is highly poetic. That *Moby-Dick*, however poetic, is not a poem may be argued; but the issue is complicated by the prose poems of writers as diverse as Amy Lowell, Karl Shapiro, and Russell Edson. Verse and prose are mediums of meaning, and either may be the medium of poetry.

GLOSSARY

Accent. Special emphasis given to a syllable in pronunciation as a result of pitch, loudness, duration, and timbre. Usually used synonymously with stress.

Accentual meter. A meter in which only the number of accents is counted.

Accentual-syllabic meter. A meter in which there is a correspondence between the number of accents and the number of syllables, either two syllables for every accent (as in iambic and trochaic) or three syllables for every accent (as in anapestic and dactylic).

Alexandrine. A line of iambic hexameter.

Alliteration. The repetition of consonant sounds.

Anapest. A three-syllable poetic foot accented on the last syllable.

Assonance. The repetition of the same vowel sound.

Blank verse. Unrhymed iambic pentameter.

Caesura. An internal pause in a line, usually but not necessarily marked off by punctuation, which does not affect the meter.

Couplet. A pair of lines, usually rhymed and usually having the same meter.

Dactyl. A three-syllable poetic foot accented on the first syllable.

Dimeter. A line of two feet.

End-stopped line. A line followed by a long pause, usually marked off by punctuation.

Enjambment. The flowing of the sense from one line into the next without interruption; the use of run-on lines.

Foot. A metrical unit containing one stressed syllable and usually one or two unstressed syllables.

Free verse. Rhythmical but nonmetrical lines used as a medium for poetry.

Heroic couplet. A rhyming iambic pentameter couplet.

Heptameter. A line of seven feet.

Hexameter. A line of six feet.

Iamb. A two-syllable poetic foot accented on the second syllable.

Meter. An ordered pattern of accents, rhythm that can be measured.

Monosyllabic foot. A poetic foot containing one syllable only.

Octameter. A line of eight feet.

Onomatopoeia. The use of words whose sounds imitate their meaning, as *hiss, bang, buzz.*

Pentameter. A line of five feet.

Pyrrhic. A substitute poetic foot consisting of two unstressed syllables, always followed by a spondee.

Scansion. The analysis of meter, usually with the aid of some graphic system of notation.

Spondee. A two-syllable substitute poetic foot in which both syllables are accented but the accent is conceived of as being divided between the two syllables.

Stanza. A repeated unit of lines with a prescribed meter and rhyme scheme.

Syllabic meter. A form of meter in which syllables only are counted; typical of Japanese verse, as in the haiku, and occasionally used by English and American poets.

Tetrameter. A line of four feet.

Trimeter. A line of three feet.

Trochee. A two-syllable poetic foot accented on the first syllable.
                                        LAURENCE PERRINE

Bibliography: Altenbernd, Lynn, and Lewis, Leslie, *A Handbook for the Study of Poetry* (1966); Chatman, Seymour, *A Theory of Meter* (1964); Fussell, Paul, Jr., *Poetic Meter and Poetic Form*, rev. ed. (1978); Gross, Harvey, *Sound and Form in Modern Poetry* (1964); Malof, Joseph, *A Manual of English Meters* (1970); Perrine, Laurence, *Sound and Sense: An Introduction to Poetry*, 5th ed. (1977); Preminger, Alex, ed., *The Princeton Encyclopedia of Poetry and Poetics*, rev. ed. (1974); Shapiro, Karl, and Beum, Robert, *A Prosody Handbook* (1965).

Verspronck, Johannes Cornelisz.   [vur-sprawnk']

The Dutch portraitist Johannes Cornelisz. Verspronck, 1597-1662, studied first with his father, Cornelis Engelsz. Verspronck. Later he became a pupil and follower of Frans Hals, making use of the balanced and circumscribed compositions Hals used in the 1630s. Verspronck did not, however, emulate the painterly and intense manner of Hals's later years but remained instead a skilled yet pedestrian portraitist. One of his best works is *A Girl in Blue* (1641; Rijksmuseum, Amsterdam), which is painted in the objective, impersonal style of most Dutch portraits prior to the late work of Rembrandt and Hals.

Bibliography: Rosenberg, Jacob, et al., *Dutch Art and Architecture, 1600-1800* (1966).

vertebrae: see SPINE.

vertebrate: see CHORDATE.

Vértesszöllös   [vair'-tes-surl-lursh]

Near the village of Vértesszöllös, 50 km (31 mi) west of Budapest, Hungary, lies an open-air campsite dating from the Middle Pleistocene Epoch, about 500,000 years ago. It is the earliest known deposit in Europe where human remains are clearly associated with abundant archaeological material of the Lower Paleolithic Period. Living floors, butchering sites, and scavenging areas containing bones and artifacts were excavated in three different localities composed of travertine basins filled with layers of lime and loess. Part of a human skull was also found, showing anatomical characteristics intermediate between the species *Homo erectus* and *Homo sapiens*. The stone industry is in the Pebble Tool tradition and includes, besides choppers and chopping tools, thousands of scrapers and other roughly chipped flake tools. Horses, deer, bison, and rhinoceroses are the principal animals that were hunted, and some of their bones seem to have been chipped and used as tools. Small layers of burned bone were also found, constituting the earliest clear evidence for domestic hearths in Europe.
                                        JACQUES BORDAZ

Bibliography: Vértes, Laszlo, "The Lower Paleolithic Site of Vértesszöllös, Hungary" in *Recent Archaeological Excavations in Europe*, ed. by Rupert Bruce-Mitford (1975).

Vertical Takeoff and Landing Aircraft: see VTOL.

vertigo

Vertigo is a hallucination of spinning, either of oneself or of one's environment, that may be experienced as a sensation of imminent loss of consciousness, as a loss of balance without abnormal sensation, or as a vague lightheadedness. It is a subjective symptom or complaint rather than a disease, and it can occur in several physical disorders, including dysfunction of the vestibular organs of the ear (organs of balance), the brain, eyes, gastrointestinal tract, or other organs. It can also occur in the absence of organic disease, as in hyperventilation brought on by anxiety; as a result of excessive use of alcohol or drugs; or as a result of motion sickness or fear of heights.
                                        PETER L. PETRAKIS

Vertov, Dziga   [vair'-tuhf]

Soviet filmmaker Dziga Vertov, pseudonym of Denis Kaufman, b. Jan. 2 (N.S.), 1896, d. Feb. 12, 1954, revolutionized the production of newsreel and documentary films. Beginning his career in 1918 as a newsreel editor for the Moscow Film Committee, Vertov displayed his new techniques to advantage in a newsreel series he produced (1922-25) and in informational films about Soviet achievements made for the Kino-Glaz group. His full-length documentary features include *The Man with the Movie Camera* (1929) and, following the introduction of sound, *Enthusiasm* (1931), *Three Songs About Lenin* (1934), and *Lullaby* (1937). Although his aesthetic leanings were disapproved of during the most repressive Stalinist years, Vertov greatly influenced Western European documentary filmmakers.

Verwey, Albert   [fair-vy']

Albert Verwey, b. May 15, 1865, d. Mar. 8, 1937, was originally a leader of the Dutch literary revival, *Beweging van Tachtig*, or '80s poets, and edited its journal, *De Nieuwe Gids* (The New Guide). Verwey grew dissatisfied with the individualism and impressionism of the movement, however, and became one of its leading opponents. In his own journal, *De Beweging* (The Movement, 1905-19), he advocated a cerebral and contemplative poetry and argued that the poet should be the spiritual leader of the community.   THEO D'HAEN

Verwoerd, Hendrik F.   [fur-vohrt']

Hendrik Verwoerd was elected prime minister of South Africa in 1958. A staunch advocate of apartheid, Verwoerd promoted the establishment of Bantu homelands and separate black universities. Prior to his political career, he had worked as a university professor and newspaper editor. Verwoerd was assassinated in 1966.

Hendrik Frensch Verwoerd, b. Sept. 8, 1901, d. Sept. 6, 1966, prime minister of South Africa (1958-66), was a leading figure in the establishment of APARTHEID in his country. As an infant he emigrated from Holland to South Africa with his parents. He later taught (1927-37) psychology and sociology at Stellenbosch University and then became editor of *Die Transvaaler*. A critic of Gen. Jan Smuts, he opposed South Africa's entry into World War II and favored a separate peace with Germany. As minister of native affairs (1950-58), he directed much apartheid legislation through parliament.

In 1958, Verwoerd was elected leader of the National party and prime minister. He stood for an uncompromising policy of apartheid and played a major part in setting up Bantu "homelands" and separate black universities, but he relinquished the National party's previous policy of repatriating the Indians. His administration suppressed antiapartheid organizations and demonstrations but also carried out major slum-clearance schemes and encouraged industrial development in the "homelands." Verwoerd was responsible for turning South Africa into a republic (1961). He died by assassination.
                                        L. H. GANN

Bibliography: Barnard, J. F., *Thirteen Years with Dr. H. F. Verwoerd* (1968); Hepple, Alexander, *Verwoerd* (1967).

Very Large Array: see NATIONAL RADIO ASTRONOMY OBSERVATORY.

Vesaas, Tarjei [vay'-sohs]

The poetic, often allegorical novels of Tarjei Vesaas, b. Aug. 20, 1897, d. Mar. 15, 1970, gained him international recognition and an important place in 20th-century Norwegian letters. His early novels treated rural problems and characters. *The Seed* (1940; Eng. trans., 1964), dramatizing the struggle between good and evil, with allegorical references to wartime Europe, marked a new, symbolic phase in his career. Both his short stories, collected in *Vindane* (Winds, 1952), and his several volumes of poetry are highly regarded.

Vesalius, Andreas [vuh-say'-lee-uhs]

Andreas Vesalius, b. Dec. 31, 1514, d. Oct. 15, 1564, was the Flemish anatomist and physician whose pioneering dissections of human cadavers and careful descriptions of human anatomy helped establish modern observational science. He is often called the father of anatomy. His major work, *De humani corporis fabrica* (On the Structure of the Human Body), a beautifully illustrated text of human anatomy, was published in 1543. Vesalius was physician to the Holy Roman emperor Charles V and to Philip II, king of Spain.

Bibliography: O'Malley, Charles D., *Andreas Vesalius of Brussels* (1964); Tarshis, Jerome, *Father of Modern Anatomy: Andreas Vesalius* (1969).

Vesey, Denmark [vee'-zee]

The leader of an American slave revolt in Charleston, S.C., Denmark Vesey, b. Africa, 1767, d. July 2, 1822, had been owned by a slave-ship captain before he purchased his freedom (1800) with $600 won in a street lottery. As a freedman in Charleston, he worked at carpentry, became a leader of his church, and read antislavery literature. Determined to strike a blow against the institution that had victimized him, he devised an intricate conspiracy for an uprising in Charleston and vicinity during the summer of 1822. Informers divulged the plot, however, and 35 blacks, including Vesey, were executed.

RONALD L. LEWIS

Bibliography: Lofton, John, *Insurrection in South Carolina: The Turbulent World of Denmark Vesey* (1964); Starobin, Robert S., ed., *Denmark Vesey: The Slave Conspiracy of 1822* (1970).

Vespasian, Roman Emperor [ves-payz'-ee-uhn]

Titus Flavius Vespasianus became Roman emperor in AD 69. During his reign Vespasian enlarged the empire by annexing parts of Germany and Anatolia, began building the Forum and Colosseum, and instituted financial reforms. His son Titus succeeded him in 79.

Vespasian, b. Nov. 17, AD 9, d. June 4, 79, Roman emperor (r. 69–79) and founder of the Flavian dynasty (69–96), pacified and strengthened the empire and pursued enlightened domestic policies. Having held many political and military offices, he was given the command against the Jewish rebels in 67. During this campaign, the eastern armies proclaimed him emperor (July 69). Having engineered the defeat of Vitellius, the last of the three imperial claimants following the death of NERO in 68, he was confirmed (December 69) by the Senate as emperor.

After satisfactorily ending the Jewish war and a Rhineland revolt, Vespasian turned to domestic reform. He eliminated Nero's treasury deficit through economy and increased taxation, while beginning construction of the COLOSSEUM and other monuments in Rome. His foreign policies included the Romanization of provincials through grants of citizenship to selected towns, and annexations of territory in Anatolia and Germany. He also strengthened Roman rule in Wales and sent troops into Scotland.

To prevent a recurrence of civil war, Vespasian designated his son TITUS as his successor and appointed him prefect of the often volatile Praetorian guard. When Vespasian died, Titus succeeded him, with the guard's and the Senate's support.

JOHN W. EADIE

Bibliography: Henderson, B. W., *Five Roman Emperors* (1927; repr. 1969); McCrum, M. W., and Woodhead, A. G., *Select Documents of the Principates of the Flavian Emperors* (1961).

vespers: see DIVINE OFFICE.

Vespucci, Amerigo [ves-poot'-chee]

Amerigo Vespucci, b. Florence, 1454, d. Feb. 22, 1512, an Italian explorer and navigator whose name was given to the New World, was the first to describe the Western Hemisphere as a previously unknown continent rather than as a part of Asia. Trained for a business career, he settled (1491) in Seville at a Medici bank branch. Of his four possible voyages to the New World between 1497 and 1504, only the second and third are certain. He claimed a 1497 voyage, under Spanish auspices, that reached the Central American mainland. His 1499 voyage, undertaken for Spain and commanded by Alonso de Ojeda, discovered Brazil and sailed northwest to Venezuela and then to Hispaniola. In 1501 he sailed to Brazil on Portugal's behalf and then continued south at least to the Río de la Plata. This voyage convinced him that he was exploring a new continent. Another expedition may have taken place in 1503–04, again to Brazil in Portugal's service.

In 1507 the German cartographer Martin Waldseemüller published an account of Vespucci's voyages, along with a map and a treatise, *Cosmographiae introductio* (Introduction to Cosmography); Waldseemüller was the first to use the name *America* for the region Vespucci had explored. The following year Vespucci was named to the prestigious post of pilot major for Spain, with responsibility for training and examining pilots and control of the master map.

BRUCE B. SOLNICK

Bibliography: Arciniegas, Germán, *Amerigo and the New World: The Life and Times of Amerigo Vespucci* (1955); Pohl, Frederick J., *Amerigo Vespucci, Pilot Major* (1944; repr. 1966).

Vesta [ves'-tuh]

In Roman mythology, Vesta was the goddess of the hearth and symbol of the home. She watched particularly over households and family activities, and families made offerings to her at mealtime. Vesta was portrayed as a robed and veiled figure holding a scepter in one hand and the PALLADIUM in the other. She was identified with the Greek goddess HESTIA.

Vesta was worshiped both in individual homes and at a public shrine, where an eternal flame was tended by six vestal virgins. If one of these maidens lost her virginity during her 30-year term of duty, she was buried alive. If she permitted the fire to go out, she was flogged. The cult of the vestal virgins lasted into the early Christian period.

vestal virgins: see VESTA.

Vestdijk, Simon [vest'-dayk]

The Dutch writer Simon Vestdijk, b. Oct. 17, 1898, d. Mar. 23, 1971, published more than 60 novels and short stories, 20 volumes of poetry, and numerous essays. Reacting against the excesses of expressionism, Vestdijk advocated ethical, social, and aesthetic concerns in literature. His major works include the eight-volume Anton Wachter series (1934–60), about a fictional alter ego, and the novel *The Garden Where the Brass Band Played* (1950; Eng. trans., 1965). THEO D'HAEN

vestments

Vestments are ceremonial garments worn by religious functionaries while performing sacred rites. In many religious traditions priests wear clothing that distinguishes them from the nonreligious; vestments, however, are associated with specific rituals and were traditionally given symbolic meanings. Among Christians, for example, the stole, a scarf adopted as the distinctive sign of the ordained minister, was traditionally viewed as a yoke, symbolizing that the wearer was a servant of God. The eucharistic vestments worn by Roman Catholics, Episcopalians, and Lutherans include the alb, a white floor-length tunic (symbolizing purity) tied at the waist with a rope cincture, over which is worn the chasuble, a full cloak put on over the head. The amice, often made in the form of a collar or hood (symbolizing the helmet of salvation), is wrapped around the neck under the alb. The maniple, a length of material worn over the left arm, was originally a napkin and symbolizes the role of the minister as servant of the people of God. All of these garments are of early Christian origin (the stole, alb, and chasuble were derived from 4th-century Roman dress) and had become the liturgical norm by the 10th century. Later, other originally nonliturgical garments entered liturgical use. The black, full-length cassock, originally the outdoor dress of clergymen, was often retained under the liturgical vestments. Today the cassock is often worn with a white surplice, a full garment originally designed to cover the fur vests needed in cold churches. The Geneva, or pulpit, gown today worn for church services by many Protestant clergy was, with the cassock, the ordinary dress of ministers in the 16th century.

Although the priests of ancient Judaism had elaborate sacerdotal vestments, prescribed in Exodus 28, these disappeared, along with the priestly function, after the destruction of the Temple in AD 70. Modern rabbis generally wear black gowns of the Protestant type during synagogue services.

The process by which ordinary clothing of earlier eras becomes the religious vestments of a later time is also seen in other religious traditions, such as Buddhism and Shinto. L. L. MITCHELL

Bibliography: Mayo, Janet, *A History of Ecclesiastical Dress* (1984).

Vestris (family) [ves'-tris]

The Vestris family, one of several important theatrical dynasties of the pre-romantic period, originated in Florence. **Teresa** (1726–1808), **Gaetano** (1728–1808), and **Angiolo** (1730–1809), children of **Tommaso Vestris**, were all dancers, of whom Gaetano, known as the God of the Dance, was the most celebrated and influential. His enormous vanity was justified by his artistry and virtuosity if not by his looks. Gaetano made his debut at the Paris Opéra in 1748, was appointed principal dancer in 1751, co-choreographer with Jean DAUBERVAL in 1761, and chief choreographer in 1770; he ceded this post to Jean Georges NOVERRE, with whom he had worked in Stuttgart, in 1776. Gaetano retired from the stage in 1782 but continued to teach in the Opéra school. His chief pupil was **Auguste** (1760–1842), his illegitimate son by the dancer Marie Allard; Auguste made his debut in 1772. When Vestris and his son appeared together in London in 1781, Parliament suspended its sessions.

Auguste was, like his father, ugly, conceited, and a technical prodigy. During the French Revolution, Auguste fled to London and worked with Noverre, returning to Paris in triumph in 1793 where he continued to dance until 1816. Auguste became a great teacher whose pupils included Charles Didelot, Jules Perrot, August Bournonville, and Marie Taglioni. Auguste's son **Armand** (1786–1825) studied with Gaetano and made his debut at the Paris Opéra at the age of 4, with his father and grandfather. Armand worked mostly in London (1809–16) as a dancer and choreographer. He was married briefly to Lucia Elisabetta Bartolozzi, the famous Madame Vestris. DAVID VAUGHAN

Bibliography: Winter, Marian Hannah, *The Pre-Romantic Ballet* (1975).

Vestris, Madame

Madame Vestris was the stage name of the English actress and theater manager Lucia Elisabetta Bartolozzi, b. London, Jan. 3, 1797, d. Aug. 8, 1856. Upon leasing (1831) London's Olympic Theatre, she transformed it into a showcase for the realistic presentation of drama by introducing, among other innovations, the three-walled "box" set with a ceiling, the first literal on-stage representation of a room. With her second husband, Charles James MATHEWS, she managed (1839–42) Covent Garden.

Bibliography: Appleton, W., *Madame Vestris and the London Stage* (1974).

Vesuvius [vuh-soo'-vee-uhs]

Mount Vesuvius (Italian: Vesuvio), the only active volcano on the mainland of Europe, is located about 15 km (9 mi) southeast of Naples on the Bay of Naples in southern Italy. The volcano's crater, approximately 600 m (2,000 ft) in diameter and 300 m (1,000 ft) deep, lies within the remains of Monte Somma, a much larger ancient volcano from the late Pleistocene Epoch. The height of the volcano, which varies with each eruption, was 1,280 m (4,199 ft) in 1970. The fertile volcanic soil on the mountainsides supports vegetable gardens and orchards near the base, vineyards on the lower slopes, and oak and chestnut forests below the lava fields.

Before AD 79, when a tremendous eruption buried the cities of HERCULANEUM, POMPEII, and Stabiae at its base, Vesuvius was thought to be extinct. From that time to 1631, when another major eruption occurred, about 10 smaller eruptions were recorded. Since 1631, Vesuvius has been continuously active, erupting 20 times; the most devastating eruptions occurred in 1794, 1872, and 1906. The volcano's activity is now carefully monitored.

Bibliography: Marx, Walter H., *Claimed by Vesuvius* (1975); Temple, F. J., *Vesuvius*, trans. by Gregory Barr (1977).

vetch

Vetch (or *tare*) is the common name for about 150 mostly north temperate and South American species of climbing or straggling, weak-stemmed, viny herbs in the genus *Vicia* of the pea family, Leguminosae. They have compound leaves and the terminal leaflets are transformed into tendrils. Some are cultivated as forage crops (hay, pasture, and silage); others are used as cover crops and as green manure, because they are legumes. OSWALD TIPPO

Veterans Administration

The Veterans Administration (VA) is an independent U.S. governmental agency created in 1930, supplanting the U.S. Veterans Bureau, the Bureau of Pensions, and the National Home for Disabled Volunteer Soldiers. In 1988 the VA was raised to cabinet rank, becoming the Department of Veterans Affairs in March 1989. The VA provides a wide range of services for veterans and their dependents, including hospital, nursing-home, and domiciliary care for eligible veterans, plus outpatient medical and dental care. It administers veteran pension plans and other forms of compensation to veterans. The VA also directs the handling of educational programs, veterans' insurance policies, veterans' burial programs, and loans to veterans for houses, farms, and business investments. It administers various rehabilitation programs for veterans as well.

In 1986 the VA operated 172 hospitals, 16 domiciliaries, 228 clinics, and 116 nursing home units throughout the United States, Puerto Rico, and the Philippines. The first benefits for veterans in America were approved by the Plymouth Colony in 1636.

Bibliography: Israel, F., ed., *Veteran's Administration* (1987); Levitan, S., and Cleary, K., *Old Wars Remain Unfinished* (1973); Starr, P., et al., *The Discarded Army* (1974); Wetle, T., and Rowe, J., eds., *Older Veterans: Linking VA and Community Resources* (1985).

Veterans Day: see MEMORIAL DAY.

Veterans of Foreign Wars

The Veterans of Foreign Wars (VFW) is a nationwide organization of U.S. veterans headquartered in Kansas City, Mo. The VFW was created in 1914 through the merger of three associations of veterans of the Spanish-American War and chartered by Congress in 1936. Membership is open to men who have served overseas in any branch of the military. A Ladies Auxiliary is open to female relatives of veterans and to women who have served overseas in the armed forces. Among the goals of the VFW are encouragement of patriotism, the provision of aid for disabled or needy veterans and their dependents, and the promotion of national security. The VFW also sponsors community-service and youth-activity programs through about 10,000 local posts, and it maintains the VFW National Home for the children of deceased or disabled members, in Eaton Rapids, Mich.

veterans' organizations

Veterans' organizations are voluntary associations of former military personnel. They are found in many countries of the world and range from purely social organizations to active political associations. In the United States the two most powerful are the AMERICAN LEGION (founded 1919) and the Veterans of Foreign Wars (VFW; created 1914). Both maintain permanent lobbies in Washington. Most veterans' groups are patriotic and have membership qualifications, such as being limited to veterans who served in one of the armed forces during wartime or to certain categories of veterans (for example, the DISABLED AMERICAN VETERANS, those who have received a certain distinction in battle, or those who have served overseas—the VFW). They have an international coordinating body, the World Veterans Federation, which currently has 160 affiliates in 52 countries.

The principal activity of most veterans' organizations is providing for the welfare of former service personnel; many have programs of vocational training, particularly for the disabled, provide funds for the needy and their dependents, and are involved in social welfare. They are especially active in promoting legislation that aids veterans. Their stands on other national policies are of considerable influence, and candidates for political office frequently seek their endorsement.

Veterans' organizations have existed for centuries. In ancient Rome veterans of the wars against the barbarians were a potent political force. Among early American groups the Society of the Cincinnati (see CINCINNATI, SOCIETY OF THE), for example, was founded in 1783 by men who had been officers in the American Revolution, and the GRAND ARMY OF THE REPUBLIC was founded by Union soldiers after the Civil War. The ranks of veterans' groups, however, increased dramatically during the 20th century. Following World War II more than 700 veterans' organizations were formed in the United States alone, although most of them did not survive long. The British Legion, founded after World War I, is open to all men and women who served in the armed forces of the United Kingdom or its allies; it has numerous branches at home and overseas. Principal French veterans' organizations are the Fédération Nationale des Anciens Combattants and the Société Nationale des Médaillés Militaires (open to recipients of French military decorations).

Bibliography: Baker, R., *The American Legion and American Foreign Policy* (1974); Minott, R. G., *Peerless Patriots* (1962).

veterinary medicine

Veterinary medicine is that part of biology that deals with the health and disease of animals (see DISEASES, ANIMAL). Traditionally, it has principally involved the cure and treatment of disease; however, the emphasis is changing. Although cures and treatment are important, promotion of health is assuming its rightful place in veterinary medicine.

Veterinary medicine is concerned with a variety of animal species other than humans in a multitude of environmental circumstances. Humans are, however, the primary beneficiary of veterinary efforts. The practice of veterinary medicine may be applied by the veterinarian at a minimum of five levels: health promotion; specific prevention or protection; early diagnosis and prompt treatment; disability limitation; and rehabilitation or salvage.

History. Veterinary practice is probably as old as the domestication of animals. There are written records from 2000 BC in ancient Egypt and Babylonia. Aristotle and others wrote extensively describing veterinary practices in the Greek city-states. (The term itself is derived from a Latin word meaning "beasts of burden.") In the pre-Christian era no sharp distinction was made between the practice of human and of animal medicine. With the development of Judeo-Christian philosophies, however, the uniqueness of humans was emphasized. This caused a sharp line to be drawn between the physician and the veterinarian.

It was not until the 18th century that the veterinary profession developed in an ordered manner, after the founding of a college in Lyon, France. It had taken the Renaissance and Reformation to advance the science and art of all medical practice. Much of the present status and prestige of the veterinary profession has been realized only in the relatively brief period since World War II. The decline in the use of animals for power because of the competition of the internal-combustion engine and the phenomenal development of animal agriculture caused the significant changes, prevalent in the Western world, in veterinary emphasis.

Education. As a consequence of changing needs and demand for veterinary service, the veterinary colleges in the United States have improved curricula and expanded facilities. A minimum of 6 years' academic preparation is now required before the student can become a doctor of veterinary medicine. The curriculum in the last 4 years includes the basic sciences, anatomy, physiology, pharmacology, pathobiology, microbiology, and the applied areas. These areas of study include basic principles and concepts as well as practical applications in diagnosis, therapy, preventive medicine, surgery, radiology, and many other areas of specialization. Only 31 colleges of veterinary medicine presently exist in the United States and Canada. Consequently, applicants must meet rigorous academic standards and must exhibit high motivation.

Profession. As of 1987 the American Veterinary Medical Association had a membership of about 43,000 veterinarians, a figure that represented 80 to 85 percent of all practicing U.S. veterinarians. Approximately 75 percent of these engage in private practice, and the remaining 25 percent are employed in governmental agencies, educational and research institutions, such industries as drug production, and a variety of miscellaneous enterprises.

About one-half of the veterinarians engaged in private practice confine their activities exclusively to pet or companion animals. The balance have what might be termed a "mixed" practice. Part of their time is spent on companion animals and part on food-producing or economic animals. Less than 10 percent of these veterinarians confine their activities to food or economic animals. Veterinarians in private practice spend most of their time with acute procedures (medical visits or calls and nonelective surgery) and preventive medical activities (routine medical visits or calls and examinations). A sizable portion of their time is spent in elective surgery, although this is a very small segment for exclusively economic-animal practitioners.

Veterinarians outside of private practice are a much more diverse group. Their efforts range from primary animal health care through human health programs, with emphasis on environmental health, and zoonotic disease programs. (Zoonotic diseases are those communicable from animals to humans.) Many are involved in teaching and research, and others in zoological work and wildlife programs. Several fields that may offer great opportunities for future veterinarians include SPACE MEDICINE, wildlife management, mariculture (cultivation of marine organisms), and marine biology.

Increased concern with human health, the environment, and food and product safety and quality has led to greatly increased research in these areas. Research programs as varied as cancer diagnosis and control, cardiovascular and respiratory health, sewage sludge use on farms, air pollution, and infectious, metabolic, and nutritional disease have been supervised by or have included veterinarians in their programs. Veterinarians historically have contributed much to basic and applied research in human medicine, zoonotic diseases, public health, and many agricultural and biological areas.

DAVID O. JONES

Bibliography: Baker, James, and Greer, William J., *Animal Health* (1979); Berrier, Harry H., *Animal Sanitation and Disease Prevention*, 2d ed. (1977); Breazile, James E., ed., *Textbook of Veterinary Physiology* (1971); Ensminger, M. Eugene, *Animal Science*, 7th ed. (1977); McHugh, Mary, *Veterinary Medicine and Animal Care Careers* (1977); Schwabe, Calvin W., *Veterinary Medicine and Human Health*, 2d ed. (1969) and *What Should a Veterinarian Do?* (1972); Siegmund, Otto H., *The Merck Veterinary Manual*, 5th ed. (1979); Smithcors, J. F., *The American Veterinary Profession* (1963) and *The Veterinarian in America, 1625–1975* (1975).

veto

A veto (Latin, "I forbid") is the right of one governmental branch (usually the executive) to refuse to assent to an act— or to negate an act—of another branch of government (usually the legislative). The veto can be absolute or limited. A limited veto is one that can be overridden in some way. An example of an absolute veto is the right of any one of the five permanent members of the United Nations Security Council to block action on nonprocedural matters.

Leaders of most modern governments have both formal and informal veto powers. The president of the United States has limited veto power granted by the U.S. Constitution (Article I, Section 7). A presidential veto can be overridden by a two-thirds majority in each house of Congress. The president can also use the so-called pocket veto: ordinarily if the president fails to act on legislation within 10 days of receiving it, it automatically becomes law; if Congress, however, adjourns before the 10 days have elapsed, the measure is automatically killed. The legislative veto (a device by which Congress grants the executive broad authority to act in a given area but reserves the right to veto any particular action taken under that authority) was declared unconstitutional by the U.S. Supreme Court in IMMIGRATION AND NATURALIZATION SERVICE V. CHADHA (1983).

In Great Britain the prime minister has an effective veto in his or her right to call for a general election before a vote is taken on a measure.

Bibliography: Jackson, Carlton, *Presidential Vetoes, 1792–1945* (1967).

viaduct [vy'-uh-duhkt]

A viaduct is a bridge that usually rests on arches with high supporting towers and that is used to carry a road or railway over a valley or the streets of a city. The Romans built long, low viaducts at Salamanca, Córdoba, and Merida in Spain, as well as many high, multitiered stone arch structures such as the Pont du Gard near Nîmes, France, which served as both aqueduct and viaduct.

From 1830 to 1860 more than 25,000 railroad bridges and viaducts were built in Great Britain alone. Isambard K. Brunel (see BRUNEL family) built a great number of timber viaducts for the Cornwall and Devon railways, with standard spans of 15 m (50 ft) and 20 m (65 ft). Although he used Baltic pine timber of the finest quality, none of his viaducts survived more than 60 years. In the last few decades reinforced concrete and

steel have replaced other materials used in viaduct construction.

SIR HUBERT SHIRLEY-SMITH

Bibliography: Joghekar, G. D., *Bridge Engineering* (1962); Sealey, Anthony, *Bridges and Aqueducts* (1976).

Vian, Boris [vee-ahn']

An iconoclastic French novelist, poet, playwright, and musician, Boris Vian, b. Mar. 10, 1920, d. June 23, 1959, was much admired in postwar France. With his first published novel, *J'irai cracher sur vos tombes* (I'll Spit on Your Graves, 1946), a parody of American hard-boiled detective fiction, he caused a scandal 'sufficient to have the book banned. Of Vian's more serious works, the surrealist *L'Écume des jours* (1947; trans. as *Mood Indigo*, 1969), a love story, is considered his best.

Vianney, Saint Jean Baptiste Marie [vee-ah-nay']

The patron saint of parish priests, Jean Baptiste Marie Vianney, b. May 8, 1786, d. Aug. 4, 1859, was the renowned priest and confessor of the French parish of Ars. He is known as the Curé of Ars. He achieved international fame as a spiritual counselor, with as many as 20,000 persons visiting him each year. He was canonized in 1925. Feast day: Aug. 4 (formerly Aug. 9).

Viardot-García, Pauline [vee-ahr-doh'-gar-see-ah']

Pauline Viardot-García, b. July 18, 1821, d. May 18, 1910, was a celebrated French mezzo-soprano and teacher and member of a notable musical family: her father, Manuel del Popolo García, was an outstanding tenor and teacher; her brother, Manuel Patricio García, a leading vocal teacher; her sister was the renowned contralto Maria Malibran. She was married to Louis Viardot, an eminent French journalist, and became the confidant of Ivan Turgenev. Pauline made her concert debut at the age of 16 and first appeared in opera at the age of 18. A mezzo-soprano with an unusually wide range, she created the roles of Fidès in Meyerbeer's *Le Prophète* (1849) and the title role in Gounod's first opera, *Sapho* (1851). After retiring from the stage in 1863, she taught at the Paris Conservatory and composed songs, chamber music, and operas (including *Le Dernier Sorcier*, 1869).

KAREN MONSON

Bibliography: Fitzlyon, April, *Price of Genius; a Life of Pauline Viardot* (1964); Pleasants, Henry, *Great Singers* (1966).

vibraphone

The vibraphone is a MARIMBA with metal bars and resonators that have a controlled vibrato caused by a motor-driven mechanism that opens and closes them, thus altering the tone color and volume. For stopping the sound, the instrument is equipped with a damper pedal. Interesting effects may be achieved through its possibilities for sustained tones and by manipulation of the damper pedal. The vibraphone is one of the few instruments developed in the United States. Berg, Messiaen, and Vaughan Williams have written for it, but it has been most popular in dance bands. The jazz musician Lionel Hampton brought it to wide public attention.

ELWYN A. WIENANDT

Vibrio [vib'-ree-oh]

Vibrio is a genus of bacteria belonging to the phylum Eubacteria and including *V. cholerae*, the agent causing CHOLERA. Vibrio are comma shaped (curved or bent rods), and all members of the group are motile and aerobic. Vibrio form endospores.

viburnum [vy-bur'-nuhm]

Viburnum, or arrowwood, is an important genus of about 225 species of ornamental shrubs and small trees in the honeysuckle family, Caprifoliaceae. Native to America, Europe, and Asia, these plants produce simple deciduous or evergreen

The viburnum species called "fragrant snowball," V. carlcephalum, justifies its name when in bloom. It also has red berries that turn black when ripe.

leaves, small white or pink flowers in flat-topped clusters, and small drupes.

Viburnums make attractive ornamentals, and many species are hardy in temperate North America. These plants enjoy sunlight, although they also do well in shade. The hobble-bush, *V. alnifolium*, is a popular deciduous shrub that turns purple-red in autumn. Many species bear fragrant flowers. Some species are grown for their hydrangealike flower heads, including the Japanese snowball, *V. plicatum*. Numerous varieties have been cultivated to accentuate these highly valued ornamental characteristics.

Vicar of Wakefield, The

The Vicar of Wakefield (1766) was Oliver GOLDSMITH's only novel. Samuel Johnson sold the novel in 1762. The £60 that it brought the impecunious Goldsmith helped him to continue writing. The novel recounts the misfortunes of an ineffective vicar, Charles Primrose, and his gentle family after they lose their income. Goldsmith was the son of a clergyman and perhaps drew on his own experience for this sentimental, pastoral portrait. Primrose bears his misfortunes with patience and dignity and finally witnesses the happy ending. The novel contains the well-known lyric "When Lovely Woman Stoops to Folly."
MARJORIE COLLINS

vice-president of the United States

The vice-presidency of the United States is one of the two positions in the government of the United States that is filled in an election open to all eligible voters in every state and the District of Columbia. The vice-president is the second highest ranking officer in the executive branch of the federal government, beneath only the president. Both serve concurrent 4-year terms. The constitutional duties of the vice-president are relatively unimportant, however, and traditionally vice-presidents have had little influence on public affairs. The Founding Fathers who wrote the U.S. Constitution in 1787 provided that all of the "executive power" would rest in the hands of the president. Almost as an afterthought, they created the office of vice-president in order to provide for a successor should the president die or resign.

The significance of the office relates almost entirely to the fact that the vice-president succeeds to the presidency if the president dies, resigns, or is removed from office through the impeachment process. Altogether, eight presidents have died in office, and one has resigned. With the adoption in 1967 of the 25TH AMENDMENT to the U.S. Constitution, it is also possible for the vice-president to assume the duties of the presidency if the president becomes disabled.

President of the Senate. The vice-president is assigned only one responsibility by the Constitution, and that is in the legislative branch, not the executive branch. The vice-president is designated as the presiding officer of the Senate of the United States and has the additional responsibility of casting a tie-breaking vote whenever the votes of the senators are evenly divided on any roll call.

The vice-president's role as president of the Senate has not proved to be significant. The rules of parliamentary procedure adopted by the Senate provide little opportunity for the presiding officer to affect the course of the deliberations or to exercise political influence. By custom, the vice-president does not speak except to issue rulings, and the members of the Senate generally discourage the vice-president from lobbying in the Senate chamber in support of a bill favored by the administration. Behind the scenes, however, some vice-presidents, particularly those who have previously served in the Senate, have been effective in winning votes for bills favored by the administration and in explaining administration policies to the members of the Senate and House of Representatives. In practice, the vice-president does not preside over the Senate with any frequency, except for ceremonial occasions. The duty is usually delegated to a junior member of the Senate.

The responsibility for casting tie-breaking votes is not a great one. First, if a vote on a measure has ended in a tie, it is regarded as defeated, and a negative vote by the vice-president would be superfluous. Thus, only if the vice-president favors a particular measure and casts an affirmative vote can the tie-breaking vote prove decisive. Second, tie votes do not occur often. For example, Richard Nixon cast only 8 votes during 8 years as vice-president. The growth in the size of the Senate has reduced the statistical likelihood that tie votes will occur. Furthermore, most issues are negotiated in advance among influential members of the Senate, so that a clear majority for or against a particular bill is usually formed before the actual vote is taken.

Nomination and Election. The U.S. Constitution as ratified in 1789 established a system for electing presidents and vice-presidents that remained in effect for only 15 years. In each presidential election the electors chosen by the states cast their ballots for president and vice-president. Each elector was permitted to vote for two candidates but was not permitted to indicate which choice he preferred for president and which for vice-president. The authors of the Constitution reasoned that an elector might well cast one vote for a resident of his own state and give the other vote to a political leader with a national reputation, and that when all of the votes were counted such a national figure would emerge with the

Lyndon Baines Johnson, who served as vice-president under President John F. Kennedy, takes the presidential oath shortly after Kennedy's assassination on Nov. 22, 1963. Jacqueline Kennedy looks on as U.S. District Court Judge Sarah Hughes administers the oath.

most votes—and, hence, the presidency. It was further reasoned that the person who received the second greatest number of votes—hence, the vice-presidency—would also be some person of national reputation and the next best qualified person to serve as president.

The formation of political parties during the 1790s undermined the logic of this system, however. Each political party began to put up two-man teams, and the electors chosen by that party would vote for both men. In 1800 the candidates of the majority party, Thomas Jefferson and Aaron Burr, each received the same number (73) of electoral votes. Because of the tie, the responsibility for choosing the president fell to the House of Representatives. Everyone knew that Jefferson was the intended choice for president and Burr for vice-president, but the ambitious Burr allowed his name to remain in the running for the presidency, and he was supported by members of the House who opposed Jefferson.

As a result, although Jefferson was ultimately chosen by the House, it was apparent that the electoral system had to be abandoned. The 12TH AMENDMENT to the Constitution, adopted in 1804, provided that the electors vote separately for the offices of president and vice-president.

The 12th Amendment created a new problem. American political parties traditionally have been composed of several factions. Parties quickly discovered a means of achieving a semblance of unity during each election campaign. After the contest for the presidential nomination was settled, the party leaders usually sought to console the losing faction by giving one of its members the nomination for vice-president, a process known as balancing the ticket.

This development, however, meant that if a president died in office it was highly possible that he would be succeeded by someone who had substantially different views on major issues. This situation arose on several occasions. As a result, the ideologically balanced ticket concept gradually fell into disfavor. Since World War II most party leaders have sought to nominate tickets composed of candidates who generally see eye-to-eye on key issues. Balance is achieved by other means, usually by nominating a candidate who comes from a different part of the country, who represents a different ethnic background, or who has acquired different kinds of experience in public service.

In modern practice the presidential nominee consults with his advisors and with party leaders at the convention and then announces his choice for his vice-president, that is, running mate. (The one exception was in 1956, when Adlai E. Stevenson allowed the delegates of the Democratic Convention to select his running mate.) The presidential nominee's choice is invariably nominated, although seldom unanimously. Because the vice-presidential nominees are often chosen in haste, failures in judgment can occur. In 1972, Sen. George McGovern chose Sen. Thomas Eagleton to be his running mate on the Democratic ticket. McGovern later learned that Eagleton had been treated for depression and persuaded him to resign from the ticket. Spiro T. Agnew, who was twice chosen (1968, 1972) by Richard Nixon as his running mate, was forced to resign in 1973 after pleading "no contest" to a charge of income tax evasion.

All major-party nominees for president and vice-president had been white males until 1984, when the Democrats nominated Geraldine Ferraro for the vice-presidency. Blacks have recently also received serious consideration for the post.

The Succession Problem. The Constitution originally provided that "In Case of the Removal of the President from Office, or of his Death, Resignation, or Inability to discharge the Powers and Duties of the said Office, the Same shall devolve on the Vice President. . . ." Years later, a controversy arose over whether "the Same" referred to "Powers and Duties" or to "Office." In 1841, when President William Henry Harrison died in office, Vice-President John Tyler took the presidential oath and subsequently asserted that he was in fact holding the office of president, not merely performing the powers and duties of the presidency. Although some contemporaries (and some constitutional scholars today) disagreed with Tyler's interpretation of the Constitution, no serious challenge was

A cartoon appearing in the May 1, 1900, edition of the New York Telegram *shows Republican senator Mark Hanna shaping the second-term ticket of William McKinley with a protesting Theodore Roosevelt as the vice-presidential candidate. Roosevelt feared that the vice-presidency would neutralize his political influence. In fact, however, the office brought him to the presidency on the assassination of McKinley in September 1901.*

made to his assumption of the presidency, and his viewpoint prevailed. In all subsequent instances in which a president had died, his successor has been accepted by the public as the president both in power and in fact.

Tyler's precedent, however, brought on another dilemma. On several occasions a president has become disabled. In each instance the vice-president has chosen not to take action in accord with the provision of the Constitution quoted herein, for fear that the disabled president might regain his health and seek to reclaim his office. If his successor was in fact president, not merely performing the powers and duties of the office, then there would be no constitutional means of returning the office to the recovered president.

The 25th Amendment to the Constitution, ratified in 1967, sought to remedy that situation. The amendment provides that if a president is disabled, the vice-president may exercise the powers and duties of the office, but only as acting president. The president, upon his recovery, may resume his duties. The authors of the amendment devised a complicated formula to help resolve any controversy that might arise between the president and vice-president over whether or not the former was physically able to perform his duties.

Before 1967 the office of vice-president had been vacant 16 times as a result of the deaths of 8 presidents and 7 vice-presidents and the resignation of one vice-president. The 25th Amendment also created a means of filling such vacancies when they occur. It provided that if the office of vice-president becomes vacant, the president must nominate someone to fill the vacancy. On approval of both houses of the Congress, the nominee is sworn in as vice-president.

During the devastating political scandals of the early 1970s, this section of the amendment was applied twice. In 1973, after Vice-President Spiro Agnew resigned, President Nixon nominated Rep. Gerald R. Ford to succeed Agnew. After a careful investigation by the Congress, Ford's nomination was approved. Vice-President Ford, in turn, succeeded to the presidency when Nixon resigned after being implicated in the Watergate affair. Ford nominated Nelson A. Rockefeller for vice-president, and the latter was approved by the Congress.

The Constitution gives the Congress the responsibility for providing for the order of succession to the presidency should the offices of both president and vice-president be vacant at the same time. The succession statute was most recently rewritten in 1947, when Congress established the succession in this order: the Speaker of the House of Representatives, the president pro tempore of the Senate, and the heads of the departments in the executive branch of the federal government, in the order in which the departments were created, beginning with the secretary of state. The succession

A contemporary cartoon (1832) portrays Martin Van Buren, rejected by the Senate for an appointive post, reaching office on the back of President Andrew Jackson. Jackson's support led to Van Buren's nomination as vice-president and later to his election as president.

has never passed below the vice-president, although this would have occurred in 1974, when Nixon resigned, had not the 25th Amendment provided for the filling of the vacancy created by Agnew's resignation a year earlier.

Political History of the Office. The most memorable event in the early history of the vice-presidency (after the Jefferson-Burr controversy) was the competition between John C. Calhoun and Martin Van Buren to succeed President Andrew Jackson. Calhoun, who was vice-president during Jackson's first term, quarreled with the president over the issue of state rights and other matters and resigned as vice-president in frustration. Jackson chose Calhoun's adversary, Van Buren, to be the vice-president for his second term and was instrumental in securing Van Buren's election to the presidency in 1836.

From 1836 to 1988 no incumbent vice-president had been elected directly to the presidency; George Bush managed this feat in 1988. Many earlier vice-presidents were relatively unknown even in their own time.

Those vice-presidents who were elevated to the highest office through the death of the president provided some memorable moments in American history. President Zachary Taylor died during the debate over the Compromise of 1850, which he opposed. He was succeeded by Millard Fillmore, who supported the compromise, which, when adopted, helped avert the outbreak of civil war for a decade. President Abraham Lincoln, who favored reconciliation between the North and South after the Civil War, was assassinated and succeeded by Andrew Johnson, who shared Lincoln's attitude but who lacked the political skill to accomplish that objective. Chester Alan Arthur, a product of the notorious spoils system, converted to the cause of civil-service reform and helped achieve its adoption after an advocate of reform, President James Garfield, was assassinated (by a disappointed office seeker).

Another reformer, Theodore Roosevelt, succeeded the assassinated William McKinley in 1901 and became a leader in the Progressive movement. Warren Harding died in 1923 immediately before the discovery of serious scandals in his administration. He was succeeded by Calvin Coolidge, whose probity helped restore public confidence.

The modern history of the vice-presidency dates from World War II, when Franklin D. Roosevelt gave Vice-President Henry A. Wallace major responsibilities involving acquisition of natural resources required for the war effort. Thereafter, the concept of the working vice-president gradually evolved. Through acts of Congress and executive orders issued by the presidents, vice-presidents have received assignments that required them to deal with such problems as race relations, the space program, and unemployment. The vice-president is also a member of the National Security Council. Nixon was the first vice-president to travel abroad extensively on diplomatic missions, and his successors have done the same. Rockefeller headed an investigation into alleged abuses by the Central Intelligence Agency.

In another trend, recent vice-presidents have become highly partisan supporters of their presidents, defending their administrations and policies in terms more vehement than presidents consider it politic to use. President Lyndon B. Johnson's conduct of the unpopular Vietnam War and Vice-President Hubert H. Humphrey's outspoken defense of the war accounted in large measure for Humphrey's defeat as the Democratic nominee for president in 1968. As the public debate over Vietnam continued into the Nixon administration, Agnew delivered speeches remarkable for their intemperance.

During his 8 months as vice-president, Ford spoke dozens of times at Republican gatherings, seeking to rally the party during the embarrassment of the Watergate scandal. Walter Mondale relied on his close ties with the Washington political establishment and with union leaders, northern blacks, and traditional liberals in his effort to unite the Democratic party behind President Carter. George Bush campaigned vigorously in 1984 for President Reagan, who in turn supported Bush and Bush's controversial choice for vice-president, Dan Quayle, in 1988.

DONALD YOUNG

Bibliography: Barzman, Sol, *Madmen and Geniuses: The Vice-Presidents of the United States* (1974); Hatch, Louis C., *A History of the Vice-Presidency of the United States*, ed. by Earl Shoup (1934; repr.

VICE-PRESIDENTS OF THE UNITED STATES

Vice-President	Term	President
1. John Adams	1789–97	Washington
2. Thomas Jefferson	1797–1801	John Adams
3. Aaron Burr	1801–05	Jefferson
4. George Clinton	1805–09	Jefferson
George Clinton*	1809–12	Madison
5. Elbridge Gerry*	1813–14	Madison
6. Daniel D. Tompkins	1817–25	Monroe
7. John C. Calhoun	1825–29	John Quincy Adams
John C. Calhoun†	1829–32	Jackson
8. Martin Van Buren	1833–37	Jackson
9. Richard M. Johnson	1837–41	Van Buren
10. John Tyler‡	1841	William Henry Harrison
11. George M. Dallas	1845–49	Polk
12. Millard Fillmore‡	1849–50	Taylor
13. William R. D. King*	1853	Pierce
14. John C. Breckinridge	1857–61	Buchanan
15. Hannibal Hamlin	1861–65	Lincoln
16. Andrew Johnson‡	1865	Lincoln
17. Schuyler Colfax	1869–73	Grant
18. Henry Wilson*	1873–75	Grant
19. William A. Wheeler	1877–81	Hayes
20. Chester A. Arthur‡	1881	Garfield
21. Thomas A. Hendricks*	1885	Cleveland
22. Levi P. Morton	1889–93	Benjamin Harrison
23. Adlai E. Stevenson	1893–97	Cleveland
24. Garret A. Hobart*	1897–99	McKinley
25. Theodore Roosevelt‡	1901	McKinley
26. Charles W. Fairbanks	1905–09	Theodore Roosevelt
27. James S. Sherman*	1909–12	Taft
28. Thomas R. Marshall	1913–21	Wilson
29. Calvin Coolidge‡	1921–23	Harding
30. Charles G. Dawes	1925–29	Coolidge
31. Charles Curtis	1929–33	Hoover
32. John N. Garner	1933–41	Franklin D. Roosevelt
33. Henry A. Wallace	1941–45	Franklin D. Roosevelt
34. Harry S. Truman‡	1945	Franklin D. Roosevelt
35. Alben W. Barkley	1949–53	Truman
36. Richard M. Nixon	1953–61	Eisenhower
37. Lyndon B. Johnson‡	1961–63	Kennedy
38. Hubert H. Humphrey	1965–69	Lyndon B. Johnson
39. Spiro T. Agnew†	1969–73	Nixon
40. Gerald R. Ford§	1973–74	Nixon
41. Nelson A. Rockefeller	1974–77	Ford
42. Walter F. Mondale	1977–81	Carter
43. George H. W. Bush	1981–89	Reagan
44. J. Danforth Quayle	1989–	Bush

*Died in office.
†Resigned.
‡Succeeded to presidency on death of president.
§Succeeded to presidency on resignation of president.

1970); Healy, Diana D., *America's Vice Presidents* (1984); Light, Paul C., *Vice-Presidential Power* (1983); Natoli, Marie D., *American Prince, American Pauper: The Contemporary Vice-Presidency in Perspective* (1985); Vexler, Robert I., *The Vice-Presidents and Cabinet Members: Biographical Sketches Arranged Chronologically by Administration,* 2 vols. (1975); Williams, Irving G., *The Rise of the Vice Presidency* (1956).

Vicente, Gil   [vee-sayn'-tuh]

Often called the father of the Portuguese theater, Gil Vicente, *c.*1470–1536, established the fundamentals of Portuguese drama. Writing in both Portuguese and Spanish, he produced short religious plays, called *autos,* and farces for the courts of Manuel I and John III. His trilogy of *autos, The Ships of Hell, Purgatory,* and *Glory* (1517–19; Eng. trans., 1929), has been called a Portuguese *Divine Comedy.* In his farces, which reflect popular poetry in their exquisite lyrics, Vicente used satire to ridicule the immoralities of his age. *Inês Pereira* (1523) is a typical example.   MARIA ISABEL ABREU

Bibliography: Parker, Jack H., *Gil Vicente* (1967).

Vicenza   [vee-chayn'-sah]

Vicenza is the capital of Vicenza province in the Veneto region of northeastern Italy, less than 60 km (40 mi) west of Venice at the confluence of the Bacchiglione and Retrone rivers. The population is 112,771 (1983 est.). Vicenza is an agricultural, commercial, and industrial center producing iron and steel, farm and textile machinery, furniture, glass, and chemicals. The city has notable buildings dating from the Middle Ages, including a 13th-century Gothic cathedral; other attractions are the 16th-century Renaissance TEATRO OLIMPICO, VILLA ROTUNDA, Basilica Palladiana, and Loggia del Capitanio, all designed by Andrea Palladio.

An ancient Ligurian town and then a Roman settlement, Vicenza became the seat of a Lombard duchy in the 6th century. It was later ruled by Verona and Milan before finally falling to Venice in 1404. Vicenza was governed by Austria from 1797 to 1866, when it joined the newly formed Kingdom of Italy.

viceroy

Viceroy is the title formerly given by Spain and Great Britain to the governor-generals of certain important dominions. Spain first used the title (Spanish, *Virrey*) in the 16th century to describe the governors of Peru and New Spain (Mexico). Traditionally, the British lord-lieutenant of Ireland was given the rank of viceroy, and after 1858 the governor-general of India was a viceroy.

Vichy   [vee-shee']

Vichy is a town on the Allier River in the Allier department of central France, about 320 km (200 mi) south of Paris. A world-famous spa at an altitude of more than 262 m (860 ft), Vichy has a population of 30,527 (1982). The city, built around the triangular Vieux Parc, has many thermal springs that produce the famous Vichy water bottled at the Source des Célestins and exported worldwide.

The Vichy springs, known to the Romans, began to attract visitors in the 17th century and were made highly fashionable by the visits of Napoleon III in the 19th century. During World War II, Vichy was the capital of unoccupied France from July 1940 until the German occupation of all of France in November 1942.

Vichy Government

The Vichy Government (1940–44), a right-wing authoritarian regime, succeeded the Third Republic in unoccupied French territory after Germany defeated France (June 1940) early in World War II.

Meeting in the resort town of Vichy, the French National Assembly, dazed by defeat and maneuvered by Vice-Premier Pierre LAVAL, voted 569 to 80 on July 10 to grant Premier Henri Philippe PÉTAIN full emergency and constitution-making

power. The new government was composed of right-wing elements hostile to the Third Republic but did not include outright Fascists. Vichy attempted haltingly to consummate a "National Revolution" of a corporate nature—eliminating divisive political party and class strife, encouraging family growth and cohesion, and favoring church and patriotic organizations. Under German pressure, anti-Semitic measures were gradually enacted and reluctantly enforced.

Toward the Nazis, Vichy pursued an uneven wait-and-see and collaborationist policy, the direction of which often depended on the course of the war and the persons in power. Premier Pétain remained relatively aloof from direct collaboration. Vice-Premier Laval, however, who was dismissed by Pétain in December 1940 but restored under German pressure in April 1942, tended more to expediency, dealing with and yielding to Nazi demands and seeking a comfortable place for France in Hitler's "new order."

Opposition to Vichy was negligible at first, but by 1943–44, Resistance forces and the rival Free French government under Charles de Gaulle isolated the regime, which had lost almost all autonomy after German troops entered unoccupied France in November 1942. Vichy ended ignominiously as a rump government in Germany after France's liberation in June 1944.   DONALD J. HARVEY

Bibliography: Paxton, Robert O., *Vichy France: Old Guard and New Order, 1940–1944* (1972; repr. 1975); Sweets, John F., *Choices in Vichy France: The French under German Occupation* (1986).

Vickers, Jon   [vik'-urz]

The operatic tenor Jon Vickers, b. Prince Albert, Saskatchewan, Oct. 29, 1926, made his debut (1956) as Aeneas in Berlioz's *Les Troyens* with London's Royal Opera. He moved into heldentenor roles as Siegmund in *Die Walküre,* at the 1958 Bayreuth Festival; his Metropolitan Opera debut was in 1960. An outstanding singing actor, Vickers is proficient in a variety of styles; apart from Wagner, he is especially celebrated as Florestan in Beethoven's *Fidelio* and as Britten's Peter Grimes.   KAREN MONSON

Bibliography: Breslin, Herbert H., ed., *Tenors* (1974).

Vicksburg   [viks'-burg]

Vicksburg (1980 pop., 25,434) is a city in western Mississippi situated on high loess bluffs overlooking the Mississippi River at the mouth of the Yazoo River. It is the seat of Warren County and an important shipping, trade, and processing center. Vicksburg, settled in 1790, was the site of a pivotal Civil War battle. The city surrendered to Union forces in 1863, after a 66-day siege, giving the Union control of the Mississippi.

Vicksburg Campaign

In the crucial Vicksburg Campaign (April–July 1863) of the U.S. Civil War, Union forces under Gen. Ulysses S. GRANT captured Vicksburg, Miss., the Confederacy's stronghold on the Mississippi River. The victory gave the Union control of the river and split the Confederacy in two. Vicksburg's capture, combined with the Union success at Gettysburg (July 1863), shifted the impetus of victory toward the North.

Foiled in several attempts to reduce Vicksburg during the previous fall and winter, Grant launched (April 1863) a combined army-navy operation. Ground forces marched south down the west bank of the Mississippi while gunboats moved past the Vicksburg batteries to transport the troops back to the east bank at Bruinsburg, south of Gen. John C. Pemberton's heavy Vicksburg defenses.

This daring move shifted the campaign to interior Mississippi as Grant, with about 33,000 men, moved inland toward Jackson. By that action, Grant drew Pemberton out of Vicksburg while separating him from Gen. Joseph E. JOHNSTON's approximately 20,000 Confederates in Jackson, whom the Union forces drove north (May 14). Grant then defeated Pemberton at Champion Hill (May 16) and Big Black River (May 17), pushing him back into Vicksburg. A siege of Vicks-

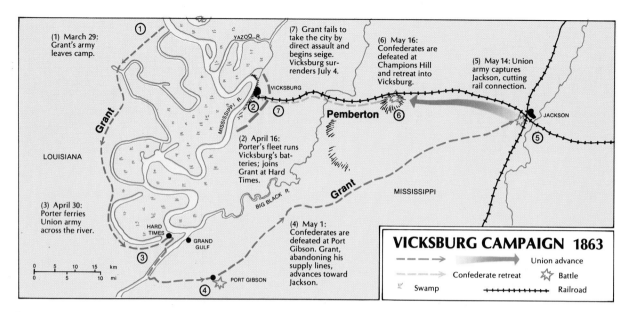

(1) March 29: Grant's army leaves camp.

YAZOO R.

(7) Grant fails to take the city by direct assault and begins siege. Vicksburg surrenders July 4.

(6) May 16: Confederates are defeated at Champions Hill and retreat into Vicksburg.

(5) May 14: Union army captures Jackson, cutting rail connection.

VICKSBURG

Grant

MISSISSIPPI R.

Pemberton

JACKSON

(2) April 16: Porter's fleet runs Vicksburg's batteries; joins Grant at Hard Times.

LOUISIANA

(3) April 30: Porter ferries Union army across the river.

BIG BLACK R.

Grant

MISSISSIPPI

HARD TIMES

GRAND GULF

(4) May 1: Confederates are defeated at Port Gibson. Grant, abandoning his supply lines, advances toward Jackson.

PORT GIBSON

0 5 10 15 km
0   5   10 mi

VICKSBURG CAMPAIGN 1863

- - - - →   Union advance
—————→   Confederate retreat   ✫ Battle
ᴠᴠ Swamp   +++++++++ Railroad

burg (May 18–July 4) ended when Pemberton, low on food and ammunition, surrendered the city and garrison.

FRANK E. VANDIVER

Bibliography: Catton, Bruce, *Grant Moves South* (1960); Meirs, Earl S., *The Web of Victory: Grant at Vicksburg* (1955); Wheeler, Richard, *The Siege of Vicksburg* (1978).

Vico, Giambattista   [vee′-koh, jahng-bah-tee′-stah]

The Italian philosopher of history Giovanni Battista, or Giambattista, Vico, b. June 23, 1668, d. Jan. 23, 1744, was the most important forerunner of the historical view known as historicism: the idea that history is the key to any science of humanity. In his *Scienza nuova* (New Science, 1725, 1730, 1744) and other writings, Vico challenged the preference of René Descartes for a natural science of deductive logic based on clear and distinct ideas and challenged as well the notions favored by Thomas Hobbes and Baruch Spinoza of a constant human nature. Vico stressed that history is the expression of human will and deeds and can therefore provide more certain knowledge about humanity than the natural sciences can. He proposed that human beings are historical entities and that human nature changes over time. He saw each epoch as a whole in which all aspects of culture—art, religion, philosophy, politics, and economics—are interrelated, and he regarded myth, poetry, and art as important means of understanding the spirit of a culture. Vico outlined a conception of historical development in which great cultures, following the pattern of Rome, go through cycles of growth and decline. Neglected in his own time, Vico was rediscovered by romantic proponents of a historical outlook, such as Jules Michelet and Thomas Carlyle, and is today regarded as one of the great historical theorists. He wrote an autobiography (Eng. trans., 1944).

GEORG G. IGGERS

Bibliography: Berlin, Isaiah, *Vico and Herder*, rev. ed. (1976); Tagliacozzo, Giorgio, ed., *Vico and Contemporary Thought* (1978); Vaughan, Frederick, *The Political Philosophy of Giambattista Vico* (1972).

Victor Amadeus II, Duke of Savoy

Victor Amadeus II, b. May 14, 1666, d. Oct. 31, 1732, duke of SAVOY, became the first king of Sardinia-Piedmont (1720–30). Son of Charles Emmanuel II, whom he succeeded as duke in 1675, he grew up under a regency headed by his mother. He ousted her in 1683, establishing an absolutist but reform-minded government. In 1690, Victor Amadeus joined the League of Augsburg against France. When his Spanish ally refused to let him have Milan, he made (1696) a separate peace with France, gaining Pinerolo. In the War of the Spanish Succession he began on France's side but in 1703 switched to the

Habsburgs. At the Peace of Utrecht (1713; see UTRECHT, PEACE OF) Victor Amadeus was elevated to the title of king and given Sicily. In 1720 he exchanged this island for Sardinia, which he turned into Italy's strongest state. He abdicated 10 years later in favor of his son, Charles Emmanuel III.

CHARLES F. DELZELL

Victor Emmanuel I, Italian King of Sardinia

Victor Emmanuel I, b. July 24, 1759, d. Jan. 10, 1824, king of Sardinia-Piedmont (1802–21), resisted the liberal reforms resulting from the Napoleonic conquests. He succeeded his brother Charles Emmanuel IV (r. 1796-1802), who abdicated. Victor Emmanuel resided (1802-14) in Sardinia during the French control of Italy, which deprived the House of SAVOY of the rest of its possessions. He regained Piedmont, Nice, and Savoy in 1814. At the Congress of Vienna in 1815, he obtained Genoa. Utterly reactionary, he suppressed secret societies seeking liberal reforms and refused to grant a constitution. Faced with an uprising, he abdicated in 1821 in favor of his brother Charles Felix.

CHARLES F. DELZELL

Bibliography: Mack Smith, Denis, ed., *The Making of Italy, 1796-1870* (1968).

Victor Emmanuel II, King of Italy

Victor Emmanuel II, originally king of Sardinia-Piedmont, became the first king of the nation of Italy after its unification by Cavour and Garibaldi. After expelling French troops from Rome, the king made the city his capital, ruling as a constitutional monarch.

Victor Emmanuel II, b. Mar. 14, 1820, d. Jan. 9, 1878, a member of the SAVOY dynasty, was king of Sardinia–Piedmont (1849–61) and of Italy (1861–78). In 1848–49 he took part in the unsuccessful wars against Austria (see REVOLUTIONS OF 1848). Ascending the throne of Sardinia after the abdication of his father, Charles Albert, Victor Emmanuel preserved the new constitution that resulted from that revolt. In 1852 he appointed as premier the conte di CAVOUR, whose maneuverings were to make Victor Emmanuel the first king of a united Italy by 1861.

In the Franco-Sardinian war against Austria in 1859, the king commanded Italian forces at Magenta and Solferino. He wisely restrained Cavour from continuing this war alone after France withdrew from it. In 1860 he secretly encouraged Giuseppe GARIBALDI to conquer Sicily and Naples. Victor Emmanuel then sent his army into papal territory, where it defeated the papal army at Castelfidardo and joined Garibaldi's force. The king took a more active part in government after Cavour died in 1861. With Prussian help, he annexed Venetia in 1866 and Rome in 1870, thereby completing the Italian RISORGIMENTO. Victor Emmanuel was succeeded as king of Italy by Humbert I, his son.
CHARLES F. DELZELL

Bibliography: Beales, D., *The Risorgimento and the Unification of Italy* (1982); Mack Smith, Denis, *Victor Emanuel, Cavour, and the Risorgimento* (1971).

Victor Emmanuel III, King of Italy

Victor Emmanuel III, b. Nov. 11, 1869, d. Dec. 28, 1947, king of Italy (1900–46), helped Benito MUSSOLINI come to power. Victor Emmanuel succeeded to the throne upon the assassination of his father, Humbert I. He revealed his dislike for liberal government in 1922 when, instead of resisting the Fascists, he invited their leader, Mussolini, to become premier and acquiesced to his dictatorship and all his wars. After the Allies invaded Sicily in 1943, however, he conspired to arrest Mussolini and set up (July 25) a royal dictatorship with Marshal Pietro BADOGLIO. The choice of Badoglio and the undignified flight of both the king and Badoglio from Rome after the armistice (September 1943) with the Allies incurred much public hostility. Victor Emmanuel was forced to relinquish all power to his son, Prince Humbert, on June 5, 1944, and formally abdicated in his favor on May 9, 1946. On June 2, however, Italy voted for a republic, forcing both kings into exile.
CHARLES F. DELZELL

Bibliography: Clark, Martin, *Modern Italy* (1984); Mack Smith, Denis, *Italy: A Modern History*, rev. ed. (1969); Salomone, A. William, *Italy from Risorgimento to Fascism* (1970).

Victoria   (Australia)

Victoria is a state in southeastern Australia; its area is 227,629 km² (87,888 mi²). Although it occupies slightly less than 3% of the country's total area, it has a population of 4,075,900 (1984 est.), second only to that of New South Wales. More than 70% live in the metropolitan area of MELBOURNE, the capital city.

Victoria is divided into four physical regions, running generally east and west. From north to south these are the plains of the Murray Basin, the Central Highlands—with a maximum elevation of 1,986 m (6,516 ft) at Mount Bogong—the Southern Plains, and the Southern Uplands. Forest covers most highland areas. The plains are largely grass, with scrubby eucalypti known as mallee in the northwest. Rainfall averages about 635 mm (25 in). Temperatures for the entire state range from 21° C (69° F) in January to 9° C (48° F) in July. Numerous streams flow from the central highlands south into Bass Strait or north into the MURRAY RIVER, Victoria's northern boundary.

The majority of the people are of British stock. Of the many persons immigrating to Victoria between 1947 and 1975, however, roughly half were of non-British origin, often eastern or southern Europeans. Melbourne, the second largest city in Australia, is Victoria's only major metropolis. Other important cities include Ballarat and Geelong.

Victoria has a diversified economy, benefiting from abun-

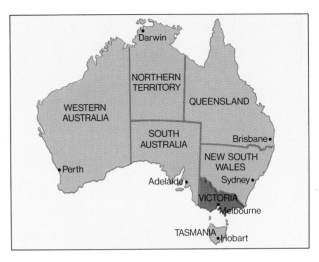

dant coal. Petroleum and natural gas are becoming increasingly important. Industries manufacture automobiles, metal products, machinery, textiles, and paper products. Agriculture is also of major importance, with leading commodities being wheat, wool, and dairy products. Melbourne is a focus of transportation routes—sea, land, and air—and almost equals Sydney as an import-export center. The state parliament consists of two elected houses: the Legislative Council (upper) and the Legislative Assembly (lower).

Explorers penetrated what is now Victoria during the 1820s, but it was not until the 1830s that permanent settlement began when Tasmanian herders crossed the Bass Strait in search of new grazing land. In 1851, Victoria, originally part of New South Wales, became a separate colony. Gold discoveries during the 1850s attracted world attention, and immigrants came by the thousands from Europe and China. Although the gold rush was short-lived, it served as the impetus for rapid development of the colony. In 1901, Victoria became a state in the Commonwealth of Australia.
CALVIN WILVERT

Victoria   (British Columbia)

Victoria is the capital city of British Columbia, Canada. Situated off the mainland on the southeast tip of Vancouver Island along the Juan de Fuca Strait, it is the island's principal city and has a population of 66,303 (1986). A major port and the base of a salmon-fishing fleet, Victoria also has shipbuilding and industries that process fish, lumber, and paper. It is connected to mainland Canada by air and ferry services. Victoria University (1902) is located in the city.

Victoria's first settlement, Fort Camosun, was established in 1843 by Sir James Douglas of the Hudson's Bay Company. Later renamed Fort Victoria in honor of Britain's queen, the city developed during the 1850s as the capital of Vancouver Island, by then a crown colony. After 1858, Victoria was a port for the gold-mining enterprises in the Cariboo Mountains. It became the capital of British Columbia in 1868, retaining this position when British Columbia joined (1871) the Canadian Confederation.

Victoria   (Hong Kong)

Victoria (1981 est. pop., 590,771) is the capital of the British crown colony of Hong Kong. It is located on the north shore of Hong Kong island and is also known as Hong Kong. A major world seaport and tourist, banking, and commercial center, the city was founded in 1843 by the British.

Victoria, Lake

Lake Victoria (or Victoria Nyanza), the largest lake in Africa and the second largest freshwater lake in the world (after Lake Superior), lies mostly within Uganda and Tanzania and borders on Kenya. Stretching over an area of 69,481 km²

(26,828 mi²), Lake Victoria's coastline is more than 3,220 km (2,000 mi) long. The lake is about 400 km (250 mi) long and approximately 240 km (150 mi) wide and is situated at an altitude of 1,134 m (3,720 ft). Lake Victoria's tributaries include the Kagera and the Mara, and it is a source of the NILE RIVER. Its only outlet is near Jinja, where a dam was built (1954) at Owen Falls to generate hydroelectric power. Ukerewe and the Sese Archipelago of 62 small islands are the most important islands.

Lake Victoria lies in a tropical area. Precipitation is well distributed and heavy, averaging more than 1,015 mm (40 in) a year. Boat-building and fishing are important occupations in the area. The first European to explore Lake Victoria was John Hanning Speke (1858); he named the lake for the British monarch, Queen Victoria.

G. N. UZOIGWE

Victoria, Queen of England, Scotland, and Ireland

Victoria, queen of Great Britain and Ireland (r. 1837–1901), the longest-reigning monarch in English history, established the monarchy as a respected and popular institution while it was irrevocably losing its place as an integral part of the British governing system.

Born in Kensington Palace, London, on May 24, 1819, Vic-

Queen Victoria, the longest reigning monarch in British history, populated most of the thrones of Europe with her descendants. Among her grandchildren were Emperor William II of Germany and Alexandra, consort of Nicholas II of Russia.

toria was the only child of Edward, duke of Kent and son of George III, and Princess Victoria, daughter of the duke of Saxe-Coburg. Emerging from a lonely, secluded childhood to take the throne on the death of her uncle, William IV, Victoria displayed a personality marked by strong prejudices and a willful stubbornness. She was strongly attached to the Whig prime minister Lord MELBOURNE; after he resigned in 1839, Sir Robert PEEL, his would-be successor, suggested that she dismiss the Whig ladies of her court. Victoria, however, refused. In part because of this "bedchamber crisis," Melbourne resumed office for two more years.

Victoria and her court were greatly transformed by her marriage to her first cousin, Prince ALBERT of Saxe-Coburg, in 1840. Although her name now designates a supposedly prudish age, it was Albert who made a point of straitlaced behavior, and it was he who introduced a strict decorum in court. He also gave a more conservative tinge to Victoria's politics, leading her to become close to Peel. Victoria and Albert had nine children.

Albert taught Victoria the need for hard work if she was to make her views felt in the cabinet, and during the prince's lifetime Victoria did, by insistently interjecting her opinions, force the ministers to take them into account. Opposing Lord PALMERSTON's policy of encouraging democratic government on the Continent, for example, she was partly responsible for his departure as foreign secretary in 1851. She also helped form cabinets. Her political importance was based, however, upon the temporarily factionalized state of Commons between 1846 and 1868, when royal intervention was needed to help glue together majority coalitions.

Always prone to self-pity, Victoria fully indulged her grief at Albert's death in 1861. She remained in mourning until her own death, making few public appearances and spending most of each year on the Isle of Wight and in the Scottish Highlands, where her closest companion was a dour Scottish servant, John Brown. Her popularity declined as a result, and republican sentiment appeared during the late 1860s.

Victoria, however, regained the people's admiration when she resumed her determined efforts to steer public affairs. She won particular esteem for defending the popular imperialist policies of the Conservative ministries of Benjamin DISRAELI, who flattered her relentlessly and made her empress of India in 1876. Conversely, she flayed William E. GLADSTONE, the Liberal prime minister, whom she intensely disliked, for ostensibly weakening the empire. Although Victoria also attacked Gladstone for encouraging democratic trends, the celebrations of her golden and diamond jubilees in 1887 and 1897 demonstrated her great popularity.

In Victoria's later career, her attempts to influence government decisions ceased to carry significant weight. The Reform Act of 1867, by doubling the electorate, strengthened party organization and eliminated the need for a mediator—the monarch—among factions in Commons.

Victoria died on Jan. 22, 1901. She was succeeded by her son, Edward VII. Her letters have been published in three series (1907; 1926–28; 1930–32).

DONALD SOUTHGATE

Bibliography: Aronson, T., *Grandmama of Europe* (1984) and *Victoria and Disraeli* (1978); Hardie, F. M., *The Political Influence of Queen Victoria* (1935; repr. 1963); Hibbert, C., *Queen Victoria in Her Letters* (1985); Longford, E., *Queen Victoria* (1965); Plowden, A., *The Young Victoria* (1981); Strachey, L., *Queen Victoria* (1921; repr. 1966); Woodham-Smith, C., *Queen Victoria* (1972).

Victoria, Tomás Luis de [veek-tohr'-ee-ah]

Tomás Luis de Victoria, b. c.1548, d. Aug. 27, 1611, was a great Spanish composer of Catholic church music who may have studied with Bartolomé Escobedo and Palestrina, but whose style is uniquely Hispanic. He shared the contrapuntal language of his age but refined it in a personal, often mystical manner that distinguishes him from his contemporaries. His first published compositions appeared in 1572, and he added steadily to his output until 1605. In Rome, where he first studied and later directed the music of the Jesuit Collegium Germanicum, Victoria gained experience as an organist and choirmaster, having competent choirs for the performance of his works. He entered the priesthood in 1575 but continued to compose and direct music in Rome until 1587, returning then to Spain. This return coincided with his appointment as chaplain to dowager empress Maria, who lived in retirement at the Royal Convent of Barefoot Clarist Nuns in Madrid. Victoria served also as director of the choir of boys and priests attached to the convent, and in the last 7 years of his life he was organist there. He wrote no secular music, but his religious works cover practically all the liturgical forms of his age—masses, motets, hymns, responsories, music for Holy Week, and a deeply moving *Officium defunctorum* for the funeral of the empress in 1603.   DENIS STEVENS

Bibliography: Reese, G., *Music in the Renaissance*, rev. ed. (1959); Stevenson, R., *Spanish Cathedral Music in the Golden Age* (1961).

Victoria, University of

Established in 1963 after being associated, as Victoria College, with McGill University (1903–15) and later with the University of British Columbia, the University of Victoria (enrollment: 11,500; library: 1,000,000 volumes) is a coeducational institution in Victoria, British Columbia, Canada. Its faculties of arts and sciences, education, fine arts, and law have undergraduate and graduate programs. The university publishes the literary quarterly *The Malahat Review.*

Victoria and Albert Museum

The Victoria and Albert Museum in London, one of the world's foremost museums of fine and applied arts, was opened by King Edward VII on June 26, 1909. At that time it included the Museum of Ornamental Art and the Art Library; a collection of British painting, sculpture, and engravings; architectural exhibits; technological models and materials; and educational facilities. Currently the museum includes the National Art Library and the National Collection of Post-Classical Sculpture (excluding modern), with major holdings of Italian and Gothic sculpture, as well as British miniatures, Italian majolica, Oriental pottery and porcelain, Early Christian and medieval ivories, medieval and Renaissance jewelry, textiles, furniture, engravings, drawings, watercolors, and English silversmiths' work. Its ceramics collection is considered among the most important in the world. The galleries underwent radical rearrangement after World War II. Since then, half of the museum's galleries—called the primary collections—have been devoted to the evolution of historic European styles.
          MAGDALENA DABROWSKI

Bibliography: Conway, M. D., *Travels in South Kensington* (1882; repr. 1977); Darby, M., et al., *The Victoria and Albert Museum* (1983).

Victoria Cross: see MEDALS AND DECORATIONS.

Victoria Falls

Victoria Falls is one of the most impressive of Africa's many natural wonders. The volume of water passing over the falls varies with the season. Victoria Falls National Park, established in 1952, is administered by the government of Zimbabwe and is among that country's leading tourist attractions.

Victoria Falls lies on the border of Zambia and Zimbabwe in south central Africa, on the middle course of the ZAMBEZI RIVER where it is more than 1,676 m (5,500 ft) wide. The falls' African name is Mosi-oa-tunya—''the smoke that thunders.'' Islands divide the falls into Devil's Cataract, Main Falls, Rainbow Falls, and Eastern Cataract. The water drops into a 122-m-deep (420-ft) chasm and hits the wall of the chasm about 25–75 m (80-240 ft) above its floor. The highest of the falls is nearly 110 m (350 ft). Great clouds of water vapor from the falls keep the surrounding vegetation green and lush all year.

A hydroelectric plant is powered by the falls. A 200-m (650-ft) railroad bridge crosses the chasm. Victoria Falls National Park surrounds the area. David Livingstone discovered the falls on Nov. 17, 1855, and named them for Queen Victoria.

Victoria Island

Victoria Island, covering an area of 212,200 km² (81,930 mi²) in the Northwest Territories, is the third largest of Canada's Arctic islands. The main settlement is Cambridge Bay (1976 pop., 612). The island was discovered by Thomas Simpson in 1838 and explored by John Rae in 1851.

Victorian literature

The first decades (1830s to 1860s) of Queen Victoria's reign produced a vigorous and varied body of literature that attempted to come to terms with the current transformations of English society, but writers in the latter decades (1870s to 1900) withdrew into AESTHETICISM, a preoccupation with sensation as an end in itself. Confronted by the shift from an agricultural to an industrial urban society and troubled by the erosion of traditional religious beliefs, the early Victorian writers held to a moral aesthetic, a belief that literature should provide both an understanding of and fresh values for a new society. Novelists of the period explored the difficulty of forming a personal identity in a world in which traditional social structures appeared to be dissolving. With compassionate realism, George ELIOT, in such works as ADAM BEDE, described the slow dissolution of a rural community. The many powerful novels of Charles DICKENS, William Makepeace THACKERAY, and Anthony TROLLOPE focused on the isolation of the individual within the city. Charlotte BRONTË in JANE EYRE dramatized the particular problems of creating a female identity. Among the writers of nonfiction, Thomas CARLYLE in *Past and Present* (1843) argued for the re-creation in industrial England of the lost sense of community between social classes. In contrast, John Stuart MILL in ON LIBERTY spoke for the fullest development of the individual through freedom from social restraint. The foremost art critic of the time, John RUSKIN, showed in *The Stones of Venice* (1851–53) the interdependence of great art and a society's moral health.

The major early Victorian poets, too, took the role of secular prophets, often expressing a longing for the free play of imaginative life. For Alfred, Lord TENNYSON, the longing found ambivalent expression in his early lyrics; his major work, *In Memoriam* (1850), translated personal grief into an affirmation of religious faith. Matthew ARNOLD, particularly in his poem *Empedocles on Etna* (1852), revealed how the spirit of his own age weakened emotional vitality. Although concerned with presenting his personal form of religious faith, Robert BROWNING used his dramatic monologues primarily to show the uniqueness of the individual personality.

By the 1870s, opposing what they now perceived as a repressive public morality, writers increasingly rejected any obligation to produce didactic art. In the influential Conclusion to *Studies in the History of the Renaissance* (1873), Walter PATER argued that moments of intense sensation are the highest good and that the function of art must be to create such moments. In poetry, Dante Gabriel ROSSETTI and Algernon Charles SWINBURNE expressed their private erotic concerns in terms shocking to the general public. Such preoccupation with sensation led to the literary decadence of the 1890s, epitomized by Oscar WILDE's play *Salomé* (1893), with illustrations by Aubrey BEARDSLEY. Along with a revitalization of prose fantasy (see William MORRIS, Robert Louis STEVENSON), the later Victorian period also saw a more searching realism, notably in such novels of Thomas HARDY's as JUDE THE OBSCURE and TESS OF THE D'URBERVILLES.   HERBERT SUSSMAN

Bibliography: Altick, R., *Victorian People and Ideas* (1973); Buckley, J., *The Victorian Temper*, new ed. (1966; repr. 1981); Houghton, W., *The Victorian Frame of Mind* (1957; repr. 1963); Kincaid, J. R., and Kuhn, A. J., eds., *Victorian Literature and Society* (1984); Levine, R. A., ed., *The Victorian Experience: The Novelists* (1976; repr. 1983), *The Victorian Experience: The Poets* (1982), and *The Victorian Experience: The Prose Writers* (1982).

Victorian style

Victorian style is a catchall term often used to describe the eclectic and revivalist trends in British architecture and design during the reign of Queen Victoria (1837–1901). At one time dismissed as a superficial and inauthentic series of revivals of historical styles, the Victorian style has received more sympathetic and serious scholarly attention in recent years, in part because of a widespread reaction against the functionalist bias of modern architecture.

In searching for a style appropriate to the new structures required by urban-industrial civilization, Victorian architects revived historical styles and reapplied them to serve modern needs. These revivals included classical, Italianate, Gothic, Elizabethan, and French Empire styles. Most significant and widespread was the GOTHIC REVIVAL, which has as its great monument the Houses of Parliament (see WESTMINSTER PALACE) in London, designed (1835) by Sir Charles BARRY and decorated by Augustus PUGIN. Among the finest examples of eclectic architecture are the Royal Courts of Justice (1874–82; London) by George Edmund Street and Saint Pancras Station (1867–74; London) by Sir George Gilbert SCOTT.

The Royal Courts of Justice in the Strand, London, is a notable example of Victorian architecture. The imposing Gothic exterior, designed by George Edmund Street (1824–81), reflects 19th-century Britain's fascination with the medieval past.

Although the leading theorists of the period, such as Pugin, William MORRIS, and John RUSKIN, looked to the past for inspiration, they anticipated modern design in stressing the idea of truth to the nature of the materials used.   DAVID CAST

Bibliography: Biddle, Gordon, *Victorian Stations* (1973); Dixon, Roger, and Muthesius, Stefan, *Victorian Architecture* (1978); Dutton, Ralph, *The Victorian Home* (1964); Girouard, Mark, *The Victorian Country House*, rev. ed. (1985); Hitchcock, Henry-Russell, *Early Victorian Architecture in Britain*, 2 vols. (1954; repr. 1970).

Victorio   [vik-tohr'-ee-oh]

Victorio, b. *c.*1825, d. Oct. 15, 1880, was a chief and military leader of the Warm Springs APACHE. During the 1870s he alternated between sporadic raiding and the bleak confinement of reservation life. Finally, in 1879, Victorio broke out from the San Carlos reservation and led his people to their beloved Black Mountains. For 15 months he kept Mexican and U.S. troops off balance by striking swiftly at different points. His

strategically located encampments permitted the enemy to use only limited numbers of attackers, comparable to his own 35 to 50 warriors. In October 1880, at Tres Castillos, on the Plains of Chihuahua, Victorio was surprised by the Mexicans. Unable to escape, he fought until his ammunition gave out and then killed himself.   FRED W. VOGET

Bibliography: Ball, Eve, *In the Days of Victorio* (1970); Thrapp, D. L., *Victorio and the Mimbres Apaches* (1974).

vicuña   [vi-koon'-yuh]

The vicuña, *Lama vicugna*, the smallest member of the camel family, Camelidae, is usually found in herds grazing on high-altitude semiarid plains of Peru, Ecuador, and Bolivia. Vicuñas stand about 85 cm (34 in) at the shoulder, are about 1.2 m (4 ft) long, and weigh about 57 kg (125 lb). Overhunted for their wool, they are now rare and protected.   EVERETT SENTMAN

The vicuña, L. vicugna, *lives in a band of 1 male and 5-15 females. The male guards his harem against predators by calling an alarm that warns away the females and by placing himself between the harem and the source of danger.*

Vicús   [vee-koos']

Vicús designates an area of northern Peru where a series of rich prehistoric cemeteries have yielded several types of pottery and metal artifacts. The area lies largely in the Piura basin, inland from the coast. One of the principal types of ceramics, called Vicús negative, is resist-decorated with black lines on a background of reddish brown. Pottery similar to early Moche ceramics (see MOCHICA) has also been found, indicating that the Vicús and Moche areas were related at various times, although the exact nature of the relationship has not been determined. Among the numerous metal artifacts from Vicús are masks, nose ornaments, and other objects fashioned of gold and of alloys of gold, copper, and silver. The goldsmiths of the area were already familiar with the technique of depletion gilding, in which the base metals were removed from these alloys, leaving a layer of relatively pure gold. The dating of Vicús, although still tentative, appears to range from about 200 BC to AD 300.   CRAIG MORRIS

Bibliography: Lumbreras, Luis, *The People and Cultures of Ancient Peru* (1974).

Vidal, Gore   [vi-dahl']

The American writer Gore Vidal, b. West Point, N.Y., Oct. 3, 1925, achieved success with his first novel, *Williwaw* (1946), inspired by his wartime service in the Aleutians. *The City and the Pillar* (1948), an account of homosexual life in the United States, and *The Judgment of Paris* (1952), a modernization of the ancient myth, won the respect of critics. *Myra Breckinridge* (1968), an outrageous spoof of Hollywood featuring a transsexual hero/heroine, brought him a much larger reading public. Vidal demonstrated his flair for dialogue and political understanding in two successful plays: *Visit to a Small Planet* (1957) and *The Best Man* (1960; film, 1964). His penchant for re-creating history in novel form led to *Julian* (1964), a fictional biography of the Roman emperor; *Burr* (1973); *Creation*

Gore Vidal, an American writer known for his cynical humor and literary eclecticism, had his greatest commercial success with Myra Breckenridge *(1968), a comic survey of American sexuality. Long a political commentator, Vidal was unsuccessful in a 1960 bid for a House of Representatives seat from New York and in a 1982 bid for the Democratic nomination for a U.S. Senate seat from California.*

Photo Jill Krementz © 1974

(1981), about the 5th century BC; *Lincoln* (1984); and *Empire* (1987). *Duluth* (1983) is a contemporary satire. Vidal's acerbic literary and political essays have been published in the collections *Homage to Daniel Shays* (1973), *Matters of Fact and Fiction* (1977), and *The Second American Revolution* (1982).

Bibliography: Dick, Bernard F., *The Apostate Angel: Gore Vidal* (1974); Kiernan, Robert F., *Gore Vidal* (1982).

Videla, Jorge Rafael   [vee-day'-lah]

Jorge Rafael Videla, b. Aug. 20, 1925, was president of Argentina from March 1976 to March 1981. A professional soldier, Videla was commissioned into the army in 1944. He became commander in chief in 1975 and the following year led the coup that overthrew President Isabel PERÓN. In 1978 he resigned from active service and the ruling junta to assume a 3-year term as president. Most of the excesses of the so-called "dirty war" against terrorism occurred during Videla's early years as president.

After Argentina returned to civilian rule in 1983, Videla and eight other top military leaders were charged with human rights abuses and tried before a civilian court. On Dec. 9, 1985, Videla and another member of his junta, Adm. Emilio Massera, were sentenced to life imprisonment. Three other defendants, including former president Roberto Eduardo Viola, received lesser sentences. The trial marked the first time in recent Latin American history that military officials were held publicly accountable by a civilian government for abuses committed during a time of military rule.

Bibliography: Simpson, John, and Bennett, Jana, *The Disappeared and the Mothers of the Plaza* (1986); Smith, Peter H., "Argentina: The Uncertain Warriors," *Current History* 78, no. 454 (February 1980).

video

The term *video* originally was used in television as a form of shorthand to denote the portion of the electrical signal representing the picture, as opposed to the sound. It was not until the 1970s, with the growth of the new visual electronic media, that it moved into the popular vocabulary, and today it is used to refer broadly to virtually all systems involving the electronic creation or re-creation of images. Television, which gave birth to video, is now one of its branches.

Video has become a dominant force in the lives of Americans. They watch television an average of more than six hours a day. As of the late 1980s, nearly 45 million households, or half the total, owned videocassette recorders. The same number (although not necessarily the same households) were connected to CABLE TV, and almost half of those were equipped to receive special "premium," or pay-TV, channels such as Home Box Office (HBO). Nearly 2 million families have backyard "dishes" to receive programs directly from COMMUNICATION SATELLITES 36,200 km (22,500 mi) above the Earth. Americans make their own videos from cameras and camcorders, or store up TV programs for later viewing, buying some 350 million blank videocassettes per year. And they buy

or rent movies or other programs on tape almost 1 billion times a year. Additional millions of Americans use office or home computers with VIDEO DISPLAY TERMINALS. Even such older media as motion pictures increasingly depend on video technology.

HISTORY

The concept of television, the transmission of images over distances, had challenged scientists even before the invention of the movies or radio. The Nipkow scanning disc, invented in 1883, was a metal disc perforated by holes arranged in a spiral. When it revolved, the disc could scan a picture placed behind it. By rapidly changing the picture, the illusion of movement could be achieved and sent, via electric wires, from a transmitter to a receiver.

The present system of electronic television was proposed in detail by a Scotsman, A. A. Campbell-Swinton, in 1908. The many other early television schemes, however, envisioned transmission through wires, not over the air. Guglielmo Marconi's invention of the wireless radio (1895) spurred efforts toward over-the-air transmission of pictures, and in the late 1920s, radio, the motion picture, and television were combined. Charles Francis JENKINS, the inventor of the modern theatrical motion picture projector, in 1928 began regular broadcasts of crude "radiomovies" in Washington, D.C., using motion-picture film as a source. John Logie Baird in 1926 developed a similar mechanical TV system in Britain, which became the basis for the British Broadcasting Corporation's (BBC) first regular television broadcasts. Also in the 1920s, Baird developed and demonstrated the first color television system and the first videodisc system, which was actually sold for several years at Selfridge's department store in London.

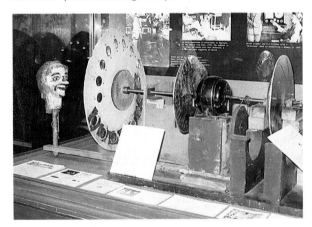

(Above) *John Logie Baird's mechanical TV scanner (1926) used perforated, rotating discs to produce a 30-line image, repeated 10 times per second and transmitted electrically to a tiny receiver screen.*

During the 1920s Vladimir K. Zworykin, a Russian-American scientist, developed a television electronic scanning device, or iconoscope. The device consists of an evacuated glass tube in which a beam of electrons scans a metal plate coated with photosensitive particles that emit electrons when light falls on them. Light from the object to be televised is thus converted into a current that varies according to the image brightness.

Electronic Television. Electronic television, which eliminated mechanical scanning discs at both the transmitting and receiving ends and substituted CATHODE RAY TUBES as receivers and transmitters, was developed simultaneously and independently in the early 1920s in the United States by Vladimir K. Zworykin and Philo T. FARNSWORTH, both of whom built on the tube developed in 1897 by Karl Ferdinand BRAUN in Germany. The first regular broadcasts of electronic television for the public began in London in 1936 using 405 horizontal scanning lines (see VIDEO TECHNOLOGY). In the United States an industry-wide engineering committee adopted standards for a 525-line system based on specifications developed by the Radio Corporation of America (RCA), and broadcasting in this black-and-white system was authorized by the Federal Communications Commission (FCC), but it was not until after World War II that regular broadcasting actually began. The U.S. system was known as NTSC, for the National Television System Committee, which developed it.

After World War II, television developed rapidly throughout the world, most of Europe choosing a 625-line system that was incompatible with the U.S. 525-line standard. The U.S. standard, however, is used in most of the Western Hemisphere and the Far East.

Color Television. Over the objections of much of the television industry, the FCC in 1950 approved a color television system developed by the Columbia Broadcasting System (CBS, Inc.) that was incompatible with the millions of black-and-white sets then in use. This 441-line system never came into widespread use, and a second NTS Committee was convened to develop a compatible color system. The 525-line NTSC color system, compatible with its black-and-white system, gained FCC approval in 1953, but it was ten years before the public responded and bought color sets in any significant numbers. In Europe, two different 625-line color systems were introduced. These U.S. and European color TV standards are the basis for most video today.

Video Recording. Television's first decade was the "era of live TV," when most original programming was televised at precisely the time that it was produced—this was not by choice, but because no satisfactory recording method except photographic film was available. Many live television shows actually were televised twice for different time zones. It was possible to make a record of a show, a film shot from the screen of a studio monitor, called a kinescope recording. These recordings were frequently made for use by stations beyond the reach of cable or microwave interconnections with the networks. Because kinescope recordings were expensive and of poor quality, almost from the inception of television broadcasting electronics engineers searched for a way to record television images on magnetic tape. Audio tape recordings were widely used on radio, and tape recorders were becoming popular on the consumer market. It seemed logical that if signals representing audio could be stored on tape, their video counterparts could also be recorded. The problem was that the video signal was far more more complex than its audio counterpart.

Much early work on videotape recording was done by Bing Crosby Laboratories, established by the singer, who was the first radio performer to pretape his programs rather than broadcast them live. RCA also spent large amounts of research money on the development of VIDEO RECORDING.

The breakthrough, however, finally came in 1956 from Ampex, the company that had introduced audio tape recording to the United States. Ampex solved the problem by mounting the recording heads on a drum that revolved at a high speed, impressing the signal crosswise on the tape, while the tape itself moved at a relatively slow pace. The Ampex-developed system was called "quad" because of its use of four recording heads; it used tape 2 inches (5.08 cm) wide, was subsequently refined to record and play back in color, and remained the standard studio broadcast video recording system for nearly 20 years.

Electronic Newsgathering. Almost from the start of the development of video recording for television studio use, electronics engineers knew that it was only a matter of time before a system would be developed for consumers. While literally dozens of "home" recording systems were developed, these met with little success before 1975. However, these early "home video" developments profoundly affected television news.

One of the many home recorders was the Sony-developed U-Matic (1971). It used a tape 0.75 inches (1.9 cm) wide, mounted in a two-reel cassette. A revolving head drum placed a track diagonally on the tape (the "helical scan" principle, used in most modern videocassette recorders). The U-Matic proved too expensive for consumers, but it was embraced by television stations and networks because its portability and good picture quality made possible electronic newsgathering, or ENG. Therefore, low-cost magnetic tape that needed no processing could be used instead of expensive photographic film that required developing and splicing before it could be shown on a news broadcast.

Just as the U-Matic revolutionized television news, videotape began to transform other aspects of TELEVISION PRODUCTION. Although film is still used, it has become the exception rather than the rule, and virtually all TV programming—including that on film—is now put on tape before being broadcast. (See also RADIO AND TELEVISION BROADCASTING.)

VIDEO TODAY

Most of the major home video media originated as adjuncts to television broadcasting. These include videotape recording, cable television, and satellite reception, all of which have become, in one way or another, competitors of, or alternatives to, broadcast television. (See TELEVISION TRANSMISSION.) It appears to be axiomatic that electronic devices and systems developed for industrial use, no matter how expensive at the start, eventually lead to versions priced low enough for the consumer market.

The Home VCR. The most spectacular success story in the history of consumer electronics is the videocassette recorder, or VCR. The VCR itself was preceded by several other video devices designed to play recorded material, but not to record. The first was the EVR, or Electronic Video Recording system, a film-based video player unveiled by CBS in 1968. Next came the LaserVision optical VIDEODISC system, developed by Philips of Holland and MCA Laboratories of the United States and introduced to the market in 1978; it later became the basis for the successful digital audio COMPACT DISC (CD) system. RCA introduced (1981) the low-cost Capacitance Electronic Disc (CED) system, which used grooves and a stylus—similar to an acoustic phonograph record—to reproduce video.

In 1975, Sony marketed Betamax, a VCR based on its U-Matic system but using tape 0.5 inches (1.27 cm) wide in a smaller cassette. It was a quick success, both in Japan and the United States. The giant Matsushita Electric Industrial Corporation soon adopted another system called VHS (for Video Home System), which had been developed by its subsidiary, the Japan Victor Company (JVC).

U.S. manufacturers and marketers of home electronic equipment contracted with Japanese makers of VCRs for a supply. When the leading U.S. manufacturer of television sets, RCA, embraced the VHS system and introduced a new version made by Matsushita with twice Beta's recording time per cassette, VHS began to surpass Beta in sales.

The economies of mass production, aided by the immediate public acceptance of the VCR and the strong competition in the U.S. and Japanese consumer electronics industries, resulted in rapidly declining prices. As a result, the two play-only videodisc systems were unable to compete with VCRs, for which a wide variety of recorded material quickly became available. RCA discontinued the manufacture of its CED system. Philips stopped making its laser-based system. Other companies, however, including Pioneer and Yamaha, continue to sell laser disc players, which have developed a small group of enthusiasts among consumers and have penetrated the industrial, commercial, and educational fields.

The Betamax Case. VCRs initially were widely advertised as "time-shift" devices that allowed owners to record broadcasts when they were shown, but watch them at their own convenience. Two major motion picture studios, MCA and Disney, filed suit in 1976 against Sony, charging that the main purpose of the VCR was the violation of copyrights. Sony and its codefendants argued that viewers had the right to record programs from the public airwaves in the privacy of their own homes. In 1984, Sony (and by implication the VCR industry) won a complete victory in the U.S. Supreme Court, whose decision gave viewers the legal right to record programs broadcast by television stations.

Cassette Sale and Rental. Although it was the first major use for VCRs, time-shifting is only one of three attractions of this popular device. With the rapid growth of the VCR population, sales and rental of recorded videocassettes—particularly motion pictures—became a huge business, giving rise to the new phenomenon of the video store, of which 25,000 now exist, slightly more than the total number of movie theater screens in the United States. Including all outlets that sell or rent videocassette programs, from convenience stores to filling stations, there are about 100,000 retail sources for such programs today. Although in the beginning the movie studios fought the VCR because of its ability to violate copyrights, films on videocassette have become a major source of income for them, and some feature films already realize more money from cassette sales than from theatrical exhibition.

The Home Video Terminal. With the growing popularity of video devices—not only VCRs but home computers and sophisticated video games—the television set or receiver has evolved into a home video terminal. With many new signal sources in addition to off-air broadcasts, monitor-receivers are replacing receive-only sets. Such monitors have special video inputs that can accept video signals from a variety of devices, bypassing the tuner, whose function is to pick up broadcast TV stations. Although any television receiver can be used to display pictures from a VCR, for example, monitors provide superior pictures. They can be used with multiple video devices. Many have special inputs for computers, and maximize the clarity and definition of computer images.

Increasingly, receiver circuits are employing digital technology. Some monitor-receivers now use digital circuits for all signal processing, and thus they are, in effect, computers that receive and display video pictures. The digital circuits are more directly compatible with such other digital devices and systems as computers and TELETEXT and VIDEOTEX information retrieval services, which provide on-screen information upon demand. Digital monitor-receivers also have the potential to deliver nearly perfect pictures, since they lend themselves to the development of such features as ghost and interference cancelers, as well as special systems to compensate for the wear of such vulnerable components as the picture tube.

The Digital Future. In 1986 the first digital videotape recorders were introduced for broadcast use. These have made possible a degree of excellence never before obtained in professional video recording, particularly when editing requires the copying of one tape on another. Instead of the gradual deterioration that occurs with standard analog recordings as multiple generations of copies are made, with digital recordings the 500th generation is indistinguishable from the first.

Digital devices are already standard in the broadcast industry for such processes as editing, special effects, and titling. Many of these digital effects are now available for consumers in advanced videorecorders (known generically as Super-VHS) and camcorders. Both incorporate digital circuitry capable of producing elaborate effects—zoom, picture-in-picture, digital art simulations, and many others—along with a sharper TV image.

The compact disc, at first available only for audio, has extended its reach to include short video sequences (CD-V), and may eventually replace videotape as the prime medium for TV recording, in the form of the erasable laserdisc.

The Video Industries. Many of the basic principles and designs for video devices and products originated in the United States and Europe—for example, the videotape recorder, video cameras, and video display terminals. Their execution and production, however, have increasingly moved to the Far East, particularly Japan. Japanese, Korean, and Taiwanese firms produce almost all black-and-white TV sets and a

This family possesses every electronic device needed for watching and recording TV; for hearing and taping music; for creating their own video images; and for making use of such systems as teletext.

large percentage of color sets, although most of them have established final assembly plants in the United States, largely as a result of U.S. restrictions against imports of finished products.

In the home VCR field, the situation is quite different. The first successful home video recorder was developed in Japan, and virtually all VCRs since then have been designed and manufactured there. Although manufacturers with U.S. brand names are leaders in the United States VCR market, they all procure their products from Japanese manufacturers.

Even industrial video equipment, such as that made for television stations, increasingly is coming from Japanese firms. Although RCA traditionally had been the dominant force in broadcast equipment, it left the field in 1985 after Sony took over the lead in that area. The picture tube has long been a U.S. product, but this area, too, is increasingly being dominated by imports from Korea and Japan.

THE IMPACT OF VIDEO

In the decade of the 1950s television threw the motion picture industry into a deep depression as people stayed home to watch the free entertainment that TV provided. The movies fought back with 3D, color, Cinerama, and CinemaScope, and for a time, they managed to hold their own. But with the coming of the VCR and the videodisc player, both of which made movies easily and cheaply available for home viewing, the industry was pushed into another crisis. In response, motion picture producers are using videocassettes to sell their products. Within a matter of months—sometimes weeks—after a film's theatrical premiere, it may show up on videocassette. Shortly after its cassette debut, it may appear on one of the new "pay-per-view" cable services. Next in sequence is a regular premium or pay channel, such as Home Box Office or Showtime. For an "A" picture, the next outlet would be network television, followed by syndication to TV stations.

Thus, movies are now made with the small-screen audience as well as theatergoers in mind. Video techniques are now used in the production and editing of movies, many producers shooting movies simultaneously with video and film cameras for the greater flexibility in editing permitted by electronic recording. In some cases, features are made on videotape and then transferred to film. With the development of high-definition television, which will provide the same detail as a 35-millimeter film, even the distribution of motion pictures promises to change. In Japan, experimental simultaneous distribution of feature films by satellite in high-definition video to hundreds of theaters is planned, with video projectors replacing photographic film equipment in the projection rooms.

As the VCR's penetration of U.S. homes increases, the opportunity for programs appealing to many different cultural levels increases. Broadway and regional theater productions, opera, and dance performances have become successful on

The most dramatic proof of the power of television to attract and influence worldwide audiences of millions was provided by the Live Aid concert, held simultaneously in London and Philadelphia on July 13, 1985, to raise money for African famine relief. Such notable stars as Paul McCartney, David Bowie, Madonna, Joan Baez, and Tina Turner were on camera for a total of 14 hours. Truly international in scope, the broadcast also featured film from other concerts given in countries around the world, and the first televised live performance of a Russian rock group. The event was simulcast to 152 countries via the largest intercontinental satellite hook-up ever attempted. There were, it is estimated, some 1.5 billion people in the TV audience, and pledged donations totaled $70 million.

videocassette. No major performance need ever be lost, since it can be easily videotaped, as an increasing number now are.

If video has affected theatrical entertainment, the new video media have also had a strong effect on the original video medium, broadcast television. The competition of cable and the VCR for the time and attention of audiences, and the wide variety of choice now available, have reduced the audiences of the broadcast television networks and thus their advertising revenues.

Video is revolutionizing education and training, as schools and colleges learn to use this visual tool. Interactive videodiscs, in which the learner actively participates, are being used increasingly for training, notably in the U.S. armed forces. Some 8,500 private firms and organizations are estimated to have spent $2.3 billion to produce video programs for employees, shareholders, and others in 1985, and one source forecasts that this private video communications market will reach $7 billion by 1990.

For the future, it seems inevitable that video will increase its presence and influence. Some significant factors should be the improvement in pictures through the adoption of high-definition standards; the increasing integration of the computer with the visual media, for more interactive forms of entertainment, education, and training; and the availability to vastly increased numbers of persons of the means of video production—especially, the camcorder and related devices—which could make creating for the electronic visual arts almost as widespread as setting pen or brush to paper or canvas.

DAVID LACHENBRUCH

Bibliography: Delson, Donn, *Delson's Dictionary of Cable, Video, and Satellite Terms* (1983); Ensign, Lynne N., and Knapton, Robyn E., *The Complete Dictionary of TV and Film* (1985); Fletcher, James, ed., *Handbook of Radio and TV Broadcasting* (1981); Hunt, Albert, *The Language of TV* (1982); Remley, Frederick M., ed., *Tomorrow's TV* (1982); Turow, Joseph, *Media Industries: The Production of News and Entertainment* (1984); Williams, Martin, *TV: The Casual Art* (1982).

GLOSSARY OF VIDEO TERMS

Note: terms followed by an asterisk (*) have separate entries in the set.

analog Information that is reproduced using a continuously varying electronic signal. In video terms, its opposite is digital.

aspect ratio The proportions of a TV or film picture, generally given as the ratio of width to height. The standard TV picture has an aspect ratio of 4 × 3, or 4:3. High-definition video systems may have aspect ratios of 5 × 3 or greater.

bandwidth The range of frequencies required for transmitting different types of electronic signals. Color TV needs a broad band—about 4.6 MHz; the telephone requires only a narrow band, less than 4 kHz.

Beta The first successful home videocassette system, using ½-inch (1.27-cm) tape.

C-band The portion of the microwave spectrum (4,000–8,000 MHz) used most widely for distribution of video programs by satellite to cable systems.

cable TV* Method of nonbroadcast distribution of video programs directly to homes, generally employing coaxial or fiber-optic cable.

camcorder One-piece combination video camera and recorder.

carrier wave An electronic signal that is capable of carrying information when the signal is modulated.

CATV Community antenna television; the predecessor of cable TV. The initials now often refer to cable TV.

CCD (charge-coupled device*) A semiconductor chip used as a highly efficient light sensor in video cameras.

CCIR International Radio Consultative Committee; a United Nations technical body that coordinates world broadcasting. The initials also refer to the 625-line, 50-frame TV system used in most European countries.

CCTV Closed-circuit television.

COMSAT Communication Satellite Corporation; providing satellite communication services and chartered by the federal government.

CRT (cathode ray tube*) The screen usually used on a TV set or on a computer terminal.

database* Computerized store of information that can be reached only via a computer.

DBS Direct Broadcast Satellite; a system that sends TV broadcasts directly from a communications satellite to home antennas, or dishes.

digital television TV transmission in the form of binary data, making possible more precise processing of the picture.

dish The parabolic antenna used for transmitting and receiving signals from communication satellites.

DOMSAT Domestic communication satellite (as opposed to one confined to military uses).

earth station The ground station that receives (downlink) and sends (uplink) signals to and from communication satellites.

edit, electronic edit The removal, or the joining together, of sections of film or videotape material. In film editing, the material is actually cut out, or pasted together mechanically. In electronic editing of videotapes, videotape recorders make the required changes electronically.

8-mm Video Videocassette format using tape 8 mm (about ⅓ in) wide, used primarily for camcorders.

ENG Electronic newsgathering; the use of video cameras and tape recorders in place of film systems for news coverage by TV stations.

ETV Educational television.

FAX (facsimile* transmission) A system that transmits pictures or print electronically.

field A set of scanning lines that, when interlaced with another set, makes up the "frame," or complete TV picture.

footprint The particular patch of the Earth's surface reached by the signal from a communications satellite.

frame A complete TV picture, comprising two fields. The U.S. transmission standard calls for 30 frames transmitted per second.

frequency* The number of cycles per second of an electromagnetic transmission. 1 hertz (Hz) = 1 cycle per second; 1 kilohertz (kHz) = 1,000; 1 megahertz (MHz) = 1,000,000; 1 gigahertz (GHz) = 1 billion.

front projection A type of projection TV system in which the picture is projected onto a reflective screen, which is viewed from the same side as the source of the projected picture.

geostationary orbit The orbit of a communications satellite that allows it to move at the precise speed at which the Earth is rotating, thus remaining at the same spot in the sky relative to the Earth. The orbit is 35,900 km (22,300 mi) above the Earth and directly over the equator.

HDTV High-definition TV; a technology aimed at producing a video picture containing as much detail as a 35-mm motion picture, with wide-screen aspect ratio and stereophonic sound.

head In video and audio, an electromagnetic device that both lays down the magnetic track on recording tape and reads an existing track.

helical scan The basis for most modern videotape recording, in which the signal is recorded as a diagonal track by recording heads on a rapidly revolving drum. The same heads, revolving at the same speed, are used for playback.

Intelsat* International Telecommunications Satellite Organization; 112-member consortium of countries formed (1964) to launch and operate communications satellites.

kinescope A TV picture tube. Also, a photographic film made from a TV transmission as it appears on the tube. Once used for recording TV programs, it has been replaced by videotape recording.

Ku-band The portion of the microwave spectrum (12,000–18,000 MHz) used in many newer video satellite transmissions, particularly in Direct Broadcast Satellite (DBS) systems designed for home reception.

LaserVision, LaserDisc Trade names for the optical videodisc* system in which picture and sound are recorded, and read out by laser.

LCD (liquid crystal* display) A thin, flat glass "sandwich" enclosing a layer of voltage-sensitive liquid. Widely used for calculator and watch displays and, more recently, for portable computer readouts and "pocket television" screens.

LPTV Low-power TV; TV station with limited broadcasting range, often built in rural areas in order to pick up and amplify distant signals. Also used for broadcast programming to specific audiences.

lux Unit of light illuminance. Used as a measure of low-light recording capacity in video cameras.

MATV Master antenna television; a distribution system in which a single antenna is used to feed broadcast TV signals to the occupants of a building or development. SMATV provides the same service but uses a dish antenna to pick up satellite transmissions.

MDS Multipoint distribution service; a method of distributing video programs from a central high point (usually a tall building) by microwave to subscribers equipped with special antennas. Sometimes called "wireless cable."

modem* A device used for accessing computer data over telephone lines.

monitor A video display used in TV studios and designed to receive direct input of video signals from studio cameras, videotapes, and other signal-producing equipment.

monitor-receiver A television receiver that has video inputs enabling it also to serve as a monitor.

MTS Multichannel TV sound; provides additional sound channels along with a single picture on a TV channel. The U.S. transmission system can include stereophonic sound as well as additional sound channels.

narrowcasting Transmission to a specific, small audience (such as Japanese-speaking people, for example), often via low-power, UHF stations.

NTSC National Television System Committee; a U.S. industry body that developed the black-and-white and color transmission standards used in most Western Hemisphere countries, in Japan, and in some other Far Eastern countries. The NTSC system uses a picture composed of 525 horizontal lines, with 30 frames (complete pictures) transmitted per second.

PAL Phase Alternation Line color system; the color TV broadcast standard used in most of Western Europe and, in modified form, in China and Brazil.

pay cable Scrambled TV pictures of premium programs, transmitted by cable, designed for viewing only by those paying a monthly fee for home decoders.

pay-per-view, PPV A form of pay TV where a specified fee is paid for watching each program selected.

pixel Picture element; the smallest area of a video picture capable of being delineated by an electrical signal. The number of pixels in a complete picture determines the amount of detail or resolution in the picture. In the United States the TV picture generally holds a maximum of 150,000 pixels.

projection television A television or video display system in which the picture is projected onto a screen, generally from three separate cathode ray tubes, one for each primary color.

pulse-code modulation One method of digitalizing an analog signal.

rear projection A projection TV system wherein the picture is projected onto a translucent screen, which is viewed from the opposite side.

resolution Standard measurement of the amount of detail that can be seen in a TV-screen image, expressed in the number of horizontal lines on a test pattern.

RF Radio frequency; the electromagnetic wave "carrier" that conveys the modulated video signal from a TV station to a home receiver.

SATCOM RCA's communication satellites.

scrambling A method of altering a cable or satellite transmission signal so that it can be seen only by those who own special decoders.

SECAM Sequentiel Couleur avec Memoire (sequential color with memory); the color TV broadcast standard used in France and its former possessions and, in modifed form, in the USSR and some Eastern European countries.

SMATV See MATV.

STV Subscription TV; broadcast TV, transmitted in scrambled form, for which a decoder is needed.

teletext* System of transmission of alphanumeric and other graphic information by TV stations along with their standard programs, for reception only by specially equipped TV receivers.

transponder Device on a communications satellite that receives electromagnetic signals and transmits them back to Earth.

TVRO TV receive-only Earth station; such as a home dish antenna.

UHF Ultra high frequencies; used by TV channels 14 to 82.

VCR Videocassette recorder; in which the tape is enclosed in a cassette and the loading within the machine is automatic.

VDT Video display terminal*; generally used with a computer.

vertical blanking interval (VBI) The 21 lines between TV frames, transmitted, like the frames, at a rate of 30 times per second. These lines are used for auxiliary information, including teletext, closed captions, and test signals.

VHD Video High Density (or Video Home Disc); a grooveless record whose video signals are read by a floating stylus.

VHF Very high frequencies; used by TV channels 2 to 13.

VHS A videocassette format, using ½-inch (1.27-cm) tape. VHS–C is a smaller VHS cassette. Super-VHS (S-VHS) incorporates advanced digital circuitry.

videodisc* A disc resembling a phonograph record that stores both picture and sound for playback.

videotex* Interactive (two-way) system for accessing written and graphic information on video screens and computer display terminals, which are linked to central computers via telephone lines.

VTR Videotape recorder, using either cassettes or open reels.

video, music

A music video is a brief performance on videotape that accompanies the recording of a single popular song. It is generally meant to embellish the song and to conceptualize it visually, and it usually features the vocalists and musicians of the recording. Music videos are available on videocassettes and are shown in nightclubs and theaters, but by far, their major outlet is television.

Although music video became a pervasive artistic and social phenomenon only in the early 1980s, televised music is as old as television itself. As far back as the late 1940s, operas were being broadcast live on TV, classical and "pop" orchestral concerts became routine on certain channels, and musical performances were an important feature on variety shows. One particular case illustrates the influence of televised music: the "Ed Sullivan Show," despite its mainstream appeal

The video for the 1984 song "You Might Think," hit of the pop-rock group The Cars, won a raft of awards for its creators, Charlex, a TV production house. In surrealistic fantasy, the song's hero appears wherever his girl friend happens to look—as here, on her alarm clock.

and a long history of notable performers, is probably best remembered for presenting two rock-music acts: Elvis Presley in the 1950s and The Beatles in 1964.

One of the first shows to target the teenage audience—a group advertisers were just beginning to recognize as major consumers—was "American Bandstand," a dance program that began airing nationally in 1957. During the 1960s and 1970s, rock artists began to make modest conceptual videos based on their recorded songs, although such videos found few outlets and were used mainly for promotional purposes.

In Europe in the late 1970s, record companies began in a serious way to utilize video in order to promote their clients. Well-produced music videos were shown in nightclubs and on TV. The sales effect of these pieces eventually persuaded U.S. record companies to attempt this type of promotion, and in June 1981 the USA Network—a cable TV company—introduced "Night Flight," a weekend program featuring music videos. Two months later, Warner Amex Satellite Entertainment Company launched Music Television, or MTV, the first 24-hour music video channel.

MTV patterned itself after Top-40 radio, using the same nonlinear, "short take" format to appeal to teenagers and young adults. Its on-air announcers, called "VJs" (video jocks), ran elaborate contests and promotions and developed playlists that showed great ingenuity in the manipulation of audience mood. MTV soon was recognized as an effective way to promote record sales and as a powerful medium for exposing such new artists as Cyndi Lauper, Madonna, and Duran Duran. The playlists, however, were criticized by black artists, who claimed—with justification—that they were not being represented. Rock videos of some heavy metal and new wave groups also came under fire for the explicit violence in their acts. (See ROCK MUSIC.) Although rock still predominates, MTV and the other channels that feature music videos now offer a variety of musical styles in an attempt to broaden their audiences.

In the competitive TV environment, videos have catered to the short attention spans of youth and tried to meet constant demands for originality, humor, and visual splendor—with mixed results. Many display groundbreaking efforts in video style. The most widely imitated examples are slick and stylized, with quick camera cuts timed to the music and, often, the use of dreamlike, fantastic imagery. Many are produced on film and then transferred to videotape, where special effects and COMPUTER GRAPHICS can be added. Some have been directed by well-known filmmakers. Music-video styles have influenced the look and pace of television shows ("Miami Vice," for example), commercials (Pepsi-Cola), and even feature films (*Flashdance, Purple Rain*). LISA LILIENTHAL

video art

Video artists combine many different ways of using video equipment in order both to create and to record a variety of artistic expression. In its simplest manifestations, it provides videotaped documents of musical, dance, and dramatic performances, of performance art, of on-the-street happenings, or even of self-portraits in motion of the artist at work. In this kind of usage, the video camera performs the same function as a motion picture camera, except that the resulting videotape can be shown on a television receiver immediately after it is shot—allowing performers, for example, to see their work in progress. Videotape editing and the addition of special effects can be done in the artist's studio, using relatively inexpensive and easily available video devices.

Most video art practitioners have come to this medium via other art forms—painting, sculpture, music, film, theater, dance, or conceptual and performance art. The field covers a wide spectrum of styles and approaches, from the use of abstract special effects to documentary and narrative themes. Techniques range from primitive black-and-white images to sophisticated, polished work in full color.

The most direct expression of video art is a comment on the machines themselves—something that Nam June PAIK, Wolf Vostell, and others have accomplished by using defunct television sets and other equipment as parts of sculptures. Paik's *V-yramid* (1983) consists of 40 television sets arranged in a pyramid. A short videotape of a dancing man in a yellow turtleneck sweater plays simultaneously on all 40 sets.

Originally a composer of electronic music, Paik was attracted to the visual possibilities of video as musical accompaniment, eventually developing his own unique methods of manipulating the electronics as well as the images of television. Paik's work, which is funny, ironic, and usually a parody of straight TV, has been shown often and successfully on broadcast television.

Beyond the simple recording of an event or the use of TV equipment to make literal, ironic, or parodic statements, there is an enormous range of possibilities in using the video screen as a canvas, "painting" on it with professional video equipment and various special devices, some of them run by computer. Bill Viola's prize-winning mixed-media installation *Room for St. John of the Cross* (1985) combines two projected video images with sound and sculpture, all positioned inside a construction. Wendy Clarke's *The Link* (1984) used two video cameras, one at the lower end of Manhattan, the other in Harlem. People were invited to "perform" for the cameras,

(Above) *Nam June Paik's* Global Groove *(1973) featured his long-time partner, cellist Charlotte Moorman. Originally a live TV performance with videotape inserts, it created many of its effects through a video synthesizer developed by Paik. (Below)* Run, It's a Long Way to Walk *(1985) is a videotape by Shalom Gorewitz, who used an image processor to alter colors and distort, bend, and twist the video shapes.*

The videotape Hatsu-Yume (First Dream) *was made in Japan by video artist Bill Viola in 1981. This still was photographed from the videotape by Kira Perov, who specializes in transforming the work of video artists into the quite different mode of still photography. "The passage from one medium to the other," she says, "from the original electronic video signal to the chemical emulsion of film, gives us new information. The image is no longer luminous. It does not emit light, but is printed only with the aid of light. Yet even without its electronic brilliance, the force of the image remains."*

Listen to the Rhythm of the Reign *(1985), by Jim Pomeroy, initially a live performance, starred Pomeroy as a mad, tyrannical professor. His flute, which actually plays, is made from plastic plumbing pipe.*

and the pictures from both cameras, superimposed on one another, were displayed on TV monitors at each site.

Some video art is meant to be seen as sculpture, or is designed to be shown as static art in a museum. Most, however, is recorded on videotape, and shares with television itself the quality of change and movement. In Paik's videotape *Allen and Allan's Complaint* (1983), for example, one sees the camera recording Allen Ginsberg as he watches a videotape of his father, whose image is superimposed on Ginsberg's forehead. (On the other hand, Paik mocks the short life of TV images in his *T.V. Buddha*, 1981, in which a statue of Buddha sits contemplating its image as it is transmitted, unchanging, over closed-circuit TV.)

As this new medium was developing in the art world, the same small, lightweight video equipment was being used by documentary makers, social activists, and community groups. Some equipment was made available through cable TV public access centers, as well as centers that were supported by government funds and private foundations. The technical advance that allowed both video artists and documentary makers to expand the potential in video art was the marketing (1971) of Sony's U-Matic tape recorder, which used ¼-inch (1.9-cm) tape inside a cassette. One-half-inch (1.27-cm) tapes became available in 1975, reducing the cost of a basic production package to about one-third that of ¼-inch tape. Video techniques were soon taught in many public school systems, community centers, and art departments in colleges and universities. Today, many video artists have grown up with television and know its techniques and much about its technology, which may be the same as broadcast television, or their own invention. David Jones, from the Experimental TV Center in Oswego, N.Y., has designed and built a number of video image-processing systems. Bill Viola was artist-in-residence with the Sony Corp. in Japan. Others work as television producers, adding their special talents to the making of standard TV programs.

Video art has always been a product of what the available equipment allowed artists to do. With the very small, lightweight 8-mm camcorders, and the graphics and animation capabilities of home computers, artists today can own many of the tools needed to produce a new generation of work in video art.   BOB DOYLE

Bibliography: Banff Centre School of Fine Arts, *The Second Link: Viewpoints on Video in the Eighties* (1983); Boyle, Deirdre, *Video Classics: A Guide to Video Art and Documentary Tapes* (1986); D'Agostino Peter, *Transmission* (1985); Hanhardt, John, *Video Culture* (1986); Marsh, Ken, *Independent Video* (1974); Schneider, Ira, and Korot, Beryl, *Video Art: An Anthology* (1976); Shamberg, Michael, *Guerrilla Television* (1971).

See also: COMPUTER GRAPHICS.

video camera

A video camera is capable of recording pictures and sound on magnetic videotape, which can then be shown on a television screen, via a videocassette recorder (VCR). Small, hand-held amateur video cameras that record only in black and white have been available since the mid-1970s. Color cameras appeared in the late 1970s. Both types require the use of a portable VCR, usually carried with a shoulder strap and connected to the camera by a cable. The large, professional studio camera, which differs considerably from the amateur camera in construction and technology, is described in VIDEO TECHNOLOGY.

The newest amateur camera technology is the camcorder, introduced in the early 1980s, which—as its name implies—is a camera and a VCR combined into one lightweight, compact device. Most camcorders have built-in playback capability, so that the operator can review the pictures already taken, or erase unusable shots while he or she is shooting. In addition, almost all camcorders can be hooked up via a cable to a television receiver, in order to screen pictures at home.

The imaging technology in amateur video cameras is quite different from that of studio cameras. In a video camera, light collected by the lens is focused on the faceplate of an imaging device. In some cameras, this may be a camera tube that contains a color stripe filter that produces the required electrical color signals. (Professional cameras, by contrast, require three separate tubes for the three primary colors.) The most recent video cameras have replaced the tube with a solid-state image sensor, usually a CHARGE-COUPLED DEVICE (CCD), that changes light energy into the electrical pulses that are recorded on videotape. The clarity and resolution of the video-taped pictures depend on the number of picture elements—tiny dots called pixels—that the CCD can create. The newest camcorders, made even smaller and lighter by the use of CCDs, can produce extremely clear, detailed pictures.

Camcorders are available with three separate types of recorder: Beta, VHS, and the relatively new 8-mm, which uses 8-mm (⅓-in) VIDEOTAPE instead of the more common ½-in (1.27-cm) tape found in most videocassettes. The newest 8-mm camcorders are extremely lightweight and record both audio and video with excellent color, clarity, and sound.

While most video cameras without built-in recorders will work compatibly with either a Beta, VHS, or 8-mm separate recorder, the cable connection between the camera and the recorder is often configured so that both must employ the same format. In the case of camcorders, only one tape format can be used. That is, 8-mm cassettes cannot be used on a Beta recorder. Nor can Beta videocamera tape cassettes be used on a home VHS videocassette recorder (see VIDEO RECORDING).

A variation of the VHS tape format, the VHS-C, is a miniature VHS cassette containing only 20 minutes of tape, played at the standard VHS speed. Its small size has enabled manufacturers to reduce the size of VHS camcorders, but in order to play these tapes on a standard VHS home VCR, a low-cost adapter housing is required. Newer camcorders can record for 60 minutes using this VHS-C cassette.

Automated features found on many video cameras and camcorders resemble those on photographic cameras; these include automatic aperture control, which eliminates the need to vary lens openings to compensate for different lighting conditions; automatic focusing; and manual or powered zoom-lens operation, to permit shooting a variety of scenes from wide-angle to close-up telephoto without changing lenses. Automatic or easily adjusted white-balance settings assure color accuracy with indoor and outdoor lighting.

Many cameras and camcorders also feature built-in electronic viewfinders—actually miniature black-and-white TV monitors that show exactly what the recorded picture will look like, and can be used for instant playback of scenes that have just been recorded. Microphones fitted to the camera pick up sound signals and record them on the appropriate section of the videotape, along with the video signals picked up by the camera itself.

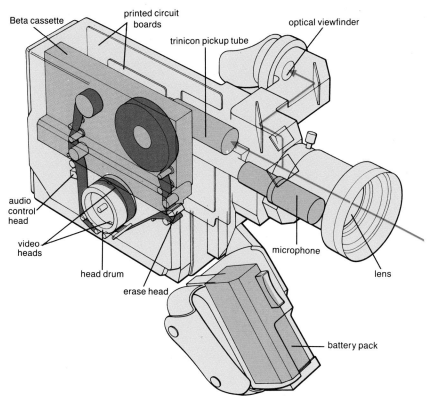

Beta cassette

printed circuit boards

trinicon pickup tube

optical viewfinder

audio control head

video heads

head drum

erase head

microphone

lens

battery pack

The camcorder combines the video camera and videocassette recorder (VCR) in one compact, lightweight unit. Camcorders are available in Beta, VHS, VHS-C, and 8-mm tape formats as well as in the high-end S-VHS and S-VHS-C configurations. The Sony Betamovie, shown here, was the first camcorder on the market. Although the Betamovie uses standard Beta cassettes, its head drum is only 44.7 mm (1.76 in) in diameter. (The standard Beta VCR's head drum is 74.5 mm/2.93 in) The drum rotates at 3,600 rpm, twice the speed of a standard VCR; with each revolution, its two heads each records information. The tape is almost completely wrapped around the drum—at a circumference of 300° instead of the usual 180°. It therefore uses less time to record a video field. To compensate, the recorded image is kept sharp by a high-speed scanning system. These design innovations produce a picture that is higher in quality than that of the standard Beta VCR, but they also prevent use of the Betamovie on the Beta VCR. Other camcorders differ in design both from the Betamovie and from each other. The VHS format, for example, uses four recording heads, records at the same speed as a standard VCR, and offers the possibility of instant playback. Many camcorders, however, use the smaller VHS-C format, which requires the use of an adapter to play the tapes in a home machine. All of the formats undergo constant refinement, however, and the limitations imposed by speed and tape-size differences may eventually be resolved.

A video camera capable of taking still pictures reached the market in 1986. Resembling a single-lens reflex film camera, this new device records 50 still pictures on a floppy disk enclosed in a cartridge. The electronic imaging sensor is a CCD that can produce 380,000 pixels, giving its pictures slightly more definition than a high-quality TV image, which has about 350,000 pixels. With its auxiliary equipment, including a printer and a digital telephone transmitter, this new camera should prove indispensable for professionals who need to produce and transmit still pictures quickly.

LEONARD FELDMAN

Bibliography: Cristol, A., *Solid State Video Cameras* (1986); Hirschman, R., and Procter, R., *How to Shoot Better Video* (1985); Millerson, G., *Video Camera Techniques* (1983); Porter, M., *The Complete Guide to Making Home Video Movies,* rev. and updated ed. (1987); Rosen, F., *Shooting Video* (1983).

video display terminal

A video display terminal (VDT) is the visual display screen of a computer. Most VDTs receive their images from a CATHODE RAY TUBE, the same type as that used in conventional television receivers, although a few employ LIQUID CRYSTAL display technology. Originally, most VDTs displayed their information in green lettering on a dark background. This combination proved difficult to read, and many newer screens use color and offer much stronger resolution.

There are millions of VDTs now in use in factories and offices, and as computerization grows more commonplace, the screen will become the standard workstation for a vast number of workers. Questions have been raised about the effects of these screens upon the health of workers. It has been suggested that they may induce high levels of stress, headaches, and eye strain, and that in the case of pregnant women, they may increase the risk of miscarriage or birth defects. Although to date no deleterious connection has been established, the National Institute for Occupational Safety and Health (NIOSH) plans an extended study of the potential health effects of VDTs.

See also: INPUT-OUTPUT DEVICES.

video game

A video game is a contest between a player and a computer-designed program on a machine equipped with a video screen and a joy stick or buttons that control the game's action. The machine may be designed to play one game, as are those in video-game arcades. On game consoles or home computers one can play any number of games, using different videotape game cartridges.

The first video games were created on mainframe computers by engineers and computer programmers in the late 1950s and early 1960s. The games traveled via a kind of programmers' network from one computer research center to another. Games such as Star Trek and Space Wars were played, with essentially the same rules, whenever there was spare computer time—usually in the middle of the night. These first games were essentially verbal—that is, the graphics, if there were any, were limited and the computer was programmed to respond primarily in words to each of the choices made by the player. Many of these games were extremely complex, although none approached the complexity of the programming involved, for instance, in computerizing a chess game.

In 1972, Nolan Bushnell, founder of Atari, produced the enormously popular Pong game, a machine in which two players attempted to hit a computerized ball into the opposition's net—all in black and white on a video screen. Space Race, Gotcha, Tank, the voracious disembodied mouth, Pacman, and—most popular of all—Space Invaders quickly followed. In Space Invaders, a movable cursor fires at an ever-oncoming line of shapes representing spaceships. Expert players, those who "zap" the largest number of ships, have their names printed in a roll of honor on the video screen, a practice that is still followed by almost all video games.

As they proliferated, video games gained color and complexity and adopted the basic theme that most of them still exhibit: the violent annihilation of an enemy (a spaceship, an alien, a man-eating crocodile) by means of one's skill at moving a lever or pushing a button (representing a gun, a bomb, an arrow, an unidentified explosive).

In "Atomic Castle," a laser disc–operated video game, the choices made by the player will change the course of the game itself. The computer-controlled laser disc combines high-resolution graphics, animation, and live actors to achieve a remarkable visual realism.

Many of the games played on home computers are more or less identical with those in video arcades. Increasingly, however, computer games are becoming more sophisticated, more difficult, and no longer dependent on elapsed time (as in arcade games, where 25¢ pays for a set number of minutes). The graphics have improved to the point where they often resemble movies rather than the rough, jagged video scenes of past games. Some of the newest games (arcade as well as home computer) generate their graphics through laser discs, which offer the most advanced technology and—given an imaginative programmer-artist—have the potential for producing an almost limitless array of exotic worlds and fantastic situations. Many include complicated sounds; some even have music. The player is the game's protagonist, the persona who must work his or her way through a web of possible actions, interacting with the game's reactions, and winning through a combination of dexterity and strategy.

There are those who feel that in order to play, one must accept the values implicit in these interactive games, which—like the often-condemned Dungeons and Dragons—may involve extremely violent or aberrant events and characters. Other types of games—especially those which use simulation (flying a plane, driving a car, escaping from a maze)—are simply highly imaginative tests of intelligence and skill. Defenders of the games claim that they help prepare children for later computer use and give them the opportunity to learn how to reach and carry out decisions quickly. (See also GAMES.) ABIGAIL REIFSNYDER

Bibliography: Cohen, Scott, *ZAP! The Rise and Fall of Atari* (1984); Levering, Robert, Katz, Michael, and Moscowitz, Milton, *The Computer Entrepreneurs* (1984); Levy, Steven, *Hackers: Heroes of the Computer Revolution* (1984).

video recording

Several technologies for recording and playing back television pictures and sound are possible today, the most popular being the use of magnetic tape. The recording of electrical TV signals may also be accomplished with VIDEODISCS, using one of the three following methods. (1) The Capacitance Electronic Disc (CED) records in narrow grooves on discs resembling ordinary phonograph records, and plays back through a TV receiver using a mechanical stylus analagous to a phonograph stylus. (2) The Video High Density (VHD) technique uses a grooveless disc over which a stylus slides, sensing electric signal variations that are converted into television signals. (3) The optical, or laser, disc records TV signals in the form of tiny pits, which form a digital code. The code is both recorded and read back by a laser.

By far the most common means of storing television pictures, however, is through the use of a videocassette recorder (VCR), which is connected to the TV receiver and which employs magnetic tape as the signal-storage medium. Magnetic VIDEOTAPE is a plastic-based tape that has been coated with tiny magnetizable particles. During recording, tape heads—either one or two pairs, mounted on a rapidly rotating head drum inside the recorder—generate a magnetic field, which is transferred to the tape in the form of magnitized patterns. During playback, these magnetic patterns are electronically processed by the heads into a standard broadcast television signal that can be viewed or heard on a conventional TV set.

All home video recording systems employ tape that moves relatively slowly from one cassette reel to the other. The high density of information storage necessary for video signal recording is achieved by having the tape heads spin over the tape at 1,800 rpm, or 30 times a second. Each rotation traces a diagonal path across the tape in a technique known as helical scan recording. Each angled, magnetized video pattern corresponds to a single "field" of a video transmission, and two fields represent a complete frame, or picture (see VIDEO TECHNOLOGY.) Thirty frames per second is the TV standard used in the United States; hence the head-drum rotational speed of 30 revolutions per second, or 1,800 rpm. The signals on magnetic videotapes can be erased, and the tape rerecorded.

The audio sound track accompanying the video signals may be recorded either as a separate, horizontal track at the top or bottom of the tape; or, in so-called HiFi videocassette recordings, as an integral part of the video signal. In the latter case, audio quality is much improved and can be recorded stereophonically, on two separate sound tracks for left and right stereo channels. The newest 8-millimeter video recording systems make provision for several types of accompanying audio recording tracks, including a stereophonic system that uses a form of digital audio recording.

The first videotape recorder was demonstrated in 1951. It used 1-inch-wide (2.54-cm) tape traveling past stationary magnetizing tape heads at 100 inches per second, producing a very poor picture. By 1956, however, a tape recorder developed by the Ampex Corporation was used for the first time by a TV network. Its quality was so much superior to that of the kinescope—quick-developing film shot from the picture on a TV screen—that it became standard in TV studios, ending the era of the use of photographic film on television.

Sony's first videotape recorder, developed in the late 1960s, employed open-reel, ½-inch-wide (1.27-cm) tape. In 1971, Sony introduced U-Matic, a ¾-inch (1.9-cm) tape format that is still very much in use for professional applications, such as newsgathering by TV reporters in the field. Betamax, another Sony invention, was a ½-inch tape enclosed in a cassette that could be used in a relatively simple home recording machine, the videocassette recorder, or VCR. Barely a year later, Japan Victor Company (JVC) produced their first VHS format (Video Home System) recorder, which, though similar in concept to the Beta machine, was incompatible with it.

The basic differences between Beta and VHS relate to the size of the tape cassettes and the method of loading, or wrapping the tape about the tape-recording head drum when a cassette is inserted in a VCR. Duration of recording differs as well. The maximum recording time for a Beta cassette (at the slowest Beta III speed) is 5 hours, whereas maximum recording time for a VHS cassette at its slowest speed, using extended-length tape on a thinner plastic base—which allows more tape to be wrapped around the cassette reel—is 8 hours.

Portable videocassette recorders, which operate on battery power, have been available since the late 1970s. When combined with a color VIDEO CAMERA, such VCRs permit the making of home movies that can be played back through any compatible VCR and viewed on a TV screen. Recently, the functions of the video camera have been combined with those of a VCR in the form of lightweight camera-recorder combinations called camcorders.

With over 35 million VCRs currently in use in homes in the United States (and some 100 million in use worldwide), video recorders have had a profound effect on the way people seek

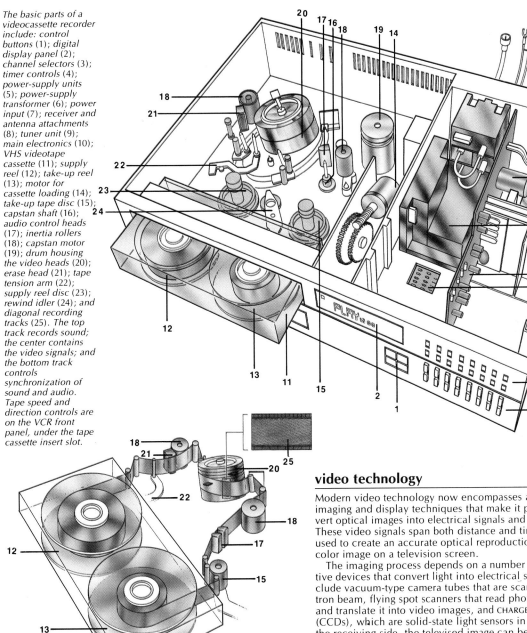

The basic parts of a videocassette recorder include: control buttons (1); digital display panel (2); channel selectors (3); timer controls (4); power-supply units (5); power-supply transformer (6); power input (7); receiver and antenna attachments (8); tuner unit (9); main electronics (10); VHS videotape cassette (11); supply reel (12); take-up reel (13); motor for cassette loading (14); take-up tape disc (15); capstan shaft (16); audio control heads (17); inertia rollers (18); capstan motor (19); drum housing the video heads (20); erase head (21); tape tension arm (22); supply reel disc (23); rewind idler (24); and diagonal recording tracks (25). The top track records sound; the center contains the video signals; and the bottom track controls synchronization of sound and audio. Tape speed and direction controls are on the VCR front panel, under the tape cassette insert slot.

entertainment. One can buy video recordings of the latest popular films, educational materials, self-help cassettes, and so forth or rent such cassettes at a nominal cost. A landmark U.S. Supreme Court decision has ruled that it is legal to record and play back programs broadcast by TV stations, so long as this is done for personal, noncommercial use. So-called time-shifting—setting VCR controls to record a program automatically, for viewing at a time later than the original broadcast—is a primary use of VCRs. Most machines can be programmed to record two or more events that will be broadcast up to four weeks later.   LEONARD FELDMAN

Bibliography: Bensinger, Charles, *The Home Video Handbook* (1980); Costello, Marjorie, and Heiss, Michael, *How to Select and Use Home Video Equipment* (1984); Utz, Peter, *The Complete Home Video Book* 2 vols. (1983).

video technology

Modern video technology now encompasses a wide range of imaging and display techniques that make it possible to convert optical images into electrical signals and vice versa. These video signals span both distance and time, and can be used to create an accurate optical reproduction of the original color image on a television screen.

The imaging process depends on a number of photosensitive devices that convert light into electrical signals. These include vacuum-type camera tubes that are scanned by an electron beam, flying spot scanners that read photographic film and translate it into video images, and CHARGE-COUPLED DEVICES (CCDs), which are solid-state light sensors in chip form. On the receiving side, the televised image can be re-created by a direct-view or projection CATHODE RAY TUBE, by a LIQUID CRYSTAL display, by large-screen luminescent panels created by gas-plasma devices, or by light-valve projectors, which employ a fixed light source and special optical systems to project video images.

Video technology also includes complex analog and digital signal processing at the source, to mix images or create special effects. A similar, although much simpler, video-signal processing can take place in the monitor or home receiver, to display multiple images on the screen or to extract data from the video signal that provides useful information, including TELETEXT and VIDEOTEX.

The distance factor is overcome by sending video images in real time from one location to another over a variety of transmission systems including electromagnetic propagation (radio waves) and hard-wire connections (cables). The time domain is overcome by video-recording devices that can capture images on magnetic tape, magnetic discs, or optical discs, and play them back at any time.

Television depends on two fundamentals of physics, the conversion of light (photons) into commensurate electrical impulses (scanning and transmission), and the electroluminescence principle that generates light output in a chemical substance in proportion to an electrical input (display).

In between these two extremities of the original and the reproduced image, there lies a vast array of signal-processing techniques that permit the video signal to be manipulated and distributed to the end viewer. The video manipulation can be done in either the analog or digital domains.

Up until the early 1970s, television signals were almost all analog, that is, the video signal representing a given optical scene was a continuously variable voltage, whose value at any point reflected the luminance (brightness) and chrominance (color hue and saturation) of the picture element being transmitted. As digital techniques developed, much of the analog video-processing circuitry was replaced by high-speed sampling methods that convert the continuously changing gradients of the video signal into binary digital bits, each representing a discrete signal level. (See DIGITAL TECHNOLOGY.)

THE PICTURE ELEMENT

The retina of the eye has an estimated 6–7 million light-sensitive receptors, which can simultaneously transfer a color image to the brain over a nerve bundle with approximately one million fibers. No practical color TV system can transfer that much information instantaneously from camera to TV screen. Instead, television depends on the methodical sequential scanning of a color image, in order to relay it over a single channel from the source to its final destinations. To do so, the original image must be broken down into picture elements called pixels. A pixel is the smallest area of a TV image that can be reproduced by an electrical signal.

For the television system to transmit properly, an exploring spot scans progressively across each picture element from the top left to the bottom right corner of the image. In scanning, the image is broken down into a series of horizontal lines (in the United States, 525 lines is the standard). In a process called interlaced scanning, the scanner ''reads'' every even line on one scan, producing one ''field.'' The second scan

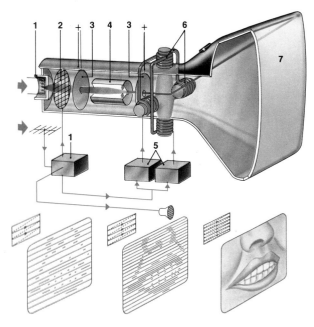

A black-and-white television set receives transmitted signals (arrow) at its antenna. A tuner (1) selects the desired channel and separates the audio signal, which is processed the same as in FM radios. The visual signal is applied to a grid (2) in the picture tube to vary the intensity of the electron beam. This beam is accelerated by two positively charged anodes (3) and magnetically focused (4). Synchronization circuits (5) control horizontal and vertical magnetic deflectors (6) that sweep the beam across the phosphor-coated screen (7). The amount of detail is determined by the number of lines.

reads the odd-numbered lines left empty during the first scan, producing the second field. The scanning process is repeated continuously, producing 30 frames, or complete scenes, per second. The continuous video signal generated by this action is interspersed by synchronizing pulses, and is relayed via a communications system to the home receiver. There, a reproducing spot, scanning the picture tube in synchronism with the scanning element in the studio, will re-create the image. The smaller the picture elements that the system can handle, the sharper the reproduced image will look. Improved cameras, using more picture elements, create color television images rivaling the quality of 35-mm film.

In existing TV broadcasting systems, the picture elements are defined by the system parameters, such as line structure and channel bandwidth. High Definition TV (HDTV), the most advanced TV transmission system, uses line structures ranging above 1,000 and bandwidths up to 30 MHz, thus allowing for sharper resolution, both horizontally and vertically. Japan is already broadcasting in HDTV, and Europe is developing its own system. It is hoped that if the United States can agree on HDTV standards—probably with Japan—U.S. transmission systems will also convert to HDTV.

THE CAMERA TUBE

The invention of the Iconoscope by Vladimir Zworykin and of the Image Dissector by Philo T. FARNSWORTH in the early 1920s led to electronic television as it is known today. Subsequent improvements in imaging-tube technology produced the Orthicon and Vidicon—which first transmitted images in black and white—and, as color television developed, the Plumbicon and Saticon were added. More recently, new imaging devices have been invented that use solid-state charge-coupled devices (CCDs) or metal oxide semiconductors (MOS) as image sensors.

Photoemission. The conversion of light into a series of electrical signals is accomplished by a variety of photosensitive devices that function as camera elements on which the scene to be televised is optically focused. The energy in the photons of light coming through the camera lens and falling on the

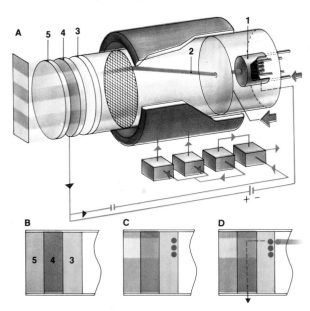

A vidicon television camera tube (A) is a glass tube in which an electron gun (1) scans an optical image with an electron beam (2). The scanned target (B) consists of a photoconductive layer (3) and a transparent, positively charged metal film (4) coated on a glass faceplate (5). Exposure (C) of the photoconductive layer to light excites electrons (dots) into a conducting state and thus decreases the layer's electrical resistance. Electrons deposited (D) by the electron beam then flow through the layer, producing a luminance signal current that varies with the light intensity of the image.

photosensitive surface is converted into free electrons in a process called photoemission.

The most common photosensitive devices used in TV cameras are vacuum-tube types, such as Vidicons, Plumbicons, and Saticons. Here, a thin layer of a complex metal alloy is placed on a substrate and located at the front end of a glass vacuum tube. An electron gun scans the rear of the substrate with an electron beam. Electrons freed from the photosensitive layer modulate the current flow from the electron gun in proportion to the light falling on the front surface of the light-sensitive metal-alloy layer. The readout of this variable current is the video signal, representing the actual brightness at each point in the scene.

Photoconduction. Another type of camera tube uses the process of photoconduction. Here the light falling on a layer of semiconducting material changes the conductivity of the material in proportion to the light intensity at a given point. A CCD is a photoconductor, a light sensor whose electrical conductivity is changed by the absorption of photons. In the CCD camera, three small solid-state chips (about $1/3 \times 1/2$ in/0.84 $\times$ 1.27 cm) replace the camera tubes and act as imagers for the red, green, and blue components of the color image. There are several varieties of semiconductor, solid-state imagers. In cameras where they are used, they have some inherent advantages over tubes: a better signal-to-noise ratio (the power of the signal relative to the internal noise in a channel); no image retention between scans; no overloading due to high light levels; and a virtually limitless life span.

Whether the image sensor is the front "window" of a camera vacuum tube, or the exposed surface of a CCD chip, the method of producing a color television image is the same. The original image is picked up by the camera lens and relayed through an optical system that includes red and blue dichroic mirrors. These mirrors essentially split light into its primary colors: the red mirror reflects red, but allows blue and green to pass through; the blue mirror reflects blue, but allows the passage of red and green. In this way, the reflected light from the scene is divided into its primary color elements, and each separate color is directed to its appropriate imaging

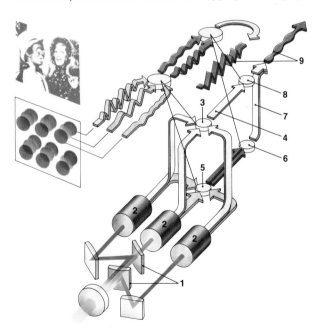

Color-television cameras use dichroic mirrors (1) to split a colored image into red, green, and blue components that are fed into separate camera tubes (2). One encoding unit (3) combines the output signals into a luminance signal (4), intended for black-and-white sets. Other encoders (5, 6) convert the signals into a chrominance signal (7) containing information for color sets. The luminance signal is then amplified (8) and combined with the color signal for transmission (9).

device. The red, blue, and green video signals generated by the image sensors are then matrixed—that is, they are cross-mixed—and signals conveying luminance (brightness) and chrominance (color hue and saturation) are added. The composite color signal now also includes horizontal and vertical synchronizing pulses.

When modulated on a radio frequency (RF) carrier on an assigned channel frequency, the signal can be picked up by a home receiver and decoded to display the original color scene on the picture tube.

THE PICTURE TUBE
On the display side, the vast majority of color television sets use a direct-view picture tube, ranging in size from 2 to 40 in (5 to 92 cm) measured diagonally. These tubes have one of two basic fluorescent-screen structures, known as the dot phosphor shadow mask, and the strip phosphor Trinitron (a trademark of the Sony Corp.).

In both cases, chemical compounds (phosphors) that convert electron-beam energy into radiant light, forming the additive primary colors (red, green, blue), are deposited on the inner face of the glass picture tube in precision arrays of dots or stripes with alternate colors. A power supply and scanning circuits provide the voltages that energize the picture tube. Processing circuitry decodes the video signal into the red, green, and blue components that drive the picture tube's electron guns. The video signal controls the intensity and position of the electron stream from the guns. As the beams scan the light-emitting phosphors in the tube, the color image is reconstructed on the face of the tube. The lag effect in the tube, and the retentivity of the human retina both contribute to the illusion of a continuous image on the screen, even with rapid motion in the picture. Finally, a separate sound detector and amplifier feed the speaker—or speakers, if the receiver has stereo components.

Sophisticated television receivers may also have teletext decoders, hard-copy printers, and direct video inputs for VCRs and home computers. Receivers with internal digital processing can add picture within picture, freeze frame, image zoom, and sequential stills. The latest improvement in such receivers is the use of noninterlaced scanning to give the appearance of doubling the horizontal line rate. The resulting image looks sharper because the space between the scanning lines is filled.

Specially designed CCD chips can also be used to cancel "ghosts" or multipath interference in television receivers, rendering much better images in mountainous terrain. In the future, the use of better encoding and decoding techniques, the use of comb filters—special circuits that sharpen resolution—and the incorporation of digital processing will produce home television images approaching studio picture quality.

Flat-Screen TV. The ultimate television set will hang on the living room wall like a picture, and be only a few inches thick. The most promising technology in this field is the liquid crystal display (LCD), which has produced pocket-size portable TV sets with up to 4-in (10.2-cm) diagonal screens. While screen diagonals up to 12 in (30.5 cm) have been demonstrated as prototypes, none have the brightness, resolution, or contrast range of a direct-view picture tube.

At the other end of the scale, very large flat screens have been built for installation at large athletic parks, where they serve as giant scoreboards or huge television screens. The largest such screen by far was built by Sony at the Tsukuba Expo 85 in Japan. Using individual triads of red, green, and blue "trini-lites" (color phosphors arrayed together inside a cell), the screen stood 14 stories high, had more than 10,000 ft^2 (930 m^2) of luminous surface (82 $\times$ 131 ft; 25 $\times$ 40 m), and could easily be seen by 50,000 viewers.

Projection Television. Larger television images can be achieved through the use of a variety of projection systems that are designed for home or professional environments. Home projection TV systems are usually the enclosed cabinet variety, with screens ranging from 40 to 50 in (92 to 127 cm) diagonally. The image comes from three high-brightness cathode ray tubes, each providing a primary color. These are projected through a folded mirror system, on the rear of the translucent screen.

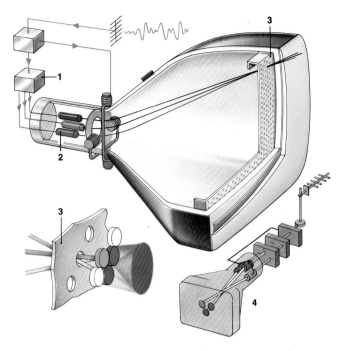

A color-television-set receiver has a decoding circuit (1) that separates the incoming signal into the red, green, and blue signals originally picked up by the camera tubes. Three electron guns (2), one for each color signal, emit beams that scan a television screen coated with phosphor dots arranged in triads. The dots fluoresce with a red, green, or blue glow when struck by an electron beam. Between the electron gun and screen is the shadow mask (3). The holes in the mask are arranged so that the electron beam from the blue gun, for instance, can bombard only the blue phosphor dots (4).

Larger screens normally employ front projection, using either CRT's or light-valve techniques, and can produce television images on theater-size screens.

DIGITAL AND ANALOG IN VIDEO TECHNOLOGY

Both the sensing of a video image and its subsequent display are basically analog, created as they are by a continuously varying electric signal. However, the processing of video signals in their transition from the camera to the receiver screen can often be improved by converting them into digital form. The major advantage of handling a video signal in digital form is that it can be manipulated with special effects, can be recorded on videotape, or used for image overlays or multiple-image mixing without any degradation in image quality. The digital signal is almost impervious to degradation. In addition, several digital signals can be interleaved (multiplexed), expediting the transmission and processing of auxiliary information.

At the present time, most television studios are analog, with "islands" of digital equipment dedicated to creating special effects and computer-assisted video graphics.

Within the home receiver, conversion to digital will improve the visual display by adding features not normally possible with analog circuits. CCD memories within the receiver will permit a "picture in picture" display, allowing the viewer to watch one channel on the full screen, with the video from another channel or from a VCR displayed in a small box in the corner of the screen. With digital circuits, the video image can be frozen or zoomed, or the screen can show up to nine sequenced still images.

Digital video techniques will continue to take over more of the TV image chain. As digital components become more plentiful and more cost effective, both TV studio equipment and consumer electronic devices will become more digitized.

TELEVISION RESOLUTION

The quality of a television image is usually rated in lines of resolution and may range from 200 to 400 depending on the sophistication of the receiver circuitry. Even the best TV mon-

itor or receiver, however, cannot display a better picture than the TV camera can produce on a given scanning system.

To improve television images beyond their fundamental limits and to create a high-definition television (HDTV) image will require a change of the basic scanning methods now in use. Several proposals have been made in the United States, Japan, and Europe for high-definition television systems using horizontal-line rates of 1,125 to 1,250, and expanding the picture to a 5:3 aspect ratio to give it a widescreen look, thus emulating the cinema screen. These HDTV systems will produce television images with 4 to 6 times the visual information content of a normal TV picture, increase the contrast ratio, and remove the visible line structure common to standard TV images. HDTV may also be used to create original programs that can be recorded on videotape, then transferred to film for motion picture theater projection.

TELEVISION TRANSMISSION

The television channel that carries pictures and sound into the home receiver is part of a very rigid system of frequency allocations made by the International Telecommunications Union (ITU) to various regions around the world. Space in the electromagnetic spectrum is so scarce and valuable that periodic global meetings are held to reexamine the needs of member nations and to maintain or change the allocations. In addition to the world body, the Federal Communications Commission (FCC) in the United States is constantly under pressure to reallocate spectrum space for emerging or growing communications services.

In North America the standard television channel is 6.0 MHz wide. Video signals are transmitted in a single sideband mode (sideband signals are present immediately above and below the carrier frequency), with the picture carrier at 1.25 MHz above the lower frequency boundary, and the sound carrier at 0.25 MHz below the upper boundary. This provides the video signal a 4.2 MHz channel, in which the color subcarrier is placed at 3.58 MHz above the picture carrier. (See also TELEVISION TRANSMISSION.)

Television signals must be transmitted in accordance with FCC regulations, with regard to the signal format, radiated power, modulation depth, and a variety of other parameters that adhere to the rules of good practice. These standards assure that the viewer will receive a stable, high-quality image and clear sound.

VIDEO RECORDING TECHNOLOGIES

A permanent record of a television image or program can be made on film, on magnetic tape or discs, on optical discs, or in a solid-state memory called a frame buffer. Up until the development of the first practical videotape recorder by Ampex Corporation in 1956, all television programs were recorded on film by kinescope recorders. Old black-and-white reruns of early TV shows made in the 1950s come from such film and attest to the limited quality of that medium. While much-better-quality color kinescope recorders are in use today, videotape has become the preferred medium for almost every·variety of programming applications.

Electronic cinematography has become the all-encompassing term for the use of television cameras to create program material, which is recorded, edited, and distributed on reels of videotape. In motion pictures there are three basic formats—35-mm professional, 16-mm industrial/educational, and Super 8-mm home movies. In the videotape world, things are not that simple. Professional videotape comes in 2-inch, 1-inch, ¾-inch, ½-inch, ¼ inch, and 8-mm widths, with enough different recording methods to create at least 15 noninterchangeable formats. In home video there are two half-inch formats, VHS and Beta, and the new 8-mm video format, none of which can play each other's tape cassettes.

Videotape Recording. VIDEOTAPE consists of a strip of plastic backing coated with a permanent layer of tiny metal particles imbedded in a durable resin. The particles are made of magnetic materials such as iron or cobalt and are capable of holding a magnetic charge imparted to them by the video recording head. When the tape is passed over the playback head, the resident magnetic charges are reproduced as the original video signal and the accompanying sound.

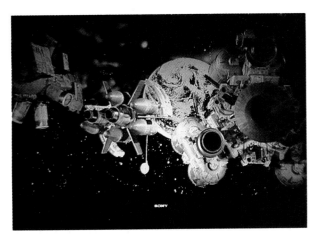

A high definition TV (HDTV) image is projected on a screen measuring 10 ft (3.05 m) diagonally. The quality of the image rivals that of film. In the future, feature films might be made in HDTV and distributed via satellite simultaneously to thousands of electronic cinemas.

In broadcast television, videotape recorders can now reproduce television programs that are virtually indistinguishable from a live show, although such machines are relatively complex and expensive. Because videotaping a TV show permits correcting any mistakes made, and allows cost-effective scheduling of TV studio facilities, most major programs are taped, then replayed at the appropriate time slot in each time zone. NBC's ''Tonight Show'' and ''CBS News'' are each recorded at least 3 hours earlier, sent by microwave or satellite to the network stations across the country, and rerecorded for local insertion. (See also TELEVISION PRODUCTION.)

Camcorders. Television crews who go out in mobile vehicles to cover the news usually carry electronic cameras that incorporate a video recorder either as a separate portable unit or as a built-in cassette recorder on the camera. These self-contained battery-operated camcorders, weighing about 7 kg (15 lb), permit very flexible coverage in tight places and make possible pictorial results of very high visual impact. The imaging and videotape recording techniques developed for broadcasting have also resulted in the production of consumer-oriented devices. Videocassette recorders are now both compact and affordable, and they are used in nearly 50% of U.S. households. By adding equally compact color cameras, electronic home movies can now be made by anyone.

Videocassette Recorders. For the last few years, home VCRs have come in two incompatible formats, the Beta system developed by Sony and the VHS made by several manufacturers. Although both systems produced comparable images, the VHS configuration has now taken over the bulk of the market and is currently the leading format in sales, availability of prerecorded movies, and variety of accessories. Extended Definition Beta and Super VHS are the latest technological improvements in the field. Both use digital circuitry to produce special effects and enhance picture quality. Camcorders are also available in these formats. Several manufacturers are also offering components that use 8-mm cassettes. (See VIDEO RECORDING.)

Optical Recorders. Video or audio signals can also be stored on optical discs by using lasers to record and play back the spiral tracks. The larger size VIDEODISC (30.5 cm/12 inches in diameter) can hold over one hour of normal television programming, one hour of a movie, or 15 minutes of high-definition TV, all with stereo sound. The COMPACT DISC can also be used for storing computer data, in which capacity it is called a CD-ROM (Read Only Memory).

The advantage of the optical, or laser-read, disc over videotape is that it is virtually indestructible, since noncontact optical readout gives it an unlimited life. It also provides rapid random access to the information on the disc. The disadvantage, at least at present, is that the user cannot record his or her own program but must buy a prerecorded disc. New, recordable discs may soon be available, however.

Optical discs have a very high information-packing density. For example, the entire *Academic American Encyclopedia* is stored on a single CD-ROM, with room to spare.

Video Still Cameras. Although they are still new and relatively untried, color cameras that record still pictures on magnetic discs have reached the market. These cameras convert the optical image into an electrical signal, then deposit the signal on circular tracks on a small magnetic disc inside the camera. Up to 50 individual video shots can be taken, and they may be displayed on a home TV receiver through a video player. Because there is no processing necessary, the pictures may be viewed immediately.

GRAPHICS TECHNOLOGY

Video Art. The development of COMPUTER GRAPHICS systems permit graphic artists to create images directly in the television medium, greatly influenced daily programming.

Electronic ''paint systems'' use a palette on which the artist renders the image with a stylus or light pen while watching a color television monitor to see the actual image being produced. The color monitor will also show the artist a wide selection of colors, a variety of print fonts, and various shapes such as circles, squares, and triangles (see PAINTBOX).

External images can also be entered through a video camera and digitized, so that they may be altered in size, position, or coloration. The more-advanced computer graphic systems will also permit animation of the images to form a moving sequence.

The TV station identification, the logos, commercial spots, and news inserts are usually created on computer graphics systems. The graphics can also be combined with live images. Major sporting events such as the Olympics or the Super Bowl will have computer graphic artists who create event-oriented graphics that are inserted into the show for ''color.''

Computer graphic systems have steadily come down in size and price. These smaller systems are capable of three-dimensional rendering of television images and can be programmed to create animated segments for assembly on a videotape recorder.

Computerized Animation. The commercials and cartoons that are being produced today for television broadcasting are often made on computer graphic systems with extended capabilities. While the individual images may be created by a system similar to the computer graphics system just described, the animation is dependent on larger computers with more memory and more capabilities. The key to generating the animation is to create a start ''key frame'' and an end ''key frame.'' By telling the computer the rate at which the begin-

The digital TV set—the newest major consumer advance in video technology—replaces some 400 analog components with a digital chip and adds a computer memory to store image information. Among its advantages is the capacity to display several channels at once.

Teletext acts as a kind of video newspaper, whose "pages" offer the latest news, sports, financial, and other data in abbreviated form. A typical front page, shown here, lists a menu of subjects from which the viewer can choose by keying a hand-held remote-control device.

ning and end images should progress, the computer will do all of the calculations, and produce the intermediate images to go smoothly from start to finish. Short animated sequences of this nature (up to 30 sec) can be stored on digital discs, from which they are transferred to tape and sequenced with past and future segments.

Video Special Effects. To achieve a high visual impact during a television show, it is necessary to manipulate images in a way that will make them appear more interesting. Because video signals can be digitized and put into a frame buffer (a color-information storage device) in pixel form, it is also possible to read out these pixels in a nonlinear form. The original image may have been rectangular, but with the proper software it can be read out as a trapezoid, circle, or some other shape. Similarly, the image may be zoomed, tumbled, overlaid with other images, or made to disappear into the horizon. These effects can be done in real time by a "joystick" and a series of function keys that select the type of effect desired. In many cases these digital video effects are recorded, and the tape is used over and over for opening a new show or for creating a promotional insert. It is also possible to use these effects during live programming to enhance the appearance of the home viewers' image.   JOSEPH ROIZEN

Bibliography: Ayers, Ralph, *Graphics for TV* (1984); Benson, K. Blair, ed., *Television Engineering Handbook* (1985); Blank, Ben, and Garcia, Mario, *Professional Graphic Video Design* (1985); Fletcher, James, ed., *Handbook of Radio and TV Broadcasting* (1981); McCavitt, William E., *Television and Technology: Alternative Communication Systems* (1983); Oakey, Virginia, *Dictionary of Film and Television Terms* (1982); Oringel, Robert, *Television Operation Handbook* (1984); Rzeszewski, T., ed., *Television Technology Today* (1985).

videocassette recorder: see VIDEO; VIDEO RECORDING.

videodisc

Videodiscs resemble phonograph recordings in appearance and size but are able to store video as well as audio programming. Several types of videodiscs have been developed. The Philips Company of the Netherlands developed the laser-optical type of videodisc in which video and audio signals are encoded in the form of microscopic pits beneath the surface of a reflective disc measuring approximately 30.50 cm (12 in) in diameter. A laser beam tracks and reads the video and audio data inscribed in this manner and translates the data into electrical video and audio signals that may then be seen and heard on a TV set or video monitor screen. (See also COMPACT DISC; VIDEO TECHNOLOGY.)

A less successful form of videodisc, employing a stylus riding in the grooves of the disc that translates variations in

electrical capacitance into video and audio signals, was developed and, for a time, marketed by RCA and others. This was known as the Capacitance Electronic Disc (CED). It was abandoned by its inventors in 1985.

A third form of videodisc, known as the Video High Density (VHD) disc, also uses changes in electrical capacitance for signal storing. It does not, however, employ record grooves. The pickup rides on the surface of the disc, guided by additional coded information and servomechanisms. This system, developed by Japan Victor Company (JVC), has not yet been made available for consumer use in the United States.

   LEONARD FELDMAN

videotape

Videotape is thin, plastic tape—usually a polyester—covered with a surface layer of metallic particles and used for storing video and audio signals. For many years videotape was used almost exclusively by the television industry for recording programs for rebroadcast. Videotape is now available to the consumer for many uses, including recording off the television at home by means of a videocassette recorder and live-action recording with a VIDEO CAMERA.

Videotape recording employs the same analog, magnetic technology of audio tapes, whereby information converted into electromagnetic form causes metallic particles embedded in tape to orient themselves in correspondence with particular frequencies and dynamics (see SOUND RECORDING AND REPRODUCTION). The metal particles used most often to coat tape are ferric oxide (doped with cobalt) and chromium dioxide.

The methodology of video recording differs from that of audio recording. In recording video signals, the tape is moved slowly past recording heads that, instead of remaining stationary, sit along the edge of a wheel that rotates in a plane perpendicular to, or on a bias with, the passing tape. This perpendicular or helical scanning places more information on the tape—a result that is necessary for reproducing complex video images. This technique also allows for video stop-action: when the tape is stopped, the playback heads can continue to scan a single piece of tape, thereby reproducing a single picture frame. Ordinarily, the top and bottom edges of videotapes contain conventional audio tracks. Some types of tape, however, incorporate the audio signal into the diagonal video tracks, producing a much higher-fidelity sound. Audio on 8-mm tape, recorded in the same tracks as the video, can also translate analog into digital stereo sound signals, and can be used for audio recording alone, with a capacity of about 12 hours of sound. In order to hear it properly, however, one must play it through a stereo-equipped television set.

Videotape used by the television industry has a standard 2-in (5.08-cm) or 1-in (2.54-cm) width and is mounted on large reels. The more well-known consumer videotapes have a 0.5-in (1.27-cm) width and are contained within plastic cassettes for easy use in VIDEO RECORDING. The even thinner, 8-mm (0.31-in) tape is marketed for use in hand-held video camera/recorders, or camcorders. This latest tape technology requires a higher-density coating of pure metal particles (rather than oxides) in order to maintain picture quality.

videotex

Videotex is an interactive electronic technology that delivers information and transactional services such as banking and shopping through a computer/telephone communications system. Users can retrieve information or conduct transactions (such as paying bills, buying airline tickets, or relaying electronic messages) using a special terminal device hooked up to a TV set, or to a personal computer, and connected—generally via telephone lines—to a host computer. Customers pay a per-use charge or a monthly subscription fee to use the service. TELETEXT, a semiinteractive, information-supplying service, is available for television viewers who own special decoders. In contrast to videotex, it offers much smaller and more-restricted information categories.

Information and service providers (such as news organizations, banks, brokerage houses, merchandisers, and travel

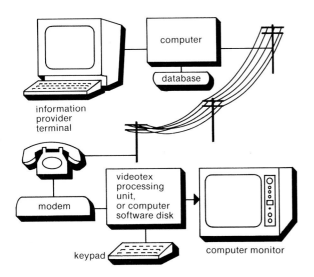

The videotex information source and the videotex user are connected by a telephone and a modem, an instrument that converts the source computer's digital signals into audio signals for transmission over telephone lines, then reconverts them back to digital signals for display on the user's computer screen. Specially modified TV receivers can also display video information. The key pad allows the user to call up specific items or pages. The videotex processing unit may be a software disc inserted into the computer itself.

packagers) supply information for videotex systems and often manage their transactions (for example, ticket or stock purchases) through "gateways" that permit computerized information to be accessed from their own computers.

Videotex growth has been much slower than was originally predicted, despite the efforts of many organizations to develop and market videotex services. In North America, major newspaper publishers, banks, and computer and telephone companies have developed and tested videotex systems. Some projects have involved cable TV or alternative transmission technologies. Several have used special personal computer software. From 1981 to 1986 about 60 videotex or hybrid videotex systems were created in the United States, most on a local or regional basis—although some offered nationwide services, such as electronic mail and coast-to-coast shopping. The most ambitious U.S. videotex ventures—few of which have succeeded—included Viewtron in Miami, Gateway in Los Angeles, and Keyfax in Chicago. All were developed by companies affiliated with major newspaper publishers.

On the other hand, videotex DATABASE systems—among them, CompuServe, The Source, and Dow Jones News/Retrieval—have attracted sizable national audiences, primarily individuals interested in services that provide such information as stock-market statistics, news reports, and business analysis.

Most videotex systems use a page-by-page format for information display, although some systems permit "scrolling" the lines of text that appear on the video screen. Although several videotex systems have used sophisticated color computer graphics displays, the expense of color terminals on consumer computers, as well as the difficulty of color transmission over telephone lines, has discouraged prospective videotex operators from investing in such systems. Most U.S. videotex systems use a computer format that transmits only words and numbers.

"Public access videotex" offers similar types of information, travel assistance, or electronic shopping through a computer-controlled kiosk in a public site, such as an airport, shopping mall, or tourist center. In addition, "private videotex" systems have been developed within corporations to provide computer-assisted information to employees who may not have computer skills.

The cost of operation and present lack of consumer appetite for electronically delivered information services have been difficult barriers for videotex development. Several outside factors have also complicated the creation of videotex systems, notably the break-up of AT&T, whose telephone lines videotex uses, and the boom-bust cycle of the home computer industry.

In Europe and Japan, government-run telecommunications agencies have developed their own videotex systems. Often these systems are related to other communications services, such as computerized electronic phone directories. In France, since 1983 the Minitel project has given away about two million inexpensive terminals to telephone subscribers who use their videotex machines to obtain free directory information or, for a fee, real-estate listings, news stories, weather forecasts, restaurant guides, and TV schedules. Britain's Prestel, West Germany's Bildschirmtext, and Japan's Captain system—all government owned—have been moderately successful.

GARY ARLEN

Bibliography: Alber, Antone F., *Videotex/Teletext: Principles and Practices* (1985); Arlen, Gary H., *International Videotex Teletext News* (periodical); Gecsei, Jan, *The Architecture of Videotex Systems* (1983); Hurly, Paul, et al., *The Videotex and Teletext Handbook* (1985); Tydeman, John, et al., *Teletext and Videotex in the United States* (1982).

Vidor, King   [vee'-dohr]

King Vidor, b. Galveston, Tex., Feb. 8, 1896, d. Nov. 1, 1982, was one of the pioneer directors of the U.S. film industry. He worked as a scriptwriter and newsreel cameraman in Hollywood before becoming an independent producer in 1918. *The Big Parade* (1925), one of the earliest films to depict World War I, was the director's first great success. Vidor's achievements as an innovative filmmaker reached their peak with *The Crowd* (1928), the all-black *Hallelujah* (1929), and *Our Daily Bread* (1934), works that display a growing interest in the editing techniques of the Soviet cinema. Also from this period were such charming light comedies as *The Patsy* (1928) and *Show People* (1928). Vidor became more stylistically conservative in such films as *The Citadel* (1938) and *Northwest Passage* (1940). Toward the end of his career he revealed a flair for melodrama in *Duel in the Sun* (1946), *The Fountainhead* (1949), and *Ruby Gentry* (1952). *War and Peace* (1956) was his last film epic.

WILLIAM S. PECHTER

Bibliography: Baxter, John, *King Vidor* (1976); Vidor, King, *A Tree Is a Tree* (1953) and *King Vidor on Film Making* (1972).

Vieira, António   [vy-ah'-ee-ruh]

The Portuguese Jesuit António Vieira, b. Feb. 6, 1608, d. July 18, 1697, was one of the most famous preachers and orators of his day, and his writings are considered models of Portuguese prose. During his long and varied life, he was court preacher and diplomat for King John IV of Portugal in the 1640s, a missionary in Brazil in the 1650s, a prisoner of the Inquisition from 1665 to 1667, and an advocate (in Rome) on behalf of the Portuguese Jews in the early 1670s.

Vieira da Silva   [vy-uh'-ee-ruh duh seel'-vuh]

Maria Helena Vieira da Silva, b. June 13, 1908, is a Portuguese painter of abstractions working in Paris. Her canvases can be characterized as grids of vivid colors that sparkle like mosaics. Vieira da Silva studied sculpture with Émile Antoine Bourdelle and Charles Despiau and painting with Áchille Émile Orthon Friesz and Fernand Léger. She has won international recognition for her paintings, which are represented in the collections of major museums of modern art. After her first postwar exhibition in New York City in 1946 she exhibited regularly in Paris (into the 1980s) and throughout Europe. Her work was included in the 1950 and 1954 Venice Biennales and in the 1954 São Paulo Bienal.

ELEANOR TUFTS

Bibliography: Lassaigne, Jacques, and Weelen, Guy, *Vieira da Silva* (1980); Russell, John, "Artist in the Family—Vieira da Silva," *Art in America* 54 (March 1966).

vielle [vee-el']

The *vielle* (German: *Geige*), the medieval French fiddle, had four fingered strings and a drone string. The Spanish *vihuela de mano* was probably a similar instrument. After the 14th century such fiddles were commonly called VIOLS. The *vielle* was played by jongleurs, who performed dance music and accompaniments for trouvère songs (see MINSTRELS, MINNESINGERS, AND TROUBADOURS). The *vielle à roue*, or HURDY-GURDY, has a rosined wheel instead of a bow.   ELWYN A. WIENANDT

Vien, Joseph Marie [vee-an']

The French painter Joseph Marie Vien, b. June 18, 1716, d. Mar. 27, 1809, introduced the stylistic reform that culminated in the pure neoclassicism of his student Jacques Louis David. Vien studied (1740–44) with Charles Natoire in Paris; he won the French Academy's Rome prize in 1743 and remained in Rome from 1744 to 1750. Later he served as the director of the French Academy in Rome (1775–81). Vien was influenced by Raphael, Michelangelo, the Carracci, and Anton Raphael Mengs (Vien's contemporary in Rome), but most of all by the classical Roman wall paintings excavated at that time. His *Selling of Cupids* (1763; Château de Fontainebleau, Ile-de-France) was inspired directly by them. Vien became (1789) director of the French Academy and exerted a powerful influence on later French painters.   NANETTE SALOMON

Bibliography: Rosenberg, P., et al., *French Painting 1774–1830* (1975); Rosenblum, R., *Transformations in Late Eighteenth Century Art* (1967).

Vienna

Vienna (German: Wein), in northeastern Austria, is located on the Danube River at an elevation of 202 m (664 ft). The capital of Austria and an autonomous province, it has a population of 1,515,666 (1981)—nearly one-quarter that of the entire country. Long the seat of the HABSBURGS dynasty (Holy Roman emperors and, later, emperors of Austria), Vienna retains its imperial style, with grand boulevards and imposing architecture.

Contemporary City. The heart of old Vienna is the Innere Stadt (Inner City), an area surrounded by a horseshoe-shaped wall that confined the city as late as the 1850s. In 1857, Emperor Francis Joseph decided to raze the wall and replace it with a 57-m-wide (187-ft) Ringstrasse (Ring Street). To line this beautifully landscaped boulevard the Viennese erected a collection of buildings of varied styles. The University of Vienna (originally founded in 1365) was rebuilt in a neo-Italian Renaissance style; across the park is the City Hall, a neo-Flemish Gothic structure. The State Opera House (Stadtsoper) is reminiscent of early French Renaissance buildings. Within the Innere Stadt is Saint Stephen's, a Gothic cathedral first built about 1135 and rebuilt, following a fire, during the 14th and 15th centuries. The oldest part of the Hofburg, the imperial palace of the Habsburgs, dates from the 13th century; the chapel (15th century) is now the home of the Vienna Boys Choir. As the strength of the empire grew, the Habsburgs moved to summer homes beyond the protection of the city walls. SCHÖNBRUNN PALACE, in the southwest part of the city, dates from the late 17th century; the Belvedere, by Johann Lukas von HILDEBRANDT, from the early 18th century.

Vienna concentrated on developing its bureaucracy and service industries while the rest of Europe passed through the Industrial Revolution. With heavy manufacturing long relegated to other sectors of the empire, Vienna never realized the industrial capability of a city its size. It does have a metallurgical industry, and it produces precision instruments and electrical appliances; it also has a reputation for hand-finished goods and for pastries and confections. The headquarters of the International Atomic Energy Agency, the Organization of Petroleum Exporting Countries, and the United Nations Industrial Development Organization are located in Vienna. Its Schwechat airport is one of Europe's busiest, and a subway system has been partially completed.

Vienna is an autonomous province of Austria as well as the capital city. Despite its imperial past, Vienna has, since 1918,

This view of Vienna's skyline shows two of the city's historic churches. On the left is the green dome of the Peterskirche, a baroque structure of the early 18th century; on the right, Saint Stephen's Cathedral, with its tall Gothic spire.

consistently elected socialist governments. In addition to providing the usual municipal services, the city operates many small businesses and is a major employer of the work force.

Vienna has one of Europe's richest musical heritages. Franz Josef Haydn began his career in the boys' choir of Saint Stephen's. Beethoven, Mozart, the Strauss family, Schubert, Brahms, Bruckner, Mahler, Schoenberg, and Richard Strauss all lived and worked in Vienna. The VIENNA PHILHARMONIC ORCHESTRA may be Europe's most respected symphonic company. Nearly 30 museums house extensive fine arts collections; these include the Historical Museum of the City of Vienna, the Museum of Fine Arts, and the ALBERTINA, in the Hofburg.

History. Originally a Celtic settlement called Vindobona, the site became a frontier encampment under the Romans. Repeatedly overrun in the great tribal migrations, the site had been resettled and fortified as Wena by the 11th century. It was chartered in 1137 and became the capital of the dukes of Austria. In 1278 the first of the Habsburgs took up residence there. The city was held (1485–90) by Matthias Corvinus of Hungary and unsuccessfully besieged by the Turks in 1529 and again in 1683. The Napoleonic Wars, during which Vienna was twice occupied (1805, 1809) by the French, ended with the Congress of Vienna (1814–15). During the late 19th century and early 20th century, Vienna flourished as a cultural, philosophical, and scientific center. Following World War I, the Austrian Empire was dismembered, leaving Vienna the capital of a small republic. In 1938, Adolf Hitler, who had studied in Vienna as a youth, annexed Austria to Germany. Badly damaged during World War II, Vienna underwent a quadripartite Allied occupation until 1955, when it was reestablished as the capital of an independent and permanently neutral Austria.   JONATHAN E. HELMREICH

Bibliography: Comini, Alessandra, *The Fantastic Art of Vienna* (1978); Edwards, Tudor, *The Blue Danube: The Vienna of Franz Josef and Its Aftermath* (1973); Hürlimann, Martin, *Vienna*, trans. by D. J. S. Thomson (1970); Moore, Charles, *Vienna—City of Melodies* (1978); Neusser-Hromatka, Maria, *Beautiful Vienna*, 10th ed. (1973); Pryce-Jones, David, *Vienna* (1978); Roth, Ernst, *A Tale of Three Cities* (1971); Schorske, Carl E., *Fin-de-Siècle Vienna: Politics and Culture* (1979); Waissenberger, Robert, *Vienna, 1890–1920* (1984).

Vienna, Congress of

The Congress of Vienna (September 1814–June 1815), convened by the states of Europe after the collapse of Napoleon I's empire, attempted to reestablish a balance of power and restore pre-Napoleonic dynasties where possible. It was an unprecedented meeting hosted by Austrian emperor Francis I (formerly Holy Roman Emperor Francis II) and attended by Emperor ALEXANDER I of Russia, King FREDERICK WILLIAM III of Prussia, and many lesser rulers. Viscount CASTLEREAGH for Great Britain, Prince Karl August von HARDENBERG for Prussia, Count Karl Robert NESSELRODE for Russia, and Prince Klemens von METTERNICH for Austria, representatives of the victorious powers, were the principal negotiators, assisted by Metternich's aide Friedrich von GENTZ, an Austrian diplomat who became secretary general of the congress.

Charles Maurice de TALLEYRAND-PÉRIGORD of France, smoothly taking advantage of differences among the four dominant powers, was eventually brought into the group to break a deadlock over the demands of Russia for all of Poland and of Prussia for all of Saxony. With Talleyrand's support, Castlereagh and Metternich forced Russia and Prussia to reduce their claims. Ultimately Prussia was given two-fifths of Saxony, and Russia received most of the grand duchy of Warsaw. The settlement in the west created barriers against French aggression. Belgium was given to the Netherlands, Prussia received the Rhineland and Westphalia, Nice and Savoy went to Sardinia, and Lombardy and Venetia were given to Austria. A loose GERMAN CONFEDERATION was established primarily for defensive purposes, and Switzerland was neutralized under international guarantee. Denmark ceded Norway to Sweden in exchange for Lauenburg. Legitimate dynasties were restored in Spain, Portugal, and Italy. The settlement as a whole remained in effect for more than 40 years and created a durable balance of power, but in ignoring nationalist yearnings it left unsolved problems that led to the REVOLUTIONS OF 1848 and later trouble.   ENNO E. KRAEHE

Bibliography: Alsop, S. M., *The Congress Dances* (1985); Gulick, E. V., *Europe's Classical Balance of Power* (1955; repr. 1967); Kissinger, H. A., *A World Restored: Metternich, Castlereagh, and the Problems of Peace, 1812–1822* (1957); Nicolson, H., *The Congress of Vienna* (1946; repr. 1970); Webster, C. K., *The Congress of Vienna, 1814–1815* (1919; repr. 1963).

See also: PARIS, TREATIES OF; QUADRUPLE ALLIANCE.

Vienna Philharmonic Orchestra

No fewer than four dates, from 1833 to 1860, may be given for the founding of the Vienna Philharmonic (*Wiener Philharmoniker*); perhaps the most significant is 1842, when the orchestra of the Royal Court Opera performed in the Redoutensaal under Otto Nicolai. The Philharmonic, which is also the orchestra of the Vienna State Opera, makes its home in the acoustically superb Musikvereinsaal. Subscriptions to its concerts have remained within families for generations and are virtually unobtainable. Among its chief conductors since Nicolai are Hans Richter, Gustav Mahler, Felix Weingartner, Wilhelm Furtwängler, Clemens Krauss, Bruno Walter, Herbert von Karajan, and, since 1971, Claudio Abbado. The sound of the orchestra is inimitable. Its musicians play Mozart with exceptional finesse, and Brahms, Bruckner, and Wagner with unexcelled richness and plangency.   LAWRENCE FUCHSBERG

Vientiane [vee-uhn-tee-en']

Vientiane is the capital and largest city of Laos, on the Mekong River in the northern part of the country, near the border of Thailand. The population is 210,000 (1981 est.). Vientiane is the major port and commercial center in Laos, serving the surrounding agricultural area. The city maintains air links with Bangkok and Ho Chi Minh City (formerly Saigon). Most buildings are wood, typical of Laotian architecture.

Vientiane became the capital in 1563, when the government was moved from Luang Prabang under pressure of a threat from Burma. The city was sacked by the Thais in 1828. The French established their administrative capital for Laos in Vientiane in 1899. After independence in 1953, Vientiane remained the administrative capital while Luang Prabang served as the royal capital. With the Communist takeover in 1975, however, the kingdom was abolished and Vientiane became the sole capital.   ASHOK K. DUTT

Viet Cong [vee'-et kawng]

In the VIETNAM WAR the insurgent guerrilla movement that fought the South Vietnamese government and its ally, the United States, was known to its enemies as the Viet Cong ("Vietnamese Communists"). The name, coined by South Vietnamese leader Ngo Dinh Diem, was inaccurate because the Communists were only one of several groups that began isolated acts of rebellion in 1957. In 1960 these groups united into the National Liberation Front of South Vietnam (NLFSV), modeled on the earlier Viet Minh, and full-scale insurrection began. Most of the insurgents were South Vietnamese, but the movement depended increasingly on North Vietnamese aid and troops. In 1969 the NLFSV formed a Provisional Revolutionary Government, which participated in the peace negotiations in Paris. The NLFSV and the PRG were dissolved soon after the war's end (1975), but several members of the latter were included in the government of the unified Vietnam.

Bibliography: Conley, Michael, *The Communist Insurgent Infrastructure in South Vietnam* (1967); Pike, Douglas, *Viet Cong* (1966) and *War, Peace, and the Viet Cong* (1969).

Viet Minh [vee'-et min]

The Viet Minh was the shortened name for the League for the Independence of Vietnam, the chief political-military organization that battled the French for independence (1946–54). It was founded in 1941 in China by the Communist-nationalist HO CHI MINH. A coalition of nationalist groups under Communist control, it was the only significant organized resistance in Vietnam during the World War II Japanese occupation. In 1946 the Viet Minh assumed the leadership of the anti-French nationalist struggle. After the French defeat at the Battle of DIEN BIEN PHU in 1954, a Communist government was established in North Vietnam, and the Viet Minh was dissolved.   RICHARD BUTWELL

Bibliography: Bodard, Lucien, *The Quicksand War: Prelude to Vietnam*, trans. by Patrick O'Brien (1967); Dunn, Peter, *The First Vietnam War* (1985); Hammer, Ellen Joy, *The Struggle for Indochina, 1940–1955* (1966).

Viète, François [vee-et']

François Viète, b. 1540, d. Dec. 13, 1603, the greatest French mathematician of his time, was the founder of modern algebra and of modern algebraic notation. Viète founded the theory of equations and discovered general solutions to cubic and quartic equations. He was the first to use algebraic rather than geometric constructions in proofs. Viète also did important work in trigonometry and left an unpublished manuscript on mathematical astronomy. Trained as a lawyer, Viète was a Huguenot sympathizer. He deciphered (1590) an elaborate code used by Philip II of Spain in his military plans against the Protestants.   STEVEN LUBAR

Bibliography: Zeller, M. C., *The Development of Trigonometry from Regiomontanus to Pitiscus* (1944).

Vietnam

Vietnam, a nation located along the eastern coast of mainland Southeast Asia, has had a turbulent history. Emerging as a distinct civilization during the first millennium BC, Vietnam was conquered by China during the early Han dynasty and subjected to 1,000 years of foreign rule. In AD 939 the Vietnamese restored their independence and gradually expanded southward along the coast from their historic homeland in the YÜAN (Red) RIVER valley. In the 19th century Vietnam was conquered once again and absorbed, along with neighboring Cambodia (now Kampuchea) and Laos, into French INDOCHINA. Patriotic elements soon began to organize national resistance to colonial rule, however, and after World War II, Communist-led VIET MINH guerrillas battled for several years to free the country from foreign subjugation. In 1954, at the GENEVA CONFERENCE, the country was divided into Communist-led North Vietnam and non-Communist South Vietnam. For the next 20 years, both North and South Vietnam were involved in the VIETNAM WAR. That conflict came to an end when Communist forces from the north occupied Saigon (now HO CHI MINH CITY) in April 1975. Today, the Vietnamese government is attempting to lead the entire nation to socialism. But domestic unrest and foreign-policy problems, compounded by renewed tensions with China over the Vietnamese occupation of Kampuchea, keep Vietnam a garrison state.

LAND AND RESOURCES
Vietnam is shaped like a giant letter ''S,'' extending some 1,600 km (1,000 mi) from the Chinese border to Point Ca Mau (Baibung) on the Gulf of Thailand. At its widest, it reaches a width of about 560 km (350 mi). In the narrow center, it is less than 50 km (30 mi) wide.

Much of Vietnam is rugged and densely forested. A chain of mountains called the Truong Son (Annamese Cordillera) extends more than 1,287 km (800 mi) from the Yüan River delta east of HANOI to the Central Highlands south of Laos. For much of that distance, these mountains form the border between Vietnam and Laos and Kampuchea. The highest point in the country, Fan Si Pan, rises to 3,143 m (10,312 ft) in the mountainous northwest, near the Chinese border. Poor soils and heavy rains make the mountainous areas relatively unsuitable for agriculture.

SOCIALIST REPUBLIC OF VIETNAM

LAND. Area: 329,556 km² (127,242 mi²). Capital: Hanoi (1985 est. pop., 2,674,400). Largest city: Ho Chi Minh City (1984 est. pop., 3,293,146).

PEOPLE. Population (1986 est.): 61,994,000. Density (1986 est.): 188 persons per km² (487 per mi²). Distribution (1986): 19% urban, 81% rural. Annual growth (1986): 2.5%. Official language: Vietnamese. Major religions: Buddhism, Caodaism, Hoa Hao, Roman Catholicism.

EDUCATION AND HEALTH. Literacy rate (1985 est.): ethnic Vietnamese—95% of adult population; minorities—70%. Universities (1981): 3. Hospital beds (1985): 205,700. Physicians (1985): 16,000. Life expectancy (1985): women—66; men—62. Infant mortality (1983): 53 per 1,000 live births.

ECONOMY. GNP (1984): $18.1 billion; $300 per capita. Labor force (1984): agriculture and fishing—73%; manufacturing—14%; commerce and services—5%. Foreign trade (1984): imports—$1,645 million; exports—$763 million; principal trade partners—USSR, Japan, India, Hong Kong, Singapore. Currency: 1 dong = 100 xu.

GOVERNMENT. Type: Communist state. Legislature: National Assembly. Political subdivisions: 36 provinces, 3 autonomous regions, 1 special area.

COMMUNICATIONS. Railroads (1983): 2,523 km (1,568 mi) total. Roads (1983): 347,243 km (215,767 mi) total. Major ports: 3. Major airfields: 3.

The large deltas of the Yüan River in the north and the MEKONG RIVER in the south are rich in alluvial basaltic soils brought down from South China and inner Southeast Asia and have abundant water resources and favorable climate that make them highly suitable for settled agriculture, particularly the cultivation of wet rice. In the Yüan delta, the climate is subtropical, ranging from 5° C (41° F) in winter to more than 38° C (100° F) in summer. The Mekong delta is almost uniformly hot, varying from 26° to 30° C (79° to 85° F) throughout the year. The monsoon season extends from early May to late October, and typhoons often cause flooding in northern coastal areas.

Most of Vietnam's hardwoods and wild animals (including buffalo, elephants, and rhinoceroses) are found in the mountains. In the north are deposits of iron ore, tin, copper, apatite (phosphate rock), and chromite. Coal, mined along the coast

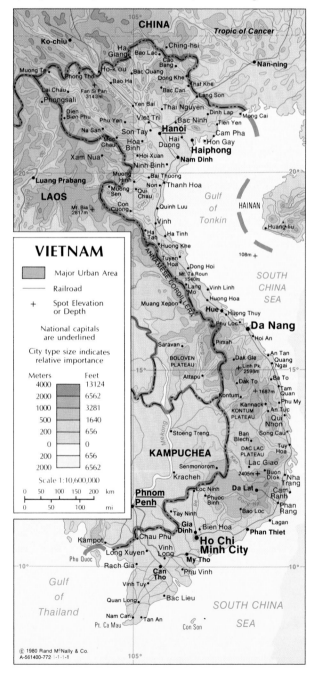

near the Chinese border, is an important export and the main source of energy, although rivers are being harnessed for hydroelectric power and the government is attempting, with Soviet assistance, to exploit modest oil reserves in the South China Sea.

PEOPLE

Vietnam is one of the most homogeneous societies in Southeast Asia. Although more than 60 different ethnic groups live in the country, ethnic Vietnamese constitute nearly 90% of the total population and are in the majority throughout the country except in the mountains. The Vietnamese are descended from peoples who settled in the Yüan delta area more than 3,000 years ago and later moved southward along the central coast into the Mekong delta. They speak Vietnamese, which exhibits many similarities to other tongues spoken in the region but is sometimes considered a separate language group (see SOUTHEAST ASIAN LANGUAGES).

The so-called overseas Chinese, descended from ethnic Chinese who migrated into the country during the 17th and 18th centuries, settled for the most part in large cities and became involved in commerce, manufacturing, fishing, and coal mining. During the traditional and colonial periods, the Chinese were placed under separate administration. Recent governments, however, have attempted to assimilate them. Thousands of ethnic Chinese fled abroad in 1978 in the wake of a government decision to nationalize commerce and industry in the south; about 2 million reportedly remain in the country.

Tribal peoples, including the MEO and the MONTAGNARDS, number about 3 million. Descended from a wide variety of ethnic backgrounds, they live primarily in the Central Highlands and in the mountains of the north, where they practice SLASH-AND-BURN AGRICULTURE. Other smaller groups are the KHMER (about 500,000) and the Cham (about 50,000), remnants

Small vegetable gardens surround homes on the outskirts of Nha Trang, a coastal city at the mouth of the Song (river) Koi in southern Vietnam. Due to Nha Trang's fine beaches on the South China Sea, the area became a resort during the period of French colonial rule.

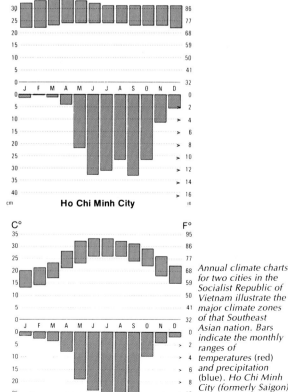

Ho Chi Minh City

Hanoi

Annual climate charts for two cities in the Socialist Republic of Vietnam illustrate the major climate zones of that Southeast Asian nation. Bars indicate the monthly ranges of temperatures (red) and precipitation (blue). Ho Chi Minh City (formerly Saigon) has a tropical wet climate. Hanoi, the nation's capital, has a subtropical humid climate.

of ancient states absorbed by the Vietnamese during their southward expansion.

Although the majority of ethnic Vietnamese traditionally considered themselves Buddhist or Confucianist, there are about 3 million Roman Catholics, most of whom now live in the south. Members of two religious sects, the Cao Dai (an amalgam of eastern and western traditions) and the Hoa Hao (a radical form of Buddhism), live mainly in the Mekong delta area and number about 1 million each. Like the ethnic minorities, these religious groups have resisted assimilation into the majority culture and today are under considerable pressure to conform to the government's socialist ideals.

The vast majority of the population live in overcrowded cities or in the densely populated delta areas and along the central coast. Large southern cities include Ho Chi Minh City, DA NANG, and HUE. Hanoi, the capital, and HAIPHONG, a port on the Gulf of Tonkin (see TONKIN, GULF OF), are the chief cities in the north.

Rapid population growth has placed considerable strain on limited health services, educational facilities, and food supplies. The government has instituted a family planning program and attempted to relieve the problem of overcrowding by resettling several million people into "new economic areas" in the sparsely populated mountains and upland plateaus. Other Vietnamese have been resettled into neighboring Kampuchea. Vietnam contends that most of the latter had lived in Kampuchea prior to 1970 and were driven or fled into exile during that country's civil war. Critics charge, however, that the resettlement program is being used to strengthen Vietnamese domination over Kampuchea, now integrated into a "special relationship" with Vietnam and Laos.

Education is under state control and is free at all levels. The leading institution of higher learning is Hanoi University. Although health facilities remain limited, there has been significant progress in health care since the reunification of the country in 1976.

For centuries, Vietnamese art and architecture were heavily influenced by Chinese and Indian forms (see SOUTHEAST ASIAN ART AND ARCHITECTURE). More recently, Vietnamese painting borrowed from French styles and techniques. Traditional handicrafts are still practiced, and poetry remains the favorite

(Left) *A patchwork of verdant rice paddies surrounds the city of Phan Rang in an aerial photograph. This rail center in the coastal lowlands of southern Vietnam, site of a U.S. military base during the Vietnam War, produces rice for domestic use and tobacco and salt for export.*

(Below) *An agricultural worker tends rice plants in a paddy along the Mekong River in southern Vietnam. The extremely fertile alluvial soils deposited in the Mekong delta on the South China Sea have made it one of the most productive rice-growing regions in Southeast Asia.*

literary genre. Vietnam's greatest poet was Nguyen Du (1765–1820).

ECONOMIC ACTIVITY

According to the evidence of contemporary archaeology, the Vietnamese were one of the first peoples of Asia to master the art of irrigation. Ever since, they have lived off the land, and their primary economic activity has been the cultivation of wet rice. During the period of French rule, the marshes of the Mekong delta were drained, leading to a significant increase in rice production. The French also developed coal mining, introduced a number of cash crops, and built a modern rail and road network, but they were determined to maintain their colonies as a market for French manufactured goods and a source of cheap raw materials and did not seriously encourage the development of a modern commercial and industrial sector. After the French departed, economic development in both North and South Vietnam was hindered by the Vietnam War, and the country remained basically preindustrial, dependent on outside assistance for essential goods and services.

The ultimate goal of the Communist regime that took power in 1975 was to transform all of Vietnam into an advanced industrial society based on socialist forms of ownership. Industry had been nationalized and agriculture collectivized in the north by the late 1950s, but Communist leaders delayed a similar socialist transformation in the south to avoid alienating the local population and to encourage economic recovery from the long years of war. In 1978, due to the slow pace of postwar economic development and fears of the growth of an unmanageable private sector in the south, government planners announced the nationalization of all industrial and commercial enterprises above the family level and began to create low-level collective organizations in the countryside. The results were disastrous. With much of the population opposed to the new policies, the economy went into a rapid decline.

In September 1979 the regime reversed course, permitting the revival of private commerce and postponing the process of collectivization in the south. During the next few years, economic production gradually recovered as emphasis shifted from heavy industry to consumer goods and farmers were allowed to sell surplus crops on the free market. But the restoration of the small private sector concerned ideological purists within the party leadership, who argued for a rapid socialist transformation. In 1985 the regime reached a compromise. Profit incentives would be temporarily retained to spur production, but the ultimate objective of eliminating the private sector on a gradual basis was reaffirmed. In the meantime, a

major campaign to improve the managerial efficiency of the state sector of the economy was launched.

At present, Vietnam continues to make halting economic progress. Despite recurrent poor weather and rapid population growth, the country is now near agricultural self-sufficiency, albeit at relatively low levels of personal consumption. Increasing pressure on arable lands has led to the recent planting of some hilly areas with cash crops such as coffee, tea, and rubber. Fishing, livestock raising, and forestry are also being encouraged. The industrial sector is showing signs of improvement, particularly in light industry and handicrafts, but consumer goods are in short supply and growth rates continue to be hampered by primitive technology, low export capacity, managerial inexperience, and shortages of energy, raw materials, and spare parts.

Vietnam suffers from a serious balance-of-payments deficit. The Soviet Union is its chief trading partner and source of foreign aid. Military expenditures are a heavy economic burden, consuming about half of the national budget.

GOVERNMENT

Vietnam is a Communist republic. A new constitution in 1980 replaced the North Vietnamese constitution of 1959, which was extended throughout the country after the formal reunification of Vietnam on July 2, 1976. On paper, Vietnam has a parliamentary form of government, with supreme power vest-

Ho Chi Minh City (formerly Saigon), the largest city in Vietnam, was the capital of South Vietnam from 1954 until the formal reunification of the country in 1976. Even today, life in the city is relatively free wheeling, and consumer goods are more abundant than in Hanoi.

ed in the unicameral National Assembly elected every five years by universal suffrage. The Assembly elects the Council of State, the collective presidency. Governmental functions are carried out by a Council of Ministers responsible to the National Assembly. In practice, real power resides in the hands of the Vietnamese Communist party.

HISTORY

The Vietnamese people first appear in history as one of several peoples living along the southern coast of China as far south as the Yüan delta. By the middle of the first millennium BC, a small state based on irrigated agriculture and calling itself Van Lang had emerged in the delta. In 101 BC, Van Lang was overrun by forces from the north and gradually absorbed into the expanding Chinese empire. Despite intensive Chinese cultural and political influence, however, the sense of cultural uniqueness did not entirely disappear, and in the 10th century rebel groups drove out the Chinese and restored national independence.

The new state, which styled itself Dai Viet (Greater Viet), accepted a tributary status with China and adopted many political and cultural institutions and values from its northern neighbor. It resisted periodic efforts to restore Chinese rule, however, and began to expand its territory, conquering the state of CHAMPA to the south and eventually seizing the Mekong delta from the declining KHMER EMPIRE.

Expansion brought problems, however. The difficulties of administering a long and narrow empire, and the cultural differences between the traditionalist and densely populated north and the sparsely settled "frontier" region in the Mekong delta, led to political tensions and, in the 17th century, to civil war. Two major aristocratic families, the Trinh and the Nguyen, squabbled for domination over the decrepit Vietnamese monarchy. This internal strife was exacerbated by the arrival of European adventurers who, in order to facilitate their commercial and missionary penetration of Southeast Asia, frequently intervened in local politics.

During the last quarter of the 18th century, a peasant rebellion led by the so-called Tay Son brothers in the south spread to the north, where the leading brother, Nguyen Hue, united the country and declared himself emperor. After his death in 1792, this dynasty rapidly declined and was overthrown by a scion of the princely house of Nguyen, who in 1802 founded a new Nguyen dynasty with its capital at Hue.

The Nguyen dynasty had come to power with French assistance, and France hoped for commercial and economic privileges. When these were not granted, the French emperor Napoleon III, under pressure from imperialist and religious

groups in France, ordered an attack on Vietnam in 1857. This resulted in a Vietnamese defeat and the ceding of several provinces in the south, which the French transformed into a new colony of COCHIN CHINA. Twenty years later the French completed their conquest of Vietnam, dividing the northern and central parts of the country into protectorates with the historic names TONKIN and ANNAM. Between 1887 and 1893, all three regions were joined with the protectorates of Laos and Cambodia into the French-dominated Union of Indochina.

French rule had a significant effect on Vietnamese society. Many traditional institutions were dismantled and replaced with others imported from the West. Western technology was introduced, and upper-class Vietnamese increasingly adopted the French language and Roman Catholicism. The economy was oriented toward the export of raw materials, and the small manufacturing and commercial sector was dominated by European and overseas Chinese interests.

Deprived of a political and economic role by the colonial administration, Vietnamese patriots turned to protest or revolt. By the late 1930s the Communist party, led by a Vietnamese revolutionary who took the name HO CHI MINH, had become the leading force in the nationalist movement.

Germany defeated France in 1940. Japan, a German ally, then occupied Vietnam, but the French Vichy Government continued to administer the country until March 1945, when the Japanese established an autonomous state of Vietnam under Annamese emperor BAO DAI. At the POTSDAM CONFERENCE in July–August, the Allies instructed Nationalist Chinese troops in the north and British troops in the south to accept the Japanese surrender. When Japan surrendered in August, however, the Viet Minh, an anti-Japanese and anti-French front founded by Ho Chi Minh in 1941, revolted and seized power. In early September, Viet Minh leaders declared the formation of the independent Democratic Republic of Vietnam (DRV). French forces returned by 1946, and in March of that year the new government reached a preliminary agreement on the formation of a Vietnamese "free state" within the FRENCH UNION, but negotiations collapsed. In December the First Indochinese War broke out between the Vietnamese and the French, who were increasingly supported by the United States. In 1954, after eight years of fighting, the Vietnamese defeated the French at DIEN BIEN PHU. Shortly after, the major powers met at Geneva and called for the departure of all foreign forces and the de facto division of Vietnam at 17° north latitude into two separate states, the Communist-dominated DRV in the north and a non-Communist state in the south, with provision for eventual reunification and elections.

The division of Vietnam lasted only two decades. In South Vietnam, the weak Bao Dai, reinstalled by the French in 1949,

Bicycles are the chief mode of transportation for most of the inhabitants of Hanoi, the capital of Vietnam. Hanoi's broad streets and architecture are reminders of an earlier time, when the city was the capital of French Indochina.

was replaced by NGO DINH DIEM. Despite support from the United States, Diem was unable to suppress a continuing guerrilla insurgency directed from Hanoi but provoked in part by his own unpopularity. In November 1963, Diem was overthrown in a military coup, and North Vietnam intensified its efforts to seek reunification under Communist rule. In 1965, with the South Vietnamese regime on the verge of collapse, the United States decided to send combat troops to South Vietnam to defeat the insurgency, whose various elements had by this time united as the Communist-dominated National Liberation Front of Vietnam (also known as the VIET CONG). But victory was elusive, and U.S. public opinion began to turn against the Vietnam War. After 1968, U.S. president Richard Nixon gradually withdrew U.S. military forces. In January 1973, over the objections of South Vietnam's NGUYEN VAN THIEU (who served as president from 1967 to 1975), a peace agreement was signed in Paris calling for a cease-fire and the total withdrawal of U.S. troops. Vague provisions for a political settlement were ignored, however, and in the spring of 1975 the Communists launched a major offensive in South Vietnam. Southern resistance rapidly collapsed, and North Vietnamese troops occupied Saigon in late April. In 1976, North and South Vietnam were formally united as the Socialist Republic of Vietnam, with PHAM VAN DONG as prime minister.

The government faced resistance to its socialist economic policies at home and a variety of pressures from abroad. Relations between North Vietnam and China, increasingly tense during the final years of the Vietnam War, reached the breaking point at war's end because of territorial disagreements and a growing rivalry over Kampuchea and Laos. In November 1978, Vietnam signed a treaty of friendship and cooperation with the Soviet Union. Less than two months later, Vietnamese forces invaded Kampuchea, overthrew the pro-Chinese KHMER ROUGE regime, and installed a new government sympathetic to Hanoi. China continued to support Khmer Rouge guerrillas in Kampuchea and cooperated with the ASEAN nations in demanding a withdrawal of Vietnamese forces from the country. Vietnam's dominant position in Kampuchea and Laos, its close ties to the Soviet Union, and the unresolved issue of U.S. soldiers missing in action during the Vietnam War hindered its efforts to improve relations with the United States. In a major government reorganization, Truong Chinh was replaced as party secretary general in 1986 (by Nguyen Van Linh) and as president in 1987 (by Vo Chi Cong). Pham Hung, who replaced Pham Van Dong as prime minister in 1987, died in March 1988; Do Muoi was named to the post in June. In 1988, facing Soviet pressure and an economic crisis caused by poor harvests, rapid population growth, a lack of foreign aid, and the costs of the occupation of Kampuchea, Vietnam announced that it would withdraw all of its forces from Kampuchea by the end of 1990.　　　WILLIAM J. DUIKER

Bibliography: Buttinger, J., *Vietnam: A Political History* (1968); Duiker, W. J., *China and Vietnam* (1986), *Vietnam since the Fall of Saigon*, 2d ed. (1985), and *Vietnam: Nation in Revolution* (1983); Fitzgerald, F., *Fire in the Lake* (1972); Gardner, L. C., *Approaching Vietnam* (1988); Harrison, J. P., *The Endless War* (1982); Hickey, G. C., *Village in Vietnam* (1964); Huynh Kim Khanh, *Vietnamese Communism, 1925–1945* (1982); Karnow, S., *Vietnam: A History* (1983); Marr, D. G., *Vietnamese Anticolonialism, 1885–1925* (1971) and *Vietnamese Tradition on Trial, 1920–1945* (1970; repr. 1983); McAlister, J. T., and Mus, P., *The Vietnamese and Their Revolution* (1970); Nguyen Khac Vien, *Tradition and Revolution in Vietnam* (1974); Pike, D., *Viet Cong* (1966); Shaplen, R., *Bitter Victory* (1986); Sully, F., ed., *We the Vietnamese* (1971); Taylor, K. W., *The Birth of Vietnam* (1983); Thayer, C., *Vietnam: Politics, Economics, and Society* (1986).

Vietnam Veterans Memorial

A v-shaped wall bearing the names of Americans killed in the Vietnam War, the Vietnam Veterans Memorial, designed by architect Maya Yang Lin, was dedicated on Nov. 13, 1982; a bronze sculpture of three soldiers designed by Frederick Hart was added to it in 1984. The memorial was sponsored by the Vietnam Veterans Memorial Fund, which raised the money to build it from private donors and persuaded Congress to provide a site for it near the Washington Monument as a belated tribute to those who fought in the Southeast Asian conflict.

A belated tribute to the Americans who fought in the Vietnam War, the Vietnam Veterans Memorial in Washington, D.C., was dedicated on Nov. 13, 1982, almost a decade after the United States withdrew from the war. The dedication was attended by thousands of veterans, many of whom were bitter at having been ignored when they returned home from the unpopular conflict. Designed by Maya Yang Lin, a Yale University architecture student, the memorial consists of two black granite walls built into the earth and meeting at an angle. Inscribed are the names of more than 58,000 Americans killed or missing in Vietnam.

Vietnam War

In the Vietnam War—which lasted from the mid-1950s until 1975—the United States and the southern-based Republic of Vietnam (RVN) opposed the southern-based revolutionary movement known as the VIET CONG and its sponsor, the Communist Democratic Republic of Vietnam (the DRV, or North Vietnam). The war was the second of two major conflicts that spread throughout Indochina, with Vietnam its focal point (see VIETNAM). The First Indochina War was a struggle between Vietnamese nationalists and the French colonial regime aided by the United States. In the second war, the United States replaced France as the major contender against Northern-based Communists and Southern insurgents. Communist victory in 1975 had profound ramifications for the United States; it was not only a setback to the containment of communism in Asia but a shock to American self-confidence.

THE ORIGINS OF THE WAR

French Indochina, which included Vietnam, Cambodia (Kampuchea), and Laos, was occupied by Japanese forces during World War II. Vietnamese Communist leader HO CHI MINH and his VIET MINH movement organized resistance against the Japanese and in 1945 declared Vietnam an independent republic. Fearing Ho's Communism, the United States supported the restoration of French rule. When fighting erupted between France and the Viet Minh in 1947, the Americans aided the French and backed the French-sponsored government of Emperor BAO DAI. By 1953 they were providing 80 percent of the cost of France's war effort.

The Partition of Vietnam. In 1954 the French, hoping to win a decisive victory, lured the Viet Minh into a set-piece battle at DIEN BIEN PHU, but were in turn besieged there. During the siege the exhausted government placed Indochina on the agenda of an international conference at Geneva (see GENEVA CONFERENCES). Defeat at Dien Bien Phu made France decide to withdraw from Indochina.

The conference terms were a mixed victory for the Viet Minh. Although it held significant areas south of the 17th parallel, Ho Chi Minh's Communist allies, the USSR and China, pressured him into accepting temporary division of Vietnam along that line, pending elections to be held in two years. Laos, Cambodia, and Vietnam were granted independence, and no foreign troops were to be stationed there. In an exchange of population, thousands of northern Vietnamese Roman Catholics moved south, while Communists moved north. Neither the United States nor the South, now led by the U.S.-backed NGO DINH DIEM in Saigon, signed the accords.

Even before the conference's conclusion, Washington, whose policy was to oppose the spread of communism, began planning a regional security pact. The result was the Southeast Asia Treaty Organization (SEATO), which provided for future U.S. intervention in the event of danger to South Vietnam; the Indochinese states did not join.

The Two Republics. Providing economic and military aid, the United States supported Diem's refusal to hold the pledged elections, apparently assuming the popular nationalist Ho would win. After a shaky start, Diem began working to destroy the remaining Communist infrastructure in the South. His military force, the Army of the Republic of Vietnam (ARVN), was advised by some 700 Americans, who replaced the French in 1956. Modeled after the U.S. Army, ARVN was trained in conventional warfare, but its leadership was selected from those loyal to Diem. Economic gains were uneven: the small urban sector benefited, but rural areas did not. Increasingly dictatorial, the Catholic Diem incurred growing opposition from the Buddhist majority. Less than 5 percent of the land was redistributed through land reforms, and many peasants who had gained land under Viet Minh rule now lost it.

In the North, the DRV developed as a Communist state with ties to China and the USSR. Harsh land reforms, in which thousands of landlords died, led to the collectivization of agriculture. Although primarily agricultural, the state did experience industrial growth. Under Ho's direction, Vietnamese communism developed independently of Soviet and Chinese models.

EARLY STAGES OF THE FIGHTING

Armed resistance to Diem was organized by former Viet Minh who became known as Viet Cong (Vietnamese Communists). Supplemented by cadres that had moved north after 1954 and

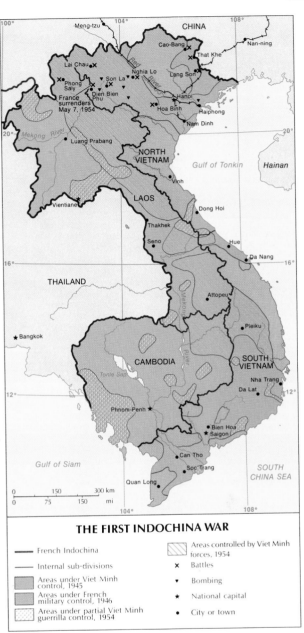

THE FIRST INDOCHINA WAR

—— French Indochina	▨ Areas controlled by Viet Minh forces, 1954
—— Internal sub-divisions	✗ Battles
▨ Areas under Viet Minh control, 1945	▼ Bombing
▨ Areas under French military control, 1946	★ National capital
▨ Areas under partial Viet Minh guerrilla control, 1954	● City or town

From 1947 to 1954 the French battled to reassert colonial control over Indochina. Their defeat by the Communist-led Vietnamese nationalists, the Viet Minh, at Dien Bien Phu (May 1954) led to their withdrawal and the partition of Vietnam by the Geneva Conference.

Vietnamese leader Ho Chi Minh (center) discusses strategy with aides prior to the attack on the French garrison at Dien Bien Phu (March–May 1954). Vo Nguyen Giap (right), the victorious general of that operation, became North Vietnam's commander in chief.

returned a few years later, the Viet Cong organized in 1960 as the National Liberation Front of South Vietnam (NLF). Communist-led and directed by Hanoi, it included all groups opposed to the Diem regime and its U.S. ally.

The NLF adopted the "people's war" strategy favored by Chinese Communist leader Mao Tse-tung: guerrillas using the civilian population as cover engaged in protracted warfare, avoiding conflict except in advantageous circumstances. Men and supplies infiltrated through Laos and Cambodia along a network of trails named for Ho Chi Minh. The Viet Cong used assassinations, terrorist activity, and military action against government-controlled villages. Diem moved peasants into "strategic hamlets" to separate them from the guerrillas. Peasant resentment at this policy aided Viet Cong recruitment, as did replacement of elected village officials with Diem appointees.

The Buddhist monk Quang Duc committed suicide by fire (June 1963) to protest against the regime of South Vietnam's Ngo Dinh Diem. The rift between the Saigon government and politically powerful Buddhists was a major factor leading to the coup that deposed and killed Diem.

U.S. intervention was based on belief in the "domino theory"—which held that if one Southeast Asian country were allowed to fall under Communist control, others would follow like a row of dominoes—and by an increasing concern for the credibility of U.S. opposition to communism after the Castro government came to power in Cuba (1959). Responding to Diem's request for help, U.S. president John F. Kennedy gradually increased the number of U.S. advisors to more than 16,000.

In Laos, the PATHET LAO guerrilla movement grew following a U.S.-sponsored right-wing coup against the neutralist regime. Kennedy accepted (1962) a Laotian settlement that brought temporary neutralization, but South Vietnam posed a more intractable problem. Introduction of helicopters and more advisors briefly boosted morale in Saigon, but ARVN lost the battle of Ap Bac in January 1963 despite advice and superior technology.

The Fall of Diem. The South Vietnamese situation became critical by mid-1963. Buddhist monks protesting religious persecution dramatized their case by immolating themselves in the Saigon streets; they attracted worldwide attention. Diem refused to placate the Buddhists, however. Frustrated and fearing the war would be lost, the United States supported a military coup that overthrew Diem on Nov. 1, 1963.

Instability marked by a series of coups in the next two years provided continued weakness for the Communists to exploit. Hanoi decided to escalate the violence and increased its strength in the South to 35–40 main force battalions of the People's Liberation Army (PLAF), in addition to some 35,000 guerrillas and 80,000 irregulars. Whereas individual members of the DRV's People's Army of Vietnam (PAVN) had infiltrated south for some time, the first complete tactical unit arrived in December, moving along the newly completed Ho Chi Minh Trail. Most forces fighting in the South continued, however, to be locally recruited; they were outnumbered by the ARVN, but guerrilla strategy was not predicated on superior numbers. Increasing Soviet as well as Chinese aid fueled the resistance.

The Tonkin Gulf Resolution. In Washington, Kennedy's successor, Lyndon B. Johnson, moved rapidly to oppose the insurgents. He authorized the CIA, using mercenaries and U.S. Army Special Forces, to conduct covert diversionary raids on the northern coast, while the U.S. Navy, in a related operation, ran electronic intelligence missions in the Gulf of Tonkin. Johnson appointed General William WESTMORELAND to head the Military Assistance Command, Vietnam (MACV), increased the number of advisors to 23,000, and expanded economic assistance. Warning Hanoi that continued support for the revolution would prompt heavy reprisals, the administration began planning bombing raids on the North.

An incident in the Gulf of Tonkin served to justify escalation of the U.S. effort. On Aug. 2, 1964, an American destroy-

er in international waters involved in electronic espionage was attacked by North Vietnamese torpedo boats. Unharmed, it was joined by a second destroyer and on August 4 the ships claimed that both had been attacked. Evidence of the second attack was weak at best (and was later found to be erroneous), but Johnson ordered retaliatory air strikes and went before Congress to urge support for the TONKIN GULF RESOLUTION, a virtual blank check to the executive to conduct retaliatory military operations. There were only two dissenting votes.

After a Viet Cong attack (February 1965) on U.S. Army barracks in Pleiku, the United States commenced Operation Rolling Thunder, a restricted but massive bombing campaign against North Vietnam. Protection of air bases then provided the rationale for introduction of 50,000 U.S. ground combat forces, which were soon increased. The American public, however, was not told when their mission and tactics changed from static defense to search-and-destroy, nor was it asked to bear the war's cost through higher taxes. Desiring both "guns and butter," Johnson dissimulated, ultimately producing a backlash that full public and congressional debate at this point might have avoided. The public never fully supported a war whose purposes were deliberately obscure.

U.S. ESCALATION OF THE WAR

The decision to escalate slowly, to bomb selected military targets while avoiding excessive civilian casualties, and to fight a war of attrition in order to avoid possible confrontations with the USSR and China seriously misjudged the nature of the enemy and the strategy of people's war. Attrition's only measure of success was a body count of the enemy dead, but Hanoi was prepared to suffer enormous casualties in a prolonged war. Because the DRV fought a total war with a totally mobilized society, it could sustain high losses yet continue infiltrating as many as 7,000 men a month virtually indefinitely. Political cadres won support from, or at least neutralized, the Southern peasantry. Weak in air power, the Viet Cong fought from tunnels and retreated to sanctuaries in Cambodia when threatened. They made mines and booby traps from unexploded U.S. ordnance and relied on ambush and sabotage of the vulnerable and increasingly extensive U.S. bases. Their intelligence penetrated the top levels of the RVN. They set the level of action, and could slip away at will.

U.S. attrition strategy depended on inflicting increasing pain through massive firepower against the North and Viet Cong–held areas until the revolutionaries found the cost too high. Territory gained was "cleared," but not held, because although ARVN, U.S., and allied forces outnumbered the enemy, the United States lacked the enormous numbers occupation would have required. In addition to bombing, the Americans and their allies—who ultimately included 70,000 South Koreans, Thais, Australians, and New Zealanders as well as 1,500,000 South Vietnamese—relied on the latest military technology, including napalm, white phosphorus, and defoliants, in an effort to hold down casualties. Agent Orange and other chemicals cleared vast areas of jungle, depriving the Viet Cong of cover as well as rice. Worldwide outcry over the use of chemical warfare and concern about its effect on the health of civilians and U.S. personnel led to discontinuance of defoliation in 1971.

In addition to conflict on the ground, water, and in the air, there was the struggle for what President Kennedy had termed the "hearts and minds" of the people. The Americans attempted to "search out and destroy" the enemy, leaving rural pacification to the poorly motivated ARVN, increasingly composed of urban elements that had little sympathy with the millions of refugees who were the by-product of the intensive bombing and defoliation. "Strategic hamlets" gave way to "revolutionary development," but the military junta headed by NGUYEN VAN THIEU, who took power in 1967, was unable to devise a successful pacification strategy. Ultimately, it resorted to Operation Phoenix, begun in 1967 to neutralize the Viet Cong infrastructure through arrests, imprisonment, and assassination. Phoenix was advised by a CIA-supported U.S. program.

As the war escalated, Johnson relied increasingly on selective service for manpower. The draft hit American youth unequally. Although student deferments ended with increasing troop call-ups, thousands of middle- and upper-class youth avoided service through a variety of stratagems, obtaining deferments that ultimately placed the heaviest burdens of combat on America's poor and minority groups. Draftees never constituted more than 40 percent of troop strength, but their use increased opposition to the war.

The Antiwar Movement. Opposition to the war grew with increased U.S. involvement. Leftist college students, members of traditional pacifist religious groups, long-time peace activists, and citizens of all ages opposed the conflict. Some were motivated by fear of being drafted, others out of commitment, some just joined the crowd, and a small minority became revolutionaries who favored a victory by Ho Chi Minh and a radical restructuring of U.S. society. College campuses became focal points for rallies and "teach-ins"—lengthy series of speeches attacking the war. Marches on Washington began in 1965 and continued sporadically, peaking in 1968 and again in 1971. Suspecting that the peace movement was infiltrated by Communists, President Johnson ordered the FBI to investigate and the CIA to conduct an illegal domestic infiltration, but they proved only that the radicalism was homegrown.

Although the antiwar movement was frequently associated with the young, support for the war was actually highest in the age group 20–29. The effectiveness of the movement is still debated. It clearly boosted North Vietnamese morale; Hanoi watched it closely and believed that ultimately America's spirit would fall victim to attrition, but the Communists were prepared to resist indefinitely anyway. The movement probably played a role in convincing Lyndon Johnson not to run for reelection in 1968, and an even larger role in the subsequent victory of Richard Nixon over the Democrat Hubert Humphrey. It may ultimately have helped set the parameters for the conflict and prevented an even wider war. Certainly its presence was an indication of the increasingly divisive effects of the war on U.S. society.

The Tet Offensive. By late 1967 the war was stalemated. Johnson urged Westmoreland to help convince a public growing more restive that the United States was winning. Although he promised "light at the end of the tunnel," increasing casualties as well as growing disbelief in public pronouncements—the "credibility gap"—fostered increasing skepticism. U.S. strategy was clearly not producing victory, and Johnson began a limited reassessment.

Meanwhile, Hanoi began planning a new offensive that involved a series of actions: first, intensified activity in the border areas including a massive attack against the base at Khe Sanh to attract ARVN and U.S. forces, followed by attacks on most provincial capitals and Saigon itself. If these were successful, regular forces poised on the outskirts of the cities would move to support a general uprising. The initial actions did draw forces away from the cities, and U.S. attention became riveted on the siege of Khe Sanh.

Attacks on cities began on Tet, the lunar holiday, Jan. 30, 1968. Hitting most provincial and district capitals and major cities, the Viet Cong also carried out a bold attack on the U.S. embassy in Saigon. The attack failed, but the attempt shocked U.S. public opinion. The Tet offensive continued for three weeks. Although they failed in their military objectives, the revolutionaries won a spectacular propaganda victory. While captured documents had indicated that the Viet Cong were planning a major offensive, its size, length, and scope were misjudged, and the Tet Offensive, as it was publicized in the U.S. media, seemed to confirm fears that the war was unwinnable. The public opposed the war in direct proportion to U.S. casualties, and these had topped a thousand dead a month. Tet appeared as a defeat, despite official pronouncements to the contrary. The media's negative assessment proved more convincing than Washington's statements of victory because it confirmed the sense of frustration that most Americans shared over the conflict.

The Significance of Tet. The Tet offensive was a major turning point in the war. Although the Communists lost 40,000 men, they had proved their ability to strike even in supposedly secure cities. Viet Cong, who had surfaced in anticipation

U.S. troops huddle around a tank in Hue during the Tet offensive of early 1968. Although the NLFSV and North Vietnamese failed to achieve their military goals, their demonstration of offensive capability disproved U.S. government claims that the war was virtually over.

of a general uprising that did not come, were decimated in the fighting or destroyed later by police, and from this point the insurgency was increasingly fought by the PAVN.

Johnson ordered a study of the Vietnam situation when Westmoreland requested 206,000 additional troops. An inquiry by Defense Secretary Clark Clifford led to the rejection of the request. However, 20,000 more troops were sent in the next three months, bringing U.S. troop strength to a peak of 549,000. At the same time, the South was urged to do more in its own defense.

Tet crystallized public dissatisfaction with the war. That the public turned against the war solely because of media coverage is doubtful; the number of "hawks" who wanted stronger action probably equaled the "doves" favoring peace, but the public as a whole clearly disapproved of the lack of progress. Further evidence of this came in March, when the antiwar senator Eugene McCarthy, running against the president, won 42 percent of the vote in New Hampshire's primary election.

On March 31, Johnson restricted bombing above the 20th parallel, paving the way for negotiations, and withdrew from a reelection bid. With Johnson's withdrawal and the assassination of Robert F. Kennedy, the Democratic nomination went to Vice-President Humphrey, who supported the war; the Republicans nominated Richard Nixon.

Communists believed in "fighting and talking"—which the United States now adopted as well. Negotiations began in May but quickly stalled over Hanoi's demands for a total bombing halt and NLF representation at the bargaining table. In November Johnson agreed to these terms. This aided Humphrey's campaign, but Nixon was victorious.

The Tet offensive demonstrated that the GVN was able to act in its own defense, yet the generally weak ARVN performance led to increasing demands for its reform. Johnson determined that primary responsibility for combat in the South henceforth should be born by ARVN. This policy—known as Vietnamization—meant pressuring the Thieu regime into a huge military buildup; the draft age was lowered to 18 and widespread evasion curtailed. Vietnamization did not curb inflation, however, and Thieu's rivalry with the flamboyant vice-premier Nguyen Cao Ky fractionalized the government. Increasing suppression of dissent brought protest from Buddhists and students, but opposition was severely punished under the martial law declared at Tet.

THE NIXON ADMINISTRATION AND VIETNAM
During the election campaign Nixon made vague promises to end the war. He was determined, however, to maintain credibility, preserve Thieu, and defeat the Communists. He and his foreign policy advisor Henry Kissinger downplayed bilateral negotiations and turned to great power diplomacy. They conceptualized a strategy of DÉTENTE, which involved harmonizing relations with the Soviets through trade and an arms-limi-

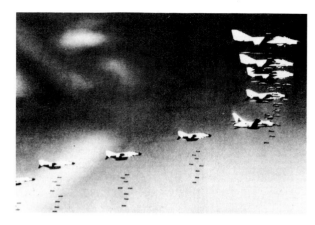

U.S. F-4C Phantoms flying in formation release their bombs over North Vietnam. The bombing of North Vietnam, begun in 1965, was cut back or halted periodically to encourage peace negotiations and then resumed, culminating in the massive strikes of Christmas 1972.

tation agreement while encouraging Moscow to abandon Hanoi. Normalizing relations with China would create a "China card" that could be played against the Soviets if they demurred. They hoped that this linkage of diplomacy could produce "peace with honor" in Vietnam and allow a face-saving U.S. departure. The Soviets, however, recognized the Provisional Revolutionary Government (PRG) formed by the NLF in June 1969.

No progress was made in the peace talks, either. The NLF and the North Vietnamese were unwilling to make concessions, and the South Vietnamese were basically opposed to negotiation. Neither side wished to lose on the diplomatic front what it thought could be gained on the battlefield.

The Vietnamization process continued: daily combat operations were turned over to the South Vietnamese, who received the latest U.S. technology and support, and bombing raids were conducted against Communist bases in Cambodia. ARVN remained poorly motivated and relatively ineffectual in combat, but its assumption of the brunt of the fighting reduced U.S. casualties and enabled the United States to begin troop withdrawals.

At home, new administration sought to lessen opposition by substituting a lottery system for selective service. President Nixon called on the "silent majority" of Americans to support his diplomatic efforts for an "honorable peace," but by the spring of 1970 public opinion was two to one against the war. When the public learned of the massacre of more than 300 civilians in the hamlet of MY LAI by U.S. troops, it reinforced beliefs that the war was a brutal, dehumanizing, and pointless affair from which the United States should withdraw.

Incursions into Cambodia and Laos. Nixon disliked confining the conflict to Vietnam instead of striking at Communist sanctuaries and supply points in neighboring neutral countries. Cambodia soon provided him the opportunity. In April 1970 a coup toppled the neutralist regime of Prince NORODOM SIHANOUK, who was replaced by the pro–U.S. LON NOL. Sihanouk had tried to preserve Cambodian neutrality by quietly accepting North Vietnamese infiltration and use of sanctuaries as well as U.S. bombing, but Lon Nol announced plans to interdict movement of Communist troops. When Hanoi then increased its pressure on Cambodia, U.S. forces were sent across the border. They were withdrawn again by June 30, but bombing raids continued until the end of the war.

The Cambodian incursion triggered protests in the United States. At Kent State and Jackson State universities, six students were killed in confrontations with police and National Guardsmen. One hundred thousand marched on Washington. Congress also protested, symbolically terminating the Tonkin Gulf Resolution. Criticism abated when U.S. troops were pulled out of Cambodia, but patience with the conflict was wearing thin. Deficit financing of the war brought uncon-

trolled inflation, which further soured the nation on the war.

Infiltration persisted despite the Cambodian incursion. Seeking to cut the Ho Chi Minh Trail, ARVN forces invaded Laos in February 1971. But intelligence provided by Communist agents within ARVN enabled the North Vietnamese to prepare a trap. The operation, intended as an example of the success of Vietnamization, escaped disaster only through U.S. air support. ARVN's casualty rate was estimated at as high as 50 percent. The campaign may have delayed a new Communist offensive, but three months later, party leaders began planning another one for the spring of 1972.

Effects of the War on U.S. Troops. Withdrawals dropped troop strength to 175,000 by the end of 1971, exacerbating effects on troop morale even as it dampened protest at home. No one wanted to be the last American to die in a war the country considered a mistake. Drug and alcohol abuse became widespread among U.S. servicemen, and morale plummeted. Search-and-destroy operations became "search-and-avoid," and officers who gave unpopular orders that exposed their troops to what they considered unacceptable risks became targets for "fraggings"—attempted murder, often by grenade. Racial conflict grew as black soldiers, stimulated by the civil rights and black power movements, increasingly resented fighting a "white man's war." Declining morale was not limited to Vietnam. The military capabilities of the army worldwide declined, and the navy and air force also suffered. Veterans of Vietnam formed their own antiwar organization.

The Easter Offensive. Heavy losses in Laos delayed a new Communist offensive, but the failure of negotiations in 1971 led to a renewed attempt at a military solution. In March 1972, Hanoi launched a major conventional invasion of the South. Its aims were to demonstrate the failure of Vietnamization, to reverse ARVN successes in the Mekong delta, and to affect U.S. morale in a presidential election year. The VC/NVA forces encountered initial success, routing ARVN troops and overrunning Quang Tri province.

The United States anticipated the spring offensive but underestimated its size and scope; U.S. forces numbered only 95,000, of whom 6,000 were combat ready. President Nixon retaliated with an intensified bombing campaign, providing air support to areas under attack in the South and striking fuel depots in the Hanoi-Haiphong area. He also informed Hanoi indirectly that he would allow Northern troops to remain in the South if they made peace before the election. When the DRV rejected this offer Nixon ordered the mining of Haiphong harbor, a naval blockade of the North, and massive sustained bombing attacks. The DRV began to evacuate Hanoi, to build a pipeline from the Chinese border, and to develop means to neutralize mines. U.S. planes bombed the Red River dikes, but damage was mitigated by constant repairs and unusually low rainfall.

Ultimately, U.S. bombing enabled ARVN to halt the offensive. The DRV won territory in the South, but its casualties from the air war were heavy. The bombing did not stop infiltration and matériel from reaching the DRV from China and the USSR. Even in victory, ARVN showed continued vulnerability: its desertion rates reached the highest levels of the war.

Negotiating and Fighting, 1971–72. Negotiations throughout 1971 made only limited progress. Kissinger offered to withdraw all U.S. troops within seven months after American POWs had been exchanged but would not abandon the Thieu regime. Meanwhile, playing on the Sino-Soviet split, the United States moved to normalize trade with China; Nixon and Kissinger both visited Peking, after which Nixon traveled to Moscow in May 1972. While improving relations with the United States, both China and the USSR nonetheless increased aid to Hanoi, in order not to be seen as abandoning their ally.

Only after the Easter Offensive did negotiations become a top priority. In three weeks of intensive negotiations in late September and October, Kissinger and North Vietnamese representative Le Duc Tho shaped an agreement withdrawing U.S. troops, returning POWs, and providing for a political settlement through establishment of a tripartite council of reconciliation. Thieu, however, rejected it because it permitted

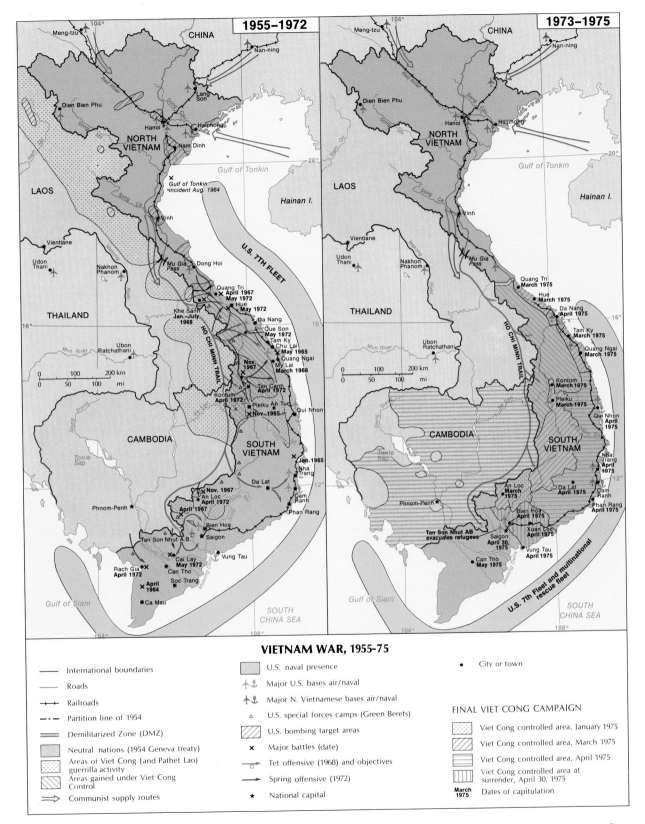

1955–1972

1973–1975

CHINA

Meng-tzu
Nan-ning
Dien Bien Phu
Lang Son
Hanoi
Haiphong
NORTH VIETNAM
Nam Dinh
Gulf of Tonkin
LAOS
Gulf of Tonkin incident Aug. 1964
Hainan I.
Vinh
Vientiane
Udon Thani
Nakhon Phanom
U.S. 7TH FLEET
Mu Gia Pass
Dong Hoi
THAILAND
Quang Tri April 1967 May 1972
Hue May 1972
Khe Sanh Jan.–July 1968
Da Nang
Que Son May 1972
Tam Ky
Chu Lai May 1965
Quang Ngai
My Lai March 1968
Nov. 1967
HO CHI MINH TRAIL
Ubon Ratchathani
Mun River
Tan Canh April 1972
Kontum April 1972
Pleiku An Tuc Nov. 1965
Qui Nhon
CAMBODIA
Sreng
Tonle Sap
SOUTH VIETNAM
Jan. 1965
Nha Trang
Da Lat
Nov. 1967 An Loc April 1972
April 1967
Cam Ranh
Phan Rang
Bien Hoa
Phnom-Penh
Tan Son Nhut A.B.
Saigon
Vung Tau
Cai Lay May 1972
Can Tho
Rach Gia April 1972
Soc Trang
April 1964
Ca Mau
Gulf of Siam
SOUTH CHINA SEA

0   100   200 km
0   50   100 mi

CHINA

Meng-tzu
Nan-ning
Dien Bien Phu
Hanoi
Haiphong
NORTH VIETNAM
Gulf of Tonkin
LAOS
Hainan I.
Vinh
Vientiane
Udon Thani
Nakhon Phanom
Mu Gia Pass
THAILAND
Quang Tri March 1975
Hue March 1975
Da Nang April 1975
Tam Ky March 1975
Quang Ngai March 1975
HO CHI MINH TRAIL
Ubon Ratchathani
Mun River
Kontum March 1975
Pleiku March 1975
Qui Nhon April 1975
CAMBODIA
Sreng
Tonle Sap
SOUTH VIETNAM
Nha Trang April 1975
An Loc March 1975
Da Lat April 1975
Cam Ranh
Phan Rang April 1975
Bien Hoa April 1975
Phnom-Penh
Tan Son Nhut AB evacuates refugees
Saigon April 30, 1975
Xuan Loc April 1975
Vung Tau April 1975
Can Tho May 1975
Gulf of Siam
U.S. 7th Fleet and multinational rescue fleet
SOUTH CHINA SEA

0   100   200 km
0   50   100 mi

VIETNAM WAR, 1955–75

—— International boundaries
—— Roads
+++ Railroads
–·–· Partition line of 1954
=== Demilitarized Zone (DMZ)
▨ Neutral nations (1954 Geneva treaty)
▨ Areas of Viet Cong (and Pathet Lao) guerrilla activity
▨ Areas gained under Viet Cong Control
⟹ Communist supply routes

▨ U.S. naval presence
⚓ Major U.S. bases air/naval
⚓ Major N. Vietnamese bases air/naval
△ U.S. special forces camps (Green Berets)
▨ U.S. bombing target areas
✕ Major battles (date)
⟶ Tet offensive (1968) and objectives
⟶ Spring offensive (1972)
★ National capital

• City or town

FINAL VIET CONG CAMPAIGN

▨ Viet Cong controlled area, January 1975
▨ Viet Cong controlled area, March 1975
▨ Viet Cong controlled area, April 1975
▨ Viet Cong controlled area at surrender, April 30, 1975
March 1975 Dates of capitulation

Between 1955 and 1965 the United States sent increasing amounts of military aid to prop up the South Vietnamese government against spreading insurrection. Then it began to deploy U.S. ground forces and aerial power on a massive scale against the insurrectionaries (Viet Cong) and their North Vietnamese allies. After 8 years of destructive but inconclusive fighting the United States withdrew its forces in 1973. Within 2 years the Viet Cong and North Vietnamese had won total control of South Vietnam and reunified the country.

(Left) *South Vietnamese president Nguyen Van Thieu and Richard Nixon address journalists following a joint strategy planning session at the U.S. base on Midway Island.*

(Right) *North Vietnam's chief negotiator, Le Duc Tho, and U.S. presidential advisor Henry Kissinger exchange handshakes and smiles during the Paris peace talks.*

Viet Cong forces to remain in place in the South, and Nixon supported him. Angered by this turn of events, the North Vietnamese released the history and text of the negotiations.

The Christmas Bombing and the Paris Peace Accords. Nixon, reelected by a huge majority in November 1972, then ordered massive bombing north of the 20th parallel. For 12 days beginning December 18, B-52s rained bombs on Hanoi and Haiphong. Women and children were evacuated and the cities defended with Russian-made surface-to-air missiles (SAMs). Fifteen B-52s were downed, 44 pilots captured, some 1,600 civilians killed, and Bach Mai hospital destroyed. More than 36,000 tons of bombs were dropped, exceeding the total for the entire 1969–71 period.

After the bombing, both sides were ready to resume negotiations: Hanoi had been seriously damaged and its stock of SAMs exhausted, while in Washington an angry Congress discussed limitations on the war. Six days of intense negotiations produced an agreement only slightly different from the October terms. Thieu was ignored. Nixon informed him that further resistance would lead to termination of U.S. aid, whereas compliance would guarantee the return of U.S. air power in case of Communist violations. Thieu refused to sign the agreement but did not actively oppose it.

The Paris Accords, signed Jan. 31, 1973, brought U.S. withdrawal and the return of the POWs but little else. Only a few civilian advisors and military personnel would remain. The Thieu government was left intact, but PAVN troops retained positions in the South. Political issues were left to negotiations between the two Vietnamese governments. A temporary four-party Joint Military Commission was to prevent a resumption of hostilities, and a four-power (Canada, Poland, Hungary, and Indonesia) International Commission of Control and Supervision was to supervise the cease-fire. The Americans agreed to aid postwar reconstruction of the DRV, a bargaining ploy the North took seriously. The accords were a "peace with honor" only by very generous interpretation: they left unresolved the major issue of the war—the question of who would govern the South.

THE RESOLUTION OF THE CONFLICT

The RVN and the DRV used the time before implementation of the peace to seize more land, and Washington sent massive amounts of aid to Thieu. Both sides quickly violated the accords. The last POWs were returned in March, but the United States halted talks with Hanoi about reconstruction aid, charging that the DRV had not ceased infiltrating troops to the South. The United States continued to bomb Cambodia and resumed reconnaissance flights over the DRV. Nixon intended to pressure China and the USSR to compel Hanoi to respect the accords and to resume B-52 flights if necessary, for he was still determined to win.

In the spring of 1973, however, Nixon's position was weakened by the involvement of his administration in the Watergate scandal. Taking advantage of this, Congress approved an amendment requiring the cessation of military operations in and over Indochina by August 15. In November 1973, Congress passed the War Powers Act, requiring the president to inform Congress within 48 hours of deployment of U.S. military forces abroad, withdrawing them within 60 days in the absence of explicit congressional endorsement. This virtually guaranteed the end of U.S. involvement in Indochina.

Both sides prepared for further war. The DRV stationed SAM missiles in areas it held in the South and turned the Ho Chi Minh Trail into an all-weather highway. Guided by the Defense Advisory Office, successor to MACV, Saigon planned new action modeled on the U.S. method of warfare, which favored the expenditure of material and use of massive firepower rather than men. Renewed fighting led Thieu to declare the start of a third Indochina War in January, confident that the United States would come to his aid. Although ARVN instituted new action, the North and the PRG won increasing victories.

By the fall of 1974 the initiative had passed to the revolution. U.S. aid fell from $2.56 billion in 1973 to $907 million in 1974 and $700 million in 1975, as Congress abandoned Vietnam for more pressing priorities elsewhere. Diminished aid hurt the RVN, but equally damaging was a 90-percent inflation rate, massive unemployment in the wake of the U.S. pullout, and increasing corruption. ARVN, bolstered by pretruce aid, looked impressive on paper, but its morale was worse than ever without U.S. air support and spare parts for U.S. equipment. Recruitment to the PRG increased in rural areas while a "third force" favoring peace developed in the cities. Thieu remained convinced that Nixon would not abandon him, but the Watergate crisis forced the latter to resign in August 1974.

In January 1975, Hanoi commenced a two-year campaign it believed necessary to defeat the South. Unexpected victory in the Central Highlands caused a speedup in the timetable. The ARVN retreat from the Highlands turned into a rout that became a disaster: troops fled south toward Saigon, anxious to protect their families. The loss of six central Vietnamese provinces led to the fall of the cities of Hué and Danang. Capitalizing on these victories, Hanoi embarked on a campaign to "liberate" Saigon. Unmoved by news of ARVN's collapse, Congress rejected President Gerald Ford's request for $300 million in supplemental aid, appropriating funds later only for humanitarian assistance and the evacuation of Americans. The rejection of the supplemental aid bill and the fall of the last resisting outpost, Xuan Loc, forced Thieu to recognize the gravity of the situation; he resigned and fled the country. Duong Van Minh became president, only to surrender unconditionally to the North on April 30.

While the world watched the dramatic evacuation of the Americans and some of their supporters from the roof of the U.S. embassy in Saigon, the other countries of Indochina fell less dramatically. Cambodia's KHMER ROUGE took Phnom Penh on April 17 and immediately evacuated the city, beginning a reign of terror that lasted for three years. The Pathet Lao had

Refugees, many of them members of the doomed South Vietnamese government, wait to board a helicopter on the roof of the U.S. embassy in Saigon on Apr. 29, 1975. Saigon was occupied by PRG and North Vietnamese troops the next day and renamed Ho Chi Minh City.

already gained participation in a coalition government in February 1973, and it took control of Laos peacefully after South Vietnam fell.

THE AFTERMATH OF THE WAR

Debate over the loss of Indochina was minimal, but the attempt to find "lessons" in the defeat engaged the United States for the next decade. The domino theory was proved invalid, as no further nations in Southeast Asia adopted communism. Isolationist in the wake of war, the United States eschewed further interventions, and even limited covert operations, until Ronald Reagan became president in 1981. Inflation caused by the war costs racked the U.S. economy for the next eight years, and the social wounds of the divisive war were slow to heal. Frustrated and angry in defeat, America at first rejected its veterans as symbols of defeat in a war generally agreed to have been a mistake.

The war's statistics were grim: 2 to 3 million Indochinese killed, 58,000 Americans dead, the expenditure of three times the amount of U.S. bombs dropped on both theaters during World War II; overwhelming devastation in Indochina. The war cost the United States over $150 billion. The Viet Cong had proved willing to take one of the highest casualty rates in proportion to population in history. That the United States never lost a major battle proved irrelevant; concentrating on military objectives, it vastly underestimated the political struggle, the nature of the enemy, and the consequences of supporting weak and unpopular regimes in the South.

By 1982 the wounds had begun to heal. The dedication of the VIETNAM VETERANS MEMORIAL in Washington, D.C., brought the veterans belated recognition for their sacrifices. The nation, recovering from its own posttraumatic shock, began embarking on new interventions against Communism. The legacy of the war embodied in the slogan "No More Vietnams" still had power, however, as opposition to these interventions demonstrated.

Vietnam was formally reunified in 1976, and Northerners quickly established dominance over the remnants of the PRG-NLF. The long-feared bloodbath did not occur, but some 200,000 supporters of the former regime were removed to "re-education" camps, where between 7,000 and 10,000 remained in 1986. Collectivization did not bring prosperity: the per capita income was only $130 in 1985. The Vietnamese proved more able soldiers than managers. The move to socialize the economy hurt many, but it especially harmed the large Chinese entrepreneurial minority in the South, whose position was further weakened when China attacked Vietnam in 1978. More than 1.4 million Vietnamese, including large numbers of ethnic Chinese, fled the country by sea; as many as 50,000 of these "boat people" may have perished in flight. Nearly a

million settled abroad, including some 725,000 in the United States.

Cambodia, renamed Kampuchea, was ruled by the despotic POL POT regime after the war. It murdered or starved some 1.5 million of its 7.5 million people and harassed its neighbor, leading the Vietnamese to invade in late 1978. Vietnam installed the HENG SAMRIN regime and retained an army of occupation. As a result of this violation of the UN charter, the United Nations ceased development aid and many Western countries followed suit, ceasing or sharply curtailing assistance. This led Vietnam to rely even more heavily on its ally the USSR, which had leased the port facilities at Cam Ranh Bay. The occupation of Kampuchea and the fate of some 2,500 Americans missing in action (MIAs) posed barriers to recognition by the United States. U.S. relations with Vietnam remained poor in the wake of the war and Hanoi's demands for reparations. By 1986, Vietnam had indicated plans to resolve two obstacles, cooperating in a resolution of the MIA issue and promising withdrawal from Kampuchea by 1990 in an effort to win U.S. recognition. But the United States, supporting its new Asian friend China, remained hostile to the Vietnamese government. Diplomatic relations existed only with the People's Republic of Laos, although progress was being made on MIAs, the last issue of the long war.

SANDRA C. TAYLOR

Bibliography: Baritz, Loren, *Backfire* (1985); Duiker, William, *The Communist Road to Power in Vietnam* (1981); Harrison, James Pinckney, *The Endless War* (1982); Herring, George, *America's Longest War*, 2d ed. (1986); Issacs, Arnold, *Without Honor: Defeat in Vietnam and Cambodia* (1983); Karnow, Stanley, *Vietnam: A History* (1983); Lewy, Guenter, *America in Vietnam* (1978); MacPherson, Myra, *Long Time Passing* (1985); Palmer, Bruce, *The Twenty-Five Year War: America's Military Role in Vietnam* (1985); Palmer, Dave Richard, *Summons of the Trumpet: US-Vietnam in Perspective* (1978); Pratt, John Clark, *Vietnam Voices: Perspectives on the War Years* (1984).

Vietnamese language: see SOUTHEAST ASIAN LANGUAGES.

Vieuxtemps, Henri   [vee-u-tahm']

The Belgian-born Henri Vieuxtemps, b. Feb. 17, 1820, d. June 6, 1881, one of the foremost violinists of 19th-century France, was called the king of the violin. He made his first concert tour at the age of 8 and from the age of 17 toured almost constantly, including triumphant visits to the United States (1844–45, 1857, and 1870). He also composed for the instrument, writing seven concertos and numerous concert pieces for violin and piano.

Viganò, Salvatore   [vee-gah-noh']

Salvatore Viganò, b. Mar. 25, 1769, d. Aug. 10, 1821, was one of the greatest choreographers of the preromantic ballet; he was the son of a dancer and nephew of the composer Luigi Boccherini, with whom he studied composition. Viganò danced in Rome, Madrid, Paris, London, Brussels, Venice, and Vienna and choreographed his first ballet, *Raoul, Signor de Créquis*, in 1791. He wrote the music for many of his own ballets, but that for *The Creatures of Prometheus*, (Vienna, 1801) was by Ludwig van Beethoven. Viganò was ballet master of La Scala, Milan (1813-21), where he choreographed numerous great dramatic ballets, many of which were admired by Stendhal.   DAVID VAUGHAN

Vigée-Lebrun, Louise Élisabeth   [vee-zhay'-luh-bruhn']

Louise Élisabeth Vigée-Lebrun, b. Apr. 16, 1755, d. Mar. 30, 1842, achieved an international reputation as a portraitist during her lifetime. She served as painter to Queen Marie Antoinette until the French Revolution forced her into an exile that lasted 12 years. Having escaped with her daughter to Italy, she continued to receive commissions as she traveled and was warmly welcomed in Europe's major capitals.

Vigée-Lebrun was introduced to painting by her father, a

pastel portraitist who recognized her talent and supported her training. At the age of 15 she was already able to support her widowed mother and her brother. At the age of 20 she married Jean Baptiste Pierre Lebrun, an art dealer, but his weakness for gambling destroyed their marriage. In 1783 she was admitted to the Académie Royale.

Her style of portraiture catches her sitters looking alert; they are generally placed within their typical surroundings. For example, *Marie Antoinette and Her Children* (1787; Versailles Palace) is set in a room of the palace, and the painter in *Hubert Robert* (1788; Louvre, Paris) is seen at work, holding his palette and brushes.

According to her own memoirs, Vigée-Lebrun painted about 900 works, of which more than 200 were landscapes and the remainder mainly portraits. ELEANOR TUFTS

Bibliography: Helm, W. H., *Vigée-Lebrun: Her Life, Works, and Friendships* (1916); Vigée-Lebrun, L. E., *Memoirs of Madame Vigée-Lebrun*, trans. by Lionel Strachey (1903).

Vigeland, Gustav [vee'-guh-lahn]

In their intense emotionalism, the works of the Norwegian sculptor Gustav Vigeland, b. Apr. 11, 1869, d. Mar. 12, 1943, are akin to those of the painter Edvard Munch, his countryman and contemporary. Both men belonged to the fin de siècle intelligentsia of Paris and Berlin, and both absorbed its nihilistic despair. Vigeland's early style was strongly influenced by Auguste Rodin; his more expressionist mode emerged only later. He spent more than four decades on his major work, the huge outdoor sculpture complex in Frogner Park, Oslo, which contains more than 200 figures. Some of his later work at Frogner Park became routine; more subtle are his early sculptured portraits of famous Norwegians.

Bibliography: Hale, Nathan Cabot, *Embrace of Life: The Sculpture of Gustav Vigeland* (1969); Stang, Ragna, *Vigeland: The Sculptor and His Works* (1980).

vigilantes

Until effective government reached the American frontier, volunteer vigilance committees—which emerged as early as the American Revolution—were formed to maintain law and order. The most famous vigilante groups were in the mining and cattle towns of the Far West, communities that attracted many lawless individuals but often could not afford either a law officer or a jail. Some committees conducted judicial proceedings; others summarily banished, whipped, or hanged those they believed guilty. In a few instances vigilantism degenerated into unrestrained, mob-dominated lynch law.

The best known of these movements were those operating in San Francisco from 1849 to 1851 and a later committee of that city, which, in 1856, claimed 8,000 members. The San Francisco vigilantes generally conducted fair public trials and held hangings attended by thousands. In the early 1860s another famous movement, in Montana, eradicated the gang of the sheriff-turned-outlaw Henry Plummer. Most vigilante groups disbanded voluntarily once adequate law enforcement was established; in any case, they rarely lasted more than 2 years. ELLIOT T. WEST

Bibliography: Brown, Richard Maxwell, *Strain of Violence* (1975); Dimsdale, Thomas J., *The Vigilantes of Montana* (1866; repr. 1985); Hollon, W. Eugene, *Frontier Violence* (1974); Lindstrom, Joyce, *Idaho's Vigilantes* (1984); Madison, Arnold, *Vigilantism in America* (1973).

Vignola, Giacomo Barozzi da [veen-yoh'-lah]

Giacomo Barozzi, called Giacomo da Vignola, b. Oct. 1, 1507, d. July 7, 1573, was an Italian architect of the Late Renaissance. He is best known for his *Regola delli cinque ordini d'architettura* (Rule of the Five Orders of Architecture, 1562), an architectural treatise that provided future generations of architects with models for the use of the classical orders and served as the basis of Vignola's influential design of the Church of Il Gesù in Rome.

After working briefly (1541–43) at the Château de FONTAINE-BLEAU, Vignola returned to Italy and began to execute his own designs, including that for the Palazzo Bocchi (1545) in Bologna. Upon being appointed (1550) papal architect to Pope Julius III, he settled in Rome, where his most important works are located. His first major Roman commission was the design of the Villa Giulia (1551–55), on which he worked with Giorgio Vasari and Bartolommeo Ammanati. Vignola probably was responsible for the classically austere main palace block and for the elegant semicircular courtyard behind it. Together with his redesign (begun 1559) of the Villa Farnese at Caprarola, the Villa Giulia reflects Vignola's ability to formulate inventive and graceful designs using classical elements.

Even more original in conception are the churches of Sant' Andrea in Via Flaminia (1550–54) and Sant'Anna dei Palafrenieri (begun 1565), whose oval-based plans represent a radical break with the Renaissance classical tradition and anticipate one of the most widely used forms in baroque architecture. Vignola departed from the oval format in building (from 1568) Il Gesù, the mother church of the Jesuit order. By eliminating side aisles he created an uncluttered and airy interior that influenced church architects for the next 200 years. The facade was designed by Giacomo della Porta.

Vignola's treatise on the classical orders, which was based on the works of the ancient Roman theorist VITRUVIUS, has from the time of its publication been regarded as the foremost authority in its field.

Vigny, Alfred de [veen-yee']

Alfred Victor, comte de Vigny, b. Mar. 27, 1797, d. Sept. 17, 1863, was the most stoical and pessimistic of the French romantic writers. In his verse, *Poèmes antiques et modernes* (Poems Ancient and Modern, 1826), in his collection of stories, *Stello* (1832), and in his play *Chatterton* (1835; Eng. trans., 1908) he deals with the condition of the poet, prophet, and genius in a noncomprehending society. Viewing the world as a place of suffering, Vigny alternates between stoicism and despair. His prose works, the novels *Cinq-Mars* (1826) and *Servitudes et grandeurs militaires* (1835; trans. as *The Military Condition*, 1964), present his belief in the brotherhood of humanity and the nobility of a military career. His adaptations and translations of Shakespeare, *Shylock* (1828) and *Othello* (1829), were presented with modest success at the Théâtre Français.

Bibliography: Doolittle, James, *Alfred de Vigny* (1967); Whitridge, A., *Alfred de Vigny* (1933; repr. 1982).

Vigo [vee'-goh]

Vigo (1981 pop., 258,724) is a port on the Vigo Estuary, an inlet of the Atlantic Ocean in northwestern Spain, about 20 km (13 mi) north of the Portuguese border. Vigo is a naval base and a major fishing port, with varied manufacturing industries producing lumber, paper, flour, soap, brandy, machinery, and tools. Known to the Romans as Vicus Spacorum, Vigo became an important naval port in the 16th century.

Vigo, Jean

Jean Vigo, b. Apr. 26, 1905, d. Oct. 5, 1934, in spite of his tragically short life, proved himself one of the great French filmmakers. The son of a celebrated anarchist who was later murdered in prison, Vigo led a disordered childhood. *À Propos de Nice* (About Nice, 1930) is a short, personal film essay mixing sharp observation and adroit camera technique. His two major films, *Zéro de conduite* (Zero for Conduct, 1933) and *L'Atalante* (Atalanta, 1934), were both commercial disasters, and at the time of his death at the age of 29, Vigo remained almost unknown. His tiny output, however, now ranks as one of the great achievements of French cinema. His work draws uniquely sensitive pictures of private worlds (those of a group of schoolboys and a newly married couple, respectively), combining a respect for reality with virtually surrealist imagery. ROY ARMES

Bibliography: Simon, William, *The Films of Jean Vigo* (1981); Simon, W. G., *The Films of Jean Vigo* (1981).

Vijayanagar [vee-juh-yuh-nuh'-gur]

Vijayanagar (City of Victory) was the capital of a Hindu empire of the same name that flourished in India from the 14th to the 16th century. The city, on the Tungabhadra River in the present state of Karnataka, extended over an area of 23 km² (9 mi²) and became the center of the largest Hindu empire in southern India.

Trade and culture flourished in the empire, a bulwark of Hindu civilization against Muslim attack from the north. In 1565, however, Muslim invaders destroyed the capital; the empire collapsed about 1614.

Viking

The Viking space project produced, during the summer of 1976, the first two successful landings on the surface of MARS. *Viking 1*, consisting of a landing craft attached to a separate vehicle that would orbit the planet, was launched on Aug. 20,

1975, and entered orbit on June 19, 1976. On July 20 the lander touched down on the slope of a dry basin in a region known as Chryse Planitia. *Viking 2*, with an identical pair of coupled spacecraft, was launched on Sept. 9, 1975, reached Martian orbit on Aug. 7, 1976, and released its lander for a Sept. 3, 1976, arrival at a rock-strewn plain in a more northerly site called Utopia Planitia.

THE ORBITERS

The Viking orbiters were equipped for photography (in color, stereo, and through filters), atmospheric water-vapor detection, and surface-temperature measurement. Each orbiter carried two slow-scan cameras using television-type vidicon tubes.

The foremost task of the orbiter cameras was to aid in the selection of safe landing sites. The cameras then moved on to the task of photographing and mapping the rest of the planet, sometimes from altitudes as low as 298 km (185 mi). The orbiters also made extremely close passes by the Martian

(Below) *The U.S. Viking spacecraft, the first probe successfully to soft-land on Mars, consisted, in its interplanetary-cruise configuration, of a lander encapsulated in an aeroshell heat shield (1), a 1.47-m-diameter (58-in) high-gain dish antenna (2), a propulsion system (3) with a 136-kg-thrust (300-lb) rocket engine (4), a low-gain antenna (5), solar panels (6) providing 600 W of power in Mars orbit, and an orbiter science payload (7)—two cameras, a water-vapor spectrometer, and an infrared-thermal mapper—mounted on a movable platform.*

(Below) *The composite 3,375-kg (7,440-lb) Viking spacecraft, broken down into component parts (right), consisted of a bioshield cap (1), sealed to prevent contamination; an aeroshell cover and parachute system (2); a lander (3); an aeroshell and heat shield (4); a bioshield base (5); and an orbiter (6) with its science payload (7) and solar panels (8). A schematic (left) indicates the spacecraft's configuration when enclosed in the nose shroud of the launch vehicle, which was a Titan IIIE with a Centaur upper stage.*

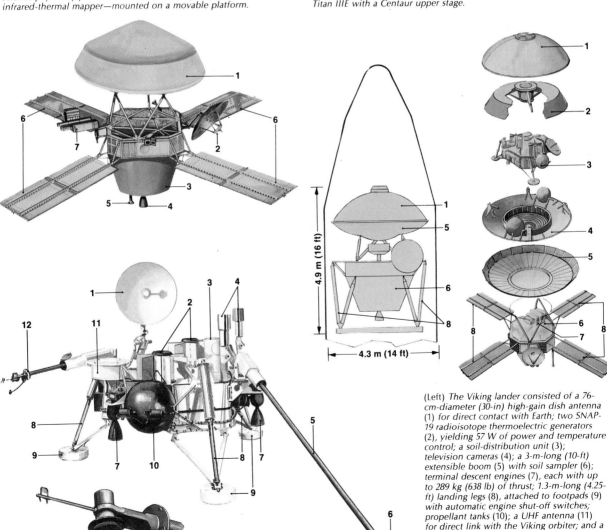

(Left) *The Viking lander consisted of a 76-cm-diameter (30-in) high-gain dish antenna (1) for direct contact with Earth; two SNAP-19 radioisotope thermoelectric generators (2), yielding 57 W of power and temperature control; a soil-distribution unit (3); television cameras (4); a 3-m-long (10-ft) extensible boom (5) with soil sampler (6); terminal descent engines (7), each with up to 289 kg (638 lb) of thrust; 1.3-m-long (4.25-ft) landing legs (8), attached to footpads (9) with automatic engine shut-off switches; propellant tanks (10); a UHF antenna (11) for direct link with the Viking orbiter; and a meteorology boom (12 and inset, lower left) that records surface temperature, humidity, and wind velocity.*

moons, PHOBOS and DEIMOS, enabling detailed photography of their surfaces and calculations of their masses based on their effects on the orbiters' trajectories.

The water-vapor detector aboard each orbiter consisted of an infrared spectrometer to measure solar infrared radiation that passed through the atmosphere after reflection from the surface of the planet. The Viking instruments showed that the water-vapor content of the atmosphere was greater than expected and that in the near-polar regions the Martian atmosphere was sometimes nearly 100 times wetter than at near-equatorial latitudes.

The infrared thermal mapper responsible for temperature measurements was a 28-channel radiometer capable of monitoring temperatures at the surface and in the upper atmosphere. Repeated measurements from successive orbits enabled investigators to calculate the thermal inertia of portions of the surface (that is, the speed at which they heat up or cool down), which can be related to the surface structure and composition.

The instrument also revealed diurnal and seasonal patterns and measured temperature differences that indicated whether visually observed cloud layers and hazes were composed of water or carbon dioxide. The residual north polar cap—the part that never disappears—was revealed to consist almost entirely of frozen water.

THE LANDERS

The Viking landers were essentially three-legged platforms, with numerous instruments atop and within the platform structure, and were powered by nuclear sources called radioisotope thermoelectric generators (see SNAP). The first measurements made by both landers came from a set of instruments—retarding potential analyzer, upper-atmosphere mass spectrometer, and pressure and temperature sensors—designed to make profile measurements of the atmosphere during the descent to the surface. The descent-phase instruments identified the presence of nitrogen (2.5% of the atmosphere) and indicated the amount of argon (1.5% of the atmosphere), whose isotopes are important in working out the planet's atmospheric evolution.

Among their surface instruments, the landers carried the first experiments ever sent from Earth with the specific intent of seeking life on another planet. Each lander carried a three-experiment biology instrument, miniaturized into less than 0.03 m³ (1 ft³) and using soil samples provided by each lander's extendable sampler arm.

A pyrolytic-release experiment searched for microorganisms that function by photosynthesis or chemical stimulation. It exposed the samples to an atmosphere containing carbon dioxide labeled with radioactive carbon-14; after an exposure period, the samples were incinerated, and the resulting gases were measured to see if the labeled atmosphere had been assimilated—a possible sign of respiration. A labeled-release experiment exposed its sample instead to a nutrient solution labeled with carbon-14; the test-chamber atmosphere was monitored for signs that the tracer in the nutrient was being given off in gaseous form, such as after some metabolic process. A gas-exchange experiment exposed a soil sample for up to 12 days in an atmosphere of helium, krypton, and carbon dioxide; changes in the test chamber's atmospheric composition (rather than the amount of radioactivity) were monitored for indications that living organisms might have taken in some materials and given off others. All three experiments on both landers showed positive indications of some kind, but more than a year and a half of analysis left the interpretation inconclusive.

The landers carried cameras, which were used not only for conventional photographs but also to measure light refraction in the atmosphere and to monitor the changing dust concentrations. A seismometer aboard Lander 1 proved impossible to free from its locked storage position, but its twin on Lander 2 showed the planet to be considerably less active than the Earth. No organic materials were found in the soil by the gas chromatograph-mass spectrometers, but X-ray fluorescence instruments analyzed the fine-grained, loose surface material, which was shown to resemble iron-rich clays. The surface material proved to be almost indistinguishable between the sites of Lander 1 (22.5° north latitude, 48.0° west longitude) and Lander 2 (47.9° north latitude, 225.7° west longitude). Meteorological instruments provided surface weather reports.

JONATHAN EBERHART

Bibliography: Arvidson, Raymond E., et al., "The Surface of Mars," *Scientific American*, March 1978; Baker, David, "Behind the Viking Scene," *Spaceflight*, February–June 1977; Burgess, Eric, *To the Red Planet* (1978); Cooper, Henry S. F., "The Search for Life on Mars," *The New Yorker*, Feb. 5 and 12, 1979; Gore, Rick, "Sifting for Life in the Sands of Mars," *National Geographic*, January 1977; Hartmann, W. K., "Viking on Mars: Exciting Results," *Astronomy*, January 1977; Horowitz, N. H., "The Search for Life on Mars," *Scientific American*, November 1977; Kaufmann, W. J., *Exploration of the Solar System* (1978); Viking Lander Imaging Team, *The Martian Landscape* (NASA SP-425; 1978).

Vikings

The Vikings were venturesome seafarers and raiders from Scandinavia who spread through Europe and the North Atlantic in the period of vigorous Scandinavian expansion (AD 800–1100) known as the Viking Age. From Norway, Sweden, and Denmark, they appeared as traders, conquerors, and settlers in Finland, Russia, Byzantium, France, England, the Netherlands, Iceland, and Greenland.

For many centuries before the year 800, such tribes as the Cimbrians, Goths, Vandals, Burgundians, and Angles had been wandering out of Scandinavia. The Vikings were different because they were sea warriors and because they carried with them a civilization that was in some ways more highly developed than those of the lands they visited. Scandinavia was rich in iron, which seems to have stimulated Viking cultural development. Iron tools cleared the forests and plowed the lands, leading to a great increase in population. Trading cities such as Birka and Hedeby appeared and became the centers of strong local kingdoms. The Viking ship, with its flexible hull and its keel and sail, was far superior to the overgrown rowboats still used by other peoples. Kings and chieftains were buried in ships (see GOKSTAD SHIP BURIAL; OSBERG SHIP BURIAL), and the rich grave goods of these and other burial sites testify to the technical expertise of the Vikings in working with textiles, stone, gold and silver, and especially iron and wood. The graves also contain Arab silver, Byzantine silks, Frankish weapons, Rhenish glass, and other products of an extensive trade. In particular, the silver kufic (or cufic) coins that flowed into the Viking lands from the caliphate further stimulated economic growth. Viking civilization flourished with its SKALDIC LITERATURE and eddic poetry, its runic inscriptions (see RUNES), its towns and markets, and, most of all, its ability to organize people under law to achieve a common task—such as an invasion.

Harold I (Harold Fairhair), the Norwegian king who gained control of and ruled most of western Norway during the late 9th century, is portrayed with the Viking chief Guthrum in this illustration from the Flateyar-bók, a 14th-century Norse saga collection.

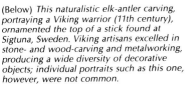

(Below) *This naturalistic elk-antler carving, portraying a Viking warrior (11th century), ornamented the top of a stick found at Sigtuna, Sweden. Viking artisans excelled in stone- and wood-carving and metalworking, producing a wide diversity of decorative objects; individual portraits such as this one, however, were not common.*

(Above) *The Oseberg ship (AD c.800) is an example of a Viking long ship. Famed as ship-builders and seafarers, the Vikings designed the ships, usually made of oak planks, with a high prow and stern, square sail, and rows of oars. The ships were traditionally carved and painted.*

The intricacy of Viking metalwork is reflected in this collection of jewelry. Three of the pieces, two worked-gold brooches and a silver ring, were discovered at Hornelund, Denmark, and date from the 10th century. A silver necklace with a pendant symbolizing Thor's hammer and a twisted gold-wire ring are also included in the group.

Expansion was apparently propelled by the search for new trading opportunities and new areas in which to settle the growing population. By the end of the 8th century, Swedish Vikings were already in the lands around the Gulf of Finland, Danish Vikings were establishing themselves along the Dutch coast, and Norwegian Vikings had colonized the Orkney and Shetland islands.

During the 9th century they expanded beyond these three bases, arriving first as rapacious raiders (looting the treasures of monasteries, for example, and capturing slaves for sale in the Middle East) but soon establishing themselves on a more permanent basis. Swedes called Rus or Varangians established fortified cities at Novgorod and then at Kiev, creating the first Russian state (see RURIK dynasty), and traded down the great rivers of Russia to Byzantium and Persia. Norwegian Vikings established kingdoms in Ireland, where they founded Dublin about 840, and in northwestern England. They settled Iceland and colonized Greenland in the 10th century and founded the short-lived North American colony called VINLAND in the early 11th century (see L'ANSE AUX MEADOWS). Great armies of Danes and Norwegians conquered the area called the DANE-LAW in England, overthrowing all the Anglo-Saxon kingdoms except King Alfred's Wessex. They attacked cities in France, Germany, the Low Countries, and Spain and, in 911, seized control of Normandy in France, where their descendants became known as the NORMANS.

After conquering and settling foreign lands, the Vikings came under the cultural influence of the conquered peoples. Originally pagan worshipers of Thor and Odin, many became Christians, and during the 10th century they brought Christianity back to Scandinavia.

The process of conquest slackened during the 10th century as civil wars raged in Scandinavia. Out of these wars emerged powerful new kingdoms with great new fortresses, including TRELLEBORG in Denmark. Soon armies of a renewed Viking age were sailing forth. In 1013, SWEYN of Denmark conquered all of England. His son, CANUTE, built an empire that included England, Denmark, and Norway.

By the second half of the 11th century, however, the emergence of stronger political systems and stronger armies in Europe, the development of new types of ships, and the redirection of military endeavor by the Crusades brought the Viking Age to an end.

J. R. CHRISTIANSON

Bibliography: Brøndsted, Johannes, *The Vikings,* trans. by Kalle Skov (1960; repr. 1971); Foote, Peter G., and Wilson, David M., *The Viking Achievement* (1970); Graham-Campbell, James, *The Viking World* (1980); Jones, Gwyn, *A History of the Vikings* (1968); Kendrick, Thomas Downing, *A History of the Vikings* (1930; repr. 1968); Kirkby, Michael, *The Vikings* (1977); Poertner, Rudolf, *The Vikings* (1975); Sawyer, P. H., *The Age of the Vikings,* 2d ed. (1972).

Vilar, Jean   [vee-lahr']

Jean Vilar, b. Mar. 25, 1912, d. May 28, 1971, revitalized France's THÉÂTRE NATIONAL POPULAIRE, which he directed from 1951 to 1963. Vilar transformed the state-subsidized theater into a popular, low-cost operation that simultaneously appealed to a mass audience and produced plays of quality, many of which he acted in and directed. In 1947, Vilar established the Avignon Festival, France's first outdoor summer theater festival.

Vilas, Guillermo   [vee'-lahs]

Guillermo Vilas, b. Aug. 17, 1952, is an Argentinean professional tennis player who possesses a powerful left-handed top-spin backhand and cool disposition. In 1974, at the age of 22, Vilas won his first major title on grass courts, a surface he normally dislikes. Later that year, at the Masters tournament in Melbourne, Australia, he defeated the Romanian star Ilie Nastase, the defending champion, in the final, his most important victory until he swept the field to win the French Open 3 years later. Vilas was ranked as the number-one player in the world by many authorities in 1977 after a spectacular season in which he won 50 consecutive matches and 10 successive tournaments, including both the French and U.S. Open titles. His exciting victory over Jimmy Connors in the U.S. Open final was among the most memorable triumphs in U.S. Open history. A reflective man, Vilas has published 2 volumes of poetry in Argentina.

STEVE FLINK

Vildrac, Charles   [veel-drahk']

Charles Vildrac, b. Nov. 23, 1882, d. June 25, 1971, was a French writer best known for his dramas, particularly *The Steamer Tenacity* (1920; Eng. trans., 1921). Like Jules Romains, he was a *unanimiste,* that is, one who studies the concept of "group spirit." He also wrote poetry, essays, and children's stories.

villa

In its earliest use—by the ancient Romans—the term *villa* referred to a country house and self-sustaining farm used from time to time as a retreat by its affluent owner. During the Italian Renaissance, in addition to the traditional *villa rustica,* there also developed the *villa urbana,* which, with its elaborate gardens, was designed not as a residence but mainly to provide recreational pleasures. In England during the 19th century the term *villa* designated a fairly luxurious, usually suburban home; today it may refer to any detached house of modest size.

Bibliography: Coffin, David Robbins, *The Villa in the Life of Renaissance Rome* (1978); Percival, John, *The Roman Villa: A Historical Introduction* (1977).

Villa, Pancho   [vee'-yah]

Francisco "Pancho" Villa, originally named Doroteo Arango, b. June 5, 1878, d. July 20, 1923, Mexican bandit and revolutionary, became a folk hero as both a Robin Hood and an advocate of social reform. After killing a man in defense of his sister around 1894 he fled to the mountains, where he became a bandit leader. He backed Francisco I. MADERO's revolution (1910–11) against dictator Porfirio Díaz and contributed to Díaz's fall.

While fighting for Madero's besieged government, Villa was condemned to death by Gen. Victoriano HUERTA, his com-

Pancho Villa, a Mexican military commander who played a key role in the Revolution of 1910, later led guerrilla forces against the Carranza government. In 1916 he raided the New Mexico town of Columbus, killing 17 Americans and provoking a U.S. punitive expedition into Mexico. Villa's exploits made him a folk hero throughout Mexico.

manding officer, in 1912, but Madero had Villa imprisoned instead. Villa soon escaped, and in 1913 he and his followers joined Venustiano CARRANZA in a revolt against Huerta, who had toppled Madero and become dictator. As provisional governor of Chihuahua and the most powerful general in northern Mexico, Villa supported the poor of that region in their demands for basic reform.

After Huerta's ouster in 1914, Villa broke with the more conservative Carranza and occupied Mexico City with Emiliano ZAPATA. Defeated at Celaya and León in 1915 by Carranza's general, Álvaro OBREGÓN, Villa withdrew to Chihuahua, where he led guerrilla raids, including several into New Mexico in retaliation for U.S. President Woodrow Wilson's recognition of Carranza in October 1915. In the resulting invasion (1916) of Mexico by U.S. troops under Gen. John J. PERSHING, Villa avoided capture and continued fighting against Carranza.

After Carranza was killed (1920) in the rebellion of Agua Prieta, which toppled his regime, Villa was given an amnesty and a hacienda in return for laying down his arms. He lived in retirement until assassinated at Parral, Chihuahua, by followers of Obregón.

ROBERT PATCH

Bibliography: Atkin, Ronald, *Revolution! Mexico, 1910–1920* (1970); Clendenen, Clarence C., *The United States and Pancho Villa: A Study in Unconventional Diplomacy* (1961; repr. 1972); Pinchón, Edgcumb, *Viva Villa!* (1933; repr. 1970).

Villa-Lobos, Heitor   [vee-lah-loh'-bohsh, ay'-tohr]

Heitor Villa-Lobos, b. Rio de Janeiro, Mar. 5, 1887, d. Nov. 17, 1959, was a world-famous Brazilian composer. In his youth he traveled widely through Brazil, absorbing folklore and popular music. His formal musical training was scanty, and he was largely self-taught in composition. Befriended by the pianist Artur Rubinstein, who played his music in the United States and Europe, Villa-Lobos was able to spend the years from 1923 to 1930 in Europe, living primarily in Paris. Audiences found his exotic compositions, such as *Rudepoema* (1923–26, for piano or orchestra) and the *Noneto* (1923), with its echoes of the Brazilian jungle, both exciting and fascinating.

After his return to Brazil he was active in music education and as organizer and director of people's choruses, while continuing his international career as composer and conductor. He was extremely prolific and has been credited with as many as 3,000 works—although that number is probably exaggerated. He composed in every category, from operas and symphonies to chamber music and songs, with many pieces for piano and several for guitar. Among his best-known works are the 9 *Bachianas Brasileiras* (1930–45) and the 14 *Chôros* (1920–28), written for a wide range of performance media, from solo guitar to full orchestra, band, and chorus. All are strongly imbued with Brazilian color. A favorite is the *Bachiana Brasileira* no. 5 (1938) for soprano and 8 cellos.

GILBERT CHASE

Bibliography: Béhague, Gerard, *Music in Latin America* (1979); Mariz, Vasco, *Heitor Villa-Lobos: Brazilian Composer* (1963); Slonimsky, Nicolas, *Music of Latin America* (1972).

Villa Rotonda

The villa La Rotonda, also called Villa Capra, on the outskirts of Vicenza, Italy, was designed by Andrea PALLADIO, the architect who gave his name to the Palladian style of neoclassical architecture. The 2-story villa is set on a high ground-floor plinth, and was built as a hilltop retreat for Mario Capra, a church dignitary. Its design is symmetrical on both axes, as to both plan and elevation, and centers on a 2-story domed circular room. Each identical facade is dominated by a pillared, pedimented temple porch, a favorite motif of Palladio that came to be the hallmark of post-Renaissance classical architecture, especially that of Great Britain and the United States during the 18th century (see COLONIAL STYLES IN NORTH AMERICA).

BETTY ELZEA

Bibliography: Ackerman, James S., *Palladio*, rev. ed. (1977); Wittkower, Rudolf, *Palladio and Palladianism* (1974).

The Villa Ròtonda (1566–67), designed by the architect Andrea Palladio, is one of the most innovative examples of Renaissance residential architecture. Situated on a hill overlooking Vicenza, Italy, the villa is distinguished by its four symmetrical pillared porticoes.

Village Voice, The

The Village Voice, a weekly publication, began as a counterculture newspaper in 1955 with a staff that included Norman Mailer and Jules Feiffer. It featured antiestablishment news, investigative reporting, and writing of literary merit. By 1970 it had evolved into a sophisticated commercial enterprise. From 1977 to 1985 the paper was owned by Rupert MURDOCH; he sold it to Leonard Stern, a businessman. *The Village Voice* has a circulation of 151,000.

ROY HALVERSON

Villahermosa [vil-ah-ayr-moh′-sah]

Villahermosa (1980 pop., 250,903), the capital of Tabasco state, lies on the Gulf coastal lowlands of southeast Mexico near Campeche Bay. Petroleum is now the major product, and the city is the principal marketing center for agricultural crops grown in the surrounding area. Villahermosa was founded by the Spanish in 1596.

villanelle [vil-uh-nel′]

The villanelle is a French verse form that consists of five three-line stanzas concluded by a quatrain. The first and third lines of the first stanza are repeated in the succeeding stanzas as a refrain and form a final couplet. The French poet Jean Passerat (1534–1602) was probably responsible for establishing the standard form. Dylan Thomas's "Do not go gentle into that good night" is a notable modern example.   J. A. CUDDON

Villanova University [vil-uh-noh′-vuh]

Established in 1842 and administered by the Augustinian Fathers, Villanova University (enrollment: 11,200; library: 500,000 volumes) is a coeducational institution in Villanova, Pa. It has colleges of arts and sciences, nursing, and commerce and finance and a school of law.

Villanovans [vil-uh-noh′-vuhnz]

The Villanovans, believed by some scholars to have been the predecessors of the ETRUSCANS, were the first people in central Italy to use iron. Their origins, like those of the Etruscans, are disputed. According to one school of thought they evolved out of the local Pianello culture, which was one of the group of URNFIELD CULTURES. Another school of thought suggests that the Villanovans were of foreign origin. They emerged during the 9th century BC and flourished between the Po and the Tiber, their earliest sites being concentrated in what is now Tuscany. From there the rich culture of the Villanovans spread to the area around Bologna, where they established an important center near the present-day village of Villanova (for which they are named).

The Villanovans worked the copper and iron mines of Tuscany and made fine metalwork that from the mid-8th century BC onward was influenced by Greek art. In early burials their terra-cotta cremation urns frequently are covered with either a crested helmet or an imitation helmet fashioned of pottery. Later Villanovan cremations were deposited in urns that were shaped to resemble wattle-and-daub huts. Little is known, however, about the actual domestic dwellings of the Villanovans.

Mystery also surrounds the eclipse of the Villanovans. In the south they were replaced by the Etruscans during the 8th century BC, but in the north they continued until the 6th century BC, producing in the Po valley an art derived from the Greek Geometric.

Rome is built on the site of an 8th-century Villanovan settlement. This is compatible with the date of 753 BC that was in Roman tradition ascribed to the foundation of the Eternal City by Romulus.

LLOYD LAING

Bibliography: Hencken, Hugh, *Tarquinia, Villanovans and Early Etruscans* (1968); Randall-MacIver, David, *Villanovans and Early Etruscans* (1924); Rose, H. J., *Primitive Culture in Italy* (1926; repr. 1971).

Villanueva, Carlos Raúl [vee-ah-nway′-vah]

Venezuela's major 20th-century architect, Carlos Raúl Villanueva, b. May 30, 1900, d. Aug. 16, 1975, was trained mainly at the École des Beaux-Arts in Paris, from which he graduated in 1928. In Venezuela since 1929, he established the National School of Architecture, where he taught for 16 years, and founded the Venezuelan Society of Architects, serving as its first president. He was also counselor to the Banco Obrero (a housing authority) and director of the National Commission on Urbanism. During the 1940s and '50s, Villanueva headed the design team that replaced the slums of Caracas with modern housing developments. He also designed the Venezuelan Pavilion at Expo 67 in Montreal.

Villanueva's most important work, the monumental structures at the Central University of Caracas (1952), epitomizes his distinctive style, which attempts to integrate art and architecture on a grand scale. This project, incorporating the work of many contemporary artists and sculptors, is probably the world's best demonstration of how architecture, painting, sculpture, and stained glass can be integrated into a new, balanced synthesis.

DONALD AND MARTHA ROBERTSON

Bibliography: Bayón, Damián, and Gasparini, Paolo, *The Changing Shape of Latin American Architecture* (1979); Damaz, P. F., *Art in Latin American Architecture* (1963); Hitchcock, Henry-Russell, *Latin American Architecture since 1945* (1972); Moholy-Nagy, Dorothea, *Carlos Raúl Villanueva and the Architecture of Venezuela* (1964).

Villanueva, Juan de

An important Spanish architect of the neoclassic style, Juan de Villanueva, b. Sept. 15, 1739, d. Aug. 22, 1811, is best known as the designer (1785-87) of the PRADO Museum in Madrid. In 1768, having spent seven years of study in Rome, Villanueva was appointed architect to the ESCORIAL. There he designed several small buildings that followed the "severe style" of the monastery. His other, later projects, all in Madrid, included the Academy of History (1788), the Observatory (begun 1790), and the north side of the Town Hall (1787-89).   EDWARD J. SULLIVAN

Bibliography: Kubler, George, and Soria, Martin, *Art and Architecture in Spain and Portugal and Their American Dominions 1500-1800* (1959).

Villard, Oswald Garrison   [vil-ard']

American newspaperman Oswald Garrison Villard, b. Wiesbaden, Germany, Mar. 13, 1872, d. Oct. 1, 1949, was an outspoken pacifist and liberal who expressed his views in the *New York Evening Post* and the *Nation,* both of which he inherited from his father, Henry Villard, in 1900. His pacifist views, including opposition to World War I, led to economic problems that forced him to sell the *Post* in 1918. He retained control of the *Nation* until 1935 and continued to champion such liberal causes as women's suffrage and black civil rights. Villard discussed 27 contemporary public figures in *Prophets, True and False* (1928) and analyzed the press at length in *Newspapers and Newspaper Men* (1923), in *The Disappearing Daily* (1944), and in his autobiography, *Fighting Years* (1939).   ERNEST C. HYNDS

Bibliography: Humes, D. Joy, *Oswald Garrison Villard, Liberal of the 1920's* (1960; repr. 1977).

Villard de Honnecourt   [vee-yar' duh ohn-koor']

The fame of the French architect Villard de Honnecourt, active c.1225-1235, rests on a notebook of drawings (Bibliothèque Nationale, Paris) that provides a rare glimpse into the aesthetics and techniques of Gothic architecture. The book was evidently intended for the edification of the people in Villard's workshop; it includes a brief text as well as technical drawings by two later hands. From the sketches of churches—real and imaginary—figures, and ornamentation, it is apparent that the author was familiar with the great cathedrals of his time—Chartres, Laon, and Reims. He himself may have been the architect of Cambrai Cathedral (no longer extant).   ROBERT NEUMAN

Bibliography: Bowie, Theodore, ed., *The Sketchbook of Villard de Honnecourt* (1959).

Villars, Claude Louis Hector, Duc de   [vee-yar']

Claude Louis Hector, duc de Villars, b. May 8, 1653, d. June 17, 1734, diplomat and soldier for Louis XIV of France, fought brilliantly during the War of the SPANISH SUCCESSION (1701-14); he was honored with the rare title of marshal general of France (1733). Villars won battles at Friedlingen (1702) and Höchstädt (1703) and pacified the rebellious French CAMISARDS. Although he lost the Battle of Malplaquet (1709) to the Anglo-imperial forces under the duke of Marlborough and Eugene of Savoy, his opponents suffered staggering casualties. Victory at Denain (1712) hastened the Peace of Utrecht (see UTRECHT, PEACE OF); Villars negotiated the component Treaty of Rastatt (1714) himself. He then served on Louis XV's Regency Council.   A. LLOYD MOOTE

Bibliography: Stargill, Claude, *Marshall Villars and the War of the Spanish Succession* (1965).

Villaurrutia, Xavier   [vee-yah-oo-roo'-tee-ah]

Xavier Villaurrutia, a Mexican poet and playwright, b. Mar. 27, 1903, d. Dec. 25, 1950, founded the important experimental theater groups *Ulises* and *Orientación,* which were respon-

sible for the renaissance of Mexican drama between 1928 and 1938. Not a popular success, Villaurrutia's theater was highly intellectual, focusing on the themes of death and personal anguish. Among his most important plays are *Parece mentira* (It Seems a Lie, 1934), *En qué piensas?* (What Are You Thinking About?, 1938), and *Invitación a la muerte* (Invitation to Death, 1947). Villaurrutia's poetic production was slight, consisting of three major books: *Reflejos* (Reflections, 1926), *Nostalgia de la muerte* (Nostalgia for Death, 1946), and *Canto a la primavera* (Song to Spring; 1948). His poetry reflects the philosophical problems also dealt with in his dramas.

Bibliography: Dayster, Frank, *Xavier Villaurrutia* (1971); Gonzáles Pēna, Carlos, *History of Mexican Literature,* 3d ed. (1968).

Villehardouin, Geoffroi de   [veel-ar-dwan']

Geoffroi de Villehardouin, c.1150-c.1213, a French historian, was a leader and chronicler of the Fourth CRUSADE (1199-1207). Marshal of Champagne from about 1185, he helped obtain ships from Venice in 1201 to transport the Crusaders, and he was involved in most of the important developments during the Crusade. After the conquest (1204) of Constantinople he was rewarded with a fief in Thrace. His unfinished account of the Crusade, usually called the *Conquête de Constantinople* (Conquest of Constantinople, published in 1585), the first important prose history in French, was a milestone in medieval historical writing.

Bibliography: Archambault, Paul, *Seven French Chroniclers* (1974).

Villella, Edward   [vil-el'-uh]

The dynamic American dancer Edward Villella, b. Bayside, N.Y., Oct. 1, 1936, has done a great deal toward making dance an acceptable career for men. Upon graduation (1956) from New York State Maritime College, where he had been a boxing champion, Villella returned to his study of ballet, interrupted since early adolescence. He joined New York City Ballet in 1957 and was immediately given leading roles. Among his most popular roles were those in *Prodigal Son, Harlequinade* (1965), and *Rubies* (1967). Jerome Robbins created the leading role for Villella in his experimental ballet *Watermill* (1972). The dancer has made frequent appearances on television and has served as consultant for many dance specials. In 1976 he won an Emmy for his children's ballet for television, *Harlequin.* He contributed to Dance Perspectives Number 40, *The Male Image.* Villella has served on the National Council of the Arts and was chairman (1978-79) of New York City's Commission on Cultural Affairs.   MICHAEL ROBERTSON

Bibliography: Gruen, John, *The Private World of Ballet* (1976); Kirstein, Lincoln, *Thirty Years: The New York City Ballet* (1978).

Villiers, George: see BUCKINGHAM, GEORGE VILLIERS, 1st DUKE OF.

Villiers de L'Isle-Adam, Philippe   [vee-lee-ay' duh leel-ah-dan']

Philippe Auguste Villiers de L'Isle-Adam, a French poet, novelist, dramatist and short-story writer, b. Feb. 28, 1838, d. Aug. 19, 1889, was a descendant of an impoverished noble family and lived in great poverty. He is best known for an esoteric symbolic play, *Axël* (1890), which was called by René Lalou "the last expression of European Romanticism, the Faust of the expiring nineteenth century." He also left two collections of short stories, *Cruel Tales* (1883; Eng. trans., 1963) and *Nouveaux contes cruels* (More Cruel Tales, 1888), and a novel, *L'Éve future* (The Eve of the Future, 1886).

Bibliography: Conroy, William T., *Villiers de L'Isle-Adam* (1978).

Villon, François   [vee-yohn']

François Villon, b. Paris, 1431, as François de Montcorbier or François des Loges, d. 1463?, was one of the finest French lyric poets. Of poor parents, he was brought up by a priest,

Guillaume de Villon, whose name he took. He did graduate study in Paris until 1452 but 3 years later was banished from the city for fatally stabbing a priest in a brawl. *Le Petit Testament* (The Small Testament), known also as *Le Lais* (The Legacy), may have been composed at this time, and Villon's other long poem, *Le Grand Testament* (The Large Testament), known also simply as *Le Testament,* soon followed.

The Testaments are written in octosyllabic lines arranged into eight-line stanzas with a rhyme scheme of *a b a b b c b c.* Villon's many ballads often consist of three ten-line stanzas followed by envois of from four to seven lines. The Testaments are mock or imaginary wills in which bequests are made alternately with compassion and with irony. For example, to the Holy Trinity, Villon leaves his soul; to the earth, his body; to a Parisian, Denis, some stolen wine; to a madman, his glasses; to a lover, all the women he wants. At least two of Villon's shorter poems—"Ballad of Hanged Men" and "I Am François, They Have Caught Me"—were composed in 1462 while the author was awaiting execution for robbery. His sentence, however, was commuted to banishment, and Villon subsequently disappeared without a trace.

Very popular during the late 19th century, Villon's poetry was translated into English by Dante Gabriel Rossetti, Algernon Swinburne, and, in the 20th century, Ezra Pound. Villon's "Ballad of the Women of Yesteryear" contains the celebrated lament on the passing of time: "Mais où sont les neiges d'antan?" ("But where are the snows of yesteryear?").

FRANCIS J. CARMODY

Bibliography: Chaney, E. F., *François Villon in His Environment* (1946); Fox, J. H., *The Poetry of Villon* (1962; repr. 1981); Lewis, D. B. Wyndham, *François Villon: A Documentary Survey* (1928); Vitz, Evelyn B., *The Crossroads of Intentions: A Study of Symbolic Expression in the Poetry of François Villon* (1974).

Villon, Jacques

The French artist Jacques Villon, b. Gaston Duchamp, July 31, 1875, d. June 9, 1963, was the brother of the Dada artist Marcel Duchamp and the sculptor Raymond Duchamp-Villon. Villon adopted his favorite poet's surname in 1895, when he went to Paris to pursue an artistic career. He was befriended by Henri de Toulouse-Lautrec, who urged him to become a graphic artist; during the next 15 years he produced numerous posters and satirical newspaper drawings and became a printmaker of the first rank. His interest turned to cubist painting in 1911, and in 1912 he helped organize the avant-garde Section d'Or (Golden Section) exhibition in Paris.

During the 1920s and '30s, Villon alternated between formal abstraction and an extremely simplified realism bordering on cubism. In his later work, such as *Portrait of Marcel Duchamp* (1951; Henie-Onstad Museum, Oslo), Villon produced an elegant synthesis of both styles.   EDWARD T. McCLELLAN

Bibliography: Cabanne, Pierre, *The Brothers Duchamp* (1976); Liebermann, W. S., *Jacques Villon, His Graphic Art* (1953); Wick, P. A., *Jacques Villon, Master of Graphic Art (1875–1963)* (1964).

Vilna   [vil'-nuh]

Vilna (Lithuanian: Vilnius), the capital of the Lithuanian Soviet Socialist Republic in the USSR, is located on the Neris River. With a population of 492,000 (1980 est.), the city is an important cultural and industrial center, accounting for about one-fourth of the manufacturing output of Lithuania. The principal products are precision instruments and electrical equipment. Vilna has the ruins of a 14th-century castle and a variety of architectural styles, ranging from Gothic to baroque. It is the seat of the Lithuanian Academy of Sciences and has a university, founded in 1579.

Settled during the 10th century, Vilna became capital of the Grand Duchy of Lithuania in 1323 and, despite destruction by the Teutonic Knights in 1377, developed into a major trading center. It declined after Lithuania was formally united with Poland in 1569. Vilna passed to Russia in 1795. After World War I, Vilna was disputed between the new governments of Lithuania and Poland, but the Poles eventually established

control. The USSR took the city in 1940 but yielded it to Lithuania, only to annex all of Lithuania later that same year. Vilna was occupied by the Germans during World War II. Vilna was an important Jewish center of Eastern Europe from the 17th century until the extermination of the Jews by the Germans during World War II.   THEODORE SHABAD

Vilnius: see VILNA.

vina   [vee'-nuh]

The South Indian vina is a tube zither; the North Indian vina is a type of lute. Both have frets, melody and drone strings, and calabash resonators. The South Indian vina has a resonator at each end and is placed on the floor for performance. The other has only a rudimentary resonator fastened to its neck and is held with the neck aloft and the resonator downward. Deviations from the fretted pitches are created by pressing the strings out of position or pulling them to the side.   ELWYN A. WIENANDT

Viña del Mar   [veen'-yah del mar]

Viña del Mar (1980 est. pop., 262,100) is a seaside and gambling resort on the coast of central Chile 8 km (5 mi) north of Valparaíso. Known for its superb gardens, a casino, a racetrack, and other recreational facilities, it also serves as an industrial and marketing center and is the site of Cerro Castillo, the summer retreat of Chilean presidents.   NEALE J. PEARSON

Vincennes   [vin-senz']

Vincennes (1980 pop., 20,875), the oldest city in Indiana, lies on the Wabash River in the southwestern part of the state. It is the seat of Knox County and an industrial and commercial center. Glass, steel, shoes, and paper products are manufactured. Landmarks include the old cathedral of Saint Francis Xavier (1825) and the Indiana Territorial Capitol (1800). Vincennes was founded in 1702 by French fur traders and ceded to the British in 1763. During the American Revolution it was captured by Americans under George Rogers Clark in 1779.

Vincennes, François Marie Bissot, Sieur de   [van-sen']

François Marie Bissot, sieur de Vincennes, b. Montreal, June 17, 1700, d. Mar. 25, 1736, a French-Canadian soldier and explorer, promoted French interests in the Wabash country in present-day Indiana. Son of the explorer Jean Baptiste Bissot, sieur de Vincennes, he erected a fort c.1722 near present-day Lafayette, Ind., and in 1731 or 1732 built another at present-day Vincennes, Ind. Vincennes was defeated in a skirmish with the hostile Chickasaw Indians, who burned him at the stake near present-day Fulton, Miss.

Vincent, John Heyl

The Methodist clergyman John Heyl Vincent, b. Tuscaloosa, Ala., Feb. 23, 1832, d. May 9, 1920, was a leader in the Sunday school movement. He attended secondary schools but was largely self-educated. Ordained an elder in 1857, he held several pastorates and began his career in Christian education in 1866 as agent and later as general secretary of the Methodist Episcopal Sunday School Union and Tract Society. He began publication of a large series of Sunday school materials. The culmination of his career came with the founding of the Chautauqua Sunday School Teachers Assembly in 1874. Out of this interdenominational project, which consisted of 8 weeks annually of summer school, developed the CHAUTAUQUA movement. Vincent was elected bishop in 1888.   FREDERICK A. NORWOOD

Bibliography: Vincent, Leon H., *John Heyl Vincent* (1925).

Vincent de Paul, Saint   [van-sahn' duh pohl']

The French priest Vincent de Paul, b. Apr. 24, 1581, d. Sept. 27, 1660, was the founder of numerous charitable organizations. Of peasant family, he began his work on behalf of the poor as a young priest by working to relieve the lot of galley slaves. He founded the Congregation of the Mission (the Vincentians or Lazarists; 1625) to preach to the rural poor and, with Saint Louise de Marillac, founded the Daughters of Charity (1633), composed of peasant women who, in ministering to the poor, were the first sisters to work outside of the convent buildings in active service. Vincent also organized several seminaries to train young men for the priesthood and inaugurated the now-standard practice of a period of spiritual preparation for men about to be ordained to the priesthood. Canonized in 1737, he is the patron of all charitable works inspired by his example, including the famous lay organization of the St. Vincent de Paul Society. Feast day: Sept. 27 (formerly July 19).   CYPRIAN DAVIS, O.S.B.

Bibliography: Coste, Pierre, *The Life and Works of Saint Vincent de Paul*, trans. by Joseph Leonard, 3 vols. (1952); Daniel-Rops, Henry, *Monsieur Vincent: The Story of St. Vincent de Paul*, trans. by Julie Kernan (1961); von Matt, Leonard, and Cognet, Louis, *St. Vincent de Paul*, trans. by Emma Craufurd (1960).

Vincent Ferrer, Saint   [vin'-sent fer'-er]

Spanish Dominican preacher Vincent Ferrer, b. c.1350, d. Apr. 5, 1419, worked to end the Great Schism (see SCHISM, GREAT). He was a protégé and friend of Pedro de Luna, whose confessor he became when de Luna was elected (1394) "antipope" at Avignon as BENEDICT XIII. In 1399, Vincent began a 10-year preaching tour through France, Spain, Switzerland, Italy, and the Low Countries, converting heretics, Jews, and Muslims. He reportedly worked wonders and was followed by thousands of flagellants. Having already tried unsuccessfully to persuade Benedict to resign, he began to denounce him publicly from about 1412 and drew support away from the Avignon papacy, thus paving the way for the end of the Schism at the Council of Constance (1417). Vincent Ferrer was canonized in 1455. Feast day: Apr. 5.

Bibliography: Allies, Mary, *Three Catholic Reformers of the Fifteenth Century* (1972).

Vincent of Beauvais   [van-sahn']

The French Dominican friar Vincent of Beauvais, c.1190-1264, was an encyclopedist whose *Speculum Majus* (Greater Mirror, c.1250) is an important compendium of medieval learning. It covers, in three parts, the entire corpus of European knowledge, including history, philosophy, theology, science, and the arts. A fourth part, dealing with morals, written between 1310 and 1325, forms part of all printed editions.

Bibliography: Gábriel, Asztrik, *The Educational Ideas of Vincent of Beauvais*, 2d ed. (1962); McCarthy, Joseph M., *Humanistic Emphasis in the Educational Thought of Vincent of Beauvais* (1976).

Vincent of Lérins, Saint   [van-sahn' lay-ran']

The Christian monk Vincent of Lérins, d. c.450, is remembered for his *Commonitorium* (Memorandum, c.434), a collection of notes in 33 chapters. One of the first to grapple with the question of doctrinal development, he offered guidelines for extracting truth from religious controversy. He held that the church can differentiate between true and false traditions by using the triple test of ecumenicity, antiquity, and consent ("what has been believed everywhere, always, by all"). This test has come to be known as the "Vincentian Canon." Feast day: May 24.

Vindication of the Rights of Women, A

Mary WOLLSTONECRAFT's *A Vindication of the Rights of Women*, written in 1792, is a milestone in the history of modern feminism. Part of the spreading debate over human rights inspired by the French Revolution and a direct response to Jean Jacques Rousseau's *Émile* (1762), it was an appeal to French leaders of the period to include women in their proposed educational reforms. Its author argued that the rights of man applied equally to both sexes and that the cause of woman's oppression lay in a faulty education that had kept her inferior. Controversial in its time, Wollstonecraft's *Vindication* represents the first major demand for the redress of feminine grievances.

vine

Plants utilizing climbing or creeping stems for support are known as vines. Rambling types rest upon other plants, often fastened with thorns or prickles, as with certain roses. English ivy has adventitious roots, whereas vines such as the morning glory climb with the entire stem coiling the host. Trailing arbutus creeps along the ground surface with rooting occurring along the hairy stem.

Vine, F. J.

The British geologist and geophysicist Frederick John Vine, b. June 17, 1939, has done important work that supports the concept of SEAFLOOR SPREADING and the theory of continental drift. Together with D. H. MATTHEWS, Vine identified the symmetrical pattern of magnetic anomalies that exists on either side of the mid-oceanic ridges and presented this as evidence that new oceanic crust is forming at the ridges and spreading away on both sides of the ridges. Vine received (1965) a Ph.D. in geophysics from the University of Cambridge and subsequently taught at Princeton University and at the School of Environmental Sciences at the University of East Anglia in Norwich, England.   ROBERT J. DELATOUR, JR.

Bibliography: Anderson, Alan H., *The Drifting Continents* (1971); Sullivan, Walter, *Continents in Motion: The New Earth Debate* (1974).

See also: PLATE TECTONICS.

vinegar

Vinegar (from the French *vinaigre*, "sour wine") is an acidic liquid obtained from the fermentation of alcohol and used either as a condiment or a preservative. Vinegar usually has an acid content of between 4 and 8 percent; in flavor it may be sharp, rich, or mellow. Vinegar is made by combining sugary materials (or materials produced by hydrolysis of starches) with vinegar or acetic acid bacteria and air. The sugars and starches are converted to alcohol by yeasts of the genus *Saccharomyces*, and the bacteria make enzymes that cause oxidation of the alcohol.

Several varieties of vinegar are manufactured. Wine vinegars, produced in grape-growing regions, are used for salad dressings and relishes and may be either reddish or white, depending on the wine used in the fermentation process. Tarragon vinegar has the distinctive flavor of the herb. Malt vinegar, popular in Great Britain, is known for its earthy quality. White vinegar, also called distilled vinegar, is made from industrial alcohol; it is often used as a preservative or in mayonnaise because of its less distinctive flavor and clear, untinted appearance. Rice vinegar, which has a piquant quality, is often used in Oriental countries for marinades and salad dressings.

Vinegar may be used as an ingredient of sweet-and-sour sauces for meat and vegetable dishes, as a minor ingredient in candies, or as an ingredient in baking, as a part of the leavening process. Vinegar is also added to milk, if sour milk is needed in a home recipe. Commercially and in the home, the most common use of vinegar is in the making of salad dressings.   MARGARET McWILLIAMS

Bibliography: Hanssen, Maurice, *Cider Vinegar: A Comprehensive Guide to Its Uses and Properties* (1975); Schierbeck, J., *The Manufacturing of Vinegar* (1951); Scott, Cyril, *Cider Vinegar*, rev. ed. (1973).

Vinet, Alexandre   [vee-nay']

Reformed theologian, moralist, and literary critic Alexandre Rudolphe Vinet, b. June 17, 1797, d. May 4, 1847, is sometimes referred to as the Swiss Friedrich Schleiermacher. A teacher of theology at Lausanne, Vinet defended separation of church and state and freedom of religious practice. His conception of Christianity was thoroughly individualistic; he believed that conscience, not dogma, is the seat of religion.

vineyard: see GRAPE; WINE.

Vinje, Aasmund Olafsson   [vin'-yeh]

The Norwegian poet and essayist Aasmund Olafsson Vinje, b. Apr. 6, 1818, d. July 30, 1870, is best remembered for his *Travelogue from the Summer of 1860* (1861; Eng. trans., 1861), recounting a hike from Oslo to Trondheim. In 1858 he had founded the journal *Dølen* (The Dalesman) in part to propagate Nynorsk, or New Norse, developed from peasant dialects.   WILLIAM MISHLER

Vinland   [vin'-luhnd]

Vinland was a VIKING, or Norse, settlement on North America's east coast in the early 11th century. The land it occupied was probably first sighted c.986, when Bjarni Herjolfsson was blown off course. Later, c.1000, LEIF ERIKSSON led an expedition that touched Helluland (probably Baffin Island) and Markland (probably Labrador) and remained a year at Vinland. His brother Thorvald went to Vinland c.1004. THORFINN KARLSEFNI (c.1010) and two brothers, Helgi and Finnbogi (c.1013), also led expeditions. Vinland was abandoned c.1015, apparently because of the hostility of the native Skraelings.

Various spots have been suggested for Vinland's location, from the Virginia Capes to Newfoundland. The L'ANSE AUX MEADOWS site (northern Newfoundland) has many Norse artifacts, but the Vinland settlement's exact location remains in doubt. Yale University's Vinland map, a world map supposedly made about 1440, includes Vinland and Greenland, but by 1974 its New World portions had been proved a modern forgery.   BRUCE B. SOLNICK

Bibliography: Haugen, Einar, *Voyage to Vinland* (1942); Ingstad, Helge, *Westward to Vinland* (1968); Magnusson, Magnus, and Palsson, Hermann, ed. and trans., *Vinland Sagas* (1966); Oleson, Tryggvi J., *Early Voyages and Northern Approaches, 1000–1632* (1964).

Vinson, Frederick M.

Frederick Moore Vinson, b. Louisa, Ky., Jan. 22, 1890, d. Sept. 8, 1953, was 13th chief justice (1946–53) of the United States. Vinson was educated at the University of Kentucky and served (1922–38) as a Democrat in the U.S. House of Representatives. In 1938, President Franklin D. Roosevelt named him to the U.S. Court of Appeals. He resigned in 1943 to head the Office of War Mobilization, and, in 1945, President Harry S. Truman appointed him secretary of the treasury. In 1946, Truman named him chief justice. On the Supreme Court, Vinson was both criticized for failing to protect individual rights and for supporting a strong federal government and praised for his record in cases involving religious freedom and the rights of blacks.

Bibliography: Pfeffer, Leo, *This Honorable Court* (1965); Swindler, William F., *Court and Constitution in the Twentieth Century* (1969).

Vinson Massif

The Vinson Massif, Antarctica's highest peak, rises to 5,140 m (16,864 ft) in the Sentinel Range of the Ellsworth Mountains near the Ronne Ice Shelf. Sighted by Lincoln Ellsworth in 1935 during an aerial survey, it was first climbed in 1966.

vinyl

Vinyl plastic is usually the common thermoplastic polyvinyl chloride (see PLASTICS). Vinyl chloride, a gas with the chemical structure $CHCl{=}CH_2$, is produced by reacting ethylene or acetylene with hydrochloric acid. The reaction replaces one hydrogen atom in ethylene with a chlorine atom; this modification makes the material nonburning. Vinyl chloride was declared a carcinogen in 1974, when the U.S. government banned its use as a propellant in aerosols and limited its concentrations in workplace air to one part in one billion. Polymerization of vinyl chloride produces polyvinyl chloride (PVC), which is not considered dangerous. PVC is a rigid plastic but is soft and flexible if compounded with plasticizing materials. It is formulated with heat and ultraviolet stabili-

zers, antioxidants, pigments, and plasticizers for impact resistance. PVC softens at temperatures above 70° C (158° F), and toward 150° C (302° F) it degrades, producing hydrogen chloride. If completely destroyed by heat, it produces hydrogen chloride and carbon dioxide and monoxide.

More polyvinyl chloride is used than any other plastic except polyethylene. Uses include house siding, window frames, electrical insulation, eaves troughs, hoses, pipe, floor tile, phonograph records, household goods, and water-resistant sheeting, such as raincoats and shower curtains.

In a chemical sense, a vinyl is any ethylene molecule with one hydrogen atom replaced by a substitute atom or group of atoms. Other vinyl plastics include polyvinyl fluoride (one fluorine atom), polyvinyl alcohol, polystyrene (polyvinyl benzene), and polyvinyl acetate. The different substitute atoms or groups result in entirely different properties; polystyrene is brittle and attacked by solvents, whereas polyvinyl fluoride is tough and resistant to solvents.   W. J. PATTON

Bibliography: Schildknecht, Calvin E., *Vinyls and Related Polymers* (1952); Sittig, Marshall, *Acrylic and Vinyl Fibers* (1972).

viol   [vy'-ul]

Viol (*viola da gamba*) is the name of a family of bowed, fretted, and stringed instruments popular during the 16th and 17th centuries and revived during the 20th century for the performance of early music. By the 14th century they had replaced the VIELLE as the principal bowed instruments of Europe; the viols in turn were superseded in the 18th century by the violin family.

Viols were extremely popular as ensemble instruments from the 15th through the 17th century, surviving into the 18th century in some baroque compositions. Unlike members of the violin family, viols have sloping shoulders, six strings, and a fretted fingerboard; they are held on or between the knees. Their deep bodies and thin strings produce a sweet tone that lacks the brilliance and power of the violin. The most common sizes were (left to right) the bass, tenor, and treble viols.

Compared with violins, viols have sloping, rather than rounded, shoulders; a deeper body; a flatter back; thinner, less-tense strings; six strings rather than four; a fretted fingerboard; a wider, flatter bridge; a wider fingerboard; and an outward-curving bow that the player holds palm upward. Viols are always held vertically, between, or resting on, the player's legs—hence the name *viola da gamba* ("leg viol"), which was later applied only to the bass instrument. The name was appropriate for the entire set except the double bass viol, from which the modern DOUBLE BASS is descended.

A set of viols, called a "chest" because of the fitted case in which they were stored, usually consisted of six instruments: two basses, two tenors (sometimes a tenor and an alto), and two trebles. The bass, or viola da gamba, was the only one with good solo capabilities, but little music survives for it because it was used mostly as a foundation instrument in realizing FIGURED BASS, and most of the solo material remained in manuscript. In addition to the three sizes of the instrument mentioned here were a smaller treble, the double bass, and the division viol, a small bass for playing variations. The lyra viol, or *viola bastarda*, midway between tenor and bass, was tuned differently from the others and used TABLATURE instead of regular notation. Two instruments in the family—the baryton, a bass instrument, and the viola d'amore, a treble—had sympathetic strings under the fingerboards to add richness to their timbre. The viola d'amore differed from the other viols in that it had no frets and it was held horizontally, like a violin.

The building and playing of viols reached a high point in Italy, but the peak of CONSORT playing was found in 17th-century England. Whole consorts, made up entirely of viols, were common; broken consorts, made up of various instruments, often called for one or more viols. The music ranged from single-movement contrapuntal pieces to suites of dances. English composers for viols included William Byrd, Orlando Gibbons, John Jenkins, and John Coperario.

ELWYN A. WIENANDT

Bibliography: Bessaraboff, N., *Ancient European Musical Instruments* (1941); Danks, Harry, *The Viola D'Amore* (1976); DeSmet, Robin, *Published Music for the Viola Da Gamba and Other Viols* (1971); Hayes, G. R., *Viols and Other Bowed Instruments* (1930); Straeten, Edmund van der, *History of the Violoncello, the Viol Da Gamba, Their Precursors, and Collateral Instruments*, 2 vols. (1915; repr. 1976).

viola   [vee-oh'-luh]

The viola is the alto of the violin family, and it has the responsibility of playing the tenor part in the string quartet. Larger and heavier than the violin, it is tuned a fifth lower and has a darker, somewhat nasal tone. Preclassical viola parts were sometimes uninteresting, but in the music of Mozart they assumed an importance that has remained. Viola concertos are few, but the instrument plays an important role in chamber music and solo sonatas. Berlioz's *Harold in Italy* is a symphony with viola solo. Concertos for the viola include those by Béla Bartók and Sir William Walton. Such modern soloists as Lionel Tertis and William Primrose have brought the instrument into prominence.   ELWYN A. WIENANDT

Bibliography: Nelson, Sheila M., *The Violin and Viola* (1972).

viola da gamba: see VIOL.

viola d'amore: see VIOL.

violet

Violets are about 500 species of temperate-zone flowers, genus *Viola*, in the violet family, Violaceae. They are low-growing herbs or subshrubs, and species bloom either annually or perennially. Violets may be stemmed—flowers and leaves growing on the same stem—or stemless—flowers and leaves growing on separate stalks. The shape of the leaves varies widely. Many species of violets produce two kinds of flowers:

The perennial sweet violet, V. odorata, has broad, heart-shaped leaves and stemless flowers—growing on separate stems from the leaves. The flowers bloom in early spring, and colors range from violet, lilac, and pink to white. Like many violet species, the petals are veined and the bottom one has a spur. Although varieties of this species are cultivated, it also grows wild in moist, slightly sunny areas of Eurasia and Africa.

showy purple, blue, pink, yellow, white, or multicolored flowers are produced in the springtime, allowing cross-pollination by insects; self-pollinating, inconspicuous green flowers without petals (cleistogamous flowers) are produced during the summer.

Although most species are wildflowers, several have been cultivated; these include the PANSY, classified as *V. tricolor* or *V. X wittrockiana* (a hybrid); Johnny-jump-up, *V. tricolor;* and sweet, or florist's, violet, *V. odorata.* Leaves of sweet violets can be added to salads, and the flowers can be candied or used to make violet jelly. Large numbers of the parma violet, *V. odorata,* var. *semperflorens,* are grown in France and Italy to produce essential oils used in perfume; more than 2 million flowers are needed to yield about half a kilogram (one pound) of the oils. In the eastern United States and Canada, common wildflower species include the woolly blue violet, *V. papilionacea,* and the bird's-foot violet, *V. pedata.* The AFRICAN VIOLET, *Saintpaulia,* is not related to the true violet.

Bibliography: Coon, Nelson, *The Complete Book of Violets* (1978); Klaber, Doretta, *Violets* (1976).

violin

The violin, the most commonly used member of the modern string family, is the highest-sounding instrument of that group. Its four strings are stretched over a high arched bridge that permits the playing of one or two strings at a time, as well as the nearly simultaneous sounding of three or four as chords. The overall length of the violin averages about 60 cm (23.5 in), whereas the sounding length of the strings, from bridge to the nut at the end of the fingerboard, is about 32 cm (12.75 in). The instrument is held on the left side of the body, while the right hand holds the bow. The wider end of the instrument is placed between the player's left shoulder and chin, while the left hand encircles its neck, the fingers stopping the strings to produce the various pitches. Sound is produced by drawing the bow across the strings to make them vibrate, or by plucking the strings (PIZZICATO). The range of the violin extends from G, the lowest open string, upward nearly four octaves.

Introduced into Europe at a time when the viol was the commonest stringed instrument, this descendant of the medieval fiddle was considered more suitable for dance music and rustic merrymaking than for the church or nobleman's chamber. By the beginning of the 17th century, Giovanni Gabrieli and Claudio Monteverdi were using the violin in their instrumental ensembles, and general acceptance of the instrument followed shortly thereafter.

The earliest important center of violin making was Brescia, where Gasparo da Saló (1540–1609) and Giovanni Paolo Maggini (1581–1630) worked. Cremona became the center of manufacture when the instruments of the Amati family, and later those of the Stradivari, Guarneri, and Ruggieri shops, at-

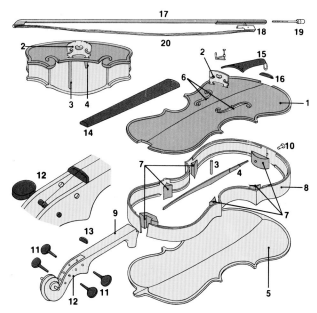

Parts of the violin are shown in this exploded view. The violin's softwood belly (1), which functions as a resonating soundboard, receives vibrations of the strings through the bridge (2). The soundpost (3) and bass bar (4), shown in cross-sectional view, carry vibrations along the belly and transmit them to the less resonant hardwood back (5). The f-shaped sound holes (6) also aid vibration. Interior blocks (7) support the ribs (8), neck (9), and button (10). The strings extend from pegs (11) in the pegbox (12) over the nut (13), fingerboard (14), and bridge to the tailpiece (15), secured over the lower nut (16) to the button. Parts of the bow include the stick (17), the nut or "frog" (18), the screw (19), and the horsehair (20).

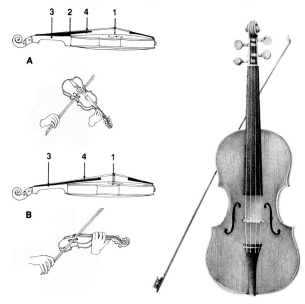

The violin, which was perfected during the early 1700s by the Italian instrument maker Antonio Stradivari, has remained virtually unchanged to the present day. Profiles of the 18th-century instrument (A) and the modern violin (B) show minor adjustments that reflect the demands of changing music and technique. The bridge (1) was raised and arched slightly during the late 18th century, increasing string tension and providing the brighter tone that was desired. In order to facilitate playing, the wedge (2) was eliminated, and the neck (3) was set at an angle to the body to support the lengthened fingerboard (4). Playing positions have also changed, from the 18th-century posture with the left hand supporting the instrument to a position with the violin held between the shoulder and chin, freeing the left hand.

tracted the attention of the public (see AMATI family; GUARNERI family; STRADIVARI family). The Italian master builders of the 17th and early 18th centuries are esteemed above all others, but makers from other areas achieved high recognition, among them the Tyrolese brothers, Jakob and Markus Stainer, the Klotz family in Bavaria, and some English and French builders. The demand for instruments brought mass production to Mittenwald, Bavaria, where the Klotzes had worked, but also a decline in quality. There the custom originated of putting labels bearing the names of famous makers, mostly Italian, into instruments, not to deceive buyers, but to identify the style of instrument that was imitated. Owners of instruments with facsimile labels sometimes mistakenly believe that they have an undiscovered masterpiece, an all but impossible dream.

Excellent violin makers exist in the United States, but the old instruments possess a special aura that is prized by performers. Because the value of old instruments increases with time, the best of them are owned and treasured by professionals or housed in special collections.

The violin is equally at home in chamber and orchestral music, in solo concertos and sonatas, in popular music and country fiddling. The instrument is extremely flexible, equally capable of playing long, sustained passages and those requiring great agility. It appears in greater numbers than the other bowed string instruments in orchestras because more violins are required to balance the corresponding viola, cello, and bass sections. In the modern symphony orchestra the concertmaster is the principal violinist. He or she plays any incidental violin solos in the music and is expected to establish the style of performance for the entire string section. Solo virtuosos have been known to every generation since the time of Corelli and Vivaldi; Paganini, Ysaÿe, Kreisler, Elman, Heifetz, Milstein, and Oistrakh are only a few among many who have attained international fame.   ELWYN A. WIENANDT

Bibliography: Boyden, David D., *The History of Violin Playing from Its Origins to 1761* (1965); Farga, Franz, *Violins and Violinists,* trans. by Egon Larsen, 2d ed. (1969); Hart, George, *The Violin and Its Music* (1976); Peterlongo, Paolo, *The Violin,* trans. by Bill Hopkins (1979); Van der Straeten, Edmund, *The History of the Violin,* 2 vols. (1933; repr. 1968).

Viollet-le-Duc, Eugène Emmanuel

The French architect Eugène Emmanuel Viollet-le-Duc, b. Jan. 27, 1814, d. Sept. 17, 1879, was known for his restorations of French medieval buildings. Among the important structures on which he worked were the Abbey Church of Vézelay (1840), the Sainte-Chapelle and Notre Dame in Paris (1845; in collaboration with Jacques Lassus), the walled city of Carcassone (1853), and the Château de Pierrefonds (1863–70).

Born into a cultured family, Viollet-le-Duc shunned the normal route of training in the conservative École des Beaux-Arts; instead, he educated himself during the 1830s through the firsthand study of buildings in France and abroad. In his theoretical writings he championed the Gothic style because he felt that its form was determined by structural necessity and its decoration both revealed and was derived from construction and materials. Thus he proposed the use of 19th-century techniques and materials, especially cast iron (see CAST-IRON ARCHITECTURE), according to the same rationalist principles employed by the Gothic masons.

ROBERT NEUMAN

Bibliography: Keating, B., "Viollet-le-Duc Re-created France's Medieval Legacy," *Smithsonian,* July 1974; Reed, Henry Hope, *The Golden City* (1959; repr. 1971); Summerson, John, *Heavenly Mansions* (1949; repr. 1963); Viollet-le-Duc, Eugène Emmanuel, *Discourses on Architecture,* trans. by Benjamin Bucknall, 2 vols. (1959).

violoncello: see CELLO.

Viotti, Giovanni Battista   [vee-oht'-tee]

Giovanni Battista Viotti, b. May 12, 1753, d. Mar. 3, 1824, was the greatest violinist of the generation before Niccolò Paganini. He studied the violin with Gaetano Pugnani and others. From 1780 to 1782, Viotti toured Europe and performed for royalty; he arrived in Paris in 1782 and entered the service of Marie Antoinette in 1784. The French Revolution forced him to flee (1792) to London, where he remained except for an exile (1798–1801) in Germany on suspicion of collaborating with the French, and an unsuccessful term (1818–1822) as director of the Italian opera in Paris. Apart from ten piano concertos, all of Viotti's compositions are for stringed instruments, the most important being his 29 violin concertos.

WILLIAM HAYS

Bibliography: Newman, William S., *The Sonata in the Classic Era* (1963).

viper

Vipers are venomous snakes in which the venom apparatus has reached its greatest development. The fang-bearing bone (maxillary) on each side of the upper jaw not only is much shorter than in most other snakes but also can be rotated. The fangs, which are hollow like hypodermic needles, are normally carried folded and rest horizontally along the roof of the mouth. When preparing to bite, a viper erects these fangs to a perpendicular position by rotating each maxillary on the front end of the supporting prefrontal bone.

The viper family, Viperidae, is usually divided into two subfamilies: the Viperinae, or true vipers, and the Crotalinae, containing the PIT VIPERS. Some classifications, however, regard the pit vipers as a separate family, the Crotalidae. The true vipers are distributed extensively in the Old World. The African Gaboon viper, *Bitis gabonica,* reaching 1.8 m (6 ft) in length, is the largest of the true vipers; the African puff adder, *B. arietans,* another large viper, is responsible for more human and livestock deaths in Africa than any other snake; the Asiatic Russell's viper, *Vipera russelli,* exceeding 1.5 m (5 ft) in length, may carry more venom than any other viper; and the saw-scaled viper, *Echis carinatus,* a 60-cm (2-ft) snake of North Africa and Asia, has the most potent venom of any viper.

Pit vipers, such as the rattlesnakes, differ from the true vipers primarily by possessing heat-sensitive pits used to detect warm-bodied prey. Pit vipers occur in North, Central, and South America and also range from Eastern Europe across Asia to Japan and the Indonesian archipelago.

An interesting relict species, Fea's viper, *Azemiops feae,* inhabits portions of the Himalayan Mountains and appears to be one of the most primitive vipers. It is intermediate between true vipers and pit vipers. It appears that the burrowing mole vipers, *Atractaspis,* arose from a colubrid rather than a viperid stock.

Most vipers are heavy bodied and terrestrial; however, some have become adapted to life in the trees and are bright green with prehensile tails (*Bothrops, Trimeresurus,* and *Atheris*). Some vipers possess interesting appendages, the functions of which are unknown. The many-horned adder, *Bitis cornuta,* and the eyelash viper, *Bothrops schlegeli,* possess raised spinelike scales over their eyes. The former is a desert species; the latter lives in tropical rain forests. A hornlike projection of the snout is found in the Patagonian viper, *Bothrops ammodytoides,* and the European sand viper, *V. ammodytes.*

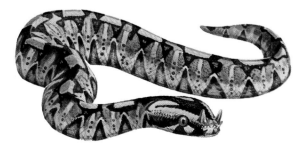

The brilliantly colored rhinoceros viper, B. nasicornis, *has two or three horns above each nostril. It inhabits central African forests.*

New World pit vipers bear living young, except for the bushmaster, *Lachesis muta,* which lays eggs. Most Old World pit vipers bear live young, although several species lay eggs; in egg-laying pit vipers, the females have a tendency to remain with the eggs until they hatch. The majority of true vipers give birth to live young, but, as in the pit vipers, a few lay eggs. In the tropics vipers may breed every year, but species inhabiting colder regions (such as the northern United States, Canada, and Europe) and at least one species from the highland tropics are unable to acquire sufficient food reserves to produce young annually. Therefore they reproduce only every other year.

JONATHAN A. CAMPBELL

Bibliography: Goin, C. J., et al., *Introduction to Herpetology,* 3d ed. (1978); Helm, T., *A World of Snakes* (1965); Minton, S. A. and M. R., *Giant Reptiles* (1973) and *Venomous Reptiles* (1969).

viperfish

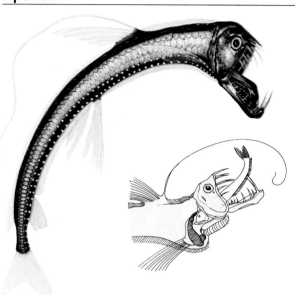

The voracious Atlantic viperfish, C. sloani, *is a deep-sea fish found at depths of up to 2,000 m (6,600 ft). It has luminous organs that act to attract prey and huge, needlelike teeth with which it spears its victims.*

Viperfish are elongated, deep-sea predators with large, expansive mouths containing several long, sharp, fanglike teeth. Making up the genus *Chauliodus,* family Chauliodontidae, viperfish are found in most oceans, usually in deep midwaters where they may make daily vertical migrations. They reach about 20 cm (8 in) in length and have adipose dorsal and ventral fins, a very elongated first dorsal spine, and many luminescent, or light-producing, organs with which they lure prey.

CAMM SWIFT

Virchow, Rudolf [fir'-koh]

Rudolf Carl Virchow, b. Schivelbein, Germany, Oct. 15, 1821, d. Sept. 5, 1902, was an important 19th-century physician who advanced the CELL theory and the science of pathology. He established a basic principle in biology that "all cells descend from other cells"; he also researched cell function in disease, especially the processes of inflammation and of tumor growth. A professor of pathological anatomy, he promoted political reform and improved public health in Germany.

Bibliography: Ackerknecht, Erwin H., *Rudolf Virchow* (1953).

Viren, Lasse [vir-eern', lahs'-suh]

Lasse Artturi Viren, b. July 22, 1949, is a Finnish long-distance runner whose feats in the 1972 and 1976 Olympic Games rank among the greatest in track-and-field history. Viren won both the 5,000- and 10,000-m (5,465- and 10,930-yd) runs in the

1972 Games, saving his most remarkable effort for the longer run, in which he not only broke the world record with a time of 27 min 38.4 sec, but did so after falling down halfway through the race. In the 1976 Olympics he became the first man ever to repeat the 5,000- and 10,000-m double victory; in those Games he ran the 5,000-m race in the Olympic-record time of 13 min 24.76 sec.

Bibliography: Moore, Kenny, "Enigma Wrapped in Glory," *Sports Illustrated*, June 27, 1977.

vireo   [vir'-ee-oh]

Vireos pluck insects from leaves. The family includes the solitary vireo, V. solitarius (top), and red-eyed vireo, V. olivaceus (bottom).

Vireos are small, mostly arboreal birds found from Canada through South America. More than 40 species, including the greenlets of South America, make up the family Vireonidae. Many are migratory, wintering in the tropics and breeding in cooler areas. Vireos are usually various shades of olive or gray above and white to gray below. Some have wing bars, eye rings, or head markings; both sexes are alike. Their beaks are somewhat hooked. They feed mostly on insects but may also eat berries. The female alone usually makes a well-constructed, lined cup nest, but the male helps in incubating the three to five white, spotted eggs and in caring for the young. The red-eyed vireo, *Vireo olivaceus,* a green-backed bird with a red eye, a white line over the eye, and a black-bordered blue gray cap, is common over its nesting range of southern Canada and the United States east of the Rocky Mountains.

WILLIAM F. SANDFORD

Virgil: see VERGIL.

virgin birth

The accounts of the birth of JESUS CHRIST in the Gospels according to Matthew and Luke, specifically the two Annunciation stories (Matt. 1:18–25; Luke 1:26–38), tell of a virginal conception by MARY through the power of the Holy Spirit. Belief that Jesus was thus conceived without a human father was more or less universal in the Christian church by the 2d century and is accepted by the Roman Catholic, Orthodox, and most Protestant churches. The origin of the tradition, however, is a controversial subject among modern scholars. Some believe it to be historical, based on information perhaps from Mary or her husband Joseph; for others it is a theological interpretation developed from extraneous sources (Hellenistic Jewish traditions about the birth of Isaac or pagan analogies). Whatever its origin, it may be recognized as a Christological affirmation denoting the divine origin of the Christ event.

REGINALD H. FULLER

Bibliography: Brown, R. E., *The Virginal Conception and Bodily Resurrection of Jesus* (1973) and *The Birth of the Messiah: A Commentary*

on the Infancy Narratives in Matthew and Luke (1977); Campenhausen, H. von, *The Virgin Birth in the Theology of the Ancient Church* (1964); Miguens, M., *The Virgin Birth: An Evaluation of Scriptural Evidence* (1975).

Virgin Islands

The Virgin Islands, a group of seven main islands and more than ninety islets and cays, lie east of Puerto Rico in the Caribbean. Their total land area is 497 km² (192 mi²). Saint Thomas, Saint Croix, Saint John, and about 50 islets belong to the United States and have a population of 95,591 (1980 pop.). Anegada, Jost Van Dyke, Tortola, Virgin Gorda, and about 32 islets are possessions of the United Kingdom; their population is 10,030 (1980 pop.). CHARLOTTE AMALIE on Saint Thomas is the capital of the U.S. Virgin Islands. Road Town on Tortola is the capital of the British Virgin Islands.

The annual rainfall averages 1,016–1,143 mm (40–45 in), and the average annual temperature is 26° C (78° F). Because freshwater is scarce, several seawater distilleries have been built.

Most Virgin Islanders are the descendants of slaves who worked colonial plantations. More recent immigrants to the islands have come from Puerto Rico, the United States, Venezuela, and the Lesser Antilles. Education and health standards are among the highest in the Caribbean. Saint Croix and Saint Thomas have divisions of the College of the Virgin Islands. Virgin Islands National Park is located on Saint John. Tourism dominates the economy. Fruits, vegetables, and coconuts are grown, and Saint Croix has petroleum refineries and bauxite-processing plants. Saint Thomas, with its large, protected harbor, has always been a commercial center.

Christopher Columbus landed at Saint Croix in 1493. The British took over the islands they now hold in 1666, and in the same year the Danes occupied Saint Thomas. In 1684 the Danes also occupied Saint John, and they acquired Saint Croix from the French in 1733. In 1917, because of the islands'

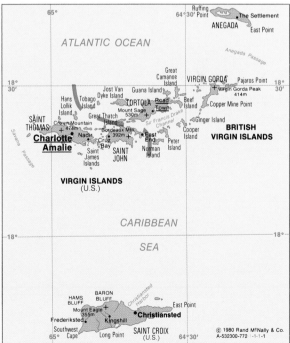

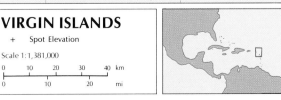

VIRGIN ISLANDS

+   Spot Elevation

Scale 1:1,381,000

0   10   20   30   40   km

0   10   20   mi

Charlotte Amalie, the capital and largest city of the U.S. Virgin Islands, is situated on the Caribbean coast of the island of Saint Thomas. Once the busiest slave market in the world, this duty-free port now bases its economy on a flourishing tourist trade.

strategic position on the approach to the Panama Canal, the United States purchased Saint Thomas, Saint Croix, and Saint John from Denmark. THOMAS G. MATHEWS

Bibliography: Harrigan, Norwell, *The Inter-Virgin Islands Conference* (1980); Moore, J. E., *Pelican Guide to the Virgin Islands* (1986).

Virgin Islands, College of the

Established in 1962, the College of the Virgin Islands (enrollment: 2,495; library: 76,961 volumes) is a coeducational liberal arts territorial school in Saint Thomas, U.S. Virgin Islands. A branch campus is at Saint Croix.

virginal

The virginal is a keyboard instrument with strings that are plucked by a mechanism like that of a HARPSICHORD. The differences between the two instruments, however, are considerable. The virginal is much smaller and has only one keyboard and a single set of strings. The strings themselves run more-or-less parallel to the front edge of the instrument. The harpsichord's strings, on the other hand, are placed at right angles to the front edge. The virginal can produce only a single timbre, whereas the harpsichord, with its several sets of strings and its "stops," can achieve a variety of tonal shades and textures. Because the longest strings of the virginal, the bass strings, are at the front, the shape of the instrument can be varied from a simple rectangle to any number of polygonal and pentagonal versions.

The smaller, simpler virginal seems to have been much more common in late medieval and Renaissance Europe (the earliest mention of the instrument occurs in Germany in 1404) than the larger and more expensive harpsichord. Certainly, painted depictions of the virginal occur far more frequently.

In England the term *virginal* included the harpsichord, and is associated with a group of composers active in the late 16th and early 17th centuries who were known as the English Vir-

The virginal, a popular keyboard instrument of 15th- to 18th-century Europe, was built in shapes ranging from simple rectangles to many-sided boxes. It was closely related to the harpsichord, and in England, virginal referred to the whole range of plucked keyboard instruments.

ginalists. The *Fitzwilliam Virginal Book* is the largest of the many collections of music for plucked keyboard instruments, and includes compositions by William Byrd, John Bull, and other Elizabethan composers. RICHARD REPHANN

Bibliography: Glyn, M. H., *Elizabethan Virginal Music and Its Composers* (1934; repr. 1977); Schott, H., ed., *The Historical Harpsichord* (1984).

Virginia

Virginia, often regarded as the gateway to the South, occupies the middle position on the Atlantic seaboard of the United States. Named for Elizabeth I, England's "Virgin Queen," the state is also known as the Old Dominion—in

VIRGINIA

LAND. Area: 105,586 km² (40,767 mi²); rank: 36th. Capital: Richmond (1986 est. pop., 217,700). Largest city: Virginia Beach (1986 est. pop., 333,400). Counties: 95. Elevations: highest—1,746 m (5,729 ft), at Mount Rogers; lowest—sea level, at the Atlantic coast.

PEOPLE. Population (1987 est.): 5,904,000; rank: 12th; density: 57.4 persons per km² (148.7 per mi²). Distribution (1986): 71.5% metropolitan, 28.5% nonmetropolitan. Average annual change (1980–87): +1.5%.

EDUCATION. Public enrollment (1986): elementary—673,237; secondary—301,898; higher—265,687. Nonpublic enrollment (1980): elementary—33,400; secondary—9,500; combined—30,000; higher (1986)—42,631. Institutions of higher education (1985): 72.

ECONOMY. State personal income (1986): $89.2 billion; rank: 11th. Median family income (1979): $20,018; rank: 23d. Nonagricultural labor distribution (1986): manufacturing—424,000 persons; wholesale and retail trade—580,000; government—521,000; services—579,000; transportation and public utilities—137,000; finance, insurance, and real estate—131,000; construction—168,000. Agriculture: income (1986)—$1.6 billion. Fishing: value (1986)—$80 million. Forestry: sawtimber volume (1987 prelim.)—67 billion board feet. Manufacturing: value added (1985)—$22.1 billion. Services: value (1982)—$10.7 billion.

GOVERNMENT (1989). Governor: Gerald L. Baliles, Democrat. U.S. Congress: Senate—1 Democrat, 1 Republican. House—5 Democrats, 5 Republicans. Electoral college votes: 12. State legislature: 40 senators, 100 representatives.

STATE SYMBOLS. Statehood: June 25, 1788; the 10th state. Nickname: Old Dominion; bird: cardinal; flower: dogwood; tree: dogwood; motto: *Sic Semper Tyrannis* ("Thus Always to Tyrants"); song: "Carry Me Back to Old Virginia."

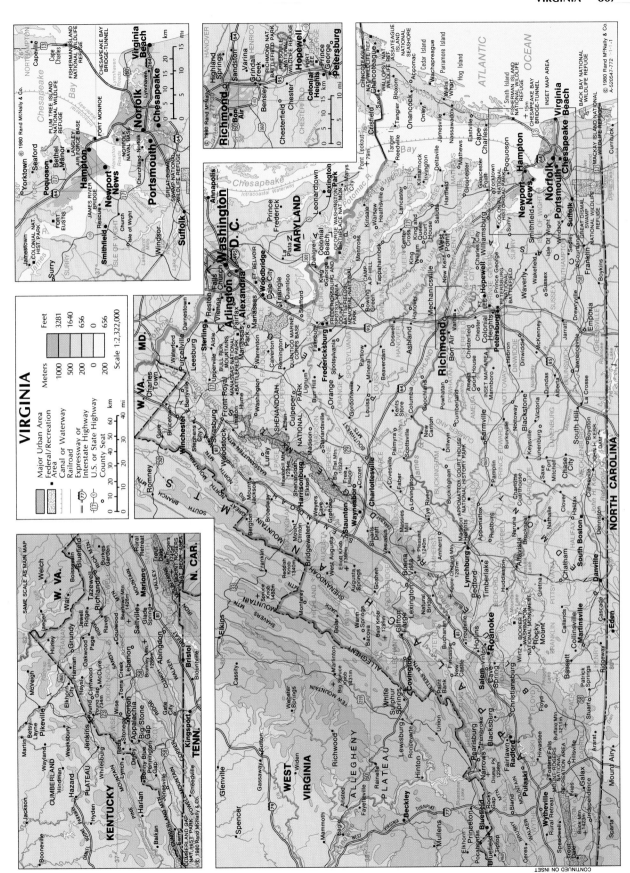

VIRGINIA

Scale 1:2,322,000

	Meters	Feet
	1000	3281
	500	1640
	200	656
	0	0
	200	656

Major Urban Area

Federal/Recreation Area

Canal or Waterway

Railroad

Expressway or Interstate Highway

U.S. or State Highway

County Seat

km 0 10 20 30 40 50 60

mi 0 10 20 30 40

© 1980 Rand McNally & Co.

recognition of the decision of Charles II to make the colony a fourth dominion of his realm, after England, Scotland, and Ireland—and as the Mother of Presidents, because it is the birthplace of eight U.S. presidents (George Washington, Thomas Jefferson, James Madison, James Monroe, William Henry Harrison, John Tyler, Zachary Taylor, and Woodrow Wilson).

Officially called the Commonwealth of Virginia, the state forms a rough triangle, with North Carolina and Tennessee to the south; Maryland, Chesapeake Bay, and the Atlantic Ocean to the northeast and east; and West Virginia and Kentucky to the northwest and west. Founded in 1607, Jamestown, near the southeastern corner of the state, represents the first permanent English settlement in North America. Virginia played a pivotal role in the American Revolution and the Civil War.

LAND AND RESOURCES

Virginia has five distinctive topographical regions. Moving in from the Atlantic coast, the Tidewater, or coastal plain, is succeeded by the Piedmont or PIEDMONT PLATEAU, the BLUE RIDGE MOUNTAINS, the ridge and valley region, and the CUMBERLAND PLATEAU. The last three are part of the APPALACHIAN MOUNTAIN system.

Tidewater Virginia, including the Eastern Shore—the southern tip of the DELMARVA PENINSULA separated from the remainder of the state by CHESAPEAKE BAY—is generally low-lying and sandy, rising to about 90 m (300 ft) as it meets the Piedmont. Broad estuaries divide the western Tidewater into a series of peninsulas reaching into the bay.

The rolling hills of Piedmont Virginia extend southwest from Alexandria in the north. The towns of Fredericksburg, Richmond, and Emporia lie on the FALL LINE. The region widens from 65 km (40 mi) at the Potomac to about 260 km (160 mi) at the North Carolina line. The continuous Blue Ridge of Precambrian rock rises from about 300 m (1,000 ft) at its base at the western edge of the Piedmont, reaching elevations of 350 m (1,200 ft) in the north to more than 1,700 m (5,500 ft) in the south. Virginia's highest point, Mount Rodgers, is found in the wider southern portion of the mountains.

The ridge and valley section of the state begins with the limestone-floored Great Valley and continues to the West Virginia border with a series of elongated hills and valleys trending northeast-southwest. In the extreme southwestern portion of Virginia lies a small part of the Cumberland Plateau of Kentucky at an average elevation of 840 m (2,750 ft).

Soils. Sandy loams dominate the Tidewater, but the Great Valley boasts dark, fertile limestone derivatives. In the mountains the thin soils are generally limestone based.

Rivers and Lakes. A series of rivers flowing east from the Blue Ridge drains most of Virginia. The POTOMAC follows Virginia's boundary with Maryland. To the south are the RAPPAHANNOCK, the York, and the JAMES RIVER, which enters Chesapeake Bay about 50 km (30 mi) north of the North Carolina line. Flowing north to join the Potomac, the SHENANDOAH RIVER drains the northern Great Valley; the western part of the state lies within the drainage basins of the Ohio and Tennessee rivers. The Roanoke drains the southwest toward North Carolina.

Virginia's only significant natural body of water, Lake Drummond (50 km²/19 mi²), lies at the center of the DISMAL SWAMP in the southeastern corner of the state. Several larger artificial lakes or reservoirs, some partly in North Carolina, have been created along the course of the Roanoke River.

Climate. Virginia has a temperate climate; although summers are hot, winters are mild, and precipitation occurs throughout the year. Elevation is the primary climatic determinant. July temperatures average 21° C (70° F) in the southwestern mountains but 27° C (80° F) in the southern Tidewater. In January the statewide average temperature drops to 4° C (39° F). The frost-free growing season varies from 140 days in the Appalachian foothills to 250 days along the Atlantic Ocean and southern Chesapeake Bay coasts. Annual precipitation ranges from 760 mm (30 in) in the northwest to 1,400 mm (55 in) in the southeast, with a state average of 1,015 mm (40 in).

Vegetation and Animal Life. Forests cover two-thirds of Virginia. Trees in the Tidewater are principally pines; in the

Wild ponies are rounded up on the last Thursday of each July—Pony Penning Day—on Assateague Island, a barrier reef off Virginia's (and Maryland's) Atlantic coast. Many of the foals are then auctioned on nearby Chincoteague Island.

(Left) The Blue Ridge Mountains, a segment of the Appalachian Mountain system, extends through Virginia from southwest to northeast. The highest point in the state, Mount Rogers (1,746 m/5,729 ft), is situated in the Blue Ridge Mountains near the North Carolina border.

Dairy cattle graze on a hillside pasture in the Shenandoah Valley of north central Virginia, near the town of New Market. Dairy products have become major agricultural commodities in the state, accounting for $194 million in the value of farm sales in 1978.

western mountains, mostly hardwoods; and in the Piedmont, a mixture. Cypress trees grow in the Dismal Swamp, and azalea, rhododendron, and mountain laurel thrive in the western mountains.

Black bears still inhabit the mountains and the Dismal Swamp, and deer can be found throughout the state. Smaller indigenous animals include foxes, rabbits, raccoons, squirrels, and opossums, and game birds such as turkeys, quail, grouse, doves, and woodcocks are found as well as such songbirds as robins, sparrows, and cardinals. Migrating ducks and geese fly across Virginia.

Resources. In the southwest, Virginia has large deposits of bituminous coal and small quantities of petroleum and natural gas. Other commercial minerals include sand and gravel, limestone (mostly in the ridge and valley region), zinc, clays,

lead, and soapstone (for talc). Groundwater resources are adequate in all sections of the state, often supplemented in the Tidewater by artesian wells.

PEOPLE

More than half of Virginia's inhabitants live in the crescent-shaped urban corridor that stretches from ARLINGTON and ALEXANDRIA in the north, through FREDERICKSBURG, the state capital RICHMOND, and PETERSBURG, to NEWPORT NEWS, HAMPTON, PORTSMOUTH, and NORFOLK. The cities of CHARLOTTESVILLE, LYNCHBURG, and ROANOKE lie to the west. The rapid influx of people to northern Virginia gave the state a growth rate from 1970 to 1980 of nearly 15%, somewhat higher than the 11.4% for the nation as a whole.

The percentage of blacks, 18.9% (1980), in Virginia's population is declining. This relative drop is attributable to an inmigration of whites rather than an out-migration of blacks. Other minorities include 66,209 Asian and Pacific Islanders and 79,873 Hispanics (1980) but few native Americans. The Baptist, Methodist, Episcopal, and Presbyterian religious denominations together have the largest numbers of adherents.

Education. Although the first free school in the United States—the Syms Free School in Hampton— was founded in 1634 and the College of William and Mary, in Williamsburg, dates from 1693, Virginia made no provision for public education until the Literary Fund was established in 1810 to assist poor children. The state constitution first provided for schools in 1869. Thomas Jefferson founded the University of Virginia in 1819 (see VIRGINIA, STATE UNIVERSITIES AND COLLEGES OF). Today Virginia has 39 public institutions of higher education and 30 private institutions of higher education—including RANDOLPH-MACON COLLEGE, WASHINGTON AND LEE UNIVERSITY, and the University of Richmond. There is also the Virginia State Community College system.

Culture. The Virginia Museum of Fine Arts, located in Richmond, is the principal state-funded cultural facility in the state, presenting drama and music as well as art exhibits. Also in Richmond are the private Valentine Museum and the Museum of the Confederacy—the latter occupying Jefferson Davis's home, the so-called White House of the Confederacy. Norfolk boasts the Chrysler Museum; Newport News has the Mariners Museum.

In addition to its many music and dance companies, Virginia has a number of orchestras. The Barter Theatre in Abingdon has won national recognition, as has the federally funded Wolf Trap Farm Park for the Performing Arts, part of the National Park System. Many local public libraries and bookmobiles can draw on the resources of the Virginia State Library in Richmond.

Graduating students file up steps of the Rotunda at the University of Virginia during commencement ceremonies. Many original buildings of this institution in Charlottesville, including the Rotunda, were designed by the university's founder, Thomas Jefferson.

Thomas Jefferson designed Monticello, his classical revival residence, and directed its construction between 1770 and 1809. Located in Albemarle County in central Virginia, the mansion, along with its surrounding estate, is maintained as a historical landmark.

Mount Vernon, once the residence of George Washington and his family, is located on the Potomac River to the south of Alexandria, Va. The Georgian colonial mansion, which was constructed during the early 18th century, is preserved as a museum of early Americana.

Historical Sites and Recreational Areas. Virginia is famous for its historic homes—particularly George Washington's at MOUNT VERNON and Thomas Jefferson's at MONTICELLO; for the carefully restored colonial settlements of JAMESTOWN, WILLIAMSBURG, and Yorktown; and for its many Civil War battlefields, including those at Chancellorsville, Fredericksburg, Spotsylvania, Manassas, Petersburg, and the Wilderness. Appomattox Court House is the site of Gen. Robert E. Lee's surrender to Ulysses S. Grant on Apr. 9, 1865.

Virginia has state park and recreation areas as well as several sites administered by the National Park Service, including Shenandoah National Park and Assateague Island National Seashore. National forests are also found within the state. Millions visit the state's beaches in summer and its mountain ski resorts in winter.

Communications. The *Virginia Gazette,* founded in 1736 by William Parks, was the colony's first newspaper; the *Alexandria Gazette* was begun in 1784. Among Virginia's leading newspapers today are the *Richmond Times-Dispatch* and *News Leader* and the *Norfolk Virginian-Pilot.* The state also has numerous radio and television broadcasting facilities as well as many cable television systems.

ECONOMIC ACTIVITY

This single most important source of income in Virginia is its government sector. Virginia has extensive military installations, and many Virginia residents work for the federal government in Washington, D.C. Manufacturing, services, and trade are also important sectors of the state's economy. Coal and timber are valuable resource industries. The millions of tourists who visit the state also contribute economically.

Agriculture. Important crops grown in Virginia are tobacco, hay, corn, soybeans, and apples. Tobacco accounts for more farm income than any other crop, but more than half of the state's farm income comes from cattle and poultry raising and dairy farming. Virginia's Shenandoah Valley is one of the nation's major apple-growing regions, and Rockingham County is a leading U.S. producer of turkeys.

Forestry and Fishing. Nearly two-thirds of Virginia's land area is forested, and about every county has some commercial forestland and supports a wood products industry. Much of the lumber harvested each year goes into making furniture. Virginia ranks among the leading U.S. fishing states. Major species caught include oysters, clams, crabs, menhaden, and alewives. Sport fishing is also popular in Virginia.

Mining. Coal and stone are the most important minerals mined in Virginia. The state's coalfields are found mainly in the Appalachian Mountains area. Limestone is found in Virginia's western valleys. Other stones produced are granite, marble, basalt, sandstone, slate, and talc. Virginia is also the nation's leading producer of kyanite.

Manufacturing. Manufacturing industries started to develop in Virginia during the 1840s but suffered a severe setback during the Civil War. Steady expansion since the late 19th century accelerated after World War II. Virginia's major industrial products include tobacco products, chemicals, foods, electrical equipment, nonelectrical machinery, transportation equipment, rubber and plastic products, printing and publishing, textiles, and furniture. Important manufacturing centers in the state are Richmond, Hopewell, Norfolk, Newport News, Lynchburg, Roanoke, and Martinsville.

Transportation. Virginia's state-operated highways, among the most extensive in the country, include long sections of interstate highways 81 and 95, two of the nation's most heavily traveled north-south arteries. Among the state's scenic roadways are the Blue Ridge Parkway, Colonial National Historical Parkway, and George Washington Memorial Parkway.

Railroad development occurred early in Virginia, and today there are a number of freight rail lines operating in the state. Amtrak provides passenger service to several cities. HAMPTON ROADS is one of the nation's leading ports. Major airports in

The Natural Bridge is a limestone formation 66 m (215 ft) high and 27 m (90 ft) long over Cedar Creek in Rockbridge County, Va. The bridge, once owned by Thomas Jefferson, is crossed by a highway.

the state are Dulles International Airport and Washington National Airport.

Energy. Major sources of electric power in Virginia are coal-fired and nuclear power plants. Most of the coal-fired plants are located in the western part of the state. Virginia Electric and Power Company (Vepco) owns the nuclear power facilities. Other energy sources are hydroelectricity, oil-fired power plants, and gas. The state is supplied with natural gas by three major pipeline companies.

GOVERNMENT AND POLITICS

Virginia's original constitution, adopted in 1776, was superseded by updated documents in 1830, 1851, 1870, 1902, and 1971. The governor serves a 4-year term and cannot hold office twice in succession. The governor administers the state through an appointed cabinet, consisting of the heads of departments of education, administration and finance, transportation, public safety, human resources, and commerce and resources.

The state general assembly—which can trace its roots to the colonial House of Burgesses, founded in 1619 and the oldest representative legislature in the country—consists of a senate, with 40 members serving 4-year terms, and a house of delegates, with 100 members serving 2-year terms. Virginia's judicial system ascends from juvenile and domestic relations courts, and general district courts, through the circuit courts to a supreme court of appeals; the legislature fills the latter with 7 judges who serve 12-year terms.

Virginia has 95 counties and 41 independent cities. Smaller towns remain part of their counties, and the inhabitants are responsible to the county as well as to the town.

In U.S. presidential elections Virginia voted for the Democratic candidate from 1932 through 1948. Since 1952, with the exception of 1964, Virginia's electoral votes have been cast for the Republican candidate. In the early 1980s, the state's congressional delegation was predominantly Republican. In 1981, however, a Democrat, Charles S. Robb, son-in-law of former president Lyndon B. Johnson, was elected governor, ending a 12-year Republican hold on that office.

HISTORY

First settled as early as 10,000 years ago, Virginia was inhabited by Indian tribes belonging to three different language families at the beginning of the 17th century. Along the coast lived the POWHATAN, of the Algonquian family; the Piedmont was occupied by tribes of the Siouan family; and the Iroquoian family was represented principally by the SUSQUEHANNA at the northern end of Chesapeake Bay, by the CHEROKEE in the southwest, and by the Nottoway in the southeast.

First European Settlements. The European history of Virginia began in 1570 with a short-lived Spanish mission probably located on the York River. In 1584, Sir Walter RALEIGH obtained a grant from Queen Elizabeth to colonize all of North America not already possessed or occupied by other Christian people. The first expedition to the vast new territory, named Virginia in honor of the queen, was sent out the same year and arrived at Roanoke Island (see ROANOKE COLONY) in 1585. More settlers came 2 years later, but by 1590—their supplies having been interrupted by England's war with Spain—all the colonists had died or disappeared.

After a few other false starts, on Dec. 20, 1606, the LONDON COMPANY, established by Shakespeare's patron, Henry Wriothesley, 3d earl of Southampton, sent out three ships—*Susan Constant, Discovery,* and *Goodspeed*—carrying 143 adventurers, most of them, according to the 18th-century Virginia writer William Byrd, "reprobates of good families." The ships landed on Apr. 26, 1607, and the settlement of Jamestown, named in honor of the king, was established May 14, 1607.

Early Trials. The colony, the first permanent English settlement in the New World, suffered from poor leadership, famine, disease, disputes with the Indians, and failure to find a marketable product.

Capt. John SMITH returned to England in 1609, and conditions grew so severe during the following winter that the colonists decided to abandon their settlement. As they set sail in June 1610, Lord DE LA WARR arrived with reinforcements and supplies.

In 1614, John ROLFE, who introduced tobacco into Virginia, married POCAHONTAS, daughter of the chief Powhatan, a union that led to a period of peace with the Indians. Under the leadership of Sir Thomas Dale and Sir George YEARDLEY, De La Warr's successors as governor, the colony began to prosper. The House of Burgesses was founded in 1619. That same year saw the importation of the first slaves to labor in the tobacco fields. In 1622 a new chief, Opechancanough, Powhatan's successor, organized a sudden attack that left 347 settlers—more than one-third of the whites—dead.

Growth of the Colony. The English crown took control of the colony in 1624, and by 1635 the population was 5,000. Although Indian raids continued, settlements were established along the rivers of the lower Tidewater. Jamestown, never a satisfactory site for a town, soon lost its preeminence to Williamsburg, to which the capital was shifted in 1699. Depressed tobacco prices, Indian uprisings, and the refusal of Gov. Sir William BERKELEY to call new elections to the House of Burgesses led in 1676 to BACON'S REBELLION.

During the early 1700s, English settlers, encouraged by Gov. Alexander SPOTSWOOD, migrated from the coastal towns westward across the Piedmont, where they met Scots-Irish and German immigrants moving southward from Pennsylvania through the Great Valley. The westward movement helped focus attention on the conflicting land claims of Virginia and France, and Gov. Robert DINWIDDIE dispatched George WASHINGTON to expel the French from FORT DUQUESNE, now Pittsburgh. Washington's mission failed, as did the disastrous expedition of Gen. Edward BRADDOCK in 1755, but the FRENCH AND INDIAN WAR (1754–63) eventually resolved the matter in favor of the British.

The American Revolution. British success against France did little to aid Virginia, however, because the western lands subsequently were closed to further settlement by the Proclamation of 1763. Friction with Britain increased, especially over the STAMP ACT and the TOWNSHEND ACTS. After the Boston Tea Party, Virginia's governor, Lord DUNMORE, dissolved the House of Burgesses to prevent its use as an antigovernment forum, but the members reassembled in Raleigh Tavern to call for a convention of all the colonies.

The First Continental Congress, as the convention was called, met in Philadelphia on Sept. 5, 1774, with Peyton Randolph (see RANDOLPH family) of Virginia presiding. A later state meeting that convened in Richmond to approve the actions of the congress received a motion from Patrick HENRY to call up the militia. The governor seized the available arms and retreated to a British warship. At the Second Continental Congress, Richard Henry Lee (see LEE family) of Virginia moved "to declare the United Colonies free and independent states," and Thomas JEFFERSON wrote the Declaration of Independence, adopted on July 4, 1776. The congress appointed Washington commander in chief of the Continental Army. Virginia became an independent commonwealth in June 1776, and adopted a constitution, including a bill of rights, drafted by George MASON.

Virginia's chief military contribution to the American Revolution was to be the provision of men and supplies to the army, although a small force under George Rogers CLARK secured the Northwest Territory in 1778–79. In 1781, Benedict Arnold laid waste to Richmond, but in May of that year Gen. Charles CORNWALLIS entered the state from the south for an unsuccessful campaign against the marquis de Lafayette, which ended with the British surrender at Yorktown on Oct. 19, 1781 (see YORKTOWN CAMPAIGN).

Early Years of the Republic. After the revolution Virginia dominated the early years of the republic, with Washington, Jefferson, Madison, and Monroe as presidents and John MARSHALL shaping the U.S. Supreme Court. Madison was also instrumental in replacing the loose Articles of Confederation with the present Constitution of the United States—although other Virginians, including Edmund PENDLETON, Patrick Henry, and Edmund Randolph, opposed the change. Later Madison drafted (1798) the Virginia Resolution supporting state rights, while Jefferson produced the similar Kentucky Resolution (see KENTUCKY AND VIRGINIA RESOLUTIONS).

Other southern states surpassed Virginia in cotton production, but the Tidewater continued to provide slaves for the rest of the South. Abolitionist sentiment was strong in the state, however, particularly in the west, and after the revolt in 1831 led by Nat TURNER, the Virginia House of Delegates almost voted to abolish slavery.

The Civil War. Conflict between the North and the South over slavery and tariffs grew during the first half of the 19th century, climaxed by John Brown's raid at Harpers Ferry in 1859 and by the election of Abraham Lincoln to the presidency in 1860. Virginia did not, however, join the Confederacy until Apr. 25, 1861, after Lincoln's call for troops. The capital of the Confederacy was moved to Richmond; thus Virginia soon became the major battleground of the war.

The fighting started at Bull Run, or Manassas, on July 21, 1861 (see BULL RUN, BATTLES OF). The following year Gen. George B. McCLELLAN attempted to come up the peninsula to Richmond but was repulsed by Gen. Robert E. LEE (see PENINSULAR CAMPAIGN). Also in 1862, Lee turned back General John POPE at the second Battle of Bull Run (August 29–30) but was himself blocked by McClellan at Antietam.

Lee defeated the Union forces at FREDERICKSBURG in December 1862 and again at CHANCELLORSVILLE the following May. Other battles took place at Petersburg (see PETERSBURG CAMPAIGN) and in the Shenandoah valley. By the time Lee surrendered to Grant at Appomattox, the state was devastated.

Reconstruction and Its Aftermath. West Virginia had separated itself from Virginia in 1863, and the remainder of the state was readmitted to the Union in 1870. The radical Republicans who ran Virginia during RECONSTRUCTION were promptly expelled from power by more conservative elements. Except for a brief period in 1881, when the so-called Readjusters, led by Gen. William Mahone, rose to power, conservatives of varying stripes have been in the ascendancy ever since, with the Democrats holding the governorship from 1883 to 1969, and then recapturing the office in 1981. Harry F. BYRD was elected governor in 1926, and although he moved on to the U.S. Senate in 1933, he continued to dominate state politics until the early 1960s.

Recent Trends. The 1950s brought Virginia into conflict with the federal government over integration. Segregation eventually yielded, however, to a new political order. A milestone occurred in 1985, when Virginia elected L. Douglas Wilder lieutenant governor—the first Southern state since Reconstruction to elect a black to a top state office.

The federal government continues to drive the state's economic growth, whether the income derives from military installations or from Virginians working for the government, many of them in adjacent Washington, D.C. Manufacturing is the second largest employer. Virginia maintains its importance in transportation. In addition to the major port of Hampton Roads and vital highway and rail networks, Washington's two major airports are in Virginia.

SAMUEL T. EMORY

Bibliography: Ashe, Dora, ed., *Four Hundred Years of Virginia, 1584–1984: An Anthology* (1985); Billings, Warren M., ed., *The Old Dominion in the Seventeenth Century: A Documentary History of Virginia, 1606–1689* (1975); Buni, Andrew, *The Negro in Virginia Politics, 1902–1965* (1967); Dabney, Virginius, *Virginia: The New Dominion* (1971; repr. 1983); Dowdey, Clifford, *The Virginia Dynasties* (1969) and *The Golden Age* (1970); Federal Writers' Project, *Virginia: A Guide to the Old Dominion* (1940; repr. 1980); Fishwick, Marshall W., *The Virginia Tradition* (1956); Gottmann, Jean, *Virginia in Our Century* (1969); Moger, Allen W., *Virginia: Bourbonism to Byrd, 1870–1925* (1968); Morgan, Edmund S., *American Slavery, American Freedom: The Ordeal of Colonial Virginia* (1975); Morris, Thomas R., and Sabato, Larry, eds., *Virginia Government and Politics: Readings and Comments*, 2d ed. (1984); Noël-Hume, Ivor, *Here Lies Virginia: An Archaeologist's View of Colonial Life and History* (1963); Rubin, Louis D., *Virginia: A Bicentennial History* (1977; repr. 1984); Tate, Thad W., et al., *Colonial Virginia: A History* (1986); Vaughan, Alden T., *American Genesis: Captain John Smith and the Founding of Virginia* (1975).

Virginia, state universities and colleges of

All but one of Virginia's state universities and colleges are coeducational, and all but three grant both undergraduate and graduate degrees. The **University of Virginia** (1819; enrollment: 16,379; library: 2,622,969 volumes), at Charlottesville, was founded by Thomas Jefferson, who also designed the Rotunda, the lawn, and the surrounding pavilions and buildings. A college of arts and sciences and schools of law, medicine, nursing, commerce, business administration, engineering, and architecture are part of the university. The library is an official depository for documents of the United Nations, United States, Nuclear Regulatory Commission, and National Aeronautics and Space Administration. **Clinch Valley College** (1954; enrollment: 1,037; library: 92,484 volumes), at Wise, is a 4-year college of the university.

The College of William and Mary, chartered in 1693 by King William III and Queen Mary of England and the second oldest college in the United States, is at Williamsburg (enrollment: 6,640; library: 966,447 volumes). PHI BETA KAPPA, the national honor society, was founded there in 1776. Sir Christopher Wren, the English architect, designed the main building, the oldest academic edifice still in use in the United States. The college, which grants bachelor's and master's degrees and the doctorate in some fields, has programs in arts and sciences, a law school (1779), the oldest in the United States, and a school of marine science, which awards a doctorate. **Christopher Newport College** (1960; enrollment: 4,268; library: 102,839 volumes), at Newport News, a 4-year college, was formerly a division of William and Mary but became independent in 1977.

Mary Washington College (1908; enrollment: 3,029; library: 280,000 volumes), an undergraduate school in Fredericksburg, was originally a part of the University of Virginia. **Old Dominion University** (1930; enrollment: 14,966; library: 1,218,725 volumes), at Norfolk, grants doctorates in engineering and in oceanography. It was once part of the College of William and Mary. **Virginia Commonwealth University** (1838; enrollment: 19,984; library: 672,637 volumes), at Richmond, has undergraduate and graduate programs in liberal arts and technology and grants doctorates in chemistry, psychology, and social work.

Other state institutions are **Longwood College** (1839; enrollment: 2,719; library: 219,980 volumes), at Farmville; **Norfolk State University** (1935; enrollment: 7,300; library: 200,000 volumes), at Norfolk; **Radford University** (1910; enrollment: 6,806; library: 300,000 volumes), at Radford; **Virginia State University** (1882; enrollment: 3,474; library: 218,309 volumes), at Petersburg; **George Mason University** (1948; enrollment: 15,548; library: 236,249 volumes), at Fairfax; and **James Madison University** (1908; enrollment: 9,320; library: 320,000 volumes), at Harrisburg. All six schools grant bachelor's and master's degrees. **Virginia Polytechnic Institute and State University** (1872; enrollment: 21,455; library: 1,400,000 volumes), a land-grant school in Blacksburg, has bachelor's, master's, and doctoral programs. **Virginia Military Institute** (1839; enrollment: 1,338; library: 266,000 volumes), a military college for men at Lexington, provides a combination of academic and military training that leads to an undergraduate degree and to a commission as second lieutenant in the U.S. Air Force, Marine Corps, Army, or Navy.

Virginia cowslip

Virginia cowslip, or bluebells, is the common name for *Mertensia virginica*, a perennial herb of the family Boraginaceae. It grows up to 60 cm (24 in), bearing handsome blue to purple, trumpet-shaped flowers in nodding clusters. Virginia cowslip occurs naturally in the rich woods and bottomlands of the region stretching from New York west to Ontario, Kansas, and Minnesota and south to Arkansas, South Carolina, and Alabama.

OSWALD TIPPO

Virginia creeper

Virginia creeper is the common name for the woody vine *Parthenocissus quinquefolia* of the family Vitaceae. Native to eastern North America, this vine climbs by means of tendrils and is sometimes used, like ivy, to cover external walls. Its leaves usually have five leaflets and turn red in autumn.

Virginia Resolutions: see KENTUCKY AND VIRGINIA RESOLUTIONS.

Virginia willow

Virginia willow, or sweetspire, is the common name for *Itea virginica* of the family Saxifragaceae. This low, deciduous shrub has small fragrant white flowers and willowlike leaves that turn brilliant red in autumn. Native to North America, it grows in swampy areas from New Jersey south to Texas and west to Oklahoma.   OSWALD TIPPO

Virgo   [vur'-goh]

Virgo, the second largest constellation and one of the earliest to be distinguished, lies on the zodiac east of Leo and, in mid-latitudes of the Northern Hemisphere, is visible above the southern horizon on spring evenings. Most of its stars are faint, except for brilliant blue white Spica, the 15th brightest star in the sky. The autumnal EQUINOX, or the position of the Sun on the first day of autumn, is located in Virgo. The constellation is noted for containing a large cluster of galaxies (see EXTRAGALACTIC SYSTEMS).   ARTHUR F. CACELLA

Bibliography: Whitney, C. A., *Whitney's Star Finder*, 4th ed. (1985).

viroid

Viroids are extremely small infectious particles that are thus far known to cause diseases only in higher plants, including the potato, tomato, cucumber, avocado, coconut, and chrysanthemum. Named by their discoverer, Swiss-born American plant pathologist Theodor O. Diener, they consist solely of RNA (see NUCLEIC ACID) and are about one-thousandth the size of the smallest known virus. Viroids can cause stunting of overall plant growth, distortions of leaf shape, discoloration of leaves, or even death of the entire plant. Infected plants never recover, and viroids can be isolated from affected tissues as long as the plants live.

Viroids can be transmitted between plant generations through both pollen and ovules. They can also be transmitted from an infected to a noninfected plant by farm implements. Their mode of reproduction in host cells, however, has not yet been determined, nor has any protein been found in host cells that could be associated with a particular viroid. It has been hypothesized that viroids represent segments of normal cellular RNA that somehow have become transmissible, disrupting the metabolism of their hosts.   LOUIS LEVINE

Bibliography: Diener, T. O., "Viroids," *Scientific American*, January 1981; Maramorosch, Karl, "The Curse of Cadang-cadang," *Natural History*, July 1987; Morse, Gardiner, "Viroids: Nature's Littlest Killers," *Science News*, Aug. 11, 1984.

virology: see VIRUS.

virtual image: see IMAGE, OPTICAL.

virus

Viruses are extremely small parasites that are able to reproduce only within the cells of their hosts, upon which they depend for many of their fundamental life processes. They are the causal agents of many INFECTIOUS DISEASES, and their study has contributed greatly to modern biological research. Many hundreds of different types of viruses exist, each of which normally grows in a restricted range of hosts; different viruses, however, have a very wide variety of hosts, including bacteria, plants, and animals.

Any given type of virus exists in several forms or stages. The free virus particle, or virion, consists of a molecule of nucleic acid—either DNA or RNA, depending on the specific virus—surrounded by protein and, in some viruses, also lipid and carbohydrate. The virion is inert, because it lacks many of the components that are necessary for independent life and reproduction; it does, however, provide for the transfer of the nucleic acid from host cell to host cell. Replication can occur only when the nucleic acid enters a host cell. Within the cell, the nucleic acid functions as genetic material and directs the synthesis of proteins. This results in the production of new virions, which then are released from the cell and can initiate new cycles of infection.

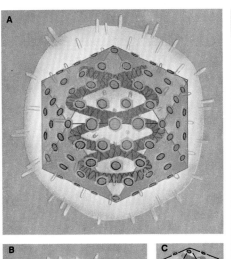

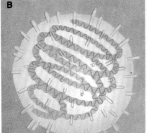

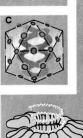

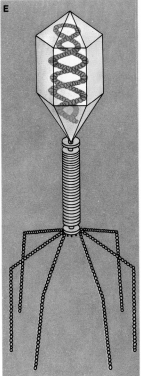

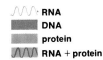

〰 **RNA**
▬ **DNA**
▨ **protein**
〰 **RNA + protein**

A complete virus particle, or virion, consists of one molecule of nucleic acid—either DNA or RNA—and a protein coat called a capsid. The DNA of a herpes virus particle (A) is enclosed by an icosahedral (20-sided) shell of 162 protein units, or capsomers, and by an outer spiked lipoprotein envelope; viruses of this type cause chicken pox and shingles in humans. A myxovirus (B), such as the influenza virus, has a protein and RNA core within a spiked lipoprotein envelope. The polyoma virus (C), which is associated with tumor induction, contains DNA in an icosahedral shell but lacks an outer envelope. Tobacco mosaic virus (D) consists of a helical strand of RNA with about 2,200 protein molecules coiled around it. The bacteriophage T2 (E) has a head—composed of DNA and a bipyramidal hexagonal (6-sided) protein shell—and a protein tail—made up of a tube core, a retractable sheath, and 6 tail fibers.

HISTORY

Viruses were discovered at the end of the 19th century, when the microorganisms responsible for many diseases were being identified (see INFECTIOUS DISEASES). In 1892, Dimitri Ivanovsky, a Russian botanist, discovered that the sap from tobacco plants affected by mosaic disease could be passed through filters so fine as to exclude all known bacteria and still retain the ability to produce the disease in new plants. In 1898, Friedrich Loeffler and Paul Frosch reported similar results for the infectious agent of foot-and-mouth disease of cattle. They also showed that an animal inoculated with a very small amount of filtered material could itself subsequently give rise to a very potent inoculum. This indicated that the infectious agent was able to reproduce itself within the infected animal. The extremely small infectious entities thus identified were known first as filterable viruses and later simply as viruses. During the next 3 decades many viruses were discovered that grow in vertebrate animals, in plants, in insects, and in bacteria. Unlike other microorganisms, none of the viruses could be propagated in the absence of host cells, which led researchers to conclude that viruses are intracellular parasites.

Beginning in the 1930s, a number of new techniques were developed for virology, or the study of viruses. The discovery that many animal viruses can be grown in mice and in chicken embryos allowed the course of viral infection to be studied under controlled laboratory conditions. Very high-speed centrifuges were developed that can cause rapid sedimentation of virions, which made possible the preparation of highly purified virions. Chemical analysis showed that viruses consist primarily of nucleic acid and protein, and the development of the electron microscope during the 1940s permitted scientists to study the size and shape of these virions in great detail.

Because of the ease with which BACTERIA can be grown and manipulated in the laboratory, many of the features of intracellular viral development were first discovered by studying bacteriophages, which are viruses that grow in bacteria. During the late 1950s techniques for growing animal cells in tissue culture were developed, making possible the detailed study of the intracellular growth of animal viruses.

CHARACTERISTICS

The virions of different viruses vary greatly in size, shape, and complexity, but those of any given virus are uniform. The simplest types are rods and regular 20-sided polygons (icosahedrons); the tobacco mosaic virus, for example, consists of a single molecule of RNA surrounded by about 2,200 molecules of a single type of protein arranged in helical fashion to produce a rod 3,000 angstroms (1/100,000 in) long.

Many virions having a simple rod or polygonal shape are composed of several types of proteins, and some of these virions are surrounded by a less regularly shaped envelope, which often includes components of the host-cell membrane. At the other extreme of complexity, bacteriophage T4 has a virion composed of at least 25 different types of protein that make up a hollow head in which a DNA molecule is enclosed, and a tubular tail by which the virion attaches to its host cell and injects its DNA into it.

Reproduction. Virus reproduction begins when the virion comes into contact with a suitable host cell. The DNA or RNA enters the host cell and begins to function as genetic information by directing the synthesis of specific types of proteins that have enzymatic and structural roles. The infectious cycle usually consists of two different stages. In the first, the proteins are produced that are required for the reproduction of the viral DNA or RNA in conjunction with components of the host cell. In the second stage, proteins that make up the virion are produced; these combine with the DNA or RNA to form mature virions, which are then released from the cell.

In some cases this release of virions involves the complete disruption and death of the cell, a process known as lysis. In other cases, individual virions are released through the cell membrane without killing the cell. In the course of a single cycle of infection, one infecting virion gives rise to hundreds or thousands of progeny virions that can then initiate new infections. In most viruses that have been studied, this process takes from about an hour to about a day to complete.

Transduction. Some viruses produce a small proportion of virions that contain host DNA in addition to or instead of viral DNA. These virions are able to transfer host genes from one

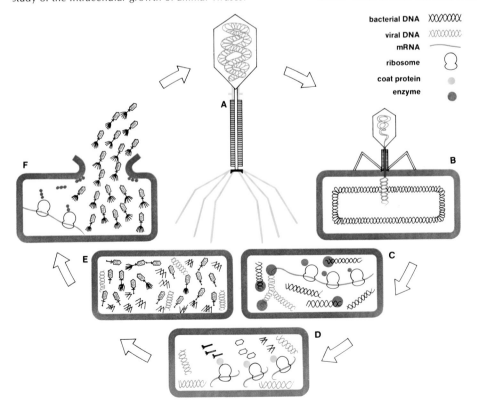

bacterial DNA	XXXXXXXX
viral DNA	XXXXXXXX
mRNA	—
ribosome	◯
coat protein	•
enzyme	⬤

A virus contains the information needed to reproduce itself coded in its nucleic acid. Because it lacks its own protein-producing machinery, however, the virus must use the machinery of a host cell in order to multiply. A bacteriophage virion (A) attaches to a bacterial cell (B) and injects its DNA into the bacterium. Using bacterial ribosomes and enzymes, the viral DNA directs the synthesis (C) of messenger RNA (mRNA), enzymes that break up bacterial DNA, and enzymes that allow replication of viral DNA. Proteins are synthesized, using mRNA, from the DNA code; these proteins form heads, tails, and tail fibers (D), and the virus parts assemble into complete virions (E). An enzyme breaks up the bacterial cell (F) and liberates the new virions, which can infect other bacterial cells.

cell to another. In bacteriophages, during the process called transduction, these genes can be incorporated into the recipient cell's chromosome, thus effecting genetic recombination.
Integration. Many viruses also interact with the host cell in such a way that the viral DNA, instead of replicating independently within the host cell, is integrated into the host-cell DNA. It is then replicated and passed on to daughter cells, as are the host cell's genes. Single or multiple copies of part or all of the viral DNA infecting animals may be incorporated into the host cell DNA. When the viral DNA is integrated, virions are not produced and the host cell is not killed. When a complete copy of viral DNA is present, the cell may return at some time to a lytic mode of virus replication with subsequent production of new virions.
RNA as Genetic Material. The RNA-containing viruses are unique among living systems because they use RNA as their primary genetic material (see NUCLEIC ACID). Some RNA-containing viruses produce enzymes that are capable of making new copies of RNA directly from the original molecule, thus circumventing DNA entirely. Retroviruses produce the enzyme called RNA-directed DNA polymerase, or reverse tran-

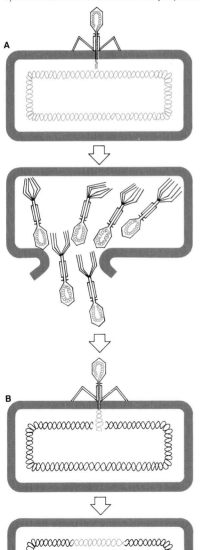

The process by which a virus transfers genetic material from one host cell to another is known as transduction. Bacteriophage replication (A) occasionally leads to the formation of virions that contain a portion of bacterial DNA (blue) in addition to or instead of viral DNA (red). This bacterial DNA is injected (B) into a new host's chromosome (black), producing a genetically altered bacterial cell. Although transduction is a relatively rare occurrence, it is commonly studied to map bacterial genes. A transducing virus may carry only a small fragment of bacterial DNA, so that only genes located near each other are transduced together. By measuring the frequency with which various genes are transduced, their relative locations on the bacterial DNA can be determined.

scriptase, which can make a DNA molecule from the RNA molecule. This DNA formed from RNA then serves as the principal genetic molecule within the infected cell (see RETROVIRUS).
IMPORTANCE OF VIRUSES
Diseases. Although many viruses are apparently harmless to their hosts, certain viruses are responsible for important diseases of humans, other animals, and plants. Such diseases as chicken pox, the common cold (see COLD, COMMON), ENCEPHALITIS, GERMAN MEASLES, HEPATITIS, genital and oral HERPES, INFLUENZA, MEASLES, viral MENINGITIS, MUMPS, POLIOMYELITIS, RABIES, SHINGLES, SMALLPOX, and YELLOW FEVER are all caused by viruses, and are due either directly or indirectly to the damaging effects of viral growth on the host cells. Of these diseases, only smallpox has been eliminated worldwide. Some of them, such as yellow fever, are caused by a class of viruses capable of growth and propagation in bloodsucking insects, where they cause no apparent harm. Such insects then act as vectors for transmitting the virus between animal hosts; in these hosts, however—including humans—the viruses cause diseases.

Viruses have been shown to cause certain types of cancer in animals. Two retroviruses have been associated with human leukemias, which are essentially cancers of T-cells (see IMMUNITY); another retrovirus has definitely been implicated with acquired immune deficiency syndrome (see AIDS). In addition, some of the PAPILLOMA viruses—the causes of various human tumors and WARTS—have been tentatively associated with diseases linked with the later development of cancer.
Vaccines. The smallpox vaccine, developed by Edward JENNER in 1796, was the first successful immunization against any infectious agent; vaccines were later found to be successful against other viral diseases, such as polio, hepatitis, influenza, and rabies. A vaccine consists of either killed virus or live virus that has been rendered incapable of causing disease. A vaccine causes the body to form antibodies, which provide protection against subsequent infections. The protection is only against the specific immunizing virus and viruses closely related to it. As an example, a new strain of the Rift Valley fever virus—borne by several species of mosquitoes and arachnids—swept eastern Africa in the late 1970s, causing epidemics that were combated by using a vaccine developed against the original strain during the 1960s. Through the use of GENETIC ENGINEERING techniques, researchers are creating various hybrid vaccines that are effective against more than one virus at a time (see VACCINATION; VACCINIA).
Interferon. Vertebrate animals also respond to viral infection by producing INTERFERON, a host-cell product that is formed and released by virus-infected cells. Interferon is taken up by uninfected cells, in which it inhibits the further growth of viruses. Once it is produced in response to one type of virus, it provides protection against a wide range of viruses.
Research. Drugs that will limit viral growth while not harming the host have been difficult to develop because of the intimate relationship of viral growth with the host cell. Some success has now been achieved with a few diseases. The study of viruses and virus-infected cells has contributed greatly to the understanding of such processes as DNA replication, protein synthesis, and enzyme action. Because virus infection results in the action of a limited number of new genes at a clearly defined time, it is often easier to study these processes in the infected cell, but it is possible to duplicate some parts of the virus life cycle in the test tube.
THE ORIGIN OF VIRUSES
Because virus genes undergo mutation and genetic recombination, viruses evolve in response to natural selection (see EVOLUTION). Two hypotheses could explain the origin of viruses: (1) they are descended from more-complex parasites that evolved to greater and greater dependence on the intracellular processes of their hosts, or (2) they are descended from blocks of host genes or messenger RNA, which acquired the capacity for independent replication and for the formation of extracellular virions. Among evidence for the latter, the cells of some organisms contain, in addition to the main chromosomal DNA, smaller DNA molecules that can be integrated into and subsequently come out of the main DNA or can be transferred among cells contacting each other. Thus viruses

may simply be at one extreme among the variety of DNA molecules that have arisen within living cells.

The existence of the viruses raises questions concerning the nature of LIFE. Although viruses reproduce and evolve, the virion itself is not a complete living organism, and the living organism within which viral reproduction occurs is clearly a larger entity than the virus itself. In addition, the only viral component that has a continuous existence is the nucleic acid. Thus, the virion is only one part of the strategy by which the nucleic acid ensures its own continuing reproduction and evolution.

JON WEIL

Bibliography: Biswas, Amita and S. B., *Introduction to Viruses*, rev. ed. (1983); Cooper, J. I., and MacCallum, F. O., *Viruses and the Environment* (1984); Galasso, G. J., et al., eds., *Antiviral Agents and Viral Diseases of Man*, 2d ed. (1984); Hughes, S. S., *The Virus: A History of the Concept* (1977); Matthews, R. E., ed., *Classification and Nomenclature of Viruses* (1982); Rigby, P. W., and Wilkie, N. M., eds., *Viruses and Cancer* (1985); Scott, Andrew, *Pirates of the Cell* (1985); Wakely, D. G., *Applied Plant Virology* (1985).

virus, slow

Slow viruses are disease agents not yet identified but assumed to exist, because the diseases resemble virus diseases in their epidemiology. Slow-virus diseases are degenerative nerve disorders that take years to develop. They include the human diseases called kuru and Creutzfeldt-Jakob disease (see NERVOUS SYSTEM, DISEASES OF THE), a fatal sheep and goat disease called scrapie (see DISEASES, ANIMAL), and possibly a recently identified cattle disease called bovine spongiform encephalopathy, among others.

Theories on the nature of slow viruses include the PRION theory that they are nothing but infectious proteins; this idea is not generally accepted. The virino theory proposes that the agents do have nucleic acids, as do known viruses, but lack proteins. A third theory suggests that the agents are viruses that simply are very adept at hiding in body systems. Several known viruses can also act slowly, such as the AIDS virus and hepatitis viruses.

Bibliography: Hotchin, J., ed., *Slow Virus Diseases* (1974); Timakov, V. D., and Zuev, V. A., *Slow Virus Infections* (1980).

visa: see PASSPORT.

Visayan: see BISAYAN.

viscacha: see CHINCHILLA.

Vischer (family) [fish'-ur]

The Vischer family, active 1453–1556 and perhaps later, were sculptors and bronze workers from Nuremberg, Germany. **Hermann the Elder**, d. 1488, founded the workshop in 1453. His major work is the bronze font (1457) in the Stadtkirche, Wittenberg; numerous bronze effigies by him have survived. **Peter the Elder**, c.1460–1529, was a master of late-Gothic naturalism. The so-called *Branch Breaker* (1490; Bayerisches Nationalmuseum, Munich), a kneeling man, reveals an interest in bodily movement than was his age, and his monumental effigy of Archbishop Ernst von Sachsen (1495; Magdeburg Cathedral) reflects his interest in monumental portraiture. Peter's large Shrine of Saint Sebald (1508–19; Saint Sebald's Church, Nuremberg) was finished by his sons, **Peter the Younger**, 1487–1528, and **Hermann the Younger**, 1486–1517. The harmonious integration of their respective contributions exemplifies the ideal of medieval craftsmanship. The younger Vischers also brought the style of the Italian Renaissance to Nuremberg in their bronze statues. The best-known works of the third brother, **Hans**, 1489–1550, are reliefs for Augsburg's Fugger Chapel (1537–40; Château Montrottier, Aunecy, France).

GIULIA BARTRUM

Bibliography: Müller, Theodor, *Sculpture in the Netherlands, Germany, France and Spain, 1400–1500* (1966); Smith, J. C., *Nuremberg: A Renaissance City* (1983).

Visconti (family) [vees-kohn'-tee]

The Visconti dynasty ruled the city of Milan and much of the surrounding region of Lombardy from 1277 to 1447. The name Visconti was formed from the family's title of viscount. The archbishop **Ottone Visconti**, b. 1207, d. Aug. 8, 1295, took possession of Milan as its signore (lord) in 1277, founding the dynasty's rule.

Archbishop **Giovanni Visconti**, b. 1290, d. Oct. 5, 1354, established unchallenged Visconti rule by expelling the rival Della Torre family. After his death, Lombardy was divided among his nephews: **Bernabò Visconti**, b. 1323, d. Dec. 19, 1385, a cruel and bizarre ruler, was given Milan; **Galeazzo II Visconti**, b. c.1320, d. Aug. 4, 1378, made his capital at Pavia. **Gian Galeazzo Visconti**, b. Oct. 16, 1351, d. Sept. 3, 1402, succeeded to rule over Pavia at the death of his father, Galeazzo II. Fearful of his uncle Bernabò's design to rule all Lombardy, Gian Galeazzo invaded Milan and probably poisoned Bernabò. Gian Galeazzo, made duke of Milan in 1395, attempted to carve out a kingdom in northern Italy. In 1387 he conquered Verona and Vicenza and briefly held Padua. During the next decade he occupied Siena, Perugia, and Bologna and even threatened Florence, which was saved only by the dissolution of his kingdom after he died of the plague.

The family recouped its fortunes under **Filippo Maria Visconti**, b. Sept. 3, 1392, d. Aug. 13, 1447, who sought to maintain Visconti control over Lombardy and opposed Venice's expansion in mainland Italy. When Filippo Maria died without a male heir, the short-lived Ambrosian Republic (1447–50) was established in Milan. Lombardy soon passed, however, to Francesco Sforza (see SFORZA family), husband of the illegitimate **Bianca Maria Visconti**, b. 1423, d. Oct. 23, 1468.

BENJAMIN G. KOHL

Bibliography: Bueno de Mesquita, D. M., *Giangaleazzo Visconti, Duke of Milan, 1321–1402* (1941); Muir, Dorothy, *A History of Milan under the Visconti* (1924).

Visconti, Luchino

An aristocrat by birth and a Marxist by inclination, Italian filmmaker Luchino Visconti, b. Nov. 2, 1906, d. Mar. 17, 1976, is known for both his contributions to NEOREALISM and his frank aestheticism. After working with Jean Renoir, he directed his first film, *Ossessione* (1942), an antecedent, and one of the masterpieces, of neorealist cinema. In the film self-destructive sexual passions are played out against a landscape of extraordinary beauty. Visconti used documentary techniques in his next film, *La Terra Trema* (The Earth Trembles, 1948), to describe the lives of peasants in a Sicilian fishing village. A favorite theme was the tension between family solidarity and the destructive power of family relationships, best expressed in *Rocco and His Brothers* (1960) and *The Damned* (1969). Visconti's first film in color, *Senso* (1953), brilliantly portraying political and sexual conflicts during the Austro-Italian war of 1866, displayed the attention to detail and love for period reconstructions that would become his hallmarks in *The Leopard* (1963), *The Stranger* (1967), *Death in Venice* (1971), and *The Innocent* (1978).

GAUTAM DASGUPTA

Bibliography: Marcini, Elaine, *Luchino Visconti* (1986); Servadio, Gaia, *Luchino Visconti* (1983); Stirling, Monica, *A Screen of Time* (1979); Tonetti, Claretta, *Luchino Visconti* (1983).

viscosity [vis-kahs'-i-tee]

Viscosity is a property of fluids (liquids or gases) that is a measure of a fluid's resistance to flow. When a fluid starts to flow under the action of a force, a shearing stress arises everywhere in the fluid that tends to oppose the motion. As one layer of the fluid moves past an adjacent layer, the fluid's molecules interact so as to transmit momentum from the faster layer to the slower layer tending to resist the relative motion. The simplest relation is in fluids for which the stress equals the coefficient of viscosity times the rate of shear. Such fluids are called Newtonian fluids, because their properties were first described by Isaac Newton. The viscosity of butter, a fluid that is non-Newtonian, decreases under a shearing stress, permitting the butter to be spread. Quicksand is a non-Newtonian fluid in which the viscosity increases when a shearing stress is applied.   R. E. STREET

viscount: see TITLES OF NOBILITY AND HONOR.

Vishinsky, Andrei Yanuarievich: see VYSHINSKY, ANDREI YANUARIEVICH.

Vishnu   [vish'-noo]

One of the two premier gods of HINDUISM, Vishnu is frequently viewed as the preserver and protector of the world. The most popular contemporary forms or incarnations (AVATARS) of Vishnu are Rama, hero of the epic RAMAYANA, and KRISHNA, hero of the BHAGAVAD GITA. A kindly deity, Vishnu is represented riding on the bird Garuda or reclining on the snake Shesha and is sometimes worshiped symbolically by a small stone called a salagrama. His female consort is Lakshmi, goddess of well-being.

The cult of Vishnu is called Vaishnavism. Particularly important sects of Vaishnavism are the Srivaisnavas of southern India, associated with the philosophy of Ramanuja (see VEDANTA); the Krishna cult of Brndaban, founded by Vallabha; and the Bengal movement, associated with the name of Caitanya (see HARE KRISHNA).   KARL H. POTTER

Bibliography: Gupta, Shakti M., *Vishnu and His Incarnations* (1974); Zimmer, Heinrich, *Myths and Symbols in Indian Art and Civilization* (1972).

Vishnu, one of the principal Hindu deities, is portrayed in one of his characteristic postures—at rest during the hiatus between the world's periodic annihilation and rebirth. Vishnu is worshiped as both Rama and Krishna, two of his ten avatars (incarnations).

Visigoths: see GOTHS.

vision: see EYE.

visionary architecture

The term *visionary architecture* is applied to a late-18th-century body of radically original architectural designs produced chiefly in France and principally by the architects Claude Nicholas LEDOUX and Étienne Louis BOULLÉE. In his works (1774–79) at the saltworks of Chaux at Arc et Senans, in his *Propylées* (customs houses) erected (1784–89) around Paris, and especially in his fantastic projects for the expansion of Chaux in his two-volume *Architecture considérée sous le rapport de l'art, des moeurs et de la législation* (The Relation of Architecture to Art, Customs, and Law, 1804 and 1847), Ledoux attempted to demonstrate a new and immediately comprehensible architectural language in which a cooper's house,

Étienne Louis Boullée's design (1784) for a monument to Sir Isaac Newton, a masonry globe representing the celestial sphere, exhibits the rationality and symbolic intent characteristic of visionary architecture. Impractical in its day, this stark geometric form is a portent of 20th-century architectural aesthetics and styles.

for example, could be made in the shape of a barrel. As part of the contemporaneous search for natural, self-evident institutions and art, Ledoux's work eventually (1850s) came to be called *architecture parlante*, or "speaking architecture."

Architecture parlante involved a radical simplification of architectural forms that Boullée developed as an end in itself in his projects of the 1780s and '90s. In his *Essai sur l'art* (n.d.; pub. 1953 as *Boullée's Treatise on Architecture*), he conceived elaborate compositions of colonnades, domes, and unadorned masses of masonry so arranged as to become huge architectural landscapes. His proposed monument (1784) to Sir Isaac Newton, for example, is an immense spherical masonry shell pierced with starlike holes patterned after the constellations; once inside, an observer could feel as if he or she were suspended in space, viewing the cosmos that Newton's laws sought to explain.

A whole generation of architects produced similar designs: Jean Jacques Lequeu and Jean Nicholas Louis Durand in France, George Dance and Sir John Soane in England, Giuseppe Valadier in Italy, and Friedrich Gilly in Germany. The formal elementarism of their designs presaged many of the concerns of modern architecture—an association strengthened by the fact that their aesthetic reaction to the French Revolution of 1789 resembles that of Walter Gropius and Mies van der Rohe to the German social upheavals of 1918–19. This identification with the French Revolution led the critic Emil Kaufmann to call their work "revolutionary architecture," but today the term *visionary* is preferred.   ANN VAN ZANTEN

Bibliography: Conrads, Ulrich, and Sperlich, H. G., *Fantastic Architecture* (1968); Kaufmann, Emil, *Three Revolutionary Architects: Boullée, Ledoux and Lequeu* (1952); Lemagny, J. C., *Visionary Architects: Boullée, Ledoux, Lequeu* (1968); Rosenau, Helen, *Boullée and Visionary Architecture* (1976) and *Ledoux and Utopian Architecture* (1977).

Visser 'T Hooft, Willem Adolf   [vis'-airt hohft]

Dutch ecumenical leader Willem Adolf Visser 'T Hooft, b. Sept. 20, 1900, d. July 4, 1985, served as secretary of the World Alliance of YMCAs (1924-31), as general secretary of the World Student Christian Federation, and as the first general secretary of the WORLD COUNCIL OF CHURCHES (1938–66). A minister of the Reformed church, he was broadly evangelical in his theology, and his many writings reflect this outlook.

VISTA: see ACTION.

Vistula River   [vis'-chu-luh]

The Vistula River is a 1,069-km-long (664-mi) river flowing across central Poland. The country's longest river, it has a drainage basin of 198,500 km^2 (76,600 mi^2). Rising in the Carpathian Mountains in southernmost Poland, it flows generally northeast past Kraków, turns northwest toward Warsaw, and then north to its outlet in the Baltic Sea at Gdańsk.

The Vistula, which is paralleled by railroads and canals along much of its route, is navigable from Gdańsk to its tributary the San in southeastern Poland. Other tributaries include the Bug, Pilica, and Dunajec. Since ancient times the Vistula has been used as a route for trade and expansion in Poland. Since World War II dams and reservoirs have been built to improve navigation.

visual magnitude: see MAGNITUDE.

vital statistics: see DEMOGRAPHY.

vitamins and minerals

Vitamins are carbon-containing substances that are required for normal metabolism but are not synthesized in the body; they are obtained, therefore, from such outside sources as food and water or are administered orally or intravenously. Exceptions to this definition include vitamin D, which is synthesized in the body to a limited extent, and vitamin B_{12}, which is synthesized by bacterial flora in the intestinal tract. Certain minerals are also considered in the same light as vitamins because they also must be obtained from outside sources.

Vitamins and minerals function as "cofactors" in the metabolism of products in the body. Most aspects of bodily metabolism proceed with the aid of specific enzymes but if additional catalysts were not present, for example, the cofactor vitamins and minerals, the reactions would proceed so slowly that they would be ineffective.

RDA. Most authorities assume that all the human vitamin and mineral requirements have been discovered; it is possible, therefore, to predict accurately the vitamin and mineral requirements of humans for health and prevention of disease. In the United States a Food and Nutrition Board was established for the purpose of determining vitamin and mineral requirements. This board is composed of distinguished scientists and nutritionists and is under the auspices of the National Research Council of the National Academy of Sciences. Since 1940 the board has periodically prepared a bro-chure listing the "Recommended Dietary Allowances" (RDA) of vitamins and other nutrients, based on existing knowledge.

These allowances are intended as a guide for nutritionists, institutional dietitians, and homemakers in planning food supplies and in the interpretation of food consumption levels. The RDA figures, however, are estimations based on the present state of knowledge of the needs of most human beings; particular requirements will be less or more, depending on numerous individual factors such as genetics, environmental influences, and presence or absence of disease processes.

Supplements. Dietary supplements of vitamins are often recommended by physicians when any of the following conditions are present: unusual diets obviously deficient in vitamins (insufficient intake); conditions or diseases causing poor intestinal absorption; and increased tissue requirements that occur in relatively healthy individuals during periods of growth, hard physical work, pregnancy, lactation, and menstruation. Some disorders, including hyperthyroidism, infectious diseases accompanied by fever, and tissue-wasting diseases, also cause increased tissue requirements.

Multivitamin Preparations. Two principal types of multivitamin preparations are available to the public and the medical profession: supplemental, or prophylactic, and therapeutic. Supplemental vitamins contain a range of one-half to one-and-a-half times the RDA requirements except for vitamin D, which should not exceed 400 international units (IU). These multivitamin preparations are designed to help prevent disease and to supplement the diet in cases of unusual stress and other such situations.

Therapeutic multivitamin preparations are prescribed by physicians only for deficiency states and for the nutritional support of severe pathological conditions.

Toxicity. Most of the water-soluble vitamins ingested in excessive amounts are rapidly excreted in the urine and thus rarely cause toxicity. The fat-soluble vitamins, on the other hand, are stored in body fat and are capable of causing severe toxicity when taken in excessive amounts, as in the case of vitamins A and D. The amounts of vitamins A and D, however, that are sold "over the counter" are regulated by the FOOD AND DRUG ADMINISTRATION (FDA).

FAT-SOLUBLE VITAMINS

Vitamin A. Vitamin A exists in a variety of forms, including

RECOMMENDED DIETARY ALLOWANCES (RDA)*

		FAT-SOLUBLE VITAMINS			WATER-SOLUBLE VITAMINS (MG)						
	Age (years)	Vitamin A Activity RE† (IU)	Vitamin D (IU)	Vitamin E Activity	Vitamin B₁ (thiamine)	Vitamin B₂ (riboflavin)	Vitamin B₃ (niacin)	Vitamin B₆	Vitamin B₁₂	Folic Acid	Vitamin C (ascorbic acid)
Infants	birth–½	420 1400	400	4	0.3	0.4	5	0.3	0.3	50	35
	½–1	400 2000	400	5	0.5	0.6	8	0.4	0.3	50	35
Children	1–3	400 2000	400	7	0.7	0.8	9	0.6	1.0	100	40
	4–6	500 2500	400	9	0.9	1.1	12	0.9	1.5	200	40
	7–10	700 3000	400	10	1.2	1.2	16	1.2	2.0	300	40
Males	11–14	1000 5000	400	12	1.4	1.5	18	1.6	3.0	400	45
	15–18	1000 5000	400	15	1.5	1.8	20	2.0	3.0	400	45
	19–22	1000 5000	400	15	1.5	1.8	20	2.0	3.0	400	45
	23–50	1000 5000	—	15	1.4	1.6	18	2.0	3.0	400	45
	51+	1000 5000	—	15	1.2	1.5	16	2.0	3.0	400	45
Females	11–14	800 4000	400	12	1.2	1.3	16	1.6	3.0	400	45
	15–18	800 4000	400	12	1.1	1.4	14	2.0	3.0	400	45
	19–22	800 4000	400	12	1.1	1.4	14	2.0	3.0	400	45
	23–50	800 4000	—	12	1.0	1.2	13	2.0	3.0	400	45
	51+	800 4000	—	12	1.0	1.1	12	2.0	3.0	400	45
Pregnant Women		1000 5000	400	15	+0.3	+0.3	+2.0	2.5	4.0	800	60
Lactating Women		1200 6000	400	15	+0.5	+0.5	+4.0	2.5	4.0	600	80

* These vitamins and minerals are the amounts that should be present in a variety of common foods, which will also contain other nutrients, the requirements of which are less well defined. The amounts given allow for variation between individuals and ordinary environmental stresses.
† Retinal equivalents.

retinol, which is currently considered the most active form. Carotene, a plant pigment present in carrots, for example, can be converted in the human body to vitamin A. Vitamin A is also highly concentrated in fish-liver oils. The normal diet contains adequate amounts of vitamin A, and therefore supplements rarely need to be administered.

Vitamin A has many important functions in the body that relate to membrane integrity, especially of epithelial cells and mucous membranes. It is also essential for bone growth, reproduction, and embryonic development. Vitamin A deficiency has long been known to result in night blindness, in which the ability of the eye to see in dim light is impaired.

Hypervitaminosis A, which results from excessive intake over a long period of time, is most common in children. Symptoms consist of irritability, vomiting, loss of appetite, headache, dry skin, and scaling of skin. Intracranial pressure is increased, and characteristic bony changes are demonstrable on X-ray examination. An extremely high plasma level of vitamin A occurs in this disorder.

Vitamin D. The active forms of vitamin D are ergocalciferol (vitamin D$_2$) and cholecalciferol (vitamin D$_3$), both of which arise in the body from ingested precursors by exposure of the skin to ultraviolet light. Vitamin D primarily regulates calcium metabolism by determining the movement of calcium from intestines to blood and from blood to bone. It interacts with parathyroid hormone and calcitonin in controlling calcium levels. In tropical countries, where exposure to sunlight is high, vitamin D deficiency is rare; it is much more common in northern regions. Ultraviolet irradiation of food products, a practice common in some countries, increases their vitamin D content. A deficiency of vitamin D results in failure to absorb calcium and phosphorus, causing faulty formation of bone. In children the syndrome is known as RICKETS and is manifested by deformities of the rib cage and skull and by bow legs as a consequence of long bones. Adult rickets, or osteomalacia, is characterized by generalized bone calcification and, eventually, gross bone deformities. Symptoms of hypervitaminosis D consist of weakness, fatigue, lassitude, headache, nausea, vomiting, and diarrhea. Urinary symptoms occur when calcium deposits build up in the kidneys.

Vitamin E. Vitamin E is chemically known as alpha tocopherol, the most active of a group of tocopherols; it is present in seed oils, especially wheat-germ oil. Few vitamins have been advocated for more diseases than has vitamin E, including such diverse disorders as coronary artery disease, muscular dystrophy, habitual abortion, and schizophrenia. No persuasive evidence, however, demonstrates that vitamin E has any therapeutic value in these or other diseases. Fortunately it is relatively nontoxic, and few adverse effects from excessive intake have been reported from its use in humans.

Vitamin K. Vitamin K is essential for synthesis by the liver of several factors necessary for the clotting of blood. Chemically, phylloquinone is the natural plant source of vitamin K, and a synthetic derivative, menadione, is used therapeutically. A wide variety of vegetables, egg yolk, liver, and fish oils contain this vitamin. Deficiency of vitamin K rarely occurs, and its human requirements have not been specified. It is never included in dietary vitamin preparations but is used medically in treating specific deficiencies that occur during anticoagulant therapy, in hemorrhagic disease of the newborn, and in hepato-cellular disease.

WATER-SOLUBLE VITAMINS

With the exception of vitamin C (ascorbic acid), water-soluble vitamins belong mainly to what has been termed the *B complex* of vitamins. The better-known B vitamins are thiamine (B$_1$), riboflavin (B$_2$), nicotinic acid (B$_3$), pyridoxine (B$_6$), pantothenic acid, lecithin, choline, inositol, and para-aminobenzoic acid (PABA). Two other members are folic acid and cyanocobalamin (B$_{12}$). Yeast and liver are natural sources of most of these vitamins.

Thiamine. Thiamine, the first B vitamin to be identified chemically (1926), consists of a complex organic molecule containing a pyrimidine and a thiazole nucleus. In the body it functions as a coenzyme in the form of thiamine pyrophosphate and is important in carbohydrate intermediary metabolism. The symptoms of thiamine deficiency are known as BERI-BERI, a syndrome consisting primarily of peripheral neuritis marked by sensory and motor paralysis of the limbs and, finally, heart failure. People of Asia who acquired beriberi as a result of a diet of mainly polished rice could be cured by adding rice polishings, which are high in thiamine. Today, thiamine deficiency results from liver damage and most often occurs in nutritionally deficient alcoholics.

Riboflavin. Riboflavin (B$_2$) is a complex organic ring structure to which the sugar ribose is joined. In the body riboflavin is conjugated by phosphate to yield riboflavin 5'-phosphate (FMN) and by adenine dinucleotide to yield flavin adenine dinucleotide (FAD), both of which serve as coenzymes for a wide variety of respiratory proteins (see METABOLISM).

Riboflavin deficiency in humans is characterized by growth failure in children; nerve degradation, particularly of the eyes; sore throat; seborrheic dermatitis of the face and extremities; and anemia. The only established use of riboflavin is in the therapy or prevention of deficiency disease.

Niacin. Two forms of niacin exist: nicotinic acid and nicotinamide. Both are related to the tobacco alkaloid nicotine; in the body they are active as nicotinamide adenine dinucleotide (NAD) and nicotinamide adenine dinucleotide phosphate (NADP) and serve as coenzymes in conjunction with protein in tissue respiration and also as dehydrogenases.

Pellagra, caused by niacin deficiency, is characterized by a cutaneous eruption, at first resembling sunburn because it affects the areas of the body exposed to sunlight. The tongue becomes red and swollen, with excessive salivary secretion, and diarrhea occurs along with nausea and vomiting. Later, central nervous system symptoms appear with headache, dizziness, insomnia, depression, and even overt psychosis with hallucinations and other mental disturbances.

The only established use of niacin is in the treatment of pellagra. MEGAVITAMIN doses have been used experimentally in the therapy of schizophrenia; because nicotinic acid in large doses lowers blood lipids, it has been extensively used in the therapy and prevention of arteriosclerotic vascular disease. Toxicity may occur in the form of liver damage with prolonged large doses.

Pyridoxine. Pyridoxine, or vitamin B$_6$, is a substituted pyridine ring structure that exists in three forms, all of which may be

RECOMMENDED DIETARY ALLOWANCES (RDA)*

MINERALS (MG)

Calcium	Phosphorus	Iodine	Iron‡	Magnesium	Zinc
360	240	35	10	60	3
540	400	45	15	70	5
800	800	60	15	200	10
800	800	80	10	250	10
800	800	110	10	350	15
1200	1200	150	18	400	15
1200	1200	140	10	350	15
800	800	130	10	350	15
800	800	110	10	350	15
800	800	115	18	300	15
1200	1200	115	18	300	15
1200	1200	115	18	300	15
800	800	100	18	300	15
800	800	100	18	300	15
800	800	80	10	300	15
1200	1200	125	18 +	450	20
1200	1200	150	18	450	25

‡ Requirement cannot be met by ordinary diet; supplemental iron needed.
SOURCE: Table is modified from the Report of the Food and Nutrition Board, National Academy of Sciences (1974).

converted in the body to pyridoxal-5-phosphate (PLP), the active coenzyme form. PLP functions in human metabolism in the conversion processes of amino acids, including decarboxylation, transamination, and racemization.

Symptoms of deficiency in humans consist of seborrhealike skin lesions of the face; increased irritability; convulsive seizures, particularly in children; and neuritis resulting in degeneration of peripheral nerves. On the other hand, excessive dosages of vitamin B_6 over a period of time can also severely damage the nerves.

Pantothenic Acid. Widely distributed in nature, pantothenic acid was first identified in 1933 as a factor necessary to cure certain skin lesions in chicks; its role in human nutrition, however, has not been clearly delineated. Biochemically, pantothenic acid is converted to coenzyme A, which serves a vital role for a variety of reactions involving transfer of 2-carbon fragments (acetyl groups) and which is essential for the production of metabolic products crucial to all living organisms. Pantothenic acid has no specific therapeutic indications but is included in multivitamin preparations.

Folic Acid. Chemically, folic acid is pteroylglutamic acid, composed of a pterin, para-aminobenzoic acid, and glutamic acid moieties. In the body folic acid is converted to folinic acid (5-formyl-tetrahydrofolic acid), the coenzyme form, which accepts 1-carbon units important in the metabolism of many body compounds. Nucleic acid synthesis cannot take place without the presence of folic acid.

Deficiency in humans results in pernicious anemia and can be produced by antivitamins such as methotrexate, which is used in cancer chemotherapy. Folic acid is present in many common foods, for example, vegetables and liver, but can be destroyed by excessive cooking. Deficiency is relatively rare unless caused by an antivitamin, tropical sprue, or pregnancy. The only therapeutic use of folic acid is in the specific deficiency, although it is included in multivitamin preparations.

Cyanocobalamin (B_{12}). Vitamin B_{12}, isolated in 1948, is chemically the most complex of all the vitamins, having a corrin nucleus linked to an aminopropanol esterified by a nucleotide and also an atom of cobalt to which is attached a cyanide group. Few vitamins are as important metabolically as B_{12}, because it is involved in many of the synthetic steps required in the manufacture of nucleoproteins and proteins. Almost all organisms need this vitamin but only in very small amounts. Vitamin B_{12} is present mainly in the liver, the kidneys, and the heart. In nature the source is believed to be solely that synthesized by microorganisms.

The ability to absorb this vitamin depends on the production by the stomach of an intrinsic factor, a glycoprotein; cases of B_{12} deficiency often involve patients with defective production of an intrinsic factor. The symptoms of deficiency are identical to the classical syndrome of pernicious anemia: ineffective manufacture of red blood cells; faulty myelin synthesis, leading to a paralyzing neuritis; and a failure to maintain the epithelium of the intestinal tract. Marked anemia and generalized debility, which eventually develop, are always fatal unless treated. Cyanocobalamin has only one established use, the treatment of this deficiency disease, but is included nevertheless in many multivitamin preparations.

Ascorbic Acid (Vitamin C). Probably the first deficiency disease to be recognized was SCURVY, and as early as 1720 fresh vegetables or fruit were found to cure the disease. James Lind, a physician in the British navy, demonstrated in 1757 that consumption of oranges and lemons could prevent the disease. As a result of his work, the British navy in 1804 made it compulsory to issue a ration of lemons or limes to sailors, who were from then on nicknamed "limeys." Chemically, ascorbic acid is a plant sugar in the acid form, hexuronic acid. In the body ascorbic acid is reduced to dehydroascorbic acid and is involved in oxidation-reduction reactions. Unlike vitamins of the B complex, it does not act as a cofactor.

The symptoms of scurvy result from the fact that ascorbic acid is essential for the formation and maintenance of intercellular ground substance and collagen. The pathology affects mainly bone and blood vessels; teeth loosen because dentin is absorbed and the gums become spongy and bleed easily.

Hemorrhages in other tissues also occur easily with the slightest trauma. Vitamin C is used to prevent and treat scurvy and many other disorders, including various dental problems. Controversy surrounds the practice of taking very large daily doses of vitamin C to prevent the common cold, because medical research has not supported this notion; intake of very large amounts for long periods of time can also be harmful, even though vitamin C has a relatively low toxicity. A sufficient daily intake of fresh orange juice provides enough vitamin C for most purposes.

Biotin, Choline, Inositol, and PABA. Biotin, a complex organic acid containing sulfur, is a coenzyme for several carboxylation reactions involving carbon dioxide fixation. It is synthesized by intestinal bacteria and is widespread in food products. A natural deficiency in humans is unknown, even in individuals on extremely deficient diets.

Choline, a simple amino alcohol, is a component of lecithin and of acetylcholine, the latter of which is one of the most important neurotransmitters. Unlike most vitamins, choline can be synthesized in the body, provided that methionine intake is sufficient. It is present in large amounts in egg yolk, milk, and seafood; human deficiency rarely occurs.

Inositol is actually an isomer of glucose, which is the common sugar of human diets and a component of certain phospholipids. No coenzyme function has been established, but inositol promotes the growth of yeast and certain lower animal forms.

Para-aminobenzoic acid (PABA) deserves brief mention not because it is a human requirement but because it is an obligatory metabolite for most microorganisms and unicellular forms such as protozoa. Sulfonamides, the first successful group of modern chemotherapeutic agents against infections, act as antagonists to para-aminobenzoic acid. In order to survive, most microorganisms need to incorporate para-aminobenzoic acid into the molecule of folic acid. Sulfonamides prevent this, and thus they are inhibitory to the growth of bacteria. They are not harmful in this sense to mammals, because these higher forms cannot synthesize folic acid and obtain it preformed in the diet.

MINERALS

Unlike sodium and potassium, which are staple elements of the diet and are present in ample amounts in all food of vegetable and animal origin, certain minerals are additional dietary requirements. Although most are present in the average diet, these minerals may not always be ingested in quantities sufficient to satisfy metabolic needs, especially during growth, stress, trauma, and blood loss, and in some diseases.

Calcium. The body's requirements for calcium are generally met by eating or drinking dairy products, especially milk. Most calcium (90 percent) is stored in bone, with a constant exchange occurring among blood, tissue, and bone. The intake is balanced by losses in urine and feces. The blood levels of calcium and its intestinal absorption, deposition, or mobilization from bone are all controlled by a complex interplay of vitamin D, parathyroid hormone, and calcitonin. Contrary to some long-held beliefs, high intakes of protein and phosphorus do not lead to a loss of calcium.

Calcium promotes bone rigidity and is important in maintaining the integrity of intracellular cement and cellular membranes. It also regulates nervous excitability and muscle contraction and may be protective against high blood pressure. During periods of growth, pregnancy, and lactation, calcium intake should be increased. Diseases of calcium metabolism include vitamin D deficiency, hypervitaminosis D, hypo- and hyperparathyroidism, and some forms of renal disease.

Phosphorus. Phosphorus plays an important role in the hemostasis of calcium and in reactions involving carbohydrates, lipids, and proteins. The chemical energy of the body is stored in "high energy phosphate" compounds.

Elemental phosphorus is extremely poisonous, but phosphorus ingested as phosphates in the diet is not toxic.

Iodine. The one important function of iodine is associated with the synthesis of thyroxine and the function of the thyroid gland. Persons living in coastal regions usually receive an adequate supply of iodine because of the high content in seafood. In geographic regions located far inland, however, a lack of iodine in food is apt to occur, causing goiter, so a small amount of iodine is often added by manufacturers of table salt (iodized salt). Elemental iodine is highly poisonous, and its only use in medicine is as an antiseptic.

Iron. Iron is a vital component of hemoglobin and also of certain respiratory enzymes. Foods high in iron content include meat (liver and heart), egg yolk, wheat germ, and most green vegetables. Increased requirements for iron occur during the growth period and pregnancy, and with excessive menses and other instances of blood loss. The average diet contains 10 to 15 mg a day, adequate for most people. Iron deficiency, resulting in anemia, can be treated by large amounts of iron in order to gain positive absorption.

Magnesium. Magnesium is an essential element in human metabolism and functions in the activities of muscles and nerves, protein synthesis, and many other reactions. Magnesium deficiency may occur in alcoholism, diabetes mellitus, pancreatitis, and renal diseases. Prolonged deficiency can cause changes in heart and skeletal muscle. Excessive retention of magnesium can occur in renal disease and results in muscle weakness and hypertension.

Zinc. Zinc serves as a cofactor of dehydrogenases and carbonic anhydrase; its lack can cause skin rashes, taste disturbances, and mental lethargy. Zinc loss occurs during such stress situations as surgical operations, and its replacement aids in wound healing. Dietary programs often promote zinc loss, and the use of concentrated zinc supplements can lead to calcium deficiency. Overingestion of zinc or inhalation of its vapors can cause depression, vomiting, and headache.

Fluorine and Trace Minerals. Fluorine as fluoride is a requirement to bind calcium in bones, and fluoridation of the water supply is the most efficient method of providing this mineral. Microamounts of such elements as chromium, chlorine, copper, manganese, molybdenum, selenium, silicon, sulfur, and vanadium are considered necessary to health. Copper deficiency, for example, has been linked with heart disease, and the onset of diabetes in older age may in some way be associated with chromium deficiency. Normal diets would appear to provide adequate amounts of the trace minerals, but effects such as the linking of high levels of fructose in the diet with copper-deficiency problems are the subject of ongoing research.   JOSEPH R. DiPALMA

Bibliography: Briggs, M. H., *Vitamins in Human Biology and Medicine* (1981); Consumer Guide, *The Vitamin Book* (1979); Dyke, S. F., *The Chemistry of the Vitamins* (1965); Kutsky, R. J., *Handbook of Vitamins, Minerals and Hormones*, 2d ed. (1981); Lewis, C. M., *Basic and Family Nutrition*, 2d ed. (1984); Passwater, Richard, *A Beginner's Introduction to Vitamins* (1983); Rennert, O. M., and Chan, Waiyee, eds., *Metabolism of Trace Metals in Man*, 2 vols. (1984); Solomons, N. W., and Rosenberg, I. H., *Absorption and Metabolism of Mineral Nutrients* (1984).

Vitoria   [vee-toh'-ree-ah]

Vitoria (1981 pop., 192,773) is the capital of Alava, one of the Basque provinces of northeastern Spain. The city underwent rapid industrialization from the late 1950s on and includes paper, furniture, leather goods, bicycles, and agricultural equipment among its products. In 1813 the duke of Wellington won a major Peninsular War victory over the French there. A 14th-century cathedral is the principal landmark. Vitoria was founded by Visigoths during the 6th century and became part of Navarre in 1181.

Vitoria, Francisco de

Spanish Dominican theologian Francisco de Vitoria, b. c.1483, d. Aug. 12, 1546, was a leading humanist scholar and international jurist. He studied in Paris and, upon returning to Spain, was elected (1526) professor at Salamanca, where he remained until his death. He advised the Spanish king Charles (Holy Roman Emperor Charles V) on policy. Each year Vitoria began classes with a public lecture on important world problems; the notes from many of these lectures were later published, and they form the basis for his reputation in interna-

tional law. In discussing Spanish colonization and Christianization of the New World, he was a staunch defender of the rights of the Indians. He also argued that war was justified only as a last resort in defense against aggression or to right a substantial wrong.   THOMAS E. MORRISSEY

Bibliography: Reidy, S. J., *Civil Authority According to Francis de Vitoria* (1959).

Vitrac, Roger   [vee'-trahk]

Roger Vitrac, b. Nov. 17, 1899, d. Jan. 22, 1952, a French dramatist and poet, was a leading exponent of surrealism. Associated with Antonin Artaud, Vitrac wrote plays that combine surrealist effects and music-hall or vaudeville elements. Like Artaud's dramas, they are designed to shock by their brutality and cynicism. They include *Les Mystères de l'amour* (Mysteries of Love, 1924) and *Le Coup de Trafalgar* (The Trafalgar Business, 1935). A collection of his poetry and prose, *Connaissance de la mort* (Recognition of Death), was published in 1926.   ROBIN BUSS

Vitruvius   [vi-troo'-vee-uhs]

The Roman architect and writer Marcus Vitruvius Pollio, active between 46 and 30 BC, wrote the sole surviving treatise on ancient architectural theory and practice; it is the most important treatise in the history of architecture. Called *De architectura*, it served Renaissance architects such as Leon Battista Alberti as their chief source of inspiration and remained influential up to the 20th century. The work consists of ten volumes: (1) the architect's training and aims, (2) materials, and the origin of architecture, (3) proportions, (4) the Greek orders and temples, (5) other civic structures, (6) domestic architecture, (7) stucco work and painting, (8) water and aqueducts, (9) astronomy, and (10) civil and military machines. Through his prefaces, Vitruvius reveals that his expertise brought him to the attention of Julius Caesar; later he worked for the emperor Augustus. Vitruvius makes little reference to buildings of his own time and takes a basically conservative approach to style.   JOHN STEPHENS CRAWFORD

Bibliography: Vitruvius, *Ten Books on Architecture*, trans. by Morris H. Morgan (1960).

Vitry, Philippe de   [vee-tree']

The French composer, poet, and theorist Philippe de Vitry, b. Oct. 31, 1291, d. June 9, 1361, is best known for his treatise *Ars Nova*, which codified the new practice of musical notation reflecting the changed treatment of rhythm and the introduction of duple (instead of only triple) time. Modern scholars apply the term *Ars Nova* to the music of the 14th century to distinguish it from the preceding *Ars Antiqua* (see MEDIEVAL MUSIC). Vitry is also credited with originating the isorhythmic MOTET, but few of his works survive.

Bibliography: Reese, Gustave, *Music in the Middle Ages* (1940); Seay, Albert, *Music in the Medieval World*, 2d ed. (1975).

Vittoria, Alessandro   [vit-toh'-ree-ah]

One of the most gifted and prolific Venetian sculptors of the 16th century, Alessandro Vittoria, b. 1525, d. May 27, 1608, began his career as an apprentice to Andrea Sansovino. His work was more Mannerist than that of his master; his skill in more than one medium soon became evident. Vittoria's best-known work is the richly sculptured stucco decoration of the Scala d'Oro (Golden Stairs; mid-16th century) of the Doge's Palace in Venice.   ROSA MARIA LETTS

Bibliography: Cessi, Francesco, *Alessandro Vittoria*, 4 vols. (1960–61).

Vittorini, Elio   [vit-toh-ree'-nee]

A leader of the Italian neorealist movement, Elio Vittorini, b. July 23, 1908, d. Feb. 14, 1966, examined the political and moral aspects of fascism in his novels *In Sicily* (1941; Eng. trans., 1949), for which he was jailed (1943); *The Twilight of the Elephant* (1947; Eng. trans., 1951); and *The Red Carnation* (1948;

Eng. trans., 1952). The critical essays in *Diario in pubblico* (Public Diary, 1957) constitute an important documentary record of his times. Also a translator, Vittorini introduced many Italians to the works of contemporary American novelists during the 1930s.

LOUIS KIBLER

Bibliography: Heiney, Donald, *Three Italian Novelists* (1968).

Vivaldi, Antonio   [vee-vahl'-dee]

The Italian baroque composer Antonio Vivaldi wrote numerous operas, oratorios, and secular cantatas but is remembered most for his 447 concertos that helped standardize the three-movement concerto form and that influenced the work of J. S. Bach.

The Italian composer and violinist Antonio Vivaldi, b. Venice, Mar. 4, 1678, d. July (buried July 28), 1741, was a major figure in BAROQUE music and exercised a considerable influence on the development of the CONCERTO. He entered the priesthood, and because of his red hair he was known as "The Red Priest." From 1704 to 1740 he was teacher, conductor, and composer for the Ospidale della Pietà, a Venetian conservatory and orphanage for girls whose musical performances were famous. He also traveled widely, producing operas in various European cities. His reputation diminished in later years, and he died destitute in Vienna.

Vivaldi's music was forgotten for a century after his death but began to arouse interest with the discovery of its influence on J. S. Bach, who arranged a number of Vivaldi's concertos for keyboard. Large quantities of his works have been found since the 1920s, and they are now widely published, performed, and recorded.

Vivaldi's output was enormous, encompassing most of the vocal and instrumental forms of his time. He claimed to have written 94 operas, of which 19 are preserved; these are rarely revived. He also wrote secular cantatas and many church works for chorus, soloists, and orchestra—oratorios, motets, and mass movements, the most popular today being the splendid *Gloria Mass*. His instrumental music, however, is the most admired. His greatest contribution lay in his nearly 450 concertos. These are in various scorings—for orchestra alone (also called *sinfonias*), orchestra with one solo instrument, and orchestra with two or more solo instruments. More than half feature the violin, but a variety of other instruments are also represented—cello, viola d'amore, mandolin, and woodwinds and brasses. Most are in three movements with spirited outer movements framing a slow lyrical one. Some are descriptive, such as the popular four that depict the four seasons. Many are routine works, but the best, such as the set entitled *L'Estro Armonico* (Harmonic Inspiration), have vigorous themes, powerful rhythmic drive, and strong structures.

ALMONTE HOWELL

Bibliography: Kendall, Alan, *Vivaldi* (1978); Kolneder, Walter, *Antonio Vivaldi: His Life and Work,* trans. by Bill Hopkins (1970); Pincherle, Marc, *Vivaldi: Genius of the Baroque,* trans. by Christopher Hatch (1975); Talbot, Michael, *Vivaldi* (1978).

Vivar, Roderigo Diaz: see EL CID.

Vivarini   (family)   [vee-vah-ree'-nee]

The Vivarini family included several 15th-century painters who operated a successful workshop in Venice for nearly a century. **Antonio,** 1415–84, used the vitreous, enameled colors of Venetian glass in his early Madonnas, like the one painted for the Oratorio dei Filippini in Padua (*c.*1440). His figures—symbols of divine splendor—show no attempt at naturalness until later, as in his *Madonna and Saint* (*c.*1445; Accademia, Venice). Here, strong contours strengthen the figures in a vain attempt to achieve plasticity. His masterpiece, the polyptych entitled *Virgin and Child Enthroned with Saints* (*c.*1450; Art Gallery, Bologna), shows the influence of his brother **Bartolomeo,** 1432–91, a coarser but bolder artist.

Antonio's son **Alvise,** 1445–1505, was a more original artist; his crisp modeling and firm outlines were inspired by Antonello da Messina. *Christ Blessing* (1498; Brera Gallery, Milan) is clearly reminiscent of Antonello; *Saint Anthony of Padua* (n.d.; Correr Museum, Venice) owes its composition to the example of Andrea Mantegna.

ROSA MARIA LETTS

Bibliography: Berenson, Bernard, *The Italian Painters of the Renaissance,* vol. 1 (1968).

Vivekananda   [vee-vuh-kuh-nuhn'-duh]

The Hindu thinker Vivekananda, b. Jan. 12, 1863, d. Jan. 4, 1902, founded the Ramakrishna order. Originally named Narendranath Datta, he became a follower of RAMAKRISHNA in 1881 and later his chief disciple. After Ramakrishna died (1886), Vivekananda traveled as a monk throughout India and went in 1893 to the World's Parliament of Religions in Chicago, where he represented Hinduism. His message of the truth of all religions made a remarkable impression. He returned to India and founded the Ramakrishna Mission at Belur, near Calcutta, in 1897. He made a second trip to the United States in 1899. Unlike Ramakrishna, Vivekananda was an erudite thinker; he wrote and lectured extensively. The philosophy he propounded was Advaita VEDANTA, which he reinterpreted in a more rationalistic and activist vein and in an eclectic manner that appealed to those who professed various faiths.

KARL H. POTTER

Bibliography: Dhar, Sailendra N., *A Comprehensive Biography of Swami Vivekananda* (1975); Srivastava, R. P., *Contemporary Indian Idealism* (1973).

Vives, Juan Luis   [vee'-vays]

Spanish humanist philosopher and scholar Juan Luis Vives, b. Mar. 6, 1492, d. May 6, 1540, is considered one of the great empiricists of the Renaissance. Vives taught at Oxford and Louvain and, during his stay in England, was imprisoned for opposing Henry VIII's divorce from Catherine of Aragon. Vives called for greater attention to observation and experiment and less reliance on ancient authorities; he criticized the philosophers of his time for failing to realize that knowledge is valuable only when used; and he advocated such social reforms as relief for the poor and education for women. His *De anima et vita libri tres* (Three Books on the Soul and Life, 1538) is an important work in the history of psychology.

Bibliography: Adams, Robert P., *The Better Part of Valor* (1963).

viviparity   [vi-vi-pair'-i-tee]

Viviparity is the giving of birth to live offspring. This contrasts with oviparity, in which young are hatched from eggs deposited and incubated outside the body. Eggs of viviparous animals lack a hard or tough protective covering and contain little yolk; protection and nourishment for the embryo are supplied by the mother's body.

PETER L. PETRAKIS

vivisection   [vi-vi-sek'-shuhn]

The term *vivisection,* most specifically referring to surgery on a living animal during scientific research, has come to mean all experimentation using live animals.

The practice of using live animals for scientific experiments has been opposed by numerous humane societies, frequently called antivivisectionists. In the 1870s a strong antivivisection movement emerged in Great Britain, culminating in the Cruelty to Animals Act of 1876. As a result of controversy concerning vivisection, the Animal Welfare Act (1970) was enforced by the United States Department of Agriculture, and the Laboratory Animal Act (1966) was enforced by the Food and Drug Administration. Voluntary controls for the benefit of laboratory animals are accreditation by the American Association for the Accreditation of Laboratory Animal Care (AAALAC), and the National Institutes of Health (NIH) policy requiring both adherence to the *Guide for the Care and Use of Laboratory Animals* by its grantees and their eventual AAALAC accreditation.

Little doubt exists in the minds of most scientists and humane-society members that vivisection benefits humanity, nor does any question arise concerning the scientist's responsibility to society in the conduct of scientific experimentation. Scientists, however, are obliged to ask themselves whether or not animals are essential to the collection of data in a given experiment that will probably benefit humanity.

EDWARD T. GREENSTEIN, D.V.M.

Bibliography: French, R., *Anti-Vivisection and Medical Science in Victorian Society* (1975); Vyvyan, J., *The Dark Face of Science* (1972).

See also: ANIMAL EXPERIMENTATION; ANIMAL RIGHTS; SOCIETY FOR THE PREVENTION OF CRUELTY TO ANIMALS.

Vix [veeks]

An exceptionally rich Celtic grave dating from the late 6th century BC was discovered at the prehistoric hillfort of Vix, near Châtillon-sur-Seine, in east central France, in 1953. The Vix burial provides evidence of Celtic trade with the Greek world. During the Early Iron Age (the HALLSTATT D period) a woman had been buried in a timber-lined rectangular shaft on a wagon with its wheels removed. The accompanying grave goods included a gold torc (neck ring), bronze and silver bowls, and an Attic Greek cup of black-figure style dating from c.520 BC. The prize piece, however, was a bronze krater (mixing bowl) more than 1.5 m (5 ft) high and with a capacity of 1,250 l (330 U.S. gal.); it is one of the finest surviving examples of early Greek metalwork.   LLOYD LAING

Vizcaíno, Sebastián [vees'-kah-ee'-noh]

Sebastián Vizcaíno, c.1550–c.1628, Spanish navigator and explorer, made the first systematic examination of the California coast (1602–03), sailing from Acapulco north to Cape Mendocino and discovering Monterey Bay. Later (1611–14), Vizcaíno sailed from Mexico to Japan and back.

vizsla [vizh'-luh]

The vizsla is a medium-sized, robust, but rather lightly built hunting dog. Sometimes known as the Hungarian pointer, it

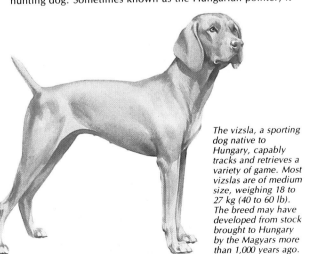

The vizsla, a sporting dog native to Hungary, capably tracks and retrieves a variety of game. Most vizslas are of medium size, weighing 18 to 27 kg (40 to 60 lb). The breed may have developed from stock brought to Hungary by the Magyars more than 1,000 years ago.

stands 52–60 cm (21–24 in) at the shoulder, has pendant ears carried flat to the side, and a docked, or shortened, tail. Its coat is smooth, short haired, and solidly colored in a distinctive rusty gold. Graceful and fast, the vizsla is a multipurpose hunting dog used on upland birds, rabbits, and waterfowl. The breed has been known in Hungary since the 14th century. Recognized by the American Kennel Club in 1960, the vizsla is now popular in the United States both as a household pet and in the field.   JOHN MANDEVILLE

Bibliography: Gottlieb, Gay, *The Hungarian Vizsla* (1985).

Vlad the Impaler, Prince of Walachia [vlahd, wah-lay'-kee-uh]

Vlad the Impaler, c.1431–c.1476, prince of Walachia (1456–62, c.1476), fought bitterly against the Turks and, because of his sadistic cruelty toward subjects and Turkish prisoners alike, became the source of the DRACULA legend. Deposed in 1462, he was later reinstated (c.1476) but soon was caught and beheaded by the Turks. His father was known as Vlad Dracul (Vlad the Devil)—hence the son's name Dracula (or son of the Devil).   K. M. SMOGORZEWSKI

Bibliography: Florescu, Radu, and McNally, R. T., *Dracula: A Biography of Vlad the Impaler, 1431–1476* (1973).

Vladimir [vluh-dee'-meer]

Vladimir is the capital of Vladimir oblast in the Russian republic of the USSR. It is situated on the Klyazma River, about 210 km (130 mi) east of Moscow. The city has a population of 331,000 (1985 est.). One of the oldest of Russia's cities, Vladimir was founded in 1108 and was the center of the early Russian realm until absorbed by the newly dominant Moscow in the 14th century. The Golden Gate, a triumphal arch built in 1164, and the Assumption Cathedral (1158–61) are preserved. Industrial development has been moderate and includes the manufacturing of plastics, tractors, and electric machinery.

THEODORE SHABAD

Vladimir I, Grand Duke of Kiev

Vladimir I, b. c.956, d. July 15, 1015, grand duke of Kiev (c.978–1015), converted from paganism to Eastern Orthodox Christianity, thereby transforming the religious history of Russia. A descendant of the Varangian rulers of Kiev and a son of SVYATOSLAV I, who sent him (970) to govern Novgorod, Vladimir became grand duke after killing his brother Yaropolk; he thus united Kiev and Novgorod. Vladimir was initially anti-Christian, but about 988 he converted and subsequently married Princess Anna, sister of Byzantine Emperor Basil II. Requiring his subjects to undergo baptism, Vladimir also advanced Christianity by building churches, promoting religious charity, and establishing canon law. He was canonized by the Russian Orthodox church. Feast day: July 15.

K. M. SMOGORZEWSKI

Bibliography: Grekov, Boris D., *Kiev Russia,* trans. by Y. Sdobnikov, ed. by Dennis Ogden (1959).

Vladivostok [vlah-dee-vuh-stawk']

Vladivostok is the capital of the Maritime krai (territory) in the Russian republic of the USSR, in far eastern Siberia. It is a major Soviet seaport on the Pacific coast and has a population of 600,000 (1985 est.). An important industrial center, Vladivostok is also the terminus of the TRANS-SIBERIAN RAILROAD and has a naval base and a commercial port for domestic trade. The city is closed to foreign shipping, which is diverted to the nearby foreign trade port of Nakhodka.

Vladivostok has shipyards and manufacturing plants and serves as a base for Soviet fishing and sealing fleets in the Pacific. The city lies in a picturesque amphitheater around a narrow, deep bay known as the Golden Horn.

Vladivostok was founded in 1860, when the region passed from China to Russia; the presence of Russian power in the region was reflected in the city's name, which means "ruler of the east.'' After the Bolshevik Revolution in 1917, Vladivostok served as a base for Japanese and U.S. interventionist forces from 1918 to 1922.   THEODORE SHABAD

Vlaminck, Maurice de [vlah-mank']

Maurice de Vlaminck's The Seine at Le Pecq *(1905) exhibits the vivid color and dynamic brushwork of van Gogh, an early influence. One of the earliest exponents of Fauvism, Vlaminck worked primarily in muted colors and an expressionist style after 1915. (Private collection.)*

The French painter Maurice de Vlaminck, b. Apr. 4, 1876, d. Oct. 11, 1958, was one of the original Fauves (''wild beasts''; see FAUVISM). The group of boldly colored and seemingly chaotic compositions that Vlaminck and his colleagues exhibited at the Salon d'Automne in 1905 ushered modern painting into the 20th century. Vlaminck's finest works employ jarring combinations of red, white, and blue with remarkable effectiveness. His *Tugboat at Chatou* (1906; private collection, New York City) exemplifies this effect.

Vlaminck, who had almost no art training, openly despised the tradition of French masters and boasted that he had never been inside the Louvre. As a racing cyclist and lover of speed, he was fascinated by the rhythms and tempo of urban life. An accomplished violinist as well, Vlaminck supported himself with his music and began to paint seriously only after he and André Derain began working together in 1899. In 1901 he was filled with enthusiasm by the van Gogh retrospective in Paris and adopted the Dutch painter's energetic brushstrokes and brilliant palette. His most characteristic works stem from the following years. By 1908 he had begun to subdue his colors, and his compositions became more orderly.   IRMA B. JAFFE

Bibliography: Heron, Patrick, *Vlaminck: Paintings, 1900–1945* (1948); MacOrlan, Pierre, *Vlaminck* (1958); Perry, Jacques, *Maurice Vlaminck* (1957); Selz, Jean, *Vlaminck,* trans. by Graham Snell (1963).

Vlorë [vlohr'-uh]

Vlorë (Italian: Valona) is a major city and seaport in southwestern Albania, with a population of 61,500 (1981 est.). The city commands the Strait of Otranto at the entrance to the Adriatic Sea and was occupied as an Italian naval base from 1914 to 1920 and again during World War II. The principal economic activities are fishing and canning, the export of refined petroleum, and the manufacture of cement. Vlorë was founded *c.*750–680 BC as the Greek colony of Aulon and changed hands many times until conquered by the Ottoman Turks in 1464. Albanian independence from Turkish rule was proclaimed there in 1912.

Vo Nguyen Giap [voh nuh-win' dee-ahp']

As the Vietnamese military and political leader who organized the victory of the Viet Minh over the French at DIEN BIEN PHU in 1954, Vo Nguyen Giap, b. 1912, also set the strategy for the ensuing successful struggle against the South Vietnamese government and the United States.

Giap was educated at a French lycée in Hue and joined the Vietnamese Communist movement in the early 1930s. In 1939 he fled to China, where, with Ho Chi Minh, he began organizing the Vietnamese revolutionary forces that marched into Hanoi in August 1945. He became a leading exponent of the theory and practice of guerrilla warfare. In 1946 he was made commander in chief of the People's Army of Vietnam. He became a deputy premier and defense minister of the Democratic Republic of Vietnam and a member of the politburo of the Lao Dong (Communist) party. He is the author of *People's War, People's Army* (1962) and *Big Victory, Great Task* (1968). Giap stepped down as minister of defense in 1980, and in 1982 he was dropped from the ruling politburo.

Bibliography: O'Neill, R. J., *General Giap: Politician and Strategist* (1969).

vocabulary: see ENGLISH LANGUAGE; LANGUAGE AND LITERATURE.

vocal cords: see LARYNX.

vocational education

Vocational education prepares students for industrial and commercial occupations that do not require a university degree. It includes training in such fields as manufacturing, building, business and health services, and agriculture. Vocational education programs are found in public and private secondary schools, community and junior colleges, industry, labor unions, penal institutions, adult education courses, and the military. Although vocational education students concentrate their efforts on learning a job-related skill, many schools require a program of academic study in order to ensure that students are competent in reading, writing, and arithmetic. In the United States in the early 1980s there were over 10 million students in secondary vocational programs and 1.7 million men and women in postsecondary programs—nearly 450,000 in public schools and more than 1.2 million in private schools.

History of Vocational Education. Before the 19th century, vocational training was typically provided by a child's father or mother or through an APPRENTICESHIP. The Industrial Revolution of the early 19th century created a need for skilled workers that was greater than apprenticeship training could fulfill. As a result, the first vocational training programs in the United States were offered during the 1820s. The Gardiner Lyceum, Gardiner, Maine (1821); the Franklin Institute, Philadelphia (1824); and the Rensselaer Institute, Troy, N.Y. (1824), were among the earliest vocational technical schools in the United States. In 1862 the MORRILL ACT provided for the establishment of LAND-GRANT COLLEGES.

Several European countries began teaching manual skills in schools during the second half of the 19th century. This training was not intended to prepare students for a specific occupation, but rather to teach them basic craft skills. In 1876, at the Centennial Exhibition in Philadelphia, the Russian government displayed the projects of students from the Moscow Imperial Technical School. This demonstration, along with reports on the other European manual-training programs, impressed several U.S. educators, especially John Runkle, president of the Massachusetts Institute of Technology, who used these ideas for shop courses at his school, and Calvin M. Woodward, who founded the St. Louis Manual Training School in 1880. During the 1880s further manual-training programs were started in U.S. schools.

Vocational Education in Public Schools. Just prior to the 20th century a few public schools began offering vocational education programs, but they were primarily in agriculture. During the early 1900s, efforts were made to obtain public support for formal vocational training in the secondary public schools, and distinctions were made between training for specific tasks and general education in practical skills. INDUSTRIAL ARTS PROGRAMS, formerly called manual-skill training courses, are designed for general education in the basic industrial processes, and strong competence in applied science and mathematics is required for TECHNICAL EDUCATION courses. Vocational education is concerned with the teaching of specific occupational skills. In an industrial arts program a student learns how to make objects out of wood, but a carpentry student in a vocational education program learns building-construction techniques.

The Smith-Hughes Act. The growing acceptance of the idea of providing job-related instructional programs in public schools gave rise to the SMITH-HUGHES ACT of 1917, which remained the basis of vocational education policy until, in 1961, President John F. Kennedy appointed a panel to conduct a comprehensive study of vocational education. Its recommendations resulted in the passage of the Vocational Education Act of 1963, which went beyond the provisions of the Smith-Hughes Act. The 1963 act did not state the specific occupational preparation programs that were eligible to receive federal support, but instead permitted federal money to be used for all vocational education programs in public secondary schools. As a result, vocational education programs and physical facilities grew rapidly during the 1960s. Later amendments (1968, 1972, 1976, 1984) to the 1963 act broadened the coverage of federal aid to include postsecondary and adult vocational programs, programs for handicapped and disadvantaged students, sanctions against sexual and racial discrimination, special programs in private institutions, and such support services as counseling and job placement. In 1981 more than 16 million students were enrolled in federally supported vocational education programs. Since 1964, vocational training for young adults has also been provided by the JOB CORPS.

Contemporary Vocational Education. Many contemporary vocational programs offer opportunities for students to gain work experience in their chosen occupation. These cooperative work-experience programs allow a student to attend school for part of the day or year and also hold a part-time job. Such programs differ from general work-experience programs, which provide job opportunities, sometimes for pay, but not in a specified occupational area. These also differ from Work Experience Career Exploration Programs (WECEP), which are an aspect of CAREER EDUCATION.

C. WILLIAM GARNER

Bibliography: Calhoun, Calfrey C., and Finch, Alton V., *Vocational and Career Education: Concepts and Operations* (1976); Christian, Nancy D., *Education in the Eighties: Vocational Education* (1982); Evans, Rupert N., and Herr, Edwin L., *Foundations of Vocational Education,* 2d ed. (1978); Finch, C. R., and McGough, R. C., *Administering and Supervising Vocational Education* (1982); National Institute of Education, *Vocational Education and Social Mobility* (1981); Roberts, Roy W., *Vocational and Practical Arts Education: History, Development and Principles,* 3d ed. (1971); Strong, Merle E., and Schaefer, Carl J., *Introduction to Trade, Industrial, and Technical Education* (1975); Thompson, John F., *Foundations of Vocational Education* (1973).

vocational guidance: SEE CAREER EDUCATION.

vocoder

A vocoder (from voice coder) is an electronic apparatus that analyzes speech, transforms it into signals that can be transmitted over limited-frequency-bandwidth communications systems, and then re-creates the speech from the signals. The telephone vocoder has a speech analyzer at the transmitting end that can isolate and control such speech components as stress, pitch, inflection, duration, and levels of sound energy. The analyzed speech is fed into multiplexing equipment that combines it with other messages and transmits it. At the receiving end, demultiplexing equipment separates and routes the messages and feeds each to a speech synthesizer.

vodka

The traditional liquor of Russia and Poland, vodka is a colorless, almost tasteless liquid made by distilling a mash of grain, sugar beets, potatoes, or other starchy food materials. The name is the Russian diminutive of *voda* ("water"). Vodka differs from WHISKEY principally in its lack of flavor (except that of alcohol itself) and color, a result of its distillation at

so high a proof that flavoring substances are eliminated. Alcohol content is reduced by adding water, and most vodkas are sold at proofs ranging from 80 to 90 (40 to 45 percent alcohol by volume). Some Russian and Polish vodkas are flavored by steeping aromatic grasses, berries, fruit peels, or seeds in the liquid. During the past 30 years vodka has gained in popularity in the United States and other Western countries, where it is used chiefly in mixed drinks (see ALCOHOL CONSUMPTION). Most U.S. vodkas are made from grain spirits purified by filtration through charcoal.

Vogel, Hermann Wilhelm [foh'-gul]

Hermann Wilhelm Vogel, b. Mar. 26, 1834, d. Dec. 17, 1898, was a German chemist whose development of orthochromatic plates greatly enhanced the range of tones in black-and-white photography and anticipated by more than 30 years the advent of panchromatic, or full-color, film. By dyeing plates with coraline he succeeded (1873) in producing an impression of yellow, which until then could not be photographed; this was the first step in the development of dyed emulsions sensitive to all colors of the spectrum. Vogel, a professor of photography at Berlin's Technische Hochschule, wrote the popular *Handbook of the Practice and Art of Photography* (1870; Eng. trans., 1871) and the more technical *Chemistry of Light and Photography* (1874; Eng. trans., 1875).

Vogel, Sir Julius [voh'-gul]

Sir Julius Vogel, b. London, Feb. 24, 1835, d. Mar. 12, 1899, was prime minister of New Zealand from 1873 to 1875 and in 1876. Vogel emigrated to Australia in 1852. In 1861 he moved to New Zealand and established the first daily paper in that colony. Elected to its Parliament in 1863, he served as opposition leader (1865–69) and as treasurer (1869–72) in the cabinet of William Fox. In 1873, as prime minister, he arranged a loan of £10 million from Great Britain for economic development through public-works projects. He was New Zealand agent-general in London from 1876 to 1880, and from 1884 to 1887 he served as treasurer and postmaster general in Sir Robert Stout's administration.

Bibliography: Burdon, Randal M., *The Life and Times of Sir Julius Vogel* (1948).

voice, singing

The voice is the instrument used for speaking and singing; its mechanism includes the diaphragm, lungs, and larynx, and the resonating areas of the head. The differences between speech and song lie in the duration, intensity, quality, and range of the pitches the voice produces in each mode, song generally requiring prolongation of the vowels and a greater range of pitches, whereas in speech little attention is paid to those qualities. Almost anyone can sing a simple song; the wide variation in kinds of singing is due not only to physiological attributes but also to differences in the singers' cultural environment or training.

In producing a singing tone, the breath is forced by the diaphragm upward from the lungs, through the larynx, and into the oral cavity. Pitches are formed by the varying tensions of the vocal cords in the larynx. The vocal cords of the adult male are longer than those of the female, which accounts for the differences in vocal range between men and women. Other variations in the physical makeup of individuals—and so, in the resulting timbre of the voice—are responsible for the difference between SOPRANO and CONTRALTO, and TENOR and BASS.

Western cultures generally use an unaffected sound in folk music, a straightforward delivery that stresses the text over vocal artistry; the result, therefore, is modified speech. Current popular music, for example, sacrifices vocal projection to the convenience of the microphone and denies the need for a common lyric style because of the interest in styling a song to project the individualized images of the various performers. Concert and opera singing, on the other hand, both have developed a standard based on tradition and aimed at an ideal far removed from the natural, untrained vocal utterance.

In classical music a difference exists between the vocal requirements of choral and solo singing; the former requires singers to subordinate their individual vocal qualities to the sound of the group, whereas the soloist develops a voice that is unique and easily identifiable among all others. In each case the singer is expected to produce a balanced sound throughout his or her range, sing on pitch with agility and sustained control, and be able to modify the character of the voice to suit various moods and types of music.

Vocal training in western Europe dates back to the 4th century, when the first schools for teaching religious song were established; but the rigorous training of the solo voice began in the 17th century with the beginning of opera. The demands of opera brought forward virtuoso singers who could execute brilliant passages, sustain long phrases on a single breath, and express a range of emotions from the pathetic to the heroic. Coupled with the dramatic needs of RECITATIVE, the rise of a lyric style called BEL CANTO attracted the attention of the musical world and brought to the fore the first great teachers, among whom Nicola Antonio Porpora (1686–1768) and Pier Francesco Tosi (1654–1732) were widely recognized during the 18th century, and Manuel Rodriguez García (1805–1906), inventor of the laryngoscope, during the 19th. During the 20th century outstanding teachers are found in a number of countries; in the United States many are associated with conservatories and universities. Emphasizing beauty of tone and brilliance of execution above dramatic content, the bel canto style was the vocal ideal during the 18th century and is still the foundation of most vocal training. Romantic opera created a need for heroic and dramatic vocal presentation, and today a variety of musical effects is demanded from the professional singer. Training is based on breath control, removal of muscular tension, production of pure vowels as the vehicles of sound, and development of a rich tone throughout the entire range of the voice.   ELWYN A. WIENANDT

Bibliography: Appelman, D. Ralph, *The Science of Vocal Pedagogy* (1967); Ostwald, Peter F., *The Semiotics of Human Sound* (1973); Rushmore, Robert, *The Singing Voice* (1971); Schafer, R. Murray, *When Words Sing* (1970); Vennard, William, *Singing*, 5th ed. (1968).

Voice of America

The Voice of America (VOA), established in 1942 as part of the Office of War Information, is (since 1953) the international radio network of the U.S. INFORMATION AGENCY (formerly the U.S. International Communications Agency). It is charged with promoting a favorable understanding of the United States abroad—principally in Communist countries—a task it fulfills with a wide range of programs, including news and music. In December 1984 the VOA announced a long-term modernization plan to increase its broadcasting languages from 42 to 60 as well as the number of its worldwide transmitters (about 110 in 1984). The USSR and other Soviet-bloc countries attempted to jam the VOA broadcasts directed to them between 1948 and 1963 and again between 1968 and 1973. The VOA has its headquarters in Washington, D.C.

voice recognition

A voice-recognition unit is a computer input device that converts spoken words into recognizable digital signals (see INPUT-OUTPUT DEVICES). It permits untrained individuals to use computers with ease, provides manufacturing workers with uninterrupted use of their hands, and allows handicapped people to control computers, typewriters, and robots.

Most voice-recognition devices decode discrete words in a noise-free environment by analyzing waveform ratios created by variations in frequency (pitch), relative amplitude (loudness), and time duration. Each speaker must "train" the unit to recognize his or her voice quality and pronunciation. Once trained, the computer eliminates the waveform variations created by emotional and physical stress.

Because of its extreme complexity, satisfactory recognition of continuous speech will not be possible until the advent of the next generation of supercomputers. Japanese researchers who are developing such computers are planning for a vocabulary of 100,000 words.   DONNA AND TOM LOGSDON

Voinovich, Vladimir   [voyn'-oh-vich]

The Russian writer Vladimir Nikolaevich Voinovich, b. Sept. 26, 1932, is known in the USSR for his short stories. His fame in the West, however, rests on his novel *The Life and Extraordinary Adventures of Private Ivan Chonkin* (1975; Eng. trans., 1977), which draws on Soviet army life. The protagonist, Ivan Chonkin, a seemingly simple-minded Russian soldier, outwits the Soviet bureaucracy, both in the army and in civilian life. Because of its ridicule of Soviet taboos, the novel was not published in the Soviet Union. His later books are *The Ivankiad* (1976; Eng. trans., 1977), *In Plain Russian: Stories* (1979; Eng. trans., 1979), and *Pretendent na Prestol: Novye Priklyucheniya Soldata Ivana Chonkina* (Pretender to The Throne: New Adventures of Private Ivan Chonkin, 1979).

LASZLO TIKOS

volcanic rock: see IGNEOUS ROCK.

volcano

A volcano is a vent in the Earth from which molten rock (magma) and gas erupt. The molten rock that erupts from the volcano (lava) forms a hill or mountain around the vent. The

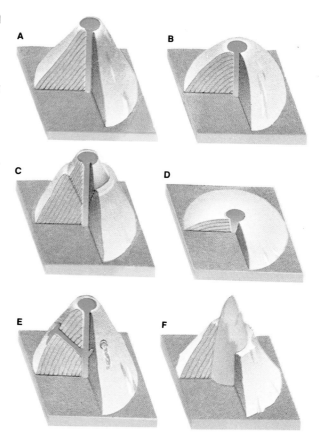

Among the main volcanic forms are: (A) the common, relatively small, steep-sided ash and cinder cone; (B) the volcanic dome that looks like an overturned bowl, usually without any sign of craters or orifices; (C) the secondary cone formed inside an old crater; (D) the shield volcano with a wide-spreading dome and gentle slopes; (E) the high, steep-sided composite volcano, which often contains parasitic cones on its slopes; and (F) the massive compact igneous rock, or plug, that remains after erosion of an extinct volcano cone.

©Gary Rosenquist/Earth Images

The explosive eruption of Mount St. Helens, 64 km (40 mi) northeast of Vancouver, Wash., on May 18, 1980, was the most violent volcanic event yet to have occurred within the continental United States. The photographic sequence shows the top of the mountain as it disappeared in a cloud of ash and smoke, reducing St. Helens by some 400 m (1,300 ft) in height and strewing large regions with the fallout. Extensive damage was done to forest and agricultural lands in the vicinity, and several people lost their lives despite warnings for weeks beforehand of an impending massive eruption. Mount St. Helens lies along the belt of volcanic and earthquake activity that surrounds the Pacific Ocean, and although it had lain dormant since 1857, geologists could give no assurance that the mountain would not erupt violently again.

lava may flow out as a viscous liquid, or it may explode from the vent as solid or liquid particles.

Types of Volcanoes. The most fluid magmas are erupted quietly and flow from the vent to form gently sloping shield volcanoes, a name derived from their resemblance to the shields of early Germanic warriors. The lava flows from shield volcanoes are usually only 1 to 10 m (3.3 to 33 ft) thick, but they may extend for great distances away from the vent. The volcanoes of Hawaii and Iceland are typical shield volcanoes.

Magmas with high gas contents and high viscosities are usually more explosive than those flowing from shield volcanoes. These gas-rich magmas in many instances are blown high into the air during an eruption. The magma falls as volcanic bombs, which accumulate around the vent and form steep-sided but relatively small cinder cones. Volcanic bombs range in size from fine-grained ash to house-size blocks. Cinder cones most commonly consist of volcanic fragments anywhere from ash to small-pebble size, less than 3 cm (1.2 in) in diameter.

Most of the tallest volcanoes are composite volcanoes (stratovolcanoes). These form from a cycle of quiet eruptions of fluid lava followed by explosive eruptions of viscous lava. The fluid lava creates an erosion-resistant shell over the explosive debris, forming strong, steep-sided volcanic cones.

In the past, great eruptions of extremely fluid basaltic lava from extensive systems of fissures in the Earth have occurred. These series of eruptions formed extensive plateaus of basaltic lava. In India the Deccan basalts cover 260,000 km² (100,000 mi²), and in Oregon and Washington the Columbia Plateau basalts cover approximately 130,000 km² (50,000 mi²). No eruptions of this extent have been observed during historic times. Even more voluminous accumulations of basaltic lava, however, are currently being formed at the mid-ocean ridges.

Types of Eruptions. A volcano may exhibit different styles of eruption at different times, and eruptions may change from one type to another as the eruption progresses. The least violent type of eruption is termed Hawaiian and is characterized by extensive fluid lava flows from central vents or fissures and occasionally accompanied by lava fountains. Strombolian eruptions are characterized by moderately fluid lava flows, usually accompanied by a violent lava-fountaining that produces an abundance of volcanic bombs and cinders. Vulcanian eruptions are characterized by viscous magmas that form short, thick flows around vents; very viscous or solid frag-

ments of lava are violently ejected from these vents. Peléan eruptions are similar to Vulcanian eruptions but have even more viscous lava; domes form over the vents, and ash flows commonly accompany the dome formation. The most violent eruptions, such as that of Washington's Mount St. Helens in 1980, are termed Plinian after Pliny the Elder, who died in the Vesuvius eruption of AD 79. They include the violent ejection of large volumes of volcanic ash, followed by collapse of the central part of the volcano (caldera collapse).

A cross section of a composite volcano reveals a steep-sided cone of ash and lava layers deposited around a cylindrically shaped conduit, or vent (1), leading from the surface to the magma source far below (2). Dikes, or sheets of lava that normally solidify along rising fissures beneath the Earth's surface (3), may sometimes serve as feeders through which lava may pass from a deep reservoir to a side vent, producing a parasitic cone (4). Magma may also solidify below the surface as thick bulges, or laccoliths (5), between sedimentary layers.

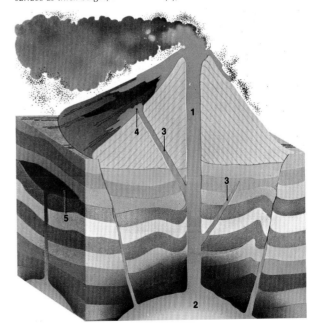

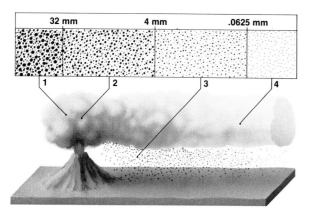

When pressurized magma reaches the Earth's surface, the reduction in pressure releases the gases. If the magma has a low viscosity, the gas merely escapes quietly or forms bubbles in the resulting rock. If the magma is viscous, however, the plastic lava may be shattered by the rapidly expanding gases. The resulting fragments may range in size from large, angular blocks to fine dust. Angular blocks and bombs (1) are fragments larger than 32 mm (1.25 in) in diameter, whereas lapilli (2) vary from 32 mm to 4 mm (0.16 in) in size. Ash particles (3) vary from 4 mm to 0.0625 mm (0.0025 in), and dust (4) from an eruption is considered to include any material smaller than 0.0625 mm.

Volcanic Origins. Most of the world's volcanoes are found along the margins of huge plates into which the Earth's crust is divided (see PLATE TECTONICS). The largest volume of volcanic material emerges at SEAFLOOR SPREADING centers between plates, such as the Mid-Atlantic Ridge. These mid-ocean ridges are usually basaltic in composition and erupt quietly onto the ocean floor. In contrast, the volcanoes formed over subduction zones may be among the most violent.

Along continental margins, chains of volcanoes such as the Andes have formed. Collisions of oceanic crust produce island arcs such as the Antilles, the Aleutians, and the Japanese Islands. In addition to these plate margin areas, volcanoes also form over "hot spots" within a plate, as in the cases of the Hawaiian Islands and the Yellowstone volcanic field.

Volcanic lava derives from deep-lying molten material (see MAGMA) that tends to rise and infiltrate the Earth's crust. The ultimate source of the magma-producing heat is commonly thought to be the decay of radioactive isotopes within the Earth, perhaps combined with residual heat from the time when the planet was formed (see EARTH, HEAT FLOW IN).

Economic Resources. Volcanic activity has yielded a variety of economic resources. Volcanoes supply both lightweight and heavy aggregates, as well as pumice for abrasives and polishing compounds, and elements such as sulfur, zinc, copper, and lead are often found in massive sulfide deposits associated with undersea volcanic activity. Recently, volcanic areas have become important sources of geothermal energy, as in New Zealand, Iceland, and California. Research into new applications for volcanic products is being pursued by various agencies, including NASA.   JAMES A. WHITNEY

Bibliography: Berger, Melvin, *Disastrous Volcanoes* (1981); Boly, William, *Fire Mountain: The Eruptions of Mount St. Helens* (1980); Cocks, L. R. M., ed., *The Evolving Earth* (1981); Fodor, R. V., *Earth Afire! Volcanoes and Their Activity* (1981); Ritchie, David, *The Ring of Fire* (1981); Scientific American, *Volcanoes and the Earth's History* (1982); Taylor, G. Jeffrey, *Volcanoes in Our Solar System* (1983); Time-Life Books, *Volcanoes* (1982).

Volcker, Paul

The American economist Paul Volcker, b. Cape May, N.J., Sept. 5, 1927, served as chairman of the Federal Reserve Board from 1979 to 1987, succeeding G. William Miller. Volcker was educated at Princeton, Harvard, and the London School of Economics. After working in several financial positions, he became a vice-president of Chase Manhattan Bank (1965–68). From 1969 to 1974 he served as undersecretary for monetary affairs in the Treasury Department and then as president of the New York Federal Reserve Bank (1975–79). Volcker's performance as head of the Federal Reserve Board was widely praised; his major achievement was curbing double-digit inflation through tight money policies.

vole   [vohl]

The water vole, Arvicola terrestris, a mouselike, stocky animal with thick fur, digs its burrow along lakes or rivers.

Voles are small, mouselike rodents found in North and Central America and northern Eurasia. About 47 species are classified in several genera, including the field voles (*Microtus*) and the red-backed voles (*Clethrionomys*), of the family Cricetidae. Voles are about 10 to 25 cm (4 to 10 in) long, including a short tail, and weigh up to 0.14 kg (5 oz). The long coat is grayish brown to black. Voles live in a wide variety of habitats, from moist meadows and semiswampy areas to woodland clearings and deserts. They often make runways under low vegetation or, where ground cover is scant, dig short burrows and build nests of shredded plant material. Some also live in rock crevices. Voles eat almost their own weight in vegetable matter each day, consuming chiefly seeds, bark, roots, and leaves. They are prolific, sometimes producing litters of up to 8 young every 3 weeks.   EVERETT SENTMAN

Volga-Baltic Waterway   [vohl'-guh-bawl'-tik]

The Volga-Baltic Waterway, completed in 1964, is a 1,060-km-long (660-mi) transportation system in the north European USSR that connects the Volga River with the Baltic Sea. Replacing the 18th-century Mariinsk Waterway, the system begins at the Rybinsk Reservoir near Cherepovets, extends north to Lake Beloye, and then follows the Kovzha River before passing via canal to the Vytegra River and on to Lake ONEGA. From there it continues as the White Sea–Baltic Waterway to Leningrad. Five hydroelectric generating complexes and seven locks have been constructed along the waterway. Ships can complete the trip between Cherepovets and Leningrad in less than 3 days. Iron ore, coal, petroleum, timber, and grain are the most common cargoes.

Volga River

The Volga, the longest river in both the European USSR and Europe as a whole, rises at an altitude of 228 m (748 ft) in the Valdai Hills, 320 km (200 mi) northwest of Moscow, and enters the Caspian Sea to the south after a course of about 3,690 km (2,290 mi). The Volga and its approximately 200 tributaries drain an area of about 1,360,000 km^2 (525,000 mi^2), or one-third of the European USSR. The river is almost entirely navigable, although obstructed by ice for 3 or 4 months in the winter. The navigation period varies from about 200 days in the north to about 260 in the south. The Volga and its 70 or more navigable tributaries carry about two-thirds of all Soviet river freight. Timber, petroleum, coal, salt, farm equipment, construction materials, fish, and fertilizers constitute the bulk of freight on the Volga. The river serves the cities of Kalinin, Rybinsk, Yaroslavl, Kuibyshev, Gorky, Kazan, Saratov, Volgograd, and Astrakhan. The construction of dams and reservoirs in the 20th century has turned the river into a series of artificial lakes between Rybinsk and Volgograd, facilitating navigation and supplying hydroelectric power.

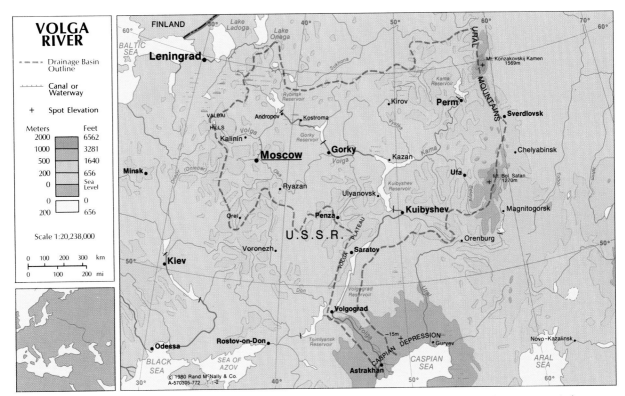

VOLGA RIVER

- – - – - Drainage Basin Outline
- ┴┴┴┴┴ Canal or Waterway
- + Spot Elevation

Meters	Feet
2000	6562
1000	3281
500	1640
200	656
0	Sea Level
0	0
200	656

Scale 1:20,238,000

0 100 200 300 km
0 100 200 mi

© 1980 Rand McNally & Co.
A-570305-772 -1-2

Rainfall along the river course is greater on the upper reaches (635 mm/25 in) than on the lower course (305 mm/12 in). Temperatures on the river's upper reaches range from −14° to −7° C (6° to 19° F) in January to 17° to 20° C (62° to 68° F) in July. On the lower river January temperatures average 0° C (32° F), and July temperatures range from 20° to 25° C (68° to 77° F).

The Upper Volga flows through the northern forests from its source to Gorky and links a number of lakes. The Middle Volga flows eastward from Gorky, where it is joined by the Oka, to just below Kazan, where it receives its largest tributary, the Kama. The Lower Volga flows southwestward to Volgograd and then southeastward to the Caspian Sea near Astrakhan. The Volga Delta encompasses more than 19,000 km² (7,330 mi²). Canals connect the Volga to the Baltic, Black, and White seas, the Sea of Azov, the Don River, and Moscow.

The river is fed mainly by melting snow and summer rains. Reservoirs have modified the perennial spring floods and fluctuations in water level. The average rate of water flow at the river's mouth is 7,680 m³ (271,186 ft³) per sec. The Volga has varied vegetation and fish, including salmon and sturgeon.

Known to the ancient Greeks and mentioned by the geographer Ptolemy (2d century AD), the Volga became an important trade route linking Scandinavia, Persia, and central Asia in the 8th and 9th centuries. In the following centuries the Volga Basin was settled by Slavs. By the end of the 16th century, Russian control extended to the entire Volga basin, with the fall of the Tatar khanates of Kazan and Astrakhan. The river's economic importance has been greatly enhanced since the 19th century with the coming of railroads, canals, dams, reservoirs, and industry.   NORMAN J. G. POUNDS

Bibliography: Shott, P., *Geographical and Cultural Portraits of the Volga-Don Region* (1986).

Volgograd   [vohl-guh-graht']

Volgograd, the capital of Volgograd oblast in the Russian republic of the USSR, is located in southern European Russia, on the right bank of the Volga River at a rail junction. The population is 974,000 (1985 est.). Principal industries include tractor manufacturing, steel and aluminum production, and petroleum refining. Woodworking plants process timber floated down the Volga. Other industries, including petrochemicals, synthetic fibers, and rubber, are found in the left-bank suburb of Volzhski (1984 est. pop., 238,000). Much of the electric power consumed by the industries is generated by the largest hydroelectric station in European Russia, completed in 1957. Volgograd extends in a narrow, 60-km-long (40-mi) strip along the Volga, from the hydroelectric dam in the north to the mouth of the Volga-Don Canal in the south. It was founded in 1589 as a fortress guarding the Volga trade route after the Russians had seized the valley from the Tatars. It was originally called Tsaritsyn, for the Tsaritsa River, a small Volga tributary. Industrial and transport growth dates from the late 19th century. The city was called Stalingrad (1925–61), and that name is associated with a historic battle of World War II, when the Red Army stopped the advancing Germans there in 1942–43 (see STALINGRAD, BATTLE OF).

THEODORE SHABAD

Volkov, Vladislav Nikolayevich   [vohl'-kawf]

The Soviet cosmonaut Vladislav Nikolayevich Volkov, b. Nov. 23, 1935, d. June 30, 1971, was a member of the three-man space crew that perished after completing the world's first space-station mission. Volkov was a civilian engineer at the Soviet manned spacecraft design bureau when he was selected into the cosmonaut program in 1966. He was the flight engineer on the 5-day SOYUZ 7 flight in October 1969. On June 6, 1971, he was launched into space on board *Soyuz 11*, together with Colonel Georgi Dobrovolsky and engineer Viktor Patsayev. The trio spent 3 weeks on board the SALYUT 1 space station and were returning to Earth when a faulty valve let the air leak out of their command module. Without spacesuits, the men suffocated quickly.   JAMES E. OBERG

Bibliography: Riabchikov, E., *Russians in Space,* trans. by G. Daniels (1971); Smolders, P., *Soviets in Space,* trans. by M. Powell (1974).

Volkova, Vera   [vohl'-kaw-vuh]

The Russian-British ballet teacher Vera Volkova, b. Saint Petersburg (now Leningrad), c.1904, d. May 5, 1975, was a major influence in shaping dancers' technique and style in Great

Britain and Denmark. Trained in Saint Petersburg, she had a brief performing career that took her from Russia to China (1920s) and then to Great Britain (1936). Teaching in London both in her own studio and for the Sadler's Wells (now Royal) Ballet school and company, she helped to develop some of the outstanding dancers of the postwar era. In 1951, Volkova went to the Royal Danish Ballet, where she extended the range of the Danish dancers to encompass the bolder technique necessary to perform the later 19th- and 20th-century works central to the international repertory.   Tobi Tobias

Bibliography: Vaughan, D., *The Royal Ballet at Covent Garden* (1975).

Volkswagen

Designed by Ferdinand Porsche in the 1930s as the German "peoples' car"—a small automobile that would be inexpensive enough for the average family—the Volkswagen was not put into large-scale production until after World War II. The decision was then made to concentrate on a single model, the Volkswagen 1200 "Beetle," and to avoid annual model changes. The Beetle recalled Henry Ford's Model T in being simple in design, plain in style, and economical to operate. It was unique in that its four-cylinder air-cooled engine was mounted over the rear axle. The car became a phenomenal success, and, by 1978 when other Volkswagen models had achieved popularity, and the series was discontinued, 19,200,000 Beetles had been produced, making it the best-selling model in history. Volkswagen became (1978) the first important foreign manufacturer to build autos in the United States, and the firm opened factories in Latin America as well. Nevertheless, the VW Rabbit, the auto that was intended to take over the Beetle's market role, never achieved the popularity of its predecessor. By the early 1980s, Volkswagen sales in its overseas markets had plummeted, overtaken by recession and competition from Japanese automakers. Volkswagen is still, however, the largest auto producer in West Germany.
        John B. Rae

Bibliography: Fry, R., *The Volkswagen Beetle* (1980); Hopfinger, K. B., *Volkswagen Story* (1971); Sloniger, J., *The Volkswagen Story* (1981).

Vollard, Ambroise   [voh-lahr']

The French art dealer and collector Ambroise Vollard, b. 1867, d. Feb. 19, 1939, contributed significantly to the development of modern art through his prescient sponsorship and tireless advocacy of postimpressionist artists. As the owner of a small art gallery in Paris, he arranged (1895) Paul Cézanne's first one-man show, a landmark event in modern painting. By the turn of the century, his shop had become a familiar rendezvous for avant-garde artists, and he was the principal agent for (and collector of works by) most of the period's leading painters. He also published (1896–99 and 1900) two albums of prints by postimpressionist painters, which helped introduce their works to the public. After 1900 he concentrated on writing and publishing art books and artists' biographies and on selling his superb collection of paintings and lithographs.   Magdalena Dabrowski

Bibliography: Druick, D. W., *Cézanne, Vollard and Lithography* (1972); Johnson, Uta, *Ambroise Vollard, Editeur* (1977); Vollard, Ambroise, *Recollections of a Picture Dealer* (1936; repr. 1978).

volleyball

Volleyball is a recreational and competitive team game that is played both in and out of doors by 2 teams of 6 players each. The object of the game is to try to score points in the course of hitting a ball with the hands across a net and within the boundaries of the court so that the opposing team cannot return the ball. In its official form volleyball is played on a rectangular court 18 m (59 ft 0.75 in) long and 9 m (29 ft 6.375 in) wide; a net placed 2.43 m (7 ft 11.625 in) high for men and 2.24 m (7 ft 4.125 in) high for women is suspended across the middle of the court. The ball weighs about 280 g (8.75–9.8 oz) when inflated and is made of supple leather or rubber.

To play, each team places 3 players—left, right, and center forwards—in the front line and 3 in the rear. The right rear

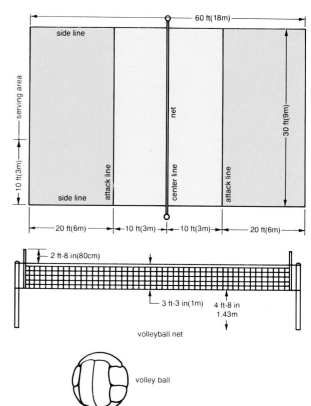

volleyball net

volley ball

In volleyball 2 teams, each consisting of 6 players, use mainly their hands to hit a ball back and forth over a net. The game is played on an 18 × 9-m court (above, top) bisected by a net 2.43 m (2.24 m for women) high. Volleyball became an Olympic sport in 1964.

player is stationed out of bounds in the service area and delivers the serve with a one-handed strike. The server hits the ball over the net, and the defensive team attempts to return service before the ball hits the surface of the court, using no more than 3 hits. The ball may not be caught in the hands, and no player may hit the ball twice in succession. If a serve goes out of bounds or fails to clear the net, play stops and the opposing team gains the serve. At each change of service the players rotate one position clockwise. This procedure allows each player a chance to serve during the course of the game. Only when serving may a team score points—1 point for each successful offensive rally—and the first team to score 15 points wins the game, except when the score is tied at 14. In this case a team must gain a 2-point advantage to win.

Volleyball was invented in 1895 by YMCA physical fitness director William G. Morgan, in Holyoke, Mass. Morgan hoped that his game of "mintonette" would be a welcome substitute for basketball, a sport too strenuous for many of the older men he instructed. After World War II volleyball skills and distinct offensive and defensive patterns came into wide use. The game gained great popularity, and in 1947 a governing body, the International Volleyball Federation, was formed.

Power volleyball, a style of play introduced by the Japanese, demanded that players dive and roll on the floor to recover shots and jump high to "spike" returns. Both the men's and women's teams of Japan, the Soviet Union, East Germany, and China have dominated international competitions using this style, but teams from other nations are fast catching up: American men and women won the gold and silver medals, respectively, at the 1984 Olympics in Los Angeles. Volleyball became an Olympic sport in 1964.   Gerald S. Couzens

Bibliography: Nicholls, Keith, *Modern Volleyball* (1976); Peck, Wilbur, *Volleyball* (1970); Slaymaker, Thomas, and Brown, Virginia H., *Power Volleyball*, 2d ed. (1976).

Volpone   [vohl-poh'-nee]

Volpone; or The Fox (1606), Ben JONSON's best-known play, is a vigorous satirical comedy set in Venice that exposes human corruption and greed. The childless Volpone pretends to be dying in order to solicit rich gifts from his three would-be heirs: Corbaccio ("The Crow"), Corvino ("The Raven"), and Voltore ("The Vulture"). He is aided by his parasitic servant, Mosca ("The Fly"), whose elaborately arranged schemes make the drama seem like a series of plays within a play. By the end Volpone's schemes are confounded, all deceivers are unmasked, and virtue is rewarded.

Volstead, Andrew J.   [vahl'-sted]

Andrew Joseph Volstead, b. Goodhue County, Minn., Oct. 31, 1860, d. Jan. 20, 1947, Republican congressman (1903–23) from Minnesota, won fame when he wrote the Volstead Act (1919), which outlawed the production, sale, and transportation of beverages containing more than one-half of one percent alcohol. The act, meant to enforce the 18TH AMENDMENT, was passed over President Woodrow Wilson's veto. Volstead also participated in efforts to check the power of big business, big cities, and labor unions. In 1922 he coauthored the Cooperative Marketing Act, which exempted farmer cooperatives from antitrust statutes. Following defeat in the 1922 elections, Volstead returned to private law practice in Granite Falls, Minn.   K. AUSTIN KERR

Bibliography: Sinclair, Andrew, *Prohibition* (1962).

volt

The volt, the unit of electromotive force (emf), is defined as the difference in electric potential that will cause a current of one ampere to flow through a resistance of one ohm. The volt is named for the Italian physicist Count Alessandro Volta of Como (1745–1827). Certain standards laboratories, such as the U.S. National Bureau of Standards, keep standard voltaic cells whose emf is very precisely maintained. These cells are used to calibrate other emf sources and instruments, usually by measuring the potential drop across a standard resistor and comparing it to the standard's potential drop. In the laboratory the potential drop, or voltage, is measured with a resistometer-galvanometer combination known as an electrodynamic VOLTMETER, and the current it draws must be so small as not to alter the voltage measurably. To measure extremely high voltages, electrostatic voltmeters are used, in which the meter reading is proportional to the charge collected on a known capacitor and, by inference, to the voltage.
                                    A.G. ENGELHARDT AND M. KRISTIANSEN

See also: OHM'S LAW.

Volta, Alessandro, Count   [vohl'-tah]

The Italian physicist Alessandro Giuseppe Antonio Anastasio Volta, b. Feb. 18, 1745, d. Mar. 5, 1827, was the inventor of the voltaic pile, the first electric battery. In 1775 he invented the electrophorus, a device that, once electrically charged by having been rubbed, could transfer charge to other objects. Between 1776 and 1778, Volta discovered and isolated methane gas. When Luigi Galvani's experiments with "animal electricity" were published (1791), Volta began experiments that led him to theorize that animal tissue was not necessary for conduction of electricity. Proof of this theory was the battery, which Volta invented in 1800. Volta taught at Como Gymnasium (1775–78) and at Pavia University (1778–1815). Napoleon made him a count in 1801. The unit of electric potential, the volt, is named in his honor.

Bibliography: Dibner, Bern, *Alessandro Volta and the Electric Battery* (1964) and *Galvani-Volta: A Controversy That Led to the Discovery of Useful Electricity* (1952).

Volta, Lake   [vohl'-tuh]

Lake Volta, one of the world's largest artificial reservoirs, is located on the Volta River in southeastern Ghana. It has a surface area of 8,482 km² (3,275 mi²) and extends 450 km (280 mi) behind the 113-m-high (370-ft) Akosombo Dam. Completed in 1965, the dam provides irrigation water for the Accra Plains and also generates hydroelectric power for Ghana's large aluminum industry, for other domestic uses, and for sale to neighboring Togo and Benin.

Volta River

The Volta River, formed at the confluence of the Black and White Volta rivers in northern Ghana, West Africa, flows southward about 465 km (290 mi) to the Gulf of Guinea at Ada. The Akosombo Dam, completed at Ajena in 1965 to form Lake Volta, now regulates the river's flow, provides electricity for Ghana, and contributes to industrial growth.

voltage regulator

A voltage regulator is an electromechanical component or electronic circuit that delivers a constant output voltage; to a specified extent, the output is independent of variations in either the input voltage or the current demand of the load. Automobiles utilize a regulator (either electromechanical or solid-state) to govern the charging rate of the battery by the vehicle's generator or alternator. Without such an arrangement the battery could be damaged by overcharging. Many automobiles use a second voltage regulator to reduce the battery voltage to a level suitable for powering temperature and fuel gauges. Electronic circuits utilize voltage regulators to deliver the various operating voltages required by the circuit.   FORREST M. MIMS III

Voltaire   [vohl-tair']

Voltaire, b. François Marie Arouet, in Paris, Nov. 21, 1694, d. May 30, 1778, was the most influential figure of the French ENLIGHTENMENT. Considered by his contemporaries as the greatest poet and dramatist of the century, he is now better known for his essays and tales. His precocious wit, his upbringing among a group of *libertins*, or freethinkers, and his predilection for aristocratic circles were to mark his life, as his classical education by the Jesuits was to form his taste.

For writing some satirical verses, he spent a year imprisoned in the Bastille (1717–18), after which he adopted the name Voltaire. Subsequently he quarreled with a nobleman, was returned briefly to the Bastille in April 1726, then went into exile in England for 3 years. There he absorbed the lessons of British liberties, deism, and literature. Still unwelcome in Paris, he lived at Cirey in Lorraine from 1734 to 1744 with the intellectual and amorous Madame du Châtelet, then at Versailles, Sceaux, and Lunéville. After Madame du Châtelet's death in childbirth in 1749, Voltaire was the honored guest of Frederick the Great at Potsdam, but increasing acrimony led to their abrupt separation in 1753. After 2 years of wandering, Voltaire settled at Les Délices, a château on the edge of Lake Geneva (and now a Voltaire museum). Then, for safety, he

Voltaire, one of the greatest literary and philosophical figures of the 18th century, embodied in his works the ideals of the French Enlightenment. Best known in his own day for his classical tragedies, Voltaire manifested a massive intellect in histories, essays, reformist tracts, poetry, and satirical tales. The Dictionnaire philosophique (1764) wittily encapsulates his religious, political, and philosophical biases.

moved (1759) to Ferney, just inside the French border, which remained his home until his triumphal return to Paris in February 1778.

Works. Voltaire was preeminent in almost every genre. He catapulted to fame in 1718 with *Oedipe* (Oedipus), but his best tragedies were *Zaïre* (1732; Eng. trans., 1736), *Alzire* (1736; Eng. trans., 1736), *Mahomet* (1741; Eng. trans., 1744), and *Mérope* (1743; Eng. trans., 1744). Voltaire's epic, *The Henriade* (1728; Eng. trans., 1732), although considered a masterpiece at the time, was uninspired, but his light satiric verse—especially his long burlesque poem, *The Maid of Orleans* (1755; Eng. trans., 1758), long condemned by both Catholics and patriots—was unsurpassed. His historical works—*History of Charles XII* (1731; Eng. trans., 1732), *Age of Louis XIV* (1751; Eng. trans., 1752), *Essay on Manners* (1753–56; Eng. trans., 1759)—are landmarks of historiography.

Most of all, however, Voltaire was, and remains, famous as a *philosophe*, a fighter for reform. His ideas were expressed in poems, tracts, pamphlets, and tales. These last, particularly *Zadig* (1747; Eng. trans., 1749), CANDIDE, and *L'Ingénu* (1766; Eng. trans., 1786), are still universally read and admired. His philosophical works include the *Traité de métaphysique* (Treatise on Metaphysics, 1734), *Le Désastre de Lisbonne* (The Disaster of Lisbon, 1756), and the influential *Philosophical Dictionary* (1764; Eng. trans., 1765), a witty compendium of his ideas.

Finally, Voltaire was the most prolific correspondent of the century. His thousands of letters portray his life and personality, reflect his wit and ideas, and describe his times. Another side of the man is revealed in his love letters to his niece, Madame Denis, who was also his mistress.

Ideas. Voltaire was the leader and chief organizer and propagandist of the reformist group called PHILOSOPHES. He strove for collaboration with the more radical of the encyclopedists—DIDEROT and d'HOLBACH—but in 1770 the two groups could not agree on the issue of atheism or on tactics. Voltaire preferred enlightened despotism for France, although favoring constitutional monarchy for Britain and a more democratic government for Switzerland. He fought not to dismantle the hierarchical *Ancien Régime* but to reform it. *Écrasez l'infâme*, "crush the infamous," was the famous slogan he raised against church, Christianity, and intolerance. Other of his targets were the horrendous systems of criminal justice and taxation and censorship of the press. Among his celebrated battles was that for the recognition of Jean Calas, a Protestant unjustly executed. Paradoxically, some consider Voltaire a fount of modern anti-Semitism. He constantly vilified the Jews, especially the ancient Hebrews, as superstitious fanatics, guilty of producing the Bible, Jesus Christ, and Christianity. However, he always opposed persecution.

Voltaire long struggled with the idea of God. He felt that God was necessary to explain the universe and life, to justify morality, and to act as a policeman for the despised common people. His increasing preoccupation with evil, with man's estrangement from a universe foreign to his needs and aspirations, made his God into a removed, inactive deity, who had set up certain natural laws and the best possible original arrangement on earth, but then left man to shift for himself.

Although Voltaire is known principally as a reformer and teller of tales, he had a keen awareness of what is now called the human predicament and the absurd. His unresolved dilemmas extended to his acceptance of determinism and his rejection of materialism; yet he did not believe in the soul—although he would not have wanted such a doctrine spread among the people and even attended mass out of prudence.

Along with Hume and Gibbon, Voltaire was one of the originators of modern historiography. Although his use of history for nonhistorical purposes—propaganda, debunking, philosophical explanations—has been justly criticized, he demanded authentic documentation and broke with tradition in his conception of history as the history of civilization—social, economic, and cultural, as well as political.

LESTER G. CROCKER

Bibliography: Aldridge, A. Owen, *Voltaire and the Century of Light* (1975); Besterman, Theodore, *Voltaire*, 3d ed. (1976); Brailsford, Henry N., *Voltaire* (1935; repr. 1963); Gay, Peter, *Voltaire's Politics: The Poet as Realist* (1959); Lanson, Gustave, *Voltaire*, trans. by Robert A. Wagoner (1966); Morley, John, *Voltaire* (1872; repr. 1973); Orieux, Jean, *Voltaire*, trans. by Barbara Bracy and Helen Lane (1979); Topazio, Virgil W., *Voltaire: A Critical Study of His Major Works* (1967); Torrey, Norman L., *The Spirit of Voltaire* (1938); Wade, Ira O., *The Intellectual Development of Voltaire* (1969).

Volterra, Daniele da   [vohl-tair'-rah]

The Italian Mannerist painter and sculptor Daniele Ricciarelli da Volterra, b. 1509, d. Apr. 4, 1566, made the well-known bronze portrait bust (c.1564) of Michelangelo, his good friend and mentor.

In Rome, Volterra painted the powerful and highly admired *Deposition* (1541) in the Cappella Orsini in the church of Trinità dei Monti. His fine draftsmanship of the nude reflects his study of Michelangelo's late works. Volterra had the misfortune to be commissioned to cover up the nudity in Michelangelo's *Last Judgment* in the Sistine Chapel, which earned him the nickname *Il Braghettone*—"the breeches maker."

ALAN P. DERR

voltmeter

The voltmeter is a device that converts electrical energy to physical energy in order to measure the electrical potential in volts. Most voltmeters are classical GALVANOMETERS that have been modified to measure the potential rather than the current. If a suitable resistor is placed in the circuit in parallel with the meter, the voltage can be determined as a product of the resistance value times the current; the meter can thus be calibrated directly in volts. In order to measure the voltage of alternating current, a rectifier must be provided, which is a device that converts alternating current into direct current.

Voltmeters are essential to electricians, scientists, and industrial workers. One basic meter movement is often used to measure volts, amperes, and resistance in ohms by providing suitable resistors and switches, and a small standard electrical source. Such a combination is called a multimeter or a Volt-Milliammeter (VOM).

LESLIE W. LEE

Volturno River   [vohl-toor'-noh]

The Volturno is the major river of south central Italy. It rises in the Apennines southeast of Rome and flows first south and then west for 175 km (110 mi) to the Gulf of Gaeta on the Tyrrhenian Sea, about 35 km (22 mi) north of Naples. Dammed above Capua, the river is used for irrigation. During World War II it served as an important German defense line until it was taken (1943) by the Allies.

volume

Volume is the measure of the capacity or space occupied or enclosed by a three-dimensional figure (a solid). The volume of a cube with edge e is e^3. If the measure of the edge is in meters (m), for example, the volume is in cubic meters (m^3).

The volume V of a rectangular parallelepiped (or simply, a box) with edges a, b, c, is $a \times b \times c$. For a right circular cylinder of radius r and height h, $V = \pi r^2 h$; for a sphere of radius r, $V = (4/3)\pi r^3$; for a pyramid of height h and area of base B, $V = (1/3) Bh$; for a cone of height h and radius of base r, $V = (1/3)\pi r^2 h$. In general, for any prismatoid (a polyhedron with all its vertices in two parallel planes) with height h, areas of bases B_1 and B_2, and plane section halfway between the bases of area M, $V = (h/6) (B_1 + 4M + B_2)$.

BRUCE E. MESERVE

volumetric analysis: see QUANTITATIVE CHEMICAL ANALYSIS.

Volunteers in Service to America: see ACTION.

Volunteers of America

Branching off from the original SALVATION ARMY based in England, the Volunteers of America became the first religious-social-welfare organization devoted to aiding the needy in the United States. Founded in 1896 in New York City's Bowery section by Ballington Booth (a son of the Salvation Army's founder, William Booth) and his wife, Maud, it has expanded to almost 600 program centers in posts throughout the nation. At present it serves more than 2 million persons every year and operates on an annual budget of $10 million, all raised from voluntary contributions.

The Volunteers of America offers both spiritual and material help, especially to the poor living in major urban areas. On the religious side, it conducts mission churches and Sunday schools in the inner city; some of its staff conduct regular worship services in prisons as well. It also runs a wide variety of social-service organizations.

The Volunteers of America is organized along military lines similar to those of the Salvation Army but is democratic in that it is governed by elected leaders.

HENRY WARNER BOWDEN

Bibliography: McMahon, John F., *The Volunteers of America* (1971).

Volvox   [vahl'-vahks]

Volvox is a genus of freshwater, colonial, plantlike flagellated protozoa. Hundreds to thousands of cells connected by strands form rolling green balls. Each cell contains two flagella, a chloroplast, an eyespot, and a nucleus. Volvox colonies foreshadow multicellular differentiation. Some specialized cells reproduce asexually, releasing daughter cells to form new colonies. Volvox colonies also reproduce sexually, with tiny sperm fertilizing eggs to form a zygote that germinates into a cell that later divides to form a new colony.

J. FORBES McCLELLAN

Volynov, Boris Valentinovich   [vahl-ee'-nawf]

The Soviet cosmonaut Boris Valentinovich Volynov, b. Dec. 18, 1934, was the command pilot on two space-docking missions. Volynov was a Soviet Air Force pilot when he was selected in the first group of cosmonauts in 1960. In January 1969 he was commander of the three-man SOYUZ 5 spacecraft, which linked up with *Soyuz 4*. Volynov's two companions walked in space to the other ship; he thus landed *Soyuz 5* alone. In July-August 1976, Volynov was commander of the two-man *Soyuz 21* spacecraft, which linked up with the SALYUT 5 space station. He and engineer Vitaly Zholobov spent 49 days in space.

JAMES E. OBERG

Bibliography: Hooper, Gordon R., "Missions to Salyut 5," *Spaceflight*, April 1977; Riabchikov, Evgeny, *Russians in Space,* trans. by Guy Daniels (1971).

Von Arx, William S.   [von arks]

William Stelling von Arx, b. Highland Mills, N.Y., Sept. 27, 1916, is an American physical oceanographer with a broad range of interests from instrument design and development to laboratory simulations of ocean and estuarine circulations. He developed a current meter that may be suspended from an anchored ship, made pioneering current measurements using towed electrodes, and devised the geomagnetic electrokinetograph (GEK). He has performed numerous laboratory experiments on flow characteristics on a rotating Earth.

ROBERT E. WILSON

von Braun, Wernher   [vuhn brown]

The German-born engineer Wernher von Braun, b. Mar. 23, 1912, d. June 23, 1977, was a driving force in the development of manned space flight and directed the development of the rockets that put humans on the Moon. Von Braun received his bachelor's degree at the Berlin Institute of Technology in 1932 and his doctorate in physics at the University of Berlin in 1934. Prior to graduating, however, his work on rocketry had won him a research grant from the German Ordnance Department. His rocket research group was reorganized (1937) at the Peenemünde Peninsula on the Baltic coast. Von Braun and a select team of engineers and technicians there developed the A-4 ballistic missile, later designated V-2 (sec-

Wernher von Braun looks at a model of a Saturn rocket in this 1960 photograph. As director of the Marshall Space Flight Center in Huntsville, Ala., von Braun supervised the development of the Saturn V rocket used to launch Apollo spacecraft for lunar landing missions.

ond vengeance weapon; see V-2) and used against Great Britain in World War II.

After the fall of the Third Reich, von Braun and more than 100 top engineers surrendered to the U.S. Army. After interrogation they were offered (1945) contracts to continue their research in the United States. This research was done first at Fort Bliss, Tex., near the White Sands Missile Range, N.Mex., and then at Redstone Arsenal at Huntsville, Ala. Under von Braun the army produced the REDSTONE battlefield rocket and the Jupiter intermediate range ballistic missile (see JUPITER, rocket). In 1958 a modified Redstone (Jupiter C) put the first U.S. satellite into orbit.

The National Aeronautics and Space Administration on July 1, 1960, acquired von Braun's army team to form the nucleus of the Marshall Space Flight Center, also located in Huntsville. At Marshall he continued development of larger rockets started by the army: the Saturn I, then the largest U.S. rocket; the Saturn IB, used to launch the Apollo spacecraft on Earth-orbit missions; and the Saturn V rocket, which put humans on the Moon (see SATURN, rocket).

In 1970, von Braun became NASA deputy associate administrator for planning. Two years later he left NASA to become vice-president for engineering and development at Fairchild Industries in Germantown, Md.

Von Braun's books include *Across the Space Frontier* (1952), *Conquest of the Moon* (1953), and *History of Rocketry and Space Travel* (rev. ed, 1975), coauthored with Frederick I. Ordway III.

DAVID DOOLING

Bibliography: Bergaust, Erik, *Reaching for the Stars* (1960); David, Heather M., *Wernher von Braun* (1967); Goodrum, John C., *Wernher von Braun: Space Pioneer* (1969); Ordway, Frederick I., and Shape, Mitchell R., *The Rocket Team* (1979).

Von Däniken, Erich   [fuhn dahn'-i-ken]

The Swiss writer Erich Von Däniken, b. Apr. 14, 1935, has attracted immense interest from the public with his highly controversial theory that extraterrestrial visitors communicated their knowledge to primitive human beings in ancient times, enabling the latter to evolve into civilized humanity. Von Däniken travels and lectures widely, and his books—*Chariots of the Gods? Unsolved Mysteries of the Past* (1968; Eng. trans., 1970), *Gods from Outer Space: Return to the Stars or Evidence of the Impossible* (1971), *The Gold of the Gods* (1973), *In Search of Ancient Gods: My Pictorial Evidence for the Impossible* (1974), and *Miracles of the Gods* (1976)—have sold 25 million copies worldwide. Scientists discount the evidence presented in his books and dispute his claims.

Bibliography: Krassa, Peter, *Disciple of the Gods: A Biography of Erich Von Däniken,* trans. by David Koblink (1978).

von Neumann, John   [vuhn noy'-mahn]

John von Neumann, b. Dec. 28, 1903, d. Feb. 8, 1957, was a Hungarian-American mathematician who made important contributions to the foundations of mathematics, logic, quantum physics, meteorology, computer science, and game theory. He was noted for a phenomenal memory and the speed with which he absorbed ideas and solved problems. In 1925 he received a B.S. diploma in chemical engineering from Zurich Institute and in 1926 a Ph.D. in mathematics from the University of Budapest. His Ph.D. dissertation on set theory was an important contribution to the subject. At the age of 20, von Neumann proposed a new definition of ordinal numbers that was universally adopted. While still in his twenties, he made many contributions in both pure and applied mathematics that established him as a mathematician of unusual depth. His *Mathematical Foundations of Quantum Mechanics* (1932) built a solid framework for the new scientific discipline. During this time he also proved the minimax theorem of GAME THEORY. He gradually expanded his work in game theory, and with coauthor Oskar Morgenstern he wrote *Theory of Games and Economic Behavior* (1944).

In 1930, von Neumann journeyed to the United States, becoming a visiting lecturer at Princeton University; he was appointed professor there in 1931. He became one of the original six mathematics professors in 1933 at the new Institute for Advanced Study in Princeton, a position he kept for the remainder of his life. He became a U.S. citizen in 1937.

During the 1940s and '50s, von Neumann was one of the pioneers of computer science. He made significant contributions to the development of logical design, advanced the theory of cellular AUTOMATA, advocated the adoption of the BIT as a measurement of computer memory, and solved problems in obtaining reliable information from unreliable computer components. Moreover, his involvement attracted the interest of fellow mathematicians to the computer field.

During and after World War II, von Neumann served as a consultant to the armed forces, where his valuable contributions included a proposal of the implosion method for making a nuclear explosion and his espousal of the development of the hydrogen bomb. In 1955 he was appointed to the Atomic Energy Commission, and in 1956 he received its Enrico Fermi Award. His many and varied scientific contributions made him one of the last generalists among contemporary scientists.

H. HOWARD FRISINGER

Bibliography: Heims, S. J., *John von Neumann and Norbert Wiener* (1980).

Von Stroheim, Erich: see STROHEIM, ERICH VON.

Von Sydow, Max   [vuhn see'-dohf]

A tall, ascetic-looking Swedish actor, Max Von Sydow, b. Apr. 10, 1929, gave memorable performances in such Ingmar Bergman films as *The Seventh Seal* (1956), *Through a Glass Darkly* (1961), and *Hour of the Wolf* (1967). Although his best work has been done as a member of Bergman's company, he gained wider American recognition in the role of Christ in *The Greatest Story Ever Told* (1965) and in such films as *Hawaii* (1966), *Three Days of the Condor* (1975), and *Hannah and Her Sisters* (1986). His performance in the award-winning Danish film *Pelle the Conqueror* (1988) was acclaimed.

Vondel, Joost van den   [vohn'-dul]

Joost van den Vondel, b. Nov. 17, 1587, d. Feb. 5, 1679, is generally regarded as the most important poet and dramatist of 17th-century Dutch literature. His early work was rooted in the tradition of the REDERIJKERS, but later writings belong to the mainstream of European literature.

The tragedy *Palamedes* (1625), attacking the stadtholder Maurits for the judicial murder of Johan van OLDENBARNEVELT, brought Vondel into conflict with the authorities. Two subsequent plays—*Gijsbreght van Aemstel* (Gijsbreght from Amsterdam, 1637), written for the inauguration of the new Amster-

dam theater, and the pastoral *Leeuwendalers* (The Lion's Share, 1647)—likewise have blameless heroes. But in *Lucifer* (1654; Eng. trans., 1898)—which Milton may have drawn upon for the portrayal of Satan in *Paradise Lost*—the central personality is defeated by his own character flaws. Vondel elaborated biblical themes in his last plays, *Jeptha* (1659), *Adam in Exile* (1664; Eng. trans., 1952), and *Noah* (1667).

Vondel's prodigious output of lyric poetry included sonnets, odes, nuptial songs, elegies, religious poems (he converted to Catholicism in 1641), and political satires denouncing corruption and intolerance. He translated many classical and Renaissance works from Greek, Latin, Italian, and French and composed a biblical epic, *Joannes de Boetgezant* (John the Baptist, 1662), in six cantos.

Vonnegut, Kurt, Jr.   [vahn'-uh-guht]

Kurt Vonnegut, Jr., one of the most popular writers in the United States during the 1960s, has often used irony and the elements of fantasy associated with the science-fiction genre to create works whose disenchantment with modern society mirrored the attitudes of the young adults of the 1960s and early '70s. The semi-autobiographical, antiwar novel Slaughterhouse-Five (1969) is one of Vonnegut's most acclaimed works.

Photo Jill Krementz © 1979

Kurt Vonnegut, Jr., b. Indianapolis, Ind., Nov. 11, 1922, combines science fiction, social satire, and black comedy in his novels, which won a wide following during the 1960s. Vonnegut's themes spring from his contemplation of 20th-century horrors: dehumanization in a technological society in *Player Piano* (1952) and *Cat's Cradle* (1963), and the random destructiveness of modern war in *Slaughterhouse-Five* (1969; film, 1972). His play *Happy Birthday, Wanda June* was first produced in 1970; more recent works include *Breakfast of Champions* (1973), *Jailbird* (1979), *Galápagos* (1985), and *Bluebeard* (1987). Although his work has been criticized as simplistic, it has equally often been praised for its comic creativity.

Bibliography: Giannone, Richard, *Vonnegut* (1977); Klinkowitz, Jerome, *Kurt Vonnegut* (1982); Schatt, Stanley, *Kurt Vonnegut, Jr.* (1976).

Vonnoh, Bessie Potter   [vahn'-oh]

Bessie Potter Vonnoh, b. St. Louis, Mo., Aug. 17, 1872, d. Aug. 8, 1955, was a sculptor of intimate figure groups. Her most popular work, *Young Mother* (1896; Art Institute of Chicago), was the source of several variations, including *Motherhood* (n.d.; Art Institute of Chicago), in which the spontaneous poses and flickering surfaces emulated the contemporary French manner. During the 1920s and '30s Vonnoh made life-sized figures of children for fountains. Her figure (1925) of a little girl holding a bowl for birds can be seen in the Roosevelt Bird Sanctuary at Oyster Bay, N.Y.

JOAN C. SIEGFRIED

Bibliography: Craven, Wayne, *Sculpture in America*, 2d ed. (1983).

voodoo

Voodoo is a religious system with followers predominantly in Haiti, the West Indies. Developed by slaves brought to Haiti by the French between the 17th and 19th centuries, it combines features of African and native West Indian religion along with some of the Roman Catholic liturgy and sacraments. The voodoo deities, called loa, are closely related to African gods and may be spirits of natural phenomena—such as fire, water, or wind—or of the dead, including eminent ancestors. A feature of the cult is that at special ceremonies the loa have the power to make their presence known. They temporarily displace the astral body of a living person and occupy his or her physical body. The individual thus possessed is said to be mounted by the loa and behaves and acts as the loa directs, usually in a manner characteristic of the loa itself. Priests called *houngans* preside over these ceremonies.

Two main groups constitute the loa: the rada, often mild and helping, and the petro, dangerous and often deadly. Graveyards, coffins, shrouds, bones, and skulls figure prominently in the symbolism of the petro cult. The bocor, or priest, is especially dreaded for his supposed ability to create the zombie, a newly dead body that he reanimates by causing it to be possessed by an elemental spirit.   BENJAMIN WALKER

Bibliography: Courlander, H., and Bastein, R., *Religion and Politics in Haiti* (1966); Davis, Wade, *The Serpent and the Rainbow* (1986) and *Passage of Darkness: The Ethnobiology of the Haitian Zombie* (1988); Deren, Maya, *Divine Horsemen* (1953; repr. 1972); Haskins, James, *Witchcraft, Mysticism and Magic in the Black World* (1974); Kerboull, Jean, *Voodoo and Magic Practices* (1978); Metraux, Alfred, *Voodoo in Haiti*, trans. by Hugo Charteris (1972).

See also: AFRO-AMERICAN CULTS.

Voronezh   [vuh-rawn'-ish]

Voronezh is the capital of Voronezh oblast in the Russian republic of the USSR. It is situated on the small Voronezh River, about 510 km (320 mi) south of Moscow. The city has a population of 860,000 (1986 est.). During the Soviet period Voronezh has developed as a diversified manufacturing center, producing a wide range of machinery as well as synthetic rubber. Voronezh was founded in 1586 as a fortress on the southern approaches to Moscow and served as an early shipbuilding center under Peter I.   THEODORE SHABAD

Voroshilov, Kliment Yefremovich   [vuh-ruh-shee'-luhf]

Kliment Yefremovich Voroshilov, b. Feb. 4 (N.S.), 1881, d. Dec. 2, 1969, a Soviet military officer and political leader who joined the Social Democratic party in 1903, fought both in the civil war (1918–20) that followed the RUSSIAN REVOLUTIONS OF 1917 and in World War II. A Red Army commander in the civil war, he skillfully defended (1919) Tsaritsyn (now Volgograd). Allied with Joseph Stalin, Voroshilov became commissar for military and naval affairs (1925–34), commissar for defense (1934–40), and a member of the Communist party's politburo (1926–60). Early in World War II he suffered repeated defeats on the northern front and spent the remainder of the war in minor posts. After Stalin's death, Voroshilov served as chairman of the presidium (1953–60), a ceremonial position. He participated in the effort to remove Nikita Khrushchev in 1957 and lost (1960) his major posts, but he was restored to central committee membership shortly before his death.
K. M. SMOGORZEWSKI

Bibliography: Haupt, Georges, and Mani, J. J., *Makers of the Russian Revolution* (1974).

Vorster, B. Johannes   [for'-stur]

Prime minister of the Republic of South Africa from 1966 to 1978 and president from 1978 to 1979, Balthazar Johannes Vorster, b. Jamestown, South Africa, Dec. 13, 1915, d. Sept. 10, 1983, graduated (1938) in law at the University of Stellenbosch. He was interned during World War II because of his pro-Nazi sentiments and his leadership of a fascist organization. After World War II he joined the Nationalist party, entered (1953) the House of Assembly, and was appointed (1961) minister of justice in Hendrik Verwoerd's government. Vorster succeeded (1966) the latter when the Nationalist leader was assassinated. On Sept. 20, 1978, Vorster resigned as prime minister, for reasons of health, and was succeeded by Pieter W. Botha. After serving as president of South Africa, a ceremonial post, for 9 months, Vorster resigned in 1979 after being implicated in a financial scandal.
K. M. SMOGORZEWSKI

Bibliography: D'Oliveira, John, *Vorster: The Man* (1977); Legum, Colin, *Vorster's Gamble for Africa* (1976).

Vorticella   [vor-ti-sel'-uh]

Vorticella is a genus of bell-shaped ciliated protozoa common in water treatment systems and also found in freshwater and in the soil. Vorticella are usually attached to other surfaces by means of a long, springlike stalk with contractile musclelike fibers. They may, however, develop cilia and become free-swimming. Winding rows of cilia on the anterior broad end sweep bacterial food into the mouth. Vorticella exhibit a type of sexual reproduction in which different-sized organisms conjugate (exchange nuclear material).   J. FORBES MCCLELLAN

vorticism   [vor'-ti-sizm]

Vorticism began as an abstract-geometric style of painting and sculpture among a few artists in London about 1912. It was publicized as a movement when the painter and writer Wyndham LEWIS published *Blast: Review of the Great English Vortex* (1914–15). *Blast*'s manifestos ridiculed many old, traditional values while praising modern technology and the dynamism of industrialized, urban society. Unlike the futurists (see FUTURISM), who embraced the speed, noise, and violence of modern life and attempted to convey them visually, the vorticists admired the hard, polished surfaces, sharp edges, and bare, precise shapes of the machine age; they strove to incorporate these attributes into their visual and literary works. The movement disintegrated after 1915, but some traces of its principles appear in the later work of Lewis and in the poetic theory and practice of Ezra POUND.   WILLIAM C. WEES

Bibliography: Cork, Richard, *Vorticism and Abstract Art in the First Machine Age*, 2 vols. (1977); Wees, W. C., *Vorticism and the English Avant-Garde* (1972).

Vosges   [vohzh]

The Vosges, a mountain range in eastern France, extend about 200 km (120 mi) through Alsace-Lorraine near the French-German border and the Rhine River. The massif has a core of ancient crystalline rock covered by sedimentary deposits from the Permian and Triassic periods. The summits of the High Vosges are gently rounded and rise above 1,220 m (4,000 ft); the Low Vosges in the north do not exceed 600 m (2,000 ft). The highest peak is Ballon de Guebwiller (1,424 m/4,672 ft).

Mostly forested, the slopes of the Vosges support beech forests to elevations of about 790 m (2,600 ft) and firs and pines above. Small glacial lakes are found throughout the range. The Moselle, Meurthe, Saar, and Ill rivers rise in the Vosges. Vineyards are cultivated on the steep Alsatian slopes; elsewhere, pulp and paper, textile, and other industries exploit the abundant water power. Automobile and rail traffic, made difficult by the relatively high passes at the heads of deep valleys, move through the principal passes of Saverne Gap, Bussang, Bonhomme, and Schlucht.

Voskhod   [vuhs-hohd']

The Soviet spacecraft Voskhod, based on modifications to the Vostok design, made two manned space missions—the first (1964) was the world's first multiperson spaceflight, and the second (1965) saw the first walk in open space by a space-suited cosmonaut. *Voskhod* in Russian means much the same thing as *vostok*, essentially a "moving upward"; the word is poorly translated as "sunrise."

The Spacecraft. In order to conduct impressive spaceflights prior to the beginning of the American GEMINI PROGRAM, Soviet chief space designer Sergei KOROLEV was ordered by Premier Nikita Khrushchev to modify the existing Vostok design to carry two additional crew members. These modifications were accomplished, despite the objections of Korolev, by removing the Vostok ejection seat and inserting three crew members into the spacecraft sideways and without spacesuits. The removal of the ejection seat eliminated any possibility of crew survival in the event of malfunction early in flight.

The Voshkod strongly resembled the Vostok spacecraft but was heavier—*Voskhod 1* weighed 5,320 kg (11,730 lb) and *Voskhod 2* weighed 5,685 kg (12,530 lb), compared to Vostok's 4,700 kg (10,400 lb). Voskhod had the same basic spherical command module as Vostok; an expanded service module, however, contained batteries, oxygen, and a rocket engine. An extra retro-rocket engine was mounted atop the command module in event of a primary-engine failure. Voskhod's additional weight required the use of a larger upper-stage rocket, although the lower stages were identical to those used to launch Vostok and Sputnik flights.

Missions. Six days after an unmanned test flight (*Cosmos 47*), the manned *Voskhod 1* was put into orbit on Oct. 12, 1964. Pilot-cosmonaut Vladimir KOMAROV was in command; he was accompanied by two nonpilots who had received only 4 months of training: medical doctor Boris YEGOROV and spacecraft designer Konstantin FEOKTISTOV. The ship returned to Earth after a flight of 24 hr 17 min 3 sec, despite rumors in Moscow that a week-long flight had been planned.

After another unmanned test flight (*Cosmos 57*) on Feb. 22, 1965, *Voskhod 2* was launched on Mar. 18, 1965, with two spacesuited crew members aboard. While pilot Pavel BELYAYEV guided the spacecraft, copilot Aleksei LEONOV crawled into a special inflatable airlock chamber and subsequently exited the ship through the outer hatch, thus becoming the first person to walk in space. The autopilot failed at the end of the mission; the crew made an off-course manual landing, coming down in a snowy pine forest in the Ural Mountains after a flight of 26 hr 2 min 17 sec. No further manned Voshkod flights were made, although a modified Voskhod (*Cosmos 110*) was launched on Feb. 22, 1966, with two dogs aboard.

JAMES E. OBERG

VOSKHOD PROGRAM FLIGHTS

Name	Launch Date	Results
Cosmos 47	Oct. 6, 1964	Reentered or decayed Oct. 7, 1964; unmanned test
Voskhod 1	Oct. 12, 1964	Cosmonauts Konstantin Feoktistov, Vladimir Komarov, and Boris Yegorov recovered after 16 orbits (24 hr 17 min)
Cosmos 57	Feb. 22, 1965	Decayed Feb. 22, 1965; probably exploded; unmanned test
Voskhod 2	Mar. 18, 1965	Cosmonauts Pavel Belyayev and Aleksei Leonov recovered after 17 orbits (26 hr 2 min); Leonov accomplished first extravehicular activity (24 min)
Cosmos 110	Feb. 22, 1966	Dogs Vetorok and Ugolyok recovered after 330 orbits (22 days)

Bibliography: Gatland, Kenneth, *Manned Spacecraft* (1967); Johnson, Nicholas L., *Handbook of Soviet Manned Space Flight* (1980); Oberg, James E., "The Voskhod Programme: Khrushchev's Folly?" *Spaceflight*, April 1974, and *Red Star in Orbit* (1981); Riabchikov, Evgeny, *Russians in Space*, trans. by Guy Daniels (1971); Shelton, William, *Soviet Space Exploration: The First Decade* (1968); Smolders, Peter, *Soviets in Space*, trans. by Marian Powell (1973); Sullivan, Peter, "The Voskhod Spacecraft," *Spaceflight*, November 1974.

Vostok [vuhs-tawk']

Vostok, the first Soviet manned spacecraft, participated in six manned spaceflights between 1961 and 1963; these flights included the orbiting of the first man and the first woman in space (*Vostok 1* and 6) and the first simultaneous flight of two manned spacecraft (*Vostok 3* and 4). The Russian word *vostok* is translated as "east" but actually connotes "upwards," making it a particularly appropriate name for manned spaceflight.

The Spacecraft. The Vostok weighed about 4,700 kg (10,400 lb) and was launched by an improved version of the same booster that had placed the first Sputnik satellites in orbit. For the Vostok program, an upper rocket stage was added. The Vostok consisted of a spherical command module measuring 2.3 m (7.5 ft) in diameter and weighing about 2.4 tons, and a 2.3-ton service module containing batteries, oxygen, and a rocket engine. The pilot remained strapped to an ejection seat that could be thrown free if a booster exploded and that catapulted the pilot from the descending capsule at the end of the mission. All the Vostok cosmonauts bailed out of their ships at an altitude of 6,100 m (20,000 ft) and descended by individual parachute, although the account of the first landing was changed for propaganda reasons to insist that the pilot rode the capsule all the way to the ground.

Missions. The Vostok program was developed under the direction of chief Soviet space engineer Sergei KOROLEV. A series of unmanned test flights in 1960 and early 1961 overcame technical problems, clearing the way for the first flight of a human being into outer space, on Apr. 12, 1961. A young air force pilot named Yuri GAGARIN rode the remote-controlled *Vostok 1* once around the Earth and landed by parachute near the Volga River. Gagarin's flight was preceded by a period of insistent rumors to the effect that earlier manned flights had taken place in secret but had not been successful, resulting in the killing or maiming of the pilots. In hindsight these stories are believed to have been groundless.

The course of the Vostok program seems to have been heavily influenced by political considerations. Soviet premier Nikita Khrushchev reportedly prevailed on Korolev to conduct a series of spectacular flights that Khrushchev could use for international diplomatic and prestige purposes but that did not truly meet standards of science or flight safety. Such considerations appear to have weighed heavily in the planning of the double Vostok mission in June 1963. Cosmonaut Valery BYKOVSKY was launched in *Vostok 5* on June 14, and 2 days later *Vostok 6*, flown by Valentina TERESHKOVA, the first woman in space, was put into a nearby orbit. The mission was appropriately spectacular, but few scientific or engineering results ever appeared.

The Vostok was heavily redesigned for the VOSKHOD pro-

VOSTOK PROGRAM FLIGHTS

Name	Launch Date	Results
Sputnik 4	May 15, 1960	Unmanned prototype decayed Sept. 5, 1962; recovery on May 19, 1960, failed as cabin went into higher orbit; cabin decayed on Oct. 15, 1965
Sputnik 5	Aug. 19, 1960	Reentered Aug. 20, 1960; cabin with dogs Belka and Strelka recovered after 18 orbits
Sputnik 6	Dec. 1, 1960	Decayed Dec. 2, 1960; recovery attempt failed, resulting in loss of cabin with dogs Pshchelka and Mushka
Sputnik 9	Mar. 9, 1961	Cabin with dog Chernushka recovered after one orbit
Sputnik 10	Mar. 25, 1961	Cabin with dog Zvezdochka recovered after one orbit
Vostok 1	Apr. 12, 1961	First manned spaceflight; cosmonaut Yury Gagarin recovered after one orbit (1 hr 48 min)
Vostok 2	Aug. 6, 1961	Cosmonaut Gherman Titov recovered after 17 orbits (25 hr 18 min)
Vostok 3	Aug. 11, 1962	Cosmonaut Andrian Nikolayev recovered after 64 orbits (94 hr 25 min)
Vostok 4	Aug. 12, 1962	Cosmonaut Pavel Popovich recovered after 48 orbits (70 hr 59 min); *Vostok 3* and *Vostok 4* formed the first group spaceflight and came within 6.5 km (4.0 mi) of each other during first orbit of *Vostok 4*
Vostok 5	June 14, 1963	Cosmonaut Valery Bykovsky recovered after 81 orbits (119 hr 6 min)
Vostok 6	June 16, 1963	Cosmonaut Valentina Tereshkova (first woman in space) recovered after 48 orbits (70 hr 50 min); *Vostok 5* and *Vostok 6* came within 5.0 km (3.1 mi) of each other during first orbit of *Vostok 6*

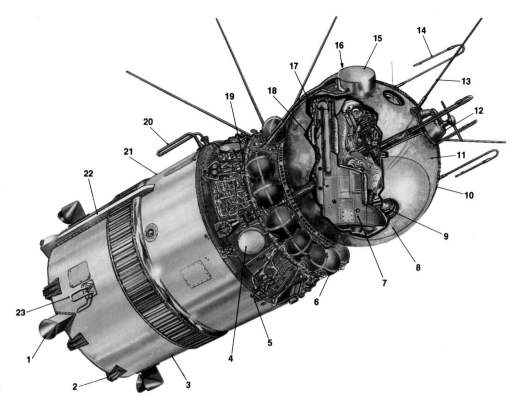

Numbers for the Vostok vehicle and the final rocket stage indicate attitude-control thrusters (1); interstage attachments (2); final-stage rocket (3); access hatch (4); vernier nozzles (5); oxygen and nitrogen bottles (6); ejection seat (7); equipment-inspection hatch (8); portholes (9); tensioning bands holding reentry capsule (10); spherical reentry capsule with ablative heatshield (11); electronics package (12); whip aerials (13); control command aerials (14); multiplex connector (15); ejection-seat hatch (16, unseen); ejection seat rails (17); ejection-seat rocket motors (18); electric harness (19); paperclip command aerial (20); rocket-stage extension (21), shrouding retrorocket of equipment module; external conduit (22); and VHF aerial (23).

gram and for a biosatellite space-medicine program that has involved joint U.S.-Soviet investigations of the effects of spaceflight on living organisms. Hundreds of unmanned Vostok-type photoreconnaissance satellites have been launched since 1962, staying in space for up to 2 weeks at a time.

JAMES F. OBERG

Bibliography: Gatland, Kenneth, *Manned Spacecraft*, 3d ed. (1967); Johnson, Nicholas L., *Handbook of Soviet Manned Space Flight* (1980); Oberg, James E., *Red Star in Orbit* (1981); Riabchikov, Evgeny, *Russians in Space*, trans. by Guy Daniels (1971); Shelton, William, *Soviet Space Exploration: The First Decade* (1968); Smolders, Peter, *Soviets in Space*, trans. by Marian Powell (1973).

voter registration

Voter registration is required in every state in the United States and in some foreign countries to maintain a list of all those qualified to vote and to preclude voting frauds. Massachusetts enacted the first registration laws in 1800, and the other New England states followed; New York instituted registration in the middle of the century, and most of the country had some statute enacted by 1900. In recent years a national system of registration by mail has been proposed.

Although guaranteed the right to vote under the 15th Amendment to the U.S. Constitution, southern blacks were long prevented from doing so by various methods ranging from poll taxes to violence. The best-known organized attempts to rectify this situation were made in Mississippi in 1962 and 1964. Ensuing federal legislation banned the poll tax and permitted federal examiners to register voters.

voting: see ELECTION.

voting machine

A voting machine is an automatic, boothlike device used to record votes in popular elections and to keep track of the number of voters who cast ballots at a polling place. Inside the machine a levered mechanism listing candidates and

questions is set at zero before voting begins. In a typical voting machine, the voter enters the booth past an open curtain and swings a large lever at the base of the machine's face in order to close the curtain and provide for a secret ballot. Small levers beside the candidates' names and beside any questions being voted on are depressed according to the voter's choice. After selections are made, and with the small levers still down, the voter swings the large lever back to its original position. This action opens the curtain, records the selections while resetting the levers, and increases by one the machine's total voter-count. When voting hours are over, officials lock the tally mechanism, record the tallies on a certificate, and seal the machine for a period specified by law, often 30 days. Voting machines, first used officially at Lockport, N.Y., in 1892, are now common in most U.S. states.

Voting Rights Act

The Voting Rights Act was passed by the U.S. Congress in 1965. In 1957 and 1960 Congress had passed laws to protect the rights of black voters, and the 24TH AMENDMENT (1964) banned the use of POLL TAXES in federal elections. Nevertheless, in the presidential elections of 1964, blacks continued to have difficulty registering to vote in many areas. Voter registration drives met with bitter, and sometimes violent, opposition. In March 1965, Martin Luther King, Jr., led a march from Selma to Montgomery, Ala., to dramatize the voting issue (see CIVIL RIGHTS). Immediately after the march, President Lyndon B. Johnson sent a voting rights bill to Congress, and it was quickly passed.

The Voting Rights Act authorized the U.S. attorney general to send federal examiners to register black voters under certain circumstances. It also suspended all literacy tests in states in which less than 50% of the voting-age population had been registered or had voted in the 1964 election. The law had an immediate impact. By the end of 1965 a quarter of a million new black voters had been registered, one third by federal examiners. The Voting Rights Act was readopted and strengthened in 1970, 1975, and 1982.

Vouet, Simon   [voo'-ay]

The painter Simon Vouet, baptized Jan. 9, 1590, d. June 30, 1649, introduced the classical baroque mode to France, where it was to become the dominant style of the 17th century. Vouet, trained by his father, Laurent, went to England to work as a portraitist at the age of 14. After traveling to Constantinople and Venice he arrived in Rome in 1613. Vouet was influenced briefly by Caravaggio and, in the 1620s, by Annibale Carracci and Guido Reni. In 1627 he was called to Paris by Louis XIII, who named him painter to the king. Vouet's large studio supplied paintings—allegories, religious scenes, and portraits—for the king, the queen, and wealthy private patrons. The *Toilet of Venus* (*c.*1637; Carnegie Institute, Pittsburgh) exemplifies his classical yet decorative style and his lush, sensual use of color.   NANETTE SALOMON

Bibliography: Crelly, William R., *The Painting of Simon Vouet* (1962).

Voyager

The identical U.S. interplanetary probes *Voyager 1* and *2* were designed to explore the outer, giant planets of the solar system and their satellites. *Voyager 1,* launched from Kennedy Space Center on Sept. 5, 1977, made its closest approach to the cloud tops of JUPITER (272,000 km/170,000 mi) on Mar. 5, 1979, and to those of SATURN (126,000 km/78,000 mi) on Nov. 12, 1980. *Voyager 2,* launched on Aug. 20, 1977, on a slower and longer trajectory, made its closest approach to Jupiter (640,000 km/400,000 mi) on July 9, 1979, and to Saturn (101,000 km/63,000 mi) on Aug. 25, 1981. *Voyager 1* then headed on a trajectory taking it above the plane of the solar system toward interstellar space. *Voyager 2* sped toward an encounter with the planet URANUS, making its closest approach (80,000 km/50,000 mi) on Jan. 24, 1986. The probe then headed for a rendezvous with Neptune in 1989.

The Spacecraft. The central part of each 815-kg (1,797-lb) Voyager is a ten-sided aluminum framework ring, about 45 cm (18 in) high and 179 cm (70 in) across. The ring contains 10 electronic packaging compartments and surrounds a titanium sphere filled with lydrazine propellant for the 16 maneuvering thrusters. Above the ring is a high-gain antenna dish, 3.7 m (12 ft) in diameter, capable of transmitting and receiving at two frequencies in the S and X bands. Each spacecraft is powered by 3 radioisotope thermoelectric generators on a boom deployed shortly after launch.

The scientific equipment on each probe comprises a radio

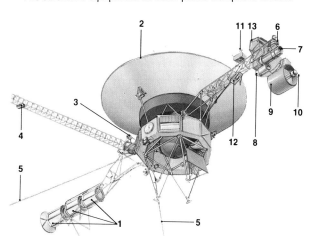

The unmanned Voyager spacecraft, developed specifically to explore the outer planets, is powered by plutonium radioisotope thermoelectric generators (1) and uses a large high-gain antenna (2) to return information to Earth. The space probe carries high- (3) and low-field (4) magnetometers, two long antennas (5) to detect planetary and plasma radio waves, wide- (6) and narrow-angle (7) television cameras, a photopolarimeter (8), infrared (9) and ultraviolet (10) spectrometers, and various instruments for detecting high-energy cosmic rays (11), low-energy charged particles (12), and plasma (13).

transmitter and 10 experiment packages, most of them located on the scan platform boom. Voyager's optical scanners include a pair of television cameras, an infrared radiometer and interferometer-spectrometer, an ultraviolet spectrometer, and a photopolarimeter. The 4 particle and field detectors measure interplanetary plasmas, low-energy charged particles, cosmic rays, and magnetic fields. Each probe also carries 4 magnetometers; the remaining instrument package is a pair of 10-m-long (33-ft-long) antennas for studying planetary and plasma radio emissions.

Results. Both Voyager probes have carried out their functions with great success during their planetary encounters, the results of which are described in the separate entries on the planets and their major satellites. *Voyager 2,* in particular, which was designed to operate at peak performance only through its Saturn encounter, required extensive reprogramming in order to maintain adequate data transmission as its distance from the Earth continued to increase. One change in performance was a process called data compression, which reduced by more than 50% the number of bits of data required to transmit an image. Because the probe had to pass through the tilted plane of Uranus's satellite system at great speed, it also had to be reprogrammed for a technique called image motion compensation—that is, rotation of the craft while the camera shutter remained open. Back on Earth, NASA also employed a method called arraying, or the use of two or more of its Deep Space Network antennas, to reinforce the very faint signals from *Voyager 2.*

Messages to Extraterrestrial Civilizations. *Voyager 1* is already headed toward interstellar space, and it will be followed by *Voyager 2* after the encounter with the planet Neptune in 1989. Because of the remote possibility that either of the probes might be recovered by some extraterrestrial civilization, scientists attached to both probes an identical gold-coated record. Encoded on the record are 117 pictures descriptive of the planet Earth and of human beings, greetings in 54 different languages, and a 90-minute selection of the world's music.   CRAIG B. WAFF

Bibliography: Berry, Richard, "Return to Jupiter," *Astronomy,* September 1979, and "Uranus: The Voyage Continues," *Astronomy,* April 1986; Cooper, Henry S. F., Jr., "Imaging Saturn," *New Yorker,* Aug. 24, 1981; Davies, J. K., "A Brief History of the Voyager Project," *Spaceflight,* February, March, May, and August-September 1981; Morrison, David, and Samz, Jane, *Voyage to Jupiter* (NASA SP-439; 1980); Sagan, Carl, et al., *Murmurs of Earth* (1978).

voyeurism   [voy-ur'-izm]

Voyeurism is deriving inordinate sexual gratification from viewing others in a state of undress or engaged in sexual acts. Most voyeurs are male—hence the term *peeping tom*—and prepared to spend considerable time in the hope of catching someone else unawares. Voyeurism probably originates as a psychological defense technique against possible negative judgment of one's own sexuality. Taking pleasure in viewing naked bodies or intercourse or in viewing one's sexual partner while making love is not considered voyeurism. Viewing becomes voyeurism when it is a compulsive need and routinely supplants other available sexual activity.

Bibliography: Coleman, J. C., and Butcher, J.N., *Abnormal Psychology and Modern Life,* 7th ed. (1984); McCary, J. L., and S.P., *McCary's Human Sexuality,* 4th ed. (1981).

Voysey, Charles Francis Annesley   [voy'-zee]

The English architect Charles Francis Annesley Voysey, b. May 28, 1857, d. Feb. 12, 1941, was noted for his domestic architecture and his designs of furniture, chintzes, and wallpapers. Between 1888 and 1900 he built a number of houses in a simple, primitive style reminiscent of Gothic forms, which he felt to be especially English. His works include Perrycroft (1893–94; Cornwall); Greyfriars (1896; the Hog's Back, Surrey); Norney (1897; Shackleford, Surrey); and the Orchard (1900–01; Chorley, Hertfordshire). Voysey's influence in both England and the United States was considerable.   DAVID CAST

Bibliography: Gray, A. Stuart, *Edwardian Architecture* (1986).

Voznesensky, Andrei   [vuhz-nuh-sayn′-skee]

The Russian poet Andrei Andreyevich Voznesensky, b. May 12, 1933, became famous during the 1960s both in the USSR and abroad for such collections of poems as *Parabola* (1960; Eng. trans., 1967) and *Antiworlds* (1964; Eng. trans., 1967). Influenced by the works of Boris Pasternak and Vladimir Mayakovsky, Voznesensky's poetry is characterized by innovations in form and a predilection for philosophical questions. Some of his more recent poems are contained in *Story under Full Sail* (1974; Eng. trans., 1974) and *Nostalgia for the Present* (1978; Eng. trans., 1978).   Laszlo Tikos

Bibliography: Kunitz, Stanley, "Voznesensky and Kunitz on Poetry," *New York Times Book Review*, Apr. 16, 1972.

Vredeman de Vries, Hans   [vray′-duh-mahn duh vrees]

The Dutch artist Hans Vredeman de Vries, 1527–*c.*1606, made countless ornamental and architectural prints, which, disseminated throughout Germany and the Netherlands, helped to shape northern European styles. His prints included fantastic architectural inventions as well as numerous variations on the structures of Cornelis Floris (see Floris family), although he rejected Floris's gracefulness. His publications, *Architectura*, 4 vols. (1565–78), *Perspectiva* (1604–05), and *Variae Architecturae* (1601), were influential in Europe far into the 17th century.   Robert F. Chirico

Bibliography: Rosenberg, Jakob, et al., *Dutch Art and Architecture: 1600-1800* (1966; repr. 1977).

Vries, Adriaen de   [vrees]

The Dutch Mannerist sculptor Adriaen de Vries, b. 1545, d. 1626, studied with Giovanni da Bologna in Florence and was one of the best assimilators of his master's bronze technique. Later, he helped to spread Italian Mannerism in Germany and Prague. His sensuous, delicate handling of the bronze medium reveals a further debt to Benvenuto Cellini. De Vries's *Mercury and Psyche* group (*c.*1593; Louvre, Paris) and its companion piece, *Psyche* (*c.*1593; Nationalmuseum, Stockholm), are perfect examples of his elaborate but exquisite sense of composition.   Rosa Maria Letts

Bibliography: Wichtenberger, Franzsepp, *Mannerism, the European Style of the Sixteenth Century,* trans. by Michael Heron (1963).

Vries, Hugo De

The Dutch botanist and geneticist Hugo De Vries, b. Feb. 16, 1848, d. May 21, 1935, the foremost botanist of his time, proposed theories on heredity and variation in plants and rediscovered Mendel's laws and the phenomenon of mutation. In 1877 he was appointed the first lecturer in plant physiology at the newly established University of Amsterdam. Vries published (1889) one of the most important books in the history of genetics, *Intracellular Pangenesis,* which proposed the theory that "pangenes" carried hereditary traits in plants. In 1903, Vries published his study of the phenomenon of variation and plant mutation, *The Mutation Theory,* the book that brought him fame. The winner of 11 honorary doctorates and 7 gold medals, Vries retired in 1918, actively contributing to scientific research until his death.

Bibliography: Allen, G. E., "Hugo De Vries and the Reception of the 'Mutation Theory,' " *Journal of the History of Biology* 2 (1969); Magner, Lois N., *History of the Life Sciences* (1979).

Vrubel, Mikhail Aleksandrovich   [vroo′-buhl]

The symbolist, proto-expressionist art of Mikhail Aleksandrovich Vrubel, b. Mar. 17 (N.S.), 1856, d. Apr. 14 (N.S.), 1910, exerted a tremendous influence on avant-garde painters in Russia during the late 19th and early 20th centuries. Vrubel, who entered the Academy of Fine Arts in Saint Petersburg in 1880, also acquired experience through the restoration of medieval art treasures during his visits to Italy. By 1890 he had turned to a highly personal style that dwelt on distant eras and places and reflected his disturbed mental state, which became progressively worse until his death in an insane asylum.   Alan C. Birnholz

Bibliography: Gray, Camilla, *The Great Experiment: Russian Art 1863-1922* (1962); Hamilton, G. H., *The Art and Architecture of Russia*, 2d ed. (1976).

Vrught, Johanna Petronella   [vrookt]

Writing under the pseudonym of Anna Blaman, the Dutch novelist and short-story writer Johanna Petronella Vrught, b. Jan. 31, 1905, d. July 13, 1960, strongly influenced 20th-century literary trends in the Netherlands through her use of realistic narratives and existential inquiries. She is best known for the novel *A Matter of Life and Death* (1954; Eng. trans., 1974).

VTOL

Britain's Hawker Siddeley Harrier, first flown in 1966, was the world's first operational V/STOL strike and reconnaissance jet. The Harrier, capable of landing and taking off in terrain inaccessible to conventional warplanes, may achieve speeds up to Mach 0.95.

Vertical Takeoff and Landing (VTOL) aircraft are a general class of aircraft capable of takeoff and landing with no ground roll. Although a wide variety of methods to achieve vertical takeoff exist and numerous prototype aircraft have demonstrated the ability to take off and land vertically, the helicopter is the only VTOL aircraft commonly used in military and commercial applications.

Jet-propelled aircraft have achieved vertical takeoff and landing by rotating the propulsion engines of the aircraft to the vertical, maintaining the fuselage level; by rotating the nozzles of the propulsion engines to deflect the jet engine exhaust downward; by using separate lifting engines; and by rotating the entire aircraft to the vertical. In propeller-driven VTOL aircraft the complete wing-propeller assembly or the propellers alone are rotated to the vertical for takeoff and landing.

In order to achieve good hovering efficiency—that is, a high value of lift or thrust per horsepower at zero forward speed—a large-diameter lifting device, whether rotor, propeller, or jet engine, must be used to move a large mass of air; the large rotor thus employed by the helicopter provides the best efficiency in hovering flight. The conventional helicopter, however, is limited in horizontal flight to about 322 km/h (200 mph), depending on its size and weight. In order to achieve high-speed flight as well as good efficiency at high speeds, a relatively small propulsion device is required, with its axis aligned with the flight direction. A VTOL aircraft capable of high horizontal flight speeds, therefore, requires a jet engine; it will tend, however, to be inefficient in hovering and vertical flight.

VTOL aircraft hold promise for military applications, in which the ability to land and take off from unprepared fields or small ships presents a distinct operational advantage. One V/STOL (vertical and short takeoff and landing) aircraft, the Hawker Harrier, is a turbojet-powered fighter with rotating nozzles for vertical lift; it is currently in service in the U.S. Marines and the Royal Air Force (see STOL).   H. C. Curtiss, Jr.

Bibliography: Campbell, J., *Vertical Takeoff and Landing Aircraft* (1962).

Vuillard, Édouard   [vwee-yahr']

Édouard Vuillard's Woman in a Blue Bodice (c.1910–13) is typical of the quiet interior scenes that elicited the application of the term Intimist, *an appellation he shared with Bonnard. Vuillard's concern with contour and flat blocks of color, reflecting the influence of Gauguin and Japanese prints, anticipated many of the elements of 20th-century abstract art. (Musée des Beaux Arts, Grenoble, France.)*

The French postimpressionist artist Édouard Vuillard, b. Nov. 11, 1868, d. June 21, 1940, is best known as one of the principal figures of the NABIS, a group of young admirers of Paul Gauguin who banded together (c.1888–1900) in a close-knit group devoted to a radically antinaturalistic and mystical theory of painting. Together with his friend Pierre Bonnard, with whom he shared a studio, Vuillard abandoned (c.1890) academic painting after coming under the influence of Gauguin and of Japanese prints. The rhythmic patterns and contrasting areas of flat color characteristic of Japanese works inspired Vuillard to explore the potential of two-dimensional compositions in which masses of color are manipulated to achieve delicate surface effects.

Less interested than the other Nabis in formulating a new theory of art based on the mystical association of images and feelings, Vuillard concentrated on small-scale decorative works featuring low-keyed, closely toned colors and blurred contours flushed with subtle light. In his best Nabis works, such as *Under the Trees* (1894; Cleveland Museum of Art, Ohio), he exhibits a delicate, brooding sensibility alive to the nuances of light and color. His remarkable series of domestic interiors (1895–1900) are notable for their intimacy and warmth. After 1900 Vuillard's works became more expansive and impressionistic, and the remainder of his career was devoted largely to portraits.   BARBARA CAVALIERE

Bibliography: Preston, Stuart, *Vuillard* (1985); Ritchie, A. C., *Edouard Vuillard* (1954; repr. 1970); Roger-Marx, Claude, *Vuillard* (1946; repr. 1976); Russell, John, *Vuillard: Drawings, 1855–1930* (1971).

Vulcan   [vuhl'-kuhn]

In Roman mythology Vulcan was a god of fire, especially the destructive fire of volcanoes, and was invoked to prevent fires. Ugly and lame, he married VENUS, but she was constantly unfaithful. Vulcan was later identified with the Greek god HEPHAESTUS and was portrayed as a smith and artificer.

vulcanization: see RUBBER.

Vulgate: see BIBLE.

vulture

Vultures are large birds of prey that live mainly as scavengers on carrion. They are divided into two groups: the New World vultures, family Cathartidae, and the Old World vultures, subfamily Aegypiinae, family Accipitridae. Both groups are placed in the order Falconiformes, together with hawks and eagles, and Old World vultures are in fact related to hawks. New World vultures, however, are of more ancient evolution-

ary origin and have been linked genetically to the storks. The combined classification resulted from superficial similarities produced by convergent evolution; thus the head and neck of all vultures are usually bare except for a thin covering of down, and both groups have weak feet adapted more for walking than clutching. Bills of New World vultures, however, are relatively weak; the Old World vultures generally have much stronger beaks.

New World vulture species include the turkey vulture, *Cathartes aura,* and black vulture, *Coragyps atratus,* both widespread in the Americas; the king vulture, *Sarcoramphus papa,* of tropical forest regions; and two South American *Cathartes* species. (In the United States, vultures are also called buzzards.) Turkey vultures have a keen sense of smell, whereas black vultures depend more on eyesight for finding carrion. The two CONDOR species include the California condor, *Gymnogyps californianus,* and Andean condor, *Vultur gryphus,* which are among the world's largest flying birds; both species are in danger of extinction.

Old World vultures inhabit the warmer parts of Europe, all of Africa, and the drier parts of Asia. They are most common in mountainous or open country and are seldom found in forests or in areas with high rainfall. All are carrion eaters except for the palm-nut vulture, *Gyphohierax angolensis,* which feeds principally on the fruit of the oil palm. The Egyptian vulture, *Neophron percnopterus,* may be the most common vulture in the Old World. It eats carrion, eggs, or insects, and often scavenges in settlements.   STEPHEN FAUER

Bibliography: Turner, Ann W., *Vultures* (1973); Weick, Friedhelm, and Brown, Leslie, *Birds of Prey of the World* (1980).

The turkey vulture, C. aura, grows to 81 cm (32 in) with a wingspan of up to 1.8 m (6 ft). The most widely distributed New World vulture, it ranges from southern Canada to southern South America.

Vyshinsky, Andrei Yanuarievich   [vish-een'-skee]

Andrei Yanuarievich Vyshinsky, b. Dec. 10 (N.S.), 1883, d. Nov. 22, 1954, was a major participant of the Stalinist terror. Chief Soviet prosecutor from 1935 to 1939, he conducted the notorious GREAT PURGE trials in Moscow and developed the theory that confession alone was the determinant of criminal guilt. He was his country's chief delegate to the United Nations (1946–54) and its foreign minister (1949–53).

Vytautas, Grand Duke of Lithuania   [vee-tow'-tahs]

Vytautas, b. 1350, d. Oct. 27, 1430, grand duke of Lithuania, expanded Lithuanian territory to its maximum breadth and helped drive the TEUTONIC KNIGHTS from the country. Initially allied with the Knights, he won recognition from Polish king Władysław II (or V; see JAGELLO dynasty) in 1392 as Lithuania's grand duke, nominally subordinate to Władysław. Later, seeing the Knights as a threat to his power, Vytautas allied himself with Władysław to halt the westward expansion of the Knights at the Battle of TANNENBERG in 1410.   ROBIN BUSS